# GERMAN
# DICTIONARY
## *Plus* GRAMMAR

HarperCollins*Publishers*

*first published in this edition 1997*

© HarperCollins Publishers 1997

**latest reprint 1999**

HarperCollins Publishers
P.O. Box, Glasgow G4 0NB, Great Britain

ISBN 0 00 472099-7

HarperCollins Publishers, Inc.
10 East 53rd Street, New York, NY 10022
ISBN 0-06-276058-0

First HarperCollins edition published 1998

Library of Congress Card Number: 98-070454

99 00 01 02 CIBM 10 9 8 7 6 5 4 3

*Dictionary text typeset by Morton Word Processing Ltd, Scarborough*
*Grammar text typeset by Tradespools Ltd, Frome, Somerset*

*A catalogue record for this book is available from the British Library*

*Printed and bound in Great Britain by*
*Caledonian International Book Manufacturing Ltd, Glasgow, G64*

| INHALT | | CONTENTS | |
|---|---|---|---|

---

Dagmar Förtsch, Hildegard Pesch, Veronika Schnorr, Gisela Moohan
Ulrike Seeberger, Lorna Sinclair, Elspeth Anderson, Val McNulty
Eva Vennebusch, Horst Kopleck, Robin Sawers, Ilse MacLean

*editorial staff*
Nicola Cooke, Joyce Littlejohn, Maree Airlie, Carol MacLeod
Anne Lindsay, Megan Thomson, Caitlin McMahon

*computing staff*
André Gautier, Raymund Carrick

*series editor*
Lorna Sinclair

*editorial management*
Vivian Marr

---

# INTRODUCTION

You may be starting to learn German, or you may wish to extend your knowledge of the language. Perhaps you want to read and study German books, newspapers and magazines, or perhaps simply have a conversation with Geman speakers. Whatever the reason, whether you're a student, a tourist or want to use German for business, this is the ideal book to help you understand and communicate. This modern, user-friendly dictionary gives priority to everyday vocabulary and the language of current affairs, business and tourism. As in all Collins dictionaries, the emphasis is firmly placed on contemporary language and expressions.

# HOW TO USE THE DICTIONARY

You will find below an outline of the way in which information is presented in your dictionary. Our aim is to give you the maximum amount of information whilst still providing a text which is clear and user-friendly.

## Entries

A typical entry in your dictionary will be made up of the following elements:

## Phonetic transcription

Phonetics appear in square brackets immediately after the headword. They are shown using the International Phonetic Alphabet (IPA), and a complete list of the symbols used in this system can be found on pages xvi and xvii.

## Grammatical information

All words belong to one of the following parts of speech: noun, verb, adjective, adverb, pronoun, article, conjunction, preposition, abbreviation. Nouns can be singular or plural and, in German, masculine, feminine, or neuter. Verbs can be transitive, intransitive, reflexive or impersonal. Parts of speech appear in *italics* immediately after the phonetic spelling of the headword. The gender of the translation appears in *italics* immediately following the key element of the translation.

Often a word can have more than one part of speech. Just as the English word **next** can be an adjective or an adverb, the German word **gut** can be an adjective ("good") or an adverb ("well"). In the same way the verb **to walk** is sometimes transitive, ie it takes an object ("to walk the dog") and sometimes intransitive, ie it doesn't take an object ("to walk to school"). To help you find the meaning you are looking for quickly and for clarity of presentation, the different part of speech categories are separated by a black lozenge ♦.

## Meaning divisions

Most words have more than one meaning. Take, for example, **punch** which can be, amongst other things, a blow with the fist or an object used for making holes. Other words are translated differently depending on the context in which they are used. The intransitive verb **to recede**, for example, can be translated by "zurückgehen" or "verschwinden" depending on *what* is receding. To help you select the most appropriate translation in every context, entries are divided according to meaning. Each different meaning is introduced by an "indicator" in *italics* and in brackets. Thus, the examples given above will be shown as follows:

> **punch** n (*blow*) Schlag m; (*tool*) Locher m
> **recede** vi (*tide*) zurückgehen; (*lights etc*) verschwinden

Likewise, some words can have a different meaning when used to talk about a specific subject area or field. For example, **bishop**, which in a religious context means a high-ranking clergyman, is also the name of a chess piece. To show English speakers which translation to use, we have added "subject field labels" in capitals and in brackets, in this case (*REL*) and (*CHESS*):

**bishop** *n* (*REL*) Bischof *m*; (*CHESS*) Läufer *m*

Field labels are often shortened to save space. You will find a complete list of abbreviations used in the dictionary on pages xii to xiv.

## Translations

Most English words have a direct translation in German and vice versa, as shown in the examples given above. Sometimes, however, no exact equivalent exists in the target language. In such cases we have given an approximate equivalent, indicated by the sign ≈. Such is the case of **high school**, the German equivalent of which is "Oberschule *f*". This is not an exact translation since the systems of the two countries in question are quite different:

**high school** *n* ≈ Oberschule *f*

On occasion it is impossible to find even an approximate equivalent. This may be the case, for example, with the names of culinary specialities like this German cake:

**Streuselkuchen** *m cake with crumble topping*

Here the translation (which doesn't exist) is replaced by an explanation. For increased clarity the explanation, or "gloss", is shown in *italics*.

It is often the case that a word, or a particular meaning of a word, cannot be translated in isolation. The translation of **Dutch**, for example, is "holländisch, niederländisch". However, the phrase **to go Dutch** is rendered by "getrennte Kasse machen". Even an expression as simple as **cake shop** needs a separate translation since it translates as "Konditorei", not "Kuchengeschäft". This is where your dictionary will prove to be particularly informative and useful since it contains an abundance of compounds, phrases and idiomatic expressions.

## Register

In English you instinctively know when to say **I'm broke** *or* **I'm a bit short of cash** and when to say **I don't have any money**. When you are trying to understand someone who is speaking German, however, or when you yourself try to speak German, it is especially important to know what is polite and what is less so. To help you with this, we have added the register labels (*umg*) and (*inf*) to colloquial or offensive expressions. Those expressions which are particularly vulgar are also given an exclamation mark (*umg!*) or (*inf!*), warning you to use them with extreme care. Please note that the register labels (*umg*) and (*inf*) are not repeated in the target language when the register of the translation matches that of the word or phrase being translated.

## Keywords

Words labelled in the text as *KEYWORDS*, such as **be** and **do** or their German equivalents **sein** and **machen**, have been given special treatment because they form the basic elements of the language. This extra help will ensure that you know how to use these complex words with confidence.

## Cultural information

Entries which appear separated from the main text by a line above and below them explain aspects of culture in German- and English-speaking countries. Subject areas covered include politics, education, media and national festivals, for example **Bundestag**, **Abitur**, **BBC** and **Hallowe'en**.

# ABKÜRZUNGEN      *ABBREVIATIONS*

| | | |
|---|---|---|
| Abkürzung | **abk, abbr** | abbreviation |
| Adjektiv | **adj** | adjective |
| Verwaltung | **ADMIN** | administration |
| Adverb | **adv** | adverb |
| Agrarwirtschaft | **AGR** | agriculture |
| Akkusativ | **akk, acc** | accusative |
| Anatomie | **ANAT** | anatomy |
| Architektur | **ARCHIT** | architecture |
| Artikel | **art** | article |
| Kunst | **ART** | |
| Astrologie | **ASTROL** | astrology |
| Astronomie | **ASTRON** | astronomy |
| attributiv | **attrib** | attributive |
| Kraftfahrzeugwesen | **AUT** | automobiles |
| Hilfsverb | **aux** | auxiliary |
| Luftfahrt | **AVIAT** | aviation |
| Bergbau | **BERGB** | mining |
| besonders | **bes** | especially |
| Biologie | **BIOL** | biology |
| Botanik | **BOT** | botany |
| britisch | **BRIT** | British |
| Kartenspiel | **CARDS** | |
| Chemie | **CHEM** | chemistry |
| Film | **CINE** | cinema |
| Handel | **COMM** | commerce |
| Komparativ | **comp** | comparative |
| Computerwesen | **COMPUT** | computers |
| Konjunktion | **conj** | conjunction |
| Bauwesen | **CONSTR** | building |
| zusammengesetztes Wort | **cpd** | compound |
| Kochen und Backen | **CULIN** | cooking |
| Dativ | **dat** | dative |
| bestimmt | **def** | definite |
| diminutiv | **dimin** | diminutive |
| dekliniert | **dekl** | declined |
| kirchlich | **ECCL** | ecclesiastical |
| Volkswirtschaft | **ECON** | economics |
| Eisenbahnwesen | **EISENB** | railways |
| Elektrizität | **ELEK, ELEC** | electricity |
| besonders | **esp** | especially |
| und so weiter | **etc** | et cetera |
| etwas | **etw** | something |
| Euphemismus | **euph** | euphemism |
| Ausruf | **excl** | exclamation |
| Femininum | **f** | feminine |
| übertragen | **fig** | figurative |
| Film | **FILM** | cinema |
| Finanzwesen | **FIN** | finance |
| formell | **form** | formal |
| 'phrasal verb', bei dem Partikel und Verb nicht getrennt werden können | **fus** | fused: phrasal verb where the particle cannot be separated from the verb |
| gehoben | **geh** | elevated |
| Genitiv | **gen** | genitive |
| Geographie | **GEOG** | geography |

| | | |
|---|---|---|
| Geologie | *GEOL* | geology |
| Geometrie | *GEOM* | geometry |
| Grammatik | *GRAM* | grammar |
| Geschichte | *HIST* | history |
| scherzhaft | *hum* | humorous |
| Imperfekt | *imperf* | imperfect |
| unpersönlich | *impers* | impersonal |
| unbestimmt | *indef* | indefinite |
| umgangssprachlich | *inf* | informal |
| untrennbares Verb | *insep* | inseparable |
| Interjektion | *interj* | interjection |
| interrogativ | *interrog* | interrogative |
| unveränderlich | *inv* | invariable |
| unregelmäßig | *irreg* | irregular |
| jemand | *jd* | somebody |
| jemandem | *jdm* | (to) somebody |
| jemanden | *jdn* | somebody |
| jemandes | *jds* | somebody's |
| Rechtswesen | *JUR* | law |
| Kartenspiel | *KARTEN* | cards |
| Kochen und Backen | *KOCH* | cooking |
| Komparativ | *komp* | comparative |
| Konjunktion | *konj* | conjunction |
| Rechtswesen | *LAW* | |
| Sprachwissenschaft | *LING* | linguistics |
| wörtlich | *lit* | literal |
| literarisch | *liter* | literary |
| Literatur | *LITER* | literature |
| Maskulinum | *m* | masculine |
| Mathematik | *MATH* | mathematics |
| Medizin | *MED* | medicine |
| Meteorologie | *MET* | meteorology |
| Militärwesen | *MIL* | military |
| Bergbau | *MIN* | mining |
| Musik | *MUS* | music |
| Substantiv | *n* | noun |
| nautisch | *NAUT* | nautical |
| Nominativ | *nom* | nominative |
| Norddeutschland | *NORDD* | North German |
| Neutrum | *nt* | neuter |
| Zahlwort | *num* | numeral |
| Objekt | *obj* | object |
| oder | *od* | or |
| veraltet | *old* | |
| sich | *o.s.* | oneself |
| Österreich | *ÖSTERR* | Austria |
| Parlament | *PARL* | parliament |
| pejorativ | *pej* | pejorative |
| Person/persönlich | *pers* | person/personal |
| Pharmazie | *PHARM* | pharmacy |
| Photographie | *PHOT* | photography |
| Physik | *PHYS* | physics |
| Physiologie | *PHYSIOL* | physiology |
| Plural | *pl* | plural |
| Politik | *POL* | politics |

# ABKÜRZUNGEN

# ABBREVIATIONS

| | | |
|---|---|---|
| possessiv | ***poss*** | possessive |
| Partizip Perfekt | ***pp*** | past participle |
| Präfix | ***präf, pref*** | prefix |
| Präposition | ***präp, prep*** | preposition |
| Präsens | ***präs, pres*** | present |
| Typographie | *PRINT* | printing |
| Pronomen | ***pron*** | pronoun |
| Psychologie | *PSYCH* | psychology |
| Imperfekt | ***pt*** | past tense |
| Radio | *RADIO* | radio |
| Eisenbahn | *RAIL* | railways |
| Relativ- | ***rel*** | relative |
| Religion | *REL* | religion |
| Rundfunk | *RUNDF* | broadcasting |
| jemand (-en, -em) | ***sb*** | somebody |
| Schulwesen | *SCH* | school |
| Naturwissenschaft | *SCI* | science |
| Schulwesen | *SCOL* | teaching |
| schottisch | *SCOT* | Scottish |
| Singular | ***sing*** | singular |
| Skisport | *SKI* | skiing |
| etwas | ***sth*** | something |
| Süddeutschland | *SÜDD* | South German |
| Suffix | ***suff*** | suffix |
| Superlativ | ***superl*** | superlative |
| Technik | *TECH* | technology |
| Nachrichtentechnik | *TEL* | telecommunications |
| Theater | *THEAT* | theatre |
| Fernsehen | *TV* | television |
| Typographie | *TYP* | typography |
| umgangssprachlich | ***umg*** | colloquial |
| Universität | *UNIV* | university |
| unpersönlich | ***unpers*** | impersonal |
| unregelmäßig | ***unreg*** | irregular |
| untrennbar | ***untr*** | inseparable |
| unveränderlich | ***unver*** | invariable |
| (nord)amerikanisch | *US* | (North) American |
| gewöhnlich | ***usu*** | usually |
| und so weiter | ***usw*** | et cetera |
| Verb | ***vb*** | verb |
| intransitives Verb | ***vi*** | intransitive verb |
| reflexives Verb | ***vr*** | reflexive verb |
| transitives Verb | ***vt*** | transitive verb |
| vulgär | ***vulg*** | vulgar |
| Wirtschaft | *WIRTS* | economy |
| Zoologie | *ZOOL* | zoology |
| zusammengesetztes Wort | ***zW*** | compound |
| zwischen zwei Sprechern | - | change of speaker |
| ungefähre Entsprechung | ≈ | cultural equivalent |
| eingetragenes Warenzeichen | ® | registered trademark |

After many noun entries on the German-English side of the dictionary, you will find two pieces of grammatical information, separated by commas, to help you with the declension of the noun, e.g. -, -n or -(e)s, -e.

The first item shows you the genitive singular form, and the second gives the plural form. The hyphen stands for the word itself and the other letters are endings. Sometimes an umlaut is shown over the hyphen, which means an umlaut must be placed on the vowel of the word, e.g.:

| dictionary entry | genitive singular | plural |
|---|---|---|
| **Mann** *m* **(e)s, ̈er** | **Mannes** *or* **Manns** | **Männer** |
| **Jacht** *f* **-, -en** | **Jacht** | **Jachten** |

This information is not given when the noun has one of the regular German noun endings below, and you should refer to this table in such cases.

Similarly, genitive and plural endings are not shown when the German entry is a compound consisting of two or more words which are to be found elsewhere in the dictionary, since the compound form takes the endings of the LAST word of which it is formed, e.g.:

| | |
|---|---|
| for **Nebenstraße** | *see* **Straße** |
| for **Schneeball** | *see* **Ball** |

## Regular German Noun Endings

| nom | | gen | pl |
|---|---|---|---|
| -ant | *m* | -anten | -anten |
| -anz | *f* | -anz | -anzen |
| -ar | *m* | -ar(e)s | -are |
| -chen | *nt* | -chens | -chen |
| -ei | *f* | -ei | -eien |
| -elle | *f* | -elle | -ellen |
| -ent | *m* | -enten | -enten |
| -enz | *f* | -enz | -enzen |
| -ette | *f* | -ette | -etten |
| -eur | *m* | -eurs | -eure |
| -euse | *f* | -euse | -eusen |
| -heit | *f* | -heit | -heiten |
| -ie | *f* | -ie | -ien |
| -ik | *f* | -ik | -iken |
| -in | *f* | -in | -innen |
| -ine | *f* | -ine | -inen |
| -ion | *f* | -ion | -ionen |
| -ist | *m* | -isten | -isten |
| -ium | *nt* | -iums | -ien |
| -ius | *m* | -ius | -iusse |
| -ive | *f* | -ive | -iven |
| -keit | *f* | -keit | -keiten |
| -lein | *nt* | -leins | -lein |
| -ling | *m* | -lings | -linge |
| -ment | *nt* | -ments | -mente |
| -mus | *m* | -mus | -men |
| -schaft | *f* | -schaft | -schaften |
| -tät | *f* | -tät | -täten |
| -tor | *m* | -tors | -toren |
| -ung | *f* | -ung | -ungen |
| -ur | *f* | -ur | -uren |

# PHONETIC SYMBOLS   LAUTSCHRIFT

NB: All vowels sounds are approximate only.

NB: Manche Laute sind nur ungefähre Entsprechungen.

## Vowels                   Vokale

| | | |
|---|---|---|
| matt | [a] | |
| Fahne | [aː] | |
| Vater | [ər] | |
| | [ɑː] | calm, part |
| | [æ] | sat |
| Rendezvous | [ã] | |
| Chance | [aː] | |
| | [ãː] | clientele |
| Etage | [e] | |
| Seele, Mehl | [eː] | |
| Wäsche, Bett | [ɛ] | egg |
| zählen | [ɛː] | |
| Teint | [ɛ̃ː] | |
| mache | [ə] | above |
| | [əː] | burn, earn |
| Kiste | [ɪ] | pit, awfully |
| Vitamin | [i] | |
| Ziel | [iː] | peat |
| Oase | [o] | |
| oben | [oː] | |
| Champignon | [õ] | |
| Salon | [õː] | |
| Most | [ɔ] | cot |
| | [ɔː] | born, jaw |
| ökonomisch | [ø] | |
| blöd | [øː] | |
| Göttin | [œ] | |
| | [ʌ] | hut |
| zuletzt | [u] | put |
| Mut | [uː] | pool |
| Mutter | [ʊ] | |
| Physik | [y] | |
| Kübel | [yː] | |
| Sünde | [ʏ] | |

## Diphthongs | Diphthonge

| | | |
|---|---|---|
| Sty̲ling | [ai] | |
| we̲i̲t | [aɪ] | bu̲y, di̲e, my̲ |
| umbau̲en | [au] | hou̲se, no̲w̲ |
| Hau̲s | [aʊ] | |
| | [eɪ] | pa̲y, ma̲te |
| | [ɛə] | pa̲i̲r, ma̲re |
| | [əu] | no̲, bo̲a̲t |
| | [ɪə] | me̲re, she̲a̲r |
| Heu̲, Häu̲ser | [ɔY] | |
| | [ɔɪ] | bo̲y̲, co̲i̲n |
| | [uə] | tou̲r, po̲o̲r |

## Consonants | Konsonanten

| | | |
|---|---|---|
| Ba̲ll | [b] | ba̲ll |
| mich̲ | [ç] | |
| | [tʃ] | ch̲ild |
| fe̲rn | [f] | fi̲eld |
| ge̲rn | [g] | good |
| Ha̲nd | [h] | ha̲nd |
| .ja̲ | [j] | y̲et, milli̲on |
| | [dʒ] | ju̲st |
| Ki̲nd | [k] | ki̲nd, ca̲tch |
| li̲nks, Pul̲t | [l] | le̲ft, li̲ttl̲e |
| ma̲tt | [m] | ma̲t |
| Ne̲st | [n] | ne̲st |
| lang̲ | [ŋ] | long̲ |
| Pa̲ar | [p] | pu̲t |
| re̲nnen | [r] | ru̲n |
| fas̲t, fass̲en | [s] | si̲t |
| Ch̲ef, St̲ein, Sch̲lag | [ʃ] | sh̲all |
| Ta̲fel | [t] | ta̲b |
| | [θ] | th̲ing |
| | [ð] | th̲is |
| we̲r | [v] | ve̲ry |
| | [w] | we̲t |
| Loch̲ | [x] | loch̲ |
| fix̲ | [ks] | box̲ |
| s̲ingen | [z] | pods̲, z̲ip |
| Za̲hn | [ts] | |
| genie̲ren | [ʒ] | meas̲ure |

## Other signs | Andere Zeichen

| | | |
|---|---|---|
| glottal stop | \| | Knacklaut |
| main stress | ['] | Hauptton |
| long vowel | [ː] | Längezeichen |

# GERMAN IRREGULAR VERBS

* with 'sein'

| Infinitive | Present Indicative 2nd pers sing ♦ 3rd pers sing | Imperfect Indicative | Past Participle |
|---|---|---|---|
| aufschrecken* | schrickst auf ♦ schrickt auf | schrak *od* schreckte auf | aufgeschreckt |
| ausbedingen | bedingst aus ♦ bedingt aus | bedang *od* bedingte aus | ausbedungen |
| backen | bäckst ♦ bäckt | backte *od* buk | gebacken |
| befehlen | befiehlst ♦ befiehlt | befahl | befohlen |
| beginnen | beginnst ♦ beginnt | begann | begonnen |
| beißen | beißt ♦ beißt | biß | gebissen |
| bergen | birgst ♦ birgt | barg | geborgen |
| bersten* | birst ♦ birst | barst | geborsten |
| bescheißen* | bescheißt ♦ bescheißt | beschiß | beschissen |
| bewegen | bewegst ♦ bewegt | bewog | bewogen |
| biegen | biegst ♦ biegt | bog | gebogen |
| bieten | bietest ♦ bietet | bot | geboten |
| binden | bindest ♦ bindet | band | gebunden |
| bitten | bittest ♦ bittet | bat | gebeten |
| blasen | bläst ♦ bläst | blies | geblasen |
| bleiben* | bleibst ♦ bleibt | blieb | geblieben |
| braten | brätst ♦ brät | briet | gebraten |
| brechen* | brichst ♦ bricht | brach | gebrochen |
| brennen | brennst ♦ brennt | brannte | gebrannt |
| bringen | bringst ♦ bringt | brachte | gebracht |
| denken | denkst ♦ denkt | dachte | gedacht |
| dreschen | drisch(e)st ♦ drischt | drasch | gedroschen |
| dringen* | dringst ♦ dringt | drang | gedrungen |
| dürfen | darfst ♦ darf | durfte | gedurft |
| empfangen | empfängst ♦ empfängt | empfing | empfangen |
| empfehlen | empfiehlst ♦ empfiehlt | empfahl | empfohlen |
| erbleichen* | erbleichst ♦ erbleicht | erbleichte | erblichen |
| erlöschen* | erlischst ♦ erlischt | erlosch | erloschen |
| erschrecken* | erschrickst ♦ erschrickt | erschrak | erschrocken |
| essen | ißt ♦ ißt | aß | gegessen |
| fahren* | fährst ♦ fährt | fuhr | gefahren |
| fallen* | fällst ♦ fällt | fiel | gefallen |
| fangen | fängst ♦ fängt | fing | gefangen |
| fechten | fichtst ♦ ficht | focht | gefochten |
| finden | findest ♦ findet | fand | gefunden |
| flechten | flichtst ♦ flicht | flocht | geflochten |
| fliegen* | fliegst ♦ fliegt | flog | geflogen |
| fliehen* | fliehst ♦ flieht | floh | geflohen |
| fließen* | fließt ♦ fließt | floß | geflossen |
| fressen | frißt ♦ frißt | fraß | gefressen |
| frieren | frierst ♦ friert | fror | gefroren |
| gären* | gärst ♦ gärt | gor | gegoren |
| gebären | gebierst ♦ gebiert | gebar | geboren |
| geben | gibst ♦ gibt | gab | gegeben |
| gedeihen* | gedeihst ♦ gedeiht | gedieh | gediehen |
| gehen* | gehst ♦ geht | ging | gegangen |

| Infinitive | Present Indicative 2nd pers sing ♦ 3rd pers sing | Imperfect Indicative | Past Participle |
|---|---|---|---|
| gelingen* | - ♦ gelingt | gelang | gelungen |
| gelten | giltst ♦ gilt | galt | gegolten |
| genesen* | gene(se)st ♦ genest | genas | genesen |
| genießen | genießt ♦ genießt | genoß | genossen |
| geraten* | gerätst ♦ gerät | geriet | geraten |
| geschehen* | - ♦ geschieht | geschah | geschehen |
| gewinnen | gewinnst ♦ gewinnt | gewann | gewonnen |
| gießen | gießt ♦ gießt | goß | gegossen |
| gleichen | gleichst ♦ gleicht | glich | geglichen |
| gleiten* | gleitest ♦ gleitet | glitt | geglitten |
| glimmen | glimmst ♦ glimmt | glomm | geglommen |
| graben | gräbst ♦ gräbt | grub | gegraben |
| greifen | greifst ♦ greift | griff | gegriffen |
| haben | hast ♦ hat | hatte | gehabt |
| halten | hältst ♦ hält | hielt | gehalten |
| hängen | hängst ♦ hängt | hing | gehangen |
| hauen | haust ♦ haut | hieb | gehauen |
| heben | hebst ♦ hebt | hob | gehoben |
| heißen | heißt ♦ heißt | hieß | geheißen |
| helfen | hilfst ♦ hilft | half | geholfen |
| kennen | kennst ♦ kennt | kannte | gekannt |
| klimmen* | klimmst ♦ klimmt | klomm | geklommen |
| klingen | klingst ♦ klingt | klang | geklungen |
| kneifen | kneifst ♦ kneift | kniff | gekniffen |
| kommen* | kommst ♦ kommt | kam | gekommen |
| können | kannst ♦ kann | konnte | gekonnt |
| kriechen* | kriechst ♦ kriecht | kroch | gekrochen |
| laden | lädst ♦ lädt | lud | geladen |
| lassen | läßt ♦ läßt | ließ | gelassen |
| laufen* | läufst ♦ läuft | lief | gelaufen |
| leiden | leidest ♦ leidet | litt | gelitten |
| leihen | leihst ♦ leiht | lieh | geliehen |
| lesen | liest ♦ liest | las | gelesen |
| liegen* | liegst ♦ liegt | lag | gelegen |
| lügen | lügst ♦ lügt | log | gelogen |
| mahlen | mahlst ♦ mahlt | mahlte | gemahlen |
| meiden | meidest ♦ meidet | mied | gemieden |
| melken | milkst ♦ milkt | molk | gemolken |
| messen | mißt ♦ mißt | maß | gemessen |
| mißlingen* | - ♦ mißlingt | mißlang | mißlungen |
| mögen | magst ♦ mag | mochte | gemocht |
| müssen | mußt ♦ muß | mußte | gemußt |
| nehmen | nimmst ♦ nimmt | nahm | genommen |
| nennen | nennst ♦ nennt | nannte | genannt |
| pfeifen | pfeifst ♦ pfeift | pfiff | gepfiffen |
| preisen | preist ♦ preist | pries | gepriesen |
| quellen* | quillst ♦ quillt | quoll | gequollen |
| raten | rätst ♦ rät | riet | geraten |
| reiben | reibst ♦ reibt | rieb | gerieben |
| reißen* | reißt ♦ reißt | riß | gerissen |
| reiten* | reitest ♦ reitet | ritt | geritten |
| rennen* | rennst ♦ rennt | rannte | gerannt |
| riechen | riechst ♦ riecht | roch | gerochen |
| ringen | ringst ♦ ringt | rang | gerungen |

| Infinitive | Present Indicative<br>2nd pers sing♦3rd<br>pers sing | Imperfect<br>Indicative | Past<br>Participle |
|---|---|---|---|
| **rinnen*** | rinnst♦rinnt | rann | geronnen |
| **rufen** | rufst♦ruft | rief | gerufen |
| **salzen** | salzt♦salzt | salzte | gesalzen |
| **saufen** | säufst♦säuft | soff | gesoffen |
| **saugen** | saugst♦saugt | sog | gesogen *od* gesaugt |
| **schaffen** | schaffst♦schafft | schuf | geschaffen |
| **schallen** | schallst♦schallt | scholl | geschollen |
| **scheiden*** | scheidest♦scheidet | schied | geschieden |
| **scheinen** | scheinst♦scheint | schien | geschienen |
| **scheißen** | scheißt♦scheißt | schiß | geschissen |
| **schelten** | schiltst♦schilt | schalt | gescholten |
| **scheren** | scherst♦schert | schor | geschoren |
| **schieben** | schiebst♦schiebt | schob | geschoben |
| **schießen** | schießt♦schießt | schoß | geschossen |
| **schinden** | schindest♦schindet | schindete | geschunden |
| **schlafen** | schläfst♦schläft | schlief | geschlafen |
| **schlagen** | schlägst♦schlägt | schlug | geschlagen |
| **schleichen*** | schleichst♦schleicht | schlich | geschlichen |
| **schleifen** | schleifst♦schleift | schliff | geschliffen |
| **schließen** | schließt♦schließt | schloß | geschlossen |
| **schlingen** | schlingst♦ schlingt | schlang | geschlungen |
| **schmeißen** | schmeißt♦schmeißt | schmiß | geschmissen |
| **schmelzen*** | schmilzt♦schmilzt | schmolz | geschmolzen |
| **schneiden** | schneidest♦schneidet | schnitt | geschnitten |
| **schreiben** | schreibst♦schreibt | schrieb | geschrieben |
| **schreien** | schreist♦schreit | schrie | geschrie(e)n |
| **schreiten** | schreitest♦schreitet | schritt | geschritten |
| **schweigen** | schweigst♦schweigt | schwieg | geschwiegen |
| **schwellen*** | schwillst♦schwillt | schwoll | geschwollen |
| **schwimmen*** | schwimmst♦schwimmt | schwamm | geschwommen |
| **schwinden*** | schwindest♦schwindet | schwand | geschwunden |
| **schwingen** | schwingst♦schwingt | schwang | geschwungen |
| **schwören** | schwörst♦schwört | schwor | geschworen |
| **sehen** | siehst♦sieht | sah | gesehen |
| **sein*** | bist♦ist | war | gewesen |
| **senden** | sendest♦sendet | sandte | gesandt |
| **singen** | singst♦singt | sang | gesungen |
| **sinken*** | sinkst♦sinkt | sank | gesunken |
| **sinnen** | sinnst♦sinnt | sann | gesonnen |
| **sitzen*** | sitzt♦sitzt | saß | gesessen |
| **sollen** | sollst♦soll | sollte | gesollt |
| **speien** | speist♦speit | spie | gespie(e)n |
| **spinnen** | spinnst♦spinnt | spann | gesponnen |
| **sprechen** | sprichst♦spricht | sprach | gesprochen |
| **sprießen*** | sprießt♦sprießt | sproß | gesprossen |
| **springen*** | springst♦springt | sprang | gesprungen |
| **stechen** | stichst♦sticht | stach | gestochen |
| **stecken** | steckst♦steckt | steckte *od* stak | gesteckt |
| **stehen** | stehst♦steht | stand | gestanden |
| **stehlen** | stiehlst♦stiehlt | stahl | gestohlen |
| **steigen*** | steigst♦steigt | stieg | gestiegen |
| **sterben*** | stirbst♦stirbt | starb | gestorben |

| Infinitive | Present Indicative<br>2nd pers sing ♦ 3rd<br>pers sing | Imperfect<br>Indicative | Past<br>Participle |
|---|---|---|---|
| **stinken** | stinkst ♦ stinkt | stank | gestunken |
| **stoßen** | stößt ♦ stößt | stieß | gestoßen |
| **streichen** | streichst ♦ streicht | strich | gestrichen |
| **streiten** | streitest ♦ streitet | stritt | gestritten |
| **tragen** | trägst ♦ trägt | trug | getragen |
| **treffen** | triffst ♦ trifft | traf | getroffen |
| **treiben\*** | treibst ♦ treibt | trieb | getrieben |
| **treten\*** | trittst ♦ tritt | trat | getreten |
| **trinken** | trinkst ♦ trinkt | trank | getrunken |
| **trügen** | trügst ♦ trügt | trog | getrogen |
| **tun** | tust ♦ tut | tat | getan |
| **verderben** | verdirbst ♦ verdirbt | verdarb | verdorben |
| **verdrießen** | verdrießt ♦ verdrießt | verdroß | verdrossen |
| **vergessen** | vergißt ♦ vergißt | vergaß | vergessen |
| **verlieren** | verlierst ♦ verliert | verlor | verloren |
| **verschleißen** | verschleißt ♦ verschleißt | verschliß | verschlissen |
| **wachsen\*** | wächst ♦ wächst | wuchs | gewachsen |
| **wägen** | wägst ♦ wägt | wog | gewogen |
| **waschen** | wäschst ♦ wäscht | wusch | gewaschen |
| **weben** | webst ♦ webt | webte od wob | gewoben |
| **weichen\*** | weichst ♦ weicht | wich | gewichen |
| **weisen** | weist ♦ weist | wies | gewiesen |
| **wenden** | wendest ♦ wendet | wendete | gewendet |
| **werben** | wirbst ♦ wirbt | warb | geworben |
| **werden\*** | wirst ♦ wird | wurde | geworden |
| **werfen** | wirfst ♦ wirft | warf | geworfen |
| **wiegen** | wiegst ♦ wiegt | wog | gewogen |
| **winden** | windest ♦ windet | wand | gewunden |
| **wissen** | weißt ♦ weiß | wußte | gewußt |
| **wollen** | willst ♦ will | wollte | gewollt |
| **wringen** | wringst ♦ wringt | wrang | gewrungen |
| **zeihen** | zeihst ♦ zeiht | zieh | geziehen |
| **ziehen\*** | ziehst ♦ zieht | zog | gezogen |
| **zwingen** | zwingst ♦ zwingt | zwang | gezwungen |

For additional information on German verb formation, see pp 6-97 of Grammar section.

# GERMAN SPELLING CHANGES

In July 1996, all German–speaking countries signed a declaration concerning the reform of German spelling, with the result that the new spelling rules can now be taught in all schools. To ensure that you have the most up–to–date information at your fingertips, the following list contains the old and new spellings of all German headwords in this dictionary which are affected by the reform.

| ALT/OLD | NEU/NEW | ALT/OLD | NEU/NEW |
|---|---|---|---|
| abend | Abend | aufeinanderfolgend | aufeinander folgend |
| **Abfluß** | Abfluss | **aufeinanderlegen** | aufeinander legen |
| **Abflußrohr** | Abflussrohr | **aufeinanderprallen** | aufeinander prallen |
| **Abguß** | Abguss | **Aufgußbeutel** | Aufgussbeutel |
| **Abriß** | Abriss | **Aufschluß** | Aufschluss |
| **Abschluß** | Abschluss | aufschlußreich | aufschlussreich |
| **Abschlußfeier** | Abschlussfeier | aufsehenerregend | Aufsehen erregend |
| **Abschlußprüfung** | Abschlussprüfung | aufsein | auf sein |
| **Abschlußrechnung** | Abschlussrechnung | aufwärtsgehen | aufwärts gehen |
| **Abschlußzeugnis** | Abschlusszeugnis | aufwendig | aufwendig |
| **Abschuß** | Abschuss | | or aufwändig |
| **Abschußliste** | Abschussliste | auseinanderbringen | auseinander bringen |
| **Abschußrampe** | Abschussrampe | auseinanderfallen | auseinander fallen |
| **Abszeß** | Abszess | auseinandergehen | auseinander gehen |
| Abtreibungsparagraph | Abtreibungsparagraph | auseinanderhalten | auseinander halten |
| | or Abtreibungsparagraf | auseinanderklaffen | auseinander klaffen |
| abwärtsgehen | abwärts gehen | auseinanderlaufen | auseinander laufen |
| **Adhäsionsverschluß** | Adhäsionsverschluss | auseinanderleben | auseinander leben |
| **Adreßbuch** | Adressbuch | auseinandernehmen | auseinander nehmen |
| alleinerziehend | allein erziehend | auseinandersetzen | auseinander setzen |
| **Alleinerziehende(r)** | Alleinerziehende(r) | **Ausfluß** | Ausfluss |
| | or allein Erziehende(r) | **Ausguß** | Ausguss |
| alleinstehend | allein stehend | **Ausschluß** | Ausschluss |
| allgemeingültig | allgemein gültig | **Ausschuß** | Ausschuss |
| allgemeinverständlich | allgemein verständlich | aussein | aus sein |
| allzugern | allzu gern | außerstande | außerstande |
| allzuviel | allzu viel | | or außer Stande |
| alphanumerisch | alphanummerisch | Autobiographie | Autobiographie |
| Alptraum | Alptraum | | or Autobiografie |
| | or Albtraum | **Baß** | Bass |
| **Amboß** | Amboss | **Baßschlüssel** | Bassschlüssel |
| **Amtsmißbrauch** | Amtsmissbrauch | | or Bass–Schlüssel |
| Andersdenkende(r) | Andersdenkende(r) | **Baßstimme** | Bassstimme |
| | or anders Denkende(r) | | or Bass–Stimme |
| andersgläubig | anders gläubig | beieinandersein | beieinander sein |
| anderslautend | anders lautend | beifallheischend | Beifall heischend |
| aneinanderfügen | aneinander fügen | bekanntgeben | bekannt geben |
| aneinandergeraten | aneinander geraten | bekanntmachen | bekannt machen |
| angepaßt | angepasst | belemmert | belämmert |
| **Anlaß** | Anlass | **Beschiß** | Beschiss |
| anläßlich | anlässlich | **Beschluß** | Beschluss |
| **Anschiß** | Anschiss | beschlußfähig | beschlussfähig |
| **Anschluß** | Anschluss | **Beschuß** | Beschuss |
| ansein | an sein | bestehenbleiben | bestehen bleiben |
| As | Ass | bewußt | bewusst |
| aufeinanderfolgen | aufeinander folgen | bewußtlos | bewusstlos |

| ALT/OLD | NEU/NEW | ALT/OLD | NEU/NEW |
|---|---|---|---|
| **Bewußtlosigkeit** | Bewusstlosigkeit | **Differentialrechnung** | Differentialrechnung |
| **bewußtmachen** | bewußt machen | | or Differenzialrechnung |
| **Bewußtsein** | Bewusstsein | **Diktaphon** | Diktaphon |
| **Bewußtseinsbildung** | Bewusstseinsbildung | | or Diktafon |
| **bewußtseinserweiternd** | bewusstseinserweiternd | **dreiviertel** | drei Viertel |
| **Bewußtseinserweiterung** | | **dünngesät** | dünn gesät |
| | Bewusstseinserweiterung | **Dünnschiß** | Dünnschiss |
| **Bibliographie** | Bibliographie | **durcheinanderbringen** | durcheinander bringen |
| | or Bibliografie | **durcheinanderreden** | durcheinander reden |
| **Biographie** | Biographie | **durcheinanderwerfen** | durcheinander werfen |
| | or Biografie | **durchnumerieren** | durchnummerieren |
| **Biß** | Biss | **Durchschuß** | Durchschuss |
| **bißchen** | bisschen | **dußlig** | dusslig |
| **blaß** | blass | **ebensogut** | ebenso gut |
| **bleibenlassen** | bleiben lassen | **ebensooft** | ebenso oft |
| **blindschreiben** | blind schreiben | **ebensoviel** | ebenso viel |
| **Bluterguß** | Bluterguss | **ebensowenig** | ebenso wenig |
| **Boß** | Boss | **ehrfurchtgebietend** | Ehrfurcht gebietend |
| **braungebrannt** | braun gebrannt | **einbleuen** | einbläuen |
| **breitgefächert** | breit gefächert | **Einfluß** | Einfluss |
| **breitmachen** | breit machen | **Einflußbereich** | Einflussbereich |
| **Büroschluß** | Büroschluss | **einflußreich** | einflussreich |
| **Chicorée** | Chicorée | **Einlaß** | Einlass |
| | or Schikoree | **Einsendeschluß** | Einsendeschluss |
| **Choreograph** | Choreograph | **ekelerregend** | Ekel erregend |
| | or Choreograf | **Elsaß** | Elsass |
| **Choreographie** | Choreographie | **Engpaß** | Engpass |
| | or Choreografie | **Entschluß** | Entschluss |
| **Coupé** | Coupé | **entschlußfreudig** | entschlussfreudig |
| | or Kupee | **Entschlußkraft** | Entschlusskraft |
| **dabeisein** | dabei sein | **epochemachend** | Epoche machend |
| **Dachgeschoß** | Dachgeschoss | **Erdgeschoß** | Erdgeschoss |
| **dafürkönnen** | dafür können | **Erdnuß** | Erdnuss |
| **dahinterklemmen** | dahinter klemmen | **erfolgversprechend** | Erfolg versprechend |
| **dahinterknien** | dahinter knien | **Erguß** | Erguss |
| **dahinterkommen** | dahinter kommen | **Erlaß** | Erlass |
| **danebensein** | daneben sein | **ernstgemeint** | ernst gemeint |
| **darauffolgend** | darauf folgend | **erstemal** | erste Mal |
| **darüberliegen** | darüber liegen | **eßbar** | essbar |
| **darunterfallen** | darunter fallen | **Eßgeschirr** | Essgeschirr |
| **daruntermischen** | darunter mischen | **Eßkastanie** | Esskastanie |
| **daruntersetzen** | darunter setzen | **Eßlöffel** | Esslöffel |
| **dasein** | da sein | **Eßtisch** | Esstisch |
| **daß** | dass | **Eßwaren** | Esswaren |
| **Dekolleté** | Dekolleté | **Eßzimmer** | Esszimmer |
| | or Dekolletee | **existentiell** | existentiell |
| **Delphin** | Delphin | | or existenziell |
| | or Delfin | **Expreßgut** | Expressgut |
| **Delphinschwimmen** | Delphinschwimmen | **Expreßzug** | Expresszug |
| | or Delfinschwimmen | **Exzeß** | Exzess |
| **Demographie** | Demographie | **fallenlassen** | fallen lassen |
| | or Demografie | **Familienanschluß** | Familienanschluss |
| **deplaziert** | deplatziert | **Faß** | Fass |
| **dessenungeachtet** | dessen ungeachtet | **faßbar** | fassbar |
| **diät** | Diät | **Faßbier** | Fassbier |
| **dichtbevölkert** | dicht bevölkert | **faßlich** | fasslich |
| **diensthabend** | Dienst habend | **Fehlschluß** | Fehlschluss |
| **diensttuend** | Dienst tuend | **fernhalten** | fern halten |

| ALT/OLD | NEU/NEW | ALT/OLD | NEU/NEW |
|---|---|---|---|
| fernliegen | fern liegen | Grammophon | Grammophon |
| fertigbringen | fertig bringen | | or Grammofon |
| fertigmachen | fertig machen | Graphik | Graphik |
| fertigstellen | fertig stellen | | or Grafik |
| festangestellt | fest angestellt | graphisch | graphisch |
| Filmriß | Filmriss | | or grafisch |
| flötengehen | flöten gehen | gräßlich | grässlich |
| Fluß | Fluss | graumeliert | grau meliert |
| flußab(wärts) | flussab(wärts) | Greuel | Gräuel |
| Flußdiagramm | Flussdiagramm | Greuelpropaganda | Gräuelpropaganda |
| flüssigmachen | flüssig machen | Greueltat | Gräueltat |
| Flußmündung | Flussmündung | greulich | gräulich |
| Flußpferd | Flusspferd | großangelegt | groß angelegt |
| Fön ® | Föhn | Grundriß | Grundriss |
| | or Fön ® | Gummigeschoß | Gummigeschoss |
| fönen | föhnen | Gummiparagraph | Gummiparagraph |
| Friedensschluß | Friedensschluss | | or Gummiparagraf |
| Friteuse | Fritteuse | Guß | Guss |
| fritieren | frittieren | Gußeisen | Gusseisen |
| frühauf | früh auf | gutgehen | gut gehen |
| frühzeitig | früh zeitig | gutgehend | gut gehend |
| Gebiß | Gebiss | gutgelaunt | gut gelaunt |
| Gebührenerlaß | Gebührenerlass | gutgemeint | gut gemeint |
| gefangenhalten | gefangen halten | gutsituiert | gut situiert |
| gefangennehmen | gefangen nehmen | guttun | gut tun |
| gefaßt | gefasst | gutunterrichtet | gut unterrichtet |
| geheimhalten | geheim halten | haftenbleiben | haften bleiben |
| Geheimtip | Geheimtipp | halboffen | halb offen |
| gehenlassen | gehen lassen | haltmachen | Halt machen |
| Gemse | Gämse | Hämorrhoiden | Hämorrhoiden |
| gemußt | gemusst | | or Hämorriden |
| genaugenommen | genau genommen | Handkuß | Handkuss |
| Genuß | Genuss | hängenbleiben | hängen bleiben |
| genüßlich | genüsslich | hängenlassen | hängen lassen |
| Genußmittel | Genussmittel | Hängeschloß | Hängeschloss |
| Geograph | Geograph | hartgekocht | hart gekocht |
| | or Geograf | Haselnuß | Haselnuss |
| Geographie | Geographie | Haß | Hass |
| | or Geografie | häßlich | hässlich |
| geographisch | geographisch | Häßlichkeit | Hässlichkeit |
| | or geografisch | Haßliebe | Hassliebe |
| geringachten | gering achten | haushalten | haushalten |
| Geschäftsabschluß | Geschäftsabschluss | | or Haus halten |
| Geschäftsschluß | Geschäftsschluss | heiligsprechen | heilig sprechen |
| Geschoß | Geschoss | heißersehnt | heiß ersehnt |
| gewinnbringend | Gewinn bringend | heißumstritten | heiß umstritten |
| gewiß | gewiss | hellicht | helllicht |
| Gewißheit | Gewissheit | heraussein | heraus sein |
| gewißlich | gewisslich | hersein | her sein |
| gewußt | gewusst | heruntersein | herunter sein |
| glattgehen | glatt gehen | Hexenschuß | Hexenschuss |
| glattrasiert | glatt rasiert | hierbehalten | hier behalten |
| glattstreichen | glatt streichen | hierbleiben | hier bleiben |
| gleichbleibend | gleich bleibend | hierhergehören | hierher gehören |
| gleichgesinnt | gleich gesinnt | hierlassen | hier lassen |
| gleichgestellt | gleich gestellt | hierzulande | hier zu Lande |
| gleichlautend | gleich lautend | hinsein | hin sein |
| Glimmstengel | Glimmstängel | hinterhersein | hinterher sein |

| ALT/OLD | NEU/NEW | ALT/OLD | NEU/NEW |
|---|---|---|---|
| **hochachten** | hoch achten | **Kreppapier** | Krepppapier |
| **hochbegabt** | hoch begabt | | or Krepp–Papier |
| **hochdotiert** | hoch dotiert | **krummnehmen** | krumm nehmen |
| **hochempfindlich** | hoch empfindlich | **kurzgefaßt** | kurz gefasst |
| **hochentwickelt** | hoch entwickelt | **kurzhalten** | kurz halten |
| **Hochgenuß** | Hochgenuss | **Kurzschluß** | Kurzschluss |
| **hochgestellt** | hoch gestellt | **kurztreten** | kurz treten |
| **Hochschulabschluß** | Hochschulabschluss | **Kuß** | Kuss |
| **Ich-Roman** | Ichroman | **Ladenschluß** | Ladenschluss |
| **Imbiß** | Imbiss | **langersehnt** | lang ersehnt |
| **Imbißhalle** | Imbisshalle | **läßlich** | lässlich |
| **Imbißstube** | Imbissstube | **Laufpaß** | Laufpass |
| | or Imbiss–Stube | **leerstehend** | leer stehend |
| **Impfpaß** | Impfpass | **leichtfallen** | leicht fallen |
| **imstande** | imstande | **leichtmachen** | leicht machen |
| | or im Stande | **leichtnehmen** | leicht nehmen |
| **ineinandergreifen** | ineinander greifen | **leichtverletzt** | leicht verletzt |
| **Ist-Bestand** | Istbestand | **Lexikographie** | Lexikographie |
| **Jahresabschluß** | Jahresabschluss | | or Lexikografie |
| **Joghurt** | Joghurt | **Lichtmeß** | Lichtmess |
| | or Jogurt | **liebgewinnen** | lieb gewinnen |
| **Kabelanschluß** | Kabelanschluss | **liebhaben** | lieb haben |
| **kahlfressen** | kahl fressen | **liegenbleiben** | liegen bleiben |
| **kahlgeschoren** | kahl geschoren | **liegenlassen** | liegen lassen |
| **kaltbleiben** | kalt bleiben | **Litfaßsäule** | Litfasssäule |
| **kaltlächelnd** | kalt lächelnd | | or Litfass–Säule |
| **Känguruh** | Känguru | **Lithographie** | Lithographie |
| **Karamel** | Karamell | | or Lithografie |
| **Katarrh** | Katarrh | **Luftschloß** | Luftschloss |
| | or Katarr | **maschineschreiben** | Maschine schreiben |
| **Kellergeschoß** | Kellergeschoss | **maßhalten** | Maß halten |
| **keß** | kess | **Megaphon** | Megaphon |
| **Kindesmißhandlung** | Kindesmisshandlung | | or Megafon |
| **klarsehen** | klar sehen | **Meßband** | Messband |
| **klarwerden** | klar werden | **meßbar** | messbar |
| **Klassenbewußtsein** | Klassenbewusstsein | **Meßbecher** | Messbecher |
| **klatschnaß** | klatschnass | **Meßbuch** | Messbuch |
| **kleinhacken** | klein hacken | **Meßdiener** | Messdiener |
| **kleinschneiden** | klein schneiden | **Meßgerät** | Messgerät |
| **Klettverschluß** | Klettverschluss | **Meßgewand** | Messgewand |
| **knapphalten** | knapp halten | **Meßstab** | Messstab |
| **Kokosnuß** | Kokosnuss | | or Mess–Stab |
| **Koloß** | Koloss | **Meßwert** | Messwert |
| **Kombinationsschloß** | Kombinationsschloss | **metallverarbeitend** | Metall verarbeitend |
| **Kommiß** | Kommiss | **Mikrophon** | Mikrophon |
| **Kommißbrot** | Kommissbrot | | or Mikrofon |
| **Kommuniqué** | Kommuniqué | **mißachten** | missachten |
| | or Kommunikee | **Mißachtung** | Missachtung |
| **Kompaß** | Kompass | **Mißbehagen** | Missbehagen |
| **Kompromiß** | Kompromiss | **Mißbildung** | Missbildung |
| **kompromißbereit** | kompromissbereit | **mißbilligen** | missbilligen |
| **Kompromißlösung** | Kompromisslösung | **Mißbilligung** | Missbilligung |
| **Kongreß** | Kongress | **Mißbrauch** | Missbrauch |
| **Kontrabaß** | Kontrabass | **mißbrauchen** | missbrauchen |
| **Kontrollampe** | Kontrolllampe | **mißdeuten** | missdeuten |
| | or Kontroll–Lampe | **Mißerfolg** | Misserfolg |
| **kraß** | krass | **Mißernte** | Missernte |
| **krebserregend** | Krebs erregend | **mißfallen** | missfallen |

| ALT/OLD | NEU/NEW | ALT/OLD | NEU/NEW |
|---|---|---|---|
| Mißfallen | Missfallen | nebeneinanderlegen | nebeneinander legen |
| Mißgeburt | Missgeburt | Nebenfluß | Nebenfluss |
| Mißgeschick | Missgeschick | Necessaire | Necessaire |
| mißglücken | missglücken | | or Nessessär |
| mißgönnen | missgönnen | Negerkuß | Negerkuss |
| Mißgriff | M.ssgriff | Netzanschluß | Netzanschluss |
| Mißgunst | Missgunst | neueröffnet | neu eröffnet |
| mißgünstig | missgünstig | neugeboren | neu geboren |
| mißhandeln | misshandeln | nichtrostend | nicht rostend |
| Mißhandlung | Misshandlung | nichtsahnend | nichts ahnend |
| Mißhelligkeit | Misshelligkeit | nichtssagend | nichts sagend |
| Mißklang | Missklang | notleidend | Not leidend |
| Mißkredit | Misskredit | numerieren | nummerieren |
| mißliebig | missliebig | numerisch | nummerisch |
| mißlingen | misslingen | Nuß | Nuss |
| Mißlingen | Misslingen | Nußbaum | Nussbaum |
| mißlungen | misslungen | Nußknacker | Nussknacker |
| Mißmut | Missmut | obenerwähnt | oben erwähnt |
| mißmutig | missmutig | Obergeschoß | Obergeschoss |
| mißraten | missraten | offenbleiben | offen bleiben |
| Mißstand | Missstand | offenhalten | offen halten |
| | or Miss–Stand | offenlassen | offen lassen |
| Mißstimmung | Missstimmung | offenstehen | offen stehen |
| | or Miss–Stimmung | Ölmeßstab | Ölmessstab |
| mißtrauen | misstrauen | | or Ölmess–Stab |
| Mißtrauen | Misstrauen | Orthographie | Orthographie |
| Mißtrauensantrag | Misstrauensantrag | | or Orthografie |
| Mißtrauensvotum | Misstrauensvotum | orthographisch | orthographisch |
| mißtrauisch | misstrauisch | | or orthografisch |
| Mißverhältnis | Missverhältnis | Panther | Panther |
| mißverständlich | missverständlich | | or Panter |
| Mißverständnis | Missverständnis | Pappmaché | Pappmaché |
| mißverstehen | missverstehen | | or Pappmaschee |
| Mißwahl | Misswahl | Paragraph | Paragraph |
| Mißwirtschaft | Misswirtschaft | | or Paragraf |
| mittag | Mittag | Paragraphenreiter | Paragraphenreiter |
| Muß | Muss | | or Paragrafenreiter |
| Mußheirat | Mussheirat | Paranuß | Paranuss |
| Musterprozeß | Musterprozess | Parlamentsausschuß | Parlamentsausschuss |
| nachhinein | Nachhinein | Parlamentsbeschluß | Parlamentsbeschluss |
| Nachlaß | Nachlass | partiell | partiell |
| Nachlaßverwalter | Nachlassverwalter | | or parziell |
| nachmittag | Nachmittag | Paß | Pass |
| nacht | Nacht | Paßamt | Passamt |
| nahebringen | nahe bringen | Paßbild | Passbild |
| nahegehen | nahe gehen | passé | passé |
| nahekommen | nahe kommen | | or passee |
| nahelegen | nahe legen | Paßfoto | Passfoto |
| naheliegen | nahe liegen | Paßkontrolle | Passkontrolle |
| naheliegend | nahe liegend | Paßstelle | Passstelle |
| näherkommen | näher kommen | | or Pass–Stelle |
| nahestehen | nahe stehen | Paßstraße | Passstraße |
| narzißtisch | narzisstisch | | or Pass–Straße |
| naß | nass | Paßzwang | Passzwang |
| naßkalt | nasskalt | patschnaß | patschnass |
| Naßrasur | Nassrasur | pflichtbewußt | pflichtbewusst |
| Nebelschlußleuchte | Nebelschlussleuchte | Pflichtbewußtsein | Pflichtbewusstsein |
| Nebenanschluß | Nebenanschluss | Phantasie | Phantasie |

| ALT/OLD | NEU/NEW | ALT/OLD | NEU/NEW |
|---|---|---|---|
| | *or* Fantasie | **Roß** | Ross |
| **Phantasiegebilde** | Phantasiegebilde | **Roßkastanie** | Rosskastanie |
| | *or* Fantasiegebilde | **Roßkur** | Rosskur |
| **phantasielos** | phantasielos | **Rückschluß** | Rückschluss |
| | *or* fantasielos | **Rußland** | Russland |
| **phantasieren** | phantasieren | **Sammelanschluß** | Sammelanschluss |
| | *or* fantasieren | **sauberhalten** | sauber halten |
| **phantasievoll** | phantasievoll | **saubermachen** | sauber machen |
| | *or* fantasievoll | **Sauregurkenzeit** | Saure-Gurken-Zeit |
| **Phantast** | Phantast | **Saxophon** | Saxophon |
| | *or* Fantast | | *or* Saxofon |
| **phantastisch** | phantastisch | **Schattenriß** | Schattenriss |
| | *or* fantastisch | **schätzenlernen** | schätzen lernen |
| **pitsch(e)naß** | pitsch(e)nass | **Schauprozeß** | Schauprozess |
| **Platitüde** | Platitüde | **Schenke** | Schenke |
| | *or* Plattitüde | | *or* Schänke |
| **platschnaß** | platschnass | **schiefgehen** | schief gehen |
| **plazieren** | platzieren | **schiefliegen** | schief liegen |
| **Pornographie** | Pornographie | **Schiß** | Schiss |
| | *or* Pornografie | **Schlangenbiß** | Schlangenbiss |
| **pornographisch** | pornographisch | **schlechtgehen** | schlecht gehen |
| | *or* pornografisch | **schlechtmachen** | schlecht machen |
| **Portemonnaie** | Portemonnaie | **Schlegel** | Schlägel |
| | *or* Portmonee | **Schloß** | Schloss |
| **Potential** | Potential | **Schloßhund** | Schlosshund |
| | *or* Potenzial | **Schluß** | Schluss |
| **potentiell** | potentiell | **Schlußfolgerung** | Schlussfolgerung |
| | *or* potenziell | **Schlußformel** | Schlussformel |
| **potthäßlich** | potthässlich | **Schlußlicht** | Schlusslicht |
| **Preisnachlaß** | Preisnachlass | **Schlußstrich** | Schlussstrich |
| **Preßluft** | Pressluft | | *or* Schluss-Strich |
| **Preßluftbohrer** | Pressluftbohrer | **Schlußverkauf** | Schlussverkauf |
| **Prozeß** | Prozess | **Schlußwort** | Schlusswort |
| **Prozeßführung** | Prozessführung | **Schmiß** | Schmiss |
| **Prozeßkosten** | Prozesskosten | **Schnappschloß** | Schnappschloss |
| **Prüfungsausschuß** | Prüfungsausschuss | **Schnappschuß** | Schnappschuss |
| **Pulverfaß** | Pulverfass | **Schnellimbiß** | Schnellimbiss |
| **quergestreift** | quer gestreift | **schneuzen** | schnäuzen |
| **querlegen** | quer legen | **Schößling** | Schössling |
| **radfahren** | Rad fahren | **Schreckschuß** | Schreckschuss |
| **Rassenhaß** | Rassenhass | **schuld** | Schuld |
| **ratsuchend** | Rat suchend | **schuldbewußt** | schuldbewusst |
| **rauh** | rau | **Schuß** | Schuss |
| **rauhbeinig** | raubeinig | **Schußbereich** | Schussbereich |
| **Rauhfasertapete** | Raufasertapete | **Schußlinie** | Schusslinie |
| **rauhhaarig** | rauhaarig | **Schußverletzung** | Schussverletzung |
| **Rauhreif** | Raureif | **Schußwaffe** | Schusswaffe |
| **raumsparend** | Raum sparend | **Schußwaffengebrauch** | Schusswaffengebrauch |
| **Redaktionsschluß** | Redaktionsschluss | **Schußwechsel** | Schusswechsel |
| **Regenguß** | Regenguss | **Schußweite** | Schussweite |
| **Regreß** | Regress | **schwererziehbar** | schwer erziehbar |
| **Regreßanspruch** | Regressanspruch | **schwerfallen** | schwer fallen |
| **reinwaschen** | rein waschen | **schwermachen** | schwer machen |
| **Reisepaß** | Reisepass | **schwernehmen** | schwer nehmen |
| **richtigstellen** | richtig stellen | **schwertun** | schwer tun |
| **Riß** | Riss | **schwerverdaulich** | schwer verdaulich |
| **Rommé** | Rommé | **schwerverdient** | schwer verdient |
| | *or* Rommee | **schwerverletzt** | schwer verletzt |

| ALT/OLD | NEU/NEW | ALT/OLD | NEU/NEW |
|---|---|---|---|
| schwerverwundet | schwer verwundet | Strafprozeßordnung | Strafprozessordnung |
| schwindelerregend | Schwindel erregend | Streifschuß | Streifschuss |
| seinlassen | sein lassen | strenggenommen | streng genommen |
| Seismograph | Seismograph | Streß | Stress |
|  | or Seismograf | streßfrei | stressfrei |
| selbständig | selbständig | Stromanschluß | Stromanschluss |
|  | or selbstständig | Stukkateur | Stuckateur |
| Selbständigkeit | Selbständigkeit | Stuß | Stuss |
|  | or Selbstständigkeit | suchterzeugend | Sucht erzeugend |
| selbstbewußt | selbstbewusst | Tankverschluß | Tankverschluss |
| Selbstbewußtsein | Selbstbewusstsein | Telegraph | Telegraph |
| selbstgemacht | selbst gemacht |  | or Telegraf |
| selbstgestrickt | selbst gestrickt | Thunfisch | Thunfisch |
| selbstverdient | selbst verdient |  | or Tunfisch |
| selbstverschuldet | selbst verschuldet | tiefgreifend | tief greifend |
| selbstverständlich | selbst verständlich | tiefschürfend | tief schürfend |
| Sendeschluß | Sendeschluss | Tintenfaß | Tintenfass |
| Seniorenpaß | Seniorenpass | Tip | Tipp |
| sequentiell | sequentiell | topographisch | topographisch |
|  | or sequenziell |  | or topografisch |
| seßhaft | sesshaft | Toresschluß | Toresschluss |
| Sicherheitsschloß | Sicherheitsschloss | Torschlußpanik | Torschlusspanik |
| Sicherheitsverschluß | Sicherheitsverschluss | Tortenguß | Tortenguss |
| sitzenbleiben | sitzen bleiben | totenblaß | totenblass |
| sitzenlassen | sitzen lassen | totgeboren | tot geboren |
| Sommerschlußverkauf | Sommerschlussverkauf | tropfnaß | tropfnass |
| sonstjemand | sonst jemand | Trugschluß | Trugschluss |
| sonstwas | sonst was | tschüs | tschüs |
| sonstwo | sonst wo |  | or tschüss |
| sonstwohin | sonst wohin | übelgelaunt | übel gelaunt |
| Spaghetti | Spaghetti | übelnehmen | übel nehmen |
|  | or Spagetti | Überdruß | Überdruss |
| spazierenfahren | spazieren fahren | übereinanderschlagen | übereinander schlagen |
| spazierengehen | spazieren gehen | Überfluß | Überfluss |
| Sproß | Spross | Überflußgesellschaft | Überflussgesellschaft |
| Sprößling | Sprössling | überhandnehmen | überhand nehmen |
| Standesbewußtsein | Standesbewusstsein | Überschuß | Überschuss |
| Statt | statt | überschwenglich | überschwänglich |
| steckenbleiben | stecken bleiben | Überschwenglichkeit | Überschwänglichkeit |
| steckenlassen | stecken lassen | übrigbleiben | übrig bleiben |
| stehenbleiben | stehen bleiben | übriglassen | übrig lassen |
| stehenlassen | stehen lassen | Umriß | Umriss |
| Steilpaß | Steilpass | Umweltbewußtsein | Umweltbewusstsein |
| Stengel | Stängel | unangepaßt | unangepasst |
| Stenograph | Stenograph | unbewußt | unbewusst |
|  | or Stenograf | unerläßlich | unerlässlich |
| Stenographie | Stenographie | unermeßlich | unermesslich |
|  | or Stenografie | unfaßbar | unfassbar |
| stenographieren | stenographieren | ungewiß | ungewiss |
|  | or stenografieren | Ungewißheit | Ungewissheit |
| Steptanz | Stepptanz | unheilbringend | Unheil bringend |
| Stewardeß | Stewardess | unmißverständlich | unmissverständlich |
| stiftengehen | stiften gehen | unpäßlich | unpässlich |
| Stilleben | Stillleben | unselbständig | unselbständig |
|  | or Still–Leben |  | or unselbstständig |
| Stillegung | Stilllegung | untengenannt | unten genannt |
|  | or Still–Legung | Unterbewußtsein | Unterbewusstsein |
| stillhalten | still halten | unterderhand | unter der Hand |

| ALT/OLD | NEU/NEW | ALT/OLD | NEU/NEW |
|---|---|---|---|
| Untergeschoß | Untergeschoss | wiedervereinigen | wieder vereinigen |
| Untersuchungsausschuß | | wieviel | wie viel |
| | Untersuchungsausschuss | Winterschlußverkauf | Winterschlussverkauf |
| unvergeßlich | unvergesslich | Wirtschaftsgeographie | Wirtschaftsgeographie |
| verantwortungsbewußt | verantwortungsbewusst | | or Wirtschaftsgeografie |
| Verdruß | Verdruss | Wißbegier(de) | Wissbegier(de) |
| vergeßlich | vergesslich | wißbegierig | wissbegierig |
| Vergeßlichkeit | Vergesslichkeit | wohlgemeint | wohl gemeint |
| Vergißmeinnicht | Vergissmeinnicht | wohltun | wohl tun |
| verhaßt | verhasst | Wurfgeschoß | Wurfgeschoss |
| Verlaß | Verlass | Xerographie | Xerographie |
| verläßlich | verlässlich | | or Xerografie |
| verlorengehen | verloren gehen | Xylophon | Xylophon |
| Vermißte(r) | Vermisste(r) | | or Xylofon |
| Vermißtenanzeige | Vermisstenanzeige | Zahlenschloß | Zahlenschloss |
| Verriß | Verriss | zartbesaitet | zart besaitet |
| Verschluß | Verschluss | Zeitlang | Zeit lang |
| verselbständigen | verselbständigen | zielbewußt | zielbewusst |
| | or verselbstständigen | Zuckerguß | Zuckerguss |
| vertrauenerweckend | Vertrauen erweckend | Zufluß | Zufluss |
| vielbeschäftigt | viel beschäftigt | zufriedengeben | zufrieden geben |
| vielgeprüft | viel geprüft | zufriedenlassen | zufrieden lassen |
| vielsagend | viel sagend | zufriedenstellen | zufrieden stellen |
| vielversprechend | viel versprechend | zugrunde | zugrunde |
| vollbringen | voll bringen | | or zu Grunde |
| vollmachen | voll machen | zugunsten | zugunsten |
| vollschreiben | voll schreiben | | or zu Gunsten |
| volltanken | voll tanken | zulande | zu Lande |
| vorgefaßt | vorgefasst | zuleide | zuleide |
| Vorhängeschloß | Vorhängeschloss | | or zu Leide |
| vorhinein | Vorhinein | zumute | zumute |
| vorliebnehmen | vorlieb nehmen | | or zu Mute |
| Vorschuß | Vorschuss | zunutze | zunutze |
| vorwärtsgehen | vorwärts gehen | | or zu Nutze |
| vorwärtskommen | vorwärts kommen | Zusammenfluß | Zusammenfluss |
| Waggon | Waggon | Zusammenschluß | Zusammenschluss |
| | or Wagon | zuschulden | zuschulden |
| Walnuß | Walnuss | | or zu Schulden |
| Walroß | Walross | Zuschuß | Zuschuss |
| warmhalten | warm halten | Zuschußbetrieb | Zuschussbetrieb |
| warmlaufen | warm laufen | zusein | zu sein |
| wasserabstoßend | Wasser abstoßend | zustande | zustande |
| weithergeholt | weit hergeholt | | or zu Stande |
| weitreichend | weit reichend | zutage | zutage |
| weitverbreitet | weit verbreitet | | or zu Tage |
| weitverzweigt | weit verzweigt | zuviel | zu viel |
| wiedergutmachen | wieder gutmachen | zuwege | zuwege |
| wiederherstellen | wieder herstellen | | or zu Wege |
| wiedersehen | wieder sehen | zuwenig | zu wenig |

# *A, a*

**A¹, a** [aː] *nt* A, a; ~ **wie Anton** ≈ A for Andrew, A for Able (*US*); **das ~ und O** the be-all and end-all; (*eines Wissensgebietes*) the basics *pl*; **wer ~ sagt, muß auch B sagen** (*Sprichwort*) in for a penny, in for a pound (*Sprichwort*).

**A²** *f abk* (= *Autobahn*) ≈ M (*BRIT*).

**a.** *abk* = **am.**

**à** [aː] *präp* (*bes COMM*) at.

**AA** *nt abk* (= *Auswärtiges Amt*) F.O. (*BRIT*).

**Aachen** [ˈaːxən] (**-s**) *nt* Aachen.

**Aal** [aːl] (**-(e)s, -e**) *m* eel.

**aalen** [ˈaːlən] (*umg*) *vr*: **sich in der Sonne ~** to bask in the sun.

**a.a.O.** *abk* (= *am angegebenen od angeführten Ort*) loc. cit.

**Aas** [aːs] (**-es, -e** *od* **Äser**) *nt* carrion; **~geier** *m* vulture.

=============== *SCHLÜSSELWORT*

**ab** [ap] *präp +dat* from; ~ **Werk** (*COMM*) ex works; **Kinder** ~ **12 Jahren** children from the age of 12; ~ **morgen** from tomorrow; ~ **sofort** as of now

♦ *adv* **1** off; **links** ~ to the left; **der Knopf ist** ~ the button has come off; ~ **nach Hause!** off home with you!; ~ **durch die Mitte!** (*umg*) beat it!

**2** (*zeitlich*): **von da** ~ from then on; **von heute** ~ from today, as of today

**3** (*auf Fahrplänen*): **München** ~ **12.20** leaving Munich 12.20

**4**: ~ **und zu** *od* **an** now and then *od* again.

**abändern** [ˈapˌɛndərn] *vt*: ~ (**in** +*akk*) to alter (to); (*Gesetzentwurf*) to amend (to); (*Strafe, Urteil*) to revise (to).

**Abänderung** *f* alteration; amendment; revision.

**Abänderungsantrag** *m* (*PARL*) proposed amendment.

**abarbeiten** [ˈapˌarbaɪtən] *vr* to slave away.

**Abart** [ˈapˌaːrt] *f* (*BIOL*) variety.

**abartig** *adj* abnormal.

**Abb.** *abk* (= *Abbildung*) illus.

**Abbau** [ˈapbaʊ] (**-(e)s**) *m* (+*gen*) dismantling; (*Verminderung*) reduction (in); (*Verfall*) decline (in); (*MIN*) mining; (*über Tage*) quarrying; (*CHEM*) decomposition.

**abbaubar** *adj*: **biologisch** ~ biodegradable.

**abbauen** *vt* to dismantle; (*verringern*) to reduce; (*MIN*) to mine; to quarry; (*CHEM*) to break down; **Arbeitsplätze** ~ to make job cuts.

**Abbaurechte** *pl* mineral rights *pl*.

**abbeißen** [ˈapbaɪsən] *unreg vt* to bite off.

**abbekommen** [ˈapbəkɔmən] *unreg vt*: **etwas** ~ to get some (of it); (*beschädigt werden*) to get damaged; (*verletzt werden*) to get hurt.

**abberufen** [ˈapbəruːfən] *unreg vt* to recall.

**Abberufung** *f* recall.

**abbestellen** [ˈapbəʃtɛlən] *vt* to cancel.

**abbezahlen** [ˈapbətsaːlən] *vt* to pay off.

**abbiegen** [ˈapbiːgən] *unreg vi* to turn off; (*Straße*) to bend ♦ *vt* to bend; (*verhindern*) to ward off.

**Abbiegespur** *f* turning lane.

**Abbild** [ˈapbɪlt] *nt* portrayal; (*einer Person*) image, likeness; **a~en** [ˈapbɪldən] *vt* to portray; **~ung** *f* illustration; (*Schaubild*) diagram.

**abbinden** [ˈapbɪndən] *unreg vt* (*MED: Arm, Bein etc*) to ligature.

**Abbitte** [ˈapbɪtə] *f*: ~ **leisten** *od* **tun** (**bei**) to make one's apologies (to).

**abblasen** [ˈapblaːzən] *unreg vt* to blow off; (*fig: umg*) to call off.

**abblättern** [ˈapblɛtərn] *vi* (*Putz, Farbe*) to flake (off).

**abblenden** [ˈapblɛndən] *vt* (*AUT*) to dip (*BRIT*), dim (*US*) ♦ *vi* to dip (*BRIT*) *od* dim (*US*) one's headlights.

**Abblendlicht** [ˈapblɛntlɪçt] *nt* dipped (*BRIT*) *od* dimmed (*US*) headlights *pl*.

**abblitzen** ['apblɪtsən] (*umg*) *vi:* **jdn ~ lassen** to send sb packing.

**abbrechen** ['apbrɛçən] *unreg vt* to break off; (*Gebäude*) to pull down; (*Zelt*) to take down; (*aufhören*) to stop; (*COMPUT*) to abort ♦ *vi* to break off; to stop; **sich** *dat* **einen ~** (*umg: sich sehr anstrengen*) to bust a gut.

**abbrennen** ['apbrɛnən] *unreg vt* to burn off; (*Feuerwerk*) to let off ♦ *vi* (*Hilfsverb sein*) to burn down; **abgebrannt sein** (*umg*) to be broke.

**abbringen** ['apbrɪŋən] *unreg vt:* **jdn von etw ~** to dissuade sb from sth; **jdn vom Weg ~** to divert sb; **ich bringe den Verschluß nicht ab** (*umg*) I can't get the top off.

**abbröckeln** ['apbrœkəln] *vi* to crumble off *od* away; (*BÖRSE: Preise*) to ease.

**Abbruch** ['apbrʊx] *m* (*von Verhandlungen etc*) breaking off; (*von Haus*) demolition; (*COMPUT*) abort; **jdm/etw ~ tun** to harm sb/sth; **~arbeiten** *pl* demolition work *sing*; **a~reif** *adj* only fit for demolition.

**abbrühen** ['apbryːən] *vt* to scald.

**abbuchen** ['apbuːxən] *vt* to debit; (*durch Dauerauftrag*): **~ (von)** to pay by standing order (from).

**abbürsten** ['apbʏrstən] *vt* to brush off.

**abbüßen** ['apbyːsən] *vt* (*Strafe*) to serve.

**ABC-Waffen** *pl abk* (= *atomare, biologische und chemische Waffen*) ABC weapons (= *atomic, biological and chemical weapons*).

**abdampfen** ['apdampfən] *vi* (*fig: umg: losgehen/-fahren*) to hit the road.

**abdanken** ['apdaŋkən] *vi* to resign; (*König*) to abdicate.

**Abdankung** *f* resignation; abdication.

**abdecken** ['apdɛkən] *vt* to uncover; (*Tisch*) to clear; (*Loch*) to cover.

**abdichten** ['apdɪçtən] *vt* to seal; (*NAUT*) to caulk.

**abdrängen** ['apdrɛŋən] *vt* to push off.

**abdrehen** ['apdreːən] *vt* (*Gas*) to turn off; (*Licht*) to switch off; (*Film*) to shoot ♦ *vi* (*Schiff*) to change course; **jdm den Hals ~** to wring sb's neck.

**abdriften** ['apdrɪftən] *vi* to drift (away).

**abdrosseln** ['apdrɔsəln] *vt* to throttle; (*AUT*) to stall; (*Produktion*) to cut back.

**Abdruck** ['apdrʊk] *m* (*Nachdrucken*) reprinting; (*Gedrucktes*) reprint; (*Gips~, Wachs~*) impression; (*Finger~*) print; **a~en** *vt* to print.

**abdrücken** ['apdrʏkən] *vt* to make an impression of; (*Waffe*) to fire; (*umg: Person*) to hug, squeeze ♦ *vr* to leave imprints; (*abstoßen*) to push o.s. away; **jdm die Luft ~** to squeeze all the breath out of sb.

**abebben** ['apɛbən] *vi* to ebb away.

**Abend** ['aːbənt] (*-s, -e*) *m* evening; **gegen ~** towards (the) evening; **den ganzen ~ (über)** the whole evening; **zu ~ essen** to have dinner *od* supper; **a~** *adv:* **heute a~** this

evening; **~anzug** *m* dinner jacket (*BRIT*), tuxedo (*US*); **~brot** *nt* supper; **~essen** *nt* supper; **a~füllend** *adj* taking up the whole evening; **~gymnasium** *nt* night school; **~kasse** *f* (*THEAT*) box office; **~kleid** *nt* evening gown; **~kurs** *m* evening classes *pl*; **~land** *nt* West; **a~lich** *adj* evening; **~mahl** *nt* Holy Communion; **~rot** *nt* sunset.

**abends** *adv* in the evening.

**Abend-** *zW:* **~vorstellung** *f* evening performance; **~zeitung** *f* evening paper.

**Abenteuer** ['aːbəntɔyər] (*-s, -*) *nt* adventure; (*Liebes~*) affair; **a~lich** *adj* adventurous; **~spielplatz** *m* adventure playground.

**Abenteurer** (*-s, -*) *m* adventurer; **~in** *f* adventuress.

**aber** ['aːbər] *konj* but; (*jedoch*) however ♦ *adv:* **tausend und ~ tausend** thousands upon thousands; **oder ~** or else; **bist du ~ braun!** aren't you brown!; **das ist ~ schön** that's really nice; **nun ist ~ Schluß!** now that's enough!; **A~** *nt* but.

**Aberglaube** ['aːbərglaʊbə] *m* superstition.

**abergläubisch** ['aːbərglɔybɪʃ] *adj* superstitious.

**aberkennen** ['ap|ɛrkɛnən] *unreg vt:* **jdm etw ~** to deprive sb of sth, take sth (away) from sb.

**Aberkennung** *f* taking away.

**abermalig** *adj* repeated.

**abermals** *adv* once again.

**Abf.** *abk* (= *Abfahrt*) dep.

**abfahren** ['apfaːrən] *unreg vi* to leave, depart ♦ *vt* to take *od* cart away; (*Film*) to start; (*FILM, TV: Kamera*) to roll; (*Strecke*) to drive; (*Reifen*) to wear; (*Fahrkarte*) to use; **der Zug ist abgefahren** (*lit*) the train has left; (*fig*) we've/you've *etc* missed the boat; **der Zug fährt um 8.00 von Bremen ab** the train leaves Bremen at 8 o'clock; **jdn ~ lassen** (*umg: abweisen*) to tell sb to get lost; **auf jdn ~** (*umg*) to really go for sb.

**Abfahrt** ['apfaːrt] *f* departure; (*Autobahn~*) exit; (*SKI*) descent; (*Piste*) run; **Vorsicht bei der ~ des Zuges!** stand clear, the train is about to leave!

**Abfahrts-** *zW:* **~lauf** *m* (*SKI*) downhill; **~tag** *m* day of departure; **~zeit** *f* departure time.

**Abfall** ['apfal] *m* waste; (*von Speisen etc*) rubbish (*BRIT*), garbage (*US*); (*Neigung*) slope; (*Verschlechterung*) decline; **~eimer** *m* rubbish bin (*BRIT*), garbage can (*US*).

**abfallen** *unreg vi* (*lit, fig*) to fall *od* drop off; (*POL, vom Glauben*) to break away; (*sich neigen*) to fall *od* drop away; **wieviel fällt bei dem Geschäft für mich ab?** (*umg*) how much do I get out of the deal?

**abfällig** ['apfɛlɪç] *adj* disparaging, deprecatory.

**Abfallprodukt** *nt* (*lit, fig*) waste product.

**abfangen** ['apfaŋən] *unreg vt* to intercept; (*Person*) to catch; (*unter Kontrolle bringen*) to check; (*Aufprall*) to absorb; (*Kunden*) to lure away.

**Abfangjäger** *m* (*MIL*) interceptor.

**abfärben** ['apfɛrbən] *vi* (*lit*) to lose its colour; (*Wäsche*) to run; (*fig*) to rub off.

**abfassen** ['apfasən] *vt* to write, draft.

**abfeiern** ['apfaɪərn] (*umg*) *vt*: **Überstunden ~** to take time off in lieu of overtime pay.

**abfertigen** ['apfɛrtɪgən] *vt* to prepare for dispatch, process; (*an der Grenze*) to clear; (*Kundschaft*) to attend to; **jdn kurz ~** to give sb short shrift.

**Abfertigung** *f* preparing for dispatch, processing; clearance; (*Bedienung: von Kunden*) service; (: *von Antragstellern*): **~ von** dealing with.

**abfeuern** ['apfɔyərn] *vt* to fire.

**abfinden** ['apfɪndən] *unreg vt* to pay off ♦ *vr* to come to terms; **sich mit jdm ~/nicht ~** to put up with/not to get on with sb; **er konnte sich nie damit ~, daß ...** he could never accept the fact that ...

**Abfindung** *f* (*von Gläubigern*) payment; (*Geld*) sum in settlement.

**abflachen** ['apflaxən] *vt* to level (off), flatten (out) ♦ *vi* (*fig: sinken*) to decline.

**abflauen** ['apflauən] *vi* (*Wind, Erregung*) to die away, subside; (*Nachfrage, Geschäft*) to fall *od* drop off.

**abfliegen** ['apfli:gən] *unreg vi* to take off ♦ *vt* (*Gebiet*) to fly over.

**abfließen** ['apfli:sən] *unreg vi* to drain away; **ins Ausland ~** (*Geld*) to flow out of the country.

**Abflug** ['apflu:k] *m* departure; (*Start*) take-off; **~zeit** *f* departure time.

**Abfluß** ['apflʊs] *m* draining away; (*Öffnung*) outlet; **~rohr** *nt* drainpipe; (*von sanitären Anlagen*) wastepipe.

**abfragen** ['apfra:gən] *vt* to test; (*COMPUT*) to call up; **jdn etw ~** to question sb on sth.

**abfrieren** ['apfri:rən] *unreg vi*: **ihm sind die Füße abgefroren** his feet got frostbitten, he got frostbite in his feet.

**Abfuhr** ['apfu:r] (**-, -en**) *f* removal; (*fig*) snub, rebuff; **sich** *dat* **eine ~ holen** to meet with a rebuff.

**abführen** ['apfy:rən] *vt* to lead away; (*Gelder, Steuern*) to pay ♦ *vi* (*MED*) to have a laxative effect.

**Abführmittel** *nt* laxative, purgative.

**Abfüllanlage** *f* bottling plant.

**abfüllen** ['apfʏlən] *vt* to draw off; (*in Flaschen*) to bottle.

**Abgabe** ['apga:bə] *f* handing in; (*von Ball*) pass; (*Steuer*) tax; (*einer Erklärung*) giving.

**abgabenfrei** *adj* tax-free.

**abgabenpflichtig** *adj* liable to tax.

**Abgabetermin** *m* closing date; (*für Dissertation etc*) submission date.

**Abgang** ['apgaŋ] *m* (*von Schule*) leaving; (*THEAT*) exit; (*MED: Ausscheiden*) passing;

(: *Fehlgeburt*) miscarriage; (*Abfahrt*) departure; (*der Post, von Waren*) dispatch.

**Abgangszeugnis** *nt* leaving certificate.

**Abgas** ['apga:s] *nt* waste gas; (*AUT*) exhaust.

**ABGB** *nt abk* (*ÖSTERR*: = *Allgemeines Bürgerliches Gesetzbuch*) *Civil Code in Austria*.

**abgeben** ['apge:bən] *unreg vt* (*Gegenstand*) to hand *od* give in; (*Ball*) to pass; (*Wärme*) to give off; (*Amt*) to hand over; (*Schuß*) to fire; (*Erklärung, Urteil*) to give; (*darstellen*) to make ♦ *vr*: **sich mit jdm/etw ~** to associate with sb/bother with sth; **„Kinderwagen abzugeben"** "pram for sale"; **jdm etw ~** (*überlassen*) to let sb have sth.

**abgebrannt** ['apgəbrant] (*umg*) *adj* broke.

**abgebrüht** ['apgəbry:t] (*umg*) *adj* (*skrupellos*) hard-boiled, hardened.

**abgedroschen** ['apgədrɔʃən] *adj* trite; (*Witz*) corny.

**abgefahren** ['apgəfa:rən] *pp von* **abfahren**.

**abgefeimt** ['apgəfaɪmt] *adj* cunning.

**abgegeben** ['apge:ge:bən] *pp von* **abgeben**.

**abgegriffen** ['apgəgrɪfən] *adj* (*Buch*) well-thumbed; (*Redensart*) trite.

**abgehackt** ['apgəhakt] *adj* clipped.

**abgehalftert** ['apgəhalftərt] *adj* (*fig: umg*) run-down, dead beat.

**abgehangen** ['apgəhaŋən] *pp von* **abhängen** ♦ *adj*: (**gut**) **~** (*Fleisch*) well-hung.

**abgehärtet** ['apgəhɛrtət] *adj* tough, hardy; (*fig*) hardened.

**abgehen** ['apge:ən] *unreg vi* to go away, leave; (*THEAT*) to exit; (*POST*) to go; (*MED*) to be passed; (*sterben*) to die; (*Knopf etc*) to come off; (*abgezogen werden*) to be taken off; (*Straße*) to branch off; (*abweichen*): **von einer Forderung ~** to give up a demand ♦ *vt* (*Strecke*) to go *od* walk along; (*MIL: Gelände*) to patrol; **von seiner Meinung ~** to change one's opinion; **davon gehen 5% ab** 5% is taken off that; **etw geht jdm ab** (*fehlt*) sb lacks sth.

**abgekämpft** ['apgəkɛmpft] *adj* exhausted.

**abgekartet** ['apgəkartət] *adj*: **ein ~es Spiel** a rigged job.

**abgeklärt** ['apgəklɛrt] *adj* serene, tranquil.

**abgelegen** ['apgəle:gən] *adj* remote.

**abgelten** ['apgɛltən] *unreg vt* (*Ansprüche*) to satisfy.

**abgemacht** ['apgəmaxt] *adj* fixed; **~!** done!

**abgemagert** ['apgəma:gərt] *adj* (*sehr dünn*) thin; (*ausgemergelt*) emaciated.

**abgeneigt** ['apgənaɪgt] *adj* averse.

**abgenutzt** ['apgənʊtst] *adj* worn, shabby; (*Reifen*) worn; (*fig: Klischees*) well-worn.

**Abgeordnete(r)** ['apgəˈɔrdnətə(r)] *f(m)* elected representative; (*von Parlament*) member of parliament.

**Abgesandte(r)** ['apgəzantə(r)] *f(m)* delegate; (*POL*) envoy.

**abgeschieden** ['apgəʃi:dən] *adj* (*einsam*):

**~ leben/wohnen** to live in seclusion.

**abgeschlagen** ['apgəʃlaːgən] *adj* (*besiegt*) defeated; (*erschöpft*) exhausted, worn-out.

**abgeschlossen** ['apgəʃlɔsən] *pp von* **abschließen ♦** *adj attrib* (*Wohnung*) self-contained.

**abgeschmackt** ['apgəʃmakt] *adj* tasteless; **A~heit** *f* lack of taste; (*Bemerkung*) tasteless remark.

**abgesehen** ['apgəzeːən] *adj:* **es auf jdn/etw ~ haben** to be after sb/sth; **~ von ...** apart from ...

**abgespannt** ['apgəʃpant] *adj* tired out.

**abgestanden** ['apgəʃtandən] *adj* stale; (*Bier*) flat.

**abgestorben** ['apgəʃtɔrbən] *adj* numb; (*BIOL, MED*) dead.

**abgestumpft** ['apgəʃtʊmpft] *adj* (*gefühllos: Person*) insensitive; (*Gefühle, Gewissen*) dulled.

**abgetakelt** ['apgətaːkəlt] *adj* (*fig*) decrepit, past it.

**abgetan** ['apgətaːn] *adj:* **damit ist die Sache ~** that settles the matter.

**abgetragen** ['apgətraːgən] *adj* worn.

**abgewinnen** ['apgəvɪnən] *unreg vt:* **jdm Geld ~** to win money from sb; **einer Sache etw/ Geschmack ~** to get sth/pleasure from sth.

**abgewogen** ['apgəvoːgən] *adj* (*Urteil, Worte*) balanced.

**abgewöhnen** ['apgəvøːnən] *vt:* **jdm/sich etw ~** to cure sb of sth/give sth up.

**abgießen** ['apgiːsən] *unreg vt* (*Flüssigkeit*) to pour off.

**Abglanz** ['apglants] *m* (*auch fig*) reflection.

**abgleiten** ['apglaɪtən] *unreg vi* to slip, slide.

**Abgott** ['apgɔt] *m* idol.

**abgöttisch** ['apgœtɪʃ] *adj:* **~ lieben** to idolize.

**abgrasen** ['apgraːzən] *vt* (*Feld*) to graze; (*umg: Thema*) to do to death.

**abgrenzen** ['apgrɛntsən] *vt* (*lit, fig*) to mark off; (*Gelände*) to fence off **♦** *vr:* **sich ~ (gegen)** to dis(as)sociate o.s. (from).

**Abgrund** ['apgrʊnt] *m* (*lit, fig*) abyss.

**abgründig** ['apgrʏndɪç] *adj* unfathomable; (*Lächeln*) cryptic.

**abgrundtief** *adj* (*Haß, Verachtung*) profound.

**abgucken** ['apgʊkən] *vt, vi* to copy.

**Abguß** ['apgʊs] *m* (*KUNST, METALLURGIE: Vorgang*) casting; (: *Form*) cast.

**abhaben** ['aphaːbən] *unreg* (*umg*) *vt* (*abbekommen*) **willst du ein Stück ~?** do you want a bit?

**abhacken** ['aphakən] *vt* to chop off.

**abhaken** ['aphaːkən] *vt* to tick off (*BRIT*), check off (*US*).

**abhalten** ['aphaltən] *unreg vt* (*Versammlung*) to hold; **jdn von etw ~** (*fernhalten*) to keep sb away from sth; (*hindern*) to keep sb from sth.

**abhandeln** ['aphandəln] *vt* (*Thema*) to deal with; **jdm die Waren/8 Mark ~** to do a deal with sb for the goods/beat sb down 8 marks.

**abhanden** [ap'handən] *adj:* **~ kommen** to get lost.

**Abhandlung** ['aphandlʊŋ] *f* treatise, discourse.

**Abhang** ['aphaŋ] *m* slope.

**abhängen** ['aphɛŋən] *unreg vt* (*Bild*) to take down; (*Anhänger*) to uncouple; (*Verfolger*) to shake off **♦** *vi* (*Fleisch*) to hang; **von jdm/etw ~** to depend on sb/sth; **das hängt ganz davon ab** it all depends; **er hat abgehängt** (*TEL: umg*) he hung up (on me *etc*).

**abhängig** ['aphɛŋɪç] *adj:* **~ (von)** dependent (on); **A~keit** *f:* **A~keit (von)** dependence (on).

**abhärten** ['aphɛrtən] *vt* to toughen up **♦** *vr* to toughen (o.s.) up; **sich gegen etw ~** to harden o.s. to sth.

**abhauen** ['aphaʊən] *unreg vt* to cut off; (*Baum*) to cut down **♦** *vi* (*umg*) to clear off *od* out; **hau ab!** beat it!

**abheben** ['apheːbən] *unreg vt* to lift (up); (*Karten*) to cut; (*Masche*) to slip; (*Geld*) to withdraw, take out **♦** *vi* (*Flugzeug*) to take off; (*Rakete*) to lift off; (*KARTEN*) to cut **♦** *vr:* **sich ~ von** to stand out from, contrast with.

**abheften** ['aphɛftən] *vt* (*Rechnungen etc*) to file away; (*NÄHEN*) to tack, baste.

**abhelfen** ['aphɛlfən] *unreg vi +dat* to remedy.

**abhetzen** ['aphɛtsən] *vr* to wear *od* tire o.s. out.

**Abhilfe** ['aphɪlfə] *f* remedy; **~ schaffen** to put things right.

**Abholmarkt** *m* cash and carry.

**abholen** ['aphoːlən] *vt* (*Gegenstand*) to fetch, collect; (*Person*) to call for; (*am Bahnhof etc*) to pick up, meet.

**abholzen** ['aphɔltsən] *vt* (*Wald*) to clear, deforest.

**abhorchen** ['aphɔrçən] *vt* (*MED*) to listen to, sound.

**abhören** ['aphøːrən] *vt* (*Vokabeln*) to test; (*Telefongespräch*) to tap; (*Tonband etc*) to listen to; **abgehört werden** (*umg*) to be bugged.

**Abhörgerät** *nt* bug.

**abhungern** ['aphʊŋərn] *vr:* **sich** *dat* **10 Kilo ~** to lose 10 kilos by going on a starvation diet.

**Abi** ['abi] (**-s, -s**) *nt* (*SCH: umg*) = **Abitur.**

**Abitur** [abi'tuːr] (**-s, -e**) *nt* German school-leaving examination, ≈ A-levels *pl* (*BRIT*); **(das) ~ machen** to take one's school-leaving exam *od* A-levels.

> The **Abitur** is the German school-leaving examination which is taken at the age of 18 or 19, after 12 or 13 years of school, by pupils at a **Gymnasium**. It is taken in four subjects and is necessary for entry to a university education.

**Abiturient(in)** [abituri'ɛnt(ɪn)] *m(f)* candidate

for school-leaving certificate.

**abkämmen** ['apkɛmən] *vt* (*Gegend*) to comb, scour.

**abkanzeln** ['apkantsəln] (*umg*) *vt*: **jdn** ~ to give sb a dressing-down.

**abkapseln** ['apkapsəln] *vr* to shut *od* cut o.s. off.

**abkarten** ['apkartən] (*umg*) *vt*: **die Sache war von vornherein abgekartet** the whole thing was a put-up job.

**abkaufen** ['apkaʊfən] *vt*: **jdm etw** ~ to buy sth from sb.

**abkehren** ['apke:rən] *vt* (*Blick*) to avert, turn away ♦ *vr* to turn away.

**abklappern** ['apklapərn] (*umg*) *vt* (*Kunden*) to call on; (: *Läden, Straße*): ~ (**nach**) to scour (for), comb (for).

**abklären** ['apklɛ:rən] *vt* (*klarstellen*) to clear up, clarify ♦ *vr* (*sich setzen*) to clarify.

**Abklatsch** ['apklatʃ] (**-es, -e**) *m* (*fig*) (poor) copy.

**abklemmen** ['apklɛmən] *vt* (*Leitung*) to clamp.

**abklingen** ['apklɪŋən] *unreg vi* to die away; (*RUNDF*) to fade out.

**abknallen** ['apknalən] (*umg*) *vt* to shoot down.

**abknöpfen** ['apknœpfən] *vt* to unbutton; **jdm etw** ~ (*umg*) to get sth off sb.

**abkochen** ['apkɔxən] *vt* to boil; (*keimfrei machen*) to sterilize (by boiling).

**abkommandieren** ['apkɔmandi:rən] *vt* (*MIL: zu Einheit*) to post; (*zu bestimmtem Dienst*): ~ **zu** to detail for.

**abkommen** ['apkɔmən] *unreg vi* to get away; (**vom Thema**) ~ to get off the subject, digress; **von der Straße/einem Plan** ~ to leave the road/give up a plan.

**Abkommen** (**-s, -**) *nt* agreement.

**abkömmlich** ['apkœmlɪç] *adj* available, free.

**Abkömmling** *m* (*Nachkomme*) descendant; (*fig*) adherent.

**abkönnen** ['apkœnən] *unreg* (*umg*) *vt* (*mögen*): **das kann ich nicht ab** I can't stand it.

**abkratzen** ['apkratsən] *vt* to scrape off ♦ *vi* (*umg*) to kick the bucket.

**abkriegen** ['apkri:gən] (*umg*) *vt* = **abbekommen**.

**abkühlen** ['apky:lən] *vt* to cool down ♦ *vr* (*Mensch*) to cool down *od* off; (*Wetter*) to get cool; (*Zuneigung*) to cool.

**Abkunft** ['apkʊnft] (**-**) *f* origin, birth.

**abkürzen** ['apkʏrtsən] *vt* to shorten; (*Wort*) to abbreviate; **den Weg** ~ to take a short cut.

**Abkürzung** *f* abbreviation; short cut.

**abladen** ['apla:dən] *unreg vi* to unload ♦ *vt* to unload; (*fig: umg*): **seinen Ärger (bei jdm)** ~ to vent one's anger (on sb).

**Ablage** ['apla:gə] *f* place to keep/put sth; (*Aktenordnung*) filing; (*für Akten*) tray.

**ablagern** ['apla:gərn] *vt* to deposit ♦ *vr* to be deposited ♦ *vi* to mature.

**Ablagerung** *f* (*abgelagerter Stoff*) deposit.

**ablassen** ['aplasən] *unreg vt* (*Wasser, Dampf*) to

let out *od* off; (*vom Preis*) to knock off ♦ *vi*: **von etw** ~ to give sth up, abandon sth.

**Ablauf** *m* (*Abfluß*) drain; (*von Ereignissen*) course; (*einer Frist, Zeit*) expiry (*BRIT*), expiration (*US*); **nach** ~ **des Jahres/dieser Zeit** at the end of the year/this time.

**ablaufen** ['aplaʊfən] *unreg vi* (*abfließen*) to drain away; (*Ereignisse*) to happen; (*Frist, Zeit, Paß*) to expire ♦ *vt* (*Sohlen*) to wear (down *od* out); ~ **lassen** (*abspulen, abspielen: Platte, Tonband*) to play; (*Film*) to run; **sich** *dat* **die Beine** *od* **Hacken nach etw** ~ (*umg*) to walk one's legs off looking for sth; **jdm den Rang** ~ to steal a march on sb.

**Ableben** ['aple:bən] *nt* (*form*) demise (*form*).

**ablegen** ['aple:gən] *vt* to put *od* lay down; (*Kleider*) to take off; (*Gewohnheit*) to get rid of; (*Prüfung*) to take, sit (*BRIT*); (*Zeugnis*) give; (*Schriftwechsel*) to file (away); (*nicht mehr tragen: Kleidung*) to discard, cast off; (*Schwur, Eid*) to swear ♦ *vi* (*Schiff*) to cast off.

**Ableger** (**-s, -**) *m* layer; (*fig*) branch, offshoot.

**ablehnen** ['aple:nən] *vt* to reject; (*mißbilligen*) to disapprove of; (*Einladung*) to decline, refuse ♦ *vi* to decline, refuse.

**Ablehnung** *f* rejection; refusal; **auf** ~ **stoßen** to meet with disapproval.

**ableisten** ['aplaɪstən] *vt* (*form: Zeit*) to serve.

**ableiten** ['aplaɪtən] *vt* (*Wasser*) to divert; (*deduzieren*) to deduce; (*Wort*) to derive.

**Ableitung** *f* diversion; deduction; derivation; (*Wort*) derivative.

**ablenken** ['aplɛŋkən] *vt* to turn away, deflect; (*zerstreuen*) to distract ♦ *vi* to change the subject; **das lenkt ab** (*zerstreut*) it takes your mind off things; (*stört*) it's distracting.

**Ablenkung** *f* deflection; distraction.

**Ablenkungsmanöver** *nt* diversionary tactic; (*um vom Thema abzulenken*) red herring.

**ablesen** ['aple:zən] *unreg vt* to read; **jdm jeden Wunsch von den Augen** ~ to anticipate sb's every wish.

**ableugnen** ['aplɔʏgnən] *vt* to deny.

**ablichten** ['aplɪçtən] *vt* to photocopy; (*fotografieren*) to photograph.

**abliefern** ['apli:fərn] *vt* to deliver; **etw bei jdm/einer Dienststelle** ~ to hand sth over to sb/in at an office.

**Ablieferung** *f* delivery.

**abliegen** ['apli:gən] *unreg vi* to be some distance away; (*fig*) to be far removed.

**ablisten** ['aplɪstən] *vt*: **jdm etw** ~ to trick *od* con sb out of sth.

**ablösen** ['aplø:zən] *vt* (*abtrennen*) to take off, remove; (*in Amt*) to take over from; (*FIN: Schuld, Hypothek*) to pay off, redeem; (*Methode, System*) to supersede ♦ *vr* (*auch: einander* ~) to take turns; (*Fahrer, Kollegen, Wachen*) to relieve each other.

**Ablösung** *f* removal; relieving.

**abluchsen** ['aplʊksən] (*umg*) *vt*: **jdm etw** ~ to

get *od* wangle sth out of sb.

**Abluft** *f* (*TECH*) used air.

**ABM** *pl abk* (= *Arbeitsbeschaffungsmaßnahmen*) *job-creation scheme.*

**abmachen** ['apmaxən] *vt* to take off; (*vereinbaren*) to agree; **etw mit sich allein ~** to sort sth out for o.s.

**Abmachung** *f* agreement.

**abmagern** ['apma:gərn] *vi* to get thinner, become emaciated.

**Abmagerungskur** *f* diet; **eine ~ machen** to go on a diet.

**Abmarsch** ['apmarʃ] *m* departure; **a~bereit** *adj* ready to start.

**abmarschieren** ['apmarʃiːrən] *vi* to march off.

**abmelden** ['apmɛldən] *vt* (*Auto*) to take off the road; (*Telefon*) to have disconnected; (*COMPUT*) to log off ♦ *vr* to give notice of one's departure; (*im Hotel*) to check out; **ein Kind von einer Schule ~** to take a child away from a school; **er/sie ist bei mir abgemeldet** (*umg*) I don't want anything to do with him/her; **jdn bei der Polizei ~** to register sb's departure with the police.

**abmessen** ['apmɛsən] *unreg vt* to measure.

**Abmessung** *f* measurement; (*Ausmaß*) dimension.

**abmontieren** ['apmɔntiːrən] *vt* to take off; (*Maschine*) to dismantle.

**ABM-Stelle** *f* temporary post created as part of a job creation scheme.

**abmühen** ['apmyːən] *vr* to wear o.s. out.

**abnabeln** ['apnaːbəln] *vt:* **jdn ~** (*auch fig*) to cut sb's umbilical cord.

**abnagen** ['apnaːgən] *vt* to gnaw off; (*Knochen*) to gnaw.

**Abnäher** ['apnɛːər] (**-s**, **-**) *m* dart.

**Abnahme** ['apnaːmə] *f* (+*gen*) removal; (*COMM*) buying; (*Verringerung*) decrease (in).

**abnehmen** ['apneːmən] *unreg vt* to take off, remove; (*Führerschein*) to take away; (*Prüfung*) to hold; (*Maschen*) to decrease; (*Hörer*) to lift, pick up; (*begutachten: Gebäude, Auto*) to inspect ♦ *vi* to decrease; (*schlanker werden*) to lose weight; **jdm etw ~** (*Geld*) to get sth out of sb; (*kaufen: auch umg: glauben*) to buy sth from sb; **kann ich dir etwas ~?** (*tragen*) can I take something for you?; **jdm Arbeit ~** to take work off sb's shoulders; **jdm ein Versprechen ~** to make sb promise sth.

**Abnehmer** (**-s**, **-**) *m* purchaser, customer; **viele/wenige ~ finden** (*COMM*) to sell well/badly.

**Abneigung** ['apnaɪɡʊŋ] *f* aversion, dislike.

**abnorm** [ap'nɔrm] *adj* abnormal.

**abnötigen** ['apnøːtɪɡən] *vt:* **jdm etw/Respekt ~** to force sth from sb/gain sb's respect.

**abnutzen** ['apnʊtsən] *vt* to wear out.

**Abnutzung** *f* wear (and tear).

**Abo** ['abo] (**-s**, **-s**) (*umg*) *nt* = **Abonnement.**

**Abonnement** [abɔn(ə)'mãː] (**-s**, **-s** *od* **-e**) *nt* subscription; (*Theater~*) season ticket.

**Abonnent(in)** [abɔ'nɛnt(ɪn)] *m(f)* subscriber.

**abonnieren** [abɔ'niːrən] *vt* to subscribe to.

**abordnen** ['apˈɔrdnən] *vt* to delegate.

**Abordnung** *f* delegation.

**Abort** [a'bɔrt] (**-(e)s**, **-e**) *m* (*veraltet*) lavatory.

**abpacken** ['appakən] *vt* to pack.

**abpassen** ['appasən] *vt* (*Person, Gelegenheit*) to wait for; (*warten auf*) to catch; (*jdm auflauern*) to waylay; **etw gut ~** to time sth well.

**abpausen** ['appaʊzən] *vt* to make a tracing of.

**abpfeifen** ['appfaɪfən] *unreg vt, vi* (*SPORT*): (**das Spiel**) **~** to blow the whistle (for the end of the game).

**Abpfiff** ['appfɪf] *m* final whistle.

**abplagen** ['appla:gən] *vr* to struggle (away).

**Abprall** ['appral] *m* rebound; (*von Kugel*) ricochet.

**abprallen** ['appralən] *vi* to bounce off; to ricochet; **an jdm ~** (*fig*) to make no impression on sb.

**abputzen** ['apputsən] *vt* to clean; (*Nase etc*) to wipe.

**abquälen** ['apkvɛːlən] *vr* to struggle (away).

**abrackern** ['aprakərn] (*umg*) *vr* to slave away.

**abraten** ['apra:tən] *unreg vi:* **jdm von etw ~** to advise sb against sth, warn sb against sth.

**abräumen** ['aprɔymən] *vt* to clear up *od* away; (*Tisch*) to clear ♦ *vi* to clear up *od* away.

**abreagieren** ['apreagiːrən] *vt:* **seinen Zorn (an jdm/etw) ~** to work one's anger off (on sb/sth) ♦ *vr* to calm down; **seinen Ärger an anderen ~** to take it out on others.

**abrechnen** ['aprɛçnən] *vt* to deduct, take off ♦ *vi* (*lit*) to settle up; (*fig*) to get even; **darf ich ~?** would you like your bill (*BRIT*) *od* check (*US*) now?

**Abrechnung** *f* settlement; (*Rechnung*) bill; (*Aufstellung*) statement; (*Bilanz*) balancing; (*fig: Rache*) revenge; **in ~ stellen** (*form: Abzug*) to deduct; **~ über** +*akk* bill/statement for.

**Abrechnungszeitraum** *m* accounting period.

**Abrede** ['apreːdə] *f:* **etw in ~ stellen** to deny *od* dispute sth.

**abregen** ['apreːgən] (*umg*) *vr* to calm *od* cool down.

**abreiben** ['apraɪbən] *unreg vt* to rub off; (*säubern*) to wipe; **jdn mit einem Handtuch ~** to towel sb down.

**Abreibung** (*umg*) *f* (*Prügel*) hiding, thrashing.

**Abreise** ['apraɪzə] *f* departure.

**abreisen** *vi* to leave, set off.

**abreißen** ['apraɪsən] *unreg vt* (*Haus*) to tear down; (*Blatt*) to tear off ♦ *vi:* **den Kontakt nicht ~ lassen** to stay in touch.

**abrichten** ['aprɪçtən] *vt* to train.

**abriegeln** ['apriːɡəln] *vt* (*Tür*) to bolt; (*Straße,*

*Gebiet*) to seal off.
**abringen** ['apriŋən] *unreg vt*: **sich** *dat* **ein Lächeln** ~ **to** force a smile.
**Abriß** ['apris] (**-sses, -sse**) *m* (*Übersicht*) outline; (*Abbruch*) demolition.
**abrollen** ['aprɔlən] *vt* (*abwickeln*) to unwind ♦ *vi* (*vonstatten gehen: Programm*) to run; (: *Veranstaltung*) to go off; (: *Ereignisse*) to unfold.
**Abruf** ['apruːf] *m*: **auf** ~ on call.
**abrufen** *unreg vt* (*Mensch*) to call away; (*COMM: Ware*) to request delivery of; (*COMPUT*) to recall, retrieve.
**abrunden** ['aprʊndən] *vt* to round off.
**abrüsten** ['aprystən] *vi* to disarm.
**Abrüstung** *f* disarmament.
**abrutschen** ['aprʊtʃən] *vi* to slip; (*AVIAT*) to sideslip.
**Abs.** *abk* = **Absender**; (= *Absatz*) par., para.
**absacken** ['apzakən] *vi* (*sinken*) to sink; (*Boden, Gebäude*) to subside.
**Absage** ['apzaːgə] (**-, -n**) *f* refusal; (*auf Einladung*) negative reply.
**absagen** *vt* to cancel, call off; (*Einladung*) to turn down ♦ *vi* to cry off; (*ablehnen*) to decline; **jdm** ~ to tell sb that one can't come.
**absägen** ['apzɛːgən] *vt* to saw off.
**absahnen** ['apzaːnən] *vt* (*lit*) to skim; **das beste für sich** ~ (*fig*) to take the cream.
**Absatz** ['apzats] *m* (*COMM*) sales *pl*; (*JUR*) section; (*Bodensatz*) deposit; (*neuer Abschnitt*) paragraph; (*Treppen*~) landing; (*Schuh*~) heel; ~**flaute** *f* slump in the market; ~**förderung** *f* sales promotion; ~**gebiet** *nt* (*COMM*) market; sales territory; ~**prognose** *f* sales forecast; ~**schwierigkeiten** *pl* sales problems *pl*; ~**ziffern** *pl* sales figures *pl*.
**absaufen** ['apzaʊfən] *unreg* (*umg*) *vi* (*ertrinken*) to drown; (: *Motor*) to flood; (: *Schiff etc*) to go down.
**absaugen** ['apzaʊgən] *vt* (*Flüssigkeit*) to suck out *od* off; (*Teppich, Sofa*) to hoover ®, vacuum.
**abschaben** ['apʃaːbən] *vt* to scrape off; (*Möhren*) to scrape.
**abschaffen** ['apʃafən] *vt* to abolish, do away with.
**Abschaffung** *f* abolition.
**abschalten** ['apʃaltən] *vt, vi* (*lit: umg*) to switch off.
**abschattieren** ['apʃatiːrən] *vt* to shade.
**abschätzen** ['apʃɛtsən] *vt* to estimate; (*Lage*) to assess; (*Person*) to size up.
**abschätzig** ['apʃɛtsɪç] *adj* disparaging, derogatory.
**Abschaum** ['apʃaʊm] (**-(e)s**) *m* scum.
**Abscheu** ['apʃɔy] (**-(e)s**) *m* loathing, repugnance; **a~erregend** *adj* repulsive, loathsome; **a~lich** *adj* abominable.
**abschicken** ['apʃɪkən] *vt* to send off.

**abschieben** ['apʃiːbən] *unreg vt* to push away; (*Person*) to pack off; (*ausweisen: Ausländer*) to deport; (*fig: Verantwortung, Schuld*): ~ **(auf** +*akk*) to shift (onto).
**Abschied** ['apʃiːt] (**-(e)s, -e**) *m* parting; (*von Armee*) discharge; (**von jdm**) ~ **nehmen** to say goodbye (to sb), take one's leave (of sb); **seinen** ~ **nehmen** (*MIL*) to apply for discharge; **zum** ~ on parting.
**Abschiedsbrief** *m* farewell letter.
**Abschiedsfeier** *f* farewell party.
**abschießen** ['apʃiːsən] *unreg vt* (*Flugzeug*) to shoot down; (*Geschoß*) to fire; (*umg: Minister*) to get rid of.
**abschirmen** ['apʃɪrmən] *vt* to screen; (*schützen*) to protect ♦ *vr* (*sich isolieren*): **sich** ~ **(gegen)** to cut o.s. off (from).
**abschlaffen** ['apʃlafən] (*umg*) *vi* to flag.
**abschlagen** ['apʃlaːgən] *unreg vt* (*abhacken, COMM*) to knock off; (*ablehnen*) to refuse; (*MIL*) to repel.
**abschlägig** ['apʃlɛːgɪç] *adj* negative; **jdn/etw** ~ **bescheiden** (*form*) to turn sb/sth down.
**Abschlagszahlung** *f* interim payment.
**abschleifen** ['apʃlaɪfən] *unreg vt* to grind down; (*Holzboden*) to sand (down) ♦ *vr* to wear off.
**Abschleppdienst** *m* (*AUT*) breakdown service (*BRIT*), towing company (*US*).
**abschleppen** ['apʃlɛpən] *vt* to (take in) tow.
**Abschleppseil** *nt* towrope.
**abschließen** ['apʃliːsən] *unreg vt* (*Tür*) to lock; (*beenden*) to conclude, finish; (*Vertrag, Handel*) to conclude; (*Versicherung*) to take out; (*Wette*) to place ♦ *vr* (*sich isolieren*) to cut o.s. off; **mit abgeschlossenem Studium** with a degree; **mit der Vergangenheit** ~ **to** break with the past.
**abschließend** *adj* concluding ♦ *adv* in conclusion, finally.
**Abschluß** ['apʃlʊs] *m* (*Beendigung*) close, conclusion; (*COMM: Bilanz*) balancing; (*von Vertrag, Handel*) conclusion; **zum** ~ in conclusion; ~**feier** *f* (*SCH*) school-leavers' ceremony; ~**prüfer** *m* accountant; ~**prüfung** *f* (*SCH*) final examination; (*UNIV*) finals *pl*; ~**rechnung** *f* final account; ~**zeugnis** *nt* (*SCH*) leaving certificate, diploma (*US*).
**abschmecken** ['apʃmɛkən] *vt* (*kosten*) to taste; (*würzen*) to season.
**abschmieren** ['apʃmiːrən] *vt* (*AUT*) to grease, lubricate.
**abschminken** ['apʃmɪŋkən] *vt*: **sich** ~ **to** remove one's make-up.
**abschmirgeln** ['apʃmɪrgəln] *vt* to sand down.
**abschnallen** ['apʃnalən] *vr* to unfasten one's seat belt ♦ *vi* (*umg: nicht mehr folgen können*) to give up; (: *fassungslos sein*) to be staggered.
**abschneiden** ['apʃnaɪdən] *unreg vt* to cut off ♦ *vi* to do, come off; **bei etw gut/schlecht** ~ (*umg*) to come off well/badly in sth.
**Abschnitt** ['apʃnɪt] *m* section; (*MIL*) sector;

(*Kontroll~*) counterfoil (*BRIT*), stub (*US*); (*MATH*) segment; (*Zeit~*) period.

**abschnüren** ['apʃnyːrən] *vt* to constrict.

**abschöpfen** ['apʃœpfən] *vt* to skim off.

**abschrauben** ['apʃraʊbən] *vt* to unscrew.

**abschrecken** ['apʃrɛkən] *vt* to deter, put off; (*mit kaltem Wasser*) to plunge into cold water.

**abschreckend** *adj* deterrent; ~**es Beispiel** warning; **eine ~e Wirkung haben, ~ wirken** to act as a deterrent.

**abschreiben** ['apʃraɪbən] *unreg vt* to copy; (*verlorengeben*) to write off; (*COMM*) to deduct; **er ist bei mir abgeschrieben** I'm finished with him.

**Abschreibung** *f* (*COMM*) deduction; (*Wertverminderung*) depreciation.

**Abschrift** ['apʃrɪft] *f* copy.

**abschuften** ['apʃʊftən] (*umg*) *vr* to slog one's guts out (*umg*).

**abschürfen** ['apʃʏrfən] *vt* to graze.

**Abschuß** ['apʃʊs] *m* (*eines Geschützes*) firing; (*Herunterschießen*) shooting down; (*Tötung*) shooting.

**abschüssig** ['apʃʏsɪç] *adj* steep.

**Abschußliste** *f*: **er steht auf der ~** (*umg*) his days are numbered.

**Abschußrampe** *f* launch(ing) pad.

**abschütteln** ['apʃʏtəln] *vt* to shake off.

**abschütten** ['apʃʏtən] *vt* (*Flüssigkeit etc*) to pour off.

**abschwächen** ['apʃvɛçən] *vt* to lessen; (*Behauptung, Kritik*) to tone down ♦ *vr* to lessen.

**abschweifen** ['apʃvaɪfən] *vi* to wander; (*Redner*) to digress.

**Abschweifung** *f* digression.

**abschwellen** ['apʃvɛlən] *unreg vi* (*Geschwulst*) to go down; (*Lärm*) to die down.

**abschwenken** ['apʃvɛŋkən] *vi* to turn away.

**abschwören** ['apʃvøːrən] *unreg vi* +*dat* to renounce.

**absehbar** ['apzeːbaːr] *adj* foreseeable; **in ~er Zeit** in the foreseeable future; **das Ende ist ~** the end is in sight.

**absehen** *unreg vt* (*Ende, Folgen*) to foresee ♦ *vi:* **von etw ~** to refrain from sth; (*nicht berücksichtigen*) to leave sth out of consideration; **jdm etw ~** (*erlernen*) to copy sth from sb.

**abseilen** ['apzaɪlən] *vt* to lower down on a rope ♦ *vr* (*Bergsteiger*) to abseil (down).

**Abseits** ['apzaɪts] *nt* (*SPORT*) offside; **im ~ stehen** to be offside; **im ~ leben** (*fig*) to live in the shadows.

**abseits** *adv* out of the way ♦ *präp* +*gen* away from.

**absenden** ['apzɛndən] *unreg vt* to send off, dispatch.

**Absender** *m* sender.

**Absendung** *f* dispatch.

**absetzbar** ['apzɛtsbaːr] *adj* (*Beamter*)

dismissible; (*Waren*) saleable; (*von Steuer*) deductible.

**absetzen** ['apzɛtsən] *vt* (*niederstellen, aussteigen lassen*) to put down; (*abnehmen; auch Theaterstück*) to take off; (*COMM: verkaufen*) to sell; (*FIN: abziehen*) to deduct; (*entlassen*) to dismiss; (*König*) to depose; (*streichen*) to drop; (*Fußballspiel, Termin*) to cancel; (*hervorheben*) to pick out ♦ *vi:* **er trank das Glas aus, ohne abzusetzen** he emptied his glass in one ♦ *vr* (*sich entfernen*) to clear off; (*sich ablagern*) to be deposited; **das kann man ~** that is tax-deductible.

**Absetzung** *f* (*FIN: Abzug*) deduction; (*Entlassung*) dismissal; (*von König*) deposing; (*Streichung*) dropping.

**absichern** ['apzɪçərn] *vt* to make safe; (*schützen*) to safeguard ♦ *vr* to protect o.s.

**Absicht** ['apzɪçt] *f* intention; **mit ~** on purpose; **a~lich** *adj* intentional, deliberate.

**absichtslos** *adj* unintentional.

**absinken** ['apzɪŋkən] *unreg vi* to sink; (*Temperatur, Geschwindigkeit*) to decrease.

**absitzen** ['apzɪtsən] *unreg vi* to dismount ♦ *vt* (*Strafe*) to serve.

**absolut** [apzoˈluːt] *adj* absolute.

**Absolutheitsanspruch** *m* claim to absolute right.

**Absolutismus** [apzoluˈtɪsmʊs] *m* absolutism.

**Absolvent(in)** *m(f):* **die ~en eines Lehrgangs** the students who have completed a course.

**absolvieren** [apzɔlˈviːrən] *vt* (*SCH*) to complete.

**absonderlich** [apˈzɔndərlɪç] *adj* odd, strange.

**absondern** *vt* to separate; (*ausscheiden*) to give off, secrete ♦ *vr* to cut o.s. off.

**Absonderung** *f* separation; (*MED*) secretion.

**absorbieren** [apzɔrˈbiːrən] *vt* (*lit, fig*) to absorb.

**abspalten** ['apʃpaltən] *vt* to split off.

**Abspannung** ['apʃpanʊŋ] *f* (*Ermüdung*) exhaustion.

**absparen** ['apʃpaːrən] *vt:* **sich** *dat* **etw ~** to scrimp and save for sth.

**abspecken** ['apʃpɛkən] (*umg*) *vt* to shed ♦ *vi* to lose weight.

**abspeisen** ['apʃpaɪzən] *vt* (*fig*) to fob off.

**abspenstig** ['apʃpɛnstɪç] *adj:* (**jdm**) ~ **machen** to lure away (from sb).

**absperren** ['apʃpɛrən] *vt* to block *od* close off; (*Tür*) to lock.

**Absperrung** *f* (*Vorgang*) blocking *od* closing off; (*Sperre*) barricade.

**abspielen** ['apʃpiːlən] *vt* (*Platte, Tonband*) to play; (*SPORT: Ball*) to pass ♦ *vr* to happen; **vom Blatt ~** (*MUS*) to sight-read.

**absplittern** ['apʃplɪtərn] *vt, vi* to chip off.

**Absprache** ['apʃpraːxə] *f* arrangement; **ohne vorherige ~** without prior consultation.

**absprechen** ['apʃprɛçən] *unreg vt* (*vereinbaren*) to arrange ♦ *vr:* **die beiden hatten sich vorher abgesprochen** they had agreed on what to

do/say *etc* in advance; **jdm etw** ~ to deny sb
sth; (*in Abrede stellen: Begabung*) to dispute
sb's sth.

**abspringen** ['apʃprɪŋən] *unreg vi* to jump
down/off; (*Farbe, Lack*) to flake off; (*AVIAT*)
to bale out; (*sich distanzieren*) to back out.

**Absprung** ['apʃpruŋ] *m* jump; **den ~ schaffen**
(*fig*) to make the break (*umg*).

**abspulen** ['apʃpuːlən] *vt* (*Kabel, Garn*) to
unwind.

**abspülen** ['apʃpyːlən] *vt* to rinse; **Geschirr ~**
to wash up (*BRIT*), do the dishes.

**abstammen** ['apʃtamən] *vi* to be descended;
(*Wort*) to be derived.

**Abstammung** *f* descent; derivation;
**französischer ~** of French extraction *od*
descent.

**Abstand** ['apʃtant] *m* distance; (*zeitlich*)
interval; **davon ~ nehmen, etw zu tun** to
refrain from doing sth; **~ halten** (*AUT*) to
keep one's distance; **~ von etw gewinnen**
(*fig*) to distance o.s. from sth; **mit großem
~ führen** to lead by a wide margin; **mit
~ der beste** by far the best.

**Abstandssumme** *f* compensation.

**abstatten** ['apʃtatən] *vt* (*form: Dank*) to give;
(: *Besuch*) to pay.

**abstauben** ['apʃtaubən] *vt, vi* to dust; (*umg:
mitgehen lassen*) to help oneself to, pinch;
**(den Ball) ~** (*SPORT*) to tuck the ball away.

**Abstauber(in)** ['apʃtaubər(ɪn)] (**-s, -**) (*umg*)
*m(f)* (*Person*) somebody on the make.

**abstechen** ['apʃtɛçən] *unreg vt* to cut; (*Tier*) to
cut the throat of ♦ *vi*: **~ gegen** *od* **von** to
contrast with.

**Abstecher** (**-s, -**) *m* detour.

**abstecken** ['apʃtɛkən] *vt* (*Fläche*) to mark out;
(*Saum*) to pin.

**abstehen** ['apʃteːən] *unreg vi* (*Ohren, Haare*) to
stick out; (*entfernt sein*) to stand away.

**Absteige** *f* cheap hotel.

**absteigen** ['apʃtaɪgən] *unreg vi* (*vom Rad etc*) to
get off, dismount; **in einem Gasthof ~** to put
up at an inn; **(in die zweite Liga) ~** to be
relegated (to the second division); **auf dem
~den Ast sein** (*umg*) to be going downhill,
be on the decline.

**abstellen** ['apʃtɛlən] *vt* (*niederstellen*) to put
down; (*entfernt stellen*) to pull out; (*hinstellen:
Auto*) to park; (*ausschalten*) to turn *od* switch
off; (*Mißstand, Unsitte*) to stop;
(*abkommandieren*) to order off; (*ausrichten*):
**~ auf** +*akk* to gear to; **das läßt sich nicht/läßt
sich ~** nothing/something can be done
about that.

**Abstellgleis** *nt* siding; **jdn aufs ~ schieben**
(*fig*) to cast sb aside.

**Abstellraum** *m* storeroom.

**abstempeln** ['apʃtɛmpəln] *vt* to stamp; (*fig*):
**~ zu** *od* **als** to brand as.

**absterben** ['apʃtɛrbən] *unreg vi* to die;
(*Körperteil*) to go numb.

**Abstieg** ['apʃtiːk] (**-(e)s, -e**) *m* descent;
(*SPORT*) relegation; (*fig*) decline.

**abstimmen** ['apʃtɪmən] *vi* to vote ♦ *vt*: **~ (auf**
+*akk*) (*Instrument*) to tune (to); (*Interessen*) to
match (with); (*Termine, Ziele*) to fit in (with)
♦ *vr* to agree.

**Abstimmung** *f* vote; (*geheime ~*) ballot.

**abstinent** [apsti'nɛnt] *adj* (*von Alkohol*)
teetotal.

**Abstinenz** [apsti'nɛnts] *f* teetotalism.

**Abstinenzler(in)** (**-s, -**) *m(f)* teetotaller.

**abstoßen** ['apʃtoːsən] *unreg vt* to push off *od*
away; (*anekeln*) to repel; (*COMM: Ware,
Aktien*) to sell off.

**abstoßend** *adj* repulsive.

**abstottern** ['apʃtɔtərn] (*umg*) *vt* to pay off in
instalments.

**abstrahieren** [apstra'hiːrən] *vt, vi* to abstract.

**abstrakt** [ap'strakt] *adj* abstract ♦ *adv*
abstractly, in the abstract.

**Abstraktion** [apstraktsi'oːn] *f* abstraction.

**Abstraktum** [ap'straktʊm] (**-s, Abstrakta**) *nt*
abstract concept; (*GRAM*) abstract noun.

**abstrampeln** ['apʃtrampəln] *vr* (*fig: umg*) to
sweat (away).

**abstreifen** ['apʃtraɪfən] *vt* (*abtreten: Schuhe,
Füße*) to wipe; (*abziehen: Schmuck*) to take
off, slip off.

**abstreiten** ['apʃtraɪtən] *unreg vt* to deny.

**Abstrich** ['apʃtrɪç] *m* (*Abzug*) cut; (*MED*)
smear; **~e machen** to lower one's sights.

**abstufen** ['apʃtuːfən] *vt* (*Hang*) to terrace;
(*Farben*) to shade; (*Gehälter*) to grade.

**abstumpfen** ['apʃtʊmpfən] *vt* (*lit, fig*) to dull,
blunt ♦ *vi* to become dulled.

**Absturz** ['apʃtʊrts] *m* fall; (*AVIAT*) crash.

**abstürzen** ['apʃtyrtsən] *vi* to fall; (*AVIAT*) to
crash.

**absuchen** ['apzuːxən] *vt* to scour, search.

**absurd** [ap'zʊrt] *adj* absurd.

**Abszeß** [aps'tsɛs] (**-sses, -sse**) *m* abscess.

**Abt** [apt] (**-(e)s, ⁻e**) *m* abbot.

**Abt.** *abk* (= *Abteilung*) dept.

**abtasten** ['aptastən] *vt* to feel, probe; (*ELEK*)
to scan; (*bei Durchsuchung*): **~ (auf** +*akk*) to
frisk (for).

**abtauen** ['aptauən] *vt, vi* to thaw; (*Kühlschrank*)
to defrost.

**Abtei** [ap'taɪ] (**-, -en**) *f* abbey.

**Abteil** [ap'taɪl] (**-(e)s, -e**) *nt* compartment.

**abteilen** ['aptaɪlən] *vt* to divide up; (*abtrennen*)
to divide off.

**Abteilung** *f* (*in Firma, Kaufhaus*) department;
(*MIL*) unit; (*in Krankenhaus, JUR*) section.

**Abteilungsleiter(in)** *m(f)* head of
department; (*in Kaufhaus*) department
manager(ess).

**abtelefonieren** ['aptelefoniːrən] (*umg*) *vi* to
telephone to say one can't make it.

**Äbtissin** [ɛp'tɪsɪn] *f* abbess.

**abtönen** ['aptøːnən] *vt* (*PHOT*) to tone down.

**abtöten** ['aptøːtən] *vt* (*lit, fig*) to destroy, kill

(off); (*Nerv*) to deaden.

**abtragen** ['aptraːgən] *unreg vt* (*Hügel, Erde*) to level down; (*Essen*) to clear away; (*Kleider*) to wear out; (*Schulden*) to pay off.

**abträglich** ['aptrɛːklɪç] *adj* (+*dat*) harmful (to).

**Abtragung** *f* (*GEOL*) erosion.

**Abtransport** (-(e)s, -e) *m* transportation; (*aus Katastrophengebiet*) evacuation.

**abtransportieren** ['aptranspɔrtiːrən] *vt* to transport; to evacuate.

**abtreiben** ['aptraɪbən] *unreg vt* (*Boot, Flugzeug*) to drive off course; (*Kind*) to abort ♦ *vi* to be driven off course; (*Frau*) to have an abortion.

**Abtreibung** *f* abortion.

**Abtreibungsparagraph** *m* abortion law.

**Abtreibungsversuch** *m* attempted abortion.

**abtrennen** ['aptrɛnən] *vt* (*lostrennen*) to detach; (*entfernen*) to take off; (*abteilen*) to separate off.

**abtreten** ['aptreːtən] *unreg vt* to wear out; (*überlassen*) to hand over, cede; (*Rechte, Ansprüche*) to transfer ♦ *vi* to go off; (*zurücktreten*) to step down; **sich** *dat* **die Füße** ~ to wipe one's feet; ~! (*MIL*) dismiss!

**Abtritt** ['aptrɪt] *m* (*Rücktritt*) resignation.

**abtrocknen** ['aptrɔknən] *vt* to dry ♦ *vi* to do the drying-up.

**abtropfen** ['aptrɔpfən] *vi:* **etw** ~ **lassen** to let sth drain.

**abtrünnig** ['aptrʏnɪç] *adj* renegade.

**abtun** ['aptuːn] *unreg vt* to take off; (*fig*) to dismiss; **etw kurz** ~ to brush sth aside.

**aburteilen** ['apˈʊrtaɪlən] *vt* to condemn.

**abverlangen** ['apfɛrlaŋən] *vt:* **jdm etw** ~ to demand sth from sb.

**abwägen** ['apvɛːgən] *unreg vt* to weigh up.

**abwählen** ['apvɛːlən] *vt* to vote out (of office); (*SCH: Fach*) to give up.

**abwälzen** ['apvɛltsən] *vt:* ~ (**auf** +*akk*) (*Schuld, Verantwortung*) to shift (onto); (*Arbeit*) to unload (onto); (*Kosten*) to pass on (to).

**abwandeln** ['apvandəln] *vt* to adapt.

**abwandern** ['apvandərn] *vi* to move away.

**Abwärme** ['apvɛrmə] *f* waste heat.

**abwarten** ['apvartən] *vt* to wait for ♦ *vi* to wait; **das Gewitter** ~ to wait till the storm is over; ~ **und Tee trinken** (*umg*) to wait and see; **eine** ~**de Haltung einnehmen** to play a waiting game.

**abwärts** ['apvɛrts] *adv* down; ~**gehen** *vi unpers* (*fig*): **mit ihm/dem Land geht es** ~ he/the country is going downhill.

**Abwasch** ['apvaʃ] (-(e)s) *m* washing-up; **du kannst das auch machen, das ist (dann) ein** ~ (*umg*) you could do that as well and kill two birds with one stone.

**abwaschen** *unreg vt* (*Schmutz*) to wash off; (*Geschirr*) to wash (up).

**Abwasser** ['apvasər] (-s, -wässer) *nt* sewage; ~**aufbereitung** *f* sewage treatment; ~**kanal** *m* sewer.

**abwechseln** ['apvɛksəln] *vi, vr* to alternate; (*Personen*) to take turns.

**abwechselnd** *adj* alternate.

**Abwechslung** *f* change; (*Zerstreuung*) diversion; **für** ~ **sorgen** to provide entertainment.

**abwechslungsreich** *adj* varied.

**Abweg** ['apveːk] *m:* **auf** ~**e geraten/führen** to go/lead astray.

**abwegig** ['apveːgɪç] *adj* wrong; (*Verdacht*) groundless.

**Abwehr** ['apveːr] (-) *f* defence; (*Schutz*) protection; (~*dienst*) counter-intelligence (service); **auf** ~ **stoßen** to be repulsed; **a**~**en** *vt* to ward off; (*Ball*) to stop; **a**~**ende Geste** dismissive gesture; ~**reaktion** *f* (*PSYCH*) defence (*BRIT*) *od* defense (*US*) reaction; ~**stoff** *m* antibody.

**abweichen** ['apvaɪçən] *unreg vi* to deviate; (*Meinung*) to differ; **vom rechten Weg** ~ (*fig*) to wander off the straight and narrow.

**abweichend** *adj* deviant; differing.

**Abweichler** (-s, -) *m* (*POL*) maverick.

**Abweichung** *f* (*zeitlich, zahlenmäßig*) allowance; **zulässige** ~ (*TECH*) tolerance.

**abweisen** ['apvaɪzən] *unreg vt* to turn away; (*Antrag*) to turn down; **er läßt sich nicht** ~ he won't take no for an answer.

**abweisend** *adj* (*Haltung*) cold.

**abwenden** ['apvɛndən] *unreg vt* to avert ♦ *vr* to turn away.

**abwerben** ['apvɛrbən] *unreg vt:* (**jdm**) ~ to woo away (from sb).

**abwerfen** ['apvɛrfən] *unreg vt* to throw off; (*Profit*) to yield; (*aus Flugzeug*) to drop; (*Spielkarte*) to discard.

**abwerten** ['apvɛrtən] *vt* (*FIN*) to devalue.

**abwertend** *adj* pejorative.

**Abwertung** *f* devaluation.

**abwesend** ['apveːzənt] *adj* absent; (*zerstreut*) far away.

**Abwesenheit** ['apveːzənhaɪt] *f* absence; **durch** ~ **glänzen** (*ironisch*) to be conspicuous by one's absence.

**abwickeln** ['apvɪkəln] *vt* to unwind; (*Geschäft*) to transact, conclude; (*fig: erledigen*) to deal with.

**Abwicklungskosten** ['apvɪkluŋskɔstən] *pl* transaction costs *pl.*

**abwiegen** ['apviːgən] *unreg vt* to weigh out.

**abwimmeln** ['apvɪməln] (*umg*) *vt* (*Person*) to get rid of; (: *Auftrag*) to get out of.

**abwinken** ['apvɪŋkən] *vi* to wave it/him *etc* aside; (*fig: ablehnen*) to say no.

**abwirtschaften** ['apvɪrtʃaftən] *vi* to go downhill.

**abwischen** ['apvɪʃən] *vt* to wipe off *od* away; (*putzen*) to wipe.

**abwracken** ['apvrakən] *vt* (*Schiff*) to break (up); **ein abgewrackter Mensch** a wreck (of a person).

**Abwurf** ['apvʊrf] *m* throwing off; (*von Bomben*

*etc*) dropping; (*von Reiter, SPORT*) throw.

**abwürgen** ['apvʏrgən] (*umg*) *vt* to scotch; (*Motor*) to stall; **etw von vornherein** ~ **to** nip sth in the bud.

**abzahlen** ['aptsaːlən] *vt* to pay off.

**abzählen** ['aptsɛːlən] *vt* to count (up); **abgezähltes Fahrgeld** exact fare.

**Abzählreim** ['aptsɛːlraɪm] *m* counting rhyme (*e.g. eeny meeny miney mo*).

**Abzahlung** *f* repayment; **auf** ~ **kaufen** to buy on hire purchase (*BRIT*) *od* the installment plan (*US*).

**abzapfen** ['aptsapfən] *vt* to draw off; **jdm Blut** ~ to take blood from sb.

**abzäunen** ['aptsɔʏnən] *vt* to fence off.

**Abzeichen** ['aptsaɪçən] *nt* badge; (*Orden*) decoration.

**abzeichnen** ['aptsaɪçnən] *vt* to draw, copy; (*unterschreiben*) to initial ♦ *vr* to stand out; (*fig: bevorstehen*) to loom.

**Abziehbild** *nt* transfer.

**abziehen** ['aptsiːən] *unreg vt* to take off; (*Tier*) to skin; (*Bett*) to strip; (*Truppen*) to withdraw; (*subtrahieren*) to take away, subtract; (*kopieren*) to run off; (*Schlüssel*) to take out, remove ♦ *vi* to go away; (*Truppen*) to withdraw; (*abdrücken*) to pull the trigger, fire.

**abzielen** ['aptsiːlən] *vi:* ~ **auf** +*akk* to be aimed at.

**Abzug** ['aptsuːk] *m* departure; (*von Truppen*) withdrawal; (*Kopie*) copy; (*Subtraktion*) subtraction; (*Betrag*) deduction; (*Rauch~*) flue; (*von Waffen*) trigger; (*Rabatt*) discount; (*Korrekturfahne*) proof; (*PHOT*) print; **jdm freien** ~ **gewähren** to grant sb safe passage.

**abzüglich** ['aptsyːklɪç] *präp* +*gen* less.

**abzweigen** ['aptsvaɪgən] *vi* to branch off ♦ *vt* to set aside.

**Abzweigung** *f* junction.

**Accessoires** [aksɛsoˈaːrs] *pl* accessories *pl*.

**ach** [ax] *interj* oh; ~ **so!** I see!; **mit A~ und Krach** by the skin of one's teeth; ~ **was** *od* **wo, das ist doch nicht so schlimm!** come on now, it's not that bad!

**Achillesferse** [aˈxɪlɛsfɛrzə] *f* Achilles heel.

**Achse** ['aksə] (-, -n) *f* axis; (*AUT*) axle; **auf** ~ **sein** (*umg*) to be on the move.

**Achsel** ['aksəl] (-, -n) *f* shoulder; ~**höhle** *f* armpit; ~**zucken** *nt* shrug (of one's shoulders).

**Achsenbruch** *m* (*AUT*) broken axle.

**Achsenkreuz** *nt* coordinate system.

**Acht**[1] [axt] (-, -en) *f* eight; (*beim Eislaufen etc*) figure (of) eight.

**Acht**[2] (-) *f* attention; **hab a~** (*MIL*) attention!; **sich in a~ nehmen** (**vor** +*dat*) to be careful (of), watch out (for); **etw außer a~ lassen** to disregard sth.

**acht** *num* eight; ~ **Tage** a week.

**achtbar** *adj* worthy.

**achte(r, s)** *adj* eighth.

**Achteck** *nt* octagon.

**Achtel** *nt* eighth; ~**note** *f* quaver, eighth note (*US*).

**achten** *vt* to respect ♦ *vi:* ~ (**auf** +*akk*) to pay attention (to); **darauf** ~, **daß** ... to be careful that ...

**ächten** ['ɛçtən] *vt* to outlaw, ban.

**Achterbahn** *f* roller coaster.

**Achterdeck** *nt* (*NAUT*) afterdeck.

**achtfach** *adj* eightfold.

**achtgeben** *unreg vi:* ~ (**auf** +*akk*) to take care (of); (*aufmerksam sein*) to pay attention (to).

**achtlos** *adj* careless; **viele gehen** ~ **daran vorbei** many people just pass by without noticing.

**achtmal** *adv* eight times.

**achtsam** *adj* attentive.

**Achtstundentag** *m* eight-hour day.

**Achtung** ['axtʊŋ] *f* attention; (*Ehrfurcht*) respect ♦ *interj* look out!; (*MIL*) attention!; **alle** ~! good for you/him etc!; ~, **fertig, los!** ready, steady, go!; „~ **Hochspannung!"** "danger, high voltage"; „~ **Lebensgefahr/ Stufe!"** "danger/mind the step!".

**Achtungserfolg** *m* reasonable success.

**achtzehn** *num* eighteen.

**achtzig** *num* eighty; **A~er(in)** (-s, -) *m(f)* octogenarian.

**ächzen** ['ɛçtsən] *vi:* ~ (**vor** +*dat*) to groan (with).

**Acker** ['akər] (-s, ̈-) *m* field; ~**bau** *m* agriculture; ~**bau und Viehzucht** farming.

**ackern** *vi* to plough; (*umg*) to slog away.

**a conto** [a ˈkɔnto] *adv* (*COMM*) on account.

**A.D.** *abk* (= *Anno Domini*) A.D.

**a.D.** *abk* = **außer Dienst**.

**a.d.** *abk* = **an der** (*bei Ortsnamen*).

**ad absurdum** [at apˈzʊrdʊm] *adv:* ~ **führen** (*Argument etc*) to reduce to absurdity.

**ADAC** (-) *m abk* (= *Allgemeiner Deutscher Automobilclub*) *German motoring organization;* ≈ AA (*BRIT*), AAA (*US*).

**ad acta** [at ˈakta] *adv:* **etw** ~ **legen** (*fig*) to consider sth finished; (*Frage, Problem*) to consider sth closed.

**Adam** ['aːdam] *m:* **bei** ~ **und Eva anfangen** (*umg*) to start right from scratch *od* from square one.

**adaptieren** [adapˈtiːrən] *vt* to adapt.

**adäquat** [adɛˈkvaːt] *adj* (*Belohnung, Übersetzung*) adequate; (*Stellung, Verhalten*) suitable.

**addieren** [aˈdiːrən] *vt* to add (up).

**Addis Abeba** ['adɪsˈaːbeba] (-, -s) *nt* Addis Ababa.

**Addition** [aditsiˈoːn] *f* addition.

**ade** *interj* bye!

**Adel** ['aːdəl] (-s) *m* nobility; ~ **verpflichtet** noblesse oblige.

**adelig** *adj* noble.

**Adelsstand** *m* nobility.

**Ader** ['aːdər] (-, -n) *f* vein; (*fig: Veranlagung*)

bent.

**Adhäsionsverschluß** [athɛzi'oːnsfɛrʃlʊs] *m* adhesive seal.

**Adjektiv** ['atjɛktiːf] (-s, -e) *nt* adjective.

**Adler** ['aːdlər] (-s, -) *m* eagle.

**adlig** *adj* = **adelig**.

**Admiral** [atmi'raːl] (-s, -e) *m* admiral.

**Admiralität** *f* admiralty.

**adoptieren** [adɔp'tiːrən] *vt* to adopt.

**Adoption** [adɔptsi'oːn] *f* adoption.

**Adoptiveltern** *pl* adoptive parents *pl*.

**Adoptivkind** *nt* adopted child.

**Adr.** *abk* (= *Adresse*) add.

**Adressant** [adre'sant] *m* sender.

**Adressat** [adrɛ'saːt] (-en, -en) *m* addressee.

**Adreßbuch** *nt* directory; (*privat*) address book.

**Adresse** [a'drɛsə] (-, -n) *f* (*auch COMPUT*) address; **an der falschen ~ sein** (*umg*) to have gone/come to the wrong person; **absolute ~** absolute address; **relative ~** relative address.

**adressieren** [adrɛ'siːrən] *vt:* ~ **(an** +*akk***)** to address (to).

**Adria** ['aːdria] (-) *f* Adriatic Sea.

**Adriatisches Meer** [adri'aːtɪʃəs meːr] *nt* (*form*) Adriatic Sea.

**Advent** [at'vɛnt] (-(e)s, -e) *m* Advent; **der erste/zweite ~** the first/second Sunday in Advent.

**Advents-** *zW:* ~**kalender** *m* Advent calendar; ~**kranz** *m* Advent wreath.

**Adverb** [at'vɛrp] *nt* adverb.

**adverbial** [atvɛrbi'aːl] *adj* adverbial.

**aero-** [aero] *präf* aero-.

**Aerobic** [ae'roːbik] (-s) *nt* aerobics *sing*.

**Affäre** [a'fɛːrə] (-, -n) *f* affair; **sich aus der ~ ziehen** (*umg*) to get (o.s.) out of it.

**Affe** ['afə] (-n, -n) *m* monkey; (*umg: Kerl*) berk (*BRIT*).

**Affekt** (-(e)s, -e) *m:* **im ~ handeln** to act in the heat of the moment.

**affektiert** [afɛk'tiːrt] *adj* affected.

**Affen-** *zW:* **a~artig** *adj* like a monkey; **mit a~artiger Geschwindigkeit** (*umg*) like a flash; **a~geil** (*umg*) *adj* magic, fantastic; ~**hitze** (*umg*) *f* incredible heat; ~**liebe** *f:* ~**liebe (zu)** blind adoration (of); ~**schande** (*umg*) *f* crying shame; ~**tempo** (*umg*) *nt:* **in** *od* **mit einem** ~**tempo** at breakneck speed; ~**theater** (*umg*) *nt:* **ein** ~**theater aufführen** to make a fuss.

**affig** ['afɪç] *adj* affected.

**Afghane** [af'gaːnə] (-n, -n) *m* Afghan.

**Afghanin** [af'gaːnɪn] *f* Afghan.

**afghanisch** *adj* Afghan.

**Afghanistan** [af'gaːnɪstaːn] (-s) *nt* Afghanistan.

**Afrika** ['aːfrika] (-s) *nt* Africa.

**Afrikaans** [afri'kaːns] (-) *nt* Afrikaans.

**Afrikaner(in)** [afri'kaːnər(ɪn)] (-s, -) *m(f)* African.

**afrikanisch** *adj* African.

**afro-amerikanisch** ['aːfro|ameri'kaːnɪʃ] *adj* Afro-American.

**After** ['aftər] (-s, -) *m* anus.

**AG** (-) *f abk* (= *Aktiengesellschaft*) ≈ plc (*BRIT*), corp., inc. (*US*).

**Ägäis** [ɛ'gɛːɪs] (-) *f* Aegean (Sea).

**Ägäisches Meer** *nt* Aegean Sea.

**Agent(in)** [a'gɛnt(ɪn)] *m(f)* agent.

**Agententätigkeit** *f* espionage.

**Agentur** [agɛn'tuːr] *f* agency; ~**bericht** *m* (news) agency report.

**Aggregat** [agre'gaːt] (-(e)s, -e) *nt* aggregate; (*TECH*) unit; ~**zustand** *m* (*PHYS*) state.

**Aggression** [agresi'oːn] *f* aggression.

**aggressiv** [agre'siːf] *adj* aggressive.

**Aggressivität** [agresivi'tɛːt] *f* aggressiveness.

**Aggressor** [a'grɛsoːr] (-s, -en) *m* aggressor.

**Agitation** [agitatsi'oːn] *f* agitation.

**Agrarpolitik** *f* agricultural policy.

**Agrarstaat** *m* agrarian state.

**AGV** *f abk* (= *Arbeitsgemeinschaft der Verbraucherverbände*) *consumer groups' association*.

**Ägypten** [ɛ'gyptən] (-s) *nt* Egypt.

**Ägypter(in)** (-s, -) *m(f)* Egyptian.

**ägyptisch** *adj* Egyptian.

**aha** [a'haː] *interj* aha!

**Aha-Erlebnis** *nt* sudden insight.

**ahd.** *abk* (= *althochdeutsch*) OHG.

**Ahn** [aːn] (-en, -en) *m* forebear.

**ahnden** ['aːndən] *vt* (*geh: Freveltat, Verbrechen*) to avenge; (*Übertretung, Verstoß*) to punish.

**ähneln** ['ɛːnəln] *vi* +*dat* to be like, resemble ♦ *vr* to be alike *od* similar.

**ahnen** ['aːnən] *vt* to suspect; (*Tod, Gefahr*) to have a presentiment of; **nichts Böses ~** to be unsuspecting; **du ahnst es nicht!** you have no idea!; **davon habe ich nichts geahnt** I didn't have the slightest inkling of it.

**Ahnenforschung** *f* genealogy.

**ähnlich** ['ɛːnlɪç] *adj* (+*dat*) similar (to); **das sieht ihm (ganz)** ~**!** (*umg*) that's just like him!, that's him all over!; **Ä~keit** *f* similarity.

**Ahnung** ['aːnʊŋ] *f* idea, suspicion; (*Vorgefühl*) presentiment.

**ahnungslos** *adj* unsuspecting.

**Ahorn** ['aːhɔrn] (-s, -e) *m* maple.

**Ähre** ['ɛːrə] (-, -n) *f* ear.

**Aids** [eːdz] (-) *nt* Aids.

**Akademie** [akade'miː] *f* academy.

**Akademiker(in)** [aka'deːmikər(ɪn)] (-s, -) *m(f)* university graduate.

**akademisch** *adj* academic.

**Akazie** [a'kaːtsiə] (-, -n) *f* acacia.

**Akk.** *abk* = **Akkusativ**.

**akklimatisieren** [aklimati'ziːrən] *vr* to become acclimatized.

**Akkord** [a'kɔrt] (-(e)s, -e) *m* (*MUS*) chord; **im ~ arbeiten** to do piecework; ~**arbeit** *f* piecework.

**Akkordeon** [a'kɔrdeɔn] (-s, -s) *nt* accordion.
**Akkordlohn** *m* piece wages *pl*, piece rate.
**Akkreditiv** [akredi'ti:f] (-s, -e) *nt* (*COMM*) letter of credit.
**Akku** ['aku] (-s, -s) (*umg*) *m* (*Akkumulator*) battery.
**akkurat** [aku'ra:t] *adj* precise; (*sorgfältig*) meticulous.
**Akkusativ** ['akuzati:f] (-s, -e) *m* accusative (case); ~**objekt** *nt* accusative *od* direct object.
**Akne** ['aknə] (-, -n) *f* acne.
**Akribie** [akri'bi:] *f* (*geh*) meticulousness.
**Akrobat(in)** [akro'ba:t(ɪn)] (-en, -en) *m(f)* acrobat.
**Akt** [akt] (-(e)s, -e) *m* act; (*KUNST*) nude.
**Akte** ['aktə] (-, -n) *f* file; **etw zu den** ~**n legen** (*lit, fig*) to file sth away.
**Akten-** *zW:* ~**deckel** *m* folder; ~**koffer** *m* attaché case; **a~kundig** *adj* on record; ~**notiz** *f* memo(randum); ~**ordner** *m* file; ~**schrank** *m* filing cabinet; ~**tasche** *f* briefcase; ~**zeichen** *nt* reference.
**Aktie** ['aktsiə] (-, -n) *f* share; **wie stehen die** ~**n?** (*hum: umg*) how are things?
**Aktien-** *zW:* ~**bank** *f* joint-stock bank; ~**emission** *f* share issue; ~**gesellschaft** *f* joint-stock company; ~**index** *m* share index; ~**kapital** *nt* share capital; ~**kurs** *m* share price.
**Aktion** [aktsi'o:n] *f* campaign; (*Polizei~, Such~*) action.
**Aktionär(in)** [aktsio'nɛ:r(ɪn)] (-s, -e) *m(f)* shareholder.
**Aktionismus** [aktsio'nɪsmʊs] *m* (*POL*) actionism.
**Aktionsradius** [aktsi'o:nzra:diʊs] (-, -ien) *m* (*AVIAT, NAUT*) range; (*fig: Wirkungsbereich*) scope.
**aktiv** [ak'ti:f] *adj* active; (*MIL*) regular; **A~** (-s) *nt* (*GRAM*) active (voice).
**Aktiva** [ak'ti:va] *pl* assets *pl*.
**aktivieren** [akti'vi:rən] *vt* to activate; (*fig: Arbeit, Kampagne*) to step up; (*Mitarbeiter*) to get moving.
**Aktivität** [aktivi'tɛ:t] *f* activity.
**Aktivposten** *m* (*lit, fig*) asset.
**Aktivsaldo** *m* (*COMM*) credit balance.
**aktualisieren** [aktuali'zi:rən] *vt* (*COMPUT*) to update.
**Aktualität** [aktuali'tɛ:t] *f* topicality; (*einer Mode*) up-to-dateness.
**aktuell** [aktu'ɛl] *adj* topical; up-to-date; **eine** ~**e Sendung** (*RUNDF, TV*) a current affairs programme.
**Akupunktur** [akupʊŋk'tu:ər] *f* acupuncture.
**Akustik** [a'kʊstɪk] *f* acoustics *pl*.
**akustisch** [a'kʊstɪʃ] *adj* acoustic; **ich habe dich rein** ~ **nicht verstanden** I simply didn't catch what you said (properly).
**akut** [a'ku:t] *adj* acute; (*Frage*) pressing, urgent.

**AKW** *nt' abk* = **Atomkraftwerk**.
**Akzent** [ak'tsɛnt] (-(e)s, -e) *m* accent; (*Betonung*) stress; ~ **e setzen** (*fig*) to bring out *od* emphasize the main points; ~**verschiebung** *f* (*fig*) shift of emphasis.
**Akzept** (-(e)s, -e) *nt* (*COMM: Wechsel*) acceptance.
**akzeptabel** [aktsɛp'ta:bl] *adj* acceptable.
**akzeptieren** [aktsɛp'ti:rən] *vt* to accept.
**AL** *f abk* (= *Alternative Liste*) *siehe* **alternativ**.
**Alarm** [a'larm] (-(e)s, -e) *m* alarm; (*Zustand*) alert; ~ **schlagen** to give *od* raise the alarm; ~**anlage** *f* alarm system; **a~bereit** *adj* standing by; ~**bereitschaft** *f* stand-by.
**alarmieren** [alar'mi:rən] *vt* to alarm.
**Alaska** [a'laska] (-s) *nt* Alaska.
**Albaner(in)** [al'ba:nər(ɪn)] (-s, -) *m(f)* Albanian.
**Albanien** [al'ba:niən] (-s) *nt* Albania.
**albanisch** *adj* Albanian.
**albern** ['albərn] *adj* silly.
**Album** ['albʊm] (-s, **Alben**) *nt* album.
**Aleuten** [ale'u:tən] *pl* Aleutian Islands *pl*.
**Alg** (*umg*) *abk* = **Arbeitslosengeld**.
**Alge** ['algə] (-, -n) *f* alga.
**Algebra** ['algebra] (-) *f* algebra.
**Algerien** [al'ge:riən] (-s) *nt* Algeria.
**Algerier(in)** [al'ge:riər(ɪn)] (-s, -) *m(f)* Algerian.
**algerisch** [al'ge:rɪʃ] *adj* Algerian.
**Algier** ['alʒiːər] (-s) *nt* Algiers.
**ALGOL** ['algɔl] (-(s)) *nt* (*COMPUT*) ALGOL.
**Algorithmus** [algo'rɪtmʊs] *m* (*COMPUT*) algorithm.
**alias** ['a:lias] *adv* alias.
**Alibi** ['a:libi] (-s, -s) *nt* alibi.
**Alimente** [ali'mɛntə] *pl* alimony *sing*.
**Alkohol** ['alkohɔl] (-s, -e) *m* alcohol; **unter** ~ **stehen** to be under the influence (of alcohol); **a~arm** *adj* low alcohol; **a~frei** *adj* non-alcoholic; ~**gehalt** *m* proof.
**Alkoholika** [alko'ho:lika] *pl* alcoholic drinks *pl*, liquor (*US*).
**Alkoholiker(in)** [alko'ho:likər(ɪn)] (-s, -) *m(f)* alcoholic.
**alkoholisch** *adj* alcoholic.
**Alkoholverbot** *nt* ban on alcohol.
**All** [al] (-s) *nt* universe; (*RAUMFAHRT*) space; (*außerhalb unseres Sternsystems*) outer space.
**allabendlich** *adj* every evening.
**allbekannt** *adj* universally known.
**alle** *adj siehe* **alle(r, s)**.
**alledem** ['alədeːm] *pron:* **bei/trotz** *etc* ~ with/in spite of *etc* all that; **zu** ~ moreover.
**Allee** [a'le:] (-, -n) *f* avenue.
**allein** [a'laɪn] *adj, adv* alone; (*ohne Hilfe*) on one's own, by oneself ♦ *konj* (*geh*) but, only; **von** ~ by oneself/itself; **nicht** ~ (*nicht nur*) not only; ~ **schon der Gedanke** the very *od* mere thought ..., the thought alone ...; ~**erziehend** *adj* single-parent; **A~erziehen-de(r)** *f(m)* single parent; **A~gang** *m:* **im A~gang** on one's own; **A~herrscher(in)** *m(f)*

autocrat; **A~hersteller(in)** *m(f)* sole manufacturer.
**alleinig** [a'lainɪç] *adj* sole.
**allein-** *zW:* **A~sein** *nt* being on one's own; (*Einsamkeit*) loneliness; **~stehend** *adj* single; **A~unterhalter(in)** *m(f)* solo entertainer; **A~vertretung** *f* (*COMM*) sole agency; **A~vertretungsvertrag** *m* (*COMM*) exclusive agency agreement.
**allemal** ['alə'ma:l] *adv* (*jedesmal*) always; (*ohne weiteres*) with no bother; **ein für ~** once and for all.
**allenfalls** ['alən'fals] *adv* at all events; (*höchstens*) at most.

===================== SCHLÜSSELWORT

**alle(r, s)** *adj* **1** (*sämtliche*) all; **wir ~** all of us; **~ Kinder waren da** all the children were there; **~ Kinder mögen ...** all children like ...; **~ beide** both of us/them; **sie kamen ~** they all came; **~s Gute** all the best; **~s in ~m** all in all; **vor ~m** above all; **das ist ~s andere als ...** that's anything but ...; **es hat ~s keinen Sinn mehr** nothing makes sense any more; **was habt ihr ~s gemacht?** what did you get up to?
**2** (*mit Zeit- oder Maßangaben*) every; **~ vier Jahre** every four years; **~ fünf Meter** every five metres
♦ *pron* everything; **~s was er sagt** everything he says, all that he says; **trotz ~m** in spite of everything
♦ *adv* (*zu Ende, aufgebraucht*) finished; **die Milch is ~** the milk's all gone, there's no milk left; **etw ~ machen** to finish sth up.

**allerbeste(r, s)** ['alər'bɛstə(r, s)] *adj* very best.
**allerdings** ['alər'dɪŋs] *adv* (*zwar*) admittedly; (*gewiß*) certainly.
**Allergie** [aler'gi:] *f* allergy.
**allergisch** [a'lɛrgɪʃ] *adj* allergic; **auf etw** *akk* **~ reagieren** to be allergic to sth.
**allerhand** (*umg*) *adj inv* all sorts of; **das ist doch ~!** that's a bit much!; **~!** (*lobend*) good show!
**Allerheiligen** *nt* All Saints' Day.

**Allerheiligen** (*All Saints' Day*) *is a public holiday in Germany and in Austria. It is a day in honour of all the saints.* **Allerseelen** (*All Souls' Day*) *is celebrated on November 2nd in the Roman Catholic Church. It is customary to visit cemeteries and place lighted candles on the graves of deceased relatives and friends.*

**aller-** *zW:* **~höchste(r, s)** *adj* very highest; **es wird ~höchste Zeit, daß ...** it's really high time that ...; **~höchstens** *adv* at the very most; **~lei** *adj inv* all sorts of; **~letzte(r, s)** *adj* very last; **der/das ist das ~letzte** (*umg*) he's/it's the absolute end!; **~neu(e)ste(r, s)** *adj* very latest; **~seits** *adv* on all sides; **prost**

**~seits!** cheers everyone!
**Allerseelen** (**-s**) *nt* All Soul's Day; *siehe auch* **Allerheiligen.**
**Allerwelts-** *in zW* (*Durchschnitts-*) common; (*nichtssagend*) commonplace.
**allerwenigste(r, s)** *adj* very least; **die ~n Menschen wissen das** very few people know that.
**Allerwerteste(r)** *m* (*hum*) posterior (*hum*).
**alles** *pron* everything; *siehe auch* **alle(r, s).**
**allesamt** *adv* all (of them/us *etc*).
**Alleskleber** (**-s, -**) *m* all-purpose adhesive.
**Allgäu** ['algɔy] *nt part of the alpine region of Bavaria.*
**allgegenwärtig** *adj* omnipresent, ubiquitous.
**allgemein** ['algəmain] *adj* general ♦ *adv:* **es ist ~ üblich** it's the general rule; **im ~en Interesse** in the common interest; **auf ~en Wunsch** by popular request; **A~bildung** *f* general *od* all-round education; **~gültig** *adj* generally accepted; **A~heit** *f* (*Menschen*) general public; **Allgemeinheiten** *pl* (*Redensarten*) general remarks *pl*; **~verständlich** *adj* generally intelligible; **A~wissen** *nt* general knowledge.
**Allheilmittel** [al'hailmɪtəl] *nt* cure-all, panacea (*bes fig*).
**Alliierte(r)** [ali'i:rtə(r)] *f(m)* ally.
**all-** *zW:* **~jährlich** *adj* annual; **~mächtig** *adj* all-powerful, omnipotent; **~mählich** *adv* gradually; **es wird ~mählich Zeit** (*umg*) it's about time; **A~radantrieb** *m* all-wheel drive; **~seitig** *adj* (*allgemein*) general; (*ausnahmslos*) universal; **A~tag** *m* everyday life; **~täglich** *adj* daily; (*gewöhnlich*) commonplace; **~tags** *adv* on weekdays.
**Allüren** [a'ly:rən] *pl* odd behaviour (*BRIT*) *od* behavior (*US*) *sing*; (*eines Stars etc*) airs and graces *pl*.
**all-** *zW:* **~wissend** *adj* omniscient; **~zu** *adv* all too; **~zugern** *adv* (*mögen*) only too much; (*bereitwillig*) only too willingly; **~zuoft** *adv* all too often; **~zuviel** *adv* too much.
**Allzweck-** ['altsvɛk-] *in zW* all-purpose.
**Alm** [alm] (**-, -en**) *f* alpine pasture.
**Almosen** ['almo:zən] (**-s, -**) *nt* alms *pl*.
**Alpen** ['alpən] *pl* Alps *pl*; **~blume** *f* alpine flower; **~veilchen** *nt* cyclamen; **~vorland** *nt* foothills *pl* of the Alps.
**Alphabet** [alfa'be:t] (**-(e)s, -e**) *nt* alphabet.
**alphabetisch** *adj* alphabetical.
**alphanumerisch** [alfanu'me:rɪʃ] *adj* (*COMPUT*) alphanumeric.
**Alptraum** ['alptraʊm] *m* nightmare.

===================== SCHLÜSSELWORT

**als** [als] *konj* **1** (*zeitlich*) when; (*gleichzeitig*) as; **damals, ~ ...** (in the days) when ...; **gerade, ~ ...** just as ...
**2** (*in der Eigenschaft*) than; **~ Antwort** as an answer; **~ Kind** as a child
**3** (*bei Vergleichen*) than; **ich kam später ~ er**

I came later than he (did) *od* later than him; **lieber ... ~ ...** rather ... than ...; **alles andere ~** anything but; **nichts ~ Ärger** nothing but trouble; **soviel/soweit ~ möglich** (*bei Vergleichen*) as much/far as possible **4: ~ ob/wenn** as if.

**alsbaldig** [als'baldıç] *konj:* „**zum ~en Verbrauch bestimmt**" "for immediate use only".

**also** ['alzo:] *konj* so; (*folglich*) therefore; **~ wie ich schon sagte** well (then), as I said before; **ich komme ~ morgen** so I'll come tomorrow; **~ gut** *od* **schön!** okay then; **~, so was!** well really!; **na ~!** there you are then!

**Alt** [alt] (**-s, -e**) *m* (*MUS*) alto.

**alt** *adj* old; **ich bin nicht mehr der ~e** I am not the man I was; **alles beim ~en lassen** to leave everything as it was; **ich werde heute nicht ~ (werden)** (*umg*) I won't last long today/tonight *etc*; **~ aussehen** (*fig: umg*) to be in a pickle.

**Altar** [al'ta:r] (**-(e)s, -äre**) *m* altar.

**alt-** *zW:* **A~bau** *m* old building; **A~bauwohnung** *f* flat (*BRIT*) *od* apartment (*US*) in an old building; **~bekannt** *adj* well-known; **~bewährt** *adj* (*Methode etc*) well-tried; (*Tradition etc*) long-standing; **A~bier** *nt* top-fermented German dark beer; **~eingesessen** *adj* old-established; **A~eisen** *nt* scrap iron.

**Altenheim** *nt* old people's home.

**Altenteil** ['altəntail] *nt:* **sich aufs ~ setzen** *od* **zurückziehen** (*fig*) to retire from public life.

**Alter** ['altər] (**-s, -**) *nt* age; (*hohes*) old age; **er ist in deinem ~** he's your age; **im ~ von** at the age of.

**älter** ['ɛltər] *adj* (*comp*) older; (*Bruder, Schwester*) elder; (*nicht mehr jung*) elderly.

**altern** ['altərn] *vi* to grow old, age.

**Alternativ-** [altɛrna'ti:f] *in zW* alternative.

**alternativ** *adj:* **A~e Liste** electoral pact between the Greens and alternative parties; **~ leben** to live an alternative way of life.

**Alternative** [altɛrna'ti:və] *f* alternative.

**Alternativ-** *zW:* **~medizin** *f* alternative medicine; **~szene** *f* alternative scene; **~-Technologie** *f* alternative technology.

**alters** ['altərs] *adv* (*geh*): **von** *od* **seit ~ (her)** from time immemorial.

**Alters-** *zW:* **a~bedingt** *adj* related to a particular age; caused by old age; **~grenze** *f* age limit; **flexible ~grenze** flexible retirement age; **~heim** *nt* old people's home; **~rente** *f* old age pension; **~ruhegeld** *nt* retirement benefit; **a~schwach** *adj* (*Mensch*) old and infirm; (*Auto, Möbel*) decrepit; **~versorgung** *f* provision for old age.

**Altertum** ['altərtu:m] *nt* antiquity.

**altertümlich** *adj* (*aus dem Altertum*) ancient; (*veraltet*) antiquated.

**alt-** *zW:* **~gedient** *adj* long-serving; **A~glas** *nt* used glass (*for recycling*), scrap glass; **A~glascontainer** *m* bottle bank; **~hergebracht** *adj* traditional; **A~herrenmannschaft** *f* (*SPORT*) team of players over thirty; **~klug** *adj* precocious; **A~lasten** *pl* legacy *sing* of dangerous waste; **A~material** *nt* scrap; **A~metall** *nt* scrap metal; **~modisch** *adj* old-fashioned; **A~papier** *nt* waste paper; **A~stadt** *f* old town.

**Altstimme** *f* alto.

**Altwarenhändler** *m* second-hand dealer.

**Altweibersommer** *m* Indian summer.

**Alu** ['a:lu] *abk* = **Arbeitslosenunterstützung**; **Aluminium**.

**Alufolie** ['a:lufo:liə] *f* tinfoil.

**Aluminium** [alu'mi:niom] (**-s**) *nt* aluminium, aluminum (*US*); **~folie** *f* tinfoil.

**Alzheimer-Krankheit** ['altshaɪmər'kraŋkhaɪt] *f* Alzheimer's disease.

**am** [am] = **an dem; ~ Sterben** on the point of dying; **~ 15. März** on March 15th; **~ letzten Sonntag** last Sunday; **~ Morgen/Abend** in the morning/evening; **~ besten/schönsten** best/most beautiful.

**Amalgam** [amal'ga:m] (**-s, -e**) *nt* amalgam.

**Amateur** [ama'tø:r] *m* amateur.

**Amazonas** [ama'tso:nas] (**-**) *m* Amazon (river).

**Ambiente** [ambi'ɛntə] (**-**) *nt* ambience.

**Ambition** [ambitsi'o:n] *f:* **~en auf etw** *akk* **haben** to have ambitions of getting sth.

**Amboß** ['ambɔs] (**-sses, -sse**) *m* anvil.

**ambulant** [ambu'lant] *adj* outpatient.

**Ameise** ['a:maɪzə] (**-, -n**) *f* ant.

**Ameisenhaufen** *m* anthill.

**Amerika** [a'me:rika] (**-s**) *nt* America.

**Amerikaner** [ameri'ka:nər] (**-s, -**) *m* American; (*Gebäck*) flat iced cake; **~in** *f* American.

**amerikanisch** *adj* American.

**Ami** ['ami] (**-s, -s**) (*umg*) *m* Yank; (*Soldat*) GI.

**Amme** ['amə] (**-, -n**) *f* (*veraltet*) foster mother; (*Nährmutter*) wet nurse.

**Ammenmärchen** ['amənmɛːrçən] *nt* fairy tale *od* story.

**Amok** ['a:mɔk] *m:* **~ laufen** to run amok *od* amuck.

**Amortisation** [amɔrtizatsi'o:n] *f* amortization.

**amortisieren** [amɔrti'zi:rən] *vr* to pay for itself.

**Ampel** ['ampəl] (**-, -n**) *f* traffic lights *pl*.

**amphibisch** [am'fi:bıʃ] *adj* amphibious.

**Ampulle** [am'pʊlə] (**-, -n**) *f* (*Behälter*) ampoule.

**amputieren** [ampu'ti:rən] *vt* to amputate.

**Amsel** ['amzəl] (**-, -n**) *f* blackbird.

**Amsterdam** [amstər'dam] *nt* (**-s**) Amsterdam.

**Amt** [amt] (**-(e)s, ¨er**) *nt* office; (*Pflicht*) duty; (*TEL*) exchange; **zum zuständigen ~ gehen**

to go to the relevant authority; **von ~s wegen** (*auf behördliche Anordnung hin*) officially.

**amtieren** [am'ti:rən] *vi* to hold office; (*fungieren*): **als ... ~** to act as ...

**amtierend** *adj* incumbent.

**amtlich** *adj* official; **~es Kennzeichen** registration (number), license number (*US*).

**Amtmann** (-(e)s, *pl* -männer *od* -leute) *m* (*VERWALTUNG*) senior civil servant.

**Amtmännin** *f* (*VERWALTUNG*) senior civil servant.

**Amts-** *zW:* **~arzt** *m* medical officer; **a~ärztlich** *adj:* **a~ärztlich untersucht werden** to have an official medical examination; **~deutsch(e)** *nt* officialese; **~eid** *m:* **den ~eid ablegen** to be sworn in, take the oath of office; **~geheimnis** *nt* (*geheime Sache*) official secret; (*Schweigepflicht*) official secrecy; **~gericht** *nt* county (*BRIT*) *od* district (*US*) court; **~mißbrauch** *m* abuse of one's position; **~periode** *f* term of office; **~person** *f* official; **~richter** *m* district judge; **~schimmel** *m* (*hum*) officialdom; **~sprache** *f* official language; **~stunden** *pl* office hours *pl*; **~träger** *m* office bearer; **~weg** *m:* **auf dem ~weg** through official channels; **~zeit** *f* period of office.

**amüsant** [amy'zant] *adj* amusing.

**Amüsement** [amyzə'mã:] *nt* amusement.

**amüsieren** [amy'zi:rən] *vt* to amuse ♦ *vr* to enjoy o.s.; **sich über etw** *akk* **~** to find sth funny; (*unfreundlich*) to make fun of sth.

================= *SCHLÜSSELWORT*

**an** [an] *präp +dat* **1** (*räumlich: wo?*) at; (*auf, bei*) on; (*nahe bei*) near; **~ diesem Ort** at this place; **~ der Wand** on the wall; **zu nahe ~ etw** too near to sth; **unten am Fluß** down by the river; **Köln liegt am Rhein** Cologne is on the Rhine; **~ der gleichen Stelle** at *od* on the same spot; **jdn ~ der Hand nehmen** to take sb by the hand; **sie wohnen Tür ~ Tür** they live next door to one another; **es ~ der Leber** *etc* **haben** (*umg*) to have a liver *etc* trouble

**2** (*zeitlich: wann?*) on; **~ diesem Tag** on this day; **~ Ostern** at Easter

**3: arm ~ Fett** low in fat; **jung ~ Jahren sein** to be young in years; **~ der ganzen Sache ist nichts** there is nothing in it; **~ etw sterben** to die of sth; **~ (und für) sich** actually ♦ *präp +akk* **1** (*räumlich: wohin?*) to; **er ging ~s Fenster** he went (over) to the window; **etw ~ die Wand hängen/schreiben** to hang/write sth on the wall; **~ die Arbeit gehen** to get down to work

**2** (*zeitlich: woran?*): **~ etw denken** to think of sth

**3** (*gerichtet an*) to; **ein Gruß/eine Frage ~ dich** greetings/a question to you

♦ *adv* **1** (*ungefähr*) about; **~ die hundert** about

a hundred; **~ die 5 DM** around 5 marks

**2** (*auf Fahrplänen*): **Frankfurt ~ 18.30** arriving Frankfurt 18.30

**3** (*ab*): **von dort/heute ~** from there/today onwards

**4** (*angeschaltet, angezogen*) on; **das Licht is ~** the light is on; **ohne etwas ~** with nothing on; *siehe auch* **am.**

**analog** [ana'lo:k] *adj* analogous.

**Analogie** [analo'gi:] *f* analogy.

**Analogrechner** [ana'lo:krɛçnər] *m* analog computer.

**Analphabet(in)** [an|alfa'be:t(ın)] (-en, -en) *m(f)* illiterate (person).

**Analyse** [ana'ly:zə] (-, -n) *f* analysis.

**analysieren** [analy'zi:rən] *vt* to analyse (*BRIT*), analyze (*US*).

**Anämie** [anɛ'mi:] (-, -n) *f* anaemia (*BRIT*), anemia (*US*).

**Ananas** ['ananas] (-, - *od* -se) *f* pineapple.

**Anarchie** [anar'çi:] *f* anarchy.

**anarchisch** [a'narçıʃ] *adj* anarchic.

**Anarchist(in)** [anar'çıst(ın)] *m(f)* (-en, -en) anarchist.

**Anästhesist(in)** [an|este'zıst(ın)] (-en, -en) *m(f)* anaesthetist (*BRIT*), anesthesiologist (*US*).

**Anatomie** [anato'mi:] *f* anatomy.

**anbahnen** ['anba:nən] *vr* to open up; (*sich andeuten*) to be in the offing; (*Unangenehmes*) to be looming ♦ *vt* to initiate.

**Anbahnung** *f* initiation.

**anbändeln** ['anbɛndəln] (*umg*) *vi* to flirt.

**Anbau** ['anbaʊ] *m* (*AGR*) cultivation; (*Gebäude*) extension.

**anbauen** *vt* (*AGR*) to cultivate; (*Gebäudeteil*) to build on.

**Anbaugebiet** *nt:* **ein gutes ~ für etw** a good area for growing sth.

**Anbaumöbel** *pl* unit furniture *sing.*

**anbehalten** ['anbəhaltən] *unreg vt* to keep on.

**anbei** [an'baı] *adv* enclosed (*form*); **~ schicken wir Ihnen ...** please find enclosed ...

**anbeißen** ['anbaısən] *unreg vt* to bite into ♦ *vi* (*lit*) to bite; (*fig*) to swallow the bait; **zum A~ aussehen** (*umg*) to look good enough to eat.

**anbelangen** ['anbəlaŋən] *vt* to concern; **was mich anbelangt** as far as I am concerned.

**anberaumen** ['anbəraʊmən] *vt* (*form*) to fix, arrange.

**anbeten** ['anbe:tən] *vt* to worship.

**Anbetracht** ['anbətraxt] *m:* **in ~** *+gen* in view of.

**Anbetung** *f* worship.

**anbiedern** ['anbi:dərn] (*pej*) *vr:* **sich ~ (bei)** to curry favour (with).

**anbieten** ['anbi:tən] *unreg vt* to offer ♦ *vr* to volunteer; **das bietet sich als Lösung an** that would provide a solution.

**anbinden** ['anbɪndən] *unreg vt* to tie up; (*verbinden*) to connect.
**Anblick** ['anblɪk] *m* sight.
**anblicken** *vt* to look at.
**anbraten** ['anbraːtən] *unreg vt* (*Fleisch*) to brown.
**anbrechen** ['anbrɛçən] *unreg vt* to start; (*Vorräte*) to break into ♦ *vi* to start; (*Tag*) to break; (*Nacht*) to fall.
**anbrennen** ['anbrɛnən] *unreg vi* to catch fire; (*KOCH*) to burn.
**anbringen** ['anbrɪŋən] *unreg vt* to bring; (*Ware*) to sell; (*festmachen*) to fasten; (*Telefon etc*) to install.
**Anbruch** ['anbrʊx] *m* beginning; ~ **des Tages** dawn; ~ **der Nacht** nightfall.
**anbrüllen** ['anbrʏlən] *vt* to roar at.
**Andacht** ['andaxt] (-, -en) *f* devotion; (*Versenkung*) rapt interest; (*Gottesdienst*) prayers *pl*; (*Ehrfurcht*) reverence.
**andächtig** ['andɛçtɪç] *adj* devout.
**andauern** ['andaʊərn] *vi* to last, go on.
**andauernd** *adj* continual.
**Anden** ['andən] *pl:* **die** ~ **the** Andes *pl.*
**Andenken** ['andɛŋkən] (-s, -) *nt* memory; (*Reise~*) souvenir; (*Erinnerungsstück*) ~ **(an** +*akk*) a memento (of), a keepsake (from).
**andere(r, s)** *adj* other; (*verschieden*) different; **am** ~**n Tage** the next day; **ein** ~**s Mal** another time; **kein** ~**r** nobody else; **alles** ~ **als zufrieden** anything but pleased, far from pleased; **von etwas** ~**m sprechen** to talk about something else; **es blieb mir nichts** ~**s übrig, als selbst hinzugehen** I had no alternative but to go myself; **unter** ~**m** among other things; **von einem Tag zum** ~**n** overnight; **sie hat einen** ~**n** she has someone else.
**andererseits** *adv* on the other hand.
**andermal** *adv:* **ein** ~ some other time.
**ändern** ['ɛndərn] *vt* to alter, change ♦ *vr* to change.
**andernfalls** *adv* otherwise.
**andernorts** ['andərn'ɔrts] *adv* elsewhere.
**anders** *adv:* ~ **(als)** differently (from); **wer** ~**?** who else?; **niemand** ~ no-one else; **wie nicht** ~ **zu erwarten** as was to be expected; **wie könnte es** ~ **sein?** how could it be otherwise?; **ich kann nicht** ~ (*kann es nicht lassen*) I can't help it; (*muß leider*) I have no choice; ~ **ausgedrückt** to put it another way; **jemand/irgendwo** ~ somebody/somewhere else; ~ **aussehen/klingen** to look/sound different.
**andersartig** *adj* different.
**Andersdenkende(r)** *f(m)* dissident, dissenter.
**anderseits** ['andər'zaɪts] *adv* = **andererseits**.
**anders-** *zW:* ~**farbig** *adj* of a different colour; ~**gläubig** *adj* of a different faith; ~**herum** *adv* the other way round; ~ **lautend** *adj attrib*

(*form*): ~**lautende Berichte** reports to the contrary; ~**wo** *adv* elsewhere; ~**woher** *adv* from elsewhere; ~**wohin** *adv* elsewhere.
**anderthalb** ['andərt'halp] *adj* one and a half.
**Änderung** ['ɛndərʊŋ] *f* alteration, change.
**Änderungsantrag** ['ɛndərʊŋs|antraːk] *m* (*PARL*) amendment.
**anderweitig** ['andər'vaɪtɪç] *adj* other ♦ *adv* otherwise; (*anderswo*) elsewhere.
**andeuten** ['andɔʏtən] *vt* to indicate; (*Wink geben*) to hint at.
**Andeutung** *f* indication; hint.
**andeutungsweise** *adv* (*als Anspielung, Anzeichen*) by way of a hint; (*als flüchtiger Hinweis*) in passing.
**andichten** ['andɪçtən] *vt:* **jdm etw** ~ (*umg: Fähigkeiten*) to credit sb with sth.
**Andorra** [an'dɔra] (-s) *nt* Andorra.
**Andorraner(in)** [andɔ'raːnər(ɪn)] *m(f)* Andorran.
**Andrang** ['andraŋ] *m* crush.
**andrehen** ['andreːən] *vt* to turn *od* switch on; **jdm etw** ~ (*umg*) to unload sth onto sb.
**androhen** ['androːən] *vt:* **jdm etw** ~ to threaten sb with sth.
**Androhung** *f:* **unter** ~ **von Gewalt** with the threat of violence.
**anecken** ['an|ɛkən] (*umg*) *vi:* **(bei jdm/allen)** ~ to rub (sb/everyone) up the wrong way.
**aneignen** ['an|aɪgnən] *vt:* **sich** *dat* **etw** ~ to acquire sth; (*widerrechtlich*) to appropriate sth; (*sich mit etw vertraut machen*) to learn sth.
**aneinander** [an|aɪ'nandər] *adv* at/on/to *etc* one another *od* each other; ~**fügen** *vt* to put together; ~**geraten** *unreg vi* to clash; ~**legen** *vt* to put together.
**anekeln** ['an|eːkəln] *vt* to disgust.
**Anemone** [ane'moːnə] (-, -n) *f* anemone.
**anerkannt** ['an|ɛrkant] *adj* recognized, acknowledged.
**anerkennen** ['an|ɛrkɛnən] *unreg vt* to recognize, acknowledge; (*würdigen*) to appreciate; **das muß man** ~ (*zugeben*) you can't argue with that; (*würdigen*) one has to appreciate that.
**anerkennend** *adj* appreciative.
**anerkennenswert** *adj* praiseworthy.
**Anerkennung** *f* recognition, acknowledgement; appreciation.
**anerzogen** ['an|ɛrtsoːgən] *adj* acquired.
**anfachen** ['anfaxən] *vt* (*lit*) to fan into flame; (*fig*) to kindle.
**anfahren** ['anfaːrən] *unreg vt* to deliver; (*fahren gegen*) to hit; (*Hafen*) to put into; (*umg*) to bawl at ♦ *vi* to drive up; (*losfahren*) to drive off.
**Anfahrt** ['anfaːrt] *f* (*~sweg, ~szeit*) journey; (*Zufahrt*) approach.
**Anfall** ['anfal] *m* (*MED*) attack; **in einem** ~ **von** (*fig*) in a fit of.
**anfallen** *unreg vt* to attack ♦ *vi* (*Arbeit*) to come

up; (*Produkt, Nebenprodukte*) to be obtained; (*Zinsen*) to accrue; (*sich anhäufen*) to accumulate; **die ~den Kosten/Reparaturen** the costs/repairs incurred.

**anfällig** ['anfɛlɪç] *adj* delicate; **~ für etw** prone to sth.

**Anfang** ['anfaŋ] (**-(e)s, -fänge**) *m* beginning, start; **von ~ an** right from the beginning; **zu ~** at the beginning; **~ Fünfzig** in one's early fifties; **~ Mai/1994** at the beginning of May/1994.

**anfangen** ['anfaŋən] *unreg vt* to begin, start; (*machen*) to do ♦ *vi* to begin, start; **damit kann ich nichts ~** (*nützt mir nichts*) that's no good to me; (*verstehe ich nicht*) it doesn't mean a thing to me; **mit dir ist heute (aber) gar nichts anzufangen!** you're no fun at all today!; **bei einer Firma ~** to start working for a firm.

**Anfänger(in)** ['anfɛŋər(ɪn)] (**-s, -**) *m(f)* beginner.

**anfänglich** ['anfɛŋlɪç] *adj* initial.

**anfangs** *adv* at first; **wie ich schon ~ erwähnte** as I mentioned in the beginning; **A~buchstabe** *m* initial *od* first letter; **A~gehalt** *nt* starting salary; **A~stadium** *nt* initial stages *pl*.

**anfassen** ['anfasən] *vt* to handle; (*berühren*) to touch ♦ *vi* to lend a hand ♦ *vr* to feel.

**anfechtbar** ['anfɛçtbaːr] *adj* contestable.

**anfechten** ['anfɛçtən] *unreg vt* to dispute; (*Meinung, Aussage*) to challenge; (*Urteil*) to appeal against; (*beunruhigen*) to trouble.

**anfeinden** ['anfaɪndən] *vt* to treat with hostility.

**anfertigen** ['anfɛrtɪgən] *vt* to make.

**anfeuchten** ['anfɔʏçtən] *vt* to moisten.

**anfeuern** ['anfɔʏərn] *vt* (*fig*) to spur on.

**anflehen** ['anfleːən] *vt* to implore.

**anfliegen** ['anfliːgən] *unreg vt* to fly to ♦ *vi* to fly up.

**Anflug** ['anfluːk] *m* (*AVIAT*) approach; (*Spur*) trace.

**anfordern** ['anfɔrdərn] *vt* to demand; (*COMM*) to requisition.

**Anforderung** *f* (*+gen*) demand (for); (*COMM*) requisition.

**Anfrage** ['anfraːgə] *f* inquiry; (*PARL*) question.

**anfragen** ['anfraːgən] *vi* to inquire.

**anfreunden** ['anfrɔʏndən] *vr* to make friends; **sich mit etw ~** (*fig*) to get to like sth.

**anfügen** ['anfyːgən] *vt* to add; (*beifügen*) to enclose.

**anfühlen** ['anfyːlən] *vt, vr* to feel.

**anführen** ['anfyːrən] *vt* to lead; (*zitieren*) to quote; (*umg: betrügen*) to lead up the garden path.

**Anführer(in)** (**-s, -**) *m(f)* leader.

**Anführung** *f* leadership; (*Zitat*) quotation.

**Anführungszeichen** *pl* quotation marks *pl*, inverted commas *pl* (*BRIT*).

**Angabe** ['angaːbə] *f* statement; (*TECH*) specification; (*umg: Prahlerei*) boasting; (*SPORT*) service; **Angaben** *pl* (*Auskunft*) particulars *pl*; **ohne ~ von Gründen** without giving any reasons; **~n zur Person** (*form*) personal details *od* particulars.

**angeben** ['angeːbən] *unreg vt* to give; (*anzeigen*) to inform on; (*bestimmen*) to set ♦ *vi* (*umg*) to boast; (*SPORT*) to serve.

**Angeber(in)** (**-s, -**) (*umg*) *m(f)* show-off.

**Angeberei** [angeːbəˈraɪ] (*umg*) *f* showing off.

**angeblich** ['angeːplɪç] *adj* alleged.

**angeboren** ['angəboːrən] *adj* (*+dat*) inborn, innate (in); (*MED, fig*): **~ (bei)** congenital (to).

**Angebot** ['angəboːt] *nt* offer; (*COMM*): **~ (an +dat*) supply (of); **im ~** (*umg*) on special offer.

**angeboten** ['angəboːtən] *pp von* **anbieten**.

**Angebotspreis** *m* offer price.

**angebracht** ['angəbraxt] *adj* appropriate.

**angebrannt** ['angəbrant] *adj*: **es riecht hier so ~** there's a smell of burning here.

**angebrochen** ['angəbrɔxən] *adj* (*Packung, Flasche*) open(ed); **was machen wir mit dem ~en Abend?** (*umg*) what shall we do with the rest of the evening?

**angebunden** ['angəbʊndən] *adj*: **kurz ~ sein** (*umg*) to be abrupt *od* curt.

**angefangen** *pp von* **anfangen**.

**angegeben** *pp von* **angeben**.

**angegossen** ['angəgɔsən] *adj*: **wie ~ sitzen** to fit like a glove.

**angegriffen** ['angəgrɪfən] *adj*: **er wirkt ~** he looks as if he's under a lot of strain.

**angehalten** ['angəhaltən] *pp von* **anhalten** ♦ *adj*: **~ sein, etw zu tun** to be required *od* obliged to do sth.

**angehaucht** ['angəhaʊxt] *adj*: **links/rechts ~ sein** to have left-/right-wing tendencies *od* leanings.

**angeheiratet** ['angəhaɪratət] *adj* related by marriage.

**angeheitert** ['angəhaɪtərt] *adj* tipsy.

**angehen** ['angeːən] *unreg vt* to concern; (*angreifen*) to attack; (*bitten*): **jdn ~ (um)** to approach sb (for) ♦ *vi* (*Feuer*) to light; (*umg: beginnen*) to begin; **das geht ihn gar nichts an** that's none of his business; **gegen jdn ~** (*entgegentreten*) to fight sb; **gegen etw ~** (*entgegentreten*) to fight sth; (*Mißstände, Zustände*) to take measures against sth.

**angehend** *adj* prospective; (*Musiker, Künstler*) budding.

**angehören** ['angəhøːrən] *vi +dat* to belong to.

**Angehörige(r)** *f(m)* relative.

**Angeklagte(r)** ['angəklaːktə(r)] *f(m)* accused, defendant.

**angeknackst** ['angəknakst] (*umg*) *adj* (*Mensch*) uptight; (: *Selbstbewußtsein*) weakened.

**angekommen** ['angəkɔmən] *pp von*

ankommen.

**Angel** ['aŋəl] (-, -n) f fishing rod; (Tür~) hinge; **die Welt aus den ~n heben** (fig) to turn the world upside down.

**Angelegenheit** ['aŋəle:gənhaɪt] f affair, matter.

**angelernt** ['aŋəlɛrnt] adj (Arbeiter) semi-skilled.

**Angelhaken** m fish hook.

**angeln** ['aŋəln] vt to catch ♦ vi to fish; **A~ (-s)** nt angling, fishing.

**Angelpunkt** m crucial od central point; (Frage) key od central issue.

**Angelrute** f fishing rod.

**Angelsachse** ['aŋəlzaksə] (-n, -n) m Anglo-Saxon.

**Angelsächsin** ['aŋəlzɛksɪn] f Anglo-Saxon.

**angelsächsisch** ['aŋəlzɛksɪʃ] adj Anglo-Saxon.

**Angelschein** m fishing permit.

**angemessen** ['aŋəmɛsən] adj appropriate, suitable; **eine der Leistung ~e Bezahlung** payment commensurate with the input.

**angenehm** ['aŋəne:m] adj pleasant; ~! (bei Vorstellung) pleased to meet you; **das A~e mit dem Nützlichen verbinden** to combine business with pleasure.

**angenommen** ['aŋənɔmən] pp von annehmen ♦ adj assumed; (Kind) adopted; ~, **wir ... assuming we ...**

**angepaßt** ['aŋəpast] adj conformist.

**angerufen** ['aŋəru:fən] pp von anrufen.

**angesäuselt** ['aŋəzɔʏzəlt] adj tipsy, merry.

**angeschlagen** ['aŋəʃla:gən] (umg) adj (Mensch, Aussehen, Nerven) shattered; (: Gesundheit) poor.

**angeschlossen** ['aŋəʃlɔsən] adj (+dat) affiliated (to od with), associated (with).

**angeschmiert** ['aŋəʃmi:rt] (umg) adj in trouble; **der/die A~e sein** to have been had.

**angeschrieben** ['aŋəʃri:bən] (umg) adj: **bei jdm gut/schlecht ~ sein** to be in sb's good/bad books.

**angesehen** ['aŋəze:ən] pp von ansehen ♦ adj respected.

**Angesicht** ['aŋəzɪçt] nt (geh) face.

**angesichts** ['aŋəzɪçts] präp +gen in view of, considering.

**angespannt** ['aŋəʃpant] adj (Aufmerksamkeit) close; (Nerven, Lage) tense, strained; (COMM: Markt) tight, overstretched; (Arbeit) hard.

**Angest.** abk = **Angestellte(r).**

**angestammt** ['aŋəʃtamt] adj (überkommen) traditional; (ererbt: Rechte) hereditary; (: Besitz) inherited.

**Angestellte(r)** ['aŋəʃtɛltə(r)] f(m) employee; (Büro~) white-collar worker.

**angestrengt** ['aŋəʃtrɛŋt] adv as hard as one can.

**angetan** ['aŋəta:n] adj: **von jdm/etw ~ sein** to be taken with sb/sth; **es jdm ~ haben** to appeal to sb.

**angetrunken** ['aŋətrʊŋkən] adj inebriated.

**angewiesen** ['aŋəvi:zən] adj: **auf jdn/etw ~ sein** to be dependent on sb/sth; **auf sich selbst ~ sein** to be left to one's own devices.

**angewöhnen** ['aŋəvø:nən] vt: **jdm/sich etw ~** to accustom sb/become accustomed to sth.

**Angewohnheit** ['aŋəvo:nhaɪt] f habit.

**angewurzelt** ['aŋəvʊrtsəlt] adj: **wie ~ dastehen** to be rooted to the spot.

**angiften** ['aŋɪftən] (pej: umg) vt to snap at.

**angleichen** ['aŋlaɪçən] unreg vt, vr to adjust.

**Angler** ['aŋlər] (-s, -) m angler.

**angliedern** ['aŋli:dərn] vt: ~ **(an +akk)** (Verein, Partei) to affiliate (to od with); (Land) to annex (to).

**Anglist(in)** [aŋ'glɪst(ɪn)] (-en, -en) m(f) English specialist; (Student) English student; (Professor etc) English lecturer/professor.

**Angola** [aŋ'go:la] (-s) nt Angola.

**angolanisch** [aŋgo'la:nɪʃ] adj Angolan.

**angreifen** ['aŋgraɪfən] unreg vt to attack; (anfassen) to touch; (Arbeit) to tackle; (beschädigen) to damage.

**Angreifer(in)** (-s, -) m(f) attacker.

**angrenzen** ['aŋgrɛntsən] vi: **an etw** akk ~ to border on etw, adjoin sth.

**Angriff** ['aŋgrɪf] m attack; **etw in ~ nehmen** to make a start on sth.

**Angriffsfläche** f: **jdm/etw eine ~ bieten** (lit, fig) to provide sb/sth with a target.

**angriffslustig** adj aggressive.

**Angst** [aŋst] (-, ⁻e) f fear; ~ **haben (vor** +dat) to be afraid od scared (of); ~ **um jdn/etw haben** to be worried about sb/sth; **jdm ~ einflößen** od **einjagen** to frighten sb; **nur keine ~!** don't be scared; **a~** adj: **jdm ist a~** sb is afraid od scared; **jdm a~ machen** to scare sb; **a~frei** adj free of fear; **~hase** (umg) m chicken, scaredy-cat.

**ängstigen** ['ɛŋstɪgən] vt to frighten ♦ vr: **sich ~ (vor** +dat od **um)** to worry (o.s.) (about).

**ängstlich** adj nervous; (besorgt) worried; (schüchtern) timid; **Ä~keit** f nervousness.

**Angstschweiß** m: **mir brach der ~ aus** I broke out in a cold sweat.

**angurten** ['aŋgʊrtən] vt, vr = **anschnallen.**

**Anh.** abk (= Anhang) app.

**anhaben** ['anha:bən] unreg vt to have on; **er kann mir nichts ~** he can't hurt me.

**anhaften** ['anhaftən] vi (lit): ~ **(an** +dat) to stick (to); (fig): ~ +dat to stick to, stay with.

**anhalten** ['anhaltən] unreg vt to stop ♦ vi to stop; (andauern) to persist; (werben): **um die Hand eines Mädchens ~** to ask for a girl's hand in marriage; **(jdm) etw ~** to hold sth up (against sb); **jdn zur Arbeit/Höflichkeit ~** to get sb to work/teach sb to be polite.

**anhaltend** adj persistent.

**Anhalter(in)** (-s, -) m(f) hitch-hiker; **per ~ fahren** to hitch-hike.

**Anhaltspunkt** m clue.

**anhand** [an'hant] *präp +gen* with.
**Anhang** ['anhaŋ] *m* appendix; (*Leute*) family; (*Anhängerschaft*) supporters *pl.*
**anhängen** ['anhɛŋən] *unreg vt* to hang up; (*Wagen*) to couple up; (*Zusatz*) to add (on); (*COMPUT*) to append; **sich an jdn** ~ to attach o.s. to sb; **jdm etw** ~ (*umg: nachsagen, anlasten*) to blame sb for sth, blame sth on sb; (: *Verdacht, Schuld*) to pin sth on sb.
**Anhänger** (-s, -) *m* supporter; (*AUT*) trailer; (*am Koffer*) tag; (*Schmuck*) pendant; ~**schaft** *f* supporters *pl.*
**Anhängeschloß** *nt* padlock.
**anhängig** *adj* (*JUR*) sub judice; **etw** ~ **machen** to start legal proceedings over sth.
**anhänglich** *adj* devoted; **A~keit** *f* devotion.
**Anhängsel** (-s, -) *nt* appendage.
**anhauen** ['anhauən] (*umg*) *vt* (*ansprechen*): **jdn** ~ (**um**) to accost sb (for).
**anhäufen** ['anhɔyfən] *vt* to accumulate, amass ♦ *vr* to accrue.
**Anhäufung** ['anhɔyfuŋ] *f* accumulation.
**anheben** ['anheːbən] *unreg vt* to lift up; (*Preise*) to raise.
**anheimelnd** ['anhaiməlnt] *adj* comfortable, cosy.
**anheimstellen** [an'haimʃtɛlən] *vt*: **jdm etw** ~ to leave sth up to sb.
**anheizen** ['anhaitsən] *vt* (*Ofen*) to light; (*fig: umg: Wirtschaft*) to stimulate; (*verschlimmern: Krise*) to aggravate.
**anheuern** ['anhɔyərn] *vt, vi* (*NAUT, fig*) to sign on *od* up.
**Anhieb** ['anhiːb] *m*: **auf** ~ straight off, first go; **es klappte auf** ~ it was an immediate success.
**anhimmeln** ['anhiməln] (*umg*) *vt* to idolize, worship.
**Anhöhe** ['anhøːə] *f* hill.
**anhören** ['anhøːrən] *vt* to listen to; (*anmerken*) to hear ♦ *vr* to sound.
**Anhörung** *f* hearing.
**Animierdame** [ani'miːrdaːmə] *f* nightclub/bar hostess.
**animieren** [ani'miːrən] *vt* to encourage, egg on.
**Anis** [a'niːs] (-es, -e) *m* aniseed.
**Ank.** *abk* (= *Ankunft*) arr.
**ankämpfen** ['ankɛmpfən] *vi*: **gegen etw** ~ to fight (against) sth; (*gegen Wind, Strömung*) to battle against sth.
**Ankara** ['aŋkara] (-s) *nt* Ankara.
**Ankauf** ['ankauf] *m*: ~ **und Verkauf von** ... we buy and sell ...; **a~en** *vt* to purchase, buy.
**Anker** ['aŋkər] (-s, -) *m* anchor; **vor** ~ **gehen** to drop anchor.
**ankern** *vt, vi* to anchor.
**Ankerplatz** *m* anchorage.
**Anklage** ['anklaːgə] *f* accusation; (*JUR*) charge; **gegen jdn** ~ **erheben** (*JUR*) to bring *od* prefer charges against sb; ~**bank** *f* dock.

**anklagen** ['anklaːgən] *vt* to accuse; **jdn (eines Verbrechens)** ~ (*JUR*) to charge sb (with a crime).
**Anklagepunkt** *m* charge.
**Ankläger(in)** ['anklɛːgər(in)] (-s, -) *m(f)* accuser.
**Anklageschrift** *f* indictment.
**anklammern** ['anklamərn] *vt* to clip, staple ♦ *vr*: **sich an etw** *akk od dat* ~ to cling to sth.
**Anklang** ['anklaŋ] *m*: **bei jdm** ~ **finden** to meet with sb's approval.
**ankleben** ['ankleːbən] *vt*: „**Plakate** ~ **verboten!**" "stick no bills".
**Ankleidekabine** *f* changing cubicle.
**ankleiden** ['anklaidən] *vt, vr* to dress.
**anklingen** ['anklinən] *vi* (*angeschnitten werden*) to be touched (up)on; (*erinnern*): ~ **an** +*akk* to be reminiscent of.
**anklopfen** ['anklɔpfən] *vi* to knock.
**anknipsen** ['anknipsən] *vt* to switch on; (*Schalter*) to flick.
**anknüpfen** ['anknypfən] *vt* to fasten *od* tie on; (*Beziehungen*) to establish; (*Gespräch*) to start up ♦ *vi* (*anschließen*): ~ **an** +*akk* to refer to.
**Anknüpfungspunkt** *m* link.
**ankommen** ['ankɔmən] *unreg vi* to arrive; (*näherkommen*) to approach; (*Anklang finden*): **bei jdm (gut)** ~ to go down well with sb ♦ *vi unpers*: **er ließ es auf einen Streit/einen Versuch** ~ he was prepared to argue about it/to give it a try; **es kommt darauf an** it depends; (*wichtig sein*) that is what matters; **es kommt auf ihn an** it depends on him; **es darauf** ~ **lassen** to let things take their course; **gegen jdn/etw** ~ to cope with sb/sth; **damit kommst du bei ihm nicht an!** you won't get anywhere with him like that.
**ankreiden** ['ankraidən] *vt* (*fig*): **jdm etw (dick** *od* **übel)** ~ to hold sth against sb.
**ankreuzen** ['ankrɔytsən] *vt* to mark with a cross.
**ankündigen** ['ankyndigən] *vt* to announce.
**Ankündigung** *f* announcement.
**Ankunft** ['ankunft] (-, -**künfte**) *f* arrival.
**Ankunftszeit** *f* time of arrival.
**ankurbeln** ['ankurbəln] *vt* (*AUT*) to crank; (*fig*) to boost.
**Anl.** *abk* (= *Anlage*) enc(l).
**anlachen** ['anlaxən] *vt* to smile at; **sich** *dat* **jdn** ~ (*umg*) to pick sb up.
**Anlage** ['anlaːgə] *f* disposition; (*Begabung*) talent; (*Park*) gardens *pl*; (*Beilage*) enclosure; (*TECH*) plant; (*Einrichtung*: MIL, ELEK) installation(s *pl*); (*Sport*~ *etc*) facilities *pl*; (*umg: Stereo*~) (stereo) system; (*FIN*) investment; (*Entwurf*) layout; **als** ~ *od* **in der** ~ **erhalten Sie** ... please find enclosed ...; ~**berater(in)** *m(f)* investment consultant; ~**kapital** *nt* fixed capital.
**Anlagenabschreibung** *f* capital allowance.
**Anlagevermögen** *nt* capital assets *pl*, fixed

assets *pl*.

**anlangen** ['anlaŋən] *vi* (*ankommen*) to arrive.

**Anlaß** ['anlas] (-**sses, -lässe**) *m*: ~ (**zu**) cause (for); (*Ereignis*) occasion; **aus** ~ +*gen* on the occasion of; ~ **zu etw geben** to give rise to sth; **beim geringsten/bei jedem** ~ for the slightest reason/at every opportunity; **etw zum** ~ **nehmen** to take the opportunity of sth.

**anlassen** *unreg vt* to leave on; (*Motor*) to start ♦ *vr* (*umg*) to start off.

**Anlasser** (-**s, -**) *m* (*AUT*) starter.

**anläßlich** ['anlɛslɪç] *präp* +*gen* on the occasion of.

**anlasten** ['anlastən] *vt*: **jdm etw** ~ to blame sb for sth.

**Anlauf** ['anlaʊf] *m* run-up; (*fig: Versuch*) attempt, try.

**anlaufen** *unreg vi* to begin; (*Film*) to be showing; (*SPORT*) to run up; (*Fenster*) to mist up; (*Metall*) to tarnish ♦ *vt* to call at; **rot** ~ to turn *od* go red; **gegen etw** ~ to run into *od* up against sth; **angelaufen kommen** to come running up.

**Anlauf-** *zW*: ~**stelle** *f* place to go (with one's problems); ~**zeit** *f* (*fig*) time to get going *od* started.

**anläuten** ['anlɔɪtən] *vi* to ring.

**anlegen** ['anleːɡən] *vt* to put; (*anziehen*) to put on; (*gestalten*) to lay out; (*Kartei, Akte*) to start; (*COMPUT: Datei*) to create; (*Geld*) to invest ♦ *vi* to dock; (*NAUT*) to berth; **etw an etw** *akk* ~ to put sth against *od* on sth; **ein Gewehr** ~ (**auf** +*akk*) to aim a weapon (at); **es auf etw** *akk* ~ to be out for sth/to do sth; **strengere Maßstäbe** ~ (**bei**) to lay down *od* impose stricter standards (in); **sich mit jdm** ~ (*umg*) to quarrel with sb.

**Anlegeplatz** *m* landing place.

**Anleger(in)** (-**s, -**) *m(f)* (*FIN*) investor.

**Anlegestelle** *f* landing place.

**anlehnen** ['anleːnən] *vt* to lean; (*Tür*) to leave ajar; (**sich**) **an etw** *akk* ~ to lean on *od* against sth.

**Anlehnung** *f* (*Imitation*): **in** ~ **an jdn/etw** following sb/sth.

**Anlehnungsbedürfnis** *nt* need of loving care.

**anleiern** ['anlaɪərn] (*umg*) *vt* to get going.

**Anleihe** ['anlaɪə] (-**, -n**) *f* (*FIN*) loan; (*Wertpapier*) bond.

**anleiten** ['anlaɪtən] *vt* to instruct.

**Anleitung** *f* instructions *pl*.

**anlernen** ['anlɛrnən] *vt* to teach, instruct.

**anlesen** ['anleːzən] *unreg vt* (*aneignen*): **sich** *dat* **etw** ~ to learn sth by reading.

**Anliegen** ['anliːɡən] (-**s, -**) *nt* matter; (*Wunsch*) wish.

**anliegen** *unreg vi* (*Kleidung*) to cling.

**anliegend** *adj* adjacent; (*beigefügt*) enclosed.

**Anlieger** (-**s, -**) *m* resident; ~ **frei** no thoroughfare - residents only.

**anlocken** ['anlɔkən] *vt* to attract; (*Tiere*) to lure.

**anlügen** ['anlyːɡən] *unreg vt* to lie to.

**Anm.** *abk* (= *Anmerkung*) n.

**anmachen** ['anmaxən] *vt* to attach; (*Elektrisches*) to put on; (*Salat*) to dress; **jdn** ~ (*umg*) to try and pick sb up.

**anmalen** ['anmaːlən] *vt* to paint ♦ *vr* (*pej: schminken*) to paint one's face *od* o.s.

**Anmarsch** ['anmarʃ] *m*: **im** ~ **sein** to be advancing; (*hum*) to be on the way; **im** ~ **sein auf** +*akk* to be advancing on.

**anmaßen** ['anmaːsən] *vt*: **sich** *dat* **etw** ~ to lay claim to sth.

**anmaßend** *adj* arrogant.

**Anmaßung** *f* presumption.

**Anmeldeformular** ['anmɛldəfɔrmulaːr] *nt* registration form.

**anmelden** *vt* to announce; (*geltend machen: Recht, Ansprüche, zu Steuerzwecken*) to declare; (*COMPUT*) to log on ♦ *vr* (*sich ankündigen*) to make an appointment; (*polizeilich, für Kurs etc*) to register; **ein Gespräch nach Deutschland** ~ (*TEL*) to book a call to Germany.

**Anmeldung** *f* announcement; appointment; registration; **nur nach vorheriger** ~ by appointment only.

**anmerken** ['anmɛrkən] *vt* to observe; (*anstreichen*) to mark; **jdm seine Verlegenheit** *etc* ~ to notice sb's embarrassment *etc*; **sich** *dat* **nichts** ~ **lassen** not to give anything away.

**Anmerkung** *f* note.

**Anmut** ['anmuːt] (-) *f* grace.

**anmuten** *vt* (*geh*): **jdn** ~ to appear *od* seem to sb.

**anmutig** *adj* charming.

**annähen** ['annɛːən] *vt* to sew on.

**annähern** ['annɛːərn] *vr* to get closer.

**annähernd** *adj* approximate; **nicht** ~ **soviel** not nearly as much.

**Annäherung** *f* approach.

**Annäherungsversuch** *m* advances *pl*.

**Annahme** ['annaːmə] (-**, -n**) *f* acceptance; (*Vermutung*) assumption; ~**stelle** *f* counter; (*für Reparaturen*) reception; ~**verweigerung** *f* refusal.

**annehmbar** ['anneːmbaːr] *adj* acceptable.

**annehmen** *unreg vt* to accept; (*Namen*) to take; (*Kind*) to adopt; (*vermuten*) to suppose, assume ♦ *vr* (+*gen*) to take care (of); **jdn an Kindes Statt** ~ to adopt sb; **angenommen, das ist so** assuming that is so.

**Annehmlichkeit** *f* comfort.

**annektieren** [anɛk'tiːrən] *vt* to annex.

**anno** ['ano] *adj*: **von** ~ **dazumal** (*umg*) from the year dot.

**Annonce** [a'nõːsə] (-**, -n**) *f* advertisement.

**annoncieren** [anõ'siːrən] *vt, vi* to advertise.

**annullieren** [anʊ'liːrən] *vt* to annul.

**Anode** [a'noːdə] (-**, -n**) *f* anode.

**anöden** ['an|ø:dən] (*umg*) *vt* to bore stiff.
**anomal** [ano'ma:l] *adj* (*regelwidrig*) unusual, abnormal; (*nicht normal*) strange, odd.
**anonym** [ano'ny:m] *adj* anonymous.
**Anorak** ['anorak] (**-s, -s**) *m* anorak.
**anordnen** ['an|ɔrdnən] *vt* to arrange; (*befehlen*) to order.
**Anordnung** *f* arrangement; order; ~**en treffen** to give orders.
**anorganisch** ['an|ɔrga:nɪʃ] *adj* (*CHEM*) inorganic.
**anpacken** ['anpakən] *vt* to grasp; (*fig*) to tackle; **mit** ~ to lend a hand.
**anpassen** ['anpasən] *vt* (*Kleidung*) to fit; (*fig*) to adapt ♦ *vr* to adapt.
**Anpassung** *f* fitting; adaptation.
**Anpassungsdruck** *m* pressure to conform (*to society*).
**anpassungsfähig** *adj* adaptable.
**anpeilen** ['anpaɪlən] *vt* (*mit Radar, Funk etc*) to take a bearing on; **etw** ~ (*fig: umg*) to have one's sights on sth.
**Anpfiff** ['anpfɪf] *m* (*SPORT*) (starting) whistle; (*Spielbeginn: Fußball etc*) kick-off; **einen** ~ **bekommen** (*umg*) to get a rocket (*BRIT*).
**anpöbeln** ['anpø:bəln] *vt* to abuse; (*umg*) to pester.
**Anprall** ['anpral] *m:* ~ **gegen** *od* **an** +*akk* impact on *od* against.
**anprangern** ['anpraŋərn] *vt* to denounce.
**anpreisen** ['anpraɪzən] *unreg vt* to extol; **sich** ~ (**als**) to sell o.s. (as); **etw** ~ to extol (the virtues of) sth; **seine Waren** ~ to cry one's wares.
**Anprobe** ['anpro:bə] *f* trying on.
**anprobieren** ['anprobi:rən] *vt* to try on.
**anpumpen** ['anpʊmpən] (*umg*) *vt* to borrow from.
**anquatschen** ['ankvatʃən] (*umg*) *vt* to speak to; (: *Mädchen*) to try to pick up.
**Anrainer** ['anraɪnər] (**-s, -**) *m* neighbour (*BRIT*), neighbor (*US*).
**anranzen** ['anrantsən] (*umg*) *vt:* **jdn** ~ to tick sb off.
**anraten** ['anra:tən] *unreg vt* to recommend; **auf A**~ **des Arztes** *etc* on the doctor's *etc* advice *od* recommendation.
**anrechnen** ['anrɛçnən] *vt* to charge; (*fig*) to count; **jdm etw hoch** ~ to think highly of sb for sth.
**Anrecht** ['anrɛçt] *nt:* ~ **auf** +*akk* right (to); **ein** ~ **auf etw haben** to be entitled to sth, have a right to sth.
**Anrede** ['anre:də] *f* form of address.
**anreden** *vt* to address.
**anregen** ['anre:gən] *vt* to stimulate; **angeregte Unterhaltung** lively discussion.
**anregend** *adj* stimulating.
**Anregung** *f* stimulation; (*Vorschlag*) suggestion.
**anreichern** ['anraɪçərn] *vt* to enrich.
**Anreise** ['anraɪzə] *f* journey there/here.

**anreisen** *vi* to arrive.
**anreißen** ['anraɪsən] *unreg vt* (*kurz zur Sprache bringen*) to touch on.
**Anreiz** ['anraɪts] *m* incentive.
**anrempeln** ['anrɛmpəln] *vt* (*anstoßen*) to bump into; (*absichtlich*) to jostle.
**anrennen** ['anrɛnən] *unreg vi:* **gegen etw** ~ (*gegen Wind etc*) to run against sth; (*MIL*) to storm sth.
**Anrichte** ['anrɪçtə] (**-, -n**) *f* sideboard.
**anrichten** *vt* to serve up; **Unheil** ~ to make mischief; **da hast du aber etwas angerichtet!** (*umg: verursacht*) you've started something there all right!; (: *angestellt*) you've really made a mess there!
**anrüchig** ['anrʏçɪç] *adj* dubious.
**anrücken** ['anrʏkən] *vi* to approach; (*MIL*) to advance.
**Anruf** ['anru:f] *m* call; ~**beantworter** *m* (telephone) answering machine, answerphone.
**anrufen** *unreg vt* to call out to; (*bitten*) to call on; (*TEL*) to ring up, phone, call.
**anrühren** ['anry:rən] *vt* to touch; (*mischen*) to mix.
**ans** [ans] = **an das.**
**Ansage** ['anza:gə] *f* announcement.
**ansagen** *vt* to announce ♦ *vr* to say one will come.
**Ansager(in)** (**-s, -**) *m(f)* announcer.
**ansammeln** ['anzaməln] *vt* to collect ♦ *vr* to accumulate; (*fig: Wut, Druck*) to build up.
**Ansammlung** *f* collection; (*Leute*) crowd.
**ansässig** ['anzɛsɪç] *adj* resident.
**Ansatz** ['anzats] *m* start; (*Haar*~) hairline; (*Hals*~) base; (*Verlängerungsstück*) extension; (*Veranschlagung*) estimate; **die ersten Ansätze zu etw** the beginnings of sth; ~**punkt** *m* starting point; ~**stück** *nt* (*TECH*) attachment.
**anschaffen** ['anʃafən] *vt* to buy, purchase ♦ *vi:* ~ **gehen** (*umg: durch Prostitution*) to be on the game; **sich** *dat* **Kinder** ~ (*umg*) to have children.
**Anschaffung** *f* purchase.
**anschalten** ['anʃaltən] *vt* to switch on.
**anschauen** ['anʃaʊən] *vt* to look at.
**anschaulich** *adj* illustrative.
**Anschauung** *f* (*Meinung*) view; **aus eigener** ~ from one's own experience.
**Anschauungsmaterial** *nt* illustrative material.
**Anschein** ['anʃaɪn] *m* appearance; **allem** ~ **nach** to all appearances; **den** ~ **haben** to seem, appear.
**anscheinend** *adj* apparent.
**anschieben** ['anʃi:bən] *unreg vt* (*Fahrzeug*) to push.
**Anschiß** ['anʃɪs] (*umg*) *m:* **einen** ~ **bekommen** to get a telling-off *od* ticking-off (*bes BRIT*).
**Anschlag** ['anʃla:k] *m* notice; (*Attentat*) attack; (*COMM*) estimate; (*auf Klavier*) touch; (*auf*

*Schreibmaschine*) keystroke; **einem ~ zum Opfer fallen** to be assassinated; **ein Gewehr im ~ haben** (*MIL*) to have a rifle at the ready; **~brett** *nt* notice board (*BRIT*), bulletin board (*US*).

**anschlagen** ['anʃlaːgən] *unreg vt* to put up; (*beschädigen*) to chip; (*Akkord*) to strike; (*Kosten*) to estimate ♦ *vi* to hit; (*wirken*) to have an effect; (*Glocke*) to ring; (*Hund*) to bark; **einen anderen Ton ~** (*fig*) to change one's tune; **an etw** *akk* **~** to hit against sth.

**anschlagfrei** *adj*: **~er Drucker** non-impact printer.

**Anschlagzettel** *m* notice.

**anschleppen** ['anʃlɛpən] (*umg*) *vt* (*unerwünscht mitbringen*) to bring along.

**anschließen** ['anʃliːsən] *unreg vt* to connect up; (*Sender*) to link up; (*in Steckdose*) to plug in; (*fig: hinzufügen*) to add ♦ *vi*: **an etw** *akk* **~** (*zeitlich*) to follow sth ♦ *vr*: **sich jdm/etw ~** to join sb/sth; (*beipflichten*) to agree with sb/ sth; **sich an etw** *akk* **~** (*angrenzen*) to adjoin sth.

**anschließend** *adj* adjacent; (*zeitlich*) subsequent ♦ *adv* afterwards; **~ an** +*akk* following.

**Anschluß** ['anʃlʊs] *m* (*ELEK, EISENB, TEL*) connection; (*weiterer Apparat*) extension; (*von Wasser etc*) supply; (*COMPUT*) port; **im ~ an** +*akk* following; **~ finden** to make friends; **~ bekommen** to get through; **kein ~ unter dieser Nummer** number unobtainable; **den ~ verpassen** (*EISENB etc*) to miss one's connection; (*fig*) to miss the boat.

**anschmiegen** ['anʃmiːgən] *vr*: **sich an jdn/etw ~** (*Kind, Hund*) to snuggle *od* nestle up to *od* against sb/sth.

**anschmiegsam** ['anʃmiːkzaːm] *adj* affectionate.

**anschmieren** ['anʃmiːrən] *vt* to smear; (*umg*) to take in.

**anschnallen** ['anʃnalən] *vt* to buckle on ♦ *vr* to fasten one's seat belt.

**Anschnallpflicht** *f*: **für Kinder besteht ~** children must wear seat belts.

**anschnauzen** ['anʃnautsən] (*umg*) *vt* to yell at.

**anschneiden** ['anʃnaɪdən] *unreg vt* to cut into; (*Thema*) to introduce.

**Anschnitt** ['anʃnɪt] *m* first slice.

**anschreiben** ['anʃraɪbən] *unreg vt* to write (up); (*COMM*) to charge up; (*benachrichtigen*) to write to; **bei jdm gut/schlecht angeschrieben sein** to be well/badly thought of by sb, be in sb's good/bad books.

**anschreien** ['anʃraɪən] *unreg vt* to shout at.

**Anschrift** ['anʃrɪft] *f* address.

**Anschriftenliste** *f* mailing list.

**Anschuldigung** ['anʃʊldɪgʊŋ] *f* accusation.

**anschwärzen** ['anʃvɛrtsən] *vt* (*fig: umg*): **jdn ~ (bei)** to blacken sb's name (with).

**anschwellen** ['anʃvɛlən] *unreg vi* to swell (up).

**anschwemmen** ['anʃvɛmən] *vt* to wash ashore.

**anschwindeln** ['anʃvɪndəln] (*umg*) *vt* to lie to.

**ansehen** ['anzeːən] *unreg vt* to look at; **jdm etw ~** to see sth (from sb's face); **jdn/etw als etw ~** to look on sb/sth as sth; **~ für** to consider; (**sich** *dat*) **etw ~** to (have a) look at sth; (*Fernsehsendung*) to watch sth; (*Film, Stück, Sportveranstaltung*) to see sth; **etw (mit) ~** to watch sth, see sth happening.

**Ansehen** (**-s**) *nt* respect; (*Ruf*) reputation; **ohne ~ der Person** (*JUR*) without respect of person.

**ansehnlich** ['anzeːnlɪç] *adj* fine-looking; (*beträchtlich*) considerable.

**anseilen** ['anzaɪlən] *vt*: **jdn/sich ~** to rope sb/ o.s. up.

**ansein** ['anzaɪn] *unreg* (*umg*) *vi* to be on.

**ansetzen** ['anzɛtsən] *vt* (*festlegen*) to fix; (*entwickeln*) to develop; (*Fett*) to put on; (*Blätter*) to grow; (*zubereiten*) to prepare ♦ *vi* (*anfangen*) to start, begin; (*Entwicklung*) to set in; (*dick werden*) to put on weight ♦ *vr* (*Rost etc*) to start to develop; **~ an** +*akk* (*anfügen*) to fit on to; (*anlegen, an Mund etc*) to put to; **zu etw ~** to prepare to do sth; **jdn/etw auf jdn/etw ~** to set sb/sth on sb/ sth.

**Ansicht** ['anzɪçt] *f* (*Anblick*) sight; (*Meinung*) view, opinion; **zur ~** on approval; **meiner ~ nach** in my opinion.

**Ansichtskarte** *f* picture postcard.

**Ansichtssache** *f* matter of opinion.

**ansiedeln** ['anziːdəln] *vt* to settle; (*Tierart*) to introduce ♦ *vr* to settle; (*Industrie etc*) to get established.

**ansonsten** [an'zɔnstən] *adv* otherwise.

**anspannen** ['anʃpanən] *vt* to harness; (*Muskel*) to strain.

**Anspannung** *f* strain.

**Anspiel** ['anʃpiːl] *nt* (*SPORT*) start of play.

**anspielen** *vt* (*SPORT*) to play the ball *etc* to ♦ *vi*: **auf etw** *akk* **~** to refer *od* allude to sth.

**Anspielung** *f*: **~ (auf** +*akk*) reference (to), allusion (to).

**Ansporn** ['anʃpɔrn] (**-(e)s**) *m* incentive.

**Ansprache** ['anʃpraːxə] *f* (*Rede*) address.

**ansprechen** ['anʃprɛçən] *unreg vt* to speak to; (*bitten, gefallen*) to appeal to; (*Eindruck machen auf*) to make an impression on ♦ *vi*: **~ (auf** +*akk*) (*Patient*) to respond (to); (*Meßgerät*) to react (to); **jdn auf etw** *akk* **(hin) ~** to ask sb about sth.

**ansprechend** *adj* attractive.

**Ansprechpartner** *m* contact.

**anspringen** ['anʃprɪŋən] *unreg vi* (*AUT*) to start ♦ *vt* (*anfallen*) to jump; (*Raubtier*) to pounce (up)on; (*Hund: hochspringen*) to jump up at.

**Anspruch** ['anʃprux] (**-s, -sprüche**) *m* (*Recht*): **~ (auf** +*akk*) claim (to); **den Ansprüchen gerecht werden** to meet the requirements; **hohe Ansprüche stellen/haben** to demand/

expect a lot; **jdn/etw in ~ nehmen** to occupy sb/take up sth.

**anspruchslos** *adj* undemanding.

**anspruchsvoll** *adj* demanding; (*COMM*) upmarket.

**anspucken** ['anʃpʊkən] *vt* to spit at.

**anstacheln** ['anʃtaxəln] *vt* to spur on.

**Anstalt** ['anʃtalt] (-, -en) *f* institution; **~en machen, etw zu tun** to prepare to do sth.

**Anstand** ['anʃtant] *m* decency; (*Manieren*) (good) manners *pl*.

**anständig** ['anʃtɛndɪç] *adj* decent; (*umg*) proper; (*groß*) considerable; **A~keit** *f* propriety, decency.

**anstandshalber** ['anʃtantshalbər] *adv* out of politeness.

**anstandslos** *adv* without any ado.

**anstarren** ['anʃtarən] *vt* to stare at.

**anstatt** [an'ʃtat] *präp* +gen instead of ♦ *konj*: **~ etw zu tun** instead of doing sth.

**anstauen** ['anʃtauən] *vr* to accumulate; (*Blut in Adern etc*) to congest; (*fig: Gefühle*) to build up.

**anstechen** ['anʃtɛçən] *unreg vt* to prick; (*Faß*) to tap.

**anstecken** ['anʃtɛkən] *vt* to pin on; (*Ring*) to put *od* slip on; (*MED*) to infect; (*Pfeife*) to light; (*Haus*) to set fire to ♦ *vr*: **ich habe mich bei ihm angesteckt** I caught it from him ♦ *vi* (*fig*) to be infectious.

**ansteckend** *adj* infectious.

**Ansteckung** *f* infection.

**anstehen** ['anʃteːən] *unreg vi* to queue (up) (*BRIT*), line up (*US*); (*Verhandlungspunkt*) to be on the agenda.

**ansteigen** ['anʃtaɪɡən] *unreg vi* to rise; (*Straße*) to climb.

**anstelle** [an'ʃtɛlə] *präp* +gen in place of.

**anstellen** ['anʃtɛlən] *vt* (*einschalten*) to turn on; (*Arbeit geben*) to employ; (*umg: Unfug treiben*) to get up to; (*: machen*) to do ♦ *vr* to queue (up) (*BRIT*), line up (*US*); (*umg*) to act; (*: sich zieren*) to make a fuss, act up.

**Anstellung** *f* employment; (*Posten*) post, position; **~ auf Lebenszeit** tenure.

**ansteuern** ['anʃtɔyərn] *vt* to make *od* steer *od* head for.

**Anstich** ['anʃtɪç] *m* (*von Faß*) tapping, broaching.

**Anstieg** ['anʃtiːk] (-(e)s, -e) *m* climb; (*fig: von Preisen etc*) increase.

**anstiften** ['anʃtɪftən] *vt* (*Unglück*) to cause; **jdn zu etw ~** to put sb up to sth.

**Anstifter** (-s, -) *m* instigator.

**Anstiftung** *f* (*von Tat*) instigation; (*von Mensch*): **~ (zu)** incitement (to).

**anstimmen** ['anʃtɪmən] *vt* (*Lied*) to strike up (with); (*Geschrei*) to set up ♦ *vi* to strike up.

**Anstoß** ['anʃtoːs] *m* impetus; (*Ärgernis*) offence (*BRIT*), offense (*US*); (*SPORT*) kick-off; **der erste ~** the initiative; **ein Stein des ~es** (*umstrittene Sache*) a bone of contention;

**~ nehmen an** +*dat* to take offence at.

**anstoßen** *unreg vt* to push; (*mit Fuß*) to kick ♦ *vi* to knock, bump; (*mit der Zunge*) to lisp; (*mit Gläsern*) to drink a toast; **an etw** *akk* **~** (*angrenzen*) to adjoin sth; **~ auf** +*akk* to drink (a toast) to.

**anstößig** ['anʃtøːsɪç] *adj* offensive, indecent; **A~keit** *f* indecency, offensiveness.

**anstrahlen** ['anʃtraːlən] *vt* to floodlight; (*strahlend ansehen*) to beam at.

**anstreben** ['anʃtreːbən] *vt* to strive for.

**anstreichen** ['anʃtraɪçən] *unreg vt* to paint; (*jdm*) **etw als Fehler ~** to mark sth wrong.

**Anstreicher(in)** (-s, -) *m(f)* painter.

**anstrengen** ['anʃtrɛŋən] *vt* to strain; (*strapazieren: jdn*) to tire out; (*: Patienten*) to fatigue; (*JUR*) to bring ♦ *vr* to make an effort; **eine Klage ~ (gegen)** (*JUR*) to initiate *od* institute proceedings (against).

**anstrengend** *adj* tiring.

**Anstrengung** *f* effort.

**Anstrich** ['anʃtrɪç] *m* coat of paint.

**Ansturm** ['anʃtʊrm] *m* rush; (*MIL*) attack.

**Ansuchen** ['anzuːxən] (-s, -) *nt* request.

**ansuchen** ['anzuːxən] *vi*: **um etw ~** to apply for sth.

**Antagonismus** [antagoˈnɪsmʊs] *m* antagonism.

**antanzen** ['antantsən] (*umg*) *vi* to turn *od* show up.

**Antarktis** [antˈʔarktɪs] (-) *f* Antarctic.

**antarktisch** *adj* Antarctic.

**antasten** ['antastən] *vt* to touch; (*Recht*) to infringe upon; (*Ehre*) to question.

**Anteil** ['antaɪl] (-s, -e) *m* share; (*Mitgefühl*) sympathy; **~ nehmen an** +*dat* to share in; (*sich interessieren*) to take an interest in; **~ an etw** *dat* **haben** (*beitragen*) to contribute to sth; (*teilnehmen*) to take part in sth.

**anteilig** *adj* proportionate, proportional.

**anteilmäßig** *adj* pro rata.

**Anteilnahme** (-) *f* sympathy.

**Antenne** [anˈtɛnə] (-, -n) *f* aerial; (*ZOOL*) antenna; **eine/keine ~ für etw haben** (*fig: umg*) to have a/no feeling for sth.

**Anthrazit** [antraˈtsiːt] (-s, -e) *m* anthracite.

**Anthropologie** [antropoloˈɡiː] (-) *f* anthropology.

**Anti-** ['anti] *in zW* anti; **~alkoholiker** *m* teetotaller; **a~autoritär** *adj* anti-authoritarian; **~babypille** *f* (contraceptive) pill; **~biotikum** (-s, -ka) *nt* antibiotic; **~held** *m* antihero.

**antik** [anˈtiːk] *adj* antique.

**Antike** (-, -n) *f* (*Zeitalter*) ancient world; (*Kunstgegenstand*) antique.

**Antikörper** *m* antibody.

**Antillen** [anˈtɪlən] *pl* Antilles *pl*.

**Antilope** [antiˈloːpə] (-, -n) *f* antelope.

**Antipathie** [antipaˈtiː] *f* antipathy.

**antippen** ['antɪpən] *vt* to tap; (*Pedal, Bremse*) to touch; (*fig: Thema*) to touch on.

**Antiquariat** [antikvari'a:t] (-(e)s, -e) *nt*
secondhand bookshop; **modernes ~**
remainder bookshop/department.

**antiquiert** [anti'kvi:rt] (*pej*) *adj* antiquated.

**Antiquitäten** [antikvi'te:tən] *pl* antiques *pl*;
**~handel** *m* antique business; **~händler(in)**
*m(f)* antique dealer.

**Antisemitismus** [antizemi'tɪsmʊs] *m* anti-
semitism.

**antiseptisch** [anti'zɛptɪʃ] *adj* antiseptic.

**Antlitz** ['antlɪts] (-es, -e) *nt* (*liter*) countenance
(*liter*), face.

**antörnen** ['antœrnən] *vt*, *vi* = **anturnen**.

**Antrag** ['antra:k] (-(e)s, -träge) *m* proposal;
(*PARL*) motion; (*Gesuch*) application; **einen
~ auf etw** *akk* **stellen** to make an application
for sth; (*JUR etc*) to file a petition/claim for
sth.

**Antragsformular** *nt* application form.

**Antragsgegner(in)** *m(f)* (*JUR*) respondent.

**Antragsteller(in)** (-s, -) *m(f)* claimant; (*für
Kredit etc*) applicant.

**antreffen** ['antrɛfən] *unreg vt* to meet.

**antreiben** ['antraɪbən] *unreg vt* to drive on;
(*Motor*) to drive; (*anschwemmen*) to wash up
♦ *vi* to be washed up; **jdn zur Eile/Arbeit ~** to
urge sb to hurry up/to work.

**Antreiber** (-s, -) *m* slave-driver (*pej*).

**antreten** ['antre:tən] *unreg vt* (*Amt*) to take up;
(*Erbschaft*) to come into; (*Beweis*) to offer;
(*Reise*) to start, begin ♦ *vi* (*MIL*) to fall in;
(*SPORT*) to line up; (*zum Dienst*) to report;
**gegen jdn ~** to play/fight against sb.

**Antrieb** ['antri:p] *m* (*lit, fig*) drive; **aus
eigenem ~** of one's own accord.

**Antriebskraft** *f* (*TECH*) power.

**antrinken** ['antrɪŋkən] *unreg vt* (*Flasche, Glas*) to
start to drink from; **sich** *dat* **Mut/einen
Rausch ~** to give o.s. Dutch courage/get
drunk; **angetrunken sein** to be tipsy.

**Antritt** ['antrɪt] *m* beginning, commencement;
(*eines Amts*) taking up.

**antun** ['antu:n] *unreg vt*: **jdm etw ~** to do sth to
sb; **sich** *dat* **Zwang ~** to force o.s.

**anturnen** ['antʊrnən] (*umg*) *vt* (*Drogen, Musik*)
to turn on ♦ *vi*: **... turnt an ...** turns you on.

**Antwerpen** [ant'vɛrpən] (-s) *nt* Antwerp.

**Antwort** ['antvɔrt] (-, -en) *f* answer, reply;
**um ~ wird gebeten** RSVP.

**antworten** *vi* to answer, reply.

**anvertrauen** ['anfertrauən] *vt*: **jdm etw ~** to
entrust sb with sth; **sich jdm ~** to confide in
sb.

**anvisieren** ['anvizi:rən] *vt* (*fig*) to set one's
sights on.

**anwachsen** ['anvaksən] *unreg vi* to grow;
(*Pflanze*) to take root.

**Anwalt** ['anvalt] (-(e)s, -wälte) *m* solicitor;
lawyer; (*fig: Fürsprecher*) advocate; (: *der
Armen etc*) champion.

**Anwältin** ['anvɛltɪn] *f siehe* **Anwalt**.

**Anwalts-** *zW*: **~honorar** *nt* retainer, retaining

fee; **~kammer** *f professional association of
lawyers*, ≈ Law Society (*BRIT*); **~kosten** *pl*
legal expenses *pl*.

**Anwandlung** ['anvandlʊŋ] *f* caprice; **eine
~ von etw** a fit of sth.

**anwärmen** ['anvɛrmən] *vt* to warm up.

**Anwärter(in)** ['anvɛrtər(ɪn)] *m(f)* candidate.

**anweisen** ['anvaɪzən] *unreg vt* to instruct;
(*zuteilen*) to assign.

**Anweisung** *f* instruction; (*COMM*)
remittance; (*Post~, Zahlungs~*) money
order.

**anwendbar** ['anvɛntba:r] *adj* practicable,
applicable.

**anwenden** ['anvɛndən] *unreg vt* to use, employ;
(*Gesetz, Regel*) to apply.

**Anwenderprogramm** *nt* (*COMPUT*)
application program.

**Anwendersoftware** *f* application package.

**Anwendung** *f* use; application.

**anwerfen** ['anvɛrfən] *unreg vt* (*TECH*) to start
up.

**anwesend** ['anve:zənt] *adj* present; **die A~en**
those present.

**Anwesenheit** *f* presence.

**Anwesenheitsliste** *f* attendance register.

**anwidern** ['anvi:dərn] *vt* to disgust.

**Anwohner(in)** ['anvo:nər(ɪn)] (-s, -) *m(f)*
resident.

**Anwuchs** ['anvu:ks] *m* growth.

**Anzahl** ['antsa:l] *f*: **~ (an** +*dat*) number (of).

**anzahlen** *vt* to pay on account.

**Anzahlung** *f* deposit, payment on account.

**anzapfen** ['antsapfən] *vt* to tap.

**Anzeichen** ['antsaɪçən] *nt* sign, indication; **alle
~ deuten darauf hin, daß ...** all the signs are
that ...

**Anzeige** ['antsaɪgə] (-, -n) *f* (*Zeitungs~*)
announcement; (*Werbung*) advertisement;
(*COMPUT*) display; (*bei Polizei*) report; **gegen
jdn ~ erstatten** to report sb (to the police).

**anzeigen** *vt* (*zu erkennen geben*) to show;
(*bekanntgeben*) to announce; (*bei Polizei*) to
report.

**Anzeigenteil** *m* advertisements *pl*.

**anzeigepflichtig** *adj* notifiable.

**Anzeiger** *m* indicator.

**anzetteln** ['antsɛtəln] (*umg*) *vt* to instigate.

**anziehen** ['antsi:ən] *unreg vt* to attract;
(*Kleidung*) to put on; (*Mensch*) to dress;
(*Schraube, Seil*) to pull tight; (*Knie*) to draw
up; (*Feuchtigkeit*) to absorb ♦ *vr* to get
dressed.

**anziehend** *adj* attractive.

**Anziehung** *f* (*Reiz*) attraction.

**Anziehungskraft** *f* power of attraction;
(*PHYS*) force of gravitation.

**Anzug** ['antsu:k] *m* suit; **im ~ sein** to be
approaching.

**anzüglich** ['antsy:klɪç] *adj* personal; (*anstößig*)
offensive; **A~keit** *f* offensiveness;
(*Bemerkung*) personal remark.

**anzünden** ['antsʏndən] *vt* to light.
**Anzünder** *m* lighter.
**anzweifeln** ['antsvaifəln] *vt* to doubt.
**AOK** (-) *f abk* (= *Allgemeine Ortskrankenkasse*)
*siehe* **Ortskrankenkasse**.

> The **AOK** (*Allgemeine Ortskrankenkasse*)
> forms part of a compulsory medical insurance
> scheme for people who are not members of a
> private scheme. The AOK has an office in every
> large town.

**APA** *f abk* (= *Austria Presse-Agentur*) *Austrian*
*news agency*.
**apart** [a'part] *adj* distinctive.
**Apartheid** [a'pa:rthait] *f* apartheid.
**Apartment** [a'partmənt] (-s, -s) *nt* flat (*BRIT*),
apartment (*bes US*).
**Apathie** [apa'ti:] *f* apathy.
**apathisch** [a'pa:tɪʃ] *adj* apathetic.
**Apenninen** [apɛ'ni:nən] *pl* Apennines *pl*.
**Apfel** ['apfəl] (-s, ̈-) *m* apple; **in den sauren**
~ **beißen** (*fig: umg*) to swallow the bitter
pill; **etw für einen ~ und ein Ei kaufen** (*umg*)
to buy sth dirt cheap *od* for a song; ~**mus** *nt*
apple purée; (*als Beilage*) apple sauce; ~**saft**
*m* apple juice.
**Apfelsine** [apfəl'zi:nə] (-, -n) *f* orange.
**Apfeltasche** *f* apple turnover.
**Apfelwein** *m* strong cider.
**apl.** *abk* = **außerplanmäßig**.
**APO, Apo** ['a:po] (-) *f abk*
(= *außerparlamentarische Opposition*)
*extraparliamentary opposition*.

> The **APO** was an extraparliamentary
> opposition group formed in West Germany in
> the late 1960s by those who felt that their
> interests were not being sufficiently
> represented in parliament. It was disbanded in
> the 1970s. Some of its members then formed
> the RAF, a terrorist organisation. Some formed
> the Green Party (**die Grünen**).

**apolitisch** ['apoli:tɪʃ] *adj* non-political,
apolitical.
**Apostel** [a'pɔstəl] (-s, -) *m* apostle.
**Apostroph** [apo'stro:f] (-s, -e) *m* apostrophe.
**Apotheke** [apo'te:kə] (-, -n) *f* chemist's
(shop) (*BRIT*), drugstore (*US*).

> The **Apotheke** is a pharmacy selling medicines
> only available on prescription. It also sells
> toiletries. The pharmacist is qualified to give
> advice on medicines and treatment.

**Apotheker(in)** (-s, -) *m(f)* pharmacist,
(dispensing) chemist (*BRIT*), druggist (*US*).
**Appalachen** [apa'laxən] *pl* Appalachian
Mountains *pl*.
**Apparat** [apa'ra:t] (-(e)s, -e) *m* piece of
apparatus; (*Foto~*) camera; (*Telefon~*)

telephone; (*RUNDF, TV*) set; (*Verwaltungs~*,
*Partei~*) machinery, apparatus; **am** ~ on the
phone; (*als Antwort*) speaking; **am** ~ **bleiben**
to hold the line.
**Apparatur** [apara'tu:r] *f* apparatus.
**Appartement** [apart(ə)'mã:] (-s, -s) *nt* flat
(*BRIT*), apartment (*bes US*).
**Appell** [a'pɛl] (-s, -e) *m* (*MIL*) muster, parade;
(*fig*) appeal; **zum** ~ **antreten** to line up for
roll call.
**appellieren** [apɛ'li:rən] *vi:* ~ (**an** +*akk*) to
appeal (to).
**Appetit** [ape'ti:t] (-(e)s, -e) *m* appetite; **guten**
~! enjoy your meal; **a**~**lich** *adj* appetizing;
~**losigkeit** *f* lack of appetite.
**Applaus** [a'plaʊs] (-es, -e) *m* applause.
**Appretur** [apre'tu:r] *f* finish;
(*Wasserundurchlässigkeit*) waterproofing.
**approbiert** [apro'bi:rt] *adj* (*Arzt*) registered,
certified.
**Apr.** *abk* (= *April*) Apr.
**Aprikose** [apri'ko:zə] (-, -n) *f* apricot.
**April** [a'prɪl] (-(s), -e) (*pl selten*) *m* April; **jdn in**
**den** ~ **schicken** to make an April fool of sb;
*siehe auch* **September**; ~**wetter** *nt* April
showers *pl*.
**apropos** [apro'po:] *adv* by the way, that
reminds me.
**Aquaplaning** [akva'pla:nɪŋ] (-(s)) *nt*
aquaplaning.
**Aquarell** [akva'rɛl] (-s, -e) *nt* watercolour
(*BRIT*), watercolor (*US*).
**Aquarium** [a'kva:riʊm] *nt* aquarium.
**Äquator** [ɛ'kva:tɔr] (-s) *m* equator.
**Äquivalent** [ɛkviva'lɛnt] (-(e)s, -e) *nt*
equivalent.
**Ar** [a:r] (-s, -e) *nt od m* (*Maß*) are (*100 m²*).
**Ära** ['ɛ:ra] (-, **Ären**) *f* era.
**Araber(in)** ['a:rabər(ɪn)] (-s, -) *m(f)* Arab.
**Arabien** [a'ra:biən] (-s) *nt* Arabia.
**arabisch** *adj* Arab; (*Arabien betreffend*)
Arabian; (*Sprache*) Arabic; **A**~**er Golf**
Arabian Gulf; **A**~**es Meer** Arabian Sea; **A**~**e**
**Wüste** Arabian Desert.
**Arbeit** ['arbait] (-, -en) *f* work *no art*; (*Stelle*)
job; (*Erzeugnis*) piece of work;
(*wissenschaftliche*) dissertation; (*Klassen~*)
test; **Tag der** ~ Labour (*BRIT*) *od* Labor (*US*)
Day; **sich an die** ~ **machen, an die** ~ **gehen**
to get down to work, start working; **jdm**
~ **machen** (*Mühe*) to put sb to trouble; **das**
**war eine** ~ that was a hard job.
**arbeiten** *vi* to work ♦ *vt* to make ♦ *vr:* **sich**
**nach oben/an die Spitze** ~ (*fig*) to work
one's way up/to the top.
**Arbeiter(in)** (-s, -) *m(f)* worker; (*ungelernt*)
labourer (*BRIT*), laborer (*US*).
**Arbeiter-** *zW:* ~**familie** *f* working-class
family; ~**kind** *nt* child from a working-class
family; ~**mitbestimmung** *f* employee
participation; ~**schaft** *f* workers *pl*, labour
(*BRIT*) *od* labor (*US*) force; ~**selbstkontrolle**

*f* workers' control; **~-und-Bauern-Staat** *m* (*DDR*) workers' and peasants' state; **~wohlfahrt** *f* workers' welfare association.
**Arbeit-** *zW:* **~geber (-s, -)** *m* employer; **~nehmer (-s, -)** *m* employee; **a~sam** *adj* industrious.
**Arbeits-** *in zW* labour (*BRIT*), labor (*US*); **~amt** *nt* employment exchange, Job Centre (*BRIT*); **~aufwand** *m* expenditure of energy; (*INDUSTRIE*) use of labour (*BRIT*) *od* labor (*US*); **~bedingungen** *pl* working conditions *pl*; **~beschaffung** *f* (*~platzbeschaffung*) job creation; **~erlaubnis** *f* work permit; **a~fähig** *adj* fit for work, able-bodied; **~gang** *m* operation; **~gemeinschaft** *f* study group; **~gericht** *nt* industrial tribunal; **a~intensiv** *adj* labour-intensive (*BRIT*), labor-intensive (*US*); **~konflikt** *m* industrial dispute; **~kraft** *f* worker; **~kräfte** *pl* workers *pl*, labour (*BRIT*), labor (*US*); **a~los** *adj* unemployed, out-of-work; **~losengeld** *nt* unemployment benefit; **~losenhilfe** *f* supplementary benefit; **~losenunterstützung** *f* unemployment benefit; **~losenversicherung** *f* compulsory insurance against unemployment; **~losigkeit** *f* unemployment; **~markt** *m* job market; **~moral** *f* attitude to work; (*in Betrieb*) work climate; **~niederlegung** *f* walkout; **~platte** *f* (*Küche*) work-top, work surface; **~platz** *m* place of work; (*Stelle*) job; **~platzrechner** *m* (*COMPUT*) work station; **~recht** *nt* industrial law; **a~scheu** *adj* workshy; **~schutz** *m* maintenance of health and safety standards at work; **~tag** *m* work(ing) day; **~teilung** *f* division of labour (*BRIT*) *od* labor (*US*); **~tier** *nt* (*fig: umg*) glutton for work, workaholic; **a~unfähig** *adj* unfit for work; **~unfall** *m* industrial accident; **~verhältnis** *nt* employee-employer relationship; **~vermittlung** *f* (*Amt*) employment exchange; (*privat*) employment agency; **~vertrag** *m* contract of employment; **~zeit** *f* working hours *pl*; **~zeitverkürzung** *f* reduction in working hours; **~zimmer** *nt* study.
**Archäologe** [arçεo'lo:gə] **(-n, -n)** *m* arch(a)eologist.
**Archäologin** [arçεo'lo:gın] *f* arch(a)eologist.
**Arche** ['arçə] **(-, -n)** *f:* **die ~ Noah** Noah's Ark.
**Architekt(in)** [arçi'tεkt(ın)] **(-en, -en)** *m(f)* architect.
**architektonisch** [arçitεk'to:nıʃ] *adj* architectural.
**Architektur** [arçitεk'tu:r] *f* architecture.
**Archiv** [ar'çi:f] **(-s, -e)** *nt* archive.

**Arena** [a're:na] **(-, Arenen)** *f* (*lit, fig*) arena; (*Zirkus~, Stierkampf~*) ring.
**arg** [ark] *adj* bad, awful ♦ *adv* awfully, very; **es zu ~ treiben** to go too far.
**Argentinien** [argεn'ti:niən] **(-s)** *nt* Argentina, the Argentine.
**Argentinier(in)** **(-s, -)** *m(f)* Argentine, Argentinian (*BRIT*), Argentinean (*US*).
**argentinisch** [argεn'ti:nıʃ] *adj* Argentine, Argentinian (*BRIT*), Argentinean (*US*).
**Ärger** ['εrgər] **(-s)** *m* (*Wut*) anger; (*Unannehmlichkeit*) trouble; **jdm ~ machen** *od* **bereiten** to cause sb a lot of trouble *od* bother; **ä~lich** *adj* (*zornig*) angry; (*lästig*) annoying, aggravating.
**ärgern** *vt* to annoy ♦ *vr* to get annoyed.
**Ärgernis** **(-ses, -se)** *nt* annoyance; (*Anstoß*) offence (*BRIT*), offense (*US*), outrage; **öffentliches ~ erregen** to be a public nuisance.
**arg-** *zW:* **~listig** *adj* cunning, insidious; **~listige Täuschung** fraud; **~los** *adj* guileless, innocent; **A~losigkeit** *f* guilelessness, innocence.
**Argument** [argu'mεnt] *nt* argument.
**argumentieren** [argumεn'ti:rən] *vi* to argue.
**Argusauge** ['argus|augə] *nt* (*geh*): **mit ~n** eagle-eyed.
**Argwohn** *m* suspicion.
**argwöhnisch** *adj* suspicious.
**Arie** ['a:riə] *f* aria.
**Aristokrat(in)** [arısto'kra:t(ın)] **(-en, -en)** *m(f)* aristocrat.
**Aristokratie** [arıstokra:'ti:] *f* aristocracy.
**aristokratisch** *adj* aristocratic.
**arithmetisch** [arıt'me:tıʃ] *adj* arithmetical; **~es Mittel** arithmetic mean.
**Arkaden** [ar'ka:dən] *pl* (*Bogengang*) arcade *sing*.
**Arktis** ['arktıs] **(-)** *f* Arctic.
**arktisch** *adj* Arctic.
**arm** [arm] *adj* poor; **~ dran sein** (*umg*) to have a hard time of it.
**Arm** **(-(e)s, -e)** *m* arm; (*Fluß~*) branch; **jdn auf den ~ nehmen** (*fig: umg*) to pull sb's leg; **jdm unter die ~e greifen** (*fig*) to help sb out; **einen langen/den längeren ~ haben** (*fig*) to have a lot of/more pull (*umg*) *od* influence.
**Armatur** [arma'tu:r] *f* (*ELEK*) armature.
**Armaturenbrett** *nt* instrument panel; (*AUT*) dashboard.
**Armband** *nt* bracelet; **~uhr** *f* (wrist) watch.
**Arme(r)** *f(m)* poor man/woman; **die ~n** the poor.
**Armee** [ar'me:] **(-, -n)** *f* army; **~korps** *nt* army corps.
**Ärmel** ['εrməl] **(-s, -)** *m* sleeve; **etw aus dem**

~ **schütteln** (*fig*) to produce sth just like that.

**Ärmelkanal** *m* (English) Channel.

**Armenien** [ar'meːniən] (**-s**) *nt* Armenia.

**Armenier(in)** [ar'meːniər(ın)] (**-s, -**) *m(f)* Armenian.

**armenisch** [ar'meːnıʃ] *adj* Armenian.

**Armenrecht** *nt* (*JUR*) legal aid.

**Armer** *m siehe* **Arme(r)**.

**Armlehne** *f* armrest.

**Armleuchter** (*pej: umg*) *m* (*Dummkopf*) twit (*BRIT*), fool.

**ärmlich** ['ɛrmlıç] *adj* poor; **aus ~en Verhältnissen** from a poor family.

**armselig** *adj* wretched, miserable; (*mitleiderregend*) pathetic, pitiful.

**Armut** ['armuːt] (**-**) *f* poverty.

**Armutsgrenze** *f* poverty line.

**Armutszeugnis** *nt* (*fig*): **jdm/sich ein ~ ausstellen** to show sb's/one's shortcomings.

**Aroma** [a'roːma] (**-s, Aromen**) *nt* aroma; **~therapie** *f* aromatherapy.

**aromatisch** [aro'maːtıʃ] *adj* aromatic.

**arrangieren** [arãː'ʒiːrən] *vt* to arrange ♦ *vr* to come to an arrangement.

**Arrest** [a'rɛst] (**-(e)s, -e**) *m* detention.

**arretieren** [are'tiːrən] *vt* (*TECH*) to lock (in place).

**arrogant** [aro'gant] *adj* arrogant.

**Arroganz** *f* arrogance.

**Arsch** [arʃ] (**-es, ̈-e**) (*umg!*) *m* arse (*!*); **leck mich am ~!** (*laß mich in Ruhe*) get stuffed! (*!*), fuck off! (*!*); **am ~ der Welt** (*umg*) in the back of beyond; **~kriecher** (*umg!*) *m* arse licker (*!*), crawler; **~loch** (*umg!*) *nt* (*Mensch*) bastard (*!*).

**Arsen** [ar'zeːn] (**-s**) *nt* arsenic.

**Art** [aːrt] (**-, -en**) *f* (*Weise*) way; (*Sorte*) kind, sort; (*BIOL*) species; **eine ~ (von) Frucht** a kind of fruit; **Häuser aller ~** houses of all kinds; **einzig in seiner ~ sein** to be the only one of its kind, be unique; **auf diese ~ und Weise** in this way; **das ist doch keine ~!** that's no way to behave!; **es ist nicht seine ~, das zu tun** it's not like him to do that; **ich mache das auf meine ~** I do that my (own) way; **Schnitzel nach ~ des Hauses** chef's special escalope.

**arten** *vi*: **nach jdm ~** to take after sb; **der Mensch ist so geartet, daß ...** human nature is such that ...

**Artenschutz** *m* protection of endangered species.

**Arterie** [ar'teːriə] *f* artery.

**Arterienverkalkung** *f* arteriosclerosis.

**Artgenosse** ['aːrtgənɔsə] *m* animal/plant of the same species; (*Mensch*) person of the same type.

**Arthritis** [ar'triːtıs] (**-, -ritiden**) *f* arthritis.

**artig** ['aːrtıç] *adj* good, well-behaved.

**Artikel** [ar'tiːkəl] (**-s, -**) *m* article.

**Artillerie** [artılə'riː] *f* artillery.

**Artischocke** [artı'ʃɔkə] (**-, -n**) *f* artichoke.

**Artistik** [ar'tıstık] (**-**) *f* artistry; (*Zirkus-/Varietékunst*) circus/variety performing.

**Arznei** [aːrts'naı] *f* medicine; **~mittel** *nt* medicine, medicament.

**Arzt** [aːrtst] (**-es, ̈-e**) *m* doctor; **praktischer ~** general practitioner, GP.

**Ärztekammer** *f* ≈ General Medical Council (*BRIT*), State Medical Board of Registration (*US*).

**Arzthelferin** *f* doctor's assistant.

**Ärztin** ['ɛːrtstın] *f* woman doctor; *siehe auch* **Arzt**.

**ärztlich** ['ɛːrtstlıç] *adj* medical.

**Arztpraxis** *f* doctor's practice; (*Räume*) doctor's surgery (*BRIT*) *od* office (*US*).

**As** [as] (**-ses, -se**) *nt* ace; (*MUS*) A flat.

**Asbest** [as'bɛst] (**-(e)s, -e**) *m* asbestos.

**Asche** ['aʃə] (**-, -n**) *f* ash.

**Aschen-** *zW*: **~bahn** *f* cinder track; **~becher** *m* ashtray; **~brödel** *nt* (*LITER, fig*) Cinderella; **~puttel** *nt* (*LITER, fig*) Cinderella.

**Aschermittwoch** *m* Ash Wednesday.

**Aserbaidschan** [azɛrbaı'dʒaːn] (**-s**) *nt* Azerbaijan.

**aserbaidschanisch** *adj* Azerbaijani.

**Asiat(in)** [azi'aːt(ın)] (**-en, -en**) *m(f)* Asian.

**asiatisch** *adj* Asian, Asiatic.

**Asien** ['aːziən] (**-s**) *nt* Asia.

**asozial** ['azotsiaːl] *adj* antisocial; (*Familie*) asocial.

**Asoziale(r)** (*pej*) *f(m)* antisocial person; **Asoziale** *pl* antisocial elements.

**Aspekt** [as'pɛkt] (**-(e)s, -e**) *m* aspect.

**Asphalt** [as'falt] (**-(e)s, -e**) *m* asphalt.

**asphaltieren** [asfal'tiːrən] *vt* to asphalt.

**Asphaltstraße** *f* asphalt road.

**aß** *etc* [aːs] *vb siehe* **essen**.

**Ass.** *abk* = **Assessor**.

**Assekurant(in)** [asekuˈrant(ın)] (**-en, -en**) *m(f)* underwriter.

**Assemblersprache** [əˈsɛmblərʃpraːxə] *f* (*COMPUT*) assembly language.

**Assessor(in)** [a'sɛsɔr(ın)] (**-s, -en**) *m(f)* graduate civil servant who has completed his/her traineeship.

**Assistent(in)** [asıs'tɛnt(ın)] *m(f)* assistant.

**Assistenzarzt** [asıs'tɛntsaːrtst] *m* houseman (*BRIT*), intern (*US*).

**Assoziation** [asotsiatsi'oːn] *f* association.

**assoziieren** [asotsi'iːrən] *vt* (*geh*) to associate.

**Ast** [ast] (**-(e)s, ̈-e**) *m* branch; **sich** *dat* **einen ~ lachen** (*umg*) to double up (with laughter).

**AStA** ['asta] (**-(s), -(s)**) *m abk* (= *Allgemeiner Studentenausschuß*) *students' association*.

**Aster** ['astər] (**-, -n**) *f* aster.

**ästhetisch** [ɛs'teːtıʃ] *adj* aesthetic (*BRIT*), esthetic (*US*).

**Asthma** ['astma] (**-s**) *nt* asthma.

**Asthmatiker(in)** [ast'maːtikər(ın)] (**-s, -**) *m(f)*

asthmatic.

**astrein** ['astraın] *adj (fig: umg: moralisch einwandfrei)* straight, on the level; *(: echt)* genuine; *(prima)* fantastic.

**Astrologe** [astro'lo:gə] (**-n, -n**) *m* astrologer.

**Astrologie** [astrolo'gi:] *f* astrology.

**Astrologin** *f* astrologer.

**Astronaut(in)** [astro'naʊt(ın)] (**-en, -en**) *m(f)* astronaut.

**Astronautik** *f* astronautics.

**Astronom(in)** [astro'no:m(ın)] (**-en, -en**) *m(f)* astronomer.

**Astronomie** [astrono'mi:] *f* astronomy.

**ASU** *f abk* (= *Arbeitsgemeinschaft selbständiger Unternehmer*) association of private traders; (= *Abgassonderuntersuchung*) exhaust emission test.

**ASW** *f abk* (= *außersinnliche Wahrnehmung*) ESP.

**Asyl** [a'zy:l] (**-s, -e**) *nt* asylum; *(Heim)* home; *(Obdachlosen~)* shelter.

**Asylant(in)** [azy'lant(ın)] (**-en, -en**) *m(f)* person seeking (political) asylum.

**Asylrecht** *nt (POL)* right of (political) asylum.

**A.T.** *abk* (= *Altes Testament*) O.T.

**Atelier** [atəli'e:] (**-s, -s**) *nt* studio.

**Atem** ['a:təm] (**-s**) *m* breath; **den ~ anhalten** to hold one's breath; **außer ~** out of breath; **jdn in ~ halten** to keep sb in suspense *od* on tenterhooks; **das verschlug mir den ~** it took my breath away; **einen langen/den längeren ~ haben** to have a lot of staying power; **a~beraubend** *adj* breathtaking; **a~los** *adj* breathless; **~pause** *f* breather; **~wege** *pl* *(ANAT)* respiratory tract; **~zug** *m* breath.

**Atheismus** [ate'ısmʊs] *m* atheism.

**Atheist(in)** *m(f)* atheist; **a~isch** *adj* atheistic.

**Athen** [a'te:n] (**-s**) *nt* Athens.

**Athener(in)** (**-s, -**) *m(f)* Athenian.

**Äther** ['ɛ:tər] (**-s, -**) *m* ether.

**Äthiopien** [ɛti'o:piən] (**-s**) *nt* Ethiopia.

**Äthiopier(in)** (**-s, -**) *m(f)* Ethiopian.

**äthiopisch** *adj* Ethiopian.

**Athlet(in)** [at'le:t(ın)] (**-en, -en**) *m(f)* athlete.

**Athletik** *f* athletics *sing*.

**Atlanten** *pl von* **Atlas**.

**Atlantik** [at'lantık] (**-s**) *m* Atlantic.

**atlantisch** *adj* Atlantic; **der A~e Ozean** the Atlantic Ocean.

**Atlas** ['atlas] (**-** *od* **-ses, -se** *od* **Atlanten**) *m* atlas; **~gebirge** *nt* Atlas Mountains *pl*.

**atmen** ['a:tmən] *vt, vi* to breathe.

**Atmosphäre** [atmo'sfɛ:rə] (**-, -n**) *f* atmosphere.

**atmosphärisch** *adj* atmospheric.

**Atmung** ['a:tmʊŋ] *f* respiration.

**Ätna** ['ɛ:tna] (**-(s)**) *m* Etna.

**Atom** [a'to:m] (**-s, -e**) *nt* atom.

**atomar** [ato'ma:r] *adj* atomic, nuclear; *(Drohung)* nuclear.

**Atom-** *zW:* **~bombe** *f* atom bomb; **~energie** *f* nuclear *od* atomic energy; **~kern** *m* atomic nucleus; **~kraft** *f* nuclear power; **~kraftwerk** *nt* nuclear power station; **~krieg** *m* nuclear *od* atomic war; **~lobby** *f* nuclear lobby; **~macht** *f* nuclear *od* atomic power; **~meiler** *m* nuclear reactor; **~müll** *m* nuclear waste; **~physik** *f* nuclear physics *sing*; **~pilz** *m* mushroom cloud; **~sperrvertrag** *m (POL)* nuclear non-proliferation treaty; **~sprengkopf** *m* nuclear *od* atomic warhead; **~strom** *m electricity generated by nuclear power*; **~test** *m* nuclear test; **~testgelände** *nt* nuclear testing range; **~waffen** *pl* nuclear *od* atomic weapons *pl*; **a~waffenfrei** *adj (Zone)* nuclear-free; **~wirtschaft** *f* nuclear industry; **~zeitalter** *nt* atomic age.

**Attacke** [a'takə] (**-, -n**) *f (Angriff)* attack.

**Attentat** [atɛn'ta:t] (**-(e)s, -e**) *nt:* **~ (auf +akk)** (attempted) assassination (of).

**Attentäter(in)** [atɛn'tɛ:tər(ın)] (**-s, -**) *m(f)* (would-be) assassin.

**Attest** [a'tɛst] (**-(e)s, -e**) *nt* certificate.

**Attraktion** [atraktsi'o:n] *f* attraction.

**attraktiv** [atrak'ti:f] *adj* attractive.

**Attrappe** [a'trapə] (**-, -n**) *f* dummy; **bei ihr ist alles ~** everything about her is false.

**Attribut** [atri'bu:t] (**-(e)s, -e**) *nt (GRAM)* attribute.

**ätzen** ['ɛtsən] *vi* to be caustic.

**ätzend** *adj (lit: Säure)* corrosive; *(Geruch)* pungent; *(fig: umg: furchtbar)* dreadful, horrible; *(: toll)* magic.

─────────── *SCHLÜSSELWORT*

**auch** [aʊx] *adv* **1** *(ebenfalls)* also, too, as well; **das ist ~ schön** that's nice too *od* as well; **er kommt - ich ~** he's coming - so am I, me too; **~ nicht** not ... either; **ich ~ nicht** nor I, me neither; **oder ~** or; **~ das noch!** not that as well!; **nicht nur ..., sondern ~ ...** not only ... but also ...

**2** *(selbst, sogar)* even; **~ wenn das Wetter schlecht ist** even if the weather is bad; **ohne ~ nur zu fragen** without even asking

**3** *(wirklich)* really; **du siehst müde aus - bin ich ~** you look tired - (so) I am; **so sieht es ~ aus** (and) that's what it looks like

**4** *(~ immer)*: **wer ~** whoever; **was ~** whatever; **wozu ~?** *(emphatisch)* whatever for?; **wie dem ~ sei** be that as it may; **wie sehr er sich ~ bemühte** however much he tried.

**Audienz** [aʊdi'ɛnts] (**-, -en**) *f (bei Papst, König etc)* audience.

**Audimax** [aʊdi'maks] *nt (UNIV: umg)* main lecture hall.

**audiovisuell** [aʊdiovizu'ɛl] *adj* audiovisual.

**Auditorium** [aʊdi'to:rium] *nt (Hörsaal)* lecture hall; *(geh: Zuhörerschaft)* audience.

=============== SCHLÜSSELWORT

**auf** [aʊf] *präp +dat* (*wo?*) on; ~ **dem Tisch** on the table; ~ **der Reise** on the way; ~ **der Post/dem Fest** at the post office/party; ~ **der Straße** on the road; ~ **dem Land/der ganzen Welt** in the country/the whole world; **was hat es damit** ~ **sich?** what does it mean?

♦ *präp +akk* **1** (*wohin?*) on(to); ~ **den Tisch** on(to) the table; ~ **die Post gehen** to go to the post office; ~ **das Land** into the country; **etw** ~ **einen Zettel schreiben** to write sth on a piece of paper; ~ **eine Tasse Kaffee/eine Zigarette(nlänge)** for a cup of coffee/a smoke; **die Nacht (von Montag)** ~ **Dienstag** Monday night; ~ **einen Polizisten kommen 1.000 Bürger** there is one policeman to every 1,000 citizens

**2**: ~ **deutsch** in German; ~ **Lebenszeit** for my/his lifetime; **bis** ~ **ihn** except for him; ~ **einmal** at once; ~ **seinen Vorschlag (hin)** at his suggestion

♦ *adv* **1** (*offen*) open; **das Fenster ist** ~ the window is open

**2** (*hinauf*) up; ~ **und ab** up and down; ~ **und davon** up and away; ~! (*los!*) come on!; **von klein** ~ from childhood onwards

**3** (*aufgestanden*) up; **ist er schon** ~? is he up yet?

♦ *konj:* ~ **daß** (so) that.

**aufarbeiten** ['aʊf|arbaɪtən] *vt* (*erledigen: Korrespondenz etc*) to catch up with.

**aufatmen** ['aʊf|a:tmən] *vi* to heave a sigh of relief.

**aufbahren** ['aʊfba:rən] *vt* to lay out.

**Aufbau** ['aʊfbaʊ] *m* (*Bauen*) building, construction; (*Struktur*) structure; (*aufgebautes Teil*) superstructure.

**aufbauen** ['aʊfbaʊən] *vt* to erect, build (up); (*Existenz*) to make; (*gestalten*) to construct; (*gründen*): ~ (**auf** *+dat*) to found (on), base (on) ♦ *vr:* **sich vor jdm** ~ to draw o.s. up to one's full height in front of sb.

**aufbäumen** ['aʊfbɔymən] *vr* to rear; (*fig*) to revolt, rebel.

**aufbauschen** ['aʊfbaʊʃən] *vt* to puff out; (*fig*) to exaggerate.

**aufbegehren** ['aʊfbəge:rən] *vi* (*geh*) to rebel.

**aufbehalten** ['aʊfbəhaltən] *unreg vt* to keep on.

**aufbekommen** ['aʊfbəkɔmən] *unreg* (*umg*) *vt* (*öffnen*) to get open; (: *Hausaufgaben*) to be given.

**aufbereiten** ['aʊfbəraɪtən] *vt* to process; (*Trinkwasser*) to purify; (*Text etc*) to work up.

**Aufbereitungsanlage** *f* processing plant.

**aufbessern** ['aʊfbɛsərn] *vt* (*Gehalt*) to increase.

**aufbewahren** ['aʊfbəva:rən] *vt* to keep; (*Gepäck*) to put in the left-luggage office.

**Aufbewahrung** *f* (safe)keeping; (*Gepäck*~)

left-luggage office (*BRIT*), baggage check (*US*); **jdm etw zur** ~ **geben** to give sb sth for safekeeping.

**Aufbewahrungsort** *m* storage place.

**aufbieten** ['aʊfbi:tən] *unreg vt* (*Kraft*) to summon (up); (*Armee, Polizei*) to mobilize.

**Aufbietung** *f:* **unter** ~ **aller Kräfte** ... summoning up all his/her *etc* strength ...

**aufbinden** ['aʊfbɪndən] *unreg vt:* **laß dir doch so etwas nicht** ~ (*fig*) don't fall for that.

**aufblähen** ['aʊfblɛːən] *vr* to blow out; (*Segel*) to billow out; (*MED*) to become swollen; (*fig: pej*) to puff o.s. up.

**aufblasen** ['aʊfbla:zən] *unreg vt* to blow up, inflate ♦ *vr* (*umg*) to become big-headed.

**aufbleiben** ['aʊfblaɪbən] *unreg vi* (*Laden*) to remain open; (*Person*) to stay up.

**aufblenden** ['aʊfblɛndən] *vt* (*Scheinwerfer*) to turn on full beam.

**aufblicken** ['aʊfblɪkən] *vi* to look up; ~ **zu** (*lit*) to look up at; (*fig*) to look up to.

**aufblühen** ['aʊfbly:ən] *vi* to blossom; (*fig*) to blossom, flourish.

**aufblühend** *adj* (*COMM*) booming.

**aufbocken** ['aʊfbɔkən] *vt* (*Auto*) to jack up.

**aufbrauchen** ['aʊfbraʊxən] *vt* to use up.

**aufbrausen** ['aʊfbraʊzən] *vi* (*fig*) to flare up.

**aufbrausend** *adj* hot-tempered.

**aufbrechen** ['aʊfbrɛçən] *unreg vt* to break open, to prise (*BRIT*) *od* pry (*US*) open ♦ *vi* to burst open; (*gehen*) to start, set off.

**aufbringen** ['aʊfbrɪŋən] *unreg vt* (*öffnen*) to open; (*in Mode*) to bring into fashion; (*beschaffen*) to procure; (*FIN*) to raise; (*ärgern*) to irritate; **Verständnis für etw** ~ to be able to understand sth.

**Aufbruch** ['aʊfbrʊx] *m* departure.

**aufbrühen** ['aʊfbry:ən] *vt* (*Tee*) to make.

**aufbrummen** ['aʊfbrʊmən] (*umg*) *vt:* **jdm die Kosten** ~ to land sb with the costs.

**aufbürden** ['aʊfbʏrdən] *vt:* **jdm etw** ~ to burden sb with sth.

**aufdecken** ['aʊfdɛkən] *vt* to uncover; (*Spielkarten*) to show.

**aufdrängen** ['aʊfdrɛŋən] *vt:* **jdm etw** ~ to force sth on sb ♦ *vr:* **sich jdm** ~ to intrude on sb.

**aufdrehen** ['aʊfdre:ən] *vt* (*Wasserhahn etc*) to turn on; (*Ventil*) to open; (*Schraubverschluß*) to unscrew; (*Radio etc*) to turn up; (*Haar*) to put in rollers.

**aufdringlich** ['aʊfdrɪŋlɪç] *adj* pushy; (*Benehmen*) obtrusive; (*Parfüm*) powerful.

**aufeinander** [aʊf|aɪ'nandər] *adv* on top of one another; (*schießen*) at each other; (*warten*) for one another; (*vertrauen*) each other; **A~folge** *f* succession, series; **~folgen** *vi* to follow one another; **~folgend** *adj* consecutive; **~legen** *vt* to lay on top of one another; **~prallen** *vi* (*Autos etc*) to collide; (*Truppen, Meinungen*) to clash.

**Aufenthalt** ['aʊf|ɛnthalt] *m* stay; (*Verzögerung*)

delay; (*EISENB: Halten*) stop; (*Ort*) haunt.
**Aufenthalts-** *zW:* ~**erlaubnis** *f*,
~**genehmigung** *f* residence permit; ~**raum**
*m* day room; (*in Betrieb*) recreation room.
**auferlegen** ['aʊf|ɛrleːɡən] *vt:* (**jdm**) ~ to
impose (upon sb).
**auferstehen** ['aʊf|ɛrʃteːən] *unreg vi untr* to rise
from the dead.
**Auferstehung** *f* resurrection.
**aufessen** ['aʊf|ɛsən] *unreg vt* to eat up.
**auffahren** ['aʊffaːrən] *unreg vi* (*herankommen*)
to draw up; (*hochfahren*) to jump up; (*wütend
werden*) to flare up; (*in den Himmel*) to
ascend ♦ *vt* (*Kanonen, Geschütz*) to bring up;
~ **auf** +*akk* (*Auto*) to run *od* crash into.
**auffahrend** *adj* hot-tempered.
**Auffahrt** *f* (*Haus*~) drive; (*Autobahn*~) slip
road (*BRIT*), entrance ramp (*US*).
**Auffahrunfall** *m* pile-up.
**auffallen** ['aʊffalən] *unreg vi* to be noticeable;
**angenehm/unangenehm** ~ to make a good/
bad impression; **jdm** ~ (*bemerkt werden*) to
strike sb.
**auffallend** *adj* striking.
**auffällig** ['aʊffɛlɪç] *adj* conspicuous, striking.
**auffangen** ['aʊffaŋən] *unreg vt* to catch;
(*Funkspruch*) to intercept; (*Preise*) to peg;
(*abfangen: Aufprall etc*) to cushion, absorb.
**Auffanglager** *nt* reception camp.
**auffassen** ['aʊffasən] *vt* to understand,
comprehend; (*auslegen*) to see, view.
**Auffassung** *f* (*Meinung*) opinion; (*Auslegung*)
view, conception; (*auch:* ~**sgabe**) grasp.
**auffindbar** ['aʊffɪntbaːr] *adj* to be found.
**aufflammen** ['aʊfflamən] *vi* (*lit, fig: Feuer,
Unruhen etc*) to flare up.
**auffliegen** ['aʊffliːɡən] *unreg vi* to fly up; (*umg:
Rauschgiftring etc*) to be busted.
**auffordern** ['aʊffɔrdərn] *vt* to challenge;
(*befehlen*) to call upon, order; (*bitten*) to ask.
**Aufforderung** *f* (*Befehl*) order; (*Einladung*)
invitation.
**aufforsten** ['aʊffɔrstən] *vt* (*Gebiet*) to
reafforest; (*Wald*) to restock.
**auffrischen** ['aʊffrɪʃən] *vt* to freshen up;
(*Kenntnisse*) to brush up; (*Erinnerungen*) to
reawaken ♦ *vi* (*Wind*) to freshen.
**aufführen** ['aʊffyːrən] *vt* (*THEAT*) to perform;
(*in einem Verzeichnis*) to list, specify ♦ *vr*
(*sich benehmen*) to behave; **einzeln** ~ to
itemize.
**Aufführung** *f* (*THEAT*) performance; (*Liste*)
specification.
**auffüllen** ['aʊffʏlən] *vt* to fill up; (*Vorräte*) to
replenish; (*Öl*) to top up.
**Aufgabe** ['aʊfgaːbə] (**-, -n**) *f* task; (*SCH*)
exercise; (*Haus*~) homework; (*Verzicht*)
giving up; (*von Gepäck*) registration; (*von
Post*) posting; (*von Inserat*) insertion; **sich** *dat*
**etw zur** ~ **machen** to make sth one's job *od*
business.
**aufgabeln** ['aʊfgaːbəln] *vt* (*fig: umg: jdn*) to

pick up; (: *Sache*) to get hold of.
**Aufgabenbereich** *m* area of responsibility.
**Aufgang** ['aʊfgaŋ] *m* ascent; (*Sonnen*~) rise;
(*Treppe*) staircase.
**aufgeben** ['aʊfgeːbən] *unreg vt* (*verzichten auf*)
to give up; (*Paket*) to send, post; (*Gepäck*) to
register; (*Bestellung*) to give; (*Inserat*) to
insert; (*Rätsel, Problem*) to set ♦ *vi* to give up.
**aufgeblasen** ['aʊfgəblaːzən] *adj* (*fig*) puffed
up, self-important.
**Aufgebot** ['aʊfgəboːt] *nt* supply; (*von Kräften*)
utilization; (*Ehe*~) banns *pl.*
**aufgedonnert** ['aʊfgədɔnərt] (*pej: umg*) *adj*
tarted up.
**aufgedreht** ['aʊfgədreːt] (*umg*) *adj* excited.
**aufgedunsen** ['aʊfgədʊnzən] *adj* swollen,
puffed up.
**aufgegeben** ['aʊfgeːɡəbən] *pp von* **aufgeben**.
**aufgehen** ['aʊfgeːən] *unreg vi* (*Sonne, Teig*) to
rise; (*sich öffnen*) to open; (*THEAT: Vorhang*)
to go up; (*Knopf, Knoten etc*) to come undone;
(*klarwerden*) to become clear; (*MATH*) to
come out exactly; ~ (**in** +*dat*) (*sich widmen*)
to be absorbed (in sth); **in Rauch/Flammen** ~ to
go up in smoke/flames.
**aufgeilen** ['aʊfgaɪlən] (*umg*) *vt* to turn on ♦ *vr*
to be turned on.
**aufgeklärt** ['aʊfgəklɛːrt] *adj* enlightened;
(*sexuell*) knowing the facts of life.
**aufgekratzt** ['aʊfgəkratst] (*umg*) *adj* in high
spirits, full of beans.
**aufgelaufen** ['aʊfgəlaʊfən] *adj:* ~**e Zinsen** *pl*
accrued interest *sing.*
**Aufgeld** *nt* premium.
**aufgelegt** ['aʊfgeːleːkt] *adj:* **gut/schlecht** ~ **sein**
to be in a good/bad mood; **zu etw** ~ **sein** to
be in the mood for sth.
**aufgenommen** ['aʊfgənɔmən] *pp von*
**aufnehmen**.
**aufgeregt** ['aʊfgəreːkt] *adj* excited.
**aufgeschlossen** ['aʊfgəʃlɔsən] *adj* open,
open-minded.
**aufgeschmissen** ['aʊfgəʃmɪsən] (*umg*) *adj* in a
fix, stuck.
**aufgeschrieben** ['aʊfgəʃriːbən] *pp von*
**aufschreiben**.
**aufgestanden** ['aʊfgəʃtandən] *pp von*
**aufstehen**.
**aufgetakelt** ['aʊfgətaːkəlt] *adj* (*fig: umg*)
dressed up to the nines.
**aufgeweckt** ['aʊfgəvɛkt] *adj* bright,
intelligent.
**aufgießen** ['aʊfgiːsən] *unreg vt* (*Wasser*) to
pour over; (*Tee*) to infuse.
**aufgliedern** ['aʊfgliːdərn] *vr:* **sich** ~ (**in** +*akk*) to
(sub)divide (into), break down (into).
**aufgreifen** ['aʊfgraɪfən] *unreg vt* (*Thema*) to
take up; (*Verdächtige*) to pick up, seize.
**aufgrund** [aʊf'grʊnt] *präp* +*gen* on the basis of;
(*wegen*) because of.
**Aufgußbeutel** ['aʊfgʊsbɔʏtəl] *m* sachet
(containing coffee/herbs *etc*) for brewing;

(*Teebeutel*) tea bag.
**aufhaben** ['aʊfhaːbən] *unreg vt* (*Hut etc*) to have on; (*Arbeit*) to have to do.
**aufhalsen** ['aʊfhalzən] (*umg*) *vt*: jdm etw ~ to saddle *od* lumber sb with sth.
**aufhalten** ['aʊfhaltən] *unreg vt* (*Person*) to detain; (*Entwicklung*) to check; (*Tür, Hand*) to hold open; (*Augen*) to keep open ♦ *vr* (*wohnen*) to live; (*bleiben*) to stay; jdn (bei etw) ~ (*abhalten, stören*) to hold *od* keep sb back (from sth); sich über etw/jdn ~ to go on about sth/sb; sich mit etw ~ to waste time over sth; sich bei etw ~ (*sich befassen*) to dwell on sth.
**aufhängen** ['aʊfhɛŋən] *unreg vt* (*Wäsche*) to hang up; (*Menschen*) to hang ♦ *vr* to hang o.s.
**Aufhänger** (-s, -) *m* (*am Mantel*) hook; (*fig*) peg.
**Aufhängung** *f* (*TECH*) suspension.
**aufheben** ['aʊfheːbən] *unreg vt* (*hochheben*) to raise, lift; (*Sitzung*) to wind up; (*Urteil*) to annul; (*Gesetz*) to repeal, abolish; (*aufbewahren*) to keep; (*ausgleichen*) to offset, make up for ♦ *vr* to cancel itself out; viel A~(s) machen (von) to make a fuss (about); bei jdm gut aufgehoben sein to be well looked after at sb's.
**aufheitern** ['aʊfhaɪtərn] *vt, vr* (*Himmel, Miene*) to brighten; (*Mensch*) to cheer up.
**Aufheiterungen** *pl* (*MET*) bright periods *pl*.
**aufheizen** ['aʊfhaɪtsən] *vt*: die Stimmung ~ to stir up feelings.
**aufhelfen** ['aʊfhɛlfən] *unreg vi* (*lit: beim Aufstehen*): jdm ~ to help sb up.
**aufhellen** ['aʊfhɛlən] *vt, vr* to clear up; (*Farbe, Haare*) to lighten.
**aufhetzen** ['aʊfhɛtsən] *vt* to stir up.
**aufheulen** ['aʊfhɔʏlən] *vi* to howl; (*Sirene*) to (start to) wail; (*Motor*) to (give a) roar.
**aufholen** ['aʊfhoːlən] *vt* to make up ♦ *vi* to catch up.
**aufhorchen** ['aʊfhɔrçən] *vi* to prick up one's ears.
**aufhören** ['aʊfhøːrən] *vi* to stop; ~, etw zu tun to stop doing sth.
**aufkaufen** ['aʊfkaʊfən] *vt* to buy up.
**aufklappen** ['aʊfklapən] *vt* to open; (*Verdeck*) to fold back.
**aufklären** ['aʊfklɛːrən] *vt* (*Geheimnis etc*) to clear up; (*Person*) to enlighten; (*sexuell*) to tell the facts of life to; (*MIL*) to reconnoitre ♦ *vr* to clear up.
**Aufklärung** *f* (*von Geheimnis*) clearing up; (*Unterrichtung, Zeitalter*) enlightenment; (*sexuell*) sex education; (*MIL, AVIAT*) reconnaissance.
**Aufklärungsarbeit** *f* educational work.
**aufkleben** ['aʊfkleːbən] *vt* to stick on.
**Aufkleber** (-s, -) *m* sticker.
**aufknöpfen** ['aʊfknœpfən] *vt* to unbutton.
**aufkochen** ['aʊfkɔxən] *vt* to bring to the boil.
**aufkommen** ['aʊfkɔmən] *unreg vi* (*Wind*) to

come up; (*Zweifel, Gefühl*) to arise; (*Mode*) to start; für jdn/etw ~ to be liable *od* responsible for sb/sth; für den Schaden ~ to pay for the damage; endlich kam Stimmung auf at last things livened up.
**aufkreuzen** ['aʊfkrɔʏtsən] (*umg*) *vi* (*erscheinen*) to turn *od* show up.
**aufkündigen** ['aʊfkʏndɪgən] *vt* (*Vertrag etc*) to terminate.
**aufladen** ['aʊflaːdən] *unreg vt* to load ♦ *vr* (*Batterie etc*) to be charged; (*neu* ~) to be recharged; jdm/sich etw ~ (*fig*) to saddle sb/o.s. with sth.
**Auflage** ['aʊflaːgə] *f* edition; (*Zeitung*) circulation; (*Bedingung*) condition; jdm etw zur ~ machen to make sth a condition for sb.
**Auflage(n)höhe** *f* (*von Buch*) number of copies published; (*von Zeitung*) circulation.
**auflassen** ['aʊflasən] *unreg vt* (*umg*) *vt* (*offen*) to leave open; (: *aufgesetzt*) to leave on; die Kinder länger ~ to let the children stay up (longer).
**auflauern** ['aʊflaʊərn] *vi*: jdm ~ to lie in wait for sb.
**Auflauf** ['aʊflaʊf] *m* (*KOCH*) pudding; (*Menschen*~) crowd.
**auflaufen** *unreg vi* (*auf Grund laufen: Schiff*) to run aground; jdn ~ lassen (*umg*) to drop sb in it.
**Auflaufform** *f* (*KOCH*) ovenproof dish.
**aufleben** ['aʊfleːbən] *vi* to revive.
**auflegen** ['aʊfleːgən] *vt* to put on; (*Hörer*) to put down; (*TYP*) to print ♦ *vi* (*TEL*) to hang up.
**auflehnen** ['aʊfleːnən] *vt* to lean on ♦ *vr* to rebel.
**Auflehnung** *f* rebellion.
**auflesen** ['aʊfleːzən] *unreg vt* to pick up.
**aufleuchten** ['aʊflɔʏçtən] *vi* to light up.
**aufliegen** ['aʊfliːgən] *unreg vi* to lie on; (*COMM*) to be available.
**auflisten** ['aʊflɪstən] *vt* (*auch COMPUT*) to list.
**auflockern** ['aʊflɔkərn] *vt* to loosen; (*fig: Eintönigkeit etc*) to liven up; (*entspannen, zwangloser machen*) to make relaxed; (*Atmosphäre*) to make more relaxed, ease.
**auflösen** ['aʊfløːzən] *vt* to dissolve; (*Mißverständnis*) to sort out; (*Konto*) to close; (*Firma*) to wind up; (*Haushalt*) to break up; in Tränen aufgelöst sein to be in tears.
**Auflösung** *f* dissolving; (*fig*) solution; (*Bildschirm*) resolution.
**aufmachen** ['aʊfmaxən] *vt* to open; (*Kleidung*) to undo; (*zurechtmachen*) to do up ♦ *vr* to set out.
**Aufmacher** *m* (*PRESSE*) lead.
**Aufmachung** *f* (*Kleidung*) outfit, get-up; (*Gestaltung*) format.
**aufmerksam** ['aʊfmɛrkzaːm] *adj* attentive; auf etw *akk* ~ werden to become aware of sth; jdn auf etw *akk* ~ machen to point sth out to

sb; **(das ist) sehr ~ von Ihnen**
(*zuvorkommend*) (that's) most kind of you;
**A~keit** *f* attention, attentiveness;
(*Geschenk*) token (gift).
**aufmöbeln** ['aʊfmøːbəln] (*umg*) *vt*
(*Gegenstand*) to do up; (: *beleben*) to buck up,
pep up.
**aufmucken** ['aʊfmʊkən] (*umg*) *vi*: **~ gegen** to
protest at *od* against.
**aufmuntern** ['aʊfmʊntərn] *vt* (*ermutigen*) to
encourage; (*erheitern*) to cheer up.
**aufmüpfig** ['aʊfmʏpfɪç] (*umg*) *adj* rebellious.
**Aufnahme** ['aʊfnaːmə] (-, -n) *f* reception;
(*Beginn*) beginning; (*in Verein etc*) admission;
(*in Liste etc*) inclusion; (*Notieren*) taking
down; (*PHOT*) shot; (*auf Tonband etc*)
recording; **~antrag** *m* application for
membership *od* admission; **a~fähig** *adj*
receptive; **~leiter** *m* (*FILM*) production
manager; (*RUNDF, TV*) producer; **~prüfung** *f*
entrance test; **~stopp** *m* (*für Flüchtlinge etc*)
freeze on immigration.
**aufnehmen** ['aʊfneːmən] *unreg vt* to receive;
(*hochheben*) to pick up; (*beginnen*) to take
up; (*in Verein etc*) to admit; (*in Liste etc*) to
include; (*fassen*) to hold; (*begreifen*) to take
in, grasp; (*beim Stricken: Maschen*) to
increase, make; (*notieren*) to take down;
(*fotografieren*) to photograph; (*auf Tonband,
Platte*) to record; (*FIN: leihen*) to take out; **es
mit jdm ~ können** to be able to compete
with sb.
**aufnötigen** ['aʊfnøːtɪgən] *vt*: **jdm etw ~** to
force sth on sb.
**aufoktroyieren** ['aʊf|ɔktroajiːrən] *vt*: **jdm etw
~** (*geh*) to impose *od* force sth on sb.
**aufopfern** ['aʊf|ɔpfərn] *vt* to sacrifice ♦ *vr* to
sacrifice o.s.
**aufopfernd** *adj* selfless.
**aufpassen** ['aʊfpasən] *vi* (*aufmerksam sein*) to
pay attention; **auf jdn/etw ~** to look after *od*
watch sb/sth; **aufgepaßt!** look out!
**Aufpasser(in)** (-s, -) (*pej*) *m(f)* (*Aufseher,
Spitzel*) spy, watchdog; (*Beobachter*)
supervisor; (*Wächter*) guard.
**aufpflanzen** ['aʊfpflantsən] *vr*: **sich vor jdm ~**
to plant o.s. in front of sb.
**aufplatzen** ['aʊfplatsən] *vi* to burst open.
**aufplustern** ['aʊfpluːstərn] *vr* (*Vogel*) to ruffle
(up) its feathers; (*Mensch*) to puff o.s. up.
**aufprägen** ['aʊfprɛːgən] *vt*: **jdm/etw seinen
Stempel ~** (*fig*) to leave one's mark on sb/
sth.
**Aufprall** ['aʊfpral] (-(e)s, -e) *m* impact.
**aufprallen** *vi* to hit, strike.
**Aufpreis** ['aʊfpraɪs] *m* extra charge.
**aufpumpen** ['aʊfpʊmpən] *vt* to pump up.
**aufputschen** ['aʊfpʊtʃən] *vt* (*aufhetzen*) to
inflame; (*erregen*) to stimulate.
**Aufputschmittel** *nt* stimulant.
**aufraffen** ['aʊfrafən] *vr* to rouse o.s.
**aufräumen** ['aʊfrɔʏmən] *vt, vi* (*Dinge*) to clear

away; (*Zimmer*) to tidy up.
**Aufräumungsarbeiten** *pl* clearing-up
operations *pl*.
**aufrecht** ['aʊfrɛçt] *adj* (*lit, fig*) upright.
**aufrechterhalten** *unreg vt* to maintain.
**aufregen** ['aʊfreːgən] *vt* to excite; (*ärgerlich
machen*) to irritate, annoy; (*nervös machen*)
to make nervous; (*beunruhigen*) to disturb
♦ *vr* to get excited.
**aufregend** *adj* exciting.
**Aufregung** *f* excitement.
**aufreiben** ['aʊfraɪbən] *unreg vt* (*Haut*) to rub
raw; (*erschöpfen*) to exhaust; (*MIL: völlig
vernichten*) to wipe out, annihilate.
**aufreibend** *adj* strenuous.
**aufreihen** ['aʊfraɪən] *vt* (*in Linie*) to line up;
(*Perlen*) to string.
**aufreißen** ['aʊfraɪsən] *unreg vt* (*Umschlag*) to
tear open; (*Augen*) to open wide; (*Tür*) to
throw open; (*Straße*) to take up; (*umg:
Mädchen*) to pick up.
**Aufreißer** (-s, -) *m* (*Person*) smooth operator.
**aufreizen** ['aʊfraɪtsən] *vt* to incite, stir up.
**aufreizend** *adj* exciting, stimulating.
**aufrichten** ['aʊfrɪçtən] *vt* to put up, erect;
(*moralisch*) to console ♦ *vr* to rise;
(*moralisch*): **sich ~ (an** +*dat*) to take heart
(from); **sich im Bett ~** to sit up in bed.
**aufrichtig** ['aʊfrɪçtɪç] *adj* sincere; honest;
**A~keit** *f* sincerity.
**aufrollen** ['aʊfrɔlən] *vt* (*zusammenrollen*) to
roll up; (*Kabel*) to coil *od* wind up; **einen
Fall/Prozeß wieder ~** to reopen a case/trial.
**aufrücken** ['aʊfrʏkən] *vi* to move up;
(*beruflich*) to be promoted.
**Aufruf** ['aʊfruːf] *m* summons; (*zur Hilfe*) call;
(*des Namens*) calling out.
**aufrufen** *unreg vt* (*Namen*) to call out;
(*auffordern*): **jdn ~ (zu)** to call upon sb (for);
**einen Schüler ~** to ask a pupil (to answer) a
question.
**Aufruhr** ['aʊfruːr] (-(e)s, -e) *m* uprising, revolt;
**in ~ sein** to be in uproar.
**Aufrührer(in)** (-s, -) *m(f)* rabble-rouser.
**aufrührerisch** ['aʊfryːrərɪʃ] *adj* rebellious.
**aufrunden** ['aʊfrʊndən] *vt* (*Summe*) to round
up.
**aufrüsten** ['aʊfrʏstən] *vt, vi* to arm.
**Aufrüstung** *f* rearmament.
**aufrütteln** ['aʊfrʏtəln] *vt* (*lit, fig*) to shake up.
**aufs** [aʊfs] = **auf das**.
**aufsagen** ['aʊfzaːgən] *vt* (*Gedicht*) to recite;
(*geh: Freundschaft*) to put an end to.
**aufsammeln** ['aʊfzaməln] *vt* to gather up.
**aufsässig** ['aʊfzɛsɪç] *adj* rebellious.
**Aufsatz** ['aʊfzats] *m* (*Geschriebenes*) essay,
composition; (*auf Schrank etc*) top.
**aufsaugen** ['aʊfzaʊgən] *unreg vt* to soak up.
**aufschauen** ['aʊfʃaʊən] *vi* to look up.
**aufscheuchen** ['aʊfʃɔʏçən] *vt* to scare,
startle.
**aufschichten** ['aʊfʃɪçtən] *vt* to stack, pile up.

**aufschieben** ['aʊfʃiːbən] *unreg vt* to push open; (*verzögern*) to put off, postpone.

**Aufschlag** ['aʊfʃlaːk] *m* (*Ärmel~*) cuff; (*Jacken~*) lapel; (*Hosen~*) turn-up (*BRIT*), cuff (*US*); (*Aufprall*) impact; (*Preis~*) surcharge; (*TENNIS*) service.

**aufschlagen** ['aʊfʃlaːgən] *unreg vt* to open; (*verwunden*) to cut; (*hochschlagen*) to turn up; (*aufbauen: Zelt, Lager*) to pitch, erect; (*Wohnsitz*) to take up ♦ *vi* (*aufprallen*) to hit; (*teurer werden*) to go up; (*TENNIS*) to serve; **schlagt Seite 111 auf** open your books at page 111.

**aufschließen** ['aʊfʃliːsən] *unreg vt* to open up, unlock ♦ *vi* (*aufrücken*) to close up.

**Aufschluß** ['aʊfʃlʊs] *m* information.

**aufschlüsseln** ['aʊfʃlʏsəln] *vt*: ~ **(nach)** to break down (into); (*klassifizieren*) to classify (according to).

**aufschlußreich** *adj* informative, illuminating.

**aufschnappen** ['aʊfʃnapən] *vt* (*umg*) to pick up ♦ *vi* to fly open.

**aufschneiden** ['aʊfʃnaɪdən] *unreg vt* to cut open; (*Brot*) to cut up; (*MED: Geschwür*) to lance ♦ *vi* (*umg*) to brag.

**Aufschneider** (-**s**, -) *m* boaster, braggart.

**Aufschnitt** ['aʊfʃnɪt] *m* (slices of) cold meat.

**aufschnüren** ['aʊfʃnyːrən] *vt* to unlace; (*Paket*) to untie.

**aufschrauben** ['aʊfʃraʊbən] *vt* (*fest~*) to screw on; (*lösen*) to unscrew.

**aufschrecken** ['aʊfʃrɛkən] *vt* to startle ♦ *vi* (*unreg*) to start up.

**Aufschrei** ['aʊfʃraɪ] *m* cry.

**aufschreiben** ['aʊfʃraɪbən] *unreg vt* to write down.

**aufschreien** *unreg vi* to cry out.

**Aufschrift** ['aʊfʃrɪft] *f* (*Inschrift*) inscription; (*Etikett*) label.

**Aufschub** ['aʊfʃuːp] (-**(e)s**, -**schübe**) *m* delay, postponement; **jdm** ~ **gewähren** to grant sb an extension.

**aufschürfen** ['aʊfʃʏrfən] *vt*: **sich** *dat* **die Haut/ das Knie** ~ to graze *od* scrape o.s./one's knee.

**aufschütten** ['aʊfʃʏtən] *vt* (*Flüssigkeit*) to pour on; (*Kohle*) to put on (the fire); (*Damm, Deich*) to throw up; **Kaffee** ~ to make coffee.

**aufschwatzen** ['aʊfʃvatsən] (*umg*) *vt*: **jdm etw** ~ to talk sb into (getting/having *etc*) sth.

**Aufschwung** ['aʊfʃvʊŋ] *m* (*Elan*) boost; (*wirtschaftlich*) upturn, boom; (*SPORT: an Gerät*) mount.

**aufsehen** ['aʊfzeːən] *unreg vi* to look up; ~ **zu** (*lit*) to look up at; (*fig*) to look up to; **A~** (-**s**) *nt* sensation, stir.

**aufsehenerregend** *adj* sensational.

**Aufseher(in)** (-**s**, -) *m(f)* guard; (*im Betrieb*) supervisor; (*Museums~*) attendant; (*Park~*) keeper.

**aufsein** ['aʊfzaɪn] *unreg* (*umg*) *vi* to be open;

(*Person*) to be up.

**aufsetzen** ['aʊfzɛtsən] *vt* to put on; (*Flugzeug*) to put down; (*Dokument*) to draw up ♦ *vr* to sit upright ♦ *vi* (*Flugzeug*) to touch down.

**Aufsicht** ['aʊfzɪçt] *f* supervision; **die** ~ **haben** to be in charge; **bei einer Prüfung** ~ **führen** to invigilate (*BRIT*) *od* supervise an exam.

**Aufsichtsrat** *m* board (of directors).

**aufsitzen** ['aʊfzɪtsən] *unreg vi* (*aufgerichtet sitzen*) to sit up; (*aufs Pferd, Motorrad*) to mount, get on; (*Schiff*) to run aground; **jdn** ~ **lassen** (*umg*) to stand sb up; **jdm** ~ (*umg*) to be taken in by sb.

**aufspalten** ['aʊfʃpaltən] *vt* to split.

**aufspannen** ['aʊfʃpanən] *vt* (*Netz, Sprungtuch*) to stretch *od* spread out; (*Schirm*) to put up, open.

**aufsparen** ['aʊfʃpaːrən] *vt* to save (up).

**aufsperren** ['aʊfʃpɛrən] *vt* to unlock; (*Mund*) to open wide; **die Ohren** ~ (*umg*) to prick up one's ears.

**aufspielen** ['aʊfʃpiːlən] *vr* to show off; **sich als etw** ~ to try to come on as sth.

**aufspießen** ['aʊfʃpiːsən] *vt* to spear.

**aufspringen** ['aʊfʃprɪŋən] *unreg vi* (*hochspringen*) to jump up; (*sich öffnen*) to spring open; (*Hände, Lippen*) to become chapped; ~ **auf** +*akk* to jump onto.

**aufspüren** ['aʊfʃpyːrən] *vt* to track down, trace.

**aufstacheln** ['aʊfʃtaxəln] *vt* to incite.

**aufstampfen** ['aʊfʃtampfən] *vi*: **mit dem Fuß** ~ to stamp one's foot.

**Aufstand** ['aʊfʃtant] *m* insurrection, rebellion.

**aufständisch** ['aʊfʃtɛndɪʃ] *adj* rebellious, mutinous.

**aufstauen** ['aʊfʃtaʊən] *vr* to collect; (*fig: Ärger*) to be bottled up.

**aufstechen** ['aʊfʃtɛçən] *unreg vt* to prick open, puncture.

**aufstecken** ['aʊfʃtɛkən] *vt* to stick on; (*mit Nadeln*) to pin up; (*umg*) to give up.

**aufstehen** ['aʊfʃteːən] *unreg vi* to get up; (*Tür*) to be open; **da mußt du früher** *od* **eher** ~! (*fig: umg*) you'll have to do better than that!

**aufsteigen** ['aʊfʃtaɪgən] *unreg vi* (*hochsteigen*) to climb; (*Rauch*) to rise; ~ **auf** +*akk* to get onto; **in jdm** ~ (*Haß, Verdacht, Erinnerung etc*) to well up in sb.

**Aufsteiger** (-**s**,) *m* (*SPORT*) promoted team; (*sozialer*) ~ social climber.

**aufstellen** ['aʊfʃtɛlən] *vt* (*aufrecht stellen*) to put up; (*Maschine*) to install; (*aufreihen*) to line up; (*Kandidaten*) to nominate; (*Forderung, Behauptung*) to put forward; (*formulieren: Programm etc*) to draw up; (*leisten: Rekord*) to set up.

**Aufstellung** *f* (*SPORT*) line-up; (*Liste*) list.

**Aufstieg** ['aʊfʃtiːk] (-**(e)s**, -**e**) *m* (*auf Berg*) ascent; (*Fortschritt*) rise; (*beruflich, SPORT*) promotion.

**Aufstiegschance** f prospect of promotion.
**aufstöbern** ['aʊfʃtøːbərn] vt (Wild) to start, flush; (umg: entdecken) to run to earth.
**aufstocken** ['aʊfʃtɔkən] vt (Vorräte) to build up.
**aufstoßen** ['aʊfʃtoːsən] unreg vt to push open ♦ vi to belch.
**aufstrebend** ['aʊfʃtreːbənd] adj ambitious; (Land) striving for progress.
**Aufstrich** ['aʊfʃtrɪç] m spread.
**aufstülpen** ['aʊfʃtʏlpən] vt (Ärmel) to turn up; (Hut) to put on.
**aufstützen** ['aʊfʃtʏtsən] vt (Körperteil) to prop, lean; (Person) to prop up ♦ vr: sich ~ auf +akk to lean on.
**aufsuchen** ['aʊfzuːxən] vt (besuchen) to visit; (konsultieren) to consult.
**auftakeln** ['aʊftaːkəln] vt (NAUT) to rig (out) ♦ vr (pej: umg) to deck o.s. out.
**Auftakt** ['aʊftakt] m (MUS) upbeat; (fig) prelude.
**auftanken** ['aʊftaŋkən] vi to get petrol (BRIT) od gas (US) ♦ vt to refuel.
**auftauchen** ['aʊftaʊxən] vi to appear; (gefunden werden, kommen) to turn up; (aus Wasser etc) to emerge; (U-Boot) to surface; (Zweifel) to arise.
**auftauen** ['aʊftaʊən] vt to thaw ♦ vi to thaw; (fig) to relax.
**aufteilen** ['aʊftaɪlən] vt to divide up; (Raum) to partition.
**Aufteilung** f division; partition.
**auftischen** ['aʊftɪʃən] vt to serve (up); (fig) to tell.
**Auftr.** abk = **Auftrag**.
**Auftrag** ['aʊftraːk] m (-(e)s, -träge) m order; (Anweisung) commission; (Aufgabe) mission; **etw in ~ geben (bei)** to order/commission sth (from); **im ~ von** on behalf of; **im ~ od i.A. J. Burnett** pp J. Burnett.
**auftragen** ['aʊftraːgən] unreg vt (Essen) to serve; (Farbe) to put on; (Kleidung) to wear out ♦ vi (dick machen): **die Jacke trägt auf** the jacket makes one look fat; **jdm etw ~** to tell sb sth; **dick ~** (umg) to exaggerate.
**Auftraggeber(in)** (-s, -) m(f) client; (COMM) customer.
**Auftragsbestätigung** f confirmation of order.
**auftreiben** ['aʊftraɪbən] unreg (umg) vt (beschaffen) to raise.
**auftrennen** ['aʊftrɛnən] vt to undo.
**auftreten** ['aʊftreːtən] unreg vi to kick open ♦ vi to appear; (mit Füßen) to tread; (sich verhalten) to behave; (fig: eintreten) to occur; (Schwierigkeiten etc) to arise; **als Vermittler etc ~** to act as intermediary etc; **geschlossen ~** to put up a united front.
**Auftreten** (-s) nt (Vorkommen) appearance; (Benehmen) behaviour (BRIT), behavior (US).
**Auftrieb** ['aʊftriːp] m (PHYS) buoyancy, lift; (fig) impetus.

**Auftritt** ['aʊftrɪt] m (des Schauspielers) entrance; (lit, fig: Szene) scene.
**auftrumpfen** ['aʊftrʊmpfən] vi to show how good one is; (mit Bemerkung) to crow.
**auftun** ['aʊftuːn] unreg vt to open ♦ vr to open up.
**auftürmen** ['aʊftʏrmən] vr (Gebirge etc) to tower up; (Schwierigkeiten) to pile od mount up.
**aufwachen** ['aʊfvaxən] vi to wake up.
**aufwachsen** ['aʊfvaksən] unreg vi to grow up.
**Aufwand** ['aʊfvant] m (-(e)s) m expenditure; (Kosten) expense; (Luxus) show; **bitte, keinen ~!** please don't go out of your way.
**Aufwandsentschädigung** f expense allowance.
**aufwärmen** ['aʊfvɛrmən] vt to warm up; (alte Geschichten) to rake up.
**aufwarten** ['aʊfvartən] vi (zu bieten haben): **mit etw ~** to offer sth.
**aufwärts** ['aʊfvɛrts] adv upwards; **A~entwicklung** f upward trend; **~gehen** unreg vi to look up.
**aufwecken** ['aʊfvɛkən] vt to wake(n) up.
**aufweichen** ['aʊfvaɪçən] vt to soften; (Brot) to soak.
**aufweisen** ['aʊfvaɪzən] unreg vt to show.
**aufwenden** ['aʊfvɛndən] unreg vt to expend; (Geld) to spend; (Sorgfalt) to devote.
**aufwendig** adj costly.
**aufwerfen** ['aʊfvɛrfən] unreg vt (Fenster etc) to throw open; (Probleme) to throw up, raise ♦ vr: **sich zu etw ~** to make o.s. out to be sth.
**aufwerten** ['aʊfvɛrtən] vt (FIN) to revalue; (fig) to raise in value.
**Aufwertung** f revaluation.
**aufwickeln** ['aʊfvɪkəln] vt (aufrollen) to roll up; (umg: Haar) to put in curlers; (lösen) to untie.
**aufwiegeln** ['aʊfviːgəln] vt to stir up, incite.
**aufwiegen** ['aʊfviːgən] unreg vt to make up for.
**Aufwind** ['aʊfvɪnt] m up-current; **neuen ~ bekommen** (fig) to get new impetus.
**aufwirbeln** ['aʊfvɪrbəln] vt to whirl up; **Staub ~** (fig) to create a stir.
**aufwischen** ['aʊfvɪʃən] vt to wipe up.
**aufwühlen** ['aʊfvyːlən] vt (lit: Erde, Meer) to churn (up); (Gefühle) to stir.
**aufzählen** ['aʊftsɛːlən] vt to count out.
**aufzeichnen** ['aʊftsaɪçnən] vt to sketch; (schriftlich) to jot down; (auf Band) to record.
**Aufzeichnung** f (schriftlich) note; (Tonband~, Film~) recording.
**aufzeigen** ['aʊftsaɪgən] vt to show, demonstrate.
**aufziehen** ['aʊftsiːən] unreg vt (hochziehen) to raise, draw up; (öffnen) to pull open; (: Reißverschluß) to undo; (Gardinen) to draw (back); (Uhr) to wind; (großziehen: Kinder) to raise, bring up; (Tiere) to rear; (umg: necken) to tease; (: veranstalten) to set up; (: Fest) to arrange ♦ vi (Gewitter, Wolken) to gather.

**Aufzucht** ['aʊftsʊxt] *f* (*das Großziehen*) rearing, raising.

**Aufzug** ['aʊftsuːk] *m* (*Fahrstuhl*) lift (*BRIT*), elevator (*US*); (*Aufmarsch*) procession, parade; (*Kleidung*) get-up; (*THEAT*) act.

**aufzwingen** ['aʊftsvɪŋən] *unreg vt:* **jdm etw ~** to force sth upon sb.

**Aug.** *abk* (= *August*) Aug.

**Augapfel** ['aʊkˌapfəl] *m* eyeball; (*fig*) apple of one's eye.

**Auge** ['aʊgə] (**-s, -n**) *nt* eye; (*Fett~*) globule of fat; **unter vier ~n** in private; **vor aller ~n** in front of everybody, for all to see; **jdn/etw mit anderen ~n (an)sehen** to see sb/sth in a different light; **ich habe kein ~ zugetan** I didn't sleep a wink; **ein ~/beide ~n zudrücken** (*umg*) to turn a blind eye; **jdn/ etw aus den ~n verlieren** to lose sight of sb/sth; (*fig*) to lose touch with sb/sth; **etw ins ~ fassen** to contemplate sth; **das kann leicht ins ~ gehen** (*fig: umg*) it might easily go wrong.

**Augenarzt** *m* eye specialist, ophthalmologist.

**Augenblick** *m* moment; **im ~** at the moment; **im ersten ~** for a moment; **a~lich** *adj* (*sofort*) instantaneous; (*gegenwärtig*) present.

**Augen-** *zW:* **~braue** *f* eyebrow; **~höhe** *f:* **in ~höhe** at eye level; **~merk** *nt* (*Aufmerksamkeit*) attention; **~schein** *m:* **jdn/ etw in ~schein nehmen** to have a close look at sb/sth; **a~scheinlich** *adj* obvious; **~weide** *f* sight for sore eyes; **~wischerei** *f* (*fig*) eye-wash; **~zeuge** *m* eye witness; **~zeugin** *f* eye witness.

**August** [aʊ'ɡʊst] (**-(e)s** *od* **-, -e**) (*pl selten*) *m* August; *siehe auch* **September**.

**Auktion** [aʊktsi'oːn] *f* auction.

**Auktionator** [aʊktsi̯o'naːtɔr] *m* auctioneer.

**Aula** ['aʊla] (**-, Aulen** *od* **-s**) *f* assembly hall.

**Aus** [aʊs] (**-**) *nt* (*SPORT*) outfield; **ins ~ gehen** to go out.

═══════════════ *SCHLÜSSELWORT*

**aus** [aʊs] *präp +dat* **1** (*räumlich*) out of; (*von ... her*) from; **er ist ~ Berlin** he's from Berlin; **~ dem Fenster** out of the window

**2** (*gemacht/hergestellt* ~) made of; **ein Herz ~ Stein** a heart of stone

**3** (*auf Ursache deutend*) out of; **~ Mitleid** out of sympathy; **~ Erfahrung** from experience; **~ Spaß** for fun

**4: ~ ihr wird nie etwas** she'll never get anywhere

♦ *adv* **1** (*zu Ende*) finished, over; **~ und vorbei** over and done with

**2** (*ausgeschaltet, ausgezogen*) off; **Licht ~!** lights out!

**3** (*in Verbindung mit von*): **von Rom ~** from Rome; **vom Fenster ~** out of the window; **von sich ~** (*selbständig*) of one's own accord; **von mir ~** as far as I'm concerned

**4 ~ und ein gehen** to come and go; (*bei jdm*) to visit frequently; **weder ~ noch ein wissen** to be at one's wits' end; **auf etw** *akk* **~ sein** to be after sth.

**ausarbeiten** ['aʊsˌarbaɪtən] *vt* to work out.

**ausarten** ['aʊsˌartən] *vi* to degenerate; (*Kind*) to become overexcited.

**ausatmen** ['aʊsˌaːtmən] *vi* to breathe out.

**ausbaden** ['aʊsbaːdən] (*umg*) *vt:* **etw ~ müssen** to carry the can for sth.

**Ausbau** ['aʊsbaʊ] *m* extension, expansion; removal.

**ausbauen** *vt* to extend, expand; (*herausnehmen*) to take out, remove.

**ausbaufähig** *adj* (*fig*) worth developing.

**ausbedingen** ['aʊsbədɪŋən] *unreg vt:* **sich** *dat* **etw ~** to insist on sth.

**ausbeißen** ['aʊsbaɪsən] *unreg vr:* **sich** *dat* **an etw** *dat* **die Zähne ~** (*fig*) to have a tough time of it with sth.

**ausbessern** ['aʊsbɛsərn] *vt* to mend, repair.

**Ausbesserungsarbeiten** *pl* repair work *sing.*

**ausbeulen** ['aʊsbɔɪlən] *vt* to beat out.

**Ausbeute** ['aʊsbɔɪtə] *f* yield; (*Gewinn*) profit, gain; (*Fische*) catch.

**ausbeuten** *vt* to exploit; (*MIN*) to work.

**ausbezahlen** ['aʊsbətsaːlən] *vt* (*Geld*) to pay out.

**ausbilden** ['aʊsbɪldən] *vt* to educate; (*Lehrling, Soldat*) to instruct, train; (*Fähigkeiten*) to develop; (*Geschmack*) to cultivate.

**Ausbilder(in)** (**-s, -**) *m(f)* instructor, instructress.

**Ausbildung** *f* education; training, instruction; development; cultivation; **er ist noch in der ~** he's still a trainee; he hasn't finished his education.

**Ausbildungs-** *zW:* **~förderung** *f* (provision of) grants for students and trainees; (*Stipendium*) grant; **~platz** *m* (*Stelle*) training vacancy.

**ausbitten** ['aʊsbɪtən] *unreg vt:* **sich** *dat* **etw ~** (*geh: erbitten*) to ask for sth; (*verlangen*) to insist on sth.

**ausblasen** ['aʊsblaːzən] *unreg vt* to blow out; (*Ei*) to blow.

**ausbleiben** ['aʊsblaɪbən] *unreg vi* (*Personen*) to stay away, not come; (*Ereignisse*) to fail to happen, not happen; **es konnte nicht ~, daß ...** it was inevitable that ...

**ausblenden** ['aʊsblɛndən] *vt, vi* (*TV etc*) to fade out.

**Ausblick** ['aʊsblɪk] *m* (*lit, fig*) prospect, outlook, view.

**ausbomben** ['aʊsbɔmbən] *vt* to bomb out.

**ausbooten** ['aʊsboːtən] (*umg*) *vt* (*jdn*) to kick *od* boot out.

**ausbrechen** ['aʊsbrɛçən] *unreg vi* to break out ♦ *vt* to break off; **in Tränen/Gelächter ~** to burst into tears/out laughing.

**Ausbrecher(in)** (**-s, -**) (*umg*) *m(f)* (*Gefangener*)

escaped prisoner, escapee.
**ausbreiten** ['aʊsbraɪtən] vt to spread (out);
(*Arme*) to stretch out ♦ vr to spread; **sich
über ein Thema** ~ to expand od enlarge on a
topic.
**ausbrennen** ['aʊsbrɛnən] unreg vt to scorch;
(*Wunde*) to cauterize ♦ vi to burn out.
**ausbringen** ['aʊsbrɪŋən] unreg vt (*ein Hoch*) to
propose.
**Ausbruch** ['aʊsbrʊx] m outbreak; (*von Vulkan*)
eruption; (*Gefühls~*) outburst; (*von
Gefangenen*) escape.
**ausbrüten** ['aʊsbryːtən] vt (*lit, fig*) to hatch.
**Ausbuchtung** ['aʊsbʊxtʊŋ] f bulge; (*Küste*)
cove.
**ausbügeln** ['aʊsbyːgəln] vt to iron out; (*umg:
Fehler, Verlust*) to make good.
**ausbuhen** ['aʊsbuːən] vt to boo.
**Ausbund** ['aʊsbʊnt] m: **ein** ~ **an** od **von
Tugend/Sparsamkeit** a paragon of virtue/a
model of thrift.
**ausbürgern** ['aʊsbyrgərn] vt to expatriate.
**ausbürsten** ['aʊsbyrstən] vt to brush out.
**Ausdauer** ['aʊsdaʊər] f stamina;
(*Beharrlichkeit*) perseverance.
**ausdauernd** adj persevering.
**ausdehnen** ['aʊsdeːnən] vt, vr (*räumlich*) to
expand; (*zeitlich, auch Gummi*) to stretch;
(*Nebel, fig: Macht*) to extend.
**ausdenken** ['aʊsdɛŋkən] unreg vt (*zu Ende
denken*) to think through; **sich** dat **etw** ~ to
think sth up; **das ist nicht auszudenken**
(*unvorstellbar*) it's inconceivable.
**ausdiskutieren** ['aʊsdɪskutiːrən] vt to talk out.
**ausdrehen** ['aʊsdreːən] vt to turn od switch
off.
**Ausdruck** ['aʊsdrʊk] (-**s**, -**drücke**) m
expression, phrase; (*Kundgabe, Gesichts~*)
expression; (*Fach~*) term; (*COMPUT*) hard
copy; **mit dem** ~ **des Bedauerns** (*form*)
expressing regret.
**ausdrucken** vt (*Text*) to print out.
**ausdrücken** ['aʊsdrʏkən] vt (*auch vr:
formulieren, zeigen*) to express; (*Zigarette*) to
put out; (*Zitrone*) to squeeze.
**ausdrücklich** adj express, explicit.
**Ausdrucks-** zW: ~**fähigkeit** f expressiveness;
(*Gewandtheit*) articulateness; **a~los** adj
expressionless, blank; **a~voll** adj
expressive; ~**weise** f mode of expression.
**Ausdünstung** ['aʊsdʏnstʊŋ] f (*Dampf*) vapour
(*BRIT*), vapor (*US*); (*Geruch*) smell.
**auseinander** [aʊsaɪˈnandər] adv (*getrennt*)
apart; **weit** ~ far apart; ~ **schreiben** to
write as separate words; ~**bringen** unreg vt to
separate; ~**fallen** unreg vi to fall apart;
~**gehen** unreg vi (*Menschen*) to separate;
(*Meinungen*) to differ; (*Gegenstand*) to fall
apart; (*umg: dick werden*) to put on weight;
~**halten** unreg vt to tell apart; ~**klaffen** vi to
gape open; (*fig: Meinungen*) to be far apart,
diverge (wildly); ~**laufen** unreg (*umg*) vi (*sich

trennen*) to break up; (*Menge*) to disperse;
~**leben** vr to drift apart; ~**nehmen** unreg vt to
take to pieces, dismantle; ~**setzen** vt
(*erklären*) to set forth, explain ♦ vr (*sich
verständigen*) to come to terms, settle; (*sich
befassen*) to concern o.s.; **sich mit jdm
~setzen** to talk with sb; (*sich streiten*) to
argue with sb; **A~setzung** f argument.
**auserkoren** ['aʊsˌɛrkoːrən] adj (*liter*) chosen,
selected.
**auserlesen** ['aʊsˌɛrleːzən] adj select, choice.
**ausersehen** ['aʊsˌɛrzeːən] unreg vt (*geh*): **dazu
~ sein, etw zu tun** to be chosen to do sth.
**ausfahrbar** adj extendable; (*Antenne,
Fahrgestell*) retractable.
**ausfahren** ['aʊsfaːrən] unreg vi to drive out;
(*NAUT*) to put out (to sea) ♦ vt to take out;
(*AUT*) to drive flat out; (*ausliefern: Waren*) to
deliver; **ausgefahrene Wege** rutted roads.
**Ausfahrt** f (*des Zuges etc*) leaving,
departure; (*Autobahn~, Garagen~*) exit, way
out; (*Spazierfahrt*) drive, excursion.
**Ausfall** ['aʊsfal] m loss; (*Nichtstattfinden*)
cancellation; (*das Versagen: TECH, MED*)
failure; (*von Motor*) breakdown;
(*Produktionsstörung*) stoppage; (*MIL*) sortie;
(*Fechten*) lunge; (*radioaktiv*) fallout.
**ausfallen** ['aʊsfalən] unreg vi (*Zähne, Haare*) to
fall od come out; (*nicht stattfinden*) to be
cancelled; (*wegbleiben*) to be omitted;
(*Person*) to drop out; (*Lohn*) to be stopped;
(*nicht funktionieren*) to break down; (*Resultat
haben*) to turn out; **wie ist das Spiel
ausgefallen?** what was the result of the
game?; **die Schule fällt morgen aus** there's
no school tomorrow.
**ausfallend** adj impertinent.
**Ausfallstraße** f arterial road.
**Ausfallzeit** f (*Maschine*) downtime.
**ausfegen** ['aʊsfeːgən] vt to sweep out.
**ausfeilen** ['aʊsfaɪlən] vt to file out; (*Stil*) to
polish up.
**ausfertigen** ['aʊsfɛrtɪgən] vt (*form*) to draw
up; (*Rechnung*) to make out; **doppelt** ~ to
duplicate.
**Ausfertigung** f (*form*) drawing up; making
out; (*Exemplar*) copy; **in doppelter/dreifacher
~** in duplicate/triplicate.
**ausfindig** ['aʊsfɪndɪç] adj: ~ **machen** to
discover.
**ausfliegen** ['aʊsfliːgən] unreg vi to fly away ♦ vt
to fly out; **sie sind ausgeflogen** (*umg*) they're
out.
**ausfließen** ['aʊsfliːsən] unreg vi: ~ (**aus**)
(*herausfließen*) to flow out (of); (*auslaufen: Öl
etc*) to leak (out of); (*Eiter etc*) to be
discharged (from).
**ausflippen** ['aʊsflɪpən] (*umg*) vi to freak out.
**Ausflucht** ['aʊsflʊxt] (-, -**flüchte**) f excuse.
**Ausflug** ['aʊsfluːk] m excursion, outing.
**Ausflügler(in)** ['aʊsflyːklər(ɪn)] (-**s**, -) m(f)
tripper (*BRIT*), excursionist (*US*).

**Ausfluß** ['aʊsflʊs] *m* outlet; (*MED*) discharge.
**ausfragen** ['aʊsfraːgən] *vt* to interrogate, question.
**ausfransen** ['aʊsfranzən] *vi* to fray.
**ausfressen** ['aʊsfrɛsən] *unreg* (*umg*) *vt* (*anstellen*) to be up to.
**Ausfuhr** ['aʊsfuːr] (-, -en) *f* export, exportation; (*Ware*) export ♦ *in zW* export.
**ausführbar** ['aʊsfyːrbaːr] *adj* feasible; (*COMM*) exportable.
**ausführen** ['aʊsfyːrən] *vt* (*verwirklichen*) to carry out; (*Person*) to take out; (*Hund*) to take for a walk; (*COMM*) to export; (*erklären*) to give details of; **die ~de Gewalt** (*POL*) the executive.
**Ausfuhrgenehmigung** *f* export licence.
**ausführlich** *adj* detailed ♦ *adv* in detail; **A~keit** *f* detail.
**Ausführung** *f* execution, performance; (*von Waren*) design; (*von Thema*) exposition; (*Durchführung*) completion; (*Herstellungsart*) version; (*Erklärung*) explanation.
**Ausfuhrzoll** *m* export duty.
**ausfüllen** ['aʊsfʏlən] *vt* to fill up; (*Fragebogen etc*) to fill in; (*Beruf*) to be fulfilling for; **jdn (ganz)** ~ (*Zeit in Anspruch nehmen*) to take (all) sb's time.
**Ausg.** *abk* (= *Ausgabe*) ed.
**Ausgabe** ['aʊsgaːbə] *f* (*Geld*) expenditure, outlay; (*Aushändigung*) giving out; (*Schalter*) counter; (*Ausführung*) version; (*Buch*) edition; (*Nummer*) issue.
**Ausgang** ['aʊsgaŋ] *m* way out, exit; (*Ende*) end; (*~spunkt*) starting point; (*Ergebnis*) result; (*Ausgehtag*) free time, time off; **ein Unfall mit tödlichem** ~ a fatal accident; **kein** ~ no exit.
**Ausgangs-** *zW*: **~basis** *f* starting point; **~punkt** *m* starting point; **~sperre** *f* curfew.
**ausgeben** ['aʊsgeːbən] *unreg vt* (*Geld*) to spend; (*austeilen*) to issue, distribute; (*COMPUT*) to output ♦ *vr*: **sich für etw/jdn** ~ to pass o.s. off as sth/sb; **ich gebe heute abend einen aus** (*umg*) it's my treat this evening.
**ausgebeult** ['aʊsgəbɔʏlt] *adj* (*Kleidung*) baggy; (*Hut*) battered.
**ausgebucht** ['aʊsgəbuːxt] *adj* fully booked.
**Ausgeburt** ['aʊsgəbuːrt] (*pej*) *f* (*der Phantasie etc*) monstrous product *od* invention.
**ausgedehnt** ['aʊsgədeːnt] *adj* (*breit, groß, fig: weitreichend*) extensive; (*Spaziergang*) long; (*zeitlich*) lengthy.
**ausgedient** ['aʊsgədiːnt] *adj* (*Soldat*) discharged; (*verbraucht*) no longer in use; ~ **haben** to have come to the end of its useful life.
**ausgefallen** ['aʊsgəfalən] *adj* (*ungewöhnlich*) exceptional.
**ausgefuchst** ['aʊsgəfʊkst] (*umg*) *adj* clever; (: *listig*) crafty.
**ausgegangen** ['aʊsgəgaŋən] *pp von* **ausgehen**.
**ausgeglichen** ['aʊsgəglɪçən] *adj* (well-)bal-

anced; **A~heit** *f* balance; (*von Mensch*) even-temperedness.
**Ausgehanzug** *m* good suit.
**ausgehen** ['aʊsgeːən] *unreg vi* (*auch Feuer, Ofen Licht*) to go out; (*zu Ende gehen*) to come to an end; (*Benzin*) to run out; (*Haare, Zähne*) to fall *od* come out; (*Strom*) to go off; (*Resultat haben*) to turn out; (*spazierengehen*) to go (out) for a walk; (*abgeschickt werden: Post*) to be sent off; **mir ging das Benzin aus** I ran out of petrol (*BRIT*) *od* gas (*US*); **auf etw** *akk* ~ to aim at sth; **von etw** ~ (*wegführen*) to lead away from sth; (*herrühren*) to come from sth; (*zugrunde legen*) to proceed from sth; **wir können davon** ~, **daß** ... we can proceed from the assumption that ..., we can take as our starting point that ...; **leer** ~ to get nothing; **schlecht** ~ to turn out badly.
**ausgehungert** ['aʊsgəhʊŋərt] *adj* starved; (*abgezehrt: Mensch etc*) emaciated.
**Ausgehverbot** *nt* curfew.
**ausgeklügelt** ['aʊsgəklyːgəlt] *adj* ingenious.
**ausgekocht** ['aʊsgəkɔxt] (*pej: umg*) *adj* (*durchtrieben*) cunning; (*fig*) out-and-out.
**ausgelassen** ['aʊsgəlasən] *adj* boisterous, high-spirited, exuberant; **A~heit** *f* boisterousness, high spirits *pl*, exuberance.
**ausgelastet** ['aʊsgəlastət] *adj* fully occupied.
**ausgeleiert** ['aʊsgəlaɪərt] *adj* worn; (*Gummiband*) stretched.
**ausgelernt** ['aʊsgəlɛrnt] *adj* trained, qualified.
**ausgemacht** ['aʊsgəmaxt] *adj* settled; (*umg: Dummkopf etc*) out-and-out, downright; **es gilt als** ~, **daß** ... it is settled that ...; **es war eine ~e Sache, daß** ... it was a foregone conclusion that ...
**ausgemergelt** ['aʊsgəmɛrgəlt] *adj* (*Gesicht*) emaciated, gaunt.
**ausgenommen** ['aʊsgənɔmən] *konj* except; **Anwesende sind** ~ present company excepted.
**ausgepowert** ['aʊsgəpoːvərt] *adj*: ~ **sein** (*umg*) to be tired, be exhausted.
**ausgeprägt** ['aʊsgəprɛːkt] *adj* prominent; (*Eigenschaft*) distinct.
**ausgerechnet** ['aʊsgərɛçnət] *adv* just, precisely; ~ **du** you of all people; ~ **heute** today of all days.
**ausgeschlossen** ['aʊsgəʃlɔsən] *pp von* **ausschließen** ♦ *adj* (*unmöglich*) impossible, out of the question; **es ist nicht** ~, **daß** ... it cannot be ruled out that ...
**ausgeschnitten** ['aʊsgəʃnɪtən] *adj* (*Kleid*) low-necked.
**ausgesehen** ['aʊsgəzeːən] *pp von* **aussehen**.
**ausgesprochen** ['aʊsgəʃprɔxən] *adj* (*Faulheit, Lüge etc*) out-and-out; (*unverkennbar*) marked ♦ *adv* decidedly.
**ausgestorben** ['aʊsgəʃtɔrbən] *adj* (*Tierart*) extinct; (*fig*) deserted.
**ausgewogen** ['aʊsgəvoːgən] *adj* balanced; (*Maß*) equal.

**ausgezeichnet** ['aʊsgətsaɪçnət] *adj* excellent.
**ausgiebig** ['aʊsgiːbɪç] *adj* (*Gebrauch*) full, good; (*Essen*) generous, lavish; ~ **schlafen** to have a good sleep.
**ausgießen** ['aʊsgiːsən] *unreg vt* (*aus einem Behälter*) to pour out; (*Behälter*) to empty; (*weggießen*) to pour away.
**Ausgleich** ['aʊsglaɪç] (-(e)s, -e) *m* balance; (*von Fehler, Mangel*) compensation; (*SPORT*): **den** ~ **erzielen** to equalize; **zum** ~ +*gen* in order to offset sth; **das ist ein guter** ~ (*entspannend*) that's very relaxing.
**ausgleichen** ['aʊsglaɪçən] *unreg vt* to balance (out); (*Konflikte*) to reconcile; (*Höhe*) to even up ♦ *vi* (*SPORT*) to equalize; **~de Gerechtigkeit** poetic justice.
**Ausgleichssport** *m* keep-fit activity.
**Ausgleichstor** *nt* equalizer.
**ausgraben** ['aʊsgraːbən] *unreg vt* to dig up; (*Leichen*) to exhume; (*fig*) to unearth.
**Ausgrabung** *f* excavation.
**ausgrenzen** ['aʊsgrɛntsən] *vt* to shut out, separate.
**Ausgrenzung** *f* shut-out, separation.
**Ausguck** ['aʊsgʊk] *m* look-out.
**Ausguß** ['aʊsgʊs] *m* (*Spüle*) sink; (*Abfluß*) outlet; (*Tülle*) spout.
**aushaben** ['aʊshaːbən] *unreg* (*umg*) *vt* (*Kleidung*) to have taken off; (*Buch*) to have finished.
**aushalten** ['aʊshaltən] *unreg vt* to bear, stand; (*umg: Geliebte*) to hold ♦ *vi* to hold out; **das ist nicht zum A~** that is unbearable; **sich von jdm** ~ **lassen** to be kept by sb.
**aushandeln** ['aʊshandəln] *vt* to negotiate.
**aushändigen** ['aʊshɛndɪgən] *vt*: **jdm etw** ~ to hand sth over to sb.
**Aushang** ['aʊshaŋ] *m* notice.
**aushängen** ['aʊshɛŋən] *unreg vt* (*Meldung*) to put up; (*Fenster*) to take off its hinges ♦ *vi* to be displayed ♦ *vr* to hang out.
**Aushängeschild** *nt* (shop) sign; (*fig*): **als** ~ **für etw dienen** to promote sth.
**ausharren** ['aʊsharən] *vi* to hold out.
**aushäusig** ['aʊshɔʏzɪç] *adj* gallivanting around, on the tiles.
**ausheben** ['aʊsheːbən] *unreg vt* (*Erde*) to lift out; (*Grube*) to hollow out; (*Tür*) to take off its hinges; (*Diebesnest*) to clear out; (*MIL*) to enlist.
**aushecken** ['aʊshɛkən] (*umg*) *vt* to concoct, think up.
**aushelfen** ['aʊshɛlfən] *unreg vi*: **jdm** ~ to help sb out.
**Aushilfe** ['aʊshɪlfə] *f* help, assistance; (*Person*) (temporary) worker.
**Aushilfs-** *zW*: **~kraft** *f* temporary worker; **~lehrer(in)** *m(f)* supply teacher; **a~weise** *adv* temporarily, as a stopgap.
**aushöhlen** ['aʊshøːlən] *vt* to hollow out; (*fig: untergraben*) to undermine.
**ausholen** ['aʊshoːlən] *vi* to swing one's arm

back; (*zur Ohrfeige*) to raise one's hand; (*beim Gehen*) to take long strides; **zum Gegenschlag** ~ (*lit, fig*) to prepare for a counter-attack.
**aushorchen** ['aʊshɔrçən] *vt* to sound out, pump.
**aushungern** ['aʊshʊŋərn] *vt* to starve out.
**auskennen** ['aʊskɛnən] *unreg vr* to know a lot; (*an einem Ort*) to know one's way about; (*in Fragen etc*) to be knowledgeable; **man kennt sich bei ihm nie aus** you never know where you are with him.
**auskippen** ['aʊskɪpən] *vt* to empty.
**ausklammern** ['aʊsklamərn] *vt* (*Thema*) to exclude, leave out.
**Ausklang** ['aʊsklaŋ] *m* (*geh*) end.
**ausklappbar** ['aʊsklapbaːr] *adj*: **dieser Tisch ist** ~ this table can be opened out.
**auskleiden** ['aʊsklaɪdən] *vr* (*geh*) to undress ♦ *vt* (*Wand*) to line.
**ausklingen** ['aʊsklɪŋən] *unreg vi* to end; (*Ton, Lied*) to die away; (*Fest*) to come to an end.
**ausklinken** ['aʊsklɪŋkən] *vt* (*Bomben*) to release ♦ *vi* (*umg*) to flip one's lid.
**ausklopfen** ['aʊsklɔpfən] *vt* (*Teppich*) to beat; (*Pfeife*) to knock out.
**auskochen** ['aʊskɔxən] *vt* to boil; (*MED*) to sterilize.
**auskommen** ['aʊskɔmən] *unreg vi*: **mit jdm** ~ to get on with sb; **mit etw** ~ to get by with sth; **A~** (-s) *nt*: **sein A~ haben** to get by; **mit ihr ist kein A~** she's impossible to get on with.
**auskosten** ['aʊskɔstən] *vt* to enjoy to the full.
**auskramen** ['aʊskraːmən] (*umg*) *vt* to dig out, unearth; (*fig: alte Geschichten etc*) to bring up.
**auskratzen** ['aʊskratsən] *vt* (*auch MED*) to scrape out.
**auskugeln** ['aʊskuːgəln] *vr*: **sich** *dat* **den Arm** ~ to dislocate one's arm.
**auskundschaften** ['aʊskʊntʃaftən] *vt* to spy out; (*Gebiet*) to reconnoitre (*BRIT*), reconnoiter (*US*).
**Auskunft** ['aʊskʊnft] (-, **-künfte**) *f* information; (*nähere*) details *pl*, particulars *pl*; (*Stelle*) information office; (*TEL*) inquiries; **jdm** ~ **erteilen** to give sb information.
**auskuppeln** ['aʊskʊpəln] *vi* to disengage the clutch.
**auskurieren** ['aʊskuriːrən] (*umg*) *vt* to cure.
**auslachen** ['aʊslaxən] *vt* to laugh at, mock.
**ausladen** ['aʊslaːdən] *unreg vt* to unload; (*umg: Gäste*) to cancel an invitation to ♦ *vi* (*Äste*) to spread.
**ausladend** *adj* (*Gebärden, Bewegung*) sweeping.
**Auslage** ['aʊslaːgə] *f* shop window (display).
**Auslagen** *pl* outlay *sing*, expenditure *sing*.
**Ausland** ['aʊslant] *nt* foreign countries *pl*; **im** ~ abroad; **ins** ~ abroad.

**Ausländer(in)** ['aʊslɛndər(ɪn)] (-s, -) *m(f)* foreigner.
**Ausländerfeindlichkeit** *f* hostility to foreigners, xenophobia.
**ausländisch** *adj* foreign.
**Auslands-** *zW:* ~**aufenthalt** *m* stay abroad; ~**gespräch** *nt* international call; ~**korrespondent(in)** *m(f)* foreign correspondent; ~**reise** *f* trip abroad; ~**schutzbrief** *m* international travel cover; ~**vertretung** *f* agency abroad; (*von Firma*) foreign branch.
**auslassen** ['aʊslasən] *unreg vt* to leave out; (*Wort etc*) to omit; (*Fett*) to melt; (*Kleidungsstück*) to let out ♦ *vr:* **sich über etw** *akk* ~ to speak one's mind about sth; **seine Wut** *etc* **an jdm** ~ to vent one's rage *etc* on sb.
**Auslassung** *f* omission.
**Auslassungszeichen** *nt* apostrophe.
**auslasten** ['aʊslastən] *vt* (*Fahrzeug*) to make full use of; (*Maschine*) to use to capacity; (*jdn*) to occupy fully.
**Auslauf** ['aʊslaʊf] *m* (*für Tiere*) run; (*Ausfluß*) outflow, outlet.
**auslaufen** *unreg vi* to run out; (*Behälter*) to leak; (*NAUT*) to put out (to sea); (*langsam aufhören*) to run down.
**Ausläufer** ['aʊslɔyfər] *m* (*von Gebirge*) spur; (*Pflanze*) runner; (*MET: von Hoch*) ridge; (*: von Tief*) trough.
**ausleeren** ['aʊsleːrən] *vt* to empty.
**auslegen** ['aʊsleːgən] *vt* (*Waren*) to lay out; (*Köder*) to put down; (*Geld*) to lend; (*bedecken*) to cover; (*Text etc*) to interpret.
**Ausleger** (-s, -) *m* (*von Kran etc*) jib, boom.
**Auslegung** *f* interpretation.
**Ausleihe** ['aʊslaɪə] (-, -n) *f* issuing; (*Stelle*) issue desk.
**ausleihen** ['aʊslaɪən] *unreg vt* (*verleihen*) to lend; **sich** *dat* **etw** ~ to borrow sth.
**auslernen** ['aʊslɛrnən] *vi* (*Lehrling*) to finish one's apprenticeship; **man lernt nie aus** (*Sprichwort*) you live and learn.
**Auslese** ['aʊsleːzə] (-, -n) *f* selection; (*Elite*) elite; (*Wein*) choice wine.
**auslesen** ['aʊsleːzən] *unreg vt* to select; (*umg: zu Ende lesen*) to finish.
**ausliefern** ['aʊsliːfərn] *vt* to hand over; (*COMM*) to deliver ♦ *vr:* **sich jdm** ~ to give o.s. up to sb; ~ (**an** +*akk*) to deliver (up) (to), hand over (to); (*an anderen Staat*) to extradite (to); **jdm/etw ausgeliefert sein** to be at the mercy of sb/sth.
**Auslieferungsabkommen** *nt* extradition treaty.
**ausliegen** ['aʊsliːgən] *unreg vi* (*zur Ansicht*) to be displayed; (*Zeitschriften etc*) to be available (to the public); (*Liste*) to be up.
**auslöschen** ['aʊslœʃən] *vt* to extinguish; (*fig*) to wipe out, obliterate.
**auslosen** ['aʊsloːzən] *vt* to draw lots for.

**auslösen** ['aʊsløːzən] *vt* (*Explosion, Schuß*) to set off; (*hervorrufen*) to cause, produce; (*Gefangene*) to ransom; (*Pfand*) to redeem.
**Auslöser** (-s, -) *m* trigger; (*PHOT*) release; (*Anlaß*) cause.
**ausloten** ['aʊsloːtən] *vt* (*NAUT: Tiefe*) to sound; (*fig geh*) to plumb.
**ausmachen** ['aʊsmaxən] *vt* (*Licht, Radio*) to turn off; (*Feuer*) to put out; (*entdecken*) to make out; (*vereinbaren*) to agree; (*beilegen*) to settle; (*Anteil darstellen, betragen*) to represent; (*bedeuten*) to matter; **das macht ihm nichts aus** it doesn't matter to him; **macht es Ihnen etwas aus, wenn ...?** would you mind if ...?
**ausmalen** ['aʊsmaːlən] *vt* to paint; (*fig*) to describe; **sich** *dat* **etw** ~ to imagine sth.
**Ausmaß** ['aʊsmaːs] *nt* dimension; (*fig*) scale.
**ausmerzen** ['aʊsmɛrtsən] *vt* to eliminate.
**ausmessen** ['aʊsmɛsən] *unreg vt* to measure.
**ausmisten** ['aʊsmɪstən] *vt* (*Stall*) to muck out; (*fig: umg: Schrank etc*) to tidy out; (*: Zimmer*) to clean out.
**ausmustern** ['aʊsmʊstərn] *vt* (*Maschine, Fahrzeug etc*) to take out of service; (*MIL: entlassen*) to invalid out.
**Ausnahme** ['aʊsnaːmə] (-, -n) *f* exception; **eine** ~ **machen** to make an exception; ~**erscheinung** *f* exception, one-off example; ~**fall** *m* exceptional case; ~**zustand** *m* state of emergency.
**ausnahmslos** *adv* without exception.
**ausnahmsweise** *adv* by way of exception, for once.
**ausnehmen** ['aʊsneːmən] *unreg vt* to take out, remove; (*Tier*) to gut; (*Nest*) to rob; (*umg: Geld abnehmen*) to clean out; (*ausschließen*) to make an exception of ♦ *vr* to look, appear
**ausnehmend** *adj* exceptional.
**ausnüchtern** ['aʊsnʏçtərn] *vt, vi* to sober up.
**Ausnüchterungszelle** *f* drying-out cell.
**ausnutzen** ['aʊsnʊtsən] *vt* (*Zeit, Gelegenheit*) to use, turn to good account; (*Einfluß*) to use; (*Mensch, Gutmütigkeit*) to exploit.
**auspacken** ['aʊspakən] *vt* to unpack ♦ *vi* (*umg. alles sagen*) to talk.
**auspfeifen** ['aʊspfaɪfən] *unreg vt* to hiss/boo at.
**ausplaudern** ['aʊsplaʊdərn] *vt* (*Geheimnis*) to blab.
**ausposaunen** ['aʊspozaʊnən] (*umg*) *vt* to tell the world about.
**ausprägen** ['aʊsprɛːgən] *vr* (*Begabung, Charaktereigenschaft*) to reveal *od* show itself.
**auspressen** ['aʊsprɛsən] *vt* (*Saft, Schwamm etc*) to squeeze out; (*Zitrone etc*) to squeeze.
**ausprobieren** ['aʊsprobiːrən] *vt* to try (out).
**Auspuff** ['aʊspʊf] (-(e)s, -e) *m* (*TECH*) exhaust; ~**rohr** *nt* exhaust (pipe); ~**topf** *m* (*AUT*) silencer (*BRIT*), muffler (*US*).
**ausquartieren** ['aʊskvartiːrən] *vt* to move out.
**ausquetschen** ['aʊskvɛtʃən] *vt* (*Zitrone etc*) to

squeeze; (*umg: ausfragen*) to grill; (: *aus Neugier*) to pump.

**ausradieren** ['aʊsradiːrən] *vt* to erase, rub out.

**ausrangieren** ['aʊsrãʒiːrən] (*umg*) *vt* to chuck out; (*Maschine, Auto*) to scrap.

**ausrauben** ['aʊsraʊbən] *vt* to rob.

**ausräumen** ['aʊsrɔʏmən] *vt* (*Dinge*) to clear away; (*Schrank, Zimmer*) to empty; (*Bedenken*) to put aside.

**ausrechnen** ['aʊsrɛçnən] *vt* to calculate, reckon.

**Ausrechnung** *f* calculation, reckoning.

**Ausrede** ['aʊsreːdə] *f* excuse.

**ausreden** ['aʊsreːdən] *vi* to have one's say ♦ *vt: jdm etw* ~ to talk sb out of sth; **er hat mich nicht mal** ~ **lassen** he didn't even let me finish (speaking).

**ausreichen** ['aʊsraɪçən] *vi* to suffice, be enough.

**ausreichend** *adj* sufficient, adequate; (*SCH*) adequate.

**Ausreise** ['aʊsraɪzə] *f* departure; **bei der** ~ when leaving the country; ~**erlaubnis** *f* exit visa.

**ausreisen** ['aʊsraɪzən] *vi* to leave the country.

**ausreißen** ['aʊsraɪsən] *unreg vt* to tear *od* pull out ♦ *vi* (*Riß bekommen*) to tear; (*umg*) to make off, scram; **er hat sich** *dat* **kein Bein ausgerissen** (*umg*) he didn't exactly overstrain himself.

**ausrenken** ['aʊsrɛŋkən] *vt* to dislocate.

**ausrichten** ['aʊsrɪçtən] *vt* (*Botschaft*) to deliver; (*Gruß*) to pass on; (*Hochzeit etc*) to arrange; (*in gerade Linie bringen*) to get in a straight line; (*angleichen*) to bring into line; (*TYP etc*) to justify; **etwas/nichts bei jdm** ~ to get somewhere/nowhere with sb; **jdm etw** ~ to take a message for sb; **ich werde es ihm** ~ I'll tell him.

**ausrotten** ['aʊsrɔtən] *vt* to stamp out, exterminate.

**ausrücken** ['aʊsrʏkən] *vi* (*MIL*) to move off; (*Feuerwehr, Polizei*) to be called out; (*umg: weglaufen*) to run away.

**Ausruf** ['aʊsruːf] *m* (*Schrei*) cry, exclamation; (*Verkünden*) proclamation.

**ausrufen** *unreg vt* to cry out, exclaim; to call out; **jdn** ~ **(lassen)** (*über Lautsprecher etc*) to page sb.

**Ausrufezeichen** *nt* exclamation mark.

**ausruhen** ['aʊsruːən] *vt, vi, vr* to rest.

**ausrüsten** ['aʊsrʏstən] *vt* to equip, fit out.

**Ausrüstung** *f* equipment.

**ausrutschen** ['aʊsrʊtʃən] *vi* to slip.

**Ausrutscher (-s, -)** (*umg*) *m* (*lit, fig*) slip.

**Aussage** ['aʊszaːɡə] (**-, -n**) *f* (*JUR*) statement; **der Angeklagte/Zeuge verweigerte die** ~ the accused/witness refused to give evidence.

**aussagekräftig** *adj* expressive, full of expression.

**aussagen** ['aʊszaːɡən] *vt* to say, state ♦ *vi* (*JUR*) to give evidence.

**Aussatz** ['aʊszats] (**-es**) *m* (*MED*) leprosy.

**aussaugen** ['aʊszaʊɡən] *vt* (*Saft etc*) to suck out; (*Wunde*) to suck the poison out of; (*fig: ausbeuten*) to drain dry.

**ausschalten** ['aʊsʃaltən] *vt* to switch off; (*fig*) to eliminate.

**Ausschank** ['aʊsʃaŋk] (**-(e)s, -schänke**) *m* dispensing, giving out; (*COMM*) selling; (*Theke*) bar.

**Ausschankerlaubnis** *f* licence (*BRIT*), license (*US*).

**Ausschau** ['aʊsʃaʊ] *f:* ~ **halten (nach)** to look out (for), watch (for).

**ausschauen** *vi:* ~ **(nach)** to look out (for), be on the look-out (for).

**ausscheiden** ['aʊsʃaɪdən] *unreg vt* (*aussondern*) to take out; (*MED*) to excrete ♦ *vi:* ~ **(aus)** to leave; (*aus einem Amt*) to retire (from); (*SPORT*) to be eliminated (from), be knocked out (of); **er scheidet für den Posten aus** he can't be considered for the job.

**Ausscheidung** *f* (*Aussondern*) removal; (*MED*) excretion; (*SPORT*) elimination.

**ausschenken** ['aʊsʃɛŋkən] *vt* to pour out; (*am Ausschank*) to serve.

**ausscheren** ['aʊsʃeːrən] *vi* (*Fahrzeug*) to leave the line *od* convoy; (*zum Überholen*) to pull out.

**ausschildern** ['aʊsʃɪldərn] *vt* to signpost.

**ausschimpfen** ['aʊsʃɪmpfən] *vt* to scold, tell off.

**ausschlachten** ['aʊsʃlaxtən] *vt* (*Auto*) to cannibalize; (*fig*) to make a meal of.

**ausschlafen** ['aʊsʃlaːfən] *unreg vi, vr* to sleep late ♦ *vt* to sleep off; **ich bin nicht ausgeschlafen** I didn't have *od* get enough sleep.

**Ausschlag** ['aʊsʃlaːk] *m* (*MED*) rash; (*Pendel~*) swing; (*von Nadel*) deflection; **den** ~ **geben** (*fig*) to tip the balance.

**ausschlagen** ['aʊsʃlaːɡən] *unreg vt* to knock out; (*auskleiden*) to deck out; (*verweigern*) to decline ♦ *vi* (*Pferd*) to kick out; (*BOT*) to sprout; (*Zeiger*) to be deflected.

**ausschlaggebend** *adj* decisive.

**ausschließen** ['aʊsʃliːsən] *unreg vt* to shut *od* lock out; (*SPORT*) to disqualify; (*Fehler, Möglichkeit etc*) to rule out; (*fig*) to exclude; **ich will mich nicht** ~ myself not excepted.

**ausschließlich** *adj* exclusive ♦ *adv* exclusively ♦ *präp +gen* excluding, exclusive of.

**ausschlüpfen** ['aʊsʃlʏpfən] *vi* to slip out; (*aus Ei, Puppe*) to hatch out.

**Ausschluß** ['aʊsʃlʊs] *m* exclusion; **unter** ~ **der Öffentlichkeit stattfinden** to be closed to the public; (*JUR*) to be held in camera.

**ausschmücken** ['aʊsʃmʏkən] *vt* to decorate; (*fig*) to embellish.

**ausschneiden** ['aʊsʃnaɪdən] *unreg vt* to cut out; (*Büsche*) to trim.

**Ausschnitt** ['ausʃnɪt] m (*Teil*) section; (*von Kleid*) neckline; (*Zeitungs~*) cutting (*BRIT*), clipping (*US*); (*aus Film etc*) excerpt.

**ausschöpfen** ['ausʃœpfən] vt to ladle out; (*fig*) to exhaust; **Wasser** *etc* **aus etw** ~ to ladle water *etc* out of sth.

**ausschreiben** ['ausʃraibən] unreg vt (*ganz schreiben*) to write out (in full); (*Scheck, Rechnung etc*) to write (out); (*Stelle, Wettbewerb etc*) to announce, advertise.

**Ausschreibung** f (*Bekanntmachung: von Wahlen*) calling; (*: von Stelle*) advertising.

**Ausschreitung** ['ausʃraitʊŋ] f excess.

**Ausschuß** ['ausʃus] m committee, board; (*Abfall*) waste, scraps pl; (*COMM: auch:* ~ware) reject.

**ausschütten** ['ausʃytən] vt to pour out; (*Eimer*) to empty; (*Geld*) to pay ♦ vr to shake (with laughter).

**Ausschüttung** f (*FIN*) distribution.

**ausschwärmen** ['ausʃvɛrmən] vi (*Bienen, Menschen*) to swarm out; (*MIL*) to fan out.

**ausschweifend** ['ausʃvaifənt] adj (*Leben*) dissipated, debauched; (*Phantasie*) extravagant.

**Ausschweifung** f excess.

**ausschweigen** ['ausʃvaigən] unreg vr to keep silent.

**ausschwitzen** ['ausʃvɪtsən] vt to sweat out.

**aussehen** ['auszeːən] unreg vi to look; **gut** ~ to look good/well; **wie sieht's aus?** (*umg: wie steht's?*) how's things?; **das sieht nach nichts aus** that doesn't look anything special; **es sieht nach Regen aus** it looks like rain; **es sieht schlecht aus** things look bad; **A~** (-**s**) nt appearance.

**aussein** ['aussain] unreg (*umg*) vi to be out; (*zu Ende*) to be over ♦ vi unpers: **es ist aus mit ihm** he is finished, he has had it.

**außen** ['ausən] adv outside; (*nach* ~) outwards; ~ **ist es rot** it's red (on the) outside.

**Außen-** zW: ~**antenne** f outside aerial; ~**arbeiten** pl work sing on the exterior; ~**aufnahme** f outdoor shot; ~**bezirk** m outlying district; ~**bordmotor** m outboard motor.

**aussenden** ['auszɛndən] unreg vt to send out, emit.

**Außen-** zW: ~**dienst** m outside od field service; (*von Diplomat*) foreign service; ~**handel** m foreign trade; ~**minister** m foreign minister; ~**ministerium** nt foreign office; ~**politik** f foreign policy; ~**seite** f outside; ~**seiter(in)** (-**s**, -) m(f) outsider; ~**spiegel** m (*AUT*) outside mirror; ~**stände** pl (*bes COMM*) outstanding debts pl, arrears pl; ~**stehende(r)** f(m) outsider; ~**stelle** f branch; ~**welt** f outside world.

**außer** ['ausər] präp +dat (*räumlich*) out of; (*abgesehen von*) except ♦ konj (*ausgenommen*) except; ~ **Gefahr sein** to be out of danger; ~ **Zweifel** beyond any doubt;

~ **Betrieb** out of order; ~ **sich** dat **sein/ geraten** to be beside o.s.; ~ **Dienst** retired; ~ **Landes** abroad; ~ **wenn** unless; ~ **daß** except; ~**amtlich** adj unofficial, private.

**außerdem** konj besides, in addition ♦ adv anyway.

**außerdienstlich** adj private.

**äußere(r, s)** ['ɔysərə(r, s)] adj outer, external; **Ä~(s)** nt exterior; (*fig: Aussehen*) outward appearance.

**außer-** zW: ~**ehelich** adj extramarital; ~**gewöhnlich** adj unusual; ~**halb** präp +gen outside ♦ adv outside; ~**irdisch** adj extraterrestrial; **A~kraftsetzung** f repeal.

**äußerlich** adj external; **rein** ~ **betrachtet** on the face of it; **Ä~keit** f (*fig*) triviality; (*Oberflächlichkeit*) superficiality; (*Formalität*) formality.

**äußern** vt to utter, express; (*zeigen*) to show ♦ vr to give one's opinion; (*sich zeigen*) to show itself.

**außer-** zW: ~**ordentlich** adj extraordinary; ~**planmäßig** adj unscheduled; ~**sinnlich** adj: ~**sinnliche Wahrnehmung** extrasensory perception.

**äußerst** ['ɔysərst] adv extremely, most.

**außerstande** [ausər'ʃtandə] adv (*nicht in der Lage*) not in a position; (*nicht fähig*) unable.

**Äußerste(s)** nt: **bis zum** ~**n gehen** to go to extremes.

**äußerste(r, s)** adj utmost; (*räumlich*) farthest; (*Termin*) last possible; (*Preis*) highest; **mein** ~**s Angebot** my final offer.

**äußerstenfalls** adv if the worst comes to the worst.

**Äußerung** f (*Bemerkung*) remark, comment; (*Behauptung*) statement; (*Zeichen*) expression.

**aussetzen** ['auszɛtsən] vt (*Kind, Tier*) to abandon; (*Boote*) to lower; (*Belohnung*) to offer; (*Urteil, Verfahren*) to postpone ♦ vi (*aufhören*) to stop; (*Pause machen*) to have a break; **jdn/sich einer Sache** dat ~ to lay sb/ o.s. open to sth; **jdm/etw ausgesetzt sein** to be exposed to sb/sth; **was haben Sie daran auszusetzen?** what's your objection to it?; **an jdm/etw etwas** ~ to find fault with sb/ sth.

**Aussicht** ['auszɪçt] f view; (*in Zukunft*) prospect; **in** ~ **sein** to be in view; **etw in** ~ **haben** to have sth in view; **jdm etw in** ~ **stellen** to promise sb sth.

**Aussichts-** zW: **a~los** adj hopeless; ~**punkt** m viewpoint; **a~reich** adj promising; ~**turm** m observation tower.

**Aussiedler(in)** ['auszi:dlər(ɪn)] (-**s**, -) m(f) (*Auswanderer*) emigrant.

---

*Aussiedler are people of German origin from East and South-East Europe who have resettled in Germany. Many come from the former Soviet Union. They are given free*

*German language tuition for 6 months and receive financial help for 15 months. The number of Aussiedler increased dramatically in the early 1990s.*

**aussöhnen** ['aʊszøːnən] *vt* to reconcile ♦ *vr* (*einander*) to become reconciled; **sich mit jdm/etw** ~ to reconcile o.s. with sb/to sth.

**Aussöhnung** *f* reconciliation.

**aussondern** ['aʊszɔndərn] *vt* to separate off, select.

**aussorgen** ['aʊszɔrgən] *vi:* **ausgesorgt haben** to have no more money worries.

**aussortieren** ['aʊszɔrtiːrən] *vt* to sort out.

**ausspannen** ['aʊsʃpanən] *vt* to spread *od* stretch out; (*Pferd*) to unharness; (*umg: Mädchen*): **jdm jdn** ~ to steal sb from sb ♦ *vi* to relax.

**aussparen** ['aʊsʃpaːrən] *vt* to leave open.

**aussperren** ['aʊsʃpɛrən] *vt* to lock out.

**Aussperrung** *f* (*INDUSTRIE*) lock-out.

**ausspielen** ['aʊsʃpiːlən] *vt* (*Karte*) to lead; (*Geldprämie*) to offer as a prize ♦ *vi* (*KARTEN*) to lead; **ausgespielt haben** to be finished; **jdn gegen jdn** ~ to play sb off against sb.

**Ausspielung** *f* (*im Lotto*) draw.

**ausspionieren** ['aʊsʃpioniːrən] *vt* (*Pläne etc*) to spy out; (*Person*) to spy on.

**Aussprache** ['aʊsʃpraːxə] *f* pronunciation; (*Unterredung*) (frank) discussion.

**aussprechen** ['aʊsʃprɛçən] *unreg vt* to pronounce; (*zu Ende sprechen*) to speak; (*äußern*) to say, express ♦ *vr* (*sich äußern*): **sich** ~ (**über** +*akk*) to speak (about); (*sich anvertrauen*) to unburden o.s. (about *od* on); (*diskutieren*) to discuss ♦ *vi* (*zu Ende sprechen*) to finish speaking; **der Regierung das Vertrauen** ~ to pass a vote of confidence in the government.

**Ausspruch** ['aʊsʃprʊx] *m* remark; (*geflügeltes Wort*) saying.

**ausspucken** ['aʊsʃpʊkən] *vt* to spit out ♦ *vi* to spit.

**ausspülen** ['aʊsʃpyːlən] *vt* to wash out; (*Mund*) to rinse.

**ausstaffieren** ['aʊsʃtafiːrən] *vt* to equip, kit out; (*Zimmer*) to furnish.

**Ausstand** ['aʊsʃtant] *m* strike; **in den** ~ **treten** to go on strike; **seinen** ~ **geben** to hold a leaving party.

**ausstatten** ['aʊsʃtatən] *vt* (*Zimmer etc*) to furnish; **jdn mit etw** ~ to equip sb *od* kit sb out with sth.

**Ausstattung** *f* (*Ausstatten*) provision; (*Kleidung*) outfit; (*Aussteuer*) dowry; (*Aufmachung*) make-up; (*Einrichtung*) furnishing.

**ausstechen** ['aʊsʃtɛçən] *unreg vt* (*Torf, Kekse*) to cut out; (*Augen*) to gouge out; (*übertreffen*) to outshine.

**ausstehen** ['aʊsʃteːən] *unreg vt* to stand, endure ♦ *vi* (*noch nicht dasein*) to be outstanding.

**aussteigen** ['aʊsʃtaɪgən] *unreg vi* to get out, alight; **alles** ~! (*von Schaffner*) all change!; **aus der Gesellschaft** ~ to drop out (of society).

**Aussteiger(in)** (*umg*) *m(f)* dropout.

**ausstellen** ['aʊsʃtɛlən] *vt* to exhibit, display; (*umg: ausschalten*) to switch off; (*Rechnung etc*) to make out; (*Paß, Zeugnis*) to issue.

**Aussteller(in)** *m(f)* (*auf Messe*) exhibitor; (*von Scheck*) drawer.

**Ausstellung** *f* exhibition; (*FIN*) drawing up; (*einer Rechnung*) making out; (*eines Passes etc*) issuing.

**Ausstellungsdatum** *nt* date of issue.

**Ausstellungsstück** *nt* (*in Ausstellung*) exhibit; (*in Schaufenster etc*) display item.

**aussterben** ['aʊsʃtɛrbən] *unreg vi* to die out; **A~** *nt* extinction.

**Aussteuer** ['aʊsʃtɔyər] *f* dowry.

**aussteuern** ['aʊsʃtɔyərn] *vt* (*Verstärker*) to adjust.

**Ausstieg** ['aʊsʃtiːk] (-(e)s, -e) *m* (*Ausgang*) exit; ~ **aus der Atomenergie** abandonment of nuclear energy.

**ausstopfen** ['aʊsʃtɔpfən] *vt* to stuff.

**ausstoßen** ['aʊsʃtoːsən] *unreg vt* (*Luft, Rauch*) to give off, emit; (*aus Verein etc*) to expel, exclude; (*herstellen: Teile, Stückzahl*) to turn out, produce.

**ausstrahlen** ['aʊsʃtraːlən] *vt, vi* to radiate; (*RUNDF*) to broadcast.

**Ausstrahlung** *f* radiation; (*fig*) charisma.

**ausstrecken** ['aʊsʃtrɛkən] *vt, vr* to stretch out.

**ausstreichen** ['aʊsʃtraɪçən] *unreg vt* to cross out; (*glätten*) to smooth out.

**ausstreuen** ['aʊsʃtrɔyən] *vt* to scatter; (*fig: Gerücht*) to spread.

**ausströmen** ['aʊsʃtrøːmən] *vi* (*Gas*) to pour out, escape ♦ *vt* to give off; (*fig*) to radiate.

**aussuchen** ['aʊszuːxən] *vt* to select, pick out.

**Austausch** ['aʊstaʊʃ] *m* exchange; **a~bar** *adj* exchangeable.

**austauschen** *vt* to exchange, swop.

**Austauschmotor** *m* replacement engine; (*gebraucht*) factory-reconditioned engine.

**Austauschstudent(in)** *m(f)* exchange student.

**austeilen** ['aʊstaɪlən] *vt* to distribute, give out.

**Auster** ['aʊstər] (-, -n) *f* oyster.

**austoben** ['aʊstoːbən] *vr* (*Kind*) to run wild; (*Erwachsene*) to let off steam; (*sich müde machen*) to tire o.s. out.

**austragen** ['aʊstraːgən] *unreg vt* (*Post*) to deliver; (*Streit etc*) to decide; (*Wettkämpfe*) to hold; **ein Kind** ~ (*nicht abtreiben*) to have a child.

**Austräger** ['aʊstrɛːgər] *m* delivery boy; (*Zeitungs*~) newspaper boy.

**Austragungsort** *m* (*SPORT*) venue.

**Australien** [aʊs'traːliən] (**-s**) *nt* Australia.
**Australier(in)** (**-s, -**) *m(f)* Australian.
**australisch** *adj* Australian.
**austreiben** ['aʊstraɪbən] *unreg vt* to drive out, expel; (*Teufel etc*) to exorcize; **jdm etw ~** to cure sb of sth; (*bes durch Schläge*) to knock sth out of sb.
**austreten** ['aʊstreːtən] *unreg vi* (*zur Toilette*) to be excused ♦ *vt* (*Feuer*) to tread out, trample; (*Schuhe*) to wear out; (*Treppe*) to wear down; **aus etw ~** to leave sth.
**austricksen** ['aʊstrɪksən] (*umg*) *vt* (*SPORT, fig*) to trick.
**austrinken** ['aʊstrɪŋkən] *unreg vt* (*Glas*) to drain; (*Getränk*) to drink up ♦ *vi* to finish one's drink, drink up.
**Austritt** ['aʊstrɪt] *m* emission; (*aus Verein, Partei etc*) retirement, withdrawal.
**austrocknen** ['aʊstrɔknən] *vt, vi* to dry up.
**austüfteln** ['aʊstyftəln] (*umg*) *vt* to work out; (*ersinnen*) to think up.
**ausüben** ['aʊs|yːbən] *vt* (*Beruf*) to practise (*BRIT*), practice (*US*), carry out; (*innehaben: Amt*) to hold; (*Funktion*) to perform; (*Einfluß*) to exert; **einen Reiz auf jdn ~** to hold an attraction for sb; **eine Wirkung auf jdn ~** to have an effect on sb.
**Ausübung** *f* practice, exercise; **in ~ seines Dienstes/seiner Pflicht** (*form*) in the execution of his duty.
**ausufern** ['aʊs|uːfərn] *vi* (*fig*) to get out of hand; (*Konflikt etc*): **~ (zu)** to escalate (into).
**Ausverkauf** ['aʊsfɛrkaʊf] *m* sale; (*fig: Verrat*) sell-out.
**ausverkaufen** *vt* to sell out; (*Geschäft*) to sell up.
**ausverkauft** *adj* (*Karten, Artikel*) sold out; (*THEAT: Haus*) full.
**auswachsen** ['aʊsvaksən] *unreg vi*: **das ist (ja) zum A~** (*umg*) it's enough to drive you mad.
**Auswahl** ['aʊsvaːl] *f*: **eine ~ (an +dat)** a selection (of), a choice (of).
**auswählen** ['aʊsvɛːlən] *vt* to select, choose.
**Auswahlmöglichkeit** *f* choice.
**Auswanderer** ['aʊsvandərər] (**-s, -**) *m* emigrant.
**Auswanderin** ['aʊsvandərɪn] *f* emigrant.
**auswandern** *vi* to emigrate.
**Auswanderung** *f* emigration.
**auswärtig** ['aʊsvɛrtɪç] *adj* (*nicht am/vom Ort*) out-of-town; (*ausländisch*) foreign; **das A~e Amt** the Foreign Office (*BRIT*), the State Department (*US*).
**auswärts** ['aʊsvɛrts] *adv* outside; (*nach außen*) outwards; **~ essen** to eat out; **A~spiel** *nt* away game.
**auswaschen** ['aʊsvaʃən] *unreg vt* to wash out; (*spülen*) to rinse (out).
**auswechseln** ['aʊsvɛksəln] *vt* to change, substitute.
**Ausweg** ['aʊsveːk] *m* way out; **der letzte ~** the last resort; **a~los** *adj* hopeless.

**ausweichen** ['aʊsvaɪçən] *unreg vi*: **jdm/etw ~** (*lit*) to move aside *od* make way for sb/sth; (*fig*) to sidestep sb/sth; **jdm/einer Begegnung ~** to avoid sb/a meeting.
**ausweichend** *adj* evasive.
**Ausweichmanöver** *nt* evasive action.
**ausweinen** ['aʊsvaɪnən] *vr* to have a (good) cry.
**Ausweis** ['aʊsvaɪs] (**-es, -e**) *m* identity card; passport; (*Mitglieds~, Bibliotheks~ etc*) card; **~, bitte** your papers, please.
**ausweisen** ['aʊsvaɪzən] *unreg vt* to expel, banish ♦ *vr* to prove one's identity.
**Ausweis-** *zW*: **~karte** *f* identity papers *pl*; **~kontrolle** *f* identity check; **~papiere** *pl* identity papers *pl*.
**Ausweisung** *f* expulsion.
**ausweiten** ['aʊsvaɪtən] *vt* to stretch.
**auswendig** ['aʊsvɛndɪç] *adv* by heart; **~ lernen** to learn by heart.
**auswerfen** ['aʊsvɛrfən] *unreg vt* (*Anker, Netz*) to cast.
**auswerten** ['aʊsvɛrtən] *vt* to evaluate.
**Auswertung** *f* evaluation, analysis; (*Nutzung*) utilization.
**auswickeln** ['aʊsvɪkəln] *vt* (*Paket, Bonbon etc*) to unwrap.
**auswirken** ['aʊsvɪrkən] *vr* to have an effect.
**Auswirkung** *f* effect.
**auswischen** ['aʊsvɪʃən] *vt* to wipe out; **jdm eins ~** (*umg*) to put one over on sb.
**Auswuchs** ['aʊsvuːks] *m* (out)growth; (*fig*) product; (*Mißstand, Übersteigerung*) excess.
**auswuchten** ['aʊsvʊxtən] *vt* (*AUT*) to balance.
**auszacken** ['aʊtsakən] *vt* (*Stoff etc*) to pink.
**auszahlen** ['aʊtsaːlən] *vt* (*Lohn, Summe*) to pay out; (*Arbeiter*) to pay off; (*Miterben*) to buy out ♦ *vr* (*sich lohnen*) to pay.
**auszählen** ['aʊtsɛːlən] *vt* (*Stimmen*) to count; (*BOXEN*) to count out.
**auszeichnen** ['aʊtsaɪçnən] *vt* to honour (*BRIT*), honor (*US*), (*MIL*) to decorate; (*COMM*) to price ♦ *vr* to distinguish o.s.; **der Wagen zeichnet sich durch ... aus** one of the car's main features is ...
**Auszeichnung** *f* distinction; (*COMM*) pricing; (*Ehrung*) awarding of decoration; (*Ehre*) honour (*BRIT*), honor (*US*); (*Orden*) decoration; **mit ~** with distinction.
**ausziehen** ['aʊtsiːən] *unreg vt* (*Kleidung*) to take off; (*Haare, Zähne, Tisch etc*) to pull out ♦ *vr* to undress ♦ *vi* (*aufbrechen*) to leave; (*aus Wohnung*) to move out.
**Auszubildende(r)** ['aʊtsʊbɪldəndə(r)] *f(m)* trainee; (*als Handwerker*) apprentice.
**Auszug** ['aʊtsuːk] *m* (*aus Wohnung*) removal; (*aus Buch etc*) extract; (*Konto~*) statement; (*Ausmarsch*) departure.
**autark** [aʊ'tark] *adj* self-sufficient (*auch fig*); (*COMM*) autarkical.
**Auto** ['aʊto] (**-s, -s**) *nt* (motor-)car, automobile (*US*); **mit dem ~ fahren** to go by car;

~ **fahren** to drive.
**Autoatlas** *m* road atlas.
**Autobahn** *f* motorway (*BRIT*), expressway
(*US*).

> **Autobahn** *is the German for a motorway. In the*
> *former West Germany there is a widespread*
> *network but in the former* **DDR** *the motorways*
> *are somewhat less extensive. There is no*
> *overall speed limit but a limit of 130 km per*
> *hour is recommended and there are lower*
> *mandatory limits on certain stretches of road.*
> *As yet there are no tolls payable on German*
> *Autobahnen.*

**Autobahndreieck** *nt* motorway (*BRIT*) *od*
expressway (*US*) junction.
**Autobahnkreuz** *nt* motorway (*BRIT*) *od*
expressway (*US*) intersection.
**Autobahnzubringer** *m* motorway feeder *od*
access road.
**Autobiographie** [aʊtobiogra'fiː] *f*
autobiography.
**Auto-** *zW:* ~**bombe** *f* car bomb; ~**bus** *m* bus;
(*Reisebus*) coach (*BRIT*), bus (*US*); ~**fähre** *f*
car ferry; ~**fahrer(in)** *m(f)* motorist, driver;
~**fahrt** *f* drive; ~**friedhof** (*umg*) *m* car
dump.
**autogen** [aʊto'geːn] *adj* autogenous; ~**es**
**Training** (*PSYCH*) relaxation through self-
hypnosis.
**Autogramm** [aʊto'gram] *nt* autograph.
**Automat** (-en, -en) *m* machine.
**Automatik** [aʊto'maːtɪk] *f* automatic
mechanism (*auch fig*); (*Gesamtanlage*)
automatic system; (*AUT*) automatic
transmission.
**automatisch** *adj* automatic.
**Automatisierung** [aʊtomati'ziːrʊŋ] *f*
automation.
**Automobilausstellung**
[aʊtomo'biːlaʊsʃtɛlʊŋ] *f* motor show.
**autonom** [aʊto'noːm] *adj* autonomous.
**Autopsie** [aʊtɔ'psiː] *f* post-mortem, autopsy.
**Autor** ['aʊtɔr] (-s, -en) *m* author.
**Auto-** *zW:* ~**radio** *nt* car radio; ~**reifen** *m* car
tyre (*BRIT*) *od* tire (*US*); ~**reisezug** *m*
motorail train; ~**rennen** *nt* motor race;
(*Sportart*) motor racing.
**Autorin** [aʊ'toːrɪn] *f* authoress.
**autoritär** [aʊtori'tɛːr] *adj* authoritarian.
**Autorität** *f* authority.
**Auto-** *zW:* ~**schalter** *m* drive-in bank
(counter); ~**telefon** *nt* car phone; ~**unfall** *m*
car *od* motor accident; ~**verleih** *m*,
~**vermietung** *f* car hire (*BRIT*) *od* rental (*US*).
**AvD** (-) *m abk* (= *Automobilclub von*
*Deutschland*) *German motoring organization,*
≈ AA (*BRIT*), AAA (*US*).
**Axt** [akst] (-, ‥e) *f* axe (*BRIT*), ax (*US*).
**AZ, Az.** *abk* (= *Aktenzeichen*) ref.
**Azoren** [a'tsoːrən] *pl* (*GEOG*) Azores *pl*.

**Azteke** [ats'teːkə] (-n, -n) *m* Aztec.
**Aztekin** *f* Aztec.
**Azubi** [a'tsuːbi] (-s, -s) (*umg*) *f(m) abk*
= **Auszubildende(r)**.


$$B, b$$


**B¹, b** [beː] *nt* (*letter*) B, b; ~ **wie Bertha** ≈ B
for Benjamin, B for Baker (*US*);
**B-Dur/b-Moll** (the key of) B flat major/
minor.
**B²** [beː] *f abk* = **Bundesstraße**.
**Baby** ['beːbi] (-s, -s) *nt* baby; ~**ausstattung** *f*
layette; ~**raum** *m* (*Flughafen etc*) nursing
room; ~**sitter** ['beːbɪsɪtər] (-s, -) *m* baby-
sitter; ~**speck** (*umg*) *m* puppy fat.
**Bach** [bax] (-(e)s, ‥e) *m* stream, brook.
**Backblech** *nt* baking tray.
**Backbord** (-(e)s, -e) *nt* (*NAUT*) port.
**Backe** (-, -n) *f* cheek.
**backen** ['bakən] *unreg vt, vi* to bake; **frisch/**
**knusprig gebackenes Brot** fresh/crusty
bread.
**Backenbart** *m* sideboards *pl*.
**Backenzahn** *m* molar.
**Bäcker(in)** ['bɛkər(ɪn)] (-s, -) *m(f)* baker.
**Bäckerei** [bɛkə'raɪ] *f* bakery; (*Bäckerladen*)
baker's (shop).
**Bäckerjunge** *m* (*Lehrling*) baker's apprentice.
**Back-** *zW:* ~**fisch** *m* fried fish; (*veraltet*)
teenager; ~**form** *f* baking tin (*BRIT*) *od* pan
(*US*); ~**hähnchen** *nt* fried chicken in
breadcrumbs; ~**obst** *nt* dried fruit; ~**ofen**
*m* oven; ~**pflaume** *f* prune; ~**pulver** *nt*
baking powder; ~**stein** *m* brick.
**bäckt** [bɛkt] *vb siehe* **backen**.
**Bad** [baːt] (-(e)s, ‥er) *nt* bath; (*Schwimmen*)
bathing; (*Ort*) spa.
**Bade-** *zW:* ~**anstalt** *f* swimming pool;
~**anzug** *m* bathing suit; ~**hose** *f* bathing *od*
swimming trunks *pl*; ~**kappe** *f* bathing cap;
~**mantel** *m* bath(ing) robe; ~**meister** *m*
swimming pool attendant.
**baden** ['baːdən] *vi* to bathe, have a bath ♦ *vt* to
bath; ~ **gehen** (*fig: umg*) to come a cropper.
**Baden-Württemberg** ['baːdən'vʏrtəmbɛrk] *nt*
Baden-Württemberg.
**Bade-** *zW:* ~**ort** *m* spa; ~**sachen** *pl* swimming
things *pl*; ~**tuch** *nt* bath towel; ~**wanne** *f*
bath(tub); ~**zimmer** *nt* bathroom.
**baff** [baf] *adj:* ~ **sein** (*umg*) to be
flabbergasted.
**BAföG, Bafög** ['baːføk] *nt abk* (= *Bundes-*
*ausbildungsförderungsgesetz*) *German stu-*
*dent grants system*.

**Bafög** *is the system which awards grants for living expenses to students at universities and certain training colleges. The amount is based on parental income. Part of the grant must be paid back a few years after graduating.*

**BAG** (-) *nt abk* (= *Bundesarbeitsgericht*) German industrial tribunal.
**Bagatelle** [baga'tɛlə] (-, -n) *f* trifle.
**Bagdad** ['bakdat] (-s) *nt* Baghdad.
**Bagger** ['bagər] (-s, -) *m* excavator; (*NAUT*) dredger.
**baggern** *vt, vi* to excavate; (*NAUT*) to dredge.
**Baggersee** *m* (flooded) gravel pit.
**Bahamas** [ba'ha:mas] *pl:* **die** ~ the Bahamas *pl.*
**Bahn** [ba:n] (-, -en) *f* railway (*BRIT*), railroad (*US*); (*Weg*) road, way; (*Spur*) lane; (*Renn~*) track; (*ASTRON*) orbit; (*Stoff~*) length; **mit der** ~ by train *od* rail/tram; **frei** ~ (*COMM*) carriage free to station of destination; **jdm/etw die** ~ **frei machen** (*fig*) to clear the way for sb/sth; **von der rechten** ~ **abkommen** to stray from the straight and narrow; **jdn aus der** ~ **werfen** (*fig*) to shatter sb; ~**beamte(r)** *m* railway (*BRIT*) *od* railroad (*US*) official; **b**~**brechend** *adj* pioneering; ~**brecher(in)** (-s, -) *m(f)* pioneer; ~**damm** *m* railway embankment.
**bahnen** *vt:* **sich einen Weg** ~ to clear a way.
**Bahnfahrt** *f* railway (*BRIT*) *od* railroad (*US*) journey.
**Bahnhof** *m* station; **auf dem** ~ at the station; **ich verstehe nur** ~ (*hum: umg*) it's all Greek to me.
**Bahnhofshalle** *f* station concourse.
**Bahnhofsmission** *f* charitable organization for helping rail travellers.

*The* **Bahnhofsmission** *is a charitable organization set up by and run jointly by various churches. At railway stations in most big cities they have an office to which people in need of advice and help can go.*

**Bahnhofswirtschaft** *f* station restaurant.
**Bahn-** *zW:* **b**~**lagernd** *adj* (*COMM*) to be collected from the station; ~**linie** *f* (railway (*BRIT*) *od* railroad (*US*)) line; ~**schranke** *f* level (*BRIT*) *od* grade (*US*) crossing barrier; ~**steig** *m* platform; ~**steigkarte** *f* platform ticket; ~**strecke** *f* railway (*BRIT*) *od* railroad (*US*) line; ~**übergang** *m* level (*BRIT*) *od* grade (*US*) crossing; **beschrankter** ~**übergang** crossing with gates; **unbeschrankter** ~**übergang** unguarded crossing; ~**wärter** *m* signalman.
**Bahrain** [ba'raɪn] (-s) *nt* Bahrain.
**Bahre** ['ba:rə] (-, -n) *f* stretcher.
**Baiser** [bɛ'ze:] (-s, -s) *nt* meringue.
**Baisse** ['bɛːsə] (-, -n) *f* (*Börse*) fall; (*plötzlich*)

slump.
**Bajonett** [bajo'nɛt] (-(e)s, -e) *nt* bayonet.
**Bakelit**® [bake'li:t] (-s) *nt* Bakelite®.
**Bakterien** [bak'te:riən] *pl* bacteria *pl.*
**Balance** [ba'lã:sə] (-, -n) *f* balance, equilibrium.
**balancieren** *vt, vi* to balance.
**bald** [balt] *adv* (*zeitlich*) soon; (*beinahe*) almost; ~ ... ~ ... now ... now ...; ~ **darauf** soon afterwards; **bis** ~! see you soon.
**baldig** ['baldɪç] *adj* early, speedy.
**baldmöglichst** *adv* as soon as possible.
**Baldrian** ['baldria:n] (-s, -e) *m* valerian.
**Balearen** [bale'a:rən] *pl:* **die** ~ the Balearics *pl.*
**Balg** [balk] (-(e)s, ̈-er) (*pej: umg*) *m od nt* (*Kind*) brat.
**balgen** ['balgən] *vr:* **sich** ~ (**um**) to scrap (over).
**Balkan** ['balka:n] *m:* **der** ~ the Balkans *pl.*
**Balken** ['balkən] (-s, -) *m* beam; (*Trag~*) girder; (*Stütz~*) prop.
**Balkon** [bal'kõ:] (-s, -s *od* -e) *m* balcony; (*THEAT*) (dress) circle.
**Ball** [bal] (-(e)s, ̈-e) *m* ball; (*Tanz*) dance, ball.
**Ballade** [ba'la:də] (-, -n) *f* ballad.
**Ballast** ['balast] (-(e)s, -e) *m* ballast; (*fig*) weight, burden; ~**stoffe** *pl* (*MED*) roughage *sing.*
**Ballen** ['balən] (-s, -) *m* bale; (*ANAT*) ball.
**ballen** *vt* (*formen*) to make into a ball; (*Faust*) to clench ♦ *vr* to build up; (*Menschen*) to gather.
**ballern** ['balərn] (*umg*) *vi* to shoot, fire.
**Ballett** [ba'lɛt] (-(e)s, -e) *nt* ballet; ~**(t)änzer(in)** *m(f)* ballet dancer.
**Ballistik** [ba'lɪstɪk] *f* ballistics *sing.*
**Balljunge** *m* ball boy.
**Ballkleid** *nt* evening dress.
**Ballon** [ba'lõ:] (-s, -s *od* -e) *m* balloon.
**Ballspiel** *nt* ball game.
**Ballung** ['baluŋ] *f* concentration; (*von Energie*) build-up.
**Ballungs-** *zW:* ~**gebiet** *nt*, ~**raum** *m* conurbation; ~**zentrum** *nt* centre (*BRIT*) *od* center (*US*) (*of population, industry etc*).
**Balsam** ['balza:m] (-s, -e) *m* balsam; (*fig*) balm.
**Balte** ['baltə] (-n, -n) *m* Balt; **er ist** ~ he comes from the Baltic.
**Baltikum** ['baltikʊm] (-s) *nt:* **das** ~ the Baltic States *pl.*
**Baltin** ['baltɪn] *f siehe* **Balte**.
**baltisch** *adj* Baltic *attrib*.
**Balz** [balts] (-, -en) *f* (*Paarungsspiel*) courtship display; (*Paarungszeit*) mating season.
**Bambus** ['bambʊs] (-ses, -se) *m* bamboo; ~**rohr** *nt* bamboo cane.
**Bammel** ['baməl] (-s) (*umg*) *m:* (**einen**) ~ **vor jdm/etw haben** to be scared of sb/sth.
**banal** [ba'na:l] *adj* banal.
**Banalität** [banali'tɛ:t] *f* banality.
**Banane** [ba'na:nə] (-, -n) *f* banana.

**Bananenschale** *f* banana skin.
**Bananenstecker** *m* jack plug.
**Banause** [ba'nauzə] (-n, -n) *m* philistine.
**Band¹** [bant] (-(e)s, ⸚e) *m* (*Buchband*) volume; **das spricht Bände** that speaks volumes.
**Band²** (-(e)s, ⸚er) *nt* (*Stoff~*) ribbon, tape; (*Fließ~*) production line; (*Faß~*) hoop; (*Ziel~, Ton~*) tape; (*ANAT*) ligament; **etw auf ~ aufnehmen** to tape sth; **am laufenden ~** (*umg*) non-stop.
**Band³** (-(e)s, -e) *nt* (*Freundschafts~ etc*) bond.
**Band⁴** [bɛnt] (-, -s) *f* band, group.
**band** *etc* [bant] *vb siehe* **binden.**
**Bandage** [ban'da:ʒə] (-, -n) *f* bandage.
**bandagieren** *vt* to bandage.
**Bandbreite** *f* (*von Meinungen etc*) range.
**Bande** ['bandə] (-, -n) *f* band; (*Straßen~*) gang.
**bändigen** ['bɛndɪgən] *vt* (*Tier*) to tame; (*Trieb, Leidenschaft*) to control, restrain.
**Bandit** [ban'di:t] (-en, -en) *m* bandit.
**Band-** *zW:* **~maß** *nt* tape measure; **~nudeln** *pl* tagliatelle *pl*; **~säge** *f* band saw; **~scheibe** *f* (*ANAT*) disc; **~scheibenschaden** *m* slipped disc; **~wurm** *m* tapeworm.
**bange** ['baŋə] *adj* scared; (*besorgt*) anxious; **jdm wird es ~** sb is becoming scared; **jdm ~ machen** to scare sb; **B~macher** (-s, -) *m* scaremonger.
**bangen** *vi:* **um jdn/etw ~** to be anxious *od* worried about sb/sth.
**Bangkok** ['baŋkɔk] (-s) *nt* Bangkok.
**Bangladesch** [baŋgla'dɛʃ] (-s) *nt* Bangladesh.
**Banjo** ['banjo, 'bɛndʒo] (-s, -s) *nt* banjo.
**Bank¹** [baŋk] (-, ⸚e) *f* (*Sitz~*) bench; (*Sand~ etc*) (sand)bank, (sand)bar; **etw auf die lange ~ schieben** (*umg*) to put sth off.
**Bank²** (- , -en) *f* (*Geld~*) bank; **bei der ~** at the bank; **Geld auf der ~ haben** to have money in the bank; **~anweisung** *f* banker's order; **~automat** *m* cash dispenser; **~beamte(r)** *m* bank clerk; **~einlage** *f* (bank) deposit.
**Bankett** [baŋ'kɛt] (-(e)s, -e) *nt* (*Essen*) banquet; (*Straßenrand*) verge (*BRIT*), shoulder (*US*).
**Bank-** *zW:* **~fach** *nt* (*Schließfach*) safe-deposit box; **~gebühr** *f* bank charge; **~geheimnis** *nt* confidentiality in banking.
**Bankier** [baŋki'e:] (-s, -s) *m* banker.
**Bank-** *zW:* **~konto** *nt* bank account; **~leitzahl** *f* bank code number; **~note** *f* banknote; **~raub** *m* bank robbery.
**bankrott** [baŋ'krɔt] *adj* bankrupt; **B~** (-(e)s, -e) *m* bankruptcy; **B~ machen** to go bankrupt; **den B~ anmelden** *od* **erklären** to declare o.s. bankrupt; **B~erklärung** *f* (*lit*) declaration of bankruptcy; (*fig: umg*) declaration of failure.
**Banküberfall** *m* bank raid.
**Bann** [ban] (-(e)s, -e) *m* (*HIST*) ban; (*Kirchen~*) excommunication; (*fig: Zauber*) spell; **b~en** *vt* (*Geister*) to exorcize; (*Gefahr*) to avert; (*bezaubern*) to enchant; (*HIST*) to banish.
**Banner** (-s, -) *nt* banner, flag.
**Bar** [ba:r] (-, -s) *f* bar.
**bar** *adj* (+*gen*) (*unbedeckt*) bare; (*frei von*) lacking (in); (*offenkundig*) utter, sheer; **~e(s) Geld** cash; **etw (in) ~ bezahlen** to pay sth (in) cash; **etw für ~e Münze nehmen** (*fig*) to take sth at face value; **~ aller Hoffnung** (*liter*) devoid of hope, completely without hope.
**Bär** [bɛ:r] (-en, -en) *m* bear; **jdm einen ~en aufbinden** (*umg*) to have sb on.
**Baracke** [ba'rakə] (-, -n) *f* hut.
**barbarisch** [bar'ba:rɪʃ] *adj* barbaric, barbarous.
**Barbestand** *m* money in hand.
**Bardame** *f* barmaid.
**Bärenhunger** (*umg*) *m:* **einen ~ haben** to be famished.
**bärenstark** (*umg*) *adj* strapping, strong as an ox; (*fig*) terrific.
**barfuß** *adj* barefoot.
**barg** *etc* [bark] *vb siehe* **bergen.**
**Bargeld** *nt* cash, ready money.
**bargeldlos** *adj* non-cash; **~er Zahlungsverkehr** non-cash *od* credit transactions *pl*.
**barhäuptig** *adj* bareheaded.
**Barhocker** *m* bar stool.
**Bariton** ['ba:ritɔn] *m* baritone.
**Barkauf** *m* cash purchase.
**Barkeeper** ['ba:rki:pər] (-s, -) *m* barman, bartender.
**Barkredit** *m* cash loan.
**Barmann** (-(e)s, *pl* -männer) *m* barman.
**barmherzig** [barm'hɛrtsɪç] *adj* merciful, compassionate; **B~keit** *f* mercy, compassion.
**Barock** [ba'rɔk] (-s *od* -) *nt od m* baroque.
**Barometer** [baro'me:tər] (-s, -) *nt* barometer; **das ~ steht auf Sturm** (*fig*) there's a storm brewing.
**Baron** [ba'ro:n] (-s, -e) *m* baron.
**Baronesse** [baro'nɛsə] (-, -n) *f* baroness.
**Baronin** *f* baroness.
**Barren** ['barən] (-s, -) *m* parallel bars *pl*; (*Gold~*) ingot.
**Barriere** [bari'ɛ:rə] (-, -n) *f* barrier.
**Barrikade** [bari'ka:də] (-, -n) *f* barricade.
**Barsch** [barʃ] (-(e)s, -e) *m* perch.
**barsch** [barʃ] *adj* brusque, gruff; **jdn ~ anfahren** to snap at sb.
**Barschaft** *f* ready money.
**Barscheck** *m* open *od* uncrossed cheque (*BRIT*), open check (*US*).
**barst** *etc* [barst] *vb siehe* **bersten.**
**Bart** [ba:rt] (-(e)s, ⸚e) *m* beard; (*Schlüssel~*) bit.
**bärtig** ['bɛ:rtɪç] *adj* bearded.
**Barvermögen** *nt* liquid assets *pl*.
**Barzahlung** *f* cash payment.

**Basar** [ba'zaːr] (**-s, -e**) m bazaar.
**Base** ['baːzə] (**-, -n**) f (CHEM) base; (Kusine) cousin.
**Basel** ['baːzəl] (**-s**) nt Basle.
**Basen** pl von **Base, Basis.**
**basieren** [ba'ziːrən] vt to base ♦ vi to be based.
**Basilikum** [ba'ziːlikʊm] (**-s**) nt basil.
**Basis** ['baːzɪs] (**-, pl Basen**) f basis; (ARCHIT, MIL, MATH) base; ~ **und Überbau** (POL, SOZIOLOGIE) foundation and superstructure; **die** ~ (umg) the grass roots.
**basisch** ['baːzɪʃ] adj (CHEM) alkaline.
**Basisgruppe** f action group.
**Baske** ['baskə] (**-n, -n**) m Basque.
**Baskenland** nt Basque region.
**Baskenmütze** f beret.
**Baskin** f Basque.
**Baß** [bas] (**Basses, pl Bässe**) m bass.
**Bassin** [ba'sɛ̃ː] (**-s, -s**) nt pool.
**Bassist** [ba'sɪst] m bass.
**Baßschlüssel** m bass clef.
**Baßstimme** f bass voice.
**Bast** [bast] (**-(e)s, -e**) m raffia.
**basta** ['basta] interj: (**und damit**) ~! (and) that's that!
**basteln** ['bastəln] vt to make ♦ vi to do handicrafts; **an etw** dat ~ (an etw herum~) to tinker with sth.
**Bastler** ['bastlər] (**-s, -**) m do-it-yourselfer; (handwerklich) handicrafts enthusiast.
**BAT** m abk (= Bundesangestelltentarif) German salary scale for employees.
**bat** etc [baːt] vb siehe **bitten.**
**Bataillon** [batal'joːn] (**-s, -e**) nt battalion.
**Batist** [ba'tɪst] (**-(e)s, -e**) m batiste.
**Batterie** [batə'riː] f battery.
**Bau** [baʊ] (**-(e)s**) m (~en) building, construction; (Auf~) structure; (Körper~) frame; (~stelle) building site; (pl ~e: Tier~) hole, burrow; (: MIN) working(s); (pl ~ten: Gebäude) building; **sich im** ~ **befinden** to be under construction; ~**arbeiten** pl (Straßen~) roadworks pl (BRIT), roadwork sing (US); building od construction work sing; ~**arbeiter** m building worker.
**Bauch** [baʊx] (**-(e)s, Bäuche**) m belly; (ANAT) stomach, abdomen; **sich** dat (**vor Lachen**) **den** ~ **halten** (umg) to split one's sides (laughing); **mit etw auf den** ~ **fallen** (umg) to come a cropper with sth; ~**ansatz** m beginning of a paunch; ~**fell** nt peritoneum.
**bauchig** adj bulging.
**Bauch-** zW: ~**landung** f: **eine** ~**landung machen** (fig) to experience a failure, to flop; ~**muskel** m abdominal muscle; ~**nabel** m navel, belly-button (umg); ~**redner** m ventriloquist; ~**schmerzen** pl stomachache sing; ~**speicheldrüse** f pancreas; ~**tanz** m belly dance; belly dancing; ~**weh** nt stomachache.
**Baud-Rate** [baʊt'raːtə] f (COMPUT) baud rate.
**bauen** ['baʊən] vt to build; (TECH) to construct; (umg: verursachen: Unfall) to cause ♦ vi to build; **auf jdn/etw** ~ to depend od count upon sb/sth; **da hast du Mist gebaut** (umg) you really messed that up.
**Bauer¹** ['baʊər] (**-n** od **-s, -n**) m farmer; (SCHACH) pawn.
**Bauer²** (**-s, -**) nt od m (Vogel~) cage.
**Bäuerchen** ['bɔyərçən] nt (Kindersprache) burp.
**Bäuerin** ['bɔyərɪn] f farmer; (Frau des Bauern) farmer's wife.
**bäuerlich** adj rustic.
**Bauern-** zW: ~**brot** nt black bread; ~**fänge'rei** f deception, confidence trick(s); ~**frühstück** nt bacon and potato omelette (BRIT) od omelet (US); ~**haus** nt farmhouse; ~**hof** m farm; ~**schaft** f farming community; ~**schläue** f native cunning, craftiness, shrewdness.
**Bau-** zW: **b**~**fällig** adj dilapidated; ~**fälligkeit** f dilapidation; ~**firma** f construction firm; ~**führer** m site foreman; ~**gelände** nt building site; ~**genehmigung** f building permit; ~**gerüst** nt scaffolding; ~**herr** m client (of construction firm); ~**ingenieur** m civil engineer.
**Bauj.** abk = Baujahr.
**Bau-** zW: ~**jahr** nt year of construction; (von Auto) year of manufacture; ~**kasten** m box of bricks; ~**klötzchen** nt (building) block; ~**kosten** pl construction costs pl; ~**land** nt building land; ~**leute** pl building workers pl; **b**~**lich** adj structural; ~**löwe** m building speculator; ~**lücke** f undeveloped building plot.
**Baum** [baʊm] (**-(e)s, pl Bäume**) m tree; **heute könnte ich Bäume ausreißen** I feel full of energy today.
**Baumarkt** m DIY superstore.
**baumeln** ['baʊməln] vi to dangle.
**bäumen** ['bɔymən] vr to rear (up).
**Baum-** zW: ~**grenze** f tree line; ~**schule** f nursery; ~**stamm** m tree trunk; ~**stumpf** m tree stump; ~**wolle** f cotton.
**Bau-** zW: ~**plan** m architect's plan; ~**platz** m building site; ~**sachverständige(r)** f(m) quantity surveyor; ~**satz** m construction kit.
**Bausch** [baʊʃ] (**-(e)s, pl Bäusche**) m (Watte~) ball, wad; **in** ~ **und Bogen** (fig) lock, stock, and barrel.
**bauschen** vt, vi, vr to puff out.
**bauschig** adj baggy, wide.
**Bau-** zW: **b**~**sparen** vi untr to save with a building society (BRIT) od a building and loan association (US); ~**sparkasse** f building society (BRIT), building and loan association (US); ~**sparvertrag** m savings contract with a building society (BRIT) od building and loan association (US); ~**stein** m building stone, freestone; ~**stelle** f building site; ~**stil** m architectural style;

**b~technisch** adj in accordance with building od construction methods; **~teil** nt prefabricated part (of building); **~ten** pl von **Bau**; **~unternehmer** m contractor, builder; **~weise** f (method of) construction; **~werk** nt building; **~zaun** m hoarding.

**b.a.w.** abk (= bis auf weiteres) until further notice.

**Bayer(in)** ['baɪər(ɪn)] (-n, -n) m(f) Bavarian.

**bay(e)risch** adj Bavarian.

**Bayern** nt Bavaria.

**Bazillus** [ba'tsɪlʊs] (-, pl **Bazillen**) m bacillus.

**Bd.** abk (= Band) vol.

**Bde.** abk (= Bände) vols.

**beabsichtigen** [bə'|apzɪçtɪgən] vt to intend.

**beachten** [bə'|axtən] vt to take note of; (Vorschrift) to obey; (Vorfahrt) to observe.

**beachtenswert** adj noteworthy.

**beachtlich** adj considerable.

**Beachtung** f notice, attention, observation; **jdm keine ~ schenken** to take no notice of sb.

**Beamte(r)** [bə'|amtə(r)] (-n, -n) m official; (Staats~) civil servant; (Bank~ etc) employee.

**Beamtenlaufbahn** f: **die ~ einschlagen** to enter the civil service.

**Beamtenverhältnis** nt: **im ~ stehen** to be a civil servant.

**beamtet** adj (form) appointed on a permanent basis (by the state).

**Beamtin** f siehe **Beamte(r)**.

**beängstigend** [bə'|ɛŋstɪgənt] adj alarming.

**beanspruchen** [bə'|anʃpruxən] vt to claim; (Zeit, Platz) to take up, occupy; **jdn ~** to take up sb's time; **etw stark ~** to put sth under a lot of stress.

**beanstanden** [bə'|anʃtandən] vt to complain about, object to; (Rechnung) to query.

**Beanstandung** f complaint.

**beantragen** [bə'|antraːgən] vt to apply for, ask for.

**beantworten** [bə'|antvɔrtən] vt to answer.

**Beantwortung** f reply.

**bearbeiten** [bə'|arbaɪtən] vt to work; (Material) to process; (Thema) to deal with; (Land) to cultivate; (CHEM) to treat; (Buch) to revise; (umg: beeinflussen wollen) to work on.

**Bearbeitung** f processing; cultivation; treatment; revision; **die ~ meines Antrags hat lange gedauert** it took a long time to deal with my claim.

**Bearbeitungsgebühr** f handling charge.

**beatmen** [bə'|aːtmən] vt: **jdn künstlich ~** to give sb artificial respiration.

**Beatmung** [bə'|aːtmʊŋ] f respiration.

**beaufsichtigen** [bə'|aʊfzɪçtɪgən] vt to supervise.

**Beaufsichtigung** f supervision.

**beauftragen** [bə'|aʊftraːgən] vt to instruct; **jdn mit etw ~** to entrust sb with sth.

**Beauftragte(r)** f(m) representative.

**bebauen** [bə'baʊən] vt to build on; (AGR) to cultivate.

**beben** ['beːbən] vi to tremble, shake; **B~ (-s -)** nt earthquake.

**bebildern** [bə'bɪldərn] vt to illustrate.

**Becher** ['bɛçər] (-s, -) m mug; (ohne Henkel) tumbler.

**bechern** ['bɛçərn] (umg) vi (trinken) to have a few (drinks).

**Becken** ['bɛkən] (-s, -) nt basin; (MUS) cymbal; (ANAT) pelvis.

**Bedacht** [bə'daxt] m: **mit ~** (vorsichtig) prudently, carefully; (absichtlich) deliberately.

**bedacht** adj thoughtful, careful; **auf etw akk ~ sein** to be concerned about sth.

**bedächtig** [bə'dɛçtɪç] adj (umsichtig) thoughtful, reflective; (langsam) slow, deliberate.

**bedanken** [bə'daŋkən] vr: **sich (bei jdm) ~** to say thank you (to sb); **ich bedanke mich herzlich** thank you very much.

**Bedarf** [bə'darf] (-(e)s) m need; (~smenge) requirements pl; (COMM) demand; supply; **alles für den häuslichen ~** all household requirements; **je nach ~** according to demand; **bei ~** if necessary; **~ an etw** dat **haben** to be in need of sth.

**Bedarfs-** zW: **~artikel** m requisite; **~deckung** f satisfaction of sb's needs; **~fall** m case of need; **~haltestelle** f request stop.

**bedauerlich** [bə'daʊərlɪç] adj regrettable.

**bedauern** [bə'daʊərn] vt to be sorry for; (bemitleiden) to pity; **wir ~, Ihnen mitteilen zu müssen, ...** we regret to have to inform you ...; **B~ (-s)** nt regret.

**bedauernswert** adj (Zustände) regrettable; (Mensch) pitiable, unfortunate.

**bedecken** [bə'dɛkən] vt to cover.

**bedeckt** adj covered; (Himmel) overcast.

**bedenken** [bə'dɛŋkən] unreg vt to think over, consider; **ich gebe zu ~, daß ...** (geh) I would ask you to consider that ...; **B~ (-s, -)** nt (Überlegen) consideration; (Zweifel) doubt; (Skrupel) scruple; **mir kommen B~** I am having second thoughts.

**bedenklich** adj doubtful; (bedrohlich) dangerous, risky.

**Bedenkzeit** f time to consider; **zwei Tage ~** two days to think about it.

**bedeuten** [bə'dɔʏtən] vt to mean; to signify; (wichtig sein) to be of importance; **das bedeutet nichts Gutes** that means trouble.

**bedeutend** adj important; (beträchtlich) considerable.

**bedeutsam** adj significant; (vielsagend) meaningful.

**Bedeutung** f meaning; significance; (Wichtigkeit) importance.

**bedeutungslos** adj insignificant, unimportant.

**bedeutungsvoll** adj momentous, significant.

**bedienen** [bə'di:nən] *vt* to serve; (*Maschine*) to
work, operate ♦ *vr* (*beim Essen*) to help o.s.;
(*gebrauchen*): **sich jds/einer Sache ~** to make
use of sb/sth; **werden Sie schon bedient?**
are you being served?; **damit sind Sie sehr
gut bedient** that should serve you very
well; **ich bin bedient!** (*umg*) I've had
enough.

**Bedienung** *f* service; (*Kellner etc*) waiter/
waitress; (*Zuschlag*) service (charge); (*von
Maschinen*) operation.

**Bedienungsanleitung** *f* operating
instructions *pl*.

**bedingen** [bə'dɪŋən] *vt* (*voraussetzen*) to
demand, involve; (*verursachen*) to cause,
occasion.

**bedingt** *adj* limited; (*Straferlaß*) conditional;
(*Reflex*) conditioned; (*nur*) **~ gelten** to be
(only) partially valid; **~ geeignet** suitable
up to a point.

**Bedingung** *f* condition; (*Voraussetzung*)
stipulation; **mit** *od* **unter der ~, daß ...** on
condition that ...; **zu günstigen ~en** (*COMM*)
on favourable (*BRIT*) *od* favorable (*US*)
terms.

**Bedingungsform** *f* (*GRAM*) conditional.

**bedingungslos** *adj* unconditional.

**bedrängen** [bə'drɛŋən] *vt* to pester, harass.

**Bedrängnis** [bə'drɛŋnɪs] *f* (*seelisch*) distress,
torment.

**Bedrängung** *f* trouble.

**bedrohen** [bə'dro:ən] *vt* to threaten.

**bedrohlich** *adj* ominous, threatening.

**Bedrohung** *f* threat, menace.

**bedrucken** [bə'drʊkən] *vt* to print on.

**bedrücken** [bə'drʏkən] *vt* to oppress, trouble.

**bedürfen** [bə'dʏrfən] *unreg vi +gen* (*geh*) to
need, require; **ohne daß es eines Hinweises
bedurft hätte, ...** without having to be asked
...

**Bedürfnis** [bə'dʏrfnɪs] (*-ses, -se*) *nt* need; **das
~ nach etw haben** to need sth; **~anstalt** *f*
(*form*) public convenience (*BRIT*), comfort
station (*US*); **b~los** *adj* frugal, modest.

**bedürftig** *adj* in need, poor, needy.

**Beefsteak** ['bi:fste:k] (*-s, -s*) *nt* steak;
**deutsches ~** hamburger.

**beehren** [bə'|e:rən] *vt* (*geh*) to honour (*BRIT*),
honor (*US*); **wir ~ uns ...** we have pleasure
in ...

**beeilen** [bə'|aɪlən] *vr* to hurry.

**beeindrucken** [bə'|aɪndrʊkən] *vt* to impress,
make an impression on.

**beeinflussen** [bə'|aɪnflʊsən] *vt* to influence.

**Beeinflussung** *f* influence.

**beeinträchtigen** [bə'|aɪntrɛçtɪgən] *vt* to affect
adversely; (*Sehvermögen*) to impair;
(*Freiheit*) to infringe upon.

**beend(ig)en** [bə'|ɛnd(ɪg)ən] *vt* to end, finish,
terminate.

**Beend(ig)ung** *f* end(ing), finish(ing).

**beengen** [bə'|ɛŋən] *vt* to cramp; (*fig*) to

hamper, inhibit; **~de Kleidung** restricting
clothing.

**beengt** *adj* cramped; (*fig*) stifled.

**beerben** [bə'|ɛrbən] *vt* to inherit from.

**beerdigen** [bə'|e:rdɪgən] *vt* to bury.

**Beerdigung** *f* funeral, burial.

**Beerdigungsunternehmer** *m* undertaker.

**Beere** ['be:rə] (*-, -n*) *f* berry; (*Trauben~*)
grape.

**Beerenauslese** *f* wine made from specially
selected grapes.

**Beet** [be:t] (*-(e)s, -e*) *nt* (*Blumen~*) bed.

**befähigen** [bə'fɛ:ɪgən] *vt* to enable.

**befähigt** *adj* (*begabt*) talented; (*fähig*): **~ (für)**
capable (of).

**Befähigung** *f* capability; (*Begabung*) talent,
aptitude; **die ~ zum Richteramt** the
qualifications to become a judge.

**befahl** *etc* [bə'fa:l] *vb siehe* **befehlen**.

**befahrbar** [bə'fa:rba:r] *adj* passable; (*NAUT*)
navigable; **nicht ~ sein** (*Straße, Weg*) to be
closed (to traffic); (*wegen Schnee etc*) to be
impassable.

**befahren** [bə'fa:rən] *unreg vt* to use, drive over;
(*NAUT*) to navigate ♦ *adj* used.

**befallen** [bə'falən] *unreg vt* to come over.

**befangen** [bə'faŋən] *adj* (*schüchtern*) shy,
self-conscious; (*voreingenommen*) bias(s)ed;
**B~heit** *f* shyness; bias.

**befassen** [bə'fasən] *vr* to concern o.s.

**Befehl** [bə'fe:l] (*-(e)s, -e*) *m* command, order;
(*COMPUT*) command; **auf ~ handeln** to act
under orders; **zu ~, Herr Hauptmann!** (*MIL*)
yes, sir; **den ~ haben** *od* **führen (über** +*akk*)
to be in command (of).

**befehlen** *unreg vt* to order ♦ *vi* to give orders;
**jdm etw ~** to order sb to do sth; **du hast mir
gar nichts zu ~** I won't take orders from
you.

**befehligen** *vt* to be in command of.

**Befehls-** *zW*: **~empfänger** *m* subordinate;
**~form** *f* (*GRAM*) imperative; **~haber (-s, -)**
*m* commanding officer; **~notstand** *m* (*JUR*)
obligation to obey orders; **~verweigerung** *f*
insubordination.

**befestigen** [bə'fɛstɪgən] *vt* to fasten; (*stärken*)
to strengthen; (*MIL*) to fortify; **~ an** +*dat* to
fasten to.

**Befestigung** *f* fastening; strengthening;
(*MIL*) fortification.

**Befestigungsanlage** *f* fortification.

**befeuchten** [bə'fɔʏçtən] *vt* to damp(en),
moisten.

**befinden** [bə'fɪndən] *unreg vr* to be; (*sich fühlen*)
to feel ♦ *vt*: **jdn/etw für** *od* **als etw ~** to deem
sb/sth to be sth ♦ *vi*: **~ (über** +*akk*) to decide
(on), adjudicate (on).

**Befinden** (*-s*) *nt* health, condition; (*Meinung*)
view, opinion.

**beflecken** [bə'flɛkən] *vt* (*lit*) to stain; (*fig geh:
Ruf, Ehre*) to besmirch.

**befliegen** [bə'fli:gən] *unreg vt* (*Strecke*) to fly.

**beflügeln** [bə'fly:gəln] vt (geh) to inspire.
**befohlen** [bə'fo:lən] pp von **befehlen**.
**befolgen** [bə'fɔlgən] vt to comply with, follow.
**befördern** [bə'fœrdərn] vt (senden) to transport, send; (beruflich) to promote; **etw mit der Post/per Bahn** ~ to send sth by post/by rail.
**Beförderung** f transport; promotion.
**Beförderungskosten** pl transport costs pl.
**befragen** [bə'fra:gən] vt to question; (um Stellungnahme bitten): ~ (über +akk) to consult (about).
**Befragung** f poll.
**befreien** [bə'fraɪən] vt to set free; (erlassen) to exempt.
**Befreier(in)** (-s, -) m(f) liberator.
**befreit** adj (erleichtert) relieved.
**Befreiung** f liberation, release; (Erlassen) exemption.
**Befreiungs-** zW: ~**bewegung** f liberation movement; ~**kampf** m struggle for liberation; ~**versuch** m escape attempt.
**befremden** [bə'frɛmdən] vt to surprise; (unangenehm) to disturb; **B~** (-s) nt surprise, astonishment.
**befreunden** [bə'frɔyndən] vr to make friends; (mit Idee etc) to acquaint o.s.
**befreundet** adj friendly; **wir sind schon lange (miteinander)** ~ we have been friends for a long time.
**befriedigen** [bə'fri:dɪgən] vt to satisfy.
**befriedigend** adj satisfactory.
**Befriedigung** f satisfaction, gratification.
**befristet** [bə'frɪstət] adj limited; (Arbeitsverhältnis, Anstellung) temporary.
**befruchten** [bə'frʊxtən] vt to fertilize; (fig) to stimulate.
**Befruchtung** f: **künstliche** ~ artificial insemination.
**Befugnis** [bə'fu:knɪs] (-, -se) f authorization, powers pl.
**befugt** adj authorized, entitled.
**befühlen** [bə'fy:lən] vt to feel, touch.
**Befund** [bə'fʊnt] (-(e)s, -e) m findings pl; (MED) diagnosis; **ohne** ~ (MED) (results) negative.
**befürchten** [bə'fʏrçtən] vt to fear.
**Befürchtung** f fear, apprehension.
**befürworten** [bə'fy:rvɔrtən] vt to support, speak in favour (BRIT) od favor (US) of.
**Befürworter(in)** (-s, -) m(f) supporter, advocate.
**Befürwortung** f support(ing), favouring (BRIT), favoring (US).
**begabt** [bə'ga:pt] adj gifted.
**Begabung** [bə'ga:bʊŋ] f talent, gift.
**begann** etc [bə'gan] vb siehe **beginnen**.
**begatten** [bə'gatən] vr to mate ♦ vt to mate od pair (with).
**begeben** [bə'ge:bən] unreg vr (gehen) to proceed; (geschehen) to occur; **sich** ~ **nach** od **zu** to proceed to to(wards); **sich in ärztliche Behandlung** ~ to undergo medical

treatment; **sich in Gefahr** ~ to expose o.s. to danger; **B~heit** f occurrence.
**begegnen** [bə'ge:gnən] vi: **jdm** ~ to meet sb; (behandeln) to treat; **Blicke** ~ **sich** eyes meet.
**Begegnung** f meeting; (SPORT) match.
**begehen** [bə'ge:ən] unreg vt (Straftat) to commit; (Weg etc) to use, negotiate; (geh: feiern) to celebrate.
**begehren** [bə'ge:rən] vt to desire.
**begehrenswert** adj desirable.
**begehrt** adj in demand; (Junggeselle) eligible.
**begeistern** [bə'gaɪstərn] vt to fill with enthusiasm; (inspirieren) to inspire ♦ vr: **sich für etw** ~ to get enthusiastic about sth; **er ist für nichts zu** ~ he's not interested in doing anything.
**begeistert** adj enthusiastic.
**Begeisterung** f enthusiasm.
**Begierde** [bə'gi:rdə] (-, -n) f desire, passion.
**begierig** [bə'gi:rɪç] adj eager, keen; (voll Verlangen) hungry, greedy.
**begießen** [bə'gi:sən] unreg vt to water; (mit Fett: Braten etc) to baste; (mit Alkohol) to drink to.
**Beginn** [bə'gɪn] (-(e)s) m beginning; **zu** ~ at the beginning.
**beginnen** unreg vt, vi to start, begin.
**beglaubigen** [bə'glaʊbɪgən] vt to countersign; (Abschrift) to authenticate; (Echtheit, Übersetzung) to certify.
**Beglaubigung** f countersignature.
**Beglaubigungsschreiben** nt credentials pl.
**begleichen** [bə'glaɪçən] unreg vt to settle, pay; **mit Ihnen habe ich noch eine Rechnung zu** ~ (fig) I've a score to settle with you.
**begleiten** [bə'glaɪtən] vt to accompany; (MIL) to escort.
**Begleiter(in)** (-s, -) m(f) companion; (zum Schutz) escort; (MUS) accompanist.
**Begleit-** zW: ~**erscheinung** f side effect; ~**musik** f accompaniment; ~**papiere** pl (COMM) accompanying documents pl; ~**schiff** nt escort vessel; ~**schreiben** nt covering letter; ~**umstände** pl attendant circumstances.
**Begleitung** f company; (MIL) escort; (MUS) accompaniment.
**beglücken** [bə'glʏkən] vt to make happy, delight.
**beglückwünschen** [bə'glʏkvʏnʃən] vt: ~ **(zu)** to congratulate (on).
**begnadet** [bə'gna:dət] adj gifted.
**begnadigen** [bə'gna:dɪgən] vt to pardon.
**Begnadigung** f pardon.
**begnügen** [bə'gny:gən] vr: **sich** ~ **mit** to be satisfied with, content o.s. with.
**Begonie** [bə'go:niə] f begonia.
**begonnen** [bə'gɔnən] pp von **beginnen**.
**begossen** [bə'gɔsən] pp von **begießen** ♦ adj: **er stand da wie ein** ~**er Pudel** (umg) he looked so sheepish.

**begraben** [bə'gra:bən] *unreg vt* to bury; (*aufgeben: Hoffnung*) to abandon; (*beenden: Streit etc*) to end; **dort möchte ich nicht ~ sein** (*umg*) I wouldn't like to be stuck in that hole.

**Begräbnis** [bə'grɛ:pnɪs] (**-ses, -se**) *nt* burial, funeral.

**begradigen** [bə'gra:dɪgən] *vt* to straighten (out).

**begreifen** [bə'graɪfən] *unreg vt* to understand, comprehend.

**begreiflich** [bə'graɪflɪç] *adj* understandable; **ich kann mich ihm nicht ~ machen** I can't make myself clear to him.

**begrenzen** [bə'grɛntsən] *vt* (*beschränken*): **~ (auf +akk)** to restrict (to), limit (to).

**Begrenztheit** [bə'grɛntsthaɪt] *f* limitation, restriction; (*fig*) narrowness.

**Begriff** [bə'grɪf] (**-(e)s, -e**) *m* concept, idea; **im ~ sein, etw zu tun** to be about to do sth; **sein Name ist mir ein/kein ~** his name means something/doesn't mean anything to me; **du machst dir keinen ~ (davon)** you've no idea; **für meine ~e** in my opinion; **schwer von ~** (*umg*) slow on the uptake.

**Begriffsbestimmung** *f* definition.

**begriffsstutzig** *adj* slow-witted, dense.

**begrub** *etc* [bə'gru:p] *vb siehe* **begraben**.

**begründen** [bə'grʏndən] *vt* (*Gründe geben*) to justify; **etw näher ~** to give specific reasons for sth.

**Begründer(in)** *f(m)* founder.

**begründet** *adj* well-founded, justified; **sachlich ~** founded on fact.

**Begründung** *f* justification, reason.

**begrünen** [bə'gry:nən] *vt* to plant with greenery.

**begrüßen** [bə'gry:sən] *vt* to greet, welcome.

**begrüßenswert** *adj* welcome.

**Begrüßung** *f* greeting, welcome.

**begünstigen** [bə'gʏnstɪgən] *vt* (*Person*) to favour (*BRIT*), favor (*US*); (*Sache*) to further, promote.

**Begünstigte(r)** *f(m)* beneficiary.

**begutachten** [bə'gu:t|axtən] *vt* to assess; (*umg: ansehen*) to have a look at.

**begütert** [bə'gy:tərt] *adj* wealthy, well-to-do.

**begütigend** *adj* (*Worte etc*) soothing; **~ auf jdn einreden** to calm sb down.

**behaart** [bə'ha:rt] *adj* hairy.

**behäbig** [bə'hɛ:bɪç] *adj* (*dick*) portly, stout; (*geruhsam*) comfortable.

**behaftet** [bə'haftət] *adj:* **mit etw ~ sein** to be afflicted by sth.

**behagen** [bə'ha:gən] *vi:* **das behagt ihm nicht** he does not like it; **B~ (-s)** *nt* comfort, ease; **mit B~ essen** to eat with relish.

**behaglich** [bə'ha:klɪç] *adj* comfortable, cosy; **B~keit** *f* comfort, cosiness.

**behält** [bə'hɛlt] *vb siehe* **behalten**.

**behalten** [bə'haltən] *unreg vt* to keep, retain; (*im Gedächtnis*) to remember; **~ Sie (doch)**

**Platz! please don't get up!**

**Behälter** [bə'hɛltər] (**-s, -**) *m* container, receptacle.

**behämmert** [bə'hɛmərt] (*umg*) *adj* screwy, crazy.

**behandeln** [bə'handəln] *vt* to treat; (*Thema*) to deal with; (*Maschine*) to handle; **der ~de Arzt** the doctor in attendance.

**Behandlung** *f* treatment; (*von Maschine*) handling.

**behängen** [bə'hɛŋən] *vt* to decorate.

**beharren** [bə'harən] *vi:* **auf etw** *dat* **~** to stick od keep to sth.

**beharrlich** [bə'harlɪç] *adj* (*ausdauernd*) steadfast, unwavering; (*hartnäckig*) tenacious, dogged; **B~keit** *f* steadfastness, tenacity.

**behaupten** [bə'haʊptən] *vt* to claim, assert, maintain; (*sein Recht*) to defend ♦ *vr* to assert o.s.; **von jdm ~, daß ...** to say (of sb) that ...; **sich auf dem Markt ~** to establish itself on the market.

**Behauptung** *f* claim, assertion.

**Behausung** [bə'haʊzʊŋ] *f* dwelling, abode; (*armselig*) hovel.

**beheben** [bə'he:bən] *unreg vt* (*beseitigen*) to remove; (*Mißstände*) to remedy; (*Schaden*) to repair; (*Störung*) to clear.

**beheimatet** [bə'haɪma:tət] *adj:* **~ (in +dat)** domiciled (at/in); (*Tier, Pflanze*) native (to).

**beheizen** [bə'haɪtsən] *vt* to heat.

**Behelf** [bə'hɛlf] (**-(e)s, -e**) *m* expedient, makeshift; **b~en** *unreg vr:* **sich mit etw b~en** to make do with sth.

**behelfsmäßig** *adj* improvised, makeshift; (*vorübergehend*) temporary.

**behelligen** [bə'hɛlɪgən] *vt* to trouble, bother.

**Behendigkeit** [bə'hɛndɪçkaɪt] *f* agility, quickness.

**beherbergen** [bə'hɛrbɛrgən] *vt* (*lit, fig*) to house.

**beherrschen** [bə'hɛrʃən] *vt* (*Volk*) to rule, govern; (*Situation*) to control; (*Sprache, Gefühle*) to master ♦ *vr* to control o.s.

**beherrscht** *adj* controlled; **B~heit** *f* self-control.

**Beherrschung** *f* rule; control; mastery; **die ~ verlieren** to lose one's temper.

**beherzigen** [bə'hɛrtsɪgən] *vt* to take to heart.

**beherzt** *adj* spirited, brave.

**behielt** *etc* [bə'hi:lt] *vb siehe* **behalten**.

**behilflich** [bə'hɪlflɪç] *adj* helpful; **jdm ~ sein (bei)** to help sb (with).

**behindern** [bə'hɪndərn] *vt* to hinder, impede.

**Behinderte(r)** *f(m)* disabled person.

**Behinderung** *f* hindrance; (*Körperbehinderung*) handicap.

**Behörde** [bə'hø:rdə] (**-, -n**) *f* authorities *pl*; (*Amtsgebäude*) office(s *pl*).

**behördlich** [bə'hø:rtlɪç] *adj* official.

**behüten** [bə'hy:tən] *vt* to guard; **jdn vor etw** *dat* **~** to preserve sb from sth.

**behütet** *adj* (*Jugend etc*) sheltered.
**behutsam** [bə'huːtzaːm] *adj* cautious, careful; **man muß es ihr ~ beibringen** it will have to be broken to her gently; **B~keit** *f* caution, carefulness.

═══════════════ *SCHLÜSSELWORT*

**bei** [baɪ] *präp +dat* **1** (*nahe* ~) near; (*zum Aufenthalt*) at, with; (*unter, zwischen*) among; **~ München** near Munich; **~ uns** at our place; **~m Friseur** at the hairdresser's; **~ seinen Eltern wohnen** to live with one's parents; **~ einer Firma arbeiten** to work for a firm; **etw ~ sich haben** to have sth on one; **jdn ~ sich haben** to have sb with one; **~ Goethe** in Goethe; **~m Militär** in the army **2** (*zeitlich*) at, on; (*während*) during; (*Zustand, Umstand*) in; **~ Nacht** at night; **~ Nebel** in fog; **~ Regen** if it rains; **~ solcher Hitze** in such heat; **~ meiner Ankunft** on my arrival; **~ der Arbeit** when I'm *etc* working; **~m Fahren** while driving; **~ offenem Fenster schlafen** to sleep with the window open; **~ Feuer Scheibe einschlagen** in case of fire break glass; **~ seinem Talent** with his talent.

**beibehalten** ['baɪbəhaltən] *unreg vt* to keep, retain.
**Beibehaltung** *f* keeping, retaining.
**Beiblatt** ['baɪblat] *nt* supplement.
**beibringen** ['baɪbrɪŋən] *unreg vt* (*Beweis, Zeugen*) to bring forward; (*Gründe*) to adduce; **jdm etw ~** (*zufügen*) to inflict sth on sb; (*zu verstehen geben*) to make sb understand sth; (*lehren*) to teach sb sth.
**Beichte** ['baɪçtə] *f* confession.
**beichten** *vt* to confess ♦ *vi* to go to confession.
**Beichtgeheimnis** *nt* secret of the confessional.
**Beichtstuhl** *m* confessional.
**beide** ['baɪdə] *pron, adj* both; **meine ~n Brüder** my two brothers, both my brothers; **die ersten ~n** the first two; **wir ~** we two; **einer von ~n** one of the two; **alles ~s** both (of them); **~mal** *adv* both times.
**beider-** *zW:* **~lei** *adj inv* of both; **~seitig** *adj* mutual, reciprocal; **~seits** *adv* mutually ♦ *präp +gen* on both sides of.
**beidhändig** ['baɪthɛndɪç] *adj* ambidextrous.
**beidrehen** ['baɪdreːən] *vi* to heave to.
**beidseitig** ['baɪtzaɪtɪç] *adj* (*auf beiden Seiten*) on both sides.
**beieinander** [baɪaɪˈnandər] *adv* together; **~sein** *unreg vi:* **gut ~sein** (*umg: gesundheitlich*) to be in good shape; (*: geistig*) to be all there.
**Beifahrer(in)** ['baɪfaːrər(ɪn)] **(-s, -)** *m(f)* passenger; **~sitz** *m* passenger seat.
**Beifall** ['baɪfal] **(-(e)s)** *m* applause; (*Zustimmung*) approval.

**beifallheischend** ['baɪfalhaɪʃənt] *adj* fishing for applause/approval.
**beifällig** ['baɪfɛlɪç] *adj* approving; (*Kommentar*) favourable (*BRIT*), favorable (*US*).
**Beifilm** ['baɪfɪlm] *m* supporting film.
**beifügen** ['baɪfyːgən] *vt* to enclose.
**Beigabe** ['baɪgaːbə] *f* addition.
**beige** ['beːʒ] *adj* beige.
**beigeben** ['baɪgeːbən] *unreg vt* (*zufügen*) to add; (*mitgeben*) to give ♦ *vi:* **klein ~** (*nachgeben*) to climb down.
**Beigeschmack** ['baɪgəʃmak] *m* aftertaste.
**Beihilfe** ['baɪhɪlfə] *f* aid, assistance; (*Studienbeihilfe*) grant; (*JUR*) aiding and abetting; **wegen ~ zum Mord** (*JUR*) because of being an accessory to the murder.
**beikommen** ['baɪkɔmən] *unreg vi +dat* to get at; (*einem Problem*) to deal with.
**Beil** [baɪl] **(-(e)s, -e)** *nt* axe (*BRIT*), ax (*US*), hatchet.
**Beilage** ['baɪlaːgə] *f* (*Buch~ etc*) supplement; (*KOCH*) accompanying vegetables; (*getrennt serviert*) side dish.
**beiläufig** ['baɪlɔyfɪç] *adj* casual, incidental ♦ *adv* casually, by the way.
**beilegen** ['baɪleːgən] *vt* (*hinzufügen*) to enclose, add; (*beimessen*) to attribute, ascribe; (*Streit*) to settle.
**beileibe** [baɪˈlaɪbə] *adv:* **~ nicht** by no means.
**Beileid** ['baɪlaɪt] *nt* condolence, sympathy; **herzliches ~** deepest sympathy.
**beiliegend** ['baɪliːgənt] *adj* (*COMM*) enclosed.
**beim** [baɪm] **= bei dem.**
**beimessen** ['baɪmɛsən] *unreg vt* to attribute, ascribe.
**Bein** [baɪn] **(-(e)s, -e)** *nt* leg; **jdm ein ~ stellen** (*lit, fig*) to trip sb up; **wir sollten uns auf die ~e machen** (*umg*) we ought to be making tracks; **jdm ~e machen** (*umg: antreiben*) to make sb get a move on; **die ~e in die Hand nehmen** (*umg*) to take to one's heels; **sich** *dat* **die ~e in den Bauch stehen** (*umg*) to stand about until one is fit to drop; **etw auf die ~e stellen** (*fig*) to get sth off the ground.
**beinah(e)** [baɪˈnaː(ə)] *adv* almost, nearly.
**Beinbruch** *m* fracture of the leg; **das ist kein ~** (*fig: umg*) it could be worse.
**beinhalten** [bəˈʔɪnhaltən] *vt* to contain.
**beipflichten** ['baɪpflɪçtən] *vi:* **jdm/etw ~** to agree with sb/sth.
**Beiprogramm** ['baɪprogram] *nt* supporting programme (*BRIT*) *od* program (*US*).
**Beirat** ['baɪraːt] *m* advisory council; (*Eltern~*) parents' council.
**beirren** [bəˈʔɪrən] *vt* to confuse, muddle; **sich nicht ~ lassen** not to let o.s. be confused.
**Beirut** [baɪˈruːt] **(-s)** *nt* Beirut.
**beisammen** [baɪˈzamən] *adv* together; **~haben** *unreg vt:* **er hat (sie) nicht alle ~** (*umg*) he's not all there; **B~sein** **(-s)** *nt* get-together.
**Beischlaf** ['baɪʃlaːf] *m* (*JUR*) sexual intercourse.

**Beisein** ['baɪzaɪn] (**-s**) *nt* presence.
**beiseite** [baɪ'zaɪtə] *adv* to one side, aside; (*stehen*) on one side, aside; **Spaß ~!** joking apart!; **etw ~ legen** (*sparen*) to put sth by; **jdn/etw ~ schaffen** to get rid of sb/sth.
**beisetzen** ['baɪzɛtsən] *vt* to bury.
**Beisetzung** *f* funeral.
**Beisitzer(in)** ['baɪzɪtsər(ɪn)] (**-s**, **-**) *m(f)* (*JUR*) assessor; (*bei Prüfung*) observer.
**Beispiel** ['baɪʃpiːl] (**-(e)s**, **-e**) *nt* example; **mit gutem ~ vorangehen** to set a good example; **sich** *dat* **an jdm ein ~ nehmen** to take sb as an example; **zum ~** for example; **b~haft** *adj* exemplary; **b~los** *adj* unprecedented.
**beispielsweise** *adv* for instance, for example.
**beispringen** ['baɪʃprɪŋən] *unreg vi* +*dat* to come to the aid of.
**beißen** ['baɪsən] *unreg vt, vi* to bite; (*stechen: Rauch, Säure*) to burn ♦ *vr* (*Farben*) to clash.
**beißend** *adj* biting, caustic; (*Geruch*) pungent, sharp; (*fig*) sarcastic.
**Beißzange** ['baɪstsaŋə] *f* pliers *pl*.
**Beistand** ['baɪʃtant] (**-(e)s**, **-̈e**) *m* support, help; (*JUR*) adviser; **jdm ~ leisten** to give sb assistance/one's support.
**beistehen** ['baɪʃteːən] *unreg vi*: **jdm ~** to stand by sb.
**Beistelltisch** ['baɪʃtɛltɪʃ] *m* occasional table.
**beisteuern** ['baɪʃtɔʏərn] *vt* to contribute.
**beistimmen** ['baɪʃtɪmən] *vi* +*dat* to agree with.
**Beistrich** ['baɪʃtrɪç] *m* comma.
**Beitrag** ['baɪtraːk] (**-(e)s**, **-̈e**) *m* contribution; (*Zahlung*) fee, subscription; (*Versicherungs~*) premium; **einen ~ zu etw leisten** to make a contribution to sth.
**beitragen** ['baɪtraːgən] *unreg vt, vi*: **~ (zu)** to contribute (to); (*mithelfen*) to help (with).
**Beitrags-** *zW*: **b~frei** *adj* non-contributory; **b~pflichtig** *adj* contributory; **b~pflichtig sein** (*Mensch*) to have to pay contributions; **~zahlende(r)** *f(m)* fee-paying member.
**beitreten** ['baɪtreːtən] *unreg vi* +*dat* to join.
**Beitritt** ['baɪtrɪt] *m* joining; membership.
**Beitrittserklärung** *f* declaration of membership.
**Beiwagen** ['baɪvaːgən] *m* (*Motorrad~*) sidecar; (*Straßenbahn~*) extra carriage.
**beiwohnen** ['baɪvoːnən] *vi* (*geh*): **einer Sache** *dat* **~** to attend *od* be present at sth.
**Beiwort** ['baɪvɔrt] *nt* adjective.
**Beize** ['baɪtsə] (**-**, **-n**) *f* (*Holz~*) stain; (*KOCH*) marinade.
**beizeiten** [baɪ'tsaɪtən] *adv* in time.
**bejahen** [bə'jaːən] *vt* (*Frage*) to say yes to, answer in the affirmative; (*gutheißen*) to agree with.
**bejahrt** [bə'jaːrt] *adj* elderly, advanced in years.
**bejammern** [bə'jamərn] *vt* to lament, bewail.
**bejammernswert** *adj* lamentable.
**bekakeln** [bə'kaːkəln] (*umg*) *vt* to discuss.

**bekam** *etc* [bə'kam] *vb siehe* **bekommen**.
**bekämpfen** [bə'kɛmpfən] *vt* (*Gegner*) to fight; (*Seuche*) to combat ♦ *vr* to fight.
**Bekämpfung** *f*: **~ (+**gen**)** fight (against), struggle (against).
**bekannt** [bə'kant] *adj* (well-)known; (*nicht fremd*) familiar; **mit jdm ~ sein** to know sb; **jdn mit jdm ~ machen** to introduce sb to sb; **sich mit etw ~ machen** to familiarize o.s. with sth; **das ist mir ~** I know that; **es/sie kommt mir ~ vor** it/she seems familiar; **durch etw ~ werden** to become famous because of sth.
**Bekannte(r)** *f(m)* friend, acquaintance.
**Bekanntenkreis** *m* circle of friends.
**bekanntermaßen** *adv* as is known.
**bekannt-** *zW*: **B~gabe** *f* announcement; **~geben** *unreg vt* to announce publicly; **B~heitsgrad** *m* degree of fame; **~lich** *adv* as is well known, as you know; **~machen** *vt* to announce; **B~machung** *f* publication; (*Anschlag etc*) announcement; **B~schaft** *f* acquaintance.
**bekehren** [bə'keːrən] *vt* to convert ♦ *vr* to be *od* become converted.
**Bekehrung** *f* conversion.
**bekennen** [bə'kɛnən] *unreg vt* to confess; (*Glauben*) to profess ♦ *vr*: **sich zu jdm/etw ~** to declare one's support for sb/sth; **Farbe ~** (*umg*) to show where one stands.
**Bekenntnis** [bə'kɛntnɪs] (**-ses**, **-se**) *nt* admission, confession; (*Religion*) confession, denomination; **ein ~ zur Demokratie ablegen** to declare one's belief in democracy; **~schule** *f* denominational school.
**beklagen** [bə'klaːgən] *vt* to deplore, lament ♦ *vr* to complain.
**beklagenswert** *adj* lamentable, pathetic; (*Mensch*) pitiful; (*Zustand*) deplorable; (*Unfall*) terrible.
**beklatschen** [bə'klatʃən] *vt* to applaud, clap.
**bekleben** [bə'kleːbən] *vt*: **etw mit Bildern ~** to stick pictures onto sth.
**bekleckern** [bə'klɛkərn] (*umg*) *vt* to stain.
**bekleiden** [bə'klaɪdən] *vt* to clothe; (*Amt*) to occupy, fill.
**Bekleidung** *f* clothing; (*form: eines Amtes*) tenure.
**Bekleidungsindustrie** *f* clothing industry, rag trade (*umg*).
**beklemmen** [bə'klɛmən] *vt* to oppress.
**Beklemmung** *f* oppressiveness; (*Gefühl der Angst*) feeling of apprehension.
**beklommen** [bə'klɔmən] *adj* anxious, uneasy; **B~heit** *f* anxiety, uneasiness.
**bekloppt** [bə'klɔpt] (*umg*) *adj* (*Mensch*) crazy; (: *Sache*) lousy.
**beknackt** [bə'knakt] (*umg*) *adj* = **bekloppt**.
**beknien** [bə'kniːən] (*umg*) *vt* (*jdn*) to beg.
**bekommen** [bə'kɔmən] *unreg vt* to get, receive; (*Kind*) to have; (*Zug*) to catch, get

◆ *vi:* **jdm** ~ to agree with sb; **es mit jdm zu tun** ~ to get into trouble with sb; **wohl bekomm's!** your health!
**bekömmlich** [bə'kœmlıç] *adj* easily digestible.
**beköstigen** [bə'kœstɪgən] *vt* to cater for.
**bekräftigen** [bə'krɛftɪgən] *vt* to confirm, corroborate.
**Bekräftigung** *f* corroboration.
**bekreuzigen** [bə'krɔʏtsɪgən] *vr* to cross o.s.
**bekritteln** [bə'krɪtəln] *vt* to criticize, pick holes in.
**bekümmern** [bə'kʏmərn] *vt* to worry, trouble.
**bekunden** [bə'kʊndən] *vt* (*sagen*) to state; (*zeigen*) to show.
**belächeln** [bə'lɛçəln] *vt* to laugh at.
**beladen** [bə'la:dən] *unreg vt* to load.
**Belag** [bə'la:k] (-(e)s, -̈e) *m* covering, coating; (*Brot~*) spread; (*auf Pizza, Brot*) topping; (*auf Tortenboden, zwischen Brotscheiben*) filling; (*Zahn~*) tartar; (*auf Zunge*) fur; (*Brems~*) lining.
**belagern** [bə'la:gərn] *vt* to besiege.
**Belagerung** *f* siege.
**Belagerungszustand** *m* state of siege.
**Belang** [bə'laŋ] (-(e)s) *m* importance.
**Belange** *pl* interests *pl*, concerns *pl*.
**belangen** *vt* (*JUR*) to take to court.
**belanglos** *adj* trivial, unimportant.
**Belanglosigkeit** *f* triviality.
**belassen** [bə'lasən] *unreg vt* (*in Zustand, Glauben*) to leave; (*in Stellung*) to retain; **es dabei** ~ to leave it at that.
**Belastbarkeit** *f* (*von Brücke, Aufzug*) load-bearing capacity; (*von Menschen, Nerven*) ability to take stress.
**belasten** [bə'lastən] *vt* (*lit*) to burden; (*fig: bedrücken*) to trouble, worry; (*COMM: Konto*) to debit; (*JUR*) to incriminate ◆ *vr* to weigh o.s. down; (*JUR*) to incriminate o.s.; **etw (mit einer Hypothek)** ~ to mortgage sth.
**belastend** *adj* (*JUR*) incriminating.
**belästigen** [bə'lɛstɪgən] *vt* to annoy, pester.
**Belästigung** *f* annoyance, pestering; (*körperlich*) molesting.
**Belastung** [bə'lastʊŋ] *f* (*lit*) load; (*fig: Sorge etc*) weight; (*COMM*) charge, debit(ing); (*mit Hypothek*): ~ (+*gen*) mortgage (on); (*JUR*) incriminating evidence.
**Belastungs-** *zW:* ~**material** *nt* (*JUR*) incriminating evidence; ~**probe** *f* capacity test; (*fig*) test; ~**zeuge** *m* witness for the prosecution.
**belaubt** [bə'laʊpt] *adj:* **dicht** ~ **sein** to have thick foliage.
**belaufen** [bə'laʊfən] *unreg vr:* **sich** ~ **auf** +*akk* to amount to.
**belauschen** [bə'laʊʃən] *vt* to eavesdrop on.
**beleben** [bə'le:bən] *vt* (*anregen*) to liven up; (*Konjunktur, jds Hoffnungen*) to stimulate.
**belebt** [bə'le:pt] *adj* (*Straße*) crowded.
**Beleg** [bə'le:k] (-(e)s, -e) *m* (*COMM*) receipt; (*Beweis*) documentary evidence, proof;

(*Beispiel*) example.
**belegen** [bə'le:gən] *vt* to cover; (*Kuchen, Brot*) to spread; (*Platz*) to reserve, book; (*Kurs, Vorlesung*) to register for; (*beweisen*) to verify, prove.
**Belegschaft** *f* personnel, staff.
**belegt** *adj* (*Zunge*) furred; (*Stimme*) hoarse; (*Zimmer*) occupied; ~**e Brote** open sandwiches.
**belehren** [bə'le:rən] *vt* to instruct, teach; **jdn eines Besseren** ~ to teach sb better; **er ist nicht zu** ~ he won't be told.
**Belehrung** *f* instruction.
**beleibt** [bə'laɪpt] *adj* stout, corpulent.
**beleidigen** [bə'laɪdɪgən] *vt* to insult; to offend.
**beleidigt** *adj* insulted; (*gekränkt*) offended; **die ~e Leberwurst spielen** (*umg*) to be in a huff.
**Beleidigung** *f* insult; (*JUR*) slander; (: *schriftlich*) libel.
**beleihen** [bə'laɪən] *unreg vt* (*COMM*) to lend money on.
**belemmert** [bə'lɛmərt] (*umg*) *adj* sheepish.
**belesen** [bə'le:zən] *adj* well-read.
**beleuchten** [bə'lɔʏçtən] *vt* to light, illuminate; (*fig*) to throw light on.
**Beleuchter(in)** (-s, -) *m(f)* lighting technician.
**Beleuchtung** *f* lighting, illumination.
**beleumdet** [bə'lɔʏmdət] *adj:* **gut/schlecht** ~ **sein** to have a good/bad reputation.
**beleumundet** [bə'lɔʏmʊndət] *adj =* **beleumdet.**
**Belgien** ['bɛlgiən] (-s) *nt* Belgium.
**Belgier(in)** (-s, -) *m(f)* Belgian.
**belgisch** *adj* Belgian.
**Belgrad** ['bɛlgraːt] (-s) *nt* Belgrade.
**belichten** [bə'lıçtən] *vt* to expose.
**Belichtung** *f* exposure.
**Belichtungsmesser** *m* exposure meter.
**Belieben** [bə'li:bən] *nt:* (**ganz**) **nach** ~ (just) as you wish.
**belieben** *vi unpers* (*geh*): **wie es Ihnen beliebt** as you wish.
**beliebig** [bə'li:bɪç] *adj* any you like, as you like; ~ **viel** as much as you like; **in** ~**er Reihenfolge** in any order whatever; **ein** ~**es Thema** any subject you like *od* want.
**beliebt** [bə'li:pt] *adj* popular; **sich bei jdm** ~ **machen** to make o.s. popular with sb; **B~heit** *f* popularity.
**beliefern** [bə'li:fərn] *vt* to supply.
**Belize** [bɛ'li:z] (-s) *nt* Belize.
**bellen** ['bɛlən] *vi* to bark.
**Belletristik** [bɛle'trɪstɪk] *f* fiction and poetry.
**belohnen** [bə'lo:nən] *vt* to reward.
**Belohnung** *f* reward.
**Belüftung** [bə'lʏftʊŋ] *f* ventilation.
**belügen** [bə'ly:gən] *unreg vt* to lie to, deceive.
**belustigen** [bə'lʊstɪgən] *vt* to amuse.
**Belustigung** *f* amusement.
**bemächtigen** [bə'mɛçtɪgən] *vr:* **sich einer Sache** *gen* ~ to take possession of sth, seize sth.
**bemalen** [bə'ma:lən] *vt* to paint ◆ *vr* (*pej:*

*schminken*) to put on one's war paint (*umg*).
**bemängeln** [bə'mɛŋəln] *vt* to criticize.
**bemannen** [bə'manən] *vt* to man.
**Bemannung** *f* manning; (*NAUT, AVIAT etc*) crew.
**bemänteln** [bə'mɛntəln] *vt* to cloak, hide.
**bemerkbar** *adj* perceptible, noticeable; **sich ~ machen** (*Person*) to make *od* get o.s. noticed; (*Unruhe*) to become noticeable.
**bemerken** [bə'mɛrkən] *vt* (*wahrnehmen*) to notice, observe; (*sagen*) to say, mention; **nebenbei bemerkt** by the way.
**bemerkenswert** *adj* remarkable, noteworthy.
**Bemerkung** *f* remark, comment; (*schriftlich*) comment, note.
**bemitleiden** [bə'mɪtlaɪdən] *vt* to pity.
**bemittelt** [bə'mɪtəlt] *adj* well-to-do, well-off.
**bemühen** [bə'myːən] *vr* to take trouble *od* pains; **sich um eine Stelle ~** to try to get a job.
**bemüht** *adj:* (*darum*) **~ sein, etw zu tun** to endeavour (*BRIT*) *od* endeavor (*US*) *od* be at pains to do sth.
**Bemühung** *f* trouble, pains *pl*, effort.
**bemüßigt** [bə'myːsɪçt] *adj:* **sich ~ fühlen/ sehen** (*geh*) to feel called upon.
**bemuttern** [bə'mʊtərn] *vt* to mother.
**benachbart** [bə'naxbaːrt] *adj* neighbouring (*BRIT*), neighboring (*US*).
**benachrichtigen** [bə'naːxrɪçtɪgən] *vt* to inform.
**Benachrichtigung** *f* notification.
**benachteiligen** [bə'naːxtaɪlɪgən] *vt* to (put at a) disadvantage, victimize.
**benehmen** [bə'neːmən] *unreg vr* to behave; **B~** (**-s**) *nt* behaviour (*BRIT*), behavior (*US*); **kein B~ haben** not to know how to behave.
**beneiden** [bə'naɪdən] *vt* to envy.
**beneidenswert** *adj* enviable.
**Beneluxländer** ['beːnelʊkslɛndər] *pl* Benelux (countries *pl*).
**Beneluxstaaten** *pl* Benelux (countries *pl*).
**benennen** [bə'nɛnən] *unreg vt* to name.
**Bengel** ['bɛŋəl] (**-s**, **-**) *m* (little) rascal *od* rogue.
**Benimm** [bə'nɪm] (**-s**) (*umg*) *m* manners *pl*.
**Benin** [be'niːn] (**-s**) *nt* Benin.
**benommen** [bə'nɔmən] *adj* dazed.
**benoten** [bə'noːtən] *vt* to mark.
**benötigen** [bə'nøːtɪgən] *vt* to need.
**benutzen** [bə'nʊtsən] *vt* to use.
**benützen** [bə'nʏtsən] *vt* to use.
**Benutzer(in)** (**-s**, **-**) *m(f)* user; **b~freundlich** *adj* user-friendly.
**Benutzung** *f* utilization, use; **jdm etw zur ~ überlassen** to put sth at sb's disposal.
**Benzin** [bɛnt'siːn] (**-s**, **-e**) *nt* (*AUT*) petrol (*BRIT*), gas(oline) (*US*); **~einspritzanlage** *f* (*AUT*) fuel injection system; **~kanister** *m* petrol (*BRIT*) *od* gas (*US*) can; **~tank** *m* petrol (*BRIT*) *od* gas (*US*) tank; **~uhr** *f* petrol

(*BRIT*) *od* gas (*US*) gauge.
**beobachten** [bə'|oːbaxtən] *vt* to observe.
**Beobachter(in)** (**-s**, **-**) *m(f)* observer; (*eines Unfalls*) witness; (*PRESSE, TV*) correspondent.
**Beobachtung** *f* observation.
**beordern** [bə'|ɔrdərn] *vt:* **jdn zu sich ~** to send for sb.
**bepacken** [bə'pakən] *vt* to load, pack.
**bepflanzen** [bə'pflantsən] *vt* to plant.
**bequatschen** [bə'kvatʃən] (*umg*) *vt* (*überreden*) to persuade; **etw ~** to talk sth over.
**bequem** [bə'kveːm] *adj* comfortable; (*Ausrede*) convenient; (*Person*) lazy, indolent.
**bequemen** [bə'kveːmən] *vr:* **sich ~, etw zu tun** to condescend to do sth.
**Bequemlichkeit** *f* convenience, comfort; (*Faulheit*) laziness, indolence.
**Ber.** *abk* = **Bericht; Beruf.**
**berät** [bə'rɛːt] *vb siehe* **beraten.**
**beraten** [bə'raːtən] *unreg vt* to advise; (*besprechen*) to discuss, debate ♦ *vr* to consult; **gut/schlecht ~ sein** to be well/ill advised; **sich ~ lassen** to get advice.
**beratend** *adj* consultative; **jdm ~ zur Seite stehen** to act in an advisory capacity to sb.
**Berater(in)** (**-s**, **-**) *m(f)* adviser; **~vertrag** *m* consultancy contract.
**beratschlagen** [bə'raːtʃlaːgən] *vi* to deliberate, confer ♦ *vt* to deliberate on, confer about.
**Beratung** *f* advice; (*Besprechung*) consultation.
**Beratungsstelle** *f* advice centre (*BRIT*) *od* center (*US*).
**berauben** [bə'raʊbən] *vt* to rob.
**berauschen** [bə'raʊʃən] *vt* (*lit, fig*) to intoxicate.
**berauschend** *adj:* **das war nicht sehr ~** (*ironisch*) that wasn't very exciting.
**berechenbar** [bə'rɛçənbaːr] *adj* calculable; (*Verhalten*) predictable.
**berechnen** [bə'rɛçnən] *vt* to calculate; (*COMM:* anrechnen) to charge.
**berechnend** *adj* (*Mensch*) calculating, scheming.
**Berechnung** *f* calculation; (*COMM*) charge.
**berechtigen** [bə'rɛçtɪgən] *vt* to entitle; (*bevollmächtigen*) to authorize; (*fig*) to justify.
**berechtigt** [bə'rɛçtɪçt] *adj* justifiable, justified.
**Berechtigung** *f* authorization; (*fig*) justification.
**bereden** [bə'reːdən] *vt* (*besprechen*) to discuss; (*überreden*) to persuade ♦ *vr* to discuss.
**beredt** [bə'reːt] *adj* eloquent.
**Bereich** [bə'raɪç] (**-(e)s**, **-e**) *m* (*Bezirk*) area; (*Ressort, Gebiet*) sphere; **im ~ des Möglichen liegen** to be within the bounds of possibility.
**bereichern** [bə'raɪçərn] *vt* to enrich ♦ *vr* to get

rich; **sich auf Kosten anderer** ~ to feather one's nest at the expense of other people.

**Bereifung** [bə'raifʊŋ] f (set of) tyres (BRIT) od tires (US) pl; (Vorgang) fitting with tyres (BRIT) od tires (US).

**bereinigen** [bə'raɪnɪgən] vt to settle.

**bereisen** [bə'raɪzən] vt to travel through; (COMM: Gebiet) to travel, cover.

**bereit** [bə'raɪt] adj ready, prepared; **zu etw** ~ **sein** to be ready for sth; **sich** ~ **erklären** to declare o.s. willing.

**bereiten** vt to prepare, make ready; (Kummer, Freude) to cause; **einer Sache** dat **ein Ende** ~ to put an end to sth.

**bereit-** zW: ~**halten** unreg vt to keep in readiness; ~**legen** vt to lay out; ~**machen** vt, vr to prepare, get ready.

**bereits** adv already.

**bereit-** zW: **B~schaft** f readiness; (Polizei) alert; **in B~schaft sein** to be on the alert od on stand-by; **B~schaftsarzt** m doctor on call; (im Krankenhaus) duty doctor; **B~schaftsdienst** m emergency service; ~**stehen** unreg vi (Person) to be prepared; (Ding) to be ready; ~**stellen** vt (Kisten, Pakete etc) to put ready; (Geld etc) to make available; (Truppen, Maschinen) to put at the ready.

**Bereitung** f preparation.

**bereitwillig** adj willing, ready; **B~keit** f willingness, readiness.

**bereuen** [bə'rɔyən] vt to regret.

**Berg** [bɛrk] (-(e)s, -e) m mountain; (kleiner) hill; **mit etw hinterm** ~ **halten** (fig) to keep quiet about sth; **über alle** ~**e sein** to be miles away; **da stehen einem ja die Haare zu** ~**e** it's enough to make your hair stand on end; **b~ab** adv downhill; **b~an** adv uphill; ~**arbeiter** m miner; **b~auf** adv uphill; ~**bahn** f mountain railway (BRIT) od railroad (US); ~**bau** m mining.

**bergen** ['bɛrgən] unreg vt (retten) to rescue; (Ladung) to salvage; (enthalten) to contain.

**Bergführer** m mountain guide.

**Berggipfel** m mountain top, peak, summit.

**bergig** ['bɛrgɪç] adj mountainous, hilly.

**Berg-** zW: ~**kamm** m crest, ridge; ~**kette** f mountain range; ~**kristall** m rock crystal; ~**mann** (-(e)s, pl ~**leute**) m miner; ~**not** f: **in** ~**not sein/geraten** to be in/get into difficulties while climbing; ~**predigt** f (REL) Sermon on the Mount; ~**rettungsdienst** m mountain rescue service; ~**rutsch** m landslide; ~**schuh** m walking boot; ~**steigen** nt mountaineering; ~**steiger(in)** m(f) mountaineer, climber; ~**und-Tal-Bahn** f big dipper, roller-coaster.

**Bergung** ['bɛrgʊŋ] f (von Menschen) rescue; (von Material) recovery; (NAUT) salvage.

**Bergwacht** f mountain rescue service.

**Bergwerk** nt mine.

**Bericht** [bə'rɪçt] (-(e)s, -e) m report, account;

**b~en** vt, vi to report; ~**erstatter** (-s, -) m reporter, (newspaper) correspondent; ~**erstattung** f reporting.

**berichtigen** [bə'rɪçtɪgən] vt to correct.

**Berichtigung** f correction.

**berieseln** [bə'ri:zəln] vt to spray with water.

**Berieselung** f watering; **die dauernde** ~ **mit Musik** ... (fig) the constant stream of music ...

**Berieselungsanlage** f sprinkler (system).

**Beringmeer** ['be:rɪŋme:r] nt Bering Sea.

**beritten** [bə'rɪtən] adj mounted.

**Berlin** [bɛr'li:n] (-s) nt Berlin.

**Berliner¹** adj attrib Berlin.

**Berliner²** (-s, -) m (Person) Berliner; (KOCH) jam doughnut.

**Berlinerin** f Berliner.

**berlinerisch** (umg) adj (Dialekt) Berlin attr.

**Bermudas** [bɛr'mu:das] pl: **auf den** ~ in Bermuda.

**Bern** [bɛrn] (-s) nt Berne.

**Bernhardiner** [bɛrnhar'di:nər] (-s, -) m Saint Bernard (dog).

**Bernstein** ['bɛrnʃtaɪn] m amber.

**bersten** ['bɛrstən] unreg vi to burst, split.

**berüchtigt** [bə'rʏçtɪçt] adj notorious, infamous.

**berücksichtigen** [bə'rʏkzɪçtɪgən] vt to consider, bear in mind.

**Berücksichtigung** f consideration; **in** od **unter** ~ **der Tatsache, daß** ... in view of the fact that ...

**Beruf** [bə'ru:f] (-(e)s, -e) m occupation, profession; (Gewerbe) trade; **was sind Sie von** ~? what is your occupation etc?, what do you do for a living?; **seinen** ~ **verfehlt haben** to have missed one's vocation.

**berufen** unreg vt (in Amt): **jdn in etw** akk ~ to appoint sb to sth ♦ vr: **sich auf jdn/etw** ~ to refer od appeal to sb/sth ♦ adj competent, qualified; (ausersehen): **zu etw** ~ **sein** to have a vocation for sth.

**beruflich** adj professional; **er ist** ~ **viel unterwegs** he is away a lot on business.

**Berufs-** zW: ~**ausbildung** f vocational od professional training; **b~bedingt** adj occupational; ~**berater** m careers adviser; ~**beratung** f vocational guidance; ~**bezeichnung** f job description; ~**erfahrung** f (professional) experience; ~**feuerwehr** f fire service; ~**geheimnis** nt professional secret; ~**krankheit** f occupational disease; ~**kriminalität** f professional crime; ~**leben** nt professional life; **im** ~**leben stehen** to be working od in employment; **b~mäßig** adj professional; ~**risiko** nt occupational hazard; ~**schule** f vocational od trade school; ~**soldat** m professional soldier, regular; ~**sportler** m professional (sportsman); **b~tätig** adj employed; **b~unfähig** adj unable to work (at one's profession); ~**unfall** m occupational accident; **~verbot** *nt:* **jdm ~verbot erteilen** to ban sb from his/her profession; (*einem Arzt, Anwalt*) to strike sb off; **~verkehr** *m* commuter traffic; **~wahl** *f* choice of a job.

**Berufung** *f* vocation, calling; (*Ernennung*) appointment; (*JUR*) appeal; **~ einlegen** to appeal; **unter ~ auf etw** *akk* (*form*) with reference to sth.

**Berufungsgericht** *nt* appeal court, court of appeal.

**beruhen** [bə'ruːən] *vi:* **auf etw** *dat* **~** to be based on sth; **etw auf sich ~ lassen** to leave sth at that; **das beruht auf Gegenseitigkeit** the feeling is mutual.

**beruhigen** [bə'ruːɪgən] *vt* to calm, pacify, soothe ♦ *vr* (*Mensch*) to calm (o.s.) down; (*Situation*) to calm down.

**beruhigend** *adj* (*Gefühl, Wissen*) reassuring; (*Worte*) comforting; (*Mittel*) tranquillizing.

**Beruhigung** *f* reassurance; (*der Nerven*) calming; **zu jds ~** to reassure sb.

**Beruhigungsmittel** *nt* sedative.

**Beruhigungspille** *f* tranquillizer.

**berühmt** [bə'ryːmt] *adj* famous; **das war nicht ~** (*umg*) it was nothing to write home about; **~-berüchtigt** *adj* infamous, notorious; **B~heit** *f* (*Ruf*) fame; (*Mensch*) celebrity.

**berühren** [bə'ryːrən] *vt* to touch; (*gefühlsmäßig bewegen*) to affect; (*flüchtig erwähnen*) to mention, touch on ♦ *vr* to meet, touch; **von etw peinlich berührt sein** to be embarrassed by sth.

**Berührung** *f* contact.

**Berührungspunkt** *m* point of contact.

**bes.** *abk* (= *besonders*) esp.

**besagen** [bə'zaːgən] *vt* to mean.

**besagt** *adj* (*form: Tag etc*) in question.

**besaiten** [bə'zaɪtən] *vt:* **neu ~** (*Instrument*) to restring.

**besänftigen** [bə'zɛnftɪgən] *vt* to soothe, calm.

**besänftigend** *adj* soothing.

**Besänftigung** *f* soothing, calming.

**besaß** etc [bə'zaːs] *vb siehe* **besitzen**.

**besät** [bə'zɛːt] *adj* covered; (*mit Blättern etc*) strewn.

**Besatz** [bə'zats] (**-es**, **-̈e**) *m* trimming, edging.

**Besatzung** *f* garrison; (*NAUT, AVIAT*) crew.

**Besatzungsmacht** *f* occupying power.

**Besatzungszone** *f* occupied zone.

**besaufen** [bə'zaʊfən] *unreg* (*umg*) *vr* to get drunk *od* stoned.

**beschädigen** [bə'ʃɛːdɪgən] *vt* to damage.

**Beschädigung** *f* damage; (*Stelle*) damaged spot.

**beschaffen** [bə'ʃafən] *vt* to get, acquire ♦ *adj* constituted; **so ~ sein wie ...** to be the same as ...; **B~heit** *f* constitution, nature; **je nach B~heit der Lage** according to the situation.

**Beschaffung** *f* acquisition.

**beschäftigen** [bə'ʃɛftɪgən] *vt* to occupy; (*beruflich*) to employ; (*innerlich*): **jdn ~** to be on sb's mind ♦ *vr* to occupy *od* concern o.s.

**beschäftigt** *adj* busy, occupied; (*angestellt*): **(bei einer Firma) ~** employed (by a firm).

**Beschäftigung** *f* (*Beruf*) employment; (*Tätigkeit*) occupation; (*geistige ~*) preoccupation; **einer ~ nachgehen** (*form*) to be employed.

**Beschäftigungsprogramm** *nt* employment scheme.

**Beschäftigungstherapie** *f* occupational therapy.

**beschämen** [bə'ʃɛːmən] *vt* to put to shame.

**beschämend** *adj* shameful; (*Hilfsbereitschaft*) shaming.

**beschämt** *adj* ashamed.

**beschatten** [bə'ʃatən] *vt* to shade; (*Verdächtige*) to shadow.

**beschaulich** [bə'ʃaʊlɪç] *adj* contemplative; (*Leben, Abend*) quiet, tranquil.

**Bescheid** [bə'ʃaɪt] (**-(e)s**, **-e**) *m* information; (*Weisung*) directions *pl*; **~ wissen (über** +*akk*) to be well-informed (about); **ich weiß ~** I know; **jdm ~ geben** *od* **sagen** to let sb know; **jdm ordentlich ~ sagen** (*umg*) to tell sb where to go.

**bescheiden** [bə'ʃaɪdən] *unreg vr* to content o.s. ♦ *vt:* **etw abschlägig ~** (*form*) to turn sth down ♦ *adj* modest; **B~heit** *f* modesty.

**bescheinen** [bə'ʃaɪnən] *unreg vt* to shine on.

**bescheinigen** [bə'ʃaɪnɪgən] *vt* to certify; (*bestätigen*) to acknowledge; **hiermit wird bescheinigt, daß ...** this is to certify that ...

**Bescheinigung** *f* certificate; (*Quittung*) receipt.

**bescheißen** [bə'ʃaɪsən] *unreg* (*umg!*) *vt* to cheat.

**beschenken** [bə'ʃɛŋkən] *vt* to give presents to.

**bescheren** [bə'ʃeːrən] *vt:* **jdm etw ~** to give sb sth as a present; **jdn ~** to give presents to sb.

**Bescherung** *f* giving of presents; (*umg*) mess; **da haben wir die ~!** (*umg*) what did I tell you!

**bescheuert** [bə'ʃɔʏɐt] (*umg*) *adj* stupid.

**beschichten** [bə'ʃɪçtən] *vt* (*TECH*) to coat, cover.

**beschießen** [bə'ʃiːsən] *unreg vt* to shoot *od* fire at.

**beschildern** [bə'ʃɪldɐn] *vt* to signpost.

**beschimpfen** [bə'ʃɪmpfən] *vt* to abuse.

**Beschimpfung** *f* abuse, insult.

**beschirmen** [bə'ʃɪrmən] *vt* (*geh: beschützen*) to shield.

**Beschiß** [bə'ʃɪs] (**-sses**) (*umg*) *m:* **das ist ~** that is a cheat.

**beschiß** etc *vb siehe* **bescheißen**.

**beschissen** *pp von* **bescheißen** ♦ *adj* (*umg!*) bloody awful, lousy.

**Beschlag** [bə'ʃlaːk] (**-(e)s**, **-̈e**) *m* (*Metallband*) fitting; (*auf Fenster*) condensation; (*auf Metall*) tarnish; finish; (*Hufeisen*) horseshoe; **jdn/etw in ~ nehmen** *od* **mit ~ belegen** to monopolize sb/sth.

**beschlagen** [bə'ʃlaːgən] *unreg vt* to cover; (*Pferd*) to shoe; (*Fenster, Metall*) to cover ♦ *vi, vr* (*Fenster etc*) to mist over; ~ **sein** (**in** *od* **auf** +*dat*) to be well versed (in).

**beschlagnahmen** *vt* to seize, confiscate.

**Beschlagnahmung** *f* confiscation.

**beschleunigen** [bə'ʃlɔɪnɪgən] *vt* to accelerate, speed up ♦ *vi* (*AUT*) to accelerate.

**Beschleunigung** *f* acceleration.

**beschließen** [bə'ʃliːsən] *unreg vt* to decide on; (*beenden*) to end, close.

**beschlossen** [bə'ʃlɔsən] *pp von* **beschließen** ♦ *adj* (*entschieden*) decided, agreed; **das ist ~e Sache** that's been settled.

**Beschluß** [bə'ʃlʊs] (-**sses**, -**schlüsse**) *m* decision, conclusion; (*Ende*) close, end; **einen ~ fassen** to pass a resolution.

**beschlußfähig** *adj*: ~ **sein** to have a quorum.

**beschmieren** [bə'ʃmiːrən] *vt* (*Wand*) to bedaub.

**beschmutzen** [bə'ʃmʊtsən] *vt* to dirty, soil.

**beschneiden** [bə'ʃnaɪdən] *unreg vt* to cut; (*stutzen*) to trim; (: *Strauch*) to prune; (*REL*) to circumcise.

**beschnuppern** [bə'ʃnʊpərn] *vr* (*Hunde*) to sniff each other; (*fig: umg*) to size each other up.

**beschönigen** [bə'ʃøːnɪgən] *vt* to gloss over; ~**der Ausdruck** euphemism.

**beschränken** [bə'ʃrɛŋkən] *vt, vr*: (**sich**) ~ (**auf** +*akk*) to limit *od* restrict (o.s.) (to).

**beschrankt** [bə'ʃraŋkt] *adj* (*Bahnübergang*) with barrier.

**beschränkt** [bə'ʃrɛŋkt] *adj* confined, narrow; (*Mensch*) limited, narrow-minded; (*pej: geistig*) dim; **Gesellschaft mit ~er Haftung** limited company (*BRIT*), corporation (*US*); **B~heit** *f* narrowness.

**Beschränkung** *f* limitation.

**beschreiben** [bə'ʃraɪbən] *unreg vt* to describe; (*Papier*) to write on.

**Beschreibung** *f* description.

**beschrieb** *etc* [bə'ʃriːp] *vb siehe* **beschreiben**.

**beschrieben** [bə'ʃriːbən] *pp von* **beschreiben**.

**beschriften** [bə'ʃrɪftən] *vt* to mark, label.

**Beschriftung** *f* lettering.

**beschuldigen** [bə'ʃʊldɪgən] *vt* to accuse.

**Beschuldigung** *f* accusation.

**beschummeln** [bə'ʃʊməln] (*umg*) *vt, vi* to cheat.

**Beschuß** [bə'ʃʊs] *m*: **jdn/etw unter ~ nehmen** (*MIL*) to (start to) bombard *od* shell sb/sth; (*fig*) to attack sb/sth; **unter ~ geraten** (*lit, fig*) to come into the firing line.

**beschützen** [bə'ʃYtsən] *vt*: ~ (**vor** +*dat*) to protect (from).

**Beschützer(in)** (-**s**, -) *m(f)* protector.

**Beschützung** *f* protection.

**beschwatzen** [bə'ʃvatsən] (*umg*) *vt* (*überreden*) to talk over.

**Beschwerde** [bə'ʃveːrdə] (-, -**n**) *f* complaint; (*Mühe*) hardship; (*INDUSTRIE*) grievance; **Beschwerden** *pl* (*Leiden*) trouble; ~ **einlegen** (*form*) to lodge a complaint; **b~frei** *adj* fit and healthy; ~**frist** *f* (*JUR*) period of time during which an appeal may be lodged.

**beschweren** [bə'ʃveːrən] *vt* to weight down; (*fig*) to burden ♦ *vr* to complain.

**beschwerlich** *adj* tiring, exhausting.

**beschwichtigen** [bə'ʃvɪçtɪgən] *vt* to soothe, pacify.

**Beschwichtigung** *f* soothing, calming.

**beschwindeln** [bə'ʃvɪndəln] *vt* (*betrügen*) to cheat; (*belügen*) to fib to.

**beschwingt** [bə'ʃvɪŋt] *adj* cheery, in high spirits.

**beschwipst** [bə'ʃvɪpst] *adj* tipsy.

**beschwören** [bə'ʃvøːrən] *unreg vt* (*Aussage*) to swear to; (*anflehen*) to implore; (*Geister*) to conjure up.

**beseelen** [bə'zeːlən] *vt* to inspire.

**besehen** [bə'zeːən] *unreg vt* to look at; **genau ~** to examine closely.

**beseitigen** [bə'zaɪtɪgən] *vt* to remove.

**Beseitigung** *f* removal.

**Besen** ['beːzən] (-**s**, -) *m* broom; (*pej: umg: Frau*) old bag; **ich fresse einen ~, wenn das stimmt** (*umg*) if that's right, I'll eat my hat; ~**stiel** *m* broomstick.

**besessen** [bə'zɛsən] *adj* possessed; (*von einer Idee etc*): ~ (**von**) obsessed (with).

**besetzen** [bə'zɛtsən] *vt* (*Haus, Land*) to occupy; (*Platz*) to take, fill; (*Posten*) to fill; (*Rolle*) to cast; (*mit Edelsteinen*) to set.

**besetzt** *adj* full; (*TEL*) engaged, busy; (*Platz*) taken; (*WC*) engaged; **B~zeichen** *nt* engaged tone (*BRIT*), busy signal (*US*).

**Besetzung** *f* occupation; (*von Stelle*) filling; (*von Rolle*) casting; (*die Schauspieler*) cast; **zweite ~** (*THEAT*) understudy.

**besichtigen** [bə'zɪçtɪgən] *vt* to visit, look at.

**Besichtigung** *f* visit.

**besiedeln** *vt*: **dicht/dünn besiedelt** densely/ thinly populated.

**Besied(e)lung** [bə'ziːd(ə)lʊŋ] *f* population.

**besiegeln** [bə'ziːgəln] *vt* to seal.

**besiegen** [bə'ziːgən] *vt* to defeat, overcome.

**Besiegte(r)** [bə'ziːktə(r)] *f(m)* loser.

**besinnen** [bə'zɪnən] *unreg vr* (*nachdenken*) to think, reflect; (*erinnern*) to remember; **sich anders ~** to change one's mind.

**besinnlich** *adj* contemplative.

**Besinnung** *f* consciousness; **bei/ohne ~ sein** to be conscious/unconscious; **zur ~ kommen** to recover consciousness; (*fig*) to come to one's senses.

**besinnungslos** *adj* unconscious; (*fig*) blind.

**Besitz** [bə'zɪts] (-**es**) *m* possession; (*Eigentum*) property; ~**anspruch** *m* claim of ownership; (*JUR*) title; **b~anzeigend** *adj* (*GRAM*) possessive.

**besitzen** *unreg vt* to possess, own; (*Eigenschaft*) to have.

**Besitzer(in)** (-s, -) *m(f)* owner, proprietor.
**Besitz-** *zW:* ~**ergreifung** *f* seizure; ~**nahme** *f* seizure; ~**tum** *nt* (*Grundbesitz*) estate(s *pl*), property; ~**urkunde** *f* title deeds *pl.*
**besoffen** [bə'zɔfən] (*umg*) *adj* sozzled.
**besohlen** [bə'zoːlən] *vt* to sole.
**Besoldung** [bə'zɔldʊŋ] *f* salary, pay.
**besondere(r, s)** [bə'zɔndərə(r, s)] *adj* special; (*eigen*) particular; (*gesondert*) separate; (*eigentümlich*) peculiar.
**Besonderheit** *f* peculiarity.
**besonders** *adv* especially, particularly; (*getrennt*) separately; **das Essen/der Film war nichts** ~ the food/film was nothing special *od* out of the ordinary; **wie geht's dir? - nicht** ~ how are you? - not too hot.
**besonnen** [bə'zɔnən] *adj* sensible, level-headed; **B~heit** *f* level-headedness.
**besorgen** [bə'zɔrgən] *vt* (*beschaffen*) to acquire; (*kaufen*) to purchase; (*erledigen: Geschäfte*) to deal with; (*sich kümmern um*) to take care of; **es jdm** ~ (*umg*) to sort sb out.
**Besorgnis** (-, -se) *f* anxiety, concern; **b~erregend** *adj* alarming, worrying.
**besorgt** [bə'zɔrkt] *adj* anxious, worried; **B~heit** *f* anxiety, worry.
**Besorgung** *f* acquisition; (*Kauf*) purchase; (*Einkauf*): ~**en machen** to do some shopping.
**bespannen** [bə'ʃpanən] *vt* (*mit Saiten, Fäden*) to string.
**bespielbar** *adj* (*Rasen etc*) playable.
**bespielen** [bə'ʃpiːlən] *vt* (*Tonband, Kassette*) to make a recording on.
**bespitzeln** [bə'ʃpɪtsəln] *vt* to spy on.
**besprechen** [bə'ʃprɛçən] *unreg vt* to discuss; (*Tonband etc*) to record, speak onto; (*Buch*) to review ♦ *vr* to discuss, consult.
**Besprechung** *f* meeting, discussion; (*von Buch*) review.
**bespringen** [bə'ʃprɪŋən] *unreg vt* (*Tier*) to mount, cover.
**bespritzen** [bə'ʃprɪtsən] *vt* to spray; (*beschmutzen*) to spatter.
**besser** ['bɛsər] *adj* better; **nur ein** ~**er** ... just a glorified ...; ~**e Leute** a better class of people; ~**gehen** *unreg vi unpers:* **es geht ihm** ~ he feels better.
**bessern** *vt* to make better, improve ♦ *vr* to improve; (*Mensch*) to reform.
**besserstehen** *unreg* (*umg*) *vr* to be better off.
**Besserung** *f* improvement; **auf dem Weg(e) der** ~ **sein** to be getting better, be improving; **gute** ~! get well soon!
**Besserwisser(in)** (-s, -) *m(f)* know-all (*BRIT*), know-it-all (*US*).
**Bestand** [bə'ʃtant] (-(e)s, ̈-e) *m* (*Fortbestehen*) duration, continuance; (*Kassenbestand*) amount, balance; (*Vorrat*) stock; **eiserner** ~ iron rations *pl*; ~ **haben, von** ~ **sein** to last long, endure.
**bestand** *etc vb siehe* **bestehen.**
**bestanden** *pp von* **bestehen** ♦ *adj:* **nach** ~**er**

**Prüfung** after passing the exam.
**beständig** [bə'ʃtɛndɪç] *adj* (*ausdauernd*) constant (*auch fig*); (*Wetter*) settled; (*Stoffe*) resistant; (*Klagen etc*) continual.
**Bestandsaufnahme** *f* stocktaking.
**Bestandsüberwachung** *f* stock control, inventory control.
**Bestandteil** *m* part, component; (*Zutat*) ingredient; **sich in seine** ~**e auflösen** to fall to pieces.
**bestärken** [bə'ʃtɛrkən] *vt:* **jdn in etw** *dat* ~ to strengthen *od* confirm sb in sth.
**bestätigen** [bə'ʃtɛːtɪgən] *vt* to confirm; (*anerkennen, COMM*) to acknowledge; **jdn (im Amt)** ~ to confirm sb's appointment.
**Bestätigung** *f* confirmation; acknowledgement.
**bestatten** [bə'ʃtatən] *vt* to bury.
**Bestatter** (-s, -) *m* undertaker.
**Bestattung** *f* funeral.
**Bestattungsinstitut** *nt* undertaker's (*BRIT*), mortician's (*US*).
**bestäuben** [bə'ʃtɔybən] *vt* to powder, dust; (*Pflanze*) to pollinate.
**beste(r, s)** ['bɛstə(r, s)] *adj* best; **sie singt am** ~**n** she sings best; **so ist es am** ~**n** it's best that way; **am** ~**n gehst du gleich** you'd better go at once; **jdn zum** ~**n haben** to pull sb's leg; **einen Witz etc zum** ~**n geben** to tell a joke *etc;* **aufs** ~ in the best possible way; **zu jds B~n** for the benefit of sb; **es steht nicht zum** ~**n** it does not look too promising.
**bestechen** [bə'ʃtɛçən] *unreg vt* to bribe ♦ *vi* (*Eindruck machen*): **(durch etw)** ~ to be impressive (because of sth).
**bestechend** *adj* (*Schönheit, Eindruck*) captivating; (*Angebot*) tempting.
**bestechlich** *adj* corruptible; **B~keit** *f* corruptibility.
**Bestechung** *f* bribery, corruption.
**Bestechungsgelder** *pl* bribe *sing.*
**Bestechungsversuch** *m* attempted bribery.
**Besteck** [bə'ʃtɛk] (-(e)s, -e) *nt* knife, fork and spoon, cutlery; (*MED*) set of instruments; ~**kasten** *m* cutlery canteen.
**bestehen** [bə'ʃteːən] *unreg vi* to exist; (*andauern*) to last ♦ *vt* (*Probe, Prüfung*) to pass; (*Kampf*) to win; **die Schwierigkeit/das Problem besteht darin, daß** ... the difficulty/problem lies in the fact that ..., the difficulty/problem is that ...; ~ **auf** +*dat* to insist on; ~ **aus** to consist of; **B~** *nt:* **seit B~ der Firma** ever since the firm came into existence *od* has existed.
**bestehenbleiben** *unreg vi* to last, endure; (*Frage, Hoffnung*) to remain.
**bestehlen** [bə'ʃteːlən] *unreg vt* to rob.
**besteigen** [bə'ʃtaɪgən] *unreg vt* to climb, ascend; (*Pferd*) to mount; (*Thron*) to ascend.
**Bestellbuch** *nt* order book.
**bestellen** [bə'ʃtɛlən] *vt* to order; (*kommen*

*lassen*) to arrange to see; (*nominieren*) to name; (*Acker*) to cultivate; (*Grüße, Auftrag*) to pass on; **wie bestellt und nicht abgeholt** (*hum: umg*) like orphan Annie; **er hat nicht viel/nichts zu** ~ he doesn't have much/any say here; **ich bin für 10 Uhr bestellt** I have an appointment for *od* at 10 o'clock; **es ist schlecht um ihn bestellt** (*fig*) he is in a bad way.

**Bestell-** *zW:* ~**formular** *nt* purchase order; ~**nummer** *f* order number; ~**schein** *m* order coupon.

**Bestellung** *f* (*COMM*) order; (*Bestellen*) ordering; (*Ernennung*) nomination, appointment.

**bestenfalls** ['bɛstən'fals] *adv* at best.

**bestens** ['bɛstəns] *adv* very well.

**besteuern** [bə'ʃtɔyərn] *vt* to tax.

**bestialisch** [bɛsti'aːlɪʃ] (*umg*) *adj* awful, beastly.

**besticken** [bə'ʃtɪkən] *vt* to embroider.

**Bestie** ['bɛstiə] *f* (*lit, fig*) beast.

**bestimmen** [bə'ʃtɪmən] *vt* (*Regeln*) to lay down; (*Tag, Ort*) to fix; (*prägen*) to characterize; (*ausersehen*) to mean; (*ernennen*) to appoint; (*definieren*) to define; (*veranlassen*) to induce ♦ *vi:* **du hast hier nicht zu** ~ you don't make the decisions here; **er kann über sein Geld allein** ~ it is up to him what he does with his money.

**bestimmend** *adj* (*Faktor, Einfluß*) determining, decisive.

**bestimmt** *adj* (*entschlossen*) firm; (*gewiß*) certain, definite; (*Artikel*) definite ♦ *adv* (*gewiß*) definitely, for sure; **suchen Sie etwas B~es?** are you looking for anything in particular?; **B~heit** *f* certainty; **in** *od* **mit aller B~heit** quite categorically.

**Bestimmung** *f* (*Verordnung*) regulation; (*Festsetzen*) determining; (*Verwendungszweck*) purpose; (*Schicksal*) fate; (*Definition*) definition.

**Bestimmungs-** *zW:* ~**bahnhof** *m* (*EISENB*) destination; **b~gemäß** *adj* as agreed; ~**hafen** *m* (port of) destination; ~**ort** *m* destination.

**Bestleistung** *f* best performance.

**bestmöglich** *adj* best possible.

**Best.-Nr.** *abk* = **Bestellnummer.**

**bestrafen** [bə'ʃtraːfən] *vt* to punish.

**Bestrafung** *f* punishment.

**bestrahlen** [bə'ʃtraːlən] *vt* to shine on; (*MED*) to treat with X-rays.

**Bestrahlung** *f* (*MED*) X-ray treatment, radiotherapy.

**Bestreben** [bə'ʃtreːbən] (**-s**) *nt* endeavour (*BRIT*), endeavor (*US*), effort.

**bestrebt** [bə'ʃtreːpt] *adj:* ~ **sein, etw zu tun** to endeavour (*BRIT*) *od* endeavor (*US*) to do sth.

**Bestrebung** [bə'ʃtreːbʊŋ] *f* = **Bestreben.**

**bestreichen** [bə'ʃtraɪçən] *unreg vt* (*Brot*) to spread.

**bestreiken** [bə'ʃtraɪkən] *vt* (*INDUSTRIE*) to black; **die Fabrik wird zur Zeit bestreikt** there's a strike on in the factory at the moment.

**bestreiten** [bə'ʃtraɪtən] *unreg vt* (*abstreiten*) to dispute; (*finanzieren*) to pay for, finance; **er hat das ganze Gespräch allein bestritten** he did all the talking.

**bestreuen** [bə'ʃtrɔyən] *vt* to sprinkle, dust; (*Straße*) to (spread with) grit.

**Bestseller** [bɛst'sɛlər] (**-s, -**) *m* best-seller.

**bestürmen** [bə'ʃtʏrmən] *vt* (*mit Fragen, Bitten etc*) to overwhelm, swamp.

**bestürzen** [bə'ʃtʏrtsən] *vt* to dismay.

**bestürzt** *adj* dismayed.

**Bestürzung** *f* consternation.

**Bestzeit** *f* (*bes SPORT*) best time.

**Besuch** [bə'zuːx] (**-(e)s, -e**) *m* visit; (*Person*) visitor; **einen** ~ **bei jdm machen** to pay sb a visit *od* call; ~ **haben** to have visitors; **bei jdm auf** *od* **zu** ~ **sein** to be visiting sb.

**besuchen** *vt* to visit; (*SCH etc*) to attend; **gut besucht** well-attended.

**Besucher(in)** (**-s, -**) *m(f)* visitor, guest.

**Besuchserlaubnis** *f* permission to visit.

**Besuchszeit** *f* visiting hours *pl*.

**besudeln** [bə'zuːdəln] *vt* (*Wände*) to smear; (*fig: Namen, Ehre*) to sully.

**betagt** [bə'taːkt] *adj* aged.

**betasten** [bə'tastən] *vt* to touch, feel.

**betätigen** [bə'tɛːtɪgən] *vt* (*bedienen*) to work, operate ♦ *vr* to involve o.s.; **sich politisch** ~ to be involved in politics; **sich als etw** ~ to work as sth.

**Betätigung** *f* activity; (*beruflich*) occupation; (*TECH*) operation.

**betäuben** [bə'tɔybən] *vt* to stun; (*fig: Gewissen*) to still; (*MED*) to anaesthetize (*BRIT*), anesthetize (*US*); **ein** ~**der Duft** an overpowering smell.

**Betäubung** *f* (*Narkose*): **örtliche** ~ local anaesthetic (*BRIT*) *od* anesthetic (*US*).

**Betäubungsmittel** *nt* anaesthetic (*BRIT*), anesthetic (*US*).

**Bete** ['beːtə] (**-, -n**) *f:* **rote** ~ beetroot (*BRIT*), beet (*US*).

**beteiligen** [bə'taɪlɪgən] *vr:* **sich (an etw** *dat*) ~ to take part (in sth), participate (in sth); (*an Geschäft: finanziell*) to have a share (in sth) ♦ *vt:* **jdn (an etw** *dat*) ~ to give sb a share *od* interest (in sth); **sich an den Unkosten** ~ to contribute to the expenses.

**Beteiligung** *f* participation; (*Anteil*) share, interest; (*Besucherzahl*) attendance.

**Beteiligungsgesellschaft** *f* associated company.

**beten** ['beːtən] *vi* to pray ♦ *vt* (*Rosenkranz*) to say.

**beteuern** [bə'tɔyərn] *vt* to assert; (*Unschuld*) to protest; **jdm etw** ~ to assure sb of sth.

**Beteuerung** *f* assertion; protestation;

assurance.

**Beton** [be'tõ:] (**-s, -s**) *m* concrete.

**betonen** [bə'to:nən] *vt* to stress.

**betonieren** [beto'ni:rən] *vt* to concrete.

**Betonmischmaschine** *f* concrete mixer.

**betont** [bə'to:nt] *adj* (*Höflichkeit*) emphatic, deliberate; (*Kühle, Sachlichkeit*) pointed.

**Betonung** *f* stress, emphasis.

**betören** [bə'tø:rən] *vt* to beguile.

**Betr.** *abk* = **Betreff.**

**betr.** *abk* (= *betreffend, betreffs*) re.

**Betracht** [bə'traxt] *m:* **in ~ kommen** to be concerned *od* relevant; **nicht in ~ kommen** to be out of the question; **etw in ~ ziehen** to consider sth; **außer ~ bleiben** not to be considered.

**betrachten** *vt* to look at; (*fig*) to consider, look at.

**Betrachter(in)** (**-s, -**) *m(f)* onlooker.

**beträchtlich** [bə'trɛçtlıç] *adj* considerable.

**Betrachtung** *f* (*Ansehen*) examination; (*Erwägung*) consideration; **über etw** *akk* **~en anstellen** to reflect on *od* contemplate sth.

**betraf** *etc* [bə'tra:f] *vb siehe* **betreffen.**

**Betrag** [bə'tra:k] (**-(e)s, ⁻e**) *m* amount, sum; **~ erhalten** (*COMM*) sum received.

**betragen** [bə'tra:gən] *unreg vt* to amount to ♦ *vr* to behave.

**Betragen** (**-s**) *nt* behaviour (*BRIT*), behavior (*US*); (*bes in Zeugnis*) conduct.

**beträgt** [bə'trɛ:kt] *vb siehe* **betragen.**

**betrat** *etc* [bə'tra:t] *vb siehe* **betreten.**

**betrauen** [bə'trauən] *vt:* **jdn mit etw ~** to entrust sb with sth.

**betrauern** [bə'trauərn] *vt* to mourn.

**beträufeln** [bə'trɔyfəln] *vt:* **den Fisch mit Zitrone ~** to sprinkle lemon juice on the fish.

**Betreff** *m:* **~: Ihr Schreiben vom ...** re *od* reference your letter of ...

**betreffen** [bə'trɛfən] *unreg vt* to concern, affect; **was mich betrifft** as for me.

**betreffend** *adj* relevant, in question.

**betreffs** [bə'trɛfs] *präp +gen* concerning, regarding.

**betreiben** [bə'traıbən] *unreg vt* (*ausüben*) to practise (*BRIT*), practice (*US*); (*Politik*) to follow; (*Studien*) to pursue; (*vorantreiben*) to push ahead; (*TECH: antreiben*) to drive; **auf jds B~** *akk* **hin** (*form*) at sb's instigation.

**betreten** [bə'tre:tən] *unreg vt* to enter; (*Bühne etc*) to step onto ♦ *adj* embarrassed; **„B~ verboten"** "keep off/out".

**betreuen** [bə'trɔyən] *vt* to look after.

**Betreuer(in)** (**-s, -**) *m(f)* carer; (*Kinderbetreuer*) child-minder.

**Betreuung** *f:* **er wurde mit der ~ der Gruppe beauftragt** he was put in charge of the group.

**Betrieb** (**-(e)s, -e**) *m* (*Firma*) firm, concern; (*Anlage*) plant; (*Tätigkeit*) operation; (*Treiben*) bustle; (*Verkehr*) traffic; **außer ~ sein** to be

out of order; **in ~ sein** to be in operation; **eine Maschine in/außer ~ setzen** to start a machine up/stop a machine; **eine Maschine/Fabrik in ~ nehmen** to put a machine/factory into operation; **in den Geschäften herrscht großer ~** the shops are very busy; **er hält den ganzen ~ auf** (*umg*) he's holding everything up.

**betrieb** *etc* [bə'tri:p] *vb siehe* **betreiben.**

**betrieben** [bə'tri:bən] *pp von* **betreiben.**

**betrieblich** *adj* company *attr* ♦ *adv* (*regeln*) within the company.

**Betriebs-** *zW:* **~anleitung** *f* operating instructions *pl;* **~ausflug** *m* firm's outing; **~ausgaben** *pl* revenue expenditure *sing;* **b~eigen** *adj* company *attr;* **~erlaubnis** *f* operating permission/licence (*BRIT*) *od* license (*US*); **b~fähig** *adj* in working order; **~ferien** *pl* company holidays *pl* (*BRIT*) *od* vacation *sing* (*US*); **~führung** *f* management; **~geheimnis** *nt* trade secret; **~kapital** *nt* capital employed; **~klima** *nt* (working) atmosphere; **~kosten** *pl* running costs; **~leitung** *f* management; **~rat** *m* workers' council; **~rente** *f* company pension; **b~sicher** *adj* safe, reliable; **~stoff** *m* fuel; **~störung** *f* breakdown; **~system** *nt* (*COMPUT*) operating system; **~unfall** *m* industrial accident; **~wirt** *m* management expert; **~wirtschaft** *f* business management.

**betrifft** [bə'trıft] *vb siehe* **betreffen.**

**betrinken** [bə'trıŋkən] *unreg vr* to get drunk.

**betritt** [bə'trıt] *vb siehe* **betreten.**

**betroffen** [bə'trɔfən] *pp von* **betreffen** ♦ *adj* (*bestürzt*) amazed, perplexed; **von etw ~ werden** *od* **sein** to be affected by sth.

**betrüben** [bə'try:bən] *vt* to grieve.

**betrübt** [bə'try:pt] *adj* sorrowful, grieved.

**Betrug** (**-(e)s**) *m* deception; (*JUR*) fraud.

**betrug** *etc* [bə'tru:k] *vb siehe* **betragen.**

**betrügen** [bə'try:gən] *unreg vt* to cheat; (*JUR*) to defraud; (*Ehepartner*) to be unfaithful to ♦ *vr* to deceive o.s.

**Betrüger(in)** (**-s, -**) *m(f)* cheat, deceiver.

**betrügerisch** *adj* deceitful; (*JUR*) fraudulent; **in ~er Absicht** with intent to defraud.

**betrunken** [bə'trʊŋkən] *adj* drunk.

**Betrunkene(r)** *f(m)* drunk.

**Bett** [bɛt] (**-(e)s, -en**) *nt* bed; **im ~ sein** in bed; **ins** *od* **zu ~ gehen** to go to bed; **~bezug** *m* duvet cover; **~decke** *f* blanket; (*Daunenbettdecke*) quilt; (*Überwurf*) bedspread.

**bettelarm** ['bɛtəl|arm] *adj* very poor, destitute.

**Bettelei** [bɛtə'laı] *f* begging.

**Bettelmönch** *m* mendicant *od* begging monk.

**betteln** *vi* to beg.

**betten** *vt* to make a bed for.

**Bett-** *zW:* **~hupferl** (*SÜDD*) *nt* bedtime sweet; **b~lägerig** *adj* bedridden; **~laken** *nt* sheet;

~**lektüre** f bedtime reading.
**Bettler(in)** ['bɛtlər(ɪn)] (-s, -) m(f) beggar.
**Bett-** zW: ~**nässer** (-s, -) m bedwetter;
~**schwere** (umg) f: **die nötige ~schwere
haben/bekommen** to be/get tired enough to
sleep; ~**(t)uch** nt sheet; ~**vorleger** m
bedside rug; ~**wäsche** f bedclothes pl,
bedding; ~**zeug** nt = **Bettwäsche**.
**betucht** [bə'tuːxt] (umg) adj well-to-do.
**betulich** [bə'tuːlɪç] adj (übertrieben besorgt)
fussing attr; (Redeweise) twee.
**betupfen** [bə'tʊpfən] vt to dab; (MED) to swab.
**Beugehaft** ['bɔʏɡəhaft] f (JUR) coercive
detention.
**beugen** ['bɔʏɡən] vt to bend; (GRAM) to inflect
♦ vr (+dat) (sich fügen) to bow (to).
**Beule** ['bɔʏlə] (-, -n) f bump.
**beunruhigen** [bə'|ʊnruːɪɡən] vt to disturb,
alarm ♦ vr to become worried.
**Beunruhigung** f worry, alarm.
**beurkunden** [bə'|uːrkʊndən] vt to attest,
verify.
**beurlauben** [bə'|uːrlaʊbən] vt to give leave od
holiday to (BRIT), grant vacation to (US);
**beurlaubt sein** to have leave of absence;
(suspendiert sein) to have been relieved of
one's duties.
**beurteilen** [bə'|ʊrtaɪlən] vt to judge; (Buch etc)
to review.
**Beurteilung** f judgement; (von Buch etc)
review; (Note) mark.
**Beute** ['bɔʏtə] (-) f booty, loot; (von Raubtieren
etc) prey.
**Beutel** (-s, -) m bag; (Geld~) purse; (Tabaks~)
pouch.
**bevölkern** [bə'fœlkərn] vt to populate.
**Bevölkerung** f population.
**Bevölkerungs-** zW: ~**explosion** f population
explosion; ~**schicht** f social stratum;
~**statistik** f vital statistics pl.
**bevollmächtigen** [bə'fɔlmɛçtɪɡən] vt to
authorize.
**Bevollmächtigte(r)** f(m) authorized agent.
**Bevollmächtigung** f authorization.
**bevor** [bə'foːr] konj before; ~**munden** vt untr to
dominate; ~**stehen** unreg vi: (jdm) ~**stehen** to
be in store (for sb); ~**stehend** adj imminent,
approaching; ~**zugen** vt untr to prefer; ~**zugt**
[bə'foːrtsuːkt] adv: **etw ~zugt abfertigen** etc
to give sth priority; **B~zugung** f
preference.
**bewachen** [bə'vaxən] vt to watch, guard.
**bewachsen** [bə'vaksən] adj overgrown.
**Bewachung** f (Bewachen) guarding; (Leute)
guard, watch.
**bewaffnen** [bə'vafnən] vt to arm.
**Bewaffnung** f (Vorgang) arming;
(Ausrüstung) armament, arms pl.
**bewahren** [bə'vaːrən] vt to keep; **jdn vor jdm/
etw ~** to save sb from sb/sth; **(Gott)
bewahre!** (umg) heaven od God forbid!
**bewähren** [bə'vɛːrən] vr to prove o.s.;

(Maschine) to prove its worth.
**bewahrheiten** [bə'vaːrhaɪtən] vr to come true.
**bewährt** adj reliable.
**Bewährung** f (JUR) probation; **ein Jahr
Gefängnis mit ~** a suspended sentence of
one year with probation.
**Bewährungs-** zW: ~**frist** f (period of)
probation; ~**helfer** m probation officer;
~**probe** f: **etw einer ~probe** dat **unterziehen**
to put sth to the test.
**bewaldet** [bə'valdət] adj wooded.
**bewältigen** [bə'vɛltɪɡən] vt to overcome;
(Arbeit) to finish; (Portion) to manage;
(Schwierigkeiten) to cope with.
**bewandert** [bə'vandərt] adj expert,
knowledgeable.
**Bewandtnis** [bə'vantnɪs] f: **damit hat es
folgende ~** the fact of the matter is this.
**bewarb** etc [bə'varp] vb siehe **bewerben**.
**bewässern** [bə'vɛsərn] vt to irrigate.
**Bewässerung** f irrigation.
**bewegen** [bə'veːɡən] vt, vr to move; **der Preis
bewegt sich um die 50 Mark** the price is
about 50 marks; **jdn zu etw ~** to induce sb
to do sth.
**Beweggrund** m motive.
**beweglich** adj movable, mobile; (flink) quick.
**bewegt** [bə'veːkt] adj (Leben) eventful; (Meer)
rough; (ergriffen) touched.
**Bewegung** f movement, motion; (innere)
emotion; (körperlich) exercise; **sich** dat
~ **machen** to take exercise.
**Bewegungsfreiheit** f freedom of
movement; (fig) freedom of action.
**bewegungslos** adj motionless.
**Beweis** [bə'vaɪs] (-es, -e) m proof; (Zeichen)
sign; ~**aufnahme** f (JUR) taking od hearing
of evidence; **b~bar** adj provable.
**beweisen** unreg vt to prove; (zeigen) to show;
**was zu ~** war QED.
**Beweis-** zW: ~**führung** f reasoning; (JUR)
presentation of one's case; ~**kraft** f weight,
conclusiveness; **b~kräftig** adj convincing,
conclusive; ~**last** f (JUR) onus, burden of
proof; ~**mittel** nt evidence; ~**not** f (JUR)
lack of evidence; ~**stück** nt exhibit.
**bewenden** [bə'vɛndən] vi: **etw dabei ~ lassen**
to leave sth at that.
**bewerben** [bə'vɛrbən] unreg vr: **sich ~ (um)** to
apply (for).
**Bewerber(in)** (-s, -) m(f) applicant.
**Bewerbung** f application.
**Bewerbungsunterlagen** pl application
documents.
**bewerkstelligen** [bə'vɛrkʃtɛlɪɡən] vt to
manage, accomplish.
**bewerten** [bə'veːrtən] vt to assess.
**bewies** etc [bə'viːs] vb siehe **beweisen**.
**bewiesen** [bə'viːzən] pp von **beweisen**.
**bewilligen** [bə'vɪlɪɡən] vt to grant, allow.
**Bewilligung** f granting.
**bewirbt** [bə'vɪrpt] vb siehe **bewerben**.

**bewirken** [bə'vɪrkən] *vt* to cause, bring about.
**bewirten** [bə'vɪrtən] *vt* to entertain.
**bewirtschaften** [bə'vɪrtʃaftən] *vt* to manage.
**Bewirtung** *f* hospitality; **die ~ so vieler Gäste** catering for so many guests.
**bewog** *etc* [bə'voːk] *vb siehe* **bewegen**.
**bewogen** [bə'voːgən] *pp von* **bewegen**.
**bewohnbar** *adj* inhabitable.
**bewohnen** [bə'voːnən] *vt* to inhabit, live in.
**Bewohner(in)** (-s, -) *m(f)* inhabitant; (*von Haus*) resident.
**bewölkt** [bə'vœlkt] *adj* cloudy, overcast.
**Bewölkung** *f* clouds *pl.*
**Bewölkungsauflockerung** *f* break-up of the cloud.
**beworben** [bə'vɔrbən] *pp von* **bewerben**.
**Bewunderer(in)** (-s, -) *m(f)* admirer.
**bewundern** [bə'vʊndərn] *vt* to admire.
**bewundernswert** *adj* admirable, wonderful.
**Bewunderung** *f* admiration.
**bewußt** [bə'vʊst] *adj* conscious; (*absichtlich*) deliberate; **sich** *dat* **einer Sache** *gen* ~ **sein** to be aware of sth; **~los** *adj* unconscious; **B~losigkeit** *f* unconsciousness; **bis zur B~losigkeit** (*umg*) ad nauseam; **~machen** *vt:* **jdm etw ~machen** to make sb conscious of sth; **sich** *dat* **etw ~machen** to realize sth; **B~sein** *nt* consciousness; **bei B~sein** conscious; **im B~sein, daß ...** in the knowledge that ...
**Bewußtseins-** *zW:* **~bildung** *f* (*POL*) shaping of political ideas; **b~erweiternd** *adj:* **b~erweiternde Drogen** mind-expanding drugs; **~erweiterung** *f* consciousness raising.
**Bez.** *abk* = **Bezirk**.
**bez.** *abk* (= *bezüglich*) re.
**bezahlen** [bə'tsaːlən] *vt* to pay (for); **es macht sich bezahlt** it will pay.
**Bezahlung** *f* payment; **ohne/gegen** *od* **für** ~ without/for payment.
**bezaubern** [bə'tsaubərn] *vt* to enchant, charm.
**bezeichnen** [bə'tsaɪçnən] *vt* (*kennzeichnen*) to mark; (*nennen*) to call; (*beschreiben*) to describe; (*zeigen*) to show, indicate.
**bezeichnend** *adj:* ~ (**für**) characteristic (of), typical (of).
**Bezeichnung** *f* (*Zeichen*) mark, sign; (*Beschreibung*) description; (*Ausdruck*) expression, term.
**bezeugen** [bə'tsɔygən] *vt* to testify to.
**bezichtigen** [bə'tsɪçtɪgən] *vt* (*+gen*) to accuse (of).
**Bezichtigung** *f* accusation.
**beziehen** [bə'tsiːən] *unreg vt* (*mit Überzug*) to cover; (*Haus, Position*) to move into; (*Standpunkt*) to take up; (*erhalten*) to receive; (*Zeitung*) to subscribe to, take ♦ *vr* (*Himmel*) to cloud over; **die Betten frisch** ~ to change the beds; **etw auf jdn/etw** ~ to relate sth to sb/sth; **sich** ~ **auf** *+akk* to refer to.
**Beziehung** *f* (*Verbindung*) connection;

(*Zusammenhang*) relation; (*Verhältnis*) relationship; (*Hinsicht*) respect; **diplomatische ~en** diplomatic relations; **seine ~en spielen lassen** to pull strings; **in jeder** ~ in every respect; **~en haben** (*vorteilhaft*) to have connections *od* contacts.
**Beziehungskiste** (*umg*) *f* relationship.
**beziehungsweise** *adv* or; (*genauer gesagt*) that is, or rather; (*im anderen Fall*) and ... respectively.
**beziffern** [bə'tsɪfərn] *vt* (*angeben*): ~ **auf** *+akk od* **mit** to estimate at.
**Bezirk** [bə'tsɪrk] (-(e)s, -e) *m* district.
**bezirzen** [bə'tsɪrtsən] (*umg*) *vt* to bewitch.
**bezogen** [bə'tsoːgən] *pp von* **beziehen**.
**Bezogene(r)** [bə'tsoːgənə(r)] *f(m)* (*von Scheck etc*) drawee.
**Bezug** [bə'tsuːk] (-(e)s, ⁻e) *m* (*Hülle*) covering; (*COMM*) ordering; (*Gehalt*) income, salary; (*Beziehung*): ~ (**zu**) relationship (to); **in b~ auf** *+akk* with reference to; **mit** *od* **unter** ~ **auf** *+akk* regarding; (*form*) with reference to; ~ **nehmen auf** *+akk* to refer to.
**bezüglich** [bə'tsyːklɪç] *präp +gen* concerning, referring to ♦ *adj* concerning; (*GRAM*) relative.
**Bezugnahme** *f:* ~ (**auf** *+akk*) reference (to).
**Bezugs-** *zW:* **~person** *f:* **die wichtigste ~person des Kleinkindes** the person to whom the small child relates most closely; **~preis** *m* retail price; **~quelle** *f* source of supply.
**bezuschussen** [bə'tsuːʃusən] *vt* to subsidize.
**bezwecken** [bə'tsvɛkən] *vt* to aim at.
**bezweifeln** [bə'tsvaɪfəln] *vt* to doubt.
**bezwingen** [bə'tsvɪŋən] *unreg vt* to conquer; (*Feind*) to defeat, overcome.
**bezwungen** [bə'tsvʊŋən] *pp von* **bezwingen**.
**Bf.** *abk* = **Bahnhof; Brief**.
**BfA** (-) *f abk* (= *Bundesversicherungsanstalt für Angestellte*) *Federal insurance company for employees*.
**BfV** (-) *nt abk* (= *Bundesamt für Verfassungsschutz*) *Federal Office for Protection of the Constitution*.
**BG** (-) *f abk* (= *Berufsgenossenschaft*) *professional association*.
**BGB** (-) *nt abk* (= *Bürgerliches Gesetzbuch*) *siehe* **bürgerlich**.
**BGH** (-) *m abk* (= *Bundesgerichtshof*) *Federal Supreme Court*.
**BGS** (-) *m abk* = **Bundesgrenzschutz**.
**BH** (-s, -(s)) *m abk* (= *Büstenhalter*) bra.
**Bhf.** *abk* = **Bahnhof**.
**BI** *f abk* = **Bürgerinitiative**.
**Biathlon** ['biːatlɔn] (-s, -s) *nt* biathlon.
**bibbern** ['bɪbərn] (*umg*) *vi* (*vor Kälte*) to shiver.
**Bibel** ['biːbəl] (-, -n) *f* Bible.
**bibelfest** *adj* well versed in the Bible.
**Biber** ['biːbər] (-s, -) *m* beaver.
**Biberbettuch** *nt* flannelette sheet.
**Bibliographie** [bibliogra'fiː] *f* bibliography.

**Bibliothek** [biblio'te:k] (-, -en) f (auch COMPUT) library.
**Bibliothekar(in)** [bibliote'ka:r(ın)] (-s, -e) m(f) librarian.
**biblisch** ['bi:blıʃ] adj biblical.
**bieder** ['bi:dər] adj upright, worthy; (pej) conventional; (Kleid etc) plain.
**Biedermann** (-(e)s, pl -männer) (pej) m (geh) petty bourgeois.
**biegbar** ['bi:kba:r] adj flexible.
**Biege** f: die ~ machen (umg) to buzz off, split.
**biegen** ['bi:gən] unreg vt, vr to turn; sich vor Lachen ~ (fig) to double up with laughter; auf B~ oder Brechen (umg) by hook or by crook.
**biegsam** ['bi:kza:m] adj supple.
**Biegung** f bend, curve.
**Biene** ['bi:nə] (-, -n) f bee; (veraltet: umg: Mädchen) bird (BRIT), chick (bes US).
**Bienen-** zW: ~honig m honey; ~korb m beehive; ~stich m (KOCH) sugar-and-almond coated cake filled with custard or cream; ~stock m beehive; ~wachs nt beeswax.
**Bier** [bi:r] (-(e)s, -e) nt beer; zwei ~, bitte! two beers, please.
**Bier-** zW: ~bauch (umg) m beer belly; ~brauer m brewer; ~deckel m beer mat; ~filz m beer mat; ~krug m beer mug; ~schinken m ham sausage; ~seidel nt beer mug; ~wurst f ham sausage.
**Biest** [bi:st] (-(e)s, -er) (pej: umg) nt (Mensch) (little) wretch; (Frau) bitch (!).
**biestig** adj beastly.
**bieten** ['bi:tən] unreg vt to offer; (bei Versteigerung) to bid ♦ vr (Gelegenheit): sich jdm ~ to present itself to sb; sich dat etw ~ lassen to put up with sth.
**Bigamie** [biga'mi:] f bigamy.
**Bikini** [bi'ki:ni] (-s, -s) m bikini.
**Bilanz** [bi'lants] f balance; (fig) outcome; eine ~ aufstellen to draw up a balance sheet; ~ ziehen (aus) to take stock (of); ~prüfer m auditor.
**bilateral** ['bi:latera:l] adj bilateral; ~er Handel bilateral trade; ~es Abkommen bilateral agreement.
**Bild** [bılt] (-(e)s, -er) nt (lit, fig) picture; photo; (Spiegel~) reflection; (fig: Vorstellung) image, picture; ein ~ machen to take a photo od picture; im ~e sein (über +akk) to be in the picture (about); ~auflösung f (TV, COMPUT) resolution; ~band m illustrated book; ~bericht m pictorial report; ~beschreibung f (SCH) description of a picture.
**bilden** ['bıldən] vt to form; (erziehen) to educate; (ausmachen) to constitute ♦ vr to arise; (durch Lesen etc) to improve one's mind; (erziehen) to educate o.s.
**bildend** adj: die ~e Kunst art.
**Bilderbuch** nt picture book.
**Bilderrahmen** m picture frame.

**Bild-** zW: ~fläche f screen; (fig) scene; von der ~fläche verschwinden (fig: umg) to disappear (from the scene); b~haft adj (Sprache) vivid; ~hauer m sculptor; b~hübsch adj lovely, pretty as a picture; b~lich adj figurative; pictorial; sich dat etw b~lich vorstellen to picture sth in one's mind's eye.
**Bildnis** ['bıltnıs] nt (liter) portrait.
**Bild-** zW: ~platte f videodisc; ~röhre f (TV) cathode ray tube; ~schirm m (TV, COMPUT) screen; ~schirmgerät nt (COMPUT) visual display unit, VDU; ~schirmtext m teletext; ≈ Ceefax ®, Oracle ®; b~schön adj lovely.
**Bildtelefon** nt videophone.
**Bildung** ['bıldʊŋ] f formation; (Wissen, Benehmen) education.
**Bildungs-** zW: ~gang m school (and university/college) career; ~gut nt cultural heritage; ~lücke f gap in one's education; ~politik f educational policy; ~roman m (LITER) Bildungsroman, novel relating hero's intellectual/spiritual development; ~urlaub m educational holiday; ~weg m: auf dem zweiten ~weg through night school/ the Open University etc; ~wesen nt education system.
**Bildweite** f (PHOT) distance.
**Bildzuschrift** f reply enclosing photograph.
**Billard** ['bıljart] (-s, -e) nt billiards; ~ball m billiard ball; ~kugel f billiard ball.
**billig** ['bılıç] adj cheap; (gerecht) fair, reasonable; ~e Handelsflagge flag of convenience; ~es Geld cheap/easy money.
**billigen** ['bılıgən] vt to approve of; etw stillschweigend ~ to condone sth.
**billigerweise** adv (veraltet) in all fairness, reasonably.
**Billigladen** m discount store.
**Billigpreis** m low price.
**Billigung** f approval.
**Billion** [bılı'o:n] f billion (BRIT), trillion (US).
**bimmeln** ['bıməln] vi to tinkle.
**Bimsstein** ['bımsʃtaın] m pumice stone.
**bin** [bın] vb siehe sein.
**binär** [bi'nɛ:r] adj binary; B~zahl f binary number.
**Binde** ['bındə] (-, -n) f bandage; (Armbinde) band; (MED) sanitary towel (BRIT) od napkin (US); sich dat einen hinter die ~ gießen od kippen (umg) to put a few drinks away.
**Binde-** zW: ~glied nt connecting link; ~hautentzündung f conjunctivitis; ~mittel nt binder.
**binden** unreg vt to bind, tie ♦ vr (sich verpflichten): sich ~ (an +akk) to commit o.s. (to).
**bindend** adj binding; (Zusage) definite; ~ für binding on.
**Bindestrich** m hyphen.
**Bindewort** nt conjunction.
**Bindfaden** m string; es regnet Bindfäden

(*umg*) it's sheeting down.
**Bindung** f bond, tie; (*SKI*) binding.
**binnen** ['bɪnən] *präp* (+*dat od gen*) within;
**B~hafen** m inland harbour (*BRIT*) *od* harbor
(*US*); **B~handel** m internal trade; **B~markt** m
home market; **Europäischer B~markt** single
European market.
**Binse** ['bɪnzə] (-, -n) f rush, reed; **in die ~n
gehen** (*fig: umg: mißlingen*) to be a wash-out.
**Binsenwahrheit** f truism.
**Biographie** [biogra'fiː] f biography.
**Bioladen** ['biolaːdən] m health food shop
(*BRIT*) *od* store (*US*).

> A **Bioladen** is a shop which specializes in
> selling environmentally-friendly products such
> as phosphate-free washing powders, recycled
> paper and organically-grown vegetables.

**Biologe** [bio'loːgə] (-n, -n) m biologist.
**Biologie** [biolo'giː] f biology.
**Biologin** f biologist.
**biologisch** [bio'loːgɪʃ] *adj* biological; **~e
Vielfalt** biodiversity; **~e Uhr** biological
clock.
**Bio-** [bio-] *zW:* **~sphäre** f biosphere; **~technik**
[bio'tɛçnɪk] f biotechnology; **~treibstoff**
['biːotraipʃtɔf] m biofuel.
**birgt** [bɪrkt] *vb siehe* **bergen**.
**Birke** ['bɪrkə] (-, -n) f birch.
**Birma** ['bɪrma] (-s) *nt* Burma.
**Birnbaum** m pear tree.
**Birne** ['bɪrnə] (-, -n) f pear; (*ELEK*) (light)
bulb.
**birst** [bɪrst] *vb siehe* **bersten**.

═══════════ *SCHLÜSSELWORT*

**bis** [bɪs] *präp* +*akk, adv* **1** (*zeitlich*) till, until; (~
*spätestens*) by; **Sie haben ~ Dienstag Zeit**
you have until *od* till Tuesday; **~ zum
Wochenende** up to *od* until the weekend;
(*spätestens*) by the weekend; **~ Dienstag
muß es fertig sein** it must be ready by
Tuesday; **~ wann ist das fertig?** when will
that be finished?; **~ auf weiteres** until
further notice; **~ in die Nacht** into the night;
**~ bald!/gleich!** see you later/soon
**2** (*räumlich*) (up) to; **ich fahre ~ Köln** I'm
going as far as Cologne; **~ an unser
Grundstück** (right *od* up) to our plot;
**~ hierher** this far; **~ zur Straße kommen** to
get as far as the road
**3** (*bei Zahlen, Angaben*) up to; **~ zu** up to;
**Gefängnis ~ zu 8 Jahren** a maximum of 8
years' imprisonment
**4** **~ auf etw** *akk* (*außer*) except sth;
(*einschließlich*) including sth
♦ *konj* **1** (*mit Zahlen*) to; **10 ~ 20** 10 to 20
**2** (*zeitlich*) till, until; **~ es dunkel wird** till *od*
until it gets dark; **von ... ~ ...** from ... to ...

**Bisamratte** ['biːzamratə] f muskrat (beaver).

**Bischof** ['bɪʃɔf] (-s, ⁼e) m bishop.
**bischöflich** ['bɪʃøːflɪç] *adj* episcopal.
**bisexuell** [bizɛksu'ɛl] *adj* bisexual.
**bisher** [bɪs'heːr] *adv* till now, hitherto.
**bisherig** [bɪs'heːrɪç] *adj* till now.
**Biskaya** [bɪs'kaːya] f: **Golf von ~** Bay of
Biscay.
**Biskuit** [bɪs'kviːt] (-(e)s, -s *od* -e) m *od* nt
biscuit; **~gebäck** nt sponge cake(s); **~teig** m
sponge mixture.
**bislang** [bɪs'laŋ] *adv* hitherto.
**Biß** (-sses, -sse) m bite.
**biß** *etc* [bɪs] *vb siehe* **beißen**.
**bißchen** ['bɪsçən] *adj, adv* bit.
**Bissen** ['bɪsən] (-s, -) m bite, morsel; **sich** *dat*
**jeden ~ vom** *od* **am Munde absparen** to
watch every penny one spends.
**bissig** ['bɪsɪç] *adj* (*Hund*) snappy; vicious;
(*Bemerkung*) cutting, biting; **„Vorsicht, ~er
Hund"** "beware of the dog".
**bist** [bɪst] *vb siehe* **sein**.
**Bistum** ['bɪstuːm] *nt* bishopric.
**bisweilen** [bɪs'vaɪlən] *adv* at times,
occasionally.
**Bit** [bɪt] (-(s), -(s)) nt (*COMPUT*) bit.
**Bittbrief** m petition.
**Bitte** ['bɪtə] (-, -n) f request; **auf seine ~ hin**
at his request; **b~** *interj* please; (*als Antwort
auf Dank*) you're welcome; **wie b~?** (I beg
your) pardon?; **b~ schön!** it was a pleasure;
**b~ schön?** (*in Geschäft*) can I help you?; **na
b~!** there you are!
**bitten** *unreg vt* to ask ♦ *vi* (*einladen*): **ich lasse ~**
would you ask him/her *etc* to come in now?;
**~ um** to ask for; **aber ich bitte dich!** not at
all; **ich bitte darum** (*form*) if you wouldn't
mind; **ich muß doch (sehr) ~!** well I must
say!
**bittend** *adj* pleading, imploring.
**bitter** ['bɪtər] *adj* bitter; (*Schokolade*) plain;
**etw ~ nötig haben** to be in dire need of sth;
**~böse** *adj* very angry; **~ernst** *adj:* **damit ist
es mir ~ernst** I am deadly serious *od* in
deadly earnest; **B~keit** f bitterness; **~lich**
*adj* bitter ♦ *adv* bitterly.
**Bittsteller(in)** (-s, -) m(f) petitioner.
**Biwak** ['biːvak] (-s, -s *od* -e) *nt* bivouac.
**Bj.** *abk* = Baujahr.
**Blabla** [blaː'blaː] (-s) (*umg*) nt waffle.
**blähen** ['blɛːən] *vt, vr* to swell, blow out ♦ *vi*
(*Speisen*) to cause flatulence *od* wind.
**Blähungen** *pl* (*MED*) wind *sing.*
**blamabel** [bla'maːbəl] *adj* disgraceful.
**Blamage** [bla'maːʒə] (-, -n) f disgrace.
**blamieren** [bla'miːrən] *vr* to make a fool of
o.s., disgrace o.s. ♦ *vt* to let down, disgrace.
**blank** [blaŋk] *adj* bright; (*unbedeckt*) bare;
(*sauber*) clean, polished; (*umg: ohne Geld*)
broke; (*offensichtlich*) blatant.
**blanko** ['blaŋko] *adv* blank; **B~scheck** m blank
cheque (*BRIT*) *od* check (*US*); **B~vollmacht** f
carte blanche.

**Bläschen** ['blɛːsçən] *nt* bubble; (*MED*) small blister.

**Blase** ['blaːzə] (-, -n) *f* bubble; (*MED*) blister; (*ANAT*) bladder.

**Blasebalg** *m* bellows *pl*.

**blasen** *unreg vt, vi* to blow; **zum Aufbruch ~** (*fig*) to say it's time to go.

**Blasenentzündung** *f* cystitis.

**Bläser(in)** ['blɛːzər(ın)] (-s, -) *m(f)* (*MUS*) wind player; **die ~** the wind (section).

**blasiert** [bla'ziːrt] (*pej*) *adj* (*geh*) blasé.

**Blas-** *zW:* **~instrument** *nt* wind instrument; **~kapelle** *f* brass band; **~musik** *f* brass band music.

**blaß** [blas] *adj* pale; (*Ausdruck*) weak, insipid; (*fig: Ahnung, Vorstellung*) faint, vague; **~ vor Neid werden** to go green with envy.

**Blässe** ['blɛsə] (-) *f* paleness, pallor.

**Blatt** [blat] (-(e)s, ̈er) *nt* leaf; (*von Papier*) sheet; (*Zeitung*) newspaper; (*KARTEN*) hand; **vom ~ singen/spielen** to sight-read; **kein ~ vor den Mund nehmen** not to mince one's words.

**blättern** ['blɛtərn] *vi:* **in etw** *dat* **~** to leaf through sth.

**Blätterteig** *m* flaky *od* puff pastry.

**Blattlaus** *f* greenfly, aphid.

**blau** [blau] *adj* blue; (*umg*) drunk, stoned; (*KOCH*) boiled; (*Auge*) black; **~er Fleck** bruise; **mit einem ~en Auge davonkommen** (*fig*) to get off lightly; **~er Brief** (*SCH*) *letter telling parents a child may have to repeat a year*; **er wird sein ~es Wunder erleben** (*umg*) he won't know what's hit him; **~äugig** *adj* blue-eyed; **B~beere** *f* bilberry.

**Blaue** *nt:* **Fahrt ins ~** mystery tour; **das ~ vom Himmel (herunter) lügen** (*umg*) to tell a pack of lies.

**blau-** *zW:* **B~helm** (*umg*) *m* UN Soldier; **B~kraut** *nt* red cabbage; **B~licht** *nt* flashing blue light; **~machen** (*umg*) *vi* to skive off work; **B~pause** *f* blueprint; **B~säure** *f* prussic acid; **B~strumpf** *m* (*fig*) bluestocking.

**Blech** [blɛç] (-(e)s, -e) *nt* tin, sheet metal; (*Back~*) baking tray; **~ reden** (*umg*) to talk rubbish *od* nonsense; **~bläser** *pl* the brass (section); **~büchse** *f* tin, can; **~dose** *f* tin, can.

**blechen** (*umg*) *vt, vi* to pay.

**Blechschaden** *m* (*AUT*) damage to bodywork.

**Blechtrommel** *f* tin drum.

**blecken** [blɛkən] *vt:* **die Zähne ~** to bare *od* show øne's teeth.

**Blei** [blai] (-(e)s, -e) *nt* lead.

**Bleibe** (-, -n) *f* roof over one's head.

**bleiben** *unreg vi* to stay, remain; **bitte, ~ Sie doch sitzen** please don't get up; **wo bleibst du so lange?** (*umg*) what's keeping you?; **das bleibt unter uns** (*fig*) that's (just) between ourselves; **~lassen** *unreg vt*

(*aufgeben*) to give up; **etw ~lassen** (*unterlassen*) to give sth a miss.

**bleich** [blaiç] *adj* faded, pale; **~en** *vt* to bleach; **B~gesicht** (*umg*) *nt* (*blasser Mensch*) pastyface.

**bleiern** *adj* leaden.

**Blei-** *zW:* **b~frei** *adj* lead-free; **~gießen** *nt New Year's Eve fortune-telling using lead shapes*; **b~haltig** *adj:* **b~haltig sein** to contain lead; **~stift** *m* pencil; **~stiftabsatz** *m* stiletto heel (*BRIT*), spike heel (*US*); **~stiftspitzer** *m* pencil sharpener; **~vergiftung** *f* lead poisoning.

**Blende** ['blɛndə] (-, -n) *f* (*PHOT*) aperture; (: *Einstellungsposition*) f-stop.

**blenden** *vt* to blind, dazzle; (*fig*) to hoodwink.

**blendend** (*umg*) *adj* grand; **~ aussehen** to look smashing.

**Blender** (-s, -) *m* con-man.

**blendfrei** ['blɛntfrai] *adj* (*Glas*) non-reflective.

**Blick** [blɪk] (-(e)s, -e) *m* (*kurz*) glance, glimpse; (*Anschauen*) look, gaze; (*Aussicht*) view; **Liebe auf den ersten ~** love at first sight; **den ~ senken** to look down; **den bösen ~ haben** to have the evil eye; **einen (guten) ~ für etw haben** to have an eye for sth; **mit einem ~** at a glance.

**blicken** *vi* to look; **das läßt tief ~** that's very revealing; **sich ~ lassen** to put in an appearance.

**Blick-** *zW:* **~fang** *m* eye-catcher; **~feld** *nt* range of vision (*auch fig*); **~kontakt** *m* visual contact; **~punkt** *m:* **im ~punkt der Öffentlichkeit stehen** to be in the public eye.

**blieb** *etc* [bliːp] *vb siehe* **bleiben.**

**blies** *etc* [bliːs] *vb siehe* **blasen.**

**blind** [blɪnt] *adj* blind; (*Glas etc*) dull; (*Alarm*) false; **~er Passagier** stowaway.

**Blinddarm** *m* appendix; **~entzündung** *f* appendicitis.

**Blindekuh** ['blɪndəkuː] *f:* **~ spielen** to play blind man's buff.

**Blindenhund** *m* guide dog.

**Blindenschrift** *f* braille.

**Blind-** *zW:* **~gänger** *m* (*MIL, fig*) dud; **~heit** *f* blindness; **mit ~heit geschlagen sein** (*fig*) to be blind; **b~lings** *adv* blindly; **~schleiche** *f* slow worm; **b~schreiben** *unreg vi* to touchtype.

**blinken** ['blɪŋkən] *vi* to twinkle, sparkle; (*Licht*) to flash, signal; (*AUT*) to indicate ♦ *vt* to flash, signal.

**Blinker** (-s, -) *m* (*AUT*) indicator.

**Blinklicht** *nt* (*AUT*) indicator.

**blinzeln** ['blɪntsəln] *vi* to blink, wink.

**Blitz** [blɪts] (-es, -e) *m* (flash of) lightning; **wie ein ~ aus heiterem Himmel** (*fig*) like a bolt from the blue; **~ableiter** *m* lightning conductor; (*fig*) vent *od* safety valve for feelings; **b~en** *vi* (*aufleuchten*) to glint, shine; **es b~t** (*MET*) there's a flash of lightning; **~gerät** *nt* (*PHOT*) flash(gun);

~**licht** nt flashlight; **b~sauber** adj spick and span; **b~schnell** adj, adv as quick as a flash; ~**würfel** m (PHOT) flashcube.

**Block** [blɔk] (-(e)s, ⸚e) m (lit, fig) block; (von Papier) pad; (POL: Staaten~) bloc; (Fraktion) faction.

**Blockade** [blɔ'ka:də] (-, -n) f blockade.

**Block-** zW: ~**buchstabe** m block letter od capital; ~**flöte** f recorder; **b~frei** adj (POL) non-aligned; ~**haus** nt log cabin; ~**hütte** f log cabin.

**blockieren** [blɔ'ki:rən] vt to block ♦ vi (Räder) to jam.

**Block-** zW: ~**schokolade** f cooking chocolate; ~**schrift** f block letters pl; ~**stunde** f double period.

**blöd** [blø:t] adj silly, stupid.

**blödeln** ['blø:dəln] (umg) vi to fool around.

**Blödheit** f stupidity.

**Blödian** ['blø:dian] (-(e)s, -e) (umg) m idiot.

**blöd-** zW: **B~mann** (-(e)s, pl **-männer**) (umg) m idiot; **B~sinn** m nonsense; ~**sinnig** adj silly, idiotic.

**blöken** ['blø:kən] vi (Schaf) to bleat.

**blond** [blɔnt] adj blond(e), fair-haired.

**Blondine** [blɔn'di:nə] f blonde.

================= *SCHLÜSSELWORT*

**bloß** [blo:s] adj **1** (unbedeckt) bare; (nackt) naked; **mit der ~en Hand** with one's bare hand; **mit ~em Auge** with the naked eye **2** (alleinig: nur) mere; **der ~e Gedanke** the very thought; ~**er Neid** sheer envy ♦ adv only, merely; **laß das ~!** just don't do that!; **wie ist das ~ passiert?** how on earth did that happen?

**Blöße** ['blø:sə] (-, -n) f bareness; nakedness; (fig) weakness; **sich** dat **eine ~ geben** (fig) to lay o.s. open to attack.

**bloßlegen** vt to expose.

**bloßstellen** vt to show up.

**blühen** ['bly:ən] vi (lit) to bloom, be in bloom; (fig) to flourish; (umg: bevorstehen): **(jdm) ~** to be in store for sb.

**blühend** adj: **wie das ~e Leben aussehen** to look the very picture of health.

**Blume** ['blu:mə] (-, -n) f flower; (von Wein) bouquet; **jdm etw durch die ~ sagen** to say sth in a roundabout way to sb.

**Blumen-** zW: ~**geschäft** nt flower shop, florist's; ~**kasten** m window box; ~**kohl** m cauliflower; ~**strauß** m bouquet, bunch of flowers; ~**topf** m flowerpot; ~**zwiebel** f bulb.

**Bluse** ['blu:zə] (-, -n) f blouse.

**Blut** [blu:t] (-(e)s) nt (lit, fig) blood; **(nur) ruhig ~** keep your shirt on (umg); **jdn/sich bis aufs ~ bekämpfen** to fight sb/fight bitterly; **b~arm** adj anaemic (BRIT), anemic (US); (fig) penniless; ~**bahn** f bloodstream; ~**bank** f blood bank; **b~befleckt** adj bloodstained;

~**bild** nt blood count; ~**buche** f copper beech; ~**druck** m blood pressure.

**Blüte** ['bly:tə] (-, -n) f blossom; (fig) prime.

**Blutegel** ['blu:t|e:gəl] m leech.

**bluten** vi to bleed.

**Blütenstaub** m pollen.

**Bluter** (-s, -) m (MED) haemophiliac (BRIT), hemophiliac (US).

**Bluterguß** m haemorrhage (BRIT), hemorrhage (US); (auf Haut) bruise.

**Blütezeit** f flowering period; (fig) prime.

**Blutgerinnsel** nt blood clot.

**Blutgruppe** f blood group.

**blutig** adj bloody; (umg: Anfänger) absolute; (: Ernst) deadly.

**Blut-** zW: **b~jung** adj very young; ~**konserve** f unit od pint of stored blood; ~**körperchen** nt blood corpuscle; ~**probe** f blood test; **b~rünstig** adj bloodthirsty; ~**schande** f incest; ~**senkung** f (MED): **eine ~senkung machen** to test the sedimentation rate of the blood; ~**spender** m blood donor; **b~stillend** adj styptic; ~**sturz** m haemorrhage (BRIT), hemorrhage (US).

**blutsverwandt** adj related by blood.

**Blutübertragung** f blood transfusion.

**Blutung** f bleeding, haemorrhage (BRIT), hemorrhage (US).

**Blut-** zW: **b~unterlaufen** adj suffused with blood; (Augen) bloodshot; ~**vergießen** nt bloodshed; ~**vergiftung** f blood poisoning; ~**wurst** f black pudding; ~**zuckerspiegel** m blood sugar level.

**BLZ** abk = **Bankleitzahl.**

**BMX-Rad** nt BMX.

**BND** (-s, -) m abk = **Bundesnachrichtendienst.**

**Bö** (-, -en) f squall.

**Boccia** ['bɔtʃa] nt od f bowls sing.

**Bock** [bɔk] (-(e)s, ⸚e) m buck, ram; (Gestell) trestle, support; (SPORT) buck; **alter ~** (umg) old goat; **den ~ zum Gärtner machen** (fig) to choose the worst possible person for the job; **einen ~ schießen** (fig: umg) to (make a) boob; ~ **haben, etw zu tun** (umg: Lust) to fancy doing sth.

**Bockbier** nt bock (beer) (type of strong beer).

**bocken** ['bɔkən] (umg) vi (Auto, Mensch) to play up.

**Bocksbeutel** m wide, rounded (dumpy) bottle containing Franconian wine.

**Bockshorn** nt: **sich von jdm ins ~ jagen lassen** to let sb upset one.

**Bocksprung** m leapfrog; (SPORT) vault.

**Bockwurst** f bockwurst (large frankfurter).

**Boden** ['bo:dən] (-s, ⸚) m ground; (Fuß~) floor; (Meeres~, Faß~) bottom; (Speicher) attic; **den ~ unter den Füßen verlieren** (lit) to lose one's footing; (fig: in Diskussion) to get out of one's depth; **ich hätte (vor Scham) im ~ versinken können** (fig) I was so ashamed, I wished the ground would swallow me up; **am ~ zerstört sein** (umg) to be shattered;

etw aus dem ~ **stampfen** (*fig*) to conjure sth
up out of nothing; (*Häuser*) to build
overnight; **auf dem ~ der Tatsachen bleiben**
(*fig: Grundlage*) to stick to the facts; **zu**
~ **fallen** to fall to the ground; **festen ~ unter**
**den Füßen haben** to be on firm ground, be
on terra firma; ~**kontrolle** *f* (*RAUMFAHRT*)
ground control; **b~los** *adj* bottomless; (*umg*)
incredible; ~**personal** *nt* (*AVIAT*) ground
personnel *pl*, ground staff; ~**satz** *m* dregs *pl*,
sediment; ~**schätze** *pl* mineral wealth *sing*.

**Bodensee** ['boːdənzeː] *m:* **der ~** Lake
Constance.

**Bodenturnen** *nt* floor exercises *pl*.

**Böe** (-, -n) *f* squall.

**bog** *etc* [boːk] *vb siehe* **biegen**.

**Bogen** ['boːgən] (-s, -) *m* (*Biegung*) curve;
(*ARCHIT*) arch; (*Waffe, MUS*) bow; (*Papier*)
sheet; **den ~ heraushaben** (*umg*) to have got
the hang of it; **einen großen ~ um jdn/etw**
**machen** (*meiden*) to give sb/sth a wide
berth; **jdn in hohem ~ hinauswerfen** (*umg*)
to fling sb out; ~**gang** *m* arcade; ~**schütze** *m*
archer.

**Bohle** ['boːlə] (-, -n) *f* plank.

**Böhme** ['bøːmə] (-n, -n) *m* Bohemian.

**Böhmen** (-s) *nt* Bohemia.

**Böhmin** *f* Bohemian woman.

**böhmisch** ['bøːmɪʃ] *adj* Bohemian; **das sind**
**für mich ~e Dörfer** (*umg*) that's all Greek to
me.

**Bohne** ['boːnə] (-, -n) *f* bean; **blaue ~** (*umg*)
bullet; **nicht die ~** not one little bit.

**Bohnen-** *zW:* ~**kaffee** *m* real coffee; ~**stange**
*f* (*fig: umg*) beanpole; ~**stroh** *nt:* **dumm wie**
~**stroh** (*umg*) (as) thick as two (short)
planks.

**bohnern** *vt* to wax, polish.

**Bohnerwachs** *nt* floor polish.

**bohren** ['boːrən] *vt* to bore; (*Loch*) to drill ♦ *vi*
to drill; (*fig: drängen*) to keep on; (*peinigen:*
*Schmerz, Zweifel etc*) to gnaw; **nach Öl/**
**Wasser ~** drill for oil/water; **in der Nase ~**
to pick one's nose.

**Bohrer** (-s, -) *m* drill.

**Bohr-** *zW:* ~**insel** *f* oil rig; ~**maschine** *f* drill;
~**turm** *m* derrick.

**Boiler** ['boylər] (-s, -) *m* water heater.

**Boje** ['boːjə] (-, -n) *f* buoy.

**Bolivianer(in)** [bolivi'aːnər(ɪn)] (-s, -) *m(f)*
Bolivian.

**Bolivien** [bo'liːviən] *nt* Bolivia.

**bolivisch** [bo'liːvɪʃ] *adj* Bolivian.

**Bollwerk** ['bɔlvɛrk] *nt* (*lit, fig*) bulwark.

**Bolschewismus** [bɔlʃe'vɪsmʊs] (-) *m*
Bolshevism.

**Bolzen** ['bɔltsən] (-s, -) *m* bolt.

**bombardieren** [bɔmbar'diːrən] *vt* to bombard;
(*aus der Luft*) to bomb.

**Bombe** ['bɔmbə] (-, -n) *f* bomb; **wie eine**
~ **einschlagen** to come as a (real)
bombshell.

**Bomben-** *zW:* ~**alarm** *m* bomb scare;
~**angriff** *m* bombing raid; ~**anschlag** *m* bomb
attack; ~**erfolg** (*umg*) *m* huge success;
~**geschäft** (*umg*) *nt:* **ein ~geschäft machen** to
do a roaring trade; **b~sicher** (*umg*) *adj* dead
certain.

**bombig** (*umg*) *adj* great, super.

**Bon** [bɔŋ] (-s, -s) *m* voucher; (*Kassenzettel*)
receipt.

**Bonbon** [bõ'bõː] (-s, -s) *nt od m* sweet.

**Bonn** [bɔn] (-s) *nt* Bonn.

**Bonze** ['bɔntsə] (-n, -n) *m* big shot (*umg*).

**Bonzenviertel** (*umg*) *nt* posh quarter (*of*
*town*).

**Boot** [boːt] (-(e)s, -e) *nt* boat.

**Bord** [bɔrt] (-(e)s, -e) *m* (*AVIAT, NAUT*) board
♦ *nt* (*Brett*) shelf; **über ~ gehen** to go
overboard; (*fig*) to go by the board; **an ~** on
board.

**Bordell** [bɔr'dɛl] (-s, -e) *nt* brothel.

**Bordfunkanlage** *f* radio.

**Bordstein** *m* kerb(stone) (*BRIT*), curb(stone)
(*US*).

**borgen** ['bɔrgən] *vt* to borrow; **jdm etw ~** to
lend sb sth.

**Borneo** ['bɔrneo] (-s) *nt* Borneo.

**borniert** [bɔr'niːrt] *adj* narrow-minded.

**Börse** ['bœrzə] (-, -n) *f* stock exchange;
(*Geld~*) purse.

**Börsen-** *zW:* ~**makler** *m* stockbroker;
**b~notiert** *adj:* **b~notierte Firma** listed
company; ~**notierung** *f* quotation (on the
stock exchange).

**Borste** ['bɔrstə] (-, -n) *f* bristle.

**Borte** ['bɔrtə] (-, -n) *f* edging; (*Band*)
trimming.

**bös** [bøːs] *adj* = **böse**; ~**artig** *adj* malicious;
(*MED*) malignant.

**Böschung** ['bœʃʊŋ] *f* slope; (*Ufer~ etc*)
embankment.

**böse** ['bøːzə] *adj* bad, evil; (*zornig*) angry; **das**
**war nicht ~ gemeint** I/he *etc* didn't mean it
nastily.

**Bösewicht** (*umg*) *m* baddy.

**boshaft** ['boːshaft] *adj* malicious, spiteful.

**Bosheit** *f* malice, spite.

**Bosnien** ['bɔsniən] (-s) *nt* Bosnia.

**Bosnien-Herzegowina**
['bɔsniənhɛrtsə'goːviːna] (-s) *nt* Bosnia-
Herzegovina.

**Bosnier(in)** (-s, -) *m(f)* Bosnian.

**bosnisch** *adj* Bosnian.

**Boß** [bɔs] (-sses, -sse) (*umg*) *m* boss.

**böswillig** ['bøːsvɪlɪç] *adj* malicious.

**bot** *etc* [boːt] *vb siehe* **bieten**.

**Botanik** [bo'taːnɪk] *f* botany.

**botanisch** [bo'taːnɪʃ] *adj* botanical.

**Bote** ['boːtə] (-n, -n) *m* messenger.

**Botengang** *m* errand.

**Botenjunge** *m* errand boy.

**Botin** ['boːtɪn] *f* messenger.

**Botschaft** *f* message, news; (*POL*) embassy;

**die Frohe ~** the Gospel; **~er (-s, -)** *m* ambassador.

**Botswana** [bɔ'tsvaːna] **(-s)** *nt* Botswana.

**Bottich** ['bɔtɪç] **(-(e)s, -e)** *m* vat, tub.

**Bouillon** [buˈljõː] **(-, -s)** *f* consommé.

**Boulevard-** [buləˈvaːr] *zW:* **~blatt** (*umg*) *nt* tabloid; **~presse** *f* tabloid press; **~stück** *nt* light play/comedy.

**Boutique** [buˈtiːk] **(-, -n)** *f* boutique.

**Bowle** ['boːlə] **(-, -n)** *f* punch.

**Bowlingbahn** ['boːlɪŋbaːn] *f* bowling alley.

**Box** [bɔks] *f* (*Lautsprecher~*) speaker.

**boxen** *vi* to box.

**Boxer (-s, -)** *m* boxer.

**Boxhandschuh** *m* boxing glove.

**Boxkampf** *m* boxing match.

**Boykott** [bɔyˈkɔt] **(-(e)s, -s)** *m* boycott.

**boykottieren** [bɔykɔˈtiːrən] *vt* to boycott.

**BR** *abk* (*= Bayerischer Rundfunk*) *German radio station*.

**brach** *etc* [braːx] *vb siehe* **brechen**.

**brachial** [braxiˈaːl] *adj:* **mit ~er Gewalt** by brute force.

**brachliegen** ['braːxliːgən] *unreg vi* (*lit, fig*) to lie fallow.

**brachte** *etc* ['braxtə] *vb siehe* **bringen**.

**Branche** ['brãːʃə] **(-, -n)** *f* line of business.

**Branchenverzeichnis** *nt* trade directory.

**Brand** [brant] **(-(e)s, ⁻e)** *m* fire; (*MED*) gangrene.

**Brandanschlag** *m* arson attack.

**branden** ['brandən] *vi* to surge; (*Meer*) to break.

**Brandenburg** ['brandənburk] **(-s)** *nt* Brandenburg.

**Brandherd** *m* source of the fire.

**brandmarken** *vt* to brand; (*fig*) to stigmatize.

**brandneu** (*umg*) *adj* brand-new.

**Brand-** *zW:* **~salbe** *f* ointment for burns; **~satz** *m* incendiary device; **~stifter** *m* arsonist, fire-raiser; **~stiftung** *f* arson.

**Brandung** *f* surf.

**Brandwunde** *f* burn.

**brannte** *etc* ['brantə] *vb siehe* **brennen**.

**Branntwein** ['brantvaɪn] *m* brandy; **~steuer** *f* tax on spirits.

**Brasilianer(in)** [braziliˈaːnɔr(ɪn)] **(-s, -)** *m(f)* Brazilian.

**brasilianisch** *adj* Brazilian.

**Brasilien** [braˈziːliən] *nt* Brazil.

**brät** [brɛt] *vb siehe* **braten**.

**Bratapfel** *m* baked apple.

**braten** ['braːtən] *unreg vt* to roast; (*in Pfanne*) to fry; **B~ (-s, -)** *m* roast, joint; **den B~ riechen** (*umg*) to smell a rat, suss something.

**Brat-** *zW:* **~hähnchen** *nt* (*SÜDD, ÖSTERR*) roast chicken; **~hendl** *nt* roast chicken; **~huhn** *nt* roast chicken; **~kartoffeln** *pl* fried/roast potatoes *pl*; **~pfanne** *f* frying pan; **~rost** *m* grill.

**Bratsche** ['braːtʃə] **(-, -n)** *f* viola.

**Bratspieß** *m* spit.

**Bratwurst** *f* grilled sausage.

**Brauch** [braux] **(-(e)s,** *pl* **Bräuche)** *m* custom.

**brauchbar** *adj* usable, serviceable; (*Person*) capable.

**brauchen** *vt* (*bedürfen*) to need; (*müssen*) to have to; (*verwenden*) to use; **wie lange braucht man, um ...?** how long does it take to ...?

**Brauchtum** *nt* customs *pl*, traditions *pl*.

**Braue** ['brauə] **(-, -n)** *f* brow.

**brauen** ['brauən] *vt* to brew.

**Brauerei** [brauəˈraɪ] *f* brewery.

**braun** [braun] *adj* brown; (*von Sonne*) tanned; (*pej*) Nazi.

**Bräune** ['brɔynə] **(-, -n)** *f* brownness; (*Sonnen~*) tan.

**bräunen** *vt* to make brown; (*Sonne*) to tan.

**braungebrannt** *adj* tanned.

**Braunkohle** *f* brown coal.

**Braunschweig** ['braunʃvaɪk] **(-s)** *nt* Brunswick.

**Brause** ['brauzə] **(-, -n)** *f* shower; (*von Gießkanne*) rose; (*Getränk*) lemonade.

**brausen** *vi* to roar; (*auch vr: duschen*) to take a shower.

**Brausepulver** *nt* lemonade powder.

**Brausetablette** *f* lemonade tablet.

**Braut** [braut] **(-,** *pl* **Bräute)** *f* bride; (*Verlobte*) fiancée.

**Bräutigam** ['brɔytɪgam] **(-s, -e)** *m* bridegroom; (*Verlobter*) fiancé.

**Braut-** *zW:* **~jungfer** *f* bridesmaid; **~kleid** *nt* wedding dress; **~paar** *nt* bride and bridegroom, bridal pair.

**brav** [braːf] *adj* (*artig*) good; (*ehrenhaft*) worthy, honest; (*bieder: Frisur, Kleid*) plain; **sei schön ~!** be a good boy/girl.

**BRD (-)** *f abk* (*= Bundesrepublik Deutschland*) FRG; **die alte ~** former West Germany.

> *The **BRD** (Bundesrepublik Deutschland) is the official name for the Federal Republic of Germany. It comprises 16 **Länder** (see **Land**). It was originally the name given to the former West Germany as opposed to East Germany (the **DDR**). The two Germanies were reunited on 3rd October 1990.*

**Brechbohne** *f* French bean.

**Brecheisen** *nt* crowbar.

**brechen** *unreg vt, vi* to break; (*Licht*) to refract; (*speien*) to vomit; **die Ehe ~** to commit adultery; **mir bricht das Herz** it breaks my heart; **~d voll sein** to be full to bursting.

**Brechmittel** *nt:* **er/das ist das reinste ~** (*umg*) he/it makes me feel ill.

**Brechreiz** *m* nausea.

**Brechung** *f* (*des Lichts*) refraction.

**Brei** [braɪ] **(-(e)s, -e)** *m* (*Masse*) pulp; (*KOCH*) gruel; (*Hafer~*) porridge (*BRIT*), oatmeal (*US*); (*für Kinder, Kranke*) mash; **um den heißen ~ herumreden** (*umg*) to beat about the bush.

**breit** [braɪt] *adj* broad; (*bei Maßangabe*) wide; **die ~e Masse** the masses *pl*; **~beinig** *adj* with one's legs apart.

**Breite** (-, -n) *f* breadth; (*bei Maßangabe*) width; (*GEOG*) latitude.

**breiten** *vt*: **etw über etw** *akk* ~ to spread sth over sth.

**Breitengrad** *m* degree of latitude.

**Breitensport** *m* popular sport.

**breit-** *zW*: **~gefächert** *adj*: **ein ~gefächertes** · **Angebot** a wide range; **~machen** *vr* to spread o.s. out; **~schlagen** *unreg* (*umg*) *vt*: **sich ~schlagen lassen** to let o.s. be talked round; **~schult(e)rig** *adj* broad-shouldered; **~treten** *unreg* (*umg*) *vt* to go on about; **B~wandfilm** *m* wide-screen film.

**Bremen** ['breːmən] (-s) *nt* Bremen.

**Bremsbelag** *m* brake lining.

**Bremse** ['brɛmzə] (-, -n) *f* brake; (*ZOOL*) horsefly.

**bremsen** *vi* to brake, apply the brakes ♦ *vt* (*Auto*) to brake; (*fig*) to slow down ♦ *vr*: **ich kann mich ~** (*umg*) not likely!

**Brems-** *zW*: **~flüssigkeit** *f* brake fluid; **~licht** *nt* brake light; **~pedal** *nt* brake pedal; **~schuh** *m* brake shoe; **~spur** *f* tyre (*BRIT*) *od* tire (*US*) marks *pl*; **~weg** *m* braking distance.

**brennbar** *adj* inflammable; **leicht ~** highly inflammable.

**Brennelement** *nt* fuel element.

**brennen** ['brɛnən] *unreg* *vi* to burn, be on fire; (*Licht, Kerze etc*) to burn ♦ *vt* (*Holz etc*) to burn; (*Ziegel, Ton*) to fire; (*Kaffee*) to roast; (*Branntwein*) to distil; **wo brennt's denn?** (*fig: umg*) what's the panic?; **darauf ~, etw zu tun** to be dying to do sth.

**Brenn-** *zW*: **~material** *nt* fuel; **~(n)essel** *f* nettle; **~ofen** *m* kiln; **~punkt** *m* (*MATH, OPTIK*) focus; **~spiritus** *m* methylated spirits *pl*; **~stoff** *m* liquid fuel.

**brenzlig** ['brɛntslɪç] *adj* smelling of burning, burnt; (*fig*) precarious.

**Bresche** ['brɛʃə] (-, -n) *f*: **in die ~ springen** (*fig*) to step into the breach.

**Bretagne** [bre'tanjə] *f*: **die ~** Brittany.

**Bretone** [bre'toːnə] (-n, -n) *m* Breton.

**Bretonin** [bre'toːnɪn] *f* Breton.

**Brett** [brɛt] (-(e)s, -er) *nt* board, plank; (*Bord*) shelf; (*Spiel~*) board; **Bretter** *pl* (*SKI*) skis *pl*; (*THEAT*) boards *pl*; **Schwarzes ~** notice board; **er hat ein ~ vor dem Kopf** (*umg*) he's really thick.

**brettern** (*umg*) *vi* to speed.

**Bretterzaun** *m* wooden fence.

**Brezel** ['breːtsəl] (-, -n) *f* pretzel.

**bricht** [brɪçt] *vb siehe* **brechen**.

**Brief** [briːf] (-(e)s, -e) *m* letter; **~beschwerer** (-s, -) *m* paperweight; **~drucksache** *f* circular; **~freund(in)** *m(f)* pen friend, pen-pal; **~kasten** *m* letter box; (*COMPUT*)

mailbox; **~kopf** *m* letterhead; **b~lich** *adj, adv* by letter; **~marke** *f* postage stamp; **~öffner** *m* letter opener; **~papier** *nt* notepaper; **~qualität** *f* (*COMPUT*) letter quality; **~tasche** *f* wallet; **~taube** *f* carrier pigeon; **~träger** *m* postman; **~umschlag** *m* envelope; **~wahl** *f* postal vote; **~wechsel** *m* correspondence.

**briet** *etc* [briːt] *vb siehe* **braten**.

**Brigade** [bri'gaːdə] (-, -n) *f* (*MIL*) brigade; (*DDR*) (work) team *od* group.

**Brikett** [bri'kɛt] (-s, -s) *nt* briquette.

**brillant** [brɪl'jant] *adj* (*fig*) sparkling, brilliant; **B~** (-en, -en) *m* brilliant, diamond.

**Brille** ['brɪlə] (-, -n) *f* spectacles *pl*; (*Schutz~*) goggles *pl*; (*Toiletten~*) (toilet) seat.

**Brillenschlange** *f* (*hum*) four-eyes.

**Brillenträger(in)** *m(f)*: **er ist ~** he wears glasses.

**bringen** ['brɪŋən] *unreg* *vt* to bring; (*mitnehmen, begleiten*) to take; (*einbringen: Profit*) to bring in; (*veröffentlichen*) to publish; (*THEAT, FILM*) to show; (*RUNDF, TV*) to broadcast; (*in einen Zustand versetzen*) to get; (*umg: tun können*) to manage; **jdn dazu ~, etw zu tun** to make sb do sth; **jdn zum Lachen/Weinen ~** to make sb laugh/cry; **es weit ~** to do very well, get far; **jdn nach Hause ~** to take sb home; **jdn um etw ~** to make sb lose sth; **jdn auf eine Idee ~** to give sb an idea.

**brisant** [bri'zant] *adj* (*fig*) controversial.

**Brisanz** [bri'zants] *f* (*fig*) controversial nature.

**Brise** ['briːzə] (-, -n) *f* breeze.

**Brite** ['briːtə] (-n, -n) *m* Briton, Britisher (*US*); **die ~n** the British.

**Britin** *f* Briton, Britisher (*US*).

**britisch** ['briːtɪʃ] *adj* British; **die B~en Inseln** the British Isles.

**bröckelig** ['brœkəlɪç] *adj* crumbly.

**Brocken** ['brɔkən] (-s, -) *m* piece, bit; (*Felsbrocken*) lump of rock; **ein paar ~ Spanisch** a smattering of Spanish; **ein harter ~** (*umg*) a tough nut to crack.

**brodeln** ['broːdəln] *vi* to bubble.

**Brokat** [bro'kaːt] (-(e)s, -e) *m* brocade.

**Brokkoli** ['brɔkoli] *pl* broccoli.

**Brombeere** ['brɔmbeːrə] *f* blackberry, bramble (*BRIT*).

**bronchial** [brɔnçi'aːl] *adj* bronchial.

**Bronchien** ['brɔnçiən] *pl* bronchial tubes *pl*.

**Bronchitis** [brɔn'çiːtɪs] (-, -tiden) *f* bronchitis.

**Bronze** ['brõːsə] (-, -n) *f* bronze.

**Brosame** ['broːzaːmə] (-, -n) *f* crumb.

**Brosche** ['brɔʃə] (-, -n) *f* brooch.

**Broschüre** [brɔ'ʃyːrə] (-, -n) *f* pamphlet.

**Brot** [broːt] (-(e)s, -e) *nt* bread; (*~laib*) loaf; **das ist ein hartes ~** (*fig*) that's a hard way to earn one's living.

**Brötchen** ['brøːtçən] *nt* roll; **kleine ~ backen** (*fig*) to set one's sights lower; **~geber** *m* (*hum*) employer, provider (*hum*).

**brotlos** ['broːtloːs] *adj* (*Person*) unemployed; (*Arbeit etc*) unprofitable.

**Brotzeit** (*SÜDD*) *f* (*Pause*) ≈ tea break.

**BRT** *abk* (= *Bruttoregistertonne*) GRT.

**Bruch** [brʊx] (-(e)s, ̈-e) *m* breakage; (*zerbrochene Stelle*) break; (*fig*) split, breach; (*MED: Eingeweide~*) rupture, hernia; (*Bein~ etc*) fracture; (*MATH*) fraction; **zu ~ gehen** to get broken; **sich einen ~ heben** to rupture o.s.; **~bude** (*umg*) *f* shack.

**brüchig** ['brʏçɪç] *adj* brittle, fragile.

**Bruch-** *zW:* **~landung** *f* crash landing; **~schaden** *m* breakage; **~stelle** *f* break; (*von Knochen*) fracture; **~strich** *m* (*MATH*) line; **~stück** *nt* fragment; **~teil** *m* fraction.

**Brücke** ['brʏkə] (-, -n) *f* bridge; (*Teppich*) rug; (*Turnen*) crab.

**Bruder** ['bruːdər] (-s, ̈-) *m* brother; **unter Brüdern** (*umg*) between friends.

**brüderlich** *adj* brotherly; **B~keit** *f* fraternity.

**Brudermord** *m* fratricide.

**Brüderschaft** *f* brotherhood, fellowship; **~ trinken** to agree to use the familiar "du" (*over a drink*).

**Brühe** ['brʏːə] (-, -n) *f* broth, stock; (*pej*) muck.

**brühwarm** ['brʏː'varm] (*umg*) *adj:* **er hat das sofort ~ weitererzählt** he promptly spread it around.

**Brühwürfel** *m* stock cube (*BRIT*), bouillon cube (*US*).

**brüllen** ['brʏlən] *vi* to bellow, roar.

**Brummbär** *m* grumbler.

**brummeln** ['brʊməln] *vt, vi* to mumble.

**brummen** *vi* (*Bär, Mensch etc*) to growl; (*Insekt, Radio*) to buzz; (*Motor*) to roar; (*murren*) to grumble ♦ *vt* to growl; **jdm brummt der Kopf** sb's head is buzzing.

**Brummer** ['brʊmər] (-s, -) (*umg*) *m* (*Lastwagen*) juggernaut.

**Brummi** ['brʊmi] (*umg*) *m* lorry, juggernaut.

**brummig** (*umg*) *adj* grumpy.

**Brummschädel** (*umg*) *m* thick head.

**brünett** [brʏ'nɛt] *adj* brunette, brown-haired.

**Brunnen** ['brʊnən] (-s, -) *m* fountain; (*tief*) well; (*natürlich*) spring; **~kresse** *f* watercress.

**Brunst** [brʊnst] *f* (*von männlichen Tieren*) rut; (*von weiblichen Tieren*) heat; **~zeit** *f* rutting season.

**brüsk** [brʏsk] *adj* abrupt, brusque.

**brüskieren** [brʏs'kiːrən] *vt* to snub.

**Brüssel** ['brʏsəl] (-s) *nt* Brussels.

**Brust** [brʊst] (-, ̈-e) *f* breast; (*Männer~*) chest; **einem Kind die ~ geben** to breast-feed (*BRIT*) *od* nurse (*US*) a baby.

**brüsten** ['brʏstən] *vr* to boast.

**Brust-** *zW:* **~fellentzündung** *f* pleurisy; **~kasten** *m* chest; **~korb** *m* (*ANAT*) thorax; **~schwimmen** *nt* breast-stroke; **~ton** *m:* **im ~ton der Überzeugung** in a tone of utter conviction.

**Brüstung** ['brʏstʊŋ] *f* parapet.

**Brustwarze** *f* nipple.

**Brut** [bruːt] (-, -en) *f* brood; (*Brüten*) hatching.

**brutal** [bru'taːl] *adj* brutal; **B~ität** *f* brutality.

**Brutapparat** *m* incubator.

**brüten** ['brʏːtən] *vi* (*auch fig*) to brood; **~de Hitze** oppressive *od* stifling heat.

**Brüter** (-s, -) *m* (*TECH*): **schneller ~** fast-breeder (reactor).

**Brutkasten** *m* incubator.

**Brutstätte** *f* (+*gen*) (*lit, fig*) breeding ground (for).

**brutto** ['brʊto] *adv* gross; **B~einkommen** *nt* gross salary; **B~gehalt** *nt* gross salary; **B~gewicht** *nt* gross weight; **B~gewinn** *m* gross profit; **B~inlandsprodukt** *nt* gross domestic product; **B~lohn** *m* gross wages *pl*; **B~sozialprodukt** *nt* gross national product.

**brutzeln** ['brʊtsəln] (*umg*) *vi* to sizzle away ♦ *vt* to fry (up).

**Btx** *abk* = **Bildschirmtext**.

**Bub** [buːp] (-en, -en) *m* boy, lad.

**Bube** ['buːbə] (-n, -n) *m* (*Schurke*) rogue; (*KARTEN*) jack.

**Bubikopf** *m* bobbed hair.

**Buch** [buːx] (-(e)s, ̈-er) *nt* book; (*COMM*) account book; **er redet wie ein ~** (*umg*) he never stops talking; **ein ~ mit sieben Siegeln** (*fig*) a closed book; **über etw** *akk* **~ führen** to keep a record of sth; **zu ~(e) schlagen** to make a significant difference, tip the balance; **~binder** *m* bookbinder; **~drucker** *m* printer.

**Buche** (-, -n) *f* beech tree.

**buchen** *vt* to book; (*Betrag*) to enter; **etw als Erfolg ~** to put sth down as a success.

**Bücherbord** ['byːçər-] *nt* bookshelf.

**Bücherbrett** *nt* bookshelf.

**Bücherei** [byːçə'raɪ] *f* library.

**Bücherregal** *nt* bookshelves *pl*, bookcase.

**Bücherschrank** *m* bookcase.

**Bücherwurm** (*umg*) *m* bookworm.

**Buchfink** ['buːxfɪŋk] *m* chaffinch.

**Buch-** *zW:* **~führung** *f* book-keeping, accounting; **~halter(in)** (-s, -) *m(f)* book-keeper; **~handel** *m* book trade; **im ~handel erhältlich** available in bookshops; **~händler(in)** *m(f)* bookseller; **~handlung** *f* bookshop; **~prüfung** *f* audit; **~rücken** *m* spine.

**Büchse** ['bʏksə] (-, -n) *f* tin, can; (*Holz~*) box; (*Gewehr*) rifle.

**Büchsenfleisch** *nt* tinned meat.

**Büchsenöffner** *m* tin *od* can opener.

**Buchstabe** (-ns, -n) *m* letter (of the alphabet).

**buchstabieren** [buːxʃta'biːrən] *vt* to spell.

**buchstäblich** ['buːxʃtɛːplɪç] *adj* literal.

**Buchstütze** *f* book end.

**Bucht** ['bʊxt] (-, -en) *f* bay.

**Buchung** ['buːxʊŋ] *f* booking; (*COMM*) entry.

**Buchweizen** *m* buckwheat.
**Buchwert** *m* book value.
**Buckel** ['bʊkəl] (**-s, -**) *m* hump; **er kann mir den** ~ **runterrutschen** (*umg*) he can (go and) take a running jump.
**buckeln** (*pej*) *vi* to bow and scrape.
**bücken** ['bʏkən] *vr* to bend; **sich nach etw** ~ **to** bend down *od* stoop to pick sth up.
**Bückling** ['bʏklɪŋ] *m* (*Fisch*) kipper; (*Verbeugung*) bow.
**Budapest** ['buːdapɛst] (**-s**) *nt* Budapest.
**buddeln** ['bʊdəln] (*umg*) *vi* to dig.
**Bude** ['buːdə] (**-, -n**) *f* booth, stall; (*umg*) digs *pl* (*BRIT*) *od* place (*US*); **jdm die** ~ **einrennen** (*umg*) to pester sb.
**Budget** [by'dʒeː] (**-s, -s**) *nt* budget.
**Büfett** [by'fɛt] (**-s, -s**) *nt* (*Anrichte*) sideboard; (*Geschirrschrank*) dresser; **kaltes** ~ cold buffet.
**Büffel** ['bʏfəl] (**-s, -**) *m* buffalo.
**büffeln** ['bʏfəln] (*umg*) *vi* to swot, cram ♦ *vt* (*Lernstoff*) to swot up.
**Bug** [buːk] (**-(e)s, -e**) *m* (*NAUT*) bow; (*AVIAT*) nose.
**Bügel** ['byːgəl] (**-s, -**) *m* (*Kleider~*) hanger; (*Steig~*) stirrup; (*Brillen~*) arm; ~**brett** *nt* ironing board; ~**eisen** *nt* iron; ~**falte** *f* crease; **b~frei** *adj* non-iron; (*Hemd*) drip-dry.
**bügeln** *vt, vi* to iron.
**Buhmann** ['buːman] (*umg*) *m* bogeyman.
**Bühne** ['byːnə] (**-, -n**) *f* stage.
**Bühnenbild** *nt* set, scenery.
**Buhruf** ['buːruːf] *m* boo.
**buk** *etc* [buːk] *vb* (*veraltet*) *siehe* **backen**.
**Bukarest** ['buːkarɛst] (**-s**) *nt* Bucharest.
**Bulette** [bu'lɛtə] *f* meatball.
**Bulgare** [bʊl'gaːrə] (**-n, -n**) *m* Bulgarian.
**Bulgarien** (**-s**) *nt* Bulgaria.
**Bulgarin** *f* Bulgarian.
**bulgarisch** *adj* Bulgarian.
**Bulimie** [buli'miː] *f* (*MED*) bulimia.
**Bull-** *zW:* ~**auge** *nt* (*NAUT*) porthole; ~**dogge** *f* bulldog; ~**dozer** ['bʊldoːzər] (**-s, -**) *m* bulldozer.
**Bulle** (**-n, -n**) *m* bull; **die** ~**n** (*pej: umg*) the fuzz *sing*, the cops.
**Bullenhitze** (*umg*) *f* sweltering heat.
**Bummel** ['bʊməl] (**-s, -**) *m* stroll; (*Schaufenster~*) window-shopping (expedition).
**Bummelant** [bʊmə'lant] *m* slowcoach.
**Bummelei** [bʊmə'laɪ] *f* wandering; dawdling; skiving.
**bummeln** *vi* to wander, stroll; (*trödeln*) to dawdle; (*faulenzen*) to skive (*BRIT*), loaf around.
**Bummelstreik** *m* go-slow (*BRIT*), slowdown (*US*).
**Bummelzug** *m* slow train.
**Bummler(in)** ['bʊmlər(ɪn)] (**-s, -**) *m(f)* (*langsamer Mensch*) dawdler (*BRIT*), slowpoke (*US*); (*Faulenzer*) idler, loafer.

**bumsen** ['bʊmzən] *vi* (*schlagen*) to thump; (*prallen, stoßen*) to bump, bang; (*umg: koitieren*) to bonk, have it off (*BRIT*).
**Bund¹** [bʊnt] (**-(e)s, ⁻e**) *m* (*Freundschafts~ etc*) bond; (*Organisation*) union; (*POL*) confederacy; (*Hosen~, Rock~*) waistband; **den** ~ **fürs Leben schließen** to take the marriage vows.
**Bund²** (**-(e)s, -e**) *nt* bunch; (*Stroh~*) bundle.
**Bündchen** ['bʏntçən] *nt* ribbing; (*Ärmel~*) cuff.
**Bündel** (**-s, -**) *nt* bundle, bale.
**bündeln** *vt* to bundle.
**Bundes-** ['bʊndəs] *in zW* Federal; ~**bahn** *f*: **die Deutsche** ~**bahn** German Federal Railways *pl*; ~**bank** *f* Federal Bank, Bundesbank; ~**bürger** *m* German citizen; (*vor 1990*) West German citizen; ~**gerichtshof** *m* Federal Supreme Court; ~**grenzschutz** *m* Federal Border Guard; ~**hauptstadt** *f* Federal capital; ~**haushalt** *m* (*POL*) National Budget; ~**kanzler** *m* Federal Chancellor.

*The **Bundeskanzler**, head of the German government, is elected for 4 years and determines government guidelines. He is formally proposed by the **Bundespräsident** but needs a majority in parliament to be elected to office.*

**Bundes-** *zW:* ~**land** *nt* state, Land; ~**liga** *f* (*SPORT*) national league; ~**nachrichten- dienst** *m* Federal Intelligence Service; ~**post** *f*: **die (Deutsche)** ~**post** the (German) Federal Post (Office).

*The **Bundespräsident** is the head of state of the Federal Republic of Germany who is elected every 5 years by the members of the **Bundestag** and by delegates of the Landtage (regional parliaments). His role is that of a figurehead who represents Germany at home and abroad. No one can be elected more than twice.*
*The **Bundesrat** is the Upper House of the German Parliament whose 68 members are not elected but nominated by the parliaments of the individual **Länder**. Its most important function is the approval of federal laws which concern jurisdiction of the Länder. It can raise objections to all other laws but can be outvoted by the Bundestag.*

**Bundes-** *zW:* ~**regierung** *f* Federal Government; ~**republik** *f* Federal Republic (of Germany); ~**staat** *m* Federal state; ~**straße** *f* Federal Highway, main road.

*The **Bundestag** is the Lower House of the German Parliament, elected by the people. There are 646 MPs, half of them elected directly from the first vote (**Erststimme**), and half from the regional list of parliamentary* *candidates resulting from the second vote* (**Zweitstimme**)*, and giving proportional representation to the parties. The Bundestag exercises parliamentary control over the government.*

**Bundes-** *zW:* ~**tagsabgeordnete(r)** *f(m)* member of the German Parliament; ~**tagswahl** *f* (Federal) parliamentary elections *pl*; ~**verfassungsgericht** *nt* Federal Constitutional Court; ~**wehr** *f* German *od* (*vor 1990*) West German Armed Forces *pl*.

*The* **Bundeswehr** *is the name for the German armed forces. It was established in 1955, first of all for volunteers, but since 1956 there has been compulsory military service for all able-bodied young men of 18 (see* **Wehrdienst**)*. In peacetime the Defence Minister is the head of the Bundeswehr, but in wartime, the* **Bundeskanzler** *takes over. The Bundeswehr comes under the jurisdiction of NATO.*

**Bundfaltenhose** *f* pleated trousers *pl*.
**Bundhose** *f* knee breeches *pl*.
**bündig** ['bʏndɪç] *adj* (*kurz*) concise.
**Bündnis** ['bʏntnɪs] (**-ses, -se**) *nt* alliance.
**Bunker** ['bʊŋkər] (**-s, -**) *m* bunker; (*Luftschutzbunker*) air-raid shelter.
**bunt** [bʊnt] *adj* coloured (*BRIT*), colored (*US*); (*gemischt*) mixed; **jdm wird es zu ~** it's getting too much for sb; **B~stift** *m* coloured (*BRIT*) *od* colored (*US*) pencil, crayon.
**Bürde** ['bʏrdə] (**-, -n**) *f* (*lit, fig*) burden.
**Burg** [bʊrk] (**-, -en**) *f* castle, fort.
**Bürge** ['bʏrgə] (**-n, -n**) *m* guarantor.
**bürgen** *vi* to vouch; **für jdn ~** (*fig*) to vouch for sb; (*FIN*) to stand surety for sb.
**Bürger(in)** (**-s, -**) *m(f)* citizen; member of the middle class; ~**initiative** *f* citizen's initiative; ~**krieg** *m* civil war; **b~lich** *adj* (*Rechte*) civil; (*Klasse*) middle-class; (*pej*) bourgeois; **gut b~liche Küche** good home cooking; **b~liches Gesetzbuch** Civil Code; ~**meister** *m* mayor; ~**recht** *nt* civil rights *pl*; ~**rechtler(in)** *m(f)* civil rights campaigner; ~**schaft** *f* population, citizens *pl*; ~**schreck** *m* bogey of the middle classes; ~**steig** *m* pavement (*BRIT*), sidewalk (*US*); ~**tum** *nt* citizens *pl*; ~**wehr** *f* vigilantes *pl*.
**Burgfriede(n)** *m* (*fig*) truce.
**Bürgin** *f* guarantor.
**Bürgschaft** *f* surety; ~ **leisten** to give security.
**Burgund** [bʊr'gʊnt] (**-(s)**) *nt* Burgundy.
**Burgunder** (**-s, -**) *m* (*Wein*) burgundy.
**Büro** [by'roː] (**-s, -s**) *nt* office; ~**angestellte(r)** *f(m)* office worker; ~**klammer** *f* paper clip; ~**kraft** *f* (office) clerk.
**Bürokrat** [byro'kraːt] (**-en, -en**) *m* bureaucrat.
**Bürokratie** [byrokra'tiː] *f* bureaucracy.
**bürokratisch** *adj* bureaucratic.

**Bürokratismus** *m* red tape.
**Büroschluß** *m* office closing time.
**Bursch** ['bʊrʃ(ə)] (**-en, -en**) *m* = **Bursche**.
**Bursche** (**-n, -n**) *m* lad, fellow; (*Diener*) servant.
**Burschenschaft** *f* student fraternity.
**burschikos** [bʊrʃi'koːs] *adj* (*jungenhaft*) (tom)boyish; (*unbekümmert*) casual.
**Bürste** ['bʏrstə] (**-, -n**) *f* brush.
**bürsten** *vt* to brush.
**Bus** [bʊs] (**-ses, -se**) *m* bus.
**Busch** [bʊʃ] (**-(e)s, ̈-e**) *m* bush, shrub; **bei jdm auf den ~ klopfen** (*umg*) to sound sb out.
**Büschel** ['bʏʃəl] (**-s, -**) *nt* tuft.
**buschig** *adj* bushy.
**Busen** ['buːzən] (**-s, -**) *m* bosom; (*Meer~*) inlet, bay; ~**freund(in)** *m(f)* bosom friend.
**Bushaltestelle** *f* bus stop.
**Bussard** ['bʊsart] (**-s, -e**) *m* buzzard.
**Buße** ['buːsə] (**-, -n**) *f* atonement, penance; (*Geld*) fine.
**büßen** ['byːsən] *vi* to do penance, atone ♦ *vt* to atone for.
**Bußgeld** *nt* fine.
**Buß- und Bettag** *m* day of prayer and repentance.
**Büste** ['bʏstə] (**-, -n**) *f* bust.
**Büstenhalter** *m* bra.
**Butan** [bu'taːn] (**-s**) *nt* butane.
**Büttenrede** ['bʏtənreːdə] *f* carnival speech.
**Butter** ['bʊtər] (**-**) *f* butter; **alles (ist) in ~** (*umg*) everything is fine *od* hunky-dory; ~**berg** (*umg*) *m* butter mountain; ~**blume** *f* buttercup; ~**brot** *nt* (piece of) bread and butter; ~**brotpapier** *nt* greaseproof paper; ~**cremetorte** *f* gateau with buttercream filling; ~**dose** *f* butter dish; ~**keks** *m* ≈ Rich Tea ® biscuit; ~**milch** *f* buttermilk; **b~weich** *adj* soft as butter; (*fig: umg*) soft.
**Butzen** ['bʊtsən] (**-s, -**) *m* core.
**BVG** *nt abk* (= *Betriebsverfassungsgesetz*) ≈ Industrial Relations Act; = **Bundesverfassungsgericht**.
**b.w.** *abk* (= *bitte wenden*) p.t.o.
**Byte** [baɪt] (**-s, -s**) *nt* (*COMPUT*) byte.
**Bz.** *abk* = **Bezirk**.
**bzgl.** *abk* (= *bezüglich*) re.
**bzw.** *abk* = **beziehungsweise**.

# C, c

**C¹, c** [tse:] *nt* C, c; ~ **wie Cäsar** ≈ C for Charlie.

**C²** [tse:] *abk* (= *Celsius*) C.

**ca.** [ka] *abk* (= *circa*) approx.

**Cabriolet** [kabrio'le:] (-**s**, -**s**) *nt* (*AUT*) convertible.

**Café** [ka'fe:] (-**s**, -**s**) *nt* café.

**Cafeteria** [kafete'ri:a] (-, -**s**) *f* cafeteria.

**cal** *abk* (= *Kalorie*) cal.

**Calais** [ka'lɛ:] (-') *nt:* **die Straße von** ~ the Straits of Dover.

**Camcorder** (-**s**, -) *m* camcorder.

**campen** ['kɛmpən] *vi* to camp.

**Camper(in)** (-**s**, -) *m(f)* camper.

**Camping** ['kɛmpɪŋ] (-**s**) *nt* camping; ~**bus** *m* camper; ~**platz** *m* camp(ing) site.

**Caravan** ['karavan] (-**s**, -**s**) *m* caravan.

**Carnet** [kar'nɛ] (-**s**) *nt* (*COMM*) international customs pass, carnet.

**Cäsium** ['tsɛ:ziʊm] *nt* caesium (*BRIT*), cesium (*US*).

**ccm** *abk* (= *Kubikzentimeter*) cc, cm³.

**CD** *f abk* (= *Compact Disc*) CD; ~-**ROM** (-, -**s**) *f* CD-ROM; ~-**Spieler** *m* CD player.

**CDU** [tse:de:'|u:] (-) *f abk* (= *Christlich-Demokratische Union (Deutschlands)*) Christian Democratic Union.

---

*The* **CDU** *(Christlich-Demokratische Union) is a Christian and conservative political party founded in 1945. It operates in all the* **Länder** *apart from Bavaria where its sister party the* **CSU** *is active. In the* **Bundestag** *the two parties form a coalition. It is the second largest party in Germany after the* **SPD***, the Social Democratic Party.*

---

**Celli** *pl von* **Cello.**

**Cellist(in)** [tʃɛ'lɪst(ɪn)] *m(f)* cellist.

**Cello** ['tʃɛlo] (-**s**, -**s** *od* **Celli**) *nt* cello.

**Celsius** ['tsɛlziʊs] *m* Celsius.

**Cembalo** ['tʃɛmbalo] (-**s**, -**s**) *nt* cembalo, harpsichord.

**Ces** [tsɛs] (-, -) *nt* (*MUS*) C flat.

**ces** [tsɛs] (-, -) *nt* (*MUS*) C flat.

**Ceylon** ['tsailɔn] (-**s**) *nt* Ceylon.

**Chamäleon** [ka'mɛ:leɔn] (-**s**, -**s**) *nt* chameleon.

**Champagner** [ʃam'panjər] (-**s**, -) *m* champagne.

**Champignon** ['ʃampɪnjõ] (-**s**, -**s**) *m* button mushroom.

**Chance** ['ʃã:s(ə)] (-, -**n**) *f* chance, opportunity.

**Chancengleichheit** *f* equality of opportunity.

**Chaos** ['ka:ɔs] (-) *nt* chaos.

**Chaot(in)** [ka'o:t(ɪn)] (-**en**, -**en**) *m(f)* (*POL: pej*) anarchist (*pej*).

**chaotisch** [ka'o:tɪʃ] *adj* chaotic.

**Charakter** [ka'raktər] (-**s**, -**e**) *m* character; **c~fest** *adj* of firm character.

**charakterisieren** [karakteri'zi:rən] *vt* to characterize.

**Charakteristik** [karakte'rɪstɪk] *f* characterization.

**charakteristisch** [karakte'rɪstɪʃ] *adj:* ~ **(für)** characteristic (of), typical (of).

**Charakter-** *zW:* **c~los** *adj* unprincipled; ~**losigkeit** *f* lack of principle; ~**schwäche** *f* weakness of character; ~**stärke** *f* strength of character; ~**zug** *m* characteristic, trait.

**charmant** [ʃar'mant] *adj* charming.

**Charme** [ʃarm] (-**s**) *m* charm.

**Charta** ['karta] (-, -**s**) *f* charter.

**Charterflug** ['tʃartərflu:k] *m* charter flight.

**Chartermaschine** ['tʃartərmaʃi:nə] *f* charter plane.

**chartern** ['tʃartərn] *vt* to charter.

**Chassis** [ʃa'si:] (-, -) *nt* chassis.

**Chauffeur** [ʃɔ'føːr] *m* chauffeur.

**Chaussee** [ʃo'se:] (-, -**n**) *f* (*veraltet*) high road.

**Chauvi** ['ʃovi] (-**s**, -**s**) (*umg*) *m* male chauvinist.

**Chauvinismus** [ʃovi'nɪsmʊs] *m* chauvinism.

**Chauvinist** [ʃovi'nɪst] *m* chauvinist.

**checken** ['tʃɛkən] *vt* (*überprüfen*) to check; (*umg: verstehen*) to get.

**Chef(in)** [ʃɛf(ɪn)] (-**s**, -**s**) *m(f)* head; (*umg*) boss; ~**arzt** *m* senior consultant; ~**etage** *f* executive floor; ~**redakteur** *m* editor-in-chief; ~**sekretärin** *f* personal assistant/ secretary; ~**visite** *f* (*MED*) consultant's round.

**Chemie** [çe'mi:] (-) *f* chemistry; ~**faser** *f* man-made fibre (*BRIT*) *od* fiber (*US*).

**Chemikalie** [çemi'ka:liə] *f* chemical.

**Chemiker(in)** ['çe:mikər(ɪn)] (-**s**, -) *m(f)* (industrial) chemist.

**chemisch** ['çe:mɪʃ] *adj* chemical; ~**e Reinigung** dry cleaning.

**Chemotherapie** [çemotera'pi:] *f* chemotherapy.

**Chicorée** [ʃiko're:] (-**s**) *f od m* chicory.

**Chiffre** ['ʃifrə] (-, -**n**) *f* (*Geheimzeichen*) cipher; (*in Zeitung*) box number.

**Chiffriermaschine** [ʃi'fri:rmaʃi:nə] *f* cipher machine.

**Chile** ['tʃi:le] (-**s**) *nt* Chile.

**Chilene** [tʃi'le:nə] (-**n**, -**n**) *m* Chilean.

**Chilenin** [tʃi'le:nɪn] *f* Chilean.

**chilenisch** *adj* Chilean.

**China** ['çi:na] (-**s**) *nt* China.

**Chinakohl** *m* Chinese leaves *pl.*

**Chinese** [çi'ne:zə] (-**n**, -**n**) *m* Chinaman, Chinese.

**Chinesin** *f* Chinese woman.
**chinesisch** *adj* Chinese.
**Chinin** [çi'niːn] *nt* quinine.
**Chipkarte** ['tʃɪpkartə] *f* smart card.
**Chips** [tʃɪps] *pl* crisps *pl* (*BRIT*), chips *pl* (*US*).
**Chirurg(in)** [çi'rʊrg(ɪn)] (**-en, -en**) *m(f)* surgeon.
**Chirurgie** [çirʊr'giː] *f* surgery.
**chirurgisch** *adj* surgical; **ein ~er Eingriff** surgery.
**Chlor** [kloːr] (**-s**) *nt* chlorine.
**Chloroform** [kloro'fɔrm] (**-s**) *nt* chloroform.
**chloroformieren** [klorofor'miːrən] *vt* to chloroform.
**Chlorophyll** [kloro'fʏl] (**-s**) *nt* chlorophyll.
**Cholera** ['koːlera] (**-**) *f* cholera.
**Choleriker(in)** [ko'leːrikər(ɪn)] (**-s, -**) *m(f)* hot-tempered person.
**cholerisch** [ko'leːrɪʃ] *adj* choleric.
**Cholesterin** [kolɛste'riːn] (**-s**) *nt* cholesterol; **~spiegel** [kolɛste'riːnʃpiɡəl] *m* cholesterol level.
**Chor** [koːr] (**-(e)s, ¨-e**) *m* choir; (*Musikstück, THEAT*) chorus.
**Choral** [ko'raːl] (**-s, -äle**) *m* chorale.
**Choreograph(in)** [koreo'graːf(ɪn)] (**-en, -en**) *m(f)* choreographer.
**Choreographie** [koreogra'fiː] *f* choreography.
**Chorgestühl** *nt* choir stalls *pl*.
**Chorknabe** *m* choirboy.
**Chose** ['ʃoːzə] (**-, -n**) (*umg*) *f* (*Angelegenheit*) thing.
**Chr.** *abk* = **Christus; Chronik.**
**Christ** [krɪst] (**-en, -en**) *m* Christian; **~baum** *m* Christmas tree.
**Christenheit** *f* Christendom.
**Christentum** (**-s**) *nt* Christianity.
**Christin** *f* Christian.
**Christkind** *nt* ≈ Father Christmas; (*Jesus*) baby Jesus.
**christlich** *adj* Christian; **C~er Verein Junger Männer** Young Men's Christian Association.
**Christus** (**Christi**) *m* Christ; **Christi Himmelfahrt** Ascension Day.
**Chrom** [kroːm] (**-s**) *nt* (*CHEM*) chromium; chrome.
**Chromosom** [kromo'zoːm] (**-s, -en**) *nt* (*BIOL*) chromosome.
**Chronik** ['kroːnɪk] *f* chronicle.
**chronisch** *adj* chronic.
**Chronologie** [kronolo'giː] *f* chronology.
**chronologisch** *adj* chronological.
**Chrysantheme** [kryzan'teːmə] (**-, -n**) *f* chrysanthemum.
**CIA** ['siːaɪ'eɪ] (**-**) *f od m abk* (= *Central Intelligence Agency*) CIA.
**circa** ['tsɪrka] *adv* (round) about.
**Cis** [tsɪs] (**-, -**) *nt* (*MUS*) C sharp.
**cis** [tsɪs] (**-, -**) *nt* (*MUS*) C sharp.
**City** ['sɪti] (**-, -s**) *f* city centre (*BRIT*); **in der ~** in the city centre (*BRIT*), downtown (*US*); **die ~ von Berlin** the (city) centre of Berlin

(*BRIT*), downtown Berlin (*US*).
**clean** [kliːn] *adj* (*DROGEN: umg*) off drugs.
**clever** ['klɛvər] *adj* clever; (*gerissen*) crafty.
**Clique** ['klɪkə] (**-, -n**) *f* set, crowd.
**Clou** [kluː] (**-s, -s**) *m* (*von Geschichte*) (whole) point; (*von Show*) highlight, high spot.
**Clown** [klaʊn] (**-s, -s**) *m* clown.
**cm** *abk* (= *Zentimeter*) cm.
**COBOL** ['koːbɔl] *nt* COBOL.
**Cockpit** ['kɔkpɪt] (**-s, -s**) *nt* cockpit.
**Cocktail** ['kɔkteːl] (**-s, -s**) *m* cocktail.
**Cola** ['koːla] (**-(s), -s**) *nt od f* Coke ®.
**Comicheft** ['kɔmɪkhɛft] *nt* comic.
**Computer** [kɔm'pjuːtər] (**-s, -**) *m* computer; **c~gesteuert** *adj* computer-controlled; **~kriminalität** *f* computer crime; **~spiel** *nt* computer game; **~technik** *f* computer technology.
**Conférencier** [kõferãsi'eː] (**-s, -s**) *m* compère.
**Container** [kɔn'teːnər] (**-s, -**) *m* container; **~schiff** *nt* container ship.
**Contergankind** [kɔntɛr'gankɪnt] (*umg*) *nt* thalidomide child.
**cool** [kuːl] (*umg*) *adj* (*gefaßt*) cool.
**Cord** [kɔrt] (**-(e)s, -e** *od* **-s**) *m* corduroy.
**Cornichon** [kɔrni'ʃõː] (**-s, -s**) *nt* gherkin.
**Costa Rica** ['kɔsta 'riːka] (**-s**) *nt* Costa Rica.
**Couch** [kaʊtʃ] (**-, -es** *od* **-en**) *f* couch; **~garnitur** ['kaʊtʃɡarniˈtuːr] *f* three-piece suite.
**Couleur** [ku'løːr] (**-s, -s**) *f* (*geh*) kind, sort.
**Coupé** [ku'peː] (**-s, -s**) *nt* (*AUT*) coupé, sports version.
**Coupon** [ku'põː] (**-s, -s**) *m* coupon, voucher; (*Stoff~*) length of cloth.
**Courage** [ku'raːzə] (**-**) *f* courage.
**Cousin** [ku'zɛ̃ː] (**-s, -s**) *m* cousin.
**Cousine** [ku'ziːnə] (**-, -n**) *f* cousin.
**Crack** [krɛk] (**-**) *nt* (*Droge*) crack.
**Creme** [krɛːm] (**-, -s**) *f* (*lit, fig*) cream; (*Schuh~*) polish; (*KOCH*) mousse; **c~farben** *adj* cream(-coloured (*BRIT*) *od* -colored (*US*)).
**cremig** ['kreːmɪç] *adj* creamy.
**Crux** [krʊks] (**-**) *f* (*Schwierigkeit*) trouble, problem.
**CSU** [tseː|ɛs'uː] (**-**) *f abk* (= *Christlich-Soziale Union*) Christian Social Union.

> The **CSU** (*Christlich-Soziale Union*) is a party founded in 1945 in Bavaria. Like its sister party the **CDU** it is a Christian, right-wing party.

**CT-Scanner** [tseː'teːskɛnər] *m* CT scanner.
**Curriculum** [kʊ'riːkulom] (**-s, -cula**) *nt* (*geh*) curriculum.
**Curry** ['kari] (**-s**) *m od nt* curry powder; **~pulver** ['karipʊlfər] *nt* curry powder; **~wurst** *f* curried sausage.
**Cursor** ['køːrsər] (**-s**) *m* (*COMPUT*) cursor.
**Cutter(in)** ['katər(ɪn)] (**-s, -**) *m(f)* (*FILM*) editor.
**CVJM** [tseːfaʊjɔt'|ɛm] (**-**) *m abk* (= *Christlicher*

*Verein Junger Männer)* YMCA.

# D, d

**D, d** [de:] *nt* D, d; ~ **wie Dora** ≈ D for David, D for Dog (*US*).

**D.** *abk* = **Doktor** (*der evangelischen Theologie*).

━━━━━━━━━━ *SCHLÜSSELWORT*

**da** [da:] *adv* **1** (*örtlich*) there; (*hier*) here; ~ **draußen** out there; ~ **bin ich** here I am; ~ **hast du dein Geld** (there you are,) there's your money; ~, **wo** where; **ist noch Milch** ~? is there any milk left?
**2** (*zeitlich*) then; (*folglich*) so; **es war niemand im Zimmer,** ~ **habe ich ...** there was nobody in the room, so I ...
**3:** ~ **haben wir Glück gehabt** we were lucky there; **was gibt's denn** ~ **zu lachen?** what's so funny about that?; ~ **kann man nichts machen** there's nothing one can do (in a case like that)
♦ *konj* (*weil*) as, since.

**d.Ä.** *abk* (= *der Ältere*) Sen., sen.

**DAAD** (-) *m abk* (= *Deutscher Akademischer Austauschdienst*) German Academic Exchange Service.

**dabehalten** *unreg vt* to keep.

**dabei** [da'baɪ] *adv* (*räumlich*) close to it; (*noch dazu*) besides; (*zusammen mit*) with them/it *etc*; (*zeitlich*) during this; (*obwohl doch*) but, however; **was ist schon** ~? what of it?; **es ist doch nichts** ~, **wenn ...** it doesn't matter if ...; **bleiben wir** ~ let's leave it at that; **es soll nicht** ~ **bleiben** this isn't the end of it; **es bleibt** ~ that's settled; **das Dumme/ Schwierige** ~ the stupid/difficult part of it; **er war gerade** ~, **zu gehen** he was just leaving; **hast du** ~ **etwas gelernt?** did you learn anything from it?; ~ **darf man nicht vergessen, daß ...** it shouldn't be forgotten that ...; **die** ~ **entstehenden Kosten** the expenses arising from this; **es kommt doch nichts** ~ **heraus** nothing will come of it; **ich finde gar nichts** ~ I don't see any harm in it; ~**sein** *unreg vi* (*anwesend*) to be present; (*beteiligt*) to be involved; **ich bin** ~! count me in!; ~**stehen** *unreg vi* to stand around.

**Dach** [dax] (-(e)s, ⁻er) *nt* roof; **unter** ~ **und Fach sein** (*abgeschlossen*) to be in the bag (*umg*); (*Vertrag, Geschäft*) to be signed and sealed; (*in Sicherheit*) to be safe; **jdm eins aufs** ~ **geben** (*umg: ausschimpfen*) to give sb a (good) talking to; ~**boden** *m* attic, loft;

~**decker** (-s, -) *m* slater, tiler; ~**fenster** *nt* skylight; (*ausgestellt*) dormer window; ~**first** *m* ridge of the roof; ~**gepäckträger** *m* (*AUT*) roof rack; ~**geschoß** *nt* attic storey (*BRIT*) *od* story (*US*); (*oberster Stock*) top floor *od* storey (*BRIT*) *od* story (*US*); ~**luke** *f* skylight; ~**pappe** *f* roofing felt; ~**rinne** *f* gutter.

**Dachs** [daks] (-es, -e) *m* badger.

**Dachschaden** (*umg*) *m:* **einen** ~ **haben** to have a screw loose.

**dachte** *etc* ['daxtə] *vb siehe* **denken**.

**Dach-** *zW:* ~**terrasse** *f* roof terrace; ~**verband** *m* umbrella organization; ~**ziegel** *m* roof tile.

**Dackel** ['dakəl] (-s, -) *m* dachshund.

**dadurch** [da'dʊrç] *adv* (*räumlich*) through it; (*durch diesen Umstand*) thereby, in that way; (*deshalb*) because of that, for that reason ♦ *konj:* ~, **daß** because.

**dafür** [da'fy:r] *adv* for it; (*anstatt*) instead; (*zum Ausgleich*): **in Latein ist er schlecht,** ~ **kann er gut Fußball spielen** he's bad at Latin but he makes up for it at football; **er ist bekannt** ~ he is well-known for that; **was bekomme ich** ~? what will I get for it?; ~ **ist er immer zu haben** he never says no to that; ~ **bin ich ja hier** that's what I'm here for; **D~halten** (-s) *nt* (*geh*): **nach meinem D~halten** in my opinion; ~**können** *unreg vt:* **er kann nichts** ~ (, **daß ...**) he can't help it (that ...).

**DAG** *f abk* (= *Deutsche Angestellten-Gewerkschaft*) Clerical and Administrative Workers' Union.

**dagegen** [da'ge:gən] *adv* against it; (*im Vergleich damit*) in comparison with it; (*bei Tausch*) for it ♦ *konj* however; **haben Sie etwas** ~, **wenn ich rauche?** do you mind if I smoke?; **ich habe nichts** ~ I don't mind; **ich war** ~ I was against it; **ich hätte nichts** ~ (*einzuwenden*) that's okay by me; ~ **kann man nichts tun** one can't do anything about it; ~**halten** *unreg vt* (*vergleichen*) to compare with it; (*entgegnen*) to put forward as an objection.

**dagewesen** ['da:gəve:zən] *pp von* **dasein**.

**daheim** [da'haɪm] *adv* at home; **bei uns** ~ back home; **D~** (-s) *nt* home.

**daher** [da'he:r] *adv* (*räumlich*) from there; (*Ursache*) from that ♦ *konj* (*deshalb*) that's why; **das kommt** ~, **daß ...** that is because ...; ~ **kommt er auch** that's where he comes from too; ~ **die Schwierigkeiten** that's what is causing the difficulties; ~**gelaufen** *adj:* **jeder** ~**gelaufene Kerl** any Tom, Dick or Harry; ~**reden** *vi* to talk away ♦ *vt* to say without thinking.

**dahin** [da'hɪn] *adv* (*räumlich*) there; (*zeitlich*) then; (*vergangen*) gone; **ist es noch weit bis** ~? is there still far to go?; **das tendiert** ~ it is tending towards that; **er bringt es noch** ~, **daß ich ...** he'll make me ...; ~**gegen** *konj* on the other hand; ~**gehen** _unreg vi_ (_Zeit_) to pass; ~**gehend** _adv_ on this matter; ~**gestellt** _adv:_ ~**gestellt bleiben** to remain to be seen; _etw_ ~**gestellt sein lassen** to leave sth open _od_ undecided; ~**schleppen** _vr_ (_lit: sich fortbewegen_) to drag o.s. along; (_fig: Verhandlungen, Zeit_) to drag on; ~**schmelzen** _vi_ to be enthralled.

**dahinten** [da'hɪntən] _adv_ over there.

**dahinter** [da'hɪntər] _adv_ behind it; ~**klemmen** (_umg_) _vr_ to put one's back into it; ~**knien** (_umg_) _vr_ to put one's back into it; ~**kommen** _unreg_ (_umg_) _vi_ to find out.

**dahinvegetieren** [da'hɪnvege'tiːrən] _vi_ to vegetate.

**Dahlie** ['daːliə] (-, -n) _f_ dahlia.

**DAK** (-) _f abk_ (= _Deutsche Angestellten-Krankenkasse_) _health insurance company for employees._

**Dakar** ['dakar] (-s) _nt_ Dakar.

**dalassen** ['daːlasən] _unreg vt_ to leave (behind).

**dalli** ['dali] (_umg_) _adv:_ ~, ~! on (_BRIT_) _od_ at (_US_) the double!

**damalig** ['daːmaːlɪç] _adj_ of that time, then.

**damals** ['daːmaːls] _adv_ at that time, then.

**Damaskus** [da'maskʊs] _nt_ Damascus.

**Damast** [da'mast] (-(e)s, -e) _m_ damask.

**Dame** ['daːmə] (-, -n) _f_ lady; (_SCHACH, KARTEN_) queen; (_Spiel_) draughts (_BRIT_), checkers (_US_).

**Damen-** _zW:_ ~**besuch** _m_ lady visitor _od_ visitors; ~**binde** _f_ sanitary towel (_BRIT_) _od_ napkin (_US_); **d**~**haft** _adj_ ladylike; ~**sattel** _m:_ **im** ~**sattel reiten** to ride side-saddle; ~**wahl** _f_ ladies' excuse-me.

**Damespiel** _nt_ draughts (_BRIT_), checkers (_US_).

**damit** [da'mɪt] _adv_ with it; (_begründend_) by that ♦ _konj_ in order that _od_ to; **was meint er** ~? what does he mean by that?; **was soll ich** ~? what am I meant to do with that?; **muß er denn immer wieder** ~ **ankommen?** must he keep on about it?; **was ist** ~? what about it?; **genug** ~! that's enough!; ~ **basta!** and that's that!; ~ **eilt es nicht** there's no hurry.

**dämlich** ['dɛːmlɪç] (_umg_) _adj_ silly, stupid.

**Damm** [dam] (-(e)s, -̈e) _m_ dyke (_BRIT_), dike (_US_); (_Stau_~) dam; (_Hafen_~) mole; (_Bahn~, Straßen~_) embankment.

**dämmen** ['dɛmən] _vt_ (_Wasser_) to dam up; (_Schmerzen_) to keep back.

**dämmerig** _adj_ dim, faint.

**Dämmerlicht** _nt_ twilight; (_abends_) dusk; (_Halbdunkel_) half-light.

**dämmern** ['dɛmərn] _vi_ (_Tag_) to dawn; (_Abend_) to fall; **es dämmerte ihm, daß ...** (_umg_) it dawned on him that ...

**Dämmerung** _f_ twilight; (_Morgen_~) dawn; (_Abend_~) dusk.

**Dämmerzustand** _m_ (_Halbschlaf_) dozy state; (_Bewußtseinstrübung_) semi-conscious state.

**Dämmung** _f_ insulation.

**Dämon** ['dɛːmɔn] (-s, -en) _m_ demon.

**dämonisch** [dɛ'moːnɪʃ] _adj_ demonic.

**Dampf** [dampf] (-(e)s, -̈e) _m_ steam; (_Dunst_) vapour (_BRIT_), vapor (_US_); **jdm** ~ **machen** (_umg_) to make sb get a move on; ~ **ablassen** (_lit, fig_) to let off steam; **d**~**en** _vi_ to steam.

**dämpfen** ['dɛmpfən] _vt_ (_KOCH_) to steam; (_bügeln_) to iron with a damp cloth; (_mit Dampfbügeleisen_) to steam iron; (_fig_) to dampen, subdue.

**Dampfer** ['dampfər] (-s, -) _m_ steamer; **auf dem falschen** ~ **sein** (_fig_) to have got the wrong idea.

**Dämpfer** (-s, -) _m_ (_MUS: bei Klavier_) damper; (_bei Geige, Trompete_) mute; **er hat einen** ~ **bekommen** (_fig_) it dampened his spirits.

**Dampf-** _zW:_ ~**kochtopf** _m_ pressure cooker; ~**maschine** _f_ steam engine; ~**schiff** _nt_ steamship; ~**walze** _f_ steamroller.

**Damwild** ['damvɪlt] _nt_ fallow deer.

**danach** [da'naːx] _adv_ after that; (_zeitlich_) afterwards; (_gemäß_) accordingly; (_laut diesem_) according to which _od_ that; **mir war nicht** ~ **(zumute)** I didn't feel like it; **er griff schnell** ~ he grabbed at it; ~ **kann man nicht gehen** you can't go by that; **er sieht** ~ **aus** he looks it.

**Däne** ['dɛːnə] (-n, -n) _m_ Dane, Danish man/boy.

**daneben** [da'neːbən] _adv_ beside it; (_im Vergleich_) in comparison; ~**benehmen** _unreg vr_ to misbehave; ~**gehen** _unreg vi_ to miss; (_Plan_) to fail; ~**greifen** _unreg vi_ to miss; (_fig: mit Schätzung etc_) to be wide of the mark; ~**sein** _unreg_ (_umg_) _vi_ (_verwirrt sein_) to be completely confused.

**Dänemark** ['dɛːnəmark] (-s) _nt_ Denmark.

**Dänin** ['dɛːnɪn] _f_ Dane, Danish woman _od_ girl.

**dänisch** _adj_ Danish.

**Dank** [daŋk] (-(e)s) _m_ thanks _pl_; **vielen** _od_ **schönen** ~ many thanks; **jdm** ~ **sagen** to thank sb; **mit (bestem)** ~ **zurück!** many thanks for the loan; **d**~ _präp_ (+_dat od gen_) thanks to; **d**~**bar** _adj_ grateful; (_Aufgabe_) rewarding; (_haltbar_) hard-wearing; ~**barkeit** _f_ gratitude.

**danke** _interj_ thank you, thanks.

**danken** _vi_ +_dat_ to thank; **nichts zu** ~! don't mention it; ~**d erhalten/ablehnen** to receive/decline with thanks.

**dankenswert** _adj_ (_Arbeit_) worthwhile; rewarding; (_Bemühung_) kind.

**Dank-** _zW:_ ~**gottesdienst** _m_ service of thanksgiving; **d**~**sagen** _vi_ to express one's thanks; ~**schreiben** _nt_ letter of thanks.

**dann** [dan] _adv_ then; ~ **und wann** now and then; ~ **eben nicht** well, in that case (there's no more to be said); **erst** ~, **wenn** ... only when ...; ~ **erst recht nicht!** in that case no way (_umg_).

**dannen** ['danən] _adv:_ **von** ~ (_liter: weg_) away.

**daran** [da'ran] _adv_ on it; (_stoßen_) against it; **es**

liegt ~, daß ... the cause of it is that ...; **gut/ schlecht** ~ **sein** to be well/badly off; **das Beste/Dümmste** ~ the best/stupidest thing about it; **ich war nahe** ~, **zu** ... I was on the point of ...; **im Anschluß** ~ (*zeitlich: danach anschließend*) following that *od* this; **wir können nichts** ~ **machen** we can't do anything about it; **es ist nichts** ~ (*ist nicht fundiert*) there's nothing in it; (*ist nichts Besonderes*) it's nothing special; **er ist** ~ **gestorben** he died *od* of it; ~**gehen** *unreg vi* to start; ~**machen** (*umg*) *vr:* **sich** ~**machen, etw zu tun** to set about doing sth; ~**setzen** *vt* to stake; **er hat alles** ~**gesetzt, von Glasgow wegzukommen** he has done his utmost to get away from Glasgow.

**darauf** [da'raʊf] *adv* (*räumlich*) on it; (*zielgerichtet*) towards it; (*danach*) afterwards; **es kommt ganz** ~, **ob** ... it depends whether ...; **seine Behauptungen stützen sich** ~, **daß** ... his claims are based on the supposition that ...; **wie kommst du** ~? what makes you think that?; **die Tage** ~ the days following *od* thereafter; **am Tag** ~ the next day; ~**folgend** *adj* (*Tag, Jahr*) next, following; ~**hin** *adv* (*im Hinblick* ~) in this respect; (*aus diesem Grund*) as a result; **wir müssen es** ~**hin prüfen, ob** ... we must test it to see whether ...; ~**legen** *vt* to lay *od* put on top.

**daraus** [da'raʊs] *adv* from it; **was ist** ~ **geworden?** what became of it?; ~ **geht hervor, daß** ... this means that ...

**darbieten** ['daːrbiːtən] *vt* (*vortragen: Lehrstoff*) to present ♦ *vr* to present itself.

**Darbietung** *f* performance.

**Dardanellen** [darda'nɛlən] *pl* Dardanelles *pl*.

**darein-** *präf* = **drein-**.

**Daressalam** [darɛsa'laːm] *nt* Dar-es-Salaam.

**darf** [darf] *vb siehe* **dürfen**.

**darin** [da'rɪn] *adv* in (there), in it; **der Unterschied liegt** ~, **daß** ... the difference is that ...

**darlegen** ['daːrleːgən] *vt* to explain, expound, set forth.

**Darlegung** *f* explanation.

**Darleh(e)n (-s, -)** *nt* loan.

**Darm** [darm] **(-(e)s, ̈-e)** *m* intestine; (*Wurst~*) skin; ~**ausgang** *m* anus; ~**grippe** *f* gastric influenza; ~**saite** *f* gut string; ~**trägheit** *f* under-activity of the intestines.

**darstellen** ['daːrʃtɛlən] *vt* (*abbilden, bedeuten*) to represent; (*THEAT*) to act; (*beschreiben*) to describe ♦ *vr* to appear to be.

**Darsteller(in) (-s, -)** *m(f)* actor, actress.

**darstellerisch** *adj:* **eine** ~**e Höchstleistung** a magnificent piece of acting.

**Darstellung** *f* portrayal, depiction.

**darüber** [da'ryːbər] *adv* (*räumlich*) over/above it; (*fahren*) over it; (*mehr*) more; (*währenddessen*) meanwhile; (*sprechen, streiten*) about it; ~ **hinweg sein** (*fig*) to have

got over it; ~ **hinaus** over and above that; ~ **geht nichts** there's nothing like it; **seine Gedanken** ~ his thoughts about *od* on it; ~**liegen** *unreg vi* (*fig*) to be higher.

**darum** [da'rʊm] *adv* (*räumlich*) round it ♦ *konj* that's why; ~ **herum** round about (it); **er bittet** ~ he is pleading for it; **es geht** ~, **daß** ... the thing is that ...; ~ **geht es mir/geht es mir nicht** that's my point/that's not the point for me; **er würde viel** ~ **geben, wenn** ... he would give a lot to ...; *siehe auch* **drum**.

**darunter** [da'rʊntər] *adv* (*räumlich*) under it; (*dazwischen*) among them; (*weniger*) less; **ein Stockwerk** ~ one floor below (it); **was verstehen Sie** ~? what do you understand by that?; ~ **kann ich mir nichts vorstellen** that doesn't mean anything to me; ~**fallen** *unreg vi* to be included; ~**mischen** *vt* (*Mehl*) to mix in ♦ *vr* to mingle; ~**setzen** *vt* (*Unterschrift*) to put to it.

**das** [das] *pron* that ♦ *def art* the; *siehe auch* **der**; ~ **heißt** that is; ~ **und** ~ such and such.

**Dasein** ['daːzaɪn] **(-s)** *nt* (*Leben*) life; (*Anwesenheit*) presence; (*Bestehen*) existence.

**dasein** *unreg vi* to be there; **ein Arzt, der immer für seine Patienten da ist** a doctor who always has time for his patients.

**Daseinsberechtigung** *f* right to exist.

**Daseinskampf** *m* struggle for survival.

**daß** [das] *konj* that.

**dasselbe** [das'zɛlbə] *nt pron* the same.

**dastehen** ['daːʃteːən] *unreg vi* to stand there; (*fig*): **gut/schlecht** ~ to be in a good/bad position; **allein** ~ to be on one's own.

**Dat.** *abk* = **Dativ**.

**Datei** [da'taɪ] *f* (*COMPUT*) file; ~**name** *m* file name; ~**verwaltung** *f* file management.

**Daten** ['daːtən] *pl* (*COMPUT*) data; (*Angaben*) data *pl*, particulars; *siehe auch* **Datum**; ~**autobahn** *f* information (super)highway; ~**bank** *f* data base; ~**erfassung** *f* data capture; ~**satz** *m* record; ~**schutz** *m* data protection; ~**sichtgerät** *nt* visual display unit, VDU; ~**träger** *m* data carrier; ~**typist(in)** *m(f)* keyboard operator, keyboarder; ~**übertragung** *f* data transmission; ~**verarbeitung** *f* data processing; ~**verarbeitungsanlage** *f* data processing equipment, DP equipment.

**datieren** [da'tiːrən] *vt* to date.

**Dativ** ['daːtiːf] **(-s, -e)** *m* dative; ~**objekt** *nt* (*GRAM*) indirect object.

**dato** ['daːto] *adv:* **bis** ~ (*COMM: umg*) to date.

**Dattel** ['datəl] **(-, -n)** *f* date.

**Datum** ['daːtʊm] **(-s, Daten)** *nt* date; **das heutige** ~ today's date.

**Datumsgrenze** *f* (*GEOG*) (international) date line.

**Dauer** ['daʊər] **(-, -n)** *f* duration; (*gewisse Zeitspanne*) length; (*Bestand, Fortbestehen*) permanence; **es war nur von kurzer** ~ **it**

didn't last long; **auf die** ~ in the long run; (*auf längere Zeit*) indefinitely; ~**auftrag** *m* standing order; **d~haft** *adj* lasting, durable; ~**haftigkeit** *f* durability; ~**karte** *f* season ticket; ~**lauf** *m* long-distance run.

**dauern** *vi* to last; **es hat sehr lang gedauert, bis er** ... it took him a long time to ...

**dauernd** *adj* constant.

**Dauer-** *zW:* ~**obst** *nt* fruit suitable for storing; ~**redner** (*pej*) *m* long-winded speaker; ~**regen** *m* continuous rain; ~**schlaf** *m* prolonged sleep; ~**stellung** *f* permanent position; ~**welle** *f* perm, permanent wave; ~**wurst** *f* German salami; ~**zustand** *m* permanent condition.

**Daumen** ['daʊmən] (**-s, -**) *m* thumb; **jdm die** ~ **drücken** *od* **halten** to keep one's fingers crossed for sb; **über den** ~ **peilen** to guess roughly; ~**lutscher** *m* thumb-sucker.

**Daune** ['daʊnə] (**-, -n**) *f* down.

**Daunendecke** *f* down duvet.

**davon** [da'fɔn] *adv* of it; (*räumlich*) away; (*weg von*) away from it; (*Grund*) because of it; (*mit Passiv*) by it; **das kommt** ~! that's what you get; ~ **abgesehen** apart from that; **wenn wir einmal** ~ **absehen, daß** ... if for once we overlook the fact that ...; ~ **sprechen/wissen** to talk/know of *od* about it; **was habe ich** ~? what's the point?; ~ **betroffen werden** to be affected by it; ~**gehen** *unreg vi* to leave, go away; ~**kommen** *unreg vi* to escape; ~**lassen** *unreg vt:* **die Finger** ~**lassen** (*umg*) to keep one's hands *od* fingers off (it); ~**laufen** *unreg vi* to run away; ~**machen** *vr* to make off; ~**tragen** *unreg vt* to carry off; (*Verletzung*) to receive.

**davor** [da'fo:r] *adv* (*räumlich*) in front of it; (*zeitlich*) before (that); ~ **warnen** to warn about it.

**dazu** [da'tsu:] *adv* (*legen, stellen*) by it; (*essen*) with it; **und** ~ **noch** and in addition; **ein Beispiel/seine Gedanken** ~ one example for/his thoughts on this; **wie komme ich denn** ~? why should I?; ... **aber ich bin nicht** ~ **gekommen** ... but I didn't get around to it; **das Recht** ~ the right to do it; ~ **bereit sein, etw zu tun** to be prepared to do sth; ~ **fähig sein** to be capable of it; **sich** ~ **äußern** to say something on it; ~**gehören** *vi* to belong to it; **das gehört** ~ (*versteht sich von selbst*) it's all part of it; **es gehört schon einiges** ~, **das zu tun** it takes a lot to do that; ~**gehörig** *adj* appropriate; ~**kommen** *unreg vi* (*Ereignisse*) to happen too; (*an einen Ort*) to come along; **kommt noch etwas** ~? will there be anything else?; ~**lernen** *vt:* **schon wieder was** ~**gelernt!** you learn something (new) every day!; ~**mal** ['da:tsuma:l] *adv* in those days; ~**tun** *unreg vt* to add; **er hat es ohne dein D~tun geschafft** he managed it without your doing *etc* anything.

**dazwischen** [da'tsvɪʃən] *adv* in between;

(*zusammen mit*) among them; **der Unterschied** ~ the difference between them; ~**fahren** *unreg vi* (*eingreifen*) to intervene; ~**funken** (*umg*) *vi* (*eingreifen*) to put one's oar in; ~**kommen** *unreg vi* (*hineingeraten*) to get caught in it; **es ist etwas** ~**gekommen** something (has) cropped up; ~**reden** *vi* (*unterbrechen*) to interrupt; (*sich einmischen*) to interfere; ~**treten** *unreg vi* to intervene.

**DB** *f abk* (= *Deutsche Bahn*) German railways.

**DBP** *f abk* = **Deutsche Bundespost.**

**DDR** (**-**) *f abk* (*früher: = Deutsche Demokratische Republik*) GDR.

---

*The **DDR** (Deutsche Demokratische Republik) was the name by which the former Communist German Democratic Republic was known. It was founded in 1949 from the Soviet-occupied zone. After the building of the Berlin Wall in 1961 it was virtually sealed off from the West until mass demonstrations and demands for reform forced the opening of the borders in 1989. It then merged in 1990 with the **BRD**.*

---

**DDT** ® *nt abk* DDT.

**Dealer(in)** ['di:lər(ɪn)] (**-s, -**) (*umg*) *m(f)* pusher.

**Debatte** [de'batə] (**-, -n**) *f* debate; **das steht hier nicht zur** ~ that's not the issue.

**debattieren** [deba'ti:rən] *vt* to debate.

**Debet** ['de:bɛt] (**-s, -s**) *nt* (*FIN*) debits *pl.*

**Debüt** [de'by:] (**-s, -s**) *nt* debut.

**dechiffrieren** [deʃɪ'fri:rən] *vt* to decode; (*Text*) to decipher.

**Deck** [dɛk] (**-(e)s, -s** *od* **-e**) *nt* deck; **an** ~ **gehen** to go on deck.

**Deckbett** *nt* feather quilt.

**Deckblatt** *nt* (*Schutzblatt*) cover.

**Decke** (**-, -n**) *f* cover; (*Bett~*) blanket; (*Tisch~*) tablecloth; (*Zimmer~*) ceiling; **unter einer** ~ **stecken** to be hand in glove; **an die** ~ **gehen** to hit the roof; **mir fällt die** ~ **auf den Kopf** (*fig*) I feel really claustrophobic.

**Deckel** (**-s, -**) *m* lid; **du kriegst gleich eins auf den** ~ (*umg*) you're going to catch it.

**decken** *vt* to cover ♦ *vr* to coincide ♦ *vi* to lay the table; **mein Bedarf ist gedeckt** I have all I need; (*fig*) I've had enough; **sich an einen gedeckten Tisch setzen** (*fig*) to be handed everything on a plate.

**Deckmantel** *m:* **unter dem** ~ **von** under the guise of.

**Deckname** *m* assumed name.

**Deckung** *f* (*das Schützen*) covering; (*Schutz*) cover; (*SPORT*) defence, defense (*US*); (*Übereinstimmen*) agreement; **zur** ~ **seiner Schulden** to meet his debts.

**deckungsgleich** *adj* congruent.

**Decoder** *m* (*TV*) decoder.

**de facto** [de: 'fakto] *adv* de facto.

**Defekt** [de'fɛkt] (**-(e)s, -e**) *m* fault, defect; **d~** *adj* faulty.

**defensiv** [defɛn'siːf] *adj* defensive.
**Defensive** *f*: **jdn in die** ~ **drängen** to force sb onto the defensive.
**definieren** [defi'niːrən] *vt* to define.
**Definition** [definitsi'oːn] *f* definition.
**definitiv** [defini'tiːf] *adj* definite.
**Defizit** ['deːfitsɪt] (**-s, -e**) *nt* deficit.
**defizitär** [defitsi'tɛːr] *adj*: **eine ~e Haushaltspolitik führen** to follow an economic policy which can only lead to deficit.
**Deflation** [deflatsi'oːn] *f* (*ECON*) deflation.
**deflationär** [deflatsio'nɛːr] *adj* deflationary.
**deftig** ['dɛftɪç] *adj* (*Essen*) large; (*Witz*) coarse.
**Degen** ['deːgən] (**-s, -**) *m* sword.
**degenerieren** [degene'riːrən] *vi* to degenerate.
**degradieren** [degra'diːrən] *vt* to degrade.
**dehnbar** ['deːnbaːr] *adj* elastic; (*fig: Begriff*) loose; **D~keit** *f* elasticity; looseness.
**dehnen** *vt, vr* to stretch.
**Dehnung** *f* stretching.
**Deich** [daɪç] (**-(e)s, -e**) *m* dyke (*BRIT*), dike (*US*).
**Deichsel** ['daɪksəl] (**-, -n**) *f* shaft.
**deichseln** *vt* (*fig: umg*) to wangle.
**dein** [daɪn] *pron* (*in Briefen: D~*) your; (*adjektivisch*): **herzliche Grüße, D~e Elke** with best wishes, yours *od* (*herzlicher*) love, Elke.
**deine(r, s)** *poss pron* yours.
**deiner** *gen von* **du** ♦ *pron* of you.
**deinerseits** *adv* on your part.
**deinesgleichen** *pron* people like you.
**deinetwegen** ['daɪnət've:gən] *adv* (*für dich*) for your sake; (*wegen dir*) on your account.
**deinetwillen** ['daɪnət'vɪlən] *adv*: **um ~** = **deinetwegen**.
**deinige** *pron*: **der/die/das ~** yours.
**dekadent** [deka'dɛnt] *adj* decadent.
**Dekadenz** *f* decadence.
**Dekan** [de'kaːn] (**-s, -e**) *m* dean.
**deklassieren** [dekla'siːrən] *vt* (*SOZIOLOGIE: herabsetzen*) to downgrade; (*SPORT: übertreffen*) to outclass.
**Deklination** [deklinatsi'oːn] *f* declension.
**deklinieren** [dekli'niːrən] *vt* to decline.
**Dekolleté** [dekɔl'teː] (**-s, -s**) *nt* low neckline.
**Dekor** [de'koːr] (**-s, -s** *od* **-e**) *m od nt* decoration.
**Dekorateur(in)** [dekora'tøːr(ɪn)] *m(f)* window dresser.
**Dekoration** [dekoratsi'oːn] *f* decoration; (*in Laden*) window dressing.
**dekorativ** [dekora'tiːf] *adj* decorative.
**dekorieren** [deko'riːrən] *vt* to decorate; (*Schaufenster*) to dress.
**Dekostoff** ['deːkoʃtɔf] *m* (*TEXTIL*) furnishing fabric.
**Dekret** [de'kreːt] (**-(e)s, -e**) *nt* decree.
**Delegation** [delegatsi'oːn] *f* delegation.
**delegieren** [dele'giːrən] *vt*: ~ (**an** +*akk*) to delegate (to).
**Delegierte(r)** *f(m)* delegate.

**Delhi** ['deːlɪ] (**-s**) *nt* Delhi.
**delikat** [deli'kaːt] *adj* (*zart, heikel*) delicate; (*köstlich*) delicious.
**Delikatesse** [delika'tɛsə] (**-, -n**) *f* delicacy.
**Delikatessengeschäft** *nt* delicatessen (shop).
**Delikt** [de'lɪkt] (**-(e)s, -e**) *nt* (*JUR*) offence (*BRIT*), offense (*US*).
**Delinquent** [delɪŋ'kvɛnt] *m* (*geh*) offender.
**Delirium** [de'liːriʊm] *nt*: **im ~ sein** to be delirious; (*umg: betrunken*) to be paralytic.
**Delle** ['dɛlə] (**-, -n**) (*umg*) *f* dent.
**Delphin** [dɛl'fiːn] (**-s, -e**) *m* dolphin.
**Delphinschwimmen** *nt* butterfly (stroke).
**Delta** ['dɛlta] (**-s, -s**) *nt* delta.
**dem** [de(ː)m] *art dat von* **der, das; wie ~ auch sei** be that as it may.
**Demagoge** [dema'goːgə] (**-n, -n**) *m* demagogue.
**Demarkationslinie** [demarkatsi'oːnzliːniə] *f* demarcation line.
**Dementi** [de'mɛnti] (**-s, -s**) *nt* denial.
**dementieren** [demɛn'tiːrən] *vt* to deny.
**dem-** *zW*: ~**entsprechend** *adj* appropriate ♦ *adv* correspondingly; (*demnach*) accordingly; ~**gemäß** *adv* accordingly; ~**nach** *adv* accordingly; ~**nächst** *adv* shortly.
**Demo** ['deːmo] (**-s, -s**) (*umg*) *f* demo.
**Demographie** [demogra'fiː] *f* demography.
**Demokrat(in)** [demo'kraːt(ɪn)] (**-en, -en**) *m(f)* democrat.
**Demokratie** [demokra'tiː] *f* democracy; ~**verständnis** *nt* understanding of (the meaning of) democracy.
**demokratisch** *adj* democratic.
**demokratisieren** [demokrati'ziːrən] *vt* to democratize.
**demolieren** [demo'liːrən] *vt* to demolish.
**Demonstrant(in)** [demɔn'strant(ɪn)] *m(f)* demonstrator.
**Demonstration** [demɔnstratsi'oːn] *f* demonstration.
**demonstrativ** [demɔnstra'tiːf] *adj* demonstrative; (*Protest*) pointed.
**demonstrieren** [demɔn'striːrən] *vt, vi* to demonstrate.
**Demontage** [demɔn'taːʒə] (**-, -n**) *f* (*lit, fig*) dismantling.
**demontieren** [demɔn'tiːrən] *vt* (*lit, fig*) to dismantle; (*Räder*) to take off.
**demoralisieren** [demorali'ziːrən] *vt* to demoralize.
**Demoskopie** [demosko'piː] *f* public opinion research.
**demselben** *dat von* **derselbe, dasselbe**.
**Demut** ['deːmuːt] (**-**) *f* humility.
**demütig** ['deːmyːtɪç] *adj* humble.
**demütigen** ['deːmyːtɪgən] *vt* to humiliate.
**Demütigung** *f* humiliation.
**demzufolge** ['deːmtsu'fɔlgə] *adv* accordingly.
**den** [de(ː)n] *art akk von* **den**.
**denen** ['deːnən] *pron dat pl von* **der, die, das**.

**Denk-** *zW:* ~**anstoß** *m:* **jdm** ~**anstöße geben** to give sb food for thought; ~**art** *f* mentality; **d**~**bar** *adj* conceivable.

**denken** ['dɛŋkən] *unreg vi* to think ♦ *vt:* **für jdn/ etw gedacht sein** to be intended *od* meant for sb/sth ♦ *vr* (*vorstellen*): **das kann ich mir** ~ I can imagine; (*beabsichtigen*): **sich** *dat* **etw bei etw** ~ to mean sth by sth; **wo** ~ **Sie hin!** what an idea!; **ich denke schon** I think so; **an jdn/etw** ~ to think of sb/sth; **daran ist gar nicht zu** ~ that's (quite) out of the question; **ich denke nicht daran, das zu tun** there's no way I'm going to do that (*umg*).

**Denken** (**-s**) *nt* thinking.

**Denker(in)** (**-s, -**) *m(f)* thinker; **das Volk der Dichter und** ~ the nation of poets and philosophers.

**Denk-** *zW:* ~**fähigkeit** *f* intelligence; **d**~**faul** *adj* mentally lazy; ~**fehler** *m* logical error; ~**horizont** *m* mental horizon.

**Denkmal** (**-s, ⁻er**) *nt* monument; ~**schutz** *m:* **etw unter** ~**schutz stellen** to classify sth as a historical monument.

**Denk-** *zW:* ~**pause** *f:* **eine** ~**pause einlegen** to have a break to think things over; ~**schrift** *f* memorandum; ~**vermögen** *nt* intellectual capacity; **d**~**würdig** *adj* memorable; ~**zettel** *m:* **jdm einen** ~**zettel verpassen** to teach sb a lesson.

**denn** [dɛn] *konj* for; (*konzessiv*): **es sei** ~**, (daß)** unless ♦ *adv* then; (*nach Komparativ*) than.

**dennoch** ['dɛnɔx] *konj* nevertheless ♦ *adv:* **und** ~**, ...** and yet ...

**denselben** *akk von* **derselbe** ♦ *dat von* **dieselben.**

**Denunziant(in)** [denʊntsi'ant(ɪn)] *m(f)* informer.

**denunzieren** [denʊn'tsiːrən] *vt* to inform against.

**Deospray** ['deːɔʃpreɪ] *nt od m* deodorant spray.

**Depesche** [de'pɛʃə] (**-, -n**) *f* dispatch.

**deplaziert** [depla'tsiːrt] *adj* out of place.

**Deponent(in)** [depo'nɛnt(ɪn)] *m(f)* depositor.

**Deponie** *f* dump, disposal site.

**deponieren** [depo'niːrən] *vt* (*COMM*) to deposit.

**deportieren** [depɔr'tiːrən] *vt* to deport.

**Depot** [de'poː] (**-s, -s**) *nt* warehouse; (*Bus~, EISENB*) depot; (*Bank~*) strongroom (*BRIT*), safe (*US*).

**Depp** [dɛp] (**-en, -en**) *m* (*Dialekt: pej*) twit.

**Depression** [deprɛsi'oːn] *f* depression.

**depressiv** *adj* depressive; (*FIN*) depressed.

**deprimieren** [depri'miːrən] *vt* to depress.

═══════════════ *SCHLÜSSELWORT*

**der** [de(ː)r] (*f* **die**, *nt* **das**) (*gen* **des, der, des,** *dat* **dem, der, dem**) (*akk* **den**) *def art* the; ~ **Rhein** the Rhine; ~ **Klaus** (*umg*) Klaus; **die Frau** (*im allgemeinen*) women; ~ **Tod/das Leben** death/life; ~ **Fuß des Berges** the foot of the hill; **gib es** ~ **Frau** give it to the woman; **er hat sich** *dat* **die Hand verletzt** he has hurt his hand

♦ *rel pron* (*bei Menschen*) who, that; (*bei Tieren, Sachen*) which, that; ~ **Mann, den ich gesehen habe** the man who *od* whom *od* that I saw

♦ *demon pron* he/she/it; (*jener, dieser*) that; (*pl*) those; ~/**die war es** it was him/her; ~ **mit** ~ **Brille** the one with the glasses; **ich will den (da)** I want that one.

**derart** ['deːr'aːrt] *adv* (*Art und Weise*) in such a way; (*Ausmaß: vor adj*) so; (: *vor vb*) so much.

**derartig** *adj* such, this sort of.

**derb** [dɛrp] *adj* sturdy; (*Kost*) solid; (*grob*) coarse; **D**~**heit** *f* sturdiness; solidity; coarseness.

**deren** ['deːrən] *rel pron* (*gen sing von die*) whose; (*von Sachen*) of which; (*gen pl von der, die, das*) their; whose; of whom.

**derentwillen** ['deːrənt'vɪlən] *adv:* **um** ~ (*rel*) for whose sake; (*von Sachen*) for the sake of which.

**dergestalt** *adv* (*geh*): ~**, daß ...** in such a way that ...

**der-** *zW:* ~**gleichen** *pron* such; (*substantivisch*): **er tat nichts** ~**gleichen** he did nothing of the kind; **und** ~**gleichen (mehr)** and suchlike; ~**jenige** *pron* he; she; it; (*rel*) the one (who); that (which); ~**maßen** *adv* to such an extent, so; ~**selbe** *m pron* the same; ~**weil(en)** *adv* in the meantime; ~**zeit** *adv* (*jetzt*) at present, at the moment; ~**zeitig** *adj* present, current; (*damalig*) then.

**des** [dɛs] *art gen von* **der.**

**Des** [dɛs] (**-**) *nt* (*MUS: auch:* **d**~) D flat.

**Deserteur** [dezɛr'tøːr] *m* deserter.

**desertieren** [dezɛr'tiːrən] *vi* to desert.

**desgl.** *abk* = **desgleichen.**

**desgleichen** ['dɛs'glaɪçən] *pron* the same.

**deshalb** ['dɛs'halp] *adv, konj* therefore, that's why.

**Design** [di'zaɪn] (**-s, -s**) *nt* design.

**designiert** [dezi'gniːrt] *adj attrib:* **der** ~**e Vorsitzende/Nachfolger** the chairman designate/prospective successor.

**Desinfektion** [dɛzɪnfɛktsi'oːn] *f* disinfection.

**Desinfektionsmittel** *nt* disinfectant.

**desinfizieren** [dɛzɪnfi'tsiːrən] *vt* to disinfect.

**Desinteresse** [dɛsˌɪntəˈrɛsə] (**-s**) *nt:* ~ **(an** +*dat*) lack of interest (in).

**desinteressiert** [dɛsˌɪntərɛˈsiːrt] *adj* uninterested.

**desselben** *gen von* **derselbe, dasselbe.**

**dessen** ['dɛsən] *pron gen von* **der, das;** ~**ungeachtet** *adv* nevertheless, regardless.

**Dessert** [dɛ'seːr] (**-s, -s**) *nt* dessert.

**Dessin** [dɛ'sɛ̃ː] (**-s, -s**) *nt* (*TEXTIL*) pattern, design.

**Destillation** [dɛstɪlatsi'oːn] *f* distillation.

**destillieren** [dɛstɪ'liːrən] *vt* to distil.

**desto** ['dɛsto] *adv* all *od* so much the; ~ **besser** all the better.

**destruktiv** [destrʊk'tiːf] *adj* destructive.
**deswegen** ['dɛs've:gən] *konj* therefore, hence.
**Detail** [de'taɪ] (**-s, -s**) *nt* detail.
**detaillieren** [deta'jiːrən] *vt* to specify, give
details of.
**Detektiv** [detɛk'tiːf] (**-s, -e**) *m* detective;
~**roman** *m* detective novel.
**Detektor** [de'tɛktɔr] *m* (*TECH*) detector.
**Detonation** [detonatsi'oːn] *f* explosion, blast.
**Deut** *m*: (**um**) **keinen** ~ not one iota *od* jot.
**deuten** ['dɔytən] *vt* to interpret; (*Zukunft*) to
read ♦ *vi*: ~ (**auf** +*akk*) to point (to *od* at).
**deutlich** *adj* clear; (*Unterschied*) distinct; **jdm
etw** ~ **zu verstehen geben** to make sth
perfectly clear *od* plain to sb; **D~keit** *f*
clarity; distinctness.
**deutsch** [dɔytʃ] *adj* German; ~**e Schrift**
Gothic script; **auf** ~ in German; **auf gut**
~ (**gesagt**) (*fig: umg*) ≈ in plain English;
**D~e Demokratische Republik** (*HIST*)
German Democratic Republic.
**Deutsche(r)** *f(m)*: **er ist** ~**r** he is (a) German.
**Deutschland** *nt* Germany; ~**lied** *nt German
national anthem*; ~**politik** *f* home *od*
domestic policy; (*von fremdem Staat*) policy
towards Germany.
**deutschsprachig** *adj* (*Bevölkerung, Gebiete*)
German-speaking; (*Zeitung, Ausgabe*)
German-language; (*Literatur*) German.
**deutschstämmig** *adj* of German origin.
**Deutung** *f* interpretation.
**Devise** [de'viːzə] (**-, -n**) *f* motto, device;
**Devisen** *pl* (*FIN*) foreign currency *od*
exchange.
**Devisenausgleich** *m* foreign exchange
offset.
**Devisenkontrolle** *f* exchange control.
**Dez.** *abk* (= *Dezember*) Dec.
**Dezember** [de'tsɛmbər] (**-(s), -**) *m* December;
*siehe auch* **September**.
**dezent** [de'tsɛnt] *adj* discreet.
**Dezentralisation** [detsɛntralizatsi'oːn] *f*
decentralization.
**Dezernat** [detsɛr'naːt] (**-(e)s, -e**) *nt*
(*VERWALTUNG*) department.
**Dezibel** [detsi'bɛl] (**-s, -**) *nt* decibel.
**dezidiert** [detsi'diːrt] *adj* firm, determined.
**dezimal** [detsi'maːl] *adj* decimal; **D~bruch** *m*
decimal (fraction); **D~system** *nt* decimal
system.
**dezimieren** [detsi'miːrən] *vt* (*fig*) to decimate
♦ *vr* to be decimated.
**DFB** *m abk* (= *Deutscher Fußball-Bund*) *German
Football Association*.
**DFG** *f abk* (= *Deutsche Forschungsgemein-
schaft*) *German Research Council*.
**DGB** *m abk* (= *Deutscher Gewerkschaftsbund*)
≈ TUC.
**dgl.** *abk* = **dergleichen.**
**d.h.** *abk* (= *das heißt*) i.e.
**Dia** ['diːa] (**-s, -s**) *nt* = **Diapositiv.**
**Diabetes** [dia'beːtɛs] (**-, -**) *m* (*MED*) diabetes.

**Diabetiker(in)** [dia'beːtikər(ɪn)] (**-s, -**) *m(f)*
diabetic.
**Diagnose** [dia'gnoːzə] (**-, -n**) *f* diagnosis.
**diagnostizieren** [diagnɔsti'tsiːrən] *vt, vi* (*MED,
fig*) to diagnose.
**diagonal** [diago'naːl] *adj* diagonal.
**Diagonale** (**-, -n**) *f* diagonal.
**Diagramm** [dia'gram] *nt* diagram.
**Diakonie** [diako'niː] *f* (*REL*) social welfare
work.
**Dialekt** [dia'lɛkt] (**-(e)s, -e**) *m* dialect;
~**ausdruck** *m* dialect expression *od* word;
**d~frei** *adj* without an accent.
**dialektisch** *adj* dialectal; (*Logik*) dialectical.
**Dialog** [dia'loːk] (**-(e)s, -e**) *m* dialogue.
**Diamant** [dia'mant] *m* diamond.
**Diapositiv** [diapozi'tiːf] (**-s, -e**) *nt* (*PHOT*) slide,
transparency.
**Diaprojektor** *m* slide projector.
**Diät** [di'ɛːt] (**-**) *f* diet; **Diäten** *pl* (*POL*)
allowance *sing*; **d~** *adv* (*kochen, essen*)
according to a diet; (*leben*) on a special diet.
**dich** [dɪç] *akk von du* ♦ *pron* you ♦ *refl pron*
yourself.
**dicht** [dɪçt] *adj* dense; (*Nebel*) thick; (*Gewebe*)
close; (*undurchlässig*) (water)tight; (*fig*)
concise; (*umg: zu*) shut, closed ♦ *adv*: ~ **an/
bei** close to; **er ist nicht ganz** ~ (*umg*) he's
crackers; ~ **machen** to make watertight/
airtight; (*Person*) to close one's mind;
~ **hintereinander** right behind one another;
~**bevölkert** *adj* densely *od* heavily
populated.
**Dichte** (**-, -n**) *f* density; thickness; closeness;
(water)tightness; (*fig*) conciseness.
**dichten** *vt* (*dicht machen*) to make watertight;
to seal; (*NAUT*) to caulk; (*LITER*) to compose,
write ♦ *vi* (*LITER*) to compose, write.
**Dichter(in)** (**-s, -**) *m(f)* poet; (*Autor*) writer;
**d~isch** *adj* poetical; **d~ische Freiheit** poetic
licence (*BRIT*) *od* license (*US*).
**dichthalten** *unreg* (*umg*) *vi* to keep one's
mouth shut.
**dichtmachen** (*umg*) *vt* (*Geschäft*) to wind up.
**Dichtung** *f* (*TECH*) washer; (*AUT*) gasket;
(*Gedichte*) poetry; (*Prosa*) (piece of) writing;
~ **und Wahrheit** (*fig*) fact and fantasy.
**dick** [dɪk] *adj* thick; (*fett*) fat; **durch** ~ **und
dünn** through thick and thin; **D~darm** *m*
(*ANAT*) colon.
**Dicke** (**-, -n**) *f* thickness; fatness.
**dickfellig** *adj* thick-skinned.
**dickflüssig** *adj* viscous.
**Dickicht** (**-s, -e**) *nt* thicket.
**dick-** *zW*: **D~kopf** *m* mule; **D~milch** *f* soured
milk; **D~schädel** *m* = **Dickkopf.**
**die** [diː] *def art* the; *siehe auch* **der.**
**Dieb(in)** [diːp, 'diːbɪn] (**-(e)s, -e**) *m(f)* thief;
**haltet den** ~! stop thief!; **d~isch** *adj*
thieving; (*umg*) immense; ~**stahl** *m* theft;
**d~stahlsicher** *adj* theft-proof.
**diejenige** ['diːjeːnɪgə] *pron siehe* **derjenige.**

**Diele** ['di:lə] (-, -n) *f* (*Brett*) board; (*Flur*) hall, lobby; (*Eis~*) ice-cream parlour (*BRIT*) *od* parlor (*US*).

**dienen** ['di:nən] *vi:* (**jdm**) ~ to serve (sb); **womit kann ich Ihnen** ~? what can I do for you?; (*in Geschäft*) can I help you?

**Diener** (-s, -) *m* servant; (*umg: Verbeugung*) bow; ~**in** *f* (maid)servant.

**dienern** *vi* (*fig*): ~ (**vor** +*dat*) to bow and scrape (to).

**Dienerschaft** *f* servants *pl*.

**dienlich** *adj* useful, helpful.

**Dienst** [di:nst] (-(**e**)**s, -e**) *m* service; (*Arbeit, Arbeitszeit*) work; ~ **am Kunden** customer service; **jdm zu** ~**en stehen** to be at sb's disposal; **außer** ~ retired; ~ **haben** to be on duty; **der öffentliche** ~ the civil service.

**Dienstag** *m* Tuesday; **am** ~ on Tuesday; ~ **in acht Tagen** *od* **in einer Woche** a week on Tuesday, Tuesday week; ~ **vor einer Woche** *od* **acht Tagen** a week (ago) last Tuesday.

**dienstags** *adv* on Tuesdays.

**Dienst-** *zW:* ~**alter** *nt* length of service; **d~beflissen** *adj* zealous; ~**bote** *m* servant; ~**boteneingang** *m* tradesmen's *od* service entrance; **d~eifrig** *adj* zealous; **d~frei** *adj* off duty; ~**gebrauch** *m* (*MIL, VERWALTUNG*): **nur für den** ~**gebrauch** for official use only; ~**geheimnis** *nt* professional secret; ~**gespräch** *nt* business call; ~**grad** *m* rank; **d~habend** *adj* (*Arzt, Offizier*) on duty; ~**leistung** *f* service; ~**leistungsbetrieb** *m* service industry business; ~**leistungsgewerbe** *nt* service industries *pl*; **d~lich** *adj* official; (*Angelegenheiten*) business *attrib*; ~**mädchen** *nt* domestic servant; ~**plan** *m* duty rota; ~**reise** *f* business trip; ~**stelle** *f* office; **d~tuend** *adj* on duty; ~**vorschrift** *f* service regulations *pl*; ~**wagen** *m* (*von Beamten*) official car; ~**weg** *m* official channels *pl*; ~**zeit** *f* office hours *pl*; (*MIL*) period of service.

**diesbezüglich** *adj* (*Frage*) on this matter.

**diese(r, s)** *pron* this (one) ♦ *adj* this; ~ **Nacht** tonight.

**Diesel** ['di:zəl] (-s) *m* (*Kraftstoff*) diesel fuel; ~**öl** ['di:zələ:l] *nt* diesel oil.

**dieselbe** [di:'zɛlbə] *f pron* the same.

**dieselben** [di:'zɛlbən] *pl pron* the same.

**diesig** *adj* drizzly.

**dies-** *zW:* ~**jährig** *adj* this year's; ~**mal** *adv* this time; **D~seits** (-) *nt* this life; ~**seits** *präp* +*gen* on this side.

**Dietrich** ['di:trɪç] (-s, -e) *m* picklock.

**Diffamierungskampagne** [dɪfa'mi:rʊŋskampanjə] *f* smear campaign.

**differential** [dɪferɛntsi'aːl] *adj* differential; **D~getriebe** *nt* differential gear; **D~rechnung** *f* differential calculus.

**Differenzbetrag** *m* difference, balance.

**differenzieren** [dɪferɛn'tsiːrən] *vt* to make distinctions in ♦ *vi:* ~ (**bei**) to make

distinctions (in).

**differenziert** *adj* complex.

**diffus** [dɪ'fuːs] *adj* (*Gedanken etc*) confused.

**Digital-** [digi'taːl-] *zW:* ~**anzeige** *f* digital display; ~**rechner** *m* digital computer; ~**uhr** *f* digital watch.

**Diktaphon** [dɪkta'foːn] *nt* dictaphone ®.

**Diktat** [dɪk'taːt] (-(**e**)**s, -e**) *nt* dictation; (*fig: Gebot*) dictate; (*POL*) diktat, dictate.

**Diktator** [dɪk'taːtɔr] *m* dictator; **d~isch** [-a'toːrɪʃ] *adj* dictatorial.

**Diktatur** [dɪkta'tuːr] *f* dictatorship.

**diktieren** [dɪk'tiːrən] *vt* to dictate.

**Diktion** [dɪktsi'oːn] *f* style.

**Dilemma** [di'lɛma] (-s, -s *od* -ta) *nt* dilemma.

**Dilettant** [dilɛ'tant] *m* dilettante, amateur; **d~isch** *adj* dilettante.

**Dimension** [dimɛnzi'oːn] *f* dimension.

**DIN** *f abk* (= *Deutsche Industrie-Norm*) German Industrial Standard; ~ **A4** A4.

**Ding** [dɪŋ] (-(**e**)**s, -e**) *nt* thing; object; **das ist ein** ~ **der Unmöglichkeit** that is totally impossible; **guter** ~**e sein** to be in good spirits; **so wie die** ~**e liegen, nach Lage der** ~**e** as things are; **es müßte nicht mit rechten** ~**en zugehen, wenn ...** it would be more than a little strange if ...; **ein krummes** ~ **drehen** to commit a crime; to do something wrong; **d~fest** *adj:* **jdn d~fest machen** to arrest sb; **d~lich** *adj* real, concrete.

**Dings** (-) (*umg*) *nt* thingummyjig (*BRIT*).

**Dingsbums** ['dɪŋsbʊms] (-) (*umg*) *nt* thingummybob (*BRIT*).

**Dingsda** (-) (*umg*) *nt* thingummyjig (*BRIT*).

**Dinosaurier** [dino'zauriər] *m* dinosaur.

**Diözese** [diø'tseːzə] (-, -n) *f* diocese.

**Diphtherie** [dɪfte'riː] *f* diphtheria.

**Dipl.-Ing.** *abk* = **Diplomingenieur.**

**Diplom** [di'ploːm] (-(**e**)**s, -e**) *nt* diploma; (*Hochschulabschluß*) degree; ~**arbeit** *f* dissertation.

**Diplomatie** [diplo'maːt] (-**en, -en**) *m* diplomat.

**Diplomatie** [diploma'tiː] *f* diplomacy.

**diplomatisch** [diplo'maːtɪʃ] *adj* diplomatic.

**Diplomingenieur** *m* academically qualified engineer.

**dir** [di:r] *dat von* **du** ♦ *pron* (to) you.

**direkt** [di'rɛkt] *adj* direct; ~ **fragen** to ask outright *od* straight out.

**Direktion** [dirɛktsi'oːn] *f* management; (*Büro*) manager's office.

**Direktmandat** *nt* (*POL*) direct mandate.

**Direktor(in)** *m(f)* director; (*von Hochschule*) principal; (*von Schule*) principal, head (teacher) (*BRIT*).

**Direktorium** [direk'toːriʊm] *nt* board of directors.

**Direktübertragung** *f* live broadcast.

**Direktverkauf** *m* direct selling.

**Dirigent(in)** [diri'gɛnt(ɪn)] *m(f)* conductor.

**dirigieren** [diri'giːrən] *vt* to direct; (*MUS*) to

conduct.

**Dirne** ['dɪrnə] (-, -n) f prostitute.

**Dis** [dɪs] (-, -) nt (MUS) D sharp.

**dis** [dɪs] (-, -) nt (MUS) D sharp.

**Disco** ['dɪsko] (-s, -s) f disco.

**Disharmonie** [dɪsharmo'ni:] f (lit, fig) discord.

**Diskette** [dɪs'kɛtə] f disk, diskette.

**Diskettenlaufwerk** nt disk drive.

**Diskont** [dɪs'kɔnt] (-s, -e) m discount; ~satz m rate of discount.

**Diskothek** [dɪsko'te:k] (-, -en) f disco(theque).

**diskreditieren** [dɪskredi'ti:rən] vt (geh) to discredit.

**Diskrepanz** [dɪskre'pants] f discrepancy.

**diskret** [dɪs'kre:t] adj discreet.

**Diskretion** [dɪskretsi'o:n] f discretion; **strengste ~ wahren** to preserve the strictest confidence.

**diskriminieren** [dɪskrimi'ni:rən] vt to discriminate against.

**Diskriminierung** f: ~ (von) discrimination (against).

**Diskussion** [dɪskusi'o:n] f discussion; **zur ~ stehen** to be under discussion.

**Diskussionsbeitrag** m contribution to the discussion.

**Diskuswerfen** ['dɪskusvɛrfən] nt throwing the discus.

**diskutabel** [dɪsku'ta:bəl] adj debatable.

**diskutieren** [dɪsku'ti:rən] vt, vi to discuss; **darüber läßt sich ~** that sounds like something we could talk about.

**disponieren** [dɪspo'ni:rən] vi (geh: planen) to make arrangements.

**Disposition** [dɪspozitsi'o:n] f (geh: Verfügung): **jdm zur** od **zu jds ~ stehen** to be at sb's disposal.

**disqualifizieren** [dɪskvalifi'tsi:rən] vt to disqualify.

**Dissertation** [dɪsɛrtatsi'o:n] f dissertation; doctoral thesis.

**Dissident(in)** [dɪsi'dɛnt(ɪn)] m(f) dissident.

**Distanz** [dɪs'tants] f distance; (fig: Abstand, Entfernung) detachment; (Zurückhaltung) reserve.

**distanzieren** [dɪstan'tsi:rən] vr: **sich von jdm/etw ~** to dissociate o.s. from sb/sth.

**distanziert** adj (Verhalten) distant.

**Distel** ['dɪstəl] (-, -n) f thistle.

**Disziplin** [dɪstsi'pli:n] (-, -en) f discipline.

**Disziplinarverfahren** [dɪstsipli'narfɛrfa:rən] nt disciplinary proceedings pl.

**dito** ['di:to] adv (COMM, hum) ditto.

**Diva** ['di:va] (-, -s) f star; (FILM) screen goddess.

**divers** [di'vɛrs] adj various.

**Diverses** pl sundries pl; „~" "miscellaneous".

**Dividende** [divi'dɛndə] (-, -n) f dividend.

**dividieren** [divi'di:rən] vt: ~ **(durch)** to divide (by).

**d.J.** abk (= der Jüngere) jun.

**Djakarta** [dʒa'karta] nt Jakarta.

**DJH** nt abk (= Deutsches Jugendherbergswerk) German Youth Hostel Association.

**DKP** f abk (= Deutsche Kommunistische Partei) German Communist Party.

**DLRG** f abk (= Deutsche Lebens-Rettungs-Gesellschaft) German lifesaving association.

**DLV** m abk (= Deutscher Leichtathletik-Verband) German track and field associaton.

**DM** f abk (= Deutsche Mark) DM.

**d.M.** abk (= dieses Monats) inst.

**D-Mark** ['de:mark] (-, -) f deutschmark, German mark.

**DNS** f abk (= Desoxyribo(se)nukleinsäure) DNA.

================ *SCHLÜSSELWORT*

**doch** [dɔx] adv **1** (dennoch) after all; (sowieso) anyway; **er kam ~ noch** he came after all; **du weißt es ja ~ besser** you know more about it (than I do) anyway; **es war ~ ganz interessant** it was actually quite interesting; **und ~, ...** and yet ...

**2** (als bejahende Antwort) yes I do/it does etc; **das ist nicht wahr - ~!** that's not true - yes it is!

**3** (auffordernd): **komm ~** do come; **laß ihn ~** just leave him; **nicht ~!** oh no!

**4**: **sie ist ~ noch so jung** but she's still so young; **Sie wissen ~, wie das ist** you know how it is(, don't you?); **wenn ~** if only

♦ konj (aber) but; (trotzdem) all the same; **und ~ hat er es getan** but still he did it.

**Docht** [dɔxt] (-(e)s, -e) m wick.

**Dock** [dɔk] (-s, -s od -e) nt dock; ~gebühren pl dock dues pl.

**Dogge** ['dɔgə] (-, -n) f bulldog; **deutsche ~** Great Dane.

**Dogma** ['dɔgma] (-s, -men) nt dogma.

**dogmatisch** [dɔ'gma:tɪʃ] adj dogmatic.

**Dohle** ['do:lə] (-, -n) f jackdaw.

**Doktor** ['dɔktɔr] (-s, -en) m doctor; **den ~ machen** (umg) to do a doctorate od Ph.D.

**Doktorand(in)** [dɔktɔ'rant (-dɪn)] (-en, -en) m(f) Ph.D. student.

**Doktor-** zW: ~**arbeit** f doctoral thesis; ~**titel** m doctorate; ~**vater** m supervisor.

**doktrinär** [dɔktri'nɛ:r] adj doctrinal; (stur) doctrinaire.

**Dokument** [doku'mɛnt] nt document.

**Dokumentar-** zW: ~**bericht** m documentary; ~**film** m documentary (film); **d~isch** adj documentary; ~**spiel** nt docudrama.

**dokumentieren** [dokumen'ti:rən] vt to document; (fig: zu erkennen geben) to reveal, show.

**Dolch** [dɔlç] (-(e)s, -e) m dagger; ~**stoß** m (bes fig) stab.

**dolmetschen** ['dɔlmɛtʃən] vt, vi to interpret.

**Dolmetscher(in)** (-s, -) m(f) interpreter.

**Dolomiten** [dolo'mi:tən] pl (GEOG): **die ~** the

Dolomites *pl.*

**Dom** [doːm] (-(e)s, -e) *m* cathedral.

**Domäne** [doˈmɛːnə] (-, -n) *f* (*fig*) domain, province.

**dominieren** [domiˈniːrən] *vt* to dominate ♦ *vi* to predominate.

**Dominikanische Republik** [dominiˈkaːnɪʃərepuˈbliːk] *f* Dominican Republic.

**Dompfaff** [ˈdoːmpfaf] (-en, -en) *m* bullfinch.

**Dompteur** [dɔmpˈtøːr] *m* (*Zirkus*) trainer.

**Dompteuse** [dɔmpˈtøːzə] *f* (*Zirkus*) trainer.

**Donau** [ˈdoːnaʊ] *f*: **die ~** the Danube.

**Donner** [ˈdɔnər] (-s, -) *m* thunder; **wie vom ~ gerührt** (*fig*) thunderstruck.

**donnern** *vi unpers* to thunder ♦ *vt* (*umg*) to slam, crash.

**Donnerschlag** *m* thunderclap.

**Donnerstag** *m* Thursday; *siehe auch* **Dienstag**.

**Donnerwetter** *nt* thunderstorm; (*fig*) dressing-down ♦ *interj* good heavens!; (*anerkennend*) my word!

**doof** [doːf] (*umg*) *adj* daft, stupid.

**Dopingkontrolle** [ˈdɔpɪŋkɔntrɔlə] *f* (*SPORT*) dope check.

**Doppel** [ˈdɔpəl] (-s, -) *nt* duplicate; (*SPORT*) doubles; **~band** *m* (*von doppeltem Umfang*) double-sized volume; (*zwei Bände*) two volumes *pl*; **~bett**.*nt* double bed; **d~bödig** *adj* (*fig*) ambiguous; **d~deutig** *adj* ambiguous; **~fenster** *nt* double glazing; **~gänger(in)** (-s, -) *m(f)* double; **~korn** *m* type of schnapps; **~punkt** *m* colon; **d~seitig** *adj* (*auch COMPUT: Diskette*) double-sided; (*Lungenentzündung*) double; **d~seitige Anzeige** double-page advertisement; **d~sinnig** *adj* ambiguous; **~stecker** *m* two-way adaptor; **~stunde** *f* (*SCH*) double period.

**doppelt** *adj* double; (*COMM: Buchführung*) double-entry; (*Staatsbürgerschaft*) dual ♦ *adv*: **die Karte habe ich ~** I have two of these cards; **~ gemoppelt** (*umg*) saying the same thing twice over; **in ~er Ausführung** in duplicate.

**Doppel-** *zW*: **~verdiener** *pl* two-income family; **~zentner** *m* 100 kilograms; **~zimmer** *nt* double room.

**Dorf** [dɔrf] (-(e)s, -er) *nt* village; **~bewohner** *m* villager.

**dörflich** [ˈdœrflɪç] *adj* village *attrib*.

**Dorn¹** [dɔrn] (-(e)s, -en) *m* (*BOT*) thorn; **das ist mir ein ~ im Auge** (*fig*) it's a thorn in my flesh.

**Dorn²** [dɔrn] (-(e)s, -e) *m* (*Schnallen~*) tongue, pin.

**dornig** *adj* thorny.

**Dornröschen** *nt* Sleeping Beauty.

**dörren** [ˈdœrən] *vt* to dry.

**Dörrobst** [ˈdœroːpst] *nt* dried fruit.

**Dorsch** [dɔrʃ] (-(e)s, -e) *m* cod.

**dort** [dɔrt] *adv* there; **~ drüben** over there; **~her** *adv* from there; **~hin** *adv* (to) there;

**~hinaus** *adv*: **frech bis ~hinaus** (*umg*) really cheeky.

**dortig** *adj* of that place; in that town.

**Dose** [ˈdoːzə] (-, -n) *f* box; (*Blech~*) tin, can; **in ~n** (*Konserven*) canned, tinned (*BRIT*).

**Dosen** *pl von* **Dose, Dosis.**

**dösen** [ˈdøːzən] (*umg*) *vi* to doze.

**Dosenmilch** *f* evaporated milk.

**Dosenöffner** *m* tin (*BRIT*) *od* can opener.

**dosieren** [doˈziːrən] *vt* (*lit, fig*) to measure out.

**Dosis** [ˈdoːzɪs] (-, **Dosen**) *f* dose.

**Dotierung** [doˈtiːrʊŋ] *f* endowment; (*von Posten*) remuneration.

**Dotter** [ˈdɔtər] (-s, -) *m* egg yolk.

**Double** [ˈduːbəl] (-s, -s) *nt* (*FILM etc*) stand-in.

**Down-Syndrom** *nt no pl* (*MED*) Down's Syndrome.

**Doz.** *abk* = **Dozent(in)**.

**Dozent(in)** [doˈtsɛnt(ɪn)] (-en, -en) *m(f)*: **~ (für)** lecturer (in), professor (of) (*US*).

**dpa** (-) *f abk* (= *Deutsche Presse-Agentur*) *German Press Agency*.

**Dr.** *abk* = **Doktor.**

**Drache** [ˈdraxə] (-n, -n) *m* (*Tier*) dragon.

**Drachen** (-s, -) *m* kite; **einen ~ steigen lassen** to fly a kite; **d~fliegen** *vi* to hang-glide; **~fliegen** *nt* (*SPORT*) hang-gliding.

**Dragée** [draˈʒeː] (-s, -s) *nt* (*PHARM*) dragee, sugar-coated pill.

**Draht** [draːt] (-(e)s, -e) *m* wire; **auf ~ sein** to be on the ball; **~esel** *m* (*hum*) trusty bicycle; **~gitter** *nt* wire grating; **d~los** *adj* cordless; (*Telefon*) mobile; **~seil** *nt* cable; **Nerven wie ~seile** (*umg*) nerves of steel; **~seilbahn** *f* cable railway; **~zange** *f* pliers *pl*; **~zieher(in)** *m(f)* (*Hug*) wire-puller.

**Drall** *m* (*fig: Hang*) tendency; **einen ~ nach links haben** (*AUT*) to pull to the left.

**drall** [dral] *adj* strapping; (*Frau*) buxom.

**Drama** [ˈdraːma] (-s, **Dramen**) *nt* drama.

**Dramatiker(in)** [draˈmaːtikər(ɪn)] (-s, -) *m(f)* dramatist.

**dramatisch** [draˈmaːtɪʃ] *adj* dramatic.

**Dramaturg(in)** [dramaˈtʊrk(-ɡɪn)] (-en, -en) *m(f)* artistic director; (*TV*) drama producer.

**dran** [dran] (*umg*) *adv* (*an der Reihe*): **jetzt bist du ~** it's your turn now; **früh/spät ~ sein** to be early/late; **ich weiß nicht, wie ich (bei ihm) ~ bin** I don't know where I stand (with him); *siehe auch* **daran**; **~bleiben** *unreg* (*umg*) *vi* to stay close; (*am Apparat*) to hang on.

**Drang** (-(e)s, -e) *m* (*Trieb*) urge, yearning; (*Druck*) pressure; **~ nach** urge *od* yearning for.

**drang** *etc* [draŋ] *vb siehe* **dringen**.

**drängeln** [ˈdrɛŋəln] *vt, vi* to push, jostle.

**drängen** [ˈdrɛŋən] *vt* (*schieben*) to push, press; (*antreiben*) to urge ♦ *vi* (*eilig sein*) to be urgent; (*Zeit*) to press; **auf etw** *akk* **~ to** press for sth.

**drangsalieren** [draŋzaˈliːrən] *vt* to pester, plague.

**dranhalten** (*umg*) *vr* to get a move on.

**drankommen** (*umg*) *unreg vi* (*an die Reihe kommen*) to have one's turn; (*SCH: beim Melden*) to be called; (*Frage, Aufgabe etc*) to come up.

**drannehmen** (*umg*) *unreg vt* (*Schüler*) to ask.

**drasch** *etc* [draːʃ] *vb siehe* **dreschen**.

**drastisch** ['drastɪʃ] *adj* drastic.

**drauf** [drauf] (*umg*) *adv*: ~ **und dran sein, etw zu tun** to be on the point of doing sth; **etw ~ haben** (*können*) to be able to do sth just like that; (*Kenntnisse*) to be well up on sth; *siehe auch* **darauf**; **D~gänger** (**-s, -**) *m* daredevil; ~**gehen** *unreg vi* (*verbraucht werden*) to be used up; (*kaputtgehen*) to be smashed up; ~**zahlen** *vi* (*fig: Einbußen erleiden*) to pay the price.

**draußen** ['drausən] *adv* outside, out-of-doors.

**Drechsler(in)** ['drɛkslər(ɪn)] (**-s, -**) *m(f)* (wood) turner.

**Dreck** [drɛk] (**-(e)s**) *m* mud, dirt; ~ **am Stecken haben** (*fig*) to have a skeleton in the cupboard; **das geht ihn einen ~ an** (*umg*) that's none of his business.

**dreckig** *adj* dirty, filthy; **es geht mir ~** (*umg*) I'm in a bad way.

**Dreckskerl** (*umg!*) *m* dirty swine (*!*).

**Dreh** [dreː] *m*: **den ~ raushaben** *od* **weghaben** (*umg*) to have got the hang of it.

**Dreh-** *zW*: ~**achse** *f* axis of rotation; ~**arbeiten** *pl* (*FILM*) shooting *sing*; ~**bank** *f* lathe; **d~bar** *adj* revolving; ~**buch** *nt* (*FILM*) script.

**drehen** *vt* to turn, rotate; (*Zigaretten*) to roll; (*Film*) to shoot ♦ *vi* to turn, rotate ♦ *vr* to turn; (*handeln von*): **sich um etw ~** to be about sth; **ein Ding ~** (*umg*) to play a prank.

**Dreher(in)** (**-s, -**) *m(f)* lathe operator.

**Dreh-** *zW*: ~**orgel** *f* barrel organ; ~**ort** *m* (*FILM*) location; ~**scheibe** *f* (*EISENB*) turntable; ~**tür** *f* revolving door.

**Drehung** *f* (*Rotation*) rotation; (*Um~ Wendung*) turn.

**Dreh-** *zW*: ~**wurm** (*umg*) *m*: **einen ~wurm haben/bekommen** to be/become dizzy; ~**zahl** *f* rate of revolution; ~**zahlmesser** *m* rev(olution) counter.

**drei** [drai] *num* three; **aller guten Dinge sind ~!** (*Sprichwort*) all good things come in threes!; (*nach zwei mißglückten Versuchen*) third time lucky!; **D~eck** *nt* triangle; ~**eckig** *adj* triangular; **D~ecksverhältnis** *nt* eternal triangle; ~**einhalb** *num* three and a half; **D~einigkeit** [-'|ainɪçkait] *f* Trinity.

**dreierlei** *adj inv* of three kinds.

**drei-** *zW*: ~**fach** *adj* triple, treble ♦ *adv* three times; **die ~fache Menge** three times the amount; **D~faltigkeit** *f* trinity; **D~fuß** *m* tripod; (*Schemel*) three-legged stool; **D~gangschaltung** *f* three-speed gear; ~**hundert** *num* three hundred; **D~käsehoch** (*umg*) *m* tiny tot; **D~königsfest** *nt* Epiphany;

~**mal** *adv* three times, thrice; ~**malig** *adj* three times.

**dreinblicken** ['drainblɪkən] *vi*: **traurig** *etc* ~ to look sad *etc*.

**dreinreden** ['drainreːdən] *vi*: **jdm ~** (*dazwischenreden*) to interrupt sb; (*sich einmischen*) to interfere with sb.

**Dreirad** *nt* tricycle.

**Dreisprung** *m* triple jump.

**dreißig** ['draisɪç] *num* thirty.

**dreist** [draist] *adj* bold, audacious.

**Dreistigkeit** *f* boldness, audacity.

**drei-** *zW*: ~**viertel** *num* three-quarters; **D~viertelstunde** *f* three-quarters of an hour; **D~vierteltakt** *m*: **im D~vierteltakt** in three-four time; ~**zehn** *num* thirteen; **jetzt schlägt's ~zehn!** (*umg*) that's a bit much.

**dreschen** ['drɛʃən] *unreg vt* to thresh; **Skat ~** (*umg*) to play skat.

**Dresden** ['dreːsdən] (**-s**) *nt* Dresden.

**dressieren** [drɛ'siːrən] *vt* to train.

**Dressur** [drɛ'suːr] *f* training; (*für ~reiten*) dressage.

**Dr.h.c.** *abk* (= *Doktor honoris causa*) honorary doctor.

**driften** ['drɪftən] *vi* (*NAUT, fig*) to drift.

**Drillbohrer** *m* light drill.

**drillen** ['drɪlən] *vt* (*bohren*) to drill, bore; (*MIL*) to drill; (*fig*) to train; **auf etw** *akk* **gedrillt sein** (*fig: umg*) to be practised (*BRIT*) *od* practiced (*US*) at doing sth.

**Drilling** *m* triplet.

**drin** [drɪn] (*umg*) *adv*: **bis jetzt ist noch alles ~** everything is still quite open; *siehe auch* **darin**.

**dringen** ['drɪŋən] *unreg vi* (*Wasser, Licht, Kälte*): ~ **(durch/in** +*akk*) to penetrate (through/into); **auf etw** *akk* ~ to insist on sth; **in jdn ~** (*geh*) to entreat sb.

**dringend** ['drɪŋənt] *adj* urgent; ~ **empfehlen** to recommend strongly.

**dringlich** ['drɪŋlɪç] *adj* = **dringend**.

**Dringlichkeit** *f* urgency.

**Dringlichkeitsstufe** *f* priority; ~ **1** top priority.

**drinnen** ['drɪnən] *adv* inside, indoors.

**drinstecken** ['drɪnʃtɛkən] (*umg*) *vi*: **da steckt eine Menge Arbeit drin** a lot of work has gone into it.

**drischt** [drɪʃt] *vb siehe* **dreschen**.

**dritt** *adv*: **wir kommen zu ~** three of us are coming together.

**dritte(r, s)** *adj* third; **D~ Welt** Third World; **im Beisein D~r** in the presence of a third party.

**Drittel** (**-s, -**) *nt* third.

**drittens** *adv* thirdly.

**drittklassig** *adj* third-rate, third-class.

**Dr.jur.** *abk* (= *Doktor der Rechtswissenschaften*) ≈ L.L.D.

**DRK** (**-**) *nt abk* (= *Deutsches Rotes Kreuz*) ≈ R.C.

**Dr.med.** *abk* (= *Doktor der Medizin*) ≈ M.D.

**droben** ['dro:bən] *adv* above, up there.
**Droge** ['dro:gə] (-, -n) *f* drug.
**dröge** ['drøgə] (*NORDD*) *adj* boring.
**Drogen-** *zW:* **d~abhängig** *adj* addicted to drugs; **~händler(in)** *m(f)* peddler, pusher; **d~süchtig** *adj* addicted to drugs.
**Drogerie** [drogə'ri:] *f* chemist's shop (*BRIT*), drugstore (*US*).

---

*The* **Drogerie** *as opposed to the* **Apotheke** *sells medicines not requiring a prescription. It tends to be cheaper and also sells cosmetics, perfume and toiletries.*

---

**Drogist(in)** [dro'gɪst(ɪn)] *m(f)* pharmacist, chemist (*BRIT*).
**Drohbrief** *m* threatening letter.
**drohen** ['dro:ən] *vi:* **(jdm)** ~ to threaten (sb).
**Drohgebärde** *f* (*lit, fig*) threatening gesture.
**Drohne** ['dro:nə] (-, -n) *f* drone.
**dröhnen** ['drø:nən] *vi* (*Motor*) to roar; (*Stimme, Musik*) to ring, resound.
**Drohung** ['dro:ʊŋ] *f* threat.
**drollig** ['drɔlɪç] *adj* droll.
**Drops** [drɔps] (-, -) *m od nt* fruit drop.
**drosch** *etc* [drɔʃ] *vb siehe* **dreschen.**
**Droschke** ['drɔʃkə] (-, -n) *f* cab.
**Droschkenkutscher** *m* cabman.
**Drossel** ['drɔsəl] (-, -n) *f* thrush.
**drosseln** ['drɔsəln] *vt* (*Motor etc*) to throttle; (*Heizung*) to turn down; (*Strom, Tempo, Produktion etc*) to cut down.
**Dr.phil.** *abk* (= *Doktor der Geisteswissenschaften*) ≈ Ph.D.
**Dr.theol.** *abk* (= *Doktor der Theologie*) ≈ D.D.
**drüben** ['dry:bən] *adv* over there, on the other side.
**drüber** ['dry:bər] (*umg*) *adv* = **darüber.**
**Druck** [drʊk] (-(e)s, -e) *m* (*PHYS, Zwang*) pressure; (*TYP: Vorgang*) printing; (: *Produkt*) print; (*fig: Belastung*) burden, weight; ~ **hinter etw** *akk* **machen** to put some pressure on sth; **~buchstabe** *m* block letter; **in ~buchstaben schreiben** to print.
**Drückeberger** ['drʏkəbergər] (-s, -) *m* shirker, dodger.
**drucken** ['drʊkən] *vt, vi* (*TYP, COMPUT*) to print.
**drücken** ['drʏkən] *vt* (*Knopf, Hand*) to press; (*zu eng sein*) to pinch; (*fig: Preise*) to keep down; (: *belasten*) to oppress, weigh down ♦ *vi* to press; to pinch ♦ *vr:* **sich vor etw** *dat* ~ to get out of (doing) sth; **jdm etw in die Hand** ~ to press sth into sb's hand.
**drückend** *adj* oppressive; (*Last, Steuern*) heavy; (*Armut*) grinding; (*Wetter, Hitze*) oppressive, close.
**Drucker** (-s, -) *m* printer.
**Drücker** (-s, -) *m* button; (*Tür~*) handle; (*Gewehr~*) trigger; **am** ~ **sein** *od* **sitzen** (*fig: umg*) to be the key person; **auf den letzten** ~ (*fig: umg*) at the last minute.

**Druckerei** [drʊkə'raɪ] *f* printing works, press.
**Druckerschwärze** *f* printer's ink.
**Druck-** *zW:* **~fahne** *f* galley(-proof); **~fehler** *m* misprint; **~knopf** *m* press stud (*BRIT*), snap fastener; **~kopf** *m* printhead; **~luft** *f* compressed air; **~mittel** *nt* leverage; **d~reif** *adj* ready for printing, passed for press; (*fig*) polished; **~sache** *f* printed matter; **~schrift** *f* printing; (*gedrucktes Werk*) pamphlet; **~taste** *f* push button; **~welle** *f* shock wave.
**drum** [drʊm] (*umg*) *adv* around; **mit allem D~ und Dran** with all the bits and pieces *pl*; (*Mahlzeit*) with all the trimmings *pl*.
**Drumherum** *nt* trappings *pl*.
**drunten** ['drʊntən] *adv* below, down there.
**Drüse** ['dry:zə] (-, -n) *f* gland.
**DSB** (-) *m abk* (= *Deutscher Sportbund*) *German Sports Association.*
**Dschungel** ['dʒʊŋəl] (-s, -) *m* jungle.
**DSD** *nt abk* (= *Duales System Deutschland*) *German waste collection and recycling service.*

---

*The* **DSD** (*Duales System Deutschland*) *is a scheme introduced in Germany for separating domestic refuse into two types so as to reduce environmental damage. Normal refuse is disposed of in the usual way by burning or dumping at land-fill sites; packets and containers with a green spot (**grüner Punkt**) imprinted on them are kept separate and are then collected for recycling.*

---

**dt.** *abk* = **deutsch.**
**DTC** (-) *m abk* (= *Deutscher Touring-Automobil-Club*) *German motoring organization.*
**DTP** (-) *nt abk* (= *Desktop publishing*) DTP.
**Dtzd.** *abk* (= *Dutzend*) doz.
**du** [du:] *pron* (*D~ in Briefen*) you; **mit jdm per** ~ **sein** to be on familiar terms with sb; **D~** *nt:* **jdm das D~ anbieten** to suggest that sb uses "du", suggest that sb uses the familiar form of address.
**Dübel** ['dy:bəl] (-s, -) *m* plug; (*Holz~*) dowel.
**dübeln** ['dy:bəln] *vt, vi* to plug.
**Dublin** ['dablɪn] *nt* Dublin.
**ducken** ['dʊkən] *vt* (*Kopf*) to duck; (*fig*) to take down a peg or two ♦ *vr* to duck.
**Duckmäuser** ['dʊkmɔʏzər] (-s, -) *m* yes-man.
**Dudelsack** ['du:dəlzak] *m* bagpipes *pl*.
**Duell** [du'ɛl] (-s, -e) *nt* duel.
**Duett** [du'ɛt] (-(e)s, -e) *nt* duet.
**Duft** [dʊft] (-(e)s, -̈e) *m* scent, odour (*BRIT*), odor (*US*); **d~en** *vi* to smell, be fragrant.
**duftig** *adj* (*Stoff, Kleid*) delicate, diaphanous; (*Muster*) fine.
**Duftnote** *f* (*von Parfüm*) scent.
**dulden** ['dʊldən] *vt* to suffer; (*zulassen*) to tolerate ♦ *vi* to suffer.
**duldsam** *adj* tolerant.
**dumm** [dʊm] *adj* stupid; **das wird mir zu** ~

that's just too much; **der D~e sein** to be the loser; **der ~e August** (*umg*) the clown; **du willst mich wohl für ~ verkaufen** you must think I'm stupid; **sich ~ und dämlich reden** (*umg*) to talk till one is blue in the face; **so etwas D~es** how stupid; what a nuisance; ~**dreist** *adj* impudent.

**dummerweise** *adv* stupidly.

**Dummheit** *f* stupidity; (*Tat*) blunder, stupid mistake.

**Dummkopf** *m* blockhead.

**dumpf** [dʊmpf] *adj* (*Ton*) hollow, dull; (*Luft*) close; (*Erinnerung, Schmerz*) vague; **D~heit** *f* hollowness, dullness; closeness; vagueness.

**dumpfig** *adj* musty.

**Dumpingpreis** ['dampɪŋpraɪs] *m* give-away price.

**Düne** ['dy:nə] (-, -n) *f* dune.

**Dung** [dʊŋ] (-(e)s) *m* manure.

**düngen** ['dyŋən] *vt* to fertilize.

**Dünger** (-s, -) *m* fertilizer; (*Dung*) manure.

**dunkel** ['dʊŋkəl] *adj* dark; (*Stimme*) deep; (*Ahnung*) vague; (*rätselhaft*) obscure; (*verdächtig*) dubious, shady; **im ~n tappen** (*fig*) to grope in the dark.

**Dünkel** ['dʏŋkəl] (-s) *m* self-conceit; **d~haft** *adj* conceited.

**Dunkelheit** *f* darkness; (*fig*) obscurity; **bei Einbruch der ~** at nightfall.

**Dunkelkammer** *f* (*PHOT*) dark room.

**dunkeln** *vi unpers* to grow dark.

**Dunkelziffer** *f* estimated number of unnotified cases.

**dünn** [dyn] *adj* thin; **D~darm** *m* small intestine; ~**flüssig** *adj* watery, thin; ~**gesät** *adj* scarce; **D~heit** *f* thinness; ~**machen** (*umg*) *vr* to make o.s. scarce; **D~schiß** (*umg*) *m* the runs.

**Dunst** [dʊnst] (-es, ⁻e) *m* vapour (*BRIT*), vapor (*US*); (*Wetter*) haze; ~**abzugshaube** *f* extractor hood.

**dünsten** ['dʏnstən] *vt* to steam.

**Dunstglocke** *f* haze; (*Smog*) pall of smog.

**dunstig** ['dʊnstɪç] *adj* vaporous; (*Wetter*) hazy, misty.

**düpieren** [dy'pi:rən] *vt* to dupe.

**Duplikat** [dupli'ka:t] (-(e)s, -e) *nt* duplicate.

**Dur** [du:r] (-, -) *nt* (*MUS*) major.

═══════════════ *SCHLÜSSELWORT*

**durch** [dʊrç] *präp +akk* **1** (*hindurch*) through; ~ **den Urwald** through the jungle; ~ **die ganze Welt reisen** to travel all over the world
**2** (*mittels*) through, by (means of); (*aufgrund*) due to, owing to; **Tod ~ Herzschlag/den Strang** death from a heart attack/by hanging; ~ **die Post** by post; ~ **seine Bemühungen** through his efforts
♦ *adj* **1** (*hin~*) through; **die ganze Nacht ~** all through the night; **den Sommer ~** during the summer; **8 Uhr ~** past 8 o'clock; ~ **und**

~ completely; **das geht mir ~ und ~ that** goes right through me
**2** (*KOCH: umg: durchgebraten*) done; **(gut)** ~ well-done.

**durcharbeiten** *vt, vi* to work through ♦ *vr*: **sich durch etw ~** to work one's way through sth.

**durchatmen** *vi* to breathe deeply.

**durchaus** [dʊrç'aʊs] *adv* completely; (*unbedingt*) definitely; ~ **nicht** (*in verneinten Sätzen: als Verstärkung*) by no means; (: *als Antwort*) not at all; **das läßt sich ~ machen** that sounds feasible; **ich bin ~ Ihrer Meinung** I quite *od* absolutely agree with you.

**durchbeißen** *unreg vt* to bite through ♦ *vr* (*fig*) to battle on.

**durchblättern** *vt* to leaf through.

**Durchblick** ['dʊrçblɪk] *m* view; (*fig*) comprehension; **den ~ haben** (*fig: umg*) to know what's what.

**durchblicken** *vi* to look through; (*umg: verstehen*): **(bei etw)** ~ to understand (sth); **etw ~ lassen** (*fig*) to hint at sth.

**Durchblutung** [dʊrç'blu:tʊŋ] *f* circulation (of blood).

**durchbohren** *vt untr* to bore through, pierce.

**durchboxen** ['dʊrçbɔksən] *vr* (*fig: umg*): **sich (durch etw)** ~ to fight one's way through (sth).

**durchbrechen¹** ['dʊrçbrɛçən] *unreg vt, vi* to break.

**durchbrechen²** [dʊrç'brɛçən] *unreg vt untr* (*Schranken*) to break through.

**durchbrennen** *unreg vi* (*Draht, Sicherung*) to burn through; (*umg*) to run away.

**durchbringen** *unreg vt* to get through; (*Geld*) to squander ♦ *vr* to make a living.

**Durchbruch** ['dʊrçbrʊx] *m* (*Öffnung*) opening; (*MIL*) breach; (*von Gefühlen etc*) eruption; (*der Zähne*) cutting; (*fig*) breakthrough; **zum ~ kommen** to break through.

**durchdacht** [dʊrç'daxt] *adj* well thought-out.

**durchdenken** *unreg vt untr* to think out.

**durch-** *zW*: ~**diskutieren** *vt* to talk over, discuss; ~**drängen** *vr* to force one's way through; ~**drehen** *vt* (*Fleisch*) to mince ♦ *vi* (*umg*) to crack up.

**durchdringen¹** ['dʊrçdrɪŋən] *unreg vi* to penetrate, get through.

**durchdringen²** [dʊrç'drɪŋən] *unreg vt untr* to penetrate.

**durchdringend** *adj* piercing; (*Kälte, Wind*) biting; (*Geruch*) pungent.

**durchdrücken** ['dʊrçdrʏkən] *vt* (*durch Presse*) to press through; (*Creme, Teig*) to pipe; (*fig: Gesetz, Reformen etc*) to push through; (*seinen Willen*) to get; (*Knie, Kreuz etc*) to straighten.

**durcheinander** [dʊrç|aɪ'nandər] *adv* in a mess, in confusion; (*verwirrt*) confused; ~ **trinken** to mix one's drinks; **D~** (-s) *nt* (*Verwirrung*) confusion; (*Unordnung*) mess; ~**bringen** *unreg vt* to mess up; (*verwirren*) to confuse; ~**reden** *vi* to talk at the same time; ~**werfen** *unreg vt* to muddle up.

**durch-** *zW:* ~**fahren** *unreg vi:* **er ist bei Rot** ~**gefahren** he jumped the lights ♦ *vt:* **die Nacht** ~**fahren** to travel through the night; **D**~**fahrt** *f* transit; (*Verkehr*) thoroughfare; **D**~**fahrt bitte freihalten!** please keep access free; **D**~**fahrt verboten!** no through road; **D**~**fall** *m* (*MED*) diarrhoea (*BRIT*), diarrhea (*US*); ~**fallen** *unreg vi* to fall through; (*in Prüfung*) to fail; ~**finden** *unreg vr* to find one's way through; ~**fliegen** *unreg* (*umg*) *vi* (*in Prüfung*): (**durch etw od in etw** *dat*) ~**fliegen** to fail (sth); **D**~**flug** *m:* **Passagiere auf dem D**~**flug** transit passengers.

**durchforschen** *vt untr* to explore.

**durchforsten** [dʊrç'fɔrstən] *vt untr* (*fig: Akten etc*) to go through.

**durchfragen** *vr* to find one's way by asking.

**durchfressen** *unreg vr* to eat one's way through.

**durchführbar** *adj* feasible, practicable.

**durchführen** ['dʊrçfyːrən] *vt* to carry out; (*Gesetz*) to implement; (*Kursus*) to run.

**Durchführung** *f* execution, performance.

**Durchgang** ['dʊrçɡaŋ] *m* passage(way); (*bei Produktion, Versuch*) run; (*SPORT*) round; (*bei Wahl*) ballot; ~ **verboten** no thoroughfare.

**durchgängig** ['dʊrçɡɛŋɪç] *adj* universal, general.

**Durchgangs-** *zW:* ~**handel** *m* transit trade; ~**lager** *nt* transit camp; ~**stadium** *nt* transitory stage; ~**verkehr** *m* through traffic.

**durchgeben** ['dʊrçɡeːbən] *unreg vt* (*RUNDF, TV: Hinweis, Wetter*) to give; (*Lottozahlen*) to announce.

**durchgefroren** ['dʊrçɡəfroːrən] *adj* (*See*) completely frozen; (*Mensch*) frozen stiff.

**durchgehen** ['dʊrçɡeːən] *unreg vt* (*behandeln*) to go over *od* through ♦ *vi* to go through; (*ausreißen: Pferd*) to break loose; (*Mensch*) to run away; **mein Temperament ging mit mir durch** my temper got the better of me; **jdm etw** ~ **lassen** to let sb get away with sth.

**durchgehend** *adj* (*Zug*) through; (*Öffnungszeiten*) continuous.

**durchgeschwitzt** ['dʊrçɡəʃvɪtst] *adj* soaked in sweat.

**durch-** *zW:* ~**greifen** *unreg vi* to take strong action; ~**halten** *unreg vi* to last out ♦ *vt* to keep up; **D**~**haltevermögen** *nt* staying power; ~**hängen** *unreg vi* (*lit, fig*) to sag; ~**hecheln** (*umg*) *vt* to gossip about; ~**kommen** *unreg vi* to get through; (*überleben*) to pull through.

**durchkreuzen** *vt untr* to thwart, frustrate.

**durchlassen** *unreg vt* (*Person*) to let through; (*Wasser*) to let in.

**durchlässig** *adj* leaky.

**Durchlaucht** ['dʊrçlaʊxt] (-, -en) *f:* (**Euer**) ~ Your Highness.

**Durchlauf** ['dʊrçlaʊf] *m* (*COMPUT*) run.

**durchlaufen** *unreg vt untr* (*Schule, Phase*) to go through.

**Durchlauferhitzer** (-s, -) *m* continuous-flow water heater.

**Durchlaufzeit** *f* (*COMPUT*) length of the run.

**durch-** *zW:* ~**leben** *vt untr* (*Zeit*) to live *od* go through; (*Jugend, Gefühl*) to experience; ~**lesen** *unreg vt* to read through; ~**leuchten** *vt untr* to X-ray; ~**löchern** *vt untr* to perforate; (*mit Löchern*) to punch holes in; (*mit Kugeln*) to riddle; ~**machen** *vt* to go through; **die Nacht** ~**machen** to make a night of it.

**Durchmarsch** *m* march through.

**Durchmesser** (-s, -) *m* diameter.

**durchnässen** *vt untr* to soak (through).

**durch-** *zW:* ~**nehmen** *unreg vt* to go over; ~**numerieren** *vt* to number consecutively; ~**organisieren** *vt* to organize down to the last detail; ~**pausen** *vt* to trace; ~**peitschen** *vt* (*lit*) to whip soundly; (*fig: Gesetzentwurf, Reform*) to force through.

**durchqueren** [dʊrç'kveːrən] *vt untr* to cross.

**durch-** *zW:* ~**rechnen** *vt* to calculate; ~**regnen** *vi unpers:* **es regnet durchs Dach** ~ the rain is coming through the roof; **D**~**reiche** (-, -n) *f* (serving) hatch, pass-through (*US*); **D**~**reise** *f* transit; **auf der D**~**reise** passing through; (*Güter*) in transit; **D**~**reisevisum** *nt* transit visa; ~**ringen** *unreg vr* to make up one's mind finally; ~**rosten** *vi* to rust through; ~**rutschen** *vi:* (**durch etw**) ~**rutschen** (*lit*) to slip through (sth); (*bei Prüfung*) to scrape through (sth).

**durchs** [dʊrçs] = **durch das**.

**Durchsage** ['dʊrçzaːɡə] *f* intercom *od* radio announcement.

**Durchsatz** ['dʊrçzats] *m* (*COMPUT, Produktion*) throughput.

**durchschauen¹** ['dʊrçʃaʊən] *vt, vi* (*lit*) to look *od* see through.

**durchschauen²** [dʊrç'ʃaʊən] *vt untr* (*Person, Lüge*) to see through.

**durchscheinen** ['dʊrçʃaɪnən] *unreg vi* to shine through.

**durchscheinend** *adj* translucent.

**durchschlafen** ['dʊrçʃlaːfən] *unreg vi* to sleep through.

**Durchschlag** ['dʊrçʃlaːk] *m* (*Doppel*) carbon copy; (*Sieb*) strainer.

**durchschlagen** *unreg vt* (*entzweischlagen*) to split (in two); (*sieben*) to sieve ♦ *vi* (*zum Vorschein kommen*) to emerge, come out ♦ *vr* to get by.

**durchschlagend** *adj* resounding; **(eine)** ~**e Wirkung haben** to be totally effective.

**Durchschlagpapier** *nt* flimsy; (*Kohlepapier*) carbon paper.

**Durchschlagskraft** *f* (*von Geschoß*) penetration; (*fig: von Argument*) decisiveness.

**durch-** *zW:* **~schlängeln** *vr* (*durch etw: Mensch*) to thread one's way through; **~schlüpfen** *vi* to slip through; **~schneiden** *unreg vt* to cut through.

**Durchschnitt** ['dʊrçʃnɪt] *m* (*Mittelwert*) average; **über/unter dem ~** above/below average; **im ~** on average; **d~lich** *adj* average ♦ *adv* on average; **d~lich begabt/groß** *etc* of average ability/height *etc.*

**Durchschnitts-** *zW:* **~geschwindigkeit** *f* average speed; **~mensch** *m* average man, man in the street; **~wert** *m* average.

**durch-** *zW:* **D~schrift** *f* copy; **D~schuß** *m* (*Loch*) bullet hole; **~schwimmen** *unreg vt untr* to swim across; **~segeln** (*umg*) *vi* (*nicht bestehen*): **durch** *od* **bei etw ~segeln** to fail *od* flunk (*umg*) (sth); **~sehen** *unreg vt* to look through.

**durchsetzen¹** ['dʊrçzɛtsən] *vt* to enforce ♦ *vr* (*Erfolg haben*) to succeed; (*sich behaupten*) to get one's way; **seinen Kopf ~** to get one's own way.

**durchsetzen²** [dʊrç'zɛtsən] *vt untr* to mix.

**Durchsicht** ['dʊrçzɪçt] *f* looking through, checking.

**durchsichtig** *adj* transparent; **D~keit** *f* transparency.

**durch-** *zW:* **~sickern** *vi* to seep through; (*fig*) to leak out; **~sieben** *vt* to sieve; **~sitzen** *unreg vt* (*Sessel etc*) to wear out (the seat of); **~spielen** *vt* to go *od* run through; **~sprechen** *unreg vt* to talk over; **~stehen** *unreg vt* to live through; **D~stehvermögen** *nt* endurance, staying power; **~stellen** *vt* (*TEL*) to put through; **~stöbern** [-'ʃtøːbərn] *vt untr* to ransack, search through; **~stoßen** *unreg vt*, *vi* to break through (*auch MIL*); **~streichen** *unreg vt* to cross out; **~stylen** *vt* to ponce up (*umg*); **~suchen** *vt untr* to search; **D~suchung** *f* search; **D~suchungsbefehl** *m* search warrant; **~trainieren** *vt* (*Sportler, Körper*): **gut ~trainiert** in superb condition; **~tränken** *vt untr* to soak; **~treten** *unreg vt* (*Pedal*) to step on; (*Starter*) to kick; **~trieben** *adj* cunning, wily; **~wachsen** *adj* (*lit: Speck*) streaky; (*fig: mittelmäßig*) so-so.

**Durchwahl** ['dʊrçvaːl] *f* (*TEL*) direct dialling; (*bei Firma*) extension.

**durch-** *zW:* **~weg** *adv* throughout, completely; **~wursteln** (*umg*) *vr* to muddle through; **~zählen** *vt* to count ♦ *vi* to count *od* number off; **~zechen** *vt untr:* **eine ~zechte Nacht** a night of drinking; **~ziehen** *unreg vt* (*Faden*) to draw through ♦ *vi* to pass through; **eine Sache ~ziehen** to finish off sth; **~zucken** *vt untr* to shoot *od* flash through; **D~zug** *m* (*Luft*) draught (*BRIT*), draft (*US*); (*von Truppen, Vögeln*) passage; **~zwängen** *vt, vr* to squeeze *od* force through.

═══════════════ *SCHLÜSSELWORT*

**dürfen** ['dʏrfən] *unreg vi* **1** (*Erlaubnis haben*) to be allowed to; **ich darf das** I'm allowed to (do that); **darf ich?** may I?; **darf ich ins Kino?** can *od* may I go to the cinema?; **es darf geraucht werden** you may smoke **2** (*in Verneinungen*): **er darf das nicht** he's not allowed to (do that); **das darf nicht geschehen** that must not happen; **da darf sie sich nicht wundern** that shouldn't surprise her; **das darf doch nicht wahr sein!** that can't be true! **3** (*in Höflichkeitsformeln*): **darf ich Sie bitten, das zu tun?** may *od* could I ask you to do that?; **wir freuen uns, Ihnen mitteilen zu ~** we are pleased to be able to tell you; **was darf es sein?** what can I get for you? **4** (*können*): **das ~ Sie mir glauben** you can believe me **5** (*Möglichkeit*): **das dürfte genug sein** that should be enough; **es dürfte Ihnen bekannte sein, daß ...** as you will probably know ...

**durfte** *etc* ['dʊrftə] *vb siehe* **dürfen.**

**dürftig** ['dʏrftɪç] *adj* (*ärmlich*) needy, poor; (*unzulänglich*) inadequate.

**dürr** [dʏr] *adj* dried-up; (*Land*) arid; (*mager*) skinny.

**Dürre** (-, -n) *f* aridity; (*Zeit*) drought.

**Durst** [dʊrst] (-(e)s) *m* thirst; **~ haben** to be thirsty; **einen über den ~ getrunken haben** (*umg*) to have had one too many.

**durstig** *adj* thirsty.

**Durststrecke** *f* hard times *pl.*

**Dusche** ['dʊʃə] (-, -n) *f* shower; **das war eine kalte ~** (*fig*) that really brought him/her *etc* down with a bump.

**duschen** *vi, vr* to have a shower.

**Duschgelegenheit** *f* shower facilities *pl.*

**Düse** ['dyːzə] (-, -n) *f* nozzle; (*Flugzeug~*) jet.

**Dusel** ['duːzəl] (*umg*) *m:* **da hat er (einen) ~ gehabt** he was lucky.

**Düsen-** *zW:* **~antrieb** *m* jet propulsion; **~flugzeug** *nt* jet (plane); **~jäger** *m* jet fighter.

**Dussel** ['dʊsəl] (-s, -) (*umg*) *m* twit, berk.

**Düsseldorf** ['dʏsəldɔrf] *nt* Dusseldorf.

**dusselig** ['dʊsəlɪç] (*umg*) *adj* stupid.

**dußlig** ['dʊslɪç] (*umg*) *adj* stupid.

**düster** ['dyːstər] *adj* dark; (*Gedanken, Zukunft*) gloomy; **D~keit** *f* darkness, gloom; gloominess.

**Dutzend** ['dʊtsənt] (-s, -e) *nt* dozen; **d~(e)mal** *adv* a dozen times; **~ware** (*pej*) *f* (*cheap*) mass-produced item; **d~weise** *adv* by the dozen.

**duzen** ['duːtsən] *vt* to address with the familiar "du" form ♦ *vr* to address each other with the familiar "du" form; *siehe auch* **siezen.**

> *There are two different forms of address in German: du and Sie.* **Duzen** *means addressing someone as 'du' and* **siezen** *means addressing someone as 'Sie'. 'Du' is used to address children, family and close friends. Students almost always use 'du' to each other. 'Sie' is used for all grown-ups and older teenagers.*

**Duzfreund** *m* good friend.

**Dynamik** [dy'na:mɪk] *f* (*PHYS*) dynamics; (*fig: Schwung*) momentum; (*von Mensch*) dynamism.

**dynamisch** [dy'na:mɪʃ] *adj* (*lit, fig*) dynamic; (*renten~*) index-linked.

**Dynamit** [dyna'mi:t] (-s) *nt* dynamite.

**Dynamo** [dy'na:mo] (-s, -s) *m* dynamo.

**dz** *abk* = **Doppelzentner.**

**D-Zug** ['de:tsu:k] *m* through train; **ein alter Mann ist doch kein ~-~** (*umg*) I am going as fast as I can.

====== *E, e* ======

**E¹, e** [e:] *nt* E, e; **~ wie Emil** ≈ E for Edward, E for Easy (*US*).

**E²** [e:] *abk* = **Eilzug; Europastraße.**

**Ebbe** ['ɛbə] (-, -n) *f* low tide; **~ und Flut** ebb and flow.

**eben** ['e:bən] *adj* level; (*glatt*) smooth ♦ *adv* just; (*bestätigend*) exactly; **das ist ~ so** that's just the way it is; **mein Bleistift war doch ~ noch da** my pencil was there (just) a minute ago; **~ deswegen** just because of that.

**Ebenbild** *nt:* **das genaue ~ seines Vaters** the spitting image of his father.

**ebenbürtig** *adj:* **jdm ~ sein** to be sb's peer.

**Ebene** (-, -n) *f* plain; (*MATH, PHYS*) plane; (*fig*) level.

**eben-** *zW:* **~erdig** *adj* at ground level; **~falls** *adv* likewise; **E~heit** *f* levelness; (*Glätte*) smoothness; **E~holz** *nt* ebony; **~so** *adv* just as; **~sogut** *adv* just as well; **~soft** *adv* just as often; **~soviel** *adv* just as much; **~soweit** *adv* just as far; **~sowenig** *adv* just as little.

**Eber** ['e:bər] (-s, -) *m* boar.

**Eberesche** *f* mountain ash, rowan.

**ebnen** ['e:bnən] *vt* to level; **jdm den Weg ~** (*fig*) to smooth the way for sb.

**Echo** ['ɛço] (-s, -s) *nt* echo; (**bei jdm) ein lebhaftes ~ finden** (*fig*) to meet with a lively response (from sb).

**Echolot** ['ɛço-lo:t] *nt* (*NAUT*) echo-sounder, sonar.

**Echse** ['ɛksə] (-, -n) *f* (*ZOOL*) lizard.

**echt** [ɛçt] *adj* genuine; (*typisch*) typical; **ich hab' ~ keine Zeit** (*umg*) I really don't have any time; **E~heit** *f* genuineness.

**Eckball** ['ɛkbal] *m* corner (kick).

**Ecke** ['ɛkə] (-, -n) *f* corner; (*MATH*) angle; **gleich um die ~** just around the corner; **an allen ~n und Enden sparen** (*umg*) to pinch and scrape; **jdn um die ~ bringen** (*umg*) to bump sb off; **mit jdm um ein paar ~n herum verwandt sein** (*umg*) to be distantly related to sb, be sb's second cousin twice removed (*hum*).

**eckig** *adj* angular.

**Eckzahn** *m* eye tooth.

**Eckzins** *m* (*FIN*) minimum lending rate.

**Ecstasy** ['ɛkstəsɪ] *nt* (*Droge*) ecstasy.

**ECU** [e'ky:] (-) (-(s), -(s)) *m* (*FIN*) ecu.

**Ecuador** [ekua'do:r] (-s) *nt* Ecuador.

**edel** ['e:dəl] *adj* noble; **E~ganove** *m* gentleman criminal; **E~gas** *nt* rare gas; **E~metall** *nt* rare metal; **E~stein** *m* precious stone.

**Edinburg(h)** ['e:dɪnbʊrk] *nt* Edinburgh.

**EDV** (-) *f abk* (= *elektronische Datenverarbeitung*) EDP.

**EEG** (-) *nt abk* (= *Elektroenzephalogramm*) EEG.

**Efeu** ['e:fɔy] (-s) *m* ivy.

**Effeff** [ɛf'|ɛf] (-) (*umg*) *nt:* **etw aus dem ~ können** to be able to do sth standing on one's head.

**Effekt** [ɛ'fɛkt] (-(e)s, -e) *m* effect.

**Effekten** [ɛ'fɛktən] *pl* stocks *pl*; **~börse** *f* Stock Exchange.

**Effekthascherei** [ɛfɛkthaʃə'raɪ] *f* sensationalism.

**effektiv** [ɛfɛk'ti:f] *adj* effective, actual.

**Effet** [ɛ'fe:] (-s) *m* spin.

**EG** (-) *f abk* (= *Europäische Gemeinschaft*) EC.

**egal** [e'ga:l] *adj* all the same; **das ist mir ganz ~** it's all the same to me.

**egalitär** [egali'tɛ:r] *adj* (*geh*) egalitarian.

**Egge** ['ɛgə] (-, -n) *f* (*AGR*) harrow.

**Egoismus** [ego'ɪsmʊs] *m* selfishness, egoism.

**Egoist(in)** *m(f)* egoist; **e~isch** *adj* selfish, egoistic.

**egozentrisch** [ego'tsɛntrɪʃ] *adj* egocentric, self-centred (*BRIT*), self-centered (*US*).

**eh** [e:] *adv:* **seit ~ und je** for ages, since the year dot (*umg*); **ich komme ~ nicht dazu** I won't get around to it anyway.

**e.h.** *abk* = **ehrenhalber.**

**Ehe** ['e:ə] (-, -n) *f* marriage; **die ~ eingehen** (*form*) to enter into matrimony; **sie leben in wilder ~** (*veraltet*) they are living in sin.

**ehe** *konj* before.

**Ehe-** *zW:* **~brecher** (-s, -) *m* adulterer; **~brecherin** *f* adulteress; **~bruch** *m* adultery; **~frau** *f* wife; **~leute** *pl* married couple *pl*; **e~lich** *adj* matrimonial; (*Kind*) legitimate.

**ehemalig** *adj* former.

**ehemals** *adv* formerly.

**Ehe-** *zW:* ~**mann** *m* married man; (*Partner*) husband; ~**paar** *nt* married couple; ~**partner** *m* husband; ~**partnerin** *f* wife.

**eher** ['eːər] *adv* (*früher*) sooner; (*lieber*) rather, sooner; (*mehr*) more; **nicht ~ als** not before; **um so ~, als** the more so because.

**Ehe-** *zW:* ~**ring** *m* wedding ring; ~**scheidung** *f* divorce; ~**schließung** *f* marriage; ~**stand** *m:* **in den ~stand treten** (*form*) to enter into matrimony.

**eheste(r, s)** ['eːəstə(r, s)] *adj* (*früheste*) first, earliest; **am ~n** (*am liebsten*) soonest; (*meist*) most; (*am wahrscheinlichsten*) most probably.

**Ehevermittlung** *f* (*Büro*) marriage bureau.

**Eheversprechen** *nt* (*JUR*) promise to marry.

**ehrbar** ['eːrbaːr] *adj* honourable (*BRIT*), honorable (*US*), respectable.

**Ehre** (-, -n) *f* honour (*BRIT*), honor (*US*); **etw in ~n halten** to treasure *od* cherish sth.

**ehren** *vt* to honour (*BRIT*), honor (*US*).

**Ehren-** *zW:* **e~amtlich** *adj* honorary; ~**bürgerrecht** *nt:* **die Stadt verlieh ihr das ~bürgerrecht** she was given the freedom of the city; ~**gast** *m* guest of honour (*BRIT*) *od* honor (*US*); **e~haft** *adj* honourable (*BRIT*), honorable (*US*); **e~halber** *adv:* **er wurde e~halber zum Vorsitzenden auf Lebenszeit ernannt** he was made honorary president for life; ~**mann** *m* man of honour (*BRIT*) *od* honor (*US*); ~**mitglied** *nt* honorary member; ~**platz** *m* place of honour (*BRIT*) *od* honor (*US*); ~**rechte** *pl* civic rights *pl*; **e~rührig** *adj* defamatory; ~**runde** *f* lap of honour (*BRIT*) *od* honor (*US*); ~**sache** *f* point of honour (*BRIT*) *od* honor (*US*); ~**sache!** (*umg*) you can count on me; ~**tag** *m* (*Geburtstag*) birthday; (*großer Tag*) big day; **e~voll** *adj* honourable (*BRIT*), honorable (*US*); ~**wort** *nt* word of honour (*BRIT*) *od* honor (*US*); **Urlaub auf ~wort** parole.

**Ehr-** *zW:* **e~erbietig** *adj* respectful; ~**furcht** *f* awe, deep respect; **e~furchtgebietend** *adj* awesome; (*Stimme*) authoritative; ~**gefühl** *nt* sense of honour (*BRIT*) *od* honor (*US*); ~**geiz** *m* ambition; **e~geizig** *adj* ambitious; **e~lich** *adj* honest; **e~lich verdientes Geld** hard-earned money; **e~lich gesagt** ... quite frankly *od* honestly ...; ~**lichkeit** *f* honesty; **e~los** *adj* dishonourable (*BRIT*), dishonorable (*US*).

**Ehrung** *f* honour(ing) (*BRIT*), honor(ing) (*US*).

**ehrwürdig** *adj* venerable.

**Ei** [aɪ] (-(e)s, -er) *nt* egg; **Eier** *pl* (*umg!: Hoden*) balls *pl* (*!*); **jdn wie ein rohes ~ behandeln** (*fig*) to handle sb with kid gloves; **wie aus dem ~ gepellt aussehen** (*umg*) to look spruce.

**ei** *interj* well, well; (*beschwichtigend*) now, now.

**Eibe** ['aɪbə] (-, -n) *f* (*BOT*) yew.

**Eichamt** ['aɪçʔamt] *nt* Office of Weights and Measures.

**Eiche** (-, -n) *f* oak (tree).

**Eichel** (-, -n) *f* acorn; (*KARTEN*) club; (*ANAT*) glans.

**eichen** *vt* to calibrate.

**Eichhörnchen** *nt* squirrel.

**Eichmaß** *nt* standard.

**Eichung** *f* standardization.

**Eid** ['aɪt] (-(e)s, -e) *m* oath; **eine Erklärung an ~es Statt abgeben** (*JUR*) to make a solemn declaration.

**Eidechse** ['aɪdɛksə] (-, -n) *f* lizard.

**eidesstattlich** *adj:* ~**e Erklärung** affidavit.

**Eid-** *zW:* ~**genosse** *m* Swiss; ~**genossenschaft** *f:* **Schweizerische ~genossenschaft** Swiss Confederation; **e~lich** *adj* (sworn) upon oath.

**Eidotter** *nt* egg yolk.

**Eier-** *zW:* ~**becher** *m* egg cup; ~**kuchen** *m* pancake; (*Omelett*) omelette (*BRIT*), omelet (*US*); ~**likör** *m* advocaat.

**eiern** ['aɪərn] (*umg*) *vi* to wobble.

**Eier-** *zW:* ~**schale** *f* eggshell; ~**stock** *m* ovary; ~**uhr** *f* egg timer.

**Eifel** ['aɪfəl] (-) *f* Eifel (Mountains).

**Eifer** ['aɪfər] (-s) *m* zeal, enthusiasm; **mit großem ~ bei der Sache sein** to put one's heart into it; **im ~ des Gefechts** (*fig*) in the heat of the moment; ~**sucht** *f* jealousy; **e~süchtig** *adj:* **e~süchtig (auf** +*akk*) jealous (of).

**eifrig** ['aɪfrɪç] *adj* zealous, enthusiastic.

**Eigelb** ['aɪgɛlp] (-(e)s, -e *od* -) *nt* egg yolk.

**eigen** ['aɪgən] *adj* own; (~*artig*) peculiar; (*ordentlich*) particular; (*übergenau*) fussy; **ich möchte kurz in ~er Sache sprechen** I would like to say something on my own account; **mit dem ihm ~en Lächeln** with that smile peculiar to him; **sich** *dat* **etw zu ~ machen** to make sth one's own; **E~art** *f* (*Besonderheit*) peculiarity; (*Eigenschaft*) characteristic; ~**artig** *adj* peculiar; **E~bau** *m:* **er fährt ein Fahrrad Marke E~bau** (*hum: umg*) he rides a home-made bike; **E~bedarf** *m* one's own requirements *pl*; **E~brötler(in)** (-s, -) *m(f)* loner, lone wolf; (*komischer Kauz*) oddball (*umg*); **E~gewicht** *nt* dead weight; ~**händig** *adj* with one's own hand; **E~heim** *nt* owner-occupied house; **E~heit** *f* peculiarity; **E~initiative** *f* initiative of one's own; **E~kapital** *nt* personal capital; (*von Firma*) company capital; **E~lob** *nt* self-praise; ~**mächtig** *adj* high-handed; (~*verantwortlich*) taken/done *etc* on one's own authority; (*unbefugt*) unauthorized; **E~name** *m* proper name; **E~nutz** *m* self-interest.

**eigens** *adv* expressly, on purpose.

**eigen-** *zW:* **E~schaft** *f* quality, property, attribute; **E~schaftswort** *nt* adjective; **E~sinn** *m* obstinacy; ~**sinnig** *adj* obstinate; ~**ständig** *adj* independent; **E~ständigkeit** *f* independence.

**eigentlich** *adj* actual, real ♦ *adv* actually, really; **was willst du ~ hier?** what do you want here anyway?

**eigen-** *zW:* **E~tor** *nt* own goal; **E~tum** *nt* property; **E~tümer(in)** (-s, -) *m(f)* owner, proprietor; **~tümlich** *adj* peculiar; **E~tümlichkeit** *f* peculiarity.

**Eigentumsdelikt** *nt* (*JUR: Diebstahl*) theft.

**Eigentumswohnung** *f* freehold flat.

**eigenwillig** *adj* with a mind of one's own.

**eignen** ['aignən] *vr* to be suited.

**Eignung** *f* suitability.

**Eignungsprüfung** *f* aptitude test.

**Eignungstest** (-(e)s, -s *od* -e) *m* aptitude test.

**Eilbote** *m* courier; **per** *od* **durch** **~n** express.

**Eilbrief** *m* express letter.

**Eile** (-) *f* haste; **es hat keine** ~ there's no hurry.

**Eileiter** ['ailaitər] *m* (*ANAT*) Fallopian tube.

**eilen** *vi* (*Mensch*) to hurry; (*dringend sein*) to be urgent.

**eilends** *adv* hastily.

**Eilgut** *nt* express goods *pl*, fast freight (*US*).

**eilig** *adj* hasty, hurried; (*dringlich*) urgent; **es** ~ **haben** to be in a hurry.

**Eil-** *zW:* **~tempo** *nt:* **etw im ~tempo machen** to do sth in a rush; **~zug** *m* fast stopping train; **~zustellung** *f* special delivery.

**Eimer** ['aimər] (-s, -) *m* bucket, pail; **im** ~ **sein** (*umg*) to be up the spout.

**ein(e)** ['ain(ə)] *num* one ♦ *indef art* a, an ♦ *adv:* **nicht** ~ **noch aus wissen** not to know what to do; **E~/Aus** (*an Geräten*) on/off; **er ist ihr** ~ **und alles** he means everything to her; **er geht bei uns** ~ **und aus** he is always round at our place.

**einander** [ai'nandər] *pron* one another, each other.

**einarbeiten** ['ain|arbaitən] *vr:* **sich (in etw** *akk*) ~ to familiarize o.s. (with sth).

**Einarbeitungszeit** *f* training period.

**einarmig** ['ain|armıç] *adj* one-armed.

**einäschern** ['ain|ɛʃərn] *vt* (*Leichnam*) to cremate; (*Stadt etc*) to reduce to ashes.

**einatmen** ['ain|a:tmən] *vt, vi* to inhale, breathe in.

**einäugig** ['ain|ɔygıç] *adj* one-eyed.

**Einbahnstraße** ['ainba:nʃtrasə] *f* one-way street.

**Einband** ['ainbant] *m* binding, cover.

**einbändig** ['ainbɛndıç] *adj* one-volume.

**einbauen** ['ainbauən] *vt* to build in; (*Motor*) to install, fit.

**Einbau-** *zW:* **~küche** *f* (fully-)fitted kitchen; **~möbel** *pl* built-in furniture *sing*; **~schrank** *m* fitted cupboard.

**einbegriffen** ['ainbəgrıfən] *adj* included, inclusive.

**einbehalten** ['ainbəhaltən] *unreg vt* to keep back.

**einberufen** *unreg vt* to convene, to call up (*BRIT*), draft (*US*).

**Einberufung** *f* convocation; call-up (*BRIT*), draft (*US*).

**Einberufungsbefehl** *m*, **Einberufungsbescheid** *m* (*MIL*) call-up (*BRIT*) *od* draft (*US*) papers *pl*.

**einbetten** ['ainbɛtən] *vt* to embed.

**Einbettzimmer** *nt* single room.

**einbeziehen** ['ainbətsi:ən] *unreg vt* to include.

**einbiegen** ['ainbi:gən] *unreg vi* to turn.

**einbilden** ['ainbıldən] *vr:* **sich** *dat* **etw** ~ to imagine sth; **sich** *dat* **viel auf etw** *akk* ~ (*stolz sein*) to be conceited about sth.

**Einbildung** *f* imagination; (*Dünkel*) conceit.

**Einbildungskraft** *f* imagination.

**einbinden** ['ainbındən] *unreg vt* to bind (up).

**einblenden** ['ainblɛndən] *vt* to fade in.

**einbleuen** ['ainblɔyən] (*umg*) *vt:* **jdm etw** ~ to hammer sth into sb.

**Einblick** ['ainblık] *m* insight; ~ **in die Akten nehmen** to examine the files; **jdm** ~ **in etw** *akk* **gewähren** to allow sb to look at sth.

**einbrechen** ['ainbrɛçən] *unreg vi* (*einstürzen*) to fall in; (*Einbruch verüben*) to break in; **bei ~der Dunkelheit** at nightfall.

**Einbrecher** (-s, -) *m* burglar.

**einbringen** ['ainbrıŋən] *unreg vt* to bring in; (*Geld, Vorteil*) to yield; (*mitbringen*) to contribute; **das bringt nichts ein** (*fig*) it's not worth it.

**einbrocken** ['ainbrɔkən] (*umg*) *vt:* **jdm/sich etwas** ~ to land sb/o.s. in it.

**Einbruch** ['ainbrʊx] *m* (*Haus~*) break-in, burglary; (*des Winters*) onset; (*Einsturz, FIN*) collapse; (*MIL: in Front*) breakthrough; **bei** ~ **der Nacht** at nightfall.

**einbruchssicher** *adj* burglar-proof.

**Einbuchtung** ['ainbʊxtʊŋ] *f* indentation; (*Bucht*) inlet, bay.

**einbürgern** ['ainbyrgərn] *vt* to naturalize ♦ *vr* to become adopted; **das hat sich so eingebürgert** that's become a custom.

**Einbürgerung** *f* naturalization.

**Einbuße** ['ainbu:sə] *f* loss, forfeiture.

**einbüßen** ['ainby:sən] *vt* to lose, forfeit.

**einchecken** ['aintʃɛkən] *vt, vi* to check in.

**eincremen** ['ainkre:mən] *vt* to put cream on.

**eindämmen** ['aindɛmən] *vt* (*Fluß*) to dam; (*fig*) to check, contain.

**eindecken** ['aindɛkən] *vr:* **sich** ~ **(mit)** to lay in stocks (of) ♦ *vt* (*umg: überhäufen*): **mit Arbeit eingedeckt sein** to be inundated with work.

**eindeutig** ['aindɔytıç] *adj* unequivocal.

**eindeutschen** ['aindɔytʃən] *vt* (*Fremdwort*) to Germanize.

**eindösen** ['aindø:zən] (*umg*) *vi* to doze off.

**eindringen** ['aindrıŋən] *unreg vi:* ~ **(in** +*akk*) to force one's way in(to); (*in Haus*) to break in(to); (*in Land*) to invade; (*Gas, Wasser*) to penetrate; **auf jdn** ~ (*mit Bitten*) to pester sb.

**eindringlich** *adj* forcible, urgent; **ich habe ihn** ~ **gebeten ...** I urged him ...

**Eindringling** *m* intruder.

**Eindruck** ['aɪndrʊk] *m* impression.
**eindrücken** ['aɪndrʏkən] *vt* to press in.
**eindrucksfähig** *adj* impressionable.
**eindrucksvoll** *adj* impressive.
**eine(r, s)** *pron* one; (*jemand*) someone; **wie kann ~r nur so dumm sein!** how could anybody be so stupid!; **es kam ~s zum anderen** it was (just) one thing after another; **sich** *dat* **~n genehmigen** (*umg*) to have a quick one.
**einebnen** ['aɪnʔeːbnən] *vt* (*lit*) to level (off); (*fig*) to level out.
**Einehe** ['aɪnʔeːə] *f* monogamy.
**eineiig** ['aɪnʔaɪɪç] *adj* (*Zwillinge*) identical.
**eineinhalb** ['aɪnʔaɪnʔhalp] *num* one and a half.
**einengen** ['aɪnʔɛŋən] *vt* to confine, restrict.
**Einer** ['aɪnər] (-) *m* (*MATH*) unit; (*Ruderboot*) single scull.
**Einerlei** ['aɪnərˈlaɪ] (-s) *nt* monotony; **e~** *adj* (*gleichartig*) the same kind of; **es ist mir e~ it** is all the same to me.
**einerseits** *adv* on the one hand.
**einfach** ['aɪnfax] *adj* simple; (*nicht mehrfach*) single ♦ *adv* simply; **E~heit** *f* simplicity.
**einfädeln** ['aɪnfɛːdəln] *vt* (*Nadel*) to thread; (*fig*) to contrive.
**einfahren** ['aɪnfaːrən] *unreg vt* to bring in; (*Barriere*) to knock down; (*Auto*) to run in ♦ *vi* to drive in; (*Zug*) to pull in; (*MIN*) to go down.
**Einfahrt** *f* (*Vorgang*) driving in; pulling in; (*MIN*) descent; (*Ort*) entrance; (*von Autobahn*) slip road (*BRIT*), entrance ramp (*US*).
**Einfall** ['aɪnfal] *m* (*Idee*) idea, notion; (*Licht~*) incidence; (*MIL*) raid.
**einfallen** *unreg vi* (*einstürzen*) to fall in, collapse; (*Licht*) to fall; (*MIL*) to raid; (*einstimmen*): **~ (in** +*akk*) to join in (with); **etw fällt jdm ein** sth occurs to sb; **das fällt mir gar nicht ein!** I wouldn't dream of it; **sich** *dat* **etwas ~ lassen** to have a good idea; **dabei fällt mir mein Onkel ein, der ...** that reminds me of my uncle who ...; **es fällt mir jetzt nicht ein** I can't think of it *od* it won't come to me at the moment.
**einfallslos** *adj* unimaginative.
**einfallsreich** *adj* imaginative.
**einfältig** ['aɪnfɛltɪç] *adj* simple(-minded).
**Einfaltspinsel** ['aɪnfaltspɪnzəl] (*umg*) *m* simpleton.
**Einfamilienhaus** [aɪnfaˈmiːliənhaʊs] *nt* detached house.
**einfangen** ['aɪnfaŋən] *unreg vt* to catch.
**einfarbig** ['aɪnfarbɪç] *adj* all one colour (*BRIT*) *od* color (*US*); (*Stoff etc*) self-coloured (*BRIT*), self-colored (*US*).
**einfassen** ['aɪnfasən] *vt* (*Edelstein*) to set; (*Beet, Stoff*) to edge.
**Einfassung** *f* setting; border.
**einfetten** ['aɪnfɛtən] *vt* to grease.
**einfinden** ['aɪnfɪndən] *unreg vr* to come, turn

up.
**einfliegen** ['aɪnfliːɡən] *unreg vt* to fly in.
**einfließen** ['aɪnfliːsən] *unreg vi* to flow in.
**einflößen** ['aɪnfløːsən] *vt:* **jdm etw ~** (*lit*) to give sb sth; (*fig*) to instil sth into sb.
**Einfluß** ['aɪnflʊs] *m* influence; **~ nehmen** to bring an influence to bear; **~bereich** *m* sphere of influence; **e~reich** *adj* influential.
**einflüstern** ['aɪnflʏstərn] *vt:* **jdm etw ~** to whisper sth to sb; (*fig*) to insinuate sth to sb.
**einförmig** ['aɪnfœrmɪç] *adj* uniform; (*eintönig*) monotonous; **E~keit** *f* uniformity; monotony.
**einfrieren** ['aɪnfriːrən] *unreg vi* to freeze (in) ♦ *vt* to freeze; (*POL: Beziehungen*) to suspend.
**einfügen** ['aɪnfyːɡən] *vt* to fit in; (*zusätzlich*) to add; (*COMPUT*) to insert.
**einfühlen** ['aɪnfyːlən] *vr:* **sich in jdn ~** to empathize with sb.
**einfühlsam** ['aɪnfyːlzaːm] *adj* sensitive.
**Einfühlungsvermögen** *nt* empathy; **mit großem ~** with a great deal of sensitivity.
**Einfuhr** ['aɪnfuːr] (-) *f* import; **~artikel** *m* imported article.
**einführen** ['aɪnfyːrən] *vt* to bring in; (*Mensch, Sitten*) to introduce; (*Ware*) to import; **jdn in sein Amt ~** to install sb (in office).
**Einfuhr-** *zW:* **~genehmigung** *f* import permit; **~kontingent** *nt* import quota; **~sperre** *f* ban on imports; **~stopp** *m* ban on imports.
**Einführung** *f* introduction.
**Einführungspreis** *m* introductory price.
**Einfuhrzoll** *m* import duty.
**einfüllen** ['aɪnfʏlən] *vt* to pour in.
**Eingabe** ['aɪngaːbə] *f* petition; (*Daten~*) input; **~/Ausgabe** (*COMPUT*) input/output.
**Eingang** ['aɪngaŋ] *m* entrance; (*COMM: Ankunft*) arrival; (*Sendung*) post; **wir bestätigen den ~ Ihres Schreibens vom ...** we acknowledge receipt of your letter of the ...
**eingängig** ['aɪngɛŋɪç] *adj* catchy.
**eingangs** *adv* at the outset ♦ *präp* +*gen* at the outset of.
**Eingangs-** *zW:* **~bestätigung** *f* acknowledgement of receipt; **~halle** *f* entrance hall; **~stempel** *m* (*COMM*) receipt stamp.
**eingeben** ['aɪngeːbən] *unreg vt* (*Arznei*) to give; (*Daten etc*) to enter; (*Gedanken*) to inspire.
**eingebettet** ['aɪngəbɛtət] *adj:* **in od zwischen Hügeln ~** nestling among the hills.
**eingebildet** ['aɪngəbɪldət] *adj* imaginary; (*eitel*) conceited; **~er Kranker** hypochondriac.
**Eingeborene(r)** ['aɪngəboːrənə(r)] *f(m)* native.
**Eingebung** *f* inspiration.
**eingedenk** ['aɪngədɛŋk] *präp* +*gen* bearing in mind.
**eingefahren** ['aɪngəfaːrən] *adj* (*Verhaltensweise*) well-worn.

**eingefallen** ['aɪngəfalən] *adj* (*Gesicht*) gaunt.

**eingefleischt** ['aɪngəflaɪʃt] *adj* inveterate; **~er Junggeselle** confirmed bachelor.

**eingefroren** ['aɪngəfroːrən] *adj* frozen.

**eingehen** ['aɪngeːən] *unreg vi* (*Aufnahme finden*) to come in; (*Sendung, Geld*) to be received; (*Tier, Pflanze*) to die; (*Firma*) to fold; (*schrumpfen*) to shrink ♦ *vt* (*abmachen*) to enter into; (*Wette*) to make; **auf etw** *akk* **~** to go into sth; **auf jdn ~** to respond to sb; **jdm ~** (*verständlich sein*) to be comprehensible to sb; **auf einen Vorschlag/Plan ~** (*zustimmen*) to go along with a suggestion/plan; **bei dieser Hitze/Kälte geht man ja ein!** (*umg*) this heat/cold is just too much.

**eingehend** *adj* in-depth, thorough.

**eingekeilt** ['aɪngəkaɪlt] *adj* hemmed in; (*fig*) trapped.

**eingekesselt** ['aɪngəkɛsəlt] *adj*: **~ sein** to be encircled *od* surrounded.

**Eingemachte(s)** ['aɪngəmaːxtə(s)] *nt* preserves *pl*.

**eingemeinden** ['aɪngəmaɪndən] *vt* to incorporate.

**eingenommen** ['aɪngənɔmən] *adj*: **~ (von)** fond (of), partial (to); **~ (gegen)** prejudiced (against).

**eingeschnappt** ['aɪngəʃnapt] (*umg*) *adj* cross; **~ sein** to be in a huff.

**eingeschrieben** ['aɪngəʃriːbən] *adj* registered.

**eingeschworen** ['aɪngəʃvoːrən] *adj* confirmed; (*Gemeinschaft*) close.

**eingesessen** ['aɪngəzɛsən] *adj* old-established.

**eingespannt** ['aɪngəʃpant] *adj* busy.

**eingespielt** ['aɪngəʃpiːlt] *adj*: **aufeinander ~ sein** to be in tune with each other.

**Eingeständnis** ['aɪngəʃtɛntnɪs] *nt* admission, confession.

**eingestehen** ['aɪngəʃteːən] *unreg vt* to confess.

**eingestellt** ['aɪngəʃtɛlt] *adj*: **ich bin im Moment nicht auf Besuch ~** I'm not prepared for visitors.

**eingetragen** ['aɪngətraːgən] *adj* (*COMM*) registered; **~er Gesellschaftssitz** registered office; **~es Warenzeichen** registered trademark.

**Eingeweide** ['aɪngəvaɪdə] (**-s, -**) *nt* innards *pl*, intestines *pl*.

**Eingeweihte(r)** ['aɪngəvaɪtə(r)] *f(m)* initiate.

**eingewöhnen** ['aɪngəvøːnən] *vr*: **sich ~ (in** +*dat*) to settle down (in).

**eingezahlt** ['aɪngətsaːlt] *adj*: **~es Kapital** paid-up capital.

**eingießen** ['aɪngiːsən] *unreg vt* to pour (out).

**eingleisig** ['aɪnglaɪzɪç] *adj* single-track; **er denkt sehr ~** (*fig*) he's completely single-minded.

**eingliedern** ['aɪngliːdərn] *vt*: **~ (in** +*akk*) to integrate (into) ♦ *vr*: **sich ~ (in** +*akk*) to integrate o.s. (into).

**eingraben** ['aɪngraːbən] *unreg vt* to dig in ♦ *vr* to dig o.s. in; **dieses Erlebnis hat sich seinem**

**Gedächtnis eingegraben** this experience has engraved itself on his memory.

**eingreifen** ['aɪngraɪfən] *unreg vi* to intervene, interfere; (*Zahnrad*) to mesh.

**eingrenzen** ['aɪngrɛntsən] *vt* to enclose; (*fig: Problem*) to delimit.

**Eingriff** ['aɪngrɪf] *m* intervention, interference; (*Operation*) operation.

**einhaken** ['aɪnhaːkən] *vt* to hook in ♦ *vr*: **sich bei jdm ~** to link arms with sb ♦ *vi* (*sich einmischen*) to intervene.

**Einhalt** ['aɪnhalt] *m*: **~ gebieten** +*dat* to put a stop to.

**einhalten** *unreg vt* (*Regel*) to keep ♦ *vi* to stop.

**einhämmern** ['aɪnhɛmərn] *vt*: **jdm etw ~** (*fig*) to hammer sth into sb.

**einhandeln** ['aɪnhandəln] *vt*: **etw gegen** *od* **für etw ~** to trade sth for sth.

**einhändig** ['aɪnhɛndɪç] *adj* one-handed.

**einhändigen** ['aɪnhɛndɪgən] *vt* to hand in.

**einhängen** ['aɪnhɛŋən] *vt* to hang; (*Telefon: auch vi*) to hang up; **sich bei jdm ~** to link arms with sb.

**einheimisch** ['aɪnhaɪmɪʃ] *adj* native.

**Einheimische(r)** *f(m)* local.

**einheimsen** (*umg*) *vt* to bring home.

**einheiraten** ['aɪnhaɪraːtən] *vi*: **in einen Betrieb ~** to marry into a business.

**Einheit** ['aɪnhaɪt] *f* unity; (*Maß, MIL*) unit; **eine geschlossene ~ bilden** to form an integrated whole; **e~lich** *adj* uniform.

**Einheits-** *zW*: **~front** *f* (*POL*) united front; **~liste** *f* (*POL*) single *od* unified list of candidates; **~preis** *m* uniform price.

**einheizen** ['aɪnhaɪtsən] *vi*: **jdm (tüchtig) ~** (*umg: die Meinung sagen*) to make things hot for sb.

**einhellig** ['aɪnhɛlɪç] *adj* unanimous ♦ *adv* unanimously.

**einholen** ['aɪnhoːlən] *vt* (*Tau*) to haul in; (*Fahne, Segel*) to lower; (*Vorsprung aufholen*) to catch up with; (*Verspätung*) to make up; (*Rat, Erlaubnis*) to ask ♦ *vi* (*einkaufen*) to buy, shop.

**Einhorn** ['aɪnhɔrn] *nt* unicorn.

**einhüllen** ['aɪnhʏlən] *vt* to wrap up.

**einhundert** ['aɪn'hʊndərt] *num* one hundred.

**einig** ['aɪnɪç] *adj* (*vereint*) united; **sich** *dat* **~ sein** to be in agreement; **~ werden** to agree.

**einige(r, s)** *adj, pron* some ♦ *pl* some; (*mehrere*) several; **mit Ausnahme ~r weniger** with a few exceptions; **vor ~n Tagen** the other day, a few days ago; **dazu ist noch ~s zu sagen** there are still one or two things to say about that.

**einigemal** *adv* a few times.

**einigen** *vt* to unite ♦ *vr*: **sich (auf etw** *akk*) **~** to agree (on sth).

**einigermaßen** *adv* somewhat; (*leidlich*) reasonably.

**einiges** *pron siehe* **einige(r, s).**

**einiggehen** *unreg vi* to agree.
**Einigkeit** *f* unity; (*Übereinstimmung*) agreement.
**Einigung** *f* agreement; (*Ver~*) unification.
**einimpfen** ['aɪnˌɪmpfən] *vt:* **jdm etw ~ to** inoculate sb with sth; (*fig*) to impress sth upon sb.
**einjagen** ['aɪnjaːgən] *vt:* **jdm Furcht/einen Schrecken ~** to give sb a fright.
**einjährig** ['aɪnjɛːrɪç] *adj* of *od* for one year; (*Alter*) one-year-old; (*Pflanze*) annual.
**einkalkulieren** ['aɪnkalkuliːrən] *vt* to take into account, allow for.
**einkassieren** ['aɪnkasiːrən] *vt* (*Geld, Schulden*) to collect.
**Einkauf** ['aɪnkaʊf] *m* purchase; (*COMM: Abteilung*) purchasing (department).
**einkaufen** *vt* to buy ♦ *vi* to shop; **~ gehen** to go shopping.
**Einkäufer(in)** ['aɪnkɔʏfər(ɪn)] *m(f)* (*COMM*) buyer.
**Einkaufs-** *zW:* **~bummel** *m:* **einen ~bummel machen** to go on a shopping spree; **~ korb** *m* shopping basket; **~leiter(in)** *m(f)* (*COMM*) chief buyer; **~netz** *nt* string bag; **~preis** *m* cost price, wholesale price; **~wagen** *m* trolley (*BRIT*), cart (*US*); **~zentrum** *nt* shopping centre.
**einkehren** ['aɪnkeːrən] *vi* (*geh: Ruhe, Frühling*) to come; **in einem Gasthof ~** to (make a) stop at an inn.
**einkerben** ['aɪnkɛrbən] *vt* to notch.
**einklagen** ['aɪnklaːgən] *vt* (*Schulden*) to sue for (the recovery of).
**einklammern** ['aɪnklamərn] *vt* to put in brackets, bracket.
**Einklang** ['aɪnklaŋ] *m* harmony.
**einkleiden** ['aɪnklaɪdən] *vt* to clothe; (*fig*) to express.
**einklemmen** ['aɪnklɛmən] *vt* to jam.
**einknicken** ['aɪnknɪkən] *vt* to bend in; (*Papier*) to fold ♦ *vi* (*Knie*) to give way.
**einkochen** ['aɪnkɔxən] *vt* to boil down; (*Obst*) to preserve, bottle.
**Einkommen** ['aɪnkɔmən] (**-s, -**) *nt* income.
**einkommensschwach** *adj* low-income *attrib.*
**einkommensstark** *adj* high-income *attrib.*
**Einkommen(s)steuer** *f* income tax; **~erklärung** *f* income tax return.
**Einkommensverhältnisse** *pl* (level of) income *sing.*
**einkreisen** ['aɪnkraɪzən] *vt* to encircle.
**einkriegen** ['aɪnkriːgən] (*umg*) *vr:* **sie konnte sich gar nicht mehr darüber ~, daß ...** she couldn't get over the fact that ...
**Einkünfte** ['aɪnkʏnftə] *pl* income *sing*, revenue *sing.*
**einladen** ['aɪnlaːdən] *unreg vt* (*Person*) to invite; (*Gegenstände*) to load; **jdn ins Kino ~** to take sb to the cinema.
**Einladung** *f* invitation.
**Einlage** ['aɪnlaːgə] *f* (*Programm~*) interlude;

(*Spar~*) deposit; (*FIN: Kapital~*) investment; (*Schuh~*) insole; (*Fußstütze*) support; (*Zahn~*) temporary filling; (*KOCH*) noodles, *vegetables etc (in clear soup)*.
**einlagern** ['aɪnlaːgərn] *vt* to store.
**Einlaß** ['aɪnlas] (**-sses, -lässe**) *m* admission; **jdm ~ gewähren** to admit sb.
**einlassen** *unreg vt* to let in; (*einsetzen*) to set in ♦ *vr:* **sich mit jdm/auf etw** *akk* **~** to get involved with sb/sth; **sich auf einen Kompromiß ~** to agree to a compromise; **ich lasse mich auf keine Diskussion ein** I'm not having any discussion about it.
**Einlauf** ['aɪnlaʊf] *m* arrival; (*von Pferden*) finish; (*MED*) enema.
**einlaufen** *unreg vi* to arrive, come in; (*SPORT*) to finish; (*Wasser*) to run in; (*Stoff*) to shrink ♦ *vt* (*Schuhe*) to break in ♦ *vr* (*SPORT*) to warm up; (*Motor, Maschine*) to run in; **jdm das Haus ~** to invade sb's house; **in den Hafen ~** to enter the harbour.
**einläuten** ['aɪnlɔʏtən] *vt* (*neues Jahr*) to ring in; (*SPORT: Runde*) to sound the bell for.
**einleben** ['aɪnleːbən] *vr* to settle down.
**Einlegearbeit** *f* inlay.
**einlegen** ['aɪnleːgən] *vt* (*einfügen: Blatt, Sohle*) to insert; (*KOCH*) to pickle; (*in Holz etc*) to inlay; (*Geld*) to deposit; (*Pause*) to have; (*Protest*) to make; (*Veto*) to use; (*Berufung*) to lodge; **ein gutes Wort bei jdm ~** to put in a good word for sb.
**Einlegesohle** *f* insole.
**einleiten** ['aɪnlaɪtən] *vt* to introduce, start; (*Geburt*) to induce.
**Einleitung** *f* introduction; induction.
**einlenken** ['aɪnlɛŋkən] *vi* (*fig*) to yield, give way.
**einlesen** ['aɪnleːzən] *unreg vr:* **sich in ein Gebiet ~** to get into a subject ♦ *vt:* **etw in etw** +*akk* **~** (*Daten*) to feed sth into sth.
**einleuchten** ['aɪnlɔʏçtən] *vi:* **(jdm) ~** to be clear *od* evident (to sb).
**einleuchtend** *adj* clear.
**einliefern** ['aɪnliːfərn] *vt:* **~** (**in** +*akk*) to take (into); **jdn ins Krankenhaus ~** to admit sb to hospital.
**Einlieferungsschein** *m* certificate of posting.
**einlochen** ['aɪnlɔxən] (*umg*) *vt* (*einsperren*) to lock up.
**einlösen** ['aɪnløːzən] *vt* (*Scheck*) to cash; (*Schuldschein, Pfand*) to redeem; (*Versprechen*) to keep.
**einmachen** ['aɪnmaxən] *vt* to preserve.
**Einmachglas** *nt* bottling jar.
**einmal** ['aɪnmaːl] *adv* once; (*erstens*) first of all, firstly; (*später*) one day; **nehmen wir ~ an** just let's suppose; **noch ~** once more; **nicht ~** not even; **auf ~** all at once; **es war ~** once upon a time there was/were; **~ ist keinmal** (*Sprichwort*) once doesn't count; **waren Sie schon ~ in Rom?** have you ever

been to Rome?

**Einmaleins** *nt* multiplication tables *pl*; (*fig*) ABC, basics *pl*.

**einmalig** *adj* unique; (*einmal geschehend*) single; (*prima*) fantastic.

**Einmannbetrieb** *m* one-man business.

**Einmannbus** *m* one-man-operated bus.

**Einmarsch** ['aınmarʃ] *m* entry; (*MIL*) invasion.

**einmarschieren** *vi* to march in.

**einmengen** ['aınmɛŋən] *vr*: **sich (in etw** +*akk*) ~ to interfere (with sth).

**einmieten** ['aınmi:tən] *vr*: **sich bei jdm** ~ to take lodgings with sb.

**einmischen** ['aınmıʃən] *vr*: **sich (in etw** +*akk*) ~ to interfere (with sth).

**einmotten** ['aınmɔtən] *vt* (*Kleider etc*) to put in mothballs.

**einmünden** ['aınmYndən] *vi*: ~ **in** +*akk* (*subj: Fluß*) to flow *od* run into, join; (: *Straße: in Platz*) to run into; (: : *in andere Straße*) to run into, join.

**einmütig** ['aınmy:tıç] *adj* unanimous.

**einnähen** ['aınnɛ:ən] *vt* (*enger machen*) to take in.

**Einnahme** ['aınna:mə] (-, -n) *f* (*Geld*) takings *pl*, revenue; (*von Medizin*) taking; (*MIL*) capture, taking; ~**n und Ausgaben** income and expenditure; ~**quelle** *f* source of income.

**einnehmen** ['aınne:mən] *unreg vt* to take; (*Stellung, Raum*) to take up; ~ **für/gegen** to persuade in favour of/against.

**einnehmend** *adj* charming.

**einnicken** ['aınnıkən] *vi* to nod off.

**einnisten** ['aınnıstən] *vr* to nest; (*fig*) to settle o.s.

**Einöde** ['aın|ø:də] (-, -n) *f* desert, wilderness.

**einordnen** ['aın|ɔrdnən] *vt* to arrange, fit in ♦ *vr* to adapt; (*AUT*) to get in(to) lane.

**einpacken** ['aınpakən] *vt* to pack (up).

**einparken** ['aınparkən] *vt, vi* to park.

**einpauken** ['aınpaukən] (*umg*) *vt*: **jdm etw** ~ to drum sth into sb.

**einpendeln** ['aınpɛndəln] *vr* to even out.

**einpennen** ['aınpɛnən] (*umg*) *vi* to drop off.

**einpferchen** ['aınpfɛrçən] *vt* to pen in; (*fig*) to coop up.

**einpflanzen** ['aınpflantsən] *vt* to plant; (*MED*) to implant.

**einplanen** ['aınpla:nən] *vt* to plan for.

**einprägen** ['aınprɛ:gən] *vt* to impress, imprint; (*beibringen*): **jdm etw** ~ to impress sth on sb; **sich** *dat* **etw** ~ to memorize sth.

**einprägsam** ['aınprɛ:kza:m] *adj* easy to remember; (*Melodie*) catchy.

**einprogrammieren** ['aınprogrami:rən] *vt* (*COMPUT*) to feed in.

**einprügeln** ['aınpry:gəln] (*umg*) *vt*: **jdm etw** ~ to din sth into sb.

**einquartieren** ['aınkvarti:rən] *vt* (*MIL*) to billet; **Gäste bei Freunden** ~ to put visitors up with friends.

**einrahmen** ['aınra:mən] *vt* to frame.

**einrasten** ['aınrastən] *vi* to engage.

**einräumen** ['aınrɔʏmən] *vt* (*ordnend*) to put away; (*überlassen: Platz*) to give up; (*zugestehen*) to admit, concede.

**einrechnen** ['aınrɛçnən] *vt* to include; (*berücksichtigen*) to take into account.

**einreden** ['aınre:dən] *vt*: **jdm/sich etw** ~ to talk sb/o.s. into believing sth ♦ *vi*: **auf jdn** ~ to keep on and on at sb.

**Einreibemittel** *nt* liniment.

**einreiben** ['aınraıbən] *unreg vt* to rub in.

**einreichen** ['aınraıçən] *vt* to hand in; (*Antrag*) to submit.

**einreihen** ['aınraıən] *vt* (*einordnen, einfügen*) to put in; (*klassifizieren*) to classify ♦ *vr* (*Auto*) to get in lane; **etw in etw** *akk* ~ to put sth into sth.

**Einreise** ['aınraızə] *f* entry; ~**bestimmungen** *pl* entry regulations *pl*; ~**erlaubnis** *f* entry permit; ~**genehmigung** *f* entry permit.

**einreisen** ['aınraızən] *vi*: **in ein Land** ~ to enter a country.

**Einreiseverbot** *nt* refusal of entry.

**Einreisevisum** *nt* entry visa.

**einreißen** ['aınraısən] *unreg vt* (*Papier*) to tear; (*Gebäude*) to pull down ♦ *vi* to tear; (*Gewohnheit werden*) to catch on.

**einrenken** ['aınrɛŋkən] *vt* (*Gelenk, Knie*) to put back in place; (*fig: umg*) to sort out ♦ *vr* (*fig: umg*) to sort itself out.

**einrichten** ['aınrıçtən] *vt* (*Haus*) to furnish; (*schaffen*) to establish, set up; (*arrangieren*) to arrange; (*möglich machen*) to manage ♦ *vr* (*in Haus*) to furnish one's house; **sich** ~ (**auf** +*akk*) (*sich vorbereiten*) to prepare o.s. (for); (*sich anpassen*) to adapt (to).

**Einrichtung** *f* (*Wohnungs*~) furnishings *pl*; (*öffentliche Anstalt*) organization; (*Dienste*) service; (*Labor*~ *etc*) equipment; (*Gewohnheit*): **zur ständigen** ~ **werden** to become an institution.

**Einrichtungsgegenstand** *m* item of furniture.

**einrosten** ['aınrɔstən] *vi* to get rusty.

**einrücken** ['aınrYkən] *vi* (*MIL: Soldat*) to join up; (: *in Land*) to move in ♦ *vt* (*Anzeige*) to insert; (*Zeile, Text*) to indent.

**Eins** [aıns] (-, -en) *f* one; **e**~ *num* one; **es ist mir alles e**~ it's all one to me; **e**~ **zu e**~ (*SPORT*) one all; **e**~ **a** (*umg*) first-rate.

**einsalzen** ['aınzaltsən] *vt* to salt.

**einsam** ['aınza:m] *adj* lonely, solitary; ~**e Klasse/Spitze** (*umg: hervorragend*) absolutely fantastic; **E**~**keit** *f* loneliness, solitude.

**einsammeln** ['aınzaməln] *vt* to collect.

**Einsatz** ['aınzats] *m* (*Teil*) insert; (*an Kleid*) insertion; (*Tisch*~) leaf; (*Verwendung*) use, employment; (*Spiel*~) stake; (*Risiko*) risk; (*MIL*) operation; (*MUS*) entry; **im** ~ in action; **etw unter** ~ **seines Lebens tun** to risk one's life to do sth; ~**befehl** *m* order to go into action; **e~bereit** adj ready for action; **~kommando** nt (MIL) task force.

**einschalten** ['aɪnʃaltən] vt (ELEK) to switch on; (einfügen) to insert; (Pause) to make; (AUT: Gang) to engage; (Anwalt) to bring in ♦ vr (dazwischentreten) to intervene.

**Einschaltquote** f (TV) viewing figures pl.

**einschärfen** ['aɪnʃɛrfən] vt: **jdm etw ~** to impress sth on sb.

**einschätzen** ['aɪnʃɛtsən] vt to estimate, assess ♦ vr to rate o.s.

**einschenken** ['aɪnʃɛŋkən] vt to pour out.

**einscheren** ['aɪnʃeːrən] vi to get back (into lane).

**einschicken** ['aɪnʃɪkən] vt to send in.

**einschieben** ['aɪnʃiːbən] unreg vt to push in; (zusätzlich) to insert; **eine Pause ~** to have a break.

**einschiffen** ['aɪnʃɪfən] vt to ship ♦ vr to embark, go on board.

**einschl.** abk (= einschließlich) inc.

**einschlafen** ['aɪnʃlaːfən] unreg vi to fall asleep, go to sleep; (fig: Freundschaft) to peter out.

**einschläfern** ['aɪnʃlɛːfərn] vt (schläfrig machen) to make sleepy; (Gewissen) to soothe; (narkotisieren) to give a soporific to; (töten: Tier) to put to sleep.

**einschläfernd** adj (MED) soporific; (langweilig) boring; (Stimme) lulling.

**Einschlag** ['aɪnʃlaːk] m impact; (AUT) lock; (fig: Beimischung) touch, hint.

**einschlagen** ['aɪnʃlaːgən] unreg vt to knock in; (Fenster) to smash, break; (Zähne, Schädel) to smash in; (Steuer) to turn; (kürzer machen) to take up; (Ware) to pack, wrap up; (Weg, Richtung) to take ♦ vi to hit; (sich einigen) to agree; (Anklang finden) to work, succeed; **es muß irgendwo eingeschlagen haben** something must have been struck by lightning; **gut ~** (umg) to go down well, be a big hit; **auf jdn ~** to hit sb.

**einschlägig** ['aɪnʃlɛːgɪç] adj relevant; **er ist ~ vorbestraft** (JUR) he has a previous conviction for a similar offence.

**einschleichen** ['aɪnʃlaɪçən] unreg vr (in Haus, fig: Fehler) to creep in, steal in; (in Vertrauen) to worm one's way in.

**einschleppen** ['aɪnʃlɛpən] vt (fig: Krankheit etc) to bring in.

**einschleusen** ['aɪnʃlɔyzən] vt: **~ (in +akk)** to smuggle in(to).

**einschließen** ['aɪnʃliːsən] unreg vt (Kind) to lock in; (Häftling) to lock up; (Gegenstand) to lock away; (Bergleute) to cut off; (umgeben) to surround; (MIL) to encircle; (fig) to include, comprise ♦ vr to lock o.s. in.

**einschließlich** adv inclusive ♦ präp +gen inclusive of, including.

**einschmeicheln** ['aɪnʃmaɪçəln] vr: **sich (bei jdm) ~** to ingratiate o.s. (with sb).

**einschmuggeln** ['aɪnʃmʊgəln] vt: **~ (in +akk)** to smuggle in(to).

**einschnappen** ['aɪnʃnapən] vi (Tür) to click to; (fig) to be touchy; **eingeschnappt sein** to be in a huff.

**einschneidend** ['aɪnʃnaɪdənt] adj incisive.

**einschneien** ['aɪnʃnaɪən] vi: **eingeschneit sein** to be snowed in.

**Einschnitt** ['aɪnʃnɪt] m (MED) incision; (im Tal, Gebirge) cleft; (im Leben) decisive point.

**einschnüren** ['aɪnʃnyːrən] vt (einengen) to cut into; **dieser Kragen schnürt mir den Hals ein** this collar is strangling me.

**einschränken** ['aɪnʃrɛŋkən] vt to limit, restrict; (Kosten) to cut down, reduce ♦ vr to cut down (on expenditure); **~d möchte ich sagen, daß ...** I'd like to qualify that by saying ...

**einschränkend** adj restrictive.

**Einschränkung** f restriction, limitation; reduction; (von Behauptung) qualification.

**Einschreib(e)brief** m registered (BRIT) od certified (US) letter.

**einschreiben** ['aɪnʃraɪbən] unreg vt to write in; (POST) to send by registered (BRIT) od certified (US) mail ♦ vr to register; (UNIV) to enrol; **E~** nt registered (BRIT) od certified (US) letter.

**einschreiten** ['aɪnʃraɪtən] unreg vi to step in, intervene; **~ gegen** to take action against.

**Einschub** ['aɪnʃuːp] (-(e)s, -̈e) m insertion.

**einschüchtern** ['aɪnʃʏçtərn] vt to intimidate.

**Einschüchterung** ['aɪnʃʏçtəruŋ] f intimidation.

**einschulen** ['aɪnʃuːlən] vt: **eingeschult werden** (Kind) to start school.

**einschweißen** ['aɪnʃvaɪsən] vt (in Plastik) to shrink-wrap; (TECH): **etw in etw akk ~** to weld sth into sth.

**einschwenken** ['aɪnʃvɛŋkən] vi: **~ (in +akk)** to turn od swing in(to).

**einsehen** ['aɪnzeːən] unreg vt (prüfen) to inspect; (Fehler etc) to recognize; (verstehen) to see; **das sehe ich nicht ein** I don't see why; **E~ (-s)** nt understanding; **ein E~ haben** to show understanding.

**einseifen** ['aɪnzaɪfən] vt to soap, lather; (fig: umg) to take in, con.

**einseitig** ['aɪnzaɪtɪç] adj one-sided; (POL) unilateral; (Ernährung) unbalanced; (Diskette) single-sided; **E~keit** f one-sidedness.

**einsenden** ['aɪnzɛndən] unreg vt to send in.

**Einsender(in)** (-s, -) m(f) sender, contributor.

**Einsendeschluß** m closing date (for entries).

**Einsendung** f sending in.

**einsetzen** ['aɪnzɛtsən] vt to put (in); (in Amt) to appoint, install; (Geld) to stake; (verwenden) to use; (MIL) to employ ♦ vi (beginnen) to set in; (MUS) to enter, come in ♦ vr to work hard; **sich für jdn/etw ~** to support sb/sth; **ich werde mich dafür ~, daß ...** I will do what I can to see that ...

**Einsicht** ['aɪnzɪçt] f insight; (in Akten) look, inspection; **zu der ~ kommen, daß ...** to

come to the conclusion that …
**einsichtig** *adj* (*Mensch*) judicious; **jdm etw**
~ **machen** to make sb understand *od* see
sth.
**Einsichtnahme** (-, -n) *f* (*form*) perusal; „**zur**
~" "for attention".
**einsichtslos** *adj* unreasonable.
**einsichtsvoll** *adj* understanding.
**Einsiedler** ['aɪnziːdlər] (-s, -) *m* hermit.
**einsilbig** ['aɪnzɪlbɪç] *adj* (*lit, fig*) monosyllabic;
E~**keit** *f* (*fig*) taciturnity.
**einsinken** ['aɪnzɪŋkən] *unreg vi* to sink in.
**Einsitzer** ['aɪnzɪtsər] (-s, -) *m* single-seater.
**einspannen** ['aɪnʃpanən] *vt* (*Werkstück, Papier*)
to put (in), insert; (*Pferde*) to harness; (*umg:
Person*) to rope in; **jdn für seine Zwecke** ~ to
use sb for one's own ends.
**einsparen** ['aɪnʃpaːrən] *vt* to save, economize
on; (*Kosten*) to cut down on; (*Posten*) to
eliminate.
**Einsparung** *f* saving.
**einspeichern** ['aɪnʃpaɪçərn] *vt*: **etw (in etw**
+akk**)** ~ (*COMPUT*) to feed sth in(to sth).
**einsperren** ['aɪnʃpɛrən] *vt* to lock up.
**einspielen** ['aɪnʃpiːlən] *vr* (*SPORT*) to warm up
♦ *vt* (*Film: Geld*) to bring in; (*Instrument*) to
play in; **sich aufeinander** ~ to become
attuned to each other; **gut eingespielt**
running smoothly.
**einsprachig** ['aɪnʃpraːxɪç] *adj* monolingual.
**einspringen** ['aɪnʃprɪŋən] *unreg vi* (*aushelfen*)
to stand in; (*mit Geld*) to help out.
**einspritzen** ['aɪnʃprɪtsən] *vt* to inject.
**Einspritzmotor** *m* (*AUT*) injection engine.
**Einspruch** ['aɪnʃprʊx] *m* protest, objection;
~ **einlegen** (*JUR*) to file an objection.
**Einspruchsfrist** *f* (*JUR*) period for filing an
objection.
**Einspruchsrecht** *nt* veto.
**einspurig** ['aɪnʃpuːrɪç] *adj* single-lane;
(*EISENB*) single-track.
**einst** [aɪnst] *adv* once; (*zukünftig*) one *od* some
day.
**Einstand** ['aɪnʃtant] *m* (*TENNIS*) deuce;
(*Antritt*) entrance (to office); **er hat gestern
seinen** ~ **gegeben** yesterday he celebrated
starting his new job.
**einstechen** ['aɪnʃtɛçən] *unreg vt* to pierce.
**einstecken** ['aɪnʃtɛkən] *vt* to stick in, insert;
(*Brief*) to post, mail (*US*); (*ELEK: Stecker*) to
plug in; (*Geld*) to pocket; (*mitnehmen*) to
take; (*überlegen sein*) to put in the shade;
(*hinnehmen*) to swallow.
**einstehen** ['aɪnʃteːən] *unreg vi*: **für jdn** ~ to
vouch for sb; **für etw** ~ to guarantee sth,
vouch for sth; (*Ersatz leisten*) to make good
sth.
**einsteigen** ['aɪnʃtaɪgən] *unreg vi* to get in *od*
on; (*in Schiff*) to go on board; (*sich beteiligen*)
to come in; (*hineinklettern*) to climb in; ~!
(*EISENB etc*) all aboard!
**Einsteiger** (-s, -) (*umg*) *m* beginner.

**einstellbar** *adj* adjustable.
**einstellen** ['aɪnʃtɛlən] *vt* (*in Firma*) to employ,
take on; (*aufhören*) to stop; (*Geräte*) to
adjust; (*Kamera etc*) to focus; (*Sender, Radio*)
to tune in to; (*unterstellen*) to put ♦ *vi* to take
on staff/workers ♦ *vr* (*anfangen*) to set in;
(*kommen*) to arrive; **Zahlungen** ~ to suspend
payment; **etw auf etw** *akk* ~ to adjust sth to
sth; to focus sth on sth; **sich auf jdn/etw** ~
to adapt to sb/prepare o.s. for sth.
**einstellig** *adj* (*Zahl*) single-digit.
**Einstellplatz** *m* (*auf Hof*) carport; (*in
Großgarage*) (covered) parking space.
**Einstellung** *f* (*Aufhören*) suspension,
cessation; (*von Gerät*) adjustment; (*von
Kamera etc*) focusing; (*von Arbeiter etc*)
appointment; (*Haltung*) attitude.
**Einstellungsgespräch** *nt* interview.
**Einstellungsstopp** *m* halt in recruitment.
**Einstieg** ['aɪnʃtiːk] (-(e)s, -e) *m* entry; (*fig*)
approach; (*von Bus, Bahn*) door; **kein** ~ exit
only.
**einstig** ['aɪnstɪç] *adj* former.
**einstimmen** ['aɪnʃtɪmən] *vi* to join in ♦ *vt*
(*MUS*) to tune; (*in Stimmung bringen*) to put
in the mood.
**einstimmig** *adj* unanimous; (*MUS*) for one
voice; E~**keit** *f* unanimity.
**einstmalig** *adj* former.
**einstmals** *adv* once, formerly.
**einstöckig** ['aɪnʃtœkɪç] *adj* two-storeyed
(*BRIT*), two-storied (*US*).
**einstöpseln** ['aɪnʃtœpsəln] *vt*: **etw (in etw**
+akk**)** ~ (*ELEK*) to plug sth in(to sth).
**einstudieren** ['aɪnʃtudiːrən] *vt* to study,
rehearse.
**einstufen** ['aɪnʃtuːfən] *vt* to classify.
**Einstufung** *f*: **nach seiner** ~ **in eine höhere
Gehaltsklasse** after he was put on a higher
salary grade.
**einstündig** ['aɪnʃtʏndɪç] *adj* one-hour *attrib*.
**einstürmen** ['aɪnʃtʏrmən] *vi*: **auf jdn** ~ to rush
at sb; (*Eindrücke*) to overwhelm sb.
**Einsturz** ['aɪnʃtʊrts] *m* collapse.
**einstürzen** ['aɪnʃtʏrtsən] *vi* to fall in, collapse;
**auf jdn** ~ (*fig*) to overwhelm sb.
**Einsturzgefahr** *f* danger of collapse.
**einstweilen** *adv* meanwhile; (*vorläufig*)
temporarily, for the time being.
**einstweilig** *adj* temporary; ~**e Verfügung**
(*JUR*) temporary *od* interim injunction.
**eintägig** ['aɪntɛːgɪç] *adj* one-day.
**Eintagsfliege** ['aɪntaːksfliːgə] *f* (*ZOOL*)
mayfly; (*fig*) nine-day wonder.
**eintauchen** ['aɪntaʊxən] *vt* to immerse, dip in
♦ *vi* to dive.
**eintauschen** ['aɪntaʊʃən] *vt* to exchange.
**eintausend** ['aɪn'taʊzənt] *num* one thousand.
**einteilen** ['aɪntaɪlən] *vt* (*in Teile*) to divide (up);
(*Menschen*) to assign.
**einteilig** *adj* one-piece.
**eintönig** ['aɪntøːnɪç] *adj* monotonous; E~**keit** *f*

monotony.

**Eintopf** ['aɪntɔpf] *m* stew.

**Eintopfgericht** ['aɪntɔpfgərɪçt] *nt* stew.

**Eintracht** ['aɪntraxt] (-) *f* concord, harmony.

**einträchtig** ['aɪntrɛçtɪç] *adj* harmonious.

**Eintrag** ['aɪntraːk] (-(e)s, ⁻e) *m* entry; **amtlicher ~** entry in the register.

**eintragen** ['aɪntraːgən] *unreg vt* (*in Buch*) to enter; (*Profit*) to yield ♦ *vr* to put one's name down; **jdm etw ~** to bring sb sth.

**einträglich** ['aɪntrɛːklɪç] *adj* profitable.

**Eintragung** *f*: **~** (**in** +*akk*) entry (in).

**eintreffen** ['aɪntrɛfən] *unreg vi* to happen; (*ankommen*) to arrive; (*fig: wahr werden*) to come true.

**eintreiben** ['aɪntraɪbən] *unreg vt* (*Geldbeträge*) to collect.

**eintreten** ['aɪntreːtən] *unreg vi* (*hineingehen*) to enter; (*sich ereignen*) to occur ♦ *vt* (*Tür*) to kick open; **in etw** *akk* **~** to enter sth; (*in Club, Partei*) to join sth; **für jdn/etw ~** to stand up for sb/sth.

**eintrichtern** ['aɪntrɪçtərn] (*umg*) *vt*: **jdm etw ~** to drum sth into sb.

**Eintritt** ['aɪntrɪt] *m* (*Betreten*) entrance; (*in Club etc*) joining; **~ frei** admission free; **„~ verboten"** "no admittance"; **bei ~ der Dunkelheit** at nightfall.

**Eintritts-** *zW*: **~geld** *nt* admission charge; **~karte** *f* (admission) ticket; **~preis** *m* admission charge.

**eintrocknen** ['aɪntrɔknən] *vi* to dry up.

**eintrudeln** ['aɪntruːdəln] (*umg*) *vi* to drift in.

**eintunken** ['aɪntʊŋkən] *vt* (*Brot*): **etw in etw** *akk* **~** to dunk sth in sth.

**einüben** ['aɪn|yːbən] *vt* to practise (*BRIT*), practice (*US*), drill.

**einverleiben** ['aɪnfɛrlaɪbən] *vt* to incorporate; (*Gebiet*) to annex; **sich** *dat* **etw ~** (*fig: geistig*) to assimilate sth.

**Einvernehmen** ['aɪnfɛrneːmən] (-s, -) *nt* agreement, understanding.

**einverstanden** ['aɪnfɛrʃtandən] *interj* agreed ♦ *adj*: **~ sein** to agree, be agreed; **sich mit etw ~ erklären** to give one's agreement to sth.

**Einverständnis** ['aɪnfɛrʃtɛntnɪs] (-ses) *nt* understanding; (*gleiche Meinung*) agreement; **im ~ mit jdm handeln** to act with sb's consent.

**Einwand** ['aɪnvant] (-(e)s, ⁻e) *m* objection; **einen ~ erheben** to raise an objection.

**Einwanderer** ['aɪnvandərər] *m* immigrant.

**Einwanderin** *f* immigrant.

**einwandern** *vi* to immigrate.

**Einwanderung** *f* immigration.

**einwandfrei** *adj* perfect; **etw ~ beweisen** to prove sth beyond doubt.

**einwärts** ['aɪnvɛrts] *adv* inwards.

**einwecken** ['aɪnvɛkən] *vt* to bottle, preserve.

**Einwegflasche** ['aɪnveːgflaʃə] *f* non-returnable bottle.

**Einwegspritze** *f* disposable (hypodermic) syringe.

**einweichen** ['aɪnvaɪçən] *vt* to soak.

**einweihen** ['aɪnvaɪən] *vt* (*Kirche*) to consecrate; (*Brücke*) to open; (*Gebäude*) to inaugurate; (*Person*): **in etw** *akk* **~** to initiate in sth; **er ist eingeweiht** (*fig*) he knows all about it.

**Einweihung** *f* consecration; opening; inauguration; initiation.

**einweisen** ['aɪnvaɪzən] *unreg vt* (*in Amt*) to install; (*in Arbeit*) to introduce; (*in Anstalt*) to send; (*in Krankenhaus*): **~ (in** +*akk*) to admit (to); (*AUT*): **~ (in** +*akk*) to guide in(to).

**Einweisung** *f* installation; introduction; sending.

**einwenden** ['aɪnvɛndən] *unreg vt*: **etwas ~ gegen** to object to, oppose.

**einwerfen** ['aɪnvɛrfən] *unreg vt* to throw in; (*Brief*) to post; (*Geld*) to put in, insert; (*Fenster*) to smash; (*äußern*) to interpose.

**einwickeln** ['aɪnvɪkəln] *vt* to wrap up; (*fig: umg*) to outsmart.

**einwilligen** ['aɪnvɪlɪgən] *vi*: (**in etw** *akk*) **~** to consent (to sth), agree (to sth).

**Einwilligung** *f* consent.

**einwirken** ['aɪnvɪrkən] *vi*: **auf jdn/etw ~** to influence sb/sth.

**Einwirkung** *f* influence.

**Einwohner(in)** ['aɪnvoːnər(ɪn)] (-s, -) *m(f)* inhabitant; **~meldeamt** *nt* registration office; **sich beim ~meldeamt (an)melden** ≈ to register with the police; **~schaft** *f* population, inhabitants *pl*.

**Einwurf** ['aɪnvʊrf] *m* (*Öffnung*) slot; (*Einwand*) objection; (*SPORT*) throw-in.

**Einzahl** ['aɪntsaːl] *f* singular.

**einzahlen** *vt* to pay in.

**Einzahlung** *f* payment; (*auf Sparkonto*) deposit.

**einzäunen** ['aɪntsɔʏnən] *vt* to fence in.

**einzeichnen** ['aɪntsaɪçnən] *vt* to draw in.

**Einzel** ['aɪntsəl] (-s, -) *nt* (*TENNIS*) singles *pl*.

**Einzel-** *zW*: **~aufstellung** *f* (*COMM*) itemized list; **~bett** *nt* single bed; **~blattzuführung** *f* sheet feed; **~fall** *m* single instance, individual case; **~gänger(in)** *m(f)* loner; **~haft** *f* solitary confinement; **~handel** *m* retail trade; **im ~handel erhältlich** available retail; **~handelsgeschäft** *nt* retail outlet; **~handelspreis** *m* retail price; **~händler** *m* retailer; **~heit** *f* particular, detail; **~kind** *nt* only child.

**Einzeller** ['aɪntsɛlər] (-s, -) *m* (*BIOL*) single-celled organism.

**einzeln** *adj* single; (*von Paar*) odd ♦ *adv* singly; **~ angeben** to specify; **~e** some (people), a few (people); **der/die ~e** the individual; **das ~e** the particular; **ins ~e gehen** to go into detail(s); **etw im ~en besprechen** to discuss sth in detail; **~ aufführen** to list separately *od* individually; **bitte ~ eintreten** please come in one (person) at a time.

**Einzelteil** *nt* individual part; (*Ersatzteil*) spare part; **etw in seine ~e zerlegen** to take sth to pieces, dismantle sth.

**Einzelzimmer** *nt* single room.

**einziehen** ['aɪntsiːən] *unreg vt* to draw in, take in; (*Kopf*) to duck; (*Fühler, Antenne, Fahrgestell*) to retract; (*Steuern, Erkundigungen*) to collect; (*MIL*) to call up, draft (*US*); (*aus dem Verkehr ziehen*) to withdraw; (*konfiszieren*) to confiscate ♦ *vi* to move in; (*Friede, Ruhe*) to come; (*Flüssigkeit*): **~ (in +*akk*)** to soak in(to).

**einzig** ['aɪntsɪç] *adj* only; (*ohnegleichen*) unique ♦ *adv*: **~ und allein** solely; **das ~e** the only thing; **der/die ~e** the only one; **kein ~es Mal** not once, not one single time; **kein ~er** nobody, not a single person; **~artig** *adj* unique.

**Einzug** ['aɪntsuːk] *m* entry, moving in.

**Einzugsauftrag** *m* (*FIN*) direct debit.

**Einzugsbereich** *m* catchment area.

**Einzugsverfahren** *nt* (*FIN*) direct debit.

**Eis** [aɪs] (-es, -) *nt* ice; (*Speise~*) ice cream; **~ am Stiel** ice lolly (*BRIT*), popsicle ® (*US*); **~bahn** *f* ice *od* skating rink; **~bär** *m* polar bear; **~becher** *m* sundae; **~bein** *nt* pig's trotters *pl*; **~berg** *m* iceberg; **~beutel** *m* ice pack; **~café** *nt* = **Eisdiele.**

**Eischnee** ['aɪʃneː] *m* (*KOCH*) beaten white of egg.

**Eisdecke** *f* sheet of ice.

**Eisdiele** *f* ice-cream parlour (*BRIT*) *od* parlor (*US*).

**Eisen** ['aɪzən] (-s, -) *nt* iron; **zum alten ~ gehören** (*fig*) to be on the scrap heap.

**Eisenbahn** *f* railway, railroad (*US*); **es ist (aller)höchste ~** (*umg*) it's high time; **~er** (-s, -) *m* railwayman, railway employee, railroader (*US*); **~netz** *nt* rail network; **~schaffner** *m* railway guard, (railroad) conductor (*US*); **~überführung** *f* footbridge; **~übergang** *m* level crossing, grade crossing (*US*); **~wagen** *m* railway *od* railroad (*US*) carriage; **~waggon** *m* (*Güterwagen*) goods wagon.

**Eisen-** *zW*: **~erz** *nt* iron ore; **e~haltig** *adj* containing iron; **~mangel** *m* iron deficiency; **~warenhandlung** *f* ironmonger's (*BRIT*), hardware store (*US*).

**eisern** ['aɪzərn] *adj* iron; (*Gesundheit*) robust; (*Energie*) unrelenting; (*Reserve*) emergency; **der E~e Vorhang** the Iron Curtain; **in etw** *dat* **~ sein** to be adamant about sth; **er ist ~ bei seinem Entschluß geblieben** he stuck firmly to his decision.

**Eis-** *zW*: **~fach** *nt* freezer compartment, icebox; **e~frei** *adj* clear of ice; **e~gekühlt** *adj* chilled; **~hockey** *nt* ice hockey.

**eisig** ['aɪzɪç] *adj* icy.

**Eis-** *zW*: **~kaffee** *m* iced coffee; **e~kalt** *adj* icy cold; **~kunstlauf** *m* figure skating; **~laufen**

*nt* ice-skating; **~läufer** *m* ice-skater; **~meer** *nt*: **Nördliches/Südliches ~meer** Arctic/Antarctic Ocean; **~pickel** *m* ice-axe (*BRIT*), ice-ax (*US*).

**Eisprung** ['aɪʃpruŋ] *m* ovulation.

**Eis-** *zW*: **~schießen** *nt* ≈ curling; **~scholle** *f* ice floe; **~schrank** *m* fridge, icebox (*US*); **~stadion** *nt* ice *od* skating rink; **~würfel** *m* ice cube; **~zapfen** *m* icicle; **~zeit** *f* Ice Age.

**eitel** ['aɪtəl] *adj* vain; **E~keit** *f* vanity.

**Eiter** ['aɪtər] (-s) *m* pus.

**eiterig** *adj* suppurating.

**eitern** *vi* to suppurate.

**Ei-** *zW*: **~weiß** (-es, -e) *nt* white of an egg; (*CHEM*) protein; **~weißgehalt** *m* protein content; **~zelle** *f* ovum.

**EKD** *f abk* (= *Evangelische Kirche in Deutschland*) *German Protestant Church.*

**Ekel¹** ['eːkəl] (-s) *m* nausea, disgust; **vor jdm/etw einen ~ haben** to loathe sb/sth.

**Ekel²** ['eːkəl] (-s, -) (*umg*) *nt* (*Mensch*) nauseating person.

**ekelerregend** *adj* nauseating, disgusting.

**ekelhaft** *adj*, **ekelig** *adj* = **ekelerregend.**

**ekeln** *vt* to disgust ♦ *vr*: **sich vor etw** *dat* **~** to loathe *od* be disgusted at sth; **es ekelt ihn** he is disgusted.

**EKG** (-) *nt abk* (= *Elektrokardiogramm*) ECG.

**Eklat** [e'klaː] (-s) *m* (*geh: Aufsehen*) sensation.

**eklig** *adj* nauseating, disgusting.

**Ekstase** [ɛk'staːzə] (-, -n) *f* ecstasy; **jdn in ~ versetzen** to send sb into ecstasies.

**Ekzem** [ɛk'tseːm] (-s, -e) *nt* (*MED*) eczema.

**Elan** [e'lãː] (-s) *m* élan.

**elastisch** [e'lastɪʃ] *adj* elastic.

**Elastizität** [elastitsi'tɛːt] *f* elasticity.

**Elbe** ['ɛlbə] *f* (*Fluß*) Elbe.

**Elch** [ɛlç] (-(e)s, -e) *m* elk.

**Elefant** [ele'fant] *m* elephant; **wie ein ~ im Porzellanladen** (*umg*) like a bull in a china shop.

**elegant** [ele'gant] *adj* elegant.

**Eleganz** [ele'gants] *f* elegance.

**Elektrifizierung** [elɛktrifi'tsiːrʊŋ] *f* electrification.

**Elektriker** [e'lɛktrikər] (-s, -) *m* electrician.

**elektrisch** [e'lɛktrɪʃ] *adj* electric.

**elektrisieren** [elɛktri'ziːrən] *vt* (*lit, fig*) to electrify; (*Mensch*) to give an electric shock to ♦ *vr* to get an electric shock.

**Elektrizität** [elɛktritsi'tɛːt] *f* electricity.

**Elektrizitätswerk** *nt* electric power station.

**Elektroartikel** [e'lɛktro|artikəl] *m* electrical appliance.

**Elektrode** [elɛk'troːdə] (-, -n) *f* electrode.

**Elektro-** *zW*: **~gerät** *nt* electrical appliance; **~herd** *m* electric cooker; **~kardiogramm** *nt* (*MED*) electrocardiogram.

**Elektrolyse** [elɛktro'lyːzə] (-, -n) *f* electrolysis.

**Elektromotor** *m* electric motor.

**Elektron** [e'lɛktrɔn] (-s, -en) *nt* electron.

**Elektronen(ge)hirn** nt electronic brain.
**Elektronenrechner** m computer.
**Elektronik** [elɛk'troːnɪk] f electronics sing; (Teile) electronics pl.
**elektronisch** adj electronic; ~**e Post** electronic mail.
**Elektro-** zW: ~**rasierer** (-s, -) m electric razor; ~**schock** m (MED) electric shock, electroshock; ~**techniker** m electrician; (Ingenieur) electrical engineer.
**Element** [ele'mɛnt] (-s, -e) nt element; (ELEK) cell, battery.
**elementar** [elemɛn'taːr] adj elementary; (naturhaft) elemental; **E**~**teilchen** nt (PHYS) elementary particle.
**Elend** ['eːlɛnt] (-(e)s) nt misery; **da kann man das heulende ~ kriegen** (umg) it's enough to make you scream; **e**~ adj miserable; **mir ist ganz e**~ I feel really awful.
**elendiglich** ['eːlɛndɪklɪç] adv miserably; ~ **zugrunde gehen** to come to a wretched end.
**Elendsviertel** nt slum.
**elf** [ɛlf] num eleven; **E**~ (-, en) f (SPORT) eleven.
**Elfe** (-, -n) f elf.
**Elfenbein** nt ivory; ~**küste** f Ivory Coast.
**Elfmeter** m (SPORT) penalty (kick).
**Elfmeterschießen** nt (SPORT) penalty shoot-out.
**eliminieren** [elimi'niːrən] vt to eliminate.
**elitär** [eli'tɛːr] adj elitist ♦ adv in an elitist fashion.
**Elite** [e'liːtə] (-, -n) f elite.
**Elixier** [elɪ'ksiːr] (-s, -e) nt elixir.
**Ellbogen** m = **Ellenbogen**.
**Elle** ['ɛlə] (-, -n) f ell; (Maß) ≈ yard.
**Ellenbogen** m elbow; **die ~ gebrauchen** (umg) to be pushy; ~**freiheit** f (fig) elbow room; ~**gesellschaft** f dog-eat-dog society.
**Ellipse** [ɛ'lɪpsə] (-, -n) f ellipse.
**E-Lok** ['eːlɔk] (-) f abk (= elektrische Lokomotive) electric locomotive od engine.
**Elsaß** ['ɛlzas] nt: **das ~** Alsace.
**Elsässer** ['ɛlzɛsər] adj Alsatian.
**Elsässer(in)** (-s, -) m(f) Alsatian, inhabitant of Alsace.
**elsässisch** adj Alsatian.
**Elster** ['ɛlstər] (-, -n) f magpie.
**elterlich** adj parental.
**Eltern** ['ɛltərn] pl parents pl; **nicht von schlechten ~ sein** (umg) to be quite something; ~**abend** m (SCH) parents' evening; ~**haus** nt home; **e**~**los** adj orphaned; ~**sprechtag** m open day (for parents); ~**teil** m parent.
**Email** [e'maːj] (-s, -s) nt enamel.
**emaillieren** [ema'jiːrən] vt to enamel.
**Emanze** (-, -n) (meist pej) f women's libber (umg).
**Emanzipation** [emantsipatsi'oːn] f emancipation.

**emanzipieren** [emantsi'piːrən] vt to emancipate.
**Embargo** [ɛm'bargo] (-s, -s) nt embargo.
**Embryo** ['ɛmbryo] (-s, -s od -nen) m embryo.
**Emigrant(in)** [emi'grant(ɪn)] m(f) emigrant.
**Emigration** [emigratsi'oːn] f emigration.
**emigrieren** [emi'griːrən] vi to emigrate.
**Emissionen** npl emissions pl.
**Emissionskurs** [emɪsi'oːnskʊrs] m (Aktien) issued price.
**EMNID** m abk (= Erforschung, Meinung, Nachrichten, Informationsdienst) opinion poll organization.
**emotional** [emotsio'naːl] adj emotional; (Ausdrucksweise) emotive.
**emotionsgeladen** [emotsi'oːnsgəlaːdən] adj emotionally-charged.
**Empf.** abk = **Empfänger**.
**empfahl** etc [ɛm'pfaːl] vb siehe **empfehlen**.
**empfand** etc [ɛm'pfant] vb siehe **empfinden**.
**Empfang** [ɛm'pfaŋ] (-(e)s, ̈-e) m reception; (Erhalten) receipt; **in ~ nehmen** to receive; (zahlbar) **nach** od **bei ~** +gen (payable) on receipt (of).
**empfangen** unreg vt to receive ♦ vi (schwanger werden) to conceive.
**Empfänger(in)** [ɛm'pfɛŋər(ɪn)] (-s, -) m(f) receiver; (COMM) addressee, consignee; ~ **unbekannt** (auf Briefen) not known at this address.
**empfänglich** adj receptive, susceptible.
**Empfängnis** (-, -se) f conception; **e**~**verhütend** adj; **e**~**verhütende Mittel** contraceptives pl; ~**verhütung** f contraception.
**Empfangs-** zW: ~**bestätigung** f (acknowledgement of) receipt; ~**chef** m (von Hotel) head porter; ~**dame** f receptionist; ~**schein** m receipt; ~**störung** f (RUNDF, TV) interference; ~**zimmer** nt reception room.
**empfehlen** [ɛm'pfeːlən] unreg vt to recommend ♦ vr to take one's leave.
**empfehlenswert** adj recommendable.
**Empfehlung** f recommendation; **auf ~ von** on the recommendation of.
**Empfehlungsschreiben** nt letter of recommendation.
**empfiehlt** [ɛm'pfiːlt] vb siehe **empfehlen**.
**empfinden** [ɛm'pfɪndən] unreg vt to feel; **etw als Beleidigung ~** to find sth insulting; **E**~ (-s) nt: **meinem E**~ **nach** to my mind.
**empfindlich** adj sensitive; (Stelle) sore; (reizbar) touchy; **deine Kritik hat ihn ~ getroffen** your criticism cut him to the quick; **E**~**keit** f sensitiveness; (Reizbarkeit) touchiness.
**empfindsam** adj sentimental; (Mensch) sensitive.
**Empfindung** f feeling, sentiment.
**empfindungslos** adj unfeeling, insensitive.
**empfing** etc [ɛm'pfɪŋ] vb siehe **empfangen**.

**empfohlen** [ɛm'pfoːlən] *pp von* **empfehlen**
♦ *adj:* ~**er Einzelhandelspreis** recommended retail price.
**empfunden** [ɛm'pfʊndən] *pp von* **empfinden.**
**empor** [ɛm'poːr] *adv* up, upwards.
**emporarbeiten** *vr (geh)* to work one's way up.
**Empore** [ɛm'poːrə] (-, -n) *f (ARCHIT)* gallery.
**empören** [ɛm'pøːrən] *vt* to make indignant; to shock ♦ *vr* to become indignant.
**empörend** *adj* outrageous.
**emporkommen** *unreg vi* to rise; (*vorankommen*) to succeed.
**Emporkömmling** *m* upstart, parvenu.
**empört** *adj:* ~ (**über** +*akk*) indignant (at), outraged (at).
**Empörung** *f* indignation.
**emsig** ['ɛmzɪç] *adj* diligent, busy.
**End-** ['ɛnt] *in zW* final; ~**auswertung** *f* final analysis; ~**bahnhof** *m* terminus; ~**betrag** *m* final amount.
**Ende** ['ɛndə] (-s, -n) *nt* end; **am** ~ at the end; (*schließlich*) in the end; **am** ~ **sein** to be at the end of one's tether; ~ **Dezember** at the end of December; **zu** ~ **sein** to be finished; **zu** ~ **gehen** to come to an end; **zu** ~ **führen** to finish (off); **letzten** ~**s** in the end, at the end of the day; **ein böses** ~ **nehmen** to come to a bad end; **ich bin mit meiner Weisheit am** ~ I'm at my wits' end; **er wohnt am** ~ **der Welt** (*umg*) he lives at the back of beyond.
**Endeffekt** *m:* **im** ~ (*umg*) when it comes down to it.
**enden** *vi* to end.
**Endergebnis** *nt* final result.
**endgültig** *adj* final, definite.
**Endivie** [ɛn'diːviə] *f* endive.
**End-** *zW:* ~**lager** *nt* permanent waste disposal site; ~**lagerung** *f* permanent disposal; **e~lich** *adj* final; (*MATH*) finite ♦ *adv* finally; **e~lich!** at last!; **hör e~lich damit auf!** will you stop that!; **e~los** *adj* endless; ~**lospapier** *nt* continuous paper; ~**produkt** *nt* end *od* final product; ~**spiel** *nt* final(s); ~**spurt** *m (SPORT)* final spurt; ~**station** *f* terminus.
**Endung** *f* ending.
**Endverbraucher** *m* consumer, end-user.
**Energie** [ɛnɛr'giː] *f* energy; ~**aufwand** *m* energy expenditure; ~**bedarf** *m* energy requirement; ~**einsparung** *f* energy saving; ~**gewinnung** *f* generation of energy; **e~los** *adj* lacking in energy, weak; ~**quelle** *f* source of energy; ~**versorgung** *f* supply of energy; ~**wirtschaft** *f* energy industry.
**energisch** [e'nɛrgɪʃ] *adj* energetic; ~ **durchgreifen** to take vigorous *od* firm action.
**eng** [ɛŋ] *adj* narrow; (*Kleidung*) tight; (*fig: Horizont*) narrow, limited; (*Freundschaft, Verhältnis*) close; ~ **an etw** *dat* close to sth; **in die** ~**ere Wahl kommen** to be short-listed

(*BRIT*).
**Engadin** ['ɛŋgadiːn] (-s) *nt:* **das** ~ the Engadine.
**Engagement** [ãgaʒə'mãː] (-s, -s) *nt* engagement; (*Verpflichtung*) commitment.
**engagieren** [ãga'ʒiːrən] *vt* to engage ♦ *vr* to commit o.s.; **ein engagierter Schriftsteller** a committed writer.
**Enge** ['ɛŋə] (-, -n) *f (lit, fig)* narrowness; (*Land~*) defile; (*Meer~*) straits *pl*; **jdn in die** ~ **treiben** to drive sb into a corner.
**Engel** ['ɛŋəl] (-s, -) *m* angel; **e~haft** *adj* angelic; ~**macher(in)** (-s, -) (*umg*) *m(f)* backstreet abortionist.
**Engelsgeduld** *f:* **sie hat eine** ~ she has the patience of a saint.
**Engelszungen** *pl:* (**wie) mit** ~ **reden** to use all one's own powers of persuasion.
**engherzig** *adj* petty.
**engl.** *abk* = **englisch.**
**England** ['ɛnlant] *nt* England.
**Engländer** ['ɛŋlɛndər] (-s, -) *m* Englishman; English boy; **die Engländer** *pl* the English, the Britishers (*US*); ~**in** *f* Englishwoman; English girl.
**englisch** ['ɛŋlɪʃ] *adj* English.
**engmaschig** ['ɛŋmaʃɪç] *adj* close-meshed.
**Engpaß** *m* defile, pass; (*fig: Verkehr*) bottleneck.
**en gros** [ã'gro] *adv* wholesale.
**engstirnig** ['ɛŋʃtɪrnɪç] *adj* narrow-minded.
**Enkel** ['ɛŋkəl] (-s, -) *m* grandson; ~**in** *f* granddaughter; ~**kind** *nt* grandchild.
**en masse** [ã'mas] *adv* en masse.
**enorm** [e'nɔrm] *adj* enormous; (*umg: herrlich, kolossal*) tremendous.
**en passant** [ãpa'sã] *adv* en passant, in passing.
**Ensemble** [ã'sãbəl] (-s, -s) *nt* ensemble.
**entarten** [ɛnt'|aːrtən] *vi* to degenerate.
**entbehren** [ɛnt'beːrən] *vt* to do without, dispense with.
**entbehrlich** *adj* superfluous.
**Entbehrung** *f* privation; ~**en auf sich** *akk* **nehmen** to make sacrifices.
**entbinden** [ɛnt'bɪndən] *unreg vt* (+*gen*) to release (from); (*MED*) to deliver ♦ *vi (MED)* to give birth.
**Entbindung** *f* release; (*MED*) delivery, birth.
**Entbindungsheim** *nt* maternity hospital.
**Entbindungsstation** *f* maternity ward.
**entblößen** [ɛnt'bløːsən] *vt* to denude, uncover; (*berauben*): **einer Sache** *gen* **entblößt** deprived of sth.
**entbrennen** [ɛnt'brɛnən] *unreg vi* (*liter: Kampf, Streit*) to flare up; (: *Liebe*) to be aroused.
**entdecken** [ɛnt'dɛkən] *vt* to discover; **jdm etw** ~ to disclose sth to sb.
**Entdecker(in)** (-s, -) *m(f)* discoverer.
**Entdeckung** *f* discovery.
**Ente** ['ɛntə] (-, -n) *f* duck; (*fig*) canard, false report; (*AUT*) Citroën 2CV, deux-chevaux.

**entehren** [ɛnt'|eːrən] vt to dishonour (BRIT), dishonor (US), disgrace.

**enteignen** [ɛnt'|aɪgnən] vt to expropriate; (Besitzer) to dispossess.

**enteisen** [ɛnt'|aɪzən] vt to de-ice; (Kühlschrank) to defrost.

**enterben** [ɛnt'|ɛrbən] vt to disinherit.

**Enterhaken** ['ɛntərhaːkən] m grappling iron od hook.

**entfachen** [ɛnt'faxən] vt to kindle.

**entfallen** [ɛnt'falən] unreg vi to drop, fall; (wegfallen) to be dropped; **jdm ~** (vergessen) to slip sb's memory; **auf jdn ~** to be allotted to sb.

**entfalten** [ɛnt'faltən] vt to unfold; (Talente) to develop ♦ vr to open; (Mensch) to develop one's potential.

**Entfaltung** f unfolding; (von Talenten) development.

**entfernen** [ɛnt'fɛrnən] vt to remove; (hinauswerfen) to expel ♦ vr to go away, retire, withdraw.

**entfernt** adj distant ♦ adv: **nicht im ~esten!** not in the slightest!; **weit davon ~ sein, etw zu tun** to be far from doing sth.

**Entfernung** f distance; (Wegschaffen) removal; **unerlaubte ~ von der Truppe** absence without leave.

**Entfernungsmesser** m (PHOT) rangefinder.

**entfesseln** [ɛnt'fɛsəln] vt (fig) to arouse.

**entfetten** [ɛnt'fɛtən] vt to take the fat from.

**entflammen** [ɛnt'flamən] vt (fig) to (a)rouse ♦ vi to burst into flames; (fig: Streit) to flare up; (: Leidenschaft) to be (a)roused od inflamed.

**entfremden** [ɛnt'frɛmdən] vt to estrange, alienate.

**Entfremdung** f estrangement, alienation.

**entfrosten** [ɛnt'frɔstən] vt to defrost.

**Entfroster** (-s, -) m (AUT) defroster.

**entführen** [ɛnt'fyːrən] vt to abduct, kidnap; (Flugzeug) to hijack.

**Entführer** (-s, -) m kidnapper (BRIT), kidnaper (US); hijacker.

**Entführung** f abduction, kidnapping (BRIT), kidnaping (US); hijacking.

**entgegen** [ɛnt'geːgən] präp +dat contrary to, against ♦ adv towards; **~bringen** unreg vt to bring; (fig): **jdm etw ~bringen** to show sb sth; **~gehen** unreg vi +dat to go to meet, go towards; **Schwierigkeiten ~gehen** to be heading for difficulties; **~gesetzt** adj opposite; (widersprechend) opposed; **~halten** unreg vt (fig): **einer Sache** dat **~halten, daß ...** to object to sth that ...; **E~kommen** nt obligingness; **~kommen** unreg vi +dat to come towards, approach; (fig): **jdm ~kommen** to accommodate sb; **das kommt unseren Plänen sehr ~** that fits in very well with our plans; **~kommend** adj obliging; **~laufen** unreg vi +dat to run towards od to meet; (fig) to run counter to; **E~nahme** f (form: Empfang)

receipt; (Annahme) acceptance; **~nehmen** unreg vt to receive, accept; **~sehen** unreg vi +dat to await; **~setzen** vt to oppose; **dem habe ich ~zusetzen, daß ...** against that I'd like to say that ...; **jdm/etw Widerstand ~setzen** to put up resistance to sb/sth; **~stehen** unreg vi: **dem steht nichts ~** there's no objection to that; **~treten** unreg vi +dat (lit) to step up to; (fig) to oppose, counter; **~wirken** vi +dat to counteract.

**entgegnen** [ɛnt'geːgnən] vt to reply, retort.

**Entgegnung** f reply, retort.

**entgehen** [ɛnt'geːən] unreg vi (fig): **jdm ~** to escape sb's notice; **sich** dat **etw ~ lassen** to miss sth.

**entgeistert** [ɛnt'gaɪstərt] adj thunderstruck.

**Entgelt** [ɛnt'gɛlt] (-(e)s, -e) nt remuneration.

**entgelten** unreg vt: **jdm etw ~** to repay sb for sth.

**entgleisen** [ɛnt'glaɪzən] vi (EISENB) to be derailed; (fig: Person) to misbehave; **~ lassen** to derail.

**Entgleisung** f derailment; (fig) faux pas, gaffe.

**entgleiten** [ɛnt'glaɪtən] unreg vi: **jdm ~** to slip from sb's hand.

**entgräten** [ɛnt'grɛːtən] vt to fillet, bone.

**Enthaarungsmittel** [ɛnt'haːrʊŋsmɪtəl] nt depilatory.

**enthält** [ɛnt'hɛlt] vb siehe **enthalten**.

**enthalten** [ɛnt'haltən] unreg vt to contain ♦ vr +gen to abstain from, refrain from; **sich (der Stimme) ~** to abstain.

**enthaltsam** [ɛnt'haltzaːm] adj abstinent, abstemious; **E~keit** f abstinence.

**enthärten** [ɛnt'hɛrtən] vt (Wasser) to soften; (Metall) to anneal.

**enthaupten** [ɛnt'haʊptən] vt to decapitate; (als Hinrichtung) to behead.

**enthäuten** [ɛnt'hɔʏtən] vt to skin.

**entheben** [ɛnt'heːbən] unreg vt: **jdn einer Sache** gen **~** to relieve sb of sth.

**enthemmen** [ɛnt'hɛmən] vt: **jdn ~** to free sb from his/her inhibitions.

**enthielt** etc [ɛnt'hiːlt] vb siehe **enthalten**.

**enthüllen** [ɛnt'hʏlən] vt to reveal, unveil.

**Enthüllung** f revelation; (von Skandal) exposure.

**Enthusiasmus** [ɛntuzi'asmʊs] m enthusiasm.

**entjungfern** [ɛnt'jʊŋfərn] vt to deflower.

**entkalken** [ɛnt'kalkən] vt to decalcify.

**entkernen** [ɛnt'kɛrnən] vt (Kernobst) to core; (Steinobst) to stone.

**entkleiden** [ɛnt'klaɪdən] vt, vr (geh) to undress.

**entkommen** [ɛnt'kɔmən] unreg vi to get away, escape; **jdm/etw od aus etw ~** to get away od escape from sb/sth.

**entkorken** [ɛnt'kɔrkən] vt to uncork.

**entkräften** [ɛnt'krɛftən] vt to weaken, exhaust; (Argument) to refute.

**entkrampfen** [ɛnt'krampfən] vt (fig) to relax,

ease.

**entladen** [ɛnt'laːdən] *unreg vt* to unload; (*ELEK*) to discharge ♦ *vr* (*ELEK, Gewehr*) to discharge; (*Ärger etc*) to vent itself.

**entlang** [ɛnt'laŋ] *präp* (+*akk od dat*) along ♦ *adv* along; ~ **dem Fluß, den Fluß** ~ along the river; **hier** ~ this way; **~gehen** *unreg vi* to walk along.

**entlarven** [ɛnt'larfən] *vt* to unmask, expose.

**entlassen** [ɛnt'lasən] *unreg vt* to discharge; (*Arbeiter*) to dismiss; (*nach Stellenabbau*) to make redundant.

**entläßt** [ɛnt'lɛst] *vb siehe* **entlassen**.

**Entlassung** *f* discharge; dismissal; **es gab 20 ~en** there were 20 redundancies.

**Entlassungszeugnis** *nt* (*SCH*) school-leaving certificate.

**entlasten** [ɛnt'lastən] *vt* to relieve; (*Arbeit abnehmen*) to take some of the load off; (*Angeklagte*) to exonerate; (*Konto*) to clear.

**Entlastung** *f* relief; (*COMM*) crediting.

**Entlastungszeuge** *m* defence (*BRIT*) *od* defense (*US*) witness.

**Entlastungszug** *m* relief train.

**entledigen** [ɛnt'leːdɪgən] *vr:* **sich jds/einer Sache** ~ to rid o.s. of sb/sth.

**entleeren** [ɛnt'leːrən] *vt* to empty; (*Darm*) to evacuate.

**entlegen** [ɛnt'leːgən] *adj* remote.

**entließ** *etc* [ɛnt'liːs] *vb siehe* **entlassen**.

**entlocken** [ɛnt'lɔkən] *vt:* **jdm etw** ~ to elicit sth from sb.

**entlohnen** *vt* to pay; (*fig*) to reward.

**entlüften** [ɛnt'lʏftən] *vt* to ventilate.

**entmachten** [ɛnt'maxtən] *vt* to deprive of power.

**entmenscht** [ɛnt'mɛnʃt] *adj* inhuman, bestial.

**entmilitarisiert** [ɛntmilitari'ziːrt] *adj* demilitarized.

**entmündigen** [ɛnt'mʏndɪgən] *vt* to certify; (*JUR*) to (legally) incapacitate, declare incapable of managing one's own affairs.

**entmutigen** [ɛnt'muːtɪgən] *vt* to discourage.

**Entnahme** [ɛnt'naːmə] (-, -**n**) *f* removal, withdrawal.

**Entnazifizierung** [ɛntnatsifi'tsiːrʊŋ] *f* denazification.

**entnehmen** [ɛnt'neːmən] *unreg vt* +*dat* to take out of, take from; (*folgern*) to infer from; **wie ich Ihren Worten entnehme,** ... I gather from what you say that ...

**entpuppen** [ɛnt'pʊpən] *vr* (*fig*) to reveal o.s., turn out; **sich als etw** ~ to turn out to be sth.

**entrahmen** [ɛnt'raːmən] *vt* to skim.

**entreißen** [ɛnt'raɪsən] *unreg vt:* **jdm etw** ~ to snatch sth (away) from sb.

**entrichten** [ɛnt'rɪçtən] *vt* (*form*) to pay.

**entrosten** [ɛnt'rɔstən] *vt* to derust.

**entrüsten** [ɛnt'rʏstən] *vt* to incense, outrage ♦ *vr* to be filled with indignation.

**entrüstet** *adj* indignant, outraged.

**Entrüstung** *f* indignation.

**Entsafter** [ɛnt'zaftər] (-**s**, -) *m* juice extractor.

**entsagen** [ɛnt'zaːgən] *vi* +*dat* to renounce.

**entschädigen** [ɛnt'ʃɛːdɪgən] *vt* to compensate.

**Entschädigung** *f* compensation.

**entschärfen** [ɛnt'ʃɛrfən] *vt* to defuse; (*Kritik*) to tone down.

**Entscheid** [ɛnt'ʃaɪt] (-(**e)s**, -**e**) *m* (*form*) decision.

**entscheiden** *unreg vt, vi, vr* to decide; **darüber habe ich nicht zu** ~ that is not for me to decide; **sich für jdn/etw** ~ to decide in favour of sb/sth; to decide on sb/sth.

**entscheidend** *adj* decisive; (*Stimme*) casting; **das E~e** the decisive *od* deciding factor.

**Entscheidung** *f* decision; **wie ist die ~ ausgefallen?** which way did the decision go?

**Entscheidungs-** *zW:* **~befugnis** *f* decision-making powers *pl*; **e~fähig** *adj* capable of deciding; **~spiel** *nt* play-off; **~träger** *m* decision-maker.

**entschied** *etc* [ɛnt'ʃiːt] *vb siehe* **entscheiden**.

**entschieden** [ɛnt'ʃiːdən] *pp von* **entscheiden** ♦ *adj* decided; (*entschlossen*) resolute; **das geht** ~ **zu weit** that's definitely going too far; **E~heit** *f* firmness, determination.

**entschlacken** [ɛnt'ʃlakən] *vt* (*MED: Körper*) to purify.

**entschließen** [ɛnt'ʃliːsən] *unreg vr* to decide; **sich zu nichts** ~ **können** to be unable to make up one's mind; **kurz entschlossen** straight away.

**Entschließungsantrag** *m* (*POL*) resolution proposal.

**entschloß** *etc* [ɛnt'ʃlɔs] *vb siehe* **entschließen**.

**entschlossen** [ɛnt'ʃlɔsən] *pp von* **entschließen** ♦ *adj* determined, resolute; **E~heit** *f* determination.

**entschlüpfen** [ɛnt'ʃlʏpfən] *vi* to escape, slip away; (*fig: Wort etc*) to slip out.

**Entschluß** [ɛnt'ʃlʊs] *m* decision; **aus eigenem ~ handeln** to act on one's own initiative; **es ist mein fester** ~ it is my firm intention.

**entschlüsseln** [ɛnt'ʃlʏsəln] *vt* to decipher; (*Funkspruch*) to decode.

**entschlußfreudig** *adj* decisive.

**Entschlußkraft** *f* determination, decisiveness.

**entschuldbar** [ɛnt'ʃʊltbaːr] *adj* excusable.

**entschuldigen** [ɛnt'ʃʊldɪgən] *vt* to excuse ♦ *vr* to apologize ♦ *vi:* ~ **Sie (bitte)!** excuse me; (*Verzeihung*) sorry; **jdn bei jdm** ~ to make sb's excuses *od* apologies to sb; **sich ~ lassen** to send one's apologies.

**entschuldigend** *adj* apologetic.

**Entschuldigung** *f* apology; (*Grund*) excuse; **jdn um** ~ **bitten** to apologize to sb; ~! excuse me; (*Verzeihung*) sorry.

**entschwefeln** [ɛnt'ʃveːfəln] *vt* to desulphurize.

**Entschwefelungsanlage** *f* desulphur-

ization plant.
**entschwinden** [ɛnt'ʃvɪndən] unreg vi to
disappear.
**entsetzen** [ɛnt'zɛtsən] vt to horrify ♦ vr to be
horrified od appalled; **E~ (-s)** nt horror,
dismay.
**entsetzlich** adj dreadful, appalling.
**entsetzt** adj horrified.
**entsichern** [ɛnt'zɪçərn] vt to release the
safety catch of.
**entsinnen** [ɛnt'zɪnən] unreg vr +gen to
remember.
**entsorgen** [ɛnt'zɔrgən] vt: **eine Stadt** ~ **to**
dispose of a town's refuse and sewage.
**Entsorgung** f waste disposal; (von
Chemikalien) disposal.
**entspannen** [ɛnt'ʃpanən] vt, vr (Körper) to
relax; (POL: Lage) to ease.
**Entspannung** f relaxation, rest; (POL)
détente.
**Entspannungspolitik** f policy of détente.
**Entspannungsübungen** pl relaxation
exercises pl.
**entspr.** abk = **entsprechend**.
**entsprach** etc [ɛnt'ʃprax] vb siehe **entsprechen**.
**entsprechen** [ɛnt'ʃprɛçən] unreg vi +dat to
correspond to; (Anforderungen, Wünschen) to
meet, comply with.
**entsprechend** adj appropriate ♦ adv
accordingly ♦ präp +dat: **er wird seiner**
**Leistung** ~ **bezahlt** he is paid according to
output.
**entspricht** [ɛnt'ʃprɪçt] vb siehe **entsprechen**.
**entspringen** [ɛnt'ʃprɪŋən] unreg vi (+dat) to
spring (from).
**entsprochen** [ɛnt'ʃprɔxən] pp von **entsprechen**.
**entstaatlichen** [ɛnt'ʃtaːtlɪçən] vt to
denationalize.
**entstammen** [ɛnt'ʃtamən] vi +dat to stem od
come from.
**entstand** etc [ɛnt'ʃtant] vb siehe **entstehen**.
**entstanden** [ɛnt'ʃtandən] pp von **entstehen**.
**entstehen** [ɛnt'ʃteːən] unreg vi: ~ **(aus** od
**durch)** to arise (from), result (from); **wir**
**wollen nicht den Eindruck** ~ **lassen,** ... we
don't want to give rise to the impression
that ...; **für** ~**den** od **entstandenen Schaden**
for damages incurred.
**Entstehung** f genesis, origin.
**entstellen** [ɛnt'ʃtɛlən] vt to disfigure;
(Wahrheit) to distort.
**Entstellung** f distortion; disfigurement.
**entstören** [ɛnt'ʃtøːrən] vt (RUNDF) to
eliminate interference from; (AUT) to
suppress.
**enttäuschen** [ɛnt'tɔʏʃən] vt to disappoint.
**Enttäuschung** f disappointment.
**entwachsen** [ɛnt'vaksən] unreg vi +dat to
outgrow, grow out of; (geh: herauswachsen
aus) to spring from.
**entwaffnen** [ɛnt'vafnən] vt (lit, fig) to disarm.
**entwaffnend** adj disarming.

**Entwarnung** [ɛnt'varnʊŋ] f all clear (signal).
**entwässern** [ɛnt'vɛsərn] vt to drain.
**Entwässerung** f drainage.
**entweder** [ɛnt'veːdər] konj either; ~ ... **oder** ...
either ... or ...
**entweichen** [ɛnt'vaɪçən] unreg vi to escape.
**entweihen** [ɛnt'vaɪən] unreg vt to desecrate.
**entwenden** [ɛnt'vɛndən] unreg vt to purloin,
steal.
**entwerfen** [ɛnt'vɛrfən] unreg vt (Zeichnung) to
sketch; (Modell) to design; (Vortrag, Gesetz
etc) to draft.
**entwerten** [ɛnt'veːrtən] vt to devalue;
(stempeln) to cancel.
**Entwerter (-s, -)** m (ticket-)cancelling (BRIT)
od canceling (US) machine.
**entwickeln** [ɛnt'vɪkəln] vt to develop (auch
PHOT); (Mut, Energie) to show, display ♦ vr to
develop.
**Entwickler (-s, -)** m developer.
**Entwicklung** [ɛnt'vɪklʊŋ] f development;
(PHOT) developing; **in der** ~ at the
development stage; (Jugendliche etc) still
developing.
**Entwicklungs-** zW: ~**abschnitt** m stage of
development; ~**helfer(in)** m(f) VSO worker
(BRIT), Peace Corps worker (US); ~**hilfe** f
aid for developing countries; ~**jahre** pl
adolescence sing; ~**land** nt developing
country; ~**zeit** f period of development;
(PHOT) developing time.
**entwirren** [ɛnt'vɪrən] vt to disentangle.
**entwischen** [ɛnt'vɪʃən] vi to escape.
**entwöhnen** [ɛnt'vøːnən] vt to wean;
(Süchtige): **(einer Sache** dat od **von etw)** ~ to
cure (of sth).
**Entwöhnung** f weaning; cure, curing.
**entwürdigend** [ɛnt'vʏrdɪgənt] adj degrading.
**Entwurf** [ɛnt'vʊrf] m outline, design;
(Vertrags~, Konzept) draft.
**entwurzeln** [ɛnt'vʊrtsəln] vt to uproot.
**entziehen** [ɛnt'tsiːən] unreg vt (+dat) to
withdraw (from), take away (from);
(Flüssigkeit) to draw (from), extract (from)
♦ vr (+dat) to escape (from); (jds Kenntnis) to
be outside od beyond; (der Pflicht) to shirk
(from); **sich jds Blicken** ~ to be hidden from
sight.
**Entziehung** f withdrawal.
**Entziehungsanstalt** f drug addiction/
alcoholism treatment centre (BRIT) od
center (US).
**Entziehungskur** f treatment for drug
addiction/alcoholism.
**entziffern** [ɛnt'tsɪfərn] vt to decipher;
(Funkspruch) to decode.
**entzücken** [ɛnt'tsʏkən] vt to delight; **E~ (-s)** nt
delight.
**entzückend** adj delightful, charming.
**Entzug** [ɛnt'tsuːk] **(-(e)s)** m (einer Lizenz etc,
MED) withdrawal.
**Entzugserscheinung** f withdrawal

symptom.

**entzündbar** *adj:* **leicht ~** highly inflammable; (*fig*) easily roused.

**entzünden** [ɛnt'tsʏndən] *vt* to light, set light to; (*fig, MED*) to inflame; (*Streit*) to spark off ♦ *vr* (*lit, fig*) to catch fire; (*Streit*) to start; (*MED*) to become inflamed.

**Entzündung** *f* (*MED*) inflammation.

**entzwei** [ɛnt'tsvaɪ] *adv* in two; broken; **~brechen** *unreg vt, vi* to break in two.

**entzweien** *vt* to set at odds ♦ *vr* to fall out.

**entzweigehen** *unreg vi* to break (in two).

**Enzian** ['ɛntsiaːn] (**-s, -e**) *m* gentian.

**Enzyklika** [ɛn'tsyːklika] (**-, -liken**) *f* (*REL*) encyclical.

**Enzyklopädie** [ɛntsyklope'diː] *f* encyclop(a)edia.

**Enzym** [ɛn'tsyːm] (**-s, -e**) *nt* enzyme.

**Epen** *pl von* **Epos.**

**Epidemie** [epide'miː] *f* epidemic.

**Epilepsie** [epile'psiː] *f* epilepsy.

**episch** ['eːpɪʃ] *adj* epic.

**Episode** [epi'zoːdə] (**-, -n**) *f* episode.

**Epoche** [e'pɔxə] (**-, -n**) *f* epoch; **e~machend** *adj* epoch-making.

**Epos** ['eːpɔs] (**-, Epen**) *nt* epic (poem).

**Equipe** [e'kɪp] (**-, -n**) *f* team.

**er** [eːr] *pron* he; it.

**erachten** [ɛr'|axtən] *vt* (*geh*): **~ für** *od* **als** to consider (to be); **meines E~s** in my opinion.

**erarbeiten** [ɛr'|arbaɪtən] *vt* to work for, acquire; (*Theorie*) to work out.

**Erbanlage** ['ɛrp|anlaːgə] *f* hereditary factor(s *pl*).

**erbarmen** [ɛr'barmən] *vr* (+*gen*) to have pity *od* mercy (on) ♦ *vt:* **er sieht zum E~ aus** he's a pitiful sight; **Herr, erbarme dich (unser!**) Lord, have mercy (upon us)!; **E~** (**-s**) *nt* pity.

**erbärmlich** [ɛr'bɛrmlɪç] *adj* wretched, pitiful; **E~keit** *f* wretchedness.

**Erbarmungs-** *zW:* **e~los** *adj* pitiless, merciless; **e~voll** *adj* compassionate; **e~würdig** *adj* pitiable, wretched.

**erbauen** [ɛr'bauən] *vt* to build, erect; (*fig*) to edify; **er ist von meinem Plan nicht besonders erbaut** (*umg*) he isn't particularly enthusiastic about my plan.

**Erbauer** (**-s, -**) *m* builder.

**erbaulich** *adj* edifying.

**Erbauung** *f* construction; (*fig*) edification.

**erbberechtigt** *adj* entitled to inherit.

**erbbiologisch** *adj:* **~es Gutachten** (*JUR*) blood test (*to establish paternity*).

**Erbe[1]** ['ɛrbə] (**-n, -n**) *m* heir; **jdn zum** *od* **als ~n einsetzen** to make sb one's/sb's heir.

**Erbe[2]** ['ɛrbə] (**-s**) *nt* inheritance; (*fig*) heritage.

**erben** *vt* to inherit; (*umg: geschenkt bekommen*) to get, be given.

**erbeuten** [ɛr'bɔytən] *vt* to carry off; (*MIL*) to capture.

**Erb-** *zW:* **~faktor** *m* gene; **~fehler** *m*

hereditary defect; **~feind** *m* traditional *od* arch enemy; **~folge** *f* (line of) succession.

**Erbin** *f* heiress.

**erbitten** [ɛr'bɪtən] *unreg vt* to ask for, request.

**erbittern** [ɛr'bɪtərn] *vt* to embitter; (*erzürnen*) to incense.

**erbittert** [ɛr'bɪtart] *adj* (*Kampf*) fierce, bitter.

**erblassen** [ɛr'blasən] *vi* to (turn) pale.

**Erblasser(in)** (**-s, -**) *m(f)* (*JUR*) *person who leaves an inheritance.*

**erbleichen** [ɛr'blaɪçən] *unreg vi* to (turn) pale.

**erblich** ['ɛrplɪç] *adj* hereditary; **er/sie ist ~ (vor)belastet** it runs in the family.

**erblichen** *pp von* **erbleichen.**

**erblicken** [ɛr'blɪkən] *vt* to see; (*erspähen*) to catch sight of.

**erblinden** [ɛr'blɪndən] *vi* to go blind.

**Erbmasse** ['ɛrpmasə] *f* estate; (*BIOL*) genotype.

**erbosen** [ɛr'boːzən] *vt* (*geh*) to anger ♦ *vr* to grow angry.

**erbrechen** [ɛr'brɛçən] *unreg vt, vr* to vomit.

**Erbrecht** *nt* hereditary right; (*Gesetze*) law of inheritance.

**Erbschaft** *f* inheritance, legacy.

**Erbschaftssteuer** *f* estate *od* death duties *pl.*

**Erbschleicher(in)** ['ɛrpʃlaɪçər(ɪn)] (**-s, -**) *m(f)* legacy-hunter.

**Erbse** ['ɛrpsə] (**-, -n**) *f* pea.

**Erb-** *zW:* **~stück** *nt* heirloom; **~sünde** *f* (*REL*) original sin; **~teil** *nt* inherited trait; (*JUR*) (portion of) inheritance.

**Erd-** *zW:* **~achse** *f* earth's axis; **~apfel** (*ÖSTERR*) *m* potato; **~atmosphäre** *f* earth's atmosphere; **~bahn** *f* orbit of the earth; **~beben** *nt* earthquake; **~beere** *f* strawberry; **~boden** *m* ground; **etw dem ~boden gleichmachen** to level sth, raze sth to the ground.

**Erde** (**-, -n**) *f* earth; **zu ebener ~** at ground level; **auf der ganzen ~** all over the world; **du wirst mich noch unter die ~ bringen** (*umg*) you'll be the death of me yet.

**erden** *vt* (*ELEK*) to earth.

**erdenkbar** [ɛr'dɛŋkbaːr] *adj* conceivable; **sich** *dat* **alle ~e Mühe geben** to take the greatest (possible) pains.

**erdenklich** [ɛr'dɛŋklɪç] *adj* = **erdenkbar.**

**Erdg.** *abk* = **Erdgeschoß.**

**Erd-** *zW:* **~gas** *nt* natural gas; **~geschoß** *nt* ground floor (*BRIT*), first floor (*US*); **~kunde** *f* geography; **~nuß** *f* peanut; **~oberfläche** *f* surface of the earth; **~öl** *nt* (mineral) oil; **~ölfeld** *nt* oilfield; **~ölindustrie** *f* oil industry; **~reich** *nt* soil, earth.

**erdreisten** [ɛr'draɪstən] *vr* to dare, have the audacity (to do sth).

**erdrosseln** [ɛr'drɔsəln] *vt* to strangle, throttle.

**erdrücken** [ɛr'drʏkən] *vt* to crush; **~de Übermacht/~des Beweismaterial** overwhelming superiority/evidence.

**Erd-** *zW:* **~rutsch** *m* landslide; **~stoß** *m*

(seismic) shock; ~**teil** m continent.
**erdulden** [ɛr'dʊldən] vt to endure, suffer.
**ereifern** [ɛr'|aɪfərn] vr to get excited.
**ereignen** [ɛr'|aɪgnən] vr to happen.
**Ereignis** [ɛr'|aɪgnɪs] (-ses, -se) nt event; **e~los** adj uneventful; **e~reich** adj eventful.
**Eremit** [ere'miːt] (-en, -en) m hermit.
**erfahren** [ɛr'faːrən] unreg vt to learn, find out; (erleben) to experience ♦ adj experienced.
**Erfahrung** f experience; ~**en sammeln** to gain experience; **etw in ~ bringen** to learn od find out sth.
**Erfahrungsaustausch** m exchange of experiences.
**erfahrungsgemäß** adv according to experience.
**erfand** etc [ɛr'fant] vb siehe **erfinden**.
**erfassen** [ɛr'fasən] vt to seize; (fig: einbeziehen) to include, register; (verstehen) to grasp.
**erfinden** [ɛr'fɪndən] unreg vt to invent; **frei erfunden** completely fictitious.
**Erfinder(in)** (-s, -) m(f) inventor; **e~isch** adj inventive.
**Erfindung** f invention.
**Erfindungsgabe** f inventiveness.
**Erfolg** [ɛr'fɔlk] (-(e)s, -e) m success; (Folge) result; **viel ~!** good luck!
**erfolgen** [ɛr'fɔlgən] vi to follow; (sich ergeben) to result; (stattfinden) to take place; (Zahlung) to be effected; **nach erfolgter Zahlung** when payment has been made.
**Erfolg-** zW: **e~los** adj unsuccessful; ~**losigkeit** f lack of success; **e~reich** adj successful.
**Erfolgserlebnis** nt feeling of success, sense of achievement.
**erfolgversprechend** adj promising.
**erforderlich** adj requisite, necessary.
**erfordern** [ɛr'fɔrdərn] vt to require, demand.
**Erfordernis** (-ses, -se) nt requirement, prerequisite.
**erforschen** [ɛr'fɔrʃən] vt (Land) to explore; (Problem) to investigate; (Gewissen) to search.
**Erforscher(in)** (-s, -) m(f) explorer; investigator.
**Erforschung** f exploration; investigation; searching.
**erfragen** [ɛr'fraːgən] vt to inquire, ascertain.
**erfreuen** [ɛr'frɔʏən] vr: **sich ~ an** +dat to enjoy ♦ vt to delight; **sich einer Sache** gen ~ (geh) to enjoy sth; **sehr erfreut!** (form: bei Vorstellung) pleased to meet you!
**erfreulich** [ɛr'frɔʏlɪç] adj pleasing, gratifying.
**erfreulicherweise** adv happily, luckily.
**erfrieren** [ɛr'friːrən] unreg vi to freeze (to death); (Glieder) to get frostbitten; (Pflanzen) to be killed by frost.
**erfrischen** [ɛr'frɪʃən] vt to refresh.
**Erfrischung** f refreshment.
**Erfrischungsraum** m snack bar, cafeteria.
**erfüllen** [ɛr'fʏlən] vt (Raum etc) to fill; (fig: Bitte

etc) to fulfil (BRIT), fulfill (US) ♦ vr to come true; **ein erfülltes Leben** a full life.
**Erfüllung** f: **in ~ gehen** to be fulfilled.
**erfunden** [ɛr'fʊndən] pp von **erfinden**.
**ergab** etc [ɛr'gaːp] vb siehe **ergeben**.
**ergänzen** [ɛr'gɛntsən] vt to supplement, complete ♦ vr to complement one another.
**Ergänzung** f completion; (Zusatz) supplement.
**ergattern** [ɛr'gatərn] (umg) vt to get hold of, hunt up.
**ergaunern** [ɛr'gaʊnərn] (umg) vt: **sich** dat **etw ~** to get hold of sth by underhand methods.
**ergeben** [ɛr'geːbən] unreg vt to yield, produce ♦ vr to surrender; (folgen) to result ♦ adj devoted; (demütig) humble; **sich einer Sache** dat ~ (sich hingeben) to give o.s. up to sth, yield to sth; **es ergab sich, daß unsere Befürchtungen ...** it turned out that our fears ...; **dem Trunk ~** addicted to drink; **E~heit** f devotion; humility.
**Ergebnis** [ɛr'geːpnɪs] (-ses, -se) nt result; **zu einem ~ kommen** to come to od reach a conclusion; **e~los** adj without result, fruitless; **e~los bleiben** od **verlaufen** to come to nothing.
**ergehen** [ɛr'geːən] unreg vi (form) to be issued, go out ♦ vi unpers: **es ergeht ihm gut/schlecht** he's faring od getting on well/badly ♦ vr: **sich in etw** dat ~ to indulge in sth; **etw über sich** akk ~ **lassen** to put up with sth; **sich (in langen Reden) über ein Thema ~** (fig) to hold forth at length on sth.
**ergiebig** [ɛr'giːbɪç] adj productive.
**ergo** ['ɛrgo] konj therefore, ergo (liter, hum).
**Ergonomie** [ɛrgono'miː] f ergonomics pl.
**ergötzen** [ɛr'gœtsən] vt to amuse, delight.
**ergrauen** [ɛr'graʊən] vi to turn od go grey (BRIT) od gray (US).
**ergreifen** [ɛr'graɪfən] unreg vt (lit, fig) to seize; (Beruf) to take up; (Maßnahmen) to resort to; (rühren) to move; **er ergriff das Wort** he began to speak.
**ergreifend** adj moving, affecting.
**ergriff** etc [ɛr'grɪf] vb siehe **ergreifen**.
**ergriffen** pp von **ergreifen** ♦ adj deeply moved.
**Ergriffenheit** f emotion.
**ergründen** [ɛr'grʏndən] vt (Sinn etc) to fathom; (Ursache, Motive) to discover.
**Erguß** [ɛr'gʊs] (-sses, -̈sse) m discharge; (fig) outpouring, effusion.
**erhaben** [ɛr'haːbən] adj (lit) raised, embossed; (fig) exalted, lofty; **über etw** akk ~ **sein** to be above sth.
**Erhalt** m: **bei** od **nach ~** on receipt.
**erhält** [ɛr'hɛlt] vb siehe **erhalten**.
**erhalten** [ɛr'haltən] unreg vt to receive; (bewahren) to preserve, maintain; **das Wort ~** to receive permission to speak; **jdn am Leben ~** to keep sb alive; **gut ~** in good condition.
**erhältlich** [ɛr'hɛltlɪç] adj obtainable, available.

**Erhaltung** *f* maintenance, preservation.
**erhängen** [ɛr'hɛŋən] *vt, vr* to hang.
**erhärten** [ɛr'hɛrtən] *vt* to harden; (*These*) to substantiate, corroborate.
**erhaschen** [ɛr'haʃən] *vt* to catch.
**erheben** [ɛr'he:bən] *unreg vt* to raise; (*Protest, Forderungen*) to make; (*Fakten*) to ascertain ♦ *vr* to rise (up); **sich über etw** *akk* ~ to rise above sth.
**erheblich** [ɛr'he:plɪç] *adj* considerable.
**erheitern** [ɛr'haitərn] *vt* to amuse, cheer (up).
**Erheiterung** *f* exhilaration; **zur allgemeinen** ~ to everybody's amusement.
**erhellen** [ɛr'hɛlən] *vt* (*lit, fig*) to illuminate; (*Geheimnis*) to shed light on ♦ *vr* (*Fenster*) to light up; (*Himmel, Miene*) to brighten (up); (*Gesicht*) to brighten up.
**erhielt** *etc* [ɛr'hi:lt] *vb siehe* **erhalten**.
**erhitzen** [ɛr'hɪtsən] *vt* to heat ♦ *vr* to heat up; (*fig*) to become heated *od* aroused.
**erhoffen** [ɛr'hɔfən] *vt* to hope for; **was erhoffst du dir davon?** what do you hope to gain from it?
**erhöhen** [ɛr'høːən] *vt* to raise; (*verstärken*) to increase; **erhöhte Temperatur haben** to have a temperature.
**Erhöhung** *f* (*Gehalt*) increment.
**erholen** [ɛr'hoːlən] *vr* to recover; (*entspannen*) to have a rest; (*fig: Preise, Aktien*) to rally, pick up.
**erholsam** *adj* restful.
**Erholung** *f* recovery; relaxation, rest.
**erholungsbedürftig** *adj* in need of a rest, run-down.
**Erholungsgebiet** *nt* holiday (*BRIT*) *od* vacation (*US*) area.
**Erholungsheim** *nt* convalescent home.
**erhören** [ɛr'høːrən] *vt* (*Gebet etc*) to hear; (*Bitte etc*) to yield to.
**Erika** ['eːrika] (-, **Eriken**) *f* heather.
**erinnern** [ɛr'ɪnərn] *vt:* ~ **(an** +*akk*) to remind (of) ♦ *vr:* **sich (an etw** *akk*) ~ to remember (sth).
**Erinnerung** *f* memory; (*Andenken*) reminder; **Erinnerungen** *pl* (*Lebens*~) reminiscences *pl*; (*LITER*) memoirs *pl*; **jdn/etw in guter** ~ **behalten** to have pleasant memories of sb/sth.
**Erinnerungsschreiben** *nt* (*COMM*) reminder.
**Erinnerungstafel** *f* commemorative plaque.
**Eritrea** [eri'treːa] (-s) *nt* Eritrea.
**erkalten** [ɛr'kaltən] *vi* to go cold, cool (down).
**erkälten** [ɛr'kɛltən] *vr* to catch cold; **sich** *dat* **die Blase** ~ to catch a chill in one's bladder.
**erkältet** *adj* with a cold; ~ **sein** to have a cold.
**Erkältung** *f* cold.
**erkämpfen** [ɛr'kɛmpfən] *vt* to win, secure.
**erkannt** [ɛr'kant] *pp von* **erkennen**.
**erkannte** *etc vb siehe* **erkennen**.
**erkennbar** *adj* recognizable.
**erkennen** [ɛr'kɛnən] *unreg vt* to recognize; (*sehen, verstehen*) to see; **jdm zu** ~ **geben,**

**daß** to give sb to understand that ...
**erkenntlich** *adj:* **sich** ~ **zeigen** to show one's appreciation; **E~keit** *f* gratitude; (*Geschenk*) token of one's gratitude.
**Erkenntnis** (-, -se) *f* knowledge; (*das Erkennen*) recognition; (*Einsicht*) insight; **zur** ~ **kommen** to realize.
**Erkennung** *f* recognition.
**Erkennungsdienst** *m* police records department.
**Erkennungsmarke** *f* identity disc.
**Erker** ['ɛrkər] (-s, -) *m* bay; ~**fenster** *nt* bay window.
**erklärbar** *adj* explicable.
**erklären** [ɛr'klɛːrən] *vt* to explain; (*Rücktritt*) to announce; (*Politiker, Pressesprecher etc*) to say; **ich kann mir nicht** ~, **warum** ... I can't understand why ...
**erklärlich** *adj* explicable; (*verständlich*) understandable.
**erklärt** *adj attrib* (*Gegner etc*) professed, avowed; (*Favorit, Liebling*) acknowledged.
**Erklärung** *f* explanation; (*Aussage*) declaration.
**erklecklich** [ɛr'klɛklɪç] *adj* considerable.
**erklimmen** [ɛr'klɪmən] *unreg vt* to climb to.
**erklingen** [ɛr'klɪŋən] *unreg vi* to resound, ring out.
**erklomm** *etc* [ɛr'klɔm] *vb siehe* **erklimmen**.
**erklommen** *pp von* **erklimmen**.
**erkranken** [ɛr'kraŋkən] *vi:* ~ **(an** +*dat*) to be taken ill (with); (*Organ, Pflanze, Tier*) to become diseased (with).
**Erkrankung** *f* illness.
**erkunden** [ɛr'kʊndən] *vt* to find out, ascertain; (*bes MIL*) to reconnoitre (*BRIT*), reconnoiter (*US*).
**erkundigen** *vr:* **sich** ~ **(nach)** to inquire (about); **ich werde mich** ~ I'll find out.
**Erkundigung** *f* inquiry; ~**en einholen** to make inquiries.
**Erkundung** *f* (*MIL*) reconnaissance, scouting.
**erlahmen** [ɛr'laːmən] *vi* to tire; (*nachlassen*) to flag, wane.
**erlangen** [ɛr'laŋən] *vt* to attain, achieve.
**Erlaß** [ɛr'las] (-sses, ⁻sse) *m* decree; (*Aufhebung*) remission.
**erlassen** *unreg vt* (*Verfügung*) to issue; (*Gesetz*) to enact; (*Strafe*) to remit; **jdm etw** ~ to release sb from sth.
**erlauben** [ɛr'laʊbən] *vt* to allow, permit ♦ *vr:* **sich** *dat* **etw** ~ (*Zigarette, Pause*) to permit o.s. sth; (*Bemerkung, Vorschlag*) to venture sth; (*sich leisten*) to afford sth; **jdm etw** ~ to allow *od* permit sb (to do) sth; ~ **Sie?** may I?; ~ **Sie mal!** do you mind!; **was** ~ **Sie sich (eigentlich)!** how dare you!
**Erlaubnis** [ɛr'laʊpnɪs] (-, -se) *f* permission.
**erläutern** [ɛr'lɔʏtərn] *vt* to explain.
**Erläuterung** *f* explanation; **zur** ~ in explanation.

**Erle** ['ɛrlə] (-, -n) *f* alder.
**erleben** [ɛr'le:bən] *vt* to experience; (*Zeit*) to live through; (*mit~*) to witness; (*noch mit~*) to live to see; **so wütend habe ich ihn noch nie erlebt** I've never seen *od* known him so furious.
**Erlebnis** [ɛr'le:pnɪs] (-ses, -se) *nt* experience.
**erledigen** [ɛr'le:dɪgən] *vt* to take care of, deal with; (*Antrag etc*) to process; (*umg: erschöpfen*) to wear out; (*ruinieren*) to finish; (*umbringen*) to do in ♦ *vr:* **das hat sich erledigt** that's all settled; **das ist erledigt** that's taken care of, that's been done; **ich habe noch einiges in der Stadt zu ~** I've still got a few things to do in town.
**erledigt** (*umg*) *adj* (*erschöpft*) shattered, done in; (: *ruiniert*) finished, ruined.
**erlegen** [ɛr'le:gən] *vt* to kill.
**erleichtern** [ɛr'laɪçtərn] *vt* to make easier; (*fig: Last*) to lighten; (*lindern, beruhigen*) to relieve.
**erleichtert** *adj* relieved; **~ aufatmen** to breathe a sigh of relief.
**Erleichterung** *f* facilitation; lightening; relief.
**erleiden** [ɛr'laɪdən] *unreg vt* to suffer, endure.
**erlernbar** *adj* learnable.
**erlernen** [ɛr'lɛrnən] *vt* to learn, acquire.
**erlesen** [ɛr'le:zən] *adj* select, choice.
**erleuchten** [ɛr'lɔʏçtən] *vt* to illuminate; (*fig*) to inspire.
**Erleuchtung** *f* (*Einfall*) inspiration.
**erliegen** [ɛr'li:gən] *unreg vi +dat* (*lit, fig*) to succumb to; (*einem Irrtum*) to be the victim of; **zum E~ kommen** to come to a standstill.
**erlischt** [ɛr'lɪʃt] *vb siehe* **erlöschen**.
**erlogen** [ɛr'lo:gən] *adj* untrue, made-up.
**Erlös** [ɛr'lø:s] (-es, -e) *m* proceeds *pl*.
**erlosch** *etc* [ɛr'lɔʃ] *vb siehe* **erlöschen**.
**erlöschen** [ɛr'lœʃən] *unreg vi* (*Feuer*) to go out; (*Interesse*) to cease, die; (*Vertrag, Recht*) to expire; **ein erloschener Vulkan** an extinct volcano.
**erlösen** [ɛr'lø:zən] *vt* to redeem, save.
**Erlöser** (-s, -) *m* (*REL*) Redeemer; (*Befreier*) saviour (*BRIT*), savior (*US*).
**Erlösung** *f* release; (*REL*) redemption.
**ermächtigen** [ɛr'mɛçtɪgən] *vt* to authorize, empower.
**Ermächtigung** *f* authorization.
**ermahnen** [ɛr'ma:nən] *vt* to admonish, exhort.
**Ermahnung** *f* admonition, exhortation.
**Ermang(e)lung** [ɛr'maŋəluŋ] *f*: **in ~** *+gen* because of the lack of.
**ermäßigen** [ɛr'mɛsɪgən] *vt* to reduce.
**Ermäßigung** *f* reduction.
**ermessen** [ɛr'mɛsən] *unreg vt* to estimate, gauge; **E~** (-s) *nt* estimation; discretion; **in jds E~** *dat* **liegen** to lie within sb's discretion; **nach meinem E~** in my judgement.
**Ermessensfrage** *f* matter of discretion.

**ermitteln** [ɛr'mɪtəln] *vt* to determine; (*Täter*) to trace ♦ *vi:* **gegen jdn ~** to investigate sb.
**Ermittlung** [ɛr'mɪtluŋ] *f* determination; (*Polizei~*) investigation; **~en anstellen (über** *+akk*) to make inquiries (about).
**Ermittlungsverfahren** *nt* (*JUR*) preliminary proceedings *pl*.
**ermöglichen** [ɛr'mø:klıçən] *vt (+dat)* to make possible (for).
**ermorden** [ɛr'mɔrdən] *vt* to murder.
**Ermordung** *f* murder.
**ermüden** [ɛr'my:dən] *vt* to tire; (*TECH*) to fatigue ♦ *vi* to tire.
**ermüdend** *adj* tiring; (*fig*) wearisome.
**Ermüdung** *f* fatigue.
**Ermüdungserscheinung** *f* sign of fatigue.
**ermuntern** [ɛr'muntərn] *vt* to rouse; (*ermutigen*) to encourage; (*beleben*) to liven up; (*aufmuntern*) to cheer up.
**ermutigen** [ɛr'mu:tɪgən] *vt* to encourage.
**ernähren** [ɛr'nɛ:rən] *vt* to feed, nourish; (*Familie*) to support ♦ *vr* to support o.s., earn a living; **sich ~ von** to live on.
**Ernährer(in)** (-s, -) *m(f)* breadwinner.
**Ernährung** *f* nourishment; (*MED*) nutrition; (*Unterhalt*) maintenance.
**ernennen** [ɛr'nɛnən] *unreg vt* to appoint.
**Ernennung** *f* appointment.
**erneuern** [ɛr'nɔʏərn] *vt* to renew; (*restaurieren*) to restore; (*renovieren*) to renovate.
**Erneuerung** *f* renewal; restoration; renovation.
**erneut** *adj* renewed, fresh ♦ *adv* once more.
**erniedrigen** [ɛr'ni:drɪgən] *vt* to humiliate, degrade.
**Ernst** [ɛrnst] (-es) *m* seriousness; **das ist mein ~** I'm quite serious; **im ~** in earnest; **~ machen mit etw** to put sth into practice; **e~** *adj* serious; **es steht e~ um ihn** things don't look too good for him; **~fall** *m* emergency; **e~gemeint** *adj* meant in earnest, serious; **e~haft** *adj* serious; **~haftigkeit** *f* seriousness; **e~lich** *adj* serious.
**Ernte** ['ɛrntə] (-, -n) *f* harvest; **~dankfest** *nt* harvest festival.
**ernten** *vt* to harvest; (*Lob etc*) to earn.
**ernüchtern** [ɛr'nʏçtərn] *vt* to sober up; (*fig*) to bring down to earth.
**Ernüchterung** *f* sobering up; (*fig*) disillusionment.
**Eroberer** [ɛr'|obərər] (-s, -) *m* conqueror.
**erobern** *vt* to conquer.
**Eroberung** *f* conquest.
**eröffnen** [ɛr'|œfnən] *vt* to open ♦ *vr* to present itself; **jdm etw ~** (*geh*) to disclose sth to sb.
**Eröffnung** *f* opening.
**Eröffnungsansprache** *f* inaugural *od* opening address.
**Eröffnungsfeier** *f* opening ceremony.
**erogen** [ɛro'ge:n] *adj* erogenous.
**erörtern** [ɛr'|œrtərn] *vt* to discuss (in detail).
**Erörterung** *f* discussion.

**Erotik** [e'ro:tɪk] *f* eroticism.
**erotisch** *adj* erotic.
**Erpel** ['ɛrpəl] (-, -) *m* drake.
**erpicht** [ɛr'pɪçt] *adj:* ~ **(auf** +*akk*) keen (on).
**erpressen** [ɛr'prɛsən] *vt* (*Geld etc*) to extort; (*jdn*) to blackmail.
**Erpresser** (**-s, -**) *m* blackmailer.
**Erpressung** *f* blackmail; extortion.
**erproben** [ɛr'pro:bən] *vt* to test; **erprobt** tried and tested.
**erraten** [ɛr'ra:tən] *unreg vt* to guess.
**errechnen** [ɛr'rɛçnən] *vt* to calculate, work out.
**erregbar** [ɛr're:kba:r] *adj* excitable; (*reizbar*) irritable; **E~keit** *f* excitability; irritability.
**erregen** [ɛr're:gən] *vt* to excite; (*sexuell*) to arouse; (*ärgern*) to infuriate; (*hervorrufen*) to arouse, provoke ♦ *vr* to get excited *od* worked up.
**Erreger** (**-s, -**) *m* causative agent.
**Erregtheit** *f* excitement; (*Beunruhigung*) agitation.
**Erregung** *f* excitement; (*sexuell*) arousal.
**erreichbar** *adj* accessible, within reach.
**erreichen** [ɛr'raɪçən] *vt* to reach; (*Zweck*) to achieve; (*Zug*) to catch; **wann kann ich Sie morgen ~?** when can I get in touch with you tomorrow?; **vom Bahnhof leicht zu ~** within easy reach of the station.
**errichten** [ɛr'rɪçtən] *vt* to erect, put up; (*gründen*) to establish, set up.
**erringen** [ɛr'rɪŋən] *unreg vt* to gain, win.
**erröten** [ɛr'rø:tən] *vi* to blush, flush.
**Errungenschaft** [ɛr'rʊŋənʃaft] *f* achievement; (*umg: Anschaffung*) acquisition.
**Ersatz** [ɛr'zats] (**-es**) *m* substitute; replacement; (*Schaden~*) compensation; (*MIL*) reinforcements *pl*; **als ~ für jdn einspringen** to stand in for sb; **~befriedigung** *f* vicarious satisfaction; **~dienst** *m* (*MIL*) alternative service; **~kasse** *f* private health insurance; **~mann** *m* replacement; (*SPORT*) substitute; **~mutter** *f* substitute mother; **e~pflichtig** *adj* liable to pay compensation; **~reifen** *m* (*AUT*) spare tyre (*BRIT*) *od* tire (*US*); **~teil** *nt* spare (part); **e~weise** *adv* as an alternative.
**ersaufen** [ɛr'zaʊfən] *unreg* (*umg*) *vi* to drown.
**ersäufen** [ɛr'zɔyfən] *vt* to drown.
**erschaffen** [ɛr'ʃafən] *unreg vt* to create.
**erscheinen** [ɛr'ʃaɪnən] *unreg vi* to appear.
**Erscheinung** *f* appearance; (*Geist*) apparition; (*Gegebenheit*) phenomenon; (*Gestalt*) figure; **in ~ treten** (*Merkmale*) to appear; (*Gefühle*) to show themselves.
**Erscheinungsform** *f* manifestation.
**Erscheinungsjahr** *nt* (*von Buch*) year of publication.
**erschien** *etc* [ɛr'ʃi:n] *vb siehe* **erscheinen**.
**erschienen** *pp von* **erscheinen**.
**erschießen** [ɛr'ʃi:sən] *unreg vt* to shoot (dead).

**erschlaffen** [ɛr'ʃlafən] *vi* to go limp; (*Mensch*) to become exhausted.
**erschlagen** [ɛr'ʃla:gən] *unreg vt* to strike dead ♦ *adj* (*umg: todmüde*) worn out, dead beat (*umg*).
**erschleichen** [ɛr'ʃlaɪçən] *unreg vt* to obtain by stealth *od* dubious methods.
**erschließen** [ɛr'ʃli:sən] *unreg vt* (*Gebiet, Absatzmarkt*) to develop, open up; (*Bodenschätze*) to tap.
**erschlossen** [ɛr'ʃlɔsən] *adj* (*Gebiet*) developed.
**erschöpfen** [ɛr'ʃœpfən] *vt* to exhaust.
**erschöpfend** *adj* exhaustive, thorough.
**erschöpft** *adj* exhausted.
**Erschöpfung** *f* exhaustion.
**erschossen** [ɛr'ʃɔsən] (*umg*) *adj:* (**völlig**) ~ **sein** to be whacked, be dead (beat).
**erschrak** *etc* [ɛr'ʃra:k] *vb siehe* **erschrecken²**.
**erschrecken¹** [ɛr'ʃrɛkən] *vt* to startle, frighten.
**erschrecken²** [ɛr'ʃrɛkən] *unreg vi* to be frightened *od* startled.
**erschreckend** *adj* alarming, frightening.
**erschrickt** [ɛr'ʃrɪkt] *vb siehe* **erschrecken²**.
**erschrocken** [ɛr'ʃrɔkən] *pp von* **erschrecken²** ♦ *adj* frightened, startled.
**erschüttern** [ɛr'ʃytərn] *vt* to shake; (*ergreifen*) to move deeply; **ihn kann nichts ~** he always keeps his cool (*umg*).
**erschütternd** *adj* shattering.
**Erschütterung** *f* (*des Bodens*) tremor; (*tiefe Ergriffenheit*) shock.
**erschweren** [ɛr'ʃve:rən] *vt* to complicate; **~de Umstände** (*JUR*) aggravating circumstances; **es kommt noch ~d hinzu, daß ...** to compound matters ...
**erschwindeln** [ɛr'ʃvɪndəln] *vt* to obtain by fraud.
**erschwinglich** *adj* affordable.
**ersehen** [ɛr'ze:ən] *unreg vt:* **aus etw ~, daß ...** to gather from sth that ...
**ersehnt** [ɛr'ze:nt] *adj* longed-for.
**ersetzbar** *adj* replaceable.
**ersetzen** [ɛr'zɛtsən] *vt* to replace; **jdm Unkosten** *etc* ~ to pay sb's expenses *etc*.
**ersichtlich** [ɛr'zɪçtlɪç] *adj* evident, obvious.
**ersparen** [ɛr'ʃpa:rən] *vt* (*Ärger etc*) to spare; (*Geld*) to save; **ihr blieb auch nichts erspart** she was spared nothing.
**Ersparnis** (**-, -se**) *f* saving.
**ersprießlich** [ɛr'ʃpri:slɪç] *adj* profitable, useful; (*angenehm*) pleasant.

================== *SCHLÜSSELWORT*

**erst** [e:rst] *adv* **1** first; **mach ~ (ein)mal die Arbeit fertig** do your work first; **wenn du das ~ (ein)mal hinter dir hast** once you've got that behind you
**2** (*nicht früher als, nur*) only; (*nicht bis*) not till; ~ **gestern** only yesterday; ~ **morgen** not until tomorrow; ~ **als** only when, not until; **wir fahren ~ später** we're not going

until later; **er ist (gerade)** ~ **angekommen** he's only just arrived

**3:** **wäre er doch** ~ **zurück!** if only he were back!; **da fange ich** ~ **gar nicht an** I simply won't bother to begin; **jetzt** ~ **recht!** that just makes me all the more determined; **da ging's** ~ **richtig los** then things really got going.

**erstarren** [ɛr'ʃtarən] *vi* to stiffen; (*vor Furcht*) to grow rigid; (*Materie*) to solidify.

**erstatten** [ɛr'ʃtatən] *vt* (*Unkosten*) to refund; **Anzeige gegen jdn** ~ to report sb; **Bericht** ~ to make a report.

**Erstattung** *f* (*von Unkosten*) reimbursement.

**Erstaufführung** ['eːrst|aʊffyːrʊŋ] *f* first performance.

**erstaunen** [ɛr'ʃtaʊnən] *vt* to astonish ♦ *vi* to be astonished; **E~** **(-s)** *nt* astonishment.

**erstaunlich** *adj* astonishing.

**Erstausgabe** *f* first edition.

**erstbeste(r, s)** *adj* first that comes along.

**erste(r, s)** *adj* first; **als** ~**s** first of all; **in** ~**r** **Linie** first and foremost; **fürs** ~ for the time being; **E~** **Hilfe** first aid.

**erstechen** [ɛr'ʃtɛçən] *unreg vt* to stab (to death).

**erstehen** [ɛr'ʃteːən] *unreg vt* to buy ♦ *vi* to (a)rise.

**ersteigen** [ɛr'ʃtaɪɡən] *unreg vt* to climb, ascend.

**ersteigern** [ɛr'ʃtaɪɡərn] *vt* to buy at an auction.

**erstellen** [ɛr'ʃtɛlən] *vt* to erect, build.

**erstemal** *adv:* **das** ~ the first time.

**erstens** *adv* firstly, in the first place.

**erstere(r, s)** *pron* (the) former.

**ersticken** [ɛr'ʃtɪkən] *vt* (*lit, fig*) to stifle; (*Mensch*) to suffocate; (*Flammen*) to smother ♦ *vi* (*Mensch*) to suffocate; (*Feuer*) to be smothered; **mit erstickter Stimme** in a choked voice; **in Arbeit** ~ to be snowed under with work.

**Erstickung** *f* suffocation.

**erst-** *zW:* ~**klassig** *adj* first-class; **E~kommunion** *f* first communion; ~**malig** *adj* first; ~**mals** *adv* for the first time; ~**rangig** *adj* first-rate.

**erstrebenswert** [ɛr'ʃtreːbənsveːrt] *adj* desirable, worthwhile.

**erstrecken** [ɛr'ʃtrɛkən] *vr* to extend, stretch.

**Erststimme** *f* first vote.

The **Erststimme** and **Zweitstimme** *(first and second vote)* system is used to elect MPs to the **Bundestag**. Each elector is given two votes. The first is to choose a candidate in his constituency; the candidate with the most votes is elected MP. The second is to choose a party. All the second votes in each **Land** are counted and a proportionate number of MPs from each party is sent to the Bundestag.

**Ersttagsbrief** *m* first-day cover.

**Ersttagsstempel** *m* first-day (date) stamp.

**erstunken** [ɛr'ʃtʊŋkən] *adj:* **das ist** ~ **und erlogen** (*umg*) that's a pack of lies.

**Erstwähler** **(-s, -)** *m* first-time voter.

**ersuchen** [ɛr'zuːxən] *vt* to request.

**ertappen** [ɛr'tapən] *vt* to catch, detect.

**erteilen** [ɛr'taɪlən] *vt* to give.

**ertönen** [ɛr'tøːnən] *vi* to sound, ring out.

**Ertrag** [ɛr'traːk] **(-(e)s, ⸚e)** *m* yield; (*Gewinn*) proceeds *pl.*

**ertragen** *unreg vt* to bear, stand.

**erträglich** [ɛr'trɛːklɪç] *adj* tolerable, bearable.

**ertragreich** *adj* (*Geschäft*) profitable, lucrative.

**ertrank** *etc* [ɛr'traŋk] *vb siehe* **ertrinken**.

**ertränken** [ɛr'trɛŋkən] *vt* to drown.

**erträumen** [ɛr'trɔʏmən] *vt:* **sich** *dat* **etw** ~ to dream of sth, imagine sth.

**ertrinken** [ɛr'trɪŋkən] *unreg vi* to drown; **E~** **(-s)** *nt* drowning.

**ertrunken** [ɛr'trʊŋkən] *pp von* **ertrinken**.

**erübrigen** [ɛr'|yːbrɪɡən] *vt* to spare ♦ *vr* to be unnecessary.

**erwachen** [ɛr'vaxən] *vi* to awake; **ein böses E~** (*fig*) a rude awakening.

**erwachsen** [ɛr'vaksən] *adj* grown-up ♦ *unreg vi:* **daraus erwuchsen ihm Unannehmlichkeiten** that caused him some trouble.

**Erwachsene(r)** *f(m)* adult.

**Erwachsenenbildung** *f* adult education.

**erwägen** [ɛr'vɛːɡən] *unreg vt* to consider.

**Erwägung** *f* consideration; **etw in** ~ **ziehen** to take sth into consideration.

**erwähnen** [ɛr'vɛːnən] *vt* to mention.

**erwähnenswert** *adj* worth mentioning.

**Erwähnung** *f* mention.

**erwarb** *etc* [ɛr'varp] *vb siehe* **erwerben**.

**erwärmen** [ɛr'vɛrmən] *vt* to warm, heat ♦ *vr* to get warm, warm up; **sich** ~ **für** to warm to.

**erwarten** [ɛr'vartən] *vt* to expect; (*warten auf*) to wait for; **etw kaum** ~ **können** to hardly be able to wait for sth.

**Erwartung** *f* expectation; **in** ~ **Ihrer baldigen Antwort** (*form*) in anticipation of your early reply.

**erwartungsgemäß** *adv* as expected.

**erwartungsvoll** *adj* expectant.

**erwecken** [ɛr'vɛkən] *vt* to rouse, awake; **den Anschein** ~ to give the impression; **etw zu neuem Leben** ~ to resurrect sth.

**erwehren** [ɛr'veːrən] *vr +gen* (*geh*) to fend off, ward off; (*des Lachens etc*) to refrain from.

**erweichen** [ɛr'vaɪçən] *vt* to soften; **sich nicht** ~ **lassen** to be unmoved.

**erweisen** [ɛr'vaɪzən] *unreg vt* to prove ♦ *vr:* **sich** ~ **als** to prove to be; **jdm einen Gefallen/ Dienst** ~ to do sb a favour/service; **sich jdm gegenüber dankbar** ~ to show one's gratitude to sb.

**erweitern** [ɛr'vaɪtərn] *vt, vr* to widen, enlarge;

(*Geschäft*) to expand; (*MED*) to dilate; (*fig: Kenntnisse*) to broaden; (*Macht*) to extend.
**Erweiterung** *f* expansion.
**Erwerb** [ɛr'vɛrp] (-(e)s, -e) *m* acquisition; (*Beruf*) trade.
**erwerben** [ɛr'vɛrbən] *unreg vt* to acquire; **er hat sich** *dat* **große Verdienste um die Firma erworben** he has done great service for the firm.
**Erwerbs-** *zW:* **e~fähig** *adj* (*form*) capable of gainful employment; **~gesellschaft** *f* acquisitive society; **e~los** *adj* unemployed; **~quelle** *f* source of income; **e~tätig** *adj* (gainfully) employed; **e~unfähig** *adj* unable to work.
**erwidern** [ɛr'viːdərn] *vt* to reply; (*vergelten*) to return.
**Erwiderung** *f:* **in ~ Ihres Schreibens vom ...** (*form*) in reply to your letter of the ...
**erwiesen** [ɛr'viːzən] *adj* proven.
**erwirbt** [ɛr'vɪrpt] *vb siehe* **erwerben**.
**erwirtschaften** [ɛr'vɪrtʃaftən] *vt* (*Gewinn etc*) to make by good management.
**erwischen** [ɛr'vɪʃən] (*umg*) *vt* to catch, get; **ihn hat's erwischt!** (*umg: verliebt*) he's got it bad; (*: krank*) he's got it; **kalt ~** (*umg*) to catch off-balance.
**erworben** [ɛr'vɔrbən] *pp von* **erwerben**.
**erwünscht** [ɛr'vʏnʃt] *adj* desired.
**erwürgen** [ɛr'vʏrgən] *vt* to strangle.
**Erz** [eːrts] (-es, -e) *nt* ore.
**erzählen** [ɛr'tsɛːlən] *vt, vi* to tell; **dem werd' ich was ~!** (*umg*) I'll have something to say to him; **~de Dichtung** narrative fiction.
**Erzähler(in)** (-s, -) *m(f)* narrator.
**Erzählung** *f* story, tale.
**Erzbischof** *m* archbishop.
**Erzengel** *m* archangel.
**erzeugen** [ɛr'tsɔʏgən] *vt* to produce; (*Strom*) to generate.
**Erzeuger** (-s, -) *m* producer; **~preis** *m* manufacturer's price.
**Erzeugnis** (-ses, -se) *nt* product, produce.
**Erzeugung** *f* production; generation.
**Erzfeind** *m* arch enemy.
**erziehbar** *adj:* **ein Heim für schwer ~e Kinder** a home for difficult children.
**erziehen** [ɛr'tsiːən] *unreg vt* to bring up; (*bilden*) to educate, train.
**Erzieher(in)** (-s, -) *m(f)* educator; (*in Kindergarten*) nursery school teacher.
**Erziehung** *f* bringing up; (*Bildung*) education.
**Erziehungs-** *zW:* **~berechtigte(r)** *f(m)* parent, legal guardian; **~geld** *nt* payment for new parents; **~heim** *nt* community home; **~urlaub** *m* leave for a new parent.
**erzielen** [ɛr'tsiːlən] *vt* to achieve, obtain; (*Tor*) to score.
**erzkonservativ** ['ɛrtskɔnzɛrva'tiːf] *adj* ultraconservative.
**erzog** *etc* [ɛr'tsoːk] *vb siehe* **erziehen**.

**erzogen** [ɛr'tsoːgən] *pp von* **erziehen**.
**erzürnen** [ɛr'tsʏrnən] *vt* (*geh*) to anger, incense.
**erzwingen** [ɛr'tsvɪŋən] *unreg vt* to force, obtain by force.
**Es** [ɛs] (-) *nt* (*MUS: Dur*) E flat.
**es** [ɛs] *nom, akk pron* it.
**Esche** ['ɛʃə] (-, -n) *f* ash.
**Esel** ['eːzəl] (-s, -) *m* donkey, ass; **ich ~!** (*umg*) silly me!
**Eselsbrücke** *f* (*Gedächtnishilfe*) mnemonic, aide-mémoire.
**Eselsohr** *nt* dog-ear.
**Eskalation** [ɛskalatsi'oːn] *f* escalation.
**eskalieren** [ɛska'liːrən] *vt, vi* to escalate.
**Eskimo** ['ɛskimo] (-s, -s) *m* eskimo.
**Eskorte** [ɛs'kɔrtə] (-, -n) *f* (*MIL*) escort.
**eskortieren** [ɛskɔr'tiːrən] *vt* (*geh*) to escort.
**Espenlaub** ['ɛspənlaʊp] *nt:* **zittern wie ~** to shake like a leaf.
**eßbar** ['ɛsbaːr] *adj* eatable, edible.
**Eßecke** *f* dining area.
**essen** ['ɛsən] *unreg vt, vi* to eat; **~ gehen** (*auswärts*) to eat out; **~ Sie gern Äpfel?** do you like apples?; **E~** (-s, -) *nt* (*Mahlzeit*) meal; (*Nahrung*) food; **E~ auf Rädern** meals on wheels.
**Essens-** *zW:* **~ausgabe** *f* serving of meals; (*Stelle*) serving counter; **~marke** *f* meal voucher; **~zeit** *f* mealtime.
**Eßgeschirr** *nt* dinner service.
**Essig** ['ɛsɪç] (-s, -e) *m* vinegar; **damit ist es ~** (*umg*) it's all off; **~gurke** *f* gherkin.
**Eßkastanie** *f* sweet chestnut.
**Eßl.** *abk* (= *Eßlöffel*) tbsp.
**Eß-** *zW:* **~löffel** *m* tablespoon; **~tisch** *m* dining table; **~waren** *pl* foodstuffs *pl*; **~zimmer** *nt* dining room.
**Establishment** [ɪs'tæblɪʃmənt] (-s, -s) *nt* establishment.
**Este** ['eːstə] (-n, -n) *m*, **Estin** *f* Estonian.
**Estland** ['eːstlant] *nt* Estonia.
**estnisch** ['eːstnɪʃ] *adj* Estonian.
**Estragon** ['ɛstragɔn] (-s) *m* tarragon.
**Estrich** ['ɛstrɪç] (-s, -e) *m* stone/clay *etc* floor.
**etablieren** [eta'bliːrən] *vr* to establish o.s.; (*COMM*) to set up.
**Etage** [e'taːʒə] (-, -n) *f* floor, storey (*BRIT*), story (*US*).
**Etagenbetten** *pl* bunk beds *pl*.
**Etagenwohnung** *f* flat (*BRIT*), apartment (*US*).
**Etappe** [e'tapə] (-, -n) *f* stage.
**etappenweise** *adv* step by step, stage by stage.
**Etat** [e'taː] (-s, -s) *m* budget; **~jahr** *nt* financial year; **~posten** *m* budget item.
**etc** *abk* (= *et cetera*) etc.
**etepetete** [eːtəpe'teːtə] (*umg*) *adj* fussy.
**Ethik** ['eːtɪk] *f* ethics *sing*.
**ethisch** ['eːtɪʃ] *adj* ethical.
**ethnisch** ['ɛtnɪʃ] *adj* ethnic; **~e Säuberung**

ethnic cleansing.

**Etikett** [eti'kɛt] (-**(e)s, -e**) nt (lit, fig) label.

**Etikette** f etiquette, manners pl.

**Etikettenschwindel** m (POL): **es ist reinster
~, wenn ...** it is just playing od juggling
with names if ...

**etikettieren** [etikɛ'tiːrən] vt to label.

**etliche(r, s)** ['ɛtlɪçə(r, s)] adj quite a lot of
♦ pron pl some, quite a few; ~**s** quite a lot.

**Etüde** [e'tyːdə] (-, -n) f (MUS) étude.

**Etui** [ɛt'viː] (-**s, -s**) nt case.

**etwa** ['ɛtva] adv (ungefähr) about; (vielleicht)
perhaps; (beispielsweise) for instance;
(entrüstet, erstaunt): **hast du ~ schon wieder
kein Geld dabei?** don't tell me you haven't
got any money again! ♦ adv (zur Bestätigung):
**Sie kommen doch, oder ~ nicht?** you are
coming, aren't you?; **nicht ~** by no means;
**willst du ~ schon gehen?** (surely) you don't
want to go already?

**etwaig** ['ɛtvaɪç] adj possible.

**etwas** pron something; (fragend, verneinend)
anything; (ein wenig) a little ♦ adv a little; **er
kann ~** he's good; **E~** nt: **das gewisse E~**
that certain something.

**Etymologie** [etymolo'giː] f etymology.

**EU** (-) f abk (= Europäische Union) EU.

**euch** [ɔʏç] pron (akk von ihr) you; yourselves;
(dat von ihr) (to/for) you ♦ refl pron
yourselves.

**euer** ['ɔʏər] pron gen von **ihr** of you ♦ adj your.

**Eule** ['ɔʏlə] (-, -n) f owl.

**Euphemismus** [ɔʏfe'mɪsmʊs] m euphemism.

**Eurasien** [ɔʏ'raːziən] nt Eurasia.

**Euratom** [ɔʏra'toːm] f abk (= Europäische
Atomgemeinschaft) Euratom.

**eure(r, s)** ['ɔʏrə(r, s)] pron yours.

**eurerseits** adv on your part.

**euresgleichen** pron people like you.

**euretwegen** ['ɔʏrət'veːgən] adv (für euch) for
your sakes; (wegen euch) on your account.

**euretwillen** ['ɔʏrət'vɪlən] adv: **um ~**
= euretwegen.

**eurige** pron: **der/die/das ~** (geh) yours.

**Eurokrat** [ɔʏro'kraːt] (-en, -en) m eurocrat.

**Europa** [ɔʏ'roːpa] (-**s**) nt Europe.

**Europäer(in)** [ɔʏro'pɛːər(ɪn)] (-**s, -**) m(f)
European.

**europäisch** adj European; **das E~e Parlament**
the European Parliament; **E~e Union**
European Union; **E~e
(Wirtschafts)gemeinschaft** European
(Economic) Community, Common Market.

**Europa-** zW: ~**meister** m European champion;
~**rat** m Council of Europe; ~**straße** f
Euroroute.

**Euroscheck** [ɔʏro'ʃɛk] m Eurocheque.

**Euter** ['ɔʏtər] (-**s, -**) nt udder.

**Euthanasie** [ɔʏtana'ziː] f euthanasia.

**E.V., e.V.** abk (= eingetragener Verein)
registered association.

**ev.** abk = **evangelisch**.

**evakuieren** [evaku'iːrən] vt to evacuate.

**evangelisch** [evaŋ'geːlɪʃ] adj Protestant.

**Evangelium** [evaŋ'geːliʊm] nt Gospel.

**Evaskostüm** nt: **im ~** in her birthday suit.

**eventuell** [evɛntu'ɛl] adj possible ♦ adv
possibly, perhaps.

**Everest** ['ɛvərɛst] (-**s**) m (Mount) Everest.

**Evolution** [evolutsi'oːn] f evolution.

**Evolutionstheorie** f theory of evolution.

**evtl.** abk = **eventuell**.

**EWG** [eːveː'geː] (-) f abk (= Europäische
Wirtschaftsgemeinschaft) EC.

**ewig** ['eːvɪç] adj eternal ♦ adv: **auf ~** forever;
**ich habe Sie ~ lange nicht gesehen** (umg) I
haven't seen you for ages; **E~keit** f
eternity; **bis in alle E~keit** forever.

**EWS** (-) nt abk (= Europäisches Währungssystem) EMS.

**EWU** (-) f abk (= Europäische Währungsunion)
EMU.

**ex** [ɛks] (umg) adv: **etw ~ trinken** to drink sth
down in one.

**exakt** [ɛ'ksakt] adj exact.

**exaltiert** [ɛksal'tiːrt] adj exaggerated,
effusive.

**Examen** [ɛ'ksaːmən] (-**s, -** od **Examina**) nt
examination.

**Examensangst** f exam nerves pl.

**Examensarbeit** f dissertation.

**Exekutionskommando**
[ɛksekutsi'oːnskɔmando] nt firing squad.

**Exekutive** [ɛkseku'tiːvə] f executive.

**Exempel** [ɛ'ksɛmpəl] (-**s, -**) nt example; **die
Probe aufs ~ machen** to put it to the test.

**Exemplar** [ɛksɛm'plaːr] (-**s, -e**) nt specimen;
(Buch~) copy; **e~isch** adj exemplary.

**exerzieren** [ɛksɛr'tsiːrən] vi to drill.

**Exhibitionist** [ɛkshibitsio'nɪst] m
exhibitionist.

**Exil** [ɛ'ksiːl] (-**s, -e**) nt exile.

**existentiell** [ɛksɪstɛntsi'ɛl] adj: **von ~er
Bedeutung** of vital significance.

**Existenz** [ɛksɪs'tɛnts] f existence; (Unterhalt)
livelihood, living; (pej: Mensch) character;
~**berechtigung** f right to exist; ~**grundlage**
f basis of one's livelihood; ~**kampf** m
struggle for existence; ~**minimum** (-**s, -ma**)
nt subsistence level.

**existieren** [ɛksɪs'tiːrən] vi to exist.

**exkl.** abk = **exklusive**.

**exklusiv** [ɛksklu'ziːf] adj exclusive; **E~bericht**
m (PRESSE) exclusive report.

**exklusive** [ɛksklu'ziːvə] präp +gen exclusive of,
not including ♦ adv exclusive of, excluding.

**Exkursion** [ɛkskʊrzi'oːn] f (study) trip.

**Exmatrikulation** [ɛksmatrikulatsi'oːn] f
(UNIV): **bei seiner ~** when he left university.

**exorzieren** [ɛksɔr'tsiːrən] vt to exorcize.

**exotisch** [ɛ'ksoːtɪʃ] adj exotic.

**expandieren** [ɛkspan'diːrən] vi (ECON) to
expand.

**Expansion** [ɛkspanzi'oːn] f expansion.

**expansiv** [ɛkspan'ziːf] *adj* expansionist; (*Wirtschaftszweige*) expanding.
**Expedition** [ɛkspeditsi'oːn] *f* expedition; (*COMM*) forwarding department.
**Experiment** [ɛksperi'mɛnt] *nt* experiment.
**experimentell** [ɛksperimɛn'tɛl] *adj* experimental.
**experimentieren** [ɛksperimɛn'tiːrən] *vi* to experiment.
**Experte** [ɛks'pɛrtə] (**-n, -n**) *m* expert, specialist.
**Expertin** [ɛks'pɛrtɪn] *f* expert, specialist.
**explodieren** [ɛksplo'diːrən] *vi* to explode.
**Explosion** [ɛksplozi'oːn] *f* explosion.
**explosiv** [ɛksplo'ziːf] *adj* explosive.
**Exponent** [ɛkspo'nɛnt] *m* exponent.
**exponieren** [ɛkspo'niːrən] *vt*: **an exponierter Stelle stehen** to be in an exposed position.
**Export** [ɛks'pɔrt] (**-(e)s, -e**) *m* export.
**Exportartikel** *m* export.
**Exporteur** [ɛkspɔr'tøːr] *m* exporter.
**Exporthandel** *m* export trade.
**Exporthaus** *nt* export house.
**exportieren** [ɛkspɔr'tiːrən] *vt* to export.
**Exportkaufmann** *m* exporter.
**Exportland** *nt* exporting country.
**Exportvertreter** *m* export agent.
**Expreßgut** [ɛks'prɛsguːt] *nt* express goods *pl od* freight.
**Expressionismus** [ɛksprɛsio'nɪsmʊs] *m* expressionism.
**Expreßzug** *m* express (train).
**extra** ['ɛkstra] *adj inv* (*umg: gesondert*) separate; (*besondere*) extra ♦ *adv* (*gesondert*) separately; (*speziell*) specially; (*absichtlich*) on purpose; (*vor Adjektiven, zusätzlich*) extra; **E~** (**-s, -s**) *nt* extra; **E~ausgabe** *f* special edition; **E~blatt** *nt* special edition.
**Extrakt** [ɛks'trakt] (**-(e)s, -e**) *m* extract.
**Extratour** *f* (*fig: umg*): **sich** *dat* **~en leisten** to do one's own thing.
**extravagant** [ɛkstrava'gant] *adj* extravagant; (*Kleidung*) flamboyant.
**Extrawurst** (*umg*) *f* (*Sonderwunsch*): **er will immer eine ~ (gebraten haben)** he always wants something different.
**Extrem** [ɛks'treːm] (**-s, -e**) *nt* extreme; **e~** *adj* extreme; **~fall** *m* extreme (case).
**Extremist(in)** *m(f)* extremist.
**Extremistenerlaß** [ɛkstre'mɪstən|ɛrlas] *m law(s) governing extremism*.
**extremistisch** [ɛkstre'mɪstɪʃ] *adj* (*POL*) extremist.
**Extremitäten** [ɛkstremi'tɛːtən] *pl* extremities *pl*.
**extrovertiert** [ɛkstrover'tiːrt] *adj* extrovert.
**Exzellenz** [ɛkstsɛ'lɛnts] *f* excellency.
**exzentrisch** [ɛks'tsɛntrɪʃ] *adj* eccentric.
**Exzeß** [ɛks'tsɛs] (**-sses, -sse**) *m* excess.

# $F, f$

**F, f¹** [ɛf] (**-, -**) *nt* F, f; **~ wie Friedrich** ≈ F for Frederick, F for Fox (*US*); **nach Schema F** (*umg*) in the usual old way.
**f²** *abk* (= *feminin*) fem.
**Fa.** *abk* (= *Firma*) co.
**Fabel** ['faːbəl] (**-, -n**) *f* fable; **f~haft** *adj* fabulous, marvellous (*BRIT*), marvelous (*US*).
**Fabrik** [fa'briːk] *f* factory; **~anlage** *f* plant; (*Gelände*) factory premises *pl*.
**Fabrikant** [fabri'kant] *m* (*Hersteller*) manufacturer; (*Besitzer*) industrialist.
**Fabrikarbeiter(in)** *m(f)* factory worker.
**Fabrikat** [fabri'kaːt] (**-(e)s, -e**) *nt* product; (*Marke*) make.
**Fabrikation** [fabriːkatsi'oːn] *f* manufacture, production.
**Fabrikbesitzer** *m* factory owner.
**Fabrikgelände** *nt* factory site.
**fabrizieren** [fabri'tsiːrən] *vt* (*geistiges Produkt*) to produce; (*Geschichte*) to concoct, fabricate.
**Fach** [fax] (**-(e)s, ̈-er**) *nt* compartment; (*in Schrank, Regal etc*) shelf; (*Sachgebiet*) subject; **ein Mann/eine Frau vom ~** an expert; **~arbeiter** *m* skilled worker; **~arzt** *m* (medical) specialist; **~ausdruck** *m* technical term; **~bereich** *m* (special) field; (*UNIV*) school, faculty; **~buch** *nt* reference book.
**Fächer** ['fɛçər] (**-s, -**) *m* fan.
**Fach-** *zW*: **~frau** *f* expert; **~gebiet** *nt* (special) field; **~geschäft** *nt* specialist shop (*BRIT*) *od* store (*US*); **~händler** *m* stockist; **~hochschule** *f* college; **~idiot** (*umg*) *m* narrow-minded specialist; **~kraft** *f* qualified employee; **~kreise** *pl*: **in ~kreisen** among experts; **f~kundig** *adj* expert, specialist; **~lehrer** *m* specialist subject teacher; **f~lich** *adj* technical; (*beruflich*) professional; **~mann** (**-(e)s, pl ~leute**) *m* expert; **f~männisch** *adj* professional; **~richtung** *f* subject area; **~schule** *f* technical college; **f~simpeln** *vi* to talk shop; **f~spezifisch** *adj* technical; **~verband** *m* trade association; **~welt** *f* profession; **~werk** *nt* timber frame; **~werkhaus** *nt* half-timbered house.
**Fackel** ['fakəl] (**-, -n**) *f* torch.
**fackeln** (*umg*) *vi* to dither.
**Fackelzug** *m* torchlight procession.
**fad(e)** *adj* insipid; (*langweilig*) dull; (*Essen*) tasteless.

**Faden** ['fa:dən] (-s, -̈) m thread; **der rote ~** (fig) the central theme; **alle Fäden laufen hier zusammen** this is the nerve centre (BRIT) od center (US) of the whole thing; **~nudeln** pl vermicelli sing; **f~scheinig** adj (lit, fig) threadbare.

**Fagott** [fa'gɔt] (-(e)s, -e) nt bassoon.

**fähig** ['fɛ:ɪç] adj: **~ (zu** od **+gen)** capable (of); able (to); **zu allem ~ sein** to be capable of anything; **F~keit** f ability.

**Fähnchen** ['fɛ:nçən] nt pennon, streamer.

**fahnden** ['fa:ndən] vi: **~ nach** to search for.

**Fahndung** f search.

**Fahndungsliste** f list of wanted criminals, wanted list.

**Fahne** ['fa:nə] (-, -n) f flag; standard; **mit fliegenden ~n zu jdm/etw überlaufen** to go over to sb/sth; **eine ~ haben** (umg) to smell of drink.

**Fahnenflucht** f desertion.

**Fahrausweis** m (form) ticket.

**Fahrbahn** f carriageway (BRIT), roadway.

**fahrbar** adj: **~er Untersatz** (hum) wheels pl.

**Fähre** ['fɛ:rə] (-, -n) f ferry.

**fahren** ['fa:rən] unreg vt to drive; (Rad) to ride; (befördern) to drive, take; (Rennen) to drive in ♦ vi (sich bewegen) to go; (Schiff) to sail; (ab~) to leave; **mit dem Auto/Zug ~** to go od travel by car/train; **mit dem Aufzug ~** to take the lift, ride the elevator (US); **links/ rechts ~** to drive on the left/right; **gegen einen Baum ~** to drive od go into a tree; **die U-Bahn fährt alle fünf Minuten** the underground goes od runs every five minutes; **mit der Hand ~ über +akk** to pass one's hand over; **(bei etw) gut/schlecht ~** (zurechtkommen) to do well/badly (with sth); **was ist (denn) in dich gefahren?** what's got (BRIT) od gotten (US) into you?; **einen ~ lassen** (umg) to fart (!).

**fahrend** adj: **~es Volk** travelling people.

**Fahrer(in)** ['fa:rər(ɪn)] (-s, -) m(f) driver; **~flucht** f hit-and-run driving.

**Fahr-** zW: **~gast** m passenger; **~geld** nt fare; **~gelegenheit** f transport; **~gestell** nt chassis; (AVIAT) undercarriage.

**fahrig** ['fa:rɪç] adj nervous; (unkonzentriert) distracted.

**Fahr-** zW: **~karte** f ticket; **~kartenausgabe** f ticket office; **~kartenautomat** m ticket machine; **~kartenschalter** m ticket office.

**fahrlässig** adj negligent; **~e Tötung** manslaughter; **F~keit** f negligence.

**Fahr-** zW: **~lehrer** m driving instructor; **~plan** m timetable; **f~planmäßig** adj (EISENB) scheduled; **~praxis** f driving experience; **~preis** m fare; **~prüfung** f driving test; **~rad** nt bicycle; **~radweg** m cycle path; **~rinne** f (NAUT) shipping channel, fairway; **~schein** m ticket; **~schule** f driving school; **~schüler** m learner (driver); **~spur** f lane; **~stuhl** m

lift (BRIT), elevator (US); **~stunde** f driving lesson.

**Fahrt** [fa:rt] (-, -en) f journey; (kurz) trip; (AUT) drive; (Geschwindigkeit) speed; **gute ~!** safe journey!; **volle ~ voraus!** (NAUT) full speed ahead!

**fährt** [fɛ:rt] vb siehe **fahren**.

**fahrtauglich** ['fa:rtauklɪç] adj fit to drive.

**Fährte** ['fɛ:rtə] (-, -n) f track, trail; **jdn auf eine falsche ~ locken** (fig) to put sb off the scent.

**Fahrtenschreiber** m tachograph.

**Fahrtkosten** pl travelling expenses pl.

**Fahrtrichtung** f course, direction.

**Fahr-** zW: **f~tüchtig** ['fa:rtʏçtɪç] adj fit to drive; **~verhalten** nt (von Fahrer) behaviour (BRIT) od behavior (US) behind the wheel; (von Wagen) road performance; **~zeug** nt vehicle; **~zeughalter** (-s, -) m owner of a vehicle; **~zeugpapiere** pl vehicle documents pl.

**Faible** ['fɛ:bl] (-s, -s) nt (geh) liking; (Schwäche) weakness; (Vorliebe) penchant.

**fair** [fɛ:r] adj fair.

**Fäkalien** [fɛ'ka:liən] pl faeces pl.

**Faksimile** [fak'zi:mile] (-s, -s) nt facsimile.

**faktisch** ['faktɪʃ] adj actual.

**Faktor** m factor.

**Faktum** (-s, -ten) nt fact.

**fakturieren** [faktu'ri:rən] vt (COMM) to invoice.

**Fakultät** [fakʊl'tɛ:t] f faculty.

**Falke** ['falkə] (-n, -n) m falcon.

**Falklandinseln** ['falklant'ɪnzəln] pl Falkland Islands, Falklands.

**Fall** [fal] (-(e)s, -̈e) m (Sturz) fall; (Sachverhalt, JUR, GRAM) case; **auf jeden ~, auf alle Fälle** in any case; (bestimmt) definitely; **gesetzt den ~** assuming (that); **jds ~ sein** (umg) to be sb's cup of tea; **klarer ~!** (umg) sure thing!, you bet!; **das mache ich auf keinen ~** there's no way I'm going to do that.

**Falle** (-, -n) f trap; (umg: Bett) bed; **jdm eine ~ stellen** to set a trap for sb.

**fallen** unreg vi to fall; (im Krieg) to fall, be killed; **etw ~ lassen** to drop sth.

**fällen** ['fɛlən] vt (Baum) to fell; (Urteil) to pass.

**fallenlassen** unreg vt (Bemerkung) to make; (Plan) to abandon, drop.

**fällig** ['fɛlɪç] adj due; (Wechsel) mature(d); **längst ~** long overdue; **F~keit** f (COMM) maturity.

**Fallobst** nt fallen fruit, windfall.

**falls** adv in case, if.

**Fall-** zW: **~schirm** m parachute; **~schirmjäger** m paratrooper; **~schirmspringer(in)** m(f) parachutist; **~schirmtruppe** f paratroops pl; **~strick** m (fig) trap, snare; **~studie** f case study.

**fällt** [fɛlt] vb siehe **fallen**.

**Falltür** f trap door.

**fallweise** adj from case to case.

**falsch** [falʃ] *adj* false; (*unrichtig*) wrong;
~ **liegen (bei** *od* **in** +*dat*) (*umg*) to be wrong
(about); ~ **liegen mit** to be wrong in; **ein ~es
Spiel (mit jdm) treiben** to play (sb) false;
**etw ~ verstehen** to misunderstand sth, get
sth wrong.
**fälschen** ['fɛlʃən] *vt* to forge.
**Fälscher(in)** (**-s, -**) *m(f)* forger.
**Falschgeld** *nt* counterfeit money.
**Falschheit** *f* falsity, falseness; (*Unrichtigkeit*)
wrongness.
**fälschlich** *adj* false.
**fälschlicherweise** *adv* mistakenly.
**Falschmeldung** *f* (*PRESSE*) false report.
**Fälschung** *f* forgery.
**fälschungssicher** *adj* forgery-proof.
**Faltblatt** *nt* leaflet; (*in Zeitschrift etc*) insert.
**Fältchen** ['fɛltçən] *nt* crease, wrinkle.
**Falte** ['faltə] (**-, -n**) *f* (*Knick*) fold, crease;
(*Haut*~) wrinkle; (*Rock*~) pleat.
**falten** *vt* to fold; (*Stirn*) to wrinkle.
**faltenlos** *adj* without folds; without wrinkles.
**Faltenrock** *m* pleated skirt.
**Falter** ['faltər] (**-s, -**) *m* (*Tag*~) butterfly;
(*Nacht*~) moth.
**faltig** ['faltıç] *adj* (*Haut*) wrinkled; (*Rock usw*)
creased.
**falzen** ['faltsən] *vt* (*Papierbogen*) to fold.
**Fam.** *abk* = **Familie.**
**familiär** [famili'ɛːr] *adj* familiar.
**Familie** [fa'miːliə] *f* family; ~ **Otto Francke**
(*als Anschrift*) Mr. & Mrs. Otto Francke and
family; **zur ~ gehören** to be one of the
family.
**Familien-** *zW:* ~**ähnlichkeit** *f* family
resemblance; ~**anschluß** *m:* **Unterkunft mit
~anschluß** *accommodation where one is
treated as one of the family;* ~**kreis** *m*
family circle; ~**mitglied** *nt* member of the
family; ~**name** *m* surname; ~**packung** *f*
family(-size) pack; ~**planung** *f* family
planning; ~**stand** *m* marital status; ~**vater**
*m* head of the family; ~**verhältnisse** *pl*
family circumstances *pl.*
**Fanatiker(in)** [fa'naːtikər(ın)] (**-s, -**) *m(f)*
fanatic.
**fanatisch** *adj* fanatical.
**Fanatismus** [fana'tısmʊs] *m* fanaticism.
**fand** *etc* [fant] *vb siehe* **finden.**
**Fang** [faŋ] (**-(e)s, -̈e**) *m* catch; (*Jagen*) hunting;
(*Kralle*) talon, claw.
**fangen** *unreg vt* to catch ♦ *vr* to get caught;
(*Flugzeug*) to level out; (*Mensch: nicht fallen*)
to steady o.s.; (*fig*) to compose o.s.; (*in
Leistung*) to get back on form.
**Fangfrage** *f* catch *od* trick question.
**Fanggründe** *pl* fishing grounds *pl.*
**fängt** [fɛŋkt] *vb siehe* **fangen.**
**Farb-** *zW:* ~**abzug** *m* coloured (*BRIT*) *od*
colored (*US*) print; ~**aufnahme** *f* colour
(*BRIT*) *od* color (*US*) photograph; ~**band** *nt*
typewriter ribbon.

**Farbe** ['faːrbə] (**-, -n**) *f* colour (*BRIT*), color
(*US*); (*zum Malen etc*) paint; (*Stoff*~) dye;
(*KARTEN*) suit.
**farbecht** ['farpˌɛçt] *adj* colourfast (*BRIT*),
colorfast (*US*).
**färben** ['fɛrbən] *vt* to colour (*BRIT*), color (*US*);
(*Stoff, Haar*) to dye.
**farben-** *zW:* ~**blind** *adj* colour-blind (*BRIT*),
color-blind (*US*); ~**froh** *adj* colourful (*BRIT*),
colorful (*US*); ~**prächtig** *adj* colourful
(*BRIT*), colorful (*US*).
**Farbfernsehen** *nt* colour (*BRIT*) *od* color (*US*)
television.
**Farbfilm** *m* colour (*BRIT*) *od* color (*US*) film.
**Farbfoto** *nt* colour (*BRIT*) *od* color (*US*) photo.
**farbig** *adj* coloured (*BRIT*), colored (*US*).
**Farbige(r)** *f(m)* coloured (*BRIT*) *od* colored
(*US*) person.
**Farb-** *zW:* ~**kasten** *m* paintbox; **f~los** *adj*
colourless (*BRIT*), colorless (*US*); ~**stift** *m*
coloured (*BRIT*) *od* colored (*US*) pencil;
~**stoff** *m* dye; (*Lebensmittel*~) (artificial)
colouring (*BRIT*) *od* coloring (*US*); ~**ton** *m*
hue, tone.
**Färbung** ['fɛrbʊŋ] *f* colouring (*BRIT*), coloring
(*US*); (*Tendenz*) bias.
**Farn** [farn] (**-(e)s, -e**) *m* fern; (*Adler*~) bracken.
**Farnkraut** [farn] *nt* = **Farn.**
**Färöer** [fɛ'røːər] *pl* Faeroe Islands *pl.*
**Fasan** [fa'zaːn] (**-(e)s, -e(n)**) *m* pheasant.
**Fasching** ['faʃıŋ] (**-s, -e** *od* **-s**) *m* carnival.
**Faschismus** [fa'ʃısmʊs] *m* fascism.
**Faschist(in)** *m(f)* fascist.
**faschistisch** [fa'ʃıstıʃ] *adj* fascist.
**faseln** ['faːzəln] *vi* to talk nonsense, drivel.
**Faser** ['faːzər] (**-, -n**) *f* fibre.
**fasern** *vi* to fray.
**Faß** [fas] (**-sses, Fässer**) *nt* vat, barrel; (*für Öl*)
drum; **Bier vom ~** draught beer; **ein ~ ohne
Boden** (*fig*) a bottomless pit.
**Fassade** [fa'saːdə] *f* (*lit, fig*) façade.
**faßbar** *adj* comprehensible.
**Faßbier** *nt* draught beer.
**fassen** ['fasən] *vt* (*ergreifen*) to grasp, take;
(*inhaltlich*) to hold; (*Entschluß etc*) to take;
(*verstehen*) to understand; (*Ring etc*) to set;
(*formulieren*) to formulate, phrase ♦ *vr* to
calm down; **nicht zu ~** unbelievable; **sich
kurz ~** to be brief.
**faßlich** ['faslıç] *adj* comprehensible.
**Fasson** [fa'sõː] (**-, -s**) *f* style; (*Art und Weise*)
way; **aus der ~ geraten** (*lit*) to lose its shape.
**Fassung** ['fasʊŋ] *f* (*Umrahmung*) mounting;
(*Lampen*~) socket; (*Wortlaut*) version;
(*Beherrschung*) composure; **jdn aus der
~ bringen** to upset sb; **völlig außer
~ geraten** to lose all self-control.
**fassungslos** *adj* speechless.
**Fassungsvermögen** *nt* capacity;
(*Verständnis*) comprehension.
**fast** [fast] *adv* almost, nearly; ~ **nie** hardly
ever.

**fasten** ['fastən] vi to fast; **F~** (-s) nt fasting; **F~zeit** f Lent.

**Fastnacht** f Shrovetide carnival.

**faszinieren** [fastsi'niːrən] vt to fascinate.

**fatal** [fa'taːl] adj fatal; (peinlich) embarrassing.

**fauchen** ['fauxən] vt, vi to hiss.

**faul** [faul] adj rotten; (Person) lazy; (Ausreden) lame; **daran ist etwas ~** there's something fishy about it.

**faulen** vi to rot.

**faulenzen** ['faulɛntsən] vi to idle.

**Faulenzer(in)** (-s, -) m(f) idler, loafer.

**Faulheit** f laziness.

**faulig** adj putrid.

**Fäulnis** ['fɔylnɪs] (-) f decay, putrefaction.

**Faulpelz** (umg) m lazybones sing.

**Faust** ['faust] (-, **Fäuste**) f fist; **das paßt wie die ~ aufs Auge** (paßt nicht) it's all wrong; **auf eigene ~** (fig) on one's own initiative.

**Fäustchen** ['fɔystçən] nt: **sich** dat **ins ~ lachen** to laugh up one's sleeve.

**faustdick** (umg) adj: **er hat es ~ hinter den Ohren** he's a crafty one.

**Fausthandschuh** m mitten.

**Faustregel** f rule of thumb.

**Favorit(in)** [favo'riːt(ɪn)] (-en, -en) m(f) favourite (BRIT), favorite (US).

**Fax** [faks] (-, -e) nt fax; **f~en** vt to fax.

**Faxen** ['faksən] pl: **~ machen** to fool around.

**Fazit** ['faːtsɪt] (-s, -s od -e) nt: **wenn wir aus diesen vier Jahren das ~ ziehen** if we take stock of these four years.

**FCKW** (-s, -s) m abk (= Fluorchlorkohlen-wasserstoff) CFC.

**FdH** (umg) abk (= Friß die Hälfte) eat less.

**FDP, F.D.P.** f abk (= Freie Demokratische Partei) Free Democratic Party.

> The **FDP** (Freie Demokratische Partei) was founded in 1948 and is Germany's centre party. It is a liberal party which has formed governing coalitions with both the **SPD** and the **CDU/CSU** at times, both in the regions and in the **Bundestag**.

**Feb.** abk (= Februar) Feb.

**Februar** ['feːbruaːr] (-(s), -e) (pl selten) m February; siehe auch **September**.

**fechten** ['fɛçtən] unreg vi to fence.

**Feder** ['feːdər] (-, -n) f feather; (Schreib~) pen nib; (TECH) spring; **in den ~n liegen** (umg) to be/stay in bed; **~ball** m shuttlecock; **~ballspiel** nt badminton; **~bett** nt continental quilt; **f~führend** adj (Behörde): **f~führend (für)** in overall charge (of); **~halter** m pen; **f~leicht** adj light as a feather; **~lesen** nt: **nicht viel ~lesens mit jdm/etw machen** to make short work of sb/sth.

**federn** vi (nachgeben) to be springy; (sich bewegen) to bounce ♦ vt to spring.

**Federung** f suspension.

**Federvieh** nt poultry.

**Federweiße(r)** m new wine.

**Federzeichnung** f pen-and-ink drawing.

**Fee** [feː] (-, -n) f fairy.

**feenhaft** ['feːənhaft] adj (liter) fairylike.

**Fegefeuer** ['feːgəfɔyər] nt purgatory.

**fegen** ['feːgən] vt to sweep.

**fehl** [feːl] adj: **~ am Platz** od **Ort** out of place; **F~anzeige** (umg) f dead loss.

**fehlen** vi to be wanting od missing; (abwesend sein) to be absent ♦ vi unpers: **es fehlte nicht viel, und ich hätte ihn verprügelt** I almost hit him; **etw fehlt jdm** sb lacks sth; **du fehlst mir** I miss you; **was fehlt ihm?** what's wrong with him?; **der/das hat mir gerade noch gefehlt!** (ironisch) he/that was all I needed; **weit gefehlt!** (fig) you're way out! (umg); (ganz im Gegenteil) far from it!; **mir ~ die Worte** words fail me; **wo fehlt es?** what's the trouble?, what's up? (umg).

**Fehlentscheidung** f wrong decision.

**Fehler** (-s, -) m mistake, error; (Mangel, Schwäche) fault; **ihr ist ein ~ unterlaufen** she's made a mistake; **~beseitigung** f (COMPUT) debugging; **f~frei** adj faultless; without any mistakes; **f~haft** adj incorrect; faulty; **f~los** adj = **fehlerfrei**; **~meldung** f (COMPUT) error message; **~suchprogramm** nt (COMPUT) debugger.

**fehl-** zW: **F~geburt** f miscarriage; **~gehen** unreg vi to go astray; **F~griff** m blunder; **F~konstruktion** f: **eine F~konstruktion sein** to be badly designed; **F~leistung** f: **Freudsche F~leistung** Freudian slip; **F~schlag** m failure; **~schlagen** unreg vi to fail; **F~schluß** m wrong conclusion; **F~start** m (SPORT) false start; **F~tritt** m false move; (fig) blunder, slip; (: Affäre) indiscretion; **F~urteil** nt miscarriage of justice; **F~zündung** f (AUT) misfire, backfire.

**Feier** ['faiər] (-, -n) f celebration; **~abend** m time to stop work; **~abend machen** to stop, knock off; **was machst du am ~abend?** what are you doing after work?; **jetzt ist ~abend!** that's enough!

**feierlich** adj solemn; **das ist ja nicht mehr ~** (umg) that's beyond a joke; **F~keit** f solemnity; **Feierlichkeiten** pl festivities pl.

**feiern** vt, vi to celebrate.

**Feiertag** m holiday.

**feig** adj cowardly.

**Feige** ['faigə] (-, -n) f fig.

**feige** adj cowardly.

**Feigheit** f cowardice.

**Feigling** m coward.

**Feile** ['failə] (-, -n) f file.

**feilen** vt, vi to file.

**feilschen** ['failʃən] vi to haggle.

**fein** [fain] adj fine; (vornehm) refined; (Gehör etc) keen; **~!** great!; **er ist ~ raus** (umg) he's sitting pretty; **sich ~ machen** to get all dressed up.

**Feind(in)** [faint, 'faindin] (-(e)s, -e) *m(f)* enemy;
~**bild** *nt* concept of an/the enemy; **f~lich** *adj*
hostile; ~**schaft** *f* enmity; **f~selig** *adj* hostile;
~**seligkeit** *f* hostility.

**Fein-** *zW:* **f~fühlend** *adj* sensitive; **f~fühlig** *adj*
sensitive; ~**gefühl** *nt* delicacy, tact; ~**heit** *f*
fineness; refinement; keenness;
~**kostgeschäft** *nt* delicatessen (shop), deli;
~**schmecker** (-s, -) *m* gourmet;
~**waschmittel** *nt* mild(-action) detergent.

**feist** [faist] *adj* fat.

**feixen** ['faiksən] (*umg*) *vi* to smirk.

**Feld** [fɛlt] (-(e)s, -er) *nt* field; (*SCHACH*) square;
(*SPORT*) pitch; **Argumente ins ~ führen** to
bring arguments to bear; **das ~ räumen**
(*fig*) to bow out; ~**arbeit** *f* (*AGR*) work in the
fields; (*GEOG etc*) fieldwork; ~**blume** *f* wild
flower; ~**herr** *m* commander; ~**jäger** *pl* (*MIL*)
the military police; ~**lazarett** *nt* (*MIL*) field
hospital; ~**salat** *m* lamb's lettuce; ~**stecher**
*m* (pair of) binoculars *pl od* field glasses *pl*.

**Feld-Wald-und-Wiesen-** (*umg*) *in zW*
common-or-garden.

**Feld-** *zW:* ~**webel** (-s, -) *m* sergeant; ~**weg** *m*
path; ~**zug** *m* (*lit, fig*) campaign.

**Felge** ['fɛlgə] (-, -n) *f* (wheel) rim.

**Felgenbremse** *f* caliper brake.

**Fell** [fɛl] (-(e)s, -e) *nt* fur; coat; (*von Schaf*)
fleece; (*von toten Tieren*) skin; **ein dickes
~ haben** to be thick-skinned, have a thick
skin; **ihm sind die ~e weggeschwommen**
(*fig*) all his hopes were dashed.

**Fels** [fɛls] (-en, -en) *m* = **Felsen.**

**Felsen** ['fɛlzən] (-s, -) *m* rock; (*Klippe*) cliff;
**f~fest** *adj* firm.

**felsig** *adj* rocky.

**Felsspalte** *f* crevice.

**Felsvorsprung** *m* ledge.

**feminin** [femi'ni:n] *adj* feminine; (*pej*)
effeminate.

**Feministin** [femi'nɪstɪn] *f* feminist.

**Fenchel** ['fɛnçəl] (-s) *m* fennel.

**Fenster** ['fɛnstər] (-s, -) *nt* window; **weg vom
~** (*umg*) out of the game, finished; ~**brett** *nt*
windowsill; ~**laden** *m* shutter; ~**leder** *nt*
chamois, shammy (leather); ~**platz** *m*
window seat; ~**putzer** (-s, -) *m* window
cleaner; ~**scheibe** *f* windowpane; ~**sims** *m*
windowsill.

**Ferien** ['fe:riən] *pl* holidays *pl*, vacation (*US*);
**die großen ~** the summer holidays (*BRIT*),
the long vacation (*US UNIV*); ~ **haben** to be
on holiday; ~**kurs** *m* holiday course; ~**reise** *f*
holiday; ~**wohnung** *f* holiday flat (*BRIT*),
vacation apartment (*US*); ~**zeit** *f* holiday
period.

**Ferkel** ['fɛrkəl] (-s, -) *nt* piglet.

**fern** [fɛrn] *adj, adv* far-off, distant; ~ **von hier** a
long way (away) from here; **F~amt** *nt* (*TEL*)
exchange; **F~bedienung** *f* remote control;
~**bleiben** *unreg vi:* ~ **bleiben (von** *od* +*dat*) to
stay away (from).

**Ferne** (-, -n) *f* distance.

**ferner** *adj, adv* further; (*weiterhin*) in future;
**unter „~ liefen" rangieren** (*umg*) to be an
also-ran.

**fern-** *zW:* **F~fahrer** *m* long-distance lorry
(*BRIT*) *od* truck driver; **F~flug** *m* long-
distance flight; **F~gespräch** *nt* long-distance
call (*BRIT*), toll call (*US*); ~**gesteuert** *adj*
remote-controlled; (*Rakete*) guided; **F~glas**
*nt* binoculars *pl*; ~**halten** *unreg vt, vr* to keep
away; **F~kopie** *f* fax; **F~kopierer** *m* fax
machine; **F~kurs(us)** *m* correspondence
course; **F~lenkung** *f* remote control;
**F~licht** *nt* (*AUT*): **mit F~licht fahren** to drive
on full beam; ~**liegen** *unreg vi:* **jdm ~liegen**
to be far from sb's mind.

**Fernmelde-** *in zW* telecommunications; (*MIL*)
signals.

**fern-** *zW:* **F~ost: aus/in F~ost** from/in the Far
East; ~**östlich** *adj* Far Eastern *attrib*; **F~rohr**
*nt* telescope; **F~schreiben** *nt* telex;
**F~schreiber** *m* teleprinter; ~**schriftlich** *adj*
by telex.

**Fernsehapparat** *m* television (set).

**fernsehen** ['fɛrnze:ən] *unreg vi* to watch
television; **F~** (-s) *nt* television; **im F~** on
television.

**Fernseher** (-s, -) *m* television (set).

**Fernseh-** *zW:* ~**gebühr** *f* television licence
(*BRIT*) *od* license (*US*) fee; ~**gerät** *nt*
television set; ~**programm** *nt* (*Kanal*)
channel, station (*US*); (*Sendung*)
programme (*BRIT*), program (*US*);
(~*zeitschrift*) (television) programme (*BRIT*)
*od* program (*US*) guide; ~**sendung** *f*
television programme (*BRIT*) *od* program
(*US*); ~**überwachungsanlage** *f* closed-
circuit television; ~**zuschauer** *m*
(television) viewer.

**Fern-** *zW:* ~**sprecher** *m* telephone;
~**sprechzelle** *f* telephone box (*BRIT*) *od*
booth (*US*); ~**steuerung** *f* remote control;
~**studium** *nt* multimedia course, ≈ Open
University course (*BRIT*); ~**verkehr** *m* long-
distance traffic; ~**weh** *nt* wanderlust.

---

**Fernstudium** *is a distance-learning degree
course where students do not go to university
but receive their tuition by letter, television or
radio programmes. There is no personal
contact between student and lecturer. The first
Fernstudium was founded in 1974. Students
are free to practise their career or to bring up a
family at the same time as studying.*

---

**Ferse** ['fɛrzə] (-, -n) *f* heel.

**Fersengeld** *nt:* ~ **geben** to take to one's
heels.

**fertig** ['fɛrtɪç] *adj* (*bereit*) ready; (*beendet*)
finished; (*gebrauchs~*) ready-made;
~ **ausgebildet** fully qualified; **mit jdm/etw
~ werden** to cope with sb/sth; **mit den**

**Nerven** ~ **sein** to be at the end of one's tether; ~ **essen/lesen** to finish eating/reading; **F~bau** m prefab(ricated house); ~**bringen** unreg vt (fähig sein) to manage, be capable of; (beenden) to finish.

**fertigen** ['fɛrtɪgən] vt to manufacture.

**fertig-** zW: **F~gericht** nt ready-to-serve meal; **F~haus** nt prefab(ricated house); **F~keit** f skill; ~**machen** vt (beenden) to finish; (umg: Person) to finish; (: körperlich) to exhaust; (: moralisch) to get down ♦ vr to get ready; ~**stellen** vt to complete.

**Fertigung** f production.

**Fertigungs-** in zW production; ~**straße** f production line.

**Fertigware** f finished product.

**fesch** [fɛʃ] (umg) adj (modisch) smart; (: hübsch) attractive.

**Fessel** ['fɛsəl] (-, -n) f fetter.

**fesseln** vt to bind; (mit F~) to fetter; (fig) to grip; **ans Bett gefesselt** (fig) confined to bed.

**fesselnd** adj gripping.

**Fest** [fɛst] (-(e)s, -e) nt (Feier) celebration; (Party) party; **man soll die ~e feiern, wie sie fallen** (Sprichwort) make hay while the sun shines.

**fest** adj firm; (Nahrung) solid; (Gehalt) regular; (Gewebe, Schuhe) strong, sturdy; (Freund(in)) steady ♦ adv (schlafen) soundly; ~ **entschlossen sein** to be absolutely determined; ~**e Kosten** (COMM) fixed costs pl.

**festangestellt** adj employed on a permanent basis.

**Festbeleuchtung** f illumination.

**festbinden** unreg vt to tie, fasten.

**festbleiben** unreg vi to stand firm.

**Festessen** nt banquet.

**festfahren** unreg vr to get stuck.

**festhalten** unreg vt to seize, hold fast; (Ereignis) to record ♦ vr: **sich** ~ **(an** +dat) to hold on (to).

**festigen** vt to strengthen.

**Festigkeit** f strength.

**fest-** zW: ~**klammern** vr: **sich** ~**klammern (an** +dat) to cling on (to); ~**klemmen** vt to wedge fast; **F~komma** nt (COMPUT) fixed point; **F~land** nt mainland; ~**legen** vt to fix ♦ vr to commit o.s.; **jdn auf etw** akk ~**legen** (~nageln) to tie sb (down) to sth; (verpflichten) to commit sb to sth.

**festlich** adj festive.

**fest-** zW: ~**liegen** unreg vi (FIN: Geld) to be tied up; ~**machen** vt to fasten; (Termin etc) to fix; ~**nageln** vt: **jdn** ~**nageln (auf** +akk) (fig: umg) to pin sb down (to); **F~nahme** (-, -n) f capture; ~**nehmen** unreg vt to capture, arrest; **F~platte** f (COMPUT) hard disk; **F~preis** m (COMM) fixed price.

**Festrede** f speech, address.

**festschnallen** vt to strap down ♦ vr to fasten one's seat belt.

**festsetzen** vt to fix, settle.

**Festspiel** nt festival.

**fest-** zW: ~**stehen** unreg vi to be certain; ~**stellbar** adj (herauszufinden) ascertainable; ~**stellen** vt to establish; (sagen) to remark; (TECH) to lock (fast); **F~stellung** f: **die F~stellung machen, daß** ... to realize that ...; (bemerken) to remark od observe that ...; **F~tag** m holiday; ~**umrissen** adj attrib clear-cut.

**Festung** f fortress.

**festverzinslich** adj fixed-interest attrib.

**Festwertspeicher** m (COMPUT) read-only memory.

**Festzelt** nt marquee.

**Fete** ['feːtə] (-, -n) f party.

**Fett** [fɛt] (-(e)s, -e) nt fat, grease; **f~** adj fat; (Essen etc) greasy; **f~arm** adj low fat; **f~en** vt to grease; ~**fleck** m grease spot od stain; **f~frei** adj fat-free; **f~gedruckt** adj bold-type; ~**gehalt** m fat content; **f~ig** adj greasy, fatty; ~**näpfchen** nt: **ins** ~**näpfchen treten** to put one's foot in it; ~**polster** nt (hum: umg): ~**polster haben** to be well-padded.

**Fetzen** ['fɛtsən] (-s, -) m scrap; ..., **daß die** ~ **fliegen** (umg) ... like mad.

**feucht** [fɔyçt] adj damp; (Luft) humid; ~**fröhlich** adj (hum) boozy.

**Feuchtigkeit** f dampness; humidity.

**Feuchtigkeitscreme** f moisturizer.

**feudal** [fɔyˈdaːl] adj (POL, HIST) feudal; (umg) plush.

**Feuer** ['fɔyər] (-s, -) nt fire; (zum Rauchen) a light; (fig: Schwung) spirit; **für jdn durchs** ~ **gehen** to go through fire and water for sb; ~ **und Flamme (für etw) sein** (umg) to be dead keen (on sth); ~ **für etw/jdn fangen** (fig) to develop a great interest in sth/sb; ~**alarm** m fire alarm; ~**eifer** m zeal; **f~fest** adj fireproof; ~**gefahr** f danger of fire; **bei** ~**gefahr** in the event of fire; **f~gefährlich** adj inflammable; ~**leiter** f fire escape ladder; ~**löscher** (-s, -) m fire extinguisher; ~**melder** (-s, -) m fire alarm.

**feuern** vt, vi (lit, fig) to fire.

**Feuer-** zW: **f~polizeilich** adj (Bestimmungen) laid down by the fire authorities; ~**probe** f acid test; **f~rot** adj fiery red.

**Feuersbrunst** f (geh) conflagration.

**Feuer-** zW: ~**schlucker** m fire-eater; ~**schutz** m (Vorbeugung) fire prevention; (MIL: Deckung) covering fire; **f~sicher** adj fireproof; ~**stein** m flint; ~**stelle** f fireplace; ~**treppe** f fire escape; ~**versicherung** f fire insurance; ~**waffe** f firearm; ~**wehr** f fire brigade; ~**wehrauto** nt fire engine; ~**werk** nt fireworks pl; ~**werkskörper** m firework; ~**zangenbowle** f red wine punch containing rum which has been flamed off; ~**zeug** nt (cigarette) lighter.

**Feuilleton** [fœjəˈtõː] (-s, -s) nt (PRESSE) feature section; (Artikel) feature (article).

**feurig** ['fɔyrɪç] *adj* fiery.
**Fiche** [fiːʃ] (-s, -s) *m od nt* (micro)fiche.
**ficht** [fɪçt] *vb siehe* **fechten**.
**Fichte** ['fɪçtə] (-, -n) *f* spruce.
**ficken** ['fɪkən] (*umg!*) *vt, vi* to fuck (*!*).
**fick(e)rig** ['fɪk(ə)rɪç] (*umg*) *adj* fidgety.
**fidel** [fi'deːl] (*umg*) *adj* jolly.
**Fidschiinseln** ['fɪdʒi|ɪnzəln] *pl* Fiji Islands.
**Fieber** ['fiːbər] (-s, -) *nt* fever, temperature;
(*Krankheit*) fever; ~ **haben** to have a
temperature; **f~haft** *adj* feverish; ~**messer**
*m* thermometer; ~**thermometer** *nt*
thermometer.
**fiel** *etc* [fiːl] *vb siehe* **fallen**.
**fies** [fiːs] (*umg*) *adj* nasty.
**Figur** [fi'guːr] (-, -en) *f* figure; (*Schach~*)
chessman, chess piece; **eine gute/**
**schlechte/traurige** ~ **abgeben** to cut a good/
poor/sorry figure.
**fiktiv** [fɪk'tiːf] *adj* fictitious.
**Filet** [fi'leː] (-s, -s) *nt* (*KOCH*) fillet; (*Rinder~*)
fillet steak; (*zum Braten*) piece of sirloin *od*
tenderloin (*US*).
**Filiale** [fili'aːlə] (-, -n) *f* (*COMM*) branch.
**Filipino** [fili'piːno] (-s, -s) *m* Filipino.
**Film** [fɪlm] (-(e)s, -e) *m* film, movie (*bes US*);
**da ist bei mir der** ~ **gerissen** (*umg*) I had a
mental blackout; ~**aufnahme** *f* shooting.
**Filmemacher(in)** *m(f)* film-maker.
**filmen** *vt, vi* to film.
**Film-** *zW:* ~**festspiele** *pl* film festival *sing*;
~**kamera** *f* cine-camera; ~**riß** (*umg*) *m*
mental blackout; ~**schauspieler(in)** *m(f)* film
*od* movie (*bes US*) actor, film *od* movie
actress; ~**verleih** *m* film distributors *pl*;
~**vorführgerät** *nt* cine-projector.
**Filter** ['fɪltər] (-s, -) *m* filter; ~**kaffee** *m* filter *od*
drip (*US*) coffee; ~**mundstück** *nt* filter tip.
**filtern** *vt* to filter.
**Filterpapier** *nt* filter paper.
**Filterzigarette** *f* tipped cigarette.
**Filz** [fɪlts] (-es, -e) *m* felt.
**filzen** *vt* (*umg*) to frisk ♦ *vi* (*Wolle*) to mat.
**Filzstift** *m* felt-tip (pen).
**Fimmel** ['fɪməl] (-s, -) (*umg*) *m*: **du hast wohl**
**einen** ~! you're crazy!
**Finale** [fi'naːlə] (-s, -(s)) *nt* finale; (*SPORT*)
final(s *pl*).
**Finanz** [fi'nants] *f* finance; **Finanzen** *pl*
finances *pl*; **das übersteigt meine** ~**en** that's
beyond my means; ~**amt** *nt* ≈ Inland
Revenue Office (*BRIT*), Internal Revenue
Office (*US*); ~**beamte(r)** *f(m)* revenue officer.
**finanziell** [finantsi'ɛl] *adj* financial.
**finanzieren** [finan'tsiːrən] *vt* to finance, to
fund.
**Finanzierung** *f* financing, funding.
**Finanz-** *zW:* ~**minister** *m* ≈ Chancellor of the
Exchequer (*BRIT*), Minister of Finance;
**f~schwach** *adj* financially weak; ~**wesen** *nt*
financial system; ~**wirtschaft** *f* public
finances *pl*.

**finden** ['fɪndən] *unreg vt* to find; (*meinen*) to
think ♦ *vr* to be (found); (*sich fassen*) to
compose o.s. ♦ *vi:* **ich finde schon allein**
**hinaus** I can see myself out; **ich finde nichts**
**dabei, wenn** ... I don't see what's wrong if
...; **das wird sich** ~ things will work out.
**Finder(in)** (-s, -) *m(f)* finder; ~**lohn** *m* reward
(for the finder).
**findig** *adj* resourceful.
**fing** *etc* [fɪŋ] *vb siehe* **fangen**.
**Finger** ['fɪŋər] (-s, -) *m* finger; **mit** ~**n auf jdn**
**zeigen** (*fig*) to look askance at sb; **das kann**
**sich jeder an den (fünf)** ~**n abzählen** (*umg*) it
sticks out a mile; **sich** *dat* **etw aus den** ~**n**
**saugen** to conjure sth up; **lange** ~ **machen**
(*umg*) to be light-fingered; ~**abdruck** *m*
fingerprint; ~**handschuh** *m* glove; ~**hut** *m*
thimble; (*BOT*) foxglove; ~**nagel** *m*
fingernail; ~**ring** *m* ring; ~**spitze** *f* fingertip;
~**spitzengefühl** *nt* sensitivity; ~**zeig**
(-(e)s, -e) *m* hint, pointer.
**fingieren** [fɪŋ'giːrən] *vt* to feign.
**fingiert** *adj* made-up, fictitious.
**Fink** ['fɪŋk] (-en, -en) *m* finch.
**Finne** ['fɪnə] (-n, -n) *m* Finn.
**Finnin** ['fɪnɪn] *f* Finn.
**finnisch** *adj* Finnish.
**Finnland** *nt* Finland.
**finster** ['fɪnstər] *adj* dark, gloomy; (*verdächtig*)
dubious; (*verdrossen*) grim; (*Gedanke*) dark;
**jdn** ~ **ansehen** to give sb a black look; **F~nis**
(-) *f* darkness, gloom.
**Finte** ['fɪntə] (-, -n) *f* feint, trick.
**Firlefanz** ['fɪrləfants] (*umg*) *m* (*Kram*)
frippery; (*Albernheit*): **mach keinen** ~ don't
clown around.
**firm** [fɪrm] *adj* well-up.
**Firma** (-, -men) *f* firm; **die** ~ **dankt** (*hum*)
much obliged (to you).
**Firmen-** *zW:* ~**inhaber** *m* proprietor (*of firm*);
~**register** *nt* register of companies; ~**schild**
*nt* (shop) sign; ~**übernahme** *f* takeover;
~**wagen** *m* company car; ~**zeichen** *nt*
trademark.
**Firmung** *f* (*REL*) confirmation.
**Firnis** ['fɪrnɪs] (-ses, -se) *m* varnish.
**Fis** [fɪs] (-, -) *nt* (*MUS*) F sharp.
**Fisch** [fɪʃ] (-(e)s, -e) *m* fish; **Fische** *pl* (*ASTROL*)
Pisces *sing*; **das sind kleine** ~**e** (*fig: umg*)
that's child's play; ~**bestand** *m* fish
population.
**fischen** *vt, vi* to fish.
**Fischer** (-s, -) *m* fisherman.
**Fischerei** [fɪʃə'rai] *f* fishing, fishery.
**Fisch-** *zW:* ~**fang** *m* fishing; ~**geschäft** *nt*
fishmonger's (shop); ~**gräte** *f* fishbone;
~**gründe** *pl* fishing grounds *pl*, fisheries *pl*;
~**stäbchen** *nt* fish finger (*BRIT*), fish stick
(*US*); ~**zucht** *f* fish-farming; ~**zug** *m* catch
of fish.
**Fisimatenten** [fizima'tɛntən] (*umg*) *pl*
(*Ausflüchte*) excuses *pl*; (*Umstände*) fuss *sing*.

**Fiskus** ['fɪskʊs] m (*fig: Staatskasse*) Treasury.

**fit** [fɪt] *adj* fit.

**Fittich** ['fɪtɪç] (**-(e)s, -e**) m (*liter*): **jdn unter seine ~e nehmen** (*hum*) to take sb under one's wing.

**fix** [fɪks] *adj* (*flink*) quick; (*Person*) alert, smart; **~e Idee** obsession, idée fixe; **~ und fertig** finished; (*erschöpft*) done in; **jdn ~ und fertig machen** (*nervös machen*) to drive sb mad.

**fixen** (*umg*) *vi* (*Drogen spritzen*) to fix.

**fixieren** [fɪ'ksiːrən] *vt* to fix; (*anstarren*) to stare at; **er ist zu stark auf seine Mutter fixiert** (*PSYCH*) he has a mother fixation.

**Fixkosten** *pl* (*COMM*) fixed costs *pl*.

**FKK** *abk* = **Freikörperkultur**.

**flach** [flax] *adj* flat; (*Gefäß*) shallow; **auf dem ~en Land** in the middle of the country.

**Fläche** ['flɛçə] (**-, -n**) f area; (*Ober~*) surface.

**Flächeninhalt** m surface area.

**Flach-** *zW:* **f~fallen** *unreg* (*umg*) *vi* to fall through; **~heit** f flatness; shallowness; **~land** *nt* lowland; **f~liegen** *unreg* (*umg*) *vi* to be laid up; **~mann** (**-(e)s,** *pl* **-männer**) (*umg*) m hip flask.

**flachsen** ['flaksən] (*umg*) *vi* to kid around.

**flackern** ['flakərn] *vi* to flare, flicker.

**Fladen** ['flaːdən] (**-s, -**) m (*KOCH*) round flat dough-cake; (*umg: Kuh~*) cowpat.

**Flagge** ['flagə] (**-, -n**) f flag; **~ zeigen** (*fig*) to nail one's colours to the mast.

**flaggen** *vi* to fly flags *od* a flag.

**flagrant** [fla'grant] *adj* flagrant; **in ~i** red-handed.

**Flak** [flak] (**-s, -**) f (= *Flug(zeug)abwehrkanone*) anti-aircraft gun; (*Einheit*) anti-aircraft unit.

**flambieren** [flam'biːrən] *vt* (*KOCH*) to flambé.

**Flame** ['flaːmə] (**-n, -n**) m Fleming.

**Flämin** ['flɛːmɪn] f Fleming.

**flämisch** ['flɛːmɪʃ] *adj* Flemish.

**Flamme** ['flamə] (**-, -n**) f flame; **in ~n stehen/aufgehen** to be in/go up in flames.

**Flandern** ['flandərn] *nt* Flanders *sing*.

**Flanell** [fla'nɛl] (**-s, -e**) m flannel.

**Flanke** ['flaŋkə] (**-, -n**) f flank; (*SPORT: Seite*) wing.

**Flasche** ['flaʃə] (**-, -n**) f bottle; (*umg: Versager*) wash-out; **zur ~ greifen** (*fig*) to hit the bottle.

**Flaschen-** *zW:* **~bier** *nt* bottled beer; **~öffner** m bottle opener; **~wein** m bottled wine; **~zug** m pulley.

**flatterhaft** *adj* flighty, fickle.

**flattern** ['flatərn] *vi* to flutter.

**flau** [flau] *adj* (*Brise, COMM*) slack; **jdm ist ~ (im Magen)** sb feels queasy.

**Flaum** [flaum] (**-(e)s**) m (*Feder*) down.

**flauschig** ['flauʃɪç] *adj* fluffy.

**Flausen** ['flauzən] *pl* silly ideas *pl*; (*Ausflüchte*) weak excuses *pl*.

**Flaute** ['flautə] (**-, -n**) f calm; (*COMM*) recession.

**Flechte** ['flɛçtə] (**-, -n**) f (*MED*) dry scab; (*BOT*) lichen.

**flechten** *unreg* *vt* to plait; (*Kranz*) to twine.

**Fleck** [flɛk] (**-(e)s, -e**) m (*Schmutz~*) stain; (*Farb~*) patch; (*Stelle*) spot; **nicht vom ~ kommen** (*lit, fig*) not to get any further; **sich nicht vom ~ rühren** not to budge; **vom ~ weg** straight away.

**Fleckchen** *nt*: **ein schönes ~ (Erde)** a lovely little spot.

**Flecken** (**-s, -**) m = **Fleck**; **f~los** *adj* spotless; **~mittel** *nt* stain remover; **~wasser** *nt* stain remover.

**fleckig** *adj* marked; (*schmutzig*) stained.

**Fledermaus** ['fleːdərmaus] f bat.

**Flegel** ['fleːgəl] (**-s, -**) m flail; (*Person*) lout; **f~haft** *adj* loutish, unmannerly; **~jahre** *pl* adolescence *sing*.

**flegeln** *vr* to loll, sprawl.

**flehen** ['fleːən] *vi* (*geh*) to implore.

**flehentlich** *adj* imploring.

**Fleisch** [flaɪʃ] (**-(e)s**) *nt* flesh; (*Essen*) meat; **sich** *dat od akk* **ins eigene ~ schneiden** to cut off one's nose to spite one's face (*Sprichwort*); **es ist mir in ~ und Blut übergegangen** it has become second nature to me; **~brühe** f meat stock.

**Fleischer** (**-s, -**) m butcher.

**Fleischerei** [flaɪʃə'raɪ] f butcher's (shop).

**fleischig** *adj* fleshy.

**Fleisch-** *zW:* **~käse** m meat loaf; **f~lich** *adj* carnal; **~pastete** f meat pie; **~salat** m diced meat salad with mayonnaise; **~vergiftung** f food poisoning (*from meat*); **~wolf** m mincer; **~wunde** f flesh wound; **~wurst** f pork sausage.

**Fleiß** [flaɪs] (**-es**) m diligence, industry; **ohne ~ kein Preis** (*Sprichwort*) success never comes easily.

**fleißig** *adj* diligent, industrious; **~ studieren/arbeiten** to study/work hard.

**flektieren** [flɛk'tiːrən] *vt* to inflect.

**flennen** ['flɛnən] (*umg*) *vi* to cry, blubber.

**fletschen** ['flɛtʃən] *vt* (*Zähne*) to show.

**Fleurop ®** ['flɔʏrɔp] f ≈ Interflora ®.

**flexibel** [flɛ'ksiːbəl] *adj* flexible.

**Flexibilität** [flɛksibili'tɛːt] f flexibility.

**flicht** [flɪçt] *vb siehe* **flechten**.

**Flicken** ['flɪkən] (**-s, -**) m patch.

**flicken** *vt* to mend.

**Flickschusterei** ['flɪkʃuːstəraɪ] f: **das ist ~** that's a patch-up job.

**Flieder** ['fliːdər] (**-s, -**) m lilac.

**Fliege** ['fliːgə] (**-, -n**) f fly; (*Schlips*) bow tie; **zwei ~n mit einer Klappe schlagen** (*Sprichwort*) to kill two birds with one stone; **ihn stört die ~ an der Wand** every little thing irritates him.

**fliegen** *unreg* *vt, vi* to fly; **auf jdn/etw ~** (*umg*) to be mad about sb/sth; **aus der Kurve ~** to skid off the bend; **aus der Firma ~** (*umg*) to get the sack.

**fliegend** *adj attrib* flying; **~e Hitze** hot flushes

*pl.*
**Fliegengewicht** *nt* (*SPORT, fig*) flyweight.
**Fliegenklatsche** ['fliːɡənklatʃə] *f* fly-swat.
**Fliegenpilz** *m* fly agaric.
**Flieger** (**-s, -**) *m* flier, airman; **~alarm** *m* air-raid warning.
**fliehen** ['fliːən] *unreg vi* to flee.
**Fliehkraft** ['fliːkraft] *f* centrifugal force.
**Fliese** ['fliːzə] (**-, -n**) *f* tile.
**Fließband** ['fliːsbant] *nt* assembly *od* production line; **am ~ arbeiten** to work on the assembly *od* production line; **~arbeit** *f* production-line work; **~produktion** *f* assembly-line production.
**fließen** *unreg vi* to flow.
**fließend** *adj* flowing; (*Rede, Deutsch*) fluent; (*Übergang*) smooth.
**Fließ-** *zW:* **~heck** *nt* fastback; **~komma** *nt* (*COMPUT*) ≈ floating point; **~papier** *nt* blotting paper (*BRIT*), fleece paper (*US*).
**Flimmerkasten** (*umg*) *m* (*Fernsehen*) box.
**Flimmerkiste** (*umg*) *f* (*Fernsehen*) box.
**flimmern** ['flɪmərn] *vi* to glimmer; **es flimmert mir vor den Augen** my head's swimming.
**flink** [flɪŋk] *adj* nimble, lively; **mit etw ~ bei der Hand sein** to be quick (off the mark) with sth; **F~heit** *f* nimbleness, liveliness.
**Flinte** ['flɪntə] (**-, -n**) *f* shotgun; **die ~ ins Korn werfen** to throw in the sponge.
**Flirt** [flœrt] (**-s, -s**) *m* flirtation; **einen ~ (mit jdm) haben** flirt (with sb).
**flirten** ['flɪrtən] *vi* to flirt.
**Flittchen** (*pej: umg*) *nt* floozy.
**Flitter** (**-s, -**) *m* (**~schmuck**) sequins *pl.*
**Flitterwochen** *pl* honeymoon *sing.*
**flitzen** ['flɪtsən] *vi* to flit.
**Flitzer** (**-s, -**) (*umg*) *m* (*Auto*) sporty car.
**floaten** ['floːtən] *vt, vi* (*FIN*) to float.
**flocht** *etc* [flɔxt] *vb siehe* **flechten**.
**Flocke** ['flɔkə] (**-, -n**) *f* flake.
**flockig** *adj* flaky.
**flog** *etc* [floːk] *vb siehe* **fliegen**.
**Floh** [floː] (**-(e)s, ꞋꞋe**) *m* flea; **jdm einen ~ ins Ohr setzen** (*umg*) to put an idea into sb's head.
**floh** *etc vb siehe* **fliehen**.
**Flohmarkt** *m* flea market.
**Flora** ['floːra] (**-, -ren**) *f* flora.
**Florenz** [floˈrɛnts] *nt* Florence.
**florieren** [floˈriːrən] *vi* to flourish.
**Florist(in)** *m(f)* florist.
**Floskel** ['flɔskəl] (**-, -n**) *f* set phrase; **f~haft** *adj* cliché-ridden, stereotyped.
**Floß** [floːs] (**-es, ꞋꞋe**) *nt* raft.
**floß** *etc* [flɔs] *vb siehe* **fließen**.
**Flosse** ['flɔsə] (**-, -n**) *f* fin; (*Taucher~*) flipper; (*umg: Hand*) paw.
**Flöte** ['fløːtə] (**-, -n**) *f* flute; (*Block~*) recorder.
**flötengehen** ['fløːtənɡeːən] (*umg*) *vi* to go for a burton.
**Flötist(in)** [fløˈtɪst(ɪn)] *m(f)* flautist, flutist (*bes US*).

**flott** [flɔt] *adj* lively; (*elegant*) smart; (*NAUT*) afloat.
**Flotte** (**-, -n**) *f* fleet.
**Flottenstützpunkt** *m* naval base.
**flottmachen** *vt* (*Schiff*) to float off; (*Auto, Fahrrad etc*) to put back on the road.
**Flöz** [fløːts] (**-es, -e**) *nt* layer, seam.
**Fluch** [fluːx] (**-(e)s, ꞋꞋe**) *m* curse; **f~en** *vi* to curse, swear.
**Flucht** [flʊxt] (**-, -en**) *f* flight; (*Fenster~*) row; (*Reihe*) range; (*Zimmer~*) suite; (*geglückt*) flight, escape; **jdn/etw in die ~ schlagen** to put sb/sth to flight.
**fluchtartig** *adj* hasty.
**flüchten** ['flʏçtən] *vi* to flee ♦ *vr* to take refuge.
**Fluchthilfe** *f:* **~ leisten** to aid an escape.
**flüchtig** *adj* fugitive; (*CHEM*) volatile; (*oberflächlich*) cursory; (*eilig*) fleeting; **~er Speicher** (*COMPUT*) volatile memory; **jdn ~ kennen** to have met sb briefly; **F~keit** *f* transitoriness; volatility; cursoriness; **F~keitsfehler** *m* careless slip.
**Flüchtling** *m* refugee.
**Flüchtlingslager** *nt* refugee camp.
**Flucht-** *zW:* **~versuch** *m* escape attempt; **~weg** *m* escape route.
**Flug** [fluːk] (**-(e)s, ꞋꞋe**) *m* flight; **im ~** airborne, in flight; **wie im ~** (*e*) (*fig*) in a flash; **~abwehr** *f* anti-aircraft defence; **~bahn** *f* flight path; (*Kreisbahn*) orbit; **~begleiter(in)** *m(f)* (*AVIAT*) flight attendant; **~blatt** *nt* pamphlet.
**Flügel** ['flyːɡəl] (**-s, -**) *m* wing; (*MUS*) grand piano; **~tür** *f* double door.
**flugfähig** *adj* able to fly; (*Flugzeug: in Ordnung*) airworthy.
**Fluggast** *m* airline passenger.
**flügge** ['flʏɡə] *adj* (fully-)fledged; **~ werden** (*lit*) to be able to fly; (*fig*) to leave the nest.
**Flug-** *zW:* **~geschwindigkeit** *f* flying *od* air speed; **~gesellschaft** *f* airline (company); **~hafen** *m* airport; **~höhe** *f* altitude (of flight); **~lotse** *m* air traffic *od* flight controller; **~plan** *m* flight schedule; **~platz** *m* airport; (*klein*) airfield; **~reise** *f* flight.
**flugs** [flʊks] *adv* speedily.
**Flug-** *zW:* **~sand** *m* drifting sand; **~schein** *m* pilot's licence (*BRIT*) *od* license (*US*); **~schreiber** *m* flight recorder; **~schrift** *f* pamphlet; **~steig** *m* gate; **~strecke** *f* air route; **~verkehr** *m* air traffic; **~wesen** *nt* aviation.
**Flugzeug** (**-(e)s, -e**) *nt* plane, aeroplane (*BRIT*), airplane (*US*); **~entführung** *f* hijacking of a plane; **~halle** *f* hangar; **~träger** *m* aircraft carrier.
**fluktuieren** [flʊktuˈiːrən] *vi* to fluctuate.
**Flunder** ['flʊndər] (**-, -n**) *f* flounder.
**flunkern** ['flʊŋkərn] *vi* to fib, tell stories.
**Fluor** ['fluːɔr] (**-s**) *nt* fluorine.
**Flur¹** [fluːr] (**-(e)s, -e**) *m* hall; (*Treppen~*) staircase.

**Flur²** [flu:r] (-, -en) f (geh) open fields pl; **allein auf weiter ~ stehen** (fig) to be out on a limb.

**Fluß** [flʊs] (-sses, ⁼sse) m river; (Fließen) flow; **im ~ sein** (fig) to be in a state of flux; **etw in ~** akk **bringen** to get sth moving; **f~ab(wärts)** adv downstream; **f~auf(wärts)** adv upstream; **~diagramm** nt flow chart.

**flüssig** ['flʏsɪç] adj liquid; (Stil) flowing; **~es Vermögen** (COMM) liquid assets pl; **F~keit** f liquid; (Zustand) liquidity; **~machen** vt (Geld) to make available.

**Flußmündung** f estuary.

**Flußpferd** nt hippopotamus.

**flüstern** ['flʏstərn] vt, vi to whisper.

**Flüsterpropaganda** f whispering campaign.

**Flut** [flu:t] (-, -en) f (lit, fig) flood; (Gezeiten) high tide; **f~en** vi to flood; **~licht** nt floodlight.

**flutschen** ['flʊtʃən] (umg) vi (rutschen) to slide; (funktionieren) to go well.

**Flutwelle** f tidal wave.

**fl.W.** abk (= fließendes Wasser) running water.

**focht** etc [fɔxt] vb siehe **fechten**.

**föderativ** [fødera'ti:f] adj federal.

**Fohlen** ['fo:lən] (-s, -) nt foal.

**Föhn** [fø:n] (-(e)s, -e) m foehn, warm dry alpine wind.

**Föhre** ['fø:rə] (-, -n) f Scots pine.

**Folge** ['fɔlgə] (-, -n) f series, sequence; (Fortsetzung) instalment (BRIT), installment (US); (TV, RUNDF) episode; (Auswirkung) result; **in rascher ~** in quick succession; **etw zur ~ haben** to result in sth; **~n haben** to have consequences; **einer Sache** dat **~ leisten** to comply with sth; **~erscheinung** f result, consequence.

**folgen** vi +dat to follow ♦ vi (gehorchen) to obey; **jdm ~ können** (fig) to follow od understand sb; **daraus folgt, daß ...** it follows from this that ...

**folgend** adj following; **im ~en** in the following; (schriftlich) below.

**folgendermaßen** ['fɔlgəndər'ma:sən] adv as follows, in the following way.

**folgenreich** adj momentous.

**folgenschwer** adj momentous.

**folgerichtig** adj logical.

**folgern** vt: **~ (aus)** to conclude (from).

**Folgerung** f conclusion.

**folgewidrig** adj illogical.

**folglich** ['fɔlklɪç] adv consequently.

**folgsam** ['fɔlkza:m] adj obedient.

**Folie** ['fo:liə] (-, -n) f foil.

**Folienschweißgerät** nt shrink-wrap machine.

**Folklore** ['fɔlklo:ər] (-) f folklore.

**Folter** ['fɔltər] (-, -n) f torture; (Gerät) rack; **jdn auf die ~ spannen** (fig) to keep sb on tenterhooks.

**foltern** vt to torture.

**Fön** ® [fø:n] (-(e)s, -e) m hair dryer.

**Fonds** [fõ:] (-, -) m (lit, fig) fund; (FIN: Schuldverschreibung) government bond.

**fönen** vt to blow-dry.

**Fontäne** [fɔn'tɛ:nə] (-, -n) f fountain.

**foppen** ['fɔpən] vt to tease.

**forcieren** [fɔr'si:rən] vt to push; (Tempo) to force; (Konsum, Produktion) to push od force up.

**Förderband** ['fœrdərbant] nt conveyor belt.

**Förderer** (-s, -) m patron.

**Fördergebiet** nt development area.

**Förderin** f patroness.

**Förderkorb** m pit cage.

**Förderleistung** f (MIN) output.

**förderlich** adj beneficial.

**fordern** ['fɔrdərn] vt to demand; (fig: kosten, Opfer) to claim; (: heraus~) to challenge.

**fördern** ['fœrdərn] vt to promote; (unterstützen) to help; (Kohle) to extract; (finanziell: Projekt) to sponsor; (jds Talent, Neigung) to encourage, foster.

**Förderplattform** f production platform.

**Förderstufe** f (SCH) first stage of secondary school where abilities are judged.

**Förderturm** m (MIN) winding tower; (auf Bohrstelle) derrick.

**Forderung** ['fɔrdərʊŋ] f demand.

**Förderung** ['fœrdərʊŋ] f promotion; help; extraction.

**Forelle** [fo'rɛlə] f trout.

**Form** [fɔrm] (-, -en) f shape; (Gestaltung) form; (Guß~) mould; (Back~) baking tin; **in ~ von** in the shape of; **in ~ sein** to be in good form od shape; **die ~ wahren** to observe the proprieties; **in aller ~** formally.

**formal** [fɔr'ma:l] adj formal; (Besitzer, Grund) technical.

**formalisieren** [fɔrmali'zi:rən] vt to formalize.

**Formalität** [fɔrmali'tɛ:t] f formality; **alle ~en erledigen** to go through all the formalities.

**Format** [fɔr'ma:t] (-(e)s, -e) nt format; (fig) quality.

**formatieren** [fɔrma'ti:rən] vt (Text, Diskette) to format.

**Formation** [fɔrmatsi'o:n] f formation.

**formbar** adj malleable.

**Formblatt** nt form.

**Formel** (-, -n) f formula; (von Eid etc) wording; (Floskel) set phrase; **f~haft** adj (Sprache, Stil) stereotyped.

**formell** [fɔr'mɛl] adj formal.

**formen** vt to form, shape.

**Formfehler** m faux pas, gaffe; (JUR) irregularity.

**formieren** [fɔr'mi:rən] vt to form ♦ vr to form up.

**förmlich** ['fœrmlɪç] adj formal; (umg) real; **F~keit** f formality.

**formlos** adj shapeless; (Benehmen etc) informal; (Antrag) unaccompanied by a form od any forms.

**Formsache** f formality.

**Formular** [fɔrmu'laːr] (**-s, -e**) *nt* form.
**formulieren** [fɔrmu'liːrən] *vt* to formulate.
**Formulierung** *f* wording.
**formvollendet** *adj* perfect; (*Vase etc*)
perfectly formed.
**forsch** [fɔrʃ] *adj* energetic, vigorous.
**forschen** [fɔrʃən] *vi* to search;
(*wissenschaftlich*) to (do) research; ~ **nach** to
search for.
**forschend** *adj* searching.
**Forscher** (**-s, -**) *m* research scientist; (*Natur~*)
explorer.
**Forschung** ['fɔrʃʊŋ] *f* research; ~ **und Lehre**
research and teaching; ~ **und Entwicklung**
research and development.
**Forschungsreise** *f* scientific expedition.
**Forst** [fɔrst] (**-(e)s, -e**) *m* forest; ~**arbeiter** *m*
forestry worker.
**Förster** ['fœrstər] (**-s, -**) *m* forester; (*für Wild*)
gamekeeper.
**Forstwesen** *nt* forestry.
**Forstwirtschaft** *f* forestry.
**fort** [fɔrt] *adv* away; (*verschwunden*) gone;
(*vorwärts*) on; **und so** ~ and so on; **in einem**
~ incessantly; ~**bestehen** *unreg vi* to
continue to exist; ~**bewegen** *vt, vr* to move
away; ~**bilden** *vr* to continue one's
education; **F~bildung** *f* further education;
~**bleiben** *unreg vi* to stay away; ~**bringen**
*unreg vt* to take away; **F~dauer** *f*
continuance; ~**dauernd** *adj* continuing; (*in
der Vergangenheit*) continued ♦ *adv*
constantly, continuously; ~**fahren** *unreg vi* to
depart; (*~setzen*) to go on, continue;
~**führen** *vt* to continue, carry on; **F~gang** *m*
(*Verlauf*) progress; (*Weggang*): **F~gang (aus)**
departure (from); ~**gehen** *unreg vi* to go
away; ~**geschritten** *adj* advanced; ~**kommen**
*unreg vi* to get on; (*wegkommen*) to get away;
~**können** *unreg vi* to be able to get away;
~**lassen** *vt* (*auslassen*) to leave out, omit;
(*weggehen lassen*): **jdn** ~**lassen** to let sb go;
~**laufend** *adj*: ~**laufend numeriert**
consecutively numbered; ~**müssen** *unreg vi*
to have to go; ~**pflanzen** *vr* to reproduce;
**F~pflanzung** *f* reproduction.
**FORTRAN** ['fɔrtran] *nt* FORTRAN.
**Forts.** *abk* = **Fortsetzung**.
**fortschaffen** *vt* to remove.
**fortschreiten** *unreg vi* to advance.
**Fortschritt** ['fɔrtʃrɪt] *m* advance; ~**e machen**
to make progress; **dem** ~ **dienen** to further
progress; **f~lich** *adj* progressive.
**fortschrittsgläubig** *adj* believing in
progress.
**fort-** *zW*: ~**setzen** *vt* to continue; **F~setzung** *f*
continuation; (*folgender Teil*) instalment
(*BRIT*), installment (*US*); **F~setzung folgt** to
be continued; **F~setzungsroman** *m*
serialized novel; ~**während** *adj* incessant,
continual; ~**wirken** *vi* to continue to have an
effect; ~**ziehen** *unreg vt* to pull away ♦ *vi* to

move on; (*umziehen*) to move away.
**Foto** ['foːto] (**-s, -s**) *nt* photo(graph); **ein**
~ **machen** to take a photo(graph); ~**album**
*nt* photograph album; ~**apparat** *m* camera;
~**graf(in)** (**-en, -en**) *m(f)* photographer;
~**grafie** *f* photography; (*Bild*) photograph;
**f~grafieren** *vt* to photograph ♦ *vi* to take
photographs; ~**kopie** *f* photocopy;
**f~kopieren** *vt* to photocopy; ~**kopierer** *m*
photocopier; ~**kopiergerät** *nt* photocopier.
**Foul** [faʊl] (**-s, -s**) *nt* foul.
**Foyer** [foa'jeː] (**-s, -s**) *nt* foyer; (*in Hotel*) lobby,
foyer.
**FPÖ** (**-**) *f* *abk* (= *Freiheitliche Partei Österreichs*)
Austrian Freedom Party.
**Fr.** *abk* (= *Frau*) Mrs, Ms.
**Fracht** [fraxt] (**-, -en**) *f* freight; (*NAUT*) cargo;
(*Preis*) carriage; ~ **zahlt Empfänger** (*COMM*)
carriage forward; ~**brief** *m* consignment
note, waybill.
**Frachter** (**-s, -**) *m* freighter.
**Fracht-** *zW*: **f~frei** *adj* (*COMM*) carriage paid
*od* free; ~**gut** *nt* freight; ~**kosten** *pl*
(*COMM*) freight charges *pl*.
**Frack** [frak] (**-(e)s, ̈-e**) *m* tails *pl*, tail coat.
**Frage** ['fraːgə] (**-, -n**) *f* question; **etw in**
~ **stellen** to question sth; **jdm eine** ~ **stellen**
to ask sb a question, put a question to sb;
**das ist gar keine** ~, **das steht außer** ~
there's no question about it; **in** ~ **kommend**
possible; (*Bewerber*) worth considering;
**nicht in** ~ **kommen** to be out of the
question; ~**bogen** *m* questionnaire.
**fragen** *vt, vi* to ask ♦ *vr* to wonder; **nach**
**Arbeit/Post** ~ to ask whether there is/was
any work/mail; **da fragst du mich zuviel**
(*umg*) I really couldn't say; **nach** *od* **wegen**
(*umg*) **jdm** ~ to ask for sb; (*nach jds Befinden*)
to ask after sb; **ohne lange zu** ~ without
asking a lot of questions.
**Fragerei** [fraːgə'raɪ] *f* questions *pl*.
**Fragestunde** *f* (*PARL*) question time.
**Fragezeichen** *nt* question mark.
**fraglich** *adj* questionable, doubtful;
(*betreffend*) in question.
**fraglos** *adv* unquestionably.
**Fragment** [fra'gmɛnt] *nt* fragment.
**fragmentarisch** [fragmɛn'taːrɪʃ] *adj*
fragmentary.
**fragwürdig** ['fraːkvʏrdɪç] *adj* questionable,
dubious.
**Fraktion** [fraktsi'oːn] *f* parliamentary party.
**Fraktionsvorsitzende(r)** *f(m)* (*POL*) party
whip.
**Fraktionszwang** *m* requirement to obey the
party whip.
**frank** [fraŋk] *adj* frank, candid.
**Franken** [1] ['fraŋkən] *nt* Franconia.
**Franken** [2] ['fraŋkən] (**-, -**) *m*: (*Schweizer*) ~
(Swiss) Franc.
**Frankfurt** ['fraŋkfʊrt] (**-s**) *nt* Frankfurt.
**Frankfurter(in)** *m(f)* native of Frankfurt ♦ *adj*

Frankfurt; ~ **Würstchen** pl frankfurters.
**frankieren** [fraŋ'kiːrən] vt to stamp, frank.
**Frankiermaschine** f franking machine.
**fränkisch** ['fraŋkɪʃ] adj Franconian.
**franko** adv carriage paid; (POST) post-paid.
**Frankreich** ['fraŋkraɪç] (-s) nt France.
**Franse** ['franzə] (-, -n) f fringe.
**fransen** vi to fray.
**franz.** abk = französisch.
**Franzbranntwein** m alcoholic liniment.
**Franzose** [fran'tsoːzə] (-n, -n) m Frenchman;
French boy.
**Französin** [fran'tsøːzɪn] f Frenchwoman;
French girl.
**französisch** adj French; ~**es Bett** double bed.
**Fräse** ['frɛːzə] (-, -n) f (Werkzeug) milling
cutter; (für Holz) moulding cutter.
**Fraß** (-es, -e) (pej: umg) m (Essen) muck.
**fraß** etc [fraːs] vb siehe **fressen**.
**Fratze** ['fratsə] (-, -n) f grimace; **eine**
~ **schneiden** to pull od make a face.
**Frau** [frau] (-, -en) f woman; (Ehe~) wife;
(Anrede) Mrs, Ms; ~ **Doktor** Doctor.
**Frauen-** zW: ~**arzt** m gynaecologist (BRIT),
gynecologist (US); ~**bewegung** f feminist
movement; **f~feindlich** adj anti-women,
misogynous; ~**haus** nt women's refuge;
~**quote** f recommended proportion of
women (employed); ~**rechtlerin** f feminist;
~**zentrum** nt women's advice centre;
~**zimmer** (pej) nt female, broad (US).
**Fräulein** ['frɔylaɪn] nt young lady; (Anrede)
Miss; (Verkäuferin) assistant (BRIT), sales
clerk (US); (Kellnerin) waitress.
**fraulich** ['fraulɪç] adj womanly.
**frech** [frɛç] adj cheeky, impudent; ~ **wie**
**Oskar sein** (umg) to be a little monkey;
**F~dachs** m cheeky monkey; **F~heit** f cheek,
impudence; **sich** dat (einige) **F~heiten**
**erlauben** to be a bit cheeky (bes BRIT) od
fresh (bes US).
**Fregatte** [fre'gatə] (-, -n) f frigate.
**frei** [fraɪ] adj free; (Stelle) vacant; (Mitarbeiter)
freelance; (Geld) available; (unbekleidet)
bare; **aus** ~**en Stücken** od ~**em Willen** of
one's own free will; ~ **nach** ... based on ...;
**für etw** ~**e Fahrt geben** (fig) to give sth the
go-ahead; **der Film ist** ~ **ab 16 (Jahren)** the
film may be seen by people of 16 years (of
age) and over; **unter** ~**em Himmel** in the
open (air); **morgen/Mittwoch ist** ~
tomorrow/Wednesday is a holiday; „**Zimmer**
~" "vacancies"; **auf** ~**er Strecke** (EISENB)
between stations; (AUT) on the road; **sich**
~ **machen** (beim Arzt) to take one's clothes
off, strip; ~**er Wettbewerb** fair/open
competition; ~ **Haus** (COMM) carriage paid;
~ **Schiff** (COMM) free on board; ~**e**
**Marktwirtschaft** free market economy; **sich**
dat **einen Tag** ~ **nehmen** to take a day off;
**von etw** ~ **sein** to be free of sth; **im F~en** in
the open air; ~ **sprechen** to talk without

notes; **F~bad** nt open-air swimming pool;
~**bekommen** unreg vt: **jdn/einen Tag**
~**bekommen** to get sb freed/get a day off;
~**beruflich** adj self-employed; **F~betrag** m
tax allowance.
**Freier** (-s, -) m suitor.
**Frei-** zW: ~**exemplar** nt free copy; **f~geben**
unreg vt: **etw zum Verkauf f~geben** to allow
sth to be sold on the open market; **f~gebig**
adj generous; ~**gebigkeit** f generosity;
~**hafen** m free port; **f~halten** unreg vt to keep
free; (bezahlen) to pay for; ~**handel** m free
trade; ~**handelszone** f free trade area;
**f~händig** adv (fahren) with no hands.
**Freiheit** f freedom; **sich** dat **die** ~ **nehmen,**
**etw zu tun** to take the liberty of doing sth;
**f~lich** adj liberal; (Verfassung) based on the
principle of liberty; (Demokratie) free.
**Freiheits-** zW: ~**beraubung** f (JUR) wrongful
deprivation of personal liberty; ~**drang** m
urge/desire for freedom; ~**kampf** m fight
for freedom; ~**kämpfer(in)** m(f) freedom
fighter; ~**rechte** pl civil liberties pl; ~**strafe**
f prison sentence.
**frei-** zW: ~**heraus** adv frankly; **F~karte** f free
ticket; ~**kaufen** vt: **jdn/sich** ~**kaufen** to buy
sb's/one's freedom; ~**kommen** unreg vi to get
free; **F~körperkultur** f nudism; ~**lassen**
unreg vt to (set) free; **F~lauf** m freewheeling;
~**laufend** adj (Hühner) free-range; ~**legen** vt
to expose; ~**lich** adv certainly, admittedly;
**ja** ~**lich!** yes of course; **F~lichtbühne** f
open-air theatre; ~**machen** vt (POST) to
frank ♦ vr to arrange to be free; **Tage**
~**machen** to take days off; **F~maurer** m
Mason, Freemason.
**freimütig** ['fraɪmyːtɪç] adj frank, honest.
**Frei-** zW: ~**raum** m: ~**raum (zu)** (fig) freedom
(for); **f~schaffend** adj attrib freelance;
~**schärler** (-s, -) m guerrilla; **f~schwimmen**
vr (fig) to learn to stand on one's own two
feet; **f~setzen** vt (Energien) to release;
**f~sinnig** adj liberal; **f~sprechen** unreg vt:
**f~sprechen (von)** to acquit (of); ~**spruch** m
acquittal; **f~stehen** unreg vi: **es steht dir f~,**
**das zu tun** you are free to do so; **das steht**
**Ihnen völlig f~** that is completely up to you;
**f~stellen** vt: **jdm etw f~stellen** to leave sth
(up) to sb; ~**stoß** m free kick; ~**stunde** f
free hour; (SCH) free period.
**Freitag** m Friday; siehe auch **Dienstag**.
**freitags** adv on Fridays.
**Frei-** zW: ~**tod** m suicide; ~**übungen** pl
(physical) exercises pl; ~**umschlag** m
reply-paid envelope; ~**wild** nt (fig) fair
game; **f~willig** adj voluntary; ~**willige(r)**
f(m) volunteer; ~**zeichen** nt (TEL) ringing
tone; ~**zeit** f spare od free time;
~**zeitgestaltung** f organization of one's
leisure time; **f~zügig** adj liberal, broad-
minded; (mit Geld) generous.
**fremd** [frɛmt] adj (unvertraut) strange;

(*ausländisch*) foreign; (*nicht eigen*) someone else's; **etw ist jdm ~** sth is foreign to sb; **ich bin hier ~** I'm a stranger here; **sich ~ fühlen** to feel like a stranger; **~artig** *adj* strange.

**Fremde** (-) *f* (*liter*): **die ~** foreign parts *pl*.

**Fremde(r)** *f(m)* stranger; (*Ausländer*) foreigner.

**Fremden-** *zW:* **~führer** *m* (tourist) guide; (*Buch*) guide (book); **~legion** *f* foreign legion; **~verkehr** *m* tourism; **~zimmer** *nt* guest room.

**fremd-** *zW:* **~gehen** *unreg* (*umg*) *vi* to be unfaithful; **F~kapital** *nt* loan capital; **F~körper** *m* foreign body; **~ländisch** *adj* foreign; **F~ling** *m* stranger; **F~sprache** *f* foreign language; **F~sprachenkorrespondentin** *f* bilingual secretary; **~sprachig** *adj attrib* foreign-language; **F~wort** *nt* foreign word.

**frenetisch** [fre'neːtɪʃ] *adj* frenetic.

**Frequenz** [fre'kvɛnts] *f* (*RUNDF*) frequency.

**Fresse** (-, -n) (*umg!*) *f* (*Mund*) gob; (*Gesicht*) mug.

**fressen** ['frɛsən] *unreg vt, vi* to eat ♦ *vr:* **sich voll** *od* **satt ~** to gorge o.s.; **einen Narren an jdm/etw gefressen haben** to dote on sb/sth.

**Freude** ['frɔydə] (-, -n) *f* joy, delight; **~ an etw** *dat* **haben** to get *od* derive pleasure from sth; **jdm eine ~ machen** *od* **bereiten** to make sb happy.

**Freudenhaus** *nt* (*veraltet*) house of ill repute.

**Freudentanz** *m:* **einen ~ aufführen** to dance with joy.

**freudestrahlend** *adj* beaming with delight.

**freudig** *adj* joyful, happy.

**freudlos** *adj* joyless.

**freuen** ['frɔyən] *vt unpers* to make happy *od* pleased ♦ *vr* to be glad *od* happy; **sich auf etw** *akk* **~** to look forward to sth; **sich über etw** *akk* **~** to be pleased about sth; **sich zu früh ~** to get one's hopes up too soon.

**Freund** ['frɔynt] (-(e)s, -e) *m* friend; (*Liebhaber*) boyfriend; **ich bin kein ~ von so etwas** I'm not one for that sort of thing; **~in** *f* friend; (*Liebhaberin*) girlfriend; **f~lich** *adj* kind, friendly; **bitte recht f~lich!** smile please!; **würden Sie bitte so f~lich sein und das tun?** would you be so kind as to do that?; **f~licherweise** *adv* kindly; **~lichkeit** *f* friendliness, kindness; **~schaft** *f* friendship; **f~schaftlich** *adj* friendly.

**Frevel** ['freːfəl] (-s, -) *m:* **~ (an** +*dat*) crime *od* offence (against); **f~haft** *adj* wicked.

**Frhr.** *abk* (= *Freiherr*) baron.

**Frieden** ['friːdən] (-s, -) *m* peace; **im ~** in peacetime; **~ schließen** to make one's peace; (*POL*) to make peace; **um des lieben ~s willen** (*umg*) for the sake of peace and quiet; **ich traue dem ~ nicht** (*umg*) something (fishy) is going on.

**Friedens-** *zW:* **~bewegung** *f* peace movement; **~richter** *m* justice of the peace;

**~schluß** *m* peace agreement; **~truppe** *f* peace-keeping force; **~verhandlungen** *pl* peace negotiations *pl*; **~vertrag** *m* peace treaty; **~zeit** *f* peacetime.

**fried-** *zW:* **~fertig** *adj* peaceable; **F~hof** *m* cemetery; **~lich** *adj* peaceful; **etw auf ~lichem Wege lösen** to solve sth by peaceful means.

**frieren** ['friːrən] *unreg vi* to freeze ♦ *vt unpers* to freeze ♦ *vi unpers:* **heute nacht hat es gefroren** it was below freezing last night; **ich friere, es friert mich** I am freezing, I'm cold; **wie ein Schneider ~** (*umg*) to be *od* get frozen to the marrow.

**Fries** [friːs] (-es, -e) *m* (*ARCHIT*) frieze.

**Friese** ['friːzə] (-n, -n) *m* Fri(e)sian.

**Friesin** ['friːzə] *f* Fri(e)sian.

**frigid(e)** *adj* frigid.

**Frikadelle** [frika'dɛlə] *f* meatball.

**frisch** [frɪʃ] *adj* fresh; (*lebhaft*) lively; **~ gestrichen!** wet paint!; **sich ~ machen** to freshen (o.s.) up; **jdn auf ~er Tat ertappen** to catch sb red-handed *od* in the act.

**Frische** (-) *f* freshness; liveliness; **in alter ~** (*umg*) as always.

**Frischhaltebeutel** *m* airtight bag.

**Frischhaltefolie** *f* clingfilm.

**frischweg** *adv* (*munter*) straight out.

**Friseur** [fri'zøːr] *m* hairdresser.

**Friseuse** [fri'zøːzə] *f* hairdresser.

**frisieren** [fri'ziːrən] *vt* (*Haar*) to do; (*fig: Abrechnung*) to fiddle, doctor ♦ *vr* to do one's hair; **jdn ~, jdm das Haar ~** to do sb's hair.

**Frisiersalon** *m* hairdressing salon.

**Frisiertisch** *m* dressing table.

**Frisör** [fri'zøːr] (-s, -e) *m* hairdresser.

**frißt** [frɪst] *vb siehe* **fressen**.

**Frist** [frɪst] (-, -en) *f* period; (*Termin*) deadline; **eine ~ einhalten/verstreichen lassen** to meet a deadline/let a deadline pass; (*bei Rechnung*) to pay/not to pay within the period stipulated; **jdm eine ~ von vier Tagen geben** to give sb four days' grace.

**fristen** *vt* (*Dasein*) to lead; (*kümmerlich*) to eke out.

**Fristenlösung** *f* abortion law (*permitting abortion in the first three months*).

**fristgerecht** *adj* within the period stipulated.

**fristlos** *adj* (*Entlassung*) instant.

**Frisur** [fri'zuːr] *f* hairdo, hairstyle.

**Friteuse** [fri'tøːzə] (-, -n) *f* chip pan (*BRIT*), deep fat fryer.

**fritieren** [fri'tiːrən] *vt* to deep fry.

**frivol** [fri'voːl] *adj* frivolous.

**Frl.** *abk* (= *Fräulein*) Miss.

**froh** [froː] *adj* happy, cheerful; **ich bin ~, daß ...** I'm glad that ...

**fröhlich** ['frøːlɪç] *adj* merry, happy; **F~keit** *f* merriment, gaiety.

**frohlocken** *vi* (*geh*) to rejoice; (*pej*) to gloat.

**Frohsinn** *m* cheerfulness.

**fromm** [frɔm] *adj* pious, good; (*Wunsch*) idle.

**Frömmelei** [frœmə'laɪ] f false piety.
**Frömmigkeit** f piety.
**frönen** ['frøːnən] vi +dat to indulge in.
**Fronleichnam** [froːn'laɪçnaːm] (-(e)s) m Corpus Christi.
**Front** [frɔnt] (-, -en) f front; **klare ~en schaffen** (fig) to clarify the position.
**frontal** [frɔn'taːl] adj frontal; **F~angriff** m frontal attack.
**fror** etc [froːr] vb siehe **frieren**.
**Frosch** [frɔʃ] (-(e)s, ⁻e) m frog; (Feuerwerk) squib; **sei kein ~!** (umg) be a sport!; **~mann** m frogman; **~perspektive** f: **etw aus der ~perspektive sehen** to get a worm's-eye view of sth; **~schenkel** m frog's leg.
**Frost** [frɔst] (-(e)s, ⁻e) m frost; **f~beständig** adj frost-resistant; **~beule** f chilblain.
**frösteln** ['frœstəln] vi to shiver.
**frostig** adj frosty.
**Frostschutzmittel** nt anti-freeze.
**Frottee** [frɔ'teː] (-(s), -s) nt od m towelling.
**frottieren** [frɔ'tiːrən] vt to rub, towel.
**Frottierhandtuch** nt towel.
**Frottiertuch** nt towel.
**frotzeln** ['frɔtsəln] (umg) vt, vi to tease.
**Frucht** [fruxt] (-, ⁻e) f (lit, fig) fruit; (Getreide) corn; (Embryo) foetus; **f~bar** adj fruitful, fertile; **~barkeit** f fertility; **~becher** m fruit sundae.
**Früchtchen** ['frʏçtçən] (umg) nt (Tunichtgut) good-for-nothing.
**fruchten** vi to be of use.
**fruchtlos** adj fruitless.
**Fruchtsaft** m fruit juice.
**früh** [fryː] adj, adv early; **heute ~** this morning; **~auf** adv: **von ~auf** from an early age; **F~aufsteher** (-s, -) m early riser; **F~dienst** m: **F~dienst haben** to be on early shift.
**Frühe** (-) f early morning; **in aller ~** at the crack of dawn.
**früher** adj earlier; (ehemalig) former ♦ adv formerly; **~ war das anders** that used to be different; **~ oder später** sooner or later.
**frühestens** adv at the earliest.
**Frühgeburt** f premature birth; (Kind) premature baby.
**Frühjahr** nt spring.
**Frühjahrsmüdigkeit** f springtime lethargy.
**Frühjahrsputz** m spring-cleaning.
**Frühling** m spring; **im ~** in spring.
**früh-** zW: **~reif** adj precocious; **F~rentner** m person who has retired early; **F~schicht** f early shift; **F~schoppen** m morning/lunchtime drink; **F~sport** m early morning exercise; **F~stück** nt breakfast; **~stücken** vi to (have) breakfast; **F~warnsystem** nt early warning system; **~zeitig** adj early; (vorzeitig) premature.
**Frust** (-(e)s) (umg) m frustration.
**frustrieren** [frʊs'triːrən] vt to frustrate.
**frz.** abk = **französisch**.
**FSV** abk (= Fußball-Sportverein) F.C.

**FU** (-) f abk (= Freie Universität Berlin) Berlin University.
**Fuchs** [fʊks] (-es, ⁻e) m fox.
**fuchsen** (umg) vt to rile, annoy ♦ vr to be annoyed.
**Füchsin** ['fʏksɪn] f vixen.
**fuchsteufelswild** adj hopping mad.
**Fuchtel** ['fʊxtl] (-, -n) f (fig: umg): **unter jds ~** under sb's control od thumb.
**fuchteln** ['fʊxtəln] vi to gesticulate wildly.
**Fuge** ['fuːgə] (-, -n) f joint; (MUS) fugue.
**fügen** ['fyːgən] vt to place, join ♦ vr unpers to happen ♦ vr: **sich ~ (in** +akk) to be obedient (to); (anpassen) to adapt o.s. (to).
**fügsam** ['fyːkzaːm] adj obedient.
**fühlbar** adj perceptible, noticeable.
**fühlen** ['fyːlən] vt, vi, vr to feel.
**Fühler** (-s, -) m feeler.
**Fühlung** f: **mit jdm in ~ bleiben/stehen** to stay/be in contact od touch with sb.
**fuhr** etc [fuːr] vb siehe **fahren**.
**Fuhre** (-, -n) f (Ladung) load.
**führen** ['fyːrən] vt to lead; (Geschäft) to run; (Name) to bear; (Buch) to keep; (im Angebot haben) to stock ♦ vi to lead ♦ vr to behave; **was führt Sie zu mir?** (form) what brings you to me?; **Geld/seine Papiere bei sich ~** (form) to carry money/one's papers on one's person; **das führt zu nichts** that will come to nothing.
**Führer(in)** ['fyːrər(ɪn)] (-s, -) m(f) leader; (Fremden~) guide; **~haus** nt cab; **~schein** m driving licence (BRIT), driver's license (US); **den ~schein machen** (AUT) to learn to drive; (die Prüfung ablegen) to take one's (driving) test; **~scheinentzug** m disqualification from driving.
**Fuhrmann** ['fuːrman] (-(e)s, pl -leute) m carter.
**Führung** ['fyːrʊŋ] f leadership; (eines Unternehmens) management; (MIL) command; (Benehmen) conduct; (Museums~) conducted tour.
**Führungs-** zW: **~kraft** f executive; **~stab** m (MIL) command; (COMM) top management; **~stil** m management style; **~zeugnis** nt certificate of good conduct.
**Fuhrunternehmen** nt haulage business.
**Fuhrwerk** nt cart.
**Fülle** ['fʏlə] (-) f wealth, abundance.
**Füllen** (-s, -) nt foal.
**füllen** vt to fill; (KOCH) to stuff ♦ vr to fill (up).
**Füller** (-s, -) m fountain pen.
**Füllfederhalter** m fountain pen.
**Füllgewicht** nt (COMM) weight at time of packing; (auf Dosen) net weight.
**füllig** ['fʏlɪç] adj (Mensch) corpulent, portly; (Figur) ample.
**Füllung** f filling; (Holz~) panel.
**fummeln** ['fʊməln] (umg) vi to fumble.
**Fund** [fʊnt] (-(e)s, -e) m find.
**Fundament** [fʊnda'mɛnt] nt foundation.

**fundamental** *adj* fundamental.
**Fundamentalismus** *m* fundamentalism.
**Fundbüro** *nt* lost property office, lost and found (*US*).
**Fundgrube** *f* (*fig*) treasure trove.
**fundieren** [fʊn'diːrən] *vt* to back up.
**fundiert** *adj* sound.
**fündig** ['fʏndɪç] *adj* (*MIN*) rich; ~ **werden** to make a strike; (*fig*) to strike it lucky.
**Fundsachen** *pl* lost property *sing*.
**fünf** [fʏnf] *num* five; **seine ~ Sinne beisammen haben** to have all one's wits about one; ~**(e) gerade sein lassen** (*umg*) to turn a blind eye; ~**hundert** *num* five hundred; ~**jährig** *adj* (*Frist, Plan*) five-year; (*Kind*) five-year-old; **F~kampf** *m* pentathlon; **F~prozentklausel** *f* (*PARL*) *clause debarring parties with less than 5% of the vote from Parliament;* **F~tagewoche** *f* five-day week.

> The **Fünfprozentklausel** is a rule in German Federal elections whereby only those parties who collect at least 5% of the second vote (**Zweitstimme**) receive a parliamentary seat. This is to avoid the parliament being made up of a large number of very small parties which, in the Weimar Republic, led to political instability.

**fünfte(r, s)** *adj* fifth.
**Fünftel** (**-s, -**) *nt* fifth.
**fünfzehn** *num* fifteen.
**fünfzig** *num* fifty.
**fungieren** [fʊŋ'giːrən] *vi* to function; (*Person*) to act.
**Funk** [fʊŋk] (**-s**) *m* radio, wireless (*BRIT old*); ~**ausstellung** *f* radio and television exhibition.
**Funke** (**-ns, -n**) *m* (*lit, fig*) spark.
**funkeln** *vi* to sparkle.
**funkelnagelneu** (*umg*) *adj* brand-new.
**Funken** (**-s, -**) *m* = **Funke**.
**funken** *vt* to radio.
**Funker** (**-s, -**) *m* radio operator.
**Funk-** *zW:* ~**gerät** *nt* radio set; ~**haus** *nt* broadcasting centre; ~**kolleg** *nt* educational radio broadcasts *pl*; ~**rufempfänger** *m* (*TELEC*) pager, paging device; ~**spot** *m* advertisement on the radio; ~**sprechgerät** *nt* radio telephone; ~**spruch** *m* radio signal; ~**station** *f* radio station; ~**stille** *f* (*fig*) ominous silence; ~**streife** *f* police radio patrol; ~**taxi** *nt* radio taxi; ~**telefon** *nt* cell phone.
**Funktion** [fʊŋktsi'oːn] *f* function; **in ~ treten/sein** to come into/be in operation.
**Funktionär(in)** [fʊŋktsio'nɛːr(ɪn)] (**-s, -e**) *m(f)* functionary, official.
**funktionieren** [fʊŋktsio'niːrən] *vi* to work, function.
**Funktions-** *zW:* **f~fähig** *adj* working; ~**taste** *f* (*COMPUT*) function key; **f~tüchtig** *adj* in

working order.
**Funzel** [fʊntsəl] (**-, -n**) (*umg*) *f* dim lamp.
**für** [fyːr] *präp +akk* for; **was ~** what kind *od* sort of; ~**s erste** for the moment; **was Sie da sagen, hat etwas ~ sich** there's something in what you're saying; **Tag ~ Tag** day after day; **Schritt ~ Schritt** step by step; **das F~ und Wider** the pros and cons *pl*; **F~bitte** *f* intercession.
**Furche** ['fʊrçə] (**-, -n**) *f* furrow.
**furchen** *vt* to furrow.
**Furcht** [fʊrçt] (**-**) *f* fear; **f~bar** *adj* terrible, awful.
**fürchten** ['fʏrçtən] *vt* to be afraid of, fear ♦ *vr:* **sich ~** (**vor** *+dat*) to be afraid (of).
**fürchterlich** *adj* awful.
**furchtlos** *adj* fearless.
**furchtsam** *adj* timorous.
**füreinander** [fyːr|aɪ'nandər] *adv* for each other.
**Furie** ['fuːriə] (**-, -n**) *f* (*MYTHOLOGIE*) fury; (*fig*) hellcat.
**Furnier** [fʊr'niːr] (**-s, -e**) *nt* veneer.
**Furore** [fu'roːrə] *f od nt:* ~ **machen** (*umg*) to cause a sensation.
**fürs** [fyːrs] = **für das**.
**Fürsorge** ['fyːrzɔrgə] *f* care; (*Sozial~*) welfare; **von der ~ leben** to live on social security (*BRIT*) *od* welfare (*US*); ~**amt** *nt* welfare office.
**Fürsorger(in)** (**-s, -**) *m(f)* welfare worker.
**Fürsorgeunterstützung** *f* social security (*BRIT*), welfare benefit (*US*).
**fürsorglich** *adj* caring.
**Fürsprache** *f* recommendation; (*um Gnade*) intercession.
**Fürsprecher** *m* advocate.
**Fürst** [fʏrst] (**-en, -en**) *m* prince.
**Fürstentum** *nt* principality.
**Fürstin** *f* princess.
**fürstlich** *adj* princely.
**Furt** [fʊrt] (**-, -en**) *f* ford.
**Furunkel** [fu'rʊŋkəl] (**-s, -**) *nt od m* boil.
**Fürwort** ['fyːrvɔrt] *nt* pronoun.
**furzen** ['fʊrtsən] (*umg!*) *vi* to fart (*!*).
**Fusion** [fuzi'oːn] *f* amalgamation; (*von Unternehmen*) merger; (*von Atomkernen, Zellen*) fusion.
**fusionieren** [fuzio'niːrən] *vt* to amalgamate.
**Fuß** [fuːs] (**-es, -̈e**) *m* foot; (*von Glas, Säule etc*) base; (*von Möbel*) leg; **zu ~** on foot; **bei ~!** heel!; **jdm etw vor die Füße werfen** (*lit*) to throw sth at sb; (*fig*) to tell sb to keep sth; **(festen) ~ fassen** (*lit, fig*) to gain a foothold; (*sich niederlassen*) to settle down; **mit jdm auf gutem ~ stehen** to be on good terms with sb; **auf großem ~ leben** to live the high life.
**Fußball** *m* football; ~**platz** *m* football pitch; ~**spiel** *nt* football match; ~**spieler** *m* footballer (*BRIT*), football player (*US*); ~**toto** *m od nt* football pools *pl*.

**Fußboden** *m* floor; **~heizung** *f* underfloor heating.

**Fußbremse** *f* (*AUT*) foot brake.

**fusselig** ['fʊsəliç] *adj*: **sich** *dat* **den Mund ~ reden** (*umg*) to talk till one is blue in the face.

**fusseln** ['fʊsəln] *vi* (*Stoff, Kleid etc*) to go bobbly (*umg*).

**fußen** *vi*: **~ auf** *+dat* to rest on, be based on.

**Fuß-** *zW*: **~ende** *nt* foot; **~gänger(in)** (*-s, -*) *m(f)* pedestrian; **~gängerüberführung** *f* pedestrian bridge; **~gängerzone** *f* pedestrian precinct; **~leiste** *f* skirting board (*BRIT*), baseboard (*US*); **~nagel** *m* toenail; **~note** *f* footnote; **~pfleger** *m* chiropodist; **~pilz** *m* (*MED*) athlete's foot; **~spur** *f* footprint; **~stapfen** (*-s, -*) *m*: **in jds ~stapfen treten** (*fig*) to follow in sb's footsteps; **~tritt** *m* kick; (*Spur*) footstep; **~volk** *nt* (*fig*): **das ~volk** the rank and file; **~weg** *m* footpath.

**futsch** [fʊtʃ] (*umg*) *adj* (*weg*) gone, vanished.

**Futter** ['fʊtər] (*-s, -*) *nt* fodder, feed; (*Stoff*) lining.

**Futteral** [fʊtə'raːl] (*-s, -e*) *nt* case.

**futtern** ['fʊtərn] *vi* (*hum: umg*) to stuff o.s. ◆ *vt* to scoff.

**füttern** ['fʏtərn] *vt* to feed; (*Kleidung*) to line; „F~ **verboten**" "do not feed the animals".

**Futur** [fu'tuːr] (*-s, -e*) *nt* future.

# G, g

**G, g¹** [geː] *nt* G, g; **~ wie Gustav** ≈ G for George.

**g²** *abk* (*ÖSTERR*) = **Groschen**; (= *Gramm*) g.

**gab** *etc* [gaːp] *vb siehe* **geben**.

**Gabe** ['gaːbə] (*-, -n*) *f* gift.

**Gabel** ['gaːbəl] (*-, -n*) *f* fork; (*TEL*) rest, cradle; **~frühstück** *nt* mid-morning light lunch; **~stapler** (*-s, -*) *m* fork-lift truck.

**gabeln** *vr* to fork.

**Gabelung** *f* fork.

**Gabentisch** ['gaːbəntɪʃ] *m* table for Christmas or birthday presents.

**Gabun** [ga'buːn] *nt* Gabon.

**gackern** ['gakərn] *vi* to cackle.

**gaffen** ['gafən] *vi* to gape.

**Gag** [gɛk] (*-s, -s*) *m* (*Film~*) gag; (*Werbe~*) gimmick.

**Gage** ['gaːʒə] (*-, -n*) *f* fee.

**gähnen** ['gɛːnən] *vi* to yawn; **~de Leere** total emptiness.

**GAL** (*-*) *f abk* (= *Grün-Alternative Liste*) electoral pact of Greens and alternative parties.

**Gala** ['gala] (*-*) *f* formal dress.

**galant** [ga'lant] *adj* gallant, courteous.

**Galavorstellung** *f* (*THEAT*) gala performance.

**Galerie** [galə'riː] *f* gallery.

**Galgen** ['galgən] (*-s, -*) *m* gallows *pl*; **~frist** *f* respite; **~humor** *m* macabre humour (*BRIT*) *od* humor (*US*); **~strick** (*umg*) *m*, **~vogel** (*umg*) *m* gallows bird.

**Galionsfigur** [gali'oːnsfiguːr] *f* figurehead.

**gälisch** ['gɛːlɪʃ] *adj* Gaelic.

**Galle** ['galə] (*-, -n*) *f* gall; (*Organ*) gall bladder; **jdm kommt die ~ hoch** sb's blood begins to boil.

**Galopp** [ga'lɔp] (*-s, -s od -e*) *m* gallop; **im ~** (*lit*) at a gallop; (*fig*) at top speed.

**galoppieren** [galɔ'piːrən] *vi* to gallop.

**galt** *etc* [galt] *vb siehe* **gelten**.

**galvanisieren** [galvani'ziːrən] *vt* to galvanize.

**Gamasche** [ga'maʃə] (*-, -n*) *f* gaiter; (*kurz*) spat.

**Gameboy** ® ['geːmbɔy] *m* (*COMPUT*) games console.

**Gammastrahlen** ['gamaʃtraːlən] *pl* gamma rays *pl*.

**gamm(e)lig** ['gam(ə)liç] (*umg*) *adj* (*Kleidung*) tatty.

**gammeln** ['gaməln] (*umg*) *vi* to loaf about.

**Gammler(in)** ['gamlər(ɪn)] (*-s, -*) *m(f)* dropout.

**Gang¹** [gaŋ] (*-(e)s, ̈-e*) *m* walk; (*Boten~*) errand; (*~art*) gait; (*Abschnitt eines Vorgangs*) operation; (*Essens~, Ablauf*) course; (*Flur etc*) corridor; (*Durch~*) passage; (*AUT, TECH*) gear; (*THEAT, AVIAT, in Kirche*) aisle; **den ersten ~ einlegen** to engage first (gear); **einen ~ machen/tun** to go on an errand/for a walk; **den ~ nach Canossa antreten** (*fig*) to eat humble pie; **seinen gewohnten ~ gehen** (*fig*) to run its usual course; **in ~ bringen** to start up; (*fig*) to get off the ground; **in ~ sein** to be in operation; (*fig*) to be under way.

**Gang²** [gɛŋ] (*-, -s*) *f* gang.

**gang** *adj*: **~ und gäbe** usual, normal.

**Gangart** *f* way of walking, walk, gait; (*von Pferd*) gait; **eine härtere ~ einschlagen** (*fig*) to apply harder tactics.

**gangbar** *adj* passable; (*Methode*) practicable.

**Gängelband** ['gɛŋəlbant] *nt*: **jdn am ~ halten** (*fig*) to spoon-feed sb.

**gängeln** *vt* to spoonfeed; **jdn ~** to treat sb like a child.

**gängig** ['gɛŋɪç] *adj* common, current; (*Ware*) in demand, selling well.

**Gangschaltung** *f* gears *pl*.

**Gangway** ['gæŋweɪ] *f* (*NAUT*) gangway; (*AVIAT*) steps *pl*.

**Ganove** [ga'noːvə] (*-n, -n*) (*umg*) *m* crook.

**Gans** [gans] (*-, ̈-e*) *f* goose.

**Gänse-** *zW*: **~blümchen** *nt* daisy; **~braten** *m* roast goose; **~füßchen** (*umg*) *pl* inverted commas *pl* (*BRIT*), quotes *pl*; ~**haut** *f* goose pimples *pl*; ~**marsch** *m*: **im** ~**marsch** in single file.

**Gänserich** (**-s, -e**) *m* gander.

**ganz** [gants] *adj* whole; (*vollständig*) complete ♦ *adv* quite; (*völlig*) completely; (*sehr*) really; (*genau*) exactly; ~ **Europa** all Europe; **im** (**großen und**) ~**en genommen** on the whole, all in all; **etw wieder** ~ **machen** to mend sth; **sein** ~**es Geld** all his money; ~ **gewiß!** absolutely; **ein** ~ **klein wenig** just a tiny bit; **das mag ich** ~ **besonders gern(e)** I'm particularly fond of that; **sie ist** ~ **die Mutter** she's just *od* exactly like her mother; ~ **und gar nicht** not at all.

**Ganze(s)** *nt*: **es geht ums** ~ everything's at stake; **aufs** ~ **gehen** to go for the lot.

**Ganzheitsmethode** ['gantshaɪtsmetoːdə] *f* (*SCH*) look-and-say method.

**gänzlich** ['gɛntslɪç] *adj* complete, entire ♦ *adv* completely, entirely.

**ganztägig** ['gantstɛːgɪç] *adj* all-day *attrib*.

**ganztags** *adv* (*arbeiten*) full time.

**gar** [gaːr] *adj* cooked, done ♦ *adv* quite; ~ **nicht/nichts/keiner** not/nothing/nobody at all; ~ **nicht schlecht** not bad at all; ~ **kein Grund** no reason whatsoever *od* at all; **er wäre** ~ **zu gern noch länger geblieben** he would really have liked to stay longer.

**Garage** [ga'raːʒə] (**-, -n**) *f* garage.

**Garantie** [garan'tiː] *f* guarantee; **das fällt noch unter die** ~ that's covered by the guarantee.

**garantieren** *vt* to guarantee.

**garantiert** *adv* guaranteed; (*umg*) I bet.

**Garantieschein** *m* guarantee.

**Garaus** ['gaːraus] (*umg*) *m*: **jdm den** ~ **machen** to do sb in.

**Garbe** ['garbə] (**-, -n**) *f* sheaf; (*MIL*) burst of fire.

**Garde** ['gardə] (**-, -n**) *f* guard(s); **die alte** ~ the old guard.

**Garderobe** [gardə'roːbə] (**-, -n**) *f* wardrobe; (*Abgabe*) cloakroom (*BRIT*), checkroom (*US*); (*Kleiderablage*) hall stand; (*THEAT: Umkleideraum*) dressing room.

**Garderobenfrau** *f* cloakroom attendant.

**Garderobenständer** *m* hall stand.

**Gardine** [gar'diːnə] (**-, -n**) *f* curtain.

**Gardinenpredigt** (*umg*) *f*: **jdm eine** ~ **halten** to give sb a talking-to.

**Gardinenstange** *f* curtain rail; (*zum Ziehen*) curtain rod.

**garen** ['gaːrən] *vt, vi* (*KOCH*) to cook.

**gären** ['gɛːrən] *unreg vi* to ferment.

**Garn** [garn] (**-(e)s, -e**) *nt* thread; (*Häkel~, fig*) yarn.

**Garnele** [gar'neːlə] (**-, -n**) *f* shrimp, prawn.

**garnieren** [gar'niːrən] *vt* to decorate; (*Speisen*) to garnish.

**Garnison** [garni'zoːn] (**-, -en**) *f* garrison.

**Garnitur** [garni'tuːr] *f* (*Satz*) set;

(*Unterwäsche*) set of (matching) underwear; **erste** ~ (*fig*) top rank; **zweite** ~ second rate.

**garstig** ['garstɪç] *adj* nasty, horrid.

**Garten** ['gartən] (**-s, ~̈**) *m* garden; ~**arbeit** *f* gardening; ~**bau** *m* horticulture; ~**fest** *nt* garden party; ~**gerät** *nt* gardening tool; ~**haus** *nt* summerhouse; ~**kresse** *f* cress; ~**laube** *f* (~*häuschen*) summerhouse; ~**lokal** *nt* beer garden; ~**schere** *f* pruning shears *pl*; ~**tür** *f* garden gate; ~**zaun** *m* garden fence; ~**zwerg** *m* garden gnome; (*pej: umg*) squirt.

**Gärtner(in)** ['gɛrtnər(ɪn)] (**-s, -**) *m(f)* gardener.

**Gärtnerei** [gɛrtnə'raɪ] *f* nursery; (*Gemüse~*) market garden (*BRIT*), truck farm (*US*).

**gärtnern** *vi* to garden.

**Gärung** ['gɛːrʊŋ] *f* fermentation.

**Gas** [gaːs] (**-es, -e**) *nt* gas; ~ **geben** (*AUT*) to accelerate, step on the gas.

**Gascogne** [gas'kɔnjə] *f* Gascony.

**Gas-** *zW*: ~**flasche** *f* bottle of gas, gas canister; **g~förmig** *adj* gaseous; ~**hahn** *m* gas tap; ~**herd** *m* gas cooker; ~**kocher** *m* gas cooker; ~**leitung** *f* gas pipeline; ~**maske** *f* gas mask; ~**pedal** *nt* accelerator, gas pedal (*US*); ~**pistole** *f* gas pistol.

**Gasse** ['gasə] (**-, -n**) *f* lane, alley.

**Gassenhauer** (**-s, -**) (*veraltet: umg*) *m* popular melody.

**Gassenjunge** *m* street urchin.

**Gast** [gast] (**-es, ~̈e**) *m* guest; **bei jdm zu** ~ **sein** to be sb's guest(s); ~**arbeiter** *m* foreign worker.

**Gäste-** *zW*: ~**bett** *nt* spare bed; ~**buch** *nt* visitors' book; ~**zimmer** *nt* guest room.

**Gast-** *zW*: **g~freundlich** *adj* hospitable; ~**freundlichkeit** *f* hospitality; ~**freundschaft** *f* hospitality; ~**geber(in)** (**-s, -**) *m(f)* host(ess); ~**haus** *nt* hotel, inn; ~**hof** *m* hotel, inn; ~**hörer(in)** *m(f)* (*UNIV*) observer, auditor (*US*).

**gastieren** [gas'tiːrən] *vi* (*THEAT*) to (appear as a) guest.

**Gast-** *zW*: ~**land** *nt* host country; **g~lich** *adj* hospitable; ~**lichkeit** *f* hospitality; ~**rolle** *f* (*THEAT*) guest role; **eine** ~**rolle spielen** to make a guest appearance.

**Gastronomie** [gastrono'miː] *f* (*form: Gaststättengewerbe*) catering trade.

**gastronomisch** [gastro'noːmɪʃ] *adj* gastronomic(al).

**Gast-** *zW*: ~**spiel** *nt* (*SPORT*) away game; **ein** ~**spiel geben** (*THEAT*) to give a guest performance; (*fig*) to put in a brief appearance; ~**stätte** *f* restaurant; (*Trinklokal*) pub; ~**wirt** *m* innkeeper; ~**wirtschaft** *f* hotel, inn; ~**zimmer** *nt* guest room.

**Gas-** *zW*: ~**vergiftung** *f* gas poisoning; ~**versorgung** *f* (*System*) gas supply; ~**werk** *nt* gasworks *sing od pl*; ~**zähler** *m* gas meter.

**Gatte** ['gatə] (**-n, -n**) *m* (*form*) husband, spouse; **die** ~**n** husband and wife.

**Gatter** ['gatər] (-s, -) nt grating; (Tür) gate.
**Gattin** f (form) wife, spouse.
**Gattung** ['gatʊŋ] f (BIOL) genus; (Sorte) kind.
**GAU** [gaʊ] m abk (= größter anzunehmender Unfall) MCA, maximum credible accident.
**Gaudi** ['gaʊdi] (SÜDD, ÖSTERR: umg) nt od f fun.
**Gaukler** ['gaʊklər] (-s, -) m (liter) travelling entertainer; (Zauberkünstler) conjurer, magician.
**Gaul** [gaʊl] (-(e)s, Gäule) (pej) m nag.
**Gaumen** ['gaʊmən] (-s, -) m palate.
**Gauner** ['gaʊnər] (-s, -) m rogue.
**Gaunerei** [gaʊnə'raɪ] f swindle.
**Gaunersprache** f underworld jargon.
**Gaze** ['ga:zə] (-, -n) f gauze.
**Geäst** [gə|'ɛst] nt branches pl.
**geb.** abk = **geboren**.
**Gebäck** [gə'bɛk] (-(e)s, -e) nt (Kekse) biscuits pl (BRIT), cookies pl (US); (Teilchen) pastries pl.
**gebacken** [gə'bakən] pp von **backen**.
**Gebälk** [gə'bɛlk] (-(e)s) nt timberwork.
**gebannt** [gə'bant] adj spellbound.
**gebar** etc [gə'ba:r] vb siehe **gebären**.
**Gebärde** [gə'bɛ:rdə] (-, -n) f gesture.
**gebärden** vr to behave.
**Gebaren** [gə'ba:rən] (-s) nt behaviour (BRIT), behavior (US); (Geschäfts~) conduct.
**gebären** [gə'bɛ:rən] unreg vt to give birth to.
**Gebärmutter** f uterus, womb.
**Gebäude** [gə'bɔydə] (-s, -) nt building; ~komplex m (building) complex; ~reinigung f (das Reinigen) commercial cleaning; (Firma) cleaning contractors pl.
**Gebein** [gə'baɪn] (-(e)s, -e) nt bones pl.
**Gebell** [gə'bɛl] (-(e)s) nt barking.
**geben** ['ge:bən] unreg vt, vi to give; (Karten) to deal ♦ vt unpers: **es gibt** there is/are; there will be ♦ vr (sich verhalten) to behave, act; (aufhören) to abate; **jdm etw** ~ to give sb sth od sth to sb; **in die Post** ~ to post; **das gibt keinen Sinn** that doesn't make sense; **er gibt Englisch** he teaches English; **viel/nicht viel auf etw** akk ~ to set great store/not much store by sth; **etw von sich** ~ (Laute etc) to utter; **ein Wort gab das andere** one angry word led to another; **ein gutes Beispiel** ~ to set a good example; ~ **Sie mir bitte Herrn Braun** (TEL) can I speak to Mr Braun please?; **ein Auto in Reparatur** ~ to have a car repaired; **was gibt's?** what's the matter?, what's up?; **was gibt's zum Mittagessen?** what's for lunch?; **das gibt's doch nicht!** that's impossible!; **sich geschlagen** ~ to admit defeat; **das wird sich schon** ~ that'll soon sort itself out.
**Gebet** [gə'be:t] (-(e)s, -e) nt prayer; **jdn ins** ~ **nehmen** (fig) to take sb to task.
**gebeten** [gə'be:tən] pp von **bitten**.
**gebeugt** [gə'bɔykt] adj (Haltung) stooped; (Kopf) bowed; (Schultern) sloping.

**gebiert** [gə'bi:rt] vb siehe **gebären**.
**Gebiet** [gə'bi:t] (-(e)s, -e) nt area; (Hoheits~) territory; (fig) field.
**gebieten** unreg vt to command, demand.
**Gebieter** (-s, -) m master; (Herrscher) ruler; ~in f mistress; g~isch adj imperious.
**Gebietshoheit** f territorial sovereignty.
**Gebilde** [gə'bɪldə] (-s, -) nt object, structure.
**gebildet** adj cultured, educated.
**Gebimmel** [gə'bɪməl] (-s) nt (continual) ringing.
**Gebirge** [gə'bɪrgə] (-s, -) nt mountains pl.
**gebirgig** adj mountainous.
**Gebirgs-** zW: ~**bahn** f railway crossing a mountain range; ~**kette** f, ~**zug** m mountain range.
**Gebiß** [gə'bɪs] (-sses, -sse) nt teeth pl; (künstlich) dentures pl.
**gebissen** pp von **beißen**.
**Gebläse** [gə'blɛ:zə] (-s, -) nt fan, blower.
**geblasen** [gə'bla:zən] pp von **blasen**.
**geblichen** [gə'blɪçən] pp von **bleichen**.
**geblieben** [gə'bli:bən] pp von **bleiben**.
**geblümt** [gə'bly:mt] adj flowered; (Stil) flowery.
**Geblüt** [gə'bly:t] (-(e)s) nt blood, race.
**gebogen** [gə'bo:gən] pp von **biegen**.
**geboren** [gə'bo:rən] pp von **gebären** ♦ adj born; (Frau) née; **wo sind Sie** ~? where were you born?
**geborgen** [gə'bɔrgən] pp von **bergen** ♦ adj secure, safe.
**geborsten** [gə'bɔrstən] pp von **bersten**.
**Gebot** (-(e)s, -e) nt (Gesetz) law; (REL) commandment; (bei Auktion) bid; **das** ~ **der Stunde** the needs of the moment.
**gebot** etc [gə'bo:t] vb siehe **gebieten**.
**geboten** [gə'bo:tən] pp von **bieten, gebieten** ♦ adj (geh: ratsam) advisable; (: notwendig) necessary; (: dringend ~) imperative.
**Gebr.** abk (= Gebrüder) Bros., bros.
**gebracht** [gə'braxt] pp von **bringen**.
**gebrannt** [gə'brant] pp von **brennen** ♦ adj: **ein** ~**es Kind scheut das Feuer** (Sprichwort) once bitten twice shy (Sprichwort).
**gebraten** [gə'bra:tən] pp von **braten**.
**Gebräu** [gə'brɔy] (-(e)s, -e) nt brew, concoction.
**Gebrauch** [gə'braʊx] (-(e)s, Gebräuche) m use; (Sitte) custom; **zum äußerlichen/innerlichen** ~ for external use/to be taken internally.
**gebrauchen** vt to use; **er/das ist zu nichts zu** ~ he's/that's (of) no use to anybody.
**gebräuchlich** [gə'brɔyçlɪç] adj usual, customary.
**Gebrauchs-** zW: ~**anweisung** f directions pl for use; ~**artikel** m article of everyday use; **g~fertig** adj ready for use; ~**gegenstand** m commodity.
**gebraucht** [gə'braʊxt] adj used; **G~wagen** m second-hand od used car.
**gebrechlich** [gə'brɛçlɪç] adj frail; **G~keit** f

frailty.

**gebrochen** [gə'brɔxən] *pp von* **brechen.**

**Gebrüder** [gə'bryːdər] *pl* brothers *pl.*

**Gebrüll** [gə'bryl] (**-(e)s**) *nt* (*von Mensch*) yelling; (*von Löwe*) roar.

**gebückt** [gə'bʏkt] *adj:* **eine** ~**e Haltung** a stoop.

**Gebühr** [gə'byːr] (**-, -en**) *f* charge; (*Post–*) postage *no pl;* (*Honorar*) fee; **zu ermäßigter** ~ at a reduced rate; ~ **(be)zahlt Empfänger** postage to be paid by addressee; **nach** ~ suitably; **über** ~ excessively.

**gebühren** *vi* (*geh*): **jdm** ~ to be sb's due *od* due to sb ♦ *vr* to be fitting.

**gebührend** *adj* (*verdient*) due; (*angemessen*) suitable.

**Gebühren-** *zW:* ~**einheit** *f* (*TEL*) tariff unit; ~**erlaß** *m* remission of fees; ~**ermäßigung** *f* reduction of fees; **g**~**frei** *adj* free of charge; **g**~**pflichtig** *adj* subject to charges; **g**~**pflichtige Verwarnung** (*JUR*) fine.

**gebunden** [gə'bʊndən] *pp von* **binden** ♦ *adj:* **vertraglich** ~ **sein** to be bound by contract.

**Geburt** [gə'buːrt] (**-, -en**) *f* birth; **das war eine schwere** ~**!** (*fig: umg*) that took some doing.

**Geburten-** *zW:* ~**kontrolle** *f* birth control; ~**regelung** *f* birth control; ~**rückgang** *m* drop in the birth rate; **g**~**schwach** *adj* (*Jahrgang*) with a low birth rate; ~**ziffer** *f* birth rate.

**gebürtig** [gə'bʏrtɪç] *adj* born in, native of; ~**e Schweizerin** native of Switzerland, Swiss-born woman.

**Geburts-** *zW:* ~**anzeige** *f* birth notice; ~**datum** *nt* date of birth; ~**fehler** *m* congenital defect; ~**helfer** *m* (*Arzt*) obstetrician; ~**helferin** *f* (*Ärztin*) obstetrician; (*Hebamme*) midwife; ~**hilfe** *f* (*als Fach*) obstetrics *sing;* (*von Hebamme*) midwifery; ~**jahr** *nt* year of birth; ~**ort** *m* birthplace; ~**tag** *m* birthday; **herzlichen Glückwunsch zum** ~**tag!** happy birthday!, many happy returns (of the day)!; ~**urkunde** *f* birth certificate.

**Gebüsch** [gə'bʏʃ] (**-(e)s, -e**) *nt* bushes *pl.*

**gedacht** [gə'daxt] *pp von* **denken, gedenken.**

**gedachte** *etc vb siehe* **gedenken.**

**Gedächtnis** [gə'dɛçtnɪs] (**-ses, -se**) *nt* memory; **wenn mich mein** ~ **nicht trügt** if my memory serves me right; ~**feier** *f* commemoration; ~**hilfe** *f* memory aid, mnemonic; ~**schwund** *m* loss of memory; ~**verlust** *m* amnesia.

**gedämpft** [gə'dɛmpft] *adj* (*Geräusch*) muffled; (*Farben, Instrument, Stimmung*) muted; (*Licht, Freude*) subdued.

**Gedanke** [gə'daŋkə] (**-ns, -n**) *m* thought; (*Idee, Plan, Einfall*) idea; (*Konzept*) concept; **sich über etw** *akk* ~**n machen** to think about sth; **jdn auf andere** ~**n bringen** to make sb think about other things; **etw ganz in** ~**n** *dat* **tun** to do sth without thinking; **auf einen** ~**n**

**kommen** to have *od* get an idea.

**Gedanken-** *zW:* ~**austausch** *m* exchange of ideas; ~**freiheit** *f* freedom of thought; **g**~**los** *adj* thoughtless; ~**losigkeit** *f* thoughtlessness; ~**sprung** *m* mental leap; ~**strich** *m* dash; ~**übertragung** *f* thought transference, telepathy; **g**~**verloren** *adj* lost in thought; **g**~**voll** *adj* thoughtful.

**Gedärme** [gə'dɛrmə] *pl* intestines *pl.*

**Gedeck** [gə'dɛk] (**-(e)s, -e**) *nt* cover(ing); (*Menü*) set meal; **ein** ~ **auflegen** to lay a place.

**gedeckt** *adj* (*Farbe*) muted.

**Gedeih** *m:* **auf** ~ **und Verderb** for better or for worse.

**gedeihen** [gə'daɪən] *unreg vi* to thrive, prosper; **die Sache ist so weit gediehen, daß ...** the matter has reached the point *od* stage where ...

**gedenken** [gə'dɛŋkən] *unreg vi +gen* (*geh: denken an*) to remember; (*beabsichtigen*) to intend; **G**~ *nt:* **zum G**~ **an jdn** in memory *od* remembrance of sb.

**Gedenk-** *zW:* ~**feier** *f* commemoration; ~**minute** *f* minute's silence; ~**stätte** *f* memorial; ~**tag** *m* remembrance day.

**Gedicht** [gə'dɪçt] (**-(e)s, -e**) *nt* poem.

**gediegen** [gə'diːgən] *adj* (*good*) quality; (*Mensch*) reliable; (*rechtschaffen*) honest; **G**~**heit** *f* quality; reliability; honesty.

**gedieh** *etc* [gə'diː] *vb siehe* **gedeihen.**

**gediehen** *pp von* **gedeihen.**

**gedr.** *abk* = **gedruckt.**

**Gedränge** [gə'drɛŋə] (**-s**) *nt* crush, crowd; **ins** ~ **kommen** (*fig*) to get into difficulties.

**gedrängt** *adj* compressed; ~ **voll** packed.

**gedroschen** [gə'drɔʃən] *pp von* **dreschen.**

**gedruckt** [gə'drʊkt] *adj* printed; **lügen wie** ~ (*umg*) to lie left, right and centre.

**gedrungen** [gə'drʊŋən] *pp von* **dringen** ♦ *adj* thickset, stocky.

**Geduld** [gə'dʊlt] (**-**) *f* patience; **mir reißt die** ~**, ich verliere die** ~ my patience is wearing thin, I'm losing my patience.

**gedulden** [gə'dʊldən] *vr* to be patient.

**geduldig** *adj* patient.

**Geduldsprobe** *f* trial of (one's) patience.

**gedungen** [gə'dʊŋən] (*pej*) *adj* (*geh: Mörder*) hired.

**gedunsen** [gə'dʊnzən] *adj* bloated.

**gedurft** [gə'dʊrft] *pp von* **dürfen.**

**geehrt** [gə'|eːrt] *adj:* **Sehr** ~**e Damen und Herren!** Ladies and Gentlemen!; (*in Briefen*) Dear Sir or Madam.

**geeignet** [gə'|aɪgnət] *adj* suitable; **im** ~**en Augenblick** at the right moment.

**Gefahr** [gə'faːr] (**-, -en**) *f* danger; ~ **laufen, etw zu tun** to run the risk of doing sth; **auf eigene** ~ at one's own risk; **außer** ~ (*nicht gefährdet*) not in danger; (*nicht mehr gefährdet*) out of danger; (*Patienten*) off the danger list.

**gefährden** [gə'fɛːrdən] vt to endanger.
**gefahren** [gə'faːrən] pp von **fahren**.
**Gefahren-** zW: **~quelle** f source of danger; **~schwelle** f threshold of danger; **~stelle** f danger spot; **~zulage** f danger money.
**gefährlich** [gə'fɛːrlɪç] adj dangerous.
**Gefährte** [gə'fɛːrtə] (-n, -n) m companion.
**Gefährtin** [gə'fɛːrtɪn] f companion.
**Gefälle** [gə'fɛlə] (-s, -) nt (von Land, Straße) slope; (Neigungsgrad) gradient; **starkes ~!** steep hill.
**Gefallen¹** [gə'falən] (-s, -) m favour; **jdm etw zu ~ tun** to do sth to please sb.
**Gefallen²** [gə'falən] (-s) nt pleasure; **an etw** dat **~ finden** to derive pleasure from sth; **an jdm ~ finden** to take to sb.
**gefallen** pp von **fallen**, **gefallen** ♦ vi (unreg): **jdm ~** to please sb; **er/es gefällt mir** I like him/it; **das gefällt mir an ihm** that's one thing I like about him; **sich** dat **etw ~ lassen** to put up with sth.
**Gefallene(r)** m soldier killed in action.
**gefällig** [gə'fɛlɪç] adj (hilfsbereit) obliging; (erfreulich) pleasant; **sonst noch etwas ~?** (veraltet, ironisch) will there be anything else?; **G~keit** f favour (BRIT), favor (US); helpfulness; **etw aus G~keit tun** to do sth as a favour (BRIT) od favor (US).
**gefälligst** (umg) adv kindly; **sei ~ still!** will you kindly keep your mouth shut!
**gefällt** [gə'fɛlt] vb siehe **gefallen**.
**gefangen** [gə'faŋən] pp von **fangen** ♦ adj captured; (fig) captivated.
**Gefangene(r)** f(m) prisoner, captive.
**Gefangenenlager** nt prisoner-of-war camp.
**gefangen-** zW: **~halten** unreg vt to keep prisoner; **G~nahme** (-, -n) f capture; **~nehmen** unreg vt to capture; **G~schaft** f captivity.
**Gefängnis** [gə'fɛŋnɪs] (-ses, -se) nt prison; **zwei Jahre ~ bekommen** to get two years' imprisonment; **~strafe** f prison sentence; **~wärter** m prison warder (BRIT) od guard.
**gefärbt** [gə'fɛrpt] adj (fig: Bericht) biased; (Lebensmittel) coloured (BRIT), colored (US).
**Gefasel** [gə'faːzəl] (-s) nt twaddle, drivel.
**Gefäß** [gə'fɛːs] (-es, -e) nt vessel (auch ANAT), container.
**gefaßt** [gə'fast] adj composed, calm; **auf etw** akk **~ sein** to be prepared od ready for sth; **er kann sich auf etwas ~ machen** (umg) I'll give him something to think about.
**Gefecht** [gə'fɛçt] (-(e)s, -e) nt fight; (MIL) engagement; **jdn/etw außer ~ setzen** (lit, fig) to put sb/sth out of action.
**gefedert** [gə'feːdərt] adj (Matratze) sprung.
**gefeiert** [gə'faɪərt] adj celebrated.
**gefeit** [gə'faɪt] adj: **gegen etw ~ sein** to be immune to sth.
**gefestigt** [gə'fɛstɪçt] adj (Charakter) steadfast.

**Gefieder** [gə'fiːdər] (-s, -) nt plumage, feathers pl.
**gefiedert** adj feathered.
**gefiel** etc [gə'fiːl] vb siehe **gefallen**.
**Geflecht** [gə'flɛçt] (-(e)s, -e) nt (lit, fig) network.
**gefleckt** [gə'flɛkt] adj spotted; (Blume, Vogel) speckled.
**Geflimmer** [gə'flɪmər] (-s) nt shimmering; (FILM, TV) flicker(ing).
**geflissentlich** [gə'flɪsəntlɪç] adj intentional ♦ adv intentionally.
**geflochten** [gə'flɔxtən] pp von **flechten**.
**geflogen** [gə'floːgən] pp von **fliegen**.
**geflohen** [gə'floːən] pp von **fliehen**.
**geflossen** [gə'flɔsən] pp von **fließen**.
**Geflügel** [gə'flyːgəl] (-s) nt poultry.
**geflügelt** adj: **~e Worte** familiar quotations.
**Geflüster** [gə'flystər] (-s) nt whispering.
**gefochten** [gə'fɔxtən] pp von **fechten**.
**Gefolge** [gə'fɔlgə] (-s, -) nt retinue.
**Gefolgschaft** [gə'fɔlkʃaft] f following.
**Gefolgsmann** (-(e)s, pl **-leute**) m follower.
**gefragt** [ge'fraːkt] adj in demand.
**gefräßig** [gə'frɛːsɪç] adj voracious.
**Gefreite(r)** [gə'fraɪtə(r)] m (MIL) lance corporal (BRIT), private first class (US); (NAUT) able seaman (BRIT), seaman apprentice (US); (AVIAT) aircraftman (BRIT), airman first class (US).
**gefressen** [gə'frɛsən] pp von **fressen** ♦ adj: **den hab(e) ich ~** (umg) I'm sick of him.
**gefrieren** [gə'friːrən] unreg vi to freeze.
**Gefrier-** zW: **~fach** nt freezer compartment; **~fleisch** nt frozen meat; **g~getrocknet** adj freeze-dried; **~punkt** m freezing point; **~schutzmittel** nt antifreeze; **~truhe** f deep-freeze.
**gefror** etc [gə'froːr] vb siehe **gefrieren**.
**gefroren** pp von **frieren**, **gefrieren**.
**Gefüge** [gə'fyːgə] (-s, -) nt structure.
**gefügig** adj submissive; (gehorsam) obedient.
**Gefühl** [gə'fyːl] (-(e)s, -e) nt feeling; **etw im ~ haben** to have a feel for sth; **g~los** adj unfeeling; (Glieder) numb.
**Gefühls-** zW: **g~betont** adj emotional; **~duselei** [-duːzə'laɪ] (pej) f mawkishness; **~leben** nt emotional life; **g~mäßig** adj instinctive; **~mensch** m emotional person.
**gefühlvoll** adj (empfindsam) sensitive; (ausdrucksvoll) expressive; (liebevoll) loving.
**gefüllt** [gə'fʏlt] adj (KOCH) stuffed; (Pralinen) with soft centres.
**gefunden** [gə'fʊndən] pp von **finden** ♦ adj: **das war ein ~es Fressen für ihn** that was handing it to him on a plate.
**gegangen** [gə'gaŋən] pp von **gehen**.
**gegeben** [gə'geːbən] pp von **geben** ♦ adj given; **zu ~er Zeit** in due course.
**gegebenenfalls** [gə'geːbənənfals] adv if need be.

===================== *SCHLÜSSELWORT*

**gegen** ['ge:gən] *präp +akk* **1** against; **nichts ~ jdn haben** to have nothing against sb; **X ~ Y** (*SPORT, JUR*) X versus Y; **ein Mittel ~ Schnupfen** something for colds **2** (*in Richtung auf*) towards; **~ Osten** to(wards) the east; **~ Abend** towards evening; **~ einen Baum fahren** to drive into a tree **3** (*ungefähr*) round about; **~ 3 Uhr** around 3 o'clock **4** (*gegenüber*) towards; (*ungefähr*) around; **gerecht ~ alle** fair to all **5** (*im Austausch für*) for; **~ bar** for cash; **~ Quittung** against a receipt **6** (*verglichen mit*) compared with.

**Gegen-** *zW:* **~angriff** *m* counter-attack; **~besuch** *m* return visit; **~beweis** *m* counter-evidence.

**Gegend** ['ge:gənt] (*-, -en*) *f* area, district.

**Gegen-** *zW:* **~darstellung** *f* (*PRESSE*) reply; **g~einander** *adv* against one another; **~fahrbahn** *f* opposite carriageway; **~frage** *f* counterquestion; **~gewicht** *nt* counterbalance; **~gift** *nt* antidote; **~kandidat** *m* rival candidate; **g~läufig** *adj* contrary; **~leistung** *f* service in return; **~lichtaufnahme** *f* back lit photograph; **~liebe** *f* requited love; (*fig: Zustimmung*) approval; **~maßnahme** *f* countermeasure; **~mittel** *nt:* **~mittel (gegen)** (*MED*) antidote (to); **~probe** *f* cross-check.

**Gegensatz** (*-es, ⁻e*) *m* contrast; **Gegensätze überbrücken** to overcome differences.

**gegensätzlich** *adj* contrary, opposite; (*widersprüchlich*) contradictory.

**Gegen-** *zW:* **~schlag** *m* counter-attack; **~seite** *f* opposite side; (*Rückseite*) reverse; **g~seitig** *adj* mutual, reciprocal; **sich g~seitig helfen** to help each other; **in g~seitigem Einverständnis** by mutual agreement; **~seitigkeit** *f* reciprocity; **~spieler** *m* opponent; **~sprechanlage** *f* (two-way) intercom; **~stand** *m* object; **g~ständlich** *adj* objective, concrete; (*KUNST*) representational; **g~standslos** *adj* (*überflüssig*) irrelevant; (*grundlos*) groundless; **~stimme** *f* vote against; **~stoß** *m* counterblow; **~stück** *nt* counterpart; **~teil** *nt* opposite; **im ~teil** on the contrary; **das ~teil bewirken** to have the opposite effect; (*Mensch*) to achieve the exact opposite; **ganz im ~teil** quite the reverse; **ins ~teil umschlagen** to swing to the other extreme; **g~teilig** *adj* opposite, contrary; **ich habe nichts ~teiliges gehört** I've heard nothing to the contrary.

**gegenüber** [ge:gən'|y:bər] *präp +dat* opposite; (*zu*) to(wards); (*in bezug auf*) with regard to; (*im Vergleich zu*) in comparison with;

(*angesichts*) in the face of ♦ *adv* opposite; **mir ~ hat er das nicht geäußert** he didn't say that to me; **G~** (*-s, -*) *nt* person opposite; (*bei Kampf*) opponent; (*bei Diskussion*) opposite number; **~liegen** *unreg vr* to face each other; **~stehen** *unreg vr* to be opposed (to each other); **~stellen** *vt* to confront; (*fig*) to contrast; **G~stellung** *f* confrontation; (*fig*) contrast; (: *Vergleich*) comparison; **~treten** *unreg vi +dat* to face.

**Gegen-** *zW:* **~veranstaltung** *f* counter-meeting; **~verkehr** *m* oncoming traffic; **~vorschlag** *m* counterproposal.

**Gegenwart** ['ge:gənvart] *f* present; **in ~ von** in the presence of.

**gegenwärtig** *adj* present ♦ *adv* at present; **das ist mir nicht mehr ~** that has slipped my mind.

**gegenwartsbezogen** *adj* (*Roman etc*) relevant to present times.

**Gegen-** *zW:* **~wert** *m* equivalent; **~wind** *m* headwind; **~wirkung** *f* reaction; **g~zeichnen** *vt* to countersign; **~zug** *m* countermove; (*EISENB*) corresponding train in the other direction.

**gegessen** [gə'gɛsən] *pp von* **essen**.

**geglichen** [gə'glɪçən] *pp von* **gleichen**.

**gegliedert** [gə'gli:dərt] *adj* jointed; (*fig*) structured.

**geglitten** [gə'glɪtən] *pp von* **gleiten**.

**geglommen** [gə'glɔmən] *pp von* **glimmen**.

**geglückt** [gə'glʏkt] *adj* (*Feier*) successful; (*Überraschung*) real.

**Gegner(in)** ['ge:gnər(ɪn)] (*-s, -*) *m(f)* opponent; **g~isch** *adj* opposing; **~schaft** *f* opposition.

**gegolten** [gə'gɔltən] *pp von* **gelten**.

**gegoren** [gə'go:rən] *pp von* **gären**.

**gegossen** [gə'gɔsən] *pp von* **gießen**.

**gegr.** *abk* (*= gegründet*) estab.

**gegraben** [gə'gra:bən] *pp von* **graben**.

**gegriffen** [gə'grɪfən] *pp von* **greifen**.

**Gehabe** [gə'ha:bə] (*-s*) (*umg*) *nt* affected behaviour (*BRIT*) *od* behavior (*US*).

**gehabt** [gə'ha:pt] *pp von* **haben**.

**Gehackte(s)** [gə'haktə(s)] *nt* mince(d meat) (*BRIT*), ground meat (*US*).

**Gehalt¹** [gə'halt] (*-(e)s, -e*) *m* content.

**Gehalt²** [gə'halt] (*-(e)s, ⁻er*) *nt* salary.

**gehalten** [gə'haltən] *pp von* **halten** ♦ *adj:* **~ sein, etw zu tun** (*form*) to be required to do sth.

**Gehalts-** *zW:* **~abrechnung** *f* salary statement; **~empfänger** *m* salary earner; **~erhöhung** *f* salary increase; **~klasse** *f* salary bracket; **~konto** *nt* current account (*BRIT*), checking account (*US*); **~zulage** *f* salary increment.

**gehaltvoll** [gə'haltfɔl] *adj* (*Speise, Buch*) substantial.

**gehandikapt** [gə'hɛndikɛpt] *adj* handicapped.

**gehangen** [gə'haŋən] *pp von* **hängen**.

**geharnischt** [gə'harnɪʃt] *adj* (*fig*) forceful, sharp.

**gehässig** [gəˈhɛsɪç] *adj* spiteful, nasty; **G~keit** *f* spite(fulness).

**gehäuft** [gəˈhɔʏft] *adj* (*Löffel*) heaped.

**Gehäuse** [gəˈhɔʏzə] (**-s, -**) *nt* case; (*Radio~, Uhr~*) casing; (*von Apfel etc*) core.

**gehbehindert** [ˈgeːbehɪndərt] *adj* disabled.

**Gehege** [gəˈheːgə] (**-s, -**) *nt* enclosure, preserve; **jdm ins ~ kommen** (*fig*) to poach on sb's preserve.

**geheim** [gəˈhaɪm] *adj* secret; (*Dokumente*) classified; **streng ~** top secret; **G~dienst** *m* secret service, intelligence service; **G~fach** *nt* secret compartment; **~halten** *unreg vt* to keep secret.

**Geheimnis** (**-ses, -se**) *nt* secret; (*rätselhaftes ~*) mystery; **~krämer** *m* mystery-monger; **g~voll** *adj* mysterious.

**Geheim-** *zW:* **~nummer** *f* (*TEL*) secret number; **~polizei** *f* secret police; **~rat** *m* privy councillor; **~ratsecken** *pl:* **er hat ~ratsecken** he is going bald at the temples; **~schrift** *f* code, secret writing; **~tip** *m* (personal) tip.

**Geheiß** [gəˈhaɪs] (**-es**) *nt* (*geh*) command; **auf jds ~** *+akk* at sb's bidding.

**geheißen** [gəˈhaɪsən] *pp von* **heißen**.

**gehemmt** [gəˈhɛmt] *adj* inhibited.

**gehen** [ˈgeːən] *unreg vi* (*auch Auto, Uhr*) to go; (*zu Fuß ~*) to walk; (*funktionieren*) to work; (*Teig*) to rise ♦ *vt* to go; to walk ♦ *vi unpers:* **wie geht es dir?** how are you *od* things?; **~ nach** (*Fenster*) to face; **in sich** *akk* **~** to think things over; **nach etw ~** (*urteilen*) to go by sth; **wieviele Leute ~ in deinen Wagen?** how many people can you get in your car?; **nichts geht über** *+akk* ... there's nothing to beat ..., there's nothing better than ...; **schwimmen/schlafen ~** to go swimming/to bed; **in die Tausende ~** to run into (the) thousands; **mir/ihm geht es gut** I'm/he's (doing) fine; **geht das?** is that possible?; **geht's noch?** can you manage?; **es geht** not too bad, O.K.; **das geht nicht** that's not on; **es geht um etw** it concerns sth, it's about sth; **laß es dir gut ~** look after yourself, take care of yourself; **so geht das, das geht so** that/this is how it's done; **darum geht es (mir) nicht** that's not the point; (*spielt keine Rolle*) that's not important to me; **morgen geht es nicht** tomorrow's no good; **wenn es nach mir ginge** ... if it were *od* was up to me ...

**gehenlassen** *unreg vr* to lose one's self-control; (*nachlässig sein*) to let o.s. go.

**gehetzt** [gəˈhɛtst] *adj* harassed.

**geheuer** [gəˈhɔʏər] *adj:* **nicht ~** eerie; (*fragwürdig*) dubious.

**Geheul** [gəˈhɔʏl] (**-(e)s**) *nt* howling.

**Gehilfe** [gəˈhɪlfə] (**-n, -n**) *m* assistant.

**Gehilfin** [gəˈhɪlfɪn] *f* assistant.

**Gehirn** [gəˈhɪrn] (**-(e)s, -e**) *nt* brain; **~erschütterung** *f* concussion; **~schlag** *m* stroke; **~wäsche** *f* brainwashing.

**gehoben** [gəˈhoːbən] *pp von* **heben** ♦ *adj:* **~er Dienst** professional and executive levels of the civil service.

**geholfen** [gəˈhɔlfən] *pp von* **helfen**.

**Gehör** [gəˈhøːr] (**-(e)s**) *nt* hearing; **musikalisches ~** ear; **absolutes ~** perfect pitch; **~ finden** to gain a hearing; **jdm ~ schenken** to give sb a hearing.

**gehorchen** [gəˈhɔrçən] *vi +dat* to obey.

**gehören** [gəˈhøːrən] *vi* to belong ♦ *vr unpers* to be right *od* proper; **das gehört nicht zur Sache** that's irrelevant; **dazu gehört (schon) einiges** *od* **etwas** that takes some doing (*umg*); **er gehört ins Bett** he should be in bed.

**gehörig** *adj* proper; **~ zu** *od +dat* (*geh*) belonging to.

**gehörlos** *adj* (*form*) deaf.

**gehorsam** [gəˈhoːrzaːm] *adj* obedient; **G~** (**-s**) *m* obedience.

**Gehörsinn** *m* sense of hearing.

**Gehsteig** [ˈgeːʃtaɪk] *m*, **Gehweg** [ˈgeːvɛk] *m* pavement (*BRIT*), sidewalk (*US*).

**Geier** [ˈgaɪər] (**-s, -**) *m* vulture; **weiß der ~!** (*umg*) God knows.

**geifern** [ˈgaɪfərn] *vi* to slaver; (*fig*) to be bursting with venom.

**Geige** [ˈgaɪgə] (**-, -n**) *f* violin; **die erste/zweite ~ spielen** (*lit*) to play first/second violin; (*fig*) to call the tune/play second fiddle.

**Geiger(in)** (**-s, -**) *m(f)* violinist.

**Geigerzähler** *m* geiger counter.

**geil** [gaɪl] *adj* randy (*BRIT*), horny (*US*); (*pej: lüstern*) lecherous; (*umg: gut*) fantastic.

**Geisel** [ˈgaɪzəl] (**-, -n**) *f* hostage; **~nahme** (**-**) *f* taking of hostages.

**Geißel** [ˈgaɪsəl] (**-, -n**) *f* scourge, whip.

**geißeln** *vt* to scourge.

**Geist** [gaɪst] (**-(e)s, -er**) *m* spirit; (*Gespenst*) ghost; (*Verstand*) mind; **von allen guten ~ern verlassen sein** (*umg*) to have taken leave of one's senses; **hier scheiden sich die ~er** this is the parting of the ways; **den** *od* **seinen ~ aufgeben** to give up the ghost.

**Geister-** *zW:* **~fahrer** (*umg*) *m* ghost-driver (*US*), *person driving in the wrong direction*; **g~haft** *adj* ghostly; **~hand** *f:* **wie von ~hand** as if by magic.

**Geistes-** *zW:* **g~abwesend** *adj* absent-minded; **~akrobat** *m* mental acrobat; **~blitz** *m* brain wave; **~gegenwart** *f* presence of mind; **g~gegenwärtig** *adj* quick-witted; **g~gestört** *adj* mentally disturbed; (*stärker*) (mentally) deranged; **~haltung** *f* mental attitude; **g~krank** *adj* mentally ill; **~kranke(r)** *f(m)* mentally ill person; **~krankheit** *f* mental illness; **~störung** *f* mental disturbance; **~verfassung** *f* frame of mind; **~wissenschaften** *pl* arts (subjects) *pl*; **~zustand** *m* state of mind; **jdn auf seinen ~zustand untersuchen** to give sb a

psychiatric examination.
**geistig** *adj* intellectual; (*PSYCH*) mental; (*Getränke*) alcoholic; ~ **behindert** mentally handicapped; ~**-seelisch** mental and spiritual.
**geistlich** *adj* spiritual; (*religiös*) religious; **G~e(r)** *m* clergyman; **G~keit** *f* clergy.
**geist-** *zW:* ~**los** uninspired, dull; ~**reich** *adj* intelligent; (*witzig*) witty; ~**tötend** *adj* soul-destroying; ~**voll** *adj* intellectual; (*weise*) wise.
**Geiz** [gaɪts] (**-es**) *m* miserliness, meanness; **g~en** *vi* to be miserly; ~**hals** *m* miser.
**geizig** *adj* miserly, mean.
**Geizkragen** *m* miser.
**gekannt** [gə'kant] *pp von* **kennen**.
**Gekicher** [gə'kɪçər] (**-s**) *nt* giggling.
**Geklapper** [gə'klapər] (**-s**) *nt* rattling.
**Geklimper** [gə'klɪmpər] (**-s**) (*umg*) *nt* (*Klavier~*) tinkling; (: *stümperhaft*) plonking; (*von Geld*) jingling.
**geklungen** [gə'kluŋən] *pp von* **klingen**.
**geknickt** [gə'knɪkt] *adj* (*fig*) dejected.
**gekniffen** [gə'knɪfən] *pp von* **kneifen**.
**gekommen** [gə'kɔmən] *pp von* **kommen**.
**gekonnt** [gə'kɔnt] *pp von* **können** ♦ *adj* skilful (*BRIT*), skillful (*US*).
**Gekritzel** [gə'krɪtsəl] (**-s**) *nt* scrawl, scribble.
**gekrochen** [gə'krɔxən] *pp von* **kriechen**.
**gekünstelt** [ge'kʏnstəlt] *adj* artificial; (*Sprache, Benehmen*) affected.
**Gel** [geːl] (**-s, -e**) *nt* gel.
**Gelaber(e)** [gə'laːbər(ə)] (**-s**) (*umg*) *nt* prattle.
**Gelächter** [gə'lɛçtər] (**-s, -**) *nt* laughter; **in** ~ **ausbrechen** to burst out laughing.
**gelackmeiert** [gə'lakmaɪərt] (*umg*) *adj* conned.
**geladen** [ge'laːdən] *pp von* **laden** ♦ *adj* loaded; (*ELEK*) live; (*fig*) furious.
**Gelage** [gə'laːgə] (**-s, -**) *nt* feast, banquet.
**gelagert** [gə'laːgərt] *adj:* **in anders/ähnlich ~en Fällen** in different/similar cases.
**gelähmt** [gə'lɛːmt] *adj* paralysed.
**Gelände** [gə'lɛndə] (**-s, -**) *nt* land, terrain; (*von Fabrik, Sport~*) grounds *pl*; (*Bau~*) site; ~**fahrzeug** *nt* cross-country vehicle; **g~gängig** *adj* able to go cross-country; ~**lauf** *m* cross-country race.
**Geländer** [gə'lɛndər] (**-s, -**) *nt* railing; (*Treppen~*) banister(s).
**gelang** *etc vb siehe* **gelingen**.
**gelangen** [gə'laŋən] *vi:* ~ **an** *+akk od* **zu** to reach; (*erwerben*) to attain; **in jds Besitz** *akk* ~ to come into sb's possession; **in die richtigen/falschen Hände** ~ to fall into the right/wrong hands.
**gelangweilt** *adj* bored.
**gelassen** [gə'lasən] *pp von* **lassen** ♦ *adj* calm; (*gefaßt*) composed; **G~heit** *f* calmness; composure.
**Gelatine** [ʒela'tiːnə] *f* gelatine.
**gelaufen** [gə'laʊfən] *pp von* **laufen**.
**geläufig** [gə'lɔʏfɪç] *adj* (*üblich*) common; **das**

**ist mir nicht** ~ I'm not familiar with that; **G~keit** *f* commonness; familiarity.
**gelaunt** [gə'laʊnt] *adj:* **schlecht/gut** ~ in a bad/good mood; **wie ist er** ~? what sort of mood is he in?
**Geläut** [gə'lɔʏt] (**-(e)s**) *nt* ringing; (*Läutwerk*) chime.
**Geläute** (**-s**) *nt* ringing.
**gelb** [gɛlp] *adj* yellow; (*Ampellicht*) amber (*BRIT*), yellow (*US*); **G~e Seiten** Yellow Pages; ~**lich** *adj* yellowish.
**Gelbsucht** *f* jaundice.
**Geld** [gɛlt] (**-(e)s, -er**) *nt* money; **etw zu** ~ **machen** to sell sth off; **er hat** ~ **wie Heu** (*umg*) he's stinking rich; **am** ~ **hängen** *od* **kleben** to be tight with money; **staatliche/ öffentliche** ~**er** state/public funds *pl od* money; ~**adel** *m:* **der** ~**adel** the moneyed aristocracy; (*hum: die Reichen*) the rich; ~**anlage** *f* investment; ~**automat** *m* cash dispenser; ~**automatenkarte** *f* cash card; ~**beutel** *m* purse; ~**börse** *f* purse; ~**einwurf** *m* slot; ~**geber** (**-s, -**) *m* financial backer; **g~gierig** *adj* avaricious; ~**institut** *nt* financial institution; ~**mittel** *pl* capital *sing*, means *pl*; ~**quelle** *f* source of income; ~**schein** *m* banknote; ~**schrank** *m* safe, strongbox; ~**strafe** *f* fine; ~**stück** *nt* coin; ~**verlegenheit** *f:* **in** ~**verlegenheit sein/kommen** to be/run short of money; ~**verleiher** *m* moneylender; ~**wäsche** *f* money-laundering; ~**wechsel** *m* exchange (of money); „~**wechsel**" "bureau de change"; ~**wert** *m* cash value; (*FIN: Kaufkraft*) currency value.
**geleckt** [gə'lɛkt] *adj:* **wie** ~ **aussehen** to be neat and tidy.
**Gelee** [ʒe'leː] (**-s, -s**) *nt od m* jelly.
**gelegen** [gə'leːgən] *pp von* **liegen** ♦ *adj* situated; (*passend*) convenient, opportune; **etw kommt jdm** ~ sth is convenient for sb; **mir ist viel/nichts daran** ~ (*wichtig*) it matters a great deal/doesn't matter to me.
**Gelegenheit** [gə'leːgənhaɪt] *f* opportunity; (*Anlaß*) occasion; **bei** ~ some time (or other); **bei jeder** ~ at every opportunity.
**Gelegenheits-** *zW:* ~**arbeit** *f* casual work; ~**arbeiter** *m* casual worker; ~**kauf** *m* bargain.
**gelegentlich** [gə'leːgəntlɪç] *adj* occasional ♦ *adv* occasionally; (*bei Gelegenheit*) some time (or other) ♦ *präp +gen* on the occasion of.
**gelehrig** [gə'leːrɪç] *adj* quick to learn.
**gelehrt** *adj* learned; **G~e(r)** *f(m)* scholar; **G~heit** *f* scholarliness.
**Geleise** [gə'laɪzə] (**-s, -**) *nt* = **Gleis**.
**Geleit** [gə'laɪt] (**-(e)s, -e**) *nt* escort; **freies** *od* **sicheres** ~ safe conduct; **g~en** *vt* to escort; ~**schutz** *m* escort.
**Gelenk** [gə'lɛŋk] (**-(e)s, -e**) *nt* joint.
**gelenkig** *adj* supple.
**gelernt** [gə'lɛrnt] *adj* skilled.

**gelesen** [gə'leːzən] *pp von* **lesen.**
**Geliebte** *f* sweetheart; (*Liebhaberin*) mistress.
**Geliebte(r)** *m* sweetheart; (*Liebhaber*) lover.
**geliefert** [gə'liːfərt] *adj:* **ich bin ~** (*umg*) I've had it.
**geliehen** [gə'liːən] *pp von* **leihen.**
**gelind** [gə'lɪnt] *adj* = **gelinde.**
**gelinde** [gə'lɪndə] *adj* (*geh*) mild; **~ gesagt** to put it mildly.
**gelingen** [gə'lɪŋən] *unreg vi* to succeed; **die Arbeit gelingt mir nicht** I'm not doing very well with this work; **es ist mir gelungen, etw zu tun** I succeeded in doing sth; **G~** *nt* (*geh: Glück*) success; (: *erfolgreiches Ergebnis*) successful outcome.
**gelitten** [gə'lɪtən] *pp von* **leiden.**
**gellen** ['gɛlən] *vi* to shrill.
**gellend** *adj* shrill, piercing.
**geloben** [gə'loːbən] *vt, vi* to vow, swear; **das Gelobte Land** (*REL*) the Promised Land.
**gelogen** [gə'loːgən] *pp von* **lügen.**
**gelten** ['gɛltən] *unreg vt* (*wert sein*) to be worth ♦ *vi* (*gültig sein*) to be valid; (*erlaubt sein*) to be allowed ♦ *vb unpers* (*geh*): **es gilt, etw zu tun** it is necessary to do sth; **was gilt die Wette?** do you want a bet?; **das gilt nicht!** that doesn't count!; (*nicht erlaubt*) that's not allowed; **etw gilt bei jdm viel/wenig** sb values sth highly/doesn't value sth very highly; **jdm viel/wenig ~** to mean a lot/not mean much to sb; **jdm ~** (*gemünzt sein auf*) to be meant for *od* aimed at sb; **etw ~ lassen** to accept sth; **für diesmal lasse ich's ~** I'll let it go this time; **als** *od* **für etw ~** to be considered to be sth; **jdm** *od* **für jdn ~** (*betreffen*) to apply to sb.
**geltend** *adj* (*Preise*) current; (*Gesetz*) in force; (*Meinung*) prevailing; **etw ~ machen** to assert sth; **sich ~ machen** to make itself/o.s. felt; **einen Einwand ~ machen** to raise an objection.
**Geltung** ['gɛltʊŋ] *f:* **~ haben** to have validity; **sich/etw** *dat* **~ verschaffen** to establish o.s./sth; **etw zur ~ bringen** to show sth to its best advantage; **zur ~ kommen** to be seen/heard *etc* to its best advantage.
**Geltungsbedürfnis** *nt* desire for admiration.
**geltungssüchtig** *adj* craving admiration.
**Gelübde** [gə'lypdə] (**-s**, **-**) *nt* vow.
**gelungen** [gə'lʊŋən] *pp von* **gelingen** ♦ *adj* successful.
**Gem.** *abk* = **Gemeinde.**
**gemächlich** [gə'mɛːçlɪç] *adj* leisurely.
**gemacht** [gə'maːxt] *adj* (*gewollt, gekünstelt*) false, contrived; **ein ~er Mann sein** to be made.
**Gemahl** [gə'maːl] (**-(e)s**, **-e**) *m* (*geh, form*) spouse, husband.
**gemahlen** [gə'maːlən] *pp von* **mahlen.**
**Gemahlin** *f* (*geh, form*) spouse, wife.
**Gemälde** [gə'mɛːldə] (**-s**, **-**) *nt* picture, painting.

**gemasert** [gə'maːzərt] *adj* (*Holz*) grained.
**gemäß** [gə'mɛːs] *präp +dat* in accordance with ♦ *adj +dat* appropriate to.
**gemäßigt** *adj* moderate; (*Klima*) temperate.
**Gemauschel** [gə'mauʃəl] (**-s**) (*umg*) *nt* scheming.
**Gemecker** [gə'mɛkər] (**-s**) *nt* (*von Ziegen*) bleating; (*umg: Nörgelei*) moaning.
**gemein** [gə'maɪn] *adj* common; (*niederträchtig*) mean; **etw ~ haben (mit)** to have sth in common (with).
**Gemeinde** [gə'maɪndə] (**-**, **-n**) *f* district; (*Bewohner*) community; (*Pfarr~*) parish; (*Kirchen~*) congregation; **~abgaben** *pl* rates and local taxes *pl*; **~ordnung** *f* by(e) laws *pl*, ordinances *pl* (*US*); **~rat** *m* district council; (*Mitglied*) district councillor; **~schwester** *f* district nurse (*BRIT*); **~steuer** *f* local rates *pl*; **~verwaltung** *f* local administration; **~vorstand** *m* local council; **~wahl** *f* local election.
**Gemein-** *zW:* **~eigentum** *nt* common property; **g~gefährlich** *adj* dangerous to the public; **~gut** *nt* public property; **~heit** *f* (*Niedertracht*) meanness; **das war eine ~heit** that was a mean thing to do/to say; **g~hin** *adv* generally; **~kosten** *pl* overheads *pl*; **~nutz** *m* public good; **g~nützig** *adj* of benefit to the public; (*wohltätig*) charitable; **~platz** *m* commonplace, platitude; **g~sam** *adj* joint, common (*auch MATH*) ♦ *adv* together; **g~same Sache mit jdm machen** to be in cahoots with sb; **der g~same Markt** the Common Market; **g~sames Konto** joint account; **etw g~sam haben** to have sth in common; **~samkeit** *f* common ground; **~schaft** *f* community; **in ~schaft mit** jointly *od* together with; **eheliche ~schaft** (*JUR*) matrimony; **~schaft Unabhängiger Staaten** Commonwealth of Independent States; **g~schaftlich** *adj* = **gemeinsam; ~schaftsantenne** *f* party aerial (*BRIT*) *od* antenna (*US*); **~schaftsarbeit** *f* teamwork; **~schaftsbesitz** *m* collective ownership; **~schaftserziehung** *f* coeducation; **~schaftskunde** *f* social studies *pl*; **~schaftsraum** *m* common room; **~sinn** *m* public spirit; **g~verständlich** *adj* generally comprehensible; **~wesen** *nt* community; **~wohl** *nt* common good.
**Gemenge** [gə'mɛŋə] (**-s**, **-**) *nt* mixture; (*Hand~*) scuffle.
**gemessen** [gə'mɛsən] *pp von* **messen** ♦ *adj* measured.
**Gemetzel** [gə'mɛtsəl] (**-s**, **-**) *nt* slaughter, carnage.
**gemieden** [gə'miːdən] *pp von* **meiden.**
**Gemisch** [gə'mɪʃ] (**-es**, **-e**) *nt* mixture.
**gemischt** *adj* mixed.
**gemocht** [gə'mɔxt] *pp von* **mögen.**
**gemolken** [gə'mɔlkən] *pp von* **melken.**

**Gemse** ['gɛmzə] (-, -n) *f* chamois.
**Gemunkel** [gə'muŋkəl] (-s) *nt* gossip.
**Gemurmel** [gə'murməl] (-s) *nt* murmur(ing).
**Gemüse** [gə'myːzə] (-s, -) *nt* vegetables *pl*;
~**garten** *m* vegetable garden; ~**händler** *m*
greengrocer (*BRIT*), vegetable dealer (*US*);
~**platte** *f* (*KOCH*): **eine** ~**platte** assorted
vegetables.
**gemußt** [gə'must] *pp von* **müssen.**
**gemustert** [gə'mustərt] *adj* patterned.
**Gemüt** [gə'myːt] (-(e)s, -er) *nt* disposition,
nature; (*fig: Mensch*) person; **sich** *dat* **etw zu**
~**e führen** (*umg*) to indulge in sth; **die** ~**er**
**erregen** to arouse strong feelings; **wir**
**müssen warten, bis sich die** ~**er beruhigt**
**haben** we must wait until feelings have
cooled down.
**gemütlich** *adj* comfortable, cosy; (*Person*)
good-natured; **wir verbrachten einen** ~**en**
**Abend** we spent a very pleasant evening;
**G**~**keit** *f* comfortableness, cosiness;
amiability.
**Gemüts-** *zW*: ~**bewegung** *f* emotion;
**g**~**krank** *adj* emotionally disturbed;
~**mensch** *m* sentimental person; ~**ruhe** *f*
composure; **in aller** ~**ruhe** (*umg*) (as) cool as
a cucumber; (*gemächlich*) at a leisurely
pace; ~**zustand** *m* state of mind.
**gemütvoll** *adj* warm, tender.
**Gen** [geːn] (-s, -e) *nt* gene.
**Gen.** *abk* = **Genossenschaft**; (= *Genitiv*) gen.
**gen.** *abk* (= *genannt*) named, called.
**genannt** [gə'nant] *pp von* **nennen.**
**genas** *etc* [gə'naːs] *vb siehe* **genesen.**
**genau** [gə'nau] *adj* exact, precise ♦ *adv*
exactly, precisely; **etw** ~ **nehmen** to take
sth seriously; **G**~**eres** further details *pl*; **etw**
~ **wissen** to know sth for certain; ~ **auf die**
**Minute, auf die Minute** ~ exactly on time;
~**genommen** *adv* strictly speaking.
**Genauigkeit** *f* exactness, accuracy.
**genauso** [gə'nauzoː] *adv* (*vor Adjektiv*) just as;
(*alleinstehend*) just *od* exactly the same.
**Gen.-Dir.** *abk* = **Generaldirektor.**
**genehm** [gə'neːm] *adj* agreeable, acceptable.
**genehmigen** *vt* to approve, authorize; **sich**
*dat* **etw** ~ to indulge in sth.
**Genehmigung** *f* approval, authorization.
**geneigt** [gə'naikt] *adj* (*geh*) well-disposed,
willing; ~ **sein, etw zu tun** to be inclined to
do sth.
**Genera** *pl von* **Genus.**
**General** [gene'raːl] (-s, -e *od* ⁻e) *m* general;
~**direktor** *m* chairman (*BRIT*), president
(*US*); ~**konsulat** *nt* consulate general;
~**probe** *f* dress rehearsal; ~**sekretär** *m*
secretary-general; ~**stabskarte** *f* ordnance
survey map; ~**streik** *m* general strike;
**g**~**überholen** *vt* to overhaul thoroughly;
~**vertretung** *f* sole agency.
**Generation** [generatsi'oːn] *f* generation.
**Generationskonflikt** *m* generation gap.

**Generator** [gene'raːtɔr] *m* generator, dynamo.
**generell** [genə'rɛl] *adj* general.
**genesen** [ge'neːzən] *unreg vi* (*geh*) to
convalesce, recover.
**Genesende(r)** *f(m)* convalescent.
**Genesung** *f* recovery, convalescence.
**Genetik** [ge'neːtɪk] *f* genetics.
**genetisch** [ge'neːtɪʃ] *adj* genetic.
**Genf** ['gɛnf] (-s) *nt* Geneva.
**Genfer** *adj attrib*: **der** ~ **See** Lake Geneva; **die**
~ **Konvention** the Geneva Convention.
**genial** [geni'aːl] *adj* brilliant.
**Genialität** [geniali'tɛːt] *f* brilliance, genius.
**Genick** [gə'nɪk] (-(e)s, -e) *nt* (back of the)
neck; **jdm/etw das** ~ **brechen** (*fig*) to finish
sb/sth; ~**starre** *f* stiff neck.
**Genie** [ʒe'niː] (-s, -s) *nt* genius.
**genieren** [ʒe'niːrən] *vr* to be embarrassed ♦ *vt*
to bother; **geniert es Sie, wenn ...?** do you
mind if ...?
**genießbar** *adj* edible; (*trinkbar*) drinkable.
**genießen** [gə'niːsən] *unreg vt* to enjoy; (*essen*)
to eat; (*trinken*) to drink; **er ist heute nicht zu**
~ (*umg*) he is unbearable today.
**Genießer(in)** (-s, -) *m(f)* connoisseur; (*des*
*Lebens*) pleasure-lover; **g**~**isch** *adj*
appreciative ♦ *adv* with relish.
**Genitalien** [geni'taːliən] *pl* genitals *pl*.
**Genitiv** ['geːnitiːf] *m* genitive.
**genommen** [gə'nɔmən] *pp von* **nehmen.**
**genoß** *etc* [gə'nɔs] *vb siehe* **genießen.**
**Genosse** [gə'nɔsə] (-n, -n) *m* comrade (*bes*
*POL*), companion.
**genossen** *pp von* **genießen.**
**Genossenschaft** *f* cooperative
(association).
**Genossin** *f* comrade (*bes POL*), companion.
**genötigt** [gə'nøːtɪçt] *adj*: **sich** ~ **sehen, etw zu**
**tun** to feel obliged to do sth.
**Genre** [ʒãːrə] (-s, -s) *nt* genre.
**Gent** [gɛnt] (-s) *nt* Ghent.
**Gentechnik** *f*, **Gentechnologie** *f* gene
technology.
**Genua** ['geːnua] (-s) *nt* Genoa.
**genug** [gə'nuːk] *adv* enough; **jetzt ist('s) aber**
~**!** that's enough!
**Genüge** [gə'nyːgə] *f*: **jdm/etw** ~ **tun** *od* **leisten**
to satisfy sb/sth; **etw zur** ~ **kennen** to know
sth well enough; (*abwertender*) to know sth
only too well.
**genügen** *vi* to be enough; (*den Anforderungen*
*etc*) to satisfy; **jdm** ~ to be enough for sb.
**genügend** *adj* enough, sufficient;
(*befriedigend*) satisfactory.
**genügsam** [gə'nyːkzaːm] *adj* modest, easily
satisfied; **G**~**keit** *f* moderation.
**Genugtuung** [gə'nuːktuːuŋ] *f* satisfaction.
**Genus** ['geːnus] (-, **Genera**) *nt* (*GRAM*) gender.
**Genuß** [gə'nus] (-sses, ⁻sse) *m* pleasure;
(*Zusichnehmen*) consumption; **etw mit**
~ **essen** to eat sth with relish; **in den** ~ **von**
**etw kommen** to receive the benefit of sth.

**genüßlich** [gə'nʏslɪç] *adv* with relish.
**Genußmittel** *pl* (semi-)luxury items *pl*.
**geöffnet** [gə'œfnət] *adj* open.
**Geograph** [geo'graːf] (-en, -en) *m* geographer.
**Geographie** [geogra'fiː] *f* geography.
**Geographin** *f* geographer.
**geographisch** *adj* geographical.
**Geologe** [geo'loːgə] (-n, -n) *m* geologist.
**Geologie** [geolo'giː] *f* geology.
**Geologin** *f* geologist.
**Geometrie** [geome'triː] *f* geometry.
**geordnet** [gə'ɔrdnət] *adj*: **in ~en Verhältnissen leben** to live a well-ordered life.
**Georgien** [ge'ɔrgiən] (-s) *nt* Georgia.
**Gepäck** [gə'pɛk] (-(e)s) *nt* luggage, baggage; **mit leichtem ~ reisen** to travel light; **~abfertigung** *f* luggage desk/office; **~annahme** *f* (*Bahnhof*) baggage office; (*Flughafen*) baggage check-in; **~aufbewahrung** *f* left-luggage office (*BRIT*), baggage check (*US*); **~ausgabe** *f* (*Bahnhof*) baggage office; (*Flughafen*) baggage reclaim; **~netz** *nt* luggage rack; **~schein** *m* luggage *od* baggage ticket; **~stück** *nt* piece of baggage; **~träger** *m* porter; (*Fahrrad*) carrier; **~wagen** *m* luggage van (*BRIT*), baggage car (*US*).
**Gepard** ['geːpart] (-(e)s, -e) *m* cheetah.
**gepfeffert** [gə'pfɛfərt] (*umg*) *adj* (*Preise*) steep; (*Fragen, Prüfung*) tough; (*Kritik*) biting.
**gepfiffen** [gə'pfɪfən] *pp von* **pfeifen**.
**gepflegt** [gə'pfleːkt] *adj* well-groomed; (*Park etc*) well looked after; (*Atmosphäre*) sophisticated; (*Ausdrucksweise, Sprache*) cultured.
**Gepflogenheit** [gə'pfloːgənhaɪt] *f* (*geh*) custom.
**Geplapper** [gə'plapər] (-s) *nt* chatter.
**Geplauder** [gə'plaʊdər] (-s) *nt* chat(ting).
**Gepolter** [gə'pɔltər] (-s) *nt* din.
**gepr.** *abk* (= *geprüft*) tested.
**gepriesen** [gə'priːzən] *pp von* **preisen**.
**gequält** [gə'kvɛːlt] *adj* (*Lächeln*) forced; (*Miene, Ausdruck*) pained; (*Gesang, Stimme*) strained.
**Gequatsche** [gə'kvatʃə] (-s) (*pej: umg*) *nt* gabbing; (*Blödsinn*) twaddle.
**gequollen** [gə'kvɔlən] *pp von* **quellen**.
**Gerade** [gə'raːdə] (-n, -n) *f* straight line.

======================= *SCHLÜSSELWORT*

**gerade** [gə'raːdə] *adj* straight; (*aufrecht*) upright; **eine ~ Zahl** an even number
♦ *adv* **1** (*genau*) just, exactly; (*speziell*) especially; **~ deshalb** that's just *od* exactly why; **das ist es ja ~!** that's just it; **~ du** you especially; **warum ~ ich?** why me (of all people)?; **jetzt ~ nicht!** not now!; **~ neben** right next to; **nicht ~ schön** not exactly beautiful
**2** (*eben, soeben*) just; **er wollte ~ aufstehen** he was just about to get up; **da wir ~ von**

**Geld sprechen ... talking of money ...; ~ erst** only just; **~ noch** (only) just.

**gerade-** *zW*: **~aus** *adv* straight ahead; **~biegen** *unreg vt* (*lit, fig*) to straighten out; **~heraus** *adv* straight out, bluntly.
**gerädert** [gə'rɛːdərt] *adj*: **wie ~ sein, sich wie ~ fühlen** to be *od* feel (absolutely) whacked (*umg*).
**geradeso** *adv* just so; **~ dumm** *etc* just as stupid *etc*; **~ wie** just as.
**geradestehen** *unreg vi* (*aufrecht stehen*) to stand up straight; **für jdn/etw ~** (*fig*) to answer *od* be answerable for sb/sth.
**geradezu** *adv* (*beinahe*) virtually, almost.
**geradlinig** *adj* straight.
**gerammelt** [gə'raməlt] *adv*: **~ voll** (*umg*) (jam-)packed.
**Geranie** [ge'raːniə] *f* geranium.
**gerannt** [gə'rant] *pp von* **rennen**.
**Gerät** [gə'rɛːt] (-(e)s, -e) *nt* device; (*Apparat*) gadget; (*elektrisches ~*) appliance; (*Werkzeug*) tool; (*SPORT*) apparatus; (*Zubehör*) equipment *no pl*.
**gerät** [gə'rɛːt] *vb siehe* **geraten**.
**geraten** [gə'raːtən] *unreg pp von* **raten, geraten**
♦ *vi* (*gedeihen*) to thrive; (*gelingen*): (**jdm**) **~** to turn out well (for sb); (*zufällig gelangen*): **~ in** +*akk* to get into; **gut/schlecht ~** to turn out well/badly; **an jdn ~** to come across sb; **an den Richtigen/Falschen ~** to come to the right/wrong person; **in Angst ~** to get frightened; **nach jdm ~** to take after sb.
**Geräteturnen** *nt* apparatus gymnastics.
**Geratewohl** [gəratə'voːl] *nt*: **aufs ~** on the off chance; (*bei Wahl*) at random.
**geraum** [gə'raʊm] *adj*: **seit ~er Zeit** for some considerable time.
**geräumig** [gə'rɔymɪç] *adj* roomy.
**Geräusch** [gə'rɔyʃ] (-(e)s, -e) *nt* sound; (*unangenehm*) noise; **g~arm** *adj* quiet; **~kulisse** *f* background noise; (*FILM, RUNDF, TV*) sound effects *pl*; **g~los** *adj* silent; **~pegel** *m* sound level; **g~voll** *adj* noisy.
**gerben** ['gɛrbən] *vt* to tan.
**Gerber** (-s, -) *m* tanner.
**Gerberei** [gɛrbə'raɪ] *f* tannery.
**gerecht** [gə'rɛçt] *adj* just, fair; **jdm/etw ~ werden** to do justice to sb/sth; **~fertigt** *adj* justified.
**Gerechtigkeit** *f* justice, fairness.
**Gerechtigkeits-** *zW*: **~fanatiker** *m* justice fanatic; **~gefühl** *nt* sense of justice; **~sinn** *m* sense of justice.
**Gerede** [gə'reːdə] (-s) *nt* talk; (*Klatsch*) gossip.
**geregelt** [gə'reːgəlt] *adj* (*Arbeit, Mahlzeiten*) regular; (*Leben*) well-ordered.
**gereizt** [gə'raɪtst] *adj* irritable; **G~heit** *f* irritation.
**Gericht** [gə'rɪçt] (-(e)s, -e) *nt* court; (*Essen*) dish; **jdn/einen Fall vor ~ bringen** to take sb/a case to court; **mit jdm ins ~ gehen** (*fig*)

to judge sb harshly; **über jdn zu ~ sitzen** to sit in judgement on sb; **das Jüngste ~** the Last Judgement; **g~lich** *adj* judicial, legal ♦ *adv* judicially, legally; **ein g~liches Nachspiel haben** to finish up in court; **g~lich gegen jdn vorgehen** to take legal proceedings against sb.

**Gerichts-** *zW:* **~akten** *pl* court records *pl*; **~barkeit** *f* jurisdiction; **~hof** *m* court (of law); **~kosten** *pl* (legal) costs *pl*; **g~medizinisch** *adj* forensic medical *attrib*; **~saal** *m* courtroom; **~stand** *m* court of jurisdiction; **~verfahren** *nt* legal proceedings *pl*; **~verhandlung** *f* court proceedings *pl*; **~vollzieher** *m* bailiff.

**gerieben** [gə'riːbən] *pp von* **reiben** ♦ *adj* grated; (*umg: schlau*) smart, wily.

**geriet** *etc* [gə'riːt] *vb siehe* **geraten**.

**gering** [gə'rɪŋ] *adj* slight, small; (*niedrig*) low; (*Zeit*) short; **~achten** *vt* to think little of; **~fügig** *adj* slight, trivial; **~schätzig** *adj* disparaging; **G~schätzung** *f* disdain.

**geringste(r, s)** *adj* slightest, least; **nicht im ~n** not in the least *od* slightest.

**gerinnen** [gə'rɪnən] *unreg vi* to congeal; (*Blut*) to clot; (*Milch*) to curdle.

**Gerinnsel** [gə'rɪnzəl] (**-s, -**) *nt* clot.

**Gerippe** [gə'rɪpə] (**-s, -**) *nt* skeleton.

**gerissen** [gə'rɪsən] *pp von* **reißen** ♦ *adj* wily, smart.

**geritten** [gə'rɪtən] *pp von* **reiten**.

**geritzt** [gə'rɪtst] (*umg*) *adj:* **die Sache ist ~** everything's fixed up *od* settled.

**Germanist(in)** [gɛrma'nɪst(ɪn)] *m(f)* Germanist, German specialist; (*Student*) German student.

**Germanistik** *f* German (studies *pl*).

**gern** [gɛrn] *adv* willingly, gladly; (**aber**) **~!** of course!; **~ haben, ~ mögen** to like; **etw ~ tun** to like doing sth; **~ geschehen!** you're welcome!, not at all!; **ein ~ gesehener Gast** a welcome visitor; **ich hätte** *od* **möchte ~ ...** I would like ...; **du kannst mich mal ~ haben!** (*umg*) (you can) go to hell!

**gerne** ['gɛrnə] *adv* = **gern**.

**Gernegroß** (**-, -e**) *m* show-off.

**gerochen** [gə'rɔxən] *pp von* **riechen**.

**Geröll** [gə'rœl] (**-(e)s, -e**) *nt* scree.

**geronnen** [gə'rɔnən] *pp von* **rinnen, gerinnen**.

**Gerste** ['gɛrstə] (**-, -n**) *f* barley.

**Gerstenkorn** *nt* (*im Auge*) stye.

**Gerte** ['gɛrtə] (**-, -n**) *f* switch, rod.

**gertenschlank** *adj* willowy.

**Geruch** [gə'rʊx] (**-(e)s, ⁻e**) *m* smell, odour (*BRIT*), odor (*US*); **g~los** *adj* odourless (*BRIT*), odorless (*US*).

**Geruchssinn** *m* sense of smell.

**Gerücht** [gə'rʏçt] (**-(e)s, -e**) *nt* rumour (*BRIT*), rumor (*US*).

**geruchtilgend** *adj* deodorant.

**gerufen** [gə'ruːfən] *pp von* **rufen**.

**geruhen** [gə'ruːən] *vi* to deign.

**geruhsam** [gə'ruːzaːm] *adj* peaceful; (*Spaziergang etc*) leisurely.

**Gerümpel** [gə'rʏmpəl] (**-s**) *nt* junk.

**gerungen** [gə'rʊŋən] *pp von* **ringen**.

**Gerüst** [gə'rʏst] (**-(e)s, -e**) *nt* (*Bau~*) scaffold(ing); (*fig*) framework.

**Ges.** *abk* (= *Gesellschaft*) Co., co.

**gesalzen** [gə'zaltsən] *pp von* **salzen** ♦ *adj* (*fig: umg: Preis, Rechnung*) steep, stiff.

**gesamt** [gə'zamt] *adj* whole, entire; (*Werke*) total; (*Kosten*) complete; **im ~en** all in all; **G~auflage** *f* gross circulation; **G~ausgabe** *f* complete edition; **G~betrag** *m* total (amount); **~deutsch** *adj* all-German; **G~eindruck** *m* general impression; **G~heit** *f* totality, whole.

**Gesamthochschule** *f* polytechnic (*BRIT*).

---

A **Gesamthochschule** *is an institution combining several different kinds of higher education organizations eg. a university, teacher training college and institute of applied science. Students can study for various degrees within the same subject area and it is easier to change course than it is in an individual institution.*

---

**Gesamt-** *zW:* **~masse** *f* (*COMM*) total assets *pl*; **~nachfrage** *f* (*COMM*) composite demand; **~schaden** *m* total damage.

**Gesamtschule** *f* ≈ comprehensive school.

---

*The* **Gesamtschule** *is a comprehensive school teaching pupils who have different aims. Traditionally pupils would go to one of three different schools, the* **Gymnasium, Realschule** *or* **Hauptschule,** *depending on ability. The Gesamtschule seeks to avoid the elitist element prevalent in many Gymnasien, but in Germany these schools are still very controversial. Many parents still prefer the traditional system.*

---

**Gesamtwertung** *f* (*SPORT*) overall placings *pl*.

**gesandt** *pp von* **senden**.

**Gesandte(r)** [gə'zantə(r)] *f(m)* envoy.

**Gesandtschaft** [gə'zantʃaft] *f* legation.

**Gesang** [gə'zaŋ] (**-(e)s, ⁻e**) *m* song; (*Singen*) singing; **~buch** *nt* (*REL*) hymn book; **~verein** *m* choral society.

**Gesäß** [gə'zɛːs] (**-es, -e**) *nt* seat, bottom.

**gesättigt** [gə'zɛtɪçt] *adj* (*CHEM*) saturated.

**gesch.** *abk* (= *geschieden*) div.

**Geschädigte(r)** [gə'ʃɛːdɪçtə(r)] *f(m)* victim.

**geschaffen** [gə'ʃafən] *pp von* **schaffen**.

**Geschäft** [gə'ʃɛft] (**-(e)s, -e**) *nt* business; (*Laden*) shop; (*~sabschluß*) deal; **mit jdm ins ~ kommen** to do business with sb; **dabei hat er ein ~ gemacht** he made a profit by it; **im ~** at work; (*im Laden*) in the shop; **sein**

~ **verrichten** to do one's business (*euph*).
**Geschäftemacher** *m* wheeler-dealer.
**geschäftig** *adj* active, busy; (*pej*) officious.
**geschäftlich** *adj* commercial ♦ *adv* on
business; ~ **unterwegs** away on business.
**Geschäfts-** *zW:* ~**abschluß** *m* business deal
*od* transaction; ~**aufgabe** *f* closure of a/the
business; ~**auflösung** *f* closure of a/the
business; ~**bedingungen** *pl* terms of
business; ~**bereich** *m* (*PARL*)
responsibilities *pl*; **Minister ohne** ~**bereich**
minister without portfolio; ~**bericht** *m*
financial report; ~**computer** *m* business
computer; ~**essen** *nt* business lunch;
~**führer** *m* manager; (*Klub*) secretary;
~**geheimnis** *nt* trade secret; ~**inhaber** *m*
owner; ~**jahr** *nt* financial year; ~**lage** *f*
business conditions *pl*; ~**leitung** *f*
management; ~**mann** (-(e)s, *pl* -leute) *m*
businessman; **g~mäßig** *adj* businesslike;
~**ordnung** *f* standing orders *pl*; **eine Frage
zur** ~**ordnung** a question on a point of
order; ~**partner** *m* partner; ~**reise** *f*
business trip; ~**schluß** *m* closing time;
~**sinn** *m* business sense; ~**stelle** *f* office(s
*pl*), place of business; **g~tüchtig** *adj*
business-minded; ~**viertel** *nt* shopping
centre (*BRIT*) *od* center (*US*); (*Banken etc*)
business quarter, commercial district;
~**wagen** *m* company car; ~**wesen** *nt*
business; ~**zeit** *f* business hours *pl*;
~**zweig** *m* branch (of a business).
**geschah** *etc* [gə'ʃaː] *vb siehe* **geschehen**.
**geschehen** [gə'ʃeːən] *unreg vi* to happen; **das
geschieht ihm (ganz) recht** it serves him
(jolly well (*umg*)) right; **was soll mit ihm/
damit** ~? what is to be done with him/it?; **es
war um ihn** ~ that was the end of him.
**gescheit** [gə'ʃaɪt] *adj* clever; (*vernünftig*)
sensible.
**Geschenk** [gə'ʃɛŋk] (-(e)s, -e) *nt* present, gift;
~**artikel** *m* gift; ~**gutschein** *m* gift voucher;
~**packung** *f* gift pack; ~**sendung** *f* gift
parcel.
**Geschichte** [gə'ʃɪçtə] (-, -n) *f* story; (*Sache*)
affair; (*Historie*) history.
**Geschichtenerzähler** *m* storyteller.
**geschichtlich** *adj* historical; (*bedeutungsvoll*)
historic.
**Geschichtsfälschung** *f* falsification of
history.
**Geschichtsschreiber** *m* historian.
**Geschick** [gə'ʃɪk] (-(e)s, -e) *nt* skill; (*geh:
Schicksal*) fate.
**Geschicklichkeit** *f* skill, dexterity.
**Geschicklichkeitsspiel** *nt* game of skill.
**geschickt** *adj* skilful (*BRIT*), skillful (*US*);
(*taktisch*) clever; (*beweglich*) agile.
**geschieden** [gə'ʃiːdən] *pp von* **scheiden** ♦ *adj*
divorced.
**geschieht** [gə'ʃiːt] *vb siehe* **geschehen**.
**geschienen** [gə'ʃiːnən] *pp von* **scheinen**.

**Geschirr** [gə'ʃɪr] (-(e)s, -e) *nt* crockery;
(*Küchen~*) pots and pans *pl*; (*Pferde~*)
harness; ~**spülmaschine** *f* dishwasher;
~**tuch** *nt* tea towel (*BRIT*), dishtowel (*US*).
**geschissen** [gə'ʃɪsən] *pp von* **scheißen**.
**geschlafen** [gə'ʃlaːfən] *pp von* **schlafen**.
**geschlagen** [gə'ʃlaːgən] *pp von* **schlagen**.
**geschlaucht** [gə'ʃlaʊxt] *adv:* ~ **sein** (*umg*) to
be exhausted *od* knackered.
**Geschlecht** [gə'ʃlɛçt] (-(e)s, -er) *nt* sex;
(*GRAM*) gender; (*Gattung*) race;
(*Abstammung*) lineage; **g~lich** *adj* sexual.
**Geschlechts-** *zW:* ~**krankheit** *f* sexually-
transmitted disease; **g~reif** *adj* sexually
mature; **g~spezifisch** *adj* (*SOZIOLOGIE*) sex-
specific; ~**teil** *nt* od *m* genitals *pl*; ~**verkehr**
*m* sexual intercourse; ~**wort** *nt* (*GRAM*)
article.
**geschlichen** [gə'ʃlɪçən] *pp von* **schleichen**.
**geschliffen** [gə'ʃlɪfən] *pp von* **schleifen**.
**geschlossen** [gə'ʃlɔsən] *pp von* **schließen** ♦ *adj:*
~**e Gesellschaft** (*Fest*) private party ♦ *adv:*
~ **hinter jdm stehen** to stand solidly behind
sb; ~**e Ortschaft** built-up area.
**geschlungen** [gə'ʃlʊŋən] *pp von* **schlingen**.
**Geschmack** [gə'ʃmak] (-(e)s, ̈-e) *m* taste; **nach
jds** ~ to sb's taste; ~ **an etw** *dat* **finden** to
(come to) like sth; **je nach** ~ to one's own
taste; **er hat einen guten** ~ (*fig*) he has good
taste; **g~los** *adj* tasteless; (*fig*) in bad taste.
**Geschmacks-** *zW:* ~**sache** *f* matter of taste;
~**sinn** *m* sense of taste; ~**verirrung** *f:* **unter
~verirrung leiden** (*ironisch*) to have no taste.
**geschmackvoll** *adj* tasteful.
**Geschmeide** [gə'ʃmaɪdə] (-s, -) *nt* jewellery
(*BRIT*), jewelry (*US*).
**geschmeidig** *adj* supple; (*formbar*) malleable.
**Geschmeiß** *nt* vermin *pl*.
**Geschmiere** [gə'ʃmiːrə] (-s) *nt* scrawl; (*Bild*)
daub.
**geschmissen** [gə'ʃmɪsən] *pp von* **schmeißen**.
**geschmolzen** [gə'ʃmɔltsən] *pp von* **schmelzen**.
**Geschnetzelte(s)** [gə'ʃnɛtsəltə(s)] *nt* (*KOCH*)
*meat cut into strips and stewed to produce
a thick sauce.*
**geschnitten** [gə'ʃnɪtən] *pp von* **schneiden**.
**geschoben** [gə'ʃoːbən] *pp von* **schieben**.
**geschollen** [gə'ʃɔlən] *pp von* **schallen**.
**gescholten** [gə'ʃɔltən] *pp von* **schelten**.
**Geschöpf** [gə'ʃœpf] (-(e)s, -e) *nt* creature.
**geschoren** [gə'ʃoːrən] *pp von* **scheren**.
**Geschoß** [gə'ʃɔs] (-sses, -sse) *nt* (*MIL*)
projectile; (*Rakete*) missile; (*Stockwerk*)
floor.
**geschossen** [gə'ʃɔsən] *pp von* **schießen**.
**geschraubt** [gə'ʃraʊpt] *adj* stilted, artificial.
**Geschrei** [gə'ʃraɪ] (-s) *nt* cries *pl*, shouting;
(*fig: Aufheben*) noise, fuss.
**geschrieben** [gə'ʃriːbən] *pp von* **schreiben**.
**geschrie(e)n** [gə'ʃriː(ə)n] *pp von* **schreien**.
**geschritten** [gə'ʃrɪtən] *pp von* **schreiten**.
**geschunden** [gə'ʃʊndən] *pp von* **schinden**.

**Geschütz** [gə'ʃʏts] (**-es, -e**) *nt* gun, piece of artillery; **ein schweres ~ auffahren** (*fig*) to bring out the big guns; **~feuer** *nt* artillery fire, gunfire.

**geschützt** *adj* protected; (*Winkel, Ecke*) sheltered.

**Geschw.** *abk* = **Geschwister.**

**Geschwader** [gə'ʃvaːdər] (**-s, -**) *nt* (*NAUT*) squadron; (*AVIAT*) group.

**Geschwafel** [gə'ʃvaːfəl] (**-s**) *nt* silly talk.

**Geschwätz** [gə'ʃvɛts] (**-es**) *nt* chatter; (*Klatsch*) gossip.

**geschwätzig** *adj* talkative; **G~keit** *f* talkativeness.

**geschweige** [gə'ʃvaɪgə] *adv:* ~ (**denn**) let alone, not to mention.

**geschwiegen** [gə'ʃviːgən] *pp von* **schweigen.**

**geschwind** [gə'ʃvɪnt] *adj* quick, swift.

**Geschwindigkeit** [gə'ʃvɪndɪçkaɪt] *f* speed, velocity.

**Geschwindigkeits-** *zW:* **~begrenzung** *f*, **~beschränkung** *f* speed limit; **~messer** *m* (*AUT*) speedometer; **~überschreitung** *f* speeding.

**Geschwister** [gə'ʃvɪstər] *pl* brothers and sisters *pl*.

**geschwollen** [gə'ʃvɔlən] *pp von* **schwellen** ♦ *adj* pompous.

**geschwommen** [gə'ʃvɔmən] *pp von* **schwimmen.**

**geschworen** [gə'ʃvoːrən] *pp von* **schwören.**

**Geschworene(r)** *f(m)* juror; **die Geschworenen** *pl* the jury.

**Geschwulst** [gə'ʃvʊlst] (**-, -̈e**) *f* growth, tumour.

**geschwunden** [gə'ʃvʊndən] *pp von* **schwinden.**

**geschwungen** [gə'ʃvʊŋən] *pp von* **schwingen** ♦ *adj* curved.

**Geschwür** [gə'ʃvyːr] (**-(e)s, -e**) *nt* ulcer; (*Furunkel*) boil.

**gesehen** [gə'zeːən] *pp von* **sehen.**

**Geselle** [gə'zɛlə] (**-n, -n**) *m* fellow; (*Handwerks~*) journeyman.

**gesellen** *vr:* **sich zu jdm ~** to join sb.

**Gesellenbrief** *m* articles *pl*.

**Gesellenprüfung** *f* examination to become a journeyman.

**gesellig** *adj* sociable; **~es Beisammensein** get-together; **G~keit** *f* sociability.

**Gesellschaft** *f* society; (*Begleitung, COMM*) company; (*Abend~ etc*) party; (*pej*) crowd (*umg*); (*Kreis von Menschen*) group of people; **in schlechte ~ geraten** to get into bad company; **geschlossene ~** private party; **jdm ~ leisten** to keep sb company.

**Gesellschafter(in)** (**-s, -**) *m(f)* shareholder; (*Partner*) partner.

**gesellschaftlich** *adj* social.

**Gesellschafts-** *zW:* **~anzug** *m* evening dress; **g~fähig** *adj* socially acceptable; **~ordnung** *f* social structure; **~reise** *f* group tour; **~schicht** *f* social stratum; **~system** *nt* social system.

**gesessen** [gə'zɛsən] *pp von* **sitzen.**

**Gesetz** [gə'zɛts] (**-es, -e**) *nt* law; (*PARL*) act; (*Satzung, Regel*) rule; **vor dem ~** in (the eyes of the) law; **nach dem ~** under the law; **das oberste ~ (der Wirtschaft** *etc*) the golden rule (of industry *etc*); **~blatt** *nt* law gazette; **~buch** *nt* statute book; **~entwurf** *m* bill.

**Gesetzeshüter** *m* (*ironisch*) guardian of the law.

**Gesetzesvorlage** *f* bill.

**Gesetz-** *zW:* **g~gebend** *adj* legislative; **~geber** (**-s, -**) *m* legislator; **~gebung** *f* legislation; **g~lich** *adj* legal, lawful; **~lichkeit** *f* legality, lawfulness; **g~los** *adj* lawless; **g~mäßig** *adj* lawful.

**gesetzt** *adj* (*Mensch*) sedate ♦ *konj:* ~ **den Fall ...** assuming (that) ...

**gesetzwidrig** *adj* illegal; (*unrechtmäßig*) unlawful.

**ges. gesch.** *abk* (= *gesetzlich geschützt*) reg.

**Gesicht** [gə'zɪçt] (**-(e)s, -er**) *nt* face; **das Zweite ~** second sight; **das ist mir nie zu ~ gekommen** I've never laid eyes on that; **jdn zu ~ bekommen** to clap eyes on sb; **jdm etw ins ~ sagen** to tell sb sth to his face; **sein wahres ~ zeigen** to show (o.s. in) one's true colours; **jdm wie aus dem ~ geschnitten sein** to be the spitting image of sb.

**Gesichts-** *zW:* **~ausdruck** *m* (facial) expression; **~farbe** *f* complexion; **~packung** *f* face pack; **~punkt** *m* point of view; **~wasser** *nt* face lotion; **~züge** *pl* features *pl*.

**Gesindel** [gə'zɪndəl] (**-s**) *nt* rabble.

**gesinnt** [gə'zɪnt] *adj* disposed, minded.

**Gesinnung** [gə'zɪnʊŋ] *f* disposition; (*Ansicht*) views *pl*.

**Gesinnungs-** *zW:* **~genosse** *m* like-minded person; **~losigkeit** *f* lack of conviction; **~schnüffelei** (*pej*) *f:* **~schnüffelei betreiben** to pry into people's political convictions; **~wandel** *m* change of opinion.

**gesittet** [gə'zɪtət] *adj* well-mannered.

**gesoffen** [gə'zɔfən] *pp von* **saufen.**

**gesogen** [gə'zoːgən] *pp von* **saugen.**

**gesollt** [gə'zɔlt] *pp von* **sollen.**

**gesondert** [gə'zɔndərt] *adj* separate.

**gesonnen** [gə'zɔnən] *pp von* **sinnen.**

**gespalten** [gə'ʃpaltən] *adj* (*Bewußtsein*) split; (*Lippe*) cleft.

**Gespann** [gə'ʃpan] (**-(e)s, -e**) *nt* team; (*umg*) couple.

**gespannt** *adj* tense, strained; (*neugierig*) curious; (*begierig*) eager; **ich bin ~, ob** I wonder if *od* whether; **auf etw/jdn ~ sein** to look forward to sth/to meeting sb; **ich bin ~ wie ein Flitzebogen** (*hum: umg*) I'm on tenterhooks.

**Gespenst** [gə'ʃpɛnst] (**-(e)s, -er**) *nt* ghost; (*fig: Gefahr*) spectre (*BRIT*), specter (*US*); **~er**

sehen (fig: umg) to imagine things.
**gespensterhaft, gespenstisch** adj ghostly.
**gespie(e)n** [gəʃpiː(ə)n] pp von **speien**.
**gespielt** [gəˈʃpiːlt] adj feigned.
**gesponnen** [gəʃpɔnən] pp von **spinnen**.
**Gespött** [gəˈʃpœt] (-(e)s) nt mockery; **zum ~ werden** to become a laughing stock.
**Gespräch** [gəˈʃprɛːç] (-(e)s, -e) nt conversation; (Diskussion) discussion; (Anruf) call; **zum ~ werden** to become a topic of conversation; **ein ~ unter vier Augen** a confidential od private talk; **mit jdm ins ~ kommen** to get into conversation with sb; (fig) to establish a dialogue with sb.
**gesprächig** adj talkative; **G~keit** f talkativeness.
**Gesprächs-** zW: **~einheit** f (TEL) unit; **~gegenstand** m topic; **~partner** m: **mein ~partner bei den Verhandlungen** my opposite number at the talks; **~stoff** m topics pl; **~thema** nt subject od topic (of conversation).
**gesprochen** [gəˈʃprɔxən] pp von **sprechen**.
**gesprossen** [gəˈʃprɔsən] pp von **sprießen**.
**gesprungen** [gəˈʃpruŋən] pp von **springen**.
**Gespür** [gəˈʃpyːr] (-s) nt feeling.
**gest.** abk (= gestorben) dec.
**Gestalt** [gəˈʃtalt] (-, -en) f form, shape; (Person) figure; (LITER: pej: Mensch) character; **in ~ von** in the form of; **~ annehmen** to take shape.
**gestalten** vt (formen) to shape, form; (organisieren) to arrange, organize ♦ vr: **sich ~ (zu)** to turn out (to be); **etw interessanter etc ~** to make sth more interesting etc.
**Gestaltung** f formation; organization.
**gestanden** [gəʃtandən] pp von **stehen**, **gestehen**.
**geständig** [gəˈʃtɛndɪç] adj: **~ sein** to have confessed.
**Geständnis** [gəˈʃtɛntnɪs] (-ses, -se) nt confession.
**Gestank** [gəˈʃtaŋk] (-(e)s) m stench.
**gestatten** [gəˈʃtatən] vt to permit, allow; **~ Sie?** may I?; **sich** dat **~, etw zu tun** to take the liberty of doing sth.
**Geste** [ˈɡɛstə] (-, -n) f gesture.
**Gesteck** [gəˈʃtɛk] (-(e)s, -e) nt flower arrangement.
**gestehen** [gəˈʃteːən] unreg vt to confess; **offen gestanden** quite frankly.
**Gestein** [gəˈʃtaɪn] (-(e)s, -e) nt rock.
**Gestell** [gəˈʃtɛl] (-(e)s, -e) nt stand; (Regal) shelf; (Bett~, Brillen~) frame.
**gestellt** adj (unecht) posed.
**gestern** [ˈɡɛstɐn] adv yesterday; **~ abend/morgen** yesterday evening/morning; **er ist nicht von ~** (umg) he wasn't born yesterday.
**gestiefelt** [gəˈʃtiːfəlt] adj: **der G~e Kater** Puss-in-Boots.
**gestiegen** [gəˈʃtiːɡən] pp von **steigen**.

**Gestik** (-) f gestures pl.
**gestikulieren** [ɡɛstikuˈliːrən] vi to gesticulate.
**Gestirn** [gəˈʃtɪrn] (-(e)s, -e) nt star.
**gestoben** [gəˈʃtoːbən] pp von **stieben**.
**Gestöber** [gəˈʃtøːbər] (-s, -) nt flurry; (länger) blizzard.
**gestochen** [gəˈʃtɔxən] pp von **stechen** ♦ adj (Handschrift) clear, neat.
**gestohlen** [gəˈʃtoːlən] pp von **stehlen** ♦ adj: **der/das kann mir ~ bleiben** (umg) he/it can go hang.
**gestorben** [gəˈʃtɔrbən] pp von **sterben**.
**gestört** [gəˈʃtøːrt] adj disturbed; (Rundfunkempfang) poor, with a lot of interference.
**gestoßen** [gəˈʃtoːsən] pp von **stoßen**.
**Gestotter** [gəˈʃtɔtər] (-s) nt stuttering, stammering.
**Gesträuch** [gəˈʃtrɔʏç] (-(e)s, -e) nt shrubbery, bushes pl.
**gestreift** [gəˈʃtraɪft] adj striped.
**gestrichen** [gəˈʃtrɪçən] pp von **streichen** ♦ adj: **~ voll** (genau voll) level; (sehr voll) full to the brim; **ein ~er Teelöffel voll** a level teaspoon(ful).
**gestrig** [ˈɡɛstrɪç] adj yesterday's.
**gestritten** [gəˈʃtrɪtən] pp von **streiten**.
**Gestrüpp** [gəˈʃtrʏp] (-(e)s, -e) nt undergrowth.
**gestunken** [gəˈʃtuŋkən] pp von **stinken**.
**Gestüt** [gəˈʃtyːt] (-(e)s, -e) nt stud farm.
**Gesuch** [gəˈzuːx] (-(e)s, -e) nt petition; (Antrag) application.
**gesucht** adj (begehrt) sought after.
**gesund** [gəˈzʊnt] adj healthy; **wieder ~ werden** to get better; **~ und munter** hale and hearty; **jdn ~ schreiben** to certify sb (as) fit; **G~heit** f health; (Sportlichkeit, fig) healthiness; **G~heit!** bless you!; **bei guter G~heit** in good health; **~heitlich** adj health attrib, physical ♦ adv physically; **wie geht es Ihnen ~heitlich?** how's your health?
**Gesundheits-** zW: **~amt** nt public health department; **~apostel** m (ironisch) health freak (umg); **~fürsorge** f health care; **~reform** f health service reforms pl; **~risiko** nt health hazard; **g~schädlich** adj unhealthy; **~wesen** nt health service; **~zeugnis** nt health certificate; **~zustand** m state of health.
**gesungen** [gəˈzʊŋən] pp von **singen**.
**gesunken** [gəˈzʊŋkən] pp von **sinken**.
**getan** [gəˈtaːn] pp von **tun** ♦ adj: **nach ~er Arbeit** when the day's work is done.
**Getier** [gəˈtiːər] (-(e)s, -e) nt (Tiere, bes Insekten) creatures pl; (einzelnes) creature.
**Getöse** [gəˈtøːzə] (-s) nt din, racket.
**getragen** [gəˈtraːɡən] pp von **tragen**.
**Getränk** [gəˈtrɛŋk] (-(e)s, -e) nt drink.
**Getränkeautomat** m drinks machine od dispenser.
**Getränkekarte** f (in Café) list of beverages; (in Restaurant) wine list.

**getrauen** [gə'trauən] *vr* to dare.
**Getreide** [gə'traɪdə] (**-s**, **-**) *nt* cereal, grain; **~speicher** *m* granary.
**getrennt** [gə'trɛnt] *adj* separate; **~ leben** to be separated, live apart.
**getreten** [gə'treːtən] *pp von* **treten**.
**getreu** [gə'trɔy] *adj* faithful.
**Getriebe** [gə'triːbə] (**-s**, **-**) *nt* (*Leute*) bustle; (*AUT*) gearbox.
**getrieben** *pp von* **treiben**.
**Getriebeöl** *nt* transmission oil.
**getroffen** [gə'trɔfən] *pp von* **treffen**.
**getrogen** [gə'troːgən] *pp von* **trügen**.
**getrost** [gə'troːst] *adv* confidently; **~ sterben** to die in peace; **du kannst dich ~ auf ihn verlassen** you need have no fears about relying on him.
**getrunken** [gə'trʊŋkən] *pp von* **trinken**.
**Getto** ['gɛto] (**-s**, **-s**) *nt* ghetto.
**Getue** [gə'tuːə] (**-s**) *nt* fuss.
**Getümmel** [gə'tʏməl] (**-s**) *nt* turmoil.
**geübt** [gə'yːpt] *adj* experienced.
**GEW** (**-**) *f abk* (= *Gewerkschaft Erziehung und Wissenschaft*) *union of employees in education and science.*
**Gew.** *abk* = **Gewerkschaft**.
**Gewächs** [gə'vɛks] (**-es**, **-e**) *nt* growth; (*Pflanze*) plant.
**gewachsen** [gə'vaksən] *pp von* **wachsen ♦** *adj:* **jdm/etw ~ sein** to be sb's equal/equal to sth.
**Gewächshaus** *nt* greenhouse.
**gewagt** [gə'vaːkt] *adj* daring, risky.
**gewählt** [gə'vɛːlt] *adj* (*Sprache*) refined, elegant.
**gewahr** [gə'vaːr] *adj:* **eine** *od* **einer Sache** *gen* **~ werden** to become aware of sth.
**Gewähr** [gə'vɛːr] (**-**) *f* guarantee; **keine ~ übernehmen für** to accept no responsibility for; **die Angabe erfolgt ohne ~** this information is supplied without liability.
**gewähren** *vt* to grant; (*geben*) to provide; **jdn ~ lassen** not to stop sb.
**gewährleisten** *vt* to guarantee.
**Gewahrsam** [gə'vaːrzaːm] (**-s**, **-e**) *m* safekeeping; (*Polizei~*) custody.
**Gewährsmann** *m* informant, source.
**Gewährung** *f* granting.
**Gewalt** [gə'valt] (**-**, **-en**) *f* power; (*große Kraft*) force; (*~taten*) violence; **mit aller ~** with all one's might; **die ausübende/gesetzgebende/richterliche ~** the executive/legislature/judiciary; **elterliche ~** parental authority; **höhere ~** acts/an act of God; **~anwendung** *f* use of force.
**Gewaltenteilung** *f* separation of powers.
**Gewaltherrschaft** *f* tyranny.
**gewaltig** *adj* tremendous; (*Irrtum*) huge; **sich ~ irren** to be very much mistaken.
**Gewalt-** *zW:* **g~los** *adj* non-violent ♦ *adv* without force/violence; **~marsch** *m* forced

march; **~monopol** *nt* monopoly on the use of force; **g~sam** *adj* forcible; **g~tätig** *adj* violent; **~verbrechen** *nt* crime of violence; **~verzicht** *m* non-aggression.
**Gewand** [gə'vant] (**-(e)s**, **-̈er**) *nt* garment.
**gewandt** [gə'vant] *pp von* **wenden ♦** *adj* deft, skilful (*BRIT*), skillful (*US*); (*erfahren*) experienced; **G~heit** *f* dexterity, skill.
**gewann** *etc* [gə'van] *vb siehe* **gewinnen**.
**gewaschen** [gə'vaʃən] *pp von* **waschen**.
**Gewässer** [gə'vɛsər] (**-s**, **-**) *nt* waters pl.
**Gewebe** [gə'veːbə] (**-s**, **-**) *nt* (*Stoff*) fabric; (*BIOL*) tissue.
**Gewehr** [gə'veːr] (**-(e)s**, **-e**) *nt* (*Flinte*) rifle; (*Schrotbüchse*) shotgun; **~lauf** *m* rifle barrel; barrel of a shotgun.
**Geweih** [gə'vaɪ] (**-(e)s**, **-e**) *nt* antlers pl.
**Gewerbe** [gə'vɛrbə] (**-s**, **-**) *nt* trade, occupation; **Handel und ~** trade and industry; **fahrendes ~** mobile trade; **~aufsichtsamt** *nt* ≈ factory inspectorate; **~schein** *m* trading licence; **~schule** *f* technical school; **g~treibend** *adj* carrying on a trade.
**gewerblich** *adj* industrial.
**gewerbsmäßig** *adj* professional.
**Gewerbszweig** *m* line of trade.
**Gewerkschaft** [gə'vɛrkʃaft] *f* trade *od* labor (*US*) union.
**Gewerkschaft(l)er(in)** *m(f)* trade *od* labor (*US*) unionist.
**gewerkschaftlich** *adj:* **wir haben uns ~ organisiert** we organized ourselves into a union.
**Gewerkschaftsbund** *m* federation of trade *od* labor (*US*) unions, ≈ Trades Union Congress (*BRIT*), Federation of Labor (*US*).
**gewesen** [gə'veːzən] *pp von* **sein**.
**gewichen** [gə'vɪçən] *pp von* **weichen**.
**Gewicht** [gə'vɪçt] (**-(e)s**, **-e**) *nt* weight; (*fig*) importance.
**gewichten** *vt* to evaluate.
**Gewichtheben** (**-s**) *nt* (*SPORT*) weight-lifting.
**gewichtig** *adj* weighty.
**Gewichtsklasse** *f* (*SPORT*) weight (category).
**gewieft** [gə'viːft] (*umg*) *adj* shrewd, cunning.
**gewiesen** [gə'viːzən] *pp von* **weisen**.
**gewillt** [gə'vɪlt] *adj* willing, prepared.
**Gewimmel** [gə'vɪməl] (**-s**) *nt* swarm; (*Menge*) crush.
**Gewinde** [gə'vɪndə] (**-s**, **-**) *nt* (*Kranz*) wreath; (*von Schraube*) thread.
**Gewinn** [gə'vɪn] (**-(e)s**, **-e**) *m* profit; (*bei Spiel*) winnings pl; **etw mit ~ verkaufen** to sell sth at a profit; **aus etw ~ schlagen** (*umg*) to make a profit out of sth; **~anteil** *m* (*COMM*) dividend; **~ausschüttung** *f* prize draw; **~beteiligung** *f* profit-sharing; **g~bringend** *adj* profitable; **~chancen** pl (*beim Wetten*) odds pl.

**gewinnen** *unreg vt* to win; (*erwerben*) to gain; (*Kohle, Öl*) to extract ♦ *vi* to win; (*profitieren*) to gain; **jdn (für etw)** ~ to win sb over (to sth); **an etw** *dat* ~ to gain in sth.

**gewinnend** *adj* winning, attractive.

**Gewinner(in)** (**-s, -**) *m(f)* winner.

**Gewinn-** *zW:* ~**(n)ummer** *f* winning number; ~**spanne** *f* profit margin; ~**sucht** *f* love of gain; ~**- und Verlustrechnung** *f* profit and loss account.

**Gewinnung** *f* (*von Kohle etc*) mining; (*von Zucker etc*) extraction.

**Gewirr** [gə'vɪr] (**-(e)s, -e**) *nt* tangle; (*von Straßen*) maze.

**gewiß** [gə'vɪs] *adj* certain ♦ *adv* certainly; **in gewissem Maße** to a certain extent.

**Gewissen** [gə'vɪsən] (**-s, -**) *nt* conscience; **jdm ins** ~ **reden** to have a serious talk with sb; **g~haft** *adj* conscientious; ~**haftigkeit** *f* conscientiousness; **g~los** *adj* unscrupulous.

**Gewissens-** *zW:* ~**bisse** *pl* pangs of conscience *pl*, qualms *pl*; ~**frage** *f* matter of conscience; ~**freiheit** *f* freedom of conscience; ~**konflikt** *m* moral conflict.

**gewissermaßen** [gəvɪsər'ma:sən] *adv* more or less, in a way.

**Gewißheit** *f* certainty; **sich** *dat* ~ **verschaffen** to find out for certain.

**gewißlich** *adv* surely.

**Gewitter** [gə'vɪtər] (**-s, -**) *nt* thunderstorm.

**gewittern** *vi unpers:* **es gewittert** there's a thunderstorm.

**gewitterschwül** *adj* sultry and thundery.

**Gewitterwolke** *f* thundercloud; (*fig: umg*) storm cloud.

**gewitzt** [gə'vɪtst] *adj* shrewd, cunning.

**gewoben** [gə'vo:bən] *pp von* **weben**.

**gewogen** [gə'vo:gən] *pp von* **wiegen** ♦ *adj (+dat)* well-disposed (towards).

**gewöhnen** [gə'vø:nən] *vt:* **jdn an etw** *akk* ~ to accustom sb to sth; (*erziehen zu*) to teach sb sth ♦ *vr:* **sich an etw** *akk* ~ to get used *od* accustomed to sth.

**Gewohnheit** [gə'vo:nhaɪt] *f* habit; (*Brauch*) custom; **aus** ~ from habit; **zur** ~ **werden** to become a habit; **sich** *dat* **etw zur** ~ **machen** to make a habit of sth.

**Gewohnheits-** *in zW* habitual; ~**mensch** *m* creature of habit; ~**recht** *nt* common law; ~**tier** (*umg*) *nt* creature of habit.

**gewöhnlich** [gə'vø:nlɪç] *adj* usual; (*durchschnittlich*) ordinary; (*pej*) common; **wie** ~ as usual.

**gewohnt** [gə'vo:nt] *adj* usual; **etw** ~ **sein** to be used to sth.

**Gewöhnung** *f:* ~ (**an** +*akk*) getting accustomed (to); (*das Angewöhnen*) training (in).

**Gewölbe** [gə'vœlbə] (**-s, -**) *nt* vault.

**gewollt** [gə'vɔlt] *pp von* **wollen** ♦ *adj* forced, artificial.

**gewonnen** [gə'vɔnən] *pp von* **gewinnen**.

**geworben** [gə'vɔrbən] *pp von* **werben**.

**geworden** [gə'vɔrdən] *pp von* **werden**.

**geworfen** [gə'vɔrfən] *pp von* **werfen**.

**gewrungen** [gə'vrʊŋən] *pp von* **wringen**.

**Gewühl** [gə'vy:l] (**-(e)s**) *nt* throng.

**gewunden** [gə'vʊndən] *pp von* **winden**.

**gewunken** [gə'vʊŋkən] *pp von* **winken**.

**Gewürz** [gə'vʏrts] (**-es, -e**) *nt* spice; (*Pfeffer, Salz*) seasoning; ~**gurke** *f* pickled gherkin; ~**nelke** *f* clove.

**gewußt** [gə'vʊst] *pp von* **wissen**.

**gez.** *abk* (= *gezeichnet*) signed.

**gezackt** [gə'tsakt] *adj* (*Fels*) jagged; (*Blatt*) serrated.

**gezähnt** [gə'tsɛːnt] *adj* serrated, toothed.

**gezeichnet** [gə'tsaɪçnət] *adj* marked.

**Gezeiten** [gə'tsaɪtən] *pl* tides *pl*.

**Gezeter** [gə'tse:tər] (**-s**) *nt* nagging.

**gezielt** [gə'tsi:lt] *adj* (*Frage, Maßnahme*) specific; (*Hilfe*) well-directed; (*Kritik*) pointed.

**geziemen** [gə'tsi:mən] *vr unpers* to be fitting.

**geziemend** *adj* proper.

**geziert** [gə'tsi:rt] *adj* affected; **G~heit** *f* affectation.

**gezogen** [gə'tso:gən] *pp von* **ziehen**.

**Gezwitscher** [gə'tsvɪtʃər] (**-s**) *nt* twitter(ing), chirping.

**gezwungen** [gə'tsvʊŋən] *pp von* **zwingen** ♦ *adj* forced; (*Atmosphäre*) strained.

**gezwungenermaßen** *adv* of necessity; **etw** ~ **tun** to be forced to do sth, do sth of necessity.

**GG** *abk* = **Grundgesetz**.

**ggf.** *abk* = **gegebenenfalls**.

**Ghana** ['ga:na] (**-s**) *nt* Ghana.

**Ghettoblaster** ['gɛtoblastər] (**-s, -s**) *m* ghettoblaster.

**Gibraltar** [gi'braltar] (**-s**) *nt* Gibraltar.

**gibst** [gi:pst] *vb siehe* **geben**.

**gibt** *vb siehe* **geben**.

**Gicht** [gɪçt] (**-**) *f* gout; **g~isch** *adj* gouty.

**Giebel** ['gi:bəl] (**-s, -**) *m* gable; ~**dach** *nt* gable(d) roof; ~**fenster** *nt* gable window.

**Gier** [gi:r] (**-**) *f* greed.

**gierig** *adj* greedy.

**Gießbach** *m* torrent.

**gießen** ['gi:sən] *unreg vt* to pour; (*Blumen*) to water; (*Metall*) to cast; (*Wachs*) to mould ♦ *vi unpers:* **es gießt in Strömen** it's pouring down.

**Gießerei** [gi:sə'raɪ] *f* foundry.

**Gießkanne** *f* watering can.

**Gift** [gɪft] (**-(e)s, -e**) *nt* poison; **das ist** ~ **für ihn** (*umg*) that is very bad for him; **darauf kannst du** ~ **nehmen** (*umg*) you can bet your life on it; **g~grün** *adj* bilious green.

**giftig** *adj* poisonous; (*fig: boshaft*) venomous.

**Gift-** *zW:* ~**müll** *m* toxic waste; ~**pilz** *m* poisonous toadstool; ~**stoff** *m* toxic substance; ~**wolke** *f* poisonous cloud; ~**zahn** *m* fang; ~**zwerg** (*umg*) *m* spiteful little devil.

**Gigabyte** ['gɪgabaɪt] *nt* (*COMPUT*) gigabyte.

**Gilde** ['gɪldə] (-, -n) *f* guild.

**gilt** [gɪlt] *vb siehe* **gelten.**

**ging** *etc* [gɪŋ] *vb siehe* **gehen.**

**Ginseng** ['gɪnzɛŋ] (-s, -s) *m* ginseng.

**Ginster** ['gɪnstər] (-s, -) *m* broom.

**Gipfel** ['gɪpfəl] (-s, -) *m* summit, peak; (*fig*) height; **das ist der ~!** (*umg*) that's the limit!; **~konferenz** *f* (*POL*) summit conference.

**gipfeln** *vi* to culminate.

**Gipfeltreffen** *nt* summit (meeting).

**Gips** [gɪps] (-es, -e) *m* plaster; (*MED*) plaster (of Paris); **~abdruck** *m* plaster cast; **~bein** (*umg*) *nt* leg in plaster; **g~en** *vt* to plaster; **~figur** *f* plaster figure; **~verband** *m* plaster (cast).

**Giraffe** [gi'rafə] (-, -n) *f* giraffe.

**Girlande** [gɪr'landə] (-, -n) *f* garland.

**Giro** ['ʒiːro] (-s, -s) *nt* giro; **~konto** *nt* current account (*BRIT*), checking account (*US*).

**girren** ['gɪrən] *vi* to coo.

**Gis** [gɪs] (-, -) *nt* (*MUS*) G sharp.

**Gischt** [gɪʃt] (-(e)s, -e) *m od f* spray, foam.

**Gitarre** [gi'tarə] (-, -n) *f* guitar.

**Gitter** ['gɪtər] (-s, -) *nt* grating, bars *pl*; (*für Pflanzen*) trellis; (*Zaun*) railing(s); **~bett** *nt* cot (*BRIT*), crib (*US*); **~fenster** *nt* barred window; **~zaun** *m* railing(s).

**Glacéhandschuh** [gla'seːhantʃuː] *m* kid glove.

**Gladiole** [gladi'oːlə] (-, -n) *f* gladiolus.

**Glanz** [glants] (-es) *m* shine, lustre (*BRIT*), luster (*US*); (*fig*) splendour (*BRIT*), splendor (*US*); **~abzug** *m* (*PHOT*) glossy *od* gloss print.

**glänzen** ['glɛntsən] *vi* to shine (*also fig*), gleam.

**glänzend** *adj* shining; (*fig*) brilliant; **wir haben uns ~ amüsiert** we had a marvellous *od* great time.

**Glanz-** *zW:* **~lack** *m* gloss (paint); **~leistung** *f* brilliant achievement; **g~los** *adj* dull; **~stück** *nt* pièce de résistance; **~zeit** *f* heyday.

**Glas** [glaːs] (-es, ̈-er) *nt* glass; (*Brillen~*) lens *sing*; **zwei ~ Wein** two glasses of wine; **~bläser** *m* glass blower; **~er** (-s, -) *m* glazier; **~faser** *f* fibreglass (*BRIT*), fiberglass (*US*); **~faserkabel** *nt* optical fibre (*BRIT*) *od* fiber (*US*) cable.

**Glasgow** ['glaːsgoʊ] *nt* Glasgow.

**glasieren** [gla'ziːrən] *vt* to glaze.

**glasig** *adj* glassy; (*Zwiebeln*) transparent.

**glasklar** *adj* crystal clear.

**Glasscheibe** *f* pane.

**Glasur** [gla'zuːr] *f* glaze; (*KOCH*) icing, frosting (*bes US*).

**glatt** [glat] *adj* smooth; (*rutschig*) slippery; (*Absage*) flat; (*Lüge*) downright; (*Haar*) straight; (*MED: Bruch*) clean; (*pej: allzu gewandt*) smooth, slick.

**Glätte** ['glɛtə] (-, -n) *f* smoothness;

slipperiness.

**Glatteis** *nt* (black) ice; **„Vorsicht ~!"** "danger, black ice!"; **jdn aufs ~ führen** (*fig*) to take sb for a ride.

**glätten** *vt* to smooth out.

**glatt-** *zW:* **~gehen** *unreg vi* to go smoothly; **~rasiert** *adj* (*Mann, Kinn*) clean-shaven; **~streichen** *unreg vt* to smooth out.

**Glatze** ['glatsə] (-, -n) *f* bald head; **eine ~ bekommen** to go bald.

**glatzköpfig** *adj* bald.

**Glaube** ['glaʊbə] (-ns, -n) *m:* **~ (an** +*akk*) faith (in); (*Überzeugung*) belief (in); **den ~n an jdn/etw verlieren** to lose faith in sb/sth.

**glauben** *vt, vi* to believe; (*meinen*) to think; **jdm ~** to believe sb; **~ an** +*akk* to believe in; **jdm (etw) aufs Wort ~** to take sb's word (for sth); **wer's glaubt, wird selig** (*ironisch*) a likely story.

**Glaubens-** *zW:* **~bekenntnis** *nt* creed; **~freiheit** *f* religious freedom; **~gemeinschaft** *f* religious sect; (*christliche*) denomination.

**glaubhaft** ['glaʊbhaft] *adj* credible; **jdm etw ~ machen** to satisfy sb of sth.

**Glaubhaftigkeit** *f* credibility.

**gläubig** ['glɔybɪç] *adj* (*REL*) devout; (*vertrauensvoll*) trustful; **G~e(r)** *f(m)* believer; **die Gläubigen** *pl* the faithful.

**Gläubiger(in)** (-s, -) *m(f)* creditor.

**glaubwürdig** ['glaʊbvʏrdɪç] *adj* credible; (*Mensch*) trustworthy; **G~keit** *f* credibility; trustworthiness.

**gleich** [glaɪç] *adj* equal; (*identisch*) (the) same, identical ♦ *adv* equally; (*sofort*) straight away; (*bald*) in a minute; (*räumlich*): **~ hinter dem Haus** just behind the house; (*zeitlich*): **~ am Anfang** at the very beginning; **es ist mir ~** it's all the same to me; **zu ~en Teilen** in equal parts; **das ~e, aber nicht dasselbe Auto** a similar car, but not the same one; **ganz ~ wer/was** *etc* no matter who/what *etc*; **2 mal 2 ~ 4** 2 times 2 is *od* equals 4; **bis ~!** see you soon!; **wie war doch ~ Ihr Name?** what was your name again?; **es ist ~ drei Uhr** it's very nearly three o'clock; **sie sind ~ groß** they are the same size; **~ nach/an** right after/at; **~altrig** *adj* of the same age; **~artig** *adj* similar; **~bedeutend** *adj* synonymous; **~berechtigt** *adj* with equal rights; **G~berechtigung** *f* equal rights *pl*; **~bleibend** *adj* constant; **bei ~bleibendem Gehalt** when one's salary stays the same.

**gleichen** *unreg vi:* **jdm/etw ~** to be like sb/sth ♦ *vr* to be alike.

**gleichermaßen** *adv* equally.

**gleich-** *zW:* **~falls** *adv* likewise; **danke ~falls!** the same to you; **G~förmigkeit** *f* uniformity; **~gesinnt** *adj* like-minded; **~gestellt** *adj:* **rechtlich ~gestellt** equal in law; **G~gewicht** *nt* equilibrium, balance; **jdn aus dem G~gewicht bringen** to throw sb off balance; ~**gültig** adj indifferent; (unbedeutend) unimportant; G~**gültigkeit** f indifference; G~**heit** f equality; (Identität) identity; (INDUSTRIE) parity; G~**heitsprinzip** nt principle of equality; G~**heitszeichen** nt (MATH) equals sign; ~**kommen** unreg vi +dat to be equal to; ~**lautend** adj identical; G~**macherei** f egalitarianism, levelling down (pej); ~**mäßig** adj even, equal; G~**mut** m equanimity.

**Gleichnis** (-ses, -se) nt parable.

**gleich-** zW: ~**rangig** adj (Probleme etc) equally important; ~**rangig (mit)** (Beamte etc) equal in rank (to), at the same level (as); ~**sam** adv as it were; ~**schalten** (pej) vt to bring into line; G~**schritt** m: **im G~schritt, marsch!** forward march!; ~**sehen** unreg vi: **jdm ~sehen** to be od look like sb; ~**stellen** vt (rechtlich etc) to treat as equal; G~**strom** m (ELEK) direct current; ~**tun** unreg vi: **es jdm ~tun** to match sb.

**Gleichung** f equation.

**gleich-** zW: ~**viel** adv no matter; ~**wertig** adj of the same value; (Leistung, Qualität) equal; (Gegner) evenly matched; ~**wohl** adv (geh) nevertheless; ~**zeitig** adj simultaneous.

**Gleis** [glaɪs] (-es, -e) nt track, rails pl; (am Bahnhof) platform (BRIT), track (US).

**gleißend** ['glaɪsənt] adj glistening, gleaming.

**gleiten** unreg vi to glide; (rutschen) to slide.

**gleitend** ['glaɪtənt] adj: ~**e Arbeitszeit** flexible working hours pl, flex(i)time.

**Gleit-** zW: ~**flug** m glide; ~**klausel** f (COMM) escalator clause; ~**komma** nt floating point; ~**zeit** f flex(i)time.

**Gletscher** ['glɛtʃər] (-s, -) m glacier; ~**spalte** f crevasse.

**glich** etc [glɪç] vb siehe **gleichen**.

**Glied** [gliːt] (-(e)s, -er) nt member; (Arm, Bein) limb; (Penis) penis; (von Kette) link; (MIL) rank(s); **der Schreck steckt ihr noch in den ~ern** she is still shaking with the shock.

**gliedern** vt to organize, structure.

**Gliederreißen** nt rheumatic pains pl.

**Gliederschmerz** m rheumatic pains pl.

**Gliederung** f structure, organization.

**Gliedmaßen** pl limbs pl.

**glimmen** ['glɪmən] unreg vi to glow.

**Glimmer** (-s, -) m (MINERAL) mica.

**Glimmstengel** (umg) m fag (BRIT), butt (US).

**glimpflich** ['glɪmpflɪç] adj mild, lenient; ~ **davonkommen** to get off lightly.

**glitschig** ['glɪtʃɪç] (umg) adj slippery, slippy.

**glitt** etc [glɪt] vb siehe **gleiten**.

**glitzern** ['glɪtsərn] vi to glitter; (Stern) to twinkle.

**global** [glo'baːl] adj (weltweit) global, worldwide; (ungefähr, pauschal) general.

**Globus** ['gloːbʊs] (- od -ses, **Globen** od -se) m globe.

**Glöckchen** ['glœkçən] nt (little) bell.

**Glocke** ['glɔkə] (-, -n) f bell; **etw an die große ~ hängen** (fig) to shout sth from the rooftops.

**Glocken-** zW: ~**geläut** nt peal of bells; ~**schlag** m stroke (of the bell); (von Uhr) chime; ~**spiel** nt chime(s); (MUS) glockenspiel; ~**turm** m belfry, bell-tower.

**glomm** etc [glɔm] vb siehe **glimmen**.

**Glorie** ['gloːriə] f glory; (von Heiligen) halo.

**glorreich** ['gloːrraɪç] adj glorious.

**Glossar** [glɔ'saːr] (-s, -e) nt glossary.

**Glosse** ['glɔsə] (-, -n) f comment.

**Glotze** (-, -n) (umg) f gogglebox (BRIT), TV set.

**glotzen** ['glɔtsən] (umg) vi to stare.

**Glück** [glyk] (-(e)s) nt luck, fortune; (Freude) happiness; ~ **haben** to be lucky; **viel ~** good luck; **zum ~** fortunately; **ein ~!** how lucky!, what a stroke of luck!; **auf gut ~** (aufs Geratewohl) on the off-chance; (unvorbereitet) trusting to luck; (wahllos) at random; **sie weiß noch nichts von ihrem ~** (ironisch) she doesn't know anything about it yet; **er kann von ~ sagen, daß ...** he can count himself lucky that ...; ~**auf** nt: „~**auf"** (Bergleute) (cry of) "good luck".

**Glucke** (-, -n) f (Bruthenne) broody hen; (mit Jungen) mother hen.

**glücken** vi to succeed; **es glückte ihm, es zu bekommen** he succeeded in getting it.

**gluckern** ['glʊkərn] vi to glug.

**glücklich** adj fortunate; (froh) happy ♦ adv happily; (umg: endlich, zu guter Letzt) finally, eventually.

**glücklicherweise** adv fortunately.

**glücklos** adj luckless.

**Glücksbringer** (-s, -) m lucky charm.

**glückselig** [glyk'zeːlɪç] adj blissful.

**Glücks-** zW: ~**fall** m stroke of luck; ~**kind** nt lucky person; ~**pilz** m lucky beggar (umg); ~**sache** f matter of luck; ~**spiel** nt game of chance; ~**stern** m lucky star; ~**strähne** f lucky streak.

**glückstrahlend** adj radiant (with happiness).

**Glückszahl** f lucky number.

**Glückwunsch** m: ~ **(zu)** congratulations pl (on), best wishes pl (on).

**Glühbirne** f light bulb.

**glühen** ['glyːən] vi to glow.

**glühend** adj glowing; (heiß~: Metall) red-hot; (Hitze) blazing; (fig: leidenschaftlich) ardent; (: Haß) burning; (Wangen) flushed, burning.

**Glüh-** zW: ~**faden** m (ELEK) filament; ~**wein** m mulled wine; ~**würmchen** nt glow-worm.

**Glut** [gluːt] (-, -en) f (Röte) glow; (Feuers~) fire; (Hitze) heat; (fig) ardour (BRIT), ardor (US).

**GmbH** (-, -s) f abk (= Gesellschaft mit beschränkter Haftung) ≈ Ltd. (BRIT), plc (BRIT), Inc. (US).

**Gnade** ['gnaːdə] (-, -n) f (Gunst) favour (BRIT), favor (US); (Erbarmen) mercy; (Milde) clemency; ~ **vor Recht ergehen lassen** to temper justice with mercy.

**gnaden** *vi:* **(dann) gnade dir Gott!** (then) God help you *od* heaven have mercy on you!

**Gnaden-** *zW:* **~brot** *nt:* **jdm/einem Tier das ~brot geben** to keep sb/an animal in his/her/its old age; **~frist** *f* reprieve; **~gesuch** *nt* petition for clemency; **g~los** *adj* merciless; **~stoß** *m* coup de grâce.

**gnädig** ['gnɛːdɪç] *adj* gracious; (*voll Erbarmen*) merciful; **~e Frau** (*form*) madam, ma'am.

**Gockel** ['gɔkəl] (-s, -) *m* (*bes SÜDD*) cock.

**Gold** [gɔlt] (-(e)s) *nt* gold; **nicht mit ~ zu bezahlen** *od* **aufzuwiegen sein** to be worth one's weight in gold; **g~en** *adj* golden; **g~ene Worte** words of wisdom; **der Tanz ums g~ene Kalb** (*fig*) the worship of Mammon; **~fisch** *m* goldfish; **~grube** *f* gold mine; **~hamster** *m* (golden) hamster.

**goldig** ['gɔldɪç] *adj* (*fig: umg: allerliebst*) sweet, cute.

**Gold-** *zW:* **~regen** *m* laburnum; (*fig*) riches *pl*; **g~richtig** (*umg*) *adj* dead right; **~schmied** *m* goldsmith; **~schnitt** *m* gilt edging; **~standard** *m* gold standard; **~stück** *nt* piece of gold; (*fig: umg*) treasure; **~waage** *f:* **jedes Wort auf die ~waage legen** (*fig*) to weigh one's words; **~währung** *f* gold standard.

**Golf¹** [gɔlf] (-(e)s, -e) *m* gulf; **der (Persische) ~** the Gulf.

**Golf²** [gɔlf] (-s) *nt* golf; **~platz** *m* golf course; **~schläger** *m* golf club; **~spieler** *m* golfer.

**Golfstaaten** *pl:* **die ~** the Gulf States *pl*.

**Golfstrom** *m* (*GEOG*) Gulf Stream.

**Gondel** ['gɔndəl] (-, -n) *f* gondola; (*von Seilbahn*) cable car.

**gondeln** (*umg*) *vi:* **durch die Welt ~** to go globetrotting.

**Gong** [gɔŋ] (-s, -s) *m* gong; (*bei Boxkampf etc*) bell.

**gönnen** ['gœnən] *vt:* **jdm etw ~** not to begrudge sb sth; **sich** *dat* **etw ~** to allow o.s. sth.

**Gönner** (-s, -) *m* patron; **g~haft** *adj* patronizing; **~in** *f* patroness; **~miene** *f* patronizing air.

**gor** *etc* [goːr] *vb siehe* **gären.**

**Gorilla** [goˈrɪla] (-s, -s) *m* gorilla; (*umg: Leibwächter*) heavy.

**goß** *etc* [gɔs] *vb siehe* **gießen.**

**Gosse** ['gɔsə] (-, -n) *f* gutter.

**Gote** ['goːtə] (-n, -n) *m* Goth.

**Gotik** ['goːtɪk] *f* (*KUNST*) Gothic (style); (*Epoche*) Gothic period.

**Gotin** ['goːtɪn] *f* Goth.

**Gott** [gɔt] (-es, ̈er) *m* god; (*als Name*) God; **um ~es Willen!** for heaven's sake!; **~ sei Dank!** thank God!; **grüß ~!** (*bes SÜDD, ÖSTERR*) hello, good morning/afternoon/evening; **den lieben ~ einen guten Mann sein lassen** (*umg*) to take things as they come; **ein Bild für die Götter** (*hum: umg*) a sight for sore eyes; **das wissen die Götter** (*umg*) God (only) knows; **über ~ und die Welt reden** (*fig*) to talk about everything under the sun; **wie ~ in Frankreich leben** (*umg*) to be in clover.

**Götterspeise** *f* (*KOCH*) jelly (*BRIT*), jello (*US*).

**Gottes-** *zW:* **~dienst** *m* service; **g~fürchtig** *adj* god-fearing; **~haus** *nt* place of worship; **~lästerung** *f* blasphemy.

**Gottheit** *f* deity.

**Göttin** ['gœtɪn] *f* goddess.

**göttlich** *adj* divine.

**Gott-** *zW:* **g~lob** *interj* thank heavens!; **g~los** *adj* godless; **g~verdammt** *adj* goddamn(ed); **g~verlassen** *adj* godforsaken; **~vertrauen** *nt* trust in God.

**Götze** ['gœtsə] (-n, -n) *m* idol.

**Grab** [graːp] (-(e)s, ̈er) *nt* grave.

**grabbeln** ['grabəln] (*NORDD: umg*) *vt* to rummage.

**Graben** ['graːbən] (-s, ̈) *m* ditch; (*MIL*) trench.

**graben** *unreg vt* to dig.

**Grabesstille** *f* (*liter*) deathly hush.

**Grab-** *zW:* **~mal** *nt* monument; (*~stein*) gravestone; **~rede** *f* funeral oration; **~stein** *m* gravestone.

**gräbt** *vb siehe* **graben.**

**Gracht** [graxt] (-, -en) *f* canal.

**Grad** [graːt] (-(e)s, -e) *m* degree; **im höchsten ~(e)** extremely; **Verbrennungen ersten ~es** (*MED*) first-degree burns; **~einteilung** *f* graduation; **g~linig** *adj* straight; **g~weise** *adv* gradually.

**Graf** [graːf] (-en, -en) *m* count, earl (*BRIT*).

**Grafik** *f siehe* **Graphik.**

**Grafiker(in)** *m(f) siehe* **Graphiker(in).**

**Gräfin** ['grɛːfɪn] *f* countess.

**grafisch** *adj siehe* **graphisch.**

**Grafschaft** *f* county.

**Grahambrot** ['graːhambroːt] *nt* type of wholemeal (*BRIT*) *od* whole-wheat (*US*) bread.

**Gralshüter** ['graːlzhyːtər] (-s, -) *m* (*fig*) guardian.

**Gram** [graːm] (-(e)s) *m* (*geh*) grief, sorrow.

**grämen** ['grɛːmən] *vr* to grieve; **sich zu Tode ~** to die of grief *od* sorrow.

**Gramm** [gram] (-s, -e) *nt* gram(me).

**Grammatik** [graˈmatɪk] *f* grammar.

**grammatisch** *adj* grammatical.

**Grammophon** [gramoˈfoːn] (-s, -e) *nt* gramophone.

**Granat** [graˈnaːt] (-(e)s, -e) *m* (*Stein*) garnet; **~apfel** *m* pomegranate.

**Granate** (-, -n) *f* (*MIL*) shell; (*Hand~*) grenade.

**grandios** [granˈdioːs] *adj* magnificent, superb.

**Granit** [graˈniːt] (-s, -e) *m* granite; **auf ~ beißen (bei ...)** to bang one's head against a brick wall (with ...).

**grantig** ['grantɪç] (*umg*) *adj* grumpy.

**Graphik** ['graːfɪk] f (COMPUT, TECH) graphics; (ART) graphic arts pl.

**Graphiker(in)** ['graːfɪkər(ɪn)] (-s, -) m(f) graphic artist; (Illustrator) illustrator.

**graphisch** ['graːfɪʃ] adj graphic; ~e Darstellung graph.

**grapschen** ['grapʃən] (umg) vt, vi to grab; (sich dat) etw ~ to grab sth.

**Gras** [graːs] (-es, ⁻er) nt (auch umg: Marihuana) grass; über etw akk ~ wachsen lassen (fig) to let the dust settle on sth; g~en vi to graze; ~halm m blade of grass.

**grasig** adj grassy.

**Grasnarbe** f turf.

**grassieren** [gra'siːrən] vi to be rampant, rage.

**gräßlich** ['grɛslɪç] adj horrible.

**Grat** [graːt] (-(e)s, -e) m ridge.

**Gräte** ['grɛːtə] (-, -n) f fish-bone.

**Gratifikation** [gratifikatsi'oːn] f bonus.

**gratis** ['graːtɪs] adj, adv free (of charge); **G~probe** f free sample.

**Grätsche** ['grɛːtʃə] (-, -n) f (SPORT) straddle.

**Gratulant(in)** [gratu'lant(ɪn)] m(f) well-wisher.

**Gratulation** [gratulatsi'oːn] f congratulation(s).

**gratulieren** [gratu'liːrən] vi: jdm (zu etw) ~ to congratulate sb (on sth); (ich) gratuliere! congratulations!

**Gratwanderung** f (fig) tightrope walk.

**grau** [grau] adj grey (BRIT), gray (US); der ~e Alltag drab reality; **G~brot** nt = Mischbrot.

**Grauen** (-s) nt horror.

**grauen** vi (Tag) to dawn ♦ vi unpers: es graut jdm vor etw sb dreads sth, sb is afraid of sth ♦ vr: sich ~ vor to dread, have a horror of.

**grauenhaft, grauenvoll** adj horrible.

**grauhaarig** adj grey-haired (BRIT), gray-haired (US).

**graumeliert** adj grey-flecked (BRIT), gray-flecked (US).

**Graupelregen** ['graupəlreːgən] m sleet.

**Graupelschauer** m sleet.

**Graupen** ['graupən] pl pearl barley sing.

**grausam** ['grauzaːm] adj cruel; **G~keit** f cruelty.

**Grausen** ['grauzən] (-s) nt horror; da kann man das kalte ~ kriegen (umg) it's enough to give you the creeps.

**grausen** vb = grauen.

**Grauzone** f (fig) grey (BRIT) od gray (US) area.

**gravieren** [gra'viːrən] vt to engrave.

**gravierend** adj grave.

**Grazie** ['graːtsiə] f grace.

**graziös** [gratsi'øːs] adj graceful.

**greifbar** adj tangible, concrete; in ~er Nähe within reach.

**greifen** ['graifən] unreg vt (nehmen) to grasp; (grapschen) to seize, grab ♦ vi (nicht rutschen, einrasten) to grip; nach etw ~ to reach for sth; um sich ~ (fig) to spread; zu etw ~ (fig)

to turn to sth; **diese Zahl ist zu niedrig gegriffen** (fig) this figure is too low; **aus dem Leben gegriffen** taken from life.

**Greifer** (-s, -) m (TECH) grab.

**Greifvogel** m bird of prey.

**Greis** [grais] (-es, -e) m old man.

**Greisenalter** nt old age.

**greisenhaft** adj very old.

**Greisin** ['graizɪn] f old woman.

**grell** [grɛl] adj harsh.

**Gremium** ['greːmium] nt body; (Ausschuß) committee.

**Grenadier** [grena'diːər] (-s, -e) m (MIL: Infanterist) infantryman.

**Grenzbeamte(r)** m frontier official.

**Grenze** (-, -n) f border; (zwischen Grundstücken, fig) boundary; (Staats~) frontier; (Schranke) limit; über die ~ gehen/fahren to cross the border; hart an der ~ des Erlaubten bordering on the limits of what is permitted.

**grenzen** vi: ~ an +akk to border on.

**grenzenlos** adj boundless.

**Grenz-** zW: ~fall m borderline case; ~gänger m (Arbeiter) international commuter (across a local border); ~gebiet nt (lit, fig) border area; ~kosten pl marginal cost sing; ~linie f boundary; ~übergang m frontier crossing; ~wert m limit; ~zwischenfall m border incident.

**Gretchenfrage** ['greːtçənfraːgə] f (fig) crunch question, sixty-four-thousand-dollar question (umg).

**Greuel** ['grɔyəl] (-s, -) m horror; (~tat) atrocity; etw ist jdm ein ~ sb loathes sth; ~propaganda f atrocity propaganda; ~tat f atrocity.

**greulich** ['grɔylɪç] adj horrible.

**Grieche** ['griːçə] (-n, -n) m Greek.

**Griechenland** nt Greece.

**Griechin** ['griːçɪn] f Greek.

**griechisch** adj Greek.

**griesgrämig** ['griːsgrɛːmɪç] adj grumpy.

**Grieß** [griːs] (-es, -e) m (KOCH) semolina; ~brei m cooked semolina.

**Griff** [grɪf] (-(e)s, -e) m grip; (Vorrichtung) handle; (das Greifen): der ~ nach etw reaching for sth; jdn/etw in den ~ bekommen (fig) to gain control of sb/sth; etw in den ~ bekommen (geistig) to get a grasp of sth.

**griff** etc vb siehe greifen.

**griffbereit** adj handy.

**Griffel** ['grɪfəl] (-s, -) m slate pencil; (BOT) style.

**griffig** ['grɪfɪç] adj (Fahrbahn etc) that has a good grip; (fig: Ausdruck) useful, handy.

**Grill** [grɪl] (-s, -s) m grill; (AUT) grille.

**Grille** ['grɪlə] (-, -n) f cricket; (fig) whim.

**grillen** vt to grill.

**Grimasse** [gri'masə] (-, -n) f grimace; ~n schneiden to make faces.

**grimmig** *adj* furious; (*heftig*) fierce, severe.
**grinsen** ['grɪnzən] *vi* to grin; (*höhnisch*) to smirk.
**Grippe** ['grɪpə] (-, -n) *f* influenza, flu.
**Grips** [grɪps] (-es, -e) (*umg*) *m* sense.
**grob** [gro:p] *adj* coarse, gross; (*Fehler, Verstoß*) gross; (*brutal, derb*) rough; (*unhöflich*) ill-mannered; ~ **geschätzt** at a rough estimate; **G~heit** *f* coarseness; (*Beschimpfung*) coarse expression.
**Grobian** ['gro:bia:n] (-s, -e) *m* ruffian.
**grobknochig** *adj* large-boned.
**groggy** ['grɔgɪ] *adj* (*BOXEN*) groggy; (*umg: erschöpft*) bushed.
**grölen** ['grø:lən] (*pej*) *vt*, *vi* to bawl.
**Groll** [grɔl] (-(e)s) *m* resentment; **g~en** *vi* (*Donner*) to rumble; **g~en (mit** *od* +*dat*) to bear ill will (towards).
**Grönland** ['grø:nlant] (-s) *nt* Greenland.
**Grönländer(in)** (-s, -) *m(f)* Greenlander.
**Groschen** ['grɔʃən] (-s, -) (*umg*) *m* 10-pfennig piece; (*ÖSTERR*) groschen; (*fig*) penny, cent (*US*); ~**roman** (*pej*) *m* cheap *od* dime (*US*) novel.
**groß** [gro:s] *adj* big, large; (*hoch*) tall; (*Freude, Werk*) great ♦ *adv* greatly; **im ~en und ganzen** on the whole; **wie ~ bist du?** how tall are you?; **die G~en** (*Erwachsene*) the grown-ups; **mit etw ~ geworden sein** to have grown up with sth; **die G~en Seen** the Great Lakes *pl*; ~**en Hunger haben** to be very hungry; ~**e Mode sein** to be all the fashion; ~ **und breit** (*fig: umg*) at great *od* enormous length; **ein Wort ~ schreiben** to write a word with a capital; **G~abnehmer** *m* (*COMM*) bulk buyer; **G~alarm** *m* red alert; ~**angelegt** *adj attrib* large-scale, on a large scale; ~**artig** *adj* great, splendid; **G~aufnahme** *f* (*FILM*) close-up; **G~britannien** (-s) *nt* (*Great*) Britain; **G~buchstabe** *m* capital (letter).
**Größe** ['grø:sə] (-, -n) *f* size; (*Länge*) height; (*fig*) greatness; **eine unbekannte ~** (*lit, fig*) an unknown quantity.
**Groß-** *zW:* ~**einkauf** *m* bulk purchase; ~**einsatz** *m:* ~**einsatz der Polizei** *etc* large-scale operation by the police *etc*; ~**eltern** *pl* grandparents *pl*.
**Größenordnung** *f* scale; (*Größe*) magnitude; (*MATH*) order (of magnitude).
**großenteils** *adv* for the most part.
**Größen-** *zW:* ~**unterschied** *m* difference in size; ~**wahn** *m*, ~**wahnsinn** *m* megalomania, delusions *pl* of grandeur.
**Groß-** *zW:* ~**format** *nt* large size; ~**handel** *m* wholesale trade; ~**handelspreisindex** *m* wholesale-price index; ~**händler** *m* wholesaler; **g~herzig** *adj* generous; ~**hirn** *nt* cerebrum; ~**industrielle(r)** *f(m)* major industrialist; **g~kotzig** (*umg*) *adj* show-offish, bragging; ~**kundgebung** *f* mass rally; ~**macht** *f* great power; ~**maul** *m*

braggart; ~**mut** (-) *f* magnanimity; **g~mütig** *adj* magnanimous; ~**mutter** *f* grandmother; ~**raum** *m:* **der ~raum München** the Munich area *od* conurbation, Greater Munich; ~**raumbüro** *nt* open-plan office; ~**rechner** *m* mainframe; ~**reinemachen** *nt* thorough cleaning, ≈ spring cleaning; **g~schreiben** *unreg vt:* **g~geschrieben werden** (*umg*) to be stressed; ~**schreibung** *f* capitalization; **g~spurig** *adj* pompous; ~**stadt** *f* city.
**größte(r, s)** [grø:stə(r, s)] *adj superl von* **groß**.
**größtenteils** *adv* for the most part.
**Groß-** *zW:* ~**tuer** (-s, -) *m* boaster; **g~tun** *unreg vi* to boast; ~**vater** *m* grandfather; ~**verbraucher** *m* (*COMM*) heavy user; ~**verdiener** *m* big earner; ~**wild** *nt* big game; **g~ziehen** *unreg vt* to raise; **g~zügig** *adj* generous; (*Planung*) on a large scale.
**grotesk** [gro'tɛsk] *adj* grotesque.
**Grotte** ['grɔtə] (-, -n) *f* grotto.
**grub** *etc* [gru:p] *vb siehe* **graben**.
**Grübchen** ['gry:pçən] *nt* dimple.
**Grube** ['gru:bə] (-, -n) *f* pit; (*Bergwerk*) mine.
**grübeln** ['gry:bəln] *vi* to brood.
**Grubenarbeiter** *m* miner.
**Grubengas** *nt* firedamp.
**Grübler** ['gry:blər] (-s, -) *m* brooder; **g~isch** *adj* brooding, pensive.
**Gruft** [gruft] (-, ⁻e) *f* tomb, vault.
**grün** [gry:n] *adj* green; (*ökologisch*) green; (*POL*): **die G~en** the Greens; **G~e Minna** (*umg*) Black Maria (*BRIT*), paddy wagon (*US*); ~**e Welle** phased traffic lights; ~**e Versicherungskarte** (*AUT*) green card; **sich ~ und blau** *od* **gelb ärgern** (*umg*) to be furious; **auf keinen ~en Zweig kommen** (*fig: umg*) to get nowhere; **jdm ~es Licht geben** to give sb the green light; **G~anlage** *f* park.
**Grund** [grʊnt] (-(e)s, ⁻e) *m* ground; (*von See, Gefäß*) bottom; (*fig*) reason; **von ~ auf** entirely, completely; **auf ~ von** on the basis of; **aus gesundheitlichen** *etc* **Gründen** for health *etc* reasons; **im ~e genommen** basically; **ich habe ~ zu der Annahme, daß ...** I have reason to believe that ...; **einer Sache** *dat* **auf den ~ gehen** (*fig*) to get to the bottom of sth; **in ~ und Boden** (*fig*) utterly, thoroughly; ~**ausbildung** *f* basic training; ~**bedeutung** *f* basic meaning; ~**bedingung** *f* fundamental condition; ~**begriff** *m* basic concept; ~**besitz** *m* land(ed property), real estate; ~**buch** *nt* land register; **g~ehrlich** *adj* thoroughly honest.
**gründen** [grɘndən] *vt* to found ♦ *vr:* **sich ~ auf** +*akk* to be based on; ~ **auf** +*akk* to base on.
**Gründer(in)** (-s, -) *m(f)* founder.
**Grund-** *zW:* **g~falsch** *adj* utterly wrong; ~**gebühr** *f* basic charge; ~**gedanke** *m* basic idea; ~**gesetz** *nt* constitution.
**Grundierung** [grʊn'di:rʊŋ] *f* (*Farbe*) primer.
**Grund-** *zW:* ~**kapital** *nt* nominal capital;

~**kurs** m basic course; ~**lage** f foundation; **jeder** ~**lage** gen **entbehren** to be completely unfounded; **g~legend** adj fundamental.

**gründlich** adj thorough; **jdm** ~ **die Meinung sagen** to give sb a piece of one's mind.

**Grund-** zW: **g~los** adj (fig) groundless; ~**mauer** f foundation wall; ~**nahrungsmittel** nt basic food(stuff).

**Gründonnerstag** m Maundy Thursday.

**Grund-** zW: ~**ordnung** f: **die freiheitlich-demokratische** ~**ordnung** (BRD POL) the German constitution based on democratic liberty; ~**rechenart** f basic arithmetical operation; ~**recht** nt basic od constitutional right; ~**regel** f basic od ground rule; ~**riß** m plan; (fig) outline; ~**satz** m principle; **g~sätzlich** adj fundamental; (Frage) of principle ♦ adv fundamentally; (prinzipiell) on principle; **das ist g~sätzlich verboten** it is absolutely forbidden; ~**satzurteil** nt judgement that establishes a principle.

**Grundschule** f primary (BRIT) od elementary school.

The **Grundschule** is a primary school which children attend for 4 years from the age of 6 to 10. There are no formal examinations in the Grundschule but parents receive a report on their child's progress twice a year. Many children attend a **Kindergarten** from 3-6 years before going to the Grundschule, but no formal instruction takes place in the Kindergarten.

**Grund-** zW: ~**stein** m foundation stone; ~**steuer** f rates pl; ~**stück** nt plot (of land); (Anwesen) estate; ~**stücksmakler** m estate agent (BRIT), realtor (US); ~**stufe** f first stage; (SCH) ≈ junior (BRIT) od grade (US) school.

**Gründung** f foundation.

**Gründungsurkunde** f (COMM) certificate of incorporation.

**Gründungsversammlung** f (Aktiengesellschaft) statutory meeting.

**Grund-** zW: **g~verschieden** adj utterly different; ~**wasser** nt ground water; ~**wasserspiegel** m water table, ground-water level; ~**zug** m characteristic; **etw in seinen** ~**zügen darstellen** to outline (the essentials of) sth.

**Grüne** (-n) nt: **im** ~**n** in the open air; **ins** ~ **fahren** to go to the country.

**Grüne(r)** f(m) (POL) Ecologist, Green; **die Grünen** pl (als Partei) the Greens.

Die **Grünen** is the name given to the Green or ecological party in Germany which was founded in 1980. Since 1993 they have been allied with the originally East German party, Bündnis 90.

The **grüner Punkt** is the green spot symbol which appears on packaging that should not be thrown into the normal household refuse but kept separate to be recycled through the DSD system. The recycling is financed by licences bought by the manufacturer from the DSD and the cost of this is often passed on to the consumer.

**Grün-** zW: ~**kohl** m kale; ~**schnabel** m greenhorn; ~**span** m verdigris; ~**streifen** m central reservation.

**grunzen** ['gruntsən] vi to grunt.

**Gruppe** ['grupə] (-, -n) f group.

**Gruppen-** zW: ~**arbeit** f teamwork; ~**dynamik** f group dynamics pl; ~**therapie** f group therapy; **g~weise** adv in groups.

**gruppieren** [gru'pi:rən] vt, vr to group.

**gruselig** adj creepy.

**gruseln** ['gru:zəln] vi unpers: **es gruselt jdm vor etw** sth gives sb the creeps ♦ vr to have the creeps.

**Gruß** [gru:s] (-es, ̈-e) m greeting; (MIL) salute; **viele Grüße** best wishes; **Grüße an** +akk regards to; **einen (schönen)** ~ **an Ihre Frau!** my regards to your wife; **mit freundlichen Grüßen** (als Briefformel) Yours sincerely.

**grüßen** ['gry:sən] vt to greet; (MIL) to salute; **jdn von jdm** ~ to give sb sb's regards; **jdn** ~ **lassen** to send sb one's regards.

**Grütze** ['grytsə] (-, -n) f (Brei) gruel; **rote** ~ (type of) red fruit jelly.

**Guatemala** [guate'ma:la] (-s) nt Guatemala.

**Guayana** [gua'ja:na] (-s) nt Guyana.

**gucken** ['gukən] vi to look.

**Guckloch** nt peephole.

**Guinea** [gi'ne:a] (-s) nt Guinea.

**Gulasch** ['gu:laʃ] (-(e)s, -e) nt goulash; ~**kanone** f (MIL: umg) field kitchen.

**gültig** ['gyltɪç] adj valid; ~ **werden** to become valid; (Gesetz, Vertrag) to come into effect; (Münze) to become legal tender; **G~keit** f validity; **G~keitsdauer** f period of validity.

**Gummi** ['gumi] (-s, -s) nt od m rubber; (~harze) gum; (umg: Kondom) rubber, Durex ®; (~band) rubber od elastic band; (Hosen~) elastic; ~**band** nt rubber od elastic band; ~**bärchen** nt jelly baby; ~**geschoß** nt rubber bullet; ~**knüppel** m rubber truncheon; ~**paragraph** m ambiguous od meaningless law od statute; ~**stiefel** m rubber boot, wellington (boot) (BRIT); ~**strumpf** m elastic stocking; ~**zelle** f padded cell.

**Gunst** [gunst] (-) f favour (BRIT), favor (US).

**günstig** ['gynstɪç] adj favourable (BRIT), favorable (US); (Angebot, Preis etc) reasonable, good; **bei** ~**er Witterung** weather permitting; **im** ~**sten Fall(e)** with luck.

**Gurgel** ['gurgəl] (-, -n) f throat.

**gurgeln** vi to gurgle; (im Rachen) to gargle.

**Gurke** ['gurkə] (-, -n) f cucumber; **saure** ~ pickled cucumber, gherkin.

**Gurt** [gʊrt] (-(e)s, -e) *m* belt.
**Gurtanlegepflicht** *f (form) obligation to wear a safety belt in vehicles.*
**Gürtel** ['gʏrtəl] (-s, -) *m* belt; *(GEOG)* zone; ~**reifen** *m* radial tyre; ~**rose** *f* shingles *sing od pl.*
**GUS** [geː|uː'|ɛs] *f abk (= Gemeinschaft Unabhängiger Staaten)* CIS.
**Guß** [gʊs] (-sses, Güsse) *m* casting; *(Regen~)* downpour; *(KOCH)* glazing; ~**eisen** *nt* cast iron.
**Gut** [guːt] (-(e)s, -er) *nt (Besitz)* possession; *(Landgut)* estate; **Güter** *pl (Waren)* goods *pl.*

================== *SCHLÜSSELWORT*

**gut** *adj* good; **das ist ~ gegen** *od* **für** *(umg)* **Husten** it's good for coughs; **sei so ~ (und) gib mir das** would you mind giving me that; **dafür ist er sich zu ~** he wouldn't stoop to that sort of thing; **das ist ja alles ~ und schön, aber ...** that's all very well but ...; **du bist ~!** *(umg)* you're a fine one!; **alles G~e** all the best; **also ~** all right then ♦ *adv* well; **du hast es ~!** you've got it made!; **~, aber ...** OK, but ...; **(na) ~, ich komme** all right, I'll come; **~ drei Stunden** a good three hours; **das kann ~ sein** that may well be; **~ und gern** easily; **laß es ~ sein** that'll do.

**Gut-** *zW:* ~**achten** (-s, -) *nt* report; ~**achter** (-s, -) *m* expert; ~**achterkommission** *f* quango; **g~artig** *adj* good-natured; *(MED)* benign; **g~bürgerlich** *adj (Küche)* (good) plain; ~**dünken** *nt:* **nach ~dünken** at one's discretion.
**Güte** ['gyːtə] (-) *f* goodness, kindness; *(Qualität)* quality; **ach du liebe** *od* **meine ~!** *(umg)* goodness me!; ~**klasse** *f (COMM)* grade; ~**klasseneinteilung** *f (COMM)* grading.
**Güter-** *zW:* ~**abfertigung** *f (EISENB)* goods office; ~**bahnhof** *m* goods station; ~**trennung** *f (JUR)* separation of property; ~**verkehr** *m* freight traffic; ~**wagen** *m* goods waggon *(BRIT)*, freight car *(US)*; ~**zug** *m* goods train *(BRIT)*, freight train *(US)*.
**Gütesiegel** *nt (COMM)* stamp of quality.
**gut-** *zW:* ~**gehen** *unreg vi unpers* to work, come off; **es geht jdm ~** sb's doing fine; **das ist noch einmal ~gegangen** it turned out all right; ~**gehend** *adj attrib* thriving; ~**gelaunt** *adj* cheerful, in a good mood; ~**gemeint** *adj* well meant; ~**gläubig** *adj* trusting; **G~haben** (-s) *nt* credit; ~**haben** *unreg vt:* **20 Mark (bei jdm) ~haben** to be in credit (with sb) to the tune of 20 marks; ~**heißen** *unreg vt* to approve (of); ~**herzig** *adj* kind(-hearted).
**gütig** ['gyːtɪç] *adj* kind.
**gütlich** ['gyːtlɪç] *adj* amicable.
**gut-** *zW:* ~**machen** *vt (in Ordnung bringen: Fehler)* to put right, correct; *(Schaden)* to make good; ~**mütig** *adj* good-natured;

**G~mütigkeit** *f* good nature.
**Gutsbesitzer(in)** *m(f)* landowner.
**Gut-** *zW:* ~**schein** *m* voucher; **g~schreiben** *unreg vt* to credit; ~**schrift** *f* credit.
**Gutsherr** *m* squire.
**Gutshof** *m* estate.
**gut-** *zW:* ~**situiert** *adj attrib* well-off; ~**tun** *unreg vi:* **jdm ~tun** to do sb good; ~**unterrichtet** *adj attrib* well-informed; ~**willig** *adj* willing.
**Gymnasiallehrer(in)** [gʏmnaziˈaːlleːrər(ɪn)] *m(f)* ≈ grammar school teacher *(BRIT)*, high school teacher *(US)*.
**Gymnasium** [gʏmˈnaːziʊm] *nt* ≈ grammar school *(BRIT)*, high school *(US)*.

> The **Gymnasium** *is a selective secondary school. There are nine years of study at a Gymnasium leading to the* **Abitur** *which gives access to higher education. Pupils who successfully complete six years automatically gain the* **mittlere Reife**.

**Gymnastik** [gʏmˈnastɪk] *f* exercises *pl*, keep-fit; ~ **machen** to do keep-fit (exercises)/ gymnastics.
**Gynäkologe** [gʏnɛkoˈloːgə] (-n, -n) *m* gynaecologist *(BRIT)*, gynecologist *(US)*.
**Gynäkologin** [gʏnɛkoˈloːgɪn] *f* gynaecologist *(BRIT)*, gynecologist *(US)*.

# H, h

**H, h** [haː] *nt* H, h; ~ **wie Heinrich** ≈ H for Harry, H for How *(US)*; *(MUS)* B.
**ha** *abk* = Hektar.
**Haag** [haːk] (-s) *m:* **Den ~** The Hague.
**Haar** [haːr] (-(e)s, -e) *nt* hair; **um ein ~** nearly; ~ **auf den Zähnen haben** to be a tough customer; **sich die ~e raufen** *(umg)* to tear one's hair; **sich** *dat* **in die ~e kriegen** *(umg)* to quarrel; **das ist an den ~en herbeigezogen** that's rather far-fetched; ~**ansatz** *m* hairline; ~**bürste** *f* hairbrush.
**haaren** *vi, vr* to lose hair.
**Haaresbreite** *f:* **um ~** by a hair's-breadth.
**Haarfestiger** (-s, -) *m* setting lotion.
**haargenau** *adv* precisely.
**haarig** *adj* hairy; *(fig)* nasty.
**Haar-** *zW:* ~**klemme** *f*, ~**klemme** *f* hair grip *(BRIT)*, barrette *(US)*; **h~klein** *adv* in minute detail; **h~los** *adj* hairless; ~**nadel** *f* hairpin; **h~scharf** *adv (beobachten)* very sharply; *(verfehlen)* by a hair's breadth; ~**schnitt** *m* haircut; ~**schopf** *m* head of hair; ~**sieb** *nt* fine sieve; ~**spalterei** *f* hair-splitting;

~**spange** f hair slide; **h~sträubend** adj hair-raising; ~**teil** nt hairpiece; ~**waschmittel** nt shampoo; ~**wasser** nt hair lotion.

**Hab** [ha:p] nt: ~ **und Gut** possessions pl, belongings pl, worldly goods pl.

**Habe** ['ha:bə] (-) f property.

**haben** ['ha:bən] unreg vt, Hilfsverb to have ♦ vr unpers: **und damit hat es sich** (umg) and that's that; **Hunger/Angst** ~ to be hungry/afraid; **da hast du 10 Mark** there's 10 Marks; **die ~'s (ja)** (umg) they can afford it; **Ferien** ~ to be on holiday; **es am Herzen** ~ (umg) to have heart trouble; **sie ist noch zu** ~ (umg: nicht verheiratet) she's still single; **für etw zu** ~ **sein** to be keen on sth; **sie werden schon merken, was sie an ihm** ~ they'll see how valuable he is; **haste was, biste was** (Sprichwort) money brings status; **wie gehabt!** some things don't change; **das hast du jetzt davon** now see what's happened; **woher hast du das?** where did you get that from?; **was hast du denn?** what's the matter (with you)?; **ich habe zu tun** I'm busy.

**Haben** (-s, -) nt (COMM) credit.

**Habenseite** f (COMM) credit side.

**Habgier** f avarice.

**habgierig** adj avaricious.

**habhaft** adj: **jds/einer Sache** ~ **werden** (geh) to get hold of sb/sth.

**Habicht** ['ha:bıçt] (-(e)s, -e) m hawk.

**Habilitation** [habilitatsi'o:n] f (Lehrberechtigung) postdoctoral lecturing qualification.

**Habseligkeiten** ['ha:pze:lıçkaɪtən] pl belongings pl.

**Habsucht** ['ha:pzʊxt] f greed.

**Hachse** ['haksə] (-, -n) f (KOCH) knuckle.

**Hackbraten** m meat loaf.

**Hackbrett** nt chopping board; (MUS) dulcimer.

**Hacke** ['hakə] (-, -n) f hoe; (Ferse) heel.

**hacken** vt to hack, chop; (Erde) to hoe.

**Hacker** ['hakər] (-s, -) m (COMPUT) hacker.

**Hackfleisch** nt mince, minced meat, ground meat (US).

**Hackordnung** f (lit, fig) pecking order.

**Häcksel** ['hɛksəl] (-s) m od nt chopped straw, chaff.

**hadern** ['ha:dərn] vi (geh): ~ **mit** to quarrel with; (unzufrieden sein) to be at odds with.

**Hafen** ['ha:fən] (-s, ̈-) m harbour, harbor (US), port; (fig) haven; ~**anlagen** pl docks pl; ~**arbeiter** m docker; ~**damm** m jetty, mole; ~**gebühren** pl harbo(u)r dues pl; ~**stadt** f port.

**Hafer** ['ha:fər] (-s, -) m oats pl; **ihn sticht der** ~ (umg) he is feeling his oats; ~**brei** m porridge (BRIT), oatmeal (US); ~**flocken** pl rolled oats pl (BRIT), oatmeal (US); ~**schleim** m gruel.

**Haff** [haf] (-s, -s od -e) nt lagoon.

**Haft** [haft] (-) f custody; ~**anstalt** f detention centre (BRIT) od center (US); **h~bar** adj liable, responsible; ~**befehl** m warrant (for arrest); **einen** ~**befehl gegen jdn ausstellen** to issue a warrant for sb's arrest.

**haften** vi to stick, cling; ~ **für** to be liable od responsible for; **für Garderobe kann nicht gehaftet werden** all articles are left at owner's risk; ~**bleiben** unreg vi: ~**bleiben (an** +dat) to stick (to).

**Häftling** ['hɛftlıŋ] m prisoner.

**Haft-** zW: ~**pflicht** f liability; ~**pflichtversicherung** f third party insurance; ~**richter** m magistrate.

**Haftschalen** pl contact lenses pl.

**Haftung** f liability.

**Hagebutte** ['ha:gəbʊtə] (-, -n) f rose hip.

**Hagedorn** m hawthorn.

**Hagel** ['ha:gəl] (-s) m hail; ~**korn** nt hailstone; (MED) eye cyst.

**hageln** vi unpers to hail.

**Hagelschauer** m (short) hailstorm.

**hager** ['ha:gər] adj gaunt.

**Häher** ['hɛ:ər] (-s, -) m jay.

**Hahn** [ha:n] (-(e)s, ̈-e) m cock; (Wasser~) tap, faucet (US); (Abzug) trigger; ~ **im Korb sein** (umg) to be cock of the walk; **danach kräht kein** ~ **mehr** (umg) no one cares two hoots about that any more.

**Hähnchen** ['hɛ:nçən] nt cockerel; (KOCH) chicken.

**Hai(fisch)** ['haı(fıʃ)] (-(e)s, -e) m shark.

**Haiti** [ha'i:ti] (-s) nt Haiti.

**Häkchen** ['hɛ:kçən] nt small hook.

**Häkelarbeit** f crochet work.

**häkeln** ['hɛ:kəln] vt to crochet.

**Häkelnadel** f crochet hook.

**Haken** ['ha:kən] (-s, -) m hook; (fig) catch; **einen** ~ **schlagen** to dart sideways; ~**kreuz** nt swastika; ~**nase** f hooked nose.

**halb** [halp] adj half ♦ adv (beinahe) almost; ~ **eins** half past twelve; **ein** ~**es Dutzend** half a dozen; **nichts H~es und nichts Ganzes** neither one thing nor the other; **(noch) ein** ~**es Kind sein** to be scarcely more than a child; **das ist** ~ **so schlimm** it's not as bad as all that; **mit jdm** ~**e-~e machen** (umg) to go halves with sb.

**halb-** zW: **H~blut** nt (Tier) crossbreed; **H~bruder** m half-brother; **H~dunkel** nt semi-darkness.

**halber** ['halbər] präp +gen (wegen) on account of; (für) for the sake of.

**Halb-** zW: **h~fett** adj medium fat; ~**finale** nt semi-final; ~**heit** f half-measure; **h~herzig** adj half-hearted.

**halbieren** [hal'bi:rən] vt to halve.

**Halb-** zW: ~**insel** f peninsula; **h~jährlich** adj half-yearly; ~**kreis** m semicircle; ~**kugel** f hemisphere; **h~lang** adj: **nun mach mal h~lang!** (umg) now wait a minute!; **h~laut** adv in an undertone; ~**leiter** m (PHYS) semiconductor; **h~mast** *adv* at half-mast; **~mond** *m* half-moon; *(fig)* crescent; **h~offen** *adj* half-open; **~pension** *f* half-board *(BRIT)*, European plan *(US)*; **~schuh** *m* shoe; **~schwester** *f* half-sister; **h~seiden** *adj (lit)* fifty per cent silk; *(fig: Dame)* fast; *(: homosexuell)* gay; **h~seitig** *adj (Anzeige)* half-page; **~starke(r)** *f(m)* hooligan, rowdy; **h~tags** *adv:* **h~tags arbeiten** to work part-time; **~tagsarbeit** *f* part-time work; **~tagskraft** *f* part-time worker; **~ton** *m* half-tone; *(MUS)* semitone; **h~trocken** *adj* medium-dry; **~waise** *f* child/person who has lost one parent; **h~wegs** *adv* half-way; **h~wegs besser** more or less better; **~welt** *f* demimonde; **~wertzeit** *f* half-life; **~wüchsige(r)** *f(m)* adolescent; **~zeit** *f (SPORT)* half; *(Pause)* half-time.

**Halde** ['haldə] *f* tip; *(Schlacken~)* slag heap.

**half** *etc* [half] *vb siehe* **helfen**.

**Hälfte** ['hɛlftə] *(-, -en) f* half; **um die ~ steigen** to increase by half.

**Halfter¹** ['halftər] *(-s, -) m od nt (für Tiere)* halter.

**Halfter²** ['halftər] *(-, -n od -s, -) f od nt (Pistolen~)* holster.

**Hall** [hal] *(-(e)s, -e) m* sound.

**Halle** ['halə] *(-, -n) f* hall; *(AVIAT)* hangar.

**hallen** *vi* to echo, resound.

**Hallen-** *in zW* indoor; **~bad** *nt* indoor swimming pool.

**hallo** [ha'lo:] *interj* hallo.

**Halluzination** [halutsinatsi'o:n] *f* hallucination.

**Halm** ['halm] *(-(e)s, -e) m* blade, stalk.

**Hals** [hals] *(-es, ⁻e) m* neck; *(Kehle)* throat; **sich** *dat* **nach jdm/etw den ~ verrenken** *(umg)* to crane one's neck to see sb/sth; **jdm um den ~ fallen** to fling one's arms around sb's neck; **aus vollem ~(e)** at the top of one's voice; **~ über Kopf** in a rush; **jdn auf dem** *od* **am ~ haben** *(umg)* to be lumbered *od* saddled with sb; **das hängt mir zum ~ raus** *(umg)* I'm sick and tired of it; **sie hat es in den falschen ~ bekommen** *(falsch verstehen)* she took it wrongly; **~abschneider** *(pej: umg) m* shark; **~band** *nt (Hundehalsband)* collar; **h~brecherisch** *adj (Tempo)* breakneck; *(Fahrt)* hair-raising; **~kette** *f* necklace; **~krause** *f* ruff; **~-Nasen-Ohren-Arzt** *m* ear, nose and throat specialist; **~schlagader** *f* carotid artery; **~schmerzen** *pl* sore throat *sing;* **h~starrig** *adj* stubborn, obstinate; **~tuch** *nt* scarf; **~- und Beinbruch** *interj* good luck; **~weh** *nt* sore throat; **~wirbel** *m* cervical vertebra.

**Halt** [halt] *(-(e)s, -e) m* stop; *(fester ~)* hold; *(innerer ~)* stability; **h~!** stop!, halt!

**hält** [hɛlt] *vb siehe* **halten**.

**Halt-** *zW:* **h~bar** *adj* durable; *(Lebensmittel)* non-perishable; *(MIL, fig)* tenable; **h~bar bis 6.11.** use by 6 Nov.; **~barkeit** *f* durability;

*(non-)perishability;* tenability; *(von Lebensmitteln)* shelf life; **~barkeitsdatum** *nt* best-before date.

**halten** ['haltən] *unreg vt* to keep; *(fest~)* to hold ♦ *vi* to hold; *(frisch bleiben)* to keep; *(stoppen)* to stop ♦ *vr (frisch bleiben)* to keep; *(sich behaupten)* to hold out; **den Mund ~** *(umg)* to keep one's mouth shut; **~ für** to regard as; **~ von** to think of; **das kannst du ~ wie du willst** that's completely up to you; **der Film hält nicht, was er verspricht** the film doesn't live up to expectations; **davon halt(e) ich nichts** I don't think much of it; **zu jdm ~** to stand *od* stick by sb; **an sich** *akk* **~** to restrain o.s.; **auf sich** *akk* **~** *(auf Äußeres achten)* to take a pride in o.s.; **er hat sich gut gehalten** *(umg)* he's well-preserved; **sich an ein Versprechen ~** to keep a promise; **sich rechts/links ~** to keep to the right/left.

**Halter** ['haltər] *(-s, -) m (Halterung)* holder.

**Haltestelle** *f* stop.

**Halteverbot** *nt:* **absolutes ~** no stopping; **eingeschränktes ~** no waiting; **hier ist ~** you cannot stop here.

**Halt-** *zW:* **h~los** *adj* unstable; **~losigkeit** *f* instability; **h~machen** *vi* to stop.

**Haltung** *f* posture; *(fig)* attitude; *(Selbstbeherrschung)* composure; **~ bewahren** to keep one's composure.

**Halunke** [ha'luŋkə] *(-n, -n) m* rascal.

**Hamburg** ['hambʊrk] *(-s) nt* Hamburg.

**Hamburger** *(-s, -) m (KOCH)* burger, hamburger.

**Hamburger(in)** *(-s, -) m(f)* native of Hamburg.

**Hameln** ['ha:məln] *nt* Hamelin.

**hämisch** ['hɛ:mɪʃ] *adj* malicious.

**Hammel** ['haməl] *(-s, ⁻ od -) m* wether; **~fleisch** *nt* mutton; **~keule** *f* leg of mutton.

**Hammelsprung** *m (PARL)* division.

**Hammer** ['hamər] *(-s, ⁻) m* hammer; **das ist ein ~!** *(umg: unerhört)* that's absurd!

**hämmern** ['hɛmərn] *vt, vi* to hammer.

**Hammondorgel** ['hæmənd|ɔrgəl] *f* electric organ.

**Hämorrhoiden** [hɛmɔro'i:dən] *pl* piles *pl,* haemorrhoids *pl (BRIT),* hemorrhoids *pl (US).*

**Hampelmann** ['hampəlman] *m (lit, fig)* puppet.

**Hamster** ['hamstər] *(-s, -) m* hamster.

**Hamsterei** [hamstə'raɪ] *f* hoarding.

**Hamsterer** *(-s, -) m* hoarder.

**hamstern** *vi* to hoard.

**Hand** [hant] *(-, ⁻e) f* hand; **etw zur ~ haben** to have sth to hand; *(Ausrede, Erklärung)* to have sth ready; **jdm zur ~ gehen** to lend sb a helping hand; **zu Händen von jdm** for the attention of sb; **in festen Händen sein** to be spoken for; **die ~ für jdn ins Feuer legen** to vouch for sb; **hinter vorgehaltener ~** on the quiet; **~ aufs Herz** cross your heart; **jdn auf Händen tragen** to cherish sb; **bei etw die** *od* **seine ~ im Spiel haben** to have a hand in sth; **eine ~ wäscht die andere** (*Sprichwort*) if you scratch my back I'll scratch yours; **das hat weder ~ noch Fuß** that doesn't make sense; **das liegt auf der ~** (*umg*) that's obvious; **an ~ eines Beispiels** by means of an example; **~arbeit** *f* manual work; (*Nadelarbeit*) needlework; **~arbeiter** *m* manual worker; **~ball** *m* handball; **~besen** *m* brush; **~betrieb** *m*: **mit ~betrieb** hand-operated; **~bewegung** *f* gesture; **~bibliothek** *f* (*in Bibliothek*) reference section; (*auf Schreibtisch*) reference books *pl*; **~bremse** *f* handbrake; **~buch** *nt* handbook, manual.

**Händedruck** *m* handshake.

**Händeklatschen** *nt* clapping, applause.

**Handel**[1] ['handəl] **(-s)** *m* trade; (*Geschäft*) transaction; **im ~ sein** to be on the market; **(mit jdm) ~ treiben** to trade (with sb); **etw in den ~ bringen/aus dem ~ ziehen** to put sth on/take sth off the market.

**Handel**[2] **(-s, ⸚)** *m* quarrel.

**handeln** ['handəln] *vi* to trade; (*tätig werden*) to act ♦ *vr unpers*: **sich ~ um** to be a question of, be about; **~ von** to be about; **ich lasse mit mir ~** I'm open to persuasion; (*in bezug auf Preis*) I'm open to offers.

**Handeln (-s)** *nt* action.

**handelnd** *adj*: **die ~en Personen in einem Drama** the characters in a drama.

**Handels-** *zW*: **~bank** *f* merchant bank (*BRIT*), commercial bank; **~bilanz** *f* balance of trade; **aktive/passive ~bilanz** balance of trade surplus/deficit; **~delegation** *f* trade mission; **h~einig** *adj*: **mit jdm h~einig werden** to conclude a deal with sb; **~gesellschaft** *f* commercial company; **~kammer** *f* chamber of commerce; **~klasse** *f* grade; **~marine** *f* merchant navy; **~marke** *f* trade name; **~name** *m* trade name; **~recht** *nt* commercial law; **~register** *nt* register of companies; **~reisende(r)** *f(m)* = **Handlungsreisende(r)** commercial traveller; **~sanktionen** *pl* trade sanctions *pl*; **~schule** *f* business school; **~spanne** *f* gross margin, mark-up; **~sperre** *f* trade embargo; **h~üblich** *adj* customary; **~vertreter** *m* sales representative; **~vertretung** *f* trade mission; **~ware** *f* commodity.

**händeringend** ['hɛndərɪŋənd] *adv* wringing one's hands; (*fig*) imploringly.

**Hand-** *zW*: **~feger** *m* brush; **~fertigkeit** *f* dexterity; **h~fest** *adj* hefty; **~fläche** *f* palm *od* flat (of one's hand); **h~gearbeitet** *adj* handmade; **~gelenk** *nt* wrist; **aus dem ~gelenk** (*umg: ohne Mühe*) effortlessly; (: *improvisiert*) off the cuff; **~gemenge** *nt* scuffle; **~gepäck** *nt* hand baggage *od* luggage; **h~geschrieben** *adj* handwritten; **~granate** *f* hand grenade; **h~greiflich** *adj* palpable; **h~greiflich werden** to become

violent; **~griff** *m* flick of the wrist; **~habe** *f*: **ich habe gegen ihn keine ~habe** (*fig*) I have no hold on him; **h~haben** *unreg vt untr* to handle; **~karren** *m* handcart; **~käse** *m* strong-smelling, round German cheese; **~kuß** *m* kiss on the hand; **~langer (-s, -)** *m* odd-job man, handyman; (*fig: Untergeordneter*) dogsbody.

**Händler** ['hɛndlər] **(-s, -)** *m* trader, dealer.

**handlich** ['hantlɪç] *adj* handy.

**Handlung** ['handluŋ] *f* action; (*Tat*) act; (*in Buch*) plot; (*Geschäft*) shop.

**Handlungs-** *zW*: **~ablauf** *m* plot; **~bevollmächtigte(r)** *f(m)* authorized agent; **h~fähig** *adj* (*Regierung*) able to act; (*JUR*) empowered to act; **~freiheit** *f* freedom of action; **h~orientiert** *adj* action-orientated; **~reisende(r)** *f(m)* commercial traveller (*BRIT*), traveling salesman (*US*); **~vollmacht** *f* proxy; **~weise** *f* manner of dealing.

**Hand-** *zW*: **~pflege** *f* manicure; **~schelle** *f* handcuff; **~schlag** *m* handshake; **keinen ~schlag tun** not to do a stroke (of work); **~schrift** *f* handwriting; (*Text*) manuscript; **h~schriftlich** *adj* handwritten ♦ *adv* (*korrigieren, einfügen*) by hand; **~schuh** *m* glove; **~schuhfach** *nt* (*AUT*) glove compartment; **~tasche** *f* handbag (*BRIT*), pocket book (*US*), purse (*US*); **~tuch** *nt* towel; **~umdrehen** *nt*: **im ~umdrehen** (*fig*) in the twinkling of an eye.

**Handwerk** *nt* trade, craft; **jdm das ~ legen** (*fig*) to put a stop to sb's game.

**Handwerker (-s, -)** *m* craftsman, artisan; **wir haben seit Wochen die ~ im Haus** we've had workmen in the house for weeks.

**Handwerkskammer** *f* trade corporation.

**Hand-** *zW*: **~werkzeug** *nt* tools *pl*; **~wörterbuch** *nt* concise dictionary; **~zeichen** *nt* signal; (*Geste*) sign; (*bei Abstimmung*) show of hands; **~zettel** *m* leaflet, handbill.

**Hanf** [hanf] **(-(e)s)** *m* hemp.

**Hang** [haŋ] **(-(e)s, ⸚e)** *m* inclination; (*Ab~*) slope.

**Hänge-** ['hɛŋə] *in zW* hanging; **~brücke** *f* suspension bridge; **~matte** *f* hammock.

**Hängen** ['hɛŋən] *nt*: **mit ~ und Würgen** (*umg*) by the skin of one's teeth.

**hängen** *unreg vi* to hang ♦ *vt*: **~ (an +akk)** to hang (on(to)); **an jdm ~** (*fig*) to be attached to sb; **den Kopf ~ lassen** (*fig*) to be downcast; **die ganze Sache hängt an ihm** it all depends on him; **sich ~ an +akk** to hang on to, cling to.

**hängenbleiben** *unreg vi* to be caught; (*fig*) to remain, stick; **~ an +dat** to catch *od* get caught on; **es bleibt ja doch alles an mir hängen** (*fig: umg*) in the end it's all down to me anyhow.

**hängend** *adj*: **mit ~er Zunge kam er**

**angelaufen** (*fig*) he came running up panting.

**hängenlassen** *unreg vt* (*vergessen*) to leave behind ♦ *vr* to let o.s. go.

**Hängeschloß** *nt* padlock.

**Hanglage** *f*: **in ~** situated on a slope.

**Hannover** [ha'no:fər] (*-s*) *nt* Hanover.

**Hannoveraner(in)** [hanovə'ra:nər(ɪn)] (*-s, -*) *m(f)* Hanoverian.

**hänseln** ['hɛnzəln] *vt* to tease.

**Hansestadt** ['hanzəʃtat] *f* Hanseatic *od* Hanse town.

**Hanswurst** [hans'vʊrst] (*-(e)s, -e od -würste*) *m* clown.

**Hantel** ['hantəl] (*-, -n*) *f* (*SPORT*) dumb-bell.

**hantieren** [han'ti:rən] *vi* to work, be busy; **mit etw ~** to handle sth.

**hapern** ['ha:pərn] *vi unpers*: **es hapert an etw** *dat* there is a lack of sth.

**Happen** ['hapən] (*-s, -*) *m* mouthful.

**happig** ['hapɪç] (*umg*) *adj* steep.

**Hardware** ['ha:dwɛə] (*-, -s*) *f* hardware.

**Harfe** ['harfə] (*-, -n*) *f* harp.

**Harke** ['harkə] (*-, -n*) *f* rake.

**harken** *vt, vi* to rake.

**harmlos** ['harmlo:s] *adj* harmless.

**Harmlosigkeit** *f* harmlessness.

**Harmonie** [harmo'ni:] *f* harmony.

**harmonieren** *vi* to harmonize.

**Harmonika** [har'mo:nika] (*-, -s*) *f* (*Zieh~*) concertina.

**harmonisch** [har'mo:nɪʃ] *adj* harmonious.

**Harmonium** [har'mo:niʊm] (*-s, -nien od -s*) *nt* harmonium.

**Harn** ['harn] (*-(e)s, -e*) *m* urine; **~blase** *f* bladder.

**Harnisch** ['harnɪʃ] (*-(e)s, -e*) *m* armour, armor (*US*); **jdn in ~ bringen** to infuriate sb; **in ~ geraten** to become angry.

**Harpune** [har'pu:nə] (*-, -n*) *f* harpoon.

**harren** ['harən] *vi*: **~ auf** +*akk* to wait for.

**Harsch** [harʃ] (*-(e)s*) *m* frozen snow.

**harschig** *adj* (*Schnee*) frozen.

**hart** [hart] *adj* hard; (*fig*) harsh ♦ *adv*: **das ist ~ an der Grenze** that's almost going too far; **~e Währung** hard currency; **~ bleiben** to stand firm; **es geht ~ auf ~** it's a tough fight.

**Härte** ['hɛrtə] (*-, -n*) *f* hardness; (*fig*) harshness; **soziale ~n** social hardships; **~fall** *m* case of hardship; (*umg: Mensch*) hardship case; **~klausel** *f* hardship clause.

**härten** *vt, vr* to harden.

**hart-** *zW*: **H~faserplatte** *f* hardboard, fiberboard (*US*); **~gekocht** *adj* hard-boiled; **~gesotten** *adj* tough, hard-boiled; **~herzig** *adj* hard-hearted; **~näckig** *adj* stubborn; **H~näckigkeit** *f* stubbornness.

**Harz¹** [ha:rts] (*-es, -e*) *nt* resin.

**Harz²** (*-es*) *m* (*GEOG*) Harz Mountains *pl*.

**Haschee** [ha'ʃeː] (*-s, -s*) *nt* hash.

**haschen** ['haʃən] *vt* to catch, snatch ♦ *vi* (*umg*)

to smoke hash.

**Haschisch** ['haʃɪʃ] (*-*) *nt* hashish.

**Hase** ['ha:zə] (*-n, -n*) *m* hare; **falscher ~** (*KOCH*) meat loaf; **wissen, wie der ~ läuft** (*fig: umg*) to know which way the wind blows; **mein Name ist ~(, ich weiß von nichts)** I don't know anything about anything.

**Haselnuß** ['ha:zəlnʊs] *f* hazelnut.

**Hasenfuß** *m* coward.

**Hasenscharte** *f* harelip.

**Haspel** (*-, -n*) *f* reel, bobbin; (*Winde*) winch.

**Haß** [has] (*-sses*) *m* hate, hatred; **einen ~ (auf jdn) haben** (*umg: Wut*) to be really mad (with sb).

**hassen** ['hasən] *vt* to hate; **etw ~ wie die Pest** (*umg*) to detest sth.

**hassenswert** *adj* hateful.

**häßlich** ['hɛslɪç] *adj* ugly; (*gemein*) nasty; **H~keit** *f* ugliness; nastiness.

**Haßliebe** *f* love-hate relationship.

**Hast** [hast] (*-*) *f* haste.

**hast** *vb siehe* **haben**.

**hasten** *vi, vr* to rush.

**hastig** *adj* hasty.

**hat** [hat] *vb siehe* **haben**.

**hätscheln** ['hɛtʃəln] *vt* to pamper; (*zärtlich*) to cuddle.

**hatte** *etc* ['hatə] *vb siehe* **haben**.

**hätte** *etc* ['hɛtə] *vb siehe* **haben**.

**Haube** ['haʊbə] (*-, -n*) *f* hood; (*Mütze*) cap; (*AUT*) bonnet (*BRIT*), hood (*US*); **unter der ~ sein/unter die ~ kommen** (*hum*) to be/get married.

**Hauch** [haʊx] (*-(e)s, -e*) *m* breath; (*Luft~*) breeze; (*fig*) trace; **h~dünn** *adj* extremely thin; (*Scheiben*) wafer-thin; (*fig: Mehrheit*) extremely narrow; **h~en** *vi* to breathe; **h~fein** *adj* very fine.

**Haue** ['haʊə] (*-, -n*) *f* hoe; (*Pickel*) pick; (*umg*) hiding.

**hauen** *unreg vt* to hew, cut; (*umg*) to thrash.

**Hauer** ['haʊər] (*-s, -*) *m* (*MIN*) face-worker.

**Häufchen** ['hɔʏfçən] *nt*: **ein ~ Unglück** *od* **Elend** a picture of misery.

**Haufen** ['haʊfən] (*-s, -*) *m* heap; (*Leute*) crowd; **ein ~ (Bücher)** (*umg*) loads *od* a lot (of books); **auf einem ~** in one heap; **etw über den ~ werfen** (*umg: verwerfen*) to chuck sth out; **jdn über den ~ rennen** *od* **fahren** *etc* (*umg*) to knock sb down.

**häufen** ['hɔʏfən] *vt* to pile up ♦ *vr* to accumulate.

**haufenweise** *adv* in heaps; in droves; **etw ~ haben** to have piles of sth.

**häufig** ['hɔʏfɪç] *adj* frequent ♦ *adv* frequently; **H~keit** *f* frequency.

**Haupt** [haʊpt] (*-(e)s, Häupter*) *nt* head; (*Ober~*) chief ♦ *in zW* main; **~akteur** *m* (*lit, fig*) leading light; (*pej*) main figure; **~aktionär** *m* major shareholder; **~bahnhof** *m* central station; **h~beruflich** *adv* as one's main occupation;

~**buch** nt (COMM) ledger; ~**darsteller(in)** m(f) leading actor, leading actress; ~**eingang** m main entrance; ~**fach** nt (SCH, UNIV) main subject, major (US); **etw im** ~**fach studieren** to study sth as one's main subject, major in sth (US); ~**film** m main film; ~**gericht** nt main course; ~**geschäftsstelle** f head office; ~**geschäftszeit** f peak (shopping) period; ~**gewinn** m first prize; **einer der** ~**gewinne** one of the main prizes; ~**leitung** f mains pl.

**Häuptling** ['hɔyptlɪŋ] m chief(tain).

**Haupt-** zW: ~**mahlzeit** f main meal; ~**mann** (-(e)s, pl -**leute**) m (MIL) captain; ~**nahrungsmittel** nt staple food; ~**person** f (im Roman usw) main character; (fig) central figure; ~**postamt** nt main post office; ~**quartier** nt headquarters pl; ~**rolle** f leading part; ~**sache** f main thing; **in der** ~**sache** in the main, mainly; **h~sächlich** adj chief ♦ adv chiefly; ~**saison** f peak od high season; ~**satz** m main clause; ~**schlagader** f aorta; ~**schlüssel** m master key.

**Hauptschule** f ≈ secondary modern (school) (BRIT), junior high (school) (US).

---

The **Hauptschule** is a non-selective school which pupils attend after the **Grundschule**. They complete five years of study and most go on to do some training in a practical subject or trade.

---

**Haupt-** zW: ~**sendezeit** f (TV) prime time; ~**stadt** f capital; ~**straße** f main street; ~**verkehrsstraße** f (in Stadt) main street; (Durchgangsstraße) main thoroughfare; (zwischen Städten) main highway, trunk road (BRIT); ~**verkehrszeit** f rush hour; ~**versammlung** f general meeting; ~**wohnsitz** m main place of residence; ~**wort** nt noun.

**hau ruck** ['hau 'rʊk] interj heave-ho.

**Haus** [haus] (-es, **Häuser**) nt house; **nach** ~**e** home; **zu** ~**e** at home; **fühl dich wie zu** ~**e!** make yourself at home!; **ein Freund des** ~**es** a friend of the family; **wir liefern frei** ~ (COMM) we offer free delivery; **das erste** ~ **am Platze** (Hotel) the best hotel in town; ~**angestellte** f domestic servant; ~**arbeit** f housework; (SCH) homework; ~**arrest** m (im Internat) detention; (JUR) house arrest; ~**arzt** m family doctor; ~**aufgabe** f (SCH) homework; ~**besetzung** f squat; ~**besitzer** m house-owner; ~**besuch** m home visit; (von Arzt) house call.

**Häuschen** ['hɔysçən] nt: **ganz aus dem** ~ **sein** (fig: umg) to be out of one's mind (with excitement/fear etc).

**Hauseigentümer** m house-owner.

**hausen** ['hauzən] vi to live (in poverty); (pej) to wreak havoc.

**Häuser-** zW: ~**block** m block (of houses); ~**makler** m estate agent (BRIT), real estate agent (US); ~**reihe** f, ~**zeile** f row of houses; (aneinandergebaut) terrace (BRIT).

**Haus-** zW: ~**frau** f housewife; ~**freund** m family friend; (umg) lover; ~**friedensbruch** m (JUR) trespass (in sb's house); ~**gebrauch** m: **für den** ~**gebrauch** (Gerät) for domestic od household use; **h~gemacht** adj home-made; ~**gemeinschaft** f household (community); ~**halt** m household; (POL) budget; **h~halten** unreg vi to keep house; (sparen) to economize; ~**hälterin** f housekeeper.

**Haushalts-** zW: ~**auflösung** f dissolution of the household; ~**buch** nt housekeeping book; ~**debatte** f (PARL) budget debate; ~**geld** nt housekeeping (money); ~**gerät** nt domestic appliance; ~**hilfe** f domestic od home help; ~**jahr** nt (POL, WIRTS) financial od fiscal year; ~**periode** f budget period; ~**plan** m budget.

**Haus-** zW: ~**haltung** f housekeeping; ~**herr** m host; (Vermieter) landlord; **h~hoch** adv: **h~hoch verlieren** to lose by a mile.

**hausieren** [hau'ziːrən] vi to peddle.

**Hausierer** (-s, -) m pedlar (BRIT), peddler (US).

**hausintern** ['haus|ɪntɛrn] adj internal company attrib.

**häuslich** ['hɔyslɪç] adj domestic; **sich irgendwo** ~ **einrichten** od **niederlassen** to settle in somewhere; **H~keit** f domesticity.

**Hausmacherart** ['hausmaxər|aːrt] f: **Wurst** etc **nach** ~ home-made-style sausage etc.

**Haus-** zW: ~**mann** (-(e)s, pl -**männer**) m (den Haushalt versorgender Mann) househusband; ~**marke** f (eigene Marke) own brand; (bevorzugte Marke) favourite (BRIT) od favorite (US) brand; ~**meister** m caretaker, janitor; ~**mittel** nt household remedy; ~**nummer** f house number; ~**ordnung** f house rules pl; ~**putz** m house cleaning; ~**ratversicherung** f (household) contents insurance; ~**schlüssel** m front-door key; ~**schuh** m slipper; ~**schwamm** m dry rot.

**Hausse** ['hoːsə] (-, -n) f (WIRTS) boom; (BÖRSE) bull market; ~ **an** +dat boom in.

**Haus-** zW: ~**segen** m: **bei ihnen hängt der** ~**segen schief** (hum) they're a bit short on domestic bliss; ~**stand** m: **einen** ~**stand gründen** to set up house od home; ~**(durch)suchung** f police raid; ~**(durch)suchungsbefehl** m search warrant; ~**tier** nt domestic animal; ~**tür** f front door; ~**verbot** nt: **jdm** ~**verbot erteilen** to ban sb from the house; ~**verwalter** m property manager; ~**verwaltung** f property management; ~**wirt** m landlord; ~**wirtschaft** f domestic science; ~**-zu-~-Verkauf** m door-to-door selling.

**Haut** [haut] (-, **Häute**) f skin; (Tier~) hide; **mit** ~ **und Haar(en)** (umg) completely; **aus der** ~ **fahren** (umg) to go through the roof;

~**arzt** *m* skin specialist, dermatologist.
**häuten** ['hɔytən] *vt* to skin ♦ *vr* to shed one's skin.
**hauteng** *adj* skintight.
**Hautfarbe** *f* complexion.
**Hautkrebs** *m* (*MED*) skin cancer.
**Havanna** [ha'vana] (-s) *nt* Havana.
**Havel** ['ha:fəl] (-) *f* (*Fluß*) Havel.
**Haxe** ['haksə] (-, -n) *f* = **Hachse**.
**Hbf.** *abk* = **Hauptbahnhof.**
**H-Bombe** ['ha:bɔmbə] *f abk* H-bomb.
**Hebamme** ['he:p|amə] *f* midwife.
**Hebel** ['he:bəl] (-s, -) *m* lever; **alle ~ in Bewegung setzen** (*umg*) to move heaven and earth; **am längeren ~ sitzen** (*umg*) to have the whip hand.
**heben** ['he:bən] *unreg vt* to raise, lift; (*steigern*) to increase; **einen ~ gehen** (*umg*) to go for a drink.
**Hebräer(in)** [he'brɛ:ər(ɪn)] (-s, -) *m(f)* Hebrew.
**hebräisch** [he'brɛ:ɪʃ] *adj* Hebrew.
**Hebriden** [he'bri:dən] *pl:* **die ~** the Hebrides *pl.*
**hecheln** ['hɛçəln] *vi* (*Hund*) to pant.
**Hecht** [hɛçt] (-(e)s, -e) *m* pike; ~**sprung** *m* (*beim Schwimmen*) racing dive; (*beim Turnen*) forward dive; (*FUSSBALL: umg*) dive.
**Heck** [hɛk] (-(e)s, -e) *nt* stern; (*von Auto*) rear.
**Hecke** ['hɛkə] (-, -n) *f* hedge.
**Heckenrose** *f* dog rose.
**Heckenschütze** *m* sniper.
**Heck-** *zW:* ~**fenster** *nt* (*AUT*) rear window; ~**klappe** *f* tailgate; ~**motor** *m* rear engine.
**heda** ['he:da] *interj* hey there.
**Heer** [he:r] (-(e)s, -e) *nt* army.
**Hefe** ['he:fə] (-, -n) *f* yeast.
**Heft** ['hɛft] (-(e)s, -e) *nt* exercise book; (*Zeitschrift*) number; (*von Messer*) haft; **jdm das ~ aus der Hand nehmen** (*fig*) to seize control *od* power from sb.
**Heftchen** *nt* (*Fahrkarten~*) book of tickets; (*Briefmarken~*) book of stamps.
**heften** *vt:* ~ (**an** +*akk*) to fasten (to); (*nähen*) to tack (on (to)); (*mit Heftmaschine*) to staple *od* fasten (to) ♦ *vr:* **sich an jds Fersen** *od* **Sohlen ~** (*fig*) to dog sb's heels.
**Hefter** (-s, -) *m* folder.
**heftig** *adj* fierce, violent; **H~keit** *f* fierceness, violence.
**Heft-** *zW:* ~**klammer** *f* staple; ~**maschine** *f* stapling machine; ~**pflaster** *nt* sticking plaster; ~**zwecke** *f* drawing pin (*BRIT*), thumb tack (*US*).
**hegen** ['he:gən] *vt* to nurse; (*fig*) to harbour (*BRIT*), harbor (*US*), foster.
**Hehl** [he:l] *m od nt:* **kein(en) ~ aus etw machen** to make no secret of sth.
**Hehler** (-s, -) *m* receiver (of stolen goods), fence.
**Heide¹** ['haɪdə] (-, -n) *f* heath, moor; (~*kraut*) heather.

**Heide²** ['haɪdə] (-n, -n) *m* heathen, pagan.
**Heidekraut** *nt* heather.
**Heidelbeere** *f* bilberry.
**Heiden-** *zW:* ~**angst** (*umg*) *f:* **eine ~angst vor etw/jdm haben** to be scared stiff of sth/sb; ~**arbeit** (*umg*) *f* real slog; **h~mäßig** (*umg*) *adj* terrific; ~**tum** *nt* paganism.
**Heidin** *f* heathen, pagan.
**heidnisch** ['haɪdnɪʃ] *adj* heathen, pagan.
**heikel** ['haɪkəl] *adj* awkward, thorny; (*wählerisch*) fussy.
**Heil** [haɪl] (-(e)s) *nt* well-being; (*Seelen~*) salvation ♦ *interj* hail; **Ski/Petri ~!** good skiing/fishing!
**heil** *adj* in one piece, intact; **mit ~er Haut davonkommen** to escape unscathed; **die ~e Welt** an ideal world (*without problems etc*).
**Heiland** (-(e)s, -e) *m* saviour (*BRIT*), savior (*US*).
**Heil-** *zW:* ~**anstalt** *f* nursing home; (*für Sucht- oder Geisteskranke*) home; ~**bad** *nt* (*Bad*) medicinal bath; (*Ort*) spa; **h~bar** *adj* curable.
**Heilbutt** ['haɪlbʊt] (-s, -e) *m* halibut.
**heilen** *vt* to cure ♦ *vi* to heal; **als geheilt entlassen werden** to be discharged with a clean bill of health.
**heilfroh** *adj* very relieved.
**Heilgymnastin** *f* physiotherapist.
**heilig** ['haɪlɪç] *adj* holy; **jdm ~ sein** (*lit, fig*) to be sacred to sb; **die H~e Schrift** the Holy Scriptures *pl*; **es ist mein ~er Ernst** I am deadly serious; **H~abend** *m* Christmas Eve.
**Heilige(r)** *f(m)* saint.
**heiligen** *vt* to sanctify, hallow; **der Zweck heiligt die Mittel** the end justifies the means.
**Heiligenschein** *m* halo.
**heilig-** *zW:* **H~keit** *f* holiness; ~**sprechen** *unreg vt* to canonize; **H~tum** *nt* shrine; (*Gegenstand*) relic.
**Heilkunde** *f* medicine.
**heillos** *adj* unholy; (*Schreck*) terrible.
**Heil-** *zW:* ~**mittel** *nt* remedy; ~**praktiker(in)** (-s, -) *m(f)* non-medical practitioner; **h~sam** *adj* (*fig*) salutary.
**Heilsarmee** *f* Salvation Army.
**Heilung** *f* cure.
**heim** [haɪm] *adv* home.
**Heim** (-(e), -e) *nt* home; (*Wohn~*) hostel.
**Heimarbeit** *f* (*INDUSTRIE*) homework, outwork.
**Heimat** ['haɪma:t] (-, -en) *f* home (town/ country *etc*); ~**film** *m sentimental film in idealized regional setting*; ~**kunde** *f* (*SCH*) local history; ~**land** *nt* homeland; **h~lich** *adj* native, home *attrib*; (*Gefühle*) nostalgic; **h~los** *adj* homeless; ~**museum** *nt* local history museum; ~**ort** *m* home town *od* area; ~**vertriebene(r)** *f(m)* displaced person.
**heimbegleiten** *vt* to accompany home.
**Heimchen** *nt:* ~ (**am Herd**) (*pej: Frau*)

housewife.
**Heimcomputer** *m* home computer.
**heimelig** ['haɪməlɪç] *adj* homely.
**Heim-** *zW:* **h~fahren** *unreg vi* to drive *od* go home; **~fahrt** *f* journey home; **~gang** *m* return home; (*Tod*) decease; **h~gehen** *unreg vi* to go home; (*sterben*) to pass away; **h~isch** *adj* (*gebürtig*) native; **sich h~isch fühlen** to feel at home; **~kehr** (-, -en) *f* homecoming; **h~kehren** *vi* to return home; **~kind** *nt* child *brought up in a home*; **h~kommen** *unreg vi* to come home; **~leiter** *m* warden of a home/hostel.
**heimlich** *adj* secret ♦ *adv:* ~, **still und leise** (*umg*) quietly, on the quiet; **H~keit** *f* secrecy; **H~tuerei** *f* secrecy.
**Heim-** *zW:* **~reise** *f* journey home; **~spiel** *nt* home game; **h~suchen** *vt* to afflict; (*Geist*) to haunt; **h~tückisch** *adj* malicious; **h~wärts** *adv* homewards; **~weg** *m* way home; **~weh** *nt* homesickness; **~weh haben** to be homesick; **~werker** *m* handyman; **h~zahlen** *vt:* **jdm etw h~zahlen** to pay back sb for sth.
**Heini** ['haɪni] (-s, -s) *m:* **blöder** ~ (*umg*) silly idiot.
**Heirat** ['haɪraːt] (-, -en) *f* marriage; **h~en** *vt, vi* to marry.
**Heirats-** *zW:* **~antrag** *m* proposal (of marriage); **~anzeige** *f* (*Annonce*) advertisement for a marriage partner; **~schwindler** *m person who makes a marriage proposal under false pretences*; **~urkunde** *f* marriage certificate.
**heiser** ['haɪzər] *adj* hoarse; **H~keit** *f* hoarseness.
**heiß** [haɪs] *adj* hot; (*Thema*) hotly disputed; (*Diskussion, Kampf*) heated, fierce; (*Begierde, Liebe, Wunsch*) burning; **es wird nichts so ~ gegessen, wie es gekocht wird** (*Sprichwort*) things are never as bad as they seem; **~er Draht** hot line; **~es Eisen** (*fig: umg*) hot potato; **~es Geld** hot money; **jdn/ etw ~ und innig lieben** to love sb/sth madly; **~blütig** *adj* hot-blooded.
**heißen** ['haɪsən] *unreg vi* to be called; (*bedeuten*) to mean ♦ *vt* to command; (*nennen*) to name ♦ *vi unpers:* **es heißt hier ...** it says here ...; **es heißt, daß ...** they say that ...; **wie ~ Sie?** what's your name?; **... und wie sie alle ~ ...** and the rest of them; **das will schon etwas ~** that's quite something; **jdn willkommen ~** to bid sb welcome; **das heißt** that is; (*mit anderen Worten*) that is to say.
**Heiß-** *zW:* **h~ersehnt** *adj* longed for; **~hunger** *m* ravenous hunger; **h~laufen** *unreg vi, vr* to overheat; **~luft** *f* hot air; **h~umstritten** *adj attrib* hotly debated; **~wasserbereiter** *m* water heater.
**heiter** ['haɪtər] *adj* cheerful; (*Wetter*) bright; **aus ~em Himmel** (*fig*) out of the blue;

**H~keit** *f* cheerfulness; (*Belustigung*) amusement.
**heizbar** *adj* heated; (*Raum*) with heating; **leicht** ~ easily heated.
**Heizdecke** *f* electric blanket.
**heizen** *vt* to heat.
**Heizer** (-s, -) *m* stoker.
**Heiz-** *zW:* **~gerät** *nt* heater; **~körper** *m* radiator; **~öl** *nt* fuel oil; **~sonne** *f* electric fire.
**Heizung** *f* heating.
**Heizungsanlage** *f* heating system.
**Hektar** [hɛk'taːr] (-s, -e) *nt od m* hectare.
**Hektik** ['hɛktɪk] *f* hectic rush; (*von Leben etc*) hectic pace.
**hektisch** ['hɛktɪʃ] *adj* hectic.
**Hektoliter** [hɛkto'liːtər] *m od nt* hectolitre (*BRIT*), hectoliter (*US*).
**Held** [hɛlt] (-en, -en) *m* hero; **h~enhaft** ['hɛldənhaft] *adj* heroic; **~in** *f* heroine.
**helfen** ['hɛlfən] *unreg vi* to help; (*nützen*) to be of use ♦ *vb unpers:* **es hilft nichts, du mußt ...** it's no use, you'll have to ...; **jdm (bei etw)** ~ to help sb (with sth); **sich** *dat* **zu ~ wissen** to be resourceful; **er weiß sich** *dat* **nicht mehr zu ~** he's at his wits' end.
**Helfer(in)** (-s, -) *m(f)* helper, assistant.
**Helfershelfer** *m* accomplice.
**Helgoland** ['hɛlgolant] (-s) *nt* Heligoland.
**hell** [hɛl] *adj* clear; (*Licht, Himmel*) bright; (*Farbe*) light; **~es Bier** ≈ lager; **von etw ~ begeistert sein** to be very enthusiastic about sth; **es wird** ~ it's getting light; **~blau** *adj* light blue; **~blond** *adj* ash-blond.
**Helle** (-) *f* clearness; brightness.
**Heller** (-s, -) *m* farthing; **auf ~ und Pfennig** (down) to the last penny.
**hellhörig** *adj* keen of hearing; (*Wand*) poorly soundproofed.
**hellicht** ['hɛllɪçt] (*getrennt* **hell-licht**) *adj:* **am ~en Tage** in broad daylight.
**Helligkeit** *f* clearness; brightness; lightness.
**hell-** *zW:* **~sehen** *vi:* **~sehen können** to be clairvoyant; **H~seher(in)** *m(f)* clairvoyant; **~wach** *adj* wide-awake.
**Helm** ['hɛlm] (-(e)s, -e) *m* helmet.
**Helsinki** ['hɛlzɪŋki] (-s) *nt* Helsinki.
**Hemd** [hɛmt] (-(e)s, -en) *nt* shirt; (*Unter~*) vest; **~bluse** *f* blouse.
**Hemdenknopf** *m* shirt button.
**hemdsärmelig** *adj* shirt-sleeved; (*fig: umg: salopp*) pally; (*Ausdrucksweise*) casual.
**Hemisphäre** [hemi'sfɛːrə] *f* hemisphere.
**hemmen** ['hɛmən] *vt* to check, hold up; **gehemmt sein** to be inhibited.
**Hemmschuh** *m* (*fig*) impediment.
**Hemmung** *f* check; (*PSYCH*) inhibition; (*Bedenken*) scruple.
**hemmungslos** *adj* unrestrained, without restraint.
**Hengst** [hɛŋst] (-es, -e) *m* stallion.
**Henkel** ['hɛŋkəl] (-s, -) *m* handle; **~krug** *m* jug;

~**mann** (_umg_) _m_ (_Gefäß_) canteen.
**henken** ['hɛŋkən] _vt_ to hang.
**Henker** (**-s, -**) _m_ hangman.
**Henne** ['hɛnə] (**-, -n**) _f_ hen.
**Hepatitis** [hepa'tiːtɪs] _f_ (**-, Hepatitiden**)
hepatitis.

=========== _SCHLÜSSELWORT_

**her** [heːr] _adv_ **1** (_Richtung_): **komm ~ zu mir**
come here (to me); **von England ~** from
England; **von weit ~** from a long way away;
**~ damit!** hand it over!; **wo bist du ~?** where
do you come from?; **wo hat er das ~?** where
did he get that from?
**2** (_Blickpunkt_): **von der Form ~** as far as the
form is concerned
**3** (_zeitlich_): **das ist 5 Jahre ~** that was 5
years ago; **ich kenne ihn von früher ~** I
know him from before.

**herab** [hɛ'rap] _adv_ down, downward(s);
~**hängen** _unreg vi_ to hang down; ~**lassen** _unreg_
_vt_ to let down ♦ _vr_ to condescend; ~**lassend**
_adj_ condescending; **H~lassung** _f_
condescension; ~**sehen** _unreg vi_: ~**sehen (auf**
**+akk**) to look down (on); ~**setzen** _vt_ to lower,
reduce; (_fig_) to belittle, disparage; **zu stark**
~**gesetzten Preisen** at greatly reduced
prices; **H~setzung** _f_ reduction;
disparagement; ~**stürzen** _vi_ to fall off;
(_Felsbrocken_) to fall down; **von etw** ~**stürzen**
to fall off sth; to fall down from sth;
~**würdigen** _vt_ to belittle, disparage.
**heran** [hɛ'ran] _adv_: **näher ~!** come closer!;
**~ zu mir!** come up to me!; ~**bilden** _vt_ to
train; ~**bringen** _unreg vt_: ~**bringen (an +akk**) to
bring up (to); ~**fahren** _unreg vi_: ~**fahren (an**
**+akk**) to drive up (to); ~**gehen** _unreg vi_: **an etw**
_akk_ ~**gehen** (_an Problem, Aufgabe_) to tackle
sth; ~**kommen** _unreg vi_: (**an jdn/etw**)
~**kommen** to approach (sb/sth), come near
((to) sb/sth); **er läßt alle Probleme an sich**
~**kommen** he always adopts a wait-and-see
attitude; ~**machen** _vr_: **sich an jdn** ~**machen**
to make up to sb; (_umg_) to approach sb;
~**wachsen** _unreg vi_ to grow up;
**H~wachsende(r)** _f(m)_ adolescent; ~**winken** _vt_
to beckon over; (_Taxi_) to hail; ~**ziehen** _unreg_
_vt_ to pull nearer; (_aufziehen_) to raise;
(_ausbilden_) to train; (_zu Hilfe holen_) to call in;
(_Literatur_) to consult; **etw zum Vergleich**
~**ziehen** to use sth by way of comparison;
**jdn zu etw** ~**ziehen** to call upon sb to help in
sth.
**herauf** [hɛ'rauf] _adv_ up, upward(s), up here;
~**beschwören** _unreg vt_ to conjure up, evoke;
~**bringen** _unreg vt_ to bring up; ~**setzen** _vt_ to
increase; ~**ziehen** _unreg vt_ to draw _od_ pull up
♦ _vi_ to approach; (_Sturm_) to gather.
**heraus** [hɛ'raus] _adv_ out; **nach vorn ~ wohnen**
to live at the front (of the house); **~ mit der**
**Sprache!** out with it!; ~**arbeiten** _vt_ to work

out; ~**bekommen** _unreg vt_ to get out; (_fig_) to
find _od_ figure out; (_Wechselgeld_) to get back;
~**bringen** _unreg vt_ to bring out; (_Geheimnis_) to
elicit; **jdn/etw ganz groß** ~**bringen** (_umg_) to
give sb/sth a big build-up; **aus ihm war kein**
**Wort** ~**zubringen** they couldn't get a single
word out of him; ~**finden** _unreg vt_ to find out;
~**fordern** _vt_ to challenge; (_provozieren_) to
provoke; **H~forderung** _f_ challenge;
provocation; ~**geben** _unreg vt_ to give up,
surrender; (_Geld_) to give back; (_Buch_) to
edit; (_veröffentlichen_) to publish ♦ _vi_
(_Wechselgeld geben_): **können Sie (mir)**
~**geben?** can you give me change?;
**H~geber** (**-s, -**) _m_ editor; (_Verleger_)
publisher; ~**gehen** _unreg vi_: **aus sich** ~**gehen**
to come out of one's shell; ~**halten** _unreg vr_:
**sich aus etw** ~**halten** to keep out of sth;
~**hängen** _unreg vt, vi_ to hang out; ~**holen** _vt_:
~**holen (aus**) to get out (of); ~**hören** _vt_
(_wahrnehmen_) to hear; (_fühlen_): ~**hören (aus**)
to detect (in); ~**kehren** _vt_ (_fig_): **den**
**Vorgesetzten** ~**kehren** to act the boss;
~**kommen** _unreg vi_ to come out; **dabei kommt**
**nichts ~** nothing will come of it; **er kam aus**
**dem Staunen nicht ~** he couldn't get over
his astonishment; **es kommt auf dasselbe ~**
it comes (down) to the same thing;
~**nehmen** _unreg vt_ to take out; **sich** _dat_
**Freiheiten** ~**nehmen** to take liberties; **Sie**
**nehmen sich zuviel ~** you're going too far;
~**putzen** _vt_: **sich** ~**putzen** to get dressed up;
~**reden** _vr_ to talk one's way out of it (_umg_);
~**reißen** _unreg vt_ to tear out; (_Zahn, Baum_) to
pull out; ~**rücken** _vt_ (_Geld_) to fork out, hand
over; **mit etw** ~**rücken** (_fig_) to come out with
sth; ~**rutschen** _vi_ to slip out; (_fig_) to obtain;
~**schlagen** _unreg_
_vt_ to knock out; (_fig_) to obtain; ~**sein** _unreg vi_:
**aus dem Gröbsten** ~**sein** to be over the
worst; ~**stellen** _vr_: **sich** ~**stellen (als**) to turn
out (to be); **das muß sich erst** ~**stellen** that
remains to be seen; ~**strecken** _vt_ to stick
out; ~**suchen** _vt_: **sich** _dat_ **jdn/etw** ~**suchen** to
pick out sb/sth; ~**treten** _unreg vi_: ~**treten**
(**aus**) to come out (of); ~**wachsen** _unreg vi_:
~**wachsen aus** to grow out of; ~**winden**
_unreg vr_ (_fig_): **sich aus etw** ~**winden** to
wriggle out of sth; ~**wollen** _vi_: **nicht mit etw**
~**wollen** (_umg: sagen wollen_) to not want to
come out with sth; ~**ziehen** _unreg vt_ to pull
out, extract.
**herb** [hɛrp] _adj_ (slightly) bitter, acid; (_Wein_)
dry; (_fig: schmerzlich_) bitter; (: _streng_) stern,
austere.
**herbei** [hɛr'baɪ] _adv_ (over) here; ~**führen** _vt_ to
bring about; ~**schaffen** _vt_ to procure;
~**sehnen** _vt_ to long for.
**herbemühen** ['heːrbəmyːən] _vr_ to take the
trouble to come.
**Herberge** ['hɛrbɛrgə] (**-, -n**) _f_ (_Jugend~ etc_)
hostel.
**Herbergsmutter** _f_ warden.

**Herbergsvater** *m* warden.
**herbitten** *unreg vt* to ask to come (here).
**herbringen** *unreg vt* to bring here.
**Herbst** [hɛrpst] (-(e)s, -e) *m* autumn, fall (*US*);
**im** ~ in autumn, in the fall (*US*); **h~lich** *adj*
autumnal.
**Herd** [heːrt] (-(e)s, -e) *m* cooker; (*fig, MED*)
focus, centre (*BRIT*), center (*US*).
**Herde** ['heːrdə] (-, -n) *f* herd; (*Schaf~*) flock.
**Herdentrieb** *m* (*lit, fig: pej*) herd instinct.
**Herdplatte** *f* (*von Elektroherd*) hotplate.
**herein** [hɛ'raɪn] *adv* in (here), here; ~! come
in!; ~**bitten** *unreg vt* to ask in; ~**brechen** *unreg*
*vi* to set in; ~**bringen** *unreg vt* to bring in;
~**dürfen** *unreg vi* to have permission to enter;
**H~fall** *m* letdown; ~**fallen** *unreg vi* to be
caught, be taken in; ~**fallen auf** *+akk* to fall
for; ~**kommen** *unreg vi* to come in; ~**lassen**
*unreg vt* to admit; ~**legen** *vt*: **jdn** ~**legen** to
take sb in; ~**platzen** *vi* to burst in;
~**schneien** (*umg*) *vi* to drop in; ~**spazieren** *vi*:
~**spaziert!** come right in!
**her-** *zW*: **H~fahrt** *f* journey here; ~**fallen**
*unreg vi*: ~**fallen über** *+akk* to fall upon;
**H~gang** *m* course of events, circumstances
*pl*; ~**geben** *unreg vt* to give, hand (over); **sich**
**zu etw** ~**geben** to lend one's name to sth;
**das Thema gibt viel/nichts** ~ there's a lot/
nothing to this topic; ~**gebracht** *adj*: **in**
~**gebrachter Weise** in the traditional way;
~**gehen** *unreg vi*: **hinter jdm** ~**gehen** to follow
sb; **es geht hoch** ~ there are a lot of
goings-on; ~**haben** *unreg* (*umg*) *vt*: **wo hat er**
**das** ~? where did he get that from?;
~**halten** *unreg vt* to hold out; ~**halten müssen**
(*umg*) to have to suffer; ~**hören** *vi* to listen;
**hör mal** ~! listen here!
**Hering** ['heːrɪŋ] (-s, -e) *m* herring; (*Zeltpflock*)
(tent) peg.
**herkommen** *unreg vi* to come; **komm mal her!**
come here!
**herkömmlich** *adj* traditional.
**Herkunft** (-, -künfte) *f* origin.
**Herkunftsland** *nt* (*COMM*) country of origin.
**her-** *zW*: ~**laufen** *unreg vi*: ~**laufen hinter** *+dat* to
run after; ~**leiten** *vr* to derive; ~**machen** *vr*:
**sich** ~**machen über** *+akk* to set about *od* upon
♦ *vt* (*umg*): **viel** ~**machen** to look impressive.
**Hermelin** [hɛrməˈliːn] (-s, -e) *m od nt* ermine.
**hermetisch** [hɛrˈmeːtɪʃ] *adj* hermetic;
~ **abgeriegelt** completely sealed off.
**her-** *zW*: ~**nach** *adv* afterwards; ~**nehmen**
*unreg vt*: **wo soll ich das** ~**nehmen?** where am
I supposed to get that from?; ~**nieder** *adv*
down.
**Heroin** [hero'iːn] (-s) *nt* heroin.
**heroisch** [he'roːɪʃ] *adj* heroic.
**Herold** ['heːrɔlt] (-(e)s, -e) *m* herald.
**Herpes** ['hɛrpɛs] *m* (-) (*MED*) herpes.
**Herr** [hɛr] (-(e)n, -en) *m* master; (*Mann*)
gentleman; (*adliger, REL*) Lord; (*vor Namen*)
Mr.; **mein** ~! sir!; **meine** ~**en!** gentlemen!;

**Lieber** ~ **A, Sehr geehrter** ~ **A** (*in Brief*) Dear
Mr. A; „~**en"** (*Toilette*) "gentlemen" (*BRIT*),
"men's room" (*US*); **die** ~**en der Schöpfung**
(*hum: Männer*) the gentlemen.
**Herrchen** (*umg*) *nt* (*von Hund*) master.
**Herren-** *zW*: ~**bekanntschaft** *f* gentleman
friend; ~**bekleidung** *f* menswear; ~**besuch**
*m* gentleman visitor *od* visitors; ~**doppel** *nt*
men's doubles; ~**einzel** *nt* men's singles;
~**haus** *nt* mansion; **h~los** *adj* ownerless;
~**magazin** *nt* men's magazine.
**Herrgott** *m*: ~ **noch mal!** (*umg*) damn it all!
**Herrgottsfrühe** *f*: **in aller** ~ (*umg*) at the
crack of dawn.
**herrichten** ['heːrrɪçtən] *vt* to prepare.
**Herrin** *f* mistress.
**herrisch** *adj* domineering.
**herrje** [hɛrˈjeː] *interj* goodness gracious!
**herrjemine** [hɛrˈjeːmine] *interj* goodness
gracious!
**herrlich** *adj* marvellous (*BRIT*), marvelous
(*US*), splendid; **H~keit** *f* splendour (*BRIT*),
splendor (*US*), magnificence.
**Herrschaft** *f* power, rule; (*Herr und Herrin*)
master and mistress; **meine** ~**en!** ladies and
gentlemen!
**herrschen** ['hɛrʃən] *vi* to rule; (*bestehen*) to
prevail, be; **hier** ~ **ja Zustände!** things are in
a pretty state round here!
**Herrscher(in)** (-s, -) *m(f)* ruler.
**Herrschsucht** *f* domineeringness.
**her-** *zW*: ~**rühren** *vi* to arise, originate;
~**sagen** *vt* to recite; ~**sehen** *unreg vi*: **hinter**
**jdm/etw** ~**sehen** to follow sb/sth with one's
eyes; ~**sein** *unreg vi*: **das ist schon 5 Jahre** ~
that was 5 years ago; **hinter jdm/etw** ~**sein**
to be after sb/sth; ~**stammen** *vi* to descend
*od* come from; ~**stellen** *vt* to make,
manufacture; (*zustande bringen*) to establish;
**H~steller** (-s, -) *m* manufacturer;
**H~stellung** *f* manufacture;
**H~stellungskosten** *pl* manufacturing costs
*pl*; ~**tragen** *unreg vt*: **etw hinter jdm** ~**tragen**
to carry sth behind sb.
**herüber** [hɛˈryːbər] *adv* over (here), across.
**herum** [hɛˈrʊm] *adv* about, (a)round; **um etw**
~ around sth; ~**ärgern** *vr*: **sich** ~**ärgern (mit)**
to get annoyed (with); ~**blättern** *vi*:
~**blättern in** *+dat* to browse *od* flick through;
~**doktern** (*umg*) *vi* to fiddle *od* tinker about;
~**drehen** *vt*: **jdm das Wort im Mund** ~**drehen**
to twist sb's words; ~**drücken** *vr* (*vermeiden*):
**sich um etw** ~**drücken** to dodge sth;
~**fahren** *unreg vi* to travel around; (*mit Auto*)
to drive around; (*sich rasch umdrehen*) to
spin (a)round; ~**führen** *vt* to show around;
~**gammeln** (*umg*) *vi* to bum around; ~**gehen**
*unreg vi* (~**spazieren**) to walk about; **um etw**
~**gehen** to walk *od* go round sth; **etw**
~**gehen lassen** to circulate sth; ~**hacken** *vi*
(*fig: umg*): **auf jdm** ~**hacken** to pick on sb;
~**irren** *vi* to wander about; ~**kommen** *unreg*

(*umg*) *vi:* **um etw ~kommen** to get out of sth; **er ist viel ~gekommen** he has been around a lot; **~kriegen** *vt* to bring *od* talk round; **~lungern** *vi* to lounge about; (*umg*) to hang around; **~quälen** *vr:* **sich mit Rheuma ~quälen** to be plagued by rheumatism; **~reißen** *unreg vt* to swing around (hard); **~schlagen** *unreg vr:* **sich mit etw ~schlagen** (*umg*) to tussle with sth; **~schleppen** *vt:* **etw mit sich ~schleppen** (*Sorge, Problem*) to be troubled by sth; (*Krankheit*) to have sth; **~sprechen** *unreg vr* to get around, be spread; **~stochern** (*umg*) *vi:* **im Essen ~stochern** to pick at one's food; **~treiben** *unreg vi, vr* to drift about; **H~treiber(in)** (**-s, -**) (*pej*) *m(f)* tramp; **~ziehen** *unreg vi, vr* to wander about.

**herunter** [hɛ'rʊntər] *adv* downward(s), down (there); **~gekommen** *adj* run-down; **~handeln** (*umg*) *vt* (*Preis*) to beat down; **~hängen** *unreg vi* to hang down; **~holen** *vt* to bring down; **~kommen** *unreg vi* to come down; (*fig*) to come down in the world; **~leiern** (*umg*) *vt* to reel off; **~machen** *vt* to take down; (*schlechtmachen*) to run down, knock; **~putzen** (*umg*) *vt:* **jdn ~putzen** to tear sb off a strip; **~sein** *unreg* (*umg*) *vi:* **mit den Nerven/der Gesundheit ~sein** to be at the end of one's tether/be run-down; **~spielen** *vt* to play down; **~wirtschaften** (*umg*) *vt* to bring to the brink of ruin.

**hervor** [hɛr'foːr] *adv* out, forth; **~brechen** *unreg vi* to burst forth, break out; **~bringen** *unreg vt* to produce; (*Wort*) to utter; **~gehen** *unreg vi* to emerge, result; **daraus geht ~, daß ...** from this it follows that ...; **~heben** *unreg vt* to stress; (*als Kontrast*) to set off; **~ragend** *adj* excellent; (*lit*) projecting; **~rufen** *unreg vt* to cause, give rise to; **~stechen** *unreg vi* (*lit; fig*) to stand out; **~stoßen** *unreg vt* (*Worte*) to gasp (out); **~treten** *unreg vi* to come out; **~tun** *unreg vr* to distinguish o.s.; (*umg: sich wichtig tun*) to show off; **sich mit etw ~tun** to show off sth.

**Herz** [hɛrts] (**-ens, -en**) *nt* heart; (*KARTEN: Farbe*) hearts *pl*; **mit ganzem ~en** wholeheartedly; **etw auf dem ~en haben** to have sth on one's mind; **sich** *dat* **etw zu ~en nehmen** to take sth to heart; **du sprichst mir aus dem ~en** that's just what I feel; **es liegt mir am ~en** I am very concerned about it; **seinem ~en Luft machen** to give vent to one's feelings; **sein ~ an jdn/etw hängen** to commit o.s. heart and soul to sb/sth; **ein ~ und eine Seele sein** to be the best of friends; **jdn/etw auf ~ und Nieren prüfen** to examine sb/sth very thoroughly; **~anfall** *m* heart attack; **~beschwerden** *pl* heart trouble *sing*.

**herzen** *vt* to caress, embrace.

**Herzenslust** *f:* **nach ~** to one's heart's content.

**Herz-** *zW:* **h~ergreifend** *adj* heart-rending;

**h~erweichend** *adj* heartrending; **~fehler** *m* heart defect; **h~haft** *adj* hearty.

**herziehen** ['heːrtsiːən] *vi:* **über jdn/etw ~** (*umg*) to pull sb/sth to pieces (*fig*).

**Herz-** *zW:* **~infarkt** *m* heart attack; **~klappe** *f* (heart) valve; **~klopfen** *nt* palpitation; **h~krank** *adj* suffering from a heart condition.

**herzlich** *adj* cordial ♦ *adv* (*sehr*): **~ gern!** with the greatest of pleasure!; **~en Glückwunsch** congratulations *pl*; **~e Grüße** best wishes; **H~keit** *f* cordiality.

**herzlos** *adj* heartless; **H~igkeit** *f* heartlessness.

**Herzog** ['hɛrtsoːk] (**-(e)s, ⁻e**) *m* duke; **~in** *f* duchess; **h~lich** *adj* ducal; **~tum** *nt* duchy.

**Herz-** *zW:* **~schlag** *m* heartbeat; (*MED*) heart attack; **~schrittmacher** *m* pacemaker; **h~zerreißend** *adj* heartrending.

**Hesse** ['hɛsə] (**-n, -n**) *m* Hessian.

**Hessen** ['hɛsən] (**-s**) *nt* Hesse.

**Hessin** *f* Hessian.

**hessisch** *adj* Hessian.

**heterogen** [hetero'geːn] *adj* heterogeneous.

**heterosexuell** [heterozɛ'ksuɛl] *adj* heterosexual.

**Hetze** ['hɛtsə] *f* (*Eile*) rush.

**hetzen** *vt* to hunt; (*verfolgen*) to chase ♦ *vi* (*eilen*) to rush; **jdn/etw auf jdn/etw ~** to set sb/sth on sb/sth; **~ gegen** to stir up feeling against; **~ zu** to agitate for.

**Hetzerei** [hɛtsə'raɪ] *f* agitation; (*Eile*) rush.

**Hetzkampagne** ['hɛtskampanjə] *f* smear campaign.

**Heu** [hɔy] (**-(e)s**) *nt* hay; **~boden** *m* hayloft.

**Heuchelei** [hɔyçə'laɪ] *f* hypocrisy.

**heucheln** ['hɔyçəln] *vt* to pretend, feign ♦ *vi* to be hypocritical.

**Heuchler(in)** [hɔyçlər(ɪn)] (**-s, -**) *m(f)* hypocrite; **h~isch** *adj* hypocritical.

**Heuer** ['hɔyər] (**-, -n**) *f* (*NAUT*) pay.

**heuer** *adv* this year.

**heuern** ['hɔyərn] *vt* to sign on, hire.

**Heugabel** *f* pitchfork.

**Heuhaufen** *m* haystack.

**heulen** ['hɔylən] *vi* to howl; (*weinen*) to cry; **das ~de Elend bekommen** to get the blues.

**heurig** ['hɔyrɪç] *adj* this year's.

**Heuschnupfen** *m* hay fever.

**Heuschrecke** *f* grasshopper; (*in heißen Ländern*) locust.

**heute** ['hɔytə] *adv* today; **~ abend/früh** this evening/morning; **~ morgen** this morning; **~ in einer Woche** a week today, today week; **von ~ auf morgen** (*fig: plötzlich*) overnight, from one day to the next; **das H~** today.

**heutig** ['hɔytɪç] *adj* today's; **unser ~es Schreiben** (*COMM*) our letter of today('s date).

**heutzutage** ['hɔyttsutaːgə] *adv* nowadays.

**Hexe** ['hɛksə] (**-, -n**) *f* witch.

**hexen** *vi* to practise witchcraft; **ich kann**

doch nicht ~ I can't work miracles.
**Hexen-** zW: **~häuschen** nt gingerbread house;
**~kessel** m (lit, fig) cauldron; **~meister** m
wizard; **~schuß** m lumbago.
**Hexerei** [hɛksə'raɪ] f witchcraft.
**HG** f abk = **Handelsgesellschaft.**
**Hg.** abk (= Herausgeber) ed.
**hg.** abk (= herausgegeben) ed.
**HGB** (-) nt abk (= Handelsgesetzbuch) statutes
of commercial law.
**Hieb** (-(e)s, -e) m blow; (Wunde) cut, gash;
(Stichelei) cutting remark; **~e bekommen** to
get a thrashing.
**hieb** etc [hi:p] vb (veraltet) siehe **hauen.**
**hieb- und stichfest** adj (fig) watertight.
**hielt** etc [hi:lt] vb siehe **halten.**
**hier** [hi:r] adv here; ~ **spricht Dr. Müller** (TEL)
this is Dr Müller (speaking); **er ist von ~**
he's a local (man).
**Hierarchie** [hierar'çi:] f hierarchy.
**hier-** zW: **~auf** adv thereupon; (danach) after
that; **~aus** adv: **~aus folgt, daß** ... from this
it follows that ...; **~behalten** unreg vt to keep
here; **~bei** adv (bei dieser Gelegenheit) on
this occasion; **~bleiben** unreg vi to stay here;
**~durch** adv by this means; (örtlich) through
here; **~her** adv this way, here; **~hergehören**
vi to belong here; (fig: relevant sein) to be
relevant; **~lassen** unreg vt to leave here;
**~mit** adv hereby; **~mit erkläre ich** ... (form) I
hereby declare ...; **~nach** adv hereafter;
**~von** adv about this, hereof; **~von
abgesehen** apart from this; **~zu** adv (dafür)
for this; (dazu) with this; (außerdem) in
addition to this, moreover; (zu diesem Punkt)
about this; **~zulande** adv in this country.
**hiesig** ['hi:zɪç] adj of this place, local.
**hieß** etc [hi:s] vb siehe **heißen.**
**Hi-Fi-Anlage** ['haɪfɪanla:gə] f hi-fi set od
system.
**High-Tech-Industrie** ['haɪtɛkɪndʊs'tri:] f high
tech od hi-tech industry.
**Hilfe** ['hɪlfə] (-, -n) f help; (für Notleidende) aid;
**Erste ~** first aid; **jdm ~ leisten** to help sb; **~!**
help!; **~leistung** f: **unterlassene ~leistung**
(JUR) denial of assistance; **~stellung** f
(SPORT, fig) support.
**Hilf-** zW: **h~los** adj helpless; **~losigkeit** f
helplessness; **h~reich** adj helpful.
**Hilfs-** zW: **~aktion** f relief action, relief
measures pl; **~arbeiter** m labourer (BRIT),
laborer (US); **h~bedürftig** adj needy;
**h~bereit** adj ready to help; **~kraft** f
assistant, helper; **~mittel** nt aid; **~schule** f
school for backward children; **~zeitwort** nt
auxiliary verb.
**hilft** [hɪlft] vb siehe **helfen.**
**Himalaja** [hi'ma:laja] (-s) m: **der ~** the
Himalayas pl.
**Himbeere** ['hɪmbe:rə] (-, -n) f raspberry.
**Himmel** ['hɪməl] (-s, -) m sky; (REL, liter)
heaven; **um ~s willen** (umg) for Heaven's

sake; **zwischen ~ und Erde** in midair;
**h~angst** adj: **es ist mir h~angst** I'm scared
to death; **~bett** nt four-poster bed; **h~blau**
adj sky-blue.
**Himmelfahrt** f Ascension.
**Himmelfahrtskommando** nt (MIL: umg)
suicide squad; (Unternehmen) suicide
mission.
**Himmelreich** nt (REL) Kingdom of Heaven.
**himmelschreiend** adj outrageous.
**Himmelsrichtung** f direction; **die vier ~en**
the four points of the compass.
**himmelweit** adj: **ein ~er Unterschied** a world
of difference.
**himmlisch** ['hɪmlɪʃ] adj heavenly.

════════════════════════ *SCHLÜSSELWORT*

**hin** [hɪn] adv **1** (Richtung): ~ **und zurück** there
and back; **einmal London ~ und zurück** a
return to London (BRIT), a roundtrip ticket
to London (US); ~ **und her** to and fro; **etw
~ und her überlegen** to turn sth over and
over in one's mind; **bis zur Mauer ~** up to
the wall; **wo ist er ~?** where has he gone?;
**nichts wie ~!** (umg) let's go then!; **nach
außen ~** (fig) outwardly; **Geld ~, Geld her**
money or no money
**2** (auf ... ~): **auf meine Bitte ~** at my request;
**auf seinen Rat ~** on the basis of his advice;
**auf meinen Brief ~** on the strength of my
letter
**3**: **mein Glück ist ~** my happiness has gone;
~ **und wieder** (every) now and again.

**hinab** [hɪ'nap] adv down; **~gehen** unreg vi to go
down; **~sehen** unreg vi to look down.
**hinarbeiten** ['hɪnarbaɪtən] vi: **auf etw** akk ~
(auf Ziel) to work towards sth.
**hinauf** [hɪ'nauf] adv up; **~arbeiten** vr to work
one's way up; **~steigen** unreg vi to climb.
**hinaus** [hɪ'naus] adv out; **hinten/vorn ~** at the
back/front; **darüber ~** over and above this;
**auf Jahre ~** for years to come; **~befördern**
vt to kick od throw out; **~fliegen** unreg (umg)
vi to be kicked out; **~führen** vi: **über etw** akk
**~führen** (lit, fig) to go beyond sth; **~gehen**
unreg vi to go out; **~gehen über** +akk to
exceed; **~laufen** unreg vi to run out; **~laufen
auf** +akk to come to, amount to; **~schieben**
unreg vt to put off, postpone; **~schießen** unreg
vi: **über das Ziel ~schießen** (fig) to overshoot
the mark; **~wachsen** unreg vi: **er wuchs über
sich selbst ~** he surpassed himself;
**~werfen** unreg vt to throw out; **~wollen** vi to
want to go out; **hoch ~wollen** to aim high;
**~wollen auf** +akk to drive at, get at; **~ziehen**
unreg vi to draw out ♦ vr to be protracted;
**~zögern** vt to delay, put off ♦ vr to be
delayed, be put off.
**hinbekommen** unreg (umg) vt: **das hast du gut
~** you've made a good job of it.
**hinblättern** (umg) vt (Geld) to fork out.

**Hinblick** ['hɪnblɪk] *m*: **in** *od* **im ~ auf** +*akk* in view of.

**hinderlich** ['hɪndərlɪç] *adj* awkward; **jds Karriere** *dat* **~ sein** to be a hindrance to sb's career.

**hindern** *vt* to hinder, hamper; **jdn an etw** *dat* **~** to prevent sb from doing sth.

**Hindernis** (**-ses, -se**) *nt* obstacle; **~lauf** *m*, **~rennen** *nt* steeplechase.

**Hinderungsgrund** *m* obstacle.

**hindeuten** ['hɪndɔʏtən] *vi*: **~ auf** +*akk* to point to.

**Hinduismus** [hɪnduˈɪsmʊs] *m* Hinduism.

**hindurch** [hɪnˈdʊrç] *adv* through; across; (*zeitlich*) over.

**hindürfen** [hɪnˈdʏrfən] *unreg vi*: **~ (zu)** to be allowed to go (to).

**hinein** [hɪˈnaɪn] *adv* in; **bis tief in die Nacht ~** well into the night; **~fallen** *unreg vi* to fall in; **~fallen in** +*akk* to fall into; **~finden** *unreg vr* (*fig: sich vertraut machen*) to find one's feet; (*sich abfinden*) to come to terms with it; **~gehen** *unreg vi* to go in; **~gehen in** +*akk* to go into, enter; **~geraten** *unreg vi*: **~geraten in** +*akk* to get into; **~knien** *vr* (*fig: umg*): **sich in etw** *akk* **~knien** to get into sth; **~lesen** *unreg vt*: **etw in etw** *akk* **~lesen** to read sth into sth; **~passen** *vi* to fit in; **~passen in** +*akk* to fit into; **~prügeln** *vt*: **etw in jdn ~prügeln** to cudgel sth into sb; **~reden** *vi*: **jdm ~reden** to interfere in sb's affairs; **~stecken** *vt*: **Geld/Arbeit in etw** *akk* **~stecken** to put money/some work into sth; **~steigern** *vr* to get worked up; **~versetzen** *vr*: **sich in jdn ~versetzen** to put o.s. in sb's position; **~ziehen** *unreg vt*: **~ziehen (in** +*akk*) to pull in (to); **jdn in etw ~ziehen** (*in Konflikt, Gespräch*) to draw sb into sth.

**hin-** *zW*: **~fahren** *unreg vi* to go; to drive ♦ *vt* to take; to drive; **H~fahrt** *f* journey there; **~fallen** *unreg vi* to fall down; **~fällig** *adj* frail, decrepit; (*Regel etc*) unnecessary; **~fliegen** *unreg vi* to fly there; (*umg: ~fallen*) to fall over; **H~flug** *m* outward flight.

**hing** *etc* [hɪŋ] *vb siehe* **hängen**.

**hin-** *zW*: **H~gabe** *f* devotion; **mit H~gabe tanzen/singen** *etc* (*fig*) to dance/sing *etc* with abandon; **~geben** *unreg vr* +*dat* to give o.s. up to, devote o.s. to; **~gebungsvoll** ['hɪŋɡeːbʊŋsfɔl] *adv* (*begeistert*) with abandon; (*lauschen*) raptly.

**hingegen** [hɪnˈɡeːɡən] *konj* however.

**hin-** *zW*: **~gehen** *unreg vi* to go; (*Zeit*) to pass; **gehst du auch ~?** are you going too?; **~gerissen** *adj*: **~gerissen sein** to be enraptured; **ich bin ganz ~- und hergerissen** (*ironisch*) that's absolutely great; **~halten** *unreg vt* to hold out; (*warten lassen*) to put off, stall; **H~haltetaktik** *f* stalling *od* delaying tactics *pl*.

**hinhauen** ['hɪnhaʊən] *unreg* (*umg*) *vi* (*klappen*) to work; (*ausreichen*) to do.

**hinhören** ['hɪnhøːrən] *vi* to listen.

**hinken** ['hɪŋkən] *vi* to limp; (*Vergleich*) to be unconvincing.

**hin-** *zW*: **~kommen** *unreg* (*umg*) *vi* (*auskommen*) to manage; (: *ausreichen, stimmen*) to be right; **~länglich** *adj* adequate ♦ *adv* adequately; **~legen** *vt* to put down ♦ *vr* to lie down; **sich der Länge nach ~legen** (*umg*) to fall flat; **~nehmen** *unreg vt* (*fig*) to put up with, take; **~reichen** *vi* to be adequate ♦ *vt*: **jdm etw ~reichen** to hand sb sth; **~reichend** *adj* adequate; (*genug*) sufficient; **H~reise** *f* journey out; **~reißen** *unreg vt* to carry away, enrapture; **sich ~reißen lassen, etw zu tun** to get carried away and do sth; **~reißend** *adj* (*Landschaft, Anblick*) enchanting; (*Schönheit, Mensch*) captivating; **~richten** *vt* to execute; **H~richtung** *f* execution; **~sehen** *unreg vi*: **bei genauerem H~sehen** on closer inspection.

**hinsein** ['hɪnzaɪn] *unreg* (*umg*) *vi* (*kaputt sein*) to have had it; (*Ruhe*) to be gone.

**hin-** *zW*: **~setzen** *vr* to sit down; **H~sicht** *f*: **in mancher** *od* **gewisser H~sicht** in some respects *od* ways; **~sichtlich** *präp* +*gen* with regard to; **~sollen** (*umg*) *vi*: **wo soll ich/das Buch ~?** where do I/does the book go?; **H~spiel** *nt* (*SPORT*) first leg; **~stellen** *vt* to put (down) ♦ *vr* to place o.s.

**hintanstellen** [hɪntˈʔanʃtɛlən] *vt* (*fig*) to ignore.

**hinten** ['hɪntən] *adv* behind; (*rückwärtig*) at the back; **~ und vorn** (*fig: betrügen*) left, right and centre; **das reicht ~ und vorn nicht** that's nowhere near enough; **~dran** (*umg*) *adv* at the back; **~herum** *adv* round the back; (*fig*) secretly.

**hinter** ['hɪntər] *präp* (+*dat od akk*) behind; (: *nach*) after; **~ jdm hersein** to be after sb; **~ die Wahrheit kommen** to get to the truth; **sich ~ jdn stellen** (*fig*) to support sb; **etw ~ sich** *dat* **haben** (*zurückgelegt haben*) to have got through sth; **sie hat viel ~ sich** she has been through a lot; **H~achse** *f* rear axle; **H~bänkler** (**-s, -**) *m* (*POL: pej*) backbencher; **H~bein** *nt* hind leg; **sich auf die H~beine stellen** to get tough; **H~bliebene(r)** *f(m)* surviving relative; **~drein** *adv* afterwards.

**hintere(r, s)** *adj* rear, back.

**hinter-** *zW*: **~'einander** *adv* one after the other; **zwei Tage ~einander** two days running; **~fotzig** (*umg*) *adj* underhanded; **~fragen** *vt untr* to analyse; **H~gedanke** *m* ulterior motive; **~gehen** *unreg vt untr* to deceive; **H~grund** *m* background; **~gründig** *adj* cryptic, enigmatic; **H~grundprogramm** *nt* (*COMPUT*) background program; **~halt** *m* ambush; **etw im H~halt haben** to have sth in reserve; **~hältig** *adj* underhand, sneaky; **~her** *adv* afterwards, after; **~hersein** *unreg vi*: **er ist ~her, daß ...** (*fig*) he sees to it that ...; **H~hof** *m* back yard; **H~kopf** *m* back of one's head; **H~land** nt hinterland; **~lassen** unreg vt untr to leave; **H~lassenschaft** f (testator's) estate; **~legen** vt untr to deposit; **H~legungsstelle** f depository; **H~list** f cunning, trickery; (Handlung) trick, dodge; **~listig** adj cunning, crafty; **H~mann** (-(e)s, pl -männer) m person behind; **die H~männer des Skandals** the men behind the scandal.

**Hintern** ['hɪntərn] (-s, -) (umg) m bottom, backside; **jdm den ~ versohlen** to smack sb's bottom.

**hinter-** zW: **H~rad** nt back wheel; **H~radantrieb** m (AUT) rear-wheel drive; **~rücks** adv from behind; **H~teil** nt behind; **H~treffen** nt: **ins H~treffen kommen** to lose ground; **~treiben** unreg vt untr to prevent, frustrate; **H~treppe** f back stairs pl; **H~tür** f back door; (fig: Ausweg) escape, loophole; **H~wäldler** (-s, -) (umg) m backwoodsman, hillbilly (bes US); **~ziehen** unreg vt untr (Steuern) to evade (paying).

**hintun** ['hɪntuːn] unreg (umg) vt: **ich weiß nicht, wo ich ihn ~ soll** (fig) I can't (quite) place him.

**hinüber** [hɪ'nyːbər] adv across, over; **~gehen** unreg vi to go over od across.

**hinunter** [hɪ'nʊntər] adv down; **~bringen** unreg vt to take down; **~schlucken** vt (lit, fig) to swallow; **~spülen** vt to flush away; (Essen, Tablette) to wash down; (fig: Ärger) to soothe; **~steigen** unreg vi to descend.

**Hinweg** ['hɪnveːk] m journey out.

**hinweg-** [hɪn'vɛk] zW: **~gehen** unreg vi: **über etw** akk **~gehen** (fig) to pass over sth; **~helfen** unreg vi: **jdm über etw** akk **~helfen** to help sb to get over sth; **~kommen** unreg vi (fig): **über etw** akk **~kommen** to get over sth; **~sehen** unreg vi: **darüber ~sehen, daß** ... to overlook the fact that ...; **~setzen** vr: **sich ~setzen über** +akk to disregard.

**Hinweis** ['hɪnvaɪs] (-es, -e) m (Andeutung) hint; (Anweisung) instruction; (Verweis) reference; **sachdienliche ~e** relevant information.

**hinweisen** unreg vi: **~ auf** +akk to point to; (verweisen) to refer to; **darauf ~, daß** ... to point out that ...; (anzeigen) to indicate that ...

**Hinweisschild** nt sign.
**Hinweistafel** f sign.

**hinwerfen** unreg vt to throw down; **eine hingeworfene Bemerkung** a casual remark.

**hinwirken** vi: **auf etw** akk **~** to work towards sth.

**Hinz** [hɪnts] m: **~ und Kunz** (umg) every Tom, Dick and Harry.

**hinziehen** unreg vr (fig) to drag on.
**hinzielen** vi: **~ auf** +akk to aim at.

**hinzu** [hɪn'tsuː] adv in addition; **~fügen** vt to add; **H~fügung** f: **unter H~fügung von etw** (form) by adding sth; **~kommen** unreg vi: **es kommt noch ~, daß** ... there is also the fact that ...; **~ziehen** unreg vt to consult.

**Hiobsbotschaft** ['hiːɔpsboːtʃaft] f bad news.

**Hirn** [hɪrn] (-(e)s, -e) nt brain(s); **~gespinst** (-(e)s, -e) nt fantasy; **~hautentzündung** f (MED) meningitis; **h~tot** adj braindead; **h~verbrannt** adj (umg) harebrained.

**Hirsch** [hɪrʃ] (-(e)s, -e) m stag.

**Hirse** ['hɪrzə] (-, -n) f millet.

**Hirt** ['hɪrt] (-en, -en) m, **Hirte** (-n, -n) m herdsman; (Schaf~, fig) shepherd.

**Hirtin** f herdswoman; (Schaf~) shepherdess.

**hissen** ['hɪsən] vt to hoist.

**Historiker** [hɪs'toːrikər] (-s, -) m historian.

**historisch** [hɪs'toːrɪʃ] adj historical.

**Hit** [hɪt] (-s, -s) m (MUS, fig: umg) hit; **~parade** f hit parade.

**Hitze** ['hɪtsə] (-) f heat; **h~beständig** adj heat-resistant; **h~frei** adj: **h~frei haben** to have time off school/work because of excessive heat; **~welle** f heat wave.

**hitzig** adj hot-tempered; (Debatte) heated.

**Hitz-** zW: **~kopf** m hothead; **h~köpfig** adj fiery, hot-headed; **~schlag** m heatstroke.

**HIV-negativ** adj HIV-negative.
**HIV-positiv** adj HIV-positive.

**hl.** abk = **heilig**.

**H-Milch** ['haːmɪlç] f long-life milk, UHT milk.

**HNO-Arzt** m ENT specialist.

**hob** etc [hoːp] vb siehe **heben**.

**Hobby** ['hɔbi] (-s, -s) nt hobby.

**Hobel** ['hoːbəl] (-s, -) m plane; **~bank** f carpenter's bench.

**hobeln** vt, vi to plane.

**Hobelspäne** pl wood shavings pl.

**hoch** [hoːx] (attrib hohe(r, s)) adj high ♦ adv: **wenn es ~ kommt** (umg) at (the) most, at the outside; **das ist mir zu ~** (umg) that's above my head; **ein hohes Tier** (umg) a big fish; **es ging ~ her** (umg) we/they etc had a whale of a time; **~ und heilig versprechen** to promise faithfully.

**Hoch** (-s, -s) nt (Ruf) cheer; (MET, fig) high.

**hoch-** zW: **~achten** vt to respect; **H~achtung** f respect, esteem; **mit vorzüglicher H~achtung** (form: Briefschluß) yours faithfully; **~achtungsvoll** adv yours faithfully; **~aktuell** adj highly topical; **H~amt** nt high mass; **~arbeiten** vr to work one's way up; **~begabt** adj extremely gifted; **~betagt** adj very old, aged; **H~betrieb** m intense activity; (COMM) peak time; **H~betrieb haben** to be at one's od its busiest; **~bringen** unreg vt to bring up; **H~burg** f stronghold; **H~deutsch** nt High German; **~dotiert** adj highly paid; **H~druck** m high pressure; **H~ebene** f plateau; **~empfindlich** adj highly sensitive; (Film) high-speed; **~entwickelt** adj attrib (Kultur, Land) highly developed; (Geräte, Methoden) sophisticated; **~erfreut** adj highly delighted; **~fahren** unreg vi (erschreckt) to jump;

~**fliegend** *adj* ambitious; (*fig*) high-flown; **H~form** *f* top form; **H~gebirge** *nt* high mountains *pl*; **H~gefühl** *nt* elation; ~**gehen** *unreg* (*umg*) *vi* (*explodieren*) to blow up; (*Bombe*) to go off; **H~genuß** *m* great *od* special treat; (*großes Vergnügen*) great pleasure; ~**geschlossen** *adj* (*Kleid etc*) high-necked; ~**gestellt** *adj attrib* (*fig: Persönlichkeit*) high-ranking; **H~glanz** *m* high polish; (*PHOT*) gloss; ~**gradig** *adj* intense, extreme; ~**halten** *unreg vt* to hold up; (*fig*) to uphold, cherish; **H~haus** *nt* multi-storey building; ~**heben** *unreg vt* to lift (up); ~**kant** *adv*: **jdn** ~**kant hinauswerfen** (*fig: umg*) to chuck sb out on his/her ear; ~**kommen** *unreg vi* (*nach oben*) to come up; (*fig: gesund werden*) to get back on one's feet; (*beruflich, gesellschaftlich*) to come up in the world; **H~konjunktur** *f* boom; ~**krempeln** *vt* to roll up; **H~land** *nt* highlands *pl*; ~**leben** *vi*: **jdn** ~**leben lassen** to give sb three cheers; **H~leistungssport** *m* competitive sport; ~**modern** *adj* very modern, ultra-modern; **H~mut** *m* pride; ~**mütig** *adj* proud, haughty; ~**näsig** *adj* stuck-up, snooty; ~**nehmen** *unreg vt* to pick up; **jdn** ~**nehmen** (*umg: verspotten*) to pull sb's leg; **H~ofen** *m* blast furnace; ~**prozentig** *adj* (*Alkohol*) strong; **H~rechnung** *f* projected result; **H~saison** *f* high season; **H~schätzung** *f* high esteem.

**Hochschulabschluß** *m* degree.
**Hochschulbildung** *f* higher education.
**Hochschule** *f* college; (*Universität*) university.
**Hochschulreife** *f*: **er hat (die)** ~ ≈ he's got his A-levels (*BRIT*), he's graduated from high school (*US*).
**hoch-** *zW*: ~**schwanger** *adj* heavily pregnant, well advanced in pregnancy; **H~seefischerei** *f* deep-sea fishing; **H~sitz** *m* (*Jagd*) (raised) hide; **H~sommer** *m* middle of summer; **H~spannung** *f* high tension; ~**spielen** *vt* (*fig*) to blow up; **H~sprache** *f* standard language; ~**springen** *unreg vi* to jump up; **H~sprung** *m* high jump.
**höchst** [høːçst] *adv* highly, extremely.
**Hochstapler** ['hoːxʃtaˌplər] (**-s,** -) *m* swindler.
**höchste(r, s)** *adj* highest; (*äußerste*) extreme; **die** ~ **Instanz** (*JUR*) the supreme court of appeal.
**höchstens** *adv* at the most.
**Höchstgeschwindigkeit** *f* maximum speed.
**Höchstgrenze** *f* upper limit.
**Hochstimmung** *f* high spirits *pl*.
**Höchst-** *zW*: ~**leistung** *f* best performance; (*bei Produktion*) maximum output; **h~persönlich** *adv* personally, in person; ~**preis** *m* maximum price; ~**stand** *m* peak; **h~wahrscheinlich** *adv* most probably.
**Hoch-** *zW*: ~**technologie** *f* high technology; **h~technologisch** *adj* high-tech; ~**temperatur-Reaktor** *m* high-temperature

reactor; ~**tour** *f*: **auf** ~**touren laufen** *od* **arbeiten** to be working flat out; **h~trabend** *adj* pompous; ~**- und Tiefbau** *m* structural and civil engineering; ~**verrat** *m* high treason; ~**wasser** *nt* high water; (*Überschwemmung*) floods *pl*; **h~wertig** *adj* high-class, first-rate; ~**würden** *m* Reverend; ~**zahl** *f* (*MATH*) exponent.
**Hochzeit** ['hɔxtsaɪt] (**-, -en**) *f* wedding; **man kann nicht auf zwei** ~**en tanzen** (*Sprichwort*) you can't have your cake and eat it.
**Hochzeitsreise** *f* honeymoon.
**Hochzeitstag** *m* wedding day; (*Jahrestag*) wedding anniversary.
**hochziehen** *unreg vt* (*Rolladen, Hose*) to pull up; (*Brauen*) to raise.
**Hocke** ['hɔkə] (**-, -n**) *f* squatting position; (*beim Turnen*) squat vault; (*beim Skilaufen*) crouch.
**hocken** ['hɔkən] *vi, vr* to squat, crouch.
**Hocker** (**-s, -**) *m* stool.
**Höcker** ['hœkər] (**-s, -**) *m* hump.
**Hockey** ['hɔki] (**-s**) *nt* hockey.
**Hoden** ['hoːdən] (**-s, -**) *m* testicle.
**Hodensack** *m* scrotum.
**Hof** [hoːf] (**-(e)s, ̈e**) *m* (*Hinter~*) yard; (*Bauern~*) farm; (*Königs~*) court; **einem Mädchen den** ~ **machen** (*veraltet*) to court a girl.
**hoffen** ['hɔfən] *vi*: ~ **(auf** +*akk*) to hope (for).
**hoffentlich** *adv* I hope, hopefully.
**Hoffnung** ['hɔfnʊŋ] *f* hope; **jdm** ~**en machen** to raise sb's hopes; **sich** *dat* ~**en machen** to have hopes; **sich** *dat* **keine** ~**en machen** not to hold out any hope(s).
**Hoffnungs-** *zW*: **h~los** *adj* hopeless; ~**losigkeit** *f* hopelessness; ~**schimmer** *m* glimmer of hope; **h~voll** *adj* hopeful.
**höflich** ['høːflɪç] *adj* courteous, polite; **H~keit** *f* courtesy, politeness.
**hohe(r, s)** ['hoːə(r, s)] *adj siehe* **hoch**.
**Höhe** ['høːə] (**-, -n**) *f* height; (*An~*) hill; **nicht auf der** ~ **sein** (*fig: umg*) to feel below par; **ein Scheck in** ~ **von** ... a cheque (*BRIT*) *od* check (*US*) for the amount of ...; **das ist doch die** ~ (*fig: umg*) that's the limit; **er geht immer gleich in die** ~ (*umg*) he always flares up; **auf der** ~ **der Zeit sein** to be up-to-date.
**Hoheit** ['hoːhaɪt] *f* (*POL*) sovereignty; (*Titel*) Highness.
**Hoheits-** *zW*: ~**gebiet** *nt* sovereign territory; ~**gewalt** *f* (national) jurisdiction; ~**gewässer** *nt* territorial waters *pl*; ~**zeichen** *nt* national emblem.
**Höhen-** *zW*: ~**angabe** *f* altitude reading; (*auf Karte*) height marking; ~**flug** *m*: **geistiger** ~**flug** intellectual flight; ~**lage** *f* altitude; ~**luft** *f* mountain air; ~**messer** *m* altimeter; ~**sonne** *f* sun lamp; ~**unterschied** *m* difference in altitude; ~**zug** *m* mountain chain.
**Höhepunkt** *m* climax; (*des Lebens*) high

point.

**höher** adj, adv higher.

**hohl** [ho:l] adj hollow; (umg: dumm) hollow(-headed).

**Höhle** ['hø:lə] (-, -n) f cave; hole; (Mund~) cavity; (fig, ZOOL) den.

**Hohl-** zW: ~**heit** f hollowness; ~**kreuz** nt (MED) hollow back; ~**maß** nt measure of volume; ~**raum** m hollow space; (Gebäude) cavity; ~**saum** m hemstitch; ~**spiegel** m concave mirror.

**Hohn** [ho:n] (-(e)s) m scorn; **das ist der reinste** ~ it's sheer mockery.

**höhnen** ['hø:nən] vt to taunt, scoff at.

**höhnisch** adj scornful, taunting.

**Hokuspokus** [ho:kus'po:kus] (-) m (Zauberformel) hey presto; (fig: Täuschung) hocus-pocus.

**hold** [holt] adj charming, sweet.

**holen** ['ho:lən] vt to get, fetch; (Atem) to take; **jdn/etw ~ lassen** to send for sb/sth; **sich** dat **eine Erkältung ~** to catch a cold.

**Holland** ['holant] (-s) nt Holland.

**Holländer** ['holɛndər] (-s, -) m Dutchman.

**Holländerin** f Dutchwoman, Dutch girl.

**holländisch** adj Dutch.

**Hölle** ['hœlə] (-, -n) f hell; **ich werde ihm die ~ heiß machen** (umg) I'll give him hell.

**Höllenangst** f: **eine ~ haben** to be scared to death.

**Höllenlärm** m infernal noise (umg).

**höllisch** ['hœlɪʃ] adj hellish, infernal.

**Hologramm** [holo'gram] (-s, -e) nt hologram.

**holperig** ['holpərɪç] adj rough, bumpy.

**holpern** ['holpərn] vi to jolt.

**Holunder** [ho'lundər] (-s, -) m elder.

**Holz** [holts] (-es, ̈-er) nt wood; **aus ~** made of wood, wooden; **aus einem anderen/demselben ~ geschnitzt sein** (fig) to be cast in a different/the same mould; **gut ~!** (Kegeln) have a good game!; ~**bläser** m woodwind player.

**hölzern** ['hœltsərn] adj (lit, fig) wooden.

**Holz-** zW: ~**fäller** (-s, -) m lumberjack, woodcutter; ~**faserplatte** f (wood) fibreboard (BRIT) od fiberboard (US); **h~frei** adj (Papier) wood-free.

**holzig** adj woody.

**Holz-** zW: ~**klotz** m wooden block; ~**kohle** f charcoal; ~**kopf** m (fig: umg) blockhead, numbskull; ~**scheit** nt log; ~**schuh** m clog; ~**weg** m (fig) wrong track; ~**wolle** f fine wood shavings pl; ~**wurm** m woodworm.

**Homecomputer** ['hoʊmkɔm'pjuːtər] (-s, -) m home computer.

**homogen** [homo'ge:n] adj homogenous.

**Homöopath** [homøo'pa:t] (-en, -en) m homeopath.

**Homöopathie** [homøopa'ti:] f homeopathy, homeopathic medicine.

**homosexuell** [homozɛksu'ɛl] adj homosexual.

**Honduras** [hon'du:ras] (-) nt Honduras.

**Hongkong** [hoŋ'koŋ] (-s) nt Hong Kong.

**Honig** ['ho:nɪç] (-s, -e) m honey; ~**lecken** nt (fig): **das ist kein ~lecken** it's no picnic; ~**melone** f honeydew melon; ~**wabe** f honeycomb.

**Honorar** [hono'ra:r] (-s, -e) nt fee.

**Honoratioren** [honoratsi'o:rən] pl dignitaries pl.

**honorieren** [hono'ri:rən] vt to remunerate; (Scheck) to honour (BRIT), honor (US).

**Hopfen** ['hopfən] (-s, -) m hops pl; **bei ihm ist ~ und Malz verloren** (umg) he's a dead loss.

**hoppla** ['hopla] interj whoops.

**hopsen** ['hopsən] vi to hop.

**Hörapparat** m hearing aid.

**hörbar** adj audible.

**horch** [horç] interj listen.

**horchen** vi to listen; (pej) to eavesdrop.

**Horcher** (-s, -) m listener; eavesdropper.

**Horde** ['hordə] (-, -n) f horde.

**hören** ['hø:rən] vt, vi to hear; **auf jdn/etw ~** to listen to sb/sth; **ich lasse von mir ~** I'll be in touch; **etwas/nichts von sich ~ lassen** to get/not to get in touch; **H~** nt: **es verging ihm H~ und Sehen** (umg) he didn't know whether he was coming or going.

**Hörensagen** nt: **vom ~** from hearsay.

**Hörer** (-s, -) m (RUNDF) listener; (UNIV) student; (Telefon~) receiver.

**Hörfunk** m radio.

**Hörgerät** nt hearing aid.

**hörig** ['hø:rɪç] adj: **sie ist ihm (sexuell) ~** he has (sexual) power over her.

**Horizont** [hori'tsont] (-(e)s, -e) m horizon; **das geht über meinen ~** (fig) that is beyond me.

**horizontal** [horitso'ta:l] adj horizontal.

**Hormon** [hɔr'moːn] (-s, -e) nt hormone.

**Hörmuschel** f (TEL) earpiece.

**Horn** [hɔrn] (-(e)s, ̈-er) nt horn; **ins gleiche** od **in jds ~ blasen** to chime in; **sich** dat **die Hörner abstoßen** (umg) to sow one's wild oats; ~**brille** f horn-rimmed spectacles pl.

**Hörnchen** ['hœrnçən] nt (Gebäck) croissant.

**Hornhaut** f horny skin; (des Auges) cornea.

**Hornisse** [hɔr'nɪsə] (-, -n) f hornet.

**Hornochs(e)** m (fig: umg) blockhead, idiot.

**Horoskop** [horo'sko:p] (-s, -e) nt horoscope.

**Hör-** zW: ~**rohr** nt ear trumpet; (MED) stethoscope; ~**saal** m lecture room; ~**spiel** nt radio play.

**Horst** [hɔrst] (-(e)s, -e) m (Nest) nest; (Adler~) eyrie.

**Hort** [hɔrt] (-(e)s, -e) m hoard; (SCH) nursery school; **h~en** vt to hoard.

**Hörweite** f: **in/außer ~** within/out of hearing od earshot.

**Hose** ['ho:zə] (-, -n) f trousers pl, pants pl (US); **in die ~ gehen** (umg) to be a complete flop.

**Hosen-** zW: ~**anzug** m trouser suit, pantsuit (US); ~**boden** m: **sich auf den ~boden setzen** (umg) to get stuck in; ~**rock** m culottes *pl*; ~**tasche** *f* trouser pocket; ~**träger** *pl* braces *pl* (*BRIT*), suspenders *pl* (*US*).

**Hostie** ['hɔstiə] *f* (*REL*) host.

**Hotel** [ho'tɛl] (**-s, -s**) *nt* hotel; ~**fach** *nt* hotel management; ~ **garni** *nt* bed and breakfast hotel.

**Hotelier** [hotɛli'e:] (**-s, -s**) *m* hotelkeeper, hotelier.

**HR** *abk* (= *Hessischer Rundfunk*) Hessen Radio.

**Hr.** *abk* (= *Herr*) Mr.

**Hrsg.** *abk* (= *Herausgeber*) ed.

**hrsg.** *abk* (= *herausgegeben*) ed.

**Hub** [hu:p] (**-(e)s, ̈-e**) *m* lift; (*TECH*) stroke.

**hüben** ['hy:bən] *adv* on this side, over here; ~ **und drüben** on both sides.

**Hubraum** *m* (*AUT*) cubic capacity.

**hübsch** [hypʃ] *adj* pretty, nice; **immer** ~ **langsam!** (*umg*) nice and easy.

**Hubschrauber** (**-s, -**) *m* helicopter.

**Hucke** ['hʊkə] (**-, -n**) *f*: **jdm die** ~ **vollhauen** (*umg*) to give sb a good hiding.

**huckepack** ['hʊkəpak] *adv* piggy-back, pick-a-back.

**hudeln** ['hu:dəln] *vi* to be sloppy.

**Huf** ['hu:f] (**-(e)s, -e**) *m* hoof; ~**eisen** *nt* horseshoe; ~**nagel** *m* horseshoe nail.

**Hüfte** ['hyftə] (**-, -n**) *f* hip.

**Hüftgürtel** *m* girdle.

**Hüfthalter** *m* girdle.

**Huftier** *nt* hoofed animal.

**Hügel** ['hy:gəl] (**-s, -**) *m* hill.

**hüg(e)lig** *adj* hilly.

**Huhn** [hu:n] (**-(e)s, ̈-er**) *nt* hen; (*KOCH*) chicken; **da lachen ja die Hühner** (*umg*) it's enough to make a cat laugh; **er sah aus wie ein gerupftes** ~ (*umg*) he looked as if he'd been dragged through a hedge backwards.

**Hühnchen** ['hy:nçən] *nt* young chicken; **mit jdm ein** ~ **zu rupfen haben** (*umg*) to have a bone to pick with sb.

**Hühner-** *zW*: ~**auge** *nt* corn; ~**brühe** *f* chicken broth; ~**klein** *nt* (*KOCH*) chicken trimmings *pl*.

**Huld** [hʊlt] (**-**) *f* favour (*BRIT*), favor (*US*).

**huldigen** ['hʊldɪgən] *vi*: **jdm** ~ to pay homage to sb.

**Huldigung** *f* homage.

**Hülle** ['hylə] (**-, -n**) *f* cover(ing); (*Zellophan*~) wrapping; **in** ~ **und Fülle** galore; **die** ~**n fallen lassen** (*fig*) to strip off.

**hüllen** *vt*: ~ (**in** +*akk*) to cover (with); to wrap (in).

**Hülse** ['hylzə] (**-, -n**) *f* husk, shell.

**Hülsenfrucht** *f* pulse.

**human** [hu'ma:n] *adj* humane.

**humanistisch** [huma'nɪstɪʃ] *adj*: ~**es Gymnasium** *secondary school with bias on Latin and Greek*.

**humanitär** [humani'tɛːr] *adj* humanitarian.

**Humanität** *f* humanity.

**Humanmedizin** *f* (human) medicine.

**Hummel** ['hʊməl] (**-, -n**) *f* bumblebee.

**Hummer** ['hʊmər] (**-s, -**) *m* lobster.

**Humor** [hu'mo:r] (**-s, -e**) *m* humour (*BRIT*), humor (*US*); ~ **haben** to have a sense of humo(u)r; ~**ist(in)** *m(f)* humorist; **h**~**istisch** *adj* humorous; **h**~**voll** *adj* humorous.

**humpeln** ['hʊmpəln] *vi* to hobble.

**Humpen** ['hʊmpən] (**-s, -**) *m* tankard.

**Humus** ['hu:mʊs] (**-**) *m* humus.

**Hund** [hʊnt] (**-(e)s, -e**) *m* dog; **auf den** ~ **kommen, vor die** ~**e gehen** (*fig: umg*) to go to the dogs; ~**e, die bellen, beißen nicht** (*Sprichwort*) empty vessels make most noise (*Sprichwort*); **er ist bekannt wie ein bunter** ~ (*umg*) everybody knows him.

**Hunde-** *zW*: **h**~**elend** (*umg*) *adj*: **mir ist h**~**elend** I feel lousy; ~**hütte** *f* (dog) kennel; ~**kuchen** *m* dog biscuit; ~**marke** *f* dog licence disc, dog tag (*US*); **h**~**müde** (*umg*) *adj* dog-tired.

**hundert** ['hʊndərt] *num* hundred; **H**~ (**-s, -e**) *nt* hundred; **H**~**e von Menschen** hundreds of people.

**Hunderter** (**-s, -**) *m* hundred; (*umg: Geldschein*) hundred (mark/pound/dollar *etc* note).

**hundert-** *zW*: **H**~**jahrfeier** *f* centenary; **H**~**meterlauf** *m* (*SPORT*): **der/ein H**~**meterlauf** the/a hundred metres (*BRIT*) *od* meters (*US*) *sing*; ~**prozentig** *adj, adv* one hundred per cent.

**hundertste(r, s)** *adj* hundredth; **von H**~**n ins Tausendste kommen** (*fig*) to get carried away.

**Hundesteuer** *f* dog licence (*BRIT*) *od* license (*US*) fee.

**Hundewetter** (*umg*) *nt* filthy weather.

**Hündin** ['hyndɪn] *f* bitch.

**Hüne** ['hy:nə] (**-n, -n**) *m*: **ein** ~ **von Mensch** a giant of a man.

**Hünengrab** *nt* megalithic tomb.

**Hunger** ['hʊŋər] (**-s**) *m* hunger; ~ **haben** to be hungry; **ich sterbe vor** ~ (*umg*) I'm starving; ~**lohn** *m* starvation wages *pl*.

**hungern** *vi* to starve.

**Hungersnot** *f* famine.

**Hungerstreik** *m* hunger strike.

**Hungertuch** *nt*: **am** ~ **nagen** (*fig*) to be starving.

**hungrig** ['hʊŋrɪç] *adj* hungry.

**Hunsrück** ['hʊnsryk] *m* Hunsruck (Mountains *pl*).

**Hupe** ['hu:pə] (**-, -n**) *f* horn.

**hupen** *vi* to hoot, sound one's horn.

**hupfen** ['hʊpfən] *vi* to hop, jump; **das ist gehupft wie gesprungen** (*umg*) it's six of one and half a dozen of the other.

**hüpfen** ['hypfən] *vi* = **hupfen.**

**Hupkonzert** (*umg*) *nt* hooting (of car horns).

**Hürde** ['hyrdə] (**-, -n**) *f* hurdle; (*für Schafe*) pen.

**Hürdenlauf** *m* hurdling.

**Hure** ['huːrə] (-, -n) f whore.
**Hurensohn** (pej: umg!) m bastard (!), son of a bitch (!).
**hurra** [hʊ'raː] interj hurray, hurrah.
**hurtig** ['hʊrtɪç] adj brisk, quick ♦ adv briskly, quickly.
**huschen** ['hʊʃən] vi to flit, scurry.
**Husten** ['huːstən] (-s) m cough; **h~** vi to cough; **auf etw** akk **h~** (umg) not to give a damn for sth; **~anfall** m coughing fit; **~bonbon** m od nt cough drop; **~saft** m cough mixture.
**Hut¹** [huːt] (-(e)s, ⁻e) m hat; **unter einen ~ bringen** (umg) to reconcile; (Termine etc) to fit in.
**Hut²** [huːt] (-) f care; **auf der ~ sein** to be on one's guard.
**hüten** ['hyːtən] vt to guard ♦ vr to watch out; **das Bett/Haus ~** to stay in bed/indoors; **sich ~, zu** to take care not to; **sich ~ vor** +dat to beware of; **ich werde mich ~**! not likely!
**Hutschnur** f: **das geht mir über die ~** (umg) that's going too far.
**Hütte** ['hytə] (-, -n) f hut; (Holz~, Block~) cabin; (Eisen~) forge; (umg: Wohnung) pad; (TECH: Hüttenwerk) iron and steel works.
**Hüttenindustrie** f iron and steel industry.
**Hüttenkäse** m cottage cheese.
**Hüttenwerk** nt iron and steel works.
**hutzelig** ['hʊtsəlıç] adj shrivelled.
**Hyäne** [hy'ɛːnə] (-, -n) f hyena.
**Hyazinthe** [hya'tsıntə] (-, -n) f hyacinth.
**Hydrant** [hy'drant] m hydrant.
**hydraulisch** [hy'draʊlıʃ] adj hydraulic.
**Hydrierung** [hy'driːrʊŋ] f hydrogenation.
**Hygiene** [hygi'eːnə] (-) f hygiene.
**hygienisch** [hygi'eːnıʃ] adj hygienic.
**Hymne** ['hymnə] (-, -n) f hymn, anthem.
**hyper-** ['hypɐ] präf hyper-.
**Hypnose** [hyp'noːzə] (-, -n) f hypnosis.
**hypnotisch** adj hypnotic.
**Hypnotiseur** [hypnoti'zøːr] m hypnotist.
**hypnotisieren** [hypnoti'ziːrən] vt to hypnotize.
**Hypotenuse** [hypote'nuːzə] (-, -n) f hypotenuse.
**Hypothek** [hypo'teːk] (-, -en) f mortgage; **eine ~ aufnehmen** to raise a mortgage; **etw mit einer ~ belasten** to mortgage sth.
**Hypothese** [hypo'teːzə] (-, -n) f hypothesis.
**hypothetisch** [hypo'teːtıʃ] adj hypothetical.
**Hysterie** [hyste'riː] f hysteria.
**hysterisch** [hys'teːrıʃ] adj hysterical; **einen ~en Anfall bekommen** (fig) to have hysterics.

# I, i

**I, i** [iː] nt I, i; **~ wie Ida** ≈ I for Isaac, I for Item (US); **das Tüpfelchen auf dem i** (fig) the final touch.
**i.** abk = **in, im**.
**i.A.** abk (= im Auftrag) p.p.
**iberisch** [i'beːrıʃ] adj Iberian; **die ~e Halbinsel** the Iberian Peninsula.
**IC** (-) m abk = **Intercity-Zug**.
**ICE** m abk (= Intercity-Expreßzug) inter-city train.
**ich** [ıç] pron I; **~ bin's!** it's me!; **I~** (-(s), -(s)) nt self; (PSYCH) ego; **I~form** f first person; **I~-Roman** m novel in the first person.
**Ideal** [ide'aːl] (-s, -e) nt ideal; **i~** adj ideal; **~fall** m: **im ~fall** ideally.
**Idealismus** [idea'lısmʊs] m idealism.
**Idealist(in)** m(f) idealist.
**idealistisch** adj idealistic.
**Idealvorstellung** f ideal.
**Idee** [i'deː] (-, -n) f idea; (ein wenig) shade, trifle; **jdn auf die ~ bringen, etw zu tun** to give sb the idea of doing sth.
**ideell** [ide'ɛl] adj ideal.
**identifizieren** [identifi'tsiːrən] vt to identify.
**identisch** [i'dɛntıʃ] adj identical.
**Identität** [identi'tɛːt] f identity.
**Ideologe** [ideo'loːgə] (-n, -n) m ideologist.
**Ideologie** [ideolo'giː] f ideology.
**Ideologin** [ideo'loːgın] f ideologist.
**ideologisch** [ideo'loːgıʃ] adj ideological.
**idiomatisch** [idio'maːtıʃ] adj idiomatic.
**Idiot** [idi'oːt] (-en, -en) m idiot.
**Idiotenhügel** m (hum: umg) beginners' od nursery slope.
**idiotensicher** (umg) adj foolproof.
**Idiotin** f idiot.
**idiotisch** adj idiotic.
**Idol** [i'doːl] nt (-s, -e) idol.
**idyllisch** [i'dylıʃ] adj idyllic.
**IG** abk (= Industriegewerkschaft) industrial trade union.
**IGB** (-) m abk (= Internationaler Gewerkschaftsbund) International Trades Union Congress.
**Igel** ['iːgəl] (-s, -) m hedgehog.
**igitt(igitt)** [i'gıt(i'gıt)] interj ugh!
**Iglu** ['iːglu] (-s, -s) m od nt igloo.
**Ignorant** [ıgno'rant] (-en, -en) m ignoramus.
**ignorieren** [ıgno'riːrən] vt to ignore.
**IHK** f abk = **Industrie- und Handelskammer**.
**ihm** [iːm] dat von er, es pers pron (to) him, (to) it; **es ist ~ nicht gut** he doesn't feel well.

**ihn** [iːn] *akk von er pers pron* him; (*bei Tieren, Dingen*) it.
**ihnen** ['iːnən] *dat pl von sie pers pron* (to) them; (*nach Präpositionen*) them.
**Ihnen** *dat von Sie pers pron* (to) you; (*nach Präpositionen*) you.

════════════ *SCHLÜSSELWORT*

**ihr** [iːr] *pron* **1** (*nom pl*) you; ~ **seid es** it's you **2** (*dat von sie*) (to) her; (*bei Tieren, Dingen*) (to) it; **gib es** ~ give it to her; **er steht neben** ~ he is standing beside her
♦ *poss pron* **1** (*sing*) her; (: *bei Tieren, Dingen*) its; ~ **Mann** her husband
**2** (*pl*) their; **die Bäume und** ~**e Blätter** the trees and their leaves.

**Ihr** *poss pron* your.
**Ihre(r, s)** *poss pron* yours; **tun Sie das** ~ (*geh*) you do your bit.
**ihre(r, s)** *poss pron* hers; (*eines Tieres*) its; (*von mehreren*) theirs; **sie taten das** ~ (*geh*) they did their bit.
**ihrer** ['iːrər] *gen von sie pers pron* (*sing*) of her; (*pl*) of them.
**Ihrer** *gen von Sie pers pron* of you.
**ihrerseits** *adv* for your part.
**ihrerseits** *adv* for her/their part.
**ihresgleichen** *pron* people like her/them; (*von Dingen*) others like it; **eine Frechheit, die** ~ **sucht!** an incredible cheek!
**ihretwegen** *adv* (*für sie*) for her/its/their sake; (*wegen ihr, ihnen*) on her/its/their account; **sie sagte,** ~ **könnten wir gehen** she said that, as far as she was concerned, we could go.
**ihretwillen** *adv:* **um** ~ for her/its/their sake.
**ihrige** ['iːrɪgə] *pron:* **der/die/das** ~ hers; its; theirs.
**i.J.** *abk* (= *im Jahre*) in (the year).
**Ikone** [i'koːnə] (-, -n) *f* icon.
**IKRK** *nt abk* (= *Internationales Komitee vom Roten Kreuz*) ICRC.
**illegal** ['ɪlegaːl] *adj* illegal.
**illegitim** ['ɪlegitiːm] *adj* illegitimate.
**Illusion** [ɪluzi'oːn] *f* illusion; **sich** *dat* ~**en machen** to delude o.s.
**illusorisch** [ɪlu'zoːrɪʃ] *adj* illusory.
**Illustration** [ɪlʊstratsi'oːn] *f* illustration.
**illustrieren** [ɪlʊs'triːrən] *vt* to illustrate.
**Illustrierte** (-n, -n) *f* picture magazine.
**Iltis** ['ɪltɪs] (-ses, -se) *m* polecat.
**im** [ɪm] = **in dem** ♦ *präp:* **etw** ~ **Liegen/Stehen tun** do sth lying down/standing up.
**Image** ['ɪmɪtʃ] (-(s), -s) *nt* image; ~**pflege** ['ɪmɪtʃpfleːgə] (*umg*) *f* image-building.
**imaginär** [imagi'nɛːr] *adj* imaginary.
**Imbiß** ['ɪmbɪs] (-sses, -sse) *m* snack; ~**halle** *f* snack bar; ~**stube** *f* snack bar.
**imitieren** [imi'tiːrən] *vt* to imitate.
**Imker** ['ɪmkər] (-s, -) *m* beekeeper.
**immanent** [ɪma'nɛnt] *adj* inherent, intrinsic.

**Immatrikulation** [ɪmatrikulatsi'oːn] *f* (*UNIV*) registration.
**immatrikulieren** [ɪmatriku'liːrən] *vi, vr* to register.
**immer** ['ɪmər] *adv* always; ~ **wieder** again and again; **etw** ~ **wieder tun** to keep on doing sth; ~ **noch** still; ~ **noch nicht** still not; **für** ~ forever; ~ **wenn ich ...** every time I ...; ~ **schöner** more and more beautiful; ~**trauriger** sadder and sadder; **was/wer (auch)** ~ whatever/whoever; ~**hin** *adv* all the same; ~**zu** *adv* all the time.
**Immigrant(in)** [ɪmi'grant(ɪn)] *m(f)* immigrant.
**Immobilien** [ɪmo'biːliən] *pl* real property (*BRIT*), real estate (*US*); (*in Zeitungsannoncen*) property *sing*; ~**händler** *m*, ~**makler** *m* estate agent (*BRIT*), realtor (*US*).
**immun** [ɪ'muːn] *adj* immune.
**immunisieren** [ɪmuni'ziːrən] *vt* to immunize.
**Immunität** [ɪmuni'tɛːt] *f* immunity.
**Immunschwäche** *f* immunodeficiency.
**Immunsystem** *nt* immune system.
**imperativ** ['ɪmperatiːf] *adj:* ~**es Mandat** imperative mandate.
**Imperativ** (-s, -e) *m* imperative.
**Imperfekt** ['ɪmpɛrfɛkt] (-s, -e) *nt* imperfect (tense).
**Imperialismus** [ɪmperia'lɪsmʊs] *m* imperialism.
**Imperialist** [ɪmperia'lɪst] *m* imperialist; **i**~**isch** *adj* imperialistic.
**impfen** ['ɪmpfən] *vt* to vaccinate.
**Impf-** *zW:* ~**paß** *m* vaccination card; ~**schutz** *m* protection given by vaccination; ~**stoff** *m* vaccine; ~**ung** *f* vaccination; ~**zwang** *m* compulsory vaccination.
**implizieren** [ɪmpli'tsiːrən] *vt* to imply.
**imponieren** [ɪmpo'niːrən] *vi +dat* to impress.
**Import** [ɪm'pɔrt] (-(e)s, -e) *m* import.
**Importeur** [ɪmpɔr'tøːr] (-s, -e) *m* importer.
**importieren** [ɪmpɔr'tiːrən] *vt* to import.
**imposant** [ɪmpo'zant] *adj* imposing.
**impotent** ['ɪmpotɛnt] *adj* impotent.
**Impotenz** ['ɪmpotɛnts] *f* impotence.
**imprägnieren** [ɪmprɛ'gniːrən] *vt* to (water)proof.
**Impressionismus** [ɪmpresio'nɪsmʊs] *m* impressionism.
**Impressum** [ɪm'prɛsʊm] (-s, -ssen) *nt* imprint; (*von Zeitung*) masthead.
**Improvisation** [ɪmprovizatsi'oːn] *f* improvisation.
**improvisieren** [ɪmprovi'ziːrən] *vt, vi* to improvise.
**Impuls** [ɪm'pʊls] (-es, -e) *m* impulse; **etw aus einem** ~ **heraus tun** to do sth on impulse.
**impulsiv** [ɪmpʊl'ziːf] *adj* impulsive.
**imstande** [ɪm'ʃtandə] *adj:* ~ **sein** to be in a position; (*fähig*) to be able; **er ist zu allem** ~ he's capable of anything.

================ **SCHLÜSSELWORT**

**in** [ɪn] *präp +akk* **1** (*räumlich: wohin*) in, into; ~ **die Stadt** into town; ~ **die Schule gehen** to go to school; ~ **die Hunderte gehen** to run into (the) hundreds
**2** (*zeitlich*): **bis** ~**s 20. Jahrhundert** into *od* up to the 20th century
♦ *präp +dat* **1** (*räumlich: wo*) in; ~ **der Stadt** in town; ~ **der Schule sein** to be at school; **es** ~ **sich haben** (*umg: Text*) to be tough; (: *Drink*) to have quite a kick
**2** (*zeitlich: wann*): ~ **diesem Jahr** this year; (*in jenem Jahr*) in that year; **heute** ~ **zwei Wochen** two weeks today.

**inaktiv** ['ɪn|aktiːf] *adj* inactive; (*Mitglied*) non-active.
**Inangriffnahme** [ɪn'|angrɪfnaːmə] (-, -n) *f* (*form*) commencement.
**Inanspruchnahme** [ɪn'|anʃpruxnaːmə] (-, -n) *f*: ~ (+*gen*) demands *pl* (on); **im Falle einer** ~ **der Arbeitslosenunterstützung** (*form*) where unemployment benefit has been sought.
**Inbegriff** ['ɪnbəgrɪf] *m* embodiment, personification.
**inbegriffen** *adv* included.
**Inbetriebnahme** ['ɪnbətriːpnaːmə] (-, -n) *f* (*form*) commissioning; (*von Gebäude, U-Bahn etc*) inauguration.
**inbrünstig** ['ɪnbrʏnstɪç] *adj* ardent.
**indem** [ɪn'deːm] *konj* while; ~ **man etw macht** (*dadurch*) by doing sth.
**Inder(in)** ['ɪndər(ɪn)] (-s, -) *m(f)* Indian.
**indes(sen)** [ɪn'dɛs(ən)] *adv* meanwhile ♦ *konj* while.
**Index** ['ɪndɛks] (-(es), -e *od* Indizes) *m*: **auf dem** ~ **stehen** (*fig*) to be banned; ~**zahl** *f* index number.
**Indianer(in)** [ɪndi'aːnər(ɪn)] (-s, -) *m(f)* (Red *od* American) Indian.
**indianisch** *adj* (Red *od* American) Indian.
**Indien** ['ɪndiən] (-s) *nt* India.
**indigniert** [ɪndɪ'gniːrt] *adj* indignant.
**Indikation** [ɪndikatsi'oːn] *f*: **medizinische/ soziale** ~ medical/social grounds *pl* for the termination of pregnancy.
**Indikativ** ['ɪndikatiːf] (-s, -e) *m* indicative.
**indirekt** ['ɪndirɛkt] *adj* indirect; ~**e Steuer** indirect tax.
**indisch** ['ɪndɪʃ] *adj* Indian; **l~er Ozean** Indian Ocean.
**indiskret** ['ɪndɪskreːt] *adj* indiscreet.
**Indiskretion** [ɪndɪskretsi'oːn] *f* indiscretion.
**indiskutabel** ['ɪndɪskutaːbəl] *adj* out of the question.
**indisponiert** ['ɪndɪsponiːrt] *adj* (*geh*) indisposed.
**Individualist** [ɪndividua'lɪst] *m* individualist.
**Individualität** [ɪndividuali'tɛt] *f* individuality.
**individuell** [ɪndividu'ɛl] *adj* individual; **etw** ~ **gestalten** to give sth a personal note.

**Individuum** [ɪndi'viːduom] (-s, -duen) *nt* individual.
**Indiz** [ɪn'diːts] (-es, -ien) *nt* (*JUR*) clue; ~ (**für**) sign (of).
**Indizes** ['ɪnditseːz] *pl von* **Index.**
**Indizienbeweis** *m* circumstantial evidence.
**indizieren** [ɪndi'tsiːrən] *vt, vi* (*COMPUT*) to index.
**Indochina** ['ɪndo'çiːna] (-s) *nt* Indochina.
**indogermanisch** ['ɪndogɛr'maːnɪʃ] *adj* Indo-Germanic, Indo-European.
**indoktrinieren** [ɪndɔktri'niːrən] *vt* to indoctrinate.
**Indonesien** [ɪndo'neːziən] (-s) *nt* Indonesia.
**Indonesier(in)** (-s, -) *m(f)* Indonesian.
**indonesisch** [ɪndo'neːzɪʃ] *adj* Indonesian.
**Indossament** [ɪndɔsa'mɛnt] *nt* (*COMM*) endorsement.
**Indossant** [ɪndɔ'sant] *m* endorser.
**Indossat** [ɪndɔ'saːt] (-en, -en) *m* endorsee.
**indossieren** *vt* to endorse.
**industrialisieren** [ɪndustriali'zɪːrən] *vt* to industrialize.
**Industrialisierung** *f* industrialization.
**Industrie** [ɪndus'triː] *f* industry; **in der** ~ **arbeiten** to be in industry; ~**gebiet** *nt* industrial area; ~**gelände** *nt* industrial *od* trading estate; ~**kaufmann** *m* industrial manager.
**industriell** [ɪndustri'ɛl] *adj* industrial; ~**e Revolution** industrial revolution.
**Industrielle(r)** *f(m)* industrialist.
**Industrie-** *zW:* ~**staat** *m* industrial nation; ~**- und Handelskammer** *f* chamber of industry and commerce; ~**zweig** *m* branch of industry.
**ineinander** [ɪn|aɪ'nandər] *adv* in(to) one another *od* each other; ~ **übergehen** to merge (into each other); ~**greifen** *unreg vi* (*lit*) to interlock; (*Zahnräder*) to mesh; (*fig: Ereignisse etc*) to overlap.
**Infanterie** [ɪnfantə'riː] *f* infantry.
**Infarkt** [ɪn'farkt] (-(e)s, -e) *m* coronary (thrombosis).
**Infektion** [ɪnfɛktsi'oːn] *f* infection.
**Infektionsherd** *m* focus of infection.
**Infektionskrankheit** *f* infectious disease.
**Infinitiv** ['ɪnfinitiːf] (-s, -e) *m* infinitive.
**infizieren** [ɪnfi'tsiːrən] *vt* to infect ♦ *vr*: **sich (bei jdm)** ~ to be infected (by sb).
**in flagranti** [ɪn fla'granti] *adv* in the act, red-handed.
**Inflation** [ɪnflatsi'oːn] *f* inflation.
**inflationär** [ɪnflatsio'nɛːr] *adj* inflationary.
**Inflationsrate** *f* rate of inflation.
**inflatorisch** [ɪnfla'toːrɪʃ] *adj* inflationary.
**Info** ['ɪnfo] (-s, -s) (*umg*) *nt* (information) leaflet.
**infolge** [ɪn'fɔlgə] *präp +gen* as a result of, owing to; ~**dessen** *adv* consequently.
**Informatik** [ɪnfɔr'maːtɪk] *f* information studies *pl*.

**Informatiker(in)** (-s, -) *m(f)* computer scientist.

**Information** [ɪnfɔrmatsi'oːn] *f* information *no pl*; **Informationen** *pl* (*COMPUT*) data; **zu Ihrer ~ for your information.

**Informationsabruf** *m* (*COMPUT*) information retrieval.

**Informationstechnik** *f* information technology.

**informativ** [ɪnfɔrma'tiːf] *adj* informative.

**informieren** [ɪnfɔr'miːrən] *vt*: **~ (über +akk)** to inform (about) ♦ *vr*: **sich ~ (über +akk)** to find out (about).

**Infrastruktur** ['ɪnfraʃtruktuːr] *f* infrastructure.

**Infusion** [ɪnfuzi'oːn] *f* infusion.

**Ing.** *abk* = **Ingenieur.**

**Ingenieur** [ɪnʒeni'øːr] *m* engineer; **~schule** *f* school of engineering.

**Ingwer** ['ɪŋvər] (-s) *m* ginger.

**Inh.** *abk* (= *Inhaber(in)*) prop.; (= *Inhalt*) cont.

**Inhaber(in)** ['ɪnhaːbər(ɪn)] (-s, -) *m(f)* owner; (*COMM*) proprietor; (*Haus~*) occupier; (*Lizenz~*) licensee, holder; (*FIN*) bearer.

**inhaftieren** [ɪnhaf'tiːrən] *vt* to take into custody.

**inhalieren** [ɪnha'liːrən] *vt, vi* to inhale.

**Inhalt** ['ɪnhalt] (-(e)s, -e) *m* contents *pl*; (*eines Buchs etc*) content; (*MATH: Flächen~*) area; (: *Raum~*) volume; **i~lich** *adj* as regards content.

**Inhalts-** *zW*: **~angabe** *f* summary; **i~los** *adj* empty; **i~reich** *adj* full; **~verzeichnis** *nt* table of contents; (*COMPUT*) directory.

**inhuman** ['ɪnhumaːn] *adj* inhuman.

**initialisieren** [initsiali'ziːrən] *vt* (*COMPUT*) to initialize.

**Initialisierung** *f* (*COMPUT*) initialization.

**Initiative** [initsia'tiːvə] *f* initiative; **die ~ ergreifen** to take the initiative.

**Initiator(in)** [initsi'aːtɔr(ɪn)] *m(f)* (*geh*) initiator.

**Injektion** [ɪnjɛktsi'oːn] *f* injection.

**injizieren** [ɪnji'tsiːrən] *vt* to inject; **jdm etw ~** to inject sb with sth.

**Inka** ['ɪŋka] (-(s), -s) *f(m)* Inca.

**Inkaufnahme** [ɪn'kaʊfnaːmə] *f* (*form*): **unter ~ finanzieller Verluste** accepting the inevitable financial losses.

**inkl.** *abk* (= *inklusive*) inc.

**inklusive** [ɪnklu'ziːvə] *präp +gen* inclusive of ♦ *adv* inclusive.

**Inklusivpreis** *m* all-in rate.

**inkognito** [ɪn'kɔɡnito] *adv* incognito.

**inkonsequent** ['ɪnkɔnzekvɛnt] *adj* inconsistent.

**inkorrekt** ['ɪnkɔrɛkt] *adj* incorrect.

**Inkrafttreten** [ɪn'krafttreːtən] (-s) *nt* coming into force.

**Inkubationszeit** [ɪnkubatsi'oːnstsaɪt] *f* (*MED*) incubation period.

**Inland** ['ɪnlant] (-(e)s) *nt* (*GEOG*) inland; (*POL, COMM*) home (country); **im ~ und Ausland** at home and abroad; **~flug** *m* domestic flight.

**Inlandsporto** *nt* inland postage.

**inmitten** [ɪn'mɪtən] *präp +gen* in the middle of; **~ von** amongst.

**innehaben** ['ɪnəhaːbən] *unreg vt* to hold.

**innehalten** ['ɪnəhaltən] *unreg vi* to pause, stop.

**innen** ['ɪnən] *adv* inside; **nach ~** inwards; **von ~** from the inside; **I~architekt** *m* interior designer; **I~aufnahme** *f* indoor photograph; **I~bahn** *f* (*SPORT*) inside lane; **I~dienst** *m*: **im I~dienst sein** to work in the office; **I~einrichtung** *f* (interior) furnishings *pl*; **I~leben** *nt* (*seelisch*) emotional life; (*umg: körperlich*) insides *pl*; **I~minister** *m* minister of the interior, Home Secretary (*BRIT*); **I~politik** *f* domestic policy; **~politisch** *adj* relating to domestic policy, domestic; **I~stadt** *f* town *od* city centre (*BRIT*) *od* center (*US*).

**innerbetrieblich** *adj* in-house; **etw ~ regeln** to settle sth within the company.

**innerdeutsch** *adj*: **~e(r) Handel** domestic trade in Germany.

**Innere(s)** *nt* inside; (*Mitte*) centre (*BRIT*), center (*US*); (*fig*) heart.

**innere(r, s)** *adj* inner; (*im Körper, inländisch*) internal.

**Innereien** [ɪnə'raɪən] *pl* innards *pl*.

**inner-** *zW*: **~halb** *adv* within; (*räumlich*) inside ♦ *prep +dat* within; inside; **~lich** *adj* internal; (*geistig*) inward; **I~lichkeit** *f* (*LITER*) inwardness; **~parteilich** *adj*: **~parteiliche Demokratie** democracy (with)in the party structure.

**Innerste(s)** *nt* heart; **bis ins ~ getroffen** hurt to the quick.

**innerste(r, s)** *adj* innermost.

**innewohnen** ['ɪnəvoːnən] *vi +dat* (*geh*) to be inherent in.

**innig** ['ɪnɪç] *adj* profound; (*Freundschaft*) intimate; **mein ~ster Wunsch** my dearest wish.

**Innung** ['ɪnʊŋ] *f* (trade) guild; **du blamierst die ganze ~** (*hum: umg*) you are letting the whole side down.

**inoffiziell** ['ɪnɔfitsiɛl] *adj* unofficial.

**ins** [ɪns] = **in das.**

**Insasse** ['ɪnzasə] (-n, -n) *m*, **Insassin** *f* (*einer Anstalt*) inmate; (*AUT*) passenger.

**insbesondere** [ɪnsbə'zɔndərə] *adv* (e)specially.

**Inschrift** ['ɪnʃrɪft] *f* inscription.

**Insekt** [ɪn'zɛkt] (-(e)s, -en) *nt* insect.

**Insektenvertilgungsmittel** *nt* insecticide.

**Insel** ['ɪnzəl] (-, -n) *f* island.

**Inserat** [ɪnze'raːt] (-(e)s, -e) *nt* advertisement.

**Inserent** [ɪnze'rɛnt] *m* advertiser.

**inserieren** [ɪnze'riːrən] *vt, vi* to advertise.

**insgeheim** [ɪnsɡə'haɪm] *adv* secretly.

**insgesamt** [ɪnsɡə'zamt] *adv* altogether, all in

all.
**Insiderhandel** *m* insider dealing *od* trading.
**insofern** [ɪnzoˈfɛrn] *adv* in this respect ♦ *konj* if; *(deshalb)* (and) so; ~ **als** in so far as.
**insolvent** [ˈɪnzɔlvɛnt] *adj* bankrupt, insolvent.
**Insolvenz** *f* (*COMM*) insolvency.
**insoweit** *adv, konj* = **insofern.**
**in spe** [ɪnˈʃpeː] (*umg*) *adj:* **unser Schwiegersohn** ~ our son-in-law to be, our future son-in-law.
**Inspektion** [ɪnspɛktsiˈoːn] *f* inspection; (*AUT*) service.
**Inspektor(in)** [ɪnˈspɛktɔr, -ˈtoːrɪn] (**-s, -en**) *m(f)* inspector.
**Inspiration** [ɪnspiratsiˈoːn] *f* inspiration.
**inspirieren** [ɪnspiˈriːrən] *vt* to inspire; **sich von etw** ~ **lassen** to get one's inspiration from sth.
**inspizieren** [ɪnspiˈtsiːrən] *vt* to inspect.
**Installateur** [ɪnstalaˈtøːr] *m* plumber; (*Elektro~*) electrician.
**installieren** [ɪnstaˈliːrən] *vt* to install (*auch fig, COMPUT*).
**Instandhaltung** [ɪnˈʃtanthaltʊŋ] *f* maintenance.
**inständig** [ɪnˈʃtɛndɪç] *adj* urgent; ~ **bitten** to beg.
**Instandsetzung** *f* overhaul; (*eines Gebäudes*) restoration.
**Instanz** [ɪnˈstants] *f* authority; (*JUR*) court; **Verhandlung in erster/zweiter** ~ first/second court case.
**Instanzenweg** *m* official channels *pl.*
**Instinkt** [ɪnˈstɪŋkt] (**-(e)s, -e**) *m* instinct.
**instinktiv** [ɪnstɪŋkˈtiːf] *adj* instinctive.
**Institut** [ɪnstiˈtuːt] (**-(e)s, -e**) *nt* institute.
**Institution** [ɪnstitutsiˈoːn] *f* institution.
**Instrument** [ɪnstruˈmɛnt] *nt* instrument.
**Insulin** [ɪnzuˈliːn] (**-s**) *nt* insulin.
**inszenieren** [ɪnstseˈniːrən] *vt* to direct; (*fig*) to stage-manage.
**Inszenierung** *f* production.
**intakt** [ɪnˈtakt] *adj* intact.
**Integralrechnung** [ɪnteˈgraːlrɛçnʊŋ] *f* integral calculus.
**Integration** [ɪntegratsiˈoːn] *f* integration.
**integrieren** [ɪnteˈgriːrən] *vt* to integrate; **integrierte Gesamtschule** comprehensive school (*BRIT*).
**Integrität** [ɪntegriˈtɛːt] *f* integrity.
**Intellekt** [ɪnteˈlɛkt] (**-(e)s**) *m* intellect.
**intellektuell** [ɪntɛlɛktuˈɛl] *adj* intellectual.
**Intellektuelle(r)** *f(m)* intellectual.
**intelligent** [ɪnteliˈgɛnt] *adj* intelligent.
**Intelligenz** [ɪnteliˈgɛnts] *f* intelligence; (*Leute*) intelligentsia *pl*; ~**quotient** *m* IQ, intelligence quotient.
**Intendant** [ɪntɛnˈdant] *m* director.
**Intensität** [ɪntɛnziˈtɛːt] *f* intensity.
**intensiv** [ɪntɛnˈziːf] *adj* intensive.
**intensivieren** [ɪntɛnziˈviːrən] *vt* to intensify.
**Intensivkurs** *m* intensive course.

**Intensivstation** *f* intensive care unit.
**interaktiv** *adj* (*COMPUT*) interactive.
**Intercity-Zug** [ɪntərˈsɪtitsuːk] *m* inter-city train.
**interessant** [ɪnterɛˈsant] *adj* interesting; **sich** ~ **machen** to attract attention.
**interessanterweise** *adv* interestingly enough.
**Interesse** [ɪnteˈrɛsə] (**-s, -n**) *nt* interest; ~ **haben an** *+dat* to be interested in.
**Interessengebiet** *nt* field of interest.
**Interessengegensatz** *m* clash of interests.
**Interessent(in)** [ɪnterɛˈsɛnt(ɪn)] *m(f)* interested party; **es haben sich mehrere** ~**en gemeldet** several people have shown interest.
**Interessenvertretung** *f* representation of interests; (*Personen*) group representing (one's) interests.
**interessieren** [ɪnterɛˈsiːrən] *vt:* **jdn (für etw** *od* **an etw** *dat*) ~ to interest sb (in sth) ♦ *vr:* **sich** ~ **für** to be interested in.
**interessiert** *adj:* **politisch** ~ interested in politics.
**Interkontinentalrakete** [ɪntərkɔntinɛnˈtaːlrakeːtə] *f* intercontinental missile.
**intern** [ɪnˈtɛrn] *adj* internal.
**Internat** [ɪntɛrˈnaːt] (**-(e)s, -e**) *nt* boarding school.
**international** [ɪntɛrnatsioˈnaːl] *adj* international.
**Internatsschüler(in)** *m(f)* boarder.
**internieren** [ɪntɛrˈniːrən] *vt* to intern.
**Internierungslager** *nt* internment camp.
**Internist(in)** *m(f)* internist.
**Interpol** [ˈɪntərpoːl] (**-**) *f abk* (= *Internationale Polizei*) Interpol.
**Interpret** [ɪntərˈpreːt] (**-en, -en**) *m:* **Lieder verschiedener** ~**en** songs by various singers.
**Interpretation** [ɪntərpretatsiˈoːn] *f* interpretation.
**interpretieren** [ɪntərpreˈtiːrən] *vt* to interpret.
**Interpretin** *f siehe* **Interpret.**
**Interpunktion** [ɪntərpʊŋktsiˈoːn] *f* punctuation.
**Intervall** [ɪntərˈval] (**-s, -e**) *nt* interval.
**intervenieren** [ɪntɛrveˈniːrən] *vi* to intervene.
**Interview** [ɪntərˈvjuː] (**-s, -s**) *nt* interview; **i~en** [-ˈvjuːən] *vt* to interview.
**intim** [ɪnˈtiːm] *adj* intimate; **I~bereich** *m* (*ANAT*) genital area.
**Intimität** [ɪntimiˈtɛːt] *f* intimacy.
**Intimsphäre** *f:* **jds** ~ **verletzen** to invade sb's privacy.
**intolerant** [ˈɪntolerant] *adj* intolerant.
**intransitiv** [ˈɪntranzitiːf] *adj* (*GRAM*) intransitive.
**Intrige** [ɪnˈtriːgə] (**-, -n**) *f* intrigue, plot.
**intrinsisch** [ɪnˈtrɪnzɪʃ] *adj:* ~**er Wert** intrinsic value.

**introvertiert** [ɪntrovɛrˈtiːrt] *adj:* ~ **sein** to be an introvert.

**intuitiv** [ɪntuiˈtiːf] *adj* intuitive.

**intus** [ˈɪntʊs] *adj:* **etw** ~ **haben** (*umg: Wissen*) to have got sth into one's head; (*Essen, Trinken*) to have got sth down one (*umg*).

**Invalide** [ɪnvaˈliːdə] (**-n, -n**) *m* disabled person, invalid.

**Invalidenrente** *f* disability pension.

**Invasion** [ɪnvaziˈoːn] *f* invasion.

**Inventar** [ɪnvɛnˈtaːr] (**-s, -e**) *nt* inventory; (*COMM*) assets and liabilities *pl*.

**Inventur** [ɪnvɛnˈtuːr] *f* stocktaking; ~ **machen** to stocktake.

**investieren** [ɪnvɛsˈtiːrən] *vt* to invest.

**investiert** *adj:* ~**es Kapital** capital employed.

**Investition** [ɪnvɛstitsiˈoːn] *f* investment.

**Investitionszulage** *f* investment grant.

**Investmentgesellschaft** [ɪnˈvɛstməntɡəzɛlʃaft] *f* unit trust.

**inwiefern** [ɪnviˈfɛrn] *adv* how far, to what extent.

**inwieweit** [ɪnviˈvaɪt] *adv* how far, to what extent.

**Inzest** [ɪnˈtsɛst] (**-(e)s, -e**) *m* incest *no pl*.

**inzwischen** [ɪnˈtsvɪʃən] *adv* meanwhile.

**IOK** *nt abk* (= *Internationales Olympisches Komitee*) IOC.

**Ion** [iˈoːn] (**-s, -en**) *nt* ion.

**ionisch** [iˈoːnɪʃ] *adj* Ionian; **I~es Meer** Ionian Sea.

**IQ** *m abk* (= *Intelligenzquotient*) IQ.

**i.R.** *abk* (= *im Ruhestand*) retd.

**IRA** *f abk* (= *Irisch-Republikanische Armee*) IRA.

**Irak** [iˈraːk] (**-s**) *m:* (**der**) ~ Iraq.

**Iraker(in)** (**-s, -**) *m(f)* Iraqi.

**irakisch** *adj* Iraqi.

**Iran** [iˈraːn] (**-s**) *m:* (**der**) ~ Iran.

**Iraner(in)** (**-s, -**) *m(f)* Iranian.

**iranisch** *adj* Iranian.

**irdisch** [ˈɪrdɪʃ] *adj* earthly; **den Weg alles Irdischen gehen** to go the way of all flesh.

**Ire** [ˈiːrə] (**-n, -n**) *m* Irishman; Irish boy; **die** ~**n** the Irish.

**irgend** [ˈɪrɡənt] *adv* at all; **wann/was/wer** ~ whenever/whatever/whoever; ~ **jemand/ etwas** somebody/something; (*fragend, verneinend*) anybody/anything; ~**ein(e, s)** *adj* some, any; **haben Sie (sonst) noch** ~**einen Wunsch?** is there anything else you would like?; ~**eine(r, s)** *pron* (*Person*) somebody; (*Ding*) something; (*fragend, verneinend*) anybody/anything; **ich will nicht bloß** ~**ein(e)s** I don't want any old one; ~**einmal** *adv* sometime or other; (*fragend*) ever; ~**wann** *adv* sometime; ~**wer** (*umg*) *pron* somebody; (*fragend, verneinend*) anybody; ~**wie** *adv* somehow; ~**wo** *adv* somewhere (*BRIT*), someplace (*US*); (*fragend, verneinend, bedingend*) anywhere (*BRIT*), any place (*US*); ~**wohin** *adv* somewhere (*BRIT*), someplace (*US*); (*fragend, verneinend, bedingend*)

anywhere (*BRIT*), any place (*US*).

**Irin** [ˈiːrɪn] *f* Irishwoman; Irish girl.

**Iris** [ˈiːrɪs] (**-, -**) *f* iris.

**irisch** *adj* Irish; **I~e See** Irish Sea.

**IRK** *nt abk* (= *Internationales Rotes Kreuz*) IRC.

**Irland** [ˈɪrlant] (**-s**) *nt* Ireland; (*Republik* ~) Eire.

**Irländer** [ˈɪrlɛndər(ɪn)] (**-s, -**) *m* = **Ire**; ~**in** *f* = **Irin**.

**Ironie** [iroˈniː] *f* irony.

**ironisch** [iˈroːnɪʃ] *adj* ironic(al).

**irre** [ˈɪrə] *adj* crazy, mad; ~ **gut** (*umg*) way out (*umg*); **I~(r)** *f(m)* lunatic; ~**führen** *vt* to mislead; **I~führung** *f* fraud.

**irrelevant** [ˈɪrelevant] *adj:* ~ (**für**) irrelevant (for *od* to).

**irremachen** *vt* to confuse.

**irren** *vi* to be mistaken; (*umher*~) to wander, stray ♦ *vr* to be mistaken; **jeder kann sich mal** ~ anyone can make a mistake; **I~anstalt** *f* (*veraltet*) lunatic asylum; **I~haus** *nt:* **hier geht es zu wie im I~haus** (*umg*) this place is an absolute madhouse.

**Irrfahrt** [ˈɪrfaːrt] *f* wandering.

**irrig** [ˈɪrɪç] *adj* incorrect, wrong.

**irritieren** [ɪriˈtiːrən] *vt* (*verwirren*) to confuse, muddle; (*ärgern*) to irritate.

**Irr-** *zW:* ~**licht** *nt* will-o'-the-wisp; ~**sinn** *m* madness; **so ein** ~**sinn, das zu tun** what a crazy thing to do!; **i~sinnig** *adj* mad, crazy; (*umg*) terrific; **i~sinnig komisch** incredibly funny; ~**tum** (**-s, -tümer**) *m* mistake, error; **im** ~**tum sein** to be wrong *od* mistaken; ~**tum!** wrong!; **i~tümlich** *adj* mistaken.

**ISBN** *f abk* (= *Internationale Standardbuchnummer*) ISBN.

**Ischias** [ˈɪʃias] (**-**) *m od nt* sciatica.

**Islam** [ˈɪslam] (**-s**) *m* Islam.

**islamisch** [ɪsˈlaːmɪʃ] *adj* Islamic.

**Island** [ˈiːslant] (**-s**) *nt* Iceland.

**Isländer(in)** [ˈiːslɛndər(ɪn)] (**-s, -**) *m(f)* Icelander.

**isländisch** *adj* Icelandic.

**Isolation** [izolatsiˈoːn] *f* isolation; (*ELEK*) insulation; (*von Häftlingen*) solitary confinement.

**Isolator** [izoˈlaːtɔr] *m* insulator.

**Isolierband** *nt* insulating tape.

**isolieren** [izoˈliːrən] *vt* to isolate; (*ELEK*) to insulate.

**Isolierstation** *f* (*MED*) isolation ward.

**Isolierung** *f* isolation; (*ELEK*) insulation.

**Israel** [ˈɪsraeːl] (**-s**) *nt* Israel.

**Israeli**[1] [ɪsraˈeːli] (**-(s), -s**) *m* Israeli.

**Israeli**[2] [ɪsraˈeːli] (**-, -(s)**) *f* Israeli.

**israelisch** *adj* Israeli.

**ißt** [ɪst] *vb siehe* **essen**.

**ist** [ɪst] *vb siehe* **sein**.

**Istanbul** [ˈɪstambuːl] (**-s**) *nt* Istanbul.

**Ist-Bestand** *m* (*Geld*) cash in hand; (*Waren*) actual stock.

**Italien** [iˈtaːliən] (**-s**) *nt* Italy.

**Italiener(in)** [itali'e:nər(ın)] (-s, -) *m(f)* Italian.
**italienisch** *adj* Italian; **die ~e Schweiz**
Italian-speaking Switzerland.
**i.V., I.V.** *abk* (= *in Vertretung*) on behalf of;
(= *in Vollmacht*) by proxy.
**IWF** *m abk* (= *Internationaler Währungsfonds*)
IMF.

# J, j

**J, j** [jɔt] *nt* J, j; **~ wie Julius** ≈ J for Jack, J
for Jig (*US*).

═══════════ *SCHLÜSSELWORT*

**ja** [ja:] *adv* **1** yes; **haben Sie das gesehen? - ~**
did you see it? - yes(, I did); **ich glaube ~**
(yes) I think so; **zu allem ~ und amen sagen**
(*umg*) to accept everything without
question

**2** (*fragend*) really; **ich habe gekündigt - ~?**
I've quit - have you?; **du kommst, ~?** you're
coming, aren't you?

**3**: **sei ~ vorsichtig** do be careful; **Sie wissen
~, daß ...** as you know, ...; **tu das ~ nicht!**
don't do that!; **sie ist ~ erst fünf** (after all)
she's only five; **Sie wissen ~, wie das so ist**
you know how it is; **ich habe es ~ gewußt** I
just knew it; **~, also ...** well you see ...

**Jacht** [jaxt] (-, -en) *f* yacht.
**Jacke** ['jakə] (-, -n) *f* jacket; (*Woll~*)
cardigan.
**Jacketkrone** ['dʒɛkıtkro:nə] *f* (*Zahnkrone*)
jacket crown.
**Jackett** [ʒa'kɛt] (-s, -s *od* -e) *nt* jacket.
**Jagd** [ja:kt] (-, -en) *f* hunt; (*Jagen*) hunting;
**~beute** *f* kill; **~flugzeug** *nt* fighter; **~gewehr**
*nt* sporting gun; **~hund** *m* hunting dog;
**~schein** *m* hunting licence (*BRIT*) *od* license
(*US*); **~wurst** *f* smoked sausage.
**jagen** ['ja:gən] *vi* to hunt; (*eilen*) to race ♦ *vt* to
hunt; (*weg~*) to drive (off); (*verfolgen*) to
chase; **mit diesem Essen kannst
du mich ~** (*umg*) I wouldn't touch that food
with a barge pole (*BRIT*) *od* ten-foot pole
(*US*).
**Jäger** ['jɛ:gər] (-s, -) *m* hunter; **~in** *f* huntress,
huntswoman; **~latein** (*umg*) *nt* hunters' tales
*pl*; **~schnitzel** *nt* (*KOCH*) *cutlet served with
mushroom sauce.*
**jäh** [jɛ:] *adj* abrupt, sudden; (*steil*) steep,
precipitous; **~lings** *adv* abruptly.
**Jahr** [ja:r] (-(e)s, -e) *nt* year; **im ~(e) 1066** in
(the year) 1066; **die sechziger ~e** the sixties
*pl*; **mit dreißig ~en** at the age of thirty; **in**

**den besten ~en sein** to be in the prime of
(one's) life; **nach ~ und Tag** after (many)
years; **zwischen den ~en** (*umg*) between
Christmas and New Year; **j~aus** *adv*: **j~aus,
j~ein** year in, year out; **~buch** *nt* annual,
year book.
**jahrelang** *adv* for years.
**Jahres-** *zW*: **~abonnement** *nt* annual
subscription; **~abschluß** *m* end of the year;
(*COMM*) annual statement of account;
**~beitrag** *m* annual subscription; **~bericht** *m*
annual report; **~hauptversammlung** *f*
(*COMM*) annual general meeting, AGM;
**~karte** *f* annual season ticket; **~tag** *m*
anniversary; **~umsatz** *m* (*COMM*) yearly
turnover; **~wechsel** *m* turn of the year;
**~zahl** *f* date, year; **~zeit** *f* season.
**Jahr-** *zW*: **~gang** *m* age group; (*von Wein*)
vintage; **er ist ~gang 1950** he was born in
1950; **~hundert** *nt* century; **~hundertfeier** *f*
centenary; **~hundertwende** *f* turn of the
century.
**jährlich** ['jɛ:rlıç] *adj, adv* yearly; **zweimal ~**
twice a year.
**Jahr-** *zW*: **~markt** *m* fair; **~tausend** *nt*
millennium; **~zehnt** *nt* decade.
**Jähzorn** ['jɛ:tsɔrn] *m* hot temper.
**jähzornig** *adj* hot-tempered.
**Jalousie** [ʒalu'zi:] *f* venetian blind.
**Jamaika** [ja'maıka] (-s) *nt* Jamaica.
**Jammer** ['jamər] (-s) *m* misery; **es ist ein ~,
daß ...** it is a crying shame that ...
**jämmerlich** ['jɛmərlıç] *adj* wretched, pathetic;
**J~keit** *f* wretchedness.
**jammern** *vi* to wail ♦ *vt unpers*: **es jammert
mich** it makes me feel sorry.
**jammerschade** *adj*: **es ist ~** it is a crying
shame.
**Jan.** *abk* (= *Januar*) Jan.
**Januar** ['janua:r] (-s, -e) (*pl selten*) *m* January;
*siehe auch* **September**.
**Japan** ['ja:pan] (-s) *nt* Japan.
**Japaner(in)** [ja'pa:nər(ın)] (-s, -) *m(f)*
Japanese.
**japanisch** *adj* Japanese.
**Jargon** [ʒar'gõ:] (-s, -s) *m* jargon.
**Jasager** ['ja:za:gər] (-s, -) (*pej*) *m* yes man.
**Jastimme** *f* vote in favour (*BRIT*) *od* favor
(*US*) (of).
**jäten** ['jɛ:tən] *vt, vi* to weed.
**Jauche** ['jaʊxə] *f* liquid manure; **~grube** *f*
cesspool, cesspit.
**jauchzen** ['jaʊxtsən] *vi* to rejoice, shout (with
joy).
**Jauchzer** (-s, -) *m* shout of joy.
**jaulen** ['jaʊlən] *vi* to howl.
**Jause** ['jaʊzə] (*ÖSTERR*) *f* snack.
**jawohl** *adv* yes (of course).
**Jawort** *nt* consent; **jdm das ~ geben** to
consent to marry sb; (*bei Trauung*) to say "I
do".
**Jazz** [dʒæz] (-) *m* jazz; **~keller** *m* jazz club.

===================== SCHLÜSSELWORT

**je** [jeː] *adv* **1** (*jemals*) ever; **hast du so was ~ gesehen?** did you ever see anything like it?
**2** (*jeweils*) every, each; **sie zahlten ~ 3 Mark** they paid 3 marks each
♦ *konj* **1**: **~ nach** depending on; **~ nachdem** it depends; **~ nachdem, ob** ... depending on whether ...
**2**: **~ eher, desto** *od* **um so besser** the sooner the better; **~ länger, ~ lieber** the longer the better.

**Jeans** [dʒiːnz] *pl* jeans *pl*; **~anzug** *m* denim suit.
**jede(r, s)** ['jeːdə(r, s)] *adj* (*einzeln*) each; (*von zweien*) either; (**~ von allen**) every ♦ *indef pron* (*einzeln*) each (one); (**~ von allen**) everyone, everybody; **ohne ~ Anstrengung** without any effort; **~r zweite** every other (one).
**jedenfalls** *adv* in any case.
**jedermann** *pron* everyone; **das ist nicht ~s Sache** it's not everyone's cup of tea.
**jederzeit** *adv* at any time.
**jedesmal** *adv* every time, each time.
**jedoch** [je'dɔx] *adv* however.
**jeher** ['jeːheːr] *adv*: **von ~** all along.
**jein** [jaɪn] *adv* (*hum*) yes no.
**jemals** ['jeːmaːls] *adv* ever.
**jemand** ['jeːmant] *indef pron* someone, somebody; (*bei Fragen, bedingenden Sätzen, Negation*) anyone, anybody.
**Jemen** ['jeːmən] (**-s**) *m* Yemen.
**Jemenit(in)** [jeme'niːt(ɪn)] (**-en, -en**) *m(f)* Yemeni.
**jemenitisch** *adj* Yemeni.
**Jenaer Glas** ® ['jeːnaːrglaːs] *nt* heatproof glass, ≈ Pyrex ®.
**jene(r, s)** ['jeːnə(r, s)] *adj* that; (*pl*) those ♦ *pron* that one; (*pl*) those; (*der Vorherige, die Vorherigen*) the former.
**jenseits** ['jeːnzaɪts] *adv* on the other side ♦ *präp +gen* on the other side of, beyond; **J~** *nt:* **das J~** the hereafter, the beyond; **jdn ins J~ befördern** (*umg*) to send sb to kingdom come.
**Jesus** ['jeːzʊs] (**Jesu**) *m* Jesus; **~ Christus** Jesus Christ.
**jetten** ['dʒɛtən] (*umg*) *vi* to jet (*inf*).
**jetzig** ['jɛtsɪç] *adj* present.
**jetzt** [jɛtst] *adv* now; **~ gleich** right now.
**jeweilig** *adj* respective; **die ~e Regierung** the government of the day.
**jeweils** *adv*: **~ zwei zusammen** two at a time; **zu ~ 5 DM** at 5 marks each; **~ das erste** the first each time; **~ am Monatsletzten** on the last day of each month.
**Jg.** *abk* = **Jahrgang**.
**Jh.** *abk* (= *Jahrhundert*) cent.
**jiddisch** ['jɪdɪʃ] *adj* Yiddish.
**Job** [dʒɔp] (**-s, -s**) (*umg*) *m* job.

**jobben** ['dʒɔbən] (*umg*) *vi* to work, have a job.
**Joch** [jɔx] (**-(e)s, -e**) *nt* yoke.
**Jochbein** *nt* cheekbone.
**Jockei** ['dʒɔke] (**-s, -s**) *m* jockey.
**Jod** [joːt] (**-(e)s**) *nt* iodine.
**jodeln** ['joːdəln] *vi* to yodel.
**joggen** ['dʒɔgən] *vi* to jog.
**Joghurt** ['joːgʊrt] (**-s, -s**) *m* od *nt* yog(h)urt.
**Johannisbeere** [jo'hanɪsbeːrə] *f*: **rote ~** redcurrant; **schwarze ~** blackcurrant.
**johlen** ['joːlən] *vi* to yell.
**Joint** [dʒɔɪnt] (**-s, -s**) (*umg*) *m* joint.
**Joint-venture** ['dʒɔɪntventʃə'] (**-, -s**) *nt* joint venture.
**Jolle** ['jɔlə] (**-, -n**) *f* dinghy.
**Jongleur** [ʒõ'gløːr] (**-s, -e**) *m* juggler.
**jonglieren** [ʒõ'gliːrən] *vi* to juggle.
**Joppe** ['jɔpə] (**-, -n**) *f* jacket.
**Jordanien** [jɔr'daːniən] (**-s**) *nt* Jordan.
**Jordanier(in)** [jɔr'daːniər(ɪn)] (**-s, -**) *m(f)* Jordanian.
**jordanisch** *adj* Jordanian.
**Journalismus** [ʒʊrna'lɪsmʊs] *m* journalism.
**Journalist(in)** [ʒʊrna'lɪst(ɪn)] *m(f)* journalist; **j~isch** *adj* journalistic.
**Jubel** ['juːbəl] (**-s**) *m* rejoicing; **~, Trubel, Heiterkeit** laughter and merriment; **~jahr** *nt:* **alle ~jahre (einmal)** (*umg*) once in a blue moon.
**jubeln** *vi* to rejoice.
**Jubilar(in)** [jubi'laːr(ɪn)] (**-s, -e**) *m(f) person celebrating an anniversary*.
**Jubiläum** [jubi'lɛːʊm] (**-s, Jubiläen**) *nt* jubilee; (*Jahrestag*) anniversary.
**jucken** ['jʊkən] *vi* to itch ♦ *vt:* **es juckt mich am Arm** my arm is itching; **das juckt mich** that's itchy; **das juckt mich doch nicht** (*umg*) I don't care.
**Juckpulver** *nt* itching powder.
**Juckreiz** *m* itch.
**Judaslohn** ['juːdaslɔːn] *m* (*liter*) blood money.
**Jude** ['juːdə] (**-n, -n**) *m* Jew.
**Juden-** *zW:* **~stern** *m* star of David; **~tum** (**-s**) *nt* (*die Juden*) Jewry; **~verfolgung** *f* persecution of the Jews.
**Jüdin** ['jyːdɪn] *f* Jewess.
**jüdisch** *adj* Jewish.
**Judo** ['juːdo] (**-(s)**) *nt* judo.
**Jugend** ['juːgənt] (**-**) *f* youth; **~amt** *nt* youth welfare department; **j~frei** *adj* suitable for young people; (*FILM*) U(-certificate), G (*US*); **~herberge** *f* youth hostel; **~hilfe** *f* youth welfare scheme; **~kriminalität** *f* juvenile crime; **j~lich** *adj* youthful; **~liche(r)** *f(m)* teenager, young person; **~liebe** *f* (*Geliebte(r)*) love of one's youth; **~richter** *m* juvenile court judge; **~schutz** *m* protection of children and young people; **~stil** *m* (*KUNST*) Art Nouveau; **~strafanstalt** *f* youth custody centre (*BRIT*); **~sünde** *f* youthful misdeed; **~zentrum** *nt* youth centre (*BRIT*) *od* center (*US*).
**Jugoslawe** [jugo'slaːvə] (**-n, -n**) *m* Yugoslav.

**Jugoslawien** [jugoˈslaːviən] (**-s**) nt
  Yugoslavia.
**Jugoslawin** [jugoˈslaːvɪn] f Yugoslav.
**jugoslawisch** adj Yugoslav(ian).
**Juli** [ˈjuːli] (**-(s)**, **-s**) (pl selten) m July; siehe auch
  **September**.
**jun.** abk (= junior) jun.
**jung** [jʊŋ] adj young.
**Junge** (**-n**, **-n**) m boy, lad ♦ nt young animal;
  (pl) young pl.
**Jünger** [ˈjʏŋər] (**-s**, **-**) m disciple.
**jünger** adj younger.
**Jungfer** (**-**, **-n**) f: alte ~ old maid.
**Jungfernfahrt** f maiden voyage.
**Jung-** zW: ~**frau** f virgin; (ASTROL) Virgo;
  ~**geselle** m bachelor; ~**gesellin** f bachelor
  girl; (älter) single woman.
**Jüngling** [ˈjʏŋlɪŋ] m youth.
**Jungsozialist** m (BRD POL) Young Socialist.
**jüngst** [jʏŋst] adv lately, recently.
**jüngste(r, s)** adj youngest; (neueste) latest;
  **das J~ Gericht** the Last Judgement; **der
  J~ Tag** Doomsday, the Day of Judgement.
**Jungwähler(in)** m(f) young voter.
**Juni** [ˈjuːni] (**-(s)**, **-s**) (pl selten) m June; siehe
  auch **September**.
**Junior** [ˈjuːniɔr] (**-s**, **-en**) m junior.
**Junta** [ˈxʊnta] (**-**, **-ten**) f (POL) junta.
**jur.** abk = juristisch.
**Jura** [ˈjuːra] no art (UNIV) law.
**Jurist(in)** [juˈrɪst(ɪn)] m(f) jurist, lawyer;
  (Student) law student; **j~isch** adj legal.
**Juso** [ˈjuːzo] (**-s**, **-s**) m abk = **Jungsozialist**.
**just** [jʊst] adv just.
**Justiz** [jʊsˈtiːts] (**-**) f justice; ~**beamte(r)** m
  judicial officer; ~**irrtum** m miscarriage of
  justice; ~**minister** m minister of justice;
  ~**mord** m judicial murder.
**Juwel** [juˈveːl] (**-s**, **-en**) m od nt jewel.
**Juwelier** [juveˈliːr] (**-s**, **-e**) m jeweller (BRIT),
  jeweler (US); ~**geschäft** nt jeweller's (BRIT)
  od jeweler's (US) (shop).
**Jux** [jʊks] (**-es**, **-e**) m joke, lark; **etw aus
  ~ tun/sagen** (umg) to do/say sth in fun.
**jwd** [jɔtveːˈdeː] adv (hum) in the back of
  beyond.

# K, k

**K, k** [kaː] nt K, k; ~ **wie Kaufmann** ≈ K for
  King.
**Kabarett** [kabaˈrɛt] (**-s**, **-e** od **-s**) nt cabaret;
  ~**ist(in)** [kabarɛˈtɪst(ɪn)] m(f) cabaret artiste.
**Kabel** [ˈkaːbəl] (**-s**, **-**) nt (ELEK) wire; (stark)
  cable; ~**anschluß** m: ~**anschluß haben** to
  have cable television; ~**fernsehen** nt cable
  television.
**Kabeljau** [ˈkaːbəljaʊ] (**-s**, **-e** od **-s**) m cod.
**kabeln** vt, vi to cable.
**Kabelsalat** (umg) m tangle of cable.
**Kabine** [kaˈbiːnə] f cabin; (Zelle) cubicle.
**Kabinett** [kabiˈnɛt] (**-s**, **-e**) nt (POL) cabinet;
  (kleines Zimmer) small room ♦ m high-quality
  German white wine.
**Kachel** [ˈkaxəl] (**-**, **-n**) f tile.
**kacheln** vt to tile.
**Kachelofen** m tiled stove.
**Kacke** [ˈkakə] (**-**, **-n**) (umg!) f crap (!).
**Kadaver** [kaˈdaːvər] (**-s**, **-**) m carcass.
**Kader** [ˈkaːdər] (**-s**, **-**) m (MIL, POL) cadre;
  (SPORT) squad; (DDR, SCHWEIZ: Fachleute)
  group of specialists; ~**schmiede** f (POL:
  umg) institution for the training of cadre
  personnel.
**Kadett** [kaˈdɛt] (**-en**, **-en**) m cadet.
**Käfer** [ˈkɛːfər] (**-s**, **-**) m beetle.
**Kaff** [kaf] (**-s**, **-s**) (umg) nt dump, hole.
**Kaffee** [ˈkafe] (**-s**, **-s**) m coffee; **zwei ~, bitte!**
  two coffees, please; **das ist kalter ~** (umg)
  that's old hat; ~**kanne** f coffeepot; ~**klatsch**
  m, ~**kränzchen** nt coffee circle; ~**löffel** m
  coffee spoon; ~**maschine** f coffee maker;
  ~**mühle** f coffee grinder; ~**satz** m coffee
  grounds pl; ~**tante** f (hum) coffee addict; (in
  Café) old biddy; ~**wärmer** m cosy (for
  coffeepot).
**Käfig** [ˈkɛːfɪç] (**-s**, **-e**) m cage.
**kahl** [kaːl] adj bald; ~**fressen** unreg vt to strip
  bare; ~**geschoren** adj shaven, shorn; **K~heit**
  f baldness; ~**köpfig** adj bald-headed;
  **K~schlag** m (in Wald) clearing.
**Kahn** [kaːn] (**-(e)s**, **⁻e**) m boat, barge.
**Kai** [kaɪ] (**-s**, **-e** od **-s**) m quay.
**Kairo** [ˈkaɪro] (**-s**) nt Cairo.
**Kaiser** [ˈkaɪzər] (**-s**, **-**) m emperor; ~**in** f
  empress; **k~lich** adj imperial; ~**reich** nt
  empire; ~**schmarren** [ˈkaɪzərʃmarən] m
  (KOCH) sugared, cut-up pancake with
  raisins; ~**schnitt** m (MED) Caesarean (BRIT)
  od Cesarean (US) (section).
**Kajak** [ˈkaːjak] (**-s**, **-s**) m or nt kayak.

**Kajüte** [ka'jy:tə] (-, -n) f cabin.
**Kakao** [ka'ka:o] (-s, -s) m cocoa; **jdn durch den
~ ziehen** (*umg: veralbern*) to make fun of sb;
(: *boshaft reden*) to run sb down.
**Kakerlak** ['ka:kərlak] (-en, -en) m cockroach.
**Kaktee** [kak'te:ə] (-, -n) f cactus.
**Kaktus** ['kaktʊs] (-, -se) m cactus.
**Kalabrien** [ka'la:briən] (-s) nt Calabria.
**Kalauer** ['ka:laʊər] (-s, -) m corny joke;
(*Wortspiel*) corny pun.
**Kalb** [kalp] (-(e)s, ̈-er) nt calf; **k~en** ['kalbən] vi
to calve; **~fleisch** nt veal.
**Kalbsleder** nt calf(skin).
**Kalender** [ka'lɛndər] (-s, -) m calendar;
(*Taschen~*) diary.
**Kali** ['ka:li] (-s, -s) nt potash.
**Kaliber** [ka'li:bər] (-s, -) nt (*lit, fig*) calibre
(*BRIT*), caliber (*US*).
**Kalifornien** [kali'fɔrniən] (-s) nt California.
**Kalk** [kalk] (-(e)s, -e) m lime; (*BIOL*) calcium;
**~stein** m limestone.
**Kalkül** [kal'ky:l] (-s, -e) m od nt (*geh*)
calculation.
**Kalkulation** [kalkulatsi'o:n] f calculation.
**Kalkulator** [kalku'la:tɔr] m cost accountant.
**kalkulieren** [kalku'li:rən] vt to calculate.
**kalkuliert** adj: **~es Risiko** calculated risk.
**Kalkutta** [kal'kʊta] (-s) nt Calcutta.
**Kalorie** [kalo'ri:] (-, -n) f calorie.
**kalorienarm** adj low-calorie.
**kalt** [kalt] adj cold; **mir ist (es) ~** I am cold; **~e
Platte** cold meat; **der K~e Krieg** the Cold
War; **etw ~ stellen** to put sth to chill; **die
Wohnung kostet ~ 980 DM** the flat costs 980
DM without heating; **~bleiben** unreg vi to be
unmoved; **~blütig** adj cold-blooded; (*ruhig*)
cool; **K~blütigkeit** f cold-bloodedness;
coolness.
**Kälte** ['kɛltə] (-) f coldness; (*Wetter*) cold;
**~einbruch** m cold spell; **~grad** m degree of
frost od below zero; **~welle** f cold spell.
**kalt-** zW: **~herzig** adj cold-hearted; **~lächelnd**
adv (*ironisch*) cool as you please; **~machen**
(*umg*) vt to do in; **K~miete** f rent exclusive
of heating; **K~schale** f (*KOCH*) cold sweet
soup; **~schnäuzig** adj cold, unfeeling;
**~stellen** vt to chill; (*fig*) to leave out in the
cold.
**Kalzium** ['kaltsiʊm] (-s) nt calcium.
**kam** etc [ka:m] vb siehe **kommen**.
**Kambodscha** [kam'bɔdʒa] nt Cambodia.
**Kamel** [ka'me:l] (-(e)s, -e) nt camel.
**Kamera** ['kamera] (-, -s) f camera; **~-
Recorder** m camcorder.
**Kamerad(in)** [kamə'ra:t,-'ra:dɪn] (-en, -en) m(f)
comrade, friend; **~schaft** f comradeship;
**k~schaftlich** adj comradely.
**Kameraführung** f camera work.
**Kameramann** (-(e)s, pl -männer) m
cameraman.
**Kamerun** ['kaməru:n] (-s) nt Cameroon.
**Kamille** [ka'mɪlə] (-, -n) f camomile.

**Kamillentee** m camomile tea.
**Kamin** [ka'mi:n] (-s, -e) m (*außen*) chimney;
(*innen*) fireside; (*Feuerstelle*) fireplace;
**~feger** (-s, -) m chimney sweep; **~kehrer**
(-s, -) m chimney sweep.
**Kamm** [kam] (-(e)s, ̈-e) m comb; (*Berg~*)
ridge; (*Hahnen~*) crest; **alle/alles über einen
~ scheren** (*fig*) to lump everyone/
everything together.
**kämmen** ['kɛmən] vt to comb.
**Kammer** ['kamər] (-, -n) f chamber; (*Zimmer*)
small bedroom; **~diener** m valet; **~jäger** m
(*Schädlingsbekämpfer*) pest controller;
**~musik** f chamber music; **~zofe** f
chambermaid.
**Kammstück** nt (*KOCH*) shoulder.
**Kampagne** [kam'panjə] (-, -n) f campaign.
**Kampf** [kampf] (-(e)s, ̈-e) m fight, battle;
(*Wettbewerb*) contest; (*fig: Anstrengung*)
struggle; **jdm/etw den ~ ansagen** (*fig*) to
declare war on sb/sth; **k~bereit** adj ready
for action.
**kämpfen** ['kɛmpfən] vi to fight; **ich habe lange
mit mir ~ müssen, ehe ...** I had a long battle
with myself before ...
**Kampfer** ['kampfər] (-s) m camphor.
**Kämpfer(in)** (-s, -) m(f) fighter, combatant.
**Kampf-** zW: **~flugzeug** nt fighter (aircraft);
**~geist** m fighting spirit; **~handlung** f
action; **~kunst** f martial arts pl; **k~los** adj
without a fight; **k~lustig** adj pugnacious;
**~platz** m battlefield; (*SPORT*) arena,
stadium; **~richter** m (*SPORT*) referee;
**~sport** m martial art.
**Kampuchea** [kampu'tʃe:a] (-s) nt Kampuchea.
**Kanada** ['kanada] (-s) nt Canada.
**Kanadier(in)** [ka'na:diər(ɪn)] (-s, -) m(f)
Canadian.
**kanadisch** [ka'na:dɪʃ] adj Canadian.
**Kanal** [ka'na:l] (-s, Kanäle) m (*Fluß*) canal;
(*Rinne*) channel; (*für Abfluß*) drain; **der ~**
(*auch*: **der Ärmelkanal**) the (English)
Channel.
**Kanalinseln** pl Channel Islands pl.
**Kanalisation** [kanalizatsi'o:n] f sewage
system.
**kanalisieren** [kanali'zi:rən] vt to provide with
a sewage system; (*fig: Energie etc*) to
channel.
**Kanaltunnel** m Channel Tunnel.
**Kanarienvogel** [ka'na:riənfo:gəl] m canary.
**Kanarische Inseln** [ka'na:rɪʃə'ɪnzəln] pl
Canary Islands pl, Canaries pl.
**Kandare** [kan'da:rə] (-, -n) f: **jdn an die
~ nehmen** (*fig*) to take sb in hand.
**Kandidat(in)** [kandi'da:t(ɪn)] (-en, -en) m(f)
candidate; **jdn als ~en aufstellen** to
nominate sb.
**Kandidatur** [kandida'tu:r] f candidature,
candidacy.
**kandidieren** [kandi'di:rən] vi (*POL*) to stand,
run.

**kandiert** [kan'diːrt] *adj* (*Frucht*) candied.
**Kandis(zucker)** ['kandıs(tsʊkər)] (-) *m* rock candy.
**Känguruh** ['kɛŋguru] (-s, -s) *nt* kangaroo.
**Kaninchen** [ka'niːnçən] *nt* rabbit.
**Kanister** [ka'nıstər] (-s, -) *m* can, canister.
**kann** [kan] *vb siehe* **können**.
**Kännchen** ['kɛnçən] *nt* pot; (*für Milch*) jug.
**Kanne** ['kanə] (-, -n) *f* (*Krug*) jug; (*Kaffee~*) pot; (*Milch~*) churn; (*Gieß~*) watering can.
**Kannibale** [kani'baːlə] (-n, -n) *m* cannibal.
**kannte** *etc* ['kantə] *vb siehe* **kennen**.
**Kanon** ['kaːnɔn] (-s, -s) *m* canon.
**Kanone** [ka'noːnə] (-, -n) *f* gun; (*HIST*) cannon; (*fig: Mensch*) ace; **das ist unter aller ~** (*umg*) that defies description.
**Kanonenfutter** (*umg*) *nt* cannon fodder.
**Kant.** *abk* = **Kanton.**
**Kantate** [kan'taːtə] (-, -n) *f* cantata.
**Kante** ['kantə] (-, -n) *f* edge; **Geld auf die hohe ~ legen** (*umg*) to put money by.
**kantig** ['kantıç] *adj* (*Holz*) edged; (*Gesicht*) angular.
**Kantine** [kan'tiːnə] *f* canteen.
**Kanton** [kan'toːn] (-s, -e) *m* canton.
**Kantor** ['kantɔr] *m* choirmaster.
**Kanu** ['kaːnu] (-s, -s) *nt* canoe.
**Kanzel** ['kantsəl] (-, -n) *f* pulpit; (*AVIAT*) cockpit.
**Kanzlei** [kants'laı] *f* chancery; (*Büro*) chambers *pl*.
**Kanzler** ['kantslər] (-s, -) *m* chancellor.
**Kap** [kap] (-s, -s) *nt* cape; **das ~ der guten Hoffnung** the Cape of Good Hope.
**Kapazität** [kapatsi'tɛːt] *f* capacity; (*Fachmann*) authority.
**Kapelle** [ka'pɛlə] *f* (*Gebäude*) chapel; (*MUS*) band.
**Kapellmeister(in)** *m(f)* director of music; (*MIL, von Tanzkapelle etc*) bandmaster, bandleader.
**Kaper** ['kaːpər] (-, -n) *f* caper.
**kapern** *vt* to capture.
**kapieren** [ka'piːrən] (*umg*) *vt, vi* to understand.
**Kapital** [kapi'taːl] (-s, -e *od* -ien) *nt* capital; **aus etw ~ schlagen** (*pej: lit, fig*) to make capital out of sth; **~anlage** *f* investment; **~aufwand** *m* capital expenditure; **~ertrag** *m* capital gains *pl*; **~ertragssteuer** *f* capital gains tax; **~flucht** *f* flight of capital; **~gesellschaft** *f* (*COMM*) joint-stock company; **~güter** *pl* capital goods *pl*; **k~intensiv** *adj* capital-intensive.
**Kapitalismus** [kapita'lısmʊs] *m* capitalism.
**Kapitalist** [kapita'lıst] *m* capitalist.
**kapitalistisch** *adj* capitalist.
**Kapital-** *zW:* **k~kräftig** *adj* wealthy; **~markt** *m* money market; **~verbrechen** *nt* serious crime; (*mit Todesstrafe*) capital crime.
**Kapitän** [kapi'tɛːn] (-s, -e) *m* captain.
**Kapitel** [ka'pıtəl] (-s, -) *nt* chapter; **ein trauriges ~** (*Angelegenheit*) a sad story.

**Kapitulation** [kapitulatsi'oːn] *f* capitulation.
**kapitulieren** [kapitu'liːrən] *vi* to capitulate.
**Kaplan** [ka'plaːn] (-s, **Kapläne**) *m* chaplain.
**Kappe** ['kapə] (-, -n) *f* cap; (*Kapuze*) hood; **das nehme ich auf meine ~** (*fig: umg*) I'll take the responsibility for that.
**kappen** *vt* to cut.
**Kapsel** ['kapsəl] (-, -n) *f* capsule.
**Kapstadt** ['kapʃtat] *nt* Cape Town.
**kaputt** [ka'pʊt] (*umg*) *adj* smashed, broken; (*Person*) exhausted, knackered; **der Fernseher ist ~** the TV's not working; **ein ~er Typ** a bum; **~gehen** *unreg vi* to break; (*Schuhe*) to fall apart; (*Firma*) to go bust; (*Stoff*) to wear out; (*sterben*) to cop it (*umg*); **~lachen** *vr* to laugh o.s. silly; **~machen** *vt* to break; (*Mensch*) to exhaust, wear out; **~schlagen** *unreg vt* to smash.
**Kapuze** [ka'puːtsə] (-, -n) *f* hood.
**Karabiner** [kara'biːnər] (-s, -) *m* (*Gewehr*) carbine.
**Karacho** [ka'raxo] (-s) *nt:* **mit ~** (*umg*) hell for leather.
**Karaffe** [ka'rafə] (-, -n) *f* carafe; (*geschliffen*) decanter.
**Karambolage** [karambo'laːʒə] (-, -n) *f* (*Zusammenstoß*) crash.
**Karamel** [kara'mɛl] (-s) *m* caramel; **~bonbon** *m od nt* toffee.
**Karat** [ka'raːt] (-(e)s, -e) *nt* carat.
**Karate** (-s) *nt* karate.
**Karawane** [kara'vaːnə] (-, -n) *f* caravan.
**Kardinal** [kardi'naːl] (-s, **Kardinäle**) *m* cardinal; **~fehler** *m* cardinal error; **~zahl** *f* cardinal number.
**Karenzzeit** [ka'rɛntstsaıt] *f* waiting period.
**Karfreitag** [kaːr'fraıtaːk] *m* Good Friday.
**karg** [kark] *adj* scanty, poor; (*Mahlzeit*) meagre (*BRIT*), meager (*US*); **etw ~ bemessen** to be mean with sth; **K~heit** *f* poverty, scantiness; meagreness (*BRIT*), meagerness (*US*).
**kärglich** ['kɛrklıç] *adj* poor, scanty.
**Kargo** ['kargo] (-s, -s) *m* (*COMM*) cargo.
**Karibik** [ka'riːbık] (-) *f:* **die ~** the Caribbean.
**karibisch** *adj* Caribbean; **das K~e Meer** the Caribbean Sea.
**kariert** [ka'riːrt] *adj* (*Stoff*) checked (*BRIT*), checkered (*US*); (*Papier*) squared; **~ reden** (*umg*) to talk rubbish *od* nonsense.
**Karies** ['kaːriɛs] (-) *f* caries.
**Karikatur** [karika'tuːr] *f* caricature; **~ist(in)** [karikatu'rıst(ın)] *m(f)* cartoonist.
**karikieren** [kari'kiːrən] *vt* to caricature.
**karitativ** [karita'tiːf] *adj* charitable.
**Karneval** ['karnəval] (-s, -e *od* -s) *m* carnival.

---

**Karneval** *is the name given to the days immediately before Lent when people gather to sing, dance, eat, drink and generally make merry before the fasting begins.* **Rosenmontag,** *the day before Shrove Tuesday, is the most* *important day of Karneval on the Rhine. Most firms take a day's holiday on that day to enjoy the parades and revelry. In South Germany Karneval is called Fasching.*

**Karnickel** [kar'nɪkəl] (**-s**, **-**) (*umg*) *nt* rabbit.

**Kärnten** ['kɛrntən] (**-s**) *nt* Carinthia.

**Karo** ['ka:ro] (**-s**, **-s**) *nt* square; (*KARTEN*) diamonds; **~-As** *nt* ace of diamonds.

**Karosse** [ka'rɔsə] (**-**, **-n**) *f* coach, carriage.

**Karosserie** [karɔsə'ri:] *f* (*AUT*) body(work).

**Karotte** [ka'rɔtə] (**-**, **-n**) *f* carrot.

**Karpaten** [kar'pa:tən] *pl* Carpathians *pl*.

**Karpfen** ['karpfən] (**-s**, **-**) *m* carp.

**Karre** ['karə] (**-**, **-n**) *f* = **Karren**.

**Karree** [ka:'re:] (**-s**, **-s**) *nt*: **einmal ums ~ gehen** (*umg*) to walk around the block.

**karren** ['karən] *vt* to cart, transport; **K~** (**-s**, **-**) *m* cart, barrow; **den K~ aus dem Dreck ziehen** (*umg*) to get things sorted out.

**Karriere** [kari'ɛ:rə] (**-**, **-n**) *f* career; **~ machen** to get on, get to the top; **~macher(in)** *m(f)* careerist.

**Karsamstag** [ka:r'zamsta:k] *m* Easter Saturday.

**Karst** [karst] (**-s**, **-e**) *m* (*GEOG, GEOL*) karst, *barren landscape*.

**Karte** ['kartə] (**-**, **-n**) *f* card; (*Land~*) map; (*Speise~*) menu; (*Eintritts~, Fahr~*) ticket; **mit offenen ~n spielen** (*fig*) to put one's cards on the table; **alles auf eine ~ setzen** to put all one's eggs in one basket.

**Kartei** [kar'taɪ] *f* card index; **~karte** *f* index card; **~leiche** (*umg*) *f* sleeping *od* non-active member; **~schrank** *m* filing cabinet.

**Kartell** [kar'tɛl] (**-s**, **-e**) *nt* cartel; **~amt** *nt* monopolies commission; **~gesetzgebung** *f* anti-trust legislation.

**Karten-** *zW*: **~haus** *nt* (*lit, fig*) house of cards; **~legen** *nt* fortune-telling (*using cards*); **~spiel** *nt* card game; (*Karten*) pack (*BRIT*) *od* deck (*US*) of cards; **~telefon** *nt* cardphone; **~vorverkauf** *m* advance sale of tickets.

**Kartoffel** [kar'tɔfəl] (**-**, **-n**) *f* potato; **~brei** *m* mashed potatoes *pl*; **~chips** *pl* potato crisps *pl* (*BRIT*), potato chips *pl* (*US*); **~püree** *nt* mashed potatoes *pl*; **~salat** *m* potato salad.

**Karton** [kar'tõ:] (**-s**, **-s**) *m* cardboard; (*Schachtel*) cardboard box.

**kartoniert** [karto'ni:rt] *adj* hardback.

**Karussell** [karu'sɛl] (**-s**, **-s**) *nt* roundabout (*BRIT*), merry-go-round.

**Karwoche** ['ka:rvɔxə] *f* Holy Week.

**Karzinom** [kartsi'no:m] (**-s**, **-e**) *nt* (*MED*) carcinoma.

**Kasachstan** [kazaxs'ta:n] (**-s**) *nt* (*GEOG*) Kazakhstan.

**Kaschemme** [ka'ʃɛmə] (**-**, **-n**) *f* dive.

**kaschieren** [ka'ʃi:rən] *vt* to conceal, cover up.

**Kaschmir** ['kaʃmi:r] (**-s**) *nt* (*GEOG*) Kashmir.

**Käse** ['kɛ:zə] (**-s**, **-**) *m* cheese; (*umg: Unsinn*) rubbish, twaddle; **~blatt** (*umg*) *nt* (*local*)

rag; **~glocke** *f* cheese cover; **~kuchen** *m* cheesecake.

**Kaserne** [ka'zɛrnə] (**-**, **-n**) *f* barracks *pl*.

**Kasernenhof** *m* parade ground.

**käsig** ['kɛ:zɪç] *adj* (*fig: umg: Gesicht, Haut*) pasty, pale; (*vor Schreck*) white; (*lit*) cheesy.

**Kasino** [ka'zi:no] (**-s**, **-s**) *nt* club; (*MIL*) officers' mess; (*Spiel~*) casino.

**Kaskoversicherung** ['kaskofɛrzɪçərʊŋ] *f* (*AUT: Teil~*) ≈ third party, fire and theft insurance; (: *Voll~*) fully comprehensive insurance.

**Kasper** ['kaspər] (**-s**, **-**) *m* Punch; (*fig*) clown.

**Kasperl(e)theater** ['kaspərl(ə)tea:tər] *nt* Punch and Judy (show).

**Kaspisches Meer** ['kaspɪʃəs'me:r] *nt* Caspian Sea.

**Kasse** ['kasə] (**-**, **-n**) *f* (*Geldkasten*) cashbox; (*in Geschäft*) till, cash register; (*Kino~, Theater~ etc*) box office; (*Kranken~*) health insurance; (*Spar~*) savings bank; **die ~ führen** to be in charge of the money; **jdn zur ~ bitten** to ask sb to pay up; **~ machen** to count the money; **getrennte ~ führen** to pay separately; **an der ~** (*in Geschäft*) at the (cash) desk; **gut bei ~ sein** to be in the money.

**Kasseler** ['kasələr] (**-s**, **-**) *nt lightly smoked pork loin.*

**Kassen-** *zW*: **~arzt** *m* ≈ National Health doctor (*BRIT*), panel doctor (*US*); **~bestand** *m* cash balance; **~führer** *m* (*COMM*) cashier; **~patient** *m* ≈ National Health patient (*BRIT*); **~prüfung** *f* audit; **~schlager** (*umg*) *m* (*THEAT etc*) box-office hit; (: *Ware*) big seller; **~sturz** *m*: **~sturz machen** to check one's money; **~wart** *m* (*von Klub etc*) treasurer; **~zettel** *m* sales slip.

**Kasserolle** [kasə'rɔlə] (**-**, **-n**) *f* casserole.

**Kassette** [ka'sɛtə] *f* small box; (*Tonband, PHOT*) cassette; (*COMPUT*) cartridge, cassette; (*Bücher~*) case.

**Kassettenrecorder** (**-s**, **-**) *m* cassette recorder.

**Kassiber** [ka'si:bər] (**-s**, **-**) *m* (*in Gefängnis*) secret message.

**kassieren** [ka'si:rən] *vt* (*Gelder etc*) to collect; (*umg: wegnehmen*) to take (away) ♦ *vi*: **darf ich ~?** would you like to pay now?

**Kassierer(in)** [ka'si:rər(ɪn)] (**-s**, **-**) *m(f)* cashier; (*von Klub*) treasurer.

**Kastanie** [kas'ta:niə] *f* chestnut.

**Kastanienbaum** *m* chestnut tree.

**Kästchen** ['kɛstçən] *nt* small box, casket.

**Kaste** ['kastə] (**-**, **-n**) *f* caste.

**Kasten** ['kastən] (**-s**, **-̈**) *m* box (*auch SPORT*), case; (*Truhe*) chest; **er hat was auf dem ~** (*umg*) he's brainy; **~form** *f* (*KOCH*) (square) baking tin (*BRIT*) *od* pan (*US*); **~wagen** *m* van.

**kastrieren** [kas'tri:rən] *vt* to castrate.

**Kat** (**-**, **-s**) *m abk* (*AUT*) = **Katalysator**.

**katalanisch** [kata'la:nɪʃ] *adj* Catalan.
**Katalog** [kata'lo:k] (**-(e)s, -e**) *m* catalogue (*BRIT*), catalog (*US*).
**katalogisieren** [katalogi'zi:rən] *vt* to catalogue (*BRIT*), catalog (*US*).
**Katalysator** [kataly'za:tɔr] *m* (*lit, fig*) catalyst; (*AUT*) catalytic converter; **~-Auto** vehicle fitted with a catalytic converter.
**Katapult** [kata'pʊlt] (**-(e)s, -e**) *nt or m* catapult.
**katapultieren** [katapʊl'ti:rən] *vt* to catapult ♦ *vr* to catapult o.s.; (*Pilot*) to eject.
**Katar** ['ka:tar] *nt* Qatar.
**Katarrh** [ka'tar] (**-s, -e**) *m* catarrh.
**Katasteramt** [ka'tastəramt] *nt* land registry.
**katastrophal** [katastro'fa:l] *adj* catastrophic.
**Katastrophe** [kata'stro:fə] (**-, -n**) *f* catastrophe, disaster.
**Katastrophen-** *zW:* **~alarm** *m* emergency alert; **~gebiet** *nt* disaster area; **~medizin** *f* medical treatment in disasters; **~schutz** *m* disaster control.
**Katechismus** [katɛ'çɪsmʊs] *m* catechism.
**Kategorie** [katego'ri:] *f* category.
**kategorisch** [kate'go:rɪʃ] *adj* categorical.
**kategorisieren** [kategori'zi:rən] *vt* to categorize.
**Kater** ['ka:tər] (**-s, -**) *m* tomcat; (*umg*) hangover; **~frühstück** *nt breakfast (of pickled herring etc) to cure a hangover.*
**kath.** *abk* = **katholisch.**
**Katheder** [ka'te:dər] (**-s, -**) *nt* (*SCH*) teacher's desk; (*UNIV*) lectern.
**Kathedrale** [kate'dra:lə] (**-, -n**) *f* cathedral.
**Katheter** [ka'te:tər] (**-s, -**) *m* (*MED*) catheter.
**Kathode** [ka'to:də] (**-, -n**) *f* cathode.
**Katholik(in)** [kato'li:k(ɪn)] (**-en, -en**) *m(f)* Catholic.
**katholisch** [ka'to:lɪʃ] *adj* Catholic.
**Katholizismus** [katoli'tsɪsmʊs] *m* Catholicism.
**katzbuckeln** ['katsbʊkəln] (*pej: umg*) *vi* to bow and scrape.
**Kätzchen** ['kɛtsçən] *nt* kitten.
**Katze** ['katsə] (**-, -n**) *f* cat; **die ~ im Sack kaufen** to buy a pig in a poke; **für die Katz** (*umg*) in vain, for nothing.
**Katzen-** *zW:* **~auge** *nt* cat's-eye (*BRIT*); (*am Fahrrad*) rear light; **~jammer** (*umg*) *m* hangover; **~musik** *f* (*fig*) caterwauling; **~sprung** (*umg*) *m* stone's throw, short distance; **~tür** *f* cat flap; **~wäsche** *f* a lick and a promise.
**Kauderwelsch** ['kaʊdərvɛlʃ] (**-(s)**) *nt* jargon; (*umg*) double Dutch (*BRIT*).
**kauen** ['kaʊən] *vt, vi* to chew.
**kauern** ['kaʊərn] *vi* to crouch.
**Kauf** [kaʊf] (**-(e)s, Käufe**) *m* purchase, buy; (**~en**) buying; **ein guter ~** a bargain; **etw in ~ nehmen** to put up with sth.
**kaufen** *vt* to buy; **dafür kann ich mir nichts ~** (*ironisch*) what use is that to me!
**Käufer(in)** ['kɔyfər(ɪn)] (**-s, -**) *m(f)* buyer.
**Kauf-** *zW:* **~frau** *f* businesswoman;

(*Einzelhandelskauffrau*) shopkeeper; **~haus** *nt* department store; **~kraft** *f* purchasing power; **~laden** *m* shop, store.
**käuflich** ['kɔyflɪç] *adj* purchasable, for sale; (*pej*) venal ♦ *adv:* **~ erwerben** to purchase.
**Kauf-** *zW:* **~lust** *f* desire to buy things; (*BÖRSE*) buying; **k~lustig** *adj* interested in buying; **~mann** (**-(e)s, pl -leute**) *m* businessman; (*Einzelhandelskaufmann*) shopkeeper; **k~männisch** *adj* commercial; **k~männischer Angestellter** clerk; **~preis** *m* purchase price; **~vertrag** *m* bill of sale; **~willige(r)** *f(m)* potential buyer; **~zwang** *m:* **kein/ohne ~zwang** no/without obligation.
**Kaugummi** ['kaʊgʊmi] *m* chewing gum.
**Kaukasus** ['kaʊkazʊs] *m:* **der ~** the Caucasus.
**Kaulquappe** ['kaʊlkvapə] (**-, -n**) *f* tadpole.
**kaum** [kaʊm] *adv* hardly, scarcely; **wohl ~, ich glaube ~** I hardly think so.
**Kausalzusammenhang** [kaʊ'za:l-tsuzamənhaŋ] *m* causal connection.
**Kaution** [kaʊtsi'o:n] *f* deposit; (*JUR*) bail.
**Kautschuk** ['kaʊtʃʊk] (**-s, -e**) *m* India rubber.
**Kauz** [kaʊts] (**-es, Käuze**) *m* owl; (*fig*) queer fellow.
**Kavalier** [kava'li:r] (**-s, -e**) *m* gentleman.
**Kavaliersdelikt** *nt* peccadillo.
**Kavallerie** [kavalə'ri:] *f* cavalry.
**Kavallerist** [kavalə'rɪst] *m* cavalryman.
**Kaviar** ['ka:viar] *m* caviar.
**KB** *nt abk* (= *Kilobyte*) KB, kbyte.
**Kcal** *abk* (= *Kilokalorie*) kcal.
**keck** [kɛk] *adj* daring, bold; **K~heit** *f* daring, boldness.
**Kegel** ['ke:gəl] (**-s, -**) *m* skittle; (*MATH*) cone; **~bahn** *f* skittle alley, bowling alley; **k~förmig** *adj* conical.
**kegeln** *vi* to play skittles.
**Kehle** ['ke:lə] (**-, -n**) *f* throat; **er hat das in die falsche ~ bekommen** (*lit*) it went down the wrong way; (*fig*) he took it the wrong way; **aus voller ~** at the top of one's voice.
**Kehl-** *zW:* **~kopf** *m* larynx; **~kopfkrebs** *m* cancer of the throat; **~laut** *m* guttural.
**Kehre** ['ke:rə] (**-, -n**) *f* turn(ing), bend.
**kehren** *vt, vi* (*wenden*) to turn; (*mit Besen*) to sweep; **sich an etw** *dat* **nicht ~** not to heed sth; **in sich** *akk* **gekehrt** (*versunken*) pensive; (*verschlossen*) introspective, introverted.
**Kehricht** (**-s**) *m* sweepings *pl*.
**Kehr-** *zW:* **~maschine** *f* sweeper; **~reim** *m* refrain; **~seite** *f* reverse, other side; (*ungünstig*) wrong *od* bad side; **die ~seite der Medaille** the other side of the coin.
**kehrtmachen** *vi* to turn about, about-turn.
**Kehrtwendung** *f* about-turn.
**keifen** ['kaɪfən] *vi* to scold, nag.
**Keil** [kaɪl] (**-(e)s, -e**) *m* wedge; (*MIL*) arrowhead; **k~en** *vt* to wedge ♦ *vr* to fight.
**Keilerei** [kaɪlə'raɪ] (*umg*) *f* punch-up.
**Keilriemen** *m* (*AUT*) fan belt.
**Keim** [kaɪm] (**-(e)s, -e**) *m* bud; (*MED, fig*) germ;

etw im ~ **ersticken** to nip sth in the bud.
**keimen** *vi* to germinate.
**Keim-** *zW:* **k~frei** *adj* sterile; **k~tötend** *adj*
antiseptic, germicidal; **~zelle** *f* (*fig*)
nucleus.
**kein(e)** ['kaɪn(ə)] *pron* none ♦ *adj* no, not any;
~ **schlechte Idee** not a bad idea; ~ **Stunde/**
**drei Monate** (*nicht einmal*) less than an
hour/three months.
**keine(r, s)** *indef pron* no one, nobody; (*von*
*Gegenstand*) none.
**keinerlei** ['kaɪnər'laɪ] *adj attrib* no ... whatever.
**keinesfalls** *adv* on no account.
**keineswegs** *adv* by no means.
**keinmal** *adv* not once.
**Keks** [keːks] (**-es, -e**) *m od nt* biscuit (*BRIT*),
cookie (*US*).
**Kelch** [kɛlç] (**-(e)s, -e**) *m* cup, goblet, chalice.
**Kelle** ['kɛlə] (**-, -n**) *f* ladle; (*Maurer~*) trowel.
**Keller** ['kɛlər] (**-s, -**) *m* cellar; **~assel** (**-, -n**) *f*
woodlouse.
**Kellerei** [kɛlə'raɪ] *f* wine cellars *pl*; (*Firma*)
wine producer.
**Kellergeschoß** *nt* basement.
**Kellerwohnung** *f* basement flat (*BRIT*) *od*
apartment (*US*).
**Kellner(in)** ['kɛlnər(ɪn)] (**-s, -**) *m(f)* waiter,
waitress.
**kellnern** (*umg*) *vi* to work as a waiter/
waitress (*BRIT*), wait on tables (*US*).
**Kelte** ['kɛltə] (**-n, -n**) *m* Celt.
**Kelter** (**-, -n**) *f* winepress; (*Obst~*) press.
**keltern** ['kɛltərn] *vt* to press.
**Keltin** ['kɛltɪn] *f* (female) Celt.
**keltisch** *adj* Celtic.
**Kenia** ['keːnia] (**-s**) *nt* Kenya.
**kennen** ['kɛnən] *unreg vt* to know; ~ **Sie sich**
**schon?** do you know each other (already)?;
**kennst du mich noch?** do you remember
me?; **~lernen** *vt* to get to know; **sich ~lernen**
to get to know each other; (*zum erstenmal*) to
meet.
**Kenner(in)** (**-s, -**) *m(f):* ~ (*von od +gen*)
connoisseur (of); expert (on).
**Kennkarte** *f* identity card.
**kenntlich** *adj* distinguishable, discernible;
**etw ~ machen** to mark sth.
**Kenntnis** (**-, -se**) *f* knowledge *no pl*; **etw zur**
~ **nehmen** to note sth; **von etw ~ nehmen** to
take notice of sth; **jdn in ~ setzen** to inform
sb; **über ~se von etw verfügen** to be
knowledgeable about sth.
**Kenn-** *zW:* **~wort** *nt* (*Chiffre*) code name;
(*Losungswort*) password, code word;
**~zeichen** *nt* mark, characteristic;
**(amtliches/polizeiliches) ~zeichen** (*AUT*)
number plate (*BRIT*), license plate (*US*);
**k~zeichnen** *vt untr* to characterize;
**k~zeichnenderweise** *adv* characteristically;
**~ziffer** *f* (code) number; (*COMM*) reference
number.
**kentern** ['kɛntərn] *vi* to capsize.

**Keramik** [ke'raːmɪk] (**-, -en**) *f* ceramics *pl*,
pottery; (*Gegenstand*) piece of ceramic
work *od* pottery.
**Kerbe** ['kɛrbə] (**-, -n**) *f* notch, groove.
**Kerbel** (**-s, -**) *m* chervil.
**kerben** *vt* to notch.
**Kerbholz** *nt:* **etw auf dem ~ haben** to have
done sth wrong.
**Kerker** ['kɛrkər] (**-s, -**) *m* prison.
**Kerl** [kɛrl] (**-s, -e**) (*umg*) *m* chap, bloke (*BRIT*),
guy; **du gemeiner ~!** you swine!
**Kern** [kɛrn] (**-(e)s, -e**) *m* (*Obst~*) pip, stone;
(*Nuß~*) kernel; (*Atom~*) nucleus; (*fig*) heart,
core; **~energie** *f* nuclear energy; **~fach** *nt*
(*SCH*) core subject; **~familie** *f* nuclear
family; **~forschung** *f* nuclear research;
**~frage** *f* central issue; **~fusion** *f* nuclear
fusion; **~gehäuse** *nt* core; **k~gesund** *adj*
thoroughly healthy, fit as a fiddle.
**kernig** *adj* robust; (*Ausspruch*) pithy.
**Kern-** *zW:* **~kraftwerk** *nt* nuclear power
station; **k~los** *adj* seedless, pipless;
**~physik** *f* nuclear physics *sing*; **~reaktion** *f*
nuclear reaction; **~reaktor** *m* nuclear
reactor; **~schmelze** *f* meltdown; **~seife** *f*
washing soap; **~spaltung** *f* nuclear fission;
**~stück** *nt* (*fig*) main item; (*von Theorie etc*)
central part, core; **~waffen** *pl* nuclear
weapons *pl*; **k~waffenfrei** *adj* nuclear-free;
**~zeit** *f* core time.
**Kerze** ['kɛrtsə] (**-, -n**) *f* candle; (*Zünd~*) plug.
**Kerzen-** *zW:* **k~gerade** *adj* straight as a die;
**~halter** *m* candlestick; **~ständer** *m* candleholder.
**keß** [kɛs] *adj* saucy.
**Kessel** ['kɛsəl] (**-s, -**) *m* kettle; (*von Lokomotive*
*etc*) boiler; (*Mulde*) basin; (*GEOG*)
depression; (*MIL*) encirclement; **~stein** *m*
scale, fur (*BRIT*); **~treiben** *nt* (*fig*) witch-
hunt.
**Kette** ['kɛtə] (**-, -n**) *f* chain; **jdn an die ~ legen**
(*fig*) to tie sb down.
**ketten** *vt* to chain.
**Ketten-** *zW:* **~fahrzeug** *nt* tracked vehicle;
**~hund** *m* watchdog; **~karussell** *nt* merry-
go-round (*with gondolas on chains*); **~laden**
*m* chain store; **~rauchen** *nt* chain smoking;
**~reaktion** *f* chain reaction.
**Ketzer(in)** ['kɛtsər(ɪn)] (**-s, -**) *m(f)* heretic; **~ei**
[kɛtsə'raɪ] *f* heresy; **k~isch** *adj* heretical.
**keuchen** ['kɔʏçən] *vi* to pant, gasp.
**Keuchhusten** *m* whooping cough.
**Keule** ['kɔʏlə] (**-, -n**) *f* club; (*KOCH*) leg.
**keusch** [kɔʏʃ] *adj* chaste; **K~heit** *f* chastity.
**Kfm.** *abk* = **Kaufmann.**
**kfm.** *abk* = **kaufmännisch.**
**Kfz** (**-(s), -(s)**) *f abk* = **Kraftfahrzeug.**
**KG** (**-, -s**) *f abk* = **Kommanditgesellschaft.**
**kg** *abk* (= *Kilogramm*) kg.
**kHz** *abk* (= *Kilohertz*) kHz.
**Kibbuz** [kɪ'buːts] (**-, Kibbuzim** *od* **-e**) *m*
kibbutz.

**kichern** ['kıçərn] *vi* to giggle.
**kicken** ['kıkən] *vt, vi* (*Fußball*) to kick.
**kidnappen** ['kıtnɛpən] *vt* to kidnap.
**Kidnapper(in)** (**-s, -**) *m(f)* kidnapper.
**Kiebitz** ['ki:bıts] (**-es, -e**) *m* peewit.
**Kiefer**[1] ['ki:fər] (**-s, -**) *m* jaw.
**Kiefer**[2] ['ki:fər] (**-, -n**) *f* pine.
**Kiefernholz** *nt* pine(wood).
**Kiefernzapfen** *m* pine cone.
**Kieferorthopäde** *m* orthodontist.
**Kieker** ['ki:kər] (**-s, -**) *m:* **jdn auf dem ~ haben** (*umg*) to have it in for sb.
**Kiel** [ki:l] (**-(e)s, -e**) *m* (*Feder~*) quill; (*NAUT*) keel; **~wasser** *nt* wake.
**Kieme** ['ki:mə] (**-, -n**) *f* gill.
**Kies** [ki:s] (**-es, -e**) *m* gravel; (*umg: Geld*) money, dough.
**Kiesel** ['ki:zəl] (**-s, -**) *m* pebble; **~stein** *m* pebble.
**Kiesgrube** *f* gravel pit.
**Kiesweg** *m* gravel path.
**Kiew** ['ki:ɛf] (**-s**) *nt* Kiev.
**kiffen** ['kıfən] (*umg*) *vt* to smoke pot *od* grass.
**Kilimandscharo** [kiliman'dʒa:ro] (**-s**) *m* Kilimanjaro.
**Killer** ['kılər(ın)] (**-s, -**) (*umg*) *m* killer, murderer; (*gedungener*) hit man; **~in** (*umg*) *f* killer, female murderer, murderess.
**Kilo** ['ki:lo] (**-s, -(s)**) *nt* kilo; **~byte** [kilo'baıt] *nt* (*COMPUT*) kilobyte; **~gramm** [kilo'gram] *nt* kilogram.
**Kilometer** [kilo'me:tər] *m* kilometre (*BRIT*), kilometer (*US*); **~fresser** (*umg*) *m* long-haul driver; **~geld** *nt* ≈ mileage (allowance); **~stand** *m* ≈ mileage; **~stein** *m* ≈ milestone; **~zähler** *m* ≈ mileometer.
**Kilowatt** [kilo'vat] *nt* kilowatt.
**Kimme** ['kımə] (**-, -n**) *f* notch; (*Gewehr*) back sight.
**Kind** [kınt] (**-(e)s, -er**) *nt* child; **sich freuen wie ein ~** to be as pleased as Punch; **mit ~ und Kegel** (*hum: umg*) with the whole family; **von ~ auf** from childhood.
**Kinderarzt** *m* paediatrician (*BRIT*), pediatrician (*US*).
**Kinderbett** *nt* cot (*BRIT*), crib (*US*).
**Kinderei** [kındə'raı] *f* childishness.
**Kindererziehung** *f* bringing up of children; (*durch Schule*) education of children.
**kinderfeindlich** *adj* anti-children; (*Architektur, Planung*) not catering for children.
**Kinderfreibetrag** *m* child allowance.
**Kindergarten** *m* nursery school.

---

*A* **Kindergarten** *is a nursery school for children aged between 3 and 6 years. The children sing, play and do handicrafts. They are not taught the three Rs at this stage. Most Kindergärten are financed by the town or the church and not by the state. Parents pay a monthly contribution towards the cost.*

---

**Kinder-** *zW:* **~gärtner(in)** *m(f)* nursery-school teacher; **~geld** *nt* child benefit (*BRIT*); **~heim** *nt* children's home; **~krankheit** *f* childhood illness; **~laden** *m* (alternative) playgroup; **~lähmung** *f* polio(myelitis); **k~leicht** *adj* childishly easy; **k~lieb** *adj* fond of children; **~lied** *nt* nursery rhyme; **k~los** *adj* childless; **~mädchen** *nt* nursemaid; **~pflegerin** *f* child minder; **k~reich** *adj* with a lot of children; **~schuh** *m:* **es steckt noch in den ~schuhen** (*fig*) it's still in its infancy; **~spiel** *nt* child's play; **ein ~spiel sein** to be a doddle; **~stube** *f:* **eine gute ~stube haben** to be well-mannered; **~tagesstätte** *f* day-nursery; **~teller** *m* children's dish; **~wagen** *m* pram (*BRIT*), baby carriage (*US*); **~zimmer** *nt* child's/children's room; (*für Kleinkinder*) nursery.
**Kindes-** *zW:* **~alter** *nt* infancy; **~beine** *pl:* **von ~beinen an** from early childhood; **~mißhandlung** *f* child abuse.
**Kind-** *zW:* **k~gemäß** *adj* suitable for a child *od* children; **~heit** *f* childhood; **k~isch** *adj* childish; **k~lich** *adj* childlike.
**kindsköpfig** *adj* childish.
**Kinkerlitzchen** ['kıŋkərlıtsçən] (*umg*) *pl* knick-knacks *pl.*
**Kinn** [kın] (**-(e)s, -e**) *nt* chin; **~haken** *m* (*BOXEN*) uppercut; **~lade** *f* jaw.
**Kino** ['ki:no] (**-s, -s**) *nt* cinema (*BRIT*), movies (*US*); **~besucher** *m,* **~gänger** *m* cinema-goer (*BRIT*), movie-goer (*US*); **~programm** *nt* film programme (*BRIT*), movie program (*US*).
**Kiosk** [ki'ɔsk] (**-(e)s, -e**) *m* kiosk.
**Kippe** ['kıpə] (**-, -n**) *f* (*umg*) cigarette end; **auf der ~ stehen** (*fig*) to be touch and go.
**kippen** *vi* to topple over, overturn ♦ *vt* to tilt.
**Kipper** ['kıpər] (**-s, -**) *m* (*AUT*) tipper, dump(er) truck.
**Kippschalter** *m* rocker switch.
**Kirche** ['kırçə] (**-, -n**) *f* church.
**Kirchen-** *zW:* **~chor** *m* church choir; **~diener** *m* churchwarden; **~fest** *nt* church festival; **~lied** *nt* hymn; **~schiff** *nt* (*Längsschiff*) nave; (*Querschiff*) transept; **~steuer** *f* church tax; **~tag** *m* church congress.
**Kirch-** *zW:* **~gänger(in)** (**-s, -**) *m(f)* churchgoer; **~hof** *m* churchyard; **k~lich** *adj* ecclesiastical; **~turm** *m* church tower, steeple; **~weih** *f* fair, kermis (*US*).
**Kirgistan** ['kırgista:n] (**-s**) *nt* (*GEOG*) Kirghizia.
**Kirmes** ['kırmɛs] (**-, -sen**) *f* (*Dialekt*) fair, kermis (*US*).
**Kirschbaum** ['kırʃbaum] *m* cherry tree; (*Holz*) cherry (wood).
**Kirsche** ['kırʃə] (**-, -n**) *f* cherry; **mit ihm ist nicht gut ~n essen** (*fig*) it's best not to tangle with him.
**Kirschtorte** *f:* **Schwarzwälder ~** Black Forest Gateau.

**Kirschwasser** *nt* kirsch.

**Kissen** ['kɪsən] (**-s, -**) *nt* cushion; (*Kopf~*) pillow; **~bezug** *m* pillow case.

**Kiste** ['kɪstə] (**-, -n**) *f* box; (*Truhe*) chest; (*umg: Bett*) sack; (: *Fernsehen*) box (*BRIT*), tube (*US*).

**Kita** ['kɪta] *f abk* = **Kindertagesstätte**.

**Kitsch** [kɪtʃ] (**-(e)s**) *m* trash.

**kitschig** *adj* trashy.

**Kitt** [kɪt] (**-(e)s, -e**) *m* putty.

**Kittchen** (*umg*) *nt* clink.

**Kittel** (**-s, -**) *m* overall; (*von Arzt, Laborant etc*) (white) coat.

**kitten** *vt* to putty; (*fig*) to patch up.

**Kitz** [kɪts] (**-es, -e**) *nt* kid; (*Reh~*) fawn.

**kitzelig** ['kɪtsəlɪç] *adj* (*lit, fig*) ticklish.

**kitzeln** *vt, vi* to tickle.

**Kiwi** ['kiːvi] (**-, -s**) *f* kiwi fruit.

**KKW** (**-, -s**) *nt abk* = **Kernkraftwerk**.

**Kl.** *abk* (= *Klasse*) cl.

**Klacks** [klaks] (**-es, -e**) (*umg*) *m* (*von Kartoffelbrei, Sahne*) dollop; (*von Senf, Farbe etc*) blob.

**Kladde** ['kladə] (**-, -n**) *f* rough book; (*Block*) scribbling pad.

**klaffen** ['klafən] *vi* to gape.

**kläffen** ['klɛfən] *vi* to yelp.

**Klage** ['klaːgə] (**-, -n**) *f* complaint; (*JUR*) action; **eine ~ gegen jdn einreichen** *od* **erheben** to institute proceedings against sb; **~lied** *nt*: **ein ~lied über jdn/etw anstimmen** (*fig*) to complain about sb/sth; **~mauer** *f*: **die ~mauer** the Wailing Wall.

**klagen** *vi* (*weh~*) to lament, wail; (*sich beschweren*) to complain; (*JUR*) to take legal action; **jdm sein Leid/seine Not ~** to pour out one's sorrow/distress to sb.

**Kläger(in)** ['klɛːgər(ɪn)] (**-s, -**) *m(f)* (*JUR: im Zivilrecht*) plaintiff; (: *im Strafrecht*) prosecuting party; (: *in Scheidung*) petitioner.

**Klageschrift** *f* (*JUR*) charge; (*bei Scheidung*) petition.

**kläglich** ['klɛːklɪç] *adj* wretched.

**Klamauk** [kla'mauk] (**-s**) (*umg*) *m* (*Alberei*) tomfoolery; (*im Theater*) slapstick.

**Klamm** [klam] (**-, -en**) *f* ravine.

**klamm** *adj* (*Finger*) numb; (*feucht*) damp.

**Klammer** ['klamər] (**-, -n**) *f* clamp; (*in Text*) bracket; (*Büro~*) clip; (*Wäsche~*) peg (*BRIT*), pin (*US*); (*Zahn~*) brace; **~ auf/zu** open/ close brackets.

**klammern** *vr*: **sich ~ an** +*akk* to cling to.

**klammheimlich** [klam'haɪmlɪç] (*umg*) *adj* secret ♦ *adv* on the quiet.

**Klamotte** [kla'mɔtə] (**-, -n**) *f* (*pej: Film etc*) rubbishy old film *etc*; **Klamotten** *pl* (*umg: Kleider*) clothes *pl*; (: *Zeug*) stuff.

**Klampfe** ['klampfə] (**-, -n**) (*umg*) *f* guitar.

**klang** *etc* [klaŋ] *vb siehe* **klingen**.

**Klang** (**-(e)s, ̈e**) *m* sound.

**klangvoll** *adj* sonorous.

**Klappbett** *nt* folding bed.

**Klappe** ['klapə] (**-, -n**) *f* valve; (*an Oboe etc*) key; (*FILM*) clapperboard; (*Ofen~*) damper; (*umg: Mund*) trap; **die ~ halten** to shut one's trap.

**klappen** *vi* (*Geräusch*) to click; (*Sitz etc*) to tip ♦ *vt* to tip ♦ *vi unpers* to work; **hat es mit den Karten/dem Job geklappt?** did you get the tickets/job O.K.?

**Klappentext** *m* blurb.

**Klapper** ['klapər] (**-, -n**) *f* rattle.

**klapperig** *adj* run-down, worn-out.

**klappern** *vi* to clatter, rattle.

**Klapperschlange** *f* rattlesnake.

**Klapperstorch** *m* stork; **er glaubt noch an den ~** he still thinks babies are found under the gooseberry bush.

**Klapp-** *zW*: **~messer** *nt* jackknife; **~rad** *nt* collapsible *od* folding bicycle; **~stuhl** *m* folding chair; **~tisch** *m* folding table.

**Klaps** [klaps] (**-es, -e**) *m* slap; **einen ~ haben** (*umg*) to have a screw loose; **k~en** *vt* to slap.

**klar** [klaːr] *adj* clear; (*NAUT*) ready to sail; (*MIL*) ready for action; **bei ~em Verstand sein** to be in full possession of one's faculties; **sich** *dat* **im ~en sein über** +*akk* to be clear about; **ins ~e kommen** to get clear.

**Kläranlage** *f* sewage plant; (*von Fabrik*) purification plant.

**Klare(r)** (*umg*) *m* schnapps.

**klären** *vt* (*Flüssigkeit*) to purify; (*Probleme*) to clarify ♦ *vr* to clear (itself) up.

**Klarheit** *f* clarity; **sich** *dat* **~ über etw** *akk* **verschaffen** to get sth straight.

**Klarinette** [klari'nɛtə] *f* clarinet.

**klar-** *zW*: **~kommen** *unreg* (*umg*) *vi*: **mit jdm/ etw ~kommen** to be able to cope with sb/ sth; **~legen** *vt* to clear up, explain; **~machen** *vt* (*Schiff*) to get ready for sea; **jdm etw ~machen** to make sth clear to sb; **~sehen** *unreg vi* to see clearly; **K~sichtfolie** *f* transparent film; **~stellen** *vt* to clarify; **K~text** *m*: **im K~text** in clear; (*fig: umg*) ≈ in plain English.

**Klärung** ['klɛːrʊŋ] *f* purification; clarification.

**klarwerden** *unreg vr*: **sich** *dat* **über etw** *akk* **~** to get sth clear in one's mind.

**Klasse** ['klasə] (**-, -n**) *f* class; (*SCH*) class, form; (*auch*: **Steuer~**) bracket; (*Güter~*) grade.

**klasse** (*umg*) *adj* smashing.

**Klassen-** *zW*: **~arbeit** *f* test; **~bewußtsein** *nt* class-consciousness; **~buch** *nt* (*SCH*) (class) register; **~gesellschaft** *f* class society; **~kamerad(in)** *m(f)* classmate; **~kampf** *m* class conflict; **~lehrer(in)** *m(f)* class teacher; **k~los** *adj* classless; **~sprecher(in)** *m(f)* class spokesperson; **~ziel** *nt*: **das ~ziel nicht erreichen** (*SCH*) not to reach the required standard (for the year); (*fig*) not to make the grade; **~zimmer** *nt* classroom.

**klassifizieren** [klasifi'tsiːrən] *vt* to classify.

**Klassifizierung** f classification.
**Klassik** ['klasık] f (Zeit) classical period; (Stil) classicism; ~**er** (-**s**, -) m classic.
**klassisch** adj (lit, fig) classical.
**Klassizismus** [klasi'tsısmʊs] m classicism.
**Klatsch** [klatʃ] (-(**e**)**s**, -**e**) m smack, crack; (Gerede) gossip; ~**base** f gossip(monger).
**klatschen** vi (tratschen) to gossip; (Beifall spenden) to applaud, to clap ♦ vt: (**jdm**) **Beifall** ~ to applaud od clap (sb).
**Klatsch-** zW: ~**mohn** m (corn) poppy; **k~naß** adj soaking wet; ~**spalte** f gossip column; ~**tante** (pej: umg) f gossip(monger).
**klauben** ['klaʊbən] vt to pick.
**Klaue** ['klaʊə] (-, -**n**) f claw; (umg: Schrift) scrawl.
**klauen** vt to claw; (umg) to pinch.
**Klause** ['klaʊzə] (-, -**n**) f cell; (von Mönch) hermitage.
**Klausel** ['klaʊzəl] (-, -**n**) f clause; (Vorbehalt) proviso.
**Klausur** [klaʊ'zuːr] f seclusion; ~**arbeit** f examination paper.
**Klaviatur** [klavia'tuːr] f keyboard.
**Klavier** [kla'viːr] (-**s**, -**e**) nt piano; ~**auszug** m piano score.
**Klebeband** nt adhesive tape.
**Klebemittel** nt glue.
**kleben** ['kleːbən] vt, vi: ~ (**an** +akk) to stick (to); **jdm eine** ~ (umg) to belt sb one.
**Klebezettel** m gummed label.
**klebrig** adj sticky.
**Klebstoff** m glue.
**Klebstreifen** m adhesive tape.
**kleckern** ['klɛkərn] vi to slobber.
**Klecks** [klɛks] (-**es**, -**e**) m blot, stain; **k~en** vi to blot; (pej) to daub.
**Klee** [kleː] (-**s**) m clover; **jdn/etw über den grünen** ~ **loben** (fig) to praise sb/sth to the skies; ~**blatt** nt cloverleaf; (fig) trio.
**Kleid** [klaɪt] (-(**e**)**s**, -**er**) nt garment; (Frauen~) dress; **Kleider** pl clothes pl.
**kleiden** ['klaɪdən] vt to clothe, dress ♦ vr to dress; **jdn** ~ to suit sb.
**Kleider-** zW: ~**bügel** m coat hanger; ~**bürste** f clothes brush; ~**schrank** m wardrobe; ~**ständer** m coat-stand.
**kleidsam** adj becoming.
**Kleidung** f clothing.
**Kleidungsstück** nt garment.
**Kleie** ['klaɪə] (-, -**n**) f bran.
**klein** [klaɪn] adj little, small; **haben Sie es nicht** ~**er?** haven't you got anything smaller?; **ein** ~**es Bier, ein K~es** (umg) ≈ half a pint, a half; **von** ~ **an** od **auf** (von Kindheit an) from childhood; (von Anfang an) from the very beginning; **das** ~**ere Übel** the lesser evil; **sein Vater war (ein)** ~**er Beamter** his father was a minor civil servant; ~ **anfangen** to start off in a small way; **ein Wort** ~ **schreiben** to write a word with a small initial letter; **K~anzeige** f small ad

(BRIT), want ad (US); **Kleinanzeigen** pl classified advertising sing; **K~arbeit** f: **in zäher/mühseliger K~arbeit** with rigorous/ painstaking attention to detail; **K~asien** nt Asia Minor; **K~bürgertum** nt petite bourgeoisie; **K~bus** m minibus.
**Kleine(r)** f(m) little one.
**klein-** zW: **K~familie** f small family, nuclear family (SOZIOLOGIE); **K~format** nt small size; **im K~format** small-scale; **K~gedruckte(s)** nt small print; **K~geld** nt small change; **das nötige K~geld haben** (fig) to have the wherewithal (umg); ~**gläubig** adj of little faith; ~**hacken** vt to chop up; **K~holz** nt firewood; **K~holz aus jdm machen** to make mincemeat of sb.
**Kleinigkeit** f trifle; **wegen** od **bei jeder** ~ for the slightest reason; **eine** ~ **essen** to have a bite to eat.
**klein-** zW: ~**kariert** adj: ~**kariert denken** to think small; **K~kind** nt infant; **K~kram** m details pl; **K~kredit** m personal loan; ~**kriegen** (umg) vt (gefügig machen) to bring into line; (unterkriegen) to get down; (körperlich) to tire out; ~**laut** adj dejected, quiet; ~**lich** adj petty, paltry; **K~lichkeit** f pettiness, paltriness; ~**mütig** adj fainthearted.
**Kleinod** ['klaɪnoːt] (-**s**, -**odien**) nt gem, jewel; (fig) treasure.
**klein-** zW: **K~rechner** m minicomputer; ~**schneiden** unreg vt to chop up; ~**schreiben** unreg vt: ~**geschrieben werden** (umg) to count for (very) little; **K~schreibung** f use of small initial letters; **K~stadt** f small town; ~**städtisch** adj provincial.
**kleinstmöglich** adj smallest possible.
**Kleinwagen** m small car.
**Kleister** ['klaɪstər] (-**s**, -) m paste.
**kleistern** vt to paste.
**Klemme** ['klɛmə] (-, -**n**) f clip; (MED) clamp; (fig) jam; **in der** ~ **sitzen** od **sein** (fig: umg) to be in a fix.
**klemmen** vt (festhalten) to jam; (quetschen) to pinch, nip ♦ vr to catch o.s.; (sich hineinzwängen) to squeeze o.s. ♦ vi (Tür) to stick, jam; **sich hinter jdn/etw** ~ to get on to sb/get down to sth.
**Klempner** ['klɛmpnər] (-**s**, -) m plumber.
**Kleptomanie** [klɛptoma'niː] f kleptomania.
**Kleriker** ['kleːrikər] (-**s**, -) m cleric.
**Klerus** ['kleːrʊs] (-) m clergy.
**Klette** ['klɛtə] (-, -**n**) f burr; **sich wie eine** ~ **an jdn hängen** to cling to sb like a limpet.
**Kletterer** ['klɛtərər] (-**s**, -) m climber.
**Klettergerüst** nt climbing frame.
**klettern** vi to climb.
**Kletterpflanze** f creeper.
**Kletterseil** nt climbing rope.
**Klettverschluß** m Velcro ® fastener.
**klicken** ['klɪkən] vi to click.
**Klient(in)** [kli'ɛnt(ɪn)] m(f) client.

**Klima** ['kliːma] (-s, -s *od* -te) *nt* climate; ~anlage *f* air conditioning.
**klimatisieren** [kliːmati'ziːrən] *vt* to air-condition.
**klimatisiert** *adj* air-conditioned.
**Klimawechsel** *m* change of air.
**Klimbim** [klɪm'bɪm] (-s) (*umg*) *m* odds and ends *pl*.
**klimpern** ['klɪmpərn] *vi* to tinkle; (*auf Gitarre*) to strum.
**Klinge** ['klɪŋə] (-, -n) *f* blade, sword; **jdn über die ~ springen lassen** (*fig: umg*) to allow sb to run into trouble.
**Klingel** ['klɪŋəl] (-, -n) *f* bell; ~beutel *m* collection bag; ~knopf *m* bell push.
**klingeln** *vi* to ring; **es hat geklingelt** (*an Tür*) somebody just rang the doorbell, the doorbell just rang.
**klingen** ['klɪŋən] *unreg vi* to sound; (*Gläser*) to clink.
**Klinik** ['kliːnɪk] *f* clinic.
**klinisch** ['kliːnɪʃ] *adj* clinical.
**Klinke** ['klɪŋkə] (-, -n) *f* handle.
**Klinker** ['klɪŋkər] (-s, -) *m* clinker.
**Klippe** ['klɪpə] (-, -n) *f* cliff; (*im Meer*) reef; (*fig*) hurdle.
**klippenreich** *adj* rocky.
**klipp und klar** ['klɪp|ʊntklaːr] *adj* clear and concise.
**Klips** [klɪps] (-es, -e) *m* clip; (*Ohr*~) earring.
**klirren** ['klɪrən] *vi* to clank, jangle; (*Gläser*) to clink; ~de Kälte biting cold.
**Klischee** [kli'ʃeː] (-s, -s) *nt* (*Druckplatte*) plate, block; (*fig*) cliché; ~vorstellung *f* stereotyped idea.
**Klitoris** ['kliːtorɪs] (-, -) *f* clitoris.
**Klo** [kloː] (-s, -s) (*umg*) *nt* loo (*BRIT*), john (*US*).
**Kloake** [klo'aːkə] (-, -n) *f* sewer.
**klobig** ['kloːbɪç] *adj* clumsy.
**Klon** [kloːn] (-s, -e) *m* clone.
**Klopapier** (*umg*) *nt* toilet paper.
**klopfen** ['klɔpfən] *vi* to knock; (*Herz*) to thump ♦ *vt* to beat; **es klopft** somebody's knocking; **jdm auf die Finger ~** (*lit, fig*) to give sb a rap on the knuckles; **jdm auf die Schulter ~** to tap sb on the shoulder.
**Klopfer** (-s, -) *m* (*Teppich*~) beater; (*Tür*~) knocker.
**Klöppel** ['klœpəl] (-s, -) *m* (*von Glocke*) clapper.
**klöppeln** *vi* to make lace.
**Klops** [klɔps] (-es, -e) *m* meatball.
**Klosett** [klo'zɛt] (-s, -e *od* -s) *nt* lavatory, toilet; ~brille *f* toilet seat; ~papier *nt* toilet paper.
**Kloß** [kloːs] (-es, ̈-e) *m* (*Erd*~) clod; (*im Hals*) lump; (*KOCH*) dumpling.
**Kloster** ['kloːstər] (-s, ̈-) *nt* (*Männer*~) monastery; (*Frauen*~) convent; **ins ~ gehen** to become a monk/nun.
**klösterlich** ['klœːstərlɪç] *adj* monastic; convent *attrib*.

**Klotz** [klɔts] (-es, ̈-e) *m* log; (*Hack*~) block; **jdm ein ~ am Bein sein** (*fig*) to be a millstone round sb's neck.
**Klub** [klʊp] (-s, -s) *m* club; ~jacke *f* blazer; ~sessel *m* easy chair.
**Kluft** [klʊft] (-, ̈-e) *f* cleft, gap; (*GEOG*) chasm; (*Uniform*) uniform; (*umg: Kleidung*) gear.
**klug** [kluːk] *adj* clever, intelligent; **ich werde daraus nicht ~** I can't make head or tail of it; **K~heit** *f* cleverness, intelligence; **K~scheißer** (*umg*) *m* smart-ass.
**Klümpchen** ['klʏmpçən] *nt* clot, blob.
**klumpen** ['klʊmpən] *vi* to go lumpy, clot.
**Klumpen** (-s, -) *m* (*KOCH*) lump; (*Erd*~) clod; (*Blut*~) clot; (*Gold*~) nugget.
**Klumpfuß** ['klʊmpfuːs] *m* club foot.
**Klüngel** ['klʏŋəl] (-s, -) (*umg*) *m* (*Clique*) clique.
**Klunker** ['klʊŋkər] (-s, -) (*umg*) *m* (*Schmuck*) rock(s *pl*).
**km** *abk* (= *Kilometer*) km.
**km/h** *abk* (= *Kilometer pro Stunde*) km/h.
**knabbern** ['knabərn] *vt, vi* to nibble; **an etw** *dat* ~ (*fig: umg*) to puzzle over sth.
**Knabe** ['knaːbə] (-n, -n) *m* boy.
**knabenhaft** *adj* boyish.
**Knäckebrot** ['knɛkəbroːt] *nt* crispbread.
**knacken** ['knakən] *vi* (*lit, fig*) to crack ♦ *vt* (*umg: Auto*) to break into.
**knackfrisch** (*umg*) *adj* oven-fresh, crispy-fresh.
**knackig** *adj* crisp.
**Knacks** [knaks] (-es, -e) *m*: **einen ~ weghaben** (*umg*) to be uptight about sth.
**Knackwurst** *f* type of frankfurter.
**Knall** [knal] (-(e)s, -e) *m* bang; (*Peitschen*~) crack; ~ auf Fall (*umg*) just like that; **einen ~ haben** (*umg*) to be crazy *od* crackers; ~bonbon *nt* cracker; ~effekt *m* surprise effect, spectacular effect; k~en *vi* to bang; to crack ♦ *vt*: jdm eine k~en (*umg*) to clout sb; ~frosch *m* jumping jack; k~hart (*umg*) *adj* really hard; (: *Worte*) hard-hitting; (: *Film*) brutal; (: *Porno*) hard-core; ~kopf (*umg*) *m* dickhead; k~rot *adj* bright red.
**knapp** [knap] *adj* tight; (*Geld*) scarce; (*kurz*) short; (*Mehrheit, Sieg*) narrow; (*Sprache*) concise; **meine Zeit ist ~ bemessen** I am short of time; **mit ~er Not** only just.
**Knappe** (-n, -n) *m* (*Edelmann*) young knight.
**knapphalten** *unreg vt*: jdn ~ (mit) to keep sb short (of).
**Knappheit** *f* tightness; scarcity; conciseness.
**Knarre** ['knarə] (-, -n) (*umg*) *f* (*Gewehr*) shooter.
**knarren** *vi* to creak.
**Knast** [knast] (-(e)s) (*umg*) *m* clink, can (*US*).
**Knatsch** [knatʃ] (-es) (*umg*) *m* trouble.
**knattern** ['knatərn] *vi* to rattle; (*Maschinengewehr*) to chatter.

**Knäuel** ['knɔYəl] (-s, -) m od nt (Woll~) ball; (Menschen~) knot.

**Knauf** [knauf] (-(e)s, Knäufe) m knob; (Schwert~) pommel.

**Knauser** ['knauzər] (-s, -) m miser.

**knauserig** adj miserly.

**knausern** vi to be mean.

**knautschen** ['knautʃən] vt, vi to crumple.

**Knebel** ['kneːbəl] (-s, -) m gag.

**knebeln** vt to gag; (NAUT) to fasten.

**Knecht** [knɛçt] (-(e)s, -e) m servant; (auf Bauernhof) farm labourer (BRIT) od laborer (US).

**knechten** vt to enslave.

**Knechtschaft** f servitude.

**kneifen** ['knaɪfən] unreg vt to pinch ♦ vi to pinch; (sich drücken) to back out; **vor etw** dat ~ to dodge sth.

**Kneifzange** f pliers pl; (kleine) pincers pl.

**Kneipe** ['knaɪpə] (-, -n) (umg) f pub (BRIT), bar, saloon (US).

**Kneippkur** ['knaɪpkuːr] f Kneipp cure, type of hydropathic treatment combined with diet, rest etc.

**Knete** ['kneːtə] (umg) f (Geld) dough.

**kneten** vt to knead; (Wachs) to mould (BRIT), mold (US).

**Knetgummi** m od nt Plasticine ®.

**Knetmasse** f Plasticine ®.

**Knick** [knɪk] (-(e)s, -e) m (Sprung) crack; (Kurve) bend; (Falte) fold.

**knicken** vt, vi (springen) to crack; (brechen) to break; (Papier) to fold; „nicht ~!" "do not bend"; **geknickt sein** to be downcast.

**Knicks** [knɪks] (-es, -e) m curts(e)y; **k~en** vi to curts(e)y.

**Knie** [kniː] (-s, -) nt knee; **in die ~ gehen** to kneel; (fig) to be brought to one's knees; ~**beuge** (-, -n) f knee bend; ~**fall** m genuflection; ~**gelenk** nt knee joint; ~**kehle** f back of the knee.

**knien** vi to kneel ♦ vr: **sich in die Arbeit ~** (fig) to get down to (one's) work.

**Kniescheibe** f kneecap.

**Kniestrumpf** m knee-length sock.

**kniff** etc [knɪf] vb siehe kneifen.

**Kniff** (-(e)s, -e) m (Zwicken) pinch; (Falte) fold; (fig) trick, knack.

**kniffelig** adj tricky.

**knipsen** ['knɪpsən] vt (Fahrkarte) to punch; (PHOT) to take a snap of, snap ♦ vi (PHOT) to take snaps/a snap.

**Knirps** [knɪrps] (-es, -e) m little chap; (®: Schirm) telescopic umbrella.

**knirschen** ['knɪrʃən] vi to crunch; **mit den Zähnen** ~ to grind one's teeth.

**knistern** ['knɪstərn] vi to crackle; (Papier, Seide) to rustle.

**Knitterfalte** f crease.

**knitterfrei** adj non-crease.

**knittern** vi to crease.

**knobeln** ['knoːbəln] vi (würfeln) to play dice;

(um eine Entscheidung) to toss for it.

**Knoblauch** ['knoːplaux] (-(e)s) m garlic.

**Knöchel** ['knœçəl] (-s, -) m knuckle; (Fuß~) ankle.

**Knochen** ['knɔxən] (-s, -) m bone; ~**arbeit** (umg) f hard work; ~**bau** m bone structure; ~**bruch** m fracture; ~**gerüst** nt skeleton; ~**mark** nt bone marrow.

**knöchern** ['knœçərn] adj bone.

**knochig** ['knɔxɪç] adj bony.

**Knödel** ['knøːdəl] (-s, -) m dumpling.

**Knolle** ['knɔlə] (-, -n) f bulb.

**Knopf** [knɔpf] (-(e)s, ⸚e) m button; ~**druck** m touch of a button.

**knöpfen** ['knœpfən] vt to button.

**Knopfloch** nt buttonhole.

**Knorpel** ['knɔrpəl] (-s, -) m cartilage, gristle.

**knorpelig** adj gristly.

**knorrig** ['knɔrɪç] adj gnarled, knotted.

**Knospe** ['knɔspə] (-, -n) f bud.

**knospen** vi to bud.

**knoten** ['knoːtən] vt to knot; **K~** (-s, -) m knot; (Haar) bun; (BOT) node; (MED) lump.

**Knotenpunkt** m junction.

**knuffen** ['knufən] (umg) vt to cuff.

**Knüller** ['knʏlər] (-s, -) (umg) m hit; (Reportage) scoop.

**knüpfen** ['knʏpfən] vt to tie; (Teppich) to knot; (Freundschaft) to form.

**Knüppel** ['knʏpəl] (-s, -) m cudgel; (Polizei~) baton, truncheon; (AVIAT) (joy)stick; **jdm ~ zwischen die Beine werfen** (fig) to put a spoke in sb's wheel; **k~dick** (umg) adj very thick; (fig) thick and fast; ~**schaltung** f (AUT) floor-mounted gear change.

**knurren** ['knurən] vi (Hund) to snarl, growl; (Magen) to rumble; (Mensch) to mutter.

**knusp(e)rig** ['knusp(ə)rɪç] adj crisp; (Keks) crunchy.

**knutschen** ['knuːtʃən] (umg) vt to snog with ♦ vi, vr to snog.

**k.o.** adj (SPORT) knocked out; (fig: umg) whacked.

**Koalition** [koalitsi'oːn] f coalition.

**Kobalt** ['koːbalt] (-s) nt cobalt.

**Kobold** ['koːbɔlt] (-(e)s, -e) m imp.

**Kobra** ['koːbra] (-, -s) f cobra.

**Koch** [kɔx] (-(e)s, ⸚e) m cook; ~**buch** nt cookery book, cookbook; **k~echt** adj (Farbe) fast.

**kochen** vi to cook; (Wasser) to boil ♦ vt (Essen) to cook; **er kochte vor Wut** (umg) he was seething; **etw auf kleiner Flamme ~** to simmer sth over a low heat.

**Kocher** (-s, -) m stove, cooker.

**Köcher** ['kœçər] (-s, -) m quiver.

**Kochgelegenheit** f cooking facilities pl.

**Köchin** ['kœçɪn] f cook.

**Koch-** zW: ~**kunst** f cooking; ~**löffel** m kitchen spoon; ~**nische** f kitchenette; ~**platte** f hotplate; ~**salz** nt cooking salt; ~**topf** m saucepan, pot; ~**wäsche** f washing

that can be boiled.
**Kode** [koːt] (-s, -s) *m* code.
**Köder** ['køːdər] (-s, -) *m* bait, lure.
**ködern** *vt* to lure, entice.
**Koexistenz** [koɛksɪs'tɛnts] *f* coexistence.
**Koffein** [kɔfe'iːn] (-s) *nt* caffeine; **k~frei** *adj* decaffeinated.
**Koffer** ['kɔfər] (-s, -) *m* suitcase; (*Schrank~*) trunk; **die ~ packen** (*lit, fig*) to pack one's bags; **~kuli** *m* (luggage) trolley (*BRIT*), cart (*US*); **~radio** *nt* portable radio; **~raum** *m* (*AUT*) boot (*BRIT*), trunk (*US*).
**Kognak** ['kɔnjak] (-s, -s) *m* brandy, cognac.
**Kohl** [koːl] (-(e)s, -e) *m* cabbage.
**Kohldampf** (*umg*) *m:* ~ **haben** to be famished.
**Kohle** ['koːlə] (-, -n) *f* coal; (*Holz~*) charcoal; (*CHEM*) carbon; (*umg: Geld*): **die ~n stimmen** the money's right; **~hydrat** (-(e)s, -e) *nt* carbohydrate; **~kraftwerk** *nt* coal-fired power station.
**kohlen** ['koːlən] (*umg*) *vi* to tell white lies.
**Kohlen-** *zW:* **~bergwerk** *nt* coal mine, pit, colliery (*BRIT*); **~dioxyd** (-(e)s, -e) *nt* carbon dioxide; **~grube** *f* coal mine, pit; **~händler** *m* coal merchant, coalman; **~säure** *f* carbon dioxide; **ein Getränk ohne ~säure** a non-fizzy *od* still drink; **~stoff** *m* carbon.
**Kohlepapier** *nt* carbon paper.
**Köhler** ['køːlər] (-s, -) *m* charcoal burner.
**Kohlestift** *m* charcoal pencil.
**Kohlezeichnung** *f* charcoal drawing.
**Kohl-** *zW:* **k~(pech)rabenschwarz** *adj* (*Haar*) jet-black; (*Nacht*) pitch-black; **~rübe** *f* turnip; **k~schwarz** *adj* coal-black.
**Koitus** ['koːitʊs] (-, - *od* -se) *m* coitus.
**Koje** ['koːjə] (-, -n) *f* cabin; (*Bett*) bunk.
**Kokain** [koka'iːn] (-s) *nt* cocaine.
**kokett** [ko'kɛt] *adj* coquettish, flirtatious.
**kokettieren** [kokɛ'tiːrən] *vi* to flirt.
**Kokosnuß** ['koːkɔsnʊs] *f* coconut.
**Koks** [koːks] (-es, -e) *m* coke.
**Kolben** ['kɔlbən] (-s, -) *m* (*Gewehr~*) butt; (*Keule*) club; (*CHEM*) flask; (*TECH*) piston; (*Mais~*) cob.
**Kolchose** [kɔl'çoːzə] (-, -n) *f* collective farm.
**Kolik** ['koːlɪk] *f* colic, gripe.
**Kollaborateur(in)** [kɔlabora'tøːr(ɪn)] *m(f)* (*POL*) collaborator.
**Kollaps** [kɔ'laps] (-es, -e) *m* collapse.
**Kolleg** [kɔl'eːk] (-s, -s *od* -ien) *nt* lecture course.
**Kollege** [kɔ'leːgə] (-n, -n) *m* colleague.
**kollegial** [kɔlegi'aːl] *adj* cooperative.
**Kollegin** [kɔ'leːgɪn] *f* colleague.
**Kollegium** *nt* board; (*SCH*) staff.
**Kollekte** [kɔ'lɛktə] (-, -n) *f* (*REL*) collection.
**Kollektion** [kɔlɛktsi'oːn] *f* collection; (*Sortiment*) range.
**kollektiv** [kɔlɛk'tiːf] *adj* collective.
**Koller** ['kɔlər] (-s, -) (*umg*) *m* (*Anfall*) funny mood; (*Wutanfall*) rage; (*Tropen~*,

*Gefängnis~*) madness.
**kollidieren** [kɔli'diːrən] *vi* to collide; (*zeitlich*) to clash.
**Kollier** [kɔli'eː] (-s, -s) *nt* necklet, necklace.
**Kollision** [kɔlizi'oːn] *f* collision; (*zeitlich*) clash.
**Kollisionskurs** *m:* **auf ~ gehen** (*fig*) to be heading for trouble.
**Köln** [kœln] (-s) *nt* Cologne.
**Kölnischwasser** *nt* eau de Cologne.
**kolonial** [koloni'aːl] *adj* colonial; **K~macht** *f* colonial power; **K~warenhändler** *m* grocer.
**Kolonie** [kolo'niː] *f* colony.
**kolonisieren** [koloni'ziːrən] *vt* to colonize.
**Kolonist(in)** [kolo'nɪst(ɪn)] *m(f)* colonist.
**Kolonne** [ko'lɔnə] (-, -n) *f* column; (*von Fahrzeugen*) convoy.
**Koloß** [ko'lɔs] (-sses, -sse) *m* colossus.
**kolossal** [kolɔ'saːl] *adj* colossal.
**Kolumbianer(in)** [kolumbi'aːnər(ɪn)] *m(f)* Columbian.
**kolumbianisch** *adj* Columbian.
**Kolumbien** [ko'lumbiən] (-s) *nt* Columbia.
**Koma** ['koːma] (-s, -s *od* -ta) *nt* (*MED*) coma.
**Kombi** ['kɔmbi] (-s, -s) *m* (*AUT*) estate (car) (*BRIT*), station wagon (*US*).
**Kombination** [kɔmbinatsi'oːn] *f* combination; (*Vermutung*) conjecture; (*Hemdhose*) combinations *pl*; (*AVIAT*) flying suit.
**Kombinationsschloß** *nt* combination lock.
**kombinieren** [kɔmbi'niːrən] *vt* to combine ♦ *vi* to deduce, work out; (*vermuten*) to guess.
**Kombiwagen** *m* (*AUT*) estate (car) (*BRIT*), station wagon (*US*).
**Kombizange** *f* (pair of) pliers.
**Komet** [ko'meːt] (-en, -en) *m* comet.
**kometenhaft** *adj* (*fig: Aufstieg*) meteoric.
**Komfort** [kɔm'foːr] (-s) *m* luxury; (*von Möbel etc*) comfort; (*von Wohnung*) amenities *pl*; (*von Auto*) luxury features *pl*; (*von Gerät*) extras *pl*.
**komfortabel** [kɔmfɔr'taːbəl] *adj* comfortable.
**Komik** ['koːmɪk] *f* humour (*BRIT*), humor (*US*), comedy; **~er** (-s, -) *m* comedian.
**komisch** ['koːmɪʃ] *adj* funny; **mir ist so ~** (*umg*) I feel funny *od* strange *od* odd; **~erweise** ['koːmɪʃər'vaɪzə] *adv* funnily enough.
**Komitee** [komi'teː] (-s, -s) *nt* committee.
**Komm.** *abk* (= *Kommission*) comm.
**Komma** ['kɔma] (-s, -s *od* -ta) *nt* comma; (*MATH*) decimal point; **fünf ~ drei** five point three.
**Kommandant** [koman'dant] *m* commander, commanding officer.
**Kommandeur** [koman'døːr] *m* commanding officer.
**kommandieren** [koman'diːrən] *vt* to command ♦ *vi* to command; (*Befehle geben*) to give orders.
**Kommanditgesellschaft** [koman'diːt-gəzɛlʃaft] *f* limited partnership.

**Kommando** [kɔ'mando] (**-s, -s**) nt command, order; (Truppe) detachment, squad; **auf ~ to** order; **~brücke** f (NAUT) bridge; **~wirtschaft** f command economy.

**kommen** ['kɔmən] unreg vi to come; (näher ~) to approach; (passieren) to happen; (gelangen, geraten) to get; (Blumen, Zähne, Tränen etc) to appear; (in die Schule, ins Gefängnis etc) to go; **was kommt diese Woche im Kino?** what's on at the cinema this week? ♦ vi unpers: **es kam eins zum anderen** one thing led to another; **~ lassen** to send for; **in Bewegung ~** to start moving; **jdn besuchen ~** to come and visit sb; **das kommt davon!** see what happens?; **du kommst mir gerade recht** (ironisch) you're just what I need; **das kommt in den Schrank** that goes in the cupboard; **an etw akk ~** (berühren) to touch sth; (sich verschaffen) to get hold of sth; **auf etw akk ~** (sich erinnern) to think of sth; (sprechen über) to get onto sth; **das kommt auf die Rechnung** that goes onto the bill; **hinter etw akk ~** (herausfinden) to find sth out; **zu sich ~** to come round od to; **zu etw ~** to acquire sth; **um etw ~** to lose sth; **nichts auf jdn/etw ~ lassen** to have nothing said against sb/sth; **jdm frech ~** to get cheeky with sb; **auf jeden vierten kommt ein Platz** there's one place to every fourth person; **mit einem Anliegen ~** to have a request (to make); **wer kommt zuerst?** who's first?; **wer zuerst kommt, mahlt zuerst** (Sprichwort) first come first served; **unter ein Auto ~** to be run over by a car; **das kommt zusammen auf 20 DM** that comes to 20 marks altogether; **und so kam es, daß ...** and that is how it happened that ...; **daher kommt es, daß ...** that's why ...

**Kommen** (**-s**) nt coming.

**kommend** adj (Jahr, Woche, Generation) coming; (Ereignisse, Montag) future; (Trend) upcoming; **(am) ~en Montag** next Monday.

**Kommentar** [kɔmɛn'taːr] m commentary; **kein ~** no comment; **k~los** adj without comment.

**Kommentator** [kɔmɛn'taːtɔr] m (TV) commentator.

**kommentieren** [kɔmɛn'tiːrən] vt to comment on; **kommentierte Ausgabe** annotated edition.

**kommerziell** [kɔmɛrtsi'ɛl] adj commercial.

**Kommilitone** [kɔmili'toːnə] (**-n, -n**) m, **Kommilitonin** f fellow student.

**Kommiß** [kɔ'mɪs] (**-sses**) m (life in the) army.

**Kommissar** [kɔmɪ'saːr] m police inspector.

**Kommißbrot** nt army bread.

**Kommission** [kɔmɪsi'oːn] f (COMM) commission; (Ausschuß) committee; **in ~ geben** to give (to a dealer) for sale on commission.

**Kommode** [kɔ'moːdə] (**-, -n**) f (chest of) drawers.

**kommunal** [kɔmu'naːl] adj local; (von Stadt) municipal; **K~abgaben** pl local rates and taxes pl; **K~politik** f local government politics; **K~verwaltung** f local government; **K~wahlen** pl local (government) elections pl.

**Kommune** [kɔ'muːnə] (**-, -n**) f commune.

**Kommunikation** [kɔmunɪkatsi'oːn] f communication.

**Kommunion** [kɔmuni'oːn] f communion.

**Kommuniqué** [kɔmyni'keː] (**-s, -s**) nt communiqué.

**Kommunismus** [kɔmu'nɪsmʊs] m communism.

**Kommunist(in)** [kɔmu'nɪst(ɪn)] m(f) communist; **k~isch** adj communist.

**kommunizieren** [kɔmuni'tsiːrən] vi to communicate; (ECCL) to receive communion.

**Komödiant** [komødi'ant] m comedian; **~in** f comedienne.

**Komödie** [ko'møːdiə] f comedy; **~ spielen** (fig) to put on an act.

**Kompagnon** [kɔmpan'jõː] (**-s, -s**) m (COMM) partner.

**kompakt** [kɔm'pakt] adj compact.

**Kompaktanlage** f (RUNDF) audio system.

**Kompanie** [kɔmpa'niː] f company.

**Komparativ** ['kɔmparatiːf] (**-s, -e**) m comparative.

**Kompaß** ['kɔmpas] (**-sses, -sse**) m compass.

**kompatibel** [kɔmpa'tiːbəl] adj (auch COMPUT) compatible.

**Kompatibilität** [kɔmpatibili'tɛːt] f (auch COMPUT) compatibility.

**kompensieren** [kɔmpɛn'ziːrən] vt to compensate for, offset.

**kompetent** [kɔmpe'tɛnt] adj competent.

**Kompetenz** f competence, authority; **~streitigkeiten** pl dispute over respective areas of responsibility.

**komplett** [kɔm'plɛt] adj complete.

**komplex** [kɔm'plɛks] adj complex; **K~** (**-es, -e**) m complex.

**Komplikation** [kɔmplikatsi'oːn] f complication.

**Kompliment** [kɔmpli'mɛnt] nt compliment.

**Komplize** [kɔm'pliːtsə] (**-n, -n**) m accomplice.

**komplizieren** [kɔmpli'tsiːrən] vt to complicate.

**kompliziert** adj complicated; (MED: Bruch) compound.

**Komplizin** [kɔm'pliːtsɪn] f accomplice.

**Komplott** [kɔm'plɔt] (**-(e)s, -e**) nt plot.

**komponieren** [kɔmpo'niːrən] vt to compose.

**Komponist(in)** [kɔmpo'nɪst(ɪn)] m(f) composer.

**Komposition** [kɔmpozitsi'oːn] f composition.

**Kompost** [kɔm'pɔst] (**-(e)s, -e**) m compost; **~haufen** m compost heap.

**Kompott** [kɔm'pɔt] (**-(e)s, -e**) nt stewed fruit.

**Kompresse** [kɔm'prɛsə] (**-, -n**) f compress.

**Kompressor** [kɔm'prɛsɔr] *m* compressor.
**Kompromiß** [kɔmpro'mɪs] **(-sses, -sse)** *m*
compromise; **einen ~ schließen** to compro-
mise; **k~bereit** *adj* willing to compromise;
**~lösung** *f* compromise solution.
**kompromittieren** [kɔmprɔmɪ'tiːrən] *vt* to
compromise.
**Kondensation** [kɔndɛnzatsi'oːn] *f*
condensation.
**Kondensator** [kɔndɛn'zaːtɔr] *m* condenser.
**kondensieren** [kɔndɛn'ziːrən] *vt* to condense.
**Kondensmilch** *f* condensed milk.
**Kondensstreifen** *m* vapour (*BRIT*) *od* vapor
(*US*) trail.
**Kondition** [kɔnditsi'oːn] *f* condition, shape;
(*Durchhaltevermögen*) stamina.
**Konditionalsatz** [kɔnditsio'naːlzats] *m*
conditional clause.
**Konditionstraining** *nt* fitness training.
**Konditor** [kɔn'diːtɔr] *m* pastry-cook.
**Konditorei** [kɔndito'raɪ] *f* cake shop; (*mit
Café*) café.
**kondolieren** [kɔndo'liːrən] *vi:* **jdm ~** to
condole with sb, offer sb one's condolences.
**Kondom** [kɔn'doːm] **(-s, -e)** *m or nt* condom.
**Konfektion** [kɔnfɛktsi'oːn] *f* (production of)
ready-to-wear *od* off-the-peg clothing.
**Konfektionsgröße** *f* clothes size.
**Konfektionskleidung** *f* ready-to-wear *od*
off-the-peg clothing.
**Konferenz** [kɔnfe'rɛnts] *f* conference;
(*Besprechung*) meeting; **~schaltung** *f* (*TEL*)
conference circuit; (*RUNDF, TV*) television
*od* radio link-up.
**konferieren** [kɔnfe'riːrən] *vi* to confer; to have
a meeting.
**Konfession** [kɔnfɛsi'oːn] *f* religion; (*christlich*)
denomination; **k~ell** [-'nɛl] *adj*
denominational.
**Konfessions-** *zW:* **k~gebunden** *adj*
denominational; **k~los** *adj* non-denomina-
tional; **~schule** *f* denominational school.
**Konfetti** [kɔn'feti] **(-s)** *nt* confetti.
**Konfiguration** [kɔnfiguratsi'oːn] *f* (*COMPUT*)
configuration.
**Konfirmand(in)** [kɔnfɪr'mant, -'mandɪn] *m(f)*
candidate for confirmation.
**Konfirmation** [kɔnfɪrmatsi'oːn] *f* (*ECCL*)
confirmation.
**konfirmieren** [kɔnfɪr'miːrən] *vt* to confirm.
**konfiszieren** [kɔnfɪs'tsiːrən] *vt* to confiscate.
**Konfitüre** [kɔnfi'tyːrə] **(-, -n)** *f* jam.
**Konflikt** [kɔn'flɪkt] **(-(e)s, -e)** *m* conflict; **~herd**
*m* (*POL*) centre (*BRIT*) *od* center (*US*) of
conflict; **~stoff** *m* cause of conflict.
**konform** [kɔn'fɔrm] *adj* concurring; **~ gehen**
to be in agreement.
**Konfrontation** [kɔnfrɔntatsi'oːn] *f*
confrontation.
**konfrontieren** [kɔnfrɔn'tiːrən] *vt* to confront.
**konfus** [kɔn'fuːs] *adj* confused.
**Kongo** ['kɔŋgo] **(-s)** *m* Congo.

**Kongreß** [kɔn'grɛs] **(-sses, -sse)** *m* congress.
**Kongruenz** [kɔŋgru'ɛnts] *f* agreement,
congruence.
**König** ['køːnɪç] **(-(e)s, -e)** *m* king.
**Königin** ['køːnɪgɪn] *f* queen.
**königlich** *adj* royal **◊** *adv:* **sich ~ amüsieren**
(*umg*) to have the time of one's life.
**Königreich** *nt* kingdom.
**Königtum** ['køːnɪçtuːm] **(-(e)s, -tümer)** *nt*
kingship; (*Reich*) kingdom.
**konisch** ['koːnɪʃ] *adj* conical.
**Konj.** *abk* (= *Konjunktiv*) conj.
**Konjugation** [kɔnjugatsi'oːn] *f* conjugation.
**konjugieren** [kɔnju'giːrən] *vt* to conjugate.
**Konjunktion** [kɔnjɔŋktsi'oːn] *f* conjunction.
**Konjunktiv** ['kɔnjɔŋktiːf] **(-s, -e)** *m*
subjunctive.
**Konjunktur** [kɔnjɔŋk'tuːr] *f* economic
situation; (*Hoch~*) boom; **steigende/fallende
~** upward/downward economic trend;
**~barometer** *nt* economic indicators *pl*; **~loch**
*nt* temporary economic dip; **~politik** *f*
*policies aimed at preventing economic
fluctuations.*
**konkav** [kɔn'kaːf] *adj* concave.
**konkret** [kɔn'kreːt] *adj* concrete.
**Konkurrent(in)** [kɔnkʊ'rɛnt(ɪn)] *m(f)*
competitor.
**Konkurrenz** [kɔnkʊ'rɛnts] *f* competition; **jdm
~ machen** (*COMM, fig*) to compete with sb;
**k~fähig** *adj* competitive; **~kampf** *m*
competition; (*umg*) rat race.
**konkurrieren** [kɔnkʊ'riːrən] *vi* to compete.
**Konkurs** [kɔn'kʊrs] **(-es, -e)** *m* bankruptcy; **in
~ gehen** to go into receivership; **~ machen**
(*umg*) to go bankrupt; **~verfahren** *nt*
bankruptcy proceedings *pl*; **~verwalter** *m*
receiver; (*von Gläubigern bevollmächtigt*)
trustee.

================== *SCHLÜSSELWORT*

**können** ['kœnən] (*pt* **konnte**, *pp* **gekonnt** *od* (*als
Hilfsverb*) **können**) *vt, vi* **1** to be able to; **ich
kann es machen** I can do it, I am able to do
it; **ich kann es nicht machen** I can't do it, I'm
not able to do it; **ich kann nicht ...** I can't ..., I
cannot ...; **was ~ Sie?** what can you do?; **ich
kann nicht mehr** I can't go on; **ich kann
nichts dafür** I can't help it; **du kannst mich
(mal)!** (*umg*) get lost!
**2** (*wissen, beherrschen*) to know; **~ Sie
Deutsch?** can you speak German?; **er kann
gut Englisch** he speaks English well; **sie
kann keine Mathematik** she can't do
mathematics
**3** (*dürfen*) to be allowed to; **kann ich gehen?**
can I go?; **könnte ich ...?** could I ...?; **kann ich
mit?** (*umg*) can I come with you?
**4** (*möglich sein*): **Sie könnten recht haben**
you may be right; **das kann sein** that's
possible; **kann sein** maybe.

**Können** (-s) *nt* ability.
**Könner** (-s, -) *m* expert.
**Konnossement** [kɔnɔsə'mɛnt] *nt* (*Export*) bill of lading.
**konnte** *etc* ['kɔntə] *vb siehe* **können**.
**konsequent** [kɔnze'kvɛnt] *adj* consistent; **ein Ziel ~ verfolgen** to pursue an objective single-mindedly.
**Konsequenz** [kɔnze'kvɛnts] *f* consistency; (*Folgerung*) conclusion; **die ~en tragen** to take the consequences; **(aus etw) die ~en ziehen** to take the appropriate steps.
**konservativ** [kɔnzɛrva'tiːf] *adj* conservative.
**Konservatorium** [kɔnzɛrva'toːriʊm] *nt* academy of music, conservatory.
**Konserve** [kɔn'zɛrvə] (-, -n) *f* tinned (*BRIT*) *od* canned food.
**Konservenbüchse** *f*, **Konservendose** *f* tin (*BRIT*), can.
**konservieren** [kɔnzɛr'viːrən] *vt* to preserve.
**Konservierung** *f* preservation.
**Konservierungsstoff** *m* preservative.
**Konsole** [kɔnzoːlə] *f* games console.
**konsolidiert** [kɔnzoli'diːrt] *adj* consolidated.
**Konsolidierung** *f* consolidation.
**Konsonant** [kɔnzo'nant] *m* consonant.
**Konsortium** [kɔn'zɔrtsiʊm] *nt* consortium, syndicate.
**konspirativ** [kɔnspira'tiːf] *adj:* **~e Wohnung** conspirators' hideaway.
**konstant** [kɔn'stant] *adj* constant.
**Konstellation** [kɔnstɛlatsi'oːn] *f* constellation; (*fig*) line-up; (*von Faktoren etc*) combination.
**Konstitution** [kɔnstitutsi'oːn] *f* constitution.
**konstitutionell** [kɔnstitutsio'nɛl] *adj* constitutional.
**konstruieren** [kɔnstru'iːrən] *vt* to construct.
**Konstrukteur(in)** [kɔnstrʊk'tøːr(ɪn)] *m(f)* designer.
**Konstruktion** [kɔnstrʊktsi'oːn] *f* construction.
**Konstruktionsfehler** *m* (*im Entwurf*) design fault; (*im Aufbau*) structural defect.
**konstruktiv** [kɔnstrʊk'tiːf] *adj* constructive.
**Konsul** ['kɔnzʊl] (-s, -n) *m* consul.
**Konsulat** [kɔnzu'laːt] (-(e)s, -e) *nt* consulate.
**konsultieren** [kɔnzʊl'tiːrən] *vt* to consult.
**Konsum¹** [kɔn'zuːm] (-s) *m* consumption.
**Konsum²** ['kɔnzuːm] (-s, -s) *m* (*Genossenschaft*) cooperative society; (*Laden*) cooperative store, co-op (*umg*).
**Konsumartikel** *m* consumer article.
**Konsument** [kɔnzu'mɛnt] *m* consumer.
**Konsumgesellschaft** *f* consumer society.
**konsumieren** [kɔnzu'miːrən] *vt* to consume.
**Konsumterror** *m* pressures *pl* of a materialistic society.
**Konsumzwang** *m* compulsion to buy.
**Kontakt** [kɔn'takt] (-(e)s, -e) *m* contact; **mit jdm ~ aufnehmen** to get in touch with sb;

**~anzeige** *f* lonely hearts ad; **k~arm** *adj* unsociable; **k~freudig** *adj* sociable.
**kontaktieren** [kɔntak'tiːrən] *vt* to contact.
**Kontakt-** *zW:* **~linsen** *pl* contact lenses *pl*; **~mann** (-(e)s, *pl* **-männer**) *m* (*Agent*) contact; **~sperre** *f* ban on visits and letters (*to a prisoner*).
**Konterfei** ['kɔntɐfaɪ] (-s, -s) *nt* likeness, portrait.
**kontern** ['kɔntɐn] *vt, vi* to counter.
**Konterrevolution** ['kɔntɐrevolutsioːn] *f* counter-revolution.
**Kontinent** [kɔnti'nɛnt] *m* continent.
**Kontingent** [kɔntɪŋ'gɛnt] (-(e)s, -e) *nt* quota; (*Truppen~*) contingent.
**kontinuierlich** [kɔntinu'iːrlɪç] *adj* continuous.
**Kontinuität** [kɔntinui'tɛːt] *f* continuity.
**Konto** ['kɔnto] (-s, **Konten**) *nt* account; **das geht auf mein ~** (*umg: ich bin schuldig*) I am to blame for this; (*ich zahle*) this is on me (*umg*); **~auszug** *m* statement (of account); **~inhaber(in)** *m(f)* account holder.
**Kontor** [kɔn'toːr] (-s, -e) *nt* office.
**Kontorist(in)** [kɔnto'rɪst(ɪn)] *m(f)* clerk, office worker.
**Kontostand** *m* bank balance.
**kontra** ['kɔntra] *präp +akk* against; (*JUR*) versus.
**Kontra** (-s, -s) *nt* (*KARTEN*) double; **jdm ~ geben** (*fig*) to contradict sb.
**Kontrabaß** *m* double bass.
**Kontrahent** [-'hɛnt] *m* contracting party; (*Gegner*) opponent.
**Kontrapunkt** *m* counterpoint.
**Kontrast** [kɔn'trast] (-(e)s, -e) *m* contrast.
**Kontrollabschnitt** *m* (*COMM*) counterfoil, stub.
**Kontrollampe** [kɔn'trɔllampə] (*getrennt Kontroll-lampe*) *f* pilot lamp; (*AUT: für Ölstand etc*) warning light.
**Kontrolle** [kɔn'trɔlə] (-, -n) *f* control, supervision; (*Paß~*) passport control.
**Kontrolleur** [kɔntrɔ'løːr] *m* inspector.
**kontrollieren** [kɔntrɔ'liːrən] *vt* to control, supervise; (*nachprüfen*) to check.
**Kontrollturm** *m* control tower.
**Kontroverse** [kɔntro'vɛrzə] (-, -n) *f* controversy.
**Kontur** [kɔn'tuːr] *f* contour.
**Konvention** [kɔnvɛntsi'oːn] *f* convention.
**Konventionalstrafe** [kɔnvɛntsio'naːlʃtraːfə] *f* penalty *od* fine (*for breach of contract*).
**konventionell** [kɔnvɛntsio'nɛl] *adj* conventional.
**Konversation** [kɔnvɛrzatsi'oːn] *f* conversation.
**Konversationslexikon** *nt* encyclopaedia.
**konvex** [kɔn'vɛks] *adj* convex.
**Konvoi** ['kɔnvɔy] (-s, -s) *m* convoy.
**Konzentrat** [kɔntsɛn'traːt] (-s, -e) *nt* concentrate.
**Konzentration** [kɔntsɛntratsi'oːn] *f*

concentration.
**Konzentrationsfähigkeit** *f* power of concentration.
**Konzentrationslager** *nt* concentration camp.
**konzentrieren** [kɔntsɛn'triːrən] *vt, vr* to concentrate.
**konzentriert** *adj* concentrated ♦ *adv* (*zuhören, arbeiten*) intently.
**Konzept** [kɔn'tsɛpt] (-(e)s, -e) *nt* rough draft; (*Plan, Programm*) plan; (*Begriff, Vorstellung*) concept; **jdn aus dem ~ bringen** to confuse sb; **~papier** *nt* rough paper.
**Konzern** [kɔn'tsɛrn] (-s, -e) *m* combine.
**Konzert** [kɔn'tsɛrt] (-(e)s, -e) *nt* concert; (*Stück*) concerto; **~saal** *m* concert hall.
**Konzession** [kɔntsɛsi'oːn] *f* licence (*BRIT*), license (*US*); (*Zugeständnis*) concession; **die ~ entziehen** +*dat* (*COMM*) to disenfranchise.
**Konzessionär** [kɔntsɛsio'nɛːr] (-s, -e) *m* concessionaire.
**konzessionieren** [kɔntsɛsio'niːrən] *vt* to license.
**Konzil** [kɔn'tsiːl] (-s, -e *od* -ien) *nt* council.
**konzipieren** [kɔntsi'piːrən] *vt* to conceive; (*entwerfen*) to design.
**kooperativ** [ko|opera'tiːf] *adj* cooperative.
**kooperieren** [ko|ope'riːrən] *vi* to cooperate.
**koordinieren** [ko|ɔrdi'niːrən] *vt* to coordinate.
**Kopenhagen** [koːpən'haːgən] (-s) *nt* Copenhagen.
**Kopf** [kɔpf] (-(e)s, ⁓e) *m* head; **~ hoch!** chin up!; **~ an ~** shoulder to shoulder; (*SPORT*) neck and neck; **pro ~** per person *od* head; **~ oder Zahl?** heads or tails?; **jdm den ~ waschen** (*fig: umg*) to give sb a piece of one's mind; **jdm über den ~ wachsen** (*lit*) to outgrow sb; (*fig: Sorgen etc*) to be more than sb can cope with; **jdn vor den ~ stoßen** to antagonize sb; **sich** *dat* **an den ~ fassen** (*fig*) to be speechless; **sich** *dat* **über etw** *akk* **den ~ zerbrechen** to rack one's brains over sth; **sich** *dat* **etw durch den ~ gehen lassen** to think about sth; **sich** *dat* **etw aus dem ~ schlagen** to put sth out of one's mind; ... **und wenn du dich auf den ~ stellst!** (*umg*) ... no matter what you say/do!; **er ist nicht auf den ~ gefallen** he's no fool; **~bahnhof** *m* terminus station; **~bedeckung** *f* headgear.
**Köpfchen** [ˈkœpfçən] *nt:* **~ haben** to be brainy.
**köpfen** [ˈkœpfən] *vt* to behead; (*Baum*) to lop; (*Ei*) to take the top off; (*Ball*) to head.
**Kopf-** *zW:* **~ende** *nt* head; **~haut** *f* scalp; **~hörer** *m* headphone; **~kissen** *nt* pillow; **k~lastig** *adj* (*fig*) completely rational; **k~los** *adj* panic-stricken; **~losigkeit** *f* panic; **k~rechnen** *vi* to do mental arithmetic; **~salat** *m* lettuce; **k~scheu** *adj* **jdn k~scheu machen** to intimidate sb; **~schmerzen** *pl* headache *sing*; **~sprung** *m* header, dive; **~stand** *m* headstand; **~steinpflaster** *nt*: **eine Straße mit ~steinpflaster** a cobbled street;

**~stütze** *f* headrest; (*im Auto*) head restraint; **~tuch** *nt* headscarf; **k~über** *adv* head-first; **~weh** *nt* headache; **~zerbrechen** *nt*: **jdm ~zerbrechen machen** to give sb a lot of headaches.
**Kopie** [ko'piː] *f* copy.
**kopieren** [ko'piːrən] *vt* to copy.
**Kopierer** (-s, -) *m* (photo)copier.
**Kopilot(in)** [ˈkoːpiloːt(ɪn)] *m(f)* co-pilot.
**Koppel¹** [ˈkɔpəl] (-, -n) *f* (*Weide*) enclosure.
**Koppel²** [ˈkɔpəl] (-s, -) *nt* (*Gürtel*) belt.
**koppeln** *vt* to couple.
**Koppelung** *f* coupling.
**Koppelungsmanöver** *nt* docking manoeuvre (*BRIT*) *od* maneuver (*US*).
**Koralle** [ko'ralə] (-, -n) *f* coral.
**Korallenkette** *f* coral necklace.
**Korallenriff** *nt* coral reef.
**Korb** [kɔrp] (-(e)s, ⁓e) *m* basket; **jdm einen ~ geben** (*fig*) to turn sb down; **~ball** *m* basketball.
**Körbchen** [ˈkœrpçən] *nt* (*von Büstenhalter*) cup.
**Korbstuhl** *m* wicker chair.
**Kord** [kɔrt] (-(e)s, -e) *m* corduroy.
**Kordel** [ˈkɔrdəl] (-, -n) *f* cord, string.
**Korea** [ko'reːa] (-s) *nt* Korea.
**Koreaner(in)** (-s, -) *m(f)* Korean.
**Korfu** [ˈkɔrfu] (-s) *nt* Corfu.
**Korinthe** [ko'rɪntə] (-, -n) *f* currant.
**Korinthenkacker** [ko'rɪntənkakər] (-s, -) (*umg*) *m* fusspot, hair-splitter.
**Kork** [kɔrk] (-(e)s, -e) *m* cork.
**Korken** (-s, -) *m* stopper, cork; **~zieher** (-s, -) *m* corkscrew.
**Korn¹** [kɔrn] (-(e)s, ⁓er) *nt* corn, grain; (*Gewehr*) sight; **etw aufs ~ nehmen** (*fig: umg*) to hit out at sth.
**Korn²** [kɔrn] (-, -s) *m* (*Kornbranntwein*) corn schnapps.
**Kornblume** *f* cornflower.
**Körnchen** [ˈkœrnçən] *nt* grain, granule.
**körnig** [ˈkœrnɪç] *adj* granular, grainy.
**Kornkammer** *f* granary.
**Körnung** [ˈkœrnʊŋ] *f* (*TECH*) grain size; (*PHOT*) granularity.
**Körper** [ˈkœrpər] (-s, -) *m* body; **~bau** *m* build; **k~behindert** *adj* disabled; **~geruch** *m* body odour (*BRIT*) *od* odor (*US*); **~gewicht** *nt* weight; **~größe** *f* height; **~haltung** *f* carriage, deportment; **k~lich** *adj* physical; **k~liche Arbeit** manual work; **~pflege** *f* personal hygiene; **~schaft** *f* corporation; **~schaft des öffentlichen Rechts** public corporation *od* body; **~schaftssteuer** *f* corporation tax; **~sprache** *f* body language; **~teil** *m* part of the body; **~verletzung** *f* (*JUR*): **schwere ~verletzung** grievous bodily harm.
**Korps** [koːr] (-, -) *nt* (*MIL*) corps; (*UNIV*) students' club.
**korpulent** [kɔrpu'lɛnt] *adj* corpulent.
**korrekt** [kɔ'rɛkt] *adj* correct; **K~heit** *f*

correctness.
**Korrektor(in)** [kɔ'rɛktɔr, -'toːrɪn] (**-s, -**) m(f)
proofreader.
**Korrektur** [kɔrɛk'tuːr] f (eines Textes)
proofreading; (Text) proof; (SCH) marking,
correction; (**bei etw**) ~ **lesen** to proofread
(sth); ~**fahne** f (TYP) proof.
**Korrespondent(in)** [kɔrɛspɔn'dɛnt(ɪn)] m(f)
correspondent.
**Korrespondenz** [kɔrɛspɔn'dɛnts] f
correspondence; ~**qualität** f (Drucker) letter
quality.
**korrespondieren** [kɔrɛspɔn'diːrən] vi to
correspond.
**Korridor** ['kɔridoːr] (**-s, -e**) m corridor.
**korrigieren** [kɔri'giːrən] vt to correct;
(Meinung, Einstellung) to change.
**Korrosion** [kɔrozi'oːn] f corrosion.
**Korrosionsschutz** m corrosion protection.
**korrumpieren** [kɔrʊm'piːrən] vt (auch
COMPUT) to corrupt.
**korrupt** [kɔ'rʊpt] adj corrupt.
**Korruption** [kɔrʊptsi'oːn] f corruption.
**Korsett** [kɔr'zɛt] (**-(e)s, -e**) nt corset.
**Korsika** ['kɔrzika] (**-s**) nt Corsica.
**Koseform** ['koːzəfɔrm] f pet form.
**kosen** vt to caress ♦ vi to bill and coo.
**Kosename** m pet name.
**Kosewort** nt term of endearment.
**Kosmetik** [kɔs'meːtɪk] f cosmetics pl.
**Kosmetikerin** f beautician.
**kosmetisch** adj cosmetic; (Chirurgie) plastic.
**kosmisch** ['kɔsmɪʃ] adj cosmic.
**Kosmonaut** [kɔsmo'naʊt] (**-en, -en**) m
cosmonaut.
**Kosmopolit** [kɔsmopo'liːt] (**-en, -en**) m
cosmopolitan; **k~isch** [-po'liːtiʃ] adj
cosmopolitan.
**Kosmos** ['kɔsmɔs] (**-**) m cosmos.
**Kost** [kɔst] (**-**) f (Nahrung) food; (Verpflegung)
board; ~ **und Logis** board and lodging.
**kostbar** adj precious; (teuer) costly,
expensive; **K~keit** f preciousness;
costliness, expensiveness; (Wertstück)
treasure.
**Kosten** pl cost(s); (Ausgaben) expenses pl; **auf**
~ **von** at the expense of; **auf seine**
~ **kommen** (fig) to get one's money's worth.
**kosten** vt to cost; (versuchen) to taste ♦ vi to
taste; **koste es, was es wolle** whatever the
cost.
**Kosten-** zW: ~**anschlag** m estimate;
**k~deckend** adj cost-effective; ~**erstattung** f
reimbursement of expenses; ~**kontrolle** f
cost control; **k~los** adj free (of charge); ~-
**Nutzen-Analyse** f cost-benefit analysis;
**k~pflichtig** adj: **ein Auto k~pflichtig**
**abschleppen** to tow away a car at the
owner's expense; ~**stelle** f (COMM) cost
centre (BRIT) od center (US); ~**voranschlag**
m (costs) estimate.
**Kostgeld** nt board.

**köstlich** ['kœstlɪç] adj precious; (Einfall)
delightful; (Essen) delicious; **sich**
~ **amüsieren** to have a marvellous time.
**Kostprobe** f taste; (fig) sample.
**kostspielig** adj expensive.
**Kostüm** [kɔs'tyːm] (**-s, -e**) nt costume;
(Damen~) suit; ~**fest** nt fancy-dress party.
**kostümieren** [kɔsty'miːrən] vt, vr to dress up.
**Kostümprobe** f (THEAT) dress rehearsal.
**Kostümverleih** m costume agency.
**Kot** [koːt] (**-(e)s**) m excrement.
**Kotelett** [kɔtə'lɛt] (**-(e)s, -e** od **-s**) nt cutlet,
chop.
**Koteletten** pl sideboards pl (BRIT), sideburns
pl (US).
**Köter** ['køːtər] (**-s, -**) m cur.
**Kotflügel** m (AUT) wing.
**kotzen** ['kɔtsən] (umg!) vi to puke (!), throw
up; **das ist zum K~** it makes you sick.
**KP** (**-, -s**) f abk (= Kommunistische Partei) C.P.
**KPÖ** (**-**) f abk (= Kommunistische Partei
Österreichs) Austrian Communist Party.
**Kr.** abk = Kreis.
**Krabbe** ['krabə] (**-, -n**) f shrimp.
**krabbeln** vi to crawl.
**Krach** [krax] (**-(e)s, -s** od **-e**) m crash;
(andauernd) noise; (umg: Streit) quarrel,
argument; ~ **schlagen** to make a fuss; **k~en**
vi to crash; (beim Brechen) to crack ♦ vr
(umg) to argue, quarrel.
**krächzen** ['krɛçtsən] vi to croak.
**Kräcker** ['krɛkər] (**-s, -**) m (KOCH) cracker.
**kraft** [kraft] präp +gen by virtue of.
**Kraft** (**-, ⁻e**) f strength; (von Stimme, fig)
power, force; (Arbeits~) worker; **mit**
**vereinten Kräften werden wir ...** if we
combine our efforts we will ...; **nach**
**(besten) Kräften** to the best of one's
abilities; **außer** ~ **sein** (JUR: Geltung) to be
no longer in force; **in** ~ **treten** to come into
effect.
**Kraft-** zW: ~**aufwand** m effort; ~**ausdruck** m
swearword; ~**brühe** f beef tea.
**Kräfteverhältnis** ['krɛftəfɛrhɛltnɪs] nt (POL)
balance of power; (von Mannschaften etc)
relative strength.
**Kraftfahrer** m motor driver.
**Kraftfahrzeug** nt motor vehicle; ~**brief** m
(AUT) logbook (BRIT), motor-vehicle
registration certificate (US); ~**schein** m
(AUT) car licence (BRIT) od license (US);
~**steuer** f ≈ road tax.
**kräftig** ['krɛftɪç] adj strong; (Suppe, Essen)
nourishing; ~**en** ['krɛftɪgən] vt to strengthen.
**Kraft-** zW: **k~los** adj weak; powerless; (JUR)
invalid; ~**meierei** (umg) f showing off of
physical strength; ~**probe** f trial of
strength; ~**rad** nt motorcycle; ~**stoff** m fuel;
~**training** nt weight training; **k~voll** adj
vigorous; ~**wagen** m motor vehicle; ~**werk**
nt power station; ~**werker** m power station
worker.

**Kragen** ['kra:gən] (-, -) *m* collar; **da ist mir der ~ geplatzt** (*umg*) I blew my top; **es geht ihm an den ~** (*umg*) he's in for it; **~weite** *f* collar size; **das ist nicht meine ~weite** (*fig: umg*) that's not my cup of tea.

**Krähe** ['krɛːə] (-, -n) *f* crow.

**krähen** *vi* to crow.

**krakeelen** [kra'keːlən] (*umg*) *vi* to make a din.

**krakelig** ['kraːkəlɪç] (*umg*) *adj* (*Schrift*) scrawly, spidery.

**Kralle** ['kralə] (-, -n) *f* claw; (*Vogel~*) talon.

**krallen** *vt* to clutch; (*krampfhaft*) to claw.

**Kram** [kraːm] (-(e)s) *m* stuff, rubbish; **den ~ hinschmeißen** (*umg*) to chuck the whole thing; **k~en** *vi* to rummage; **~laden** (*pej*) *m* small shop.

**Krampf** [krampf] (-(e)s, ̈-e) *m* cramp; (*zuckend*) spasm; (*Unsinn*) rubbish; **~ader** *f* varicose vein; **k~haft** *adj* convulsive; (*fig: Versuche*) desperate.

**Kran** [kraːn] (-(e)s, ̈-e) *m* crane; (*Wasser~*) tap (*BRIT*), faucet (*US*).

**Kranich** ['kraːnɪç] (-s, -e) *m* (*ZOOL*) crane.

**krank** [krank] *adj* ill, sick; **sich ~ melden** to let one's boss *etc* know that one is ill; (*telefonisch*) to phone in sick; (*bes MIL*) to report sick; **jdn ~ schreiben** to give sb a medical certificate; (*bes MIL*) to put sb on the sick list; **das macht mich ~!** (*umg*) it gets on my nerves!, it drives me round the bend!; **sich ~ stellen** to pretend to be ill, malinger.

**Kranke(r)** *f(m)* sick person, invalid; (*Patient*) patient.

**kränkeln** ['krɛŋkəln] *vi* to be in bad health.

**kranken** ['krankən] *vi*: **an etw** *dat* **~** (*fig*) to suffer from sth.

**kränken** ['krɛŋkən] *vt* to hurt.

**Kranken-** *zW*: **~bericht** *m* medical report; **~besuch** *m* visit to a sick person; **~geld** *nt* sick pay; **~geschichte** *f* medical history; **~gymnastik** *f* physiotherapy; **~haus** *nt* hospital; **~kasse** *f* health insurance; **~pfleger** *m* orderly; (*mit Schwesternausbildung*) male nurse; **~pflegerin** *f* nurse; **~schein** *m* medical insurance certificate; **~schwester** *f* nurse; **~versicherung** *f* health insurance; **~wagen** *m* ambulance.

**krankfeiern** (*umg*) *vi* to be off sick; (*vortäuschend*) to skive (*BRIT*).

**krankhaft** *adj* diseased; (*Angst etc*) morbid; **sein Geiz ist schon ~** his meanness is almost pathological.

**Krankheit** *f* illness; disease; **nach langer schwerer ~** after a long serious illness.

**Krankheitserreger** *m* disease-causing agent.

**kränklich** ['krɛŋklɪç] *adj* sickly.

**Kränkung** *f* insult, offence (*BRIT*), offense (*US*).

**Kranz** [krants] (-es, ̈-e) *m* wreath, garland.

**Kränzchen** ['krɛntsçən] *nt* small wreath; (*fig: Kaffee~*) coffee circle.

**Krapfen** ['krapfən] (-s, -) *m* fritter; (*Berliner*) doughnut (*BRIT*), donut (*US*).

**kraß** [kras] *adj* crass; (*Unterschied*) extreme.

**Krater** ['kraːtər] (-s, -) *m* crater.

**Kratzbürste** ['kratsbyrstə] *f* (*fig*) crosspatch.

**Krätze** ['krɛtsə] *f* (*MED*) scabies *sing*.

**kratzen** ['kratsən] *vt*, *vi* to scratch; (*ab~*): **etw von etw ~** to scrape sth off sth.

**Kratzer** (-s, -) *m* scratch; (*Werkzeug*) scraper.

**Kraul** [kraʊl] (-s) *nt* (*auch*: **~schwimmen**) crawl; **k~en** *vi* (*schwimmen*) to do the crawl ♦ *vt* (*streicheln*) to tickle.

**kraus** [kraʊs] *adj* crinkly; (*Haar*) frizzy; (*Stirn*) wrinkled.

**Krause** ['kraʊzə] (-, -n) *f* frill, ruffle.

**kräuseln** ['krɔʏzəln] *vt* (*Haar*) to make frizzy; (*Stoff*) to gather; (*Stirn*) to wrinkle ♦ *vr* (*Haar*) to go frizzy; (*Stirn*) to wrinkle; (*Wasser*) to ripple.

**Kraut** [kraʊt] (-(e)s, **Kräuter**) *nt* plant; (*Gewürz*) herb; (*Gemüse*) cabbage; **dagegen ist kein ~ gewachsen** (*fig*) there's nothing anyone can do about that; **ins ~ schießen** (*lit*) to run to seed; (*fig*) to get out of control; **wie ~ und Rüben** (*umg*) extremely untidy.

**Kräutertee** ['krɔʏtərteː] *m* herb tea.

**Krawall** [kra'val] (-s, -e) *m* row, uproar.

**Krawatte** [kra'vatə] (-, -n) *f* tie.

**kreativ** [krea'tiːf] *adj* creative.

**Kreativität** [kreativi'tɛːt] *f* creativity.

**Kreatur** [krea'tuːr] *f* creature.

**Krebs** [kreːps] (-es, -e) *m* crab; (*MED*) cancer; (*ASTROL*) Cancer; **k~erregend** *adj* carcinogenic; **k~krank** *adj* suffering from cancer; **k~krank sein** to have cancer; **~kranke(r)** *f(m)* cancer victim; (*Patient*) cancer patient; **k~rot** *adj* red as a lobster.

**Kredit** [kre'diːt] (-(e)s, -e) *m* credit; (*Darlehen*) loan; (*fig*) standing; **~drosselung** *f* credit squeeze; **k~fähig** *adj* creditworthy; **~grenze** *f* credit limit; **~hai** (*umg*) *m* loan-shark; **~karte** *f* credit card; **~konto** *nt* credit account; **~politik** *f* lending policy; **k~würdig** *adj* creditworthy; **~würdigkeit** *f* creditworthiness, credit status.

**Kreide** ['kraɪdə] (-, -n) *f* chalk; **bei jdm (tief) in der ~ stehen** to be (deep) in debt to sb; **k~bleich** *adj* as white as a sheet.

**Kreis** [kraɪs] (-es, -e) *m* circle; (*Stadt~ etc*) district; **im ~ gehen** (*lit, fig*) to go round in circles; **(weite) ~e ziehen** (*fig*) to have (wide) repercussions; **weite ~e der Bevölkerung** wide sections of the population; **eine Feier im kleinen ~e** a celebration for a few close friends and relatives.

**kreischen** ['kraɪʃən] *vi* to shriek, screech.

**Kreisel** ['kraɪzəl] (-s, -) *m* top; (*Verkehrs~*) roundabout (*BRIT*), traffic circle (*US*).

**kreisen** ['kraɪzən] *vi* to spin; (*fig: Gedanken, Gespräch*): **~ um** to revolve around.

**Kreis-** *zW*: **k~förmig** *adj* circular; **~lauf** *m*

(*MED*) circulation; (*fig: der Natur etc*) cycle;
~**laufkollaps** *m* circulatory collapse;
~**laufstörungen** *pl* circulation trouble *sing*;
~**säge** *f* circular saw.
**Kreißsaal** ['kraɪsza:l] *m* delivery room.
**Kreisstadt** *f* ≈ county town.
**Kreisverkehr** *m* roundabout (*BRIT*), traffic
circle (*US*).
**Krematorium** [krema'to:riʊm] *nt*
crematorium.
**Kreml** ['krɛml] (**-s**) *m*: **der** ~ the Kremlin.
**Krempe** ['krɛmpə] (**-, -n**) *f* brim.
**Krempel** (**-s**) (*umg*) *m* rubbish.
**krepieren** [kre'pi:rən] (*umg*) *vi* (*sterben*) to die,
kick the bucket.
**Krepp** [krɛp] (**-s, -s** *od* **-e**) *m* crêpe.
**Kreppapier** (*getrennt Krepp-papier*) *nt* crêpe
paper.
**Kreppsohle** *f* crêpe sole.
**Kresse** ['krɛsə] (**-, -n**) *f* cress.
**Kreta** ['kre:ta] (**-s**) *nt* Crete.
**Kreter(in)** [kre:tər(ɪn)] (**-s, -**) *m(f)* Cretan.
**kretisch** *adj* Cretan.
**kreuz** [krɔʏts] *adj*: ~ **und quer** all over.
**Kreuz** (**-es, -e**) *nt* cross; (*ANAT*) small of the
back; (*KARTEN*) clubs; (*MUS*) sharp;
(*Autobahn~*) intersection; **zu** ~**e kriechen**
(*fig*) to eat humble pie, eat crow (*US*); **jdn**
**aufs** ~ **legen** to throw sb on his back; (*fig:
umg*) to take sb for a ride.
**kreuzen** *vt* to cross ♦ *vr* to cross; (*Meinungen
etc*) to clash ♦ *vi* (*NAUT*) to cruise; **die Arme**
~ to fold one's arms.
**Kreuzer** (**-s, -**) *m* (*Schiff*) cruiser.
**Kreuz-** *zW*: ~**fahrt** *f* cruise; ~**feuer** *nt* (*fig*): **im**
~**feuer stehen** to be caught in the crossfire;
~**gang** *m* cloisters *pl*.
**kreuzigen** *vt* to crucify.
**Kreuzigung** *f* crucifixion.
**Kreuzotter** *f* adder.
**Kreuzschmerzen** *pl* backache *sing*.
**Kreuzung** *f* (*Verkehrs~*) crossing, junction;
(*Züchtung*) cross.
**Kreuz-** *zW*: **k~unglücklich** *adj* absolutely
miserable; ~**verhör** *nt* cross-examination;
**ins** ~**verhör nehmen** to cross-examine;
~**weg** *m* crossroads; (*REL*) Way of the Cross;
~**worträtsel** *nt* crossword puzzle; ~**zeichen**
*nt* sign of the cross; ~**zug** *m* crusade.
**kribb(e)lig** ['krɪb(ə)lɪç] (*umg*) *adj* fidgety;
(*kribbelnd*) tingly.
**kribbeln** ['krɪbəln] *vi* (*jucken*) to itch; (*prickeln*)
to tingle.
**kriechen** ['kri:çən] *unreg vi* to crawl, creep;
(*pej*) to grovel, crawl.
**Kriecher** (**-s, -**) *m* crawler.
**kriecherisch** *adj* grovelling (*BRIT*), groveling
(*US*).
**Kriechspur** *f* crawler lane (*BRIT*).
**Kriechtier** *nt* reptile.
**Krieg** [kri:k] (**-(e)s, -e**) *m* war; ~ **führen** (**mit** *od*
**gegen**) to wage war (on).

**kriegen** ['kri:gən] (*umg*) *vt* to get.
**Krieger** (**-s, -**) *m* warrior; ~**denkmal** *nt* war
memorial; **k~isch** *adj* warlike.
**Kriegführung** *f* warfare.
**Kriegs-** *zW*: ~**beil** *nt*: **das** ~**beil begraben** (*fig*)
to bury the hatchet; ~**bemalung** *f* war
paint; ~**dienstverweigerer** *m* conscientious
objector; ~**erklärung** *f* declaration of war;
~**fuß** *m*: **mit jdm/etw auf** ~**fuß stehen** to be
at loggerheads with sb/not to get on with
sth; ~**gefangene(r)** *f(m)* prisoner of war;
~**gefangenschaft** *f* captivity; ~**gericht** *nt*
court-martial; ~**rat** *m* council of war;
~**recht** *nt* (*MIL*) martial law; ~**schauplatz** *m*
theatre (*BRIT*) *od* theater (*US*) of war;
~**schiff** *nt* warship; ~**schuld** *f* war guilt;
~**verbrecher** *m* war criminal; ~**versehrte(r)**
*f(m)* person disabled in the war; ~**zustand** *m*
state of war.
**Krim** [krɪm] *f*: **die** ~ the Crimea.
**Krimi** ['kri:mi] (**-s, -s**) (*umg*) *m* thriller.
**kriminal** [krimi'na:l] *adj* criminal;
**K~beamte(r)** *m* detective; **K~film** *m* crime
thriller *od* movie (*bes US*).
**Kriminalität** [kriminali'tɛ:t] *f* criminality.
**Kriminalpolizei** *f* ≈ Criminal Investigation
Department (*BRIT*), Federal Bureau of
Investigation (*US*).
**Kriminalroman** *m* detective story.
**kriminell** [krimi'nɛl] *adj* criminal.
**Kriminelle(r)** *f(m)* criminal.
**Krimskrams** ['krɪmskrams] (**-es**) (*umg*) *m* odds
and ends *pl*.
**Kringel** ['krɪŋəl] (**-s, -**) *m* (*der Schrift*) squiggle;
(*KOCH*) ring.
**kringelig** *adj*: **sich** ~ **lachen** (*umg*) to kill o.s.
laughing.
**Kripo** ['kri:po] (**-, -s**) *f abk* (= *Kriminalpolizei*)
≈ CID (*BRIT*), ≈ FBI (*US*).
**Krippe** ['krɪpə] (**-, -n**) *f* manger, crib;
(*Kinder~*) crèche.
**Krippenspiel** *nt* nativity play.
**Krippentod** *m* cot death.
**Krise** ['kri:zə] (**-, -n**) *f* crisis.
**kriseln** *vi*: **es kriselt** there's a crisis looming,
there is trouble brewing.
**Krisen-** *zW*: **k~fest** *adj* stable; ~**herd** *m* flash
point; trouble spot; ~**stab** *m* action *od* crisis
committee.
**Kristall**[1] [krɪs'tal] (**-s, -e**) *m* crystal.
**Kristall**[2] (**-s**) *nt* (*Glas*) crystal; ~**zucker** *m*
refined sugar crystals *pl*.
**Kriterium** [kri'te:riʊm] *nt* criterion.
**Kritik** [kri'ti:k] *f* criticism; (*Zeitungs~*)
review, write-up; **an jdm/etw** ~ **üben** to
criticize sb/sth; **unter aller** ~ **sein** (*umg*) to
be beneath contempt.
**Kritiker(in)** ['kri:tikər(ɪn)] (**-s, -**) *m(f)* critic.
**kritiklos** *adj* uncritical.
**kritisch** ['kri:tɪʃ] *adj* critical.
**kritisieren** [kriti'zi:rən] *vt, vi* to criticize.
**kritteln** ['krɪtəln] *vi* to find fault, carp.

**kritzeln** ['krɪtsəln] *vt, vi* to scribble, scrawl.
**Kroate** [kro'aːtə] (**-n, -n**) *m* Croat.
**Kroatien** [kro'aːtsiən] (**-s**) *nt* Croatia.
**Kroatin** *f* Croat.
**kroatisch** *adj* Croatian.
**kroch** *etc* [krɔx] *vb siehe* **kriechen**.
**Krokodil** [kroko'diːl] (**-s, -e**) *nt* crocodile.
**Krokodilstränen** *pl* crocodile tears *pl.*
**Krokus** ['kroːkʊs] (**-, -** *od* **-se**) *m* crocus.
**Krone** ['kroːnə] (**-, -n**) *f* crown; (*Baum~*) top;
  **einen in der ~ haben** (*umg*) to be tipsy.
**krönen** ['krøːnən] *vt* to crown.
**Kron-** *zW:* **~korken** *m* bottle top; **~leuchter** *m*
  chandelier; **~prinz** *m* crown prince.
**Krönung** ['krøːnʊŋ] *f* coronation.
**Kronzeuge** *m* (*JUR*) person who turns
  Queen's/King's (*BRIT*) *od* State's (*US*)
  evidence; (*Hauptzeuge*) principal witness.
**Kropf** [krɔpf] (**-(e)s, ⁻e**) *m* (*MED*) goitre (*BRIT*),
  goiter (*US*); (*von Vogel*) crop.
**Krösus** ['krøːzʊs] (**-ses, -se**) *m*: **ich bin doch
  kein ~** (*umg*) I'm not made of money.
**Kröte** ['krøːtə] (**-, -n**) *f* toad; **Kröten** *pl* (*umg:
  Geld*) pennies *pl.*
**Krs.** *abk* = **Kreis**.
**Krücke** ['krʏkə] (**-, -n**) *f* crutch.
**Krug** [kruːk] (**-(e)s, ⁻e**) *m* jug; (*Bier~*) mug.
**Krümel** ['kryːməl] (**-s, -**) *m* crumb.
**krümeln** *vt, vi* to crumble.
**krumm** [krʊm] *adj* (*lit, fig*) crooked; (*kurvig*)
  curved; **sich ~ und schief lachen** (*umg*) to
  fall about laughing; **keinen Finger ~ machen**
  (*umg*) not to lift a finger; **ein ~es Ding
  drehen** (*umg*) to do something crooked;
  **~beinig** *adj* bandy-legged.
**krümmen** ['krʏmən] *vt* to bend ♦ *vr* to bend,
  curve.
**krummlachen** (*umg*) *vr* to laugh o.s. silly.
**krummnehmen** *unreg vt*: **jdm etw ~** (*umg*) to
  take sth amiss.
**Krümmung** *f* bend, curve.
**Krüppel** ['krʏpəl] (**-s, -**) *m* cripple.
**Kruste** ['krʊstə] (**-, -n**) *f* crust.
**Kruzifix** [krutsi'fɪks] (**-es, -e**) *nt* crucifix.
**Kt.** *abk* = **Kanton**.
**Kto.** *abk* (= *Konto*) a/c.
**Kuba** ['kuːba] (**-s**) *nt* Cuba.
**Kubaner(in)** [ku'baːnər(ɪn)] (**-s, -**) *m(f)* Cuban.
**kubanisch** [ku'baːnɪʃ] *adj* Cuban.
**Kübel** ['kyːbəl] (**-s, -**) *m* tub; (*Eimer*) pail.
**Kubik-** [ku'biːk] *in zW* cubic; **~meter** *m* cubic
  metre (*BRIT*) *od* meter (*US*).
**Küche** ['kʏçə] (**-, -n**) *f* kitchen; (*Kochen*)
  cooking, cuisine.
**Kuchen** ['kuːxən] (**-s, -**) *m* cake; **~blech** *nt*
  baking tray; **~form** *f* baking tin (*BRIT*) *od*
  pan (*US*); **~gabel** *f* pastry fork.
**Küchen-** *zW:* **~gerät** *nt* kitchen utensil;
  (*elektrisch*) kitchen appliance; **~herd** *m*
  cooker, stove; **~maschine** *f* food processor;
  **~messer** *nt* kitchen knife; **~schabe** *f*
  cockroach; **~schrank** *m* kitchen cabinet.

**Kuchenteig** *m* cake mixture.
**Kuckuck** ['kʊkʊk] (**-s, -e**) *m* cuckoo; (*umg:
  Siegel des Gerichtsvollziehers*) bailiff's seal
  (*for distraint of goods*); **das weiß der ~**
  heaven (only) knows.
**Kuckucksuhr** *f* cuckoo clock.
**Kuddelmuddel** ['kʊdəlmʊdəl] (**-s**) (*umg*) *m od*
  *nt* mess.
**Kufe** ['kuːfə] (**-, -n**) *f* (*Faß~*) vat; (*Schlitten~*)
  runner; (*AVIAT*) skid.
**Kugel** ['kuːgəl] (**-, -n**) *f* ball; (*MATH*) sphere;
  (*MIL*) bullet; (*Erd~*) globe; (*SPORT*) shot; **eine
  ruhige ~ schieben** (*umg*) to have a cushy
  number; **k~förmig** *adj* spherical; **~kopf** *m*
  (*Schreibmaschine*) golf ball;
  **~kopfschreibmaschine** *f* golf-ball
  typewriter; **~lager** *nt* ball bearing.
**kugeln** *vt* to roll; (*SPORT*) to bowl ♦ *vr* (*vor
  Lachen*) to double up.
**Kugel-** *zW:* **k~rund** *adj* (*Gegenstand*) round;
  (*umg: Person*) tubby; **~schreiber** *m* ball-point
  (pen), Biro ®; **k~sicher** *adj* bulletproof;
  **~stoßen** (**-s**) *nt* shot put.
**Kuh** [kuː] (**-, ⁻e**) *f* cow; **~dorf** (*pej: umg*) *nt*
  one-horse town; **~handel** (*pej: umg*) *m*
  horse-trading; **~haut** *f*: **das geht auf keine
  ~haut** (*fig: umg*) that's absolutely
  incredible.
**kühl** [kyːl] *adj* (*lit, fig*) cool; **K~anlage** *f*
  refrigeration plant.
**Kühle** (**-**) *f* coolness.
**kühlen** *vt* to cool.
**Kühler** (**-s, -**) *m* (*AUT*) radiator; **~haube** *f*
  (*AUT*) bonnet (*BRIT*), hood (*US*).
**Kühl-** *zW:* **~flüssigkeit** *f* coolant; **~haus** *nt*
  cold-storage depot; **~raum** *m* cold-storage
  chamber; **~schrank** *m* refrigerator;
  **~tasche** *f* cool bag; **~truhe** *f* freezer.
**Kühlung** *f* cooling.
**Kühlwagen** *m* (*EISENB, Lastwagen*)
  refrigerator van.
**Kühlwasser** *nt* coolant.
**kühn** [kyːn] *adj* bold, daring; **K~heit** *f*
  boldness.
**Kuhstall** *m* cow-shed.
**k.u.k.** *abk* (= *kaiserlich und königlich*) imperial
  and royal.
**Küken** ['kyːkən] (**-s, -**) *nt* chicken; (*umg:
  Nesthäkchen*) baby of the family.
**kulant** [ku'lant] *adj* obliging.
**Kulanz** [ku'lants] *f* accommodating attitude,
  generousness.
**Kuli** ['kuːli] (**-s, -s**) *m* coolie; (*umg:
  Kugelschreiber*) Biro ®.
**kulinarisch** [kuli'naːrɪʃ] *adj* culinary.
**Kulisse** [ku'lɪsə] (**-, -n**) *f* scene.
**Kulissenschieber(in)** *m(f)* stagehand.
**Kulleraugen** ['kʊləraʊgən] (*umg*) *pl* wide eyes
  *pl.*
**kullern** ['kʊlərn] *vi* to roll.
**Kult** [kʊlt] (**-(e)s, -e**) *m* worship, cult; **mit etw
  ~ treiben** to make a cult out of sth.

**kultivieren** [kʊltiˈviːrən] *vt* to cultivate.
**kultiviert** *adj* cultivated, refined.
**Kultstätte** *f* place of worship.
**Kultur** [kʊlˈtuːr] *f* culture; (*Lebensform*) civilization; (*des Bodens*) cultivation; **~banause** (*umg*) *m* philistine, low-brow; **~betrieb** *m* culture industry; **~beutel** *m* toilet bag (*BRIT*), washbag.
**kulturell** [kʊltuˈrɛl] *adj* cultural.
**Kulturfilm** *m* documentary film.
**Kulturteil** *m* (*von Zeitung*) arts section.
**Kultusminister** [ˈkʊltʊsministər] *m* minister of education and the arts.
**Kümmel** [ˈkʏməl] (*-s, -*) *m* caraway seed; (*Branntwein*) kümmel.
**Kummer** [ˈkʊmər] (*-s*) *m* grief, sorrow.
**kümmerlich** [ˈkʏmərlɪç] *adj* miserable, wretched.
**kümmern** *vr*: **sich um jdn ~** to look after sb ♦ *vt* to concern; **sich um etw ~** to see to sth; **das kümmert mich nicht** that doesn't worry me.
**Kumpan(in)** [kʊmˈpaːn(ɪn)] (*-s, -e*) *m(f)* mate; (*pej*) accomplice.
**Kumpel** [ˈkʊmpəl] (*-s, -*) (*umg*) *m* mate.
**kündbar** [ˈkʏntbaːr] *adj* redeemable, recallable; (*Vertrag*) terminable.
**Kunde¹** [ˈkʊndə] (*-n, -n*) *m* customer.
**Kunde²** [ˈkʊndə] (*-, -n*) *f* (*Botschaft*) news.
**Kunden-** *zW*: **~beratung** *f* customer advisory service; **~dienst** *m* after-sales service; **~fang** (*pej*) *m*: **auf ~fang sein** to be touting for customers; **~fänger** *m* tout (*umg*); **~konto** *nt* charge account; **~kreis** *m* customers *pl*, clientele; **~werbung** *f* publicity (*aimed at attracting custom or customers*).
**Kund-** *zW*: **~gabe** *f* announcement; **k~geben** *unreg vt* to announce; **~gebung** *f* announcement; (*Versammlung*) rally.
**kundig** *adj* expert, experienced.
**kündigen** [ˈkʏndɪgən] *vi* to give in one's notice ♦ *vt* to cancel; **jdm ~** to give sb his notice; **zum 1. April ~** to give one's notice for April 1st; (*Mieter*) to give notice for April 1st; (*bei Mitgliedschaft*) to cancel one's membership as of April 1st; (*jdm*) **die Stellung ~** to give (sb) notice; **sie hat ihm die Freundschaft gekündigt** she has broken off their friendship.
**Kündigung** *f* notice.
**Kündigungsfrist** *f* period of notice.
**Kündigungsschutz** *m* protection against wrongful dismissal.
**Kundin** *f* customer.
**Kundschaft** *f* customers *pl*, clientele.
**Kundschafter** (*-s, -*) *m* spy; (*MIL*) scout.
**künftig** [ˈkʏnftɪç] *adj* future ♦ *adv* in future.
**Kunst** [kʊnst] (*-, -̈e*) *f* (*auch SCH*) art; (*Können*) skill; **das ist doch keine ~** it's easy; **mit seiner ~ am Ende sein** to be at one's wits' end; **das ist eine brotlose ~** there's no

money in that; **~akademie** *f* academy of art; **~druck** *m* art print; **~dünger** *m* artificial manure; **~erziehung** *f* (*SCH*) art; **~faser** *f* synthetic fibre (*BRIT*) *od* fiber (*US*); **~fehler** *m* professional error; (*weniger ernst*) slip; **~fertigkeit** *f* skilfulness (*BRIT*), skillfulness (*US*); **~flieger** *m* stunt flyer; **k~gerecht** *adj* skilful (*BRIT*), skillful (*US*); **~geschichte** *f* history of art; **~gewerbe** *nt* arts and crafts *pl*; **~griff** *m* trick, knack; **~händler** *m* art dealer; **~harz** *nt* artificial resin; **~leder** *nt* artificial leather.
**Künstler(in)** [ˈkʏnstlər(ɪn)] (*-s, -*) *m(f)* artist; **k~isch** *adj* artistic; **~name** *m* pseudonym; (*von Schauspieler*) stage name; **~pech** (*umg*) *nt* hard luck.
**künstlich** [ˈkʏnstlɪç] *adj* artificial; **~e Intelligenz** (*COMPUT*) artificial intelligence; **sich ~ aufregen** (*umg*) to get all worked up about nothing.
**Kunst-** *zW*: **~sammler** *m* art collector; **~seide** *f* artificial silk; **~stoff** *m* synthetic material; **~stopfen** (*-s*) *nt* invisible mending; **~stück** *nt* trick; **das ist kein ~stück** (*fig*) there's nothing to it; **~turnen** *nt* gymnastics *sing*; **k~voll** *adj* artistic; **~werk** *nt* work of art.
**kunterbunt** [ˈkʊntərbʊnt] *adj* higgledy-piggledy.
**Kupfer** [ˈkʊpfər] (*-s, -*) *nt* copper; **~geld** *nt* coppers *pl*.
**kupfern** *adj* copper ♦ *vt* (*fig: umg*) to plagiarize, copy, imitate.
**Kupferstich** *m* copperplate engraving.
**Kuppe** [ˈkʊpə] (*-, -n*) *f* (*Berg~*) top; (*Finger~*) tip.
**Kuppel** (*-, -n*) *f* cupola, dome.
**Kuppelei** [kʊpəˈlaɪ] *f* (*JUR*) procuring.
**kuppeln** *vi* (*JUR*) to procure; (*AUT*) to declutch ♦ *vt* to join.
**Kuppler** [ˈkʊplər] (*-s, -*) *m* procurer; **~in** *f* procuress.
**Kupplung** *f* (*auch TECH*) coupling; (*AUT etc*) clutch; **die ~ (durch)treten** to disengage the clutch.
**Kur** [kuːr] (*-, -en*) *f* (*im Kurort*) (health) cure, (course of) treatment; (*Schlankheitskur*) diet; **eine ~ machen** to take a cure (in a health resort).
**Kür** [kyːr] (*-, -en*) *f* (*SPORT*) free exercises *pl*.
**Kuratorium** [kuraˈtoːriʊm] *nt* (*Vereinigung*) committee.
**Kurbel** [ˈkʊrbəl] (*-, -n*) *f* crank, winder; (*AUT*) starting handle; **~welle** *f* crankshaft.
**Kürbis** [ˈkʏrbɪs] (*-ses, -se*) *m* pumpkin; (*exotisch*) gourd.
**Kurde** [ˈkʊrdə] (*-n, -n*) *m*, **Kurdin** *f* Kurd.
**Kurfürst** [ˈkuːrfʏrst] *m* Elector, electoral prince.
**Kurgast** *m* visitor (to a health resort).
**Kurier** [kuˈriːr] (*-s, -e*) *m* courier, messenger.
**kurieren** [kuˈriːrən] *vt* to cure.
**kurios** [kuriˈoːs] *adj* curious, odd.

**Kuriosität** [kuriozi'tɛːt] *f* curiosity.
**Kur-** *zW:* ~**konzert** *nt* concert (*at a health resort*); ~**ort** *m* health resort; ~**pfuscher** *m* quack.
**Kurs** [kʊrs] (**-es, -e**) *m* course; (*FIN*) rate; **hoch im ~ stehen** (*fig*) to be highly thought of; **einen ~ besuchen** *od* **mitmachen** to attend a class; **harter/weicher ~** (*POL*) hard/soft line; ~**änderung** *f* (*lit, fig*) change of course; ~**buch** *nt* timetable.
**Kürschner(in)** ['kʏrʃnər(ın)] (**-s, -**) *m(f)* furrier.
**kursieren** [kʊr'ziːrən] *vi* to circulate.
**kursiv** *adv* in italics.
**Kursnotierung** *f* quotation.
**Kursus** ['kʊrzʊs] (**-, Kurse**) *m* course.
**Kurswagen** *m* (*EISENB*) through carriage.
**Kurswert** *m* (*FIN*) market value.
**Kurtaxe** *f* spa tax (*paid by visitors*).
**Kurve** ['kʊrvə] (**-, -n**) *f* curve; (*Straßen~*) bend; (*statistisch, Fieber~ etc*) graph; **die ~ nicht kriegen** (*umg*) not to get around to it.
**kurvenreich** *adj:* „~**e Strecke**" "bends".
**kurvig** *adj* (*Straße*) bendy.
**kurz** [kʊrts] *adj* short ♦ *adv:* ~ **und bündig** concisely; **zu ~ kommen** to come off badly; **den kürzeren ziehen** to get the worst of it; ~ **und gut** in short; **über ~ oder lang** sooner or later; **eine Sache ~ abtun** to dismiss sth out of hand; **sich ~ fassen** to be brief; **darf ich mal ~ stören?** could I just interrupt for a moment?
**Kurzarbeit** *f* short-time work.

---

**Kurzarbeit** *is the term used to describe a shorter working week made necessary by a lack of work. It has been introduced in recent years as a preferable alternative to redundancy. It has to be approved by the* **Arbeitsamt,** *the job centre, which pays some compensation to the worker for loss of pay.*

---

**kurzärm(e)lig** *adj* short-sleeved.
**kurzatmig** *adj* (*fig*) feeble, lame; (*MED*) short-winded.
**Kürze** ['kʏrtsə] (**-, -n**) *f* shortness, brevity.
**kürzen** *vt* to cut short; (*in der Länge*) to shorten; (*Gehalt*) to reduce.
**kurzerhand** ['kʊrtsər'hant] *adv* without further ado; (*entlassen*) on the spot.
**kurz-** *zW:* **K~fassung** *f* shortened version; ~**fristig** *adj* short-term; ~**fristige Verbindlichkeiten** current liabilities *pl*; ~**gefaßt** *adj* concise; **K~geschichte** *f* short story; ~**halten** *unreg vt* to keep short; ~**lebig** *adj* short-lived.
**kürzlich** ['kʏrtslıc] *adv* lately, recently.
**Kurz-** *zW:* ~**meldung** *f* news flash; ~**parker** *m* short-stay parker; ~**schluß** *m* (*ELEK*) short circuit; ~**schlußhandlung** *f* (*fig*) rash action; ~**schrift** *f* shorthand; **k~sichtig** *adj* short-sighted; ~**strecken-** *in zW* short-range;

~**streckenläufer(in)** *m(f)* sprinter; **k~treten** *unreg vi* (*fig: umg*) to go easy; **k~um** *adv* in a word.
**Kürzung** *f* cutback.
**Kurzwaren** *pl* haberdashery (*BRIT*), notions *pl* (*US*).
**Kurzwelle** *f* short wave.
**kuschelig** *adj* cuddly.
**kuscheln** ['kʊʃəln] *vr* to snuggle up.
**kuschen** ['kʊʃən] *vi, vr* (*Hund etc*) to get down; (*fig*) to knuckle under.
**Kusine** [ku'ziːnə] *f* cousin.
**Kuß** [kʊs] (**-sses, ⸚sse**) *m* kiss.
**küssen** ['kʏsən] *vt, vr* to kiss.
**Küste** ['kʏstə] (**-, -n**) *f* coast, shore.
**Küsten-** *zW:* ~**gewässer** *pl* coastal waters *pl*; ~**schiff** *nt* coaster; ~**wache** *f* coastguard (station).
**Küster** ['kʏstər] (**-s, -**) *m* sexton, verger.
**Kutsche** ['kʊtʃə] (**-, -n**) *f* coach, carriage.
**Kutscher** (**-s, -**) *m* coachman.
**kutschieren** [kʊ'tʃiːrən] *vi:* **durch die Gegend ~** (*umg*) to drive around.
**Kutte** ['kʊtə] (**-, -n**) *f* cowl.
**Kuvert** [ku'vɛrt] (**-s, -e** *od* **-s**) *nt* envelope; (*Gedeck*) cover.
**Kuwait** [ku'vait] (**-s**) *nt* Kuwait.
**KV** *abk* (*MUS:* = *Köchelverzeichnis*): ~ **280** K. (number) 280.
**KW** *abk* (= *Kurzwelle*) SW.
**kW** *abk* (= *Kilowatt*) kW.
**Kybernetik** [kybɛr'neːtık] *f* cybernetics *sing.*
**kybernetisch** [kybɛr'neːtıʃ] *adj* cybernetic.
**KZ** (**-s, -s**) *nt abk* = **Konzentrationslager.**

---

# *L, l*

**L, l¹** [ɛl] *nt* L, l; ~ **wie Ludwig** ≈ L for Lucy, L for Love (*US*).
**l²** [ɛl] *abk* (= *Liter*) l.
**laben** ['laːbən] *vt* to refresh ♦ *vr* to refresh o.s.; (*fig*): **sich an etw** *dat* ~ to relish sth.
**labern** ['laːbərn] (*umg*) *vi* to prattle (on) ♦ *vt* to talk.
**labil** [la'biːl] *adj* (*physisch: Gesundheit*) delicate; (*: Kreislauf*) poor; (*psychisch*) unstable.
**Labor** [la'boːr] (**-s, -e** *od* **-s**) *nt* lab(oratory).
**Laborant(in)** [labo'rant(ın)] *m(f)* lab(oratory) assistant.
**Laboratorium** [labora'toːriʊm] *nt* lab(oratory).
**Labyrinth** [laby'rınt] (**-s, -e**) *nt* labyrinth.
**Lache** ['laxə] (**-, -n**) *f* (*Wasser*) pool, puddle; (*umg: Gelächter*) laugh.
**lächeln** ['lɛçəln] *vi* to smile; **L~** (**-s**) *nt* smile.

**lachen** ['laxən] *vi* to laugh; **mir ist nicht zum L~ (zumute)** I'm in no laughing mood; **daß ich nicht lache!** (*umg*) don't make me laugh!; **das wäre doch gelacht** it would be ridiculous; **L~** *nt*: **dir wird das L~ schon noch vergehen!** you'll soon be laughing on the other side of your face.

**Lacher** (**-s, -**) *m*: **die ~ auf seiner Seite haben** to have the last laugh.

**lächerlich** ['lɛçərlɪç] *adj* ridiculous; **L~keit** *f* absurdity.

**Lach-** *zW*: **~gas** *nt* laughing gas; **l~haft** *adj* laughable; **~krampf** *m*: **einen ~krampf bekommen** to go into fits of laughter.

**Lachs** [laks] (**-es, -e**) *m* salmon.

**Lachsalve** ['laxzalvə] *f* burst *od* roar of laughter.

**Lachsschinken** *m* smoked, rolled fillet of ham.

**Lack** [lak] (**-(e)s, -e**) *m* lacquer, varnish; (*von Auto*) paint.

**lackieren** [la'ki:rən] *vt* to varnish; (*Auto*) to spray.

**Lackierer** [la'ki:rər] (**-s, -**) *m* varnisher.

**Lackleder** *nt* patent leather.

**Lackmus** ['lakmʊs] (**-**) *m od nt* litmus.

**Lade** ['la:də] (**-, -n**) *f* box, chest; **~baum** *m* derrick; **~fähigkeit** *f* load capacity; **~fläche** *f* load area; **~gewicht** *nt* tonnage; **~hemmung** *f*: **das Gewehr hat ~hemmung** the gun is jammed.

**Laden** ['la:dən] (**-s, -̈**) *m* shop; (*Fenster~*) shutter; (*umg: Betrieb*) outfit; **der ~ läuft** (*umg*) business is good.

**laden** ['la:dən] *unreg vt* (*Lasten, COMPUT*) to load; (*JUR*) to summon; (*ein~*) to invite; **eine schwere Schuld auf sich** *akk* **~** to place o.s. under a heavy burden of guilt.

**Laden-** *zW*: **~aufsicht** *f* shopwalker (*BRIT*), floorwalker (*US*); **~besitzer** *m* shopkeeper; **~dieb** *m* shoplifter; **~diebstahl** *m* shoplifting; **~hüter** (**-s, -**) *m* unsaleable item; **~preis** *m* retail price; **~schluß** *m*, **~schlußzeit** *f* closing time; **~tisch** *m* counter.

**Laderampe** *f* loading ramp.

**Laderaum** *m* (*NAUT*) hold.

**lädieren** [lɛ'di:rən] *vt* to damage.

**lädt** [lɛːt] *vb siehe* **laden**.

**Ladung** ['la:dʊŋ] *f* (*Last*) cargo, load; (*Beladen*) loading; (*JUR*) summons; (*Ein~*) invitation; (*Spreng~*) charge.

**lag** *etc* [la:k] *vb siehe* **liegen**.

**Lage** ['la:gə] (**-, -n**) *f* position, situation; (*Schicht*) layer; **in der ~ sein** to be in a position; **eine gute/ruhige ~ haben** to be in a good/peaceful location; **Herr der ~ sein** to be in control of the situation; **~bericht** *m* report; (*MIL*) situation report; **~beurteilung** *f* situation assessment.

**lagenweise** *adv* in layers.

**Lager** ['la:gər] (**-s, -**) *nt* camp; (*COMM*) warehouse; (*Schlaf~*) bed; (*von Tier*) lair; (*TECH*) bearing; **etw auf ~ haben** to have sth in stock; **~arbeiter** *m* storehand; **~bestand** *m* stocks *pl*; **~feuer** *nt* camp fire; **~geld** *nt* storage (charges *pl*); **~haus** *nt* warehouse, store.

**Lagerist(in)** [la:gə'rɪst(ɪn)] *m(f)* storeman, storewoman.

**lagern** ['la:gərn] *vi* (*Dinge*) to be stored; (*Menschen*) to camp; (*auch vr: rasten*) to lie down ♦ *vt* to store; (*betten*) to lay down; (*Maschine*) to bed.

**Lager-** *zW*: **~raum** *m* storeroom; (*in Geschäft*) stockroom; **~schuppen** *m* store shed; **~stätte** *f* resting place.

**Lagerung** *f* storage.

**Lagune** [la'gu:nə] (**-, -n**) *f* lagoon.

**lahm** [la:m] *adj* lame; (*umg: langsam, langweilig*) dreary, dull; (*Geschäftsgang*) slow, sluggish; **eine ~e Ente sein** (*umg*) to have no zip; **~arschig** ['la:m|arʃɪç] (*umg*) *adj* bloody *od* damn (*!*) slow.

**lahmen** *vi* to be lame, limp.

**lähmen** ['lɛ:mən], **lahmlegen** ['la:mle:gən] *vt* to paralyse (*BRIT*), paralyze (*US*).

**Lähmung** *f* paralysis.

**Lahn** [la:n] (**-**) *f* (*Fluß*) Lahn.

**Laib** [laip] (**-s, -e**) *m* loaf.

**Laich** [laiç] (**-(e)s, -e**) *m* spawn; **l~en** *vi* to spawn.

**Laie** ['laiə] (**-n, -n**) *m* layman; (*fig, THEAT*) amateur.

**laienhaft** *adj* amateurish.

**Lakai** [la'kai] (**-en, -en**) *m* lackey.

**Laken** ['la:kən] (**-s, -**) *nt* sheet.

**Lakritze** [la'krɪtsə] (**-, -n**) *f* liquorice.

**lala** ['la'la] (*umg*) *adv*: **so ~** so-so, not too bad.

**lallen** ['lalən] *vt, vi* to slur; (*Baby*) to babble.

**Lama** ['la:ma] (**-s, -s**) *nt* llama.

**Lamelle** [la'mɛlə] *f* lamella; (*ELEK*) lamina; (*TECH*) plate.

**lamentieren** [lamɛn'ti:rən] *vi* to lament.

**Lametta** [la'mɛta] (**-s**) *nt* tinsel.

**Lamm** [lam] (**-(e)s, -̈er**) *nt* lamb; **~fell** *nt* lambskin; **l~fromm** *adj* like a lamb; **~wolle** *f* lambswool.

**Lampe** ['lampə] (**-, -n**) *f* lamp.

**Lampenfieber** *nt* stage fright.

**Lampenschirm** *m* lampshade.

**Lampion** [lampi'õ:] (**-s, -s**) *m*: Chinese lantern.

**Land** [lant] (**-(e)s, -̈er**) *nt* land; (*Nation, nicht Stadt*) country; (*Bundes~*) state; **auf dem ~(e)** in the country; **an ~ gehen** to go ashore; **endlich sehe ich ~** (*fig*) at last I can see the light at the end of the tunnel; **einen Auftrag an ~ ziehen** (*umg*) to land an order; **aus aller Herren Länder** from all over the world.

*A **Land** (plural **Länder**) is a member state of the* **BRD.** *There are 16 Länder, namely Baden-Württemberg, Bayern, Berlin, Brandenburg,*

*Bremen, Hamburg, Hessen, Mecklenburg-Vorpommern, Niedersachsen, Nordrhein-Westfalen, Rheinland-Pfalz, Saarland, Sachsen, Sachsen-Anhalt, Schleswig-Holstein and Thüringen. Each Land has its own parliament and constitution.*

**Landarbeiter** *m* farm *od* agricultural worker.
**Landbesitz** *m* landed property.
**Landbesitzer** *m* landowner.
**Landebahn** *f* runway.
**Landeerlaubnis** *f* permission to land.
**landeinwärts** [lant'|aɪnvɛrts] *adv* inland.
**landen** ['landən] *vt, vi* to land; **mit deinen Komplimenten kannst du bei mir nicht ~** your compliments won't get you anywhere with me.
**Ländereien** [lɛndə'raɪən] *pl* estates *pl*.
**Länderspiel** *nt* international (match).
**Landes-** *zW:* **~farben** *pl* national colours *pl* (*BRIT*) *od* colors *pl* (*US*); **~grenze** *f* (national) frontier; (*von Bundesland*) state boundary; **~innere(s)** *nt* inland region; **~kind** *nt* native of a German state; **~kunde** *f* regional studies *pl*; **~tracht** *f* national costume; **l~üblich** *adj* customary; **~verrat** *m* high treason; **~verweisung** *f* banishment; **~währung** *f* national currency; **l~weit** *adj* countrywide.
**Landeverbot** *nt* refusal of permission to land.
**Land-** *zW:* **~flucht** *f* emigration to the cities; **~gut** *nt* estate; **~haus** *nt* country house; **~karte** *f* map; **~kreis** *m* administrative region; **l~läufig** *adj* customary.
**ländlich** ['lɛntlɪç] *adj* rural.
**Land-** *zW:* **~rat** *m* head of administration of a Landkreis; **~schaft** *f* countryside; (*KUNST*) landscape; **die politische ~schaft** the political scene; **l~schaftlich** *adj* scenic; (*Besonderheiten*) regional.
**Landsmann** (**-(e)s**, *pl* **-leute**) *m* compatriot, fellow countryman.
**Landsmännin** *f* compatriot, fellow countrywoman.
**Land-** *zW:* **~straße** *f* country road; **~streicher** (**-s**, **-**) *m* tramp; **~strich** *m* region; **~tag** *m* (*POL*) regional parliament.
**Landung** ['landʊŋ] *f* landing.
**Landungs-** *zW:* **~boot** *nt* landing craft; **~brücke** *f* jetty, pier; **~stelle** *f* landing place.
**Landurlaub** *m* shore leave.
**Landvermesser** *m* surveyor.
**landw.** *abk* (= *landwirtschaftlich*) agricultural.
**Land-** *zW:* **~wirt** *m* farmer; **~wirtschaft** *f* agriculture; **~wirtschaft betreiben** to farm; **~zunge** *f* spit.
**lang** [laŋ] *adj* long; (*umg: Mensch*) tall ♦ *adv:* **~ anhaltender Beifall** prolonged applause; **hier wird mir die Zeit nicht ~** I won't get

bored here; **er machte ein ~es Gesicht** his face fell; **~ und breit** at great length; **~atmig** *adj* long-winded.
**lange** *adv* for a long time; (*dauern, brauchen*) a long time; **~ nicht so ...** not nearly as ...; **wenn der das schafft, kannst du das schon ~** if he can do it, you can do it easily.
**Länge** ['lɛŋə] (**-, -n**) *f* length; (*GEOG*) longitude; **etw der ~ nach falten** to fold sth lengthways; **etw in die ~ ziehen** to drag sth out (*umg*); **der ~ nach hinfallen** to fall flat (on one's face).
**langen** ['laŋən] *vi* (*ausreichen*) to do, suffice; (*fassen*): **~ nach** to reach for; **es langt mir** I've had enough; **jdm eine ~** (*umg*) to give sb a clip on the ear.
**Längengrad** *m* longitude.
**Längenmaß** *nt* linear measure.
**langersehnt** ['laŋ|ɛrzeːnt] *adj attrib* longed-for.
**Langeweile** *f* boredom.
**lang-** *zW:* **~fristig** *adj* long-term ♦ *adv* in the long term; (*planen*) for the long term; **~fristige Verbindlichkeiten** long-term liabilities *pl*; **~jährig** *adj* (*Freundschaft, Gewohnheit*) long-standing; (*Erfahrung, Verhandlungen*) many years of; (*Mitarbeiter*) of many years' standing; **L~lauf** *m* (*SKI*) cross-country skiing; **~lebig** *adj* long-lived; **~lebige Gebrauchsgüter** consumer durables *pl*.
**länglich** *adj* longish.
**Langmut** *f* forbearance, patience.
**langmütig** *adj* forbearing.
**längs** [lɛŋs] *präp* (*+gen od dat*) along ♦ *adv* lengthways.
**langsam** *adj* slow; **immer schön ~!** (*umg*) easy does it!; **ich muß jetzt ~ gehen** I must be getting on my way; **~ (aber sicher) reicht es mir** I've just about had enough; **L~keit** *f* slowness.
**Langschläfer** *m* late riser.
**Langspielplatte** *f* long-playing record.
**längsseit(s)** *adv* alongside ♦ *präp +gen* alongside.
**längst** [lɛŋst] *adv:* **das ist ~ fertig** that was finished a long time ago, that has been finished for a long time.
**längste(r, s)** *adj* longest.
**Langstrecken-** *in zW* long-distance; **~flugzeug** *nt* long-range aircraft.
**Languste** [laŋ'gʊstə] (**-, -n**) *f* crayfish, crawfish (*US*).
**lang-** *zW:* **~weilen** *vt untr* to bore ♦ *vr untr* to be *od* get bored; **L~weiler** (**-s**, **-**) *m* bore; **~weilig** *adj* boring, tedious; **L~welle** *f* long wave; **~wierig** *adj* lengthy, long-drawn-out.
**Lanze** ['lantsə] (**-, -n**) *f* lance.
**Lanzette** [lan'tsɛtə] *f* lancet.
**Laos** ['laːɔs] (**-**) *nt* Laos.
**Laote** [la'oːtə] (**-n, -n**) *m*, **Laotin** *f* Laotian.
**laotisch** [la'oːtɪʃ] *adj* Laotian.
**lapidar** [lapi'daːr] *adj* terse, pithy.

**Lappalie** [la'pa:liə] *f* trifle.
**Lappe** ['lapə] (**-n, -n**) *m* Lapp, Laplander.
**Lappen** (**-s, -**) *m* cloth, rag; (*ANAT*) lobe; **jdm durch die ~ gehen** (*umg*) to slip through sb's fingers.
**läppern** ['lɛpərn] (*umg*) *vr unpers:* **es läppert sich zusammen** it (all) mounts up.
**Lappin** *f* Lapp, Laplander.
**läppisch** ['lɛpɪʃ] *adj* foolish.
**Lappland** ['laplant] (**-s**) *nt* Lapland.
**Lappländer(in)** ['laplɛndər(ɪn)] (**-s, -**) *m(f)* Lapp, Laplander.
**lappländisch** *adj* Lapp.
**Lapsus** ['lapsus] (**-, -**) *m* slip.
**Laptop** ['lɛptɔp] (**-s, -s**) *m* laptop.
**Lärche** ['lɛrçə] (**-, -n**) *f* larch.
**Lärm** [lɛrm] (**-(e)s**) *m* noise; **~belästigung** *f* noise nuisance; **l~en** *vi* to be noisy, make a noise.
**Larve** ['larfə] (**-, -n**) *f* mask; (*BIOL*) larva.
**las** *etc* [la:s] *vb siehe* **lesen**.
**Lasagne** [la'zanjə] *pl* lasagne *sing*.
**lasch** [laʃ] *adj* slack; (*Geschmack*) tasteless.
**Lasche** ['laʃə] (**-, -n**) *f* (*Schuh~*) tongue; (*EISENB*) fishplate.
**Laser** ['le:zər] (**-s, -**) *m* laser; **~drucker** *m* laser printer.

================ *SCHLÜSSELWORT*

**lassen** ['lasən] (*pt* **ließ,** *pp* **gelassen** *od (als Hilfsverb)* **lassen**) *vt* **1** (*unter~*) to stop; (*momentan*) to leave; **laß das (sein)!** don't (do it)!; (*hör auf*) stop it!; **laß mich!** leave me alone!; **~ wir das!** let's leave it!; **er kann das Trinken nicht ~** he can't stop drinking; **tu, was du nicht ~ kannst!** if you must, you must!
**2** (*zurück~*) to leave; **etw ~, wie es ist** to leave sth (just) as it is
**3** (*erlauben*) to let, allow; **laß ihn doch** let him; **jdn ins Haus ~** to let sb into the house; **das muß man ihr ~** (*zugestehen*) you've got to grant her that
♦ *vi:* **laß mal, ich mache das schon** leave it, I'll do it
♦ *Hilfsverb* **1** (*veran~*): **etw machen ~** to have *od* get sth done; **jdn etw machen ~** to get sb to do sth; (*durch Befehl usw*) to make sb do sth; **er ließ mich warten** he kept me waiting; **mein Vater wollte mich studieren ~** my father wanted me to study; **sich** *dat* **etw schicken ~** to have sth sent (to one)
**2** (*zu~*): **jdn etw wissen ~** to let sb know sth; **das Licht brennen ~** to leave the light on; **einen Bart wachsen ~** to grow a beard; **laß es dir gutgehen!** take care of yourself!
**3: laß uns gehen** let's go
♦ *vr:* **das läßt sich machen** that can be done; **es läßt sich schwer sagen** it's difficult to say.

**lässig** ['lɛsɪç] *adj* casual; **L~keit** *f* casualness.

**läßlich** ['lɛslɪç] *adj* pardonable, venial.
**läßt** [lɛst] *vb siehe* **lassen**.
**Last** [last] (**-, -en**) *f* load; (*Trag~*) burden; (*NAUT, AVIAT*) cargo; (*meist pl: Gebühr*) charge; **jdm zur ~ fallen** to be a burden to sb; **~auto** *nt* lorry (*BRIT*), truck.
**lasten** *vi:* **~ auf** +*dat* to weigh on.
**Lastenaufzug** *m* hoist, goods lift (*BRIT*) *od* elevator (*US*).
**Lastenausgleichsgesetz** *nt* law on financial compensation for losses suffered in WWII.
**Laster** ['lastər] (**-s, -**) *nt* vice ♦ *m* (*umg*) lorry (*BRIT*), truck.
**Lästerer** ['lɛstərər] (**-s, -**) *m* mocker; (*Gottes~*) blasphemer.
**lasterhaft** *adj* immoral.
**lästerlich** *adj* scandalous.
**lästern** ['lɛstərn] *vt, vi* (*Gott*) to blaspheme; (*schlecht sprechen*) to mock.
**Lästerung** *f* jibe; (*Gottes~*) blasphemy.
**lästig** ['lɛstɪç] *adj* troublesome, tiresome; **(jdm) ~ werden** to become a nuisance (to sb); (*zum Ärgernis werden*) to get annoying (to sb).
**Last-** *zW:* **~kahn** *m* barge; **~kraftwagen** *m* heavy goods vehicle; **~schrift** *f* debiting; (*Eintrag*) debit item; **~tier** *nt* beast of burden; **~träger** *m* porter; **~wagen** *m* lorry (*BRIT*), truck; **~zug** *m* truck and trailer.
**Latein** [la'tain] (**-s**) *nt* Latin; **mit seinem ~ am Ende sein** (*fig*) to be stumped (*umg*); **~amerika** *nt* Latin America; **l~amerikanisch** *adj* Latin-American; **l~isch** *adj* Latin.
**latent** [la'tɛnt] *adj* latent.
**Laterne** [la'tɛrnə] (**-, -n**) *f* lantern; (*Straßen~*) lamp, light.
**Laternenpfahl** *m* lamppost.
**Latinum** [la'ti:nom] (**-s**) *nt:* **kleines/großes ~** ≈ Latin O-/A-level exams (*BRIT*).
**Latrine** [la'tri:nə] *f* latrine.
**Latsche** ['latʃə] (**-, -n**) *f* dwarf pine.
**Latschen** ['la:tʃən] (*umg*) *m* (*Hausschuh*) slipper; (*pej: Schuh*) worn-out shoe.
**latschen** (*umg*) *vi* (*gehen*) to wander, go; (*lässig*) to slouch.
**Latte** ['latə] (**-, -n**) *f* lath; (*SPORT*) goalpost; (*quer*) crossbar.
**Lattenzaun** *m* lattice fence.
**Latz** [lats] (**-es, ⁻e**) *m* bib; (*Hosen~*) front flap.
**Lätzchen** ['lɛtsçən] *nt* bib.
**Latzhose** *f* dungarees *pl*.
**lau** [lau] *adj* (*Nacht*) balmy; (*Wasser*) lukewarm; (*fig: Haltung*) half-hearted.
**Laub** [laup] (**-(e)s**) *nt* foliage; **~baum** *m* deciduous tree.
**Laube** ['laubə] (**-, -n**) *f* arbour (*BRIT*), arbor (*US*); (*Gartenhäuschen*) summerhouse.
**Laub-** *zW:* **~frosch** *m* tree frog; **~säge** *f* fretsaw; **~wald** *m* deciduous forest.
**Lauch** [laux] (**-(e)s, -e**) *m* leek.
**Lauer** ['lauər] *f:* **auf der ~ sein** *od* **liegen** to lie in wait.

**lauern** *vi* to lie in wait; (*Gefahr*) to lurk.

**Lauf** [lauf] (-(e)s, Läufe) *m* run; (*Wett~*) race; (*Entwicklung, ASTRON*) course; (*Gewehr~*) barrel; **im ~e des Gesprächs** during the conversation; **sie ließ ihren Gefühlen freien ~** she gave way to her feelings; **einer Sache** *dat* **ihren ~ lassen** to let sth take its course; **~bahn** *f* career; **eine ~bahn einschlagen** to embark on a career; **~bursche** *m* errand boy.

**laufen** ['laufən] *unreg vi* to run; (*umg: gehen*) to walk; (*Uhr*) to go; (*funktionieren*) to work; (*Elektrogerät: eingeschaltet sein*) to be on; (*gezeigt werden: Film, Stück*) to be on; (*Bewerbung, Antrag*) to be under consideration ♦ *vt* to run; **es lief mir eiskalt über den Rücken** a chill ran up my spine; **ihm läuft die Nase** he's got a runny nose; **die Dinge ~ lassen** to let things slide; **die Sache ist gelaufen** (*umg*) it's in the bag; **das Auto läuft auf meinen Namen** the car is in my name; **Ski/Schlittschuh/Rollschuh** *etc* **~** to ski/skate/rollerskate *etc*.

**laufend** *adj* running; (*Monat, Ausgaben*) current; **auf dem ~en sein/halten** to be/keep up to date; **am ~en Band** (*fig*) continuously; **~e Nummer** serial number; (*von Konto*) number; **~e Kosten** running costs *pl*.

**laufenlassen** *unreg vt* (*Person*) to let go.

**Läufer** ['lɔyfər] (-s, -) *m* (*Teppich, SPORT*) runner; (*Fußball*) half-back; (*Schach*) bishop.

**Lauferei** [laufə'rai] (*umg*) *f* running about.

**Läuferin** *f* (*SPORT*) runner.

**Lauf-** *zW:* **~feuer** *nt:* **sich wie ein ~feuer verbreiten** to spread like wildfire; **~kundschaft** *f* passing trade; **~masche** *f* run, ladder (*BRIT*); **~paß** *m:* **jdm den ~paß geben** (*umg*) to give sb his/her marching orders; **~schritt** *m:* **im ~schritt** at a run; **~stall** *m* playpen; **~steg** *m* catwalk.

**läuft** [lɔyft] *vb siehe* **laufen**.

**Lauf-** *zW:* **~werk** *nt* running gear; (*COMPUT*) drive; **~zeit** *f* (*von Wechsel, Vertrag*) period of validity; (*von Maschine*) life; **~zettel** *m* circular.

**Lauge** ['laugə] (-, -n) *f* soapy water; (*CHEM*) alkaline solution.

**Laune** ['launə] (-, -n) *f* mood, humour (*BRIT*), humor (*US*); (*Einfall*) caprice; (*schlechte ~*) temper.

**launenhaft** *adj* capricious, changeable.

**launisch** *adj* moody.

**Laus** [laus] (-, Läuse) *f* louse; **ihm ist (wohl) eine ~ über die Leber gelaufen** (*umg*) something's biting him; **~bub** *m* rascal, imp.

**Lauschangriff** *m:* **~ (gegen)** bugging operation (on).

**lauschen** ['lauʃən] *vi* to eavesdrop, listen in.

**Lauscher(in)** (-s, -) *m(f)* eavesdropper.

**lauschig** ['lauʃɪç] *adj* snug.

**Lausejunge** (*umg*) *m* little devil; (*wohlwollend*) rascal.

**lausen** ['lauzən] *vt* to delouse; **ich denk', mich laust der Affe!** (*umg*) well blow me down!

**lausig** ['lauzɪç] (*umg*) *adj* lousy; (*Kälte*) perishing ♦ *adv* awfully.

**laut** [laut] *adj* loud ♦ *adv* loudly; (*lesen*) aloud ♦ *präp* (*+gen od dat*) according to.

**Laut** (-(e)s, -e) *m* sound.

**Laute** ['lautə] (-, -n) *f* lute.

**lauten** ['lautən] *vi* to say; (*Urteil*) to be.

**läuten** ['lɔytən] *vt, vi* to ring, sound; **er hat davon (etwas) ~ hören** (*umg*) he has heard something about it.

**lauter** ['lautər] *adj* (*Wasser*) clear, pure; (*Wahrheit, Charakter*) honest ♦ *adj inv* (*Freude, Dummheit etc*) sheer ♦ *adv* (*nur*) nothing but, only; **L~keit** *f* purity; honesty, integrity.

**läutern** ['lɔytərn] *vt* to purify.

**Läuterung** *f* purification.

**laut-** *zW:* **~hals** *adv* at the top of one's voice; **~los** *adj* noiseless, silent; **~malend** *adj* onomatopoeic; **L~schrift** *f* phonetics *pl*; **L~sprecher** *m* loudspeaker; **L~sprecheranlage** *f:* **öffentliche L~sprecheranlage** public-address *od* PA system; **L~sprecherwagen** *m* loudspeaker van; **~stark** *adj* vociferous; **L~stärke** *f* (*RUNDF*) volume.

**lauwarm** ['lauvarm] *adj* (*lit, fig*) lukewarm.

**Lava** ['laːva] (-, Laven) *f* lava.

**Lavendel** [la'vɛndəl] (-s, -) *m* lavender.

**Lawine** [la'viːnə] *f* avalanche.

**Lawinengefahr** *f* danger of avalanches.

**lax** [laks] *adj* lax.

**Layout** ['leːaut] (-s, -s) *nt* layout.

**Lazarett** [latsa'rɛt] (-(e)s, -e) *nt* (*MIL*) hospital, infirmary.

**Ldkrs.** *abk* = **Landkreis**.

**leasen** ['liːzən] *vt* to lease.

**Leasing** ['liːzɪŋ] (-s, -s) *nt* (*COMM*) leasing.

**Lebehoch** *nt* three cheers *pl*.

**Lebemann** (-(e)s, *pl* -männer) *m* man about town.

**Leben** ['leːbən] (-s, -) *nt* life; **am ~ sein/ bleiben** to be/stay alive; **ums ~ kommen** to die; **etw ins ~ rufen** to bring sth into being; **seines ~s nicht mehr sicher sein** to fear for one's life; **etw für sein ~ gern tun** to love doing sth.

**leben** *vt, vi* to live.

**lebend** *adj* living; **~es Inventar** livestock.

**lebendig** [le'bɛndɪç] *adj* living, alive; (*lebhaft*) lively; **L~keit** *f* liveliness.

**Lebens-** *zW:* **~abend** *m* old age; **~alter** *nt* age; **~anschauung** *f* philosophy of life; **~art** *f* way of life; **l~bejahend** *adj* positive; **~dauer** *f* life (span); (*von Maschine*) life; **~erfahrung** *f* experience of life; **~erwartung** *f* life expectancy; **l~fähig** *adj* able to live; **l~froh** *adj* full of the joys of life; **~gefahr** *f:* **~gefahr!** danger!; **in ~gefahr** critically *od* dangerously ill; **l~gefährlich** *adj* dangerous; (*Krankheit, Verletzung*) critical; **~gefährte** *m:*

ihr ~**gefährte** the man she lives with; ~**gefährtin** f: **seine ~gefährtin** the woman he lives with; ~**größe** f: **in ~größe** life-size(d); ~**haltungskosten** pl cost of living sing; ~**inhalt** m purpose in life; ~**jahr** nt year of life; ~**künstler** m master in the art of living; ~**lage** f situation in life; l~**länglich** adj (Strafe) for life; l~**lauf** m curriculum vitae, CV; l~**lustig** adj cheerful, lively; ~**mittel** pl food sing; ~**mittelgeschäft** nt grocer's; ~**mittelvergiftung** f food poisoning; l~**müde** adj tired of life; ~**qualität** f quality of life; ~**raum** m (POL) Lebensraum; (BIOL) biosphere; ~**retter** m lifesaver; ~**standard** m standard of living; ~**stellung** f permanent post; ~**stil** m life style; ~**unterhalt** m livelihood; ~**versicherung** f life insurance; ~**wandel** m way of life; ~**weise** f way of life, habits pl; ~**weisheit** f maxim; (~**erfahrung**) wisdom; ~**wichtig** adj vital; ~**zeichen** m sign of life; ~**zeit** f lifetime; **Beamter auf ~zeit** permanent civil servant.

**Leber** ['le:bər] (-, -n) f liver; **frei** od **frisch von der ~ weg reden** (umg) to speak out frankly; ~**fleck** m mole; ~**käse** m ≈ meat loaf; ~**tran** m cod-liver oil; ~**wurst** f liver sausage.

**Lebewesen** nt creature.

**Lebewohl** nt farewell, goodbye.

**leb-** zW: ~**haft** adj lively, vivacious; **L~haftigkeit** f liveliness, vivacity; **L~kuchen** m gingerbread; ~**los** adj lifeless; **L~tag** m (fig): **das werde ich mein L~tag nicht vergessen** I'll never forget that as long as I live; **L~zeiten** pl: **zu jds L~zeiten** (Leben) in sb's lifetime.

**lechzen** ['lɛçtsən] vi: **nach etw ~** to long for sth.

**leck** [lɛk] adj leaky, leaking; **L~** (-(e)s, -e) nt leak.

**lecken¹** vi (Loch haben) to leak.

**lecken²** vt, vi (schlecken) to lick.

**lecker** ['lɛkər] adj delicious, tasty; **L~bissen** m dainty morsel; **L~maul** nt: **ein L~maul sein** to enjoy one's food.

**led.** abk = **ledig.**

**Leder** ['le:dər] (-s, -) nt leather; (umg: Fußball) ball; ~**hose** f leather trousers pl; (von Tracht) leather shorts pl.

**ledern** adj leather.

**Lederwaren** pl leather goods pl.

**ledig** ['le:dɪç] adj single; **einer Sache** gen **~ sein** to be free of sth; ~**lich** adv merely, solely.

**leer** [le:r] adj empty; (Blick) vacant.

**Leere** (-) f emptiness; **(eine) gähnende ~** a gaping void.

**leeren** vt to empty ♦ vr to (become) empty.

**leer-** zW: ~**gefegt** adj (Straße) deserted; **L~gewicht** nt unladen weight; **L~gut** nt empties pl; **L~lauf** m (AUT) neutral; ~**stehend** adj empty; **L~taste** f

(Schreibmaschine) space-bar.

**Leerung** f emptying; (POST) collection.

**legal** [le'ga:l] adj legal, lawful.

**legalisieren** [legali'zi:rən] vt to legalize.

**Legalität** [legali'tɛ:t] f legality; **(etwas) außerhalb der ~** (euph) (slightly) outside the law.

**Legasthenie** [legaste'ni:] f dyslexia.

**Legastheniker(in)** [legas'te:nikər(ɪn)] (-s, -) m(f) dyslexic.

**Legebatterie** f laying battery.

**legen** ['le:gən] vt to lay, put, place; (Ei) to lay ♦ vr to lie down; (fig) to subside; **sich ins Bett ~** to go to bed.

**Legende** [le'gɛndə] (-, -n) f legend.

**leger** [le'ʒɛ:r] adj casual.

**legieren** [le'gi:rən] vt to alloy.

**Legierung** f alloy.

**Legislative** [legɪsla'ti:və] f legislature.

**Legislaturperiode** [legɪsla'tu:rperio:də] f parliamentary (BRIT) od congressional (US) term.

**legitim** [legi'ti:m] adj legitimate.

**Legitimation** [legiti:matsi'o:n] f legitimation.

**legitimieren** [legiti'mi:rən] vt to legitimate ♦ vr to prove one's identity.

**Legitimität** [legitimi'tɛ:t] f legitimacy.

**Lehm** [le:m] (-(e)s, -e) m loam.

**lehmig** adj loamy.

**Lehne** ['le:nə] (-, -n) f arm; (Rücken~) back.

**lehnen** vt, vr to lean.

**Lehnstuhl** m armchair.

**Lehr-** zW: ~**amt** nt teaching profession; ~**befähigung** f teaching qualification; ~**brief** m indentures pl; ~**buch** nt textbook.

**Lehre** ['le:rə] (-, -n) f teaching, doctrine; (beruflich) apprenticeship; (moralisch) lesson; (TECH) gauge; **bei jdm in die ~ gehen** to serve one's apprenticeship with sb.

**lehren** vt to teach.

**Lehrer(in)** (-s, -) m(f) teacher; ~**ausbildung** f teacher training; ~**kollegium** nt teaching staff; ~**zimmer** nt staff room.

**Lehr-** zW: ~**gang** m course; ~**geld** nt: ~**geld für etw zahlen müssen** (fig) to pay dearly for sth; ~**jahre** pl apprenticeship sing; ~**kraft** f (form) teacher; ~**ling** m apprentice; trainee; ~**mittel** nt teaching aid; ~**plan** m syllabus; ~**probe** f demonstration lesson, crit (umg); l~**reich** adj instructive; ~**satz** m proposition; ~**stelle** f apprenticeship; ~**stuhl** m chair; ~**zeit** f apprenticeship.

**Leib** [laip] (-(e)s, -er) m body; **halt ihn mir vom ~!** keep him away from me!; **etw am eigenen ~(e) spüren** to experience sth for o.s.

**leiben** ['laibən] vi: **wie er leibt und lebt** to a T (umg).

**Leibes-** zW: ~**erziehung** f physical education; ~**kraft** f: **aus ~kraft schreien** etc to shout etc with all one's might; ~**übung** f physical exercise; ~**visitation** f body search.

**Leibgericht** nt favourite (*BRIT*) od favorite (*US*) meal.

**Leib-** zW: l~**haftig** adj personified; (*Teufel*) incarnate; l~**lich** adj bodily; (*Vater etc*) natural; ~**rente** f life annuity; ~**wache** f bodyguard.

**Leiche** ['laɪçə] (-, -n) f corpse; **er geht über** ~**n** (*umg*) he'd stick at nothing.

**Leichen-** zW: ~**beschauer** (-s, -) m doctor conducting a post-mortem; ~**halle** f mortuary; ~**hemd** nt shroud; ~**träger** m bearer; ~**wagen** m hearse.

**Leichnam** ['laɪçnaːm] (-(e)s, -e) m corpse.

**leicht** [laɪçt] adj light; (*einfach*) easy ♦ adv: ~ **zerbrechlich** very fragile; **nichts** ~**er als das!** nothing (could be) simpler!; L~**athletik** f athletics sing; ~**fallen** unreg vi: **jdm** ~**fallen** to be easy for sb; ~**fertig** adj thoughtless; ~**gläubig** adj gullible, credulous; L~**gläubigkeit** f gullibility, credulity; ~**hin** adv lightly.

**Leichtigkeit** f easiness; **mit** ~ with ease.

**leicht-** zW: ~**lebig** adj easy-going; ~**machen** vt: **es sich** dat ~**machen** to make things easy for o.s.; (*nicht gewissenhaft sein*) to take the easy way out; L~**matrose** m ordinary seaman; L~**metall** nt light alloy; ~**nehmen** unreg vt to take lightly; L~**sinn** m carelessness; **sträflicher** L~**sinn** criminal negligence; ~**sinnig** adj careless; ~**verletzt** adj attrib slightly injured.

**Leid** [laɪt] (-(e)s) nt grief, sorrow; **jdm sein** ~ **klagen** to tell sb one's troubles.

**leid** adj: **etw** ~ **haben** od **sein** to be tired of sth; **es tut mir/ihm** ~ I am/he is sorry; **er/ das tut mir** ~ I am sorry for him/about it; **sie kann einem** ~ **tun** you can't help feeling sorry for her.

**leiden** ['laɪdən] unreg vt to suffer; (*erlauben*) to permit ♦ vi to suffer; **jdn/etw nicht** ~ **können** not to be able to stand sb/sth; L~ (-s, -) nt suffering; (*Krankheit*) complaint.

**Leidenschaft** f passion; l~**lich** adj passionate.

**Leidens-** zW: ~**genosse** m, ~**genossin** f fellow sufferer; ~**geschichte** f: **die** ~**geschichte (Christi)** (*REL*) Christ's Passion.

**leider** ['laɪdər] adv unfortunately; **ja,** ~ yes, I'm afraid so; ~ **nicht** I'm afraid not.

**leidig** ['laɪdɪç] adj miserable, tiresome.

**leidlich** [laɪtlɪç] adj tolerable ♦ adv tolerably.

**Leidtragende(r)** f(m) bereaved; (*Benachteiligter*) one who suffers.

**Leidwesen** nt: **zu jds** ~ to sb's dismay.

**Leier** ['laɪər] (-, -n) f lyre; (*fig*) old story.

**Leierkasten** m barrel organ.

**leiern** vt (*Kurbel*) to turn; (*umg: Gedicht*) to rattle off ♦ vi (*drehen*): ~ **an** +dat to crank.

**Leiharbeit** f subcontracted labour; ~**arbeiter(in)** m(f) subcontracted worker; ~**bibliothek** f, ~**bücherei** f lending library.

**leihen** ['laɪən] unreg vt to lend; **sich** dat **etw** ~ to borrow sth.

**Leih-** zW: ~**gabe** f loan; ~**gebühr** f hire charge; ~**haus** nt pawnshop; ~**mutter** f surrogate mother; ~**schein** m pawn ticket; (*in der Bibliothek*) borrowing slip; ~**unternehmen** nt hire service; (*Arbeitsmarkt*) temp service; ~**wagen** m hired car (*BRIT*), rental car (*US*); ~**weise** adv on loan.

**Leim** [laɪm] (-(e)s, -e) m glue; **jdm auf den** ~ **gehen** to be taken in by sb; l~**en** vt to glue.

**Leine** ['laɪnə] (-, -n) f line, cord; (*Hunde~*) leash, lead; ~ **ziehen** (*umg*) to clear out.

**Leinen** (-s, -) nt linen; (*grob, segeltuchartig*) canvas; (*als Bucheinband*) cloth.

**leinen** adj linen.

**Lein-** zW: ~**samen** m linseed; ~**tuch** nt linen cloth; (*Bettuch*) sheet; ~**wand** f (*KUNST*) canvas; (*FILM*) screen.

**leise** ['laɪzə] adj quiet; (*sanft*) soft, gentle; **mit** ~**r Stimme** in a low voice; **nicht die** ~**ste Ahnung haben** not to have the slightest (idea).

**Leisetreter** (*pej: umg*) m pussyfoot(er).

**Leiste** ['laɪstə] (-, -n) f ledge; (*Zier~*) strip; (*ANAT*) groin.

**leisten** ['laɪstən] vt (*Arbeit*) to do; (*Gesellschaft*) to keep; (*Ersatz*) to supply; (*vollbringen*) to achieve; **sich** dat **etw** ~ to allow o.s. sth; (*sich gönnen*) to treat o.s. to sth; **sich** dat **etw** ~ **können** to be able to afford sth.

**Leistenbruch** m (*MED*) hernia, rupture.

**Leistung** f performance; (*gute*) achievement; (*eines Motors*) power; (*von Krankenkasse etc*) benefit; (*Zahlung*) payment.

**Leistungs-** zW: ~**abfall** m (in bezug auf Qualität) drop in performance; (in bezug auf Quantität) drop in productivity; ~**beurteilung** f performance appraisal; ~**druck** m pressure; l~**fähig** adj efficient; ~**fähigkeit** f efficiency; ~**gesellschaft** f meritocracy; ~**kurs** m (*SCH*) set; l~**orientiert** adj performance-orientated; ~**prinzip** nt achievement principle; ~**sport** m competitive sport; ~**zulage** f productivity bonus.

**Leitartikel** m leader.

**Leitbild** nt model.

**leiten** ['laɪtən] vt to lead; (*Firma*) to manage; (*in eine Richtung*) to direct; (*ELEK*) to conduct; **sich von jdm/etw** ~ **lassen** (*lit, fig*) to (let o.s.) be guided by sb/sth.

**leitend** adj leading; (*Gedanke, Idee*) dominant; (*Stellung, Position*) managerial; (*Ingenieur, Beamter*) in charge; (*PHYS*) conductive; ~**er Angestellter** executive.

**Leiter**[1] ['laɪtər] (-s, -) m leader, head; (*ELEK*) conductor.

**Leiter**[2] ['laɪtər] (-, -n) f ladder.

**Leiterin** f leader, head.

**Leiterplatte** f (*COMPUT*) circuit board.

**Leit-** zW: ~**faden** m guide; ~**fähigkeit** f

conductivity; ~**gedanke** m central idea;
~**motiv** nt leitmotiv; ~**planke** f crash
barrier; ~**spruch** m motto.

**Leitung** f (Führung) direction; (FILM, THEAT
etc) production; (von Firma) management;
directors pl; (Wasser~) pipe; (Kabel) cable;
**eine lange ~ haben** to be slow on the
uptake; **da ist jemand in der ~** (umg) there's
somebody else on the line.

**Leitungs-** zW: ~**draht** m wire; ~**mast** m
telegraph pole; ~**rohr** nt pipe; ~**wasser** nt
tap water.

**Leitwerk** nt (AVIAT) tail unit.

**Leitzins** m (FIN) base rate.

**Lektion** [lɛktsi'oːn] f lesson; **jdm eine
~ erteilen** (fig) to teach sb a lesson.

**Lektor(in)** ['lɛktɔr, lɛk'toːrɪn] m(f) (UNIV)
lector; (Verlag) editor.

**Lektüre** [lɛk'tyːrə] (-, -n) f (Lesen) reading;
(Lesestoff) reading matter.

**Lende** ['lɛndə] (-, -n) f loin.

**Lendenbraten** m roast sirloin.

**Lendenstück** nt fillet.

**lenkbar** ['lɛŋkbaːr] adj (Fahrzeug) steerable;
(Kind) manageable.

**lenken** vt to steer; (Kind) to guide; (Gespräch)
to lead; ~ **auf** +akk (Blick, Aufmerksamkeit) to
direct at; (Verdacht) to throw on(to); (: auf
sich) to draw onto.

**Lenkrad** nt steering wheel.

**Lenkstange** f handlebars pl.

**Lenkung** f steering; (Führung) direction.

**Lenz** [lɛnts] (-es, -e) m (liter) spring; **sich** dat
**einen (faulen) ~ machen** (umg) to laze
about, swing the lead.

**Leopard** [leo'part] (-en, -en) m leopard.

**Lepra** ['leːpra] (-) f leprosy; ~**kranke(r)** f(m)
leper.

**Lerche** ['lɛrçə] (-, -n) f lark.

**lernbegierig** adj eager to learn.

**lernbehindert** adj educationally handicapped
(BRIT) od handicapped (US).

**lernen** vt to learn ♦ vi: **er lernt bei der Firma
Braun** he's training at Braun's.

**Lernhilfe** f educational aid.

**lesbar** ['leːsbaːr] adj legible.

**Lesbierin** ['lɛsbiərɪn] f lesbian.

**lesbisch** adj lesbian.

**Lese** ['leːzə] (-, -n) f (Wein~) harvest.

**Lesebuch** nt reading book, reader.

**lesen** unreg vt to read; (ernten) to gather, pick
♦ vi to read; ~/**schreiben** (COMPUT) to read/
write.

**Leser(in)** (-s, -) m(f) reader.

**Leseratte** ['leːzəratə] (umg) f bookworm.

**Leser-** zW: ~**brief** m reader's letter; „~**briefe**"
"letters to the editor"; ~**kreis** m readership;
**l~lich** adj legible.

**Lese-** zW: ~**saal** m reading room; ~**stoff** m
reading material; ~**zeichen** nt bookmark;
~**zirkel** m magazine club.

**Lesotho** [le'zoːto] (-s) nt Lesotho.

**Lesung** ['leːzʊŋ] f (PARL) reading; (ECCL)
lesson.

**lethargisch** [le'targɪʃ] adj (MED, fig)
lethargic.

**Lette** ['lɛtə] (-n, -n) m, **Lettin** f Latvian.

**lettisch** adj Latvian.

**Lettland** ['lɛtlant] (-s) nt Latvia.

**Letzt** f: **zu guter ~** finally, in the end.

**letzte(r, s)** ['lɛtstə(r, s)] adj last; (neueste)
latest; **der L~ Wille** the last will and
testament; **bis zum ~n** to the utmost; **in ~r
Zeit** recently.

**Letzte(s)** nt: **das ist ja das ~!** (umg) that
really is the limit!

**letztenmal** adv: **zum ~** for the last time.

**letztens** adv lately.

**letztere(r, s)** adj the latter.

**letztlich** adv in the end.

**Leuchte** ['lɔʏçtə] (-, -n) f lamp, light; (umg:
Mensch) genius.

**leuchten** vi to shine, gleam.

**Leuchter** (-s, -) m candlestick.

**Leucht-** zW: ~**farbe** f fluorescent colour
(BRIT) od color (US); ~**feuer** nt beacon;
~**käfer** m glow-worm; ~**kugel** f flare;
~**pistole** f flare pistol; ~**rakete** f flare;
~**reklame** f neon sign; ~**röhre** f strip light;
~**turm** m lighthouse; ~**zifferblatt** nt
luminous dial.

**leugnen** ['lɔʏgnən] vt, vi to deny.

**Leugnung** f denial.

**Leukämie** [lɔʏkɛ'miː] f leukaemia (BRIT),
leukemia (US).

**Leukoplast** ® [lɔʏko'plast] (-(e)s, -e) nt
Elastoplast ®.

**Leumund** ['lɔʏmʊnt] (-(e)s, -e) m reputation.

**Leumundszeugnis** nt character reference.

**Leute** ['lɔʏtə] pl people pl; **kleine ~** (fig)
ordinary people; **etw unter die ~ bringen**
(umg: Gerücht etc) to spread sth around.

**Leutnant** ['lɔʏtnant] (-s, -s od -e) m
lieutenant.

**leutselig** ['lɔʏtzeːlıç] adj affable; **L~keit** f
affability.

**Leviten** [le'viːtən] pl: **jdm die ~ lesen** (umg) to
haul sb over the coals.

**lexikalisch** [lɛksi'kaːlıʃ] adj lexical.

**Lexikographie** [lɛksikogra'fiː] f
lexicography.

**Lexikon** ['lɛksikɔn] (-s, Lexiken od Lexika) nt
encyclopedia.

**lfd.** abk = **laufend**.

**Libanese** [liba'neːzə] (-n, -n) m, **Libanesin** f
Lebanese.

**libanesisch** adj Lebanese.

**Libanon** ['liːbanɔn] (-s) m: **der ~** the Lebanon.

**Libelle** [li'bɛlə] (-, -n) f dragonfly; (TECH)
spirit level.

**liberal** [libe'raːl] adj liberal.

**Liberale(r)** f(m) (POL) Liberal.

**Liberalisierung** [liberali'ziːrʊŋ] f
liberalization.

**Liberalismus** [libera'lɪsmʊs] *m* liberalism.
**Liberia** [li'beːria] (**-s**) *nt* Liberia.
**Liberianer(in)** [liberi'aːnər(ɪn)] (**-s, -**) *m(f)* Liberian.
**liberianisch** *adj* Liberian.
**Libero** ['liːbero] (**-s, -s**) *m* (*FUSSBALL*) sweeper.
**Libyen** ['liːbyən] (**-s**) *nt* Libya.
**Libyer(in)** (**-s, -**) *m(f)* Libyan.
**libyisch** *adj* Libyan.
**Licht** [lɪçt] (**-(e)s, -er**) *nt* light; ~ **machen** (*anschalten*) to turn on a light; (*anzünden*) to light a candle *etc*; **mir geht ein ~ auf** it's dawned on me; **jdn hinters ~ führen** (*fig*) to lead sb up the garden path.
**licht** *adj* light, bright.
**Licht-** *zW:* ~**bild** *nt* photograph; (*Dia*) slide; ~**blick** *m* cheering prospect; **l~empfindlich** *adj* sensitive to light.
**lichten** ['lɪçtən] *vt* to clear; (*Anker*) to weigh ♦ *vr* (*Nebel*) to clear; (*Haar*) to thin.
**lichterloh** ['lɪçtər'loː] *adv:* ~ **brennen** to blaze.
**Licht-** *zW:* ~**geschwindigkeit** *f* speed of light; ~**griffel** *m* (*COMPUT*) light pen; ~**hupe** *f* flashing of headlights; ~**jahr** *nt* light year; ~**maschine** *f* dynamo; ~**meß** (**-**) *f* Candlemas; ~**pause** *f* photocopy; (*bei Blaupausverfahren*) blueprint; ~**schalter** *m* light switch; **l~scheu** *adj* averse to light; (*fig: Gesindel*) shady.
**Lichtung** *f* clearing, glade.
**Lid** [liːt] (**-(e)s, -er**) *nt* eyelid; ~**schatten** *m* eyeshadow.
**lieb** [liːp] *adj* dear; (*viele*) ~**e Grüße, Deine Silvia** love, Silvia; **L~e Anna,** ~**er Klaus! ...** Dear Anna and Klaus, ...; **am** ~**sten lese ich Kriminalromane** best of all I like detective novels; **den** ~**en langen Tag** (*umg*) all the livelong day; **sich bei jdm ~ Kind machen** (*pej*) to suck up to sb (*umg*).
**liebäugeln** ['liːpʔɔygəln] *vi untr:* **mit dem Gedanken ~, etw zu tun** to toy with the idea of doing sth.
**Liebe** ['liːbə] (**-, -n**) *f* love; **l~bedürftig** *adj:* **l~bedürftig sein** to need love.
**Liebelei** *f* flirtation.
**lieben** ['liːbən] *vt* to love; (*weniger stark*) to like; **etw ~d gern tun** to love to do sth.
**liebens-** *zW:* ~**wert** *adj* loveable; ~**würdig** *adj* kind; ~**würdigerweise** *adv* kindly; **L~würdigkeit** *f* kindness.
**lieber** ['liːbər] *adv* rather, preferably; **ich gehe ~ nicht** I'd rather not go; **ich trinke ~ Wein als Bier** I prefer wine to beer; **bleib ~ im Bett** you'd better stay in bed.
**Liebes-** *zW:* ~**brief** *m* love letter; ~**dienst** *m* good turn; ~**kummer** *m:* ~**kummer haben** to be lovesick; ~**paar** *nt* courting couple, lovers *pl*; ~**roman** *m* romantic novel.
**liebevoll** *adj* loving.
**lieb-** *zW:* ~**gewinnen** *unreg vt* to get fond of; ~**haben** *unreg vt* to love; (*weniger stark*) to be

(*very*) fond of; **L~haber(in)** (**-s, -**) *m(f)* lover; (*Sammler*) collector; **L~haberei** *f* hobby; ~**kosen** *vt untr* to caress; ~**lich** *adj* lovely, charming; (*Duft, Wein*) sweet.
**Liebling** *m* darling.
**Lieblings-** *in zW* favourite (*BRIT*), favorite (*US*).
**lieblos** *adj* unloving.
**Liebschaft** *f* love affair.
**Liechtenstein** ['lɪçtənʃtain] (**-s**) *nt* Liechtenstein.
**Lied** [liːt] (**-(e)s, -er**) *nt* song; (*ECCL*) hymn; **davon kann ich ein ~ singen** (*fig*) I could tell you a thing or two about that (*umg*).
**Liederbuch** *nt* songbook; (*REL*) hymn book.
**liederlich** ['liːdərlɪç] *adj* slovenly; (*Lebenswandel*) loose, immoral; **L~keit** *f* slovenliness; immorality.
**lief** *etc* [liːf] *vb siehe* **laufen**.
**Lieferant** [liːfə'rant] *m* supplier.
**Lieferanteneingang** *m* tradesmen's entrance; (*von Warenhaus etc*) goods entrance.
**lieferbar** *adj* (*vorrätig*) available.
**Lieferbedingungen** *pl* terms of delivery.
**Lieferfrist** *f* delivery period.
**liefern** ['liːfərn] *vt* to deliver; (*versorgen mit*) to supply; (*Beweis*) to produce.
**Lieferschein** *m* delivery note.
**Liefertermin** *m* delivery date.
**Lieferung** *f* delivery; (*Versorgung*) supply.
**Lieferwagen** *m* (delivery) van, panel truck (*US*).
**Lieferzeit** *f* delivery period; ~ **6 Monate** delivery six months.
**Liege** ['liːgə] (**-, -n**) *f* bed; (*Camping~*) camp bed (*BRIT*), cot (*US*); ~**geld** *nt* (*Hafen, Flughafen*) demurrage.
**liegen** ['liːgən] *unreg vi* to lie; (*sich befinden*) to be (situated); **mir liegt nichts/viel daran** it doesn't matter to me/it matters a lot to me; **es liegt bei Ihnen, ob ...** it rests with you whether ...; **Sprachen ~ mir nicht** languages are not my line; **woran liegt es?** what's the cause?; **so, wie die Dinge jetzt ~** as things stand at the moment; **an mir soll es nicht ~, wenn die Sache schiefgeht** it won't be my fault if things go wrong; ~**bleiben** *unreg vi* (*Person*) to stay in bed; (*nicht aufstehen*) to stay lying down; (*Ding*) to be left (behind); (*nicht ausgeführt werden*) to be left (undone); ~**lassen** *unreg vt* (*vergessen*) to leave behind; **L~schaft** *f* real estate.
**Liege-** *zW:* ~**platz** *m* (*auf Schiff, in Zug etc*) berth; (*Ankerplatz*) moorings *pl*; ~**sitz** *m* (*AUT*) reclining seat; ~**stuhl** *m* deck chair; ~**stütz** *m* (*SPORT*) press-up (*BRIT*), push-up (*US*); ~**wagen** *m* (*EISENB*) couchette car; ~**wiese** *f* lawn (*for sunbathing*).
**lieh** *etc* [liː] *vb siehe* **leihen**.
**ließ** *etc* [liːs] *vb siehe* **lassen**.
**liest** [liːst] *vb siehe* **lesen**.

**Lift** [lɪft] (-(e)s, -e *od* -s) *m* lift.
**Liga** ['liːga] (-, **Ligen**) *f* (*SPORT*) league.
**liieren** [li'iːrən] *vt*: **liiert sein** (*Firmen etc*) to be working together; (*ein Verhältnis haben*) to have a relationship.
**Likör** [li'køːr] (-s, -e) *m* liqueur.
**lila** ['liːla] *adj inv* purple; **L~** (-s, -s) *nt* (*Farbe*) purple.
**Lilie** ['liːliə] *f* lily.
**Liliputaner(in)** [lilipu'taːnər(ɪn)] (-s, -) *m(f)* midget.
**Limit** ['lɪmɪt] (-s, -s *od* -e) *nt* limit; (*FIN*) ceiling.
**Limonade** [limo'naːdə] (-, -n) *f* lemonade.
**lind** [lɪnt] *adj* gentle, mild.
**Linde** ['lɪndə] (-, -n) *f* lime tree, linden.
**lindern** ['lɪndərn] *vt* to alleviate, soothe.
**Linderung** *f* alleviation.
**lindgrün** *adj* lime green.
**Lineal** [line'aːl] (-s, -e) *nt* ruler.
**linear** [line'aːr] *adj* linear.
**Linguist(in)** [lɪŋgu'ɪst(ɪn)] *m(f)* linguist.
**Linguistik** *f* linguistics *sing*.
**Linie** ['liːniə] *f* line; **in erster ~** first and foremost; **auf die ~ achten** to watch one's figure; **fahren Sie mit der ~ 2** take the number 2 (bus *etc*).
**Linien-** *zW*: **~blatt** *nt* ruled sheet; **~bus** *m* service bus; **~flug** *m* scheduled flight; **~richter** *m* (*SPORT*) linesman; **l~treu** *adj* loyal to the (party) line.
**liniieren** [lini'iːrən] *vt* to line.
**Linke** ['lɪŋkə] (-, -n) *f* left side; left hand; (*POL*) left.
**Linke(r)** *f(m)* (*POL*) left-winger, leftie (*pej*).
**linke(r, s)** *adj* left; **~ Masche** purl; **das mache ich mit der ~n Hand** (*umg*) I can do that with my eyes shut.
**linkisch** *adj* awkward, gauche.
**links** *adv* left; to *od* on the left; **~ von mir** on *od* to my left; **~ von der Mitte** left of centre; **jdn ~ liegenlassen** (*fig: umg*) to ignore sb; **L~abbieger** *m* motorist/vehicle turning left; **L~außen** (-s, -) *m* (*SPORT*) outside left; **L~händer(in)** (-s, -) *m(f)* left-handed person; **L~kurve** *f* left-hand bend; **~lastig** *adj*: **~lastig sein** to list *od* lean to the left; **~radikal** *adj* (*POL*) radically left-wing; **L~rutsch** *m* (*POL*) swing to the left; **L~steuerung** *f* (*AUT*) left-hand drive; **L~verkehr** *m* driving on the left.
**Linoleum** [li'noːleum] (-s) *nt* lino(leum).
**Linse** ['lɪnzə] (-, -n) *f* lentil; (*optisch*) lens.
**linsen** (*umg*) *vi* to peak.
**Lippe** ['lɪpə] (-, -n) *f* lip.
**Lippenbekenntnis** *nt* lip service.
**Lippenstift** *m* lipstick.
**Liquidation** [likvidatsi'oːn] *f* liquidation.
**Liquidationswert** *m* break-up value.
**Liquidator** [likvi'daːtor] *m* liquidator.
**liquid(e)** [lik'viːt, lik'viːdə] *adj* (*Firma*) solvent.
**liquidieren** [likvi'diːrən] *vt* to liquidate.

**Liquidität** [likvidi'tɛːt] *f* liquidity.
**lispeln** ['lɪspəln] *vi* to lisp.
**Lissabon** ['lɪsabɔn] *nt* Lisbon.
**List** [lɪst] (-, -en) *f* cunning; (*Plan*) trick, ruse; **mit ~ und Tücke** (*umg*) with a lot of coaxing.
**Liste** ['lɪstə] (-, -n) *f* list.
**Listenplatz** *m* (*POL*) place on the party list.
**Listenpreis** *m* list price.
**listig** *adj* cunning, sly.
**Litanei** [lita'naɪ] *f* litany.
**Litauen** ['liːtauən] (-s) *nt* Lithuania.
**Litauer(in)** (-s, -) *m(f)* Lithuanian.
**litauisch** *adj* Lithuanian.
**Liter** ['liːtər] (-s, -) *m od nt* litre (*BRIT*), liter (*US*).
**literarisch** [lɪte'raːrɪʃ] *adj* literary.
**Literatur** [lɪtera'tuːr] *f* literature; **~preis** *m* award *od* prize for literature; **~wissenschaft** *f* literary studies *pl*.
**literweise** ['liːtərvaɪzə] *adv* (*lit*) by the litre (*BRIT*) *od* liter (*US*); (*fig*) by the gallon.
**Litfaßsäule** ['lɪtfaszɔylə] *f* advertising (*BRIT*) *od* advertizing (*US*) pillar.
**Lithographie** [litogra'fiː] *f* lithography.
**litt** *etc* [lɪt] *vb siehe* **leiden**.
**Liturgie** [litur'giː] *f* liturgy.
**liturgisch** [li'turgɪʃ] *adj* liturgical.
**Litze** ['lɪtsə] (-, -n) *f* braid; (*ELEK*) flex.
**live** [laɪf] *adj, adv* (*RUNDF, TV*) live.
**Livree** [li'vreː] (-, -n) *f* livery.
**Lizenz** [li'tsɛnts] *f* licence (*BRIT*), license (*US*); **~ausgabe** *f* licensed edition; **~gebühr** *f* licence fee; (*im Verlagswesen*) royalty.
**LKW, Lkw** (-(s), -(s)) *m abk* = **Lastkraftwagen**.
**l.M.** *abk* (= *laufenden Monats*) inst.
**Lob** [loːp] (-(e)s) *nt* praise.
**Lobby** ['lɔbi] (-, -s *od* **Lobbies**) *f* lobby.
**loben** ['loːbən] *vt* to praise; **das lob ich mir** that's what I like (to see/hear *etc*).
**lobenswert** *adj* praiseworthy.
**löblich** ['løːplɪç] *adj* praiseworthy, laudable.
**Loblied** *nt*: **ein ~ auf jdn/etw singen** to sing sb's/sth's praises.
**Lobrede** *f* eulogy.
**Loch** [lɔx] (-(e)s, -̈er) *nt* hole; **l~en** *vt* to punch holes in; **~er** (-s, -) *m* punch.
**löcherig** ['lœçərɪç] *adj* full of holes.
**löchern** (*umg*) *vt*: **jdn ~** to pester sb with questions.
**Loch-** *zW*: **~karte** *f* punch card; **~streifen** *m* punch tape; **~zange** *f* punch.
**Locke** ['lɔkə] (-, -n) *f* lock, curl.
**locken** *vt* to entice; (*Haare*) to curl.
**lockend** *adj* tempting.
**Lockenwickler** (-s, -) *m* curler.
**locker** ['lɔkər] *adj* loose; (*Kuchen, Schaum*) light; (*umg*) cool; **~lassen** *unreg vi*: **nicht ~lassen** not to let up.
**lockern** *vt* to loosen ♦ *vr* (*Atmosphäre*) to get more relaxed.
**Lockerungsübung** *f* loosening-up exercise;

(*zur Warmwerden*) limbering-up exercise.
**lockig** ['lɔkɪç] *adj* curly.
**Lockmittel** *nt* lure.
**Lockruf** *m* call.
**Lockung** *f* enticement.
**Lockvogel** *m* decoy, bait; ~**angebot** *nt*
(*COMM*) loss leader.
**Lodenmantel** ['loːdənmantəl] *m* thick woollen
coat.
**lodern** ['loːdərn] *vi* to blaze.
**Löffel** ['lœfəl] (**-s**, **-**) *m* spoon.
**löffeln** *vt* to spoon.
**löffelweise** *adv* by the spoonful.
**log** *etc* [loːk] *vb siehe* **lügen.**
**Logarithmentafel** [loga'rɪtmənta:fəl] *f*
log(arithm) tables *pl.*
**Logarithmus** [loga'rɪtmʊs] *m* logarithm.
**Loge** ['loːʒə] (**-**, **-n**) *f* (*THEAT*) box;
(*Freimaurer~*) (masonic) lodge; (*Pförtner~*)
office.
**logieren** [lo'ʒiːrən] *vi* to lodge, stay.
**Logik** ['loːgɪk] *f* logic.
**Logis** [lo'ʒiː] (**-**, **-**) *nt*: **Kost und** ~ board and
lodging.
**logisch** ['loːgɪʃ] *adj* logical; (*umg:*
*selbstverständlich*): **gehst du auch hin? -** ~
are you going too? - of course.
**logo** ['logo] (*umg*) *interj* obvious!
**Logopäde** [logo'pɛːdə] (**-n**, **-n**) *m* speech
therapist.
**Logopädin** [logo'pɛːdɪn] *f* speech therapist.
**Lohn** [loːn] (**-(e)s**, **-̈e**) *m* reward; (*Arbeits~*)
pay, wages *pl*; ~**abrechnung** *f* labour;
~**ausfall** *m* loss of earnings; ~**büro** *nt* wages
office; ~**diktat** *nt* wage dictate; ~**empfänger**
*m* wage earner.
**lohnen** ['loːnən] *vt* (*liter*): **jdm etw** ~ to reward
sb for sth ♦ *vr unpers* to be worth it.
**lohnend** *adj* worthwhile.
**Lohn-** *zW:* ~**erhöhung** *f* wage increase, pay
rise; ~**forderung** *f* wage claim;
~**fortzahlung** *f* continued payment of
wages; ~**fortzahlungsgesetz** *nt law on*
*continued payment of wages*; ~**gefälle** *nt*
wage differential; ~**kosten** *pl* labour (*BRIT*)
*od* labor (*US*) costs; ~**politik** *f* wages
policy; ~**runde** *f* pay round; ~**steuer** *f*
income tax; ~**steuerjahresausgleich** *m*
income tax return; ~**steuerkarte** *f* (*income*)
tax card; ~**stopp** *m* pay freeze; ~**streifen** *m*
pay slip; ~**tüte** *f* pay packet.
**Lok** [lɔk] (**-**, **-s**) *f abk* (= *Lokomotive*) loco
(*umg*).
**lokal** [lo'ka:l] *adj* local.
**Lokal** (**-(e)s**, **-e**) *nt* pub(lic house) (*BRIT*).
**Lokalblatt** (*umg*) *nt* local paper.
**lokalisieren** [loka:li'zi:rən] *vt* to localize.
**Lokalisierung** *f* localization.
**Lokalität** [lokali'tɛːt] *f* locality; (*Raum*)
premises *pl.*
**Lokal-** *zW:* ~**presse** *f* local press; ~**teil** *m*
(*Zeitung*) local section; ~**termin** *m* (*JUR*)

visit to the scene of the crime.
**Lokomotive** [lokomo'tiːvə] (**-**, **-n**) *f*
locomotive.
**Lokomotivführer** *m* engine driver (*BRIT*),
engineer (*US*).
**Lombardei** [lɔmbar'daɪ] *f* Lombardy.
**London** ['lɔndɔn] (**-s**) *nt* London.
**Londoner** *adj attrib* London.
**Londoner(in)** (**-s**, **-**) *m(f)* Londoner.
**Lorbeer** ['lɔrbeːr] (**-s**, **-en**) *m* (*lit, fig*) laurel;
~**blatt** *nt* (*KOCH*) bay leaf.
**Lore** ['loːrə] (**-**, **-n**) *f* (*MIN*) truck.
**Los** [loːs] (**-es**, **-e**) *nt* (*Schicksal*) lot, fate; (*in der*
*Lotterie*) lottery ticket; **das große** ~ **ziehen**
(*lit, fig*) to hit the jackpot; **etw durch das**
~ **entscheiden** to decide sth by drawing
lots.
**los** *adj* loose ♦ *adv:* ~**!** go on!; **etw** ~ **sein** to be
rid of sth; **was ist** ~**?** what's the matter?;
**dort ist nichts/viel** ~ there's nothing/a lot
going on there; **ich bin mein ganzes Geld** ~
(*umg*) I'm cleaned out; **irgendwas ist mit**
**ihm** ~ there's something wrong with him;
**wir wollen früh** ~ we want to be off early;
**nichts wie** ~**!** let's get going; ~**binden** *unreg*
*vt* to untie; ~**brechen** *unreg vi* (*Sturm, Gewitter*)
to break.
**losch** *etc* [lɔʃ] *vb siehe* **löschen.**
**Löschblatt** ['lœʃblat] *nt* sheet of blotting
paper.
**löschen** ['lœʃən] *vt* (*Feuer, Licht*) to put out,
extinguish; (*Durst*) to quench; (*COMM*) to
cancel; (*Tonband*) to erase; (*Fracht*) to
unload; (*COMPUT*) to delete; (*Tinte*) to blot
♦ *vi* (*Feuerwehr*) to put out a fire; (*Papier*) to
blot.
**Lösch-** *zW:* ~**fahrzeug** *nt* fire engine; ~**gerät**
*nt* fire extinguisher; ~**papier** *nt* blotting
paper; ~**taste** *f* (*COMPUT*) delete key.
**Löschung** *f* extinguishing; (*COMM*)
cancellation; (*Fracht*) unloading.
**lose** ['loːzə] *adj* loose.
**Lösegeld** *nt* ransom.
**losen** ['loːzən] *vi* to draw lots.
**lösen** ['løːzən] *vt* to loosen; (*Handbremse*) to
release; (*Husten, Krampf*) to ease; (*Rätsel etc*)
to solve; (*Verlobung*) to call off; (*CHEM*) to
dissolve; (*Partnerschaft*) to break up;
(*Fahrkarte*) to buy ♦ *vr* (*aufgehen*) to come
loose; (*Schuß*) to go off; (*Zucker etc*) to
dissolve; (*Problem, Schwierigkeit*) to (re)solve
itself.
**los-** *zW:* ~**fahren** *unreg vi* to leave; ~**gehen** *unreg*
*vi* to set out; (*anfangen*) to start; (*Bombe*) to
go off; **jetzt geht's** ~**!** here we go!; **nach**
**hinten** ~**gehen** (*umg*) to backfire; **auf jdn**
~**gehen** to go for sb; ~**kaufen** *vt* (*Gefangene,*
*Geiseln*) to pay ransom for; ~**kommen** *unreg*
*vi* (*sich befreien*) to free o.s.; **von etw**
~**kommen** to get away from sth; ~**lassen**
*unreg vt* (*Seil etc*) to let go of; **der Gedanke**
**läßt mich nicht mehr** ~ the thought haunts

me; ~**laufen** *unreg vi* to run off; ~**legen** (*umg*) *vi*: **nun leg mal** ~ **und erzähl(e)** ... now come on and tell me/us ...

**löslich** ['løːslɪç] *adj* soluble; **L~keit** *f* solubility.

**loslösen** *vt* to free ♦ *vr*: **sich (von etw)** ~ to detach o.s. (from sth).

**losmachen** *vt* to loosen; (*Boot*) to unmoor ♦ *vr* to get free.

**Losnummer** *f* ticket number.

**los-** *zW*: ~**sagen** *vr*: **sich von jdm/etw** ~**sagen** to renounce sb/sth; ~**schießen** *unreg vi*: **schieß** ~! (*fig: umg*) fire away!; ~**schrauben** *vt* to unscrew; ~**sprechen** *unreg vt* to absolve; ~**stürzen** *vi*: **auf jdn/etw** ~**stürzen** to pounce on sb/sth.

**Losung** ['loːzʊŋ] *f* watchword, slogan.

**Lösung** ['løːzʊŋ] *f* (*Lockermachen*) loosening; (*eines Rätsels, CHEM*) solution.

**Lösungsmittel** *nt* solvent.

**loswerden** *unreg vt* to get rid of.

**losziehen** *unreg vi* (*sich aufmachen*) to set out; **gegen jdn** ~ (*fig*) to run sb down.

**Lot** [loːt] (-(e)s, -e) *nt* plumbline; (*MATH*) perpendicular; **im** ~ vertical; (*fig*) on an even keel; **die Sache ist wieder im** ~ things have been straightened out; **l~en** *vt* to plumb, sound.

**löten** ['løːtən] *vt* to solder.

**Lothringen** ['loːtrɪŋən] (-s) *nt* Lorraine.

**Lötkolben** *m* soldering iron.

**Lotse** ['loːtsə] (-n, -n) *m* pilot; (*AVIAT*) air traffic controller.

**lotsen** *vt* to pilot; (*umg*) to lure.

**Lotterie** [lɔtə'riː] *f* lottery.

**Lotterleben** ['lɔtərleːbən] (*umg*) *nt* dissolute life.

**Lotto** ['lɔto] (-s, -s) *nt* ≈ National Lottery.

**Lottozahlen** *pl* winning Lotto numbers *pl*.

**Löwe** ['løːvə] (-n, -n) *m* lion; (*ASTROL*) Leo.

**Löwen-** *zW*: ~**anteil** *m* lion's share; ~**maul** *nt*, ~**mäulchen** *nt* antirrhinum, snapdragon; ~**zahn** *m* dandelion.

**Löwin** ['løːvɪn] *f* lioness.

**loyal** [loa'jaːl] *adj* loyal.

**Loyalität** [loajali'tɛːt] *f* loyalty.

**LP** (-, -s) *f abk* (= *Langspielplatte*) LP.

**LSD** (-(s)) *nt abk* (= *Lysergsäurediäthylamid*) LSD.

**lt.** *abk* = **laut.**

**Luchs** [lʊks] (-es, -e) *m* lynx.

**Lücke** ['lʏkə] (-, -n) *f* gap; (*Gesetzes~*) loophole; (*in Versorgung*) break.

**Lücken-** *zW*: ~**büßer** (-s, -) *m* stopgap; **l~haft** *adj* full of gaps; (*Versorgung*) deficient; **l~los** *adj* complete.

**lud** *etc* [luːt] *vb siehe* **laden.**

**Luder** ['luːdər] (-s, -) (*pej*) *nt* (*Frau*) hussy; (*bedauernswert*) poor wretch.

**Luft** [lʊft] (-, ̈-e) *f* air; (*Atem*) breath; **die** ~ **anhalten** (*lit*) to hold one's breath; **seinem Herzen** ~ **machen** to get everything off

one's chest; **in der** ~ **liegen** to be in the air; **dicke** ~ (*umg*) a bad atmosphere; **(frische)** ~ **schnappen** (*umg*) to get some fresh air; **in die** ~ **fliegen** (*umg*) to explode; **diese Behauptung ist aus der** ~ **gegriffen** this statement is (a) pure invention; **die** ~ **ist rein** (*umg*) the coast is clear; **jdn an die (frische)** ~ **setzen** (*umg*) to show sb the door; **er ist** ~ **für mich** I'm not speaking to him; **jdn wie** ~ **behandeln** to ignore sb; ~**angriff** *m* air raid; ~**aufnahme** *f* aerial photo; ~**ballon** *m* balloon; ~**blase** *f* air bubble; ~**brücke** *f* airlift; **l~dicht** *adj* airtight; ~**druck** *m* atmospheric pressure; **l~durchlässig** *adj* pervious to air.

**lüften** ['lʏftən] *vt* to air; (*Hut*) to lift, raise ♦ *vi* to let some air in.

**Luft-** *zW*: ~**fahrt** *f* aviation; ~**feuchtigkeit** *f* humidity; ~**fracht** *f* air cargo; **l~gekühlt** *adj* air-cooled; ~**gewehr** *nt* air rifle.

**luftig** *adj* (*Ort*) breezy; (*Raum*) airy; (*Kleider*) summery.

**Luft-** *zW*: ~**kissenfahrzeug** *nt* hovercraft; ~**krieg** *m* war in the air, aerial warfare; ~**kurort** *m* health resort; **l~leer** *adj*: **l~leerer Raum** vacuum; ~**linie** *f*: **in der** ~**linie** as the crow flies; ~**loch** *nt* air hole; (*AVIAT*) air pocket; ~**matratze** *f* Lilo ® (*BRIT*), air mattress; ~**pirat** *m* hijacker; ~**post** *f* airmail; ~**pumpe** *f* (*für Fahrrad*) (bicycle) pump; ~**raum** *m* air space; ~**röhre** *f* (*ANAT*) windpipe; ~**schlange** *f* streamer; ~**schloß** *nt* (*fig*) castle in the air; ~**schutz** *m* anti-aircraft defence (*BRIT*) *od* defense (*US*); ~**schutzbunker** *m*, ~**schutzkeller** *m* air-raid shelter; ~**sprung** *m* (*fig*): **einen** ~**sprung machen** to jump for joy.

**Lüftung** ['lʏftʊŋ] *f* ventilation.

**Luft-** *zW*: ~**veränderung** *f* change of air; ~**verkehr** *m* air traffic; ~**verschmutzung** *f* air pollution; ~**waffe** *f* air force; ~**weg** *m*: **etw auf dem** ~**weg befördern** to transport sth by air; ~**zufuhr** *f* air supply; ~**zug** *m* draught (*BRIT*), draft (*US*).

**Lüge** ['lyːgə] (-, -n) *f* lie; **jdn/etw** ~**n strafen** to give the lie to sb/sth.

**lügen** ['lyːgən] *unreg vi* to lie; **wie gedruckt** ~ (*umg*) to lie like mad.

**Lügendetektor** ['lyːgəndetɛktɔr] *m* lie detector.

**Lügner(in)** (-s, -) *m(f)* liar.

**Luke** ['luːkə] (-, -n) *f* hatch; (*Dach~*) skylight.

**lukrativ** [lukra'tiːf] *adj* lucrative.

**Lümmel** ['lʏməl] (-s, -) *m* lout.

**lümmeln** *vr* to lounge (about).

**Lump** [lʊmp] (-en, -en) *m* scamp, rascal.

**lumpen** ['lʊmpən] *vt*: **sich nicht** ~ **lassen** not to be mean.

**Lumpen** (-s, -) *m* rag.

**Lumpensammler** *m* rag and bone man.

**lumpig** ['lʊmpɪç] *adj* shabby; ~**e 10 Mark** (*umg*) 10 measly marks.

**Lüneburger Heide** ['ly:nəbʊrgər 'haɪdə] *f*
Lüneburg Heath.
**Lunge** ['lʊŋə] (-, -n) *f* lung.
**Lungen-** *zW:* ~**entzündung** *f* pneumonia;
**l~krank** *adj* suffering from a lung disease;
~**krankheit** *f* lung disease.
**lungern** ['lʊŋərn] *vi* to hang about.
**Lunte** ['lʊntə] (-, -n) *f* fuse; ~ **riechen** to smell
a rat.
**Lupe** ['lu:pə] (-, -n) *f* magnifying glass; **unter
die ~ nehmen** (*fig*) to scrutinize.
**lupenrein** *adj* (*lit: Edelstein*) flawless.
**Lupine** [lu'pi:nə] *f* lupin.
**Lurch** [lʊrç] (-(e)s, -e) *m* amphibian.
**Lust** [lʊst] (-, ⁻e) *f* joy, delight; (*Neigung*)
desire; (*sexuell*) lust (*pej*); ~ **haben zu** *od* **auf
etw** *akk/***etw zu tun** to feel like sth/doing
sth; **hast du ~?** how about it?; **er hat die
~ daran verloren** he has lost all interest in
it; **je nach ~ und Laune** just depending on
how I *od* you *etc* feel; **l~betont** *adj* pleasure-
orientated.
**lüstern** ['lystərn] *adj* lustful, lecherous.
**Lustgefühl** *nt* pleasurable feeling.
**Lustgewinn** *m* pleasure.
**lustig** ['lʊstɪç] *adj* (*komisch*) amusing, funny;
(*fröhlich*) cheerful; **sich über jdn/etw
~ machen** to make fun of sb/sth.
**Lüstling** *m* lecher.
**Lust-** *zW:* **l~los** *adj* unenthusiastic; ~**mord** *m*
sex(ual) murder; ~**prinzip** *nt* (*PSYCH*)
pleasure principle; ~**spiel** *nt* comedy;
**l~wandeln** *vi* to stroll about.
**luth.** *abk* =**lutherisch**
**Lutheraner(in)** [lʊtə'ra:nər(ɪn)] *m(f)* Lutheran.
**lutherisch** ['lʊtərɪʃ] *adj* Lutheran.
**lutschen** ['lʊtʃən] *vt, vi* to suck; **am Daumen ~**
to suck one's thumb.
**Lutscher** (-s, -) *m* lollipop.
**Luxemburg** ['lʊksəmbʊrk] (-s) *nt*
Luxembourg.
**Luxemburger(in)** ['lʊksəmburgər(ɪn)] (-s, -)
*m(f)* citizen of Luxembourg, Luxembourger.
**luxemburgisch** *adj* Luxembourgian.
**luxuriös** [lʊksuri'ø:s] *adj* luxurious.
**Luxus** ['lʊksʊs] (-) *m* luxury; ~**artikel** *pl* luxury
goods *pl*; ~**ausführung** *f* de luxe model;
~**dampfer** *m* luxury cruise ship; ~**hotel** *nt*
luxury hotel; ~**steuer** *f* tax on luxuries.
**LVA** (-) *f abk* (= *Landesversicherungsanstalt*)
county insurance company.
**LW** *abk* (= *Langwelle*) LW.
**Lycra** ['ly:kra] (-(s)) *no pl nt* Lycra ®.
**Lymphe** ['lymfə] (-, -n) *f* lymph.
**Lymphknoten** *m* lymph(atic) gland.
**lynchen** ['lynçən] *vt* to lynch.
**Lynchjustiz** *f* lynch law.
**Lyrik** ['ly:rɪk] *f* lyric poetry; ~**er(in)** (-s, -) *m(f)*
lyric poet.
**lyrisch** ['ly:rɪʃ] *adj* lyrical.

# M, m

**M, m¹** [ɛm] *nt* M, m; ~ **wie Martha** ≈ M for
Mary, M for Mike (*US*).
**m²** *abk* (= *Meter*) m; (=*männlich*) m.
**M.** *abk* = *Monat.*
**MA.** *abk* = **Mittelalter.**
**Maat** [ma:t] (-s, -e *od* -en) *m* (*NAUT*) (ship's)
mate.
**Machart** *f* make.
**machbar** *adj* feasible.
**Mache** (-) (*umg*) *f* show, sham; **jdn in der
~ haben** to be having a go at sb.

══════════════════ SCHLÜSSELWORT

**machen** ['maxən] *vt* **1** to do; **was machst du
da?** what are you doing there?; **das ist nicht
zu ~** that can't be done; **was ~ Sie
(beruflich)?** what do you do for a living?;
**mach, daß du hier verschwindest!** (you just)
get out of here!; **mit mir kann man's ja ~!**
(*umg*) the things I put up with!; **das läßt er
nicht mit sich ~** he won't stand for that;
**eine Prüfung ~** to take an exam
**2** (*herstellen*) to make; **das Radio leiser ~** to
turn the radio down; **aus Holz gemacht**
made of wood; **das Essen ~** to get the meal;
**Schluß ~** to finish (off)
**3** (*verursachen, bewirken*) to make; **jdm Angst
~** to make sb afraid; **das macht die Kälte** it's
the cold that does that
**4** (*aus~*) to matter; **das macht nichts** that
doesn't matter; **die Kälte macht mir nichts** I
don't mind the cold
**5** (*kosten: ergeben*) to be; **3 und 5 macht 8** 3
and 5 is *od* are 8; **was** *od* **wieviel macht das?**
how much does that come to?
**6: was macht die Arbeit?** how's the work
going?; **was macht dein Bruder?** how is your
brother doing?; **das Auto ~ lassen** to have
the car done; **mach's gut!** take care!; (*viel
Glück*) good luck!
♦ *vi:* **mach schnell!** hurry up!; **mach schon!**
come on!; **jetzt macht sie auf große Dame**
(*umg*) she's playing the lady now; **laß mich
mal ~** (*umg*) let me do it; (*ich bringe das in
Ordnung*) I'll deal with it; **groß/klein ~** (*umg:
Notdurft*) to do a big/little job; **sich** *dat* **in die
Hose ~** to wet o.s.; **ins Bett ~** to wet one's
bed; **das macht müde** it makes you tired; **in
etw** *dat* **~** to be *od* deal in sth
♦ *vr* to come along (nicely); **sich an etw** *akk*
**~** to set about sth; **sich verständlich ~** to
make o.s. understood; **sich** *dat* **viel aus jdm/**

etw ~ to like sb/sth; **mach dir nichts daraus** don't let it bother you; **sich auf den Weg ~** to get going; **sich an etw** akk ~ to set about sth.

**Machenschaften** pl wheelings and dealings pl.

**Macher** (-s, -) (umg) m man of action.

**macho** ['matʃo] (umg) adj macho.

**Macho** (-s, -s) (umg) m macho type.

**Macht** [maxt] (-, ⁻e) f power; **mit aller ~** with all one's might; **an der ~ sein** to be in power; **alles in unserer ~ Stehende** everything in our power; **~ergreifung** f seizure of power; **~haber** (-s, -) m ruler.

**mächtig** ['mɛçtɪç] adj powerful, mighty; (umg: ungeheuer) enormous.

**Macht-** zW: **m~los** adj powerless; **~probe** f trial of strength; **~stellung** f position of power; **~wort** nt: **ein ~wort sprechen** to lay down the law.

**Machwerk** nt work; (schlechte Arbeit) botched-up job.

**Macke** ['makə] (-, -n) (umg) f (Tick, Knall) quirk; (Fehler) fault.

**Macker** (-s, -) (umg) m fellow, guy.

**MAD** (-) m abk (= Militärischer Abschirmdienst) ≈ MI5 (BRIT), CIA (US).

**Madagaskar** [mada'gaskar] (-s) nt Madagascar.

**Mädchen** ['mɛːtçən] nt girl; **ein ~ für alles** (umg) a dogsbody; (im Büro etc) a girl Friday; **m~haft** adj girlish; **~name** m maiden name.

**Made** ['maːdə] (-, -n) f maggot.

**Madeira**[1] [ma'deːra] (-s) nt (GEOG) Madeira.

**Madeira**[2] (-s, -s) m (Wein) Madeira.

**Mädel** ['mɛːdl] (-s, -(s)) nt (Dialekt) lass, girl.

**madig** ['maːdɪç] adj maggoty; **jdm etw ~ machen** to spoil sth for sb.

**Madrid** [ma'drɪt] (-s) nt Madrid.

**mag** [maːk] vb siehe **mögen**.

**Mag.** abk = **Magister**.

**Magazin** [maga'tsiːn] (-s, -e) nt (Zeitschrift, am Gewehr) magazine; (Lager) storeroom; (Bibliotheks~) stockroom.

**Magd** [maːkt] (-, ⁻e) f maid(servant).

**Magen** ['maːgən] (-s, - od ⁻) m stomach; **jdm auf den ~ schlagen** (umg) to upset sb's stomach; (fig) to upset sb; **sich** dat **den ~ verderben** to upset one's stomach; **~bitter** m bitters pl; **~geschwür** nt stomach ulcer; **~schmerzen** pl stomach-ache sing; **~verstimmung** f stomach upset.

**mager** ['maːgər] adj lean; (dünn) thin; **M~keit** f leanness; thinness; **M~milch** f skimmed milk; **M~quark** m low-fat soft cheese; **M~sucht** f (MED) anorexia; **~süchtig** adj anorexic.

**Magie** [ma'giː] f magic.

**Magier** ['maːgiər] (-s, -) m magician.

**magisch** ['maːgɪʃ] adj magical.

**Magister** [ma'gɪstər] (-s, -) m (UNIV) M.A., Master of Arts.

**Magistrat** [magɪs'traːt] (-(e)s, -e) m municipal authorities pl.

**Magnat** [ma'gnaːt] (-en, -en) m magnate.

**Magnet** [ma'gneːt] (-s od -en, -en) m magnet; **~bahn** f magnetic railway; **~band** nt (COMPUT) magnetic tape; **m~isch** adj magnetic.

**magnetisieren** [magneti'ziːrən] vt to magnetize.

**Magnetnadel** f magnetic needle.

**Magnettafel** f magnetic board.

**Mahagoni** [maha'goːni] (-s) nt mahogany.

**Mähdrescher** (-s, -) m combine (harvester).

**mähen** ['mɛːən] vt, vi to mow.

**Mahl** [maːl] (-(e)s, -e) nt meal.

**mahlen** unreg vt to grind.

**Mahlstein** m grindstone.

**Mahlzeit** f meal ♦ interj enjoy your meal!

**Mähne** ['mɛːnə] (-, -n) f mane.

**mahnen** ['maːnən] vt to remind; (warnend) to warn; (wegen Schuld) to demand payment from; **jdn zur Eile/Geduld** etc ~ (auffordern) to urge sb to hurry/be patient etc.

**Mahn-** zW: **~gebühr** f reminder fee; **~mal** nt memorial; **~schreiben** nt reminder.

**Mahnung** f admonition, warning; (Mahnbrief) reminder.

**Mähre** ['mɛːrə] (-, -n) f mare.

**Mähren** ['mɛːrən] (-s) nt Moravia.

**Mai** [mai] (-(e)s, -e) (pl selten) m May; siehe auch **September**; **~baum** m maypole; **~bowle** f white wine punch (flavoured with woodruff); **~glöckchen** nt lily of the valley; **~käfer** m cockchafer.

**Mailand** ['mailant] (-s) nt Milan.

**Main** [main] (-(e)s) m (Fluß) Main.

**Mais** [mais] (-es, -e) m maize, corn (US); **~kolben** m corncob.

**Majestät** [majɛs'tɛːt] f majesty.

**majestätisch** adj majestic.

**Majestätsbeleidigung** f lese-majesty.

**Major** [ma'joːr] (-s, -e) m (MIL) major; (AVIAT) squadron leader.

**Majoran** [majo'raːn] (-s, -e) m marjoram.

**makaber** [ma'kaːbər] adj macabre.

**Makedonien** [make'doːniən] (-s) nt Macedonia.

**makedonisch** adj Macedonian.

**Makel** ['maːkəl] (-s, -) m blemish; (moralisch) stain; **ohne ~** flawless; **m~los** adj immaculate, spotless.

**mäkeln** ['mɛːkəln] vi to find fault.

**Make-up** [meːk'|ap] (-s, -s) nt make-up; (flüssig) foundation.

**Makkaroni** [maka'roːni] pl macaroni sing.

**Makler** ['maːklər] (-s, -) m broker; (Grundstücks~) estate agent (BRIT), realtor (US); **~gebühr** f broker's commission, brokerage.

**Makrele** [ma'kre:lə] (-, -n) *f* mackerel.
**Makro-** *in zW* macro-.
**Makrone** [ma'kro:nə] (-, -n) *f* macaroon.
**Makroökonomie** *f* macroeconomics *sing.*
**Mal** [ma:l] (-(e)s, -e) *nt* mark, sign; (*Zeitpunkt*) time; **ein für alle** ~ once and for all; **mit einem** ~(e) all of a sudden.
**mal** *adv* times.
**-mal** *suff* -times.
**Malaie** [ma'laɪə] (-n, -n) *m*, **Malaiin** *f* Malay.
**malaiisch** *adj* Malayan.
**Malawi** [ma'la:vi] (-s) *nt* Malawi.
**Malaysia** [ma'laɪzia] (-s) *nt* Malaysia.
**Malaysier(in)** (-s, -) *m(f)* Malaysian.
**malaysisch** *adj* Malaysian.
**Malediven** [male'di:vən] *pl:* **die** ~ the Maldive Islands.
**malen** *vt, vi* to paint.
**Maler** (-s, -) *m* painter.
**Malerei** [ma:lə'raɪ] *f* painting.
**malerisch** *adj* picturesque.
**Malkasten** *m* paintbox.
**Mallorca** [ma'lɔrka] (-s) *nt* Majorca.
**Mallorquiner(in)** [malɔr'ki:nər(ɪn)] (-s, -) *m(f)* Majorcan.
**mallorquinisch** *adj* Majorcan.
**malnehmen** *unreg vt, vi* to multiply.
**Malta** ['malta] (-s) *nt* Malta.
**Malteser(in)** [mal'te:zər(ɪn)] (-s, -) *m(f)* Maltese.
**Malteser-Hilfsdienst** *m* ≈ St. John's Ambulance Brigade (*BRIT*).
**maltesisch** *adj* Maltese.
**malträtieren** [maltrɛ'ti:rən] *vt* to ill-treat, maltreat.
**Malz** [malts] (-es) *nt* malt; ~**bonbon** *nt or m* cough drop; ~**kaffee** *m* coffee substitute made from malt barley.
**Mama** ['mama:] (-, -s) (*umg*) *f* mum(my) (*BRIT*), mom(my) (*US*).
**Mami** ['mami] (-, -s) *f* = **Mama**.
**Mammographie** [mamɔgra'fi:] *f* (*MED*) mammography.
**Mammut** ['mamʊt] (-s, -e *od* -s) *nt* mammoth ♦ *in zW* mammoth, giant; ~**anlagen** *pl* (*INDUSTRIE*) mammoth plants.
**mampfen** ['mampfən] (*umg*) *vt, vi* to munch, chomp.
**man** [man] *pron* one, you, people *pl;* ~ **hat mir gesagt** ... I was told ...
**managen** ['mɛnɪdʒən] *vt* to manage; **ich manage das schon!** (*umg*) I'll fix it somehow!
**Manager(in)** (-s, -) *m(f)* manager.
**manch** [manç] *pron:* ~ **ein(e)** ... many a ...; ~ **eine(r)** many a person.
**manche(r, s)** *adj* many a; (*pl*) a number of ♦ *pron* some.
**mancherlei** [mançər'laɪ] *adj inv* various ♦ *pron* a variety of things.
**manchmal** *adv* sometimes.
**Mandant(in)** [man'dant(ɪn)] *m(f)* (*JUR*) client.

**Mandarine** [manda'ri:nə] *f* mandarin, tangerine.
**Mandat** [man'da:t] (-(e)s, -e) *nt* mandate; **sein** ~ **niederlegen** (*PARL*) to resign one's seat.
**Mandel** ['mandəl] (-, -n) *f* almond; (*ANAT*) tonsil; ~**entzündung** *f* tonsillitis.
**Mandschurei** (-) [mandʒu'raɪ] *f:* **die** ~ Manchuria.
**Manege** [ma'nɛ:ʒə] (-, -n) *f* ring, arena.
**Mangel¹** ['maŋəl] (-, -n) *f* mangle; **durch die** ~ **drehen** (*fig: umg*) to put through it; (*Prüfling etc*) to put through the mill.
**Mangel²** ['maŋəl] (-s, ⁻) *m* lack; (*Knappheit*) shortage; (*Fehler*) defect, fault; ~ **an** +*dat* shortage of.
**Mängelbericht** ['mɛŋəlbərɪçt] *m* list of faults.
**Mängelerscheinung** *f* deficiency symptom.
**mangelhaft** *adj* poor; (*fehlerhaft*) defective, faulty; (*Schulnote*) unsatisfactory.
**mangeln** *vi unpers:* **es mangelt jdm an etw** *dat* sb lacks sth ♦ *vt* (*Wäsche*) to mangle.
**mangels** *präp* +*gen* for lack of.
**Mangelware** *f* scarce commodity.
**Manie** [ma'ni:] *f* mania.
**Manier** [ma'ni:r] (-) *f* manner; (*Stil*) style; (*pej*) mannerism.
**Manieren** *pl* manners *pl;* (*pej*) mannerisms *pl.*
**maniriert** [mani'ri:rt] *adj* mannered, affected.
**manierlich** *adj* well-mannered.
**Manifest** [mani'fɛst] (-es, -e) *nt* manifesto.
**Maniküre** [mani'ky:rə] (-, -n) *f* manicure.
**maniküren** *vt* to manicure.
**Manipulation** [manipulatsi'o:n] *f* manipulation; (*Trick*) manoeuvre (*BRIT*), maneuver (*US*).
**manipulieren** [manipu'li:rən] *vt* to manipulate.
**Manko** ['maŋko] (-s, -s) *nt* deficiency; (*COMM*) deficit.
**Mann** [man] (-(e)s, ⁻er *od* (*NAUT*) **Leute**) *m* man; (*Ehe*~) husband; (*NAUT*) hand; **pro** ~ per head; **mit** ~ **und Maus untergehen** to go down with all hands; (*Passagierschiff*) to go down with no survivors; **seinen** ~ **stehen** to hold one's own; **etw an den** ~ **bringen** (*umg*) to get rid of sth; **einen kleinen** ~ **im Ohr haben** (*hum: umg*) to be crazy.
**Männchen** ['mɛnçən] *nt* little man; (*Tier*) male; ~ **machen** (*Hund*) to (sit up and) beg.
**Mannequin** [manə'kɛ̃:] (-s, -s) *nt* fashion model.
**Männersache** ['mɛnərzaxə] *f* (*Angelegenheit*) man's business; (*Arbeit*) man's job.
**mannigfaltig** ['manɪçfaltɪç] *adj* various, varied; **M~keit** *f* variety.
**männlich** ['mɛnlɪç] *adj* (*BIOL*) male; (*fig, GRAM*) masculine.
**Mannsbild** *nt* (*veraltet: pej*) fellow.
**Mannschaft** *f* (*SPORT, fig*) team; (*NAUT, AVIAT*) crew; (*MIL*) other ranks *pl.*
**Mannschaftsgeist** *m* team spirit.
**Mannsleute** (*umg*) *pl* menfolk *pl.*

**Mannweib** (*pej*) *nt* mannish woman.
**Manometer** [mano'me:tər] *nt* (*TECH*) pressure gauge; ~! (*umg*) wow!
**Manöver** [ma'nø:vər] (-s, -) *nt* manoeuvre (*BRIT*), maneuver (*US*).
**manövrieren** [manø'vri:rən] *vt, vi* to manoeuvre (*BRIT*), maneuver (*US*).
**Mansarde** [man'zardə] (-, -n) *f* attic.
**Manschette** [man'ʃɛtə] *f* cuff; (*Papier~*) paper frill; (*TECH*) sleeve.
**Manschettenknopf** *m* cufflink.
**Mantel** ['mantəl] (-s, ̈) *m* coat; (*TECH*) casing, jacket; ~**tarif** *m* general terms of employment; ~**tarifvertrag** *m* general agreement on conditions of employment.
**Manuskript** [manu'skrɪpt] (-(e)s, -e) *nt* manuscript.
**Mappe** ['mapə] (-, -n) *f* briefcase; (*Akten~*) folder.
**Marathonlauf** ['ma:ratɔnlaʊf] *m* marathon.
**Märchen** ['mɛːrçən] *nt* fairy tale; **m~haft** *adj* fabulous; ~**prinz** *m* prince charming.
**Marder** ['mardər] (-s, -) *m* marten.
**Margarine** [marga'ri:nə] *f* margarine.
**Marge** ['marʒə] (-, -n) *f* (*COMM*) margin.
**Maria** [ma'ri:a] (-) *f* Mary.
**Marienbild** *nt* picture of the Virgin Mary.
**Marienkäfer** *m* ladybird.
**Marihuana** [marihu'a:na] (-s) *nt* marijuana.
**Marinade** [mari'na:də] (-, -n) *f* (*KOCH*) marinade; (*Soße*) mayonnaise-based sauce.
**Marine** [ma'ri:nə] *f* navy; **m~blau** *adj* navy-blue.
**marinieren** [mari'ni:rən] *vt* to marinate.
**Marionette** [mario'nɛtə] *f* puppet.
**Mark¹** [mark] (-, -) *f* (*Geld*) mark.
**Mark²** [mark] (-(e)s *nt* (*Knochen~*) marrow; **jdn bis ins ~ treffen** (*fig*) to cut sb to the quick; **jdm durch ~ und Bein gehen** to go right through sb.
**markant** [mar'kant] *adj* striking.
**Marke** ['markə] (-, -n) *f* mark; (*Warensorte*) brand; (*Fabrikat*) make; (*Rabatt~, Brief~*) stamp; (*Essen(s)~*) luncheon voucher; (*aus Metall etc*) token, disc.
**Marken-** *zW:* ~**artikel** *m* proprietary article; ~**butter** *f* best quality butter; ~**zeichen** *nt* trademark.
**Marketing** ['markətɪŋ] (-s) *nt* marketing.
**markieren** [mar'ki:rən] *vt* to mark; (*umg*) to act ♦ *vi* (*umg*) to act it.
**Markierung** *f* marking.
**markig** ['markɪç] *adj* (*fig*) pithy.
**Markise** [mar'ki:zə] (-, -n) *f* awning.
**Markstück** *nt* one-mark piece.
**Markt** [markt] (-(e)s, ̈-e) *m* market; ~**analyse** *f* market analysis; ~**anteil** *m* market share; **m~fähig** *adj* marketable; ~**forschung** *f* market research; **m~gängig** *adj* marketable; **m~gerecht** *adj* geared to market requirements; ~**lücke** *f* gap in the market; ~**platz** *m* market place; ~**preis** *m* market

price; ~**wert** *m* market value; ~**wirtschaft** *f* market economy; **m~wirtschaftlich** *adj* free enterprise.
**Marmelade** [marmə'la:də] (-, -n) *f* jam.
**Marmor** ['marmɔr] (-s, -e) *m* marble.
**marmorieren** [marmo'ri:rən] *vt* to marble.
**Marmorkuchen** *m* marble cake.
**marmorn** *adj* marble.
**Marokkaner(in)** [marɔ'ka:nər(ɪn)] (-s, -) *m(f)* Moroccan.
**marokkanisch** *adj* Moroccan.
**Marokko** [ma'rɔko] (-s) *nt* Morocco.
**Marone** [ma'ro:nə] (-, -n) *f* chestnut.
**Marotte** [ma'rɔtə] (-, -n) *f* fad, quirk.
**Marsch¹** [marʃ] (-, -en) *f* marsh.
**Marsch²** (-(e)s, ̈-e) *m* march; **jdm den ~ blasen** (*umg*) to give sb a rocket ♦ **m~** *interj* march; **m~ ins Bett!** off to bed with you!
**Marschbefehl** *m* marching orders *pl*.
**marschbereit** *adj* ready to move.
**marschieren** [mar'ʃi:rən] *vi* to march.
**Marschverpflegung** *f* rations *pl*; (*MIL*) field rations *pl*.
**Marseille** [mar'sɛːj] (-s) *nt* Marseilles.
**Marsmensch** ['marsmɛnʃ] *m* Martian.
**Marter** ['martər] (-, -n) *f* torment.
**martern** *vt* to torture.
**Martinshorn** ['marti:nshɔrn] *nt* siren (*of police etc*).
**Märtyrer(in)** ['mɛrtyrər(ɪn)] (-s, -) *m(f)* martyr.
**Martyrium** [mar'ty:riʊm] *nt* (*fig*) ordeal.
**Marxismus** [mar'ksɪsmʊs] *m* Marxism.
**März** [mɛrts] (-(es), -e) (*pl selten*) *m* March; *siehe auch* **September**.
**Marzipan** [martsi'pa:n] (-s, -e) *nt* marzipan.
**Masche** ['maʃə] (-, -n) *f* mesh; (*Strick~*) stitch; **das ist die neueste ~** that's the latest dodge; **durch die ~n schlüpfen** to slip through the net.
**Maschendraht** *m* wire mesh.
**maschenfest** *adj* runproof.
**Maschine** [ma'ʃi:nə] *f* machine; (*Motor*) engine.
**maschinell** [maʃi'nɛl] *adj* machine(-), mechanical.
**Maschinen-** *zW:* ~**ausfallzeit** *f* machine downtime; ~**bauer** *m* mechanical engineer; ~**führer** *m* machinist; **m~geschrieben** *adj* typewritten; ~**gewehr** *nt* machine gun; **m~lesbar** *adj* (*COMPUT*) machine-readable; ~**pistole** *f* submachine gun; ~**raum** *m* plant room; (*NAUT*) engine room; ~**saal** *m* machine shop; ~**schaden** *m* mechanical fault; ~**schlosser** *m* fitter; ~**schrift** *f* typescript; ~**sprache** *f* (*COMPUT*) machine language.
**Maschinerie** [maʃinə'ri:] *f* (*fig*) machinery.
**maschineschreiben** *unreg vi* to type.
**Maschinist(in)** [maʃi'nɪst(ɪn)] *m(f)* engineer.
**Maser** ['ma:zər] (-, -n) *f* grain.
**Masern** *pl* (*MED*) measles *sing*.

**Maserung** *f* grain(ing).
**Maske** ['maskə] (-, -n) *f* mask.
**Maskenball** *m* fancy-dress ball.
**Maskenbildner(in)** *m(f)* make-up artist.
**Maskerade** [maskə'raːdə] *f* masquerade.
**maskieren** [mas'kiːrən] *vt* to mask; (*verkleiden*) to dress up ♦ *vr* to disguise o.s., dress up.
**Maskottchen** [mas'kɔtçən] *nt* (lucky) mascot.
**Maskulinum** [masku'liːnʊm] (-s, **Maskulina**) *nt* (*GRAM*) masculine noun.
**Masochist** [mazo'xɪst] (-en, -en) *m* masochist.
**Maß¹** [maːs] (-es, -e) *nt* measure; (*Mäßigung*) moderation; (*Grad*) degree, extent; **über alle ~en** (*liter*) extremely, beyond measure; **mit zweierlei ~ messen** (*fig*) to operate a double standard; **sich** *dat* **etw nach ~ anfertigen lassen** to have sth made to measure *od* order (*US*); **in besonderem ~e** especially; **das ~ ist voll** (*fig*) that's enough (of that).
**Maß²** (-, -(e)) *f* litre (*BRIT*) *od* liter (*US*) of beer.
**maß** *etc vb siehe* **messen**.
**Massage** [ma'saːʒə] (-, -n) *f* massage.
**Massaker** [ma'saːkər] (-s, -) *nt* massacre.
**Maßanzug** *m* made-to-measure suit.
**Maßarbeit** *f* (*fig*) neat piece of work.
**Masse** ['masə] (-, -n) *f* mass; **eine ganze ~** (*umg*) a great deal.
**Maßeinheit** *f* unit of measurement.
**Massen-** *zW:* **~artikel** *m* mass-produced article; **~blatt** *nt* tabloid; **~grab** *nt* mass grave; **m~haft** *adj* masses of; **~medien** *pl* mass media *pl*; **~produktion** *f* mass production; **~veranstaltung** *f* mass meeting; **~vernichtungswaffen** *pl* weapons of mass destruction *od* extermination; **~ware** *f* mass-produced article; **m~weise** *adv* in huge numbers.
**Masseur** [ma'søːr] *m* masseur.
**Masseuse** [ma'søːzə] *f* masseuse.
**Maß-** *zW:* **m~gebend** *adj* authoritative; **m~gebende Kreise** influential circles; **m~geblich** *adj* definitive; **m~geschneidert** *adj* (*Anzug*) made-to-measure, made-to-order (*US*), custom *attrib* (*US*); **m~halten** *unreg vi* to exercise moderation.
**massieren** [ma'siːrən] *vt* to massage; (*MIL*) to mass.
**massig** ['masɪç] *adj* massive; (*umg*) a massive amount of.
**mäßig** ['mɛːsɪç] *adj* moderate; **~en** ['mɛːsɪgən] *vt* to restrain, moderate; **sein Tempo ~en** to slacken one's pace; **M~keit** *f* moderation.
**massiv** [ma'siːf] *adj* solid; (*fig*) heavy, rough; **~ werden** (*umg*) to turn nasty; **M~** (-s, -e) *nt* massif.
**Maß-** *zW:* **~krug** *m* tankard; **m~los** *adj* (*Verschwendung, Essen, Trinken*) excessive, immoderate; (*Enttäuschung, Ärger etc*) extreme; **~nahme** (-, -n) *f* measure, step; **m~regeln** *vt untr* to reprimand.
**Maßstab** *m* rule, measure; (*fig*) standard;

(*GEOG*) scale; **als ~ dienen** to serve as a model.
**maßstab(s)getreu** *adj* (true) to scale.
**maßvoll** *adj* moderate.
**Mast** [mast] (-(e)s, -e(n)) *m* mast; (*ELEK*) pylon.
**Mastdarm** *m* rectum.
**mästen** ['mɛstən] *vt* to fatten.
**masturbieren** [mastʊr'biːrən] *vi* to masturbate.
**Material** [materi'aːl] (-s, -ien) *nt* material(s); **~fehler** *m* material defect.
**Materialismus** [materia'lismʊs] *m* materialism.
**Materialist(in)** *m(f)* materialist; **m~isch** *adj* materialistic.
**Materialkosten** *pl* cost *sing* of materials.
**Materialprüfung** *f* material(s) control.
**Materie** [ma'teːriə] *f* matter, substance.
**materiell** [materi'ɛl] *adj* material.
**Mathe** ['matə] (-) *f* (*SCH: umg*) maths (*BRIT*), math (*US*).
**Mathematik** [matema'tiːk] *f* mathematics *sing*; **~er(in)** [mate'maːtɪkər(ɪn)] (-s, -) *m(f)* mathematician.
**mathematisch** [mate'maːtɪʃ] *adj* mathematical.
**Matjeshering** ['matjəsheːrɪŋ] (*umg*) *m* salted young herring.
**Matratze** [ma'tratsə] (-, -n) *f* mattress.
**Matrixdrucker** *m* dot-matrix printer.
**Matrixzeichen** *nt* matrix character.
**Matrize** [ma'triːtsə] (-, -n) *f* matrix; (*zum Abziehen*) stencil.
**Matrose** [ma'troːzə] (-n, -n) *m* sailor.
**Matsch** [matʃ] (-(e)s) *m* mud; (*Schnee~*) slush.
**matschig** *adj* muddy; slushy.
**matt** [mat] *adj* weak; (*glanzlos*) dull; (*PHOT*) matt; (*SCHACH*) mate; **jdn ~ setzen** (*auch fig*) to checkmate sb; **M~** (-s, -s) *nt* (*SCHACH*) checkmate.
**Matte** ['matə] (-, -n) *f* mat; **auf der ~ stehen** (*am Arbeitsplatz etc*) to be in.
**Mattigkeit** *f* weakness; dullness.
**Mattscheibe** *f* (*TV*) screen; **~ haben** (*umg*) to be not quite with it.
**Matura** [ma'tuːra] (-) (*ÖSTERR, SCHWEIZ*) *f* = **Abitur**.
**Mätzchen** ['mɛtsçən] (*umg*) *nt* antics *pl*; **~ machen** to fool around.
**mau** [maʊ] (*umg*) *adj* poor, bad.
**Mauer** ['maʊər] (-, -n) *f* wall; **~blümchen** (*umg*) *nt* (*fig*) wallflower.
**mauern** *vi* to build, lay bricks ♦ *vt* to build.
**Mauer-** *zW:* **~schwalbe** *f* swift; **~segler** *m* swift; **~werk** *nt* brickwork; (*Stein*) masonry.
**Maul** [maʊl] (-(e)s, **Mäuler**) *nt* mouth; **ein loses** *od* **lockeres ~ haben** (*umg: frech sein*) to be an impudent so-and-so; (: *indiskret sein*) to be a blabbermouth; **halt's ~!** (*umg*) shut your face (!); **darüber werden sich die Leute das ~ zerreißen** (*umg*) that will start people's tongues wagging; **dem Volk** *od* **den Leuten**

**aufs ~ schauen** (*umg*) to listen to what ordinary people say; **m~en** (*umg*) *vi* to grumble; **~esel** *m* mule; **~korb** *m* muzzle; **~sperre** *f* lockjaw; **~tier** *nt* mule; **~- und Klauenseuche** *f* (*Tiere*) foot-and-mouth disease.

**Maulwurf** *m* mole.

**Maulwurfshaufen** *m* molehill.

**Maurer** ['maʊrər] (**-s, -**) *m* bricklayer; **pünktlich wie die ~** (*hum*) super-punctual.

**Mauretanien** [maʊrə'taːniən] (**-s**) *nt* Mauritania.

**Mauritius** [maʊ'riːtsiʊs] (**-**) *nt* Mauritius.

**Maus** [maʊs] (**-, Mäuse**) *f* (*auch COMPUT*) mouse; **Mäuse** *pl* (*umg: Geld*) bread *sing*, dough *sing*.

**mauscheln** ['maʊʃəln] (*umg*) *vt, vi* (*manipulieren*) to fiddle.

**mäuschenstill** ['mɔʏsçən'ʃtɪl] *adj* very quiet.

**Mausefalle** *f* mousetrap.

**mausen** *vt* (*umg*) to pinch ♦ *vi* to catch mice.

**mausern** *vr* to moult (*BRIT*), molt (*US*).

**maus(e)tot** *adj* stone dead.

**Maut** [maʊt] (**-, -en**) *f* toll.

**max.** *abk* (= *maximal*) max.

**maximal** [maksi'maːl] *adj* maximum.

**Maxime** [ma'ksiːmə] (**-, -n**) *f* maxim.

**maximieren** [maksi'miːrən] *vt* to maximize.

**Maximierung** *f* (*WIRTS*) maximization.

**Maximum** ['maksimʊm] (**-s, Maxima**) *nt* maximum.

**Mayonnaise** [majɔ'nɛːzə] (**-, -n**) *f* mayonnaise.

**Mazedonien** [matse'doːniən] (**-s**) *nt* Macedonia.

**Mäzen** [mɛ'tseːn] (**-s, -e**) *m* (*gen*) patron, sponsor.

**MdB** *nt abk* (= *Mitglied des Bundestages*) member of the Bundestag, ≈ MP.

**MdL** *nt abk* (= *Mitglied des Landtags*) member of the Landtag.

**m.E.** *abk* (= *meines Erachtens*) in my opinion.

**Mechanik** [me'çaːnɪk] *f* mechanics *sing*; (*Getriebe*) mechanics *pl*; **~er** (**-s, -**) *m* mechanic, engineer.

**mechanisch** *adj* mechanical.

**mechanisieren** [meçani|zi:rən] *vt* to mechanize.

**Mechanisierung** *f* mechanization.

**Mechanismus** [meça'nɪsmʊs] *m* mechanism.

**meckern** ['mɛkərn] *vi* to bleat; (*umg*) to moan.

**Mecklenburg** ['meː:klənbʊrk] (**-s**) *nt* Mecklenburg.

**Mecklenburg-Vorpommern** (**-s**) *nt* (state of) Mecklenburg-Vorpommern.

**Medaille** [me'daljə] (**-, -n**) *f* medal.

**Medaillon** [medal'jõː] (**-s, -s**) *nt* (*Schmuck*) locket.

**Medien** ['meːdiən] *pl* media *pl*; **~forschung** *f* media research.

**Medikament** [medika'mɛnt] *nt* medicine.

**Meditation** [meditatsi'oːn] *f* meditation.

**meditieren** [medi'tiːrən] *vi* to meditate.

**Medium** ['meːdiʊm] *nt* medium.

**Medizin** [medi'tsiːn] (**-, -en**) *f* medicine.

**Mediziner(in)** (**-s, -**) *m(f)* doctor; (*UNIV*) medic (*umg*).

**medizinisch** *adj* medical; **~-technische Assistentin** medical assistant.

**Meer** [meːr] (**-(e)s, -e**) *nt* sea; **am ~(e)** by the sea; **ans ~ fahren** to go to the sea(side); **~busen** *m* bay, gulf; **~enge** *f* straits *pl*.

**Meeres-** *zW*: **~früchte** *pl* seafood; **~klima** *nt* maritime climate; **~spiegel** *m* sea level.

**Meer-** *zW*: **~jungfrau** *f* mermaid; **~rettich** *m* horseradish; **~schweinchen** *nt* guinea pig; **~wasser** *nt* sea water.

**Mega-, mega-** [mɛga-] *in zW* mega-; **~byte** [mega'baɪt] *nt* megabyte; **~phon** [mega'foːn] (**-s, -e**) *nt* megaphone; **~watt** [mɛga'vat] *nt* megawatt.

**Mehl** [m'eːl] (**-(e)s, -e**) *nt* flour.

**mehlig** *adj* floury.

**Mehlschwitze** *f* (*KOCH*) roux.

**mehr** [meːr] *adv* more; **nie ~** never again, nevermore (*liter*); **es war niemand ~ da** there was no one left; **nicht ~ lange** not much longer; **M~aufwand** *m* additional expenditure; **M~belastung** *f* excess load; (*fig*) additional burden; **~deutig** *adj* ambiguous.

**mehrere** *indef pron* several; (*verschiedene*) various; **~s** several things.

**mehrfach** *adj* multiple; (*wiederholt*) repeated.

**Mehrheit** *f* majority.

**Mehrheitsprinzip** *nt* principle of majority rule.

**Mehrheitswahlrecht** *nt* first-past-the-post voting system.

**mehr-** *zW*: **~jährig** *adj attrib* of several years; **M~kosten** *pl* additional costs *pl*; **~malig** *adj* repeated; **~mals** *adv* repeatedly; **M~parteiensystem** *nt* multi-party system; **M~platzsystem** *nt* (*COMPUT*) multi-user system; **M~programmbetrieb** *m* (*COMPUT*) multiprogramming; **~sprachig** *adj* multilingual; **~stimmig** *adj* for several voices; **~stimmig singen** to harmonize; **M~wegflasche** *f* returnable bottle; **M~wertsteuer** *f* value added tax, VAT; **M~zahl** *f* majority; (*GRAM*) plural.

**Mehrzweck-** *in zW* multipurpose.

**meiden** ['maɪdən] *unreg vt* to avoid.

**Meile** ['maɪlə] (**-, -n**) *f* mile; **das riecht man drei ~n gegen den Wind** (*umg*) you can smell that a mile off.

**Meilenstein** *m* milestone.

**meilenweit** *adj* for miles.

**mein** [maɪn] *pron* my.

**meine(r, s)** *poss pron* mine.

**Meineid** ['maɪn|aɪt] *m* perjury.

**meinen** ['maɪnən] *vt* to think; (*sagen*) to say; (*sagen wollen*) to mean ♦ *vi* to think; **wie Sie ~!** as you wish; **damit bin ich gemeint** that refers to me; **das will ich ~** I should think so.

**meiner** *gen von* **ich** ♦ *pron* of me.

**meinerseits** *adv* for my part.

**meinesgleichen** ['maɪnəs'glaɪçən] *pron* people like me.

**meinetwegen** ['maɪnət've:gən] *adv* (*für mich*) for my sake; (*wegen mir*) on my account; (*von mir aus*) as far as I'm concerned; (*ich habe nichts dagegen*) I don't care *od* mind.

**meinetwillen** ['maɪnət'vɪlən] *adv*: **um ~** = **meinetwegen**.

**meinige** *pron*: **der/die/das ~** mine.

**meins** [maɪns] *pron* mine.

**Meinung** ['maɪnʊŋ] *f* opinion; **meiner ~ nach** in my opinion; **einer ~ sein** to think the same; **jdm die ~ sagen** to give sb a piece of one's mind.

**Meinungs-** *zW*: **~austausch** *m* exchange of views; **~forscher(in)** *m(f)* pollster; **~forschungsinstitut** *nt* opinion research institute; **~freiheit** *f* freedom of speech; **~umfrage** *f* opinion poll; **~verschiedenheit** *f* difference of opinion.

**Meise** ['maɪzə] (*-, -n*) *f* tit(mouse); **eine ~ haben** (*umg*) to be crackers.

**Meißel** ['maɪsəl] (*-s, -*) *m* chisel.

**meißeln** *vt* to chisel.

**meist** [maɪst] *adj* most ♦ *adv* mostly; **M~begünstigungsklausel** *f* (*COMM*) most-favoured-nation clause; **~bietend** *adj*: **~bietend versteigern** to sell to the highest bidder.

**meiste(r, s)** *superl von* **viel**.

**meistens** *adv* mostly.

**Meister** ['maɪstər] (*-s, -*) *m* master; (*SPORT*) champion; **seinen ~ machen** to take one's master craftsman's diploma; **es ist noch kein ~ vom Himmel gefallen** (*Sprichwort*) no one is born an expert; **~brief** *m* master craftsman's diploma; **m~haft** *adj* masterly.

**Meisterin** *f* (*auf einem Gebiet*) master, expert; (*SPORT*) (woman) champion.

**meistern** *vt* to master; **sein Leben ~** to come to grips with one's life.

**Meister-** *zW*: **~schaft** *f* mastery; (*SPORT*) championship; **~stück** *nt* masterpiece; **~werk** *nt* masterpiece.

**meistgekauft** *adj attrib* best-selling.

**Mekka** ['mɛka] (*-s, -s*) *nt* (*GEOG, fig*) Mecca.

**Melancholie** [melaŋko'li:] *f* melancholy.

**melancholisch** [melaŋ'ko:lɪʃ] *adj* melancholy.

**Meldebehörde** *f* registration authorities *pl*.

**Meldefrist** *f* registration period.

**melden** *vt* to report; (*registrieren*) to register ♦ *vr* to report; to register; (*SCH*) to put one's hand up; (*freiwillig*) to volunteer; (*auf etw, am Telefon*) to answer; **nichts zu ~ haben** (*umg*) to have no say; **wen darf ich ~?** who shall I say (is here)?; **sich ~ bei** to report to; to register with; **sich auf eine Anzeige ~** to answer an advertisement; **es meldet sich**

**niemand** there's no answer; **sich zu Wort ~** to ask to speak.

**Meldepflicht** *f* obligation to register with the police.

**Meldestelle** *f* registration office.

**Meldung** ['mɛldʊŋ] *f* announcement; (*Bericht*) report.

**meliert** [me'li:rt] *adj* mottled, speckled.

**melken** ['mɛlkən] *unreg vt* to milk.

**Melodie** [melo'di:] *f* melody, tune.

**melodisch** [me'lo:dɪʃ] *adj* melodious, tuneful.

**melodramatisch** [melodra'ma:tɪʃ] *adj* (*auch fig*) melodramatic.

**Melone** [me'lo:nə] (*-, -n*) *f* melon; (*Hut*) bowler (hat).

**Membran** [mem'bra:n] (*-, -en*) *f* (*TECH*) diaphragm; (*ANAT*) membrane.

**Memme** ['mɛmə] (*-, -n*) (*umg*) *f* cissy, yellow-belly.

**Memoiren** [memo'a:rən] *pl* memoirs *pl*.

**Menge** ['mɛŋə] (*-, -n*) *f* quantity; (*Menschen~*) crowd; (*große Anzahl*) lot (of); **jede ~** (*umg*) masses *pl*, loads *pl*.

**mengen** *vt* to mix ♦ *vr*: **sich ~ in** +*akk* to meddle with.

**Mengen-** *zW*: **~einkauf** *m* bulk buying; **~lehre** *f* (*MATH*) set theory; **~rabatt** *m* bulk discount.

**Menorca** [me'nɔrka] (*-s*) *nt* Menorca.

**Mensa** ['mɛnza] (*-, -s od* **Mensen**) *f* (*UNIV*) refectory (*BRIT*), commons (*US*).

**Mensch** [mɛnʃ] (*-en, -en*) *m* human being, man; (*Person*) person; **kein ~** nobody; **ich bin auch nur ein ~!** I'm only human; **~ ärgere dich nicht** *nt* (*Spiel*) ludo.

**Menschen-** *zW*: **~alter** *nt* generation; **~feind** *m* misanthrope; **m~freundlich** *adj* philanthropical; **~gedenken** *nt*: **der kälteste Winter seit ~gedenken** the coldest winter in living memory; **~handel** *m* slave trade; (*JUR*) trafficking in human beings; **~kenner** *m* judge of human nature; **~kenntnis** *f* knowledge of human nature; **m~leer** *adj* deserted; **~liebe** *f* philanthropy; **~masse** *f* crowd (of people); **~menge** *f* crowd of people); **m~möglich** *adj* humanly possible; **~rechte** *pl* human rights *pl*; **m~scheu** *adj* shy; **~schlag** (*umg*) *m* kind of people; **~seele** *f*: **keine ~seele** (*fig*) not a soul.

**Menschenskind** *interj* good heavens!

**Menschen-** *zW*: **m~unwürdig** *adj* degrading; **~verachtung** *f* contempt for human beings *od* of mankind; **~verstand** *m*: **gesunder ~verstand** common sense; **~würde** *f* human dignity; **m~würdig** *adj* (*Behandlung*) humane; (*Unterkunft*) fit for human habitation.

**Mensch-** *zW*: **~heit** *f* humanity, mankind; **m~lich** *adj* human; (*human*) humane; **~lichkeit** *f* humanity.

**Menstruation** [mɛnstruatsi'o:n] *f* menstruation.

**Mentalität** [mɛntali'tɛːt] f mentality.
**Menü** [me'nyː] (-s, -s) nt (auch COMPUT) menu; **m~gesteuert** adj (COMPUT) menu-driven.
**Merkblatt** nt instruction sheet od leaflet.
**merken** ['mɛrkən] vt to notice; **sich** dat **etw ~** to remember sth; **sich** dat **eine Autonummer ~** to make a (mental) note of a licence (BRIT) od license (US) number.
**merklich** adj noticeable.
**Merkmal** nt sign, characteristic.
**merkwürdig** adj odd.
**meschugge** [me'ʃʊgə] (umg) adj nuts, meshuga (US).
**Meß-** zW: **~band** nt tape measure; **m~bar** adj measurable; **~becher** m measuring cup.
**Meßbuch** nt missal.
**Meßdiener** m (REL) server, acolyte (form).
**Messe** ['mɛsə] (-, -n) f fair; (ECCL) mass; (MIL) mess; **auf der ~** at the fair; **~gelände** nt exhibition centre (BRIT) od center (US).
**messen** unreg vt to measure ♦ vr to compete.
**Messer** (-s, -) nt knife; **auf des ~s Schneide stehen** (fig) to hang in the balance; **jdm ins offene ~ laufen** (fig) to walk into a trap; **m~scharf** adj (fig): **m~scharf schließen** to conclude with incredible logic (ironisch); **~spitze** f knife point; (in Rezept) pinch; **~stecherei** f knife fight.
**Messestadt** f (town with an) exhibition centre (BRIT) od center (US).
**Messestand** m exhibition stand.
**Meßgerät** nt measuring device, gauge.
**Meßgewand** nt chasuble.
**Messing** ['mɛsɪŋ] (-s) nt brass.
**Meßstab** m (AUT: Öl- etc) dipstick.
**Messung** f (das Messen) measuring; (von Blutdruck) taking; (Meßergebnis) measurement.
**Meßwert** m measurement; (Ableseergebnis) reading.
**Metall** [me'tal] (-s, -e) nt metal; **m~en** adj metallic; **m~isch** adj metallic; **m~verarbeitend** adj: **die m~verarbeitende Industrie** the metal-processing industry.
**Metallurgie** [metalʊr'giː] f metallurgy.
**Metapher** [me'tafər] (-, -n) f metaphor.
**metaphorisch** [meta'foːrɪʃ] adj metaphorical.
**Metaphysik** [metafy'ziːk] f metaphysics sing.
**Metastase** [meta'staːzə] (-, -n) f (MED) secondary growth.
**Meteor** [mete'oːr] (-s, -e) m meteor.
**Meteorologe** [meteoro'loːgə] (-n, -n) m meteorologist.
**Meter** ['meːtər] (-s, -) m od nt metre (BRIT), meter (US); **in 500 ~ Höhe** at a height of 500 metres; **~maß** nt tape measure; **~ware** f (TEXTIL) piece goods.
**Methode** [me'toːdə] (-, -n) f method.
**Methodik** [me'toːdɪk] f methodology.
**methodisch** [me'toːdɪʃ] adj methodical.
**Metier** [meti'eː] (-s, -s) nt (hum) job,
profession.
**metrisch** ['meːtrɪʃ] adj metric, metrical.
**Metropole** [metro'poːlə] (-, -n) f metropolis.
**Mettwurst** ['mɛtvʊrst] f (smoked) pork/beef sausage.
**Metzger** ['mɛtsgər] (-s, -) m butcher.
**Metzgerei** [mɛtsgə'rai] f butcher's (shop).
**Meuchelmord** ['mɔyçəlmɔrt] m assassination.
**Meute** ['mɔytə] (-, -n) f pack.
**Meuterei** [mɔytə'rai] f mutiny.
**Meuterer** (-s, -) m mutineer.
**meutern** vi to mutiny.
**Mexikaner(in)** [mɛksi'kaːnər(ɪn)] (-s, -) m(f) Mexican.
**mexikanisch** adj Mexican.
**Mexiko** ['mɛksiko] (-s) nt Mexico.
**MEZ** abk (= mitteleuropäische Zeit) C.E.T.
**MFG** abk = **Mitfahrgelegenheit.**
**MG** (-(s), -(s)) nt abk = **Maschinengewehr.**
**mg** abk (= Milligramm) mg.
**mhd.** abk (= mittelhochdeutsch) MHG.
**MHz** abk (= Megahertz) MHz.
**miauen** [mi'auən] vi to miaow.
**mich** [mɪç] akk von **ich** ♦ pron me; (reflexiv) myself.
**mick(e)rig** ['mɪk(ə)rɪç] (umg) adj pathetic; (altes Männchen) puny.
**mied** etc [miːt] vb siehe **meiden.**
**Miederwaren** ['miːdərvaːrən] pl corsetry sing.
**Mief** [miːf] (-s) (umg) m fug; (muffig) stale air; (Gestank) stink, pong (BRIT).
**miefig** (umg) adj smelly, pongy (BRIT).
**Miene** ['miːnə] (-, -n) f look, expression; **gute ~ zum bösen Spiel machen** to grin and bear it.
**Mienenspiel** nt facial expressions pl.
**mies** [miːs] (umg) adj lousy.
**Miese** ['miːzə] (umg) pl: **in den ~n sein** to be in the red.
**Miesmacher(in)** (umg) m(f) killjoy.
**Mietauto** nt hired car (BRIT), rental car (US).
**Miete** ['miːtə] (-, -n) f rent; **zur ~ wohnen** to live in rented accommodation od accommodations (US).
**mieten** vt to rent; (Auto) to hire (BRIT), rent.
**Mieter(in)** (-s, -) m(f) tenant; **~schutz** m rent control.
**Mietshaus** nt tenement, block of flats (BRIT) od apartments (US).
**Miet-** zW: **~verhältnis** nt tenancy; **~vertrag** m tenancy agreement; **~wagen** m = **~auto**; **~wucher** m the charging of exorbitant rent(s).
**Mieze** ['miːtsə] (-, -n) (umg) f (Katze) pussy; (Mädchen) chick, bird (BRIT).
**Migräne** [mi'grɛːnə] (-, -n) f migraine.
**Mikado** [mi'kaːdo] (-s) nt (Spiel) pick-a-stick.
**Mikro-** ['miːkro] in zW micro-.
**Mikrobe** [mi'kroːbə] (-, -n) f microbe.
**Mikro-** zW: **~chip** m microchip; **~computer** m microcomputer; **~fiche** m od nt microfiche; **~film** m microfilm.

**Mikrofon** [mikro'foːn] (**-s, e**) *nt* microphone.
**Mikroökonomie** *f* microeconomics *pl*.
**Mikrophon** [mikro'foːn] (**-s, -e**) *nt* microphone.
**Mikroprozessor** (**-s, -oren**) *m* microprocessor.
**Mikroskop** [mikro'skoːp] (**-s, -e**) *nt* microscope; **m~isch** *adj* microscopic.
**Mikrowelle** ['miːkrovɛlə] *f* microwave.
**Mikrowellenherd** *m* microwave (oven).
**Milbe** ['mɪlbə] (**-, -n**) *f* mite.
**Milch** [mɪlç] (**-**) *f* milk; (*Fisch~*) milt, roe; **~drüse** *f* mammary gland; **~glas** *nt* frosted glass.
**milchig** *adj* milky.
**Milch-** *zW:* **~kaffee** *m* white coffee; **~mixgetränk** *nt* milk shake; **~pulver** *nt* powdered milk; **~straße** *f* Milky Way; **~tüte** *f* milk carton; **~zahn** *m* milk tooth.
**mild** [mɪlt] *adj* mild; (*Richter*) lenient; (*freundlich*) kind, charitable.
**Milde** ['mɪldə] (**-, -n**) *f* mildness; leniency.
**mildern** *vt* to mitigate, soften; (*Schmerz*) to alleviate; **~de Umstände** extenuating circumstances.
**Milieu** [mili'øː] (**-s, -s**) *nt* background, environment; **m~geschädigt** *adj* maladjusted.
**militant** [mili'tant] *adj* militant.
**Militär** [mili'tɛːr] (**-s**) *nt* military, army; **~dienst** *m* military service; **~gericht** *nt* military court; **m~isch** *adj* military.
**Militarismus** [milita'rɪsmʊs] *m* militarism.
**militaristisch** *adj* militaristic.
**Militärpflicht** *f* (compulsory) military service.
**Mill.** *abk* (= *Million(en)*) m.
**Milli-** *in zW* milli-.
**Milliardär(in)** [mɪliar'dɛːr(ɪn)] (**-s, -e**) *m(f)* multimillionaire.
**Milliarde** [mɪli'ardə] (**-, -n**) *f* milliard, billion (*bes US*).
**Millimeter** *m* millimetre (*BRIT*), millimeter (*US*); **~papier** *nt* graph paper.
**Million** [mɪli'oːn] (**-, -en**) *f* million.
**Millionär(in)** [mɪlio'nɛːr(ɪn)] (**-s, -e**) *m(f)* millionaire.
**millionenschwer** (*umg*) *adj* worth a few million.
**Milz** [mɪlts] (**-, -en**) *f* spleen.
**Mimik** ['miːmɪk] *f* mime.
**Mimose** [mi'moːzə] (**-, -n**) *f* mimosa; (*fig*) sensitive person.
**minder** ['mɪndər] *adj* inferior ♦ *adv* less; **~begabt** *adj* less able; **~bemittelt** *adj:* geistig **~bemittelt** (*ironisch*) intellectually challenged.
**Minderheit** *f* minority.
**Minderheitsbeteiligung** *f* (*Aktien*) minority interest.
**Minderheitsregierung** *f* minority government.

**minderjährig** *adj* minor; **M~jährige(r)** *f(m)* minor; **M~keit** *f* minority.
**mindern** *vt, vr* to decrease, diminish.
**Minderung** *f* decrease.
**minder-** *zW:* **~wertig** *adj* inferior; **M~wertigkeitsgefühl** *nt* inferiority complex; **M~wertigkeitskomplex** (**-es, -e**) *m* inferiority complex.
**Mindestalter** *nt* minimum age.
**Mindestbetrag** *m* minimum amount.
**mindeste(r, s)** *adj* least.
**mindestens** *adv* at least.
**Mindest-** *zW:* **~lohn** *m* minimum wage; **~maß** *nt* minimum; **~stand** *m* (*COMM*) minimum stock; **~umtausch** *m* minimum obligatory exchange.
**Mine** ['miːnə] (**-, -n**) *f* mine; (*Bleistift~*) lead; (*Kugelschreiber~*) refill.
**Minenfeld** *nt* minefield.
**Minensuchboot** *nt* minesweeper.
**Mineral** [mine'raːl] (**-s, -e** *od* **-ien**) *nt* mineral; **m~isch** *adj* mineral; **~ölsteuer** *f* tax on oil and petrol (*BRIT*) *od* gasoline (*US*); **~wasser** *nt* mineral water.
**Miniatur** [minia'tuːr] *f* miniature.
**Minigolf** ['mɪnigɔlf] *nt* miniature golf.
**minimal** [mini'maːl] *adj* minimal.
**Minimum** ['miːnimʊm] (**-s, Minima**) *nt* minimum.
**Minirock** ['mɪnirɔk] *m* miniskirt.
**Minister(in)** [mi'nɪstər(ɪn)] (**-s, -**) *m(f)* (*POL*) minister.
**ministeriell** [minɪsteri'ɛl] *adj* ministerial.
**Ministerium** [minɪs'teːriʊm] *nt* ministry.
**Ministerpräsident(in)** *m(f)* prime minister.
**Minna** ['mɪna] *f:* **jdn zur ~ machen** (*umg*) to give sb a piece of one's mind.
**minus** ['miːnʊs] *adv* minus; **M~** (**-, -**) *nt* deficit; **M~pol** *m* negative pole; **M~zeichen** *nt* minus sign.
**Minute** [mi'nuːtə] (**-, -n**) *f* minute; **auf die ~** (**genau** *od* **pünktlich**) (right) on the dot.
**Minutenzeiger** *m* minute hand.
**Mio.** *abk* (= *Million(en)*) m.
**mir** [miːr] *dat von* **ich** ♦ *pron* (to) me; **von ~ aus!** I don't mind; **wie du ~, so ich dir** (*Sprichwort*) tit for tat (*umg*); (*als Drohung*) I'll get my own back; **~ nichts, dir nichts** just like that.
**Mirabelle** [mira'bɛlə] *f* mirabelle, *small yellow plum*.
**Misch-** *zW:* **~batterie** *f* mixer tap; **~brot** *nt bread made from more than one kind of flour*; **~ehe** *f* mixed marriage.
**mischen** *vt* to mix; (*COMPUT: Datei, Text*) to merge; (*Karten*) to shuffle ♦ *vi* (*Karten*) to shuffle.
**Misch-** *zW:* **~konzern** *m* conglomerate; **~ling** *m* half-caste; **~masch** (*umg*) *m* hotchpotch; (*Essen*) concoction; **~pult** *nt* (*RUNDF, TV*) mixing panel.
**Mischung** *f* mixture.

**Mischwald** *m* mixed (deciduous and coniferous) woodland.

**miserabel** [mizə'ra:bəl] (*umg*) *adj* lousy; (*Gesundheit*) wretched; (*Benehmen*) dreadful.

**Misere** [mi'ze:rə] (-, -n) *f* (*von Leuten, Wirtschaft etc*) plight; (*von Hunger, Krieg etc*) misery, miseries *pl*.

**Miß-** *zW*: **m~achten** *vt untr* to disregard; **~achtung** *f* disregard; **~behagen** *nt* uneasiness; (*~fallen*) discontent; **~bildung** *f* deformity; **m~billigen** *vt untr* to disapprove of; **~billigung** *f* disapproval; **~brauch** *m* abuse; (*falscher Gebrauch*) misuse; **m~brauchen** *vt untr* to abuse; to misuse; (*vergewaltigen*) to assault; **jdn zu** *od* **für etw m~brauchen** to use sb for *od* to do sth; **m~deuten** *vt untr* to misinterpret.

**missen** *vt* to do without; (*Erfahrung*) to miss.

**Mißerfolg** *m* failure.

**Mißernte** *f* crop failure.

**Missetat** ['mɪsəta:t] *f* misdeed.

**Missetäter** *m* criminal; (*umg*) scoundrel.

**Miß-** *zW*: **m~fallen** *vt untr*: **jdm m~fallen** to displease sb; **~fallen** (-s) *nt* displeasure; **~geburt** *f* freak; (*fig*) failure; **~geschick** *nt* misfortune; **m~glücken** *vi untr* to fail; **jdm m~glückt etw** *sb* does not succeed with sth; **m~gönnen** *vt untr*: **jdm etw m~gönnen** to (be)grudge sb sth; **~griff** *m* mistake; **~gunst** *f* envy; **m~günstig** *adj* envious; **m~handeln** *vt untr* to ill-treat; **~handlung** *f* ill-treatment; **~helligkeit** *f*: **~helligkeiten haben** to be at variance.

**Mission** [mɪsi'o:n] *f* mission.

**Missionar(in)** [mɪsio'na:r(ɪn)] *m(f)* missionary.

**Mißklang** *m* discord.

**Mißkredit** *m* discredit.

**mißlang** *etc* [mɪs'laŋ] *vb siehe* **mißlingen**.

**mißliebig** *adj* unpopular.

**mißlingen** [mɪs'lɪŋən] *unreg vi untr* to fail; **M~** (-s) *nt* failure.

**mißlungen** [mɪs'lʊŋən] *pp von* **mißlingen**.

**Miß-** *zW*: **~mut** *m* bad temper; **m~mutig** *adj* cross; **m~raten** *unreg vi untr* to turn out badly ♦ *adj* ill-bred; **~stand** *m* deplorable state of affairs; **~stimmung** *f* discord; (*~mut*) ill feeling.

**mißt** *vb siehe* **messen**.

**Miß-** *zW*: **m~trauen** *vi untr* to mistrust; **~trauen** (-s) *nt*: **~trauen** (**gegenüber**) distrust (of), suspicion (of); **~trauensantrag** *m* (*POL*) motion of no confidence; **~trauensvotum** *nt* (*POL*) vote of no confidence; **m~trauisch** *adj* distrustful, suspicious; **~verhältnis** *nt* disproportion; **m~verständlich** *adj* unclear; **~verständnis** *nt* misunderstanding; **m~verstehen** *unreg vt untr* to misunderstand.

**Mißwahl, Misswahl** ['mɪsva:l] *f* beauty contest.

**Mißwirtschaft** *f* mismanagement.

**Mist** [mɪst] (-(e)s) *m* dung; (*umg*) rubbish; **~!** (*umg*) blast!; **das ist nicht auf seinem ~ gewachsen** (*umg*) he didn't think that up himself.

**Mistel** (-, -n) *f* mistletoe.

**Mist-** *zW*: **~gabel** *f* pitchfork (*used for shifting manure*); **~haufen** *m* dungheap; **~stück** (*umg!*) *nt*, **~vieh** (*umg!*) *nt* (*Mann*) bastard (*!*); (*Frau*) bitch (*!*).

**mit** [mɪt] *präp +dat* with; (*mittels*) by ♦ *adv* along, too; **~ der Bahn** by train; **~ dem nächsten Flugzeug/Bus kommen** to come on the next plane/bus; **~ Bleistift schreiben** to write in pencil; **~ Verlust** at a loss; **er ist ~ der Beste in der Gruppe** he is among the best in the group; **wie wär's ~ einem Bier?** (*umg*) how about a beer?; **~ 10 Jahren** at the age of 10; **wollen Sie ~?** do you want to come along?

**Mitarbeit** ['mɪt|arbaɪt] *f* cooperation; **m~en** *vi*: **m~en (an** +*dat*) to cooperate (on), collaborate (on).

**Mitarbeiter(in)** *m(f)* (*an Projekt*) collaborator; (*Kollege*) colleague; (*Angestellter*) member of staff ♦ *pl* staff; **~stab** *m* staff.

**mit-** *zW*: **~bekommen** *unreg vt* to get *od* be given; (*umg: verstehen*) to get; **~bestimmen** *vi*: (**bei etw**) **~bestimmen** to have a say (in sth) ♦ *vt* to have an influence on; **M~bestimmung** *f* participation in decision-making; (*POL*) determination; **~bringen** *unreg vt* to bring along; **M~bringsel** ['mɪtbrɪŋzəl] (-s, -) *nt* (*Geschenk*) small present; (*Andenken*) souvenir; **M~bürger(in)** *m(f)* fellow citizen; **~denken** *unreg vi* to follow; **du hast ja ~gedacht!** good thinking!; **~dürfen** *unreg vi*: **wir durften nicht ~** we weren't allowed to go along; **M~eigentümer** *m* joint owner.

**miteinander** [mɪt|aɪ'nandər] *adv* together, with one another.

**miterleben** *vt* to see, witness.

**Mitesser** ['mɪt|esər] (-s, -) *m* blackhead.

**mit-** *zW*: **~fahren** *unreg vi*: (**mit jdm**) **~fahren** to go (with sb); (*auf Reise auch*) to go *od* travel (with sb); **M~fahrerzentrale** *f* agency for arranging lifts; **M~fahrgelegenheit** *f* lift; **~fühlen** *vi*: **~ jdm/etw ~fühlen** to sympathize with sb/sth; **~fühlend** *adj* sympathetic; **~führen** *vt* (*Papiere, Ware etc*) to carry (with one); (*Fluß*) to carry along; **~geben** *unreg vt* to give; **M~gefühl** *nt* sympathy; **~gehen** *unreg vi* to go *od* come along; **etw ~gehen lassen** (*umg*) to pinch sth; **~genommen** *adj* done in, in a bad way; **M~gift** *f* dowry.

**Mitglied** ['mɪtgli:t] *nt* member.

**Mitgliedsbeitrag** *m* membership fee, subscription.

**Mitgliedschaft** *f* membership.

**mit-** *zW*: **~haben** *unreg vt*: **etw ~haben** to have sth (with one); **~halten** *unreg vi* to keep up;

~**helfen** *vi unreg* to help, lend a hand; **bei etw** ~**helfen** to help with sth; **M**~**hilfe** *f* help, assistance; ~**hören** *vt* to listen in to; ~**kommen** *unreg vi* to come along; (*verstehen*) to keep up, follow; **M**~**läufer** *m* hanger-on; (*POL*) fellow traveller.

**Mitleid** *nt* sympathy; (*Erbarmen*) compassion.

**Mitleidenschaft** *f:* **in** ~ **ziehen** to affect.

**mitleidig** *adj* sympathetic.

**mitleidlos** *adj* pitiless, merciless.

**mit-** *zW:* ~**machen** *vt* to join in, take part in; (*umg: einverstanden sein*): **da macht mein Chef nicht** ~ my boss won't go along with that; **M**~**mensch** *m* fellow man; ~**mischen** (*umg*) *vi* (*sich beteiligen*): ~**mischen (in** +*dat od* **bei)** to be involved (in); (*sich einmischen*) to interfere (in); ~**nehmen** *unreg vt* to take along *od* away; (*anstrengen*) to wear out, exhaust; ~**genommen aussehen** to look the worse for wear; ~**reden** *vi* (*Meinung äußern*): **(bei etw)** ~**reden** to join in (sth); (~*bestimmen*) to have a say (in sth) ♦ *vt:* **Sie haben hier nichts** ~**zureden** this is none of your concern; ~**reißen** *vt unreg* to sweep away; (*fig: begeistern*) to carry away; ~**reißend** *adj* (*Rhythmus*) infectious; (*Reden*) rousing; (*Film, Fußballspiel*) thrilling, exciting.

**mitsamt** [mɪt'zamt] *präp* +*dat* together with.

**mitschneiden** *vt unreg* to record.

**Mitschnitt** ['mɪtʃnɪt] (-(e)s, -e) *m* recording.

**mitschreiben** *unreg vt* to write *od* take down ♦ *vi* to take notes.

**Mitschuld** *f* complicity.

**mitschuldig** *adj:* ~ **(an** +*dat*) implicated (in); (*an Unfall*) partly responsible (for).

**Mitschuldige(r)** *f(m)* accomplice.

**mit-** *zW:* **M**~**schüler(in)** *m(f)* schoolmate; ~**spielen** *vi* to join in, take part; **er hat ihr übel** *od* **hart** ~**gespielt** (*Schaden zufügen*) he has treated her badly; **M**~**spieler(in)** *m(f)* partner; **M**~**spracherecht** *nt* voice, say.

**Mittag** ['mɪtaːk] (-(e)s, -e) *m* midday, noon, lunchtime; ~ **machen** to take one's lunch hour; **(zu)** ~ **essen** to have lunch; **m**~ *adv* at lunchtime *od* noon; ~**essen** *nt* lunch, dinner.

**mittags** *adv* at lunchtime *od* noon.

**Mittags-** *zW:* ~**pause** *f* lunch break; ~**ruhe** *f* period of quiet (after lunch); (*in Geschäft*) midday closing; ~**schlaf** *m* early afternoon nap, siesta; ~**zeit** *f:* **während** *od* **in der** ~**zeit** at lunchtime.

**Mittäter(in)** ['mɪttɛːtər(ɪn)] *m(f)* accomplice.

**Mitte** ['mɪtə] (-, -n) *f* middle; **aus unserer** ~ from our midst.

**mitteilen** ['mɪttaɪlən] *vt:* **jdm etw** ~ to inform sb of sth, communicate sth to sb ♦ *vr:* **sich (jdm)** ~ to communicate (with sb).

**mitteilsam** *adj* communicative.

**Mitteilung** *f* communication; **jdm (eine)** ~ **von etw machen** (*form*) to inform sb of sth; (*bekanntgeben*) to announce sth

to sb.

**Mitteilungsbedürfnis** *nt* need to talk to other people.

**Mittel** ['mɪtəl] (-s, -) *nt* means; (*Methode*) method; (*MATH*) average; (*MED*) medicine; **kein** ~ **unversucht lassen** to try everything; **als letztes** ~ as a last resort; **ein** ~ **zum Zweck** a means to an end; ~**alter** *nt* Middle Ages *pl*; **m**~**alterlich** *adj* medieval; ~**amerika** *nt* Central America (and the Caribbean); **m**~**amerikanisch** *adj* Central American; **m**~**bar** *adj* indirect; ~**ding** *nt* (*Mischung*) cross; ~**europa** *nt* Central Europe; ~**europäer(in)** *m(f)* Central European; **m**~**europäisch** *adj* Central European; **m**~**fristig** *adj* (*Finanzplanung, Kredite*) medium-term; ~**gebirge** *nt* low mountain range; **m**~**groß** *adj* medium-sized; **m**~**los** *adj* without means; ~**maß** *nt:* **das (gesunde)** ~**maß** the happy medium; **m**~**mäßig** *adj* mediocre, middling; ~**mäßigkeit** *f* mediocrity; ~**meer** *nt* Mediterranean (Sea); **m**~**prächtig** *adj* not bad; ~**punkt** *m* centre (*BRIT*), center (*US*); **im** ~**punkt stehen** to be centre-stage.

**mittels** *präp* +*gen* by means of.

**Mittelschicht** *f* middle class.

**Mittelsmann** (-(e)s, *pl* **Mittelsmänner** *od* **Mittelsleute**) *m* intermediary.

**Mittel-** *zW:* ~**stand** *m* middle class; ~**streckenrakete** *f* medium-range missile; ~**streifen** *m* central reservation (*BRIT*), median strip (*US*); ~**stufe** *f* (*SCH*) middle school (*BRIT*), junior high (*US*); ~**stürmer** *m* centre forward; ~**weg** *m* middle course; ~**welle** *f* (*RUNDF*) medium wave; ~**wert** *m* average value, mean.

**mitten** ['mɪtən] *adv* in the middle; ~ **auf der Straße/in der Nacht** in the middle of the street/night; ~**drin** *adv* (right) in the middle of it; ~**durch** *adv* (right) through the middle.

**Mitternacht** ['mɪtərnaxt] *f* midnight.

**mittlere(r, s)** ['mɪtlərə(r, s)] *adj* middle; (*durchschnittlich*) medium, average; **der Mittlere Osten** the Middle East; **mittleres Management** middle management.

---

*The* **mittlere Reife** *is the standard certificate achieved at a* **Realschule** *on successful completion of 6 years' education there. If a pupil at a Realschule attains good results in several subjects he is allowed to enter the 11th class of a Gymnasium to study for the* **Abitur.**

---

**mittlerweile** ['mɪtlər'vaɪlə] *adv* meanwhile.

**Mittwoch** ['mɪtvɔx] (-(e)s, -e) *m* Wednesday; *siehe auch* **Dienstag.**

**mittwochs** *adv* on Wednesdays.

**mitunter** [mɪt'ʊntər] *adv* occasionally, sometimes.

**mit-** *zW:* ~**verantwortlich** *adj* also responsible; ~**verdienen** *vi* to (go out to) work as well;

M~**verfasser** *m* co-author; M~**verschulden** *nt* contributory negligence; ~**wirken** *vi:* (**bei etw**) ~**wirken** to contribute (to sth); (*THEAT*) to take part (in sth); M~**wirkende(r)** *f(m):* **die M~wirkenden** (*THEAT*) the cast; M~**wirkung** *f* contribution; participation; **unter M~wirkung von** with the help of; M~**wisser** (**-s, -**) *m:* M~**wisser (einer Sache** *gen*) **sein** to be in the know (about sth); **jdn zum M~wisser machen** to tell sb (all) about it.

**Mixer** ['mɪksər] (**-s, -**) *m* (*Bar~*) cocktail waiter; (*Küchen~*) blender; (*Rührmaschine, RUNDF, TV*) mixer.

**ml** *abk* (= *Milliliter*) ml.

**mm** *abk* (= *Millimeter*) mm.

**Mnemonik** [mne'mo:nɪk] *f* (*auch COMPUT*) mnemonic.

**Möbel** ['mø:bəl] (**-s, -**) *nt* (piece of) furniture; ~**packer** *m* removal man (*BRIT*), (furniture) mover (*US*); ~**wagen** *m* furniture *od* removal van (*BRIT*), moving van (*US*).

**mobil** [mo'bi:l] *adj* mobile; (*MIL*) mobilized.

**Mobilfunk** *m* cellular telephone service.

**Mobiliar** [mobili'a:r] (**-s, -e**) *nt* movable assets *pl.*

**mobilisieren** [mobili'zi:rən] *vt* (*MIL*) to mobilize.

**Mobilmachung** *f* mobilization.

**Mobiltelefon** *nt* (*TELEC*) mobile phone.

**möbl.** *abk* = **möbliert.**

**möblieren** [mø'bli:rən] *vt* to furnish; **möbliert wohnen** to live in furnished accommodation.

**mochte** *etc* ['mɔxtə] *vb siehe* **mögen.**

**Möchtegern-** ['mœçtəgɛrn] *in zW* (*ironisch*) would-be.

**Modalität** [modali'tɛ:t] *f* (*von Plan, Vertrag etc*) arrangement.

**Mode** ['mo:də] (**-, -n**) *f* fashion; ~**farbe** *f* in colour (*BRIT*) *od* color (*US*); ~**heft** *nt* fashion magazine; ~**journal** *nt* fashion magazine.

**Modell** [mo'dɛl] (**-s, -e**) *nt* model; ~**eisenbahn** *f* model railway; (*als Spielzeug*) train set; ~**fall** *m* textbook case.

**modellieren** [modɛ'li:rən] *vt* to model.

**Modellversuch** *m* (*bes SCH*) pilot scheme.

**Modem** ['mo:dɛm] (**-s, -s**) *nt* (*COMPUT*) modem.

**Modenschau** *f* fashion show.

**Modepapst** *m* high priest of fashion.

**Moder** ['mo:dər] (**-s**) *m* mustiness; (*Schimmel*) mildew.

**moderat** [modeˈra:t] *adj* moderate.

**Moderator(in)** [mode'ra:tɔr, -a'to:rɪn] *m(f)* presenter.

**moderieren** [mode'ri:rən] *vt, vi* (*RUNDF, TV*) to present.

**modern** [mo'dɛrn] *adj* modern; (*modisch*) fashionable.

**modernisieren** [modɛrni'zi:rən] *vt* to modernize.

**Mode-** *zW:* ~**schmuck** *m* fashion jewellery (*BRIT*) *od* jewelry (*US*); ~**schöpfer(in)** *m(f)* fashion designer; ~**wort** *nt* fashionable word.

**modifizieren** [modifi'tsi:rən] *vt* to modify.

**modisch** ['mo:dɪʃ] *adj* fashionable.

**Modul** ['mo:dʊl] (**-s, -n**) *nt* (*COMPUT*) module.

**Modus** ['mo:dʊs] (**-, Modi**) *m* way; (*GRAM*) mood; (*COMPUT*) mode.

**Mofa** ['mo:fa] (**-s, -s**) *nt* (= *Motorfahrrad*) small moped.

**Mogadischu** (**-s**) [moga'dɪʃu] *nt* Mogadishu.

**mogeln** ['mo:gəln] (*umg*) *vi* to cheat.

═══════════════════════ *SCHLÜSSELWORT*

**mögen** ['mø:gən] (*pt* **mochte**, *pp* **gemocht** *od* (*als Hilfsverb*) **mögen**) *vt, vi* to like; **magst du/ mögen Sie ihn?** do you like him?; **ich möchte ...** I would like ...; I'd like ...; **er möchte in die Stadt** he'd like to go into town; **ich möchte nicht, daß du ...** I wouldn't like you to ...; **ich mag nicht mehr** I've had enough; (*bin am Ende*) I can't take any more; **man möchte meinen, daß ...** you would think that ...

♦ *Hilfsverb* to like to; (*wollen*) to want; **möchtest du etwas essen?** would you like something to eat?; **sie mag nicht bleiben** she doesn't want to stay; **das mag wohl sein** that may very well be; **was mag das heißen?** what might that mean?; **Sie möchten zu Hause anrufen** could you please call home?

─────────────────────────────

**möglich** ['mø:klɪç] *adj* possible; **er tat sein ~stes** he did his utmost.

**möglicherweise** *adv* possibly.

**Möglichkeit** *f* possibility; **nach ~** if possible.

**möglichst** *adv* as ... as possible.

**Mohammedaner(in)** [mohame'da:nər(ɪn)] (**-s, -**) *m(f)* Mohammedan, Muslim.

**Mohikaner** [mohi'ka:nər] (**-s, -**) *m:* **der letzte ~** (*hum: umg*) the very last one.

**Mohn** [mo:n] (**-(e)s, -e**) *m* (~*blume*) poppy; (~*samen*) poppy seed.

**Möhre** ['mø:rə] (**-, -n**) *f* carrot.

**Mohrenkopf** ['mo:rənkɔpf] *m* chocolate-covered marshmallow.

**Mohrrübe** *f* carrot.

**mokieren** [mo'ki:rən] *vr:* **sich über etw** *akk* ~ to make fun of sth.

**Mokka** ['mɔka] (**-s**) *m* mocha, *strong coffee.*

**Moldau** ['mɔldau] *f:* **die ~** the Vltava.

**Moldawien** [mɔl'da:viən] (**-s**) *nt* Moldavia.

**moldawisch** *adj* Moldavian.

**Mole** ['mo:lə] (**-, -n**) *f* (*NAUT*) mole.

**Molekül** [mole'ky:l] (**-s, -e**) *nt* molecule.

**molk** *etc* [mɔlk] *vb siehe* **melken.**

**Molkerei** [mɔlkə'rai] *f* dairy; ~**butter** *f* blended butter.

**Moll** [mɔl] (**-, -**) *nt* (*MUS*) minor (key).

**mollig** *adj* cosy; (*dicklich*) plump.

**Molotowcocktail** ['moːlotɔfkɔktəːl] *m* Molotov cocktail.

**Moment** [mo'mɛnt] (-(e)s, -e) *m* moment ♦ *nt* factor, element; **im** ~ at the moment; ~ **mal!** just a minute!; **im ersten** ~ for a moment.

**momentan** [momɛn'taːn] *adj* momentary ♦ *adv* at the moment.

**Monaco** ['moːnako] (-s) *nt* Monaco.

**Monarch** [mo'narç] (-en, -en) *m* monarch.

**Monarchie** [monar'çiː] *f* monarchy.

**Monat** ['moːnat] (-(e)s, -e) *m* month; **sie ist im sechsten** ~ **(schwanger)** she's five months pregnant; **was verdient er im** ~**?** how much does he earn a month?

**monatelang** *adv* for months.

**monatlich** *adj* monthly.

**Monats-** *zW:* ~**blutung** *f* menstrual period; ~**karte** *f* monthly ticket; ~**rate** *f* monthly instalment (*BRIT*) *od* installment (*US*).

**Mönch** [mœnç] (-(e)s, -e) *m* monk.

**Mond** [moːnt] (-(e)s, -e) *m* moon; **auf** *od* **hinter dem** ~ **leben** (*umg*) to be behind the times; ~**fähre** *f* lunar (excursion) module; ~**finsternis** *f* eclipse of the moon; **m**~**hell** *adj* moonlit; ~**landung** *f* moon landing; ~**schein** *m* moonlight; ~**sonde** *f* moon probe.

**Monegasse** [mone'gasə] (-n, -n) *m* Monegasque.

**Monegassin** [mone'gasɪn] *f* Monegasque.

**monegassisch** *adj* Monegasque.

**Monetarismus** [moneta'rɪsmʊs] *m* (*ECON*) monetarism.

**Monetarist** *m* monetarist.

**Moneten** [mo'neːtən] (*umg*) *pl* (*Geld*) bread *sing*, dough *sing*.

**Mongole** [mɔŋ'goːlə] (-n, -n) *m* Mongolian, Mongol.

**Mongolei** [mɔŋgo'laɪ] *f:* **die** ~ Mongolia.

**Mongolin** *f* Mongolian, Mongol.

**mongolisch** [mɔŋ'goːlɪʃ] *adj* Mongolian.

**mongoloid** [mɔŋgolo'iːt] *adj* (*MED*) mongoloid.

**monieren** [mo'niːrən] *vt* to complain about ♦ *vi* to complain.

**Monitor** ['moːnitɔr] *m* (*Bildschirm*) monitor.

**Mono-** [mono] *in zW* mono.

**monogam** [mono'gaːm] *adj* monogamous.

**Monogamie** [monogs'miː] *f* monogamy.

**Monolog** [mono'loːk] (-s, -e) *m* monologue.

**Monopol** (-s, -e) *nt* monopoly.

**monopolisieren** [monopoli'ziːrən] *vt* to monopolize.

**Monopolstellung** *f* monopoly.

**monoton** [mono'toːn] *adj* monotonous.

**Monotonie** [monoto'niː] *f* monotony.

**Monstrum** ['mɔnstrʊm] (-s, **Monstren**) *nt* (*lit, fig*) monster; **ein** ~ **von einem/einer** ... a hulking great ...

**Monsun** [mɔn'zuːn] (-s, -e) *m* monsoon.

**Montag** ['moːntaːk] (-(e)s, -e) *m* Monday; *siehe*

*auch* **Dienstag.**

**Montage** [mɔn'taːʒə] (-, -n) *f* (*PHOT etc*) montage; (*TECH*) assembly; (*Einbauen*) fitting.

**montags** *adv* on Mondays.

**Montanindustrie** [mɔn'taːnɪndʊstriː] *f* coal and steel industry.

**Montblanc** [mõ'blãː] *m* Mont Blanc.

**Monte Carlo** ['mɔntə 'karlo] (-s) *nt* Monte Carlo.

**Montenegro** [mɔnte'neːgro] (-s) *nt* Montenegro.

**Monteur** [mɔn'tøːr] *m* fitter, assembly man.

**montieren** [mɔn'tiːrən] *vt* to assemble, set up.

**Montur** [mɔn'tuːr] (*umg*) *f* (*Spezialkleidung*) gear, rig-out.

**Monument** [monu'mɛnt] *nt* monument.

**monumental** [monumɛn'taːl] *adj* monumental.

**Moor** [moːr] (-(e)s, -e) *nt* moor; ~**bad** *nt* mud bath.

**Moos** [moːs] (-es, -e) *nt* moss.

**Moped** ['moːpɛt] (-s, -s) *nt* moped.

**Mops** [mɔps] (-es, -e) *m* (*Hund*) pug.

**Moral** [mo'raːl] (-, -en) *f* morality; (*einer Geschichte*) moral; (*Disziplin: von Volk, Soldaten*) morale; ~**apostel** *m* upholder of moral standards; **m**~**isch** *adj* moral; **einen** *od* **den** ~**ischen haben** (*umg*) to have (a fit of) the blues.

**Moräne** [mo'rɛːnə] (-, -n) *f* moraine.

**Morast** [mo'rast] (-(e)s, -e) *m* morass, mire.

**morastig** *adj* boggy.

**Mord** [mɔrt] (-(e)s, -e) *m* murder; **dann gibt es** ~ **und Totschlag** (*umg*) there'll be hell to pay; ~**anschlag** *m* murder attempt.

**Mörder** ['mœrdər] (-s, -) *m* murderer; ~**in** *f* murderess.

**mörderisch** *adj* (*fig: schrecklich*) dreadful, terrible; (*Preise*) exorbitant; (*Konkurrenzkampf*) cut-throat ♦ *adv* (*umg: entsetzlich*) dreadfully, terribly.

**Mordkommission** *f* murder squad.

**Mords-** *zW:* ~**ding** (*umg*) *nt* whopper; ~**glück** (*umg*) *nt* amazing luck; ~**kerl** *m* (*verwegen*) hell of a guy; **m**~**mäßig** (*umg*) *adj* terrific, enormous; ~**schreck** (*umg*) *m* terrible fright.

**Mord-** *zW:* ~**verdacht** *m* suspicion of murder; ~**versuch** *m* murder attempt; ~**waffe** *f* murder weapon.

**morgen** ['mɔrgən] *adv* tomorrow; **bis** ~**!** see you tomorrow!; ~ **in acht Tagen** a week (from) tomorrow; ~ **um diese Zeit** this time tomorrow; ~ **früh** tomorrow morning; **M**~ (-s, -) *m* morning; (*Maß*) ≈ acre; **am M**~ in the morning; **guten M**~**!** good morning!

**Morgen-** *zW:* ~**grauen** *nt* dawn, daybreak; ~**mantel** *m* dressing gown; ~**rock** *m* dressing gown; ~**rot** *nt*, ~**röte** *f* dawn.

**morgens** *adv* in the morning; **von** ~ **bis abends** from morning to night.

**Morgenstunde** *f:* **Morgenstund(e) hat Gold**

im Mund(e) (*Sprichwort*) the early bird catches the worm (*Sprichwort*).

**morgig** ['mɔrgɪç] *adj* tomorrow's; **der ~e Tag** tomorrow.

**Morphium** ['mɔrfiʊm] *nt* morphine.

**morsch** [mɔrʃ] *adj* rotten.

**Morsealphabet** ['mɔrzəʔalfabeːt] *nt* Morse code.

**morsen** *vi* to send a message by Morse code.

**Mörser** ['mœrzər] (-) *m* mortar (*auch MIL*).

**Mörtel** ['mœrtəl] (-s, -) *m* mortar.

**Mosaik** [moza'iːk] (-s, -en *od* -e) *nt* mosaic.

**Mosambik** [mosam'biːk] (-s) *nt* Mozambique.

**Moschee** [mɔ'ʃeː] (-, -n) *f* mosque.

**Mosel**[1] ['moːzəl] *f* (*GEOG*) Moselle.

**Mosel**[2] (-s, -) *m* (*auch*: ~**wein**) Moselle (wine).

**mosern** ['moːzərn] (*umg*) *vi* to gripe, bellyache.

**Moskau** ['mɔskaʊ] (-s) *nt* Moscow.

**Moskauer** *adj* Moscow *attrib*.

**Moskauer(in)** (-s, -) *m(f)* Muscovite.

**Moskito** [mɔs'kiːto] (-s, -s) *m* mosquito.

**Moslem** ['mɔslɛm] (-s, -s) *m* Muslim.

**moslemisch** [mɔs'leːmɪʃ] *adj* Muslim.

**Most** [mɔst] (-(e)s, -e) *m* (unfermented) fruit juice; (*Apfelwein*) cider.

**Motel** [mo'tɛl] (-s, -s) *nt* motel.

**Motiv** [mo'tiːf] (-s, -e) *nt* motive; (*MUS*) theme.

**Motivation** [motivatsi'oːn] *f* motivation.

**motivieren** [moti'viːrən] *vt* to motivate.

**Motivierung** *f* motivation.

**Motor** ['moːtɔr] (-s, -en) *m* engine; (*bes ELEK*) motor; ~**boot** *nt* motorboat.

**Motorenöl** *nt* engine oil.

**Motorhaube** *f* (*AUT*) bonnet (*BRIT*), hood (*US*).

**motorisch** *adj* (*PHYSIOLOGIE*) motor *attrib*.

**motorisieren** [motori'ziːrən] *vt* to motorize.

**Motor-** *zW:* ~**rad** *nt* motorcycle; ~**radfahrer** *m* motorcyclist; ~**roller** *m* motor scooter; ~**schaden** *m* engine trouble *od* failure; ~**sport** *m* motor sport.

**Motte** ['mɔtə] (-, -n) *f* moth.

**Motten-** *zW:* **m~fest** *adj* mothproof; ~**kiste** *f:* **etw aus der ~kiste hervorholen** (*fig*) to dig sth out; ~**kugel** *f* mothball.

**Motto** ['mɔto] (-s, -s) *nt* motto.

**motzen** ['mɔtsən] (*umg*) *vi* to grouse, beef.

**Mountain-Bike** *nt* mountain bike.

**Möwe** ['møːvə] (-, -n) *f* seagull.

**MP** (-) *f abk* = **Maschinenpistole**.

**Mrd.** *abk* = **Milliarde(n)**.

**MS** *abk* (= *Motorschiff*) motor vessel, MV; (= *multiple Sklerose*) MS.

**MTA** (-, -s) *f abk* (= *medizinisch-technische Assistentin*) medical assistant.

**mtl.** *abk* = **monatlich**.

**Mucke** ['mʊkə] (-, -n) *f* (*meist pl*) caprice; (*von Ding*) snag, bug; **seine ~n haben** to be temperamental.

**Mücke** ['mʏkə] (-, -n) *f* midge, gnat; **aus einer ~ einen Elefanten machen** (*umg*) to make a mountain out of a molehill.

**Muckefuck** ['mʊkəfʊk] (-s) (*umg*) *m* coffee substitute.

**mucken** *vi:* **ohne zu ~** without a murmur.

**Mückenstich** *m* midge *od* gnat bite.

**Mucks** [mʊks] (-es, -e) *m:* **keinen ~ sagen** not to make a sound; (*nicht widersprechen*) not to say a word.

**mucksen** (*umg*) *vr* to budge; (*Laut geben*) to open one's mouth.

**mucksmäuschenstill** ['mʊks'mɔʏsçənʃtɪl] (*umg*) *adj* (as) quiet as a mouse.

**müde** ['myːdə] *adj* tired; **nicht ~ werden, etw zu tun** never to tire of doing something.

**Müdigkeit** ['myːdɪçkaɪt] *f* tiredness; **nur keine ~ vorschützen!** (*umg*) don't (you) tell me you're tired.

**Muff** [mʊf] (-(e)s, -e) *m* (*Handwärmer*) muff.

**Muffel** (-s, -) (*umg*) *m* killjoy, sourpuss.

**muffig** *adj* (*Luft*) musty.

**Mühe** ['myːə] (-, -n) *f* trouble, pains *pl*; **mit Müh(e) und Not** with great difficulty; **sich** *dat* ~ **geben** to go to a lot of trouble; **m~los** *adj* effortless, easy.

**muhen** ['muːən] *vi* to low, moo.

**mühevoll** *adj* laborious, arduous.

**Mühle** ['myːlə] (-, -n) *f* mill; (*Kaffee~*) grinder; (~*spiel*) nine men's morris.

**Mühlrad** *nt* millwheel.

**Mühlstein** *m* millstone.

**Mühsal** (-, -e) *f* tribulation.

**mühsam** *adj* arduous, troublesome ◊ *adv* with difficulty.

**mühselig** *adj* arduous, laborious.

**Mulatte** [mu'latə] (-, -n) *m* mulatto.

**Mulattin** *f* mulatto.

**Mulde** ['mʊldə] (-, -n) *f* hollow, depression.

**Mull** [mʊl] (-(e)s, -e) *m* thin muslin.

**Müll** [mʏl] (-(e)s) *m* refuse, rubbish, garbage (*US*); ~**abfuhr** *f* refuse *od* garbage (*US*) collection; (*Leute*) dustmen *pl* (*BRIT*), garbage collectors *pl* (*US*); ~**abladeplatz** *m* rubbish dump; ~**beutel** *m* bin liner (*BRIT*), trashcan liner (*US*).

**Mullbinde** *f* gauze bandage.

**Mülldeponie** *f* waste disposal site, rubbish tip.

**Mülleimer** *m* rubbish bin (*BRIT*), garbage can (*US*).

**Müller** (-s, -) *m* miller.

**Müll-** *zW:* ~**halde** *f*, ~**haufen** *m* rubbish *od* garbage (*US*) heap; ~**mann** (-(e)s, *pl* ~**männer**) (*umg*) *m* dustman (*BRIT*), garbage collector (*US*); ~**sack** *m* rubbish *od* garbage (*US*) bag; ~**schlucker** *m* waste (*BRIT*) *od* garbage (*US*) disposal unit; ~**tonne** *f* dustbin (*BRIT*), trashcan (*US*); ~**verbrennung** *f* rubbish *od* garbage (*US*) incineration; ~**verbrennungsanlage** *f* incinerator, incinerating plant; ~**wagen** *m*

dustcart (*BRIT*), garbage truck (*US*).
**mulmig** ['mʊlmɪç] *adj* rotten; (*umg*)
uncomfortable; **jdm ist ~ sein** sb feels funny.
**Multi** ['mʊlti] (**-s, -s**) (*umg*) *m* multinational
(organization).
**multi-** *in zW* multi; **~lateral** *adj*: **~lateraler
Handel** multilateral trade; **~national** *adj*
multinational; **~nationaler Konzern**
multinational organization.
**multiple Sklerose** [mʊl'tiːplə skle'roːzə] *f*
multiple sclerosis.
**multiplizieren** [mʊltipli'tsiːrən] *vt* to multiply.
**Mumie** ['muːmiə] *f* (*Leiche*) mummy.
**Mumm** [mʊm] (**-s**) (*umg*) *m* gumption, nerve.
**Mumps** [mʊmps] (**-**) *m od f* mumps *sing*.
**München** ['mʏnçən] *nt* Munich.
**Münch(e)ner(in)** (**-s, -**) *m(f)* person from
Munich.
**Mund** [mʊnt] (**-(e)s, ̈-er**) *m* mouth; **den
~ aufmachen** (*fig: seine Meinung sagen*) to
speak up; **sie ist nicht auf den ~ gefallen**
(*umg*) she's never at a loss for words; **~art** *f*
dialect.
**Mündel** ['mʏndəl] (**-s, -**) *nt* (*JUR*) ward.
**münden** ['mʏndən] *vi*: **in etw** *akk* **~** to flow into
sth.
**Mund-** *zW*: **m~faul** *adj* uncommunicative;
**m~gerecht** *adj* bite-sized; **~geruch** *m* bad
breath; **~harmonika** *f* mouth organ.
**mündig** ['mʏndɪç] *adj* of age; **M~keit** *f*
majority.
**mündlich** ['mʏntlɪç] *adj* oral; **~e Prüfung**
oral (exam); **~e Verhandlung** (*JUR*) hearing;
**alles weitere ~!** let's talk about it more
when I see you.
**Mund-** *zW*: **~raub** *m* (*JUR*) theft of food for
personal consumption; **~stück** *nt*
mouthpiece; (*von Zigarette*) tip; **m~tot** *adj*:
**jdn m~tot machen** to muzzle sb.
**Mündung** ['mʏndʊŋ] *f* estuary; (*von Fluß,
Rohr etc*) mouth; (*Gewehr~*) muzzle.
**Mund-** *zW*: **~wasser** *nt* mouthwash; **~werk** *nt*:
**ein großes ~werk haben** to have a big
mouth; **~winkel** *m* corner of the mouth; **~-
zu-~-Beatmung** *f* mouth-to-mouth
resuscitation.
**Munition** [munitsi'oːn] *f* ammunition.
**Munitionslager** *nt* ammunition dump.
**munkeln** ['mʊŋkəln] *vi* to whisper, mutter;
**man munkelt, daß ...** there's a rumour
(*BRIT*) *od* rumor (*US*) that ...
**Münster** ['mʏnstər] (**-s, -**) *nt* minster.
**munter** ['mʊntər] *adj* lively; (*wach*) awake;
(*aufgestanden*) up and about; **M~keit** *f*
liveliness.
**Münzanstalt** *f* mint.
**Münzautomat** *m* slot machine.
**Münze** ['mʏntsə] (**-, -n**) *f* coin.
**münzen** *vt* to coin, mint; **auf jdn gemünzt
sein** to be aimed at sb.
**Münzfernsprecher** ['mʏntsfɛrnʃprɛçər] *m*
callbox (*BRIT*), pay phone (*US*).

**Münzwechsler** *m* change machine.
**mürb(e)** ['mʏrb(ə)] *adj* (*Gestein*) crumbly;
(*Holz*) rotten; (*Gebäck*) crisp; **jdn ~ machen**
to wear sb down.
**Mürb(e)teig** *m* shortcrust pastry.
**Murmel** ['mʊrməl] (**-, -n**) *f* marble.
**murmeln** *vt, vi* to murmur, mutter.
**Murmeltier** ['mʊrməltiːr] *nt* marmot; **schlafen
wie ein ~** to sleep like a log.
**murren** ['mʊrən] *vi* to grumble, grouse.
**mürrisch** ['mʏrɪʃ] *adj* sullen.
**Mus** [muːs] (**-es, -e**) *nt* purée.
**Muschel** ['mʊʃəl] (**-, -n**) *f* mussel; (*~schale*)
shell; (*Telefon~*) receiver.
**Muse** ['muːzə] (**-, -n**) *f* muse.
**Museum** [mu'zeːʊm] (**-s, Museen**) *nt* museum.
**museumsreif** *adj*: **~ sein** to be almost a
museum piece.
**Musik** [mu'ziːk] *f* music; (*Kapelle*) band.
**musikalisch** [muzi'kaːlɪʃ] *adj* musical.
**Musikbox** *f* jukebox.
**Musiker(in)** ['muːzikər(ɪn)] (**-s, -**) *m(f)*
musician.
**Musik-** *zW*: **~hochschule** *f* music school;
**~instrument** *nt* musical instrument;
**~kapelle** *f* band; **~stück** *nt* piece of music;
**~stunde** *f* music lesson.
**musisch** ['muːzɪʃ] *adj* artistic.
**musizieren** [muzi'tsiːrən] *vi* to make music.
**Muskat** [mʊs'kaːt] (**-(e)s, -e**) *m* nutmeg.
**Muskel** ['mʊskəl] (**-s, -n**) *m* muscle;
**~dystrophie** *f* muscular dystrophy; **~kater**
*m*: **einen ~kater haben** to be stiff; **~paket**
(*umg*) *nt* muscleman; **~zerrung** (*umg*) *f*
pulled muscle.
**Muskulatur** [mʊskula'tuːr] *f* muscular
system.
**muskulös** [mʊsku'løːs] *adj* muscular.
**Müsli** ['myːsli] (**-s, -**) *nt* muesli.
**Muß** [mʊs] (**-**) *nt* necessity, must.
**muß** *vb siehe* **müssen**.
**Muße** ['muːsə] (**-**) *f* leisure.

==================== *SCHLÜSSELWORT*

**müssen** ['mʏsən] (*pt* **mußte**, *pp* **gemußt** *od* (*als
Hilfsverb*) **müssen**) *vi* **1** (*Zwang*) must (*nur im
Präsens*), to have to; **ich muß es tun** I must
do it, I have to do it; **ich mußte es tun** I had
to do it; **er muß es nicht tun** he doesn't have
to do it; **muß ich?** must I?, do I have to?;
**wann müßt ihr zur Schule?** when do you
have to go to school?; **der Brief muß heute
noch zur Post** the letter must be posted
(*BRIT*) *od* mailed (*US*) today; **er hat gehen ~**
he (has) had to go; **muß das sein?** is that
really necessary?; **wenn es (unbedingt) sein
muß** if it's absolutely necessary; **ich muß
mal** (*umg*) I need to go to the loo (*BRIT*) *od*
bathroom (*US*)
**2** (*sollen*): **das mußt du nicht tun!** you
oughtn't to *od* shouldn't do that; **das
müßtest du eigentlich wissen** you ought to

od you should know that; **Sie hätten ihn fragen** ~ you should have asked him
**3: es muß geregnet haben** it must have rained; **es muß nicht wahr sein** it needn't be true.

**Mußheirat** (*umg*) *f* shotgun wedding.
**müßig** ['myːsɪç] *adj* idle; **M~gang** *m* idleness.
**mußt** [mʊst] *vb siehe* **müssen**.
**mußte** *etc* ['mʊstə] *vb siehe* **müssen**.
**Muster** ['mʊstər] (**-s, -**) *nt* model; (*Dessin*) pattern; (*Probe*) sample; ~ **ohne Wert** free sample; **~beispiel** *nt* classic example; **m~gültig** *adj* exemplary; **m~haft** *adj* exemplary.
**mustern** *vt* (*betrachten, MIL*) to examine; (*Truppen*) to inspect.
**Musterprozeß** *m* test case.
**Musterschüler** *m* model pupil.
**Musterung** *f* (*von Stoff*) pattern; (*MIL*) inspection.
**Mut** [muːt] *m* courage; **nur ~!** cheer up!; **jdm ~ machen** to encourage sb; ~ **fassen** to pluck up courage.
**mutig** *adj* courageous.
**mutlos** *adj* discouraged, despondent.
**mutmaßen** *vt untr* to conjecture ♦ *vi untr* to conjecture.
**mutmaßlich** ['muːtmaːslɪç] *adj* presumed ♦ *adv* probably.
**Mutprobe** *f* test of courage.
**Mutter¹** ['mʊtər] (**-, -n**) *f* (*Schrauben~*) nut.
**Mutter²** ['mʊtər] (**-, ⁻**) *f* mother; **~freuden** *pl* the joys *pl* of motherhood; **~gesellschaft** *f* (*COMM*) parent company; **~kuchen** *m* (*ANAT*) placenta; **~land** *nt* mother country; **~leib** *m* womb.
**mütterlich** ['mʏtərlɪç] *adj* motherly.
**mütterlicherseits** *adv* on the mother's side.
**Mutter-** *zW:* **~liebe** *f* motherly love; **~mal** *nt* birthmark; **~milch** *f* mother's milk.
**Mutterschaft** *f* motherhood.
**Mutterschaftsgeld** *nt* maternity benefit.
**Mutterschaftsurlaub** *m* maternity leave.
**Mutter-** *zW:* **~schutz** *m* maternity regulations *pl*; **m~seelenallein** *adj* all alone; **~sprache** *f* native language; **~tag** *m* Mother's Day.
**Mutti** (**-, -s**) (*umg*) *f* mum(my) (*BRIT*), mom(my) (*US*).
**mutwillig** ['muːtvɪlɪç] *adj* malicious, deliberate.
**Mütze** ['mʏtsə] (**-, -n**) *f* cap.
**MV** *f abk* (= *Mitgliederversammlung*) general meeting.
**MW** *abk* (= *Mittelwelle*) MW.
**MWSt, MwSt** *abk* (= *Mehrwertsteuer*) VAT.
**mysteriös** [mʏsteriˈøːs] *adj* mysterious.
**Mystik** ['mʏstɪk] *f* mysticism.
**Mystiker(in)** (**-s, -**) *m(f)* mystic.
**mystisch** ['mʏstɪʃ] *adj* mystical; (*rätselhaft*) mysterious.
**Mythologie** [mytoloˈgiː] *f* mythology.

**Mythos** ['myːtɔs] (**-, Mythen**) *m* myth.

# *N, n*

**N¹, n** [ɛn] *nt* N, n; ~ **wie Nordpol** ≈ N for Nellie, N for Nan (*US*).
**N²** [ɛn] *abk* (= *Norden*) N.
**na** [na] *interj* well; ~ **gut** (*umg*) all right, OK; ~ **also!** (well,) there you are (then)!; ~ **so was!** well, I never!; ~ **und?** so what?
**Nabel** ['naːbəl] (**-s, -**) *m* navel; **der ~ der Welt** (*fig*) the hub of the universe; **~schnur** *f* umbilical cord.

SCHLÜSSELWORT

**nach** [naːx] *präp +dat* **1** (*örtlich*) to; ~ **Berlin** to Berlin; ~ **links/rechts** (to the) left/right; ~ **oben/hinten** up/back; **er ist schon** ~ **London abgefahren** he has already left for London
**2** (*zeitlich*) after; **einer** ~ **dem anderen** one after the other; ~ **Ihnen!** after you!; **zehn (Minuten)** ~ **drei** ten (minutes) past *od* after (*US*) three
**3** (*gemäß*) according to; ~ **dem Gesetz** according to the law; **die Uhr** ~ **dem Radio stellen** to put a clock right by the radio; **ihrer Sprache** ~ **(zu urteilen)** judging by her language; **dem Namen** ~ judging by his/her name; ~ **allem, was ich weiß** as far as I know
♦ *adv*: **ihm ~!** after him!; ~ **und** ~ gradually, little by little; ~ **wie vor** still.

**nachäffen** ['naːxɛfən] *vt* to ape.
**nachahmen** ['naːxaːmən] *vt* to imitate.
**nachahmenswert** *adj* exemplary.
**Nachahmung** *f* imitation; **etw zur ~ empfehlen** to recommend sth as an example.
**Nachbar(in)** ['naxbaːr(ɪn)] (**-s, -n**) *m(f)* neighbour (*BRIT*), neighbor (*US*); **~haus** *nt*: **im ~haus** next door; **n~lich** *adj* neighbourly (*BRIT*), neighborly (*US*); **~schaft** *f* neighbourhood (*BRIT*), neighborhood (*US*); **~staat** *m* neighbouring (*BRIT*) *od* neighboring (*US*) state.
**nach-** *zW:* **N~behandlung** *f* (*MED*) follow-up treatment; **~bestellen** *vt* to order again; **N~bestellung** *f* (*COMM*) repeat order; **~beten** (*pej: umg*) *vt* to repeat parrot-fashion; **~bezahlen** *vt* to pay; (*später*) to pay later; **~bilden** *vt* to copy; **N~bildung** *f* imitation, copy; **~blicken** *vi* to look *od* gaze after; **~datieren** *vt* to postdate.

**nachdem** [naːxˈdeːm] *konj* after; (*weil*) since; **je ~ (ob)** it depends (whether).

**nach-** *zW:* **~denken** *unreg vi:* **über etw** *akk* **~denken** to think about sth; **darüber darf man gar nicht ~denken** it doesn't bear thinking about; **N~denken** *nt* reflection, meditation; **~denklich** *adj* thoughtful, pensive; **~denklich gestimmt sein** to be in a thoughtful mood.

**Nachdruck** [ˈnaːxdrʊk] *m* emphasis; (*TYP*) reprint, reproduction; **besonderen ~ darauf legen, daß ...** to stress *od* emphasize particularly that ...

**nachdrücklich** [ˈnaːxdrʏklɪç] *adj* emphatic; **~ auf etw** *dat* **bestehen** to insist firmly (up)on sth.

**nacheifern** [ˈnaːxˌaɪfərn] *vi:* **jdm ~** to emulate sb.

**nacheinander** [naːxˌaɪˈnandər] *adv* one after the other; **kurz ~** shortly after each other; **drei Tage ~** three days running, three days on the trot (*umg*).

**nachempfinden** [ˈnaːxˌɛmpfɪndən] *unreg vt:* **jdm etw ~** to feel sth with sb.

**nacherzählen** [ˈnaːxˌɛɐtseːlən] *vt* to retell.

**Nacherzählung** *f* reproduction (of a story).

**Nachf.** *abk* = **Nachfolger**.

**Nachfahr** [ˈnaːxfaːr] (**-en, -en**) *m* descendant.

**Nachfolge** [ˈnaːxfɔlgə] *f* succession; **die/jds ~ antreten** to succeed/succeed sb.

**nachfolgen** *vi* (*lit*): **jdm/etw ~** to follow sb/sth.

**nachfolgend** *adj* following.

**Nachfolger(in)** (**-s, -**) *m(f)* successor.

**nachforschen** *vt, vi* to investigate.

**Nachforschung** *f* investigation; **~en anstellen** to make enquiries.

**Nachfrage** [ˈnaːxfraːgə] *f* inquiry; (*COMM*) demand; **es besteht eine rege ~** (*COMM*) there is a great demand; **danke der ~** (*form*) thank you for your concern; (*umg*) nice of you to ask; **n~mäßig** *adj* according to demand.

**nachfragen** *vi* to inquire.

**nach-** *zW:* **~fühlen** *vt* = **nachempfinden**; **~füllen** *vt* to refill; **~geben** *unreg vi* to give way, yield.

**Nachgebühr** *f* surcharge; (*POST*) excess postage.

**Nachgeburt** *f* afterbirth.

**nachgehen** [ˈnaːxgeːən] *unreg vi* (+*dat*) to follow; (*erforschen*) to inquire (into); (*Uhr*) to be slow; **einer geregelten Arbeit ~** to have a steady job.

**Nachgeschmack** [ˈnaːxgəʃmak] *m* aftertaste.

**nachgiebig** [ˈnaːxgiːbɪç] *adj* soft, accommodating; **N~keit** *f* softness.

**nachgrübeln** [ˈnaːxgryːbəln] *vi:* **über etw** *akk* **~** to think about sth; (*sich Gedanken machen*) to ponder on sth.

**nachgucken** [ˈnaːxgʊkən] *vt, vi* = **nachsehen**.

**nachhaken** [ˈnaːxhaːkən] (*umg*) *vi* to dig

deeper.

**Nachhall** [ˈnaːxhal] *m* resonance.

**nachhallen** *vi* to resound.

**nachhaltig** [ˈnaːxhaltɪç] *adj* lasting; (*Widerstand*) persistent.

**nachhängen** [ˈnaːxhɛŋən] *unreg vi:* **seinen Erinnerungen ~** to lose o.s. in one's memories.

**Nachhauseweg** [naːxˈhaʊzəveːk] *m* way home.

**nachhelfen** [ˈnaːxhɛlfən] *unreg vi:* **jdm ~** to help *od* assist sb; **er hat dem Glück ein bißchen nachgeholfen** he engineered himself a little luck.

**nachher** [naːxˈheːr] *adv* afterwards; **bis ~** see you later!

**Nachhilfe** [ˈnaːxhɪlfə] *f* (*auch:* **~unterricht**) extra (private) tuition.

**nachhinein** [ˈnaːxhɪnaɪn] *adv:* **im ~** afterwards; (*rückblickend*) in retrospect.

**Nachholbedarf** *m:* **einen ~ an etw** *dat* **haben** to have a lot of sth to catch up on.

**nachholen** [ˈnaːxhoːlən] *vt* to catch up with; (*Versäumtes*) to make up for.

**Nachkomme** [ˈnaːxkɔmə] (**-, -n**) *m* descendant.

**nachkommen** *unreg vi* to follow; (*einer Verpflichtung*) to fulfil; **Sie können Ihr Gepäck ~ lassen** you can have your luggage sent on (after).

**Nachkommenschaft** *f* descendants *pl*.

**Nachkriegs-** [ˈnaːxkriːks] *in zW* postwar; **~zeit** *f* postwar period.

**Nach-** *zW:* **~laß** (**-lasses, -lässe**) *m* (*COMM*) discount, rebate; (*Erbe*) estate; **n~lassen** *unreg vt* (*Strafe*) to remit; (*Summe*) to take off; (*Schulden*) to cancel ♦ *vi* to decrease, ease off; (*Sturm*) to die down; (*schlechter werden*) to deteriorate; **er hat n~gelassen** he has got worse; **n~lässig** *adj* negligent, careless; **~lässigkeit** *f* negligence, carelessness; **~laßsteuer** *f* death duty; **~laßverwalter** *m* executor.

**nachlaufen** [ˈnaːxlaʊfən] *unreg vi:* **jdm ~** to run after *od* chase sb.

**nachliefern** [ˈnaːxliːfərn] *vt* (*später liefern*) to deliver at a later date; (*zuzüglich liefern*) to make a further delivery of.

**nachlösen** [ˈnaːxløːzən] *vi* to pay on the train/ when one gets off; (*zur Weiterfahrt*) to pay the extra.

**nachm.** *abk* (= *nachmittags*) p.m.

**nachmachen** [ˈnaːxmaxən] *vt* to imitate, copy; (*fälschen*) to counterfeit; **jdm etw ~** to copy sth from sb; **das soll erst mal einer ~!** I'd like to see anyone else do that!

**Nachmieter(in)** [ˈnaːxmiːtər(ɪn)] *m(f):* **wir müssen einen ~ finden** we have to find someone to take over the flat *etc*.

**Nachmittag** [ˈnaːxmɪtaːk] *m* afternoon; **am ~** in the afternoon; **n~** *adv:* **gestern/heute n~** yesterday/this afternoon.

**achmittags** *adv* in the afternoon.
**lachmittagsvorstellung** *f* matinée (performance).
**lachn.** *abk* = **Nachnahme.**
**lachnahme** (-, -n) *f* cash on delivery (*BRIT*), collect on delivery (*US*); **per ~** C.O.D.
**lachname** *m* surname.
**lachporto** *nt* excess postage.
**achprüfbar** ['na:xpry:fba:r] *adj* verifiable.
**achprüfen** ['na:xpry:fən] *vt* to check, verify.
**achrechnen** ['na:xrɛçnən] *vt* to check.
**lachrede** ['na:xre:də] *f:* **üble ~** (*JUR*) defamation of character.
**achreichen** ['na:xraɪçən] *vt* to hand in later.
**lachricht** ['na:xrɪçt] (-, -en) *f* (piece of) news *sing*; (*Mitteilung*) message.
**lachrichten** *pl* news *sing*; **~agentur** *f* news agency; **~dienst** *m* (*MIL*) intelligence service; **~satellit** *m* (tele)communications satellite; **~sperre** *f* news blackout; **~sprecher(in)** *m(f)* newsreader; **~technik** *f* telecommunications *sing*.
**achrücken** ['na:xrʏkən] *vi* to move up.
**lachruf** ['na:xru:f] *m* obituary (notice).
**achrüsten** ['na:xrʏstən] *vt* (*Kraftwerk etc*) to modernize; (*Auto etc*) to refit; (*Waffen*) to keep up to date ♦ *vi* (*MIL*) to deploy new arms.
**achsagen** ['na:xza:gən] *vt* to repeat; **jdm etw ~** to say sth of sb; **das lasse ich mir nicht ~!** I'm not having that said of me!
**lachsaison** ['na:xzɛzõ:] *f* off season.
**achschenken** ['na:xʃɛŋkən] *vt, vi:* **darf ich Ihnen noch (etwas) ~?** may I top up your glass?
**achschicken** ['na:xʃɪkən] *vt* to forward.
**achschlagen** ['na:xʃla:gən] *unreg vt* to look up ♦ *vi:* **jdm ~** to take after sb.
**lachschlagewerk** *nt* reference book.
**lachschlüssel** *m* master key.
**achschmeiß en** ['na:xʃmaɪsən] *unreg* (*umg*) *vt:* **das ist ja nachgeschmissen!** it's a real bargain!
**achschrift** ['na:xʃrɪft] *f* postscript.
**achschub** ['na:xʃu:p] *m* supplies *pl*; (*Truppen*) reinforcements *pl*.
**achsehen** ['na:xze:ən] *unreg vt* (*prüfen*) to check ♦ *vi* (*erforschen*) to look and see; **jdm etw ~** to forgive sb sth; **jdm ~** to gaze after sb.
**achsehen** *nt:* **das ~ haben** to be left empty-handed.
**achsenden** ['na:xzɛndən] *unreg vt* to send on, forward.
**achsicht** ['na:xzɪçt] (-) *f* indulgence, leniency.
**achsichtig** *adj* indulgent, lenient.
**achsilbe** ['na:xzɪlbə] *f* suffix.
**achsitzen** ['na:xzɪtsən] *unreg vi* (*SCH*) to be kept in.
**achsorge** ['na:xzɔrgə] *f* (*MED*) aftercare.
**achspann** ['na:xʃpan] *m* credits *pl*.

**Nachspeise** ['na:xʃpaɪzə] *f* dessert, sweet (*BRIT*).
**Nachspiel** ['na:xʃpi:l] *nt* epilogue; (*fig*) sequel.
**nachspionieren** ['na:xʃpioni:rən] (*umg*) *vi:* **jdm ~** to spy on sb.
**nachsprechen** ['na:xʃprɛçən] *unreg vt:* **(jdm) ~** to repeat (after sb).
**nächst** [nɛːçst] *präp +dat* (*räumlich*) next to; (*außer*) apart from; **~beste(r, s)** *adj* first that comes along; (*zweitbeste*) next-best.
**Nächste(r, s)** *f(m)* neighbour (*BRIT*), neighbor (*US*).
**nächste(r, s)** *adj* next; (*nächstgelegen*) nearest; **aus ~r Nähe** from close by; (*betrachten*) at close quarters; **Ende ~n Monats** at the end of next month; **am ~n Tag** (the) next day; **bei ~r Gelegenheit** at the earliest opportunity; **in ~r Zeit** some time soon; **der ~ Angehörige** the next of kin.
**nachstehen** ['na:xʃte:ən] *unreg vi:* **jdm in nichts ~** to be sb's equal in every way.
**nachstehend** *adj attrib* following.
**nachstellen** ['na:xʃtɛlən] *vi:* **jdm ~** to follow sb; (*aufdringlich umwerben*) to pester sb.
**Nächstenliebe** *f* love for one's fellow men.
**nächstens** *adv* shortly, soon.
**nächstliegend** *adj* (*lit*) nearest; (*fig*) obvious.
**nächstmöglich** *adj* next possible.
**nachsuchen** ['na:xzu:xən] *vi:* **um etw ~** to ask *od* apply for sth.
**Nacht** [naxt] (-, ̈-e) *f* night; **gute ~!** good night!; **in der ~** at night; **in der ~ auf Dienstag** during Monday night; **in der ~ vom 12. zum 13. April** during the night of April 12th to 13th; **über ~** (*auch fig*) overnight; **bei ~ und Nebel** (*umg*) at dead of night; **sich** *dat* **die ~ um die Ohren schlagen** (*umg*) to stay up all night; (*mit Feiern, arbeiten*) to make a night of it.
**nacht** *adv:* **heute ~** tonight.
**Nachtdienst** *m* night duty.
**Nachteil** ['na:xtaɪl] *m* disadvantage; **im ~ sein** to be at a disadvantage.
**nachteilig** *adj* disadvantageous.
**Nachtfalter** *m* moth.
**Nachthemd** *nt* (*Herren~*) nightshirt; nightdress (*BRIT*), nightgown.
**Nachtigall** ['naxtɪgal] (-, -en) *f* nightingale.
**Nachtisch** ['na:xtɪʃ] *m* = **Nachspeise.**
**Nachtleben** *nt* night life.
**nächtlich** ['nɛçtlɪç] *adj* nightly.
**Nacht-** *zW:* **~lokal** *nt* night club; **~mensch** ['naxtmɛnʃ] *m* night person; **~portier** *m* night porter.
**nach-** *zW:* **N~trag** ['na:xtra:k] (-(e)s, -träge) *m* supplement; **~tragen** *unreg vt* (*zufügen*) to add; **jdm etw ~tragen** to carry sth after sb; (*fig*) to hold sth against sb; **~tragend** *adj* resentful; **~träglich** *adj* later, subsequent; (*zusätzlich*) additional ♦ *adv* later, subsequently; (*zusätzlich*) additionally;

**~trauern** *vi:* **jdm/etw ~trauern** to mourn the loss of sb/sth.

**Nachtruhe** ['naxtruːə] *f* sleep.

**nachts** *adv* by night.

**Nachtschicht** *f* night shift.

**Nachtschwester** *f* night nurse.

**nachtsüber** *adv* during the night.

**Nacht-** *zW:* **~tarif** *m* off-peak tariff; **~tisch** *m* bedside table; **~topf** *m* chamber pot; **~wache** *f* night watch; (*im Krankenhaus*) night duty; **~wächter** *m* night watchman.

**Nach-** *zW:* **~untersuchung** *f* checkup; **n~vollziehen** *unreg vt* to understand, comprehend; **n~wachsen** *unreg vi* to grow again; **~wahl** *f* ≈ by-election (*bes BRIT*); **~wehen** *pl* afterpains *pl*; (*fig*) aftereffects *pl*; **n~weinen** *vi* +*dat* to mourn ♦ *vt:* **dieser Sache** *dat* **weine ich keine Träne n~** I won't shed any tears over that.

**Nachweis** ['naːxvaɪs] (**-es, -e**) *m* proof; **den ~ für etw erbringen** *od* **liefern** to furnish proof of sth; **n~bar** *adj* provable, demonstrable; **n~en** ['naːxvaɪzən] *unreg vt* to prove; **jdm etw n~en** to point sth out to sb; **n~lich** *adj* evident, demonstrable.

**nach-** *zW:* **N~welt** *f:* **die N~welt** posterity; **~winken** *vi:* **jdm ~winken** to wave after sb; **~wirken** *vi* to have aftereffects; **N~wirkung** *f* aftereffect; **N~wort** *nt* appendix; **N~wuchs** *m* offspring; (*beruflich etc*) new recruits *pl*; **~zahlen** *vt, vi* to pay extra; **~zählen** *vt* to count again; **N~zahlung** *f* additional payment; (*zurückdatiert*) back pay.

**nachziehen** ['naːxtsiːən] *unreg vt* (*Linie*) to go over; (*Lippen*) to paint; (*Augenbrauen*) to pencil in; (*hinterherziehen*): **etw ~** to drag sth behind one.

**Nachzügler** (**-s, -**) *m* straggler.

**Nackedei** ['nakədaɪ] (**-(e)s, -e** *od* **-s**) *m* (*hum: umg: Kind*) little bare monkey.

**Nacken** ['nakən] (**-s, -**) *m* nape of the neck; **jdm im ~ sitzen** (*umg*) to breathe down sb's neck.

**nackt** [nakt] *adj* naked; (*Tatsachen*) plain, bare; **N~heit** *f* nakedness; **N~kultur** *f* nudism.

**Nadel** ['naːdəl] (**-, -n**) *f* needle; (*Steck~*) pin; **~baum** *m* conifer; **~kissen** *nt* pincushion; **~öhr** *nt* eye of a needle; **~wald** *m* coniferous forest.

**Nagel** ['naːgəl] (**-s, -̈**) *m* nail; **sich** *dat* **etw unter den ~ reißen** (*umg*) to pinch sth; **etw an den ~ hängen** (*fig*) to chuck sth in (*umg*); **Nägel mit Köpfen machen** (*umg*) to do the job properly; **~bürste** *f* nailbrush; **~feile** *f* nailfile; **~haut** *f* cuticle; **~lack** *m* nail varnish (*BRIT*) *od* polish; **~lackentferner** (**-s, -**) *m* nail polish remover.

**nageln** *vt, vi* to nail.

**nagelneu** *adj* brand-new.

**Nagelschere** *f* nail scissors *pl*.

**nagen** ['naːgən] *vt, vi* to gnaw.

**Nagetier** ['naːgətiːr] *nt* rodent.

**nah** *adj* = **nahe.**

**Nahaufnahme** *f* close-up.

**Nahe** *f* (*Fluß*) Nahe.

**nahe** *adj* (*räumlich*) near(by); (*Verwandte*) near, close; (*Freunde*) close; (*zeitlich*) near, close ♦ *adv:* **von nah und fern** from near and far ♦ *präp* +*dat* near (to), close to; **von ~m** at close quarters; **der N~ Osten** the Middle East; **jdm zu ~ treten** (*fig*) to offend sb; **mit jdm ~ verwandt sein** to be closely related to sb.

**Nähe** ['nɛːə] (**-**) *f* nearness, proximity; (*Umgebung*) vicinity; **in der ~** close by; at hand; **aus der ~** from close to.

**nahe-** *zW:* **~bei** *adv* nearby; **~bringen** *unreg vt* +*dat* (*fig*): **jdm etw ~bringen** to bring sth home to sb; **~gehen** *unreg vi:* **jdm ~gehen** to grieve sb; **~kommen** *unreg vi:* **jdm ~kommen** to get close to sb; **~legen** *vt:* **jdm etw ~legen** to suggest sth to sb; **~liegen** *unreg vi* to be obvious; **der Verdacht liegt ~, daß ... i** seems reasonable to suspect that ...; **~liegend** *adj* obvious.

**nahen** *vi, vr* to approach, draw near.

**nähen** ['nɛːən] *vt, vi* to sew.

**näher** *adj* nearer; (*Erklärung, Erkundigung*) more detailed ♦ *adv* nearer; in greater detail; **ich kenne ihn nicht ~** I don't know him well.

**Nähere(s)** *nt* details *pl*, particulars *pl*.

**Näherei** [nɛːə'raɪ] *f* sewing, needlework.

**Naherholungsgebiet** *nt* recreational area (*close to a centre of population*).

**Näherin** *f* seamstress.

**näherkommen** *unreg vi, vr* to get closer.

**nähern** *vr* to approach.

**Näherungswert** *m* approximate value.

**nahe-** *zW:* **~stehen** *unreg vi:* **jdm ~stehen** to be close to sb; **einer Sache ~stehen** to sympathize with sth; **~stehend** *adj* close; **~zu** *adv* nearly.

**Nähgarn** *nt* thread.

**Nahkampf** *m* hand-to-hand fighting.

**Nähkasten** *m* workbox, sewing basket.

**nahm** *etc* [naːm] *vb siehe* **nehmen.**

**Nähmaschine** *f* sewing machine.

**Nähnadel** *f* (sewing) needle.

**Nahost** [naː'ɔst] *m:* **aus ~** from the Middle East.

**Nährboden** *m* (*lit*) fertile soil; (*fig*) breeding ground.

**nähren** ['nɛːrən] *vt* to feed ♦ *vr* (*Person*) to fee o.s.; (*Tier*) to feed; **er sieht gut genährt aus** he looks well fed.

**Nährgehalt** ['nɛːrgəhalt] *m* nutritional value.

**nahrhaft** ['naːrhaft] *adj* (*Essen*) nourishing.

**Nährstoffe** *pl* nutrients *pl*.

**Nahrung** ['naːruŋ] *f* food; (*fig*) sustenance.

**Nahrungs-** *zW:* **~aufnahme** *f:* **die ~aufnahme verweigern** to refuse food; **~kette** *f* food chain; **~mittel** *nt* food(stuff); **~mittelindustrie** *f* food industry; **~suche** *f* search for food.

**Nährwert** m nutritional value.

**Naht** [naːt] (-, -̈e) f seam; (MED) suture; (TECH) join; **aus allen Nähten platzen** (umg) to be bursting at the seams; **n~los** adj seamless; **n~los ineinander übergehen** to follow without a gap.

**Nahverkehr** m local traffic.

**Nahverkehrszug** m local train.

**Nähzeug** nt sewing kit, sewing things pl.

**Nahziel** nt immediate objective.

**naiv** [naˈiːf] adj naïve.

**Naivität** [naivɪˈtɛːt] f naïveté, naïvety.

**Name** ['naːmə] (-ns, -n) m name; **im ~n von** on behalf of; **dem ~n nach müßte sie Deutsche sein** judging by her name she must be German; **die Dinge beim ~n nennen** (fig) to call a spade a spade; **ich kenne das Stück nur dem ~n nach** I've heard of the play but that's all.

**namens** adv by the name of.

**Namensänderung** f change of name.

**Namenstag** m name day, saint's day.

---

In catholic areas of Germany the **Namenstag** is often a more important celebration than a birthday. It is the day dedicated to the saint after whom a person is called, and on that day the person receives presents and invites relatives and friends round to celebrate.

---

**namentlich** ['naːməntlɪç] adj by name ♦ adv particularly, especially.

**namhaft** ['naːmhaft] adj (berühmt) famed, renowned; (beträchtlich) considerable; **~ machen** to name, identify.

**Namibia** [naˈmiːbia] (-s) nt Namibia.

**nämlich** ['nɛːmlɪç] adv that is to say, namely; (denn) since; **der/die/das ~e** the same.

**nannte** etc ['nantə] vb siehe **nennen**.

**nanu** [naˈnuː] interj well I never!

**Napalm** ['naːpalm] (-s) nt napalm.

**Napf** [napf] (-(e)s, -̈e) m bowl, dish; **~kuchen** m ≈ ring-shaped pound cake.

**Narbe** ['narbə] (-, -n) f scar.

**narbig** ['narbɪç] adj scarred.

**Narkose** [narˈkoːzə] (-, -n) f anaesthetic (BRIT), anesthetic (US).

**Narr** [nar] (-en, -en) m fool; **jdn zum ~en halten** to make a fool of sb; **n~en** vt to fool.

**Narrenfreiheit** f: **sie hat bei ihm ~** he gives her (a) free rein.

**narrensicher** adj foolproof.

**Narrheit** f foolishness.

**Närrin** ['nɛrɪn] f fool.

**närrisch** adj foolish, crazy; **die ~en Tage** Fasching and the period leading up to it.

**Narzisse** [narˈtsɪsə] (-, -n) f narcissus.

**narzißtisch** [narˈtsɪstɪʃ] adj narcissistic.

**NASA** ['naːza] (-) f abk (= National Aeronautics and Space Administration) NASA.

**naschen** ['naʃən] vt to nibble; (heimlich) to eat secretly ♦ vi to nibble sweet things; **~ von** od **an** +dat to nibble at.

**naschhaft** adj sweet-toothed.

**Nase** ['naːzə] (-, -n) f nose; **sich** dat **die ~ putzen** to wipe one's nose; (sich schneuzen) to blow one's nose; **jdm auf der ~ herumtanzen** (umg) to play sb up; **jdm etw vor der ~ wegschnappen** (umg) to just beat sb to sth; **die ~ voll haben** (umg) to have had enough; **jdm etw auf die ~ binden** (umg) to tell sb all about sth; **(immer) der ~ nachgehen** (umg) to follow one's nose; **jdn an der ~ herumführen** (als Täuschung) to lead sb by the nose; (als Scherz) to pull sb's leg.

**Nasen-** zW: **~bluten** (-s) nt nosebleed; **~loch** nt nostril; **~rücken** m bridge of the nose; **~tropfen** pl nose drops pl.

**naseweis** adj pert, cheeky; (neugierig) nosey.

**Nashorn** ['naːshɔrn] nt rhinoceros.

**naß** [nas] adj wet.

**Nassauer** ['nasaʊər] (-s, -) (umg) m scrounger.

**Nässe** ['nɛsə] (-) f wetness.

**nässen** vt to wet.

**naßkalt** adj wet and cold.

**Naßrasur** f wet shave.

**Nation** [natsiˈoːn] f nation.

**national** [natsioˈnaːl] adj national; **N~elf** f international (football) team; **N~feiertag** m national holiday; **N~hymne** f national anthem.

**nationalisieren** [natsionaliˈziːrən] vt to nationalize.

**Nationalisierung** f nationalization.

**Nationalismus** [natsionaˈlɪsmʊs] m nationalism.

**nationalistisch** [natsionaˈlɪstɪʃ] adj nationalistic.

**Nationalität** [natsionaliˈtɛːt] f nationality.

**National-** zW: **~mannschaft** f international team; **~sozialismus** m National Socialism; **~sozialist** m National Socialist.

**NATO, Nato** ['naːto] (-) f abk: **die ~** NATO.

**Natrium** ['naːtriʊm] (-s) nt sodium.

**Natron** ['naːtrɔn] (-s) nt soda.

**Natter** ['natər] (-, -n) f adder.

**Natur** [naˈtuːr] f nature; (körperlich) constitution; (freies Land) countryside; **das geht gegen meine ~** it goes against the grain.

**Naturalien** [natuˈraːliən] pl natural produce sing; **in ~** in kind.

**Naturalismus** [naturaˈlɪsmʊs] m naturalism.

**Naturell** [natuˈrɛl] (-s, -e) nt temperament, disposition.

**Natur-** zW: **~erscheinung** f natural phenomenon od event; **n~farben** adj natural-coloured (BRIT) od -colored (US); **~forscher** m natural scientist; **~freak** (-s, -s) (umg) m back-to-nature freak; **n~gemäß** adj natural; **~geschichte** f natural history; **~gesetz** nt law of nature; **n~getreu** adj true

to life; ~**heilverfahren** *nt* natural cure;
~**katastrophe** *f* natural disaster;
~**kostladen** *m* health food shop; ~**kunde** *f*
natural history; ~**lehrpfad** *m* nature trail.
**natürlich** [na'tyːrlɪç] *adj* natural ♦ *adv*
naturally; **eines ~en Todes sterben** to die of
natural causes.
**natürlicherweise** [na'tyːrlɪçər'vaɪzə] *adv*
naturally, of course.
**Natürlichkeit** *f* naturalness.
**Natur-** *zW:* ~**produkt** *nt* natural product;
**n~rein** *adj* natural, pure; ~**schutz** *m:* **unter**
~**schutz stehen** to be legally protected;
~**schutzgebiet** *nt* nature reserve (*BRIT*),
national park (*US*); ~**talent** *nt* natural
prodigy; **n~verbunden** *adj* nature-loving;
~**wissenschaft** *f* natural science;
~**wissenschaftler** *m* scientist; ~**zustand** *m*
natural state.
**Nautik** ['naʊtɪk] *f* nautical science,
navigation.
**nautisch** ['naʊtɪʃ] *adj* nautical.
**Navelorange** ['naːvəloraːʒə] *f* navel orange.
**Navigation** [navigatsi'oːn] *f* navigation.
**Navigationsfehler** *m* navigational error.
**Navigationsinstrumente** *pl* navigation
instruments *pl*.
**Nazi** ['naːtsi] (**-s, -s**) *m* Nazi.
**NB** *abk* (= *nota bene*) NB.
**n.Br.** *abk* (= *nördlicher Breite*) northern
latitude.
**NC** *m abk* (= *numerus clausus*) *siehe* **Numerus.**
**Nchf.** *abk* = **Nachfolger.**
**n.Chr.** *abk* (= *nach Christus*) A.D.
**NDR** (**-**) *m abk* (= *Norddeutscher Rundfunk*)
North German Radio.
**Neapel** [ne'aːpəl] (**-s**) *nt* Naples.
**Neapolitaner(in)** [neapoli'taːnər(ın)] (**-s, -**) *m(f)*
Neapolitan.
**neapolitanisch** [neapoli'taːnɪʃ] *adj*
Neapolitan.
**Nebel** ['neːbəl] (**-s, -**) *m* fog, mist.
**nebelig** *adj* foggy, misty.
**Nebel-** *zW:* ~**leuchte** *f* (*AUT*) rear fog-light;
~**scheinwerfer** *m* fog-lamp; ~**schlußleuchte**
*f* (*AUT*) rear fog-light.
**neben** ['neːbən] *präp +akk* next to ♦ *präp +dat*
next to; (*außer*) apart from, besides; ~**an**
[neːbən'|an] *adv* next door; **N~anschluß** *m*
(*TEL*) extension; **N~ausgaben** *pl* incidental
expenses *pl*; ~**bei** [neːbən'baɪ] *adv* at the
same time; (*außerdem*) additionally;
(*beiläufig*) incidentally; ~**bei bemerkt** *od*
**gesagt** by the way, incidentally; **N~beruf** *m*
second occupation; **er ist im N~beruf** ... he
has a second job as a ...; **N~beschäftigung** *f*
sideline; (*Zweitberuf*) extra job; **N~buhler(in)**
(**-s, -**) *m(f)* rival; ~**einander** [neːbənaɪ'nandər]
*adv* side by side; ~**einanderlegen** *vt* to put
next to each other; **N~eingang** *m* side
entrance; **N~einkünfte** *pl*, **N~einnahmen** *pl*
supplementary income *sing*; **N~erscheinung**

*f* side effect; **N~fach** *nt* subsidiary subject;
**N~fluß** *m* tributary; **N~geräusch** *nt* (*RUNDF*)
atmospherics *pl*, interference; **N~handlung**
*f* (*LITER*) subplot; ~**her** [neːbən'heːr] *adv*
(*zusätzlich*) besides; (*gleichzeitig*) at the same
time; (*daneben*) alongside; ~**herfahren** *unreg*
*vi* to drive alongside; **N~kläger** *m* (*JUR*) joint
plaintiff; **N~kosten** *pl* extra charges *pl*,
extras *pl*; **N~mann** (**-(e)s,** *pl* **-männer**) *m:* **Ihr**
**N~mann** the person next to you;
**N~produkt** *nt* by-product; **N~rolle** *f* minor
part; **N~sache** *f* trifle, side issue; ~**sächlich**
*adj* minor, peripheral; **N~saison** *f* low
season; **N~satz** *m* (*GRAM*) subordinate
clause; ~**stehend** *adj:* ~**stehende Abbildung**
illustration opposite; **N~straße** *f* side
street; **N~strecke** *f* (*EISENB*) branch *od*
local line; **N~verdienst** *m* secondary
income; **N~zimmer** *nt* adjoining room.
**neblig** ['neːblɪç] *adj* = **nebelig.**
**nebst** [neːpst] *präp +dat* together with.
**Necessaire** [nesɛ'sɛːr] (**-s, -s**) *nt* (*Näh~*)
needlework box; (*Nagel~*) manicure case.
**Neckar** ['nɛkar] (**-s**) *m* (*Fluß*) Neckar.
**necken** ['nɛkən] *vt* to tease.
**Neckerei** [nɛkə'raɪ] *f* teasing.
**neckisch** *adj* coy; (*Einfall, Lied*) amusing.
**nee** [neː] (*umg*) *adv* no, nope.
**Neffe** ['nɛfə] (**-n, -n**) *m* nephew.
**negativ** ['neːgatiːf] *adj* negative; **N~** (**-s, -e**) *nt*
(*PHOT*) negative.
**Neger** ['neːgər] (**-s, -**) *m* negro; ~**in** *f* negress;
~**kuß** *m* chocolate-covered marshmallow.
**negieren** [ne'giːrən] *vt* (*bestreiten*) to deny;
(*verneinen*) to negate.
**nehmen** ['neːmən] *unreg vt, vi* to take; **etw zu**
**sich ~** to take sth, partake of sth (*liter*); **jdm**
**etw ~** to take sth (away) from sb; **sich ernst**
~ to take o.s. seriously; ~ **Sie sich doch**
**bitte** help yourself; **man nehme ...** (*KOCH*)
take ...; **wie man's nimmt** depending on
your point of view; **die Mauer nimmt einem**
**die ganze Sicht** the wall blocks the whole
view; **er ließ es sich** *dat* **nicht ~, es**
**persönlich zu tun** he insisted on doing it
himself.
**Nehrung** ['neːrʊŋ] *f* (*GEOG*) spit (of land).
**Neid** [naɪt] (**-(e)s**) *m* envy.
**Neider** ['naɪdər] (**-s, -**) *m* envier.
**Neidhammel** (*umg*) *m* envious person.
**neidisch** *adj* envious, jealous.
**Neige** (**-, -n**) *f* (*geh: Ende*): **die Vorräte gehen**
**zur ~** the provisions are fast becoming
exhausted.
**neigen** ['naɪgən] *vt* to incline, lean; (*Kopf*) to
bow ♦ *vi*: **zu etw ~** to tend to sth.
**Neigung** *f* (*des Geländes*) slope; (*Tendenz*)
tendency, inclination; (*Vorliebe*) liking;
(*Zuneigung*) affection.
**Neigungswinkel** *m* angle of inclination.
**nein** [naɪn] *adv* no.
**Nelke** ['nɛlkə] (**-, -n**) *f* carnation, pink;

(*Gewürz~*) clove.

**ennen** ['nɛnən] *unreg vt* to name; (*mit Namen*) to call; **das nenne ich Mut!** that's what I call courage!

**ennenswert** *adj* worth mentioning.

**lenner** (**-s, -**) *m* denominator; **etw auf einen ~ bringen** (*lit, fig*) to reduce sth to a common denominator.

**lennung** *f* naming.

**ennwert** *m* nominal value; (*COMM*) par.

**eon** ['neːɔn] (**-s**) *nt* neon.

**eo-Nazi** [neoˈnaːtsi] *m* Neonazi.

**eon-** *zW:* **~licht** *nt* neon light; **~reklame** *f* neon sign; **~röhre** *f* neon tube.

**epal** ['neːpal] (**-s**) *nt* Nepal.

**epp** [nɛp] (**-s**) (*umg*) *m:* **der reinste ~** daylight robbery, a rip-off.

**erv** [nɛrf] (**-s, -en**) *m* nerve; **die ~en sind mit ihm durchgegangen** he lost control, he snapped (*umg*); **jdm auf die ~en gehen** to get on sb's nerves.

**erven** (*umg*) *vt:* **jdn ~** to get on sb's nerves.

**erven-** *zW:* **~aufreibend** *adj* nerve-racking; **~bündel** *nt* bundle of nerves; **~gas** *nt* (*MIL*) nerve gas; **~heilanstalt** *f* mental hospital; **~klinik** *f* psychiatric clinic; **n~krank** *adj* mentally ill; **~säge** (*umg*) *f* pain (in the neck); **~schwäche** *f* neurasthenia; **~system** *nt* nervous system; **~zusammenbruch** *m* nervous breakdown.

**ervig** ['nɛrvɪç] (*umg*) *adj* exasperating, annoying.

**ervös** [nɛrˈvøːs] *adj* nervous.

**ervosität** [nɛrvoziˈtɛːt] *f* nervousness.

**ervtötend** *adj* nerve-racking; (*Arbeit*) soul-destroying.

**erz** [nɛrts] (**-es, -e**) *m* mink.

**essel** ['nɛsəl] (**-, -n**) *f* nettle; **sich in die ~n setzen** (*fig: umg*) to put o.s. in a spot.

**est** [nɛst] (**-(e)s, -er**) *nt* nest; (*umg: Ort*) dump; (*fig: Bett*) bed; (: *Schlupfwinkel*) hideout, lair; **da hat er sich ins warme ~ gesetzt** (*umg*) he's got it made; **~beschmutzung** (*pej*) *f* running-down (*umg*) *od* denigration (of one's family/country).

**esteln** *vi:* **an etw** +*dat* **~** to fumble *od* fiddle about with sth.

**esthäkchen** ['nɛsthɛːkçən] *nt* baby of the family.

**ett** [nɛt] *adj* nice; **sei so ~ und räum auf!** would you mind clearing up?

**etterweise** ['nɛtərˈvaɪzə] *adv* kindly.

**etto** *adv* net; **N~einkommen** *nt* net income; **N~gewicht** *nt* net weight; **N~gewinn** *m* net profit; **N~gewinnspanne** *f* net margin; **N~lohn** *m* take-home pay.

**etz** [nɛts] (**-es, -e**) *nt* net; (*Gepäck~*) rack; (*Einkaufs~*) string bag; (*Spinnen~*) web; (*System, auch COMPUT*) network; (*Strom~*) mains *sing od pl*; **das soziale ~** the social security network; **jdm ins ~ gehen** (*fig*) to fall into sb's trap; **~anschluß** *m* mains

connection; **~haut** *f* retina; **~karte** *f* (*EISENB*) runabout ticket (*BRIT*); **~plantechnik** *f* network analysis; **~spannung** *f* mains voltage.

**neu** [nɔy] *adj* new; (*Sprache, Geschichte*) modern; **der/die N~e** the new person, the newcomer; **seit ~estem** (since) recently; **~ schreiben** to rewrite, write again; **auf ein ~es!** (*Aufmunterung*) let's try again; **was gibt's N~es?** (*umg*) what's the latest?; **von ~em** (*von vorn*) from the beginning; (*wieder*) again; **sich ~ einkleiden** to buy o.s. a new set of clothes; **N~ankömmling** *m* newcomer; **N~anschaffung** *f* new purchase *od* acquisition; **~artig** *adj* new kind of; **N~auflage** *f* new edition; **N~ausgabe** *f* new edition; **N~bau** (**-(e)s, -ten**) *m* new building; **N~bauwohnung** *f* newly-built flat; **N~bearbeitung** *f* revised edition; (*das Neubearbeiten*) revision, reworking; **N~druck** *m* reprint; **N~emission** *f* (*Aktien*) new issue.

**neuerdings** *adv* (*kürzlich*) (since) recently; (*von neuem*) again.

**neueröffnet** *adj attrib* newly-opened; (*wiedergeöffnet*) reopened.

**Neuerscheinung** *f* (*Buch*) new publication; (*Schallplatte*) new release.

**Neuerung** *f* innovation, new departure.

**Neufassung** *f* revised version.

**Neufundland** [nɔyˈfʊntlant] *nt* Newfoundland; **Neufundländer(in)** (**-s, -**) *m(f)* Newfoundlander; **neufundländisch** *adj* Newfoundland *attrib*.

**neugeboren** *adj* newborn; **sich wie ~ fühlen** to feel (like) a new man/woman.

**Neugier** *f* curiosity.

**Neugierde** (**-**) *f:* **aus ~** out of curiosity.

**neugierig** *adj* curious.

**Neuguinea** [nɔygiˈneːa] (**-s**) *nt* New Guinea.

**Neuheit** *f* novelty; (*neuartige Ware*) new thing.

**Neuigkeit** *f* news *sing*.

**neu-** *zW:* **N~jahr** *nt* New Year; **N~land** *nt* virgin land; (*fig*) new ground; **~lich** *adv* recently, the other day; **N~ling** *m* novice; **~modisch** *adj* fashionable; (*pej*) newfangled; **N~mond** *m* new moon.

**neun** [nɔyn] *num* nine; **N~** (**-, -en**) *f* nine; **ach du grüne N~e!** (*umg*) well I'm blowed!

**neunmalklug** *adj* (*ironisch*) smart-aleck *attrib*.

**neunzehn** *num* nineteen.

**neunzig** *num* ninety.

**Neureg(e)lung** *f* adjustment.

**neureich** *adj* nouveau riche; **N~e(r)** *f(m)* nouveau riche.

**Neurologie** [nɔyroloˈgiː] *f* neurology.

**neurologisch** [nɔyroˈloːgɪʃ] *adj* neurological.

**Neurose** [nɔyˈroːzə] (**-, -n**) *f* neurosis.

**Neurotiker(in)** [nɔyˈroːtikər(ɪn)] (**-s, -**) *m(f)* neurotic.

**neurotisch** *adj* neurotic.

**Neu-** *zW:* ~**schnee** *m* fresh snow; ~**seeland** [nɔy'tseːlant] *nt* New Zealand; ~**seeländer(in)** (**-s, -**) *m(f)* New Zealander; **n~seeländisch** *adj* New Zealand *attrib;* **n~sprachlich** *adj:* **n~sprachliches Gymnasium** grammar school (*BRIT*) *od* high school (*bes US*) stressing modern languages.
**neutral** [nɔy'traːl] *adj* neutral.
**neutralisieren** [nɔytrali'ziːrən] *vt* to neutralize.
**Neutralität** [nɔytrali'tɛːt] *f* neutrality.
**Neutron** ['nɔytrɔn] (**-s, -en**) *nt* neutron.
**Neutrum** ['nɔytrum] (**-s, Neutra** *od* **Neutren**) *nt* neuter.
**Neu-** *zW:* ~**wert** *m* purchase price; **n~wertig** *adj* as new; ~**zeit** *f* modern age; **n~zeitlich** *adj* modern, recent.
**N.H.** *abk* (= *Normalhöhenpunkt*) normal peak (level).
**nhd.** *abk* (= *neuhochdeutsch*) NHG.
**Nicaragua** [nika'raːgua] (**-s**) *nt* Nicaragua; ~**ner(in)** [nikaragu'aːnər(ɪn)] (**-s, -**) *m(f)* Nicaraguan; **n~nisch** [nikaragu'aːnɪʃ] *adj* Nicaraguan.

=============== *SCHLÜSSELWORT*

**nicht** [nɪçt] *adv* **1** (*Verneinung*) not; **er ist es ~** it's not him, it isn't him; **er raucht ~** (*gerade*) he isn't smoking; (*gewöhnlich*) he doesn't smoke; **ich kann das ~ - ich auch ~** I can't do it - neither *od* nor can I; **es regnet ~ mehr** it's not raining any more; **~ mehr als** no more than
**2** (*Bitte, Verbot*): **~!** don't!, no!; **~ berühren!** do not touch!; **~ doch!** don't!
**3** (*rhetorisch*): **du bist müde, ~ (wahr)?** you're tired, aren't you?; **das ist schön, ~ (wahr)?** it's nice, isn't it?
**4: was du ~ sagst!** the things you say!
♦ *präf* non-.

**Nicht-** *zW:* ~**achtung** *f* disregard; ~**anerkennung** *f* repudiation; ~**angriffspakt** *m* non-aggression pact.
**Nichte** ['nɪçtə] (**-, -n**) *f* niece.
**Nicht-** *zW:* ~**einhaltung** *f* (+*gen*) non-compliance (with); ~**einmischung** *f* (*POL*) nonintervention; ~**gefallen** *nt:* **bei** ~**gefallen (zurück)** if not satisfied (return).
**nichtig** ['nɪçtɪç] *adj* (*ungültig*) null, void; (*wertlos*) futile; **N~keit** *f* nullity, invalidity; (*Sinnlosigkeit*) futility.
**Nichtraucher** *m* nonsmoker; **ich bin ~** I don't smoke.
**nichtrostend** *adj* stainless.
**nichts** [nɪçts] *pron* nothing; ~ **als** nothing but; ~ **da!** (*ausgeschlossen*) nothing doing (*umg*); ~ **wie raus/hin** *etc* (*umg*) let's get out/over there *etc* (on the double); **für ~ und wieder ~** for nothing at all; **N~** (**-s**) *nt* nothingness; (*pej: Person*) nonentity; **n~ahnend** *adj* unsuspecting.

**Nichtschwimmer** (**-s, -**) *m* nonswimmer.
**nichts-** *zW:* ~**destotrotz** *adv* notwithstanding (*form*), nonetheless; ~**destoweniger** *adv* nevertheless; **N~nutz** (**-es, -e**) *m* good-for-nothing; ~**nutzig** *adj* worthless, useless; ~**sagend** *adj* meaningless; **N~tun** (**-s**) *nt* idleness.
**Nichtzutreffende(s)** *nt:* ~ **(bitte) streichen** (please) delete as applicable.
**Nickel** ['nɪkəl] (**-s**) *nt* nickel; ~**brille** *f* metal-rimmed glasses *pl.*
**nicken** ['nɪkən] *vi* to nod.
**Nickerchen** ['nɪkərçən] *nt* nap; **ein ~ machen** (*umg*) to have forty winks.
**Nicki** ['nɪki] (**-s, -s**) *m* velours pullover.
**nie** [niː] *adv* never; ~ **wieder** *od* **mehr** never again; ~ **und nimmer** never ever; **fast ~** hardly ever.
**nieder** ['niːdər] *adj* low; (*gering*) inferior ♦ *adv* down; ~**deutsch** *adj* (*LING*) Low-German; **N~gang** *m* decline; ~**gedrückt** *adj* depresse~ ~**gehen** *unreg vi* to descend; (*AVIAT*) to come down; (*Regen*) to fall; (*Boxer*) to go down; ~**geschlagen** *adj* depressed, dejected; **N~geschlagenheit** *f* depression, dejection; **N~kunft** *f* (*veraltet*) delivery, giving birth; **N~lage** *f* defeat.
**Niederlande** ['niːdərlandə] *pl:* **die ~** the Netherlands *pl.*
**Niederländer(in)** ['niːdərlɛndər(ɪn)] (**-s, -**) *m(f* Dutchman, Dutchwoman.
**niederländisch** *adj* Dutch, Netherlands *attrib*
**nieder-** *zW:* ~**lassen** *unreg vr* (*sich setzen*) to si~ down; (*an Ort*) to settle (down); (*Arzt, Rechtsanwalt*) to set up in practice; **N~lassung** *f* settlement; (*COMM*) branch; ~**legen** *vt* to lay down; (*Arbeit*) to stop; (*Am* to resign; ~**machen** *vt* to mow down; **N~österreich** *nt* Lower Austria; **N~rhein** *m* Lower Rhine; ~**rheinisch** *adj* Lower Rhine *attrib;* **N~sachsen** *nt* Lower Saxony; **N~schlag** *m* (*CHEM*) precipitate; (*Bodensatz*) sediment; (*MET*) precipitation (*form*), rainfall; (*BOXEN*) knockdown; **radioaktiver N~schlag** (radioactive) fallout; ~**schlagen** *unreg vt* (*Gegner*) to beat down; (*Gegenstand* to knock down; (*Augen*) to lower; (*JUR: Prozeß*) to dismiss; (*Aufstand*) to put down ♦ *vr* (*CHEM*) to precipitate; **sich in etw** *dat* ~**schlagen** (*Erfahrungen etc*) to find expression in sth; ~**schlagsfrei** ['niːdərʃlaːksfraɪ] *adj* dry, without precipitation (*form*); ~**schmetternd** *adj* (*Nachricht, Ergebnis*) shattering; ~**schreiben** *unreg vt* to write down; **N~schrift** *f* transcription; ~**tourig** *adj* (*Motor*) low-revving; ~**trächtig** *adj* base, mean; **N~trächtigkeit** *f* despicable *od* malicious behaviour.
**Niederung** *f* (*GEOG*) depression.
**niederwalzen** ['niːdərvaltsən] *vt:* **jdn/etw ~**

(*umg*) to mow sb/sth down.
**niederwerfen** ['ni:dərvɛrfən] *unreg vt* to throw down; (*fig*) to overcome; (*Aufstand*) to suppress.
**niedlich** ['ni:tlıç] *adj* sweet, nice, cute.
**niedrig** ['ni:drıç] *adj* low; (*Stand*) lowly, humble; (*Gesinnung*) mean.
**niemals** ['ni:ma:ls] *adv* never.
**niemand** ['ni:mant] *pron* nobody, no-one.
**Niemandsland** ['ni:mantslant] *nt* no-man's-land.
**Niere** ['ni:rə] (-, -n) *f* kidney; **künstliche ~** kidney machine.
**Nierenentzündung** *f* kidney infection.
**nieseln** ['ni:zəln] *vi* to drizzle.
**Nieselregen** *m* drizzle.
**niesen** ['ni:zən] *vi* to sneeze.
**Niespulver** *nt* sneezing powder.
**Niet** [ni:t] (-(e)s, -e) *m* (*TECH*) rivet.
**Niete** ['ni:tə] (-, -n) *f* (*TECH*) rivet; (*Los*) blank; (*Reinfall*) flop; (*Mensch*) failure.
**nieten** *vt* to rivet.
**Nietenhose** *f* (pair of) studded jeans *pl*.
**niet- und nagelfest** (*umg*) *adj* nailed down.
**Niger¹** ['ni:gər] (-s) *nt* (*Staat*) Niger.
**Niger²** ['ni:gər] (-s) *m* (*Fluß*) Niger.
**Nigeria** [ni'ge:ria] (-s) *nt* Nigeria; **~ner(in)** [nigeri'a:nər(ın)] *m(f)* Nigerian; **n~nisch** [nige:ri'a:nıʃ] *adj* Nigerian.
**Nihilismus** [nihi'lısmʊs] *m* nihilism.
**Nihilist** [nihi'lıst] *m* nihilist; **n~isch** *adj* nihilistic.
**Nikolaus** ['ni:kolaʊs] (-, -e *od* (*hum: umg*) **-läuse**) *m* ≈ Santa Claus, Father Christmas.
**Nikosia** [niko'zi:a] (-s) *nt* Nicosia.
**Nikotin** [niko'ti:n] (-s) *nt* nicotine; **n~arm** *adj* low-nicotine.
**Nil** [ni:l] (-s) *m* Nile; **~pferd** *nt* hippopotamus.
**Nimbus** ['nımbʊs] (-, -se) *m* (*Heiligenschein*) halo; (*fig*) aura.
**nimmersatt** ['nımərzat] *adj* insatiable; **N~** (-(e)s, -e) *m* glutton.
**Nimmerwiedersehen** (*umg*) *nt*: **auf ~!** I never want to see you again.
**nimmt** [nımt] *vb siehe* **nehmen**.
**nippen** ['nıpən] *vt, vi* to sip.
**Nippes** ['nıpəs] *pl* knick-knacks *pl*, bric-a-brac *sing*.
**Nippsachen** ['nıpzaxən] *pl* knick-knacks *pl*.
**nirgends** ['nırgənts] *adv* nowhere; **überall und ~** here, there and everywhere.
**nirgendwo** ['nırgəntvo] *adv* = **nirgends**.
**nirgendwohin** *adv* nowhere.
**Nische** ['ni:ʃə] (-, -n) *f* niche.
**nisten** ['nıstən] *vi* to nest.
**Nitrat** [ni'tra:t] (-(e)s, -e) *nt* nitrate.
**Niveau** [ni'vo:] (-s, -s) *nt* level; **diese Schule hat ein hohes ~** this school has high standards; **unter meinem ~** beneath me.
**Nivellierung** [nivɛ'li:rʊŋ] *f* (*Ausgleichung*) levelling out.
**nix** [nıks] (*umg*) *pron* = **nichts**.

**Nixe** ['nıksə] (-, -n) *f* water nymph.
**Nizza** ['nıtsa] (-s) *nt* Nice.
**n.J.** *abk* (= *nächsten Jahres*) next year.
**n.M.** *abk* (= *nächsten Monats*) next month.
**NN** *abk* (= *Normalnull*) m.s.l.
**N.N.** *abk* = **NN**.
**NO** *abk* (= *Nordost*) NE.
**no.** *abk* (= *netto*) net.
**nobel** ['no:bəl] *adj* (*großzügig*) generous; (*elegant*) posh (*umg*).
**Nobelpreis** [no'bɛlprais] *m* Nobel prize; **~träger(in)** *m(f)* Nobel prize winner.

====================================== *SCHLÜSSELWORT*

**noch** [nɔx] *adv* **1** (*weiterhin*) still; **~ nicht** not yet; **~ nie** never (yet); **~ immer** *od* **immer ~** still; **bleiben Sie doch ~** stay a bit longer; **ich gehe kaum ~ aus** I hardly go out any more
**2** (*in Zukunft*) still, yet; (*irgendwann einmal*) one day; **das kann ~ passieren** that might still happen; **er wird ~ kommen** he'll come (yet); **das wirst du ~ bereuen** you'll come to regret it (one day)
**3** (*nicht später als*): **~ vor einer Woche** only a week ago; **~ am selben Tag** the very same day; **~ im 19. Jahrhundert** as late as the 19th century; **~ heute** today
**4** (*zusätzlich*): **wer war ~ da?** who else was there?; **~ einmal** once more, again; **~ dreimal** three more times; **~ einer** another one; **und es regnete auch ~** and on top of that it was raining
**5** (*bei Vergleichen*): **~ größer** even bigger; **das ist ~ besser** that's better still; **und wenn es ~ so schwer ist** however hard it is
**6**: **Geld ~ und ~** heaps (and heaps) of money; **sie hat ~ und ~ versucht, ...** she tried again and again to ...
♦ *konj*: **weder A ~ B** neither A nor B.

**nochmal(s)** *adv* again, once more.
**nochmalig** *adj* repeated.
**Nockenwelle** ['nɔkənvɛlə] *f* camshaft.
**NOK** *nt abk* (= *Nationales Olympisches Komitee*) National Olympic Committee.
**Nom.** *abk* = **Nominativ**.
**Nominalwert** [nomi'na:lve:rt] *m* (*FIN*) nominal *od* par value.
**Nominativ** ['no:minati:f] (-s, -e) *m* nominative.
**nominell** [nomi'nɛl] *adj* nominal.
**nominieren** [nomi'ni:rən] *vt* to nominate.
**Nonne** ['nɔnə] (-, -n) *f* nun.
**Nonnenkloster** *nt* convent.
**Nonplusultra** [nɔnplʊs'|ʊltra] (-s) *nt* ultimate.
**Nord** [nɔrt] (-s) *m* north; **~afrika** ['nɔrt|a:frika] *nt* North Africa; **~amerika** *nt* North America; **n~amerikanisch** ['nɔrt|ameri'ka:nıʃ] *adj* North American.
**nordd.** *abk* = **norddeutsch**.
**norddeutsch** *adj* North German.

**Norddeutschland** *nt* North(ern) Germany.
**Norden** ['nɔrdən] *m* north.
**Nord-** *zW:* ~**england** *nt* the North of England;
~**irland** *nt* Northern Ireland, Ulster; **n~isch**
*adj* northern; **n~ische Kombination** (*SKI*)
nordic combination; ~**kap** *nt* North Cape;
~**korea** ['nɔrtkoˈreːa] *nt* North Korea.
**nördlich** ['nœrtlɪç] *adj* northerly, northern
♦ *präp* +*gen* (to the) north of; **der ~e**
**Polarkreis** the Arctic Circle; **N~es Eismeer**
Arctic Ocean; ~ **von** north of.
**Nord-** *zW:* ~**licht** *nt* northern lights *pl*, aurora
borealis; ~**-Ostsee-Kanal** *m* Kiel Canal;
~**pol** *m* North Pole; ~**polargebiet** *nt* Arctic
(Zone).
**Nordrhein-Westfalen** ['nɔrtraɪnvɛstˈfaːlən]
(-s) *nt* North Rhine-Westphalia.
**Nordsee** *f* North Sea.
**nordwärts** *adv* northwards.
**Nörgelei** [nœrgəˈlaɪ] *f* grumbling.
**nörgeln** *vi* to grumble.
**Nörgler(in)** (-s, -) *m(f)* grumbler.
**Norm** [nɔrm] (-, -en) *f* norm; (*Leistungssoll*)
quota; (*Größenvorschrift*) standard
(specification).
**normal** [nɔrˈmaːl] *adj* normal; **bist du noch ~?**
(*umg*) have you gone mad?; **N~benzin** *nt*
two-star petrol (*BRIT veraltet*), regular gas
(*US*).
**normalerweise** *adv* normally.
**Normalfall** *m:* **im ~** normally.
**Normalgewicht** *nt* normal weight; (*genormt*)
standard weight.
**normalisieren** [nɔrmaliˈziːrən] *vt* to normalize
♦ *vr* to return to normal.
**Normalzeit** *f* (*GEOG*) standard time.
**Normandie** [nɔrmanˈdiː] *f* Normandy.
**normen** *vt* to standardize.
**Norwegen** ['nɔrveːgən] (-s) *nt* Norway.
**Norweger(in)** (-s, -) *m(f)* Norwegian.
**norwegisch** *adj* Norwegian.
**Nostalgie** [nɔstalˈgiː] *f* nostalgia.
**Not** [noːt] (-, ⁻e) *f* need; (*Mangel*) want;
(*Mühe*) trouble; (*Zwang*) necessity; **zur ~** if
necessary; (*gerade noch*) just about; **wenn**
**~ am Mann ist** if you/they *etc* are short
(*umg*); (*im Notfall*) in an emergency; **er hat**
**seine liebe ~ mit ihr/damit** he really has
problems with her/it; **in seiner ~** in his hour
of need.
**Notar(in)** [noˈtaːr(ɪn)] (-s, -e) *m(f)* notary;
**n~iell** *adj* notarial; **n~iell beglaubigt** attested
by a notary.
**Not-** *zW:* ~**arzt** *m* doctor on emergency call;
~**ausgang** *m* emergency exit; ~**behelf** *m*
stopgap; ~**bremse** *f* emergency brake;
~**dienst** *m:* ~**dienst haben** (*Apotheke*) to be
open 24 hours; (*Arzt*) to be on call;
**n~dürftig** *adj* scanty; (*behelfsmäßig*)
makeshift; **sich n~dürftig verständigen**
**können** to be abe to communicate to some
extent.

**Note** ['noːtə] (-, -n) *f* note; (*SCH*) mark (*BRIT*),
grade (*US*); **Noten** *pl* (*MUS*) music *sing*; **eine**
**persönliche ~** a personal touch.
**Noten-** *zW:* ~**bank** *f* issuing bank; ~**blatt** *nt*
sheet of music; ~**schlüssel** *m* clef;
~**ständer** *m* music stand.
**Not-** *zW:* ~**fall** *m* (case of) emergency; **n~falls**
*adv* if need be; **n~gedrungen** *adj* necessary,
unavoidable; **etw n~gedrungen machen** to
be forced to do sth; ~**groschen** ['noːtgrɔʃən]
*m* nest egg.
**notieren** [noˈtiːrən] *vt* to note; (*COMM*) to
quote.
**Notierung** *f* (*COMM*) quotation.
**nötig** ['nøːtɪç] *adj* necessary ♦ *adv* (*dringend*):
**etw ~ brauchen** to need sth urgently; **etw**
**~ haben** to need sth; **das habe ich nicht ~!** I
can do without that!
**nötigen** *vt* to compel, force; ~**falls** *adv* if
necessary.
**Nötigung** *f* compulsion, coercion (*JUR*).
**Notiz** [noˈtiːts] (-, -en) *f* note; (*Zeitungs~*)
item; ~ **nehmen** to take notice; ~**block** *m*
notepad; ~**buch** *nt* notebook; ~**zettel** *m* piece
of paper.
**Not-** *zW:* ~**lage** *f* crisis, emergency;
**n~landen** *vi* to make a forced *od* emergency
landing; ~**landung** *f* forced *od* emergency
landing; **n~leidend** *adj* needy; ~**lösung** *f*
temporary solution; ~**lüge** *f* white lie.
**notorisch** [noˈtoːrɪʃ] *adj* notorious.
**Not-** *zW:* ~**ruf** *m* emergency call; ~**rufsäule** *f*
emergency telephone; **n~schlachten** *vt*
(*Tiere*) to destroy; ~**stand** *m* state of
emergency; ~**standsgebiet** *nt* (*wirtschaftlich*)
depressed area; (*bei Katastrophen*) disaster
area; ~**standsgesetz** *nt* emergency law;
~**unterkunft** *f* emergency accommodation;
~**verband** *m* emergency dressing; ~**wehr**
(-) *f* self-defence; **n~wendig** *adj* necessary;
~**wendigkeit** *f* necessity; ~**zucht** *f* rape.
**Nov.** *abk* (= *November*) Nov.
**Novelle** [noˈvɛlə] (-, -n) *f* novella; (*JUR*)
amendment.
**November** [noˈvɛmbər] (-(s), -) *m* November;
*siehe auch* **September.**
**Novum** ['noːvʊm] (-s, **Nova**) *nt* novelty.
**NPD** (-) *f abk* (= *Nationaldemokratische Partei*
*Deutschlands*) National Democratic Party.
**Nr.** *abk* (= *Nummer*) no.
**NRW** *abk* = **Nordrhein-Westfalen.**
**NS** *abk* = **Nachschrift; Nationalsozialismus.**
**NS-** *in zW* Nazi.
**N.T.** *abk* (= *Neues Testament*) N.T.
**Nu** [nuː] *m:* **im ~** in an instant.
**Nuance** [nyˈãːsə] (-, -n) *f* nuance; (*Kleinigkeit*)
shade.
**nüchtern** ['nʏçtərn] *adj* sober; (*Magen*) empty;
(*Urteil*) prudent; **N~heit** *f* sobriety.
**Nudel** ['nuːdəl] (-, -n) *f* noodle; (*umg: Mensch:*
*dick*) dumpling; (: : *komisch*) character;
~**holz** *nt* rolling pin.

**Nugat** ['nu:gat] (**-s, -s**) *m od nt* nougat.
**nuklear** [nukle'a:r] *adj attrib* nuclear.
**null** [nʊl] *num* zero; (*Fehler*) no; ~ **Uhr**
  midnight; ~ **und nichtig** null and void; **N~**
  (**-, -en**) *f* nought, zero; (*pej: Mensch*) dead
  loss; **in N~ Komma nichts** (*umg*) in less than
  no time; **die Stunde N~** the new starting
  point; **gleich N~ sein** to be absolutely nil;
  ~**achtfünfzehn** (*umg*) *adj* run-of-the-mill;
  **N~diät** *f* starvation diet; **N~(l)ösung** *f*
  (*POL*) zero option; **N~punkt** *m* zero; **auf dem**
  **N~punkt** at zero; **N~tarif** *m* (*für*
  *Verkehrsmittel*) free travel; **zum N~tarif** free
  of charge.
**numerieren** [nume'ri:rən] *vt* to number.
**numerisch** [nu'me:rɪʃ] *adj* numerical; ~**es**
  **Tastenfeld** (*COMPUT*) numeric pad.
**Numerus** ['nu:merʊs] (**-, Numeri**) *m* (*GRAM*)
  number; ~ **clausus** (*UNIV*) restricted entry.
**Nummer** ['nʊmər] (**-, -n**) *f* number; **auf**
  ~ **Sicher gehen** (*umg*) to play (it) safe.
**Nummern-** *zW:* ~**konto** *nt* numbered bank
  account; ~**scheibe** *f* telephone dial;
  ~**schild** *nt* (*AUT*) number *od* license (*US*)
  plate.
**nun** [nu:n] *adv* now ♦ *interj* well.
**nur** [nu:r] *adv* just, only; **nicht** ~ **..., sondern**
  **auch ...** not only ... but also ...; **alle,** ~ **ich**
  **nicht** everyone but me; **ich hab' das** ~ **so**
  **gesagt** I was just talking.
**Nürnberg** ['nʏrnbɛrk] (**-s**) *nt* Nuremberg.
**nuscheln** ['nʊʃəln] (*umg*) *vt, vi* to mutter,
  mumble.
**Nuß** [nʊs] (**-, Nüsse**) *f* nut; **eine doofe** ~ (*umg*)
  a stupid twit; **eine harte** ~ a hard nut (to
  crack); ~**baum** *m* walnut tree; ~**knacker**
  (**-s, -**) *m* nutcracker.
**Nüster** ['nʏːstər] (**-, -n**) *f* nostril.
**Nutte** ['nʊtə] (**-, -n**) *f* tart (*BRIT*), hooker (*US*).
**nutz** [nʊts] *adj* = **nütze**; ~**bar** *adj:* ~**bar machen**
  to utilize; **N~barmachung** *f* utilization;
  ~**bringend** *adj* profitable; **etw** ~**bringend**
  **anwenden** to use sth to good effect, put sth
  to good use.
**nütze** ['nʏtsə] *adj:* **zu nichts** ~ **sein** to be
  useless.
**nutzen** *vi* to be of use ♦ *vt:* (**zu etw**) ~ to use
  (for sth); **was nutzt es?** what's the use?,
  what use is it?; **N~** (**-s**) *nt* usefulness;
  (*Gewinn*) profit; **von N~** useful
**nützen** *vt, vi* = **nutzen**.
**Nutz-** *zW:* ~**fahrzeug** *nt farm od military*
  *vehicle etc*; (*COMM*) commercial vehicle;
  ~**fläche** *f* us(e)able floor space; (*AGR*)
  productive land; ~**last** *f* maximum load,
  payload.
**nützlich** ['nʏtslɪç] *adj* useful; **N~keit** *f*
  usefulness.
**Nutz-** *zW:* **n~los** *adj* useless; (*unnötig*)
  needless; ~**losigkeit** *f* uselessness;
  ~**nießer** (**-s, -**) *m* beneficiary.
**Nutzung** *f* (*Gebrauch*) use; (*das Ausnutzen*)

exploitation.
**NW** *abk* (= *Nordwest*) NW.
**Nylon** ['naɪlɔn] (**-s**) *nt* nylon.
**Nymphe** ['nʏmfə] (**-, -n**) *f* nymph.

# O, o

**O¹, o** [o:] *nt* O, o; ~ **wie Otto** ≈ O for Olive, O
  for Oboe (*US*).
**O²** [o:] *abk* (= *Osten*) E.
**o.ä.** *abk* (= *oder ähnliche(s)*) or similar.
**Oase** [o'a:zə] (**-, -n**) *f* oasis.
**OB** (**-s, -s**) *m abk* = **Oberbürgermeister**.
**ob** [ɔp] *konj* if, whether; ~ **das wohl wahr ist?**
  can that be true?; ~ **ich (nicht) lieber gehe?**
  maybe I'd better go; **(so) tun als** ~ (*umg*) to
  pretend; **und** ~! you bet!
**Obacht** ['o:baxt] *f:* ~ **geben** to pay attention.
**Obdach** ['ɔpdax] (**-(e)s**) *nt* shelter, lodging;
  **o~los** *adj* homeless; ~**losenasyl** *nt* hostel *od*
  shelter for the homeless; ~**losenheim** *nt*
  = **Obdachlosenasyl**; ~**lose(r)** *f(m)* homeless
  person.
**Obduktion** [ɔpdʊktsi'o:n] *f* postmortem.
**obduzieren** [ɔpdu'tsi:rən] *vt* to do a
  postmortem on.
**O-Beine** ['o:baɪnə] *pl* bow *od* bandy legs *pl*.
**oben** ['o:bən] *adv* above; (*in Haus*) upstairs;
  (*am oberen Ende*) at the top; **nach** ~ up; **von**
  ~ **down; siehe** ~ see above; **ganz** ~ right at
  the top; ~ **ohne** topless; **die Abbildung**
  ~ **links** *od* **links** ~ the illustration in the top
  left-hand corner; **jdn von** ~ **herab**
  **behandeln** to treat sb condescendingly; **jdn**
  **von** ~ **bis unten ansehen** to look sb up and
  down; **Befehl von** ~ orders from above; **die**
  **da** ~ (*umg: die Vorgesetzten*) the powers that
  be; ~'**an** *adv* at the top; ~'**auf** *adv* up above,
  on the top ♦ *adj* (*munter*) in form; ~'**drein** *adv*
  into the bargain; ~**erwähnt** *adj* above-
  mentioned; ~**genannt** *adj* above-mentioned;
  ~'**hin** *adv* cursorily, superficially.
**Ober** ['o:bər] (**-s, -**) *m* waiter.
**Ober-** *zW:* ~**arm** *m* upper arm; ~**arzt** *m* senior
  physician; ~**aufsicht** *f* supervision;
  ~**bayern** *nt* Upper Bavaria; ~**befehl** *m*
  supreme command; ~**befehlshaber** *m*
  commander-in-chief; ~**begriff** *m* generic
  term; ~**bekleidung** *f* outer clothing; ~**bett**
  *nt* quilt; ~**bürgermeister** *m* lord mayor;
  ~**deck** *nt* upper *od* top deck.
**obere(r, s)** *adj* upper; **die O~n** the bosses;
  (*ECCL*) the superiors; **die ~n Zehntausend**
  (*umg*) high society.
**Ober-** *zW:* ~**fläche** *f* surface; **o~flächlich** *adj*

superficial; **bei o~flächlicher Betrachtung** at a quick glance; **jdn (nur) o~flächlich kennen** to know sb (only) slightly; **~geschoß** *nt* upper storey *od* story (*US*); **im zweiten ~geschoß** on the second floor (*BRIT*), on the third floor (*US*); **o~halb** *adv* above ♦ *präp +gen* above; **~hand** *f* (*fig*): **die ~hand gewinnen (über** *+akk*) to get the upper hand (over); **~haupt** *nt* head, chief; **~haus** *nt* (*BRIT POL*) upper house, House of Lords, **~hemd** *nt* shirt; **~herrschaft** *f* supremacy, sovereignty.

**Oberin** *f* matron; (*ECCL*) Mother Superior.

**Ober-** *zW:* **o~irdisch** *adj* above ground; (*Leitung*) overhead; **~italien** *nt* Northern Italy; **~kellner** *m* head waiter; **~kiefer** *m* upper jaw; **~kommando** *nt* supreme command; **~körper** *m* upper part of body; **~lauf** *m:* **am ~lauf des Rheins** in the upper reaches of the Rhine; **~leitung** *f* (*ELEK*) overhead cable; **~licht** *nt* skylight; **~lippe** *f* upper lip; **~österreich** *nt* Upper Austria; **~prima** *f* *final year of German secondary school;* **~schenkel** *m* thigh; **~schicht** *f* upper classes *pl;* **~schule** *f* grammar school (*BRIT*), high school (*US*); **~schwester** *f* (*MED*) matron; **~seite** *f* top (side); **~sekunda** *f* *seventh year of German secondary school.*

**Oberst** ['oːbərst] (**-en** *od* **-s, -en** *od* **-e**) *m* colonel.

**oberste(r, s)** *adj* very top, topmost.

**Ober-** *zW:* **~stübchen** (*umg*) *nt:* **er ist nicht ganz richtig im ~stübchen** he's not quite right up top; **~stufe** *f* upper school; **~teil** *nt* upper part; **~tertia** *f* *fifth year of German secondary school;* **~wasser** *nt:* **~wasser haben/bekommen** to be/get on top (of things); **~weite** *f* bust *od* chest measurement.

**obgleich** [ɔp'ɡlaɪç] *konj* although.

**Obhut** ['ɔphuːt] (**-**) *f* care, protection; **in jds ~** *dat* **sein** to be in sb's care.

**obig** ['oːbɪç] *adj* above.

**Objekt** [ɔp'jɛkt] (**-(e)s, -e**) *nt* object.

**objektiv** [ɔpjɛk'tiːf] *adj* objective.

**Objektiv** (**-s, -e**) *nt* lens *sing.*

**Objektivität** [ɔpjɛktivi'tɛːt] *f* objectivity.

**Oblate** [o'blaːtə] (**-, -n**) *f* (*Gebäck*) wafer; (*ECCL*) host.

**obligatorisch** [obliga'toːrɪʃ] *adj* compulsory, obligatory.

**Oboe** [o'boːə] (**-, -n**) *f* oboe.

**Obrigkeit** ['oːbrɪçkaɪt] *f* (*Behörden*) authorities *pl*, administration; (*Regierung*) government.

**Obrigkeitsdenken** *nt* acceptance of authority.

**obschon** [ɔp'ʃoːn] *konj* although.

**Observatorium** [ɔpzɛrva'toːriʊm] *nt* observatory.

**obskur** [ɔps'kuːr] *adj* obscure; (*verdächtig*) dubious.

**Obst** [oːpst] (**-(e)s**) *nt* fruit; **~bau** *m* fruit-growing; **~baum** *m* fruit tree; **~garten** *m* orchard; **~händler** *m* fruiterer (*BRIT*), fruit merchant; **~kuchen** *m* fruit tart; **~saft** *m* fruit juice; **~salat** *m* fruit salad.

**obszön** [ɔps'tsøːn] *adj* obscene.

**Obszönität** [ɔpstøni'tɛːt] *f* obscenity.

**Obus** ['oːbʊs] (**-ses, -se**) (*umg*) *m* trolleybus.

**obwohl** [ɔp'voːl] *konj* although.

**Ochse** ['ɔksə] (**-n, -n**) *m* ox; (*umg: Dummkopf*) twit; **er stand da wie der ~ vorm Berg** (*umg*) he stood there utterly bewildered.

**ochsen** (*umg*) *vt, vi* to cram, swot (*BRIT*).

**Ochsenschwanzsuppe** *f* oxtail soup.

**Ochsenzunge** *f* ox tongue.

**Ocker** ['ɔkər] (**-s, -**) *m od nt* ochre (*BRIT*), ocher (*US*).

**öd** [øːt(ə)] *adj* = **öde.**

**öde** *adj* (*Land*) waste, barren; (*fig*) dull; **~ und leer** dreary and desolate.

**Öde** (**-, -n**) *f* desert, waste(land); (*fig*) tedium.

**oder** ['oːdər] *konj* or; **entweder ... ~** either ... or; **du kommst doch, ~?** you're coming, aren't you?

**Ofen** ['oːfən] (**-s, -̈**) *m* oven; (*Heiz~*) fire, heater; (*Kohle~*) stove; (*Hoch~*) furnace; (*Herd*) cooker, stove; **jetzt ist der ~ aus** (*umg*) that does it!; **~rohr** *nt* stovepipe.

**offen** ['ɔfən] *adj* open; (*aufrichtig*) frank; (*Stelle*) vacant; (*Bein*) ulcerated; (*Haare*) loose; **~er Wein** wine by the carafe *od* glass; **auf ~er Strecke** (*Straße*) on the open road; (*EISENB*) between stations; **Tag der ~en Tür** open day (*BRIT*), open house (*US*); **~e Handelsgesellschaft** (*COMM*) general *od* ordinary (*US*) partnership; **seine Meinung ~ sagen** to speak one's mind; **ein ~es Wort mit jdm reden** to have a frank talk with sb; **~ gesagt** to be honest.

**offenbar** *adj* obvious; (*vermutlich*) apparently.

**offenbaren** [ɔfən'baːrən] *vt* to reveal, manifest.

**Offenbarung** *f* (*REL*) revelation.

**Offenbarungseid** *m* (*JUR*) oath of disclosure.

**offen-** *zW:* **~bleiben** *unreg vi* (*Fenster*) to stay open; (*Frage, Entscheidung*) to remain open; **~halten** *unreg vt* to keep open; **O~heit** *f* candour (*BRIT*), candor (*US*), frankness; **~herzig** *adj* candid, frank; (*hum: Kleid*) revealing; **O~herzigkeit** *f* frankness; **~kundig** *adj* well-known; (*klar*) evident; **~lassen** *unreg vt* to leave open; **~sichtlich** *adj* evident, obvious.

**offensiv** [ɔfɛn'ziːf] *adj* offensive.

**Offensive** (**-, -n**) *f* offensive.

**offenstehen** *unreg vi* to be open; (*Rechnung*) to be unpaid; **es steht Ihnen offen, es zu tun** you are at liberty to do it; **die (ganze) Welt steht ihm offen** he has the (whole) world at his feet.

**öffentlich** ['œfəntlɪç] *adj* public; **die ~e Hand** (central/local) government; **Anstalt des ~en Rechts** public institution; **Ausgaben der ~en Hand** public spending *sing*.

**Öffentlichkeit** *f* (*Leute*) public; (*einer Versammlung etc*) public nature; **in aller ~ in** public; **an die ~ dringen** to reach the public ear; **unter Ausschluß der ~** in secret; (*JUR*) in camera.

**Öffentlichkeitsarbeit** *f* public relations work.

**öffentlich-rechtlich** *adj attrib* (under) public law.

**offerieren** [ɔfe'riːrən] *vt* to offer.

**Offerte** [ɔ'fɛrtə] (-, -n) *f* offer.

**offiziell** [ɔfitsi'ɛl] *adj* official.

**Offizier** [ɔfi'tsiːr] (-s, -e) *m* officer.

**Offizierskasino** *nt* officers' mess.

**öffnen** ['œfnən] *vt, vr* to open; **jdm die Tür ~ to** open the door for sb.

**Öffner** ['œfnər] (-s, -) *m* opener.

**Öffnung** ['œfnʊŋ] *f* opening.

**Öffnungszeiten** *pl* opening times *pl*.

**Offsetdruck** ['ɔfsɛtdrʊk] *m* offset (printing).

**oft** [ɔft] *adv* often.

**öfter** ['œftər] *adv* more often *od* frequently; **des ~en** quite frequently; **~ mal was Neues** (*umg*) variety is the spice of life (*Sprichwort*).

**öfters** *adv* often, frequently.

**oftmals** *adv* often, frequently.

**o.G.** *abk* (= *ohne Gewähr*) without liability.

**OHG** *f abk* (= *offene Handelsgesellschaft*) *siehe* **offen**.

**ohne** ['oːnə] *präp +akk, konj* without; **das Darlehen ist ~ weiteres bewilligt worden** the loan was granted without any problem; **das kann man nicht ~ weiteres voraussetzen** you can't just assume that automatically; **das ist nicht ~** (*umg*) it's not bad; **~ weiteres** without a second thought; (*sofort*) immediately; **~dies** *adv* anyway; **~einander** [oːnə|aɪ'nandər] *adv* without each other; **~gleichen** *adj* unsurpassed, without equal; **es ist ~hin** *adv* anyway, in any case; **es ist ~hin schon spät** it's late enough already.

**Ohnmacht** ['oːnmaxt] *f* faint; (*fig*) impotence; **in ~ fallen** to faint.

**ohnmächtig** ['oːnmɛçtɪç] *adj* in a faint, unconscious; (*fig*) weak, impotent; **sie ist ~** she has fainted; **~e Wut, ~er Zorn** helpless rage; **einer Sache** *dat* **~ gegenüberstehen** to be helpless in the face of sth.

**Ohr** [oːr] (-(e)s, -en) *nt* ear; (*Gehör*) hearing; **sich aufs ~ legen** *od* **hauen** (*umg*) to kip down; **jdm die ~en langziehen** (*umg*) to tweak sb's ear(s); **jdm in den ~en liegen** to keep on at sb; **jdn übers ~ hauen** (*umg*) to pull a fast one on sb; **auf dem ~ bin ich taub** (*fig*) nothing doing (*umg*); **schreib es dir hinter die ~en** (*umg*) will you (finally) get that into your (thick) head!; **bis über die** *od*

**beide ~en verliebt sein** to be head over heels in love; **viel um die ~en haben** (*umg*) to have a lot on (one's plate); **halt die ~en steif!** keep a stiff upper lip!

**Öhr** [øːr] (-(e)s, -e) *nt* eye.

**Ohren-** *zW:* **~arzt** *m* ear specialist; **o~betäubend** *adj* deafening; **~sausen** *nt* (*MED*) buzzing in one's ears; **~schmalz** *nt* earwax; **~schmerzen** *pl* earache *sing*; **~schützer** (-s, -) *m* earmuff.

**Ohr-** *zW:* **~feige** *f* slap on the face; (*als Strafe*) box on the ears; **o~feigen** *vt untr:* **jdn o~feigen** to slap sb's face; to box sb's ears; **ich könnte mich selbst o~feigen, daß ich das gemacht habe** I could kick myself for doing that; **~läppchen** *nt* ear lobe; **~ringe** *pl* earrings *pl*; **~wurm** *m* earwig; (*MUS*) catchy tune.

**o.J.** *abk* (= *ohne Jahr*) no year given.

**okkupieren** [ɔku'piːrən] *vt* to occupy.

**Öko-** ['øko-] *in zW* eco-, ecological; **~laden** ['øːkola:dən] *m* wholefood shop.

**Ökologie** [økolo'giː] *f* ecology.

**ökologisch** [øko'loːgɪʃ] *adj* ecological, environmental.

**Ökonometrie** [økonome'triː] *f* econometrics *pl*.

**Ökonomie** [økono'miː] *f* economy; (*als Wissenschaft*) economics *sing*.

**ökonomisch** [øko'noːmɪʃ] *adj* economical.

**Ökopaxe** [øko'paksə] (-n, -n) (*umg*) *m* environmentalist.

**Ökosystem** ['øːkozystɛm] *nt* ecosystem.

**Okt.** *abk* (= *Oktober*) Oct.

**Oktan** [ɔk'taːn] (-s, -e) *nt* octane; **~zahl** *f* octane rating.

**Oktave** [ɔk'taːvə] (-, -n) *f* octave.

**Oktober** [ɔk'toːbər] (-(s), -) *m* October; *siehe auch* **September**.

---

*The annual October beer festival, the* **Oktoberfest,** *takes place in Munich on a huge field where beer tents, roller coasters and many other amusements are set up. People sit at long wooden tables, drink beer from enormous litre beer mugs, eat pretzels and listen to brass bands. It is a great attraction for tourists and locals alike.*

---

**ökumenisch** [øku'meːnɪʃ] *adj* ecumenical.

**Öl** [øːl] (-(e)s, -e) *nt* oil; **auf ~ stoßen** to strike oil.

**Öl-** *zW:* **~baum** *m* olive tree; **ö~en** *vt* to oil; (*TECH*) to lubricate; **wie ein geölter Blitz** (*umg*) like greased lightning; **~farbe** *f* oil paint; **~feld** *nt* oilfield; **~film** *m* film of oil; **~heizung** *f* oil-fired central heating.

**ölig** *adj* oily.

**Oligopol** [oligo'poːl] (-s, -e) *nt* oligopoly.

**oliv** [o'liːf] *adj* olive-green.

**Olive** [o'liːvə] (-, -n) *f* olive.

**Olivenöl** *nt* olive oil.

**Öljacke** f oilskin jacket.
**oll** [ɔl] (_umg_) _adj_ old; **das sind ~e Kamellen** that's old hat.
**Öl-** _zW:_ **~meßstab** m dipstick; **~pest** f oil pollution; **~plattform** f oil rig; **~sardine** f sardine; **~scheich** m oil sheik; **~stand** m oil level; **~standanzeiger** m (_AUT_) oil level indicator; **~tanker** m oil tanker; **~teppich** m oil slick.
**Ölung** f oiling; (_ECCL_) anointment; **die Letzte ~** Extreme Unction.
**Ölwanne** f (_AUT_) sump (_BRIT_), oil pan (_US_).
**Ölwechsel** m oil change.
**Olymp** [o'lʏmp] (**-s**) m (_Berg_) Mount Olympus.
**Olympiade** [olʏmpi'a:də] (**-, -n**) f Olympic Games _pl_.
**Olympiasieger(in)** [o'lʏmpiazi:gər(ɪn)] m(f) Olympic champion.
**olympisch** [o'lʏmpɪʃ] _adj_ Olympic.
**Ölzeug** nt oilskins _pl_.
**Oma** ['o:ma] (**-, -s**) (_umg_) f granny.
**Oman** [o'ma:n] (**-s**) nt Oman.
**Omelett** [ɔm(ə)'lɛt] (**-(e)s, -s**) nt omelette (_BRIT_), omelet (_US_).
**Omelette** [ɔm(ə)'lɛt] f = **Omelett**.
**Omen** ['o:mɛn] (**-s, -** _od_ **Omina**) nt omen.
**Omnibus** ['ɔmnibʊs] m (omni)bus.
**Onanie** [ona'ni:] f masturbation.
**onanieren** _vi_ to masturbate.
**ondulieren** [ɔndu'li:rən] _vt, vi_ to crimp.
**Onkel** ['ɔŋkəl] (**-s, -**) m uncle.
**OP** m _abk_ = **Operationssaal**.
**Opa** ['o:pa] (**-s, -s**) (_umg_) m grandpa.
**Opal** [o'pa:l] (**-s, -e**) m opal.
**Oper** ['o:pər] (**-, -n**) f opera; (_Opernhaus_) opera house.
**Operation** [operatsi'o:n] f operation.
**Operationssaal** m operating theatre (_BRIT_) _od_ theater (_US_).
**operativ** [opəra'ti:f] _adv_ (_MED_): **eine Geschwulst ~ entfernen** to remove a growth by surgery.
**Operette** [ope'rɛtə] f operetta.
**operieren** [ope'ri:rən] _vt, vi_ to operate; **sich ~ lassen** to have an operation.
**Opern-** _zW:_ **~glas** nt opera glasses _pl_; **~haus** nt opera house; **~sänger(in)** m(f) opera singer.
**Opfer** ['ɔpfər] (**-s, -**) nt sacrifice; (_Mensch_) victim; **~bereitschaft** f readiness to make sacrifices.
**opfern** _vt_ to sacrifice.
**Opferstock** m (_ECCL_) offertory box.
**Opferung** f sacrifice; (_ECCL_) offertory.
**Opium** ['o:piʊm] (**-s**) nt opium.
**opponieren** [ɔpo'ni:rən] _vi:_ **gegen jdn/etw ~** to oppose sb/sth.
**opportun** [ɔpɔr'tu:n] _adj_ opportune; **O~ismus** [-'nɪsmʊs] m opportunism; **O~ist(in)** [-'nɪst(ɪn)] m(f) opportunist.
**Opposition** [ɔpozitsi'o:n] f opposition.
**oppositionell** [ɔpozitsio:'nɛl] _adj_ opposing.

**Oppositionsführer** m leader of the opposition.
**optieren** [ɔp'ti:rən] _vi_ (_POL: form_): **~ für** to opt for.
**Optik** ['ɔptɪk] f optics _sing_.
**Optiker(in)** (**-s, -**) m(f) optician.
**optimal** [ɔpti'ma:l] _adj_ optimal, optimum.
**Optimismus** [ɔpti'mɪsmʊs] m optimism.
**Optimist(in)** [ɔpti'mɪst(ɪn)] m(f) optimist; **o~isch** _adj_ optimistic.
**optisch** ['ɔptɪʃ] _adj_ optical; **~e Täuschung** optical illusion.
**Orakel** [o'ra:kəl] (**-s, -**) nt oracle.
**Orange** [o'rã:ʒə] (**-, -n**) f orange; **o~** _adj_ orange.
**Orangeade** [orã'ʒa:də] (**-, -n**) f orangeade.
**Orangeat** [orã'ʒa:t] (**-s, -e**) nt candied peel.
**Orangen-** _zW:_ **~marmelade** f marmalade; **~saft** m orange juice; **~schale** f orange peel.
**Oratorium** [ora'to:riʊm] nt (_MUS_) oratorio.
**Orchester** [ɔr'kɛstər] (**-s, -**) nt orchestra.
**Orchidee** [ɔrçi'de:ə] (**-, -n**) f orchid.
**Orden** ['ɔrdən] (**-s, -**) m (_ECCL_) order; (_MIL_) decoration.
**Ordensgemeinschaft** f religious order.
**Ordensschwester** f nun.
**ordentlich** ['ɔrdəntlıç] _adj_ (_anständig_) decent, respectable; (_geordnet_) tidy, neat; (_umg: annehmbar_) not bad; (: _tüchtig_) real, proper; (_Leistung_) reasonable; **~es Mitglied** full member; **~er Professor** (full) professor; **eine ~e Tracht Prügel** a proper hiding; **~ arbeiten** to be a thorough and precise worker; **O~keit** f respectability; tidiness, neatness.
**Order** (**-, -s** _od_ **-n**) f (_COMM: Auftrag_) order.
**ordern** _vt_ (_COMM_) to order.
**Ordinalzahl** [ɔrdi'na:ltsa:l] f ordinal number.
**ordinär** [ɔrdi'nɛ:r] _adj_ common, vulgar.
**Ordinarius** [ɔrdi'na:riʊs] (**-, Ordinarien**) m (_UNIV_): **~ (für)** professor (of).
**ordnen** ['ɔrdnən] _vt_ to order, put in order.
**Ordner** (**-s, -**) m steward; (_COMM_) file.
**Ordnung** f order; (_Ordnen_) ordering; (_Geordnetsein_) tidiness; **geht in ~** (_umg_) that's all right _od_ OK (_umg_); **~ schaffen, für ~ sorgen** to put things in order, tidy things up; **jdn zur ~ rufen** to call sb to order; **bei ihm muß alles seine ~ haben** (_räumlich_) he has to have everything in its proper place; (_zeitlich_) he has to do everything according to a fixed schedule; **das Kind braucht seine ~** the child needs a routine.
**Ordnungs-** _zW:_ **~amt** nt ≈ town clerk's office; **o~gemäß** _adj_ proper, according to the rules; **o~halber** _adv_ as a matter of form; **~liebe** f tidiness, orderliness; **~strafe** f fine; **o~widrig** _adj_ contrary to the rules, irregular; **~widrigkeit** f infringement (_of law or rule_); **~zahl** f ordinal number.
**ORF** (**-**) m _abk_ = **Österreichischer Rundfunk**.

**Organ** [ɔr'gaːn] (-s, -e) nt organ; (*Stimme*) voice.
**Organisation** [ɔrganizatsi'oːn] f organization.
**Organisationstalent** nt organizing ability; (*Person*) good organizer.
**Organisator** [ɔrgani'zaːtɔr] m organizer.
**organisch** [ɔr'gaːnɪʃ] adj organic; (*Erkrankung, Leiden*) physical.
**organisieren** [ɔrgani'ziːrən] vt to organize, arrange; (*umg: beschaffen*) to acquire ♦ vr to organize.
**Organismus** [ɔrga'nɪsmʊs] m organism.
**Organist** [ɔrga'nɪst] m organist.
**Organspender** m donor (of an organ).
**Organspenderausweis** m donor card.
**Organverpflanzung** f transplantation (of an organ).
**Orgasmus** [ɔr'gasmʊs] m orgasm.
**Orgel** ['ɔrgəl] (-, -n) f organ; ~**pfeife** f organ pipe; **wie die ~pfeifen stehen** to stand in order of height.
**Orgie** ['ɔrgiə] f orgy.
**Orient** ['oːriɛnt] (-s) m Orient, east; **der Vordere** ~ the Near East.
**Orientale** [oːriɛn'taːlə] (-n, -n) m Oriental.
**Orientalin** [oːriɛn'taːlɪn] f Oriental.
**orientalisch** adj oriental.
**orientieren** [oːriɛn'tiːrən] vt (*örtlich*) to locate; (*fig*) to inform ♦ vr to find one's way od bearings; (*fig*) to inform o.s.
**Orientierung** [oːriɛn'tiːrʊŋ] f orientation; (*fig*) information; **die ~ verlieren** to lose one's bearings.
**Orientierungssinn** m sense of direction.

> The **Orientierungsstufe** *is the name given to the first two years spent in a* **Realschule** *or* **Gymnasium**, *during which a child is assessed as to his or her suitability for that type of school. At the end of the two years it may be decided to transfer the child to a school more suited to his or her ability.*

**original** [origi'naːl] adj original; ~ **Meißener Porzellan** genuine Meissen porcelain; **O~** (-s, -e) nt original; (*Mensch*) character; **O~ausgabe** f first edition; **O~fassung** f original version.
**Originalität** [originali'tɛːt] f originality.
**Originalübertragung** f live broadcast.
**originell** [origi'nɛl] adj original.
**Orkan** [ɔr'kaːn] (-(e)s, -e) m hurricane; **o~artig** adj (*Wind*) gale-force; (*Beifall*) thunderous.
**Orkneyinseln** ['ɔːkni|ɪnzəln] pl Orkney Islands pl, Orkneys pl.
**Ornament** [ɔrna'mɛnt] nt decoration, ornament.
**ornamental** [ɔrnamɛn'taːl] adj decorative, ornamental.
**Ornithologe** [ɔrnito'loːgə] (-n, -n) m ornithologist.
**Ornithologin** [ɔrnito'loːgɪn] f ornithologist.

**Ort¹** [ɔrt] (-(e)s, -e) m place; **an ~ und Stelle** on the spot; **am ~** in the place; **am angegebenen ~** in the place quoted, loc. cit.; ~ **der Handlung** (*THEAT*) scene of the action; **das ist höheren ~(e)s entschieden worden** (*hum: form*) the decision came from above.
**Ort²** [ɔrt] (-(e)s, -̈er) m: **vor ~** at the (coal) face; (*auch fig*) on the spot.
**Örtchen** ['œrtçən] (*umg*) nt loo (*BRIT*), john (*US*).
**orten** vt to locate.
**orthodox** [ɔrto'dɔks] adj orthodox.
**Orthographie** [ɔrtogra'fiː] f spelling, orthography.
**orthographisch** [ɔrto'graːfɪʃ] adj orthographic.
**Orthopäde** [ɔrto'pɛːdə] (-n, -n) m orthopaedic (*BRIT*) od orthopedic (*US*) specialist, orthopaedist (*BRIT*), orthopedist (*US*).
**Orthopädie** [ɔrtopɛ'diː] f orthopaedics sing (*BRIT*), orthopedics sing (*US*).
**orthopädisch** adj orthopaedic (*BRIT*), orthopedic (*US*).
**örtlich** ['œrtlɪç] adj local; **jdn ~ betäuben** to give sb a local anaesthetic (*BRIT*) od anesthetic (*US*); **Ö~keit** f locality; **sich mit den Ö~keiten vertraut machen** to get to know the place.
**Ortsangabe** f (name of the) town; **ohne ~** (*Buch*) no place of publication indicated.
**ortsansässig** adj local.
**Ortschaft** f village, small town; **geschlossene ~** built-up area.
**Orts-** zW: **o~fremd** adj nonlocal; ~**fremde(r)** f(m) stranger; ~**gespräch** nt local (phone) call; ~**gruppe** f local branch od group; ~**kenntnis** f: (**gute**) ~**kenntnisse haben** to know one's way around (well); ~**krankenkasse** f: **Allgemeine ~krankenkasse** compulsory medical insurance scheme; **o~kundig** adj familiar with the place; **o~kundig sein** to know one's way around; ~**name** m place name; ~**netz** nt (*TEL*) local telephone exchange area; ~**netzkennzahl** f (*TEL*) dialling (*BRIT*) od area (*US*) code; ~**schild** nt place name sign; ~**sinn** m sense of direction; ~**tarif** m (*TEL*) charge for local calls; ~**vorschriften** pl by(e)-laws pl; ~**zeit** f local time; ~**zuschlag** m (local) weighting allowance.
**Ortung** f locating.
**öS.** abk = **österreichischer Schilling**.
**Öse** ['øːzə] (-, -n) f loop; (*an Kleidung*) eye.
**Oslo** ['ɔslo] (-s) nt Oslo.
**Ossi** ['ɔsi] (-s, -s) (*umg*) m East German.

> **Ossi** *is a colloquial and often derogatory word used to describe a German from the former DDR.*

**öst.** abk (= *österreichisch*) Aust.

**Ost-** *zW:* ~**afrika** *nt* East Africa; **o~deutsch**
  *adj* East German; ~**deutsche(r)** *f(m)* East
  German; ~**deutschland** *nt* (*POL: früher*) East
  Germany; (*GEOG*) Eastern Germany.
**Osten** (**-s**) *m* east; **der Ferne** ~ the Far East;
  **der Nahe** ~ the Middle East, the Near East.
**ostentativ** [ɔstɛnta'tiːf] *adj* pointed,
  ostentatious.
**Oster-** *zW:* ~**ei** *nt* Easter egg; ~**fest** *nt* Easter;
  ~**glocke** *f* daffodil; ~**hase** *m* Easter bunny;
  ~**insel** *f* Easter Island; ~**marsch** *m* Easter
  demonstration; ~**montag** *m* Easter
  Monday.
**Ostern** (**-s, -**) *nt* Easter; **frohe** *od* **fröhliche** ~!
  Happy Easter!; **zu** ~ at Easter.
**Österreich** ['øːstəraiç] (**-s**) *nt* Austria.
**Österreicher(in)** (**-s, -**) *m(f)* Austrian.
**österreichisch** *adj* Austrian.
**Ostersonntag** *m* Easter Day *od* Sunday.
**Osteuropa** *nt* East(ern) Europe.
**osteuropäisch** *adj* East European.
**östlich** ['œstliç] *adj* eastern, easterly.
**Östrogen** [œstro'geːn] (**-s, -e**) *nt* oestrogen
  (*BRIT*), estrogen (*US*).
**Ost-** *zW:* ~**see** *f* Baltic Sea; **o~wärts** *adv*
  eastwards; ~**wind** *m* east wind.
**oszillieren** [ɔstsɪ'liːrən] *vi* to oscillate.
**Otter**[1] ['ɔtər] (**-s, -**) *m* otter.
**Otter**[2] ['ɔtər] (**-, -n**) *f* (*Schlange*) adder.
**ÖTV** (**-**) *f abk* (= *Gewerkschaft öffentliche
  Dienste, Transport und Verkehr*) ≈ Transport
  and General Workers' Union.
**Ouvertüre** [uvɛr'tyːrə] (**-, -n**) *f* overture.
**oval** [o'vaːl] *adj* oval.
**Ovation** [ovatsi'oːn] *f* ovation.
**Overall** ['ouvərɔːl] (**-s, -s**) *m* (*Schutzanzug*)
  overalls *pl.*
**ÖVP** (**-**) *f abk* (= *Österreichische Volkspartei*)
  Austrian People's Party.
**Ovulation** [ovulatsi'oːn] *f* ovulation.
**Oxyd** [ɔ'ksyːt] (**-(e)s, -e**) *nt* oxide.
**oxydieren** [ɔksy'diːrən] *vt, vi* to oxidize.
**Oxydierung** *f* oxidization.
**Ozean** ['oːtseaːn] (**-s, -e**) *m* ocean; ~**dampfer** *m*
  (ocean-going) liner.
**Ozeanien** [otse'aːniən] (**-s**) *nt* Oceania.
**ozeanisch** [otse'aːnɪʃ] *adj* oceanic; (*Sprachen*)
  Oceanic.
**Ozeanriese** (*umg*) *m* ocean liner.
**Ozon** [o'tsoːn] (**-s**) *nt* ozone; ~**loch** *nt* hole in
  the ozone layer; ~**schicht** *f* ozone layer.

# $P, p$

**P, p** [peː] *nt* P, p; ~ **wie Peter** ≈ P for Peter.
**P.** *abk* = **Pastor; Pater.**
**Paar** [paːr] (**-(e)s, -e**) *nt* pair; (*Liebes~*) couple.
**paar** *adj inv:* **ein** ~ a few; (*zwei oder drei*) a
  couple of.
**paaren** *vt, vr* (*Tiere*) to mate, pair.
**Paar-** *zW:* ~**hufer** *pl* (*ZOOL*) cloven-hoofed
  animals *pl;* ~**lauf** *m* pair skating; **p~mal** *adv:*
  **ein p~mal** a few times.
**Paarung** *f* combination; (*von Tieren*) mating.
**paarweise** *adv* in pairs; in couples.
**Pacht** [paxt] (**-, -en**) *f* lease; (*Entgelt*) rent;
  **p~en** *vt* to lease; **du hast das Sofa doch nicht
  für dich gepachtet** (*umg*) don't hog the sofa.
**Pächter(in)** ['pɛçtər(ɪn)] (**-s, -**) *m(f)*
  leaseholder; tenant.
**Pachtvertrag** *m* lease.
**Pack**[1] [pak] (**-(e)s, -e** *od* **-̈e**) *m* bundle, pack.
**Pack**[2] [pak] (**-(e)s**) (*pej*) *nt* mob, rabble.
**Päckchen** ['pɛkçən] *nt* small package;
  (*Zigaretten*) packet; (*Post~*) small parcel.
**Packeis** *nt* pack ice.
**Packen** (**-s, -**) *m* bundle; (*fig: Menge*) heaps
  (of); **p~** *vt, vi* (*auch COMPUT*) to pack;
  (*fassen*) to grasp, seize; (*umg: schaffen*) to
  manage; (*fig: fesseln*) to grip; **p~ wir's!** (*umg:
  gehen*) let's go.
**Packer(in)** (**-s, -**) *m(f)* packer.
**Packesel** *m* pack mule; (*fig*) packhorse.
**Packpapier** *nt* brown paper, wrapping paper.
**Packung** *f* packet; (*Pralinen~*) box; (*MED*)
  compress.
**Packzettel** *m* (*COMM*) packing slip.
**Pädagoge** [pɛda'goːgə] (**-n, -n**) *m*
  educationalist.
**Pädagogik** *f* education.
**Pädagogin** [pɛda'goːgɪn] *f* educationalist.
**pädagogisch** *adj* educational, pedagogical;
  **P~e Hochschule** college of education.
**Paddel** ['padəl] (**-s, -**) *nt* paddle; ~**boot** *nt*
  canoe.
**paddeln** *vi* to paddle.
**pädophil** [pɛdo'fiːl] *adj* paedophile (*BRIT*),
  pedophile (*US*).
**Pädophilie** [pɛdofɪ'liː] *f* paedophilia (*BRIT*),
  pedophilia (*US*).
**paffen** ['pafən] *vt, vi* to puff.
**Page** ['paːʒə] (**-n, -n**) *m* page(boy).
**Pagenkopf** *m* pageboy cut.
**paginieren** [pagi'niːrən] *vt* to paginate.
**Paginierung** *f* pagination.
**Paillette** [paɪ'jɛtə] *f* sequin.

**Paket** [pa'keːt] (-(e)s, -e) *nt* packet; (*Post~*) parcel; **~annahme** *f* parcels office; **~ausgabe** *f* parcels office; **~karte** *f* dispatch note; **~post** *f* parcel post; **~schalter** *m* parcels counter.

**Pakistan** ['paːkɪstaːn] (-s) *nt* Pakistan.

**Pakistaner(in)** [pakɪs'taːnər(ɪn)] (-s, -) *m(f)* Pakistani.

**Pakistani** [pakɪs'taːni] (-(s), -(s)) *m* Pakistani.

**pakistanisch** *adj* Pakistani.

**Pakt** [pakt] (-(e)s, -e) *m* pact.

**Paläontologie** [palɛɔntolo'giː] *f* palaeontology (*BRIT*), paleontology (*US*).

**Palast** [pa'last] (-es, **Paläste**) *m* palace.

**Palästina** [palɛ'stiːna] (-s) *nt* Palestine.

**Palästinenser(in)** [palɛsti'nɛnzər(ɪn)] (-s, -) *m(f)* Palestinian.

**palästinensisch** *adj* Palestinian.

**Palaver** [pa'laːvər] (-s, -) *nt* (*auch fig: umg*) palaver.

**Palette** [pa'lɛtə] *f* palette; (*fig*) range; (*Lade~*) pallet.

**Palme** ['palmə] (-, -n) *f* palm (tree); **jdn auf die ~ bringen** (*umg*) to make sb see red.

**Palmsonntag** *m* Palm Sunday.

**Pampelmuse** ['pampəlmuːzə] (-, -n) *f* grapefruit.

**pampig** ['pampɪç] (*umg*) *adj* (*frech*) fresh.

**Panama** ['panama] (-s) *nt* Panama; **~kanal** *m* Panama Canal.

**Panflöte** ['paːnfløːtə] *f* panpipes *pl*, Pan's pipes *pl*.

**panieren** [pa'niːrən] *vt* (*KOCH*) to coat with egg and breadcrumbs.

**Paniermehl** [pa'niːrmeːl] *nt* breadcrumbs *pl*.

**Panik** ['paːnɪk] *f* panic; **nur keine ~**! don't panic!; **in ~ ausbrechen** to panic.

**Panikkäufe** *pl* panic buying *sing*; **~mache** (*umg*) *f* panicmongering.

**panisch** ['paːnɪʃ] *adj* panic-stricken.

**Panne** ['panə] (-, -n) *f* (*AUT etc*) breakdown; (*Mißgeschick*) slip; **uns ist eine ~ passiert** we've boobed (*BRIT*) (*umg*) *od* goofed (*US*) (*umg*).

**Pannendienst** *m* breakdown service.

**Pannenhilfe** *f* breakdown service.

**Panorama** [pano'raːma] (-s, -men) *nt* panorama.

**panschen** ['panʃən] *vi* to splash about ♦ *vt* to water down.

**Panther** ['pantər] (-s, -) *m* panther.

**Pantoffel** [pan'tɔfəl] (-s, -n) *m* slipper; **~held** (*umg*) *m* henpecked husband.

**Pantomime** [panto'miːmə] (-, -n) *f* mime.

**Panzer** ['pantsər] (-s, -) *m* armour (*BRIT*), armor (*US*); (*fig*) shield; (*Platte*) armo(u)r plate; (*Fahrzeug*) tank; **~faust** *f* bazooka; **~glas** *nt* bulletproof glass; **~grenadier** *m* armoured (*BRIT*) *od* armored (*US*) infantryman.

**panzern** *vt* to armour (*BRIT*) *od* armor (*US*) plate ♦ *vr* (*fig*) to arm o.s.

**Panzerschrank** *m* strongbox.

**Panzerwagen** *m* armoured (*BRIT*) *od* armored (*US*) car.

**Papa** [pa'paː] (-s, -s) (*umg*) *m* dad(dy), pa.

**Papagei** [papa'gaɪ] (-s, -en) *m* parrot.

**Papier** [pa'piːr] (-s, -e) *nt* paper; (*Wert~*) share; **Papiere** *pl* (identity) papers *pl*; (*Urkunden*) documents *pl*; **seine ~e bekommen** (*entlassen werden*) to get one's cards; **~fabrik** *f* paper mill; **~geld** *nt* paper money; **~korb** *m* wastepaper basket; **~kram** (*umg*) *m* bumf (*BRIT*) (*umg*); **~krieg** *m* red tape; **~tüte** *f* paper bag; **~vorschub** *m* (*Drucker*) paper advance.

**Pappbecher** *m* paper cup.

**Pappdeckel** (-, -n) *m* cardboard.

**Pappe** ['papə] *f* cardboard; **das ist nicht von ~** (*umg*) that is really something.

**Pappeinband** *m* pasteboard.

**Pappel** (-, -n) *f* poplar.

**pappen** (*umg*) *vt, vi* to stick.

**Pappenheimer** *pl*: **ich kenne meine ~** (*umg*) I know you lot/that lot (inside out).

**Pappenstiel** (*umg*) *m*: **keinen ~ wert sein** not to be worth a thing; **für einen ~ bekommen** to get for a song.

**papperlapapp** [papərla'pap] *interj* rubbish!

**pappig** *adj* sticky.

**Pappmaché** [papma'ʃeː] (-s, -s) *nt* papier-mâché.

**Pappteller** *m* paper plate.

**Paprika** ['paprika] (-s, -s) *m* (*Gewürz*) paprika; (*~schote*) pepper; **~schote** *f* pepper; **gefüllte ~schoten** stuffed peppers.

**Papst** [paːpst] (-(e)s, -̈e) *m* pope.

**päpstlich** ['pɛːpstlɪç] *adj* papal; **~er als der Papst sein** to be more Catholic than the Pope.

**Parabel** [pa'raːbəl] (-, -n) *f* parable; (*MATH*) parabola.

**Parabolantenne** [para'boːlʔantɛnə] *f* (*TV*) satellite dish.

**Parade** [pa'raːdə] (-, -n) *f* (*MIL*) parade, review; (*SPORT*) parry; **~beispiel** *nt* prime example; **~marsch** *m* march past; **~schritt** *m* goose step.

**Paradies** [para'diːs] (-es, -e) *nt* paradise; **p~isch** *adj* heavenly.

**Paradox** [para'dɔks] (-es, -e) *nt* paradox; **p~** *adj* paradoxical.

**Paraffin** [para'fiːn] (-s, -e) *nt* (*CHEM*: *~öl*) paraffin (*BRIT*), kerosene (*US*); (*~wachs*) paraffin wax.

**Paragraph** [para'graːf] (-en, -en) *m* paragraph; (*JUR*) section.

**Paragraphenreiter** (*umg*) *m* pedant.

**Paraguay** [paragu'aːi] (-s) *nt* Paraguay.

**Paraguayer(in)** [paragu'aːjər(ɪn)] (-s, -) *m(f)* Paraguayan.

**paraguayisch** *adj* Paraguayan.

**parallel** [para'leːl] *adj* parallel; **~ schalten** (*ELEK*) to connect in parallel.

**Parallele** (-, -n) *f* parallel.
**Parameter** [pa'ra:metər] *m* parameter.
**paramilitärisch** [paramili'tɛːrɪʃ] *adj* paramilitary.
**Paranuß** ['pa:ranʊs] *f* Brazil nut.
**paraphieren** [para'fi:rən] *vt* (*Vertrag*) to initial.
**Parasit** [para'zi:t] (-en, -en) *m* (*lit, fig*) parasite.
**parat** [pa'ra:t] *adj* ready.
**Pärchen** ['pɛ:rçən] *nt* couple.
**Parcours** [par'ku:r] (-, -) *m* showjumping course; (*Sportart*) showjumping.
**Pardon** [par'dõ:] (-s) (*umg*) *m od nt:* ~! (*Verzeihung*) sorry!; **kein ~ kennen** to be ruthless.
**Parfüm** [par'fy:m] (-s, -s *od* -e) *nt* perfume.
**Parfümerie** [parfymə'ri:] *f* perfumery.
**Parfümflasche** *f* scent bottle.
**parfümieren** [parfy'mi:rən] *vt* to scent, perfume.
**parieren** [pa'ri:rən] *vt* to parry ♦ *vi* (*umg*) to obey.
**Paris** [pa'ri:s] (-) *nt* Paris.
**Pariser** [pa'ri:zər] (-s, -) *m* Parisian; (*umg: Kondom*) rubber ♦ *adj attrib* Parisian, Paris *attrib*.
**Pariserin** *f* Parisian.
**Parität** [pari'tɛ:t] *f* parity; **p~isch** *adj:* **p~ische Mitbestimmung** equal representation.
**Pariwert** ['pa:rive:rt] *m* par value, parity.
**Park** [park] (-s, -s) *m* park.
**Parka** ['parka] (-(s), -s) *m* parka.
**Parkanlage** *f* park; (*um Gebäude*) grounds *pl*.
**Parkbucht** *f* parking bay.
**parken** *vt, vi* to park; „**P~ verboten!**“ "No Parking".
**Parkett** [par'kɛt] (-(e)s, -e) *nt* parquet (floor); (*THEAT*) stalls *pl* (*BRIT*), orchestra (*US*).
**Park-** *zW:* **~haus** *nt* multistorey car park; **~lücke** *f* parking space; **~platz** *m* car park, parking lot (*US*); parking place; **~scheibe** *f* parking disc; **~uhr** *f* parking meter; **~verbot** *nt* parking ban.
**Parlament** [parla'mɛnt] *nt* parliament.
**Parlamentarier** [parlamɛn'ta:riər] (-s, -) *m* parliamentarian.
**parlamentarisch** *adj* parliamentary.
**Parlaments-** *zW:* **~ausschuß** *m* parliamentary committee; **~beschluß** *m* vote of parliament; **~ferien** *pl* recess *sing*; **~mitglied** *nt* Member of Parliament (*BRIT*), Congressman (*US*); **~sitzung** *f* sitting (of parliament).
**Parodie** [paro'di:] *f* parody.
**parodieren** *vt* to parody.
**Parodontose** [parodɔn'to:zə] (-, -n) *f* shrinking gums *pl*.
**Parole** [pa'ro:lə] (-, -n) *f* password; (*Wahlspruch*) motto.
**Partei** [par'tai] *f* party; (*im Mietshaus*) tenant, party (*form*); **für jdn ~ ergreifen** to take sb's side; **~buch** *nt* party membership book; **~führung** *f* party leadership; **~genosse** *m*

party member; **p~isch** *adj* partial, bias(s)ed; **p~lich** *adj* party *attrib*; **~linie** *f* party line; **p~los** *adj* neutral; **~nahme** (-, -n) *f* partisanship; **p~politisch** *adj* party political; **~programm** *nt* (party) manifesto; **~tag** *m* party conference; **~vorsitzende(r)** *f(m)* party leader.
**Parterre** [par'tɛr] (-s, -s) *nt* ground floor; (*THEAT*) stalls *pl* (*BRIT*), orchestra (*US*).
**Partie** [par'ti:] *f* part; (*Spiel*) game; (*Ausflug*) outing; (*Mann, Frau*) catch; (*COMM*) lot; **mit von der ~ sein** to join in.
**partiell** [partsi'ɛl] *adj* partial.
**Partikel** [par'ti:kəl] (-, -n) *f* particle.
**Partisan(in)** [parti'za:n(ɪn)] (-s *od* -en, -en) *m(f)* partisan.
**Partitur** [parti'tu:r] *f* (*MUS*) score.
**Partizip** [parti'tsi:p] (-s, -ien) *nt* participle; **~ Präsens/Perfekt** (*GRAM*) present/past participle.
**Partner(in)** ['partnər(ɪn)] (-s, -) *m(f)* partner; **~schaft** *f* partnership; (*Städtepartnerschaft*) twinning; **p~schaftlich** *adj* as partners; **~stadt** *f* twin town (*BRIT*).
**partout** [par'tu:] *adv:* **er will ~ ins Kino gehen** he insists on going to the cinema.
**Party** ['pa:rti] (-, -s *od* **Parties**) *f* party.
**Parzelle** [par'tsɛlə] *f* plot, lot.
**Pascha** ['paʃa] (-s, -s) *m:* **wie ein ~** like Lord Muck (*BRIT*) (*umg*).
**Paß** [pas] (-sses, ̈-sse) *m* pass; (*Ausweis*) passport.
**passabel** [pa'sa:bəl] *adj* passable, reasonable.
**Passage** [pa'sa:ʒə] (-, -n) *f* passage; (*Ladenstraße*) arcade.
**Passagier** [pasa'ʒi:r] (-s, -e) *m* passenger; **~dampfer** *m* passenger steamer; **~flugzeug** *nt* airliner.
**Passah(fest)** ['pasa(fɛst)] *nt* (Feast of the) Passover.
**Paßamt** *nt* passport office.
**Passant(in)** [pa'sant(ɪn)] *m(f)* passer-by.
**Paßbild** *nt* passport photo(graph).
**passé** [pa'se:] *adj:* **diese Mode ist längst ~** this fashion went out long ago.
**passen** ['pasən] *vi* to fit; (*auf Frage, KARTEN*) to pass; **~ zu** (*Farbe etc*) to go with; **Sonntag paßt uns nicht** Sunday is no good for us; **die Schuhe ~ (mir) gut** the shoes are a good fit (for me); **zu jdm ~** (*Mensch*) to suit sb; **das paßt mir nicht** that doesn't suit me; **er paßt nicht zu dir** he's not right for you; **das könnte dir so ~!** (*umg*) you'd like that, wouldn't you?
**passend** *adj* suitable; (*zusammen~*) matching; (*angebracht*) fitting; (*Zeit*) convenient; **haben Sie es ~?** (*Geld*) have you got the right money?
**Paßfoto** *nt* passport photo(graph).
**passierbar** [pa'si:rba:r] *adj* passable; (*Fluß, Kanal*) negotiable.
**passieren** *vt* to pass; (*durch Sieb*) to strain ♦ *vi*

(*Hilfsverb sein*) to happen; **es ist ein Unfall passiert** there has been an accident.

**Passierschein** *m* pass, permit.

**Passion** [pasi'o:n] *f* passion.

**passioniert** [pasio:'ni:rt] *adj* enthusiastic, passionate.

**Passionsfrucht** *f* passion fruit.

**Passionsspiel** *nt* Passion Play.

**Passionszeit** *f* Passiontide.

**passiv** ['pasi:f] *adj* passive; **~es Rauchen** passive smoking; **P~** (**-s, -e**) *nt* passive.

**Passiva** [pa'si:va] *pl* (*COMM*) liabilities *pl*.

**Passivität** [pasivi'tɛːt] *f* passiveness.

**Passivposten** *m* (*COMM*) debit entry.

**Paß-** *zW:* **~kontrolle** *f* passport control; **~stelle** *f* passport office; **~straße** *f* (mountain) pass; **~zwang** *m* requirement to carry a passport.

**Paste** ['pastə] (**-, -n**) *f* paste.

**Pastell** [pas'tɛl] (**-(e)s, -e**) *nt* pastel; **~farbe** *f* pastel colour (*BRIT*) *od* color (*US*); **p~farben** *adj* pastel-colo(u)red.

**Pastete** [pas'te:tə] (**-, -n**) *f* pie; (*Pastetchen*) vol-au-vent; (: *ungefüllt*) vol-au-vent case.

**pasteurisieren** [pastøri'zi:rən] *vt* to pasteurize.

**Pastor** ['pastɔr] *m* vicar; pastor, minister.

**Pate** ['pa:tə] (**-n, -n**) *m* godfather; **bei etw ~ gestanden haben** (*fig*) to be the force behind sth.

**Patenkind** *nt* godchild.

**Patenstadt** *f* twin town (*BRIT*).

**patent** [pa'tɛnt] *adj* clever.

**Patent** (**-(e)s, -e**) *nt* patent; (*MIL*) commission; **etw als** *od* **zum ~ anmelden** to apply for a patent on sth.

**Patentamt** *nt* patent office.

**patentieren** [patɛn'ti:rən] *vt* to patent.

**Patent-** *zW:* **~inhaber** *m* patentee; **~lösung** *f* (*fig*) patent remedy; **~schutz** *m* patent right; **~urkunde** *f* letters patent *pl*.

**Pater** ['pa:tər] (**-s, - ** *od* **Patres**) *m* (*ECCL*) Father.

**Paternoster** [patər'nɔstər] (**-s, -**) *m* (*Aufzug*) paternoster.

**pathetisch** [pa'te:tɪʃ] *adj* emotional.

**Pathologe** [pato'lo:gə] (**-n, -n**) *m* pathologist.

**Pathologin** [pato'lo:gɪn] *f* pathologist.

**pathologisch** *adj* pathological.

**Pathos** ['pa:tɔs] (**-**) *nt* emotiveness, emotionalism.

**Patience** [pasi'ã:s] (**-, -n**) *f:* **~n legen** to play patience.

**Patient(in)** [patsi'ɛnt(ɪn)] *m(f)* patient.

**Patin** ['pa:tɪn] *f* godmother.

**Patina** ['pa:tina] (**-**) *f* patina.

**Patriarch** [patri'arç] (**-en, -en**) *m* patriarch.

**patriarchalisch** [patriar'ça:lɪʃ] *adj* patriarchal.

**Patriot(in)** [patri'o:t(ɪn)] (**-en, -en**) *m(f)* patriot; **p~isch** *adj* patriotic.

**Patriotismus** [patrio'tɪsmʊs] *m* patriotism.

**Patron** [pa'tro:n] (**-s, -e**) *m* patron; (*ECCL*) patron saint.

**Patrone** (**-, -n**) *f* cartridge.

**Patronenhülse** *f* cartridge case.

**Patronin** *f* patroness; (*ECCL*) patron saint.

**Patrouille** [pa'trʊljə] (**-, -n**) *f* patrol.

**patrouillieren** [patrʊl'ji:rən] *vi* to patrol.

**patsch** [patʃ] *interj* splash!

**Patsche** (**-, -n**) (*umg*) *f* (*Händchen*) paw; (*Fliegen~*) swat; (*Feuer~*) beater; (*Bedrängnis*) mess, jam.

**patschen** *vi* to smack, slap; (*im Wasser*) to splash.

**patschnaß** *adj* soaking wet.

**Patt** [pat] (**-s, -s**) *nt* (*lit, fig*) stalemate.

**patzen** ['patsən] (*umg*) *vi* to boob (*BRIT*), goof (*US*).

**patzig** ['patsɪç] (*umg*) *adj* cheeky, saucy.

**Pauke** ['paʊkə] (**-, -n**) *f* kettledrum; **auf die ~ hauen** to live it up; **mit ~n und Trompeten durchfallen** (*umg*) to fail dismally.

**pauken** *vt, vi* (*SCH*) to swot (*BRIT*), cram.

**Pauker** (**-s, -**) (*umg*) *m* teacher.

**pausbäckig** ['paʊsbɛkɪç] *adj* chubby-cheeked.

**pauschal** [paʊ'ʃa:l] *adj* (*Kosten*) inclusive; (*einheitlich*) flat-rate *attrib*; (*Urteil*) sweeping; **die Werkstatt berechnet ~ pro Inspektion 250 DM** the garage has a flat rate of 250 marks per service.

**Pauschale** (**-, -n**) *f* flat rate; (*vorläufig geschätzter Betrag*) estimated amount.

**Pauschal-** *zW:* **~gebühr** *f* flat rate; **~preis** *m* all-in price; **~reise** *f* package tour; **~summe** *f* lump sum; **~versicherung** *f* comprehensive insurance.

**Pause** ['paʊzə] (**-, -n**) *f* break; (*THEAT*) interval; (*das Innehalten*) pause; (*MUS*) rest; (*Kopie*) tracing.

**pausen** *vt* to trace.

**Pausen-** *zW:* **~brot** *nt* sandwich (*to eat at break*); **~hof** *m* playground, schoolyard (*US*); **p~los** *adj* nonstop; **~zeichen** *nt* (*RUNDF*) call sign; (*MUS*) rest.

**pausieren** [paʊ'si:rən] *vi* to make a break.

**Pauspapier** ['paʊspapi:r] *nt* tracing paper.

**Pavian** ['pa:via:n] (**-s, -e**) *m* baboon.

**Pazifik** [pa'tsi:fɪk] (**-s**) *m* Pacific.

**pazifisch** *adj* Pacific; **der P~e Ozean** the Pacific (Ocean).

**Pazifist(in)** [patsi'fɪst(ɪn)] *m(f)* pacifist; **p~isch** *adj* pacifist.

**PC** *m abk* (= *Personalcomputer*) PC.

**PDS** *f abk* (= *Partei des Demokratischen Sozialismus*) German Socialist Party.

---

*The* **PDS** *(Partei des Demokratischen Sozialismus) was founded in 1989 as the successor of the SED, the former East German Communist Party. Its aims are the establishment of a democratic socialist society and to hold a position in the German political scene left of the* **SPD**.

**Pech** [pɛç] (-s, -e) nt pitch; (fig) bad luck; ~ **haben** to be unlucky; **die beiden halten zusammen wie** ~ **und Schwefel** (umg) the two are inseparable; ~ **gehabt!** tough! (umg); **p~schwarz** adj pitch-black; ~**strähne** (umg) f unlucky patch; ~**vogel** (umg) m unlucky person.

**Pedal** [pe'daːl] (-s, -e) nt pedal; **in die** ~**e treten** to pedal (hard).

**Pedant** [pe'dant] m pedant.

**Pedanterie** [pedantə'riː] f pedantry.

**pedantisch** adj pedantic.

**Peddigrohr** ['pɛdɪçroːr] nt cane.

**Pediküre** [pedi'kyːrə] (-, -n) f (Fußpflege) pedicure; (Fußpflegerin) chiropodist.

**Pegel** ['peːgəl] (-s, -) m water gauge; (Geräusch~) noise level; ~**stand** m water level.

**peilen** ['paɪlən] vt to get a fix on; **die Lage** ~ (umg) to see how the land lies.

**Pein** [paɪn] (-) f agony, suffering.

**peinigen** vt to torture; (plagen) to torment.

**peinlich** adj (unangenehm) embarrassing, awkward, painful; (genau) painstaking; **in seinem Zimmer herrschte** ~**e Ordnung** his room was meticulously tidy; **er vermied es** ~**st, davon zu sprechen** he was at pains not to talk about it; **P~keit** f painfulness, awkwardness; (Genauigkeit) scrupulousness.

**Peitsche** ['paɪtʃə] (-, -n) f whip.

**peitschen** vt to whip; (Regen) to lash.

**Peitschenhieb** m lash.

**Pekinese** [peki'neːzə] (-n, -n) m Pekinese, peke (umg).

**Peking** ['peːkɪŋ] (-s) nt Peking.

**Pelikan** ['peːlikaːn] (-s, -e) m pelican.

**Pelle** ['pɛlə] (-, -n) f skin; **der Chef sitzt mir auf der** ~ (umg) I've got the boss on my back.

**pellen** vt to skin, peel.

**Pellkartoffeln** pl jacket potatoes pl.

**Pelz** [pɛlts] (-es, -e) m fur.

**Pendel** ['pɛndəl] (-s, -) nt pendulum.

**pendeln** vi (schwingen) to swing (to and fro); (Zug, Fähre etc) to shuttle; (Mensch) to commute; (fig) to fluctuate.

**Pendelverkehr** m shuttle service; (Berufsverkehr) commuter traffic.

**Pendler(in)** ['pɛndlər(ɪn)] (-s, -) m(f) commuter.

**penetrant** [pene'trant] adj sharp; (Person) pushing; **das schmeckt/riecht** ~ **nach Knoblauch** it has a very strong taste/smell of garlic.

**penibel** [pe'niːbəl] adj pernickety (BRIT) (umg), persnickety (US) (umg), precise.

**Penis** ['peːnɪs] (-, -se) m penis.

**Pennbruder** ['pɛnbruːdər] (umg) m tramp (BRIT), hobo (US).

**Penne** (-, -n) (umg) f (SCH) school.

**pennen** (umg) vi to kip.

**Penner** (-s, -) (pej: umg) m tramp (BRIT), hobo (US).

**Pension** [pɛnzi'oːn] f (Geld) pension; (Ruhestand) retirement; (für Gäste) boarding house, guesthouse; **halbe/volle** ~ half/full board; **in** ~ **gehen** to retire.

**Pensionär(in)** [pɛnzio'nɛːr(ɪn)] (-s, -e) m(f) pensioner.

**Pensionat** (-(e)s, -e) nt boarding school.

**pensionieren** [pɛnzio'niːrən] vt to pension (off); **sich** ~ **lassen** to retire.

**pensioniert** adj retired.

**Pensionierung** f retirement.

**Pensions-** zW: **p~berechtigt** adj entitled to a pension; ~**gast** m boarder, paying guest; **p~reif** (umg) adj ready for retirement.

**Pensum** ['pɛnzʊm] (-s, **Pensen**) nt quota; (SCH) curriculum.

**Peperoni** [pepe'roːni] pl chillies pl.

**per** [pɛr] präp +akk by, per; (pro) by; ~ **Adresse** (COMM) care of, c/o; **mit jdm** ~ **du sein** (umg) to be on first-name terms with sb.

**Perfekt** ['pɛrfɛkt] (-(e)s, -e) nt perfect.

**perfekt** [pɛr'fɛkt] adj perfect; (abgemacht) settled; **die Sache** ~ **machen** to clinch the deal; **der Vertrag ist** ~ the contract is all settled.

**perfektionieren** [pɛrfɛktsio'niːrən] vt to perfect.

**Perfektionismus** [pɛrfɛktsio'nɪsmʊs] m perfectionism.

**perforieren** [pɛrfo'riːrən] vt to perforate.

**Pergament** [pɛrga'mɛnt] nt parchment; ~**papier** nt greaseproof paper (BRIT), wax(ed) paper (US).

**Pergola** ['pɛrgola] (-, **Pergolen**) f pergola, arbour (BRIT), arbor (US).

**Periode** [peri'oːdə] (-, -n) f period; **0,33** ~ 0.33 recurring.

**periodisch** [peri'oːdɪʃ] adj periodic; (dezimal) recurring.

**Peripherie** [perife'riː] f periphery; (um Stadt) outskirts pl; (MATH) circumference; ~**gerät** nt (COMPUT) peripheral.

**Perle** ['pɛrlə] (-, -n) f (lit, fig) pearl; (Glas~, Holz~, Tropfen) bead; (veraltet: umg: Hausgehilfin) maid.

**perlen** vi to sparkle; (Tropfen) to trickle.

**Perlenkette** f pearl necklace.

**Perlhuhn** nt guinea fowl.

**Perlmutt** ['pɛrlmʊt] (-s) nt mother-of-pearl.

**Perlon** ® ['pɛrlɔn] (-s) nt ≈ nylon.

**Perlwein** m sparkling wine.

**perplex** [pɛr'plɛks] adj dumbfounded.

**Perser** ['pɛrzər] (-s, -) m (Person) Persian; (umg: Teppich) Persian carpet.

**Perserin** f Persian.

**Persianer** [pɛrzi'aːnər] (-s, -) m Persian lamb (coat).

**Persien** ['pɛrziən] (-s) nt Persia.

**Persiflage** [pɛrzi'flaːʒə] (-, -n) f: ~ (+gen od auf +akk) pastiche (of), satire (on).

**persisch** adj Persian; **P~er Golf** Persian Gulf.

**Person** [pɛr'zoːn] (-, -en) f person; (pej: Frau) female; **sie ist Köchin und Haushälterin in einer** ~ she is cook and housekeeper rolled into one; **ich für meine** ~ personally I.

**Personal** [pɛrzo'naːl] (-s) nt personnel; (Bedienung) servants pl; ~abbau m staff cuts pl; ~akte f personal file; ~angaben pl particulars pl; ~ausweis m identity card; ~bogen m personal record; ~büro nt personnel (department); ~chef m personnel manager; ~computer m personal computer.

**Personalien** [pɛrzo'naːliən] pl particulars pl.

**Personalität** [pɛrzonali'tɛːt] f personality.

**Personal-** zW: ~kosten pl staff costs; ~mangel m staff shortage; ~pronomen nt personal pronoun; ~reduzierung f staff reduction.

**personell** [pɛrzo'nɛl] adj staff attrib; ~e Veränderungen changes in personnel.

**Personen-** zW: ~aufzug m lift, elevator (US); ~beschreibung f (personal) description; ~gedächtnis nt memory for faces; ~gesellschaft f partnership; ~kraftwagen m private motorcar, automobile (US); ~kreis m group of people; ~kult m personality cult; ~schaden m injury to persons; ~verkehr m passenger services pl; ~waage f scales pl; ~zug m stopping train; passenger train.

**personifizieren** [pɛrzonifi'tsiːrən] vt to personify.

**persönlich** [pɛr'zøːnlıç] adj personal ♦ adv in person; personally; (auf Briefen) private (and confidential); ~ **haften** (COMM) to be personally liable; **P~keit** f personality; **P~keiten des öffentlichen Lebens** public figures.

**Perspektive** [pɛrspɛk'tiːvə] f perspective; **das eröffnet ganz neue** ~**n für uns** that opens new horizons for us.

**Pers. Ref.** abk (= Persönlicher Referent) personal representative.

**Peru** [pe'ruː] (-s) nt Peru.

**Peruaner(in)** [peru'aːnər(ın)] (-s, -) m(f) Peruvian.

**peruanisch** adj Peruvian.

**Perücke** [pe'rykə] (-, -n) f wig.

**pervers** [pɛr'vɛrs] adj perverse.

**Perversität** [pɛrvɛrzi'tɛːt] f perversity.

**Pessar** [pɛ'saːr] (-s, -e) nt pessary; (zur Empfängnisverhütung) cap, diaphragm.

**Pessimismus** [pɛsi'mısmʊs] m pessimism.

**Pessimist(in)** [pɛsi'mıst(ın)] m(f) pessimist; **p~isch** adj pessimistic.

**Pest** [pɛst] (-) f plague; **jdn/etw wie die** ~ **hassen** (umg) to loathe (and detest) sb/sth.

**Petersilie** [petər'ziːliə] f parsley.

**Petrochemie** [petroːçe'miː] f petrochemistry.

**Petrodollar** [petro'dɔlar] m petrodollar.

**Petroleum** [pe'troːleʊm] (-s) nt paraffin (BRIT), kerosene (US).

**petzen** ['pɛtsən] (umg) vi to tell tales; **er petzt immer** he always tells.

**Pf** abk = **Pfennig.**

**Pfad** [pfaːt] (-(e)s, -e) m path; ~finder m Boy Scout; **er ist bei den** ~findern he's in the (Boy) Scouts; ~finderin f Girl Guide.

**Pfaffe** ['pfafə] (-n, -n) (pej) m cleric, parson.

**Pfahl** [pfaːl] (-(e)s, ⁀e) m post, stake; ~bau m pile dwelling.

**Pfalz** [pfalts] (-, -en) f (GEOG) Palatinate.

**Pfälzer(in)** ['pfɛltsər(ın)] (-s, -) m(f) person from the Palatinate.

**pfälzisch** adj Palatine, of the (Rhineland) Palatinate.

**Pfand** [pfant] (-(e)s, ⁀er) nt pledge, security; (Flaschen~) deposit; (im Spiel) forfeit; (fig: der Liebe etc) pledge; ~brief m bond.

**pfänden** ['pfɛndən] vt to seize, impound.

**Pfänderspiel** nt game of forfeits.

**Pfand-** zW: ~haus nt pawnshop; ~leiher (-s, -) m pawnbroker; ~recht nt lien; ~schein m pawn ticket.

**Pfändung** ['pfɛndʊŋ] f seizure, distraint (form).

**Pfanne** ['pfanə] (-, -n) f (frying) pan; **jdn in die** ~ **hauen** (umg) to tear a strip off sb.

**Pfannkuchen** m pancake; (Berliner) doughnut (BRIT), donut (US).

**Pfarrei** [pfar'raı] f parish.

**Pfarrer** (-s, -) m priest; (evangelisch) vicar; (von Freikirchen) minister.

**Pfarrhaus** nt vicarage.

**Pfau** [pfaʊ] (-(e)s, -en) m peacock.

**Pfauenauge** nt peacock butterfly.

**Pfd.** abk (= Pfund) ≈ lb.

**Pfeffer** ['pfɛfər] (-s, -) m pepper; **er soll bleiben, wo der** ~ **wächst!** (umg) he can take a running jump; ~korn nt peppercorn; ~kuchen m gingerbread; ~minz (-es, -e) nt peppermint; ~minze f peppermint (plant); ~mühle f pepper mill.

**pfeffern** vt to pepper; (umg: werfen) to fling; **gepfefferte Preise/Witze** steep prices/spicy jokes.

**Pfeife** ['pfaıfə] (-, -n) f whistle; (Tabak~, Orgel~) pipe; **nach jds** ~ **tanzen** to dance to sb's tune.

**pfeifen** unreg vt, vi to whistle; **auf dem letzten Loch** ~ (umg: erschöpft sein) to be on one's last legs; (: finanziell) to be on one's beam ends; **ich pfeif(e) drauf!** (umg) I don't give a damn!; **P~stopfer** m tamper.

**Pfeifer** (-s, -) m piper.

**Pfeifkonzert** nt catcalls pl.

**Pfeil** [pfaıl] (-(e)s, -e) m arrow.

**Pfeiler** ['pfaılər] (-s, -) m pillar, prop; (Brücken~) pier.

**Pfennig** ['pfɛnıç] (-(e)s, -e) m pfennig (hundredth part of a mark); ~absatz m stiletto

heel; **~fuchser (-s, -)** (*umg*) *m* skinflint.
**pferchen** ['pfɛrçən] *vt* to cram, pack.
**Pferd** [pfeːrt] **(-(e)s, -e)** *nt* horse; **wie ein
~ arbeiten** (*umg*) to work like a Trojan; **mit
ihm kann man ~e stehlen** (*umg*) he's a great
sport; **auf das falsche/richtige ~ setzen** (*lit,
fig*) to back the wrong/right horse.
**Pferde-** *zW:* **~äpfel** *pl* horse droppings *pl od*
dung *sing*; **~fuß** *m:* **die Sache hat aber einen
~fuß** there's just one snag; **~rennen** *nt*
horse-race; (*Sportart*) horse-racing;
**~schwanz** *m* (*Frisur*) ponytail; **~stall** *m*
stable; **~stärke** *f* horsepower.
**Pfiff (-(e)s, -e)** *m* whistle; (*Kniff*) trick.
**pfiff** *etc* [pfɪf] *vb siehe* **pfeifen.**
**Pfifferling** ['pfɪfərlɪŋ] *m* yellow chanterelle;
**keinen ~ wert** not worth a thing.
**pfiffig** *adj* smart.
**Pfingsten** ['pfɪŋstən] **(-, -)** *nt* Whitsun.
**Pfingstrose** *f* peony.
**Pfingstsonntag** *m* Whit Sunday, Pentecost
(*REL*).
**Pfirsich** ['pfɪrzɪç] **(-s, -e)** *m* peach.
**Pflanze** ['pflantsə] **(-, -n)** *f* plant.
**pflanzen** *vt* to plant ♦ *vr* (*umg*) to plonk o.s.
**Pflanzenfett** *nt* vegetable fat.
**Pflanzenschutzmittel** *nt* pesticide.
**pflanzlich** *adj* vegetable.
**Pflanzung** *f* plantation.
**Pflaster** ['pflastər] **(-s, -)** *nt* plaster; (*Straßen~*)
pavement (*BRIT*), sidewalk (*US*); **ein teures
~** (*umg*) a pricey place; **ein heißes ~** a
dangerous *od* unsafe place; **p~müde** *adj*
dead on one's feet.
**pflastern** *vt* to pave.
**Pflasterstein** *m* paving stone.
**Pflaume** ['pflaumə] **(-, -n)** *f* plum; (*umg:
Mensch*) twit (*BRIT*).
**Pflaumenmus** *nt* plum jam.
**Pflege** ['pfleːgə] **(-, -n)** *f* care; (*von Idee*)
cultivation; (*Kranken~*) nursing; **jdn/etw in
~ nehmen** to look after sb/sth; **in ~ sein**
(*Kind*) to be fostered out; **p~bedürftig** *adj*
needing care; **~eltern** *pl* foster parents *pl*;
**~fall** *m* case for nursing; **~geld** *nt* (*für
~kinder*) boarding-out allowance; (*für
Kranke*) attendance allowance; **~heim** *nt*
nursing home; **~kind** *nt* foster child;
**p~leicht** *adj* easy-care; **~mutter** *f* foster
mother.
**pflegen** *vt* to look after; (*Kranke*) to nurse;
(*Beziehungen*) to foster ♦ *vi* (*gewöhnlich tun*):
**sie pflegte zu sagen** she used to say.
**Pfleger** **(-s, -)** *m* (*im Krankenhaus*) orderly;
(*voll qualifiziert*) male nurse; **~in** *f* nurse.
**Pflegesatz** *m* hospital and nursing charges
*pl*.
**Pflegevater** *m* foster father.
**Pflegeversicherung** *f* geriatric care
insurance.
**Pflicht** [pflɪçt] **(-, -en)** *f* duty; (*SPORT*)
compulsory section; **Rechte und ~en** rights

and responsibilities; **p~bewußt** *adj*
conscientious; **~bewußtsein** *nt* sense of
duty; **~fach** *nt* (*SCH*) compulsory subject;
**~gefühl** *nt* sense of duty; **p~gemäß** *adj*
dutiful **p~vergessen** *adj* irresponsible;
**~versicherung** *f* compulsory insurance.
**Pflock** [pflɔk] **(-(e)s, ⁝e)** *m* peg; (*für Tiere*)
stake.
**pflog** *etc* [pfloːk] *vb* (*veraltet*) *siehe* **pflegen.**
**pflücken** ['pflʏkən] *vt* to pick.
**Pflug** [pfluːk] **(-(e)s, ⁝e)** *m* plough (*BRIT*), plow
(*US*).
**pflügen** ['pflyːgən] *vt* to plough (*BRIT*), plow
(*US*).
**Pflugschar** *f* ploughshare (*BRIT*), plowshare
(*US*).
**Pforte** ['pfɔrtə] **(-, -n)** *f* (*Tor*) gate.
**Pförtner** ['pfœrtnər] **(-s, -)** *m* porter,
doorkeeper, doorman.
**Pförtnerin** *f* doorkeeper, porter.
**Pfosten** ['pfɔstən] **(-s, -)** *m* post; (*senkrechter
Balken*) upright.
**Pfote** ['pfoːtə] **(-, -n)** *f* paw; (*umg: Schrift*)
scrawl.
**Pfropf** [pfrɔpf] **(-(e)s, -e)** *m* (*Flaschen~*)
stopper; (*Blut~*) clot.
**Pfropfen (-s, -)** *m* = **Pfropf.**
**pfropfen** *vt* (*stopfen*) to cram; (*Baum*) to graft;
**gepfropft voll** crammed full.
**pfui** [pfʊi] *interj* ugh!; (*na na*) tut tut!; (*Buhruf*)
boo!; **~ Teufel!** (*umg*) ugh!, yuck!
**Pfund** [pfʊnt] **(-(e)s, -e)** *nt* (*Gewicht, FIN*)
pound; **das ~ sinkt** sterling *od* the pound is
falling.
**pfundig** (*umg*) *adj* great.
**Pfundskerl** ['pfʊntskɛrl] (*umg*) *m* great guy.
**pfundweise** *adv* by the pound.
**pfuschen** ['pfʊʃən] *vi* to bungle; (*einen Fehler
machen*) to slip up.
**Pfuscher(in)** ['pfʊʃər(ɪn)] **(-s, -)** (*umg*) *m(f)*
sloppy worker; (*Kur~*) quack.
**Pfuscherei** [pfʊʃəˈraɪ] (*umg*) *f* sloppy work;
(*Kur~*) quackery.
**Pfütze** ['pfʏtsə] **(-, -n)** *f* puddle.
**PH (-, -s)** *f abk* = **Pädagogische Hochschule.**
**Phänomen** [fɛnoˈmeːn] **(-s, -e)** *nt*
phenomenon; **p~al** [-'naːl] *adj* phenomenal.
**Phantasie** [fantaˈziː] *f* imagination; **in seiner
~** in his mind; **~gebilde** *nt* (*Einbildung*)
figment of the imagination; **p~los** *adj*
unimaginative.
**phantasieren** [fantaˈziːrən] *vi* to fantasize;
(*MED*) to be delirious.
**phantasievoll** *adj* imaginative.
**Phantast** [fanˈtast] **(-en, -en)** *m* dreamer,
visionary.
**phantastisch** *adj* fantastic.
**Phantom** [fanˈtoːm] **(-s, -e)** *nt* (*Trugbild*)
phantom; **einem ~ nachjagen** (*fig*) to tilt at
windmills; **~bild** *nt* Identikit ® picture.
**Pharisäer** [fariˈzɛːər] **(-s, -)** *m* (*lit, fig*) pharisee.
**Pharmazeut(in)** [farmaˈtsɔyt(ɪn)] **(-en, -en)**

*m(f)* pharmacist.

**pharmazeutisch** *adj* pharmaceutical.

**Pharmazie** *f* pharmacy, pharmaceutics *sing*.

**Phase** ['fa:zə] (-, -n) *f* phase.

**Philanthrop** [filan'tro:p] (-en, -en) *m* philanthropist; **p~isch** *adj* philanthropic.

**Philharmoniker** [fɪlhar'mo:nikər] (-s, -) *m*: **die** ~ the philharmonic (orchestra) *sing*.

**Philatelist(in)** [filate'lɪst(ɪn)] (-en, -en) *m(f)* philatelist.

**Philippine** [fɪlɪ'pi:nə] (-n, -n) *m* Filipino.

**Philippinen** *pl* Philippines *pl*, Philippine Islands *pl*.

**Philippinin** *f* Filipino.

**philippinisch** *adj* Filipino.

**Philologe** [filo'lo:gə] (-n, -n) *m* philologist.

**Philologie** [filolo'gi:] *f* philology.

**Philologin** *f* philologist.

**Philosoph(in)** [filo'zo:f(ɪn)] (-en, -en) *m(f)* philosopher.

**Philosophie** [filozo'fi:] *f* philosophy.

**philosophieren** [filozo'fi:rən] *vi*: ~ **(über** +*akk*) to philosophize (about).

**philosophisch** *adj* philosophical.

**Phlegma** ['flɛgma] (-s) *nt* lethargy.

**phlegmatisch** [flɛ'gma:tɪʃ] *adj* lethargic.

**Phobie** [fo'bi:] *f*: ~ **(vor** +*dat*) phobia (about).

**Phonetik** [fo'ne:tɪk] *f* phonetics *sing*.

**phonetisch** *adj* phonetic.

**Phonotypistin** [fonoty'pɪstɪn] *f* audiotypist.

**Phosphat** [fɔs'fa:t] (-(e)s, -e) *nt* phosphate.

**Phosphor** ['fɔsfɔr] (-s) *m* phosphorus.

**phosphoreszieren** [fɔsfɔres'tsi:rən] *vt* to phosphoresce.

**Photo** *etc* ['fo:to] = **Foto** *etc*.

**Phrase** ['fra:zə] (-, -n) *f* phrase; (*pej*) hollow phrase; ~**n dreschen** (*umg*) to churn out one cliché after another.

**pH-Wert** [pe:'ha:vert] *m* pH value.

**Physik** [fy'zi:k] *f* physics *sing*.

**physikalisch** [fyzi'ka:lɪʃ] *adj* of physics.

**Physiker(in)** ['fy:zikər(ɪn)] (-s, -) *m(f)* physicist.

**Physikum** ['fy:zikʊm] (-s) *nt* (*UNIV*) *preliminary examination in medicine*.

**Physiologe** [fyzio'lo:gə] (-n, -n) *m* physiologist.

**Physiologie** [fyziolo'gi:] *f* physiology.

**Physiologin** *f* physiologist.

**physisch** ['fy:zɪʃ] *adj* physical.

**Pianist(in)** [pia'nɪst(ɪn)] *m(f)* pianist.

**picheln** ['pɪçəln] (*umg*) *vi* to booze.

**Pickel** ['pɪkəl] (-s, -) *m* pimple; (*Werkzeug*) pickaxe; (*Berg~*) ice axe.

**pick(e)lig** *adj* pimply.

**picken** ['pɪkən] *vt* to peck ♦ *vi*: ~ **(nach)** to peck (at).

**Picknick** ['pɪknɪk] (-s, -e *od* -s) *nt* picnic; ~ **machen** to have a picnic.

**piekfein** ['pi:k'faɪn] (*umg*) *adj* posh.

**Piemont** [pie'mɔnt] (-s) *nt* Piedmont.

**piepen** ['pi:pən] *vi* to chirp; (*Funkgerät etc*) to

bleep; **bei dir piept's wohl!** (*umg*) are you off your head?; **es war zum P~!** (*umg*) it was a scream!

**piepsen** ['pi:psən] *vi* = **piepen**.

**Piepser** (*umg*) *m* pager, paging device.

**Piepsstimme** *f* squeaky voice.

**Piepton** *m* bleep.

**Pier** [pi:ər] (-s, -s *od* -e) *m* jetty, pier.

**piesacken** ['pi:zakən] (*umg*) *vt* to torment.

**Pietät** [pie'tɛ:t] *f* piety; reverence; **p~los** *adj* impious, irreverent.

**Pigment** [pɪg'mɛnt] (-(e)s, -e) *nt* pigment.

**Pik** [pi:k] (-s, -s) *nt* (*KARTEN*) spades; **einen** ~ **auf jdn haben** (*umg*) to have it in for sb.

**pikant** [pi'kant] *adj* spicy, piquant; (*anzüglich*) suggestive.

**Pike** (-, -n) *f*: **etw von der** ~ **auf lernen** (*fig*) to learn sth from the bottom up.

**pikiert** [pi'ki:rt] *adj* offended.

**Pikkolo** ['pɪkolo] (-s, -s) *m* trainee waiter; (*auch*: ~**flasche**) *quarter bottle of champagne*; (*MUS*: *auch*: ~**flöte**) piccolo.

**Piktogramm** [pɪkto'gram] *nt* pictogram.

**Pilger(in)** ['pɪlgər(ɪn)] (-s, -) *m(f)* pilgrim; ~**fahrt** *f* pilgrimage.

**pilgern** *vi* to make a pilgrimage; (*umg*: *gehen*) to wend one's way.

**Pille** ['pɪlə] (-, -n) *f* pill.

**Pilot(in)** [pi'lo:t(ɪn)] (-en, -en) *m(f)* pilot; ~**enschein** *m* pilot's licence (*BRIT*) *od* license (*US*).

**Pils** [pɪls] (-, -) *nt* Pilsner (lager).

**Pils(e)ner** [pɪlz(ə)nər] (-s, -) *nt* Pilsner (lager).

**Pilz** [pɪlts] (-es, -e) *m* fungus; (*eßbar*) mushroom; (*giftig*) toadstool; **wie** ~**e aus dem Boden schießen** (*fig*) to mushroom; ~**krankheit** *f* fungal disease.

**Pimmel** ['pɪməl] (-s, -) (*umg*) *m* (*Penis*) willie.

**pingelig** ['pɪŋəlɪç] (*umg*) *adj* fussy.

**Pinguin** ['pɪŋgui:n] (-s, -e) *m* penguin.

**Pinie** ['pi:niə] *f* pine.

**Pinkel** (-s, -) (*umg*) *m*: **ein feiner** *od* **vornehmer** ~ a swell, Lord Muck (*BRIT*) (*umg*).

**pinkeln** ['pɪŋkəln] (*umg*) *vi* to pee.

**Pinnwand** ['pɪnvant] *f* pinboard.

**Pinsel** ['pɪnzəl] (-s, -) *m* paintbrush.

**pinseln** (*umg*) *vt*, *vi* to paint; (*pej*: *malen*) to daub.

**Pinte** ['pɪntə] (-, -n) (*umg*) *f* (*Lokal*) boozer (*BRIT*).

**Pinzette** [pɪn'tsɛtə] *f* tweezers *pl*.

**Pionier** [pio'ni:r] (-s, -e) *m* pioneer; (*MIL*) sapper, engineer; ~**arbeit** *f* pioneering work; ~**unternehmen** *nt* pioneer company.

**Pipi** [pi'pi:] (-s, -s) *nt od m* (*Kindersprache*) wee(-wee).

**Pirat** [pi'ra:t] (-en, -en) *m* pirate.

**Piratensender** *m* pirate radio station.

**Pirsch** [pɪrʃ] (-) *f* stalking.

**pissen** ['pɪsən] (*umg!*) *vi* to (have a) piss (*!*); (*regnen*) to piss down (*!*).

**Pistazie** [pɪs'ta:tsiə] (-, -n) *f* pistachio.

**Piste** ['pɪstə] (-, -n) f (SKI) run, piste; (AVIAT) runway.

**Pistole** [pɪs'toːlə] (-, -n) f pistol; **wie aus der ~ geschossen** (fig) like a shot; **jdm die ~ auf die Brust setzen** (fig) to hold a pistol to sb's head.

**pitsch(e)naß** ['pɪtʃ(ə)'nas] (umg) adj soaking (wet).

**Pizza** ['pɪtsa] (-, -s) f pizza.

**PKW** m abk = **Pkw.**

**Pkw** (-(s), -(s)) m abk = **Personenkraftwagen.**

**Pl.** abk (= Plural) pl.; (= Platz) Sq.

**Plackerei** [plakə'raɪ] f drudgery.

**plädieren** [plɛ'diːrən] vi to plead.

**Plädoyer** [plɛdoa'jeː] (-s, -s) nt speech for the defence; (fig) plea.

**Plage** ['plaːgə] (-, -n) f plague; (Mühe) nuisance; **~geist** m pest, nuisance.

**plagen** vt to torment ♦ vr to toil, slave.

**Plagiat** [plagi'aːt] (-(e)s, -e) nt plagiarism.

**Plakat** [pla'kaːt] (-(e)s, -e) nt poster; (aus Pappe) placard.

**plakativ** [plaka'tiːf] adj striking, bold.

**Plakatwand** f hoarding, billboard (US).

**Plakette** [pla'kɛtə] (-, -n) f (Abzeichen) badge; (Münze) commemorative coin; (an Wänden) plaque.

**Plan** [plaːn] (-(e)s, ⁻e) m plan; (Karte) map; **Pläne schmieden** to make plans; **nach ~ verlaufen** to go according to plan; **jdn auf den ~ rufen** (fig) to bring sb into the arena.

**Plane** (-, -n) f tarpaulin.

**planen** vt to plan; (Mord etc) to plot.

**Planer(in)** (-s, -) m(f) planner.

**Planet** [pla'neːt] (-en, -en) m planet.

**Planetenbahn** f orbit (of a planet).

**planieren** [pla'niːrən] vt to level off.

**Planierraupe** f bulldozer.

**Planke** ['plaŋkə] (-, -n) f plank.

**Plänkelei** [plɛŋkə'laɪ] f skirmish(ing).

**plänkeln** ['plɛŋkəln] vi to skirmish.

**Plankton** ['plaŋktɔn] (-s) nt plankton.

**planlos** adj (Vorgehen) unsystematic; (Umherlaufen) aimless.

**planmäßig** adj according to plan; (methodisch) systematic; (EISENB) scheduled.

**Planschbecken** ['planʃbɛkən] nt paddling pool.

**planschen** vi to splash.

**Plansoll** nt output target.

**Planstelle** f post.

**Plantage** [plan'taːʒə] (-, -n) f plantation.

**Planung** f planning.

**Planwagen** m covered wagon.

**Planwirtschaft** f planned economy.

**Plappermaul** (umg) nt (Kind) chatterbox.

**plappern** ['plapərn] vi to chatter.

**plärren** ['plɛrən] vi (Mensch) to cry, whine; (Radio) to blare.

**Plasma** ['plasma] (-s, Plasmen) nt plasma.

**Plastik¹** ['plastɪk] f sculpture.

**Plastik²** ['plastɪk] (-s) nt (Kunststoff) plastic; **~folie** f plastic film; **~geschoß** nt plastic bullet; **~tüte** f plastic bag.

**Plastilin** [plasti'liːn] (-s) nt Plasticine ®.

**plastisch** ['plastɪʃ] adj plastic; **stell dir das ~ vor!** just picture it!

**Platane** [pla'taːnə] (-, -n) f plane (tree).

**Platin** ['plaːtiːn] (-s) nt platinum.

**Platitüde** [plati'tyːdə] (-, -n) f platitude.

**platonisch** [pla'toːnɪʃ] adj platonic.

**platsch** [platʃ] interj splash!

**platschen** vi to splash.

**plätschern** ['plɛtʃərn] vi to babble.

**platschnaß** adj drenched.

**platt** [plat] adj flat; (umg: überrascht) flabbergasted; (fig: geistlos) flat, boring; **einen P~en haben** to have a flat (umg), have a flat tyre (BRIT) od tire (US).

**plattdeutsch** adj Low German.

**Platte** (-, -n) f (Speisen~, PHOT, TECH) plate; (Stein~) flag; (Kachel) tile; (Schall~) record; **kalte ~** cold dish; **die ~ kenne ich schon** (umg) I've heard all that before.

**Plätteisen** nt iron.

**plätten** vt, vi to iron.

**Platten-** zW: **~leger** (-s, -) m paver; **~spieler** m record player; **~teller** m turntable.

**Plattform** f platform; (fig: Grundlage) basis.

**Plattfuß** m flat foot; (Reifen) flat tyre (BRIT) od tire (US).

**Platz** [plats] (-es, ⁻e) m place; (Sitz~) seat; (Raum) space, room; (in Stadt) square; (Sport~) playing field; **~ machen** to get out of the way; **~ nehmen** to take a seat; **jdm ~ machen** to make room for sb; **auf ~ zwei** in second place; **fehl am ~e sein** to be out of place; **seinen ~ behaupten** to stand one's ground; **das erste Hotel am ~** the best hotel in town; **auf die Plätze, fertig, los!** (beim Sport) on your marks, get set, go!; **einen Spieler vom ~ stellen** od **verweisen** (SPORT) to send a player off; **~angst** f (MED) agoraphobia; (umg) claustrophobia; **~angst haben/bekommen** (umg) to feel/get claustrophobic; **~anweiser(in)** (-s, -) m(f) usher(ette).

**Plätzchen** ['plɛtsçən] nt spot; (Gebäck) biscuit.

**platzen** vi (Hilfsverb sein) to burst; (Bombe) to explode; (Naht, Hose, Haut) to split; (umg: scheitern: Geschäft) to fall through; (: Freundschaft) to break up; (: Theorie, Verschwörung) to collapse; (: Wechsel) to bounce; **vor Wut ~** (umg) to be bursting with anger.

**Platz-** zW: **~karte** f seat reservation; **~konzert** nt open-air concert; **~mangel** m lack of space; **~patrone** f blank cartridge; **~regen** m downpour; **~sparend** adj space-saving; **~verweis** m sending-off; **~wart** m (SPORT) groundsman (BRIT), groundskeeper (US); **~wunde** f cut.

**Plauderei** [plaʊdə'raɪ] f chat, conversation.

**plaudern** ['plaʊdərn] *vi* to chat, talk.
**Plausch** [plaʊʃ] (-(e)s, -e) (*umg*) *m* chat.
**plausibel** [plaʊ'ziːbəl] *adj* plausible.
**Playback** ['pleɪbæk] (-s, -s) *nt* (*Verfahren: Schallplatte*) double-tracking; (*TV*) miming.
**plazieren** [pla'tsiːrən] *vt* to place ♦ *vr* (*SPORT*) to be placed; (*TENNIS*) to be seeded; (*umg: sich setzen, stellen*) to plant o.s.
**Plebejer(in)** [ple'beːjər(ɪn)] (-s, -) *m(f)* plebeian.
**plebejisch** [ple'beːjɪʃ] *adj* plebeian.
**pleite** ['plaɪtə] (*umg*) *adj* broke; **P~** (-, -n) *f* bankruptcy; (*umg: Reinfall*) flop; **P~ machen** to go bust.
**Pleitegeier** (*umg*) *m* (*drohende Pleite*) vulture; (*Bankrotteur*) bankrupt.
**plemplem** [plɛm'plɛm] (*umg*) *adj* nuts.
**Plenarsitzung** [ple'naːrzɪtsʊŋ] *f* plenary session.
**Plenum** ['pleːnʊm] (-s, Plenen) *nt* plenum.
**Pleuelstange** ['plɔʏəlʃtaŋə] *f* connecting rod.
**Plissee** [plɪ'seː] (-s, -s) *nt* pleat.
**Plombe** ['plɔmbə] (-, -n) *f* lead seal; (*Zahn~*) filling.
**plombieren** [plɔm'biːrən] *vt* to seal; (*Zahn*) to fill.
**Plotter** ['plɔtər] (-s, -s) *m* (*COMPUT*) plotter.
**plötzlich** ['plœtslɪç] *adj* sudden ♦ *adv* suddenly; **~er Kindstod** SIDS= *sudden infant death syndrome*.
**Pluderhose** ['pluːdərhoːzə] *f* harem trousers *pl*.
**plump** [plʊmp] *adj* clumsy; (*Hände*) coarse; (*Körper*) shapeless; **~e Annäherungsversuche** very obvious advances.
**plumpsen** (*umg*) *vi* to plump down, fall.
**Plumpsklo(sett)** (*umg*) *nt* earth closet.
**Plunder** ['plʊndər] (-s) *m* junk, rubbish.
**Plundergebäck** *nt* flaky pastry.
**plündern** ['plʏndərn] *vt* to plunder; (*Stadt*) to sack ♦ *vi* to plunder.
**Plünderung** ['plʏndərʊŋ] *f* plundering, sack, pillage.
**Plural** ['pluːraːl] (-s, -e) *m* plural; **im ~ stehen** to be (in the) plural.
**pluralistisch** [plura'lɪstɪʃ] *adj* pluralistic.
**plus** [plʊs] *adv* plus; **mit ~ minus null abschließen** (*COMM*) to break even; **P~** (-, -) *nt* plus; (*FIN*) profit; (*Vorteil*) advantage.
**Plüsch** [plyːʃ] (-(e)s, -e) *m* plush; **~tier** *nt* ≈ soft toy.
**Plus-** *zW:* **~pol** *m* (*ELEK*) positive pole; **~punkt** *m* (*SPORT*) point; (*fig*) point in sb's favour; **~quamperfekt** *nt* pluperfect.
**Plutonium** [plu'toːnium] (-s) *nt* plutonium.
**PLZ** *abk* = **Postleitzahl**.
**Pneu** [pnɔʏ] (-s, -s) *m abk* (= *Pneumatik*) tyre (*BRIT*), tire (*US*).
**Po** [poː] (-s, -s) (*umg*) *m* bum (*BRIT*), fanny (*US*).
**Pöbel** ['pøːbəl] (-s) *m* mob, rabble.
**Pöbelei** [pøːbə'laɪ] *f* vulgarity.

**pöbelhaft** *adj* low, vulgar.
**pochen** ['pɔxən] *vi* to knock; (*Herz*) to pound; **auf etw** *akk* **~** (*fig*) to insist on sth.
**Pocken** ['pɔkən] *pl* smallpox *sing*.
**Pocken(schutz)impfung** *f* smallpox vaccination.
**Podest** [po'dɛst] (-(e)s, -e) *nt od m* (*Sockel, fig*) pedestal; (*Podium*) platform.
**Podium** ['poːdiʊm] *nt* podium.
**Podiumsdiskussion** *f* panel discussion.
**Poesie** [poe'ziː] *f* poetry.
**Poet** [po'eːt] (-en, -en) *m* poet; **p~isch** *adj* poetic.
**pofen** ['poːfən] (*umg*) *vi* to kip (*BRIT*), doss.
**Pointe** [po'ɛ̃ːtə] (-, -n) *f* point; (*eines Witzes*) punch line.
**pointiert** [poɛ̃'tiːrt] *adj* trenchant, pithy.
**Pokal** [po'kaːl] (-s, -e) *m* goblet; (*SPORT*) cup; **~spiel** *nt* cup tie.
**Pökelfleisch** ['pøːkəlflaɪʃ] *nt* salt meat.
**pökeln** *vt* (*Fleisch, Fisch*) to pickle, salt.
**Poker** ['poːkər] (-s) *nt* poker.
**pokern** ['poːkərn] *vi* to play poker.
**Pol** [poːl] (-s, -e) *m* pole; **der ruhende ~** (*fig*) the calming influence.
**pol.** *abk* = **politisch; polizeilich**.
**polar** [po'laːr] *adj* polar.
**polarisieren** [polari'ziːrən] *vt, vr* to polarize.
**Polarkreis** *m* polar circle; **nördlicher/ südlicher ~** Arctic/Antarctic Circle.
**Polarstern** *m* Pole Star.
**Pole** ['poːlə] (-n, -n) *m* Pole.
**Polemik** [po'leːmɪk] (-, -en) *f* polemics *sing*.
**polemisch** *adj* polemical.
**polemisieren** [polemi'ziːrən] *vi* to polemicize.
**Polen** ['poːlən] (-s) *nt* Poland.
**Polente** (-) (*veraltet: umg*) *f* cops *pl*.
**Police** [po'liːs(ə)] (-, -n) *f* insurance policy.
**Polier** [po'liːr] (-s, -e) *m* foreman.
**polieren** *vt* to polish.
**Poliklinik** [poli'kliːnɪk] *f* outpatients (department) *sing*.
**Polin** *f* Pole, Polish woman.
**Politesse** [poli'tɛsə] (-, -n) *f* (*Frau*) ≈ traffic warden (*BRIT*).
**Politik** [poli'tiːk] *f* politics *sing*; (*eine bestimmte*) policy; **in die ~ gehen** to go into politics; **eine ~ verfolgen** to pursue a policy.
**Politiker(in)** [po'liːtikər(ɪn)] (-s, -) *m(f)* politician.
**politisch** [po'liːtɪʃ] *adj* political.
**politisieren** [politi'ziːrən] *vi* to talk politics ♦ *vt* to politicize; **jdn ~** to make sb politically aware.
**Politur** [poli'tuːr] *f* polish.
**Polizei** [poli'tsaɪ] *f* police; **~aufsicht** *f:* **unter ~aufsicht stehen** to have to report regularly to the police; **~beamte(r)** *m* police officer; **p~lich** *adj* police *attrib*; **sich p~lich melden** to register with the police; **p~liches Führungszeugnis** *certificate of "no criminal record" issued by the police*; **~präsidium** *nt*

police headquarters *pl*; ~**revier** *nt* police station; ~**spitzel** *m* police spy, informer; ~**staat** *m* police state; ~**streife** *f* police patrol; ~**stunde** *f* closing time; ~**wache** *f* police station; **p**~**widrig** *adj* illegal.

**Polizist(in)** [poli'tsɪst(ɪn)] (**-en, -en**) *m(f)* policeman/-woman.

**Pollen** ['pɔlən] (**-s, -**) *m* pollen.

**poln.** *abk* = **polnisch.**

**polnisch** ['pɔlnɪʃ] *adj* Polish.

**Polohemd** ['poːlohɛmt] *nt* polo shirt.

**Polster** ['pɔlstər] (**-s, -**) *nt* çushion; (~*ung*) upholstery; (*in Kleidung*) padding; (*fig: Geld*) reserves *pl*; ~**er** (**-s, -**) *m* upholsterer; ~**garnitur** *f* three-piece suite; ~**möbel** *pl* upholstered furniture *sing*.

**polstern** *vt* to upholster; (*Kleidung*) to pad; **sie ist gut gepolstert** (*umg*) she's well padded; (: *finanziell*) she's not short of the odd penny.

**Polsterung** *f* upholstery.

**Polterabend** ['pɔltəraːbənt] *m party on the eve of a wedding.*

**poltern** *vi* (*Krach machen*) to crash; (*schimpfen*) to rant.

**Polygamie** [polyga'miː] *f* polygamy.

**Polynesien** [poly'neːziən] (**-s**) *nt* Polynesia.

**Polynesier(in)** [poly'neːziər(ɪn)] (**-s, -**) *m(f)* Polynesian.

**polynesisch** *adj* Polynesian.

**Polyp** [po'lyːp] (**-en, -en**) *m* polyp; (*umg*) cop; **Polypen** *pl* (*MED*) adenoids *pl*.

**Polytechnikum** [poly'tɛçnikʊm] (**-s, Polytechnika**) *nt* polytechnic, poly (*umg*).

**Pomade** [po'maːdə] *f* pomade.

**Pommern** ['pɔmərn] (**-s**) *nt* Pomerania.

**Pommes frites** [pɔm'frɪt] *pl* chips *pl* (*BRIT*), French fried potatoes *pl* (*BRIT*), French fries *pl* (*US*).

**Pomp** [pɔmp] (**-(e)s**) *m* pomp.

**pompös** [pɔm'pøːs] *adj* grandiose.

**Pontius** ['pɔntsiʊs] *m:* **von ~ zu Pilatus** from pillar to post.

**Pony** ['pɔni] (**-s, -s**) *m* (*Frisur*) fringe (*BRIT*), bangs *pl* (*US*) ♦ *nt* (*Pferd*) pony.

**Pop** [pɔp] (**-s**) *m* (*MUS*) pop; (*KUNST*) pop art.

**Popelin** [popə'liːn] (**-s, -e**) *m* poplin.

**Popeline** (**-, -n**) *f* poplin.

**Popkonzert** *nt* pop concert.

**Popmusik** *f* pop music.

**Popo** [po'poː] (**-s, -s**) (*umg*) *m* bottom, bum (*BRIT*).

**populär** [popu'lɛːr] *adj* popular.

**Popularität** [populari'tɛːt] *f* popularity.

**populärwissenschaftlich** *adj* popular science.

**Pore** ['poːrə] (**-, -n**) *f* pore.

**Porno** ['pɔrno] (**-s, no pl**) (*umg*) *m* porn.

**Pornographie** [pɔrnogra'fiː] *f* pornography.

**pornographisch** [pɔrno'graːfɪʃ] *adj* pornographic.

**porös** [po'røːs] *adj* porous.

**Porree** ['pɔre] (**-s, -s**) *m* leek.

**Portal** [pɔr'taːl] (**-s, -e**) *nt* portal.

**Portefeuille** [pɔrt(ə)'føːj] (**-s, -s**) *nt* (*POL, FIN*) portfolio.

**Portemonnaie** [pɔrtmɔ'neː] (**-s, -s**) *nt* purse.

**Portier** [pɔrti'eː] (**-s, -s**) *m* porter; (*Pförtner*) porter, doorkeeper, doorman.

**Portion** [pɔrtsi'oːn] *f* portion, helping; (*umg: Anteil*) amount; **eine halbe ~** (*fig: umg: Person*) a half-pint; **eine ~ Kaffee** a pot of coffee.

**Porto** ['pɔrto] (**-s, -s od Porti**) *nt* postage; **~ zahlt Empfänger** postage paid; **p~frei** *adj* post-free, (postage) prepaid.

**Porträt** [pɔr'trɛː] (**-s, -s**) *nt* portrait.

**porträtieren** [pɔrtrɛ'tiːrən] *vt* to paint (a portrait of); (*fig*) to portray.

**Portugal** ['pɔrtugal] (**-s**) *nt* Portugal.

**Portugiese** [portu'giːzə] (**-n, -n**) *m* Portuguese.

**Portugiesin** *f* Portuguese.

**portugiesisch** *adj* Portuguese.

**Portwein** ['pɔrtvain] *m* port.

**Porzellan** [pɔrtsɛ'laːn] (**-s, -e**) *nt* china, porcelain; (*Geschirr*) china.

**Posaune** [po'zaunə] (**-, -n**) *f* trombone.

**Pose** ['poːzə] (**-, -n**) *f* pose.

**posieren** [po'ziːrən] *vi* to pose.

**Position** [pozitsi'oːn] *f* position; (*COMM: auf Liste*) item.

**Positionslichter** *pl* navigation lights *pl*.

**positiv** ['poːzitiːf] *adj* positive; **~ zu etw stehen** to be in favour (*BRIT*) *od* favor (*US*) of sth; **P~** (**-s, -e**) *nt* (*PHOT*) positive.

**Positur** [pozi'tuːr] *f* posture, attitude; **sich in ~ setzen** *od* **stellen** to adopt a posture.

**Posse** ['pɔsə] (**-, -n**) *f* farce.

**possessiv** ['pɔsɛsiːf] *adj* possessive; **P~** (**-s, -e**) *nt* possessive pronoun; **P~pronomen** (**-s, -e**) *nt* possessive pronoun.

**possierlich** [pɔ'siːrlɪç] *adj* funny.

**Post** [pɔst] (**-, -en**) *f* post (office); (*Briefe*) post, mail; **ist ~ für mich da?** are there any letters for me?; **mit getrennter ~** under separate cover; **etw auf die ~ geben** to post (*BRIT*) *od* mail sth; **auf die** *od* **zur ~ gehen** to go to the post office; **~amt** *nt* post office; **~anweisung** *f* postal order (*BRIT*), money order; **~bote** *m* postman (*BRIT*), mailman (*US*).

**Posten** (**-s, -**) *m* post, position; (*COMM*) item; (: *Warenmenge*) quantity, lot; (*auf Liste*) entry; (*MIL*) sentry; (*Streik~*) picket; **~ beziehen** to take up one's post; **nicht ganz auf dem ~ sein** (*nicht gesund sein*) to be off-colour (*BRIT*) *od* off-color (*US*).

**Poster** ['pɔstər] (**-s, -(s)**) *nt* poster.

**Postf.** *abk* (= *Postfach*) PO Box.

**Post-** *zW:* ~**fach** *nt* post office box; ~**karte** *f* postcard; **p~lagernd** *adv* poste restante; ~**leitzahl** *f* postal code.

**postmodern** [pɔstmo'dɛrn] *adj* postmodern.

**Post-** *zW:* ~**scheckkonto** *nt* Post Office Giro account (*BRIT*); ~**sparbuch** *nt* post office savings book (*Brit*); ~**sparkasse** *f* post office savings bank; ~**stempel** *m* postmark; **p~wendend** *adv* by return (of post); ~**wertzeichen** *nt* (*form*) postage stamp; ~**wurfsendung** *f* direct mail advertising.

**potent** [po'tɛnt] *adj* potent; (*fig*) high-powered.

**Potential** [potɛntsi'aːl] (**-s, -e**) *nt* potential.

**potentiell** [potɛntsi'ɛl] *adj* potential.

**Potenz** [po'tɛnts] *f* power; (*eines Mannes*) potency.

**potenzieren** [potɛn'tsiːrən] *vt* (*MATH*) to raise to the power of.

**Potpourri** ['pɔtpuri] (**-s, -s**) *nt*: ~ (**aus**) (*MUS*) medley (of); (*fig*) assortment (of).

**Pott** [pɔt] (**-(e)s, ⁼e**) (*umg*) *m* pot; **p~häßlich** (*umg*) *adj* ugly as sin.

**pp., ppa.** *abk* (= *per procura*) p.p.

**Präambel** [prɛ'|ambəl] (**-, -n**) *f* (+*gen*) preamble (to).

**Pracht** [praxt] (**-**) *f* splendour (*BRIT*), splendor (*US*), magnificence; **es ist eine wahre** ~ it's (really) marvellous; ~**exemplar** *nt* beauty (*umg*); (*fig: Mensch*) fine specimen.

**prächtig** ['prɛçtɪç] *adj* splendid.

**Prachtstück** *nt* showpiece.

**prachtvoll** *adj* splendid, magnificent.

**prädestinieren** [prɛdɛsti'niːrən] *vt* to predestine.

**Prädikat** [prɛdi'kaːt] (**-(e)s, -e**) *nt* title; (*GRAM*) predicate; (*Zensur*) distinction; **Wein mit** ~ special quality wine.

**Prag** [praːk] (**-s**) *nt* Prague.

**prägen** ['prɛːɡən] *vt* to stamp; (*Münze*) to mint; (*Ausdruck*) to coin; (*Charakter*) to form; (*kennzeichnen: Stadtbild*) to characterize; **das Erlebnis prägte ihn** the experience left its mark on him.

**prägend** *adj* having a forming *od* shaping influence.

**pragmatisch** [pra'ɡmaːtɪʃ] *adj* pragmatic.

**prägnant** [prɛ'ɡnant] *adj* concise, terse.

**Prägnanz** *f* conciseness, terseness.

**Prägung** ['prɛːɡʊŋ] *f* minting; forming; (*Eigenart*) character, stamp.

**prahlen** ['praːlən] *vi* to boast, brag.

**Prahlerei** [praːlə'raɪ] *f* boasting.

**prahlerisch** *adj* boastful.

**Praktik** ['praktɪk] *f* practice.

**praktikabel** [praktɪ'kaːbəl] *adj* practicable.

**Praktikant(in)** [praktɪ'kant(ɪn)] *m(f)* trainee.

**Praktikum** (**-s, Praktika** *od* **Praktiken**) *nt* practical training.

**praktisch** ['praktɪʃ] *adj* practical, handy; ~**er Arzt** general practitioner; ~**es Beispiel** concrete example.

**praktizieren** [praktɪ'tsiːrən] *vt, vi* to practise (*BRIT*), practice (*US*).

**Praline** [pra'liːnə] *f* chocolate.

**prall** [pral] *adj* firmly rounded; (*Segel*) taut; (*Arme*) plump; (*Sonne*) blazing.

**prallen** *vi* to bounce, rebound; (*Sonne*) to blaze.

**prallvoll** *adj* full to bursting; (*Brieftasche*) bulging.

**Prämie** ['prɛːmiə] *f* premium; (*Belohnung*) award, prize.

**prämienbegünstigt** *adj* with benefit of premiums.

**prämiensparen** *vi* to save in a bonus scheme.

**prämieren** [prɛ'miːrən] *vt* to give an award to.

**Pranger** ['praŋər] (**-s, -**) *m* (*HIST*) pillory; **jdn an den** ~ **stellen** (*fig*) to pillory sb.

**Pranke** ['praŋkə] (**-, -n**) *f* (*Tier~*: *umg: Hand*) paw.

**Präparat** [prɛpa'raːt] (**-(e)s, -e**) *nt* (*BIOL*) preparation; (*MED*) medicine.

**präparieren** *vt* (*konservieren*) to preserve; (*MED: zerlegen*) to dissect.

**Präposition** [prɛpozitsi'oːn] *f* preposition.

**Prärie** [prɛ'riː] *f* prairie.

**Präs.** *abk* = **Präsens; Präsident**.

**Präsens** ['prɛːzɛns] (**-**) *nt* present tense.

**präsent** *adj*: **etw** ~ **haben** to have sth at hand.

**präsentieren** [prɛzɛn'tiːrən] *vt* to present.

**Präsenzbibliothek** *f* reference library.

**Präservativ** [prɛzɛrva'tiːf] (**-s, -e**) *nt* condom, sheath.

**Präsident(in)** [prɛzi'dɛnt(ɪn)] *m(f)* president; ~**schaft** *f* presidency; ~**schaftskandidat** *m* presidential candidate.

**Präsidium** [prɛ'ziːdiʊm] *nt* presidency, chairmanship; (*Polizei~*) police headquarters *pl*.

**prasseln** ['prasəln] *vi* (*Feuer*) to crackle; (*Hagel*) to drum; (*Wörter*) to rain down.

**prassen** ['prasən] *vi* to live it up.

**Präteritum** [prɛ'teːritʊm] (**-s, Präterita**) *nt* preterite.

**Pratze** ['pratsə] (**-, -n**) *f* paw.

**Präventiv-** [prɛvɛn'tiːf] *in zW* preventive.

**Praxis** ['praksɪs] (**-, Praxen**) *f* practice; (*Erfahrung*) experience; (*Behandlungsraum*) surgery; (*von Anwalt*) office; **die** ~ **sieht anders aus** the reality is different; **ein Beispiel aus der** ~ an example from real life.

**Präzedenzfall** [prɛtse'dɛntsfal] *m* precedent.

**präzis** [prɛ'tsiːs] *adj* precise.

**Präzision** [prɛtsizi'oːn] *f* precision.

**PR-Chef** *m* PR officer.

**predigen** ['preːdɪɡən] *vt, vi* to preach.

**Prediger** (**-s, -**) *m* preacher.

**Predigt** ['preːdɪçt] (**-, -en**) *f* sermon.

**Preis** [praɪs] (**-es, -e**) *m* price; (*Sieges~*) prize; (*Auszeichnung*) award; **um keinen** ~ not at any price; **um jeden** ~ at all costs; ~**angebot** *nt* quotation; ~**ausschreiben** *nt* competition; ~**bindung** *f* price-fixing; ~**brecher** *m* (*Firma*) undercutter.

**Preiselbeere** *f* cranberry.

**preisempfindlich** *adj* price-sensitive.

**preisen** [ˈpraɪzən] *unreg vt* to praise; **sich glücklich ~** (*geh*) to count o.s. lucky.

**Preis-** *zW:* **~entwicklung** *f* price trend; **~erhöhung** *f* price increase; **~frage** *f* question of price; (*Wettbewerb*) prize question.

**preisgeben** *unreg vt* to abandon; (*opfern*) to sacrifice; (*zeigen*) to expose.

**Preis-** *zW:* **~gefälle** *nt* price gap; **p~gekrönt** *adj* prizewinning; **~gericht** *nt* jury; **p~günstig** *adj* inexpensive; **~index** *m* price index; **~krieg** *m* price war; **~lage** *f* price range; **p~lich** *adj* price *attr*, in price; **~liste** *f* price list, tariff; **~nachlaß** *m* discount; **~schild** *nt* price tag; **~spanne** *f* price range; **~sturz** *m* price slump; **~träger** *m* prizewinner; **p~wert** *adj* inexpensive.

**prekär** [preˈkɛːr] *adj* precarious.

**Prellbock** [ˈprɛlbɔk] *m* buffers *pl*.

**prellen** *vt* to bruise; (*fig*) to cheat, swindle.

**Prellung** *f* bruise.

**Premiere** [prəmiˈɛːrə] (-, -n) *f* premiere.

**Premierminister(in)** [prəmiˈeːmɪnɪstər(ɪn)] *m(f)* prime minister, premier.

**Presse** [ˈprɛsə] (-, -n) *f* press; **~agentur** *f* press *od* news agency; **~ausweis** *m* press pass; **~erklärung** *f* press release; **~freiheit** *f* freedom of the press; **~konferenz** *f* press conference; **~meldung** *f* press report.

**pressen** *vt* to press.

**Presse-** *zW:* **~sprecher(in)** *m(f)* spokesperson, press officer; **~stelle** *f* press office; **~verlautbarung** *f* press release.

**pressieren** [prɛˈsiːrən] *vi* to be in a hurry; **es pressiert** it's urgent.

**Preßluft** [ˈprɛslʊft] *f* compressed air; **~bohrer** *m* pneumatic drill.

**Prestige** [prɛsˈtiːʒə] (-s) *nt* prestige; **~verlust** *m* loss of prestige.

**Preuße** [ˈprɔʏsə] (-n, -n) *m* Prussian.

**Preußen** (-s) *nt* Prussia.

**Preußin** *f* Prussian.

**preußisch** *adj* Prussian.

**prickeln** [ˈprɪkəln] *vi* to tingle; (*kitzeln*) to tickle; (*Bläschen bilden*) to sparkle, bubble ♦ *vt* to tickle.

**pries** *etc* [priːs] *vb siehe* **preisen**.

**Priester** [ˈpriːstər] (-s, -) *m* priest.

**Priesterin** *f* priestess.

**Priesterweihe** *f* ordination (to the priesthood).

**Prima** [ˈpriːma] (-, Primen) *f* eighth and ninth year of German secondary school.

**prima** *adj inv* first-class, excellent.

**primär** [priˈmɛːr] *adj* primary; **P~daten** *pl* primary data *pl*.

**Primel** [ˈpriːməl] (-, -n) *f* primrose.

**primitiv** [primiˈtiːf] *adj* primitive.

**Primzahl** [ˈpriːmtsaːl] *f* prime (number).

**Prinz** [prɪnts] (-en, -en) *m* prince.

**Prinzessin** [prɪnˈtsɛsɪn] *f* princess.

**Prinzip** [prɪnˈtsiːp] (-s, -ien) *nt* principle; **aus ~** on principle; **im ~** in principle.

**prinzipiell** [prɪntsiˈpiɛl] *adj* on principle.

**prinzipienlos** *adj* unprincipled.

**Priorität** [prioriˈtɛːt] *f* priority; **Prioritäten** *pl* (*COMM*) preference shares *pl*, preferred stock *sing* (*US*); **~en setzen** to establish one's priorities.

**Prise** [ˈpriːzə] (-, -n) *f* pinch.

**Prisma** [ˈprɪsma] (-s, Prismen) *nt* prism.

**privat** [priˈvaːt] *adj* private; **jdn ~ sprechen** to speak to sb in private; **P~besitz** *m* private property; **P~dozent** *m* outside lecturer; **P~fernsehen** *nt* commercial television; **P~gespräch** *nt* private conversation; (*am Telefon*) private call.

**privatisieren** [privatiˈziːrən] *vt* to privatize.

**Privatschule** *f* private school.

**Privatwirtschaft** *f* private sector.

**Privileg** [priviˈleːk] (-(e)s, -ien) *nt* privilege.

**Pro** [proː] (-) *nt* pro.

**pro** *präp +akk* per; **~ Stück** each, apiece.

**Probe** [ˈproːbə] (-, -n) *f* test; (*Teststück*) sample; (*THEAT*) rehearsal; **jdn auf die ~ stellen** to put sb to the test; **er ist auf ~ angestellt** he's employed for a probationary period; **zur ~** to try out; **~bohrung** *f* (*Öl*) exploration well; **~exemplar** *nt* specimen copy; **~fahrt** *f* test drive; **~lauf** *m* trial run.

**proben** *vt* to try; (*THEAT*) to rehearse.

**Probe-** *zW:* **~stück** *nt* specimen; **p~weise** *adv* on approval; **~zeit** *f* probation period.

**probieren** [proˈbiːrən] *vt* to try; (*Wein, Speise*) to taste, sample ♦ *vi* to try; to taste.

**Problem** [proˈbleːm] (-s, -e) *nt* problem; **vor einem ~ stehen** to be faced with a problem.

**Problematik** [probleˈmaːtɪk] *f* problem.

**problematisch** [probleˈmaːtɪʃ] *adj* problematic.

**problemlos** *adj* problem-free.

**Problemstellung** *f* way of looking at a problem.

**Produkt** [proˈdʊkt] (-(e)s, -e) *nt* product; (*AGR*) produce *no pl*.

**Produktion** [prodʊktsiˈoːn] *f* production.

**Produktionsleiter** *m* production manager.

**Produktionsstätte** *f* (*Halle*) shop floor.

**produktiv** [prodʊkˈtiːf] *adj* productive.

**Produktivität** [prodʊktiviˈtɛːt] *f* productivity.

**Produzent** [produˈtsɛnt] *m* manufacturer; (*FILM*) producer.

**produzieren** [produˈtsiːrən] *vt* to produce ♦ *vr* to show off.

**Prof.** [prof] *abk* (= *Professor*) Prof.

**profan** [proˈfaːn] *adj* (*weltlich*) secular, profane; (*gewöhnlich*) mundane.

**professionell** [profesioˈnɛl] *adj* professional.

**Professor(in)** [proˈfɛsɔr, profeˈsoːrɪn] *m(f)* professor; (*ÖSTERR: Gymnasiallehrer*) grammar school teacher (*BRIT*), high school teacher (*US*).

**Professur** [profeˈsuːr] *f:* **~ (für)** chair (of).

**Profi** ['proːfi] (**-s, -s**) *m abk* (= *Professional*) pro.
**Profil** [proˈfiːl] (**-s, -e**) *nt* profile; (*fig*) image;
(*Querschnitt*) cross section; (*Längsschnitt*)
vertical section; (*von Reifen, Schuhsohle*)
tread.
**profilieren** [profiˈliːrən] *vr* to create an image
for o.s.
**Profilsohle** *f* sole with a tread.
**Profit** [proˈfiːt] (**-(e)s, -e**) *m* profit.
**profitieren** [profiˈtiːrən] *vi*: ~ **(von)** to profit
(from).
**Profitmacherei** (*umg*) *f* profiteering.
**pro forma** *adv* as a matter of form.
**Pro-forma-Rechnung** *f* pro forma invoice.
**Prognose** [proˈgnoːzə] (**-, -n**) *f* prediction,
prognosis.
**Programm** [proˈgram] (**-s, -e**) *nt* programme
(*BRIT*), program (*US*); (*COMPUT*) program;
(*TV: Sender*) channel; (*Kollektion*) range; **nach**
~ as planned; **p~gemäß** *adj* according to
plan; **~fehler** *m* (*COMPUT*) bug; **~hinweis** *m*
(*RUNDF, TV*) programme (*BRIT*) *od* program
(*US*) announcement.
**programmieren** [progra'miːrən] *vt* to
programme (*BRIT*), program (*US*);
(*COMPUT*) to program; **auf etw** *akk*
**programmiert sein** (*fig*) to be geared to sth.
**Programmierer(in)** [progra'miːrər(ɪn)] *m(f)* programmer.
**Programmiersprache** *f* (*COMPUT*)
programming language.
**Programmierung** *f* (*COMPUT*)
programming.
**Programmvorschau** *f* preview; (*FILM*)
trailer.
**progressiv** [progre'siːf] *adj* progressive.
**Projekt** [proˈjɛkt] (**-(e)s, -e**) *nt* project.
**Projektleiter(in)** *m(f)* project manager(ess).
**Projektor** [proˈjɛktɔr] *m* projector.
**projizieren** [proji'tsiːrən] *vt* to project.
**proklamieren** [prokla'miːrən] *vt* to proclaim.
**Pro-Kopf-Einkommen** *nt* per capita income.
**Prokura** [proˈkuːra] (**-, Prokuren**) *f* (*form*)
power of attorney.
**Prokurist(in)** [proku'rɪst(ɪn)] *m(f)* attorney.
**Prolet** [proˈleːt] (**-en, -en**) *m* prole, pleb.
**Proletariat** [proletari'aːt] (**-(e)s, -e**) *nt*
proletariat.
**Proletarier** [prole'taːriər] (**-s, -**) *m* proletarian.
**Prolog** [proˈloːk] (**-(e)s, -e**) *m* prologue.
**Promenade** [proməˈnaːdə] (**-, -n**) *f*
promenade.
**Promenadenmischung** *f* (*hum*) mongrel.
**Promille** [proˈmɪlə] (**-(s), -**) (*umg*) *nt* alcohol
level; **~grenze** *f* legal (alcohol) limit.
**prominent** [promi'nɛnt] *adj* prominent.
**Prominenz** [promi'nɛnts] *f* VIPs *pl*.
**Promoter** [proˈmoːtər] (**-s, -**) *m* promoter.
**Promotion** [promotsi'oːn] *f* doctorate, Ph.D.
**promovieren** [promo'viːrən] *vi* to receive a
doctorate *etc*.
**prompt** [prɔmpt] *adj* prompt.
**Pronomen** [proˈnoːmɛn] (**-s, -**) *nt* pronoun.

**Propaganda** [propaˈganda] (**-**) *f* propaganda.
**propagieren** [propa'giːrən] *vt* to propagate.
**Propangas** [pro'paːngaːs] *nt* propane gas.
**Propeller** [proˈpɛlər] (**-s, -**) *m* propeller.
**proper** ['prɔpər] (*umg*) *adj* neat, tidy.
**Prophet(in)** [proˈfeːt(ɪn)] (**-en, -en**) *m(f)*
prophet(ess).
**prophezeien** [profe'tsaɪən] *vt* to prophesy.
**Prophezeiung** *f* prophecy.
**prophylaktisch** [profy'laktɪʃ] *adj* prophylactic
(*form*), preventive.
**Proportion** [proportsi'oːn] *f* proportion.
**proportional** [proportsio'naːl] *adj*
proportional; **P~schrift** *f* (*COMPUT*)
proportional printing.
**proportioniert** [proportsio'niːrt] *adj*: **gut/**
**schlecht** ~ well/badly proportioned.
**Proporz** [proˈpɔrts] (**-es, -e**) *m* proportional
representation.
**Prosa** ['proːza] (**-**) *f* prose.
**prosaisch** [pro'zaːɪʃ] *adj* prosaic.
**prosit** ['proːzit] *interj* cheers!; **P~ Neujahr!**
happy New Year!
**Prospekt** [proˈspɛkt] (**-(e)s, -e**) *m* leaflet,
brochure.
**prost** [proːst] *interj* cheers!
**Prostata** ['prɔstata] (**-**) *f* prostate gland.
**Prostituierte** [prostitu'iːrtə] (**-, -n**) *f*
prostitute.
**Prostitution** [prostitutsi'oːn] *f* prostitution.
**prot.** [prot] *abk* = **protestantisch**.
**Protektionismus** [protɛktsio'nɪsmʊs] *m*
protectionism.
**Protektorat** [protɛkto'raːt] (**-(e)s, -e**) *nt*
(*Schirmherrschaft*) patronage; (*Schutzgebiet*)
protectorate.
**Protest** [proˈtɛst] (**-(e)s, -e**) *m* protest.
**Protestant(in)** [protɛs'tant(ɪn)] *m(f)*
Protestant; **p~isch** *adj* Protestant.
**Protestbewegung** *f* protest movement.
**protestieren** [protɛs'tiːrən] *vi* to protest.
**Protestkundgebung** *f* (protest) rally.
**Prothese** [pro'teːzə] (**-, -n**) *f* artificial limb;
(*Zahn~*) dentures *pl*.
**Protokoll** [proto'kɔl] (**-s, -e**) *nt* register;
(*Niederschrift*) record; (*von Sitzung*) minutes
*pl*; (*diplomatisch*) protocol; (*Polizei~*)
statement; (*Strafzettel*) ticket; **(das)** ~ **führen**
(*bei Sitzung*) to take the minutes; (*bei*
*Gericht*) to make a transcript of the
proceedings; **etw zu** ~ **geben** to have sth
put on record; (*bei Polizei*) to say sth in one's
statement; **~führer** *m* secretary; (*JUR*) clerk
(of the court).
**protokollieren** [protoko'liːrən] *vt* to take
down; (*Bemerkung*) to enter in the minutes.
**Proton** ['proːtɔn] (**-s, -en**) *nt* proton.
**Prototyp** *m* prototype.
**Protz** ['prɔts] (**-es, -e**) *m* swank; **p~en** *vi* to
show off.
**protzig** *adj* ostentatious.
**Proviant** [provi'ant] (**-s, -e**) *m* provisions *pl*,

supplies *pl.*

**Provinz** [pro'vɪnts] (-, -en) *f* province; **das ist finsterste ~** (*pej*) it's a cultural backwater.

**provinziell** [provɪn'tsiɛl] *adj* provincial.

**Provision** [provizi'o:n] *f* (*COMM*) commission.

**provisorisch** [provi'zo:rɪʃ] *adj* provisional.

**Provisorium** [provi'zo:riʊm] (-s, -ien) *nt* provisional arrangement.

**Provokation** [provokatsi'o:n] *f* provocation.

**provokativ** [provoka'ti:f] *adj* provocative, provoking.

**provokatorisch** [provoka'to:rɪʃ] *adj* provocative, provoking.

**provozieren** [provo'tsi:rən] *vt* to provoke.

**Proz.** *abk* (= *Prozent*) pc.

**Prozedur** [protse'du:r] *f* procedure; (*pej*) carry-on; **die ~ beim Zahnarzt** the ordeal at the dentist's.

**Prozent** [pro'tsɛnt] (-(e)s, -e) *nt* per cent, percentage; **~rechnung** *f* percentage calculation; **~satz** *m* percentage.

**prozentual** [protsɛntu'a:l] *adj* percentage; *attrib.*

**Prozeß** [pro'tsɛs] (-sses, -sse) *m* trial, case; (*Vorgang*) process; **es zum ~ kommen lassen** to go to court; **mit jdm/etw kurzen ~ machen** (*fig: umg*) to make short work of sb/sth; **~anwalt** *m* barrister, counsel; **~führung** *f* handling of a case.

**prozessieren** [protse'si:rən] *vi:* **~ (mit)** to bring an action (against), go to law (with *od* against).

**Prozession** [protsesi'o:n] *f* procession.

**Prozeßkosten** *pl* (legal) costs *pl*.

**prüde** ['pry:də] *adj* prudish.

**Prüderie** [pry:də'ri:] *f* prudery.

**prüfen** ['pry:fən] *vt* to examine, test; (*nach~*) to check; (*erwägen*) to consider; (*Geschäftsbücher*) to audit; (*mustern*) to scrutinize.

**Prüfer(in)** (-s, -) *m(f)* examiner.

**Prüfling** *m* examinee.

**Prüfstein** *m* touchstone.

**Prüfung** *f* (*SCH, UNIV*) examination, exam; (*Über~*) checking; **eine ~ machen** to take *od* sit (*BRIT*) an exam(ination); **durch eine ~ fallen** to fail an exam(ination).

**Prüfungs-** *zW:* **~ausschuß** *m* examining board; **~kommission** *f* examining board; **~ordnung** *f* exam(ination) regulations *pl*.

**Prügel** ['pry:gəl] (-s, -) *m* cudgel ♦ *pl* beating *sing*.

**Prügelei** [pry:gə'laɪ] *f* fight.

**Prügelknabe** *m* scapegoat.

**prügeln** *vt* to beat ♦ *vr* to fight.

**Prügelstrafe** *f* corporal punishment.

**Prunk** [prʊŋk] (-(e)s) *m* pomp, show; **p~voll** *adj* splendid, magnificent.

**prusten** ['pru:stən] (*umg*) *vi* to snort.

**PS** *abk* (= *Pferdestärke*) hp; (= *Postskript(um)*) PS.

**Psalm** [psalm] (-s, -en) *m* psalm.

**PSchA** *nt abk* (= *Postscheckamt*) National Giro Office.

**pseudo-** [psɔydo] *in zW* pseudo.

**Psychiater** [psy'çia:tər] (-s, -) *m* psychiatrist.

**Psychiatrie** [psyçia'tri:] *f* psychiatry.

**psychiatrisch** [psy'çia:trɪʃ] *adj* psychiatric; **~e Klinik** mental *od* psychiatric hospital.

**psychisch** ['psy:çɪʃ] *adj* psychological; **~ gestört** emotionally *od* psychologically disturbed.

**Psychoanalyse** [psyçoana'ly:zə] *f* psychoanalysis.

**Psychologe** [psyço'lo:gə] (-n, -n) *m* psychologist.

**Psychologie** *f* psychology.

**Psychologin** *f* psychologist.

**psychologisch** *adj* psychological.

**Psychotherapie** *f* psychotherapy.

**PTT** (*SCHWEIZ*) *abk* (= *Post, Telefon, Telegraf*) *postal and telecommunication services.*

**Pubertät** [puber'tɛ:t] *f* puberty.

**publik** [pu'bli:k] *adj:* **~ werden** to become public knowledge.

**Publikum** ['pu:blikʊm] (-s) *nt* audience; (*SPORT*) crowd; **das ~ in dieser Bar ist sehr gemischt** you get a very mixed group of people using this bar.

**Publikumserfolg** *m* popular success.

**Publikumsverkehr** *m:* **„heute kein ~"** "closed today for public business".

**publizieren** [publi'tsi:rən] *vt* to publish.

**Pudding** ['pʊdɪŋ] (-s, -e *od* -s) *m* blancmange; **~pulver** *nt* custard powder.

**Pudel** ['pu:dəl] (-s, -) *m* poodle; **das also ist des ~s Kern** (*fig*) that's what it's really all about.

**pudelwohl** (*umg*) *adj:* **sich ~ fühlen** to feel on top of the world.

**Puder** ['pu:dər] (-s, -) *m* powder; **~dose** *f* powder compact.

**pudern** *vt* to powder.

**Puderzucker** *m* icing sugar (*BRIT*), confectioner's sugar (*US*).

**Puertoricaner(in)** [puertori'ka:nər(ɪn)] (-s, -) *m(f)* Puerto Rican.

**puertoricanisch** *adj* Puerto Rican.

**Puerto Rico** [pu'ɛrto'ri:ko] (-s) *nt* Puerto Rico.

**Puff¹** [pʊf] (-(e)s, -e) *m* (*Wäsche~*) linen basket; (*Sitz~*) pouf.

**Puff²** (-(e)s, ¨e) (*umg*) *m* (*Stoß*) push.

**Puff³** (-s, -s) (*umg*) *m od nt* (*Bordell*) brothel.

**Puffer** (-s, -) *m* (*auch COMPUT*) buffer; **~speicher** *m* (*COMPUT*) cache; **~staat** *m* buffer state; **~zone** *f* buffer zone.

**Puffreis** *m* puffed rice.

**Pulle** ['pʊlə] (-, -n) (*umg*) *f* bottle; **volle ~ fahren** (*umg*) to drive flat out.

**Pulli** ['pʊli] (-s, -s) (*umg*) *m* sweater, jumper (*BRIT*).

**Pullover** [pʊ'lo:vər] (-s, -) *m* sweater, jumper (*BRIT*).

**Pullunder** [pʊ'lʊndər] (-s, -) *m* slipover.

**Puls** [pʊls] (**-es, -e**) *m* pulse; **~ader** *f* artery; **sich** *dat* **die ~ader(n) aufschneiden** to slash one's wrists.

**pulsieren** [pʊl'ziːrən] *vi* to throb, pulsate.

**Pult** [pʊlt] (**-(e)s, -e**) *nt* desk.

**Pulver** ['pʊlfər] (**-s, -**) *nt* powder; **~faß** *nt* powder keg; **(wie) auf einem ~faß sitzen** (*fig*) to be sitting on (top of) a volcano.

**pulverig** *adj* powdery.

**pulverisieren** [pʊlveri'ziːrən] *vt* to pulverize.

**Pulverkaffee** *m* instant coffee.

**Pulverschnee** *m* powdery snow.

**pummelig** ['pʊməlɪç] *adj* chubby.

**Pump** (**-(e)s**) (*umg*) *m:* **auf ~ kaufen** to buy on tick (*BRIT*) *od* credit.

**Pumpe** ['pʊmpə] (**-, -n**) *f* pump; (*umg: Herz*) ticker.

**pumpen** *vt* to pump; (*umg*) to lend; (: *entleihen*) to borrow.

**Pumphose** *f* knickerbockers *pl*.

**puncto** ['pʊŋkto] *präp +gen:* **in ~ X** where X is concerned.

**Punkt** [pʊŋkt] (**-(e)s, -e**) *m* point; (*bei Muster*) dot; (*Satzzeichen*) full stop, period (*bes US*); **~ 12 Uhr** at 12 o'clock on the dot; **nun mach aber mal einen ~!** (*umg*) come off it!; **p~gleich** *adj* (*SPORT*) level.

**punktieren** [pʊŋk'tiːrən] *vt* to dot; (*MED*) to aspirate.

**pünktlich** ['pʏŋktlɪç] *adj* punctual; **P~keit** *f* punctuality.

**Punkt-** *zW:* **~matrix** *f* dot matrix; **~richter** *m* (*SPORT*) judge; **~sieg** *m* victory on points; **~wertung** *f* points system; **~zahl** *f* score.

**Punsch** [pʊnʃ] (**-(e)s, -e**) *m* (hot) punch.

**Pupille** [pu'pɪlə] (**-, -n**) *f* (*im Auge*) pupil.

**Puppe** ['pʊpə] (**-, -n**) *f* doll; (*Marionette*) puppet; (*Insekten~*) pupa, chrysalis; (*Schaufenster~, MIL: Übungs~*) dummy; (*umg: Mädchen*) doll, bird (*bes BRIT*).

**Puppen-** *zW:* **~haus** *nt* doll's house, dollhouse (*US*); **~spieler** *m* puppeteer; **~stube** *f* (single-room) doll's house *od* dollhouse (*US*); **~theater** *nt* puppet theatre (*BRIT*) *od* theater (*US*); **~wagen** *m* doll's pram.

**pupsen** ['puːpsən] (*umg*) *vi* to make a rude noise/smell.

**pur** [puːr] *adj* pure; (*völlig*) sheer; (*Whisky*) neat.

**Püree** [py're:] (**-s, -s**) *nt* purée; (*Kartoffel~*) mashed potatoes *pl*.

**Purpur** ['pʊrpʊr] (**-s**) *m* crimson.

**Purzelbaum** ['pʊrtsəlbaʊm] *m* somersault.

**purzeln** *vi* to tumble.

**Puste** ['puːstə] (**-**) (*umg*) *f* puff; (*fig*) steam.

**Pusteblume** (*umg*) *f* dandelion.

**Pustel** ['pʊstəl] (**-, -n**) *f* pustule.

**pusteln** *vi* to puff, blow.

**pusten** ['puːstən] (*umg*) *vi* to puff.

**Pute** ['puːtə] (**-, -n**) *f* turkey hen.

**Puter** (**-s, -**) *m* turkey cock; **p~rot** *adj* scarlet.

**Putsch** [pʊtʃ] (**-(e)s, -e**) *m* revolt, putsch;

**p~en** *vi* to revolt; **~ist** *m* rebel; **~versuch** *m* attempted coup (d'état).

**Putte** ['pʊtə] (**-, -n**) *f* (*KUNST*) cherub.

**Putz** [pʊts] (**-es**) *m* (*Mörtel*) plaster, roughcast; **eine Mauer mit ~ verkleiden** to roughcast a wall.

**putzen** *vt* to clean; (*Nase*) to wipe, blow ♦ *vr* to clean o.s.; (*veraltet: sich schmücken*) to dress o.s. up.

**Putzfrau** *f* cleaning lady, charwoman (*BRIT*).

**putzig** *adj* quaint, funny.

**Putzlappen** *m* cloth.

**putzmunter** (*umg*) *adj* full of beans.

**Putz-** *zW:* **~tag** *m* cleaning day; **~teufel** (*umg*) *m* maniac for housework; **~zeug** *nt* cleaning things *pl*.

**Puzzle** ['pasəl] (**-s, -s**) *nt* jigsaw (puzzle).

**PVC** [peːfau'tseː] (**-(s)**) *nt abk* PVC.

**Pygmäe** [pʏ'ɡmɛːə] (**-n, -n**) *m* Pygmy.

**Pyjama** [pi'dʒaːma] (**-s, -s**) *m* pyjamas *pl* (*BRIT*), pajamas *pl* (*US*).

**Pyramide** [pyra'miːdə] (**-, -n**) *f* pyramid.

**Pyrenäen** [pyre'nɛːən] *pl:* **die ~** the Pyrenees *pl*.

**Python** ['pyːtɔn] (**-s, -s**) *m* python; **~schlange** *f* python.

# Q, q

**Q, q** [kuː] *nt* Q, q; **~ wie Quelle** ≈ Q for Queen.

**qcm** *abk* (= *Quadratzentimeter*) cm².

**qkm** *abk* (= *Quadratkilometer*) km².

**qm** *abk* (= *Quadratmeter*) m².

**quabb(e)lig** ['kvab(ə)lɪç] *adj* wobbly; (*Frosch*) slimy.

**Quacksalber** ['kvakzalbər] (**-s, -**) *m* quack (doctor).

**Quader** ['kvaːdər] (**-s, -**) *m* square stone block; (*MATH*) cuboid.

**Quadrat** [kva'draːt] (**-(e)s, -e**) *nt* square; **q~isch** *adj* square; **~latschen** *pl* (*hum: umg: Schuhe*) clodhoppers *pl*; **~meter** *m* square metre (*BRIT*) *od* meter (*US*).

**quadrieren** [kva'driːrən] *vt* to square.

**quaken** ['kvaːkən] *vi* to croak; (*Ente*) to quack.

**quäken** ['kvɛːkən] *vi* to screech.

**quäkend** *adj* screeching.

**Quäker(in)** (**-s, -**) *m(f)* Quaker.

**Qual** [kvaːl] (**-, -en**) *f* pain, agony; (*seelisch*) anguish; **er machte ihr das Leben zur ~** he made her life a misery.

**quälen** ['kvɛːlən] *vt* to torment ♦ *vr* (*sich abmühen*) to struggle; (*geistig*) to torment o.s.; **~de Ungewißheit** agonizing uncertainty.

**Quälerei** [kvɛːlə'raɪ] f torture, torment.
**Quälgeist** (*umg*) m pest.
**Qualifikation** [kvalifikatsi'oːn] f qualification.
**qualifizieren** [kvalifi'tsiːrən] vt to qualify;
  (*einstufen*) to label ♦ vr to qualify.
**qualifiziert** adj (*Arbeiter, Nachwuchs*)
  qualified; (*Arbeit*) professional; (*POL:
  Mehrheit*) requisite.
**Qualität** [kvali'tɛːt] f quality; **von
  ausgezeichneter** ~ (of) top quality.
**qualitativ** [kvalita'tiːf] adj qualitative.
**Qualitätskontrolle** f quality control.
**Qualitätsware** f article of high quality.
**Qualle** ['kvalə] (-, -n) f jellyfish.
**Qualm** [kvalm] (-(e)s) m thick smoke.
**qualmen** vt, vi to smoke.
**qualvoll** ['kvaːlfɔl] adj painful; (*Schmerzen*)
  excruciating, agonizing.
**Quantensprung** m quantum leap.
**Quantentheorie** ['kvantənteori:] f quantum
  theory.
**Quantität** [kvanti'tɛːt] f quantity.
**quantitativ** [kvantita'tiːf] adj quantitative.
**Quantum** ['kvantʊm] (-s, Quanten) nt
  quantity, amount.
**Quarantäne** [karan'tɛːnə] (-, -n) f quarantine.
**Quark¹** [kvark] (-s) m curd cheese, quark;
  (*umg*) rubbish.
**Quark²** [kvark] (-s, -s) nt (*PHYS*) quark.
**Quarta** ['kvarta] (-, Quarten) f *third year of
  German secondary school*.
**Quartal** [kvar'taːl] (-s, -e) nt quarter (year);
  **Kündigung zum** ~ quarterly notice date.
**Quartett** [kvar'tɛt] (-(e)s, -e) nt (*MUS*) quartet;
  (*KARTEN*) set of four cards; (: *Spiel*)
  ≈ happy families.
**Quartier** [kvar'tiːr] (-s, -e) nt accommodation
  (*BRIT*), accommodations pl (*US*); (*MIL*)
  quarters pl; (*Stadt~*) district.
**Quarz** [kvaːrts] (-es, -e) m quartz.
**quasi** ['kvaːzi] adv virtually ♦ präf quasi.
**quasseln** ['kvasəln] (*umg*) vi to natter.
**Quaste** ['kvastə] (-, -n) f (*Troddel*) tassel; (*von
  Pinsel*) bristles pl.
**Quästur** [kvɛs'tuːr] f (*UNIV*) bursary.
**Quatsch** [kvatʃ] (-es) (*umg*) m rubbish,
  hogwash; **hört doch endlich auf mit dem** ~!
  stop being so stupid!; ~ **machen** to mess
  about.
**quatschen** vi to chat, natter.
**Quatschkopf** (*umg*) m (*pej: Schwätzer*)
  windbag; (*Dummkopf*) twit (*BRIT*).
**Quecksilber** ['kvɛksɪlbər] nt mercury.
**Quelle** ['kvɛlə] (-, -n) f spring; (*eines Flusses,
  COMPUT*) source; **an der** ~ **sitzen** (*fig*) to be
  well placed; **aus zuverlässiger** ~ from a
  reliable source.
**quellen** vi (*hervor~*) to pour od gush forth;
  (*schwellen*) to swell.
**Quellenangabe** f reference.
**Quellsprache** f source language.
**Quengelei** [kvɛŋə'laɪ] (*umg*) f whining.

**quengelig** (*umg*) adj whining.
**quengeln** (*umg*) vi to whine.
**quer** [kveːr] adv crossways, diagonally;
  (*rechtwinklig*) at right angles; ~ **auf dem Bett**
  across the bed; **Q~balken** m crossbeam;
  **Q~denker** m maverick.
**Quere** ['kveːrə] f: **jdm in die** ~ **kommen** to
  cross sb's path.
**quer-** zW: ~**feldein** adv across country;
  **Q~feldeinrennen** nt cross-country; (*mit
  Motorrädern*) motocross; (*Radrennen*) cyclo-
  cross; **Q~flöte** f flute; **Q~format** nt oblong
  format; ~**gestreift** adj attrib horizontally
  striped; **Q~kopf** m awkward customer;
  ~**legen** vr (*fig: umg*) to be awkward;
  **Q~schiff** nt transept; **Q~schläger** (*umg*) m
  ricochet; **Q~schnitt** m cross section;
  ~**schnittsgelähmt** adj paraplegic, paralysed
  below the waist; **Q~schnittslähmung** f
  paraplegia; **Q~straße** f intersecting road;
  **Q~strich** m (horizontal) stroke od line;
  **Q~summe** f (*MATH*) sum of digits of a
  number; **Q~treiber** (-s, -) m obstructionist.
**Querulant(in)** [kveru'lant(ɪn)] (-en, -en) m(f)
  grumbler.
**Querverbindung** f connection, link.
**Querverweis** m cross-reference.
**quetschen** ['kvɛtʃən] vt to squash, crush;
  (*MED*) to bruise ♦ vr (*sich klemmen*) to be
  caught; (*sich zwängen*) to squeeze (o.s.).
**Quetschung** f bruise, contusion (*form*).
**Queue** [køː] (-s, -s) nt (*BILLIARD*) cue.
**quicklebendig** ['kvɪkle'bɛndɪç] (*umg*) adj
  (*Kind*) lively, active; (*ältere Person*) spry.
**quieken** ['kviːkən] vi to squeak.
**quietschen** ['kviːtʃən] vi to squeak.
**quietschvergnügt** ['kviːtʃfɛrgnyːkt] (*umg*) adj
  happy as a sandboy.
**quillt** [kvɪlt] vb siehe **quellen**.
**Quinta** ['kvɪnta] (-, Quinten) f *second year in
  German secondary school*.
**Quintessenz** ['kvɪntesɛnts] f quintessence.
**Quintett** [kvɪn'tɛt] (-(e)s, -e) nt quintet.
**Quirl** [kvɪrl] (-(e)s, -e) m whisk.
**quirlig** ['kvɪrlɪç] adj lively, frisky.
**quitt** [kvɪt] adj quits, even.
**Quitte** (-, -n) f quince.
**quittieren** [kvɪ'tiːrən] vt to give a receipt for;
  (*Dienst*) to leave.
**Quittung** f receipt; **er hat seine**
  ~ **bekommen** he's paid the penalty od
  price.
**Quiz** [kvɪs] (-, -) nt quiz.
**quoll** etc [kvɔl] vb siehe **quellen**.
**Quote** ['kvoːtə] (-, -n) f proportion; (*Rate*)
  rate.
**Quotenregelung** f quota system (*for
  ensuring adequate representation of women*).
**Quotierung** [kvo'tiːrʊŋ] f (*COMM*) quotation.

# R, r

**R¹, r** nt R, r; ~ **wie Richard** ≈ R for Robert, R for Roger (US).

**R², r** abk (= Radius) r.

**r.** abk (= rechts) r.

**Rabatt** [ra'bat] (-(e)s, -e) m discount.

**Rabatte** (-, -n) f flower bed, border.

**Rabattmarke** f trading stamp.

**Rabatz** [ra'bats] (-es) (umg) m row, din.

**Rabe** ['ra:bə] (-n, -n) m raven.

**Rabenmutter** f bad mother.

**rabenschwarz** adj pitch-black.

**rabiat** [rabi'a:t] adj furious.

**Rache** ['raxə] (-) f revenge, vengeance.

**Rachen** (-s, -) m throat.

**rächen** ['rɛçən] vt to avenge, revenge ♦ vr to take (one's) revenge; **das wird sich** ~ you'll pay for that.

**Rachitis** [ra'xi:tɪs] (-) f rickets sing.

**Rachsucht** f vindictiveness.

**rachsüchtig** adj vindictive.

**Racker** ['rakər] (-s, -) m rascal, scamp.

**Rad** [ra:t] (-(e)s, ̈er) nt wheel; (Fahr~) bike; **unter die Räder kommen** (umg) to fall into bad ways; **das fünfte** ~ **am Wagen sein** (umg) to be in the way.

**Radar** ['ra:da:r] (-s) m od nt radar; ~**falle** f speed trap; ~**kontrolle** f radar-controlled speed check.

**Radau** [ra'dau] (-s) (umg) m row; ~ **machen** to kick up a row; (Unruhe stiften) to cause trouble.

**Raddampfer** m paddle steamer.

**radebrechen** ['ra:dəbrɛçən] vi untr: **deutsch** etc ~ to speak broken German etc.

**radeln** vi (Hilfsverb sein) to cycle.

**Rädelsführer** ['rɛ:dəlsfy:rər] (-s, -) m ringleader.

**Rad-** zW: **r~fahren** unreg vi to cycle; ~**fahrer** m cyclist; (pej: umg) crawler; ~**fahrweg** m cycle track od path.

**radieren** [ra'di:rən] vt to rub out, erase; (ART) to etch.

**Radiergummi** m rubber (BRIT), eraser (bes US).

**Radierung** f etching.

**Radieschen** [ra'di:sçən] nt radish.

**radikal** [radi'ka:l] adj radical; ~ **gegen etw vorgehen** to take radical steps against sth.

**Radikale(r)** f(m) radical.

**Radikalisierung** [radikali'zi:rʊŋ] f radicalization.

**Radikalkur** (umg) f drastic remedy.

**Radio** ['ra:dio] (-s, -s) nt radio, wireless (bes BRIT); **im** ~ on the radio; **r~aktiv** adj radioactive; **r~aktiver Niederschlag** (radioactive) fallout; ~**aktivität** f radioactivity; ~**apparat** m radio (set); ~**recorder** m radio-cassette recorder.

**Radium** ['ra:diʊm] (-s) nt radium.

**Radius** ['ra:diʊs] (-, **Radien**) m radius.

**Radkappe** f (AUT) hub cap.

**Radler(in)** (-s, -) m(f) cyclist.

**Rad-** zW: ~**rennbahn** f cycling (race)track; ~**rennen** nt cycle race; (Sportart) cycle racing; ~**sport** m cycling.

**RAF** (-) f abk (= Rote Armee Fraktion) Red Army Faction.

**raffen** ['rafən] vt to snatch, pick up; (Stoff) to gather (up); (Geld) to pile up, rake in; (umg: verstehen) to catch on to.

**Raffgier** f greed, avarice.

**Raffinade** [rafi'na:də] f refined sugar.

**Raffinesse** [rafi'nɛsə] (-) f (Feinheit) refinement; (Schlauheit) cunning.

**raffinieren** [rafi'ni:rən] vt to refine.

**raffiniert** adj crafty, cunning; (Zucker) refined.

**Rage** ['ra:ʒə] (-) f (Wut) rage, fury.

**ragen** ['ra:gən] vi to tower, rise.

**Rahm** [ra:m] (-s) m cream.

**Rahmen** (-s, -) m frame(work); **aus dem** ~ **fallen** to go too far; **im** ~ **des Möglichen** within the bounds of possibility; **r~** vt to frame; ~**handlung** f (LITER) background story; ~**plan** m outline plan; ~**richtlinien** pl guidelines pl.

**rahmig** adj creamy.

**Rakete** [ra'ke:tə] (-, -n) f rocket; **ferngelenkte** ~ guided missile.

**Raketenstützpunkt** m missile base.

**Rallye** ['rali] (-, -s) f rally.

**rammdösig** ['ramdø:zɪç] (umg) adj giddy, dizzy.

**rammen** ['ramən] vt to ram.

**Rampe** ['rampə] (-, -n) f ramp.

**Rampenlicht** nt (THEAT) footlights pl; **sie möchte immer im** ~ **stehen** (fig) she always wants to be in the limelight.

**ramponieren** [rampo'ni:rən] (umg) vt to damage.

**Ramsch** [ramʃ] (-(e)s, -e) m junk.

**ran** [ran] (umg) adv = **heran**.

**Rand** [rant] (-(e)s, ̈er) m edge; (von Brille, Tasse etc) rim; (Hut~) brim; (auf Papier) margin; (Schmutz~, unter Augen) ring; (fig) verge, brink; **außer** ~ **und Band** wild; **am** ~**e bemerkt** mentioned in passing; **am** ~**e der Stadt** on the outskirts of the town; **etw am** ~**e miterleben** to experience sth from the sidelines.

**randalieren** [randa'li:rən] vi to (go on the) rampage.

**Rand-** zW: ~**bemerkung** f marginal note; (fig) odd comment; ~**erscheinung** f unimportant side effect, marginal phenomenon; ~**figur** f minor figure; ~**gebiet** nt (GEOG) fringe; (POL) border territory; (fig) subsidiary; ~**streifen** m (der Straße) verge (BRIT), berm (US); (der Autobahn) hard shoulder (BRIT), shoulder (US); **r~voll** adj full to the brim.

**rang** etc [raŋ] vb siehe **ringen**.

**Rang** (-(e)s, ⁻e) m rank; (Stand) standing; (Wert) quality; (THEAT) circle; **ein Mann ohne ~ und Namen** a man without any standing; **erster/zweiter ~** dress/upper circle.

**Rangabzeichen** nt badge of rank.

**Rangälteste(r)** m senior officer.

**rangeln** ['raŋəln] (umg) vi to scrap; (um Posten): ~ **(um)** to wrangle (for).

**Rangfolge** f order of rank (bes MIL).

**Rangierbahnhof** [rã'ʒiːrbaːnhoːf] m marshalling yard.

**rangieren** vt (EISENB) to shunt, switch (US) ♦ vi to rank, be classed.

**Rangiergleis** nt siding.

**Rangliste** f (SPORT) ranking list, rankings pl.

**Rangordnung** f hierarchy; (MIL) rank.

**Rangunterschied** m social distinction; (MIL) difference in rank.

**rank** [raŋk] adj: ~ **und schlank** (liter) slender and supple.

**Ranke** ['raŋkə] (-, -n) f tendril, shoot.

**Ränke** ['rɛŋkə] pl intrigues pl; ~**schmied** m (liter) intriguer.

**ranken** ['raŋkən] vr to trail, grow; **sich um etw** ~ to twine around sth.

**ränkevoll** adj scheming.

**ranklotzen** ['raŋklɔtsən] (umg) vi to put one's nose to the grindstone.

**ranlassen** unreg (umg) vt: **jdn** ~ to let sb have a go.

**rann** etc [ran] vb siehe **rinnen**.

**rannte** etc ['rantə] vb siehe **rennen**.

**Ranzen** ['rantsən] (-s, -) m satchel; (umg: Bauch) belly, gut.

**ranzig** ['rantsɪç] adj rancid.

**Rappe** ['rapə] (-n, -n) m black horse.

**Rappel** ['rapəl] (-s, -) (umg) m (Fimmel) craze; (Wutanfall): **einen ~ kriegen** to throw a fit.

**Rappen** ['rapən] (-s, -) (SCHWEIZ) m (Geld) centime, rappen.

**Raps** [raps] (-es, -e) m (BOT) rape; ~**öl** nt rapeseed oil.

**rar** [raːr] adj rare; **sich ~ machen** (umg) to stay away.

**Rarität** [rari'tɛːt] f rarity; (Sammelobjekt) curio.

**rasant** [ra'zant] adj quick, rapid.

**rasch** [raʃ] adj quick.

**rascheln** vi to rustle.

**rasen** ['raːzən] vi to rave; (sich schnell bewegen) to race.

**Rasen** (-s, -) m grass; (gepflegt) lawn.

**rasend** adj furious; ~**e Kopfschmerzen** a splitting headache.

**Rasen-** zW: ~**mäher** (-s, -) m lawnmower; ~**mähmaschine** f lawnmower; ~**platz** m lawn; ~**sprenger** m (lawn) sprinkler.

**Raserei** [raːzə'raɪ] f raving, ranting; (Schnelle) reckless speeding.

**Rasier-** zW: ~**apparat** m shaver; ~**creme** f shaving cream; **r~en** vt, vr to shave; ~**klinge** f razor blade; ~**messer** nt razor; ~**pinsel** m shaving brush; ~**seife** f shaving soap od stick; ~**wasser** nt aftershave.

**raspeln** ['raspəln] vt to grate; (Holz) to rasp.

**Rasse** ['rasə] (-, -n) f race; (Tier~) breed; ~**hund** m thoroughbred dog.

**Rassel** (-, -n) f rattle.

**rasseln** vi to rattle, clatter.

**Rassenhaß** m race od racial hatred.

**Rassentrennung** f racial segregation.

**rassig** ['rasɪç] adj (Pferd, Auto) sleek; (Frau) vivacious; (Wein) spirited, lively.

**Rassismus** [ra'sɪsmʊs] (-) m racialism, racism.

**rassistisch** [ra'sɪstɪʃ] adj racialist, racist.

**Rast** [rast] (-, -en) f rest; **r~en** vi to rest.

**Raster** ['rastər] (-s, -) m (ARCHIT) grid; (PHOT: Gitter) screen; (TV) raster; (fig) framework.

**Rast-** zW: ~**haus** nt (AUT) service area, services pl; ~**hof** m (motorway) motel; (mit Tankstelle) service area (with a motel); **r~los** adj tireless; (unruhig) restless; ~**platz** m (AUT) lay-by (BRIT); ~**stätte** f service area, services pl.

**Rasur** [ra'zuːr] f shave; (das Rasieren) shaving.

**Rat** [raːt] (-(e)s, -schläge) m (piece of) advice; **jdn zu ~e ziehen** to consult sb; **jdm mit ~ und Tat zur Seite stehen** to support sb in (both) word and deed; **(sich** dat**) keinen ~ wissen** not to know what to do.

**rät** [rɛːt] vb siehe **raten**.

**Rate** (-, -n) f instalment (BRIT), installment (US); **auf ~n kaufen** to buy on hire purchase (BRIT) od on the installment plan (US); **in ~n zahlen** to pay in instalments (BRIT) od installments (US).

**raten** unreg vt, vi to guess; (empfehlen): **jdm ~** to advise sb; **dreimal darfst du ~** I'll give you three guesses (auch ironisch).

**ratenweise** adv by instalments (BRIT) od installments (US).

**Ratenzahlung** f hire purchase (BRIT), installment plan (US).

**Ratespiel** nt guessing game; (TV) quiz; (: Beruferaten etc) panel game.

**Ratgeber** (-s, -) m adviser.

**Rathaus** nt town hall; (einer Großstadt) city hall (bes US).

**ratifizieren** [ratifi'tsiːrən] vt to ratify.

**Ratifizierung** f ratification.

**Ration** [ratsi'oːn] f ration.

**rational** [ratsio'naːl] adj rational.

**rationalisieren** [ratsionali'ziːrən] vt to rationalize.

**rationell** [ratsio'nɛl] *adj* efficient.
**rationieren** [ratsio'niːrən] *vt* to ration.
**ratlos** *adj* at a loss, helpless.
**Ratlosigkeit** *f* helplessness.
**rätoromanisch** [rɛtoro'maːnɪʃ] *adj* Rhaetian.
**ratsam** *adj* advisable.
**Ratschlag** *m* (piece of) advice.
**Rätsel** ['rɛːtsəl] (-s, -) *nt* puzzle; (*Wort~*) riddle; **vor einem ~ stehen** to be baffled; **r~haft** *adj* mysterious; **es ist mir r~haft** it's a mystery to me; **r~n** *vi* to puzzle; **~raten** *nt* guessing game.
**Ratsherr** *m* councillor (*BRIT*), councilor (*US*).
**Ratskeller** *m* town-hall restaurant.
**ratsuchend** *adj:* **sich ~ an jdn wenden** to turn to sb for advice.
**Ratte** ['ratə] (-, -n) *f* rat.
**Rattenfänger** (-s, -) *m* rat-catcher.
**rattern** ['ratərn] *vi* to rattle, clatter.
**Raub** [raʊp] (-(e)s) *m* robbery; (*Beute*) loot, booty; **~bau** *m* overexploitation; **~druck** *m* pirate(d) edition; **r~en** ['raʊbən] *vt* to rob; (*jdn*) to kidnap, abduct.
**Räuber** ['rɔʏbər] (-s, -) *m* robber; **r~isch** *adj* thieving.
**Raub-** *zW:* **~fisch** *m* predatory fish; **r~gierig** *adj* rapacious; **~kassette** *f* pirate cassette; **~mord** *m* robbery with murder; **~tier** *nt* predator; **~überfall** *m* robbery with violence; **~vogel** *m* bird of prey.
**Rauch** [raʊx] (-(e)s) *m* smoke; **~abzug** *m* smoke outlet.
**rauchen** *vt, vi* to smoke; **mir raucht der Kopf** (*fig*) my head's spinning; „R~ verboten" "no smoking".
**Raucher(in)** (-s, -) *m(f)* smoker; **~abteil** *nt* (*EISENB*) smoker.
**räuchern** ['rɔʏçərn] *vt* to smoke, cure.
**Räucherspeck** *m* ≈ smoked bacon.
**Räucherstäbchen** *nt* joss stick.
**Rauch-** *zW:* **~fahne** *f* smoke trail; **~fang** *m* chimney hood; **~fleisch** *nt* smoked meat.
**rauchig** *adj* smoky.
**Rauchschwaden** *pl* drifts of smoke *pl*.
**räudig** ['rɔʏdɪç] *adj* mangy.
**rauf** [raʊf] (*umg*) *adv* = **herauf; hinauf.**
**Raufbold** (-(e)s, -e) *m* thug, hooligan.
**raufen** *vt* (*Haare*) to pull out ♦ *vi, vr* to fight.
**Rauferei** [raʊfə'raɪ] *f* brawl, fight.
**rauflustig** *adj* ready for a fight, pugnacious.
**rauh** [raʊ] *adj* rough, coarse; (*Wetter*) harsh; **in ~en Mengen** (*umg*) by the ton, galore; **~beinig** *adj* rough-and-ready; **R~fasertapete** *f* woodchip paper; **~haarig** *adj* wire-haired; **R~reif** *m* hoarfrost.
**Raum** [raʊm] (-(e)s, Räume) *m* space; (*Zimmer, Platz*) room; (*Gebiet*) area; **eine Frage im ~ stehen lassen** to leave a question unresolved; **~ausstatter(in)** *m(f)* interior decorator.
**räumen** ['rɔʏmən] *vt* to clear; (*Wohnung, Platz*) to vacate, move out of; (*verlassen: Gebäude,*

*Gebiet*) to evacuate; (*wegbringen*) to shift, move; (*in Schrank etc*) to put away.
**Raum-** *zW:* **~fähre** *f* space shuttle; **~fahrer** *m* astronaut; (*sowjetisch*) cosmonaut; **~fahrt** *f* space travel.
**Räumfahrzeug** ['rɔʏmfaːrtsɔʏk] *nt* bulldozer; (*für Schnee*) snow-clearer.
**Rauminhalt** *m* cubic capacity, volume.
**Raumkapsel** *f* space capsule.
**räumlich** ['rɔʏmlɪç] *adj* spatial; **R~keiten** *pl* premises *pl*.
**Raum-** *zW:* **~mangel** *m* lack of space; **~maß** *nt* unit of volume; cubic measurement; **~meter** *m* cubic metre (*BRIT*) *od* meter (*US*); **~pflegerin** *f* cleaner; **~schiff** *nt* spaceship; **~schiffahrt** *f* space travel; **r~sparend** *adj* space-saving; **~station** *f* space station; **~transporter** *m* space shuttle.
**Räumung** ['rɔʏmʊŋ] *f* clearing (away); (*von Haus etc*) vacating; (*wegen Gefahr*) evacuation; (*unter Zwang*) eviction.
**Räumungs-** *zW:* **~befehl** *m* eviction order; **~klage** *f* action for eviction; **~verkauf** *m* clearance sale.
**raunen** ['raʊnən] *vt, vi* to whisper.
**Raupe** ['raʊpə] (-, -n) *f* caterpillar; (*Raupenkette*) (caterpillar) track.
**Raupenschlepper** *m* caterpillar tractor.
**raus** [raʊs] (*umg*) *adv* = **heraus; hinaus.**
**Rausch** [raʊʃ] (-(e), *pl* Räusche) *m* intoxication; **einen ~ haben** to be drunk.
**rauschen** *vi* (*Wasser*) to rush; (*Baum*) to rustle; (*Radio etc*) to hiss; (*Mensch*) to sweep, sail.
**rauschend** *adj* (*Beifall*) thunderous; (*Fest*) sumptuous.
**Rauschgift** *nt* drug; **~handel** *m* drug traffic; **~süchtige(r)** *f(m)* drug addict.
**rausfliegen** *unreg* (*umg*) *vi* to be chucked out.
**räuspern** ['rɔʏspərn] *vr* to clear one's throat.
**Rausschmeißer** ['raʊsʃmaɪsər] (-s, -) (*umg*) *m* bouncer.
**Raute** ['raʊtə] (-, -n) *f* diamond; (*MATH*) rhombus.
**rautenförmig** *adj* rhombic.
**Razzia** ['ratsia] (-, Razzien) *f* raid.
**Reagenzglas** [rea'gɛntsglaːs] *nt* test tube.
**reagieren** [rea'giːrən] *vi:* **~ (auf +akk)** to react (to).
**Reaktion** [reaktsi'oːn] *f* reaction.
**reaktionär** [reaktsio'nɛːr] *adj* reactionary.
**Reaktionsfähigkeit** *f* reactions *pl*.
**Reaktionsgeschwindigkeit** *f* speed of reaction.
**Reaktor** [re'aktɔr] *m* reactor; **~kern** *m* reactor core; **~unglück** *nt* nuclear accident.
**real** [re'aːl] *adj* real, material; **R~einkommen** *nt* real income.
**realisierbar** [reali'ziːrbaːr] *adj* practicable, feasible.
**Realismus** [rea'lɪsmʊs] *m* realism.
**Realist(in)** [rea'lɪst(ɪn)] *m(f)* realist; **r~isch** *adj*

realistic.

**Realität** [reali'tɛːt] *f* reality; **Realitäten** *pl*
(*Gegebenheiten*) facts *pl*.

**realitätsfremd** *adj* out of touch with reality.

**Realpolitik** *f* political realism.

**Realschule** *f* ≈ middle school (*BRIT*), junior
high school (*US*).

---

*The* **Realschule** *is one of the choices of
secondary schools available to a German
schoolchild after the* **Grundschule***. At the end
of six years schooling in the Realschule pupils
gain the* **mittlere Reife** *and usually go on to
some kind of training or to a college of further
education.*

---

**Realzeit** *f* real time.

**Rebe** ['reːbə] (-, -n) *f* vine.

**Rebell(in)** [re'bɛl(ɪn)] (-en, -en) *m(f)* rebel.

**rebellieren** [rebe'liːrən] *vi* to rebel.

**Rebellion** [rebɛli'oːn] *f* rebellion.

**rebellisch** [re'bɛlɪʃ] *adj* rebellious.

**Rebensaft** *m* wine.

**Reb-** [rep] *zW:* **~huhn** *nt* partridge; **~laus** *f*
vine pest; **~stock** *m* vine.

**Rechen** ['rɛçən] (-s, -) *m* rake; **r~** *vt, vi* to rake.

**Rechen-** *zW:* **~aufgabe** *f* sum, mathematical
problem; **~fehler** *m* miscalculation;
**~maschine** *f* adding machine.

**Rechenschaft** *f* account; **jdm über etw** *akk*
**~ ablegen** to account to sb for sth; **jdn zur
~ ziehen (für)** to call sb to account (for *od*
over); **jdm ~ schulden** to be accountable to
sb.

**Rechenschaftsbericht** *m* report.

**Rechenschieber** *m* slide rule.

**Rechenzentrum** *nt* computer centre (*BRIT*)
*od* center (*US*).

**recherchieren** [reʃɛr'ʃiːrən] *vt, vi* to
investigate.

**rechnen** ['rɛçnən] *vt, vi* to calculate;
(*veranschlagen*) to estimate, reckon; **jdn/etw
zu etw ~** to count sb/sth among sth; **~ mit**
to reckon with; **~ auf** +*akk* to count on.

**Rechnen** *nt* arithmetic; (*bes SCH*) sums *pl*.

**Rechner** (-s, -) *m* calculator; (*COMPUT*)
computer; **r~abhängig** *adj* (*COMPUT*) on line;
**r~fern** *adj* (*COMPUT*) remote; **r~isch** *adj*
arithmetical; **r~unabhängig** *adj* (*COMPUT*)
off line.

**Rechnung** *f* calculation(s); (*COMM*) bill
(*BRIT*), check (*US*); **auf eigene ~** on one's
own account; **(jdm) etw in ~ stellen** to
charge (sb) for sth; **jdm/etw ~ tragen** to
take sb/sth into account.

**Rechnungs-** *zW:* **~aufstellung** *f* statement;
**~buch** *nt* account book; **~hof** *m* ≈ Auditor-
General's office (*BRIT*), audit division (*US*);
**~jahr** *nt* financial year; **~prüfer** *m* auditor;
**~prüfung** *f* audit(ing).

**recht** [rɛçt] *adj* right ♦ *adv* (*vor Adjektiv*) really,
quite; **das ist mir ~** that suits me; **jetzt erst**

~ now more than ever; **alles, was ~ ist**
(*empört*) fair's fair; (*anerkennend*) you can't
deny it; **nach dem R~en sehen** to see that
everything's O.K.; **~ haben** to be right; **jdm
~ geben** to agree with sb, admit that sb is
right; **du kommst gerade ~, um ...** you're
just in time to ...; **gehe ich ~ in der
Annahme, daß ...?** am I correct in assuming
that ...?; **~ herzlichen Dank** thank you very
much indeed.

**Recht** (-(e)s, -e) *nt* right; (*JUR*) law;
**~ sprechen** to administer justice; **mit** *od* **zu
~** rightly, justly; **von ~s wegen** by rights;
**zu seinem ~ kommen** (*lit*) to gain one's
rights; (*fig*) to come into one's own; **gleiches
~ für alle!** equal rights for all!

**Rechte** *f* right (hand); (*POL*) Right.

**Rechte(r, s)** *f(m)* (*POL*) right-winger ♦ *nt*
right thing; **etwas/nichts ~s** something/
nothing proper.

**rechte(r, s)** *adj* right; (*POL*) right-wing.

**recht-** *zW:* **R~eck** (-(e)s, -e) *nt* rectangle;
**~eckig** *adj* rectangular; **~fertigen** *vt untr* to
justify ♦ *vr untr* to justify o.s.; **R~fertigung** *f*
justification; **~haberisch** *adj* dogmatic;
**~lich** *adj* legal, lawful; **~lich nicht zulässig**
not permissible in law, illegal; **~mäßig** *adj*
legal, lawful.

**rechts** [rɛçts] *adv* on *od* to the right; **~ stehen**
*od* **sein** (*POL*) to be right-wing; **~ stricken** to
knit (plain); **R~abbieger** (-s, -) *m*: **die Spur
für R~abbieger** the right-hand turn-off lane;
**R~anspruch** *m*: **einen R~anspruch auf etw**
*akk* **haben** to be legally entitled to sth;
**R~anwalt** *m*, **R~anwältin** *f* lawyer,
barrister; **R~außen** (-, -) *m* (*SPORT*) outside
right; **R~beistand** *m* legal adviser.

**rechtschaffen** *adj* upright.

**Rechtschreibung** *f* spelling.

**Rechts-** *zW:* **~drehung** *f* clockwise rotation;
**~extremismus** *m* right-wing extremism;
**~extremist** *m* right-wing extremist; **~fall** *m*
(law) case; **~frage** *f* legal question;
**r~gültig** *adj* legally valid; **~händer(in)** (-s, -)
*m(f)* right-handed person; **r~kräftig** *adj* valid,
legal; **~kurve** *f* right-hand bend; **~lage** *f*
legal position; **r~lastig** *adj* listing to the
right; (*fig*) leaning to the right; **~pflege** *f*
administration of justice; **~pfleger** *m*
*official with certain judicial powers.*

**Rechtsprechung** ['rɛçtʃprɛçʊŋ] *f*
(*Gerichtsbarkeit*) jurisdiction; (*richterliche
Tätigkeit*) dispensation of justice.

**Rechts-** *zW:* **r~radikal** *adj* (*POL*) extreme
right-wing; **~schutz** *m* legal protection;
**~spruch** *m* verdict; **~staat** *m* state under the
rule of law; **~streit** *m* lawsuit; **~titel** *m* title;
**r~verbindlich** *adj* legally binding; **~verkehr**
*m* driving on the right; **~weg** *m*: **der ~weg
ist ausgeschlossen** ≈ the judges' decision is
final; **r~widrig** *adj* illegal; **~wissenschaft** *f*
jurisprudence.

**rechtwinklig** *adj* right-angled.
**rechtzeitig** *adj* timely ♦ *adv* in time.
**Reck** [rɛk] (-(e)s, -e) *nt* horizontal bar.
**recken** *vt, vr* to stretch.
**recyceln** [riː'saikəln] *vt* to recycle.
**Recycling** [ri'sailkɪŋ] (-s) *nt* recycling.
**Red.** *abk* = **Redaktion**; (= *Redakteur(in)*) ed.
**Redakteur(in)** [redak'tøːr(ɪn)] *m(f)* editor.
**Redaktion** [redaktsi'oːn] *f* editing; (*Leute*)
   editorial staff; (*Büro*) editorial office(s *pl*).
**Redaktionsschluß** *m* time of going to press;
   (*Einsendeschluß*) copy deadline.
**Rede** ['reːdə] (-, -n) *f* speech; (*Gespräch*) talk;
   **jdn zur ~ stellen** to take sb to task; **eine**
   **~ halten** to make a speech; **das ist nicht der**
   **~ wert** it's not worth mentioning; **davon**
   **kann keine ~ sein** it's out of the question;
   **~freiheit** *f* freedom of speech; **r~gewandt**
   *adj* eloquent.
**Reden** (-s) *nt* talking, speech.
**reden** *vi* to talk, speak ♦ *vt* to say; (*Unsinn etc*)
   to talk; **(viel) von sich ~ machen** to become
   (very much) a talking point; **darüber läßt**
   **sich ~** that's a possibility; (*über Preis,*
   *Bedingungen*) I think we could discuss that;
   **er läßt mit sich ~** he could be persuaded; (*in*
   *bezug auf Preis*) he's open to offers;
   (*gesprächsbereit*) he's open to discussion.
**Redensart** *f* set phrase.
**Redeschwall** *m* torrent of words.
**Redewendung** *f* expression, idiom.
**redlich** ['reːtlɪç] *adj* honest; **R~keit** *f* honesty.
**Redner(in)** (-s, -) *m(f)* speaker, orator.
**redselig** ['reːtzeːlɪç] *adj* talkative, loquacious;
   **R~keit** *f* talkativeness, loquacity.
**redundant** [redʊn'dant] *adj* redundant.
**Redundanz** [redʊn'dants] (-) *f* redundancy.
**reduzieren** [redu'tsiːrən] *vt* to reduce.
**Reduzierung** *f* reduction.
**Reede** ['reːdə] (-, -n) *f* protected anchorage.
**Reeder** (-s, -) *m* shipowner.
**Reederei** [reːdə'rai] *f* shipping line *od* firm.
**reell** [re'ɛl] *adj* fair, honest; (*Preis*) fair;
   (*COMM: Geschäft*) sound; (*MATH*) real.
**Reetdach** ['reːtdax] *nt* thatched roof.
**Ref.** *abk* = **Referendar(in)**; **Referent(in)**.
**Referat** [refe'raːt] (-(e)s, -e) *nt* report; (*Vortrag*)
   paper; (*Gebiet*) section; (*VERWALTUNG:*
   *Ressort*) department; **ein ~ halten** to present
   a seminar paper.
**Referendar(in)** [referɛn'darɪn)] *m(f)* trainee
   (in civil service); (*Studien~*) trainee
   teacher; (*Gerichts~*) articled clerk.
**Referendum** [refe'rɛndʊm] (-s, Referenden) *nt*
   referendum.
**Referent(in)** [refe'rɛnt(ɪn)] *m(f)* speaker;
   (*Berichterstatter*) reporter; (*Sachbearbeiter*)
   expert.
**Referenz** [refe'rɛnts] *f* reference.
**referieren** [refe'riːrən] *vi:* **~ über** +*akk* to speak
   *od* talk on.
**reflektieren** [reflek'tiːrən] *vt, vi* to reflect;

   **~ auf** +*akk* to be interested in.
**Reflex** [re'flɛks] (-es, -e) *m* reflex; **~bewegung**
   *f* reflex action.
**reflexiv** [reflɛ'ksiːf] *adj* (*GRAM*) reflexive.
**Reform** [re'fɔrm] (-, -en) *f* reform.
**Reformation** [refɔrmatsi'oːn] *f* reformation.
**Reformator** [refɔr'maːtɔr] *m* reformer; **r~isch**
   *adj* reformatory, reforming.
**reform-** *zW:* **~bedürftig** *adj* in need of reform;
   **~freudig** *adj* avid for reform; **R~haus** *nt*
   health food shop.
**reformieren** [refɔr'miːrən] *vt* to reform.
**Refrain** [rə'frɛː] (-s, -s) *m* refrain, chorus.
**Reg.** *abk* (= *Regierungs-*) gov.; (= *Register*)
   reg.
**Regal** [re'gaːl] (-s, -e) *nt* (book)shelves *pl*,
   bookcase; (*TYP*) stand, rack.
**Regatta** [re'gata] (-, Regatten) *f* regatta.
**Reg.-Bez.** *abk* = **Regierungsbezirk**.
**rege** ['reːgə] *adj* lively, active; (*Geschäft*)
   brisk.
**Regel** ['reːgəl] (-, -n) *f* rule; (*MED*) period; **in**
   **der ~** as a rule; **nach allen ~n der Kunst** (*fig*)
   thoroughly; **sich** *dat* **etw zur ~ machen** to
   make a habit of sth; **r~los** *adj* irregular,
   unsystematic; **r~mäßig** *adj* regular;
   **~mäßigkeit** *f* regularity.
**regeln** *vt* to regulate, control; (*Angelegenheit*)
   to settle ♦ *vr:* **sich von selbst ~** to take care
   of itself; **gesetzlich geregelt sein** to be laid
   down by law.
**regelrecht** *adj* proper, thorough.
**Regelung** *f* regulation; settlement.
**regelwidrig** *adj* irregular, against the rules.
**regen** ['reːgən] *vt* to move ♦ *vr* to move, stir.
**Regen** (-s, -) *m* rain; **vom ~ in die Traufe**
   **kommen** (*Sprichwort*) to jump out of the
   frying pan into the fire (*Sprichwort*).
**Regenbogen** *m* rainbow; **~haut** *f* (*ANAT*)
   iris; **~presse** *f* trashy magazines *pl*.
**regenerieren** [regene'riːrən] *vr* (*BIOL*) to
   regenerate; (*fig*) to revitalize *od* regenerate
   o.s. *od* itself; (*nach Anstrengung, Schock etc*)
   to recover.
**Regen-** *zW:* **~guß** *m* downpour; **~mantel** *m*
   raincoat, mac(kintosh); **~menge** *f* rainfall;
   **~schauer** *m* shower (of rain); **~schirm** *m*
   umbrella.
**Regent(in)** [re'gɛnt(ɪn)] *m(f)* regent.
**Regentag** *m* rainy day.
**Regentropfen** *m* raindrop.
**Regentschaft** *f* regency.
**Regen-** *zW:* **~wald** *m* (*GEOG*) rain forest;
   **~wetter** *nt:* **er macht ein Gesicht wie drei** *od*
   **sieben Tage ~wetter** (*umg*) he's got a face
   as long as a month of Sundays; **~wurm** *m*
   earthworm; **~zeit** *f* rainy season, rains *pl*.
**Regie** [re'ʒiː] *f* (*FILM etc*) direction; (*THEAT*)
   production; **unter der ~ von** directed *od*
   produced by; **~anweisung** *f* (stage)
   direction.
**regieren** [re'giːrən] *vt, vi* to govern, rule.

**Regierung** f government; (*Monarchie*) reign; **an die ~ kommen** to come to power.

**Regierungs-** zW: **~bezirk** m ≈ county (*BRIT, US*), region (*SCOT*); **~erklärung** f inaugural speech; (*in Großbritannien*) Queen's/King's Speech; **~sprecher** m government spokesman; **~vorlage** f government bill; **~wechsel** m change of government; **~zeit** f period in government; (*von König*) reign.

**Regiment** [regi'mɛnt] (-s, -er) nt regiment.

**Region** [regi'o:n] f region.

**Regionalplanung** [regio'na:lpla:nʊŋ] f regional planning.

**Regionalprogramm** nt (*RUNDF, TV*) regional programme (*BRIT*) od program (*US*).

**Regisseur(in)** [reʒɪ'sø:r(ɪn)] m(f) director; (*THEAT*) (stage) producer.

**Register** [re'gɪstər] (-s, -) nt register; (*in Buch*) table of contents, index; **alle ~ ziehen** to pull out all the stops; **~führer** m registrar.

**Registratur** [regɪstra'tu:r] f registry, records office.

**registrieren** [regɪs'tri:rən] vt to register; (*umg: zur Kenntnis nehmen*) to note.

**Registrierkasse** f cash register.

**Regler** ['re:glər] (-s, -) m regulator, governor.

**reglos** ['re:klo:s] adj motionless.

**regnen** ['re:gnən] vi unpers to rain ♦ vt unpers: **es regnet Glückwünsche** congratulations are pouring in; **es regnet in Strömen** it's pouring (with rain).

**regnerisch** adj rainy.

**Regreß** [re'grɛs] (-sses, -sse) m (*JUR*) recourse, redress; **~anspruch** m (*JUR*) claim for compensation.

**regsam** ['re:kza:m] adj active.

**regulär** [regu'lɛ:r] adj regular.

**regulieren** [regu'li:rən] vt to regulate; (*COMM*) to settle; **sich von selbst ~** to be self-regulating.

**Regung** ['re:gʊŋ] f motion; (*Gefühl*) feeling, impulse.

**regungslos** adj motionless.

**Reh** [re:] (-(e)s, -e) nt deer; (*weiblich*) roe deer.

**rehabilitieren** [rehabili'ti:rən] vt to rehabilitate; (*Ruf, Ehre*) to vindicate ♦ vr to rehabilitate (*form*) od vindicate o.s.

**Rehabilitierung** f rehabilitation.

**Reh-** zW: **~bock** m roebuck; **~braten** m roast venison; **~kalb** nt fawn; **~kitz** nt fawn.

**Reibach** ['raɪbax] (-s) m: **einen ~ machen** (*umg*) to make a killing.

**Reibe** ['raɪbə] (-, -n) f grater.

**Reibeisen** ['raɪpˌaɪzən] nt grater.

**Reibekuchen** m (*KOCH*) ≈ potato waffle.

**reiben** unreg vt to rub; (*KOCH*) to grate.

**Reiberei** [raɪbə'raɪ] f friction no pl.

**Reibfläche** f rough surface.

**Reibung** f friction.

**reibungslos** adj smooth; **~ verlaufen** to go off smoothly.

**Reich** [raɪç] (-(e)s, -e) nt empire, kingdom;

(*fig*) realm; **das Dritte ~** the Third Reich.

**reich** adj rich ♦ adv: **eine ~ ausgestattete Bibliothek** a well-stocked library.

**reichen** vi to reach; (*genügen*) to be enough od sufficient ♦ vt to hold out; (*geben*) to pass, hand; (*anbieten*) to offer; **so weit das Auge reicht** as far as the eye can see; **jdm ~** (*genügen*) to be enough od sufficient for sb; **mir reichts!** I've had enough!

**reich-** zW: **~haltig** adj ample, rich; **~lich** adj ample, plenty of; **R~tum** (-s, -tümer) m wealth; **R~weite** f range; **jd ist in R~weite** sb is nearby.

**reif** [raɪf] adj ripe; (*Mensch, Urteil*) mature; **für etw ~ sein** (*umg*) to be ready for sth.

**Reif¹** (-(e)s) m hoarfrost.

**Reif²** (-(e)s, -e) m (*Ring*) ring, hoop.

**Reife** (-) f ripeness; maturity; **mittlere ~** (*SCH*) *first public examination in secondary school*, ≈ O-Levels pl (*BRIT*).

**Reifen** (-s, -) m ring, hoop; (*Fahrzeug~*) tyre (*BRIT*), tire (*US*).

**reifen** vi to mature; (*Obst*) to ripen.

**Reifen-** zW: **~druck** m tyre (*BRIT*) od tire (*US*) pressure; **~panne** f puncture, flat; **~profil** nt tyre (*BRIT*) od tire (*US*) tread; **~schaden** m puncture, flat.

**Reifeprüfung** f school-leaving exam.

**Reifezeugnis** nt school-leaving certificate.

**reiflich** ['raɪflɪç] adj thorough, careful.

**Reihe** ['raɪə] (-, -n) f row; (*von Tagen etc: umg: Anzahl*) series sing; **eine ganze ~ (von)** (*unbestimmte Anzahl*) a whole lot (of); **der ~ nach** in turn; **er ist an der ~** it's his turn; **an die ~ kommen** to have one's turn; **außer der ~** out of turn; (*ausnahmsweise*) out of the usual way of things; **aus der ~ tanzen** (*fig: umg*) to be different; (*gegen Konventionen verstoßen*) to step out of line; **ich kriege heute nichts auf die ~** I can't get my act together today.

**reihen** vt to set in a row; to arrange in series; (*Perlen*) to string.

**Reihen-** zW: **~folge** f sequence; **alphabetische ~folge** alphabetical order; **~haus** nt terraced (*BRIT*) od row (*US*) house; **~untersuchung** f mass screening; **r~weise** adv (*in Reihen*) in rows; (*fig: in großer Anzahl*) by the dozen.

**Reiher** (-s, -) m heron.

**reihum** [raɪ'ʊm] adv: **etw ~ gehen lassen** to pass sth around.

**Reim** [raɪm] (-(e)s, -e) m rhyme; **sich** dat **einen ~ auf etw** akk **machen** (*umg*) to make sense of sth; **r~en** vt to rhyme.

**rein¹** [raɪn] (*umg*) adv = **herein; hinein.**

**rein²** [raɪn] adj pure; (*sauber*) clean ♦ adv purely; **das ist die ~ste Freude/der ~ste Hohn** etc it's pure od sheer joy/mockery etc; **etw ins ~e schreiben** to make a fair copy of sth; **etw ins ~e bringen** to clear sth up; **~en Tisch machen** (*fig*) to get things straight;

~ **unmöglich** (*umg: ganz, völlig*) absolutely impossible.

**Rein-** *in zW* (*COMM*) net(t).

**Rein(e)machefrau** *f* cleaning lady, charwoman (*BRIT*).

**rein(e)weg** (*umg*) *adv* completely, absolutely.

**rein-** *zW:* **R~fall** (*umg*) *m* let-down; (*Mißerfolg*) flop; **~fallen** *vi:* **auf jdn/etw ~fallen** to be taken in by sb/sth; **R~gewinn** *m* net profit; **R~heit** *f* purity; cleanness.

**reinigen** ['raɪnɪɡən] *vt* to clean; (*Wasser*) to purify.

**Reiniger** (**-s, -**) *m* cleaner.

**Reinigung** *f* cleaning; purification; (*Geschäft*) cleaner's; **chemische ~** dry-cleaning; (*Geschäft*) dry-cleaner's.

**Reinigungsmittel** *nt* cleansing agent.

**rein-** *zW:* **~lich** *adj* clean; **R~lichkeit** *f* cleanliness; **~rassig** *adj* pedigree; **~reiten** *unreg vt:* **jdn ~reiten** to get sb into a mess; **R~schrift** *f* fair copy; **R~vermögen** *nt* net assets *pl;* **~waschen** *unreg vr* to clear o.s.

**Reis¹** [raɪs] (**-es, -e**) *m* rice.

**Reis²** [raɪs] (**-es, -er**) *nt* twig, sprig.

**Reise** ['raɪzə] (**-, -n**) *f* journey; (*Schiffs~*) voyage; **Reisen** *pl* travels *pl;* **gute ~!** bon voyage!, have a good journey!; **auf ~n sein** to be away (travelling (*BRIT*) *od* traveling (*US*)); **er ist viel auf ~n** he does a lot of travelling (*BRIT*) *od* traveling (*US*); **~andenken** *nt* souvenir; **~apotheke** *f* first-aid kit; **~bericht** *m* account of one's journey; (*Buch*) travel story; (*Film*) travelogue (*BRIT*), travelog (*US*); **~büro** *nt* travel agency; **~diplomatie** *f* shuttle diplomacy; **~erleichterungen** *pl* easing *sing* of travel restrictions; **r~fertig** *adj* ready to start; **~fieber** *nt* (*fig*) travel nerves *pl;* **~führer** *m* guide(book); (*Mensch*) (travel) guide; **~gepäck** *nt* luggage; **~gesellschaft** *f* party of travellers (*BRIT*) *od* travelers (*US*); **~kosten** *pl* travelling (*BRIT*) *od* traveling (*US*) expenses *pl;* **~leiter** *m* courier; **~lektüre** *f* reading for the journey; **~lust** *f* wanderlust.

**reisen** *vi* to travel; **~ nach** to go to.

**Reisende(r)** *f(m)* traveller (*BRIT*), traveler (*US*).

**Reise-** *zW:* **~paß** *m* passport; **~pläne** *pl* plans *pl* for a *od* the journey; **~proviant** *m* provisions *pl* for the journey; **~route** *f* itinerary; **~scheck** *m* traveller's cheque (*BRIT*), traveler's check (*US*); **~schreibmaschine** *f* portable typewriter; **~tasche** *f* travelling (*BRIT*) *od* traveling (*US*) bag *od* case; **~veranstalter** *m* tour operator; **~verkehr** *m* tourist *od* holiday traffic; **~wetter** *nt* holiday weather; **~ziel** *nt* destination.

**Reisig** ['raɪzɪç] (**-s**) *nt* brushwood.

**Reißaus** *m:* **~ nehmen** to run away, flee.

**Reißbrett** *nt* drawing board; **~stift** *m* drawing

pin (*BRIT*), thumbtack (*US*).

**reißen** ['raɪsən] *unreg vt* to tear; (*ziehen*) to pull, drag; (*Witz*) to crack ♦ *vi* to tear; to pull, drag; **etw an sich ~** to snatch sth up; (*fig*) to take sth over; **sich um etw ~** to scramble for sth; **hin und her gerissen sein** (*fig*) to be torn; **wenn alle Stricke ~** (*fig: umg*) if the worst comes to the worst.

**Reißen** *nt* (*Gewichtheben: Disziplin*) snatch; (*umg: Glieder~*) ache.

**reißend** *adj* (*Fluß*) torrential; (*COMM*) rapid; **~en Absatz finden** to sell like hot cakes (*umg*).

**Reißer** (**-s, -**) (*umg*) *m* thriller; **r~isch** *adj* sensational.

**Reiß-** *zW:* **~leine** *f* (*AVIAT*) ripcord; **~nagel** *m* drawing pin (*BRIT*), thumbtack (*US*); **~schiene** *f* T-square; **~verschluß** *m* zip (fastener) (*BRIT*), zipper (*US*); **~wolf** *m* shredder; **durch den ~wolf geben** (*Dokumente*) to shred; **~zeug** *nt* geometry set; **~zwecke** *f* = **Reißnagel**.

**reiten** ['raɪtən] *unreg vt, vi* to ride.

**Reiter** (**-s, -**) *m* rider; (*MIL*) cavalryman, trooper.

**Reiterei** [raɪtə'raɪ] *f* cavalry.

**Reiterin** *f* rider.

**Reit-** *zW:* **~hose** *f* riding breeches *pl;* **~pferd** *nt* saddle horse; **~schule** *f* riding school; **~stiefel** *m* riding boot; **~turnier** *nt* horse show; **~weg** *m* bridle path; **~zeug** *nt* riding outfit.

**Reiz** [raɪts] (**-es, -e**) *m* stimulus; (*angenehm*) charm; (*Verlockung*) attraction.

**reizbar** *adj* irritable; **R~keit** *f* irritability.

**reizen** *vt* to stimulate; (*unangenehm*) to irritate; (*verlocken*) to appeal to, attract; (*KARTEN*) to bid ♦ *vi:* **zum Widerspruch ~** to invite contradiction.

**reizend** *adj* charming.

**Reiz-** *zW:* **~gas** *nt* tear gas, CS gas; **~husten** *m* chesty cough; **r~los** *adj* unattractive; **r~voll** *adj* attractive; **~wäsche** *f* sexy underwear; **~wort** *nt* emotive word.

**rekapitulieren** [rekapitu'liːrən] *vt* to recapitulate.

**rekeln** ['reːkəln] *vr* to stretch out; (*lümmeln*) to lounge *od* loll about.

**Reklamation** [reklamatsi'oːn] *f* complaint.

**Reklame** [re'klaːmə] (**-, -n**) *f* advertising; (*Anzeige*) advertisement; **mit etw ~ machen** (*pej*) to show off about sth; **für etw ~ machen** to advertise sth; **~trommel** *f:* **die ~trommel für jdn/etw rühren** (*umg*) to beat the (big) drum for sb/sth; **~wand** *f* notice (*BRIT*) *od* bulletin (*US*) board.

**reklamieren** [rekla'miːrən] *vi* to complain ♦ *vt* to complain about; (*zurückfordern*) to reclaim.

**rekonstruieren** [rekɔnstru'iːrən] *vt* to reconstruct.

**Rekonvaleszenz** [rekɔnvales'tsɛnts] *f*

convalescence.

**Rekord** [re'kɔrt] (**-(e)s, -e**) *m* record; **~leistung** *f* record performance.

**Rekrut** [re'kruːt] (**-en, -en**) *m* recruit.

**rekrutieren** [rekru'tiːrən] *vt* to recruit ♦ *vr* to be recruited.

**Rektor** ['rɛktɔr] *m* (*UNIV*) rector, vice-chancellor; (*SCH*) head teacher (*BRIT*), principal (*US*).

**Rektorat** [rɛktɔ'raːt] (**-(e)s, -e**) *nt* rectorate, vice-chancellorship; headship (*BRIT*), principalship (*US*); (*Zimmer*) rector's *etc* office.

**Rektorin** [rɛk'toːrɪn] *f* (*SCH*) head teacher (*BRIT*), principal (*US*).

**Rel.** *abk* (= *Religion*) rel.

**Relais** [rə'lɛː] (**-, -**) *nt* relay.

**Relation** [relatsi'oːn] *f* relation.

**relativ** [rela'tiːf] *adj* relative.

**Relativität** [relativi'tɛːt] *f* relativity.

**Relativpronomen** *nt* (*GRAM*) relative pronoun.

**relevant** [rele'vant] *adj* relevant.

**Relevanz** *f* relevance.

**Relief** [reli'ɛf] (**-s, -s**) *nt* relief.

**Religion** [religi'oːn] *f* religion.

**Religions-** *zW*: **~freiheit** *f* freedom of worship; **~lehre** *f* religious education; **~unterricht** *m* religious education.

**religiös** [religi'øːs] *adj* religious.

**Relikt** [re'lɪkt] (**-(e)s, -e**) *nt* relic.

**Reling** ['reːlɪŋ] (**-, -s**) *f* (*NAUT*) rail.

**Reliquie** [re'liːkviə] *f* relic.

**Reminiszenz** [reminɪs'tsɛnts] *f* reminiscence, recollection.

**Remis** [rə'miː] (**-, - od -en**) *nt* (*SCHACH, SPORT*) draw.

**Remittende** [remɪ'tɛndə] (**-, -n**) *f* (*COMM*) return.

**Remittent** *m* (*FIN*) payee.

**remittieren** *vt* (*COMM: Waren*) to return; (*Geld*) to remit.

**Remmidemmi** ['rɛmidɛmi] (**-s**) (*umg*) *nt* (*Krach*) row, rumpus; (*Trubel*) rave-up.

**Remoulade** [remu'laːdə] (**-, -n**) *f* remoulade.

**rempeln** ['rɛmpəln] (*umg*) *vt* to jostle, elbow; (*SPORT*) to barge into; (*foulen*) to push.

**Ren** [rɛn] (**-s, -s od -e**) *nt* reindeer.

**Renaissance** [rənɛ'sãːs] (**-, -n**) *f* (*HIST*) renaissance; (*fig*) revival, rebirth.

**Rendezvous** [rãde'vuː] (**-, -**) *nt* rendezvous.

**Rendite** [rɛn'diːtə] (**-, -n**) *f* (*FIN*) yield, return on capital.

**Rennbahn** *f* racecourse; (*AUT*) circuit, racetrack.

**rennen** ['rɛnən] *unreg vt, vi* to run, race; **um die Wette ~** to have a race; **R~** (**-s, -**) *nt* running; (*Wettbewerb*) race; **das R~ machen** (*lit, fig*) to win (the race).

**Renner** (**-s, -**) (*umg*) *m* winner, worldbeater.

**Renn-** *zW*: **~fahrer** *m* racing driver (*BRIT*), race car driver (*US*); **~pferd** *nt* racehorse;

**~platz** *m* racecourse; **~rad** *nt* racing cycle; **~sport** *m* racing; **~wagen** *m* racing car (*BRIT*), race car (*US*).

**renommiert** [reno'miːrt] *adj*: **~ (wegen)** renowned (for), famous (for).

**renovieren** [reno'viːrən] *vt* to renovate.

**Renovierung** *f* renovation.

**rentabel** [rɛn'taːbəl] *adj* profitable, lucrative.

**Rentabilität** [rɛntabili'tɛːt] *f* profitability.

**Rente** ['rɛntə] (**-, -n**) *f* pension.

**Renten-** *zW*: **~basis** *f* annuity basis; **~empfänger** *m* pensioner; **~papier** *nt* (*FIN*) fixed-interest security; **~versicherung** *f* pension scheme.

**Rentier** ['rɛntiːr] *nt* reindeer.

**rentieren** [rɛn'tiːrən] *vi, vr* to pay, be profitable; **das rentiert (sich) nicht** it's not worth it.

**Rentner(in)** ['rɛntnər(ɪn)] (**-s, -**) *m(f)* pensioner.

**Reparation** [reparatsi'oːn] *f* reparation.

**Reparatur** [repara'tuːr] *f* repairing; repair; **etw in ~ geben** to have sth repaired; **r~bedürftig** *adj* in need of repair; **~werkstatt** *f* repair shop; (*AUT*) garage.

**reparieren** [repa'riːrən] *vt* to repair.

**Repertoire** [reperto'aːr] (**-s, -s**) *nt* repertoire.

**Reportage** [repɔr'taːʒə] (**-, -n**) *f* report.

**Reporter(in)** [re'pɔrtər(ɪn)] (**-s, -**) *m(f)* reporter, commentator.

**Repräsentant(in)** [reprɛzɛn'tant(ɪn)] *m(f)* representative.

**repräsentativ** [reprɛzɛnta'tiːf] *adj* representative; (*Geschenk etc*) prestigious; **die ~en Pflichten eines Botschafters** the social duties of an ambassador.

**repräsentieren** [reprɛzɛn'tiːrən] *vt* to represent ♦ *vi* to perform official duties.

**Repressalien** [reprɛ'saːliən] *pl* reprisals *pl*.

**reprivatisieren** [reprivati'ziːrən] *vt* to denationalize.

**Reprivatisierung** *f* denationalization.

**Reproduktion** [reprodʊktsi'oːn] *f* reproduction.

**reproduzieren** [reprodu'tsiːrən] *vt* to reproduce.

**Reptil** [rɛp'tiːl] (**-s, -ien**) *nt* reptile.

**Republik** [repu'bliːk] *f* republic.

**Republikaner** [republi'kaːnər] (**-s, -**) *m* republican.

**republikanisch** *adj* republican.

**Requisiten** *pl* (*THEAT*) props *pl*, properties *pl* (*form*).

**Reservat** [rezɛr'vaːt] (**-(e)s, -e**) *nt* reservation.

**Reserve** [re'zɛrvə] (**-, -n**) *f* reserve; **jdn aus der ~ locken** to bring sb out of his/her shell; **~rad** *nt* (*AUT*) spare wheel; **~spieler** *m* reserve; **~tank** *m* reserve tank.

**reservieren** [rezɛr'viːrən] *vt* to reserve.

**reserviert** *adj* (*Platz, Mensch*) reserved.

**Reservist** [rezɛr'vɪst] *m* reservist.

**Reservoir** [rezɛrvo'aːr] (**-s, -e**) *nt* reservoir.

**Residenz** [rezi'dɛnts] *f* residence, seat.

**residieren** [rezi'di:rən] *vi* to reside.
**Resignation** [rezɪgnatsi'o:n] *f* resignation.
**resignieren** [rezɪ'gni:rən] *vi* to resign.
**resolut** [rezo'lu:t] *adj* resolute.
**Resolution** [rezolutsi'o:n] *f* resolution;
(*Bittschrift*) petition.
**Resonanz** [rezo'nants] *f* (*lit, fig*) resonance;
~**boden** *m* sounding board; ~**kasten** *m*
soundbox.
**Resopal** ® [rezo'pa:l] (**-s**) *nt* Formica ®.
**resozialisieren** [rezotsiali'zi:rən] *vt* to
rehabilitate.
**Resozialisierung** *f* rehabilitation.
**Respekt** [rɛ'spɛkt] (**-(e)s**) *m* respect; (*Angst*)
fear; **bei allem ~ (vor jdm/etw)** with all due
respect (to sb/for sth).
**respektabel** [rɛspɛk'ta:bəl] *adj* respectable.
**respektieren** [rɛspɛk'ti:rən] *vt* to respect.
**respektlos** *adj* disrespectful.
**Respektsperson** *f* person commanding
respect.
**respektvoll** *adj* respectful.
**Ressentiment** [rɛsãti'mã:] (**-s, -s**) *nt*
resentment.
**Ressort** [rɛ'so:r] (**-s, -s**) *nt* department; **in das**
**~ von jdm fallen** (*lit, fig*) to be sb's
department.
**Ressourcen** [rɛ'sursən] *pl* resources *pl*.
**Rest** [rɛst] (**-(e)s, -e**) *m* remainder, rest;
(*Über~*) remains *pl*; **Reste** *pl* (*COMM*)
remnants *pl*; **das hat mir den ~ gegeben**
(*umg*) that finished me off.
**Restaurant** [rɛsto'rã:] (**-s, -s**) *nt* restaurant.
**Restauration** [rɛstauratsi'o:n] *f* restoration.
**restaurieren** [rɛstau'ri:rən] *vt* to restore.
**Restaurierung** *f* restoration.
**Rest-** *zW*: ~**betrag** *m* remainder, outstanding
sum; **r~lich** *adj* remaining; **r~los** *adj*
complete; ~**posten** *m* (*COMM*) remaining
stock.
**Resultat** [rezul'ta:t] (**-(e)s, -e**) *nt* result.
**Retorte** [re'tortə] (**-, -n**) *f* retort; **aus der ~**
(*umg*) synthetic.
**Retortenbaby** *nt* test-tube baby.
**retour** [re'tu:r] *adv* (*veraltet*) back.
**Retouren** *pl* (*Waren*) returns *pl*.
**retten** ['rɛtən] *vt* to save, rescue ♦ *vr* to
escape; **bist du noch zu ~?** (*umg*) are you
out of your mind?; **sich vor etw** *dat* **nicht**
**mehr ~ können** (*fig*) to be swamped with
sth.
**Retter(in)** (**-s, -**) *m(f)* rescuer, saviour (*BRIT*),
savior (*US*).
**Rettich** ['rɛtɪç] (**-s, -e**) *m* radish.
**Rettung** *f* rescue; (*Hilfe*) help; **seine letzte ~**
his last hope.
**Rettungs-** *zW*: ~**aktion** *f* rescue operation;
~**boot** *nt* lifeboat; ~**dienst** *m* rescue service;
~**gürtel** *m* lifebelt, life preserver (*US*);
**r~los** *adj* hopeless; ~**ring** *m*
= **Rettungsgürtel**; ~**schwimmer** *m* lifesaver;
(*am Strand*) lifeguard; ~**wagen** *m*

ambulance.
**Return-Taste** [ri'tø:rntastə] *f* (*COMPUT*)
return key.
**retuschieren** [retu'ʃi:rən] *vt* (*PHOT*) to
retouch.
**Reue** ['rɔyə] (**-**) *f* remorse; (*Bedauern*) regret.
**reuen** *vt*: **es reut ihn** he regrets it, he is sorry
about it.
**reuig** ['rɔyɪç] *adj* penitent.
**reumütig** *adj* remorseful; (*Sünder*) contrite.
**Reuse** ['rɔyzə] (**-, -n**) *f* fish trap.
**Revanche** [re'vã:ʃə] (**-, -n**) *f* revenge; (*SPORT*)
return match.
**revanchieren** [revã'ʃi:rən] *vr* (*sich rächen*) to
get one's own back, have one's revenge;
(*erwidern*) to reciprocate, return the
compliment.
**Revers** [re've:r] (**-, -**) *nt or m* lapel.
**revidieren** [revi'di:rən] *vt* to revise; (*COMM*) to
audit.
**Revier** [re'vi:r] (**-s, -e**) *nt* district; (*MIN:*
*Kohlen~*) (coal)mine; (*Jagd~*) preserve;
(*Polizei~*) police station, station house (*US*);
(*Dienstbereich*) beat (*BRIT*), precinct (*US*);
(*MIL*) sick bay.
**Revision** [revizi'o:n] *f* revision; (*COMM*)
auditing; (*JUR*) appeal.
**Revisionsverhandlung** *f* appeal hearing.
**Revisor** [re'vi:zor] (**-s, -en**) *m* (*COMM*) auditor.
**Revolte** [re'voltə] (**-, -n**) *f* revolt.
**Revolution** [revolutsi'o:n] *f* revolution.
**revolutionär** [revolutsio'nɛ:r] *adj*
revolutionary.
**Revolutionär(in)** [revolutsio'nɛ:r(ɪn)] (**-s, -e**)
*m(f)* revolutionary.
**revolutionieren** [revolutsio'ni:rən] *vt* to
revolutionize.
**Revoluzzer** [revo'lutsər] (**-s, -**) (*pej*) *m* would-
be revolutionary.
**Revolver** [re'volvər] (**-s, -**) *m* revolver.
**Revue** [rə'vy:] (**-, -n**) *f*: **etw ~ passieren lassen**
(*fig*) to pass sth in review.
**Reykjavik** ['raɪkjavi:k] (**-s**) *nt* Reykjavik.
**Rezensent** [retsɛn'zɛnt] *m* reviewer, critic.
**rezensieren** [retsɛn'zi:rən] *vt* to review.
**Rezension** *f* review.
**Rezept** [re'tsɛpt] (**-(e)s, -e**) *nt* (*KOCH*) recipe;
(*MED*) prescription.
**Rezeption** [retsɛptsi'o:n] *f* (*von Hotel:*
*Empfang*) reception.
**rezeptpflichtig** *adj* available only on
prescription.
**Rezession** [retsɛsi'o:n] *f* (*FIN*) recession.
**rezitieren** [retsi'ti:rən] *vt* to recite.
**R-Gespräch** ['ɛrgəʃprɛ:ç] *nt* (*TEL*) reverse
charge call (*BRIT*), collect call (*US*).
**Rh** *abk* (= *Rhesus(faktor) positiv*) Rh positive.
**rh** *abk* (= *Rhesus(faktor) negativ*) Rh negative.
**Rhabarber** [ra'barbər] (**-s**) *m* rhubarb.
**Rhein** [raɪn] (**-(e)s**) *m* Rhine.
**rhein.** *abk* = *rheinisch*.
**Rheingau** *m* wine-growing area along the

*Rhine.*

**Rheinhessen** *nt* wine-growing area along the *Rhine.*

**rheinisch** *adj attrib* Rhenish, Rhineland.

**Rheinland** *nt* Rhineland.

**Rheinländer(in)** *m(f)* Rhinelander.

**Rheinland-Pfalz** *nt* Rhineland-Palatinate.

**Rhesusfaktor** ['reːzusfaktɔr] *m* rhesus factor.

**Rhetorik** [re'toːrɪk] *f* rhetoric.

**rhetorisch** [re'toːrɪʃ] *adj* rhetorical.

**Rheuma** ['rɔyma] (**-s**) *nt* rheumatism.

**Rheumatismus** [rɔyma'tɪsmʊs] *m* rheumatism.

**Rhinozeros** [ri'noːtserɔs] (**-** *od* **-ses, -se**) *nt* rhinoceros; (*umg: Dummkopf*) fool.

**Rhld.** *abk* = **Rheinland**.

**Rhodesien** [ro'deːziən] (**-s**) *nt* Rhodesia.

**Rhodos** ['roːdɔs] (**-**) *nt* Rhodes.

**rhythmisch** ['rytmɪʃ] *adj* rythmical.

**Rhythmus** *m* rhythm.

**RIAS** ['riːas] (**-**) *m abk* (= *Rundfunk im amerikanischen Sektor (Berlin)*) broadcasting station in the former American sector of *Berlin.*

**Richtantenne** ['rɪçt|antɛnə] (**-, -n**) *f* directional aerial (*bes BRIT*) *od* antenna.

**richten** ['rɪçtən] *vt* to direct; (*Waffe*) to aim; (*einstellen*) to adjust; (*instand setzen*) to repair; (*zurechtmachen*) to prepare, get ready; (*adressieren: Briefe, Anfragen*) to address; (*Bitten, Forderungen*) to make; (*in Ordnung bringen*) to do, fix; (*bestrafen*) to pass judgement on ♦ *vr:* **sich ~ nach** to go by; **~ an** +*akk* to direct at; (*fig*) to direct to; (*Briefe etc*) to address to; (*Bitten etc*) to make to; **~ auf** +*akk* to aim at; **wir ~ uns ganz nach unseren Kunden** we are guided entirely by our customers' wishes.

**Richter(in)** (**-s, -**) *m(f)* judge; **sich zum ~ machen** (*fig*) to set (o.s.) up in judgement; **r~lich** *adj* judicial.

**Richtgeschwindigkeit** *f* recommended speed.

**richtig** *adj* right, correct; (*echt*) proper ♦ *adv* correctly, right; (*umg: sehr*) really; **der/die R~e** the right one *od* person; **das R~e** the right thing; **die Uhr geht ~** the clock is right; **R~keit** *f* correctness; **das hat schon seine R~keit** it's right enough; **~stellen** *vt* to correct; **R~stellung** *f* correction, rectification.

**Richt-** *zW:* **~linie** *f* guideline; **~preis** *m* recommended price; **~schnur** *f* (*fig: Grundsatz*) guiding principle.

**Richtung** *f* direction; (*Tendenz*) tendency, orientation; **in jeder ~** each way.

**richtungweisend** *adj:* **~ sein** to point the way (ahead).

**rieb** *etc* [riːp] *vb siehe* **reiben**.

**riechen** ['riːçən] *unreg vt, vi* to smell; **an etw** *dat* **~** to smell sth; **es riecht nach Gas** there's a smell of gas; **ich kann das/ihn nicht ~** (*umg*)

I can't stand it/him; **das konnte ich doch nicht ~!** (*umg*) how was I (supposed) to know?

**Riecher** (**-s, -**) *m:* **einen guten** *od* **den richtigen ~ für etw haben** (*umg*) to have a nose for sth.

**Ried** [riːt] (**-(e)s, -e**) *nt* reed; (*Moor*) marsh.

**rief** *etc* [riːf] *vb siehe* **rufen**.

**Riege** ['riːgə] (**-, -n**) *f* team, squad.

**Riegel** ['riːgəl] (**-s, -**) *m* bolt, bar; **einer Sache** *dat* **einen ~ vorschieben** (*fig*) to clamp down on sth.

**Riemen** ['riːmən] (**-s, -**) *m* strap; (*Gürtel, TECH*) belt; (*NAUT*) oar; **sich am ~ reißen** (*fig: umg*) to get a grip on o.s.; **~antrieb** *m* belt drive.

**Riese** ['riːzə] (**-n, -n**) *m* giant.

**rieseln** *vi* to trickle; (*Schnee*) to fall gently.

**Riesen-** *zW:* **~erfolg** *m* enormous success; **~gebirge** *nt* (*GEOG*) Sudeten Mountains *pl*; **r~groß** *adj*, **r~haft** *adj* colossal, gigantic, huge; **~rad** *nt* big *od* Ferris wheel; **~schritt** *m:* **sich mit ~schritten nähern** (*fig*) to be drawing on apace; **~slalom** *m* (*SKI*) giant slalom.

**riesig** ['riːzɪç] *adj* enormous, huge, vast.

**Riesin** *f* giantess.

**riet** *etc* [riːt] *vb siehe* **raten**.

**Riff** [rɪf] (**-(e)s, -e**) *nt* reef.

**rigoros** [rigo'roːs] *adj* rigorous.

**Rille** ['rɪlə] (**-, -n**) *f* groove.

**Rind** [rɪnt] (**-(e)s, -er**) *nt* ox; (*Kuh*) cow; (*KOCH*) beef; **Rinder** *pl* cattle *pl*; **vom ~** beef.

**Rinde** ['rɪndə] (**-, -n**) *f* rind; (*Baum~*) bark; (*Brot~*) crust.

**Rinderbraten** *m* roast beef.

**Rinderwahn** ['rɪndərvaːn] *m* mad cow disease.

**Rindfleisch** *nt* beef.

**Rindvieh** *nt* cattle *pl*; (*umg*) blockhead, stupid oaf.

**Ring** [rɪŋ] (**-(e)s, -e**) *m* ring; **~buch** *nt* ring binder.

**ringeln** ['rɪŋəln] *vt* (*Pflanze*) to (en)twine; (*Schwanz etc*) to curl ♦ *vr* to go curly, curl; (*Rauch*) to curl up(wards).

**Ringelnatter** *f* grass snake.

**Ringeltaube** *f* wood pigeon.

**ringen** *unreg vi* to wrestle; **nach** *od* **um etw ~** (*streben*) to struggle for sth; **R~** (**-s**) *nt* wrestling.

**Ringer** (**-s, -**) *m* wrestler.

**Ring-** *zW:* **~finger** *m* ring finger; **r~förmig** *adj* ring-shaped; **~kampf** *m* wrestling bout; **~richter** *m* referee.

**rings** *adv:* **~ um** round; **~ herum** *adv* round about.

**Ringstraße** *f* ring road.

**ringsum(her)** [rɪŋs'|ʊm, 'rɪŋs|ʊm'heːr] *adv* (*rundherum*) round about; (*überall*) all round.

**Rinne** ['rɪnə] (**-, -n**) *f* gutter, drain.

**rinnen** *unreg vi* to run, trickle.

**Rinnsal** (**-s, -e**) *nt* trickle of water.

**Rinnstein** *m* gutter.

**Rippchen** ['rɪpçən] *nt* small rib; cutlet.
**Rippe** ['rɪpə] (-, -n) *f* rib.
**Rippen-** *zW:* ~**fellentzündung** *f* pleurisy; ~**speer** *m od nt* (*KOCH*): **Kasseler ~speer** *slightly cured pork spare rib*; ~**stoß** *m* dig in the ribs.
**Risiko** ['riːziko] (-s, -s *od* Risiken) *nt* risk; r~**behaftet** *adj* fraught with risk; ~**investition** *f* sunk cost.
**riskant** [rɪs'kant] *adj* risky, hazardous.
**riskieren** [rɪs'kiːrən] *vt* to risk.
**riß** *etc* [rɪs] *vb siehe* **reißen**.
**Riß** (-sses, -sse) *m* tear; (*in Mauer, Tasse etc*) crack; (*in Haut*) scratch; (*TECH*) design.
**rissig** ['rɪsɪç] *adj* torn; cracked; scratched.
**ritt** *etc* [rɪt] *vb siehe* **reiten**.
**Ritt** (-(e)s, -e) *m* ride.
**Ritter** (-s, -) *m* knight; **jdn zum ~ schlagen** to knight sb; **arme ~** *pl* (*KOCH*) *sweet French toast, made with bread soaked in milk*; r~**lich** *adj* chivalrous; ~**schlag** *m* knighting; ~**tum** (-s) *nt* chivalry; ~**zeit** *f* age of chivalry.
**rittlings** *adv* astride.
**Ritual** [ritu'aːl] (-s, -e *od* -ien) *nt* (*lit, fig*) ritual.
**rituell** [ritu'ɛl] *adj* ritual.
**Ritus** ['riːtus] (-, Riten) *m* rite.
**Ritze** ['rɪtsə] (-, -n) *f* crack, chink.
**ritzen** *vt* to scratch; **die Sache ist geritzt** (*umg*) it's all fixed up.
**Rivale** [ri'vaːlə] (-n, -n) *m*, **Rivalin** *f* rival.
**rivalisieren** [rivali'ziːrən] *vi*: **mit jdm ~** to compete with sb.
**Rivalität** [rivali'tɛːt] *f* rivalry.
**Riviera** [rivi'eːra] (-) *f* Riviera.
**Rizinusöl** ['riːtsinus|øːl] *nt* castor oil.
**r.-k.** *abk* (= römisch-katholisch) R.C.
**Robbe** ['rɔbə] (-, -n) *f* seal.
**robben** ['rɔbən] *vi* (*Hilfsverb sein: auch MIL*) to crawl (*using elbows*).
**Robbenfang** *m* seal hunting.
**Robe** ['roːbə] (-, -n) *f* robe.
**Roboter** ['rɔbɔtər] (-s, -) *m* robot; ~**technik** *f* robotics *sing*.
**Robotik** ['rɔbɔtɪk] *f* robotics *sing*.
**robust** [ro'bʊst] *adj* (*Mensch, Gesundheit*) robust; (*Material*) tough.
**roch** *etc* [rɔx] *vb siehe* **riechen**.
**Rochade** [rɔ'xaːdə] (-, -n) *f* (*SCHACH*): **die kleine/große ~** castling king's side/queen's side.
**röcheln** ['rœçəln] *vi* to wheeze; (*Sterbender*) to give the death rattle.
**Rock¹** [rɔk] (-(e)s, ⁻e) *m* skirt; (*Jackett*) jacket; (*Uniform~*) tunic.
**Rock²** [rɔk] (-(s), -(s)) *m* (*MUS*) rock; ~**musik** *f* rock music.
**Rockzipfel** *m*: **an Mutters ~ hängen** (*umg*) to cling to (one's) mother's skirts.
**Rodel** ['roːdəl] (-s, -) *m* toboggan; ~**bahn** *f* toboggan run.
**rodeln** *vi* to toboggan.

**roden** ['roːdən] *vt, vi* to clear.
**Rogen** ['roːgən] (-s, -) *m* roe.
**Roggen** ['rɔgən] (-s, -) *m* rye; ~**brot** *nt* rye bread; (*Vollkornbrot*) black bread.
**roh** [roː] *adj* raw; (*Mensch*) coarse, crude; ~**e Gewalt** brute force; R~**bau** *m* shell of a building; R~**eisen** *nt* pig iron; R~**fassung** *f* rough draft; R~**kost** *f* raw fruit and vegetables *pl*; R~**ling** *m* ruffian; R~**material** *nt* raw material; R~**öl** *nt* crude oil.
**Rohr** [roːr] (-(e)s, -e) *nt* pipe, tube; (*BOT*) cane; (*Schilf*) reed; (*Gewehr~*) barrel; ~**bruch** *m* burst pipe.
**Röhre** ['røːrə] (-, -n) *f* tube, pipe; (*RUNDF etc*) valve; (*Back~*) oven.
**Rohr-** *zW:* ~**geflecht** *nt* wickerwork; ~**leger** (-s, -) *m* plumber; ~**leitung** *f* pipeline; ~**post** *f* pneumatic post; ~**spatz** *m*: **schimpfen wie ein ~spatz** (*umg*) to curse and swear; ~**stock** *m* cane; ~**stuhl** *m* basket chair; ~**zucker** *m* cane sugar.
**Rohseide** *f* raw silk.
**Rohstoff** *m* raw material.
**Rokoko** ['rɔkoko] (-s) *nt* rococo.
**Rollbahn** *f* (*AVIAT*) runway.
**Rolle** ['rɔlə] (-, -n) *f* roll; (*THEAT, SOZIOLOGIE*) role; (*Garn~ etc*) reel, spool; (*Walze*) roller; (*Wäsche~*) mangle, wringer; **bei** *od* **in etw** *dat* **eine ~ spielen** to play a part in sth; **aus der ~ fallen** (*fig*) to forget o.s.; **keine ~ spielen** not to matter.
**rollen** *vi* to roll; (*AVIAT*) to taxi ♦ *vt* to roll; (*Wäsche*) to mangle, put through the wringer; **den Stein ins R~ bringen** (*fig*) to start the ball rolling.
**Rollen-** *zW:* ~**besetzung** *f* (*THEAT*) cast; ~**konflikt** *m* (*PSYCH*) role conflict; ~**spiel** *nt* role-play; ~**tausch** *m* exchange of roles; (*SOZIOLOGIE*) role reversal.
**Roller** (-s, -) *m* scooter; (*Welle*) roller.
**Roll-** *zW:* ~**feld** *nt* runway; ~**kragen** *m* roll *od* polo neck; ~**(l)aden** *m* shutter; ~**mops** *m* pickled herring.
**Rollo** ['rɔlo] (-, -s) *nt* (roller) blind.
**Roll-** *zW:* ~**schrank** *m* roll-fronted cupboard; ~**schuh** *m* roller skate; ~**schuhlaufen** *nt* roller skating; ~**splitt** *m* grit; ~**stuhl** *m* wheelchair; ~**treppe** *f* escalator.
**Rom** [roːm] (-s) *nt* Rome; **das sind Zustände wie im alten ~** (*umg: unmoralisch*) it's disgraceful; (: *primitiv*) it's medieval (*umg*).
**röm.** *abk* = **römisch**.
**Roman** [ro'maːn] (-s, -e) *m* novel; **(jdm) einen ganzen ~ erzählen** (*umg*) to give (sb) a long rigmarole; ~**heft** *nt* pulp novel.
**romanisch** *adj* (*Volk, Sprache*) Romance; (*KUNST*) Romanesque.
**Romanistik** [roma'nɪstɪk] *f* (*UNIV*) Romance languages and literature.
**Romanschreiber** *m* novelist.
**Romanschriftsteller** *m* novelist.
**Romantik** [ro'mantɪk] *f* romanticism.

**Romantiker(in)** **(-s, -)** *m(f)* romanticist.
**romantisch** *adj* romantic.
**Romanze** [ro'mantsə] **(-, -n)** *f* romance.
**Römer** ['røːmər] **(-s, -)** *m* wineglass; (*Mensch*) Roman; **~topf** ® *m* (*KOCH*) ≈ (chicken) brick.
**römisch** ['røːmɪʃ] *adj* Roman; **~-katholisch** *adj* Roman Catholic.
**röm.-kath.** *abk* (= *römisch-katholisch*) R.C.
**Rommé** [rɔ'meː] **(-s, -s)** *nt* rummy.
**röntgen** ['rœntgən] *vt* to X-ray; **R~aufnahme** *f* X-ray; **R~bild** *nt* X-ray; **R~strahlen** *pl* X-rays *pl*.
**rosa** ['roːza] *adj inv* pink, rose(-coloured).
**Rose** ['roːzə] **(-, -n)** *f* rose.
**Rosé** [ro'zeː] **(-s, -s)** *m* rosé.
**Rosenkohl** *m* Brussels sprouts *pl*.
**Rosenkranz** *m* rosary.
**Rosenmontag** *m* Monday of Shrovetide; *siehe auch* **Karneval.**
**Rosette** [ro'zɛtə] *f* rosette.
**rosig** ['roːzɪç] *adj* rosy.
**Rosine** [ro'ziːnə] *f* raisin; **(große) ~n im Kopf haben** (*umg*) to have big ideas.
**Rosmarin** ['roːsmariːn] **(-s)** *m* rosemary.
**Roß** [rɔs] **(-sses, -sse)** *nt* horse, steed; **auf dem hohen ~ sitzen** (*fig*) to be on one's high horse; **~kastanie** *f* horse chestnut; **~kur** (*umg*) *f* kill-or-cure remedy.
**Rost** [rɔst] **(-(e)s, -e)** *m* rust; (*Gitter*) grill, gridiron; (*Bett~*) springs *pl*; **~braten** *m* roast(ed) meat, roast; **~bratwurst** *f* grilled *od* barbecued sausage.
**rosten** *vi* to rust.
**rösten** ['røːstən] *vt* to roast; (*Brot*) to toast
**rostfrei** *adj* (*Stahl*) stainless.
**rostig** *adj* rusty.
**Röstkartoffeln** *pl* fried potatoes *pl*.
**Rostschutz** *m* rustproofing.
**rot** [roːt] *adj* red; **~ werden, einen ~en Kopf bekommen** to blush, go red; **~ sehen** (*umg*) to see red, become angry; **die R~e Armee** the Red Army; **das R~e Kreuz** the Red Cross; **das R~e Meer** the Red Sea.
**Rotation** [rotatsi'oːn] *f* rotation.
**rot-** *zW:* **~bäckig** *adj* red-cheeked; **R~barsch** *m* rosefish; **~blond** *adj* strawberry blond.
**Röte** ['røːtə] **(-)** *f* redness.
**Röteln** *pl* German measles *sing*.
**röten** *vt, vr* to redden.
**rothaarig** *adj* red-haired.
**rotieren** [ro'tiːrən] *vi* to rotate.
**Rot-** *zW:* **~käppchen** *nt* Little Red Riding Hood; **~kehlchen** *nt* robin; **~kohl** *m* red cabbage; **~kraut** *nt* red cabbage; **~stift** *m* red pencil; **~wein** *m* red wine.
**Rotz** [rɔts] **(-es, -e)** (*umg*) *m* snot; **r~frech** (*umg*) *adj* cocky; **r~näsig** (*umg*) *adj* snotty-nosed.
**Rouge** [ruːʒ] **(-s, -s)** *nt* rouge.
**Roulade** [ru'laːdə] **(-, -n)** *f* (*KOCH*) beef olive.
**Roulett(e)** [ru'lɛt(ə)] **(-s, -s)** *nt* roulette.

**Route** ['ruːtə] **(-, -n)** *f* route.
**Routine** [ru'tiːnə] *f* experience; (*Gewohnheit*) routine.
**routiniert** [ruti'niːərt] *adj* experienced.
**Rowdy** ['raʊdɪ] **(-s, -s** *od* **Rowdies)** *m* hooligan; (*zerstörerisch*) vandal; (*lärmend*) rowdy (type).
**Ruanda** [ru'anda] *nt* Rwanda.
**ruandisch** *adj* Rwandan.
**rubbeln** ['rʊbəln] (*umg*) *vt, vi* to rub.
**Rübe** ['ryːbə] **(-, -n)** *f* turnip; **gelbe ~** carrot; **rote ~** beetroot (*BRIT*), beet (*US*).
**Rübenzucker** *m* beet sugar.
**Rubin** [ru'biːn] **(-s, -e)** *m* ruby.
**Rubrik** [ru'briːk] *f* heading; (*Spalte*) column.
**Ruck** [rʊk] **(-(e)s, -e)** *m* jerk, jolt; **sich** *dat* **einen ~ geben** (*fig: umg*) to make an effort.
**ruck** *adv:* **das geht ~, zuck** it won't take a second.
**Rückantwort** *f* reply, answer; **um ~ wird gebeten** please reply.
**ruckartig** *adj:* **er stand ~ auf** he shot to his feet.
**Rück-** *zW:* **~besinnung** *f* recollection; **r~bezüglich** *adj* reflexive; **~blende** *f* flashback; **r~blenden** *vi* to flash back; **~blick** *m:* **im ~blick auf etw** *akk* looking back on sth; **r~blickend** *adj* retrospective ♦ *adv* in retrospect; **r~datieren** *vt* to backdate.
**Rücken** **(-s, -)** *m* back; (*Berg~*) ridge; **jdm in den ~ fallen** (*fig*) to stab sb in the back.
**rücken** *vt, vi* to move.
**Rücken-** *zW:* **~deckung** *f* backing; **~lage** *f* supine position; **~lehne** *f* back (of chair); **~mark** *nt* spinal cord; **~schwimmen** *nt* backstroke; **~stärkung** *f* (*fig*) moral support; **~wind** *m* following wind.
**Rück-** *zW:* **~erstattung** *f* return, restitution; **~fahrkarte** *f* return ticket (*BRIT*), round-trip ticket (*US*); **~fahrt** *f* return journey; **~fall** *m* relapse; **r~fällig** *adj* relapsed; **r~fällig werden** to relapse; **~flug** *m* return flight; **~frage** *f* question; **nach ~frage bei der zuständigen Behörde ...** after checking this with the appropriate authority ...; **r~fragen** *vi* to inquire; (*nachprüfen*) to check; **~führung** *f* (*von Menschen*) repatriation, return; **~gabe** *f* return; **gegen ~gabe** (*+gen*) on return (of); **~gang** *m* decline, fall; **r~gängig** *adj:* **etw ~gängig machen** (*widerrufen*) to undo sth; (*Bestellung*) to cancel sth; **~gewinnung** *f* recovery; (*von Land, Gebiet*) reclaiming; (*aus verbrauchten Stoffen*) recycling.
**Rückgrat** *nt* spine, backbone.
**Rück-** *zW:* **~griff** *m* recourse; **~halt** *m* backing; (*Einschränkung*) reserve; **r~haltlos** *adj* unreserved; **~hand** *f* (*SPORT*) backhand; **r~kaufbar** *adj* redeemable; **~kehr** **(-, -en)** *f* return; **~koppelung** *f* feedback; **~lage** *f* reserve, savings *pl*; **~lauf** *m* reverse running; (*beim Tonband*)

rewind; (*von Maschinenteil*) return travel; **r~läufig** *adj* declining, falling; **eine r~läufige Entwicklung** a decline; **~licht** *nt* rear light; **r~lings** *adv* from behind; (*rückwärts*) backwards; **~meldung** *f* (*UNIV*) reregistration; **~nahme** (-, -n) *f* taking back; **~porto** *nt* return postage; **~reise** *f* return journey; (*NAUT*) home voyage; **~ruf** *m* recall.

**Rucksack** ['rʊkzak] *m* rucksack.

**Rück-** *zW:* **~schau** *f* reflection; **r~schauend** *adj* = **rückblickend**; **~schlag** *m* setback; **~schluß** *m* conclusion; **~schritt** *m* retrogression; **r~schrittlich** *adj* reactionary; (*Entwicklung*) retrograde; **~seite** *f* back; (*von Münze etc*) reverse; **siehe ~seite** see over(leaf); **r~setzen** *vt* (*COMPUT*) to reset.

**Rücksicht** *f* consideration; **~ nehmen auf** +*akk* to show consideration for; **~nahme** *f* consideration.

**rücksichtslos** *adj* inconsiderate; (*Fahren*) reckless; (*unbarmherzig*) ruthless.

**Rücksichtslosigkeit** *f* lack of consideration; (*beim Fahren*) recklessness; (*Unbarmherzigkeit*) ruthlessness.

**rücksichtsvoll** *adj* considerate.

**Rück-** *zW:* **~sitz** *m* back seat; **~spiegel** *m* (*AUT*) rear-view mirror; **~spiel** *nt* return match; **~sprache** *f* further discussion *od* talk; **~sprache mit jdm nehmen** to confer with sb; **~stand** *m* arrears *pl*; (*Verzug*) delay; **r~ständig** *adj* backward, out-of-date; (*Zahlungen*) in arrears; **~stau** *m* (*AUT*) tailback (*BRIT*), line of cars; **~stoß** *m* recoil; **~strahler** (-s, -) *m* rear reflector; **~strom** *m* (*von Menschen, Fahrzeugen*) return; **~taste** *f* (*an Schreibmaschine*) backspace key; **~tritt** *m* resignation; **~trittbremse** *f* backpedal brake; **~trittsklausel** *f* (*Vertrag*) escape clause; **~vergütung** *f* repayment; (*COMM*) refund; **r~versichern** *vt, vi* to reinsure ♦ *vr* to check (up *od* back); **~versicherung** *f* reinsurance; **r~wärtig** *adj* rear; **r~wärts** *adv* backward(s), back; **~wärtsgang** *m* (*AUT*) reverse gear; **im ~wärtsgang fahren** to reverse; **~weg** *m* return journey, way back; **r~wirkend** *adj* retroactive; **~wirkung** *f* repercussion; **eine Zahlung mit ~wirkung vom ...** a payment backdated to ...; **eine Gesetzesänderung mit ~wirkung vom ...** an amendment made retrospective to ...; **~zahlung** *f* repayment; **~zieher** (*umg*) *m:* **einen ~zieher machen** to back out; **~zug** *m* retreat; **~zugsgefecht** *nt* (*MIL, fig*) rearguard action.

**rüde** ['ry:də] *adj* blunt, gruff.

**Rüde** (-n, -n) *m* male dog.

**Rudel** ['ru:dəl] (-s, -) *nt* pack; (*von Hirschen*) herd.

**Ruder** ['ru:dər] (-s, -) *nt* oar; (*Steuer*) rudder; **das ~ fest in der Hand haben** (*fig*) to be in control of the situation; **~boot** *nt* rowing

boat; **~er** (-s, -) *m* rower, oarsman.

**rudern** *vt, vi* to row; **mit den Armen ~** (*fig*) to flail one's arms about.

**Ruf** [ru:f] (-(e)s, -e) *m* call, cry; (*Ansehen*) reputation; (*UNIV: Berufung*) offer of a chair.

**rufen** *unreg vt, vi* to call; (*aus~*) to cry; **um Hilfe ~** to call for help; **das kommt mir wie gerufen** that's just what I needed.

**Rüffel** ['rʏfəl] (-s, -) (*umg*) *m* telling-off, ticking-off.

**Ruf-** *zW:* **~mord** *m* character assassination; **~name** *m* usual (first) name; **~nummer** *f* (tele)phone number; **~säule** *f* (*für Taxi*) telephone; (*an Autobahn*) emergency telephone; **~zeichen** *nt* (*RUNDF*) call sign; (*TEL*) ringing tone.

**Rüge** ['ry:gə] (-, -n) *f* reprimand, rebuke.

**rügen** *vt* to reprimand.

**Ruhe** ['ru:ə] (-) *f* rest; (*Ungestörtheit*) peace, quiet; (*Gelassenheit, Stille*) calm; (*Schweigen*) silence; **~!** be quiet!, silence!; **angenehme ~!** sleep well!; **~ bewahren** to stay cool *od* calm; **das läßt ihm keine ~** he can't stop thinking about it; **sich zur ~ setzen** to retire; **die ~ weghaben** (*umg*) to be unflappable; **immer mit der ~** (*umg*) don't panic; **die letzte ~ finden** (*liter*) to be laid to rest; **~lage** *f* (*von Mensch*) reclining position; (*MED: bei Bruch*) immobile position; **r~los** *adj* restless.

**ruhen** *vi* to rest; (*Verkehr*) to cease; (*Arbeit*) to stop, cease; (*Waffen*) to be laid down; (*begraben sein*) to lie, be buried.

**Ruhe-** *zW:* **~pause** *f* break; **~platz** *m* resting place; **~stand** *m* retirement; **~stätte** *f:* **letzte ~stätte** final resting place; **~störung** *f* breach of the peace; **~tag** *m* closing day.

**ruhig** ['ru:ɪç] *adj* quiet; (*bewegungslos*) still; (*Hand*) steady; (*gelassen, friedlich*) calm; (*Gewissen*) clear; **tu das ~** feel free to do that; **etw ~ mitansehen** (*gleichgültig*) to stand by and watch sth; **du könntest ~ mal etwas für mich tun!** it's about time you did something for me!

**Ruhm** [ru:m] (-(e)s) *m* fame, glory.

**rühmen** ['ry:mən] *vt* to praise ♦ *vr* to boast.

**rühmlich** *adj* praiseworthy; (*Ausnahme*) notable.

**ruhmlos** *adj* inglorious.

**ruhmreich** *adj* glorious.

**Ruhr** [ru:r] (-) *f* dysentery.

**Rührei** ['ry:r|ai] *nt* scrambled egg.

**rühren** *vt* (*lit, fig*) to move, stir (*auch KOCH*) ♦ *vr* (*lit, fig*) to move, stir ♦ *vi:* **~ von** to come *od* stem from; **~ an** +*akk* to touch; (*fig*) to touch on.

**rührend** *adj* touching, moving; **das ist ~ von Ihnen** that is sweet of you.

**Ruhrgebiet** *nt* Ruhr (area).

**rührig** *adj* active, lively.

**rührselig** *adj* sentimental, emotional.

**Rührung** *f* emotion.

**Ruin** [ru'i:n] (-s) *m* ruin; **vor dem ~ stehen** to be on the brink *od* verge of ruin.
**Ruine** (-, -n) *f* (*lit, fig*) ruin.
**ruinieren** [rui'ni:rən] *vt* to ruin.
**rülpsen** ['rʏlpsən] *vi* to burp, belch.
**Rum** [rʊm] (-s, -s) *m* rum.
**rum** (*umg*) *adv* = **herum**.
**Rumäne** [ru'mɛ:nə] (-n, -n) *m* Romanian.
**Rumänien** (-s) *nt* Romania.
**Rumänin** *f* Romanian.
**rumänisch** *adj* Romanian.
**rumfuhrwerken** ['rʊmfu:rvɛrkən] (*umg*) *vt* to bustle around.
**Rummel** ['rʊməl] (-s) (*umg*) *m* hurly-burly; (*Jahrmarkt*) fair; **~platz** *m* fairground, fair.
**rumoren** [ru'mo:rən] *vi* to be noisy, make a noise.
**Rumpelkammer** ['rʊmpəlkamər] *f* junk room.
**rumpeln** *vi* to rumble; (*holpern*) to jolt.
**Rumpf** [rʊmpf] (-(e)s, ⁻e) *m* trunk, torso; (*AVIAT*) fuselage; (*NAUT*) hull.
**rümpfen** ['rʏmpfən] *vt* (*Nase*) to turn up.
**Rumtopf** *m soft fruit in rum.*
**rund** [rʊnt] *adj* round ♦ *adv* (*etwa*) around; **~ um etw** round sth; **jetzt geht's ~** (*umg*) this is where the fun starts; **wenn er das erfährt, geht's ~** (*umg*) there'll be a to-do when he finds out; **R~bogen** *m* Norman *od* Romanesque arch; **R~brief** *m* circular.
**Runde** ['rʊndə] (-, -n) *f* round; (*in Rennen*) lap; (*Gesellschaft*) circle; **die ~ machen** to do the rounds; (*herumgegeben werden*) to be passed round; **über die ~n kommen** (*SPORT, fig*) to pull through; **eine ~ spendieren** *od* **schmeißen** (*umg: Getränke*) to stand a round.
**runden** *vt* to make round ♦ *vr* (*fig*) to take shape.
**rund-** *zW:* **~erneuert** *adj* (*Reifen*) remoulded (*BRIT*), remolded (*US*); **R~fahrt** *f* (round) trip; **R~frage** *f:* **R~frage (unter** +*dat*) survey (of).
**Rundfunk** ['rʊntfʊŋk] (-(e)s) *m* broadcasting; (*bes Hörfunk*) radio; (*~anstalt*) broadcasting corporation; **im ~** on the radio; **~anstalt** *f* broadcasting corporation; **~empfang** *m* reception; **~gebühr** *f* licence (*BRIT*), license (*US*); **~gerät** *nt* radio set; **~sendung** *f* broadcast, radio programme (*BRIT*) *od* program (*US*).
**Rund-** *zW:* **~gang** *m* (*Spaziergang*) walk; (*von Wachmann*) rounds *pl*; (*von Briefträger etc*) round; (*zur Besichtigung*): **~gang (durch)** tour (of); **r~heraus** *adv* straight out, bluntly; **r~herum** *adv* all round; (*fig: umg: völlig*) totally; **r~lich** *adj* plump, rounded; **~reise** *f* round trip; **~schreiben** *nt* (*COMM*) circular; **r~um** *adv* all around; (*fig*) completely.
**Rundung** *f* curve, roundness.
**rundweg** *adv* straight out.
**runter** ['rʊntər] (*umg*) *adv* = **herunter; hinunter; ~würgen** (*umg*) *vt* (*Ärger*) to

swallow.
**Runzel** ['rʊntsəl] (-, -n) *f* wrinkle.
**runz(e)lig** *adj* wrinkled.
**runzeln** *vt* to wrinkle; **die Stirn ~** to frown.
**Rüpel** ['ry:pəl] (-s, -) *m* lout; **r~haft** *adj* loutish.
**rupfen** ['rʊpfən] *vt* to pluck; **wie ein gerupftes Huhn aussehen** to look like a shorn sheep.
**Rupfen** (-s, -) *m* sackcloth.
**ruppig** ['rʊpɪç] *adj* rough, gruff.
**Rüsche** ['ry:ʃə] (-, -n) *f* frill.
**Ruß** [ru:s] (-es) *m* soot.
**Russe** ['rʊsə] (-n, -n) *m* Russian.
**Rüssel** ['rʏsəl] (-s, -) *m* snout; (*Elefanten~*) trunk.
**rußen** *vi* to smoke; (*Ofen*) to be sooty.
**rußig** *adj* sooty.
**Russin** *f* Russian.
**russisch** *adj* Russian; **~e Eier** (*KOCH*) egg(s) mayonnaise.
**Rußland** (-s) *nt* Russia.
**rüsten** ['rʏstən] *vt, vi, vr* to prepare; (*MIL*) to arm.
**rüstig** ['rʏstɪç] *adj* sprightly, vigorous; **R~keit** *f* sprightliness, vigour (*BRIT*), vigor (*US*).
**rustikal** [rʊsti'ka:l] *adj:* **sich ~ einrichten** to furnish one's home in a rustic style.
**Rüstung** ['rʏstʊŋ] *f* preparation; (*MIL*) arming; (*Ritter~*) armour (*BRIT*), armor (*US*); (*Waffen etc*) armaments *pl*.
**Rüstungs-** *zW:* **~gegner** *m* opponent of the arms race; **~industrie** *f* armaments industry; **~kontrolle** *f* arms control; **~wettlauf** *m* arms race.
**Rüstzeug** *nt* tools *pl*; (*fig*) capacity.
**Rute** ['ru:tə] (-, -n) *f* rod, switch.
**Rutsch** [rʊtʃ] (-(e)s, -e) *m* slide; (*Erd~*) landslide; **guten ~!** (*umg*) have a good New Year!; **~bahn** *f* slide.
**rutschen** *vi* to slide; (*aus~*) to slip; **auf dem Stuhl hin und her ~** to fidget around on one's chair.
**rutschfest** *adj* non-slip.
**rutschig** *adj* slippery.
**rütteln** ['rʏtəln] *vt, vi* to shake, jolt; **daran ist nicht zu ~** (*fig: umg: an Grundsätzen*) there's no doubt about that.
**Rüttelschwelle** *f* (*AUT*) rumble strips *pl*.

# S, s

**S¹, s¹** [ɛs] *nt* S, s; ~ **wie Samuel** ≈ S for Sugar.

**S²** [ɛs] *abk* (= *Süden*) S; (= *Seite*) p; (= *Schilling*) S.

**s²** *abk* (= *Sekunde*) sec.; (= *siehe*) v., vid.

**SA** (-) *f abk* (= *Sturmabteilung*) SA.

**s.a.** *abk* (= *siehe auch*) see also.

**Saal** [zaːl] (-(e)s, **Säle**) *m* hall; (*für Sitzungen etc*) room.

**Saarland** ['zaːrlant] (-s) *nt* Saarland.

**Saat** [zaːt] (-, -**en**) *f* seed; (*Pflanzen*) crop; (*Säen*) sowing; ~**gut** *nt* seed(s *pl*).

**Sabbat** ['zabat] (-s, -e) *m* sabbath.

**sabbern** ['zabərn] (*umg*) *vi* to dribble.

**Säbel** ['zɛːbəl] (-s, -) *m* sabre (*BRIT*), saber (*US*); ~**rasseln** *nt* sabre-rattling.

**Sabotage** [zabo'taːʒə] (-, -n) *f* sabotage.

**sabotieren** [zabo'tiːrən] *vt* to sabotage.

**Saccharin** [zaxa'riːn] (-s) *nt* saccharin.

**Sachanlagen** ['zax|anlaːgən] *pl* tangible assets *pl*.

**Sachbearbeiter(in)** *m(f)*: ~ **(für)** (*Beamter*) official in charge (of).

**Sachbuch** *nt* non-fiction book.

**sachdienlich** *adj* relevant, helpful.

**Sache** ['zaxə] (-, -n) *f* thing; (*Angelegenheit*) affair, business; (*Frage*) matter; (*Pflicht*) task; (*Thema*) subject; (*JUR*) case; (*Aufgabe*) job; (*Ideal*) cause; (*umg: km/h*): **mit 60/100** ~**n** ≈ at 40/60 (mph); **ich habe mir die** ~ **anders vorgestellt** I had imagined things differently; **er versteht seine** ~ he knows what he's doing; **das ist so eine** ~ (*umg*) it's a bit tricky; **mach keine** ~**n!** (*umg*) don't be daft!; **bei der** ~ **bleiben** (*bei Diskussion*) to keep to the point; **bei der** ~ **sein** to be with it (*umg*); **das ist** ~ **der Polizei** this is a matter for the police; **zur** ~ to the point; **das ist eine runde** ~ that is well-balanced *od* rounded-off.

**Sachertorte** ['zaxərtɔrtə] *f* rich chocolate cake, sachertorte.

**Sach-** *zW*: **s~gemäß** *adj* appropriate, suitable; ~**kenntnis** *f* (*in bezug auf Wissensgebiet*) knowledge of the/his *etc* subject; (*in bezug auf* ~**lage**) knowledge of the facts; **s~kundig** *adj* (well-)informed; **sich s~kundig machen** to inform oneself; ~**lage** *f* situation, state of affairs; ~**leistung** *f* payment in kind; **s~lich** *adj* matter-of-fact; (*Kritik etc*) objective; (*Irrtum, Angabe*) factual; **bleiben Sie bitte s~lich** don't get carried away (*umg*); (*nicht persönlich werden*) please stay objective.

**sächlich** ['zɛxlɪç] *adj* neuter.

**Sachregister** *nt* subject index.

**Sachschaden** *m* material damage.

**Sachse** ['zaksə] (-n, -n) *m* Saxon.

**Sachsen** (-s) *nt* Saxony; ~-**Anhalt** (-s) *nt* Saxony Anhalt.

**Sächsin** ['zɛksɪn] *f* Saxon.

**sächsisch** ['zɛksɪʃ] *adj* Saxon.

**sacht(e)** *adv* softly, gently.

**Sach-** *zW*: ~**verhalt** (-(e)s, -e) *m* facts *pl* (of the case); **s~verständig** *adj* (*Urteil*) expert; (*Publikum*) informed; ~**verständige(r)** *f(m)* expert; ~**zwang** *m* force of circumstances.

**Sack** [zak] (-(e)s, ⁻e) *m* sack; (*aus Papier, Plastik*) bag; (*ANAT, ZOOL*) sac; (*umg!: Hoden*) balls *pl* (*!*); (: *Kerl, Bursche*) bastard (*!*); **mit** ~ **und Pack** (*umg*) with bag and baggage.

**sacken** *vi* to sag, sink.

**Sackgasse** *f* cul-de-sac, dead-end street (*US*).

**Sackhüpfen** *nt* sack race.

**Sadismus** [za'dɪsmʊs] *m* sadism.

**Sadist(in)** [za'dɪst(ɪn)] *m(f)* sadist; **s~isch** *adj* sadistic.

**Sadomasochismus** [zadomazɔ'xɪsmʊs] *m* sadomasochism.

**säen** ['zɛːən] *vt, vi* to sow; **dünn gesät** (*fig*) thin on the ground, few and far between.

**Safari** [za'faːri] (-, -s) *f* safari.

**Safe** [zeːf] (-s, -s) *m od nt* safe.

**Saft** [zaft] (-(e)s, ⁻e) *m* juice; (*BOT*) sap; **ohne** ~ **und Kraft** (*fig*) wishy-washy (*umg*), effete.

**saftig** *adj* juicy; (*Grün*) lush; (*umg: Rechnung, Ohrfeige*) hefty; (*Brief, Antwort*) hard-hitting.

**Saftladen** (*pej: umg*) *m* rum joint.

**saftlos** *adj* dry.

**Sage** ['zaːgə] (-, -n) *f* saga.

**Säge** ['zɛːgə] (-, -n) *f* saw; ~**blatt** *nt* saw blade; ~**mehl** *nt* sawdust.

**sagen** ['zaːgən] *vt, vi*: **(jdm etw)** ~ to say (sth to sb), tell (sb sth); **unter uns gesagt** between you and me (and the gatepost (*hum umg*)); **laß dir das gesagt sein** take it from me; **das hat nichts zu** ~ that doesn't mean anything; **sagt dir der Name etwas?** does the name mean anything to you?; **das ist nicht gesagt** that's by no means certain; **sage und schreibe** (whether you) believe it or not.

**sägen** *vt, vi* to saw; (*hum: umg: schnarchen*) to snore, saw wood (*US*).

**sagenhaft** *adj* legendary; (*umg*) great, smashing.

**sagenumwoben** *adj* legendary.

**Sägespäne** *pl* wood shavings *pl*.

**Sägewerk** *nt* sawmill.

**sah** *etc* [zaː] *vb siehe* **sehen**.

**Sahara** [za'haːra] *f* Sahara (Desert).

**Sahne** ['zaːnə] (-) *f* cream.

**Saison** [zɛ'zõː] (-, -s) *f* season.

**saisonal** [zɛzoˈnaːl] *adj* seasonal.
**Saisonarbeiter** *m* seasonal worker.
**saisonbedingt** *adj* seasonal.
**Saite** [ˈzaɪtə] (-, -n) *f* string; **andere ~n aufziehen** (*umg*) to get tough.
**Saiteninstrument** *nt* string(ed) instrument.
**Sakko** [ˈzako] (-s, -s) *m od nt* jacket.
**Sakrament** [zakraˈmɛnt] *nt* sacrament.
**Sakristei** [zakrısˈtaɪ] *f* sacristy.
**Salami** [zaˈlaːmi] (-, -s) *f* salami.
**Salat** [zaˈlaːt] (-(e)s, -e) *m* salad; (*Kopf~*) lettuce; **da haben wir den ~!** (*umg*) now we're in a fine mess; **~besteck** *nt* salad servers *pl*; **~platte** *f* salad; **~soße** *f* salad dressing.
**Salbe** [ˈzalbə] (-, -n) *f* ointment.
**Salbei** [ˈzalbaɪ] (-s) *m* sage.
**salben** *vt* to anoint.
**Salbung** *f* anointing.
**salbungsvoll** *adj* unctuous.
**saldieren** [zalˈdiːrən] *vt* (*COMM*) to balance.
**Saldo** [ˈzaldo] (-s, **Salden**) *m* balance; **~übertrag** *m* balance brought *od* carried forward; **~vortrag** *m* balance brought *od* carried forward.
**Säle** [ˈzɛːlə] *pl von* **Saal**.
**Salmiak** [zalmiˈak] (-s) *m* sal ammoniac; **~geist** *m* liquid ammonia.
**Salmonellen** [zalmoˈnɛlən] *pl* salmonellae *pl*.
**Salon** [zaˈlõ:] (-s, -s) *m* salon; **~löwe** *m* lounge lizard.
**salopp** [zaˈlɔp] *adj* casual; (*Manieren*) slovenly; (*Sprache*) slangy.
**Salpeter** [zalˈpeːtər] (-s) *m* saltpetre (*BRIT*), saltpeter (*US*); **~säure** *f* nitric acid.
**Salto** [ˈzalto] (-s, -s *od* **Salti**) *m* somersault.
**Salut** [zaˈluːt] (-(e)s, -e) *m* salute.
**salutieren** [zaluˈtiːrən] *vi* to salute.
**Salve** [ˈzalvə] (-, -n) *f* salvo.
**Salz** [zalts] (-es, -e) *nt* salt; **s~arm** *adj* (*KOCH*) low-salt; **~bergwerk** *nt* salt mine.
**salzen** *unreg vt* to salt.
**salzig** *adj* salty.
**Salz-** *zW:* **~kartoffeln** *pl* boiled potatoes *pl*; **~säule** *f:* **zur ~säule erstarren** (*fig*) to stand (as though) rooted to the spot; **~säure** *f* hydrochloric acid; **~stange** *f* pretzel stick; **~streuer** *m* salt cellar *od* shaker (*US*); **~wasser** *nt* salt water.
**Sambia** [ˈzambia] (-s) *nt* Zambia.
**sambisch** *adj* Zambian.
**Samen** [ˈzaːmən] (-s, -) *m* seed; (*ANAT*) sperm; **~bank** *f* sperm bank; **~handlung** *f* seed shop.
**sämig** [ˈzɛːmɪç] *adj* thick, creamy.
**Sammel-** *zW:* **~anschluß** *m* (*TEL*) private (branch) exchange; (*von Privathäusern*) party line; **~antrag** *m* composite motion; **~band** *m* anthology; **~becken** *nt* reservoir; (*fig*): **~becken (von)** melting pot (for); **~begriff** *m* collective term; **~bestellung** *f* collective order; **~büchse** *f* collecting tin;

**~mappe** *f* folder.
**sammeln** *vt* to collect ♦ *vr* to assemble, gather; (*sich konzentrieren*) to collect one's thoughts.
**Sammelname** *m* collective term.
**Sammelnummer** *f* (*TEL*) private exchange number, switchboard number.
**Sammelsurium** [zaməlˈzuːriʊm] *nt* hotchpotch (*BRIT*), hodgepodge (*US*).
**Sammler(in)** (-s, -) *m(f)* collector.
**Sammlung** [ˈzamlʊŋ] *f* collection; (*Konzentration*) composure.
**Samstag** [ˈzamstaːk] *m* Saturday; *siehe auch* **Dienstag**.
**samstags** *adv* (on) Saturdays.
**samt** [zamt] *präp +dat* (along) with, together with; **~ und sonders** each and every one (of them); **S~** (-(e)s, -e) *m* velvet; **in S~ und Seide** (*liter*) in silks and satins.
**Samthandschuh** *m:* **jdn mit ~en anfassen** (*umg*) to handle sb with kid gloves.
**sämtlich** [ˈzɛmtlɪç] *adj* (*alle*) all (the); (*vollständig*) complete; **Schillers ~e Werke** the complete works of Schiller.
**Sanatorium** [zanaˈtoːriʊm] *nt* sanatorium (*BRIT*), sanitarium (*US*).
**Sand** [zant] (-(e)s, -e) *m* sand; **das/die gibt's wie ~ am Meer** (*umg*) there are piles of it/ heaps of them; **im ~e verlaufen** to peter out.
**Sandale** [zanˈdaːlə] (-, -n) *f* sandal.
**Sandbank** *f* sandbank.
**Sandelholz** [ˈzandəlhɔlts] (-es) *nt* sandalwood.
**sandig** [ˈzandɪç] *adj* sandy.
**Sand-** *zW:* **~kasten** *m* sandpit; **~kastenspiele** *pl* (*MIL*) sand-table exercises *pl*; (*fig*) tactical manoeuvrings *pl* (*BRIT*) *od* maneuverings *pl* (*US*); **~kuchen** *m* Madeira cake; **~mann** *m*, **~männchen** *nt* (*in Geschichten*) sandman; **~papier** *nt* sandpaper; **~stein** *m* sandstone; **s~strahlen** *vt, vi untr* to sandblast
**sandte** *etc* [ˈzantə] *vb siehe* **senden**.
**Sanduhr** *f* hourglass; (*Eieruhr*) egg timer.
**sanft** [zanft] *adj* soft, gentle; **~mütig** *adj* gentle, meek.
**sang** *etc* [zaŋ] *vb siehe* **singen**.
**Sänger(in)** [ˈzɛŋər(ın)] (-s, -) *m(f)* singer.
**sang- und klanglos** (*umg*) *adv* without any ado, quietly.
**Sani** [ˈzani] (-s, -s) (*umg*) *m* = **Sanitäter**.
**sanieren** [zaˈniːrən] *vt* to redevelop; (*Betrieb*) to make financially sound; (*Haus*) to renovate ♦ *vr* to line one's pockets; (*Unternehmen*) to become financially sound.
**Sanierung** *f* redevelopment; renovation.
**sanitär** [zaniˈtɛːr] *adj* sanitary; **~e Anlagen** sanitation *sing*.
**Sanitäter** [zaniˈtɛːtər] (-s, -) *m* first-aid attendant; (*in Krankenwagen*) ambulance man; (*MIL*) (medical) orderly.
**Sanitätsauto** *nt* ambulance.
**sank** *etc* [zaŋk] *vb siehe* **sinken**.
**Sanktion** [zaŋktsiˈoːn] *f* sanction.

**sanktionieren** [zaŋktsio'ni:rən] *vt* to sanction.
**sann** *etc* [zan] *vb siehe* **sinnen.**
**Saphir** ['za:fi:r] (**-s, -e**) *m* sapphire.
**Sarde** ['zardə] (**-n, -n**) *m* Sardinian.
**Sardelle** [zar'dɛlə] *f* anchovy.
**Sardine** [zar'di:nə] *f* sardine.
**Sardinien** [zar'di:niən] (**-s**) *nt* Sardinia.
**Sardinier(in)** (**-s, -**) *m(f)* Sardinian.
**sardinisch** *adj* Sardinian.
**sardisch** *adj* Sardinian.
**Sarg** [zark] (**-(e)s, ⁻e**) *m* coffin; **~nagel** (*umg*) *m* (*Zigarette*) coffin nail.
**Sarkasmus** [zar'kasmʊs] *m* sarcasm.
**sarkastisch** [zar'kastɪʃ] *adj* sarcastic.
**saß** *etc* [zas] *vb siehe* **sitzen.**
**Satan** ['za:tan] (**-s, -e**) *m* Satan; (*fig*) devil.
**Satansbraten** *m* (*hum: umg*) young devil.
**Satellit** [zatɛ'li:t] (**-en, -en**) *m* satellite.
**Satelliten-** *zW:* **~antenne** *f* satellite dish; **~fernsehen** *nt* satellite television; **~foto** *nt* satellite picture; **~schüssel** *f* satellite dish; **~station** *f* space station.
**Satin** [za'tɛ̃:] (**-s, -s**) *m* satin.
**Satire** [za'ti:rə] (**-, -n**) *f:* **~ (auf** +*akk*) satire (on).
**Satiriker** [za'ti:rikər] (**-s, -**) *m* satirist.
**satirisch** [za'ti:rɪʃ] *adj* satirical.
**satt** [zat] *adj* full; (*Farbe*) rich, deep; (*blasiert, übersättigt*) well-fed; (*selbstgefällig*) smug; **jdn/etw ~ sein** *od* **haben** to be fed-up with sb/sth; **sich ~ hören/sehen an** +*dat* to see/hear enough of; **sich ~ essen** to eat one's fill; **~ machen** to be filling.
**Sattel** ['zatəl] (**-s, ⁻**) *m* saddle; (*Berg*) ridge; **s~fest** *adj* (*fig*) proficient.
**satteln** *vt* to saddle.
**Sattelschlepper** *m* articulated lorry (*BRIT*), artic (*BRIT umg*), semitrailer (*US*), semi (*US umg*).
**Satteltasche** *f* saddlebag; (*Gepäcktasche am Fahrrad*) pannier.
**sättigen** ['zɛtɪgən] *vt* to satisfy; (*CHEM*) to saturate.
**Sattler** (**-s, -**) *m* saddler; (*Polsterer*) upholsterer.
**Satz** [zats] (**-es, ⁻e**) *m* (*GRAM*) sentence; (*Neben~, Adverbial~*) clause; (*Theorem*) theorem; (*der gesetzte Text*) type; (*MUS*) movement; (*COMPUT*) record; (*TENNIS, Briefmarken, Zusammengehöriges*) set; (*Kaffee~*) grounds *pl*; (*Boden~*) dregs *pl*; (*Spesen~*) allowance; (*COMM*) rate; (*Sprung*) jump; **~bau** *m* sentence construction; **~gegenstand** *m* (*GRAM*) subject; **~lehre** *f* syntax; **~teil** *m* constituent (of a sentence).
**Satzung** *f* statute, rule; (*Firma*) (memorandum and) articles of association.
**satzungsgemäß** *adj* statutory.
**Satzzeichen** *nt* punctuation mark.
**Sau** [zau] (**-, Säue**) *f* sow; (*umg*) dirty pig; **die ~ rauslassen** (*fig: umg*) to let it all hang out.
**sauber** ['zaubər] *adj* clean; (*anständig*) honest, upstanding; (*umg: großartig*) fantastic, great; (: *ironisch*) fine; **~ sein** (*Kind*) to be (potty-)trained; (*Hund etc*) to be house-trained; **~halten** *unreg vt* to keep clean; **S~keit** *f* cleanness; (*einer Person*) cleanliness.
**säuberlich** ['zɔybərlɪç] *adv* neatly.
**saubermachen** *vt* to clean.
**säubern** *vt* to clean; (*POL etc*) to purge.
**Säuberung** *f* cleaning; purge.
**Säuberungsaktion** *f* cleaning-up operation; (*POL*) purge.
**saublöd** (*umg*) *adj* bloody (*BRIT!*) *od* damn (*!*) stupid.
**Saubohne** *f* broad bean.
**Sauce** ['zo:sə] (**-, -n**) *f* = **Soße.**
**Sauciere** [zosi'e:rə] (**-, -n**) *f* sauce boat.
**Saudi-** [zaudi-] *zW:* **~araber(in)** *m(f)* Saudi; **~-Arabien** (**-s**) *nt* Saudi Arabia; **s~arabisch** *adj* Saudi(-Arabian).
**sauer** ['zauər] *adj* sour; (*CHEM*) acid; (*umg*) cross; **Saurer Regen** acid rain; **~ werden** (*Milch, Sahne*) to go sour, turn; **jdm das Leben ~ machen** to make sb's life a misery; **S~braten** *m braised beef (marinaded in vinegar)*, sauerbraten (*US*).
**Sauerei** [zauə'rai] (*umg*) *f* rotten state of affairs, scandal; (*Schmutz etc*) mess; (*Unanständigkeit*) obscenity.
**Sauerkirsche** *f* sour cherry.
**Sauerkraut** (**-(e)s**) *nt* sauerkraut, pickled cabbage.
**säuerlich** ['zɔyərlɪç] *adj* sourish, tart.
**Sauer-** *zW:* **~milch** *f* sour milk; **~stoff** *m* oxygen; **~stoffgerät** *nt* breathing apparatus; **~teig** *m* leaven.
**saufen** ['zaufən] *unreg* (*umg*) *vt, vi* to drink, booze; **wie ein Loch ~** (*umg*) to drink like a fish.
**Säufer(in)** ['zɔyfər(ɪn)] (**-s, -**) (*umg*) *m(f)* boozer, drunkard.
**Sauferei** [zaufə'rai] *f* drinking, boozing; (*Saufgelage*) booze-up.
**Saufgelage** (*pej: umg*) *nt* drinking bout, booze-up.
**säuft** [zɔyft] *vb siehe* **saufen.**
**saugen** ['zaugən] *unreg vt, vi* to suck.
**säugen** ['zɔygən] *vt* to suckle.
**Sauger** ['zaugər] (**-s, -**) *m* dummy (*BRIT*), pacifier (*US*); (*auf Flasche*) teat; (*Staub~*) vacuum cleaner, hoover ® (*BRIT*).
**Säugetier** *nt* mammal.
**saugfähig** *adj* absorbent.
**Säugling** *m* infant, baby.
**Säuglingsschwester** *f* infant nurse.
**Sau-** *zW:* **~haufen** (*umg*) *m* bunch of layabouts; **s~kalt** (*umg*) *adj* bloody (*BRIT!*) *od* damn (*!*) cold; **s~klaue** (*umg*) *f* scrawl.
**Säule** ['zɔylə] (**-, -n**) *f* column, pillar.
**Säulengang** *m* arcade.
**Saum** [zaum] (**-(e)s, Säume**) *m* hem; (*Naht*) seam.

**saumäßig** (*umg*) *adj* lousy ♦ *adv* lousily.
**säumen** ['zɔymən] *vt* to hem; to seam ♦ *vi* to delay, hesitate.
**säumig** ['zɔymɪç] *adj* (*geh: Schuldner*) defaulting; (*Zahlung*) outstanding, overdue.
**Sauna** ['zaʊna] (-, -s) *f* sauna.
**Säure** ['zɔyrə] (-, -n) *f* acid; (*Geschmack*) sourness, acidity; **s~beständig** *adj* acid-proof.
**Sauregurkenzeit** (-) *f* (*hum: umg*) bad time *od* period; (*in den Medien*) silly season.
**säurehaltig** *adj* acidic.
**Saurier** ['zaʊriər] (-s, -) *m* dinosaur.
**Saus** [zaʊs] (-es) *m*: **in ~ und Braus leben** to live like a lord.
**säuseln** ['zɔyzəln] *vi* to murmur; (*Blätter*) to rustle ♦ *vt* to murmur.
**sausen** ['zaʊzən] *vi* to blow; (*umg: eilen*) to rush; (*Ohren*) to buzz; **etw ~ lassen** (*umg*) not to bother with sth.
**Sau-** *zW*: **~stall** (*umg*) *m* pigsty; **~wetter** (*umg*) *nt* bloody (*BRIT!*) *od* damn (*!*) awful weather; **s~wohl** (*umg*) *adj*: **ich fühle mich s~wohl** I feel bloody (*BRIT!*) *od* really good.
**Saxophon** [zakso'foːn] (-s, -e) *nt* saxophone.
**SB** *abk* = **Selbstbedienung**.
**S-Bahn** *f abk* (= *Schnellbahn*) high-speed suburban railway or railroad (*US*).
**SBB** *abk* (= *Schweizerische Bundesbahnen*) Swiss Railways.
**s. Br.** *abk* (= *südlicher Breite*) southern latitude.
**Schabe** ['ʃaːbə] (-, -n) *f* cockroach.
**schaben** *vt* to scrape.
**Schaber** (-s, -) *m* scraper.
**Schabernack** (-(e)s, -e) *m* trick, prank.
**schäbig** ['ʃɛːbɪç] *adj* shabby; (*Mensch*) mean; **S~keit** *f* shabbiness.
**Schablone** [ʃa'bloːnə] (-, -n) *f* stencil; (*Muster*) pattern; (*fig*) convention.
**schablonenhaft** *adj* stereotyped, conventional.
**Schach** [ʃax] (-s, -s) *nt* chess; (*Stellung*) check; **im ~ stehen** to be in check; **jdn in ~ halten** (*fig*) to stall sb; **~brett** *nt* chessboard.
**schachern** (*pej*) *vi*: **um etw ~** to haggle over sth.
**Schach-** *zW*: **~figur** *f* chessman; **s~matt** *adj* checkmate; **jdn s~matt setzen** (*lit*) to (check)mate sb; (*fig*) to snooker sb (*umg*); **~partie** *f* game of chess; **~spiel** *nt* game of chess.
**Schacht** [ʃaxt] (-(e)s, -e) *m* shaft.
**Schachtel** (-, -n) *f* box; (*pej: Frau*) bag, cow (*BRIT*); **~satz** *m* complicated *od* multi-clause sentence.
**Schachzug** *m* (*auch fig*) move.
**schade** ['ʃaːdə] *adj* a pity *od* shame ♦ *interj* (what a) pity *od* shame; **sich** *dat* **für etw zu ~ sein** to consider o.s. too good for sth; **um sie ist es nicht ~** she's no great loss.
**Schädel** ['ʃɛːdəl] (-s, -) *m* skull; **einen dicken**

**~ haben** (*fig: umg*) to be stubborn; **~bruch** *m* fractured skull.
**Schaden** (-s, ̈-) *m* damage; (*Verletzung*) injury; (*Nachteil*) disadvantage; **zu ~ kommen** to suffer; (*physisch*) to be injured; **jdm ~ zufügen** to harm sb.
**schaden** ['ʃaːdən] *vi +dat* to hurt; **einer Sache ~** to damage sth.
**Schaden-** *zW*: **~ersatz** *m* compensation, damages *pl*; **~ersatz leisten** to pay compensation; **~ersatzanspruch** *m* claim for compensation; **s~ersatzpflichtig** *adj* liable for damages; **~freiheitsrabatt** *m* (*Versicherung*) no-claim(s) bonus; **~freude** *f* malicious delight; **s~froh** *adj* gloating.
**schadhaft** ['ʃaːthaft] *adj* faulty, damaged.
**schädigen** ['ʃɛdɪɡən] *vt* to damage; (*Person*) to do harm to, harm.
**Schädigung** *f* damage; harm.
**schädlich** *adj*: **~ (für)** harmful (to); **S~keit** *f* harmfulness.
**Schädling** *m* pest.
**Schädlingsbekämpfungsmittel** *nt* pesticide.
**schadlos** ['ʃaːtloːs] *adj*: **sich ~ halten an** +*dat* to take advantage of.
**Schadstoff** (-(e)s, -e) *m* pollutant; **s~arm** *adj* low in pollutants; **s~haltig** *adj* containing pollutants.
**Schaf** [ʃaːf] (-(e)s, -e) *nt* sheep; (*umg: Dummkopf*) twit (*BRIT*), dope; **~bock** *m* ram.
**Schäfchen** ['ʃɛːfçən] *nt* lamb; **sein ~ ins Trockene bringen** (*Sprichwort*) to see o.s. all right (*umg*); **~wolken** *pl* cirrus clouds *pl*.
**Schäfer** ['ʃɛːfər] (-s, -) *m* shepherd; **~hund** *m* Alsatian (dog) (*BRIT*), German shepherd (dog) (*US*); **~in** *f* shepherdess.
**Schaffen** ['ʃafən] (-s) *nt* (creative) activity.
**schaffen¹** *unreg vt* to create; (*Platz*) to make; **sich** *dat* **etw ~** to get o.s. sth; **dafür ist er wie geschaffen** he's just made for it.
**schaffen²** ['ʃafən] *vt* (*erreichen*) to manage, do; (*erledigen*) to finish; (*Prüfung*) to pass; (*transportieren*) to take ♦ *vi* (*tun*) to do; (*umg: arbeiten*) to work; **das ist nicht zu ~** that can't be done; **das hat mich geschafft** it took it out of me; (*nervlich*) it got on top of me; **ich habe damit nichts zu ~** that has nothing to do with me; **jdm (schwer) zu ~ machen** (*zusetzen*) to cause sb (a lot of) trouble; (*bekümmern*) to worry sb (a lot); **sich** *dat* **an etw** *dat* **zu ~ machen** to busy o.s. with sth.
**Schaffensdrang** *m* energy; (*von Künstler*) creative urge.
**Schaffenskraft** *f* creativity.
**Schaffner(in)** ['ʃafnər(ɪn)] (-s, -) *m(f)* (*Bus~*) conductor, conductress; (*EISENB*) guard (*BRIT*), conductor (*US*).
**Schaffung** *f* creation.
**Schafskäse** *m* sheep's *od* ewe's milk cheese.
**Schaft** [ʃaft] (-(e)s, -e) *m* shaft; (*von Gewehr*) stock; (*von Stiefel*) leg; (*BOT*) stalk; (*von

*Baum*) tree trunk; ~**stiefel** *m* high boot.
**Schakal** [ʃa'kaːl] (-**s**, -**e**) *m* jackal.
**Schäker(in)** ['ʃɛːkər(ɪn)] (-**s**, -) *m(f)* flirt;
(*Witzbold*) joker.
**schäkern** *vi* to flirt; to joke.
**Schal** [ʃaːl] (-**s**, -**s** *od* -**e**) *m* scarf.
**schal** *adj* flat; (*fig*) insipid.
**Schälchen** ['ʃɛːlçən] *nt* bowl.
**Schale** ['ʃaːlə] (-, -**n**) *f* skin; (*abgeschält*) peel;
(*Nuß~, Muschel~, Eier~*) shell; (*Geschirr*)
dish, bowl; **sich in ~ werfen** (*umg*) to get
dressed up.
**schälen** ['ʃɛːlən] *vt* to peel; to shell ♦ *vr* to
peel.
**Schalk** [ʃalk] (-**s**, -**e** *od* -̈**e**) *m* (*veraltet*) joker.
**Schall** [ʃal] (-(**e**)**s**, -**e**) *m* sound; **Name ist**
**~ und Rauch** what's in a name?;
**s~dämmend** *adj* sound-deadening;
~**dämpfer** *m* (*AUT*) silencer (*BRIT*), muffler
(*US*); **s~dicht** *adj* soundproof.
**schallen** *vi* to (re)sound.
**schallend** *adj* resounding, loud.
**Schall-** *zW:* ~**geschwindigkeit** *f* speed of
sound; ~**grenze** *f* sound barrier; ~**mauer** *f*
sound barrier; ~**platte** *f* record.
**schalt** *etc* [ʃalt] *vb siehe* **schelten.**
**Schaltbild** *nt* circuit diagram.
**Schaltbrett** *nt* switchboard.
**schalten** ['ʃaltən] *vt* to switch, turn ♦ *vi* (*AUT*)
to change (gear); (*umg: begreifen*) to catch
on; (*reagieren*) to react; **in Reihe/parallel ~**
(*ELEK*) to connect in series/in parallel;
**~ und walten** to do as one pleases.
**Schalter** (-**s**, -) *m* counter; (*an Gerät*) switch;
~**beamte(r)** *m* counter clerk; ~**stunden** *pl*
hours of business *pl*.
**Schalt-** *zW:* ~**hebel** *m* switch; (*AUT*) gear
lever (*BRIT*), gearshift (*US*); ~**jahr** *nt* leap
year; ~**knüppel** *m* (*AUT*) gear lever (*BRIT*),
gearshift (*US*); (*AVIAT, COMPUT*) joystick;
~**kreis** *m* (switching) circuit; ~**plan** *m*
circuit diagram; ~**pult** *nt* control desk;
~**stelle** *f* (*fig*) coordinating point; ~**uhr** *f*
time switch.
**Schaltung** *f* switching; (*ELEK*) circuit; (*AUT*)
gear change.
**Scham** [ʃaːm] (-) *f* shame; (~*gefühl*) modesty;
(*Organe*) private parts *pl*.
**schämen** ['ʃɛːmən] *vr* to be ashamed.
**Scham-** *zW:* ~**gefühl** *nt* sense of shame;
~**haare** *pl* pubic hair *sing*; **s~haft** *adj* modest;
bashful; ~**lippen** *pl* labia *pl*, lips *pl* of the
vulva; **s~los** *adj* shameless; (*unanständig*)
indecent; (*Lüge*) brazen, barefaced.
**Schampus** ['ʃampʊs] (-, *no pl*) (*umg*) *m*
champagne, champers (*BRIT*).
**Schande** ['ʃandə] (-) *f* disgrace; **zu meiner**
**~ muß ich gestehen, daß ...** to my shame I
have to admit that ...
**schänden** ['ʃɛndən] *vt* to violate.
**Schandfleck** ['ʃantflɛk] *m:* **er war der ~ der**
**Familie** he was the disgrace of his family.

**schändlich** ['ʃɛntlɪç] *adj* disgraceful,
shameful; **S~keit** *f* disgracefulness,
shamefulness.
**Schandtat** (*umg*) *f* escapade, shenanigan.
**Schändung** *f* violation, defilement.
**Schank-** *zW:* ~**erlaubnis** *f*, ~**konzession** *f*
(publican's) licence (*BRIT*), excise license
(*US*); ~**tisch** *m* bar.
**Schanze** ['ʃantsə] (-, -**n**) *f* (*MIL*) fieldwork,
earthworks *pl*; (*Sprung~*) ski jump.
**Schar** [ʃaːr] (-, -**en**) *f* band, company; (*Vögel*)
flock; (*Menge*) crowd; **in ~en** in droves.
**Scharade** [ʃa'raːdə] (-, -**n**) *f* charade.
**scharen** *vr* to assemble, rally.
**scharenweise** *adv* in droves.
**scharf** [ʃarf] *adj* sharp; (*Verstand, Augen*) keen;
(*Kälte, Wind*) biting; (*Protest*) fierce; (*Ton*)
piercing, shrill; (*Essen*) hot, spicy;
(*Munition*) live; (*Maßnahmen*) severe;
(*Bewachung*) close, tight; (*Geruch,*
*Geschmack*) pungent, acrid; (*umg: geil*)
randy (*BRIT*), horny; (*Film*) sexy, blue *attrib*;
~ **nachdenken** to think hard; ~ **aufpassen/**
**zuhören** to pay close attention/listen
closely; **etw ~ einstellen** (*Bild, Diaprojektor*
*etc*) to bring sth into focus; **mit ~em Blick**
(*fig*) with penetrating insight; **auf etw** *akk*
~ **sein** (*umg*) to be keen on sth; ~**e Sachen**
(*umg*) hard stuff.
**Scharfblick** *m* (*fig*) penetration.
**Schärfe** ['ʃɛrfə] (-, -**n**) *f* sharpness; (*Strenge*)
rigour (*BRIT*), rigor (*US*); (*an Kamera,*
*Fernsehen*) focus.
**schärfen** *vt* to sharpen.
**Schärfentiefe** *f* (*PHOT*) depth of focus.
**Scharf-** *zW:* **s~machen** (*umg*) *vt* to stir up;
~**richter** *m* executioner; ~**schießen** *nt*
shooting with live ammunition; ~**schütze** *m*
marksman, sharpshooter; ~**sinn** *m*
astuteness, shrewdness; **s~sinnig** *adj*
astute, shrewd.
**Scharlach** ['ʃarlax] (-**s**, -**e**) *m* scarlet;
(*Krankheit*) scarlet fever; ~**fieber** *nt* scarlet
fever.
**Scharlatan** ['ʃarlatan] (-**s**, -**e**) *m* charlatan.
**Scharmützel** [ʃar'mʏtsəl] (-**s**, -) *nt* skirmish.
**Scharnier** [ʃar'niːr] (-**s**, -**e**) *nt* hinge.
**Schärpe** ['ʃɛrpə] (-, -**n**) *f* sash.
**scharren** ['ʃarən] *vt, vi* to scrape, scratch.
**Scharte** ['ʃartə] (-, -**n**) *f* notch, nick; (*Berg*)
wind gap.
**schartig** ['ʃartɪç] *adj* jagged.
**Schaschlik** ['ʃaʃlɪk] (-**s**, -**s**) *m od nt* (shish)
kebab.
**Schatten** ['ʃatən] (-**s**, -) *m* shadow; (*schattige*
*Stelle*) shade; **jdn/etw in den ~ stellen** (*fig*)
to put sb/sth in the shade; ~**bild** *nt*
silhouette; **s~haft** *adj* shadowy.
**Schattenmorelle** (-, -**n**) *f* morello cherry.
**Schatten-** *zW:* ~**riß** *m* silhouette; ~**seite** *f*
shady side; (*von Planeten*) dark side; (*fig:*
*Nachteil*) drawback; ~**wirtschaft** *f* black

economy.
**schattieren** [ʃa'tiːrən] *vt, vi* to shade.
**Schattierung** *f* shading.
**schattig** ['ʃatɪç] *adj* shady.
**Schatulle** [ʃa'tʊlə] (-, -n) *f* casket; (*Geld~*) coffer.
**Schatz** [ʃats] (-es, ⁻e) *m* treasure; (*Person*) darling; ~**amt** *nt* treasury.
**schätzbar** ['ʃɛtsbaːr] *adj* assessable.
**Schätzchen** *nt* darling, love.
**schätzen** *vt* (*ab~*) to estimate; (*Gegenstand*) to value; (*würdigen*) to value, esteem; (*vermuten*) to reckon; **etw zu ~ wissen** to appreciate sth; **sich glücklich ~** to consider o.s. lucky; ~**lernen** *vt* to learn to appreciate.
**Schatzkammer** *f* treasure chamber *od* vault.
**Schatzmeister** *m* treasurer.
**Schätzung** *f* estimate; estimation; valuation; **nach meiner ~ ...** I reckon that ...
**schätzungsweise** *adv* (*ungefähr*) approximately; (*so vermutet man*) it is thought.
**Schätzwert** *m* estimated value.
**Schau** [ʃaʊ] (-) *f* show; (*Ausstellung*) display, exhibition; **etw zur ~ stellen** to make a show of sth, show sth off; **eine ~ abziehen** (*umg*) to put on a show; ~**bild** *nt* diagram.
**Schauder** ['ʃaʊdər] (-s, -) *m* shudder; (*wegen Kälte*) shiver; s~**haft** *adj* horrible.
**schaudern** *vi* to shudder; (*wegen Kälte*) to shiver.
**schauen** ['ʃaʊən] *vi* to look; **da schau her!** well, well!
**Schauer** ['ʃaʊər] (-s, -) *m* (*Regen~*) shower; (*Schreck*) shudder; ~**geschichte** *f* horror story; s~**lich** *adj* horrific, spine-chilling; ~**märchen** *nt* horror story.
**Schaufel** ['ʃaʊfəl] (-, -n) *f* shovel; (*Kehricht~*) dustpan; (*von Turbine*) vane; (*NAUT*) paddle; (*TECH*) scoop.
**schaufeln** *vt* to shovel; (*Grab, Grube*) to dig ♦ *vi* to shovel.
**Schaufenster** *nt* shop window; ~**auslage** *f* window display; ~**bummel** *m* window-shopping (expedition); ~**dekorateur(in)** *m(f)* window dresser; ~**puppe** *f* display dummy.
**Schaugeschäft** *nt* show business.
**Schaukasten** *m* showcase.
**Schaukel** ['ʃaʊkəl] (-, -n) *f* swing.
**schaukeln** *vi* to swing, rock ♦ *vt* to rock; **wir werden das Kind od das schon ~** (*fig: umg*) we'll manage it.
**Schaukelpferd** *nt* rocking horse.
**Schaukelstuhl** *m* rocking chair.
**Schaulustige(r)** ['ʃaʊlʊstɪgə(r)] *f(m)* onlooker.
**Schaum** [ʃaʊm] (-(e)s, Schäume) *m* foam; (*Seifen~*) lather; (*von Getränken*) froth; (*von Bier*) head; ~**bad** *nt* bubble bath.
**schäumen** ['ʃɔymən] *vi* to foam.
**Schaumgummi** *m* foam (rubber).
**schaumig** *adj* frothy, foamy.

**Schaum-** *zW:* ~**krone** *f* whitecap; ~**schläger** *m* (*fig*) windbag; ~**schlägerei** *f* (*fig: umg*) hot air; ~**stoff** *m* foam material; ~**wein** *m* sparkling wine.
**Schauplatz** *m* scene.
**Schauprozeß** *m* show trial.
**schaurig** *adj* horrific, dreadful.
**Schauspiel** *nt* spectacle; (*THEAT*) play.
**Schauspieler(in)** *m(f)* actor, actress; s~**isch** *adj* (*Können, Leistung*) acting.
**schauspielern** *vi untr* to act.
**Schauspielhaus** *nt* playhouse, theatre (*BRIT*), theater (*US*).
**Schauspielschule** *f* drama school.
**Schausteller** ['ʃaʊʃtɛlər] (-s, -) *m person who owns or runs a fairground ride/sideshow etc*.
**Scheck** [ʃɛk] (-s, -s) *m* cheque (*BRIT*), check (*US*); ~**buch** *nt*, ~**heft** *nt* cheque book (*BRIT*), check book (*US*).
**scheckig** *adj* dappled, piebald.
**Scheckkarte** *f* cheque (*BRIT*) *od* check (*US*) card, banker's card.
**scheel** [ʃeːl] (*umg*) *adj* dirty; **jdn ~ ansehen** to give sb a dirty look.
**scheffeln** ['ʃɛfəln] *vt* to amass.
**Scheibe** ['ʃaɪbə] (-, -n) *f* disc (*BRIT*), disk (*US*); (*Brot etc*) slice; (*Glas~*) pane; (*MIL*) target; (*Eishockey*) puck; (*Töpfer~*) wheel; (*umg: Schallplatte*) disc (*BRIT*), disk (*US*); **von ihm könntest du dir eine ~ abschneiden** (*fig: umg*) you could take a leaf out of his book.
**Scheiben-** *zW:* ~**bremse** *f* (*AUT*) disc brake; ~**kleister** *interj* (*euph: umg*) sugar!; ~**waschanlage** *f* (*AUT*) windscreen (*BRIT*) *od* windshield (*US*) washers *pl*; ~**wischer** *m* (*AUT*) windscreen (*BRIT*) *od* windshield (*US*) wiper.
**Scheich** [ʃaɪç] (-s, -e *od* -s) *m* sheik(h).
**Scheide** ['ʃaɪdə] (-, -n) *f* sheath; (*ANAT*) vagina.
**scheiden** *unreg vt* to separate; (*Ehe*) to dissolve ♦ *vi* to depart; (*sich trennen*) to part ♦ *vr* (*Wege*) to divide; (*Meinungen*) to diverge; **sich ~ lassen** to get a divorce; **von dem Moment an waren wir (zwei) geschiedene Leute** (*umg*) after that it was the parting of the ways for us; **aus dem Leben ~** to depart this life.
**Scheideweg** *m* (*fig*) crossroads *sing*.
**Scheidung** *f* (*Ehe~*) divorce; **die ~ einreichen** to file a petition for divorce.
**Scheidungsgrund** *m* grounds *pl* for divorce.
**Scheidungsklage** *f* divorce suit.
**Schein** [ʃaɪn] (-(e)s, -e) *m* light; (*An~*) appearance; (*Geld~*) (bank)note; (*Bescheinigung*) certificate; **den ~ wahren** to keep up appearances; **etw zum ~ tun** to pretend to do sth, make a pretence (*BRIT*) *od* pretense (*US*) of doing sth; s~**bar** *adj* apparent.
**scheinen** *unreg vi* to shine; (*Anschein haben*) to

seem.

**Schein-** *zW:* **s~heilig** *adj* hypocritical; **~tod** *m* apparent death; **~werfer (-s, -)** *m* floodlight; (*THEAT*) spotlight; (*Suchscheinwerfer*) searchlight; (*AUT*) headlight.

**Scheiß** [ʃaɪs] (-, *no pl*) (*umg*) *m* bullshit (*!*).

**Scheiß-** ['ʃaɪs-] (*umg*) *in zW* bloody (*BRIT!*); **~dreck** (*umg!*) *m* shit (*!*), crap (*!*); **das geht dich einen ~dreck an** it's got bugger-all to do with you (*!*).

**Scheiße** ['ʃaɪsə] (-) (*umg!*) *f* shit (*!*).

**scheißegal** (*umg!*) *adj:* **das ist mir doch ~!** I don't give a damn (*!*).

**scheißen** (*umg!*) *vi* to shit (*!*).

**scheißfreundlich** (*pej: umg*) *adj* as nice as pie (*ironisch*).

**Scheißkerl** (*umg!*) *m* bastard (*!*), son-of-a-bitch (*US!*).

**Scheit** [ʃaɪt] (-(e)s, -e *od* -er) *nt* log.

**Scheitel** ['ʃaɪtəl] (-s, -) *m* top; (*Haar*) parting (*BRIT*), part (*US*).

**scheiteln** *vt* to part.

**Scheitelpunkt** *m* zenith, apex.

**Scheiterhaufen** ['ʃaɪtərhaʊfən] *m* (funeral) pyre; (*HIST: zur Hinrichtung*) stake.

**scheitern** ['ʃaɪtərn] *vi* to fail.

**Schelle** ['ʃɛlə] (-, -n) *f* small bell.

**schellen** *vi* to ring; **es hat geschellt** the bell has gone.

**Schellfisch** ['ʃɛlfɪʃ] *m* haddock.

**Schelm** [ʃɛlm] (-(e)s, -e) *m* rogue.

**Schelmenroman** *m* picaresque novel.

**schelmisch** *adj* mischievous, roguish.

**Schelte** ['ʃɛltə] (-, -n) *f* scolding.

**schelten** *unreg vt* to scold.

**Schema** ['ʃeːma] (-s, -s *od* -ta) *nt* scheme, plan; (*Darstellung*) schema; **nach ~ F** quite mechanically.

**schematisch** [ʃe'maːtɪʃ] *adj* schematic; (*pej*) mechanical.

**Schemel** ['ʃeːməl] (-s, -) *m* (foot)stool.

**schemenhaft** *adj* shadowy.

**Schenke** (-, -n) *f* tavern, inn.

**Schenkel** ['ʃɛŋkəl] (-s, -) *m* thigh; (*MATH: von Winkel*) side.

**schenken** ['ʃɛŋkən] *vt* (*lit, fig*) to give; (*Getränk*) to pour; **ich möchte nichts geschenkt haben!** (*lit*) I don't want any presents!; (*fig: bevorzugt werden*) I don't want any special treatment!; **sich** *dat* **etw ~** (*umg*) to skip sth; **jdm etw ~** (*erlassen*) to let sb off sth; **ihm ist nie etwas geschenkt worden** (*fig*) he never had it easy; **das ist geschenkt!** (*billig*) that's a giveaway!; (*nichts wert*) that's worthless!

**Schenkung** *f* gift.

**Schenkungsurkunde** *f* deed of gift.

**scheppern** ['ʃɛpərn] (*umg*) *vi* to clatter.

**Scherbe** ['ʃɛrbə] (-, -n) *f* broken piece, fragment; (*archäologisch*) potsherd.

**Schere** ['ʃeːrə] (-, -n) *f* scissors *pl*; (*groß*) shears *pl*; (*ZOOL*) pincer; (*von Hummer, Krebs etc*) pincer, claw; **eine ~** a pair of scissors.

**scheren** *unreg vt* to cut; (*Schaf*) to shear; (*stören*) to bother ♦ *vr* (*sich kümmern*) to care; **scher dich (zum Teufel)!** get lost!

**Scherenschleifer** (-s, -) *m* knife grinder.

**Scherenschnitt** *m* silhouette.

**Schererei** [ʃeːrə'raɪ] (*umg*) *f* bother, trouble.

**Scherflein** ['ʃɛrflaɪn] *nt* mite, bit.

**Scherz** [ʃɛrts] (-es, -e) *m* joke; fun; **s~en** *vi* to joke; (*albern*) to banter; **~frage** *f* conundrum; **s~haft** *adj* joking, jocular.

**Scheu** [ʃɔy] (-) *f* shyness; (*Ehrfurcht*) awe; (*Angst*): **~ (vor** +*dat*) fear (of).

**scheu** [ʃɔy] *adj* shy.

**Scheuche** (-, -n) *f* scarecrow.

**scheuchen** ['ʃɔyçən] *vt* to scare (off).

**scheuen** *vr:* **sich ~ vor** +*dat* to be afraid of, shrink from ♦ *vt* to shun ♦ *vi* (*Pferd*) to shy; **weder Mühe noch Kosten ~** to spare neither trouble nor expense.

**Scheuer** ['ʃɔyər] (-, -n) *f* barn.

**Scheuer-** *zW:* **~bürste** *f* scrubbing brush; **~lappen** *m* floorcloth (*BRIT*), scrubbing rag (*US*); **~leiste** *f* skirting board.

**scheuern** *vt* to scour; (*mit Bürste*) to scrub ♦ *vr:* **sich** *akk* **(wund) ~** to chafe o.s.; **jdm eine ~** (*umg*) to clout sb one.

**Scheuklappe** *f* blinker.

**Scheune** ['ʃɔynə] (-, -n) *f* barn.

**Scheunendrescher** (-s, -) *m:* **er frißt wie ein ~** (*umg*) he eats like a horse.

**Scheusal** ['ʃɔyzaːl] (-s, -e) *nt* monster.

**scheußlich** ['ʃɔyslɪç] *adj* dreadful, frightful; **S~keit** *f* dreadfulness.

**Schi** [ʃiː] *m* = **Ski**.

**Schicht** [ʃɪçt] (-, -en) *f* layer; (*Klasse*) class, level; (*in Fabrik etc*) shift; **~arbeit** *f* shift work.

**schichten** *vt* to layer, stack.

**Schichtwechsel** *m* change of shifts.

**schick** [ʃɪk] *adj* stylish, chic.

**schicken** *vt* to send ♦ *vr:* **sich ~ (in** +*akk*) to resign o.s. (to) ♦ *vb unpers* (*anständig sein*) to be fitting.

**Schickeria** [ʃɪkə'riːa] *f* (*ironisch*) in-people *pl*.

**Schicki(micki)** ['ʃɪkɪ('mɪkɪ)] (-s, -s) (*umg*) *m* trendy.

**schicklich** *adj* proper, fitting.

**Schicksal** (-s, -e) *nt* fate.

**schicksalhaft** *adj* fateful.

**Schicksalsschlag** *m* great misfortune, blow.

**Schickse** ['ʃɪksə] (-, -n) (*umg*) *f* floozy, shiksa (*US*).

**Schiebedach** *nt* (*AUT*) sunroof, sunshine roof.

**schieben** ['ʃiːbən] *unreg vt* (*auch Drogen*) to push; (*Schuld*) to put; (*umg: handeln mit*) to traffic in; **die Schuld auf jdn ~** to put the blame on (to) sb; **etw vor sich** *dat* **her ~** (*fig*) to put sth off.

**Schieber** (-s, -) *m* slide; (*Besteckteil*) pusher; (*Person*) profiteer; (*umg: Schwarzhändler*) black marketeer; (: *Waffen~*) gunrunner; (: *Drogen~*) pusher.

**Schiebetür** *f* sliding door.

**Schieblehre** *f* (*MATH*) calliper (*BRIT*) *od* caliper (*US*) rule.

**Schiebung** *f* fiddle; **das war doch ~** (*umg*) that was rigged *od* a fix.

**schied** *etc* [ʃiːt] *vb siehe* **scheiden**.

**Schieds-** *zW:* **~gericht** *nt* court of arbitration; **~mann** (-(e)s, *pl* **-männer**) *m* arbitrator; **~richter** *m* referee, umpire; (*Schlichter*) arbitrator; **s~richtern** *vi untr* to referee, umpire; to arbitrate; **~spruch** *m* arbitration award; **~verfahren** *nt* arbitration.

**schief** [ʃiːf] *adj* crooked; (*Ebene*) sloping; (*Turm*) leaning; (*Winkel*) oblique; (*Blick*) wry; (*Vergleich*) distorted ♦ *adv* crookedly; (*ansehen*) askance; **auf die ~e Bahn geraten** (*fig*) to leave the straight and narrow; **etw ~ stellen** to slope sth.

**Schiefer** ['ʃiːfər] (-s, -) *m* slate; **~dach** *nt* slate roof; **~tafel** *f* (child's) slate.

**schief-** *zW:* **~gehen** *unreg* (*umg*) *vi* to go wrong; **es wird schon ~gehen!** (*hum*) it'll be O.K.; **~lachen** (*umg*) *vr* to kill o.s. laughing; **~liegen** *unreg* (*umg*) *vi* to be wrong, be on the wrong track (*umg*).

**schielen** ['ʃiːlən] *vi* to squint; **nach etw ~** (*fig*) to eye sth up.

**schien** *etc* [ʃiːn] *vb siehe* **scheinen**.

**Schienbein** *nt* shinbone.

**Schiene** ['ʃiːnə] *f* rail; (*MED*) splint.

**schienen** *vt* to put in splints.

**Schienenbus** *m* railcar.

**Schienenstrang** *m* (*EISENB etc*) (section of) track.

**schier** [ʃiːr] *adj* pure; (*fig*) sheer ♦ *adv* nearly, almost.

**Schießbude** *f* shooting gallery.

**Schießbudenfigur** (*umg*) *f* clown, ludicrous figure.

**schießen** ['ʃiːsən] *unreg vi* to shoot; (*Salat etc*) to run to seed ♦ *vt* to shoot; (*Ball*) to kick; (*Geschoß*) to fire; **~ auf** +*akk* to shoot at; **aus dem Boden ~** (*lit, fig*) to spring *od* sprout up; **jdm durch den Kopf ~** (*fig*) to flash through sb's mind.

**Schießerei** [ʃiːsəˈraɪ] *f* shoot-out, gun battle.

**Schieß-** *zW:* **~gewehr** *nt* (*hum*) gun; **~hund** *m:* **wie ein ~hund aufpassen** (*umg*) to watch like a hawk; **~platz** *m* firing range; **~pulver** *nt* gunpowder; **~scharte** *f* embrasure; **~stand** *m* rifle *od* shooting range.

**Schiff** [ʃɪf] (-(e)s, -e) *nt* ship, vessel; (*Kirchen~*) nave; **s~bar** *adj* navigable; **~bau** *m* shipbuilding; **~bruch** *m* shipwreck; **~bruch erleiden** (*lit*) to be shipwrecked; (*fig*) to fail; (*Unternehmen*) to founder; **s~brüchig** *adj* shipwrecked.

**Schiffchen** *nt* small boat; (*WEBEN*) shuttle; (*Mütze*) forage cap.

**Schiffer** (-s, -) *m* boatman, sailor; (*von Lastkahn*) bargee.

**Schiff-** *zW:* **~(f)ahrt** *f* shipping; (*Reise*) voyage; **~(f)ahrtslinie** *f* shipping route; **~schaukel** *f* swing boat.

**Schiffs-** *zW:* **~junge** *m* cabin boy; **~körper** *m* hull; **~ladung** *f* cargo, shipload; **~planke** *f* gangplank; **~schraube** *f* ship's propeller.

**Schiit** [ʃiˈiːt] (-en, -en) *m* Shiite; **s~isch** *adj* Shiite.

**Schikane** [ʃiˈkaːnə] (-, -n) *f* harassment; dirty trick; **mit allen ~n** with all the trimmings; **das hat er aus reiner ~ gemacht** he did it out of sheer bloody-mindedness.

**schikanieren** [ʃikaˈniːrən] *vt* to harass; (*Ehepartner*) to mess around; (*Mitschüler*) to bully.

**schikanös** [ʃikaˈnøːs] *adj* (*Mensch*) bloody-minded; (*Maßnahme etc*) harassing.

**Schild¹** [ʃɪlt] (-(e)s, -e) *m* shield; (*Mützen~*) peak, visor; **etwas im ~e führen** to be up to something.

**Schild²** [ʃɪlt] (-(e)s, -er) *nt* sign; (*Namens~*) nameplate; (*an Monument, Haus, Grab*) plaque; (*Etikett*) label.

**Schildbürger** *m* duffer, blockhead.

**Schilddrüse** *f* thyroid gland.

**schildern** ['ʃɪldərn] *vt* to describe; (*Menschen etc*) to portray; (*skizzieren*) to outline.

**Schilderung** *f* description; portrayal.

**Schildkröte** *f* tortoise; (*Wasser~*) turtle.

**Schildkrötensuppe** *f* turtle soup.

**Schilf** [ʃɪlf] (-(e)s, -e) *nt*, **Schilfrohr** *nt* (*Pflanze*) reed; (*Material*) reeds *pl*, rushes *pl*.

**Schillerlocke** ['ʃɪlɔrlɔkə] *f* (*Gebäck*) cream horn; (*Räucherfisch*) strip of smoked rock salmon.

**schillern** ['ʃɪlɔrn] *vi* to shimmer.

**schillernd** *adj* iridescent; (*fig: Charakter*) enigmatic.

**Schilling** ['ʃɪlɪŋ] (-s, - *od* (*Schillingstücke*) -e) (*ÖSTERR*) *m* schilling.

**schilt** [ʃɪlt] *vb siehe* **schelten**.

**Schimmel** ['ʃɪməl] (-s, -) *m* mould (*BRIT*), mold (*US*); (*Pferd*) white horse.

**schimm(e)lig** *adj* mouldy (*BRIT*), moldy (*US*).

**schimmeln** *vi* to go mouldy (*BRIT*) *od* moldy (*US*).

**Schimmer** ['ʃɪmər] (-s) *m* glimmer; **keinen (blassen) ~ von etw haben** (*umg*) not to have the slightest idea about sth.

**schimmern** *vi* to glimmer; (*Seide, Perlen*) to shimmer.

**Schimpanse** [ʃɪmˈpanzə] (-n, -n) *m* chimpanzee.

**Schimpf** [ʃɪmpf] (-(e)s, -e) *m* disgrace; **mit ~ und Schande** in disgrace.

**schimpfen** *vi* (*sich beklagen*) to grumble; (*fluchen*) to curse.

**Schimpfkanonade** *f* barrage of abuse.

**Schimpfwort** *nt* term of abuse.

**Schindel** ['ʃɪndəl] (-, -n) *f* shingle.

**schinden** ['ʃɪndən] *unreg vt* to maltreat, drive too hard ♦ *vr:* **sich ~ (mit)** to sweat and strain (at), toil away (at); **Eindruck ~** (*umg*) to create an impression.

**Schinder** (**-s, -**) *m* knacker; (*fig*) slave driver.

**Schinderei** [ʃɪndə'raɪ] *f* grind, drudgery.

**Schindluder** ['ʃɪntluːdər] *nt:* **mit etw ~ treiben** to muck *od* mess sth about; (*Vorrecht*) to abuse sth.

**Schinken** ['ʃɪŋkən] (**-s, -**) *m* ham; (*gekocht und geräuchert*) gammon; (*pej: umg: Theaterstück etc*) hackneyed and clichéd play *etc*; **~speck** *m* bacon.

**Schippe** ['ʃɪpə] (**-, -n**) *f* shovel; **jdn auf die ~ nehmen** (*fig: umg*) to pull sb's leg.

**schippen** *vt* to shovel.

**Schirm** [ʃɪrm] (**-(e)s, -e**) *m* (*Regen~*) umbrella; (*Sonnen~*) parasol, sunshade; (*Wand~, Bild~*) screen; (*Lampen~*) (lamp)shade; (*Mützen~*) peak; (*Pilz~*) cap; **~bildaufnahme** *f* X-ray; **~herr(in)** *m(f)* patron(ess); **~herrschaft** *f* patronage; **~mütze** *f* peaked cap; **~ständer** *m* umbrella stand.

**Schiß** *m:* **~ haben** (*umg*) to be shit scared (*!*).

**schiß** *etc* [ʃɪs] *vb siehe* **scheißen**.

**schizophren** [ʃitso'freːn] *adj* schizophrenic.

**Schizophrenie** [ʃitsofre'niː] *f* schizophrenia.

**schlabbern** ['ʃlabərn] (*umg*) *vt, vi* to slurp.

**Schlacht** [ʃlaxt] (**-, -en**) *f* battle.

**schlachten** *vt* to slaughter, kill.

**Schlachtenbummler** (*umg*) *m* visiting football fan.

**Schlachter** (**-s, -**) *m* butcher.

**Schlacht-** *zW:* **~feld** *nt* battlefield; **~fest** *nt country feast at which freshly slaughtered meat is served*; **~haus** *nt*, **~hof** *m* slaughterhouse, abattoir (*BRIT*); **~opfer** *nt* sacrifice; (*Mensch*) human sacrifice; **~plan** *m* battle plan; (*fig*) plan of action; **~ruf** *m* battle cry, war cry; **~schiff** *nt* battleship; **~vieh** *nt* animals *pl* kept for meat.

**Schlacke** ['ʃlakə] (**-, -n**) *f* slag.

**schlackern** (*umg*) *vi* to tremble; (*Kleidung*) to hang loosely, be baggy; **mit den Ohren ~** (*fig*) to be (left) speechless.

**Schlaf** [ʃlaːf] (**-(e)s**) *m* sleep; **um seinen ~ kommen** *od* **gebracht werden** to lose sleep; **~anzug** *m* pyjamas *pl* (*BRIT*), pajamas *pl* (*US*).

**Schläfchen** ['ʃlɛːfçən] *nt* nap.

**Schläfe** (**-, -n**) *f* (*ANAT*) temple.

**schlafen** *unreg vi* to sleep; (*umg: nicht aufpassen*) to be asleep; **bei jdm ~** to stay overnight with sb; **S~gehen** *nt* going to bed.

**Schlafenszeit** *f* bedtime.

**Schläfer(in)** ['ʃlɛːfər(ɪn)] (**-s, -**) *m(f)* sleeper.

**schlaff** [ʃlaf] *adj* slack; (*Haut*) loose; (*Muskeln*) flabby; (*energielos*) limp; (*erschöpft*) exhausted; **S~heit** *f* slackness; looseness; flabbiness; limpness; exhaustion.

**Schlafgelegenheit** *f* place to sleep.

**Schlafittchen** [ʃla'fɪtçən] (*umg*) *nt:* **jdn am** *od*

**beim ~ nehmen** to take sb by the scruff of the neck.

**Schlaf-** *zW:* **~krankheit** *f* sleeping sickness; **~lied** *nt* lullaby; **s~los** *adj* sleepless; **~losigkeit** *f* sleeplessness, insomnia; **~mittel** *nt* sleeping drug; (*fig, ironisch*) soporific; **~mütze** (*umg*) *f* dope.

**schläfrig** ['ʃlɛːfrɪç] *adj* sleepy.

**Schlaf-** *zW:* **~rock** *m* dressing gown; **Apfel im ~rock** baked apple in puff pastry; **~saal** *m* dormitory; **~sack** *m* sleeping bag.

**schläft** [ʃlɛːft] *vb siehe* **schlafen**.

**Schlaf-** *zW:* **~tablette** *f* sleeping pill; **s~trunken** *adj* drowsy, half-asleep; **~wagen** *m* sleeping car, sleeper; **s~wandeln** *vi untr* to sleepwalk; **~wandler(in)** (**-s, -**) *m(f)* sleepwalker; **~zimmer** *nt* bedroom.

**Schlag** [ʃlaːk] (**-(e)s, ⁻e**) *m* (*lit, fig*) blow; (*auch MED*) stroke; (*Puls~, Herz~*) beat; (*ELEK*) shock; (*Blitz~*) bolt, stroke; (*Glocken~*) chime; (*Autotür*) car door; (*gegen: Portion*) helping; (*: Art*) kind, type; **Schläge** *pl* (*Tracht Prügel*) beating *sing*; **~ acht Uhr** (*umg*) on the stroke of eight; **mit einem ~** all at once; **~ auf ~** in rapid succession; **die haben keinen ~ getan** (*umg*) they haven't done a stroke (of work); **ich dachte, mich trifft der ~** (*umg*) I was thunderstruck; **vom gleichen ~ sein** to be cast in the same mould (*BRIT*) *od* mold (*US*); (*pej*) to be tarred with the same brush; **ein ~ ins Wasser** (*umg*) a wash-out; **~abtausch** *m* (*BOXEN*) exchange of blows; (*fig*) (verbal) exchange; **~ader** *f* artery; **~anfall** *m* stroke; **s~artig** *adj* sudden, without warning; **~baum** *m* barrier; **~bohrer** *m* percussion drill.

**schlagen** ['ʃlaːgən] *unreg vt* to strike, hit; (*wiederholt ~, besiegen*) to beat; (*Glocke*) to ring; (*Stunde*) to strike; (*Kreis, Bogen*) to describe; (*Purzelbaum*) to do; (*Sahne*) to whip; (*Schlacht*) to fight; (*einwickeln*) to wrap ♦ *vi* to strike, hit; to beat; to ring; to strike ♦ *vr* to fight; **um sich ~** to lash out; **ein Ei in die Pfanne ~** to crack an egg into the pan; **eine geschlagene Stunde** a full hour; **na ja, ehe ich mich ~ lasse!** (*hum: umg*) I suppose you could twist my arm; **nach jdm ~** (*fig*) to take after sb; **sich gut ~** (*fig*) to do well; **sich nach links/Norden ~** to strike out to the left/(for the) north; **sich auf jds Seite** *akk* **~** to side with sb; (*die Fronten wechseln*) to go over to sb.

**schlagend** *adj* (*Beweis*) convincing; **~e Wetter** (*MIN*) firedamp.

**Schlager** ['ʃlaːgər] (**-s, -**) *m* (*MUS, fig*) hit.

**Schläger** ['ʃlɛːgər] (**-s, -**) *m* brawler; (*SPORT*) bat; (*TENNIS etc*) racket; (*GOLF*) club; (*Hockey~*) hockey stick.

**Schlägerei** [ʃlɛːgə'raɪ] *f* fight, punch-up.

**Schlagersänger** *m* pop singer.

**Schlägertyp** (*umg*) *m* thug.

**Schlag-** *zW:* **s~fertig** *adj* quick-witted;

~**fertigkeit** f ready wit, quickness of repartee; ~**instrument** nt percussion instrument; ~**kraft** f (lit, fig) power; (MIL) strike power; (BOXEN) punch(ing power); s~**kräftig** adj powerful; (Beweise) clear-cut; ~**loch** nt pothole; ~**obers** (-, -) (ÖSTERR) nt, ~**rahm** m, ~**sahne** f (whipped) cream; ~**seite** f (NAUT) list; ~**stock** m (form) truncheon (BRIT), nightstick (US).

**schlägt** [ʃlɛːkt] vb siehe **schlagen**.

**Schlag-** zW: ~**wort** nt slogan, catch phrase; ~**zeile** f headline; ~**zeilen machen** (umg) to hit the headlines; ~**zeug** nt drums pl; (in Orchester) percussion; ~**zeuger** (-s, -) m drummer; percussionist.

**schlaksig** [ˈʃlaːksɪç] (umg) adj gangling, gawky.

**Schlamassel** [ʃlaˈmasəl] (-s, -) (umg) m mess.

**Schlamm** [ʃlam] (-(e)s, -e) m mud.

**schlammig** adj muddy.

**Schlampe** [ˈʃlampə] (-, -n) (umg) f slattern, slut.

**schlampen** (umg) vi to be sloppy.

**Schlamperei** [ʃlampəˈraɪ] (umg) f disorder, untidiness; (schlechte Arbeit) sloppy work.

**schlampig** (umg) adj slovenly, sloppy.

**schlang** etc [ʃlaŋ] vb siehe **schlingen**.

**Schlange** [ˈʃlaŋə] (-, -n) f snake; (Menschen~) queue (BRIT), line (US); ~ **stehen** to (form a) queue (BRIT), stand in line (US); **eine falsche** ~ a snake in the grass.

**schlängeln** [ˈʃlɛŋəln] vr to twist, wind; (Fluß) to meander.

**Schlangen-** zW: ~**biß** m snake bite; ~**gift** nt snake venom; ~**linie** f wavy line.

**schlank** [ʃlaŋk] adj slim, slender; **S~heit** f slimness, slenderness; **S~heitskur** f diet.

**schlapp** [ʃlap] adj limp; (locker) slack; (umg: energielos) listless; (nach Krankheit etc) run-down.

**Schlappe** (-, -n) (umg) f setback.

**Schlappen** (-s, -) (umg) m slipper.

**schlapp-** zW: **S~heit** f limpness; slackness; **S~hut** m slouch hat; ~**machen** (umg) vi to wilt, droop; **S~schwanz** (pej: umg) m weakling, softy.

**Schlaraffenland** [ʃlaˈrafənlant] nt land of milk and honey.

**schlau** [ʃlaʊ] adj crafty, cunning; **ich werde nicht** ~ **aus ihm** I don't know what to make of him; **S~berger** (-s, -) (umg) m clever Dick.

**Schlauch** [ʃlaʊx] (-(e)s, Schläuche) m hose; (in Reifen) inner tube; (umg: Anstrengung) grind; **auf dem** ~ **stehen** (umg) to be in a jam od fix; ~**boot** nt rubber dinghy.

**schlauchen** (umg) vt to tell on, exhaust.

**schlauchlos** adj (Reifen) tubeless.

**Schläue** [ˈʃlɔʏə] (-) f cunning.

**Schlaufe** [ˈʃlaʊfə] (-, -n) f loop; (Aufhänger) hanger.

**Schlauheit** f cunning.

**Schlaukopf** m clever Dick.

**Schlawiner** [ʃlaˈviːnər] (-s, -) m (hum: umg) villain, rogue.

**schlecht** [ʃlɛçt] adj bad; (ungenießbar) bad, off (BRIT) ♦ adv: **er kann** ~ **nein sagen** he finds it hard to say no, he can't say no; **jdm ist** ~ sb feels sick od ill; ~ **und recht** after a fashion; **auf jdn** ~ **zu sprechen sein** not to have a good word to say for sb; **er hat nicht** ~ **gestaunt** (umg) he wasn't half surprised.

**schlechterdings** adv simply.

**schlecht-** zW: ~**gehen** unreg vi unpers: **jdm geht es** ~ sb is in a bad way; **heute geht es** ~ today is not very convenient; **S~heit** f badness; ~**hin** adv simply; **der Dramatiker** ~**hin** THE playwright.

**Schlechtigkeit** f badness; (Tat) bad deed.

**schlechtmachen** vt to run down, denigrate.

**schlecken** [ˈʃlɛkən] vt, vi to lick.

**Schlegel** [ˈʃleːɡəl] (-s, -) m (drum)stick; (Hammer) hammer; (KOCH) leg.

**schleichen** [ˈʃlaɪçən] unreg vi to creep, crawl.

**schleichend** adj creeping; (Krankheit, Gift) insidious.

**Schleichweg** m: **auf** ~**en** (fig) on the quiet.

**Schleichwerbung** f: **eine** ~ a plug.

**Schleie** [ˈʃlaɪə] (-, -n) f tench.

**Schleier** [ˈʃlaɪər] (-s, -) m veil; ~**eule** f barn owl; s~**haft** (umg) adj: **jdm s~haft sein** to be a mystery to sb.

**Schleife** [ˈʃlaɪfə] (-, -n) f (auch COMPUT) loop; (Band) bow; (Kranz~) ribbon.

**schleifen¹** vt to drag; (MIL: Festung) to raze ♦ vi to drag; **die Kupplung** ~ **lassen** (AUT) to slip the clutch.

**schleifen²** unreg vt to grind; (Edelstein) to cut; (MIL: Soldaten) to drill.

**Schleifmaschine** f sander; (in Fabrik) grinding machine.

**Schleifstein** m grindstone.

**Schleim** [ʃlaɪm] (-(e)s, -e) m slime; (MED) mucus; (KOCH) gruel; ~**haut** f mucous membrane.

**schleimig** adj slimy.

**schlemmen** [ˈʃlɛmən] vi to feast.

**Schlemmer(in)** (-s, -) m(f) gourmet, bon vivant.

**Schlemmerei** [ʃlɛməˈraɪ] f feasting.

**schlendern** [ˈʃlɛndərn] vi to stroll.

**Schlendrian** [ˈʃlɛndriaːn] (-(e)s) m sloppy way of working.

**Schlenker** [ˈʃlɛŋkər] (-s, -) m swerve.

**schlenkern** vt, vi to swing, dangle.

**Schleppe** [ˈʃlɛpə] (-, -n) f train.

**schleppen** vt to drag; (Auto, Schiff) to tow; (tragen) to lug.

**schleppend** adj dragging; (Bedienung, Abfertigung) sluggish, slow.

**Schlepper** (-s, -) m tractor; (Schiff) tug.

**Schleppkahn** m (canal) barge.

**Schlepptau** nt towrope; **jdn ins** ~ **nehmen** (fig) to take sb in tow.

**Schlesien** ['ʃleːziən] (-s) nt Silesia.
**Schlesier(in)** (-s, -) m(f) Silesian.
**schlesisch** adj Silesian.
**Schleswig-Holstein** ['ʃleːsvɪç'hɔlʃtain] (-s) nt Schleswig-Holstein.
**Schleuder** ['ʃlɔydər] (-, -n) f catapult; (Wäsche~) spin-dryer; (Zentrifuge) centrifuge; ~honig m extracted honey.
**schleudern** vt to hurl; (Wäsche) to spin-dry ♦ vi (AUT) to skid; **ins S~ kommen** (AUT) to go into a skid; (fig: umg) to run into trouble.
**Schleuder-** zW: ~**preis** m give-away price; ~**sitz** m (AVIAT) ejector seat; (fig) hot seat; ~**ware** f cut-price (BRIT) od cut-rate (US) goods pl.
**schleunig** ['ʃlɔynɪç] adj prompt, speedy; (Schritte) quick.
**schleunigst** adv straight away.
**Schleuse** ['ʃlɔyzə] (-, -n) f lock; (Schleusentor) sluice.
**schleusen** vt (Schiffe) to pass through a lock, lock; (Wasser) to channel; (Menschen) to filter; (fig: heimlich) to smuggle.
**Schlich** (-(e)s, -e) m dodge, trick; **jdm auf die ~e kommen** to get wise to sb.
**schlich** etc [ʃlɪç] vb siehe **schleichen**.
**schlicht** [ʃlɪçt] adj simple, plain.
**schlichten** vt to smooth; (beilegen) to settle; (Streit: vermitteln) to mediate, arbitrate.
**Schlichter(in)** (-s, -) m(f) mediator, arbitrator.
**Schlichtheit** f simplicity, plainness.
**Schlichtung** f settlement; arbitration.
**Schlick** [ʃlɪk] (-(e)s, -e) m mud; (Öl~) slick.
**schlief** etc [ʃliːf] vb siehe **schlafen**.
**Schließe** ['ʃliːsə] (-, -n) f fastener.
**schließen** ['ʃliːsən] unreg vt to close, shut; (beenden) to close; (Freundschaft, Bündnis, Ehe) to enter into; (COMPUT: Datei) to close; (folgern): ~ **(aus)** to infer (from) ♦ vi, vr to close, shut; **auf etw** akk ~ **lassen** to suggest sth; **jdn/etw in sein Herz** ~ to take sb/sth to one's heart; **etw in sich** ~ to include sth; „**geschlossen**" "closed".
**Schließfach** nt locker.
**schließlich** adv finally; (~ doch) after all.
**Schliff** (-(e)s, -e) m cut(ting); (fig) polish; **einer Sache den letzten** ~ **geben** (fig) to put the finishing touch(es) to sth.
**schliff** etc [ʃlɪf] vb siehe **schleifen**.
**schlimm** [ʃlɪm] adj bad; **das war** ~ that was terrible; **das ist halb so** ~! that's not so bad!; ~**er** adj worse; ~**ste(r, s)** adj worst.
**schlimmstenfalls** adv at (the) worst.
**Schlinge** ['ʃlɪŋə] (-, -n) f loop; (an Galgen) noose; (Falle) snare; (MED) sling.
**Schlingel** (-s, -) m rascal.
**schlingen** unreg vt to wind ♦ vi (essen) to bolt one's food, gobble.
**schlingern** vi to roll.
**Schlingpflanze** f creeper.
**Schlips** [ʃlɪps] (-es, -e) m tie, necktie (US);

**sich auf den** ~ **getreten fühlen** (fig: umg) to feel offended.
**Schlitten** ['ʃlɪtən] (-s, -) m sledge, sled; (Pferde~) sleigh; **mit jdm** ~ **fahren** (umg) to give sb a rough time; ~**bahn** f toboggan run; ~**fahren** (-s) nt tobogganing.
**schlittern** ['ʃlɪtərn] vi to slide; (Wagen) to skid.
**Schlittschuh** ['ʃlɪtʃuː] m skate; ~ **laufen** to skate; ~**bahn** f skating rink; ~**läufer** m skater.
**Schlitz** [ʃlɪts] (-es, -e) m slit; (für Münze) slot; (Hosen~) flies pl; **s~äugig** adj slant-eyed; **s~en** vt to slit; ~**ohr** nt (fig) sly fox.
**schlohweiß** ['ʃloːvais] adj snow-white.
**Schlokal** nt gourmet restaurant.
**Schloß** (-sses, -sser) nt lock, padlock; (an Schmuck etc) clasp; (Bau) castle; (Palast) palace; **ins** ~ **fallen** to lock (itself).
**schloß** etc [ʃlɔs] vb siehe **schließen**.
**Schlosser** ['ʃlɔsər] (-s, -) m (Auto~) fitter; (für Schlüssel etc) locksmith.
**Schlosserei** [ʃlɔsə'rai] f metal(working) shop.
**Schloßhund** m: **heulen wie ein** ~ to howl one's head off.
**Schlot** [ʃloːt] (-(e)s, -e) m chimney; (NAUT) funnel.
**schlottern** ['ʃlɔtərn] vi to shake; (vor Angst) to tremble; (Kleidung) to be baggy.
**Schlucht** [ʃlʊxt] (-, -en) f gorge, ravine.
**schluchzen** ['ʃlʊxtsən] vi to sob.
**Schluck** [ʃlʊk] (-(e)s, -e) m swallow; (größer) gulp; (kleiner) sip; (ein bißchen) drop.
**Schluckauf** (-s) m hiccups pl.
**schlucken** vt to swallow; (umg: Alkohol, Benzin) to guzzle; (: verschlingen) to swallow up ♦ vi to swallow.
**Schlucker** (-s, -) (umg) m: **armer** ~ poor devil.
**Schluckimpfung** f oral vaccination.
**schlud(e)rig** ['ʃluːdrɪç] (umg) adj slipshod.
**schludern** ['ʃluːdərn] (umg) vi to do slipshod work.
**schlug** etc [ʃluːk] vb siehe **schlagen**.
**Schlummer** ['ʃlʊmər] (-s) m slumber.
**schlummern** vi to slumber.
**Schlund** [ʃlʊnt] (-(e)s, -e) m gullet; (fig) jaw.
**schlüpfen** ['ʃlʏpfən] vi to slip; (Vogel etc) to hatch (out).
**Schlüpfer** ['ʃlʏpfər] (-s, -) m panties pl, knickers pl.
**Schlupfloch** ['ʃlʊpflɔx] nt hole; (Versteck) hide-out; (fig) loophole.
**schlüpfrig** ['ʃlʏpfrɪç] adj slippery; (fig) lewd; **S~keit** f slipperiness; lewdness.
**Schlupfwinkel** m hiding place; (fig) quiet corner.
**schlurfen** ['ʃlʊrfən] vi to shuffle.
**schlürfen** ['ʃlʏrfən] vt, vi to slurp.
**Schluß** [ʃlʊs] (-sses, -̈sse) m end; (~folgerung) conclusion; **am** ~ at the end; ~ **für heute!** that'll do for today; ~ **jetzt!** that's enough

now!; ~ **machen mit** to finish with.
**Schlüssel** ['ʃlʏsəl] **(-s, -)** m (*lit, fig*) key;
(*Schraub~*) spanner, wrench; (*MUS*) clef;
~**bein** nt collarbone; ~**blume** f cowslip,
primrose; ~**bund** m bunch of keys;
~**erlebnis** nt (*PSYCH*) crucial experience;
~**kind** nt latchkey child; ~**loch** nt keyhole;
~**position** f key position; ~**wort** nt safe
combination; (*COMPUT*) keyword.
**Schlußfolgerung** f conclusion, inference.
**Schlußformel** f (*in Brief*) closing formula;
(*bei Vertrag*) final clause.
**schlüssig** ['ʃlʏsɪç] adj conclusive; **sich** dat
(**über etw** akk) ~ **sein** to have made up one's
mind (about sth).
**Schluß-** zW: ~**licht** nt rear light (*BRIT*),
taillight (*US*); (*fig*) tail ender; ~**strich** m (*fig*)
final stroke; **einen** ~**strich unter etw** akk
**ziehen** to consider sth finished; ~**verkauf** m
clearance sale; ~**wort** nt concluding words
pl.
**Schmach** [ʃmaːx] **(-)** f disgrace, ignominy.
**schmachten** ['ʃmaxtən] vi to languish; **nach
jdm** ~ to pine for sb.
**schmächtig** ['ʃmɛçtɪç] adj slight.
**schmachvoll** adj ignominious, humiliating.
**schmackhaft** ['ʃmakhaft] adj tasty; **jdm etw**
~ **machen** (*fig*) to make sth palatable to sb.
**schmähen** ['ʃmɛːən] vt to abuse, revile.
**schmählich** adj ignominious, shameful.
**Schmähung** f abuse.
**schmal** [ʃmaːl] adj narrow; (*Person, Buch etc*)
slender, slim; (*karg*) meagre (*BRIT*), meager
(*US*); ~**brüstig** adj narrow-chested.
**schmälern** ['ʃmɛːlərn] vt to diminish; (*fig*) to
belittle.
**Schmalfilm** m cine (*BRIT*) od movie (*US*) film.
**Schmalspur** f narrow gauge.
**Schmalspur-** (*pej*) in zW small-time.
**Schmalz** [ʃmalts] **(-es, -e)** nt dripping;
(*Schweine~*) lard; (*fig*) sentiment, schmaltz.
**schmalzig** adj (*fig*) schmaltzy, slushy.
**schmarotzen** [ʃmaˈrɔtsən] vi (*BIOL*) to be
parasitic; (*fig*) to sponge.
**Schmarotzer** **(-s, -)** m (*auch fig*) parasite.
**Schmarren** ['ʃmarən] **(-s, -)** m (*ÖSTERR*) small
pieces of pancake; (*fig*) rubbish, tripe.
**schmatzen** ['ʃmatsən] vi to eat noisily.
**Schmaus** [ʃmaʊs] **(-es, Schmäuse)** m feast;
**s~en** vi to feast.
**schmecken** ['ʃmɛkən] vt, vi to taste; **es
schmeckt ihm** he likes it; **schmeckt es
Ihnen?** is it good?, are you enjoying your
food od meal?; **das schmeckt nach mehr!**
(*umg*) it's very moreish (*hum*); **es sich**
~ **lassen** to tuck in.
**Schmeichelei** [ʃmaɪçəˈlaɪ] f flattery.
**schmeichelhaft** ['ʃmaɪçəlhaft] adj flattering.
**schmeicheln** vi to flatter.
**Schmeichler(in)** **(-s, -)** m(f) flatterer.
**schmeißen** ['ʃmaɪsən] unreg (*umg*) vt to throw,
chuck; (*spendieren*): **eine Runde** od **Lage** ~ to

stand a round.
**Schmeißfliege** f bluebottle.
**Schmelz** [ʃmɛlts] **(-es, -e)** m enamel; (*Glasur*)
glaze; (*von Stimme*) melodiousness; **s~bar**
adj fusible.
**schmelzen** unreg vt to melt; (*Erz*) to smelt ♦ vi
to melt.
**Schmelz-** zW: ~**hütte** f smelting works pl;
~**käse** m cheese spread; (*in Scheiben*)
processed cheese; ~**ofen** m melting
furnace; (*für Erze*) smelting furnace;
~**punkt** m melting point; ~**tiegel** m (*lit, fig*)
melting pot; ~**wasser** nt melted snow.
**Schmerbauch** ['ʃmeːrbaʊx] (*umg*) m paunch,
potbelly.
**Schmerz** [ʃmɛrts] **(-es, -en)** m pain; (*Trauer*)
grief no pl; ~**en haben** to be in pain;
**s~empfindlich** adj sensitive to pain.
**schmerzen** vt, vi to hurt.
**Schmerzensgeld** nt compensation.
**Schmerz-** zW: **s~haft** adj painful; **s~lich** adj
painful; **s~lindernd** adj pain-relieving;
**s~los** adj painless; ~**mittel** nt painkiller,
analgesic; **s~stillend** adj pain-killing,
analgesic; ~**tablette** f pain-killing tablet.
**Schmetterling** ['ʃmɛtərlɪŋ] m butterfly.
**Schmetterlingsstil** m (*SCHWIMMEN*)
butterfly stroke.
**schmettern** ['ʃmɛtərn] vt to smash; (*Melodie*)
to sing loudly, bellow out ♦ vi to smash
(*SPORT*); (*Trompete*) to blare.
**Schmied** [ʃmiːt] **(-(e)s, -e)** m blacksmith.
**Schmiede** ['ʃmiːdə] **(-, -n)** f smithy, forge;
~'**eisen** nt wrought iron.
**schmieden** vt to forge; (*Pläne*) to devise,
concoct.
**schmiegen** ['ʃmiːgən] vt to press, nestle ♦ vr:
**sich** ~ **an** +akk to cuddle up to, nestle up to.
**schmiegsam** ['ʃmiːkzaːm] adj flexible, pliable.
**Schmiere** ['ʃmiːrə] f grease; (*THEAT*)
greasepaint, make-up; (*pej: schlechtes
Theater*) fleapit; ~ **stehen** (*umg*) to be the
look-out.
**schmieren** vt to smear; (*ölen*) to lubricate,
grease; (*bestechen*) to bribe ♦ vi (*schreiben*)
to scrawl; **es läuft wie geschmiert** it's going
like clockwork; **jdm eine** ~ (*umg*) to clout sb
one.
**Schmierenkomödiant** (*pej*) m ham (actor).
**Schmier-** zW: ~**fett** nt grease; ~**fink** m messy
person; ~**geld** nt bribe; ~**heft** nt jotter.
**schmierig** adj greasy.
**Schmiermittel** nt lubricant.
**Schmierseife** f soft soap.
**schmilzt** [ʃmɪltst] vb siehe **schmelzen**.
**Schminke** ['ʃmɪŋkə] **(-, -n)** f make-up.
**schminken** vt, vr to make up.
**schmirgeln** ['ʃmɪrgəln] vt to sand (down).
**Schmirgelpapier** (-s) nt emery paper.
**Schmiß** **(-sses, -sse)** m (*Narbe*) duelling (*BRIT*)
od dueling (*US*) scar; (*veraltet: Schwung*)
dash, élan.

**schmiß** *etc* [ʃmɪs] *vb siehe* **schmeißen.**

**Schmöker** ['ʃmøːkər] (**-s, -**) (*umg*) *m* (trashy) old book.

**schmökern** *vi* to bury o.s. in a book; (*umg*) to browse.

**schmollen** ['ʃmɔlən] *vi* to pout; (*gekränkt*) to sulk.

**schmollend** *adj* sulky.

**Schmollmund** *m* pout.

**schmolz** *etc* [ʃmɔlts] *vb siehe* **schmelzen.**

**Schmorbraten** *m* stewed *od* braised meat.

**schmoren** ['ʃmoːrən] *vt* to braise.

**Schmu** [ʃmuː] (**-s**) (*umg*) *m* cheating.

**Schmuck** [ʃmʊk] (**-(e)s, -e**) *m* jewellery (*BRIT*), jewelry (*US*); (*Verzierung*) decoration.

**schmücken** ['ʃmʏkən] *vt* to decorate.

**Schmuck-** *zW:* **s~los** *adj* unadorned, plain; **~losigkeit** *f* simplicity; **~sachen** *pl* jewels *pl*, jewellery *sing* (*BRIT*), jewelry *sing* (*US*); **~stück** *nt* (*Ring etc*) piece of jewellery (*BRIT*) *od* jewelry (*US*); (*fig: Prachtstück*) gem.

**schmudd(e)lig** ['ʃmʊd(ə)lɪç] *adj* messy; (*schmutzig*) dirty; (*schmierig, unsauber*) filthy.

**Schmuggel** ['ʃmʊgəl] (**-s**) *m* smuggling.

**schmuggeln** *vt, vi* to smuggle.

**Schmuggelware** *f* contraband.

**Schmuggler(in)** (**-s, -**) *m(f)* smuggler.

**schmunzeln** ['ʃmʊntsəln] *vi* to smile benignly.

**schmusen** ['ʃmuːzən] (*umg*) *vi* (*zärtlich sein*) to cuddle; **mit jdm ~** to cuddle sb.

**Schmutz** [ʃmʊts] (**-es**) *m* dirt; (*fig*) filth; **s~en** *vi* to get dirty; **~fink** *m* filthy creature; **~fleck** *m* stain.

**schmutzig** *adj* dirty; **~e Wäsche waschen** (*fig*) to wash one's dirty linen in public.

**Schnabel** ['ʃnaːbəl] (**-s, -̈**) *m* beak, bill; (*Ausguß*) spout; (*umg: Mund*) mouth; **reden, wie einem der ~ gewachsen ist** to say exactly what comes into one's head; (*unaffektiert*) to talk naturally.

**schnacken** ['ʃnakən] (*NORDD: umg*) *vi* to chat.

**Schnake** ['ʃnaːkə] (**-, -n**) *f* crane fly; (*Stechmücke*) gnat.

**Schnalle** ['ʃnalə] (**-, -n**) *f* buckle; (*an Handtasche, Buch*) clasp.

**schnallen** *vt* to buckle.

**schnalzen** ['ʃnaltsən] *vi* to snap; (*mit Zunge*) to click.

**Schnäppchen** ['ʃnɛpçən] (*umg*) *nt* bargain, snip.

**schnappen** ['ʃnapən] *vt* to grab, catch; (*umg: ergreifen*) to snatch ♦ *vi* to snap.

**Schnappschloß** *nt* spring lock.

**Schnappschuß** *m* (*PHOT*) snapshot.

**Schnaps** [ʃnaps] (**-es, -̈e**) *m* schnapps; (*umg: Branntwein*) spirits *pl*; **~idee** (*umg*) *f* crackpot idea; **~leiche** (*umg*) *f* drunk.

**schnarchen** ['ʃnarçən] *vi* to snore.

**schnattern** ['ʃnatərn] *vi* to chatter; (*zittern*) to shiver.

**schnauben** ['ʃnaʊbən] *vi* to snort ♦ *vr* to blow one's nose.

**schnaufen** ['ʃnaʊfən] *vi* to puff, pant.

**Schnaufer** (**-s, -**) (*umg*) *m* breath.

**Schnauzbart** ['ʃnaʊtsbaːrt] *m* moustache (*BRIT*), mustache (*US*).

**Schnauze** (**-, -n**) *f* snout, muzzle; (*Ausguß*) spout; (*umg*) gob; **auf die ~ fallen** (*fig*) to come a cropper (*umg*); **etw frei nach ~ machen** to do sth any old how.

**Schnecke** ['ʃnɛkə] (**-, -n**) *f* snail; (*Nackt~*) slug; (*KOCH: Gebäck*) ≈ Chelsea bun; **jdn zur ~ machen** (*umg*) to give sb a real bawling out.

**Schneckenhaus** *nt* snail's shell.

**Schneckentempo** (*umg*) *nt:* **im ~** at a snail's pace.

**Schnee** [ʃneː] (**-s**) *m* snow; (*Ei~*) beaten egg white; **~ von gestern** old hat; **water under the bridge; ~ball** *m* snowball; **~besen** *m* (*KOCH*) whisk; **~fall** *m* snowfall; **~flocke** *f* snowflake; **~gestöber** *nt* snowstorm; **~glöckchen** *nt* snowdrop; **~grenze** *f* snowline; **~kette** *f* (*AUT*) snow chain; **~könig** *m:* **sich freuen wie ein ~könig** to be as pleased as Punch; **~mann** *m* snowman; **~pflug** *m* snowplough (*BRIT*), snowplow (*US*); **~regen** *m* sleet; **~schmelze** *f* thaw; **~treiben** *nt* driving snow; **~wehe** *f* snowdrift; **~wittchen** *nt* Snow White.

**Schneid** [ʃnaɪt] (**-(e)s**) (*umg*) *m* pluck.

**Schneidbrenner** (**-s, -**) *m* (*TECH*) oxyacetylene cutter.

**Schneide** ['ʃnaɪdə] (**-, -n**) *f* edge; (*Klinge*) blade.

**schneiden** *unreg vt* to cut; (*Film, Tonband*) to edit; (*kreuzen*) to cross, intersect ♦ *vr* to cut o.s.; (*umg: sich täuschen*): **da hat er sich aber geschnitten!** he's very much mistaken; **die Luft ist zum S~** (*fig: umg*) the air is very bad.

**schneidend** *adj* cutting.

**Schneider** (**-s, -**) *m* tailor; **frieren wie ein ~** (*umg*) to be frozen to the marrow; **aus dem ~ sein** (*fig*) to be out of the woods.

**Schneiderei** [ʃnaɪdəˈraɪ] *f* tailor's shop; (*einer Schneiderin*) dressmaker's shop.

**Schneiderin** *f* dressmaker.

**schneidern** *vt* to make ♦ *vi* to be a tailor.

**Schneidersitz** (**-es**) *m:* **im ~ sitzen** to sit cross-legged.

**Schneidezahn** *m* incisor.

**schneidig** *adj* dashing; (*mutig*) plucky.

**schneien** ['ʃnaɪən] *vi* to snow; **jdm ins Haus ~** (*umg: Besuch*) to drop in on sb; (: *Rechnung, Brief*) to come in the post (*BRIT*) *od* mail (*US*).

**Schneise** ['ʃnaɪzə] (**-, -n**) *f* (*Wald~*) clearing.

**schnell** [ʃnɛl] *adj* quick, fast ♦ *adv* quick(ly), fast; **das ging ~** that was quick; **S~boot** *nt* speedboat.

**Schnelle** (**-**) *f:* **etw auf die ~ machen** to do sth in a rush.

**schnellen** *vi* to shoot.

**Schnellgericht** nt (*JUR*) summary court; (*KOCH*) convenience food.
**Schnellhefter** m loose-leaf binder.
**Schnelligkeit** f speed.
**Schnell-** zW: **~imbiß** m (*Essen*) (quick) snack; (*Raum*) snack bar; **~kochtopf** m (*Dampfkochtopf*) pressure cooker; **~reinigung** f express cleaner's.
**schnellstens** adv as quickly as possible.
**Schnellstraße** f expressway.
**Schnellzug** m fast od express train.
**schneuzen** ['ʃnɔytsən] vr to blow one's nose.
**Schnickschnack** ['ʃnɪkʃnak] (**-(e)s**) (*umg*) m twaddle.
**Schnippchen** ['ʃnɪpçən] nt: **jdm ein ~ schlagen** to play a trick on sb.
**schnippeln** ['ʃnɪpəln] (*umg*) vt to snip; (*mit Messer*) to hack ♦ vi: **~ an** +dat to snip at; to hack at.
**schnippen** ['ʃnɪpən] vi: **mit den Fingern ~** to snap one's fingers.
**schnippisch** ['ʃnɪpɪʃ] adj sharp-tongued.
**Schnipsel** ['ʃnɪpsəl] (**-s, -**) (*umg*) m od nt scrap; (*Papier~*) scrap of paper.
**Schnitt** (**-(e)s, -e**) m cut(ting); (*~punkt*) intersection; (*Quer~*) (cross) section; (*Durch~*) average; (*~muster*) pattern; (*Ernte*) crop; (*an Buch*) edge; (*umg: Gewinn*) profit; **~**: **L. Schwarz** (*FILM*) editor - L. Schwarz; **im ~** on average.
**schnitt** etc [ʃnɪt] vb siehe **schneiden**.
**Schnittblumen** pl cut flowers pl.
**Schnittbohnen** pl French od green beans pl.
**Schnitte** (**-, -n**) f slice; (*belegt*) sandwich.
**schnittfest** adj (*Tomaten*) firm.
**Schnittfläche** f section.
**schnittig** ['ʃnɪtɪç] adj smart; (*Auto, Formen*) stylish.
**Schnitt-** zW: **~lauch** m chive; **~muster** nt pattern; **~punkt** m (point of) intersection; **~stelle** f (*COMPUT*) interface; **~wunde** f cut.
**Schnitzarbeit** f wood carving.
**Schnitzel** (**-s, -**) nt scrap; (*KOCH*) escalope; **~jagd** f paperchase.
**schnitzen** ['ʃnɪtsən] vt to carve.
**Schnitzer** (**-s, -**) m carver; (*umg*) blunder.
**Schnitzerei** [ʃnɪtsə'raɪ] f wood carving.
**schnodderig** ['ʃnɔdərɪç] (*umg*) adj snotty.
**schnöde** ['ʃnøːdə] adj base, mean.
**Schnorchel** ['ʃnɔrçəl] (**-s, -**) m snorkel.
**schnorcheln** vi to go snorkelling.
**Schnörkel** ['ʃnœrkəl] (**-s, -**) m flourish; (*ARCHIT*) scroll.
**schnorren** ['ʃnɔrən] vt, vi to cadge (*BRIT*).
**Schnorrer** (**-s, -**) (*umg*) m cadger (*BRIT*).
**Schnösel** ['ʃnøːzəl] (**-s, -**) (*umg*) m snotty(-nosed) little upstart.
**schnuckelig** ['ʃnʊkəlɪç] (*umg*) adj (*gemütlich*) snug, cosy; (*Person*) sweet.
**schnüffeln** ['ʃnyfəln] vi to sniff; (*fig: umg: spionieren*) to snoop around; **S~** nt (*von*

*Klebstoff etc*) glue-sniffing etc.
**Schnüffler(in)** (**-s, -**) m(f) snooper.
**Schnuller** ['ʃnʊlər] (**-s, -**) m dummy (*BRIT*), pacifier (*US*).
**Schnulze** ['ʃnʊltsə] (**-, -n**) (*umg*) f schmaltzy film/book/song.
**Schnupfen** ['ʃnʊpfən] (**-s, -**) m cold.
**Schnupftabak** m snuff.
**schnuppe** ['ʃnʊpə] (*umg*) adj: **jdm ~ sein** to be all the same to sb.
**schnuppern** ['ʃnʊpərn] vi to sniff.
**Schnur** [ʃnuːr] (**-, -̈e**) f string; (*Kordel*) cord; (*ELEK*) flex.
**Schnürchen** ['ʃnyːrçən] nt: **es läuft od klappt (alles) wie am ~** everything's going like clockwork.
**schnüren** ['ʃnyːrən] vt to tie.
**schnurgerade** adj straight (as a die od an arrow).
**Schnurrbart** ['ʃnʊrbaːrt] m moustache (*BRIT*), mustache (*US*).
**schnurren** ['ʃnʊrən] vi to purr; (*Kreisel*) to hum.
**Schnürschuh** m lace-up (shoe).
**Schnürsenkel** m shoelace.
**schnurstracks** adv straight (away); **~ auf jdn/etw zugehen** to make a beeline for sb/sth (*umg*).
**schob** etc [ʃoːp] vb siehe **schieben**.
**Schock** [ʃɔk] (**-(e)s, -e**) m shock; **unter ~ stehen** to be in (a state of) shock.
**schocken** (*umg*) vt to shock.
**Schocker** (**-s, -**) (*umg*) m shocking film/novel, shocker.
**schockieren** vt to shock, outrage.
**Schöffe** ['ʃœfə] (**-n, -n**) m lay magistrate.
**Schöffengericht** nt magistrates' court.
**Schöffin** f lay magistrate.
**Schokolade** [ʃoko'laːdə] (**-, -n**) f chocolate.
**scholl** etc [ʃɔl] vb siehe **schallen**.
**Scholle** ['ʃɔlə] (**-, -n**) f clod; (*Eis~*) ice floe; (*Fisch*) plaice.
**Scholli** ['ʃɔlɪ] (*umg*) m: **mein lieber ~!** (*drohend*) now look here!

═════════════════════════ *SCHLÜSSELWORT*

**schon** [ʃoːn] adv **1** (*bereits*) already; **er ist ~ da** he's there/here already, he's already there/here; **ist er ~ da?** is he there/here yet?; **warst du ~ einmal dort?** have you ever been there?; **ich war ~ einmal dort** I've been there before; **das war ~ immer so** that has always been the case; **hast du ~ gehört?** have you heard?; **~ 1920** as early as 1920; **~ vor 100 Jahren** as far back as 100 years ago; **er wollte ~ die Hoffnung aufgeben, als** ... he was just about to give up hope when ...; **wartest du ~ lange?** have you been waiting (for) long?; **wie lang so oft** as so often (before); **was, ~ wieder?** what - again?

**2** (*bestimmt*) all right; **du wirst ~ sehen**

you'll see (all right); **das wird ~ noch gutgehen** that should turn out OK (in the end)

**3** (bloß) just; **allein ~ das Gefühl** ... just the very feeling ...; **~ der Gedanke** the mere od very thought; **wenn ich das ~ höre** I only have to hear that

**4** (einschränkend): **ja ~, aber** ... yes (well), but ...

**5: das ist ~ möglich** that's quite possible; **~ gut** OK; **du weißt ~** you know; **komm ~** come on; **hör ~ auf damit!** will you stop that!; **was macht das ~, wenn ...?** what does it matter if ...?; **und wenn ~!** (umg) so what?

**schön** [ʃøːn] adj beautiful; (Mann) handsome; (nett) nice ♦ adv: **sich ganz ~ ärgern** to be very angry; **da hast du etwas S~es angerichtet** you've made a fine od nice mess; **~e Grüße** best wishes; **~en Dank** (many) thanks; **~ weich/warm** nice and soft/warm.

**schonen** ['ʃoːnən] vt to look after; (jds Nerven) to spare; (Gegner, Kind) to be easy on; (Teppich, Füße) to save ♦ vr to take it easy.

**schonend** adj careful, gentle; **jdm etw ~ beibringen** to break sth to sb gently.

**Schoner** ['ʃoːnər] (-s, -) m (NAUT) schooner; (Sessel~) cover.

**Schönfärberei** f (fig) glossing things over.

**Schonfrist** f period of grace.

**Schöngeist** m cultured person, aesthete (BRIT), esthete (US).

**Schönheit** f beauty.

**Schönheits-** zW: **~fehler** m blemish, flaw; **~operation** f cosmetic surgery; **~wettbewerb** m beauty contest.

**Schonkost** (-) f light diet.

**schönmachen** vr to make o.s. look nice.

**Schönschrift** f: **in ~** in one's best (hand)writing.

**schöntun** unreg vi: **jdm ~** (schmeicheln) to flatter od soft-soap sb, play up to sb.

**Schonung** f good care; (Nachsicht) consideration; (Forst) plantation of young trees.

**schonungslos** adj ruthless, harsh.

**Schonzeit** f close season.

**Schopf** [ʃɔpf] (-(e)s, -e) m: **eine Gelegenheit beim ~ ergreifen od fassen** to seize od grasp an opportunity with both hands.

**schöpfen** ['ʃœpfən] vt to scoop; (Suppe) to ladle; (Mut) to summon up; (Luft) to breathe in; (Hoffnung) to find.

**Schöpfer** (-s, -) m creator; (Gott) Creator; (umg: Schöpfkelle) ladle; **s~isch** adj creative.

**Schöpfkelle** f ladle.

**Schöpflöffel** m skimmer, scoop.

**Schöpfung** f creation.

**Schoppen** ['ʃɔpən] (-s, -) m (Glas Wein) glass of wine; **~wein** m wine by the glass.

**schor** etc [ʃoːr] vb siehe **scheren**.

**Schorf** [ʃɔrf] (-(e)s, -e) m scab.

**Schorle** ['ʃɔrlə] (-, -n) f spritzer, wine and soda water or lemonade.

**Schornstein** ['ʃɔrnʃtaɪn] m chimney; (NAUT) funnel; **~feger** (-s, -) m chimney sweep.

**Schoß** (-es, -e) m lap; (Rock~) coat tail; **im ~e der Familie** in the bosom of one's family.

**schoß** etc [ʃɔs] vb siehe **schießen**.

**Schoßhund** m lapdog.

**.Schößling** ['ʃœslɪŋ] m (BOT) shoot.

**Schote** ['ʃoːtə] (-, -n) f pod.

**Schotte** ['ʃɔtə] (-n, -n) m Scot, Scotsman.

**Schottenrock** ['ʃɔtənrɔk] m kilt; (für Frauen) tartan skirt.

**Schotter** ['ʃɔtər] (-s) m gravel; (im Straßenbau) road metal; (EISENB) ballast.

**Schottin** ['ʃɔtɪn] f Scot, Scotswoman.

**schottisch** ['ʃɔtɪʃ] adj Scottish, Scots; **das ~e Hochland** the Scottish Highlands pl.

**Schottland** (-s) nt Scotland.

**schraffieren** [ʃraˈfiːrən] vt to hatch.

**schräg** [ʃrɛːk] adj slanting; (schief, geneigt) sloping; (nicht gerade od parallel) oblique ♦ adv: **~ gedruckt** in italics; **etw ~ stellen** to put sth at an angle; **~ gegenüber** diagonally opposite.

**Schräge** ['ʃrɛːgə] (-, -n) f slant.

**Schräg-** zW: **~kante** f bevelled (BRIT) od beveled (US) edge; **~schrift** f italics pl; **~streifen** m bias binding; **~strich** m oblique stroke.

**Schramme** ['ʃramə] (-, -n) f scratch.

**schrammen** vt to scratch.

**Schrank** [ʃraŋk] (-(e)s, -e) m cupboard (BRIT), closet (US); (Kleider~) wardrobe.

**Schranke** (-, -n) f barrier; (fig: Grenze) limit; (: Hindernis) barrier; **jdn in seine ~n (ver)weisen** (fig) to put sb in his place.

**schrankenlos** adj boundless; (zügellos) unrestrained.

**Schrankenwärter** m (EISENB) level-crossing (BRIT) od grade-crossing (US) attendant.

**Schrankkoffer** m wardrobe trunk.

**Schrankwand** f wall unit.

**Schraube** ['ʃraubə] (-, -n) f screw.

**schrauben** vt to screw; **etw in die Höhe ~** (fig: Preise, Rekorde) to push sth up; (: Ansprüche) to raise sth.

**Schraubenschlüssel** m spanner (BRIT), wrench (US).

**Schraubenzieher** (-s, -) m screwdriver.

**Schraubstock** ['ʃraupʃtɔk] m (TECH) vice (BRIT), vise (US).

**Schrebergarten** ['ʃreːbərgartən] m allotment (BRIT).

**Schreck** [ʃrɛk] (-(e)s, -e) m fright; **o ~ laß nach** (hum: umg) for goodness' sake!

**Schrecken** (-s, -) m terror; (Schreck) fright; **s~** vt to frighten, scare ♦ vi: **aus dem Schlaf s~** to be startled out of one's sleep.

**schreckensbleich** adj as white as a sheet od ghost.

**Schreckensherrschaft** f (reign of) terror.
**Schreck-** zW: ~**gespenst** nt nightmare;
s~**haft** adj jumpy, easily frightened; s~**lich**
adj terrible, dreadful; s~**lich gerne!** (umg)
I'd absolutely love to; ~**schraube** (pej: umg)
f (old) battle-axe; ~**schuß** m shot fired in
the air; ~**sekunde** f moment of shock.
**Schrei** [ʃraɪ] (-(e)s, -e) m scream; (Ruf) shout;
**der letzte** ~ (umg) the latest thing, all the
rage.
**Schreibbedarf** m writing materials pl,
stationery.
**Schreibblock** m writing pad.
**schreiben** ['ʃraɪbən] unreg vt to write; (mit
Schreibmaschine) to type out; (berichten:
Zeitung etc) to say; (buchstabieren) to spell
♦ vi to write; to type; to say; to spell ♦ vr: **wie
schreibt sich das?** how is that spelt?; **S~**
(-s, -) nt letter, communication.
**Schreiber(in)** (-s, -) m(f) writer; (Büro~)
clerk.
**Schreib-** zW: s~**faul** adj lazy about writing
letters; ~**fehler** m spelling mistake; ~**kraft**
f typist; ~**maschine** f typewriter; ~**papier**
nt notepaper; ~**schrift** f running
handwriting; (TYP) script; ~**schutz** m
(COMPUT) write-protect; ~**stube** f orderly
room; ~**tisch** m desk; ~**tischtäter** m wire od
string puller.
**Schreibung** f spelling.
**Schreib-** zW: ~**unterlage** f pad; ~**waren** pl
stationery sing; ~**warengeschäft** nt
stationer's (shop) (BRIT), stationery store
(US); ~**weise** f spelling; (Stil) style;
s~**wütig** adj crazy about writing; ~**zentrale**
f typing pool; ~**zeug** nt writing materials pl.
**schreien** ['ʃraɪən] unreg vt, vi to scream; (rufen)
to shout; **es war zum S~** (umg) it was a
scream od a hoot; **nach etw** ~ (fig) to cry
out for sth.
**schreiend** adj (fig) glaring; (: Farbe) loud.
**Schreihals** (umg) m (Baby) bawler;
(Unruhestifter) noisy troublemaker.
**Schreikrampf** m screaming fit.
**Schreiner** ['ʃraɪnər] (-s, -) m joiner;
(Zimmermann) carpenter; (Möbel~)
cabinetmaker.
**Schreinerei** [ʃraɪnə'raɪ] f joiner's workshop.
**schreiten** ['ʃraɪtən] unreg vi to stride.
**schrie** etc [ʃriː] vb siehe schreien.
**Schrieb** (-(e)s, -e) (umg) m missive (hum).
**schrieb** etc [ʃriːp] vb siehe schreiben.
**Schrift** [ʃrɪft] (-, -en) f writing; (Hand~)
handwriting; (~art) script; (TYP) typeface;
(Buch) work; ~**art** f (Hand~) script; (TYP)
typeface; ~**bild** nt script; (COMPUT)
typeface; ~**deutsch** nt written German;
~**führer** m secretary; s~**lich** adj written ♦ adv
in writing; **das kann ich Ihnen** s~**lich geben**
(fig: umg) I can tell you that for free;
~**probe** f (Hand~) specimen of one's
handwriting; ~**satz** m (TYP) fount (BRIT),

font (US); ~**setzer** m compositor; ~**sprache** f
written language.
**Schriftsteller(in)** (-s, -) m(f) writer; s~**isch** adj
literary.
**Schrift-** zW: ~**stück** nt document; ~**verkehr** m
correspondence; ~**wechsel** m
correspondence.
**schrill** [ʃrɪl] adj shrill; ~**en** vi (Stimme) to
sound shrilly; (Telefon) to ring shrilly.
**Schritt** (-(e)s, -e) m step; (Gangart) walk;
(Tempo) pace; (von Hose) crotch, crutch
(BRIT); **auf** ~ **und Tritt** (lit, fig) wherever od
everywhere one goes; „~ **fahren**" "dead
slow"; **mit zehn** ~**en Abstand** at a distance
of ten paces; **den ersten** ~ **tun** (fig) to make
the first move; (: etw beginnen) to take the
first step.
**schritt** etc [ʃrɪt] vb siehe schreiten.
**Schritt-** zW: ~**macher** m pacemaker;
~**(t)empo** nt: **im** ~**(t)empo** at a walking pace;
s~**weise** adv gradually, little by little.
**schroff** [ʃrɔf] adj steep; (zackig) jagged; (fig)
brusque; (ungeduldig) abrupt.
**schröpfen** ['ʃrœpfən] vt (fig) to fleece.
**Schrot** [ʃroːt] (-(e)s, -e) m od nt (Blei) (small)
shot; (Getreide) coarsely ground grain,
groats pl; ~**flinte** f shotgun.
**Schrott** [ʃrɔt] (-(e)s, -e) m scrap metal; **ein
Auto zu** ~ **fahren** to write off a car;
~**händler** m scrap merchant; ~**haufen** m
scrap heap; s~**reif** adj ready for the scrap
heap; ~**wert** m scrap value.
**schrubben** ['ʃrʊbən] vt to scrub.
**Schrubber** (-s, -) m scrubbing brush.
**Schrulle** ['ʃrʊlə] (-, -n) f eccentricity, quirk.
**schrullig** adj cranky.
**schrumpfen** ['ʃrʊmpfən] vi (Hilfsverb sein) to
shrink; (Apfel) to shrivel; (Leber, Niere) to
atrophy.
**Schub** [ʃuːp] (-(e)s, ̈e) m (Stoß) push, shove;
(Gruppe, Anzahl) batch; ~**fach** nt drawer;
~**karren** m wheelbarrow; ~**lade** f drawer.
**Schubs** [ʃuːps] (-es, -e) (umg) m shove, push;
s~**en** (umg) vt, vi to shove, push.
**schüchtern** ['ʃʏçtərn] adj shy; **S~heit** f
shyness.
**schuf** etc [ʃuːf] vb siehe schaffen.
**Schuft** [ʃʊft] (-(e)s, -e) m scoundrel.
**schuften** (umg) vi to graft, slave away.
**Schuh** [ʃuː] (-(e)s, -e) m shoe; **jdm etw in die**
~**e schieben** (fig: umg) to put the blame for
sth on sb; **wo drückt der** ~**?** (fig) what's
troubling you?; ~**band** nt shoelace; ~**creme** f
shoe polish; ~**größe** f shoe size; ~**löffel** m
shoehorn; ~**macher** m shoemaker; ~**werk** nt
footwear.
**Schukosteckdose**® ['ʃʊkoʃtɛkdoːzə] f
safety socket.
**Schukostecker**® m safety plug.
**Schul-** zW: ~**aufgaben** pl homework sing;
~**bank** f: **die** ~**bank drücken** (umg) to go to
school; ~**behörde** f education authority;

~**besuch** m school attendance; ~**buch** nt
schoolbook; ~**buchverlag** m educational
publisher.

**Schuld** [ʃʊlt] (-, -en) f guilt; (FIN) debt;
(Verschulden) fault; **jdm die ~ geben** od
**zuschieben** to blame sb; **ich bin mir keiner
~ bewußt** I'm not aware of having done
anything wrong; **~ und Sühne** crime and
punishment; **ich stehe tief in seiner ~** (fig)
I'm deeply indebted to him; ~**en machen** to
run up debts; **s~** adj: **s~ sein** od **haben (an**
+dat) to be to blame (for); **er ist** od **hat s~** it's
his fault; **jdm s~ geben** to blame sb.
**schuldbewußt** adj (Mensch) feeling guilty;
(Miene) guilty.
**schulden** [ˈʃʊldən] vt to owe.
**schuldenfrei** adj free from debt.
**Schuldgefühl** nt feeling of guilt.
**schuldhaft** adj (JUR) culpable.
**Schuldienst** (-(e)s) m (school)teaching.
**schuldig** adj guilty; (gebührend) due; **an etw**
dat ~ **sein** to be guilty of sth; **jdm etw ~ sein**
od **bleiben** to owe sb sth; **jdn ~ sprechen** to
find sb guilty; **~ geschieden sein** to be the
guilty party in a divorce; **S~keit** f duty.
**schuldlos** adj innocent, blameless.
**Schuldner(in)** (-s, -) m(f) debtor.
**Schuld-** zW: ~**prinzip** nt (JUR) principle of the
guilty party; ~**schein** m promissory note,
IOU; ~**spruch** m verdict of guilty.
**Schule** [ˈʃuːlə] (-, -n) f school; **auf** od **in der ~**
at school; **in die ~ kommen/gehen** to start
school/go to school; **~ machen** (fig) to
become the accepted thing.
**schulen** vt to train, school.
**Schüler(in)** [ˈʃyːlər(ɪn)] (-s, -) m(f) pupil;
~**ausweis** m (school) student card; ~**lotse** m
pupil acting as a road-crossing warden;
~**mitverwaltung** f school od student
council.
**Schul-** zW: ~**ferien** pl school holidays pl (BRIT)
od vacation sing (US); ~**fernsehen** nt schools'
od educational television; **s~frei** adj: **die
Kinder haben morgen s~frei** the children
don't have to go to school tomorrow; ~**funk**
m schools' broadcasts pl; ~**geld** nt school
fees pl, tuition (US); ~**heft** nt exercise book;
~**hof** m playground, schoolyard.
**schulisch** [ˈʃuːlɪʃ] adj (Leistungen, Probleme) at
school; (Angelegenheiten) school attrib.
**Schul-** zW: ~**jahr** nt school year; ~**junge** m
schoolboy; ~**kind** nt schoolchild; ~**leiter** m
headmaster (bes BRIT), principal; ~**leiterin** f
headmistress (bes BRIT), principal;
~**mädchen** nt schoolgirl; ~**medizin** f
orthodox medicine; ~**pflicht** f compulsory
school attendance; **s~pflichtig** adj of school
age; ~**reife** f: **die ~reife haben** to be ready to
go to school; ~**schiff** nt (NAUT) training
ship; ~**sprecher(in)** m(f) head boy/girl (BRIT);
~**stunde** f period, lesson; ~**tasche** f school
bag.

**Schulter** [ˈʃʊltər] (-, -n) f shoulder; **auf die
leichte ~ nehmen** to take lightly; ~**blatt** nt
shoulder blade.
**schultern** vt to shoulder.
**Schultüte** f bag of sweets given to children
on the first day at school.
**Schulung** f education, schooling.
**Schul-** zW: **weg** m way to school; ~**wesen** nt
educational system; ~**zeugnis** nt school
report.
**schummeln** [ˈʃʊməln] (umg) vi: **(bei etw) ~** to
cheat (at sth).
**schumm(e)rig** [ˈʃʊm(ə)rɪç] adj (Beleuchtung)
dim; (Raum) dimly-lit.
**Schund** (-(e)s) m trash, garbage.
**schund** etc [ʃʊnt] vb siehe **schinden.**
**Schundroman** m trashy novel.
**Schupo** [ˈʃuːpo] (-s, -s) m abk (veraltet:
= Schutzpolizist) cop.
**Schuppe** [ˈʃʊpə] (-, -n) f scale; **Schuppen** pl
(Haarschuppen) dandruff.
**Schuppen** (-s, -) m shed; (umg: übles Lokal)
dive; siehe auch **Schuppe.**
**schuppen** vt to scale ♦ vr to peel.
**schuppig** [ˈʃʊpɪç] adj scaly.
**Schur** [ʃuːr] (-, -en) f shearing.
**Schüreisen** nt poker.
**schüren** [ˈʃyːrən] vt to rake; (fig) to stir up.
**schürfen** [ˈʃʏrfən] vt, vi to scrape, scratch;
(MIN) to prospect; to dig.
**Schürfung** f abrasion; (MIN) prospecting.
**Schürhaken** m poker.
**Schurke** [ˈʃʊrkə] (-n, -n) m rogue.
**Schurwolle** f: **„reine ~"** "pure new wool".
**Schurz** [ʃʊrts] (-es, -e) m apron.
**Schürze** [ˈʃʏrtsə] (-, -n) f apron.
**Schürzenjäger** (umg) m philanderer, one for
the girls.
**Schuß** [ʃʊs] (-sses, ̈-sse) m shot; (FUSSBALL)
kick; (Spritzer: von Wein, Essig etc) dash;
(WEBEN) weft; **(gut) in ~ sein** (umg) to be in
good shape od nick; (Mensch) to be in form;
**etw in ~ halten** to keep sth in good shape;
**weitab vom ~ sein** (fig: umg) to be miles
from where the action is; **der goldene ~** ≈ a
lethal dose of a drug; **ein ~ in den Ofen**
(umg) a complete waste of time, a failure;
~**bereich** m effective range.
**Schüssel** [ˈʃʏsəl] (-, -n) f bowl, basin;
(Servier~, umg: Satelliten~) dish; (Wasch~)
basin.
**schusselig** [ˈʃʊsəlɪç] (umg) adj (zerstreut)
scatterbrained, muddle-headed (umg).
**Schuß-** zW: ~**linie** f line of fire; ~**verletzung**
f bullet wound; ~**waffe** f firearm;
~**waffengebrauch** m (form) use of firearms;
~**wechsel** m exchange of shots; ~**weite** f
range (of fire).
**Schuster** [ˈʃuːstər] (-s, -) m cobbler,
shoemaker.
**Schutt** [ʃʊt] (-(e)s) m rubbish; (Bau~) rubble;
**„~ abladen verboten"** "no tipping";

~**abladeplatz** *m* refuse dump.
**Schüttelfrost** *m* shivering.
**schütteln** ['ʃytəln] *vt* to shake ♦ *vr* to shake o.s.; **sich vor Kälte** ~ to shiver with cold; **sich vor Ekel** ~ to shudder with *od* in disgust.
**schütten** ['ʃytən] *vt* to pour; (*Zucker, Kies etc*) to tip; (*ver*~) to spill ♦ *vi unpers* to pour (down).
**schütter** *adj* (*Haare*) sparse, thin.
**Schutthalde** *f* dump.
**Schutthaufen** *m* heap of rubble.
**Schutz** [ʃʊts] (**-es**) *m* protection; (*Unterschlupf*) shelter; **jdn in** ~ **nehmen** to stand up for sb; ~**anzug** *m* overalls *pl*; **s**~**bedürftig** *adj* in need of protection; ~**befohlene(r)** *f(m)* charge; ~**blech** *nt* mudguard; ~**brief** *m* (*Versicherung*) (international) travel cover; ~**brille** *f* goggles *pl*.
**Schütze** ['ʃytsə] (**-n, -n**) *m* gunman; (*Gewehr*~) rifleman; (*Scharf*~, *Sport*~) marksman; (*ASTROL*) Sagittarius.
**schützen** ['ʃytsən] *vt* to protect ♦ *vr* to protect o.s.; **(sich)** ~ **vor** +*dat od* **gegen** to protect (o.s.) from *od* against; **gesetzlich geschützt** registered; **urheberrechtlich geschützt** protected by copyright; **vor Nässe** ~**!** keep dry.
**Schützenfest** *nt fair featuring shooting matches*.
**Schutzengel** *m* guardian angel.
**Schützen-** *zW:* ~**graben** *m* trench; ~**hilfe** *f* (*fig*) support; ~**verein** *m* shooting club.
**Schutz-** *zW:* ~**gebiet** *nt* protectorate; (*Naturschutzgebiet*) reserve; ~**gebühr** *f* (token) fee; ~**haft** *f* protective custody; ~**heilige(r)** *f(m)* patron saint; ~**helm** *m* safety helmet; ~**impfung** *f* immunization.
**Schützling** ['ʃytslɪŋ] *m* protégé; (*bes Kind*) charge.
**Schutz-** *zW:* **s**~**los** *adj* defenceless (*BRIT*), defenseless (*US*); ~**mann** (**-(e)s**, *pl* **-leute** *od* **-männer**) *m* policeman; ~**marke** *f* trademark; ~**maßnahme** *f* precaution; ~**patron** *m* patron saint; ~**schirm** *m* (*TECH*) protective screen; ~**umschlag** *m* (book) jacket; ~**verband** *m* (*MED*) protective bandage *od* dressing; ~**vorrichtung** *f* safety device.
**Schw.** *abk* = **Schwester.**
**schwabbelig** ['ʃvab(ə)lɪç] (*umg*) *adj* (*Körperteil*) flabby; (: *Gelee*) wobbly.
**Schwabe** ['ʃvaːbə] (**-n, -n**) *m* Swabian.
**Schwaben** (**-s**) *nt* Swabia.
**Schwäbin** ['ʃvɛːbɪn] *f* Swabian.
**schwäbisch** ['ʃvɛːbɪʃ] *adj* Swabian.
**schwach** [ʃvax] *adj* weak, feeble; (*Gedächtnis, Gesundheit*) poor; (*Hoffnung*) faint; ~ **werden** to weaken; **das ist ein** ~**es Bild** (*umg*) *od* **eine** ~**e Leistung** (*umg*) that's a poor show; **ein**

~**er Trost** cold *od* small comfort; **mach mich nicht** ~**!** (*umg*) don't say that!; **auf** ~**en Beinen** *od* **Füßen stehen** (*fig*) to be on shaky ground; (: *Theorie*) to be shaky.
**Schwäche** ['ʃvɛçə] (**-, -n**) *f* weakness.
**schwächen** *vt* to weaken.
**schwach-** *zW:* **S**~**heit** *f* weakness; **S**~**kopf** (*umg*) *m* dimwit, idiot; ~**köpfig** *adj* silly, daft (*BRIT*).
**schwächlich** *adj* weakly, delicate.
**Schwächling** *m* weakling.
**Schwach-** *zW:* ~**sinn** *m* (*MED*) mental deficiency, feeble-mindedness (*veraltet*); (*umg: Quatsch*) rubbish; (*fig: umg: unsinnige Tat*) idiocy; **s**~**sinnig** *adj* mentally deficient; (*Idee*) idiotic; ~**stelle** *f* weak point; ~**strom** *m* weak current.
**Schwächung** ['ʃvɛçʊŋ] *f* weakening.
**Schwaden** ['ʃvaːdən] (**-s, -**) *m* cloud.
**schwafeln** ['ʃvaːfəln] (*umg*) *vi* to blather, drivel; (*in einer Prüfung*) to waffle.
**Schwager** ['ʃvaːgər] (**-s, ⁻**) *m* brother-in-law.
**Schwägerin** ['ʃvɛːgərɪn] *f* sister-in-law.
**Schwalbe** ['ʃvalbə] (**-, -n**) *f* swallow.
**Schwall** [ʃval] (**-(e)s, -e**) *m* surge; (*Worte*) flood, torrent.
**Schwamm** (**-(e)s, ⁻e**) *m* sponge; (*Pilz*) fungus; ~ **drüber!** (*umg*) (let's) forget it!
**schwamm** *etc* [ʃvam] *vb siehe* **schwimmen**.
**schwammig** *adj* spongy; (*Gesicht*) puffy; (*vage: Begriff*) woolly (*BRIT*), wooly (*US*).
**Schwan** [ʃvaːn] (**-(e)s, ⁻e**) *m* swan.
**schwand** *etc* [ʃvant] *vb siehe* **schwinden**.
**schwanen** *vi unpers:* **jdm schwant es** sb has a foreboding *od* forebodings; **jdm schwant etwas** sb senses something might happen.
**schwang** *etc* [ʃvaŋ] *vb siehe* **schwingen**.
**schwanger** ['ʃvaŋər] *adj* pregnant.
**schwängern** ['ʃvɛŋərn] *vt* to make pregnant.
**Schwangerschaft** *f* pregnancy.
**Schwangerschaftsabbruch** *m* termination of pregnancy, abortion.
**Schwank** [ʃvaŋk] (**-(e)s, ⁻e**) *m* funny story; (*LITER*) merry *od* comical tale; (*THEAT*) farce.
**schwanken** *vi* to sway; (*taumeln*) to stagger, reel; (*Preise, Zahlen*) to fluctuate; (*zögern*) to hesitate; (*Überzeugung etc*) to begin to waver; **ins S**~ **kommen** (*Baum, Gebäude etc*) to start to sway; (*Preise, Kurs etc*) to start to fluctuate *od* vary.
**Schwankung** *f* fluctuation.
**Schwanz** [ʃvants] (**-es, ⁻e**) *m* tail; (*umg!: Penis*) prick (*!*); **kein** ~ (*umg*) not a (blessed) soul.
**schwänzen** ['ʃvɛntsən] (*umg*) *vt* (*Stunde, Vorlesung*) to skip ♦ *vi* to play truant.
**Schwänzer** ['ʃvɛntsər] (**-s, -**) (*umg*) *m* truant.
**schwappen** ['ʃvapən] *vi* (*über*~) to splash, slosh.
**Schwarm** [ʃvarm] (**-(e)s, ⁻e**) *m* swarm; (*umg*) heart-throb, idol.

**schwärmen** ['ʃvɛrmən] *vi* to swarm; ~ **für** to be mad *od* wild about.
**Schwärmerei** [ʃvɛrmə'raɪ] *f* enthusiasm.
**schwärmerisch** *adj* impassioned, effusive.
**Schwarte** ['ʃvartə] (-, -n) *f* hard skin; (*Speck~*) rind; (*umg: Buch*) tome (*hum*).
**Schwartenmagen** (-s) *m* (*KOCH*) brawn.
**schwarz** [ʃvarts] *adj* black; (*umg: ungesetzlich*) illicit; (: *katholisch*) Catholic, Papist (*pej*); (*POL*) Christian Democrat; **ins S~e treffen** (*lit, fig*) to hit the bull's-eye; **das S~e Brett** the notice (*BRIT*) *od* bulletin (*US*) board; ~**e Liste** blacklist; ~**es Loch** black hole; **das S~e Meer** the Black Sea; **S~er Peter** (*KARTEN*) *children's card game*; **jdm den S~en Peter zuschieben** (*fig: die Verantwortung abschieben*) to pass the buck to sb (*umg*); **sich ~ ärgern** to get extremely annoyed; **dort wählen alle ~** they all vote conservative there; **in den ~en Zahlen** in the black; **S~arbeit** *f* illicit work, moonlighting; **S~arbeiter** *m* moonlighter; **S~brot** *nt* (*Pumpernickel*) black bread, pumpernickel; (*braun*) brown rye bread.
**Schwärze** ['ʃvɛrtsə] (-, -n) *f* blackness; (*Farbe*) blacking; (*Drucker~*) printer's ink.
**Schwarze(r)** *f(m)* (*Neger*) black; (*umg: Katholik*) Papist; (*POL: umg*) Christian Democrat.
**schwärzen** *vt* to blacken.
**Schwarz-** *zW:* **s~fahren** *unreg vi* to travel without paying; (*ohne Führerschein*) to drive without a licence (*BRIT*) *od* license (*US*); ~**fahrer** *m* (*Bus etc*) fare dodger (*umg*); ~**handel** *m* black market (trade); ~**händler** *m* black-market operator; **s~hören** *vi* to listen to the radio without a licence (*BRIT*) *od* license (*US*).
**schwärzlich** ['ʃvɛrtslɪç] *adj* blackish, darkish.
**Schwarz-** *zW:* **s~malen** *vi* to be pessimistic ♦ *vt* to be pessimistic about; ~**markt** *m* black market; **s~sehen** *unreg* (*umg*) *vi* to see the gloomy side of things; (*TV*) to watch TV without a licence (*BRIT*) *od* license (*US*); ~**seher** *m* pessimist; (*TV*) viewer without a licence (*BRIT*) *od* license (*US*); ~**wald** *m* Black Forest; ~**wälder Kirschtorte** *f* Black Forest gâteau; **s~weiß** *adj* black and white; ~**weiß-** in *zW* black and white; ~**wurzel** *f* (*KOCH*) salsify.
**Schwatz** [ʃvats] (-es, -e) *m* chat.
**schwatzen** ['ʃvatsən] *vi* to chat; (*schnell, unaufhörlich*) to chatter; (*über belanglose Dinge*) to prattle; (*Unsinn reden*) to blether (*umg*).
**schwätzen** ['ʃvɛtsən] *vi* = **schwatzen**.
**Schwätzer(in)** ['ʃvɛtsər(ɪn)] (-s, -) *m(f)* chatterbox; (*Schwafler*) gasbag (*umg*); (*Klatschbase*) gossip.
**schwatzhaft** *adj* talkative, gossipy.
**Schwebe** ['ʃveːbə] *f:* **in der ~** (*fig*) in abeyance; (*JUR, COMM*) pending.

**Schwebebahn** *f* overhead railway (*BRIT*) *od* railroad (*US*).
**Schwebebalken** *m* (*SPORT*) beam.
**schweben** *vi* to drift, float; (*hoch*) to soar; (*unentschieden sein*) to be in the balance; **es schwebte mir vor Augen** (*Bild*) I saw it in my mind's eye.
**schwebend** *adj* (*TECH, CHEM*) suspended; (*fig*) undecided, unresolved; ~**es Verfahren** (*JUR*) pending case.
**schwed.** *abk* = **schwedisch.**
**Schwede** ['ʃveːdə] (-n, -n) *m* Swede.
**Schweden** (-s) *nt* Sweden.
**Schwedin** ['ʃveːdɪn] *f* Swede.
**schwedisch** *adj* Swedish.
**Schwefel** ['ʃveːfəl] (-s) *m* sulphur (*BRIT*), sulfur (*US*); ~**dioxid** *nt* sulphur dioxide.
**schwefelig** *adj* sulphurous (*BRIT*), sulfurous (*US*).
**Schwefelsäure** *f* sulphuric (*BRIT*) *od* sulfuric (*US*) acid.
**Schweif** [ʃvaɪf] (-(e)s, -e) *m* tail.
**schweifen** *vi* to wander, roam.
**Schweigegeld** *nt* hush money.
**Schweigeminute** *f* one minute('s) silence.
**schweigen** ['ʃvaɪɡən] *unreg vi* to be silent; (*still sein*) to keep quiet; **kannst du ~?** can you keep a secret?; **ganz zu ~ von ...** to say nothing of ...; **S~** (-s) *nt* silence.
**schweigend** *adj* silent.
**Schweigepflicht** *f* pledge of secrecy; (*von Anwalt etc*) requirement of confidentiality.
**schweigsam** ['ʃvaɪkzaːm] *adj* silent; (*als Charaktereigenschaft*) taciturn; **S~keit** *f* silence; taciturnity.
**Schwein** [ʃvaɪn] (-(e)s, -e) *nt* pig; (*fig: umg*) (good) luck; **kein ~** (*umg*) nobody, not a single person.
**Schweine-** *zW:* ~**braten** *m* joint of pork; (*gekocht*) roast pork; ~**fleisch** *nt* pork; ~**geld** (*umg*) *nt:* **ein ~geld** a packet; ~**hund** (*umg*) *m* stinker, swine.
**Schweinerei** [ʃvaɪnə'raɪ] *f* mess; (*Gemeinheit*) dirty trick; **so eine ~!** (*umg*) how disgusting!
**Schweineschmalz** *nt* dripping; (*als Kochfett*) lard.
**Schweinestall** *m* pigsty.
**schweinisch** *adj* filthy.
**Schweinsleder** *nt* pigskin.
**Schweinsohr** *nt* pig's ear; (*Gebäck*) (kidney-shaped) pastry.
**Schweiß** [ʃvaɪs] (-es) *m* sweat, perspiration; ~**band** *nt* sweatband.
**Schweißbrenner** (-s, -) *m* (*TECH*) welding torch.
**schweißen** *vt, vi* to weld.
**Schweißer** (-s, -) *m* welder.
**Schweiß-** *zW:* ~**füße** *pl* sweaty feet *pl*; ~**naht** *f* weld; **s~naß** *adj* sweaty.
**Schweiz** [ʃvaɪts] *f:* **die ~** Switzerland.
**schweiz.** *abk* = **schweizerisch.**

**Schweizer** ['ʃvaɪtsər] (-s, -) m Swiss ♦ adj attrib Swiss; ~**deutsch** nt Swiss German; ~**in** f Swiss; **s~isch** adj Swiss.

**schwelen** ['ʃveːlən] vi to smoulder (BRIT), smolder (US).

**schwelgen** ['ʃvɛlgən] vi to indulge o.s.; ~ **in** +dat to indulge in.

**Schwelle** ['ʃvɛlə] (-, -n) f (auch fig) threshold; (EISENB) sleeper (BRIT), tie (US).

**schwellen** unreg vi to swell.

**Schwellenland** nt threshold country.

**Schwellung** f swelling.

**Schwemme** ['ʃvɛmə] f: **eine** ~ **an** +dat a glut of.

**schwemmen** ['ʃvɛmən] vt (treiben: Sand etc) to wash.

**Schwengel** ['ʃvɛŋəl] (-s, -) m pump handle; (Glocken~) clapper.

**Schwenk** [ʃvɛŋk] (-(e)s, -s) m (FILM) pan, panning shot.

**Schwenkarm** m swivel arm.

**schwenkbar** adj swivel-mounted.

**schwenken** vt to swing; (Kamera) to pan; (Fahne) to wave; (Kartoffeln) to toss; (abspülen) to rinse ♦ vi to turn, swivel; (MIL) to wheel.

**Schwenkung** f turn; (MIL) wheel.

**schwer** [ʃveːr] adj heavy; (schwierig) difficult, hard; (schlimm) serious, bad ♦ adv (sehr) very (much); (verletzt etc) seriously, badly; ~ **erkältet sein** to have a heavy cold; **er lernt** ~ he's a slow learner; **er ist** ~ **in Ordnung** (umg) he's a good bloke (BRIT) od guy; ~ **hören** to be hard of hearing; **S~arbeiter** m labourer (BRIT), laborer (US); **S~behinderte(r)** f(m), **S~beschädigte(r)** f(m) (veraltet) severely handicapped person.

**Schwere** (-, -n) f weight; heaviness; (PHYS) gravity; **s~los** adj weightless; ~**losigkeit** f weightlessness.

**schwer-** zW: ~**erziehbar** adj maladjusted; ~**fallen** unreg vi: **jdm** ~**fallen** to be difficult for sb; ~**fällig** adj (auch Stil) ponderous; (Gang) clumsy, awkward; (Verstand) slow; **S~gewicht** nt heavyweight; (fig) emphasis; ~**gewichtig** adj heavyweight; ~**hörig** adj hard of hearing; **S~industrie** f heavy industry; **S~kraft** f gravity; **S~kranke(r)** f(m) person who is seriously ill; ~**lich** adv hardly; ~**machen** vt: **jdm/sich etw** ~**machen** to make sth difficult for sb/o.s.; **S~metall** nt heavy metal; ~**mütig** adj melancholy; ~**nehmen** unreg vt to take to heart; **S~punkt** m centre (BRIT) od center (US) of gravity; (fig) emphasis, crucial point; **S~punktstreik** m pinpoint strike; ~**reich** (umg) adj attrib stinking rich.

**Schwert** [ʃveːrt] (-(e)s, -er) nt sword; ~**lilie** f iris.

**schwer-** zW: ~**tun** unreg vi: **sich** dat od akk ~**tun** to have difficulties; **S~verbrecher** m criminal; ~**verdaulich** adj indigestible; (fig) heavy; ~**verdient** adj attrib (Geld) hard-earned; ~**verletzt** adj seriously od badly injured; **S~verletzte(r)** f(m) serious casualty; ~**verwundet** adj seriously wounded; ~**wiegend** adj weighty, important.

**Schwester** ['ʃvɛstər] (-, -n) f sister; (MED) nurse; **s~lich** adj sisterly.

**schwieg** etc [ʃviːk] vb siehe **schweigen**.

**Schwieger-** zW: ~**eltern** pl parents-in-law pl; ~**mutter** f mother-in-law; ~**sohn** m son-in-law; ~**tochter** f daughter-in-law; ~**vater** m father-in-law.

**Schwiele** ['ʃviːlə] (-, -n) f callus.

**schwierig** ['ʃviːrɪç] adj difficult, hard; **S~keit** f difficulty; **S~keitsgrad** m degree of difficulty.

**schwillt** [ʃvɪlt] vb siehe **schwellen**.

**Schwimmbad** nt swimming baths pl.

**Schwimmbecken** nt swimming pool.

**schwimmen** unreg vi to swim; (treiben, nicht sinken) to float; (fig: unsicher sein) to be all at sea; **im Geld** ~ (umg) to be rolling in money; **mir schwimmt es vor den Augen** I feel dizzy.

**Schwimmer** (-s, -) m swimmer; (ANGELN) float.

**Schwimmerin** f swimmer.

**Schwimm-** zW: ~**flosse** f (von Taucher) flipper; ~**haut** f (ORNITHOLOGIE) web; ~**lehrer** m swimming instructor; ~**sport** m swimming; ~**weste** f life jacket.

**Schwindel** ['ʃvɪndəl] (-s) m dizziness; (Betrug) swindle, fraud; (Zeug) stuff; **s~erregend** adj: **in s~erregender Höhe** at a dizzy height; **s~frei** adj free from giddiness.

**schwindeln** vi (umg: lügen) to fib; **mir schwindelt** I feel dizzy; **jdm schwindelt es** sb feels dizzy.

**schwinden** ['ʃvɪndən] unreg vi to disappear; (Kräfte) to fade, fail; (sich verringern) to decrease.

**Schwindler** (-s, -) m swindler; (Hochstapler) con man, fraud; (Lügner) liar.

**schwindlig** adj dizzy; **mir ist** ~ I feel dizzy.

**Schwindsucht** f (veraltet) consumption.

**schwingen** ['ʃvɪŋən] unreg vt to swing; (Waffe etc) to brandish ♦ vi to swing; (vibrieren) to vibrate; (klingen) to sound.

**Schwinger** (-s, -) m (BOXEN) swing.

**Schwingtor** nt up-and-over door.

**Schwingtür** f swing door(s pl) (BRIT), swinging door(s pl) (US).

**Schwingung** f vibration; (PHYS) oscillation.

**Schwips** [ʃvɪps] (-es, -e) m: **einen** ~ **haben** to be tipsy.

**schwirren** ['ʃvɪrən] vi to buzz.

**Schwitze** ['ʃvɪtsə] (-, -n) f (KOCH) roux.

**schwitzen** vi to sweat, perspire.

**schwofen** ['ʃvoːfən] (umg) vi to dance.

**schwoll** etc [ʃvɔl] vb siehe **schwellen**.

**schwören** ['ʃvøːrən] unreg vt, vi to swear; **auf**

**jdn/etw** ~ (*fig*) to swear by sb/sth.
**schwul** [ʃvuːl] (*umg*) *adj* gay, queer (*pej*).
**schwül** [ʃvyːl] *adj* sultry, close.
**Schwule(r)** (*umg*) *m* gay, queer (*pej*), fag (*US pej*).
**Schwüle** (-) *f* sultriness, closeness.
**Schwulität** [ʃvuliˈtɛːt] (*umg*) *f* trouble, difficulty.
**Schwulst** [ʃvʊlst] (-(e)s) *m* bombast.
**schwülstig** [ˈʃvʏlstɪç] *adj* pompous.
**Schwund** [ʃvʊnt] (-(e)s) *m* (+*gen*) decrease (in), decline (in), dwindling (of); (*MED*) atrophy; (*Schrumpfen*) shrinkage.
**Schwung** [ʃvʊŋ] (-(e)s, ̈-e) *m* swing; (*Triebkraft*) momentum; (*fig: Energie*) verve, energy; (*umg: Menge*) batch; **in** ~ **sein** (*fig*) to be in full swing; ~ **in die Sache bringen** (*umg*) to liven things up; **s~haft** *adj* brisk, lively; ~**rad** *nt* flywheel; **s~voll** *adj* vigorous.
**Schwur** (-(e)s, ̈-e) *m* oath.
**schwur** *etc* [ʃvuːr] *vb siehe* **schwören**.
**Schwurgericht** *nt* court with a jury.
**SDR** (-) *m abk* (= *Süddeutscher Rundfunk*) South German Radio.
**sechs** [zɛks] *num* six; **S~eck** *nt* hexagon; ~**hundert** *num* six hundred.
**sechste(r, s)** *adj* sixth.
**Sechstel** [ˈzɛkstəl] (-s, -) *nt* sixth.
**sechzehn** [ˈzɛçtseːn] *num* sixteen.
**sechzig** [ˈzɛçtsɪç] *num* sixty.
**See¹** [zeː] (-, -n) *f* sea; **an der** ~ by the sea, at the seaside; **in** ~ **stechen** to put to sea; **auf hoher** ~ on the high seas.
**See²** [zeː] (-s, -n) *m* lake.
**See-** *zW:* ~**bad** *nt* seaside resort; ~**bär** *m* (*hum: umg*) seadog; (*ZOOL*) fur seal; ~**fahrt** *f* seafaring; (*Reise*) voyage; **s~fest** *adj* (*Mensch*) not subject to seasickness; ~**gang** *m* (motion of the) sea; ~**gras** *nt* seaweed; ~**hund** *m* seal; ~**igel** *m* sea urchin; ~**karte** *f* chart; **s~krank** *adj* seasick; ~**krankheit** *f* seasickness; ~**lachs** *m* rock salmon.
**Seele** [ˈzeːlə] (-, -n) *f* soul; (*Mittelpunkt*) life and soul; **jdm aus der** ~ **sprechen** to express exactly what sb feels; **das liegt mir auf der** ~ it weighs heavily on my mind; **eine** ~ **von Mensch** an absolute dear.
**Seelen-** *zW:* ~**amt** *nt* (*REL*) requiem; ~**friede(n)** *m* peace of mind; ~**heil** *nt* salvation of one's soul; (*fig*) spiritual welfare; ~**ruhe** *f:* **in aller** ~**ruhe** calmly; (*kaltblütig*) as cool as you please; **s~ruhig** *adv* calmly.
**Seeleute** [ˈzeːlɔytə] *pl* seamen *pl*.
**Seel-** *zW:* **s~isch** *adj* (*REL*) spiritual; (*Belastung*) emotional; ~**sorge** *f* pastoral duties *pl*; ~**sorger** (-s, -) *m* clergyman.
**See-** *zW:* ~**macht** *f* naval power; ~**mann** (-(e)s, *pl* -**leute**) *m* seaman, sailor; ~**meile** *f* nautical mile.
**Seengebiet** [ˈzeːəngəbiːt] *nt* lakeland district.
**See-** *zW:* ~**not** *f:* **in** ~**not** (*Schiff etc*) in

distress; ~**pferd(chen)** *nt* sea horse; ~**räuber** *m* pirate; ~**recht** *nt* maritime law; ~**rose** *f* waterlily; ~**stern** *m* starfish; ~**tang** *m* seaweed; **s~tüchtig** *adj* seaworthy; ~**versicherung** *f* marine insurance; ~**weg** *m* sea route; **auf dem** ~**weg** by sea; ~**zunge** *f* sole.
**Segel** [ˈzeːɡəl] (-s, -) *nt* sail; **mit vollen** ~**n** under full sail *od* canvas; (*fig*) with gusto; **die** ~ **streichen** (*fig*) to give in; ~**boot** *nt* yacht; ~**fliegen** (-s) *nt* gliding; ~**flieger** *m* glider pilot; ~**flugzeug** *nt* glider.
**segeln** *vt, vi* to sail; **durch eine Prüfung** ~ (*umg*) to flop in an exam, fail (in) an exam.
**Segel-** *zW:* ~**schiff** *nt* sailing vessel; ~**sport** *m* sailing; ~**tuch** *nt* canvas.
**Segen** [ˈzeːɡən] (-s, -) *m* blessing.
**segensreich** *adj* beneficial.
**Segler** [ˈzeːɡlər] (-s, -) *m* sailor, yachtsman; (*Boot*) sailing boat.
**Seglerin** *f* yachtswoman.
**segnen** [ˈzeːɡnən] *vt* to bless.
**sehen** [ˈzeːən] *unreg vt, vi* to see; (*in bestimmte Richtung*) to look; (*Fernsehsendung*) to watch; **sieht man das?** does it show?; **da sieht man('s) mal wieder!** that's typical!; **du siehst das nicht richtig** you've got it wrong; **so gesehen** looked at in this way; **sich** ~ **lassen** to put in an appearance, appear; **das neue Rathaus kann sich** ~ **lassen** the new town hall is certainly something to be proud of; **siehe oben/unten** see above/below; **da kann man mal** ~ that just shows (you) *od* just goes to show (*umg*); **mal** ~! we'll see; **darauf** ~, **daß** ... to make sure (that) ...; **jdn kommen** ~ to see sb coming.
**sehenswert** *adj* worth seeing.
**Sehenswürdigkeiten** *pl* sights *pl* (of a town).
**Seher** (-s, -) *m* seer.
**Sehfehler** *m* sight defect.
**Sehkraft** *f* (eye)sight.
**Sehne** [ˈzeːnə] (-, -n) *f* sinew; (*an Bogen*) string.
**sehnen** *vr:* **sich** ~ **nach** to long *od* yearn for.
**Sehnenscheidenentzündung** *f* (*MED*) tendovaginitis.
**Sehnerv** *m* optic nerve.
**sehnig** *adj* sinewy.
**sehnlich** *adj* ardent.
**Sehnsucht** *f* longing.
**sehnsüchtig** *adj* longing; (*Erwartung*) eager.
**sehnsuchtsvoll** *adv* longingly, yearningly.
**sehr** [zeːr] *adv* (*vor adj, adv*) very; (*mit Verben*) a lot, (very) much; **zu** ~ too much; **er ist** ~ **dafür/dagegen** he is all for it/very much against it; **wie** ~ **er sich auch bemühte** ... however much he tried ...
**Sehvermögen** [ˈzeːfɛrmøːɡən] (-s) *nt* powers *pl* of vision.
**seicht** [zaɪçt] *adj* (*lit, fig*) shallow.
**seid** [zaɪt] *vb siehe* **sein**.
**Seide** [ˈzaɪdə] (-, -n) *f* silk.

**Seidel** (-s, -) *nt* tankard, beer mug.
**seiden** *adj* silk; **S~papier** *nt* tissue paper.
**seidig** ['zaɪdɪç] *adj* silky.
**Seife** ['zaɪfə] (-, -n) *f* soap.
**Seifen-** *zW:* **~blase** *f* soap bubble; (*fig*) bubble; **~lauge** *f* soapsuds *pl*; **~schale** *f* soap dish; **~schaum** *m* lather.
**seifig** ['zaɪfɪç] *adj* soapy.
**seihen** ['zaɪən] *vt* to strain, filter.
**Seil** [zaɪl] (-(e)s, -e) *nt* rope; (*Kabel*) cable; **~bahn** *f* cable railway; **~hüpfen** (-s) *nt* skipping; **~springen** (-s) *nt* skipping; **~tänzer(in)** *m(f)* tightrope walker; **~zug** *m* tackle.

================= *SCHLÜSSELWORT*

**sein** [zaɪn] (*pt* **war,** *pp* **gewesen**) *vi* **1** to be; **ich bin I** am; **du bist you** are; **er/sie/es ist** he/she/it is; **wir sind/ihr seid/sie sind** we/you/they are; **wir waren** we were; **wir sind gewesen** we have been
**2: seien Sie nicht böse** don't be angry; **sei so gut und ...** be so kind as to ...; **das wäre gut** that would *od* that'd be a good thing; **wenn ich Sie wäre** if I were *od* was you; **das wär's** that's all, that's it; **morgen bin ich in Rom** tomorrow I'll *od* I will *od* I shall be in Rome; **waren Sie mal in Rom?** have you ever been to Rome?
**3: wie ist das zu verstehen?** how is that to be understood?; **er ist nicht zu ersetzen** he cannot be replaced; **mit ihr ist nicht zu reden** you can't talk to her
**4: mir ist kalt** I'm cold; **mir ist, als hätte ich ihn früher schon einmal gesehen** I've a feeling I've seen him before; **was ist?** what's the matter?, what is it?; **ist was?** is something the matter?; **es sei denn(, daß ...)** unless ...; **wie dem auch sei** be that as it may; **wie wäre es mit ...?** how *od* what about ...?; **laß das ~!** stop that!; **es ist an dir, zu ...** it's up to you to ...; **was sind Sie (beruflich)?** what do you do?; **das kann schon ~** that may well be
♦ *pron* his; (*bei Dingen*) its.

**Sein** (-s) *nt:* **~ oder Nichtsein** to be or not to be.
**seine(r, s)** *poss pron* his; its; **er ist gut ~ zwei Meter** (*umg*) he's a good two metres (*BRIT*) *od* meters (*US*); **die S~n** (*geh*) his family, his people; **jedem das S~** to each his own.
**seiner** *gen von* **er, es** ♦ *pron* of him; of it.
**seinerseits** *adv* for his part.
**seinerzeit** *adv* in those days, formerly.
**seinesgleichen** *pron* people like him.
**seinetwegen** *adv* (*für ihn*) for his sake; (*wegen ihm*) on his account; (*von ihm aus*) as far as he is concerned.
**seinetwillen** *adv:* **um ~ = seinetwegen.**
**seinige** *pron:* **der/die/das ~** his.
**seinlassen** *unreg vt:* **etw ~** (*aufhören*) to stop

(doing) sth; (*nicht tun*) to drop sth, leave sth.
**Seismograph** [zaɪsmoˈɡraːf] (-en, -en) *m* seismograph.
**seit** [zaɪt] *präp +dat* since; (*Zeitdauer*) for, in (*bes US*) ♦ *konj* since; **er ist ~ einer Woche hier** he has been here for a week; **~ langem** for a long time; **~dem** *adv, konj* since.
**Seite** ['zaɪtə] (-, -n) *f* side; (*Buch~*) page; (*MIL*) flank; **~ an ~** side by side; **jdm zur ~ stehen** (*fig*) to stand by sb's side; **jdn zur ~ nehmen** to take sb aside *od* on one side; **auf der einen ~ ..., auf der anderen (~) ...** on the one hand ..., on the other (hand) ...; **einer Sache** *dat* **die beste ~ abgewinnen** to make the best *od* most of sth.
**seiten** *präp +gen:* **auf** *od* **von ~** on the part of.
**Seiten-** *zW:* **~ansicht** *f* side view; **~hieb** *m* (*fig*) passing shot, dig; **s~lang** *adj* several pages long, going on for pages; **~ruder** *nt* (*AVIAT*) rudder.
**seitens** *präp +gen* on the part of.
**Seiten-** *zW:* **~schiff** *nt* aisle; **~sprung** *m* extramarital escapade; **~stechen** *nt* (a) stitch; **~straße** *f* side road; **~streifen** *m* (*der Straße*) verge (*BRIT*), berm (*US*); (*der Autobahn*) hard shoulder (*BRIT*), shoulder (*US*); **s~verkehrt** *adj* the wrong way round; **~wagen** *m* sidecar; **~wind** *m* crosswind; **~zahl** *f* page number; (*Gesamtzahl*) number of pages.
**seit-** *zW:* **~her** [zaɪtˈheːr] *adv, konj* since (then); **~lich** *adv* on one/the side ♦ *adj* side *attrib*; **~wärts** *adv* sideways.
**sek, Sek.** *abk* (= *Sekunde*) sec.
**Sekretär** [zekreˈtɛːr] *m* secretary; (*Möbel*) bureau.
**Sekretariat** [zekretariˈaːt] (-(e)s, -e) *nt* secretary's office, secretariat.
**Sekretärin** *f* secretary.
**Sekt** [zɛkt] (-(e)s, -e) *m* sparkling wine.
**Sekte** (-, -n) *f* sect.
**Sektor** ['zɛktɔr] *m* sector; (*Sachgebiet*) field.
**Sekunda** [zeˈkʊnda] (-, **Sekunden**) *f* (*SCH: Unter~/Ober~*) sixth/seventh year of German secondary school.
**sekundär** [zekʊnˈdɛːr] *adj* secondary; **S~literatur** *f* secondary literature.
**Sekunde** [zeˈkʊndə] (-, -n) *f* second.
**Sekunden-** *zW:* **~kleber** *m* superglue; **~schnelle** *f:* **in ~schnelle** in a matter of seconds; **~zeiger** *m* second hand.
**sel.** *abk* = **selig.**
**selber** ['zɛlbər] *demon pron* = **selbst; S~machen** *nt* do-it-yourself, DIY (*BRIT*); (*von Kleidern etc*) making one's own.
**Selbst** [zɛlpst] (-) *nt* self.

================= *SCHLÜSSELWORT*

**selbst** [zɛlpst] *pron* **1: ich/er/wir ~** I myself/he himself/we ourselves; **sie ist die Tugend ~** she's virtue itself; **er braut sein Bier ~** he brews his own beer; **das muß er ~ wissen**

it's up to him; **wie geht's?** - **gut, und ~?** how
are things? - fine, and yourself?
**2** (*ohne Hilfe*) alone, on my/his/one's *etc* own;
**von ~** by itself; **er kam von ~** he came of
his own accord; **~ ist der Mann/die Frau!**
self-reliance is the name of the game (*umg*)
♦ *adv* even; **~ wenn** even if; **~ Gott** even
God (himself).

**Selbstachtung** *f* self-respect.
**selbständig** ['zɛlpʃtɛndɪç] *adj* independent;
**sich ~ machen** (*beruflich*) to set up on one's
own, start one's own business; **S~keit** *f*
independence.
**Selbst-** *zW*: **~anzeige** *f*: **~anzeige erstatten** to
come forward oneself; **der Dieb hat
~anzeige erstattet** the thief has come
forward; **~auslöser** *m* (*PHOT*) delayed-
action shutter release; **~bedienung** *f* self-
service; **~befriedigung** *f* masturbation;
(*fig*) self-gratification; **~beherrschung** *f*
self-control; **~bestätigung** *f* self-
affirmation; **s~bewußt** *adj* self-confident;
(*selbstsicher*) self-assured; **~bewußtsein** *nt*
self-confidence; **~bildnis** *nt* self-portrait;
**~erhaltung** *f* self-preservation;
**~erkenntnis** *f* self-knowledge; **~fahrer** *m*
(*AUT*): **Autovermietung für ~fahrer** self-
drive car hire (*BRIT*) *od* rental; **s~gefällig**
*adj* smug, self-satisfied; **s~gemacht** *adj*
home-made; **s~gerecht** *adj* self-righteous;
**~gespräch** *nt* conversation with o.s.;
**s~gestrickt** *adj* hand-knitted; (*umg: Methode
etc*) homespun, amateurish; **s~gewiß** *adj*
confident; **s~herrlich** *adj* high-handed;
(*selbstgerecht*) self-satisfied; **~hilfe** *f* self-
help; **zur ~hilfe greifen** to take matters into
one's own hands; **s~klebend** *adj* self-
adhesive; **~kostenpreis** *m* cost price; **s~los**
*adj* unselfish, selfless; **~mord** *m* suicide;
**~mörder(in)** *m(f)* (*Person*) suicide;
**s~mörderisch** *adj* suicidal; **s~sicher** *adj*
self-assured; **~sicherheit** *f* self-assurance;
**~studium** *nt* private study; **s~süchtig** *adj*
selfish; **s~tätig** *adj* automatic;
**~überwindung** *f* willpower; **s~verdient** *adj*:
**s~verdientes Geld** money one has earned
o.s.; **s~vergessen** *adj* absent-minded; (*Blick*)
faraway; **s~verschuldet** *adj*: **wenn der Unfall
s~verschuldet ist** if there is personal
responsibility for the accident; **~versorger**
*m*: **~versorger sein** to be self-sufficient *od*
self-reliant; **Urlaub für ~versorger** self-
catering holiday.
**selbstverständlich** *adj* obvious ♦ *adv*
naturally; **ich halte das für ~** I take that for
granted.
**Selbstverständlichkeit** *f* (*Unbefangenheit*)
naturalness; (*natürliche Voraussetzung*)
matter of course.
**Selbst-** *zW*: **~verständnis** *nt*: **nach seinem
eigenen ~verständnis** as he sees himself;

**~verteidigung** *f* self-defence (*BRIT*), self-
defense (*US*); **~vertrauen** *nt* self-
confidence; **~verwaltung** *f* autonomy, self-
government; **~wählferndienst** *m* (*TEL*)
automatic dialling service, subscriber
trunk dialling (*BRIT*), STD (*BRIT*), direct
distance dialing (*US*); **~wertgefühl** *nt*
feeling of one's own worth *od* value, self-
esteem; **s~zufrieden** *adj* self-satisfied;
**~zweck** *m* end in itself.
**selig** ['ze:lɪç] *adj* happy, blissful; (*REL*)
blessed; (*tot*) late; **S~keit** *f* bliss.
**Sellerie** ['zɛləri:] (**-s, -(s)** *od* **-, -n**) *m od f*
celery.
**selten** ['zɛltən] *adj* rare ♦ *adv* seldom, rarely;
**S~heit** *f* rarity; **S~heitswert** (**-(e)s**) *m* rarity
value.
**Selterswasser** ['zɛltɐsvasɐ] *nt* soda water.
**seltsam** ['zɛltza:m] *adj* curious, strange.
**seltsamerweise** *adv* curiously, strangely.
**Seltsamkeit** *f* strangeness.
**Semester** [ze'mɛstɐ] (**-s, -**) *nt* semester; **ein
älteres ~** a senior student.
**Semi-** [zemi] *in zW* semi-.
**Semikolon** [-'ko:lɔn] (**-s, -s**) *nt* semicolon.
**Seminar** [zemi'na:r] (**-s, -e**) *nt* seminary;
(*Kurs*) seminar; (*UNIV: Ort*) department
building.
**semitisch** [ze'mi:tɪʃ] *adj* Semitic.
**Semmel** ['zɛməl] (**-, -n**) *f* roll; **~brösel(n)** *pl*
breadcrumbs *pl*; **~knödel** (*SÜDD, ÖSTERR*) *m*
bread dumpling.
**sen.** *abk* (= *senior*) sen.
**Senat** [ze'na:t] (**-(e)s, -e**) *m* senate.
**Sendebereich** *m* transmission range.
**Sendefolge** *f* (*Serie*) series.
**senden¹** *unreg vt* to send.
**senden²** *vt, vi* (*RUNDF, TV*) to transmit,
broadcast.
**Sendenetz** *nt* network.
**Sendepause** *f* (*RUNDF, TV*) interval.
**Sender** (**-s, -**) *m* station; (*Anlage*) transmitter.
**Sende-** *zW*: **~reihe** *f* series (of broadcasts);
**~schluß** *m* (*RUNDF, TV*) closedown;
**~station** *f* transmitting station; **~stelle** *f*
transmitting station; **~zeit** *f* broadcasting
time, air time.
**Sendung** ['zɛndʊŋ] *f* consignment; (*Aufgabe*)
mission; (*RUNDF, TV*) transmission;
(*Programm*) programme (*BRIT*), program
(*US*).
**Senegal** ['ze:negal] (**-s**) *nt* Senegal.
**Senf** [zɛnf] (**-(e)s, -e**) *m* mustard; **seinen
~ dazugeben** (*umg*) to put one's oar in;
**~korn** *nt* mustard seed.
**sengen** ['zɛŋən] *vt* to singe ♦ *vi* to scorch.
**senil** [ze'ni:l] (*pej*) *adj* senile.
**Senior** ['ze:niɔr] (**-s, -en**) *m* (*Rentner*) senior
citizen; (*Geschäftspartner*) senior partner.
**Seniorenpaß** [zeni'o:rənpas] *m* senior
citizen's travel pass (*BRIT*).
**Senkblei** ['zɛŋkblaɪ] *nt* plumb.

**Senke** (-, -n) *f* depression.
**Senkel** (-s, -) *m* (shoe)lace.
**senken** *vt* to lower; (*Kopf*) to bow; (*TECH*) to sink ♦ *vr* to sink; (*Stimme*) to drop.
**Senk-** *zW:* ~**fuß** *m* flat foot; ~**grube** *f* cesspit; **s~recht** *adj* vertical, perpendicular; ~**rechte** *f* perpendicular; ~**rechtstarter** *m* (*AVIAT*) vertical takeoff plane; (*fig: Person*) high-flier.
**Senner(in)** ['zɛnər(ɪn)] (-s, -) *m(f)* (Alpine) dairyman, dairymaid.
**Sensation** [zɛnzatsi'oːn] *f* sensation.
**sensationell** [zɛnzatsio'nɛl] *adj* sensational.
**Sensationsblatt** *nt* sensational paper.
**Sensationssucht** *f* sensationalism.
**Sense** ['zɛnzə] (-, -n) *f* scythe; **dann ist ~!** (*umg*) that's the end!
**sensibel** [zɛn'ziːbəl] *adj* sensitive.
**sensibilisieren** [zɛnzibili'ziːrən] *vt* to sensitize.
**Sensibilität** [zɛnzibili'tɛːt] *f* sensitivity.
**sentimental** [zɛntimɛn'taːl] *adj* sentimental.
**Sentimentalität** [zɛntimɛntali'tɛːt] *f* sentimentality.
**separat** [zepa'raːt] *adj* separate; (*Wohnung, Zimmer*) self-contained.
**Sept.** *abk* (= *September*) Sept.
**September** [zɛp'tɛmbər] (-(s), -) *m* September; **im ~** in September; **im Monat ~** in the month of September; **heute ist der zweite ~** today is the second of September *od* September second (*US*); (*geschrieben*) today is 2nd September; **in diesem ~** this September; **Anfang/Ende/Mitte ~** at the beginning/end/in the middle of September.
**septisch** ['zɛptɪʃ] *adj* septic.
**sequentiell** [zekvɛntsi'ɛl] *adj* (*COMPUT*) sequential; ~**er Zugriff** sequential access.
**Sequenz** [ze'kvɛnts] *f* sequence.
**Serbe** ['zɛrbə] (-n, -n) *m* Serbian.
**Serbien** (-s) *nt* Serbia.
**Serbin** *f* Serbian.
**serbisch** *adj* Serbian.
**Serbokroatisch(e)** *nt* Serbo-Croat.
**Serie** ['zeːriə] *f* series.
**seriell** [zeri'ɛl] *adj* (*COMPUT*) serial; ~**e Daten** serial data *pl*; ~**er Anschluß** serial port; ~**er Drucker** serial printer.
**Serien-** *zW:* ~**anfertigung** *f*, ~**herstellung** *f* series production; **s~mäßig** *adj* (*Ausstattung*) standard; (*Herstellung*) series *attrib* ♦ *adv* (*herstellen*) in series; ~**nummer** *f* serial number; **s~weise** *adv* in series.
**seriös** [zeri'øːs] *adj* serious; (*anständig*) respectable.
**Serpentine** [zɛrpɛn'tiːnə] *f* hairpin (bend).
**Serum** ['zeːrum] (-s, Seren) *nt* serum.
**Service**[1] [zɛr'viːs] (-(s), -) *nt* (*Gläser~*) set; (*Geschirr*) service.
**Service**[2] ['səːvɪs] (-, -s) *m* (*COMM, SPORT*) service.
**servieren** [zɛr'viːrən] *vt*, *vi* to serve.

**Serviererin** [zɛr'viːrərɪn] *f* waitress.
**Servierwagen** *m* trolley.
**Serviette** [zɛrvi'ɛtə] *f* napkin, serviette.
**Servolenkung** ['zɛrvo-] *f* power steering.
**Servomotor** *m* servo motor.
**Servus** ['zɛrvʊs] (*ÖSTERR, SÜDD*) *interj* hello; (*beim Abschied*) goodbye, so long (*umg*).
**Sesam** ['zeːzam] (-s, -s) *m* sesame.
**Sessel** ['zɛsəl] (-s, -) *m* armchair; ~**lift** *m* chairlift.
**seßhaft** ['zɛshaft] *adj* settled; (*ansässig*) resident.
**Set** [zɛt] (-s, -s) *nt od m* set; (*Deckchen*) tablemat.
**setzen** ['zɛtsən] *vt* to put, place, set; (*Baum etc*) to plant; (*Segel, TYP*) to set ♦ *vr* (*Platz nehmen*) to sit down; (*Kaffee, Tee*) to settle ♦ *vi* to leap; (*wetten*) to bet; (*TYP*) to set; **jdm ein Denkmal ~** to build a monument to sb; **sich zu jdm ~** to sit with sb.
**Setzer** ['zɛtsər] (-s, -) *m* (*TYP*) typesetter.
**Setzerei** [zɛtsə'raɪ] *f* caseroom; (*Firma*) typesetting firm.
**Setz-** *zW:* ~**kasten** *m* (*TYP*) case; (*an Wand*) ornament shelf; ~**ling** *m* young plant; ~**maschine** *f* (*TYP*) typesetting machine.
**Seuche** ['zɔʏçə] (-, -n) *f* epidemic.
**Seuchengebiet** *nt* infected area.
**seufzen** ['zɔʏftsən] *vt*, *vi* to sigh.
**Seufzer** ['zɔʏftsər] (-s, -) *m* sigh.
**Sex** [zɛks] (-(es)) *m* sex.
**Sexta** ['zɛksta] (-, Sexten) *f* first year of German secondary school.
**Sexualerziehung** [zɛksu'aːlɛrtsiːʊŋ] *f* sex education.
**Sexualität** [zɛksuali'tɛːt] *f* sex, sexuality.
**Sexual-** *zW:* ~**kunde** [zɛksu'aːlkʊndə] *f* sex education; ~**leben** *nt* sex life; ~**objekt** *nt* sex object.
**sexuell** [zɛksu'ɛl] *adj* sexual.
**Seychellen** [ze'ʃɛlən] *pl* Seychelles *pl*.
**sezieren** [ze'tsiːrən] *vt* to dissect.
**SFB** (-) *m abk* (= *Sender Freies Berlin*) Radio Free Berlin.
**Sfr, sFr** *abk* (= *Schweizer Franken*) sfr.
**Shampoo** [ʃam'puː] (-s, -s) *nt* shampoo.
**Shetlandinseln** ['ʃɛtlant|ɪnzəln] *pl* Shetland, Shetland Isles *pl*.
**Shorts** [ʃɔːrts] *pl* shorts *pl*.
**Showmaster** ['ʃoʊmaːstər] (-s, -) *m* compère, MC.
**siamesisch** [zia'meːzɪʃ] *adj:* ~**e Zwillinge** Siamese twins.
**Siamkatze** *f* Siamese (cat).
**Sibirien** [zi'biːriən] (-s) *nt* Siberia.
**sibirisch** *adj* Siberian.

========================== *SCHLÜSSELWORT*

**sich** [zɪç] *pron* **1** (*akk*): **er/sie/es ... ~** he/she/it ... himself/herself/itself; **sie** *pl*/**man ... ~** they/one ... themselves/oneself; **Sie ... ~** you ... yourself/yourselves *pl*; ~ **wiederholen** to repeat oneself/itself

**2** (*dat*): **er/sie/es** ... ~ he/she/it ... to himself/ herself/itself; **sie** *pl/***man** ... ~ they/one ... to themselves/oneself; **Sie** ... ~ you ... to yourself/yourselves *pl*; **sie hat** ~ **einen Pullover gekauft** she bought herself a jumper; ~ **die Haare waschen** to wash one's hair

**3** (*mit Präposition*): **haben Sie Ihren Ausweis bei** ~**?** do you have your pass on you?; **er hat nichts bei** ~ he's got nothing on him; **sie bleiben gern unter** ~ they keep themselves to themselves

**4** (*einander*) each other, one another; **sie bekämpfen** ~ they fight each other *od* one another.

**5**: **dieses Auto fährt** ~ **gut** this car drives well; **hier sitzt es** ~ **gut** it's good to sit here.

**Sichel** ['zɪçəl] (**-, -n**) *f* sickle; (*Mond~*) crescent.

**sicher** ['zɪçər] *adj* safe; (*gewiß*) certain; (*Hand, Job*) steady; (*zuverlässig*) secure, reliable; (*selbst~*) confident; (*Stellung*) secure ♦ *adv* (*natürlich*): **du hast dich** ~ **verrechnet** you must have counted wrongly; **vor jdm/etw** ~ **sein** to be safe from sb/sth; **sich** *dat* **einer Sache/jds** ~ **sein** to be sure of sth/sb; ~ **ist** ~ you can't be too sure.

**sichergehen** *unreg vi* to make sure.

**Sicherheit** ['zɪçərhaɪt] *f* safety; (*auch FIN*) security; (*Gewißheit*) certainty; (*Selbst~*) confidence; **die öffentliche** ~ public security; ~ **im Straßenverkehr** road safety; ~ **leisten** (*COMM*) to offer security.

**Sicherheits-** *zW*: ~**abstand** *m* safe distance; ~**bestimmungen** *pl* safety regulations *pl*; (*betrieblich, POL etc*) security controls *pl*; ~**einrichtungen** *pl* security equipment *sing*, security devices *pl*; ~**glas** *nt* safety glass; ~**gurt** *m* seat belt; **s~halber** *adv* to be on the safe side; ~**nadel** *f* safety pin; ~**rat** *m* Security Council; ~**schloß** *nt* safety lock; ~**spanne** *f* (*COMM*) margin of safety; ~**verschluß** *m* safety clasp; ~**vorkehrung** *f* safety precaution.

**sicherlich** *adv* certainly, surely.

**sichern** *vt* to secure; (*schützen*) to protect; (*Bergsteiger etc*) to belay; (*Waffe*) to put the safety catch on; (*COMPUT: Daten*) to back up; **jdm/sich etw** ~ to secure sth for sb/for o.s.

**sicherstellen** *vt* to impound; (*garantieren*) to guarantee.

**Sicherung** *f* (*Sichern*) securing; (*Vorrichtung*) safety device; (*an Waffen*) safety catch; (*ELEK*) fuse; **da ist (bei) ihm die** ~ **durchgebrannt** (*fig: umg*) he blew a fuse.

**Sicherungskopie** *f* backup copy.

**Sicht** [zɪçt] (**-**) *f* sight; (*Aus~*) view; (*Sehweite*) visibility; **auf** *od* **nach** ~ (*FIN*) at sight; **auf lange** ~ on a long-term basis; **s~bar** *adj*

visible; ~**barkeit** *f* visibility.

**sichten** *vt* to sight; (*auswählen*) to sort out; (*ordnen*) to sift through.

**Sicht-** *zW*: **s~lich** *adj* evident, obvious; ~**verhältnisse** *pl* visibility *sing*; ~**vermerk** *m* visa; ~**weite** *f* visibility; **außer** ~**weite** out of sight.

**sickern** ['zɪkərn] *vi* (*Hilfsverb sein*) to seep; (*in Tropfen*) to drip.

**Sie** [ziː] *nom, akk pron* you.

**sie** *pron* (*sing: nom*) she; (: *akk*) her; (*pl: nom*) they; (: *akk*) them.

**Sieb** [ziːp] (**-(e)s, -e**) *nt* sieve; (*KOCH*) strainer; (*Gemüse~*) colander.

**sieben**[1] ['ziːbən] *vt* to sieve, sift; (*Flüssigkeit*) to strain ♦ *vi*: **bei der Prüfung wird stark gesiebt** (*fig: umg*) the exam will weed a lot of people out.

**sieben**[2] ['ziːbən] *num* seven; **S~gebirge** *nt*: **das S~gebirge** the Seven Mountains *pl* (*near Bonn*); ~**hundert** *num* seven hundred; **S~meter** *m* (*SPORT*) penalty; **S~sachen** *pl* belongings *pl*; **S~schläfer** *m* (*ZOOL*) dormouse.

**siebte(r, s)** ['ziːptə(r, s)] *adj* seventh.

**Siebtel** (**-s, -**) *nt* seventh.

**siebzehn** ['ziːptseːn] *num* seventeen.

**siebzig** ['ziːptsɪç] *num* seventy.

**siedeln** ['ziːdəln] *vi* to settle.

**sieden** ['ziːdən] *vt, vi* to boil.

**Siedepunkt** *m* boiling point.

**Siedler** (**-s, -**) *m* settler.

**Siedlung** *f* settlement; (*Häuser~*) housing estate (*BRIT*) *od* development (*US*).

**Sieg** [ziːk] (**-(e)s, -e**) *m* victory.

**Siegel** ['ziːgəl] (**-s, -**) *nt* seal; ~**lack** *m* sealing wax; ~**ring** *m* signet ring.

**siegen** ['ziːgən] *vi* to be victorious; (*SPORT*) to win; **über jdn/etw** ~ (*fig*) to triumph over sb/sth; (*in Wettkampf*) to beat sb/sth.

**Sieger(in)** (**-s, -**) *m(f)* victor; (*SPORT etc*) winner; ~**ehrung** *f* (*SPORT*) presentation ceremony.

**siegessicher** *adj* sure of victory.

**Siegeszug** *m* triumphal procession.

**siegreich** *adj* victorious.

**siehe** ['ziːə] *Imperativ* see; (~ **da**) behold.

**siehst** [ziːst] *vb siehe* **sehen**.

**sieht** [ziːt] *vb siehe* **sehen**.

**Siel** [ziːl] (**-(e)s, -e**) *nt od m* (*Schleuse*) sluice; (*Abwasserkanal*) sewer.

**siezen** ['ziːtsən] *vt* to address as "Sie"; *siehe auch* **duzen**.

**Signal** [zɪ'gnaːl] (**-s, -e**) *nt* signal; ~**anlage** *f* signals *pl*, set of signals.

**signalisieren** [zɪgnali'ziːrən] *vt* (*lit, fig*) to signal.

**Signatur** [zɪgna'tuːr] *f* signature; (*Bibliotheks~*) shelf mark.

**Silbe** ['zɪlbə] (**-, -n**) *f* syllable; **er hat es mit keiner** ~ **erwähnt** he didn't say a word about it.

**Silber** ['zɪlbər] (**-s**) *nt* silver; **~bergwerk** *nt* silver mine; **~blick** *m*: **einen ~blick haben** to have a slight squint; **~hochzeit** *f* silver wedding.

**silbern** *adj* silver.

**Silberpapier** *nt* silver paper.

**Silhouette** [zilu'ɛtə] *f* silhouette.

**Silikonchip** [zili'koːntʃɪp] *m* silicon chip.

**Silikonplättchen** [zili'koːnplɛtçən] *nt* silicon chip.

**Silo** ['ziːlo] (**-s, -s**) *nt od m* silo.

**Silvester** [zɪl'vɛstər] (**-s, -**) *m or nt* New Year's Eve, Hogmanay (*SCOT*).

> **Silvester** *is the German name for New Year's Eve. Although not an official holiday most businesses close early and shops shut at midday. Most Germans celebrate in the evening, and at midnight they let off fireworks and rockets; the revelry usually lasts until the early hours of the morning.*

**Simbabwe** [zɪm'baːbvə] (**-s**) *nt* Zimbabwe.

**simpel** ['zɪmpəl] *adj* simple; **S~** (**-s, -**) (*umg*) *m* simpleton.

**Sims** [zɪms] (**-es, -e**) *nt od m* (*Kamin~*) mantelpiece; (*Fenster~*) (window)sill.

**Simulant(in)** [zimu'lant(ɪn)] (**-en, -en**) *m(f)* malingerer.

**simulieren** [zimu'liːrən] *vt* to simulate; (*vortäuschen*) to feign ♦ *vi* to feign illness.

**simultan** [zimʊl'taːn] *adj* simultaneous; **S~dolmetscher** *m* simultaneous interpreter.

**sind** [zɪnt] *vb siehe* **sein**.

**Sinfonie** [zɪnfo'niː] *f* symphony.

**Singapur** ['zɪŋgapuːr] (**-s**) *nt* Singapore.

**singen** ['zɪŋən] *unreg vt, vi* to sing.

**Single¹** ['sɪŋgəl] (**-s, -s**) *m* (*Alleinlebender*) single person.

**Single²** ['sɪŋgəl] (**-, -s**) *f* (*MUS*) single.

**Singsang** *m* (*Gesang*) monotonous singing.

**Singstimme** *f* vocal part.

**Singular** ['zɪŋgulaːr] *m* singular.

**Singvogel** ['zɪŋfoːgəl] *m* songbird.

**sinken** ['zɪŋkən] *unreg vi* to sink; (*Boden, Gebäude*) to subside; (*Fundament*) to settle; (*Preise etc*) to fall, go down; **den Mut/die Hoffnung ~ lassen** to lose courage/hope.

**Sinn** [zɪn] (**-(e)s, -e**) *m* mind; (*Wahrnehmungs~*) sense; (*Bedeutung*) sense, meaning; **im ~e des Gesetzes** according to the spirit of the law; **~ für etw** sense of sth; **im ~e des Verstorbenen** in accordance with the wishes of the deceased; **von ~en sein** to be out of one's mind; **das ist nicht der ~ der Sache** that is not the point; **das hat keinen ~** there is no point in that; **~bild** *nt* symbol; **s~bildlich** *adj* symbolic.

**sinnen** *unreg vi* to ponder; **auf etw** *akk* **~** to contemplate sth.

**Sinnenmensch** *m* sensualist.

**Sinnes-** *zW:* **~organ** *nt* sense organ;

**~täuschung** *f* illusion; **~wandel** *m* change of mind.

**sinngemäß** *adj* faithful; (*Wiedergabe*) in one's own words.

**sinnig** *adj* apt; (*ironisch*) clever.

**Sinn-** *zW:* **s~lich** *adj* sensual, sensuous; (*Wahrnehmung*) sensory; **~lichkeit** *f* sensuality; **s~los** *adj* senseless, meaningless; **s~los betrunken** blind drunk; **~losigkeit** *f* senselessness, meaninglessness; **s~verwandt** *adj* synonymous; **s~voll** *adj* meaningful; (*vernünftig*) sensible.

**Sinologe** [zino'loːgə] (**-n, -n**) *m* Sinologist.

**Sinologin** *f* Sinologist.

**Sintflut** ['zɪntfluːt] *f* Flood; **nach uns die ~** (*umg*) it doesn't matter what happens after we've gone; **s~artig** *adj*: **s~artige Regenfälle** torrential rain *sing*.

**Sinus** ['ziːnʊs] (**-, - od -se**) *m* (*ANAT*) sinus; (*MATH*) sine.

**Siphon** [zi'fõː] (**-s, -s**) *m* siphon.

**Sippe** ['zɪpə] (**-, -n**) *f* (extended) family; (*umg: Verwandtschaft*) clan.

**Sippschaft** ['zɪpʃaft] (*pej*) *f* tribe; (*Bande*) gang.

**Sirene** [zi'reːnə] (**-, -n**) *f* siren.

**Sirup** ['ziːrʊp] (**-s, -e**) *m* syrup.

**Sit-in** [sɪt'|ɪn] (**-(s), -s**) *nt*: **ein ~ machen** to stage a sit-in.

**Sitte** ['zɪtə] (**-, -n**) *f* custom; **Sitten** *pl* morals *pl*; **was sind denn das für ~n?** what sort of way is that to behave?

**Sitten-** *zW:* **~polizei** *f* vice squad; **~strolch** (*umg*) *m* sex fiend; **~wächter** *m* (*ironisch*) guardian of public morals; **s~widrig** *adj* (*form*) immoral.

**Sittich** ['zɪtɪç] (**-(e)s, -e**) *m* parakeet.

**Sitt-** *zW:* **s~lich** *adj* moral; **~lichkeit** *f* morality; **~lichkeitsverbrechen** *nt* sex offence (*BRIT*) *od* offense (*US*); **s~sam** *adj* modest, demure.

**Situation** [zituatsi'oːn] *f* situation.

**situiert** [zitu'iːrt] *adj*: **gut ~ sein** to be well off.

**Sitz** [zɪts] (**-es, -e**) *m* seat; (*von Firma, Verwaltung*) headquarters *pl*; **der Anzug hat einen guten ~** the suit sits well.

**sitzen** *unreg vi* to sit; (*Bemerkung, Schlag*) to strike home; (*Gelerntes*) to have sunk in; (*umg: im Gefängnis ~*) to be inside; **locker ~** to be loose; **~ Sie bequem?** are you comfortable?; **einen ~ haben** (*umg*) to have had one too many; **er sitzt im Kultusministerium** (*umg: sein*) he's in the Ministry of Education; **~ bleiben** to remain seated.

**sitzenbleiben** *unreg vi* (*SCH*) to have to repeat a year; **auf etw** *dat* **~** to be lumbered with sth.

**sitzend** *adj* (*Tätigkeit*) sedentary.

**sitzenlassen** *unreg vt* (*SCH*) to keep down a year; (*Mädchen*) to jilt; (*Wartenden*) to stand

up; **etw auf sich** *dat* ~ to take sth lying down.
**Sitz-** *zW:* ~**fleisch** (*umg*) *nt:* ~**fleisch haben** to be able to sit still; ~**gelegenheit** *f* seats *pl;* ~**ordnung** *f* seating plan; ~**platz** *m* seat; ~**streik** *m* sit-down strike.
**Sitzung** *f* meeting.
**Sizilianer(in)** [zitsili'a:nər(ɪn)] (-s, -) *m(f)* Sicilian.
**sizilianisch** *adj* Sicilian.
**Sizilien** [zi'tsi:liən] (-s) *nt* Sicily.
**Skala** ['ska:la] (-, **Skalen**) *f* scale; (*fig*) range.
**Skalpell** [skal'pɛl] (-s, -e) *nt* scalpel.
**skalpieren** [skal'pi:rən] *vt* to scalp.
**Skandal** [skan'da:l] (-s, -e) *m* scandal.
**skandalös** [skanda'lø:s] *adj* scandalous.
**Skandinavien** [skandi'na:viən] (-s) *nt* Scandinavia.
**Skandinavier(in)** (-s, -) *m(f)* Scandinavian.
**skandinavisch** *adj* Scandinavian.
**Skat** [ska:t] (-(e)s, -e *od* -s) *m* (*KARTEN*) skat.
**Skelett** [ske'lɛt] (-(e)s, -e) *nt* skeleton.
**Skepsis** ['skɛpsɪs] (-) *f* scepticism (*BRIT*), skepticism (*US*).
**skeptisch** ['skɛptɪʃ] *adj* sceptical (*BRIT*), skeptical (*US*).
**Ski** [ʃi:] (-s, -er) *m* ski; ~ **laufen** *od* **fahren** to ski; ~**fahrer** *m* skier; ~**hütte** *f* ski hut *od* lodge (*US*); ~**läufer** *m* skier; ~**lehrer** *m* ski instructor; ~**lift** *m* ski lift; ~**springen** *nt* ski jumping; ~**stiefel** *m* ski boot; ~**stock** *m* ski pole.
**Skizze** ['skɪtsə] (-, -n) *f* sketch.
**skizzieren** [skɪ'tsi:rən] *vt* to sketch; (*fig: Plan etc*) to outline ♦ *vi* to sketch.
**Sklave** ['skla:və] (-n, -n) *m* slave.
**Sklaventreiber** (-s, -) (*pej*) *m* slave-driver.
**Sklaverei** [skla:və'raɪ] *f* slavery.
**Sklavin** *f* slave.
**sklavisch** *adj* slavish.
**Skonto** ['skɔnto] (-s, -s) *nt od m* discount.
**Skorbut** [skɔr'bu:t] (-(e)s) *m* scurvy.
**Skorpion** [skɔrpi'o:n] (-s, -e) *m* scorpion; (*ASTROL*) Scorpio.
**Skrupel** ['skru:pəl] (-s, -) *m* scruple; **s~los** *adj* unscrupulous.
**Skulptur** [skʊlp'tu:r] *f* sculpture.
**skurril** [skʊ'ri:l] *adj* (*geh*) droll, comical.
**Slalom** ['sla:lɔm] (-s, -s) *m* slalom.
**Slawe** ['sla:və] (-n, -n) *m* Slav.
**Slawin** *f* Slav.
**slawisch** *adj* Slavonic, Slavic.
**Slip** [slɪp] (-s, -s) *m* (pair of) briefs *pl.*
**Slowake** [slo'va:kə] (-n, -n) *m* Slovak.
**Slowakei** [slova'kaɪ] *f* Slovakia.
**Slowakin** *f* Slovak.
**Slowakisch** [slo'va:kɪʃ] *nt* (*LING*) Slovak; **s~** *adj* Slovak.
**Slowenien** [slo've:niən] (-s) *nt* Slovenia.
**slowenisch** *adj* Slovene.
**S.M.** *abk* (= *Seine Majestät*) H.M.
**Smaragd** [sma'rakt] (-(e)s, -e) *m* emerald.

**Smoking** ['smo:kɪŋ] (-s, -s) *m* dinner jacket (*BRIT*), tuxedo (*US*).
**SMV** (-, -s) *f abk* = **Schülermitverwaltung.**
**Snob** [snɔp] (-s, -s) *m* snob.
**SO** *abk* (= *Südost(en)*) SE.

═══════════ *SCHLÜSSELWORT*

**so** [zo:] *adv* **1** (*sosehr*) so; ~ **groß/schön** *etc* so big/nice *etc;* ~ **groß/schön wie** ... as big/nice as ...; **das hat ihn** ~ **geärgert, daß** ... that annoyed him so much that ...
**2** (*auf diese Weise*) like this; **mach es nicht** ~ don't do it like that; ~ **oder** ~ (in) one way or the other; ... **oder so** or something (like that); **und** ~ **weiter** and so on; ~ **ein** ... such a ...; ~ **einer wie ich** somebody like me; ~ **(et)was** something like this/that; **na** ~ **was!** well I never!; **das ist gut** ~ that's fine; **sie ist nun einmal** ~ that's just the way she is; **das habe ich nur** ~ **gesagt** I didn't really mean it
**3** (*umg: umsonst*): **ich habe es** ~ **bekommen** I got it for nothing
**4** (*als Füllwort: nicht übersetzt*): ~ **mancher** a number of people *pl*
♦ *konj:* ~ **daß** so that; ~ **wie es jetzt ist** as things are at the moment
♦ *interj:* ~? really?; ~, **das wär's** right, that's it then.

**s.o.** *abk* (= *siehe oben*) see above.
**sobald** [zo'balt] *konj* as soon as.
**Söckchen** [zœkçən] *nt* ankle sock.
**Socke** ['zɔkə] (-, -n) *f* sock; **sich auf die** ~**n machen** (*umg*) to get going.
**Sockel** ['zɔkəl] (-s, -) *m* pedestal, base.
**Sodawasser** ['zo:davasər] *nt* soda water.
**Sodbrennen** ['zo:tbrenən] (-s) *nt* heartburn.
**Sodomie** [zodo'mi:] *f* bestiality.
**soeben** [zo'e:bən] *adv* just (now).
**Sofa** ['zo:fa] (-s, -s) *nt* sofa.
**Sofabett** *nt* sofa bed, bed settee.
**sofern** [zo'fɛrn] *konj* if, provided (that).
**soff** *etc* [zɔf] *vb siehe* **saufen.**
**sofort** [zo'fɔrt] *adv* immediately, at once; **(ich) komme** ~! (I'm) just coming!; **S~hilfe** *f* emergency relief *od* aid; **S~hilfegesetz** *nt* law on emergency aid.
**sofortig** *adj* immediate.
**Sofortmaßnahme** *f* immediate measure.
**Softeis** ['sɔftʔaɪs] (-es) *nt* soft ice-cream.
**Softie** ['zɔftiː] (-s, -s) (*umg*) *m* softy.
**Software** ['zɔftwɛːər] (-, -s) *f* software; **s~kompatibel** *adj* software compatible; ~**paket** *nt* software package.
**Sog** (-(e)s, -e) *m* suction; (*von Strudel*) vortex; (*fig*) maelstrom.
**sog** *etc* [zo:k] *vb siehe* **saugen.**
**sog.** *abk* = **sogenannt.**
**sogar** [zo'ga:r] *adv* even.
**sogenannt** ['zo:gənant] *adj* so-called.
**sogleich** [zo'glaɪç] *adv* straight away, at once.

**Sogwirkung** *f* suction; (*fig*) knock-on effect.
**Sohle** ['zo:lə] (-, -n) *f* (*Fuß~*) sole; (*Tal~ etc*) bottom; (*MIN*) level; **auf leisen ~n** (*fig*) softly, noiselessly.
**Sohn** [zo:n] (-(e)s, ⁼e) *m* son.
**Sojasoße** ['zo:jazo:sə] *f* soy *od* soya sauce.
**solang(e)** *konj* as *od* so long as.
**Solar-** [zo'la:r] *in zW* solar; **~energie** *f* solar energy.
**Solarium** [zo'la:riʊm] *nt* solarium.
**Solbad** ['zo:lba:t] *nt* saltwater bath.
**solch** [zɔlç] *adj inv* such.
**solche(r, s)** *adj* such; **ein ~r Mensch** such a person.
**Sold** [zɔlt] (-(e)s, -e) *m* pay.
**Soldat** [zɔl'da:t] (-en, -en) *m* soldier; **s~isch** *adj* soldierly.
**Söldner** ['zœldnər] (-s, -) *m* mercenary.
**Sole** ['zo:lə] (-, -n) *f* brine, salt water.
**Solei** ['zo:laɪ] *nt* pickled egg.
**Soli** ['zo:li] *pl von* **Solo.**
**solid(e)** [zo'li:d(ə)] *adj* solid; (*Arbeit, Wissen*) sound; (*Leben, Person*) staid, respectable.
**solidarisch** [zoli'da:rɪʃ] *adj* in *od* with solidarity; **sich ~ erklären** to declare one's solidarity.
**solidarisieren** [zolidari'zi:rən] *vr:* **sich ~ mit** to show (one's) solidarity with.
**Solidarität** [zolidari'tɛːt] *f* solidarity.
**Solidaritätsstreik** *m* sympathy strike.
**Solist(in)** [zo'lɪst(ɪn)] *m(f)* (*MUS*) soloist.
**Soll** [zɔl] (-(s), -(s)) *nt* (*FIN*) debit (side); (*Arbeitsmenge*) quota, target; **~ und Haben** debit and credit.
**soll** *vb siehe* **sollen.**

========= *SCHLÜSSELWORT*

**sollen** ['zɔlən] (*pt* **sollte**, *pp* **gesollt** *od (als Hilfsverb)* **sollen**) *Hilfsverb* **1** (*Pflicht, Befehl*) be supposed to; **du hättest nicht gehen ~** you shouldn't have gone, you oughtn't to have gone; **er sollte eigentlich morgen kommen** he was supposed to come tomorrow; **soll ich?** shall I?; **soll ich dir helfen?** shall I help you?; **sag ihm, er soll warten** tell him he's to wait; **was soll ich machen?** what should I do?; **mir soll es gleich sein** it's all the same to me; **er sollte sie nie wiedersehen** he was never to see her again

**2** (*Vermutung*): **sie soll verheiratet sein** she's said to be married; **was soll das heißen?** what's that supposed to mean?; **man sollte glauben, daß ...** you would think that ...; **sollte das passieren, ...** if that should happen ...

♦ *vt, vi:* **was soll das?** what's all this about *od* in aid of?; **das sollst du nicht** you shouldn't do that; **was soll's?** what the hell!

**sollte** *etc* ['zɔltə] *vb siehe* **sollen.**
**Solo** ['zo:lo] (-s, -s *od* **Soli**) *nt* solo.
**solo** *adv* (*MUS*) solo; (*fig: umg*) on one's own, alone.
**solvent** [zɔl'vɛnt] *adj* (*FIN*) solvent.
**Solvenz** [zɔl'vɛnts] *f* (*FIN*) solvency.
**Somalia** [zo'ma:lia] (-s) *nt* Somalia.
**somit** [zo'mɪt] *konj* and so, therefore.
**Sommer** ['zɔmər] (-s, -) *m* summer; **~ wie Winter** all year round; **~ferien** *pl* summer holidays *pl* (*BRIT*) *od* vacation *sing* (*US*); (*JUR, PARL*) summer recess *sing*; **s~lich** *adj* summer *attrib*; (*sommerartig*) summery; **~loch** *nt* silly season; **~reifen** *m* normal tyre (*BRIT*) *od* tire (*US*); **~schlußverkauf** *m* summer sale; **~semester** *nt* (*UNIV*) summer semester (*bes US*), ≈ summer term (*BRIT*); **~sprossen** *pl* freckles *pl*; **~zeit** *f* summertime.
**Sonate** [zo'na:tə] (-, -n) *f* sonata.
**Sonde** ['zɔndə] (-, -n) *f* probe.
**Sonder-** ['zɔndər] *in zW* special; **~anfertigung** *f* special model; **~angebot** *nt* special offer; **~ausgabe** *f* special edition; **s~bar** *adj* strange, odd; **~beauftragte(r)** *f(m)* (*POL*) special emissary; **~beitrag** *m* (special) feature; **~fahrt** *f* special trip; **~fall** *m* special case; **s~gleichen** *adj inv* without parallel, unparalleled; **eine Frechheit s~gleichen** the height of cheek; **s~lich** *adj* particular; (*außergewöhnlich*) remarkable; (*eigenartig*) peculiar; **~ling** *m* eccentric; **~marke** *f* special issue (stamp); **~müll** *m* dangerous waste.
**sondern** *konj* but ♦ *vt* to separate; **nicht nur ..., ~ auch** not only ..., but also.
**Sonder-** *zW:* **~preis** *m* special price; **~regelung** *f* special provision; **~schule** *f* special school; **~vergünstigungen** *pl* perquisites *pl*, perks *pl* (*bes BRIT*); **~wünsche** *pl* special requests *pl*; **~zug** *m* special train.
**sondieren** [zɔn'di:rən] *vt* to suss out; (*Gelände*) to scout out.
**Sonett** [zo'nɛt] (-(e)s, -e) *nt* sonnet.
**Sonnabend** ['zɔn|a:bənt] *m* Saturday; *siehe auch* **Dienstag.**
**Sonne** ['zɔnə] (-, -n) *f* sun; **an die ~ gehen** to go out in the sun.
**sonnen** *vr* to sun o.s.; **sich in etw** *dat* **~** (*fig*) to bask in sth.
**Sonnen-** *zW:* **~aufgang** *m* sunrise; **s~baden** *vi* to sunbathe; **~blume** *f* sunflower; **~brand** *m* sunburn; **~brille** *f* sunglasses *pl*; **~creme** *f* suntan lotion; **~energie** *f* solar energy; **~finsternis** *f* solar eclipse; **~fleck** *m* sunspot; **s~gebräunt** *adj* suntanned; **s~klar** *adj* crystal-clear; **~kollektor** *m* solar panel; **~kraftwerk** *nt* solar power station; **~milch** *f* suntan lotion; **~öl** *nt* suntan oil; **~schein** *m* sunshine; **~schirm** *m* sunshade; **~schutzmittel** *nt* sunscreen; **~stich** *m* sunstroke; **du hast wohl einen ~stich!** (*hum; umg*) you must have been out in the sun too long!; **~system** *nt* solar system; **~uhr** *f*

sundial; **~untergang** m sunset; **~wende** f
solstice.
**sonnig** ['zɔnɪç] adj sunny.
**Sonntag** ['zɔntaːk] m Sunday; siehe auch
**Dienstag.**
**sonntäglich** adj attrib: ~ **gekleidet** dressed in
one's Sunday best.
**sonntags** adv (on) Sundays.
**Sonntagsdienst** m: ~ **haben** (Apotheke) to be
open on Sundays.
**Sonntagsfahrer** (pej) m Sunday driver.
**sonst** [zɔnst] adv otherwise; (mit pron, in
Fragen) else; (zu anderer Zeit) at other times;
(gewöhnlich) usually, normally ♦ konj
otherwise; **er denkt, er ist** ~ **wer** (umg) he
thinks he's somebody special; ~ **geht's dir
gut?** (ironisch: umg) are you feeling okay?;
**wenn ich Ihnen** ~ **noch behilflich sein kann**
if I can help you in any other way; ~ **noch
etwas?** anything else?; ~ **nichts** nothing
else.
**sonstig** adj other; „S~es" "other".
**sonst-** zW: ~**jemand** (umg) pron anybody (at
all); ~**was** (umg) pron: **da kann ja** ~**was
passieren** anything could happen; ~**wo**
(umg) adv somewhere else; ~**woher** (umg)
adv from somewhere else; ~**wohin** (umg)
adv somewhere else.
**sooft** [zo'|ɔft] konj whenever.
**Sopran** [zo'praːn] (-s, -e) m soprano (voice).
**Sopranistin** [zopra'nɪstɪn] f soprano (singer).
**Sorge** ['zɔrgə] (-, -n) f care, worry; **dafür**
~ **tragen, daß** ... (geh) to see to it that ...
**sorgen** vi: **für jdn** ~ to look after sb ♦ vr: **sich**
~ **(um)** to worry (about); **für etw** ~ to take
care of od see to sth; **dafür** ~, **daß** ... to see
to it that ...; **dafür ist gesorgt** that's taken
care of.
**Sorgen-** zW: **s~frei** adj carefree; ~**kind** nt
problem child; **s~voll** adj troubled, worried.
**Sorgerecht** (-(e)s) nt custody (of a child).
**Sorgfalt** ['zɔrkfalt] (-) f care(fulness); **viel**
~ **auf etw** akk **verwenden** to take a lot of
care over sth.
**sorgfältig** adj careful.
**sorglos** adj careless; (ohne Sorgen) carefree.
**sorgsam** adj careful.
**Sorte** ['zɔrtə] (-, -n) f sort; (Waren~) brand;
**Sorten** pl (FIN) foreign currency sing.
**sortieren** [zɔr'tiːrən] vt to sort (out);
(COMPUT) to sort.
**Sortiermaschine** f sorting machine.
**Sortiment** [zɔrti'mɛnt] nt assortment.
**SOS** [ɛs|oː'|ɛs] nt abk SOS.
**sosehr** [zo'zeːr] konj as much as.
**soso** [zo'zoː] interj: ~! I see!; (erstaunt) well,
well!; (drohend) well!
**Soße** ['zoːsə] (-, -n) f sauce; (Braten~) gravy.
**Souffleur** [zu'fløːr] m prompter.
**Souffleuse** [zu'fløːzə] f prompter.
**soufflieren** [zu'fliːrən] vt, vi to prompt.
**soundso** ['zoː|ʊntzoː] adv: ~ **lange** for such

and such a time.
**soundsoviele(r, s)** adj: **am S~n** (Datum) on
such and such a date.
**Souterrain** [zutɛ'rɛ̃ː] (-s, -s) nt basement.
**Souvenir** [zuvə'niːr] (-s, -s) nt souvenir.
**souverän** [zuvə'rɛːn] adj sovereign;
(überlegen) superior; (fig) supremely good.
**soviel** [zo'fiːl] konj as far as ♦ pron: ~ **(wie)** as
much (as); **rede nicht** ~ don't talk so much.
**soweit** [zo'vait] konj as far as ♦ adv: ~ **sein** to
be ready; ~ **wie** od **als möglich** as far as
possible; **ich bin** ~ **zufrieden** by and large
I'm quite satisfied; **es ist bald** ~ it's nearly
time.
**sowenig** [zo'veːnɪç] adv: ~ **(wie)** no more
(than), not any more (than) ♦ konj however
little; ~ **wie möglich** as little as possible.
**sowie** [zo'viː] konj (sobald) as soon as;
(ebenso) as well as.
**sowieso** [zovi'zoː] adv anyway.
**Sowjetbürger** m (früher) Soviet citizen.
**sowjetisch** [zɔ'vjɛtɪʃ] adj (früher) Soviet.
**Sowjet-** zW (früher): ~**republik** f Soviet
Republic; ~**russe** m Soviet Russian;
~**union** f Soviet Union.
**sowohl** [zo'voːl] konj: ~ ... **als** od **wie auch** ...
both ... and ...
**soz.** abk = **sozial; sozialistisch.**
**sozial** [zotsi'aːl] adj social; ~ **eingestellt**
public-spirited; ~**er Wohnungsbau** public-
sector housing (programme); **S~abbau** m
public-spending cuts pl; **S~abgaben** pl
National Insurance contributions pl (BRIT),
Social Security contributions pl (US);
**S~amt** nt (social) welfare office; **S~arbeiter**
m social worker; **S~beruf** m caring
profession; **S~demokrat** m social democrat;
**S~hilfe** f welfare (aid).
**Sozialisation** [zotsializatsi'oːn] f (PSYCH,
SOZIOLOGIE) socialization.
**sozialisieren** [zotsiali'ziːrən] vt to socialize.
**Sozialismus** [zotsia'lɪsmʊs] m socialism.
**Sozialist(in)** [zotsia'lɪst(ɪn)] m(f) socialist.
**sozialistisch** adj socialist.
**Sozial-** zW: ~**kunde** f social studies sing;
~**leistungen** pl social security contributions
(from the state and employer); ~**plan** m
redundancy payments scheme; ~**politik** f
social welfare policy; ~**produkt** nt (gross od
net) national product; ~**staat** m welfare
state; ~**versicherung** f national insurance
(BRIT), social security (US); ~**wohnung** f
≈ council flat (BRIT), state-subsidized
apartment.

A **Sozialwohnung** is a council house or flat let
at a fairly low rent to people on low incomes.
They are built from public funds (in 1993 there
was a cash injection of DM 2 million into this
housing fund). People applying for a
Sozialwohnung have to prove their entitlement.

**Soziologe** [zotsio'lo:gə] (**-n, -n**) *m* sociologist.
**Soziologie** [zotsiolo'gi:] *f* sociology.
**Soziologin** [zotsio'lo:gɪn] *f* sociologist.
**soziologisch** [zotsio'lo:gɪʃ] *adj* sociological.
**Sozius** ['zo:tsius] (**-, -se**) *m* (*COMM*) partner;
(*Motorrad*) pillion rider; **~sitz** *m* pillion
(seat).
**sozusagen** [zotsu'za:gən] *adv* so to speak.
**Spachtel** ['ʃpaxtəl] (**-s, -**) *m* spatula.
**spachteln** *vt* (*Mauerfugen, Ritzen*) to fill (in)
♦ *vi* (*umg: essen*) to tuck in.
**Spagat** [ʃpa'ga:t] (**-(e)s, -e**) *m od nt* splits *pl*.
**Spaghetti** [ʃpa'gɛti] *pl* spaghetti *sing*.
**spähen** ['ʃpɛ:ən] *vi* to peep, peek.
**Spalier** [ʃpa'li:r] (**-s, -e**) *nt* (*Gerüst*) trellis;
(*Leute*) guard of honour (*BRIT*) *od* honor
(*US*); **~ stehen, ein ~ bilden** to form a guard
of honour (*BRIT*) or honor (*US*).
**Spalt** [ʃpalt] (**-(e)s, -e**) *m* crack; (*Tür~*) chink;
(*fig: Kluft*) split.
**Spalte** (**-, -n**) *f* crack, fissure; (*Gletscher~*)
crevasse; (*in Text*) column.
**spalten** *vt, vr* (*lit, fig*) to split.
**Spaltung** *f* splitting.
**Span** [ʃpa:n] (**-(e)s, -̈e**) *m* shaving.
**Spanferkel** *nt* sucking pig.
**Spange** ['ʃpaŋə] (**-, -n**) *f* clasp; (*Haar~*) hair
slide; (*Schnalle*) buckle; (*Arm~*) bangle.
**Spaniel** ['ʃpa:niəl] (**-s, -s**) *m* spaniel.
**Spanien** ['ʃpa:niən] (**-s**) *nt* Spain.
**Spanier(in)** (**-s, -**) *m(f)* Spaniard.
**spanisch** *adj* Spanish; **das kommt mir ~ vor**
(*umg*) that seems odd to me; **~e Wand**
(folding) screen.
**Spann** (**-(e)s, -̈e**) *m* instep.
**spann** *etc* [ʃpan] *vb siehe* **spinnen**.
**Spannbeton** (**-s**) *m* prestressed concrete.
**Spanne** (**-, -n**) *f* (*Zeit~*) space; (*Differenz*) gap;
*siehe auch* **Spann**.
**spannen** *vt* (*straffen*) to tighten, tauten;
(*befestigen*) to brace ♦ *vi* to be tight.
**spannend** *adj* exciting, gripping; **mach's
nicht so ~!** (*umg*) don't keep me *etc* in
suspense.
**Spanner** (**-s, -**) (*umg*) *m* (*Voyeur*) peeping
Tom.
**Spannkraft** *f* elasticity; (*fig*) energy.
**Spannung** *f* tension; (*ELEK*) voltage; (*fig*)
suspense; (*unangenehm*) tension.
**Spannungsgebiet** *nt* (*POL*) flashpoint, area
of tension.
**Spannungsprüfer** *m* voltage detector.
**Spannweite** *f* (*von Flügeln, AVIAT*)
(wing)span.
**Spanplatte** *f* chipboard.
**Sparbuch** *nt* savings book.
**Sparbüchse** *f* moneybox.
**sparen** ['ʃpa:rən] *vt, vi* to save; **sich** *dat* **etw ~**
to save o.s. sth; (*Bemerkung*) to keep sth to
o.s.; **mit etw ~** to be sparing with sth; **an
etw** *dat* **~** to economize on sth.
**Sparer(in)** (**-s, -**) *m(f)* (*bei Bank etc*) saver.

**Sparflamme** *f* low flame; **auf ~** (*fig: umg*)
just ticking over.
**Spargel** ['ʃpargəl] (**-s, -**) *m* asparagus.
**Spar-** *zW*: **~groschen** *m* nest egg; **~kasse** *f*
savings bank; **~konto** *nt* savings account.
**spärlich** ['ʃpɛ:rlɪç] *adj* meagre (*BRIT*), meager
(*US*); (*Bekleidung*) scanty; (*Beleuchtung*)
poor.
**Spar-** *zW*: **~maßnahme** *f* economy measure;
**~packung** *f* economy size; **s~sam** *adj*
economical, thrifty; **s~sam im Verbrauch**
economical; **~samkeit** *f* thrift,
economizing; **~schwein** *nt* piggy bank.
**Sparte** ['ʃpartə] (**-, -n**) *f* field; (*COMM*) line of
business; (*PRESSE*) column.
**Sparvertrag** *m* savings agreement.
**Spaß** [ʃpa:s] (**-es, -̈e**) *m* joke; (*Freude*) fun;
**~ muß sein** there's no harm in a joke; **jdm
~ machen** to be fun (for sb); **s~en** *vi* to joke;
**mit ihm ist nicht zu s~en** you can't take
liberties with him.
**spaßeshalber** *adv* for the fun of it.
**spaßig** *adj* funny, droll.
**Spaß-** *zW*: **~macher** *m* joker, funny man;
**~verderber** (**-s, -**) *m* spoilsport; **~vogel** *m*
joker.
**Spastiker(in)** ['ʃpastikər(ɪn)] *m(f)* (*MED*)
spastic.
**spät** [ʃpɛ:t] *adj, adv* late; **heute abend wird es
~** it'll be a late night tonight.
**Spaten** ['ʃpa:tən] (**-s, -**) *m* spade; **~stich** *m:* **den
ersten ~stich tun** to turn the first sod.
**Spätentwickler** *m* late developer.
**später** *adj, adv* later; **an ~ denken** to think of
the future; **bis ~!** see you later!
**spätestens** *adv* at the latest.
**Spätlese** *f* late vintage.
**Spatz** [ʃpats] (**-en, -en**) *m* sparrow.
**spazieren** [ʃpa'tsi:rən] *vi* (*Hilfsverb sein*) to
stroll; **~fahren** *unreg vi* to go for a drive;
**~gehen** *unreg vi* to go for a walk.
**Spazier-** *zW*: **~gang** *m* walk; **einen ~gang
machen** to go for a walk; **~gänger(in)** *m(f)*
stroller; **~stock** *m* walking stick; **~weg** *m*
path, walk.
**SPD** (**-**) *f abk* (*= Sozialdemokratische Partei
Deutschlands*) German Social Democratic
Party.

---

*The* **SPD** *(Sozialdemokratische Partei
Deutschlands), the German Social Democratic
Party, was newly formed in 1945. It is the
largest political party in Germany. It shared in
the government with the* **CDU/CSU** *from
1966-69 and governed from 1969-82 along with
the* **FDP** *in a socialist-liberal coalition.*

---

**Specht** [ʃpɛçt] (**-(e)s, -e**) *m* woodpecker.
**Speck** [ʃpɛk] (**-(e)s, -e**) *m* bacon; **mit ~ fängt
man Mäuse** (*Sprichwort*) you need a sprat to
catch a mackerel; **'ran an den ~** (*umg*) let's
get stuck in.

**Spediteur** [ʃpedi'tøːr] m carrier; (*Möbel~*) furniture remover.

**Spedition** [ʃpeditsi'oːn] f carriage; (*~sfirma*) road haulage contractor; (*Umzugsfirma*) removal (*BRIT*) od moving (*US*) firm.

**Speer** [ʃpeːr] (**-(e)s, -e**) m spear; (*SPORT*) javelin; **~werfen** nt: **das ~werfen** throwing the javelin.

**Speiche** ['ʃpaɪçə] (**-, -n**) f spoke.

**Speichel** ['ʃpaɪçəl] (**-s**) m saliva, spit(tle); **~lecker** (*pej: umg*) m bootlicker.

**Speicher** ['ʃpaɪçər] (**-s, -**) m storehouse; (*Dach~*) attic, loft; (*Korn~*) granary; (*Wasser~*) tank; (*TECH*) store; (*COMPUT*) memory; **~auszug** m (*COMPUT*) dump.

**speichern** vt (*auch COMPUT*) to store.

**speien** ['ʃpaɪən] unreg vt, vi to spit; (*erbrechen*) to vomit; (*Vulkan*) to spew.

**Speise** ['ʃpaɪzə] (**-, -n**) f food; **kalte und warme ~n** hot and cold meals; **~eis** nt ice-cream; **~fett** nt cooking fat; **~kammer** f larder, pantry; **~karte** f menu.

**speisen** vt to feed; to eat ♦ vi to dine.

**Speise-** zW: **~öl** nt salad oil; (*zum Braten*) cooking oil; **~röhre** f (*ANAT*) gullet, oesophagus (*BRIT*), esophagus (*US*); **~saal** m dining room; **~wagen** m dining car; **~zettel** m menu.

**Spektakel** [ʃpɛk'taːkəl] (**-s, -**) m (*umg: Lärm*) row ♦ nt (**-s, -**) spectacle.

**spektakulär** [ʃpɛktaku'lɛːr] adj spectacular.

**Spektrum** ['ʃpɛktrʊm] (**-s, -tren**) nt spectrum.

**Spekulant(in)** [ʃpeku'lant(ɪn)] m(f) speculator.

**Spekulation** [ʃpekulatsi'oːn] f speculation.

**Spekulatius** [ʃpeku'laːtsiʊs] (**-, -**) m spiced biscuit (*BRIT*) od cookie (*US*).

**spekulieren** [ʃpeku'liːrən] vi (*fig*) to speculate; **auf etw** akk **~** to have hopes of sth.

**Spelunke** [ʃpe'lʊŋkə] (**-, -n**) f dive.

**spendabel** [ʃpɛn'daːbəl] (*umg*) adj generous, open-handed.

**Spende** ['ʃpɛndə] (**-, -n**) f donation.

**spenden** vt to donate, give; **S~konto** nt donations account; **S~waschanlage** f donation-laundering organization.

**Spender(in)** (**-s, -**) m(f) donator; (*MED*) donor.

**spendieren** [ʃpɛn'diːrən] vt to pay for, buy; **jdm etw ~** to treat sb to sth, stand sb sth.

**Sperling** ['ʃpɛrlɪŋ] m sparrow.

**Sperma** ['ʃpɛrma] (**-s, Spermen**) nt sperm.

**sperrangelweit** ['ʃpɛr|aŋəl'vaɪt] adj wide-open.

**Sperrbezirk** m no-go area.

**Sperre** (**-, -n**) f barrier; (*Verbot*) ban; (*Polizei~*) roadblock.

**sperren** ['ʃpɛrən] vt to block; (*COMM: Konto*) to freeze; (*COMPUT: Daten*) to disable; (*SPORT*) to suspend, bar; (: *vom Ball*) to obstruct; (*einschließen*) to lock; (*verbieten*) to ban ♦ vr to baulk, jibe, jib.

**Sperr-** zW: **~feuer** nt (*MIL, fig*) barrage; **~frist** f (*auch JUR*) waiting period; (*SPORT*)

(period of) suspension; **~gebiet** nt prohibited area; **~gut** nt bulky freight; **~holz** nt plywood.

**sperrig** adj bulky.

**Sperr-** zW: **~konto** nt blocked account; **~müll** m bulky refuse; **~sitz** m (*THEAT*) stalls pl (*BRIT*), orchestra (*US*); **~stunde** f closing time; **~zeit** f closing time; **~zone** f exclusion zone.

**Spesen** ['ʃpeːzən] pl expenses pl; **~abrechnung** f expense account.

**Spessart** ['ʃpɛsart] (**-s**) m Spessart (Mountains pl).

**Spezi** ['ʃpeːtsi] (**-s, -s**) (*umg*) m pal, mate (*BRIT*).

**Spezial-** [ʃpetsi'aːl] in zW special; **s~angefertigt** adj custom-built; **~ausbildung** f specialized training.

**spezialisieren** [ʃpetsiali'ziːrən] vr to specialize.

**Spezialisierung** f specialization.

**Spezialist(in)** [ʃpetsia'lɪst(ɪn)] m(f): **~ (für)** specialist (in).

**Spezialität** [ʃpetsiali'tɛːt] f speciality (*BRIT*), specialty (*US*).

**speziell** [ʃpetsi'ɛl] adj special.

**Spezifikation** [ʃpetsifikatsi'oːn] f specification.

**spezifisch** [ʃpe'tsiːfɪʃ] adj specific.

**Sphäre** ['sfɛːrə] (**-, -n**) f sphere.

**spicken** ['ʃpɪkən] vt to lard ♦ vi (*SCH*) to copy, crib.

**Spickzettel** m (*SCH: umg*) crib.

**spie** etc [ʃpiː] vb siehe **speien**.

**Spiegel** ['ʃpiːgəl] (**-s, -**) m mirror; (*Wasser~*) level; (*MIL*) tab; **~bild** nt reflection; **s~bildlich** adj reversed.

**Spiegelei** ['ʃpiːgəl|aɪ] nt fried egg.

**spiegeln** vt to mirror, reflect ♦ vr to be reflected ♦ vi to gleam; (*wider~*) to be reflective.

**Spiegelreflexkamera** f reflex camera.

**Spiegelschrift** f mirror writing.

**Spiegelung** f reflection.

**spiegelverkehrt** adj in mirror image.

**Spiel** [ʃpiːl] (**-(e)s, -e**) nt game; (*Schau~*) play; (*Tätigkeit*) play(ing); (*KARTEN*) pack (*BRIT*), deck (*US*); (*TECH*) (free) play; **leichtes ~ (bei od mit jdm) haben** to have an easy job of it (with sb); **die Hand** od **Finger im ~ haben** to have a hand in affairs; **jdn/etw aus dem ~ lassen** to leave sb/sth out of it; **auf dem ~(e) stehen** to be at stake; **~automat** m gambling machine; (*zum Geldgewinnen*) fruit machine (*BRIT*); **~bank** f casino; **~dose** f musical box (*BRIT*), music box (*US*).

**spielen** vt, vi to play; (*um Geld*) to gamble; (*THEAT*) to perform, act; **was wird hier gespielt?** (*umg*) what's going on here?

**spielend** adv easily.

**Spieler(in)** (**-s, -**) m(f) player; (*um Geld*)

gambler.

**Spielerei** [ʃpiːləˈraɪ] *f* (*Kinderspiel*) child's play.

**spielerisch** *adj* playful; (*Leichtigkeit*) effortless; ~**es Können** skill as a player; (*THEAT*) acting ability.

**Spiel-** *zW:* ~**feld** *nt* pitch, field; ~**film** *m* feature film; ~**geld** *nt* (*Einsatz*) stake; (*unechtes Geld*) toy money; ~**karte** *f* playing card; ~**mannszug** *m* (brass) band; ~**plan** *m* (*THEAT*) programme (*BRIT*), program (*US*); ~**platz** *m* playground; ~**raum** *m* room to manoeuvre (*BRIT*) od maneuver (*US*), scope; ~**regel** *f* (*lit, fig*) rule of the game; ~**sachen** *pl* toys *pl*; ~**show** *f* gameshow; ~**stand** *m* score; ~**straße** *f* play street; ~**sucht** *f* addiction to gambling; ~**verderber** (**-s, -**) *m* spoilsport; ~**waren** *pl* toys *pl*; ~**zeit** *f* (*Saison*) season; (~*dauer*) playing time; ~**zeug** *nt* toy; (~*sachen*) toys *pl*.

**Spieß** [ʃpiːs] (**-es, -e**) *m* spear; (*Brat*~) spit; (*MIL: umg*) sarge; **den ~ umdrehen** (*fig*) to turn the tables; **wie am ~(e) schreien** (*umg*) to squeal like a stuck pig; ~**braten** *m* joint roasted on a spit.

**Spießbürger** (**-s, -**) *m* bourgeois.

**Spießer** (**-s, -**) *m* bourgeois.

**Spikes** [spaɪks] *pl* (*SPORT*) spikes *pl*; (*AUT*) studs *pl*; ~**reifen** *m* studded tyre (*BRIT*) od tire (*US*).

**Spinat** [ʃpiˈnaːt] (**-(e)s, -e**) *m* spinach.

**Spind** [ʃpɪnt] (**-(e)s, -e**) *m* od *nt* locker.

**spindeldürr** [ˈʃpɪndəlˈdʏr] (*pej*) *adj* spindly, thin as a rake.

**Spinne** [ˈʃpɪnə] (**-, -n**) *f* spider; **s~feind** (*umg*) *adj:* **sich** od **einander** *dat* **s~feind sein** to be deadly enemies.

**spinnen** *unreg vt* to spin ♦ *vi* (*umg*) to talk rubbish; (*verrückt*) to be crazy od mad; **ich denk' ich spinne** (*umg*) I don't believe it.

**Spinnengewebe** *nt* cobweb.

**Spinner(in)** (**-s, -**) *m(f)* (*fig: umg*) screwball, crackpot.

**Spinnerei** [ʃpɪnəˈraɪ] *f* spinning mill.

**Spinn-** *zW:* ~**gewebe** *nt* cobweb; ~**rad** *nt* spinning wheel; ~**webe** *f* cobweb.

**Spion** [ʃpiˈoːn] (**-s, -e**) *m* spy; (*in Tür*) spyhole.

**Spionage** [ʃpioˈnaːʒə] (**-**) *f* espionage; ~**abwehr** *f* counterintelligence; ~**satellit** *m* spy satellite.

**spionieren** [ʃpioˈniːrən] *vi* to spy.

**Spionin** *f* (woman) spy.

**Spirale** [ʃpiˈraːlə] (**-, -n**) *f* spiral; (*MED*) coil.

**Spirituosen** [ʃpirituˈoːzən] *pl* spirits *pl*.

**Spiritus** [ˈʃpiritus] (**-, -se**) *m* (methylated) spirits *pl*; ~**kocher** *m* spirit stove.

**Spitz** [ʃpɪts] (**-es, -e**) *m* (*Hund*) spitz.

**spitz** *adj* pointed; (*Winkel*) acute; (*fig: Zunge*) sharp; (: *Bemerkung*) caustic.

**Spitz-** *zW:* **s~bekommen** *unreg vt:* **etw s~bekommen** (*umg*) to get wise to sth; ~**bogen** *m* pointed arch; ~**bube** *m* rogue.

**Spitze** (**-, -n**) *f* point, tip; (*Berg*~) peak; (*Bemerkung*) taunt; (*fig: Stichelei*) dig; (*erster Platz*) lead, top; (*meist pl: Gewebe*) lace; (*umg: prima*) great; **etw auf die ~ treiben** to carry sth too far.

**Spitzel** (**-s, -**) *m* police informer.

**spitzen** *vt* to sharpen; (*Lippen, Mund*) to purse; (*lit, fig: Ohren*) to prick up.

**Spitzen-** *in zW* top; ~**leistung** *f* top performance; ~**lohn** *m* top wages *pl*; ~**marke** *f* brand leader; **s~mäßig** *adj* really great; ~**position** *f* leading position; ~**reiter** *m* (*SPORT*) leader; (*fig: Kandidat*) front runner; (*Ware*) top seller; (*Schlager*) number one; ~**sportler** *m* top-class sportsman; ~**verband** *m* leading organization.

**Spitzer** (**-s, -**) *m* sharpener.

**spitzfindig** *adj* (over)subtle.

**Spitzmaus** *f* shrew.

**Spitzname** *m* nickname.

**Spleen** [ʃpliːn] (**-s, -e** od **-s**) *m* (*Angewohnheit*) crazy habit; (*Idee*) crazy idea; (*Fimmel*) obsession.

**Splitt** [ʃplɪt] (**-s, -e**) *m* stone chippings *pl*; (*Streumittel*) grit.

**Splitter** (**-s, -**) *m* splinter; ~**gruppe** *f* (*POL*) splinter group; **s~nackt** *adj* stark naked.

**SPÖ** (**-**) *f abk* (= *Sozialistische Partei Österreichs*) Austrian Socialist Party.

**sponsern** [ˈʃpɔnzərn] *vt* to sponsor.

**Sponsor** [ˈʃpɔnzɔr] (**-s, -en**) *m* sponsor.

**spontan** [ʃpɔnˈtaːn] *adj* spontaneous.

**sporadisch** [ʃpoˈraːdɪʃ] *adj* sporadic.

**Sporen** [ˈʃpoːrən] *pl* (*auch BOT, ZOOL*) spurs *pl*.

**Sport** [ʃpɔrt] (**-(e)s, -e**) *m* sport; (*fig*) hobby; **treiben Sie ~?** do you do any sport?; ~**abzeichen** *nt* sports certificate; ~**artikel** *pl* sports equipment *sing*; ~**fest** *nt* sports gala; (*SCH*) sports day (*BRIT*); ~**geist** *m* sportsmanship; ~**halle** *f* sports hall; ~**klub** *m* sports club; ~**lehrer** *m* games od P.E. teacher.

**Sportler(in)** (**-s, -**) *m(f)* sportsman, sportswoman.

**Sport-** *zW:* **s~lich** *adj* sporting; (*Mensch*) sporty; (*durchtrainiert*) athletic; (*Kleidung*) smart but casual; ~**medizin** *f* sports medicine; ~**platz** *m* playing od sports field; ~**schuh** *m* sports shoe; (*sportlicher Schuh*) casual shoe.

**Sportsfreund** *m* (*fig: umg*) buddy.

**Sport-** *zW:* ~**verein** *m* sports club; ~**wagen** *m* sports car; ~**zeug** *nt* sports gear.

**Spot** [spɔt] (**-s, -s**) *m* commercial, advertisement.

**Spott** [ʃpɔt] (**-(e)s**) *m* mockery, ridicule; **s~billig** *adj* dirt-cheap; **s~en** *vi* to mock; **s~en über** +*akk* to mock (at), ridicule; **das s~et jeder Beschreibung** that simply defies description.

**spöttisch** [ˈʃpœtɪʃ] *adj* mocking.

**Spottpreis** *m* ridiculously low price.

**sprach** *etc* [ʃpraːx] *vb siehe* **sprechen**.
**sprachbegabt** *adj* good at languages.
**Sprache** (-, -n) *f* language; **heraus mit der ~!**
(*umg*) come on, out with it!; **zur ~ kommen**
to be mentioned; **in französischer ~ in**
French.
**Sprachenschule** *f* language school.
**Sprach-** *zW:* **~fehler** *m* speech defect;
**~fertigkeit** *f* fluency; **~führer** *m* phrase
book; **~gebrauch** *m* (linguistic) usage;
**~gefühl** *nt* feeling for language;
**~kenntnisse** *pl:* **mit englischen ~kenntnissen**
with a knowledge of English; **~kurs** *m*
language course; **~labor** *nt* language
laboratory; **s~lich** *adj* linguistic; **s~los** *adj*
speechless; **~rohr** *nt* megaphone; (*fig*)
mouthpiece; **~störung** *f* speech disorder;
**~wissenschaft** *f* linguistics *sing*.
**sprang** *etc* [ʃpraŋ] *vb siehe* **springen**.
**Spray** [spreː] (-s, -s) *m od nt* spray; **~dose** *f*
aerosol (can), spray.
**sprayen** *vt, vi* to spray.
**Sprechanlage** *f* intercom.
**Sprechblase** *f* speech balloon.
**sprechen** [ˈʃprɛçən] *unreg vi* to speak, talk ♦ *vt*
to say; (*Sprache*) to speak; (*Person*) to speak
to; **mit jdm ~** to speak *od* talk to sb; **das**
**spricht für ihn** that's a point in his favour;
**frei ~** to extemporize; **nicht gut auf jdn zu**
**~ sein** to be on bad terms with sb; **es spricht**
**vieles dafür, daß ...** there is every reason to
believe that ...; **hier spricht man Spanisch**
Spanish spoken; **wir ~ uns noch!** you
haven't heard the last of this!
**Sprecher(in)** (-s, -) *m(f)* speaker; (*für Gruppe*)
spokesman, spokeswoman; (*RUNDF, TV*)
announcer.
**Sprech-** *zW:* **~funkgerät** *nt* radio telephone;
**~rolle** *f* speaking part; **~stunde** *f*
consultation (hour); (*von Arzt*) (doctor's)
surgery (*BRIT*); **~stundenhilfe** *f* (doctor's)
receptionist; **~zimmer** *nt* consulting room,
surgery (*BRIT*).
**spreizen** [ˈʃpraitsən] *vt* to spread ♦ *vr* to put on
airs.
**Sprengarbeiten** *pl* blasting operations *pl*.
**sprengen** [ˈʃprɛŋən] *vt* to sprinkle; (*mit*
*Sprengstoff*) to blow up; (*Gestein*) to blast;
(*Versammlung*) to break up.
**Spreng-** *zW:* **~kopf** *m* warhead; **~ladung** *f*
explosive charge; **~satz** *m* explosive
device; **~stoff** *m* explosive(s *pl*);
**~stoffanschlag** *m* bomb attack.
**Spreu** [ʃprɔy] (-) *f* chaff.
**spricht** [ʃprɪçt] *vb siehe* **sprechen**.
**Sprichwort** *nt* proverb.
**sprichwörtlich** *adj* proverbial.
**sprießen** [ˈʃpriːsən] *vi* (*aus der Erde*) to spring
up; (*Knospen*) to shoot.
**Springbrunnen** *m* fountain.
**springen** [ˈʃprɪŋən] *unreg vi* to jump, leap;
(*Glas*) to crack; (*mit Kopfsprung*) to dive; **etw**

**~ lassen** (*umg*) to fork out for sth.
**springend** *adj:* **der ~e Punkt** the crucial
point.
**Springer** (-s, -) *m* jumper; (*SCHACH*) knight.
**Springreiten** *nt* show jumping.
**Springseil** *nt* skipping rope.
**Sprinkler** [ˈʃprɪŋklər] (-s, -) *m* sprinkler.
**Sprit** [ʃprɪt] (-(e)s, -e) (*umg*) *m* petrol (*BRIT*),
gas(oline) (*US*), fuel.
**Spritzbeutel** *m* icing bag.
**Spritze** [ˈʃprɪtsə] (-, -n) *f* syringe; (*Injektion*)
injection; (*an Schlauch*) nozzle.
**spritzen** *vt* to spray; (*Wein*) to dilute with
soda water/lemonade; (*MED*) to inject ♦ *vi* to
splash; (*heißes Fett*) to spit; (*heraus~*) to
spurt; (*aus einer Tube etc*) to squirt; (*MED*) to
give injections.
**Spritzer** (-s, -) *m* (*Farb~, Wasser~*) splash.
**Spritzpistole** *f* spray gun.
**Spritztour** (*umg*) *f* spin.
**spröde** [ˈʃprøːdə] *adj* brittle; (*Person*)
reserved; (*Haut*) rough.
**Sproß** (-sses, -sse) *m* shoot.
**sproß** *etc* [ʃprɔs] *vb siehe* **sprießen**.
**Sprosse** [ˈʃprɔsə] (-, -n) *f* rung.
**Sprossenwand** *f* (*SPORT*) wall bars *pl*.
**Sprößling** [ˈʃprœslɪŋ] *m* offspring *no pl*.
**Spruch** [ʃprʊx] (-(e)s, -̈e) *m* saying, maxim;
(*JUR*) judgement; **Sprüche klopfen** (*umg*) to
talk fancy; **~band** *nt* banner.
**Sprüchemacher** [ˈʃprʏçəmaxər] (*umg*) *m*
patter-merchant.
**spruchreif** *adj:* **die Sache ist noch nicht ~** it's
not definite yet.
**Sprudel** [ˈʃpruːdəl] (-s, -) *m* mineral water;
(*süß*) lemonade.
**sprudeln** *vi* to bubble.
**Sprüh-** *zW:* **~dose** *f* aerosol (can); **s~en** *vi* to
spray; (*fig*) to sparkle ♦ *vt* to spray; **~regen**
*m* drizzle.
**Sprung** [ʃprʊŋ] (-(e)s, -̈e) *m* jump;
(*schwungvoll, fig: Gedanken~*) leap; (*Riß*)
crack; **immer auf dem ~ sein** (*umg*) to be
always on the go; **jdm auf die Sprünge**
**helfen** (*wohlwollend*) to give sb a (helping)
hand; **auf einen ~ bei jdm vorbeikommen**
(*umg*) to drop in to see sb; **damit kann man**
**keine großen Sprünge machen** (*umg*) you
can't exactly live it up on that; **~brett** *nt*
springboard; **~feder** *f* spring; **s~haft** *adj*
erratic; (*Aufstieg*) rapid; **~schanze** *f* ski
jump; **~turm** *m* diving platform.
**Spucke** [ˈʃpʊkə] (-) *f* spit.
**spucken** *vt, vi* to spit; **in die Hände ~** (*fig*) to
roll up one's sleeves.
**Spucknapf** *m* spittoon.
**Spucktüte** *f* sickbag.
**Spuk** [ʃpuːk] (-(e)s, -e) *m* haunting; (*fig*)
nightmare; **s~en** *vi* to haunt; **hier s~t es** this
place is haunted.
**Spülbecken** [ˈʃpyːlbɛkən] *nt* sink.
**Spule** [ˈʃpuːlə] (-, -n) *f* spool; (*ELEK*) coil.

**Spüle** ['ʃpyːlə] (-, -n) f (kitchen) sink.

**spülen** vt to rinse; (Geschirr) to wash, do; (Toilette) to flush ♦ vi to rinse; to wash up (BRIT), do the dishes; to flush; **etw an Land** ~ to wash sth ashore.

**Spül-** zW: **~maschine** f dishwasher; **~mittel** nt washing-up liquid (BRIT), dish-washing liquid; **~stein** m sink.

**Spülung** f rinsing; (Wasser~) flush; (MED) irrigation.

**Spund** [ʃpʊnt] (-(e)s, -e) m: **junger** ~ (veraltet: umg) young pup.

**Spur** [ʃpuːr] (-, -en) f trace; (Fuß~, Rad~, Tonband~) track; (Fährte) trail; (Fahr~) lane; **jdm auf die** ~ **kommen** to get onto sb; **(seine) ~en hinterlassen** (fig) to leave its mark; **keine** ~ (umg) not/nothing at all.

**spürbar** adj noticeable, perceptible.

**spuren** (umg) vi to obey; (sich fügen) to toe the line.

**spüren** ['ʃpyːrən] vt to feel; **etw zu** ~ **bekommen** (lit) to feel sth; (fig) to feel the (full) force of sth.

**Spurenelement** nt trace element.

**Spurensicherung** f securing of evidence.

**Spürhund** m tracker dog; (fig) sleuth.

**spurlos** adv without (a) trace; ~ **an jdm vorübergehen** to have no effect on sb.

**Spurt** [ʃpʊrt] (-(e)s, -s od -e) m spurt.

**spurten** vi (Hilfsverb sein: SPORT) to spurt; (umg: rennen) to sprint.

**Squash** [skvɔʃ] (-) nt (SPORT) squash.

**sputen** ['ʃpuːtən] vr to make haste.

**SS** (-) f abk (= Schutzstaffel) SS ♦ nt abk = **Sommersemester**.

**s. S.** abk (= siehe Seite) see p.

**SSV** abk = **Sommerschlußverkauf**.

**st** abk (= Stunde) h.

**St.** abk = **Stück**; (= Stunde) h.; (= Sankt) St.

**Staat** [ʃtaːt] (-(e)s, -en) m state; (Prunk) show; (Kleidung) finery; **mit etw** ~ **machen** to show off od parade sth.

**staatenlos** adj stateless.

**staatl.** abk = **staatlich**.

**staatlich** adj state attrib; state-run ♦ adv: ~ **geprüft** state-certified.

**Staats-** zW: **~affäre** f (lit) affair of state; (fig) major operation; **~angehörige(r)** f(m) national; **~angehörigkeit** f nationality; **~anleihe** f government bond; **~anwalt** m public prosecutor; **~bürger** m citizen; **~dienst** m civil service; **s~eigen** adj state-owned; **~eigentum** nt public ownership; **~examen** nt (UNIV) degree; **s~feindlich** adj subversive; **~geheimnis** nt (lit, fig hum) state secret; **~haushalt** m budget; **~kosten** pl public expenses pl; **~mann** (-(e)s, pl -männer) m statesman; **s~männisch** adj statesmanlike; **~oberhaupt** nt head of state; **~schuld** f (FIN) national debt; **~sekretär** m secretary of state; **~streich** m coup (d'état); **~verschuldung** f national

debt.

**Stab** [ʃtaːp] (-(e)s, ⸚e) m rod; (für ~hochsprung) pole; (für Staffellauf) baton; (Gitter~) bar; (Menschen) staff; (von Experten) panel.

**Stäbchen** ['ʃtɛːpçən] nt (Eß~) chopstick.

**Stabhochsprung** m pole vault.

**stabil** [ʃtaˈbiːl] adj stable; (Möbel) sturdy.

**Stabilisator** [ʃtabiliˈzaːtɔr] m stabilizer.

**stabilisieren** [ʃtabiliˈziːrən] vt to stabilize.

**Stabilisierung** f stabilization.

**Stabilität** [ʃtabiliˈtɛːt] f stability.

**Stabreim** m alliteration.

**Stabsarzt** m (MIL) captain in the medical corps.

**stach** etc [ʃtaːx] vb siehe **stechen**.

**Stachel** ['ʃtaxəl] (-s, -n) m spike; (von Tier) spine; (von Insekten) sting; **~beere** f gooseberry; **~draht** m barbed wire.

**stach(e)lig** adj prickly.

**Stachelschwein** nt porcupine.

**Stadion** ['ʃtaːdiɔn] (-s, Stadien) nt stadium.

**Stadium** ['ʃtaːdiʊm] nt stage, phase.

**Stadt** [ʃtat] (-, ⸚e) f town; (Groß~) city; (~verwaltung) (town/city) council; **~bad** nt municipal swimming baths pl; **s~bekannt** adj known all over town; **~bezirk** m municipal district.

**Städtchen** ['ʃtɛːtçən] nt small town.

**Städtebau** (-(e)s) m town planning.

**Städter(in)** (-s, -) m(f) town/city dweller, townie.

**Stadtgespräch** nt: (das) ~ **sein** to be the talk of the town.

**Stadtguerilla** f urban guerrilla.

**städtisch** adj municipal; (nicht ländlich) urban.

**Stadt-** zW: **~kasse** f town/city treasury; **~kern** m = **Stadtzentrum**; **~kreis** m town/city borough; **~mauer** f city wall(s pl); **~mitte** f town/city centre (BRIT) od center (US); **~park** m municipal park; **~plan** m street map; **~rand** m outskirts pl; **~rat** m (Behörde) (town/city) council; **~streicher** m street vagrant; **~streicherin** f bag lady; **~teil** m district, part of town; **~verwaltung** f (Behörde) municipal authority; **~viertel** m district od part of a town; **~zentrum** nt town/city centre (BRIT) od center (US).

**Staffel** ['ʃtafəl] (-, -n) f rung; (SPORT) relay (team); (AVIAT) squadron.

**Staffelei** [ʃtafəˈlaɪ] f easel.

**Staffellauf** m relay race.

**staffeln** vt to graduate.

**Staffelung** f graduation.

**Stagnation** [ʃtagnatsiˈoːn] f stagnation.

**stagnieren** [ʃtaˈgniːrən] vi to stagnate.

**Stahl** (-(e)s, ⸚e) m steel.

**stahl** etc [ʃtaːl] vb siehe **stehlen**.

**Stahlhelm** m steel helmet.

**stak** etc [ʃtaːk] vb siehe **stecken**.

**Stall** [ʃtal] (-(e)s, ⸚e) m stable; (Kaninchen~) hutch; (Schweine~) sty; (Hühner~) henhouse.

**Stallung** f stables pl.

**Stamm** [ʃtam] (-(e)s, ˝-e) m (Baum~) trunk; (Menschen~) tribe; (GRAM) stem; (Bakterien~) strain; ~aktie f ordinary share, common stock (US); ~baum m family tree; (von Tier) pedigree; ~buch nt book of family events with legal documents, ≈ family bible.

**stammeln** vt, vi to stammer.

**stammen** vi: ~ von od aus to come from.

**Stamm-** zW: ~form f base form; ~gast m regular (customer); ~halter m son and heir.

**stämmig** [ʃtɛmɪç] adj sturdy; (Mensch) stocky; **S~keit** f sturdiness; stockiness.

**Stamm-** zW: ~kapital nt (FIN) ordinary share od common stock (US) capital; ~kunde m, ~kundin f regular (customer); ~lokal nt favourite (BRIT) od favorite (US) café/ restaurant etc; (Kneipe) local (BRIT); ~platz m usual seat; ~tisch m (Tisch in Gasthaus) table reserved for the regulars.

**stampfen** [ʃtampfən] vi to stamp; (stapfen) to tramp ♦ vt (mit Stampfer) to mash.

**Stampfer** (-s, -) m (Stampfgerät) masher.

**Stand** (-(e)s, ˝-e) m position; (Wasser~, Benzin~ etc) level; (Zähler~ etc) reading; (Stehen) standing position; (Zustand) state; (Spiel~) score; (Messe~ etc) stand; (Klasse) class; (Beruf) profession; **bei jdm** od **gegen jdn einen schweren ~ haben** (fig) to have a hard time of it with sb; **etw auf den neuesten ~ bringen** to bring sth up to date.

**stand** etc [ʃtant] vb siehe **stehen**.

**Standard** [ʃtandart] (-s, -s) m standard; ~ausführung f standard design.

**standardisieren** [ʃtandardi'ziːrən] vt to standardize.

**Standarte** (-, -n) f (MIL, POL) standard.

**Standbild** nt statue.

**Ständchen** [ʃtɛntçən] nt serenade.

**Ständer** (-s, -) m stand.

**Standes-** zW: ~amt nt registry office (BRIT), city/county clerk's office (US); **s~amtlich** adj: **s~amtliche Trauung** registry office wedding (BRIT), civil marriage ceremony; ~beamte(r) m registrar; ~bewußtsein nt status consciousness; ~dünkel m snobbery; **s~gemäß** adj, adv according to one's social position; ~unterschied m social difference.

**Stand-** zW: **s~fest** adj (Tisch, Leiter) stable, steady; (fig) steadfast; **s~haft** adj steadfast; ~haftigkeit f steadfastness; **s~halten** unreg vi: **(jdm/etw) s~halten** to stand firm (against sb/sth), resist (sb/sth).

**ständig** [ʃtɛndɪç] adj permanent; (ununterbrochen) constant, continual.

**Stand-** zW: ~licht nt sidelights pl (BRIT), parking lights pl (US); ~ort m location; (MIL) garrison; ~pause (umg) f: **jdm eine ~pause halten** to give sb a lecture; ~punkt m standpoint; **s~rechtlich** adj: **s~rechtlich erschießen** to put before a firing squad;

~spur f (AUT) hard shoulder (BRIT), berm (US).

**Stange** [ʃtaŋə] (-, -n) f stick; (Stab) pole; (Quer~) bar; (Zigaretten) carton; **von der ~** (COMM) off the peg (BRIT) od rack (US); **eine ~ Geld** quite a packet; **jdm die ~ halten** (umg) to stick up for sb; **bei der ~ bleiben** (umg) to stick at od to sth.

**Stangenbohne** f runner bean.

**Stangenbrot** nt French bread; (Laib) French stick (loaf).

**stank** etc [ʃtaŋk] vb siehe **stinken**.

**stänkern** [ʃtɛŋkərn] (umg) vi to stir things up.

**Stanniol** [ʃtani'oːl] (-s, -e) nt tinfoil.

**Stanze** [ʃtantsə] (-, -n) f stanza; (TECH) stamp.

**stanzen** vt to stamp; (Löcher) to punch.

**Stapel** [ʃtaːpəl] (-s, -) m pile; (NAUT) stocks pl; ~lauf m launch.

**stapeln** vt to pile (up).

**Stapelverarbeitung** f (COMPUT) batch processing.

**stapfen** [ʃtapfən] vi to trudge, plod.

**Star¹** [ʃtaːr] (-(e)s, -e) m starling; **grauer/ grüner ~** (MED) cataract/glaucoma.

**Star²** [ʃtaːr] (-s, -s) m (Film~ etc) star.

**starb** etc [ʃtarp] vb siehe **sterben**.

**stark** [ʃtark] adj strong; (heftig, groß) heavy; (Maßangabe) thick; (umg: hervorragend) great ♦ adv very; (beschädigt etc) badly; (vergrößert, verkleinert) greatly; **das ist ein ~es Stück!** (umg) that's a bit much!; **sich für etw ~ machen** (umg) to stand up for sth; **er ist ~ erkältet** he has a bad cold.

**Stärke** [ʃtɛrkə] (-, -n) f strength (auch fig); heaviness; thickness; (von Mannschaft) size; (KOCH, Wäsche~) starch; ~mehl nt (KOCH) thickening agent.

**stärken** vt (lit, fig) to strengthen; (Wäsche) to starch; (Selbstbewußtsein) to boost; (Gesundheit) to improve; (erfrischen) to fortify ♦ vi to be fortifying; ~des Mittel tonic.

**Starkstrom** m heavy current.

**Stärkung** [ʃtɛrkʊŋ] f strengthening; (Essen) refreshment.

**Stärkungsmittel** nt tonic.

**starr** [ʃtar] adj stiff; (unnachgiebig) rigid; (Blick) staring.

**starren** vi to stare; ~ **vor** +dat od **von** (voll von) to be covered in; (Waffen) to be bristling with; **vor sich** akk **hin ~** to stare straight ahead.

**starr-** zW: **S~heit** f rigidity; ~köpfig adj stubborn; **S~sinn** m obstinacy.

**Start** [ʃtart] (-(e)s, -e) m start; (AVIAT) takeoff; ~automatik f (AUT) automatic choke; ~bahn f runway; **s~en** vi to start; (AVIAT) to take off ♦ vt to start; ~er (-s, -) m starter; ~erlaubnis f takeoff clearance; ~hilfe f (AVIAT) rocket-assisted takeoff; (fig) initial aid; **jdm ~hilfe geben** to help sb get off the ground; ~**hilfekabel** nt jump leads pl (BRIT), jumper cables pl (US); **s~klar** adj (AVIAT) clear for takeoff; (SPORT) ready to start; ~**kommando** nt (SPORT) starting signal; ~**zeichen** nt start signal.

**Stasi** ['ʃtaːzi] (-s) (umg) f abk (früher: = Staatssicherheitsdienst der DDR) Stasi.

> Stasi, an abbreviation of Staatssicherheitsdienst, the **DDR** secret service, was founded in 1950 and disbanded in 1989. The Stasi organized an extensive spy network of full-time and part-time workers who often held positions of trust in both the DDR and the **BRD**. They held personal files on 6 million people.

**Station** [ʃtatsi'oːn] f station; (Kranken~) hospital ward; (Haltestelle) stop; ~ **machen** to stop off.

**stationär** [ʃtatsio'nɛːr] adj stationary; (MED) in-patient attrib.

**stationieren** [ʃtatsio'niːrən] vt to station; (Atomwaffen etc) to deploy.

**Stations-** zW: ~**arzt** m ward doctor; ~**ärztin** f ward doctor; ~**vorsteher** m (EISENB) stationmaster.

**statisch** ['ʃtaːtɪʃ] adj static.

**Statist(in)** [ʃta'tɪst(ɪn)] m(f) (FILM) extra; (THEAT) supernumerary.

**Statistik** f statistic; (Wissenschaft) statistics sing.

**Statistiker(in)** (-s, -) m(f) statistician.

**statistisch** adj statistical.

**Stativ** [ʃta'tiːf] (-s, -e) nt tripod.

**Statt** [ʃtat] (-) f place.

**statt** konj instead of ♦ präp (+dat od gen) instead of; ~ **dessen** instead.

**Stätte** ['ʃtɛtə] (-, -n) f place.

**statt-** zW: ~**finden** unreg vi to take place; ~**haft** adj admissible; **S~halter** m governor; ~**lich** adj imposing, handsome; (Bursche) strapping; (Sammlung) impressive; (Familie) large; (Summe) handsome.

**Statue** ['ʃtaːtuə] (-, -n) f statue.

**Statur** [ʃta'tuːr] f build.

**Status** ['ʃtaːtʊs] (-, -) m status; ~**symbol** nt status symbol.

**Statuten** [ʃta'tuːtən] pl by(e)-law(s pl).

**Stau** [ʃtaʊ] (-(e)s, -e) m blockage; (Verkehrs~) (traffic) jam.

**Staub** [ʃtaʊp] (-(e)s) m dust; ~ **wischen** to dust; **sich aus dem** ~ **machen** (umg) to clear off.

**stauben** ['ʃtaʊbən] vi to be dusty.

**Staubfaden** m (BOT) stamen.

**staubig** ['ʃtaʊbɪç] adj dusty.

**Staub-** zW: ~**lappen** m duster; ~**lunge** f (MED) dust on the lung; **s~saugen** (pp **s~gesaugt**) vi untr to vacuum; ~**sauger** m vacuum cleaner; ~**tuch** nt duster.

**Staudamm** m dam.

**Staude** ['ʃtaʊdə] (-, -n) f shrub.

**stauen** ['ʃtaʊən] vt (Wasser) to dam up; (Blut) to stop the flow of ♦ vr (Wasser) to become dammed up; (MED, Verkehr) to become congested; (Menschen) to collect together; (Gefühle) to build up.

**staunen** ['ʃtaʊnən] vi to be astonished; **da kann man nur noch** ~ it's just amazing; **S~** (-s) nt amazement.

**Stausee** ['ʃtaʊzeː] m reservoir; artificial lake.

**Stauung** ['ʃtaʊʊŋ] f (von Wasser) damming-up; (von Blut, Verkehr) congestion.

**Std., Stde.** abk (= Stunde) h.

**stdl.** abk = **stündlich**.

**Steak** [ʃteːk] (-s, -s) nt steak.

**Stechen** ['ʃtɛçən] (-s, -) nt (SPORT) play-off; (Springreiten) jump-off; (Schmerz) sharp pain.

**stechen** unreg vt (mit Nadel etc) to prick; (mit Messer) to stab; (mit Finger) to poke; (Biene etc) to sting; (Mücke) to bite; (KARTEN) to take; (KUNST) to engrave; (Torf, Spargel) to cut ♦ vi (Sonne) to beat down; (mit Stechkarte) to clock in ♦ vr: **sich** akk od dat **in den Finger** ~ to prick one's finger; **es sticht** it is prickly; **in See** ~ to put to sea.

**stechend** adj piercing, stabbing; (Geruch) pungent.

**Stech-** zW: ~**ginster** m gorse; ~**karte** f clocking-in card; ~**mücke** f gnat; ~**palme** f holly; ~**uhr** f time clock.

**Steck-** zW: ~**brief** m "wanted" poster; **s~brieflich** adv: **s~brieflich gesucht werden** to be wanted; ~**dose** f (wall) socket.

**stecken** ['ʃtɛkən] vt to put; (einführen) to insert; (Nadel) to stick; (Pflanzen) to plant; (beim Nähen) to pin ♦ vi (auch unreg) to be; (festsitzen) to be stuck; (Nadeln) to stick; **etw in etw** akk ~ (umg: Geld, Mühe) to put sth into sth; (: Zeit) to devote sth to sth; **der Schlüssel steckt** the key is in the lock; **wo steckt er?** where has he got to?; **zeigen, was in einem steckt** to show what one is made of; ~**bleiben** unreg vi to get stuck; ~**lassen** unreg vt to leave in.

**Steckenpferd** nt hobbyhorse.

**Stecker** (-s, -) m (ELEK) plug.

**Steck-** zW: ~**nadel** f pin; ~**rübe** f swede, turnip; ~**schlüssel** m box spanner (BRIT) od wrench (US); ~**zwiebel** f bulb.

**Steg** [ʃteːk] (-(e)s, -e) m small bridge; (Anlege~) landing stage.

**Stegreif** m: **aus dem** ~ just like that.

**Stehaufmännchen** ['ʃteː|aʊfmɛnçən] nt (Spielzeug) tumbler.

**stehen** ['ʃteːən] unreg vi to stand; (sich befinden) to be; (in Zeitung) to say; (angehalten haben) to have stopped ♦ vi unpers: **es steht schlecht um ...** things are bad for ... ♦ vr: **sich gut/schlecht** ~ to be well-off/badly off; **zu jdm/etw** ~ to stand by sb/sth; **jdm** ~ to suit sb; **ich tue, was in meinen**

**Kräften steht** I'll do everything I can; **es steht 2:1 für München** the score is 2-1 to Munich; **mit dem Dativ ~** (*GRAM*) to take the dative; **auf Betrug steht eine Gefängnisstrafe** the penalty for fraud is imprisonment; **wie ~ Sie dazu?** what are your views on that?; **wie steht's?** how are things?; (*SPORT*) what's the score?; **wie steht es damit?** how about it?; (*Uhr*) to stop; (*Zeit*) to stand still; (*Auto, Zug*) to stand; (*Fehler*) to stay as it is; (*Verkehr, Produktion etc*) to come to a standstill *od* stop.

**stehend** *adj attrib* (*Fahrzeug*) stationary; (*Gewässer*) stagnant; (*ständig: Heer*) regular.

**stehenlassen** *unreg vt* to leave; (*Bart*) to grow; **alles stehen- und liegenlassen** to drop everything.

**Stehlampe** *f* standard lamp (*BRIT*), floor lamp (*US*).

**stehlen** ['ʃteːlən] *unreg vt* to steal.

**Stehplatz** *m*: **ein ~ kostet 10 Mark** a standing ticket costs 10 marks.

**Stehvermögen** *nt* staying power, stamina.

**Steiermark** ['ʃtaɪrmark] *f*: **die ~** Styria.

**steif** [ʃtaɪf] *adj* stiff; **~ und fest auf etw** *dat* **beharren** to insist stubbornly on sth.

**Steifftier** ® ['ʃtaɪftiːr] *nt soft toy animal*.

**Steifheit** *f* stiffness.

**Steigbügel** ['ʃtaɪkbyːgəl] *m* stirrup.

**Steigeisen** *nt* crampon.

**steigen** *unreg vi* to rise; (*klettern*) to climb ♦ *vt* (*Treppen, Stufen*) to climb (up); **das Blut stieg ihm in den Kopf** the blood rushed to his head; **~ in** +*akk*/**auf** +*akk* to get in/on.

**Steiger** (**-s, -**) *m* (*MIN*) pit foreman.

**steigern** *vt* to raise; (*GRAM*) to compare ♦ *vi* (*Auktion*) to bid ♦ *vr* to increase.

**Steigerung** *f* raising; (*GRAM*) comparison.

**Steigung** *f* incline, gradient, rise.

**steil** [ʃtaɪl] *adj* steep; **S~hang** *m* steep slope; **S~paß** *m* (*SPORT*) through ball.

**Stein** [ʃtaɪn] (**-(e)s, -e**) *m* stone; (*in Uhr*) jewel; **mir fällt ein ~ vom Herzen!** (*fig*) that's a load off my mind!; **bei jdm einen ~ im Brett haben** (*fig: umg*) to be well in with sb; **jdm ~e in den Weg legen** to make things difficult for sb; **~adler** *m* golden eagle; **s~alt** *adj* ancient; **~bock** *m* (*ASTROL*) Capricorn; **~bruch** *m* quarry.

**steinern** *adj* (made of) stone; (*fig*) stony.

**Stein-** *zW*: **~erweichen** *nt*: **zum ~erweichen weinen** to cry heartbreakingly; **~garten** *m* rockery; **~gut** *nt* stoneware; **s~hart** *adj* hard as stone.

**steinig** *adj* stony.

**steinigen** *vt* to stone.

**Stein-** *zW*: **~kohle** *f* mineral coal; **~metz** (**-es, -e**) *m* stonemason; **s~reich** (*umg*) *adj* stinking rich; **~schlag** *m*: „**Achtung ~schlag**" "danger - falling stones"; **~wurf** *m* (*fig*) stone's throw; **~zeit** *f* Stone Age.

**Steiß** [ʃtaɪs] (**-es, -e**) *m* rump; **~bein** *nt* (*ANAT*) coccyx.

**Stelle** ['ʃtɛlə] (**-, -n**) *f* place; (*Arbeit*) post, job; (*Amt*) office; (*Abschnitt*) passage; (*Text~, bes beim Zitieren*) reference; **drei ~n hinter dem Komma** (*MATH*) three decimal places; **eine freie** *od* **offene ~** a vacancy; **an dieser ~** in this place, here; **an anderer ~** elsewhere; **nicht von der ~ kommen** not to make any progress; **auf der ~** (*fig: sofort*) on the spot.

**stellen** *vt* to put; (*Uhr etc*) to set; (*zur Verfügung ~*) to supply; (*fassen: Dieb*) to apprehend; (*Antrag, Forderung*) to make; (*Aufnahme*) to pose; (*arrangieren: Szene*) to arrange ♦ *vr* (*sich auf~*) to stand; (*sich einfinden*) to present o.s.; (*bei Polizei*) to give o.s. up; (*vorgeben*) to pretend (to be); **das Radio lauter/leiser ~** to turn the radio up/down; **auf sich** *akk* **selbst gestellt sein** (*fig*) to have to fend for o.s.; **sich hinter jdn/etw ~** (*fig*) to support sb/sth; **sich einer Herausforderung ~** to take up a challenge; **sich zu etw ~** to have an opinion of sth.

**Stellen-** *zW*: **~angebot** *nt* offer of a post; (*in Zeitung*): „**~angebote**" "vacancies"; **~anzeige** *f* job advertisement *od* ad (*umg*); **~gesuch** *nt* application for a post; „**~gesuche**" "situations wanted"; **~markt** *m* job market; (*in Zeitung*) appointments section; **~nachweis** *m* employment agency; **~vermittlung** *f* employment agency; **s~weise** *adv* in places; **~wert** *m* (*fig*) status.

**Stellung** *f* position; (*MIL*) line; **~ nehmen zu** to comment on.

**Stellungnahme** *f* comment.

**stellungslos** *adj* unemployed.

**stellv.** *abk* = **stellvertretend**.

**Stell-** *zW*: **s~vertretend** *adj* deputy *attrib*, acting *attrib*; **~vertreter** *m* (*von Amts wegen*) deputy, representative; **~werk** *nt* (*EISENB*) signal box.

**Stelze** ['ʃtɛltsə] (**-, -n**) *f* stilt.

**stelzen** (*umg*) *vi* to stalk.

**Stemmbogen** *m* (*SKI*) stem turn.

**Stemmeisen** *nt* crowbar.

**stemmen** ['ʃtɛmən] *vt* to lift (up); (*drücken*) to press; **sich ~ gegen** (*fig*) to resist, oppose.

**Stempel** ['ʃtɛmpəl] (**-s, -**) *m* stamp; (*Post~*) postmark; (*TECH: Präge~*) die; (*BOT*) pistil; **~gebühr** *f* stamp duty; **~kissen** *nt* inkpad.

**stempeln** *vt* to stamp; (*Briefmarke*) to cancel ♦ *vi* (*umg: Stempeluhr betätigen*) to clock in/out; **~ gehen** (*umg*) to be *od* go on the dole (*BRIT*) *od* on welfare (*US*).

**Stengel** ['ʃtɛŋəl] (**-s, -**) *m* stalk; **vom ~ fallen** (*umg: überrascht sein*) to be staggered.

**Steno** ['ʃteno] (*umg*) *f* shorthand; **~gramm** [-'gram] *nt* text in shorthand; **~graph(in)** [-graːf(ɪn)] *m(f)* (*im Büro*) shorthand secretary; **~graphie** [-graˈfiː] *f* shorthand; **s~graphieren** [-graˈfiːrən] *vt, vi* to write (in) shorthand; **~typist(in)** [-tyˈpɪst(ɪn)] *m(f)*

shorthand typist (*BRIT*), stenographer (*US*).
**Steppdecke** *f* quilt.
**Steppe** (-, -n) *f* steppe.
**steppen** ['ʃtɛpən] *vt* to stitch ♦ *vi* to tap-dance.
**Steptanz** *m* tap-dance.
**Sterbe-** *zW:* ~**bett** *nt* deathbed; ~**fall** *m* death;
~**hilfe** *f* euthanasia; ~**kasse** *f* death benefit
fund.
**sterben** ['ʃtɛrbən] *unreg vi* to die; **an einer
Krankheit/Verletzung** ~ to die of an illness/
from an injury; **er ist für mich gestorben**
(*fig: umg*) he might as well be dead.
**Sterben** *nt:* **im** ~ **liegen** to be dying.
**sterbenslangweilig** (*umg*) *adj* deadly boring.
**Sterbenswörtchen** (*umg*) *nt:* **er hat kein**
~ **gesagt** he didn't say a word.
**Sterbeurkunde** *f* death certificate.
**sterblich** ['ʃtɛrplɪç] *adj* mortal; **S~keit** *f*
mortality; **S~keitsziffer** *f* death rate.
**stereo-** ['ste:reo] *in zW* stereo(-); **S~anlage** *f*
stereo unit; ~**typ** *adj* stereotyped.
**steril** [ʃte'ri:l] *adj* sterile.
**sterilisieren** [ʃterili'zi:rən] *vt* to sterilize.
**Sterilisierung** *f* sterilization.
**Stern** [ʃtɛrn] (-(e)s, -e) *m* star; **das steht (noch)
in den** ~**en** (*fig*) it's in the lap of the gods;
~**bild** *nt* constellation; ~**chen** *nt* asterisk;
~**enbanner** *nt* Stars and Stripes *sing*;
**s~hagelvoll** (*umg*) *adj* legless; ~**schnuppe**
(-, -n) *f* meteor, falling star; ~**stunde** *f*
historic moment; ~**warte** *f* observatory;
~**zeichen** *nt* (*ASTROL*) sign of the zodiac.
**stet** [ʃte:t] *adj* steady.
**Stethoskop** [ʃteto'sko:p] (-(e)s, -e) *nt*
stethoscope.
**stetig** *adj* constant, continual; (*MATH:
Funktion*) continuous.
**stets** *adv* continually, always.
**Steuer**¹ ['ʃtɔyər] (-s, -) *nt* (*NAUT*) helm;
(~*ruder*) rudder; (*AUT*) steering wheel; **am**
~ **sitzen** (*AUT*) to be at the wheel; (*AVIAT*) to
be at the controls.
**Steuer**² (-, -n) *f* tax.
**Steuer-** *zW:* ~**befreiung** *f* tax exemption;
**s~begünstigt** *adj* (*Investitionen, Hypothek*)
tax-deductible; (*Waren*) taxed at a lower
rate; ~**berater(in)** *m(f)* tax consultant;
~**bescheid** *m* tax assessment; ~**bord** *nt*
starboard; ~**erhöhung** *f* tax increase;
~**erklärung** *f* tax return; **s~frei** *adj* tax-free;
~**freibetrag** *m* tax allowance;
~**hinterziehung** *f* tax evasion; ~**jahr** *nt*
fiscal *od* tax year; ~**karte** *f* tax notice;
~**klasse** *f* tax group; ~**knüppel** *m*
control column; (*AVIAT, COMPUT*)
joystick; **s~lich** *adj* tax *attrib*; ~**mann**
(-(e)s, *pl* -**männer** *od* -**leute**) *m* helmsman.
**steuern** *vt* to steer; (*Flugzeug*) to pilot;
(*Entwicklung, Tonstärke*) to control ♦ *vi* to
steer; (*in Flugzeug etc*) to be at the controls;
(*bei Entwicklung etc*) to be in control.
**Steuer-** *zW:* ~**nummer** *f* ≈ National

Insurance Number (*BRIT*), Social Security
Number (*US*); ~**paradies** *nt* tax haven;
**s~pflichtig** *adj* taxable; (*Person*) liable to pay
tax; ~**progression** *f* progressive taxation;
~**prüfung** *f* tax inspector's investigation;
~**rad** *nt* steering wheel; ~**rückvergütung** *f*
tax rebate; ~**senkung** *f* tax cut.
**Steuerung** *f* steering (*auch AUT*); piloting;
control; (*Vorrichtung*) controls *pl*;
**automatische** ~ (*AVIAT*) autopilot; (*TECH*)
automatic steering (device).
**Steuer-** *zW:* ~**vergünstigung** *f* tax relief;
~**zahler** *m* taxpayer; ~**zuschlag** *m* additional
tax.
**Steward** ['stju:ərt] (-s, -s) *m* steward.
**Stewardeß** ['stju:ərdɛs] (-, -essen) *f*
stewardess.
**StGB** (-s) *nt abk* = **Strafgesetzbuch.**
**stibitzen** [ʃti'bɪtsən] (*umg*) *vt* to pilfer, pinch
(*umg*).
**Stich** [ʃtɪç] (-(e)s, -e) *m* (*Insekten~*) sting;
(*Messer~*) stab; (*beim Nähen*) stitch;
(*Färbung*) tinge; (*KARTEN*) trick; (*ART*)
engraving; (*fig*) pang; **ein** ~ **ins Rote** a tinge
of red; **einen** ~ **haben** (*umg: Eßwaren*) to be
bad *od* off (*BRIT*); (: *Mensch: verrückt sein*) to
be nuts; **jdn im** ~ **lassen** to leave sb in the
lurch.
**Stichel** (-s, -) *m* engraving tool, style.
**Stichelei** [ʃtɪçə'laɪ] *f* jibe, taunt.
**sticheln** *vi* (*fig*) to jibe; (*pej: umg*) to make
snide remarks.
**Stich-** *zW:* ~**flamme** *f* tongue of flame;
**s~haltig** *adj* valid; (*Beweis*) conclusive;
~**probe** *f* spot check.
**sticht** [ʃtɪçt] *vb siehe* **stechen.**
**Stichtag** *m* qualifying date.
**Stichwahl** *f* final ballot.
**Stichwort** *nt* (*pl* -**worte**) cue; (: *für Vortrag*)
note; (*pl* -**wörter**: *in Wörterbuch*) headword;
~**katalog** *m* classified catalogue (*BRIT*) *od*
catalog (*US*); ~**verzeichnis** *nt* index.
**Stichwunde** *f* stab wound.
**sticken** ['ʃtɪkən] *vt, vi* to embroider.
**Stickerei** [ʃtɪkə'raɪ] *f* embroidery.
**stickig** *adj* stuffy, close.
**Stickstoff** (-(e)s) *m* nitrogen.
**stieben** ['ʃti:bən] *vi* (*geh: sprühen*) to fly.
**Stief-** ['ʃti:f] *in zW* step-.
**Stiefel** ['ʃti:fəl] (-s, -) *m* boot; (*Trinkgefäß*)
*large boot-shaped beer glass.*
**Stief-** *zW:* ~**kind** *nt* stepchild; (*fig*) Cinderella;
~**mutter** *f* stepmother; ~**mütterchen** *nt*
pansy; **s~mütterlich** *adj* (*fig*): **jdn/etw
s~mütterlich behandeln** to pay little
attention to sb/sth; ~**vater** *m* stepfather.
**stieg** *etc* [ʃti:k] *vb siehe* **steigen.**
**Stiege** ['ʃti:gə] (-, -n) *f* staircase.
**Stieglitz** ['ʃti:glɪts] (-es, -e) *m* goldfinch.
**stiehlt** [ʃti:lt] *vb siehe* **stehlen.**
**Stiel** [ʃti:l] (-(e)s, -e) *m* handle; (*BOT*) stalk.
**Stielaugen** *pl* (*fig: umg*): **er machte** ~ his eyes

(nearly) popped out of his head.
**Stier** (-(e)s, -e) m bull; (*ASTROL*) Taurus.
**stier** [ʃtiːr] adj staring, fixed.
**stieren** vi to stare.
**Stierkampf** m bullfight.
**stieß** etc [ʃtiːs] vb siehe **stoßen.**
**Stift** [ʃtɪft] (-(e)s, -e) m peg; (*Nagel*) tack; (*Bunt~*) crayon; (*Blei~*) pencil; (*umg: Lehrling*) apprentice (boy).
**stiften** vt to found; (*Unruhe*) to cause; (*spenden*) to contribute; **~gehen** unreg (*umg*) vi to hop it.
**Stifter(in)** (-s, -) m(f) founder.
**Stiftung** f donation; (*Organisation*) foundation.
**Stiftzahn** m post crown.
**Stil** [ʃtiːl] (-(e)s, -e) m style; (*Eigenart*) way, manner; **~blüte** f howler; **~bruch** m stylistic incongruity.
**stilistisch** [ʃtiˈlɪstɪʃ] adj stylistic.
**still** [ʃtɪl] adj quiet; (*unbewegt*) still; (*heimlich*) secret; **ich dachte mir im ~en** I thought to myself; **er ist ein ~es Wasser** he's a deep one; **~er Teilhaber** (*COMM*) sleeping (*BRIT*) od silent (*US*) partner; **der S~e Ozean** the Pacific (Ocean).
**Stille** (-, -n) f quietness; stillness; **in aller ~** quietly.
**Stilleben** nt siehe **Still(l)eben.**
**Stillegung** f siehe **Still(l)egung.**
**stillen** vt to stop; (*befriedigen*) to satisfy; (*Säugling*) to breast-feed.
**still-** zW: **~gestanden** interj attention!; **S~halteabkommen** nt (*FIN, fig*) moratorium; **~halten** unreg vi to keep still; **S~(l)leben** nt still life; **~(l)legen** vt to close down; **S~(l)legung** f (*Betrieb*) shut-down, closure; **~(l)liegen** unreg vi (*außer Betrieb sein*) to be shut down; (*lahmliegen*) to be at a standstill; **S~schweigen** nt silence; **~schweigen** unreg vi to be silent; **~schweigend** adj silent; (*Einverständnis*) tacit ♦ adv silently; tacitly; **S~stand** m standstill; **~stehen** unreg vi to stand still.
**Stilmöbel** pl reproduction od (*antik*) period furniture sing.
**stilvoll** adj stylish.
**Stimm-** zW: **~abgabe** f voting; **~bänder** pl vocal cords pl; **s~berechtigt** adj entitled to vote; **~bruch** m: **er ist im ~bruch** his voice is breaking.
**Stimme** [ʃtɪmə] (-, -n) f voice; (*Wahl~*) vote; (*MUS: Rolle*) part; **mit leiser/lauter ~** in a soft/loud voice; **seine ~ abgeben** to vote.
**stimmen** vi (*richtig sein*) to be right; (*wählen*) to vote ♦ vt (*Instrument*) to tune; **stimmt so!** that's all right; **für/gegen etw ~** to vote for/against sth; **jdn traurig ~** to make sb feel sad.
**Stimmen-** zW: **~gewirr** nt babble of voices; **~gleichheit** f tied vote; **~mehrheit** f majority (of votes).

**Stimm-** zW: **~enthaltung** f abstention; **~gabel** f tuning fork; **s~haft** adj voiced.
**stimmig** adj harmonious.
**Stimm-** zW: **s~los** adj (*LING*) unvoiced; **~recht** nt right to vote; **s~rechtslos** adj: **s~rechtslose Aktien** "A" shares.
**Stimmung** f mood; (*Atmosphäre*) atmosphere; (*Moral*) morale; **in ~ kommen** to liven up; **~ gegen/für jdn/etw machen** to stir up (public) opinion against/in favour of sb/sth.
**Stimmungs-** zW: **~kanone** (*umg*) f life and soul of the party; **~mache** (*pej*) f cheap propaganda; **s~voll** adj (*Atmosphäre*) enjoyable; (*Gedicht*) full of atmosphere.
**Stimmzettel** m ballot paper.
**stinken** [ʃtɪŋkən] unreg vi to stink; **die Sache stinkt mir** (*umg*) I'm fed-up to the back teeth (with it).
**Stink-** zW: **s~faul** (*umg*) adj bone-lazy; **s~langweilig** (*umg*) adj deadly boring; **~tier** nt skunk; **~wut** (*umg*) f: **eine ~wut (auf jdn) haben** to be livid (with sb).
**Stipendium** [ʃtiˈpɛndiʊm] nt grant; (*als Auszeichnung*) scholarship.
**Stippvisite** [ˈʃtɪpviˈziːtə] (*umg*) f flying visit.
**stirbt** [ʃtɪrpt] vb siehe **sterben.**
**Stirn** [ʃtɪrn] (-, -en) f forehead, brow; (*Frechheit*) impudence; **die ~ haben zu ...** to have the nerve to ...; **~band** nt headband; **~höhle** f sinus; **~runzeln** (-s) nt frown.
**stob** etc [ʃtoːp] vb siehe **stieben.**
**stöbern** [ˈʃtøːbərn] vi to rummage.
**stochern** [ˈʃtɔxərn] vi to poke (about).
**Stock¹** [ʃtɔk] (-(e)s, ⸚e) m stick; (*Rohr~*) cane; (*Zeige~*) pointer; (*BOT*) stock; **über ~ und Stein** up hill and down dale.
**Stock²** [ʃtɔk] (-(e)s, - od -werke) m storey (*BRIT*), story (*US*); **im ersten ~** on the first (*BRIT*) od second (*US*) floor.
**stock-** in zW (*vor adj: umg*) completely.
**Stöckelschuh** [ˈʃtœkəlʃuː] m stiletto-heeled shoe.
**stocken** vi to stop, pause; (*Arbeit, Entwicklung*) to make no progress; (*im Satz*) to break off; (*Verkehr*) to be held up.
**stockend** adj halting.
**stockfinster** (*umg*) adj pitch-dark.
**Stockholm** [ˈʃtɔkhɔlm] (-s) nt Stockholm.
**stocksauer** (*umg*) adj pissed-off (*!*).
**stocktaub** adj stone-deaf.
**Stockung** f stoppage.
**Stockwerk** nt storey (*BRIT*), story (*US*), floor.
**Stoff** [ʃtɔf] (-(e)s, -e) m (*Gewebe*) material, cloth; (*Materie*) matter; (*von Buch etc*) subject (matter); (*umg: Rauschgift*) dope.
**Stoffel** (-s, -) (*pej: umg*) m lout, boor.
**Stoff-** zW: **s~lich** adj with regard to subject matter; **~rest** m remnant; **~tier** nt soft toy; **~wechsel** m metabolism.
**stöhnen** [ˈʃtøːnən] vi to groan.
**stoisch** [ˈʃtoːɪʃ] adj stoical.

**Stola** ['ʃtoːla] (-, **Stolen**) f stole.
**Stollen** ['ʃtɔlən] (-s, -) m (MIN) gallery; (KOCH) stollen, *cake eaten at Christmas*; (von Schuhen) stud.
**stolpern** ['ʃtɔlpərn] vi to stumble, trip; (fig: zu Fall kommen) to come a cropper (umg).
**stolz** [ʃtɔlts] adj proud; (imposant: Bauwerk) majestic; (ironisch: Preis) princely; **S~** (-es) m pride.
**stolzieren** [ʃtɔl'tsiːrən] vi to strut.
**stopfen** ['ʃtɔpfən] vt (hinein~) to stuff; (voll~) to fill (up); (nähen) to darn ♦ vi (MED) to cause constipation; **jdm das Maul ~** (umg) to silence sb.
**Stopfgarn** nt darning thread.
**Stopp** [ʃtɔp] (-s, -s) m stop, halt; (Lohn~) freeze.
**Stoppel** ['ʃtɔpəl] (-, -n) f stubble.
**stoppen** vt to stop; (mit Uhr) to time ♦ vi to stop.
**Stoppschild** nt stop sign.
**Stoppuhr** f stopwatch.
**Stöpsel** ['ʃtœpsəl] (-s, -) m plug; (für Flaschen) stopper.
**Stör** [ʃtøːr] (-(e)s, -e) m sturgeon.
**Störaktion** f disruptive action.
**störanfällig** adj susceptible to interference od breakdown.
**Storch** [ʃtɔrç] (-(e)s, ⁻e) m stork.
**Store** [ʃtoːr] (-s, -s) m net curtain.
**stören** ['ʃtøːrən] vt to disturb; (behindern, RUNDF) to interfere with ♦ vr: **sich an etw** dat **~** to let sth bother one ♦ vi to get in the way; **was mich an ihm/daran stört** what I don't like about him/it; **stört es Sie, wenn ich rauche?** do you mind if I smoke?; **ich möchte nicht ~** I don't want to be in the way.
**störend** adj disturbing, annoying.
**Störenfried** (-(e)s, -e) m troublemaker.
**Störfall** m (in Kraftwerk etc) malfunction, accident.
**stornieren** [ʃtɔr'niːrən] vt (COMM: Auftrag) to cancel; (: Buchungsfehler) to reverse.
**Storno** ['ʃtɔrno] (-s) m od nt (COMM: von Buchungsfehler) reversal; (: von Auftrag) cancellation (BRIT), cancelation (US).
**störrisch** ['ʃtœrɪʃ] adj stubborn, perverse.
**Störsender** m jammer, jamming transmitter.
**Störung** f disturbance; interference; (TECH) fault; (MED) disorder.
**Störungsstelle** f (TEL) faults service.
**Stoß** [ʃtoːs] (-es, ⁻e) m (Schub) push; (leicht) poke; (Schlag) blow; (mit Schwert) thrust; (mit Ellbogen) nudge; (mit Fuß) kick; (Erd~) shock; (Haufen) pile; **seinem Herzen einen ~ geben** to pluck up courage; **~dämpfer** m shock absorber.
**Stößel** ['ʃtøːsəl] (-s, -) m pestle; (AUT: Ventil~) tappet.
**stoßen** unreg vt (mit Druck) to shove, push; (mit Schlag) to knock, bump; (mit Ellbogen) to nudge; (mit Fuß) to kick; (mit Schwert) to thrust; (an~: Kopf etc) to bump; (zerkleinern) to pulverize ♦ vr to get a knock ♦ vi: **~ an** od **auf** +akk to bump into; (finden) to come across; (angrenzen) to be next to; **sich ~ an** +dat (fig) to take exception to; **zu jdm ~** to meet up with sb.
**Stoßgebet** nt quick prayer.
**Stoßstange** f (AUT) bumper.
**stößt** [ʃtøːst] vb siehe **stoßen.**
**Stoß-** zW: **~verkehr** m rush-hour traffic; **~zahn** m tusk; **~zeit** f (im Verkehr) rush hour; (in Geschäft etc) peak period.
**Stotterer** (-s, -) m stutterer.
**Stotterin** f stutterer.
**stottern** ['ʃtɔtərn] vt, vi to stutter.
**Stövchen** ['ʃtøːfçən] nt (teapot- etc) warmer.
**StPO** abk = **Strafprozeßordnung.**
**Str.** abk (= Straße) St.
**stracks** [ʃtraks] adv straight.
**Straf-** zW: **~anstalt** f penal institution; **~arbeit** f (SCH) lines pl, punishment exercise; **~bank** f (SPORT) penalty bench; **s~bar** adj punishable; **sich s~bar machen** to commit an offence (BRIT) od offense (US); **~barkeit** f criminal nature.
**Strafe** ['ʃtraːfə] (-, -n) f punishment; (JUR) penalty; (Gefängnis~) sentence; (Geld~) fine; **... bei ~ verboten** ... forbidden; **100 Dollar ~ zahlen** to pay a $100 fine; **er hat seine ~ weg** (umg) he's had his punishment.
**strafen** vt, vi to punish; **mit etw gestraft sein** to be cursed with sth.
**strafend** adj attrib punitive; (Blick) reproachful.
**straff** [ʃtraf] adj tight; (streng) strict; (Stil etc) concise; (Haltung) erect.
**straffällig** ['ʃtraːffɛlɪç] adj: **~ werden** to commit a criminal offence (BRIT) od offense (US).
**straffen** vt to tighten.
**Straf-** zW: **s~frei** adj: **s~frei ausgehen** to go unpunished; **~gefangene(r)** f(m) prisoner, convict; **~gesetzbuch** nt penal code; **~kolonie** f penal colony.
**sträflich** ['ʃtrɛːflɪç] adj criminal ♦ adv (vernachlässigen etc) criminally.
**Sträfling** m convict.
**Straf-** zW: **~mandat** nt ticket; **~maß** nt sentence; **s~mildernd** adj mitigating; **~porto** nt excess postage (charge); **~predigt** f severe lecture; **~prozeßordnung** f code of criminal procedure; **~raum** m (SPORT) penalty area; **~recht** nt criminal law; **s~rechtlich** adj criminal; **~stoß** m (SPORT) penalty (kick); **~tat** f punishable act; **s~versetzen** vt untr (Beamte) to transfer for disciplinary reasons; **~vollzug** m penal system; **~zettel** (umg) m ticket.
**Strahl** [ʃtraːl] (-(e)s, -en) m ray, beam;

(*Wasser~*) jet.
**strahlen** *vi* (*Kernreaktor*) to radiate; (*Sonne, Licht*) to shine; (*fig*) to beam.
**Strahlenbehandlung** *f* radiotherapy.
**Strahlenbelastung** *f* (effects of) radiation.
**strahlend** *adj* (*Wetter*) glorious; (*Lächeln, Schönheit*) radiant.
**Strahlen-** *zW:* ~**dosis** *f* radiation dose; **s~geschädigt** *adj* suffering from radiation damage; ~**opfer** *nt* victim of radiation; ~**schutz** *m* radiation protection; ~**therapie** *f* radiotherapy.
**Strahlung** *f* radiation.
**Strähnchen** ['ʃtrɛːnçən] *pl* strands (of hair); (*gefärbt*) highlights.
**Strähne** ['ʃtrɛːnə] (-, -n) *f* strand.
**strähnig** *adj* (*Haar*) straggly.
**stramm** [ʃtram] *adj* tight; (*Haltung*) erect; (*Mensch*) robust; ~**stehen** *unreg vi* (*MIL*) to stand to attention.
**Strampelhöschen** *nt* rompers *pl*.
**strampeln** ['ʃtrampəln] *vi* to kick (about), fidget.
**Strand** [ʃtrant] (-(e)s, -̈e) *m* shore; (*Meeres~*) beach; **am** ~ on the beach; ~**bad** *nt* open-air swimming pool; (*Badeort*) bathing resort.
**stranden** ['ʃtrandən] *vi* to run aground; (*fig: Mensch*) to fail.
**Strandgut** *nt* flotsam and jetsam.
**Strandkorb** *m* beach chair.
**Strang** [ʃtraŋ] (-(e)s, -̈e) *m* (*Nerven~, Muskel~*) cord; (*Schienen~*) track; **über die Stränge schlagen** to run riot (*umg*); **an einem** ~ **ziehen** (*fig*) to be in the same boat.
**strangulieren** [ʃtraŋguˈliːrən] *vt* to strangle.
**Strapaze** [ʃtraˈpaːtsə] (-, -n) *f* strain.
**strapazieren** [ʃtrapaˈtsiːrən] *vt* (*Material*) to be hard on, punish; (*jdn*) to be a strain on; (*erschöpfen*) to wear out, exhaust.
**strapazierfähig** *adj* hard-wearing.
**strapaziös** [ʃtrapatsiˈøːs] *adj* exhausting, tough.
**Straßburg** ['ʃtraːsbʊrk] (-s) *nt* Strasbourg.
**Straße** ['ʃtraːsə] (-, -n) *f* road; (*in Stadt, Dorf*) street; **auf der** ~ **liegen** (*fig: umg*) to be out of work; **auf die** ~ **gesetzt werden** (*umg*) to be turned out (onto the streets).
**Straßen-** *zW:* ~**bahn** *f* tram (*BRIT*), streetcar (*US*); ~**bauarbeiten** *pl* roadworks *pl* (*BRIT*), roadwork *sing* (*US*); ~**beleuchtung** *f* street lighting; ~**feger** (-s, -) *m* roadsweeper; ~**glätte** *f* slippery road surface; ~**junge** (*pej*) *m* street urchin; ~**karte** *f* road map; ~**kehrer** (-s, -) *m* roadsweeper; ~**kind** *nt* child of the streets; ~**kreuzer** (*umg*) *m* limousine; ~**mädchen** *nt* streetwalker; ~**rand** *m* road side; ~**sperre** *f* roadblock; ~**überführung** *f* footbridge; ~**verkehr** *m* road traffic; ~**verkehrsordnung** *f* Highway Code (*BRIT*); ~**zustandsbericht** *m* road report.

**Stratege** [ʃtraˈteːgə] (-n, -n) *m* strategist.
**Strategie** [ʃtrateˈgiː] *f* strategy.
**strategisch** *adj* strategic.
**Stratosphäre** [ʃtratoˈsfɛːrə] (-) *f* stratosphere.
**sträuben** ['ʃtrɔybən] *vt* to ruffle ♦ *vr* to bristle; (*Mensch*): **sich (gegen etw)** ~ to resist (sth).
**Strauch** [ʃtraʊx] (-(e)s, Sträucher) *m* bush, shrub.
**straucheln** ['ʃtraʊxəln] *vi* to stumble, stagger.
**Strauß**[1] [ʃtraʊs] (-es, Sträuße) *m* (*Blumen~*) bouquet, bunch.
**Strauß**[2] [ʃtraʊs] (-es, -e) *m* ostrich.
**Strebe** ['ʃtreːbə] (-, -n) *f* strut.
**Strebebalken** *m* buttress.
**streben** *vi* to strive, endeavour (*BRIT*), endeavor (*US*); ~ **nach** to strive for; ~ **zu** *od* **nach** (*sich bewegen*) to make for.
**Strebepfeiler** *m* buttress.
**Streber** (-s, -) *m* (*pej*) pushy person; (*SCH*) swot (*BRIT*).
**strebsam** *adj* industrious; **S~keit** *f* industry.
**Strecke** ['ʃtrɛkə] (-, -n) *f* stretch; (*Entfernung*) distance; (*EISENB, MATH*) line; **auf der** ~ **Paris-Brüssel** on the way from Paris to Brussels; **auf der** ~ **bleiben** (*fig*) to fall by the wayside; **zur** ~ **bringen** (*Jagd*) to bag.
**strecken** *vt* to stretch; (*Waffen*) to lay down; (*KOCH*) to eke out ♦ *vr* to stretch (o.s.).
**streckenweise** *adv* in parts.
**Streich** [ʃtraɪç] (-(e)s, -e) *m* trick, prank; (*Hieb*) blow; **jdm einen** ~ **spielen** (*Person*) to play a trick on sb.
**streicheln** *vt* to stroke.
**streichen** *unreg vt* (*berühren*) to stroke; (*auftragen*) to spread; (*anmalen*) to paint; (*durch~*) to delete; (*nicht genehmigen*) to cancel; (*Schulden*) to write off; (*Zuschuß etc*) to cut ♦ *vi* (*berühren*) to brush past; (*schleichen*) to prowl; **etw glatt** ~ to smooth sth (out).
**Streicher** *pl* (*MUS*) strings *pl*.
**Streich-** *zW:* ~**holz** *nt* match; ~**holzschachtel** *f* matchbox; ~**instrument** *nt* string(ed) instrument; ~**käse** *m* cheese spread.
**Streifband** *nt* wrapper; ~**zeitung** *f* newspaper sent at printed paper rate.
**Streife** (-, -n) *f* patrol.
**streifen** ['ʃtraɪfən] *vt* (*leicht berühren*) to brush against, graze; (*Blick*) to skim over; (*Thema, Problem*) to touch on; (*ab~*) to take off ♦ *vi* (*gehen*) to roam.
**Streifen** (-s, -) *m* (*Linie*) stripe; (*Stück*) strip; (*Film*) film.
**Streifendienst** *m* patrol duty.
**Streifenwagen** *m* patrol car.
**Streifschuß** *m* graze, grazing shot.
**Streifzug** *m* scouting trip; (*Bummel*) expedition; (*fig: kurzer Überblick*): ~ **(durch)** brief survey (of).
**Streik** [ʃtraɪk] (-(e)s, -s) *m* strike; **in den** ~ **treten** to come out on strike, strike;

~**brecher** *m* blackleg (*BRIT*), strikebreaker; **s~en** *vi* to strike; **der Computer s~t** the computer's packed up (*umg*), the computer's on the blink (*umg*); **da s~e ich** (*umg*) I refuse!; ~**kasse** *f* strike fund; ~**maßnahmen** *pl* industrial action *sing*; ~**posten** *m* (peaceful) picket.

**Streit** [ʃtraɪt] (-(e)s, -e) *m* argument; (*Auseinandersetzung*) dispute.

**streiten** *unreg vi, vr* to argue; to dispute; **darüber läßt sich ~** that's debatable.

**Streitfrage** *f* point at issue.

**Streitgespräch** *nt* debate.

**streitig** *adj:* **jdm etw ~ machen** to dispute sb's right to sth; **S~keiten** *pl* quarrel *sing*, dispute *sing*.

**Streit-** *zW:* ~**kräfte** *pl* (*MIL*) armed forces *pl*; **s~lustig** *adj* quarrelsome; ~**punkt** *m* contentious issue; ~**sucht** *f* quarrelsomeness.

**streng** [ʃtrɛŋ] *adj* severe; (*Lehrer, Maßnahme*) strict; (*Geruch etc*) sharp; ~ **geheim** top-secret; ~ **verboten!** strictly prohibited.

**Strenge** (-) *f* severity; strictness; sharpness.

**strenggenommen** *adv* strictly speaking.

**strenggläubig** *adj* strict.

**strengstens** *adv* strictly.

**Streß** [ʃtrɛs] (-sses, -sse) *m* stress.

**stressen** *vt* to put under stress.

**streßfrei** *adj* without stress.

**stressig** *adj* stressful.

**Streu** [ʃtrɔy] (-, -en) *f* litter, bed of straw.

**streuen** *vt* to strew, scatter, spread ♦ *vi* (*mit Streupulver*) to grit; (*mit Salz*) to put down salt.

**Streuer** (-s, -) *m* shaker; (*Salz~*) cellar; (*Pfeffer~*) pot.

**Streufahrzeug** *nt* gritter (*BRIT*), sander.

**streunen** *vi* to roam about; (*Hund, Katze*) to stray.

**Streupulver** (-s) *nt* grit *od* sand for road.

**Streuselkuchen** [ʃtrɔyzəlkuːxən] *m cake with crumble topping.*

**Streuung** *f* dispersion; (*Statistik*) mean variation; (*PHYS*) scattering.

**Strich** (-(e)s, -e) *m* (*Linie*) line; (*Feder~, Pinsel~*) stroke; (*von Geweben*) nap; (*von Fell*) pile; (*Quer~*) dash; (*Schräg~*) oblique, slash (*bes US*); **einen ~ machen durch** (*lit*) to cross out; (*fig*) to foil; **jdm einen ~ durch die Rechnung machen** to thwart *od* foil sb's plans; **einen ~ unter etw** *akk* **machen** (*fig*) to forget sth; **nach ~ und Faden** (*umg*) good and proper; **auf den ~ gehen** (*umg*) to walk the streets; **jdm gegen den ~ gehen** to rub sb up the wrong way.

**strich** *etc* [ʃtrɪç] *vb siehe* **streichen**.

**Strichcode** *m* = **Strichkode**.

**Stricheinteilung** *f* calibration.

**stricheln** [ʃtrɪçəln] *vt:* **eine gestrichelte Linie** a broken line.

**Strich-** *zW:* ~**junge** (*umg*) *m* male prostitute;

~**kode** *m* bar code (*BRIT*), universal product code (*US*); ~**mädchen** *nt* streetwalker; ~**punkt** *m* semicolon; **s~weise** *adv* here and there; **s~weise Regen** (*MET*) rain in places.

**Strick** [ʃtrɪk] (-(e)s, -e) *m* rope; **jdm aus etw einen ~ drehen** to use sth against sb.

**stricken** *vt, vi* to knit.

**Strick-** *zW:* ~**jacke** *f* cardigan; ~**leiter** *f* rope ladder; ~**nadel** *f* knitting needle; ~**waren** *pl* knitwear *sing*.

**striegeln** [ʃtriːɡəln] (*umg*) *vr* to spruce o.s. up.

**Strieme** [ʃtriːmə] (-, -n) *f* weal.

**strikt** [strɪkt] *adj* strict.

**Strippe** [ʃtrɪpə] (-, -n) *f* (*TEL: umg*): **jdn an der ~ haben** to have sb on the line.

**Stripper(in)** (-s, -) *m(f)* stripper.

**stritt** *etc* [ʃtrɪt] *vb siehe* **streiten**.

**strittig** [ʃtrɪtɪç] *adj* disputed, in dispute.

**Stroh** [ʃtroː] (-(e)s) *nt* straw; ~**blume** *f* everlasting flower; ~**dach** *nt* thatched roof; **s~dumm** (*umg*) *adj* thick; ~**feuer** *nt:* **ein ~feuer sein** (*fig*) to be a passing fancy; ~**halm** *m* (drinking) straw; ~**mann** (-(e)s, *pl* -**männer**) *m* (*COMM*) dummy; ~**witwe** *f* grass widow; ~**witwer** *m* grass widower.

**Strolch** [ʃtrɔlç] (-(e)s, -e) (*pej*) *m* rogue, rascal.

**Strom** [ʃtroːm] (-(e)s, ⁻e) *m* river; (*fig*) stream; (*ELEK*) current; **unter ~ stehen** (*ELEK*) to be live; (*fig*) to be excited; **der Wein floß in Strömen** the wine flowed like water; **in Strömen regnen** to be pouring with rain; **s~abwärts** *adv* downstream; ~**anschluß** *m:* ~**anschluß haben** to be connected to the electricity mains; **s~aufwärts** *adv* upstream; ~**ausfall** *m* power failure.

**strömen** [ʃtrøːmən] *vi* to stream, pour.

**Strom-** *zW:* ~**kabel** *nt* electric cable; ~**kreis** *m* (electrical) circuit; **s~linienförmig** *adj* streamlined; ~**netz** *nt* power supply system; ~**rechnung** *f* electricity bill; ~**schnelle** *f* rapids *pl*; ~**sperre** *f* power cut; ~**stärke** *f* amperage.

**Strömung** [ʃtrøːmʊŋ] *f* current.

**Stromzähler** *m* electricity meter.

**Strophe** [ʃtroːfə] (-, -n) *f* verse.

**strotzen** [ʃtrɔtsən] *vi:* ~ **vor** +*dat od* **von** to abound in, be full of.

**Strudel** [ʃtruːdəl] (-s, -) *m* whirlpool, vortex; (*KOCH*) strudel.

**strudeln** *vi* to swirl, eddy.

**Struktur** [ʃtrʊkˈtuːr] *f* structure.

**strukturell** [ʃtrʊktuˈrɛl] *adj* structural.

**strukturieren** [ʃtrʊktuˈriːrən] *vt* to structure.

**Strumpf** [ʃtrʊmpf] (-(e)s, ⁻e) *m* stocking; ~**band** *nt* garter; ~**halter** *m* suspender (*BRIT*), garter (*US*); ~**hose** *f* (pair of) tights *pl* (*BRIT*) *od* pantihose *pl* (*US*).

**Strunk** [ʃtrʊŋk] (-(e)s, ⁻e) *m* stump.

**struppig** [ʃtrʊpɪç] *adj* shaggy, unkempt.

**Stube** ['ʃtuːbə] (-, -n) f room; **die gute ~** (veraltet) the parlour (BRIT) od parlor (US).

**Stuben-** zW: **~arrest** m confinement to one's room; (MIL) confinement to quarters; **~fliege** f (common) housefly; **~hocker** (umg) m stay-at-home; **s~rein** adj house-trained.

**Stuck** [ʃtuk] (-(e)s) m stucco.

**Stück** [ʃtʏk] (-(e)s, -e) nt piece; (etwas) bit; (THEAT) play; **am ~** in one piece; **das ist ein starkes ~!** (umg) that's a bit much!; **große ~e auf jdn halten** to think highly of sb; **~arbeit** f piecework; **~gut** nt (EISENB) parcel service; **~kosten** pl unit cost sing; **~lohn** m piecework rates pl; **s~weise** adv bit by bit, piecemeal; (COMM) individually; **~werk** nt bits and pieces pl.

**Student(in)** [ʃtu'dɛnt(ɪn)] m(f) student.

**Studenten-** zW: **~ausweis** m student card; **~futter** nt nuts and raisins pl; **~werk** nt student administration; **~wohnheim** nt hall of residence (BRIT), dormitory (US).

**studentisch** adj student attrib.

**Studie** ['ʃtuːdiə] f study.

**Studien-** zW: **~beratung** f course guidance service; **~buch** nt (UNIV) book in which the courses one has attended are entered; **~fahrt** f study trip; **~platz** m university place; **~rat** m, **~rätin** f teacher at a secondary (BRIT) od high (US) school.

**studieren** [ʃtu'diːrən] vt, vi to study; **bei jdm ~** to study under sb.

**Studio** ['ʃtuːdio] (-s, -s) nt studio.

**Studium** ['ʃtuːdiʊm] nt studies pl.

**Stufe** ['ʃtuːfə] (-, -n) f step; (Entwicklungs~) stage; (Niveau) level.

**Stufen-** zW: **~heck** nt (AUT) notchback; **~leiter** f (fig) ladder; **s~los** adj (TECH) infinitely variable; **s~los verstellbar** continuously adjustable; **~plan** m graduated plan; **~schnitt** m (Frisur) layered cut; **s~weise** adv gradually.

**Stuhl** [ʃtuːl] (-(e)s, -̈e) m chair; **zwischen zwei Stühlen sitzen** (fig) to fall between two stools.

**Stuhlgang** m bowel movement.

**Stukkateur** [ʃtuka'tøːr] m (ornamental) plasterer.

**stülpen** ['ʃtʏlpən] vt (bedecken) to put; **etw über etw** akk **~** to put sth over sth; **den Kragen nach oben ~** to turn up one's collar.

**stumm** [ʃtum] adj silent; (MED) dumb.

**Stummel** (-s, -) m stump; (Zigaretten~) stub.

**Stummfilm** m silent film (BRIT) od movie (US).

**Stümper(in)** ['ʃtʏmpər(ɪn)] (-s, -) m(f) incompetent, duffer; **s~haft** adj bungling, incompetent.

**stümpern** (umg) vi to bungle.

**Stumpf** [ʃtumpf] (-(e)s, -̈e) m stump; **etw mit ~ und Stiel ausrotten** to eradicate sth root and branch.

**stumpf** adj blunt; (teilnahmslos, glanzlos) dull; (Winkel) obtuse.

**Stumpfsinn** (-(e)s) m tediousness.

**stumpfsinnig** adj dull.

**Stunde** ['ʃtundə] (-, -n) f hour; (Augenblick, Zeitpunkt) time; (SCH) lesson, period (BRIT); **~ um ~** hour after hour; **80 Kilometer in der ~ ≈** 50 miles per hour.

**stunden** vt: **jdm etw ~** to give sb time to pay sth.

**Stunden-** zW: **~geschwindigkeit** f average speed (per hour); **~kilometer** pl kilometres (BRIT) od kilometers (US) per hour; **s~lang** adj for hours; **~lohn** m hourly wage; **~plan** m timetable; **s~weise** adv by the hour; (stündlich) every hour.

**stündlich** ['ʃtʏntlɪç] adj hourly.

**Stunk** [ʃtuŋk] (-s, no pl) m: **~ machen** (umg) to kick up a stink.

**stupide** [ʃtu'piːdə] adj mindless.

**Stups** [ʃtups] (-es, -e) (umg) m push.

**stupsen** vt to nudge.

**Stupsnase** f snub nose.

**stur** [ʃtuːr] adj obstinate, stubborn; (Nein, Arbeiten) dogged; **er fuhr ~ geradeaus** he just carried straight on; **sich ~ stellen, auf ~ stellen** (umg) to dig one's heels in; **ein ~er Bock** (umg) a pig-headed fellow.

**Sturm** [ʃturm] (-(e)s, -̈e) m storm; (Wind) gale; (MIL etc) attack, assault; **~ läuten** to keep one's finger on the doorbell; **gegen etw ~ laufen** (fig) to be up in arms against sth.

**stürmen** ['ʃtʏrmən] vi (Wind) to blow hard, to rage; (rennen) to storm ♦ vt (MIL, fig) to storm ♦ vi unpers: **es stürmt** there's a gale blowing.

**Stürmer** (-s, -) m (SPORT) forward.

**sturmfrei** adj (MIL) unassailable; **eine ~e Bude** (umg) a room free from disturbance.

**stürmisch** adj stormy; (fig) tempestuous; (Entwicklung) rapid; (Liebhaber) passionate; (Beifall) tumultuous; **nicht so ~** take it easy.

**Sturm-** zW: **~schritt** m (MIL, fig): **im ~schritt** at the double; **~warnung** f gale warning; **~wind** m gale.

**Sturz** [ʃturts] (-es, -̈e) m fall; (POL) overthrow; (in Temperatur, Preis) drop.

**stürzen** ['ʃtʏrtsən] vt (werfen) to hurl; (POL) to overthrow; (umkehren) to overturn ♦ vr to rush; (hinein~) to plunge ♦ vi to fall; (AVIAT) to dive; (rennen) to dash; **jdn ins Unglück ~** to bring disaster upon sb; **„nicht ~"** "this side up"; **sich auf jdn/etw ~** to pounce on sb/sth; **sich in Unkosten ~** to go to great expense.

**Sturzflug** m nose dive.

**Sturzhelm** m crash helmet.

**Stuß** [ʃtus] (Stusses) (umg) m nonsense, rubbish.

**Stute** ['ʃtuːtə] (-, -n) f mare.

**Stuttgart** ['ʃtutgart] (-s) nt Stuttgart.

**Stützbalken** m brace, joist.

**Stütze** [ˈʃtʏtsə] (-, -n) f support; (*Hilfe*) help; **die ~n der Gesellschaft** the pillars of society.

**stutzen** [ˈʃtʊtsən] vt to trim; (*Ohr, Schwanz*) to dock; (*Flügel*) to clip ♦ vi to hesitate; (*argwöhnisch werden*) to become suspicious.

**stützen** vt (*lit, fig*) to support; (*Ellbogen etc*) to prop up ♦ vr: **sich auf jdn/etw ~** (*lit*) to lean on sb/sth; (*Beweise, Theorie*) to be based on sb/sth.

**stutzig** adj perplexed, puzzled; (*mißtrauisch*) suspicious.

**Stützmauer** f supporting wall.

**Stützpunkt** m point of support; (*von Hebel*) fulcrum; (*MIL, fig*) base.

**Stützungskäufe** pl (*FIN*) support buying sing.

**StVO** abk = **Straßenverkehrsordnung**.

**stylen** [ˈstaɪlən] vt to style; (*Wohnung*) to design.

**Styling** [ˈstaɪlɪŋ] (-s, no pl) nt styling.

**Styropor** ® [ʃtyroˈpoːr] (-s) nt (expanded) polystyrene.

**s.u.** abk (= *siehe unten*) see below.

**Suaheli** [zuaˈheːli] (-(s)) nt Swahili.

**Subjekt** [zʊpˈjɛkt] (-(e)s, -e) nt subject; (*pej: Mensch*) character (*umg*).

**subjektiv** [zʊpjɛkˈtiːf] adj subjective.

**Subjektivität** [zʊpjɛktiviˈtɛːt] f subjectivity.

**Subkultur** [ˈzʊpkʊltuːr] f subculture.

**sublimieren** [zubliˈmiːrən] vt (*CHEM, PSYCH*) to sublimate.

**Submissionsangebot** [zʊpmɪsiˈoːns-|aŋɡəboːt] nt sealed-bid tender.

**Subroutine** [ˈzʊprutiːnə] f (*COMPUT*) subroutine.

**Subskription** [zʊpskrɪptsiˈoːn] f subscription.

**Substantiv** [zʊpstanˈtiːf] (-s, -e) nt noun.

**Substanz** [zʊpˈstants] f substance; **von der ~ zehren** to live on one's capital.

**subtil** [zʊpˈtiːl] adj subtle.

**subtrahieren** [zʊptraˈhiːrən] vt to subtract.

**subtropisch** [ˈzʊptroːpɪʃ] adj subtropical.

**Subunternehmer** m subcontractor.

**Subvention** [zʊpvɛntsiˈoːn] f subsidy.

**subventionieren** [zʊpvɛntsioˈniːrən] vt to subsidize.

**subversiv** [zʊpvɛrˈziːf] adj subversive.

**Suchaktion** f search.

**Suchdienst** m missing persons tracing service.

**Suche** (-, -n) f search.

**suchen** [ˈzuːxən] vt to look for, seek; (*versuchen*) to try ♦ vi to seek, search; **du hast hier nichts zu ~** you have no business being here; **nach Worten ~** to search for words; (*sprachlos sein*) to be at a loss for words; **such!** (*zu Hund*) seek!, find!; **~ und ersetzen** (*COMPUT*) search and replace.

**Sucher** (-s, -) m seeker, searcher; (*PHOT*) viewfinder.

**Suchmeldung** f missing od wanted person announcement.

**Suchscheinwerfer** m searchlight.

**Sucht** [zʊxt] (-, ⁼e) f mania; (*MED*) addiction; **~droge** f addictive drug; **s~erzeugend** adj addictive.

**süchtig** [ˈzʏçtɪç] adj addicted.

**Süchtige(r)** f(m) addict.

**Süd** [zyːt] (-(e)s) m south; **~afrika** nt South Africa; **~amerika** nt South America.

**Sudan** [zuˈdaːn] (-s) m: **der ~** the Sudan.

**Sudanese** [zudaˈneːzə] (-n, -n) m Sudanese.

**Sudanesin** f Sudanese.

**südd.** abk = **süddeutsch**.

**süddeutsch** adj South German.

**Süddeutschland** nt South(ern) Germany.

**Süden** [ˈzyːdən] (-s) m south.

**Süd-** zW: **~europa** nt Southern Europe; **~früchte** pl Mediterranean fruit; **~korea** nt South Korea; **s~ländisch** adj southern; (*italienisch, spanisch etc*) Latin; **s~lich** adj southern; **s~lich von** (to the) south of; **~ostasien** nt South-East Asia; **~pol** m South Pole; **~polarmeer** nt Antarctic Ocean; **~see** f South Seas pl, South Pacific; **~tirol** nt South Tyrol; **s~wärts** adv southwards; **~westafrika** nt South West Africa, Namibia.

**Sueskanal** [ˈzuːɛskanaːl] (-s) m Suez Canal.

**Suff** [zʊf] m: **etw im ~ sagen** (*umg*) to say sth while under the influence.

**süffig** [ˈzʏfɪç] adj (*Wein*) very drinkable.

**süffisant** [zyfiˈzant] adj smug.

**suggerieren** [zʊɡeˈriːrən] vt to suggest.

**Suggestivfrage** [zʊɡɛsˈtiːffraːɡə] f suggestive question.

**suhlen** [ˈzuːlən] vr (*lit, fig*) to wallow.

**Sühne** [ˈzyːnə] (-, -n) f atonement, expiation.

**sühnen** vt to atone for, expiate.

**Sühnetermin** m (*JUR*) conciliatory hearing.

**Suite** [ˈsviːtə] f suite.

**Sulfat** [zʊlˈfaːt] (-(e)s, -e) nt sulphate (*BRIT*), sulfate (*US*).

**Sultan** [ˈzʊltan] (-s, -e) m sultan.

**Sultanine** [zʊltaˈniːnə] f sultana.

**Sülze** [ˈzʏltsə] (-, -n) f brawn (*BRIT*), headcheese (*US*); (*Aspik*) aspic.

**summarisch** [zʊˈmaːrɪʃ] adj summary.

**Sümmchen** [ˈzʏmçən] nt: **ein hübsches ~** a tidy sum.

**Summe** (-, -n) f sum, total.

**summen** vi to buzz ♦ vt (*Lied*) to hum.

**Summer** (-s, -) m buzzer.

**summieren** [zʊˈmiːrən] vt to add up ♦ vr to mount up.

**Sumpf** [zʊmpf] (-(e)s, ⁼e) m swamp, marsh.

**sumpfig** adj marshy.

**Sund** [zʊnt] (-(e)s, -e) m sound, straits pl.

**Sünde** [ˈzʏndə] (-, -n) f sin.

**Sünden-** zW: **~bock** m (*fig*) scapegoat; **~fall** m (*REL*) Fall; **~register** nt (*fig*) list of sins.

**Sünder(in)** (-s, -) m(f) sinner.

**sündhaft** adj (*lit*) sinful; (*fig: umg: Preise*) wicked.

**sündigen** [ˈzʏndɪɡən] vi to sin; (*hum*) to

indulge; ~ **an** +dat to sin against.
**Super** ['zu:pər] (-s) nt (Benzin) four-star
(petrol) (BRIT), premium (US).
**super** (umg) adj super ♦ adv incredibly well.
**Superlativ** ['zu:pərlati:f] (-s, -e) m superlative.
**Supermarkt** m supermarket.
**Superstar** m superstar.
**Suppe** ['zupə] (-, -n) f soup; (mit Einlage)
broth; (klare Brühe) bouillon; (fig: umg: Nebel)
peasouper (BRIT), pea soup (US); **jdm die**
~ **versalzen** (umg) to put a spoke in sb's
wheel.
**Suppen-** zW: ~**fleisch** nt meat for making
soup; ~**grün** nt herbs and vegetables for
making soup; ~**kasper** (umg) m poor eater;
~**teller** m soup plate.
**Surfbrett** ['zø:rfbrɛt] nt surfboard.
**surfen** ['zø:rfən] vi to surf.
**Surfer(in)** m(f) surfer.
**Surrealismus** [zorea'lısmʊs] m surrealism.
**surren** ['zorən] vi to buzz; (Insekt) to hum.
**Surrogat** [zoro'ga:t] (-(e)s, -e) nt substitute,
surrogate.
**suspekt** [zʊs'pɛkt] adj suspect.
**suspendieren** [zʊspɛn'di:rən] vt: ~ **(von)** to
suspend (from).
**Suspendierung** f suspension.
**süß** [zy:s] adj sweet.
**Süße** (-) f sweetness.
**süßen** vt to sweeten.
**Süßholz** nt: ~ **raspeln** (fig) to turn on the
blarney.
**Süßigkeit** f sweetness; (Bonbon etc) sweet
(BRIT), candy (US).
**süß-** zW: ~**lich** adj sweetish; (fig) sugary;
~**sauer** adj sweet-and-sour; (fig: gezwungen:
Lächeln) forced; (Gurken etc) pickled; (Miene)
artificially friendly; **S~speise** f pudding,
sweet (BRIT); **S~stoff** m sweetener;
**S~waren** pl confectionery sing; **S~wasser** nt
fresh water.
**SV** (-) m abk = **Sportverein**.
**SW** abk (= Südwest(en)) SW.
**Swasiland** ['sva:zilant] (-s) nt Swaziland.
**SWF** (-) m abk (= Südwestfunk) South West
German Radio.
**Sylvester** [zyl'vɛstər] (-s, -) nt = **Silvester**.
**Symbol** [zym'bo:l] (-s, -e) nt symbol.
**Symbolik** f symbolism.
**symbolisch** adj symbolic(al).
**symbolisieren** [zymboli'zi:rən] vt to
symbolize.
**Symmetrie** [zyme'tri:] f symmetry; ~**achse** f
symmetric axis.
**symmetrisch** [zy'me:trıʃ] adj symmetrical.
**Sympathie** [zympa'ti:] f liking; sympathy; **er**
**hat sich** dat **alle ~(n) verscherzt** he has
turned everyone against him;
~**kundgebung** f demonstration of support;
~**streik** m sympathy strike.
**Sympathisant(in)** m(f) sympathizer.
**sympathisch** [zym'pa:tıʃ] adj likeable,

congenial; **er ist mir** ~ I like him.
**sympathisieren** [zympati'zi:rən] vi to
sympathize.
**Symphonie** [zymfo'ni:] f symphony.
**Symptom** [zymp'to:m] (-s, -e) nt symptom.
**symptomatisch** [zympto'ma:tıʃ] adj
symptomatic.
**Synagoge** [zyna'go:gə] (-, -n) f synagogue.
**synchron** [zyn'kro:n] adj synchronous;
**S~getriebe** nt synchromesh gearbox (BRIT)
od transmission (US).
**synchronisieren** [zynkroni'zi:rən] vt to
synchronize; (Film) to dub.
**Synchronschwimmen** nt synchronized
swimming.
**Syndikat** [zyndi'ka:t] (-(e)s, -e) nt combine,
syndicate.
**Syndrom** [zyn'dro:m] (-s, -e) nt syndrome.
**Synkope** [zyn'ko:pə] (-, -n) f (MUS)
syncopation.
**Synode** [zy'no:də] (-, -n) f (REL) synod.
**Synonym** [zyno'ny:m] (-s, -e) nt synonym; **s~**
adj synonymous.
**Syntax** ['zyntaks] (-, -en) f syntax.
**Synthese** [zyn'te:zə] (-, -n) f synthesis.
**synthetisch** adj synthetic.
**Syphilis** ['zy:filıs] (-) f syphilis.
**Syrer(in)** ['zy:rər(ın)] (-s, -) m(f) Syrian.
**Syrien** (-s) nt Syria.
**syrisch** adj Syrian.
**System** [zys'te:m] (-s, -e) nt system; ~**analyse**
f systems analysis; ~**analytiker(in)** m(f)
systems analyst.
**Systematik** f system.
**systematisch** [zyste'ma:tıʃ] adj systematic.
**systematisieren** [zystemati'zi:rən] vt to
systematize.
**System-** zW: ~**kritiker** m critic of the system;
~**platte** f (COMPUT) system disk; ~**zwang**
m obligation to conform (to the system).
**Szenarium** [stse'na:rıʊm] nt scenario.
**Szene** ['stse:nə] (-, -n) f scene; **sich in der**
~ **auskennen** (umg) to know the scene; **sich**
**in** ~ **setzen** to play to the gallery.
**Szenenwechsel** m scene change.
**Szenerie** [stsenə'ri:] f scenery.

# T, t

**T, t¹** [te:] *nt* T, t; ~ **wie Theodor** ≈ T for Tommy.

**t²** *abk* (= *Tonne*) t.

**Tabak** ['ta:bak] (**-s, -e**) *m* tobacco; ~**laden** *m* tobacconist's (*BRIT*), tobacco store (*US*).

**tabellarisch** [tabɛ'la:rɪʃ] *adj* tabular.

**Tabelle** (**-, -n**) *f* table.

**Tabellenführer** *m* (*SPORT*) top of the table, league leader.

**Tabernakel** [tabɛr'na:kəl] (**-s, -**) *nt* tabernacle.

**Tabl.** *abk* = **Tablette(n)**.

**Tablett** (**-(e)s, -s** *od* **-e**) *nt* tray.

**Tablette** [ta'blɛtə] (**-, -n**) *f* tablet, pill.

**Tabu** [ta'bu:] (**-s, -s**) *nt* taboo.

**tabuisieren** [tabui'zi:rən] *vt* to make taboo.

**Tabulator** [tabu'la:tɔr] *m* tabulator, tab (*umg*).

**tabulieren** *vt* to tab.

**Tacho** ['taxo] (**-s, -s**) (*umg*) *m* speedo (*BRIT*).

**Tachometer** [taxo'me:tər] (**-s, -**) *m* (*AUT*) speedometer.

**Tadel** ['ta:dəl] (**-s, -**) *m* censure, scolding; (*Fehler*) fault; (*Makel*) blemish; **t~los** *adj* faultless, irreproachable.

**tadeln** *vt* to scold.

**tadelnswert** *adj* blameworthy.

**Tadschikistan** [ta'dʒi:kista:n] (**-s**) *nt* Tajikistan.

**Tafel** ['ta:fəl] (**-, -n**) *f* (*form: festlicher Speisetisch, MATH*) table; (*Festmahl*) meal; (*Anschlag~*) board; (*Wand~*) blackboard; (*Schiefer~*) slate; (*Gedenk~*) plaque; (*Illustration*) plate; (*Schalt~*) panel; (*Schokoladen~ etc*) bar; **t~fertig** *adj* ready to serve.

**täfeln** ['tɛ:fəln] *vt* to panel.

**Tafelöl** *nt* cooking oil; salad oil.

**Täfelung** *f* panelling (*BRIT*), paneling (*US*).

**Tafelwasser** *nt* table water.

**Taft** [taft] (**-(e)s, -e**) *m* taffeta.

**Tag** [ta:k] (**-(e)s, -e**) *m* day; (*Tageslicht*) daylight; **am** ~ during the day; **für** *od* **auf ein paar** ~**e** for a few days; **in den** ~ **hinein leben** to take each day as it comes; **bei** ~**(e)** (*ankommen*) while it's light; (*arbeiten, reisen*) during the day; **unter** ~ (*MIN*) underground; **über** ~**e** (*MIN*) on the surface; **an den** ~ **kommen** to come to light; **er legte großes Interesse an den** ~ he showed great interest; **auf den** ~ (**genau**) to the day; **auf seine alten** ~**e** at his age; **guten** ~**!** good morning/afternoon!; **t~aus** *adv:* **t~aus, t~ein** day in, day out; ~**dienst** *m* day duty.

**Tage-** *zW:* ~**bau** *m* (*MIN*) open-cast mining; ~**buch** *nt* diary; ~**dieb** *m* idler; ~**geld** *nt* daily allowance; **t~lang** *adv* for days.

**tagen** *vi* to sit, meet ♦ *vi unpers:* **es tagt** dawn is breaking.

**Tages-** *zW:* ~**ablauf** *m* daily routine; ~**anbruch** *m* dawn; ~**ausflug** *m* day trip; ~**decke** *f* bedspread; ~**fahrt** *f* day trip; ~**karte** *f* (*Eintrittskarte*) day ticket; (*Speisekarte*) menu of the day; ~**kasse** *f* (*COMM*) day's takings *pl*; (*THEAT*) box office; ~**licht** *nt* daylight; ~**mutter** *f* child minder; ~**ordnung** *f* agenda; **an der** ~**ordnung sein** (*fig*) to be the order of the day; ~**rückfahrkarte** *f* day return (ticket); ~**satz** *m* daily rate; ~**schau** *f* (*TV*) television news (programme (*BRIT*) *od* program (*US*)); ~**stätte** *f* day nursery (*BRIT*), daycare center (*US*); ~**wert** *m* (*FIN*) present value; ~**zeit** *f* time of day; **zu jeder** ~- **und Nachtzeit** at all hours of the day and night; ~**zeitung** *f* daily (paper).

**tägl.** *abk* = **täglich**.

**täglich** ['tɛ:klɪç] *adj, adv* daily; **einmal** ~ once a day.

**tags** [ta:ks] *adv:* ~ **darauf** *od* **danach** the next *od* following day; ~**über** *adv* during the day.

**tagtäglich** *adj* daily ♦ *adv* every (single) day.

**Tagung** *f* conference.

**Tagungsort** *m* venue (of a conference).

**Tahiti** [ta'hi:ti] (**-s**) *nt* Tahiti.

**Taifun** [tai'fu:n] (**-s, -e**) *m* typhoon.

**Taille** ['taljə] (**-, -n**) *f* waist.

**tailliert** [ta'ji:rt] *adj* waisted, gathered at the waist.

**Taiwan** ['taivan] (**-s**) *nt* Taiwan.

**Takel** ['ta:kəl] (**-s, -**) *nt* tackle.

**takeln** *vt* to rig.

**Takt** [takt] (**-(e)s, -e**) *m* tact; (*MUS*) time; ~**gefühl** *nt* tact.

**Taktik** *f* tactics *pl*.

**Taktiker(in)** *m(f)* tactician.

**taktisch** *adj* tactical.

**Takt-** *zW:* **t~los** *adj* tactless; ~**losigkeit** *f* tactlessness; ~**stock** *m* (conductor's) baton; ~**strich** *m* (*MUS*) bar (line); **t~voll** *adj* tactful.

**Tal** [ta:l] (**-(e)s, -̈er**) *nt* valley.

**Talar** [ta'la:r] (**-s, -e**) *m* (*JUR*) robe; (*UNIV*) gown.

**Talbrücke** *f* bridge over a valley.

**Talent** [ta'lɛnt] (**-(e)s, -e**) *nt* talent.

**talentiert** [talɛn'ti:rt] *adj* talented, gifted.

**Talfahrt** *f* descent; (*fig*) decline.

**Talg** [talk] (**-(e)s, -e**) *m* tallow.

**Talgdrüse** *f* sebaceous gland.

**Talisman** ['ta:lɪsman] (**-s, -e**) *m* talisman.

**Tal-** *zW:* ~**sohle** *f* bottom of a valley; ~**sperre** *f* dam; **t~wärts** *adv* down to the valley.

**Tamburin** [tambu'ri:n] (**-s, -e**) *nt* tambourine.

**Tamile** [ta'mi:lə] (**-n, -n**) *m*, **Tamilin** *f* Tamil.

**tamilisch** *adj* Tamil.

**Tampon** ['tampɔn] (-s, -s) m tampon.

**Tamtam** [tam'tam] (-s, -s) nt (MUS) tomtom; (umg: Wirbel) fuss, ballyhoo; (Lärm) din.

**Tang** [taŋ] (-(e)s, -e) m seaweed.

**Tangente** [taŋ'gɛntə] (-, -n) f tangent.

**Tanger** ['taŋər] (-s) nt Tangier(s).

**tangieren** [taŋ'giːrən] vt (Problem) to touch on; (fig) to affect.

**Tank** [taŋk] (-s, -s) m tank.

**tanken** vt (Wagen etc) to fill up with petrol (BRIT) od gas (US); (Benzin etc) to fill up with; (AVIAT) to (re)fuel; (umg: frische Luft, neue Kräfte) to get ♦ vi to fill up (with petrol od gas); to (re)fuel.

**Tanker** (-s, -) m tanker.

**Tank-** zW: **~laster** m tanker; **~schiff** nt tanker; **~stelle** f petrol (BRIT) od gas (US) station; **~uhr** f fuel gauge; **~verschluß** m fuel cap; **~wart** m petrol pump (BRIT) od gas station (US) attendant.

**Tanne** ['tanə] (-, -n) f fir.

**Tannenbaum** m fir tree.

**Tannenzapfen** m fir cone.

**Tansania** [tan'zaːnia] (-s) nt Tanzania.

**Tante** ['tantə] (-, -n) f aunt; **~-Emma-Laden** (umg) m corner shop.

**Tantieme** [tãti'eːmə] (-, -n) f fee; (für Künstler etc) royalty.

**Tanz** [tants] (-es, -e) m dance.

**tänzeln** ['tɛntsəln] vi to dance along.

**tanzen** vt, vi to dance.

**Tänzer(in)** (-s, -) m(f) dancer.

**Tanz-** zW: **~fläche** f (dance) floor; **~lokal** nt café/restaurant with dancing; **~schule** f dancing school.

**Tapet** (umg) nt: etw aufs ~ bringen to bring sth up.

**Tapete** [ta'peːtə] (-, -n) f wallpaper.

**Tapetenwechsel** m (fig) change of scenery.

**tapezieren** [tape'tsiːrən] vt to (wall)paper.

**Tapezierer** (-s, -) m (interior) decorator.

**tapfer** ['tapfər] adj brave; sich ~ schlagen (umg) to put on a brave show; **T~keit** f courage, bravery.

**tappen** ['tapən] vi to walk uncertainly od clumsily; im dunkeln ~ (fig) to grope in the dark.

**täppisch** ['tɛpɪʃ] adj clumsy.

**Tara** ['taːra] (-, **Taren**) f tare.

**Tarantel** [ta'rantəl] (-, -n) f: wie von der ~ gestochen as if stung by a bee.

**Tarif** [ta'riːf] (-s, -e) m tariff, (scale of) fares/charges; nach/über/unter ~ bezahlen to pay according to/above/below the (union) rate(s); **~autonomie** f free collective bargaining; **~gruppe** f grade; **t~lich** adj agreed, union; **~lohn** m standard wage rate; **~ordnung** f wage od salary scale; **~partner** m: die ~partner union and management; **~vereinbarung** f labour (BRIT) od labor (US) agreement; **~verhandlungen** pl collective bargaining sing; **~vertrag** m pay agreement.

**tarnen** ['tarnən] vt to camouflage; (Person, Absicht) to disguise.

**Tarnfarbe** f camouflage paint.

**Tarnmanöver** nt (lit, fig) feint, covering ploy.

**Tarnung** f camouflaging; disguising.

**Tarock** [ta'rɔk] (-s, s) m od nt tarot.

**Tasche** ['taʃə] (-, -n) f pocket; (Hand~) handbag; in die eigene ~ wirtschaften to line one's own pockets; jdm auf der ~ liegen (umg) to live off sb.

**Taschen-** zW: **~buch** nt paperback; **~dieb** m pickpocket; **~geld** nt pocket money; **~lampe** f (electric) torch, flashlight (US); **~messer** nt penknife; **~rechner** m pocket calculator; **~spieler** m conjurer; **~tuch** nt handkerchief.

**Tasmanien** [tas'maːnian] (-s) nt Tasmania.

**Tasse** ['tasə] (-, -n) f cup; er hat nicht alle ~n im Schrank (umg) he's not all there.

**Tastatur** [tasta'tuːr] f keyboard.

**Taste** ['tastə] (-, -n) f push-button control; (an Schreibmaschine) key.

**tasten** vt to feel, touch; (drücken) to press ♦ vi to feel, grope ♦ vr to feel one's way.

**Tastentelefon** nt push-button telephone.

**Tastsinn** m sense of touch.

**Tat** (-, -en) f act, deed, action; in der ~ indeed, as a matter of fact; etw in die ~ umsetzen to put sth into action.

**tat** etc [taːt] vb siehe **tun**.

**Tatbestand** m facts pl of the case.

**Tatendrang** m energy.

**tatenlos** adj inactive.

**Täter(in)** ['tɛːtər(ɪn)] (-s, -) m(f) perpetrator, culprit; **~schaft** f guilt.

**tätig** adj active; **~er Teilhaber** active partner; in einer Firma ~ sein to work for a firm.

**tätigen** vt (COMM) to conclude; (geh: Einkäufe, Anruf) to make.

**Tätigkeit** f activity; (Beruf) occupation.

**Tätigkeitsbereich** m field of activity.

**tatkräftig** adj energetic; (Hilfe) active.

**tätlich** adj violent; **T~keit** f violence; es kam zu T~keiten there were violent scenes.

**Tatort** (-(e)s, -e) m scene of the crime.

**tätowieren** [tɛto'viːrən] vt to tattoo.

**Tätowierung** f tattooing; (Ergebnis) tattoo.

**Tatsache** f fact; jdn vor vollendete ~n stellen to present sb with a fait accompli.

**Tatsachenbericht** m documentary (report).

**tatsächlich** adj actual ♦ adv really.

**tatverdächtig** adj suspected.

**Tatze** ['tatsə] (-, -n) f paw.

**Tau¹** [tau] (-(e)s, -e) nt rope.

**Tau²** (-(e)s) m dew.

**taub** [taup] adj deaf; (Nuß) hollow; sich ~ stellen to pretend not to hear.

**Taube** ['taubə] (-, -n) f (ZOOL) pigeon; (fig) dove.

**Taubenschlag** m dovecote; hier geht es zu wie im ~ (fig: umg) it's like Waterloo Station here (BRIT), it's like Grand Central Station

here (*US*).
**Taubheit** *f* deafness.
**taubstumm** *adj* deaf-mute.
**tauchen** ['tauxən] *vt* to dip ♦ *vi* to dive; (*NAUT*) to submerge.
**Taucher** (-s, -) *m* diver; ~**anzug** *m* diving suit.
**Tauchsieder** (-s, -) *m* portable immersion heater.
**Tauchstation** *f:* **auf** ~ **gehen** (*U-Boot*) to dive.
**tauen** ['tauən] *vt, vi* to thaw ♦ *vi unpers:* **es taut** it's thawing.
**Taufbecken** *nt* font.
**Taufe** ['taufə] (-, -n) *f* baptism.
**taufen** *vt* to baptize; (*nennen*) to christen.
**Tauf-** *zW:* ~**name** *m* Christian name; ~**pate** *m* godfather; ~**patin** *f* godmother; ~**schein** *m* certificate of baptism.
**taugen** ['taugən] *vi* to be of use; ~ **für** to do *od* be good for; **nicht** ~ to be no good *od* useless.
**Taugenichts** (-es, -e) *m* good-for-nothing.
**tauglich** ['tauklıç] *adj* suitable; (*MIL*) fit (for service); **T~keit** *f* suitability; fitness.
**Taumel** ['tauməl] (-s) *m* dizziness; (*fig*) frenzy.
**taumelig** *adj* giddy, reeling.
**taumeln** *vi* to reel, stagger.
**Taunus** ['taunus] (-) *m* Taunus (Mountains *pl*).
**Tausch** [tauʃ] (-(e)s, -e) *m* exchange; **einen guten/schlechten** ~ **machen** to get a good/ bad deal.
**tauschen** *vt* to exchange, swap ♦ *vi:* **ich möchte nicht mit ihm** ~ I wouldn't like to be in his place.
**täuschen** ['tɔyʃən] *vt* to deceive ♦ *vi* to be deceptive ♦ *vr* to be wrong; **wenn mich nicht alles täuscht** unless I'm completely wrong.
**täuschend** *adj* deceptive.
**Tauschhandel** *m* barter.
**Täuschung** *f* deception; (*optisch*) illusion.
**Täuschungsmanöver** *nt* (*SPORT*) feint; (*fig*) ploy.
**tausend** ['tauzənt] *num* a *od* one thousand; **T~** (-, -en) *f* (*Zahl*) thousand.
**Tausender** (-s, -) *m* (*Geldschein*) thousand.
**Tausendfüßler** (-s, -) *m* centipede.
**Tau-** *zW:* ~**tropfen** *m* dew drop; ~**wetter** *nt* thaw; ~**ziehen** *nt* tug-of-war.
**Taxe** ['taksə] (-, -n) *f* taxi, cab.
**Taxi** ['taksi] (-(s), -(s)) *nt* taxi, cab.
**taxieren** [ta'ksi:rən] *vt* (*Preis, Wert*) to estimate; (*Haus, Gemälde*) to value; (*mustern*) to look up and down.
**Taxi-** *zW:* ~**fahrer** *m* taxi driver; ~**stand** *m* taxi rank (*BRIT*) *od* stand (*US*).
**Tb, Tbc** *f abk* (= *Tuberkulose*) TB.
**Teamarbeit** ['ti:m|arbait] *f* teamwork.
**Technik** ['tɛçnık] *f* technology; (*Methode, Kunstfertigkeit*) technique.
**Techniker(in)** (-s -) *m(f)* technician.
**technisch** *adj* technical; **T~e Hochschule** ≈ polytechnic.
**Technologie** [tɛçnolo'gi:] *f* technology.

**technologisch** [tɛçno'lo:gıʃ] *adj* technological.
**Techtelmechtel** [tɛçtəl'mɛçtəl] (-s, -) (*umg*) *nt* (*Liebschaft*) affair, carry-on.
**TEE** *abk* (= *Trans-Europ-Express*) Trans-Europe-Express.
**Tee** [te:] (-s, -s) *m* tea; ~**beutel** *m* tea bag; ~**kanne** *f* teapot; ~**licht** *nt* night-light; ~**löffel** *m* teaspoon; ~**mischung** *f* blend of tea.
**Teer** [te:r] (-(e)s, -e) *m* tar; **t~en** *vt* to tar.
**Teesieb** *nt* tea strainer.
**Teewagen** *m* tea trolley.
**Teflon** ® ['tɛflo:n] (-s) *nt* Teflon ®.
**Teheran** ['te:həra:n] (-s) *nt* Teheran.
**Teich** [taiç] (-(e)s, -e) *m* pond.
**Teig** [taik] (-(e)s, -e) *m* dough.
**teigig** ['taigıç] *adj* doughy.
**Teigwaren** *pl* pasta *sing*.
**Teil** [tail] (-(e)s, -e) *m od nt* part; (*Anteil*) share ♦ *nt* (*Bestand~*) component, part; (*Ersatz~*) spare (part); **zum** ~ partly; **ich für mein(en)** ~ ... I, for my part ...; **sich** *dat* **sein** ~ **denken** (*umg*) to draw one's own conclusions; **er hat sein(en)** ~ **dazu beigetragen** he did his bit *od* share; **t~bar** *adj* divisible; ~**betrag** *m* instalment (*BRIT*), installment (*US*); ~**chen** *nt* (atomic) particle.
**teilen** *vt* to divide; (*mit jdm*) to share ♦ *vr* to divide; (*in Gruppen*) to split up.
**Teil-** *zW:* **t~entrahmt** *adj* semi-skimmed; ~**gebiet** *nt* (*Bereich*) branch; (*räumlich*) area; **t~haben** *unreg vi:* **an etw** *dat* **t~haben** to share in sth; ~**haber** (-s, -) *m* partner; ~**kaskoversicherung** *f* third party, fire and theft insurance.
**Teilnahme** (-, -n) *f* participation; (*Mitleid*) sympathy; **jdm seine herzliche** ~ **aussprechen** to offer sb one's heartfelt sympathy.
**teilnahmslos** *adj* disinterested, apathetic.
**teilnehmen** *unreg vi:* **an etw** *dat* ~ to take part in sth.
**Teilnehmer(in)** (-s, -) *m(f)* participant.
**teils** *adv* partly.
**Teilschaden** *m* partial loss.
**Teilstrecke** *f* stage; (*von Straße*) stretch; (*bei Bus etc*) fare stage.
**Teilung** *f* division.
**Teil-** *zW:* **t~weise** *adv* partially, in part; ~**zahlung** *f* payment by instalments (*BRIT*) *od* installments (*US*); ~**zeitarbeit** *f* part-time job *od* work.
**Teint** [tɛ̃:] (-s, -s) *m* complexion.
**Telebrief** ['te:lebri:f] *m* facsimile, fax.
**Telefax** ['te:lefaks] (-) *nt* telefax.
**Telefon** [tele'fo:n] (-s, -e) *nt* (tele)phone; **ans** ~ **gehen** to answer the phone; ~**amt** *nt* telephone exchange; ~**anruf** *m* (tele)phone call.
**Telefonat** [telefo'na:t] (-(e)s, -e) *nt* (tele)phone call.

**Telefon-** *zW:* **~buch** *nt* (tele)phone directory; **~gebühr** *f* call charge; (*Grundgebühr*) (tele)phone rental; **~gespräch** *nt* (tele)phone call; **~häuschen** (*umg*) *nt* = **Telefonzelle.**

**telefonieren** [telefo'ni:rən] *vi* to (tele)phone; **bei jdm ~** to use sb's phone; **mit jdm ~** to speak to sb on the phone.

**telefonisch** [tele'fo:nɪʃ] *adj* telephone; (*Benachrichtigung*) by telephone; **ich bin ~ zu erreichen** I can be reached by phone.

**Telefonist(in)** [telefo'nɪst(ɪn)] *m(f)* telephonist.

**Telefon-** *zW:* **~karte** *f* phone card; **~nummer** *f* (tele)phone number; **~seelsorge** *f:* **die ~seelsorge** ≈ the Samaritans; **~verbindung** *f* telephone connection; **~zelle** *f* telephone box (*BRIT*) *od* booth (*US*), callbox (*BRIT*); **~zentrale** *f* telephone exchange.

**Telegraf** [tele'gra:f] (**-en, -en**) *m* telegraph.

**Telegrafenleitung** *f* telegraph line.

**Telegrafenmast** *m* telegraph pole.

**Telegrafie** [telegra'fi:] *f* telegraphy.

**telegrafieren** [telegra'fi:rən] *vt, vi* to telegraph, cable, wire.

**telegrafisch** [tele'gra:fɪʃ] *adj* telegraphic; **jdm ~ Geld überweisen** to cable sb money.

**Telegramm** [tele'gram] (**-s, -e**) *nt* telegram, cable; **~adresse** *f* telegraphic address; **~formular** *nt* telegram form.

**Telegraph** *m* = **Telegraf.**

**Telekolleg** ['te:ləkɔle:k] *nt* ≈ Open University (*BRIT*).

**Teleobjektiv** ['te:lə|ɔpjɛkti:f] *nt* telephoto lens.

**Telepathie** [telepa'ti:] *f* telepathy.

**telepathisch** [tele'pa:tɪʃ] *adj* telepathic.

**Telephon** *nt* = **Telefon.**

**Teleskop** [tele'sko:p] (**-s, -e**) *nt* telescope.

**Telespiel** *nt* video game.

**Telex** ['te:lɛks] (**-, -(e)**) *nt* telex.

**Teller** ['tɛlər] (**-s, -**) *m* plate.

**Tempel** ['tɛmpəl] (**-s, -**) *m* temple.

**Temperafarbe** ['tɛmperafarbə] *f* distemper.

**Temperament** [tɛmpera'mɛnt] *nt* temperament; (*Schwung*) vivacity, vitality; **sein ~ ist mit ihm durchgegangen** he went over the top; **t~los** *adj* spiritless; **t~voll** *adj* high-spirited, lively.

**Temperatur** [tɛmpera'tu:r] *f* temperature; **erhöhte ~ haben** to have a temperature.

**Tempo¹** ['tɛmpo] (**-s, -s**) *nt* speed, pace; **~!** get a move on!

**Tempo²** ['tɛmpo] (**-s, Tempi**) *nt* (*MUS*) tempo; **das ~ angeben** (*fig*) to set the pace; **~limit** *nt* speed limit.

**temporär** [tɛmpo'rɛ:r] *adj* temporary.

**Tempotaschentuch** ® *nt* paper handkerchief.

**Tendenz** [tɛn'dɛnts] *f* tendency; (*Absicht*) intention.

**tendenziell** [tɛndɛntsi'ɛl] *adj:* **nur ~e Unterschiede** merely differences in emphasis.

**tendenziös** [tɛndɛntsi'ø:s] *adj* bias(s)ed, tendentious.

**tendieren** [tɛn'di:rən] *vi:* **zu etw ~** to show a tendency to(wards) sth, incline to(wards) sth.

**Teneriffa** [tene'rɪfa] (**-s**) *nt* Tenerife.

**Tenne** ['tɛnə] (**-, -n**) *f* threshing floor.

**Tennis** ['tɛnɪs] (**-**) *nt* tennis; **~platz** *m* tennis court; **~schläger** *m* tennis racket; **~spieler** *m* tennis player.

**Tenor** [te'no:r] (**-s, -̈e**) *m* tenor.

**Teppich** ['tɛpɪç] (**-s, -e**) *m* carpet; **~boden** *m* wall-to-wall carpeting; **~kehrmaschine** *f* carpet sweeper; **~klopfer** *m* carpet beater.

**Termin** [tɛr'mi:n] (**-s, -e**) *m* (*Zeitpunkt*) date; (*Frist*) deadline; (*Arzt~ etc*) appointment; (*JUR: Verhandlung*) hearing; **sich** *dat* **einen ~ geben lassen** to make an appointment; **t~gerecht** *adj* on schedule.

**terminieren** [tɛrmi'ni:rən] *vt* (*befristen*) to limit; (*festsetzen*) to set a date for.

**Terminkalender** *m* diary, appointments book.

**Terminologie** [tɛrminolo'gi:] *f* terminology.

**Termite** [tɛr'mi:tə] (**-, -n**) *f* termite.

**Terpentin** [tɛrpɛn'ti:n] (**-s, -e**) *nt* turpentine, turps *sing*.

**Terrain** [tɛ'rɛ̃:] (**-s, -s**) *nt* land, terrain; (*fig*) territory; **das ~ sondieren** (*MIL*) to reconnoitre the terrain; (*fig*) to see how the land lies.

**Terrasse** [tɛ'rasə] (**-, -n**) *f* terrace.

**Terrine** [tɛ'ri:nə] *f* tureen.

**territorial** [tɛritori'a:l] *adj* territorial.

**Territorium** [tɛri'to:riʊm] *nt* territory.

**Terror** ['tɛrɔr] (**-s**) *m* terror; (**~herrschaft**) reign of terror; **blanker ~** sheer terror; **~anschlag** *m* terrorist attack.

**terrorisieren** [tɛrori'zi:rən] *vt* to terrorize.

**Terrorismus** [tɛro'rɪsmʊs] *m* terrorism.

**Terrorist(in)** [tɛro'rɪst(ɪn)] *m(f)* terrorist.

**terroristisch** *adj* terrorist *attr*.

**Terrororganisation** *f* terrorist organization.

**Tertia** ['tɛrtsia] (**-, Tertien**) *f* (*SCH: Unter~/ Ober~*) *fourth/fifth year of German secondary school.*

**Terz** [tɛrts] (**-, -en**) *f* (*MUS*) third.

**Terzett** [tɛr'tsɛt] (**-(e)s, -e**) *nt* (*MUS*) trio.

**Tesafilm** ® ['te:zafɪlm] *m* Sellotape ® (*BRIT*), Scotch tape ® (*US*).

**Test** [tɛst] (**-s, -s**) *m* test.

**Testament** [testa'mɛnt] *nt* will, testament; (*REL*) Testament; **Altes/Neues ~** Old/New Testament.

**testamentarisch** [testamɛn'ta:rɪʃ] *adj* testamentary.

**Testamentsvollstrecker(in)** (**-s, -**) *m(f)* executor (of a will).

**Testat** [tɛs'ta:t] (**-(e)s, -e**) *nt* certificate.

**Testator** [tɛs'ta:tɔr] *m* testator.

**Test-** *zW:* **~bild** *nt* (*TV*) test card; **t~en** *vt* to test; **~fall** *m* test case; **~person** *f* subject (of a test); **~stoppabkommen** *nt* nuclear test ban agreement.

**Tetanus** ['te:tanʊs] (-) *m* tetanus; **~impfung** *f* (anti-)tetanus injection.

**teuer** ['tɔyər] *adj* dear, expensive; **teures Geld** good money; **das wird ihn ~ zu stehen kommen** (*fig*) that will cost him dear.

**Teuerung** *f* increase in prices.

**Teuerungszulage** *f* cost-of-living bonus.

**Teufel** ['tɔyfəl] (-s, -) *m* devil; **den ~ an die Wand malen** (*schwarzmalen*) to imagine the worst; (*Unheil heraufbeschwören*) to tempt fate *od* providence; **in ~s Küche kommen** to get into a mess; **jdn zum ~ jagen** (*umg*) to send sb packing.

**Teufelei** [tɔyfə'lai] *f* devilment.

**Teufels-** *zW:* **~austreibung** *f* exorcism; **~brut** (*umg*) *f* devil's brood; **~kreis** *m* vicious circle.

**teuflisch** ['tɔyflɪʃ] *adj* fiendish, diabolic.

**Text** [tɛkst] (-(e)s, -e) *m* text; (*Lieder~*) words *pl*; (: *von Schlager*) lyrics *pl*; **~dichter** *m* songwriter; **t~en** *vi* to write the words.

**textil** [tɛks'ti:l] *adj* textile; **T~branche** *f* textile trade.

**Textilien** *pl* textiles *pl*.

**Textilindustrie** *f* textile industry.

**Textilwaren** *pl* textiles *pl*.

**Textstelle** *f* passage.

**Textverarbeitungssystem** *nt* word processor.

**TH** (-, -s) *f abk* (= *Technische Hochschule*) *siehe* **technisch**.

**Thailand** ['tailant] (-s) *nt* Thailand.

**Thailänder(in)** ['tailɛndər(ɪn)] (-s, -) *m(f)* Thai.

**Theater** [te'a:tər] (-s, -) *nt* theatre (*BRIT*), theater (*US*); (*umg*) fuss; (**ein**) **~ machen** to make a (big) fuss; **~ spielen** to act; (*fig*) to put on an act; **~besucher** *m* playgoer; **~kasse** *f* box office; **~stück** *nt* (stage) play.

**theatralisch** [tea'tra:lɪʃ] *adj* theatrical.

**Theke** ['te:kə] (-, -n) *f* (*Schanktisch*) bar; (*Ladentisch*) counter.

**Thema** ['te:ma] (-s, **Themen** *od* **-ta**) *nt* (*MUS, Leitgedanke*) theme; topic, subject; **beim ~ bleiben/vom ~ abschweifen** to stick to/ wander off the subject.

**thematisch** [te'ma:tɪʃ] *adj* thematic.

**Themenkreis** *m* topic.

**Themenpark** *m* theme park.

**Themse** ['tɛmzə] *f:* **die ~** the Thames.

**Theologe** [teo'lo:gə] (-n, -n) *m* theologian.

**Theologie** [teolo'gi:] *f* theology.

**Theologin** *f* theologian.

**theologisch** [teo'lo:gɪʃ] *adj* theological.

**Theoretiker(in)** [teo're:tikər(ɪn)] (-s, -) *m(f)* theorist.

**theoretisch** *adj* theoretical; **~ gesehen** in theory, theoretically.

**Theorie** [teo'ri:] *f* theory.

**Therapeut** [tera'pɔyt] (-en, -en) *m* therapist.

**therapeutisch** *adj* therapeutic.

**Therapie** [tera'pi:] *f* therapy.

**Thermalbad** [tɛr'ma:lba:t] *nt* thermal bath; (*Badeort*) thermal spa.

**Thermalquelle** *f* thermal spring.

**Thermometer** [tɛrmo'me:tər] (-s, -) *nt* thermometer.

**Thermosflasche** ® ['tɛrmɔsflaʃə] *f* Thermos ® flask.

**Thermostat** [tɛrmo'sta:t] (-(e)s *od* -en, -e(n)) *m* thermostat.

**These** ['te:zə] (-, -n) *f* thesis.

**Thrombose** [trɔm'bo:sə] (-, -n) *f* thrombosis.

**Thron** [tro:n] (-(e)s, -e) *m* throne; **~besteigung** *f* accession (to the throne).

**thronen** *vi* to sit enthroned; (*fig*) to sit in state.

**Thronerbe** *m* heir to the throne.

**Thronfolge** *f* succession (to the throne).

**Thunfisch** ['tu:nfɪʃ] *m* tuna (fish).

**Thüringen** ['ty:rɪŋən] (-s) *nt* Thuringia.

**Thymian** ['ty:mia:n] (-s, -e) *m* thyme.

**Tibet** ['ti:bɛt] (-s) *nt* Tibet.

**Tick** [tɪk] (-(e)s, -s) *m* tic; (*Eigenart*) quirk; (*Fimmel*) craze.

**ticken** *vi* to tick; **nicht richtig ~** (*umg*) to be off one's rocker.

**Ticket** ['tɪkət] (-s, -s) *nt* ticket.

**tief** [ti:f] *adj* deep; (*~sinnig*) profound; (*Ausschnitt, Ton*) low; **~er Teller** soup plate; **bis ~ in die Nacht hinein** late into the night; **T~** (-s, -s) *nt* (*MET*) depression; (*fig*) low; **T~bau** *m* civil engineering (*at or below ground level*); **T~druck** *m* (*MET*) low pressure.

**Tiefe** (-, -n) *f* depth.

**Tiefebene** ['ti:f|e:bənə] *f* plain.

**Tiefenpsychologie** *f* depth psychology.

**Tiefenschärfe** *f* (*PHOT*) depth of focus.

**tief-** *zW:* **~ernst** *adj* very grave *od* solemn; **T~flug** *m* low-level *od* low-altitude flight; **T~gang** *m* (*NAUT*) draught (*BRIT*), draft (*US*); (*geistig*) depth; **T~garage** *f* underground car park (*BRIT*) *od* parking lot (*US*); **~gekühlt** *adj* frozen; **~greifend** *adj* far-reaching; **T~kühlfach** *nt* freezer compartment; **T~kühlkost** *f* frozen food; **T~kühltruhe** *f* freezer, deep freezer (*US*); **T~lader** (-s, -) *m* low-loader; **T~land** *nt* lowlands *pl*; **T~parterre** *f* basement; **T~punkt** *m* low point; (*fig*) low ebb; **T~schlag** *m* (*BOXEN, fig*) blow below the belt; **~schürfend** *adj* profound; **T~see** *f* deep parts of the sea; **T~sinn** *m* profundity; **~sinnig** *adj* profound; (*umg*) melancholy; **T~stand** *m* low level; **~stapeln** *vi* to be overmodest; **T~start** *m* (*SPORT*) crouch start.

**Tiefstwert** *m* minimum *od* lowest value.

**Tiegel** ['ti:gəl] (-s, -) *m* saucepan; (*CHEM*) crucible.

**Tier** [ti:r] (-(e)s, -e) *nt* animal; **~arzt** *m*, **~ärztin**

*f* vet(erinary surgeon) (*BRIT*), veterinarian (*US*); ~**freund** *m* animal lover; ~**garten** *m* zoo, zoological gardens *pl*; ~**handlung** *f* pet shop (*BRIT*) *od* store (*US*); **t~isch** *adj* animal *attrib*; (*lit, fig*) brutish; (*fig: Ernst etc*) deadly; ~**kreis** *m* zodiac; ~**kunde** *f* zoology; **t~lieb** *adj*, **t~liebend** *adj* fond of animals; ~**quälerei** *f* cruelty to animals; ~**reich** *nt* animal kingdom; ~**schutz** *m* protection of animals; ~**schutzverein** *m* society for the prevention of cruelty to animals; ~**versuch** *m* animal experiment; ~**welt** *f* animal kingdom.

**Tiger** ['ti:gər] (**-s, -**) *m* tiger; ~**in** *f* tigress.

**tilgen** ['tɪlgən] *vt* to erase; (*Sünden*) to expiate; (*Schulden*) to pay off.

**Tilgung** *f* erasing, blotting out; expiation; repayment.

**Tilgungsfonds** *m* (*COMM*) sinking fund.

**tingeln** ['tɪŋgəln] (*umg*) *vi* to appear in small night clubs.

**Tinktur** [tɪŋk'tu:r] *f* tincture.

**Tinte** ['tɪntə] (**-, -n**) *f* ink.

**Tinten-** *zW*: ~**faß** *nt* inkwell; ~**fisch** *m* cuttlefish; (*achtarmig*) octopus; ~**fleck** *m* ink stain *od* blot; ~**stift** *m* indelible pencil; ~**strahldrucker** *m* ink-jet printer.

**Tip** [tɪp] (**-s, -s**) *m* (*SPORT, BÖRSE*) tip; (*Andeutung*) hint; (*an Polizei*) tip-off.

**Tippelbruder** (*umg*) *m* tramp, gentleman of the road (*BRIT*), hobo (*US*).

**tippen** ['tɪpən] *vi* to tap, touch; (*umg: schreiben*) to type; (*im Lotto etc*) to bet ♦ *vt* to type; to bet; **auf jdn ~** (*umg: raten*) to tip sb, put one's money on sb (*fig*).

**Tippfehler** (*umg*) *m* typing error.

**Tippse** (**-, -n**) (*umg*) *f* typist.

**tipptopp** ['tɪp'tɔp] (*umg*) *adj* tiptop.

**Tippzettel** *m* (pools) coupon.

**Tirade** [ti'ra:də] (**-, -n**) *f* tirade.

**Tirol** [ti'ro:l] (**-s**) *nt* the Tyrol.

**Tiroler(in)** (**-s, -**) *m(f)* Tyrolese, Tyrolean.

**tirolerisch** *adj* Tyrolese, Tyrolean.

**Tisch** [tɪʃ] (**-(e)s, -e**) *m* table; **bitte zu ~!** lunch *od* dinner is served; **bei ~** at table; **vor/nach ~** before/after eating; **unter den ~ fallen** (*fig*) to be dropped; ~**decke** *f* tablecloth.

**Tischler** (**-s, -**) *m* carpenter, joiner.

**Tischlerei** [tɪʃlə'raɪ] *f* joiner's workshop; (*Arbeit*) carpentry, joinery.

**Tischlerhandwerk** *nt* cabinetmaking.

**tischlern** *vi* to do carpentry *etc*.

**Tisch-** *zW*: ~**nachbar** *m* neighbour (*BRIT*) *od* neighbor (*US*) (at table); ~**rechner** *m* desk calculator; ~**rede** *f* after-dinner speech; ~**tennis** *nt* table tennis; ~**tuch** *nt* tablecloth.

**Titel** ['ti:təl] (**-s, -**) *m* title; ~**anwärter** *m* (*SPORT*) challenger; ~**bild** *nt* cover (picture); (*von Buch*) frontispiece; ~**geschichte** *f* headline story; ~**rolle** *f* title role; ~**seite** *f* cover; (*Buch~*) title page; ~**verteidiger** *m* defending champion, title holder.

**Titte** ['tɪtə] (**-, -n**) (*umg*) *f* (*weibliche Brust*) boob, tit (*umg*).

**titulieren** [titu'li:rən] *vt* to entitle; (*anreden*) to address.

**tja** [tja] *interj* well!

**Toast** [to:st] (**-(e)s, -s** *od* **-e**) *m* toast.

**toasten** *vi* to drink a toast ♦ *vt* (*Brot*) to toast; **auf jdn ~** to toast sb, drink a toast to sb.

**Toaster** (**-s, -**) *m* toaster.

**toben** ['to:bən] *vi* to rage; (*Kinder*) to romp about.

**tob-** *zW*: **T~sucht** *f* raving madness; ~**süchtig** *adj* maniacal; **T~suchtsanfall** *m* maniacal fit.

**Tochter** ['tɔxtər] (**-, ⁓**) *f* daughter; ~**gesellschaft** *f* subsidiary (company).

**Tod** [to:t] (**-(e)s, -e**) *m* death; **zu ~e betrübt sein** to be in the depths of despair; **eines natürlichen/gewaltsamen ~es sterben** to die of natural causes/die a violent death; **t~ernst** (*umg*) *adj* deadly serious ♦ *adv* in dead earnest.

**Todes-** *zW*: ~**angst** *f* mortal fear; ~**ängste ausstehen** (*umg*) to be scared to death; ~**anzeige** *f* obituary (notice); ~**fall** *m* death; ~**kampf** *m* death throes *pl*; ~**opfer** *nt* death, casualty, fatality; ~**qualen** *pl*: ~**qualen ausstehen** (*fig*) to suffer agonies; ~**stoß** *m* deathblow; ~**strafe** *f* death penalty; ~**tag** *m* anniversary of death; ~**ursache** *f* cause of death; ~**urteil** *nt* death sentence; ~**verachtung** *f* utter disgust.

**Todfeind** *m* deadly *od* mortal enemy.

**todkrank** *adj* dangerously ill.

**tödlich** ['tø:tlɪç] *adj* fatal; (*Gift*) deadly, lethal.

**tod-** *zW*: ~**müde** *adj* dead tired; ~**schick** (*umg*) *adj* smart, classy; ~**sicher** (*umg*) *adj* absolutely *od* dead certain; **T~sünde** *f* deadly sin; ~**traurig** *adj* extremely sad.

**Tofu** ['to:fu] (**-(s)**) *m* tofu.

**Togo** ['to:go] (**-s**) *nt* Togo.

**Toilette** [toa'lɛtə] *f* toilet, lavatory (*BRIT*), john (*US*); (*Frisiertisch*) dressing table; (*Kleidung*) outfit; **auf die ~ gehen/auf der ~ sein** to go to/be in the toilet.

**Toiletten-** *zW*: ~**artikel** *pl* toiletries *pl*, toilet articles *pl*; ~**papier** *nt* toilet paper; ~**tisch** *m* dressing table.

**toi, toi, toi** ['tɔy'tɔy'tɔy] (*umg*) *interj* good luck; (*unberufen*) touch wood.

**Tokio** ['to:kjo] (**-s**) *nt* Tokyo.

**tolerant** [tole'rant] *adj* tolerant.

**Toleranz** *f* tolerance.

**tolerieren** [tole'ri:rən] *vt* to tolerate.

**toll** [tɔl] *adj* mad; (*Treiben*) wild; (*umg*) terrific.

**tollen** *vi* to romp.

**toll-** *zW*: **T~heit** *f* madness, wildness; **T~kirsche** *f* deadly nightshade; ~**kühn** *adj* daring; **T~wut** *f* rabies.

**Tölpel** ['tœlpəl] (**-s, -**) *m* oaf, clod.

**Tomate** [to'ma:tə] (**-, -n**) *f* tomato; **du treulose ~!** (*umg*) you're a fine friend!

**Tomatenmark** (-(e)s) *nt* tomato purée.

**Tombola** ['tɔmbola] (-, -s *od* **Tombolen**) *f* tombola.

**Ton**[1] [toːn] (-(e)s, -e) *m* (*Erde*) clay.

**Ton**[2] [toːn] (-(e)s, ̈-e) *m* (*Laut*) sound; (*MUS*) note; (*Redeweise*) tone; (*Farb~, Nuance*) shade; (*Betonung*) stress; **keinen ~ herausbringen** not to be able to say a word; **den ~ angeben** (*MUS*) to give an A; (*fig: Mensch*) to set the tone; **~abnehmer** *m* pick-up; **t~angebend** *adj* leading; **~arm** *m* pick-up arm; **~art** *f* (musical) key; **~band** *nt* tape; **~bandaufnahme** *f* tape recording; **~bandgerät** *nt* tape recorder.

**tönen** ['tøːnən] *vi* to sound ♦ *vt* to shade; (*Haare*) to tint.

**tönern** ['tøːnərn] *adj* clay.

**Ton-** *zW:* **~fall** *m* intonation; **~film** *m* sound film; **~höhe** *f* pitch.

**Tonika** ['toːnika] (-, -iken) *f* (*MUS*) tonic.

**Tonikum** (-s, -ika) *nt* (*MED*) tonic.

**Ton-** *zW:* **~ingenieur** *m* sound engineer; **~kopf** *m* recording head; **~künstler** *m* musician; **~leiter** *f* (*MUS*) scale; **t~los** *adj* soundless.

**Tonne** ['tɔnə] (-, -n) *f* barrel; (*Maß*) ton.

**Ton-** *zW:* **~spur** *f* soundtrack; **~taube** *f* clay pigeon; **~waren** *pl* pottery *sing*, earthenware *sing*.

**Topf** [tɔpf] (-(e)s, ̈-e) *m* pot; **alles in einen ~ werfen** (*fig*) to lump everything together; **~blume** *f* pot plant.

**Töpfer(in)** ['tœpfər(ɪn)] (-s, -) *m(f)* potter.

**Töpferei** [tœpfə'raɪ] *f* (*Töpferware*) pottery; (*Werkstatt*) pottery, potter's workshop.

**töpfern** *vi* to do pottery.

**Töpferscheibe** *f* potter's wheel.

**topfit** ['tɔp'fɪt] *adj* in top form.

**Topflappen** *m* ovencloth.

**topographisch** [topo'graːfɪʃ] *adj* topographic.

**topp** [tɔp] *interj* O.K.

**Tor**[1] [toːr] (-en, -en) *m* fool.

**Tor**[2] (-(e)s, -e) *nt* gate; (*SPORT*) goal; **~bogen** *m* archway; **~einfahrt** *f* entrance gate.

**Toresschluß** *m:* **(kurz) vor ~** right at the last minute.

**Torf** [tɔrf] (-(e)s) *m* peat; **~stechen** *nt* peat-cutting.

**Torheit** *f* foolishness; (*törichte Handlung*) foolish deed.

**Torhüter** (-s, -) *m* goalkeeper.

**töricht** ['tøːrɪçt] *adj* foolish.

**torkeln** ['tɔrkəln] *vi* to stagger, reel.

**torpedieren** [tɔrpe'diːrən] *vt* (*lit, fig*) to torpedo.

**Torpedo** [tɔr'peːdo] (-s, -s) *m* torpedo.

**Torschlußpanik** ['toːrʃlʊspaːnɪk] (*umg*) *f* (*von Unverheirateten*) fear of being left on the shelf.

**Torte** ['tɔrtə] (-, -n) *f* cake; (*Obst~*) flan, tart.

**Tortenguß** *m* glaze.

**Tortenheber** *m* cake slice.

**Tortur** [tɔr'tuːr] *f* ordeal.

**Torverhältnis** *nt* goal average.

**Torwart** (-(e)s, -e) *m* goalkeeper.

**tosen** ['toːzən] *vi* to roar.

**Toskana** [tɔs'kaːna] *f* Tuscany.

**tot** [toːt] *adj* dead; **er war auf der Stelle ~** he died instantly; **der ~e Winkel** the blind spot; **einen ~en Punkt haben** to be at one's lowest; **das T~e Meer** the Dead Sea.

**total** [to'taːl] *adj* total; **T~ausverkauf** *m* clearance sale.

**totalitär** [totali'tɛːr] *adj* totalitarian.

**Totaloperation** *f* extirpation; (*von Gebärmutter*) hysterectomy.

**Totalschaden** *m* (*AUT*) complete write-off.

**totarbeiten** *vr* to work o.s. to death.

**totärgern** (*umg*) *vr* to get really annoyed.

**Tote(r)** *f(m)* dead person.

**töten** ['tøːtən] *vt, vi* to kill.

**Toten-** *zW:* **~bett** *nt* deathbed; **t~blaß** *adj* deathly pale, white as a sheet; **~gräber** (-s, -) *m* gravedigger; **~hemd** *nt* shroud; **~kopf** *m* skull; **~messe** *f* requiem mass; **~schein** *m* death certificate; **~stille** *f* deathly silence; **~tanz** *m* danse macabre; **~wache** *f* wake.

**tot-** *zW:* **~fahren** *unreg vt* to run over; **~geboren** *adj* stillborn; **~kriegen** (*umg*) *vt:* **nicht ~zukriegen sein** to go on for ever; **~lachen** (*umg*) *vr* to laugh one's head off.

**Toto** ['toːto] (-s, -s) *m od nt* ≈ pools *pl*; **~schein** *m* ≈ pools coupon.

**tot-** *zW:* **~sagen** *vt:* **jdn ~sagen** to say that sb is dead; **T~schlag** *m* (*JUR*) manslaughter, second degree murder (*US*); **~schlagen** *unreg vt* (*lit, fig*) to kill; **T~schläger** *m* (*Waffe*) cosh (*BRIT*), blackjack (*US*); **~schweigen** *unreg vt* to hush up; **~stellen** *vr* to pretend to be dead; **~treten** *unreg vt* to trample to death.

**Tötung** ['tøːtʊŋ] *f* killing.

**Toupet** [tu'peː] (-s, -s) *nt* toupee.

**toupieren** [tu'piːrən] *vt* to backcomb.

**Tour** [tuːr] (-, -en) *f* tour, trip; (*Umdrehung*) revolution; (*Verhaltensart*) way; **auf ~en kommen** (*AUT*) to reach top speed; (*fig*) to get into top gear; **auf vollen ~en laufen** (*lit*) to run at full speed; (*fig*) to be in full swing; **auf die krumme ~** by dishonest means; **in einer ~** incessantly.

**Tourenzahl** *f* number of revolutions.

**Tourenzähler** *m* rev counter.

**Tourismus** [tu'rɪsmʊs] *m* tourism.

**Tourist(in)** *m(f)* tourist.

**Touristenklasse** *f* tourist class.

**Touristik** [tu'rɪstɪk] *f* tourism.

**touristisch** *adj* tourist *attr*.

**Tournee** [tur'neː] (-, -s *od* -n) *f* (*THEAT etc*) tour; **auf ~ gehen** to go on tour.

**Trab** [traːp] (-(e)s) *m* trot; **auf ~ sein** (*umg*) to be on the go.

**Trabant** [tra'bant] *m* satellite.

**Trabantenstadt** f satellite town.
**traben** ['traːbən] vi to trot.
**Tracht** [traxt] (-, -en) f (Kleidung) costume, dress; **eine ~ Prügel** a sound thrashing.
**trachten** vi to strive, endeavour (BRIT), endeavor (US); **danach ~, etw zu tun to** strive to do sth; **jdm nach dem Leben ~ to** seek to kill sb.
**trächtig** ['trɛçtıç] adj (Tier) pregnant.
**Tradition** [traditsi'oːn] f tradition.
**traditionell** [traditsio'nɛl] adj traditional.
**traf** etc [traːf] vb siehe **treffen.**
**Tragbahre** f stretcher.
**tragbar** adj (Gerät) portable; (Kleidung) wearable; (erträglich) bearable.
**träge** ['trɛːgə] adj sluggish, slow; (PHYS) inert.
**tragen** ['traːgən] unreg vt to carry; (Kleidung, Brille) to wear; (Namen, Früchte) to bear; (erdulden) to endure ♦ vi (schwanger sein) to be pregnant; (Eis) to hold; **schwer an etw** dat **~** (lit) to have a job carrying sth; (fig) to find sth hard to bear; **zum T~ kommen** to come to fruition; (nützlich werden) to come in useful.
**tragend** adj (Säule, Bauteil) load-bearing; (Idee, Motiv) fundamental.
**Träger** ['trɛːgər] (-s, -) m carrier; wearer; bearer; (Ordens~) holder; (an Kleidung) (shoulder) strap; (Körperschaft etc) sponsor; (Holz~, Beton~) (supporting) beam; (Stahl~, Eisen~) girder; (TECH: Stütze von Brücken etc) support.
**Trägerin** f (Person) siehe **Träger.**
**Träger-** zW: **~kleid** nt pinafore dress (BRIT), jumper (US); **~rakete** f launch vehicle; **~rock** m skirt with shoulder straps.
**Tragetasche** f carrier bag (BRIT), carry-all (US).
**Trag-** zW: **~fähigkeit** f load-bearing capacity; **~fläche** f (AVIAT) wing; **~flügelboot** nt hydrofoil.
**Trägheit** ['trɛːkhait] f laziness; (PHYS) inertia.
**Tragik** ['traːgık] f tragedy.
**tragikomisch** [tragi'koːmıʃ] adj tragi-comic.
**tragisch** adj tragic; **etw ~ nehmen** (umg) to take sth to heart.
**Traglast** f load.
**Tragödie** [tra'gøːdiə] f tragedy.
**trägt** [trɛːkt] vb siehe **tragen.**
**Tragweite** f range; (fig) scope; **von großer ~ sein** to have far-reaching consequences.
**Tragwerk** nt wing assembly.
**Trainer(in)** ['trɛːnər(ın)] (-s, -) m(f) (SPORT) trainer, coach; (FUSSBALL) manager.
**trainieren** [trɛ'niːrən] vt to train; (Übung) to practise (BRIT), practice (US) ♦ vi to train; **Fußball ~** to do football practice.
**Training** (-s, -s) nt training.
**Trainingsanzug** m track suit.
**Trakt** [trakt] (-(e)s, -e) m (Gebäudeteil) section; (Flügel) wing.

**Traktat** [trak'taːt] (-(e)s, -e) m od nt (Abhandlung) treatise; (Flugschrift, religiöse Schrift) tract.
**traktieren** (umg) vt (schlecht behandeln) to maltreat; (quälen) to torment.
**Traktor** ['traktor] m tractor; (von Drucker) tractor feed.
**trällern** ['trɛlərn] vt, vi to warble; (Vogel) to trill, warble.
**trampeln** ['trampəln] vt to trample; (abschütteln) to stamp ♦ vi to stamp.
**Trampelpfad** m track, path.
**Trampeltier** nt (ZOOL) (Bactrian) camel; (fig: umg) clumsy oaf.
**trampen** ['trɛmpən] vi to hitchhike.
**Tramper(in)** [trɛmpər(ın)] (-s, -) m(f) hitchhiker.
**Trampolin** [trampo'liːn] (-s, -e) nt trampoline.
**Tranchierbesteck** nt pair of carvers, carvers pl.
**tranchieren** [trã'ʃiːrən] vt to carve.
**Träne** ['trɛːnə] (-, -n) f tear.
**tränen** vi to water.
**Tränengas** nt tear gas.
**tranig** ['traːnıç] (umg) adj slow, sluggish.
**trank** etc [trank] vb siehe **trinken.**
**Tränke** ['trɛŋkə] (-, -n) f watering place.
**tränken** vt (naß machen) to soak; (Tiere) to water.
**Transaktion** [transaktsi'oːn] f transaction.
**Transformator** [transfor'maːtor] m transformer.
**Transfusion** [transfuzi'oːn] f transfusion.
**Transistor** [tran'zıstor] m transistor.
**transitiv** ['tranzitiːf] adj transitive.
**Transitverkehr** [tran'ziːtfɛrkeːr] m transit traffic.
**transparent** [transpa'rɛnt] adj transparent; **T~** (-(e)s, -e) nt (Bild) transparency; (Spruchband) banner.
**transpirieren** [transpi'riːrən] vi to perspire.
**Transplantation** [transplantatsi'oːn] f transplantation; (Haut~) graft(ing).
**Transport** [trans'port] (-(e)s, -e) m transport; (Fracht) consignment, shipment; **t~fähig** adj moveable.
**transportieren** [transpor'tiːrən] vt to transport.
**Transport-** zW: **~kosten** pl transport charges pl, carriage sing; **~mittel** nt means sing of transport; **~unternehmen** nt carrier.
**transsexuell** [transzɛksu'ɛl] adj transsexual.
**transusig** ['transuːzıç] (umg) adj sluggish.
**Transvestit** [transvɛs'tiːt] (-en, -en) m transvestite.
**Trapez** [tra'peːts] (-es, -e) nt trapeze; (MATH) trapezium.
**Trara** [tra'raː] (-s) nt: **mit viel ~ (um)** (fig: umg) with a great hullabaloo (about).
**trat** etc [traːt] vb siehe **treten.**
**Tratsch** [traːtʃ] (-(e)s) (umg) m gossip.
**tratschen** ['traːtʃən] (umg) vi to gossip.

**Tratte** ['tratə] (-, -n) *f* (*FIN*) draft.
**Traube** ['traubə] (-, -n) *f* grape; (*ganze Frucht*) bunch (of grapes).
**Traubenlese** *f* grape harvest.
**Traubenzucker** *m* glucose.
**trauen** ['trauən] *vi* +*dat* to trust ♦ *vr* to dare ♦ *vt* to marry; **jdm/etw** ~ to trust sb/sth.
**Trauer** ['trauər] (-) *f* sorrow; (*für Verstorbenen*) mourning; ~**fall** *m* death, bereavement; ~**feier** *f* funeral service; ~**flor** (-s, -e) *m* black ribbon; ~**gemeinde** *f* mourners *pl*; ~**marsch** *m* funeral march.
**trauern** *vi* to mourn; **um jdn** ~ to mourn (for) sb.
**Trauer-** *zW:* ~**rand** *m* black border; ~**spiel** *nt* tragedy; ~**weide** *f* weeping willow.
**Traufe** ['traufə] (-, -n) *f* eaves *pl*.
**träufeln** ['trɔyfəln] *vt, vi* to drip.
**traulich** ['traulɪç] *adj* cosy, intimate.
**Traum** [traum] (-(e)s, Träume) *m* dream; **aus der** ~! it's all over!
**Trauma** (-s, -men) *nt* trauma.
**traumatisieren** [traumati'ziːrən] *vt* to traumatize.
**Traumbild** *nt* vision.
**Traumdeutung** *f* interpretation of dreams.
**träumen** ['trɔymən] *vt, vi* to dream; **das hätte ich mir nicht** ~ **lassen** I'd never have thought it possible.
**Träumer(in)** (-s, -) *m(f)* dreamer.
**Träumerei** [trɔymə'rai] *f* dreaming.
**träumerisch** *adj* dreamy.
**traumhaft** *adj* dreamlike; (*fig*) wonderful.
**Traumtänzer** *m* dreamer.
**traurig** ['traurɪç] *adj* sad; **T~keit** *f* sadness.
**Trauring** *m* wedding ring.
**Trauschein** *m* marriage certificate.
**Trauung** *f* wedding ceremony.
**Trauzeuge** *m* witness (to a marriage).
**treffen** ['trɛfən] *unreg vt* to strike, hit; (*Bemerkung*) to hurt; (*begegnen*) to meet; (*Entscheidung etc*) to make; (*Maßnahmen*) to take ♦ *vi* to hit ♦ *vr* to meet; **er hat es gut getroffen** he did well; **er fühlte sich getroffen** he took it personally; ~ **auf** +*akk* to come across, meet; **es traf sich, daß** ... it so happened that ...; **es trifft sich gut** it's convenient.
**Treffen** (-s, -) *nt* meeting.
**treffend** *adj* pertinent, apposite.
**Treffer** (-s, -) *m* hit; (*Tor*) goal; (*Los*) winner.
**trefflich** *adj* excellent.
**Treffpunkt** *m* meeting place.
**Treibeis** *nt* drift ice.
**treiben** ['traibən] *unreg vt* to drive; (*Studien etc*) to pursue; (*SPORT*) to do, go in for ♦ *vi* (*Schiff etc*) to drift; (*Pflanzen*) to sprout; (*KOCH: aufgehen*) to rise; (*Medikamente*) to be diuretic; **die** ~**de Kraft** (*fig*) the driving force; **Handel mit etw/jdm** ~ to trade in sth/with sb; **es zu weit** ~ to go too far; **Unsinn** ~ to fool around; **T~** (-s) *nt* activity.

**Treib-** *zW:* ~**gut** *nt* flotsam and jetsam; ~**haus** *nt* greenhouse; ~**hauseffekt** *m* greenhouse effect; ~**hausgas** *nt* greenhouse gas; ~**jagd** *f* shoot (*in which game is sent up*); (*fig*) witchhunt; ~**sand** *m* quicksand; ~**stoff** *m* fuel.
**Trend** [trɛnt] (-s, -s) *m* trend; ~**wende** *f* new trend.
**trennbar** *adj* separable.
**trennen** ['trɛnən] *vt* to separate; (*teilen*) to divide ♦ *vr* to separate; **sich** ~ **von** to part with.
**Trennschärfe** *f* (*RUNDF*) selectivity.
**Trennung** *f* separation.
**Trennungsstrich** *m* hyphen.
**Trennwand** *f* partition (wall).
**treppab** *adv* downstairs.
**treppauf** *adv* upstairs.
**Treppe** ['trɛpə] (-, -n) *f* stairs *pl*, staircase; (*im Freien*) steps *pl*; **eine** ~ a staircase, a flight of stairs *od* steps; **sie wohnt zwei** ~**n hoch/höher** she lives two flights up/higher up.
**Treppengeländer** *nt* banister.
**Treppenhaus** *nt* staircase.
**Tresen** ['treːzən] (-s, -) *m* (*Theke*) bar; (*Ladentisch*) counter.
**Tresor** [tre'zoːr] (-s, -e) *m* safe.
**Tretboot** *nt* pedal boat, pedalo.
**treten** ['treːtən] *unreg vi* to step; (*Tränen, Schweiß*) to appear ♦ *vt* (*mit Fußtritt*) to kick; (*nieder*~) to tread, trample; ~ **nach** to kick at; ~ **in** +*akk* to step in(to); **in Verbindung** ~ to get in contact; **in Erscheinung** ~ to appear; **der Fluß trat über die Ufer** the river overflowed its banks; **in Streik** ~ to go on strike.
**Treter** ['treːtər] (*umg*) *pl* (*Schuhe*) casual shoes *pl*.
**Tretmine** *f* (*MIL*) (anti-personnel) mine.
**Tretmühle** *f* (*fig*) daily grind.
**treu** [trɔy] *adj* faithful, true; ~**doof** (*umg*) *adj* naïve.
**Treue** (-) *f* loyalty, faithfulness.
**Treuhand** (*umg*) *f,* **Treuhandanstalt** *f* trustee organization (*overseeing the privatization of former GDR state-owned firms*).

---

*The* **Treuhandanstalt** *is a now defunct organization set up in 1990 to take over the nationally-owned companies of the former* **DDR**, *to break them down into smaller units and to privatize them. It was based in Berlin and had nine branches. Many companies were closed down by the Treuhandanstalt because of their outdated equipment and inability to compete with the western firms. This resulted in a rise in unemployment.*

---

**Treuhänder** (-s, -) *m* trustee.
**Treuhandgesellschaft** *f* trust company.
**treu-** *zW:* ~**herzig** *adj* innocent; ~**lich** *adv*

faithfully; **~los** adj faithless; **~los an jdm handeln** to fail sb.

**Triathlon** ['tri:atlɔn] (-s, -s) nt triathlon.

**Tribüne** [tri'by:nə] (-, -n) f grandstand; (Redner~) platform.

**Tribut** [tri'bu:t] (-(e)s, -e) m tribute.

**Trichter** ['trıçtər] (-s, -) m funnel; (Bomben~) crater.

**Trick** [trık] (-s, -e od -s) m trick; **~film** m cartoon.

**Trieb** (-(e)s, -e) m urge, drive; (Neigung) inclination; (BOT) shoot.

**trieb** etc [tri:p] vb siehe **treiben.**

**Trieb-** zW: **~feder** f (fig) motivating force; **t~haft** adj impulsive; **~kraft** f (fig) drive; **~täter** m sex offender; **~wagen** m (EISENB) railcar; **~werk** nt engine.

**triefen** ['tri:fən] vi to drip.

**trifft** [trıft] vb siehe **treffen.**

**triftig** ['trıftıç] adj convincing; (Grund etc) good.

**Trigonometrie** [trigonome'tri:] f trigonometry.

**Trikot** [tri'ko:] (-s, -s) nt vest; (SPORT) shirt ♦ m (Gewebe) tricot.

**Triller** ['trılər] (-s, -) m (MUS) trill.

**trillern** vi to trill, warble.

**Trillerpfeife** f whistle.

**Trilogie** [trilo'gi:] f trilogy.

**Trimester** [tri'mɛstər] (-s, -) nt term.

**Trimm-Aktion** f keep-fit campaign.

**Trimm-dich-Pfad** m keep-fit trail.

**trimmen** vt (Hund) to trim; (umg: Mensch, Tier) to teach, train ♦ vr to keep fit.

**trinkbar** adj drinkable.

**trinken** ['trıŋkən] unreg vt, vi to drink.

**Trinker(in)** (-s, -) m(f) drinker.

**Trink-** zW: **t~fest** adj: **ich bin nicht sehr t~fest** I can't hold my drink very well; **~geld** nt tip; **~halle** f (Kiosk) refreshment kiosk; **~halm** m (drinking) straw; **~milch** f milk; **~spruch** m toast; **~wasser** nt drinking water.

**Trio** ['tri:o] (-s, -s) nt trio.

**trippeln** ['trıpəln] vi to toddle.

**Tripper** ['trıpər] (-s, -) m gonorrhoea (BRIT), gonorrhea (US).

**trist** [trıst] adj dreary, dismal; (Farbe) dull.

**tritt** [trıt] vb siehe **treten.**

**Tritt** (-(e)s, -e) m step; (Fuß~) kick.

**Trittbrett** nt (EISENB) step; (AUT) running board.

**Trittleiter** f stepladder.

**Triumph** [tri'umf] (-(e)s, -e) m triumph; **~bogen** m triumphal arch.

**triumphieren** [trium'fi:rən] vi to triumph; (jubeln) to exult.

**trivial** [trivi'a:l] adj trivial; **T~literatur** f light fiction.

**trocken** ['trɔkən] adj dry; **sich ~ rasieren** to use an electric razor; **T~automat** m tumble dryer; **T~dock** nt dry dock; **T~eis** nt dry ice;

**T~element** nt dry cell; **T~haube** f hairdryer; **T~heit** f dryness; **~legen** vt (Sumpf) to drain; (Kind) to put a clean nappy (BRIT) od diaper (US) on; **T~milch** f dried milk; **T~zeit** f (Jahreszeit) dry season.

**trocknen** vt, vi to dry.

**Trockner** (-s, -) m dryer.

**Troddel** ['trɔdəl] (-, -n) f tassel.

**Trödel** ['trø:dəl] (-s) (umg) m junk; **~markt** m flea market.

**trödeln** (umg) vi to dawdle.

**Trödler** (-s, -) m secondhand dealer.

**Trog** (-(e)s, ⁻e) m trough.

**trog** etc [tro:k] vb siehe **trügen.**

**trollen** ['trɔlən] (umg) vr to push off.

**Trommel** ['trɔməl] (-, -n) f drum; **die ~ rühren** (fig: umg) to drum up support; **~fell** nt eardrum; **~feuer** nt drumfire, heavy barrage.

**trommeln** vt, vi to drum.

**Trommelrevolver** m revolver.

**Trommelwaschmaschine** f tumble-action washing machine.

**Trommler(in)** ['trɔmlər(ın)] (-s, -) m(f) drummer.

**Trompete** [trɔm'pe:tə] (-, -n) f trumpet.

**Trompeter** (-s, -) m trumpeter.

**Tropen** ['tro:pən] pl tropics pl; **t~beständig** adj suitable for the tropics; **~helm** m topee, sun helmet.

**Tropf¹** [trɔpf] (-(e)s, ⁻e) (umg) m rogue; **armer ~** poor devil.

**Tropf²** (-(e)s) (umg) m (MED: Infusion) drip (umg); **am ~ hängen** to be on a drip.

**tröpfeln** ['trœpfəln] vi to drip, trickle.

**Tropfen** (-s, -) m drop; **ein guter** od **edler ~** a good wine; **ein ~ auf den heißen Stein** (fig: umg) a drop in the ocean.

**tropfen** vt, vi to drip ♦ vi unpers: **es tropft** a few raindrops are falling.

**tropfenweise** adv in drops.

**tropfnaß** adj dripping wet.

**Tropfsteinhöhle** f stalactite cave.

**Trophäe** [tro'fɛ:ə] (-, -n) f trophy.

**tropisch** ['tro:pıʃ] adj tropical.

**Trost** [tro:st] (-es) m consolation, comfort; **t~bedürftig** adj in need of consolation.

**trösten** ['trø:stən] vt to console, comfort.

**Tröster(in)** (-s, -) m(f) comfort(er).

**tröstlich** adj comforting.

**trost-** zW: **~los** adj bleak; (Verhältnisse) wretched; **T~pflaster** nt (fig) consolation; **T~preis** m consolation prize; **~reich** adj comforting.

**Tröstung** ['trø:stuŋ] f comfort, consolation.

**Trott** [trɔt] (-(e)s, -e) m trot; (Routine) routine.

**Trottel** (-s, -) (umg) m fool, dope.

**trotten** vi to trot.

**Trottoir** [trɔto'a:r] (-s, -s od -e) nt (veraltet) pavement (BRIT), sidewalk (US).

**trotz** [trɔts] präp (+gen od dat) in spite of.

**Trotz** (-es) m pig-headedness; **etw aus ~ tun**

to do sth just to show them; **jdm zum** ~ **in defiance of sb.**

**Trotzalter** *nt* obstinate phase.

**trotzdem** *adv* nevertheless ♦ *konj* although.

**trotzen** *vi +dat* to defy; (*der Kälte, dem Klima etc*) to withstand; (*der Gefahr*) to brave; (*trotzig sein*) to be awkward.

**trotzig** *adj* defiant; (*Kind*) difficult, awkward.

**Trotzkopf** *m* obstinate child.

**Trotzreaktion** *f* fit of pique.

**trüb** [try:p] *adj* dull; (*Flüssigkeit, Glas*) cloudy; (*fig*) gloomy; ~**e Tasse** (*umg*) drip.

**Trubel** ['tru:bəl] (-**s**) *m* hurly-burly.

**trüben** ['try:bən] *vt* to cloud ♦ *vr* to become clouded.

**Trübheit** *f* dullness; cloudiness; gloom.

**Trübsal** (-, -**e**) *f* distress; ~ **blasen** (*umg*) to mope.

**trüb-** *zW:* ~**selig** *adj* sad, melancholy; **T~sinn** *m* depression; ~**sinnig** *adj* depressed, gloomy.

**trudeln** ['tru:dəln] *vi* (*AVIAT*) to (go into a) spin.

**Trüffel** ['tryfəl] (-, -**n**) *f* truffle.

**Trug** (-(**e**)**s**) *m* (*liter*) deception; (*der Sinne*) illusion.

**trug** *etc* [tru:k] *vb siehe* **tragen.**

**trügen** ['try:gən] *unreg vt* to deceive ♦ *vi* to be deceptive; **wenn mich nicht alles trügt** unless I am very much mistaken.

**trügerisch** *adj* deceptive.

**Trugschluß** ['tru:kʃlus] *m* false conclusion.

**Truhe** ['tru:ə] (-, -**n**) *f* chest.

**Trümmer** ['trʏmər] *pl* wreckage *sing*; (*Bau~*) ruins *pl*; ~**feld** *nt* expanse of rubble *od* ruins; (*fig*) scene of devastation; ~**frauen** *pl* (*German*) women who cleared away the rubble after the war; ~**haufen** *m* heap of rubble.

**Trumpf** [trʊmpf] (-(**e**)**s**, -**e**) *m* (*lit, fig*) trump; **t~en** *vt, vi* to trump.

**Trunk** [trʊŋk] (-(**e**)**s**, -**e**) *m* drink.

**trunken** *adj* intoxicated; **T~bold** (-(**e**)**s**, -**e**) *m* drunkard; **T~heit** *f* intoxication; **T~heit am Steuer** drink-driving.

**Trunksucht** *f* alcoholism.

**Trupp** [trʊp] (-**s**, -**s**) *m* troop.

**Truppe** (-, -**n**) *f* troop; (*Waffengattung*) force; (*Schauspiel~*) troupe; **nicht von der schnellen** ~ **sein** (*umg*) to be slow.

**Truppen** *pl* troops *pl*; ~**abbau** *m* cutback in troop numbers; ~**führer** *m* (*military*) commander; ~**teil** *m* unit; ~**übungsplatz** *m* training area.

**Trust** [trast] (-(**e**)**s**, -**e** *od* -**s**) *m* trust.

**Truthahn** ['tru:tha:n] *m* turkey.

**Tschad** [tʃat] (-**s**) *m*: **der** ~ Chad.

**Tscheche** ['tʃɛçə] (-**n**, -**n**) *m*, **Tschechin** *f* Czech.

**tschechisch** *adj* Czech; **die T~e Republik** the Czech Republic.

**Tschechoslowakei** [tʃɛçoslova:'kai] *f*

(*früher*): **die** ~ Czechoslovakia.

**tschüs** [tʃʏs] (*umg*) *interj* cheerio (*BRIT*), so long (*US*).

**T-Shirt** ['ti:ʃə:t] (-**s**, -**s**) *nt* T-shirt.

**TU** (-) *f abk* (= *Technische Universität*) ≈ polytechnic.

**Tuba** ['tu:ba] (-, **Tuben**) *f* (*MUS*) tuba.

**Tube** ['tu:bə] (-, -**n**) *f* tube.

**Tuberkulose** [tubɛrku'lo:zə] (-, -**n**) *f* tuberculosis.

**Tuch** [tu:x] (-(**e**)**s**, -**er**) *nt* cloth; (*Hals~*) scarf; (*Kopf~*) (head)scarf; (*Hand~*) towel; ~**fühlung** *f* physical contact.

**tüchtig** ['tʏçtɪç] *adj* efficient; (*fähig*) able, capable; (*umg: kräftig*) good, sound; **etwas T~es lernen/werden** (*umg*) to get a proper training/job; **T~keit** *f* efficiency; ability.

**Tücke** ['tʏkə] (-, -**n**) *f* (*Arglist*) malice; (*Trick*) trick; (*Schwierigkeit*) difficulty, problem; **seine** ~**n haben** to be temperamental.

**tückisch** *adj* treacherous; (*böswillig*) malicious.

**tüfteln** ['tʏftəln] (*umg*) *vi* to puzzle; (*basteln*) to fiddle about.

**Tugend** ['tu:gənt] (-, -**en**) *f* virtue; **t~haft** *adj* virtuous.

**Tüll** [tʏl] (-**s**, -**e**) *m* tulle.

**Tülle** (-, -**n**) *f* spout.

**Tulpe** ['tʊlpə] (-, -**n**) *f* tulip.

**tummeln** ['tʊməln] *vr* to romp (about); (*sich beeilen*) to hurry.

**Tummelplatz** *m* play area; (*fig*) hotbed.

**Tumor** ['tu:mor] (-**s**, -**e**) *m* tumour (*BRIT*), tumor (*US*).

**Tümpel** ['tʏmpəl] (-**s**, -) *m* pond.

**Tumult** [tu'mʊlt] (-(**e**)**s**, -**e**) *m* tumult.

**tun** [tu:n] *unreg vt* (*machen*) to do; (*legen*) to put ♦ *vi* to act ♦ *vr*: **es tut sich etwas/viel** something/a lot is happening; **jdm etw** ~ **to** do sth to sb; **etw tut es auch** sth will do; **das tut nichts** that doesn't matter; **das tut nichts zur Sache** that's neither here nor there; **du kannst** ~ **und lassen, was du willst** you can do as you please; **so** ~, **als ob** to act as if; **zu** ~ **haben** (*beschäftigt sein*) to be busy, have things *od* something to do.

**Tünche** ['tʏnçə] (-, -**n**) *f* whitewash.

**tünchen** *vt* to whitewash.

**Tunesien** [tu'ne:ziən] (-**s**) *nt* Tunisia.

**Tunesier(in)** (-**s**, -) *m(f)* Tunisian.

**tunesisch** *adj* Tunisian.

**Tunke** ['tʊŋkə] (-, -**n**) *f* sauce.

**tunken** *vt* to dip, dunk.

**tunlichst** ['tu:nlɪçst] *adv* if at all possible; ~ **bald** as soon as possible.

**Tunnel** ['tʊnəl] (-**s**, -**s** *od* -) *m* tunnel.

**Tunte** ['tʊntə] (-, -**n**) (*pej: umg*) *f* fairy (*pej*).

**Tüpfel** ['tʏpfəl] (-**s**, -) *m* dot; ~**chen** *nt* (small) dot.

**tüpfeln** ['tʏpfəln] *vt* to dab.

**tupfen** ['tʊpfən] *vt* to dab; (*mit Farbe*) to dot; **T~** (-**s**, -) *m* dot, spot.

**Tupfer** (-s, -) *m* swab.
**Tür** [ty:r] (-, -en) *f* door; **an die ~ gehen**
to answer the door; **zwischen ~ und
Angel** in passing; **Weihnachten steht vor
der ~** (*fig*) Christmas is just around the
corner; **mit der ~ ins Haus fallen** (*umg*)
to blurt it *od* things out; **~angel** *f* (door)
hinge.
**Turbine** [tʊrˈbiːnə] *f* turbine.
**turbulent** [tʊrbuˈlɛnt] *adj* turbulent.
**Türke** [ˈtʏrkə] (-n, -n) *m* Turk.
**Türkei** [tʏrˈkaɪ] *f*: **die ~** Turkey.
**Türkin** *f* Turk.
**Türkis** [tʏrˈkiːs] (-es, -e) *m* turquoise; **t~** *adj*
turquoise.
**türkisch** *adj* Turkish.
**Türklinke** *f* door handle.
**Turm** [tʊrm] (-(e)s, ̈-e) *m* tower; (*Kirch~*)
steeple; (*Sprung~*) diving platform;
(*SCHACH*) castle, rook.
**türmen** [ˈtʏrmən] *vr* to tower up ♦ *vt* to heap
up ♦ *vi* (*umg*) to scarper, bolt.
**Turmuhr** *f* clock (on a tower); (*Kirch~*)
church clock.
**Turnanzug** *m* gym costume.
**turnen** [ˈtʊrnən] *vi* to do gymnastic exercises;
(*herumklettern*) to climb about; (*Kind*) to
romp ♦ *vt* to perform; **T~** (-s) *nt*
gymnastics *sing*; (*SCH*) physical education,
P.E.
**Turner(in)** (-s, -) *m(f)* gymnast.
**Turnhalle** *f* gym(nasium).
**Turnhose** *f* gym shorts *pl*.
**Turnier** [tʊrˈniːr] (-s, -e) *nt* tournament.
**Turn-** *zW*: **~lehrer(in)** *m(f)* gym *od* PE teacher;
**~schuh** *m* gym shoe; **~stunde** *f* gym *od* PE
lesson.
**Turnus** [ˈtʊrnʊs] (-, -se) *m* rota; **im ~** in
rotation.
**Turnverein** *m* gymnastics club.
**Turnzeug** *nt* gym kit.
**Türöffner** *m* buzzer.
**turteln** [ˈtʊrtəln] (*umg*) *vi* to bill and coo; (*fig*)
to whisper sweet nothings.
**Tusch** [tʊʃ] (-(e)s, -e) *m* (*MUS*) flourish.
**Tusche** [ˈtʊʃə] (-, -n) *f* Indian ink.
**tuscheln** [ˈtʊʃəln] *vt, vi* to whisper.
**Tuschkasten** *m* paintbox.
**Tussi** [ˈtʊsi] (-, -s) (*umg*) *f* (*Frau, Freundin*)
bird (*BRIT*), chick (*US*).
**tust** [tuːst] *vb siehe* **tun**.
**tut** [tuːt] *vb siehe* **tun**.
**Tüte** [ˈtyːtə] (-, -n) *f* bag; **in die ~ blasen**
(*umg*) to be breathalyzed; **das kommt nicht
in die ~!** (*umg*) no way!
**tuten** [ˈtuːtən] *vi* (*AUT*) to hoot (*BRIT*), honk
(*US*); **von T~ und Blasen keine Ahnung
haben** (*umg*) not to have a clue.
**TÜV** [tʏf] *m abk* (= *Technischer Über-
wachungs-Verein*) ≈ MOT (*BRIT*); **durch den
~ kommen** (*AUT*) to pass its test *od* MOT
(*Brit*).

> *The* **TÜV** (= *Technischer Überwachungs-
> Verein*) *is the organization responsible for
> checking the safety of machinery, particularly
> vehicles. Cars over three years old have to be
> examined every two years for their safety and
> for their exhaust emissions. The TÜV is the
> German equivalent of the MOT.*

**TV** (-) *nt abk* (= *Television*) TV ♦ *m abk*
= **Turnverein**.
**Twen** [tvɛn] (-(s), -s) *m person in his/her
twenties*.
**Typ** [ty:p] (-s, -en) *m* type.
**Type** (-, -n) *f* (*TYP*) type.
**Typenrad** *nt* (*Drucker*) daisywheel; **~drucker**
*m* daisywheel printer.
**Typhus** [ˈtyːfʊs] (-) *m* typhoid (fever).
**typisch** [ˈtyːpɪʃ] *adj*: **~ (für)** typical (of).
**Tyrann** [tyˈran] (-en, -en) *m(f)* tyrant.
**Tyrannei** [tyraˈnaɪ] *f* tyranny.
**Tyrannin** *f* tyrant.
**tyrannisch** *adj* tyrannical.
**tyrannisieren** [tyraniˈziːrən] *vt* to tyrannize.
**tyrrhenisch** [tyˈreːnɪʃ] *adj* Tyrrhenian; **T~es
Meer** Tyrrhenian Sea.

# $U, u$

**U, u** [u:] *nt* U, u; **~ wie Ulrich** ≈ U for Uncle.
**u.** *abk* = **und**.
**u.a.** *abk* (= *und andere(s)*) and others; (= *unter
anderem*) amongst other things.
**u.ä.** *abk* (= *und ähnliche(s)*) and similar.
**u.A.w.g.** *abk* (= *um Antwort wird gebeten*)
R.S.V.P.
**U-Bahn** [ˈuːbaːn] *f abk* (= *Untergrundbahn*)
underground (*BRIT*), subway (*US*).
**übel** [ˈyːbəl] *adj* bad; **jdm ist ~** sb feels sick;
**Ü~** (-s, -) *nt* evil; (*Krankheit*) disease; **zu
allem Ü~** ... to make matters worse ...;
**~gelaunt** *adj attrib* bad-tempered, sullen;
**Ü~keit** *f* nausea; **~nehmen** *unreg vt*: **jdm eine
Bemerkung** *etc* **~nehmen** to be offended at
sb's remark *etc*; **Ü~stand** *m* bad state of
affairs; **Ü~täter** *m* wrongdoer; **~wollend** *adj*
malevolent.
**üben** [ˈyːbən] *vt, vi, vr* to practise (*BRIT*),
practice (*US*); (*Gedächtnis, Muskeln*) to
exercise; **Kritik an etw** *dat* **~** to criticize sth.

=================== *SCHLÜSSELWORT*

**über** [ˈyːbər] *präp +dat* **1** (*räumlich*) over, above;
**zwei Grad ~ Null** two degrees above zero
**2** (*zeitlich*) over; **~ der Arbeit einschlafen** to

fall asleep over one's work
♦ *präp +akk* **1** (*räumlich*) over; (*hoch* ~) above; (*quer* ~) across; **er lachte ~ das ganze Gesicht** he was beaming all over his face; **Macht ~ jdn haben** to have power over sb **2** (*zeitlich*) over; **~ Weihnachten** over Christmas; **~ kurz oder lang** sooner or later **3** (*auf dem Wege*) via; **nach Köln ~ Aachen** to Cologne via Aachen; **ich habe es ~ die Auskunft erfahren** I found out from information **4** (*betreffend*) about; **ein Buch ~** ... a book about *od* on ...; **~ jdn/etw lachen** to laugh about *od* at sb/sth; **ein Scheck ~ 200 Mark** a cheque for 200 marks **5**: **Fehler ~ Fehler** mistake after mistake ♦ *adv* **1** (*mehr als*) over, more than; **Kinder ~ 12 Jahren** children over *od* above 12 years of age; **sie liebt ihn ~ alles** she loves him more than anything **2**: **~ und ~** over and over; **den ganzen Tag/ die ganze Zeit ~** all day long/all the time; **jdm in etw** *dat* **~ sein** to be superior to sb in sth.

**überall** [y:bər'|al] *adv* everywhere; **~hin** *adv* everywhere.

**überaltert** [y:bər'|altərt] *adj* obsolete.

**Überangebot** ['y:bər|angəbo:t] *nt*: **~ (an** +*dat*) surplus (of).

**überanstrengen** [y:bər'|anʃtrɛŋən] *vt untr* to overexert ♦ *vr untr* to overexert o.s.

**überantworten** [y:bər'|antvɔrtən] *vt untr* to hand over, deliver (up).

**überarbeiten** [y:bər'|arbaɪtən] *vt untr* to revise, rework ♦ *vr untr* to overwork (o.s.).

**überaus** ['y:bər|aus] *adv* exceedingly.

**überbacken** [y:bər'bakən] *unreg vt untr* to put in the oven/under the grill.

**Überbau** ['y:bərbau] *m* (*Gebäude, Philosophie*) superstructure.

**überbeanspruchen** ['y:bərbə|anʃpruxən] *vt untr* (*Menschen, Körper, Maschine*) to overtax.

**überbelichten** ['y:bərbəliçtən] *vt untr* (*PHOT*) to overexpose.

**Überbesetzung** ['y:bərbəzɛtsuŋ] *f* overmanning.

**überbewerten** ['y:bərbəve:rtən] *vt untr* (*fig*) to overrate; (*Äußerungen*) to attach too much importance to.

**überbieten** [y:bər'bi:tən] *unreg vt untr* to outbid; (*übertreffen*) to surpass; (*Rekord*) to break ♦ *vr untr*: **sich in etw** *dat* **(gegenseitig) ~** to vie with each other in sth.

**Überbleibsel** ['y:bərblaɪpsəl] (**-s, -**) *nt* residue, remainder.

**Überblick** ['y:bərblɪk] *m* view; (*fig: Darstellung*) survey, overview; (*Fähigkeit*): **~ (über** +*akk*) overall view (of), grasp (of); **den ~ verlieren** to lose track (of things); **sich** *dat* **einen ~ verschaffen** to get a general idea.

**überblicken** [y:bər'blɪkən] *vt untr* to survey;

(*fig*) to see; (: *Lage etc*) to grasp.

**überbringen** [y:bər'brɪŋən] *unreg vt untr* to deliver, hand over.

**Überbringer** (**-s, -**) *m* bearer.

**Überbringung** *f* delivery.

**überbrücken** [y:bər'brʏkən] *vt untr* to bridge.

**Überbrückung** *f*: **100 Mark zur ~** 100 marks to tide me/him *etc* over.

**Überbrückungskredit** *m* bridging loan.

**überbuchen** ['y:bərbu:xən] *vt* to overbook.

**überdauern** [y:bər'dauərn] *vt untr* to outlast.

**überdenken** [y:bər'dɛŋkən] *unreg vt untr* to think over.

**überdies** [y:bər'di:s] *adv* besides.

**überdimensional** ['y:bərdimenziona:l] *adj* oversize.

**Überdosis** ['y:bərdo:zɪs] *f* overdose, OD (*umg*); (*zu große Zumessung*) excessive amount.

**überdrehen** [y:bər'dre:ən] *vt untr* (*Uhr etc*) to overwind.

**überdreht** *adj*: **~ sein** (*fig*) to be hyped up, be overexcited.

**Überdruck** ['y:bərdrʊk] *m* (*TECH*) excess pressure.

**Überdruß** ['y:bərdrʊs] (**-sses**) *m* weariness; **bis zum ~** ad nauseam.

**überdrüssig** ['y:bərdrʏsɪç] *adj* +*gen* tired of, sick of.

**überdurchschnittlich** ['y:bərdʊrçʃnɪtlɪç] *adj* above-average ♦ *adv* exceptionally.

**übereifrig** ['y:bər|aɪfrɪç] *adj* overzealous.

**übereignen** [y:bər'|aɪgnən] *vt untr*: **jdm etw ~** (*geh*) to make sth over to sb.

**übereilen** [y:bər'|aɪlən] *vt untr* to hurry.

**übereilt** *adj* (over)hasty.

**übereinander** [y:bər|aɪ'nandər] *adv* one upon the other; (*sprechen*) about each other; **~schlagen** *unreg vt* (*Arme*) to fold; (*Beine*) to cross.

**übereinkommen** [y:bər'|aɪnkɔmən] *unreg vi* to agree.

**Übereinkunft** [y:bər'|aɪnkunft] (**-, -künfte**) *f* agreement.

**übereinstimmen** [y:bər'|aɪnʃtɪmən] *vi* to agree; (*Angaben, Meßwerte etc*) to tally; (*mit Tatsachen*) to fit.

**Übereinstimmung** *f* agreement.

**überempfindlich** ['y:bər|ɛmpfɪntlɪç] *adj* hypersensitive.

**überfahren¹** ['y:bərfa:rən] *unreg vt* to take across ♦ *vi* to cross, go across.

**überfahren²** [y:bər'fa:rən] *unreg vt untr* (*AUT*) to run over; (*fig*) to walk all over.

**Überfahrt** ['y:bərfa:rt] *f* crossing.

**Überfall** ['y:bərfal] *m* (*Bank~, MIL*) raid; (*auf jdn*) assault.

**überfallen** [y:bər'falən] *unreg vt untr* to attack; (*Bank*) to raid; (*besuchen*) to drop in on, descend (up)on.

**überfällig** ['y:bərfɛlɪç] *adj* overdue.

**Überfallkommando** *nt* flying squad.

**überfliegen** [y:bər'fli:gən] *unreg vt untr* to fly over, overfly; (*Buch*) to skim through.
**Überflieger** *m* (*fig*) high-flier.
**überflügeln** [y:bər'fly:gəln] *vt untr* to outdo.
**Überfluß** ['y:bərflʊs] *m:* ~ (**an** +*dat*) (super)abundance (of), excess (of); **zu allem** *od* **zum** ~ (*unnötigerweise*) superfluously; (*obendrein*) to crown it all (*umg*); ~**gesellschaft** *f* affluent society.
**überflüssig** ['y:bərflʏsɪç] *adj* superfluous.
**überfluten** [y:bər'flu:tən] *vt untr* (*lit*) to flood; (*fig*) to flood, inundate.
**überfordern** [y:bər'fɔrdərn] *vt untr* to demand too much of; (*Kräfte etc*) to overtax.
**überfragt** [y:bər'fra:kt] *adj:* **da bin ich** ~ there you've got me, you've got me there.
**überführen¹** ['y:bərfy:rən] *vt* to transfer; (*Leiche etc*) to transport.
**überführen²** [y:bər'fy:rən] *vt untr* (*Täter*) to have convicted.
**Überführung** *f* (*siehe vbs*) transfer; transport; conviction; (*Brücke*) bridge, overpass.
**überfüllt** [y:bər'fʏlt] *adj* overcrowded; (*Kurs*) oversubscribed.
**Übergabe** ['y:bərga:bə] *f* handing over; (*MIL*) surrender.
**Übergang** ['y:bərgaŋ] *m* crossing; (*Wandel, Überleitung*) transition.
**Übergangs-** *zW:* ~**erscheinung** *f* transitory phenomenon; ~**finanzierung** *f* (*FIN*) accommodation; **ü**~**los** *adj* without a transition; ~**lösung** *f* provisional solution, stopgap; ~**stadium** *nt* state of transition; ~**zeit** *f* transitional period.
**übergeben** [y:bər'ge:bən] *unreg vt untr* to hand over; (*MIL*) to surrender ♦ *vr untr* to be sick; **dem Verkehr** ~ to open to traffic.
**übergehen¹** ['y:bərge:ən] *unreg vi* (*Besitz*) to pass; (*zum Feind etc*) to go over, defect; (*überwechseln*): (**zu etw**) ~ to go on (to sth); ~ **in** +*akk* to turn into.
**übergehen²** [y:bər'ge:ən] *unreg vt untr* to pass over, omit.
**übergeordnet** ['y:bərgə|ɔrdnət] *adj* (*Behörde*) higher.
**Übergepäck** ['y:bərgəpɛk] *nt* excess baggage.
**übergeschnappt** ['y:bərgəʃnapt] (*umg*) *adj* crazy.
**Übergewicht** ['y:bərgəvɪçt] *nt* excess weight; (*fig*) preponderance.
**übergießen** [y:bər'gi:sən] *unreg vt untr* to pour over; (*Braten*) to baste.
**überglücklich** ['y:bərglʏklɪç] *adj* overjoyed.
**übergreifen** ['y:bərgraɪfən] *unreg vi:* ~ (**auf** +*akk*) (*auf Rechte etc*) to encroach (on); (*Feuer, Streik, Krankheit etc*) to spread (to); **ineinander** ~ to overlap.
**übergroß** ['y:bərgro:s] *adj* outsize, huge.
**Übergröße** ['y:bərgrø:sə] *f* oversize.
**überhaben** ['y:bərha:bən] *unreg* (*umg*) *vt* to be fed up with.

**überhandnehmen** [y:bər'hantne:mən] *unreg vi* to gain the ascendancy.
**überhängen** ['y:bərhɛŋən] *unreg vi* to overhang.
**überhäufen** [y:bər'hɔyfən] *vt untr:* **jdn mit Geschenken/Vorwürfen** ~ to heap presents/reproaches on sb.
**überhaupt** [y:bər'haupt] *adv* at all; (*im allgemeinen*) in general; (*besonders*) especially; ~ **nicht** not at all; **wer sind Sie** ~**?** who do you think you are?
**überheblich** [y:bər'he:plıç] *adj* arrogant; **Ü**~**keit** *f* arrogance.
**überhöht** [y:bər'hø:t] *adj* (*Forderungen, Preise*) exorbitant, excessive.
**überholen** [y:bər'ho:lən] *vt untr* to overtake; (*TECH*) to overhaul.
**Überholspur** *f* overtaking lane.
**überholt** *adj* out-of-date, obsolete.
**Überholverbot** [y:bər'ho:lfɛrbo:t] *nt* overtaking (*BRIT*) *od* passing ban.
**überhören** [y:bər'hø:rən] *vt untr* to not hear; (*absichtlich*) to ignore; **das möchte ich überhört haben!** (I'll pretend) I didn't hear that!
**Über-Ich** ['y:bər|ıç] (**-s**) *nt* superego.
**überirdisch** ['y:bər|ırdɪʃ] *adj* supernatural, unearthly.
**überkapitalisieren** ['y:bərkapitali'zi:rən] *vt untr* to overcapitalize.
**überkochen** ['y:bərkɔxən] *vi* to boil over.
**überkompensieren** ['y:bərkɔmpɛnzi:rən] *vt untr* to overcompensate for.
**überladen** [y:bər'la:dən] *unreg vt untr* to overload ♦ *adj* (*fig*) cluttered.
**überlassen** [y:bər'lasən] *unreg vt untr:* **jdm etw** ~ to leave sth to sb ♦ *vr untr:* **sich einer Sache** *dat* ~ to give o.s. over to sth; **das bleibt Ihnen** ~ that's up to you; **jdn sich** *dat* **selbst** ~ to leave sb to his/her own devices.
**überlasten** [y:bər'lastən] *vt untr* to overload; (*jdn*) to overtax.
**überlaufen¹** ['y:bərlaufən] *unreg vi* (*Flüssigkeit*) to flow over; (*zum Feind etc*) to go over, defect.
**überlaufen²** [y:bər'laufən] *unreg vt untr* (*Schauer etc*) to come over ♦ *adj* overcrowded; ~ **sein** to be inundated *od* besieged.
**Überläufer** ['y:bərlɔyfər] *m* deserter.
**überleben** [y:bər'le:bən] *vt untr* to survive.
**Überlebende(r)** *f(m)* survivor.
**überlebensgroß** *adj* larger-than-life.
**überlegen** [y:bər'le:gən] *vt untr* to consider ♦ *adj* superior; **ich habe es mir anders** *od* **noch einmal überlegt** I've changed my mind; **Ü**~**heit** *f* superiority.
**Überlegung** *f* consideration, deliberation.
**überleiten** ['y:bərlaɪtən] *vt* (*Abschnitt etc*): ~ **in** +*akk* to link up with.
**überlesen** [y:bər'le:zən] *unreg vt untr* (*übersehen*) to overlook, miss.

**überliefern** [y:bər'li:fərn] *vt untr* to hand down, transmit.

**Überlieferung** *f* tradition; **schriftliche ~en** (written) records.

**überlisten** [y:bər'lıstən] *vt untr* to outwit.

**überm** ['y:bərm] = **über dem**.

**Übermacht** ['y:bərmaxt] *f* superior force, superiority.

**übermächtig** ['y:bərmɛçtıç] *adj* superior (in strength); (*Gefühl etc*) overwhelming.

**übermannen** [y:bər'manən] *vt untr* to overcome.

**Übermaß** ['y:bərma:s] *nt:* ~ **(an +***dat*) excess (of).

**übermäßig** ['y:bərmɛ:sıç] *adj* excessive.

**Übermensch** ['y:bərmɛnʃ] *m* superman; **ü~lich** *adj* superhuman.

**übermitteln** [y:bər'mıtəln] *vt untr* to convey.

**übermorgen** ['y:bərmɔrgən] *adv* the day after tomorrow.

**Übermüdung** [y:bər'my:duŋ] *f* overtiredness.

**Übermut** ['y:bərmu:t] *m* exuberance.

**übermütig** ['y:bərmy:tıç] *adj* exuberant, high-spirited; ~ **werden** to get overconfident.

**übernächste(r, s)** ['y:bərnɛːçstə(r, s)] *adj* next ... but one; (*Woche, Jahr etc*) after next.

**übernachten** [y:bər'naxtən] *vi untr:* **(bei jdm)** ~ to spend the night (at sb's place).

**übernächtigt** [y:bər'nɛçtıçt] *adj* sleepy, tired.

**Übernachtung** *f:* ~ **mit Frühstück** bed and breakfast.

**Übernahme** ['y:bərna:mə] (-, -n) *f* taking over *od* on; (*von Verantwortung*) acceptance; ~**angebot** *nt* takeover bid.

**übernatürlich** ['y:bərnaty:rlıç] *adj* supernatural.

**übernehmen** [y:bər'ne:mən] *unreg vt untr* to take on, accept; (*Amt, Geschäft*) to take over ♦ *vr untr* to take on too much; (*sich überanstrengen*) to overdo it.

**überparteilich** ['y:bərpartaılıç] *adj* (*Zeitung*) independent; (*Amt, Präsident etc*) above party politics.

**überprüfen** [y:bər'pry:fən] *vt untr* to examine, check; (*POL: jdn*) to screen.

**Überprüfung** *f* examination.

**überqueren** [y:bər'kve:rən] *vt untr* to cross.

**überragen** [y:bər'ra:gən] *vt untr* to tower above; (*fig*) to surpass.

**überragend** *adj* outstanding; (*Bedeutung*) paramount.

**überraschen** [y:bər'raʃən] *vt untr* to surprise.

**Überraschung** *f* surprise.

**überreden** [y:bər're:dən] *vt untr* to persuade; **jdn zu etw** ~ to talk sb into sth.

**Überredungskunst** *f* powers *pl* of persuasion.

**überregional** ['y:bərregiona:l] *adj* national; (*Zeitung, Sender*) nationwide.

**überreichen** [y:bər'raıçən] *vt untr* to hand over;

(*feierlich*) to present.

**überreichlich** *adj* (more than) ample.

**überreizt** [y:bər'raıtst] *adj* overwrought.

**Überreste** ['y:bərrɛstə] *pl* remains *pl*, remnants *pl*.

**überrumpeln** [y:bər'rumpəln] *vt untr* to take by surprise; (*umg: überwältigen*) to overpower.

**überrunden** [y:bər'rundən] *vt untr* (*SPORT*) to lap.

**übers** ['y:bərs] = **über das**.

**übersättigen** [y:bər'zɛtıgən] *vt untr* to satiate.

**Überschall-** ['y:bərʃal] *in zW* supersonic; ~**flugzeug** *nt* supersonic jet; ~**geschwindigkeit** *f* supersonic speed.

**überschatten** [y:bər'ʃatən] *vt untr* to overshadow.

**überschätzen** [y:bər'ʃɛtsən] *vt untr, vr untr* to overestimate.

**überschaubar** [y:bər'ʃauba:r] *adj* (*Plan*) easily comprehensible, clear.

**überschäumen** ['y:bərʃɔymən] *vi* to froth over; (*fig*) to bubble over.

**überschlafen** [y:bər'ʃla:fən] *unreg vt untr* (*Problem*) to sleep on.

**Überschlag** ['y:bərʃla:k] *m* (*FIN*) estimate; (*SPORT*) somersault.

**überschlagen¹** [y:bər'ʃla:gən] *unreg vt untr* (*berechnen*) to estimate; (*auslassen: Seite*) to omit ♦ *vr untr* to somersault; (*Stimme*) to crack; (*AVIAT*) to loop the loop ♦ *adj* lukewarm, tepid.

**überschlagen²** ['y:bərʃla:gən] *unreg vt* (*Beine*) to cross; (*Arme*) to fold ♦ *vi* (*Hilfsverb sein: Wellen*) to break; (: *Funken*) to flash over; **in etw** *akk* ~ (*Stimmung etc*) to turn into sth.

**überschnappen** ['y:bərʃnapən] *vi* (*Stimme*) to crack; (*umg: Mensch*) to flip one's lid.

**überschneiden** [y:bər'ʃnaıdən] *unreg vr untr* (*lit, fig*) to overlap; (*Linien*) to intersect.

**überschreiben** [y:bər'ʃraıbən] *unreg vt untr* to provide with a heading; (*COMPUT*) to overwrite; **jdm etw** ~ to transfer *od* make over sth to sb.

**überschreiten** [y:bər'ʃraıtən] *unreg vt untr* to cross over; (*fig*) to exceed; (*verletzen*) to transgress.

**Überschrift** ['y:bərʃrıft] *f* heading, title.

**überschuldet** [y:bər'ʃuldət] *adj* heavily in debt; (*Grundstück*) heavily mortgaged.

**Überschuß** ['y:bərʃus] *m:* ~ **(an +***dat*) surplus (of).

**überschüssig** ['y:bərʃysıç] *adj* surplus, excess.

**überschütten** [y:bər'ʃytən] *vt untr:* **jdn/etw mit etw** ~ (*lit*) to pour sth over sb/sth; **jdn mit etw** ~ (*fig*) to shower sb with sth.

**Überschwang** ['y:bərʃvaŋ] *m* exuberance.

**überschwappen** ['y:bərʃvapən] *vi* to splash over.

**überschwemmen** [y:bər'ʃvɛmən] *vt untr* to flood.

**Überschwemmung** *f* flood.

**überschwenglich** ['y:bərʃvɛŋlıç] *adj* effusive; Ü~keit *f* effusion.
**Übersee** ['y:bərze:] *f:* nach/in ~ overseas.
**überseeisch** *adj* overseas.
**übersehbar** [y:bər'ze:ba:r] *adj (fig: Folgen, Zusammenhänge etc)* clear; *(Kosten, Dauer etc)* assessable.
**übersehen** [y:bər'ze:ən] *unreg vt untr* to look (out) over; *(fig: Folgen)* to see, get an overall view of; *(: nicht beachten)* to overlook.
**übersenden** [y:bər'zɛndən] *unreg vt untr* to send, forward.
**übersetzen¹** [y:bər'zɛtsən] *vt untr, vi untr* to translate.
**übersetzen²** ['y:bərzɛtsən] *vi (Hilfsverb sein)* to cross.
**Übersetzer(in)** [y:bər'zɛtsər(ın)] (-s, -) *m(f)* translator.
**Übersetzung** [y:bər'zɛtsʊŋ] *f* translation; *(TECH)* gear ratio.
**Übersicht** ['y:bərzıçt] *f* overall view; *(Darstellung)* survey; die ~ verlieren to lose track; ü~lich *adj* clear; *(Gelände)* open; ~lichkeit *f* clarity, lucidity.
**übersiedeln¹** ['y:bərzi:dəln] *vi* to move.
**übersiedeln²** [y:bər'zi:dəln] *vi untr* to move.
**überspannen** [y:bər'ʃpanən] *vt untr (zu sehr spannen)* to overstretch; *(überdecken)* to cover.
**überspannt** *adj* eccentric; *(Idee)* wild, crazy; Ü~heit *f* eccentricity.
**überspielen** [y:bər'ʃpi:lən] *vt untr (verbergen)* to cover (up); *(übertragen: Aufnahme)* to transfer.
**überspitzt** [y:bər'ʃpıtst] *adj* exaggerated.
**überspringen** [y:bər'ʃprıŋən] *unreg vt untr* to jump over; *(fig)* to skip.
**übersprudeln** ['y:bərʃpru:dəln] *vi* to bubble over.
**überstehen¹** [y:bər'ʃte:ən] *unreg vt untr* to overcome, get over; *(Winter etc)* to survive, get through.
**überstehen²** ['y:bərʃte:ən] *unreg vi* to project.
**übersteigen** [y:bər'ʃtaıgən] *unreg vt untr* to climb over; *(fig)* to exceed.
**übersteigert** [y:bər'ʃtaıgərt] *adj* excessive.
**überstimmen** [y:ber'ʃtımən] *vt untr* to outvote.
**überstrapazieren** ['y:bərʃtrapatsi:rən] *vt untr* to wear out ♦ *vr* to wear o.s. out.
**überstreifen** ['y:bərʃtraıfən] *vt:* (sich *dat*) etw ~ to slip sth on.
**überströmen¹** [y:bər'ʃtrø:mən] *vt untr:* von Blut überströmt sein to be streaming with blood.
**überströmen²** ['y:bərʃtrø:mən] *vi (lit, fig):* ~ (vor +dat) to overflow (with).
**Überstunden** ['y:bərʃtʊndən] *pl* overtime *sing.*
**überstürzen** [y:bər'ʃtʏrtsən] *vt untr* to rush ♦ *vr untr* to follow (one another) in rapid succession.
**überstürzt** *adj* (over)hasty.
**übertariflich** ['y:bərtarıflıç] *adj, adv* above the

agreed *od* union rate.
**übertölpeln** [y:bər'tœlpəln] *vt untr* to dupe.
**übertönen** [y:bər'tø:nən] *vt untr* to drown (out).
**Übertrag** ['y:bərtra:k] (-(e)s, -träge) *m (COMM)* amount brought forward.
**übertragbar** [y:bər'tra:kba:r] *adj* transferable; *(MED)* infectious.
**übertragen** [y:bər'tra:gən] *unreg vt untr* to transfer; *(RUNDF)* to broadcast; *(anwenden: Methode)* to apply; *(übersetzen)* to render; *(Krankheit)* to transmit ♦ *vr untr* to spread ♦ *adj* figurative; ~ auf +akk to transfer to; to apply to; sich ~ auf +akk to spread to; jdm etw ~ to assign sth to sb; *(Verantwortung etc)* to give sb sth *od* sth to sb.
**Übertragung** *f (siehe vb)* transference; broadcast; rendering; transmission.
**übertreffen** [y:bər'trɛfən] *unreg vt untr* to surpass.
**übertreiben** [y:bər'traıbən] *unreg vt untr* to exaggerate; man kann es auch ~ you can overdo things.
**Übertreibung** *f* exaggeration.
**übertreten¹** [y:bər'tre:tən] *unreg vt untr* to cross; *(Gebot etc)* to break.
**übertreten²** ['y:bərtre:tən] *unreg vi (über Linie, Gebiet)* to step (over); *(SPORT)* to overstep; *(zu anderem Glauben)* to be converted; ~ (in +akk) *(POL)* to go over (to).
**Übertretung** [y:bər'tre:tʊŋ] *f* violation, transgression.
**übertrieben** [y:bər'tri:bən] *adj* exaggerated, excessive.
**Übertritt** ['y:bərtrıt] *m (zu anderem Glauben)* conversion; *(bes zu anderer Partei)* defection.
**übertrumpfen** [y:bər'trʊmpfən] *vt untr* to outdo; *(KARTEN)* to overtrump.
**übertünchen** [y:bər'tʏnçən] *vt untr* to whitewash; *(fig)* to cover up, whitewash.
**übervölkert** [y:bər'fœlkərt] *adj* overpopulated.
**übervoll** ['y:bərfɔl] *adj* overfull.
**übervorteilen** [y:bər'fɔrtaılən] *vt untr* to dupe, cheat.
**überwachen** [y:bər'vaxən] *vt untr* to supervise; *(Verdächtigen)* to keep under surveillance.
**Überwachung** *f* supervision; surveillance.
**überwältigen** [y:bər'vɛltıgən] *vt untr* to overpower.
**überwältigend** *adj* overwhelming.
**überwechseln** ['y:bərvɛksəln] *vi:* ~ (in +akk) to move (to); *(zu Partei etc):* ~ (zu) to go over (to).
**überweisen** [y:bər'vaızən] *unreg vt untr* to transfer; *(Patienten)* to refer.
**Überweisung** *f* transfer; *(von Patient)* referral.
**überwerfen¹** ['y:bərvɛrfən] *unreg vt (Kleidungsstück)* to put on; *(sehr rasch)* to throw on.
**überwerfen²** [y:bər'vɛrfən] *unreg vr untr:* sich

**(mit jdm)** ~ to fall out (with sb).
**überwiegen** [yːbər'viːgən] *unreg vi untr* to
  predominate.
**überwiegend** *adj* predominant.
**überwinden** [yːbər'vɪndən] *unreg vt untr* to
  overcome ♦ *vr untr:* **sich** ~, **etw zu tun** to
  make an effort to do sth, bring o.s. to do
  sth.
**Überwindung** *f* overcoming; *(Selbst~)*
  effort of will.
**überwintern** [yːbər'vɪntərn] *vi untr* to (spend
  the) winter; *(umg: Winterschlaf halten)* to
  hibernate.
**Überwurf** ['yːbərvʊrf] *m* wrap.
**Überzahl** ['yːbərtsaːl] *f* superior numbers *pl*,
  superiority; **in der** ~ **sein** to be numerically
  superior.
**überzählig** ['yːbərtsɛːlɪç] *adj* surplus.
**überzeugen** [yːbər'tsɔʏgən] *vt untr* to
  convince.
**überzeugend** *adj* convincing.
**überzeugt** *adj attrib (Anhänger etc)* dedicated;
  *(Vegetarier)* strict; *(Christ, Moslem)* devout.
**Überzeugung** *f* conviction; **zu der** ~ **gelangen, daß** ... to become convinced that ...
**Überzeugungskraft** *f* power of persuasion.
**überziehen¹** ['yːbərtsiːən] *unreg vt* to put on.
**überziehen²** [yːbər'tsiːən] *unreg vt untr* to
  cover; *(Konto)* to overdraw; *(Redezeit etc)* to
  overrun ♦ *vr untr (Himmel)* to cloud over; **ein
  Bett frisch** ~ to change a bed, change the
  sheets (on a bed).
**Überziehungskredit** *m* overdraft.
**überzüchten** [yːbər'tsʏçtən] *vt untr* to
  overbreed.
**Überzug** ['yːbərtsuːk] *m* cover; *(Belag)*
  coating.
**üblich** ['yːplɪç] *adj* usual; **allgemein** ~ **sein** to
  be common practice.
**U-Boot** ['uːboːt] *nt* U-boat, submarine.
**übrig** ['yːbrɪç] *adj* remaining; **für jdn etwas**
  ~ **haben** *(umg)* to be fond of sb; **die** ~**en** the
  others; **das** ~**e** the rest; **im** ~**en** besides;
  ~**bleiben** *unreg vi* to remain, be left (over).
**übrigens** ['yːbrɪgəns] *adv* besides; *(nebenbei
  bemerkt)* by the way.
**übriglassen** ['yːbrɪglasən] *unreg vt* to leave
  (over); **einiges/viel zu wünschen** ~ *(umg)* to
  leave something/a lot to be desired.
**Übung** ['yːbʊŋ] *f* practice; *(Turn~, Aufgabe
  etc)* exercise; ~ **macht den Meister**
  *(Sprichwort)* practice makes perfect.
**Übungsarbeit** *f (SCH)* mock test.
**Übungsplatz** *m* training ground; *(MIL)* drill
  ground.
**u.d.M.** *abk (= unter dem Meeresspiegel)* below
  sea level.
**ü.d.M.** *abk (= über dem Meeresspiegel)* above
  sea level.
**u.E.** *abk (= unseres Erachtens)* in our opinion.
**Ufer** ['uːfər] *(-s, -)* *nt* bank; *(Meeres~)* shore;
  ~**befestigung** *f* embankment; **u**~**los** *adj*

endless; *(grenzenlos)* boundless; **ins u**~**lose
gehen** *(Kosten)* to go up and up; *(Debatte etc)*
to go on forever.
**UFO, Ufo** ['uːfo] *(-(s), -s)* *nt abk (= unbekanntes
  Flugobjekt)* UFO, ufo.
**Uganda** [u'ganda] *(-s)* *nt* Uganda.
**Ugander(in)** *(-s, -)* *m(f)* Ugandan.
**ugandisch** *adj* Ugandan.
**U-Haft** ['uːhaft] *f abk =* **Untersuchungshaft**.
**Uhr** [uːr] *(-, -en)* *f* clock; *(Armband~)* watch;
  **wieviel** ~ **ist es?** what time is it?; **um wieviel**
  ~**?** at what time?; **1** ~ 1 o'clock; **20** ~ 8
  o'clock, 20.00 (twenty hundred) hours;
  ~**band** *nt* watchstrap; ~**(en)gehäuse** *nt* clock
  case; watch case; ~**kette** *f* watch chain;
  ~**macher** *m* watchmaker; ~**werk** *nt (auch fig)*
  clockwork mechanism; ~**zeiger** *m* hand;
  ~**zeigersinn** *m:* **im** ~**zeigersinn** clockwise;
  **entgegen dem** ~**zeigersinn** anticlockwise;
  ~**zeit** *f* time (of day).
**Uhu** ['uːhu] *(-s, -s)* *nt* eagle owl.
**Ukraine** [ukra'iːnə] *f* Ukraine.
**Ukrainer(in)** [ukra'iːnər(ɪn)] *(-s, -)* *m(f)*
  Ukrainian.
**ukrainisch** *adj* Ukrainian.
**UKW** *abk (= Ultrakurzwelle)* VHF.
**Ulk** [ʊlk] *(-s, -e)* *m* lark.
**ulkig** ['ʊlkɪç] *adj* funny.
**Ulme** ['ʊlmə] *(-, -n)* *f* elm.
**Ulster** ['ʊlstər] *(-s)* *nt* Ulster.
**Ultimatum** [ʊlti'maːtʊm] *(-s, Ultimaten)* *nt*
  ultimatum; **jdm ein** ~ **stellen** to give sb an
  ultimatum.
**Ultra-** *zW:* ~**kurzwelle** *f* very high frequency;
  ~**leichtflugzeug** *nt* microlight; ~**schall** *m*
  *(PHYS)* ultrasound; **u**~**violett** *adj* ultraviolet.

═══════════════════ *SCHLÜSSELWORT*

**um** [ʊm] *präp +akk* **1** *(~ herum)* (a)round;
  ~ **Weihnachten** around Christmas; **er schlug**
  ~ **sich** he hit about him
  **2** *(mit Zeitangabe)* at; ~ **acht (Uhr)** at eight
  (o'clock)
  **3** *(mit Größenangabe)* by; **etw** ~ **4 cm kürzen**
  to shorten sth by 4 cm; ~ **10% teurer** 10%
  more expensive; ~ **vieles besser** better by
  far; ~ **nichts besser** not in the least bit
  better; ~ **so besser** so much the better;
  ~ **so mehr, als** ... all the more considering ...
  **4:** **der Kampf** ~ **den Titel** the battle for the
  title; ~ **Geld spielen** to play for money; **es
  geht** ~ **das Prinzip** it's a question of
  principle; **Stunde** ~ **Stunde** hour after hour;
  **Auge** ~ **Auge** an eye for an eye
  ♦ *präp +gen:* ~ ... **willen** for the sake of ...;
  ~ **Gottes willen** for goodness *od (stärker)*
  God's sake
  ♦ *konj:* ~ ... **zu** (in order) to ...; **zu klug,** ~ **zu**
  ... too clever to ...; ~ **so besser/schlimmer** so
  much the better/worse
  ♦ *adv* **1** *(ungefähr)* about; ~ **(die) 30 Leute**
  about *od* around 30 people

**2** (*vorbei*): **die zwei Stunden sind ~** the two hours are up.

**umadressieren** [ˈʊm|adrɛsiːrən] *vt untr* to readdress.

**umändern** [ˈʊm|ɛndərn] *vt* to alter.

**Umänderung** *f* alteration.

**umarbeiten** [ˈʊm|arbaɪtən] *vt* to remodel; (*Buch etc*) to revise, rework.

**umarmen** [ʊmˈ|armən] *vt untr* to embrace.

**Umbau** [ˈʊmbaʊ] **(-(e)s, -e** *od* **-ten)** *m* reconstruction, alteration(s *pl*).

**umbauen** [ˈʊmbaʊən] *vt* to rebuild, reconstruct.

**umbenennen** [ˈʊmbənɛnən] *unreg vt untr* to rename.

**umbesetzen** [ˈʊmbəzɛtsən] *vt untr* (*THEAT*) to recast; (*Mannschaft*) to change; (*Posten, Stelle*) to find someone else for.

**umbiegen** [ˈʊmbiːgən] *unreg vt* to bend (over).

**umbilden** [ˈʊmbɪldən] *vt* to reorganize; (*POL: Kabinett*) to reshuffle.

**umbinden**[1] [ˈʊmbɪndən] *unreg vt* (*Krawatte etc*) to put on.

**umbinden**[2] [ʊmˈbɪndən] *unreg vt untr*: **etw mit etw ~** to tie sth round sth.

**umblättern** [ˈʊmblɛtərn] *vt* to turn over.

**umblicken** [ˈʊmblɪkən] *vr* to look around.

**umbringen** [ˈʊmbrɪŋən] *unreg vt* to kill.

**Umbruch** [ˈʊmbrʊx] *m* radical change; (*TYP*) make-up (into page).

**umbuchen** [ˈʊmbuːxən] *vi* to change one's reservation *od* flight *etc* ♦ *vt* to change.

**umdenken** [ˈʊmdɛŋkən] *unreg vi* to adjust one's views.

**umdisponieren** [ˈʊmdɪsponiːrən] *vi untr* to change one's plans.

**umdrängen** [ʊmˈdrɛŋən] *vt untr* to crowd round.

**umdrehen** [ˈʊmdreːən] *vt* to turn (round); (*Hals*) to wring ♦ *vr* to turn (round); **jdm den Arm ~** to twist sb's arm.

**Umdrehung** *f* turn; (*PHYS*) revolution, rotation.

**umeinander** [ʊm|aɪˈnandər] *adv* round one another; (*füreinander*) for one another.

**umerziehen** [ˈʊm|ɛrtsiːən] *unreg vt* (*POL: euph*): **jdn (zu etw) ~** to re-educate sb (to become sth).

**umfahren**[1] [ˈʊmfaːrən] *unreg vt* to run over.

**umfahren**[2] [ʊmˈfaːrən] *unreg vt untr* to drive round; (*die Welt*) to sail round.

**umfallen** [ˈʊmfalən] *unreg vi* to fall down *od* over; (*fig: umg: nachgeben*) to give in.

**Umfang** [ˈʊmfaŋ] *m* extent; (*von Buch*) size; (*Reichweite*) range; (*Fläche*) area; (*MATH*) circumference; **in großem ~** on a large scale; **u~reich** *adj* extensive; (*Buch etc*) voluminous.

**umfassen** [ʊmˈfasən] *vt untr* to embrace; (*umgeben*) to surround; (*enthalten*) to include.

**umfassend** *adj* comprehensive; (*umfangreich*) extensive.

**Umfeld** [ˈʊmfɛlt] *nt*: **zum ~ von etw gehören** to be associated with sth.

**umformatieren** [ˈʊmfɔrmatiːrən] *vt untr* (*COMPUT*) to reformat.

**umformen** [ˈʊmfɔrmən] *vi* to transform.

**Umformer (-s, -)** *m* (*ELEK*) converter.

**umformulieren** [ˈʊmfɔrmuliːrən] *vt untr* to redraft.

**Umfrage** [ˈʊmfraːgə] *f* poll; **~ halten** to ask around.

**umfüllen** [ˈʊmfʏlən] *vt* to transfer; (*Wein*) to decant.

**umfunktionieren** [ˈʊmfʊŋktsioniːrən] *vt untr* to convert.

**umg** *abk* (= *umgangssprachlich*) colloquial.

**Umgang** [ˈʊmgaŋ] *m* company; (*mit jdm*) dealings *pl*; (*Behandlung*) dealing.

**umgänglich** [ˈʊmgɛŋlɪç] *adj* sociable.

**Umgangs-** *zW*: **~formen** *pl* manners *pl*; **~sprache** *f* colloquial language; **u~sprachlich** *adj* colloquial.

**umgeben** [ʊmˈgeːbən] *unreg vt untr* to surround.

**Umgebung** *f* surroundings *pl*; (*Milieu*) environment; (*Personen*) people in one's circle; **in der näheren/weiteren ~ Münchens** on the outskirts/in the environs of Munich.

**umgehen**[1] [ˈʊmgeːən] *unreg vi* to go (a)round; **im Schlosse ~** to haunt the castle; **mit jdm/ etw ~ können** to know how to handle sb/sth; **mit jdm grob** *etc* **~** to treat sb roughly *etc*; **mit Geld sparsam ~** to be careful with one's money.

**umgehen**[2] [ʊmˈgeːən] *unreg vt untr* to bypass; (*MIL*) to outflank; (*Gesetz, Vorschrift etc*) to circumvent; (*vermeiden*) to avoid.

**umgehend** *adj* immediate.

**Umgehung** *f* (*siehe vb*) bypassing; outflanking; circumvention; avoidance.

**Umgehungsstraße** *f* bypass.

**umgekehrt** [ˈʊmgəkeːrt] *adj* reverse(d); (*gegenteilig*) opposite ♦ *adv* the other way around; **und ~** and vice versa.

**umgestalten** [ˈʊmgəʃtaltən] *vt untr* to alter; (*reorganisieren*) to reorganize; (*umordnen*) to rearrange.

**umgewöhnen** [ˈʊmgəvøːnən] *vr* to readapt.

**umgraben** [ˈʊmgraːbən] *unreg vt* to dig up.

**umgruppieren** [ˈʊmgrʊpiːrən] *vt untr* to regroup.

**Umhang** [ˈʊmhaŋ] *m* wrap, cape.

**umhängen** [ˈʊmhɛŋən] *vt* (*Bild*) to hang somewhere else; **jdm etw ~** to put sth on sb.

**Umhängetasche** *f* shoulder bag.

**umhauen** [ˈʊmhaʊən] *vt* to fell; (*fig*) to bowl over.

**umher** [ʊmˈheːr] *adv* about, around; **~gehen** *unreg vi* to walk about; **~irren** *vi* to wander around; (*Blick, Augen*) to roam about; **~reisen** *vi* to travel about; **~schweifen** *vi* to roam about; ~**ziehen** *unreg vi* to wander from place to place.

**umhinkönnen** [ʊm'hɪnkœnən] *unreg vi:* **ich kann nicht umhin, das zu tun** I can't help doing it.

**umhören** ['ʊmhøːrən] *vr* to ask around.

**umkämpfen** [ʊm'kɛmpfən] *vt untr* (*Entscheidung*) to dispute; (*Wahlkreis, Sieg*) to contest.

**Umkehr** ['ʊmkeːr] (-) *f* turning back; (*Änderung*) change.

**umkehren** *vi* to turn back; (*fig*) to change one's ways ♦ *vt* to turn round, reverse; (*Tasche etc*) to turn inside out; (*Gefäß etc*) to turn upside down.

**umkippen** ['ʊmkɪpən] *vt* to tip over ♦ *vi* to overturn; (*umg: ohnmächtig werden*) to keel over; (*fig: Meinung ändern*) to change one's mind.

**umklammern** [ʊm'klamərn] *vt untr* (*mit Händen*) to clasp; (*festhalten*) to cling to.

**umklappen** ['ʊmklapən] *vt* to fold down.

**Umkleidekabine** ['ʊmklaɪdəkabiːnə] *f* changing cubicle (*BRIT*), dressing room (*US*).

**Umkleideraum** ['ʊmklaɪdəraʊm] *m* changing room; (*US, THEAT*) dressing room.

**umknicken** ['ʊmknɪkən] *vt* (*Ast*) to snap; (*Papier*) to fold (over) ♦ *vi:* **mit dem Fuß** ~ to twist one's ankle.

**umkommen** ['ʊmkɔmən] *unreg vi* to die, perish; (*Lebensmittel*) to go bad.

**Umkreis** ['ʊmkraɪs] *m* neighbourhood (*BRIT*), neighborhood (*US*); **im** ~ **von** within a radius of.

**umkreisen** [ʊm'kraɪzən] *vt untr* to circle (round); (*Satellit*) to orbit.

**umkrempeln** ['ʊmkrɛmpəln] *vt* to turn up; (*mehrmals*) to roll up; (*umg: Betrieb*) to shake up.

**umladen** ['ʊmlaːdən] *unreg vt* to transfer, reload.

**Umlage** ['ʊmlaːgə] *f* share of the costs.

**Umlauf** *m* (*Geld~*) circulation; (*von Gestirn*) revolution; (*Schreiben*) circular; **in** ~ **bringen** to circulate; ~**bahn** *f* orbit.

**umlaufen** ['ʊmlaʊfən] *unreg vi* to circulate.

**Umlaufkapital** *nt* working capital.

**Umlaufvermögen** *nt* current assets *pl*.

**Umlaut** ['ʊmlaʊt] *m* umlaut.

**umlegen** ['ʊmleːgən] *vt* to put on; (*verlegen*) to move, shift; (*Kosten*) to share out; (*umkippen*) to tip over; (*umg: töten*) to bump off.

**umleiten** ['ʊmlaɪtən] *vt* to divert.

**Umleitung** *f* diversion.

**umlernen** ['ʊmlɛrnən] *vi* to learn something new; (*fig*) to adjust one's views.

**umliegend** ['ʊmliːgənt] *adj* surrounding.

**ummelden** ['ʊmmɛldən] *vt, vr:* **jdn/sich** ~ to notify (the police of) a change in sb's/one's address.

**Umnachtung** [ʊm'naxtʊŋ] *f* mental derangement.

**umorganisieren** ['ʊm|ɔrganiziːrən] *vt untr* to reorganize.

**umpflanzen** ['ʊmpflantsən] *vt* to transplant.

**umquartieren** ['ʊmkvartiːrən] *vt untr* to move; (*Truppen*) to requarter.

**umrahmen** [ʊm'raːmən] *vt untr* to frame.

**umranden** [ʊm'randən] *vt untr* to border, edge.

**umräumen** ['ʊmrɔymən] *vt* (*anders anordnen*) to rearrange ♦ *vi* to rearrange things, move things around.

**umrechnen** ['ʊmrɛçnən] *vt* to convert.

**Umrechnung** *f* conversion.

**Umrechnungskurs** *m* rate of exchange.

**umreißen** [ʊm'raɪsən] *unreg vt untr* to outline.

**umrennen** ['ʊmrɛnən] *unreg vt* to (run into and) knock down.

**umringen** [ʊm'rɪŋən] *vt untr* to surround.

**Umriß** ['ʊmrɪs] *m* outline.

**umrühren** ['ʊmryːrən] *vt, vi* to stir.

**umrüsten** ['ʊmrʏstən] *vt* (*TECH*) to adapt; (*MIL*) to re-equip; ~ **auf** +*akk* to adapt to.

**ums** [ʊms] = **um das.**

**umsatteln** ['ʊmzatəln] (*umg*) *vi* to change one's occupation, switch jobs.

**Umsatz** ['ʊmzats] *m* turnover; ~**beteiligung** *f* commission; ~**einbuße** *f* loss of profit; ~**steuer** *f* turnover tax.

**umschalten** ['ʊmʃaltən] *vt* to switch ♦ *vi* to push/pull a lever; (*auf anderen Sender*): ~ (**auf** +*akk*) to change over (to); (*AUT*): ~ **in** +*akk* to change (*BRIT*) *od* shift into; **„wir schalten jetzt um nach Hamburg"** "and now we go over to Hamburg".

**Umschalttaste** *f* shift key.

**Umschau** *f* look(ing) round; ~ **halten nach** to look around for.

**umschauen** ['ʊmʃaʊən] *vr* to look round.

**Umschlag** ['ʊmʃlaːk] *m* cover; (*Buch~*) jacket, cover; (*MED*) compress; (*Brief~*) envelope; (*Gütermenge*) volume of traffic; (*Wechsel*) change; (*von Hose*) turn-up (*BRIT*), cuff (*US*).

**umschlagen** ['ʊmʃlaːgən] *unreg vi* to change; (*NAUT*) to capsize ♦ *vt* to knock over; (*Ärmel*) to turn up; (*Seite*) to turn over; (*Waren*) to transfer.

**Umschlag-** *zW:* ~**hafen** *m* port of transshipment; ~**platz** *m* (*COMM*) distribution centre (*BRIT*) *od* center (*US*); ~**seite** *f* cover page.

**umschlingen** [ʊm'ʃlɪŋən] *unreg vt untr* (*Pflanze*) to twine around; (*jdn*) to embrace.

**umschreiben¹** ['ʊmʃraɪbən] *unreg vt* (*neu* ~) to rewrite; (*übertragen*) to transfer; ~ **auf** +*akk* to transfer to.

**umschreiben²** [ʊm'ʃraɪbən] *unreg vt untr* to paraphrase; (*abgrenzen*) to circumscribe, define.

**Umschuldung** ['ʊmʃʊldʊŋ] *f* rescheduling (of debts).

**umschulen** ['ʊmʃuːlən] *vt* to retrain; (*Kind*) to

send to another school.

**umschwärmen** [ʊmˈʃvɛrmən] *vt untr* to swarm round; (*fig*) to surround, idolize.

**Umschweife** [ˈʊmʃvaifə] *pl:* **ohne** ~ without beating about the bush, straight out.

**umschwenken** [ˈʊmʃvɛnkən] *vi* (*Kran*) to swing out; (*fig*) to do an about-turn (*BRIT*) *od* about-face (*US*); (*Wind*) to veer.

**Umschwung** [ˈʊmʃvʊŋ] *m* (*GYMNASTIK*) circle; (*fig: ins Gegenteil*) change (around).

**umsegeln** [ʊmˈzeːgəln] *vt untr* to sail around; (*Erde*) to circumnavigate.

**umsehen** [ˈʊmzeːən] *unreg vr* to look around *od* about; (*suchen*): **sich** ~ **(nach)** to look out (for); **ich möchte mich nur mal** ~ (*in Geschäft*) I'm just looking.

**umseitig** [ˈʊmzaitiç] *adv* overleaf.

**umsetzen** [ˈʊmzɛtsən] *vt* (*Waren*) to turn over ♦ *vr* (*Schüler*) to change places; **etw in die Tat** ~ to translate sth into action.

**Umsicht** [ˈʊmzɪçt] *f* prudence, caution.

**umsichtig** *adj* prudent, cautious.

**umsiedeln** [ˈʊmziːdəln] *vt* to resettle.

**Umsiedler(in)** (-s, -) *m(f)* resettler.

**umsonst** [ʊmˈzɔnst] *adv* in vain; (*gratis*) for nothing.

**umspringen** [ˈʊmʃprɪŋən] *unreg vi* to change; **mit jdm** ~ to treat sb badly.

**Umstand** [ˈʊmʃtant] *m* circumstance; **Umstände** *pl* (*fig: Schwierigkeiten*) fuss *sing*; **in anderen Umständen sein** to be pregnant; **Umstände machen** to go to a lot of trouble; **den Umständen entsprechend** much as one would expect (under the circumstances); **die näheren Umstände** further details; **unter Umständen** possibly; **mildernde Umstände** (*JUR*) extenuating circumstances.

**umständehalber** *adv* owing to circumstances.

**umständlich** [ˈʊmʃtɛntlɪç] *adj* (*Methode*) cumbersome, complicated; (*Ausdrucksweise, Erklärung*) long-winded; (*ungeschickt*) ponderous; **etw** ~ **machen** to make heavy weather of (doing) sth.

**Umstandskleid** *nt* maternity dress.

**Umstandswort** *nt* adverb.

**umstehend** [ˈʊmʃteːənt] *adj attrib* (*umseitig*) overleaf; **die U~en** *pl* the bystanders *pl*.

**Umsteigekarte** *f* transfer ticket.

**umsteigen** [ˈʊmʃtaigən] *unreg vi* (*EISENB*) to change; (*fig: umg*): ~ **(auf +akk)** to change over (to), switch (over) (to).

**umstellen¹** [ˈʊmʃtɛlən] *vt* (*an anderen Ort*) to change round, rearrange; (*TECH*) to convert ♦ *vr:* **sich** ~ **(auf +akk)** to adapt o.s. (to).

**umstellen²** [ʊmˈʃtɛlən] *vt untr* to surround.

**Umstellung** *f* change; (*Umgewöhnung*) adjustment; (*TECH*) conversion.

**umstimmen** [ˈʊmʃtɪmən] *vt* (*MUS*) to retune; **jdn** ~ to make sb change his mind.

**umstoßen** [ˈʊmʃtoːsən] *unreg vt* (*lit*) to overturn; (*Plan etc*) to change, upset.

**umstritten** [ʊmˈʃtrɪtən] *adj* disputed; (*fraglich*) controversial.

**Umsturz** [ˈʊmʃtʊrts] *m* overthrow.

**umstürzen** [ˈʊmʃtʏrtsən] *vt* (*umwerfen*) to overturn ♦ *vi* to collapse, fall down; (*Wagen*) to overturn.

**umstürzlerisch** *adj* revolutionary.

**Umtausch** [ˈʊmtauʃ] *m* exchange; **diese Waren sind vom** ~ **ausgeschlossen** these goods cannot be exchanged.

**umtauschen** *vt* to exchange.

**Umtriebe** [ˈʊmtriːbə] *pl* machinations *pl*, intrigues *pl*.

**umtun** [ˈʊmtuːn] *unreg vr:* **sich nach etw** ~ to look for sth.

**umverteilen** [ˈʊmfɛrtailən] *vt untr* to redistribute.

**umwälzend** [ˈʊmvɛltsənt] *adj* (*fig*) radical; (*Veränderungen*) sweeping; (*Ereignisse*) revolutionary.

**Umwälzung** *f* (*fig*) radical change.

**umwandeln** [ˈʊmvandəln] *vt* to change, convert; (*ELEK*) to transform.

**umwechseln** [ˈʊmvɛksəln] *vt* to change.

**Umweg** [ˈʊmveːk] *m* detour; (*fig*) roundabout way.

**Umwelt** [ˈʊmvɛlt] *f* environment; ~**auto** (*umg*) *nt* environment-friendly vehicle; ~**belastung** *f* environmental pollution; ~**bewußtsein** *nt* environmental awareness; **u~freundlich** *adj* environment-friendly; ~**kriminalität** *f* crimes *pl* against the environment; ~**ministerium** *nt* Ministry of the Environment; **u~schädlich** *adj* harmful to the environment; ~**schutz** *m* environmental protection; ~**schützer** (-s, -) *m* environmentalist; ~**verschmutzung** *f* pollution (of the environment).

**umwenden** [ˈʊmvɛndən] *unreg vt, vr* to turn (round).

**umwerben** [ʊmˈvɛrbən] *unreg vt untr* to court, woo.

**umwerfen** [ˈʊmvɛrfən] *unreg vt* (*lit*) to upset, overturn; (*Mantel*) to throw on; (*fig: erschüttern*) to upset, throw.

**umwerfend** (*umg*) *adj* fantastic.

**umziehen** [ˈʊmtsiːən] *unreg vt, vr* to change ♦ *vi* to move.

**umzingeln** [ʊmˈtsɪŋəln] *vt untr* to surround, encircle.

**Umzug** [ˈʊmtsuːk] *m* procession; (*Wohnungs~*) move, removal.

**UN** *pl abk* (= *United Nations*): **die** ~ the UN *sing*.

**un-** *zW:* ~**abänderlich** *adj* irreversible, unalterable; ~**abänderlich feststehen** to be absolutely certain; ~**abdingbar** *adj* indispensable, essential; (*Recht*) inalienable; ~**abhängig** *adj* independent; **U~abhängigkeit** *f* independence; ~**abkömmlich** *adj* indispensable; **zur Zeit** ~**abkömmlich** not free at the moment;

~**ablässig** *adj* incessant, constant;
~**absehbar** *adj* immeasurable; (*Folgen*)
unforeseeable; (*Kosten*) incalculable;
~**absichtlich** *adj* unintentional; ~**abwendbar**
*adj* inevitable.

**unachtsam** ['ʊn|axtzaːm] *adj* careless; **U~keit**
*f* carelessness.

**un-** *zW:* ~**anfechtbar** *adj* indisputable;
~**angebracht** *adj* uncalled-for;
~**angefochten** *adj* unchallenged; (*Testament,
Wahlkandidat, Urteil*) uncontested;
~**angemeldet** *adj* unannounced; (*Besucher*)
unexpected; ~**angemessen** *adj* inadequate;
~**angenehm** *adj* unpleasant; (*peinlich*)
embarrassing; ~**angepaßt** *adj*
nonconformist; **U~annehmlichkeit** *f*
inconvenience; **Unannehmlichkeiten** *pl*
trouble *sing*; ~**ansehnlich** *adj* unsightly;
~**anständig** *adj* indecent, improper;
**U~anständigkeit** *f* indecency, impropriety;
~**antastbar** *adj* inviolable, sacrosanct.

**unappetitlich** ['ʊn|apetiːtlɪç] *adj* unsavoury
(*BRIT*), unsavory (*US*).

**Unart** ['ʊn|aːrt] *f* bad manners *pl*;
(*Angewohnheit*) bad habit.

**unartig** *adj* naughty, badly behaved.

**un-** *zW:* ~**aufdringlich** *adj* unobtrusive;
(*Parfüm*) discreet; (*Mensch*) unassuming;
~**auffällig** *adj* unobtrusive; (*Kleidung*)
inconspicuous; ~**auffindbar** *adj* not to be
found; ~**aufgefordert** *adj* unsolicited ♦ *adv*
unasked, spontaneously; ~**aufgefordert
zugesandte Manuskripte** unsolicited
manuscripts; ~**aufhaltsam** *adj* irresistible;
~**aufhörlich** *adj* incessant, continuous;
~**aufmerksam** *adj* inattentive; ~**aufrichtig**
*adj* insincere.

**un-** *zW:* ~**ausbleiblich** *adj* inevitable,
unavoidable; ~**ausgeglichen** *adj* volatile;
~**ausgegoren** *adj* immature; (*Idee, Plan*)
half-baked; ~**ausgesetzt** *adj* incessant,
constant; ~**ausgewogen** *adj* unbalanced;
~**aussprechlich** *adj* inexpressible;
~**ausstehlich** *adj* intolerable; ~**ausweichlich**
*adj* inescapable, ineluctable.

**unbändig** ['ʊnbɛndɪç] *adj* extreme, excessive.

**unbarmherzig** ['ʊnbarmhɛrtsɪç] *adj* pitiless,
merciless.

**unbeabsichtigt** ['ʊnbə|apzɪçtɪçt] *adj*
unintentional.

**unbeachtet** ['ʊnbə|axtət] *adj* unnoticed;
(*Warnung*) ignored.

**unbedacht** ['ʊnbədaxt] *adj* rash.

**unbedarft** ['ʊnbədarft] (*umg*) *adj* clueless.

**unbedenklich** ['ʊnbədɛŋklɪç] *adj* unhesitating;
(*Plan*) unobjectionable ♦ *adv* without
hesitation.

**unbedeutend** ['ʊnbədɔytənt] *adj* insignificant,
unimportant; (*Fehler*) slight.

**unbedingt** ['ʊnbədɪŋt] *adj* unconditional ♦ *adv*
absolutely; **mußt du ~ gehen?** do you really
have to go?; **nicht ~** not necessarily.

**unbefangen** ['ʊnbəfaŋən] *adj* impartial,
unprejudiced; (*ohne Hemmungen*)
uninhibited; **U~heit** *f* impartiality;
uninhibitedness.

**unbefriedigend** ['ʊnbəfriːdɪgənd] *adj*
unsatisfactory.

**unbefriedigt** ['ʊnbəfriːdɪçt] *adj* unsatisfied;
(*unzufrieden*) dissatisfied; (*unerfüllt*)
unfulfilled.

**unbefristet** ['ʊnbəfrɪstət] *adj* permanent.

**unbefugt** ['ʊnbəfʊːkt] *adj* unauthorized; **U~en
ist der Eintritt verboten** no admittance to
unauthorized persons.

**unbegabt** ['ʊnbəgaːpt] *adj* untalented.

**unbegreiflich** [ʊnbə'graɪflɪç] *adj*
inconceivable.

**unbegrenzt** ['ʊnbəgrɛntst] *adj* unlimited.

**unbegründet** ['ʊnbəgrʏndət] *adj* unfounded.

**Unbehagen** ['ʊnbəhaːgən] *nt* discomfort.

**unbehaglich** ['ʊnbəha:klɪç] *adj*
uncomfortable; (*Gefühl*) uneasy.

**unbeherrscht** ['ʊnbəhɛrʃt] *adj* uncontrolled;
(*Mensch*) lacking self-control.

**unbeholfen** ['ʊnbəhɔlfən] *adj* awkward,
clumsy; **U~heit** *f* awkwardness,
clumsiness.

**unbeirrt** ['ʊnbə|ɪrt] *adj* imperturbable.

**unbekannt** ['ʊnbəkant] *adj* unknown; ~**e
Größe** (*MATH, fig*) unknown quantity.

**unbekannterweise** *adv:* **grüß(e) sie ~ von
mir** give her my regards although I don't
know her.

**unbekümmert** ['ʊnbəkʏmərt] *adj*
unconcerned.

**unbelehrbar** [ʊnbə'leːrbaːr] *adj* fixed in one's
views; (*Rassist etc*) dyed-in-the-wool *attrib*.

**unbeliebt** ['ʊnbəliːpt] *adj* unpopular; **U~heit** *f*
unpopularity.

**unbemannt** ['ʊnbəmant] *adj* (*Raumflug*)
unmanned; (*Flugzeug*) pilotless.

**unbemerkt** ['ʊnbəmɛrkt] *adj* unnoticed.

**unbenommen** [ʊnbə'nɔmən] *adj* (*form*): **es
bleibt** *od* **ist Ihnen ~, zu ...** you are at liberty
to ...

**unbequem** ['ʊnbəkveːm] *adj* (*Stuhl*)
uncomfortable; (*Mensch*) bothersome;
(*Regelung*) inconvenient.

**unberechenbar** [ʊnbə'rɛçənbaːr] *adj*
incalculable; (*Mensch, Verhalten*)
unpredictable.

**unberechtigt** ['ʊnbərɛçtɪçt] *adj* unjustified;
(*nicht erlaubt*) unauthorized.

**unberücksichtigt** [ʊnbə'rʏkzɪçtɪçt] *adj:* **etw
~ lassen** not to consider sth.

**unberufen** [ʊnbə'ruːfən] *interj* touch wood!

**unberührt** ['ʊnbəryːrt] *adj* untouched; (*Natur*)
unspoiled; **sie ist noch ~** she is still a virgin.

**unbeschadet** [ʊnbə'ʃaːdət] *präp +gen* (*form*)
regardless of.

**unbescheiden** ['ʊnbəʃaɪdən] *adj*
presumptuous.

**unbescholten** ['ʊnbəʃɔltən] *adj* respectable;

*(Ruf)* spotless.
**unbeschrankt** ['ʊnbəʃraŋkt] *adj*
*(Bahnübergang)* unguarded.
**unbeschränkt** [ʊnbə'ʃrɛŋkt] *adj* unlimited.
**unbeschreiblich** [ʊnbə'ʃraɪplɪç] *adj*
indescribable.
**unbeschwert** ['ʊnbəʃveːrt] *adj (sorgenfrei)*
carefree; *(Melodien)* light.
**unbesehen** [ʊnbə'zeːən] *adv* indiscriminately;
*(ohne es anzusehen)* without looking at it.
**unbesonnen** ['ʊnbəzɔnən] *adj* unwise, rash,
imprudent.
**unbesorgt** ['ʊnbəzɔrkt] *adj* unconcerned; **Sie
können ganz ~ sein** you can set your mind
at rest.
**unbespielt** ['ʊnbəʃpiːlt] *adj (Kassette)* blank.
**unbest.** *abk =* **unbestimmt.**
**unbeständig** ['ʊnbəʃtɛndɪç] *adj (Mensch)*
inconstant; *(Wetter)* unsettled; *(Lage)*
unstable.
**unbestechlich** [ʊnbə'ʃtɛçlɪç] *adj*
incorruptible.
**unbestimmt** ['ʊnbəʃtɪmt] *adj* indefinite;
*(Zukunft)* uncertain; **U~heit** *f* vagueness.
**unbestritten** [ʊnbə'ʃtrɪtən] *adj* undisputed.
**unbeteiligt** [ʊnbə'taɪlɪçt] *adj* unconcerned;
*(uninteressiert)* indifferent.
**unbeugsam** ['ʊnbɔykzaːm] *adj* stubborn,
inflexible; *(Wille)* unbending.
**unbewacht** ['ʊnbəvaxt] *adj* unguarded,
unwatched.
**unbewaffnet** ['ʊnbəvafnət] *adj* unarmed.
**unbeweglich** ['ʊnbəveːklɪç] *adj* immovable.
**unbewegt** *adj* motionless; *(fig: unberührt)*
unmoved.
**unbewohnt** ['ʊnbəvoːnt] *adj (Gegend)*
uninhabited; *(Haus)* unoccupied.
**unbewußt** ['ʊnbəvʊst] *adj* unconscious.
**unbezahlbar** [ʊnbə'tsaːlbaːr] *adj* prohibitively
expensive; *(fig)* priceless; *(nützlich)*
invaluable.
**unbezahlt** ['ʊnbətsaːlt] *adj* unpaid.
**unblutig** ['ʊnbluːtɪç] *adj* bloodless.
**unbrauchbar** ['ʊnbrauxbaːr] *adj (nutzlos)*
useless; *(Gerät)* unusable; **U~keit** *f*
uselessness.
**unbürokratisch** ['ʊnbyrokratɪʃ] *adj* without
any red tape.
**und** [ʊnt] *konj* and; **~ so weiter** and so on.
**Undank** ['ʊndaŋk] *m* ingratitude; **u~bar** *adj*
ungrateful; **~barkeit** *f* ingratitude.
**undefinierbar** [ʊndefi'niːrbaːr] *adj* indefinable.
**undenkbar** [ʊn'dɛŋkbaːr] *adj* inconceivable.
**undeutlich** ['ʊndɔytlɪç] *adj* indistinct; *(Schrift)*
illegible; *(Ausdrucksweise)* unclear.
**undicht** ['ʊndɪçt] *adj* leaky.
**undifferenziert** ['ʊndɪfərɛntsiːrt] *adj*
simplistic.
**Unding** ['ʊndɪŋ] *nt* absurdity.
**unduldsam** ['ʊndʊldsaːm] *adj* intolerant.
**un-** *zW:* **~durchdringlich** *adj (Urwald)*
impenetrable; *(Gesicht)* inscrutable;

**~durchführbar** *adj* impracticable;
**~durchlässig** *adj* impervious; *(wasserundurch-
lässig)* waterproof, impermeable; **~durch-
schaubar** *adj* inscrutable; **~durchsichtig** *adj*
opaque; *(Motive)* obscure; *(fig: pej: Mensch,
Methoden)* devious.
**uneben** ['ʊn|eːbən] *adj* uneven.
**unecht** ['ʊn|ɛçt] *adj* artificial, fake; *(pej:
Freundschaft, Lächeln)* false.
**unehelich** ['ʊn|eːəlɪç] *adj* illegitimate.
**uneigennützig** ['ʊn|aɪɡənnʏtsɪç] *adj* unselfish.
**uneinbringlich** [ʊn|aɪn'brɪŋlɪç] *adj:* **~e
Forderungen** *(COMM)* bad debts *pl.*
**uneingeschränkt** ['ʊn|aɪnɡəʃrɛŋkt] *adj*
absolute, total; *(Rechte, Handel)*
unrestricted; *(Zustimmung)* unqualified.
**uneinig** ['ʊn|aɪnɪç] *adj* divided; **~ sein** to
disagree; **U~keit** *f* discord, dissension.
**uneinnehmbar** [ʊn|aɪn'neːmbaːr] *adj*
impregnable.
**uneins** ['ʊn|aɪns] *adj* at variance, at odds.
**unempfänglich** ['ʊn|ɛmpfɛŋlɪç] *adj:* **~ (für)** not
susceptible (to).
**unempfindlich** ['ʊn|ɛmpfɪntlɪç] *adj*
insensitive; **U~keit** *f* insensitivity.
**unendlich** [ʊn'|ɛntlɪç] *adj* infinite ♦ *adv*
endlessly; *(fig: sehr)* terribly; **U~keit** *f*
infinity.
**un-** *zW:* **~entbehrlich** *adj* indispensable;
**~entgeltlich** *adj* free (of charge);
**~entschieden** *adj* undecided; **~entschieden
enden** *(SPORT)* to end in a draw;
**~entschlossen** *adj* undecided; *(entschlußlos)*
irresolute; **~entwegt** *adj* unswerving;
*(unaufhörlich)* incessant.
**un-** *zW:* **~erbittlich** *adj* unyielding, inexorable;
**~erfahren** *adj* inexperienced; **~erfreulich** *adj*
unpleasant; **U~erfreuliches** *(schlechte
Nachrichten)* bad news *sing;* *(Übles)* bad
things *pl;* **~erfüllt** *adj* unfulfilled; **~ergiebig**
*adj (Quelle, Thema)* unproductive; *(Ernte,
Nachschlagewerk)* poor; **~ergründlich** *adj*
unfathomable; **~erheblich** *adj* unimportant;
**~erhört** *adj* unheard-of; *(unverschämt)*
outrageous; *(Bitte)* unanswered; **~erläßlich**
*adj* indispensable; **~erlaubt** *adj*
unauthorized; **~erledigt** *adj* unfinished;
*(Post)* unanswered; *(Rechnung)* outstanding;
*(schwebend)* pending; **~ermeßlich** *adj*
immeasurable, immense; **~ermüdlich** *adj*
indefatigable; **~ersättlich** *adj* insatiable;
**~erschlossen** *adj (Land)* undeveloped;
*(Boden)* unexploited; *(Vorkommen, Markt)*
untapped; **~erschöpflich** *adj* inexhaustible;
**~erschrocken** *adj* intrepid, courageous;
**~erschütterlich** *adj* unshakeable;
**~erschwinglich** *adj (Preis)* prohibitive;
**~ersetzlich** *adj* irreplaceable; **~erträglich** *adj*
unbearable; *(Frechheit)* insufferable;
**~erwartet** *adj* unexpected; **~erwünscht** *adj*
undesirable, unwelcome; **~erzogen** *adj* ill-
bred, rude.

**unfähig** ['ʊnfɛːɪç] *adj* incapable; (*attrib*) incompetent; **zu etw ~ sein** to be incapable of sth; **U~keit** *f* inability; incompetence.

**unfair** ['ʊnfɛːr] *adj* unfair.

**Unfall** ['ʊnfal] *m* accident; **~flucht** *f* hit-and-run (driving); **~opfer** *nt* casualty; **~station** *f* emergency ward; **~stelle** *f* scene of the accident; **~versicherung** *f* accident insurance; **~wagen** *m car involved in an accident*; (*umg: Rettungswagen*) ambulance.

**unfaßbar** [ʊn'fasbaːr] *adj* inconceivable.

**unfehlbar** [ʊn'feːlbaːr] *adj* infallible ♦ *adv* without fail; **U~keit** *f* infallibility.

**unfertig** ['ʊnfɛrtɪç] *adj* unfinished, incomplete; (*Mensch*) immature.

**unflätig** ['ʊnflɛːtɪç] *adj* rude.

**unfolgsam** ['ʊnfɔlkzaːm] *adj* disobedient.

**unförmig** ['ʊnfœrmɪç] *adj* (*formlos*) shapeless; (*groß*) cumbersome; (*Füße, Nase*) unshapely.

**unfrankiert** ['ʊnfraŋkiːrt] *adj* unfranked.

**unfrei** ['ʊnfraɪ] *adj* not free.

**unfreiwillig** *adj* involuntary.

**unfreundlich** ['ʊnfrɔʏntlɪç] *adj* unfriendly; **U~keit** *f* unfriendliness.

**Unfriede(n)** ['ʊnfriːdə(n)] *m* dissension, strife.

**unfruchtbar** ['ʊnfrʊxtbaːr] *adj* infertile; (*Gespräche*) fruitless; **U~keit** *f* infertility; fruitlessness.

**Unfug** ['ʊnfuːk] (**-s**) *m* (*Benehmen*) mischief; (*Unsinn*) nonsense; **grober ~** (*JUR*) gross misconduct.

**Ungar(in)** ['ʊŋgar(ɪn)] (**-n, -n**) *m(f)* Hungarian; **u~isch** *adj* Hungarian.

**Ungarn** (**-s**) *nt* Hungary.

**ungeachtet** ['ʊŋgə|axtət] *präp +gen* notwithstanding.

**ungeahndet** ['ʊŋgə|aːndət] *adj* (*JUR*) unpunished.

**ungeahnt** ['ʊŋgə|aːnt] *adj* unsuspected, undreamt-of.

**ungebeten** ['ʊŋgəbeːtən] *adj* uninvited.

**ungebildet** ['ʊŋgəbɪldət] *adj* uncultured; (*ohne Bildung*) uneducated.

**ungeboren** ['ʊŋgəboːrən] *adj* unborn.

**ungebräuchlich** ['ʊŋgəbrɔʏçlɪç] *adj* unusual, uncommon.

**ungebraucht** ['ʊŋgəbraʊxt] *adj* unused.

**ungebührlich** ['ʊŋgəbyːrlɪç] *adj*: **sich ~ aufregen** to get unduly excited.

**ungebunden** ['ʊŋgəbʊndən] *adj* (*Buch*) unbound; (*Leben*) (fancy-)free; (*ohne festen Partner*) unattached; (*POL*) independent.

**ungedeckt** ['ʊŋgədɛkt] *adj* (*schutzlos*) unprotected; (*Scheck*) uncovered.

**Ungeduld** ['ʊŋgədʊlt] *f* impatience.

**ungeduldig** ['ʊŋgədʊldɪç] *adj* impatient.

**ungeeignet** ['ʊŋgə|aɪgnət] *adj* unsuitable.

**ungefähr** ['ʊŋgəfɛːr] *adj* rough, approximate ♦ *adv* roughly, approximately; **so ~!** more or less!; **das kommt nicht von ~** that's hardly surprising.

**ungefährlich** ['ʊŋgəfɛːrlɪç] *adj* not dangerous, harmless.

**ungehalten** ['ʊŋgəhaltən] *adj* indignant.

**ungeheuer** ['ʊŋgəhɔʏər] *adj* huge ♦ *adv* (*umg*) enormously; **U~** (**-s, -**) *nt* monster; **~lich** [ʊŋgə'hɔʏərlɪç] *adj* monstrous.

**ungehindert** ['ʊŋgəhɪndərt] *adj* unimpeded.

**ungehobelt** ['ʊŋgəhoːbəlt] *adj* (*fig*) uncouth.

**ungehörig** ['ʊŋgəhøːrɪç] *adj* impertinent, improper; **U~keit** *f* impertinence.

**ungehorsam** ['ʊŋgəhoːrzaːm] *adj* disobedient; **U~** *m* disobedience.

**ungeklärt** ['ʊŋgəklɛːrt] *adj* not cleared up; (*Rätsel*) unsolved; (*Abwasser*) untreated.

**ungekürzt** ['ʊŋgəkʏrtst] *adj* not shortened; (*Film*) uncut.

**ungeladen** ['ʊŋgəlaːdən] *adj* not loaded; (*ELEK*) uncharged; (*Gast*) uninvited.

**ungelegen** ['ʊŋgəleːgən] *adj* inconvenient; **komme ich (Ihnen) ~?** is this an inconvenient time for you?

**ungelernt** ['ʊŋgəlernt] *adj* unskilled.

**ungelogen** ['ʊŋgəloːgən] *adv* really, honestly.

**ungemein** ['ʊŋgəmaɪn] *adj* immense.

**ungemütlich** ['ʊŋgəmyːtlɪç] *adj* uncomfortable; (*Person*) disagreeable; **er kann ~ werden** he can get nasty.

**ungenau** ['ʊŋgənaʊ] *adj* inaccurate. **Ungenauigkeit** *f* inaccuracy.

**ungeniert** ['ʊŋʒeniːrt] *adj* free and easy; (*bedenkenlos, taktlos*) uninhibited ♦ *adv* without embarrassment, freely.

**ungenießbar** ['ʊŋgəniːsbaːr] *adj* inedible; (*nicht zu trinken*) undrinkable; (*umg*) unbearable.

**ungenügend** ['ʊŋgənyːgənt] *adj* insufficient, inadequate; (*SCH*) unsatisfactory.

**ungenutzt** ['ʊŋgənʊtst] *adj*: **eine Chance ~ lassen** to miss an opportunity.

**ungepflegt** ['ʊŋgəpfleːkt] *adj* (*Garten etc*) untended; (*Person*) unkempt; (*Hände*) neglected.

**ungerade** ['ʊŋgəraːdə] *adj* odd, uneven (*US*).

**ungerecht** ['ʊŋgərɛçt] *adj* unjust.

**ungerechtfertigt** *adj* unjustified.

**Ungerechtigkeit** *f* unfairness, injustice.

**ungeregelt** ['ʊŋgəreːgəlt] *adj* irregular.

**ungereimt** ['ʊŋgəraɪmt] *adj* (*Verse*) unrhymed; (*fig*) inconsistent.

**ungern** ['ʊŋgɛrn] *adv* unwillingly, reluctantly.

**ungerufen** ['ʊŋgəruːfən] *adj* without being called.

**ungeschehen** ['ʊŋgəʃeːən] *adj*: **~ machen** to undo.

**Ungeschicklichkeit** ['ʊŋgəʃɪklɪçkaɪt] *f* clumsiness.

**ungeschickt** *adj* awkward, clumsy.

**ungeschliffen** ['ʊŋgəʃlɪfən] *adj* (*Edelstein*) uncut; (*Messer etc*) blunt; (*fig: Benehmen*) uncouth.

**ungeschmälert** ['ʊŋgəʃmɛːlərt] *adj* undiminished.

**ungeschminkt** ['ʊŋgəʃmɪŋkt] *adj* without

make-up; (*fig*) unvarnished.
**ungeschoren** ['ʊngəʃoːrən] *adj*: **jdn ~ lassen**
(*umg*) to spare sb; (*ungestraft*) to let sb off.
**ungesetzlich** ['ʊngəzɛtslɪç] *adj* illegal.
**ungestempelt** ['ʊngəʃtɛmpəlt] *adj* (*Briefmarke*)
unfranked, mint.
**ungestört** ['ʊngəʃtøːrt] *adj* undisturbed.
**ungestraft** ['ʊngəʃtraːft] *adv* with impunity.
**ungestüm** ['ʊngəʃtyːm] *adj* impetuous; **U~**
**(-(e)s)** *nt* impetuosity.
**ungesund** ['ʊngəzʊnt] *adj* unhealthy.
**ungetrübt** ['ʊngətryːpt] *adj* clear; (*fig*)
untroubled; (*Freude*) unalloyed.
**Ungetüm** ['ʊngətyːm] *nt* (-(e)s, -e) *nt* monster.
**ungeübt** ['ʊngə|yːpt] *adj* unpractical (*BRIT*),
unpracticed (*US*); (*Mensch*) out of practice.
**ungewiß** ['ʊngəvɪs] *adj* uncertain; **U~heit** *f*
uncertainty.
**ungewöhnlich** ['ʊngəvøːnlɪç] *adj* unusual.
**ungewohnt** ['ʊngəvoːnt] *adj* unusual.
**ungewollt** ['ʊngəvɔlt] *adj* unintentional.
**Ungeziefer** ['ʊngətsiːfər] (-s) *nt* vermin *pl*.
**ungezogen** ['ʊngətsoːgən] *adj* rude,
impertinent; **U~heit** *f* rudeness,
impertinence.
**ungezwungen** ['ʊngətsvʊŋən] *adj* natural,
unconstrained.
**ungläubig** ['ʊnglɔybɪç] *adj* unbelieving; **ein**
**~er Thomas** a doubting Thomas; **die U~en**
the infidel(s *pl*).
**unglaublich** [ʊn'glaʊplɪç] *adj* incredible.
**unglaubwürdig** ['ʊnglaʊpvyrdɪç] *adj*
untrustworthy, unreliable; (*Geschichte*)
improbable; **sich ~ machen** to lose
credibility.
**ungleich** ['ʊnglaɪç] *adj* dissimilar; (*Mittel,*
*Waffen*) unequal ♦ *adv* incomparably; **~artig**
*adj* different; **U~behandlung** *f* (*von Frauen,*
*Ausländern*) unequal treatment; **U~heit** *f*
dissimilarity; inequality; **~mäßig** *adj*
uneven; (*Atemzüge, Gesichtszüge, Puls*)
irregular.
**Unglück** ['ʊnglʏk] *nt* misfortune; (*Pech*) bad
luck; (*~sfall*) calamity, disaster; (*Verkehrs~*)
accident; **zu allem ~** to make matters
worse; **u~lich** *adj* unhappy; (*erfolglos*)
unlucky; (*unerfreulich*) unfortunate;
**u~licherweise** *adv* unfortunately; **u~selig** *adj*
calamitous; (*Person*) unfortunate.
**Unglücksfall** *m* accident, mishap.
**Unglücksrabe** (*umg*) *m* unlucky thing.
**Ungnade** ['ʊngnaːdə] *f*: **bei jdm in ~ fallen** to
fall out of favour (*BRIT*) *od* favor (*US*) with
sb.
**ungültig** ['ʊngʏltɪç] *adj* invalid; **etw für**
**~ erklären** to declare sth null and void;
**U~keit** *f* invalidity.
**ungünstig** ['ʊngʏnstɪç] *adj* unfavourable
(*BRIT*), unfavorable (*US*); (*Termin*)
inconvenient; (*Augenblick, Wetter*) bad; (*nicht*
*preiswert*) expensive.
**ungut** ['ʊnguːt] *adj* (*Gefühl*) uneasy; **nichts für**

**~! no offence!**
**unhaltbar** ['ʊnhaltbaːr] *adj* untenable.
**unhandlich** ['ʊnhantlɪç] *adj* unwieldy.
**Unheil** ['ʊnhaɪl] *nt* evil; (*Unglück*) misfortune;
**~ anrichten** to cause mischief.
**unheilbar** [ʊn'haɪlbaːr] *adj* incurable.
**unheilbringend** *adj* fatal, fateful.
**unheilvoll** *adj* disastrous.
**unheimlich** ['ʊnhaɪmlɪç] *adj* weird, uncanny
♦ *adv* (*umg*) tremendously; **das/er ist mir ~**
it/he gives me the creeps (*umg*).
**unhöflich** ['ʊnhøːflɪç] *adj* impolite; **U~keit** *f*
impoliteness.
**unhörbar** [ʊn'høːrbaːr] *adj* silent; (*Frequenzen*)
inaudible.
**unhygienisch** ['ʊnhygieːnɪʃ] *adj* unhygienic.
**Uni** ['ʊni] (-, -s) (*umg*) *f* university.
**uni** ['yni] *adj* self-coloured (*BRIT*), self-
colored (*US*).
**Uniform** [uni'fɔrm] (-, -en) *f* uniform.
**uniformiert** [unifɔr'miːrt] *adj* uniformed.
**Unikum** ['uːnikʊm] (-s, -s *od* Unika) (*umg*) *nt*
real character.
**uninteressant** ['ʊn|ɪnteresant] *adj*
uninteresting.
**uninteressiert** ['ʊn|ɪntərə'siːrt] *adj*: **~ (an +**
*dat*) uninterested (in), not interested (in).
**Union** [uni'oːn] *f* union.
**Unionsparteien** *pl* (*BRD POL*) CDU and CSU
parties *pl*.
**universal** [univer'zaːl] *adj* universal.
**universell** [univer'zɛl] *adj* universal.
**Universität** [univerzi'tɛːt] *f* university; **auf**
**die ~ gehen, die ~ besuchen** to go to
university.
**Universum** [uni'vɛrzʊm] (-s) *nt* universe.
**unkenntlich** ['ʊnkɛntlɪç] *adj* unrecognizable;
**U~keit** *f*: **bis zur U~keit** beyond recognition.
**Unkenntnis** ['ʊnkɛntnɪs] *f* ignorance.
**unklar** ['ʊnklaːr] *adj* unclear; **im ~en sein über**
+*akk* to be in the dark about; **U~heit** *f*
unclarity; (*Unentschiedenheit*) uncertainty.
**unklug** ['ʊnkluːk] *adj* unwise.
**unkompliziert** ['ʊnkɔmplitsiːrt] *adj*
straightforward, uncomplicated.
**unkontrolliert** ['ʊnkɔntrɔliːrt] *adj* unchecked.
**unkonzentriert** ['ʊnkɔntsɛntriːrt] *adj* lacking
in concentration.
**Unkosten** ['ʊnkɔstən] *pl* expense(s *pl*); **sich in**
**~ stürzen** (*umg*) to go to a lot of expense.
**Unkraut** ['ʊnkraʊt] *nt* weed; weeds *pl*;
**~ vergeht nicht** (*Sprichwort*) it would take
more than that to finish me/him *etc* off;
**~vertilgungsmittel** *nt* weedkiller.
**unlängst** ['ʊnlɛŋst] *adv* not long ago.
**unlauter** ['ʊnlaʊtər] *adj* unfair.
**unleserlich** ['ʊnleːzərlɪç] *adj* illegible.
**unleugbar** ['ʊnlɔykbaːr] *adj* undeniable,
indisputable.
**unlogisch** ['ʊnloːgɪʃ] *adj* illogical.
**unlösbar** [ʊn'løːsbaːr] *adj* insoluble.
**unlöslich** [ʊn'løːslɪç] *adj* insoluble.

**Unlust** ['ʊnlʊst] f lack of enthusiasm.
**unlustig** adj unenthusiastic ♦ adv without enthusiasm.
**unmännlich** ['ʊnmɛnlɪç] adj unmanly.
**Unmasse** ['ʊnmasə] (umg) f load.
**unmäßig** ['ʊnmɛːsɪç] adj immoderate.
**Unmenge** ['ʊnmɛŋə] f tremendous number, vast number.
**Unmensch** ['ʊnmɛnʃ] m ogre, brute; **u~lich** adj inhuman, brutal; (ungeheuer) awful.
**unmerklich** [ʊn'mɛrklɪç] adj imperceptible.
**unmißverständlich** ['ʊnmɪsfɛrʃtɛntlɪç] adj unmistakable.
**unmittelbar** ['ʊnmɪtəlbaːr] adj immediate; **~er Kostenaufwand** direct expense.
**unmöbliert** ['ʊnmøbliːrt] adj unfurnished.
**unmöglich** ['ʊnmøːklɪç] adj impossible; **ich kann es ~ tun** I can't possibly do it; **~ aussehen** (umg) to look ridiculous; **U~keit** f impossibility.
**unmoralisch** ['ʊnmoraːlɪʃ] adj immoral.
**unmotiviert** ['ʊnmotiviːrt] adj unmotivated.
**unmündig** ['ʊnmyndɪç] adj (minderjährig) underage.
**Unmut** ['ʊnmuːt] m ill humour (BRIT) od humor (US).
**unnachahmlich** ['ʊnnaːxˌaːmlɪç] adj inimitable.
**unnachgiebig** ['ʊnnaːxgiːbɪç] adj unyielding.
**unnahbar** [ʊn'naːbaːr] adj unapproachable.
**unnatürlich** ['ʊnnatyːrlɪç] adj unnatural.
**unnormal** ['ʊnnɔrmaːl] adj abnormal.
**unnötig** ['ʊnnøːtɪç] adj unnecessary.
**unnötigerweise** adv unnecessarily.
**unnütz** ['ʊnnʏts] adj useless.
**UNO** ['uːno] f abk (= United Nations Organization): **die ~** the UN.
**unordentlich** ['ʊnˌɔrdəntlɪç] adj untidy.
**Unordnung** ['ʊnˌɔrdnʊŋ] f disorder; (Durcheinander) mess.
**unorganisiert** ['ʊnˌɔrganiziːrt] adj disorganized.
**unparteiisch** ['ʊnpartaıʃ] adj impartial.
**Unparteiische(r)** f(m) umpire; (FUSSBALL) referee.
**unpassend** ['ʊnpasənt] adj inappropriate; (Zeit) inopportune.
**unpäßlich** ['ʊnpɛslɪç] adj unwell.
**unpersönlich** ['ʊnpɛrzøːnlɪç] adj impersonal.
**unpolitisch** ['ʊnpoliːtɪʃ] adj apolitical.
**unpraktisch** ['ʊnpraktɪʃ] adj impractical, unpractical.
**unproduktiv** ['ʊnprodʊktiːf] adj unproductive.
**unproportioniert** ['ʊnproˌpɔrtsioniːrt] adj out of proportion.
**unpünktlich** ['ʊnpʏŋktlɪç] adj unpunctual.
**unqualifiziert** ['ʊnkvalifitsiːrt] adj unqualified; (Äußerung) incompetent.
**unrasiert** ['ʊnraziːrt] adj unshaven.
**Unrat** ['ʊnraːt] (-(e)s) m (geh) refuse; (fig) filth.
**unrationell** ['ʊnratsionɛl] adj inefficient.

**unrecht** ['ʊnrɛçt] adj wrong; **das ist mir gar nicht so ~** I don't really mind; **U~** nt wrong; **zu U~** wrongly; **nicht zu U~** not without good reason; **U~ haben, im U~ sein** to be wrong.
**unrechtmäßig** adj unlawful, illegal.
**unredlich** ['ʊnreːtlɪç] adj dishonest; **U~keit** f dishonesty.
**unreell** ['ʊnreɛl] adj unfair; (unredlich) dishonest; (Preis) unreasonable.
**unregelmäßig** ['ʊnreːgəlmɛːsɪç] adj irregular; **U~keit** f irregularity.
**unreif** ['ʊnraɪf] adj (Obst) unripe; (fig) immature.
**Unreife** f immaturity.
**unrein** ['ʊnraɪn] adj not clean; (Ton, Gedanken, Taten) impure; (Atem, Haut) bad.
**unrentabel** ['ʊnrɛntaːbəl] adj unprofitable.
**unrichtig** ['ʊnrɪçtɪç] adj incorrect, wrong.
**Unruh** ['ʊnruː] (-, -en) f (von Uhr) balance.
**Unruhe** (-, -n) f unrest; **~herd** m trouble spot; **~stifter** m troublemaker.
**unruhig** adj restless; (nervös) fidgety; (belebt) noisy; (Schlaf) fitful; (Zeit etc, Meer) troubled.
**unrühmlich** ['ʊnryːmlɪç] adj inglorious.
**uns** [ʊns] pron akk, dat von **wir** us; (reflexiv) ourselves.
**unsachgemäß** ['ʊnzaxgəmɛːs] adj improper.
**unsachlich** ['ʊnzaxlɪç] adj not to the point, irrelevant; (persönlich) personal.
**unsagbar** [ʊn'zaːkbaːr] adj indescribable.
**unsäglich** [ʊn'zɛːklɪç] adj indescribable.
**unsanft** ['ʊnzanft] adj rough.
**unsauber** ['ʊnzaʊbər] adj (schmutzig) dirty; (fig) crooked; (: Klang) impure.
**unschädlich** ['ʊnʃɛːtlɪç] adj harmless; **jdn/etw ~ machen** to render sb/sth harmless.
**unscharf** ['ʊnʃarf] adj indistinct; (Bild etc) out of focus, blurred.
**unschätzbar** [ʊn'ʃɛtsbaːr] adj incalculable; (Hilfe) invaluable.
**unscheinbar** ['ʊnʃaınbaːr] adj insignificant; (Aussehen, Haus etc) unprepossessing.
**unschlagbar** [ʊn'ʃlaːkbaːr] adj invincible.
**unschlüssig** ['ʊnʃlʏsɪç] adj undecided.
**unschön** ['ʊnʃøːn] adj unsightly; (lit, fig: Szene) ugly; (Vorfall) unpleasant.
**Unschuld** ['ʊnʃʊlt] f innocence.
**unschuldig** ['ʊnʃʊldɪç] adj innocent.
**Unschuldsmiene** f innocent expression.
**unschwer** ['ʊnʃveːr] adv easily, without difficulty.
**unselbständig** ['ʊnzɛlpʃtɛndɪç] adj dependent, over-reliant on others.
**unselig** ['ʊnzeːlɪç] adj unfortunate; (verhängnisvoll) ill-fated.
**unser** ['ʊnzər] poss pron our ♦ pron gen von **wir** of us.
**unsere(r, s)** poss pron ours; **wir tun das U~** (geh) we are doing our bit.
**unsereiner** pron the likes of us.
**unsereins** pron the likes of us.

**unser(er)seits** ['ʊnzər(ər)'zaɪts] *adv* on our part.

**unseresgleichen** *pron* the likes of us.

**unserige(r, s)** *poss pron:* **der/die/das** ~ ours.

**unseriös** ['ʊnzeriøːs] *adj (unehrlich)* not straight, untrustworthy.

**unsertwegen** ['ʊnzərt've:gən] *adv (für uns)* for our sake; *(wegen uns)* on our account.

**unsertwillen** ['ʊnzərt'vɪlən] *adv:* **um** ~ = **unsertwegen.**

**unsicher** ['ʊnzɪçər] *adj* uncertain; *(Mensch)* insecure; **die Gegend** ~ **machen** *(fig: umg)* to knock about the district; **U~heit** *f* uncertainty; insecurity.

**unsichtbar** ['ʊnzɪçtbaːr] *adj* invisible; **U~keit** *f* invisibility.

**Unsinn** ['ʊnzɪn] *m* nonsense.

**unsinnig** *adj* nonsensical.

**Unsitte** ['ʊnzɪtə] *f* deplorable habit.

**unsittlich** ['ʊnzɪtlɪç] *adj* indecent; **U~keit** *f* indecency.

**unsolide** ['ʊnzoliːdə] *adj (Mensch, Leben)* loose; *(Firma)* unreliable.

**unsozial** ['ʊnzotsiaːl] *adj (Verhalten)* antisocial; *(Politik)* unsocial.

**unsportlich** ['ʊnʃpɔrtlɪç] *adj* not sporty; *(Verhalten)* unsporting.

**unsre** *etc* ['ʊnzrə] *poss pron* = **unsere** *etc; siehe auch* **unser.**

**unsrige(r, s)** ['ʊnzrɪgə(r, s)] *poss pron* = **unserige.**

**unsterblich** ['ʊnʃtɛrplɪç] *adj* immortal; **U~keit** *f* immortality.

**unstet** ['ʊnʃteːt] *adj (Mensch)* restless; *(wankelmütig)* changeable; *(Leben)* unsettled.

**Unstimmigkeit** ['ʊnʃtɪmɪçkaɪt] *f* inconsistency; *(Streit)* disagreement.

**Unsumme** ['ʊnzʊmə] *f* vast sum.

**unsympathisch** ['ʊnzʏmpatɪʃ] *adj* unpleasant; **er ist mir** ~ I don't like him.

**untad(e)lig** ['ʊntaːd(ə)lɪç] *adj* impeccable; *(Mensch)* beyond reproach.

**Untat** ['ʊntaːt] *f* atrocity.

**untätig** ['ʊntɛːtɪç] *adj* idle.

**untauglich** ['ʊntaʊklɪç] *adj* unsuitable; *(MIL)* unfit; **U~keit** *f* unsuitability; unfitness.

**unteilbar** ['ʊntaɪlbaːr] *adj* indivisible.

**unten** ['ʊntən] *adv* below; *(im Haus)* downstairs; *(an der Treppe etc)* at the bottom; **siehe** ~ see below; **nach** ~ down; ~ **am Berg** *etc* at the bottom of the mountain *etc;* **er ist bei mir** ~ **durch** *(umg)* I'm through with him; ~**an** *adv (am unteren Ende)* at the far end; *(lit, fig)* at the bottom; ~**genannt** *adj* undermentioned.

=================== *SCHLÜSSELWORT*

**unter** ['ʊntər] *präp +dat* **1** *(räumlich)* under; *(drunter)* underneath, below
**2** *(zwischen)* among(st); **sie waren** ~ **sich** they were by themselves; **einer** ~ **ihnen** one of them; ~ **anderem** among other things

♦ *präp +akk* under, below
♦ *adv (weniger als)* under; **Mädchen** ~ **18 Jahren** girls under *od* less than 18 (years of age).

**Unter-** *zW:* ~**abteilung** *f* subdivision; ~**arm** *m* forearm; **u~belegt** *adj (Kurs)* undersubscribed; *(Hotel etc)* not full.

**unterbelichten** ['ʊntərbəlɪçtən] *vt untr (PHOT)* to underexpose.

**Unterbeschäftigung** ['ʊntərbəʃɛːftɪgʊn] *f* underemployment.

**unterbesetzt** ['ʊntərbəzɛtst] *adj* understaffed.

**Unterbewußtsein** ['ʊntərbəvʊstzaɪn] *nt* subconscious.

**unterbezahlt** ['ʊntərbətsaːlt] *adj* underpaid.

**unterbieten** [ʊntər'biːtən] *unreg vt untr (COMM)* to undercut; *(fig)* to surpass.

**unterbinden** [ʊntər'bɪndən] *unreg vt untr* to stop, call a halt to.

**unterbleiben** [ʊntər'blaɪbən] *unreg vi untr (aufhören)* to stop; *(versäumt werden)* to be omitted.

**Unterbodenschutz** [ʊntər'boːdənʃʊts] *m (AUT)* underseal.

**unterbrechen** [ʊntər'brɛçən] *unreg vt untr* to interrupt.

**Unterbrechung** *f* interruption.

**unterbreiten** [ʊntər'braɪtən] *vt untr (Plan)* to present.

**unterbringen** ['ʊntərbrɪŋən] *unreg vt (in Koffer)* to stow; *(in Zeitung)* to place; *(Person: in Hotel etc)* to accommodate, put up; *(: beruflich):* ~ **(bei)** to fix up (with).

**unterbuttern** ['ʊntərbʊtərn] *(umg) vt (zuschießen)* to throw in; *(unterdrücken)* to ride roughshod over.

**unterderhand** [ʊntərder'hant] *adv* secretly; *(verkaufen)* privately.

**unterdessen** [ʊntər'dɛsən] *adv* meanwhile.

**Unterdruck** ['ʊntərdrʊk] *m (TECH)* below atmospheric pressure.

**unterdrücken** [ʊntər'drʏkən] *vt untr* to suppress; *(Leute)* to oppress.

**untere(r, s)** ['ʊntərə(r, s)] *adj* lower.

**untereinander** [ʊntəraɪ'nandər] *adv (gegenseitig)* each other; *(miteinander)* among themselves *etc.*

**unterentwickelt** ['ʊntərˌɛntvɪkəlt] *adj* underdeveloped.

**unterernährt** ['ʊntərˌɛrnɛːrt] *adj* undernourished.

**Unterernährung** *f* malnutrition.

**Unterfangen** [ʊntər'faŋən] *nt* undertaking.

**Unterführung** [ʊntər'fyːrʊŋ] *f* subway, underpass.

**Untergang** ['ʊntərgaŋ] *m* (down)fall, decline; *(NAUT)* sinking; *(von Gestirn)* setting; **dem** ~ **geweiht sein** to be doomed.

**untergeben** [ʊntər'geːbən] *adj* subordinate.

**Untergebene(r)** *f(m)* subordinate.

**untergehen** ['ʊntərgeːən] *unreg vi* to go down;

(*Sonne*) to set, go down; (*Staat*) to fall; (*Volk*) to perish; (*Welt*) to come to an end; (*im Lärm*) to be drowned.

**untergeordnet** ['ʊntərgə|ɔrdnət] *adj* (*Dienststelle*) subordinate; (*Bedeutung*) secondary.

**Untergeschoß** ['ʊntərgəʃɔs] *nt* basement.

**Untergewicht** ['ʊntərgəvɪçt] *nt:* **(10 Kilo) ~ haben** to be (10 kilos) underweight.

**untergliedern** [ʊntər'gliːdərn] *vt untr* to subdivide.

**untergraben** [ʊntər'graːbən] *unreg vt untr* to undermine.

**Untergrund** ['ʊntərgrʊnt] *m* foundation; (*POL*) underground; **~bahn** *f* underground (*BRIT*), subway (*US*); **~bewegung** *f* underground (movement).

**unterhaken** ['ʊntərhaːkən] *vr:* **sich bei jdm ~** to link arms with sb.

**unterhalb** ['ʊntərhalp] *präp +gen* below ♦ *adv* below; **~ von** below.

**Unterhalt** ['ʊntərhalt] *m* maintenance; **seinen ~ verdienen** to earn one's living.

**unterhalten** [ʊntər'haltən] *unreg vt untr* to maintain; (*belustigen*) to entertain; (*versorgen*) to support; (*Geschäft, Kfz*) to run; (*Konto*) to have ♦ *vr untr* to talk; (*sich belustigen*) to enjoy o.s.

**unterhaltend, unterhaltsam** [ʊntər'haltzaːm] *adj* entertaining.

**Unterhaltskosten** *pl* maintenance costs *pl*.

**Unterhaltszahlung** *f* maintenance payment.

**Unterhaltung** *f* maintenance; (*Belustigung*) entertainment, amusement; (*Gespräch*) talk.

**Unterhaltungskosten** *pl* running costs *pl*.

**Unterhaltungsmusik** *f* light music.

**Unterhändler** ['ʊntərhɛntlər] *m* negotiator.

**Unterhaus** ['ʊntərhaus] *nt* House of Commons (*BRIT*), House of Representatives (*US*), Lower House.

**Unterhemd** ['ʊntərhɛmt] *nt* vest (*BRIT*), undershirt (*US*).

**unterhöhlen** [ʊntər'høːlən] *vt untr* (*lit, fig*) to undermine.

**Unterholz** ['ʊntərhɔlts] *nt* undergrowth.

**Unterhose** ['ʊntərhoːzə] *f* underpants *pl*.

**unterirdisch** ['ʊntər|ɪrdɪʃ] *adj* underground.

**unterjubeln** ['ʊntərjuːbəln] (*umg*) *vt:* **jdm etw ~** to palm sth off on sb.

**unterkapitalisiert** ['ʊntərkapitali'ziːrt] *adj* undercapitalized.

**unterkellern** [ʊntər'kɛlərn] *vt untr* to build with a cellar.

**Unterkiefer** ['ʊntərkiːfər] *m* lower jaw.

**unterkommen** ['ʊntərkɔmən] *unreg vi* to find shelter; (*Stelle finden*) to find work; **das ist mir noch nie untergekommen** I've never met with that; **bei jdm ~** to stay at sb's (place).

**unterkriegen** ['ʊntərkriːgən] (*umg*) *vt:* **sich nicht ~ lassen** not to let things get one

down.

**unterkühlt** [ʊntər'kyːlt] *adj* (*Körper*) affected by hypothermia; (*fig: Mensch, Atmosphäre*) cool.

**Unterkunft** ['ʊntərkʊnft] (**-, -künfte**) *f* accommodation (*BRIT*), accommodations *pl* (*US*); **~ und Verpflegung** board and lodging.

**Unterlage** ['ʊntərlaːgə] *f* foundation; (*Beleg*) document; (*Schreib~ etc*) pad.

**unterlassen** [ʊntər'lasən] *unreg vt untr* (*versäumen*) to fail to do; (*sich enthalten*) to refrain from.

**unterlaufen** [ʊntər'laufən] *unreg vi untr* to happen ♦ *adj:* **mit Blut ~** suffused with blood; (*Augen*) bloodshot; **mir ist ein Fehler ~** I made a mistake.

**unterlegen¹** ['ʊntərleːgən] *vt* to lay *od* put under.

**unterlegen²** [ʊntər'leːgən] *adj* inferior; (*besiegt*) defeated.

**Unterleib** ['ʊntərlaip] *m* abdomen.

**unterliegen** [ʊntər'liːgən] *unreg vi untr +dat* to be defeated *od* overcome (by); (*unterworfen sein*) to be subject (to).

**Unterlippe** ['ʊntərlɪpə] *f* bottom *od* lower lip.

**unterm** = **unter dem**.

**untermalen** [ʊntər'maːlən] *vt untr* (*mit Musik*) to provide with background music.

**Untermalung** *f:* **musikalische ~** background music.

**untermauern** [ʊntər'mauərn] *vt untr* (*Gebäude, fig*) to underpin.

**Untermiete** [ʊntər'miːtə] *f* subtenancy; **bei jdm zur ~ wohnen** to rent a room from sb.

**Untermieter(in)** *m(f)* lodger.

**untern** = **unter den**.

**unternehmen** [ʊntər'neːmən] *unreg vt untr* to do; (*durchführen*) to undertake; (*Versuch, Reise*) to make; **U~** (**-s, -**) *nt* undertaking, enterprise (*auch COMM*); (*Firma*) business.

**unternehmend** *adj* enterprising, daring.

**Unternehmensberater** *m* management consultant.

**Unternehmensplanung** *f* corporate planning, management planning.

**Unternehmer(in)** [ʊntər'neːmər(ɪn)] (**-s, -**) *m(f)* (*business*) employer; (*alten Stils*) entrepreneur; **~verband** *m* employers' association.

**Unternehmungsgeist** *m* spirit of enterprise.

**unternehmungslustig** *adj* enterprising.

**Unteroffizier** ['ʊntər|ɔfitsiːr] *m* noncommissioned officer, NCO.

**unterordnen** ['ʊntər|ɔrdnən] *vt:* **~** (**+dat**) to subordinate (to).

**Unterordnung** *f* subordination.

**Unterprima** ['ʊntərpriːma] *f* eighth year of German secondary school.

**Unterprogramm** ['ʊntərprogram] *nt* (*COMPUT*) subroutine.

**Unterredung** [ʊntər'reːdʊŋ] *f* discussion,

talk.
**Unterricht** ['ʊntərrɪçt] (-(e)s) *m* teaching;
(*Stunden*) lessons *pl*; **jdm ~ (in etw** *dat*)
**geben** to teach sb (sth).
**unterrichten** [ʊntər'rɪçtən] *vt untr* to instruct;
(*SCH*) to teach ♦ *vr untr:* **sich ~ (über** +*akk*) to
inform o.s. (about), obtain information
(about).
**Unterrichts-** *zW:* **~gegenstand** *m* topic,
subject; **~methode** *f* teaching method;
**~stoff** *m* teaching material; **~stunde** *f*
lesson; **~zwecke** *pl:* **zu ~zwecken** for
teaching purposes.
**Unterrock** ['ʊntərrɔk] *m* petticoat, slip.
**unters** = **unter das.**
**untersagen** [ʊntər'za:gən] *vt untr* to forbid;
**jdm etw ~** to forbid sb to do sth.
**Untersatz** ['ʊntərzats] *m* mat; (*für Blumentöpfe*
*etc*) base.
**unterschätzen** [ʊntər'ʃɛtsən] *vt untr* to
underestimate.
**unterscheiden** [ʊntər'ʃaɪdən] *unreg vt untr* to
distinguish ♦ *vr untr* to differ.
**Unterscheidung** *f* (*Unterschied*) distinction;
(*Unterscheiden*) differentiation.
**Unterschenkel** ['ʊntərʃɛŋkəl] *m* lower leg.
**Unterschicht** ['ʊntərʃɪçt] *f* lower class.
**unterschieben** ['ʊntərʃiːbən] *unreg vt* (*fig*): **jdm**
**etw ~** to foist sth on sb.
**Unterschied** ['ʊntərʃiːt] (-(e)s, -e) *m*
difference, distinction; **im ~ zu** as distinct
from; **u~lich** *adj* varying, differing;
(*diskriminierend*) discriminatory.
**unterschiedslos** *adv* indiscriminately.
**unterschlagen** [ʊntər'ʃlaːgən] *unreg vt untr* to
embezzle; (*verheimlichen*) to suppress.
**Unterschlagung** *f* embezzlement; (*von*
*Briefen, Beweis*) withholding.
**Unterschlupf** ['ʊntərʃlʊpf] (-(e)s, -schlüpfe) *m*
refuge.
**unterschlüpfen** ['ʊntərʃlʏpfən] (*umg*) *vi* to
take cover *od* shelter; (*Versteck finden*): **(bei**
**jdm) ~** to hide out (at sb's) (*umg*).
**unterschreiben** [ʊntər'ʃraɪbən] *unreg vt untr* to
sign.
**Unterschrift** ['ʊntərʃrɪft] *f* signature; (*Bild~*)
caption.
**unterschwellig** ['ʊntərʃvɛlɪç] *adj* subliminal.
**Unterseeboot** ['ʊntərzeːboːt] *nt* submarine.
**Unterseite** ['ʊntərzaɪtə] *f* underside.
**Untersekunda** ['ʊntərzekunda] *f* sixth year of
German secondary school.
**Untersetzer** ['ʊntərzɛtsər] *m* tablemat; (*für*
*Gläser*) coaster.
**untersetzt** [ʊntər'zɛtst] *adj* stocky.
**unterste(r, s)** ['ʊntərstə(r, s)] *adj* lowest,
bottom.
**unterstehen¹** [ʊntər'ʃteːən] *unreg vi untr* +*dat* to
be under ♦ *vr untr* to dare.
**unterstehen²** ['ʊntərʃteːən] *unreg vi* to
shelter.
**unterstellen¹** [ʊntər'ʃtɛlən] *vt untr* to

subordinate; (*fig*) to impute; **jdm/etw**
**unterstellt sein** to be under sb/sth; (*in Firma*)
to report to sb/sth.
**unterstellen²** ['ʊntərʃtɛlən] *vt* (*Auto*) to
garage, park ♦ *vr* to take shelter.
**Unterstellung** *f* (*falsche Behauptung*)
misrepresentation; (*Andeutung*) insinuation.
**unterstreichen** [ʊntər'ʃtraɪçən] *unreg vt untr* (*lit,*
*fig*) to underline.
**Unterstufe** ['ʊntərʃtuːfə] *f* lower grade.
**unterstützen** [ʊntər'ʃtʏtsən] *vt untr* to support.
**Unterstützung** *f* support, assistance.
**untersuchen** [ʊntər'zuːxən] *vt untr* (*MED*) to
examine; (*Polizei*) to investigate; **sich**
**ärztlich ~ lassen** to have a medical (*BRIT*) *od*
physical (*US*) (examination), have a check-
up.
**Untersuchung** *f* examination; investigation,
inquiry.
**Untersuchungs-** *zW:* **~ausschuß** *m*
committee of inquiry; **~ergebnis** *nt* (*JUR*)
findings *pl*; (*MED*) result of an examination;
**~haft** *f* custody; **in ~haft sein** to be
remanded in custody; **~richter** *m*
examining magistrate.
**Untertagebau** [ʊntər'taːgəbau] *m*
underground mining.
**Untertan** ['ʊntərtaːn] (-s, -en) *m* subject.
**untertänig** ['ʊntərtɛːnɪç] *adj* submissive,
humble.
**Untertasse** ['ʊntərtasə] *f* saucer.
**untertauchen** ['ʊntərtauxən] *vi* to dive; (*fig*) to
disappear, go underground.
**Unterteil** ['ʊntərtaɪl] *nt od m* lower part,
bottom.
**unterteilen** [ʊntər'taɪlən] *vt untr* to divide up.
**Untertertia** ['ʊntərtɛrtsia] *f* fourth year of
German secondary school.
**Untertitel** ['ʊntərtiːtəl] *m* subtitle; (*für Bild*)
caption.
**unterwandern** [ʊntər'vandərn] *vt untr* to
infiltrate.
**Unterwäsche** ['ʊntərvɛʃə] *f* underwear.
**unterwegs** [ʊntər'veːks] *adv* on the way; (*auf*
*Reisen*) away.
**unterweisen** [ʊntər'vaɪzən] *unreg vt untr* to
instruct.
**Unterwelt** ['ʊntərvɛlt] *f* (*lit, fig*) underworld.
**unterwerfen** [ʊntər'vɛrfən] *unreg vt untr* to
subject; (*Volk*) to subjugate ♦ *vr untr* to
submit.
**unterwürfig** [ʊntər'vʏrfɪç] *adj* obsequious.
**unterzeichnen** [ʊntər'tsaɪçnən] *vt untr* to sign.
**Unterzeichner** *m* signatory.
**unterziehen** [ʊntər'tsiːən] *unreg vt untr* +*dat* to
subject ♦ *vr untr* +*dat* to undergo; (*einer*
*Prüfung*) to take.
**Untiefe** ['ʊntiːfə] *f* shallow.
**Untier** ['ʊntiːr] *nt* monster.
**untragbar** [ʊn'traːkbaːr] *adj* intolerable,
unbearable.
**untreu** [ʊntrɔy] *adj* unfaithful; **sich** *dat* **selbst**

~ **werden** to be untrue to o.s.
**Untreue** *f* unfaithfulness.
**untröstlich** [ʊn'trøːstlɪç] *adj* inconsolable.
**Untugend** ['ʊntuːgənt] *f* vice; (*Angewohnheit*)
bad habit.

**un-** *zW:* ~**überbrückbar** *adj* (*fig: Gegensätze etc*)
irreconcilable; (*Kluft*) unbridgeable;
~**überlegt** *adj* ill-considered ♦ *adv* without
thinking; ~**übersehbar** *adj* (*Schaden etc*)
incalculable; (*Menge*) vast, immense;
(*auffällig: Fehler etc*) obvious; ~**übersichtlich**
*adj* (*Gelände*) broken; (*Kurve*) blind; (*System,
Plan*) confused; ~**übertroffen** *adj*
unsurpassed.

**un-** *zW:* ~**umgänglich** *adj* indispensable, vital;
~**umstößlich** *adj* (*Tatsache*) incontrovertible;
(*Entschluß*) irrevocable; ~**umstritten** *adj*
undisputed; ~**umwunden** [-ʊm'vʊndən] *adj*
candid ♦ *adv* straight out.
**ununterbrochen** ['ʊn|ʊntərbrɔxən] *adj*
uninterrupted.

**un-** *zW:* ~**veränderlich** *adj* unchangeable;
~**verantwortlich** *adj* irresponsible;
(~*entschuldbar*) inexcusable;
~**verarbeitet** *adj* (*lit, fig*) raw; ~**veräußerlich**
[-fɛr'ɔysərlɪç] *adj* inalienable; (*Besitz*)
unmarketable; ~**verbesserlich** *adj*
incorrigible; ~**verbindlich** *adj* not binding;
(*Antwort*) curt ♦ *adv* (*COMM*) without
obligation; ~**verbleit** [-fɛrblaıt] *adj* (*Benzin*)
unleaded; ~**verblümt** [-fɛr'blyːmt] *adj* plain,
blunt ♦ *adv* plainly, bluntly; ~**verdaulich** *adj*
indigestible; ~**verdorben** *adj* unspoilt;
~**verdrossen** *adj* undeterred; (~*ermüdlich*)
untiring; ~**vereinbar** *adj* incompatible;
~**verfälscht** [-fɛrfɛlʃt] *adj* (*auch fig*)
unadulterated; (*Dialekt*) pure; (*Natürlichkeit*)
unaffected; ~**verfänglich** *adj* harmless;
~**verfroren** *adj* impudent; ~**vergänglich** *adj*
immortal; (*Eindruck, Erinnerung*) everlasting;
~**vergeßlich** *adj* unforgettable;
~**vergleichlich** *adj* unique, incomparable;
~**verhältnismäßig** *adv* disproportionately;
(*übermäßig*) excessively; ~**verheiratet** *adj*
unmarried; ~**verhofft** *adj* unexpected;
~**verhohlen** [-fɛrhoːlən] *adj* open, uncon-
cealed; ~**verkäuflich** *adj*: „~**verkäuflich**"
"not for sale"; ~**verkennbar** *adj*
unmistakable; ~**verletzlich** *adj* (*fig: Rechte*)
inviolable; (*lit*) invulnerable; ~**verletzt** *adj*
uninjured; ~**vermeidlich** *adj* unavoidable;
~**vermittelt** *adj* (*plötzlich*) sudden,
unexpected; **U**~**vermögen** *nt* inability;
~**vermutet** *adj* unexpected; ~**vernünftig** *adj*
foolish; ~**verrichtet** *adj*: ~**verrichteter Dinge**
empty-handed; ~**verschämt** *adj* impudent;
**U**~**verschämtheit** *f* impudence, insolence;
~**verschuldet** *adj* occurring through no fault
of one's own; ~**versehens** *adv* all of a
sudden; ~**versehrt** [-fɛrzeːrt] *adj* uninjured;
~**versöhnlich** *adj* irreconcilable;
**U**~**verstand** *m* lack of judgement; (*Torheit*)

folly; ~**verständlich** *adj* unintelligible;
~**versucht** *adj*: **nichts ~versucht lassen** to try
everything; ~**verträglich** *adj* quarrelsome;
(*Meinungen, MED*) incompatible;
~**verwechselbar** *adj* unmistakable,
distinctive; ~**verwüstlich** *adj* indestructible;
(*Mensch*) irrepressible; ~**verzeihlich** *adj*
unpardonable; ~**verzinslich** *adj* interest-
free; ~**verzüglich** [-fɛr'tsyːklɪç] *adj*
immediate; ~**vollendet** *adj* unfinished;
~**vollkommen** *adj* imperfect; ~**vollständig**
*adj* incomplete; ~**vorbereitet** *adj* unprepared;
~**voreingenommen** *adj* unbiased;
~**vorhergesehen** *adj* unforeseen;
~**vorsichtig** *adj* careless, imprudent;
~**vorstellbar** *adj* inconceivable; ~**vorteilhaft**
*adj* disadvantageous.

**unwahr** ['ʊnvaːr] *adj* untrue; ~**haftig** *adj*
untruthful; **U**~**heit** *f* untruth; **die U**~**heit**
**sagen** not to tell the truth; ~**scheinlich** *adj*
improbable, unlikely ♦ *adv* (*umg*) incredibly;
**U**~**scheinlichkeit** *f* improbability,
unlikelihood.

**unwegsam** ['ʊnveːkzaːm] *adj* (*Gelände etc*)
rough.
**unweigerlich** [ʊn'vaıgərlıç] *adj* unquestioning
♦ *adv* without fail.
**unweit** ['ʊnvaıt] *präp +gen* not far from ♦ *adv*
not far.
**Unwesen** ['ʊnveːzən] *nt* nuisance; (*Unfug*)
mischief; **sein ~ treiben** to wreak havoc;
(*Mörder etc*) to be at large.
**unwesentlich** *adj* inessential, unimportant;
~ **besser** marginally better.
**Unwetter** ['ʊnvɛtər] *nt* thunderstorm.
**unwichtig** ['ʊnvıçtıç] *adj* unimportant.
**un-** *zW:* ~**widerlegbar** *adj* irrefutable;
~**widerruflich** *adj* irrevocable;
~**widerstehlich** [-viːdər'ʃteːlıç] *adj*
irresistible.
**unwiederbringlich** [ʊnviːdər'brıŋlıç] *adj* (*geh*)
irretrievable.
**Unwille(n)** ['ʊnvılə(n)] *m* indignation.
**unwillig** *adj* indignant; (*widerwillig*) reluctant.
**unwillkürlich** ['ʊnvılkyːrlıç] *adj* involuntary
♦ *adv* instinctively; (*lachen*) involuntarily.
**unwirklich** ['ʊnvırklıç] *adj* unreal.
**unwirksam** ['ʊnvırkzaːm] *adj* ineffective.
**unwirsch** ['ʊnvırʃ] *adj* cross, surly.
**unwirtlich** ['ʊnvırtlıç] *adj* inhospitable.
**unwirtschaftlich** ['ʊnvırtʃaftlıç] *adj*
uneconomical.
**unwissend** ['ʊnvısənt] *adj* ignorant.
**Unwissenheit** *f* ignorance.
**unwissenschaftlich** *adj* unscientific.
**unwissentlich** *adv* unwittingly,
unknowingly.
**unwohl** ['ʊnvoːl] *adj* unwell, ill; **U**~**sein** (-s) *nt*
indisposition.
**unwürdig** ['ʊnvyrdıç] *adj* unworthy.
**Unzahl** ['ʊntsaːl] *f:* **eine ~ von** ... a whole host
of ...

**unzählig** ['ʊn'tsɛːlɪç] adj innumerable, countless.

**unzeitgemäß** ['ʊntsaɪtɡəmɛːs] adj (altmodisch) old-fashioned.

**un-** zW: ~**zerbrechlich** adj unbreakable; ~**zerreißbar** adj untearable; ~**zerstörbar** adj indestructible; ~**zertrennlich** adj inseparable.

**Unzucht** ['ʊntsʊxt] f sexual offence.

**unzüchtig** ['ʊntsʏçtɪç] adj immoral.

**un-** zW: ~**zufrieden** adj dissatisfied; **U~zufriedenheit** f discontent; ~**zugänglich** adj (Gegend) inaccessible; (Mensch) inapproachable; ~**zulänglich** adj inadequate; ~**zulässig** adj inadmissible; ~**zumutbar** adj unreasonable; ~**zurechnungsfähig** adj irresponsible; **jdn für** ~**zurechnungsfähig erklären lassen** (JUR) to have sb certified (insane); ~**zusammenhängend** adj disconnected; (Äußerung) incoherent; ~**zustellbar** adj: **falls** ~**zustellbar, bitte an Absender zurück** if undelivered, please return to sender; ~**zutreffend** adj incorrect; „~**zutreffendes bitte streichen"** "delete as applicable"; ~**zuverlässig** adj unreliable.

**unzweckmäßig** ['ʊntsvɛkmɛːsɪç] adj (nicht ratsam) inadvisable; (unpraktisch) impractical; (ungeeignet) unsuitable.

**unzweideutig** ['ʊntsvaɪdɔʏtɪç] adj unambiguous.

**unzweifelhaft** ['ʊntsvaɪfəlhaft] adj indubitable.

**üppig** ['ʏpɪç] adj (Frau) curvaceous; (Essen) sumptuous, lavish; (Vegetation) luxuriant, lush; (Haar) thick.

**Ur-** ['uːr] in zW: original.

**Urabstimmung** ['uːr|apʃtɪmʊŋ] f ballot.

**Ural** [u'raːl] (-s) m: **der** ~ the Ural mountains pl, the Urals pl; ~**gebirge** nt Ural mountains pl.

**uralt** ['uːr|alt] adj ancient, very old.

**Uran** [u'raːn] (-s) nt uranium.

**Uraufführung** f first performance.

**urbar** adj: **die Wüste/Land** ~ **machen** to reclaim the desert/cultivate land.

**Urdu** ['ʊrdu] (-) nt Urdu.

**Ur-** zW: ~**einwohner** m original inhabitant; ~**eltern** pl ancestors pl; ~**enkel(in)** m(f) great-grandchild; ~**fassung** f original version; ~**großmutter** f great-grandmother; ~**großvater** m great-grandfather.

**Urheber** (-s, -) m originator; (Autor) author; ~**recht** nt: ~**recht (an** +dat) copyright (on); **u~rechtlich** adv: **u~rechtlich geschützt** copyright.

**urig** ['uːrɪç] (umg) adj (Mensch, Atmosphäre) earthy.

**Urin** [u'riːn] (-s, -e) m urine.

**urkomisch** adj incredibly funny.

**Urkunde** f document; (Kauf~) deed.

**urkundlich** ['uːrkʊntlɪç] adj documentary.

**urladen** ['uːrlaːdən] vt (COMPUT) to boot.

**Urlader** m (COMPUT) bootstrap.

**Urlaub** ['uːrlaʊp] (-(e)s, -e) m holiday(s pl) (BRIT), vacation (US); (MIL etc) leave; ~**er** (-s, -) m holiday-maker (BRIT), vacationer (US).

**Urlaubs-** zW: ~**geld** nt holiday (BRIT) od vacation (US) money; ~**ort** m holiday (BRIT) od vacation (US) resort; **u~reif** adj in need of a holiday (BRIT) od vacation (US).

**Urmensch** m primitive man.

**Urne** ['ʊrnə] (-, -n) f urn; **zur** ~ **gehen** to go to the polls.

**urplötzlich** ['uːr'plœtslɪç] (umg) adv all of a sudden.

**Ursache** ['uːrzaxə] f cause; **keine** ~! (auf Dank) don't mention it, you're welcome; (auf Entschuldigung) that's all right.

**ursächlich** ['uːrzɛçlɪç] adj causal.

**Urschrei** ['uːrʃraɪ] m (PSYCH) primal scream.

**Ursprung** ['uːrʃprʊŋ] m origin, source; (von Fluß) source.

**ursprünglich** ['uːrʃprʏŋlɪç] adj original ♦ adv originally.

**Ursprungsland** nt (COMM) country of origin.

**Ursprungszeugnis** nt certificate of origin.

**Urteil** ['ʊrtaɪl] (-s, -e) nt opinion; (JUR) sentence, judgement; **sich** dat **ein** ~ **über etw** akk **erlauben** to pass judgement on sth; **ein** ~ **über etw** akk **fällen** to pass judgement on sth; **u~en** vi to judge.

**Urteilsbegründung** f (JUR) opinion.

**Urteilsspruch** m sentence; verdict.

**Urtrieb** ['ʊrtriːp] (-(e)s, -e) m basic drive.

**Uruguay** [uru'guaːi] (-s) nt Uruguay.

**Uruguayer(in)** (-s, -) m(f) Uruguayan.

**uruguayisch** adj Uruguayan.

**Ur-** zW: ~**wald** m jungle; **u~wüchsig** adj natural; (Landschaft) unspoilt; (Humor) earthy; ~**zeit** f prehistoric times pl.

**USA** [uː'ɛs'|aː] pl abk: **die** ~ the USA sing.

**Usbekistan** [ʊs'beːkistaːn] (-s) nt Uzbekistan.

**usw** abk (= und so weiter) etc.

**Utensilien** [utɛn'ziːliən] pl utensils pl.

**Utopie** [uto'piː] f pipe dream.

**utopisch** [u'toːpɪʃ] adj utopian.

**u.U.** abk (= unter Umständen) possibly.

**UV** abk (= ultraviolett) U.V.

**u.v.a.** abk (= und viele(s) andere) and much/many more.

**u.v.a.m.** abk (= und viele(s) andere mehr) and much/many more.

**u.W.** abk (= unseres Wissens) to our knowledge.

**Ü-Wagen** m (RUNDF, TV) outside broadcast vehicle.

**uzen** ['uːtsən] (umg) vt, vi to tease, kid.

**u.zw.** abk = und zwar.

# *V, v*

**V¹, v** [fau] *nt* V, v; ~ **wie Viktor** ≈ V for Victor.
**V²** [fau] *abk* (= *Volt*) v.
**VAE** *pl abk* (= *Vereinigte Arabische Emirate*) UAE.
**vag(e)** *adj* vague.
**Vagina** [va'gi:na] (-, **Vaginen**) *f* vagina.
**Vakuum** ['va:kuʊm] (-s, **Vakua** *od* **Vakuen**) *nt* vacuum; **v~verpackt** *adj* vacuum-packed.
**Vandalismus** [vanda'lısmʊs] *m* vandalism.
**Vanille** [va'nıljə] (-) *f* vanilla; ~**zucker** *m* vanilla sugar.
**Vanillinzucker** *m* vanilla sugar.
**variabel** [vari'a:bəl] *adj:* **variable Kosten** variable costs.
**Variable** [vari'a:blə] (-, **-n**) *f* variable.
**Variante** [vari'antə] (-, **-n**) *f:* ~ **(zu)** variant (on).
**Variation** [variatsi'o:n] *f* variation.
**variieren** [vari'i:rən] *vt, vi* to vary.
**Vase** ['va:zə] (-, **-n**) *f* vase.
**Vater** ['fa:tər] (-s, ≈) *m* father; ~ **Staat** (*umg*) the State; ~**land** *nt* native country; (*bes Deutschland*) Fatherland; ~**landsliebe** *f* patriotism.
**väterlich** ['fɛ:tərlıç] *adj* fatherly.
**väterlicherseits** *adv* on the father's side.
**Vaterschaft** *f* paternity.
**Vaterschaftsklage** *f* paternity suit.
**Vaterstelle** *f:* ~ **bei jdm vertreten** to take the place of sb's father.
**Vaterunser** (-s, -) *nt* Lord's Prayer.
**Vati** ['fa:ti] (-s, -s) (*umg*) *m* dad(dy).
**Vatikan** [vati'ka:n] (-s) *m* Vatican.
**V-Ausschnitt** ['fau|aʊsʃnıt] *m* V-neck.
**VB** *abk* (= *Verhandlungsbasis*) o.i.r.o.
**v. Chr.** *abk* (= *vor Christus*) B.C.
**Vegetarier(in)** [vege'ta:riər(ın)] (-s, -) *m(f)* vegetarian.
**vegetarisch** *adj* vegetarian.
**Vegetation** [vegetatsi'o:n] *f* vegetation.
**vegetativ** [vegeta'ti:f] *adj* (*BIOL*) vegetative; (*MED*) autonomic.
**vegetieren** [vege'ti:rən] *vi* to vegetate; (*kärglich leben*) to eke out a bare existence.
**Vehikel** [ve'hi:kəl] (-s, -) (*pej: umg*) *nt* boneshaker.
**Veilchen** ['faɪlçən] *nt* violet; (*umg: blaues Auge*) shiner, black eye.
**Velours** (-, -) *nt* suede; ~**leder** *nt* suede.
**Vene** ['ve:nə] (-, **-n**) *f* vein.
**Venedig** [ve'ne:dıç] (-s) *nt* Venice.

**Venezianer(in)** [venetsi'a:nər(ın)] (-s, -) *m(f)* Venetian.
**venezianisch** [venetsi'a:nıʃ] *adj* Venetian.
**Venezolaner(in)** [venetso'la:nər(ın)] (-s, -) *m(f)* Venezuelan.
**venezolanisch** *adj* Venezuelan.
**Venezuela** [venetsu'e:la] (-s) *nt* Venezuela.
**Ventil** [vɛn'ti:l] (-s, **-e**) *nt* valve.
**Ventilator** [vɛnti'la:tɔr] *m* ventilator.
**verabreden** [fɛr'|apre:dən] *vt* to arrange; (*Termin*) to agree upon ♦ *vr* to arrange to meet; **sich (mit jdm)** ~ to arrange to meet (sb); **schon verabredet sein** to have a prior engagement (*form*), have something else on.
**Verabredung** *f* arrangement; (*Treffen*) appointment; **ich habe eine** ~ I'm meeting somebody.
**verabreichen** [fɛr'|apraıçən] *vt* (*Tracht Prügel etc*) to give; (*Arznei*) to administer (*form*).
**verabscheuen** [fɛr'|apʃɔyən] *vt* to detest, abhor.
**verabschieden** [fɛr'|apʃi:dən] *vt* (*Gäste*) to say goodbye to; (*entlassen*) to discharge; (*Gesetz*) to pass ♦ *vr:* **sich** ~ **(von)** to take one's leave (of).
**Verabschiedung** *f* (*von Beamten etc*) discharge; (*von Gesetz*) passing.
**verachten** [fɛr'|axtən] *vt* to despise; **nicht zu** ~ (*umg*) not to be scoffed at.
**verächtlich** [fɛr'|ɛçtlıç] *adj* contemptuous; (*verachtenswert*) contemptible; **jdn** ~ **machen** to run sb down.
**Verachtung** *f* contempt; **jdn mit** ~ **strafen** to treat sb with contempt.
**veralbern** [fɛr'|albərn] (*umg*) *vt* to make fun of.
**verallgemeinern** [fɛr|algə'maınərn] *vt* to generalize.
**Verallgemeinerung** *f* generalization.
**veralten** [fɛr'|altən] *vi* to become obsolete *od* out-of-date.
**Veranda** [ve'randa] (-, **Veranden**) *f* veranda.
**veränderlich** [fɛr'|ɛndərlıç] *adj* variable; (*Wetter*) changeable; **V~keit** *f* variability; changeability.
**verändern** *vt, vr* to change.
**Veränderung** *f* change; **eine berufliche** ~ a change of job.
**verängstigen** [fɛr'|ɛŋstıgən] *vt* (*erschrecken*) to frighten; (*einschüchtern*) to intimidate.
**verankern** [fɛr'|aŋkərn] *vt* (*NAUT, TECH*) to anchor; (*fig*): ~ **(in +*dat*)** to embed (in).
**veranlagen** [fɛr'|anla:gən] *vt:* **etw** ~ **(mit)** to assess sth (at).
**veranlagt** *adj:* **praktisch** ~ **sein** to be practically-minded; **zu** *od* **für etw** ~ **sein** to be cut out for sth.
**Veranlagung** *f* disposition, aptitude.
**veranlassen** [fɛr'|anlasən] *vt* to cause; **Maßnahmen** ~ to take measures; **sich veranlaßt sehen** to feel prompted; **etw** ~ to arrange for sth; (*befehlen*) to order sth.

**Veranlassung** f cause; motive; **auf jds** ~ akk
(**hin**) at sb's instigation.
**veranschaulichen** [fɛr'|anʃaʊlıçən] vt to
illustrate.
**veranschlagen** [fɛr'|anʃlaːgən] vt to estimate.
**veranstalten** [fɛr'|anʃtaltən] vt to organize,
arrange.
**Veranstalter(in)** (-s, -) m(f) organizer;
(COMM: von Konzerten etc) promoter.
**Veranstaltung** f (Veranstalten) organizing;
(Veranstaltetes) event; (feierlich, öffentlich)
function.
**verantworten** [fɛr'|antvɔrtən] vt to accept
responsibility for; (Folgen etc) to answer for
♦ vr to justify o.s.; **etw vor jdm** ~ to answer
to sb for sth.
**verantwortlich** adj responsible.
**Verantwortung** f responsibility; **jdn zur**
~ **ziehen** to call sb to account.
**verantwortungs-** zW: **~bewußt** adj
responsible; **V~gefühl** nt sense of
responsibility; **~los** adj irresponsible;
**~voll** adj responsible.
**verarbeiten** [fɛr'|arbaıtən] vt to process;
(geistig) to assimilate; (Erlebnis etc) to digest;
**etw zu etw** ~ to make sth into sth; **~de
Industrie** processing industries pl.
**verarbeitet** adj: **gut** ~ (Kleid etc) well finished.
**Verarbeitung** f processing; assimilation.
**verärgern** [fɛr'|ɛrgərn] vt to annoy.
**verarmen** [fɛr'|armən] vi (lit, fig) to become
impoverished.
**verarschen** [fɛr'|arʃən] (umg!) vt: **jdn** ~ to take
the mickey out of sb.
**verarzten** [fɛr'|aːrtstən] vt to fix up (umg).
**verausgaben** [fɛr'|aʊsgaːbən] vr to run out of
money; (fig) to exhaust o.s.
**veräußern** [fɛr'|ɔysərn] vt (form: verkaufen) to
dispose of.
**Verb** [vɛrp] (-s, -en) nt verb.
**Verb.** abk (= Verband) assoc.
**Verband** [fɛr'bant] (-(e)s, ⁻e) m (MED)
bandage, dressing; (Bund) association,
society; (MIL) unit.
**verband** etc vb siehe **verbinden**.
**Verband-** zW: ~**(s)kasten** m medicine chest,
first-aid box; ~**(s)päckchen** nt gauze
bandage; ~**stoff** m, ~**zeug** nt bandage,
dressing material.
**verbannen** [fɛr'banən] vt to banish.
**Verbannung** f exile.
**verbarrikadieren** [fɛrbarika'diːrən] vt to
barricade ♦ vr to barricade o.s. in.
**verbauen** [fɛr'baʊən] vt: **sich** dat **alle Chancen**
~ to spoil one's chances.
**verbergen** [fɛr'bɛrgən] unreg vt, vr: (**sich**) ~ (**vor**
+dat) to hide (from).
**verbessern** [fɛr'bɛsərn] vt to improve;
(berichtigen) to correct ♦ vr to improve; to
correct o.s.
**verbessert** adj revised; improved; **eine neue,**
~**e Auflage** a new revised edition.

**Verbesserung** f improvement; correction.
**verbeugen** [fɛr'bɔygən] vr to bow.
**Verbeugung** f bow.
**verbiegen** [fɛr'biːgən] unreg vi to bend.
**verbiestert** [fɛr'biːstərt] (umg) adj crotchety.
**verbieten** [fɛr'biːtən] unreg vt to forbid;
(amtlich) to prohibit; (Zeitung, Partei) to ban;
**jdm etw** ~ to forbid sb to do sth.
**verbilligen** [fɛr'bılıgən] vt to reduce (the price
of) ♦ vr to become cheaper, go down.
**verbinden** [fɛr'bındən] unreg vt to connect;
(kombinieren) to combine; (MED) to bandage
♦ vr to combine (auch CHEM), join (together);
**jdm die Augen** ~ to blindfold sb.
**verbindlich** [fɛr'bıntlıç] adj binding;
(freundlich) obliging; ~ **zusagen** to accept
definitely; **V~keit** f obligation; (Höflichkeit)
civility; **Verbindlichkeiten** pl (JUR)
obligations pl; (COMM) liabilities pl.
**Verbindung** f connection;
(Zusammensetzung) combination; (CHEM)
compound; (UNIV) club; (TEL: Anschluß) line;
**mit jdm in** ~ **stehen** to be in touch od
contact with sb; ~ **mit jdm aufnehmen** to
contact sb.
**Verbindungsmann** (-(e)s, pl -männer
od -leute) m intermediary; (Agent) contact.
**verbissen** [fɛr'bısən] adj grim; (Arbeiter)
dogged; **V~heit** f grimness; doggedness.
**verbitten** [fɛr'bıtən] unreg vt: **sich** dat **etw** ~ not
to tolerate sth, not to stand for sth.
**verbittern** [fɛr'bıtərn] vt to embitter ♦ vi to get
bitter.
**verblassen** [fɛr'blasən] vi to fade.
**Verbleib** [fɛr'blaıp] (-(e)s) m whereabouts pl.
**verbleiben** [fɛr'blaıbən] unreg vi to remain; **wir
sind so verblieben, daß wir ...** we agreed
to ...
**verbleit** [fɛr'blaıt] adj leaded.
**Verblendung** [fɛr'blɛndʊŋ] f (fig) delusion.
**verblöden** [fɛr'bløːdən] vi (Hilfsverb sein) to
get stupid.
**verblüffen** [fɛr'blʏfən] vt to amaze; (verwirren)
to baffle.
**Verblüffung** f stupefaction.
**verblühen** [fɛr'blyːən] vi to wither, fade.
**verbluten** [fɛr'bluːtən] vi to bleed to death.
**verbohren** [fɛr'boːrən] (umg) vr: **sich in etw**
akk ~ to become obsessed with sth.
**verbohrt** adj (Haltung) stubborn, obstinate.
**verborgen** [fɛr'bɔrgən] adj hidden; ~**e Mängel**
latent defects pl.
**Verbot** [fɛr'boːt] (-(e)s, -e) nt prohibition, ban.
**verboten** adj forbidden; **Rauchen** ~! no
smoking; **er sah** ~ **aus** (umg) he looked a
real sight.
**verbotenerweise** adv though it is forbidden.
**Verbotsschild** nt prohibitory sign.
**verbrämen** [fɛr'brɛːmən] vt (fig) to gloss over;
(Kritik): ~ (**mit**) to veil (in).
**Verbrauch** [fɛr'braʊx] (-(e)s) m consumption.
**verbrauchen** vt to use up; **der Wagen**

**verbraucht 10 Liter Benzin auf 100 km** the car does 10 kms to the litre (*BRIT*) *od* liter (*US*).

**Verbraucher(in)** (-s, -) *m(f)* consumer; **~markt** *m* hypermarket; **v~nah** *adj* consumer-friendly; **~schutz** *m* consumer protection; **~verband** *m* consumer council.

**Verbrauchsgüter** *pl* consumer goods *pl*.

**verbraucht** *adj* used up, finished; (*Luft*) stale; (*Mensch*) worn-out.

**Verbrechen** [fɛr'brɛçən] (-s, -) *nt* crime.

**Verbrecher(in)** (-s, -) *m(f)* criminal; **v~isch** *adj* criminal; **~kartei** *f* file of offenders, ≈ rogues' gallery; **~tum** (-s) *nt* criminality.

**verbreiten** [fɛr'braɪtən] *vt* to spread; (*Licht*) to shed; (*Wärme, Ruhe*) to radiate ♦ *vr* to spread; **eine (weit) verbreitete Ansicht** a widely held opinion; **sich über etw** *akk* **~** to expound on sth.

**verbreitern** [fɛr'braɪtərn] *vt* to broaden.

**Verbreitung** *f* spread(ing); shedding; radiation.

**verbrennbar** *adj* combustible.

**verbrennen** [fɛr'brɛnən] *unreg vt* to burn; (*Leiche*) to cremate; (*versengen*) to scorch; (*Haar*) to singe; (*verbrühen*) to scald.

**Verbrennung** *f* burning; (*in Motor*) combustion; (*von Leiche*) cremation.

**Verbrennungsanlage** *f* incineration plant.

**Verbrennungsmotor** *m* internal-combustion engine.

**verbriefen** [fɛr'briːfən] *vt* to document.

**verbringen** [fɛr'brɪŋən] *unreg vt* to spend.

**Verbrüderung** [fɛr'bryːdərʊŋ] *f* fraternization.

**verbrühen** [fɛr'bryːən] *vt* to scald.

**verbuchen** [fɛr'buːxən] *vt* (*FIN*) to register; (*Erfolg*) to enjoy; (*Mißerfolg*) to suffer.

**verbummeln** [fɛr'bʊməln] (*umg*) *vt* (*verlieren*) to lose; (*Zeit*) to waste, fritter away; (*Verabredung*) to miss.

**verbunden** [fɛr'bʊndən] *adj* connected; **jdm ~ sein** to be obliged *od* indebted to sb; **ich/er** *etc* **war falsch ~** (*TEL*) it was a wrong number.

**verbünden** [fɛr'bʏndən] *vr* to form an alliance.

**Verbundenheit** *f* bond, relationship.

**Verbündete(r)** *f(m)* ally.

**Verbundglas** [fɛr'bʊntglaːs] *nt* laminated glass.

**verbürgen** [fɛr'bʏrgən] *vr*: **sich ~ für** to vouch for; **ein verbürgtes Recht** an established right.

**verbüßen** [fɛr'byːsən] *vt*: **eine Strafe ~** to serve a sentence.

**verchromt** [fɛr'kroːmt] *adj* chromium-plated.

**Verdacht** [fɛr'daxt] (-(e)s) *m* suspicion; **~ schöpfen (gegen jdn)** to become suspicious (of sb); **jdn in ~ haben** to suspect sb; **es besteht ~ auf Krebs** *akk* cancer is suspected.

**verdächtig** *adj* suspicious.

**verdächtigen** [fɛr'dɛçtɪgən] *vt* to suspect.

**Verdächtigung** *f* suspicion.

**verdammen** [fɛr'damən] *vt* to damn, condemn.

**Verdammnis** (-) *f* perdition, damnation.

**verdammt** (*umg*) *adj, adv* damned; **~ noch mal!** bloody hell (*!*), damn (*!*).

**verdampfen** [fɛr'dampfən] *vt, vi* (*vi Hilfsverb sein*) to vaporize; (*KOCH*) to boil away.

**verdanken** [fɛr'daŋkən] *vt*: **jdm etw ~** to owe sb sth.

**verdarb** *etc* [fɛr'darp] *vb siehe* **verderben**.

**verdattert** [fɛr'datərt] (*umg*) *adj, adv* flabbergasted.

**verdauen** [fɛr'dauən] *vt* (*lit, fig*) to digest ♦ *vi* (*lit*) to digest.

**verdaulich** [fɛr'daulɪç] *adj* digestible; **das ist schwer ~** that is hard to digest.

**Verdauung** *f* digestion.

**Verdauungsspaziergang** *m* constitutional.

**Verdauungsstörung** *f* indigestion.

**Verdeck** [fɛr'dɛk] (-(e)s, -e) *nt* (*AUT*) soft top; (*NAUT*) deck.

**verdecken** *vt* to cover (up); (*verbergen*) to hide.

**verdenken** [fɛr'dɛŋkən] *unreg vt*: **jdm etw ~** to blame sb for sth, hold sth against sb.

**verderben** [fɛr'dɛrbən] *unreg vt* to spoil; (*schädigen*) to ruin; (*moralisch*) to corrupt ♦ *vi* (*Essen*) to spoil, rot; (*Mensch*) to go to the bad; **es mit jdm ~** to get into sb's bad books.

**Verderben** (-s) *nt* ruin.

**verderblich** *adj* (*Einfluß*) pernicious; (*Lebensmittel*) perishable.

**verderbt** *adj* (*veraltet*) depraved; **V~heit** *f* depravity.

**verdeutlichen** [fɛr'dɔʏtlɪçən] *vt* to make clear.

**verdichten** [fɛr'dɪçtən] *vt* (*PHYS, fig*) to compress ♦ *vr* to thicken; (*Verdacht, Eindruck*) to deepen.

**verdienen** [fɛr'diːnən] *vt* to earn; (*moralisch*) to deserve ♦ *vi* (*Gewinn machen*): **~ (an** +*dat*) to make (a profit) (on).

**Verdienst** [fɛr'diːnst] (-(e)s, -e) *m* earnings *pl* ♦ *nt* merit; (*Dank*) credit; (*Leistung*): **~ (um)** service (to), contribution (to); **v~voll** *adj* commendable.

**verdient** [fɛr'diːnt] *adj* well-earned; (*Person*) of outstanding merit; (*Lohn, Strafe*) rightful; **sich um etw ~ machen** to do a lot for sth.

**verdirbst** [fɛr'dɪrpst] *vb siehe* **verderben**.

**verdirbt** [fɛr'dɪrpt] *vb siehe* **verderben**.

**verdonnern** [fɛr'dɔnərn] (*umg*) *vt* (*zu Haft etc*): **~ (zu)** to sentence (to); **jdn zu etw ~** to order sb to do sth.

**verdoppeln** [fɛr'dɔpəln] *vt* to double.

**Verdopp(e)lung** *f* doubling.

**verdorben** [fɛr'dɔrbən] *pp von* **verderben** ♦ *adj* spoilt; (*geschädigt*) ruined; (*moralisch*) corrupt.

**verdorren** [fɛr'dɔrən] *vi* to wither.
**verdrängen** [fɛr'drɛŋən] *vt* to oust; (*auch PHYS*) to displace; (*PSYCH*) to repress.
**Verdrängung** *f* displacement; (*PSYCH*) repression.
**verdrehen** [fɛr'dre:ən] *vt* (*lit, fig*) to twist; (*Augen*) to roll; **jdm den Kopf ~** (*fig*) to turn sb's head.
**verdreht** (*umg*) *adj* crazy; (*Bericht*) confused.
**verdreifachen** [fɛr'draɪfaxən] *vt* to treble.
**verdrießen** [fɛr'dri:sən] *unreg vt* to annoy.
**verdrießlich** [fɛr'dri:slɪç] *adj* peevish, annoyed.
**verdroß** *etc* [fɛr'drɔs] *vb siehe* **verdrießen**.
**verdrossen** [fɛr'drɔsən] *pp von* **verdrießen** ♦ *adj* cross, sulky.
**verdrücken** [fɛr'drʏkən] (*umg*) *vt* to put away, eat ♦ *vr* to disappear.
**Verdruß** [fɛr'drʊs] (*-sses, -sse*) *m* frustration; **zu jds ~** to sb's annoyance.
**verduften** [fɛr'dʊftən] *vi* to evaporate; (*umg*) to disappear.
**verdummen** [fɛr'dʊmən] *vt* to make stupid ♦ *vi* to grow stupid.
**verdunkeln** [fɛr'dʊŋkəln] *vt* to darken; (*fig*) to obscure ♦ *vr* to darken.
**Verdunk(e)lung** *f* blackout; (*fig*) obscuring.
**verdünnen** [fɛr'dʏnən] *vt* to dilute.
**Verdünner** (*-s, -*) *m* thinner.
**verdünnisieren** [fɛrdʏni'zi:rən] (*umg*) *vr* to make o.s. scarce.
**verdunsten** [fɛr'dʊnstən] *vi* to evaporate.
**verdursten** [fɛr'dʊrstən] *vi* to die of thirst.
**verdutzt** [fɛr'dʊtst] *adj* nonplussed (*BRIT*), nonplused (*US*), taken aback.
**verebben** [fɛr'|ɛbən] *vi* to subside.
**veredeln** [fɛr'|e:dəln] *vt* (*Metalle, Erdöl*) to refine; (*Fasern*) to finish; (*BOT*) to graft.
**verehren** [fɛr'|e:rən] *vt* to venerate, worship (*auch REL*); **jdm etw ~** to present sb with sth.
**Verehrer(in)** (*-s, -*) *m(f)* admirer, worshipper (*BRIT*), worshiper (*US*).
**verehrt** *adj* esteemed; **(sehr) ~e Anwesende/ ~es Publikum** Ladies and Gentlemen.
**Verehrung** *f* respect; (*REL*) worship.
**vereidigen** [fɛr'|aɪdɪgən] *vt* to put on oath; **jdn auf etw** *akk* **~** to make sb swear on sth.
**Vereidigung** *f* swearing in.
**Verein** [fɛr'|aɪn] (*-(e)s, -e*) *m* club, association; **ein wohltätiger ~** a charity.
**vereinbar** *adj* compatible.
**vereinbaren** [fɛr'|aɪnba:rən] *vt* to agree upon.
**Vereinbarkeit** *f* compatibility.
**Vereinbarung** *f* agreement.
**vereinfachen** [fɛr'|aɪnfaxən] *vt* to simplify.
**Vereinfachung** *f* simplification.
**vereinheitlichen** [fɛr'|aɪnhaɪtlɪçən] *vt* to standardize.
**vereinigen** [fɛr'|aɪnɪgən] *vt, vr* to unite.
**vereinigt** [fɛr'|aɪnɪçt] *adj* united; **V~e Arabische Emirate** *pl* United Arab Emirates;

**V~es Königreich** *nt* United Kingdom; **V~e Staaten** *pl* United States.
**Vereinigung** *f* union; (*Verein*) association.
**vereinnahmen** [fɛr'|aɪnna:mən] *vt* (*geh*) to take; **jdn ~** (*fig*) to make demands on sb.
**vereinsamen** [fɛr'|aɪnza:mən] *vi* to become lonely.
**vereint** [fɛr'|aɪnt] *adj* united; **V~e Nationen** *pl* United Nations.
**vereinzelt** [fɛr'|aɪntsəlt] *adj* isolated.
**vereisen** [fɛr'|aɪzən] *vi* to freeze, ice over ♦ *vt* (*MED*) to freeze.
**vereiteln** [fɛr'|aɪtəln] *vt* to frustrate.
**vereitern** [fɛr'|aɪtərn] *vi* to suppurate, fester.
**Verelendung** [fɛr'|e:lɛndʊŋ] *f* impoverishment.
**verenden** [fɛr'|ɛndən] *vi* to perish, die.
**verengen** [fɛr'|ɛŋən] *vr* to narrow.
**vererben** [fɛr'|ɛrbən] *vt* to bequeath; (*BIOL*) to transmit ♦ *vr* to be hereditary.
**vererblich** [fɛr'|ɛrplɪç] *adj* hereditary.
**Vererbung** *f* bequeathing; (*BIOL*) transmission; **das ist ~** (*umg*) it's hereditary.
**verewigen** [fɛr'|e:vɪgən] *vt* to immortalize ♦ *vr* (*umg*) to leave one's name.
**Verf.** *abk* = **Verfasser**.
**verfahren** [fɛr'fa:rən] *unreg vi* to act ♦ *vr* to get lost ♦ *adj* tangled; **~ mit** to deal with.
**Verfahren** (*-s, -*) *nt* procedure; (*TECH*) process; (*JUR*) proceedings *pl*.
**Verfahrenstechnik** *f* (*Methode*) process.
**Verfahrensweise** *f* procedure.
**Verfall** [fɛr'fal] (*-(e)s*) *m* decline; (*von Haus*) dilapidation; (*FIN*) expiry.
**verfallen** *unreg vi* to decline; (*Haus*) to be falling down; (*FIN*) to lapse ♦ *adj* (*Gebäude*) dilapidated, ruined; (*Karten, Briefmarken*) invalid; (*Strafe*) lapsed; (*Paß*) expired; **~ in** *+akk* to lapse into; **~ auf** *+akk* to hit upon; **einem Laster ~ sein** to be addicted to a vice; **jdm völlig ~ sein** to be completely under sb's spell.
**Verfallsdatum** *nt* expiry date; (*der Haltbarkeit*) best-before date.
**verfänglich** [fɛr'fɛŋlɪç] *adj* awkward, tricky; (*Aussage, Beweismaterial etc*) incriminating; (*gefährlich*) dangerous.
**verfärben** [fɛr'fɛrbən] *vr* to change colour (*BRIT*) *od* color (*US*).
**verfassen** [fɛr'fasən] *vt* to write; (*Gesetz, Urkunde*) to draw up.
**Verfasser(in)** (*-s, -*) *m(f)* author, writer.
**Verfassung** *f* constitution (*auch POL*); (*körperlich*) state of health; (*seelisch*) state of mind; **sie ist in guter/schlechter ~** she is in good/bad shape.
**Verfassungs-** *zW:* **v~feindlich** *adj* anticonstitutional; **~gericht** *nt* constitutional court; **v~mäßig** *adj* constitutional; **~schutz** *m* (*Aufgabe*) defence of the constitution; (*Amt*) *office responsible for defending the*

constitution; ~**schützer(in)** *m(f)* defender of the constitution; **v~widrig** *adj* unconstitutional.

**verfaulen** [fɛr'faʊlən] *vi* to rot.

**verfechten** [fɛr'fɛçtən] *unreg vt* to defend; (*Lehre*) to advocate.

**Verfechter(in)** [fɛr'fɛçtər(ɪn)] (**-s, -**) *m(f)* champion; defender.

**verfehlen** [fɛr'feːlən] *vt* to miss; **das Thema ~** to be completely off the subject.

**verfehlt** *adj* unsuccessful; (*unangebracht*) inappropriate; **etw für ~ halten** to regard sth as mistaken.

**Verfehlung** *f* (*Vergehen*) misdemeanour (*BRIT*), misdemeanor (*US*); (*Sünde*) transgression.

**verfeinern** [fɛr'faɪnərn] *vt* to refine.

**Verfettung** [fɛr'fɛtʊŋ] *f* (*von Organ, Muskeln*) fatty degeneration.

**verfeuern** [fɛr'fɔʏərn] *vt* to burn; (*Munition*) to fire; (*umg*) to use up.

**verfilmen** [fɛr'fɪlmən] *vt* to film, make a film of.

**Verfilmung** *f* film (version).

**Verfilzung** [fɛr'fɪltsʊŋ] *f* (*fig: von Firmen, Parteien*) entanglements *pl*.

**verflachen** [fɛr'flaxən] *vi* to flatten out; (*fig: Diskussion*) to become superficial.

**verfliegen** [fɛr'fliːgən] *unreg vi* to evaporate; (*Zeit*) to pass, fly ♦ *vr* to stray (past).

**verflixt** [fɛr'flɪkst] (*umg*) *adj, adv* darned.

**verflossen** [fɛr'flɔsən] *adj* past, former.

**verfluchen** [fɛr'fluːxən] *vt* to curse.

**verflüchtigen** [fɛr'flʏçtɪgən] *vr* to evaporate; (*Geruch*) to fade.

**verflüssigen** [fɛr'flʏsɪgən] *vr* to become liquid.

**verfolgen** [fɛr'fɔlgən] *vt* to pursue; (*gerichtlich*) to prosecute; (*grausam, bes POL*) to persecute.

**Verfolger(in)** (**-s, -**) *m(f)* pursuer.

**Verfolgte(r)** *f(m)* (*politisch*) victim of persecution.

**Verfolgung** *f* pursuit; persecution; **strafrechtliche ~** prosecution.

**Verfolgungswahn** *m* persecution mania.

**verfrachten** [fɛr'fraxtən] *vt* to ship.

**verfremden** [fɛr'frɛmdən] *vt* to alienate, distance.

**verfressen** [fɛr'frɛsən] (*umg*) *adj* greedy.

**verfrüht** [fɛr'fryːt] *adj* premature.

**verfügbar** *adj* available.

**verfügen** [fɛr'fyːgən] *vt* to direct, order ♦ *vr* to proceed ♦ *vi:* ~ **über** +*akk* to have at one's disposal; **über etw** *akk* **frei ~ können** to be able to do as one wants with sth.

**Verfügung** *f* direction, order; (*JUR*) writ; **zur ~** at one's disposal; **jdm zur ~ stehen** to be available to sb.

**Verfügungsgewalt** *f* (*JUR*) right of disposal.

**verführen** [fɛr'fyːrən] *vt* to tempt; (*sexuell*) to seduce; (*die Jugend, das Volk etc*) to lead astray.

**Verführer** *m* tempter; seducer.

**Verführerin** *f* temptress; seductress.

**verführerisch** *adj* seductive.

**Verführung** *f* seduction; (*Versuchung*) temptation.

**Vergabe** [fɛr'gaːbə] *f* (*von Arbeiten*) allocation; (*von Stipendium, Auftrag etc*) award.

**vergällen** [fɛr'gɛlən] *vt* (*geh*): **jdm die Freude/ das Leben ~** to spoil sb's fun/sour sb's life.

**vergaloppieren** [fɛrgalɔ'piːrən] (*umg*) *vr* (*sich irren*) to be on the wrong track.

**vergammeln** [fɛr'gaməln] (*umg*) *vi* to go to seed; (*Nahrung*) to go off; (*Zeit*) to waste.

**vergangen** [fɛr'gaŋən] *adj* past; **V~heit** *f* past; **V~heitsbewältigung** *f* coming to terms with the past.

**vergänglich** [fɛr'gɛŋlɪç] *adj* transitory; **V~keit** *f* transitoriness, impermanence.

**vergasen** [fɛr'gaːzən] *vt* to gasify; (*töten*) to gas.

**Vergaser** (**-s, -**) *m* (*AUT*) carburettor (*BRIT*), carburetor (*US*).

**vergaß** *etc* [fɛr'gaːs] *vb siehe* **vergessen**.

**vergeben** [fɛr'geːbən] *unreg vt* to forgive; (*weggeben*) to give away; (*fig: Chance*) to throw away; (*Auftrag, Preis*) to award; (*Studienplätze, Stellen*) to allocate; **jdm (etw) ~** to forgive sb (sth); ~ **an** +*akk* to award to; to allocate to; ~ **sein** to be occupied; (*umg: Mädchen*) to be spoken for.

**vergebens** *adv* in vain.

**vergeblich** [fɛr'geːplɪç] *adv* in vain ♦ *adj* vain, futile.

**Vergebung** *f* forgiveness.

**vergegenwärtigen** [fɛrgeːgən'vɛrtɪgən] *vr:* **sich** *dat* **etw ~** to visualize sth; (*erinnern*) to recall sth.

**vergehen** [fɛr'geːən] *unreg vi* to pass by *od* away ♦ *vr* to commit an offence (*BRIT*) *od* offense (*US*); **vor Angst ~** to be scared to death; **jdm vergeht etw** sb loses sth; **sich an jdm ~** to (sexually) assault sb; **V~** (**-s, -**) *nt* offence (*BRIT*), offense (*US*).

**vergeigen** [fɛr'gaɪgən] (*umg*) *vt* to cock up.

**vergeistigt** [fɛr'gaɪstɪçt] *adj* spiritual.

**vergelten** [fɛr'gɛltən] *unreg vt:* **jdm etw ~** to pay sb back for sth, repay sb for sth.

**Vergeltung** *f* retaliation, reprisal.

**Vergeltungsmaßnahme** *f* retaliatory measure.

**Vergeltungsschlag** *m* (*MIL*) reprisal.

**vergesellschaften** [fɛrgə'zɛlʃaftən] *vt* (*POL*) to nationalize.

**vergessen** [fɛr'gɛsən] *unreg vt* to forget; **V~heit** *f* oblivion; **in V~heit geraten** to fall into oblivion.

**vergeßlich** [fɛr'gɛslɪç] *adj* forgetful; **V~keit** *f* forgetfulness.

**vergeuden** [fɛr'gɔʏdən] *vt* to squander, waste.

**vergewaltigen** [fɛrgəˈvaltɪgən] *vt* to rape; (*fig*) to violate.
**Vergewaltigung** *f* rape.
**vergewissern** [fɛrgəˈvɪsərn] *vr* to make sure; **sich einer Sache** *gen od* **über etw** *akk* ~ to make sure of sth.
**vergießen** [fɛrˈgiːsən] *unreg vt* to shed.
**vergiften** [fɛrˈgɪftən] *vt* to poison.
**Vergiftung** *f* poisoning.
**vergilbt** [fɛrˈgɪlpt] *adj* yellowed.
**Vergißmeinnicht** [fɛrˈgɪsmaɪnnɪçt] (**-(e)s, -e**) *nt* forget-me-not.
**vergißt** [fɛrˈgɪst] *vb siehe* **vergessen**.
**vergittert** [fɛrˈgɪtərt] *adj:* ~**e Fenster** barred windows.
**verglasen** [fɛrˈglaːzən] *vt* to glaze.
**Vergleich** [fɛrˈglaɪç] (**-(e)s, -e**) *m* comparison; (*JUR*) settlement; **einen** ~ **schließen** (*JUR*) to reach a settlement; **in keinem** ~ **zu etw stehen** to be out of all proportion to sth; **im** ~ **mit** *od* **zu** compared with *od* to; **v**~**bar** *adj* comparable.
**vergleichen** *unreg vt* to compare ♦ *vr* (*JUR*) to reach a settlement.
**vergleichsweise** *adv* comparatively.
**verglühen** [fɛrˈglyːən] *vi* (*Feuer*) to die away; (*Draht*) to burn out; (*Raumkapsel, Meteor etc*) to burn up.
**vergnügen** [fɛrˈgnyːgən] *vr* to enjoy *od* amuse o.s.; **V**~ (**-s, -**) *nt* pleasure; **das war ein teures V**~ (*umg*) that was an expensive bit of fun; **viel V**~! enjoy yourself!
**vergnüglich** *adj* enjoyable.
**vergnügt** [fɛrˈgnyːkt] *adj* cheerful.
**Vergnügung** *f* pleasure, amusement.
**Vergnügungs-** *zW:* ~**park** *m* amusement park; **v**~**süchtig** *adj* pleasure-loving; ~**viertel** *nt* entertainments district.
**vergolden** [fɛrˈgɔldən] *vt* to gild.
**vergönnen** [fɛrˈgœnən] *vt* to grant.
**vergöttern** [fɛrˈgœtərn] *vt* to idolize.
**vergraben** [fɛrˈgraːbən] *unreg vt* to bury.
**vergrämt** [fɛrˈgrɛːmt] *adj* (*Gesicht*) troubled.
**vergreifen** [fɛrˈgraɪfən] *unreg vr:* **sich an jdm** ~ to lay hands on sb; **sich an etw** *dat* ~ to misappropriate sth; **sich im Ton** ~ to say the wrong thing.
**vergriffen** [fɛrˈgrɪfən] *adj* (*Buch*) out of print; (*Ware*) out of stock.
**vergrößern** [fɛrˈgrøːsərn] *vt* to enlarge; (*mengenmäßig*) to increase; (*Lupe*) to magnify.
**Vergrößerung** *f* enlargement; increase; magnification.
**Vergrößerungsglas** *nt* magnifying glass.
**vergünstigt** *adj* (*Lage*) improved; (*Preis*) reduced.
**Vergünstigung** [fɛrˈgʏnstɪgʊŋ] *f* concession; (*Vorteil*) privilege.
**vergüten** [fɛrˈgyːtən] *vt:* **jdm etw** ~ to compensate sb for sth; (*Arbeit, Leistung*) to pay sb for sth.

**Vergütung** *f* compensation; payment.
**verh.** *abk* = **verheiratet**.
**verhaften** [fɛrˈhaftən] *vt* to arrest.
**Verhaftete(r)** *f(m)* prisoner.
**Verhaftung** *f* arrest.
**verhallen** [fɛrˈhalən] *vi* to die away.
**verhalten** [fɛrˈhaltən] *unreg vr* (*Sache*) to be, stand; (*sich benehmen*) to behave; (*MATH*) to be in proportion to ♦ *vr unpers:* **wie verhält es sich damit?** (*wie ist die Lage?*) how do things stand?; (*wie wird das gehandhabt?*) how do you go about it? ♦ *adj* restrained; **sich ruhig** ~ to keep quiet; (*sich nicht bewegen*) to keep still; **wenn sich das so verhält** ... if that is the case ...; **V**~ (**-s**) *nt* behaviour (*BRIT*), behavior (*US*).
**Verhaltens-** *zW:* ~**forschung** *f* behavioural (*BRIT*) *od* behavioral (*US*) science; **v**~**gestört** *adj* disturbed; ~**maßregel** *f* rule of conduct.
**Verhältnis** [fɛrˈhɛltnɪs] (**-ses, -se**) *nt* relationship; (*Liebes*~) affair; (*MATH*) proportion, ratio; (*Einstellung*): ~ (**zu**) attitude (to); **Verhältnisse** *pl* (*Umstände*) conditions *pl*; **aus was für** ~**sen kommt er?** what sort of background does he come from?; **für klare** ~**se sorgen, klare** ~**se schaffen** to get things straight; **über seine** ~**se leben** to live beyond one's means; **v**~**mäßig** *adj* relative, comparative ♦ *adv* relatively, comparatively; ~**wahl** *f* proportional representation; ~**wahlrecht** *nt* (system of) proportional representation.
**verhandeln** [fɛrˈhandəln] *vi* to negotiate; (*JUR*) to hold proceedings ♦ *vt* to discuss; (*JUR*) to hear; **über etw** *akk* ~ to negotiate sth *od* about sth.
**Verhandlung** *f* negotiation; (*JUR*) proceedings *pl*; ~**en führen** to negotiate.
**Verhandlungspaket** *nt* (*COMM*) package deal.
**Verhandlungstisch** *m* negotiating table.
**verhangen** [fɛrˈhaŋən] *adj* overcast.
**verhängen** [fɛrˈhɛŋən] *vt* (*fig*) to impose, inflict.
**Verhängnis** [fɛrˈhɛŋnɪs] (**-ses, -se**) *nt* fate; **jdm zum** ~ **werden** to be sb's undoing; **v**~**voll** *adj* fatal, disastrous.
**verharmlosen** [fɛrˈharmloːzən] *vt* to make light of, play down.
**verharren** [fɛrˈharən] *vi* to remain; (*hartnäckig*) to persist.
**verhärten** [fɛrˈhɛrtən] *vr* to harden.
**verhaspeln** [fɛrˈhaspəln] (*umg*) *vr* to get into a muddle *od* tangle.
**verhaßt** [fɛrˈhast] *adj* odious, hateful.
**verhätscheln** [fɛrˈhɛːtʃəln] *vt* to spoil, pamper.
**Verhau** [fɛrˈhaʊ] (**-(e)s, -e**) *m* (*zur Absperrung*) barrier; (*Käfig*) coop.
**verhauen** *unreg* (*umg*) *vt* (*verprügeln*) to beat up; (*Prüfung etc*) to muff.

**verheben** [fɛr'he:bən] *unreg vr* to hurt o.s. lifting sth.

**verheerend** [fɛr'he:rənt] *adj* disastrous, devastating.

**verhehlen** [fɛr'he:lən] *vt* to conceal.

**verheilen** [fɛr'haɪlən] *vi* to heal.

**verheimlichen** [fɛr'haɪmlɪçən] *vt:* **(jdm) etw** ~ to keep sth secret (from sb).

**verheiratet** [fɛr'haɪra:tət] *adj* married.

**verheißen** [fɛr'haɪsən] *unreg vt:* **jdm etw** ~ to promise sb sth.

**verheißungsvoll** *adj* promising.

**verheizen** [fɛr'haɪtsən] *vt* to burn, use as fuel.

**verhelfen** [fɛr'hɛlfən] *unreg vi:* **jdm zu etw** ~ to help sb to get sth.

**verherrlichen** [fɛr'hɛrlɪçən] *vt* to glorify.

**verheult** [fɛr'hɔʏlt] *adj* (*Augen, Gesicht*) puffy (*from crying*).

**verhexen** [fɛr'hɛksən] *vt* to bewitch; **es ist wie verhext** it's jinxed.

**verhindern** [fɛr'hɪndərn] *vt* to prevent; **verhindert sein** to be unable to make it; **das läßt sich leider nicht** ~ it can't be helped, unfortunately; **ein verhinderter Politiker** (*umg*) a would-be politician.

**Verhinderung** *f* prevention.

**verhöhnen** [fɛr'hø:nən] *vt* to mock, sneer at.

**verhohnepipeln** [fɛr'ho:nəpi:pəln] (*umg*) *vt* to send up (*BRIT*), ridicule.

**verhökern** [fɛr'hø:kərn] (*umg*) *vt* to turn into cash.

**Verhör** [fɛr'hø:r] (-(e)s, -e) *nt* interrogation; (*gerichtlich*) (cross-)examination.

**verhören** *vt* to interrogate; to (cross-)examine ♦ *vr* to mishear.

**verhüllen** [fɛr'hʏlən] *vt* to veil; (*Haupt, Körperteil*) to cover.

**verhungern** [fɛr'hʊŋərn] *vi* to starve, die of hunger.

**verhunzen** [fɛr'hʊntsən] (*umg*) *vt* to ruin.

**verhüten** [fɛr'hy:tən] *vt* to prevent, avert.

**Verhütung** *f* prevention.

**Verhütungsmittel** *nt* contraceptive.

**verifizieren** [verifi'tsi:rən] *vt* to verify.

**verinnerlichen** [fɛr'|ɪnərlɪçən] *vt* to internalize.

**verirren** [fɛr'|ɪrən] *vr* to get lost, lose one's way; (*fig*) to go astray; (*Tier, Kugel*) to stray.

**verjagen** [fɛr'ja:gən] *vt* to drive away *od* out.

**verjähren** [fɛr'jɛ:rən] *vi* to come under the statute of limitations; (*Anspruch*) to lapse.

**Verjährungsfrist** *f* limitation period.

**verjubeln** [fɛr'ju:bəln] (*umg*) *vt* (*Geld*) to blow.

**verjüngen** [fɛr'jʏŋən] *vt* to rejuvenate ♦ *vr* to taper.

**verkabeln** [fɛr'ka:bəln] *vt* (*TV*) to link up to the cable network.

**Verkabelung** *f* (*TV*) linking up to the cable network.

**verkalken** [fɛr'kalkən] *vi* to calcify; (*umg*) to become senile.

**verkalkulieren** [fɛrkalku'li:rən] *vr* to miscalculate.

**verkannt** [fɛr'kant] *adj* unappreciated.

**verkatert** [fɛr'ka:tərt] (*umg*) *adj* hung over.

**Verkauf** [fɛr'kauf] *m* sale; **zum** ~ **stehen** to be up for sale.

**verkaufen** *vt, vi* to sell; **„zu** ~**"** "for sale".

**Verkäufer(in)** [fɛr'kɔʏfər(ɪn)] (-**s**, -) *m(f)* seller; (*im Außendienst*) salesman, saleswoman; (*in Laden*) shop assistant (*BRIT*), sales clerk (*US*).

**verkäuflich** [fɛr'kɔʏflɪç] *adj* saleable.

**Verkaufs-** *zW:* ~**abteilung** *f* sales department; ~**automat** *m* slot machine; ~**bedingungen** *pl* (*COMM*) terms and conditions of sale; ~**kampagne** *f* sales drive; ~**leiter** *m* sales manager; **v**~**offen** *adj:* **v**~**offener Samstag** *Saturday on which the shops are open all day*; ~**schlager** *m* big seller; ~**stelle** *f* outlet; ~**tüchtigkeit** *f* salesmanship.

**Verkehr** [fɛr'ke:r] (-**s**, -**e**) *m* traffic; (*Umgang, bes sexuell*) intercourse; (*Umlauf*) circulation; **aus dem** ~ **ziehen** to withdraw from service; **für den** ~ **freigeben** (*Straße etc*) to open to traffic; (*Transportmittel*) to bring into service.

**verkehren** *vi* (*Fahrzeug*) to ply, run ♦ *vt, vr* to turn, transform; ~ **mit** to associate with; **mit jdm brieflich** *od* **schriftlich** ~ (*form*) to correspond with sb; **bei jdm** ~ to visit sb regularly.

**Verkehrs-** *zW:* ~**ampel** *f* traffic lights *pl*; ~**amt** *nt* tourist (information) office; ~**aufkommen** *nt* volume of traffic; **v**~**beruhigt** *adj* traffic-calmed; ~**beruhigung** *f* traffic-calming; ~**betriebe** *pl* transport services *pl*; ~**delikt** *nt* traffic offence (*BRIT*) *od* violation (*US*); ~**erziehung** *f* road safety training; **v**~**günstig** *adj* convenient; ~**insel** *f* traffic island; ~**knotenpunkt** *m* traffic junction; ~**mittel** *nt:* **öffentliche/private** ~**mittel** public/private transport *sing*; ~**schild** *nt* road sign; **v**~**sicher** *adj* (*Fahrzeug*) roadworthy; ~**sicherheit** *f* road safety; ~**stockung** *f* traffic jam, stoppage; ~**sünder** (*umg*) *m* traffic offender; ~**teilnehmer** *m* road user; **v**~**tüchtig** *adj* (*Fahrzeug*) roadworthy; (*Mensch*) fit to drive; ~**unfall** *m* traffic accident; ~**verein** *m* tourist information office; **v**~**widrig** *adj* contrary to traffic regulations; ~**zeichen** *nt* road sign.

**verkehrt** *adj* wrong; (*umgekehrt*) the wrong way round.

**verkennen** [fɛr'kɛnən] *unreg vt* to misjudge; (*unterschätzen*) to underestimate.

**Verkettung** [fɛr'kɛtʊŋ] *f:* **eine** ~ **unglücklicher Umstände** an unfortunate chain of events.

**verklagen** [fɛr'kla:gən] *vt* to take to court.

**verklappen** [fɛr'klapən] *vt* to dump (at sea).

**verklären** [fɛr'klɛ:rən] *vt* to transfigure; **verklärt lächeln** to smile radiantly.

**verklausulieren** [fɛrklaʊzu'liːrən] vt (*Vertrag*) to hedge in with (restrictive) clauses.
**verkleben** [fɛr'kleːbən] vt to glue up, stick ♦ vi to stick together.
**verkleiden** [fɛr'klaɪdən] vt to disguise; (*kostümieren*) to dress up; (*Schacht, Tunnel*) to line; (*vertäfeln*) to panel; (*Heizkörper*) to cover in ♦ vr to disguise o.s.; to dress up.
**Verkleidung** f disguise; (*ARCHIT*) panelling (*BRIT*), paneling (*US*).
**verkleinern** [fɛr'klaɪnərn] vt to make smaller, reduce in size.
**verklemmt** [fɛr'klɛmt] adj (*fig*) inhibited.
**verklickern** [fɛr'klɪkərn] (*umg*) vt: **jdm etw** ~ to make sth clear to sb.
**verklingen** [fɛr'klɪŋən] unreg vi to die away.
**verknacksen** [fɛr'knaksən] (*umg*) vt: **sich** dat **den Fuß** ~ to twist one's ankle.
**verknallen** [fɛr'knalən] (*umg*) vr: **sich in jdn** ~ to fall for sb.
**verkneifen** [fɛr'knaɪfən] (*umg*) vt: **sich** dat **etw** ~ to stop o.s. from doing sth; **ich konnte mir das Lachen nicht** ~ I couldn't help laughing.
**verknöchert** [fɛr'knœçərt] adj (*fig*) fossilized.
**verknüpfen** [fɛr'knypfən] vt to tie (up), knot; (*fig*) to connect.
**Verknüpfung** f connection.
**verkochen** [fɛr'kɔxən] vt, vi (*Flüssigkeit*) to boil away.
**verkohlen** [fɛr'koːlən] vi to carbonize ♦ vt to carbonize; (*umg*): **jdn** ~ to have sb on.
**verkommen** [fɛr'kɔmən] unreg vi to deteriorate, decay; (*Mensch*) to go downhill, come down in the world ♦ adj (*moralisch*) dissolute, depraved; **V~heit** f depravity.
**verkorksen** [fɛr'kɔrksən] (*umg*) vt to ruin, mess up.
**verkörpern** [fɛr'kœrpərn] vt to embody, personify.
**verköstigen** [fɛr'kœstɪgən] vt to feed.
**verkrachen** [fɛr'kraxən] (*umg*) vr: **sich (mit jdm)** ~ to fall out (with sb).
**verkracht** (*umg*) adj (*Leben*) ruined.
**verkraften** [fɛr'kraftən] vt to cope with.
**verkrampfen** [fɛr'krampfən] vr (*Muskeln*) to go tense.
**verkrampft** [fɛr'krampft] adj (*fig*) tense.
**verkriechen** [fɛr'kriːçən] unreg vr to creep away, creep into a corner.
**verkrümeln** [fɛr'kryːməln] (*umg*) vr to disappear.
**verkrümmt** [fɛr'krymt] adj crooked.
**Verkrümmung** f bend, warp; (*ANAT*) curvature.
**verkrüppelt** [fɛr'krypəlt] adj crippled.
**verkrustet** [fɛr'krʊstət] adj encrusted.
**verkühlen** [fɛr'kyːlən] vr to get a chill.
**verkümmern** [fɛr'kymərn] vi to waste away; **emotionell/geistig** ~ to become emotionally/intellectually stunted.
**verkünden** [fɛr'kyndən] vt to proclaim; (*Urteil*) to pronounce.

**verkündigen** [fɛr'kyndɪgən] vt to proclaim; (*ironisch*) to announce; (*Evangelium*) to preach.
**verkuppeln** [fɛr'kʊpəln] vt: **jdn an jdn** ~ (*Zuhälter*) to procure sb for sb.
**verkürzen** [fɛr'kyrtsən] vt to shorten; (*Wort*) to abbreviate; **sich** dat **die Zeit** ~ to while away the time; **verkürzte Arbeitszeit** shorter working hours pl.
**Verkürzung** f shortening; abbreviation.
**Verl.** abk (= *Verlag*) publ.
**verladen** [fɛr'laːdən] unreg vt to load.
**Verlag** [fɛr'laːk] (-(e)s, -e) m publishing firm.
**verlagern** [fɛr'laːgərn] vt, vr (*lit, fig*) to shift.
**Verlagsanstalt** f publishing firm.
**Verlagswesen** nt publishing.
**verlangen** [fɛr'laŋən] vt to demand; (*wollen*) to want ♦ vi: ~ **nach** to ask for; **Sie werden am Telefon verlangt** you are wanted on the phone; ~ **Sie Herrn X** ask for Mr X; **V~** (-s, -) nt: **V~ (nach)** desire (for); **auf jds V~** akk (**hin**) at sb's request.
**verlängern** [fɛr'lɛŋərn] vt to extend; (*länger machen*) to lengthen; (*zeitlich*) to prolong; (*Paß, Abonnement etc*) to renew; **ein verlängertes Wochenende** a long weekend.
**Verlängerung** f extension; (*SPORT*) extra time.
**Verlängerungsschnur** f extension cable.
**verlangsamen** [fɛr'laŋzaːmən] vt, vr to decelerate, slow down.
**Verlaß** [fɛr'las] m: **auf ihn/das ist kein** ~ he/it cannot be relied upon.
**verlassen** [fɛr'lasən] unreg vt to leave ♦ vr: **sich** ~ **auf** +akk to depend on ♦ adj desolate; (*Mensch*) abandoned; **einsam und** ~ **so** all alone; **V~heit** f loneliness (*BRIT*), lonesomeness (*US*).
**verläßlich** [fɛr'lɛslɪç] adj reliable.
**Verlauf** [fɛr'laʊf] m course; **einen guten/ schlechten** ~ **nehmen** to go well/badly.
**verlaufen** unreg vi (*zeitlich*) to pass; (*Farben*) to run ♦ vr to get lost; (*Menschenmenge*) to disperse.
**Verlautbarung** f announcement.
**verlauten** [fɛr'laʊtən] vi: **etw** ~ **lassen** to disclose sth; **wie verlautet** as reported.
**verleben** [fɛr'leːbən] vt to spend.
**verlebt** [fɛr'leːpt] adj dissipated, worn-out.
**verlegen** [fɛr'leːgən] vt to move; (*verlieren*) to mislay; (*Kabel, Fliesen etc*) to lay; (*Buch*) to publish; (*verschieben*): ~ (**auf** +akk) to postpone (until) ♦ vr: **sich auf etw** akk ~ to resort to sth ♦ adj embarrassed; **nicht** ~ **um** never at a loss for; **V~heit** f embarrassment; (*Situation*) difficulty, scrape.
**Verleger** [fɛr'leːgər] (-s, -) m publisher.
**verleiden** [fɛr'laɪdən] vt: **jdm etw** ~ to put sb off sth.
**Verleih** [fɛr'laɪ] (-(e)s, -e) m hire service; (*das ~en*) renting (out), hiring (out) (*BRIT*);

(*Film~*) distribution.

**verleihen** *unreg vt:* **etw (an jdn)** ~ to lend sth (to sb), lend (sb) sth; (*gegen Gebühr*) to rent sth (out) (to sb), hire sth (out) (to sb) (*BRIT*); (*Kraft, Anschein*) to confer sth (on sb), bestow sth (on sb); (*Preis, Medaille*) to award sth (to sb), award (sb) sth.

**Verleiher** (-s, -) *m* hire (*BRIT*) *od* rental firm; (*von Filmen*) distributor; (*von Büchern*) lender.

**Verleihung** *f* lending; (*von Kraft etc*) bestowal; (*von Preis*) award.

**verleiten** [fɛr'laɪtən] *vt* to lead astray; ~ **zu** to talk into, tempt into.

**verlernen** [fɛr'lɛrnən] *vt* to forget, unlearn.

**verlesen** [fɛr'le:zən] *unreg vt* to read out; (*aussondern*) to sort out ♦ *vr* to make a mistake in reading.

**verletzbar** *adj* vulnerable.

**verletzen** [fɛr'lɛtsən] *vt* (*lit, fig*) to injure, hurt; (*Gesetz etc*) to violate.

**verletzend** *adj* (*fig: Worte*) hurtful.

**verletzlich** *adj* vulnerable.

**Verletzte(r)** *f(m)* injured person.

**Verletzung** *f* injury; (*Verstoß*) violation, infringement.

**verleugnen** [fɛr'lɔɪɡnən] *vt* to deny; (*Menschen*) to disown; **er läßt sich immer** ~ he always pretends not to be there.

**Verleugnung** *f* denial.

**verleumden** [fɛr'lɔɪmdən] *vt* to slander; (*schriftlich*) to libel.

**verleumderisch** *adj* slanderous; libellous (*BRIT*), libelous (*US*).

**Verleumdung** *f* slander; libel.

**verlieben** *vr:* **sich** ~ **(in** +*akk*) to fall in love (with).

**verliebt** [fɛr'li:pt] *adj* in love; **V~heit** *f* being in love.

**verlieren** [fɛr'li:rən] *unreg vt, vi* to lose ♦ *vr* to get lost; (*verschwinden*) to disappear; **das/er hat hier nichts verloren** (*umg*) that/he has no business to be here.

**Verlierer(in)** (-s, -) *m(f)* loser.

**Verlies** [fɛr'li:s] (-es, -e) *nt* dungeon.

**verloben** [fɛr'lo:bən] *vr:* **sich** ~ **(mit)** to get engaged (to); **verlobt sein** to be engaged.

**Verlobte(r)** [fɛr'lo:ptə(r)] *f(m):* **mein ~r** my fiancé; **meine** ~ my fiancée.

**Verlobung** *f* engagement.

**verlocken** [fɛr'lɔkən] *vt* to entice, lure.

**verlockend** *adj* (*Angebot, Idee*) tempting.

**Verlockung** *f* temptation, attraction.

**verlogen** [fɛr'lo:ɡən] *adj* untruthful; (*Komplimente, Versprechungen*) false; (*Moral, Gesellschaft*) hypocritical; **V~heit** *f* untruthfulness.

**verlor** *etc* [fɛr'lo:r] *vb siehe* **verlieren**.

**verloren** *pp von* **verlieren** ♦ *adj* lost; (*Eier*) poached; **der** ~**e Sohn** the prodigal son; **auf ~em Posten kämpfen** *od* **stehen** to be fighting a losing battle; **etw** ~ **geben** to give

sth up for lost; ~**gehen** *unreg vi* to get lost; **an ihm ist ein Sänger** ~**gegangen** he would have made a (good) singer.

**verlöschen** [fɛr'lœʃən] *vi* (*Hilfsverb sein*) to go out; (*Inschrift, Farbe, Erinnerung*) to fade.

**verlosen** [fɛr'lo:zən] *vt* to raffle (off), draw lots for.

**Verlosung** *f* raffle, lottery.

**verlottern** [fɛr'lɔtərn] (*umg*) *vi* to go to the dogs.

**verludern** [fɛr'lu:dərn] (*umg*) *vi* to go to the dogs.

**Verlust** [fɛr'lʊst] (-(e)s, -e) *m* loss; (*MIL*) casualty; **mit** ~ **verkaufen** to sell at a loss; ~**anzeige** *f* "lost" notice; ~**geschäft** *nt:* **das war ein ~geschäft** I/he *etc* made a loss; ~**zeit** *f* (*INDUSTRIE*) waiting time.

**vermachen** [fɛr'maxən] *vt* to bequeath, leave.

**Vermächtnis** [fɛr'mɛçtnɪs] (-ses, -se) *nt* legacy.

**vermählen** [fɛr'mɛ:lən] *vr* to marry.

**Vermählung** *f* wedding, marriage.

**vermarkten** [fɛr'marktən] *vt* to market; (*fig: Persönlichkeit*) to promote.

**Vermarktung** [fɛr'marktʊŋ] *f* marketing.

**vermasseln** [fɛr'masəln] (*umg*) *vt* to mess up.

**vermehren** [fɛr'me:rən] *vt, vr* to multiply; (*Menge*) to increase.

**Vermehrung** *f* multiplying; increase.

**vermeiden** [fɛr'maɪdən] *unreg vt* to avoid.

**vermeidlich** *adj* avoidable.

**vermeintlich** [fɛr'maɪntlɪç] *adj* supposed.

**vermengen** [fɛr'mɛŋən] *vt* to mix; (*fig*) to mix up, confuse.

**Vermenschlichung** [fɛr'mɛnʃlɪçʊŋ] *f* humanization.

**Vermerk** [fɛr'mɛrk] (-(e)s, -e) *m* note; (*in Ausweis*) endorsement.

**vermerken** *vt* to note.

**vermessen** [fɛr'mɛsən] *unreg vt* to survey ♦ *vr* (*falsch messen*) to measure incorrectly ♦ *adj* presumptuous, bold; **V~heit** *f* presumptuousness.

**Vermessung** *f* survey(ing).

**Vermessungsamt** *nt* land survey(ing) office.

**Vermessungsingenieur** *m* land surveyor.

**vermiesen** [fɛr'mi:zən] (*umg*) *vt* to spoil.

**vermieten** [fɛr'mi:tən] *vt* to let (*BRIT*), rent (out); (*Auto*) to hire out, rent.

**Vermieter(in)** (-s, -) *m(f)* landlord, landlady.

**Vermietung** *f* letting, renting (out); (*von Autos*) hiring (out), rental.

**vermindern** [fɛr'mɪndərn] *vt, vr* to lessen, decrease.

**Verminderung** *f* reduction.

**verminen** [fɛr'mi:nən] *vt* to mine.

**vermischen** [fɛr'mɪʃən] *vt, vr* to mix; (*Teesorten etc*) to blend; **vermischte Schriften** miscellaneous writings.

**vermissen** [fɛr'mɪsən] *vt* to miss; **vermißt sein, als vermißt gemeldet sein** to be reported missing; **wir haben dich bei der Party vermißt** we didn't see you at the party.

**Vermißte(r)** *f(m)* missing person.

**Vermißtenanzeige** *f* missing persons report.

**vermitteln** [fɛr'mɪtəln] *vi* to mediate ♦ *vt* to arrange; (*Gespräch*) to connect; (*Stelle*) to find; (*Gefühl, Bild, Idee etc*) to convey; (*Wissen*) to impart; **~de Worte** conciliatory words; **jdm etw ~** to help sb to obtain sth; (*Stelle*) to find sth for sb.

**Vermittler(in)** [fɛr'mɪtlər(ɪn)] (**-s, -**) *m(f)* (*COMM*) agent; (*Schlichter*) mediator.

**Vermittlung** *f* procurement; (*Stellen~*) agency; (*TEL*) exchange; (*Schlichtung*) mediation.

**Vermittlungsgebühr** *f* commission.

**vermögen** [fɛr'møːgən] *unreg vt* to be capable of; **~ zu** to be able to; **V~** (**-s, -**) *nt* wealth; (*Fähigkeit*) ability; **mein ganzes V~ besteht aus** ... my entire assets consist of ...; **ein V~ kosten** to cost a fortune.

**vermögend** *adj* wealthy.

**Vermögens-** *zW:* **~steuer** *f* property tax, wealth tax; **~wert** *m* asset; **v~wirksam** *adj:* **sein Geld v~wirksam anlegen** to invest one's money profitably; **v~wirksame Leistungen** *employers' contributions to tax-deductible savings scheme.*

**vermummen** [fɛr'mumən] *vr* to wrap up (warm); (*sich verkleiden*) to disguise.

**Vermummungsverbot** (**-(e)s**) *nt law against disguising o.s. at demonstrations.*

**vermurksen** [fɛr'murksən] (*umg*) *vt* to make a mess of.

**vermuten** [fɛr'muːtən] *vt* to suppose; (*argwöhnen*) to suspect.

**vermutlich** *adj* supposed, presumed ♦ *adv* probably.

**Vermutung** *f* supposition; suspicion; **die ~ liegt nahe, daß** ... there are grounds for assuming that ...

**vernachlässigen** [fɛr'naːxlɛsɪgən] *vt* to neglect ♦ *vr* to neglect o.s. *od* one's appearance.

**Vernachlässigung** *f* neglect.

**vernarben** [fɛr'narbən] *vi* to heal up.

**vernarren** [fɛr'narən] (*umg*) *vr:* **in jdn/etw vernarrt sein** to be crazy about sb/sth.

**vernaschen** [fɛr'naʃən] *vt* (*Geld*) to spend on sweets; (*umg: Mädchen, Mann*) to make it with.

**vernehmen** [fɛr'neːmən] *unreg vt* to hear, perceive; (*erfahren*) to learn; (*JUR*) to (cross-)examine; (*Polizei*) to question; **V~** *nt:* **dem V~ nach** from what I/we *etc* hear.

**vernehmlich** *adj* audible.

**Vernehmung** *f* (cross-)examination.

**vernehmungsfähig** *adj* in a condition to be (cross-)examined.

**verneigen** [fɛr'naɪgən] *vr* to bow.

**verneinen** [fɛr'naɪnən] *vt* (*Frage*) to answer in the negative; (*ablehnen*) to deny; (*GRAM*) to negate.

**verneinend** *adj* negative.

**Verneinung** *f* negation.

**vernichten** [fɛr'nɪçtən] *vt* to destroy, annihilate.

**vernichtend** *adj* (*fig*) crushing; (*Blick*) withering; (*Kritik*) scathing.

**Vernichtung** *f* destruction, annihilation.

**Vernichtungsschlag** *m* devastating blow.

**verniedlichen** [fɛr'niːtlɪçən] *vt* to play down.

**Vernunft** [fɛr'nunft] (**-**) *f* reason; **~ annehmen** to see reason; **~ehe** *f*, **~heirat** *f* marriage of convenience.

**vernünftig** [fɛr'nynftɪç] *adj* sensible, reasonable.

**Vernunftmensch** *m* rational person.

**veröden** [fɛr'øːdən] *vi* to become desolate ♦ *vt* (*MED*) to remove.

**veröffentlichen** [fɛr'|œfəntlɪçən] *vt* to publish.

**Veröffentlichung** *f* publication.

**verordnen** [fɛr'|ɔrdnən] *vt* (*MED*) to prescribe.

**Verordnung** *f* order, decree; (*MED*) prescription.

**verpachten** [fɛr'paxtən] *vt* to lease (out).

**verpacken** [fɛr'pakən] *vt* to pack; (*verbrauchergerecht*) to package; (*einwickeln*) to wrap.

**Verpackung** *f* packing; packaging; wrapping.

**verpassen** [fɛr'pasən] *vt* to miss; **jdm eine Ohrfeige ~** (*umg*) to give sb a clip round the ear.

**verpatzen** [fɛr'patsən] (*umg*) *vt* to spoil, mess up.

**verpennen** [fɛr'pɛnən] (*umg*) *vi, vr* to oversleep.

**verpesten** [fɛr'pɛstən] *vt* to pollute.

**verpetzen** [fɛr'pɛtsən] (*umg*) *vt:* **jdn ~ (bei)** to tell on sb (to).

**verpfänden** [fɛr'pfɛndən] *vt* to pawn; (*JUR*) to mortgage.

**verpfeifen** [fɛr'pfaɪfən] *unreg* (*umg*) *vt:* **jdn ~ (bei)** to grass on sb (to).

**verpflanzen** [fɛr'pflantsən] *vt* to transplant.

**Verpflanzung** *f* transplanting; (*MED*) transplant.

**verpflegen** [fɛr'pfleːgən] *vt* to feed, cater for (*BRIT*).

**Verpflegung** *f* catering; (*Kost*) food; (*in Hotel*) board.

**verpflichten** [fɛr'pflɪçtən] *vt* to oblige, bind; (*anstellen*) to engage ♦ *vr* to undertake; (*MIL*) to sign on ♦ *vi* to carry obligations; **jdm verpflichtet sein** to be under an obligation to sb; **sich zu etw ~** to commit o.s. to doing sth; **jdm zu Dank verpflichtet sein** to be obliged to sb.

**verpflichtend** *adj* (*Zusage*) binding.

**Verpflichtung** *f* obligation; (*Aufgabe*) duty.

**verpfuschen** [fɛr'pfuʃən] (*umg*) *vt* to bungle,

make a mess of.
**verplanen** [fɛr'plaːnən] *vt* (*Zeit*) to book up; (*Geld*) to budget.
**verplappern** [fɛr'plapərn] (*umg*) *vr* to open one's big mouth.
**verplempern** [fɛr'plɛmpərn] (*umg*) *vt* to waste.
**verpönt** [fɛr'pøːnt] *adj*: ~ **(bei)** frowned upon (by).
**verprassen** [fɛr'prasən] *vt* to squander.
**verprügeln** [fɛr'pryːgəln] (*umg*) *vt* to beat up.
**verpuffen** [fɛr'pʊfən] *vi* to (go) pop; (*fig*) to fall flat.
**Verputz** [fɛr'pʊts] *m* plaster; (*Rauhputz*) roughcast; **v~en** *vt* to plaster; (*umg: Essen*) to put away.
**verqualmen** [fɛr'kvalmən] *vt* (*Zimmer*) to fill with smoke.
**verquollen** [fɛr'kvɔlən] *adj* swollen; (*Holz*) warped.
**verrammeln** [fɛr'ramɛln] *vt* to barricade.
**Verrat** [fɛr'raːt] (*-(e)s*) *m* treachery; (*POL*) treason; ~ **an jdm üben** to betray sb.
**verraten** *unreg vt* to betray; (*fig: erkennen lassen*) to show; (*Geheimnis*) to divulge ♦ *vr* to give o.s. away.
**Verräter(in)** [fɛr'rɛːtər(ɪn)] (*-s, -*) *m(f)* traitor, traitress; **v~isch** *adj* treacherous.
**verrauchen** [fɛr'rauxən] *vi* (*fig: Zorn*) to blow over.
**verrechnen** [fɛr'rɛçnən] *vt*: ~ **mit** to set off against ♦ *vr* to miscalculate.
**Verrechnung** *f*: **nur zur** ~ (*auf Scheck*) a/c payee only.
**Verrechnungsscheck** *m* crossed cheque (*BRIT*).
**verregnet** [fɛr'reːgnət] *adj* rainy, spoilt by rain.
**verreisen** [fɛr'raizən] *vi* to go away (on a journey); **er ist geschäftlich verreist** he's away on business.
**verreißen** [fɛr'raisən] *unreg vt* to pull to pieces.
**verrenken** [fɛr'rɛŋkən] *vt* to contort; (*MED*) to dislocate; **sich** *dat* **den Knöchel** ~ to sprain one's ankle.
**Verrenkung** *f* contortion; (*MED*) dislocation.
**verrennen** [fɛr'rɛnən] *unreg vr*: **sich in etw** *akk* ~ to get stuck on sth.
**verrichten** [fɛr'rɪçtən] *vt* (*Arbeit*) to do, perform.
**verriegeln** [fɛr'riːgəln] *vt* to bolt.
**verringern** [fɛr'rɪŋərn] *vt* to reduce ♦ *vr* to decrease.
**Verringerung** *f* reduction; decrease.
**verrinnen** [fɛr'rɪnən] *unreg vi* to run out *od* away; (*Zeit*) to elapse.
**Verriß** [fɛr'rɪs] *m* slating review.
**verrohen** [fɛr'roːən] *vi* to become brutalized.
**verrosten** [fɛr'rɔstən] *vi* to rust.
**verrotten** [fɛr'rɔtən] *vi* to rot.
**verrucht** [fɛr'ruːxt] *adj* despicable; (*verrufen*) disreputable.
**verrücken** [fɛr'rʏkən] *vt* to move, shift.

**verrückt** *adj* crazy, mad; **V~e(r)** *f(m)* lunatic; **V~heit** *f* madness, lunacy.
**Verruf** [fɛr'ruːf] *m*: **in** ~ **geraten/bringen** to fall/bring into disrepute.
**verrufen** *adj* disreputable.
**verrutschen** [fɛr'rʊtʃən] *vi* to slip.
**Vers** [fɛrs] (*-es, -e*) *m* verse.
**versacken** [fɛr'zakən] *vi* (*lit*) to sink; (*fig: umg: herunterkommen*) to go downhill; (: *lange zechen*) to get involved in a booze-up (*BRIT*) *od* a drinking spree.
**versagen** [fɛr'zaːgən] *vt*: **jdm/sich etw** ~ to deny sb/o.s. sth ♦ *vi* to fail; **V~** (*-s*) *nt* failure; **menschliches V~** human error.
**Versager** (*-s, -*) *m* failure.
**versalzen** [fɛr'zaltsən] *vt* to put too much salt in; (*fig*) to spoil.
**versammeln** [fɛr'zaməln] *vt, vr* to assemble, gather.
**Versammlung** *f* meeting, gathering.
**Versammlungsfreiheit** *f* freedom of assembly.
**Versand** [fɛr'zant] (*-(e)s*) *m* dispatch; (~*abteilung*) dispatch department; ~**bahnhof** *m* dispatch station; ~**haus** *nt* mail-order firm; ~**kosten** *pl* transport(ation) costs *pl*; ~**weg** *m*: **auf dem** ~**weg** by mail order.
**versäumen** [fɛr'zɔymən] *vt* to miss; (*Pflicht*) to neglect; (*Zeit*) to lose.
**Versäumnis** (*-ses, -se*) *nt* neglect; (*Unterlassung*) omission.
**verschachern** [fɛr'ʃaxərn] (*umg*) *vt* to sell off.
**verschachtelt** [fɛr'ʃaxtəlt] *adj* (*Satz*) complex.
**verschaffen** [fɛr'ʃafən] *vt*: **jdm/sich etw** ~ to get *od* procure sth for sb/o.s.
**verschämt** [fɛr'ʃɛːmt] *adj* bashful.
**verschandeln** [fɛr'ʃandəln] (*umg*) *vt* to spoil.
**verschanzen** [fɛr'ʃantsən] *vr*: **sich hinter etw** *dat* ~ to dig in behind sth; (*fig*) to take refuge behind sth.
**verschärfen** [fɛr'ʃɛrfən] *vt* to intensify; (*Lage*) to aggravate; (*strenger machen: Kontrollen, Gesetze*) to tighten up ♦ *vr* to intensify; to become aggravated; to become tighter.
**Verschärfung** *f* intensification; (*der Lage*) aggravation; (*von Kontrollen etc*) tightening.
**verscharren** [fɛr'ʃarən] *vt* to bury.
**verschätzen** [fɛr'ʃɛtsən] *vr* to miscalculate.
**verschenken** [fɛr'ʃɛŋkən] *vt* to give away.
**verscherzen** [fɛr'ʃɛrtsən] *vt*: **sich** *dat* **etw** ~ to lose sth, throw sth away.
**verscheuchen** [fɛr'ʃɔyçən] *vt* to frighten away.
**verschicken** [fɛr'ʃɪkən] *vt* to send off; (*Sträfling*) to transport.
**verschieben** [fɛr'ʃiːbən] *unreg vt* to shift; (*EISENB*) to shunt; (*Termin*) to postpone; (*umg: Waren, Devisen*) to traffic in.
**Verschiebung** *f* shift, displacement; shunting; postponement.
**verschieden** [fɛr'ʃiːdən] *adj* different; **das ist**

**ganz** ~ (wird ~ gehandhabt) that varies, that just depends; **sie sind ~ groß** they are of different sizes; **~artig** adj various, of different kinds; **zwei so ~artige** ... two such differing ...; **~e** pron pl various people; various things pl; **~es** pron various things pl; **etwas V~es** something different; **V~heit** f difference.

**verschiedentlich** adv several times.

**verschiffen** [fɛr'ʃɪfən] vt to ship; (Sträfling) to transport.

**verschimmeln** [fɛr'ʃɪməln] vi (Nahrungsmittel) to go mouldy (BRIT) od moldy (US); (Leder, Papier etc) to become mildewed.

**verschlafen** [fɛr'ʃlaːfən] unreg vt to sleep through; (fig: versäumen) to miss ♦ vi, vr to oversleep ♦ adj sleepy.

**Verschlag** [fɛr'ʃlaːk] m shed.

**verschlagen** [fɛr'ʃlaːgən] unreg vt to board up; (TENNIS) to hit out of play; (Buchseite) to lose ♦ adj cunning; **jdm den Atem ~** to take sb's breath away; **an einen Ort ~ werden** to wind up in a place.

**verschlampen** [fɛr'ʃlampən] vi (Hilfsverb sein: Mensch) to go to seed (umg) ♦ vt to lose, mislay.

**verschlechtern** [fɛr'ʃlɛçtərn] vt to make worse ♦ vr to deteriorate, get worse; (gehaltlich) to take a lower-paid job.

**Verschlechterung** f deterioration.

**Verschleierung** [fɛr'ʃlaɪərʊŋ] f veiling; (fig) concealment; (MIL) screening.

**Verschleierungstaktik** f smoke-screen tactics pl.

**Verschleiß** [fɛr'ʃlaɪs] (-es, -e) m wear and tear.

**verschleißen** unreg vt, vi, vr to wear out.

**verschleppen** [fɛr'ʃlɛpən] vt to carry off, abduct; (zeitlich) to drag out, delay; (verbreiten: Seuche) to spread.

**verschleudern** [fɛr'ʃlɔʏdərn] vt to squander; (COMM) to sell dirt-cheap.

**verschließbar** adj lockable.

**verschließen** [fɛr'ʃliːsən] unreg vt to lock ♦ vr: **sich einer Sache** dat ~ to close one's mind to sth.

**verschlimmern** [fɛr'ʃlɪmərn] vt to make worse, aggravate ♦ vr to get worse, deteriorate.

**Verschlimmerung** f deterioration.

**verschlingen** [fɛr'ʃlɪŋən] unreg vt to devour, swallow up; (Fäden) to twist.

**verschliß** etc [fɛr'ʃlɪs] vb siehe **verschleißen**.

**verschlissen** [fɛr'ʃlɪsən] pp von **verschleißen** ♦ adj worn(-out).

**verschlossen** [fɛr'ʃlɔsən] adj locked; (fig) reserved; (schweigsam) tight-lipped; **V~heit** f reserve.

**verschlucken** [fɛr'ʃlʊkən] vt to swallow ♦ vr to choke.

**Verschluß** [fɛr'ʃlʊs] m lock; (von Kleid etc) fastener; (PHOT) shutter; (Stöpsel) plug;

**unter** ~ **halten** to keep under lock and key.

**verschlüsseln** [fɛr'ʃlʏsəln] vt to encode.

**verschmachten** [fɛr'ʃmaxtən] vi: ~ (vor +dat) to languish (for); **vor Durst ~** to be dying of thirst.

**verschmähen** [fɛr'ʃmɛːən] vt to scorn, disdain.

**verschmelzen** [fɛr'ʃmɛltsən] unreg vt, vi to merge, blend.

**verschmerzen** [fɛr'ʃmɛrtsən] vt to get over.

**verschmiert** [fɛr'ʃmiːrt] adj (Hände) smeary; (Schminke) smudged.

**verschmitzt** [fɛr'ʃmɪtst] adj mischievous.

**verschmutzen** [fɛr'ʃmʊtsən] vt to soil; (Umwelt) to pollute.

**verschnaufen** [fɛr'ʃnaʊfən] (umg) vi, vr to have a breather.

**verschneiden** [fɛr'ʃnaɪdən] vt (Whisky etc) to blend.

**verschneit** [fɛr'ʃnaɪt] adj covered in snow, snowed up.

**Verschnitt** [fɛr'ʃnɪt] m (von Whisky etc) blend.

**verschnörkelt** [fɛr'ʃnœrkəlt] adj ornate.

**verschnupft** [fɛr'ʃnʊpft] (umg) adj: ~ **sein** to have a cold; (beleidigt) to be peeved (umg).

**verschnüren** [fɛr'ʃnyːrən] vt to tie up.

**verschollen** [fɛr'ʃɔlən] adj lost, missing.

**verschonen** [fɛr'ʃoːnən] vt: **jdn mit etw ~** to spare sb sth; **von etw verschont bleiben** to escape sth.

**verschönern** [fɛr'ʃøːnərn] vt to decorate; (verbessern) to improve.

**verschossen** [fɛr'ʃɔsən] adj: ~ **sein** (fig: umg) to be in love.

**verschränken** [fɛr'ʃrɛŋkən] vt to cross; (Arme) to fold.

**verschreckt** [fɛr'ʃrɛkt] adj frightened, scared.

**verschreiben** [fɛr'ʃraɪbən] unreg vt (Papier) to use up; (MED) to prescribe ♦ vr to make a mistake (in writing); **sich einer Sache** dat ~ to devote o.s. to sth.

**verschrie(e)n** [fɛr'ʃriː(ə)n] adj notorious.

**verschroben** [fɛr'ʃroːbən] adj eccentric, odd.

**verschrotten** [fɛr'ʃrɔtən] vt to scrap.

**verschüchtert** [fɛr'ʃʏçtərt] adj subdued, intimidated.

**verschulden** [fɛr'ʃʊldən] vt to be guilty of ♦ vi (in Schulden geraten) to get into debt; **V~ (-s)** nt fault.

**verschuldet** adj in debt.

**Verschuldung** f debts pl.

**verschütten** [fɛr'ʃʏtən] vt to spill; (zuschütten) to fill; (unter Trümmer) to bury.

**verschwand** etc [fɛr'ʃvant] vb siehe **verschwinden**.

**verschweigen** [fɛr'ʃvaɪgən] unreg vt to keep secret; **jdm etw ~** to keep sth from sb.

**verschwenden** [fɛr'ʃvɛndən] vt to squander.

**Verschwender(in) (-s, -)** m(f) spendthrift; **v~isch** adj wasteful; (Leben) extravagant.

**Verschwendung** f waste.

**verschwiegen** [fɛr'ʃviːgən] adj discreet; (Ort)

secluded; **V~heit** f discretion; seclusion;
**zur V~heit verpflichtet** bound to secrecy.
**verschwimmen** [fɛr'ʃvɪmən] unreg vi to grow
hazy, become blurred.
**verschwinden** [fɛr'ʃvɪndən] unreg vi to
disappear, vanish; **verschwinde!** clear off!
(umg); **V~ (-s)** nt disappearance.
**verschwindend** adj (Anzahl, Menge)
insignificant.
**verschwitzen** [fɛr'ʃvɪtsən] vt to stain with
sweat; (umg) to forget.
**verschwitzt** adj (Kleidung) sweat-stained;
(Mensch) sweaty.
**verschwommen** [fɛr'ʃvɔmən] adj hazy,
vague.
**verschworen** [fɛr'ʃvoːrən] adj (Gesellschaft)
sworn.
**verschwören** [fɛr'ʃvøːrən] unreg vr to
conspire, plot.
**Verschwörer(in) (-s, -)** m(f) conspirator.
**Verschwörung** f conspiracy, plot.
**verschwunden** [fɛr'ʃvʊndən] pp von
**verschwinden ♦** adj missing.
**versehen** [fɛr'zeːən] unreg vt to supply,
provide; (Pflicht) to carry out; (Amt) to fill;
(Haushalt) to keep ♦ vr (fig) to make a
mistake; **ehe er (es) sich ~ hatte ...** before
he knew it ...; **V~ (-s, -)** nt oversight; **aus V~**
by mistake.
**versehentlich** adv by mistake.
**Versehrte(r)** [fɛr'zeːrtə(r)] f(m) disabled
person.
**verselbständigen** [fɛr'zɛlpʃtɛndɪgən] vr to
become independent.
**versenden** [fɛr'zɛndən] unreg vt to send;
(COMM) to forward.
**versengen** [fɛr'zɛŋən] vt to scorch; (Feuer) to
singe; (umg: verprügeln) to wallop.
**versenken** [fɛr'zɛŋkən] vt to sink ♦ vr: **sich
~ in** +akk to become engrossed in.
**versessen** [fɛr'zɛsən] adj: **~ auf** +akk mad
about, hellbent on.
**versetzen** [fɛr'zɛtsən] vt to transfer;
(verpfänden) to pawn; (umg: vergeblich warten
lassen) to stand up; (nicht geradlinig
anordnen) to stagger; (SCH: in höhere Klasse)
to move up ♦ vr: **sich in jdn** od **in jds Lage ~**
to put o.s. in sb's place; **jdm einen Tritt/
Schlag ~** to kick/hit sb; **etw mit etw ~** to
mix sth with sth; **jdm einen Stich ~** (fig) to
cut sb to the quick, wound sb (deeply); **jdn
in gute Laune ~** to put sb in a good mood.
**Versetzung** f transfer; **seine ~ ist gefährdet**
(SCH) he's in danger of having to repeat a
year.
**verseuchen** [fɛr'zɔʏçən] vt to contaminate.
**Versicherer (-s, -)** m insurer; (bei Schiffen)
underwriter.
**versichern** [fɛr'zɪçərn] vt to assure; (mit Geld)
to insure ♦ vr: **sich ~** +gen to make sure of.
**Versicherte(r)** f(m) insured.
**Versicherung** f assurance; insurance.

**Versicherungs-** zW: **~beitrag** m insurance
premium; (bei staatlicher Versicherung etc)
social security contribution; **~gesellschaft** f
insurance company; **~nehmer (-s, -)** m
(form) insured, policy holder; **~police** f
insurance policy; **~schutz** m insurance
cover; **~summe** f sum insured; **~träger** m
insurer.
**versickern** [fɛr'zɪkərn] vi to seep away; (fig:
Interesse etc) to peter out.
**versiegeln** [fɛr'ziːgəln] vt to seal (up).
**versiegen** [fɛr'ziːgən] vi to dry up.
**versiert** [vɛr'ziːrt] adj: **in etw** dat **~ sein** to be
experienced od well versed in sth.
**versilbert** [fɛr'zɪlbərt] adj silver-plated.
**versinken** [fɛr'zɪŋkən] unreg vi to sink; **ich
hätte im Boden** od **vor Scham ~ mögen** I
wished the ground would swallow me up.
**versinnbildlichen** [fɛr'zɪnbɪltlɪçən] vt to
symbolize.
**Version** [vɛrzi'oːn] f version.
**Versmaß** ['fɛrsmaːs] nt metre (BRIT), meter
(US).
**versohlen** [fɛr'zoːlən] (umg) vt to belt.
**versöhnen** [fɛr'zøːnən] vt to reconcile ♦ vr to
become reconciled.
**versöhnlich** adj (Ton, Worte) conciliatory;
(Ende) happy.
**Versöhnung** f reconciliation.
**versonnen** [fɛr'zɔnən] adj (Gesichtsausdruck)
pensive, thoughtful; (träumerisch: Blick)
dreamy.
**versorgen** [fɛr'zɔrgən] vt to provide, supply;
(Familie etc) to look after ♦ vr to look after
o.s.
**Versorger(in) (-s, -)** m(f) (Ernährer) provider,
breadwinner; (Belieferer) supplier.
**Versorgung** f provision; (Unterhalt)
maintenance; (Alters~ etc) benefit,
assistance.
**Versorgungs-** zW: **~amt** nt pension office;
**~betrieb** m public utility; **~netz** nt
(Wasserversorgung etc) (supply) grid; (von
Waren) supply network.
**verspannen** [fɛr'ʃpanən] vr (Muskeln) to tense
up.
**verspäten** [fɛr'ʃpɛːtən] vr to be late.
**verspätet** adj late.
**Verspätung** f delay; **~ haben** to be late; **mit
zwanzig Minuten ~** twenty minutes late.
**versperren** [fɛr'ʃpɛrən] vt to bar, obstruct.
**verspielen** [fɛr'ʃpiːlən] vt, vi to lose; **(bei jdm)
verspielt haben** to have had it (as far as sb
is concerned).
**verspielt** [fɛr'ʃpiːlt] adj playful.
**versponnen** [fɛr'ʃpɔnən] adj crackpot.
**verspotten** [fɛr'ʃpɔtən] vt to ridicule, scoff at.
**versprach** etc [fɛr'ʃprax] vb siehe **versprechen.**
**versprechen** [fɛr'ʃprɛçən] unreg vt to promise
♦ vr (etwas Nicht-Gemeintes sagen) to make a
slip of the tongue; **sich** dat **etw von etw ~** to
expect sth from sth; **V~ (-s, -)** nt promise.

**Versprecher** (-s, -) (*umg*) *m* slip (of the tongue).

**verspricht** [fɛr'ʃprɪçt] *vb siehe* **versprechen**.

**verspüren** [fɛr'ʃpyːrən] *vt* to feel, be conscious of.

**verstaatlichen** [fɛr'ʃtaːtlɪçən] *vt* to nationalize.

**verstaatlicht** *adj:* ~**er Industriezweig** nationalized industry.

**Verstaatlichung** *f* nationalization.

**Verstand** [fɛr'ʃtant] *m* intelligence; (*Intellekt*) mind; (*Fähigkeit zu denken*) reason; **den** ~ **verlieren** to go out of one's mind; **über jds** ~ *akk* **gehen** to be beyond sb.

**verstand** *etc vb siehe* **verstehen**.

**verstanden** [fɛr'ʃtandən] *pp von* **verstehen**.

**verstandesmäßig** *adj* rational.

**verständig** [fɛr'ʃtɛndɪç] *adj* sensible.

**verständigen** [fɛr'ʃtɛndɪgən] *vt* to inform ♦ *vr* to communicate; (*sich einigen*) to come to an understanding.

**Verständigkeit** *f* good sense.

**Verständigung** *f* communication; (*Benachrichtigung*) informing; (*Einigung*) agreement.

**verständlich** [fɛr'ʃtɛntlɪç] *adj* understandable, comprehensible; (*hörbar*) audible; **sich** ~ **machen** to make o.s. understood; (*sich klar ausdrücken*) to make o.s. clear.

**verständlicherweise** *adv* understandably (enough).

**Verständlichkeit** *f* clarity, intelligibility.

**Verständnis** (-ses, -se) *nt* understanding; **für etw kein** ~ **haben** to have no understanding *od* sympathy for sth; (*für Kunst etc*) to have no appreciation of sth; **v~los** *adj* uncomprehending; **v~voll** *adj* understanding, sympathetic.

**verstärken** [fɛr'ʃtɛrkən] *vt* to strengthen; (*Ton*) to amplify; (*erhöhen*) to intensify ♦ *vr* to intensify.

**Verstärker** (-s, -) *m* amplifier.

**Verstärkung** *f* strengthening; (*Hilfe*) reinforcements *pl*; (*von Ton*) amplification.

**verstaubt** [fɛr'ʃtaupt] *adj* dusty; (*fig: Ansichten*) fuddy-duddy (*umg*).

**verstauchen** [fɛr'ʃtauxən] *vt* to sprain.

**verstauen** [fɛr'ʃtauən] *vt* to stow away.

**Versteck** [fɛr'ʃtɛk] (-(e)s, -e) *nt* hiding (place).

**verstecken** *vt, vr* to hide.

**versteckt** *adj* hidden; (*Tür*) concealed; (*fig: Lächeln, Blick*) furtive; (*Andeutung*) veiled.

**verstehen** [fɛr'ʃteːən] *unreg vt, vi* to understand; (*können, beherrschen*) to know ♦ *vr* (*auskommen*) to get on; **das ist nicht wörtlich zu** ~ that isn't to be taken literally; **das versteht sich von selbst** that goes without saying; **die Preise** ~ **sich einschließlich Lieferung** prices are inclusive of delivery; **sich auf etw** *akk* ~ to be an expert at sth.

**versteifen** [fɛr'ʃtaifən] *vt* to stiffen, brace ♦ *vr*

(*fig*): **sich** ~ **auf** +*akk* to insist on.

**versteigen** [fɛr'ʃtaigən] *unreg vr:* **sie hat sich zu der Behauptung verstiegen, daß ...** she presumed to claim that ...

**versteigern** [fɛr'ʃtaigərn] *vt* to auction.

**Versteigerung** *f* auction.

**verstellbar** *adj* adjustable, variable.

**verstellen** [fɛr'ʃtɛlən] *vt* to move, shift; (*Uhr*) to adjust; (*versperren*) to block; (*fig*) to disguise ♦ *vr* to pretend, put on an act.

**Verstellung** *f* pretence (*BRIT*), pretense (*US*).

**versteuern** [fɛr'ʃtɔyərn] *vt* to pay tax on; **zu** ~ taxable.

**verstiegen** [fɛr'ʃtiːgən] *adj* exaggerated.

**verstimmt** [fɛr'ʃtɪmt] *adj* out of tune; (*fig*) cross, put out; (*: Magen*) upset.

**Verstimmung** *f* (*fig*) disgruntled state, peevishness.

**verstockt** [fɛr'ʃtɔkt] *adj* stubborn; **V~heit** *f* stubbornness.

**verstohlen** [fɛr'ʃtoːlən] *adj* stealthy.

**verstopfen** [fɛr'ʃtɔpfən] *vt* to block, stop up; (*MED*) to constipate.

**Verstopfung** *f* obstruction; (*MED*) constipation.

**verstorben** [fɛr'ʃtɔrbən] *adj* deceased, late.

**Verstorbene(r)** *f(m)* deceased.

**verstört** [fɛr'ʃtøːrt] *adj* (*Mensch*) distraught.

**Verstoß** [fɛr'ʃtoːs] *m:* ~ **(gegen)** infringement (of), violation (of).

**verstoßen** *unreg vt* to disown, reject ♦ *vi:* ~ **gegen** to offend against.

**Verstrebung** [fɛr'ʃtreːbʊŋ] *f* (*Strebebalken*) support(ing beam).

**verstreichen** [fɛr'ʃtraiçən] *unreg vt* to spread ♦ *vi* to elapse; (*Zeit*) to pass (by); (*Frist*) to expire.

**verstreuen** [fɛr'ʃtrɔyən] *vt* to scatter (about).

**verstricken** [fɛr'ʃtrɪkən] *vt* (*fig*) to entangle, ensnare ♦ *vr:* **sich** ~ **in** +*akk* to get entangled in.

**verströmen** [fɛr'ʃtrøːmən] *vt* to exude.

**verstümmeln** [fɛr'ʃtʏməln] *vt* to maim, mutilate (*auch fig*).

**verstummen** [fɛr'ʃtʊmən] *vi* to go silent; (*Lärm*) to die away.

**Versuch** [fɛr'zuːx] (-(e)s, -e) *m* attempt; (*CHEM etc*) experiment; **das käme auf einen** ~ **an** we'll have to have a try.

**versuchen** *vt* to try; (*verlocken*) to tempt ♦ *vr:* **sich an etw** *dat* ~ to try one's hand at sth.

**Versuchs-** *zW:* ~**anstalt** *f* research institute; ~**bohrung** *f* experimental drilling; ~**kaninchen** *nt* guinea pig; ~**objekt** *nt* test object; (*fig: Mensch*) guinea pig; ~**reihe** *f* series of experiments; **v~weise** *adv* tentatively.

**Versuchung** *f* temptation.

**versumpfen** [fɛr'zʊmpfən] *vi* (*Gebiet*) to become marshy; (*fig: umg*) to go to pot; (*lange zechen*) to get involved in a booze-up

(*BRIT*) *od* drinking spree (*US*).

**versündigen** [fɛr'zʏndɪgən] *vr* (*geh*): **sich an jdm/etw** ~ to sin against sb/sth.

**versunken** [fɛr'zʊŋkən] *adj* sunken; ~ **sein in** +*akk* to be absorbed *od* engrossed in; **V~heit** *f* absorption.

**versüßen** [fɛr'zy:sən] *vt*: **jdm etw** ~ (*fig*) to make sth more pleasant for sb.

**vertagen** [fɛr'ta:gən] *vt, vi* to adjourn. **Vertagung** *f* adjournment.

**vertauschen** [fɛr'tauʃən] *vt* to exchange; (*versehentlich*) to mix up; **vertauschte Rollen** reversed roles.

**verteidigen** [fɛr'taɪdɪgən] *vt* to defend ♦ *vr* to defend o.s.; (*vor Gericht*) to conduct one's own defence (*BRIT*) *od* defense (*US*).

**Verteidiger(in)** (-s, -) *m(f)* defender; (*Anwalt*) defence (*BRIT*) *od* defense (*US*) lawyer.

**Verteidigung** *f* defence (*BRIT*), defense (*US*).

**Verteidigungsfähigkeit** *f* ability to defend.

**Verteidigungsminister** *m* Minister of Defence (*BRIT*), Defense Secretary (*US*).

**verteilen** [fɛr'taɪlən] *vt* to distribute; (*Rollen*) to assign; (*Salbe*) to spread.

**Verteiler** (-s, -) *m* (*COMM, AUT*) distributor.

**Verteilung** *f* distribution.

**Verteuerung** [fɛr'tɔyərʊŋ] *f* increase in price.

**verteufeln** [fɛr'tɔyfəln] *vt* to condemn.

**verteufelt** (*umg*) *adj* awful, devilish ♦ *adv* awfully, devilishly.

**vertiefen** [fɛr'ti:fən] *vt* to deepen; (*SCH*) to consolidate ♦ *vr*: **sich in etw** *akk* ~ to become engrossed *od* absorbed in sth.

**Vertiefung** *f* depression.

**vertikal** [vɛrti'ka:l] *adj* vertical.

**vertilgen** [fɛr'tɪlgən] *vt* to exterminate; (*umg*) to eat up, consume.

**Vertilgungsmittel** *nt* weedkiller; ⟨*Insekten~*⟩ pesticide.

**vertippen** [fɛr'tɪpən] *vr* to make a typing mistake.

**vertonen** [fɛr'to:nən] *vt* to set to music; (*Film etc*) to add a soundtrack to.

**vertrackt** [fɛr'trakt] *adj* awkward, tricky, complex.

**Vertrag** [fɛr'tra:k] (-(e)s, -̈e) *m* contract, agreement; (*POL*) treaty.

**vertragen** [fɛr'tra:gən] *unreg vt* to tolerate, stand ♦ *vr* to get along; (*sich aussöhnen*) to become reconciled; **viel** ~ **können** (*umg: Alkohol*) to be able to hold one's drink; **sich mit etw** ~ (*Nahrungsmittel, Farbe*) to go with sth; (*Aussage, Verhalten*) to be consistent with sth.

**vertraglich** *adj* contractual.

**verträglich** [fɛr'trɛ:klɪç] *adj* good-natured; (*Speisen*) easily digested; (*MED*) easily tolerated; **V~keit** *f* good nature; digestibility.

**Vertrags-** *zW*: ~**bruch** *m* breach of contract;

~**brüchig** *adj* in breach of contract; **v~fähig** *adj* (*JUR*) competent to contract; **v~mäßig** *adj, adv* (as) stipulated, according to contract; ~**partner** *m* party to a contract; ~**spieler** *m* (*SPORT*) player under contract; **v~widrig** *adj, adv* contrary to contract.

**vertrauen** [fɛr'trauən] *vi*: **jdm** ~ to trust sb; ~ **auf** +*akk* to rely on; **V~** (-s) *nt* confidence; **jdn ins V~ ziehen** to take sb into one's confidence; **V~ zu jdm fassen** to gain confidence in sb.

**vertrauenerweckend** *adj* inspiring trust.

**Vertrauens-** *zW*: ~**mann** (-(e)s, *pl* -**männer** *od* -**leute**) *m* intermediary; ~**sache** *f* (*vertrauliche Angelegenheit*) confidential matter; (*Frage des Vertrauens*) question of trust; **v~selig** *adj* trusting; **v~voll** *adj* trustful; ~**votum** *nt* (*PARL*) vote of confidence; **v~würdig** *adj* trustworthy.

**vertraulich** [fɛr'traulɪç] *adj* familiar; (*geheim*) confidential; **V~keit** *f* familiarity; confidentiality.

**verträumt** [fɛr'trɔymt] *adj* dreamy; (*Städtchen etc*) sleepy.

**vertraut** [fɛr'traut] *adj* familiar; **sich mit dem Gedanken** ~ **machen, daß** ... to get used to the idea that ...

**Vertraute(r)** *f(m)* confidant(e), close friend.

**Vertrautheit** *f* familiarity.

**vertreiben** [fɛr'traɪbən] *unreg vt* to drive away; (*aus Land*) to expel; (*COMM*) to sell; (*Zeit*) to pass.

**Vertreibung** *f* expulsion.

**vertretbar** *adj* justifiable; (*Theorie, Argument*) tenable.

**vertreten** [fɛr'tre:tən] *unreg vt* to represent; (*Ansicht*) to hold, advocate; (*ersetzen*) to replace; (*Kollegen*) to cover for; (*COMM*) to be the agent for; **sich** *dat* **die Beine** ~ to stretch one's legs.

**Vertreter(in)** (-s, -) *m(f)* representative; (*Verfechter*) advocate; (*COMM: Firma*) agent; ~**provision** *f* agent's commission.

**Vertretung** *f* representation; advocacy; **die** ~ **übernehmen (für)** to stand in (for).

**Vertretungsstunde** *f* (*SCH*) cover lesson.

**Vertrieb** [fɛr'tri:p] (-(e)s, -e) *m* marketing; **den** ~ **für eine Firma haben** to have the (selling) agency for a firm.

**Vertriebene(r)** [fɛr'tri:bənə(r)] *f(m)* exile.

**Vertriebskosten** *pl* marketing costs *pl.*

**vertrocknen** [fɛr'trɔknən] *vi* to dry up.

**vertrödeln** [fɛr'trø:dəln] (*umg*) *vt* to fritter away.

**vertrösten** [fɛr'trø:stən] *vt* to put off.

**vertun** [fɛr'tu:n] *unreg vt* to waste ♦ *vr* (*umg*) to make a mistake.

**vertuschen** [fɛr'tuʃən] *vt* to hush *od* cover up.

**verübeln** [fɛr'y:bəln] *vt*: **jdm etw** ~ to be cross *od* offended with sb on account of sth.

**verüben** [fɛr'y:bən] *vt* to commit.

**verulken** [fɛr'ʊlkən] (*umg*) *vt* to make fun of.

**verunglimpfen** [fɛrˈʊnɡlɪmpfən] *vt* to disparage.

**verunglücken** [fɛrˈʊnɡlʏkən] *vi* to have an accident; (*fig: umg: mißlingen*) to go wrong; **tödlich** ~ to be killed in an accident.

**Verunglückte(r)** *f(m)* accident victim.

**verunreinigen** [fɛrˈʊnraɪnɪɡən] *vt* to soil; (*Umwelt*) to pollute.

**verunsichern** [fɛrˈʊnzɪçərn] *vt* to rattle (*fig*).

**verunstalten** [fɛrˈʊnʃtaltən] *vt* to disfigure; (*Gebäude etc*) to deface.

**veruntreuen** [fɛrˈʊntrɔyən] *vt* to embezzle.

**verursachen** [fɛrˈuːrzaxən] *vt* to cause.

**verurteilen** [fɛrˈuːrtaɪlən] *vt* to condemn; (*zu Strafe*) to sentence; (*für schuldig befinden*): **jdn ~ (für)** to convict sb (of).

**Verurteilung** *f* condemnation; (*JUR*) sentence; conviction.

**vervielfachen** [fɛrˈfiːlfaxən] *vt* to multiply.

**vervielfältigen** [fɛrˈfiːlfɛltɪɡən] *vt* to duplicate, copy.

**Vervielfältigung** *f* duplication, copying.

**vervollkommnen** [fɛrˈfɔlkɔmnən] *vt* to perfect.

**vervollständigen** [fɛrˈfɔlʃtɛndɪɡən] *vt* to complete.

**verw.** *abk* = **verwitwet**.

**verwachsen** [fɛrˈvaksən] *adj* (*Mensch*) deformed; (*verkümmert*) stunted; (*überwuchert*) overgrown.

**verwackeln** [fɛrˈvakəln] *vt* (*Photo*) to blur.

**verwählen** [fɛrˈvɛːlən] *vr* (*TEL*) to dial the wrong number.

**verwahren** [fɛrˈvaːrən] *vt* to keep (safe) ♦ *vr* to protest.

**verwahrlosen** *vi* to become neglected; (*moralisch*) to go to the bad.

**verwahrlost** *adj* neglected; (*moralisch*) wayward.

**Verwahrung** *f* (*von Geld etc*) keeping; (*von Täter*) custody, detention; **jdn in ~ nehmen** to take sb into custody.

**verwaist** [fɛrˈvaɪst] *adj* orphaned.

**verwalten** [fɛrˈvaltən] *vt* to manage; (*Behörde*) to administer.

**Verwalter(in)** **(-s, -)** *m(f)* adminstrator; (*Vermögens~*) trustee.

**Verwaltung** *f* management; administration.

**Verwaltungs-** *zW:* **~apparat** *m* administrative machinery; **~bezirk** *m* administrative district; **~gericht** *nt* Administrative Court.

**verwandeln** [fɛrˈvandəln] *vt* to change, transform ♦ *vr* to change.

**Verwandlung** *f* change, transformation.

**verwandt** [fɛrˈvant] *adj:* ~ **(mit)** related (to); **geistig ~ sein** (*fig*) to be kindred spirits.

**Verwandte(r)** *f(m)* relative, relation.

**Verwandtschaft** *f* relationship; (*Menschen*) relatives *pl*, relations *pl*; (*fig*) affinity.

**verwarnen** [fɛrˈvarnən] *vt* to caution.

**Verwarnung** *f* caution.

**verwaschen** [fɛrˈvaʃən] *adj* faded; (*fig*) vague.

**verwässern** [fɛrˈvɛsərn] *vt* to dilute, water down.

**verwechseln** [fɛrˈvɛksəln] *vt:* ~ **mit** to confuse with; **zum V~ ähnlich** as like as two peas.

**Verwechslung** *f* confusion, mixing up; **das muß eine ~ sein** there must be some mistake.

**verwegen** [fɛrˈveːɡən] *adj* daring, bold; **V~heit** *f* daring, audacity, boldness.

**verwehren** [fɛrˈveːrən] *vt* (*geh*): **jdm etw ~** to refuse *od* deny sb sth.

**Verwehung** [fɛrˈveːʊŋ] *f* (*Schnee~*) snowdrift; (*Sand~*) sanddrift.

**verweichlichen** [fɛrˈvaɪçlɪçən] *vt* to mollycoddle.

**verweichlicht** *adj* effeminate, soft.

**verweigern** [fɛrˈvaɪɡərn] *vt:* **jdm etw ~** to refuse sb sth; **den Gehorsam/die Aussage ~** to refuse to obey/testify.

**Verweigerung** *f* refusal.

**verweilen** [fɛrˈvaɪlən] *vi* to stay; (*fig*): ~ **bei** to dwell on.

**verweint** [fɛrˈvaɪnt] *adj* (*Augen*) swollen with tears *od* with crying; (*Gesicht*) tear-stained.

**Verweis** [fɛrˈvaɪs] **(-es, -e)** *m* reprimand, rebuke; (*Hinweis*) reference.

**verweisen** [fɛrˈvaɪzən] *unreg vt* to refer; **jdn auf etw** *akk***/an jdn ~** (*hinweisen*) to refer sb to sth/sb; **jdn vom Platz** *od* **des Spielfeldes ~** (*SPORT*) to send sb off; **jdn von der Schule ~** to expel sb (from school); **jdn des Landes ~** to deport sb.

**Verweisung** *f* reference; (*Landes~*) deportation.

**verwelken** [fɛrˈvɛlkən] *vi* to fade; (*Blumen*) to wilt.

**verweltlichen** [fɛrˈvɛltlɪçən] *vt* to secularize.

**verwendbar** [fɛrˈvɛndbaːr] *adj* usable.

**verwenden** [fɛrˈvɛndən] *unreg vt* to use; (*Mühe, Zeit, Arbeit*) to spend ♦ *vr* to intercede.

**Verwendung** *f* use.

**Verwendungsmöglichkeit** *f* (possible) use.

**verwerfen** [fɛrˈvɛrfən] *unreg vt* to reject; (*Urteil*) to quash; (*kritisieren: Handlungsweise*) to condemn.

**verwerflich** [fɛrˈvɛrflɪç] *adj* reprehensible.

**verwertbar** *adj* usable.

**verwerten** [fɛrˈveːrtən] *vt* to utilize.

**Verwertung** *f* utilization.

**verwesen** [fɛrˈveːzən] *vi* to decay.

**Verwesung** *f* decomposition.

**verwickeln** [fɛrˈvɪkəln] *vt* to tangle (up); (*fig*) to involve ♦ *vr* to get tangled (up); **jdn ~ in** *+akk* to involve sb in, get sb involved in; **sich ~ in** *+akk* to get involved in.

**verwickelt** *adj* involved.

**Verwicklung** *f* entanglement, complication.

**verwildern** [fɛrˈvɪldərn] *vi* to run wild.

**verwildert** *adj* wild; (*Garten*) overgrown; (*jds Aussehen*) unkempt.

**verwinden** [fɛr'vɪndən] *unreg vt* to get over.
**verwirken** [fɛr'vɪrkən] *vt* (*geh*) to forfeit.
**verwirklichen** [fɛr'vɪrklɪçən] *vt* to realize, put into effect.
**Verwirklichung** *f* realization.
**verwirren** [fɛr'vɪrən] *vt* to tangle (up); (*fig*) to confuse.
**Verwirrspiel** *nt* confusing tactics *pl*.
**Verwirrung** *f* confusion.
**verwischen** [fɛr'vɪʃən] *vt* (*verschmieren*) to smudge; (*lit, fig: Spuren*) to cover over; (*fig: Erinnerungen*) to blur.
**verwittern** [fɛr'vɪtərn] *vi* to weather.
**verwitwet** [fɛr'vɪtvət] *adj* widowed.
**verwöhnen** [fɛr'vøːnən] *vt* to spoil, pamper.
**Verwöhnung** *f* spoiling, pampering.
**verworfen** [fɛr'vɔrfən] *adj* depraved; **V~heit** *f* depravity.
**verworren** [fɛr'vɔrən] *adj* confused.
**verwundbar** [fɛr'vʊndbaːr] *adj* vulnerable.
**verwunden** [fɛr'vʊndən] *vt* to wound.
**verwunderlich** [fɛr'vʊndərlɪç] *adj* surprising; (*stärker*) astonishing.
**verwundern** *vt* to astonish ♦ *vr*: **sich ~ über** +*akk* to be astonished at.
**Verwunderung** *f* astonishment.
**Verwundete(r)** *f(m)* injured person; **die ~n** the injured; (*MIL*) the wounded.
**Verwundung** *f* wound, injury.
**verwünschen** [fɛr'vʏnʃən] *vt* to curse.
**verwurzelt** [fɛr'vʊrtsəlt] *adj*: **(fest) in etw** *dat* *od* **mit etw ~** (*fig*) deeply rooted in sth.
**verwüsten** [fɛr'vyːstən] *vt* to devastate.
**Verwüstung** *f* devastation.
**Verz.** *abk* = **Verzeichnis**.
**verzagen** [fɛr'tsaːgən] *vi* to despair.
**verzagt** [fɛr'tsaːkt] *adj* disheartened.
**verzählen** [fɛr'tsɛːlən] *vr* to miscount.
**verzahnen** [fɛr'tsaːnən] *vt* to dovetail; (*Zahnräder*) to cut teeth in.
**verzapfen** [fɛr'tsapfən] (*umg*) *vt*: **Unsinn ~** to talk nonsense.
**verzaubern** [fɛr'tsaubərn] *vt* (*lit*) to cast a spell on; (*fig: jdn*) to enchant.
**verzehren** [fɛr'tseːrən] *vt* to consume.
**verzeichnen** [fɛr'tsaiçnən] *vt* to list; (*Niederlage, Verlust*) to register.
**Verzeichnis** (**-ses, -se**) *nt* list, catalogue (*BRIT*), catalog (*US*); (*in Buch*) index; (*COMPUT*) directory.
**verzeihen** [fɛr'tsaiən] *unreg vt, vi* to forgive; **jdm etw ~** to forgive sb (for) sth; **~ Sie!** excuse me!
**verzeihlich** *adj* pardonable.
**Verzeihung** *f* forgiveness, pardon; **~!** sorry!, excuse me!; (**jdn**) **um ~ bitten** to apologize (to sb).
**verzerren** [fɛr'tsɛrən] *vt* to distort; (*Sehne, Muskel*) to strain, pull.
**verzetteln** [fɛr'tsɛtəln] *vr* to waste a lot of time.
**Verzicht** [fɛr'tsɪçt] (**-(e)s, -e**) *m*: **~ (auf** +*akk*)

renunciation (of); **v~en** *vi*: **v~en auf** +*akk* to forego, give up.
**verziehen** [fɛr'tsiːən] *unreg vi* (*Hilfsverb sein*) to move ♦ *vt* to put out of shape; (*Kind*) to spoil; (*Pflanzen*) to thin out ♦ *vr* to go out of shape; (*Gesicht*) to contort; (*verschwinden*) to disappear; **verzogen** (*Vermerk*) no longer at this address; **keine Miene ~** not to turn a hair; **das Gesicht ~** to pull a face.
**verzieren** [fɛr'tsiːrən] *vt* to decorate.
**Verzierung** *f* decoration.
**verzinsen** [fɛr'tsɪnzən] *vt* to pay interest on.
**verzinslich** *adj*: **(fest) ~ sein** to yield (a fixed rate of) interest.
**verzogen** [fɛr'tsoːgən] *adj* (*Kind*) spoilt; *siehe auch* **verziehen**.
**verzögern** [fɛr'tsøːgərn] *vt* to delay.
**Verzögerung** *f* delay.
**Verzögerungstaktik** *f* delaying tactics *pl*.
**verzollen** [fɛr'tsɔlən] *vt* to pay duty on; **haben Sie etwas zu ~?** have you anything to declare?
**verzücken** [fɛr'tsʏkən] *vt* to send into ecstasies, enrapture.
**Verzug** [fɛr'tsuːk] *m* delay; (*FIN*) arrears *pl*; **mit etw in ~ geraten** to fall behind with sth.
**verzweifeln** [fɛr'tsvaifəln] *vi* to despair.
**verzweifelt** *adj* desperate.
**Verzweiflung** *f* despair.
**verzweigen** [fɛr'tsvaigən] *vr* to branch out.
**verzwickt** [fɛr'tsvɪkt] (*umg*) *adj* awkward, complicated.
**Vesper** ['fɛspər] (**-, -n**) *f* vespers *pl*.
**Vesuv** [ve'zuːf] (**-(s)**) *m* Vesuvius.
**Veto** ['veːto] (**-s, -s**) *nt* veto.
**Vetter** ['fɛtər] (**-s, -n**) *m* cousin.
**vgl.** *abk* (= *vergleiche*) cf.
**v.H.** *abk* (= *vom Hundert*) pc.
**VHS** (-) *f abk* = **Volkshochschule**.
**Viadukt** [via'dʊkt] (**-(e)s, -e**) *m* viaduct.
**Vibrator** [vi'braːtər] *m* vibrator.
**vibrieren** [vi'briːrən] *vi* to vibrate.
**Video** ['viːdeo] (**-s, -s**) *nt* video; **~aufnahme** *f* video (recording); **~kamera** *f* video camera; **~recorder** *m* video recorder; **~spiel** *nt* video game; **~text** *m* teletext.
**Vieh** [fiː] (**-(e)s**) *nt* cattle *pl*; (*Nutztiere*) livestock; (*umg: Tier*) animal; **v~isch** *adj* bestial; **~zucht** *f* (live)stock *od* cattle breeding.
**viel** [fiːl] *adj* a lot of, much ♦ *adv* a lot, much; **in ~em** in many respects; **noch (ein)mal so ~** (*Zeit etc*) as much (time *etc*) again; **einer zu ~** one too many; **~ zuwenig** much too little; **~beschäftigt** *adj attrib* very busy; **~e** *pl* a lot of, many; **gleich ~e (Angestellte/Anteile** *etc*) the same number (of employees/shares *etc*).
**vielerlei** *adj* a great variety of.
**vielerorts** *adv* in many places.
**viel-** *zW*: **~fach** *adj, adv* many times; **auf ~fachen Wunsch** at the request of many people; **V~fache(s)** *nt* (*MATH*) multiple; **um**

ein V~**faches** many times over; **V~falt** (-) f variety; ~**fältig** adj varied, many-sided; **V~fraß** m glutton; ~**geprüft** adj attrib (hum) sorely tried.

**vielleicht** [fi'laɪçt] adv perhaps; (in Bitten) by any chance; **du bist** ~ **ein Idiot!** (umg) you really are an idiot!

**viel-** zW: ~**mal(s)** adv many times; **danke** ~**mals** many thanks; **ich bitte** ~**mals um Entschuldigung!** I do apologize!; ~**mehr** adv rather, on the contrary; ~**sagend** adj significant; ~**schichtig** adj (fig) complex; ~**seitig** adj many-sided; (Ausbildung) all-round attrib; (Interessen) varied; (Mensch, Gerät) versatile; ~**versprechend** adj promising; **V~völkerstaat** m multinational state.

**vier** [fiːr] num four; **alle** ~**e von sich strecken** (umg) to stretch out; **V~beiner** m (hum) four-legged friend; **V~eck** (-(e)s, -e) nt four-sided figure; (gleichseitig) square; ~**eckig** adj four-sided; square; ~**hundert** num four hundred; ~**kant** adj, adv (NAUT) square; ~**köpfig** adj: **eine** ~**köpfige Familie** a family of four; **V~mächteabkommen** nt four-power agreement.

**viert** adj: **wir gingen zu** ~ four of us went.

**Viertaktmotor** m four-stroke engine.

**vierte(r, s)** ['fiːrtə(r, s)] adj fourth.

**vierteilen** vt to quarter.

**Viertel** ['fɪrtəl] (-s, -) nt quarter; **ein** ~ **Leberwurst** a quarter of liver sausage; ~**finale** nt quarter finals pl; ~**jahr** nt three months pl, quarter (COMM, FIN); ~**jahresschrift** f quarterly; **v~jährlich** adj quarterly; ~**note** f crotchet (BRIT), quarter note (US); ~**stunde** f quarter of an hour.

**vier-** zW: ~**türig** adj four-door attr; **V~waldstättersee** m Lake Lucerne; ~**zehn** ['fɪrtseːn] num fourteen; **in** ~**zehn Tagen** in a fortnight (BRIT), in two weeks (US); ~**zehntägig** adj fortnightly; ~**zehnte(r, s)** adj fourteenth.

**vierzig** ['fɪrtsɪç] num forty; **V~stundenwoche** f forty-hour week.

**Vierzimmerwohnung** f four-room flat (BRIT) od apartment (US).

**Vietnam** [viɛt'nam] (-s) nt Vietnam.

**Vietnamese** [viɛtna'meːzə] (-n, -n) m, **Vietnamesin** f Vietnamese.

**vietnamesisch** adj Vietnamese.

**Vikar** [vi'kaːr] (-s, -e) m curate.

**Villa** ['vɪla] (-, **Villen**) f villa.

**Villenviertel** nt (prosperous) residential area.

**violett** [vio'lɛt] adj violet.

**Violinbogen** m violin bow.

**Violine** [vio'liːnə] (-, -n) f violin.

**Violinkonzert** nt violin concerto.

**Violinschlüssel** m treble clef.

**virtuell** [vɪrtu'ɛl] adj (COMPUT) virtual; ~**e Realität** virtual reality.

**virtuos** [vɪrtu'oːs] adj virtuoso attrib.

**Virtuose** [vɪrtu'oːzə] (-n, -n) m virtuoso.

**Virtuosin** [vɪrtu'oːzɪn] f virtuoso.

**Virtuosität** [vɪrtuozi'tɛt] f virtuosity.

**Virus** ['viːrus] (-, **Viren**) m od nt (also COMPUT) virus.

**Virus-** in zW viral; ~**infektion** f virus infection.

**Visage** [vi'zaːʒə] (-, -n) (pej) f face, (ugly) mug (umg).

**Visagist(in)** [viza'ʒɪst(ɪn)] m(f) make-up artist.

**vis-à-vis** [viza'viː] adv (veraltet): ~ **(von)** opposite (to) ♦ präp +dat opposite (to).

**Visier** [vi'ziːr] (-s, -e) nt gunsight; (am Helm) visor.

**Vision** [vizi'oːn] f vision.

**Visite** [vi'ziːtə] (-, -n) f (MED) visit.

**Visitenkarte** f visiting card.

**visuell** [vizu'ɛl] adj visual.

**Visum** ['viːzum] (-s, **Visa** od **Visen**) nt visa; ~**zwang** m obligation to hold a visa.

**vital** [vi'taːl] adj lively, full of life; (lebenswichtig) vital.

**Vitamin** [vita'miːn] (-s, -e) nt vitamin; ~**mangel** m vitamin deficiency.

**Vitrine** [vi'triːnə] (-, -n) f (Schrank) glass cabinet; (Schaukasten) showcase, display case.

**Vivisektion** [vivizɛktsi'oːn] f vivisection.

**Vize** ['fiːtsə] m (umg) number two; (: ~**meister**) runner-up ♦ in zW vice-.

**v.J.** abk (= vorigen Jahres) of the previous od last year.

**Vlies** [fliːs] (-es, -e) nt fleece.

**v.M.** abk (= vorigen Monats) ult.

**V-Mann** m abk = **Verbindungsmann**; **Vertrauensmann**.

**VN** pl abk (= Vereinte Nationen) UN.

**VO** abk = **Verordnung**.

**Vogel** ['foːgəl] (-s, ˵) m bird; **einen** ~ **haben** (umg) to have bats in the belfry; **den** ~ **abschießen** (umg) to surpass everyone (ironisch); ~**bauer** nt birdcage; ~**beerbaum** m rowan (tree); ~**dreck** m bird droppings pl; ~**perspektive** f bird's-eye view; ~**schau** f bird's-eye view; ~**scheuche** f scarecrow; ~**schutzgebiet** nt bird sanctuary; ~-**Strauß-Politik** f head-in-the-sand policy.

**Vogesen** [vo'geːzən] pl Vosges pl.

**Vokabel** [vo'kaːbəl] (-, -n) f word.

**Vokabular** [vokabu'laːr] (-s, -e) nt vocabulary.

**Vokal** [vo'kaːl] (-s, -e) m vowel.

**Volk** [fɔlk] (-(e)s, ˵-er) nt people; (Nation) nation; **etw unters** ~ **bringen** (Nachricht) to spread sth.

**Völker-** zW: ~**bund** m League of Nations; ~**kunde** f ethnology; ~**mord** m genocide; ~**recht** nt international law; **v~rechtlich** adj according to international law; ~**verständigung** f international understanding; ~**wanderung** f migration.

**Volks-** zW: ~**abstimmung** f referendum;

~**armee** *f* People's Army; ~**begehren** *nt* petition for a referendum; ~**deutsche(r)** *f(m)* ethnic German; **v~eigen** *adj* (*DDR*) nationally-owned; ~**feind** *m* enemy of the people; ~**fest** *nt* popular festival; (*Jahrmarkt*) fair.

**Volkshochschule** *f* adult education classes *pl.*

> *The Volkshochschule (VHS) is an institution which offers Adult Education classes. No set qualifications are necessary to attend. For a small fee adults can attend both vocational and non-vocational classes in the day-time or evening.*

**Volks-** *zW:* ~**lauf** *m* fun run; ~**lied** *nt* folk song; ~**mund** *m* vernacular; ~**polizei** *f* (*DDR*) People's Police; ~**republik** *f* people's republic; ~**schule** *f* ≈ primary school (*BRIT*), elementary school (*US*); ~**seuche** *f* epidemic; ~**stamm** *m* tribe; ~**stück** *nt* folk play in dialect; ~**tanz** *m* folk dance; ~**trauertag** *m* ≈ Remembrance Day (*BRIT*), Memorial Day (*US*); **v~tümlich** *adj* popular; ~**wirtschaft** *f* national economy; (*Fach*) economics *sing*, political economy; ~**wirtschaftler** *m* economist; ~**zählung** *f* (national) census.

**voll** [fɔl] *adj* full ♦ *adv* fully; **jdn für ~ nehmen** (*umg*) to take sb seriously; **aus dem ~en schöpfen** to draw on unlimited resources; **in ~er Größe** (*Bild*) life-size(d); (*bei plötzlicher Erscheinung etc*) large as life; ~ **sein** (*umg: satt*) to be full (up); (: *betrunken*) to be plastered; ~ **und ganz** completely.

**vollauf** [fɔl'|aʊf] *adv* amply; ~ **zu tun haben** to have quite enough to do.

**voll-** *zW:* **V~bad** *nt* (proper) bath; **V~bart** *m* full beard; **V~beschäftigung** *f* full employment; **V~besitz** *m:* **im V~besitz** +*gen* in full possession of; **V~blut** *nt* thoroughbred; ~**blütig** *adj* full-blooded; **V~bremsung** *f* emergency stop; ~**bringen** *unreg vt untr* to accomplish; **V~dampf** *m* (*NAUT*): **mit V~dampf** at full steam; ~**enden** *vt untr* to finish, complete; ~**endet** *adj* (*vollkommen*) perfect; (*Tänzer etc*) accomplished; ~**ends** *adv* completely; **V~endung** *f* completion.

**voller** *adj* fuller; ~ **Flecken/Ideen** full of stains/ideas.

**Völlerei** [fœlə'raɪ] *f* gluttony.

**Volleyball** ['vɔlibal] (-(e)s) *m* volleyball.

**voll-** *zW:* ~**fett** *adj* full-fat; **V~gas** *nt:* **mit V~gas** at full throttle; **V~gas geben** to step on it.

**völlig** ['fœlɪç] *adj* complete ♦ *adv* completely.

**voll-** *zW:* ~**jährig** *adj* of age; **V~kaskoversicherung** *f* fully comprehensive insurance; ~**kommen** *adj* perfect; (*völlig*) complete, absolute;

**V~kommenheit** *f* perfection; **V~kornbrot** *nt* wholemeal (*BRIT*) *od* whole-wheat (*US*) bread; ~**(l)aufen** *unreg vi:* **etw ~(l)aufen lassen** to fill sth up; ~**machen** *vt* to fill (up); **V~macht** *f* authority, power of attorney; **V~matrose** *m* able-bodied seaman; **V~milch** *f* full-cream milk; **V~mond** *m* full moon; **V~narkose** *f* general anaesthetic (*BRIT*) *od* anesthetic (*US*); **V~pension** *f* full board; ~**schlank** *adj* plump, stout; ~**schreiben** *unreg vt* (*Heft, Seite*) to fill; (*Tafel*) to cover (with writing); ~**ständig** *adj* complete; ~**strecken** *vt untr* to execute; ~**tanken** *vt, vi* to fill up; **V~treffer** *m* (*lit, fig*) bull's-eye; **V~versammlung** *f* general meeting; **V~waise** *f* orphan; ~**wertig** *adj* full *attrib*; (*Stellung*) equal; **V~wertkost** *f* wholefoods *pl*; ~**zählig** *adj* complete; (*anwesend*) in full number; ~**ziehen** *unreg vt untr* to carry out ♦ *vr untr* to happen; **V~zug** *m* execution.

**Volontär(in)** [vɔlɔn'tɛːr(ɪn)] (-s, -e) *m(f)* trainee.

**Volt** [vɔlt] (- *od* -(e)s, -) *nt* volt.

**Volumen** [vo'luːmən] (-s, - *od* **Volumina**) *nt* volume.

**vom** [fɔm] = **von dem.**

**von** [fɔn] *präp +dat* **1** (*Ausgangspunkt*) from; ~ ... **bis** from ... to; ~ **morgens bis abends** from morning till night; ~ ... **nach** ... from ... to ...; ~ ... **an** from ...; ~ ... **aus** from ...; ~ **dort aus** from there; **etw** ~ **sich aus tun** to do sth of one's own accord; ~ **mir aus** (*umg*) if you like, I don't mind; ~ **wo/wann** ...? where/when ... from?

**2** (*Ursache, im Passiv*) by; **ein Gedicht** ~ **Schiller** a poem by Schiller; ~ **etw müde** tired from sth

**3** (*als Genitiv*) of; **ein Freund** ~ **mir** a friend of mine; **nett** ~ **dir** nice of you; **jeweils zwei** ~ **zehn** two out of every ten

**4** (*über*) about; **er erzählte vom Urlaub** he talked about his holiday

**5**: ~ **wegen!** (*umg*) no way!

**voneinander** *adv* from each other.

**vonstatten** [fɔn'ʃtatən] *adv:* ~ **gehen** to proceed, go.

**vor** [foːr] *präp +dat* **1** (*räumlich*) in front of **2** (*zeitlich, Reihenfolge*) before; **ich war** ~ **ihm da** I was there before him; **X kommt** ~ **Y** X comes before Y; ~ **zwei Tagen** two days ago; **5 (Minuten)** ~ **4** 5 (minutes) to 4; ~ **kurzem** a little while ago

**3** (*Ursache*) with; ~ **Wut/Liebe** with rage/ love; ~ **Hunger sterben** to die of hunger; ~ **lauter Arbeit** because of work

**4**: ~ **allem,** ~ **allen Dingen** above all ♦ *präp +akk* (*räumlich*) in front of; ~ **sich hin**

**summen** to hum to oneself
♦ *adv:* ~ **und zurück** backwards and forwards.

**Vor-** *zW:* ~**abdruck** *m* preprint; ~**abend** *m* evening before, eve; ~**ahnung** *f* presentiment, premonition.

**voran** [fo'ran] *adv* before, ahead; ~**bringen** *unreg vt* to make progress with; ~**gehen** *unreg vi* to go ahead; **einer Sache** *dat* ~**gehen** to precede sth; ~**gehend** *adj* previous; ~**kommen** *unreg vi* to make progress, come along.

**Voranschlag** ['foːr|anʃlaːk] *m* estimate.

**voranstellen** [fo'ranʃtɛlən] *vt +dat* to put in front (of); (*fig*) to give precedence (over).

**Vorarbeiter** ['foːr|arbaɪtər] *m* foreman.

**voraus** [fo'raus] *adv* ahead; (*zeitlich*) in advance; **jdm** ~ **sein** to be ahead of sb; **im** ~ in advance; ~**bezahlen** *vt* to pay in advance; ~**gehen** *unreg vi* to go (on) ahead; (*fig*) to precede; ~**haben** *unreg vt:* **jdm etw** ~**haben** to have the edge on sb in sth; **V**~**sage** *f* prediction; ~**sagen** *vt* to predict; ~**sehen** *unreg vt* to foresee; ~**setzen** *vt* to assume; (*sicher annehmen*) to take for granted; (*erfordern: Kenntnisse, Geduld*) to require, demand; ~**gesetzt, daß** ... provided that ...; **V**~**setzung** *f* requirement, prerequisite; **unter der V**~**setzung, daß** ... on condition that ...; **V**~**sicht** *f* foresight; **aller V**~**sicht nach** in all probability; **in der V**~**sicht, daß** ... anticipating that ...; ~**sichtlich** *adv* probably; **V**~**zahlung** *f* advance payment.

**Vorbau** ['foːrbau] (**-(e)s, -ten**) *m* porch; (*Balkon*) balcony.

**vorbauen** ['foːrbauən] *vt* to build up in front ♦ *vi +dat* to take precautions (against).

**Vorbedacht** ['foːrbədaxt] *m:* **mit/ohne** ~ (*Überlegung*) with/without due consideration; (*Absicht*) intentionally/unintentionally.

**Vorbedingung** ['foːrbədɪŋʊŋ] *f* precondition.

**Vorbehalt** ['foːrbəhalt] *m* reservation, proviso; **unter dem** ~**, daß** ... with the reservation that ...

**vorbehalten** *unreg vt:* **sich/jdm etw** ~ to reserve sth (for o.s.)/for sb; **alle Rechte** ~ all rights reserved.

**vorbehaltlich** *präp +gen* (*form*) subject to.

**vorbehaltlos** *adj* unconditional ♦ *adv* unconditionally.

**vorbei** [fɔr'baɪ] *adv* by, past; **aus und** ~ over and done with; **damit ist es nun** ~ that's all over now; ~**bringen** *unreg* (*umg*) *vt* to drop off; ~**gehen** *unreg vi* to pass by, go past; ~**kommen** *unreg vi:* **bei jdm** ~**kommen** to drop call in on sb; ~**reden** *vi:* **an etw** *dat* ~**reden** to talk around sth.

**vorbelastet** ['foːrbəlastət] *adj* (*fig*) handicapped (*BRIT*), handicaped (*US*).

**Vorbemerkung** ['foːrbəmɛrkʊŋ] *f* introductory remark.

**vorbereiten** ['foːrbərаɪtən] *vt* to prepare.

**Vorbereitung** *f* preparation.

**vorbestellen** ['foːrbəʃtɛlən] *vt* to book (in advance), reserve.

**Vorbestellung** *f* advance booking.

**vorbestraft** ['foːrbəʃtraft] *adj* previously convicted, with a record.

**Vorbeugehaft** *f* preventive custody.

**vorbeugen** ['foːrbɔygən] *vt, vr* to lean forward ♦ *vi +dat* to prevent.

**vorbeugend** *adj* preventive.

**Vorbeugung** *f* prevention; **zur** ~ **gegen** for the prevention of.

**Vorbild** ['foːrbɪlt] *nt* model; **sich** *dat* **jdn zum** ~ **nehmen** to model o.s. on sb; **v**~**lich** *adj* model, ideal.

**Vorbildung** ['foːrbɪldʊŋ] *f* educational background.

**Vorbote** ['foːrboːtə] *m* (*fig*) herald.

**vorbringen** ['foːrbrɪŋən] *unreg vt* to voice; (*Meinung etc*) to advance, state; (*umg: nach vorne*) to bring to the front.

**vordatieren** ['foːrdatiːrən] *vt* (*Schreiben*) to postdate.

**Vorder-** *zW:* ~**achse** *f* front axle; ~**ansicht** *f* front view; ~**asien** *nt* Near East.

**vordere(r, s)** *adj* front.

**Vorder-** *zW:* ~**grund** *m* foreground; **im** ~**grund stehen** (*fig*) to be to the fore; ~**grundprogramm** *nt* (*COMPUT*) foreground program; **v**~**hand** *adv* for the present; ~**mann** (**-(e)s**, *pl* **-männer**) *m* man in front; **jdn auf** ~**mann bringen** (*umg*) to get sb to shape up; ~**seite** *f* front (side); ~**sitz** *m* front seat.

**vorderste(r, s)** *adj* front.

**vordrängen** ['foːrdrɛŋən] *vr* to push to the front.

**vordringen** ['foːrdrɪŋən] *unreg vi:* **bis zu jdm/ etw** ~ to get as far as sb/sth.

**vordringlich** *adj* urgent.

**Vordruck** ['foːrdrʊk] *m* form.

**vorehelich** ['foːr|eːəlɪç] *adj* premarital.

**voreilig** ['foːr|aɪlɪç] *adj* hasty, rash; ~**e Schlüsse ziehen** to jump to conclusions.

**voreinander** ['foːr|aɪ'nandər] *adv* (*räumlich*) in front of each other; (*einander gegenüber*) face to face.

**voreingenommen** ['foːr|aɪngənɔmən] *adj* bias(s)ed; **V**~**heit** *f* bias.

**voreingestellt** ['foːr|aɪngəʃtɛlt] *adj:* ~**er Parameter** (*COMPUT*) default (parameter).

**vorenthalten** ['foːr|ɛnthaltən] *unreg vt:* **jdm etw** ~ to withhold sth from sb.

**Vorentscheidung** ['foːr|ɛntʃaɪdʊŋ] *f* preliminary decision.

**vorerst** ['foːr|eːrst] *adv* for the moment *od* present.

**Vorfahr** ['foːrfaːr] (**-en, -en**) *m* ancestor.

**vorfahren** *unreg vi* to drive (on) ahead; (*vors Haus etc*) to drive up.

**Vorfahrt** *f* (*AUT*) right of way;
„~ **(be)achten"** "give way" (*BRIT*), "yield"
(*US*).
**Vorfahrts-** *zW:* ~**regel** *f* rule of right of way;
~**schild** *nt* "give way" (*BRIT*) *od* "yield" (*US*)
sign; ~**straße** *f* major road.
**Vorfall** ['foːrfal] *m* incident.
**vorfallen** *unreg vi* to occur.
**Vorfeld** ['foːrfɛlt] *nt* (*fig*): **im** ~ (+*gen*) in the
run-up (to).
**Vorfilm** ['foːrfɪlm] *m* short.
**vorfinden** ['foːrfɪndən] *unreg vt* to find.
**Vorfreude** ['foːrfrɔydə] *f* anticipation.
**vorfühlen** ['foːrfyːlən] *vi* (*fig*) to put out
feelers.
**vorführen** ['foːrfyːrən] *vt* to show, display;
(*Theaterstück, Kunststücke*): **(jdm) etw** ~ to
perform sth (to *od* in front of sb); **dem
Gericht** ~ to bring before the court.
**Vorgabe** ['foːrgaːbə] *f* (*SPORT*) handicap.
**Vorgang** ['foːrgaŋ] *m* (*Ereignis*) event; (*Ablauf*)
course of events; (*CHEM etc*) process.
**Vorgänger(in)** ['foːrgɛŋər(ɪn)] (-**s**, -) *m(f)*
predecessor.
**vorgaukeln** ['foːrgaʊkəln] *vt:* **jdm etw** ~ to
lead sb to believe in sth.
**vorgeben** ['foːrgeːbən] *unreg vt* to pretend, use
as a pretext; (*SPORT*) to give an advantage
*od* a start of.
**Vorgebirge** ['foːrgəbɪrgə] *nt* foothills *pl*.
**vorgefaßt** ['foːrgəfast] *adj* preconceived.
**vorgefertigt** ['foːrgəfɛrtɪçt] *adj* prefabricated.
**Vorgefühl** ['foːrgəfyːl] *nt* anticipation; (*etwas
Böses*) presentiment.
**vorgehen** ['foːrgeːən] *unreg vi* (*voraus*) to go
(on) ahead; (*nach vorn*) to go forward;
(*handeln*) to act, proceed; (*Uhr*) to be fast;
(*Vorrang haben*) to take precedence; (*Uhr*)
(*passieren*) to go on.
**Vorgehen** (-**s**) *nt* action.
**Vorgehensweise** *f* proceedings *pl*.
**vorgerückt** ['foːrgərʏkt] *adj* (*Stunde*) late;
(*Alter*) advanced.
**Vorgeschichte** ['foːrgəʃɪçtə] *f* prehistory;
(*von Fall, Krankheit*) past history.
**Vorgeschmack** ['foːrgəʃmak] *m* foretaste.
**Vorgesetzte(r)** ['foːrgəzɛtstə(r)] *f(m)* superior.
**vorgestern** ['foːrgɛstərn] *adv* the day before
yesterday; **von** ~ (*fig*) antiquated.
**vorgreifen** ['foːrgraɪfən] *unreg vi* +*dat* to
anticipate; **jdm** ~ to forestall sb.
**vorhaben** ['foːrhaːbən] *unreg vt* to intend; **hast
du schon was vor?** have you got anything
on?
**Vorhaben** (-**s**, -) *nt* intention.
**Vorhalle** ['foːrhalə] *f* (*Diele*) entrance hall;
(*von Parlament*) lobby.
**vorhalten** ['foːrhaltən] *unreg vt* to hold *od* put
up ♦ *vi* to last; **jdm etw** ~ to reproach sb for
sth.
**Vorhaltung** *f* reproach.
**Vorhand** ['foːrhant] *f* forehand.

**vorhanden** [foːrˈhandən] *adj* existing;
(*erhältlich*) available; **V~sein** (-**s**) *nt*
existence, presence.
**Vorhang** ['foːrhaŋ] *m* curtain.
**Vorhängeschloß** ['foːrhɛŋəʃlɔs] *nt* padlock.
**Vorhaut** ['foːrhaʊt] *f* (*ANAT*) foreskin.
**vorher** [foːrˈheːr] *adv* before(hand);
~**bestimmen** *vt* (*Schicksal*) to preordain;
~**gehen** *unreg vi* to precede.
**vorherig** [foːrˈheːrɪç] *adj* previous.
**Vorherrschaft** ['foːrhɛrʃaft] *f* predominance,
supremacy.
**vorherrschen** *vi* to predominate.
**vorher-** *zW:* **V~sage** *f* forecast; ~**sagen** *vt* to
forecast, predict; ~**sehbar** *adj* predictable;
~**sehen** *unreg vt* to foresee.
**vorhin** [foːrˈhɪn] *adv* not long ago, just now.
**vorhinein** ['foːrhɪnaɪn] *adv:* **im** ~ beforehand.
**Vorhof** ['foːrhoːf] *m* forecourt.
**vorig** ['foːrɪç] *adj* previous, last.
**Vorjahr** ['foːrjaːr] *nt* previous year, year
before.
**vorjährig** ['foːrjɛːrɪç] *adj* of the previous year.
**vorjammern** ['foːrjamərn] *vt, vi:* **jdm (etwas)** ~
to moan to sb (about sth).
**Vorkämpfer(in)** ['foːrkɛmpfər(ɪn)] *m(f)*
pioneer.
**Vorkaufsrecht** ['foːrkaʊfsrɛçt] *nt* option to
buy.
**Vorkehrung** ['foːrkeːrʊŋ] *f* precaution.
**Vorkenntnis** ['foːrkɛntnɪs] *f* previous
knowledge.
**vorknöpfen** ['foːrknœpfən] *vt* (*fig: umg*): **sich**
*dat* **jdn** ~ to take sb to task.
**vorkommen** ['foːrkɔmən] *unreg vi* to come
forward; (*geschehen, sich finden*) to occur;
(*scheinen*) to seem (to be); **so was soll** ~!
that's life!; **sich** *dat* **dumm** *etc* ~ to feel
stupid *etc*.
**Vorkommen** *nt* occurrence; (*MIN*) deposit.
**Vorkommnis** ['foːrkɔmnɪs] (-**ses**, -**se**) *nt*
occurrence.
**Vorkriegs-** ['foːrkriːks] *in zW* pre-war.
**vorladen** ['foːrlaːdən] *unreg vt* (*bei Gericht*) to
summons.
**Vorladung** *f* summons.
**Vorlage** ['foːrlaːgə] *f* model, pattern; (*das
Vorlegen*) presentation; (*von Beweismaterial*)
submission; (*Gesetzes*~) bill; (*SPORT*) pass.
**vorlassen** ['foːrlasən] *unreg vt* to admit;
(*überholen lassen*) to let pass; (*vorgehen
lassen*) to allow to go in front.
**Vorlauf** ['foːrlaʊf] *m* (preliminary) heat (*of
running event*).
**Vorläufer** *m* forerunner.
**vorläufig** ['foːrlɔyfɪç] *adj* temporary;
(*provisorisch*) provisional.
**vorlaut** ['foːrlaʊt] *adj* impertinent, cheeky.
**Vorleben** ['foːrleːbən] *nt* past (life).
**vorlegen** ['foːrleːgən] *vt* to put in front,
present; (*Beweismaterial etc*) to produce,
submit; **jdm etw** ~ to put sth before sb.

**Vorleger** (**-s**, **-**) *m* mat.
**Vorleistung** ['fo:rlaɪstʊŋ] *f* (*FIN: Vorausbezahlung*) advance (payment); (*Vorarbeit*) preliminary work; (*POL*) prior concession.
**vorlesen** ['fo:rle:zən] *unreg vt* to read (out).
**Vorlesung** *f* (*UNIV*) lecture.
**Vorlesungsverzeichnis** *nt* lecture timetable.
**vorletzte(r, s)** ['fo:rlɛtstə(r, s)] *adj* last but one, penultimate.
**Vorliebe** ['fo:rli:bə] *f* preference, special liking; **etw mit ~ tun** to particularly like doing sth.
**vorliebnehmen** [fo:r'li:pne:mən] *unreg vi:* **~ mit** to make do with.
**vorliegen** ['fo:rli:gən] *unreg vi* to be (here); **etw liegt jdm vor** sb has sth; **etw liegt gegen jdn vor** sb is charged with sth.
**vorliegend** *adj* present, at issue.
**vorm.** *abk* (= *vormittags*) a.m.; (= *vormals*) formerly.
**vormachen** ['fo:rmaxən] *vt:* **jdm etw ~** to show sb how to do sth; **jdm etwas ~** (*fig*) to fool sb; **mach mir doch nichts vor** don't try and fool me.
**Vormachtstellung** ['fo:rmaxtʃtɛlʊŋ] *f* supremacy.
**vormals** ['fo:rmals] *adv* formerly.
**Vormarsch** ['fo:rmarʃ] *m* advance.
**vormerken** ['fo:rmɛrkən] *vt* to book; (*notieren*) to make note of; (*bei Bestellung*) to take an order for.
**Vormittag** ['fo:rmɪta:k] *m* morning; **am ~** in the morning.
**vormittags** *adv* in the morning, before noon.
**Vormund** ['fo:rmʊnt] (**-(e)s, -e** *od* **-münder**) *m* guardian.
**vorn** [fɔrn] *adv* in front; **von ~ anfangen** to start at the beginning; **nach ~** to the front; **er betrügt sie von ~ bis hinten** he deceives her right, left and centre.
**Vorname** ['fo:rna:mə] *m* first *od* Christian name.
**vornan** [fɔrn'|an] *adv* at the front.
**vorne** ['fɔrnə] = **vorn.**
**vornehm** ['fo:rne:m] *adj* distinguished; (*Manieren etc*) refined; (*Kleid*) elegant; **in ~en Kreisen** in polite society.
**vornehmen** *unreg vt* (*fig*) to carry out; **sich** *dat* **etw ~** to start on sth; (*beschließen*) to decide to do sth; **sich** *dat* **zuviel ~** to take on too much; **sich** *dat* **jdn ~** to tell sb off.
**vornehmlich** *adv* chiefly, specially.
**vorn(e)weg** ['fɔrn(ə)vɛk] *adv* in front; (*als erstes*) first.
**vornherein** ['fɔrnhɛraɪn] *adv:* **von ~** from the start.
**Vorort** ['fo:r|ɔrt] *m* suburb; **~zug** *m* commuter train.
**vorprogrammiert** ['fo:rprogrami:rt] *adj* (*Erfolg, Antwort*) automatic.

**Vorrang** ['fo:rraŋ] *m* precedence, priority.
**vorrangig** *adj* of prime importance, primary.
**Vorrat** ['fo:rra:t] *m* stock, supply; **solange der ~ reicht** (*COMM*) while stocks last.
**vorrätig** ['fo:rrɛ:tɪç] *adj* in stock.
**Vorratskammer** *f* store cupboard; (*für Lebensmittel*) larder.
**Vorraum** *m* anteroom; (*Büro*) outer office.
**vorrechnen** ['fo:rrɛçnən] *vt:* **jdm etw ~** to calculate sth for sb; (*als Kritik*) to point sth out to sb.
**Vorrecht** ['fo:rrɛçt] *nt* privilege.
**Vorrede** ['fo:rre:də] *f* introductory speech; (*THEAT*) prologue (*BRIT*), prolog (*US*).
**Vorrichtung** ['fo:rrɪçtʊŋ] *f* device, gadget.
**vorrücken** ['fo:rrʏkən] *vi* to advance ♦ *vt* to move forward.
**Vorruhestand** ['fo:rru:əʃtant] *m* early retirement.
**Vorrunde** ['fo:rrʊndə] *f* (*SPORT*) preliminary round.
**Vors.** *abk* = **Vorsitzende(r).**
**vorsagen** ['fo:rza:gən] *vt* to recite; (*SCH: zuflüstern*) to tell secretly, prompt.
**Vorsaison** ['fo:rzɛzõ:] *f* early season, low season.
**Vorsatz** ['fo:rzats] *m* intention; (*JUR*) intent; **einen ~ fassen** to make a resolution.
**vorsätzlich** ['fo:rzɛtslɪç] *adj* intentional; (*JUR*) premeditated ♦ *adv* intentionally.
**Vorschau** ['fo:rʃaʊ] *f* (*RUNDF, TV*) (programme (*BRIT*) *od* program (*US*)) preview; (*Film*) trailer.
**Vorschein** ['fo:rʃaɪn] *m:* **zum ~ kommen** (*lit: sichtbar werden*) to appear; (*fig: entdeckt werden*) to come to light.
**vorschieben** ['fo:rʃi:bən] *unreg vt* to push forward; (*vor etw*) to push across; (*fig*) to put forward as an excuse; **jdn ~** to use sb as a front.
**vorschießen** ['fo:rʃi:sən] *unreg* (*umg*) *vt:* **jdm Geld ~** to advance sb money.
**Vorschlag** ['fo:rʃla:k] *m* suggestion, proposal.
**vorschlagen** ['fo:rʃla:gən] *unreg vt* to suggest, propose.
**Vorschlaghammer** *m* sledgehammer.
**vorschnell** ['fo:rʃnɛl] *adj* hasty, too quick.
**vorschreiben** ['fo:rʃraɪbən] *unreg vt* (*Dosis*) to prescribe; (*befehlen*) to specify; (**jdm**) **etw ~** (*lit*) to write sth out (for sb); **ich lasse mir nichts ~** I won't be dictated to.
**Vorschrift** ['fo:rʃrɪft] *f* regulation(s *pl*), rule(s *pl*); (*Anweisungen*) instruction(s *pl*); **jdm ~en machen** to give sb orders; **Dienst nach ~** work-to-rule (*BRIT*), slowdown (*US*).
**vorschriftsmäßig** *adv* as per regulations/instructions.
**Vorschub** ['fo:rʃu:p] *m:* **jdm/einer Sache ~ leisten** to encourage sb/sth.
**Vorschule** ['fo:rʃu:lə] *f* nursery school.
**vorschulisch** ['fo:rʃu:lɪʃ] *adj* preschool *attr*.
**Vorschuß** ['fo:rʃʊs] *m* advance.

**vorschützen** ['foːrʃʏtsən] *vt* to put forward as a pretext; (*Unwissenheit*) to plead.

**vorschweben** ['foːrʃveːbən] *vi:* **jdm schwebt etw vor** sb has sth in mind.

**vorsehen** ['foːrzeːən] *unreg vt* to provide for; (*planen*) to plan ♦ *vr* to take care, be careful.

**Vorsehung** *f* providence.

**vorsetzen** ['foːrzɛtsən] *vt* to move forward; (*davorsetzen*): ~ **vor** +*akk* to put in front of; (*anbieten*): **jdm etw** ~ to offer sb sth.

**Vorsicht** ['foːrzɪçt] *f* caution, care; ~! look out!, take care!; (*auf Schildern*) caution!, danger!; ~, **Stufe!** mind the step!; **etw mit** ~ **genießen** (*umg*) to take sth with a pinch of salt.

**vorsichtig** *adj* cautious, careful.

**vorsichtshalber** *adv* just in case.

**Vorsichtsmaßnahme** *f* precaution.

**Vorsilbe** ['foːrzɪlbə] *f* prefix.

**vorsintflutlich** ['foːrzɪntfluːtlɪç] (*umg*) *adj* antiquated.

**Vorsitz** ['foːrzɪts] *m* chair(manship); **den** ~ **führen** to chair the meeting.

**Vorsitzende(r)** *f(m)* chairman/-woman, chair(person).

**Vorsorge** ['foːrzɔrgə] *f* precaution(s *pl*); (*Fürsorge*) provision(s *pl*).

**vorsorgen** *vi:* ~ **für** to make provision(s *pl*) for.

**Vorsorgeuntersuchung** ['foːrzɔrgə-|ʊntərzuːxʊŋ] *f* medical check-up.

**vorsorglich** ['foːrzɔrklɪç] *adv* as a precaution.

**Vorspann** ['foːrʃpan] *m* (*FILM, TV*) opening credits *pl*; (*PRESSE*) opening paragraph.

**vorspannen** *vt* (*Pferde*) to harness.

**Vorspeise** ['foːrʃpaɪzə] *f* hors d'œuvre, starter.

**Vorspiegelung** ['foːrʃpiːgəlʊŋ] *f:* **das ist (eine)** ~ **falscher Tatsachen** it's all sham.

**Vorspiel** ['foːrʃpiːl] *nt* prelude; (*bei Geschlechtsverkehr*) foreplay.

**vorspielen** *vt:* **jdm etw** ~ (*MUS*) to play sth to sb; (*THEAT*) to act sth to sb; (*fig*) to act out a sham of sth in front of sb.

**vorsprechen** ['foːrʃprɛçən] *unreg vt* to say out loud; (*vortragen*) to recite ♦ *vi* (*THEAT*) to audition; **bei jdm** ~ to call on sb.

**vorspringend** ['foːrʃprɪŋənt] *adj* projecting; (*Nase, Kinn*) prominent.

**Vorsprung** ['foːrʃprʊŋ] *m* projection; (*Fels*~) ledge; (*fig*) advantage, start.

**Vorstadt** ['foːrʃtat] *f* suburbs *pl*.

**Vorstand** ['foːrʃtant] *m* executive committee; (*COMM*) board (of directors); (*Person*) director; (*Leiter*) head.

**Vorstandssitzung** *f* (*von Firma*) board meeting.

**Vorstandsvorsitzende(r)** *f(m)* chairperson.

**vorstehen** ['foːrʃteːən] *unreg vi* to project; **einer Sache** *dat* ~ (*fig*) to be the head of sth.

**Vorsteher(in)** (-s, -) *m(f)* (*von Abteilung*) head; (*von Gefängnis*) governor; (*Bahnhofs*~)

stationmaster.

**vorstellbar** *adj* conceivable.

**vorstellen** ['foːrʃtɛlən] *vt* to put forward; (*vor etw*) to put in front; (*bekannt machen*) to introduce; (*darstellen*) to represent ♦ *vr* to introduce o.s.; (*bei Bewerbung*) to go for an interview; **sich** *dat* **etw** ~ to imagine sth; **stell dir das nicht so einfach vor** don't think it's so easy.

**Vorstellung** *f* (*Bekanntmachen*) introduction; (*THEAT etc*) performance; (*Gedanke*) idea, thought.

**Vorstellungsgespräch** *nt* interview.

**Vorstellungsvermögen** *nt* powers of imagination *pl*.

**Vorstoß** ['foːrʃtoːs] *m* advance; (*fig: Versuch*) attempt.

**vorstoßen** *unreg vt, vi* to push forward.

**Vorstrafe** ['foːrʃtraːfə] *f* previous conviction.

**vorstrecken** ['foːrʃtrɛkən] *vt* to stretch out; (*Geld*) to advance.

**Vorstufe** ['foːrʃtuːfə] *f* first step(s *pl*).

**Vortag** ['foːrtak] *m:* **am** ~ **einer Sache** *gen* on the day before sth.

**vortasten** ['foːrtastən] *vr:* **sich langsam zu etw** ~ to approach sth carefully.

**vortäuschen** ['foːrtɔʏʃən] *vt* to pretend, feign.

**Vortäuschung** *f:* **unter** ~ **falscher Tatsachen** under false pretences (*BRIT*) *od* pretenses (*US*).

**Vorteil** ['foːrtaɪl] (**-s, -e**) *m:* ~ (**gegenüber**) advantage (over); **im** ~ **sein** to have the advantage; **die Vor- und Nachteile** the pros and cons; **v~haft** *adj* advantageous; (*Kleider*) flattering; (*Geschäft*) lucrative.

**Vortr.** *abk* = **Vortrag**.

**Vortrag** ['foːrtraːk] (**-(e)s, Vorträge**) *m* talk, lecture; (~*sart*) delivery; (*von Gedicht*) rendering; (*COMM*) balance carried forward; **einen** ~ **halten** to give a lecture *od* talk.

**vortragen** ['foːrtraːgən] *unreg vt* to carry forward (*auch COMM*); (*fig*) to recite; (*Rede*) to deliver; (*Lied*) to perform; (*Meinung etc*) to express.

**Vortragsabend** *m* lecture evening; (*mit Musik*) recital; (*mit Gedichten*) poetry reading.

**Vortragsreihe** *f* series of lectures.

**vortrefflich** [foːr'trɛflɪç] *adj* excellent.

**vortreten** ['foːrtreːtən] *unreg vi* to step forward; (*Augen etc*) to protrude.

**Vortritt** ['foːrtrɪt] *m:* **jdm den** ~ **lassen** (*lit, fig*) to let sb go first.

**vorüber** [fo'ryːbər] *adv* past, over; ~**gehen** *unreg vi* to pass (by); ~**gehen an** +*dat* (*fig*) to pass over; ~**gehend** *adj* temporary, passing.

**Voruntersuchung** ['foːr|ʊntərzuːxʊŋ] *f* (*MED*) preliminary examination; (*JUR*) preliminary investigation.

**Vorurteil** ['foːr|ʊrtaɪl] *nt* prejudice.

**vorurteilsfrei** *adj* unprejudiced, open-minded.

**Vorverkauf** ['foːrfɛrkauf] *m* advance booking.

**Vorverkaufsstelle** *f* advance booking office.

**vorverlegen** ['foːrfɛrleːgən] *vt* (*Termin*) to bring forward.

**Vorw.** *abk* = **Vorwort**.

**vorwagen** ['foːrvaːgən] *vr* to venture forward.

**Vorwahl** ['foːrvaːl] *f* preliminary election; (*TEL*) dialling (*BRIT*) *od* area (*US*) code.

**Vorwand** ['foːrvant] (**-(e)s, Vorwände**) *m* pretext.

**Vorwarnung** ['foːrvarnʊŋ] *f* (advance) warning.

**vorwärts** ['foːrvɛrts] *adv* forward; ~! (*umg*) let's go!; (*MIL*) forward march!; **V~gang** *m* (*AUT etc*) forward gear; ~**gehen** *unreg vi* to progress; ~**kommen** *unreg vi* to get on, make progress.

**Vorwäsche** *f* prewash.

**Vorwaschgang** *m* prewash.

**vorweg** [foːr'vɛk] *adv* in advance; **V~nahme** (**-, -n**) *f* anticipation; ~**nehmen** *unreg vt* to anticipate.

**vorweisen** ['foːrvaɪzən] *unreg vt* to show, produce.

**vorwerfen** ['foːrvɛrfən] *unreg vt*: **jdm etw** ~ **to** reproach sb for sth, accuse sb of sth; **sich** *dat* **nichts vorzuwerfen haben** to have nothing to reproach o.s. with; **das wirft er mir heute noch vor** he still holds it against me; **Tieren/Gefangenen etw** ~ (*lit*) to throw sth down for the animals/prisoners.

**vorwiegend** ['foːrviːgənt] *adj* predominant ♦ *adv* predominantly.

**vorwitzig** *adj* saucy, cheeky.

**Vorwort** ['foːrvɔrt] (**-(e)s, -e**) *nt* preface.

**Vorwurf** ['foːrvʊrf] (**-(e)s, ¨e**) *m* reproach; **jdm/sich Vorwürfe machen** to reproach sb/o.s.

**vorwurfsvoll** *adj* reproachful.

**Vorzeichen** ['foːrtsaɪçən] *nt* (*Omen*) omen; (*MED*) early symptom; (*MATH*) sign.

**vorzeigen** ['foːrtsaɪgən] *vt* to show, produce.

**Vorzeit** ['foːrtsaɪt] *f* prehistoric times *pl*.

**vorzeitig** *adj* premature.

**vorziehen** ['foːrtsiːən] *unreg vt* to pull forward; (*Gardinen*) to draw; (*zuerst behandeln, abfertigen*) to give priority to; (*lieber haben*) to prefer.

**Vorzimmer** ['foːrtsɪmər] *nt* anteroom; (*Büro*) outer office.

**Vorzug** ['foːrtsuːk] *m* preference; (*gute Eigenschaft*) merit, good quality; (*Vorteil*) advantage; (*EISENB*) relief train; **einer Sache** *dat* **den** ~ **geben** (*form*) to prefer sth; (*Vorrang geben*) to give sth precedence.

**vorzüglich** [foːr'tsyːklɪç] *adj* excellent, first-rate.

**Vorzugsaktien** *pl* preference shares (*BRIT*), preferred stock (*US*).

**vorzugsweise** *adv* preferably; (*hauptsächlich*) chiefly.

**Votum** ['voːtʊm] (**-s, Voten**) *nt* vote.

**Voyeur** [voa'jøːr] (**-s, -e**) *m* voyeur.

**Voyeurismus** [voajøˈrɪsmʊs] *m* voyeurism.

**v.T.** *abk* (= *vom Tausend*) per thousand.

**vulgär** [vʊlˈgɛːr] *adj* vulgar.

**Vulkan** [vʊlˈkaːn] (**-s, -e**) *m* volcano; ~**ausbruch** *m* volcanic eruption.

**vulkanisieren** [vʊlkaniˈziːrən] *vt* to vulcanize.

**v.u.Z.** *abk* (= *vor unserer Zeitrechnung*) B.C.

# $W, w$

**W, w** [veː] *nt* W, w; ~ **wie Wilhelm** ≈ W for William.

**W.** *abk* (= *West(en)*) W.

**w.** *abk* = **wenden; werktags; westlich;** (= *weiblich*) f.

**Waage** ['vaːgə] (**-, -n**) *f* scales *pl*; (*ASTROL*) Libra; **sich** *dat* **die** ~ **halten** (*fig*) to balance one another; **w~recht** *adj* horizontal.

**Waagschale** *f* (scale) pan; (**schwer**) **in die** ~ **fallen** (*fig*) to carry weight.

**wabb(e)lig** ['vab(ə)lɪç] *adj* wobbly.

**Wabe** ['vaːbə] (**-, -n**) *f* honeycomb.

**wach** [vax] *adj* awake; (*fig*) alert; ~ **werden** to wake up.

**Wachablösung** *f* changing of the guard; (*Mensch*) relief guard; (*fig: Regierungswechsel*) change of government.

**Wache** (**-, -n**) *f* guard, watch; ~ **halten** to keep watch; ~ **stehen** *od* **schieben** (*umg*) to be on guard (duty).

**wachen** *vi* to be awake; (*Wache halten*) to keep watch; **bei jdm** ~ to sit up with sb.

**wachhabend** *adj attrib* duty.

**Wachhund** *m* watchdog, guard dog; (*fig*) watchdog.

**Wacholder** [vaˈxɔldər] (**-s, -**) *m* juniper.

**wachrütteln** ['vaxrʏtəln] *vt* (*fig*) to (a)rouse.

**Wachs** [vaks] (**-es, -e**) *nt* wax.

**wachsam** ['vaxzaːm] *adj* watchful, vigilant, alert; **W~keit** *f* vigilance.

**wachsen¹** *unreg vi* to grow.

**wachsen²** *vt* (*Skier*) to wax.

**Wachsfigurenkabinett** *nt* waxworks (exhibition).

**Wachs(mal)stift** *m* wax crayon.

**wächst** [vɛkst] *vb siehe* **wachsen¹**.

**Wachstuch** ['vakstuːx] *nt* oilcloth.

**Wachstum** ['vakstuːm] (**-s**) *nt* growth.

**Wachstums-** *zW:* ~**branche** *f* growth industry; ~**grenze** *f* limits of growth; **w~hemmend** *adj* growth-inhibiting; ~**rate** *f* growth rate; ~**schmerzen** *pl* growing pains; ~**störung** *f* disturbance of growth.

**Wachtel** ['vaxtəl] (**-, -n**) *f* quail.
**Wächter** ['vɛçtər] (**-s, -**) *m* guard; (*Park*~) warden, keeper; (*Museums~, Parkplatz*~) attendant.
**Wachtmeister** *m* officer.
**Wachtposten** *m* guard, sentry.
**Wach(t)turm** *m* watchtower.
**Wach- und Schließgesellschaft** *f* security corps.
**wack(e)lig** *adj* shaky, wobbly; **auf ~en Beinen stehen** to be wobbly on one's legs; (*fig*) to be unsteady.
**Wackelkontakt** *m* loose connection.
**wackeln** *vi* to shake; (*fig: Position*) to be shaky; **mit den Hüften/Schwanz ~** to wiggle one's hips/wag its tail.
**wacker** ['vakər] *adj* valiant, stout; **sich ~ schlagen** (*umg*) to put up a brave fight.
**Wade** ['vaːdə] (**-, -n**) *f* (*ANAT*) calf.
**Waffe** ['vafə] (**-, -n**) *f* weapon; **jdn mit seinen eigenen ~n schlagen** (*fig*) to beat sb at his own game.
**Waffel** ['vafəl] (**-, -n**) *f* waffle; (*Eis*~) wafer.
**Waffen-** *zW:* ~**gewalt** *f:* **mit ~gewalt** by force of arms; ~**lager** *nt* (*von Armee*) ordnance depot; (*von Terroristen*) cache; ~**schein** *m* firearms *od* gun licence (*BRIT*), firearms license (*US*); ~**schmuggel** *m* gunrunning, arms smuggling; ~**stillstand** *m* armistice, truce.
**Wagemut** ['vaːgəmuːt] *m* daring.
**Wagen** ['vaːgən] (**-s, -**) *m* vehicle; (*Auto*) car, automobile (*US*); (*EISENB*) car, carriage (*BRIT*); (*Pferde*~) wag(g)on, cart.
**wagen** *vt* to venture, dare.
**Wagen-** *zW:* ~**führer** *m* driver; ~**heber** (**-s, -**) *m* jack; ~**park** *m* fleet of cars; ~**rückholtaste** *f* (*Schreibmaschine*) carriage return (key); ~**rücklauf** *m* carriage return.
**Waggon** [va'gõː] (**-s, -s**) *m* wag(g)on; (*Güter*~) goods van (*BRIT*), freight truck (*US*).
**waghalsig** ['vaːkhalzɪç] *adj* foolhardy.
**Wagnis** ['vaːknɪs] (**-ses, -se**) *nt* risk.
**Wahl** [vaːl] (**-, -en**) *f* choice; (*POL*) election; **erste ~** (*Qualität*) top quality; (*Gemüse, Eier*) grade one; **zweite ~** (*COMM*) seconds *pl*; **aus freier ~** of one's own free choice; **wer die ~ hat, hat die Qual** (*Sprichwort*) he is *od* you are *etc* spoilt for choice; **die ~ fiel auf ihn** he was chosen; **sich zur ~ stellen** (*POL etc*) to stand (*BRIT*) *od* run (for parliament *etc*).
**wählbar** *adj* eligible.
**Wahl-** *zW:* **w~berechtigt** *adj* entitled to vote; ~**beteiligung** *f* poll, turnout; ~**bezirk** *m* (*POL*) ward.
**wählen** ['vɛːlən] *vt* to choose; (*POL*) to elect, vote for; (*TEL*) to dial ♦ *vi* to choose; (*POL*) to vote; (*TEL*) to dial.
**Wähler(in)** (**-s, -**) *m(f)* voter; ~**abwanderung** *f* voter drift; **w~isch** *adj* fastidious, particular; ~**schaft** *f* electorate.
**Wahl-** *zW:* ~**fach** *nt* optional subject; **w~frei**

*adj:* **w~freier Zugriff** (*COMPUT*) random access; ~**gang** *m* ballot; ~**geschenk** *nt* pre-election vote-catching gimmick; ~**heimat** *f* country of adoption; ~**helfer** *m* (*im ~kampf*) election assistant; (*bei der ~*) polling officer; ~**kabine** *f* polling booth; ~**kampf** *m* election campaign; ~**kreis** *m* constituency; ~**leiter** *m* returning officer; ~**liste** *f* electoral register; ~**lokal** *nt* polling station; **w~los** *adv* at random; (*nicht wählerisch*) indiscriminately; ~**recht** *nt* franchise; **allgemeines ~recht** universal franchise; **das aktive ~recht** the right to vote; **das passive ~recht** eligibility (for political office); ~**spruch** *m* motto; ~**urne** *f* ballot box; **w~weise** *adv* alternatively.
**Wählzeichen** *nt* (*TEL*) dialling tone (*BRIT*), dial tone (*US*).
**Wahn** [vaːn] (**-(e)s**) *m* delusion; ~**sinn** *m* madness; **w~sinnig** *adj* insane, mad ♦ *adv* (*umg*) incredibly; **w~witzig** *adj* crazy *attrib* ♦ *adv* terribly.
**wahr** [vaːr] *adj* true; **da ist (et)was W~es dran** there's some truth in that.
**wahren** *vt* to maintain, keep.
**währen** ['vɛːrən] *vi* to last.
**während** *präp +gen* during ♦ *konj* while; ~**dessen** *adv* meanwhile.
**wahr-** *zW:* ~**haben** *unreg vt:* **etw nicht ~haben wollen** to refuse to admit sth; ~**haft** *adv* (*tatsächlich*) truly; ~**haftig** *adj* true, real ♦ *adv* really.
**Wahrheit** *f* truth; **die ~ sagen** to tell the truth.
**wahrheitsgetreu** *adj* (*Bericht*) truthful; (*Darstellung*) faithful.
**wahrnehmen** *unreg vt* to perceive; (*Frist*) to observe; (*Veränderungen etc*) to be aware of; (*Gelegenheit*) to take; (*Interessen, Rechte*) to look after.
**Wahrnehmung** *f* perception; observing; awareness; taking; looking after.
**wahrsagen** *vi* to predict the future, tell fortunes.
**Wahrsager** *m* fortune-teller.
**wahrscheinlich** [vaːr'ʃaɪnlɪç] *adj* probable ♦ *adv* probably; **W~keit** *f* probability; **aller W~keit nach** in all probability.
**Währung** ['vɛːrʊŋ] *f* currency.
**Währungs-** *zW:* ~**einheit** *f* monetary unit; ~**politik** *f* monetary policy; ~**reserven** *pl* official reserves *pl*; ~**union** *f* monetary union.
**Wahrzeichen** *nt* (*Gebäude, Turm etc*) symbol; (*von Stadt, Verein*) emblem.
**Waise** ['vaɪzə] (**-, -n**) *f* orphan.
**Waisen-** *zW:* ~**haus** *nt* orphanage; ~**kind** *nt* orphan; ~**knabe** *m:* **gegen dich ist er ein ~knabe** (*umg*) he's no match for you; ~**rente** *f* orphan's allowance.
**Wal** [vaːl] (**-(e)s, -e**) *m* whale.
**Wald** [valt] (**-(e)s, -̈er**) *m* wood(s *pl*); (*groß*)

forest; ~**brand** m forest fire.
**Wäldchen** ['vɛltçən] nt copse, grove.
**Waldhorn** nt (MUS) French horn.
**waldig** ['valdıç] adj wooded.
**Wald-** zW: ~**lehrpfad** m nature trail; ~**meister** m (BOT) woodruff; ~**sterben** nt loss of trees due to pollution.
**Wald- und Wiesen-** (umg) in zW common-or-garden.
**Waldweg** m woodland od forest path.
**Wales** [weılz] nt Wales.
**Walfang** ['va:lfaŋ] m whaling.
**Walfisch** ['valfıʃ] m whale.
**Waliser(in)** [va'li:zər(ın)] (-s, -) m(f) Welshman, Welshwoman.
**walisisch** adj Welsh.
**Walkman** ® ['wɔ:kman] (-s, Walkmen) m Walkman ®, personal stereo.
**Wall** [val] (-(e)s, ⁻e) m embankment; (Bollwerk) rampart.
**wallfahren** vi untr to go on a pilgrimage.
**Wallfahrer(in)** m(f) pilgrim.
**Wallfahrt** f pilgrimage.
**Wallis** ['valıs] (-) nt: das ~ Valais.
**Wallone** [va'lo:nə] (-n, -n) m, **Wallonin** f Walloon.
**Walnuß** ['valnʊs] f walnut.
**Walroß** ['valrɔs] nt walrus.
**walten** ['valtən] vi (geh): **Vernunft** ~ **lassen** to let reason prevail.
**Walzblech** (-(e)s) nt sheet metal.
**Walze** ['valtsə] (-, -n) f (Gerät) cylinder; (Fahrzeug) roller.
**walzen** vt to roll (out).
**wälzen** ['vɛltsən] vt to roll (over); (Bücher) to hunt through; (Probleme) to deliberate on ♦ vr to wallow; (vor Schmerzen) to roll about; (im Bett) to toss and turn.
**Walzer** ['valtsər] (-s, -) m waltz.
**Wälzer** ['vɛltsər] (-s, -) (umg) m tome.
**Wampe** ['vampə] (-, -n) (umg) f paunch.
**Wand** (-, ⁻e) f wall; (Trenn~) partition; (Berg~) precipice; (Fels~) (rock) face; (fig) barrier; **weiß wie die** ~ as white as a sheet; **jdn an die** ~ **spielen** to put sb in the shade; (SPORT) to outplay sb.
**wand** etc [vant] vb siehe **winden**.
**Wandel** ['vandəl] (-s) m change; **w~bar** adj changeable, variable.
**Wandelhalle** f foyer.
**wandeln** vt, vr to change ♦ vi (gehen) to walk.
**Wanderausstellung** f touring exhibition.
**Wanderbühne** f touring theatre (BRIT) od theater (US).
**Wanderer** (-s, -) m hiker, rambler.
**Wanderin** f hiker, rambler.
**Wanderkarte** f hiker's map.
**Wanderlied** nt hiking song.
**wandern** vi to hike; (Blick) to wander; (Gedanken) to stray; (umg: in den Papierkorb etc) to land.
**Wanderpreis** m challenge trophy.

**Wanderschaft** f travelling (BRIT), traveling (US).
**Wanderung** f walk, hike; (von Tieren, Völkern) migration.
**Wanderweg** m trail, (foot)path.
**Wandgemälde** nt mural.
**Wandlung** f change; (völlige Um~) transformation; (REL) transubstantiation.
**Wand-** zW: ~**malerei** f mural painting; ~**schirm** m (folding) screen; ~**schrank** m cupboard.
**wandte** etc ['vantə] vb siehe **wenden**.
**Wandteppich** m tapestry.
**Wandverkleidung** f panelling.
**Wange** ['vaŋə] (-, -n) f cheek.
**wankelmütig** ['vaŋkəlmy:tıç] adj fickle, inconstant.
**wanken** ['vankən] vi to stagger; (fig) to waver.
**wann** [van] adv when; **seit** ~ **bist/hast du ...?** how long have you been/have you had ...?
**Wanne** ['vanə] (-, -n) f tub.
**Wanze** ['vantsə] (-, -n) f (ZOOL, Abhörgerät) bug.
**Wappen** ['vapən] (-s, -) nt coat of arms, crest; ~**kunde** f heraldry.
**wappnen** vr (fig) to prepare o.s.; **gewappnet sein** to be forearmed.
**war** etc [va:r] vb siehe **sein**.
**warb** etc [varp] vb siehe **werben**.
**Ware** ['va:rə] (-, -n) f ware; **Waren** pl goods pl.
**wäre** etc ['vɛ:rə] vb siehe **sein**.
**Waren-** zW: ~**bestand** m stock; ~**haus** nt department store; ~**lager** nt stock, store; ~**muster** nt sample; ~**probe** f sample; ~**rückstände** pl backlog sing; ~**sendung** f trade sample (sent by post); ~**zeichen** nt trademark.
**warf** etc [varf] vb siehe **werfen**.
**warm** [varm] adj warm; (Essen) hot; (umg: homosexuell) queer; **mir ist** ~ I'm warm; **mit jdm** ~ **werden** (umg) to get close to sb.
**Wärme** ['vɛrmə] (-, -n) f warmth; **10 Grad** ~ 10 degrees above zero.
**wärmen** vt, vr to warm (up), heat (up).
**Wärmflasche** f hot-water bottle.
**warm-** zW: **W~front** f (MET) warm front; ~**halten** unreg vt: **sich** dat **jdn** ~**halten** (fig) to keep in with sb; ~**herzig** adj warm-hearted; ~**laufen** unreg vi (AUT) to warm up; **W~wassertank** m hot-water tank.
**Warnblinkanlage** f (AUT) hazard warning lights pl.
**Warndreieck** nt warning triangle.
**warnen** ['varnən] vt to warn.
**Warnstreik** m token strike.
**Warnung** f warning.
**Warschau** ['varʃaʊ] (-s) nt Warsaw; ~**er Pakt** m Warsaw Pact.
**Warte** (-, -n) f observation point; (fig) viewpoint.
**warten** ['vartən] vi to wait ♦ vt (Auto, Maschine) to service; ~ **auf** +akk to wait for;

**auf sich ~ lassen** to take a long time; **warte mal!** wait a minute!; (*überlegend*) let me see; **mit dem Essen auf jdn ~** to wait for sb before eating.

**Wärter(in)** ['vɛrtər(ɪn)] **(-s, -)** *m(f)* attendant.

**Wartesaal** *m* (*EISENB*) waiting room.

**Wartezimmer** *nt* (*bes beim Arzt*) waiting room.

**Wartung** *f* (*von Auto, Maschine*) servicing; **~ und Instandhaltung** maintenance.

**warum** [va'rʊm] *adv* why; **~ nicht gleich so!** that's better.

**Warze** ['vartsə] **(-, -n)** *f* wart.

**was** [vas] *pron* what; (*umg: etwas*) something; **das, ~** ... that which ...; **~ für** ...? what sort *od* kind of ...?

**Wasch-** *zW*: **~anlage** *f* (*für Autos*) car wash; **w~bar** *adj* washable; **~becken** *nt* washbasin.

**Wäsche** ['vɛʃə] **(-, -n)** *f* wash(ing); (*Bett~*) linen; (*Unter~*) underwear; **dumm aus der ~ gucken** (*umg*) to look stupid.

**waschecht** *adj* (*Farbe*) fast; (*fig*) genuine.

**Wäsche-** *zW*: **~klammer** *f* clothes peg (*BRIT*), clothespin (*US*); **~korb** *m* dirty clothes basket; **~leine** *f* washing line (*BRIT*), clothes line (*US*).

**waschen** ['vaʃən] *unreg vt, vi* to wash ♦ *vr* to (have a) wash; **sich** *dat* **die Hände ~** to wash one's hands; **~ und legen** (*Haare*) to shampoo and set.

**Wäscherei** [vɛʃə'raɪ] *f* laundry.

**Wäscheschleuder** *f* spin-dryer.

**Wasch-** *zW*: **~gang** *m* stage of the washing programme (*BRIT*) *od* program (*US*); **~küche** *f* laundry room; **~lappen** *m* face cloth *od* flannel (*BRIT*), washcloth (*US*); (*umg*) softy; **~maschine** *f* washing machine; **w~maschinenfest** *adj* machine-washable; **~mittel** *nt* detergent; **~pulver** *nt* washing powder; **~salon** *m* Launderette ® (*BRIT*), Laundromat ® (*US*).

**wäscht** [vɛʃt] *vb siehe* **waschen**.

**Waschtisch** *m* washstand.

**Washington** ['wɔʃɪŋtən] **(-s)** *nt* Washington.

**Wasser¹** ['vasər] **(-s, -)** *nt* water; **dort wird auch nur mit ~ gekocht** (*fig*) they're no different from anybody else (there); **ins ~ fallen** (*fig*) to fall through; **mit allen ~n gewaschen sein** (*umg*) to be a shrewd customer; **~ lassen** (*euph*) to pass water; **jdm das ~ abgraben** (*fig*) to take the bread from sb's mouth, take away sb's livelihood.

**Wasser²** **(-s, ⁼)** *nt* (*Flüssigkeit*) water; (*MED*) lotion; (*Parfüm*) cologne; (*Mineral~*) mineral water.

**wasserabstoßend** *adj* water-repellent.

**Wässerchen** *nt: er sieht aus, als ob er kein ~ trüben könnte* he looks as if butter wouldn't melt in his mouth.

**Wasser-** *zW*: **w~dicht** *adj* watertight; (*Stoff, Uhr*) waterproof; **~fall** *m* waterfall; **~farbe** *f* watercolour (*BRIT*), watercolor (*US*);

**w~gekühlt** *adj* (*AUT*) water-cooled; **~graben** *m* (*SPORT*) water jump; (*um Burg*) moat; **~hahn** *m* tap, faucet (*US*).

**wässerig** ['vɛsərɪç] *adj* watery.

**Wasser-** *zW*: **~kessel** *m* kettle; (*TECH*) boiler; **~kraftwerk** *nt* hydroelectric power station; **~leitung** *f* water pipe; (*Anlagen*) plumbing; **~mann** *m* (*ASTROL*) Aquarius.

**wassern** *vi* to land on the water.

**wässern** ['vɛsərn] *vt, vi* to water.

**Wasser-** *zW*: **~scheide** *f* watershed; **w~scheu** *adj* afraid of water; **~schutzpolizei** *f* (*auf Flüssen*) river police; (*im Hafen*) harbour (*BRIT*) *od* harbor (*US*) police; (*auf der See*) coastguard service; **~ski** *nt* water-skiing; **~spiegel** *m* (*Oberfläche*) surface of the water; (*~stand*) water level; **~stand** *m* water level; **~stoff** *m* hydrogen; **~stoffbombe** *f* hydrogen bomb; **~verbrauch** *m* water consumption; **~waage** *f* spirit level; **~welle** *f* shampoo and set; **~werfer** **(-s, -)** *m* water cannon; **~werk** *nt* waterworks; **~zeichen** *nt* watermark.

**waten** ['va:tən] *vi* to wade.

**watscheln** ['va:tʃəln] *vi* to waddle.

**Watt¹** [vat] **(-(e)s, -en)** *nt* mud flats *pl*.

**Watt²** **(-s, -)** *nt* (*ELEK*) watt.

**Watte** **(-, -n)** *f* cotton wool (*BRIT*), absorbent cotton (*US*).

**Wattenmeer** **(-(e)s)** *nt* mud flats *pl*.

**Wattestäbchen** *nt* cotton(-wool) swab.

**wattieren** [va'ti:rən] *vt* to pad.

**WC** [ve:'tse:] **(-s, -s)** *nt abk* (= *Wasserklosett*) WC.

**WDR** **(-)** *m abk* (= *Westdeutscher Rundfunk*) *West German Radio*.

**weben** ['ve:bən] *unreg vt* to weave.

**Weber(in)** **(-s, -)** *m(f)* weaver.

**Weberei** [ve:bə'raɪ] *f* (*Betrieb*) weaving mill.

**Webstuhl** ['ve:pʃtu:l] *m* loom.

**Wechsel** ['vɛksəl] **(-s, -)** *m* change; (*Geld~*) exchange; (*COMM*) bill of exchange; **~bäder** *pl* alternating hot and cold baths *pl*; **~beziehung** *f* correlation; **~forderungen** *pl* (*COMM*) bills receivable *pl*; **~geld** *nt* change; **w~haft** *adj* (*Wetter*) variable; **~inhaber** *m* bearer; **~jahre** *pl* change of life, menopause; **in die ~jahre kommen** to start the change; **~kurs** *m* rate of exchange; **~kursmechanismus** *m* Exchange Rate Mechanism, ERM.

**wechseln** *vt* to change; (*Blicke*) to exchange ♦ *vi* to change; (*einander ablösen*) to alternate.

**wechselnd** *adj* changing; (*Stimmungen*) changeable; (*Winde, Bewölkung*) variable.

**Wechsel-** *zW*: **w~seitig** *adj* reciprocal; **~sprechanlage** *f* two-way intercom; **~strom** *m* alternating current; **~stube** *f* currency exchange, bureau de change; **~verbindlichkeiten** *pl* bills payable *pl*; **w~weise** *adv* alternately; **~wirkung** *f* interaction.

**wecken** ['vɛkən] vt to wake (up); (fig) to arouse; (Bedarf) to create; (Erinnerungen) to revive.

**Wecker** (-s, -) m alarm clock; **jdm auf den ~ fallen** (umg) to get on sb's nerves.

**Weckglas** ® nt preserving jar.

**Weckruf** m (TEL) alarm call.

**wedeln** ['ve:dəln] vi (mit Schwanz) to wag; (mit Fächer) to fan; (SKI) to wedel.

**weder** ['ve:dər] konj neither; **~ ... noch ...** neither ... nor ...

**Weg** [ve:k] (-(e)s, -e) m way; (Pfad) path; (Route) route; **sich auf den ~ machen** to be on one's way; **jdm aus dem ~ gehen** to keep out of sb's way; **jdm nicht über den ~ trauen** (fig) not to trust sb an inch; **den ~ des geringsten Widerstandes gehen** to follow the line of least resistance; **etw in die ~e leiten** to arrange sth; **jdm Steine in den ~ legen** (fig) to put obstacles in sb's way.

**weg** [vɛk] adv away, off; **über etw** akk **~ sein** to be over sth; **er war schon ~** he had already left; **nichts wie** od **nur ~ von hier!** let's get out of here!; **~ damit!** (mit Schere etc) put it/them away!; **Finger ~!** hands off!

**Wegbereiter** (-s, -) m pioneer.

**wegblasen** unreg vt to blow away; **wie weggeblasen sein** (fig) to have vanished.

**wegbleiben** unreg vi to stay away; **mir bleibt die Spucke weg!** (umg) I am absolutely flabbergasted!

**wegen** ['ve:gən] präp +gen od (umg) +dat because of; **von ~!** you must be joking!

**weg-** zW: **~fahren** unreg vi to drive away; (abfahren) to leave; **~fallen** unreg vi to be left out; (Ferien, Bezahlung) to be cancelled; (aufhören) to cease; **~gehen** unreg vi to go away, leave; (umg: Ware) to sell; **~hören** vi to turn a deaf ear; **~jagen** vt to chase away; **~kommen** unreg vi: **(bei etw) gut/schlecht ~kommen** (umg) to come off well/badly (with sth); **~lassen** unreg vt to leave out; **~laufen** unreg vi to run away od off; **das läuft (dir) nicht ~!** (fig hum) that can wait; **~legen** vt to put aside; **~machen** (umg) vt to get rid of; **~müssen** unreg (umg) vi to have to go; **~nehmen** unreg vt to take away.

**Wegrand** ['ve:krant] m wayside.

**weg-** zW: **~räumen** vt to clear away; **~schaffen** vt to clear away; **~schließen** unreg vt to lock away; **~schnappen** vt: **(jdm) etw ~schnappen** to snatch sth away (from sb); **~stecken** vt to put away; (umg: verkraften) to cope with; **~treten** unreg vi (MIL): **~treten!** dismiss!; **geistig ~getreten sein** (umg: geistesabwesend) to be away with the fairies; **~tun** unreg vt to put away.

**wegweisend** ['ve:gvaɪzənt] adj pioneering attrib, revolutionary.

**Wegweiser** ['ve:gvaɪzər] (-s, -) m road sign,

signpost; (fig: Buch etc) guide.

**Wegwerf-** ['vɛkvɛrf] in zW disposable.

**weg-** zW: **~werfen** unreg vt to throw away; **~werfend** adj disparaging; **W~werfgesellschaft** f throw-away society; **~wollen** unreg vi (verreisen) to want to go away; **~ziehen** unreg vi to move away.

**weh** [ve:] adj sore; **~ tun** to hurt, be sore; **jdm/sich ~ tun** to hurt sb/o.s.

**Wehe** ['ve:ə] (-, -n) f drift.

**wehe** interj: **~, wenn du ...** you'll regret it if you ...; **~ dir!** you dare!

**Wehen** pl (MED) contractions pl; **in den ~ liegen** to be in labour (BRIT) od labor (US).

**wehen** vt, vi to blow; (Fahnen) to flutter.

**weh-** zW: **~klagen** vi untr to wail; **~leidig** adj oversensitive to pain; (jammernd) whiny, whining; **W~mut** f melancholy; **~mütig** adj melancholy.

**Wehr¹** [ve:r] (-(e)s, -e) nt weir.

**Wehr²** [ve:r] (-, -en) f (Feuer~) fire brigade (BRIT) od department (US) ♦ in zW defence (BRIT), defense (US); **sich zur ~ setzen** to defend o.s.

**Wehrdienst** m military service.

---

**Wehrdienst** is military service which is still compulsory in Germany. All young men receive their call-up papers at 18 and all who are pronounced physically fit are required to spend ten months in the **Bundeswehr**. Conscientious objectors are allowed to do **Zivildienst** as an alternative, on attending a hearing and presenting their case.

---

**Wehrdienstverweigerer** m ≈ conscientious objector.

**wehren** vr to defend o.s.

**Wehr-** zW: **w~los** adj defenceless (BRIT), defenseless (US); **jdm w~los ausgeliefert sein** to be at sb's mercy; **~macht** f armed forces pl; **~pflicht** f conscription; **w~pflichtig** adj liable for military service; **~übung** f reserve duty training exercise.

**Wehwehchen** (umg) nt (minor) complaint.

**Weib** [vaɪp] (-(e)s, -er) nt woman, female (pej).

**Weibchen** nt (Ehefrau) little woman; (ZOOL) female.

**weibisch** ['vaɪbɪʃ] adj effeminate.

**weiblich** adj feminine.

**weich** [vaɪç] adj soft; (Ei) soft-boiled; **~e Währung** soft currency.

**Weiche** (-, -n) f (EISENB) points pl; **die ~n stellen** (lit) to switch the points; (fig) to set the course.

**weichen** unreg vi to yield, give way; **(nicht) von jdm** od **von jds Seite ~** (not) to leave sb's side.

**Weichensteller** (-s, -) m pointsman.

**weich-** zW: **W~heit** f softness; **W~käse** m soft cheese; **~lich** adj soft, namby-pamby; **W~ling** m wimp; **W~spüler** (-s, -) m fabric conditioner; **W~teile** *pl* soft parts *pl*; **W~tier** *nt* mollusc (*BRIT*), mollusk (*US*).

**Weide** ['vaɪdə] (-, -n) *f* (*Baum*) willow; (*Gras*) pasture.

**weiden** *vi* to graze ♦ *vr*: **sich an etw** *dat* ~ to delight in sth.

**Weidenkätzchen** *nt* willow catkin.

**weidlich** ['vaɪtlɪç] *adv* thoroughly.

**weigern** ['vaɪgərn] *vr* to refuse.

**Weigerung** ['vaɪgəruŋ] *f* refusal.

**Weihe** ['vaɪə] (-, -n) *f* consecration; (*Priester~*) ordination.

**weihen** *vt* to consecrate; (*widmen*) to dedicate; **dem Untergang geweiht** (*liter*) doomed.

**Weiher** (-s, -) *m* pond.

**Weihnachten** (-) *nt* Christmas; **fröhliche ~!** happy *od* merry Christmas!; **w~** *vi unpers*: **es weihnachtet sehr** (*poetisch, ironisch*) Christmas is very much in evidence.

**weihnachtlich** *adj* Christmas(sy).

**Weihnachts-** *zW*: **~abend** *m* Christmas Eve; **~baum** *m* Christmas tree; **~geld** *nt* Christmas bonus; **~geschenk** *nt* Christmas present; **~lied** *nt* Christmas carol; **~mann** *m* Father Christmas (*BRIT*), Santa Claus.

**Weihnachtsmarkt** *m* Christmas fair.

---

*The* **Weihnachtsmarkt** *is a market held in most large towns in Germany in the weeks prior to Christmas. People visit it to buy presents, toys and Christmas decorations, and to enjoy the festive atmosphere. Food and drink associated with the Christmas festivities can also be eaten and drunk there, for example, gingerbread and mulled wine.*

---

**Weihnachtstag** *m*: (**erster**) ~ Christmas day; **zweiter** ~ Boxing Day (*BRIT*).

**Weihrauch** *m* incense.

**Weihwasser** *nt* holy water.

**weil** [vaɪl] *konj* because.

**Weile** ['vaɪlə] (-) *f* while, short time.

**Weiler** ['vaɪlər] (-s, -) *m* hamlet.

**Weimarer Republik** ['vaɪmarər repu'bliːk] *f* Weimar Republic.

**Wein** [vaɪn] (-(e)s, -e) *m* wine; (*Pflanze*) vine; **jdm reinen ~ einschenken** (*fig*) to tell sb the truth; **~bau** *m* cultivation of vines; **~bauer** *m* wine-grower; **~beere** *f* grape; **~berg** *m* vineyard; **~bergschnecke** *f* snail; **~brand** *m* brandy.

**weinen** *vt*, *vi* to cry; **das ist zum W~** it's enough to make you cry *od* weep.

**weinerlich** *adj* tearful.

**Wein-** *zW*: **~gegend** *f* wine-growing area; **~geist** *m* (ethyl) alcohol; **~glas** *nt* wine glass; **~gut** *nt* wine-growing estate; **~karte** *f* wine list.

**Weinkrampf** *m* crying fit.

**Wein-** *zW*: **~lese** *f* vintage; **~probe** *f* wine tasting; **~rebe** *f* vine; **w~rot** *adj* (*Farbe*)

claret; **w~selig** *adj* merry with wine; **~stein** *m* tartar; **~stock** *m* vine; **~stube** *f* wine bar; **~traube** *f* grape.

**weise** ['vaɪzə] *adj* wise.

**Weise** (-, -n) *f* manner, way; (*Lied*) tune; **auf diese ~** in this way.

**Weise(r)** *f(m)* wise man, wise woman, sage.

**weisen** *unreg vt* to show; **etw (weit) von sich ~** (*fig*) to reject sth (emphatically).

**Weisheit** ['vaɪshaɪt] *f* wisdom.

**Weisheitszahn** *m* wisdom tooth.

**weismachen** ['vaɪsmaxən] *vt*: **er wollte uns ~ daß ...** he would have us believe that ...

**weiß¹** [vaɪs] *vb siehe* **wissen**.

**weiß²** *adj* white; **W~blech** *nt* tin plate; **W~brot** *nt* white bread; **~en** *vt* to whitewash; **W~glut** *f* (*TECH*) incandescence; **jdn zur W~glut bringen** (*fig*) to make sb see red; **W~kohl** *m* (white) cabbage.

**Weißrußland** *nt* B(y)elorussia.

**weißt** [vaɪst] *vb siehe* **wissen**.

**Weiß-** *zW*: **~waren** *pl* linen *sing*; **~wein** *m* white wine; **~wurst** *f* veal sausage.

**Weisung** ['vaɪzuŋ] *f* instruction.

**weit** [vaɪt] *adj* wide; (*Begriff*) broad; (*Reise, Wurf*) long ♦ *adv* far; **in ~er Ferne** in the far distance; **wie ~ ist es ...?** how far is it ...?; **das geht zu ~** that's going too far; **~ und breit** for miles around; **~ gefehlt!** far from it; **es so ~ bringen, daß ...** to bring it about that ...; **~ zurückliegen** to be far behind; **von ~em** from a long way off; **~ab** *adv*: **~ab von** far (away) from; **~aus** *adv* by far; **W~blick** *m* (*fig*) far-sightedness; **~blickend** *adj* far-seeing.

**Weite** (-, -n) *f* width; (*Raum*) space; (*von Entfernung*) distance.

**weiten** *vt*, *vr* to widen.

**weiter** ['vaɪtər] *adj* wider; (*zusätzlich*) further ♦ *adv* further; **wenn es ~ nichts ist ...** well, if that's all (it is), ...; **das hat ~ nichts zu sagen** that doesn't really matter; **immer ~** on and on; (*Anweisung*) keep on (going); **~ nichts/niemand** nothing/nobody else; **~arbeiten** *vi* to go on working; **~bilden** *vr* to continue one's studies; **W~bildung** *f* further education.

**Weitere(s)** *nt* further details *pl*; **bis auf w~s** for the time being; **ohne w~s** without further ado, just like that.

**weiter-** *zW*: **~empfehlen** *unreg vt* to recommend (to others); **~erzählen** *vt* (*Geheimnis*) to pass on; **~fahrt** *f* continuation of the journey; **~führend** *adj* (*Schule*) secondary (*BRIT*), high (*US*); **~gehen** *unreg vi* to go on; **~hin** *adv*: **etw ~hin tun** to go on doing sth; **~kommen** *unreg vi*: **nicht ~kommen** (*fig*) to be bogged down; **~leiten** *vt* to pass on; **~machen** *vt*, *vi* to continue; **~reisen** *vi* to continue one's journey; **~sagen** *vt*: **nicht ~sagen!** don't tell anyone!; ~**sehen** *unreg vi:* **dann sehen wir** ~ then we'll see; ~**verarbeiten** *vt* to process; ~**wissen** *unreg vi:* **nicht (mehr)** ~**wissen** (*verzweifelt sein*) to be at one's wits' end.

**weit-** *zW:* ~**gehend** *adj* considerable ♦ *adv* largely; ~**hergeholt** *adj attrib* far-fetched; ~**hin** *adv* widely; (~*gehend*) to a large extent; ~**läufig** *adj* (*Gebäude*) spacious; (*Erklärung*) lengthy; (*Verwandter*) distant; ~**reichend** *adj* (*fig*) far-reaching; ~**schweifig** *adj* long-winded; ~**sichtig** *adj* (*lit*) long-sighted (*BRIT*), far-sighted (*US*); (*fig*) far-sighted; **W**~**sprung** *m* long jump; ~**verbreitet** *adj* widespread; ~**verzweigt** *adj attrib* (*Straßensystem*) extensive; **W**~**winkelobjektiv** *nt* (*PHOT*) wide-angle lens.

**Weizen** ['vaɪtzən] (**-s, -**) *m* wheat; ~**bier** *nt* light, fizzy wheat beer; ~**keime** *pl* (*KOCH*) wheatgerm *sing.*

**welch** [vɛlç] *pron:* ~ **ein(e)** ... what a ...

═══════════ *SCHLÜSSELWORT*

**welche(r, s)** *interrog pron* which; ~**r von beiden?** which (one) of the two?; ~**n hast du genommen?** which (one) did you take?; ~ **Freude!** what joy!

♦ *indef pron* some; (*in Fragen*) any; **ich habe** ~ I have some; **haben Sie** ~? do you have any?

♦ *rel pron* (*bei Menschen*) who; (*bei Sachen*) which, that; ~**(r, s) auch immer** whoever/ whichever/whatever.

─────────────────────────────

**welk** [vɛlk] *adj* withered; ~**en** *vi* to wither.
**Wellblech** *nt* corrugated iron.
**Welle** ['vɛlə] (**-, -n**) *f* wave; (*TECH*) shaft; **(hohe)** ~**n schlagen** (*fig*) to create (quite) a stir.
**Wellen-** *zW:* ~**bereich** *m* waveband; ~**brecher** *m* breakwater; ~**gang** *m:* **starker** ~**gang** heavy sea(s) *od* swell; ~**länge** *f* (*lit, fig*) wavelength; **mit jdm auf einer** ~**länge sein** (*fig*) to be on the same wavelength as sb; ~**linie** *f* wavy line.
**Wellensittich** *m* budgerigar.
**Wellpappe** *f* corrugated cardboard.
**Welpe** ['vɛlpə] (**-n, -n**) *m* pup, whelp; (*von Wolf etc*) cub.
**Welt** [vɛlt] (**-, -en**) *f* world; **aus der** ~ **schaffen** to eliminate; **in aller** ~ all over the world; **vor aller** ~ in front of everybody; **auf die** ~ **kommen** to be born; ~**all** *nt* universe; ~**anschauung** *f* philosophy of life; **w**~**berühmt** *adj* world-famous; **w**~**bewegend** *adj* world-shattering; ~**bild** *nt* conception of the world; (*jds Ansichten*) philosophy.
**Weltenbummler(in)** *m(f)* globetrotter.
**Weltergewicht** ['vɛltərɡəvɪçt] *nt* (*SPORT*) welterweight.
**weltfremd** *adj* unworldly.

**Weltgesundheitsorganisation** *f* World Health Organization.
**Welt-** *zW:* **w**~**gewandt** *adj* sophisticated; ~**kirchenrat** *m* World Council of Churches; ~**krieg** *m* world war; **w**~**lich** *adj* worldly; (*nicht kirchlich*) secular; ~**literatur** *f* world literature; ~**macht** *f* world power; **w**~**männisch** *adj* sophisticated; ~**meister** *m* world champion; ~**meisterschaft** *f* world *od* world's (*US*) championship; (*FUSSBALL etc*) World Cup; ~**rang** *m:* **von** ~**rang** world-famous; ~**raum** *m* space; ~**raumforschung** *f* space research; ~**raumstation** *f* space station; ~**reise** *f* trip round the world; ~**ruf** *m* world-wide reputation; ~**sicherheitsrat** *m* (*POL*) United Nations Security Council; ~**stadt** *f* metropolis; ~**untergang** *m* (*lit, fig*) end of the world; **w**~**weit** *adj* world-wide; ~**wirtschaft** *f* world economy; ~**wirtschaftskrise** *f* world economic crisis; ~**wunder** *nt* wonder of the world.
**wem** [veːm] *dat von* **wer** ♦ *pron* to whom.
**wen** [veːn] *akk von* **wer** ♦ *pron* whom.
**Wende** ['vɛndə] (**-, -n**) *f* turn; (*Veränderung*) change; **die** ~ (*POL*) (the) reunification (of Germany); ~**kreis** *m* (*GEOG*) tropic; (*AUT*) turning circle.
**Wendeltreppe** *f* spiral staircase.
**wenden** *unreg vt, vi, vr* to turn; **bitte** ~! please turn over; **sich an jdn** ~ to go/come to sb.
**Wendepunkt** *m* turning point.
**wendig** *adj* (*lit, fig*) agile; (*Auto etc*) manoeuvrable (*BRIT*), maneuverable (*US*).
**Wendung** *f* turn; (*Rede*~) idiom.
**wenig** ['veːnɪç] *adj, adv* little; **ein** ~ a little; **er hat zu** ~ **Geld** he doesn't have enough money; **ein Exemplar zu** ~ one copy too few.
**wenige** ['veːnɪɡə] *pl* few *pl*; **in** ~**n Tagen** in (just) a few days.
**weniger** *adj* less; (*mit pl*) fewer ♦ *adv* less.
**Wenigkeit** *f* trifle; **meine** ~ (*umg*) little me.
**wenigste(r, s)** *adj* least.
**wenigstens** *adv* at least.
**wenn** [vɛn] *konj* if; (*zeitlich*) when; ~ **auch** ... even if ...; ~ **ich doch** ... if only I ...; ~ **wir erst die neue Wohnung haben** once we get the new flat.
**Wenn** *nt:* **ohne** ~ **und Aber** unequivocally.
**wennschon** *adv:* **na** ~ so what?; ~, **dennschon** in for a penny, in for a pound!
**wer** [veːr] *pron* who.
**Werbe-** *zW:* ~**agentur** *f* advertising agency; ~**aktion** *f* advertising campaign; ~**antwort** *f* business reply card; ~**fernsehen** *nt* commercial television; ~**film** *m* promotional film; ~**geschenk** *nt* promotional gift, freebie (*umg*); (*zu Gekauftem*) free gift; ~**grafiker(in)** *m(f)* commercial artist; ~**kampagne** *f* advertising campaign.
**werben** ['vɛrbən] *unreg vt* to win; (*Mitglied*) to recruit ♦ *vi* to advertise; **um jdn/etw** ~ to

try to win sb/sth; **für jdn/etw** ~ to promote sb/sth.

**Werbe-** *zW:* ~**spot** *m* commercial; ~**texter (-s, -)** *m* copywriter; ~**trommel** *f:* **die ~trommel (für etw) rühren** (*umg*) to beat the big drum (for sth); **w~wirksam** *adj:* **w~wirksam sein** to be good publicity.

**Werbung** *f* advertising; (*von Mitgliedern*) recruitment; (*TV etc: Werbeblock*) commercial break; ~ **um jdn/etw** promotion of sb/sth.

**Werbungskosten** *pl* professional *od* business expenses *pl.*

**Werdegang** ['veːrdəgaŋ] *m* development; (*beruflich*) career.

═══════════════ *SCHLÜSSELWORT*

**werden** ['veːrdən] *unreg* (*pt* **wurde,** *pp* **geworden** *od* (*bei Passiv*) **worden**) *vi* to become; **was ist aus ihm/aus der Sache geworden?** what became of him/it; **es ist nichts/gut geworden** it came to nothing/turned out well; **es wird Nacht/Tage** it's getting dark/light; **es wird bald ein Jahr, daß ...** it's almost a year since ...; **er wird am 8. Mai 36** he will be 36 on the 8th May; **mir wird kalt** I'm getting cold; **mir wird schlecht** I feel ill; **Erster** ~ to come *od* be first; **das muß anders** ~ that will have to change; **rot/zu Eis** ~ to turn red/to ice; **was willst du (mal)** ~? what do you want to be?; **die Fotos sind gut geworden** the photos turned out well

♦ *Hilfsverb* **1** (*bei Futur*): **er wird es tun** he will *od* he'll do it; **er wird das nicht tun** he will not *od* he won't do it; **es wird gleich regnen** it's going to rain any moment

**2** (*bei Konjunktiv*): **ich würde ...** I would ...; **er würde gern ...** he would *od* he'd like to ...; **ich würde lieber** I would *od* I'd rather ...

**3** (*bei Vermutung*): **sie wird in der Küche sein** she will be in the kitchen

**4** (*bei Passiv*): **gebraucht** ~ to be used; **er ist erschossen worden** he has *od* he's been shot; **mir wurde gesagt, daß** I was told that ...

**werdend** *adj:* ~**e Mutter** expectant mother.
**werfen** ['vɛrfən] *unreg vt* to throw ♦ *vi* (*Tier*) to have its young; „**nicht** ~" "handle with care".
**Werft** [vɛrft] **(-, -en)** *f* shipyard; (*für Flugzeuge*) hangar.
**Werk** [vɛrk] **(-(e)s, -e)** *nt* work; (*Tätigkeit*) job; (*Fabrik, Mechanismus*) works *pl;* **ans** ~ **gehen** to set to work; **das ist sein** ~ this is his doing; **ab** ~ (*COMM*) ex works.
**werkeln** ['vɛrkəln] (*umg*) *vi* to potter about (*BRIT*), putter around (*US*).
**Werken (-s)** *nt* (*SCH*) handicrafts *pl.*
**Werkschutz** *m* works security service.
**Werksgelände** *nt* factory premises *pl.*

**Werk-** *zW:* ~**statt (-, -stätten)** *f* workshop; (*AUT*) garage; ~**stoff** *m* material; ~**student** *m* self-supporting student; ~**tag** *m* working day; **w~tags** *adv* on working days; **w~tätig** *adj* working; ~**zeug** *nt* tool; ~**zeugkasten** *m* toolbox; ~**zeugmaschine** *f* machine tool; ~**zeugschrank** *m* tool chest.
**Wermut** ['veːrmuːt] **(-(e)s, -s)** *m* wormwood; (*Wein*) vermouth.
**Wermutstropfen** *m* (*fig*) drop of bitterness.
**Wert** [veːrt] **(-(e)s, -e)** *m* worth; (*FIN*) value; ~ **legen auf** *+akk* to attach importance to; **es hat doch keinen** ~ it's useless; **im** ~**e von** to the value of.
**wert** [veːrt] *adj* worth; (*geschätzt*) dear; (*würdig*) worthy; **das ist nichts/viel** ~ it's not worth anything/it's worth a lot; **das ist es/er mir** ~ it's/he's worth that to me; **ein Auto ist viel** ~ (*nützlich*) a car is very useful.
**Wertangabe** *f* declaration of value.
**wertbeständig** *adj* stable in value.
**werten** *vt* to rate; (*beurteilen*) to judge; (*SPORT: als gültig* ~) to allow; ~ **als** to rate as; to judge to be.
**Wert-** *zW:* ~**gegenstand** *m* article of value; **w~los** *adj* worthless; ~**losigkeit** *f* worthlessness; ~**maßstab** *m* standard; ~**papier** *nt* security; ~**steigerung** *f* appreciation.
**Wertung** *f* (*SPORT*) score.
**Wert-** *zW:* **w~voll** *adj* valuable; ~**vorstellung** *f* moral concept; ~**zuwachs** *m* appreciation.
**Wesen** ['veːzən] **(-s, -)** *nt* (*Geschöpf*) being; (*Natur, Character*) nature.
**wesentlich** *adj* significant; (*beträchtlich*) considerable; **im** ~**en** essentially; (*im großen*) in the main.
**weshalb** [vɛs'halp] *adv* why.
**Wespe** ['vɛspə] **(-, -n)** *f* wasp.
**wessen** ['vɛsən] *gen von* **wer** ♦ *pron* whose.
**Wessi** ['vɛsɪ] **(-s, -s)** (*umg*) *m* West German.

┌─────────────────────────────────────┐
*A* **Wessi** *is a colloquial and often derogatory word used to describe a German from the former West Germany. The expression 'Besserwessi' is used by East Germans to describe a West German who is considered to be a know-all.*
└─────────────────────────────────────┘

**West-** *zW:* **w~deutsch** *adj* West German; ~**deutsche(r)** *f(m)* West German; ~**deutschland** *nt* (*POL: früher*) West Germany; (*GEOG*) Western Germany.
**Weste** ['vɛstə] **(-, -n)** *f* waistcoat, vest (*US*); **eine reine** ~ **haben** (*fig*) to have a clean slate.
**Westen (-s)** *m* west.
**Westentasche** *f:* **etw wie seine** ~ **kennen** (*umg*) to know sth like the back of one's hand.
**Westerwald** ['vɛstərvalt] **(-s)** *m* Westerwald (Mountains *pl*).

**Westeuropa** nt Western Europe.
**westeuropäisch** ['vɛst|ɔyrɔ'pɛːɪʃ] adj
West(ern) European; ~e Zeit Greenwich
Mean Time.
**Westfale** [vɛst'faːlə] (-n, -n) m Westphalian.
**Westfalen** (-s) nt Westphalia.
**Westfälin** [vɛst'fɛːlɪn] f Westphalian.
**westfälisch** adj Westphalian.
**Westindien** ['vɛst|ɪndɪən] (-s) nt West Indies
pl.
**westindisch** adj West Indian; die ~en Inseln
the West Indies.
**west-** zW: ~lich adj western ♦ adv to the west;
W~mächte pl (POL: früher): die W~mächte
the Western powers pl; ~wärts adv
westwards.
**weswegen** [vɛs've:gən] adv why.
**wett** [vɛt] adj even; ~ sein to be quits.
**Wettbewerb** m competition.
**Wettbewerbsbeschränkung** f restraint of
trade.
**wettbewerbsfähig** adj competitive.
**Wette** (-, -n) f bet, wager; um die ~ laufen to
run a race (with each other).
**Wetteifer** m rivalry.
**wetteifern** vi untr: mit jdm um etw wetteifern
to compete with sb for sth.
**wetten** ['vɛtən] vt, vi to bet; so haben wir nicht
gewettet! that's not part of the bargain!
**Wetter** ['vɛtər] (-s, -) nt weather; (MIN) air;
~amt nt meteorological office; ~aussichten
pl weather outlook sing; ~bericht m weather
report; ~dienst m meteorological service;
w~fest adj weatherproof; w~fühlig adj
sensitive to changes in the weather; ~karte
f weather chart; ~lage f (weather)
situation.
**wettern** ['vɛtərn] vi to curse and swear.
**Wetter-** zW: ~umschlag m sudden change in
the weather; ~vorhersage f weather
forecast; ~warte f weather station;
w~wendisch adj capricious.
**Wett-** zW: ~kampf m contest; ~lauf m race;
ein ~lauf mit der Zeit a race against time.
**wettmachen** vt to make good.
**Wett-** zW: ~rüsten nt arms race; ~spiel nt
match; ~streit m contest.
**wetzen** ['vɛtsən] vt to sharpen ♦ vi (umg) to
scoot.
**WEU** f abk (= Westeuropäische Union) WEU.
**WEZ** abk (= westeuropäische Zeit) GMT.
**WG** abk = Wohngemeinschaft.
**Whisky** ['vɪski] (-s, -s) m whisky (BRIT),
whiskey (US, Ireland).
**WHO** (-) f abk (= World Health Organization)
WHO.
**wich** etc [vɪç] vb siehe **weichen**.
**wichsen** ['vɪksən] vt (Schuhe) to polish ♦ vi
(umg!: onanieren) to jerk od toss off (!).
**Wichser** (umg!) m wanker (!).
**Wicht** [vɪçt] (-(e)s, -e) m titch; (pej) worthless
creature.

**wichtig** adj important; sich selbst/etw (zu)
~ nehmen to take o.s./sth (too) seriously;
W~keit f importance; W~tuer(in) (pej) m(f)
pompous ass (umg).
**Wicke** ['vɪkə] (-, -n) f (BOT) vetch; (Garten~)
sweet pea.
**Wickelkleid** nt wrap-around dress.
**wickeln** ['vɪkəln] vt to wind; (Haare) to set;
(Kind) to change; da bist du schief gewickelt!
(fig: umg) you're very much mistaken; jdn/
etw in etw akk ~ to wrap sb/sth in sth.
**Wickeltisch** m baby's changing table.
**Widder** ['vɪdər] (-s, -) m ram; (ASTROL) Aries.
**wider** ['vi:dər] präp +akk against.
**widerfahren** unreg vi untr: jdm widerfahren to
happen to sb.
**Widerhaken** ['vi:dərha:kən] m barb.
**Widerhall** ['vi:dərhal] m echo; keinen ~ (bei
jdm) finden (Interesse) to meet with no
response (from sb).
**widerlegen** vt untr to refute.
**widerlich** ['vi:dərlɪç] adj disgusting, repulsive;
W~keit f repulsiveness.
**widerrechtlich** adj unlawful.
**Widerrede** f contradiction; keine ~! don't
argue!
**Widerruf** ['vi:dərruːf] m retraction;
countermanding; bis auf ~ until revoked.
**widerrufen** unreg vt untr to retract;
(Anordnung) to revoke; (Befehl) to
countermand.
**Widersacher(in)** ['vi:dərzaxər(ɪn)] (-s, -) m(f)
adversary.
**widersetzen** vr untr: sich jdm widersetzen to
oppose sb; (der Polizei) to resist sb; sich einer
Sache widersetzen to oppose sth; (einem
Befehl) to refuse to comply with sth.
**widerspenstig** ['vi:dərʃpɛnstɪç] adj wilful
(BRIT), willful (US); W~keit f wilfulness
(BRIT), willfulness (US).
**widerspiegeln** ['vi:dərʃpi:gəln] vt to reflect.
**widersprechen** unreg vi untr: jdm
widersprechen to contradict sb.
**widersprechend** adj contradictory.
**Widerspruch** ['vi:dərʃprʊx] m contradiction;
ein ~ in sich a contradiction in terms.
**widersprüchlich** ['vi:dərʃprʏçlɪç] adj
contradictory, inconsistent.
**widerspruchslos** adv without arguing.
**Widerstand** ['vi:dərʃtant] m resistance; der
Weg des geringsten ~es the line of least
resistance; jdm/etw ~ leisten to resist sb/
sth.
**Widerstands-** zW: ~bewegung f resistance
(movement); w~fähig adj resistant, tough;
w~los adj unresisting.
**widerstehen** unreg vi untr: jdm/etw
widerstehen to withstand sb/sth.
**widerstreben** vi untr: es widerstrebt mir, so
etwas zu tun I am reluctant to do anything
like that.
**widerstrebend** adj reluctant; (gegensätzlich)

conflicting.

**Wider-** *zW:* **~streit** *m* conflict; **w~wärtig** *adj* nasty, horrid; **~wille** *m:* **~wille (gegen)** aversion (to); (*Abneigung*) distaste (for); (*~streben*) reluctance; **w~willig** *adj* unwilling, reluctant; **~worte** *pl* answering back *sing*.

**widmen** ['vɪtmən] *vt* to dedicate ♦ *vr* to devote o.s.

**Widmung** *f* dedication.

**widrig** ['viːdrɪç] *adj* (*Umstände*) adverse; (*Mensch*) repulsive.

════════════ *SCHLÜSSELWORT*

**wie** [viː] *adv* how; **~ groß/schnell?** how big/ fast?; **~ wär's?** how about it?; **~ wär's mit einem Whisky?** (*umg*) how about a whisky?; **~ nennt man das?** what is that called?; **~ ist er?** what's he like?; **~ gut du das kannst!** you're very good at it; **~ bitte?** pardon? (*BRIT*), pardon me? (*US*); (*entrüstet*) I beg your pardon!; **und ~!** and how!

♦ *konj* **1** (*bei Vergleichen*): **so schön ~** ... as beautiful as ...; **~ ich schon sagte** as I said; **~ noch nie** as never before; **~ du** like you; **singen ~ ein** ... to sing like a ...; **~ (zum Beispiel)** such as (for example)

**2** (*zeitlich*): **~ er das hörte, ging er** when he heard that he left; **er hörte, ~ der Regen fiel** he heard the rain falling.

**wieder** ['viːdər] *adv* again; **~ da sein** to be back (again); **gehst du schon ~?** are you off again?; **~ ein(e)** ... another ...; **das ist auch ~ wahr** that's true enough; **da sieht man mal ~** ... it just shows ...

**wieder-** *zW:* **W~aufbau** [-'|aʊfbaʊ] *m* rebuilding; **~aufbereiten** *vt* to recycle; (*Atommüll*) to reprocess; **W~aufbereitungsanlage** *f* reprocessing plant; **W~aufnahme** [-'|aʊfnaːmə] *f* resumption; **~aufnehmen** *unreg vt* to resume; (*Gedanken, Hobby*) to take up again; (*Thema*) to revert to; (*JUR: Verfahren*) to reopen; **~bekommen** *unreg vt* to get back; **~beleben** *vt* to revive; **~bringen** *unreg vt* to bring back; **~erkennen** *unreg vt* to recognize; **W~erstattung** *f* reimbursement; **~finden** *unreg vt* (*fig: Selbstachtung etc*) to regain.

**Wiedergabe** *f* (*von Rede, Ereignis*) account; (*Wiederholung*) repetition; (*Darbietung*) performance; (*Reproduktion*) reproduction; **~gerät** *nt* playback unit.

**wieder-** *zW:* **~geben** *unreg vt* (*zurückgeben*) to return; (*Erzählung etc*) to repeat; (*Gefühle etc*) to convey; **W~geburt** *f* rebirth; **~gutmachen** [-'guːtmaxən] *vt* to make up for; (*Fehler*) to put right; **W~gutmachung** *f* reparation; **~herstellen** *vt* to restore.

**wiederholen** *vt untr* to repeat.

**wiederholt** *adj:* **zum ~en Male** once again.

**Wiederholung** *f* repetition.

**Wiederholungstäter(in)** *m(f)* (*JUR*) second-time offender; (*mehrmalig*) persistent offender.

**wieder-** *zW:* **W~hören** *nt:* **auf W~hören** (*TEL*) goodbye; **~käuen** *vi* to ruminate ♦ *vt* to ruminate; (*fig: umg*) to go over again and again; **W~kehr** (-) *f* return; (*von Vorfall*) repetition, recurrence; **~kehrend** *adj* recurrent; **W~kunft** (-, ̈-e) *f* return; **~sehen** *unreg vt* to see again; **auf W~sehen** goodbye; **~um** *adv* again; (*seinerseits etc*) in turn; (*andererseits*) on the other hand; **~vereinigen** *vt* to reunite; **W~vereinigung** *f* reunification; **W~verkäufer** *m* distributor; **W~wahl** *f* re-election.

**Wiege** ['viːgə] (-, -n) *f* cradle.

**wiegen¹** *vt* (*schaukeln*) to rock; (*Kopf*) to shake.

**wiegen²** *unreg vt, vi* to weigh; **schwer ~** (*fig*) to carry a lot of weight; (*Irrtum*) to be serious.

**wiehern** ['viːərn] *vi* to neigh, whinny.

**Wien** [viːn] (-s) *nt* Vienna.

**Wiener(in)** (-s, -) *m(f)* Viennese ♦ *adj attrib* Viennese; **~ Schnitzel** Wiener schnitzel.

**wies** *etc* [viːs] *vb siehe* **weisen**.

**Wiese** ['viːzə] (-, -n) *f* meadow.

**Wiesel** ['viːzəl] (-s, -) *nt* weasel; **schnell od flink wie ein ~** quick as a flash.

**wieso** [viː'zoː] *adv* why.

**wieviel** [viː'fiːl] *adv* how much; **~ Menschen** how many people; **~mal** *adv* how often.

**wievielte(r, s)** *adj:* **zum ~n Mal?** how many times?; **den W~n haben wir?** what's the date?; **an ~r Stelle?** in what place?; **der ~ Besucher war er?** how many visitors were there before him?

**wieweit** [viː'vaɪt] *adv* to what extent.

**Wikinger** ['viːkɪŋər] (-s, -) *m* Viking.

**wild** [vɪlt] *adj* wild; **~er Streik** unofficial strike; **in ~er Ehe leben** (*veraltet, hum*) to live in sin; **~ entschlossen** (*umg*) dead set.

**Wild** (-(e)s) *nt* game.

**Wild-** *zW:* **~bahn** *f:* **in freier ~bahn** in the wild; **~bret** *nt* game; (*von Rotwild*) venison; **~dieb** *m* poacher.

**Wilde(r)** ['vɪldə(r)] *f(m)* savage.

**wildern** ['vɪldərn] *vi* to poach.

**wild-** *zW:* **W~fang** *m* little rascal; **~fremd** ['vɪlt'frɛmt] (*umg*) *adj* quite strange *od* unknown; **W~heit** *f* wildness; **W~leder** *nt* suede.

**Wildnis** (-, -se) *f* wilderness.

**Wild-** *zW:* **~schwein** *nt* (wild) boar; **~wechsel** *m:* „~wechsel" "wild animals"; **~westroman** *m* western.

**will** [vɪl] *vb siehe* **wollen**.

**Wille** ['vɪlə] (-ns, -n) *m* will; **jdm seinen ~n lassen** to let sb have his own way; **seinen eigenen ~n haben** to be self-willed.

**willen** *präp +gen:* **um ... ~** for the sake of ...

**willenlos** *adj* weak-willed.

**willens** *adj* (*geh*): ~ **sein** to be willing.
**willensstark** *adj* strong-willed.
**willentlich** ['vɪləntlıç] *adj* wilful (*BRIT*), willful (*US*), deliberate.
**willig** *adj* willing.
**willkommen** [vɪl'kɔmən] *adj* welcome; **jdn** ~ **heißen** to welcome sb; **herzlich** ~ (**in** +*dat*) welcome (to); **W**~ (**-s, -**) *nt* welcome.
**willkürlich** *adj* arbitrary; (*Bewegung*) voluntary.
**willst** [vɪlst] *vb siehe* **wollen**.
**Wilna** ['vɪlna] (**-s**) *nt* Vilnius.
**wimmeln** ['vɪməln] *vi*: ~ (**von**) to swarm (with).
**wimmern** ['vɪmɐrn] *vi* to whimper.
**Wimper** ['vɪmpɐr] (**-, -n**) *f* eyelash; **ohne mit der** ~ **zu zucken** (*fig*) without batting an eyelid.
**Wimperntusche** *f* mascara.
**Wind** [vɪnt] (**-(e)s, -e**) *m* wind; **den Mantel** *od* **das Fähnchen nach dem** ~ **hängen** to trim one's sails to the wind; **etw in den** ~ **schlagen** to turn a deaf ear to sth.
**Windbeutel** *m* cream puff; (*fig*) windbag.
**Winde** ['vɪndə] (**-, -n**) *f* (*TECH*) winch, windlass; (*BOT*) bindweed.
**Windel** ['vɪndəl] (**-, -n**) *f* nappy (*BRIT*), diaper (*US*).
**windelweich** *adj*: **jdn** ~ **schlagen** (*umg*) to beat the living daylights out of sb.
**winden¹** ['vɪndən] *vi unpers* to be windy.
**winden²** *unreg vt* to wind; (*Kranz*) to weave; (*ent~*) to twist ♦ *vr* to wind; (*Person*) to writhe; (*fig: ausweichen*) to try to wriggle out.
**Windenergie** *f* wind power.
**Windeseile** *f*: **sich in** *od* **mit Windeseile verbreiten** to spread like wildfire.
**Windhose** *f* whirlwind.
**Windhund** *m* greyhound; (*Mensch*) fly-by-night.
**windig** ['vɪndıç] *adj* windy; (*fig*) dubious.
**Wind-** *zW*: ~**jacke** *f* windcheater, windbreaker (*US*); ~**kanal** *m* (*TECH*) wind tunnel; ~**kraft** *f* wind power; ~**kraftanlage** *f* wind power station; ~**mühle** *f* windmill; **gegen** ~**mühlen (an)kämpfen** (*fig*) to tilt at windmills; ~**park** *m* wind farm.
**Windpocken** *pl* chickenpox *sing*.
**Wind-** *zW*: ~**rose** *f* (*NAUT*) compass card; (*MET*) wind rose; ~**schatten** *m* lee; (*von Fahrzeugen*) slipstream; ~**schutzscheibe** *f* (*AUT*) windscreen (*BRIT*), windshield (*US*); ~**stärke** *f* wind force; **w**~**still** *adj* (*Tag*) windless; **es ist w**~**still** there's no wind; ~**stille** *f* calm; ~**stoß** *m* gust of wind; ~**surfen** *nt* windsurfing.
**Windung** *f* (*von Weg, Fluß etc*) meander; (*von Schlange, Spule*) coil; (*von Schraube*) thread.
**Wink** [vɪŋk] (**-(e)s, -e**) *m* (*mit Kopf*) nod; (*mit Hand*) wave; (*Tip, Hinweis*) hint; **ein** ~ **mit dem Zaunpfahl** a broad hint.

**Winkel** ['vɪŋkəl] (**-s, -**) *m* (*MATH*) angle; (*Gerät*) set square; (*in Raum*) corner; ~**advokat** (*pej*) *m* incompetent lawyer; ~**messer** *m* protractor; ~**zug** *m*: **mach keine** ~**züge** stop evading the issue.
**winken** ['vɪŋkən] *vt, vi* to wave; **dem Sieger winkt eine Reise nach Italien** the (lucky) winner will receive a trip to Italy.
**winseln** ['vɪnzəln] *vi* to whine.
**Winter** ['vɪntɐr] (**-s, -**) *m* winter; ~**garten** *m* conservatory; **w**~**lich** *adj* wintry; ~**reifen** *m* winter tyre (*BRIT*) *od* tire (*US*); ~**schlaf** *m* (*ZOOL*) hibernation; ~**schlußverkauf** *m* winter sale; ~**semester** *nt* (*UNIV*) winter semester (*bes US*), ≈ autumn term (*BRIT*); ~**spiele** *pl*: (**Olympische**) ~**spiele** Winter Olympics *pl*; ~**sport** *m* winter sports *pl*.
**Winzer(in)** ['vɪntsɐr(ɪn)] (**-s, -**) *m(f)* wine-grower.
**winzig** ['vɪntsıç] *adj* tiny.
**Wipfel** ['vɪpfəl] (**-s, -**) *m* treetop.
**Wippe** ['vɪpə] (**-, -n**) *f* seesaw.
**wir** [viːr] *pron* we; ~ **alle** all of us, we all.
**Wirbel** ['vɪrbəl] (**-s, -**) *m* whirl, swirl; (*Trubel*) hurly-burly; (*Aufsehen*) fuss; (*ANAT*) vertebra; ~ **um jdn/etw machen** to make a fuss about sb/sth.
**wirbellos** *adj* (*ZOOL*) invertebrate.
**wirbeln** *vi* to whirl, swirl.
**Wirbel-** *zW*: ~**säule** *f* spine; ~**tier** *nt* vertebrate; ~**wind** *m* whirlwind.
**wirbst** *vb siehe* **werben**.
**wirbt** [vɪrpt] *vb siehe* **werben**.
**wird** [vɪrt] *vb siehe* **werden**.
**wirfst** *vb siehe* **werfen**.
**wirft** [vɪrft] *vb siehe* **werfen**.
**wirken** ['vɪrkən] *vi* to have an effect; (*erfolgreich sein*) to work; (*scheinen*) to seem ♦ *vt* (*Wunder*) to work; **etw auf sich** *akk* ~ **lassen** to take sth in.
**wirklich** ['vɪrklıç] *adj* real; **W**~**keit** *f* reality; ~**keitsgetreu** *adj* realistic.
**wirksam** ['vɪrkzaːm] *adj* effective; **W**~**keit** *f* effectiveness.
**Wirkstoff** *m* active substance.
**Wirkung** ['vɪrkʊŋ] *f* effect.
**Wirkungs-** *zW*: ~**bereich** *m* field (of activity *od* interest *etc*); (*Domäne*) domain; **w**~**los** *adj* ineffective; **w**~**los bleiben** to have no effect; **w**~**voll** *adj* effective.
**wirr** [vɪr] *adj* confused; (*unrealistisch*) wild; (*Haare etc*) tangled.
**Wirren** *pl* disturbances *pl*.
**Wirrwarr** ['vɪrvar] (**-s**) *m* disorder, chaos; (*von Stimmen*) hubbub; (*von Fäden, Haaren etc*) tangle.
**Wirsing(kohl)** ['vɪrzɪŋ(koːl)] (**-s**) *m* savoy cabbage.
**wirst** [vɪrst] *vb siehe* **werden**.
**Wirt(in)** ['vɪrt(ɪn)] (**-(e)s, -e**) *m(f)* landlord, landlady.
**Wirtschaft** ['vɪrtʃaft] *f* (*Gaststätte*) pub;

(*Haushalt*) housekeeping; (*eines Landes*) economy; (*Geschäftsleben*) industry and commerce; (*umg: Durcheinander*) mess; **w~en** *vi* (*sparsam sein*): **gut w~en können** to be economical; **~er** *m* (*Verwalter*) manager; **~erin** *f* (*im Haushalt, Heim etc*) housekeeper; **w~lich** *adj* economical; (*POL*) economic; **~lichkeit** *f* economy; (*von Betrieb*) viability.

**Wirtschafts-** *zW:* **~geld** *nt* housekeeping (money); **~geographie** *f* economic geography; **~hilfe** *f* economic aid; **~krise** *f* economic crisis; **~minister** *m* minister of economic affairs; **~ordnung** *f* economic system; **~politik** *f* economic policy; **~prüfer** *m* chartered accountant (*BRIT*), certified public accountant (*US*); **~spionage** *f* industrial espionage; **~wachstum** *nt* economic growth; **~wissenschaft** *f* economics *sing*; **~wunder** *nt* economic miracle; **~zweig** *m* branch of industry.

**Wirtshaus** *nt* inn.

**Wisch** [vɪʃ] (**-(e)s, -e**) *m* scrap of paper.

**wischen** *vt* to wipe.

**Wischer** (**-s, -**) *m* (*AUT*) wiper.

**Wischiwaschi** [vɪʃiːˈvaʃiː] (**-s**) (*pej: umg*) *nt* drivel.

**Wisent** ['viːzɛnt] (**-s, -e**) *m* bison.

**WiSo** ['vizo] *abk* (= *Wirtschafts- und Sozialwissenschaften*) economics and social sciences.

**wispern** ['vɪspərn] *vt, vi* to whisper.

**Wiss.** *abk* = **Wissenschaft**.

**wiss.** *abk* = **wissenschaftlich**.

**Wißbegier(de)** ['vɪsbəɡiːr(də)] *f* thirst for knowledge.

**wißbegierig** *adj* eager for knowledge.

**wissen** ['vɪsən] *unreg vt, vi* to know; **von jdm/etw nichts ~ wollen** not to be interested in sb/sth; **sie hält sich für wer weiß wie klug** (*umg*) she doesn't half think she's clever; **gewußt wie/wo!** *etc* sheer brilliance!; **ich weiß seine Adresse nicht mehr** (*sich erinnern*) I can't remember his address; **W~** (**-s**) *nt* knowledge; **etw gegen (sein) besseres W~ tun** to do sth against one's better judgement; **nach bestem W~ und Gewissen** to the best of one's knowledge and belief.

**Wissenschaft** ['vɪsənʃaft] *f* science.

**Wissenschaftler(in)** (**-s, -**) *m(f)* scientist; (*Geistes~*) academic.

**wissenschaftlich** *adj* scientific; **W~er Assistent** assistant lecturer.

**wissenswert** *adj* worth knowing.

**wissentlich** *adj* knowing.

**wittern** ['vɪtərn] *vt* to scent; (*fig*) to suspect.

**Witterung** *f* weather; (*Geruch*) scent.

**Witwe** ['vɪtvə] (**-, -n**) *f* widow.

**Witwer** (**-s, -**) *m* widower.

**Witz** [vɪts] (**-es, -e**) *m* joke; **der ~ an der Sache ist, daß ...** the great thing about it is that ...; **~bold** (**-(e)s, -e**) *m* joker.

**witzeln** *vi* to joke.

**witzig** *adj* funny.

**witzlos** (*umg*) *adj* (*unsinnig*) pointless, futile.

**WM** (**-**) *f abk* = **Weltmeisterschaft**.

**wo** [voː] *adv* where; (*umg: irgend~*) somewhere ♦ *konj* (*wenn*) if; **im Augenblick, ~ ...** the moment (that) ...; **die Zeit, ~ ...** the time when ...

**woanders** [voːˈʔandərs] *adv* elsewhere.

**wob** *etc* [voːp] *vb siehe* **weben**.

**wobei** [voːˈbaɪ] *adv* (*rel*) ... in/by/with which; (*interrog*) how; what ... in/by/with; **~ mir gerade einfällt ...** which reminds me ...

**Woche** ['vɔxə] (**-, -n**) *f* week.

**Wochenbett** *nt:* **im ~ sterben** to die in childbirth.

**Wochen-** *zW:* **~ende** *nt* weekend; **~endhaus** *nt* weekend house; **~karte** *f* weekly ticket; **w~lang** *adj* lasting weeks ♦ *adv* for weeks; **~schau** *f* newsreel; **~tag** *m* weekday.

**wöchentlich** ['vœçəntlɪç] *adj, adv* weekly.

**Wochenzeitung** *f* weekly (paper).

**Wöchnerin** ['vœçnərɪn] *f woman who has recently given birth*.

**wodurch** [voːˈdʊrç] *adv* (*rel*) through which; (*interrog*) what ... through.

**wofür** [voːˈfyːr] *adv* (*rel*) for which; (*interrog*) what ... for.

**Wodka** ['vɔtka] (**-s, -s**) *m* vodka.

**wog** *etc* [voːk] *vb siehe* **wiegen²**.

**Woge** ['voːɡə] (**-, -n**) *f* wave.

**wogegen** [voˈɡeːɡən] *adv* (*rel*) against which; (*interrog*) what ... against.

**wogen** *vi* to heave, surge.

**woher** [voˈheːr] *adv* where ... from; **~ kommt es eigentlich, daß ...?** how is it that ...?

**wohin** [voˈhɪn] *adv* where ... to; **~ man auch schaut** wherever you look.

**wohingegen** *konj* whereas, while.

**Wohl** (**-(e)s**) *nt* welfare; **zum ~!** cheers!

===================== *SCHLÜSSELWORT*

**wohl** [voːl] *adv* **1** well; (*behaglich*) at ease, comfortable; **sich ~ fühlen** (*zufrieden*) to feel happy; (*gesundheitlich*) to feel well; **bei dem Gedanken ist mir nicht ~** I'm not very happy at the thought; **~ oder übel** whether one likes it or not; **er weiß das sehr ~** he knows that perfectly well

**2** (*wahrscheinlich*) probably; (*vermutlich*) I suppose; (*gewiß*) certainly; (*vielleicht*) perhaps; **sie ist ~ zu Hause** she's probably at home; **sie wird ~ das Haus verkaufen** I suppose *od* presumably she's going to sell the house; **das ist doch ~ nicht dein Ernst!** surely you're not serious!; **das mag ~ sein** that may well be; **ob das ~ stimmt?** I wonder if that's true.

**wohl-** *zW:* **~auf** [voːlˈʔaʊf] *adj* well, in good health; **W~befinden** *nt* well-being; **W~behagen** *nt* comfort; **~behalten** *adj* safe and sound; **W~ergehen** *nt* welfare; **W~fahrt** *f* welfare; **W~fahrtsstaat** *m* welfare state; **W~gefallen** *nt*: **sich in W~gefallen auflösen** (*hum: Gegenstände, Probleme*) to vanish into thin air; (*zerfallen*) to fall apart; **~gemeint** *adj* well-intentioned; **~gemerkt** *adv* mark you; **~habend** *adj* wealthy.

**wohlig** *adj* contented; (*gemütlich*) comfortable.

**wohl-** *zW*: **W~klang** *m* melodious sound; **~meinend** *adj* well-meaning; **~schmeckend** *adj* delicious; **W~stand** *m* prosperity; **W~standsgesellschaft** *f* affluent society; **W~tat** *f* (*Gefallen*) favour (*BRIT*), favor (*US*); (*gute Tat*) good deed; (*Erleichterung*) relief; **W~täter** *m* benefactor; **~tätig** *adj* charitable; **W~tätigkeit** *f* charity; **~tuend** *adj* pleasant; **~tun** *unreg vi*: **jdm ~tun** to do sb good; **~verdient** *adj* (*Ruhe*) well-earned; (*Strafe*) well-deserved; **~weislich** *adv* prudently; **W~wollen (-s)** *nt* good will; **~wollend** *adj* benevolent.

**Wohnblock** ['vo:nblɔk] **(-s, -s)** *m* block of flats (*BRIT*), apartment house (*US*).

**wohnen** ['vo:nən] *vi* to live.

**wohn-** *zW*: **W~fläche** *f* living space; **W~geld** *nt* housing benefit; **W~gemeinschaft** *f* people sharing a flat (*BRIT*) *od* apartment (*US*); (*von Hippies*) commune; **~haft** *adj* resident; **W~heim** *nt* (*für Studenten*) hall (of residence), dormitory (*US*); (*für Senioren*) home; (*bes für Arbeiter*) hostel; **W~komfort** *m*: **mit sämtlichem W~komfort** with all mod cons (*BRIT*); **~lich** *adj* comfortable; **W~mobil** *nt* motor caravan (*BRIT*), motor home (*US*); **W~ort** *m* domicile; **W~silo** *nt* concrete block of flats (*BRIT*) *od* apartment block (*US*); **W~sitz** *m* place of residence; **ohne festen W~sitz** of no fixed abode.

**Wohnung** *f* house; (*Etagen~*) flat (*BRIT*), apartment (*US*).

**Wohnungs-** *zW*: **~amt** *nt* housing office; **~bau** *m* house-building; **~markt** *m* housing market; **~not** *f* housing shortage.

**wohn-** *zW*: **W~viertel** *nt* residential area; **W~wagen** *m* caravan (*BRIT*), trailer (*US*); **W~zimmer** *nt* living room.

**wölben** ['vœlbən] *vt, vr* to curve.

**Wölbung** *f* curve.

**Wolf** [vɔlf] **(-(e)s, ¨e)** *m* wolf; (*TECH*) shredder; (*Fleisch~*) mincer (*BRIT*), grinder (*US*).

**Wölfin** ['vœlfɪn] *f* she-wolf.

**Wolke** ['vɔlkə] **(-, -n)** *f* cloud; **aus allen ~n fallen** (*fig*) to be flabbergasted (*umg*).

**Wolken-** *zW*: **~bruch** *m* cloudburst; **w~bruchartig** *adj* torrential; **~kratzer** *m* skyscraper; **~kuckucksheim** *nt* cloud-cuckoo-land (*BRIT*), cloudland (*US*); **w~los** *adj* cloudless.

**wolkig** ['vɔlkɪç] *adj* cloudy.

**Wolle** ['vɔlə] **(-, -n)** *f* wool; **sich mit jdm in die**

**~ kriegen** (*fig: umg*) to start squabbling with sb.

**wollen¹** ['vɔlən] *unreg* (*pt* **wollte**, *pp* **gewollt** *od* (*als Hilfsverb*) **wollen**) *vt, vi* to want; **ich will nach Hause** I want to go home; **er will nicht** he doesn't want to; **sie wollte das nicht** she didn't want it; **wenn du willst** if you like; **ich will, daß du mir zuhörst** I want you to listen to me; **oh, das hab ich nicht gewollt** oh, I didn't mean to do that; **ich weiß nicht, was er will** (*verstehe ihn nicht*) I don't know what he's on about

♦ *Hilfsverb*: **er will ein Haus kaufen** he wants to buy a house; **ich wollte, ich wäre ...** I wish I were ...; **etw gerade tun ~** to be just about to *od* going to do sth; **und so jemand** *od* **etwas will Lehrer sein!** (*umg*) and he calls himself a teacher!; **das will alles gut überlegt sein** that needs a lot of thought.

**wollen²** *adj* woollen (*BRIT*), woolen (*US*).

**Wollsachen** *pl* wool(l)ens *pl*.

**wollüstig** ['vɔlystɪç] *adj* lusty, sensual.

**wo-** *zW*: **~mit** [vo'mɪt] *adv* (*rel*) with which; (*interrog*) what ... with; **~mit kann ich dienen?** what can I do for you?; **~möglich** [vo'mø:klɪç] *adv* probably, I suppose; **~nach** [vo'na:x] *adv* (*rel*) after/for which; (*interrog*) what ... after.

**Wonne** ['vɔnə] **(-, -n)** *f* joy, bliss.

**woran** [vo'ran] *adv* (*rel*) on/at which; (*interrog*) what ... on/at; **~ liegt das?** what's the reason for it?

**worauf** [vo'rauf] *adv* (*rel*) on which; (*interrog*) what ... on; (*zeitlich*) whereupon; **~ du dich verlassen kannst** of that you can be sure.

**woraus** [vo'raus] *adv* (*rel*) from/out of which; (*interrog*) what ... from/out of.

**worin** [vo'rɪn] *adv* (*rel*) in which; (*interrog*) what ... in.

**Wort** [vɔrt] **(-(e)s, ¨er** *od* **-e)** *nt* word; **jdn beim ~ nehmen** to take sb at his word; **ein ernstes ~ mit jdm reden** to have a serious talk with sb; **man kann sein eigenes ~ nicht (mehr) verstehen** you can't hear yourself speak; **jdm aufs ~ gehorchen** to obey sb's every word; **zu ~ kommen** to get a chance to speak; **jdm das ~ erteilen** to allow sb to speak; **~art** *f* (*GRAM*) part of speech; **w~brüchig** *adj* not true to one's word.

**Wörtchen** *nt*: **da habe ich wohl ein ~ mitzureden** (*umg*) I think I have some say in that.

**Wörterbuch** ['vœrtərbu:x] *nt* dictionary.

**Wort-** *zW*: **~fetzen** *pl* snatches *pl* of conversation; **~führer** *m* spokesman; **w~getreu** *adj* true to one's word; (*Übersetzung*) literal; **w~gewaltig** *adj* eloquent; **w~karg** *adj* taciturn; **~laut** *m* wording; **im ~laut** verbatim.

**wörtlich** ['vœrtlɪç] *adj* literal.

**Wort-** *zW:* **w~los** *adj* mute; **~meldung** *f:* **wenn es keine weiteren ~meldungen gibt,** ... if nobody else wishes to speak ...; **w~reich** *adj* wordy, verbose; **~schatz** *m* vocabulary; **~spiel** *nt* play on words, pun; **~wechsel** *m* dispute; **w~wörtlich** *adj* word-for-word ♦ *adv* quite literally.

**worüber** [vo'ry:bər] *adv* (*rel*) over/about which; (*interrog*) what ... over/about.

**worum** [vo'rʊm] *adv* (*rel*) about/round which; (*interrog*) what ... about/round; **~ handelt es sich?** what's it about?

**worunter** [vo'rʊntər] *adv* (*rel*) under which; (*interrog*) what ... under.

**wo-** *zW:* **~von** [vo'fɔn] *adv* (*rel*) from which; (*interrog*) what ... from; **~vor** [vo'fɔr] *adv* (*rel*) in front of/before which; (*interrog*) in front of/before what; **~zu** [vo'tsu] *adv* (*rel*) to/for which; (*interrog*) what ... for/to; (*warum*) why; **~zu soll das gut sein?** what's the point of that?

**Wrack** [vrak] (*-(e)s, -s*) *nt* wreck.

**wrang** *etc* [vraŋ] *vb siehe* **wringen.**

**wringen** ['vrɪŋgən] *unreg vt* to wring.

**WS** *abk* = **Wintersemester.**

**WSV** *abk* = **Winterschlußverkauf.**

**Wucher** ['vu:xər] (*-s*) *m* profiteering; **~er** (*-s, -*) *m*, **~in** *f* profiteer; **w~isch** *adj* profiteering.

**wuchern** *vi* (*Pflanzen*) to grow wild.

**Wucherpreis** *m* exorbitant price.

**Wucherung** *f* (*MED*) growth.

**Wuchs** [vu:ks] (*-es*) *m* (*Wachstum*) growth; (*Statur*) build.

**wuchs** *etc vb siehe* **wachsen¹.**

**Wucht** [vʊxt] (*-*) *f* force.

**wuchtig** *adj* massive, solid.

**wühlen** ['vy:lən] *vi* to scrabble; (*Tier*) to root; (*Maulwurf*) to burrow; (*umg: arbeiten*) to slave away ♦ *vt* to dig.

**Wühlmaus** *f* vole.

**Wühltisch** *m* (*in Kaufhaus*) bargain counter.

**Wulst** [vʊlst] (*-es, ⁓e*) *m* bulge; (*an Wunde*) swelling.

**wulstig** *adj* bulging; (*Rand, Lippen*) thick.

**wund** [vʊnt] *adj* sore; **sich** *dat* **die Füße ~ laufen** (*lit*) to get sore feet from walking; (*fig*) to walk one's legs off; **ein ~er Punkt** a sore point; **W~brand** *m* gangrene.

**Wunde** ['vʊndə] (*-, -n*) *f* wound; **alte ~n wieder aufreißen** (*fig*) to open up old wounds.

**wunder** ['vʊndər] *adv:* **meine Eltern denken ~ was passiert ist** my parents think goodness knows what has happened.

**Wunder** (*-s, -*) *nt* miracle; **es ist kein ~** it's no wonder; **w~bar** *adj* wonderful, marvellous (*BRIT*), marvelous (*US*); **~kerze** *f* sparkler; **~kind** *nt* child prodigy; **w~lich** *adj* odd, peculiar.

**wundern** *vt* to surprise ♦ *vr:* **sich ~ über** *+akk*
to be surprised at.

**Wunder-** *zW:* **w~schön** *adj* beautiful; **~tüte** *f* lucky bag; **w~voll** *adj* wonderful.

**Wundfieber** (*-s*) *nt* traumatic fever.

**Wundstarrkrampf** ['vʊntʃtarkrampf] *m* tetanus, lockjaw.

**Wunsch** [vʊnʃ] (*-(e)s, ⁓e*) *m* wish; **haben Sie (sonst) noch einen ~?** (*beim Einkauf etc*) is there anything else you'd like?; **auf jds (besonderen/ausdrücklichen) ~ hin** at sb's (special/express) request; **~denken** *nt* wishful thinking.

**Wünschelrute** ['vʏnʃəlru:tə] *f* divining rod.

**wünschen** ['vʏnʃən] *vt* to wish ♦ *vi:* **zu ~/viel zu ~ übrig lassen** to leave something/a great deal to be desired; **sich** *dat* **etw ~** to want sth, wish for sth; **was ~ Sie?** (*in Geschäft*) what can I do for you?; (*in Restaurant*) what would you like?

**wünschenswert** *adj* desirable.

**Wunsch-** *zW:* **~kind** *nt* planned child; **~konzert** *nt* (*RUNDF*) musical request programme (*BRIT*) *od* program (*US*); **w~los** *adj:* **w~los glücklich** perfectly happy; **~traum** *m* dream; (*unrealistisch*) pipe dream; **~zettel** *m* list of things one would like.

**wurde** *etc* ['vʊrdə] *vb siehe* **werden.**

**Würde** ['vʏrdə] (*-, -n*) *f* dignity; (*Stellung*) honour (*BRIT*), honor (*US*); **unter aller ~ sein** to be beneath contempt.

**Würdenträger** *m* dignitary.

**würdevoll** *adj* dignified.

**würdig** ['vʏrdɪç] *adj* worthy; (*würdevoll*) dignified.

**würdigen** ['vʏrdɪgən] *vt* to appreciate; **etw zu ~ wissen** to appreciate sth; **jdn keines Blickes ~** not to so much as look at sb.

**Wurf** [vʊrf] (*-(e)s, ⁓e*) *m* throw; (*Junge*) litter.

**Würfel** ['vʏrfəl] (*-s, -*) *m* dice; (*MATH*) cube; **die ~ sind gefallen** the die is cast; **~becher** ´*m* (dice) cup.

**würfeln** *vi* to play dice ♦ *vt* to dice.

**Würfelspiel** *nt* game of dice.

**Würfelzucker** *m* lump sugar.

**Wurf-** *zW:* **~geschoß** *nt* projectile; **~sendung** *f* circular; **~sendungen** *pl* (*Reklame*) junk mail.

**Würgegriff** (*-(e)s*) *m* (*lit, fig*) stranglehold.

**würgen** ['vʏrgən] *vt, vi* to choke; **mit Hängen und W~** by the skin of one's teeth.

**Wurm** [vʊrm] (*-(e)s, ⁓er*) *m* worm; **da steckt der ~ drin** (*fig: umg*) there's something wrong somewhere; (*verdächtig*) there's something fishy about it (*umg*).

**wurmen** (*umg*) *vt* to rile, nettle.

**Wurmfortsatz** *m* (*MED*) appendix.

**wurmig** *adj* worm-eaten.

**wurmstichig** *adj* worm-ridden.

**Wurst** [vʊrst] (*-, ⁓e*) *f* sausage; **das ist mir ~** (*umg*) I don't care, I don't give a damn; **jetzt geht es um die ~** (*fig: umg*) the moment of truth has come.

**Würstchen** ['vyrstçən] *nt* frankfurter, hot dog sausage; **~bude** *f*, **~stand** *m* hot dog stall.
**Württemberg** ['vyrtəmberk] *nt* Württemberg.
**Würze** ['vyrtsə] (-, -n) *f* seasoning.
**Wurzel** ['vortsəl] (-, -n) *f* root; **~n schlagen** (*lit*) to root; (*fig*) to put down roots; **die ~ aus 4 ist 2** (*MATH*) the square root of 4 is 2.
**würzen** *vt* to season; (*würzig machen*) to spice.
**würzig** *adj* spicy.
**wusch** *etc* [vu:ʃ] *vb siehe* **waschen**.
**wußte** *etc* ['vostə] *vb siehe* **wissen**.
**Wust** [vu:st] (-(e)s) (*umg*) *m* (*Durcheinander*) jumble; (*Menge*) pile.
**wüst** [vy:st] *adj* untidy, messy; (*ausschweifend*) wild; (*öde*) waste; (*umg: heftig*) terrible; **jdn ~ beschimpfen** to use vile language to sb.
**Wüste** (-, -n) *f* desert; **die ~ Gobi** the Gobi Desert; **jdn in die ~ schicken** (*fig*) to send sb packing.
**Wut** [vu:t] (-) *f* rage, fury; **eine ~ (auf jdn/ etw) haben** to be furious (with sb/sth); **~anfall** *m* fit of rage.
**wüten** ['vy:tən] *vi* to rage.
**wütend** *adj* furious, enraged.
**wutentbrannt** *adj* furious, enraged.
**Wz** *abk* (= *Warenzeichen*) ®.

# X, x

**X, x** [ɪks] *nt* X, x; **~ wie Xanthippe** ≈ X for Xmas; **jdm ein ~ für ein U vormachen** to put one over on sb (*umg*).
**X-Beine** ['ɪksbaɪnə] *pl* knock-knees *pl*.
**x-beliebig** [ɪksbə'li:biç] *adj* any (... whatever).
**Xerographie** [kseroɡra'fi:] *f* xerography.
**xerokopieren** [kseroko'pi:rən] *vt* to xerox, photocopy.
**x-fach** ['ɪksfax] *adj:* **die ~e Menge** (*MATH*) n times the amount.
**x-mal** ['ɪksma:l] *adv* any number of times, n times.
**x-te** ['ɪkstə] *adj* (*MATH: umg*) nth; **zum ~n Male** (*umg*) for the nth *od* umpteenth time.
**Xylophon** [ksylo'fo:n] (-s, -e) *nt* xylophone.

# Y, y

**Y, y** ['ʏpsilɔn] *nt* Y, y; **~ wie Ypsilon** ≈ Y for Yellow, Y for Yoke (*US*).
**Yen** [jɛn] (-(s), -(s)) *m* yen.
**Yoga** ['jo:ɡa] (-(s)) *m od nt* yoga.
**Ypsilon** ['ʏpsilɔn] (-(s), -s) *nt* the letter Y.

# Z, z

**Z, z** [tsɛt] *nt* Z, z; **~ wie Zacharias** ≈ Z for Zebra.
**Zack** [tsak] *m:* **auf ~ sein** (*umg*) to be on the ball.
**Zacke** ['tsakə] (-, -n) *f* point; (*Berg~*) jagged peak; (*Gabel~*) prong; (*Kamm~*) tooth.
**zackig** ['tsakɪç] *adj* jagged; (*umg*) smart; (: *Tempo*) brisk.
**zaghaft** ['tsa:khaft] *adj* timid.
**Zaghaftigkeit** *f* timidity.
**Zagreb** ['za:ɡrɛp] (-s) *nt* Zagreb.
**zäh** [tsɛ:] *adj* tough; (*Mensch*) tenacious; (*Flüssigkeit*) thick; (*schleppend*) sluggish; **~flüssig** *adj* viscous; (*Verkehr*) slow-moving.
**Zähigkeit** *f* toughness; tenacity.
**Zahl** [tsa:l] (-, -en) *f* number.
**zahlbar** *adj* payable.
**zahlen** *vt, vi* to pay; **~ bitte!** the bill *od* check (*US*) please!
**zählen** ['tsɛ:lən] *vt* to count ♦ *vi* (*sich verlassen*): **~ auf** +*akk* to count on; **seine Tage sind gezählt** his days are numbered; **~ zu** to be numbered among.
**Zahlen-** *zW:* **~angabe** *f* figure; **~kombination** *f* combination of figures; **z~mäßig** *adj* numerical; **~schloß** *nt* combination lock.
**Zahler** (-s, -) *m* payer.
**Zähler** (-s, -) *m* (*TECH*) meter; (*MATH*) numerator; **~stand** *m* meter reading.
**Zahl-** *zW:* **~grenze** *f* fare stage; **~karte** *f* transfer form; **z~los** *adj* countless; **~meister** *m* (*NAUT*) purser; **z~reich** *adj* numerous; **~tag** *m* payday.
**Zahlung** *f* payment; **in ~ geben/nehmen** to give/take in part exchange.
**Zahlungs-** *zW:* **~anweisung** *f* transfer order; **~aufforderung** *f* request for payment;

**z~fähig** *adj* solvent; **~mittel** *nt* means *sing* of payment; (*Münzen, Banknoten*) currency; **~rückstände** *pl* arrears *pl*; **z~unfähig** *adj* insolvent; **~verzug** *m* default.
**Zahlwort** *nt* numeral.
**zahm** [tsa:m] *adj* tame.
**zähmen** ['tsɛ:mən] *vt* to tame; (*fig*) to curb.
**Zahn** [tsa:n] (-(e)s, ⁻e) *m* tooth; **die dritten Zähne** (*umg*) false teeth *pl*; **einen ~ drauf haben** (*umg: Geschwindigkeit*) to be going like the clappers (*BRIT*) *od* like crazy (*US*); **jdm auf den ~ fühlen** (*fig*) to sound sb out; **einen ~ zulegen** (*fig*) to get a move on; **~arzt** *m*, **~ärztin** *f* dentist; **~belag** *m* plaque; **~bürste** *f* toothbrush; **~creme** *f* toothpaste; **z~en** *vi* to teethe; **~ersatz** *m* denture; **~fäule** (-) *f* tooth decay, caries *sing*; **~fleisch** *nt* gums *pl*; **auf dem ~fleisch gehen** (*fig: umg*) to be all in, be at the end of one's tether; **z~los** *adj* toothless; **~medizin** *f* dentistry; **~pasta** *f*, **~paste** *f* toothpaste; **~rad** *nt* cog(wheel); **~radbahn** *f* rack railway; **~schmelz** *m* (tooth) enamel; **~schmerzen** *pl* toothache *sing*; **~seide** *f* dental floss; **~spange** *f* brace; **~stein** *m* tartar; **~stocher** (-s, -) *m* toothpick; **~techniker(in)** *m(f)* dental technician; **~weh** *nt* toothache.
**Zaire** [za'i:r] (-s) *nt* Zaire.
**Zange** ['tsaŋə] (-, -n) *f* pliers *pl*; (*Zucker~ etc*) tongs *pl*; (*Beiß~, ZOOL*) pincers *pl*; (*MED*) forceps *pl*; **jdn in die ~ nehmen** (*fig*) to put the screws on sb (*umg*).
**Zangengeburt** *f* forceps delivery.
**Zankapfel** *m* bone of contention.
**zanken** ['tsaŋkən] *vi, vr* to quarrel.
**zänkisch** ['tsɛŋkɪʃ] *adj* quarrelsome.
**Zäpfchen** ['tsɛpfçən] *nt* (*ANAT*) uvula; (*MED*) suppository.
**Zapfen** ['tsapfən] (-s, -) *m* plug; (*BOT*) cone; (*Eis~*) icicle.
**zapfen** *vt* to tap.
**Zapfenstreich** *m* (*MIL*) tattoo.
**Zapfsäule** *f* petrol (*BRIT*) *od* gas (*US*) pump.
**zappelig** ['tsapəlıç] *adj* wriggly; (*unruhig*) fidgety.
**zappeln** ['tsapəln] *vi* to wriggle; to fidget; **jdn ~ lassen** (*fig: umg*) to keep sb in suspense.
**Zar** [tsa:r] (-en, -en) *m* tzar, czar.
**zart** [tsart] *adj* (*weich, leise*) soft; (*Braten etc*) tender; (*fein, schwächlich*) delicate; **~besaitet** *adj attrib* highly sensitive; **~bitter** *adj* (*Schokolade*) plain (*BRIT*), bittersweet (*US*); **Z~gefühl** *nt* tact; **Z~heit** *f* softness; tenderness; delicacy.
**zärtlich** ['tsɛ:rtlıç] *adj* tender, affectionate; **Z~keit** *f* tenderness; **Zärtlichkeiten** *pl* caresses *pl*.
**Zäsur** [tsɛ'zu:r] *f* caesura; (*fig*) break.
**Zauber** ['tsaʊbər] (-s, -) *m* magic; (*~bann*) spell; **fauler ~** (*umg*) humbug.
**Zauberei** [tsaʊbə'raɪ] *f* magic.

**Zauberer** (-s, -) *m* magician; (*Zauberkünstler*) conjurer.
**Zauber-** *zW:* **z~haft** *adj* magical, enchanting; **~in** *f* magician; conjurer; **~künstler** *m* conjurer; **~kunststück** *nt* conjuring trick; **~mittel** *nt* magical cure; (*Trank*) magic potion.
**zaubern** *vi* to conjure, do magic.
**Zauberspruch** *m* (magic) spell.
**Zauberstab** *m* magic wand.
**zaudern** ['tsaʊdərn] *vi* to hesitate.
**Zaum** [tsaʊm] (-(e)s, Zäume) *m* bridle; **etw im ~ halten** to keep sth in check.
**Zaun** [tsaʊn] (-(e)s, Zäune) *m* fence; **vom ~(e) brechen** (*fig*) to start; **~gast** *m* (*Person*) mere onlooker; **~könig** *m* wren.
**z.B.** *abk* (= *zum Beispiel*) e.g.
**z.d.A.** *abk* (= *zu den Akten*) to be filed.

The **ZDF** (*Zweites Deutsches Fernsehen*) is the second German television channel. It was founded in 1961 and is based in Mainz. It is financed by licence fees and advertising. About 40% of its transmissions are news and education programmes.

**Zebra** ['tse:bra] (-s, -s) *nt* zebra; **~streifen** *m* pedestrian crossing (*BRIT*), crosswalk (*US*).
**Zeche** ['tsɛçə] (-, -n) *f* (*Rechnung*) bill, check (*US*); (*Bergbau*) mine.
**zechen** *vi* to booze (*umg*).
**Zechprellerei** [tsɛçprɛlə'raɪ] *f* skipping payment in restaurants etc.
**Zecke** ['tsɛkə] (-, -n) *f* tick.
**Zeder** ['tse:dər] (-, -n) *f* cedar.
**Zeh** [tse:] (-s, -en) *m* toe.
**Zehe** ['tse:ə] (-, -n) *f* toe; (*Knoblauch~*) clove.
**Zehenspitze** *f*: **auf ~n** on tiptoe.
**zehn** [tse:n] *num* ten.
**Zehnerpackung** *f* packet of ten.
**Zehnfingersystem** *nt* touch-typing method.
**Zehnkampf** *m* (*SPORT*) decathlon.
**zehnte(r, s)** *adj* tenth.
**Zehntel** (-s, -) *nt* tenth (part).
**zehren** ['tse:rən] *vi:* **an jdm/etw ~** (*an Mensch, Kraft*) to wear sb/sth out.
**Zeichen** ['tsaıçən] (-s, -) *nt* sign; (*COMPUT*) character; **jdm ein ~ geben** to give sb a signal; **unser/Ihr ~** (*COMM*) our/your reference; **~block** *m* sketch pad; **~code** *m* (*COMPUT*) character code; **~erklärung** *f* key; (*auf Karten*) legend; **~folge** *f* (*COMPUT*) string; **~kette** *f* (*COMPUT*) character string; **~satz** *m* (*COMPUT*) character set; **~setzung** *f* punctuation; **~trickfilm** *m* (animated) cartoon.
**zeichnen** *vt* to draw; (*kenn~*) to mark; (*unter~*) to sign ♦ *vi* to draw; to sign.
**Zeichner(in)** (-s, -) *m(f)* artist; **technischer ~** draughtsman (*BRIT*), draftsman (*US*).
**Zeichnung** *f* drawing; (*Markierung*) marking *pl*.

**zeichnungsberechtigt** adj authorized to sign.

**Zeigefinger** m index finger.

**zeigen** ['tsaɪgən] vt to show ♦ vi to point ♦ vr to show o.s.; ~ **auf** +akk to point to; **es wird sich** ~ time will tell; **es zeigte sich, daß ...** it turned out that ...

**Zeiger** (-s, -) m pointer; (Uhr~) hand.

**Zeile** ['tsaɪlə] (-, -n) f line; (Häuser~) row.

**Zeilen-** zW: ~**abstand** m line spacing; ~**ausrichtung** f justification; ~**drucker** m line printer; ~**umbruch** m (COMPUT) wraparound; ~**vorschub** m (COMPUT) line feed.

**zeit** [tsaɪt] präp +gen: ~ **meines Lebens** in my lifetime.

**Zeit** (-, -en) f time; (GRAM) tense; **zur** ~ at the moment; **sich** dat ~ **lassen** to take one's time; **eine Stunde** ~ **haben** to have an hour (to spare); **sich** dat **für jdn/etw** ~ **nehmen** to devote time to sb/sth; **von** ~ **zu** ~ from time to time; **in letzter** ~ recently; **nach** ~ **bezahlt werden** to be paid by the hour; **zu der** ~, **als ...** (at the time) when ...

**Zeit-** zW: ~**alter** nt age; ~**ansage** f (RUNDF) time check; (TEL) speaking clock; ~**arbeit** f temporary work; ~**aufwand** m time (needed for a task); ~**bombe** f time bomb; ~**druck** m: **unter** ~**druck stehen** to be under pressure; ~**geist** m spirit of the times; z~**gemäß** adj in keeping with the times; ~**genosse** m contemporary; z~**genössisch** ['tsaɪtgənœsɪʃ] adj contemporary.

**Zeit-** zW: ~**karte** f season ticket; z~**kritisch** adj (Aufsatz) commenting on contemporary issues; ~**lang** f: **eine** ~**lang** a while, a time; z~**lebens** adv all one's life; z~**lich** adj temporal ♦ adv: **das kann sie** z~**lich nicht einrichten** she can't find (the) time for that; **das** ~**liche segnen** (euph) to depart this life; z~**los** adj timeless; ~**lupe** f slow motion; ~**lupentempo** nt: **im** ~**lupentempo** at a snail's pace; ~**not** f: **in** ~**not geraten** to run short of time; ~**plan** m schedule; ~**punkt** m moment, point in time; ~**raffer** (-s) m time-lapse photography; z~**raubend** adj time-consuming; ~**raum** m period; ~**rechnung** f time, era; **nach/vor unserer** ~**rechnung** A.D./B.C.; ~**schrift** f periodical; ~**tafel** f chronological table.

**Zeitung** f newspaper.

**Zeitungs-** zW: ~**anzeige** f newspaper advertisement; ~**ausschnitt** m press cutting; ~**händler** m newsagent (BRIT), newsdealer (US); ~**papier** nt newsprint.

**Zeit-** zW: ~**verschwendung** f waste of time; ~**vertreib** m pastime, diversion; z~**weilig** adj temporary; z~**weise** adv for a time; ~**wort** nt verb; ~**zeichen** nt (RUNDF) time signal; ~**zone** f time zone; ~**zünder** m time fuse.

**Zelle** ['tsɛlə] (-, -n) f cell; (Telefon~) callbox

(BRIT), booth.

**Zellkern** m cell, nucleus.

**Zellophan** [tsɛlo'faːn] (-s) nt cellophane.

**Zellstoff** m cellulose.

**Zellteilung** f cell division.

**Zelt** [tsɛlt] (-(e)s, -e) nt tent; **seine** ~**e aufschlagen/abbrechen** to settle down/pack one's bags; ~**bahn** f groundsheet; z~**en** vi to camp; ~**lager** nt camp; ~**platz** m camp site.

**Zement** [tse'mɛnt] (-(e)s, -e) m cement.

**zementieren** [tsemɛn'tiːrən] vt to cement.

**Zementmaschine** f cement mixer.

**Zenit** [tse'niːt] (-(e)s) m (lit, fig) zenith.

**zensieren** [tsɛn'ziːrən] vt to censor; (SCH) to mark.

**Zensur** [tsɛn'zuːr] f censorship; (SCH) mark.

**Zensus** ['tsɛnzʊs] (-, -) m census.

**Zentimeter** [tsɛnti'meːtər] m od nt centimetre (BRIT), centimeter (US); ~**maß** nt (metric) tape measure.

**Zentner** ['tsɛntnər] (-s, -) m hundredweight.

**zentral** [tsɛn'traːl] adj central.

**Zentrale** (-, -n) f central office; (TEL) exchange.

**Zentraleinheit** f (COMPUT) central processing unit.

**Zentralheizung** f central heating.

**zentralisieren** [tsɛntrali'ziːrən] vt to centralize.

**Zentralverriegelung** f (AUT) central locking.

**Zentrifugalkraft** [tsɛntrifu'gaːlkraft] f centrifugal force.

**Zentrifuge** [tsɛntri'fuːgə] (-, -n) f centrifuge; (für Wäsche) spin-dryer.

**Zentrum** ['tsɛntrʊm] (-s, Zentren) nt centre (BRIT), center (US).

**Zepter** ['tsɛptər] (-s, -) nt sceptre (BRIT), scepter (US).

**zerbrechen** unreg vt, vi to break.

**zerbrechlich** adj fragile.

**zerbröckeln** [tsɛr'brœkəln] vt, vi to crumble (to pieces).

**zerdeppern** [tsɛr'dɛpərn] vt to smash.

**zerdrücken** vt to squash; to crush; (Kartoffeln) to mash.

**Zeremonie** [tseremo'niː] f ceremony.

**Zeremoniell** [tseremoni'ɛl] (-s, -e) nt ceremonial.

**zerfahren** adj scatterbrained, distracted.

**Zerfall** m decay, disintegration; (von Kultur, Gesundheit) decline; z~**en** unreg vi to disintegrate, decay; (sich gliedern): z~**en in** +akk to fall into.

**zerfetzen** [tsɛr'fɛtsən] vt to tear to pieces.

**zerfleischen** [tsɛr'flaɪʃən] vt to tear to pieces.

**zerfließen** unreg vi to dissolve, melt away.

**zerfressen** unreg vt to eat away; (Motten, Mäuse etc) to eat.

**zergehen** unreg vi to melt, dissolve.

**zerkleinern** [tsɛr'klaɪnərn] vt to reduce to small pieces.

**zerklüftet** [tsɛr'klyftət] *adj:* **tief ~es Gestein** deeply fissured rock.

**zerknirscht** [tsɛr'knɪrʃt] *adj* overcome with remorse.

**zerknüllen** [tsɛr'knylən] *vt* to crumple up.

**zerlaufen** *unreg vi* to melt.

**zerlegbar** [tsɛr'le:kba:r] *adj* able to be dismantled.

**zerlegen** *vt* to take to pieces; (*Fleisch*) to carve; (*Satz*) to analyse.

**zerlumpt** [tsɛr'lʊmpt] *adj* ragged.

**zermalmen** [tsɛr'malmən] *vt* to crush.

**zermürben** [tsɛr'myrbən] *vt* to wear down.

**zerpflücken** *vt* (*lit, fig*) to pick to pieces.

**zerplatzen** *vi* to burst.

**zerquetschen** *vt* to squash.

**Zerrbild** ['tsɛrbɪlt] *nt* (*fig*) caricature, distorted picture.

**zerreden** *vt* (*Problem*) to flog to death.

**zerreiben** *unreg vt* to grind down.

**zerreißen** *unreg vt* to tear to pieces ♦ *vi* to tear, rip.

**Zerreißprobe** *f* (*lit*) pull test; (*fig*) real test.

**zerren** ['tsɛrən] *vt* to drag ♦ *vi:* ~ **(an** +*dat*) to tug (at).

**zerrinnen** *unreg vi* to melt away; (*Geld*) to disappear.

**zerrissen** [tsɛr'rɪsən] *pp von* **zerreißen** ♦ *adj* torn, tattered; **Z~heit** *f* tattered state; (*POL*) disunion, discord; (*innere*) disintegration.

**Zerrspiegel** ['tsɛrʃpi:gəl] *m* (*lit*) distorting mirror; (*fig*) travesty.

**Zerrung** *f:* **eine ~** a pulled ligament/muscle.

**zerrütten** [tsɛr'rytən] *vt* to wreck, destroy.

**zerrüttet** *adj* wrecked, shattered.

**Zerrüttungsprinzip** *nt* (*bei Ehescheidung*) principle of irretrievable breakdown.

**zerschellen** [tsɛr'ʃɛlən] *vi* (*Schiff, Flugzeug*) to be smashed to pieces.

**zerschießen** *unreg vt* to shoot to pieces.

**zerschlagen** *unreg vt* to shatter, smash; (*fig: Opposition*) to crush; (: *Vereinigung*) to break up ♦ *vr* to fall through.

**zerschleißen** [tsɛr'ʃlaɪsən] *unreg vt, vi* to wear out.

**zerschmelzen** *unreg vi* to melt.

**zerschmettern** [tsɛr'ʃmɛtərn] *unreg vt* to shatter; (*Feind*) to crush ♦ *vi* to shatter.

**zerschneiden** *unreg vt* to cut up.

**zersetzen** *vt, vr* to decompose, dissolve.

**zersetzend** *adj* (*fig*) subversive.

**zersplittern** [tsɛr'ʃplɪtərn] *vt, vi* to split (into pieces); (*Glas*) to shatter.

**zerspringen** *unreg vi* to shatter ♦ *vi* (*fig*) to burst.

**zerstäuben** [tsɛr'ʃtɔybən] *vt* to spray.

**Zerstäuber** (**-s, -**) *m* atomizer.

**zerstören** *vt* to destroy.

**Zerstörer** (**-s, -**) *m* (*NAUT*) destroyer.

**Zerstörung** *f* destruction.

**Zerstörungswut** *f* destructive mania.

**zerstoßen** *unreg vt* to pound, pulverize.

**zerstreiten** *unreg vr* to fall out, break up.

**zerstreuen** *vt* to disperse, scatter; (*Zweifel etc*) to dispel ♦ *vr* (*sich verteilen*) to scatter; (*fig*) to be dispelled; (*sich ablenken*) to take one's mind off things.

**zerstreut** *adj* scattered; (*Mensch*) absent-minded; **Z~heit** *f* absent-mindedness.

**Zerstreuung** *f* dispersion; (*Ablenkung*) diversion.

**zerstritten** *adj:* **mit jdm zerstritten sein** to be on very bad terms with sb.

**zerstückeln** [tsɛr'ʃtykəln] *vt* to cut into pieces.

**zerteilen** *vt* to divide into parts.

**Zertifikat** [tsɛrtifi'ka:t] (**-(e)s, -e**) *nt* certificate.

**zertreten** *unreg vt* to crush underfoot.

**zertrümmern** [tsɛr'trymərn] *vt* to shatter; (*Gebäude etc*) to demolish.

**zerwühlen** *vt* to ruffle up, tousle; (*Bett*) to rumple (up).

**Zerwürfnis** [tsɛr'vyrfnɪs] (**-ses, -se**) *nt* dissension, quarrel.

**zerzausen** [tsɛr'tsauzən] *vt* (*Haare*) to ruffle up, tousle.

**zetern** ['tse:tərn] (*pej*) *vi* to clamour (*BRIT*), clamor (*US*); (*keifen*) to scold.

**Zettel** ['tsɛtəl] (**-s, -**) *m* piece *od* slip of paper; (*Notiz~*) note; (*Formular*) form; „~ **ankleben verboten"** "stick no bills"; ~**kasten** *m* card index (box); ~**wirtschaft** (*pej*) *f:* **eine ~wirtschaft haben** to have bits of paper everywhere.

**Zeug** [tsɔyk] (**-(e)s, -e**) (*umg*) *nt* stuff; (*Ausrüstung*) gear; **dummes ~** (stupid) nonsense; **das ~ haben zu** to have the makings of; **sich ins ~ legen** to put one's shoulder to the wheel; **was das ~ hält** for all one is worth; **jdm am ~ flicken** to find fault with sb.

**Zeuge** ['tsɔygə] (**-n, -n**) *m* witness.

**zeugen** *vi* to bear witness, testify ♦ *vt* (*Kind*) to father; **es zeugt von ...** it testifies to ...

**Zeugenaussage** *f* evidence.

**Zeugenstand** *m* witness box (*BRIT*) *od* stand (*US*).

**Zeugin** *f* witness.

**Zeugnis** ['tsɔygnɪs] (**-ses, -se**) *nt* certificate; (*SCH*) report; (*Referenz*) reference; (*Aussage*) evidence, testimony; ~ **geben von** to be evidence of, testify to; ~**konferenz** *f* (*SCH*) staff meeting to decide on marks *etc*.

**Zeugung** ['tsɔygʊŋ] *f* procreation.

**zeugungsunfähig** *adj* sterile.

**ZH** *abk* = **Zentralheizung**.

**z.H., z.Hd.** *abk* (= *zu Händen*) att., attn.

**Zicken** ['tsɪkən] (*umg*) *pl:* ~ **machen** to make trouble.

**zickig** *adj* (*albern*) silly; (*prüde*) prudish.

**Zickzack** ['tsɪktsak] (**-(e)s, -e**) *m* zigzag.

**Ziege** ['tsi:gə] (**-, -n**) *f* goat; (*pej: umg: Frau*) cow (*!*).

**Ziegel** ['tsi:gəl] (**-s, -**) *m* brick; (*Dach~*) tile.

**Ziegelei** [tsi:gə'laɪ] *f* brickworks.

**Ziegelstein** m brick.
**Ziegenbock** m billy goat.
**Ziegenleder** nt kid.
**Ziegenpeter** m mumps sing.
**Ziehbrunnen** m well.
**ziehen** ['tsi:ən] unreg vt to draw; (zerren) to pull; (SCHACH etc) to move; (züchten) to rear ♦ vi to draw; (um~, wandern) to move; (Rauch, Wolke etc) to drift; (reißen) to pull ♦ vb unpers: **es zieht** there is a draught (BRIT) od draft (US), it's draughty (BRIT) od drafty (US) ♦ vr (Gummi) to stretch; (Grenze etc) to run; (Gespräche) to be drawn out; **etw nach sich ~** to lead to sth, entail sth; **etw ins Lächerliche ~** to ridicule sth; **so was zieht bei mir nicht** I don't like that sort of thing; **zu jdm ~** to move in with sb; **mir zieht's im Rücken** my back hurts; **Z~** (-s, -) nt (Schmerz) ache; (im Unterleib) dragging pain.
**Ziehharmonika** ['tsi:harmo:nika] f concertina.
**Ziehung** ['tsi:uŋ] f (Los~) drawing.
**Ziel** [tsi:l] (-(e)s, -e) nt (einer Reise) destination; (SPORT) finish; (MIL) target; (Absicht) goal, aim; **jdm/sich ein ~ stecken** to set sb/o.s. a goal; **am ~ sein** to be at one's destination; (fig) to have reached one's goal; **über das ~ hinausschießen** (fig) to overshoot the mark; **z~bewußt** adj purposeful; **z~en** vi: **z~en (auf +akk)** to aim (at); **~fernrohr** nt telescopic sight; **~foto** nt (SPORT) photo-finish, photograph; **~gruppe** f target group; **~linie** f (SPORT) finishing line; **z~los** adj aimless; **~ort** m destination; **~scheibe** f target; **z~strebig** adj purposeful.
**ziemen** ['tsi:mən] vr unpers (geh): **das ziemt sich nicht (für dich)** it is not proper (for you).
**ziemlich** ['tsi:mlıç] adj attrib (Anzahl) fair ♦ adv quite, pretty (umg); (beinahe) almost, nearly; **eine ~e Anstrengung** quite an effort; **~ lange** quite a long time; **~ fertig** almost od nearly ready.
**Zierde** ['tsi:rdə] (-, -n) f ornament, decoration; (Schmuckstück) adornment.
**zieren** ['tsi:rən] vr to act coy.
**Zierleiste** f border; (an Wand, Möbeln) moulding (BRIT), molding (US); (an Auto) trim.
**zierlich** adj dainty; **Z~keit** f daintiness.
**Zierstrauch** m flowering shrub.
**Ziffer** ['tsıfər] (-, -n) f figure, digit; **römische/ arabische ~n** roman/arabic numerals; **~blatt** nt dial, (clock od watch) face.
**zig** [tsık] (umg) adj umpteen.
**Zigarette** [tsiga'rɛtə] f cigarette.
**Zigaretten-** zW: **~automat** m cigarette machine; **~pause** f break for a cigarette; **~schachtel** f cigarette packet od pack (US); **~spitze** f cigarette holder.
**Zigarillo** [tsiga'rılo] (-s, -s) nt od m cigarillo.
**Zigarre** [tsi'garə] (-, -n) f cigar.

**Zigeuner(in)** [tsi'gɔynər(ın)] (-s, -) m(f) gipsy; **~schnitzel** nt (KOCH) cutlet served in a spicy sauce with green and red peppers; **~sprache** f Romany, Romany od Gypsy language.
**Zimmer** ['tsımər] (-s, -) nt room; **~antenne** f indoor aerial; **~decke** f ceiling; **~lautstärke** f reasonable volume; **~mädchen** nt chambermaid; **~mann** (-(e)s, pl -leute) m carpenter.
**zimmern** vt to make from wood.
**Zimmer-** zW: **~nachweis** m accommodation service; **~pflanze** f indoor plant; **~vermittlung** f accommodation (BRIT) od accommodations (US) service.
**zimperlich** ['tsımpərlıç] adj squeamish; (pingelig) fussy, finicky.
**Zimt** [tsımt] (-(e)s, -e) m cinnamon; **~stange** f cinnamon stick.
**Zink** [tsıŋk] (-(e)s) nt zinc.
**Zinke** (-, -n) f (Gabel~) prong; (Kamm~) tooth.
**Zinken** (-s, -) (umg) m (Nase) hooter.
**zinken** vt (Karten) to mark.
**Zinksalbe** f zinc ointment.
**Zinn** [tsın] (-(e)s) nt (Element) tin; (in ~waren) pewter; **~becher** m pewter tankard.
**zinnoberrot** [tsı'no:bərrot] adj vermilion.
**Zinnsoldat** m tin soldier.
**Zinnwaren** pl pewter sing.
**Zins** [tsıns] (-es, -en) m interest.
**Zinseszins** m compound interest.
**Zins-** zW: **~fuß** m rate of interest; **z~los** adj interest-free; **~satz** m rate of interest.
**Zionismus** [tsio'nısmus] m Zionism.
**Zipfel** ['tsıpfəl] (-s, -) m corner; (von Land) tip; (Hemd~) tail; (Wurst~) end; **~mütze** f pointed cap.
**zirka** ['tsırka] adv (round) about.
**Zirkel** ['tsırkəl] (-s, -) m circle; (MATH) pair of compasses; **~kasten** m geometry set.
**zirkulieren** [tsırku'li:rən] vi to circulate.
**Zirkus** ['tsırkus] (-, -se) m circus; (umg: Getue) fuss, to-do.
**zirpen** ['tsırpən] vi to chirp, cheep.
**Zirrhose** ['tsı'ro:zə] (-, -n) f cirrhosis.
**zischeln** ['tsıʃəln] vt, vi to whisper.
**zischen** ['tsıʃən] vi to hiss; (Limonade) to fizz; (Fett) to sizzle.
**Zitat** [tsi'ta:t] (-(e)s, -e) nt quotation, quote.
**zitieren** [tsi'ti:rən] vt to quote; (vorladen, rufen): **~ (vor +akk)** to summon (before).
**Zitronat** [tsitro'na:t] (-(e)s, -e) nt candied lemon peel.
**Zitrone** [tsi'tro:nə] (-, -n) f lemon.
**Zitronen-** zW: **~limonade** f lemonade; **~saft** m lemon juice; **~säure** f citric acid; **~scheibe** f lemon slice.
**zitt(e)rig** ['tsıt(ə)rıç] adj shaky.
**zittern** ['tsıtərn] vi to tremble; **vor jdm ~** to be terrified of sb.
**Zitze** ['tsıtsə] (-, -n) f teat, dug.

**Zivi** ['tsivi] (**-s**, **-s**) *m abk* = **Zivildienstleistender**.

**zivil** [tsi'viːl] *adj* civilian; (*anständig*) civil; (*Preis*) moderate; **~er Ungehorsam** civil disobedience; **Z~** (**-s**) *nt* plain clothes *pl*; (*MIL*) civilian clothing; **Z~bevölkerung** *f* civilian population; **Z~courage** *f* courage of one's convictions.

**Zivildienst** *m alternative service (for conscientious objectors)*.

---

A young German has to complete his 13 months' **Zivildienst** or community service if he has opted out of military service as a conscientious objector. This service is usually done in a hospital or old-people's home. About 18% of young Germans choose to do this as an alternative to the **Wehrdienst**, although it lasts three months longer.

---

**Zivildienstleistender** *m conscientious objector doing alternative community service.*

**Zivilisation** [tsivilizatsi'oːn] *f* civilization.

**Zivilisationserscheinung** *f* phenomenon of civilization.

**Zivilisationskrankheit** *f* disease of civilized man.

**zivilisieren** [tsivili'ziːrən] *vt* to civilize.

**zivilisiert** *adj* civilized.

**Zivilist** [tsivi'lɪst] *m* civilian.

**Zivilrecht** *nt* civil law.

**ZK** (**-s**, **-s**) *nt abk* (= *Zentralkomitee*) central committee.

**Zobel** ['tsoːbəl] (**-s**, **-**) *m* (*auch:* ~**pelz**) sable (fur).

**Zofe** ['tsoːfə] (**-**, **-n**) *f* lady's maid; (*von Königin*) lady-in-waiting.

**zog** *etc* [tsoːk] *vb siehe* **ziehen**.

**zögern** ['tsøːgərn] *vi* to hesitate.

**Zölibat** [tsøli'baːt] (**-(e)s**) *nt od m* celibacy.

**Zoll¹** [tsɔl] (**-(e)s**, **-**) *m* (*Maß*) inch.

**Zoll²** (**-(e)s**, **ᵈe**) *m* customs *pl*; (*Abgabe*) duty; ~**abfertigung** *f* customs clearance; ~**amt** *nt* customs office; ~**beamte(r)** *m* customs official; ~**erklärung** *f* customs declaration; **z~frei** *adj* duty-free; ~**gutlager** *nt* bonded warehouse; ~**kontrolle** *f* customs (check); **z~pflichtig** *adj* liable to duty, dutiable.

**Zollstock** *m* inch rule.

**Zone** ['tsoːnə] (**-**, **-n**) *f* zone; (*von Fahrkarte*) fare stage.

**Zoo** [tsoː] (**-s**, **-s**) *m* zoo; ~**handlung** *f* pet shop.

**Zoologe** [tsoo'loːgə] (**-n**, **-n**) *m* zoologist.

**Zoologie** *f* zoology.

**Zoologin** *f* zoologist.

**zoologisch** *adj* zoological.

**Zoom** [zuːm] (**-s**, **-s**) *nt* zoom shot; (*Objektiv*) zoom lens.

**Zopf** [tsɔpf] (**-(e)s**, **ᵈe**) *m* plait; pigtail; **alter ~** antiquated custom.

**Zorn** [tsɔrn] (**-(e)s**) *m* anger.

**zornig** *adj* angry.

**Zote** ['tsoːtə] (**-**, **-n**) *f* smutty joke/remark.

**zottig** ['tsɔtɪç] *adj* shaggy.

**ZPO** *abk* (= *Zivilprozeßordnung*) ≈ General Practice Act (*US*).

**z.T.** *abk* = **zum Teil**.

=========== *SCHLÜSSELWORT*

**zu** [tsuː] *präp +dat* **1** (*örtlich*) to; **~m Bahnhof/ Arzt gehen** to go to the station/doctor; **~r Schule/Kirche gehen** to go to school/church; **sollen wir ~ Euch gehen?** shall we go to your place?; **sie sah ~ ihm hin** she looked towards him; **~m Fenster herein** through the window; **~ meiner Linken** to *od* on my left

**2** (*zeitlich*) at; **~ Ostern** at Easter; **bis ~m 1. Mai** until May 1st; (*nicht später als*) by May 1st; **~ meiner Zeit** in my time

**3** (*Zusatz*) with; **Wein ~m Essen trinken** to drink wine with one's meal; **sich ~ jdm setzen** to sit down beside sb; **setz dich doch ~ uns** (come and) sit with us; **Anmerkungen ~ etw** notes on sth

**4** (*Zweck*) for; **Wasser ~m Waschen** water for washing; **Papier ~m Schreiben** paper to write on; **etw ~m Geburtstag bekommen** to get sth for one's birthday; **es ist ~ seinem Besten** it's for his own good

**5** (*Veränderung*) into; **~ etw werden** to turn into sth; **jdn ~ etw machen** to make sb (into) sth; **~ Asche verbrennen** to burn to ashes

**6** (*mit Zahlen*): **3 ~ 2** (*SPORT*) 3-2; **das Stück ~ 2 Mark** at 2 marks each; **~m ersten Mal** for the first time

**7**: **~ meiner Freude** *etc* to my joy *etc*; **~m Glück** luckily; **~ Fuß** on foot; **es ist ~m Weinen** it's enough to make you cry

♦ *konj* to; **etw ~ essen** sth to eat; **um besser sehen ~ können** in order to see better; **ohne es ~ wissen** without knowing it; **noch ~ bezahlende Rechnungen** outstanding bills

♦ *adv* **1** (*allzu*) too; **~ sehr** too much

**2** (*örtlich*) toward(s); **er kam auf mich ~** he came towards *od* up to me

**3** (*geschlossen*) shut; closed; **die Geschäfte haben ~** the shops are closed; **auf/zu** (*Wasserhahn etc*) on/off

**4** (*umg: los*): **nur ~!** just keep at it!; **mach ~!** hurry up!

**zuallererst** *adv* first of all.

**zuallerletzt** *adv* last of all.

**zubauen** ['tsuːbauən] *vt* (*Lücke*) to fill in; (*Platz, Gebäude*) to build up.

**Zubehör** ['tsuːbəhøːr] (**-(e)s**, **-e**) *nt* accessories *pl*.

**Zuber** ['tsuːbər] (**-s**, **-**) *m* tub.

**zubereiten** ['tsuːbəraɪtən] *vt* to prepare.

**zubilligen** ['tsuːbɪlɪgən] *vt* to grant.

**zubinden** ['tsuːbɪndən] *unreg vt* to tie up; **jdm**

die Augen ~ to blindfold sb.
**zubleiben** ['tsu:blaɪbən] *unreg vi* to stay shut.
**zubringen** ['tsu:brɪŋən] *unreg vt* to spend; (*herbeibringen*) to bring, take; (*umg: Tür*) to get shut.
**Zubringer** (-s, -) *m* (*TECH*) feeder, conveyor; (*Verkehrsmittel*) shuttle; (*zum Flughafen*) airport bus; ~**(bus)** *m* shuttle (bus); ~**straße** *f* slip road (*BRIT*), entrance ramp (*US*).
**Zucchini** [tsu'ki:ni:] *pl* courgettes *pl* (*BRIT*), zucchini(s) *pl* (*US*).
**Zucht** [tsʊxt] (-, -en) *f* (*von Tieren*) breeding; (*von Pflanzen*) cultivation; (*Rasse*) breed; (*Erziehung*) raising; (*Disziplin*) discipline; ~**bulle** *m* breeding bull.
**züchten** ['tsʏçtən] *vt* (*Tiere*) to breed; (*Pflanzen*) to cultivate, grow.
**Züchter(in)** (-s, -) *m(f)* breeder; grower.
**Zuchthaus** *nt* prison, penitentiary (*US*).
**Zuchthengst** *m* stallion, stud.
**züchtig** ['tsʏçtɪç] *adj* modest, demure.
**züchtigen** ['tsʏçtɪgən] *vt* to chastise.
**Züchtigung** *f* chastisement; **körperliche ~** corporal punishment.
**Zuchtperle** *f* cultured pearl.
**Züchtung** *f* (*von Tieren*) breeding; (*von Pflanzen*) cultivation; (*Zuchtart: von Tier*) breed; (: *von Pflanze*) strain.
**zucken** ['tsʊkən] *vi* to jerk, twitch; (*Strahl etc*) to flicker ♦ *vt* to shrug; **der Schmerz zuckte (mir) durch den ganzen Körper** the pain shot right through my body.
**zücken** ['tsʏkən] *vt* (*Schwert*) to draw; (*Geldbeutel*) to pull out.
**Zucker** ['tsʊkɐ] (-s, -) *m* sugar; (*MED*) diabetes; ~ **haben** (*umg*) to be a diabetic; ~**dose** *f* sugar bowl; ~**erbse** *f* mangetout (*BRIT*), sugar pea (*US*); ~**guß** *m* icing; ~**hut** *m* sugar loaf; **z**~**krank** *adj* diabetic; ~**krankheit** *f* diabetes *sing*; ~**lecken** *nt*: **das ist kein** ~**lecken** it's no picnic.
**zuckern** *vt* to sugar.
**Zucker-** *zW*: ~**rohr** *nt* sugar cane; ~**rübe** *f* sugar beet; ~**spiegel** *m* (*MED*) (blood) sugar level; **z**~**süß** *adj* sugary; ~**watte** *f* candy floss (*BRIT*), cotton candy (*US*).
**Zuckung** *f* convulsion, spasm; (*leicht*) twitch.
**zudecken** ['tsu:dekən] *vt* to cover (up); (*im Bett*) to tuck up *od* in.
**zudem** [tsu'de:m] *adv* in addition (to this).
**zudrehen** ['tsu:dre:ən] *vt* to turn off.
**zudringlich** ['tsu:drɪŋlɪç] *adj* forward, pushy; (*Nachbar etc*) intrusive; ~ **werden** to make advances; **Z**~**keit** *f* forwardness; intrusiveness.
**zudrücken** ['tsu:drʏkən] *vt* to close; **jdm die Kehle** ~ to throttle sb; **ein Auge** ~ to turn a blind eye.
**zueinander** [tsuaɪ'nandɐ] *adv* to one other; (*in Verbverbindung*) together.
**zuerkennen** ['tsu:ɛrkɛnən] *unreg vt*: **jdm etw** ~ to award sth to sb, award sb sth.

**zuerst** [tsu'ʔeːrst] *adv* first; (*zu Anfang*) at first; ~ **einmal** first of all.
**Zufahrt** ['tsu:fa:rt] *f* approach; „**keine ~ zum Krankenhaus"** "no access to hospital".
**Zufahrtsstraße** *f* approach road; (*von Autobahn etc*) slip road (*BRIT*), entrance ramp (*US*).
**Zufall** ['tsu:fal] *m* chance; (*Ereignis*) coincidence; **durch** ~ by accident; **so ein** ~! what a coincidence!
**zufallen** *unreg vi* to close, shut; (*Anteil, Aufgabe*): **jdm** ~ to fall to sb.
**zufällig** ['tsu:fɛlɪç] *adj* chance ♦ *adv* by chance; (*in Frage*) by any chance.
**Zufallstreffer** *m* fluke.
**zufassen** ['tsu:fasən] *vi* (*zugreifen*) to take hold (of it *od* them); (*fig: schnell handeln*) to seize the opportunity; (*helfen*) to lend a hand.
**zufliegen** ['tsu:fli:gən] *unreg vi*: **ihm fliegt alles nur so zu** (*fig*) everything comes so easily to him.
**Zuflucht** ['tsu:flʊxt] *f* recourse; (*Ort*) refuge; **zu etw** ~ **nehmen** (*fig*) to resort to sth.
**Zufluchtsort** *m*, **Zufluchtsstätte** *f* place of refuge.
**Zufluß** ['tsu:flʊs] *m* (*Zufließen*) inflow, influx; (*GEOG*) tributary; (*COMM*) supply.
**zufolge** [tsu'fɔlgə] *präp +dat od +gen* judging by; (*laut*) according to; (*aufgrund*) as a result of.
**zufrieden** [tsu'fri:dən] *adj* content(ed); **er ist mit nichts** ~ nothing pleases him; ~**geben** *unreg vr*: **sich mit etw** ~**geben** to be satisfied with sth; **Z**~**heit** *f* contentedness; (*Befriedigtsein*) satisfaction; ~**lassen** *unreg vt*: **laß mich damit** ~! (*umg*) shut up about it!; ~**stellen** *vt* to satisfy; ~**stellend** *adj* satisfactory.
**zufrieren** ['tsu:fri:rən] *unreg vi* to freeze up *od* over.
**zufügen** ['tsu:fy:gən] *vt* to add; (*Leid etc*): **jdm etw** ~ to cause sb sth.
**Zufuhr** ['tsu:fu:r] (-, -en) *f* (*Herbeibringen*) supplying; (*MET*) influx; (*MIL*) supplies *pl*.
**zuführen** ['tsu:fy:rən] *vt* (*bringen*) to bring; (*transportieren*) to convey; (*versorgen*) to supply ♦ *vi*: **auf etw** *akk* ~ to lead to sth.
**Zug** [tsu:k] (-(e)s, -̈e) *m* (*Eisenbahn*~) train; (*Luft*~) draught (*BRIT*), draft (*US*); (*Ziehen*) pull(ing); (*Gesichts*~) feature; (*SCHACH etc*) move; (*Klingel*~) pull; (*Schrift*~, *beim Schwimmen*) stroke; (*Atem*~) breath; (*Charakter*~) trait; (*an Zigarette*) puff, pull, drag; (*Schluck*) gulp; (*Menschengruppe*) procession; (*von Vögeln*) migration; (*MIL*) platoon; **etw in vollen Zügen genießen** to enjoy sth to the full; **in den letzten Zügen liegen** (*umg*) to be at one's last gasp; **im** ~**(e)** *+gen* (*im Verlauf*) in the course of; ~ **um** ~ (*fig*) step by step; **zum** ~**(e) kommen** (*umg*) to get a look-in; **etw in groben Zügen darstellen** *od* **umreißen** to outline sth; **das war kein schöner** ~ **von dir** that wasn't nice

of you.

**Zugabe** ['tsu:ga:bə] f extra; (in Konzert etc) encore.

**Zugabteil** nt train compartment.

**Zugang** ['tsu:gaŋ] m entrance; (Zutritt, fig) access.

**zugänglich** ['tsu:gɛŋlɪç] adj accessible; (öffentliche Einrichtungen) open; (Mensch) approachable.

**Zugbegleiter** m (EISENB) guard (BRIT), conductor (US).

**Zugbrücke** f drawbridge.

**zugeben** ['tsu:ge:bən] unreg vt (beifügen) to add, throw in; (zugestehen) to admit; (erlauben) to permit; **zugegeben ... granted ...**

**zugegebenermaßen** ['tsu:gega:bənər'ma:sən] adv admittedly.

**zugegen** [tsu:'ge:gən] adv (geh): **~ sein** to be present.

**zugehen** ['tsu:ge:ən] unreg vi (schließen) to shut ♦ vi unpers (sich ereignen) to go on, happen; **auf jdn/etw ~** to walk towards sb/sth; **dem Ende ~** to be finishing; **er geht schon auf die Siebzig zu** he's getting on for seventy; **hier geht es nicht mit rechten Dingen zu** there's something odd going on here; **dort geht es ... zu** things are ... there.

**Zugehörigkeit** ['tsu:gəhø:rɪçkaɪt] f: **~ (zu)** membership (of), belonging (to).

**Zugehörigkeitsgefühl** nt feeling of belonging.

**zugeknöpft** ['tsu:gəknœpft] (umg) adj reserved, stand-offish.

**Zügel** ['tsy:gəl] (-s, -) m rein, reins pl; (fig) rein, curb; **die ~ locker lassen** to slacken one's hold on the reins; **die ~ locker lassen bei** (fig) to give free rein to.

**zugelassen** ['tsu:gəlasən] adj authorized; (Heilpraktiker) registered; (Kfz) licensed.

**zügellos** adj unrestrained; (sexuell) licentious.

**Zügellosigkeit** f lack of restraint; licentiousness.

**zügeln** vt to curb; (Pferd) to rein in.

**zugesellen** vr: **sich jdm ~** to join sb, join up with sb.

**Zugeständnis** ['tsu:gəʃtɛntnɪs] (-ses, -se) nt concession; **~se machen** to make allowances.

**zugestehen** unreg vt to admit; (Rechte) to concede.

**zugetan** ['tsu:gəta:n] adj: **jdm/etw ~ sein** to be fond of sb/sth.

**Zugewinn** (-(e)s) m (JUR) property acquired during marriage.

**Zugezogene(r)** ['tsu:gətso:gənə(r)] f(m) newcomer.

**Zugführer** m (EISENB) chief guard (BRIT) od conductor (US); (MIL) platoon commander.

**zugig** adj draughty (BRIT), drafty (US).

**zügig** ['tsy:gɪç] adj speedy, swift.

**zugkräftig** adj (fig: Werbetext, Titel) eye-catching; (Schauspieler) crowd-pulling attr, popular.

**zugleich** [tsu:'glaɪç] adv (zur gleichen Zeit) at the same time; (ebenso) both.

**Zugluft** f draught (BRIT), draft (US).

**Zugmaschine** f traction engine, tractor.

**zugreifen** ['tsu:graɪfən] unreg vi to seize od grab it/them; (helfen) to help; (beim Essen) to help o.s.

**Zugriff** ['tsu:grɪf] m (COMPUT) access; **sich dem ~ der Polizei entziehen** (fig) to evade justice.

**zugrunde** [tsu:'grʊndə] adv: **~ gehen** to collapse; (Mensch) to perish; **er wird daran nicht ~ gehen** he'll survive; (finanziell) it won't ruin him; **einer Sache dat etw ~ legen** to base sth on sth; **einer Sache dat ~ liegen** to be based on sth; **~ richten** to ruin, destroy.

**zugunsten** [tsu:'gʊnstən] präp +gen od +dat in favour (BRIT) od favor (US) of.

**zugute** [tsu:'gu:tə] adv: **jdm etw ~ halten** to concede sth to sb; **jdm ~ kommen** to be of assistance to sb.

**Zug-** zW: **~verbindung** f train connection; **~vogel** m migratory bird; **~zwang** m (SCHACH) zugzwang; **unter ~zwang stehen** (fig) to be in a tight spot.

**zuhalten** ['tsu:haltən] unreg vt to hold shut ♦ vi: **auf jdn/etw ~** to make for sb/sth; **sich dat die Nase ~** to hold one's nose.

**Zuhälter** ['tsu:hɛltər] (-s, -) m pimp.

**zuhause** [tsu:'haʊzə] adv at home.

**Zuhause** (-s) nt home.

**Zuhilfenahme** [tsu:'hɪlfəna:mə] f: **unter ~ von** with the help of.

**zuhören** ['tsu:hø:rən] vi to listen.

**Zuhörer** (-s, -) m listener; **~schaft** f audience.

**zujubeln** ['tsu:ju:bəln] vi: **jdm ~** to cheer sb.

**zukehren** ['tsu:ke:rən] vt (zuwenden) to turn.

**zuklappen** ['tsu:klapən] vt (Buch, Deckel) to close ♦ vi (Hilfsverb sein: Tür etc) to click shut.

**zukleben** ['tsu:kle:bən] vt to paste up.

**zukneifen** ['tsu:knaɪfən] vt (Augen) to screw up; (Mund) to shut tight(ly).

**zuknöpfen** ['tsu:knœpfən] vt to button (up), fasten (up).

**zukommen** ['tsu:kɔmən] unreg vi to come up; **auf jdn ~** to come up to sb; **jdm ~** (sich gehören) to be fitting for sb; **diesem Treffen kommt große Bedeutung zu** this meeting is of the utmost importance; **jdm etw ~ lassen** to give sb sth; **die Dinge auf sich akk ~ lassen** to take things as they come.

**Zukunft** ['tsu:kʊnft] (-, no pl) f future.

**zukünftig** ['tsu:kynftɪç] adj future ♦ adv in future; **mein ~er Mann** my husband-to-be.

**Zukunfts-** zW: **~aussichten** pl future prospects pl; **~musik** (umg) f wishful thinking; **~roman** m science-fiction novel;

z~**trächtig** adj promising for the future;
z~**weisend** adj trend-setting.
**Zulage** ['tsu:la:gə] f bonus.
**zulande** [tsu'landə] adv: **bei uns ~** in our
country.
**zulangen** ['tsu:laŋən] (umg) vi (Dieb, beim
Essen) to help o.s.
**zulassen** ['tsu:lasən] unreg vt (hereinlassen) to
admit; (erlauben) to permit; (Auto) to
license; (umg: nicht öffnen) to keep shut.
**zulässig** ['tsu:lɛsɪç] adj permissible,
permitted; ~**e Höchstgeschwindigkeit**
(upper) speed limit.
**Zulassung** f (amtlich) authorization;
licensing; (von Kfz) (als praktizierender Arzt)
registration.
**Zulauf** m: **großen ~ haben** (Geschäft) to be
very popular.
**zulaufen** ['tsu:laʊfən] unreg vi: ~ **auf** +akk to run
towards; **jdm ~** (Tier) to adopt sb; **spitz ~** to
come to a point.
**zulegen** ['tsu:le:gən] vt to add; (Geld) to put in;
(Tempo) to accelerate, quicken; (schließen)
to cover over; **sich** dat **etw ~** (umg) to get
oneself sth.
**zuleide** [tsu'laɪdə] adj: **jdm etw ~ tun** to harm
sb.
**zuleiten** ['tsu:laɪtən] vt (Wasser) to supply;
(schicken) to send.
**Zuleitung** f (TECH) supply.
**zuletzt** [tsu'lɛtst] adv finally, at last; **wir**
**blieben bis ~** we stayed to the very end;
**nicht ~ wegen** not least because of.
**zuliebe** [tsu'li:bə] adv: **jdm ~** (in order) to
please sb.
**Zulieferbetrieb** ['tsu:li:fərbətri:p] m (COMM)
supplier.
**zum** [tsʊm] = **zu dem**; ~ **dritten Mal** for the
third time; ~ **Scherz** as a joke; ~ **Trinken**
for drinking; **bis ~ 15. April** until 15th April;
(nicht später als) by 15th April; ~ **ersten**
**Mal(e)** for the first time; **es ist ~ Weinen** it's
enough to make you (want to) weep;
~ **Glück** luckily.
**zumachen** ['tsu:maxən] vt to shut; (Kleidung)
to do up, fasten ♦ vi to shut; (umg) to hurry
up.
**zumal** [tsu'ma:l] konj especially (as).
**zumeist** [tsu'maɪst] adv mostly.
**zumessen** ['tsu:mɛsən] unreg vt (+dat) (Zeit) to
allocate (for); (Bedeutung) to attach (to).
**zumindest** [tsu'mɪndəst] adv at least.
**zumutbar** [tsu'mu:tba:r] adj reasonable.
**zumute** [tsu'mu:tə] adv: **wie ist ihm ~?** how
does he feel?
**zumuten** ['tsu:mu:tən] vt: **(jdm) etw ~** to
expect od ask sth (of sb); **sich** dat **zuviel ~** to
take on too much.
**Zumutung** f unreasonable expectation od
demand; (Unverschämtheit) impertinence;
**das ist eine ~!** that's a bit much!
**zunächst** [tsu'nɛ:çst] adv first of all; ~ **einmal**

to start with.
**zunageln** ['tsu:na:gəln] vt (Fenster etc) to nail
up; (Kiste etc) to nail down.
**zunähen** ['tsu:nɛ:ən] vt to sew up.
**Zunahme** ['tsu:na:mə] (-, -n) f increase.
**Zuname** ['tsu:na:mə] m surname.
**zünden** ['tsyndən] vi (Feuer) to light, ignite;
(Motor) to fire; (fig) to kindle enthusiasm
♦ vt to ignite; (Rakete) to fire.
**zündend** adj fiery.
**Zünder** (-s, -) m fuse; (MIL) detonator.
**Zünd-** zW: ~**holz** nt match; ~**kabel** nt (AUT)
plug lead; ~**kerze** f (AUT) spark(ing) plug;
~**plättchen** nt cap; ~**schlüssel** m ignition
key; ~**schnur** f fuse wire; ~**stoff** m fuel;
(fig) dynamite.
**Zündung** f ignition.
**zunehmen** ['tsu:ne:mən] unreg vi to increase,
grow; (Mensch) to put on weight.
**zunehmend** adj: **mit ~em Alter** with
advancing age.
**zuneigen** ['tsu:naɪgən] vi to incline, lean; **sich**
**dem Ende ~** to draw to a close; **einer**
**Auffassung ~** to incline towards a view; **jdm**
**zugeneigt sein** to be attracted to sb.
**Zuneigung** f affection.
**Zunft** [tsʊnft] (-, ¨-e) f guild.
**zünftig** ['tsynftɪç] adj (Arbeit) professional;
(umg: ordentlich) proper, real.
**Zunge** ['tsʊŋə] f tongue; (Fisch) sole; **böse ~n**
**behaupten, ...** malicious gossip has it ...
**züngeln** ['tsyŋəln] vi (Flammen) to lick.
**Zungenbrecher** m tongue-twister.
**zungenfertig** adj glib.
**Zünglein** ['tsyŋlaɪn] nt: **das ~ an der Waage**
**sein** (fig) to tip the scales.
**zunichte** [tsu'nɪçtə] adv: ~ **machen** to ruin,
destroy; ~ **werden** to come to nothing.
**zunutze** [tsu'nʊtsə] adv: **sich** dat **etw ~ machen**
to make use of sth.
**zuoberst** [tsu'|o:bərst] adv at the top.
**zuordnen** ['tsu:|ɔrdnən] vt to assign.
**zupacken** ['tsu:pakən] (umg) vi (zugreifen) to
make a grab for it; (bei der Arbeit) to get
down to it; **mit ~** (helfen) to give me/them
etc a hand.
**zupfen** ['tsʊpfən] vt to pull, pick, pluck;
(Gitarre) to pluck.
**zur** [tsu:r] = **zu der**.
**zurechnungsfähig** ['tsu:rɛçnʊŋsfɛ:ɪç] adj
(JUR) responsible, of sound mind; **Z~keit** f
responsibility, accountability.
**zurecht-** zW: ~**biegen** unreg vt to bend into
shape; (fig) to twist; ~**finden** unreg vr to find
one's way (about); ~**kommen** unreg vi
(rechtzeitig kommen) to come in time;
(schaffen) to cope; (finanziell) to manage;
~**legen** vt to get ready; (Ausrede etc) to have
ready; ~**machen** vt to prepare ♦ vr to get
ready; (sich schminken) to put on one's
make-up; ~**weisen** unreg vt to reprimand;
**Z~weisung** f reprimand, rebuff.

**zureden** ['tsu:re:dən] *vi:* **jdm** ~ to persuade sb, urge sb.

**zureiten** ['tsuraɪtən] *unreg vt* (*Pferd*) to break in.

**Zürich** ['tsy:rɪç] (**-s**) *nt* Zurich.

**zurichten** ['tsu:rɪçtən] *vt* (*Essen*) to prepare; (*beschädigen*) to batter, bash up.

**zürnen** ['tsyrnən] *vi:* **jdm** ~ to be angry with sb.

**zurück** [tsu'rʏk] *adv* back; (*mit Zahlungen*) behind; (*fig: ~geblieben: von Kind*) backward; ~! get back!; ~**behalten** *unreg vt* to keep back; **er hat Schäden ~behalten** he suffered lasting damage; ~**bekommen** *unreg vt* to get back; ~**bezahlen** *vt* to repay, pay back; ~**bleiben** *unreg vi* (*Mensch*) to remain behind; (*nicht nachkommen*) to fall behind, lag; (*Schaden*) to remain; ~**bringen** *unreg vt* to bring back; ~**datieren** *vt* to backdate; ~**drängen** *vt* (*Gefühle*) to repress; (*Feind*) to push back; ~**drehen** *vt* to turn back; ~**erobern** *vt* to reconquer; ~**erstatten** *vt* to refund; ~**fahren** *unreg vi* to travel back; (*vor Schreck*) to recoil ◆ *vt* to drive back; ~**fallen** *unreg vi* to fall back; (*in Laster*) to relapse; (*in Leistungen*) to fall behind; (*an Besitzer*): ~**fallen an** *+akk* to revert to; ~**finden** *unreg vi* to find one's way back; ~**fordern** *vt* to demand back; ~**führen** *vt* to lead back; **etw auf etw** *akk* ~**führen** to trace sth back to sth; ~**geben** *unreg vt* to give back; (*antworten*) to retort with; ~**geblieben** *adj* retarded; ~**gehen** *unreg vi* to go back; (*fallen*) to go down, fall; (*zeitlich*): ~**gehen (auf** *+akk*) (*zeitlich*) to go back (to); **Waren** ~**gehen lassen** to send back goods; ~**gezogen** *adj* retired, withdrawn; ~**greifen** *unreg vi:* ~**greifen (auf** *+akk*) (*fig*) to fall back (upon); (*zeitlich*) to go back (to); ~**halten** *unreg vt* to hold back; (*Mensch*) to restrain; (*hindern*) to prevent ◆ *vr* (*reserviert sein*) to be reserved; (*im Essen*) to hold back; (*im Hintergrund bleiben*) to keep in the background; (*bei Verhandlung*) to keep a low profile; ~**haltend** *adj* reserved; **Z~haltung** *f* reserve; ~**holen** *vt* (*COMPUT: Daten*) to retrieve; ~**kehren** *vi* to return; ~**kommen** *unreg vi* to come back; **auf etw** *akk* ~**kommen** to return to sth; ~**lassen** *unreg vt* to leave behind; ~**legen** *vt* to put back; (*Geld*) to put by; (*reservieren*) to keep back; (*Strecke*) to cover ◆ *vr* to lie back; ~**liegen** *unreg vi:* **der Unfall liegt etwa eine Woche** ~ the accident was about a week ago; ~**nehmen** *unreg vt* to take back; ~**reichen** *vi* (*Tradition etc*): ~**reichen (in** *+akk*) to go back (to); ~**rufen** *unreg vt, vi* to call back; **etw ins Gedächtnis** ~**rufen** to recall sth; ~**schrauben** *vt:* **seine Ansprüche** ~**schrauben** to lower one's sights; ~**schrecken** *vi:* ~**schrecken vor** *+dat* to shrink from; **vor nichts** ~**schrecken** to stop at nothing; ~**setzen** *vt* to put back; (*im Preis*) to reduce;

(*benachteiligen*) to put at a disadvantage ◆ *vi* (*mit Fahrzeug*) to reverse, back; ~**stecken** *vt* to put back ◆ *vi* (*fig*) to moderate one's wishes; ~**stellen** *vt* to put back, replace; (*aufschieben*) to put off, postpone; (*MIL*) to turn down; (*Interessen*) to defer; (*Ware*) to keep; **persönliche Interessen hinter etw** *dat* ~**stellen** to put sth before one's personal interests; ~**stoßen** *unreg vt* to repulse; ~**stufen** *vt* to downgrade; ~**treten** *unreg vi* to step back; (*vom Amt*) to retire; (*von einem Vertrag etc*): ~**treten (von)** to withdraw (from); **gegenüber** *od* **hinter etw** *dat* ~**treten** to diminish in importance in view of sth; **bitte** ~**treten!** stand back, please!; ~**verfolgen** *vt* (*fig*) to trace back; ~**versetzen** *vt* (*in alten Zustand*): ~**versetzen (in** *+akk*) to restore (to) ◆ *vr:* **sich** ~**versetzen (in** *+akk*) to think back (to); ~**weichen** *unreg vi:* ~**weichen (vor** *+dat*) to shrink back (from); ~**weisen** *unreg vt* to turn down; (*Mensch*) to reject; ~**werfen** *unreg vt* (*Ball, Kopf*) to throw back; (*Strahlen, Schall*) to reflect; (*fig: Feind*) to repel; (: *wirtschaftlich*): ~**werfen (um)** to set back (by); ~**zahlen** *vt* to pay back, repay; **Z~zahlung** *f* repayment; ~**ziehen** *unreg vt* to pull back; (*Angebot*) to withdraw ◆ *vr* to retire.

**Zuruf** ['tsu:ru:f] *m* shout, cry.

**zus.** *abk* = zusammen; zusätzlich.

**Zusage** ['tsu:za:gə] *f* promise; (*Annahme*) consent.

**zusagen** *vt* to promise ◆ *vi* to accept; **jdm etw auf den Kopf** ~ (*umg*) to tell sb sth outright; **jdm** ~ (*gefallen*) to appeal to *od* please sb.

**zusammen** [tsu'zamən] *adv* together; **Z~arbeit** *f* cooperation; ~**arbeiten** *vi* to cooperate; **Z~ballung** *f* accumulation; ~**bauen** *vt* to assemble; ~**beißen** *unreg vt* (*Zähne*) to clench; ~**bleiben** *unreg vi* to stay together; ~**brauen** (*umg*) *vt* to concoct ◆ *vr* (*Gewitter, Unheil etc*) to be brewing; ~**brechen** *unreg vi* (*Hilfsverb sein*) to collapse; (*Mensch*) to break down, collapse; (*Verkehr etc*) to come to a standstill; ~**bringen** *unreg vt* to bring *od* get together; (*Geld*) to get; (*Sätze*) to put together; **Z~bruch** *m* collapse; (*COMPUT*) crash; ~**fahren** *unreg vi* to collide; (*erschrecken*) to start; ~**fallen** *unreg vi* (*einstürzen*) to collapse; (*Ereignisse*) to coincide; ~**fassen** *vt* to summarize; (*vereinigen*) to unite; ~**fassend** *adj* summarizing ◆ *adv* to summarize; **Z~fassung** *f* summary, résumé; ~**finden** *unreg vi, vr* to meet (together); ~**fließen** *unreg vi* to flow together, meet; **Z~fluß** *m* confluence; ~**fügen** *vt* to join (together), unite; ~**führen** *vt* to bring together; (*Familie*) to reunite; ~**gehören** *vi* to belong together; (*Paar*) to match; **Z~gehörigkeitsgefühl** *nt* sense of belonging; ~**gesetzt** *adj* compound, composite; ~**gewürfelt** *adj* motley; ~**halten**

unreg vt to hold together ♦ vi to hold together; (Freunde, fig) to stick together; Z~hang m connection; im/aus dem Z~hang in/out of context; etw aus dem Z~hang reißen to take sth out of its context; ~hängen unreg vi to be connected od linked; ~hängend adj (Erzählung) coherent; ~hang(s)los adj incoherent; ~klappbar adj folding, collapsible; ~klappen vt (Messer etc) to fold ♦ vi (umg: Mensch) to flake out; ~knüllen vt to crumple up; ~kommen unreg vi to meet, assemble; (sich ereignen) to occur at once od together; ~kramen vt to gather (together); Z~kunft (-, -künfte) f meeting; ~laufen unreg vi to run od come together; (Straßen, Flüsse etc) to converge, meet; (Farben) to run into one another; ~legen vt to put together; (stapeln) to pile up; (falten) to fold; (verbinden) to combine, unite; (Termine, Feste) to combine; (Geld) to collect; ~nehmen unreg vt to summon up ♦ vr to pull o.s. together; alles ~genommen all in all; ~passen vi to go well together, match; Z~prall m (lit) collision; (fig) clash; ~prallen vi (Hilfsverb sein) to collide; ~reimen (umg) vt: das kann ich mir nicht ~reimen I can't make head nor tail of this; ~reißen unreg vr to pull o.s. together; ~rotten unreg (pej) vr to gang up; ~schlagen unreg vt (jdn) to beat up; (Dinge) to smash up; (falten) to fold; (Hände) to clap; (Hacken) to click; ~schließen unreg vt, vr to join (together); Z~schluß m amalgamation; ~schmelzen unreg vi (verschmelzen) to fuse; (zerschmelzen) to melt (away); (Anzahl) to dwindle; ~schrecken unreg vi to start; ~schreiben unreg vt to write together; (Bericht) to put together; ~schrumpfen vi (Hilfsverb sein) to shrink, shrivel up; Z~sein (-s) nt get-together; ~setzen vt to put together ♦ vr: sich ~setzen aus to consist of; Z~setzung f composition; Z~spiel nt teamwork; (von Kräften etc) interaction; ~stellen vt to put together; Z~stellung f list; (Vorgang) compilation; Z~stoß m collision; ~stoßen unreg vi (Hilfsverb sein) to collide; ~strömen vi (Hilfsverb sein: Menschen) to flock together; ~tragen unreg vt to collect; Z~treffen nt meeting; (Zufall) coincidence; ~treffen unreg vi (Hilfsverb sein) to coincide; (Menschen) to meet; ~treten unreg vi (Verein etc) to meet; ~wachsen unreg vi to grow together; ~wirken vi to combine; ~zählen vt to add up; ~ziehen unreg vt (verengern) to draw together; (vereinigen) to bring together; (addieren) to add up ♦ vr to shrink; (sich bilden) to form, develop; ~zucken vi (Hilfsverb sein) to start.

**Zusatz** ['tsuːzats] m addition; ~antrag m (POL) amendment; ~gerät nt attachment; **zusätzlich** ['tsuːzetslɪç] adj additional.
**Zusatzmittel** nt additive.

**zuschauen** ['tsuːʃauən] vi to watch, look on.
**Zuschauer** (-s, -) m spectator ♦ pl (THEAT) audience sing.
**zuschicken** ['tsuːʃɪkən] vt: jdm etw ~ to send od forward sth to sb.
**zuschießen** ['tsuːʃiːsən] unreg vt to fire; (Geld) to put in ♦ vi: ~ auf +akk to rush towards.
**Zuschlag** ['tsuːʃlaːk] m extra charge; (Erhöhung) surcharge; (EISENB) supplement.
**zuschlagen** ['tsuːʃlaːgən] unreg vt (Tür) to slam; (Ball) to hit; (bei Auktion) to knock down; (Steine etc) to knock into shape ♦ vi (Fenster, Tür) to shut; (Mensch) to hit, punch.
**zuschlagfrei** adj (EISENB) not subject to a supplement.
**zuschlagpflichtig** adj subject to surcharge.
**Zuschlagskarte** f (EISENB) supplementary ticket.
**zuschließen** ['tsuːʃliːsən] unreg vt to lock (up).
**zuschmeißen** ['tsuːʃmaɪsən] unreg (umg) vt to slam, bang shut.
**zuschmieren** ['tsuːʃmiːrən] vt to smear over; (Löcher) to fill in.
**zuschneiden** ['tsuːʃnaɪdən] unreg vt to cut to size; (NÄHEN) to cut out; auf etw akk zugeschnitten sein (fig) to be geared to sth.
**zuschnüren** ['tsuːʃnyːrən] vt to tie up; die Angst schnürte ihm die Kehle zu (fig) he was choked with fear.
**zuschrauben** ['tsuːʃraubən] vt to screw shut.
**zuschreiben** ['tsuːʃraibən] unreg vt (fig) to ascribe, attribute; (COMM) to credit; das hast du dir selbst zuzuschreiben you've only got yourself to blame.
**Zuschrift** ['tsuːʃrɪft] f letter, reply.
**zuschulden** [tsuːˈʃuldən] adv: sich dat etw ~ kommen lassen to make o.s. guilty of sth.
**Zuschuß** ['tsuːʃus] m subsidy.
**Zuschußbetrieb** m loss-making concern.
**zuschütten** ['tsuːʃytən] vt to fill up.
**zusehen** ['tsuːzeːən] unreg vi to watch; (dafür sorgen) to take care; (etw dulden) to sit back (and watch); jdm/etw ~ to watch sb/sth.
**zusehends** adv visibly.
**zusein** ['tsuːzain] unreg vi to be closed.
**zusenden** ['tsuːzendən] unreg vt to forward, send on.
**zusetzen** ['tsuːzetsən] vt (beifügen) to add; (Geld) to lose ♦ vi: jdm ~ to harass sb; (Krankheit) to take a lot out of sb; (unter Druck setzen) to lean on sb (umg); (schwer treffen) to hit sb hard.
**zusichern** ['tsuːzɪçərn] vt: jdm etw ~ to assure sb of sth.
**Zusicherung** f assurance.
**zusperren** ['tsuːʃperən] vt to bar.
**zuspielen** ['tsuːʃpiːlən] vt, vi to pass; jdm etw ~ to pass sth to sb; (fig) to pass sth on to sb; etw der Presse ~ to leak sth to the press.
**zuspitzen** ['tsuːʃpitsən] vt to sharpen ♦ vr (Lage) to become critical.
**zusprechen** ['tsuːʃprɛçən] unreg vt

(*zuerkennen*): **jdm etw** ~ to award sb sth, award sth to sb ♦ *vi:* **jdm** ~ to speak to sb; **jdm Trost** ~ to comfort sb; **dem Essen/ Alkohol** ~ to eat/drink a lot.

**Zuspruch** ['tsu:ʃprʊx] *m* encouragement; (*Anklang*) popularity.

**Zustand** ['tsu:ʃtant] *m* state, condition; **in gutem/schlechtem** ~ in good/poor condition; (*Haus*) in good/bad repair; **Zustände bekommen** *od* **kriegen** (*umg*) to have a fit.

**zustande** [tsu'ʃtandə] *adv:* ~ **bringen** to bring about; ~ **kommen** to come about.

**zuständig** ['tsu:ʃtɛndɪç] *adj* competent, responsible; **Z~keit** *f* competence, responsibility; **Z~keitsbereich** *m* area of responsibility.

**zustatten** [tsu'ʃtatən] *adj:* **jdm** ~ **kommen** (*geh*) to come in useful for sb.

**zustehen** ['tsu:ʃte:ən] *unreg vi:* **jdm** ~ to be sb's right.

**zusteigen** ['tsu:ʃtaɪgən] *unreg vi:* **noch jemand zugestiegen?** (*in Zug*) any more tickets?

**zustellen** ['tsu:ʃtɛlən] *vt* (*verstellen*) to block; (*Post etc*) to send.

**Zustellung** *f* delivery.

**zusteuern** ['tsu:ʃtɔʏərn] *vi:* **auf etw** *akk* ~ to head for sth; (*beim Gespräch*) to steer towards sth ♦ *vt* (*beitragen*) to contribute.

**zustimmen** ['tsu:ʃtɪmən] *vi* to agree.

**Zustimmung** *f* agreement; (*Einwilligung*) consent; **allgemeine** ~ **finden** to meet with general approval.

**zustoßen** ['tsu:ʃto:sən] *unreg vi* (*fig*): **jdm** ~ to happen to sb.

**Zustrom** ['tsu:ʃtro:m] *m* (*fig: Menschenmenge*) stream (of visitors *etc*); (*hineinströmend*) influx; (*MET*) inflow.

**zustürzen** ['tsu:ʃtʏrtsən] *vi:* **auf jdn/etw** ~ to rush up to sb/sth.

**zutage** [tsu'ta:gə] *adv:* ~ **bringen** to bring to light; ~ **treten** to come to light.

**Zutaten** ['tsu:ta:tən] *pl* ingredients *pl*; (*fig*) accessories *pl*.

**zuteil** [tsu'taɪl] *adv* (*geh*): **jdm wird etw** ~ sb is granted sth, sth is granted to sb.

**zuteilen** ['tsu:taɪlən] *vt* to allocate, assign.

**zutiefst** [tsu'ti:fst] *adv* deeply.

**zutragen** ['tsu:tra:gən] *unreg vt:* **jdm etw** ~ to bring sb sth, bring sth to sb ♦ *vt* (*Klatsch*) to tell sb sth ♦ *vr* to happen.

**zuträglich** ['tsu:trɛ:klɪç] *adj* beneficial.

**zutrauen** ['tsu:traʊən] *vt:* **jdm etw** ~ to credit sb with sth; **sich** *dat* **nichts** ~ to have no confidence in o.s.; **jdm viel** ~ to think a lot of sb; **jdm wenig** ~ not to think much of sb; **Z~** (-s) *nt:* **Z~** (**zu**) trust (in); **zu jdm Z~ fassen** to begin to trust sb.

**zutraulich** *adj* trusting; (*Tier*) friendly; **Z~keit** *f* trust.

**zutreffen** ['tsu:trɛfən] *unreg vi* to be correct; (*gelten*) to apply.

**zutreffend** *adj* (*richtig*) accurate; **Z~es bitte unterstreichen** please underline where applicable.

**zutrinken** ['tsu:trɪŋkən] *unreg vi:* **jdm** ~ to drink to sb.

**Zutritt** ['tsu:trɪt] *m* access; (*Einlaß*) admittance; **kein** ~, ~ **verboten** no admittance.

**zutun** ['tsu:tu:n] *unreg vt* to add; (*schließen*) to shut.

**Zutun** (-s) *nt* assistance.

**zuunterst** [tsu'|ʊntərst] *adv* right at the bottom.

**zuverlässig** ['tsu:fɛrlɛsɪç] *adj* reliable; **Z~keit** *f* reliability.

**Zuversicht** ['tsu:fɛrzɪçt] (-) *f* confidence; **z~lich** *adj* confident; **~lichkeit** *f* confidence.

**zuviel** [tsu'fi:l] *adv* too much; (*umg: zu viele*) too many; **er kriegt** ~ (*umg*) he gets annoyed.

**zuvor** [tsu'fo:r] *adv* before, previously.

**zuvorderst** [tsu'fɔrdərst] *adv* right at the front.

**zuvorkommen** *unreg vi* +*dat* to anticipate; (*Gefahr etc*) to forestall; **jdm** ~ to beat sb to it.

**zuvorkommend** *adj* courteous; (*gefällig*) obliging.

**Zuwachs** ['tsu:vaks] (-es) *m* increase, growth; (*umg*) addition.

**zuwachsen** *unreg vi* to become overgrown; (*Wunde*) to heal (up).

**Zuwachsrate** *f* rate of increase.

**zuwandern** ['tsu:vandərn] *vi* to immigrate.

**zuwege** [tsu've:gə] *adv:* **etw** ~ **bringen** to accomplish sth; **mit etw** ~ **kommen** to manage sth; **gut** ~ **sein** to be (doing) well.

**zuweilen** [tsu'vaɪlən] *adv* at times, now and then.

**zuweisen** ['tsu:vaɪzən] *unreg vt* to assign, allocate.

**zuwenden** ['tsu:vɛndən] *unreg vt* +*dat* to turn towards ♦ *vr* +*dat* to turn to; (*sich widmen*) to devote o.s. to; **jdm seine Aufmerksamkeit** ~ to give sb one's attention.

**Zuwendung** *f* (*Geld*) financial contribution; (*Liebe*) love and care.

**zuwenig** [tsu've:nɪç] *adv* too little; (*umg: zu wenige*) too few.

**zuwerfen** ['tsu:vɛrfən] *unreg vt:* **jdm etw** ~ to throw sth to sb, throw sth sb.

**zuwider** [tsu'vi:dər] *adv:* **etw ist jdm** ~ sb loathes sth, sb finds sth repugnant ♦ *präp* +*dat* contrary to; **~handeln** *vi* +*dat* to act contrary to; **einem Gesetz ~handeln** to contravene a law; **Z~handlung** *f* contravention; **~laufen** *unreg vi:* **einer Sache** *dat* **~laufen** to run counter to sth.

**zuz.** *abk* = **zuzüglich.**

**zuzahlen** ['tsu:tsa:lən] *vt:* **10 Mark** ~ to pay another 10 marks.

**zuziehen** ['tsu:tsi:ən] *unreg vt* (*schließen:*

*Vorhang*) to draw, close; (*herbeirufen: Experten*) to call in ♦ *vi* to move in, come; **sich** *dat* **etw** ~ (*Krankheit*) to catch sth; (*Zorn*) to incur sth; **sich** *dat* **eine Verletzung** ~ (*form*) to sustain an injury.

**Zuzug** ['tsu:tsuk] (-(e)s) *m* (*Zustrom*) influx; (*von Familie etc*): ~ **nach** move to.

**zuzüglich** ['tsu:tsy:klɪç] *präp +gen* plus, with the addition of.

**zuzwinkern** ['tsu:tsvɪnkɐrn] *vi:* **jdm** ~ to wink at sb.

**ZVS** *f abk* (= *Zentralstelle für die Vergabe von Studienplätzen*) *central body organizing the granting of places at university.*

**Zwang** (-(e)s, ⁻e) *m* compulsion; (*Gewalt*) coercion; **gesellschaftliche Zwänge** social constraints; **tu dir keinen** ~ **an** don't feel you have to be polite.

**zwang** *etc* [tsvaŋ] *vb siehe* **zwingen**.

**zwängen** ['tsvɛŋən] *vt, vr* to squeeze.

**Zwang-** *zW:* **z~haft** *adj* compulsive; **z~los** *adj* informal; **~losigkeit** *f* informality.

**Zwangs-** *zW:* **~abgabe** *f* (*COMM*) compulsory levy; **~arbeit** *f* forced labour (*BRIT*) *od* labor (*US*); **~ernährung** *f* force-feeding; **~jacke** *f* straitjacket; **~lage** *f* predicament, tight corner; **z~läufig** *adj* inevitable; **~maßnahme** *f* compulsory measure; (*POL*) sanction; **~vollstreckung** *f* execution; **~vorstellung** *f* (*PSYCH*) obsession; **z~weise** *adv* compulsorily.

**zwanzig** ['tsvantsɪç] *num* twenty.

**zwanzigste(r, s)** *adj* twentieth.

**zwar** [tsva:r] *adv* to be sure, indeed; **das ist** ~ ..., **aber** ... that may be ... but ...; **und** ~ in fact, actually; **und** ~ **am Sonntag** on Sunday to be precise; **und** ~ **so schnell, daß** ... in fact so quickly that ...

**Zweck** [tsvɛk] (-(e)s, -e) *m* purpose, aim; **es hat keinen** ~, **darüber zu reden** there is no point (in) talking about it; **z~dienlich** *adj* practical; (*nützlich*) useful; **z~dienliche Hinweise** (any) relevant information.

**Zwecke** (-, -n) *f* hobnail; (*Heft~*) drawing pin (*BRIT*), thumbtack (*US*).

**Zweck-** *zW:* **z~entfremden** *vt untr* to use for another purpose; **~entfremdung** *f* misuse; **z~frei** *adj* (*Forschung etc*) pure; **z~los** *adj* pointless; **z~mäßig** *adj* suitable, appropriate; **~mäßigkeit** *f* suitability.

**zwecks** *präp +gen* (*form*) for (the purpose of). .

**zweckwidrig** *adj* unsuitable.

**zwei** [tsvaɪ] *num* two; **Z~bettzimmer** *nt* twin-bedded room; **~deutig** *adj* ambiguous; (*unanständig*) suggestive; **Z~drittelmehrheit** *f* (*PARL*) two-thirds majority; **~eiig** *adj* (*Zwillinge*) non-identical.

**zweierlei** ['tsvaɪɐr'laɪ] *adj* two kinds *od* sorts of; ~ **Stoff** two different kinds of material; ~ **zu tun haben** to have two different things to do.

**zweifach** *adj* double.

**Zweifel** ['tsvaɪfəl] (-s, -) *m* doubt; **ich bin mir darüber im** ~ I'm in two minds about it; **z~haft** *adj* doubtful, dubious; **z~los** *adj* doubtless.

**zweifeln** *vi:* (**an etw** *dat*) ~ to doubt (sth).

**Zweifelsfall** *m:* **im** ~ in case of doubt.

**Zweifrontenkrieg** *m* war(fare) on two fronts.

**Zweig** [tsvaɪk] (-(e)s, -e) *m* branch; **~geschäft** *nt* (*COMM*) branch.

**zweigleisig** ['tsvaɪglaɪzɪç] *adj:* ~ **argumentieren** to argue along two different lines.

**Zweigstelle** *f* branch (office).

**zwei-** *zW:* **~händig** *adj* two-handed; (*MUS*) for two hands; **Z~heit** *f* duality; **~hundert** *num* two hundred; **Z~kampf** *m* duel; **~mal** *adv* twice; **das lasse ich mir nicht** ~**mal sagen** I don't have to be told twice; **~motorig** *adj* twin-engined; **~reihig** *adj* (*Anzug*) double-breasted; **Z~samkeit** *f* togetherness; **~schneidig** *adj* (*fig*) double-edged; **Z~sitzer** (-s, -) *m* two-seater; **~sprachig** *adj* bilingual; **~spurig** *adj* (*AUT*) two-lane; **Z~spur(tonband)gerät** *nt* twin-track (tape) recorder; **~stellig** *adj* (*Zahl*) two-digit *attrib*, with two digits; **~stimmig** *adj* for two voices.

**zweit** [tsvaɪt] *adv:* **zu** ~ (*in Paaren*) in twos.

**Zweitaktmotor** *m* two-stroke engine.

**zweitbeste(r, s)** *adj* second best.

**zweite(r, s)** *adj* second; **Bürger** ~**r Klasse** second-class citizen(s *pl*).

**zweiteilig** ['tsvaɪtaɪlɪç] *adj* (*Buch, Film etc*) in two parts; (*Kleidung*) two-piece.

**zweitens** *adv* secondly.

**zweit-** *zW:* **~größte(r, s)** *adj* second largest; **~klassig** *adj* second-class; **~letzte(r, s)** *adj* last but one, penultimate; **~rangig** *adj* second-rate; **Z~schlüssel** *m* duplicate key; **Z~stimme** *f* second vote; *siehe auch* **Erststimme**.

**zweitürig** ['tsvaɪtyrɪç] *adj* two-door.

**Zweitwagen** *m* second car.

**Zweitwohnung** *f* second home.

**zweizeilig** *adj* two-lined; (*TYP: Abstand*) double-spaced.

**Zweizimmerwohnung** *f* two-room(ed) flat (*BRIT*) *od* apartment (*US*).

**Zwerchfell** ['tsvɛrçfɛl] *nt* diaphragm.

**Zwerg(in)** [tsvɛrk, 'tsvɛrgɪn] (-(e)s, -e) *m(f)* dwarf; (*fig: Knirps*) midget; **~schule** (*umg*) *f* village school.

**Zwetschge** ['tsvɛtʃgə] (-, -n) *f* plum.

**Zwickel** ['tsvɪkəl] (-s, -) *m* gusset.

**zwicken** ['tsvɪkən] *vt* to pinch, nip.

**Zwickmühle** ['tsvɪkmy:lə] *f:* **in der** ~ **sitzen** (*fig*) to be in a dilemma.

**Zwieback** ['tsvi:bak] (-(e)s, -e *od* -bäcke) *m* rusk.

**Zwiebel** ['tsvi:bəl] (-, -n) *f* onion; (*Blumen~*) bulb; **z~artig** *adj* bulbous; **~turm** *m* (tower with an) onion dome.

**Zwie-** *zW:* ~**gespräch** *nt* dialogue (*BRIT*), dialog (*US*); ~**licht** *nt* twilight; **ins** ~**licht geraten sein** (*fig*) to appear in an unfavourable (*BRIT*) *od* unfavorable (*US*) light; **z**~**lichtig** *adj* shady, dubious; ~**spalt** *m* conflict; (*zwischen Menschen*) rift, gulf; **z**~**spältig** *adj* (*Gefühle*) conflicting; (*Charakter*) contradictory; ~**tracht** *f* discord, dissension.

**Zwilling** ['tsvɪlɪŋ] (**-s, -e**) *m* twin; **Zwillinge** *pl* (*ASTROL*) Gemini.

**zwingen** ['tsvɪŋən] *unreg vt* to force.

**zwingend** *adj* (*Grund etc*) compelling; (*logisch notwendig*) necessary; (*Schluß, Beweis*) conclusive.

**Zwinger** (**-s, -**) *m* (*Käfig*) cage; (*Hunde*~) run.

**zwinkern** ['tsvɪŋkərn] *vi* to blink; (*absichtlich*) to wink.

**Zwirn** [tsvɪrn] (**-(e)s, -e**) *m* thread.

**zwischen** ['tsvɪʃən] *präp* (*+akk od dat*) between; (*bei mehreren*) among; **Z**~**aufenthalt** *m* stopover; **Z**~**bemerkung** *f* (incidental) remark; **Z**~**bilanz** *f* (*COMM*) interim balance; ~**blenden** *vt* (*FILM, RUNDF, TV*) to insert; **Z**~**ding** *nt* cross; **Z**~**dividende** *f* interim dividend; ~**durch** *adv* in between; (*räumlich*) here and there; **Z**~**ergebnis** *nt* intermediate result; **Z**~**fall** *m* incident; **Z**~**frage** *f* question; **Z**~**größe** *f* in-between size; **Z**~**handel** *m* wholesaling; **Z**~**händler** *m* middleman, agent; **Z**~**lagerung** *f* temporary storage; **Z**~**landung** *f* (*AVIAT*) stopover; **Z**~**lösung** *f* temporary solution; ~**mahlzeit** *f* snack (*between meals*); ~**menschlich** *adj* interpersonal; **Z**~**prüfung** *f* intermediate examination; **Z**~**raum** *m* gap, space; **Z**~**ruf** *m*

interjection, interruption; **Zwischenrufe** *pl* heckling *sing*; **Z**~**saison** *f* low season; **Z**~**spiel** *nt* (*THEAT, fig*) interlude; (*MUS*) intermezzo; ~**staatlich** *adj* interstate; (*international*) international; **Z**~**station** *f* intermediate station; **Z**~**stecker** *m* (*ELEK*) adapter; **Z**~**stück** *nt* connecting piece; **Z**~**summe** *f* subtotal; **Z**~**wand** *f* partition; **Z**~**zeit** *f* interval; **in der Z**~**zeit** in the interim, meanwhile; **Z**~**zeugnis** *nt* (*SCH*) interim report.

**Zwist** [tsvɪst] (**-es, -e**) *m* dispute.

**zwitschern** ['tsvɪtʃərn] *vt, vi* to twitter, chirp; **einen** ~ (*umg*) to have a drink.

**Zwitter** ['tsvɪtər] (**-s, -**) *m* hermaphrodite.

**zwo** [tsvoː] *num* (*TEL, MIL*) two.

**zwölf** [tsvœlf] *num* twelve; **fünf Minuten vor** ~ (*fig*) at the eleventh hour.

**Zwölffingerdarm** (**-(e)s**) *m* duodenum.

**Zyankali** [tsyaːnˈkaːli] (**-s**) *nt* (*CHEM*) potassium cyanide.

**Zyklon** [tsyˈkloːn] (**-s, -e**) *m* cyclone.

**Zyklus** ['tsyːklus] (**-, Zyklen**) *m* cycle.

**Zylinder** [tsiˈlɪndər] (**-s, -**) *m* cylinder; (*Hut*) top hat; **z**~**förmig** *adj* cylindrical.

**Zyniker(in)** ['tsyːnikər(ɪn)] (**-s, -**) *m(f)* cynic.

**zynisch** ['tsyːnɪʃ] *adj* cynical.

**Zynismus** [tsyˈnɪsmus] *m* cynicism.

**Zypern** ['tsyːpərn] (**-s**) *nt* Cyprus.

**Zypresse** [tsyˈprɛsə] (**-, -n**) *f* (*BOT*) cypress.

**Zypriot(in)** [tsypriˈoːt(ɪn)] (**-en, -en**) *m(f)* Cypriot.

**zypriotisch** *adj* Cypriot, Cyprian.

**zyprisch** ['tsyːprɪʃ] *adj* Cypriot, Cyprian.

**Zyste** ['tsystə] (**-, -n**) *f* cyst.

**z.Z(t).** *abk = zur Zeit.*

# A, a

**A¹, a** [eɪ] *n* (*letter*) A *nt*, a *nt*; (*SCOL*) ≈ Eins *f*, Sehr gut *nt*; ~ **for Andrew**, (*US*) ~ **for Able** ≈ A wie Anton; ~ **road** (*BRIT: AUT*) Hauptverkehrsstraße *f*; ~ **shares** (*BRIT: STOCK EXCHANGE*) stimmrechtslose Aktien *pl*.

**A²** [eɪ] *n* (*MUS*) A *nt*, a *nt*.

**a** [ə] (*before vowel or silent h:* **an**) *indef art* **1** ein; (*before feminine noun*) eine; ~ **book** ein Buch; ~ **lamp** eine Lampe; **she's ~ doctor** sie ist Ärztin; **I haven't got ~ car** ich habe kein Auto; ~ **hundred/thousand** *etc* **pounds** einhundert/eintausend *etc* Pfund

**2** (*in expressing ratios, prices etc*) pro; **3** ~ **day/week** 3 pro Tag/Woche, 3 am Tag/in der Woche; **10 km an hour** 10 km pro Stunde.

**a.** *abbr* = **acre**.

**AA** *n abbr* (*BRIT:* = *Automobile Association*) Autofahrerorganisation, ≈ ADAC *m*; (*US:* = *Associate in/of Arts*) akademischer Grad für Geisteswissenschaftler; (= *Alcoholics Anonymous*) Anonyme Alkoholiker *pl*, AA *pl*; = **anti-aircraft**.

**AAA** *n abbr* (= *American Automobile Association*) Autofahrerorganisation, ≈ ADAC *m*; (*BRIT:* = *Amateur Athletics Association*) Leichtathletikverband der Amateure.

**A & R** *n abbr* (*MUS:* = *artists and repertoire*): ~ **person** Talentsucher(in) *m(f)*.

**AAUP** *n abbr* (= *American Association of University Professors*) Verband amerikanischer Universitätsprofessoren.

**AB** *abbr* (*BRIT*) = **able-bodied seaman**; (*CANADA:* = *Alberta*).

**abaci** ['æbəsaɪ] *npl of* **abacus**.

**aback** [ə'bæk] *adv:* **to be taken** ~ verblüfft sein.

**abacus** ['æbəkəs] (*pl* **abaci**) *n* Abakus *m*.

**abandon** [ə'bændən] *vt* verlassen; (*child*) aussetzen; (*give up*) aufgeben ♦ *n* (*wild behaviour*): **with** ~ selbstvergessen; **to** ~ **ship** das Schiff verlassen.

**abandoned** [ə'bændənd] *adj* verlassen; (*child*) ausgesetzt; (*unrestrained*) selbstvergessen.

**abase** [ə'beɪs] *vt:* **to** ~ **o.s.** sich erniedrigen; **to** ~ **o.s. so far as to do sth** sich dazu erniedrigen, etw zu tun.

**abashed** [ə'bæʃt] *adj* verlegen.

**abate** [ə'beɪt] *vi* nachlassen, sich legen.

**abatement** [ə'beɪtmənt] *n:* **noise** ~ **society** Gesellschaft *f* zur Lärmbekämpfung.

**abattoir** ['æbətwɑː] (*BRIT*) *n* Schlachthof *m*.

**abbey** ['æbɪ] *n* Abtei *f*.

**abbot** ['æbət] *n* Abt *m*.

**abbreviate** [ə'briːvɪeɪt] *vt* abkürzen; (*essay etc*) kürzen.

**abbreviation** [əbriːvɪ'eɪʃən] *n* Abkürzung *f*.

**ABC** *n abbr* (= *American Broadcasting Companies*) Fernsehsender.

**abdicate** ['æbdɪkeɪt] *vt* verzichten auf +*acc* ♦ *vi* (*monarch*) abdanken.

**abdication** [æbdɪ'keɪʃən] *n* (*see vb*) Verzicht *m*; Abdankung *f*.

**abdomen** ['æbdəmen] *n* Unterleib *m*.

**abdominal** [æb'dɒmɪnl] *adj* (*pain etc*) Unterleibs-.

**abduct** [æb'dʌkt] *vt* entführen.

**abduction** [æb'dʌkʃən] *n* Entführung *f*.

**Aberdonian** [æbə'dəʊnɪən] *adj* (*GEOG*) Aberdeener *inv* ♦ *n* Aberdeener(in) *m(f)*.

**aberration** [æbə'reɪʃən] *n* Anomalie *f*; **in a moment of mental** ~ in einem Augenblick geistiger Verwirrung.

**abet** [ə'bet] *vt see* **aid**.

**abeyance** [ə'beɪəns] *n:* **in** ~ (*law*) außer Kraft; (*matter*) ruhend.

**abhor** [əb'hɔː] *vt* verabscheuen.

**abhorrent** [əb'hɒrənt] *adj* abscheulich.

**abide** [ə'baɪd] *vt:* **I can't** ~ **it/him** ich kann es/

ihn nicht ausstehen.

▶**abide by** vt fus sich halten an +acc.

**abiding** [ə'baɪdɪŋ] adj (memory, impression) bleibend.

**ability** [ə'bɪlɪtɪ] n Fähigkeit f; **to the best of my ~** so gut ich es kann.

**abject** ['æbdʒɛkt] adj (poverty) bitter; (apology) demütig; (coward) erbärmlich.

**ablaze** [ə'bleɪz] adj in Flammen; **~ with light** hell erleuchtet.

**able** ['eɪbl] adj fähig; **to be ~ to do sth** etw tun können.

**able-bodied** ['eɪbl'bɒdɪd] adj kräftig; **~ seaman** (BRIT) Vollmatrose m.

**ablutions** [ə'bluːʃənz] npl Waschungen pl.

**ably** ['eɪblɪ] adv gekonnt.

**ABM** n abbr (= antiballistic missile) Anti-Raketen-Rakete f.

**abnormal** [æb'nɔːməl] adj abnorm; (child) anormal.

**abnormality** [æbnɔː'mælɪtɪ] n Abnormität f.

**aboard** [ə'bɔːd] adv (NAUT, AVIAT) an Bord ♦ prep an Bord +gen; **~ the train/bus** im Zug/Bus.

**abode** [ə'bəʊd] n (LAW): **of no fixed ~** ohne festen Wohnsitz.

**abolish** [ə'bɒlɪʃ] vt abschaffen.

**abolition** [æbə'lɪʃən] n Abschaffung f.

**abominable** [ə'bɒmɪnəbl] adj scheußlich.

**abominably** [ə'bɒmɪnəblɪ] adv scheußlich.

**Aborigine** [æbə'rɪdʒɪnɪ] n Ureinwohner(in) m(f) Australiens.

**abort** [ə'bɔːt] vt abtreiben; (MED: miscarry) fehlgebären; (COMPUT) abbrechen.

**abortion** [ə'bɔːʃən] n Abtreibung f; (miscarriage) Fehlgeburt f; **to have an ~** abtreiben lassen.

**abortionist** [ə'bɔːʃənɪst] n Abtreibungshelfer(in) m(f).

**abortive** [ə'bɔːtɪv] adj mißlungen.

**abound** [ə'baʊnd] vi im Überfluß vorhanden sein; **to ~ in** or **with** reich sein an +dat.

================= *KEYWORD*

**about** [ə'baʊt] adv 1 (approximately) etwa, ungefähr; **~ a hundred/thousand** etc etwa hundert/tausend etc; **at ~ 2 o'clock** etwa um 2 Uhr; **I've just ~ finished** ich bin gerade fertig

2 (referring to place) herum; **to run/walk** etc **~** herumlaufen/-gehen etc; **is Paul ~?** ist Paul da?

3: **to be ~ to do sth** im Begriff sein, etw zu tun; **he was ~ to cry** er fing fast an zu weinen; **she was ~ to leave/wash the dishes** sie wollte gerade gehen/das Geschirr spülen

♦ prep 1 (relating to) über +acc; **what is it ~?** worum geht es?; (book etc) wovon handelt es?; **we talked ~ it** wir haben darüber geredet; **what** or **how ~ going to the cinema?** wollen wir ins Kino gehen?

2 (referring to place) um ... herum; **to walk ~ the town** durch die Stadt gehen; **her clothes were scattered ~ the room** ihre Kleider waren über das ganze Zimmer verstreut.

**about-face** [ə'baʊt'feɪs] (US) n = about-turn.

**about-turn** [ə'baʊt'tɜːn] (BRIT) n Kehrtwendung f.

**above** [ə'bʌv] adv oben; (greater, more) darüber ♦ prep über +dat; **to cost ~ £10** mehr als £10 kosten; **mentioned ~** obengenannt; **he's not ~ a bit of blackmail** er ist sich dat nicht zu gut für eine kleine Erpressung; **~ all** vor allem.

**above board** adj korrekt.

**abrasion** [ə'breɪʒən] n Abschürfung f.

**abrasive** [ə'breɪzɪv] adj (substance) Scheuer-; (person, manner) aggressiv.

**abreast** [ə'brɛst] adv nebeneinander; **three ~** zu dritt nebeneinander; **to keep ~ of** (fig) auf dem laufenden bleiben mit.

**abridge** [ə'brɪdʒ] vt kürzen.

**abroad** [ə'brɔːd] adv (be) im Ausland; (go) ins Ausland; **there is a rumour ~ that ...** (fig) ein Gerücht geht um or kursiert, daß ...

**abrupt** [ə'brʌpt] adj abrupt; (person, behaviour) schroff.

**abruptly** [ə'brʌptlɪ] adv abrupt.

**abscess** ['æbsɪs] n Abszeß m.

**abscond** [əb'skɒnd] vi: **to ~ with** sich davonmachen mit; **to ~ (from)** fliehen (aus).

**abseil** ['æbseɪl] vi sich abseilen.

**absence** ['æbsəns] n Abwesenheit f; **in the ~ of** (person) in Abwesenheit +gen; (thing) in Ermangelung +gen.

**absent** ['æbsənt] adj abwesend, nicht da ♦ vt: **to ~ o.s. from** fernbleiben +dat; **to be ~** fehlen; **to be ~ without leave** (MIL) sich unerlaubt von der Truppe entfernen.

**absentee** [æbsən'tiː] n Abwesende(r) f(m).

**absenteeism** [æbsən'tiːɪzəm] n (from school) Schwänzen nt; (from work) Nichterscheinen nt am Arbeitsplatz.

**absent-minded** ['æbsənt'maɪndɪd] adj zerstreut.

**absent-mindedly** ['æbsənt'maɪndɪdlɪ] adv zerstreut; (look) abwesend.

**absent-mindedness** ['æbsənt'maɪndɪdnɪs] n Zerstreutheit f.

**absolute** ['æbsəluːt] adj absolut; (power) uneingeschränkt.

**absolutely** [æbsə'luːtlɪ] adv absolut; (agree) vollkommen; **~! genau!**

**absolution** [æbsə'luːʃən] n Lossprechung f.

**absolve** [əb'zɒlv] vt: **to ~ sb (from)** jdn lossprechen (von); (responsibility) jdn entbinden (von).

**absorb** [əb'zɔːb] vt aufnehmen (also fig); (light, heat) absorbieren; (group, business) übernehmen; **to be ~ed in a book** in ein Buch vertieft sein.

**absorbent** [əb'zɔːbənt] adj saugfähig.
**absorbent cotton** (US) n Watte f.
**absorbing** [əb'zɔːbɪŋ] adj saugfähig; (book, film, work etc) fesselnd.
**absorption** [əb'sɔːpʃən] n (see vb) Aufnahme f; Absorption f; Übernahme f; (interest) Faszination f.
**abstain** [əb'steɪn] vi (voting) sich (der Stimme) enthalten; **to ~ (from)** (eating, drinking etc) sich enthalten (+gen).
**abstemious** [əb'stiːmɪəs] adj enthaltsam.
**abstention** [əb'stɛnʃən] n (Stimm)enthaltung f.
**abstinence** ['æbstɪnəns] n Enthaltsamkeit f.
**abstract** ['æbstrækt] adj abstrakt ♦ n (summary) Zusammenfassung f ♦ vt: **to ~ sth (from)** (summarize) etw entnehmen (aus); (remove) etw entfernen (aus).
**abstruse** [æb'struːs] adj abstrus.
**absurd** [əb'sɔːd] adj absurd.
**absurdity** [əb'sɔːdɪtɪ] n Absurdität f.
**ABTA** ['æbtə] n abbr (= Association of British Travel Agents) Verband der Reiseveranstalter.
**Abu Dhabi** ['æbuː'dɑːbɪ] n (GEOG) Abu Dhabi nt.
**abundance** [ə'bʌndəns] n Reichtum m; **an ~ of** eine Fülle von; **in ~** in Hülle und Fülle.
**abundant** [ə'bʌndənt] adj reichlich.
**abundantly** [ə'bʌndəntlɪ] adv reichlich; **~ clear** völlig klar.
**abuse** [ə'bjuːs] n (insults) Beschimpfungen pl; (ill-treatment) Mißhandlung f; (misuse) Mißbrauch m ♦ vt (see n) beschimpfen; mißhandeln; mißbrauchen; **to be open to ~** sich leicht mißbrauchen lassen.
**abuser** [ə'bjuːzə'] n (drug abuser) jd, der Drogen mißbraucht; (child abuser) jd, der Kinder mißbraucht oder mißhandelt.
**abusive** [ə'bjuːsɪv] adj beleidigend.
**abysmal** [ə'bɪzməl] adj entsetzlich; (ignorance etc) grenzenlos.
**abysmally** [ə'bɪzməlɪ] adv (see adj) entsetzlich; grenzenlos.
**abyss** [ə'bɪs] n Abgrund m.
**AC** abbr = **alternating current**; (US: = athletic club) ≈ SV m.
**a/c** abbr (BANKING etc) = **account**; (= account current) Girokonto nt.
**academic** [ækə'dɛmɪk] adj akademisch (also pej); (work) wissenschaftlich; (person) intellektuell ♦ n Akademiker(in) m(f).
**academic year** n (university year) Universitätsjahr nt; (school year) Schuljahr nt.
**academy** [ə'kædəmɪ] n Akademie f; (school) Hochschule f; **~ of music** Musikhochschule f; **military/naval ~** Militär-/Marineakademie f.
**ACAS** ['eɪkæs] (BRIT) n abbr (= Advisory, Conciliation and Arbitration Service) Schlichtungsstelle für Arbeitskonflikte.

**accede** [æk'siːd] vi: **to ~ to** zustimmen +dat.
**accelerate** [æk'sɛləreɪt] vt beschleunigen ♦ vi (AUT) Gas geben.
**acceleration** [æksɛlə'reɪʃən] n Beschleunigung f.
**accelerator** [æk'sɛləreɪtə'] n Gaspedal nt.
**accent** ['æksɛnt] n Akzent m; (fig: emphasis, stress) Betonung f; **to speak with an Irish ~** mit einem irischen Akzent sprechen; **to have a strong ~** einen starken Akzent haben.
**accentuate** [æk'sɛntjueɪt] vt betonen; (need, difference etc) hervorheben.
**accept** [ək'sɛpt] vt annehmen; (fact, situation) sich abfinden mit; (risk) in Kauf nehmen; (responsibility) übernehmen; (blame) auf sich acc nehmen.
**acceptable** [ək'sɛptəbl] adj annehmbar.
**acceptance** [ək'sɛptəns] n Annahme f; **to meet with general ~** allgemeine Anerkennung finden.
**access** ['æksɛs] n Zugang m ♦ vt (COMPUT) zugreifen auf +dat; **the burglars gained ~ through a window** die Einbrecher gelangten durch ein Fenster hinein.
**accessible** [æk'sɛsəbl] adj erreichbar; (knowledge, art etc) zugänglich.
**accession** [æk'sɛʃən] n Antritt m; (of monarch) Thronbesteigung f; (to library) Neuanschaffung f.
**accessory** [æk'sɛsərɪ] n Zubehörteil nt; (DRESS) Accessoire nt; (LAW): **~ to** Mitschuldige(r) f(m) an +dat; **accessories** npl Zubehör nt; **toilet accessories** (BRIT) Toilettenartikel pl.
**access road** n Zufahrt(sstraße) f.
**access time** n (COMPUT) Zugriffszeit f.
**accident** ['æksɪdənt] n Zufall m; (mishap, disaster) Unfall m; **to meet with** or **to have an ~** einen Unfall haben, verunglücken; **~s at work** Arbeitsunfälle pl; **by ~** zufällig.
**accidental** [æksɪ'dɛntl] adj zufällig; (death, damage) Unfall-.
**accidentally** [æksɪ'dɛntəlɪ] adv zufällig.
**accident insurance** n Unfallversicherung f.
**accident-prone** ['æksɪdənt'prəun] adj vom Pech verfolgt.
**acclaim** [ə'kleɪm] n Beifall m ♦ vt: **to be ~ed for one's achievements** für seine Leistungen gefeiert werden.
**acclamation** [æklə'meɪʃən] n Anerkennung f; (applause) Beifall m.
**acclimate** [ə'klaɪmət] (US) vt = **acclimatize**.
**acclimatize** [ə'klaɪmətaɪz], (US) **acclimate** [ə'klaɪmət] vt: **to become ~d** sich akklimatisieren; **to become ~d to** sich gewöhnen an +acc.
**accolade** ['ækəleɪd] n (fig) Auszeichnung f.
**accommodate** [ə'kɔmədeɪt] vt unterbringen; (subj: car, hotel etc) Platz bieten +dat; (oblige, help) entgegenkommen +dat; **to ~ one's plans to** seine Pläne anpassen an +acc.

**accommodating** [əˈkɔmədeɪtɪŋ] *adj* entgegenkommend.

**accommodation** [əkɔməˈdeɪʃən] *n* Unterkunft *f*; **accommodations** (*US*) *npl* Unterkunft *f*; **have you any ~?** haben Sie eine Unterkunft?; **"~ to let"** „Zimmer zu vermieten"; **they have ~ for 500** sie können 500 Personen unterbringen; **the hall has seating ~ for 600** (*BRIT*) in dem Saal können 600 Personen sitzen.

**accompaniment** [əˈkʌmpənɪmənt] *n* Begleitung *f*.

**accompanist** [əˈkʌmpənɪst] *n* Begleiter(in) *m(f)*.

**accompany** [əˈkʌmpənɪ] *vt* begleiten.

**accomplice** [əˈkʌmplɪs] *n* Komplize *m*, Komplizin *f*.

**accomplish** [əˈkʌmplɪʃ] *vt* vollenden; (*achieve*) erreichen.

**accomplished** [əˈkʌmplɪʃt] *adj* ausgezeichnet.

**accomplishment** [əˈkʌmplɪʃmənt] *n* Vollendung *f*; (*achievement*) Leistung *f*; (*skill: gen pl*) Fähigkeit *f*.

**accord** [əˈkɔːd] *n* Übereinstimmung *f*; (*treaty*) Vertrag *m* ♦ *vt* gewähren; **of his own ~** freiwillig; **with one ~** geschlossen; **to be in ~** übereinstimmen.

**accordance** [əˈkɔːdəns] *n*: **in ~ with** in Übereinstimmung mit.

**according** [əˈkɔːdɪŋ] *prep*: **~ to** zufolge +*dat*; **~ to plan** wie geplant.

**accordingly** [əˈkɔːdɪŋlɪ] *adv* entsprechend; (*as a result*) folglich.

**accordion** [əˈkɔːdɪən] *n* Akkordeon *nt*.

**accost** [əˈkɔst] *vt* ansprechen.

**account** [əˈkaʊnt] *n* (*COMM: bill*) Rechnung *f*; (*in bank, department store*) Konto *nt*; (*report*) Bericht *m*; **accounts** *npl* (*COMM*) Buchhaltung *f*; (*BOOKKEEPING*) (Geschäfts)bücher *pl*; **"~ payee only"** (*BRIT*) „nur zur Verrechnung"; **to keep an ~ of** Buch führen über +*acc*; **to bring sb to ~ for sth/for having embezzled £50,000** jdn für etw/für die Unterschlagung von £50.000 zur Rechenschaft ziehen; **by all ~s** nach allem, was man hört; **of no ~** ohne Bedeutung; **on ~** auf Kredit; **to pay £5 on ~** eine Anzahlung von £5 leisten; **on no ~** auf keinen Fall; **on ~ of** wegen +*gen*; **to take into ~, take ~ of** berücksichtigen.

▶**account for** *vt fus* erklären; (*expenditure*) Rechenschaft ablegen für; (*represent*) ausmachen; **all the children were ~ed for** man wußte, wo alle Kinder waren; **4 people are still not ~ed for** 4 Personen werden immer noch vermißt.

**accountability** [əˈkaʊntəˈbɪlɪtɪ] *n* Verantwortlichkeit *f*.

**accountable** [əˈkaʊntəbl] *adj*: **~ (to)** verantwortlich (gegenüber +*dat*); **to be held ~ for sth** für etw verantwortlich gemacht werden.

**accountancy** [əˈkaʊntənsɪ] *n* Buchhaltung *f*.

**accountant** [əˈkaʊntənt] *n* Buchhalter(in) *m(f)*.

**accounting** [əˈkaʊntɪŋ] *n* Buchhaltung *f*.

**accounting period** *n* Abrechnungszeitraum *m*.

**account number** *n* Kontonummer *f*.

**accounts payable** *npl* Verbindlichkeiten *pl*.

**accounts receivable** *npl* Forderungen *pl*.

**accredited** [əˈkrɛdɪtɪd] *adj* anerkannt.

**accretion** [əˈkriːʃən] *n* Ablagerung *f*.

**accrue** [əˈkruː] *vi* sich ansammeln; **to ~ to** zufließen +*dat*.

**accrued interest** *n* aufgelaufene Zinsen *pl*.

**accumulate** [əˈkjuːmjuleɪt] *vt* ansammeln ♦ *vi* sich ansammeln.

**accumulation** [əkjuːmjuˈleɪʃən] *n* Ansammlung *f*.

**accuracy** [ˈækjʊrəsɪ] *n* Genauigkeit *f*.

**accurate** [ˈækjʊrɪt] *adj* genau.

**accurately** [ˈækjʊrɪtlɪ] *adv* genau; (*answer*) richtig.

**accusation** [ækjuˈzeɪʃən] *n* Vorwurf *m*; (*instance*) Beschuldigung *f*; (*LAW*) Anklage *f*.

**accusative** [əˈkjuːzətɪv] *n* Akkusativ *m*.

**accuse** [əˈkjuːz] *vt*: **to ~ sb (of sth)** jdn (einer Sache *gen*) beschuldigen; (*LAW*) jdn (wegen etw *dat*) anklagen.

**accused** [əˈkjuːzd] *n* (*LAW*): **the ~** der/die Angeklagte.

**accuser** [əˈkjuːzəʳ] *n* Ankläger(in) *m(f)*.

**accusing** [əˈkjuːzɪŋ] *adj* anklagend.

**accustom** [əˈkʌstəm] *vt* gewöhnen; **to ~ o.s. to sth** sich an etw *acc* gewöhnen.

**accustomed** [əˈkʌstəmd] *adj* gewohnt; (*in the habit*): **~ to** gewohnt an +*acc*.

**AC/DC** *abbr* (= *alternating current/direct current*) WS/GS.

**ACE** [eɪs] *n abbr* (= *American Council on Education*) *akademischer Verband für das Erziehungswesen*.

**ace** [eɪs] *n* As *nt*.

**acerbic** [əˈsəːbɪk] *adj* scharf.

**acetate** [ˈæsɪteɪt] *n* Acetat *nt*.

**ache** [eɪk] *n* Schmerz *m* ♦ *vi* schmerzen, weh tun; (*yearn*): **to ~ to do sth** sich danach sehnen, etw zu tun; **I've got (a) stomach ~** ich habe Magenschmerzen; **I'm aching all over** mir tut alles weh; **my head ~s** mir tut der Kopf weh.

**achieve** [əˈtʃiːv] *vt* (*aim, result*) erreichen; (*success*) erzielen; (*victory*) erringen.

**achievement** [əˈtʃiːvmənt] *n* (*act of achieving*) Erreichen *nt*; (*success, feat*) Leistung *f*.

**Achilles heel** [əˈkɪliːz-] *n* Achillesferse *f*.

**acid** [ˈæsɪd] *adj* sauer ♦ *n* (*CHEM*) Säure *f*; (*inf: LSD*) Acid *nt*.

**Acid House** *n* Acid House *nt*, *elektronische Funk-Diskomusik*.

**acidic** [əˈsɪdɪk] *adj* sauer.

**acidity** [əˈsɪdɪtɪ] *n* Säure *f*.

**acid rain** *n* saurer Regen *m*.

**acid test** *n* (*fig*) Feuerprobe *f*.

**acknowledge** [ək'nɒlɪdʒ] *vt* (*also:* ~ **receipt of**) den Empfang +*gen* bestätigen; (*fact*) zugeben; (*situation*) zur Kenntnis nehmen; (*person*) grüßen.

**acknowledgement** [ək'nɒlɪdʒmənt] *n* Empfangsbestätigung *f*; **acknowledgements** *npl* (*in book*) ≈ Danksagung *f*.

**ACLU** *n abbr* (= *American Civil Liberties Union*) Bürgerrechtsverband.

**acme** ['ækmɪ] *n* Gipfel *m*, Höhepunkt *m*.

**acne** ['æknɪ] *n* Akne *f*.

**acorn** ['eɪkɔːn] *n* Eichel *f*.

**acoustic** [ə'kuːstɪk] *adj* akustisch.

**acoustic coupler** *n* (*COMPUT*) Akustikkoppler *m*.

**acoustics** [ə'kuːstɪks] *n* Akustik *f*.

**acoustic screen** *n* Trennwand *f* zur Schalldämpfung.

**acquaint** [ə'kweɪnt] *vt*: **to** ~ **sb with sth** jdn mit etw vertraut machen; **to be** ~**ed with** (*person*) bekannt sein mit; (*fact*) vertraut sein mit.

**acquaintance** [ə'kweɪntəns] *n* Bekannte(r) *f(m)*; (*with person*) Bekanntschaft *f*; (*with subject*) Kenntnis *f*; **to make sb's** ~ jds Bekanntschaft machen.

**acquiesce** [ækwɪ'ɛs] *vi* einwilligen; **to** ~ **(to)** (*demand, arrangement, request*) einwilligen (in +*acc*).

**acquire** [ə'kwaɪəʳ] *vt* erwerben; (*interest*) entwickeln; (*habit*) annehmen.

**acquired** [ə'kwaɪəd] *adj* erworben; **whisky is an** ~ **taste** man muß sich an Whisky erst gewöhnen.

**acquisition** [ækwɪ'zɪʃən] *n* (*see vb*) Erwerb *m*, Entwicklung *f*, Annahme *f*; (*thing acquired*) Errungenschaft *f*.

**acquisitive** [ə'kwɪzɪtɪv] *adj* habgierig; **the** ~ **society** die Erwerbsgesellschaft.

**acquit** [ə'kwɪt] *vt* freisprechen; **to** ~ **o.s. well** seine Sache gut machen.

**acquittal** [ə'kwɪtl] *n* Freispruch *m*.

**acre** ['eɪkəʳ] *n* Morgen *m*.

**acreage** ['eɪkərɪdʒ] *n* Fläche *f*.

**acrid** ['ækrɪd] *adj* bitter; (*smoke, fig*) beißend.

**acrimonious** [ækrɪ'məunɪəs] *adj* bitter; (*dispute*) erbittert.

**acrimony** ['ækrɪmənɪ] *n* Erbitterung *f*.

**acrobat** ['ækrəbæt] *n* Akrobat(in) *m(f)*.

**acrobatic** [ækrə'bætɪk] *adj* akrobatisch.

**acrobatics** [ækrə'bætɪks] *npl* Akrobatik *f*.

**acronym** ['ækrənɪm] *n* Akronym *nt*.

**Acropolis** [ə'krɒpəlɪs] *n*: **the** ~ (*GEOG*) die Akropolis.

**across** [ə'krɒs] *prep* über +*acc*; (*on the other side of*) auf der anderen Seite +*gen* ♦ *adv* (*direction*) hinüber, herüber; (*measurement*) breit; **to take sb** ~ **the road** jdn über die Straße bringen; **a road** ~ **the wood** eine Straße durch den Wald; **the lake is 12 km** ~ der See ist 12 km breit; ~ **from** gegenüber +*dat*; **to get sth** ~ **(to sb)** (jdm) etw

klarmachen.

**acrylic** [ə'krɪlɪk] *adj* (*acid, paint, blanket*) Acryl- ♦ *n* Acryl *nt*; **acrylics** *npl*: **he paints in** ~**s** er malt mit Acrylfarbe.

**ACT** *n abbr* (= *American College Test*) Eignungstest *für Studienbewerber.

**act** [ækt] *n* Tat *f*; (*of play*) Akt *m*; (*in a show etc*) Nummer *f*; (*LAW*) Gesetz *nt* ♦ *vi* handeln; (*behave*) sich verhalten; (*have effect*) wirken; (*THEAT*) spielen ♦ *vt* spielen; **it's only an** ~ es ist nur Schau; ~ **of God** (*LAW*) höhere Gewalt *f*; **to be in the** ~ **of doing sth** dabei sein, etw zu tun; **to catch sb in the** ~ jdn auf frischer Tat ertappen; **to** ~ **the fool** (*BRIT*) herumalbern; **he is only** ~**ing** er tut (doch) nur so; **to** ~ **as** fungieren als; **it** ~**s as a deterrent** es dient zur Abschreckung.

▶**act on** *vt*: **to** ~ **on sth** (*take action*) auf etw +*acc* hin handeln.

▶**act out** *vt* (*event*) durchspielen; (*fantasies*) zum Ausdruck bringen.

**acting** ['æktɪŋ] *adj* stellvertretend ♦ *n* (*profession*) Schauspielkunst *f*; (*activity*) Spielen *nt*; ~ **in my capacity as chairman** ... in meiner Eigenschaft als Vorsitzender ...

**action** ['ækʃən] *n* Tat *f*; (*motion*) Bewegung *f*; (*MIL*) Kampf *m*, Gefecht *nt*; (*LAW*) Klage *f*; **to bring an** ~ **against sb** (*LAW*) eine Klage gegen jdn anstrengen; **killed in** ~ (*MIL*) gefallen; **out of** ~ (*person*) nicht einsatzfähig; (*thing*) außer Betrieb; **to take** ~ etwas unternehmen; **to put a plan into** ~ einen Plan in die Tat umsetzen.

**action replay** *n* (*TV*) Wiederholung *f*.

**activate** ['æktɪveɪt] *vt* in Betrieb setzen; (*CHEM, PHYS*) aktivieren.

**active** ['æktɪv] *adj* aktiv; (*volcano*) tätig; **to play an** ~ **part in sth** sich aktiv an etw *dat* beteiligen.

**active duty** (*US*) *n* (*MIL*) Einsatz *m*.

**actively** ['æktɪvlɪ] *adv* aktiv; (*dislike*) offen.

**active partner** *n* (*COMM*) tätiger Teilhaber *m*.

**active service** (*BRIT*) *n* (*MIL*) Einsatz *m*.

**active suspension** *n* (*AUT*) aktives *or* computergesteuertes Fahrwerk *nt*.

**activist** ['æktɪvɪst] *n* Aktivist(in) *m(f)*.

**activity** [æk'tɪvɪtɪ] *n* Aktivität *f*; (*pastime, pursuit*) Betätigung *f*.

**actor** ['æktəʳ] *n* Schauspieler *m*.

**actress** ['æktrɪs] *n* Schauspielerin *f*.

**actual** ['æktjuəl] *adj* wirklich; (*emphatic use*) eigentlich.

**actually** ['æktjuəlɪ] *adv* wirklich; (*in fact*) tatsächlich; (*even*) sogar.

**actuary** ['æktjuərɪ] *n* Aktuar *m*.

**actuate** ['æktjueɪt] *vt* auslösen.

**acuity** [ə'kjuːɪtɪ] *n* Schärfe *f*.

**acumen** ['ækjumən] *n* Scharfsinn *m*; **business** ~ Geschäftssinn *m*.

**acupuncture** ['ækjupʌŋktʃəʳ] *n* Akupunktur *f*.

**acute** [ə'kjuːt] *adj* akut; (*anxiety*) heftig; (*mind*) scharf; (*person*) scharfsinnig; (*MATH: angle*) spitz; (*LING*): ~ **accent** Akut *m*.

**AD** *adv abbr* (= *Anno Domini*) n. Chr. ♦ *n abbr* (*US: MIL*) = **active duty.**

**ad** [æd] (*inf*) *n abbr* = **advertisement.**

**adage** ['ædɪdʒ] *n* Sprichwort *nt*.

**adamant** ['ædəmənt] *adj:* **to be** ~ **that ...** darauf bestehen, daß ...; **to be** ~ **about sth** auf etw *dat* bestehen.

**Adam's apple** ['ædəmz-] *n* Adamsapfel *m*.

**adapt** [ə'dæpt] *vt* anpassen; (*novel etc*) bearbeiten ♦ *vi:* **to** ~ **(to)** sich anpassen (an +*acc*).

**adaptability** [ədæptə'bɪlɪtɪ] *n* Anpassungsfähigkeit *f*.

**adaptable** [ə'dæptəbl] *adj* anpassungsfähig; (*device*) vielseitig.

**adaptation** [ædæp'teɪʃən] *n* (*of novel etc*) Bearbeitung *f*; (*of machine etc*) Umstellung *f*.

**adapter** [ə'dæptə'] *n* (*ELEC*) Adapter *m*; (: *for several plugs*) Mehrfachsteckdose *f*.

**adaptor** [ə'dæptə'] *n* = **adapter.**

**ADC** *n abbr* (*MIL*) = **aide-de-camp;** (*US:* = *Aid to Dependent Children*) Beihilfe für sozialschwache Familien.

**add** [æd] *vt* hinzufügen; (*figures: also:* ~ **up**) zusammenzählen ♦ *vi:* **to** ~ **to** (*increase*) beitragen zu.

▶**add on** *vt* (*amount*) dazurechnen; (*room*) anbauen.

▶**add up** *vt* (*figures*) zusammenzählen ♦ *vi* (*fig*): **it doesn't** ~ **up** es ergibt keinen Sinn; **it doesn't** ~ **up to much** (*fig*) das ist nicht berühmt (*inf*).

**addenda** [ə'dɛndə] *npl of* **addendum.**

**addendum** [ə'dɛndəm] (*pl* **addenda**) *n* Nachtrag *m*.

**adder** ['ædə'] *n* Kreuzotter *f*, Viper *f*.

**addict** ['ædɪkt] *n* Süchtige(r) *f(m)*; (*enthusiast*) Anhänger(in) *m(f)*.

**addicted** [ə'dɪktɪd] *adj:* **to be** ~ **to drugs/drink** drogensüchtig/alkoholsüchtig sein; **to be** ~ **to football** (*fig*) ohne Fußball nicht mehr leben können.

**addiction** [ə'dɪkʃən] *n* Sucht *f*.

**addictive** [ə'dɪktɪv] *adj:* **to be** ~ (*drug*) süchtig machen; (*activity*) zur Sucht werden können.

**adding machine** ['ædɪŋ-] *n* Addiermaschine *f*.

**Addis Ababa** ['ædɪs'æbəbə] *n* (*GEOG*) Addis Abeba *nt*.

**addition** [ə'dɪʃən] *n* (*adding up*) Zusammenzählen *nt*; (*thing added*) Zusatz *m*; (: *to payment, bill*) Zuschlag *m*; (: *to building*) Anbau *m*; **in** ~ **(to)** zusätzlich (zu).

**additional** [ə'dɪʃənl] *adj* zusätzlich.

**additive** ['ædɪtɪv] *n* Zusatz *m*.

**addled** ['ædld] *adj* (*BRIT: egg*) faul; (*brain*) verwirrt.

**address** [ə'drɛs] *n* Adresse *f*; (*speech*) Ansprache *f* ♦ *vt* adressieren; (*speak to: person*) ansprechen; (: *audience*) sprechen

zu; **form of** ~ (Form *f* der) Anrede *f*; **what form of** ~ **do you use for ...?** wie redet man ... an?; **absolute/relative** ~ (*COMPUT*) absolute/relative Adresse; **to** ~ **(o.s. to)** (*problem*) sich befassen mit.

**address book** *n* Adreßbuch *nt*.

**addressee** [ædrɛ'siː] *n* Empfänger(in) *m(f)*.

**Aden** ['eɪdən] *n* (*GEOG*): **Gulf of** ~ Golf *m* von Aden.

**adenoids** ['ædɪnɔɪdz] *npl* Rachenmandeln *pl*.

**adept** ['ædɛpt] *adj:* **to be** ~ **at** gut sein in +*dat*.

**adequacy** ['ædɪkwəsɪ] *n* (*of resources*) Adäquatheit *f*; (*of performance, proposals etc*) Angemessenheit *f*.

**adequate** ['ædɪkwɪt] *adj* ausreichend, adäquat; (*satisfactory*) angemessen.

**adequately** ['ædɪkwɪtlɪ] *adv* ausreichend; (*satisfactorily*) zufriedenstellend.

**adhere** [əd'hɪə'] *vi:* **to** ~ **to** haften an +*dat*; (*fig: abide by*) sich halten an +*acc*; (: *hold to*) festhalten an +*dat*.

**adhesion** [əd'hiːʒən] *n* Haften *nt*, Haftung *f*.

**adhesive** [əd'hiːzɪv] *adj* klebend, Klebe- ♦ *n* Klebstoff *m*.

**adhesive tape** *n* (*BRIT*) Klebstreifen *m*; (*US: MED*) Heftpflaster *nt*.

**ad hoc** [æd'hɔk] *adj* (*committee, decision*) Ad-hoc- ♦ *adv* ad hoc.

**ad infinitum** ['ædɪnfɪ'naɪtəm] *adv* ad infinitum.

**adjacent** [ə'dʒeɪsənt] *adj:* ~ **to** neben +*dat*.

**adjective** ['ædʒɛktɪv] *n* Adjektiv *nt*, Eigenschaftswort *nt*.

**adjoin** [ə'dʒɔɪn] *vt:* **the hotel** ~**ing the station** das Hotel neben dem Bahnhof.

**adjoining** [ə'dʒɔɪnɪŋ] *adj* benachbart, Neben-.

**adjourn** [ə'dʒəːn] *vt* vertagen ♦ *vi* sich vertagen; **to** ~ **a meeting till the following week** eine Besprechung auf die nächste Woche vertagen; **they** ~**ed to the pub** (*BRIT: inf*) sie begaben sich in die Kneipe.

**adjournment** [ə'dʒəːnmənt] *n* Unterbrechung *f*.

**Adjt.** *abbr* (*MIL*) = **adjutant.**

**adjudicate** [ə'dʒuːdɪkeɪt] *vt* (*contest*) Preisrichter sein bei; (*claim*) entscheiden ♦ *vi* entscheiden; **to** ~ **on** urteilen bei +*dat*.

**adjudication** [ədʒuːdɪ'keɪʃən] *n* Entscheidung *f*.

**adjudicator** [ə'dʒuːdɪkeɪtə'] *n* Schiedsrichter(in) *m(f)*; (*in contest*) Preisrichter(in) *m(f)*.

**adjust** [ə'dʒʌst] *vt* anpassen; (*change*) ändern; (*clothing*) zurechtrücken; (*machine etc*) einstellen; (*INSURANCE*) regulieren ♦ *vi:* **to** ~ **(to)** sich anpassen (an +*acc*).

**adjustable** [ə'dʒʌstəbl] *adj* verstellbar.

**adjuster** [ə'dʒʌstə'] *n see* **loss.**

**adjustment** [ə'dʒʌstmənt] *n* Anpassung *f*; (*to machine*) Einstellung *f*.

**adjutant** ['ædʒətənt] *n* Adjutant *m*.

**ad-lib** [æd'lɪb] *vi, vt* improvisieren ♦ *adv:* **ad lib** aus dem Stegreif.

**adman** ['ædmæn] (*inf: irreg: like* **man**) *n*

Werbefachmann m.

**admin** ['ædmɪn] (*inf*) n abbr = **administration**.

**administer** [əd'mɪnɪstə*] vt (*country, department*) verwalten; (*justice*) sprechen; (*oath*) abnehmen; (*MED: drug*) verabreichen.

**administration** [ədmɪnɪs'treɪʃən] n (*management*) Verwaltung f; (*government*) Regierung f; **the A~** (*US*) die Regierung.

**administrative** [əd'mɪnɪstrətɪv] adj (*department, reform etc*) Verwaltungs-.

**administrator** [əd'mɪnɪstreɪtə*] n Verwaltungsbeamte(r) f(m).

**admirable** ['ædmərəbl] adj bewundernswert.

**admiral** ['ædmərəl] n Admiral m.

**Admiralty** ['ædmərəltɪ] (*BRIT*) n: **the ~** (*also:* **the ~ Board**) das Marineministerium.

**admiration** [ædmə'reɪʃən] n Bewunderung f; **to have great ~ for sb/sth** jdn/etw sehr bewundern.

**admire** [əd'maɪə*] vt bewundern.

**admirer** [əd'maɪərə*] n (*suitor*) Verehrer m; (*fan*) Bewunderer m, Bewunderin f.

**admiring** [əd'maɪərɪŋ] adj bewundernd.

**admissible** [əd'mɪsəbl] adj (*evidence, as evidence*) zulässig.

**admission** [əd'mɪʃən] n (*admittance*) Zutritt m; (*to exhibition, night club etc*) Einlaß m; (*to club, hospital*) Aufnahme f; (*entry fee*) Eintritt(spreis) m; (*confession*) Geständnis nt; "**~ free**", "**free ~**" „Eintritt frei"; **by his own ~** nach eigenem Eingeständnis.

**admit** [əd'mɪt] vt (*confess*) gestehen; (*permit to enter*) einlassen; (*to club, hospital*) aufnehmen; (*responsibility etc*) anerkennen; "**children not ~ted**" „kein Zutritt für Kinder"; **this ticket ~s two** diese Karte ist für zwei Personen; **I must ~ that** ... ich muß zugeben, daß ...; **to ~ defeat** sich geschlagen geben.

▶**admit of** vt fus (*interpretation etc*) erlauben.

▶**admit to** vt fus (*murder etc*) gestehen.

**admittance** [əd'mɪtəns] n Zutritt m; "**no ~**" „kein Zutritt".

**admittedly** [əd'mɪtɪdlɪ] adv zugegebenermaßen.

**admonish** [əd'mɒnɪʃ] vt ermahnen.

**ad nauseam** [æd'nɔ:sɪæm] adv (*talk*) endlos; (*repeat*) bis zum Gehtnichtmehr (*inf*).

**ado** [ə'du:] n: **without (any) more ~** ohne weitere Umstände.

**adolescence** [ædəu'lɛsns] n Jugend f.

**adolescent** [ædəu'lɛsnt] adj heranwachsend; (*remark, behaviour*) pubertär ♦ n Jugendliche(r) f(m).

**adopt** [ə'dɒpt] vt adoptieren; (*POL: candidate*) aufstellen; (*policy, attitude, accent*) annehmen.

**adopted** [ə'dɒptɪd] adj (*child*) adoptiert.

**adoption** [ə'dɒpʃən] n (*see vb*) Adoption f; Aufstellung f; Annahme f.

**adoptive** [ə'dɒptɪv] adj (*parents etc*) Adoptiv-; **~ country** Wahlheimat f.

**adorable** [ə'dɔ:rəbl] adj entzückend.

**adoration** [ædə'reɪʃən] n (*of person*) Verehrung f.

**adore** [ə'dɔ:*] vt (*person*) verehren; (*film, activity etc*) schwärmen für.

**adoring** [ə'dɔ:rɪŋ] adj (*fans etc*) ihn/sie bewundernd; (*husband/wife*) sie/ihn innig liebend.

**adoringly** [ə'dɔ:rɪŋlɪ] adv (*look, gaze*) bewundernd.

**adorn** [ə'dɔ:n] vt schmücken.

**adornment** [ə'dɔ:nmənt] n Schmuck m.

**ADP** n abbr = **automatic data processing**.

**adrenalin** [ə'drɛnəlɪn] n Adrenalin nt; **it gets the ~ going** das bringt einen in Fahrt.

**Adriatic** [eɪdrɪ'ætɪk] n: **the ~ (Sea)** (*GEOG*) die Adria, das Adriatische Meer.

**adrift** [ə'drɪft] adv (*NAUT*) treibend; (*fig*) ziellos; **to be ~** (*NAUT*) treiben; **to come ~** (*boat*) sich losmachen; (*fastening etc*) sich lösen.

**adroit** [ə'drɔɪt] adj gewandt.

**adroitly** [ə'drɔɪtlɪ] adv gewandt.

**ADT** (*US*) abbr (= *Atlantic Daylight Time*) atlantische Sommerzeit.

**adulation** [ædju'leɪʃən] n Verherrlichung f.

**adult** ['ædʌlt] n Erwachsene(r) f(m) ♦ adj erwachsen; (*animal*) ausgewachsen; (*literature etc*) für Erwachsene.

**adult education** n Erwachsenenbildung f.

**adulterate** [ə'dʌltəreɪt] vt verunreinigen; (*with water*) panschen.

**adulterer** [ə'dʌltərə*] n Ehebrecher m.

**adulteress** [ə'dʌltərɪs] n Ehebrecherin f.

**adultery** [ə'dʌltərɪ] n Ehebruch m.

**adulthood** ['ædʌlthud] n Erwachsenenalter nt.

**advance** [əd'vɑ:ns] n (*movement*) Vorrücken nt; (*progress*) Fortschritt m; (*money*) Vorschuß m ♦ vt (*money*) vorschießen; (*theory, idea*) vorbringen ♦ vi (*move forward*) vorrücken; (*make progress*) Fortschritte machen ♦ adj: **~ booking** Vorverkauf m; **to make ~s (to sb)** Annäherungsversuche (bei jdm) machen; **in ~** im voraus; **to give sb ~ notice** jdm frühzeitig Bescheid sagen; **to give sb ~ warning** jdn vorwarnen.

**advanced** [əd'vɑ:nst] adj (*SCOL: studies*) für Fortgeschrittene; (*country*) fortgeschritten; (*child*) weit entwickelt; (*ideas*) fortschrittlich; **~ in years** in fortgeschrittenem Alter.

**advancement** [əd'vɑ:nsmənt] n (*improvement*) Förderung f; (*in job, rank*) Aufstieg m.

**advantage** [əd'vɑ:ntɪdʒ] n Vorteil m; **to take ~ of** ausnutzen; (*opportunity*) nutzen; **it's to our ~ (to)** es ist für uns von Vorteil(, wenn wir).

**advantageous** [ædvən'teɪdʒəs] adj: **~ (to)** vorteilhaft (für), von Vorteil (für).

**advent** ['ædvənt] n (*of innovation*) Aufkommen nt; (*REL*): **A~** Advent m.

**Advent calendar** n Adventskalender m.

**adventure** [əd'vɛntʃəˈ] *n* Abenteuer *nt*.

**adventure playground** *n* Abenteuerspielplatz *m*.

**adventurous** [əd'vɛntʃərəs] *adj* abenteuerlustig; (*bold*) mutig.

**adverb** ['ædvəːb] *n* Adverb *nt*.

**adversarial** [ædvəˈsɛərɪəl] *adj* (*relationship*) konfliktreich.

**adversary** ['ædvəsərɪ] *n* Widersacher(in) *m(f)*.

**adverse** ['ædvəːs] *adj* ungünstig; **in ~ circumstances** unter widrigen Umständen; **~ to** ablehnend gegenüber +*dat*.

**adversity** [əd'vəːsɪtɪ] *n* Widrigkeit *f*.

**advert** ['ædvəːt] (*BRIT*) *n abbr* = **advertisement**.

**advertise** ['ædvətaɪz] *vi* (*COMM*) werben; (*in newspaper*) annoncieren, inserieren ♦ *vt* (*product, event*) werben für; (*job*) ausschreiben; **to ~ for** (*staff, accommodation etc*) (per Anzeige) suchen.

**advertisement** [əd'vəːtɪsmənt] *n* (*COMM*) Werbung *f*, Reklame *f*; (*in classified ads*) Anzeige *f*, Inserat *nt*.

**advertiser** ['ædvətaɪzəˈ] *n* (*in newspaper*) Inserent(in) *m(f)*; (*on television etc*) Firma, die im Fernsehen *etc* wirbt.

**advertising** ['ædvətaɪzɪŋ] *n* Werbung *f*.

**advertising agency** *n* Werbeagentur *f*.

**advertising campaign** *n* Werbekampagne *f*.

**advice** [əd'vaɪs] *n* Rat *m*; (*notification*) Benachrichtigung *f*, Avis *m* or *nt* (*COMM*); **a piece of ~** ein Rat(schlag); **to ask sb for ~** jdn um Rat fragen; **to take legal ~** einen Rechtsanwalt zu Rate ziehen.

**advice note** (*BRIT*) *n* (*COMM*) Avis *m* or *nt*.

**advisable** [əd'vaɪzəbl] *adj* ratsam.

**advise** [əd'vaɪz] *vt* (*person*) raten +*dat*; (*company etc*) beraten; **to ~ sb of sth** jdn von etw in Kenntnis setzen; **to ~ against sth** von etw abraten; **to ~ against doing sth** davon abraten, etw zu tun; **you would be well-/ill-~d to go** Sie wären gut/schlecht beraten, wenn Sie gingen.

**advisedly** [əd'vaɪzɪdlɪ] *adv* bewußt.

**adviser** [əd'vaɪzəˈ] *n* Berater(in) *m(f)*.

**advisor** [əd'vaɪzəˈ] *n* = **adviser**.

**advisory** [əd'vaɪzərɪ] *adj* beratend, Beratungs-; **in an ~ capacity** in beratender Funktion.

**advocate** ['ædvəkɪt] *vt* befürworten ♦ *n* (*LAW*) (Rechts)anwalt *m*, (Rechts)anwältin *f*; (*supporter, upholder*): **~ of** Befürworter(in) *m(f)* +*gen*; **to be an ~ of sth** etw befürworten.

**advt.** *abbr* = **advertisement**.

**AEA** (*BRIT*) *n abbr* (= *Atomic Energy Authority*) *britische Atomenergiebehörde*.

**AEC** (*US*) *n abbr* (= *Atomic Energy Commission*) *amerikanische Atomenergiebehörde*.

**AEEU** (*BRIT*) *n abbr* (= *Amalgamated Engineering and Electrical Union*) *Gewerkschaft der Ingenieure und Elektriker*.

**Aegean** [iːˈdʒiːən] *n*: **the ~ (Sea)** (*GEOG*) die Ägäis, das Ägäische Meer.

**aegis** ['iːdʒɪs] *n*: **under the ~ of** unter der Schirmherrschaft +*gen*.

**aeon** ['iːən] *n* Äon *m*, Ewigkeit *f*.

**aerial** ['ɛərɪəl] *n* Antenne *f* ♦ *adj* (*view, bombardment etc*) Luft-.

**aero...** [ɛərə(ʊ)] *pref* Luft-.

**aerobatics** [ˈɛərəʊˈbætɪks] *npl* fliegerische Kunststücke *pl*.

**aerobics** [ɛəˈrəʊbɪks] *n* Aerobic *nt*.

**aerodrome** ['ɛərədrəʊm] (*BRIT*) *n* Flugplatz *m*.

**aerodynamic** ['ɛərəʊdaɪˈnæmɪk] *adj* aerodynamisch.

**aeronautics** [ɛərəˈnɔːtɪks] *n* Luftfahrt *f*, Aeronautik *f*.

**aeroplane** ['ɛərəpleɪn] (*BRIT*) *n* Flugzeug *nt*.

**aerosol** ['ɛərəsɔl] *n* Sprühdose *f*.

**aerospace industry** ['ɛərəʊspeɪs-] *n* Raumfahrtindustrie *f*.

**aesthetic** [iːsˈθɛtɪk] *adj* ästhetisch.

**aesthetically** [iːsˈθɛtɪklɪ] *adv* ästhetisch.

**afar** [əˈfɑːˈ] *adv*: **from ~** aus der Ferne.

**AFB** (*US*) *n abbr* (= *Air Force Base*) Luftwaffenstützpunkt *m*.

**AFDC** (*US*) *n abbr* (= *Aid to Families with Dependent Children*) *Beihilfe für sozialschwache Familien*.

**affable** ['æfəbl] *adj* umgänglich, freundlich.

**affair** [əˈfɛəˈ] *n* Angelegenheit *f*; (*romance: also:* **love ~**) Verhältnis *nt*; **affairs** *npl* Geschäfte *pl*.

**affect** [əˈfɛkt] *vt* (*influence*) sich auswirken auf +*acc*; (*subj: disease*) befallen; (*move deeply*) bewegen; (*concern*) betreffen; (*feign*) vortäuschen; **to be ~ed by sth** von etw beeinflußt werden.

**affectation** [æfɛkˈteɪʃən] *n* Affektiertheit *f*.

**affected** [əˈfɛktɪd] *adj* affektiert.

**affection** [əˈfɛkʃən] *n* Zuneigung *f*.

**affectionate** [əˈfɛkʃənɪt] *adj* liebevoll, zärtlich; (*animal*) anhänglich.

**affectionately** [əˈfɛkʃənɪtlɪ] *adv* liebevoll, zärtlich.

**affidavit** [æfɪˈdeɪvɪt] *n* (*LAW*) eidesstattliche Erklärung *f*.

**affiliated** [əˈfɪlɪeɪtɪd] *adj* angeschlossen.

**affinity** [əˈfɪnɪtɪ] *n*: **to have an ~ with** or **for** sich verbunden fühlen mit; (*resemblance*): **to have an ~ with** verwandt sein mit.

**affirm** [əˈfəːm] *vt* versichern; (*profess*) sich bekennen zu.

**affirmation** [æfəˈmeɪʃən] *n* (*of facts*) Bestätigung *f*; (*of beliefs*) Bekenntnis *nt*.

**affirmative** [əˈfəːmətɪv] *adj* bejahend ♦ *n*: **to reply in the ~** mit „ja" antworten.

**affix** [əˈfɪks] *vt* aufkleben.

**afflict** [əˈflɪkt] *vt* quälen; (*misfortune*) heimsuchen.

**affliction** [əˈflɪkʃən] *n* Leiden *nt*.

**affluence** ['æfluəns] *n* Wohlstand *m*.

**affluent** ['æfluənt] *adj* wohlhabend; **the ~ society** die Wohlstandsgesellschaft.

**afford** [əˈfɔːd] vt sich dat leisten; (time) aufbringen; (provide) bieten; **can we ~ a car?** können wir uns ein Auto leisten?; **I can't ~ the time** ich habe einfach nicht die Zeit.

**affordable** [əˈfɔːdəbl] adj erschwinglich.

**affray** [əˈfreɪ] (BRIT) n Schlägerei f.

**affront** [əˈfrʌnt] n Beleidigung f.

**affronted** [əˈfrʌntɪd] adj beleidigt.

**Afghan** [ˈæfgæn] adj afghanisch ♦ n Afghane m, Afghanin f.

**Afghanistan** [æfˈgænɪstæn] n Afghanistan nt.

**afield** [əˈfiːld] adv: **far ~** weit fort; **from far ~** aus weiter Ferne.

**AFL-CIO** n abbr (= American Federation of Labor and Congress of Industrial Organizations) amerikanischer Gewerkschafts-Dachverband.

**afloat** [əˈfləʊt] adv auf dem Wasser ♦ adj: **to be ~** schwimmen; **to stay ~** sich über Wasser halten; **to keep/get a business ~** ein Geschäft über Wasser halten/auf die Beine stellen.

**afoot** [əˈfʊt] adv: **there is something ~** da ist etwas im Gang.

**aforementioned** [əˈfɔːmenʃənd] adj obenerwähnt.

**aforesaid** [əˈfɔːsed] adj = aforementioned.

**afraid** [əˈfreɪd] adj ängstlich; **to be ~ of** Angst haben vor +dat; **to be ~ of doing sth** or **to do sth** Angst davor haben, etw zu tun; **I am ~ that ...** leider ...; **I am ~ so/not** leider ja/nein.

**afresh** [əˈfreʃ] adv von neuem, neu.

**Africa** [ˈæfrɪkə] n Afrika nt.

**African** [ˈæfrɪkən] adj afrikanisch ♦ n Afrikaner(in) m(f).

**Afrikaans** [æfrɪˈkɑːns] n Afrikaans nt.

**Afrikaner** [æfrɪˈkɑːnəˈ] n Afrika(a)nder(in) m(f).

**Afro-American** [ˈæfrəʊəˈmerɪkən] adj afroamerikanisch.

**AFT** (US) n abbr (= American Federation of Teachers) Lehrergewerkschaft.

**aft** [ɑːft] adv (be) achtern; (go) nach achtern.

**after** [ˈɑːftəˈ] prep nach +dat; (of place) hinter +dat ♦ adv danach ♦ conj nachdem; **~ dinner** nach dem Essen; **the day ~ tomorrow** übermorgen; **what are you ~?** was willst du; **who are you ~?** wen suchst du?; **the police are ~ him** die Polizei ist hinter ihm her; **to name sb ~ sb** jdn nach jdm nennen; **it's twenty ~ eight** (US) es ist zwanzig nach acht; **to ask ~ sb** nach jdm fragen; **~ all** schließlich; **~ you!** nach Ihnen!; **~ he left** nachdem er gegangen war; **~ having shaved** nachdem er sich rasiert hatte.

**afterbirth** [ˈɑːftəbɜːθ] n Nachgeburt f.

**aftercare** [ˈɑːftəkeəˈ] (BRIT) n Nachbehandlung f.

**aftereffects** [ˈɑːftərɪfekts] npl Nachwirkungen pl.

**afterlife** [ˈɑːftəlaɪf] n Leben nt nach dem Tod.

**aftermath** [ˈɑːftəmɑːθ] n Auswirkungen pl; **in the ~ of** nach +dat.

**afternoon** [ˈɑːftəˈnuːn] n Nachmittag m.

**afters** [ˈɑːftəz] (BRIT: inf) n Nachtisch m.

**after-sales service** [ɑːftəˈseɪlz-] (BRIT) n Kundendienst m.

**aftershave (lotion)** [ˈɑːftəʃeɪv-] n Rasierwasser nt.

**aftershock** [ˈɑːftəʃɔk] n Nachbeben nt.

**aftertaste** [ˈɑːftəteɪst] n Nachgeschmack m.

**afterthought** [ˈɑːftəθɔːt] n: **as an ~** nachträglich; **I had an ~** mir ist noch etwas eingefallen.

**afterwards,** (US) **afterward** [ˈɑːftəwəd(z)] adv danach.

**again** [əˈgen] adv (once more) noch einmal; (repeatedly) wieder; **not him ~!** nicht schon wieder er!; **to do sth ~** etw noch einmal tun; **to begin ~** noch einmal anfangen; **to see ~** wieder sehen; **he's opened it ~** er hat er schon wieder geöffnet; **~ and ~** immer wieder; **now and ~** ab und zu, hin und wieder.

**against** [əˈgenst] prep gegen +acc; (leaning on) an +acc; (compared to) gegenüber +dat; **~ a blue background** vor einem blauen Hintergrund; **(as) ~** gegenüber +dat.

**age** [eɪdʒ] n Alter nt; (period) Zeitalter nt ♦ vi altern, alt werden ♦ vt alt machen; **what ~ is he?** wie alt ist er?; **20 years of ~** 20 Jahre alt; **under ~** minderjährig; **to come of ~** mündig werden; **it's been ~s since ...** es ist ewig her, seit ...

**aged¹** [eɪdʒd] adj: **~ ten** zehn Jahre alt, zehnjährig.

**aged²** [ˈeɪdʒɪd] npl: **the ~** die Alten pl.

**age group** n Altersgruppe f; **the 40 to 50 ~** die Gruppe der Vierzig- bis Fünfzigjährigen.

**ageing** [ˈeɪdʒɪŋ] adj (person, population) alternd; (thing) älter werdend; (system, technology) veraltend.

**ageless** [ˈeɪdʒlɪs] adj zeitlos.

**age limit** n Altersgrenze f.

**agency** [ˈeɪdʒənsɪ] n Agentur f; (government body) Behörde f; **through** or **by the ~ of** durch die Vermittlung von.

**agenda** [əˈdʒendə] n Tagesordnung f.

**agent** [ˈeɪdʒənt] n (COMM) Vertreter(in) m(f); (representative, spy) Agent(in) m(f); (CHEM) Mittel nt; (fig) Kraft f.

**aggravate** [ˈægrəveɪt] vt verschlimmern; (inf: annoy) ärgern.

**aggravating** [ˈægrəveɪtɪŋ] (inf) adj ärgerlich.

**aggravation** [ægrəˈveɪʃən] (inf) n Ärger m.

**aggregate** [ˈægrɪgɪt] n Gesamtmenge f ♦ vt zusammenzählen; **on ~** (SPORT) nach Toren.

**aggression** [əˈgreʃən] n Aggression f.

**aggressive** [əˈgresɪv] adj aggressiv.

**aggressiveness** [əˈgresɪvnɪs] n Aggressivität

*f.*

**aggressor** [ə'grɛsəʳ] *n* Aggressor(in) *m(f)*, Angreifer(in) *m(f)*.

**aggrieved** [ə'griːvd] *adj* verärgert.

**aggro** ['ægrəu] (*BRIT: inf*) *n* (*hassle*) Ärger *m*, Theater *nt*; (*aggressive behaviour*) Aggressivität *f.*

**aghast** [ə'gɑːst] *adj* entsetzt.

**agile** ['ædʒaɪl] *adj* beweglich, wendig.

**agility** [ə'dʒɪlɪtɪ] *n* Beweglichkeit *f,* Wendigkeit *f*; (*of mind*) (geistige) Beweglichkeit *f.*

**agitate** ['ædʒɪteɪt] *vt* aufregen; (*liquid: stir*) aufrühren; (: *shake*) schütteln ♦ *vi:* **to ~ for/ against sth** für/gegen etw agitieren.

**agitated** ['ædʒɪteɪtɪd] *adj* aufgeregt.

**agitator** ['ædʒɪteɪtəʳ] *n* Agitator(in) *m(f)*.

**AGM** *n abbr* (= *annual general meeting*) JHV *f.*

**agnostic** [æg'nɒstɪk] *n* Agnostiker(in) *m(f)*.

**ago** [ə'gəu] *adv:* **2 days ~** vor 2 Tagen; **not long ~** vor kurzem; **as long ~ as 1960** schon 1960; **how long ~?** wie lange ist das her?

**agog** [ə'gɒg] *adj* gespannt.

**agonize** ['ægənaɪz] *vi:* **to ~ over sth** sich *dat* den Kopf über etw *acc* zermartern.

**agonizing** ['ægənaɪzɪŋ] *adj* qualvoll; (*pain etc*) quälend.

**agony** ['ægənɪ] *n* (*pain*) Schmerz *m*; (*torment*) Qual *f*; **to be in ~** Qualen leiden.

**agony aunt** (*BRIT: inf*) *n* Briefkastentante *f.*

**agony column** *n* Kummerkasten *m.*

**agree** [ə'griː] *vt* (*price, date*) vereinbaren ♦ *vi* übereinstimmen; (*consent*) zustimmen; **to ~ with sb** (*subj: person*) jdm zustimmen; (: *food*) jdm bekommen; **to ~ to sth** einer Sache *dat* zustimmen; **to ~ to do sth** sich bereit erklären, etw zu tun; **to ~ on sth** sich auf etw *acc* einigen; **to ~ that** (*admit*) zugeben, daß; **garlic doesn't ~ with me** Knoblauch vertrage ich nicht; **it was ~d that ...** es wurde beschlossen, daß ...; **they ~d on this** sie haben sich in diesem Punkt geeinigt; **they ~d on going** sie einigten sich darauf, zu gehen; **they ~d on a price** sie vereinbarten einen Preis.

**agreeable** [ə'griːəbl] *adj* angenehm; (*willing*) einverstanden; **are you ~ to this?** sind Sie hiermit einverstanden?

**agreed** [ə'griːd] *adj* vereinbart; **to be ~** sich *dat* einig sein.

**agreement** [ə'griːmənt] *n* (*concurrence*) Übereinstimmung *f*; (*consent*) Zustimmung *f*; (*arrangement*) Abmachung *f*; (*contract*) Vertrag *m*; **to be in ~ (with sb)** (mit jdm) einer Meinung sein; **by mutual ~** in gegenseitigem Einverständnis.

**agricultural** [ægrɪ'kʌltʃərəl] *adj* landwirtschaftlich; (*show*) Landwirtschafts-.

**agriculture** ['ægrɪkʌltʃəʳ] *n* Landwirtschaft *f.*

**aground** [ə'graund] *adv:* **to run ~** auf Grund laufen.

**ahead** [ə'hɛd] *adv* vor uns/ihnen *etc*; **~ of** (*in advance of*) vor +*dat*; **to be ~ of sb** (*in progress, ranking*) vor jdm liegen; **to be ~ of schedule** schneller als geplant vorankommen; **~ of time** zeitlich voraus; **to arrive ~ of time** zu früh ankommen; **go right** *or* **straight ~** gehen/fahren Sie geradeaus; **go ~!** (*fig*) machen Sie nur!, nur zu!; **they were (right) ~ of us** sie waren (genau) vor uns.

**AI** *n abbr* (= *Amnesty International*) AI *no art*; (*COMPUT*) = **artificial intelligence.**

**AIB** (*BRIT*) *n abbr* (= *Accident Investigation Bureau*) Untersuchungsstelle für Unglücksfälle.

**AID** *n abbr* (= *artificial insemination by donor*) künstliche Besamung durch Samenspender; (*US:* = *Agency for International Development*) Abteilung zur Koordination von Entwicklungshilfe und Außenpolitik.

**aid** [eɪd] *n* Hilfe *f*; (*to less developed country*) Entwicklungshilfe *f*; (*device*) Hilfsmittel *nt* ♦ *vt* (*help*) helfen, unterstützen; **with the ~ of mit** Hilfe von; **in ~ of** zugunsten +*gen*; **to ~ and abet** Beihilfe leisten; *see also* **hearing aid.**

**aide** [eɪd] *n* Berater(in) *m(f)*; (*MIL*) Adjutant *m.*

**aide-de-camp** ['eɪddə'kɔ̃] *n* (*MIL*) Adjutant *m.*

**AIDS** [eɪdz] *n abbr* (= *acquired immune deficiency syndrome*) AIDS *nt.*

**AIH** *n abbr* (= *artificial insemination by husband*) künstliche Besamung durch den Ehemann/ Partner.

**ailing** ['eɪlɪŋ] *adj* kränklich; (*economy, industry etc*) krank.

**ailment** ['eɪlmənt] *n* Leiden *nt.*

**aim** [eɪm] *vt:* **to ~ at** (*gun, missile, camera*) richten auf +*acc*; (*blow*) zielen auf +*acc*; (*remark*) richten an +*acc* ♦ *vi* (*also:* **take ~**) zielen ♦ *n* (*objective*) Ziel *nt*; (*in shooting*) Zielsicherheit *f*; **to ~ at** zielen auf +*acc*; (*objective*) anstreben +*acc*; **to ~ to do sth** vorhaben, etw zu tun.

**aimless** ['eɪmlɪs] *adj* ziellos.

**aimlessly** ['eɪmlɪslɪ] *adv* ziellos.

**ain't** [eɪnt] (*inf*) = **am not; aren't; isn't.**

**air** [ɛəʳ] *n* Luft *f*; (*tune*) Melodie *f*; (*appearance*) Auftreten *nt*; (*demeanour*) Haltung *f*; (*of house etc*) Atmosphäre *f* ♦ *vt* lüften; (*grievances, views*) Luft machen +*dat*; (*knowledge*) zur Schau stellen; (*ideas*) darlegen ♦ *cpd* Luft-; **into the ~** in die Luft; **by ~** mit dem Flugzeug; **to be on the ~** (*RADIO, TV: programme*) gesendet werden; (: *station*) senden; (: *person*) auf Sendung sein.

**air base** *n* Luftwaffenstützpunkt *m.*

**air bed** (*BRIT*) *n* Luftmatratze *f.*

**airborne** ['ɛəbɔːn] *adj* in der Luft; (*plane, particles*) in der Luft befindlich; (*troops*)

Luftlande-.
**air cargo** n Luftfracht f.
**air-conditioned** ['ɛəkən'dɪʃənd] adj
klimatisiert.
**air conditioning** n Klimaanlage f.
**air-cooled** ['ɛəkuːld] adj (engine) luftgekühlt.
**aircraft** ['ɛəkrɑːft] n inv Flugzeug nt.
**aircraft carrier** n Flugzeugträger m.
**air cushion** n Luftkissen nt.
**airfield** ['ɛəfiːld] n Flugplatz m.
**Air Force** n Luftwaffe f.
**air freight** n Luftfracht f.
**air freshener** n Raumspray nt.
**air gun** n Luftgewehr nt.
**air hostess** (BRIT) n Stewardeß f.
**airily** ['ɛərɪlɪ] adv leichtfertig.
**airing** ['ɛərɪŋ] n: **to give an ~ to** (fig: ideas)
darlegen; (: views) Luft machen +dat.
**air letter** (BRIT) n Luftpostbrief m.
**airlift** ['ɛəlɪft] n Luftbrücke f.
**airline** ['ɛəlaɪn] n Fluggesellschaft f.
**airliner** ['ɛəlaɪnə'] n Verkehrsflugzeug nt.
**airlock** ['ɛəlɔk] n (in pipe etc) Luftblase f;
(compartment) Luftschleuse f.
**air mail** n: **by ~** per or mit Luftpost.
**air mattress** n Luftmatratze f.
**airplane** ['ɛəpleɪn] (US) n Flugzeug nt.
**air pocket** n Luftloch nt.
**airport** ['ɛəpɔːt] n Flughafen m.
**air raid** n Luftangriff m.
**air rifle** n Luftgewehr nt.
**airsick** ['ɛəsɪk] adj luftkrank.
**airspace** ['ɛəspeɪs] n Luftraum m.
**airspeed** ['ɛəspiːd] n Fluggeschwindigkeit f.
**airstrip** ['ɛəstrɪp] n Start- und Lande-Bahn f.
**air terminal** n Terminal m or nt.
**airtight** ['ɛətaɪt] adj luftdicht.
**airtime** ['ɛətaɪm] n (RADIO, TV) Sendezeit f.
**air-traffic control** ['ɛətræfɪk-] n
Flugsicherung f.
**air-traffic controller** ['ɛətræfɪk-] n Fluglotse
m.
**air waybill** n Luftfrachtbrief m.
**airy** ['ɛərɪ] adj luftig; (casual) lässig.
**aisle** [aɪl] n Gang m; (section of church)
Seitenschiff nt.
**ajar** [ə'dʒɑː'] adj angelehnt.
**AK** (US) abbr (POST: = Alaska).
**a.k.a.** abbr (= also known as) alias.
**akin** [ə'kɪn] adj: **~ to** ähnlich +dat.
**AL** (US) abbr (POST: = Alabama).
**ALA** n abbr (= American Library Association)
akademischer Verband für das
Bibliothekswesen.
**Ala.** (US) abbr (POST: = Alabama).
**alabaster** ['æləbɑːstə'] n Alabaster m.
**à la carte** adv à la carte.
**alacrity** [ə'lækrɪtɪ] n Bereitwilligkeit f; **with ~**
ohne zu zögern.
**alarm** [ə'lɑːm] n (anxiety) Besorgnis f; (in shop,
bank) Alarmanlage f ♦ vt (worry)
beunruhigen; (frighten) erschrecken.

**alarm call** n Weckruf m.
**alarm clock** n Wecker m.
**alarmed** [ə'lɑːmd] adj beunruhigt; **don't be ~**
erschrecken Sie nicht.
**alarming** [ə'lɑːmɪŋ] adj (worrying)
beunruhigend; (frightening) erschreckend.
**alarmingly** [ə'lɑːmɪŋlɪ] adv erschreckend.
**alarmist** [ə'lɑːmɪst] n Panikmacher(in) m(f).
**alas** [ə'læs] excl leider.
**Alaska** [ə'læskə] n Alaska nt.
**Albania** [æl'beɪnɪə] n Albanien nt.
**Albanian** [æl'beɪnɪən] adj albanisch ♦ n (LING)
Albanisch nt.
**albatross** ['ælbətrɔs] n Albatros m.
**albeit** [ɔːl'biːɪt] conj wenn auch.
**album** ['ælbəm] n Album nt.
**albumen** ['ælbjumɪn] n Albumen nt.
**alchemy** ['ælkɪmɪ] n Alchimie f, Alchemie f.
**alcohol** ['ælkəhɔl] n Alkohol m.
**alcoholic** [ælkə'hɔlɪk] adj alkoholisch ♦ n
Alkoholiker(in) m(f).
**alcoholism** ['ælkəhɔlɪzəm] n Alkoholismus m.
**alcove** ['ælkəuv] n Alkoven m, Nische f.
**Ald.** abbr = **alderman**.
**alderman** ['ɔːldəmən] (irreg: like **man**) n
≈ Stadtrat m.
**ale** [eɪl] n Ale nt.
**alert** [ə'ləːt] adj aufmerksam ♦ n Alarm m ♦ vt
alarmieren; **to be ~ to** (danger, opportunity)
sich dat bewußt sein +gen; **to be on the ~**
wachsam sein; **to ~ sb (to sth)** jdn (vor etw
dat) warnen.
**Aleutian Islands** [ə'luːʃən-] npl Aleuten pl.
**A level** (BRIT) n ≈ Abschluß m der
Sekundarstufe 2, Abitur nt.
**Alexandria** [ælɪg'zɑːndrɪə] n Alexandria nt.
**alfresco** [æl'freskəu] adj, adv im Freien.
**algebra** ['ældʒɪbrə] n Algebra f.
**Algeria** [æl'dʒɪərɪə] n Algerien nt.
**Algerian** [æl'dʒɪərɪən] adj algerisch ♦ n
Algerier(in) m(f).
**Algiers** [æl'dʒɪəz] n Algier nt.
**algorithm** ['ælgərɪðəm] n Algorithmus m.
**alias** ['eɪlɪəs] adv alias ♦ n Deckname m.
**alibi** ['ælɪbaɪ] n Alibi nt.
**alien** ['eɪlɪən] n Ausländer(in) m(f);
(extraterrestrial) außerirdisches Wesen nt
♦ adj: **~ (to)** fremd (+dat).
**alienate** ['eɪlɪəneɪt] vt entfremden;
(antagonize) befremden.
**alienation** [eɪlɪə'neɪʃən] n Entfremdung f.
**alight** [ə'laɪt] adj brennend; (eyes, expression)
leuchtend ♦ vi (bird) sich niederlassen;
(passenger) aussteigen.
**align** [ə'laɪn] vt ausrichten.
**alignment** [ə'laɪnmənt] n Ausrichtung f; **it's
out of ~ (with)** es ist nicht richtig
ausgerichtet (nach).
**alike** [ə'laɪk] adj ähnlich ♦ adv (similarly)
ähnlich; (equally) gleich; **to look ~** sich dat
ähnlich sehen; **winter and summer ~**
Sommer wie Winter.

**alimony** ['ælɪmənɪ] n Unterhalt m.
**alive** [ə'laɪv] adj (*living*) lebend; (*lively*) lebendig; (*active*) lebhaft; ~ **with** erfüllt von; **to be ~ to sth** sich dat einer Sache gen bewußt sein.
**alkali** ['ælkəlaɪ] n Base f, Lauge f.
**alkaline** ['ælkəlaɪn] adj basisch, alkalisch.

================================= *KEYWORD*

**all** [ɔːl] adj alle(r, s); ~ **day/night** den ganzen Tag/die ganze Nacht (über); ~ **men are equal** alle Menschen sind gleich; ~ **five came** alle fünf kamen; ~ **the books** die ganzen Bücher, alle Bücher; ~ **the food** das ganze Essen; ~ **the time** die ganze Zeit (über); ~ **his life** sein ganzes Leben (lang)
♦ pron **1** alles; **I ate it ~, I ate ~ of it** ich habe alles gegessen; ~ **of us/the boys went** wir alle/alle Jungen gingen; **we ~ sat down** wir setzten uns alle; **is that ~?** ist das alles?; (*in shop*) sonst noch etwas?
**2** (*in phrases*): **above ~** vor allem; **after ~** schließlich; ~ **in ~** alles in allem
♦ adv ganz; ~ **alone** ganz allein; **it's not as hard as ~ that** so schwer ist es nun auch wieder nicht; ~ **the more/the better** um so mehr/besser; ~ **but** (*all except for*) alle außer; (*almost*) fast; **the score is 2 ~** der Spielstand ist 2 zu 2.

**allay** [ə'leɪ] vt (*fears*) zerstreuen.
**all clear** n Entwarnung f.
**allegation** [ælɪ'geɪʃən] n Behauptung f.
**allege** [ə'lɛdʒ] vt behaupten; **he is ~d to have said that ...** er soll angeblich gesagt haben, daß ...
**alleged** [ə'lɛdʒd] adj angeblich.
**allegedly** [ə'lɛdʒɪdlɪ] adv angeblich.
**allegiance** [ə'liːdʒəns] n Treue f.
**allegory** ['ælɪgərɪ] n Allegorie f.
**all-embracing** ['ɔːlɪm'breɪsɪŋ] adj (all)umfassend.
**allergic** [ə'lɜːdʒɪk] adj (*rash, reaction*) allergisch; (*person*): ~ **to** allergisch gegen.
**allergy** ['ælədʒɪ] n Allergie f.
**alleviate** [ə'liːvɪeɪt] vt lindern.
**alley** ['ælɪ] n Gasse f.
**alleyway** ['ælɪweɪ] n Durchgang m.
**alliance** [ə'laɪəns] n Bündnis nt.
**allied** ['ælaɪd] adj verbündet, alliiert; (*products, industries*) verwandt.
**alligator** ['ælɪgeɪtə*] n Alligator m.
**all-important** ['ɔːlɪm'pɔːtənt] adj entscheidend, äußerst wichtig.
**all in** (*BRIT*) adv inklusive.
**all-in** ['ɔːlɪn] (*BRIT*) adj (*price*) Inklusiv-.
**all-in wrestling** n (*esp BRIT*) Freistilringen nt.
**alliteration** [əlɪtə'reɪʃən] n Alliteration f.
**all-night** ['ɔːl'naɪt] adj (*café, cinema*) die ganze Nacht geöffnet; (*party*) die ganze Nacht dauernd.

**allocate** ['æləkeɪt] vt zuteilen.
**allocation** [æləu'keɪʃən] n Verteilung f; (*of money, resources*) Zuteilung f.
**allot** [ə'lɒt] vt: **to ~ (to)** zuteilen (+dat); **in the ~ed time** in der vorgesehenen Zeit.
**allotment** [ə'lɒtmənt] n (*share*) Anteil m; (*garden*) Schrebergarten m.
**all-out** [ə'laut] adj (*effort, dedication etc*) äußerste(r, s); (*strike*) total ♦ adv: **all out** mit aller Kraft; **to go all out for** sein Letztes or Äußerstes geben für.
**allow** [ə'lau] vt erlauben; (*behaviour*) zulassen; (*sum, time*) einplanen; (*claim, goal*) anerkennen; (*concede*): **to ~ that** annehmen, daß; **to ~ sb to do sth** jdm erlauben, etw zu tun; **he is ~ed to ...** er darf ...; **smoking is not ~ed** Rauchen ist nicht gestattet; **we must ~ 3 days for the journey** wir müssen für die Reise 3 Tage einplanen.
▶**allow for** vt fus einplanen, berücksichtigen.
**allowance** [ə'lauəns] n finanzielle Unterstützung f; (*welfare payment*) Beihilfe f; (*pocket money*) Taschengeld nt; (*tax allowance*) Freibetrag m; **to make ~s for** (*person*) Zugeständnisse machen für; (*thing*) berücksichtigen.
**alloy** ['ælɔɪ] n Legierung f.
**all right** adv (*well*) gut; (*correctly*) richtig; (*as answer*) okay, in Ordnung.
**all-rounder** [ɔːl'raundə*] n Allrounder m; (*athlete etc*) Allroundsportler(in) m(f).
**allspice** ['ɔːlspaɪs] n Piment m or nt.
**all-time** ['ɔːl'taɪm] adj aller Zeiten.
**allude** [ə'luːd] vi: **to ~ to** anspielen auf +acc.
**alluring** [ə'ljuərɪŋ] adj verführerisch.
**allusion** [ə'luːʒən] n Anspielung f.
**alluvium** [ə'luːvɪəm] n Anschwemmung f.
**ally** ['ælaɪ] n Verbündete(r) f(m); (*during wars*) Alliierte(r) f(m) ♦ vt: **to ~ o.s. with** sich verbünden mit.
**almighty** [ɔːl'maɪtɪ] adj allmächtig; (*tremendous*) mächtig.
**almond** ['ɑːmənd] n Mandel f; (*tree*) Mandelbaum m.
**almost** ['ɔːlməust] adv fast, beinahe; **he ~ fell** er wäre beinahe gefallen.
**alms** [ɑːmz] npl Almosen pl.
**aloft** [ə'lɒft] adv (*hold, carry*) empor.
**alone** [ə'ləun] adj, adv allein; **to leave sb ~** jdn in Ruhe lassen; **to leave sth ~** die Finger von etw lassen; **let ~ ...** geschweige denn ...
**along** [ə'lɒŋ] prep entlang +acc ♦ adv: **is he coming ~ with us?** kommt er mit?; **he was hopping/limping ~** er hüpfte/humpelte daher; ~ **with** (*together with*) zusammen mit; **all ~** (*all the time*) die ganze Zeit.
**alongside** [ə'lɒŋ'saɪd] prep neben +dat; (*ship*) längsseits +gen ♦ adv (*come*) nebendran; (*be*) daneben; **we brought our boat ~** wir brachten unser Boot heran; **a car drew up ~** ein Auto fuhr neben mich/ihn etc heran.
**aloof** [ə'luːf] adj unnahbar ♦ adv: **to stand ~**

abseits stehen.
**aloofness** [ə'luːfnɪs] n Unnahbarkeit f.
**aloud** [ə'laud] adv laut.
**alphabet** ['ælfəbɛt] n Alphabet nt.
**alphabetical** [ælfə'bɛtɪkl] adj alphabetisch; **in ~ order** in alphabetischer Reihenfolge.
**alphanumeric** ['ælfənjuː'mɛrɪk] adj alphanumerisch.
**alpine** ['ælpaɪn] adj alpin, Alpen-.
**Alps** [ælps] npl: **the ~** die Alpen.
**already** [ɔːl'rɛdɪ] adv schon.
**alright** ['ɔːl'raɪt] (BRIT) adv = **all right**.
**Alsace** ['ælsæs] n Elsaß nt.
**Alsatian** [æl'seɪʃən] (BRIT) n (dog) Schäferhund m.
**also** ['ɔːlsəu] adv (too) auch; (moreover) außerdem.
**altar** ['ɔːltə*] n Altar m.
**alter** ['ɔːltə*] vt ändern; (clothes) umändern ♦ vi sich (ver)ändern.
**alteration** [ɔːltə'reɪʃən] n Änderung f; (to clothes) Umänderung f; (to building) Umbau m; **alterations** npl (SEWING) Änderungen pl; (ARCHIT) Umbau m.
**altercation** [ɔːltə'keɪʃən] n Auseinandersetzung f.
**alternate** [adj ɔl'təːnɪt, vi 'ɔltəneɪt] adj abwechselnd; (US: alternative: plans etc) Alternativ- ♦ vi: **to ~ (with)** sich abwechseln (mit); **on ~ days** jeden zweiten Tag.
**alternately** [ɔl'təːnɪtlɪ] adv abwechselnd.
**alternating current** ['ɔltəːneɪtɪŋ-] n Wechselstrom m.
**alternative** [ɔl'təːnətɪv] adj alternativ; (solution etc) Alternativ- ♦ n Alternative f.
**alternative energy** n Alternativenergie f.
**alternatively** [ɔl'təːnətɪvlɪ] adv: **~ one could ...** oder man könnte ...
**alternative medicine** n Alternativmedizin f.
**alternative society** n Alternativgesellschaft f.
**alternator** ['ɔltəːneɪtə*] n (AUT) Lichtmaschine f.
**although** [ɔːl'ðəu] conj obwohl.
**altitude** ['æltɪtjuːd] n Höhe f.
**alto** ['æltəu] n Alt m.
**altogether** [ɔːltə'gɛðə*] adv ganz; (on the whole, in all) im ganzen, insgesamt; **how much is that ~?** was macht das zusammen?
**altruism** ['æltruɪzəm] n Altruismus m.
**altruistic** [æltruː'ɪstɪk] adj uneigennützig, altruistisch.
**aluminium** [ælju'mɪnɪəm], (US) **aluminum** [ə'luːmɪnəm] n Aluminium nt.
**always** ['ɔːlweɪz] adv immer; **we can ~ ...** (if all else fails) wir können ja auch ...
**Alzheimer's (disease)** n (MED) Alzheimer-Krankheit f.
**AM** abbr (= amplitude modulation) AM, ≈ MW.
**am** [æm] vb see **be**.
**a.m.** adv abbr (= ante meridiem) morgens; (later) vormittags.

**AMA** n abbr (= American Medical Association) Medizinerverband.
**amalgam** [ə'mælgəm] n Amalgam nt; (fig) Mischung f.
**amalgamate** [ə'mælgəmeɪt] vi, vt fusionieren.
**amalgamation** [əmælgə'meɪʃən] n Fusion f.
**amass** [ə'mæs] vt anhäufen; (evidence) zusammentragen.
**amateur** ['æmətə*] n Amateur m ♦ adj (SPORT: player, athlete) Amateur-; **~ dramatics** Laientheater nt.
**amateurish** ['æmətərɪʃ] adj (pej) dilettantisch, stümperhaft.
**amaze** [ə'meɪz] vt erstaunen; **to be ~d (at)** erstaunt sein (über +acc).
**amazement** [ə'meɪzmənt] n Erstaunen nt.
**amazing** [ə'meɪzɪŋ] adj erstaunlich; (bargain, offer) sensationell.
**amazingly** [ə'meɪzɪŋlɪ] adv erstaunlich.
**Amazon** ['æməzən] n (river) Amazonas m; (MYTHOLOGY) Amazone f; **the ~ basin** das Amazonastiefland; **the ~ jungle** der Amazonas-Regenwald.
**Amazonian** [æmə'zəunɪən] adj amazonisch.
**ambassador** [æm'bæsədə*] n Botschafter(in) m(f).
**amber** ['æmbə*] n Bernstein m; **at ~** (BRIT: traffic lights) auf Gelb; (: move off) bei Gelb.
**ambidextrous** [æmbɪ'dɛkstrəs] adj beidhändig.
**ambience** ['æmbɪəns] n Atmosphäre f.
**ambiguity** [æmbɪ'gjuɪtɪ] n Zweideutigkeit f; (lack of clarity) Unklarheit f.
**ambiguous** [æm'bɪgjuəs] adj zweideutig; (not clear) unklar.
**ambition** [æm'bɪʃən] n Ehrgeiz m; (desire) Ambition f; **to achieve one's ~** seine Ambitionen erfüllen.
**ambitious** [æm'bɪʃəs] adj ehrgeizig.
**ambivalence** [æm'bɪvələns] n Ambivalenz f.
**ambivalent** [æm'bɪvələnt] adj ambivalent.
**amble** ['æmbl] vi schleudern.
**ambulance** ['æmbjuləns] n Krankenwagen m.
**ambulanceman** ['æmbjulənsmən] (irreg: like man) n Sanitäter m.
**ambush** ['æmbuʃ] n Hinterhalt m; (attack) Überfall m aus dem Hinterhalt ♦ vt (aus dem Hinterhalt) überfallen.
**ameba** [ə'miːbə] (US) n = **amoeba**.
**ameliorate** [ə'miːlɪəreɪt] vt verbessern.
**amen** ['ɑː'mɛn] excl amen.
**amenable** [ə'miːnəbl] adj: **~ to** zugänglich +dat; (to flattery etc) empfänglich für; **~ to the law** dem Gesetz verantwortlich.
**amend** [ə'mɛnd] vt ändern; (habits, behaviour) bessern.
**amendment** [ə'mɛndmənt] n Änderung f; (to law) Amendement nt.
**amends** [ə'mɛndz] npl: **to make ~** es wiedergutmachen; **to make ~ for sth** etw wiedergutmachen.
**amenities** [ə'miːnɪtɪz] npl Einkaufs-, Unter-

*haltungs- und Transportmöglichkeiten.*
**amenity** [ə'miːnɪtɪ] *n* (Freizeit)einrichtung *f*.
**America** [ə'merɪkə] *n* Amerika *nt*.
**American** [ə'merɪkən] *adj* amerikanisch ♦ *n* Amerikaner(in) *m(f)*.
**Americanize** [ə'merɪkənaɪz] *vt* amerikanisieren.
**amethyst** ['æmɪθɪst] *n* Amethyst *m*.
**Amex** ['æmeks] *n abbr* (= *American Stock Exchange*) *US-Börse*; (= *American Express* ®) *Kreditkarte.*
**amiable** ['eɪmɪəbl] *adj* liebenswürdig.
**amiably** ['eɪmɪəblɪ] *adv* liebenswürdig.
**amicable** ['æmɪkəbl] *adj* freundschaftlich; (*settlement*) gütlich.
**amicably** ['æmɪkəblɪ] *adv* (*part, discuss*) in aller Freundschaft; (*settle*) gütlich.
**amid(st)** [ə'mɪd(st)] *prep* inmitten +*gen*.
**amiss** [ə'mɪs] *adj, adv:* **to take sth** ~ etw übelnehmen; **there's something** ~ da stimmt irgend etwas nicht.
**ammeter** ['æmɪtə*] *n* Amperemeter *nt*.
**ammo** ['æməu] (*inf*) *n abbr* = **ammunition**.
**ammonia** [ə'məunɪə] *n* Ammoniak *nt*.
**ammunition** [æmju'nɪʃən] *n* Munition *f*.
**ammunition dump** *n* Munitionslager *nt*.
**amnesia** [æm'niːzɪə] *n* Amnesie *f*, Gedächtnisschwund *m*.
**amnesty** ['æmnɪstɪ] *n* Amnestie *f*; **to grant an** ~ **to** amnestieren.
**Amnesty International** *n* Amnesty International *no art*.
**amoeba**, (*US*) **ameba** [ə'miːbə] *n* Amöbe *f*.
**amok** [ə'mɔk] *adv:* **to run** ~ Amok laufen.
**among(st)** [ə'mʌŋ(st)] *prep* unter +*dat*.
**amoral** [æ'mɔrəl] *adj* unmoralisch.
**amorous** ['æmərəs] *adj* amourös.
**amorphous** [ə'mɔːfəs] *adj* formlos, gestaltlos.
**amortization** [əmɔːtaɪ'zeɪʃən] *n* Amortisation *f*.
**amount** [ə'maunt] *n* (*quantity*) Menge *f*; (*sum of money*) Betrag *m*; (*total*) Summe *f*; (*of bill etc*) Höhe *f* ♦ *vi:* **to** ~ **to** (*total*) sich belaufen auf +*acc*; (*be same as*) gleichkommen +*dat*; **the total** ~ (*of money*) die Gesamtsumme.
**amp(ère)** ['æmp(εə*)] *n* Ampere *nt*; **a 3** ~ **fuse** eine Sicherung von 3 Ampere; **a 13** ~ **plug** ein Stecker mit einer Sicherung von 13 Ampere.
**ampersand** ['æmpəsænd] *n* Et-Zeichen *nt*, Und-Zeichen *nt*.
**amphetamine** [æm'fɛtəmiːn] *n* Amphetamin *nt*.
**amphibian** [æm'fɪbɪən] *n* Amphibie *f*.
**amphibious** [æm'fɪbɪəs] *adj* amphibisch; (*vehicle*) Amphibien-.
**amphitheatre**, (*US*) **amphitheater** ['æmfɪθɪətə*] *n* Amphitheater *nt*.
**ample** ['æmpl] *adj* (*large*) üppig; (*abundant*) reichlich; (*enough*) genügend; **this is** ~ **das ist reichlich; to have** ~ **time/room** genügend Zeit/Platz haben.

**amplifier** ['æmplɪfaɪə*] *n* Verstärker *m*.
**amplify** ['æmplɪfaɪ] *vt* verstärken; (*expand: idea etc*) genauer ausführen.
**amply** ['æmplɪ] *adv* reichlich.
**ampoule**, (*US*) **ampule** ['æmpuːl] *n* Ampulle *f*.
**amputate** ['æmpjuteɪt] *vt* amputieren.
**amputation** [æmpju'teɪʃən] *n* Amputation *f*.
**amputee** [æmpju'tiː] *n* Amputierte(r) *f(m)*.
**Amsterdam** ['æmstədæm] *n* Amsterdam *nt*.
**amt** *abbr* = **amount**.
**amuck** [ə'mʌk] *adv* = **amok**.
**amuse** [ə'mjuːz] *vt* (*entertain*) unterhalten; (*make smile*) amüsieren, belustigen; **to** ~ **o.s. with sth/by doing sth** sich die Zeit mit etw vertreiben/damit vertreiben, etw zu tun; **to be** ~**d at** sich amüsieren über +*acc*; **he was not** ~**d** er fand das gar nicht komisch *or* zum Lachen.
**amusement** [ə'mjuːzmənt] *n* (*mirth*) Vergnügen *nt*; (*pleasure*) Unterhaltung *f*; (*pastime*) Zeitvertreib *m*; **much to my** ~ zu meiner großen Belustigung.
**amusement arcade** *n* Spielhalle *f*.
**amusement park** *n* Vergnügungspark *m*.
**amusing** [ə'mjuːzɪŋ] *adj* amüsant, unterhaltsam.
**an** [æn, ən] *indef art see* **a**.
**ANA** *n abbr* (= *American Newspaper Association*) *amerikanischer Zeitungsverband*; (= *American Nurses Association*) *Verband amerikanischer Krankenschwestern und Krankenpfleger.*
**anachronism** [ə'nækrənɪzəm] *n* Anachronismus *m*.
**anaemia**, (*US*) **anemia** [ə'niːmɪə] *n* Anämie *f*.
**anaemic**, (*US*) **anemic** [ə'niːmɪk] *adj* blutarm.
**anaesthetic**, (*US*) **anesthetic** [ænɪs'θetɪk] *n* Betäubungsmittel *nt*; **under (the)** ~ unter Narkose; **local** ~ örtliche Betäubung *f*; **general** ~ Vollnarkose *f*.
**anaesthetist** [æ'niːsθɪtɪst] *n* Anästhesist(in) *m(f)*.
**anagram** ['ænəgræm] *n* Anagramm *nt*.
**anal** ['eɪnl] *adj* anal, Anal-.
**analgesic** [ænæl'dʒiːsɪk] *adj* schmerzstillend ♦ *n* Schmerzmittel *nt*, schmerzstillendes Mittel *nt*.
**analogous** [ə'næləgəs] *adj:* ~ **(to** *or* **with)** analog (zu).
**analogue**, (*US*) **analog** ['ænəlɔg] *adj* (*watch, computer*) Analog-.
**analogy** [ə'nælədʒɪ] *n* Analogie *f*; **to draw an** ~ **between** eine Analogie herstellen zwischen +*dat*; **by** ~ durch einen Analogieschluß.
**analyse**, (*US*) **analyze** ['ænəlaɪz] *vt* analysieren; (*CHEM, MED*) untersuchen; (*person*) psychoanalytisch behandeln.
**analyses** [ə'næləsiːz] *npl of* **analysis**.
**analysis** [ə'næləsɪs] (*pl* **analyses**) *n* (*see vb*) Analyse *f*; Untersuchung *f*; Psychoanalyse *f*;

**in the last** ~ letzten Endes.
**analyst** ['ænəlɪst] *n* Analytiker(in) *m(f)*; (*US*)
Psychoanalytiker(in) *m(f)*.
**analytic(al)** [ænə'lɪtɪk(l)] *adj* analytisch.
**analyze** ['ænəlaɪz] (*US*) *vt* = **analyse**.
**anarchic** [æ'nɑːkɪk] *adj* anarchisch.
**anarchist** ['ænəkɪst] *adj* anarchistisch ◊ *n*
Anarchist(in) *m(f)*.
**anarchy** ['ænəkɪ] *n* Anarchie *f*.
**anathema** [ə'næθɪmə] *n*: **that is** ~ **to him** das
ist ihm ein Greuel.
**anatomical** [ænə'tɔmɪkl] *adj* anatomisch.
**anatomy** [ə'nætəmɪ] *n* Anatomie *f*; (*body*)
Körper *m*.
**ANC** *n abbr* (= *African National Congress*) ANC
*m*.
**ancestor** ['ænsɪstə*] *n* Vorfahr(in) *m(f)*.
**ancestral** [æn'sɛstrəl] *adj* angestammt;
~ **home** Stammsitz *m*.
**ancestry** ['ænsɪstrɪ] *n* Abstammung *f*.
**anchor** ['æŋkə*] *n* Anker *m* ◊ *vi* (*also*: **to drop**
~) ankern, vor Anker gehen ◊ *vt* (*fig*): **to**
~ **sth to** etw verankern in +*dat*; **to weigh** ~
den Anker lichten.
**anchorage** ['æŋkərɪdʒ] *n* Ankerplatz *m*.
**anchorman** [æŋkəmæn] (*irreg: like* **man**) *n* (*TV,
RADIO*) ≈ Moderator *m*.
**anchorwoman** [æŋkəwumən] (*irreg: like*
**woman**) *n* (*TV, RADIO*) ≈ Moderatorin *f*.
**anchovy** ['æntʃəvɪ] *n* Sardelle *f*, An(s)chovis *f*.
**ancient** ['eɪnʃənt] *adj* alt; (*person, car*) uralt.
**ancient monument** *n* historisches Denkmal
*nt*.
**ancillary** [æn'sɪlərɪ] *adj* Hilfs-.
**and** [ænd] *conj* und; ~ **so on** und so weiter; **try**
~ **come please** bitte versuche zu kommen;
**better** ~ **better** immer besser.
**Andes** ['ændiːz] *npl*: **the** ~ die Anden *pl*.
**Andorra** [æn'dɔːrə] *n* Andorra *nt*.
**anecdote** ['ænɪkdəut] *n* Anekdote *f*.
**anemia** *etc* [ə'niːmɪə] (*US*) = **anaemia** *etc*.
**anemone** [ə'nɛmənɪ] *n* (*BOT*) Anemone *f*,
Buschwindröschen *nt*.
**anesthetic** *etc* [ænɪs'θɛtɪk] (*US*) = **anaesthetic**
*etc*.
**anew** [ə'njuː] *adv* von neuem.
**angel** ['eɪndʒəl] *n* Engel *m*.
**angel dust** (*inf*) *n* als halluzinogene Droge
mißbrauchtes Medikament.
**angelic** [æn'dʒɛlɪk] *adj* engelhaft.
**anger** ['æŋgə*] *n* Zorn *m* ◊ *vt* ärgern; (*enrage*)
erzürnen; **red with** ~ rot vor Wut.
**angina** [æn'dʒaɪnə] *n* Angina pectoris *f*.
**angle** ['æŋgl] *n* Winkel *m*; (*viewpoint*): **from
their** ~ von ihrem Standpunkt aus ◊ *vi*: **to**
~ **for** (*invitation*) aussein auf +*acc*;
(*compliments*) fischen nach ◊ *vt*: **to** ~ **sth
towards** *or* **to** etw ausrichten auf +*acc*.
**angler** ['æŋglə*] *n* Angler(in) *m(f)*.
**Anglican** ['æŋglɪkən] *adj* anglikanisch ◊ *n*
Anglikaner(in) *m(f)*.
**anglicize** ['æŋglɪsaɪz] *vt* anglisieren.

**angling** ['æŋglɪŋ] *n* Angeln *nt*.
**Anglo-** ['æŋgləu] *pref* Anglo-, anglo-.
**Anglo-German** ['æŋgləu'dʒɜːmən] *adj*
englisch-deutsch.
**Anglo-Saxon** ['æŋgləu'sæksən] *adj*
angelsächsisch ◊ *n* Angelsachse *m*,
Angelsächsin *f*.
**Angola** [æŋ'gəulə] *n* Angola *nt*.
**Angolan** [æŋ'gəulən] *adj* angolanisch ◊ *n*
Angolaner(in) *m(f)*.
**angrily** ['æŋgrɪlɪ] *adv* verärgert.
**angry** ['æŋgrɪ] *adj* verärgert; (*wound*)
entzündet; **to be** ~ **with sb** auf jdn böse
sein; **to be** ~ **at sth** über etw *acc* verärgert
sein; **to get** ~ wütend werden; **to make sb** ~
jdn wütend machen.
**anguish** ['æŋgwɪʃ] *n* Qual *f*.
**anguished** ['æŋgwɪʃt] *adj* gequält.
**angular** ['æŋgjulə*] *adj* eckig; (*features*) kantig.
**animal** ['ænɪml] *n* Tier *nt*; (*living creature*)
Lebewesen *nt*; (*pej: person*) Bestie *f* ◊ *adj*
tierhaft; (*attraction etc*) animalisch.
**animal spirits** *npl* Vitalität *f*.
**animate** [*vt* 'ænɪmeɪt, *adj* 'ænɪmɪt] *vt* beleben
◊ *adj* lebend.
**animated** ['ænɪmeɪtɪd] *adj* lebhaft; (*film*)
Zeichentrick-.
**animation** [ænɪ'meɪʃən] *n* (*liveliness*)
Lebhaftigkeit *f*; (*film*) Animation *f*.
**animosity** [ænɪ'mɔsɪtɪ] *n* Feindseligkeit *f*.
**aniseed** ['ænɪsiːd] *n* Anis *m*.
**Ankara** ['æŋkərə] *n* Ankara *nt*.
**ankle** ['æŋkl] *n* Knöchel *m*.
**ankle sock** (*BRIT*) *n* Söckchen *nt*.
**annex** ['ænɛks] *n* (*also*: ~**e**: *BRIT*) Anhang *m*;
(*building*) Nebengebäude *nt*; (*extension*)
Anbau *m* ◊ *vt* (*take over*) annektieren.
**annexation** [ænɛk'seɪʃən] *n* Annexion *f*.
**annihilate** [ə'naɪəleɪt] *vt* (*also fig*) vernichten.
**annihilation** [ənaɪə'leɪʃən] *n* Vernichtung *f*.
**anniversary** [ænɪ'vɜːsərɪ] *n* Jahrestag *m*.
**anno Domini** *adv* Anno Domini, nach
Christus.
**annotate** ['ænəuteɪt] *vt* kommentieren.
**announce** [ə'nauns] *vt* ankündigen; (*birth,
death etc*) anzeigen; **he** ~**d that he wasn't
going** er verkündete, daß er nicht gehen
würde.
**announcement** [ə'naunsmənt] *n*
Ankündigung *f*; (*official*) Bekanntmachung *f*;
(*of birth, death etc*) Anzeige *f*; **I'd like to make
an** ~ ich möchte etwas bekanntgeben.
**announcer** [ə'naunsə*] *n* Ansager(in) *m(f)*.
**annoy** [ə'nɔɪ] *vt* ärgern; **to be** ~**ed (at sth/
with sb)** sich (über etw/jdn) ärgern; **don't
get** ~**ed!** reg' dich nicht auf!
**annoyance** [ə'nɔɪəns] *n* Ärger *m*.
**annoying** [ə'nɔɪɪŋ] *adj* ärgerlich; (*person,
habit*) lästig.
**annual** ['ænjuəl] *adj* jährlich; (*income*) Jahres-
◊ *n* (*BOT*) einjährige Pflanze *f*; (*book*)
Jahresband *m*.

**annual general meeting** (*BRIT*) *n* Jahreshauptversammlung *f*.
**annually** ['ænjuəlɪ] *adv* jährlich.
**annual report** *n* Geschäftsbericht *m*.
**annuity** [ə'njuːɪtɪ] *n* Rente *f*; **life** ~ Rente *f* auf Lebenszeit.
**annul** [ə'nʌl] *vt* annullieren; (*law*) aufheben.
**annulment** [ə'nʌlmənt] *n* (*see vb*) Annullierung *f*; Aufhebung *f*.
**annum** ['ænəm] *n see* **per.**
**Annunciation** [ənʌnsɪ'eɪʃən] *n* Mariä Verkündigung *f*.
**anode** ['ænəud] *n* Anode *f*.
**anodyne** ['ænədaɪn] (*fig*) *n* Wohltat *f* ♦ *adj* schmerzlos.
**anoint** [ə'nɔɪnt] *vt* salben.
**anomalous** [ə'nɔmələs] *adj* anomal.
**anomaly** [ə'nɔmalɪ] *n* Anomalie *f*.
**anon.** [ə'nɔn] *abbr* = **anonymous.**
**anonymity** [ænə'nɪmɪtɪ] *n* Anonymität *f*.
**anonymous** [ə'nɔnɪməs] *adj* anonym.
**anorak** ['ænəræk] *n* Anorak *m*.
**anorexia** [ænə'rɛksɪə] *n* Magersucht *f*, Anorexie *f*.
**anorexic** [ænə'rɛksɪk] *adj* magersüchtig.
**another** [ə'nʌðə'] *pron* (*additional*) noch eine(r, s); (*different*) ein(e) andere(r, s) ♦ *adj:* ~ **book** (*one more*) noch ein Buch; (*a different one*) ein anderes Buch; ~ **drink?** noch etwas zu trinken?; **in** ~ **5 years** in weiteren 5 Jahren; *see also* **one.**
**ANSI** [eɪɛnɛs'aɪ] *n abbr* (= *American National Standards Institute*) *amerikanischer Normenausschuß.*
**answer** ['ɑːnsə'] *n* Antwort *f*; (*to problem*) Lösung *f* ♦ *vi* antworten; (*TEL*) sich melden ♦ *vt* (*reply to: person*) antworten +*dat*; (: *letter, question*) beantworten; (*problem*) lösen; (*prayer*) erhören; **in** ~ **to your letter** in Beantwortung Ihres Schreibens; **to** ~ **the phone** ans Telefon gehen; **to** ~ **the bell** *or* **the door** die Tür aufmachen.
▶**answer back** *vi* widersprechen; (*child*) frech sein.
▶**answer for** *vt fus* (*person*) verantwortlich sein für, sich verbürgen für.
▶**answer to** *vt fus* (*description*) entsprechen +*dat*.
**answerable** ['ɑːnsərəbl] *adj:* **to be** ~ **to sb for sth** jdm gegenüber für etw verantwortlich sein; **I am** ~ **to no-one** ich brauche mich vor niemandem zu verantworten.
**answering machine** ['ɑːnsərɪŋ-] *n* Anrufbeantworter *m*.
**ant** [ænt] *n* Ameise *f*.
**ANTA** *n abbr* (= *American National Theater and Academy*) *Nationaltheater und Schauspielerakademie.*
**antagonism** [æn'tægənɪzəm] *n* Feindseligkeit *f*, Antagonismus *m*.
**antagonist** [æn'tægənɪst] *n* Gegner(in) *m(f)*, Antagonist(in) *m(f)*.

**antagonistic** [æntægə'nɪstɪk] *adj* feindselig.
**antagonize** [æn'tægənaɪz] *vt* gegen sich aufbringen.
**Antarctic** [ænt'ɑːktɪk] *n:* **the** ~ die Antarktis.
**Antarctica** [ænt'ɑːktɪkə] *n* Antarktik *f*.
**Antarctic Circle** *n:* **the** ~ der südliche Polarkreis.
**Antarctic Ocean** *n:* **the** ~ das Südpolarmeer.
**ante** ['æntɪ] *n:* **to up the** ~ den Einsatz erhöhen.
**ante...** ['æntɪ] *pref* vor-.
**anteater** ['æntiːtə'] *n* Ameisenbär *m*.
**antecedent** [æntɪ'siːdənt] *n* Vorläufer *m*; (*of living creature*) Vorfahr *m*; **antecedents** *npl* Herkunft *f*.
**antechamber** ['æntɪtʃeɪmbə'] *n* Vorzimmer *nt*.
**antelope** ['æntɪləup] *n* Antilope *f*.
**antenatal** ['æntɪ'neɪtl] *adj* vor der Geburt, Schwangerschafts-.
**antenatal clinic** *n* Sprechstunde *f* für werdende Mütter.
**antenna** [æn'tɛnə] (*pl* ~e) *n* (*of insect*) Fühler *m*; (*RADIO, TV*) Antenne *f*.
**antennae** [æn'tɛniː] *npl of* **antenna.**
**anteroom** ['æntɪrum] *n* Vorzimmer *nt*.
**anthem** ['ænθəm] *n:* **national** ~ Nationalhymne *f*.
**ant hill** *n* Ameisenhaufen *m*.
**anthology** [æn'θɔlədʒɪ] *n* Anthologie *f*.
**anthropologist** [ænθrə'pɔlədʒɪst] *n* Anthropologe *m*, Anthropologin *f*.
**anthropology** [ænθrə'pɔlədʒɪ] *n* Anthropologie *f*.
**anti...** ['æntɪ] *pref* Anti-, anti-.
**anti-aircraft** ['æntɪ'ɛəkrɑːft] *adj* (*gun, rocket*) Flugabwehr-.
**anti-aircraft defence** *n* Luftverteidigung *f*.
**antiballistic** ['æntɪbə'lɪstɪk] *adj* (*missile*) Anti-Raketen-.
**antibiotic** ['æntɪbaɪ'ɔtɪk] *n* Antibiotikum *nt*.
**antibody** ['æntɪbɔdɪ] *n* Antikörper *m*.
**anticipate** [æn'tɪsɪpeɪt] *vt* erwarten; (*foresee*) vorhersehen; (*look forward to*) sich freuen auf +*acc*; (*forestall*) vorwegnehmen; **this is worse than I** ~**d** es ist schlimmer, als ich erwartet hatte; **as** ~**d** wie erwartet.
**anticipation** [æntɪsɪ'peɪʃən] *n* Erwartung *f*; (*eagerness*) Vorfreude *f*; **thanking you in** ~ vielen Dank im voraus.
**anticlimax** ['æntɪ'klaɪmæks] *n* Enttäuschung *f*.
**anticlockwise** ['æntɪ'klɔkwaɪz] (*BRIT*) *adv* gegen den Uhrzeigersinn.
**antics** ['æntɪks] *npl* Mätzchen *pl*; (*of politicians etc*) Gehabe *nt*.
**anticyclone** ['æntɪ'saɪkləun] *n* Hoch(druckgebiet) *nt*.
**antidote** ['æntɪdəut] *n* Gegenmittel *nt*.
**antifreeze** ['æntɪfriːz] *n* Frostschutzmittel *nt*.
**antihistamine** ['æntɪ'hɪstəmɪn] *n* Antihistamin(ikum) *nt*.
**Antilles** [æn'tɪliːz] *npl:* **the** ~ die Antillen *pl*.
**antipathy** [æn'tɪpəθɪ] *n* Antipathie *f*,

Abneigung f.
**antiperspirant** ['æntɪ'pəːspɪrənt] n
Antitranspirant nt.
**Antipodean** [æntɪpə'diːən] adj antipodisch.
**Antipodes** [æn'tɪpədiːz] npl: **the** ~ Australien
und Neuseeland nt.
**antiquarian** [æntɪ'kwɛərɪən] n (collector)
Antiquitätensammler(in) m(f); (seller)
Antiquitätenhändler(in) m(f) ♦ adj:
~ **bookshop** Antiquariat nt.
**antiquated** ['æntɪkweɪtɪd] adj antiquiert.
**antique** [æn'tiːk] n Antiquität f ♦ adj antik.
**antique dealer** n Antiquitätenhändler(in)
m(f).
**antique shop** n Antiquitätenladen m.
**antiquity** [æn'tɪkwɪtɪ] n (period) Antike f;
**antiquities** npl (objects) Altertümer pl.
**anti-Semitic** ['æntɪsɪ'mɪtɪk] adj antisemitisch.
**anti-Semitism** ['æntɪ'semɪtɪzəm] n
Antisemitismus m.
**antiseptic** [æntɪ'septɪk] n Antiseptikum nt
♦ adj antiseptisch.
**antisocial** ['æntɪ'səuʃəl] adj unsozial; (person)
ungesellig.
**antitank** ['æntɪ'tæŋk] adj (gun, fire)
Panzerabwehr-.
**antitheses** [æn'tɪθɪsiːz] npl of **antithesis**.
**antithesis** [æn'tɪθɪsɪs] (pl **antitheses**) n
Gegensatz m; **she's the** ~ **of a good cook** sie
ist das genaue Gegenteil einer guten
Köchin.
**antitrust** ['æntɪ'trʌst] (US) adj: ~ **legislation**
Kartellgesetzgebung f.
**antlers** ['æntləz] npl Geweih nt.
**Antwerp** ['æntwəːp] n Antwerpen nt.
**anus** ['eɪnəs] n After m.
**anvil** ['ænvɪl] n Amboß m.
**anxiety** [æŋ'zaɪətɪ] n (worry) Sorge f; (MED)
Angstzustand m; (eagerness): ~ **to do sth**
Verlangen (danach), etw zu tun.
**anxious** ['æŋkʃəs] adj (worried) besorgt;
(situation) angsteinflößend; (question,
moments) bang(e); (keen): **to be** ~ **to do sth**
etw unbedingt tun wollen; **I'm very** ~ **about**
**you** ich mache mir große Sorgen um dich.
**anxiously** ['æŋkʃəslɪ] adv besorgt.

═══════════════════════ KEYWORD

**any** ['enɪ] adj **1** (in questions etc): **have you**
~ **butter/children?** haben Sie Butter/
Kinder?; **if there are** ~ **tickets left** falls noch
Karten da sind
**2** (with negative) kein(e); **I haven't**
~ **money/books** ich habe kein Geld/keine
Bücher
**3** (no matter which) irgendein(e); **choose**
~ **book you like** nehmen Sie irgendein Buch
or ein beliebiges Buch
**4** (in phrases): **in** ~ **case** in jedem Fall; ~ **day**
**now** jeden Tag; **at** ~ **moment** jeden
Moment; **at** ~ **rate** auf jeden Fall; ~ **time** (at
any moment) jeden Moment; (whenever)

jederzeit
♦ pron **1** (in questions etc) **have you got** ~?
haben Sie welche?; **can** ~ **of you sing?** kann
(irgend)einer von euch singen?
**2** (with negative) **I haven't** ~ **(of them)** ich
habe keine (davon)
**3** (no matter which one(s)) egal welche; **take**
~ **of those books (you like)** nehmen Sie
irgendwelche von diesen Büchern
♦ adv **1** (in questions etc): **do you want**
~ **more soup/sandwiches?** möchtest du
noch Suppe/Butterbrote?; **are you feeling**
~ **better?** geht es Ihnen etwas besser?
**2** (with negative): **I can't hear him** ~ **more** ich
kann ihn nicht mehr hören; **don't wait**
~ **longer** warte nicht noch länger.

**anybody** ['enɪbɔdɪ] pron = **anyone**.

═══════════════════════ KEYWORD

**anyhow** ['enɪhau] adv **1** (at any rate) sowieso,
ohnehin; **I shall go** ~ ich gehe auf jeden Fall
**2** (haphazard): **do it** ~ **you like** machen Sie
es, wie Sie wollen.

═══════════════════════ KEYWORD

**anyone** ['enɪwʌn] pron **1** (in questions etc)
(irgend) jemand; **can you see** ~? siehst du
jemanden?
**2** (with negative) keine(r); **I can't see** ~ ich
kann keinen or niemanden sehen
**3** (no matter who) jede(r); ~ **could do it** das
kann jeder.

**anyplace** ['enɪpleɪs] (US) adv = **anywhere**.

═══════════════════════ KEYWORD

**anything** ['enɪθɪŋ] pron **1** (in questions etc)
(irgend) etwas; **can you see** ~? kannst du
etwas sehen?
**2** (with negative) nichts; **I can't see** ~ ich
kann nichts sehen
**3** (no matter what) irgend etwas; **you can say**
~ **you like** du kannst sagen, was du willst;
~ **between 15 and 20 pounds** (ungefähr)
zwischen 15 und 20 Pfund.

═══════════════════════ KEYWORD

**anyway** ['enɪweɪ] adv **1** (at any rate) sowieso,
ohnehin; **I shall go** ~ ich gehe auf jeden Fall
**2** (besides): ~, **I can't come** jedenfalls kann
ich nicht kommen; **why are you phoning,** ~?
warum rufst du überhaupt or eigentlich an?

═══════════════════════ KEYWORD

**anywhere** ['enɪwɛəʳ] adv **1** (in questions etc)
irgendwo; **can you see him** ~? kannst du ihn
irgendwo sehen?
**2** (with negative) nirgendwo, nirgends; **I can't**

**see him** ~ ich kann ihn nirgendwo *or* nirgends sehen **3** (*no matter where*) irgendwo; **put the books down** ~ legen Sie die Bücher irgendwohin.

**Anzac** ['ænzæk] *n abbr* (= *Australia-New Zealand Army Corps*) (*soldier*) australischer/ neuseeländischer Soldat *m*.

**Anzac Day**, *der 25. April, ist in Australien und Neuseeland ein Feiertag zum Gedenken an die Landung der australischen und neuseeländischen Truppen in Gallipoli im ersten Weltkrieg (1915).*

**apace** [ə'peɪs] *adv:* **to continue** ~ (*negotiations, preparations etc*) rasch vorangehen.

**apart** [ə'pɑːt] *adv* (*be*) entfernt; (*move*) auseinander; (*aside*) beiseite; (*separately*) getrennt; **10 miles** ~ 10 Meilen voneinander entfernt; **a long way** ~ weit auseinander; **they are living** ~ sie leben getrennt; **with one's legs** ~ mit gespreizten Beinen; **to take** ~ auseinandernehmen; ~ **from** (*excepting*) abgesehen von; (*in addition*) außerdem.

**apartheid** [ə'pɑːteɪt] *n* Apartheid *f*.

**apartment** [ə'pɑːtmənt] *n* (*US: flat*) Wohnung *f*; (*room*) Raum *m*, Zimmer *nt*.

**apartment building** (*US*) *n* Wohnblock *m*.

**apathetic** [æpə'θetɪk] *adj* apathisch, teilnahmslos.

**apathy** ['æpəθɪ] *n* Apathie *f*, Teilnahmslosigkeit *f*.

**APB** (*US*) *n abbr* (= *all points bulletin*) *polizeiliche Fahndung*.

**ape** [eɪp] *n* (*Menschen*)affe *m* ♦ *vt* nachahmen.

**Apennines** ['æpənaɪnz] *npl:* **the** ~ die Apenninen *pl*, der Apennin.

**apéritif** *n* Aperitif *m*.

**aperture** ['æpətʃjuə*] *n* Öffnung *f*; (*PHOT*) Blende *f*.

**APEX** ['eɪpɛks] *n abbr* (*AVIAT, RAIL:* = *advance purchase excursion*) APEX.

**apex** ['eɪpɛks] *n* Spitze *f*.

**aphid** ['eɪfɪd] *n* Blattlaus *f*.

**aphorism** ['æfərɪzəm] *n* Aphorismus *m*.

**aphrodisiac** [æfrəʊ'dɪzɪæk] *adj* aphrodisisch ♦ *n* Aphrodisiakum *nt*.

**API** *n abbr* (= *American Press Institute*) *amerikanischer Presseverband*.

**apiece** [ə'piːs] *adv* (*each person*) pro Person; (*each thing*) pro Stück.

**aplomb** [ə'plɒm] *n* Gelassenheit *f*.

**APO** (*US*) *n abbr* (= *Army Post Office*) *Poststelle der Armee*.

**apocalypse** [ə'pɒkəlɪps] *n* Apokalypse *f*.

**apolitical** [eɪpə'lɪtɪkl] *adj* apolitisch.

**apologetic** [əpɒlə'dʒetɪk] *adj* entschuldigend; **to be very** ~ (**about sth**) sich (wegen etw *gen*) sehr entschuldigen.

**apologize** [ə'pɒlədʒaɪz] *vi:* **to** ~ (**for sth to sb**) sich (für etw bei jdm) entschuldigen.

**apology** [ə'pɒlədʒɪ] *n* Entschuldigung *f*; **to send one's apologies** sich entschuldigen lassen; **please accept my apologies** ich bitte um Verzeihung.

**apoplectic** [æpə'plɛktɪk] *adj* (*MED*) apoplektisch; (*fig*): **to be** ~ **with rage** vor Wut fast platzen.

**apoplexy** ['æpəplɛksɪ] *n* Schlaganfall *m*.

**apostle** [ə'pɒsl] *n* Apostel *m*.

**apostrophe** [ə'pɒstrəfɪ] *n* Apostroph *m*, Auslassungszeichen *nt*.

**apotheosis** [əpɒθɪ'əʊsɪs] *n* Apotheose *f*.

**appal** [ə'pɔːl] *vt* entsetzen; **to be** ~**led by** entsetzt sein über +*acc*.

**Appalachian Mountains** [æpə'leɪʃən-] *npl:* **the** ~ die Appalachen *pl*.

**appalling** [ə'pɔːlɪŋ] *adj* entsetzlich; **she's an** ~ **cook** sie kann überhaupt nicht kochen.

**apparatus** [æpə'reɪtəs] *n* Gerät *nt*; (*in gymnasium*) Geräte *pl*; (*of organization*) Apparat *m*; **a piece of** ~ ein Gerät *nt*.

**apparel** [ə'pærəl] (*US*) *n* Kleidung *f*.

**apparent** [ə'pærənt] *adj* (*seeming*) scheinbar; (*obvious*) offensichtlich; **it is** ~ **that** ... es ist klar, daß ...

**apparently** [ə'pærəntlɪ] *adv* anscheinend.

**apparition** [æpə'rɪʃən] *n* Erscheinung *f*.

**appeal** [ə'piːl] *vi* (*LAW*) Berufung einlegen ♦ *n* (*LAW*) Berufung *f*; (*plea*) Aufruf *m*; (*charm*) Reiz *m*; **to** ~ (**to sb**) **for** (jdn) bitten um; **to** ~ **to** (*be attractive to*) gefallen +*dat*; **it doesn't** ~ **to me** es reizt mich nicht; **right of** ~ (*LAW*) Berufungsrecht *nt*; **on** ~ (*LAW*) in der Berufung.

**appealing** [ə'piːlɪŋ] *adj* ansprechend; (*touching*) rührend.

**appear** [ə'pɪə*] *vi* erscheinen; (*seem*) scheinen; **to** ~ **on TV/in "Hamlet"** im Fernsehen/in „Hamlet" auftreten; **it would** ~ **that** ... anscheinend ...

**appearance** [ə'pɪərəns] *n* Erscheinen *nt*; (*look*) Aussehen *nt*; (*in public, on TV*) Auftritt *m*; **to put in** *or* **make an** ~ sich sehen lassen; **in** *or* **by order of** ~ (*THEAT etc*) in der Reihenfolge ihres Auftritts; **to keep up** ~**s** den (äußeren) Schein wahren; **to all** ~**s** allem Anschein nach.

**appease** [ə'piːz] *vt* beschwichtigen.

**appeasement** [ə'piːzmənt] *n* Beschwichtigung *f*.

**append** [ə'pɛnd] *vt* (*COMPUT*) anhängen.

**appendage** [ə'pɛndɪdʒ] *n* Anhängsel *nt*.

**appendices** [ə'pɛndɪsiːz] *npl of* **appendix**.

**appendicitis** [əpɛndɪ'saɪtɪs] *n* Blinddarmentzündung *f*.

**appendix** [ə'pɛndɪks] (*pl* **appendices**) *n* (*ANAT*) Blinddarm *m*; (*to publication*) Anhang *m*; **to have one's** ~ **out** sich *dat* den Blinddarm herausnehmen lassen.

**appetite** ['æpɪtaɪt] *n* Appetit *m*; (*fig*) Lust *f*; **that walk has given me an** ~ von dem

Spaziergang habe ich Appetit bekommen.
**appetizer** [ˈæpɪtaɪzəˊ] n (*food*) Appetithappen m; (*drink*) appetitanregendes Getränk nt.

**appetizing** [ˈæpɪtaɪzɪŋ] adj appetitanregend.

**applaud** [əˈplɔːd] vi applaudieren, klatschen ♦ vt (*actor etc*) applaudieren +dat, Beifall spenden or klatschen +dat; (*action, attitude*) loben; (*decision*) begrüßen.

**applause** [əˈplɔːz] n Applaus m, Beifall m.

**apple** [ˈæpl] n Apfel m; **he's the ~ of her eye** er ist ihr ein und alles.

**apple tree** n Apfelbaum m.

**apple turnover** n Apfeltasche f.

**appliance** [əˈplaɪəns] n Gerät nt.

**applicable** [əˈplɪkəbl] adj: ~ **(to)** anwendbar (auf +acc); (*on official forms*) zutreffend (auf +acc); **the law is ~ from January** das Gesetz gilt ab Januar.

**applicant** [ˈæplɪkənt] n Bewerber(in) m(f).

**application** [æplɪˈkeɪʃən] n (*for job*) Bewerbung f; (*for grant etc*) Antrag m; (*hard work*) Fleiß m; (*applying: of paint etc*) Auftragen nt; **on ~** auf Antrag.

**application form** n (*for a job*) Bewerbungsformular nt; (*for a grant etc*) Antragsformular nt.

**application program** n (*COMPUT*) Anwendungsprogramm nt.

**applications package** n (*COMPUT*) Anwendungspaket nt.

**applied** [əˈplaɪd] adj angewandt.

**apply** [əˈplaɪ] vt anwenden; (*paint etc*) auftragen ♦ vi: **to ~ (to)** (*be applicable*) gelten (für); **to ~ the brakes** die Bremse betätigen, bremsen; **to ~ o.s. to sth** sich bei etw anstrengen; **to ~ to** (*ask*) sich wenden an +acc; **to ~ for** (*permit, grant*) beantragen; (*job*) sich bewerben um.

**appoint** [əˈpɔɪnt] vt ernennen; (*date, place*) festlegen, festsetzen.

**appointed** [əˈpɔɪntɪd] adj: **at the ~ time** zur festgesetzten Zeit.

**appointee** [əpɔɪnˈtiː] n Ernannte(r) f(m).

**appointment** [əˈpɔɪntmənt] n Ernennung f; (*post*) Stelle f; (*arranged meeting*) Termin m; **to make an ~ (with sb)** einen Termin (mit jdm) vereinbaren; **by ~** nach Anmeldung, mit Voranmeldung.

**apportion** [əˈpɔːʃən] vt aufteilen; (*blame*) zuweisen; **to ~ sth to sb** jdm etw zuteilen.

**apposition** [æpəˈzɪʃən] n Apposition f, Beifügung f; **A is in ~ to B** A ist eine Apposition zu B.

**appraisal** [əˈpreɪzl] n Beurteilung f.

**appraise** [əˈpreɪz] vt beurteilen.

**appreciable** [əˈpriːʃəbl] adj merklich, deutlich.

**appreciably** [əˈpriːʃəblɪ] adv merklich.

**appreciate** [əˈpriːʃɪeɪt] vt (*like*) schätzen; (*be grateful for*) zu schätzen wissen; (*understand*) verstehen; (*be aware of*) sich dat bewußt sein +gen ♦ vi (*COMM: currency, shares*) im Wert

steigen; **I ~ your help** ich weiß Ihre Hilfe zu schätzen.

**appreciation** [əpriːʃɪˈeɪʃən] n (*enjoyment*) Wertschätzung f; (*understanding*) Verständnis nt; (*gratitude*) Dankbarkeit f; (*COMM: in value*) (Wert)steigerung f.

**appreciative** [əˈpriːʃɪətɪv] adj dankbar; (*comment*) anerkennend.

**apprehend** [æprɪˈhend] vt (*arrest*) festnehmen; (*understand*) verstehen.

**apprehension** [æprɪˈhenʃən] n (*fear*) Besorgnis f; (*arrest*) Festnahme f.

**apprehensive** [æprɪˈhensɪv] adj ängstlich; **to be ~ about sth** sich dat Gedanken or Sorgen um etw machen.

**apprentice** [əˈprentɪs] n Lehrling m, Auszubildende(r) f(m) ♦ vt: **to be ~d to sb** jdm in der Lehre sein.

**apprenticeship** [əˈprentɪsʃɪp] n Lehre f, Lehrzeit f; **to serve one's ~** seine Lehre machen.

**appro.** [ˈæprəʊ] (*BRIT: inf*) abbr (*COMM*: = *approval*): **on ~** zur Ansicht.

**approach** [əˈprəʊtʃ] vi sich nähern; (*event*) nahen ♦ vt (*come to*) sich nähern +dat; (*ask, apply to: person*) herantreten an +acc, ansprechen; (*situation, problem*) herangehen an +acc, angehen ♦ n (*advance*) (Heran)nahen nt; (*access*) Zugang m; (*: for vehicles*) Zufahrt f; (*to problem etc*) Ansatz m; **to ~ sb about sth** jdn wegen etw ansprechen.

**approachable** [əˈprəʊtʃəbl] adj (*person*) umgänglich; (*place*) zugänglich.

**approach road** n Zufahrtsstraße f.

**approbation** [æprəˈbeɪʃən] n Zustimmung f.

**appropriate** [adj əˈprəʊprɪɪt, vt əˈprəʊprɪeɪt] adj (*apt*) angebracht; (*relevant*) entsprechend ♦ vt sich dat aneignen; **it would not be ~ for me to comment** es wäre nicht angebracht, wenn ich mich dazu äußern würde.

**appropriately** [əˈprəʊprɪɪtlɪ] adv entsprechend.

**appropriation** [əprəʊprɪˈeɪʃən] n Zuteilung f, Zuweisung f.

**approval** [əˈpruːvəl] n (*approbation*) Zustimmung f, Billigung f; (*permission*) Einverständnis f; **to meet with sb's ~** jds Zustimmung or Beifall finden; **on ~** (*COMM*) zur Probe.

**approve** [əˈpruːv] vt billigen; (*motion, decision*) annehmen.

▶**approve of** vt fus etwas halten von; **I don't ~ of it/him** ich halte nichts davon/von ihm.

**approved school** [əˈpruːvd-] (*BRIT*) n Erziehungsheim nt.

**approvingly** [əˈpruːvɪŋlɪ] adv zustimmend.

**approx.** abbr = **approximately**.

**approximate** [adj əˈprɒksɪmɪt, vb əˈprɒksɪmeɪt] adj ungefähr ♦ vt, vi: **to ~ (to)** nahekommen +dat.

**approximately** [əˈprɒksɪmɪtlɪ] adv ungefähr.

**approximation** [əˈprɒksɪˈmeɪʃən] n

Annäherung *f*.
**APR** *n abbr* (= *annual(ized) percentage rate*)
Jahreszinssatz *m*.
**Apr.** *abbr* = **April.**
**apricot** ['eɪprɪkɔt] *n* Aprikose *f*.
**April** ['eɪprəl] *n* April *m*; ~ **fool!** April, April!;
*see also* **July.**
**apron** ['eɪprən] *n* Schürze *f*; (*AVIAT*) Vorfeld *nt*.
**apse** [æps] *n* Apsis *f*.
**APT** (*BRIT*) *n abbr* (= *Advanced Passenger Train*)
Hochgeschwindigkeitszug *m*.
**Apt.** *abbr* = **apartment.**
**apt** [æpt] *adj* (*suitable*) passend, treffend;
(*likely*): **to be** ~ **to do sth** dazu neigen, etw
zu tun.
**aptitude** ['æptɪtjuːd] *n* Begabung *f*.
**aptitude test** *n* Eignungstest *m*.
**aptly** ['æptlɪ] *adv* passend, treffend.
**aqualung** ['ækwəlʌŋ] *n* Tauchgerät *nt*.
**aquarium** [ə'kwɛərɪəm] *n* Aquarium *nt*.
**Aquarius** [ə'kwɛərɪəs] *n* Wassermann *m*; **to be**
~ (ein) Wassermann sein.
**aquatic** [ə'kwætɪk] *adj* (*plants etc*) Wasser-;
(*life*) im Wasser.
**aqueduct** ['ækwɪdʌkt] *n* Aquädukt *m or nt*.
**AR** (*US*) *abbr* (*POST*: = *Arkansas*).
**ARA** (*BRIT*) *n abbr* (= *Associate of the Royal
Academy*) Qualifikationsnachweis im
*künstlerischen Bereich*.
**Arab** ['ærəb] *adj* arabisch ♦ *n* Araber(in) *m(f)*.
**Arabia** [ə'reɪbɪə] *n* Arabien *nt*.
**Arabian** [ə'reɪbɪən] *adj* arabisch.
**Arabian Desert** *n*: **the** ~ die Arabische
Wüste.
**Arabian Sea** *n*: **the** ~ das Arabische Meer.
**Arabic** ['ærəbɪk] *adj* arabisch ♦ *n* (*LING*)
Arabisch *nt*.
**arable** ['ærəbl] *adj* (*land*) bebaubar; ~ **farm**
*Bauernhof, der ausschließlich Ackerbau
betreibt*.
**ARAM** (*BRIT*) *n abbr* (= *Associate of the Royal
Academy of Music*) Qualifikationsnachweis
*in Musik*.
**arbiter** ['ɑːbɪtə*] *n* Vermittler *m*.
**arbitrary** ['ɑːbɪtrərɪ] *adj* willkürlich.
**arbitrate** ['ɑːbɪtreɪt] *vi* vermitteln.
**arbitration** [ɑːbɪ'treɪʃən] *n* Schlichtung *f*; **the
dispute went to** ~ der Streit wurde vor eine
Schlichtungskommission gebracht.
**arbitrator** ['ɑːbɪtreɪtə*] *n* Vermittler(in) *m(f)*;
(*INDUSTRY*) Schlichter(in) *m(f)*.
**ARC** *n abbr* (= *American Red Cross*) ≈ DRK *nt*.
**arc** [ɑːk] *n* Bogen *m*.
**arcade** [ɑː'keɪd] *n* Arkade *f*; (*shopping mall*)
Passage *f*.
**arch** [ɑːtʃ] *n* Bogen *m*; (*of foot*) Gewölbe *nt* ♦ *vt*
(*back*) krümmen ♦ *adj* schelmisch ♦ *pref*
Erz-.
**archaeological** [ɑːkɪə'lɔdʒɪkl] *adj*
archäologisch.
**archaeologist** [ɑːkɪ'ɔlədʒɪst] *n* Archäologe *m*,
Archäologin *f*.

**archaeology,** (*US*) **archeology** [ɑːkɪ'ɔlədʒɪ] *n*
Archäologie *f*.
**archaic** [ɑː'keɪɪk] *adj* altertümlich; (*language*)
veraltet, archaisch.
**archangel** ['ɑːkeɪndʒəl] *n* Erzengel *m*.
**archbishop** [ɑːtʃ'bɪʃəp] *n* Erzbischof *m*.
**archenemy** ['ɑːtʃ'enəmɪ] *n* Erzfeind(in) *m(f)*.
**archeology** *etc* [ɑːkɪ'ɔlədʒɪ] (*US*)
= **archaeology** *etc*.
**archery** ['ɑːtʃərɪ] *n* Bogenschießen *nt*.
**archetypal** ['ɑːkɪtaɪpəl] *adj* (*arche*)typisch.
**archetype** ['ɑːkɪtaɪp] *n* Urbild *nt*, Urtyp *m*.
**archipelago** [ɑːkɪ'pɛlɪgəu] *n* Archipel *m*.
**architect** ['ɑːkɪtɛkt] *n* Architekt(in) *m(f)*.
**architectural** [ɑːkɪ'tɛktʃərəl] *adj*
architektonisch.
**architecture** ['ɑːkɪtɛktʃə*] *n* Architektur *f*.
**archive file** *n* (*COMPUT*) Archivdatei *f*.
**archives** ['ɑːkaɪvz] *npl* Archiv *nt*.
**archivist** ['ɑːkɪvɪst] *n* Archivar(in) *m(f)*.
**archway** ['ɑːtʃweɪ] *n* Torbogen *m*.
**ARCM** (*BRIT*) *n abbr* (= *Associate of the Royal
College of Music*) Qualifikationsnachweis in
*Musik*.
**Arctic** ['ɑːktɪk] *adj* arktisch ♦ *n*: **the** ~ die
Arktis.
**Arctic Circle** *n*: **the** ~ der nördliche
Polarkreis.
**Arctic Ocean** *n*: **the** ~ das Nordpolarmeer.
**ARD** (*US*) *n abbr* (*MED*: = *acute respiratory
disease*) akute Erkrankung der Atemwege.
**ardent** ['ɑːdənt] *adj* leidenschaftlich; (*admirer*)
glühend.
**ardour,** (*US*) **ardor** ['ɑːdə*] *n* Leidenschaft *f*.
**arduous** ['ɑːdjuəs] *adj* mühsam.
**are** [ɑː*] *vb see* **be.**
**area** ['ɛərɪə] *n* Gebiet *nt*; (*GEOM etc*) Fläche *f*;
(*dining area etc*) Bereich *m*; **in the London** ~
im Raum London.
**area code** (*US*) *n* Vorwahl(nummer) *f*.
**arena** [ə'riːnə] *n* Arena *f*.
**aren't** [ɑːnt] = **are not.**
**Argentina** [ɑːdʒən'tiːnə] *n* Argentinien *nt*.
**Argentinian** [ɑːdʒən'tɪnɪən] *adj* argentinisch
♦ *n* Argentinier(in) *m(f)*.
**arguable** ['ɑːgjuəbl] *adj*: **it is** ~ **whether ...** es
ist (noch) die Frage, ob ...; **it is** ~ **that ...**
man kann (wohl) sagen, daß ...
**arguably** ['ɑːgjuəblɪ] *adv* wohl; **it is** ~ **...**
dürfte wohl ... sein.
**argue** ['ɑːgjuː] *vi* (*quarrel*) sich streiten;
(*reason*) diskutieren ♦ *vt* (*debate*)
diskutieren, erörtern; **to** ~ **that ...** den
Standpunkt vertreten, daß ...; **to** ~ **about
sth** sich über etw *acc* streiten; **to** ~ **for/
against sth** sich für/gegen etw aussprechen.
**argument** ['ɑːgjumənt] *n* (*reasons*) Argument
*nt*; (*quarrel*) Streit *m*, Auseinandersetzung *f*;
(*debate*) Diskussion *f*; ~ **for/against**
Argument für/gegen; **to have an** ~ sich
streiten.
**argumentative** [ɑːgju'mɛntətɪv] *adj*

streitlustig.

**aria** ['ɑːrɪə] n Arie f.

**ARIBA** [[ə'riːbə]] (BRIT) n abbr (= Associate of the Royal Institute of British Architects) Qualifikationsnachweis in Architektur.

**arid** ['ærɪd] adj (land) dürr; (subject) trocken.

**aridity** [ə'rɪdɪtɪ] n Dürre f, Trockenheit f.

**Aries** ['ɛərɪz] n Widder m; **to be ~** (ein) Widder sein.

**arise** [ə'raɪz] (pt **arose**, pp **arisen**) vi (difficulty etc) sich ergeben; (question) sich stellen; **to ~ from** sich ergeben aus, herrühren von; **should the need ~** falls es nötig wird.

**arisen** [ə'rɪzn] pp of **arise**.

**aristocracy** [ærɪs'tɔkrəsɪ] n Aristokratie f, Adel m.

**aristocrat** ['ærɪstəkræt] n Aristokrat(in) m(f), Ad(e)lige(r) f(m).

**aristocratic** [ærɪstə'krætɪk] adj aristokratisch, ad(e)lig.

**arithmetic** [ə'rɪθmətɪk] n Rechnen nt; (calculation) Rechnung f.

**arithmetical** [ærɪθ'mɛtɪkl] adj rechnerisch, arithmetisch.

**Ariz.** (US) abbr (POST: = Arizona).

**ark** [ɑːk] n: **Noah's A~** die Arche Noah.

**arm** [ɑːm] n Arm m; (of clothing) Ärmel m; (of chair) Armlehne f; (of organization etc) Zweig m ♦ vt bewaffnen; **arms** npl (weapons) Waffen pl; (HERALDRY) Wappen nt.

**armaments** ['ɑːməmənts] npl (weapons) (Aus)rüstung f.

**armband** ['ɑːmbænd] n Armbinde f.

**armchair** ['ɑːmtʃɛə*] n Sessel m, Lehnstuhl m.

**armed** [ɑːmd] adj bewaffnet; **the ~ forces** die Streitkräfte pl.

**armed robbery** n bewaffneter Raubüberfall m.

**Armenia** [ɑː'miːnɪə] n Armenien nt.

**Armenian** [ɑː'miːnɪən] adj armenisch ♦ n Armenier(in) m(f); (LING) Armenisch nt.

**armful** ['ɑːmful] n Armvoll m.

**armistice** ['ɑːmɪstɪs] n Waffenstillstand m.

**armour**, (US) **armor** ['ɑːmə*] n (HIST) Rüstung f; (also: ~-plating) Panzerplatte f; (MIL: tanks) Panzerfahrzeuge pl.

**armoured car** ['ɑːməd-] n Panzerwagen m.

**armoury** ['ɑːmərɪ] n (storeroom) Waffenlager nt.

**armpit** ['ɑːmpɪt] n Achselhöhle f.

**armrest** ['ɑːmrɛst] n Armlehne f.

**arms control** [ɑːmz-] n Rüstungskontrolle f.

**arms race** [ɑːmz-] n: **the ~** das Wettrüsten nt.

**army** ['ɑːmɪ] n Armee f, Heer nt; (fig: host) Heer.

**aroma** [ə'rəumə] n Aroma nt, Duft m.

**aromatherapy** [ərəumə'θɛrəpɪ] n Aromatherapie f.

**aromatic** [ærə'mætɪk] adj aromatisch, duftend.

**arose** [ə'rəuz] pt of **arise**.

**around** [ə'raund] adv (about) herum; (in the area) in der Nähe ♦ prep (encircling) um ... herum; (near) in der Nähe von; (fig: about: dimensions) etwa; (: : time) gegen; (: : date) um; **is he ~?** ist er da?; **~ £5** um die £5, etwa £5; **~ 3 o'clock** gegen 3 Uhr.

**arousal** [ə'rauzəl] n (sexual) Erregung f; (of feelings, interest) Weckung f.

**arouse** [ə'rauz] vt (feelings, interest) wecken.

**arpeggio** [ɑː'pɛdʒɪəu] n Arpeggio nt.

**arrange** [ə'reɪndʒ] vt (meeting etc) vereinbaren; (tour etc) planen; (books etc) anordnen; (flowers) arrangieren; (MUS) arrangieren, bearbeiten ♦ vi: **we have ~d for a car to pick you up** wir haben veranlaßt, daß Sie mit dem Auto abgeholt werden; **it was ~d that ...** es wurde vereinbart, daß ...; **to ~ to do sth** vereinbaren or ausmachen, etw zu tun.

**arrangement** [ə'reɪndʒmənt] n (agreement) Vereinbarung f; (layout) Anordnung f; (MUS) Arrangement nt, Bearbeitung f; **arrangements** npl Pläne pl; (preparations) Vorbereitungen pl; **to come to an ~ with sb** eine Regelung mit jdm treffen; **home deliveries by ~** nach Vereinbarung Lieferung ins Haus; **I'll make ~s for you to be met** ich werde veranlassen, daß Sie abgeholt werden.

**arrant** ['ærənt] adj (coward, fool etc) Erz-; (nonsense) total.

**array** [ə'reɪ] n: **an ~ of** (things) eine Reihe von; (people) Aufgebot an +dat; (MATH, COMPUT) (Daten)feld nt.

**arrears** [ə'rɪəz] npl Rückstand m; **to be in ~ with one's rent** mit seiner Miete im Rückstand sein.

**arrest** [ə'rɛst] vt (person) verhaften; (sb's attention) erregen ♦ n Verhaftung f; **under ~** verhaftet.

**arresting** [ə'rɛstɪŋ] adj (fig) atemberaubend.

**arrival** [ə'raɪvl] n Ankunft f; (COMM: of goods) Sendung f; **new ~** (person) Neuankömmling m; (baby) Neugeborene(s) nt.

**arrive** [ə'raɪv] vi ankommen.
▶**arrive at** vt fus (fig: conclusion) kommen zu; (: situation) es bringen zu.

**arrogance** ['ærəgəns] n Arroganz f, Überheblichkeit f.

**arrogant** ['ærəgənt] adj arrogant, überheblich.

**arrow** ['ærəu] n Pfeil m.

**arse** [ɑːs] (BRIT: inf!) n Arsch m (!).

**arsenal** ['ɑːsɪnl] n Waffenlager nt; (stockpile) Arsenal nt.

**arsenic** ['ɑːsnɪk] n Arsen nt.

**arson** ['ɑːsn] n Brandstiftung f.

**art** [ɑːt] n Kunst f; **Arts** npl (SCOL) Geisteswissenschaften pl; **work of ~** Kunstwerk nt.

**artefact** ['ɑːtɪfækt] n Artefakt nt.

**arterial** [ɑː'tɪərɪəl] adj arteriell; **~ road** Fernverkehrsstraße f; **~ line** (RAIL) Hauptstrecke f.

**artery** ['ɑːtərɪ] *n* Arterie *f*, Schlagader *f*; (*fig*) Verkehrsader *f*.
**artful** ['ɑːtful] *adj* raffiniert.
**art gallery** *n* Kunstgalerie *f*.
**arthritic** [ɑː'θrɪtɪk] *adj* arthritisch.
**arthritis** [ɑː'θraɪtɪs] *n* Arthritis *f*.
**artichoke** ['ɑːtɪtʃəuk] *n* (*also*: **globe** ~) Artischocke *f*; (*also*: **Jerusalem** ~) Topinambur *m*.
**article** ['ɑːtɪkl] *n* Artikel *m*; (*object, item*) Gegenstand *m*; **articles** (*BRIT*) *npl* (*LAW*) (Rechts)referendarzeit *f*; ~ **of clothing** Kleidungsstück *nt*.
**articles of association** *npl* (*COMM*) Gesellschaftsvertrag *m*.
**articulate** [*adj* ɑː'tɪkjulɪt, *vt, vi* ɑː'tɪkjuleɪt] *adj* (*speech, writing*) klar; (*speaker*) redegewandt ♦ *vt* darlegen ♦ *vi* artikulieren; **to be** ~ (*person*) sich gut ausdrücken können.
**articulated lorry** (*BRIT*) *n* Sattelschlepper *m*.
**artifice** ['ɑːtɪfɪs] *n* List *f*.
**artificial** [ɑːtɪ'fɪʃəl] *adj* künstlich; (*manner*) gekünstelt; **to be** ~ (*person*) gekünstelt *or* unnatürlich wirken.
**artificial insemination** [-ɪnsɛmɪ'neɪʃən] *n* künstliche Besamung *f*.
**artificial intelligence** *n* künstliche Intelligenz *f*.
**artificial respiration** *n* künstliche Beatmung *f*.
**artillery** [ɑː'tɪlərɪ] *n* Artillerie *f*.
**artisan** ['ɑːtɪzæn] *n* Handwerker *m*.
**artist** ['ɑːtɪst] *n* Künstler(in) *m(f)*.
**artistic** [ɑː'tɪstɪk] *adj* künstlerisch.
**artistry** ['ɑːtɪstrɪ] *n* künstlerisches Geschick *nt*.
**artless** ['ɑːtlɪs] *adj* arglos.
**art school** *n* Kunstakademie *f*, Kunsthochschule *f*.
**artwork** ['ɑːtwɔːk] *n* (*for advert etc, material for printing*) Druckvorlage *f*; (*in book*) Bildmaterial *nt*.
**ARV** *n abbr* (*BIBLE*: = *American Revised Version*) *amerikanische revidierte Bibelübersetzung.*
**AS** (*US*) *n abbr* (= *Associate in/of Science*) *akademischer Grad in Natur- wissenschaften* ♦ *abbr* (*POST*: = *American Samoa*).

===================================== *KEYWORD*

**as** [æz] *conj* **1** (*referring to time*) als; ~ **the years went by** mit den Jahren; **he came in** ~ **I was leaving** als er hereinkam, ging ich gerade; ~ **from tomorrow** ab morgen
**2** (*in comparisons*): ~ **big** ~ so groß wie; **twice** ~ **big** ~ zweimal so groß wie; ~ **much/many** ~ soviel/so viele wie; ~ **soon** ~ sobald; **much** ~ **I admire her** ... so sehr ich sie auch bewundere ...
**3** (*since, because*) da, weil; ~ **you can't come I'll go without you** da du nicht mitkommen

kannst, gehe ich ohne dich
**4** (*referring to manner, way*) wie; **do** ~ **you wish** mach, was du willst; ~ **she said** wie sie sagte; **he gave it to me** ~ **a present** er gab es mir als Geschenk; ~ **it were** sozusagen
**5** (*in the capacity of*) als; **he works** ~ **a driver** er arbeitet als Fahrer
**6** (*concerning*): ~ **for** *or* **to that** was das betrifft *or* angeht
**7**: ~ **if** *or* **though** als ob; *see also* **long, such, well.**

───────────────────────────

**ASA** *n abbr* (= *American Standards Association*) *amerikanischer Normenausschuß.*
**a.s.a.p.** *adv abbr* (= *as soon as possible*) baldmöglichst.
**asbestos** [æz'bɛstəs] *n* Asbest *m*.
**ascend** [ə'sɛnd] *vt* hinaufsteigen; (*throne*) besteigen.
**ascendancy** [ə'sɛndənsɪ] *n* Vormachtstellung *f*; ~ **over sb** Vorherrschaft über jdn.
**ascendant** [ə'sɛndənt] *n*: **to be in the** ~ im Aufstieg begriffen sein.
**ascension** [ə'sɛnʃən] *n*: **the A**~ (*REL*) die Himmelfahrt *f* (Christi).
**Ascension Island** *n* Ascension *nt*.
**ascent** [ə'sɛnt] *n* Aufstieg *m*.
**ascertain** [æsə'teɪn] *vt* feststellen.
**ascetic** [ə'sɛtɪk] *adj* asketisch.
**asceticism** [ə'sɛtɪsɪzəm] *n* Askese *f*.
**ASCII** ['æskiː] *n abbr* (*COMPUT*: = *American Standard Code for Information Interchange*) ASCII.
**ascribe** [ə'skraɪb] *vt*: **to** ~ **sth to** etw zuschreiben +*dat*; (*cause*) etw zurückführen auf +*acc*.
**ASCU** (*US*) *n abbr* (= *Association of State Colleges and Universities*) *Verband staatlicher Bildungseinrichtungen.*
**ASEAN** ['æsɪæn] *n abbr* (= *Association of Southeast Asian Nations*) ASEAN *f* (*Gemeinschaft südostasiatischer Staaten*).
**ASH** [æʃ] (*BRIT*) *n abbr* (= *Action on Smoking and Health*) *Anti-Raucher-Initiative.*
**ash** [æʃ] *n* Asche *f*; (*wood, tree*) Esche *f*.
**ashamed** [ə'ʃeɪmd] *adj* beschämt; **to be** ~ **of** sich schämen für; **to be** ~ **of o.s. for having done sth** sich schämen, daß man etw getan hat.
**A shares** *npl* stimmrechtslose Aktien *pl*.
**ashen** ['æʃən] *adj* (*face*) aschfahl.
**ashore** [ə'ʃɔː'] *adv* an Land.
**ashtray** ['æʃtreɪ] *n* Aschenbecher *m*.
**Ash Wednesday** *n* Aschermittwoch *m*.
**Asia** ['eɪʃə] *n* Asien *nt*.
**Asia Minor** *n* Kleinasien *nt*.
**Asian** ['eɪʃən] *adj* asiatisch ♦ *n* Asiat(in) *m(f)*.
**Asiatic** [eɪsɪ'ætɪk] *adj* asiatisch.
**aside** [ə'saɪd] *adv* zur Seite; (*take*) beiseite ♦ *n* beiseite gesprochene Worte *pl*; **to brush objections** ~ Einwände beiseite schieben.
**aside from** *prep* außer +*dat*.

**ask** [ɑːsk] *vt* fragen; (*invite*) einladen; **to ~ sb to do sth** jdn bitten, etw zu tun; **to ~ (sb) sth** (jdn) etw fragen; **to ~ sb a question** jdm eine Frage stellen; **to ~ sb the time** jdn nach der Uhrzeit fragen; **to ~ sb about sth** jdn nach etw fragen; **to ~ sb out to dinner** jdn zum Essen einladen.
▶**ask after** *vt fus* fragen nach.
▶**ask for** *vt fus* bitten um; (*trouble*) haben wollen; **it's just ~ing for trouble/it** das kann ja nicht gutgehen.

**askance** [ə'skɑːns] *adv:* **to look ~ at sb** jdn mißtrauisch ansehen; **to look ~ at sth** etw mit Mißtrauen betrachten.

**askew** [ə'skjuː] *adv* schief.

**asking price** ['ɑːskɪŋ-] *n:* **the ~** der geforderte Preis.

**asleep** [ə'sliːp] *adj* schlafend; **to be ~** schlafen; **to fall ~** einschlafen.

**ASLEF** ['æzlɛf] (*BRIT*) *n abbr* (= *Associated Society of Locomotive Engineers and Firemen*) *Eisenbahnergewerkschaft.*

**asp** [æsp] *n* Natter *f.*

**asparagus** [əs'pærəgəs] *n* Spargel *m.*

**asparagus tips** *npl* Spargelspitzen *pl.*

**ASPCA** *n abbr* (= *American Society for the Prevention of Cruelty to Animals*) *Tierschutzverein.*

**aspect** ['æspɛkt] *n* (*of subject*) Aspekt *m;* (*of building etc*) Lage *f;* (*quality, air*) Erscheinung *f;* **to have a south-westerly ~** nach Südwesten liegen.

**aspersions** [əs'pəːʃənz] *npl:* **to cast ~ on** sich abfällig äußern über +*acc.*

**asphalt** ['æsfælt] *n* Asphalt *m.*

**asphyxiate** [æs'fɪksɪeɪt] *vt* ersticken.

**asphyxiation** [æsfɪksɪ'eɪʃən] *n* Erstickung *f.*

**aspirate** ['æspəreɪt] *vt* aspirieren, behauchen.

**aspirations** [æspə'reɪʃənz] *npl* Hoffnungen *pl;* **to have ~ to(wards) sth** etw anstreben.

**aspire** [əs'paɪəʳ] *vi:* **to ~ to** streben nach.

**aspirin** ['æsprɪn] *n* Kopfschmerztablette *f,* Aspirin ® *nt.*

**aspiring** [əs'paɪərɪŋ] *adj* aufstrebend.

**ass** [æs] *n* (*also fig*) Esel *m;* (*US: inf!*) Arsch! *m.*

**assail** [ə'seɪl] *vt* angreifen; (*fig*): **to be ~ed by doubts** von Zweifeln geplagt werden.

**assailant** [ə'seɪlənt] *n* Angreifer(in) *m(f).*

**assassin** [ə'sæsɪn] *n* Attentäter(in) *m(f).*

**assassinate** [ə'sæsɪneɪt] *vt* ermorden, ein Attentat verüben auf +*acc.*

**assassination** [əsæsɪ'neɪʃən] *n* Ermordung *f,* (geglücktes) Attentat *nt.*

**assault** [ə'sɔːlt] *n* Angriff *m* ♦ *vt* angreifen; (*sexually*) vergewaltigen; **~ and battery** (*LAW*) Körperverletzung *f.*

**assemble** [ə'sɛmbl] *vt* versammeln; (*car, machine*) montieren; (*furniture etc*) zusammenbauen ♦ *vi* sich versammeln.

**assembly** [ə'sɛmblɪ] *n* Versammlung *f;* (*of car, machine*) Montage *f;* (*of furniture*) Zusammenbau *m.*

**assembly language** *n* (*COMPUT*) Assemblersprache *f.*

**assembly line** *n* Fließband *nt.*

**assent** [ə'sɛnt] *n* Zustimmung *f* ♦ *vi:* **to ~ (to)** zustimmen (+*dat*).

**assert** [ə'səːt] *vt* behaupten; (*innocence*) beteuern; (*authority*) geltend machen; **to ~ o.s.** sich durchsetzen.

**assertion** [ə'səːʃən] *n* Behauptung *f.*

**assertive** [ə'səːtɪv] *adj* (*person*) selbstbewußt; (*manner*) bestimmt.

**assess** [ə'sɛs] *vt* (*situation*) einschätzen; (*abilities etc*) beurteilen; (*tax*) festsetzen; (*damages, property etc*) schätzen.

**assessment** [ə'sɛsmənt] *n* (*see vt*) Einschätzung *f;* Beurteilung *f;* Festsetzung *f;* Schätzung *f.*

**assessor** [ə'sɛsəʳ] *n* (*LAW: expert*) Gutachter(in) *m(f).*

**asset** ['æsɛt] *n* Vorteil *m;* (*person*) Stütze *f;* **assets** *npl* (*property, funds*) Vermögen *nt;* (*COMM*) Aktiva *pl.*

**asset-stripping** ['æsɛt'strɪpɪŋ] *n* (*COMM*) *Aufkauf von finanziell gefährdeten Firmen und anschließender Verkauf ihrer Vermögenswerte.*

**assiduous** [ə'sɪdjuəs] *adj* gewissenhaft.

**assign** [ə'saɪn] *vt:* **to ~ (to)** (*date*) zuweisen (+*dat*); (*task*) übertragen (+*dat*); (*person*) einteilen (für); (*cause*) zuschreiben (+*dat*); (*meaning*) zuordnen (+*dat*); **to ~ sb to do sth** jdn damit beauftragen, etw zu tun.

**assignment** [ə'saɪnmənt] *n* Aufgabe *f.*

**assimilate** [ə'sɪmɪleɪt] *vt* aufnehmen; (*immigrants*) integrieren.

**assimilation** [əsɪmɪ'leɪʃən] *n* (*see vt*) Aufnahme *f;* Integration *f.*

**assist** [ə'sɪst] *vt* helfen; (*with money etc*) unterstützen.

**assistance** [ə'sɪstəns] *n* Hilfe *f;* (*with money etc*) Unterstützung *f.*

**assistant** [ə'sɪstənt] *n* Assistent(in) *m(f);* (*BRIT: also: shop ~*) Verkäufer(in) *m(f).*

**assistant manager** *n* stellvertretender Geschäftsführer *m,* stellvertretende Geschäftsführerin *f.*

**assizes** [ə'saɪzɪz] (*BRIT*) *npl* Gerichtstage *pl.*

**associate** [*adj, n* ə'səʊʃɪɪt, *vt, vi* ə'səʊʃɪeɪt] *adj* (*director*) assoziiert; (*member, professor*) außerordentlich ♦ *n* (*at work*) Kollege *m,* Kollegin *f* ♦ *vt* in Verbindung bringen ♦ *vi:* **to ~ with sb** mit jdm verkehren.

**associated company** [ə'səʊʃɪeɪtɪd-] *n* Partnerfirma *f.*

**association** [əsəʊsɪ'eɪʃən] *n* (*group*) Verband *m;* (*involvement*) Verbindung *f;* (*PSYCH*) Assoziation *f;* **in ~ with** in Zusammenarbeit mit.

**association football** *n* Fußball *m.*

**assorted** [ə'sɔːtɪd] *adj* gemischt; (*various*) diverse(r, s); **in ~ sizes** in verschiedenen Größen.

**assortment** [ə'sɔːtmənt] *n* Mischung *f*; (*of books, people etc*) Ansammlung *f*.

**Asst** *abbr* = **assistant**.

**assuage** [ə'sweɪdʒ] *vt* (*grief, pain*) lindern; (*thirst, appetite*) stillen, befriedigen.

**assume** [ə'sjuːm] *vt* annehmen; (*responsibilities etc*) übernehmen.

**assumed name** [ə'sjuːmd-] *n* Deckname *m*.

**assumption** [ə'sʌmpʃən] *n* Annahme *f*; (*of power etc*) Übernahme *f*; **on the ~ that** ... vorausgesetzt, daß ...

**assurance** [ə'ʃuərəns] *n* Versicherung *f*; (*promise*) Zusicherung *f*; (*confidence*) Zuversicht *f*; **I can give you no ~s** ich kann Ihnen nichts versprechen.

**assure** [ə'ʃuə•] *vt* versichern; (*guarantee*) sichern.

**assured** [ə'ʃuəd] *n* (*BRIT*) Versicherte(r) *f(m)* ♦ *adj* sicher.

**AST** (*US*) *abbr* (= *Atlantic Standard Time*) Ortszeit in Ostkanada.

**asterisk** ['æstərɪsk] *n* Sternchen *nt*.

**astern** [ə'stɜːn] *adv* achtern.

**asteroid** ['æstərɔɪd] *n* Asteroid *m*.

**asthma** ['æsmə] *n* Asthma *nt*.

**asthmatic** [æs'mætɪk] *adj* asthmatisch ♦ *n* Asthmatiker(in) *m(f)*.

**astigmatism** [ə'stɪgmətɪzəm] *n* Astigmatismus *m*.

**astir** [ə'stɜː•] *adv*: **to be ~** (*out of bed*) auf sein.

**astonish** [ə'stɔnɪʃ] *vt* erstaunen.

**astonishing** [ə'stɔnɪʃɪŋ] *adj* erstaunlich; **I find it ~ that** ... es überrascht mich, daß ...

**astonishingly** [ə'stɔnɪʃɪŋlɪ] *adv* erstaunlich; **~, ...** erstaunlicherweise ...

**astonishment** [ə'stɔnɪʃmənt] *n* Erstaunen *nt*.

**astound** [ə'staund] *vt* verblüffen, sehr erstaunen.

**astounded** [ə'staundɪd] *adj* (höchst) erstaunt.

**astounding** [ə'staundɪŋ] *adj* erstaunlich.

**astray** [ə'streɪ] *adv*: **to go ~** (*letter*) verlorengehen; (*fig*) auf Abwege geraten; **to lead ~** auf Abwege bringen; **to go ~ in one's calculations** sich verrechnen.

**astride** [ə'straɪd] *adv* (*sit, ride*) rittlings; (*stand*) breitbeinig ♦ *prep* rittlings auf +*dat*; breitbeinig über +*dat*.

**astringent** [əs'trɪndʒənt] *adj* adstringierend; (*fig: caustic*) ätzend, beißend ♦ *n* Adstringens *nt*.

**astrologer** [əs'trɔlədʒə•] *n* Astrologe *m*, Astrologin *f*.

**astrology** [əs'trɔlədʒɪ] *n* Astrologie *f*.

**astronaut** ['æstrənɔːt] *n* Astronaut(in) *m(f)*.

**astronomer** [əs'trɔnəmə•] *n* Astronom(in) *m(f)*.

**astronomical** [æstrə'nɔmɪkl] *adj* (*also fig*) astronomisch.

**astronomy** [əs'trɔnəmɪ] *n* Astronomie *f*.

**astrophysics** ['æstrəu'fɪzɪks] *n* Astrophysik *f*.

**astute** [əs'tjuːt] *adj* scharfsinnig; (*operator, behaviour*) geschickt.

**asunder** [ə'sʌndə•] *adv*: **to tear ~** auseinanderreißen.

**ASV** *n abbr* (*BIBLE*: = *American Standard Version*) amerikanische Standard-Bibelübersetzung.

**asylum** [ə'saɪləm] *n* Asyl *nt*; (*mental hospital*) psychiatrische Klinik *f*; **to seek political ~** um (politisches) Asyl bitten.

**asymmetrical** [eɪsɪ'metrɪkl] *adj* asymmetrisch.

═══════════════════════════════════ *KEYWORD*

**at** [æt] *prep* **1** (*referring to position, direction*) an +*dat*, in +*dat*; **~ the top** an der Spitze; **~ home** zu Hause; **~ school** in der Schule; **~ the baker's** beim Bäcker; **to look ~ sth** auf etw *acc* blicken

**2** (*referring to time*): **~ 4 o'clock** um 4 Uhr; **~ night/dawn** bei Nacht/Tagesanbruch; **~ Christmas** zu Weihnachten; **~ times** zuweilen

**3** (*referring to rates, speed etc*): **~ £2 a kilo** zu £2 pro Kilo; **two ~ a time** zwei auf einmal; **~ 50 km/h** mit 50 km/h

**4** (*referring to activity*): **to be ~ work** (*in office etc*) auf der Arbeit sein; **to play ~ cowboys** Cowboy spielen; **to be good ~ sth** gut in etw *dat* sein

**5** (*referring to cause*): **shocked/surprised/annoyed ~ sth** schockiert/überrascht/verärgert über etw *acc*; **I went ~ his suggestion** ich ging auf seinen Vorschlag hin

**6**: **not ~ all** (*in answer to question*) überhaupt nicht, ganz und gar nicht; (*in answer to thanks*) nichts zu danken, keine Ursache; **I'm not ~ all tired** ich bin überhaupt nicht müde; **anything ~ all** irgend etwas.

**ate** [eɪt] *pt of* **eat**.

**atheism** ['eɪθiɪzəm] *n* Atheismus *m*.

**atheist** ['eɪθiɪst] *n* Atheist(in) *m(f)*.

**Athenian** [ə'θiːnɪən] *adj* Athener ♦ *n* Athener(in) *m(f)*.

**Athens** ['æθɪnz] *n* Athen *nt*.

**athlete** ['æθliːt] *n* Athlet(in) *m(f)*.

**athletic** [æθ'letɪk] *adj* sportlich; (*muscular*) athletisch.

**athletics** [æθ'letɪks] *n* Leichtathletik *f*.

**Atlantic** [ət'læntɪk] *adj* atlantisch; (*coast etc*) Atlantik- ♦ *n*: **the ~ (Ocean)** der Atlantik.

**atlas** ['ætləs] *n* Atlas *m*.

**Atlas Mountains** *npl*: **the ~** der Atlas, das Atlas-Gebirge.

**ATM** *abbr* (= *automated telling machine*) Geldautomat *m*.

**atmosphere** ['ætməsfɪə•] *n* Atmosphäre *f*; (*air*) Luft *f*.

**atmospheric** [ætməs'ferɪk] *adj* atmosphärisch.

**atmospherics** [ætməs'ferɪks] *npl* atmosphärische Störungen *pl*.

**atoll** ['ætɔl] *n* Atoll *nt*.

**atom** ['ætəm] n Atom nt.

**atomic** [ə'tɔmɪk] adj atomar; (energy, weapons) Atom-.

**atom(ic) bomb** n Atombombe f.

**atomizer** ['ætəmaɪzə°] n Zerstäuber m.

**atone** [ə'təun] vi: **to ~ for** büßen für.

**atonement** [ə'təunmənt] n Buße f.

**A to Z** ® n Stadtplan m.

**ATP** n abbr (= Association of Tennis Professionals) Tennis-Profiverband.

**atrocious** [ə'trəuʃəs] adj grauenhaft.

**atrocity** [ə'trɔsɪtɪ] n Greueltat f.

**atrophy** ['ætrəfɪ] n Schwund m, Atrophie f ♦ vt schwinden lassen ♦ vi schwinden, verkümmern.

**attach** [ə'tætʃ] vt befestigen; (document, letter)·anheften, beiheften; (employee, troops) zuteilen; (importance etc) beimessen; **to be ~ed to sb/sth** (like) an jdm/etw hängen; (be connected with) mit jdm/etw zu tun haben; **the ~ed letter** der beiliegende Brief.

**attaché** [ə'tæʃeɪ] n Attaché m.

**attaché case** n Aktenkoffer m.

**attachment** [ə'tætʃmənt] n (tool) Zubehörteil nt; (love): ~ **(to sb)** Zuneigung f (zu jdm).

**attack** [ə'tæk] vt angreifen; (subj: criminal) überfallen; (task, problem etc) in Angriff nehmen ♦ n (also fig) Angriff m; (on sb's life) Anschlag m; (of illness) Anfall m; **heart ~** Herzanfall m, Herzinfarkt m.

**attacker** [ə'tækə°] n Angreifer(in) m(f).

**attain** [ə'teɪn] vt (also: ~ **to**) erreichen; (knowledge) erlangen.

**attainments** [ə'teɪnmənts] npl Fähigkeiten pl.

**attempt** [ə'tɛmpt] n Versuch m ♦ vt versuchen; **to make an ~ on sb's life** einen Anschlag auf jdn verüben.

**attempted** [ə'tɛmptɪd] adj versucht; ~ **murder/suicide** Mord-/Selbstmordversuch m; ~ **theft** versuchter Diebstahl.

**attend** [ə'tɛnd] vt besuchen; (patient) behandeln.

**attend to** vt fus sich kümmern um; (needs) nachkommen +dat; (customer) bedienen.

**attendance** [ə'tɛndəns] n Anwesenheit f; (people present) Besucherzahl f; (SPORT) Zuschauerzahl f.

**attendant** [ə'tɛndənt] n (helper) Begleiter(in) m(f); (in garage) Tankwart m; (in museum) Aufseher(in) m(f) ♦ adj damit verbunden.

**attention** [ə'tɛnʃən] n Aufmerksamkeit f; (care) Fürsorge f ♦ excl (MIL) Achtung!; **attentions** npl (acts of courtesy) Aufmerksamkeiten pl; **for the ~ of ...** zu Händen von ...; **it has come to my ~ that ...** ich bin darauf aufmerksam geworden, daß ...; **to stand to or at ~** (MIL) stillstehen.

**attentive** [ə'tɛntɪv] adj aufmerksam.

**attentively** [ə'tɛntɪvlɪ] adv aufmerksam.

**attenuate** [ə'tɛnjueɪt] vt abschwächen ♦ vi schwächer werden.

**attest** [ə'tɛst] vt, vi: **to ~ (to)** bezeugen.

**attic** ['ætɪk] n Dachboden m.

**attire** [ə'taɪə°] n Kleidung f.

**attitude** ['ætɪtjuːd] n (posture, manner) Haltung f; (mental): ~ **to** or **towards** Einstellung f zu.

**attorney** [ə'tɔːnɪ] n (US: lawyer) (Rechts)anwalt m, (Rechts)anwältin f; (having proxy) Bevollmächtigte(r) f(m); **power of ~** Vollmacht f.

**Attorney General** n (BRIT) ≈ Justizminister(in) m(f); (US) ≈ Generalbundesanwalt m, Generalbundesanwältin f.

**attract** [ə'trækt] vt (draw) anziehen; (interest) auf sich acc lenken; (attention) erregen.

**attraction** [ə'trækʃən] n Anziehungskraft f; (of house, city) Reiz m; (gen pl: amusements) Attraktion f; (fig) **to feel an ~ towards sb/sth** sich von jdm/etw angezogen fühlen.

**attractive** [ə'træktɪv] adj attraktiv; (price, idea, offer) verlockend, reizvoll.

**attribute** [n 'ætrɪbjuːt, vt ə'trɪbjuːt] n Eigenschaft f ♦ vt: **to ~ sth to** (cause) etw zurückführen auf +acc; (poem, painting) etw zuschreiben +dat; (quality) etw beimessen +dat.

**attribution** [ætrɪ'bjuːʃən] n (see vt) Zurückführung f; Zuschreibung f; Beimessung f.

**attrition** [ə'trɪʃən] n: **war of ~** Zermürbungskrieg m.

**Atty. Gen.** abbr = **Attorney General**.

**ATV** n abbr (= all-terrain vehicle) Geländefahrzeug nt.

**atypical** [eɪ'tɪpɪkl] adj atypisch.

**aubergine** ['əubəʒiːn] n Aubergine f; (colour) Aubergine nt.

**auburn** ['ɔːbən] adj rotbraun.

**auction** ['ɔːkʃən] n (also: **sale by ~**) Versteigerung f, Auktion f ♦ vt versteigern.

**auctioneer** [ɔːkʃə'nɪə°] n Versteigerer m.

**auction room** n Auktionssaal m.

**audacious** [ɔː'deɪʃəs] adj wagemutig, kühn.

**audacity** [ɔː'dæsɪtɪ] n Kühnheit f, Verwegenheit f; (pej: impudence) Dreistigkeit f.

**audible** ['ɔːdɪbl] adj hörbar.

**audience** ['ɔːdɪəns] n Publikum nt; (RADIO) Zuhörer pl; (TV) Zuschauer pl; (with queen etc) Audienz f.

**audiotypist** ['ɔːdɪəʊtaɪpɪst] n Phonotypist(in) m(f).

**audiovisual** ['ɔːdɪəu'vɪzjuəl] adj audiovisuell.

**audiovisual aid** n audiovisuelles Lehrmittel nt.

**audit** ['ɔːdɪt] vt (COMM) prüfen ♦ n Buchprüfung f, Rechnungsprüfung f.

**audition** [ɔː'dɪʃən] n Vorsprechprobe f ♦ vi: **to ~ (for)** vorsprechen (für).

**auditor** ['ɔːdɪtə°] n Buchprüfer(in) m(f), Rechnungsprüfer(in) m(f).

**auditorium** [ɔːdɪ'tɔːrɪəm] n (building) Auditorium nt; (audience area)

Zuschauerraum *m*.

**Aug.** *abbr* = **August.**

**augment** [ɔːgˈmɛnt] *vt* vermehren; (*income, diet*) verbessern.

**augur** [ˈɔːgə*] *vi*: **it ~s well** das ist ein gutes Zeichen *or* Omen.

**August** [ˈɔːgəst] *n* August *m*; *see also* **July.**

**august** [ɔːˈgʌst] *adj* erhaben.

**aunt** [ɑːnt] *n* Tante *f*.

**auntie** [ˈɑːntɪ] *n dimin of* **aunt.**

**aunty** [ˈɑːntɪ] *n dimin of* **aunt.**

**au pair** [ˈəʊˈpɛə*] *n* (*also*: ~ **girl**) Au-Pair (-Mädchen) *nt*.

**aura** [ˈɔːrə] *n* Aura *f*.

**auspices** [ˈɔːspɪsɪz] *npl*: **under the ~ of** unter der Schirmherrschaft +*gen*.

**auspicious** [ɔːsˈpɪʃəs] *adj* verheißungsvoll; (*opening, start*) vielversprechend.

**austere** [ɒsˈtɪə*] *adj* streng; (*room, decoration*) schmucklos; (*person, lifestyle*) asketisch.

**austerity** [ɒsˈtɛrɪtɪ] *n* Strenge *f*; (*of room etc*) Schmucklosigkeit *f*; (*hardship*) Entbehrung *f*.

**Australasia** [ɔːstrəˈleɪzɪə] *n* Australien und Ozeanien *nt*.

**Australasian** [ɔːstrəˈleɪzɪən] *adj* ozeanisch, südwestpazifisch.

**Australia** [ɒsˈtreɪlɪə] *n* Australien *nt*.

**Australian** [ɒsˈtreɪlɪən] *adj* australisch ◆ *n* Australier(in) *m(f)*.

**Austria** [ˈɒstrɪə] *n* Österreich *nt*.

**Austrian** [ˈɒstrɪən] *adj* österreichisch ◆ *n* Österreicher(in) *m(f)*.

**AUT** (*BRIT*) *n abbr* (= *Association of University Teachers*) *Gewerkschaft der Universitätsdozenten.*

**authentic** [ɔːˈθɛntɪk] *adj* authentisch.

**authenticate** [ɔːˈθɛntɪkeɪt] *vt* beglaubigen.

**authenticity** [ɔːθɛnˈtɪsɪtɪ] *n* Echtheit *f*.

**author** [ˈɔːθə*] *n* (*of text*) Verfasser(in) *m(f)*; (*profession*) Autor(in) *m(f)*, Schriftsteller(in) *m(f)*; (*creator*) Urheber(in) *m(f)*; (: *of plan*) Initiator(in) *m(f)*.

**authoritarian** [ɔːθɒrɪˈtɛərɪən] *adj* autoritär.

**authoritative** [ɔːˈθɒrɪtətɪv] *adj* (*person, manner*) bestimmt, entschieden; (*source, account*) zuverlässig; (*study, treatise*) maßgeblich, maßgebend.

**authority** [ɔːˈθɒrɪtɪ] *n* Autorität *f*; (*government body*) Behörde *f*, Amt *nt*; (*official permission*) Genehmigung *f*; **the authorities** *npl* (*ruling body*) die Behörden *pl*; **to have the ~ to do sth** befugt sein, etw zu tun.

**authorization** [ɔːθəraɪˈzeɪʃən] *n* Genehmigung *f*.

**authorize** [ˈɔːθəraɪz] *vt* genehmigen; **to ~ sb to do sth** jdn ermächtigen, etw zu tun.

**authorized capital** [ˈɔːθəraɪzd-] *n* autorisiertes Aktienkapital *nt*.

**authorship** [ˈɔːθəʃɪp] *n* Autorschaft *f*, Verfasserschaft *f*.

**autistic** [ɔːˈtɪstɪk] *adj* autistisch.

**auto** [ˈɔːtəʊ] (*US*) *n* Auto *nt*, Wagen *m*.

**autobiographical** [ɔːtəbaɪəˈgræfɪkl] *adj* autobiographisch.

**autobiography** [ɔːtəbaɪˈɒgrəfɪ] *n* Autobiographie *f*.

**autocratic** [ɔːtəˈkrætɪk] *adj* autokratisch.

**Autocue** ® [ˈɔːtəʊkjuː] *n* Teleprompter *m*.

**autograph** [ˈɔːtəgraːf] *n* Autogramm *nt* ◆ *vt* signieren.

**autoimmune** [ɔːtəʊɪˈmjuːn] *adj* (*disease*) Autoimmun-.

**automat** [ˈɔːtəmæt] *n* Automat *m*; (*US*) Automatenrestaurant *nt*.

**automata** [ɔːˈtɒmətə] *npl of* **automaton.**

**automate** [ˈɔːtəmeɪt] *vt* automatisieren.

**automatic** [ɔːtəˈmætɪk] *adj* automatisch ◆ *n* (*gun*) automatische Waffe; (*washing machine*) Waschautomat *m*; (*car*) Automatikwagen *m*.

**automatically** [ɔːtəˈmætɪklɪ] *adv* automatisch.

**automatic data processing** *n* automatische Datenverarbeitung *f*.

**automation** [ɔːtəˈmeɪʃən] *n* Automatisierung *f*.

**automaton** [ɔːˈtɒmətən] (*pl* **automata**) *n* Roboter *m*.

**automobile** [ˈɔːtəməbiːl] (*US*) *n* Auto(mobil) *nt*.

**autonomous** [ɔːˈtɒnəməs] *adj* autonom.

**autonomy** [ɔːˈtɒnəmɪ] *n* Autonomie *f*.

**autopsy** [ˈɔːtɒpsɪ] *n* Autopsie *f*.

**autumn** [ˈɔːtəm] *n* Herbst *m*; **in ~** im Herbst.

**autumnal** [ɔːˈtʌmnəl] *adj* herbstlich.

**auxiliary** [ɔːgˈzɪlɪərɪ] *adj* (*tool, verb*) Hilfs- ◆ *n* (*assistant*) Hilfskraft *f*.

**AV** *n abbr* (*BIBLE*: = *Authorized Version*) *englische Bibelübersetzung von 1611* ◆ *abbr* = **audiovisual.**

**Av.** *abbr* = **avenue.**

**avail** [əˈveɪl] *vt*: **to ~ o.s. of** Gebrauch machen von ◆ *n*: **to no ~** vergeblich, erfolglos.

**availability** [əveɪləˈbɪlɪtɪ] *n* Erhältlichkeit *f*; (*of staff*) Vorhandensein *nt*.

**available** [əˈveɪləbl] *adj* erhältlich; (*person: unoccupied*) frei, abkömmlich; (: *unattached*) zu haben; (*time*) frei, verfügbar; **every ~ means alle verfügbaren Mittel**; **is the manager ~?** ist der Geschäftsführer zu sprechen?; **to make sth ~ to sb** jdm etw zur Verfügung stellen.

**avalanche** [ˈævəlɑːnʃ] *n* (*also fig*) Lawine *f*.

**avant-garde** [ˈævɑ̃ŋˈgɑːd] *adj* avantgardistisch.

**avarice** [ˈævərɪs] *n* Habsucht *f*.

**avaricious** [ævəˈrɪʃəs] *adj* habsüchtig.

**avdp.** *abbr* (= *avoirdupois*) *Handelsgewicht.*

**Ave** *abbr* = **avenue.**

**avenge** [əˈvɛndʒ] *vt* rächen.

**avenue** [ˈævənjuː] *n* Straße *f*; (*drive*) Auffahrt *f*; (*means*) Weg *m*.

**average** [ˈævərɪdʒ] *n* Durchschnitt *m* ◆ *adj* durchschnittlich, Durchschnitts- ◆ *vt* (*reach an average of*) einen Durchschnitt erreichen von; **on** ~ im Durchschnitt, durchschnittlich; **above/below (the)** ~ über/unter dem Durchschnitt.

▶**average out** vi: **to** ~ **out at** durchschnittlich ausmachen.

**averse** [ə'vəːs] adj: **to be** ~ **to sth/doing sth** eine Abneigung gegen etw haben/dagegen haben, etw zu tun; **I wouldn't be** ~ **to a drink** ich hätte nichts gegen einen Drink.

**aversion** [ə'vəːʃən] n Abneigung f; **to have an** ~ **to sb/sth** eine Abneigung gegen jdn/etw haben.

**avert** [ə'vəːt] vt (prevent) verhindern; (ward off) abwehren; (turn away) abwenden.

**aviary** ['eɪvɪərɪ] n Vogelhaus nt.

**aviation** [eɪvɪ'eɪʃən] n Luftfahrt f.

**avid** ['ævɪd] adj begeistert, eifrig.

**avidly** ['ævɪdlɪ] adv begeistert, eifrig.

**avocado** [ævə'kɑːdəu] (BRIT) n (also: ~ **pear**) Avocado f.

**avoid** [ə'vɔɪd] vt (person, obstacle) ausweichen +dat; (trouble) vermeiden; (danger) meiden.

**avoidable** [ə'vɔɪdəbl] adj vermeidbar.

**avoidance** [ə'vɔɪdəns] n (of tax) Umgehung f; (of issue) Vermeidung f.

**avowed** [ə'vaud] adj erklärt.

**AVP** (US) n abbr (= assistant vice president) stellvertretender Vizepräsident.

**avuncular** [ə'vʌŋkjulə•] adj onkelhaft.

**AWACS** ['eɪwæks] n abbr (= airborne warning and control system) AWACS.

**await** [ə'weɪt] vt warten auf +acc; ~**ing attention/delivery** zur Bearbeitung/ Lieferung bestimmt; **long** ~**ed** langersehnt.

**awake** [ə'weɪk] (pt awoke, pp awoken or awaked) adj wach ♦ vt wecken ♦ vi erwachen, aufwachen; ~ **to** sich dat bewußt werden +gen.

**awakening** [ə'weɪknɪŋ] n (also fig) Erwachen nt.

**award** [ə'wɔːd] n Preis m; (for bravery) Auszeichnung f; (damages) Entschädigung(ssumme) f ♦ vt (prize) verleihen; (damages) zusprechen.

**aware** [ə'wɛə•] adj: ~ (**of**) bewußt +gen; **to become** ~ **of** sich dat bewußt werden +gen; **to become** ~ **that** ... sich dat bewußt werden, daß ...; **politically/socially** ~ politik-/ sozialbewußt; **I am fully** ~ **that** es ist mir völlig klar or bewußt, daß.

**awareness** [ə'wɛənɪs] n Bewußtsein nt; **to develop people's** ~ **of sth** den Menschen etw zu Bewußtsein bringen.

**awash** [ə'wɔʃ] adj (also fig) überflutet.

**away** [ə'weɪ] adv weg, fort; (position) entfernt; **two kilometres** ~ zwei Kilometer entfernt; **two hours** ~ **by car** zwei Autostunden entfernt; **the holiday was two weeks** ~ es war noch zwei Wochen bis zum Urlaub; **he's** ~ **for a week** er ist eine Woche nicht da; **he's** ~ **in Milan** er ist in Mailand; **to take** ~ **(from)** (remove) entfernen (von); (subtract)

abziehen (von); **to work/pedal** etc ~ unablässig arbeiten/strampeln etc; **to fade** ~ (colour, light) verblassen; (sound) verhallen; (enthusiasm) schwinden.

**away game** n Auswärtsspiel nt.

**awe** [ɔː] n Ehrfurcht f.

**awe-inspiring** ['ɔːɪnspaɪərɪŋ] adj ehrfurchtgebietend.

**awesome** ['ɔːsəm] adj ehrfurchtgebietend; (fig: inf) überwältigend.

**awe-struck** ['ɔːstrʌk] adj von Ehrfurcht ergriffen.

**awful** ['ɔːfəl] adj furchtbar, schrecklich; **an** ~ **lot (of)** furchtbar viel(e).

**awfully** ['ɔːfəlɪ] adv furchtbar, schrecklich.

**awhile** [ə'waɪl] adv eine Weile.

**awkward** ['ɔːkwəd] adj (clumsy) unbeholfen; (inconvenient, difficult) ungünstig; (embarrassing) peinlich.

**awkwardness** ['ɔːkwədnɪs] n (see adj) Unbeholfenheit f; Ungünstigkeit f; Peinlichkeit f.

**awl** [ɔːl] n Ahle f, Pfriem m.

**awning** ['ɔːnɪŋ] n (of tent, caravan) Vordach nt; (of shop etc) Markise f.

**awoke** [ə'wəuk] pt of **awake**.

**awoken** [ə'wəukən] pp of **awake**.

**AWOL** ['eɪwɔl] abbr (MIL: = absent without leave) see **absent**.

**awry** [ə'raɪ] adv: **to be** ~ (clothes) schief sitzen; **to go** ~ schiefgehen.

**axe**, (US) **ax** [æks] n Axt f, Beil nt ♦ vt (employee) entlassen; (project, jobs etc) streichen; **to have an** ~ **to grind** (fig) ein persönliches Interesse haben.

**axes**[1] ['æksɪz] npl of **ax(e)**.

**axes**[2] ['æksiːz] npl of **axis**.

**axiom** ['æksɪəm] n Axiom nt, Grundsatz m.

**axiomatic** [æksɪəu'mætɪk] adj axiomatisch.

**axis** ['æksɪs] (pl **axes**[2]) n Achse f.

**axle** ['æksl] n (also: ~**tree**) Achse f.

**aye** [aɪ] excl (yes) ja ♦ n: **the** ~**s** die Jastimmen pl.

**AYH** n abbr (= American Youth Hostels) Jugendherbergsverband, ≈ DJHV m.

**AZ** (US) abbr (POST: = Arizona).

**azalea** [ə'zeɪlɪə] n Azalee f.

**Azerbaijan** [æzəbaɪ'dʒɑːn] n Aserbaidschan nt.

**Azerbaijani** [æzəbaɪ'dʒɑːnɪ], **Azeri** [ə'zeərɪ] adj aserbaidschanisch ♦ n Aserbaidschaner(in) m(f).

**Azores** [ə'zɔːz] npl: **the** ~ die Azoren pl.

**AZT** n abbr (= azidothymidine) AZT nt.

**Aztec** ['æztɛk] adj aztekisch ♦ n Azteke m, Aztekin f.

**azure** ['eɪʒə•] adj azurblau, tiefblau.

# *B, b*

**B¹, b** [biː] *n* (*letter*) B *nt*, b *nt*; (*SCOL*) ≈ Zwei *f*,
Gut *nt*; ~ **for Benjamin**, (*US*) ~ **for Baker** ≈ B
wie Bertha; ~ **road** (*BRIT*) Landstraße *f*.
**B²** [biː] *n* (*MUS*) H *nt*, h *nt*.
**b.** *abbr* = **born**.
**BA** *n abbr* (= *Bachelor of Arts*) *see* **bachelor**;
(= *British Academy*) *Verband zur Förderung
der Künste und Geisteswissenschaften*.
**babble** ['bæbl] *vi* schwatzen; (*baby*) plappern;
(*brook*) plätschern ♦ *n:* **a** ~ **of voices** ein
Stimmengewirr *nt*.
**babe** [beɪb] *n* (*liter*) Kindlein *nt*; (*esp US:
address*) Schätzchen *nt*; ~ **in arms** Säugling
*m*.
**baboon** [bə'buːn] *n* Pavian *m*.
**baby** ['beɪbɪ] *n* Baby *nt*; (*US: inf: darling*) Schatz
*m*, Schätzchen *nt*.
**baby carriage** (*US*) *n* Kinderwagen *m*.
**baby grand** *n* (*also:* ~ **piano**) Stutzflügel *m*.
**babyhood** ['beɪbɪhud] *n* frühe Kindheit *f*.
**babyish** ['beɪbɪɪʃ] *adj* kindlich.
**baby-minder** ['beɪbɪˈmaɪndəˀ] (*BRIT*) *n*
Tagesmutter *f*.
**baby-sit** ['beɪbɪsɪt] *vi* babysitten.
**baby-sitter** ['beɪbɪsɪtəˀ] *n* Babysitter(in) *m(f)*.
**bachelor** ['bætʃələˀ] *n* Junggeselle *m*; **B~ of
Arts/Science (degree)** ≈ Magister *m* der
philosophischen Fakultät/der
Naturwissenschaften.
**bachelorhood** ['bætʃələhud] *n*
Junggesellentum *nt*.
**bachelor party** (*US*) *n* Junggesellenparty *f*.

---

**Bachelor's Degree** *ist der akademische Grad,
den man nach drei- oder vierjährigem
erfolgreich abgeschlossenem Universitäts-
studium erhält. Die am häufigsten verliehenen
Grade sind* **BA** (*Bachelor of Arts = Magister der
Geisteswissenschaften*), **BSc** (*Bachelor of
Science = Magister der Naturwissenschaften*),
**BEd** (*Bachelor of Education = Magister der
Erziehungswissenschaften*) *und* **LLB** (*Bachelor
of Laws = Magister der Rechtswissenschaften*).
*Siehe auch* **master's degree**, **doctorate**.

---

**back** [bæk] *n* Rücken *m*; (*of house, page*)
Rückseite *f*; (*of chair*) (Rücken)lehne *f*; (*of
train*) Ende *nt*; (*FOOTBALL*) Verteidiger *m* ♦ *vt*
(*candidate: also:* ~ **up**) unterstützen; (*horse*)
setzen *or* wetten auf +*acc*; (*car*)
zurücksetzen, zurückfahren ♦ *vi* (*also:* ~ **up:**
*person*) rückwärts gehen; (*car etc*)
zurücksetzen, zurückfahren ♦ *cpd* (*payment,
rent*) ausstehend ♦ *adv* hinten; **in the** ~ (**of
the car**) hinten (im Auto); **at the** ~ **of the
book/crowd/audience** hinten im Buch/in
der Menge/im Publikum; ~ **to front**
verkehrt herum; **to break the** ~ **of a job**
(*BRIT*) mit einer Arbeit über den Berg sein;
**to have one's** ~ **to the wall** (*fig*) in die Enge
getrieben sein; ~ **room** Hinterzimmer *nt*;
~ **garden** Garten *m* (hinter dem Haus);
~ **seat** (*AUT*) Rücksitz *m*; **to take a** ~ **seat**
(*fig*) sich zurückhalten; ~ **wheels**
Hinterräder *pl*; **he's** ~ er ist zurück *or*
wieder da; **throw the ball** ~ wirf den Ball
zurück; **he called** ~ er rief zurück; **he ran** ~
er rannte zurück; **when will you be** ~? 
wann kommen Sie wieder?; **can I have it** ~?
kann ich es zurückhaben *or* wiederhaben?
►**back down** *vi* nachgeben.
►**back on to** *vt fus:* **the house** ~**s on to the
golf course** das Haus grenzt hinten an den
Golfplatz an.
►**back out** *vi* (*of promise*) einen Rückzieher
machen.
►**back up** *vt* (*support*) unterstützen;
(*COMPUT*) sichern.
**backache** ['bækeɪk] *n* Rückenschmerzen *pl*.

---

**Back bench** *bezeichnet im britischen
Unterhaus die am weitesten vom Mittelgang
entfernten Bänke, im Gegensatz zur* **front
bench**. *Auf diesen hinteren Bänken sitzen
diejenigen Unterhausabgeordneten (auch*
**backbenchers** *genannt), die kein
Regierungsamt bzw. keine wichtige Stellung in
der Opposition innehaben.*

---

**backbencher** ['bæk'bɛntʃəˀ] (*BRIT*) *n*
Abgeordnete(r) *f(m)* (*in den hinteren Reihen
im britischen Parlament*), Hinterbänkler(in)
*m(f)* (*pej*); *see also* **back bench**.
**backbiting** ['bækbaɪtɪŋ] *n* Lästern *nt*.
**backbone** ['bækbəun] *n* (*also fig*) Rückgrat *nt*.
**backchat** ['bæktʃæt] (*BRIT: inf*) *n* Widerrede *f*.
**backcloth** ['bækklɔθ] (*BRIT*) *n* Hintergrund *m*.
**backcomb** ['bækkəum] (*BRIT*) *vt* toupieren.
**backdate** [bæk'deɪt] *vt* (zu)rückdatieren; ~**d
pay rise** rückwirkend geltende
Gehaltserhöhung *f*.
**backdrop** ['bækdrɔp] *n* = **backcloth**.
**backer** ['bækəˀ] *n* (*COMM*) Geldgeber *m*.
**backfire** [bæk'faɪəˀ] *vi* (*AUT*) Fehlzündungen
haben; (*plans*) ins Auge gehen.
**backgammon** ['bækgæmən] *n* Backgammon
*nt*.
**background** ['bækgraund] *n* Hintergrund *m*;
(*basic knowledge*) Grundkenntnisse *pl*;
(*experience*) Erfahrung *f* ♦ *cpd* (*music*)
Hintergrund-; **family** ~ Herkunft *f*; ~ **noise**
Geräuschkulisse *f*; ~ **reading** vertiefende
Lektüre *f*.
**backhand** ['bækhænd] *n* (*TENNIS: also:*

~ **stroke**) Rückhand f.
**backhanded** ['bæk'hændɪd] adj (fig: compliment) zweifelhaft.
**backhander** ['bæk'hændə*] (BRIT) n Schmiergeld nt.
**backing** ['bækɪŋ] n (fig, COMM) Unterstützung f; (MUS) Begleitung f.
**backlash** ['bæklæʃ] n (fig) Gegenreaktion f.
**backlog** ['bæklɔg] n: to have a ~ of work mit der Arbeit im Rückstand sein.
**back number** n alte Ausgabe f or Nummer f.
**backpack** ['bækpæk] n Rucksack m.
**backpacker** ['bækpækə*] n Rucksacktourist(in) m(f).
**back pay** n Nachzahlung f.
**back-pedal** ['bækpedl] vi (fig) einen Rückzieher machen.
**back-seat driver** n Mitfahrer, der dem Fahrer dazwischenredet.
**backside** ['bæksaɪd] (inf) n Hintern m.
**backslash** ['bækslæʃ] n Backslash m.
**backslide** ['bækslaɪd] vi rückfällig werden.
**backspace** ['bækspeɪs] vi (in typing) die Rücktaste betätigen.
**backstage** [bæk'steɪdʒ] adv (THEAT) hinter den Kulissen; (: in dressing-room area) in der Garderobe.
**backstreet** ['bækstriːt] n Seitenstraße f ♦ cpd: ~ **abortionist** Engelmacher(in) m(f).
**backstroke** ['bækstrəuk] n Rückenschwimmen nt.
**backtrack** ['bæktræk] vi (fig) einen Rückzieher machen.
**backup** ['bækʌp] adj (train, plane) Entlastungs-; (COMPUT: copy etc) Sicherungs- ♦ n (support) Unterstützung f; (COMPUT: also: ~ **disk**, ~ **file**) Sicherungskopie f, Backup nt.
**backward** ['bækwəd] adj (movement) Rückwärts-; (person) zurückgeblieben; (country) rückständig; ~ **and forward movement** Vor- und Zurückbewegung f; ~ **step/glance** Blick m/Schritt m zurück.
**backwards** ['bækwədz] adv rückwärts; (read) von hinten nach vorne; (fall) nach hinten; (in time) zurück; to know sth ~ or (US) ~ **and forwards** etw in- und auswendig kennen.
**backwater** ['bækwɔːtə*] n (fig) Kaff nt.
**back yard** n Hinterhof m.
**bacon** ['beɪkən] n (Frühstücks)speck m, (Schinken)speck m.
**bacteria** [bæk'tɪərɪə] npl Bakterien pl.
**bacteriology** [bæktɪərɪ'ɔlədʒɪ] n Bakteriologie f.
**bad** [bæd] adj schlecht; (naughty) unartig, ungezogen; (mistake, accident, injury) schwer; **his ~ leg** sein schlimmes Bein; **to go ~** verderben, schlecht werden; **to have a ~ time of it** es schwer haben; **I feel ~ about it** es tut mir leid; **in ~ faith** mit böser Absicht.
**bad debt** n uneinbringliche Forderung f.

**baddy** ['bædɪ] (inf) n Bösewicht m.
**bade** [bæd] pt of bid.
**badge** [bædʒ] n Plakette f; (stick-on) Aufkleber m; (fig) Merkmal nt.
**badger** ['bædʒə*] n Dachs m ♦ vt zusetzen +dat.
**badly** ['bædlɪ] adv schlecht; ~ **wounded** schwer verletzt; **he needs it** ~ er braucht es dringend; **things are going** ~ es sieht schlecht or nicht gut aus; **to be ~ off (for money)** wenig Geld haben.
**bad-mannered** ['bæd'mænəd] adj ungezogen, unhöflich.
**badminton** ['bædmɪntən] n Federball m.
**bad-tempered** ['bæd'tɛmpəd] adj schlecht gelaunt; (by nature) übellaunig.
**baffle** ['bæfl] vt verblüffen.
**baffling** ['bæflɪŋ] adj rätselhaft, verwirrend.
**bag** [bæg] n Tasche f; (made of paper, plastic) Tüte f; (handbag) (Hand)tasche f; (satchel) Schultasche f; (case) Reisetasche f; (of hunter) Jagdbeute f; (pej: woman) Schachtel f; ~**s of** (inf: lots of) jede Menge; **to pack one's ~s** die Koffer packen; ~**s under the eyes** Ringe pl unter den Augen.
**bagful** ['bægful] n: **a ~ of** eine Tasche/Tüte voll.
**baggage** ['bægɪdʒ] n Gepäck nt.
**baggage car** (US) n Gepäckwagen m.
**baggage claim** n Gepäckausgabe f.
**baggy** ['bægɪ] adj weit; (out of shape) ausgebeult.
**Baghdad** [bæg'dæd] n Bagdad nt.
**bag lady** (esp US) n Stadtstreicherin f.
**bagpipes** ['bægpaɪps] npl Dudelsack m.
**bag-snatcher** ['bægsnætʃə*] (BRIT) n Handtaschendieb(in) m(f).
**Bahamas** [bə'hɑːməz] npl: **the ~** die Bahamas pl, die Bahamainseln pl.
**Bahrain** [bɑː'reɪn] n Bahrain nt.
**bail** [beɪl] n (LAW: payment) Kaution f; (: release) Freilassung f gegen Kaution ♦ vt (prisoner) gegen Kaution freilassen; (boat: also: ~ **out**) ausschöpfen; **to be on ~** gegen Kaution freigelassen sein; **to be released on ~** gegen Kaution freigelassen werden; see also **bale.**
▶**bail out** vt (prisoner) gegen Kaution freibekommen; (firm, friend) aus der Patsche helfen +dat.
**bailiff** ['beɪlɪf] n (LAW: BRIT) Gerichtsvollzieher(in) m(f); (: US) Gerichtsdiener(in) m(f); (BRIT: factor) (Guts)verwalter(in) m(f).
**bait** [beɪt] n Köder m ♦ vt (hook, trap) mit einem Köder versehen; (tease) necken.
**baize** [beɪz] n Flausch m; **green ~** Billardtuch nt.
**bake** [beɪk] vt backen; (clay etc) brennen ♦ vi backen.
**baked beans** [beɪkt-] npl gebackene Bohnen pl (in Tomatensauce).
**baker** ['beɪkə*] n Bäcker(in) m(f).

**baker's dozen** *n* dreizehn (Stück).
**bakery** ['beɪkərɪ] *n* Bäckerei *f.*
**baking** ['beɪkɪŋ] *n* Backen *nt;* (*batch*)
Ofenladung *f* ♦ *adj* (*inf: hot*) wie im
Backofen.
**baking powder** *n* Backpulver *nt.*
**baking tin** *n* Backform *f.*
**baking tray** *n* Backblech *nt.*
**balaclava** [bælə'klɑːvə] *n* (*also:* ~ **helmet**)
Kapuzenmütze *f.*
**balance** ['bæləns] *n* (*equilibrium*)
Gleichgewicht *nt;* (*COMM: sum*) Saldo *m;*
(*remainder*) Restbetrag *m;* (*scales*) Waage *f*
♦ *vt* ausgleichen; (*AUT: wheels*) auswuchten;
(*pros and cons*) (gegeneinander) abwägen;
**on** ~ alles in allem; ~ **of trade/payments**
Handels-/Zahlungsbilanz *f;* ~ **carried**
**forward** *or* **brought forward** (*COMM*)
Saldovortrag *m,* Saldoübertrag *m;* **to** ~ **the**
**books** (*COMM*) die Bilanz ziehen *or* machen.
**balanced** ['bælənst] *adj* ausgeglichen; (*report*)
ausgewogen.
**balance sheet** *n* Bilanz *f.*
**balance wheel** *n* Unruh *f.*
**balcony** ['bælkənɪ] *n* Balkon *m;* (*in theatre*)
oberster Rang *m.*
**bald** [bɔːld] *adj* kahl; (*tyre*) abgefahren;
(*statement*) knapp.
**baldness** ['bɔːldnɪs] *n* Kahlheit *f.*
**bale** [beɪl] *n* (*AGR*) Bündel *nt;* (*of papers etc*)
Packen *m.*
▶**bale out** *vi* (*of a plane*) abspringen ♦ *vt*
(*water*) schöpfen; (*boat*) ausschöpfen.
**Balearic Islands** [bælɪ'ærɪk-] *npl:* **the** ~ die
Balearen *pl.*
**baleful** ['beɪlful] *adj* böse.
**balk** [bɔːk] *vi:* **to** ~ (**at**) (*subj: person*)
zurückschrecken (vor +*dat*); (: *horse*)
scheuen (vor +*dat*).
**Balkan** ['bɔːlkən] *adj* (*countries etc*) Balkan-
♦ *n:* **the** ~**s** der Balkan, die Balkanländer *pl.*
**ball** [bɔːl] *n* Ball *m;* (*of wool, string*) Knäuel *m or*
*nt;* **to set the** ~ **rolling** (*fig*) den Stein ins
Rollen bringen; **to play** ~ (**with sb**) (*fig*) (mit
jdm) mitspielen; **to be on the** ~ (*fig:*
*competent*) am Ball sein; (: *alert*) auf Draht
*or* Zack sein; **the** ~ **is in their court** (*fig*) sie
sind am Ball.
**ballad** ['bæləd] *n* Ballade *f.*
**ballast** ['bæləst] *n* Ballast *m.*
**ball bearing** *npl* Kugellager *nt;* (*individual ball*)
Kugellagerkugel *f.*
**ball cock** *n* Schwimmerhahn *m.*
**ballerina** [bælə'riːnə] *n* Ballerina *f.*
**ballet** ['bæleɪ] *n* Ballett *nt.*
**ballet dancer** *n* Ballettänzer(in) *m(f).*
**ballistic** [bə'lɪstɪk] *adj* ballistisch.
**ballistic missile** *n* Raketengeschoß *nt.*
**ballistics** [bə'lɪstɪks] *n* Ballistik *f.*
**balloon** [bə'luːn] *n* (Luft)ballon *m;* (*hot air*
*balloon*) Heißluftballon *m;* (*in comic strip*)
Sprechblase *f.*

**balloonist** [bə'luːnɪst] *n* Ballonfahrer(in) *m(f).*
**ballot** ['bælət] *n* (geheime) Abstimmung *f.*
**ballot box** *n* Wahlurne *f.*
**ballot paper** *n* Stimmzettel *m.*
**ballpark** ['bɔːlpɑːk] (*US*) *n* (*SPORT*)
Baseballstadion *nt.*
**ballpark figure** (*inf*) *n* Richtzahl *f.*
**ballpoint (pen)** ['bɔːlpɔɪnt(-)] *n*
Kugelschreiber *m.*
**ballroom** ['bɔːlrum] *n* Tanzsaal *m.*
**balls** [bɔːlz] (*inf!*) *npl* (*testicles*) Eier *pl* (*!*);
(*courage*) Schneid *m,* Mumm *m* ♦ *excl* red
keinen Scheiß! (*!*).
**balm** [bɑːm] *n* Balsam *m.*
**balmy** ['bɑːmɪ] *adj* (*breeze*) sanft; (*air*) lau,
lind; (*BRIT: inf*) = **barmy.**
**BALPA** ['bælpə] *n abbr* (= *British Airline Pilots'*
*Association*) *Flugpilotengewerkschaft.*
**balsam** ['bɔːlsəm] *n* Balsam *m.*
**balsa (wood)** ['bɔːlsə-] *n* Balsaholz *nt.*
**Baltic** ['bɔːltɪk] *n:* **the** ~ **(Sea)** die Ostsee.
**balustrade** [bæləs'treɪd] *n* Balustrade *f.*
**bamboo** [bæm'buː] *n* Bambus *m.*
**bamboozle** [bæm'buːzl] (*inf*) *vt* hereinlegen;
**to** ~ **sb into doing sth** jdn durch Tricks
dazu bringen, etw zu tun.
**ban** [bæn] *n* Verbot *nt* ♦ *vt* verbieten; **he was**
~**ned from driving** (*BRIT*) ihm wurde
Fahrverbot erteilt.
**banal** [bə'nɑːl] *adj* banal.
**banana** [bə'nɑːnə] *n* Banane *f.*
**band** [bænd] *n* (*group*) Gruppe *f,* Schar *f;*
(*MUS: jazz, rock etc*) Band *f;* (: *military etc*)
(Musik)kapelle *f;* (*strip, range*) Band *nt;*
(*stripe*) Streifen *m.*
▶**band together** *vi* sich zusammenschließen.
**bandage** ['bændɪdʒ] *n* Verband *m* ♦ *vt*
verbinden.
**Band-Aid** ® ['bændeɪd] (*US*) *n* Heftpflaster *nt.*
**B & B** *n abbr* = **bed and breakfast.**
**bandit** ['bændɪt] *n* Bandit *m.*
**bandstand** ['bændstænd] *n* Musikpavillion *m.*
**bandwagon** ['bændwægən] *n:* **to jump on the**
~ (*fig*) auf den fahrenden Zug aufspringen.
**bandy** ['bændɪ] *vt* (*jokes*) sich erzählen; (*ideas*)
diskutieren; (*insults*) sich an den Kopf
werfen.
▶**bandy about** *vt* (*word, expression*) immer
wieder gebrauchen; (*name*) immer wieder
nennen.
**bandy-legged** ['bændɪ'lɛgɪd] *adj* O-beinig.
**bane** [beɪn] *n:* **it/he is the** ~ **of my life** das/er
ist noch mal mein Ende.
**bang** [bæŋ] *n* (*of door*) Knallen *nt;* (*of gun,*
*exhaust*) Knall *m;* (*blow*) Schlag *m* ♦ *excl* peng
♦ *vt* (*door*) zuschlagen, zuknallen; (*one's*
*head etc*) sich *dat* stoßen +*acc* ♦ *vi* knallen
♦ *adv:* **to be** ~ **on time** (*BRIT: inf*) auf die
Sekunde pünktlich sein; **to** ~ **at the door**
gegen die Tür hämmern; **to** ~ **into sth** sich
an etw *dat* stoßen.
**banger** ['bæŋə*] (*BRIT: inf*) *n* (*car: also:* **old** ~)

Klapperkiste *f*; (*sausage*) Würstchen *nt*;
(*firework*) Knallkörper *m*.
**Bangkok** [bæŋ'kɔk] *n* Bangkok *nt*.
**Bangladesh** [bæŋglə'deʃ] *n* Bangladesch *nt*.
**bangle** ['bæŋgl] *n* Armreif(en) *m*.
**bangs** [bæŋz] (*US*) *npl* (*fringe*) Pony *m*.
**banish** ['bænɪʃ] *vt* verbannen.
**banister(s)** ['bænɪstə(z)] *n(pl)* Geländer *nt*.
**banjo** ['bændʒəu] (*pl* ~**es** *or* ~**s**) *n* Banjo *nt*.
**bank** [bæŋk] *n* Bank *f*; (*of river, lake*) Ufer *nt*;
(*of earth*) Wall *m*; (*of switches*) Reihe *f* ♦ *vi*
(*AVIAT*) sich in die Kurve legen; (*COMM*):
**they ~ with Pitt's** sie haben ihr Konto bei
Pitt's.
▶**bank on** *vt fus* sich verlassen auf +*acc*.
**bank account** *n* Bankkonto *nt*.
**bank balance** *n* Kontostand *m*.
**bank card** *n* Scheckkarte *f*.
**bank charges** (*BRIT*) *npl* Konto-
führungsgebühren *pl*.
**bank draft** *n* Bankanweisung *f*.
**banker** ['bæŋkə*] *n* Bankier *m*.
**banker's card** (*BRIT*) *n* = **bank card**.
**banker's order** (*BRIT*) *n* Dauerauftrag *m*.
**bank giro** *n* Banküberweisung *f*.
**bank holiday** (*BRIT*) *n* (öffentlicher) Feiertag
*m*.

---

*Als* **bank holiday** *wird in Großbritannien ein
gesetzlicher Feiertag bezeichnet, an dem die
Banken geschlossen sind. Die meisten dieser
Feiertage, abgesehen von Weihnachten und
Ostern, fallen auf Montage im Mai und August.
An diesen langen Wochenenden (bank holiday
weekends) fahren viele Briten in Urlaub, so
daß dann auf den Straßen, Flughäfen und bei
der Bahn sehr viel Betrieb ist.*

---

**banking** ['bæŋkɪŋ] *n* Bankwesen *nt*.
**banking hours** *npl* Schalterstunden *pl*.
**bank loan** *n* Bankkredit *m*.
**bank manager** *n* Filialleiter(in) *m(f)* (einer
Bank).
**banknote** ['bæŋknəut] *n* Geldschein *m*,
Banknote *f*.
**bank rate** *n* Diskontsatz *m*.
**bankrupt** ['bæŋkrʌpt] *adj* bankrott ♦ *n*
Bankrotteur(in) *m(f)*; **to go ~** Bankrott
machen.
**bankruptcy** ['bæŋkrʌptsɪ] *n* (*COMM, fig*)
Bankrott *m*.
**bank statement** *n* Kontoauszug *m*.
**banner** ['bænə*] *n* Banner *nt*; (*in demonstration*)
Spruchband *nt*.
**banner headline** *n* Schlagzeile *f*.
**bannister(s)** ['bænɪstə(z)] *n(pl)* = **banister(s)**.
**banns** [bænz] *npl* Aufgebot *nt*.
**banquet** ['bæŋkwɪt] *n* Bankett *nt*.
**bantamweight** ['bæntəmweɪt] *n*
Bantamgewicht *nt*.
**banter** ['bæntə*] *n* Geplänkel *nt*.
**BAOR** *n abbr* (= *British Army of the Rhine*)

britische Rheinarmee.
**baptism** ['bæptɪzəm] *n* Taufe *f*.
**Baptist** ['bæptɪst] *n* Baptist(in) *m(f)*.
**baptize** [bæp'taɪz] *vt* taufen.
**bar** [bɑː*] *n* (*for drinking*) Lokal *nt*; (*counter*)
Theke *f*; (*rod*) Stange *f*; (*on window etc*)
(Gitter)stab *m*; (*slab: of chocolate*) Tafel *f*;
(*fig: obstacle*) Hindernis *nt*; (*prohibition*)
Verbot *nt*; (*MUS*) Takt *m* ♦ *vt* (*road*)
blockieren, versperren; (*window*)
verriegeln; (*person*) ausschließen; (*activity*)
verbieten; ~ **of soap** Stück *nt* Seife; **behind
~s** hinter Gittern; **the B~** (*LAW*) die
Anwaltschaft; ~ **none** ohne Ausnahme.
**Barbados** [bɑː'beɪdɔs] *n* Barbados *nt*.
**barbaric** [bɑː'bærɪk] *adj* barbarisch.
**barbarous** ['bɑːbərəs] *adj* barbarisch.
**barbecue** ['bɑːbɪkjuː] *n* Grill *m*; (*meal, party*)
Barbecue *nt*.
**barbed wire** ['bɑːbd-] *n* Stacheldraht *m*.
**barber** ['bɑːbə*] *n* (Herren)friseur *m*.
**barbiturate** [bɑː'bɪtjurɪt] *n* Schlafmittel *nt*,
Barbiturat *nt*.
**Barcelona** [bɑːsə'ləunə] *n* Barcelona *nt*.
**bar chart** *n* Balkendiagramm *nt*.
**bar code** *n* Strichkode *m*.
**bare** [bɛə*] *adj* nackt; (*trees, countryside*) kahl;
(*minimum*) absolut ♦ *vt* entblößen; (*teeth*)
blecken; **the ~ essentials, the ~ necessities**
das Allernotwendigste; **to ~ one's soul** sein
Innerstes entblößen.
**bareback** ['bɛəbæk] *adv* ohne Sattel.
**barefaced** ['bɛəfeɪst] *adj* (*fig*) unverfroren,
schamlos.
**barefoot** ['bɛəfut] *adj* barfüßig ♦ *adv* barfuß.
**bareheaded** [bɛə'hɛdɪd] *adj* barhäuptig ♦ *adv*
ohne Kopfbedeckung.
**barely** ['bɛəlɪ] *adv* kaum.
**Barents Sea** ['bærənts-] *n:* **the ~** die
Barentssee.
**bargain** ['bɑːgɪn] *n* (*deal*) Geschäft *nt*;
(*transaction*) Handel *m*; (*good offer*)
Sonderangebot *nt*; (*good buy*) guter Kauf *m*
♦ *vi:* **to ~ (with sb)** (mit jdm) verhandeln;
(*haggle*) (mit jdm) handeln; **into the ~**
obendrein.
▶**bargain for** *vt fus:* **he got more than he ~ed
for** er bekam mehr, als er erwartet hatte.
**bargaining** ['bɑːgənɪŋ] *n* Verhandeln *nt*.
**bargaining position** *n* Verhandlungs-
position *f*.
**barge** [bɑːdʒ] *n* Lastkahn *m*, Frachtkahn *m*.
▶**barge in** *vi* (*enter*) hereinplatzen; (*interrupt*)
unterbrechen.
▶**barge into** *vt fus* (*place*) hereinplatzen;
(*person*) anrempeln.
**bargepole** ['bɑːdʒpəul] *n:* **I wouldn't touch it
with a ~** (*fig*) das würde ich nicht mal mit
der Kneifzange anfassen.
**baritone** ['bærɪtəun] *n* Bariton *m*.
**barium meal** ['bɛərɪəm-] *n* Kontrastbrei *m*.
**bark** [bɑːk] *n* (*of tree*) Rinde *f*; (*of dog*) Bellen

*nt* ♦ *vi* bellen; **she's ~ing up the wrong tree**
(*fig*) sie ist auf dem Holzweg.
**barley** ['bɑːlɪ] *n* Gerste *f*.
**barley sugar** *n* Malzbonbon *nt or m*.
**barmaid** ['bɑːmeɪd] *n* Bardame *f*.
**barman** ['bɑːmən] (*irreg: like* **man**) *n* Barmann
*m*.
**barmy** ['bɑːmɪ] (*BRIT: inf*) *adj* bekloppt.
**barn** [bɑːn] *n* Scheune *f*.
**barnacle** ['bɑːnəkl] *n* Rankenfußkrebs *m*.
**barn owl** *n* Schleiereule *f*.
**barometer** [bə'rɒmɪtə*] *n* Barometer *nt*.
**baron** ['bærən] *n* Baron *m*; **industrial ~**
Industriemagnat *m*; **press ~** Pressezar *m*.
**baroness** ['bærənɪs] *n* (*baron's wife*) Baronin *f*;
(*baron's daughter*) Baroneß *f*, Baronesse *f*.
**baronet** ['bærənɪt] *n* Baronet *m*.
**barracking** ['bærəkɪŋ] *n* Buhrufe *pl*.
**barracks** ['bærəks] *npl* Kaserne *f*.
**barrage** ['bærɑːʒ] *n* (*MIL*) Sperrfeuer *nt*; (*dam*)
Staustufe *f*; (*fig: of criticism, questions etc*)
Hagel *m*.
**barrel** ['bærəl] *n* Faß *nt*; (*of oil*) Barrel *nt*; (*of
gun*) Lauf *m*.
**barrel organ** *n* Drehorgel *f*.
**barren** ['bærən] *adj* unfruchtbar.
**barricade** [bærɪ'keɪd] *n* Barrikade *f* ♦ *vt* (*road,
entrance*) verbarrikadieren; **to ~ o.s. (in)**
sich verbarrikadieren.
**barrier** ['bærɪə*] *n* (*at frontier, entrance*)
Schranke *f*; (*BRIT: also:* **crash ~**) Leitplanke *f*;
(*fig*) Barriere *f*, (: *to progress etc*) Hindernis
*nt*.
**barrier cream** (*BRIT*) *n* Hautschutzcreme *f*.
**barring** ['bɑːrɪŋ] *prep* außer im Falle +*gen*.
**barrister** ['bærɪstə*] (*BRIT*) *n* Rechtsanwalt *m*,
Rechtsanwältin *f*.

---

**Barrister** *oder* **barrister-at-law** *ist in England die*
*Bezeichnung für einen Rechtsanwalt, der seine*
*Klienten vor allem vor Gericht vertritt; im*
*Gegensatz zum* **solicitor**, *der nicht vor Gericht*
*auftritt, sondern einen barrister mit dieser*
*Aufgabe beauftragt.*

---

**barrow** ['bærəu] *n* Schubkarre *f*, Schubkarren
*m*; (*cart*) Karren *m*.
**bar stool** *n* Barhocker *m*.
**Bart.** (*BRIT*) *abbr* = **baronet**.
**bartender** ['bɑːtɛndə*] (*US*) *n* Barmann *m*.
**barter** ['bɑːtə*] *n* Tauschhandel *m* ♦ *vt*: **to
~ sth for sth** etw gegen etw tauschen.
**base** [beɪs] *n* (*of tree etc*) Fuß *m*; (*of cup, box
etc*) Boden *m*; (*foundation*) Grundlage *f*;
(*centre*) Stützpunkt *m*, Standort *m*; (*for
organization*) Sitz *m* ♦ *adj* gemein,
niederträchtig ♦ *vt*: **to ~ sth on** etw gründen
*or* basieren auf +*acc*; **to be ~d at** (*troops*)
stationiert sein in +*dat*; (*employee*) arbeiten
in +*dat*; **I'm ~d in London** ich wohne in
London; **a Paris-~d firm** eine Firma mit Sitz
in Paris; **coffee-~d** auf Kaffeebasis.

**baseball** ['beɪsbɔːl] *n* Baseball *m*.
**baseboard** ['beɪsbɔːd] (*US*) *n* Fußleiste *f*.
**base camp** *n* Basislager *nt*,
Versorgungslager *nt*.
**Basel** [bɑːl] *n* = **Basle**.
**baseline** ['beɪslaɪn] *n* (*TENNIS*) Grundlinie *f*;
(*fig: standard*) Ausgangspunkt *m*.
**basement** ['beɪsmənt] *n* Keller *m*.
**base rate** *n* Eckzins *m*, Leitzins *m*.
**bases**[1] ['beɪsɪz] *npl of* **base**.
**bases**[2] ['beɪsiːz] *npl of* **basis**.
**bash** [bæʃ] (*inf*) *vt* schlagen, hauen ♦ *n*: **I'll
have a ~ (at it)** (*BRIT*) ich probier's mal.
►**bash up** *vt* (*car*) demolieren; (*BRIT: person*)
vermöbeln.
**bashful** ['bæʃful] *adj* schüchtern.
**bashing** ['bæʃɪŋ] (*inf*) *n* Prügel *pl*; **Paki-/
queer-~** Überfälle *pl* auf Pakistaner/
Schwule.
**BASIC** ['beɪsɪk] *n* (*COMPUT*) BASIC *nt*.
**basic** ['beɪsɪk] *adj* (*method, needs etc*) Grund-;
(*principles*) grundlegend; (*problem*)
grundsätzlich; (*knowledge*) elementar;
(*facilities*) primitiv.
**basically** ['beɪsɪklɪ] *adv* im Grunde.
**basic rate** *n* Eingangssteuersatz *m*.
**basics** ['beɪsɪks] *npl*: **the ~** das Wesentliche.
**basil** ['bæzl] *n* Basilikum *nt*.
**basin** ['beɪsn] *n* Gefäß *nt*; (*BRIT: for food*)
Schüssel *f*; (*also:* **wash ~**) (Wasch)becken *nt*;
(*of river, lake*) Becken *nt*.
**basis** ['beɪsɪs] (*pl* **bases**) *n* Basis *f*, Grundlage *f*;
**on a part-time ~** stundenweise; **on a trial ~**
zur Probe; **on the ~ of what you've said** auf
Grund dessen, was Sie gesagt haben.
**bask** [bɑːsk] *vi*: **to ~ in the sun** sich sonnen.
**basket** ['bɑːskɪt] *n* Korb *m*; (*smaller*) Körbchen
*nt*.
**basketball** ['bɑːskɪtbɔːl] *n* Basketball *m*.
**basketball player** *n* Basketballspieler(in)
*m(f)*.
**Basle** [bɑːl] *n* Basel *nt*.
**basmati rice** [bəz'mætɪ-] *n* Basmatireis *m*.
**Basque** [bæsk] *adj* baskisch ♦ *n* Baske *m*,
Baskin *f*.
**bass** [beɪs] *n* Baß *m*.
**bass clef** *n* Baßschlüssel *m*.
**bassoon** [bə'suːn] *n* Fagott *nt*.
**bastard** ['bɑːstəd] *n* uneheliches Kind *nt*; (*inf!*)
Arschloch *nt* (*!*).
**baste** [beɪst] *vt* (*CULIN*) (mit Fett und
Bratensaft) begießen; (*SEWING*) heften,
reihen.
**bastion** ['bæstɪən] *n* Bastion *f*.
**bat** [bæt] *n* (*ZOOL*) Fledermaus *f*; (*for cricket,
baseball etc*) Schlagholz *nt*; (*BRIT: for table
tennis*) Schläger *m* ♦ *vt*: **he didn't ~ an eyelid**
er hat nicht mit der Wimper gezuckt; **off
one's own ~** auf eigene Faust.
**batch** [bætʃ] *n* (*of bread*) Schub *m*; (*of letters,
papers*) Stoß *m*, Stapel *m*; (*of applicants*)
Gruppe *f*; (*of work*) Schwung *m*; (*of goods*)

Ladung *f*, Sendung *f*.
**batch processing** *n* (*COMPUT*)
Stapelverarbeitung *f*.
**bated** ['beɪtɪd] *adj*: **with ~ breath** mit
angehaltenem Atem.
**bath** [bɑːθ] *n* Bad *nt*; (*bathtub*) (Bade)wanne *f*
♦ *vt* baden; **to have a ~** baden, ein Bad
nehmen; *see also* **baths**.
**bathe** [beɪð] *vi*, *vt* (*also fig*) baden.
**bather** ['beɪðə'] *n* Badende(r) *f(m)*.
**bathing** ['beɪðɪŋ] *n* Baden *nt*.
**bathing cap** *n* Bademütze *f*, Badekappe *f*.
**bathing costume,** (*US*) **bathing suit** *n*
Badeanzug *m*.
**bath mat** *n* Bademattte *f*, Badevorleger *m*.
**bathrobe** ['bɑːθrəʊb] *n* Bademantel *m*.
**bathroom** ['bɑːθrʊm] *n* Bad(ezimmer) *nt*.
**baths** [bɑːðz] *npl* (*also*: **swimming ~**)
(Schwimm)bad *nt*.
**bath towel** *n* Badetuch *nt*.
**bathtub** ['bɑːθtʌb] *n* (Bade)wanne *f*.
**batman** ['bætmən] (*irreg: like* **man**) (*BRIT*) *n*
(*MIL*) (Offiziers)bursche *m*.
**baton** ['bætən] *n* (*MUS*) Taktstock *m*;
(*ATHLETICS*) Staffelholz *nt*; (*policeman's*)
Schlagstock *m*.
**battalion** [bə'tælɪən] *n* Bataillon *nt*.
**batten** ['bætn] *n* Leiste *f*, Latte *f*; (*NAUT: on
sail*) Segellatte *f*.
►**batten down** *vt* (*NAUT*): **to ~ down the
hatches** die Luken dicht machen.
**batter** ['bætə'] *vt* schlagen, mißhandeln; (*subj:
rain*) schlagen; (*wind*) rütteln ♦ *n* (*CULIN*)
Teig *m*; (*for frying*) (Ausback)teig *m*.
**battered** ['bætəd] *adj* (*hat, pan*) verbeult;
**~ wife** mißhandelte Ehefrau; **~ child**
mißhandeltes Kind.
**battering ram** ['bætərɪŋ-] *n* Rammbock *m*.
**battery** ['bætərɪ] *n* Batterie *f*; (*of tests,
reporters*) Reihe *f*.
**battery charger** *n* (Batterie)ladegerät *nt*.
**battery farming** *n* Batteriehaltung *f*.
**battle** ['bætl] *n* (*MIL*) Schlacht *f*; (*fig*) Kampf *m*
♦ *vi* kämpfen; **that's half the ~** damit ist
schon viel gewonnen; **it's a losing ~, we're
fighting a losing ~** (*fig*) es ist ein
aussichtsloser Kampf.
**battledress** ['bætldrɛs] *n* Kampfanzug *m*.
**battlefield** ['bætlfiːld] *n* Schlachtfeld *nt*.
**battlements** ['bætlmənts] *npl* Zinnen *pl*.
**battleship** ['bætlʃɪp] *n* Schlachtschiff *nt*.
**batty** ['bætɪ] (*inf*) *adj* verrückt.
**bauble** ['bɔːbl] *n* Flitter *m*.
**baud** [bɔːd] *n* (*COMPUT*) Baud *nt*.
**baud rate** *n* (*COMPUT*) Baudrate *f*.
**baulk** [bɔːlk] *vi* = **balk**.
**bauxite** ['bɔːksaɪt] *n* Bauxit *m*.
**Bavaria** [bə'vɛərɪə] *n* Bayern *nt*.
**Bavarian** [bə'vɛərɪən] *adj* bay(e)risch ♦ *n*
Bayer(in) *m(f)*.
**bawdy** ['bɔːdɪ] *adj* derb, obszön.
**bawl** [bɔːl] *vi* brüllen, schreien.

**bay** [beɪ] *n* Bucht *f*; (*BRIT: for parking*)
Parkbucht *f*; (: *for loading*) Ladeplatz *m*;
(*horse*) Braune(r) *m*; **to hold sb at ~** jdn in
Schach halten.
**bay leaf** *n* Lorbeerblatt *nt*.
**bayonet** ['beɪənɪt] *n* Bajonett *nt*.
**bay tree** *n* Lorbeerbaum *m*.
**bay window** *n* Erkerfenster *nt*.
**bazaar** [bə'zɑː'] *n* Basar *m*.
**bazooka** [bə'zuːkə] *n* Panzerfaust *f*.
**BB** (*BRIT*) *n abbr* (= *Boys' Brigade*)
*Jugendorganisation für Jungen*.
**BBB** (*US*) *n abbr* (= *Better Business Bureau*)
*amerikanische Verbraucherbehörde*.
**BBC** *n abbr* BBC *f*.

> **BBC** (*Abkürzung für British Broadcasting
Corporation*) ist die staatliche britische
Rundfunk- und Fernsehanstalt. Die
Fernsehsender BBC1 und BBC2 bieten beide
ein umfangreiches Fernsehprogramm, wobei
BBC1 mehr Sendungen von allgemeinem
Interesse wie z.B. leichte Unterhaltung, Sport,
Aktuelles, Kinderprogramme und
Außenübertragungen zeigt. BBC2
berücksichtigt Reisesendungen, Drama, Musik
und internationale Filme. Die 5 landesweiten
Radiosender bieten von Popmusik bis Kricket
etwas für jeden Geschmack; dazu gibt es noch
37 regionale Radiosender. Der BBC World
Service ist auf der ganzen Welt auf Englisch
oder in einer von 35 anderen Sprachen zu
empfangen. Finanziert wird die BBC vor allem
durch Fernsehgebühren und ins Ausland
verkaufte Sendungen. Obwohl die BBC dem
Parlament verantwortlich ist, werden die
Sendungen nicht vom Staat kontrolliert.

**BC** *adv abbr* (= *before Christ*) v. Chr. ♦ *abbr*
(*CANADA*: = *British Columbia*) Britisch-
Kolumbien *nt*.
**BCG** *n abbr* (= *bacille Calmette-Guérin*) BCG *m*.
**BD** *n abbr* (= *Bachelor of Divinity*)
*akademischer Grad in Theologie*.
**B/D** *abbr* = **bank draft**.
**BDS** *n abbr* (= *Bachelor of Dental Surgery*)
*akademischer Grad in Zahnmedizin*.
**B/E** *abbr* = **bill of exchange**.

═══════════════════════════ *KEYWORD*

**be** [biː] (*pt* **was, were**, *pp* **been**) *aux vb* **1** (*with
present participle: forming continuous tenses*):
**what are you doing?** was machst du?; **it is
raining** es regnet; **have you been to Rome?**
waren Sie schon einmal in Rom?
**2** (*with pp: forming passives*) werden; **to
~ killed** getötet werden; **the box had been
opened** die Kiste war geöffnet worden
**3** (*in tag questions*): **he's good-looking, isn't
he?** er sieht gut aus, nicht (wahr)?; **she's
back again, is she?** sie ist wieder da, oder?
**4** (+ *to* + *infinitive*): **the house is to ~ sold** das

Haus soll verkauft werden; **he's not to open it** er darf es nicht öffnen
♦ *vb + complement* **1** sein; **I'm tired/English** ich bin müde/Engländer(in); **I'm hot/cold** mir ist heiß/kalt; **2 and 2 are 4** 2 und 2 ist *or* macht 4; **she's tall/pretty** sie ist groß/hübsch; ~ **careful/quiet** sei vorsichtig/ruhig
**2** (*of health*): **how are you?** wie geht es Ihnen?
**3** (*of age*): **how old are you?** wie alt bist du?; **I'm sixteen (years old)** ich bin sechzehn (Jahre alt)
**4** (*cost*) kosten; **how much was the meal?** was hat das Essen gekostet?; **that'll ~ 5 pounds please** das macht 5 Pfund, bitte
♦ *vi* **1** (*exist, occur etc*) sein; **there is/are** es gibt; **is there a God?** gibt es einen Gott?; ~ **that as it may** wie dem auch sei; **so ~ it** gut (und schön)
**2** (*referring to place*) sein, liegen; **Edinburgh is in Scotland** Edinburgh liegt *or* ist in Schottland; **I won't ~ here tomorrow** morgen bin ich nicht da
**3** (*referring to movement*) sein; **where have you been?** wo warst du?
♦ *impers vb* **1** (*referring to time, distance, weather*) sein; **it's 5 o'clock** es ist 5 Uhr; **it's 10 km to the village** es sind 10 km bis zum Dorf; **it's too hot/cold** es ist zu heiß/kalt
**2** (*emphatic*): **it's only me** ich bin's nur; **it's only the postman** es ist nur der Briefträger.

**beach** [biːtʃ] *n* Strand *m* ♦ *vt* (*boat*) auf (den) Strand setzen.
**beach buggy** *n* Strandbuggy *m*.
**beachcomber** ['biːtʃkəumə*] *n* Strandgutsammler *m*.
**beachwear** ['biːtʃweə*] *n* Strandkleidung *f*.
**beacon** ['biːkən] *n* Leuchtfeuer *nt*; (*marker*) Bake *f*; (*also:* **radio ~**) Funkfeuer *nt*.
**bead** [biːd] *n* Perle *f*; **beads** *npl* (*necklace*) Perlenkette *f*.
**beady** ['biːdɪ] *adj*: ~ **eyes** Knopfaugen *pl*.
**beagle** ['biːgl] *n* Beagle *m*.
**beak** [biːk] *n* Schnabel *m*.
**beaker** ['biːkə*] *n* Becher *m*.
**beam** [biːm] *n* (*ARCHIT*) Balken *m*; (*of light*) Strahl *m*; (*RADIO*) Leitstrahl *m* ♦ *vi* (*smile*) strahlen ♦ *vt* ausstrahlen, senden; **to ~ at sb** jdn anstrahlen; **to drive on full** *or* **main** *or* **high ~** mit Fernlicht fahren.
**beaming** ['biːmɪŋ] *adj* strahlend.
**bean** [biːn] *n* Bohne *f*; **runner ~** Stangenbohne *f*; **broad ~** dicke Bohne; **coffee ~** Kaffeebohne *f*.
**beanpole** ['biːnpəul] *n* (*lit, fig*) Bohnenstange *f*.
**beanshoots** ['biːnʃuːts] *npl* Sojabohnensprossen *pl*.
**beansprouts** ['biːnsprauts] *npl* = **beanshoots**.
**bear** [bɛə*] (*pt* **bore**, *pp* **borne**) *n* Bär *m*; (*STOCK EXCHANGE*) Baissier *m* ♦ *vt* tragen; (*tolerate,*

*endure*) ertragen; (*examination*) standhalten +*dat*; (*traces, signs*) aufweisen, zeigen; (*COMM: interest*) tragen, bringen; (*produce: children*) gebären; (: *fruit*) tragen ♦ *vi*: **to ~ right/left** (*AUT*) sich rechts/links halten; **to ~ the responsibility of** die Verantwortung tragen für; **to ~ comparison with** einen Vergleich standhalten mit; **I can't ~ him** ich kann ihn nicht ausstehen; **to bring pressure to ~ on sb** Druck auf jdn ausüben.
▶**bear out** *vt* (*person, suspicions etc*) bestätigen.
▶**bear up** *vi* Haltung bewahren; **he bore up well** er hat sich gut gehalten.
▶**bear with** *vt fus* Nachsicht haben mit; ~ **with me a minute** bitte gedulden Sie sich einen Moment.
**bearable** ['bɛərəbl] *adj* erträglich.
**beard** [bɪəd] *n* Bart *m*.
**bearded** ['bɪədɪd] *adj* bärtig.
**bearer** ['bɛərə*] *n* (*of letter, news*) Überbringer(in) *m(f)*; (*of cheque, passport, title etc*) Inhaber(in) *m(f)*.
**bearing** ['bɛərɪŋ] *n* (*posture*) Haltung *f*; (*air*) Auftreten *nt*; (*connection*) Bezug *m*; (*TECH*) Lager *nt*; **bearings** *npl* (*also:* **ball ~s**) Kugellager *nt*; **to take a ~ with a compass** den Kompaßkurs feststellen; **to get one's ~s** sich zurechtfinden.
**beast** [biːst] *n* (*animal*) Tier *nt*; (*inf: person*) Biest *nt*.
**beastly** ['biːstlɪ] *adj* scheußlich.
**beat** [biːt] (*pt* **beat**, *pp* **beaten**) *n* (*of heart*) Schlag *m*; (*MUS*) Takt *m*; (*of policeman*) Revier *nt* ♦ *vt* schlagen; (*record*) brechen ♦ *vi* schlagen; **to ~ time** den Takt schlagen; **to ~ it** (*inf*) abhauen, verschwinden; **that ~s everything** das ist doch wirklich der Gipfel *or* die Höhe; **to ~ about the bush** um den heißen Brei herumreden; **off the ~en track** abgelegen.
▶**beat down** *vt* (*door*) einschlagen; (*price*) herunterhandeln; (*seller*) einen niedrigeren Preis aushandeln mit ♦ *vi* (*rain*) herunterprasseln; (*sun*) herunterbrennen.
▶**beat off** *vt* (*attack, attacker*) abwehren.
▶**beat up** *vt* (*person*) zusammenschlagen; (*mixture, eggs*) schlagen.
**beater** ['biːtə*] *n* (*for eggs, cream*) Schneebesen *m*.
**beating** ['biːtɪŋ] *n* Schläge *pl*, Prügel *pl*; **to take a ~** (*fig*) eine Schlappe einstecken.
**beat-up** ['biːtʌp] (*inf*) *adj* zerbeult, ramponiert.
**beautician** [bjuːˈtɪʃən] *n* Kosmetiker(in) *m(f)*.
**beautiful** ['bjuːtɪful] *adj* schön.
**beautifully** ['bjuːtɪflɪ] *adv* (*play, sing, drive etc*) hervorragend; (*quiet, empty etc*) schön.
**beautify** ['bjuːtɪfaɪ] *vt* verschönern.
**beauty** ['bjuːtɪ] *n* Schönheit *f*; (*fig: attraction*) Schöne *nt*; **the ~ of it is that** ... das Schöne

daran ist, daß ...

**beauty contest** n Schönheitswettbewerb m.

**beauty queen** n Schönheitskönigin f.

**beauty salon** n Kosmetiksalon m.

**beauty sleep** n (Schönheits)schlaf m.

**beauty spot** (BRIT) n besonders schöner Ort m.

**beaver** ['biːvəʳ] n Biber m.

**becalmed** [bɪ'kɑːmd] adj: **to be ~** (sailing ship) in eine Flaute geraten.

**became** [bɪ'keɪm] pt of **become**.

**because** [bɪ'kɔz] conj weil; **~ of** wegen +gen or (inf) +dat.

**beck** [bɛk] n: **to be at sb's ~ and call** nach jds Pfeife tanzen.

**beckon** ['bɛkən] vt (also: **~ to**) winken ♦ vi locken.

**become** [bɪ'kʌm] (irreg: like **come**) vi werden; **it became known that** es wurde bekannt, daß; **what has ~ of him?** was ist aus ihm geworden?

**becoming** [bɪ'kʌmɪŋ] adj (behaviour) schicklich; (clothes) kleidsam.

**BECTU** ['bɛktu] (BRIT) n abbr (= Broadcasting, Entertainment, Cinematographic and Theatre Union) Gewerkschaft für Beschäftigte in der Unterhaltungsindustrie.

**BEd** n abbr (= Bachelor of Education) akademischer Grad im Erziehungswesen.

**bed** [bɛd] n Bett nt; (of coal) Flöz nt; (of clay) Schicht f; (of river) (Fluß)bett nt; (of sea) (Meeres)boden m, (Meeres)grund m; (of flowers) Beet nt; **to go to ~** ins or zu Bett gehen.

▶**bed down** vi sein Lager aufschlagen.

**bed and breakfast** n (place) (Frühstücks)pension f; (terms) Übernachtung f mit Frühstück.

---

Bed and Breakfast bedeutet 'Übernachtung mit Frühstück', wobei sich dies in Großbritannien nicht auf Hotels, sondern auf kleinere Pensionen, Privathäuser und Bauernhöfe bezieht, wo man wesentlich preisgünstiger übernachten kann als in Hotels. Oft wird für Bed and Breakfast, auch **B & B** genannt, durch ein entsprechendes Schild im Garten oder an der Einfahrt geworben.

---

**bedbug** ['bɛdbʌg] n Wanze f.

**bedclothes** ['bɛdkləʊðz] npl Bettzeug nt.

**bedding** ['bɛdɪŋ] n Bettzeug nt.

**bedevil** [bɪ'dɛvl] vt (person) heimsuchen; (plans) komplizieren; **to be ~led by misfortune/bad luck** vom Schicksal/Pech verfolgt sein.

**bedfellow** ['bɛdfɛləʊ] n: **they are strange ~s** (fig) sie sind ein merkwürdiges Gespann.

**bedlam** ['bɛdləm] n Chaos nt.

**bedpan** ['bɛdpæn] n Bettpfanne f, Bettschüssel f.

**bedpost** ['bɛdpəʊst] n Bettpfosten m.

**bedraggled** [bɪ'drægld] adj (wet) triefnaß, tropfnaß; (dirty) verdreckt.

**bedridden** ['bɛdrɪdn] adj bettlägerig.

**bedrock** ['bɛdrɔk] n (fig) Fundament nt; (GEOG) Grundgebirge nt, Grundgestein nt.

**bedroom** ['bɛdrum] n Schlafzimmer nt.

**Beds** [bɛdz] (BRIT) abbr (POST: = Bedfordshire).

**bed settee** n Sofabett nt.

**bedside** ['bɛdsaɪd] n: **at sb's ~** an jds Bett; **~ lamp** Nachttischlampe f; **~ book** Bettlektüre f.

**bedsit(ter)** ['bɛdsɪt(əʳ)] (BRIT) n möbliertes Zimmer nt.

**bedspread** ['bɛdsprɛd] n Tagesdecke f.

**bedtime** ['bɛdtaɪm] n Schlafenszeit f; **it's ~** es ist Zeit, ins Bett zu gehen.

**bee** [biː] n Biene f; **to have a ~ in one's bonnet about cleanliness** einen Sauberkeitsfimmel or Sauberkeitstick haben.

**beech** [biːtʃ] n Buche f.

**beef** [biːf] n Rind(fleisch) nt; **roast ~** Rinderbraten m.

▶**beef up** (inf) vt aufmotzen; (essay) auswalzen.

**beefburger** ['biːfbəːgəʳ] n Hamburger m.

**beefeater** ['biːfiːtəʳ] n Beefeater m.

**beehive** ['biːhaɪv] n Bienenstock m.

**beekeeping** ['biːkiːpɪŋ] n Bienenzucht f, Imkerei f.

**beeline** ['biːlaɪn] n: **to make a ~ for** schnurstracks zugehen auf +acc.

**been** [biːn] pp of **be**.

**beep** [biːp] (inf) n Tut(tut) nt ♦ vi tuten ♦ vt: **~ one's horn** hupen.

**beer** [bɪəʳ] n Bier nt.

**beer belly** (inf) n Bierbauch m.

**beer can** n Bierdose f.

**beet** [biːt] n Rübe f; (US: also: **red ~**) rote Bete f.

**beetle** ['biːtl] n Käfer m.

**beetroot** ['biːtruːt] (BRIT) n rote Bete f.

**befall** [bɪ'fɔːl] (irreg: like **fall**) vi sich zutragen ♦ vt widerfahren +dat.

**befit** [bɪ'fɪt] vt sich gehören für.

**before** [bɪ'fɔːʳ] prep vor +dat; (with movement) vor +acc ♦ conj bevor ♦ adv (time) vorher; (space) davor; **~ going** bevor er/sie etc geht/ging; **~ she goes** bevor sie geht; **the week ~** die Woche davor; **I've never seen it ~** ich habe es noch nie gesehen.

**beforehand** [bɪ'fɔːhænd] adv vorher.

**befriend** [bɪ'frɛnd] vt sich annehmen +gen.

**befuddled** [bɪ'fʌdld] adj: **to be ~** verwirrt sein.

**beg** [bɛg] vi betteln ♦ vt (food, money) betteln um; (favour, forgiveness etc) bitten um; **to ~ for** (food etc) betteln um; (forgiveness, mercy etc) bitten um; **to ~ sb to do sth** jdn bitten, etw zu tun; **I ~ your pardon** (apologizing) entschuldigen Sie bitte; (: not hearing) (wie) bitte?; **to ~ the question** der Frage ausweichen; see also **pardon**.

**began** [bɪ'gæn] *pt of* **begin**.

**beggar** ['bɛɡə*] *n* Bettler(in) *m(f)*.

**begin** [bɪ'ɡɪn] (*pt* **began**, *pp* **begun**) *vt, vi* beginnen, anfangen; **to ~ doing** *or* **to do sth** anfangen, etw zu tun; **~ning (from) Monday** ab Montag; **I can't ~ to thank you** ich kann Ihnen gar nicht genug danken; **we'll have soup to ~ with** als Vorspeise hätten wir gern Suppe; **to ~ with, I'd like to know ...** zunächst einmal möchte ich wissen, ...

**beginner** [bɪ'ɡɪnə*] *n* Anfänger(in) *m(f)*.

**beginning** [bɪ'ɡɪnɪŋ] *n* Anfang *m*; **right from the ~** von Anfang an.

**begrudge** [bɪ'ɡrʌdʒ] *vt:* **to ~ sb sth** jdm etw mißgönnen *or* nicht gönnen.

**beguile** [bɪ'ɡaɪl] *vt* betören.

**beguiling** [bɪ'ɡaɪlɪŋ] *adj* (*charming*) verführerisch; (*deluding*) betörend.

**begun** [bɪ'ɡʌn] *pp of* **begin**.

**behalf** [bɪ'hɑːf] *n:* **on ~ of**, (*US*) **in ~ of** (*as representative of*) im Namen von; (*for benefit of*) zugunsten von; **on my/his ~** in meinem/ seinem Namen; zu meinen/seinen Gunsten.

**behave** [bɪ'heɪv] *vi* (*person*) sich verhalten, sich benehmen; (*thing*) funktionieren; (*also:* **~ o.s.**) sich benehmen.

**behaviour,** (*US*) **behavior** [bɪ'heɪvjə*] *n* Verhalten *nt*; (*manner*) Benehmen *nt*.

**behead** [bɪ'hɛd] *vt* enthaupten.

**beheld** [bɪ'hɛld] *pt, pp of* **behold**.

**behind** [bɪ'haɪnd] *prep* hinter ♦ *adv* (*at/towards the back*) hinten ♦ *n* (*buttocks*) Hintern *m*, Hinterteil *nt*; **~ the scenes** (*fig*) hinter den Kulissen; **we're ~ them in technology** auf dem Gebiet der Technologie liegen wir hinter ihnen zurück; **to be ~** (*schedule*) im Rückstand *or* Verzug sein; **to leave/stay ~** zurücklassen/-bleiben.

**behold** [bɪ'həuld] (*irreg: like* **hold**) *vt* sehen, erblicken.

**beige** [beɪʒ] *adj* beige.

**Beijing** ['beɪ'dʒɪŋ] *n* Peking *nt*.

**being** ['biːɪŋ] *n* (*creature*) (Lebe)wesen *nt*; (*existence*) Leben *nt*, (Da)sein *nt*; **to come into ~** entstehen.

**Beirut** [beɪ'ruːt] *n* Beirut *nt*.

**Belarus** [bɛlə'rus] *n* Weißrußland *nt*.

**Belarussian** *adj* belarussisch, weißrussisch ♦ *n* Weißrusse *m*, Weißrussin *f*; (*LING*) Weißrussisch *nt*.

**belated** [bɪ'leɪtɪd] *adj* verspätet.

**belch** [bɛltʃ] *vi* rülpsen ♦ *vt* (*also:* **belch out:** *smoke etc*) ausstoßen.

**beleaguered** [bɪ'liːɡɪd] *adj* (*city*) belagert; (*army*) eingekesselt; (*fig*) geplagt.

**Belfast** ['bɛlfɑːst] *n* Belfast *nt*.

**belfry** ['bɛlfrɪ] *n* Glockenstube *f*.

**Belgian** ['bɛldʒən] *adj* belgisch ♦ *n* Belgier(in) *m(f)*.

**Belgium** ['bɛldʒəm] *n* Belgien *nt*.

**Belgrade** [bɛl'ɡreɪd] *n* Belgrad *nt*.

**belie** [bɪ'laɪ] *vt* (*contradict*) im Widerspruch stehen zu; (*give false impression of*) hinwegtäuschen über +*acc*; (*disprove*) widerlegen, Lügen strafen.

**belief** [bɪ'liːf] *n* Glaube *m*; (*opinion*) Überzeugung *f*; **it's beyond ~** es ist unglaublich *or* nicht zu glauben; **in the ~ that** im Glauben, daß.

**believable** [bɪ'liːvəbl] *adj* glaubhaft.

**believe** [bɪ'liːv] *vt* glauben ♦ *vi* (an Gott) glauben; **he is ~d to be abroad** es heißt, daß er im Ausland ist; **to ~ in** (*God, ghosts*) glauben an +*acc*; (*method etc*) Vertrauen haben zu; **I don't ~ in corporal punishment** ich halte nicht viel von der Prügelstrafe.

**believer** [bɪ'liːvə*] *n* (*in idea, activity*) Anhänger(in) *m(f)*; (*REL*) Gläubige(r) *f(m)*; **she's a great ~ in healthy eating** sie ist sehr für eine gesunde Ernährung.

**belittle** [bɪ'lɪtl] *vt* herabsetzen.

**Belize** [bɛ'liːz] *n* Belize *nt*.

**bell** [bɛl] *n* Glocke *f*; (*small*) Glöckchen *nt*, Schelle *f*; (*on door*) Klingel *f*; **that rings a ~** (*fig*) das kommt mir bekannt vor.

**bell-bottoms** ['bɛlbɔtəmz] *npl* Hose *f* mit Schlag.

**bellboy** ['bɛlbɔɪ] (*BRIT*) *n* Page *m*, Hoteljunge *m*.

**bellhop** ['bɛlhɔp] (*US*) *n* = **bellboy**.

**belligerence** [bɪ'lɪdʒərəns] *n* Angriffslust *f*.

**belligerent** [bɪ'lɪdʒərənt] *adj* angriffslustig.

**bellow** ['bɛləu] *vi, vt* brüllen.

**bellows** ['bɛləuz] *npl* Blasebalg *m*.

**bell push** (*BRIT*) *n* Klingel *f*.

**belly** ['bɛlɪ] *n* Bauch *m*.

**bellyache** ['bɛlɪeɪk] (*inf*) *n* Bauchschmerzen *pl* ♦ *vi* murren.

**bellybutton** ['bɛlɪbʌtn] *n* Bauchnabel *m*.

**bellyful** ['bɛlɪful] (*inf*) *n:* **I've had a ~ of that** davon habe ich die Nase voll.

**belong** [bɪ'lɔŋ] *vi:* **to ~ to** (*person*) gehören +*dat*; (*club etc*) angehören +*dat*; **this book ~s here** dieses Buch gehört hierher.

**belongings** [bɪ'lɔŋɪŋz] *npl* Sachen *pl*, Habe *f*; **personal ~** persönlicher Besitz *m*, persönliches Eigentum *nt*.

**Belorussia** [bɛluːˈrʌʃə] *n* Weißrußland *nt*.

**Belorussian** [bɛluːˈrʌʃən] *adj, n* = **Belarussian**.

**beloved** [bɪ'lʌvɪd] *adj* geliebt ♦ *n* Geliebte(r) *f(m)*.

**below** [bɪ'ləu] *prep* (*beneath*) unterhalb +*gen*; (*less than*) unter +*dat* ♦ *adv* (*beneath*) unten; **see ~** siehe unten; **temperatures ~ normal** Temperaturen unter dem Durchschnitt.

**belt** [bɛlt] *n* Gürtel *m*; (*TECH*) (Treib)riemen *m* ♦ *vt* schlagen ♦ *vi* (*BRIT: inf*): **to ~ along** rasen; **to ~ down/into** hinunter-/ hineinrasen; **industrial ~** Industriegebiet *nt*.

▶**belt out** *vt* (*song*) schmettern.

▶**belt up** (*BRIT: inf*) *vi* den Mund *or* die Klappe halten.

**beltway** ['bɛltweɪ] (*US*) *n* Umgehungsstraße *f*, Ringstraße *f*; (*motorway*)

Umgehungsautobahn f.

**bemoan** [bɪ'məʊn] vt beklagen.

**bemused** [bɪ'mjuːzd] adj verwirrt.

**bench** [bɛntʃ] n Bank f; (work bench)
Werkbank f; **the B~** (LAW: judges) die
Richter pl, der Richterstand.

**benchmark** ['bɛntʃmɑːk] n (fig) Maßstab m.

**bend** [bɛnd] (pt, pp **bent**) vt (leg, arm) beugen;
(pipe) biegen ♦ vi (person) sich beugen ♦ n
(BRIT: in road) Kurve f; (in pipe, river)
Biegung f; **bends** npl (MED): **the ~s** die
Taucherkrankheit.

▶**bend down** vi sich bücken.

▶**bend over** vi sich bücken.

**beneath** [bɪ'niːθ] prep unter +dat ♦ adv
darunter.

**benefactor** ['bɛnɪfæktə'] n Wohltäter m.

**benefactress** ['bɛnɪfæktrɪs] n Wohltäterin f.

**beneficial** [bɛnɪ'fɪʃəl] adj (effect) nützlich;
(influence) vorteilhaft; **~ (to)** gut (für).

**beneficiary** [bɛnɪ'fɪʃərɪ] n (LAW)
Nutznießer(in) m(f).

**benefit** ['bɛnɪfɪt] n (advantage) Vorteil m;
(money) Beihilfe f; (also: **~ concert, ~ match**)
Benefizveranstaltung f ♦ vt nützen +dat,
zugute kommen +dat ♦ vi: **he'll ~ from it** er
wird davon profitieren.

**Benelux** ['bɛnɪlʌks] n die Beneluxstaaten pl.

**benevolent** [bɪ'nɛvələnt] adj wohlwollend;
(organization) Wohltätigkeits-.

**BEng** n abbr (= Bachelor of Engineering)
akademischer Grad für Ingenieure.

**benign** [bɪ'naɪn] adj gütig; (MED) gutartig.

**bent** [bɛnt] pt, pp of **bend** ♦ n Neigung f ♦ adj
(wire, pipe) gebogen; (inf: dishonest) korrupt;
(: pej: homosexual) andersrum; **to be ~ on**
entschlossen sein zu.

**bequeath** [bɪ'kwiːð] vt vermachen.

**bequest** [bɪ'kwɛst] n Vermächtnis nt, Legat nt.

**bereaved** [bɪ'riːvd] adj leidtragend ♦ npl: **the ~**
die Hinterbliebenen pl.

**bereavement** [bɪ'riːvmənt] n schmerzlicher
Verlust m.

**bereft** [bɪ'rɛft] adj: **~ of** beraubt +gen.

**beret** ['bɛreɪ] n Baskenmütze f.

**Bering Sea** ['beɪrɪŋ-] n: **the ~** das
Beringmeer.

**berk** [bɜːk] (inf) n Dussel m.

**Berks** [bɑːks] (BRIT) abbr (POST: = Berkshire).

**Berlin** [bɜː'lɪn] n Berlin nt; **East/West ~**
(formerly) Ost-/Westberlin nt.

**berm** [bɜːm] (US) n Seitenstreifen m.

**Bermuda** [bɜː'mjuːdə] n Bermuda nt, die
Bermudinseln pl.

**Bermuda shorts** npl Bermudashorts pl.

**Bern** [bɜːn] n Bern nt.

**berry** ['bɛrɪ] n Beere f.

**berserk** [bə'sɜːk] adj: **to go ~** wild werden.

**berth** [bɜːθ] n (bed) Bett nt; (on ship) Koje f;
(on train) Schlafwagenbett nt; (for ship)
Liegeplatz m ♦ vi anlegen; **to give sb a wide
~** (fig) einen großen Bogen um jdn machen.

**beseech** [bɪ'siːtʃ] (pt, pp **besought**) vt anflehen.

**beset** [bɪ'sɛt] (pt, pp **beset**) vt (subj: difficulties)
bedrängen; (: fears, doubts) befallen; **~ with**
(problems, dangers etc) voller +dat.

**beside** [bɪ'saɪd] prep neben +dat; (with
movement) neben +acc; **to be ~ o.s.** außer
sich sein; **that's ~ the point** das hat damit
nichts zu tun.

**besides** [bɪ'saɪdz] adv außerdem ♦ prep außer
+dat.

**besiege** [bɪ'siːdʒ] vt belagern; (fig) belagern,
bedrängen.

**besmirch** [bɪ'smɜːtʃ] vt besudeln.

**besotted** [bɪ'sɔtɪd] (BRIT) adj: **~ with** vernarrt
in +acc.

**besought** [bɪ'sɔːt] pt, pp of **beseech**.

**bespectacled** [bɪ'spɛktɪkld] adj bebrillt.

**bespoke** [bɪ'spəʊk] (BRIT) adj (garment)
maßgeschneidert; (suit) Maß-; **~ tailor**
Maßschneider m.

**best** [bɛst] adj beste(r, s) ♦ adv am besten ♦ n:
**at ~** bestenfalls; **the ~ thing to do is ...** das
beste ist ...; **the ~ part of** der größte Teil
+gen; **to make the ~ of sth** das Beste aus etw
machen; **to do one's ~** sein Bestes tun; **to
the ~ of my knowledge** meines Wissens; **to
the ~ of my ability** so gut ich kann; **he's not
exactly patient at the ~ of times** er ist schon
normalerweise ziemlich ungeduldig.

**bestial** ['bɛstɪəl] adj bestialisch.

**best man** n Trauzeuge m (des Bräutigams).

**bestow** [bɪ'stəʊ] vt schenken; **to ~ sth on sb**
(honour, praise) jdm etw zuteil werden
lassen; (title) jdm etw verleihen.

**best seller** n Bestseller m.

**bet** [bɛt] (pt, pp **bet** or **betted**) n Wette f ♦ vi
wetten ♦ vt: **to ~ sb sth** mit jdm um etw
wetten; **it's a safe ~** (fig) es ist so gut wie
sicher; **to ~ money on sth** Geld auf etw acc
setzen.

**Bethlehem** ['bɛθlɪhɛm] n Bethlehem nt.

**betray** [bɪ'treɪ] vt verraten; (trust, confidence)
mißbrauchen.

**betrayal** [bɪ'treɪəl] n Verrat m.

**better** ['bɛtə'] adj, adv besser ♦ vt verbessern
♦ n: **to get the ~ of sb** jdn unterkriegen;
(curiosity) über jdn siegen; **I had ~ go** ich
gehe jetzt (wohl) besser; **you had ~ do it**
tun Sie es lieber; **he thought ~ of it** er
überlegte es sich dat anders; **to get ~**
gesund werden; **that's ~!** so ist es besser!; **a
change for the ~** eine Wendung zum Guten.

**better off** adj (wealthier) besser gestellt;
(more comfortable etc) besser dran; (fig):
**you'd be ~ this way** so wäre es besser für
Sie.

**betting** ['bɛtɪŋ] n Wetten nt.

**betting shop** (BRIT) n Wettbüro nt.

**between** [bɪ'twiːn] prep zwischen +dat; (with
movement) zwischen +acc; (amongst) unter
+acc or dat ♦ adv dazwischen; **the road ~ here
and London** die Straße zwischen hier und

London; **we only had £5 ~ us** wir hatten zusammen nur £5.

**bevel** ['bɛvəl] n (also: **~ edge**) abgeschrägte Kante f.

**bevelled** ['bɛvəld] adj: **a ~ edge** eine Schrägkante, eine abgeschrägte Kante.

**beverage** ['bɛvərɪdʒ] n Getränk nt.

**bevy** ['bɛvɪ] n: **a ~ of** eine Schar +gen.

**bewail** [bɪ'weɪl] vt beklagen.

**beware** [bɪ'wɛə*] vi: **to ~ (of)** sich in acht nehmen (vor +dat); **"~ of the dog"** „Vorsicht, bissiger Hund".

**bewildered** [bɪ'wɪldəd] adj verwirrt.

**bewildering** [bɪ'wɪldrɪŋ] adj verwirrend.

**bewitching** [bɪ'wɪtʃɪŋ] adj bezaubernd, hinreißend.

**beyond** [bɪ'jɔnd] prep (in space) jenseits +gen; (exceeding) über +acc ... hinaus; (after) nach; (above) über +dat ♦ adv (in space) dahinter; (in time) darüber hinaus; **it is ~ doubt** es steht außer Zweifel; **~ repair** nicht mehr zu reparieren; **it is ~ my understanding** es übersteigt mein Begriffsvermögen; **it's ~ me** das geht über meinen Verstand.

**b/f** abbr (COMM: = brought forward) Übertr.

**BFPO** n abbr (= British Forces Post Office) Postbehörde der britischen Armee.

**bhp** n abbr (AUT: = brake horsepower) Bremsleistung f.

**bi...** [baɪ] pref Bi-, bi-.

**biannual** [baɪ'ænjuəl] adj zweimal jährlich.

**bias** ['baɪəs] n (prejudice) Vorurteil nt; (preference) Vorliebe f.

**bias(s)ed** ['baɪəst] adj voreingenommen; **to be ~ against** voreingenommen sein gegen.

**biathlon** [baɪ'æθlən] n Biathlon nt.

**bib** [bɪb] n Latz m.

**Bible** ['baɪbl] n Bibel f.

**biblical** ['bɪblɪkl] adj biblisch.

**bibliography** [bɪblɪ'ɔgrəfɪ] n Bibliographie f.

**bicarbonate of soda** [baɪ'kɑːbənɪt-] n Natron nt.

**bicentenary** [baɪsɛn'tiːnərɪ] n Zweihundertjahrfeier f.

**bicentennial** [baɪsɛn'tɛnɪəl] (US) n = bicentenary.

**biceps** ['baɪsɛps] n Bizeps m.

**bicker** ['bɪkə*] vi sich zanken.

**bickering** ['bɪkərɪŋ] n Zankerei f.

**bicycle** ['baɪsɪkl] n Fahrrad nt.

**bicycle path** n (Fahr)radweg m.

**bicycle pump** n Luftpumpe f.

**bicycle track** n (Fahr)radweg m.

**bid** [bɪd] (pt **bade** or **bid**, pp **bidden** or **bid**) n (at auction) Gebot nt; (in tender) Angebot nt; (attempt) Versuch m ♦ vi bieten; (CARDS) bieten, reizen ♦ vt bieten; **to ~ sb good day** jdm einen guten Tag wünschen.

**bidder** ['bɪdə*] n: **the highest ~** der/die Höchstbietende or Meistbietende.

**bidding** ['bɪdɪŋ] n Steigern nt, Bieten nt; (order, command): **to do sb's ~** tun, was jd

einem sagt.

**bide** [baɪd] vt: **to ~ one's time** den rechten Augenblick abwarten.

**bidet** ['biːdeɪ] n Bidet nt.

**bidirectional** ['baɪdɪ'rɛkʃənl] adj (COMPUT) bidirektional.

**biennial** [baɪ'ɛnɪəl] adj zweijährlich ♦ n zweijährige Pflanze f.

**bier** [bɪə*] n Bahre f.

**bifocals** [baɪ'fəuklz] npl Bifokalbrille f.

**big** [bɪg] adj groß; **to do things in a ~ way** alles im großen Stil tun.

**bigamist** ['bɪgəmɪst] n Bigamist(in) m(f).

**bigamous** ['bɪgəməs] adj bigamistisch.

**bigamy** ['bɪgəmɪ] n Bigamie f.

**big dipper** [-'dɪpə*] n Achterbahn f.

**big end** n (AUT) Pleuelfuß m, Schubstangenkopf m.

**biggish** ['bɪgɪʃ] adj ziemlich groß.

**bigheaded** ['bɪg'hɛdɪd] adj eingebildet.

**big-hearted** ['bɪg'hɑːtɪd] adj großherzig.

**bigot** ['bɪgət] n Eiferer m; (about religion) bigotter Mensch m.

**bigoted** ['bɪgətɪd] adj (see n) eifernd; bigott.

**bigotry** ['bɪgətrɪ] n (see n) eifernde Borniertheit f; Bigotterie f.

**big toe** n große Zehe f.

**big top** n Zirkuszelt nt.

**big wheel** n Riesenrad nt.

**bigwig** ['bɪgwɪg] (inf) n hohes Tier nt.

**bike** [baɪk] n (Fahr)rad nt; (motorcycle) Motorrad nt.

**bikini** [bɪ'kiːnɪ] n Bikini m.

**bilateral** [baɪ'lætərəl] adj bilateral.

**bile** [baɪl] n Galle(nflüssigkeit) f; (fig: invective) Beschimpfungen pl.

**bilingual** [baɪ'lɪŋgwəl] adj zweisprachig.

**bilious** ['bɪlɪəs] adj unwohl; (fig: colour) widerlich; **he felt ~** ihm war schlecht or übel.

**bill** [bɪl] n Rechnung f; (POL) (Gesetz)entwurf m, (Gesetzes)vorlage f; (US: banknote) Banknote f, (Geld)schein m; (of bird) Schnabel m ♦ vt (item) in Rechnung stellen, berechnen; (customer) eine Rechnung ausstellen +dat; **"post no ~s"** „Plakate ankleben verboten"; **on the ~** (THEAT) auf dem Programm; **to fit** or **fill the ~** (fig) der/die/das richtige sein; **~ of exchange** Wechsel m, Tratte f; **~ of fare** Speisekarte f; **~ of lading** Seefrachtbrief m, Konnossement nt; **~ of sale** Verkaufsurkunde f.

**billboard** ['bɪlbɔːd] n Reklametafel f.

**billet** ['bɪlɪt] (MIL) n Quartier nt ♦ vt einquartieren.

**billfold** ['bɪlfəuld] (US) n Brieftasche f.

**billiards** ['bɪljədz] n Billard nt.

**billion** ['bɪljən] n (BRIT) Billion f; (US) Milliarde f.

**billionaire** [bɪljə'nɛə*] n Milliardär(in) m(f).

**billow** ['bɪləu] n (of smoke) Schwaden m ♦ vi

(*smoke*) in Schwaden aufsteigen; (*sail*) sich blähen.

**billy goat** ['bɪlɪ-] *n* Ziegenbock *m*.

**bimbo** ['bɪmbəu] (*inf: pej*) *n* (*woman*) Puppe *f*, Häschen *nt*.

**bin** [bɪn] *n* (*BRIT*) Mülleimer *m*; (*container*) Behälter *m*.

**binary** ['baɪnərɪ] *adj* binär.

**bind** [baɪnd] (*pt, pp* **bound**) *vt* binden; (*tie together: hands and feet*) fesseln; (*constrain, oblige*) verpflichten ♦ *n* (*inf: nuisance*) Last *f*.

▶**bind over** *vt* rechtlich verpflichten.

▶**bind up** *vt* (*wound*) verbinden; **to be bound up in** sehr beschäftigt sein mit; **to be bound up with** verbunden *or* verknüpft sein mit.

**binder** ['baɪndə\*] *n* (*file*) Hefter *m*; (*for magazines*) Mappe *f*.

**binding** ['baɪndɪŋ] *adj* bindend, verbindlich ♦ *n* (*of book*) Einband *m*.

**binge** [bɪndʒ] (*inf*) *n*: **to go on a** ~ auf eine Sauftour gehen.

**bingo** ['bɪŋgəu] *n* Bingo *nt*.

**bin liner** *n* Müllbeutel *m*.

**binoculars** [bɪ'nɔkjuləz] *npl* Fernglas *nt*.

**biochemistry** [baɪə'kemɪstrɪ] *n* Biochemie *f*.

**biodegradable** ['baɪəudɪ'greɪdəbl] *adj* biologisch abbaubar.

**biodiversity** ['baɪəudaɪ'vɜːsɪtɪ] *n* biologische Vielfalt *f*.

**biofuel** *n* Biotreibstoff *m*.

**biographer** [baɪ'ɔgrəfə\*] *n* Biograph(in) *m(f)*.

**biographic(al)** [baɪə'græfɪk(l)] *adj* biographisch.

**biography** [baɪ'ɔgrəfɪ] *n* Biographie *f*.

**biological** [baɪə'lɔdʒɪkl] *adj* biologisch.

**biological clock** *n* biologische Uhr *f*.

**biologist** [baɪ'ɔlədʒɪst] *n* Biologe *m*, Biologin *f*.

**biology** [baɪ'ɔlədʒɪ] *n* Biologie *f*.

**biophysics** ['baɪəu'fɪzɪks] *n* Biophysik *f*.

**biopic** ['baɪəupɪk] *n* Filmbiographie *f*.

**biopsy** ['baɪɔpsɪ] *n* Biopsie *f*.

**biosphere** ['baɪəsfɪə\*] *n* Biosphäre *f*.

**biotechnology** ['baɪəutek'nɔlədʒɪ] *n* Biotechnik *f*.

**biped** ['baɪped] *n* Zweifüßer *m*.

**birch** [bɜːtʃ] *n* Birke *f*.

**bird** [bɜːd] *n* Vogel *m*; (*BRIT: inf: girl*) Biene *f*.

**bird of prey** *n* Raubvogel *m*.

**bird's-eye view** ['bɜːdzaɪ-] *n* Vogelperspektive *f*; (*overview*) Überblick *m*.

**bird-watcher** ['bɜːdwɔtʃə\*] *n* Vogelbeobachter(in) *m(f)*.

**Biro** ® ['baɪərəu] *n* Kugelschreiber *m*, Kuli *m* (*inf*).

**birth** [bɜːθ] *n* Geburt *f*; **to give** ~ **to** (*subj: woman*) gebären, entbunden werden von; (: *animal*) werfen.

**birth certificate** *n* Geburtsurkunde *f*.

**birth control** *n* Geburtenkontrolle *f*, Geburtenregelung *f*.

**birthday** ['bɜːθdeɪ] *n* Geburtstag *m* ♦ *cpd* Geburtstags-; *see also* **happy**.

**birthmark** ['bɜːθmɑːk] *n* Muttermal *nt*.

**birthplace** ['bɜːθpleɪs] *n* Geburtsort *m*; (*house*) Geburtshaus *nt*; (*fig*) Entstehungsort *m*.

**birth rate** ['bɜːθreɪt] *n* Geburtenrate *f*, Geburtenziffer *f*.

**Biscay** ['bɪskeɪ] *n*: **the Bay of** ~ der Golf von Biskaya.

**biscuit** ['bɪskɪt] *n* (*BRIT*) Keks *m or nt*; (*US*) Brötchen *nt*.

**bisect** [baɪ'sekt] *vt* halbieren.

**bisexual** ['baɪ'seksjuəl] *adj* bisexuell ♦ *n* Bisexuelle(r) *f(m)*.

**bishop** ['bɪʃəp] *n* (*REL*) Bischof *m*; (*CHESS*) Läufer *m*.

**bistro** ['biːstrəu] *n* Bistro *nt*.

**bit** [bɪt] *pt of* **bite** ♦ *n* (*piece*) Stück *nt*; (*of drill*) (Bohr)einsatz *m*, Bohrer *m*; (*of plane*) (Hobel)messer *nt*; (*COMPUT*) Bit *nt*; (*of horse*) Gebiß *nt*; (*US*): **two/four/six** ~**s** 25/50/75 Cent(s); **a** ~ **of** ein bißchen; **a** ~ **mad** ein bißchen verrückt; **a** ~ **dangerous** etwas gefährlich; ~ **by** ~ nach und nach; **to come to** ~**s** kaputtgehen; **bring all your** ~**s and pieces** bringen Sie Ihre (Sieben)sachen mit; **to do one's** ~ sein(en) Teil tun *or* beitragen.

**bitch** [bɪtʃ] *n* (*dog*) Hündin *f*; (*inf!: woman*) Miststück *nt*.

**bite** [baɪt] (*pt* **bit**, *pp* **bitten**) *vt, vi* beißen; (*subj: insect etc*) stechen ♦ *n* (*insect bite*) Stich *m*; (*mouthful*) Bissen *m*; **to** ~ **one's nails** an seinen Nägeln kauen; **let's have a** ~ (**to eat**) (*inf*) laßt uns eine Kleinigkeit essen.

**biting** ['baɪtɪŋ] *adj* (*wind*) schneidend; (*wit*) scharf.

**bit part** *n* kleine Nebenrolle *f*.

**bitten** ['bɪtn] *pp of* **bite**.

**bitter** ['bɪtə\*] *adj* bitter; (*person*) verbittert; (*wind, weather*) bitterkalt, eisig; (*criticism*) scharf ♦ *n* (*BRIT: beer*) halbdunkles obergäriges Bier; **to the** ~ **end** bis zum bitteren Ende.

**bitterly** ['bɪtəlɪ] *adv* (*complain, weep*) bitterlich; (*oppose*) erbittert; (*criticize*) scharf; (*disappointed*) bitter; (*jealous*) sehr; **it's** ~ **cold** es ist bitter kalt.

**bitterness** ['bɪtənɪs] *n* Bitterkeit *f*.

**bittersweet** ['bɪtəswiːt] *adj* bittersüß.

**bitty** ['bɪtɪ] (*BRIT: inf*) *adj* zusammen-gestoppelt, zusammengestückelt.

**bitumen** ['bɪtjumɪn] *n* Bitumen *nt*.

**bivouac** ['bɪvuæk] *n* Biwak *nt*.

**bizarre** [bɪ'zɑː\*] *adj* bizarr.

**bk** *abbr* = **bank**; **book**.

**BL** *n abbr* (= *Bachelor of Law*) *akademischer Grad für Juristen*; (= *Bachelor of Letters*) *akademischer Grad für Literaturwissenschaftler*; (*US:* = *Bachelor of Literature*) *akademischer Grad für Literaturwissenschaftler*.

**b.l.** *abbr* = **bill of lading**.

**blab** [blæb] (*inf*) *vi* quatschen.

**black** [blæk] *adj* schwarz ♦ *vt* (*BRIT: INDUSTRY*)

boykottieren ♦ *n* Schwarz *nt*; (*person*): **B~**
Schwarze(r) *f(m)*; **to give sb a ~ eye** jdm ein
blaues Auge schlagen; **~ and blue** grün und
blau; **there it is in ~ and white** (*fig*) da steht
es schwarz auf weiß; **to be in the ~** in den
schwarzen Zahlen sein.

▶**black out** *vi* (*faint*) ohnmächtig werden.

**black belt** *n* (*US*) Gebiet in den Südstaaten
*der USA, das vorwiegend von Schwarzen*
*bewohnt wird*; (*JUDO*) schwarzer Gürtel *m*.

**blackberry** ['blækbəɪ] *n* Brombeere *f*.

**blackbird** ['blækbɔːd] *n* Amsel *f*.

**blackboard** ['blækbɔːd] *n* Tafel *f*.

**black box** *n* (*AVIAT*) Flugschreiber *m*.

**black coffee** *n* schwarzer Kaffee *m*.

**Black Country** (*BRIT*) *n*: **the ~**
*Industriegebiet in den englischen Midlands.*

**blackcurrant** ['blæk'kʌrənt] *n* Johannisbeere
*f*.

**black economy** *n*: **the ~** die
Schattenwirtschaft.

**blacken** ['blækn] *vt*: **to ~ sb's name/reputation**
(*fig*) jdn verunglimpfen.

**Black Forest** *n*: **the ~** der Schwarzwald.

**blackhead** ['blækhɛd] *n* Mitesser *m*.

**black hole** *n* schwarzes Loch *nt*.

**black ice** *n* Glatteis *nt*.

**blackjack** ['blækdʒæk] *n* (*CARDS*)
Siebzehnundvier *nt*; (*US: truncheon*)
Schlagstock *m*.

**blackleg** ['blæklɛg] (*BRIT*) *n* Streikbrecher(in)
*m(f)*.

**blacklist** ['blæklɪst] *n* schwarze Liste *f* ♦ *vt* auf
die schwarze Liste setzen.

**blackmail** ['blækmeɪl] *n* Erpressung *f* ♦ *vt*
erpressen.

**blackmailer** ['blækmeɪlə*] *n* Erpresser(in) *m(f)*.

**black market** *n* Schwarzmarkt *m*.

**blackout** ['blækaut] *n* (*in wartime*)
Verdunkelung *f*; (*power cut*) Stromausfall *m*;
(*TV, RADIO*) Ausfall *m*; (*faint*)
Ohnmachtsanfall *m*.

**black pepper** *n* schwarzer Pfeffer *m*.

**Black Sea** *n*: **the ~** das Schwarze Meer.

**black sheep** *n* (*fig*) schwarzes Schaf *nt*.

**blacksmith** ['blæksmɪθ] *n* Schmied *m*.

**black spot** *n* (*AUT*) Gefahrenstelle *f*; (*for*
*unemployment etc*) Gebiet, in dem ein
Problem besonders ausgeprägt ist.

**bladder** ['blædə*] *n* Blase *f*.

**blade** [bleɪd] *n* (*of knife etc*) Klinge *f*; (*of oar,*
*propeller*) Blatt *nt*; **a ~ of grass** ein Grashalm
*m*.

**blame** [bleɪm] *n* Schuld *f* ♦ *vt*: **to ~ sb for sth**
jdm die Schuld an etw *dat* geben; **to be to ~**
schuld daran haben *or* sein; **who's to ~?**
wer hat *or* ist schuld?; **I'm not to ~** es ist
nicht meine Schuld.

**blameless** ['bleɪmlɪs] *adj* schuldlos.

**blanch** [blɑːntʃ] *vi* blaß werden ♦ *vt* (*CULIN*)
blanchieren.

**blancmange** [blə'mɒnʒ] *n* Pudding *m*.

**bland** [blænd] *adj* (*taste, food*) fade.

**blank** [blæŋk] *adj* (*paper*) leer, unbeschrieben;
(*look*) ausdruckslos ♦ *n* (*on form*) Lücke *f*;
(*cartridge*) Platzpatrone *f*; **my mind was a ~**
ich hatte ein Brett vor dem Kopf; **we drew**
**a ~** (*fig*) wir hatten kein Glück.

**blank cheque** *n* Blankoscheck *m*; **to give sb a**
**~ to do sth** (*fig*) jdm freie Hand geben, etw
zu tun.

**blanket** ['blæŋkɪt] *n* Decke *f* ♦ *adj* (*statement*)
pauschal; (*agreement*) Pauschal-.

**blanket cover** *n* (*INSURANCE*) umfassende
Versicherung *f*.

**blare** [blɛə*] *vi* (*brass band*) schmettern; (*horn*)
tuten; (*radio*) plärren.

▶**blare out** *vi* (*radio, stereo*) plärren.

**blarney** ['blɑːnɪ] *n* Schmeichelei *f*.

**blasé** ['blɑːzeɪ] *adj* blasiert.

**blaspheme** [blæs'fiːm] *vi* Gott lästern.

**blasphemous** ['blæsfɪməs] *adj* lästerlich,
blasphemisch.

**blasphemy** ['blæsfɪmɪ] *n* (*Gottes*)lästerung *f*,
Blasphemie *f*.

**blast** [blɑːst] *n* (*of wind*) Windstoß *m*; (*of*
*whistle*) Trillern *nt*; (*shock wave*) Druckwelle
*f*; (*of air, steam*) Schwall *m*; (*of explosive*)
Explosion *f* ♦ *vt* (*blow up*) sprengen ♦ *excl*
(*BRIT: inf*) verdammt!, so ein Mist!); **at full ~**
(*play music*) mit voller Lautstärke; (*move,*
*work*) auf Hochtouren.

▶**blast off** *vi* (*SPACE*) abheben, starten.

**blast furnace** *n* Hochofen *m*.

**blastoff** ['blɑːstɔf] *n* (*SPACE*) Abschuß *m*.

**blatant** ['bleɪtənt] *adj* offensichtlich.

**blatantly** ['bleɪtəntlɪ] *adv* (*lie*) unverfroren;
**it's ~ obvious** es ist überdeutlich.

**blaze** [bleɪz] *n* (*fire*) Feuer *nt*, Brand *m*; (*fig: of*
*colour*) Farbenpracht *f*; (: *of glory*) Glanz *m*
♦ *vi* (*fire*) lodern; (*guns*) feuern; (*fig: eyes*)
glühen ♦ *vt*: **to ~ a trail** (*fig*) den Weg
bahnen; **in a ~ of publicity** mit viel
Publicity.

**blazer** ['bleɪzə*] *n* Blazer *m*.

**bleach** [bliːtʃ] *n* (*also*: **household ~**)
≈ Reinigungsmittel *nt* ♦ *vt* bleichen.

**bleached** [bliːtʃt] *adj* gebleicht.

**bleachers** ['bliːtʃəz] (*US*) *npl* unüberdachte
Zuschauertribüne *f*.

**bleak** [bliːk] *adj* (*countryside*) öde; (*weather,*
*situation*) trostlos; (*prospect*) trüb;
(*expression, voice*) deprimiert.

**bleary-eyed** ['blɪərɪ'aɪd] *adj* triefäugig.

**bleat** [bliːt] *vi* (*goat*) meckern; (*sheep*) blöken
♦ *n* Meckern *nt*; Blöken *nt*.

**bled** [blɛd] *pt, pp* **of bleed.**

**bleed** [bliːd] (*pt, pp* **bled**) *vi* bluten; (*colour*)
auslaufen ♦ *vt* (*brakes, radiator*) entlüften;
**my nose is ~ing** ich habe Nasenbluten.

**bleep** [bliːp] *n* Piepton *m* ♦ *vi* piepen ♦ *vt*
(*doctor etc*) rufen, anpiepen (*inf*).

**bleeper** ['bliːpə*] *n* Piepser *m* (*inf*),
Funkrufempfänger *m*.

**blemish** ['blɛmɪʃ] n Makel m.

**blend** [blɛnd] n Mischung f ♦ vt (CULIN) mischen, mixen; (colours, styles, flavours etc) vermischen ♦ vi (colours etc: also: ~ **in**) harmonieren.

**blender** ['blɛndə*] n (CULIN) Mixer m.

**bless** [blɛs] (pt, pp **blessed** or **blest**) vt segnen; **to be ~ed with** gesegnet sein mit; ~ **you!** (after sneeze) Gesundheit!

**blessed** ['blɛsɪd] adj heilig; (happy) selig; **it rains every ~ day** (inf) es regnet aber auch jeden Tag.

**blessing** ['blɛsɪŋ] n (approval) Zustimmung f; (REL, fig) Segen m; **to count one's ~s** von Glück sagen können; **it was a ~ in disguise** es war schließlich doch ein Segen.

**blew** [blu:] pt of **blow**.

**blight** [blaɪt] vt zerstören; (hopes) vereiteln; (life) verderben ♦ n (of plants) Brand m.

**blimey** ['blaɪmɪ] (BRIT: inf) excl Mensch!

**blind** [blaɪnd] adj blind ♦ n (for window) Rollo nt, Rouleau nt; (also: **Venetian ~**) Jalousie f ♦ vt blind machen; (dazzle) blenden; (deceive: with facts etc) verblenden; **the blind** npl (blind people) die Blinden pl; **to turn a ~ eye** (on or to) ein Auge zudrücken (bei); **to be ~ to sth** (fig) blind für etw sein.

**blind alley** n (fig) Sackgasse f.

**blind corner** (BRIT) n unübersichtliche Ecke f.

**blind date** n Rendezvous nt mit einem/einer Unbekannten.

**blinders** ['blaɪndəz] (US) npl = **blinkers**.

**blindfold** ['blaɪndfəuld] n Augenbinde f ♦ adj, adv mit verbundenen Augen ♦ vt die Augen verbinden +dat.

**blinding** ['blaɪndɪŋ] adj (dazzling) blendend; (remarkable) bemerkenswert.

**blindly** ['blaɪndlɪ] adv (without seeing) wie blind; (without thinking) blindlings.

**blindness** ['blaɪndnɪs] n Blindheit f.

**blind spot** n (AUT) toter Winkel m; (fig: weak spot) schwacher Punkt m.

**blink** [blɪŋk] vi blinzeln; (light) blinken ♦ n: **the TV's on the ~** (inf) der Fernseher ist kaputt.

**blinkers** ['blɪŋkəz] npl Scheuklappen pl.

**blinking** ['blɪŋkɪŋ] (BRIT: inf) adj: **this ~ ...** diese(r, s) verflixte ...

**blip** [blɪp] n (on radar screen) leuchtender Punkt m; (in a straight line) Ausschlag m; (fig) (zeitweilige) Abweichung f.

**bliss** [blɪs] n Glück nt, Seligkeit f.

**blissful** ['blɪsful] adj (event, day) herrlich; (smile) selig; **a ~ sigh** ein wohliger Seufzer m; **in ~ ignorance** in herrlicher Ahnungslosigkeit.

**blissfully** ['blɪsfəlɪ] adv selig; ~ **happy** überglücklich; ~ **unaware of** ... ohne auch nur zu ahnen, daß ...

**blister** ['blɪstə*] n Blase f ♦ vi (paint) Blasen werfen.

**blithely** ['blaɪðlɪ] adv (unconcernedly)

unbekümmert, munter; (joyfully) fröhlich.

**blithering** ['blɪðərɪŋ] (inf) adj: **this ~ idiot** dieser Trottel.

**BLit(t)** n abbr (= Bachelor of Literature; Bachelor of Letters) akademischer Grad für Literaturwissenschaftler.

**blitz** [blɪts] n (MIL) Luftangriff m; **to have a ~ on sth** (fig) einen Großangriff auf etw acc starten.

**blizzard** ['blɪzəd] n Schneesturm m.

**BLM** (US) n abbr (= Bureau of Land Management) Behörde zur Verwaltung von Grund und Boden.

**bloated** ['bləutɪd] adj aufgedunsen; (full) (über)satt.

**blob** [blɔb] n Tropfen m; (sth indistinct) verschwommener Fleck m.

**bloc** [blɔk] n Block m; **the Eastern ~** (HIST) der Ostblock.

**block** [blɔk] n Block m; (toy) Bauklotz m; (in pipes) Verstopfung f ♦ vt blockieren; (progress) aufhalten; (COMPUT) blocken; ~ **of flats** (BRIT) Wohnblock m; **3 ~s from here** 3 Blocks or Straßen weiter; **mental ~** geistige Sperre f, Mattscheibe f (inf); ~ **and tackle** Flaschenzug m.

▸**block up** vt, vi verstopfen.

**blockade** [blɔ'keɪd] n Blockade f ♦ vt blockieren.

**blockage** ['blɔkɪdʒ] n Verstopfung f.

**block booking** n Gruppenbuchung f.

**blockbuster** ['blɔkbʌstə*] n Knüller m.

**block capitals** npl Blockschrift f.

**blockhead** ['blɔkhɛd] (inf) n Dummkopf m.

**block letters** npl Blockschrift f.

**block release** (BRIT) n blockweise Freistellung von Auszubildenden zur Weiterbildung.

**block vote** (BRIT) n Stimmenblock m.

**bloke** [bləuk] (BRIT: inf) n Typ m.

**blond(e)** [blɔnd] adj blond ♦ n: ~ (woman) Blondine f.

**blood** [blʌd] n Blut nt; **new ~** (fig) frisches Blut nt.

**blood bank** n Blutbank f.

**blood bath** n Blutbad nt.

**blood count** n Blutbild nt.

**bloodcurdling** ['blʌdkə:dlɪŋ] adj grauenerregend.

**blood donor** n Blutspender(in) m(f).

**blood group** n Blutgruppe f.

**bloodhound** ['blʌdhaund] n Bluthund m.

**bloodless** ['blʌdlɪs] adj (victory) unblutig; (pale) blutleer.

**blood-letting** ['blʌdlɛtɪŋ] n (also fig) Aderlaß m.

**blood poisoning** n Blutvergiftung f.

**blood pressure** n Blutdruck m; **to have high/low ~** hohen/niedrigen Blutdruck haben.

**bloodshed** ['blʌdʃɛd] n Blutvergießen nt.

**bloodshot** ['blʌdʃɔt] adj (eyes)

blutunterlaufen.

**blood sport** n Jagdsport m (*und andere Sportarten, bei denen Tiere getötet werden*).

**bloodstained** ['blʌdsteɪnd] adj blutbefleckt.

**bloodstream** ['blʌdstriːm] n Blut nt, Blutkreislauf m.

**blood test** n Blutprobe f.

**bloodthirsty** ['blʌdθɜːstɪ] adj blutrünstig.

**blood transfusion** n Blutübertragung f, (Blut)transfusion f.

**blood type** n Blutgruppe f.

**blood vessel** n Blutgefäß nt.

**bloody** ['blʌdɪ] adj blutig; (*BRIT: inf!*): **this** ~ ... diese(r, s) verdammte ...; ~ **strong** (*inf!*) verdammt stark; ~ **good** (*inf!*) echt gut.

**bloody-minded** ['blʌdɪ'maɪndɪd] (*BRIT: inf*) adj stur.

**bloom** [bluːm] n Blüte f ♦ vi blühen; **to be in** ~ in Blüte stehen.

**blooming** ['bluːmɪŋ] (*BRIT: inf*) adj: **this** ~ ... diese(r, s) verflixte ...

**blossom** ['blɒsəm] n Blüte f ♦ vi blühen; (*fig*): **to** ~ **into** erblühen or aufblühen zu.

**blot** [blɒt] n Klecks m; (*fig: on name etc*) Makel m ♦ vt (*liquid*) aufsaugen; (*make blot on*) beklecksen; **to be a** ~ **on the landscape** ein Schandfleck in der Landschaft sein; **to** ~ **one's copy book** (*fig*) sich unmöglich machen.

▶**blot out** vt (*view*) verdecken; (*memory*) auslöschen.

**blotchy** ['blɒtʃɪ] adj fleckig.

**blotter** ['blɒtə*] n (Tinten)löscher m.

**blotting paper** ['blɒtɪŋ-] n Löschpapier nt.

**blotto** ['blɒtəʊ] (*inf*) adj (*drunk*) sternhagelvoll.

**blouse** [blauz] n Bluse f.

**blow** [bləʊ] (*pt* blew, *pp* blown) n (*also fig*) Schlag m ♦ vi (*wind*) wehen; (*person*) blasen ♦ vt (*subj: wind*) wehen; (*instrument, whistle*) blasen; (*fuse*) durchbrennen lassen; **to come to ~s** handgreiflich werden; **to** ~ **off course** (*ship*) vom Kurs abgetrieben werden; **to** ~ **one's nose** sich dat die Nase putzen; **to** ~ **a whistle** pfeifen.

▶**blow away** vt wegblasen ♦ vi wegfliegen.

▶**blow down** vt umwehen.

▶**blow off** vt wegwehen ♦ vi wegfliegen.

▶**blow out** vi ausgehen.

▶**blow over** vi sich legen.

▶**blow up** vi ausbrechen ♦ vt (*bridge*) in die Luft jagen; (*tyre*) aufblasen; (*PHOT*) vergrößern.

**blow-dry** ['bləʊdraɪ] vt fönen ♦ n: **to have a** ~ sich fönen lassen.

**blowlamp** ['bləʊlæmp] (*BRIT*) n Lötlampe f.

**blown** [bləʊn] pp of **blow**.

**blowout** ['bləʊaʊt] n Reifenpanne f; (*inf: big meal*) Schlemmerei f; (*of oil-well*) Ölausbruch m.

**blowtorch** ['bləʊtɔːtʃ] n = **blowlamp**.

**blow-up** ['bləʊʌp] n Vergrößerung f.

**blowzy** ['blauzɪ] (*BRIT*) adj schlampig.

**BLS** (*US*) n abbr (= *Bureau of Labor Statistics*) Amt für Arbeitsstatistik.

**blubber** ['blʌbə*] n Walfischspeck m ♦ vi (*pej*) heulen.

**bludgeon** ['blʌdʒən] vt niederknüppeln; (*fig*): **to** ~ **sb into doing sth** jdm so lange zusetzen, bis er etw tut.

**blue** [bluː] adj blau; (*depressed*) deprimiert, niedergeschlagen ♦ n: **out of the** ~ (*fig*) aus heiterem Himmel; **blues** n (*MUS*): **the ~s** der Blues; ~ **film** Pornofilm m; ~ **joke** schlüpfriger Witz m; (**only**) **once in a** ~ **moon** (nur) alle Jubeljahre einmal; **to have the ~s** deprimiert or niedergeschlagen sein.

**blue baby** n Baby nt mit angeborenem Herzfehler.

**bluebell** ['bluːbɛl] n Glockenblume f.

**bluebottle** ['bluːbɒtl] n Schmeißfliege f.

**blue cheese** n Blauschimmelkäse m.

**blue-chip** ['bluːtʃɪp] adj: ~ **investment** sichere Geldanlage f.

**blue-collar worker** ['bluːkɒlə*-] n Arbeiter(in) m(f).

**blue jeans** npl (Blue)jeans pl.

**blueprint** ['bluːprɪnt] n (*fig*): **a** ~ (**for**) ein Plan m or Entwurf m (für).

**bluff** [blʌf] vi bluffen ♦ n Bluff m; (*cliff*) Klippe f; (*promontory*) Felsvorsprung m; **to call sb's** ~ es darauf ankommen lassen.

**blunder** ['blʌndə*] n (dummer) Fehler m ♦ vi einen (dummen) Fehler machen; **to** ~ **into sb** mit jdm zusammenstoßen; **to** ~ **into sth** in etw acc (hinein)tappen.

**blunt** [blʌnt] adj stumpf; (*person*) direkt; (*talk*) unverblümt ♦ vt stumpf machen; ~ **instrument** (*LAW*) stumpfer Gegenstand m.

**bluntly** ['blʌntlɪ] adv (*speak*) unverblümt.

**bluntness** ['blʌntnɪs] n (*of person*) Direktheit f.

**blur** [blɜː*] n (*shape*) verschwommener Fleck m; (*scene etc*) verschwommenes Bild nt; (*memory*) verschwommene Erinnerung f ♦ vt (*vision*) trüben; (*distinction*) verwischen.

**blurb** [blɜːb] n Informationsmaterial nt.

**blurred** [blɜːd] adj (*photograph, TV picture etc*) verschwommen; (*distinction*) verwischt.

**blurt out** [blɜːt-] vt herausplatzen mit.

**blush** [blʌʃ] vi erröten ♦ n Röte f.

**blusher** ['blʌʃə*] n Rouge nt.

**bluster** ['blʌstə*] n Toben nt, Geschrei nt ♦ vi toben.

**blustering** ['blʌstərɪŋ] adj polternd.

**blustery** ['blʌstərɪ] adj stürmisch.

**Blvd** abbr = **boulevard**.

**BM** n abbr (= *British Museum*) Britisches Museum nt; (= *Bachelor of Medicine*) akademischer Grad für Mediziner.

**BMA** n abbr (= *British Medical Association*) Dachverband der Ärzte.

**BMJ** n abbr (= *British Medical Journal*) vom

*BMA herausgegebene Zeitschrift.*

**BMus** *n abbr* (= *Bachelor of Music*)
*akademischer Grad für
Musikwissenschaftler.*

**BMX** *n abbr* (= *bicycle motocross*): ~ **bike**
BMX-Rad *nt.*

**BO** *n abbr* (*inf:* = *body odour*) Körpergeruch *m*;
(*US*) = **box office.**

**boar** [bɔː'] *n* (*male pig*) Eber *m*; (*wild pig*)
Keiler *m.*

**board** [bɔːd] *n* Brett *nt*; (*cardboard*) Pappe *f*;
(*committee*) Ausschuß *m*; (*in firm*) Vorstand
*m* ♦ *vt* (*ship*) an Bord +*gen* gehen; (*train*)
einsteigen in +*acc*; **on** ~ (*NAUT, AVIAT*) an
Bord; **full/half** ~ (*BRIT*) Voll-/Halbpension *f*;
~ **and lodging** Unterkunft und Verpflegung
*f*; **to go by the** ~ (*fig*) unter den Tisch fallen;
**above** ~ (*fig*) korrekt; **across the** ~ (*fig*)
allgemein; (: *criticize, reject*) pauschal.
▶**board up** *vt* mit Brettern vernageln.

**boarder** ['bɔːdə'] *n* Internatsschüler(in) *m(f).*

**board game** *n* Brettspiel *nt.*

**boarding card** ['bɔːdɪŋ-] *n* (*AVIAT, NAUT*)
= **boarding pass.**

**boarding house** ['bɔːdɪŋ-] *n* Pension *f.*

**boarding party** ['bɔːdɪŋ-] *n* (*NAUT*)
Enterkommando *nt.*

**boarding pass** ['bɔːdɪŋ-] *n* Bordkarte *f.*

**boarding school** ['bɔːdɪŋ-] *n* Internat *nt.*

**board meeting** *n* Vorstandssitzung *f.*

**boardroom** ['bɔːdruːm] *n* Sitzungssaal *m.*

**boardwalk** ['bɔːdwɔːk] (*US*) *n* Holzsteg *m.*

**boast** [bəust] *vi* prahlen ♦ *vt* (*fig: possess*) sich
rühmen +*gen*, besitzen; **to** ~ **about** *or* **of**
prahlen mit.

**boastful** ['bəustful] *adj* prahlerisch.

**boastfulness** ['bəustfulnɪs] *n* Prahlerei *f.*

**boat** [bəut] *n* Boot *nt*; (*ship*) Schiff *nt*; **to go by**
~ mit dem Schiff fahren; **to be in the same**
~ (*fig*) in einem Boot *or* im gleichen Boot
sitzen.

**boater** ['bəutə'] *n* steifer Strohhut *m*,
Kreissäge *f* (*inf*).

**boating** ['bəutɪŋ] *n* Bootfahren *nt.*

**boat people** *npl* Bootsflüchtlinge *pl.*

**boatswain** ['bəusn] *n* Bootsmann *m.*

**bob** [bɔb] *vi* (*also:* ~ **up and down**) sich auf
und ab bewegen ♦ *n* (*BRIT: inf*) = **shilling.**
▶**bob up** *vi* auftauchen.

**bobbin** ['bɔbɪn] *n* Spule *f.*

**bobby** ['bɔbɪ] (*BRIT: inf*) *n* Bobby *m*, Polizist *m.*

**bobsleigh** ['bɔbsleɪ] *n* Bob *m.*

**bode** [bəud] *vi:* **to** ~ **well/ill (for)** ein gutes/
schlechtes Zeichen sein (für).

**bodice** ['bɔdɪs] *n* (*of dress*) Oberteil *m.*

**bodily** ['bɔdɪlɪ] *adj* körperlich; (*needs*) leiblich
♦ *adv* (*lift, carry*) mit aller Kraft.

**body** ['bɔdɪ] *n* Körper *m*; (*corpse*) Leiche *f*;
(*main part*) Hauptteil *m*; (*of car*) Karosserie *f*;
(*of plane*) Rumpf *m*; (*group*) Gruppe *f*;
(*organization*) Organ *nt*; **ruling** ~
amtierendes Organ; **in a** ~ geschlossen; **a**

~ **of facts** Tatsachenmaterial *nt.*

**body blow** *n* (*fig: setback*) schwerer Schlag
*m.*

**body building** *n* Bodybuilding *nt.*

**body double** *n* (*FILM, TV*) Double für Szenen,
*in denen Körperpartien in Nahaufnahme
gezeigt werden.*

**bodyguard** ['bɔdɪgɑːd] *n* (*group*) Leibwache *f*;
(*one person*) Leibwächter *m.*

**body language** *n* Körpersprache *f.*

**body repairs** *npl* (*AUT*) Karosseriearbeiten
*pl.*

**body search** *n* Leibesvisitation *f.*

**body stocking** *n* Body(stocking) *m.*

**bodywork** ['bɔdɪwɜːk] *n* Karosserie *f.*

**boffin** ['bɔfɪn] (*BRIT*) *n* Fachidiot *m.*

**bog** [bɔg] *n* Sumpf *m* ♦ *vt:* **to get** ~**ged down**
(*fig*) sich verzetteln.

**bogey** ['bəugɪ] *n* Schreckgespenst *nt*; (*also:*
~**man**) Butzemann *m*, Schwarzer Mann *m.*

**boggle** ['bɔgl] *vi:* **the mind** ~**s** das ist nicht *or*
kaum auszumalen.

**bogie** ['bəugɪ] *n* Drehgestell *nt*; (*trolley*)
Draisine *f.*

**Bogotá** [bəugə'tɑː] *n* Bogotá *nt.*

**bogus** ['bəugəs] *adj* (*workman etc*) falsch;
(*claim*) erfunden.

**Bohemia** [bəu'hiːmɪə] *n* Böhmen *nt.*

**Bohemian** [bəu'hiːmɪən] *adj* böhmisch ♦ *n*
Böhme *m*, Böhmin *f*; (*also:* **b**~) Bohemien *m.*

**boil** [bɔɪl] *vt, vi* kochen ♦ *n* (*MED*) Furunkel *nt or*
*m*; **to come to the** (*BRIT*) *or* **a** (*US*) ~ zu
kochen anfangen.
▶**boil down to** *vt fus* (*fig*) hinauslaufen auf
+*acc.*
▶**boil over** *vi* überkochen.

**boiled egg** [bɔɪld-] *n* gekochtes Ei *nt.*

**boiled potatoes** *npl* Salzkartoffeln *pl.*

**boiler** ['bɔɪlə'] *n* Boiler *m.*

**boiler suit** (*BRIT*) *n* Overall *m.*

**boiling** ['bɔɪlɪŋ] *adj:* **I'm** ~ (**hot**) (*inf*) mir ist
fürchterlich heiß; **it's** ~ es ist eine
Affenhitze (*inf*).

**boiling point** *n* Siedepunkt *m.*

**boil-in-the-bag** [bɔɪlɪnðə'bæg] *adj* (*meals*)
Kochbeutel-.

**boisterous** ['bɔɪstərəs] *adj* ausgelassen.

**bold** [bəuld] *adj* (*brave*) mutig; (*pej: cheeky*)
dreist; (*pattern, colours*) kräftig.

**boldly** ['bəuldlɪ] *adv* (*see adj*) mutig; dreist;
kräftig.

**boldness** ['bəuldnɪs] *n* Mut *m*; (*cheekiness*)
Dreistigkeit *f.*

**bold type** *n* Fettdruck *m.*

**Bolivia** [bə'lɪvɪə] *n* Bolivien *nt.*

**Bolivian** [bə'lɪvɪən] *adj* bolivisch, bolivianisch
♦ *n* Bolivier(in) *m(f)*, Bolivianer(in) *m(f).*

**bollard** ['bɔləd] (*BRIT*) *n* Poller *m.*

**bolshy** ['bɔlʃɪ] (*BRIT: inf*) *adj* (*stroppy*) pampig.

**bolster** ['bəulstə'] *n* Nackenrolle *f.*
▶**bolster up** *vt* stützen; (*case*) untermauern.

**bolt** [bəult] *n* Riegel *m*; (*with nut*) Schraube *f*;

(*of lightning*) Blitz(strahl) *m* ♦ *vt* (*door*) verriegeln; (*also:* ~ **together**) verschrauben; (*food*) hinunterschlingen ♦ *vi* (*run away: person*) weglaufen; (: *horse*) durchgehen ♦ *adv:* ~ **upright** kerzengerade; **a ~ from the blue** (*fig*) ein Blitz aus heiterem Himmel.

**bomb** [bɔm] *n* Bombe *f* ♦ *vt* bombardieren; (*plant bomb in or near*) einen Bombenanschlag verüben auf +*acc.*

**bombard** [bɔm'baːd] *vt* (*also fig*) bombardieren.

**bombardment** [bɔm'baːdmənt] *n* Bombardierung *f*, Bombardement *nt.*

**bombastic** [bɔm'bæstɪk] *adj* bombastisch.

**bomb disposal** *n:* ~ **unit** Bombenräumkommando *nt;* ~ **expert** Bombenräumexperte *m*, Bombenräumexpertin *f.*

**bomber** ['bɔmə*] *n* Bomber *m;* (*terrorist*) Bombenattentäter(in) *m(f).*

**bombing** ['bɔmɪŋ] *n* Bombenangriff *m.*

**bomb scare** *n* Bombenalarm *m.*

**bombshell** ['bɔmʃɛl] *n* (*fig: revelation*) Bombe *f.*

**bomb site** *n* Trümmergrundstück *nt.*

**bona fide** ['bəʊnə'faɪdɪ] *adj* echt; ~ **offer** Angebot *nt* auf Treu und Glauben.

**bonanza** [bə'nænzə] *n* (*ECON*) Boom *m.*

**bond** [bɔnd] *n* Band *nt*, Bindung *f*, (*FIN*) festverzinsliches Wertpapier *nt*, Bond *m;* (*COMM*): **in** ~ unter Zollverschluß.

**bondage** ['bɔndɪdʒ] *n* Sklaverei *f.*

**bonded warehouse** ['bɔndɪd] *n* Zollager *nt.*

**bone** [bəʊn] *n* Knochen *m;* (*of fish*) Gräte *f* ♦ *vt* (*meat*) die Knochen herauslösen aus; (*fish*) entgräten; **I've got a ~ to pick with you** ich habe mit Ihnen (noch) ein Hühnchen zu rupfen.

**bone china** *n* ≈ feines Porzellan *nt.*

**bone-dry** ['bəʊn'draɪ] *adj* knochentrocken.

**bone idle** *adj* stinkfaul.

**bone marrow** *n* Knochenmark *nt.*

**boner** ['bəʊnə*] (*US*) *n* Schnitzer *m.*

**bonfire** ['bɔnfaɪə*] *n* Feuer *nt.*

**bonk** [bɔŋk] (*inf*) *vt, vi* (*have sex (with)*) bumsen.

**bonkers** ['bɔŋkəz] (*BRIT: inf*) *adj* (*mad*) verrückt.

**Bonn** [bɔn] *n* Bonn *nt.*

**bonnet** ['bɔnɪt] *n* Haube *f;* (*for baby*) Häubchen *nt;* (*BRIT: of car*) Motorhaube *f.*

**bonny** ['bɔnɪ] (*SCOT, Northern English*) *adj* schön, hübsch.

**bonus** ['bəʊnəs] *n* Prämie *f;* (*on wages*) Zulage *f;* (*at Christmas*) Gratifikation *f;* (*fig: additional benefit*) Plus *nt.*

**bony** ['bəʊnɪ] *adj* knochig; (*MED*) knöchern; (*tissue*) knochenartig; (*meat*) mit viel Knochen; (*fish*) mit viel Gräten.

**boo** [buː] *excl* buh ♦ *vt* auspfeifen, ausbuhen.

**boob** [buːb] (*inf*) *n* (*breast*) Brust *f;* (*BRIT: mistake*) Schnitzer *m.*

**booby prize** ['buːbɪ-] *n Scherzpreis für den*

*schlechtesten Teilnehmer.*

**booby trap** ['buːbɪ-] *n* versteckte Bombe *f;* (*fig: joke etc*) *als Schabernack versteckt angebrachte Falle.*

**booby-trapped** ['buːbɪtræpt] *adj:* **a ~ car** ein Auto, in dem eine Bombe versteckt ist.

**book** [bʊk] *n* Buch *nt;* (*of stamps, tickets*) Heftchen *nt* ♦ *vt* bestellen; (*seat, room*) buchen, reservieren lassen; (*subj: traffic warden, policeman*) aufschreiben; (: *referee*) verwarnen; **books** *npl* (*COMM: accounts*) Bücher *pl;* **to keep the ~s** die Bücher führen; **by the** ~ nach Vorschrift; **to throw the** ~ **at sb** jdn nach allen Regeln der Kunst fertigmachen.

▶**book in** (*BRIT*) *vi* sich eintragen.

▶**book up** *vt:* **all seats are** ~**ed up** es ist bis auf den letzten Platz ausverkauft; **the hotel is** ~**ed up** das Hotel ist ausgebucht.

**bookable** ['bʊkəbl] *adj:* **all seats are** ~ Karten für alle Plätze können vorbestellt werden.

**bookcase** ['bʊkkeɪs] *n* Bücherregal *nt.*

**book ends** *npl* Bücherstützen *pl.*

**booking** ['bʊkɪŋ] (*BRIT*) *n* Bestellung *f;* (*of seat, room*) Buchung *f*, Reservierung *f.*

**booking office** (*BRIT*) *n* (*RAIL*) Fahrkartenschalter *m;* (*THEAT*) Vorverkaufsstelle *f*, Vorverkaufskasse *f.*

**book-keeping** ['bʊk'kiːpɪŋ] *n* Buchhaltung *f*, Buchführung *f.*

**booklet** ['bʊklɪt] *n* Broschüre *f.*

**bookmaker** ['bʊkmeɪkə*] *n* Buchmacher *m.*

**bookseller** ['bʊksɛlə*] *n* Buchhändler(in) *m(f).*

**bookshelf** ['bʊkʃɛlf] *n* Bücherbord *nt;* **bookshelves** *npl* Bücherregal *nt.*

**bookshop** ['bʊkʃɔp] *n* Buchhandlung *f.*

**bookstall** ['bʊkstɔːl] *n* Bücher- und Zeitungskiosk *m.*

**book store** *n* = **bookshop.**

**book token** *n* Buchgutschein *m.*

**book value** *n* Buchwert *m*, Bilanzwert *m.*

**bookworm** ['bʊkwɜːm] *n* (*fig*) Bücherwurm *m.*

**boom** [buːm] *n* Donnern *nt*, Dröhnen *nt;* (*in prices, population etc*) rapider Anstieg *m;* (*ECON*) Hochkonjunktur *f;* (*busy period*) Boom *m* ♦ *vi* (*guns*) donnern; (*thunder*) hallen; (*voice*) dröhnen; (*business*) florieren.

**boomerang** ['buːməræŋ] *n* Bumerang *m* ♦ *vi* (*fig*) einen Bumerangeffekt haben; **to ~ on sb** sich für jdn als Bumerang erweisen.

**boom town** *n* Goldgräberstadt *f.*

**boon** [buːn] *n* Segen *m.*

**boorish** ['bʊərɪʃ] *adj* rüpelhaft.

**boost** [buːst] *n* Auftrieb *m* ♦ *vt* (*confidence*) stärken; (*sales, economy etc*) ankurbeln; **to give a ~ to sb/sb's spirits** jdm Auftrieb geben.

**booster** ['buːstə*] *n* (*MED*) Wiederholungsimpfung *f;* (*TV*) Zusatzgleichrichter *m;* (*ELEC*) Puffersatz *m;* (*also:* ~ **rocket**) Booster *m*, Startrakete *f.*

**booster seat** n (AUT) Sitzerhöhung f.
**boot** [buːt] n Stiefel m; (ankle boot) hoher
Schuh m; (BRIT: of car) Kofferraum m ♦ vt
(COMPUT) laden; ... **to ~** (in addition)
obendrein ...; **to give sb the ~** (inf) jdn
rauswerfen or rausschmeißen.
**booth** [buːð] n (at fair) Bude f, Stand m;
(telephone booth) Zelle f; (voting booth)
Kabine f.
**bootleg** ['buːtlɛg] adj (alcohol) schwarz
gebrannt; (fuel) schwarz hergestellt; (tape
etc) schwarz mitgeschnitten.
**bootlegger** ['buːtlɛgəʳ] n Bootlegger m,
Schwarzhändler m.
**booty** ['buːtɪ] n Beute f.
**booze** [buːz] (inf) n Alkohol m ♦ vi saufen.
**boozer** ['buːzəʳ] (inf) n (person) Säufer(in) m(f);
(BRIT: pub) Kneipe f.
**border** ['bɔːdəʳ] n Grenze f; (for flowers)
Rabatte f; (on cloth etc) Bordüre f ♦ vt (road)
säumen; (another country: also: ~ **on**) grenzen
an +acc; **Borders**: **the B~s** das Grenzgebiet
zwischen England und Schottland.
▶**border on** vt fus (fig) grenzen an +acc.
**borderline** ['bɔːdəlaɪn] n (fig): **on the ~** an der
Grenze.
**borderline case** n Grenzfall m.
**bore** [bɔːʳ] pt of **bear** ♦ vt bohren; (person)
langweilen ♦ n Langweiler m; (of gun)
Kaliber nt; **to be ~d** sich langweilen; **he's
~d to tears** or **~d to death** or **~d stiff** er
langweilt sich zu Tode.
**boredom** ['bɔːdəm] n Langeweile f; (boring
quality) Langweiligkeit f.
**boring** ['bɔːrɪŋ] adj langweilig.
**born** [bɔːn] adj: **to be ~** geboren werden; **I was
~ in 1960** ich bin or wurde 1960 geboren;
**~ blind** blind geboren, von Geburt (an)
blind; **a ~ comedian** ein geborener
Komiker.
**born-again** [bɔːnə'gɛn] adj wiedergeboren.
**borne** [bɔːn] pp of **bear**.
**Borneo** ['bɔːnɪəu] n Borneo nt.
**borough** ['bʌrə] n Bezirk m, Stadtgemeinde f.
**borrow** ['bɔrəu] vt: **to ~ sth** etw borgen, sich
dat etw leihen; (from library) sich dat etw
ausleihen; **may I ~ your car?** kann ich
deinen Wagen leihen?
**borrower** ['bɔrəuəʳ] n (of loan etc)
Kreditnehmer(in) m(f).
**borrowing** ['bɔrəuɪŋ] n Kreditaufnahme f.
**borstal** ['bɔːstl] (BRIT) n (formerly)
Besserungsanstalt f.
**Bosnia** ['bɔznɪə] n Bosnien nt.
**Bosnia-Herzegovina** n Bosnien-
Herzegowina nt.
**Bosnian** ['bɔznɪən] adj bosnisch ♦ n
Bosnier(in) m(f).
**bosom** ['buzəm] n Busen m; (fig: of family)
Schoß m.
**bosom friend** n Busenfreund(in) m(f).
**boss** [bɔs] n Chef(in) m(f); (leader) Boß m ♦ vt

(also: ~ **around,** ~ **about**) herumkommandieren; **stop ~ing everyone about!**
hör auf mit dem ständigen
Herumkommandieren!
**bossy** ['bɔsɪ] adj herrisch.
**bosun** ['bəusn] n Bootsmann m.
**botanical** [bə'tænɪkl] adj botanisch.
**botanist** ['bɔtənɪst] n Botaniker(in) m(f).
**botany** ['bɔtənɪ] n Botanik f.
**botch** [bɔtʃ] vt (also: ~ **up**) verpfuschen.
**both** [bəuθ] adj beide ♦ pron beide; (two
different things) beides ♦ adv: ~ **A and B**
sowohl A als auch B; ~ (of them) (alle)
beide; ~ **of us went, we ~ went** wir gingen
beide; **they sell ~ the fabric and the finished
curtains** sie verkaufen sowohl den Stoff als
auch die fertigen Vorhänge.
**bother** ['bɔðəʳ] vt Sorgen machen +dat;
(disturb) stören ♦ vi (also: ~ **o.s.**) sich dat
Sorgen or Gedanken machen ♦ n (trouble)
Mühe f; (nuisance) Plage f ♦ excl Mist! (inf);
**don't ~ phoning** du brauchst nicht
anzurufen; **I'm sorry to ~ you** es tut mir
leid, daß ich Sie belästigen muß; **I can't be
~ed** ich habe keine Lust; **please don't ~**
bitte machen Sie sich keine Umstände;
**don't ~!** laß es!; **it is a ~ to have to shave
every morning** es ist wirklich lästig, sich
jeden Morgen rasieren zu müssen; **it's no ~**
es ist kein Problem.
**Botswana** [bɔt'swɑːnə] n Botswana nt.
**bottle** ['bɔtl] n Flasche f; (BRIT: courage)
Mumm m ♦ vt in Flaschen abfüllen; (fruit)
einmachen; **a ~ of wine/milk** eine Flasche
Wein/Milch; **wine/milk ~** Wein-/
Milchflasche f.
▶**bottle up** vt in sich dat aufstauen.
**bottle bank** n Altglascontainer m.
**bottle-fed** ['bɔtlfɛd] adj mit der Flasche
ernährt.
**bottleneck** ['bɔtlnɛk] n (also fig) Engpaß m.
**bottle-opener** ['bɔtləupnəʳ] n Flaschenöffner
m.
**bottom** ['bɔtəm] n Boden m; (buttocks)
Hintern m; (of page, list) Ende nt; (of chair)
Sitz m; (of mountain, tree) Fuß m ♦ adj (lower)
untere(r, s); (last) unterste(r, s); **at the ~ of**
unten an/in +dat; **at the ~ of the page/list**
unten auf der Seite/Liste; **to be at the ~ of
the class** der/die Letzte in der Klasse sein;
**to get to the ~ of sth** (fig) einer Sache dat
auf den Grund kommen.
**bottomless** ['bɔtəmlɪs] adj (fig)
unerschöpflich.
**bottom line** n (of accounts) Saldo m; (fig):
**that's the ~** (of it) (what it amounts to) darauf
läuft es im Endeffekt hinaus.
**botulism** ['bɔtjulɪzəm] n Botulismus m,
Nahrungsmittelvergiftung f.
**bough** [bau] n Ast m.
**bought** [bɔːt] pt, pp of **buy**.
**boulder** ['bəuldəʳ] n Felsblock m.

**boulevard** ['buːləvɑːd] *n* Boulevard *m*.
**bounce** [bauns] *vi* (auf)springen; (*cheque*) platzen ♦ *vt* (*ball*) (auf)springen lassen; (*signal*) reflektieren ♦ *n* Aufprall *m*; **he's got plenty of ~** (*fig*) er hat viel Schwung.
**bouncer** ['baunsə*] (*inf*) *n* Rausschmeißer *m*.
**bouncy castle** ['baunsɪ-] *n aufblasbare Spielfläche in Form eines Schlosses, auf dem Kinder herumspringen können.*
**bound** [baund] *pt, pp of* **bind** ♦ *n* Sprung *m*; (*gen pl: limit*) Grenze *f* ♦ *vi* springen ♦ *vt* begrenzen ♦ *adj:* ~ **by** gebunden durch; **to be ~ to do sth** (*obliged*) verpflichtet sein, etw zu tun; (*very likely*) etw bestimmt tun; **he's ~ to fail** es kann ihm ja gar nicht gelingen; ~ **for** nach; **the area is out of ~s** das Betreten des Gebiets ist verboten.
**boundary** ['baundrɪ] *n* Grenze *f*.
**boundless** ['baundlɪs] *adj* grenzenlos.
**bountiful** ['bauntɪful] *adj* großzügig; (*God*) gütig; (*supply*) reichlich.
**bounty** ['bauntɪ] *n* Freigebigkeit *f*; (*reward*) Kopfgeld *nt*.
**bounty hunter** *n* Kopfgeldjäger *m*.
**bouquet** ['bukeɪ] *n* (Blumen)strauß *m*; (*of wine*) Bukett *nt*, Blume *f*.
**bourbon** ['buəbən] (*US*) *n* (*also:* ~ **whiskey**) Bourbon *m*.
**bourgeois** ['buəʒwɑː] *adj* bürgerlich, spießig (*pej*) ♦ *n* Bürger(in) *m(f)*, Bourgeois *m*.
**bout** [baut] *n* Anfall *m*; (*BOXING etc*) Kampf *m*.
**boutique** [buːˈtiːk] *n* Boutique *f*.
**bow¹** [bəu] *n* Schleife *f*; (*weapon, MUS*) Bogen *m*.
**bow²** [bau] *n* Verbeugung *f*; (*NAUT: also:* ~**s**) Bug *m* ♦ *vi* sich verbeugen; (*yield*): **to ~ to** *or* **before** sich beugen +*dat*; **to ~ to the inevitable** sich in das Unvermeidliche fügen.
**bowels** ['bauəlz] *npl* Darm *m*; (*of the earth etc*) Innere *nt*.
**bowl** [bəul] *n* Schüssel *f*; (*shallower*) Schale *f*; (*ball*) Kugel *f*; (*of pipe*) Kopf *m*; (*US: stadium*) Stadion *nt* ♦ *vi* werfen.
▶**bowl over** *vt* (*fig*) überwältigen.
**bow-legged** ['bəuˈlɛgɪd] *adj* O-beinig.
**bowler** ['bəulə*] *n* Werfer(in) *m(f)*; (*BRIT: also:* ~ **hat**) Melone *f*.
**bowling** ['bəulɪŋ] *n* Kegeln *nt*; (*on grass*) Bowling *nt*.
**bowling alley** *n* Kegelbahn *f*.
**bowling green** *n* Bowlingrasen *m*.
**bowls** [bəulz] *n* Bowling *nt*.
**bow tie** [bəu-] *n* Fliege *f*.
**box** [bɔks] *n* Schachtel *f*; (*cardboard box*) Karton *m*; (*crate*) Kiste *f*; (*THEAT*) Loge *f*; (*BRIT: AUT*) gelb schraffierter Kreuzungsbereich; (*on form*) Feld *nt* ♦ *vt* (in eine Schachtel *etc*) verpacken; (*fighter*) boxen ♦ *vi* boxen; **to ~ sb's ears** jdm eine Ohrfeige geben.
▶**box in** *vt* einkeilen.

▶**box off** *vt* abtrennen.
**boxer** ['bɔksə*] *n* (*person, dog*) Boxer *m*.
**box file** *n* Sammelordner *m*.
**boxing** ['bɔksɪŋ] *n* Boxen *nt*.
**Boxing Day** (*BRIT*) *n* zweiter Weihnachts(feier)tag *m*.

---

**Boxing Day** *ist ein Feiertag in Großbritannien. Wenn Weihnachten auf ein Wochenende fällt, wird der Feiertag am nächsten darauffolgenden Wochentag nachgeholt. Der Name geht auf einen alten Brauch zurück; früher erhielten Händler und Lieferanten an diesem Tag ein Geschenk, die sogenannte Christmas Box.*

---

**boxing gloves** *npl* Boxhandschuhe *pl*.
**boxing ring** *n* Boxring *m*.
**box number** *n* Chiffre *f*.
**box office** *n* Kasse *f*.
**boxroom** ['bɔksrum] *n* Abstellraum *m*.
**boy** [bɔɪ] *n* Junge *m*.
**boycott** ['bɔɪkɔt] *n* Boykott *m* ♦ *vt* boykottieren.
**boyfriend** ['bɔɪfrɛnd] *n* Freund *m*.
**boyish** ['bɔɪɪʃ] *adj* jungenhaft; (*woman*) knabenhaft.
**boy scout** *n* Pfadfinder *m*.
**Bp** *abbr* = **bishop**.
**BR** *abbr* = **British Rail**.
**bra** [brɑː] *n* BH *m*.
**brace** [breɪs] *n* (*on teeth*) (Zahn)klammer *f*, (Zahn)spange *f*; (*tool*) (Hand)bohrer *m*; (*also:* ~ **bracket**) geschweifte Klammer *f* ♦ *vt* spannen; **braces** *npl* (*BRIT*) Hosenträger *pl*; **to ~ o.s.** (*for weight*) sich stützen; (*for shock*) sich innerlich vorbereiten.
**bracelet** ['breɪslɪt] *n* Armband *nt*.
**bracing** ['breɪsɪŋ] *adj* belebend.
**bracken** ['brækən] *n* Farn *m*.
**bracket** ['brækɪt] *n* Träger *m*; (*group, range*) Gruppe *f*; (*also:* **round** ~) (runde) Klammer *f*; (*also:* **brace** ~) geschweifte Klammer *f*; (*also:* **square** ~) eckige Klammer *f* ♦ *vt* (*also:* ~ **together**) zusammenfassen; (*word, phrase*) einklammern; **income** ~ Einkommensgruppe *f*; **in ~s** in Klammern.
**brackish** ['brækɪʃ] *adj* brackig.
**brag** [bræg] *vi* prahlen.
**braid** [breɪd] *n* Borte *f*; (*of hair*) Zopf *m*.
**Braille** [breɪl] *n* Blindenschrift *f*, Brailleschrift *f*.
**brain** [breɪn] *n* Gehirn *nt*; **brains** *npl* (*CULIN*) Hirn *nt*; (*intelligence*) Intelligenz *f*; **he's got ~s** er hat Köpfchen *or* Grips.
**brainchild** ['breɪntʃaɪld] *n* Geistesprodukt *nt*.
**braindead** ['breɪndɛd] *adj* hirntot; (*inf*) hirnlos.
**brain drain** *n:* **the** ~ *die Abwanderung von Wissenschaftlern, Akademikern etc.*
**brainless** ['breɪnlɪs] *adj* dumm.
**brainstorm** ['breɪnstɔːm] *n* (*fig*) Anfall *m* geistiger Umnachtung; (*US: brain wave*)

Geistesblitz m.

**brainwash** ['breɪnwɔʃ] vt einer Gehirnwäsche dat unterziehen.

**brain wave** n Geistesblitz m.

**brainy** ['breɪnɪ] adj intelligent.

**braise** [breɪz] vt schmoren.

**brake** [breɪk] n Bremse f ♦ vi bremsen.

**brake fluid** n Bremsflüssigkeit f.

**brake light** n Bremslicht nt.

**brake pedal** n Bremspedal nt.

**bramble** ['bræmbl] n Brombeerstrauch m; (fruit) Brombeere f.

**bran** [bræn] n Kleie f.

**branch** [brɑːntʃ] n Ast m; (of family, organization) Zweig m; (COMM) Filiale f, Zweigstelle f, (: bank, company etc) Geschäftsstelle f ♦ vi sich gabeln.

▶**branch out** vi (fig): **to ~ out into** seinen (Geschäfts)bereich erweitern auf +acc.

**branch line** n (RAIL) Zweiglinie f, Nebenlinie f.

**branch manager** n Zweigstellenleiter(in) m(f), Filialleiter(in) m(f).

**brand** [brænd] n (also: ~ **name**) Marke f; (fig: type) Art f ♦ vt mit einem Brandzeichen kennzeichnen; (fig: pej): **to ~ sb a communist** jdn als Kommunist brandmarken.

**brandish** ['brændɪʃ] vt schwingen.

**brand name** n Markenname m.

**brand-new** ['brænd'njuː] adj nagelneu, brandneu.

**brandy** ['brændɪ] n Weinbrand m.

**brash** [bræʃ] adj dreist.

**Brasilia** [brə'zɪlɪə] n Brasilia nt.

**brass** [brɑːs] n Messing nt; **the ~** (MUS) die Blechbläser pl.

**brass band** n Blaskapelle f.

**brassière** ['bræsɪə*] n Büstenhalter m.

**brass tacks** npl: **to get down to ~** zur Sache kommen.

**brassy** ['brɑːsɪ] adj (colour) messingfarben; (sound) blechern; (appearance, behaviour) auffällig.

**brat** [bræt] (pej) n Balg m or nt, Gör nt.

**bravado** [brə'vɑːdəʊ] n Draufgängertum nt.

**brave** [breɪv] adj mutig; (attempt, smile) tapfer ♦ n (indianischer) Krieger m ♦ vt trotzen +dat.

**bravely** ['breɪvlɪ] adv (see adj) mutig; tapfer.

**bravery** ['breɪvərɪ] n (see adj) Mut m; Tapferkeit f.

**bravo** [brɑː'vəʊ] excl bravo.

**brawl** [brɔːl] n Schlägerei f ♦ vi sich schlagen.

**brawn** [brɔːn] n Muskeln pl; (meat) Schweinskopfsülze f.

**brawny** ['brɔːnɪ] adj muskulös, kräftig.

**bray** [breɪ] vi schreien ♦ n (Esels)schrei m.

**brazen** ['breɪzn] adj unverschämt, dreist; (lie) schamlos ♦ vt: **to ~ it out** durchhalten.

**brazier** ['breɪzɪə*] n (container) Kohlenbecken nt.

**Brazil** [brə'zɪl] n Brasilien nt.

**Brazilian** [brə'zɪljən] adj brasilianisch ♦ n Brasilianer(in) m(f).

**Brazil nut** n Paranuß f.

**breach** [briːtʃ] vt (defence) durchbrechen; (wall) eine Bresche schlagen in +acc ♦ n (gap) Bresche f; (estrangement) Bruch m; (breaking): **~ of contract** Vertragsbruch m; **~ of the peace** öffentliche Ruhestörung f; **~ of trust** Vertrauensbruch m.

**bread** [brɛd] n Brot nt; (inf: money) Moos nt, Kies m; **to earn one's keep ~** sein Brot verdienen; **to know which side one's ~ is buttered (on)** wissen, wo etwas zu holen ist.

**bread and butter** n Butterbrot nt; (fig) Broterwerb m.

**bread bin** (BRIT) n Brotkasten m.

**breadboard** ['brɛdbɔːd] n Brot(schneide)brett nt; (COMPUT) Leiterplatte f.

**bread box** (US) n Brotkasten m.

**breadcrumbs** ['brɛdkrʌmz] npl Brotkrumen pl; (CULIN) Paniermehl nt.

**breadline** ['brɛdlaɪn] n: **to be on the ~** nur das Allernotwendigste zum Leben haben.

**breadth** [brɛtθ] n (also fig) Breite f.

**breadwinner** ['brɛdwɪnə*] n Ernährer(in) m(f).

**break** [breɪk] (pt **broke**, pp **broken**) vt zerbrechen; (leg, arm) sich dat brechen; (promise, record) brechen; (law) verstoßen gegen ♦ vi zerbrechen, kaputtgehen; (storm) losbrechen; (weather) umschlagen; (dawn) anbrechen; (story, news) bekanntwerden ♦ n Pause f; (gap) Lücke f; (fracture) Bruch m; (chance) Chance f, Gelegenheit f; (holiday) Urlaub m; **to ~ the news to sb** es jdm sagen; **to ~ even** seine (Un)kosten decken; **to ~ with sb** mit jdm brechen, sich von jdm trennen; **to ~ free** or **loose** sich losreißen; **to take a ~** (eine) Pause machen; (holiday) Urlaub machen; **without a ~** ohne Unterbrechung or Pause, ununterbrochen; **a lucky ~** ein Durchbruch m.

▶**break down** vt (figures, data) aufschlüsseln; (door etc) einrennen ♦ vi (car) eine Panne haben; (machine) kaputtgehen; (person, resistance) zusammenbrechen; (talks) scheitern.

▶**break in** vt (horse) zureiten ♦ vi einbrechen; (interrupt) unterbrechen.

▶**break into** vt fus einbrechen in +acc.

▶**break off** vi abbrechen ♦ vt (talks) abbrechen; (engagement) lösen.

▶**break open** vt, vi aufbrechen.

▶**break out** vi ausbrechen; **to ~ out in spots/a rash** Pickel/einen Ausschlag bekommen.

▶**break through** vi: **the sun broke through** die Sonne kam durch ♦ vt fus durchbrechen.

▶**break up** vi (ship) zerbersten; (crowd, meeting, partnership) sich auflösen; (marriage) scheitern; (friends) sich trennen; (SCOL) in die Ferien gehen ♦ vt zerbrechen; (journey, *fight etc*) unterbrechen; (*meeting*) auflösen; (*marriage*) zerstören.

**breakable** ['breɪkəbl] *adj* zerbrechlich ♦ *n:* ~**s** zerbrechliche Ware *f*.

**breakage** ['breɪkɪdʒ] *n* Bruch *m*; **to pay for** ~**s** für zerbrochene Ware *or* für Bruch bezahlen.

**breakaway** ['breɪkəweɪ] *adj* (*group etc*) Splitter-.

**break dancing** *n* Breakdance *m*.

**breakdown** ['breɪkdaun] *n* (*AUT*) Panne *f*; (*in communications*) Zusammenbruch *m*; (*of marriage*) Scheitern *nt*; (*also:* **nervous** ~) (Nerven)zusammenbruch *m*; (*of statistics*) Aufschlüsselung *f*.

**breakdown service** (*BRIT*) *n* Pannendienst *m*.

**breakdown van** (*BRIT*) *n* Abschleppwagen *m*.

**breaker** ['breɪkə*] *n* (*wave*) Brecher *m*.

**breakeven** ['breɪk'iːvn] *cpd:* ~ **chart** Gewinnschwellen-Diagramm *nt*; ~ **point** Gewinnschwelle *f*.

**breakfast** ['brɛkfəst] *n* Frühstück *nt* ♦ *vi* frühstücken.

**breakfast cereal** *n* Getreideflocken *pl*.

**break-in** ['breɪkɪn] *n* Einbruch *m*.

**breaking and entering** ['breɪkɪŋən'ɛntrɪŋ] *n* (*LAW*) Einbruch *m*.

**breaking point** ['breɪkɪŋ-] *n* (*fig*): **to reach** ~ völlig am Ende sein.

**breakthrough** ['breɪkθruː] *n* Durchbruch *m*.

**break-up** ['breɪkʌp] *n* (*of partnership*) Auflösung *f*; (*of marriage*) Scheitern *nt*.

**break-up value** *n* (*COMM*) Liquidationswert *m*.

**breakwater** ['breɪkwɔːtə*] *n* Wellenbrecher *m*.

**breast** [brɛst] *n* Brust *f*; (*of meat*) Brust *f*, Bruststück *nt*.

**breast-feed** ['brɛstfiːd] (*irreg: like* **feed**) *vt, vi* stillen.

**breast pocket** *n* Brusttasche *f*.

**breaststroke** ['brɛststrəuk] *n* Brustschwimmen *nt*.

**breath** [brɛθ] *n* Atem *m*; (*a breath*) Atemzug *m*; **to go out for a** ~ **of air** an die frische Luft gehen, frische Luft schnappen gehen; **out of** ~ außer Atem, atemlos; **to get one's** ~ **back** wieder zu Atem kommen.

**breathalyse** ['brɛθəlaɪz] *vt* blasen lassen (*inf*).

**Breathalyser** ® ['brɛθəlaɪzə*] *n* Promillemesser *m*.

**breathe** [briːð] *vt, vi* atmen; **I won't** ~ **a word about it** ich werde kein Sterbenswörtchen darüber sagen.

▶**breathe in** *vt, vi* einatmen.

▶**breathe out** *vt, vi* ausatmen.

**breather** ['briːðə*] *n* Atempause *f*, Verschnaufpause *f*.

**breathing** ['briːðɪŋ] *n* Atmung *f*.

**breathing space** *n* (*fig*) Atempause *f*, Ruhepause *f*.

**breathless** ['brɛθlɪs] *adj* atemlos, außer Atem; (*MED*) an Atemnot leidend; **I was** ~ **with**

**excitement** die Aufregung verschlug mir den Atem.

**breathtaking** ['brɛθteɪkɪŋ] *adj* atemberaubend.

**breath test** *n* Atemalkoholtest *m*.

**bred** [brɛd] *pt, pp of* **breed**.

**-bred** *suff:* **well/ill-**~ gut/schlecht erzogen.

**breed** [briːd] (*pt, pp* **bred**) *vt* züchten; (*fig: give rise to*) erzeugen; (: : hate, suspicion) hervorrufen ♦ *vi* Junge haben ♦ *n* Rasse *f*; (*type, class*) Art *f*.

**breeder** ['briːdə*] *n* Züchter(in) *m(f)*; (*also:* ~ **reactor**) Brutreaktor *m*, Brüter *m*.

**breeding** ['briːdɪŋ] *n* Erziehung *f*.

**breeding ground** *n* (*also fig*) Brutstätte *f*.

**breeze** [briːz] *n* Brise *f*.

**breeze block** (*BRIT*) *n* Ytong ® *m*.

**breezy** ['briːzɪ] *adj* (*manner, tone*) munter; (*weather*) windig.

**Breton** ['brɛtən] *adj* bretonisch ♦ *n* Bretone *m*, Bretonin *f*.

**brevity** ['brɛvɪtɪ] *n* Kürze *f*.

**brew** [bruː] *vt* (*tea*) aufbrühen, kochen; (*beer*) brauen ♦ *vi* (*tea*) ziehen; (*beer*) gären; (*storm, fig*) sich zusammenbrauen.

**brewer** ['bruːə*] *n* Brauer *m*.

**brewery** ['bruːərɪ] *n* Brauerei *f*.

**briar** ['braɪə*] *n* Dornbusch *m*; (*wild rose*) wilde Rose *f*.

**bribe** [braɪb] *n* Bestechungsgeld *nt* ♦ *vt* bestechen; **to** ~ **sb to do sth** jdn bestechen, damit er etw tut.

**bribery** ['braɪbərɪ] *n* Bestechung *f*.

**bric-a-brac** ['brɪkəbræk] *n* Nippes *pl*, Nippsachen *pl*.

**brick** [brɪk] *n* Ziegelstein *m*, Backstein *m*; (*of ice cream*) Block *m*.

**bricklayer** ['brɪkleɪə*] *n* Maurer(in) *m(f)*.

**brickwork** ['brɪkwɔːk] *n* Mauerwerk *nt*.

**bridal** ['braɪdl] *adj* (*gown, veil etc*) Braut-.

**bride** [braɪd] *n* Braut *f*.

**bridegroom** ['braɪdgruːm] *n* Bräutigam *m*.

**bridesmaid** ['braɪdzmeɪd] *n* Brautjungfer *f*.

**bridge** [brɪdʒ] *n* Brücke *f*; (*NAUT*) (Kommando)brücke *f*; (*of nose*) Sattel *m*; (*CARDS*) Bridge *nt* ♦ *vt* (*river*) eine Brücke schlagen *or* bauen über +*acc*; (*fig*) überbrücken.

**bridging loan** ['brɪdʒɪŋ-] (*BRIT*) *n* Überbrückungskredit *m*.

**bridle** ['braɪdl] *n* Zaum *m* ♦ *vt* aufzäumen ♦ *vi:* **to** ~ (**at**) sich entrüstet wehren (gegen).

**bridle path** *n* Reitweg *m*.

**brief** [briːf] *adj* kurz ♦ *n* (*LAW*) Auftrag *m*; (*task*) Aufgabe *f* ♦ *vt* instruieren; (*MIL etc*): **to** ~ **sb** (**about**) jdn instruieren (über +*acc*); **briefs** *npl* Slip *m*; **in** ~ ... kurz (gesagt) ...

**briefcase** ['briːfkeɪs] *n* Aktentasche *f*.

**briefing** ['briːfɪŋ] *n* Briefing *nt*, Lagebespechung *f*.

**briefly** ['briːflɪ] *adv* kurz; **to glimpse sth** ~ einen flüchtigen Blick von etw erhaschen.

**Brig.** *abbr* = **brigadier.**
**brigade** [brɪˈgeɪd] *n* Brigade *f*.
**brigadier** [brɪgəˈdɪəʳ] *n* Brigadegeneral *m*.
**bright** [braɪt] *adj* (*light, room*) hell; (*weather*)
heiter; (*clever*) intelligent; (*lively*) heiter,
fröhlich; (*colour*) leuchtend; (*outlook, future*)
glänzend; **to look on the ~ side** die Dinge
von der positiven Seite betrachten.
**brighten** [ˈbraɪtn] (*also:* **~ up**) *vt* aufheitern;
(*event*) beleben ♦ *vi* (*weather, face*) sich
aufheitern; (*person*) fröhlicher werden;
(*prospects*) sich verbessern.
**brightly** [ˈbraɪtlɪ] *adv* (*shine*) hell; (*smile*)
fröhlich; (*talk*) heiter.
**brill** [brɪl] (*BRIT: inf*) *adj* toll.
**brilliance** [ˈbrɪljəns] *n* Strahlen *nt*; (*of person*)
Genialität *f*, Brillanz *f*; (*of talent, skill*)
Großartigkeit *f*.
**brilliant** [ˈbrɪljənt] *adj* strahlend; (*person, idea*)
genial, brillant; (*career*) großartig; (*inf:
holiday etc*) phantastisch.
**brilliantly** [ˈbrɪljəntlɪ] *adv* (*see adj*) strahlend;
genial, brillant; großartig; phantastisch.
**brim** [brɪm] *n* Rand *m*; (*of hat*) Krempe *f*.
**brimful** [ˈbrɪmˈful] *adj*: **~ (of)** randvoll (mit);
(*fig*) voll (von).
**brine** [braɪn] *n* Lake *f*.
**bring** [brɪŋ] (*pt, pp* **brought**) *vt* bringen; (*with
you*) mitbringen; **to ~ sth to an end** etw zu
Ende bringen; **I can't ~ myself to fire him**
ich kann es nicht über mich bringen, ihn zu
entlassen.
▸**bring about** *vt* herbeiführen.
▸**bring back** *vt* (*restore*) wieder einführen;
(*return*) zurückbringen.
▸**bring down** *vt* (*government*) zu Fall
bringen; (*plane*) herunterholen; (*price*)
senken.
▸**bring forward** *vt* (*meeting*) vorverlegen;
(*proposal*) vorbringen; (*BOOKKEEPING*)
übertragen.
▸**bring in** *vt* (*money*) (ein)bringen; (*include*)
einbeziehen; (*person*) einschalten;
(*legislation*) einbringen; (*verdict*) fällen.
▸**bring off** *vt* (*plan*) durchführen; (*deal*)
zustande bringen.
▸**bring out** *vt* herausholen; (*meaning, book,
album*) herausbringen.
▸**bring round** *vt* (*after faint*) wieder zu
Bewußtsein bringen.
▸**bring up** *vt* heraufbringen; (*educate*)
erziehen; (*question, subject*) zur Sprache
bringen; (*food*) erbrechen.
**bring-and-buy sale** *n* Basar *m* (*wo
mitgebrachte Sachen verkauft werden*).
**brink** [brɪŋk] *n* Rand *m*; **on the ~ of doing sth**
nahe daran, etw zu tun; **she was on the ~ of
tears** sie war den Tränen nahe.
**brisk** [brɪsk] *adj* (*abrupt: person, tone*) forsch;
(*pace*) flott; (*trade*) lebhaft, rege; **to go for a
~ walk** einen ordentlichen Spaziergang
machen; **business is ~** das Geschäft ist

rege.
**bristle** [ˈbrɪsl] *n* Borste *f*; (*of beard*) Stoppel *f*
♦ *vi* zornig werden; **bristling with** strotzend
von.
**bristly** [ˈbrɪslɪ] *adj* borstig; (*chin*) stoppelig.
**Brit** [brɪt] (*inf*) *n abbr* (= *British person*) Brite *m*,
Britin *f*.
**Britain** [ˈbrɪtən] *n* (*also:* **Great ~**)
Großbritannien *nt*.
**British** [ˈbrɪtɪʃ] *adj* britisch ♦ *npl*: **the ~** die
Briten *pl*.
**British Isles** *npl*: **the ~** die Britischen Inseln.
**British Rail** *n* britische *Eisenbahn-
gesellschaft*.
**British Summer Time** *n* britische
Sommerzeit *f*.
**Briton** [ˈbrɪtən] *n* Brite *m*, Britin *f*.
**Brittany** [ˈbrɪtənɪ] *n* die Bretagne.
**brittle** [ˈbrɪtl] *adj* spröde; (*glass*) zerbrechlich;
(*bones*) schwach.
**Br(o).** *abbr* (*REL*) = **brother.**
**broach** [brəutʃ] *vt* (*subject*) anschneiden.
**broad** [brɔːd] *adj* breit; (*general*) allgemein;
(*accent*) stark ♦ *n* (*US: inf*) Frau *f*; **in
~ daylight** am hellichten Tag; **~ hint**
deutlicher Wink *m*.
**broad bean** *n* dicke Bohne *f*, Saubohne *f*.
**broadcast** [ˈbrɔːdkɑːst] (*pt, pp* **broadcast**) *n*
Sendung *f* ♦ *vt, vi* senden.
**broadcaster** [ˈbrɔːdkɑːstəʳ] *n* (*RADIO, TV*)
Rundfunk-/Fernsehpersönlichkeit *f*.
**broadcasting** [ˈbrɔːdkɑːstɪŋ] *n* (*RADIO*)
Rundfunk *m*; (*TV*) Fernsehen *nt*.
**broadcasting station** *n* (*RADIO*)
Rundfunkstation *f*; (*TV*) Fernsehstation *f*.
**broaden** [ˈbrɔːdn] *vt* erweitern ♦ *vi* breiter
werden, sich verbreitern; **to ~ one's mind**
seinen Horizont erweitern.
**broadly** [ˈbrɔːdlɪ] *adv* (*in general terms*) in
großen Zügen; **~ speaking** allgemein *or*
generell gesagt.
**broad-minded** [ˈbrɔːdˈmaɪndɪd] *adj* tolerant.
**broadsheet** [ˈbrɔːdʃiːt] *n* (*newspaper*)
großformatige Zeitung *f*.
**broccoli** [ˈbrɔkəlɪ] *n* Brokkoli *pl*, Spargelkohl
*m*.
**brochure** [ˈbrəuʃjuəʳ] *n* Broschüre *f*.
**brogue** [brəug] *n* Akzent *m*; (*shoe*) fester
Schuh *m*.
**broil** [brɔɪl] (*US*) *vt* grillen.
**broiler** [ˈbrɔɪləʳ] *n* Brathähnchen *nt*.
**broke** [brəuk] *pt of* **break** ♦ *adj* (*inf*) pleite; **to go
~** pleite gehen.
**broken** [ˈbrəukn] *pp of* **break** ♦ *adj* zerbrochen;
(*machine: also:* **~ down**) kaputt; (*promise,
vow*) gebrochen; **a ~ leg** ein gebrochenes
Bein; **a ~ marriage** eine gescheiterte Ehe; **a
~ home** zerrüttete Familienverhältnisse *pl*;
**in ~ English/German** in gebrochenem
Englisch/Deutsch.
**broken-down** [ˈbrəuknˈdaun] *adj* kaputt;
(*house*) baufällig.

**brokenhearted** [brəukn'ha:tɪd] *adj* untröstlich.

**broker** ['brəukə*] *n* Makler(in) *m(f)*.

**brokerage** ['brəukrɪdʒ] *n* (*commission*) Maklergebühr *f*; (*business*) Maklergeschäft *nt*.

**brolly** ['brɒlɪ] (*BRIT: inf*) *n* (Regen)schirm *m*.

**bronchitis** [brɒŋ'kaɪtɪs] *n* Bronchitis *f*.

**bronze** [brɒnz] *n* Bronze *f*.

**bronzed** [brɒnzd] *adj* braun, (sonnen)gebräunt.

**brooch** [brəutʃ] *n* Brosche *f*.

**brood** [bru:d] *n* Brut *f* ♦ *vi* (*hen*) brüten; (*person*) grübeln.

▶**brood on** *vt fus* nachgrübeln über +*acc*.

▶**brood over** *vt fus* = **brood on.**

**broody** ['bru:dɪ] *adj* (*person*) grüblerisch; (*hen*) brütig.

**brook** [bruk] *n* Bach *m*.

**broom** [brum] *n* Besen *m*; (*BOT*) Ginster *m*.

**broomstick** ['brumstɪk] *n* Besenstiel *m*.

**Bros.** *abbr* (*COMM:* = *brothers*) Gebr.

**broth** [brɒθ] *n* Suppe *f*, Fleischbrühe *f*.

**brothel** ['brɒθl] *n* Bordell *nt*.

**brother** ['brʌðə*] *n* Bruder *m*; (*in trade union, society etc*) Kollege *m*.

**brotherhood** ['brʌðəhud] *n* Brüderlichkeit *f*.

**brother-in-law** ['brʌðərɪn'lɔ:] *n* Schwager *m*.

**brotherly** ['brʌðəlɪ] *adj* brüderlich.

**brought** [brɔ:t] *pt, pp of* **bring.**

**brought forward** *adj* (*COMM*) vorgetragen.

**brow** [brau] *n* Stirn *f*; (*eyebrow*) (Augen)braue *f*; (*of hill*) (Berg)kuppe *f*.

**browbeat** ['braubi:t] *vt*: **to ~ sb (into doing sth)** jdn (so) unter Druck setzen(, daß er etw tut).

**brown** [braun] *adj* braun ♦ *n* Braun *nt* ♦ *vt* (*CULIN*) (an)bräunen; **to go ~** braun werden.

**brown bread** *n* Graubrot *nt*, Mischbrot *nt*.

**Brownie** ['braunɪ] *n* (*also:* ~ **Guide**) Wichtel *m*.

**brownie** ['braunɪ] (*US*) *n* kleiner Schokoladenkuchen.

**brown paper** *n* Packpapier *nt*.

**brown rice** *n* Naturreis *m*.

**brown sugar** *n* brauner Zucker *m*.

**browse** [brauz] *vi* (*in shop*) sich umsehen; (*animal*) weiden; (: *deer*) äsen ♦ *n*: **to have a ~ (around)** sich umsehen; **to ~ through a book** in einem Buch schmökern.

**bruise** [bru:z] *n* blauer Fleck *m*, Bluterguß *m*; (*on fruit*) Druckstelle *f* ♦ *vt* (*arm, leg etc*) sich *dat* stoßen; (*person*) einen blauen Fleck schlagen; (*fruit*) beschädigen ♦ *vi* (*fruit*) eine Druckstelle bekommen; **to ~ one's arm** sich *dat* den Arm stoßen, sich *dat* einen blauen Fleck am Arm holen.

**bruising** ['bru:zɪŋ] *adj* (*experience, encounter*) schmerzhaft ♦ *n* Quetschung *f*.

**Brum** [brʌm] (*BRIT: inf*) *n abbr* (= *Birmingham*).

**Brummie** ['brʌmɪ] (*inf*) *n aus Birmingham stammende oder dort wohnhafte Person,* Birminghamer(in) *m(f)*.

**brunch** [brʌntʃ] *n* Brunch *m*.

**brunette** [bru:'nɛt] *n* Brünette *f*.

**brunt** [brʌnt] *n*: **to bear the ~ of** die volle Wucht +*gen* tragen.

**brush** [brʌʃ] *n* Bürste *f*; (*for painting, shaving etc*) Pinsel *m*; (*quarrel*) Auseinandersetzung *f* ♦ *vt* fegen; (*groom*) bürsten; (*teeth*) putzen; (*also:* ~ **against**) streifen; **to have a ~ with sb** (*verbally*) sich mit jdm streiten; (*physically*) mit jdm aneinandergeraten; **to have a ~ with the police** mit der Polizei aneinandergeraten.

▶**brush aside** *vt* abtun.

▶**brush past** *vt* streifen.

▶**brush up** *vt* auffrischen.

**brushed** [brʌʃt] *adj* (*steel, chrome etc*) gebürstet; (*denim etc*) aufgerauht; ~ **nylon** Nylon-Velours *m*.

**brushoff** ['brʌʃɔf] (*inf*) *n*: **to give sb the ~** jdm eine Abfuhr erteilen.

**brushwood** ['brʌʃwud] *n* Reisig *nt*.

**brusque** [bru:sk] *adj* brüsk; (*tone*) schroff.

**Brussels** ['brʌslz] *n* Brüssel *nt*.

**Brussels sprouts** *npl* Rosenkohl *m*.

**brutal** ['bru:tl] *adj* brutal.

**brutality** [bru:'tælɪtɪ] *n* Brutalität *f*.

**brutalize** ['bru:təlaɪz] *vt* brutalisieren; (*ill-treat*) brutal behandeln.

**brute** [bru:t] *n* brutaler Kerl *m*; (*animal*) Tier *nt* ♦ *adj*: **by ~ force** mit roher Gewalt.

**brutish** ['bru:tɪʃ] *adj* tierisch.

**BS** (*US*) *n abbr* (= *Bachelor of Science*) *akademischer Grad für Naturwissenschaftler.*

**bs** *abbr* = **bill of sale.**

**BSA** *n abbr* (= *Boy Scouts of America*) *amerikanische Pfadfinderorganisation.*

**BSc** *abbr* (= *Bachelor of Science*) *akademischer Grad für Naturwissenschaftler.*

**BSE** *n abbr* (= *bovine spongiform encephalopathy*) BSE *f*.

**BSI** *n abbr* (= *British Standards Institution*) *britischer Normenausschuß.*

**BST** *abbr* = **British Summer Time.**

**Bt** (*BRIT*) *abbr* = **baronet.**

**btu** *n abbr* (= *British thermal unit*) *britische Wärmeeinheit.*

**bubble** ['bʌbl] *n* Blase *f* ♦ *vi* sprudeln; (*sparkle*) perlen; (*fig: person*) übersprudeln.

**bubble bath** *n* Schaumbad *nt*.

**bubble gum** *n* Bubble-Gum *m*.

**bubble-jet printer** *n* Bubble-Jet-Drucker *m*.

**bubble pack** *n* (Klar)sichtpackung *f*.

**bubbly** ['bʌblɪ] *adj* (*person*) lebendig; (*liquid*) sprudelnd ♦ *n* (*inf: champagne*) Schampus *m*.

**Bucharest** [bu:kə'rɛst] *n* Bukarest *nt*.

**buck** [bʌk] *n* (*rabbit*) Rammler *m*; (*deer*) Bock *m*; (*US: inf*) Dollar *m* ♦ *vi* bocken; **to pass the ~** die Verantwortung abschieben; **to pass the ~ to sb** jdm die Verantwortung zuschieben.

►**buck up** vi (cheer up) aufleben ♦ vt: to ~ one's ideas up sich zusammenreißen.

**bucket** ['bʌkɪt] n Eimer m ♦ vi (BRIT: inf): **the rain is ~ing (down)** es gießt or schüttet (wie aus Kübeln).

**Buckingham Palace** ist die offizielle Londoner Residenz der britischen Monarchen und liegt am St James Park. Der Palast wurde 1703 für den Herzog von Buckingham erbaut, 1762 von Georg III gekauft, zwischen 1821 und 1836 von John Nash umgebaut, und Anfang des 20. Jahrhunderts teilweise neu gestaltet. Teile des Buckingham Palace sind heute der Öffentlichkeit zugänglich.

**buckle** ['bʌkl] n Schnalle f ♦ vt zuschnallen; (wheel) verbiegen ♦ vi sich verbiegen.

►**buckle down** vi sich dahinterklemmen; **to ~ down to sth** sich hinter etw acc klemmen.

**Bucks** [bʌks] (BRIT) abbr (POST: = Buckinghamshire).

**bud** [bʌd] n Knospe f ♦ vi knospen, Knospen treiben.

**Budapest** [bjuːdə'pɛst] n Budapest nt.

**Buddha** ['budə] n Buddha m.

**Buddhism** ['budɪzəm] n Buddhismus m.

**Buddhist** ['budɪst] adj buddhistisch ♦ n Buddhist(in) m(f).

**budding** ['bʌdɪŋ] adj angehend.

**buddy** ['bʌdɪ] (US) n Kumpel m.

**budge** [bʌdʒ] vt (von der Stelle) bewegen; (fig) zum Nachgeben bewegen ♦ vi sich von der Stelle rühren; (fig) nachgeben.

**budgerigar** ['bʌdʒərɪgɑː'] n Wellensittich m.

**budget** ['bʌdʒɪt] n Budget nt, Etat m, Haushalt m ♦ vi haushalten, wirtschaften; **I'm on a tight ~** ich habe nicht viel Geld zur Verfügung; **she works out her ~ every month** sie macht (sich dat) jeden Monat einen Haushaltsplan; **to ~ for sth** etw kostenmäßig einplanen.

**budgie** ['bʌdʒɪ] n = budgerigar.

**Buenos Aires** ['bweɪnɔs'aɪrɪz] n Buenos Aires nt.

**buff** [bʌf] adj gelbbraun ♦ n (inf) Fan m.

**buffalo** ['bʌfələu] (pl ~ or ~es) n (BRIT) Büffel m; (US) Bison m.

**buffer** ['bʌfə'] n (COMPUT) Puffer m, Pufferspeicher m; (RAIL) Prellbock m; (fig) Polster nt.

**buffering** ['bʌfərɪŋ] n (COMPUT) Pufferung f.

**buffer state** n Pufferstaat m.

**buffer zone** n Pufferzone f.

**buffet¹** ['bufeɪ] (BRIT) n Büfett nt, Bahnhofsrestaurant nt; (food) kaltes Buffet nt.

**buffet²** ['bʌfɪt] vt (subj: sea) hin und her werfen; (: wind) schütteln.

**buffet car** (BRIT) n Speisewagen m.

**buffet lunch** n Buffet nt.

**buffoon** [bə'fuːn] n Clown m.

**bug** [bʌg] n (esp US) Insekt nt; (COMPUT: of program) Programmfehler m; (: of equipment) Fehler m; (fig: germ) Bazillus m; (hidden microphone) Wanze f ♦ vt (inf) nerven; (telephone etc) abhören; (room) verwanzen; **I've got the travel ~** (fig) mich hat die Reiselust gepackt.

**bugbear** ['bʌgbɛə'] n Schreckgespenst nt.

**bugger** ['bʌgə'] (inf!) n Scheißkerl m, Arschloch nt ♦ vb: ~ **off!** hau ab!; ~ **(it)!** Scheiße!

**buggy** ['bʌgɪ] n (for baby) Sportwagen m.

**bugle** ['bjuːgl] n Bügelhorn nt.

**build** [bɪld] (pt, pp built) n Körperbau m ♦ vt bauen.

►**build on** vt fus (fig) aufbauen auf +dat.

►**build up** vt aufbauen; (production) steigern; (morale) stärken; (stocks) anlegen; **don't ~ your hopes up too soon** mach dir nicht zu früh Hoffnungen.

**builder** ['bɪldə'] n Bauunternehmer m.

**building** ['bɪldɪŋ] n (industry) Bauindustrie f; (construction) Bau m; (structure) Gebäude nt, Bau.

**building contractor** n Bauunternehmer m.

**building industry** n Bauindustrie f.

**building site** n Baustelle f.

**building society** (BRIT) n Bausparkasse f.

**building trade** n = building industry.

**build-up** ['bɪldʌp] n Ansammlung f; (publicity): **to give sb/sth a good ~** jdn/etw ganz groß herausbringen.

**built** [bɪlt] pt, pp of build ♦ adj: ~**-in** eingebaut, Einbau-; (safeguards) eingebaut; **well-~** gut gebaut.

**built-up area** ['bɪltʌp-] n bebautes Gebiet nt.

**bulb** [bʌlb] n (Blumen)zwiebel f; (ELEC) (Glüh)birne f.

**bulbous** ['bʌlbəs] adj knollig.

**Bulgaria** [bʌl'gɛərɪə] n Bulgarien nt.

**Bulgarian** [bʌl'gɛərɪən] adj bulgarisch ♦ n Bulgare m, Bulgarin f; (LING) Bulgarisch nt.

**bulge** [bʌldʒ] n Wölbung f; (in birth rate, sales) Zunahme f ♦ vi (pocket) prall gefüllt sein; (cheeks) voll sein; (file) (zum Bersten) voll sein; **to be bulging with** prall gefüllt sein mit.

**bulimia** [bə'lɪmɪə] n Bulimie f.

**bulk** [bʌlk] n (of thing) massige Form f; (of person) massige Gestalt f; **in ~** im großen, en gros; **the ~ of** der Großteil +gen.

**bulk buying** [-'baɪɪŋ] n Mengeneinkauf m, Großeinkauf m.

**bulk carrier** n Bulkcarrier m.

**bulkhead** ['bʌlkhɛd] n Schott nt.

**bulky** ['bʌlkɪ] adj sperrig.

**bull** [bul] n Stier m; (male elephant or whale) Bulle m; (STOCK EXCHANGE) Haussier m, Haussespekulant m; (REL) Bulle f.

**bulldog** ['buldɔg] n Bulldogge f.

**bulldoze** ['buldəuz] vt mit Bulldozern wegräumen; (building) mit Bulldozern abreißen; **I was ~d into it** (*fig: inf*) ich wurde gezwungen *or* unter Druck gesetzt, es zu tun.

**bulldozer** ['buldəʊzəʳ] *n* Bulldozer *m*, Planierraupe *f*.

**bullet** ['bulɪt] *n* Kugel *f*.

**bulletin** ['bulɪtɪn] *n* (*TV etc*) Kurznachrichten *pl*; (*journal*) Bulletin *nt*.

**bulletin board** *n* (*COMPUT*) Schwarzes Brett *nt*.

**bulletproof** ['bulɪtpru:f] *adj* kugelsicher.

**bullfight** ['bulfaɪt] *n* Stierkampf *m*.

**bullfighter** ['bulfaɪtəʳ] *n* Stierkämpfer *m*.

**bullfighting** ['bulfaɪtɪŋ] *n* Stierkampf *m*.

**bullion** ['buljən] *n*: **gold/silver ~** Barrengold *nt*/-silber *nt*.

**bullock** ['bulək] *n* Ochse *m*.

**bullring** ['bulrɪŋ] *n* Stierkampfarena *f*.

**bull's-eye** ['bulzaɪ] *n* (*on a target*): **the ~** der Scheibenmittelpunkt, das Schwarze.

**bullshit** ['bulʃɪt] (*inf!*) *n* Scheiß *m*, Quatsch *m* ♦ *vi* Scheiß erzählen; **~!** Quatsch!

**bully** ['bulɪ] *n* Tyrann *m* ♦ *vt* tyrannisieren; (*frighten*) einschüchtern.

**bullying** ['bulɪŋ] *n* Tyrannisieren *nt*.

**bum** [bʌm] (*inf*) *n* Hintern *m*; (*esp US: good-for-nothing*) Rumtreiber *m*; (*tramp*) Penner *m*.

►**bum around** (*inf*) *vi* herumgammeln.

**bumblebee** ['bʌmblbi:] *n* Hummel *f*.

**bumf** [bʌmf] (*inf*) *n* Papierkram *m*.

**bump** [bʌmp] *n* Zusammenstoß *m*; (*jolt*) Erschütterung *f*; (*swelling*) Beule *f*; (*on road*) Unebenheit *f* ♦ *vt* stoßen; (*car*) eine Delle fahren in +*acc*.

►**bump along** *vi* entlangholpern.

►**bump into** *vt fus* (*obstacle*) stoßen gegen; (*inf: person*) treffen.

**bumper** ['bʌmpəʳ] *n* Stoßstange *f* ♦ *adj*: **~ crop, ~ harvest** Rekordernte *f*.

**bumper cars** *npl* Autoscooter *pl*.

**bumper sticker** *n* Aufkleber *m*.

**bumph** [bʌmf] *n* = **bumf**.

**bumptious** ['bʌmpʃəs] *adj* wichtigtuerisch.

**bumpy** ['bʌmpɪ] *adj* holperig; **it was a ~ flight/ride** während des Fluges/auf der Fahrt wurden wir tüchtig durchgerüttelt.

**bun** [bʌn] *n* Brötchen *nt*; (*of hair*) Knoten *m*.

**bunch** [bʌntʃ] *n* Strauß *m*; (*of keys*) Bund *m*; (*of bananas*) Büschel *nt*; (*of people*) Haufen *m*; **bunches** *npl* (*in hair*) Zöpfe *pl*; **~ of grapes** Weintraube *f*.

**bundle** ['bʌndl] *n* Bündel *nt* ♦ *vt* (*also: ~ up*) bündeln; (*put*): **to ~ sth into** etw stopfen *or* packen in +*acc*; **to ~ sb into** jdn schaffen in +*acc*.

►**bundle off** *vt* schaffen.

►**bundle out** *vt* herausschaffen.

**bun fight** (*BRIT: inf*) *n* Festivitäten *pl*; (*tea party*) Teegesellschaft *f*.

**bung** [bʌŋ] *n* Spund *m*, Spundzapfen *m* ♦ *vt* (*BRIT: inf: also: ~ in*) schmeißen; (*also: ~ up*)

verstopfen; **my nose is ~ed up** meine Nase ist verstopft.

**bungalow** ['bʌŋgələʊ] *n* Bungalow *m*.

**bungee jumping** ['bʌndʒi:'dʒʌmpɪŋ] *n* Bungee-Springen *nt*.

**bungle** ['bʌŋgl] *vt* verpfuschen.

**bunion** ['bʌnjən] *n* entzündeter Ballen *m*.

**bunk** [bʌŋk] *n* Bett *nt*, Koje *f*; **to do a ~** (*inf*) abhauen.

►**bunk off** (*inf*) *vi* abhauen.

**bunk beds** *npl* Etagenbett *nt*.

**bunker** ['bʌŋkəʳ] *n* Kohlenbunker *m*; (*MIL, GOLF*) Bunker *m*.

**bunny** ['bʌnɪ] *n* (*also: ~ rabbit*) Hase *m*, Häschen *nt*.

**bunny girl** (*BRIT*) *n* Häschen *nt*.

**bunny hill** (*US*) *n* (*SKI*) Anfängerhügel *m*.

**bunting** ['bʌntɪŋ] *n* (*flags*) Wimpel *pl*, Fähnchen *pl*.

**buoy** [bɔɪ] *n* Boje *f*.

►**buoy up** *vt* (*fig*) Auftrieb geben +*dat*.

**buoyancy** ['bɔɪənsɪ] *n* (*of ship, object*) Schwimmfähigkeit *f*.

**buoyant** ['bɔɪənt] *adj* (*ship, object*) schwimmfähig; (*market*) fest; (*economy*) stabil; (*prices, currency*) fest, stabil; (*person, nature*) heiter.

**burden** ['bə:dn] *n* Belastung *f*; (*load*) Last *f* ♦ *vt*: **to ~ sb with sth** jdn mit etw belasten; **to be a ~ to sb** jdm zur Last fallen.

**bureau** ['bjʊərəʊ] (*pl ~x*) *n* (*BRIT: writing desk*) Sekretär *m*; (*US: chest of drawers*) Kommode *f*; (*office*) Büro *nt*.

**bureaucracy** [bjʊə'rɔkrəsɪ] *n* Bürokratie *f*.

**bureaucrat** ['bjʊərəkræt] *n* Bürokrat(in) *m(f)*.

**bureaucratic** [bjʊərə'krætɪk] *adj* bürokratisch.

**bureaux** ['bjʊərəʊz] *npl of* **bureau**.

**burgeon** ['bə:dʒən] *vi* hervorsprießen.

**burger** ['bə:gəʳ] (*inf*) *n* Hamburger *m*.

**burglar** ['bə:gləʳ] *n* Einbrecher(in) *m(f)*.

**burglar alarm** *n* Alarmanlage *f*.

**burglarize** ['bə:gləraɪz] (*US*) *vt* einbrechen in +*acc*.

**burglary** ['bə:glərɪ] *n* Einbruch *m*.

**burgle** ['bə:gl] *vt* einbrechen in +*acc*.

**Burgundy** ['bə:gəndɪ] *n* Burgund *nt*.

**burial** ['bɛrɪəl] *n* Beerdigung *f*.

**burial ground** *n* Begräbnisstätte *f*.

**burlesque** [bə:'lɛsk] *n* (*parody*) Persiflage *f*; (*US: THEAT*) Burleske *f*.

**burly** ['bə:lɪ] *adj* kräftig, stämmig.

**Burma** ['bə:mə] *n* Birma *m*, Burma *nt*.

**Burmese** [bə:'mi:z] *adj* birmanisch, burmesisch ♦ *n inv* Birmane *m*, Burmese *m*, Birmanin *f*, Burmesin *f* ♦ *n* (*LING*) Birmanisch *nt*, Burmesisch *nt*.

**burn** [bə:n] (*pt, pp* **burned** *or* **burnt**) *vt* verbrennen; (*fuel*) als Brennstoff verwenden; (*food*) anbrennen lassen; (*house etc*) niederbrennen ♦ *vi* brennen; (*food*) anbrennen ♦ *n* Verbrennung *f*; **the cigarette ~t a hole in her dress** die Zigarette brannte

ein Loch in ihr Kleid; **I've ~t myself!** ich habe mich verbrannt!
▶**burn down** vt abbrennen.
▶**burn out** vt: **to ~ o.s. out** (writer etc) sich völlig verausgaben; **the fire ~t itself out** das Feuer brannte aus.
**burner** ['bɜːnə*] n Brenner m.
**burning** ['bɜːnɪŋ] adj brennend; (sand, desert) glühend heiß.
**burnish** ['bɜːnɪʃ] vt polieren.

---

Burns' Night ist der am 25. Januar begangene Gedenktag für den schottischen Dichter Robert Burns (1759-1796). Wo Schotten leben, sei es in Schottland oder im Ausland, wird dieser Tag mit einem Abendessen gefeiert, bei dem es als Hauptgericht **Haggis** gibt, der mit Dudelsackbegleitung aufgetischt wird. Dazu ißt man Steckrüben- und Kartoffelpüree und trinkt Whisky. Während des Essens werden Burns' Gedichte vorgelesen, seine Lieder gesungen, bestimmte Reden gehalten und Trinksprüche ausgegeben.

---

**burnt** [bɜːnt] pt, pp of **burn**.
**burnt sugar** (BRIT) n Karamel m.
**burp** [bɜːp] (inf) n Rülpser m ♦ vt (baby) aufstoßen lassen ♦ vi rülpsen.
**burrow** ['bʌrəʊ] n Bau m ♦ vi graben; (rummage) wühlen.
**bursar** ['bɜːsə*] n Schatzmeister m, Finanzverwalter m.
**bursary** ['bɜːsərɪ] (BRIT) n Stipendium nt.
**burst** [bɜːst] (pt, pp burst) vt zum Platzen bringen, platzen lassen ♦ vi platzen ♦ n Salve f; (also: ~ **pipe**) (Rohr)bruch m; **the river has ~ its banks** der Fluß ist über die Ufer getreten; **to ~ into flames** in Flammen aufgehen; **to ~ into tears** in Tränen ausbrechen; **to ~ out laughing** in Lachen ausbrechen; **~ blood vessel** geplatzte Ader f; **to be ~ing with** zum Bersten voll sein mit; (pride) fast platzen vor +dat; **to ~ open** aufspringen; **a ~ of energy** ein Ausbruch m von Energie; **a ~ of enthusiasm** ein Begeisterungsausbruch m; **a ~ of speed** ein Spurt m; **~ of laughter** Lachsalve f; **~ of applause** Beifallssturm m.
▶**burst in on** vt fus: **to ~ in on sb** bei jdm hereinplatzen.
▶**burst into** vt fus (into room) platzen in +acc.
▶**burst out of** vt fus (of room) stürmen or stürzen aus.
**bury** ['berɪ] vt begraben; (at funeral) beerdigen; **to ~ one's face in one's hands** das Gesicht in den Händen vergraben; **to ~ one's head in the sand** (fig) den Kopf in den Sand stecken; **to ~ the hatchet** (fig) das Kriegsbeil begraben.
**bus** [bʌs] n (Auto)bus m, (Omni)bus m; (double decker) Doppeldecker m (inf).
**bus boy** (US) n Bedienungshilfe f.

**bush** [bʊʃ] n Busch m, Strauch m; (scrubland) Busch; **to beat about the ~** um den heißen Brei herumreden.
**bushed** [bʊʃt] (inf) adj (exhausted) groggy.
**bushel** ['bʊʃl] n Scheffel m.
**bushfire** n Buschfeuer nt.
**bushy** ['bʊʃɪ] adj buschig.
**busily** ['bɪzɪlɪ] adv eifrig; **to be ~ doing sth** eifrig etw tun.
**business** ['bɪznɪs] n (matter) Angelegenheit f; (trading) Geschäft nt; (firm) Firma f, Betrieb m; (occupation) Beruf m; **to be away on ~** geschäftlich unterwegs sein; **I'm here on ~** ich bin geschäftlich hier; **he's in the insurance/transport ~** er arbeitet in der Versicherungs-/Transportbranche; **to do ~ with sb** Geschäfte pl mit jdm machen; **it's my ~ to ...** es ist meine Aufgabe, zu ...; **it's none of my ~** es geht mich nichts an; **he means ~** er meint es ernst.
**business address** n Geschäftsadresse f.
**business card** n (Visiten)karte f.
**businesslike** ['bɪznɪslaɪk] adj geschäftsmäßig.
**businessman** ['bɪznɪsmən] (irreg: like man) n Geschäftsmann m.
**business trip** n Geschäftsreise f.
**businesswoman** ['bɪznɪswʊmən] (irreg: like woman) n Geschäftsfrau f.
**busker** ['bʌskə*] (BRIT) n Straßenmusikant(in) m(f).
**bus lane** (BRIT) n Busspur f.
**bus shelter** n Wartehäuschen nt.
**bus station** n Busbahnhof m.
**bus stop** n Bushaltestelle f.
**bust** [bʌst] n Busen m; (measurement) Oberweite f; (sculpture) Büste f ♦ adj (inf) kaputt ♦ vt (inf) verhaften; **to go ~** pleite gehen.
**bustle** ['bʌsl] n Betrieb m ♦ vi eilig herumlaufen.
**bustling** ['bʌslɪŋ] adj belebt.
**bust-up** ['bʌstʌp] (BRIT: inf) n Krach m.
**busty** ['bʌstɪ] adj (woman) vollbusig.
**BUSWE** (BRIT) n abbr (= British Union of Social Work Employees) Sozialarbeiter-gewerkschaft.
**busy** ['bɪzɪ] adj (person) beschäftigt; (shop, street) belebt; (TEL: esp US) besetzt ♦ vt: **to ~ o.s. with** sich beschäftigen mit; **he's a ~ man** er ist ein vielbeschäftigter Mann; **he's ~** er hat (zur Zeit) viel zu tun.
**busybody** ['bɪzɪbɒdɪ] n: **to be a ~** sich ständig einmischen.
**busy signal** (US) n (TEL) Besetztzeichen nt.

═══════════════════════ — KEYWORD

**but** [bʌt] conj **1** (yet) aber; **not blue ~ red** nicht blau, sondern rot; **he's not very bright, ~ he's hard-working** er ist nicht sehr intelligent, aber er ist fleißig
**2** (however): **I'd love to come, ~ I'm busy** ich würde gern kommen, bin aber beschäftigt

**3** (*showing disagreement, surprise etc*):
~ **that's far too expensive!** aber das ist viel
zu teuer!; ~ **that's fantastic!** das ist doch
toll!
♦ *prep* (*apart from, except*) außer +*dat*; **nothing**
~ **trouble** nichts als Ärger; **no-one** ~ **him
can do it** keiner außer ihm kann es machen;
~ **for you** wenn Sie nicht gewesen wären;
~ **for your help** ohne Ihre Hilfe; **I'll do
anything** ~ **that** ich mache alles, nur nicht
das; **the last house** ~ **one** das vorletzte
Haus; **the next street** ~ **one** die übernächste
Straße
♦ *adv* (*just, only*) nur; **she's** ~ **a child** sie ist
doch noch ein Kind; **I can** ~ **try** ich kann es
ja versuchen.

**butane** ['bjuːteɪn] *n* (*also*: ~ **gas**) Butan(gas)
*nt.*
**butch** [butʃ] (*inf*) *adj* maskulin.
**butcher** ['butʃə'] *n* Fleischer *m*, Metzger *m*;
(*pej: murderer*) Schlächter *m* ♦ *vt* schlachten;
(*prisoners etc*) abschlachten.
**butcher's (shop)** ['butʃəz-] *n* Fleischerei *f*,
Metzgerei *f.*
**butler** ['bʌtlə'] *n* Butler *m.*
**butt** [bʌt] *n* großes Faß *nt*, Tonne *f*; (*thick end*)
dickes Ende *nt*; (*of gun*) Kolben *m*; (*of
cigarette*) Kippe *f*; (*BRIT, fig: target*)
Zielscheibe *f*; (*US: inf!*) Arsch *m* ♦ *vt* (*goat*)
mit den Hörnern stoßen; (*person*) mit dem
Kopf stoßen.
▶**butt in** *vi* sich einmischen,
dazwischenfunken (*inf*).
**butter** ['bʌtə'] *n* Butter *f* ♦ *vt* buttern.
**buttercup** ['bʌtəkʌp] *n* Butterblume *f.*
**butter dish** *n* Butterdose *f.*
**butterfingers** ['bʌtəfɪŋgəz] (*inf*) *n* Schussel *m.*
**butterfly** ['bʌtəflaɪ] *n* Schmetterling *m*;
(*SWIMMING: also:* ~ **stroke**)
Schmetterlingsstil *m*, Butterfly *m.*
**buttocks** ['bʌtəks] *npl* Gesäß *nt.*
**button** ['bʌtn] *n* Knopf *m*; (*US: badge*)
Plakette *f* ♦ *vt* (*also:* ~ **up**) zuknöpfen ♦ *vi*
geknöpft werden.
**buttonhole** ['bʌtnhəul] *n* Knopfloch *nt*;
(*flower*) Blume *f* im Knopfloch ♦ *vt* zu fassen
bekommen, sich *dat* schnappen (*inf*).
**buttress** ['bʌtrɪs] *n* Strebepfeiler *m.*
**buxom** ['bʌksəm] *adj* drall.
**buy** [baɪ] (*pt, pp* bought) *vt* kaufen; (*company*)
aufkaufen ♦ *n* Kauf *m*; **that was a good/bad**
~ das war ein guter/schlechter Kauf; **to**
~ **sb sth** jdm etw kaufen; **to** ~ **sth from sb**
etw bei jdm kaufen; (*from individual*) jdm
etw abkaufen; **to** ~ **sb a drink** jdm einen
ausgeben (*inf*).
▶**buy back** *vt* zurückkaufen.
▶**buy in** (*BRIT*) *vt* einkaufen.
▶**buy into** (*BRIT*) *vt fus* sich einkaufen in +*acc.*
▶**buy off** *vt* kaufen.
▶**buy out** *vt* (*partner*) auszahlen; (*business*)

aufkaufen.
▶**buy up** *vt* aufkaufen.
**buyer** ['baɪə'] *n* Käufer(in) *m(f)*; (*COMM*)
Einkäufer(in) *m(f).*
**buyer's market** ['baɪəz-] *n* Käufermarkt *m.*
**buyout** ['baɪaut] *n* (*of firm: by workers,
management*) Aufkauf *m.*
**buzz** [bʌz] *vi* summen, brummen; (*saw*)
kreischen ♦ *vt* rufen; (*with buzzer*) (mit dem
Summer) rufen; (*AVIAT: plane, building*)
dicht vorbeifliegen an +*dat* ♦ *n* Summen *nt*,
Brummen *nt*; (*inf*): **to give sb a** ~ jdn
anrufen; **my head is** ~**ing** mir schwirrt der
Kopf.
▶**buzz off** (*inf*) *vi* abhauen.
**buzzard** ['bʌzəd] *n* Bussard *m.*
**buzzer** ['bʌzə'] *n* Summer *m.*
**buzz word** (*inf*) *n* Modewort *nt.*

━━━━━━━━━━━━━━━━━━━━ *KEYWORD*

**by** [baɪ] *prep* **1** (*referring to cause, agent*) von
+*dat*, durch +*acc*; **killed** ~ **lightning** vom Blitz
*or* durch einen Blitz getötet; **a painting**
~ **Picasso** ein Bild von Picasso
**2** (*referring to method, manner, means*):
~ **bus/car/train** mit dem Bus/Auto/Zug; **to
pay** ~ **cheque** mit *or* per Scheck bezahlen;
~ **saving hard, he was able to ...** indem er
eisern sparte, konnte er ...
**3** (*via, through*) über +*acc*; **we came** ~ **Dover**
wir sind über Dover gekommen
**4** (*close to*) bei +*dat*, an +*dat*; **the house** ~ **the
river** das Haus am Fluß
**5** (*past*) an ... *dat* vorbei; **she rushed** ~ **me** sie
eilte an mir vorbei
**6** (*not later than*) bis +*acc*; ~ **4 o'clock** bis 4
Uhr; ~ **this time tomorrow** morgen um
diese Zeit
**7** (*amount*): ~ **the kilo/metre** kilo-/
meterweise; **to be paid** ~ **the hour**
stundenweise bezahlt werden
**8** (*MATH, measure*): **to divide** ~ **3** durch 3
teilen; **to multiply** ~ **3** mit 3 malnehmen; **it
missed me** ~ **inches** es hat mich um
Zentimeter verfehlt
**9** (*according to*): **to play** ~ **the rules** sich an
die Regeln halten; **it's all right** ~ **me** von
mir aus ist es in Ordnung
**10**: (*all*) ~ **myself/himself** *etc* (ganz) allein
**11**: ~ **the way** übrigens
♦ *adv* **1** *see* **go, pass** *etc*
**2**: ~ **and** ~ irgendwann
**3**: ~ **and large** im großen und ganzen.

**bye(-bye)** ['baɪ('baɪ)] *excl* (auf) Wiedersehen,
tschüs (*inf*).
**bye-law** ['baɪlɔː] *n* Verordnung *f.*
**by-election** ['baɪɪlekʃən] (*BRIT*) *n* Nachwahl *f.*
**Byelorussia** [bjɛləu'rʌʃə] *n* = **Belorussia.**
**Byelorussian** [bjɛləu'rʌʃən] *adj, n*
= **Belarussian.**
**bygone** ['baɪgɔn] *adj* (längst) vergangen ♦ *n*:

let ~s be ~s wir sollten die Vergangenheit ruhen lassen.

**by-law** ['baɪlɔː] n = **bye-law**.

**bypass** ['baɪpɑːs] n Umgehungsstraße f; (MED) Bypass-Operation f ♦ vt (also fig) umgehen.

**by-product** ['baɪprɔdʌkt] n Nebenprodukt nt.

**byre** ['baɪə'] (BRIT) n Kuhstall m.

**bystander** ['baɪstændə'] n Zuschauer(in) m(f).

**byte** [baɪt] n (COMPUT) Byte nt.

**byway** ['baɪweɪ] n Seitenweg m.

**byword** ['baɪwəːd] n: **to be a ~ for** der Inbegriff +gen sein, gleichbedeutend sein mit.

**by-your-leave** ['baɪjɔː'liːv] n: **without so much as a ~** ohne auch nur (um Erlaubnis) zu fragen.

# C, c

**C¹, c¹** [siː] n (letter) C nt, c nt; (SCOL) ≈ Drei f, Befriedigend nt; ~ **for Charlie** ≈ C wie Cäsar.

**C²** [siː] n (MUS) C nt, c nt.

**C³** [siː] abbr = **Celsius; centigrade**.

**c²** abbr = **century**; (= circa) ca.; (US etc: = cent(s)) Cent.

**CA** n abbr (BRIT) = **chartered accountant** ♦ abbr = **Central America**; (US: POST: = California).

**C/A** abbr (COMM) = **capital account; credit account; current account**.

**ca.** abbr (= circa) ca.

**CAA** n abbr (BRIT) = **Civil Aviation Authority**; (US: = Civil Aeronautics Authority) Zivilluftfahrtbehörde.

**CAB** (BRIT) n abbr = **Citizens' Advice Bureau**.

**cab** [kæb] n Taxi nt; (of truck, train etc) Führerhaus nt; (horse-drawn) Droschke f.

**cabaret** ['kæbəreɪ] n Kabarett nt.

**cabbage** ['kæbɪdʒ] n Kohl m.

**cabbie, cabby** ['kæbɪ] n Taxifahrer(in) m(f).

**cab driver** n Taxifahrer(in) m(f).

**cabin** ['kæbɪn] n Kabine f; (house) Hütte f.

**cabin cruiser** n Kajütboot nt.

**cabinet** ['kæbɪnɪt] n kleiner Schrank m; (also: display ~) Vitrine f; (POL) Kabinett nt.

**cabinet-maker** ['kæbɪnɪt'meɪkə'] n Möbeltischler m.

**cabinet minister** n Mitglied nt des Kabinetts, Minister(in) m(f).

**cable** ['keɪbl] n Kabel nt ♦ vt kabeln.

**cable car** n (Draht)seilbahn f.

**cablegram** ['keɪblgræm] n (Übersee)telegramm nt, Kabel nt.

**cable railway** n Seilbahn f.

**cable television** n Kabelfernsehen nt.

**cable TV** n = **cable television**.

**cache** [kæʃ] n Versteck nt, geheimes Lager nt; **a ~ of food** ein geheimes Proviantlager.

**cackle** ['kækl] vi (person: laugh) meckernd lachen; (hen) gackern.

**cacti** ['kæktaɪ] npl of **cactus**.

**cactus** ['kæktəs] (pl cacti) n Kaktus m.

**CAD** n abbr (= computer-aided design) CAD nt.

**caddie** ['kædɪ] n (GOLF) Caddie m.

**caddy** ['kædɪ] n = **caddie**.

**cadence** ['keɪdəns] n (of voice) Tonfall m.

**cadet** [kə'dɛt] n Kadett m; **police ~** Polizeianwärter(in) m(f).

**cadge** [kædʒ] (inf) vt: **to ~ (from or off)** schnorren (bei or von +dat); **to ~ a lift with sb** von jdm mitgenommen werden.

**cadger** ['kædʒə'] (BRIT: inf) n Schnorrer(in) m(f).

**cadre** ['kædrɪ] n Kader m.

**Caesarean** [siː'zɛərɪən] n: ~ **(section)** Kaiserschnitt m.

**CAF** (BRIT) abbr (= cost and freight) cf.

**café** ['kæfeɪ] n Café nt.

**cafeteria** [kæfɪ'tɪərɪə] n Cafeteria f.

**caffein(e)** ['kæfiːn] n Koffein nt.

**cage** [keɪdʒ] n Käfig m; (of lift) Fahrkorb m ♦ vt einsperren.

**cagey** ['keɪdʒɪ] (inf) adj vorsichtig; (evasive) ausweichend.

**cagoule** [kə'guːl] n Regenjacke f.

**cahoots** [kə'huːts] (inf) n: **to be in ~ with** unter einer Decke stecken mit.

**CAI** n abbr (= computer-aided instruction) CAI nt.

**Cairo** ['kaɪərəu] n Kairo nt.

**cajole** [kə'dʒəul] vt: **to ~ sb into doing sth** jdn bereden, etw zu tun.

**cake** [keɪk] n Kuchen m; (small) Gebäckstück nt; (of soap) Stück nt; **it's a piece of ~** (inf) das ist ein Kinderspiel or ein Klacks; **he wants to have his ~ and eat it (too)** (fig) er will das eine, ohne das andere zu lassen.

**caked** [keɪkt] adj: ~ **with** (mud, blood) verkrustet mit.

**cake shop** n Konditorei f.

**Cal.** (US) abbr (POST: = California).

**calamine lotion** ['kæləmaɪn-] n Galmeilotion f.

**calamitous** [kə'læmɪtəs] adj katastrophal.

**calamity** [kə'læmɪtɪ] n Katastrophe f.

**calcium** ['kælsɪəm] n Kalzium nt.

**calculate** ['kælkjuleɪt] vt (work out) berechnen; (estimate) abschätzen.

▶**calculate on** vt fus: **to ~ on sth** mit etw rechnen; **to ~ on doing sth** damit rechnen, etw zu tun.

**calculated** ['kælkjuleɪtɪd] adj (insult) bewußt; (action) vorsätzlich; **a ~ risk** ein kalkuliertes Risiko.

**calculating** ['kælkjuleɪtɪŋ] adj (scheming) berechnend.

**calculation** [kælkjuˈleɪʃən] n (*see vt*)
Berechnung f; Abschätzung f; (*sum*)
Rechnung f.

**calculator** [ˈkælkjuleɪtə*] n Rechner m.

**calculus** [ˈkælkjuləs] n Infinitesimalrechnung
f; **integral/differential** ~ Integral-/
Differentialrechnung f.

**calendar** [ˈkæləndə*] n Kalender m; (*timetable, schedule*) (Termin)kalender m.

**calendar month** n Kalendermonat m.

**calendar year** n Kalenderjahr nt.

**calf** [kɑːf] (*pl* **calves**) n Kalb nt; (*of elephant, seal etc*) Junge(s) nt; (*also*: ~**skin**) Kalb(s)leder nt; (*ANAT*) Wade f.

**caliber** [ˈkælɪbə*] (*US*) n = **calibre**.

**calibrate** [ˈkælɪbreɪt] vt (*gun etc*) kalibrieren; (*scale of measuring instrument*) eichen.

**calibre,** (*US*) **caliber** [ˈkælɪbə*] n Kaliber nt; (*of person*) Format nt.

**calico** [ˈkælɪkəu] n (*BRIT*) Kattun m, Kaliko m; (*US*) bedruckter Kattun.

**Calif.** (*US*) abbr (*POST*: = *California*).

**California** [kælɪˈfɔːnɪə] n Kalifornien nt.

**calipers** [ˈkælɪpəz] (*US*) npl = **callipers**.

**call** [kɔːl] vt (*name, consider*) nennen; (*shout out, summon*) rufen; (*TEL*) anrufen; (*witness, flight*) aufrufen; (*meeting*) einberufen; (*strike*) ausrufen ♦ vi rufen; (*TEL*) anrufen; (*visit: also*: ~ **in,** ~ **round**) vorbeigehen, vorbeikommen ♦ n Ruf m; (*TEL*) Anruf m; (*visit*) Besuch m; (*for a service etc*) Nachfrage f; (*for flight etc*) Aufruf m; (*fig: lure*) Ruf m, Verlockung f; **to be** ~**ed** (*named*) heißen; **who is** ~**ing?** (*TEL*) wer spricht da bitte?; **London** ~**ing** (*RADIO*) hier ist London; **please give me a** ~ **at 7** rufen Sie mich bitte um 7 an; **to make a** ~ ein (Telefon)gespräch führen; **to pay a** ~ **on sb** jdn besuchen; **to be on** ~ einsatzbereit sein; (*doctor etc*) Bereitschaftsdienst haben; **there's not much** ~ **for these items** es besteht keine große Nachfrage nach diesen Dingen.

►**call at** vt fus (*subj: ship*) anlaufen; (*: train*) halten in +dat.

►**call back** vi (*return*) wiederkommen; (*TEL*) zurückrufen ♦ vt (*TEL*) zurückrufen.

►**call for** vt fus (*demand*) fordern; (*fetch*) abholen.

►**call in** vt (*doctor, expert, police*) zu Rate ziehen; (*books, cars, stock etc*) aus dem Verkehr ziehen ♦ vi vorbeigehen, vorbeikommen.

►**call off** vt absagen.

►**call on** vt fus besuchen; (*appeal to*) appellieren an +acc; **to** ~ **on sb to do sth** jdn bitten or auffordern, etw zu tun.

►**call out** vi rufen ♦ vt rufen; (*police, troops*) alarmieren.

►**call up** vt (*MIL*) einberufen; (*TEL*) anrufen.

**Callanetics** ® n sing Callanetics f.

**call box** (*BRIT*) n Telefonzelle f.

**caller** [ˈkɔːlə*] n Besucher(in) m(f); (*TEL*)

Anrufer(in) m(f); **hold the line,** ~**!** (*TEL*) bitte bleiben Sie am Apparat!

**call girl** n Callgirl nt.

**call-in** [ˈkɔːlɪn] (*US*) n (*RADIO, TV*) Phone-in nt.

**calling** [ˈkɔːlɪŋ] n (*trade*) Beruf m; (*vocation*) Berufung f.

**calling card** (*US*) n Visitenkarte f.

**callipers,** (*US*) **calipers** [ˈkælɪpəz] npl (*MATH*) Tastzirkel m; (*MED*) Schiene f.

**callous** [ˈkæləs] adj herzlos.

**callousness** [ˈkæləsnɪs] n Herzlosigkeit f.

**callow** [ˈkæləu] adj unreif.

**calm** [kɑːm] adj ruhig; (*unworried*) gelassen ♦ n Ruhe f ♦ vt beruhigen; (*fears*) zerstreuen; (*grief*) lindern.

►**calm down** vt beruhigen ♦ vi sich beruhigen.

**calmly** [ˈkɑːmlɪ] adv (*see adj*) ruhig; gelassen.

**calmness** [ˈkɑːmnɪs] n (*see adj*) Ruhe f; Gelassenheit f.

**Calor gas** ® [ˈkælə*-] n Butangas nt.

**calorie** [ˈkælərɪ] n Kalorie f; **low-**~ **product** kalorienarmes Produkt nt.

**calve** [kɑːv] vi kalben.

**calves** [kɑːvz] npl of **calf**.

**CAM** n abbr (= *computer-aided manufacture*) CAM nt.

**camber** [ˈkæmbə*] n Wölbung f.

**Cambodia** [kæmˈbəudɪə] n Kambodscha nt.

**Cambodian** [kæmˈbəudɪən] adj kambodschanisch ♦ n Kambodschaner(in) m(f).

**Cambs** (*BRIT*) abbr (*POST*: = *Cambridgeshire*).

**camcorder** [ˈkæmkɔːdə*] n Camcorder m, Kamera-Recorder m.

**came** [keɪm] pt of **come**.

**camel** [ˈkæməl] n Kamel nt.

**cameo** [ˈkæmɪəu] n Kamee f; (*THEAT, LITER*) Miniatur f.

**camera** [ˈkæmərə] n (*CINE, PHOT*) Kamera f; (*also*: **cine** ~, **movie** ~) Filmkamera f; **35 mm** ~ Kleinbildkamera f; **in** ~ (*LAW*) unter Ausschluß der Öffentlichkeit.

**cameraman** [ˈkæmərəmæn] (*irreg: like* **man**) n Kameramann m.

**Cameroon** [kæməˈruːn] n Kamerun nt.

**Cameroun** [kæməˈruːn] n = **Cameroon**.

**camomile** [ˈkæməumaɪl] n Kamille f.

**camouflage** [ˈkæməflɑːʒ] n Tarnung f ♦ vt tarnen.

**camp** [kæmp] n Lager nt; (*barracks*) Kaserne f ♦ vi zelten ♦ adj (*effeminate*) tuntenhaft (*inf*).

**campaign** [kæmˈpeɪn] n (*MIL*) Feldzug m; (*POL etc*) Kampagne f ♦ vi kämpfen; **to** ~ **for/against** sich einsetzen für/gegen.

**campaigner** [kæmˈpeɪnə*] n: ~ **for** Befürworter(in) m(f) +gen; ~ **against** Gegner(in) m(f) +gen.

**camp bed** (*BRIT*) n Campingliege f.

**camper** [ˈkæmpə*] n (*person*) Camper m; (*vehicle*) Wohnmobil nt.

**camping** [ˈkæmpɪŋ] n Camping nt; **to go** ~

zelten gehen, campen.
**camp(ing) site** n Campingplatz m.
**campus** ['kæmpəs] n (UNIV)
Universitätsgelände nt, Campus m.
**camshaft** ['kæmʃɑːft] n Nockenwelle f.
**can¹** [kæn] n Büchse f, Dose f; (for oil, water)
Kanister m ♦ vt eindosen, in Büchsen or
Dosen einmachen; **a ~ of beer** eine Dose
Bier; **he had to carry the ~** (BRIT: inf) er
mußte die Sache ausbaden.

=================================== KEYWORD

**can²** (negative **cannot, can't**, conditional and pt
**could**) aux vb **1** (be able to, know how to)
können; **you ~ do it if you try** du kannst es,
wenn du es nur versuchst; **I can't see you**
ich kann dich nicht sehen; **I ~ swim/drive**
ich kann schwimmen/Auto fahren; **~ you
speak English?** sprechen Sie Englisch?
**2** (may) können, dürfen; **~ I use your phone?**
kann or darf ich Ihr Telefon benutzen?;
**could I have a word with you?** könnte ich
Sie mal sprechen?
**3** (expressing disbelief, puzzlement): **it can't be
true!** das darf doch nicht wahr sein!
**4** (expressing possibility, suggestion, etc): **he
could be in the library** er könnte in der
Bibliothek sein.

**Canada** ['kænədə] n Kanada nt.
**Canadian** [kə'neɪdɪən] adj kanadisch ♦ n
Kanadier(in) m(f).
**canal** [kə'næl] n (also ANAT) Kanal m.
**Canaries** [kə'nɛərɪz] npl = **Canary Islands**.
**canary** [kə'nɛərɪ] n Kanarienvogel m.
**Canary Islands** [kə'nɛərɪ 'aɪləndz] npl: **the ~**
die Kanarischen Inseln pl.
**Canberra** ['kænbərə] n Canberra nt.
**cancel** ['kænsəl] vt absagen; (reservation)
abbestellen; (train, flight) ausfallen lassen;
(contract) annullieren; (order) stornieren;
(cross out) durchstreichen; (stamp)
entwerten; (cheque) ungültig machen.
▶**cancel out** vt aufheben; **they ~ each other
out** sie heben sich gegenseitig auf.
**cancellation** [kænsə'leɪʃən] n Absage f; (of
reservation) Abbestellung f; (of train, flight)
Ausfall m; (TOURISM) Rücktritt m.
**cancer** ['kænsə•] n (also: C~: ASTROL) Krebs m;
**to be C~** (ein) Krebs sein.
**cancerous** ['kænsrəs] adj krebsartig.
**cancer patient** n Krebskranke(r) f(m).
**cancer research** n Krebsforschung f.
**c and f** (BRIT) abbr (COMM: = cost and freight)
cf.
**candid** ['kændɪd] adj offen, ehrlich.
**candidacy** ['kændɪdəsɪ] n Kandidatur f.
**candidate** ['kændɪdeɪt] n Kandidat(in) m(f);
(for job) Bewerber(in) m(f).
**candidature** ['kændɪdətʃə•] (BRIT) n
= **candidacy**.
**candied** ['kændɪd] adj kandiert; **~ apple** (US)

kandierter Apfel m.
**candle** ['kændl] n Kerze f; (of tallow) Talglicht
nt.
**candleholder** ['kændlhəuldə•] n see
**candlestick**.
**candlelight** ['kændllaɪt] n: **by ~** bei
Kerzenlicht.
**candlestick** ['kændlstɪk] n (also: **candleholder**)
Kerzenhalter m; (bigger, ornate)
Kerzenleuchter m.
**candour,** (US) **candor** ['kændə•] n Offenheit f.
**C & W** n abbr = **country and western (music)**.
**candy** ['kændɪ] n (also: **sugar-~**)
Kandis(zucker) m; (US) Bonbon nt or m.
**candyfloss** ['kændɪflɔs] (BRIT) n Zuckerwatte
f.
**candy store** (US) n Süßwarenhandlung f.
**cane** [keɪn] n Rohr nt; (stick) Stock m; (: for
walking) (Spazier)stock m ♦ vt (BRIT: SCOL)
mit dem Stock schlagen.
**canine** ['keɪnaɪn] adj (species) Hunde-.
**canister** ['kænɪstə•] n Dose f; (pressurized
container) Sprühdose f; (of gas, chemicals etc)
Kanister m.
**cannabis** ['kænəbɪs] n Haschisch nt; (also:
**~ plant**) Hanf m, Cannabis m.
**canned** [kænd] adj Dosen-; (inf: music) aus der
Konserve; (US: inf: worker) entlassen,
rausgeschmissen inf.
**cannibal** ['kænɪbəl] n Kannibale m, Kannibalin
f.
**cannibalism** ['kænɪbəlɪzəm] n Kannibalismus
m.
**cannon** ['kænən] n (pl ~ or ~s) Kanone f.
**cannonball** ['kænənbɔːl] n Kanonenkugel f.
**cannon fodder** n Kanonenfutter nt.
**cannot** ['kænɔt] = **can not**.
**canny** ['kænɪ] adj schlau.
**canoe** [kə'nuː] n Kanu nt.
**canoeing** [kə'nuːɪŋ] n Kanusport m.
**canon** ['kænən] n Kanon m; (clergyman)
Kanoniker m, Kanonikus m.
**canonize** ['kænənaɪz] vt kanonisieren,
heiligsprechen.
**can-opener** ['kænəupnə•] n Dosenöffner m,
Büchsenöffner m.
**canopy** ['kænəpɪ] n (also fig) Baldachin m.
**cant** [kænt] n scheinheiliges Gerede nt.
**can't** [kænt] = **can not**.
**Cantab.** (BRIT) abbr (in degree titles:
= Cantabrigiensis) der Universität
Cambridge.
**cantankerous** [kæn'tæŋkərəs] adj mürrisch.
**canteen** [kæn'tiːn] n (in school, workplace)
Kantine f; (: mobile) Feldküche f; (BRIT: of
cutlery) Besteckkasten m.
**canter** ['kæntə•] vi leicht galoppieren, kantern
♦ n leichter Galopp m, Kanter m.
**cantilever** ['kæntɪliːvə•] n Ausleger m.
**canvas** ['kænvəs] n Leinwand f; (painting)
Gemälde nt; (NAUT) Segeltuch nt; **under ~**
im Zelt.

**canvass** ['kænvəs] *vt* (*opinions, views*)
erforschen; (*person*) für seine Partei zu
gewinnen suchen; (*place*) Wahlwerbung
machen in +*dat* ♦ *vi:* **to ~ for** ... (*POL*) um
Stimmen für ... werben.

**canvasser** ['kænvəsəˀ] *n* (*POL*) Wahlhelfer(in)
*m(f)*.

**canvassing** ['kænvəsɪŋ] *n* (*POL*) Wahlwerbung
*f*.

**canyon** ['kænjən] *n* Cañon *m*.

**CAP** *n abbr* (= *Common Agricultural Policy*)
gemeinsame Agrarpolitik *f* der EG.

**cap** [kæp] *n* Mütze *f*, Kappe *f*; (*of pen*)
(Verschluß)kappe *f*; (*of bottle*) Verschluß *m*,
Deckel *m*; (*contraceptive: also:* **Dutch ~**)
Pessar *nt*; (*for toy gun*) Zündplättchen *nt*; (*for
swimming*) Bademütze *f*, Badekappe *f*;
(*SPORT*) Ehrenkappe, *die Nationalspielern
verliehen wird* ♦ *vt* (*outdo*) überbieten;
(*SPORT*) für die Nationalmannschaft
aufstellen; **~ped with** ... mit ... obendrauf;
**and to ~ it all,** ... und obendrein ...

**capability** [keɪpə'bɪlɪtɪ] *n* Fähigkeit *f*; (*MIL*)
Potential *nt*.

**capable** ['keɪpəbl] *adj* fähig; **to be ~ of doing
sth** etw tun können, fähig sein, etw zu tun;
**to be ~ of sth** (*interpretation etc*) etw
zulassen.

**capacious** [kə'peɪʃəs] *adj* geräumig.

**capacity** [kə'pæsɪtɪ] *n* Fassungsvermögen *nt*;
(*of lift etc*) Höchstlast *f*; (*capability*) Fähigkeit
*f*; (*position, role*) Eigenschaft *f*; (*of factory*)
Kapazität *f*; **filled to ~** randvoll; (*stadium etc*)
bis auf den letzten Platz besetzt; **in his ~ as**
... in seiner Eigenschaft als ...; **this work is
beyond my ~** zu dieser Arbeit bin ich nicht
fähig; **in an advisory ~** in beratender
Funktion; **to work at full ~** voll ausgelastet
sein.

**cape** [keɪp] *n* Kap *nt*; (*cloak*) Cape *nt*, Umhang
*m*.

**Cape of Good Hope** *n:* **the ~** das Kap der
guten Hoffnung.

**caper** ['keɪpəˀ] *n* (*CULIN: usu pl*) Kaper *f*;
(*prank*) Eskapade *f*, Kapriole *f*.

**Cape Town** *n* Kapstadt *nt*.

**capita** ['kæpɪtə] *see* **per capita**.

**capital** ['kæpɪtl] *n* (*also:* **~ city**) Hauptstadt *f*;
(*money*) Kapital *nt*; (*also:* **~ letter**)
Großbuchstabe *m*.

**capital account** *n* Kapitalverkehrsbilanz *f*;
(*of country*) Kapitalkonto *nt*.

**capital allowance** *n* (Anlage)abschreibung *f*.

**capital assets** *npl* Kapitalvermögen *nt*.

**capital expenditure** *n* Kapital-
aufwendungen *pl*.

**capital gains tax** *n* Kapitalertragssteuer *f*.

**capital goods** *npl* Investitionsgüter *pl*.

**capital-intensive** ['kæpɪtlɪn'tɛnsɪv] *adj*
kapitalintensiv.

**capitalism** ['kæpɪtəlɪzəm] *n* Kapitalismus *m*.

**capitalist** ['kæpɪtəlɪst] *adj* kapitalistisch ♦ *n*

Kapitalist(in) *m(f)*.

**capitalize** ['kæpɪtəlaɪz] *vt* (*COMM*)
kapitalisieren ♦ *vi:* **to ~ on** Kapital schlagen
aus.

**capital punishment** *n* Todesstrafe *f*.

**capital transfer tax** (*BRIT*) *n* Erbschafts- und
Schenkungssteuer *f*.

**Capitol** ['kæpɪtl] *n:* **the ~** das Kapitol.

---

Capitol *ist das Gebäude in Washington auf dem
Capitol Hill, in dem der Kongreß der USA
zusammentritt. Die Bezeichnung wird in vielen
amerikanischen Bundesstaaten auch für das
Parlamentsgebäude des jeweiligen Staates
verwendet.*

---

**capitulate** [kə'pɪtjuleɪt] *vi* kapitulieren.

**capitulation** [kəpɪtju'leɪʃən] *n* Kapitulation *f*.

**capricious** [kə'prɪʃəs] *adj* launisch.

**Capricorn** ['kæprɪkɔːn] *n* (*ASTROL*) Steinbock
*m*; **to be ~** (ein) Steinbock sein.

**caps** [kæps] *abbr* (= *capital letters*)
Großbuchstaben *pl*.

**capsize** [kæp'saɪz] *vt* zum Kentern bringen
♦ *vi* kentern.

**capstan** ['kæpstən] *n* Poller *m*.

**capsule** ['kæpsjuːl] *n* Kapsel *f*.

**Capt.** *abbr* (*MIL*) = **captain**.

**captain** ['kæptɪn] *n* Kapitän *m*; (*of plane*)
(Flug)kapitän *m*; (*in army*) Hauptmann *m* ♦ *vt*
(*ship*) befehligen; (*team*) anführen.

**caption** ['kæpʃən] *n* Bildunterschrift *f*.

**captivate** ['kæptɪveɪt] *vt* fesseln.

**captive** ['kæptɪv] *adj* gefangen ♦ *n*
Gefangene(r) *f(m)*.

**captivity** [kæp'tɪvɪtɪ] *n* Gefangenschaft *f*.

**captor** ['kæptəˀ] *n:* **his ~s** diejenigen, die ihn
gefangennahmen.

**capture** ['kæptʃəˀ] *vt* (*animal*) (ein)fangen;
(*person*) gefangennehmen; (*town, country,
share of market*) erobern; (*attention*) erregen;
(*COMPUT*) erfassen ♦ *n* (*of animal*)
Einfangen *nt*; (*of person*) Gefangennahme *f*;
(*of town etc*) Eroberung *f*; (*data capture*)
Erfassung *f*.

**car** [kɑːˀ] *n* Auto *nt*, Wagen *m*; (*RAIL*) Wagen *m*;
**by ~** mit dem Auto *or* Wagen.

**Caracas** [kə'rækəs] *n* Caracas *nt*.

**carafe** [kə'ræf] *n* Karaffe *f*.

**caramel** ['kærəməl] *n* Karamelle *f*,
Karamelbonbon *m or nt*; (*burnt sugar*)
Karamel *m*.

**carat** ['kærət] *n* Karat *nt*; **18 ~ gold**
achtzehnkarätiges Gold.

**caravan** ['kærəvæn] *n* (*BRIT*) Wohnwagen *m*;
(*in desert*) Karawane *f*.

**caravan site** (*BRIT*) *n* Campingplatz *m* für
Wohnwagen.

**caraway seed** *n* Kümmel *m*.

**carbohydrate** [kɑːbəʊ'haɪdreɪt] *n*
Kohle(n)hydrat *nt*.

**carbolic acid** [kɑː'bɒlɪk-] *n* Karbolsäure *f*.

**car bomb** n Autobombe f.
**carbon** ['kɑːbən] n Kohlenstoff m.
**carbonated** ['kɑːbəneɪtɪd] adj mit
   Kohlensäure (versetzt).
**carbon copy** n Durchschlag m.
**carbon dioxide** n Kohlendioxyd nt.
**carbon monoxide** [mɔ'nɔksaɪd] n
   Kohlenmonoxyd nt.
**carbon paper** n Kohlepapier nt.
**carbon ribbon** n Kohlefarbband nt.
**car-boot sale** n auf einem Parkplatz
   stattfindender Flohmarkt mit dem
   Kofferraum als Auslage.
**carburettor**, (US) **carburetor** [kɑːbjuˈrɛtə•] n
   Vergaser m.
**carcass** ['kɑːkəs] n Kadaver m.
**carcinogenic** [kɑːsɪnəˈdʒɛnɪk] adj
   krebserregend, karzinogen.
**card** [kɑːd] n Karte f; (material) (dünne) Pappe
   f, Karton m; (record card, index card etc)
   (Kartei)karte f; (membership card)
   (Mitglieds)ausweis m; (playing card)
   (Spiel)karte f; (visiting card) (Visiten)karte f;
   **to play** ~s Karten spielen.
**cardamom** ['kɑːdəməm] n Kardamom m.
**cardboard** ['kɑːdbɔːd] n Pappe f.
**cardboard box** n (Papp)karton m.
**card-carrying** ['kɑːd'kærɪɪŋ] adj: ~ **member**
   eingetragenes Mitglied nt.
**card game** n Kartenspiel nt.
**cardiac** ['kɑːdɪæk] adj (failure, patient) Herz-.
**cardigan** ['kɑːdɪgən] n Strickjacke f.
**cardinal** ['kɑːdɪnl] adj (principle, importance)
   Haupt- ♦ n Kardinal m; ~ **number**
   Kardinalzahl f; ~ **sin** Todsünde f.
**card index** n Kartei f.
**cardphone** n Kartentelefon nt.
**cardsharp** ['kɑːdʃɑːp] n Falschspieler m.
**card vote** (BRIT) n Abstimmung f durch
   Wahlmänner.
**CARE** [kɛə•] n abbr (= Cooperative for American
   Relief Everywhere) karitative Organisation.
**care** [kɛə•] n (attention) Versorgung f; (worry)
   Sorge f; (charge) Obhut f, Fürsorge f ♦ vi: **to**
   ~ **about** sich kümmern um; ~ **of** bei;
   **"handle with** ~**"** „Vorsicht, zerbrechlich";
   **in sb's** ~ in jds dat Obhut; **to take** ~
   aufpassen; **to take** ~ **to do sth** sich
   bemühen, etw zu tun; **to take** ~ **of** sich
   kümmern um; **the child has been taken into**
   ~ das Kind ist in Pflege genommen worden;
   **would you** ~ **to/for** ...? möchten Sie gerne
   ...?; **I wouldn't** ~ **to do it** ich möchte es nicht
   gern tun; **I don't** ~ es ist mir egal or
   gleichgültig; **I couldn't** ~ **less** es ist mir
   völlig egal or gleichgültig.
▶**care for** vt fus (look after) sich kümmern um;
   (like) mögen.
**career** [kəˈrɪə•] n Karriere f; (job, profession)
   Beruf m; (life) Laufbahn f ♦ vi (also: ~ **along**)
   rasen.
**career girl** n Karrierefrau f.

**careers officer** [kəˈrɪəz-] n Berufsberater(in)
   m(f).
**career woman** n Karrierefrau f.
**carefree** ['kɛəfriː] adj sorglos.
**careful** ['kɛəful] adj vorsichtig; (thorough)
   sorgfältig; **(be)** ~! Vorsicht!, paß auf!; **to be**
   ~ **with one's money** sein Geld gut
   zusammenhalten.
**carefully** ['kɛəfəlɪ] adv vorsichtig;
   (methodically) sorgfältig.
**careless** ['kɛəlɪs] adj leichtsinnig; (negligent)
   nachlässig; (remark) gedankenlos.
**carelessly** ['kɛəlɪslɪ] adv (see adj) leichtsinnig;
   nachlässig; gedankenlos.
**carelessness** ['kɛəlɪsnɪs] n (see adj)
   Leichtsinn m; Nachlässigkeit f;
   Gedankenlosigkeit f.
**caress** [kəˈrɛs] n Streicheln nt ♦ vt streicheln.
**caretaker** ['kɛəteɪkə•] n Hausmeister(in) m(f).
**caretaker government** (BRIT) n
   geschäftsführende Regierung f.
**car ferry** n Autofähre f.
**cargo** ['kɑːgəu] (pl ~**es**) n Fracht f, Ladung f.
**cargo boat** n Frachter m, Frachtschiff nt.
**cargo plane** n Transportflugzeug nt.
**car hire** (BRIT) n Autovermietung f.
**Caribbean** [kærɪˈbiːən] adj karibisch ♦ n: **the**
   ~ **(Sea)** die Karibik, das Karibische Meer.
**caricature** ['kærɪkətjuə•] n Karikatur f.
**caring** ['kɛərɪŋ] adj liebevoll; (society,
   organization) sozial; (behaviour) fürsorglich.
**carjacking** n Angriff durch Banditen, die
   gewaltsam in PKWs eindringen und den
   Wagen samt Insassen entführen.
**carnage** ['kɑːnɪdʒ] n (MIL) Blutbad nt,
   Gemetzel nt.
**carnal** ['kɑːnl] adj fleischlich, sinnlich.
**carnation** [kɑːˈneɪʃən] n Nelke f.
**carnival** ['kɑːnɪvl] n Karneval m; (US: funfair)
   Kirmes f.
**carnivorous** [kɑːˈnɪvərəs] adj fleischfressend.
**carol** ['kærəl] n: **(Christmas)** ~ Weihnachtslied
   nt.
**carouse** [kəˈrauz] vi zechen.
**carousel** [kærəˈsɛl] (US) n Karussell nt.
**carp** [kɑːp] n Karpfen m.
▶**carp at** vt fus herumnörgeln an +dat.
**car park** (BRIT) n Parkplatz m; (building)
   Parkhaus nt.
**carpenter** ['kɑːpɪntə•] n Zimmermann m.
**carpentry** ['kɑːpɪntrɪ] n Zimmerhandwerk nt;
   (school subject, hobby) Tischlern nt.
**carpet** ['kɑːpɪt] n (also fig) Teppich m ♦ vt (mit
   Teppichen/Teppichboden) auslegen; **fitted**
   ~ (BRIT) Teppichboden m.
**carpet bombing** n Flächenbombardierung f.
**carpet slippers** npl Pantoffeln pl.
**carpet-sweeper** ['kɑːpɪtswiːpə•] n
   Teppichkehrer m.
**car phone** n (TELEC) Autotelefon nt.
**carport** ['kɑːpɔːt] n Einstellplatz m.
**car rental** n Autovermietung f.

**carriage** ['kærɪdʒ] n (*RAIL, of typewriter*)
Wagen m; (*horse-drawn vehicle*) Kutsche f; (*of goods*) Beförderung f; (*transport costs*)
Beförderungskosten pl; ~ **forward** Fracht
zahlt Empfänger; ~ **free** frachtfrei; ~ **paid**
frei Haus.
**carriage return** n (*on typewriter*)
Wagenrücklauf m; (*COMPUT*) Return nt.
**carriageway** ['kærɪdʒweɪ] (*BRIT*) n Fahrbahn f.
**carrier** ['kærɪə*] n Spediteur m,
Transportunternehmer m; (*MED*)
Überträger m.
**carrier bag** (*BRIT*) n Tragetasche f, Tragetüte f.
**carrier pigeon** n Brieftaube f.
**carrion** ['kærɪən] n Aas nt.
**carrot** ['kærət] n Möhre f, Mohrrübe f, Karotte f; (*fig*) Köder m.
**carry** ['kærɪ] vt tragen; (*transport*)
transportieren; (*a motion, bill*) annehmen;
(*reponsibilities etc*) mit sich bringen; (*disease, virus*) übertragen ♦ vi (*sound*) tragen; **to get carried away** (*fig*) sich hinreißen lassen; **this loan carries 10% interest** dieses Darlehen wird mit 10% verzinst.
▶**carry forward** vt übertragen, vortragen.
▶**carry on** vi weitermachen; (*inf: make a fuss*)
(ein) Theater machen ♦ vt fortführen; **to ~ on with sth** mit etw weitermachen; **to ~ on singing/eating** weitersingen/-essen.
▶**carry out** vt (*orders*) ausführen;
(*investigation*) durchführen; (*idea*) in die Tat umsetzen; (*threat*) wahrmachen.
**carrycot** ['kærɪkɔt] (*BRIT*) n Babytragetasche f.
**carry-on** ['kærɪ'ɔn] (*inf*) n Theater nt.
**cart** [kɑːt] n Wagen m, Karren m; (*for passengers*) Wagen m; (*handcart*)
(Hand)wagen m ♦ vt (*inf*) mit sich
herumschleppen.
**carte blanche** ['kɑːt'blɔŋʃ] n: **to give sb ~** jdm
Carte Blanche or (eine) Blankovollmacht
geben.
**cartel** [kɑː'tɛl] n Kartell nt.
**cartilage** ['kɑːtɪlɪdʒ] n Knorpel m.
**cartographer** [kɑː'tɔgrəfə*] n Kartograph(in) m(f).
**cartography** [kɑː'tɔgrəfɪ] n Kartographie f.
**carton** ['kɑːtən] n (*Papp*)karton m; (*of yogurt*)
Becher m; (*of milk*) Tüte f; (*of cigarettes*)
Stange f.
**cartoon** [kɑː'tuːn] n (*drawing*) Karikatur f;
(*BRIT: comic strip*) Cartoon m; (*CINE*)
Zeichentrickfilm m.
**cartoonist** [kɑː'tuːnɪst] n Karikaturist(in) m(f).
**cartridge** ['kɑːtrɪdʒ] n (*for gun, pen*) Patrone f;
(*music tape, for camera*) Kassette f; (*of record-player*) Tonabnehmer m.
**cartwheel** ['kɑːtwiːl] n Rad nt; **to turn a ~**
radschlagen.
**carve** [kɑːv] vt (*meat*) (ab)schneiden; (*wood*)
schnitzen; (*stone*) meißeln; (*initials, design*)

einritzen.
▶**carve up** vt (*land etc*) aufteilen; (*meat*)
aufschneiden.
**carving** ['kɑːvɪŋ] n Skulptur f; (*in wood etc*)
Schnitzerei f.
**carving knife** n Tranchiermesser nt.
**car wash** n Autowaschanlage f.
**Casablanca** [kæsə'blæŋkə] n Casablanca nt.
**cascade** [kæs'keɪd] n Wasserfall m, Kaskade f;
(*of money*) Regen m; (*of hair*) wallende Fülle
f ♦ vi (in Kaskaden) herabfallen; (*hair etc*)
wallen; (*people*) strömen.
**case** [keɪs] n Fall m; (*for spectacles etc*) Etui nt;
(*BRIT: also:* **suit~**) Koffer m; (*of wine, whisky etc*) Kiste f; (*TYP*): **lower/upper ~** klein/groß
geschrieben; **to have a good ~** gute
Chancen haben, durchzukommen; **there's a strong ~ for reform** es spricht viel für eine
Reform; **in ~** ... **falls** ...; **in ~ of fire** bei
Feuer; **in ~ of emergency** im Notfall; **in ~ he comes** falls er kommt; **in any ~**
sowieso; **just in ~** für alle Fälle.
**case-hardened** ['keɪshɑːdnd] adj (*fig*)
abgebrüht (*inf*).
**case history** n (*MED*) Krankengeschichte f.
**case study** n Fallstudie f.
**cash** [kæʃ] n (Bar)geld nt ♦ vt (*cheque etc*)
einlösen; **to pay (in) ~** bar bezahlen; ~ **on delivery** per Nachnahme; ~ **with order**
zahlbar bei Bestellung.
▶**cash in** vt einlösen.
▶**cash in on** vt fus Kapital schlagen aus.
**cash account** n Kassenbuch nt.
**cash-and-carry** [kæʃən'kærɪ] n Abholmarkt m.
**cash-book** ['kæʃbuk] n Kassenkonto nt.
**cash box** n (Geld)kassette f.
**cash card** (*BRIT*) n (Geld)automatenkarte f.
**cash crop** n zum Verkauf bestimmte Ernte f.
**cash desk** (*BRIT*) n Kasse f.
**cash discount** n Skonto m or nt.
**cash dispenser** (*BRIT*) n Geldautomat m.
**cashew** [kæ'ʃuː] n (*also:* ~ **nut**) Cashewnuß f.
**cash flow** n Cash-flow m.
**cashier** [kæ'ʃɪə*] n Kassierer(in) m(f).
**cashmere** ['kæʃmɪə*] n Kaschmir m.
**cash point** n Geldautomat m.
**cash price** n Bar(zahlungs)preis m.
**cash register** n Registrierkasse f.
**cash sale** n Barverkauf m.
**casing** ['keɪsɪŋ] n Gehäuse nt.
**casino** [kə'siːnəu] n Kasino nt.
**cask** [kɑːsk] n Faß nt.
**casket** ['kɑːskɪt] n Schatulle f; (*US: coffin*) Sarg m.
**Caspian Sea** ['kæspɪən-] n: **the ~** das
Kaspische Meer.
**casserole** ['kæsərəul] n Auflauf m; (*pot, container*) Kasserolle f.
**cassette** [kæ'sɛt] n Kassette f.
**cassette deck** n Kassettendeck nt.
**cassette player** n Kassettenrekorder m.
**cassette recorder** n Kassettenrekorder m.

**cast** [kɑːst] (*pt, pp* **cast**) *vt* werfen; (*net, fishing-line*) auswerfen; (*metal, statue*) gießen ♦ *vi* die Angel auswerfen ♦ *n* (*THEAT*) Besetzung *f*; (*mould*) (Guß)form *f*; (*also*: **plaster** ~) Gipsverband *m*; **to** ~ **sb as Hamlet** (*THEAT*) die Rolle des Hamlet mit jdm besetzen; **to** ~ **one's vote** seine Stimme abgeben; **to** ~ **one's eyes over sth** einen Blick auf etw *acc* werfen; **to** ~ **aspersions on sb/sth** abfällige Bemerkungen über jdn/etw machen; **to** ~ **doubts on sth** etw in Zweifel ziehen; **to** ~ **a spell on sb/sth** jdn/etw verzaubern; **to** ~ **its skin** sich häuten.
►**cast aside** *vt* fallenlassen.
►**cast off** *vi* (*NAUT*) losmachen; (*KNITTING*) abketten ♦ *vt* abketten.
►**cast on** *vi, vt* (*KNITTING*) anschlagen, aufschlagen.
**castaway** ['kɑːstəweɪ] *n* Schiffbrüchige(r) *f(m)*.
**caste** [kɑːst] *n* Kaste *f*; (*system*) Kastenwesen *nt*.
**caster sugar** ['kɑːstə-] (*BRIT*) *n* Raffinade *f*.
**casting vote** ['kɑːstɪŋ-] (*BRIT*) *n* ausschlaggebende Stimme *f*.
**cast iron** *n* Gußeisen *nt* ♦ *adj*: **cast-iron** (*fig: will*) eisern; (: *alibi, excuse etc*) hieb- und stichfest.
**castle** ['kɑːsl] *n* Schloß *nt*; (*manor*) Herrenhaus *nt*; (*fortified*) Burg *f*; (*CHESS*) Turm *m*.
**cast off** *n* abgelegtes Kleidungsstück *nt*.
**castor** ['kɑːstə•] *n* Rolle *f*.
**castor oil** *n* Rizinusöl *nt*.
**castrate** [kæs'treɪt] *vt* kastrieren.
**casual** ['kæʒjul] *adj* (*by chance*) zufällig; (*work etc*) Gelegenheits-; (*unconcerned*) lässig, gleichgültig; (*clothes*) leger; ~ **wear** Freizeitkleidung *f*.
**casual labour** *n* Gelegenheitsarbeit *f*.
**casually** ['kæʒjuli] *adv* lässig; (*glance*) beiläufig; (*dress*) leger; (*by chance*) zufällig.
**casualty** ['kæʒjultɪ] *n* (*of war etc*) Opfer *nt*; (*someone injured*) Verletzte(r) *f(m)*; (*someone killed*) Tote(r) *f(m)*; (*MED*) Unfallstation *f*; **heavy casualties** (*MIL*) schwere Verluste *pl*.
**casualty ward** (*BRIT*) *n* Unfallstation *f*.
**cat** [kæt] *n* Katze *f*; (*lion etc*) (Raub)katze *f*.
**catacombs** ['kætəkuːmz] *npl* Katakomben *pl*.
**catalogue, (US) catalog** ['kætəlɔg] *n* Katalog *m* ♦ *vt* katalogisieren.
**catalyst** ['kætəlɪst] *n* Katalysator *m*.
**catalytic converter** [kætə'lɪtɪk kən'vəːtə•] *n* (*AUT*) Katalysator *m*.
**catapult** ['kætəpʌlt] (*BRIT*) *n* Schleuder *f*; (*MIL*) Katapult *nt* or *m* ♦ *vi* geschleudert or katapultiert werden ♦ *vt* schleudern, katapultieren.
**cataract** ['kætərækt] *n* (*MED*) grauer Star *m*.
**catarrh** [kə'tɑː•] *n* Katarrh *m*.
**catastrophe** [kə'tæstrəfi] *n* Katastrophe *f*.
**catastrophic** [kætə'strɔfɪk] *adj* katastrophal.

**catcalls** ['kætkɔːlz] *npl* Pfiffe und Buhrufe *pl*.
**catch-22** ['kætʃtwɛntɪ'tuː] *n*: **it's a** ~ **situation** es ist eine Zwickmühle.
**catch** [kætʃ] (*pt, pp* **caught**) *vt* fangen; (*take: bus, train etc*) nehmen; (*arrest*) festnehmen; (*surprise*) erwischen, ertappen; (*breath*) holen; (*attention*) erregen; (*hit*) treffen; (*hear*) mitbekommen; (*illness*) sich *dat* zuziehen or holen; (*person: also*: ~ **up**) einholen ♦ *vi* (*fire*) (anfangen zu) brennen; (*become trapped*) hängenbleiben ♦ *n* Fang *m*; (*trick, hidden problem*) Haken *m*; (*of lock*) Riegel *m*; (*game*) Fangen *nt*; **to** ~ **sb's attention/eye** jdn auf sich *acc* aufmerksam machen; **to** ~ **fire** Feuer fangen; **to** ~ **sight of** erblicken.
►**catch on** *vi* (*grow popular*) sich durchsetzen; **to** ~ **on (to sth)** (etw) kapieren.
►**catch out** (*BRIT*) *vt* (*fig*) hereinlegen.
►**catch up** *vi* (*fig: with person*) mitkommen; (: *on work*) aufholen ♦ *vt*: **to** ~ **sb up, to** ~ **up with sb** jdn einholen.
**catching** ['kætʃɪŋ] *adj* ansteckend.
**catchment area** ['kætʃmənt-] (*BRIT*) *n* Einzugsgebiet *nt*.
**catch phrase** *n* Schlagwort *nt*, Slogan *m*.
**catchy** ['kætʃɪ] *adj* (*tune*) eingängig.
**catechism** ['kætɪkɪzəm] *n* Katechismus *m*.
**categoric(al)** [kætɪ'gɔrɪk(l)] *adj* kategorisch.
**categorize** ['kætɪgəraɪz] *vt* kategorisieren.
**category** ['kætɪgərɪ] *n* Kategorie *f*.
**cater** ['keɪtə•] *vi*: **to** ~ **(for)** die Speisen und Getränke liefern (für).
►**cater for** (*BRIT*) *vt fus* (*needs, tastes*) gerecht werden +*dat*; (*readers, consumers*) eingestellt or ausgerichtet sein auf +*acc*.
**caterer** ['keɪtərə•] *n* Lieferant(in) *m(f)* von Speisen und Getränken; (*company*) Lieferfirma *f* für Speisen und Getränke.
**catering** ['keɪtərɪŋ] *n* Gastronomie *f*.
**caterpillar** ['kætəpɪlə•] *n* Raupe *f* ♦ *cpd* (*vehicle*) Raupen-.
**caterpillar track** *n* Raupenkette *f*, Gleiskette *f*.
**cat flap** *n* Katzentür *f*.
**cathedral** [kə'θiːdrəl] *n* Kathedrale *f*, Dom *m*.
**cathode** ['kæθəud] *n* Kathode *f*.
**cathode-ray tube** [kæθəud'reɪ-] *n* Kathodenstrahlröhre *f*.
**Catholic** ['kæθəlɪk] *adj* katholisch ♦ *n* Katholik(in) *m(f)*.
**catholic** ['kæθəlɪk] *adj* vielseitig.
**CAT scanner** *n abbr* (*MED*: = *computerized axial tomography scanner*) CAT-Scanner *m*.
**Catseye** ® ['kætsaɪ] (*BRIT*) *n* (*AUT*) Katzenauge *nt*.
**catsup** ['kætsəp] (*US*) *n* Ketchup *m or nt*.
**cattle** ['kætl] *npl* Vieh *nt*.
**catty** ['kætɪ] *adj* gehässig.
**catwalk** ['kætwɔːk] *n* Steg *m*; (*for models*) Laufsteg *m*.
**Caucasian** [kɔː'keɪzɪən] *adj* kaukasisch ♦ *n*

# Caucasus – cement

Kaukasier(in) *m(f)*.
**Caucasus** ['kɔːkəsəs] *n* Kaukasus *m*.
**caucus** ['kɔːkəs] *n* (*group*) Gremium *nt*, Ausschuß *m*; (*US*) Parteiversammlung *f*.

> **Caucus** bedeutet vor allem in den USA ein privates Treffen von Parteifunktionären, bei dem z.B. Kandidaten ausgewählt oder Grundsatzentscheidungen getroffen werden. Meist wird ein solches Treffen vor einer öffentlichen Parteiversammlung abgehalten. Der Begriff bezieht sich im weiteren Sinne auch auf den kleinen, aber mächtigen Kreis von Parteifunktionären, der beim caucus zusammentrifft.

**caught** [kɔːt] *pt, pp of* **catch**.
**cauliflower** ['kɔlɪflauə*] *n* Blumenkohl *m*.
**cause** [kɔːz] *n* Ursache *f*; (*reason*) Grund *m*; (*aim*) Sache *f* ♦ *vt* verursachen; **there is no ~ for concern** es besteht kein Grund zur Sorge; **to ~ sth to be done** veranlassen, daß etw getan wird; **to ~ sb to do sth** jdn veranlassen, etw zu tun.
**causeway** ['kɔːzweɪ] *n* Damm *m*.
**caustic** ['kɔːstɪk] *adj* ätzend, kaustisch; (*remark*) bissig.
**cauterize** ['kɔːtəraɪz] *vt* kauterisieren.
**caution** ['kɔːʃən] *n* Vorsicht *f*; (*warning*) Warnung *f*; (: *LAW*) Verwarnung *f* ♦ *vt* warnen; (*LAW*) verwarnen.
**cautious** ['kɔːʃəs] *adj* vorsichtig.
**cautiously** ['kɔːʃəslɪ] *adv* vorsichtig.
**cautiousness** ['kɔːʃəsnɪs] *n* Vorsicht *f*.
**cavalier** [kævə'lɪə*] *adj* unbekümmert.
**cavalry** ['kævəlrɪ] *n* Kavallerie *f*.
**cave** [keɪv] *n* Höhle *f* ♦ *vi*: **to go caving** auf Höhlenexpedition(en) gehen.
▶**cave in** *vi* einstürzen; (*to demands*) nachgeben.
**caveman** ['keɪvmæn] (*irreg: like* **man**) *n* Höhlenmensch *m*.
**cavern** ['kævən] *n* Höhle *f*.
**caviar(e)** ['kævɪɑː*] *n* Kaviar *m*.
**cavity** ['kævɪtɪ] *n* Hohlraum *m*; (*in tooth*) Loch *nt*.
**cavity wall insulation** *n* Schaumisolierung *f*.
**cavort** [kə'vɔːt] *vi* tollen, toben.
**cayenne** [keɪ'ɛn] *n* (*also:* **~ pepper**) Cayennepfeffer *m*.
**CB** *n abbr* (= *Citizens' Band (Radio)*) CB-Funk *m*.
**CBC** *n abbr* (= *Canadian Broadcasting Corporation*) kanadische Rundfunkgesellschaft.
**CBE** (*BRIT*) *n abbr* (= *Commander of (the Order of) the British Empire*) britischer Ordenstitel.
**CBI** *n abbr* (= *Confederation of British Industry*) britischer Unternehmerverband, ≈ BDI *m*.
**CBS** (*US*) *n abbr* (= *Columbia Broadcasting System*) Rundfunkgesellschaft.
**CC** (*BRIT*) *abbr* = **county council**.
**cc** *abbr* (= *cubic centimetre*) ccm; = **carbon copy**.

**CCA** (*US*) *n abbr* (= *Circuit Court of Appeals*) Berufungsgericht *nt*.
**CCU** (*US*) *n abbr* (= *cardiac or coronary care unit*) Intensivstation für Herzpatienten.
**CD** *abbr* (*BRIT*: = *Corps Diplomatique*) CD ♦ *n abbr* (*MIL*: *BRIT*: = *Civil Defence (Corps)*) Zivilschutz *m*; (: *US*: = *Civil Defense*) Zivilschutz *m*; (= *compact disk*) CD *f*; **~ player** CD-Spieler *m*.
**CDC** (*US*) *n abbr* (= *Center for Disease Control*) Seuchenkontrollbehörde.
**CD-I** *n abbr* (= *Compact Disk Interactive*) CD-I *f*.
**Cdr** *abbr* (*MIL*) = **commander**.
**CD-ROM** *n abbr* (= *compact disc read-only memory*) CD-ROM *f*.
**CDT** (*US*) *abbr* (= *Central Daylight Time*) mittelamerikanische Sommerzeit.
**cease** [siːs] *vt* beenden ♦ *vi* aufhören.
**ceasefire** ['siːsfaɪə*] *n* Waffenruhe *f*.
**ceaseless** ['siːslɪs] *adj* endlos, unaufhörlich.
**CED** (*US*) *n abbr* (= *Committee for Economic Development*) Komitee für wirtschaftliche Entwicklung.
**cedar** ['siːdə*] *n* Zeder *f*; (*wood*) Zedernholz *nt*.
**cede** [siːd] *vt* abtreten.
**cedilla** [sɪ'dɪlə] *n* Cedille *f*.
**CEEB** (*US*) *n abbr* (= *College Entry Examination Board*) akademische Zulassungsstelle.
**ceilidh** ['keɪlɪ] (*SCOT*) *n* Fest mit Volksmusik, Gesang und Tanz.
**ceiling** ['siːlɪŋ] *n* Decke *f*; (*upper limit*) Obergrenze *f*, Höchstgrenze *f*.
**celebrate** ['sɛlɪbreɪt] *vt* feiern; (*mass*) zelebrieren ♦ *vi* feiern.
**celebrated** ['sɛlɪbreɪtɪd] *adj* gefeiert.
**celebration** [sɛlɪ'breɪʃən] *n* Feier *f*.
**celebrity** [sɪ'lɛbrɪtɪ] *n* berühmte Persönlichkeit *f*.
**celeriac** [sə'lɛrɪæk] *n* (Knollen)sellerie *f*.
**celery** ['sɛlərɪ] *n* (Stangen)sellerie *f*.
**celestial** [sɪ'lɛstɪəl] *adj* himmlisch.
**celibacy** ['sɛlɪbəsɪ] *n* Zölibat *nt or m*.
**cell** [sɛl] *n* Zelle *f*.
**cellar** ['sɛlə*] *n* Keller *m*; (*for wine*) (Wein)keller *m*.
**cellist** ['tʃɛlɪst] *n* Cellist(in) *m(f)*.
**cello** ['tʃɛləu] *n* Cello *nt*.
**cellophane** ['sɛləfeɪn] *n* Cellophan *nt*.
**cellphone** ['sɛlfəun] *n* Funktelefon *nt*.
**cellular** ['sɛljulə*] *adj* (*BIOL*) zellular, Zell-; (*fabrics*) aus porösem Material.
**Celluloid**® ['sɛljulɔɪd] *n* Zelluloid *nt*.
**cellulose** ['sɛljuləus] *n* Zellulose *f*, Zellstoff *m*.
**Celsius** ['sɛlsɪəs] *adj* (*scale*) Celsius-.
**Celt** [kɛlt] *n* Kelte *m*, Keltin *f*.
**Celtic** ['kɛltɪk] *adj* keltisch ♦ *n* (*LING*) Keltisch *nt*.
**cement** [sə'mɛnt] *n* Zement *m*; (*concrete*) Beton *m*; (*glue*) Klebstoff *m* ♦ *vt* zementieren; (*stick, glue*) kleben; (*fig*) festigen.

**cement mixer** n Betonmischmaschine f.
**cemetery** ['sɛmɪtrɪ] n Friedhof m.
**cenotaph** ['sɛnətɑːf] n Ehrenmal nt.
**censor** ['sɛnsə'] n Zensor(in) m(f) ♦ vt
zensieren.
**censorship** ['sɛnsəʃɪp] n Zensur f.
**censure** ['sɛnʃə'] vt tadeln ♦ n Tadel m.
**census** ['sɛnsəs] n Volkszählung f.
**cent** [sɛnt] n (US: coin) Cent m; see also **per
cent.**
**centenary** [sɛn'tiːnərɪ] n hundertster
Jahrestag m.
**centennial** [sɛn'tɛnɪəl] (US) n = **centenary.**
**center** etc ['sɛntə'] (US) = **centre** etc.
**centigrade** ['sɛntɪɡreɪd] adj (scale) Celsius-.
**centilitre,** (US) **centiliter** ['sɛntɪliːtə'] n
Zentiliter m or nt.
**centimetre,** (US) **centimeter** ['sɛntɪmiːtə'] n
Zentimeter m or nt.
**centipede** ['sɛntɪpiːd] n Tausendfüßler m.
**central** ['sɛntrəl] adj zentral; (committee,
government) Zentral-; (idea) wesentlich.
**Central African Republic** n
Zentralafrikanische Republik f.
**Central America** n Mittelamerika nt.
**central heating** n Zentralheizung f.
**centralize** ['sɛntrəlaɪz] vt zentralisieren.
**central processing unit** n (COMPUT)
Zentraleinheit f.
**central reservation** (BRIT) n Mittelstreifen
m.
**centre,** (US) **center** ['sɛntə'] n Mitte f, (health
centre etc, town centre) Zentrum nt; (of
attention, interest) Mittelpunkt m; (of action,
belief etc) Kern m ♦ vt zentrieren; (ball) zur
Mitte spielen ♦ vi (concentrate): **to ~ on** sich
konzentrieren auf +acc.
**centrefold,** (US) **centerfold** ['sɛntəfəʊld] n
doppelseitiges Bild in der Mitte einer
Zeitschrift.
**centre forward** n Mittelstürmer(in) m(f).
**centre half** n Stopper(in) m(f).
**centrepiece,** (US) **centerpiece** ['sɛntəpiːs] n
Tafelaufsatz m; (fig) Kernstück nt.
**centre spread** (BRIT) n Doppelseite in der
Mitte einer Zeitschrift.
**centre-stage** [sɛntə'steɪdʒ] (fig) adv: **to be ~**
im Mittelpunkt stehen ♦ n **to take centre
stage** in den Mittelpunkt rücken.
**centrifugal** [sɛn'trɪfjʊɡl] adj (force)
Zentrifugal-.
**centrifuge** ['sɛntrɪfjuːʒ] n Zentrifuge f,
Schleuder f.
**century** ['sɛntjʊrɪ] n Jahrhundert nt;
(CRICKET) Hundert f; **in the twentieth ~** im
zwanzigsten Jahrhundert.
**CEO** (US) n abbr = **chief executive officer.**
**ceramic** [sɪ'ræmɪk] adj keramisch; (tiles)
Keramik-.
**ceramics** [sɪ'ræmɪks] npl Keramiken pl.
**cereal** ['sɪːrɪəl] n Getreide nt; (food)
Getreideflocken pl (Cornflakes etc).

**cerebral** ['sɛrɪbrəl] adj (MED) zerebral;
(intellectual) geistig.
**ceremonial** [sɛrɪ'məʊnɪəl] n Zeremoniell nt
♦ adj zeremoniell.
**ceremony** ['sɛrɪmənɪ] n Zeremonie f,
(behaviour) Förmlichkeit f; **to stand on ~**
förmlich sein.
**cert** [səːt] (BRIT: inf) n: **it's a dead ~** es ist
todsicher.
**certain** ['səːtən] adj sicher; **a ~ Mr Smith** ein
gewisser Herr Smith; **~ days/places**
bestimmte Tage/Orte; **a ~ coldness** eine
gewisse Kälte; **to make ~ of** sich
vergewissern +gen; **for ~** ganz sicher, ganz
genau.
**certainly** ['səːtənlɪ] adv bestimmt; (of course)
sicherlich; **~!** (aber) sicher!
**certainty** ['səːtəntɪ] n Sicherheit f,
(inevitability) Gewißheit f.
**certificate** [sə'tɪfɪkɪt] n Urkunde f; (diploma)
Zeugnis nt.
**certified letter** ['səːtɪfaɪd-] (US) n
Einschreibebrief m.
**certified mail** (US) n Einschreiben nt.
**certified public accountant** ['səːtɪfaɪd-] (US)
n geprüfter Buchhalter m, geprüfte
Buchhalterin f.
**certify** ['səːtɪfaɪ] vt bescheinigen; (award a
diploma to) ein Zeugnis verleihen +dat;
(declare insane) für unzurechnungsfähig
erklären ♦ vi: **to ~ to** sich verbürgen für.
**cervical** ['səːvɪkl] adj: **~ cancer**
Gebärmutterhalskrebs m; **~ smear**
Abstrich m.
**cervix** ['səːvɪks] n Gebärmutterhals m.
**Cesarean** [sɪ'zɛərɪən] (US) n = **Caesarean.**
**cessation** [sə'seɪʃən] n (of hostilities etc)
Einstellung f, Ende nt.
**cesspit** ['sɛspɪt] n (sewage tank) Senkgrube f.
**CET** abbr (= Central European Time) MEZ.
**Ceylon** [sɪ'lɔn] n Ceylon nt.
**cf.** abbr (= compare) vgl.
**c/f** abbr (COMM: = carried forward) Übertr.
**CFC** n abbr (= chlorofluorocarbon) FCKW m.
**CG** (US) n abbr = **coastguard.**
**cg** abbr (= centigram) cg.
**CH** (BRIT) n abbr (= Companion of Honour)
britischer Ordenstitel.
**ch.** abbr (= chapter) Kap.
**c.h.** (BRIT) abbr (= central heating) ZH.
**Chad** [tʃæd] n Tschad m.
**chafe** [tʃeɪf] vt (wund)reiben ♦ vi (fig): **to
~ against** sich ärgern über +acc.
**chaffinch** ['tʃæfɪntʃ] n Buchfink m.
**chagrin** ['ʃæɡrɪn] n Ärger m.
**chain** [tʃeɪn] n Kette f ♦ vt (also: ~ **up:** prisoner)
anketten; (: dog) an die Kette legen.
**chain reaction** n Kettenreaktion f.
**chain-smoke** ['tʃeɪnsməʊk] vi eine Zigarette
nach der anderen rauchen, kettenrauchen.
**chain store** n Kettenladen m.
**chair** [tʃɛə'] n Stuhl m; (armchair) Sessel m; (of

*university)* Lehrstuhl *m*; (*of meeting, committee)* Vorsitz *m* ♦ *vt* den Vorsitz führen bei; **the ~** (*US*) der elektrische Stuhl.
**chair lift** *n* Sessellift *m*.
**chairman** ['tʃɛəmən] (*irreg: like* **man**) *n* Vorsitzende(r) *f(m)*; (*BRIT: of company*) Präsident *m*.
**chairperson** ['tʃɛəpəːsn] *n* Vorsitzende(r) *f(m)*.
**chairwoman** ['tʃɛəwumən] (*irreg: like* **woman**) *n* Vorsitzende *f*.
**chalet** ['ʃæleɪ] *n* Chalet *nt*.
**chalice** ['tʃælɪs] *n* Kelch *m*.
**chalk** [tʃɔːk] *n* Kalkstein *m*, Kreide *f*; (*for writing*) Kreide *f*.
►**chalk up** *vt* aufschreiben, notieren; (*fig: success etc*) verbuchen.
**challenge** ['tʃælɪndʒ] *n* (*of new job*) Anforderungen *pl*; (*of unknown etc*) Reiz *m*; (*to authority etc*) Infragestellung *f*; (*dare*) Herausforderung *f* ♦ *vt* herausfordern; (*authority, right, idea etc*) in Frage stellen; **to ~ sb to do sth** jdn dazu auffordern, etw zu tun; **to ~ sb to a fight/game** jdn zu einem Kampf/Spiel herausfordern.
**challenger** ['tʃælɪndʒə'] *n* Herausforderer *m*, Herausforderin *f*.
**challenging** ['tʃælɪndʒɪŋ] *adj* (*career, task*) anspruchsvoll; (*tone, look etc*) herausfordernd.
**chamber** ['tʃeɪmbə'] *n* Kammer *f*; (*BRIT: LAW: gen pl: of barristers*) Kanzlei *f*; (: *of judge*) Amtszimmer *nt*; **~ of commerce** Handelskammer *f*.
**chambermaid** ['tʃeɪmbəmeɪd] *n* Zimmermädchen *nt*.
**chamber music** *n* Kammermusik *f*.
**chamber pot** *n* Nachttopf *m*.
**chameleon** [kə'miːliən] *n* Chamäleon *nt*.
**chamois** ['ʃæmwɑː] *n* Gemse *f*; (*cloth*) Ledertuch *nt*, Fensterleder *nt*.
**chamois leather** ['ʃæmɪ-] *n* Ledertuch *nt*, Fensterleder *nt*.
**champagne** [ʃæm'peɪn] *n* Champagner *m*.
**champers** ['ʃæmpəz] (*inf*) *n* (*champagne*) Schampus *m*.
**champion** ['tʃæmpɪən] *n* Meister(in) *m(f)*; (*of cause, principle*) Verfechter(in) *m(f)*; (*of person*) Fürsprecher(in) *m(f)* ♦ *vt* eintreten für, sich engagieren für.
**championship** ['tʃæmpɪənʃɪp] *n* Meisterschaft *f*; (*title*) Titel *m*.
**chance** [tʃɑːns] *n* (*hope*) Aussicht *f*; (*likelihood, possibility*) Möglichkeit *f*; (*opportunity*) Gelegenheit *f*; (*risk*) Risiko *nt* ♦ *vt* riskieren ♦ *adj* zufällig; **the ~s are that** ... aller Wahrscheinlichkeit nach ..., wahrscheinlich ...; **there is little ~ of his coming** es ist unwahrscheinlich, daß er kommt; **to take a ~** es darauf ankommen lassen; **by ~** durch Zufall, zufällig; **it's the ~ of a lifetime** es ist eine einmalige Chance; **to ~ to do sth** zufällig etw tun; **to ~ it** es riskieren.

►**chance (up)on** *vt fus* (*person*) zufällig begegnen +*dat*, zufällig treffen; (*thing*) zufällig stoßen auf +*acc*.
**chancel** ['tʃɑːnsəl] *n* Altarraum *m*.
**chancellor** ['tʃɑːnsələ'] *n* Kanzler *m*.
**Chancellor of the Exchequer** (*BRIT*) *n* Schatzkanzler *m*, Finanzminister *m*.
**chancy** ['tʃɑːnsɪ] *adj* riskant.
**chandelier** [ʃændə'lɪə'] *n* Kronleuchter *m*.
**change** [tʃeɪndʒ] *vt* ändern; (*wheel, job, money, baby's nappy*) wechseln; (*bulb*) auswechseln; (*baby*) wickeln ♦ *vi* sich verändern; (*traffic lights*) umspringen ♦ *n* Veränderung *f*; (*difference*) Abwechslung *f*; (*coins*) Kleingeld *nt*; (*money returned*) Wechselgeld *nt*; **to ~ sb into** jdn verwandeln in +*acc*; **to ~ gear** (*AUT*) schalten; **to ~ one's mind** seine Meinung ändern, es sich *dat* anders überlegen; **to ~ hands** den Besitzer wechseln; **to ~ (trains/buses/planes** *etc*) umsteigen; **to ~ (one's clothes)** sich umziehen; **to ~ into** (*be transformed*) sich verwandeln in +*acc*; **she ~d into an old skirt** sie zog einen alten Rock an; **a ~ of clothes** Kleidung *f* zum Wechseln; **~ of government/climate/job** Regierungs-/Klima-/Berufswechsel *m*; **small ~** Kleingeld *nt*; **to give sb ~ for or of £10** jdm £10 wechseln; **keep the ~** das stimmt so, der Rest ist für Sie; **for a ~** zur Abwechslung.
**changeable** ['tʃeɪndʒəbl] *adj* (*weather*) wechselhaft, veränderlich; (*mood*) wechselnd; (*person*) unbeständig.
**change machine** *n* (Geld)wechselautomat *m*.
**changeover** ['tʃeɪndʒəuvə'] *n* Umstellung *f*.
**changing** ['tʃeɪndʒɪŋ] *adj* sich verändernd.
**changing room** (*BRIT*) *n* (Umkleide)kabine *f*; (*SPORT*) Umkleideraum *m*.
**channel** ['tʃænl] *n* (*TV*) Kanal *m*; (*of river, waterway*) (Fluß)bett *nt*; (*for boats*) Fahrrinne *f*; (*groove*) Rille *f*; (*fig: means*) Weg *m* ♦ *vt* leiten; (*fig*): **to ~ into** lenken auf +*acc*; **through the usual ~s** auf dem üblichen Wege; **green ~** (*CUSTOMS*) „nichts zu verzollen"; **red ~** (*CUSTOMS*) „Waren zu verzollen"; **the (English) C~** der Ärmelkanal; **the C~ Islands** die Kanalinseln *pl*.
**Channel Tunnel** *n*: **the ~** der Kanaltunnel.
**chant** [tʃɑːnt] *n* Sprechchor *m*; (*REL*) Gesang *m* ♦ *vt* im (Sprech)chor rufen; (*REL*) singen ♦ *vi* Sprechchöre anstimmen; (*REL*) singen; **the demonstrators ~ed their disapproval** die Demonstranten machten ihrem Unmut in Sprechchören Luft.
**chaos** ['keɪɔs] *n* Chaos *nt*, Durcheinander *nt*.
**chaos theory** *n* Chaostheorie *f*.
**chaotic** [keɪ'ɔtɪk] *adj* chaotisch.
**chap** [tʃæp] (*BRIT: inf*) *n* Kerl *m*, Typ *m*; **old ~** alter Knabe *or* Junge.
**chapel** ['tʃæpl] *n* Kapelle *f*; (*BRIT: nonconformist chapel*) Sektenkirche *f*; (: *of union*) *Betriebsgruppe innerhalb der*

*Gewerkschaft der Drucker und Journalisten.*

**chaperone** ['ʃæpərəun] n Anstandsdame f ♦ vt begleiten.

**chaplain** ['tʃæplɪn] n Pfarrer(in) m(f); (Roman Catholic) Kaplan m.

**chapped** [tʃæpt] adj aufgesprungen, rauh.

**chapter** ['tʃæptə*] n Kapitel nt; a ~ of accidents eine Serie von Unfällen.

**char** [tʃɑː'] vt verkohlen ♦ vi (BRIT) putzen gehen ♦ n (BRIT) = **charlady**.

**character** ['kærɪktə*] n Charakter m; (personality) Persönlichkeit f; (in novel, film) Figur f, Gestalt f; (eccentric) Original nt; (letter: also COMPUT) Zeichen nt; **a person of good** ~ ein guter Mensch.

**character code** n (COMPUT) Zeichencode m.

**characteristic** [kærɪktə'rɪstɪk] n Merkmal nt ♦ adj: ~ (of) charakteristisch (für), typisch (für).

**characterize** ['kærɪktəraɪz] vt kennzeichnen, charakterisieren; (describe the character of): **to** ~ **(as)** beschreiben (als).

**charade** [ʃə'rɑːd] n Scharade f.

**charcoal** ['tʃɑːkəul] n Holzkohle f; (for drawing) Kohle f, Kohlestift m.

**charge** [tʃɑːdʒ] n (fee) Gebühr f; (accusation) Anklage f; (responsibility) Verantwortung f; (attack) Angriff m ♦ vt (customer) berechnen +dat; (sum) berechnen; (battery) (auf)laden; (gun) laden; (enemy) angreifen; (sb with task) beauftragen ♦ vi angreifen; (usu with: up, along etc) stürmen; **charges** npl Gebühren pl; **labour** ~**s** Arbeitskosten pl; **to reverse the** ~**s** (BRIT: TEL) ein R-Gespräch führen; **is there a** ~? kostet das etwas?; **there's no** ~ es ist umsonst, es kostet nichts; **at no extra** ~ ohne Aufpreis; **free of** ~ kostenlos, gratis; **to take** ~ **of** (child) sich kümmern um; (company) übernehmen; **to be in** ~ **of** die Verantwortung haben für; (business) leiten; **they** ~**d us £10 for the meal** das Essen kostete £10; **how much do you** ~? was verlangen Sie?; **to** ~ **an expense (up) to sb's account** eine Ausgabe auf jds Rechnung acc setzen; **to** ~ **sb (with)** (LAW) jdn anklagen (wegen).

**charge account** n Kunden(kredit)konto nt.

**charge card** n Kundenkreditkarte f.

**chargé d'affaires** n Chargé d'affaires m.

**charge hand** (BRIT) n Vorarbeiter(in) m(f).

**charger** ['tʃɑːdʒə*] n (also: **battery** ~) Ladegerät nt; (warhorse) (Schlacht)roß nt.

**chariot** ['tʃærɪət] n (Streit)wagen m.

**charisma** [kæ'rɪsmə] n Charisma nt.

**charitable** ['tʃærɪtəbl] adj (organization) karitativ, Wohltätigkeits-; (remark) freundlich.

**charity** ['tʃærɪtɪ] n (organization) karitative Organisation f, Wohltätigkeitsverein m; (kindness, generosity) Menschenfreundlichkeit f; (money, gifts) Almosen nt.

**charlady** ['tʃɑːleɪdɪ] (irreg: like **lady**) (BRIT) n Putzfrau f, Reinemachefrau f.

**charlatan** ['ʃɑːlətən] n Scharlatan m.

**charm** [tʃɑːm] n Charme m; (to bring good luck) Talisman m; (on bracelet etc) Anhänger m ♦ vt bezaubern.

**charm bracelet** n Armband nt mit Anhängern.

**charming** ['tʃɑːmɪŋ] adj reizend, charmant; (place) bezaubernd.

**chart** [tʃɑːt] n Schaubild nt, Diagramm nt; (map) Karte f; (weather chart) Wetterkarte f ♦ vt (course) planen; (progress) aufzeichnen; **charts** npl (hit parade) Hitliste f.

**charter** ['tʃɑːtə*] vt chartern ♦ n Charta f; (of university, company) Gründungsurkunde f; **on** ~ gechartert.

**chartered accountant** ['tʃɑːtəd-] (BRIT) n Wirtschaftsprüfer(in) m(f).

**charter flight** n Charterflug m.

**charwoman** ['tʃɑːwumən] (irreg: like **woman**) n Putzfrau f, Reinemachefrau f.

**chary** ['tʃɛərɪ] adj: **to be** ~ **of doing sth** zögern, etw zu tun.

**chase** [tʃeɪs] vt jagen, verfolgen; (also: ~ **away**) wegjagen, vertreiben; (business, job etc) hersein hinter +dat (inf) ♦ n Verfolgungsjagd f.

▶**chase down** (US) vt = **chase up**.

▶**chase up** (BRIT) vt (person) rankriegen (inf); (information) ranschaffen (inf).

**chasm** ['kæzəm] n Kluft f.

**chassis** ['ʃæsɪ] n Fahrgestell nt.

**chaste** [tʃeɪst] adj keusch.

**chastened** ['tʃeɪsnd] adj zur Einsicht gebracht.

**chastening** ['tʃeɪsnɪŋ] adj ernüchternd.

**chastise** [tʃæs'taɪz] vt (scold) schelten.

**chastity** ['tʃæstɪtɪ] n Keuschheit f.

**chat** [tʃæt] vi (also: **have a** ~) plaudern, sich unterhalten ♦ n Plauderei f, Unterhaltung f.

▶**chat up** (BRIT: inf) vt anmachen.

**chatline** ['tʃætlaɪn] n Telefondienst, der Anrufern die Teilnahme an einer Gesprächsrunde ermöglicht.

**chat show** (BRIT) n Talkshow f.

**chattel** ['tʃætl] n: **goods and** ~**s** see **good**.

**chatter** ['tʃætə*] vi schwatzen; (monkey) schnattern; (teeth) klappern ♦ n (see vi) Schwatzen nt; Schnattern nt; Klappern nt; **my teeth are** ~**ing** mir klappern die Zähne.

**chatterbox** ['tʃætəbɒks] (inf) n Quasselstrippe f.

**chattering classes** ['tʃætərɪŋ 'klɑːsɪz] npl: **the** ~ die intellektuellen Schwätzer pl.

**chatty** ['tʃætɪ] adj geschwätzig; (letter) im Plauderton.

**chauffeur** ['ʃəufə*] n Chauffeur m, Fahrer m.

**chauvinism** ['ʃəuvɪnɪzəm] n (also: **male** ~) Chauvinismus m.

**chauvinist** ['ʃəuvɪnɪst] n Chauvinist m.

**chauvinistic** [ʃəuvɪ'nɪstɪk] adj chauvinistisch.

**ChE** *abbr* (= *chemical engineer*) *Titel für* Chemotechniker.

**cheap** [tʃiːp] *adj* billig; (*reduced*) ermäßigt; (*poor quality*) billig, minderwertig; (*behaviour, joke*) ordinär ♦ *adv*: **to buy/sell sth** ~ etw billig kaufen/verkaufen.

**cheapen** ['tʃiːpn] *vt* entwürdigen.

**cheaper** ['tʃiːpəʳ] *adj* billiger.

**cheaply** ['tʃiːplɪ] *adv* billig.

**cheat** [tʃiːt] *vi* mogeln (*inf*), schummeln (*inf*) ♦ *n* Betrüger(in) *m(f)* ♦ *vt*: **to** ~ **sb (out of sth)** jdn (um etw) betrügen; **to** ~ **on sb** (*inf*) jdn betrügen.

**cheating** ['tʃiːtɪŋ] *n* Mogeln *nt* (*inf*), Schummeln *nt* (*inf*).

**check** [tʃɛk] *vt* überprüfen; (*passport, ticket*) kontrollieren; (*facts*) nachprüfen; (*enemy, disease*) aufhalten; (*impulse*) unterdrücken; (*person*) zurückhalten ♦ *vi* nachprüfen ♦ *n* Kontrolle *f*; (*curb*) Beschränkung *f*; (*US*) = **cheque**; (: *bill*) Rechnung *f*; (*pattern: gen pl*) Karo(muster) *nt* ♦ *adj* kariert; **to** ~ **o.s.** sich beherrschen; **to** ~ **with sb** bei jdm nachfragen; **to keep a** ~ **on sb/sth** jdn/etw kontrollieren.

►**check in** *vi* (*at hotel*) sich anmelden; (*at airport*) einchecken ♦ *vt* (*luggage*) abfertigen lassen.

►**check off** *vt* abhaken.

►**check out** *vi* (*of hotel*) abreisen ♦ *vt* (*luggage*) abfertigen; (*investigate*) überprüfen.

►**check up** *vi*: **to** ~ **up on sth** etw überprüfen; **to** ~ **up on sb** Nachforschungen über jdn anstellen.

**checkered** ['tʃɛkəd] (*US*) *adj* = **chequered**.

**checkers** ['tʃɛkəz] (*US*) *npl* Damespiel *nt*.

**check guarantee card** (*US*) *n* Scheckkarte *f*.

**check-in (desk)** ['tʃɛkɪn-] *n* (*at airport*) Abfertigung *f*, Abfertigungsschalter *m*.

**checking account** ['tʃɛkɪŋ-] (*US*) *n* Girokonto *nt*.

**check list** *n* Prüfliste *f*, Checkliste *f*.

**checkmate** ['tʃɛkmeɪt] *n* Schachmatt *nt*.

**checkout** ['tʃɛkaut] *n* Kasse *f*.

**checkpoint** ['tʃɛkpɔɪnt] *n* Kontrollpunkt *m*.

**checkroom** ['tʃɛkrum] (*US*) *n* (*left-luggage office*) Gepäckaufbewahrung *f*.

**checkup** ['tʃɛkʌp] *n* Untersuchung *f*.

**cheek** [tʃiːk] *n* Backe *f*; (*impudence*) Frechheit *f*; (*nerve*) Unverschämtheit *f*.

**cheekbone** ['tʃiːkbəun] *n* Backenknochen *m*.

**cheeky** ['tʃiːkɪ] *adj* frech.

**cheep** [tʃiːp] *vi* (*bird*) piep(s)en ♦ *n* Piep(s) *m*, Piepser *m*.

**cheer** [tʃɪəʳ] *vt* zujubeln +*dat*; (*gladden*) aufmuntern, aufheitern ♦ *vi* jubeln, hurra rufen ♦ *n* (*gen pl*) Hurraruf *m*, Beifallsruf *m*; **cheers** *npl* Hurrageschrei *nt*, Jubel *m*; ~**s!** prost!

►**cheer on** *vt* ansporen, anfeuern.

►**cheer up** *vi* vergnügter *or* fröhlicher werden ♦ *vt* aufmuntern, aufheitern.

**cheerful** ['tʃɪəful] *adj* fröhlich.

**cheerfulness** ['tʃɪəfulnɪs] *n* Fröhlichkeit *f*.

**cheerio** [tʃɪərɪˈəu] (*BRIT*) *excl* tschüs (*inf*).

**cheerleader** ['tʃɪəliːdəʳ] *n* jd, der bei Sportveranstaltungen etc die Zuschauer zu Beifallsrufen anfeuert.

**cheerless** ['tʃɪəlɪs] *adj* freudlos, trüb; (*room*) trostlos.

**cheese** [tʃiːz] *n* Käse *m*.

**cheeseboard** ['tʃiːzbɔːd] *n* Käsebrett *nt*; (*with cheese on it*) Käseplatte *f*.

**cheeseburger** ['tʃiːzbəːgəʳ] *n* Cheeseburger *m*.

**cheesecake** ['tʃiːzkeɪk] *n* Käsekuchen *m*.

**cheetah** ['tʃiːtə] *n* Gepard *m*.

**chef** [ʃɛf] *n* Küchenchef(in) *m(f)*.

**chemical** ['kɛmɪkl] *adj* chemisch ♦ *n* Chemikalie *f*.

**chemical engineering** *n* Chemotechnik *f*.

**chemist** ['kɛmɪst] *n* (*BRIT: pharmacist*) Apotheker(in) *m(f)*; (*scientist*) Chemiker(in) *m(f)*.

**chemistry** ['kɛmɪstrɪ] *n* Chemie *f*.

**chemist's (shop)** ['kɛmɪsts-] (*BRIT*) *n* Drogerie *f*; (*also*: **dispensing chemist's**) Apotheke *f*.

**chemotherapy** [kiːməuˈθɛrəpɪ] *n* Chemotherapie *f*.

**cheque** [tʃɛk] (*BRIT*) *n* Scheck *m*; **to pay by** ~ mit (einem) Scheck bezahlen.

**chequebook** ['tʃɛkbuk] *n* Scheckbuch *nt*.

**cheque card** (*BRIT*) *n* Scheckkarte *f*.

**chequered,** (*US*) **checkered** ['tʃɛkəd] *adj* (*fig*) bewegt.

**cherish** ['tʃɛrɪʃ] *vt* (*person*) liebevoll sorgen für; (*memory*) in Ehren halten; (*dream*) sich hingeben +*dat*; (*hope*) hegen.

**cheroot** [ʃəˈruːt] *n* Stumpen *m*.

**cherry** ['tʃɛrɪ] *n* Kirsche *f*; (*also*: ~ **tree**) Kirschbaum *m*.

**chervil** ['tʃəːvɪl] *n* Kerbel *m*.

**Ches.** (*BRIT*) *abbr* (*POST*: = *Cheshire*).

**chess** [tʃɛs] *n* Schach(spiel) *nt*.

**chessboard** ['tʃɛsbɔːd] *n* Schachbrett *nt*.

**chessman** ['tʃɛsmən] (*irreg: like* **man**) *n* Schachfigur *f*.

**chess player** *n* Schachspieler(in) *m(f)*.

**chest** [tʃɛst] *n* Brust *f*, Brustkorb *m*; (*box*) Kiste *f*, Truhe *f*; **to get sth off one's** ~ (*inf*) sich *dat* etw von der Seele reden.

**chest measurement** *n* Brustweite *f*, Brustumfang *m*.

**chestnut** ['tʃɛsnʌt] *n* Kastanie *f* ♦ *adj* kastanienbraun.

**chest of drawers** *n* Kommode *f*.

**chesty** ['tʃɛstɪ] *adj* (*cough*) tief sitzend.

**chew** [tʃuː] *vt* kauen.

**chewing gum** ['tʃuːɪŋ-] *n* Kaugummi *m*.

**chic** [ʃiːk] *adj* schick, elegant.

**chick** [tʃɪk] *n* Küken *nt*; (*inf: girl*) Mieze *f*.

**chicken** ['tʃɪkɪn] *n* Huhn *nt*; (*meat*) Hähnchen

nt; (*inf: coward*) Feigling *m*.
▶**chicken out** (*inf*) *vi*: **to ~ out of doing sth** davor kneifen, etw zu tun.
**chicken feed** *n* ein paar Pfennige *pl*; (*as salary*) ein Hungerlohn *m*.
**chickenpox** ['tʃɪkɪnpɔks] *n* Windpocken *pl*.
**chickpea** ['tʃɪkpiː] *n* Kichererbse *f*.
**chicory** ['tʃɪkərɪ] *n* (*in coffee*) Zichorie *f*; (*salad vegetable*) Chicorée *f or m*.
**chide** [tʃaɪd] *vt*: **to ~ sb (for)** jdn schelten (wegen).
**chief** [tʃiːf] *n* Häuptling *m*; (*of organization, department*) Leiter(in) *m(f)*, Chef(in) *m(f)* ♦ *adj* Haupt-, wichtigste(r, s).
**chief constable** (*BRIT*) *n* Polizeipräsident *m*, Polizeichef *m*.
**chief executive**, (*US*) **chief executive officer** *n* Generaldirektor(in) *m(f)*.
**chiefly** ['tʃiːflɪ] *adv* hauptsächlich.
**Chief of Staff** *n* Stabschef *m*.
**chiffon** ['ʃɪfɔn] *n* Chiffon *m*.
**chilblain** ['tʃɪlbleɪn] *n* Frostbeule *f*.
**child** [tʃaɪld] (*pl* ~**ren**) *n* Kind *nt*; **do you have any ~ren?** haben Sie Kinder?
**child benefit** (*BRIT*) *n* Kindergeld *nt*.
**childbirth** ['tʃaɪldbɜːθ] *n* Geburt *f*, Entbindung *f*.
**childhood** ['tʃaɪldhud] *n* Kindheit *f*.
**childish** ['tʃaɪldɪʃ] *adj* kindisch.
**childless** ['tʃaɪldlɪs] *adj* kinderlos.
**childlike** ['tʃaɪldlaɪk] *adj* kindlich.
**child minder** (*BRIT*) *n* Tagesmutter *f*.
**child prodigy** *n* Wunderkind *nt*.
**children** ['tʃɪldrən] *npl of* **child**.
**children's home** ['tʃɪldrənz-] *n* Kinderheim *nt*.
**child's play** ['tʃaɪldz-] *n*: **it was ~** es war ein Kinderspiel.
**Chile** ['tʃɪlɪ] *n* Chile *nt*.
**Chilean** ['tʃɪlɪən] *adj* chilenisch ♦ *n* Chilene *m*, Chilenin *f*.
**chill** [tʃɪl] *n* Kühle *f*; (*illness*) Erkältung *f* ♦ *adj* kühl; (*fig: reminder*) erschreckend ♦ *vt* kühlen; (*person*) frösteln *or* frieren lassen; **"serve ~ed"** „gekühlt servieren".
**chilli**, (*US*) **chili** ['tʃɪlɪ] *n* Peperoni *pl*.
**chilling** ['tʃɪlɪŋ] *adj* (*wind, morning*) eisig; (*fig: effect, prospect etc*) beängstigend.
**chill out** (*inf*) *vi* sich entspannen, relaxen.
**chilly** ['tʃɪlɪ] *adj* kühl; (*person, response, look*) kühl, frostig; **to feel ~** frösteln, frieren.
**chime** [tʃaɪm] *n* Glockenspiel *nt* ♦ *vi* läuten.
**chimney** ['tʃɪmnɪ] *n* Schornstein *m*.
**chimney sweep** *n* Schornsteinfeger(in) *m(f)*.
**chimpanzee** [tʃɪmpæn'ziː] *n* Schimpanse *m*.
**chin** [tʃɪn] *n* Kinn *nt*.
**China** ['tʃaɪnə] *n* China *nt*.
**china** ['tʃaɪnə] *n* Porzellan *nt*.
**Chinese** [tʃaɪ'niːz] *adj* chinesisch ♦ *n inv* Chinese *m*, Chinesin *f*; (*LING*) Chinesisch *nt*.
**chink** [tʃɪŋk] *n* (*in door, wall etc*) Ritze *f*, Spalt *m*; (*of bottles etc*) Klirren *nt*.

**chintz** [tʃɪnts] *n* Chintz *m*.
**chinwag** ['tʃɪnwæg] (*BRIT: inf*) *n* Schwatz *m*.
**chip** [tʃɪp] *n* (*gen pl*) Pommes frites *pl*; (*US: also:* **potato ~**) Chip *m*; (*of wood*) Span *m*; (*of glass, stone*) Splitter *m*; (*in glass, cup etc*) abgestoßene Stelle *f*; (*in gambling*) Chip *m*, Spielmarke *f*; (*COMPUT: also:* **microchip**) Chip *m* ♦ *vt* (*cup, plate*) anschlagen; **when the ~s are down** (*fig*) wenn es drauf ankommt.
▶**chip in** (*inf*) *vi* (*contribute*) etwas beisteuern; (*interrupt*) sich einschalten.
**chipboard** ['tʃɪpbɔːd] *n* Spanplatte *f*.
**chipmunk** ['tʃɪpmʌŋk] *n* Backenhörnchen *nt*.
**chippings** ['tʃɪpɪŋz] *npl*: **loose ~** (*on road*) Schotter *m*.

> Chip shop, *auch* fish-and-chip shop, *ist die traditionelle britische Imbißbude, in der vor allem fritierte Fischfilets und Pommes frites, aber auch andere einfache Mahlzeiten angeboten werden. Früher wurde das Essen zum Mitnehmen in Zeitungspapier verpackt. Manche* chip shops *haben auch einen Eßraum.*

**chiropodist** [kɪ'rɔpədɪst] (*BRIT*) *n* Fußpfleger(in) *m(f)*.
**chiropody** [kɪ'rɔpədɪ] (*BRIT*) *n* Fußpflege *f*.
**chirp** [tʃɜːp] *vi* (*bird*) zwitschern; (*crickets*) zirpen.
**chirpy** ['tʃɜːpɪ] (*inf*) *adj* munter.
**chisel** ['tʃɪzl] *n* (*for stone*) Meißel *m*; (*for wood*) Beitel *m*.
**chit** [tʃɪt] *n* Zettel *m*.
**chitchat** ['tʃɪttʃæt] *n* Plauderei *f*.
**chivalrous** ['ʃɪvəlrəs] *adj* ritterlich.
**chivalry** ['ʃɪvəlrɪ] *n* Ritterlichkeit *f*.
**chives** [tʃaɪvz] *npl* Schnittlauch *m*.
**chloride** ['klɔːraɪd] *n* Chlorid *nt*.
**chlorinate** ['klɔrɪneɪt] *vt* chloren.
**chlorine** ['klɔːriːn] *n* Chlor *nt*.
**chock** [tʃɔk] *n* Bremskeil *m*, Bremsklotz *m*.
**chock-a-block** ['tʃɔkə'blɔk] *adj* gerammelt voll.
**chock-full** [tʃɔk'ful] *adj* = **chock-a-block**.
**chocolate** ['tʃɔklɪt] *n* Schokolade *f*; (*drink*) Kakao *m*, Schokolade *f*; (*sweet*) Praline *f* ♦ *cpd* Schokoladen-.
**choice** [tʃɔɪs] *n* Auswahl *f*; (*option*) Möglichkeit *f*; (*preference*) Wahl *f* ♦ *adj* Qualitäts-, erstklassig; **I did it by** *or* **from ~** ich habe es mir so ausgesucht; **a wide ~** eine große Auswahl.
**choir** ['kwaɪə*] *n* Chor *m*.
**choirboy** ['kwaɪəbɔɪ] *n* Chorknabe *m*.
**choke** [tʃəuk] *vi* ersticken; (*with smoke, dust, anger etc*) keine Luft mehr bekommen ♦ *vt* erwürgen, erdrosseln ♦ *n* (*AUT*) Choke *m*, Starterklappe *f*; **to be ~d (with)** verstopft sein (mit).
**cholera** ['kɔlərə] *n* Cholera *f*.
**cholesterol** [kə'lɛstərɔl] *n* Cholesterin *nt*.
**choose** [tʃuːz] (*pt* **chose**, *pp* **chosen**) *vt*

(aus)wählen; (*profession, friend*) sich *dat* aussuchen ♦ *vi:* **to ~ between** wählen zwischen +*dat*, eine Wahl treffen zwischen +*dat*; **to ~ from** wählen aus *or* unter +*dat*, eine Wahl treffen aus *or* unter +*dat*; **to ~ to do sth** beschließen, etw zu tun.

**choosy** ['tʃuːzı] *adj* wählerisch.

**chop** [tʃɔp] *vt* (*wood*) hacken; (*also:* ~ **up:** *vegetables, fruit, meat*) kleinschneiden ♦ *n* Kotelett *nt*; **chops** (*inf*) *npl* (*of animal*) Maul *nt*; (*of person*) Mund *m*; **to get the ~** (*BRIT: inf: project*) dem Rotstift zum Opfer fallen; (: : *be sacked*) rausgeschmissen werden.

▶**chop down** *vt* (*tree*) fällen.

**chopper** ['tʃɔpə˙] (*inf*) *n* Hubschrauber *m*.

**choppy** ['tʃɔpı] *adj* (*sea*) kabbelig, bewegt.

**chopsticks** ['tʃɔpstıks] *npl* Stäbchen *pl*.

**choral** ['kɔːrəl] *adj* (*singing*) Chor-; (*society*) Gesang-.

**chord** [kɔːd] *n* Akkord *m*; (*MATH*) Sehne *f*.

**chore** [tʃɔː˙] *n* Hausarbeit *f*; (*routine task*) lästige Routinearbeit *f*; **household ~s** Hausarbeit.

**choreographer** [kɔrı'ɔɡrəfə˙] *n* Choreograph(in) *m(f)*.

**choreography** [kɔrı'ɔɡrəfı] *n* Choreographie *f*.

**chorister** ['kɔrıstə˙] *n* Chorsänger(in) *m(f)*.

**chortle** ['tʃɔːtl] *vi* glucksen.

**chorus** ['kɔːrəs] *n* Chor *m*; (*refrain*) Refrain *m*; (*of complaints*) Flut *f*.

**chose** [tʃəuz] *pt of* **choose**.

**chosen** ['tʃəuzn] *pp of* **choose**.

**chow** [tʃau] *n* Chow-Chow *m*.

**chowder** ['tʃaudə˙] *n* (sämige) Fischsuppe *f*.

**Christ** [kraıst] *n* Christus *m*.

**christen** ['krısn] *vt* taufen.

**christening** ['krısnıŋ] *n* Taufe *f*.

**Christian** ['krıstıən] *adj* christlich ♦ *n* Christ(in) *m(f)*.

**Christianity** [krıstı'ænıtı] *n* Christentum *nt*.

**Christian name** *n* Vorname *m*.

**Christmas** ['krısməs] *n* Weihnachten *nt*; **Happy** *or* **Merry ~!** frohe *or* fröhliche Weihnachten!

**Christmas card** *n* Weihnachtskarte *f*.

**Christmas Day** *n* der erste Weihnachtstag.

**Christmas Eve** *n* Heiligabend *m*.

**Christmas Island** *n* Weihnachtsinsel *f*.

**Christmas tree** *n* Weihnachtsbaum *m*, Christbaum *m*.

**chrome** [krəum] *n* = **chromium**.

**chromium** ['krəumıəm] *n* Chrom *nt*; (*also:* ~ **plating**) Verchromung *f*.

**chromosome** ['krəuməsəum] *n* Chromosom *nt*.

**chronic** ['krɔnık] *adj* (*also fig*) chronisch; (*severe*) schlimm.

**chronicle** ['krɔnıkl] *n* Chronik *f*.

**chronological** [krɔnə'lɔdʒıkl] *adj* chronologisch.

**chrysanthemum** [krı'sænθəməm] *n*

Chrysantheme *f*.

**chubby** ['tʃʌbı] *adj* pummelig; **~ cheeks** Pausbacken *pl*.

**chuck** [tʃʌk] (*inf*) *vt* werfen, schmeißen; (*BRIT: also:* ~ **up**, ~ **in**) (*job*) hinschmeißen; (: *person*) Schluß machen mit.

▶**chuck out** *vt* (*person*) rausschmeißen; (*rubbish etc*) wegschmeißen.

**chuckle** ['tʃʌkl] *vi* leise in sich *acc* hineinlachen.

**chuffed** [tʃʌft] (*BRIT: inf*) *adj* vergnügt und zufrieden; (*flattered*) gebauchpinselt.

**chug** [tʃʌɡ] *vi* (*also:* ~ **along**) tuckern.

**chum** [tʃʌm] *n* Kumpel *m*.

**chump** [tʃʌmp] (*inf*) *n* Trottel *m*.

**chunk** [tʃʌŋk] *n* großes Stück *nt*.

**chunky** ['tʃʌŋkı] *adj* (*furniture etc*) klobig; (*person*) stämmig, untersetzt; (*knitwear*) dick.

**church** [tʃəːtʃ] *n* Kirche *f*; **the C~ of England** die Anglikanische Kirche.

**churchyard** ['tʃəːtʃjaːd] *n* Friedhof *m*.

**churlish** ['tʃəːlıʃ] *adj* griesgrämig; (*behaviour*) ungehobelt.

**churn** [tʃəːn] *n* Butterfaß *nt*; (*also:* **milk ~**) Milchkanne *f*.

▶**churn out** *vt* am laufenden Band produzieren.

**chute** [ʃuːt] *n* (*also:* **rubbish ~**) Müllschlucker *m*; (*for coal, parcels etc*) Rutsche *f*; (*BRIT: slide*) Rutschbahn *f*, Rutsche *f*.

**chutney** ['tʃʌtnı] *n* Chutney *nt*.

**CIA** (*US*) *n abbr* (= *Central Intelligence Agency*) CIA *f or m*.

**cicada** [sı'kaːdə] *n* Zikade *f*.

**CID** (*BRIT*) *n abbr* = **Criminal Investigation Department**.

**cider** ['saıdə˙] *n* Apfelwein *m*.

**c.i.f.** *abbr* (*COMM:* = *cost, insurance and freight*) cif.

**cigar** [sı'ɡaː˙] *n* Zigarre *f*.

**cigarette** [sıɡə'rɛt] *n* Zigarette *f*.

**cigarette case** *n* Zigarettenetui *nt*.

**cigarette end** *n* Zigarettenstummel *m*.

**cigarette holder** *n* Zigarettenspitze *f*.

**C in C** *abbr* (*MIL*) = **commander in chief**.

**cinch** [sıntʃ] (*inf*) *n*: **it's a ~** das ist ein Kinderspiel *or* ein Klacks.

**Cinderella** [sındə'rɛlə] *n* Aschenputtel *nt*, Aschenbrödel *nt*.

**cinders** ['sındəz] *npl* Asche *f*.

**cine camera** ['sını-] (*BRIT*) *n* (Schmal)filmkamera *f*.

**cine film** (*BRIT*) *n* Schmalfilm *m*.

**cinema** ['sınəmə] *n* Kino *nt*; (*film-making*) Film *m*.

**cine projector** (*BRIT*) *n* Filmprojektor *m*.

**cinnamon** ['sınəmən] *n* Zimt *m*.

**cipher** ['saıfə˙] *n* (*code*) Chiffre *f*; (*fig*) Niemand *m*; **in ~** chiffriert.

**circa** ['səːkə] *prep* zirka, circa.

**circle** ['səːkl] *n* Kreis *m*; (*in cinema, theatre*)

Rang m ♦ vi kreisen ♦ vt kreisen um; (surround) umgeben.

**circuit** ['sɜːkɪt] n Runde f; (ELEC) Stromkreis m; (track) Rennbahn f.

**circuit board** n (COMPUT, ELEC) Platine f, Leiterplatte f.

**circuitous** [sɜː'kjuːɪtəs] adj umständlich.

**circular** ['sɜːkjulə*] adj rund; (route) Rund- ♦ n (letter) Rundschreiben nt, Rundbrief m; (as advertisement) Wurfsendung f; ~ argument Zirkelschluß m.

**circulate** ['sɜːkjuleɪt] vi (traffic) fließen; (blood, report) zirkulieren; (news, rumour) kursieren, in Umlauf sein; (person) die Runde machen ♦ vt herumgehen or zirkulieren lassen.

**circulating capital** [sɜːkju'leɪtɪŋ-] n (COMM) flüssiges Kapital nt, Umlaufkapital nt.

**circulation** [sɜːkju'leɪʃən] n (of traffic) Fluß m; (of air etc) Zirkulation f; (of newspaper) Auflage f; (MED: of blood) Kreislauf m.

**circumcise** ['sɜːkəmsaɪz] vt beschneiden.

**circumference** [sə'kʌmfərəns] n Umfang m; (edge) Rand m.

**circumflex** ['sɜːkəmfleks] n (also: ~ accent) Zirkumflex m.

**circumscribe** ['sɜːkəmskraɪb] vt (MATH) einen Kreis umbeschreiben; (fig) eingrenzen.

**circumspect** ['sɜːkəmspekt] adj umsichtig.

**circumstances** ['sɜːkəmstənsɪz] npl Umstände pl; (financial condition) (finanzielle) Verhältnisse pl; **in the** ~ unter diesen Umständen; **under no** ~ unter (gar) keinen Umständen, auf keinen Fall.

**circumstantial** [sɜːkəm'stænʃl] adj ausführlich; ~ **evidence** Inizienbeweis m.

**circumvent** [sɜːkəm'vent] vt umgehen.

**circus** ['sɜːkəs] n Zirkus m; (also: C~: in place names) Platz m.

**cirrhosis** [sɪ'rəʊsɪs] n (also: ~ **of the liver**) Leberzirrhose f.

**CIS** n abbr (= Commonwealth of Independent States) GUS f.

**cissy** ['sɪsɪ] n, adj see sissy.

**cistern** ['sɪstən] n Zisterne f; (of toilet) Spülkasten m.

**citation** [saɪ'teɪʃən] n Zitat nt; (US) Belobigung f, (LAW) Vorladung f (vor Gericht).

**cite** [saɪt] vt zitieren; (example) anführen; (LAW) vorladen.

**citizen** ['sɪtɪzn] n Staatsbürger(in) m(f); (of town) Bürger(in) m(f).

**Citizens' Advice Bureau** ['sɪtɪznz-] n ≈ Bürgerberatungsstelle f.

**citizenship** ['sɪtɪznʃɪp] n Staatsbürgerschaft f.

**citric acid** ['sɪtrɪk-] n Zitronensäure f.

**citrus fruit** ['sɪtrəs-] n Zitrusfrucht f.

**city** ['sɪtɪ] n (Groß)stadt f; **the C~** (FIN) die City, das Londoner Banken- und Börsenviertel.

**city centre** n Stadtzentrum nt, Innenstadt f.

**City Hall** n Rathaus nt; (US: municipal government) Stadtverwaltung f.

**civic** ['sɪvɪk] adj (authorities etc) Stadt-, städtisch; (duties, pride) Bürger-, bürgerlich.

**civic centre** (BRIT) n Stadtverwaltung f.

**civil** ['sɪvɪl] adj (disturbances, rights) Bürger-; (liberties, law) bürgerlich; (polite) höflich.

**Civil Aviation Authority** (BRIT) n Behörde f für Zivilluftfahrt.

**civil defence** n Zivilschutz m.

**civil disobedience** n ziviler Ungehorsam m.

**civil engineer** n Bauingenieur(in) m(f).

**civil engineering** n Hoch- und Tiefbau m.

**civilian** [sɪ'vɪlɪən] adj (population) Zivil- ♦ n Zivilist m; ~ **casualties** Verluste pl unter der Zivilbevölkerung.

**civilization** [sɪvɪlaɪ'zeɪʃən] n Zivilisation f; (a society) Kultur f.

**civilized** ['sɪvɪlaɪzd] adj zivilisiert; (person) kultiviert; (place, experience) gepflegt.

**civil law** n Zivilrecht nt, bürgerliches Recht nt.

**civil liberties** n (bürgerliche) Freiheitsrechte pl.

**civil rights** npl Bürgerrechte pl.

**civil servant** n (Staats)beamter m, (Staats)beamtin f.

**Civil Service** n Beamtenschaft f.

**civil war** n Bürgerkrieg m.

**civvies** ['sɪvɪz] (inf) npl Zivilklamotten pl.

**cl** abbr (= centilitre) cl.

**clad** [klæd] adj: ~ (in) gekleidet (in +acc).

**claim** [kleɪm] vt (assert) behaupten; (responsibility) übernehmen; (credit) in Anspruch nehmen; (rights, inheritance) Anspruch erheben auf +acc; (expenses) sich dat zurückerstatten lassen; (compensation, damages) verlangen ♦ vi (for insurance) Ansprüche geltend machen ♦ n (assertion) Behauptung f; (for pension, wage rise, compensation) Forderung f; (right: to inheritance, land) Anspruch m; (for expenses) Spesenabrechnung f; **(insurance)** ~ (Versicherungs)anspruch m; **to put in a** ~ **for** beantragen.

**claimant** ['kleɪmənt] n Antragsteller(in) m(f).

**claim form** n Antragsformular nt.

**clairvoyant** [kleə'vɔɪənt] n Hellseher(in) m(f).

**clam** [klæm] n Venusmuschel f.

▶**clam up** (inf) vi keinen Piep (mehr) sagen.

**clamber** ['klæmbə*] vi klettern.

**clammy** ['klæmɪ] adj feucht.

**clamour**, (US) **clamor** ['klæmə*] n Lärm m; (protest) Protest m, Aufschrei m ♦ vi: **to** ~ **for** schreien nach.

**clamp** [klæmp] n Schraubzwinge f, Klemme f ♦ vt (two things together) zusammen-klemmen; (one thing on another) klemmen; (wheel) krallen.

▶**clamp down on** vt fus rigoros vorgehen gegen.

**clampdown** ['klæmpdaun] *n:* ~ **(on)** hartes Durchgreifen *nt* (gegen).

**clan** [klæn] *n* Clan *m*.

**clandestine** [klæn'dɛstɪn] *adj* geheim, Geheim-.

**clang** [klæŋ] *vi* klappern; (*bell*) läuten ♦ *n* (*see vi*) Klappern *nt*; Läuten *nt*.

**clanger** ['klæŋə'] (*BRIT: inf*) *n* Fauxpas *m*; **to drop a** ~ ins Fettnäpfchen treten.

**clansman** ['klænzmən] *n* (*irreg: like* **man**) Clanmitglied *nt*.

**clap** [klæp] *vi* (Beifall) klatschen ♦ *vt:* **to** ~ **(one's hands)** (in die Hände) klatschen ♦ *n:* **a** ~ **of thunder** ein Donnerschlag *m*.

**clapping** ['klæpɪŋ] *n* Beifall *m*.

**claptrap** ['klæptræp] (*inf*) *n* Geschwafel *nt*.

**claret** ['klærət] *n* roter Bordeaux(wein) *m*.

**clarification** [klærɪfɪ'keɪʃən] *n* Klärung *f*.

**clarify** ['klærɪfaɪ] *vt* klären.

**clarinet** [klærɪ'nɛt] *n* Klarinette *f*.

**clarity** ['klærɪtɪ] *n* Klarheit *f*.

**clash** [klæʃ] *n* (*fight*) Zusammenstoß *m*; (*disagreement*) Streit *m*, Auseinandersetzung *f*; (*of beliefs, ideas, views*) Konflikt *m*; (*of colours, styles, personalities*) Unverträglichkeit *f*; (*of events, dates, appointments*) Überschneidung *f*; (*noise*) Klirren *nt* ♦ *vi* (*fight*) zusammenstoßen; (*disagree*) sich streiten, eine Auseinandersetzung haben; (*beliefs, ideas, views*) aufeinanderprallen; (*colours*) sich beißen; (*styles, personalities*) nicht zusammenpassen; (*two events, dates, appointments*) sich überschneiden; (*make noise*) klirrend aneinanderschlagen.

**clasp** [klɑːsp] *n* Griff *m*; (*embrace*) Umklammerung *f*; (*of necklace, bag*) Verschluß *m* ♦ *vt* (er)greifen; (*embrace*) umklammern.

**class** [klɑːs] *n* Klasse *f*; (*lesson*) (Unterrichts)stunde *f* ♦ *adj* (*struggle, distinction*) Klassen- ♦ *vt* einordnen, einstufen.

**class-conscious** ['klɑːs'kɒnʃəs] *adj* klassenbewußt, standesbewußt.

**class-consciousness** ['klɑːs'kɒnʃəsnɪs] *n* Klassenbewußtsein *nt*, Standesbewußtsein *nt*.

**classic** ['klæsɪk] *adj* klassisch ♦ *n* Klassiker *m*; (*race*) *bedeutendes Pferderennen für dreijährige Pferde*; **classics** *npl* (*SCOL*) Altphilologie *f*.

**classical** ['klæsɪkl] *adj* klassisch.

**classification** [klæsɪfɪ'keɪʃən] *n* Klassifikation *f*; (*category*) Klasse *f*; (*system*) Einteilung *f*.

**classified** ['klæsɪfaɪd] *adj* geheim.

**classified advertisement** *n* Kleinanzeige *f*.

**classify** ['klæsɪfaɪ] *vt* klassifizieren, (ein)ordnen.

**classless** ['klɑːslɪs] *adj:* ~ **society** klassenlose Gesellschaft *f*.

**classmate** ['klɑːsmeɪt] *n* Klassenkamerad(in) *m(f)*.

**classroom** ['klɑːsrum] *n* Klassenzimmer *nt*.

**classy** ['klɑːsɪ] (*inf*) *adj* nobel, exklusiv; (*person*) todschick.

**clatter** ['klætə'] *n* Klappern *nt*; (*of hooves*) Trappeln *nt* ♦ *vi* (*see n*) klappern; trappeln.

**clause** [klɔːz] *n* (*LAW*) Klausel *f*; (*LING*) Satz *m*.

**claustrophobia** [klɔːstrə'fəubɪə] *n* Klaustrophobie *f*, Platzangst *f*.

**claustrophobic** [klɔːstrə'fəubɪk] *adj* (*place, situation*) beengend; (*person*): **to be/feel** ~ Platzangst haben/bekommen.

**claw** [klɔː] *n* Kralle *f*; (*of lobster*) Schere *f*, Zange *f*.

▶**claw at** *vt fus* sich krallen an +*acc*.

**clay** [kleɪ] *n* Ton *m*; (*soil*) Lehm *m*.

**clean** [kliːn] *adj* sauber; (*fight*) fair; (*record, reputation*) einwandfrei; (*joke, story*) stubenrein, anständig; (*edge, MED: fracture*) glatt ♦ *vt* saubermachen; (*car, hands, face etc*) waschen ♦ *adv*: **he** ~ **forgot** er hat es glatt(weg) vergessen; **to have a** ~ **driving licence** *or* (*US*) **record** keine Strafpunkte haben; **to** ~ **one's teeth** (*BRIT*) sich *dat* die Zähne putzen; **the thief got** ~ **away** der Dieb konnte entkommen; **to come** ~ (*inf*) auspacken.

▶**clean off** *vt* abwaschen, abwischen.

▶**clean out** *vt* gründlich saubermachen; (*inf: person*) ausnehmen.

▶**clean up** *vt* aufräumen; (*child*) saubermachen; (*fig*) für Ordnung sorgen in +*dat* ♦ *vi* aufräumen, saubermachen; (*inf: make profit*) absahnen.

**clean-cut** ['kliːn'kʌt] *adj* gepflegt; (*situation*) klar.

**cleaner** ['kliːnə'] *n* Raumpfleger(in) *m(f)*; (*woman*) Putzfrau *f*; (*substance*) Reinigungsmittel *nt*, Putzmittel *nt*.

**cleaner's** ['kliːnəz] *n* (*also:* **dry** ~) Reinigung *f*.

**cleaning** ['kliːnɪŋ] *n* Putzen *nt*.

**cleaning lady** *n* Putzfrau *f*, Reinemachefrau *f*.

**cleanliness** ['klɛnlɪnɪs] *n* Sauberkeit *f*, Reinlichkeit *f*.

**cleanly** ['kliːnlɪ] *adv* sauber.

**cleanse** [klɛnz] *vt* (*purify*) läutern; (*face, cut*) reinigen.

**cleanser** ['klɛnzə'] *n* (*for face*) Reinigungscreme *f*, Reinigungsmilch *f*.

**clean-shaven** ['kliːn'ʃeɪvn] *adj* glattrasiert.

**cleansing department** ['klɛnzɪŋ-] (*BRIT*) *n* ≈ Stadtreinigung *f*.

**clean sweep** *n:* **to make a** ~ (*SPORT*) alle Preise einstecken.

**clean-up** ['kliːnʌp] *n:* **to give sth a** ~ etw gründlich saubermachen.

**clear** [klɪə'] *adj* klar; (*footprint*) deutlich; (*photograph*) scharf; (*commitment*) eindeutig; (*glass, plastic*) durchsichtig; (*road, way, floor etc*) frei; (*conscience, skin*) rein ♦ *vt* (*room*) ausräumen; (*trees*) abholzen; (*weeds*

etc) entfernen; (*slums etc, stock*) räumen; (*LAW*) freisprechen; (*fence, wall*) überspringen; (*cheque*) verrechnen ♦ *vi* (*weather, sky*) aufklaren; (*fog, smoke*) sich auflösen; (*room etc*) sich leeren ♦ *adv:* **to be ~ of the ground** den Boden nicht berühren ♦ *n:* **to be in the ~** (*out of debt*) schuldenfrei sein; (*free of suspicion*) von jedem Verdacht frei sein; (*out of danger*) außer Gefahr sein; **~ profit** Reingewinn *m*; **I have a ~ day tomorrow** (*BRIT*) ich habe morgen nichts vor; **to make o.s. ~** sich klar ausdrücken; **to make it ~ to sb that ...** es jdm (unmißverständlich) klarmachen, daß ...; **to ~ the table** den Tisch abräumen; **to ~ a space (for sth)** (für etw) Platz schaffen; **to ~ one's throat** sich räuspern; **to ~ a profit** einen Gewinn machen; **to keep ~ of sb** jdm aus dem Weg gehen; **to keep ~ of sth** etw meiden; **to keep ~ of trouble** allem Ärger aus dem Weg gehen.
►**clear off** (*inf*) *vi* abhauen, verschwinden.
►**clear up** *vt* aufräumen; (*mystery*) aufklären; (*problem*) lösen ♦ *vi* (*bad weather*) sich aufklären; (*illness*) sich bessern.
**clearance** ['klɪərəns] *n* (*of slums*) Räumung *f*; (*of trees*) Abholzung *f*; (*permission*) Genehmigung *f*; (*free space*) lichte Höhe *f*.
**clearance sale** *n* Räumungsverkauf *m*.
**clear-cut** ['klɪə'kʌt] *adj* klar.
**clearing** ['klɪərɪŋ] *n* Lichtung *f*; (*BRIT: BANKING*) Clearing *nt*.
**clearing bank** (*BRIT*) *n* Clearingbank *f*.
**clearing house** *n* (*COMM*) Clearingstelle *f*.
**clearly** ['klɪəlɪ] *adv* klar; (*obviously*) eindeutig.
**clearway** ['klɪəweɪ] (*BRIT*) *n* Straße *f* mit Halteverbot.
**cleavage** [kli:vɪdʒ] *n* (*of woman's breasts*) Dekolleté *nt*.
**cleaver** ['kli:və'] *n* Hackbeil *nt*.
**clef** [klef] *n* (Noten)schlüssel *m*.
**cleft** [kleft] *n* Spalte *f*.
**cleft palate** *n* (*MED*) Gaumenspalte *f*.
**clemency** ['klemənsɪ] *n* Milde *f*.
**clement** ['klemənt] *adj* mild.
**clench** [klentʃ] *vt* (*fist*) ballen; (*teeth*) zusammenbeißen.
**clergy** ['klɜːdʒɪ] *n* Klerus *m*, Geistlichkeit *f*.
**clergyman** ['klɜːdʒɪmən] (*irreg: like* **man**) *n* Geistliche(r) *m*.
**clerical** ['klerɪkl] *adj* (*job, worker*) Büro-; (*error*) Schreib-; (*REL*) geistlich.
**clerk** [klɑːk, (*US*) klɜːrk] *n* (*BRIT*) Büroangestellte(r) *f(m)*; (*US: sales person*) Verkäufer(in) *m(f)*.
**Clerk of Court** *n* Protokollführer(in) *m(f)*.
**clever** ['klevə'] *adj* klug; (*deft, crafty*) schlau, clever (*inf*); (*device, arrangement*) raffiniert.
**cleverly** ['klevəlɪ] *adv* geschickt.
**clew** [klu:] (*US*) *n* = **clue**.
**cliché** ['kli:ʃeɪ] *n* Klischee *nt*.
**click** [klɪk] *vi* klicken ♦ *vt:* **to ~ one's tongue**

mit der Zunge schnalzen; **to ~ one's heels** die Hacken zusammenschlagen.
**client** ['klaɪənt] *n* Kunde *m*, Kundin *f*; (*of bank, lawyer*) Klient(in) *m(f)*; (*of restaurant*) Gast *m*.
**clientele** [kli:ɑ̃ːn'tɛl] *n* Kundschaft *f*.
**cliff** [klɪf] *n* Kliff *nt*.
**cliffhanger** ['klɪfhæŋə'] *n* spannungsgeladene Szene am Ende einer Filmepisode, Cliffhanger *m*.
**climactic** [klaɪ'mæktɪk] *adj:* **~ point** Höhepunkt *m*.
**climate** ['klaɪmɪt] *n* Klima *nt*.
**climax** ['klaɪmæks] *n* (*also:* **sexual**) Höhepunkt *m*.
**climb** [klaɪm] *vi* klettern; (*plane, sun, prices, shares*) steigen ♦ *vt* (*stairs, ladder*) hochsteigen, hinaufsteigen; (*tree*) klettern auf +*acc*; (*hill*) steigen auf +*acc* ♦ *n* Aufstieg *m*; (*of prices etc*) Anstieg *m*; **to ~ over a wall/into a car** über eine Mauer/in ein Auto steigen *or* klettern.
►**climb down** (*BRIT*) *vi* (*fig*) nachgeben.
**climb-down** ['klaɪmdaun] *n* Nachgeben *nt*, Rückzieher *m* (*inf*).
**climber** ['klaɪmə'] *n* Bergsteiger(in) *m(f)*; (*plant*) Kletterpflanze *f*.
**climbing** ['klaɪmɪŋ] *n* Bergsteigen *nt*.
**clinch** [klɪntʃ] *vt* (*deal*) perfekt machen; (*argument*) zum Abschluß bringen.
**clincher** ['klɪntʃə'] *n* ausschlaggebender Faktor *m*.
**cling** [klɪŋ] (*pt, pp* **clung**) *vi:* **to ~ to** (*mother, support*) sich festklammern an +*dat*; (*idea, belief*) festhalten an +*dat*; (*subj: clothes, dress*) sich anschmiegen +*dat*.
**clingfilm** ['klɪŋfɪlm] *n* Frischhaltefolie *f*.
**clinic** ['klɪnɪk] *n* Klinik *f*; (*session*) Sprechstunde *f*; (: *SPORT*) Trainingstunde *f*.
**clinical** ['klɪnɪkl] *adj* klinisch; (*fig*) nüchtern, kühl; (: *building, room*) steril.
**clink** [klɪŋk] *vi* klirren.
**clip** [klɪp] *n* (*also:* **paper ~**) Büroklammer *f*; (*BRIT: also:* **bulldog ~**) Klammer *f*; (*holding wire, hose etc*) Klemme *f*; (*for hair*) Spange *f*; (*TV, CINE*) Ausschnitt *m* ♦ *vt* festklemmen; (*also:* **~ together**) zusammenheften; (*cut*) schneiden.
**clippers** ['klɪpəz] *npl* (*for gardening*) Schere *f*; (*also:* **nail ~**) Nagelzange *f*.
**clipping** ['klɪpɪŋ] *n* (*from newspaper*) Ausschnitt *m*.
**clique** [kli:k] *n* Clique *f*, Gruppe *f*.
**clitoris** ['klɪtərɪs] *n* Klitoris *f*.
**cloak** [kləuk] *n* Umhang *m* ♦ *vt* (*fig*) hüllen.
**cloakroom** ['kləukrum] *n* Garderobe *f*; (*BRIT: WC*) Toilette *f*.
**clobber** ['klɔbə'] (*inf*) *n* Klamotten *pl* ♦ *vt* (*hit*) hauen, schlagen; (*defeat*) in die Pfanne hauen.
**clock** [klɔk] *n* Uhr *f*; **round the ~** rund um die Uhr; **30,000 on the ~** (*BRIT: AUT*) ein Tachostand von 30.000; **to work against the**

~ gegen die Uhr arbeiten.
►**clock in** (*BRIT*) *vi* (den Arbeitsbeginn) stempeln *or* stechen.
►**clock off** (*BRIT*) *vi* (das Arbeitsende) stempeln *or* stechen.
►**clock on** (*BRIT*) *vi* = **clock in.**
►**clock out** (*BRIT*) *vi* = **clock off.**
►**clock up** *vt* (*miles*) fahren; (*hours*) arbeiten.
**clockwise** ['klɔkwaɪz] *adv* im Uhrzeigersinn.
**clockwork** ['klɔkwɜ:k] *n* Uhrwerk *nt* ♦ *adj* aufziehbar, zum Aufziehen; **like** ~ wie am Schnürchen.
**clog** [klɔg] *n* Clog *m*; (*wooden*) Holzschuh *m* ♦ *vt* verstopfen ♦ *vi* (*also:* ~ **up**) verstopfen.
**cloister** ['klɔɪstə*] *n* Kreuzgang *m*.
**clone** [kləun] *n* Klon *m*.
**close**[1] [kləus] *adj* (*writing, friend, contact*) eng; (*texture*) dicht, fest; (*relative*) nahe; (*examination*) genau, gründlich; (*watch*) streng, scharf; (*contest*) knapp; (*weather*) schwül; (*room*) stickig ♦ *adv* nahe; ~ **(to)** nahe (+*gen*); ~ **to** in der Nähe +*gen*; ~ **by,** ~ **at hand** in der Nähe; **how** ~ **is Edinburgh to Glasgow?** wie weit ist Edinburgh von Glasgow entfernt?; **a** ~ **friend** ein guter *or* enger Freund; **to have a** ~ **shave** (*fig*) gerade noch davonkommen; **at** ~ **quarters** aus der Nähe.
**close**[2] [kləuz] *vt* schließen, zumachen; (*sale, deal, case*) abschließen; (*speech*) schließen, beenden ♦ *vi* schließen, zumachen; (*door, lid*) sich schließen, zugehen; (*end*) aufhören ♦ *n* Ende *nt*, Schluß *m*; **to bring sth to a** ~ etw beenden.
►**close down** *vi* (*factory*) stillgelegt werden; (*magazine etc*) eingestellt werden.
►**close in** *vi* (*night*) hereinbrechen; (*fog*) sich verdichten; **to** ~ **in on sb/sth** jdm/etw auf den Leib rücken; **the days are closing in** die Tage werden kürzer.
►**close off** *vt* (*area*) abriegeln; (*road*) sperren.
**closed** [kləuzd] *adj* geschlossen; (*road*) gesperrt.
**closed-circuit television** *n* Fernseh-überwachungsanlage *f*.
**closed shop** *n* Betrieb *m* mit Gewerk-schaftszwang.
**close-knit** ['kləus'nɪt] *adj* eng zusammen-gewachsen.
**closely** ['kləuslɪ] *adv* (*examine, watch*) genau; (*connected*) eng; **we are** ~ **related** wir sind nah verwandt; **a** ~ **guarded secret** ein streng gehütetes Geheimnis.
**close season** ['kləus-] *n* Schonzeit *f*; (*SPORT*) Sommerpause *f*.
**closet** ['klɔzɪt] *n* Wandschrank *m*.
**close-up** ['kləusʌp] *n* Nahaufnahme *f*.
**closing** ['kləuzɪŋ] *adj* (*stages*) Schluß-; (*remarks*) abschließend.
**closing price** *n* (*STOCK EXCHANGE*) Schlußkurs *m*, Schlußnotierung *f*.
**closing time** (*BRIT*) *n* (*in pub*) Polizeistunde *f*,

Sperrstunde *f*.
**closure** ['kləuʒə*] *n* (*of factory*) Stillegung *f*; (*of magazine*) Einstellung *f*; (*of road*) Sperrung *f*; (*of border*) Schließung *f*.
**clot** [klɔt] *n* (*blood clot*) (Blut)gerinnsel *nt*; (*inf: idiot*) Trottel *m* ♦ *vi* gerinnen; (*external bleeding*) zum Stillstand kommen.
**cloth** [klɔθ] *n* (*material*) Stoff *m*, Tuch *nt*; (*rag*) Lappen *m*; (*BRIT: also:* **teacloth**) (Spül)tuch *nt*; (*also:* **tablecloth**) Tischtuch *nt*, Tischdecke *f*.
**clothe** [kləuð] *vt* anziehen, kleiden.
**clothes** [kləuðz] *npl* Kleidung *f*, Kleider *pl*; **to put one's** ~ **on** sich anziehen; **to take one's** ~ **off** sich ausziehen.
**clothes brush** *n* Kleiderbürste *f*.
**clothesline** ['kləuðzlaɪn] *n* Wäscheleine *f*.
**clothes peg,** (*US*) **clothes pin** *n* Wäscheklammer *f*.
**clothing** ['kləuðɪŋ] *n* = **clothes.**
**clotted cream** ['klɔtɪd-] (*BRIT*) *n* Sahne aus erhitzter Milch.
**cloud** [klaud] *n* Wolke *f* ♦ *vt* trüben; **every** ~ **has a silver lining** (*proverb*) auf Regen folgt Sonnenschein; **to** ~ **the issue** es unnötig kompliziert machen; (*deliberately*) die Angelegenheit verschleiern.
►**cloud over** *vi* (*sky*) sich bewölken, sich bedecken; (*face, eyes*) sich verfinstern.
**cloudburst** ['klaudbɜ:st] *n* Wolkenbruch *m*.
**cloud-cuckoo-land** [klaud'kuku:lænd] (*BRIT*) *n* Wolkenkuckucksheim *nt*.
**cloudy** ['klaudɪ] *adj* wolkig, bewölkt; (*liquid*) trüb.
**clout** [klaut] *vt* schlagen, hauen ♦ *n* (*fig*) Schlagkraft *f*.
**clove** [kləuv] *n* Gewürznelke *f*; ~ **of garlic** Knoblauchzehe *f*.
**clover** ['kləuvə*] *n* Klee *m*.
**cloverleaf** ['kləuvəli:f] *n* Kleeblatt *nt*.
**clown** [klaun] *n* Clown *m* ♦ *vi* (*also:* ~ **about,** ~ **around**) herumblödeln, herumkaspern.
**cloying** ['klɔɪɪŋ] *adj* süßlich.
**club** [klʌb] *n* Klub *m*, Verein *m*; (*weapon*) Keule *f*, Knüppel *m*; (*also:* **golf** ~: *object*) Golfschläger *m* ♦ *vt* knüppeln ♦ *vi*: **to** ~ **together** zusammenlegen; **clubs** *npl* (*CARDS*) Kreuz *nt*.
**club car** (*US*) *n* Speisewagen *m*.
**club class** *n* Club-Klasse *f*.
**clubhouse** ['klʌbhaus] *n* Klubhaus *nt*.
**club soda** (*US*) *n* (*soda water*) Sodawasser *nt*.
**cluck** [klʌk] *vi* glucken.
**clue** [klu:] *n* Hinweis *m*, Anhaltspunkt *m*; (*in crossword*) Frage *f*; **I haven't a** ~ ich habe keine Ahnung.
**clued-up** ['klu:dʌp], (*US*) **clued in** (*inf*) *adj*: **to be** ~ **on sth** über *acc* etw im Bilde sein.
**clueless** ['klu:lɪs] *adj* ahnungslos, unbedarft.
**clump** [klʌmp] *n* Gruppe *f*.
**clumsy** ['klʌmzɪ] *adj* ungeschickt; (*object*) unförmig; (*effort, attempt*) plump.
**clung** [klʌŋ] *pt, pp of* **cling.**

**cluster** ['klʌstə'] n Gruppe f ♦ vi (people) sich scharen; (houses) sich drängen.

**clutch** [klʌtʃ] n Griff m; (AUT) Kupplung f ♦ vt (purse, hand) umklammern; (stick) sich festklammern an +dat ♦ vi: **to ~ at** sich klammern an +acc.

**clutter** ['klʌtə'] vt (also: ~ **up**: room) vollstopfen; (: table) vollstellen ♦ n Kram m (inf).

**CM** (US) abbr (POST: = North Mariana Islands).

**cm** abbr (= centimetre) cm.

**CNAA** (BRIT) n abbr (= Council for National Academic Awards) Zentralstelle zur Vergabe von Qualifikationsnachweisen.

**CND** n abbr (= Campaign for Nuclear Disarmament) Organisation für atomare Abrüstung.

**CO** n abbr = **commanding officer**; (BRIT: = Commonwealth Office) Regierungsstelle für Angelegenheiten des Commonwealth ♦ abbr (US: POST: = Colorado).

**Co.** abbr = **company; county**.

**c/o** abbr (= care of) bei, c/o.

**coach** [kəutʃ] n (Reise)bus m; (horse-drawn) Kutsche f; (of train) Wagen m; (SPORT) Trainer m; (SCOL) Nachhilfelehrer(in) m(f) ♦ vt trainieren; (student) Nachhilfeunterricht geben +dat.

**coach trip** n Busfahrt f.

**coagulate** [kəu'ægjuleɪt] vi (blood) gerinnen; (paint etc) eindicken ♦ vt (blood) gerinnen lassen; (paint) dick werden lassen.

**coal** [kəul] n Kohle f.

**coalface** ['kəulfeɪs] n Streb m.

**coalfield** ['kəulfiːld] n Kohlenrevier nt.

**coalition** [kəuə'lɪʃən] n (POL) Koalition f; (of pressure groups etc) Zusammenschluß m.

**coalman** ['kəulmən] (irreg: like **man**) n Kohlenhändler m.

**coal merchant** n = **coalman**.

**coal mine** n Kohlenbergwerk nt, Zeche f.

**coal miner** n Bergmann m, Kumpel m (inf).

**coal mining** n (Kohlen)bergbau m.

**coarse** [kɔːs] adj (texture) grob; (vulgar) gewöhnlich, derb; (salt, sand etc) grobkörnig.

**coast** [kəust] n Küste f ♦ vi (im Leerlauf) fahren.

**coastal** ['kəustl] adj Küsten-.

**coaster** ['kəustə'] n (NAUT) Küstenfahrzeug nt; (for glass) Untersetzer m.

**coastguard** ['kəustgɑːd] n (officer) Küstenwächter m; (service) Küstenwacht f.

**coastline** ['kəustlaɪn] n Küste f.

**coat** [kəut] n Mantel m; (of animal) Fell nt; (layer) Schicht f; (: of paint) Anstrich m ♦ vt überziehen.

**coat hanger** n Kleiderbügel m.

**coating** ['kəutɪŋ] n (of chocolate etc) Überzug m; (of dust etc) Schicht f.

**coat of arms** n Wappen nt.

**coauthor** ['kəu'ɔːθə'] n Mitautor(in) m(f),

Mitverfasser(in) m(f).

**coax** [kəuks] vt (person) überreden.

**cob** [kɔb] n see **corn**.

**cobbler** ['kɔblə'] n Schuster m.

**cobbles** ['kɔblz] npl Kopfsteinpflaster nt.

**cobblestones** ['kɔblstəunz] npl = **cobbles**.

**COBOL** ['kəubɔl] n COBOL nt.

**cobra** ['kəubrə] n Kobra f.

**cobweb** ['kɔbwɛb] n Spinnennetz nt.

**cocaine** [kə'keɪn] n Kokain nt.

**cock** [kɔk] n Hahn m; (male bird) Männchen nt ♦ vt (gun) entsichern; **to ~ one's ears** (fig) die Ohren spitzen.

**cock-a-hoop** [kɔkə'huːp] adj ganz aus dem Häuschen.

**cockerel** ['kɔkərl] n junger Hahn m.

**cock-eyed** ['kɔkaɪd] adj (fig) verrückt, widersinnig.

**cockle** ['kɔkl] n Herzmuschel f.

**cockney** ['kɔknɪ] n Cockney m, echter Londoner m; (LING) Cockney nt.

**cockpit** ['kɔkpɪt] n Cockpit nt.

**cockroach** ['kɔkrəutʃ] n Küchenschabe f, Kakerlak m.

**cocktail** ['kɔkteɪl] n Cocktail m; **fruit ~** Obstsalat m; **prawn ~** Krabbencocktail m.

**cocktail cabinet** n Hausbar f.

**cocktail party** n Cocktailparty f.

**cocktail shaker** [-'ʃeɪkə'] n Mixbecher m.

**cock-up** ['kɔkʌp] (inf!) n Schlamassel m.

**cocky** ['kɔkɪ] adj großspurig.

**cocoa** ['kəukəu] n Kakao m.

**coconut** ['kəukənʌt] n Kokosnuß f.

**cocoon** [kə'kuːn] n Puppe f, Kokon m; (fig) schützende Umgebung f.

**COD** abbr (BRIT) = **cash on delivery**; (US) = **collect on delivery**.

**cod** [kɔd] n Kabeljau m.

**code** [kəud] n (cipher) Chiffre f; (dialling code) Vorwahl f; (post code) Postleitzahl f; **~ of behaviour** Sittenkodex m; **~ of practice** Verfahrensregeln pl.

**codeine** ['kəudiːn] n Kodein nt.

**codger** ['kɔdʒə'] (inf) n: **old ~** komischer Kauz m.

**codicil** ['kɔdɪsɪl] n (LAW) Kodizill nt.

**codify** ['kəudɪfaɪ] vt kodifizieren.

**cod-liver oil** ['kɔdlɪvə-] n Lebertran m.

**co-driver** ['kəu'draɪvə'] n Beifahrer(in) m(f).

**co-ed** ['kəu'ɛd] (SCOL) adj abbr = **coeducational** ♦ n abbr (US: female pupil/student) Schülerin/ Studentin an einer gemischten Schule/ Universität; (BRIT: school) gemischte Schule f.

**coeducational** ['kəuɛdjuː'keɪʃənl] adj (school) Koedukations-, gemischt.

**coerce** [kəu'ɔːs] vt zwingen.

**coercion** [kəu'ɔːʃən] n Zwang m.

**coexistence** ['kəuɪg'zɪstəns] n Koexistenz f.

**C of C** n abbr = **chamber of commerce**.

**C of E** abbr = **Church of England**.

**coffee** ['kɔfɪ] n Kaffee m; **black ~** schwarzer

Kaffee *m*; **white** ~ Kaffee mit Milch; ~ **with cream** Kaffee mit Sahne.

**coffee bar** (*BRIT*) *n* Café *nt*.

**coffee bean** *n* Kaffeebohne *f*.

**coffee break** *n* Kaffeepause *f*.

**coffee cake** (*US*) *n* Kuchen *m* zum Kaffee.

**coffee cup** *n* Kaffeetasse *f*.

**coffeepot** ['kɔfɪpɔt] *n* Kaffeekanne *f*.

**coffee table** *n* Couchtisch *m*.

**coffin** ['kɔfɪn] *n* Sarg *m*.

**C of I** *abbr* (= *Church of Ireland*) *anglikanische Kirche Irlands*.

**C of S** *abbr* (= *Church of Scotland*) *presbyterianische Kirche in Schottland*.

**cog** [kɔg] *n* (*wheel*) Zahnrad *nt*; (*tooth*) Zahn *m*.

**cogent** ['kaudʒənt] *adj* stichhaltig, zwingend.

**cognac** ['kɔnjæk] *n* Kognak *m*.

**cogwheel** ['kɔgwiːl] *n* Zahnrad *nt*.

**cohabit** [kəu'hæbɪt] *vi* (*formal*) in eheähnlicher Gemeinschaft leben; **to** ~ **(with sb)** (mit jdm) zusammenleben.

**coherent** [kəu'hɪərənt] *adj* (*speech*) zusammenhängend; (*answer, theory*) schlüssig; (*person*) bei klarem Verstand.

**cohesion** [kəu'hiːʒən] *n* Geschlossenheit *f*.

**cohesive** [kəu'hiːsɪv] *adj* geschlossen.

**COI** (*BRIT*) *n abbr* (= *Central Office of Information*) *regierungsamtliche Informationsstelle*.

**coil** [kɔɪl] *n* Rolle *f*; (*one loop*) Windung *f*; (*of smoke*) Kringel *m*; (*AUT, ELEC*) Spule *f*; (*contraceptive*) Spirale *f* ♦ *vt* aufrollen, aufwickeln.

**coin** [kɔɪn] *n* Münze *f* ♦ *vt* prägen.

**coinage** ['kɔɪnɪdʒ] *n* Münzen *pl*; (*LING*) Prägung *f*.

**coin box** (*BRIT*) *n* Münzfernsprecher *m*.

**coincide** [kəuɪn'saɪd] *vi* (*events*) zusammenfallen; (*ideas, views*) übereinstimmen.

**coincidence** [kəu'ɪnsɪdəns] *n* Zufall *m*.

**coin-operated** ['kɔɪn'ɔpəreɪtɪd] *adj* Münz-.

**Coke** ® [kəuk] *n* Coca-Cola ® *nt or f*, Coke ® *nt*.

**coke** [kəuk] *n* Koks *m*.

**Col.** *abbr* = **colonel**.

**COLA** (*US*) *n abbr* (= *cost-of-living adjustment*) *Anpassung der Löhne und Gehälter an steigende Lebenshaltungskosten*.

**colander** ['kɔləndə*] *n* Durchschlag *m*.

**cold** [kəuld] *adj* kalt; (*unemotional*) kalt, kühl ♦ *n* Kälte *f*; (*MED*) Erkältung *f*; **it's** ~ es ist kalt; **to be/feel** ~ (*person*) frieren; (*object*) kalt sein; **in** ~ **blood** kaltblütig; **to have** ~ **feet** (*fig*) kalte Füße bekommen; **to give sb the** ~ **shoulder** jdm die kalte Schulter zeigen; **to catch** ~, **to catch a** ~ sich erkälten.

**cold-blooded** ['kəuld'blʌdɪd] *adj* kaltblütig.

**cold cream** *n* (halbfette) Feuchtigkeitscreme *f*.

**coldly** ['kəuldlɪ] *adv* kalt, kühl.

**cold-shoulder** [kəuld'ʃəuldə*] *vt* die kalte

Schulter zeigen +*dat*.

**cold sore** *n* Bläschenausschlag *m*.

**cold sweat** *n*: **to come out in a** ~ **(about sth)** (wegen etw) in kalten Schweiß ausbrechen.

**cold turkey** *n*: **to do** ~ Totalentzug machen.

**Cold War** *n*: **the** ~ der kalte Krieg.

**coleslaw** ['kəulslɔː] *n* Krautsalat *m*.

**colic** ['kɔlɪk] *n* Kolik *f*.

**colicky** ['kɔlɪkɪ] *adj*: **to be** ~ Kolik *f or* Leibschmerzen *pl* haben.

**collaborate** [kə'læbəreɪt] *vi* zusammenarbeiten; (*with enemy*) kollaborieren.

**collaboration** [kəlæbə'reɪʃən] *n* (*see vb*) Zusammenarbeit *f*; Kollaboration *f*.

**collaborator** [kə'læbəreɪtə*] *n* (*see vb*) Mitarbeiter(in) *m(f)*; Kollaborateur(in) *m(f)*.

**collage** [kɔ'lɔːʒ] *n* Collage *f*.

**collagen** ['kɔlədʒən] *n* Kollagen *nt*.

**collapse** [kə'læps] *vi* zusammenbrechen; (*building*) einstürzen; (*plans*) scheitern; (*government*) stürzen ♦ *n* (*see vb*) Zusammenbruch *m*; Einsturz *m*; Scheitern *nt*; Sturz *m*.

**collapsible** [kə'læpsəbl] *adj* Klapp-, zusammenklappbar.

**collar** ['kɔlə*] *n* Kragen *m*; (*of dog, cat*) Halsband *nt*; (*TECH*) Bund *m* ♦ *vt* (*inf*) schnappen.

**collarbone** ['kɔləbəun] *n* Schlüsselbein *nt*.

**collate** [kɔ'leɪt] *vt* vergleichen.

**collateral** [kə'lætərl] *n* (*COMM*) (zusätzliche) Sicherheit *f*.

**collateral damage** *n* (*MIL*) Schäden *pl* in Wohngebieten; (: *casualties*) Opfer *pl* unter der Zivilbevölkerung.

**collation** [kə'leɪʃən] *n* Vergleich *m*; (*CULIN*): **a cold** ~ ein kalter Imbiß *m*.

**colleague** ['kɔliːg] *n* Kollege *m*, Kollegin *f*.

**collect** [kə'lɛkt] *vt* sammeln; (*mail, BRIT: fetch*) abholen; (*debts*) eintreiben; (*taxes*) einziehen ♦ *vi* sich ansammeln ♦ *adv* (*US: TEL*): **to call** ~ ein R-Gespräch führen; **to** ~ **one's thoughts** seine Gedanken ordnen, sich sammeln; ~ **on delivery** (*US: COMM*) per Nachnahme.

**collected** [kə'lɛktɪd] *adj*: ~ **works** gesammelte Werke *pl*.

**collection** [kə'lɛkʃən] *n* Sammlung *f*; (*from place, person, or mail*) Abholung *f*; (*in church*) Kollekte *f*.

**collective** [kə'lɛktɪv] *adj* kollektiv, gemeinsam ♦ *n* Kollektiv *nt*; ~ **farm** landwirtschaftliche Produktionsgenossenschaft *f*.

**collective bargaining** *n* Tarifverhandlungen *pl*.

**collector** [kə'lɛktə*] *n* Sammler(in) *m(f)*; (*of taxes etc*) Einnehmer(in) *m(f)*; (*of rent, cash*) Kassierer(in) *m(f)*; ~**'s item** *or* **piece** Sammlerstück *nt*, Liebhaberstück *nt*.

**college** ['kɔlɪdʒ] *n* College *nt*; (*of agriculture, technology*) Fachhochschule *f*; **to go to** ~

studieren; ~ **of education** Pädagogische
Hochschule *f.*
**collide** [kə'laɪd] *vi:* **to ~ (with)**
zusammenstoßen (mit); (*fig: clash*) eine
heftige Auseinandersetzung haben (mit).
**collie** ['kɒlɪ] *n* Collie *m.*
**colliery** ['kɒlɪərɪ] (*BRIT*) *n* (Kohlen)bergwerk
*nt,* Zeche *f.*
**collision** [kə'lɪʒən] *n* Zusammenstoß *m;* **to be
on a ~ course** (*also fig*) auf Kollisionskurs
sein.
**collision damage waiver** *n* (*INSURANCE*)
Verzicht auf Haftungsbeschränkung bei
Unfällen mit Mietwagen.
**colloquial** [kə'ləʊkwɪəl] *adj*
umgangssprachlich.
**collusion** [kə'luːʒən] *n* (geheime) Absprache *f;*
**to be in ~ with** gemeinsame Sache machen
mit.
**Colo.** (*US*) *abbr* (*POST:* = *Colorado*).
**Cologne** [kə'ləʊn] *n* Köln *nt.*
**cologne** [kə'ləʊn] *n* (*also:* **eau de ~**)
Kölnischwasser *nt,* Eau de Cologne *nt.*
**Colombia** [kə'lɒmbɪə] *n* Kolumbien *nt.*
**Colombian** [kə'lɒmbɪən] *adj* kolumbianisch
♦ *n* Kolumbianer(in) *m(f).*
**colon** ['kəʊlən] *n* Doppelpunkt *m;* (*ANAT*)
Dickdarm *m.*
**colonel** ['kɜːnl] *n* Oberst *m.*
**colonial** [kə'ləʊnɪəl] *adj* Kolonial-.
**colonize** ['kɒlənaɪz] *vt* kolonisieren.
**colony** ['kɒlənɪ] *n* Kolonie *f.*
**color** *etc* ['kʌlə*] (*US*) = **colour** *etc.*
**Colorado beetle** [kɒlə'rɑːdəʊ-] *n*
Kartoffelkäfer *m.*
**colossal** [kə'lɒsl] *adj* riesig, kolossal.
**colour,** (*US*) **color** ['kʌlə*] *n* Farbe *f;* (*skin
colour*) Hautfarbe *f;* (*of spectacle etc*)
Atmosphäre *f* ♦ *vt* bemalen; (*with crayons*)
ausmalen; (*dye*) färben; (*fig*) beeinflussen
♦ *vi* (*blush*) erröten, rot werden ♦ *cpd* Farb-;
**colours** *npl* (*of party, club etc*) Farben *pl;* **in ~**
(*film*) in Farbe; (*illustrations*) bunt.
▶**colour in** *vt* ausmalen.
**colour bar** *n* Rassenschranke *f.*
**colour-blind** ['kʌləblaɪnd] *adj* farbenblind.
**coloured** ['kʌləd] *adj* farbig; (*photo*) Farb-;
(*illustration etc*) bunt.
**colour film** *n* Farbfilm *m.*
**colourful** ['kʌləful] *adj* bunt; (*account, story*)
farbig, anschaulich; (*personality*) schillernd.
**colouring** ['kʌlərɪŋ] *n* Gesichtsfarbe *f,* Teint
*m;* (*in food*) Farbstoff *m.*
**colour scheme** *n* Farbzusammenstellung *f.*
**colour supplement** (*BRIT*) *n* Farbbeilage *f,*
Magazin *nt.*
**colour television** *n* Farbfernsehen *nt;* (*set*)
Farbfernseher *m.*
**colt** [kəʊlt] *n* Hengstfohlen *nt.*
**column** ['kɒləm] *n* Säule *f;* (*of people*) Kolonne
*f;* (*of print*) Spalte *f;* (*gossip/sports column*)
Kolumne *f;* **the editorial ~** der Leitartikel.

**columnist** ['kɒləmnɪst] *n* Kolumnist(in) *m(f).*
**coma** ['kəʊmə] *n* Koma *nt;* **to be in a ~** im
Koma liegen.
**comb** [kəʊm] *n* Kamm *m* ♦ *vt* kämmen; (*area*)
durchkämmen.
**combat** ['kɒmbæt] *n* Kampf *m* ♦ *vt* bekämpfen.
**combination** [kɒmbɪ'neɪʃən] *n* Kombination *f.*
**combination lock** *n* Kombinationsschloß *nt.*
**combine** [*vti* kəm'baɪn, *n* 'kɒmbaɪn] *vt*
verbinden ♦ *vi* sich zusammenschließen;
(*CHEM*) sich verbinden ♦ *n* Konzern *m;*
(*AGR*) = **combine harvester;** **~d effort**
vereintes Unternehmen.
**combine harvester** *n* Mähdrescher *m.*
**combo** ['kɒmbəʊ] *n* Combo *f.*
**combustible** [kəm'bʌstɪbl] *adj* brennbar.
**combustion** [kəm'bʌstʃən] *n* Verbrennung *f.*

═══════════════════════════ *KEYWORD*

**come** [kʌm] (*pt* **came,** *pp* **come**) *vi* **1** (*movement
towards*) kommen; **~ with me** kommen Sie
mit mir; **to ~ running** angelaufen kommen;
**coming!** ich komme!
**2** (*arrive*) kommen; **they came to a river** sie
kamen an einen Fluß; **to ~ home** nach
Hause kommen
**3** (*reach*): **to ~ to** kommen an +*acc;* **her hair
came to her waist** ihr Haar reichte ihr bis
zur Hüfte; **to ~ to a decision** zu einer
Entscheidung kommen
**4** (*occur*): **an idea came to me** mir kam eine
Idee
**5** (*be, become*) werden; **I've ~ to like him**
mittlerweile mag ich ihn; **if it ~s to it** wenn
es darauf ankommt
▶**come about** *vi* geschehen.
▶**come across** *vt fus* (*find: person, thing*)
stoßen auf +*acc* ♦ *vi:* **to ~ across well/badly**
(*idea etc*) gut/schlecht ankommen; (*meaning*)
gut/schlecht verstanden werden.
▶**come along** *vi* (*arrive*) daherkommen;
(*make progress*) vorankommen; **~ along!**
komm schon!
▶**come apart** *vi* (*break in pieces*)
auseinandergehen.
▶**come away** *vi* (*leave*) weggehen; (*become
detached*) abgehen.
▶**come back** *vi* (*return*) zurückkommen;: **to
~ back into fashion** wieder in Mode
kommen.
▶**come by** *vt fus* (*acquire*) kommen zu.
▶**come down** *vi* (*price*) sinken, fallen;
(*building: be demolished*) abgerissen werden;
(*tree: during storm*) umstürzen.
▶**come forward** *vi* (*volunteer*) sich melden.
▶**come from** *vt fus* kommen von, stammen
aus; (*person*) kommen aus.
▶**come in** *vi* (*enter*) hereinkommen; (*report,
news*) eintreffen; (*on deal etc*) sich
beteiligen; **~ in!** herein!
▶**come in for** *vt fus* (*criticism etc*) einstecken
müssen.

▶**come into** *vt fus* (*inherit: money*) erben; **to ~ into fashion** in Mode kommen; **money doesn't ~ into it** Geld hat nichts damit zu tun.

▶**come off** *vi* (*become detached: button, handle*) sich lösen; (*succeed: attempt, plan*) klappen ♦ *vt fus* (*inf*): **~ off it!** mach mal halblang!

▶**come on** *vi* (*pupil, work, project*) vorankommen; (*lights etc*) angehen; **~ on!** (*hurry up*) mach schon!; (*giving encouragement*) los!

▶**come out** *vi* herauskommen; (*stain*) herausgehen; **to ~ out (on strike)** in den Streik treten.

▶**come over** *vt fus*: **I don't know what's ~ over him!** ich weiß nicht, was in ihn gefahren ist.

▶**come round** *vi* (*after faint, operation*) wieder zu sich kommen; (*visit*) vorbeikommen; (*agree*) zustimmen.

▶**come through** *vi* (*survive*) durchkommen; (*telephone call*) (durch)kommen ♦ *vt fus* (*illness etc*) überstehen.

▶**come to** *vi* (*regain consciousness*) wieder zu sich kommen ♦ *vt fus* (*add up to*): **how much does it ~ to?** was macht das zusammen?

▶**come under** *vt fus* (*heading*) kommen unter +*acc*; (*criticism, pressure, attack*) geraten unter +*acc*.

▶**come up** *vi* (*approach*) herankommen; (*sun*) aufgehen; (*problem*) auftauchen; (*event*) bevorstehen; (*in conversation*) genannt werden; **something's come up** etwas ist dazwischengekommen.

▶**come up against** *vt fus* (*resistance, difficulties*) stoßen auf +*acc*.

▶**come upon** *vt fus* (*find*) stoßen auf +*acc*.

▶**come up to** *vt fus*: **the film didn't come up to our expectations** der Film entsprach nicht unseren Erwartungen; **it's coming up to 10 o'clock** es ist gleich 10 Uhr.

▶**come up with** *vt fus* (*idea*) aufwarten mit; (*money*) aufbringen.

**comeback** ['kʌmbæk] *n* (*of film star etc*) Comeback *nt*; (*reaction, response*) Reaktion *f*.

**Comecon** ['kɔmɪkɔn] *n abbr* (= *Council for Mutual Economic Assistance*) Comecon *m*.

**comedian** [kə'miːdɪən] *n* Komiker *m*.

**comedienne** [kəmiːdɪ'ɛn] *n* Komikerin *f*.

**comedown** ['kʌmdaun] (*inf*) *n* Enttäuschung *f*; (*professional*) Abstieg *m*.

**comedy** ['kɔmɪdɪ] *n* Komödie *f*; (*humour*) Witz *m*.

**comet** ['kɔmɪt] *n* Komet *m*.

**comeuppance** [kʌm'ʌpəns] *n*: **to get one's ~** die Quittung bekommen.

**comfort** ['kʌmfət] *n* (*physical*) Behaglichkeit *f*; (*material*) Komfort *m*; (*solace, relief*) Trost *m* ♦ *vt* trösten; **comforts** *npl* (*of home etc*) Komfort *m*, Annehmlichkeiten *pl*.

**comfortable** ['kʌmfətəbl] *adj* bequem; (*room*) komfortabel; (*walk, climb etc*) geruhsam; (*income*) ausreichend; (*majority*) sicher; **to be ~** (*physically*) sich wohl fühlen; (*financially*) sehr angenehm leben; **the patient is ~** dem Patienten geht es den Umständen entsprechend gut; **I don't feel very ~ about it** mir ist nicht ganz wohl bei der Sache.

**comfortably** ['kʌmfətəblɪ] *adv* (*sit*) bequem; (*live*) angenehm.

**comforter** ['kʌmfətə*] (*US*) *n* Schnuller *m*.

**comfort station** (*US*) *n* öffentliche Toilette *f*.

**comic** ['kɔmɪk] *adj* (*also: ~al*) komisch ♦ *n* Komiker(in) *m(f)*; (*BRIT: magazine*) Comicheft *nt*.

**comical** ['kɔmɪkl] *adj* komisch.

**comic strip** *n* Comic strip *m*.

**coming** ['kʌmɪŋ] *n* Ankunft *f*, Kommen *nt* ♦ *adj* kommend; (*next*) nächste(r, s); **in the ~ weeks** in den nächsten Wochen.

**coming(s) and going(s)** *n(pl)* Kommen und Gehen *nt*.

**Comintern** ['kɔmɪntəːn] *n* (*POL*) Komintern *f*.

**comma** ['kɔmə] *n* Komma *nt*.

**command** [kə'mɑːnd] *n* (*also COMPUT*) Befehl *m*; (*control, charge*) Führung *f*; (*MIL: authority*) Kommando *nt*, Befehlsgewalt *f*; (*mastery*) Beherrschung *f* ♦ *vt* (*troops*) befehligen, kommandieren; (*be able to get*) verfügen über +*acc*; (*deserve: respect, admiration etc*) verdient haben; **to be in ~ of** das Kommando *or* den (Ober)befehl haben über +*acc*; **to have ~ of** das Kommando haben über +*acc*; **to take ~ of** das Kommando übernehmen +*gen*; **to have at one's ~** verfügen über +*acc*; **to ~ sb to do sth** jdm befehlen, etw zu tun.

**commandant** ['kɔməndænt] *n* Kommandant *m*.

**command economy** *n* Kommandowirtschaft *f*.

**commandeer** [kɔmən'dɪə*] *vt* requirieren, beschlagnahmen; (*fig*) sich aneignen.

**commander** [kə'mɑːndə*] *n* Befehlshaber *m*, Kommandant *m*.

**commander in chief** *n* Oberbefehlshaber *m*.

**commanding** [kə'mɑːndɪŋ] *adj* (*appearance*) imposant; (*voice, tone*) gebieterisch; (*lead*) entscheidend; (*position*) vorherrschend.

**commanding officer** *n* befehlshabender Offizier *m*.

**commandment** [kə'mɑːndmənt] *n* Gebot *nt*.

**command module** *n* Kommandokapsel *f*.

**commando** [kə'mɑːndəu] *n* Kommando *nt*, Kommandotrupp *m*; (*soldier*) Angehörige(r) *m* eines Kommando(trupp)s.

**commemorate** [kə'mɛmərɛit] *vt* gedenken +*gen*.

**commemoration** [kəmɛmə'reɪʃən] *n* Gedenken *nt*.

**commemorative** [kə'mɛmərətɪv] *adj* Gedenk-.

**commence** [kə'mɛns] *vt, vi* beginnen.
**commend** [kə'mɛnd] *vt* loben; **to ~ sth to sb** jdm etw empfehlen.
**commendable** [kə'mɛndəbl] *adj* lobenswert.
**commendation** [kɔmɛn'deɪʃən] *n* Auszeichnung *f*.
**commensurate** [kə'mɛnʃərɪt] *adj*: **~ with** *or* **to** entsprechend +*dat*.
**comment** ['kɔmɛnt] *n* Bemerkung *f*; (*on situation etc*) Kommentar *m* ♦ *vi*: **to ~ (on)** sich äußern (über +*acc or* zu); (*on situation etc*) einen Kommentar abgeben (zu); **"no ~"** „kein Kommentar!"; **to ~ that ...** bemerken, daß ...
**commentary** ['kɔməntərɪ] *n* Kommentar *m*; (*SPORT*) Reportage *f*.
**commentator** ['kɔmənteɪtə*] *n* Kommentator(in) *m(f)*; (*SPORT*) Reporter(in) *m(f)*.
**commerce** ['kɔmɔːs] *n* Handel *m*.
**commercial** [kə'mɔːʃəl] *adj* kommerziell; (*organization*) Wirtschafts- ♦ *n* (*advertisement*) Werbespot *m*.
**commercial bank** *n* Handelsbank *f*.
**commercial break** *n* Werbung *f*.
**commercial college** *n* Fachschule *f* für kaufmännische Berufe.
**commercialism** [kə'mɔːʃəlɪzəm] *n* Kommerzialisierung *f*.
**commercialize** [kə'mɔːʃəlaɪz] *vt* kommerzialisieren.
**commercialized** [kə'mɔːʃəlaɪzd] (*pej*) *adj* kommerzialisiert.
**commercial radio** *n* kommerzielles Radio *nt*.
**commercial television** *n* kommerzielles Fernsehen *nt*.
**commercial traveller** *n* Handels-vertreter(in) *m(f)*.
**commercial vehicle** *n* Lieferwagen *m*.
**commiserate** [kə'mɪzəreɪt] *vi*: **to ~ with sb** jdm sein Mitgefühl zeigen.
**commission** [kə'mɪʃən] *n* (*order for work*) Auftrag *m*; (*COMM*) Provision *f*; (*committee*) Kommission *f*; (*MIL*) Offizierspatent *nt* ♦ *vt* (*work of art*) in Auftrag geben; (*MIL*) (zum Offizier) ernennen; **out of ~** außer Betrieb; (*NAUT*) nicht im Dienst; **I get 10% ~** ich bekomme 10% Provision; **~ of inquiry** Untersuchungsausschuß *m*, Untersuchungskommission *f*; **to ~ sb to do sth** jdn damit beauftragen, etw zu tun; **to ~ sth from sb** jdm etw in Auftrag geben.
**commissionaire** [kəmɪʃə'nɛə*] (*BRIT*) *n* Portier *m*.
**commissioner** [kə'mɪʃənə*] *n* Polizeipräsident *m*.
**commit** [kə'mɪt] *vt* (*crime*) begehen; (*money, resources*) einsetzen; (*to sb's care*) anvertrauen; **to ~ o.s.** sich festlegen; **to ~ o.s. to do sth** sich (dazu) verpflichten, etw zu tun; **to ~ suicide** Selbstmord begehen; **to ~ to writing** zu Papier bringen;

**to ~ sb for trial** jdn einem Gericht überstellen.
**commitment** [kə'mɪtmənt] *n* Verpflichtung *f*; (*to ideology, system*) Engagement *nt*.
**committed** [kə'mɪtɪd] *adj* engagiert.
**committee** [kə'mɪtɪ] *n* Ausschuß *m*, Komitee *nt*; **to be on a ~** in einem Ausschuß *or* Komitee sein *or* sitzen.
**committee meeting** *n* Ausschußsitzung *f*.
**commodity** [kə'mɔdɪtɪ] *n* Ware *f*; (*food*) Nahrungsmittel *nt*.
**common** ['kɔmən] *adj* (*shared by all*) gemeinsam; (*good*) Gemein-; (*property*) Gemeinschafts-; (*usual, ordinary*) häufig; (*vulgar*) gewöhnlich ♦ *n* Gemeindeland *nt*; **the Commons** (*BRIT: POL*) *npl* das Unterhaus; **in ~ use** allgemein gebräuchlich; **it's ~ knowledge that** es ist allgemein bekannt, daß; **to the ~ good** für das Gemeinwohl; **to have sth in ~ (with sb)** etw (mit jdm) gemein haben.
**common cold** *n* Schnupfen *m*.
**common denominator** *n* (*MATH, fig*) gemeinsamer Nenner *m*.
**commoner** ['kɔmənə*] *n* Bürgerliche(r) *f(m)*.
**common ground** *n* (*fig*) gemeinsame Basis *f*.
**common land** *n* Gemeindeland *nt*.
**common law** *n* Gewohnheitsrecht *nt*.
**common-law** ['kɔmənlɔː] *adj*: **she is his ~ wife** sie lebt mit ihm in eheähnlicher Gemeinschaft.
**commonly** ['kɔmənlɪ] *adv* häufig.
**Common Market** *n*: **the ~** der Gemeinsame Markt.
**commonplace** ['kɔmənpleɪs] *adj* alltäglich.
**common room** *n* Aufenthaltsraum *m*, Tagesraum *m*.
**common sense** *n* gesunder Menschenverstand *m*.
**Commonwealth** ['kɔmənwɛlθ] (*BRIT*) *n*: **the ~** das Commonwealth.

---

*Das* **Commonwealth**, *offiziell Commonwealth of Nations, ist ein lockerer Zusammenschluß aus souveränen Staaten, die früher unter britischer Regierung standen, und von Großbritannien abhängigen Gebieten. Die Mitgliedsstaaten erkennen den britischen Monarchen als Oberhaupt des Commonwealth an. Bei der Commonwealth Conference, einem Treffen der Staatsoberhäupter der Commonwealthländer, werden Angelegenheiten von gemeinsamem Interesse diskutiert.*

---

**commotion** [kə'məʊʃən] *n* Tumult *m*.
**communal** ['kɔmjuːnl] *adj* gemeinsam, Gemeinschafts-; (*life*) Gemeinschafts-.
**commune** [*n* 'kɔmjuːn, *vi* kə'mjuːn] *n* Kommune *f* ♦ *vi*: **to ~ with** Zwiesprache halten mit.
**communicate** [kə'mjuːnɪkeɪt] *vt* mitteilen;

(*idea, feeling*) vermitteln ♦ *vi:* **to ~ (with)** (*by speech, gesture*) sich verständigen (mit); (*in writing*) in Verbindung *or* Kontakt stehen (mit).

**communication** [kəmjuːnɪˈkeɪʃən] *n* Kommunikation *f*; (*letter, call*) Mitteilung *f*.

**communication cord** (*BRIT*) *n* Notbremse *f*.

**communications network** [kəmjuːnɪˈkeɪʃənz-] *n* Kommunikationsnetz *nt*.

**communications satellite** *n* Kommunikationssatellit *m*, Nachrichtensatellit *m*.

**communicative** [kəˈmjuːnɪkətɪv] *adj* gesprächig, mitteilsam.

**communion** [kəˈmjuːnɪən] *n* (*also:* **Holy C~**: *Catholic*) Kommunion *f*; (: *Protestant*) Abendmahl *nt*.

**communiqué** [kəˈmjuːnɪkeɪ] *n* Kommuniqué *nt*, (amtliche) Verlautbarung *f*.

**communism** [ˈkɔmjunɪzəm] *n* Kommunismus *m*.

**communist** [ˈkɔmjunɪst] *adj* kommunistisch ♦ *n* Kommunist(in) *m(f)*.

**community** [kəˈmjuːnɪtɪ] *n* Gemeinschaft *f*; (*within larger group*) Bevölkerungsgruppe *f*.

**community centre** *n* Gemeindezentrum *nt*.

**community charge** (*BRIT*) *n* (*formerly*) Gemeindesteuer *f*.

**community chest** (*US*) *n* Wohltätigkeitsfonds *m*, Hilfsfonds *m*.

**community health centre** *n* Gemeinde-Ärztezentrum *nt*.

**community home** (*BRIT*) *n* Erziehungsheim *nt*.

**community service** *n* Sozialdienst *m*.

**community spirit** *n* Gemeinschaftssinn *m*.

**commutation ticket** [kɔmjuˈteɪʃən-] (*US*) *n* Zeitkarte *f*.

**commute** [kəˈmjuːt] *vi* pendeln ♦ *vt* (*LAW, MATH*) umwandeln.

**commuter** [kəˈmjuːtəˈ] *n* Pendler(in) *m(f)*.

**compact** [*adj* kəmˈpækt, *n* ˈkɔmpækt] *adj* kompakt ♦ *n* (*also:* **powder ~**) Puderdose *f*.

**compact disc** *n* Compact Disk *f*, CD *f*.

**compact disc player** *n* CD-Spieler *m*.

**companion** [kəmˈpænjən] *n* Begleiter(in) *m(f)*.

**companionship** [kəmˈpænjənʃɪp] *n* Gesellschaft *f*.

**companionway** [kəmˈpænjənweɪ] *n* (*NAUT*) Niedergang *m*.

**company** [ˈkʌmpənɪ] *n* Firma *f*; (*THEAT*) (Schauspiel)truppe *f*; (*MIL*) Kompanie *f*; (*companionship*) Gesellschaft *f*; **he's good ~** seine Gesellschaft ist angenehm; **to keep sb ~** jdm Gesellschaft leisten; **to part ~ with** sich trennen von; **Smith and C~** Smith & Co.

**company car** *n* Firmenwagen *m*.

**company director** *n* Direktor(in) *m(f)*, Firmenchef(in) *m(f)*.

**company secretary** (*BRIT*) *n* ≈ Prokurist(in) *m(f)*.

**comparable** [ˈkɔmpərəbl] *adj* vergleichbar.

**comparative** [kəmˈpærətɪv] *adj* relativ; (*study, literature*) vergleichend; (*LING*) komparativ.

**comparatively** [kəmˈpærətɪvlɪ] *adv* relativ.

**compare** [kəmˈpeəˈ] *vt:* **to ~ (with** *or* **to)** vergleichen (mit) ♦ *vi:* **to ~ (with)** sich vergleichen lassen (mit); **how do the prices ~?** wie lassen sich die Preise vergleichen?; **~d with** *or* **to** im Vergleich zu, verglichen mit.

**comparison** [kəmˈpærɪsn] *n* Vergleich *m*; **in ~ (with)** im Vergleich (zu).

**compartment** [kəmˈpɑːtmənt] *n* (*RAIL*) Abteil *nt*; (*section*) Fach *nt*.

**compass** [ˈkʌmpəs] *n* Kompaß *m*; (*fig: scope*) Bereich *m*; **compasses** *npl* (*also:* **pair of ~es**) Zirkel *m*; **within the ~ of** im Rahmen *or* Bereich +*gen*; **beyond the ~ of** über den Rahmen *or* Bereich +*gen* hinaus.

**compassion** [kəmˈpæʃən] *n* Mitgefühl *nt*.

**compassionate** [kəmˈpæʃənɪt] *adj* mitfühlend; **on ~ grounds** aus familiären Gründen.

**compassionate leave** *n* (*esp MIL*) Beurlaubung wegen Krankheit oder Trauerfall in der Familie.

**compatibility** [kəmpætɪˈbɪlɪtɪ] *n* (*see adj*) Vereinbarkeit *f*; Zueinanderpassen *nt*; Kompatibilität *f*.

**compatible** [kəmˈpætɪbl] *adj* (*ideas etc*) vereinbar; (*people*) zueinander passend; (*COMPUT*) kompatibel.

**compel** [kəmˈpɛl] *vt* zwingen.

**compelling** [kəmˈpɛlɪŋ] *adj* zwingend.

**compendium** [kəmˈpɛndɪəm] *n* Kompendium *nt*.

**compensate** [ˈkɔmpənseɪt] *vt* entschädigen ♦ *vi:* **to ~ for** (*loss*) ersetzen; (*disappointment, change etc*) (wieder) ausgleichen.

**compensation** [kɔmpənˈseɪʃən] *n* (*see vb*) Entschädigung *f*; Ersatz *m*; Ausgleich *m*; (*money*) Schaden(s)ersatz *m*.

**compère** [ˈkɔmpeəˈ] *n* Conférencier *m*.

**compete** [kəmˈpiːt] *vi* (*in contest, game*) teilnehmen; (*two theories, statements*) unvereinbar sein; **to ~ (with)** (*companies, rivals*) konkurrieren (mit).

**competence** [ˈkɔmpɪtəns] *n* Fähigkeit *f*.

**competent** [ˈkɔmpɪtənt] *adj* fähig.

**competing** [kəmˈpiːtɪŋ] *adj* konkurrierend.

**competition** [kɔmpɪˈtɪʃən] *n* Konkurrenz *f*; (*contest*) Wettbewerb *m*; **in ~ with** im Wettbewerb mit.

**competitive** [kəmˈpɛtɪtɪv] *adj* (*industry, society*) wettbewerbsbetont, wettbewerbsorientiert; (*person*) vom Konkurrenzdenken geprägt; (*price, product*) wettbewerbsfähig, konkurrenzfähig; (*sport*) (Wett)kampf-.

**competitive examination** *n* (*for places*) Auswahlprüfung *f*; (*for prizes*) Wettbewerb *m*.

**competitor** [kəmˈpɛtɪtəˈ] *n* Konkurrent(in)

*m(f)*; (*participant*) Teilnehmer(in) *m(f)*.
**compilation** [kɔmpɪ'leɪʃən] *n*
Zusammenstellung *f*.
**compile** [kəm'paɪl] *vt* zusammenstellen;
(*book*) verfassen.
**complacency** [kəm'pleɪsnsɪ] *n*
Selbstzufriedenheit *f*, Selbstgefälligkeit *f*.
**complacent** [kəm'pleɪsnt] *adj* selbstzufrieden,
selbstgefällig.
**complain** [kəm'pleɪn] *vi* (*protest*) sich
beschweren; **to ~ (about)** sich beklagen
(über *+acc*); **to ~ of** (*headache etc*) klagen
über *+acc*.
**complaint** [kəm'pleɪnt] *n* Klage *f*; (*in shop etc*)
Beschwerde *f*; (*illness*) Beschwerden *pl*.
**complement** ['kɔmplɪmənt] *n* Ergänzung *f*;
(*esp ship's crew*) Besatzung *f* ♦ *vt* ergänzen;
**to have a full ~ of** ... (*people*) die volle
Stärke an ... *dat* haben; (*items*) die volle Zahl
an ... *dat* haben.
**complementary** [kɔmplɪ'mɛntərɪ] *adj*
komplementär, einander ergänzend.
**complete** [kəm'pliːt] *adj* (*total: silence*)
vollkommen; (: *change*) völlig; (: *success*)
voll; (*whole*) ganz; (: *set*) vollständig;
(: *edition*) Gesamt-; (*finished*) fertig ♦ *vt*
fertigstellen; (*task*) beenden; (*set, group etc*)
vervollständigen; (*fill in*) ausfüllen; **it's a
~ disaster** es ist eine totale Katastrophe.
**completely** [kəm'pliːtlɪ] *adv* völlig,
vollkommen.
**completion** [kəm'pliːʃən] *n* Fertigstellung *f*;
(*of contract*) Abschluß *m*; **to be nearing ~**
kurz vor dem Abschluß sein *or* stehen; **on
~ of the contract** bei Vertragsabschluß.
**complex** ['kɔmplɛks] *adj* kompliziert ♦ *n*
Komplex *m*.
**complexion** [kəm'plɛkʃən] *n* Teint *m*,
Gesichtsfarbe *f*, (*of event etc*) Charakter *m*;
(*political, religious*) Anschauung *f*; **to put a
different ~ on sth** etw in einem anderen
Licht erscheinen lassen.
**complexity** [kəm'plɛksɪtɪ] *n* Kompliziertheit *f*.
**compliance** [kəm'plaɪəns] *n* Fügsamkeit *f*;
(*agreement*) Einverständnis *nt*; **~ with**
Einverständnis mit, Zustimmung *f* zu; **in
~ with** gemäß *+dat*.
**compliant** [kəm'plaɪənt] *adj* gefällig,
entgegenkommend.
**complicate** ['kɔmplɪkeɪt] *vt* komplizieren.
**complicated** ['kɔmplɪkeɪtɪd] *adj* kompliziert.
**complication** [kɔmplɪ'keɪʃən] *n* Komplikation
*f*.
**complicity** [kəm'plɪsɪtɪ] *n* Mittäterschaft *f*.
**compliment** [*n* 'kɔmplɪmənt, *vt* 'kɔmplɪmɛnt] *n*
Kompliment *nt* ♦ *vt* ein Kompliment/
Komplimente machen; *compliments npl*
(*regards*) Grüße *pl*; **to pay sb a ~** jdm ein
Kompliment machen; **to ~ sb (on sth)** jdm
Komplimente (wegen etw) machen; **to ~ sb
on doing sth** jdm Komplimente machen,
daß er/sie etw getan hat.

**complimentary** [kɔmplɪ'mɛntərɪ] *adj*
schmeichelhaft; (*ticket, copy of book etc*)
Frei-.
**compliments slip** *n* Empfehlungszettel *m*.
**comply** [kəm'plaɪ] *vi*: **to ~ with** (*law*) einhalten
*+acc*; (*ruling*) sich richten nach.
**component** [kəm'pəunənt] *adj* einzeln ♦ *n*
Bestandteil *m*.
**compose** [kəm'pəuz] *vt* (*music*) komponieren;
(*poem*) verfassen; (*letter*) abfassen; **to be ~d
of** bestehen aus; **to ~ o.s.** sich sammeln.
**composed** [kəm'pəuzd] *adj* ruhig, gelassen.
**composer** [kəm'pəuzə*] *n* Komponist(in) *m(f)*.
**composite** ['kɔmpəzɪt] *adj* zusammengesetzt;
(*BOT*) Korbblütler-; (*MATH*) teilbar; (*BOT*):
**~ plant** Korbblütler *m*.
**composition** [kɔmpə'zɪʃən] *n*
Zusammensetzung *f*; (*essay*) Aufsatz *m*;
(*MUS*) Komposition *f*.
**compositor** [kəm'pɔzɪtə*] *n*
(Schrift)setzer(in) *m(f)*.
**compos mentis** ['kɔmpɔs 'mɛntɪs] *adj*
zurechnungsfähig.
**compost** ['kɔmpɔst] *n* Kompost *m*; (*also:
potting ~*) Blumenerde *f*.
**composure** [kəm'pəuʒə*] *n* Fassung *f*,
Beherrschung *f*.
**compound** [*n, adj* 'kɔmpaund, *vt* kəm'paund] *n*
(*CHEM*) Verbindung *f*; (*enclosure*) umzäuntes
Gebiet *or* Gelände *nt*; (*LING*) Kompositum *nt*
♦ *adj* zusammengesetzt; (*eye*) Facetten- ♦ *vt*
verschlimmern, vergrößern.
**compound fracture** *n* komplizierter Bruch
*m*.
**compound interest** *n* Zinseszins *m*.
**comprehend** [kɔmprɪ'hɛnd] *vt* begreifen,
verstehen.
**comprehension** [kɔmprɪ'hɛnʃən] *n*
Verständnis *nt*.
**comprehensive** [kɔmprɪ'hɛnsɪv] *adj*
umfassend; (*insurance*) Vollkasko- ♦ *n*
= **comprehensive school**.
**comprehensive school** (*BRIT*) *n*
Gesamtschule *f*.

**Comprehensive school** ist in Großbritannien
eine nicht selektive weiterführende Schule, an
der alle Kinder aus einem Einzugsgebiet
gemeinsam unterrichtet werden. An einer
solchen Gesamtschule können alle
Schulabschlüsse gemacht werden. Die meisten
staatlichen Schulen in Großbritannien sind
*comprehensive schools*.

**compress** [*vt* kəm'prɛs, *n* 'kɔmprɛs] *vt*
(*information etc*) verdichten; (*air*)
komprimieren; (*cotton, paper etc*)
zusammenpressen ♦ *n* (*MED*) Kompresse *f*.
**compressed air** [kəm'prɛst-] *n* Druckluft *f*,
Preßluft *f*.
**compression** [kəm'prɛʃən] *n* (*see vb*)
Verdichtung *f*; Kompression *f*;

Zusammenpressen *nt*.

**comprise** [kəm'praɪz] *vt* (*also*: **be ~d of**) bestehen aus; (*constitute*) bilden, ausmachen.

**compromise** ['kɔmprəmaɪz] *n* Kompromiß *m* ♦ *vt* (*beliefs, principles*) verraten; (*person*) kompromittieren ♦ *vi* Kompromisse schließen ♦ *cpd* (*solution etc*) Kompromiß-.

**compulsion** [kəm'pʌlʃən] *n* Zwang *m*; (*force*) Druck *m*, Zwang *m*; **under ~** unter Druck *or* Zwang.

**compulsive** [kəm'pʌlsɪv] *adj* zwanghaft; **it makes ~ viewing/reading** das muß man einfach sehen/lesen; **he's a ~ smoker** das Rauchen ist bei ihm zur Sucht geworden.

**compulsory** [kəm'pʌlsərɪ] *adj* obligatorisch; (*retirement*) Zwangs-.

**compulsory purchase** *n* Enteignung *f*.

**compunction** [kəm'pʌŋkʃən] *n* Schuldgefühle *pl*, Gewissensbisse *pl*; **to have no ~ about doing sth** etw tun, ohne sich schuldig zu fühlen.

**computer** [kəm'pjuːtə*] *n* Computer *m*, Rechner *m* ♦ *cpd* Computer-; **the process is done by ~** das Verfahren wird per Computer durchgeführt.

**computer game** *n* Computerspiel *nt*.

**computerization** [kəmpjuːtəraɪ'zeɪʃən] *n* Computerisierung *f*.

**computerize** [kəm'pjuːtəraɪz] *vt* auf Computer umstellen; (*information*) computerisieren.

**computer literate** *adj*: **to be ~** Computerkenntnisse haben.

**computer programmer** *n* Programmierer(in) *m(f)*.

**computer programming** *n* Programmieren *nt*.

**computer science** *n* Informatik *f*.

**computer scientist** *n* Informatiker(in) *m(f)*.

**computing** [kəm'pjuːtɪŋ] *n* Informatik *f*; (*activity*) Computerarbeit *f*.

**comrade** ['kɔmrɪd] *n* Genosse *m*, Genossin *f*; (*friend*) Kamerad(in) *m(f)*.

**comradeship** ['kɔmrɪdʃɪp] *n* Kameradschaft *f*.

**comsat** ['kɔmsæt] *n abbr* = **communications satellite**.

**con** [kɔn] *vt* betrügen; (*cheat*) hereinlegen ♦ *n* Schwindel *m*; **to ~ sb into doing sth** jdn durch einen Trick dazu bringen, daß er/sie etw tut.

**concave** ['kɔnkeɪv] *adj* konkav.

**conceal** [kən'siːl] *vt* verbergen; (*information*) verheimlichen.

**concede** [kən'siːd] *vt* zugeben ♦ *vi* nachgeben; (*admit defeat*) sich geschlagen geben; **to ~ defeat** sich geschlagen geben; **to ~ a point to sb** jdm in einem Punkt recht geben.

**conceit** [kən'siːt] *n* Einbildung *f*.

**conceited** [kən'siːtɪd] *adj* eingebildet.

**conceivable** [kən'siːvəbl] *adj* denkbar,

vorstellbar; **it is ~ that** ... es ist denkbar, daß ...

**conceivably** [kən'siːvəblɪ] *adv*: **he may ~ be right** es ist durchaus denkbar, daß er recht hat.

**conceive** [kən'siːv] *vt* (*child*) empfangen; (*plan*) kommen auf +*acc*; (*policy*) konzipieren ♦ *vi* empfangen; **to ~ of sth** sich *dat* etw vorstellen; **to ~ of doing sth** sich *dat* vorstellen, etw zu tun.

**concentrate** ['kɔnsəntreɪt] *vi* sich konzentrieren ♦ *vt* konzentrieren.

**concentration** [kɔnsən'treɪʃən] *n* Konzentration *f*.

**concentration camp** *n* Konzentrationslager *nt*, KZ *nt*.

**concentric** [kən'sɛntrɪk] *adj* konzentrisch.

**concept** ['kɔnsɛpt] *n* Vorstellung *f*; (*principle*) Begriff *m*.

**conception** [kən'sɛpʃən] *n* Vorstellung *f*; (*of child*) Empfängnis *f*.

**concern** [kən'səːn] *n* Angelegenheit *f*, (*anxiety, worry*) Sorge *f*; (COMM) Konzern *m* ♦ *vt* Sorgen machen +*dat*; (*involve*) angehen; (*relate to*) betreffen; **to be ~ed (about)** sich *dat* Sorgen machen (um); **"to whom it may ~"** (*on certificate*) „Bestätigung"; (*on reference*) „Zeugnis"; **as far as I am ~ed** was mich betrifft; **to be ~ed with** sich interessieren für; **the department ~ed** (*under discussion*) die betreffende Abteilung; (*involved*) die zuständige Abteilung.

**concerning** [kən'səːnɪŋ] *prep* bezüglich +*gen*, hinsichtlich +*gen*.

**concert** ['kɔnsət] *n* Konzert *nt*; **in ~** (MUS) live; (*activities, actions etc*) gemeinsam.

**concerted** [kən'səːtɪd] *adj* gemeinsam.

**concert hall** *n* Konzerthalle *f*, Konzertsaal *m*.

**concertina** [kɔnsə'tiːnə] *n* Konzertina *f* ♦ *vi* sich wie eine Ziehharmonika zusammenschieben.

**concerto** [kən'tʃəːtəu] *n* Konzert *nt*.

**concession** [kən'sɛʃən] *n* Zugeständnis *nt*, Konzession *f*; (COMM) Konzession; **tax ~** Steuervergünstigung *f*.

**concessionaire** [kənsɛʃə'nɛə*] *n* Konzessionär *m*.

**concessionary** [kən'sɛʃənrɪ] *adj* ermäßigt.

**conciliation** [kənsɪlɪ'eɪʃən] *n* Schlichtung *f*.

**conciliatory** [kən'sɪlɪətrɪ] *adj* versöhnlich.

**concise** [kən'saɪs] *adj* kurzgefaßt, prägnant.

**conclave** ['kɔnkleɪv] *n* Klausur *f*; (REL) Konklave *f*.

**conclude** [kən'kluːd] *vt* beenden, schließen; (*treaty, deal etc*) abschließen; (*decide*) schließen, folgern ♦ *vi* schließen; (*events*): **to ~ (with)** enden (mit); **"That," he ~d, "is why we did it."** „Darum", schloß er, „haben wir es getan"; **I ~ that** ... ich komme zu dem Schluß, daß ...

**concluding** [kən'kluːdɪŋ] *adj* (*remarks etc*)

abschließend, Schluß-.

**conclusion** [kən'kluːʒən] n (see vb) Ende nt; Schluß m; Abschluß m; Folgerung f; **to come to the ~ that** ... zu dem Schluß kommen, daß ...

**conclusive** [kən'kluːsɪv] adj (evidence) schlüssig; (defeat) endgültig.

**concoct** [kən'kɔkt] vt (excuse etc) sich dat ausdenken; (meal, sauce) improvisieren.

**concoction** [kən'kɔkʃən] n Zusammenstellung f; (drink) Gebräu nt.

**concord** ['kɔŋkɔːd] n Eintracht f; (treaty) Vertrag m.

**concourse** ['kɔŋkɔːs] n (Eingangs)halle f; (crowd) Menge f.

**concrete** ['kɔŋkriːt] n Beton m ♦ adj (ceiling, block) Beton-; (proposal, idea) konkret.

**concrete mixer** n Betonmischmaschine f.

**concur** [kən'kəː'] vi übereinstimmen; **to ~ with** beipflichten ♦ dat.

**concurrently** [kən'kʌrntlɪ] adv gleichzeitig.

**concussion** [kən'kʌʃən] n Gehirnerschütterung f.

**condemn** [kən'dɛm] vt verurteilen; (building) für abbruchreif erklären.

**condemnation** [kɔndɛm'neɪʃən] n Verurteilung f.

**condensation** [kɔndɛn'seɪʃən] n Kondenswasser nt.

**condense** [kən'dɛns] vi kondensieren, sich niederschlagen ♦ vt zusammenfassen.

**condensed milk** [kən'dɛnst-] n Kondensmilch f, Büchsenmilch f.

**condescend** [kɔndɪ'sɛnd] vi herablassend sein; **to ~ to do sth** sich dazu herablassen, etw zu tun.

**condescending** [kɔndɪ'sɛndɪŋ] adj herablassend.

**condition** [kən'dɪʃən] n Zustand m; (requirement) Bedingung f; (illness) Leiden nt ♦ vt konditionieren; (hair) in Form bringen; **conditions** npl (circumstances) Verhältnisse pl; **in good/poor ~** (person) in guter/ schlechter Verfassung; (thing) in gutem/ schlechtem Zustand; **a heart ~** ein Herzleiden nt; **weather ~s** die Wetterlage; **on ~ that** ... unter der Bedingung, daß ...

**conditional** [kən'dɪʃənl] adj bedingt; **to be ~ upon** abhängen von.

**conditioner** [kən'dɪʃənə'] n (for hair) Pflegespülung f; (for fabrics) Weichspüler m.

**condo** ['kɔndəu] (US: inf) n abbr = **condominium**.

**condolences** [kən'dəulənsɪz] npl Beileid nt.

**condom** ['kɔndəm] n Kondom m or nt.

**condominium** [kɔndə'mɪnɪəm] (US) n Haus nt mit Eigentumswohnungen; (rooms) Eigentumswohnung f.

**condone** [kən'dəun] vt gutheißen.

**conducive** [kən'djuːsɪv] adj: **~ to** förderlich ♦ dat.

**conduct** [n 'kɔndʌkt, vt kən'dʌkt] n Verhalten nt ♦ vt (investigation etc) durchführen; (manage) führen; (orchestra, choir etc) dirigieren; (heat, electricity) leiten; **to ~ o.s.** sich verhalten.

**conducted tour** [kən'dʌktɪd-] n Führung f.

**conductor** [kən'dʌktə'] n (of orchestra) Dirigent(in) m(f); (on bus) Schaffner m; (US: on train) Zugführer(in) m(f); (ELEC) Leiter m.

**conductress** [kən'dʌktrɪs] n (on bus) Schaffnerin f.

**conduit** ['kɔndjuɪt] n (TECH) Leitungsrohr nt; (ELEC) Isolierrohr nt.

**cone** [kəun] n Kegel m; (on road) Leitkegel m; (BOT) Zapfen m; (ice cream cornet) (Eis)tüte f.

**confectioner** [kən'fɛkʃənə'] n (maker) Süßwarensteller(in) m(f); (seller) Süßwarenhändler(in) m(f); (of cakes) Konditor(in) m(f).

**confectioner's (shop)** [kən'fɛkʃənəz-] n Süßwarenladen m; (cake shop) Konditorei f.

**confectionery** [kən'fɛkʃənrɪ] n Süßwaren pl, Süßigkeiten pl; (cakes) Konditorwaren pl.

**confederate** [kən'fɛdrɪt] adj verbündet ♦ n (pej) Komplize m, Komplizin f; (US: HIST) **the C~s** die Konföderierten pl.

**confederation** [kənfɛdə'reɪʃən] n Bund m; (POL) Bündnis nt; (COMM) Verband m.

**confer** [kən'fəː'] vt: **to ~ sth (on sb)** (jdm) etw verleihen ♦ vi sich beraten; **to ~ with sb about sth** sich mit jdm über etw acc beraten, etw mit jdm besprechen.

**conference** ['kɔnfərəns] n Konferenz f; (more informal) Besprechung f; **to be in ~** in or bei einer Konferenz/Besprechung sein.

**conference room** n Konferenzraum m; (smaller) Besprechungszimmer nt.

**confess** [kən'fɛs] vt bekennen; (sin) beichten; (crime) zugeben, gestehen ♦ vi (admit) gestehen; **to ~ to sth** (crime) etw gestehen; (weakness etc) sich zu etw bekennen; **I must ~ that I didn't enjoy it at all** ich muß sagen, daß es mir überhaupt keinen Spaß gemacht hat.

**confession** [kən'fɛʃən] n Geständnis nt; (REL) Beichte f; **to make a ~** ein Geständnis ablegen.

**confessor** [kən'fɛsə'] n Beichtvater m.

**confetti** [kən'fɛtɪ] n Konfetti nt.

**confide** [kən'faɪd] vi: **to ~ in** sich anvertrauen ♦ dat.

**confidence** ['kɔnfɪdns] n Vertrauen nt; (self-assurance) Selbstvertrauen nt; (secret) vertrauliche Mitteilung f, Geheimnis nt; **to have ~ in sb/sth** Vertrauen zu jdm/etw haben; **to have (every) ~ that** ... ganz zuversichtlich sein, daß ...; **motion of no ~** Mißtrauensantrag m; **to tell sb sth in strict ~** jdm etw ganz im Vertrauen sagen; **in ~** vertraulich.

**confidence trick** n Schwindel m.

**confident** ['kɔnfɪdənt] adj (selbst)sicher; (positive) zuversichtlich.

**confidential** [kɒnfɪ'denʃəl] *adj* vertraulich; (*secretary*) Privat-.
**confidentiality** [kɒnfɪdenʃɪ'ælɪtɪ] *n* Vertraulichkeit *f*.
**configuration** [kənfɪgju'reɪʃən] *n* Anordnung *f*; (*COMPUT*) Konfiguration *f*.
**confine** [kən'faɪn] *vt* (*shut up*) einsperren; **to ~ (to)** beschränken (auf +*acc*); **to ~ o.s. to sth** sich auf etw *acc* beschränken; **to ~ o.s. to doing sth** sich darauf beschränken, etw zu tun.
**confined** [kən'faɪnd] *adj* begrenzt.
**confinement** [kən'faɪnmənt] *n* Haft *f*; (*MED*) Entbindung *f*.
**confines** ['kɒnfaɪnz] *npl* Grenzen *pl*; (*of situation*) Rahmen *m*.
**confirm** [kən'fɜːm] *vt* bestätigen; **to be ~ed** (*REL*) konfirmiert werden.
**confirmation** [kɒnfə'meɪʃən] *n* Bestätigung *f*; (*REL*) Konfirmation *f*.
**confirmed** [kən'fɜːmd] *adj* (*bachelor*) eingefleischt; (*teetotaller*) überzeugt.
**confiscate** ['kɒnfɪskeɪt] *vt* beschlagnahmen, konfiszieren.
**confiscation** [kɒnfɪs'keɪʃən] *n* Beschlagnahme *f*, Konfiszierung *f*.
**conflagration** [kɒnflə'greɪʃən] *n* Feuersbrunst *f*.
**conflict** ['kɒnflɪkt] *n* Konflikt *m*; (*fighting*) Zusammenstoß *m*, Kampf *m* ♦ *vi:* **to ~ (with)** im Widerspruch stehen (zu).
**conflicting** [kən'flɪktɪŋ] *adj* widersprüchlich.
**conform** [kən'fɔːm] *vi* sich anpassen; **to ~ to** entsprechen +*dat*.
**conformist** [kən'fɔːmɪst] *n* Konformist(in) *m(f)*.
**confound** [kən'faund] *vt* verwirren; (*amaze*) verblüffen.
**confounded** [kən'faundɪd] *adj* verdammt, verflixt (*inf*).
**confront** [kən'frʌnt] *vt* (*problems, task*) sich stellen +*dat*; (*enemy, danger*) gegenübertreten +*dat*.
**confrontation** [kɒnfrən'teɪʃən] *n* Konfrontation *f*.
**confuse** [kən'fjuːz] *vt* verwirren; (*mix up*) verwechseln; (*complicate*) durcheinanderbringen.
**confused** [kən'fjuːzd] *adj* (*person*) verwirrt; (*situation*) verworren, konfus; **to get ~** konfus werden.
**confusing** [kən'fjuːzɪŋ] *adj* verwirrend.
**confusion** [kən'fjuːʒən] *n* (*mix-up*) Verwechslung *f*; (*perplexity*) Verwirrung *f*; (*disorder*) Durcheinander *nt*.
**congeal** [kən'dʒiːl] *vi* (*blood*) gerinnen; (*sauce, oil*) erstarren.
**congenial** [kən'dʒiːnɪəl] *adj* ansprechend, sympathisch; (*atmosphere, place, work, company*) angenehm.
**congenital** [kən'dʒenɪtl] *adj* angeboren.
**conger eel** ['kɒŋɡər-] *n* Seeaal *m*.

**congested** [kən'dʒestɪd] *adj* (*road*) verstopft; (*area*) überfüllt; (*nose*) verstopft; **his lungs are ~** in seiner Lunge hat sich Blut angestaut.
**congestion** [kən'dʒestʃən] *n* (*MED*) Blutstau *m*; (*of road*) Verstopfung *f*; (*of area*) Überfüllung *f*.
**conglomerate** [kən'ɡlɒmərɪt] *n* (*COMM*) Konglomerat *nt*.
**conglomeration** [kənɡlɒmə'reɪʃən] *n* Ansammlung *f*.
**Congo** ['kɒŋɡəu] *n* (*state*) Kongo *m*.
**congratulate** [kən'ɡrætjuleɪt] *vt* gratulieren; **to ~ sb (on sth)** jdm (zu etw) gratulieren.
**congratulations** [kənɡrætju'leɪʃənz] *npl* Glückwunsch *m*, Glückwünsche *pl*; **~!** Herzlichen Glückwunsch!; **~ on** Glückwünsche zu.
**congregate** ['kɒŋɡrɪɡeɪt] *vi* sich versammeln.
**congregation** [kɒŋɡrɪ'ɡeɪʃən] *n* Gemeinde *f*.
**congress** ['kɒŋɡres] *n* Kongreß *m*; (*US*): **C~** der Kongreß.

*Der **Congress** ist die nationale gesetzgebende Versammlung der USA, die in Washington im Capitol zusammentritt. Der Kongreß besteht aus dem Repräsentantenhaus (435 Abgeordnete, entsprechend den Bevölkerungszahlen auf die einzelnen Bundesstaaten verteilt und jeweils für 2 Jahre gewählt) und dem Senat (100 Senatoren, 2 für jeden Bundesstaat, für 6 Jahre gewählt, wobei ein Drittel alle zwei Jahre neu gewählt wird). Sowohl die Abgeordneten als auch die Senatoren werden in direkter Wahl vom Volk gewählt.*

**congressman** ['kɒŋɡresmən] (*US*) *n* (*irreg: like* **man**) Kongreßabgeordnete(r) *m*.
**congresswoman** ['kɒŋɡreswumən] (*US*) (*irreg: like* **woman**) *n* Kongreßabgeordnete *f*.
**conical** ['kɒnɪkl] *adj* kegelförmig, konisch.
**conifer** ['kɒnɪfə'] *n* Nadelbaum *m*.
**coniferous** [kə'nɪfərəs] *adj* Nadel-.
**conjecture** [kən'dʒektʃə'] *n* Vermutung *f*, Mutmaßung *f* ♦ *vi* vermuten, mutmaßen.
**conjugal** ['kɒndʒuɡl] *adj* ehelich.
**conjugate** ['kɒndʒuɡeɪt] *vt* konjugieren.
**conjugation** [kɒndʒə'ɡeɪʃən] *n* Konjugation *f*.
**conjunction** [kən'dʒʌŋkʃən] *n* Konjunktion *f*; **in ~ with** zusammen mit, in Verbindung mit.
**conjunctivitis** [kəndʒʌŋktɪ'vaɪtɪs] *n* Bindehautentzündung *f*.
**conjure** ['kʌndʒə'] *vi* zaubern ♦ *vt* (*also fig*) hervorzaubern.
►**conjure up** *vt* (*ghost, spirit*) beschwören; (*memories*) heraufbeschwören.
**conjurer** ['kʌndʒərə'] *n* Zauberer *m*, Zauberkünstler(in) *m(f)*.
**conjuring trick** ['kʌndʒərɪŋ-] *n* Zaubertrick *m*, Zauberkunststück *nt*.

**conker** ['kɒŋkə*] (*BRIT*) *n* (Roß)kastanie *f*.
**conk out** [kɒŋk-] (*inf*) *vi* den Geist aufgeben.
**con man** *n* Schwindler *m*.
**Conn.** (*US*) *abbr* (*POST:* = Connecticut).
**connect** [kə'nɛkt] *vt* verbinden; (*ELEC*)
anschließen; (*TEL: caller*) verbinden;
(: *subscriber*) anschließen; (*fig: associate*) in
Zusammenhang bringen ♦ *vi:* **to** ~ **with**
(*train, plane etc*) Anschluß haben an +acc; **to**
~ **sth to sth** etw mit einer Sache verbinden;
**to be** ~**ed with** (*associated*) in einer
Beziehung *or* in Verbindung stehen zu;
(*have dealings with*) zu tun haben mit; **I am**
**trying to** ~ **you** (*TEL*) ich versuche, Sie zu
verbinden.
**connection** [kə'nɛkʃən] *n* Verbindung *f*;
(*ELEC*) Kontakt *m*; (*train, plane etc, TEL:*
*subscriber*) Anschluß *m*; (*fig: association*)
Beziehung *f*, Zusammenhang *m*; **in** ~ **with** in
Zusammenhang mit; **what is the** ~ **between**
**them?** welche Verbindung besteht
zwischen ihnen?; **business** ~**s**
Geschäftsbeziehungen *pl*; **to get/miss one's**
~ seinen Anschluß erreichen/verpassen.
**connexion** [kə'nɛkʃən] (*BRIT*) *n* = **connection**.
**conning tower** ['kɒnɪŋ-] *n* Kommandoturm
*m*.
**connive** [kə'naɪv] *vi:* **to** ~ **at** stillschweigend
dulden.
**connoisseur** [kɒnɪ'sə:*] *n* Kenner(in) *m(f)*.
**connotation** [kɒnə'teɪʃən] *n* Konnotation *f*.
**connubial** [kə'nju:bɪəl] *adj* ehelich.
**conquer** ['kɒŋkə*] *vt* erobern; (*enemy, fear,*
*feelings*) besiegen.
**conqueror** ['kɒŋkərə*] *n* Eroberer *m*.
**conquest** ['kɒŋkwɛst] *n* Eroberung *f*.
**cons** [kɒnz] *npl see* **convenience, pro.**
**conscience** ['kɒnʃəns] *n* Gewissen *nt*; **to have**
**a guilty/clear** ~ ein schlechtes/gutes
Gewissen haben; **in all** ~ allen Ernstes.
**conscientious** [kɒnʃɪ'ɛnʃəs] *adj* gewissenhaft.
**conscientious objector** *n* Wehrdienst- *or*
Kriegsdienstverweigerer *m* (*aus*
*Gewissensgründen*).
**conscious** ['kɒnʃəs] *adj* bewußt; (*awake*) bei
Bewußtsein; **to become** ~ **of sth** sich *dat*
einer Sache *gen* bewußt werden; **to become**
~ **that** ... sich *dat* bewußt werden, daß ...
**consciousness** ['kɒnʃəsnɪs] *n* Bewußtsein *nt*;
**to lose** ~ bewußtlos werden; **to regain** ~
wieder zu sich kommen.
**conscript** ['kɒnskrɪpt] *n* Wehrpflichtige(r) *m*.
**conscription** [kən'skrɪpʃən] *n* Wehrpflicht *f*.
**consecrate** ['kɒnsɪkreɪt] *vt* weihen.
**consecutive** [kən'sɛkjutɪv] *adj* aufeinander-
folgend; **on three** ~ **occasions** dreimal
hintereinander.
**consensus** [kən'sɛnsəs] *n* Übereinstimmung *f*;
**the** ~ **(of opinion)** die allgemeine Meinung.
**consent** [kən'sɛnt] *n* Zustimmung *f* ♦ *vi:* **to**
~ **to** zustimmen +dat; **age of** ~
Ehemündigkeitsalter *nt*; **by common** ~ auf

allgemeinen Wunsch.
**consenting** [kən'sɛntɪŋ] *adj:* **between** ~ **adults**
≈ zwischen Erwachsenen.
**consequence** ['kɒnsɪkwəns] *n* Folge *f*; **of** ~
bedeutend, wichtig; **it's of little** ~ es spielt
kaum eine Rolle; **in** ~ folglich.
**consequently** ['kɒnsɪkwəntlɪ] *adv* folglich.
**conservation** [kɒnsə'veɪʃən] *n* Erhaltung *f*,
Schutz *m*; (*of energy*) Sparen *nt*; (*also:* **nature**
~) Umweltschutz *m*; (*of paintings, books*)
Erhaltung *f*, Konservierung *f*; **energy** ~
Energieeinsparung *f*.
**conservationist** [kɒnsə'veɪʃnɪst] *n*
Umweltschützer(in) *m(f)*.
**conservative** [kən'sə:vətɪv] *adj* konservativ;
(*cautious*) vorsichtig; (*BRIT: POL*): **C**~
konservativ ♦ *n* (*BRIT: POL*): **C**~
Konservative(r) *f(m)*.
**Conservative Party** *n:* **the** ~ die
Konservative Partei *f*.
**conservatory** [kən'sə:vətrɪ] *n* Wintergarten
*m*; (*MUS*) Konservatorium *nt*.
**conserve** [kən'sə:v] *vt* erhalten; (*supplies,*
*energy*) sparen ♦ *n* Konfitüre *f*.
**consider** [kən'sɪdə*] *vt* (*study*) sich *dat*
überlegen; (*take into account*) in Betracht
ziehen; **to** ~ **that** ... der Meinung sein, daß
...; **to** ~ **sb/sth as** ... jdn/etw für ... halten; **to**
~ **doing sth** in Erwägung ziehen, etw zu
tun; **they** ~ **themselves to be superior** sie
halten sich für etwas Besseres; **she** ~**ed it a**
**disaster** sie betrachtete es als eine
Katastrophe; ~ **yourself lucky** Sie können
sich glücklich schätzen; **all things** ~**ed** alles
in allem.
**considerable** [kən'sɪdərəbl] *adj* beträchtlich.
**considerably** [kən'sɪdərəblɪ] *adv* beträchtlich;
(*bigger, smaller etc*) um einiges.
**considerate** [kən'sɪdərɪt] *adj* rücksichtsvoll.
**consideration** [kənsɪdə'reɪʃən] *n* Überlegung
*f*; (*factor*) Gesichtspunkt *m*, Faktor *m*;
(*thoughtfulness*) Rücksicht *f*; (*reward*)
Entgelt *nt*; **out of** ~ **for** aus Rücksicht auf
+acc; **to be under** ~ geprüft werden; **my first**
~ **is my family** ich denke zuerst an meine
Familie.
**considered** [kən'sɪdəd] *adj:* ~ **opinion**
ernsthafte Überzeugung.
**considering** [kən'sɪdərɪŋ] *prep* in Anbetracht
+gen; ~ **(that)** wenn man bedenkt(, daß).
**consign** [kən'saɪn] *vt:* **to** ~ **to** (*object: to place*)
verbannen in +acc; (*person: to sb's care*)
anvertrauen +dat; (: *to poverty*) verurteilen
zu; (*send*) versenden an +acc.
**consignment** [kən'saɪnmənt] *n* Sendung *f*,
Lieferung *f*.
**consignment note** *n* Frachtbrief *m*.
**consist** [kən'sɪst] *vi:* **to** ~ **of** bestehen aus.
**consistency** [kən'sɪstənsɪ] *n* (*of actions etc*)
Konsequenz *f*; (*of cream etc*) Konsistenz *f*,
Dicke *f*.
**consistent** [kən'sɪstənt] *adj* konsequent;

(*argument, idea*) logisch, folgerichtig; **to be** ~ **with** entsprechen +*dat.*

**consolation** [kɔnsə'leɪʃən] *n* Trost *m*.

**console** [kən'səul] *vt* trösten ♦ *n* (*panel*) Schalttafel *f*.

**consolidate** [kən'sɔlɪdeɪt] *vt* festigen.

**consols** ['kɔnsɔlz] (*BRIT*) *npl* (*STOCK EXCHANGE*) Konsols *pl*, konsolidierte Staatsanleihen *pl.*

**consommé** [kən'sɔmeɪ] *n* Kraftbrühe *f*, Consommé *f.*

**consonant** ['kɔnsənənt] *n* Konsonant *m*, Mitlaut *m.*

**consort** ['kɔnsɔːt] *n* Gemahl(in) *m(f)*, Gatte *m*, Gattin *f* ♦ *vi:* **to** ~ **with sb** mit jdm verkehren; **prince** ~ Prinzgemahl *m.*

**consortium** [kən'sɔːtɪəm] *n* Konsortium *nt.*

**conspicuous** [kən'spɪkjuəs] *adj* auffallend; **to make o.s.** ~ auffallen.

**conspiracy** [kən'spɪrəsɪ] *n* Verschwörung *f*, Komplott *nt.*

**conspiratorial** [kənspɪrə'tɔːrɪəl] *adj* verschwörerisch.

**conspire** [kən'spaɪə*] *vi* sich verschwören; (*events*) zusammenkommen.

**constable** ['kʌnstəbl] (*BRIT*) *n* Polizist *m*; **chief** ~ Polizeipräsident *m*, Polizeichef *m.*

**constabulary** [kən'stæbjulərɪ] (*BRIT*) *n* Polizei *f.*

**constant** ['kɔnstənt] *adj* dauernd, ständig; (*fixed*) konstant, gleichbleibend.

**constantly** ['kɔnstəntlɪ] *adv* (an)dauernd, ständig.

**constellation** [kɔnstə'leɪʃən] *n* Sternbild *nt.*

**consternation** [kɔnstə'neɪʃən] *n* Bestürzung *f.*

**constipated** ['kɔnstɪpeɪtɪd] *adj:* **to be** ~ Verstopfung haben, verstopft sein.

**constipation** [kɔnstɪ'peɪʃən] *n* Verstopfung *f.*

**constituency** [kən'stɪtjuənsɪ] *n* (*POL*) Wahlkreis *m*; (*electors*) Wähler *pl* (*eines Wahlkreises*).

**constituency party** *n* Parteiorganisation in einem Wahlkreis.

**constituent** [kən'stɪtjuənt] *n* (*POL*) Wähler(in) *m(f)*; (*component*) Bestandteil *m.*

**constitute** ['kɔnstɪtjuːt] *vt* (*represent*) darstellen; (*make up*) bilden, ausmachen.

**constitution** [kɔnstɪ'tjuːʃən] *n* (*POL*) Verfassung *f*; (*of club etc*) Satzung *f*; (*health*) Konstitution *f*, Gesundheit *f*; (*make-up*) Zusammensetzung *f.*

**constitutional** [kɔnstɪ'tjuːʃnl] *adj* (*government*) verfassungsmäßig; (*reform etc*) Verfassungs-.

**constitutional monarchy** *n* konstitutionelle Monarchie *f.*

**constrain** [kən'streɪn] *vt* zwingen.

**constrained** [kən'streɪnd] *adj* gezwungen.

**constraint** [kən'streɪnt] *n* Beschränkung *f*, Einschränkung *f*; (*compulsion*) Zwang *m*; (*embarrassment*) Befangenheit *f.*

**constrict** [kən'strɪkt] *vt* einschnüren; (*blood vessel*) verengen; (*limit, restrict*) einschränken.

**constriction** [kən'strɪkʃən] *n* Einschränkung *f*; (*tightness*) Verengung *f*; (*squeezing*) Einschnürung *f.*

**construct** [kən'strʌkt] *vt* bauen; (*machine*) konstruieren; (*theory, argument*) entwickeln.

**construction** [kən'strʌkʃən] *n* Bau *m*; (*structure*) Konstruktion *f*; (*fig: interpretation*) Deutung *f*; **under** ~ in *or* im Bau.

**construction industry** *n* Bauindustrie *f.*

**constructive** [kən'strʌktɪv] *adj* konstruktiv.

**construe** [kən'struː] *vt* auslegen, deuten.

**consul** ['kɔnsl] *n* Konsul(in) *m(f)*.

**consulate** ['kɔnsjulɪt] *n* Konsulat *nt.*

**consult** [kən'sʌlt] *vt* (*doctor, lawyer*) konsultieren; (*friend*) sich beraten *or* besprechen mit; (*reference book*) nachschlagen in +*dat*; **to** ~ **sb (about sth)** jdn (wegen etw) fragen.

**consultancy** [kən'sʌltənsɪ] *n* Beratungsbüro *nt*; (*MED: job*) Facharztstelle *f.*

**consultant** [kən'sʌltənt] *n* (*MED*) Facharzt *m*, Fachärztin *f*; (*other specialist*) Berater(in) *m(f)* ♦ *cpd:* ~ **engineer** beratender Ingenieur *m*; ~ **paediatrician** Facharzt/-ärztin *m/f* für Pädiatrie *or* Kinderheilkunde; **legal/ management** ~ Rechts-/ Unternehmensberater(in) *m(f).*

**consultation** [kɔnsəl'teɪʃən] *n* (*MED, LAW*) Konsultation *f*; (*discussion*) Beratung *f*, Besprechung *f*; **in** ~ **with** in gemeinsamer Beratung mit.

**consultative** [kən'sʌltətɪv] *adj* beratend.

**consulting room** [kən'sʌltɪŋ-] (*BRIT*) *n* Sprechzimmer *nt.*

**consume** [kən'sjuːm] *vt* (*food, drink*) zu sich nehmen, konsumieren; (*fuel, energy*) verbrauchen; (*time*) in Anspruch nehmen; (*subj: emotion*) verzehren; (*: fire*) vernichten.

**consumer** [kən'sjuːmə*] *n* Verbraucher(in) *m(f).*

**consumer credit** *n* Verbraucherkredit *m.*

**consumer durables** *npl* (langlebige) Gebrauchsgüter *pl.*

**consumer goods** *npl* Konsumgüter *pl.*

**consumerism** [kən'sjuːmərɪzəm] *n* Verbraucherschutz *m.*

**consumer society** *n* Konsumgesellschaft *f.*

**consumer watchdog** *n* Verbraucherschutzorganisation *f.*

**consummate** ['kɔnsʌmeɪt] *vt* (*marriage*) vollziehen; (*ambition etc*) erfüllen.

**consumption** [kən'sʌmpʃən] *n* Verbrauch *m*; (*of food*) Verzehr *m*; (*of drinks, buying*) Konsum *m*; (*MED*) Schwindsucht *f*; **not fit for human** ~ zum Verzehr ungeeignet.

**cont.** *abbr* (= *continued*) Forts.

**contact** ['kɔntækt] *n* Kontakt *m*; (*touch*) Berührung *f*; (*person*) Kontaktperson *f* ♦ *vt* sich in Verbindung setzen mit; **to be in** ~ **with sb/sth** mit jdm/etw in Verbindung or

Kontakt stehen; (*touch*) jdn/etw berühren;
**business ~s** Geschäftsverbindungen *pl*.
**contact lenses** *npl* Kontaktlinsen *pl*.
**contagious** [kən'teɪdʒəs] *adj* ansteckend.
**contain** [kən'teɪn] *vt* enthalten; (*growth,
spread*) in Grenzen halten; (*feeling*)
beherrschen; **to ~ o.s.** an sich *acc* halten.
**container** [kən'teɪnə*] *n* Behälter *m*; (*for
shipping etc*) Container *m* ♦ *cpd* Container-.
**containerize** [kən'teɪnəraɪz] *vt* in Container
verpacken; (*port*) auf Container umstellen.
**container ship** *n* Containerschiff *nt*.
**contaminate** [kən'tæmɪneɪt] *vt* (*water, food*)
verunreinigen; (*soil etc*) verseuchen.
**contamination** [kəntæmɪ'neɪʃən] *n* (*see vb*)
Verunreinigung *f*; Verseuchung *f*.
**cont'd** *abbr* (= *continued*) Forts.
**contemplate** ['kɔntəmpleɪt] *vt* nachdenken
über *+acc*; (*course of action*) in Erwägung
ziehen; (*person, painting etc*) betrachten.
**contemplation** [kɔntəm'pleɪʃən] *n*
Betrachtung *f*.
**contemporary** [kən'tɛmpərərɪ] *adj*
zeitgenössisch; (*present-day*) modern ♦ *n*
Altersgenosse *m*, Altersgenossin *f*; **Samuel
Pepys and his contemporaries** Samuel
Pepys und seine Zeitgenossen.
**contempt** [kən'tɛmpt] *n* Verachtung *f*; **~ of
court** (*LAW*) Mißachtung *f* (der Würde) des
Gerichts, Ungebühr *f* vor Gericht; **to have
~ for sb/sth** jdn/etw verachten; **to hold sb
in ~** jdn verachten.
**contemptible** [kən'tɛmptəbl] *adj*
verachtenswert.
**contemptuous** [kən'tɛmptjuəs] *adj*
verächtlich, geringschätzig.
**contend** [kən'tɛnd] *vt*: **to ~ that ...** behaupten,
daß ...; **to ~ with** fertigwerden mit; **to ~ for**
kämpfen um; **to have to ~ with** es zu tun
haben mit; **he has a lot to ~ with** er hat viel
um die Ohren.
**contender** [kən'tɛndə*] *n* (*SPORT*)
Wettkämpfer(in) *m(f)*; (*for title*) Anwärter(in)
*m(f)*; (*POL*) Kandidat(in) *m(f)*.
**content** [*adj, vt* kən'tɛnt, *n* 'kɔntɛnt] *adj*
zufrieden ♦ *vt* zufriedenstellen ♦ *n* Inhalt *m*;
(*fat content, moisture content etc*) Gehalt *m*;
**contents** *npl* Inhalt; **(table of) ~s**
Inhaltsverzeichnis *nt*; **to be ~ with**
zufrieden sein mit; **to ~ o.s. with sth** sich
mit etw zufriedengeben *or* begnügen; **to
~ o.s. with doing sth** sich damit
zufriedengeben *or* begnügen, etw zu tun.
**contented** [kən'tɛntɪd] *adj* zufrieden.
**contentedly** [kən'tɛntɪdlɪ] *adv* zufrieden.
**contention** [kən'tɛnʃən] *n* Behauptung *f*;
(*disagreement, argument*) Streit *m*; **bone of ~**
Zankapfel *m*.
**contentious** [kən'tɛnʃəs] *adj* strittig,
umstritten.
**contentment** [kən'tɛntmənt] *n* Zufriedenheit
*f*.

**contest** [*n* 'kɔntɛst, *vt* kən'tɛst] *n* (*competition*)
Wettkampf *m*; (*for control, power etc*) Kampf
*m* ♦ *vt* (*election, competition*) teilnehmen an
*+dat*; (*compete for*) kämpfen um; (*statement*)
bestreiten; (*decision*) angreifen; (*LAW*)
anfechten.
**contestant** [kən'tɛstənt] *n* (*in quiz*)
Kandidat(in) *m(f)*; (*in competition*)
Teilnehmer(in) *m(f)*; (*in fight*) Kämpfer(in)
*m(f)*.
**context** ['kɔntɛkst] *n* Zusammenhang *m*,
Kontext *m*; **in ~** im Zusammenhang; **out of
~** aus dem Zusammenhang gerissen.
**continent** ['kɔntɪnənt] *n* Kontinent *m*, Erdteil
*m*; **the C~** (*BRIT*) (Kontinental)europa *nt*; **on
the C~** in (Kontinental)europa, auf dem
Kontinent.
**continental** [kɔntɪ'nɛntl] *adj* kontinental;
(*European*) europäisch ♦ *n* (*BRIT*)
(Festlands)europäer(in) *m(f)*.
**continental breakfast** *n* kleines Frühstück
*nt*.
**continental quilt** (*BRIT*) *n* Steppdecke *f*.
**contingency** [kən'tɪndʒənsɪ] *n* möglicher Fall
*m*, Eventualität *f*.
**contingency plan** *n* Plan *m* für den
Eventualfall.
**contingent** [kən'tɪndʒənt] *n* Kontingent *nt*
♦ *adj*: **to be ~ upon** abhängen von.
**continual** [kən'tɪnjuəl] *adj* ständig; (*process*)
ununterbrochen.
**continually** [kən'tɪnjuəlɪ] *adv* (*see adj*) ständig;
ununterbrochen.
**continuation** [kəntɪnju'eɪʃən] *n* Fortsetzung *f*;
(*extension*) Weiterführung *f*.
**continue** [kən'tɪnju:] *vi* andauern;
(*performance, road*) weitergehen; (*person:
talking*) fortfahren ♦ *vt* fortsetzen; **to ~ to do
sth/doing sth** etw weiter tun; **"to be ~d"**
„Fortsetzung folgt"; **"~d on page 10"**
„Fortsetzung auf Seite 10".
**continuing education** [kən'tɪnjuɪŋ-] *n*
Erwachsenenbildung *f*.
**continuity** [kɔntɪ'nju:ɪtɪ] *n* Kontinuität *f* ♦ *cpd*
(*TV*): **~ announcer** Ansager(in) *m(f)*; **~ studio**
Ansagestudio *nt*.
**continuous** [kən'tɪnjuəs] *adj* ununterbrochen;
(*growth etc*) kontinuierlich; **~ form** (*LING*)
Verlaufsform *f*; **~ performance** (*CINE*)
durchgehende Vorstellung *f*.
**continuously** [kən'tɪnjuəslɪ] *adv* dauernd,
ständig; (*uninterruptedly*) ununterbrochen.
**continuous stationery** *n* (*COMPUT*)
Endlospapier *nt*.
**contort** [kən'tɔːt] *vt* (*body*) verrenken,
verdrehen; (*face*) verziehen.
**contortion** [kən'tɔːʃən] *n* Verrenkung *f*.
**contortionist** [kən'tɔːʃənɪst] *n*
Schlangenmensch *m*.
**contour** ['kɔntuə*] *n* (*also:* **~ line**) Höhenlinie *f*;
(*shape, outline: gen pl*) Kontur *f*, Umriß *m*.
**contraband** ['kɔntrəbænd] *n* Schmuggelware *f*

♦ *adj* Schmuggel-.
**contraception** [kɔntrə'sɛpʃən] *n*
Empfängnisverhütung *f.*
**contraceptive** [kɔntrə'sɛptɪv] *adj*
empfängnisverhütend ♦ *n* Verhütungsmittel
*nt.*
**contract** [*n, cpd* 'kɔntrækt, *vb* kɔn'trækt] *n*
Vertrag *m* ♦ *vi* schrumpfen; (*metal, muscle*)
sich zusammenziehen ♦ *vt* (*illness*)
erkranken an +*dat* ♦ *cpd* vertraglich
festgelegt; (*work*) Auftrags-; ~ **of**
**employment/service** Arbeitsvertrag *m*; **to**
~ **to do sth** (*COMM*) sich vertraglich
verpflichten, etw zu tun.
▶**contract in** (*BRIT*) *vi* beitreten.
▶**contract out** (*BRIT*) *vi* austreten.
**contraction** [kɔn'trækʃən] *n* Zusammenziehen
*nt*; (*LING*) Kontraktion *f*; (*MED*) Wehe *f.*
**contractor** [kən'træktə•] *n* Auftragnehmer *m*;
(*building contractor*) Bauunternehmer *m.*
**contractual** [kən'træktʃuəl] *adj* vertraglich.
**contradict** [kɔntrə'dɪkt] *vt* widersprechen
+*dat.*
**contradiction** [kɔntrə'dɪkʃən] *n* Widerspruch
*m*; **to be in** ~ **with** im Widerspruch stehen
zu; **a** ~ **in terms** ein Widerspruch in sich.
**contradictory** [kɔntrə'dɪktərɪ] *adj*
widersprüchlich.
**contralto** [kən'træltəu] *n* (*MUS*) Altistin *f*;
(: *voice*) Alt *m.*
**contraption** [kən'træpʃən] (*pej*) *n* (*device*)
Vorrichtung *f*; (*machine*) Gerät *nt*, Apparat
*m.*
**contrary**[1] ['kɔntrərɪ] *adj* entgegengesetzt;
(*ideas, opinions*) gegensätzlich;
(*unfavourable*) widrig ♦ *n* Gegenteil *nt*; ~ **to**
**what we thought** im Gegensatz zu dem,
was wir dachten; **on the** ~ im Gegenteil;
**unless you hear to the** ~ sofern Sie nichts
Gegenteiliges hören.
**contrary**[2] [kən'trɛərɪ] *adj* widerspenstig.
**contrast** ['kɔntrɑːst] *n* Gegensatz *m*, Kontrast
*m* ♦ *vt* vergleichen, gegenüberstellen; **in**
~ **to** *or* **with** im Gegensatz zu.
**contrasting** [kən'trɑːstɪŋ] *adj* (*colours*)
kontrastierend; (*attitudes*) gegensätzlich.
**contravene** [kɔntrə'viːn] *vt* verstoßen gegen.
**contravention** [kɔntrə'vɛnʃən] *n* Verstoß *m*;
**to be in** ~ **of sth** gegen etw verstoßen.
**contribute** [kən'trɪbjuːt] *vi* beitragen ♦ *vt*: **to**
~ **£10/an article to** £10/einen Artikel
beisteuern zu; **to** ~ **to** (*charity*) spenden für;
(*newspaper*) schreiben für; (*discussion,*
*problem etc*) beitragen zu.
**contribution** [kɔntrɪ'bjuːʃən] *n* Beitrag *m*;
(*donation*) Spende *f.*
**contributor** [kən'trɪbjutə•] *n* (*to appeal*)
Spender(in) *m(f)*; (*to newspaper*)
Mitarbeiter(in) *m(f).*
**contributory** [kən'trɪbjutərɪ] *adj*: **a** ~ **cause**
ein Faktor, der mit eine Rolle spielt; **it was**
**a** ~ **factor in** ... es trug zu ... bei.

**contributory pension scheme** (*BRIT*) *n*
beitragspflichtige Rentenversicherung *f.*
**contrite** ['kɔntraɪt] *adj* zerknirscht.
**contrivance** [kən'traɪvəns] *n* (*scheme*) List *f*;
(*device*) Vorrichtung *f.*
**contrive** [kən'traɪv] *vt* (*meeting*) arrangieren
♦ *vi*: **to** ~ **to do sth** es fertigbringen, etw zu
tun.
**control** [kən'trəul] *vt* (*country*) regieren;
(*organization*) leiten; (*machinery, process*)
steuern; (*wages, prices*) kontrollieren;
(*temper*) zügeln; (*disease, fire*) unter
Kontrolle bringen ♦ *n* (*of country*) Kontrolle
*f*; (*of organization*) Leitung *f*; (*of oneself,*
*emotions*) Beherrschung *f*; (*SCI: also:*
~ **group**) Kontrollgruppe *f*; **controls** *npl* (*of*
*vehicle*) Steuerung *f*; (*on radio, television etc*)
Bedienungsfeld *nt*; (*governmental*) Kontrolle
*f*; **to** ~ **o.s.** sich beherrschen; **to take** ~ **of**
die Kontrolle übernehmen über +*acc*;
(*COMM*) übernehmen; **to be in** ~ **of** unter
Kontrolle haben; (*in charge of*) unter sich *dat*
haben; **out of/under** ~ außer/unter
Kontrolle; **everything is under** ~ ich habe/
wir haben *etc* die Sache im Griff (*inf*); **the**
**car went out of** ~ der Fahrer verlor die
Kontrolle über den Wagen; **circumstances**
**beyond our** ~ unvorhersehbare Umstände.
**control key** *n* (*COMPUT*) Control-Taste *f.*
**controller** [kən'trəulə•] *n* (*RADIO, TV*)
Intendant(in) *m(f).*
**controlling interest** [kən'trəulɪŋ-] *n*
Mehrheitsanteil *m.*
**control panel** *n* Schalttafel *f*; (*on television*)
Bedienungsfeld *nt.*
**control point** *n* Kontrollpunkt *m*,
Kontrollstelle *f.*
**control room** *n* (*NAUT*) Kommandoraum *m*;
(*MIL*) (Operations)zentrale *f*; (*RADIO, TV*)
Regieraum *m.*
**control tower** *n* Kontrollturm *m.*
**control unit** *n* (*COMPUT*) Steuereinheit *f.*
**controversial** [kɔntrə'vəːʃl] *adj* umstritten,
kontrovers.
**controversy** ['kɔntrəvəːsɪ] *n* Streit *m*,
Kontroverse *f.*
**conurbation** [kɔnə'beɪʃən] *n* Ballungsgebiet
*nt*, Ballungsraum *m.*
**convalesce** [kɔnvə'lɛs] *vi* genesen.
**convalescence** [kɔnvə'lɛsns] *n* Genesungszeit
*f.*
**convalescent** [kɔnvə'lɛsnt] *adj* (*leave etc*)
Genesungs-, Kur- ♦ *n* Genesende(r) *f(m).*
**convector** [kən'vɛktə•] *n* Heizlüfter *m.*
**convene** [kən'viːn] *vt* einberufen ♦ *vi*
zusammentreten.
**convener** [kən'viːnə•] *n* (*organizer*)
Organisator(in) *m(f)*; (*chairperson*)
Vorsitzende(r) *f(m).*
**convenience** [kən'viːnɪəns] *n* Annehmlichkeit
*f*; (*suitability*): **the** ~ **of this arrangement/**
**location** diese günstige Vereinbarung/Lage;

**I like the ~ of having a shower** mir gefällt, wie angenehm es ist, eine Dusche zu haben; **I like the ~ of living in the city** mir gefällt, wie praktisch es ist, in der Stadt zu wohnen; **at your ~** wann es Ihnen paßt; **at your earliest ~** möglichst bald, baldmöglichst; **with all modern ~s** or (BRIT) **all mod cons** mit allem modernen Komfort; see also **public convenience.**

**convenience foods** npl Fertiggerichte pl.

**convenient** [kən'viːnɪənt] adj günstig; (handy) praktisch; (house etc) günstig gelegen; **if it is ~ to you** wenn es Ihnen (so) paßt, wenn es Ihnen keine Umstände macht.

**conveniently** [kən'viːnɪəntlɪ] adv (happen) günstigerweise; (situated) günstig.

**convenor** [kən'viːnə*] n = **convener.**

**convent** ['kɒnvənt] n Kloster nt.

**convention** [kən'vɛnʃən] n Konvention f; (conference) Tagung f, Konferenz f; (agreement) Abkommen nt.

**conventional** [kən'vɛnʃənl] adj konventionell.

**convent school** n Klosterschule f.

**converge** [kən'vɜːdʒ] vi (roads) zusammenlaufen ♦ vi sich einander annähern; **to ~ on sb/a place** (people) von überallher zu jdm/an einen Ort strömen.

**conversant** [kən'vɜːsnt] adj: **to be ~ with** vertraut sein mit.

**conversation** [kɒnvə'seɪʃən] n Gespräch nt, Unterhaltung f.

**conversational** [kɒnvə'seɪʃənl] adj (tone, style) Unterhaltungs-; (language) gesprochen; **~ mode** (COMPUT) Dialogbetrieb m.

**conversationalist** [kɒnvə'seɪʃnəlɪst] n Unterhalter(in) m(f), Gesprächspartner(in) m(f).

**converse** [n 'kɒnvɜːs, vi kən'vɜːs] n Gegenteil nt ♦ vi: **to ~ (with sb) (about sth)** sich (mit jdm) (über etw) unterhalten.

**conversely** [kɒn'vɜːslɪ] adv umgekehrt.

**conversion** [kən'vɜːʃən] n Umwandlung f; (of weights etc) Umrechnung f; (REL) Bekehrung f; (BRIT: of house) Umbau m.

**conversion table** n Umrechnungstabelle f.

**convert** [vt kən'vɜːt, n 'kɒnvɜːt] vt umwandeln; (person) bekehren; (building) umbauen; (vehicle) umrüsten; (COMM) konvertieren; (RUGBY) verwandeln ♦ n Bekehrte(r) f(m).

**convertible** [kən'vɜːtəbl] adj (currency) konvertierbar ♦ n (AUT) Kabriolett nt.

**convex** ['kɒnvɛks] adj konvex.

**convey** [kən'veɪ] vt (information etc) vermitteln; (cargo, traveller) befördern; (thanks) übermitteln.

**conveyance** [kən'veɪəns] n Beförderung f, Spedition f; (vehicle) Gefährt nt.

**conveyancing** [kən'veɪənsɪŋ] n (Eigentums)übertragung f.

**conveyor belt** n Fließband nt.

**convict** [vt kən'vɪkt, n 'kɒnvɪkt] vt verurteilen ♦ n Sträfling m.

**conviction** [kən'vɪkʃən] n Überzeugung f; (LAW) Verurteilung f.

**convince** [kən'vɪns] vt überzeugen; **to ~ sb (of sth)** jdn (von etw) überzeugen; **to ~ sb that** ... jdn davon überzeugen, daß ...

**convinced** [kən'vɪnst] adj: **~ (of)** überzeugt (von); **~ that** ... überzeugt davon, daß ...

**convincing** [kən'vɪnsɪŋ] adj überzeugend.

**convincingly** [kən'vɪnsɪŋlɪ] adv überzeugend.

**convivial** [kən'vɪvɪəl] adj freundlich; (event) gesellig.

**convoluted** ['kɒnvəluːtɪd] adj verwickelt, kompliziert; (shape) gewunden.

**convoy** ['kɒnvɔɪ] n Konvoi m.

**convulse** [kən'vʌls] vt: **to be ~d with laughter/pain** sich vor Lachen schütteln/Schmerzen krümmen.

**convulsion** [kən'vʌlʃən] n Schüttelkrampf m.

**coo** [kuː] vi gurren.

**cook** [kuk] vt kochen, zubereiten ♦ vi (person, food) kochen; (fry, roast) braten; (pie) backen ♦ n Koch m, Köchin f.

▶**cook up** (inf) vt sich dat einfallen lassen, zurechtbasteln.

**cookbook** ['kukbuk] n Kochbuch nt.

**cook-chill** ['kuktʃɪl] adj durch rasches Kühlen haltbar gemacht.

**cooker** ['kukə*] n Herd m.

**cookery** ['kukərɪ] n Kochen nt, Kochkunst f.

**cookery book** (BRIT) n = **cookbook.**

**cookie** ['kukɪ] (US) n Keks m or nt, Plätzchen nt.

**cooking** ['kukɪŋ] n Kochen nt; (food) Essen nt ♦ cpd Koch-; (chocolate) Block-.

**cookout** ['kukaut] (US) n ≈ Grillparty f.

**cool** [kuːl] adj kühl; (dress, clothes) leicht, luftig; (person: calm) besonnen; (: unfriendly) kühl ♦ vt kühlen ♦ vi abkühlen; **it's ~** es ist kühl; **to keep sth ~** or **in a ~ place** etw kühl aufbewahren; **to keep one's ~** die Ruhe bewahren.

▶**cool down** vi abkühlen; (fig) sich beruhigen.

**coolant** ['kuːlənt] n Kühlflüssigkeit f.

**cool box** n Kühlbox f.

**cooler** ['kuːlə*] (US) n = **cool box.**

**cooling** ['kuːlɪŋ] adj (drink, shower) kühlend; (feeling, emotion) abkühlend.

**cooling tower** ['kuːlɪŋ-] n Kühlturm m.

**coolly** ['kuːlɪ] adv (calmly) besonnen, ruhig; (in unfriendly way) kühl.

**coolness** ['kuːlnɪs] n (see adj) Kühle f; Leichtigkeit f, Luftigkeit f; Besonnenheit f.

**coop** [kuːp] n (for rabbits) Kaninchenstall m; (for poultry) Hühnerstall m ♦ vt: **to ~ up** (fig) einsperren.

**co-op** ['kəuɔp] n abbr (= cooperative (society)) Genossenschaft f.

**cooperate** [kəu'ɔpəreɪt] vi zusammenarbeiten; (assist) mitmachen, kooperieren; **to ~ with sb** mit jdm zusammenarbeiten.

**cooperation** [kəʊɒpə'reɪʃən] *n* (*see vb*) Zusammenarbeit *f*; Mitarbeit *f*, Kooperation *f*.

**cooperative** [kəʊ'ɒpərətɪv] *adj* (*farm, business*) auf Genossenschaftsbasis; (*person*) kooperativ; (: *helpful*) hilfsbereit ♦ *n* Genossenschaft *f*, Kooperative *f*.

**coopt** [kəʊ'ɒpt] *vt:* to ~ **sb onto a committee** jdn in ein Komitee hinzuwählen *or* kooptieren.

**coordinate** [kəʊ'ɔːdɪneɪt] *vt* koordinieren ♦ *n* (*MATH*) Koordinate *f*; **coordinates** *npl* (*clothes*) Kleidung *f* zum Kombinieren.

**coordination** [kəʊɔːdɪ'neɪʃən] *n* Koordinierung *f*, Koordination *f*.

**coownership** [kəʊ'əʊnəʃɪp] *n* Mitbesitz *m*.

**cop** [kɒp] (*inf*) *n* Polizist(in) *m(f)*, Bulle *m* (*pej*).

**cope** [kəʊp] *vi* zurechtkommen; **to ~ with** fertigwerden mit.

**Copenhagen** ['kəʊpn'heɪgən] *n* Kopenhagen *nt.*

**copier** ['kɒpɪə*] *n* (*also:* **photocopier**) Kopiergerät *nt*, Kopierer *m.*

**copilot** ['kəʊpaɪlət] *n* Kopilot(in) *m(f)*.

**copious** ['kəʊpɪəs] *adj* reichlich.

**copper** ['kɒpə*] *n* Kupfer *nt*; (*BRIT: inf*) Polizist(in) *m(f)*, Bulle *m* (*pej*); **coppers** *npl* (*small change, coins*) Kleingeld *nt.*

**coppice** ['kɒpɪs] *n* Wäldchen *nt.*

**copse** [kɒps] *n* = **coppice.**

**copulate** ['kɒpjʊleɪt] *vi* kopulieren.

**copy** ['kɒpɪ] *n* Kopie *f*; (*of book, record, newspaper*) Exemplar *nt*; (*for printing*) Artikel *m* ♦ *vt* (*person*) nachahmen; (*idea etc*) nachmachen; (*something written*) abschreiben; **this murder story will make good ~** (*PRESS*) aus diesem Mord kann man etwas machen.

▶**copy out** *vt* abschreiben.

**copycat** ['kɒpɪkæt] (*pej*) *n* Nachahmer(in) *m(f)*.

**copyright** ['kɒpɪraɪt] *n* Copyright *nt*, Urheberrecht *nt*; **~ reserved** urheberrechtlich geschützt.

**copy typist** *n* Schreibkraft *f* (*die mit Textvorlagen arbeitet*).

**copywriter** ['kɒpɪraɪtə*] *n* Werbetexter(in) *m(f)*.

**coral** ['kɒrəl] *n* Koralle *f.*

**coral reef** *n* Korallenriff *nt.*

**Coral Sea** *n:* **the ~** das Korallenmeer.

**cord** [kɔːd] *n* Schnur *f*; (*string*) Kordel *f*; (*ELEC*) Kabel *nt*, Schnur *f*; (*fabric*) Kord(samt) *m*; **cords** *npl* (*trousers*) Kordhosen *pl.*

**cordial** ['kɔːdɪəl] *adj* herzlich ♦ *n* (*BRIT*) Fruchtsaftkonzentrat *nt.*

**cordless** ['kɔːdlɪs] *adj* schnurlos.

**cordon** ['kɔːdn] *n* Kordon *m*, Absperrkette *f.*

▶**cordon off** *vt* (*area*) absperren, abriegeln; (*crowd*) mit einer Absperrkette zurückhalten.

**corduroy** ['kɔːdərɔɪ] *n* Kord(samt) *m.*

**CORE** [kɔː*] (*US*) *n abbr* (= *Congress for Racial Equality*) Ausschuß für Rassengleichheit.

**core** [kɔː*] *n* Kern *m*; (*of fruit*) Kerngehäuse *nt* ♦ *vt* das Kerngehäuse ausschneiden aus; **rotten to the ~** durch und durch schlecht.

**Corfu** [kɔː'fuː] *n* Korfu *nt.*

**coriander** [kɒrɪ'ændə*] *n* Koriander *m.*

**cork** [kɔːk] *n* (*stopper*) Korken *m*; (*substance*) Kork *m.*

**corkage** ['kɔːkɪdʒ] *n* Korkengeld *nt.*

**corked** [kɔːkt] *adj:* **the wine is ~** der Wein schmeckt nach Kork.

**corkscrew** ['kɔːkskruː] *n* Korkenzieher *m.*

**corky** ['kɔːkɪ] (*US*) *adj* = **corked.**

**corm** [kɔːm] *n* Knolle *f.*

**cormorant** ['kɔːmərnt] *n* Kormoran *m.*

**Corn** (*BRIT*) *abbr* (*POST:* = *Cornwall*).

**corn** [kɔːn] *n* (*BRIT*) Getreide *nt*, Korn *nt*; (*US*) Mais *m*; (*on foot*) Hühnerauge *nt*; **~ on the cob** Maiskolben *m.*

**cornea** ['kɔːnɪə] *n* Hornhaut *f.*

**corned beef** ['kɔːnd-] *n* Corned beef *nt.*

**corner** ['kɔːnə*] *n* Ecke *f*; (*bend*) Kurve *f* ♦ *vt* in die Enge treiben; (*COMM: market*) monopolisieren ♦ *vi* (*in car*) die Kurve nehmen; **to cut ~s** (*fig*) das Verfahren abkürzen.

**corner flag** *n* Eckfahne *f.*

**corner kick** *n* Eckball *m.*

**cornerstone** ['kɔːnəstəʊn] *n* (*fig*) Grundstein *m*, Eckstein *m.*

**cornet** ['kɔːnɪt] *n* (*MUS*) Kornett *nt*; (*BRIT: for ice cream*) Eistüte *f.*

**cornflakes** ['kɔːnfleɪks] *npl* Corn-flakes *pl.*

**cornflour** ['kɔːnflaʊə*] (*BRIT*) *n* Stärkemehl *nt.*

**cornice** ['kɔːnɪs] *n* (Ge)sims *nt.*

**Cornish** ['kɔːnɪʃ] *adj* kornisch, aus Cornwall.

**corn oil** *n* (Mais)keimöl *nt.*

**cornstarch** ['kɔːnstɑːtʃ] (*US*) *n* = **cornflour.**

**cornucopia** [kɔːnju'kəʊpɪə] *n* Fülle *f.*

**Cornwall** ['kɔːnwəl] *n* Cornwall *nt.*

**corny** ['kɔːnɪ] (*inf*) *adj* (*joke*) blöd.

**corollary** [kə'rɒlərɪ] *n* (*logische*) Folge *f.*

**coronary** ['kɒrənərɪ] *n* (*also:* ~ **thrombosis**) Herzinfarkt *m.*

**coronation** [kɒrə'neɪʃən] *n* Krönung *f.*

**coroner** ['kɒrənə*] *n* Beamter, der Todesfälle untersucht, die nicht eindeutig eine natürliche Ursache haben.

**coronet** ['kɒrənɪt] *n* Krone *f.*

**Corp.** *abbr* = **corporation**; (*MIL*) = **corporal.**

**corporal** ['kɔːpərl] *n* Stabsunteroffizier *m.*

**corporal punishment** *n* Prügelstrafe *f.*

**corporate** ['kɔːpərɪt] *adj* (*organization*) körperschaftlich; (*action, effort, ownership*) gemeinschaftlich; (*finance*) Unternehmens-; (*image, identity*) Firmen-.

**corporate hospitality** *n* Empfänge, Diners etc auf Kosten der ausrichtenden Firma.

**corporation** [kɔːpə'reɪʃən] *n* (*COMM*) Körperschaft *f*; (*of town*) Gemeinde *f*, Stadt *f.*

**corporation tax** *n* Körperschaftssteuer *f.*

**corps** [kɔːʳ] (pl ~) n Korps nt; **the press** ~ die Presse.

**corpse** [kɔːps] n Leiche f.

**corpuscle** ['kɔːpʌsl] n Blutkörperchen nt.

**corral** [kə'rɑːl] n Korral m.

**correct** [kə'rɛkt] adj richtig; (proper) korrekt ♦ vt korrigieren; (mistake) berichtigen, verbessern; **you are** ~ Sie haben recht.

**correction** [kə'rɛkʃən] n (see vb) Korrektur f; Berichtigung f, Verbesserung f.

**correctly** [kə'rɛktlɪ] adv (see adj) richtig; korrekt.

**correlate** ['kɔrɪleɪt] vt zueinander in Beziehung setzen ♦ vi: **to** ~ **with** in einer Beziehung stehen zu.

**correlation** [kɔrɪ'leɪʃən] n Beziehung f, Zusammenhang m.

**correspond** [kɔrɪs'pɔnd] vi: **to** ~ (**with**) (write) korrespondieren (mit); (be in accordance) übereinstimmen (mit); **to** ~ **to** (be equivalent) entsprechen +dat.

**correspondence** [kɔrɪs'pɔndəns] n Korrespondenz f, Briefwechsel m; (relationship) Beziehung f.

**correspondence column** n Leserbriefspalte f.

**correspondence course** n Fernkurs m.

**correspondent** [kɔrɪs'pɔndənt] n Korrespondent(in) m(f).

**corresponding** [kɔrɪs'pɔndɪŋ] adj entsprechend.

**corridor** ['kɔrɪdɔːʳ] n Korridor m; (in train) Gang m.

**corroborate** [kə'rɔbəreɪt] vt bestätigen.

**corrode** [kə'rəud] vt zerfressen ♦ vi korrodieren.

**corrosion** [kə'rəuʒən] n Korrosion f.

**corrosive** [kə'rəuzɪv] adj korrosiv.

**corrugated** ['kɔrəgeɪtɪd] adj (roof) gewellt; (cardboard) Well-.

**corrugated iron** n Wellblech nt.

**corrupt** [kə'rʌpt] adj korrupt; (depraved) verdorben ♦ vt korrumpieren; (morally) verderben; ~ **practices** Korruption f.

**corruption** [kə'rʌpʃən] n Korruption f.

**corset** ['kɔːsɪt] n Korsett nt; (MED) Stützkorsett nt.

**Corsica** ['kɔːsɪkə] n Korsika nt.

**Corsican** ['kɔːsɪkən] adj korsisch ♦ n Korse m, Korsin f.

**cortège** [kɔː'teɪʒ] n (also: **funeral** ~) Leichenzug m.

**cortisone** ['kɔːtɪzəun] n Kortison nt.

**coruscating** ['kɔrəskeɪtɪŋ] adj sprühend.

**c.o.s.** abbr (= cash on shipment) Barzahlung bei Versand.

**cosh** [kɔʃ] (BRIT) n Totschläger m.

**cosignatory** ['kəu'sɪgnətərɪ] n Mitunterzeichner(in) m(f).

**cosiness** ['kəuzɪnɪs] n Gemütlichkeit f, Behaglichkeit f.

**cos lettuce** ['kɔs-] n römischer Salat m.

**cosmetic** [kɔz'mɛtɪk] n Kosmetikum nt ♦ adj kosmetisch; ~ **surgery** (MED) kosmetische Chirurgie f.

**cosmic** ['kɔzmɪk] adj kosmisch.

**cosmonaut** ['kɔzmənɔːt] n Kosmonaut(in) m(f).

**cosmopolitan** [kɔzmə'pɔlɪtn] adj kosmopolitisch.

**cosmos** ['kɔzmɔs] n: **the** ~ der Kosmos.

**cosset** ['kɔsɪt] vt verwöhnen.

**cost** [kɔst] (pt, pp cost) n Kosten pl; (fig: loss, damage etc) Preis m ♦ vt kosten; (find out cost of) (pt, pp costed) veranschlagen; **costs** npl (COMM, LAW) Kosten pl; **the** ~ **of living** die Lebenshaltungskosten pl; **at all** ~**s** um jeden Preis; **how much does it** ~? wieviel or was kostet es?; **it** ~**s £5/too much** es kostet £5/ ist zu teuer; **what will it** ~ **to have it repaired?** wieviel kostet die Reparatur?; **to** ~ **sb time/effort** jdn Zeit/Mühe kosten; **it** ~ **him his life/job** es kostete ihn das Leben/ seine Stelle.

**cost accountant** n Kostenbuchhalter(in) m(f).

**co-star** ['kəustɑːʳ] n einer der Hauptdarsteller m, eine der Hauptdarstellerinnen f; **she was Sean Connery's** ~ **in ...** sie spielte neben Sean Connery in ...

**Costa Rica** ['kɔstə'riːkə] n Costa Rica nt.

**cost centre** n Kostenstelle f.

**cost control** n Kostenkontrolle f.

**cost-effective** ['kɔstɪ'fɛktɪv] adj rentabel; (COMM) kostengünstig.

**cost-effectiveness** ['kɔstɪ'fɛktɪvnɪs] n Rentabilität f.

**costing** ['kɔstɪŋ] n Kalkulation f.

**costly** ['kɔstlɪ] adj teuer, kostspielig; (in time, effort) aufwendig.

**cost-of-living** ['kɔstəv'lɪvɪŋ] adj Lebenshaltungskosten-; (index) Lebenshaltungs-.

**cost price** n (BRIT) Selbstkostenpreis m; **to sell/buy at** ~ zum Selbstkostenpreis verkaufen/kaufen.

**costume** ['kɔstjuːm] n Kostüm nt; (BRIT: also: swimming ~) Badeanzug m.

**costume jewellery** n Modeschmuck m.

**cosy,** (US) **cozy** ['kəuzɪ] adj gemütlich, behaglich; (bed, scarf, gloves) warm; (chat, evening) gemütlich; **I'm very** ~ **here** ich fühle mich hier sehr wohl, ich finde es hier sehr gemütlich.

**cot** [kɔt] n (BRIT) Kinderbett nt; (US: campbed) Feldbett nt.

**cot death** n Krippentod m, plötzlicher Kindstod m.

**Cotswolds** ['kɔtswəuldz] npl: **the** ~ die Cotswolds pl.

**cottage** ['kɔtɪdʒ] n Cottage nt, Häuschen nt.

**cottage cheese** n Hüttenkäse m.

**cottage industry** n Heimindustrie f.

**cottage pie** n Hackfleisch mit Kartoffelbrei überbacken.

**cotton** ['kɔtn] n (*fabric*) Baumwollstoff m; (*plant*) Baumwollstrauch m; (*thread*) (Baumwoll)garn nt ♦ cpd (*dress etc*) Baumwoll-.
►**cotton on** (*inf*) vi: **to ~ on** es kapieren or schnallen; **to ~ on to sth** etw kapieren or schnallen.
**cotton candy** (*US*) n Zuckerwatte f.
**cotton wool** (*BRIT*) n Watte f.
**couch** [kautʃ] n Couch f ♦ vt formulieren.
**couchette** [kuːˈʃɛt] n Liegewagen(platz) m.
**couch potato** (*esp US: inf*) n Dauerglotzer(in) m(f).
**cough** [kɔf] vi husten; (*engine*) stottern ♦ n Husten m.
**cough drop** n Hustenpastille f.
**cough mixture** n Hustensaft m.
**cough syrup** n = **cough mixture**.
**could** [kud] pt of **can²**.
**couldn't** ['kudnt] = **could not**.
**council** ['kaunsl] n Rat m; **city/town ~** Stadtrat m; **C~ of Europe** Europarat m.
**council estate** (*BRIT*) n Siedlung f mit Sozialwohnungen.
**council house** (*BRIT*) n Sozialwohnung f.
**council housing** n sozialer Wohnungsbau m; (*accommodation*) Sozialwohnungen pl.
**councillor** ['kaunslə*] n Stadtrat m, Stadträtin f.
**council tax** (*BRIT*) n Gemeindesteuer f.
**counsel** ['kaunsl] n Rat(schlag) m; (*lawyer*) Rechtsanwalt m, Rechtsanwältin f ♦ vt beraten; **to ~ sth** etw raten or empfehlen; **to ~ sb to do sth** jdm raten or empfehlen, etw zu tun; **~ for the defence** Verteidiger(in) m(f); **~ for the prosecution** Vertreter(in) m(f) der Anklage.
**counsellor** ['kaunslə*] n Berater(in) m(f); (*US: lawyer*) Rechtsanwalt m, Rechtsanwältin f.
**count** [kaunt] vt zählen; (*include*) mitrechnen, mitzählen ♦ vi zählen; (*be considered*) betrachtet or angesehen werden ♦ n Zählung f; (*level*) Zahl f; (*nobleman*) Graf m; **to ~ (up) to 10** bis 10 zählen; **not ~ing the children** die Kinder nicht mitgerechnet; **10 ~ing him** 10, wenn man ihn mitrechnet; **to ~ the cost of sth** die Folgen von etw abschätzen; **it ~s for very little** es zählt nicht viel; **~ yourself lucky** Sie können sich glücklich schätzen; **to keep ~ of sth** die Übersicht über etw acc behalten; **blood ~** Blutbild nt; **cholesterol/alcohol ~** Cholesterin-/Alkoholspiegel m.
►**count on** vt fus rechnen mit; (*depend on*) sich verlassen auf +acc; **to ~ on doing sth** die feste Absicht haben, etw zu tun.
►**count up** vt zusammenzählen, zusammenrechnen.
**countdown** ['kauntdaun] n Countdown m.
**countenance** ['kauntɪnəns] n Gesicht nt ♦ vt gutheißen.
**counter** ['kauntə*] n (*in shop*) Ladentisch m; (*in café*) Theke f; (*in bank, post office*) Schalter m; (*in game*) Spielmarke f; (*TECH*) Zähler m ♦ vt (*oppose: sth said, sth done*) begegnen +dat; (*blow*) kontern ♦ adv: **~ to** gegen +acc; **to buy sth under the ~** (*fig*) etw unter dem Ladentisch bekommen; **to ~ sth with sth** auf etw acc mit etw antworten; **to ~ sth by doing sth** einer Sache damit begegnen, daß man etw tut.
**counteract** ['kauntər'ækt] vt entgegenwirken +dat; (*effect*) neutralisieren.
**counterattack** ['kauntərə'tæk] n Gegenangriff m ♦ vi einen Gegenangriff starten.
**counterbalance** ['kauntə'bæləns] vt Gegengewicht nt.
**counterclockwise** ['kauntə'klɔkwaɪz] adv gegen den Uhrzeigersinn.
**counterespionage** ['kauntər'ɛspɪənaːʒ] n Gegenspionage f, Spionageabwehr f.
**counterfeit** ['kauntəfɪt] n Fälschung f ♦ vt fälschen ♦ adj (*coin*) Falsch-.
**counterfoil** ['kauntəfɔɪl] n Kontrollabschnitt m.
**counterintelligence** ['kauntərɪn'tɛlɪdʒəns] n Gegenspionage f, Spionageabwehr f.
**countermand** ['kauntəmaːnd] vt aufheben, widerrufen.
**countermeasure** ['kauntəmɛʒə*] n Gegenmaßnahme f.
**counteroffensive** ['kauntərə'fɛnsɪv] n Gegenoffensive f.
**counterpane** ['kauntəpeɪn] n Tagesdecke f.
**counterpart** ['kauntəpaːt] n Gegenüber nt; (*of document etc*) Gegenstück nt, Pendant nt.
**counterproductive** ['kauntəprə'dʌktɪv] adj widersinnig.
**counterproposal** ['kauntəprə'pəuzl] n Gegenvorschlag m.
**countersign** ['kauntəsaɪn] vt gegenzeichnen.
**countersink** ['kauntəsɪŋk] vt senken.
**countess** ['kauntɪs] n Gräfin f.
**countless** ['kauntlɪs] adj unzählig, zahllos.
**countrified** ['kʌntrɪfaɪd] adj ländlich.
**country** ['kʌntrɪ] n Land nt; (*native land*) Heimatland nt; **in the ~** auf dem Land; **mountainous ~** gebirgige Landschaft f.
**country and western (music)** n Country-und-Western-Musik f.
**country dancing** (*BRIT*) n Volkstanz m.
**country house** n Landhaus nt.
**countryman** ['kʌntrɪmən] (*irreg: like* **man**) n (*compatriot*) Landsmann m; (*country dweller*) Landmann m.
**countryside** ['kʌntrɪsaɪd] n Land nt; (*scenery*) Landschaft f, Gegend f.
**country-wide** ['kʌntrɪ'waɪd] adj, adv landesweit.
**county** ['kauntɪ] n (*BRIT*) Grafschaft f; (*US*) (Verwaltungs)bezirk m.
**county council** (*BRIT*) n Gemeinderat m (*einer Grafschaft*).

**county town** (*BRIT*) *n* Hauptstadt einer
Grafschaft.

**coup** [kuː] (*pl* ~s) *n* (*also*: ~ **d'état**) Staats-
streich *m*; Coup d'Etat *m*; (*achievement*)
Coup *m*.

**coupé** [kuː'peɪ] *n* Coupé *nt*.

**couple** ['kʌpl] *n* Paar *nt*; (*married couple*)
Ehepaar *nt* ♦ *vt* verbinden; (*vehicles*)
koppeln; **a ~ of** (*two*) zwei; (*a few*) ein paar.

**couplet** ['kʌplɪt] *n* Verspaar *nt*.

**coupling** ['kʌplɪŋ] *n* Kupplung *f*.

**coupon** ['kuːpɔn] *n* Gutschein *m*; (*detachable
form*) Abschnitt *m*; (*COMM*) Coupon *m*.

**courage** ['kʌrɪdʒ] *n* Mut *m*.

**courageous** [kə'reɪdʒəs] *adj* mutig.

**courgette** [kuə'ʒet] (*BRIT*) *n* Zucchino *m*.

**courier** ['kurɪə*] *n* (*messenger*) Kurier(in) *m(f)*;
(*for tourists*) Reiseleiter(in) *m(f)*.

**course** [kɔːs] *n* (*SCOL*) Kurs(us) *m*; (*of ship*)
Kurs *m*; (*of life, events, time etc, of river*) Lauf
*m*; (*of argument*) Richtung *f*; (*part of meal*)
Gang *m*; (*for golf*) Platz *m*; **of ~** natürlich; **of
~!** (*aber*) natürlich!, (*aber*)
selbstverständlich!; **(no) of ~** **not!** natürlich
nicht!; **in the ~ of the next few days**
während *or* im Laufe der nächsten paar
Tage; **in due ~** zu gegebener Zeit; **~ (of
action)** Vorgehensweise *f*; **the best ~ would
be to** ... das beste wäre es, zu ...; **we have no
other ~ but to** ... es bleibt uns nichts
anderes übrig, als zu ...; **~ of lectures**
Vorlesungsreihe *f*; **~ of treatment** (*MED*)
Behandlung *f*; **first/last ~** erster/letzter
Gang, Vor-/Nachspeise *f*.

**court** [kɔːt] *n* Hof *m*; (*LAW*) Gericht *nt*; (*for
tennis, badminton etc*) Platz *m* ♦ *vt* den Hof
machen +*dat*; (*favour, popularity*) werben um;
(*death, disaster*) herausfordern; **out of ~**
(*LAW*) außergerichtlich; **to take to ~** (*LAW*)
verklagen, vor Gericht bringen.

**courteous** ['kəːtɪəs] *adj* höflich.

**courtesan** [kɔːtɪ'zæn] *n* Kurtisane *f*.

**courtesy** ['kəːtəsɪ] *n* Höflichkeit *f*; **(by) ~ of**
freundlicherweise zur Verfügung gestellt
von.

**courtesy coach** *n* gebührenfreier Bus *m*.

**courtesy light** *n* Innenleuchte *f*.

**courthouse** ['kɔːthaus] (*US*) *n* Gerichts-
gebäude *nt*.

**courtier** ['kɔːtɪə*] *n* Höfling *m*.

**court martial** (*pl* **courts martial**) *n*
Militärgericht *nt*.

**court of appeal** (*pl* **courts of appeal**) *n*
Berufungsgericht *nt*.

**court of inquiry** (*pl* **courts of inquiry**) *n*
Untersuchungskommission *f*.

**courtroom** ['kɔːtrum] *n* Gerichtssaal *m*.

**court shoe** *n* Pumps *m*.

**courtyard** ['kɔːtjɑːd] *n* Hof *m*.

**cousin** ['kʌzn] *n* (*male*) Cousin *m*, Vetter *m*;
(*female*) Cousine *f*, Kusine *f*; **first ~**
Cousin(e) ersten Grades.

**cove** [kəuv] *n* (kleine) Bucht *f*.

**covenant** ['kʌvənənt] *n* Schwur *m* ♦ *vt*: **to
~ £200 per year to a charity** sich vertraglich
verpflichten, £200 im Jahr für wohltätige
Zwecke zu spenden.

**Coventry** ['kɔvəntrɪ] *n*: **to send sb to ~** (*fig*)
jdn schneiden (*inf*).

**cover** ['kʌvə*] *vt* bedecken; (*distance*)
zurücklegen; (*INSURANCE*) versichern;
(*topic*) behandeln; (*include*) erfassen;
(*PRESS: report on*) berichten über +*acc* ♦ *n*
(*for furniture*) Bezug *m*; (*for typewriter, PC etc*)
Hülle *f*; (*of book, magazine*) Umschlag *m*;
(*shelter*) Schutz *m*; (*INSURANCE*)
Versicherung *f*; (*fig: for illegal activities*)
Tarnung *f*; **to be ~ed in** *or* **with** bedeckt sein
mit; **£10 will ~ my expenses** £10 decken
meine Unkosten; **to take ~** (*from rain*) sich
unterstellen; **under ~** geschützt; **under ~ of
darkness** im Schutz(e) der Dunkelheit;
**under separate ~** getrennt.

▶**cover up** *vt* zudecken; (*fig: facts, feelings*)
verheimlichen; (: *mistakes*) vertuschen ♦ *vi*
(*fig*): **to ~ up for sb** jdn decken.

**coverage** ['kʌvərɪdʒ] *n* Berichterstattung *f*;
**television ~ of the conference**
Fernsehberichte *pl* über die Konferenz; **to
give full ~ to** ausführlich berichten über
+*acc*.

**coveralls** ['kʌvərɔːlz] (*US*) *npl* Overall *m*.

**cover charge** *n* Kosten *pl* für ein Gedeck.

**covering** ['kʌvərɪŋ] *n* Schicht *f*; (*of snow, dust
etc*) Decke *f*.

**covering letter,** (*US*) **cover letter** *n*
Begleitbrief *m*.

**cover note** *n* (*INSURANCE*) Deckungszusage
*f*.

**cover price** *n* Einzel(exemplar)preis *m*.

**covert** ['kʌvət] *adj* versteckt; (*glance*)
verstohlen.

**cover-up** ['kʌvərʌp] *n* Vertuschung *f*,
Verschleierung *f*.

**covet** ['kʌvɪt] *vt* begehren.

**cow** [kau] *n* (*animal, infl: woman*) Kuh *f* ♦ *cpd*
Kuh- ♦ *vt* einschüchtern.

**coward** ['kauəd] *n* Feigling *m*.

**cowardice** ['kauədɪs] *n* Feigheit *f*.

**cowardly** ['kauədlɪ] *adj* feige.

**cowboy** ['kaubɔɪ] *n* (*in US*) Cowboy *m*; (*pej:
tradesman*) Pfuscher *m*.

**cow elephant** *n* Elefantenkuh *f*.

**cower** ['kauə*] *vi* sich ducken; (*squatting*)
kauern.

**cowshed** ['kauʃed] *n* Kuhstall *m*.

**cowslip** ['kauslɪp] *n* Schlüsselblume *f*.

**cox** [kɔks] *n abbr* = **coxswain**.

**coxswain** ['kɔksn] *n* Steuermann *m*; (*of ship*)
Boot(s)führer *m*.

**coy** [kɔɪ] *adj* verschämt.

**coyote** [kɔɪ'əutɪ] *n* Kojote *m*.

**cozy** ['kəuzɪ] (*US*) *adj* = **cosy**.

**CP** *n abbr* (= *Communist Party*) KP *f*.

**cp.** abbr (= compare) vgl.

**c/p** (BRIT) abbr = **carriage paid.**

**CPA** (US) n abbr = **certified public accountant.**

**CPI** n abbr (= Consumer Price Index) (Verbraucher)preisindex m.

**Cpl** abbr (MIL) = **corporal.**

**CP/M** n abbr (= Control Program for Microprocessors) CP/M nt.

**cps** abbr (COMPUT, TYP: = characters per second) cps, Zeichen pl pro Sekunde.

**CPSA** (BRIT) n abbr (= Civil and Public Services Association) Gewerkschaft im öffentlichen Dienst.

**CPU** n abbr (COMPUT) = **central processing unit.**

**cr.** abbr = **credit; creditor.**

**crab** [kræb] n Krabbe f, Krebs m; (meat) Krabbe f.

**crab apple** n Holzapfel m.

**crack** [kræk] n (noise) Knall m; (of wood breaking) Knacks m; (gap) Spalte f; (in bone, dish, glass) Sprung m; (in wall) Riß m; (joke) Witz m; (DRUGS) Crack nt ♦ vt (whip) knallen mit; (twig) knacken mit; (dish, glass) einen Sprung machen in +acc; (bone) anbrechen; (nut, code) knacken; (wall) rissig machen; (problem) lösen; (joke) reißen ♦ adj erstklassig; **to have a ~ at sth** (inf) etw mal probieren; **to ~ jokes** (inf) Witze reißen; **to get ~ing** (inf) loslegen.

►**crack down on** vt fus hart durchgreifen gegen.

►**crack up** vi durchdrehen, zusammenbrechen.

**crackdown** ['krækdaun] n: ~ **(on)** scharfes Durchgreifen nt (gegen).

**cracked** [krækt] (inf) adj übergeschnappt.

**cracker** ['kræka⁺] n (biscuit) Kräcker m; (Christmas cracker) Knallbonbon nt; (firework) Knallkörper m, Kracher m; **a ~ of a ...** (BRIT: inf) ein(e) tolle(r, s) ...; **he's ~s** (BRIT: inf) er ist übergeschnappt.

**crackle** ['krækl] vi (fire) knistern, prasseln; (twig) knacken.

**crackling** ['kræklɪŋ] n (of fire) Knistern nt, Prasseln nt; (of twig, on radio, telephone) Knacken nt; (of pork) Kruste f (des Schweinebratens).

**crackpot** ['krækpɔt] (inf) n Spinner(in) m(f) ♦ adj verrückt.

**cradle** ['kreɪdl] n Wiege f ♦ vt fest in den Armen halten.

**craft** [krɑːft] n (skill) Geschicklichkeit f; (art) Kunsthandwerk nt; (trade) Handwerk nt; (pl inv: boat) Boot nt; (pl inv: plane) Flugzeug nt.

**craftsman** ['krɑːftsmən] (irreg: like man) n Handwerker m.

**craftsmanship** ['krɑːftsmənʃɪp] n handwerkliche Ausführung f.

**crafty** ['krɑːftɪ] adj schlau, clever.

**crag** [kræg] n Fels m.

**craggy** ['krægɪ] adj (mountain) zerklüftet;

(cliff) felsig; (face) kantig.

**cram** [kræm] vt vollstopfen ♦ vi pauken (inf), büffeln (inf); **to ~ with** vollstopfen mit; **to ~ sth into** etw hineinstopfen in +acc.

**cramming** ['kræmɪŋ] n (for exams) Pauken nt, Büffeln nt.

**cramp** [kræmp] n Krampf m ♦ vt hemmen.

**cramped** [kræmpt] adj eng.

**crampon** ['kræmpən] n Steigeisen nt.

**cranberry** ['krænbərɪ] n Preiselbeere f.

**crane** [kreɪn] n Kran m; (bird) Kranich m ♦ vt: **to ~ one's neck** den Hals recken ♦ vi: **to ~ forward** den Hals recken.

**crania** ['kreɪnɪə] npl of **cranium.**

**cranium** ['kreɪnɪəm] (pl **crania**) n Schädel m.

**crank** [kræŋk] n Spinner(in) m(f); (handle) Kurbel f.

**crankshaft** ['kræŋkʃɑːft] n Kurbelwelle f.

**cranky** ['kræŋkɪ] adj verrückt.

**cranny** ['krænɪ] n see **nook.**

**crap** [kræp] (inf!) n Scheiße f (!) ♦ vi scheißen (!); **to have a ~** scheißen (!).

**crappy** ['kræpɪ] (inf!) adj beschissen (!).

**crash** [kræʃ] n (noise) Krachen nt; (of car) Unfall m; (of plane etc) Unglück nt; (collision) Zusammenstoß m; (of stock market, business etc) Zusammenbruch m ♦ vt (car) einen Unfall haben mit; (plane etc) abstürzen mit ♦ vi (plane) abstürzen; (car) einen Unfall haben; (two cars) zusammenstoßen; (market) zusammenbrechen; (firm) Pleite machen; **to ~ into** krachen or knallen gegen; **he ~ed the car into a wall** er fuhr mit dem Auto gegen eine Mauer.

**crash barrier** (BRIT) n Leitplanke f.

**crash course** n Schnellkurs m, Intensivkurs m.

**crash helmet** n Sturzhelm m.

**crash-landing** ['kræʃlændɪŋ] n Bruchlandung f.

**crass** [kræs] adj kraß; (behaviour) unfein, derb.

**crate** [kreɪt] n (also inf) Kiste f; (for bottles) Kasten m.

**crater** ['kreɪtə⁺] n Krater m.

**cravat** [krə'væt] n Halstuch nt.

**crave** [kreɪv] vt, vi: **to ~ (for)** sich sehnen nach.

**craven** ['kreɪvən] adj feige.

**craving** ['kreɪvɪŋ] n: ~ **(for)** Verlangen nt (nach).

**crawl** [krɔːl] vi kriechen; (child) krabbeln ♦ n (SWIMMING) Kraulstil m, Kraul(en) nt; **to ~ to sb** (inf) vor jdm kriechen; **to drive along at a ~** im Schneckentempo or Kriechtempo vorankommen.

**crawler lane** (BRIT) n (AUT) Kriechspur f.

**crayfish** ['kreɪfɪʃ] n inv (freshwater) Flußkrebs m; (saltwater) Languste f.

**crayon** ['kreɪən] n Buntstift m.

**craze** [kreɪz] n Fimmel m; **to be all the ~** große Mode sein.

**crazed** [kreɪzd] adj wahnsinnig; (pottery, glaze) rissig.

**crazy** ['kreɪzɪ] *adj* wahnsinnig, verrückt; ~ **about sb/sth** (*inf*) verrückt *or* wild auf jdn/etw; **to go** ~ wahnsinnig *or* verrückt werden.

**crazy paving** (*BRIT*) *n* Mosaikpflaster *nt*.

**creak** [kri:k] *vi* knarren.

**cream** [kri:m] *n* Sahne *f*, Rahm *m* (*S Ger*); (*artificial cream, cosmetic*) Creme *f*; (*élite*) Crème *f*, Elite *f* ♦ *adj* cremefarben; **whipped** ~ Schlagsahne *f*.

▶**cream off** *vt* absahnen (*inf*).

**cream cake** *n* Sahnetorte *f*; (*small*) Sahnetörtchen *nt*.

**cream cheese** *n* (Doppelrahm)frischkäse *m*.

**creamery** ['kri:mərɪ] *n* (*shop*) Milchgeschäft *nt*; (*factory*) Molkerei *f*.

**creamy** ['kri:mɪ] *adj* (*colour*) cremefarben; (*taste*) sahnig.

**crease** [kri:s] *n* Falte *f*; (*in trousers*) Bügelfalte *f* ♦ *vt* zerknittern; (*forehead*) runzeln ♦ *vi* knittern; (*forehead*) sich runzeln.

**crease-resistant** ['kri:srɪzɪstənt] *adj* knitterfrei.

**create** [kri:'eɪt] *vt* schaffen; (*interest*) hervorrufen; (*problems*) verursachen; (*produce*) herstellen; (*design*) entwerfen, kreieren; (*impression, fuss vb*) machen.

**creation** [kri:'eɪʃən] *n* (*see vb*) Schaffung *f*; Hervorrufen *nt*; Verursachung *f*; Herstellung *f*; Entwurf *m*, Kreation *f*; (*REL*) Schöpfung *f*.

**creative** [kri:'eɪtɪv] *adj* kreativ, schöpferisch.

**creativity** [kri:eɪ'tɪvɪtɪ] *n* Kreativität *f*.

**creator** [kri:'eɪtə*] *n* Schöpfer(in) *m(f)*.

**creature** ['kri:tʃə*] *n* Geschöpf *nt*; (*living animal*) Lebewesen *nt*.

**creature comforts** [- 'kʌmfəts] *npl* Lebensgenüsse *pl*.

**crèche** [krɛʃ] *n* (Kinder)krippe *f*; (*all day*) (Kinder)tagesstätte *f*.

**credence** ['kri:dns] *n*: **to lend** *or* **give** ~ **to sth** etw glaubwürdig erscheinen lassen *or* machen.

**credentials** [krɪ'dɛnʃlz] *npl* Referenzen *pl*, Zeugnisse *pl*; (*papers of identity*) (Ausweis)papiere *pl*.

**credibility** [krɛdɪ'bɪlɪtɪ] *n* Glaubwürdigkeit *f*.

**credible** ['krɛdɪbl] *adj* glaubwürdig.

**credit** ['krɛdɪt] *n* (*loan*) Kredit *m*; (*recognition*) Anerkennung *f*; (*SCOL*) Schein *m* ♦ *adj* (*COMM: terms etc*) Kredit- ♦ *vt* (*COMM*) gutschreiben; (*believe: also*: **give** ~ **to**) glauben; **credits** *npl* (*CINE, TV: at beginning*) Vorspann *m*; (: *at end*) Nachspann *m*; **to be in** ~ (*person*) Geld auf dem Konto haben; (*bank account*) im Haben sein; **on** ~ auf Kredit; **it is to his** ~ **that** ... es ehrt ihn, daß ...; **to take the** ~ **for** das Verdienst in Anspruch nehmen für; **it does him** ~ es spricht für ihn; **he's a** ~ **to his family** er macht seiner Familie Ehre; **to** ~ **sb with sth** (*fig*) jdm etw zuschreiben; **to** ~ **£5 to sb** jdm £5 gutschreiben.

**creditable** ['krɛdɪtəbl] *adj* lobenswert, anerkennenswert.

**credit account** *n* Kreditkonto *nt*.

**credit agency** (*BRIT*) *n* Kreditauskunftei *f*.

**credit balance** *n* Kontostand *m*.

**credit bureau** (*US*) *n* = **credit agency**.

**credit card** *n* Kreditkarte *f*.

**credit control** *n* Kreditüberwachung *f*.

**credit facilities** *npl* (*COMM*) Kreditmöglichkeiten *pl*.

**credit limit** *n* Kreditgrenze *f*.

**credit note** (*BRIT*) *n* Gutschrift *f*.

**creditor** ['krɛdɪtə*] *n* Gläubiger *m*.

**credit transfer** *n* Banküberweisung *f*.

**creditworthy** ['krɛdɪt'wə:ðɪ] *adj* kreditwürdig.

**credulity** [krɪ'dju:lɪtɪ] *n* Leichtgläubigkeit *f*.

**creed** [kri:d] *n* Glaubensbekenntnis *nt*.

**creek** [kri:k] *n* (kleine) Bucht *f*; (*US: stream*) Bach *m*; **to be up the** ~ (*inf*) in der Tinte sitzen.

**creel** [kri:l] *n* (*also*: **lobster** ~) Hummer-(fang)korb *m*.

**creep** [kri:p] (*pt, pp* **crept**) *vi* schleichen; (*plant: horizontally*) kriechen; (: *vertically*) klettern ♦ *n* (*inf*) Kriecher *m*; **to** ~ **up on sb** sich an jdn heranschleichen; (*time etc*) langsam auf jdn zukommen; **he's a** ~ er ist ein widerlicher *or* fieser Typ; **it gives me the** ~**s** davon kriege ich das kalte Grausen.

**creeper** ['kri:pə*] *n* Kletterpflanze *f*.

**creepers** ['kri:pəz] (*US*) *npl* Schuhe mit weichen Sohlen.

**creepy** ['kri:pɪ] *adj* gruselig; (*experience*) unheimlich, gruselig.

**creepy-crawly** ['kri:pɪ'krɔ:lɪ] (*inf*) *n* Krabbeltier *nt*.

**cremate** [krɪ'meɪt] *vt* einäschern.

**cremation** [krɪ'meɪʃən] *n* Einäscherung *f*, Kremation *f*.

**crematoria** [krɛmə'tɔ:rɪə] *npl of* **crematorium**.

**crematorium** [krɛmə'tɔ:rɪəm] (*pl* **crematoria**) *n* Krematorium *nt*.

**creosote** ['krɪəsəut] *n* Kreosot *nt*.

**crepe** [kreɪp] *n* Krepp *m*, Crêpe *m*; (*rubber*) Krepp(gummi) *m*.

**crepe bandage** (*BRIT*) *n* elastische Binde *f*.

**crepe paper** *n* Kreppapier *nt*.

**crepe sole** *n* Kreppsohle *f*.

**crept** [krɛpt] *pt, pp of* **creep**.

**crescendo** [krɪ'ʃɛndəu] *n* Höhepunkt *m*; (*MUS*) Crescendo *nt*.

**crescent** ['krɛsnt] *n* Halbmond *m*; (*street*) halbkreisförmig verlaufende Straße.

**cress** [krɛs] *n* Kresse *f*.

**crest** [krɛst] *n* (*of hill*) Kamm *m*; (*of bird*) Haube *f*; (*coat of arms*) Wappen *nt*.

**crestfallen** ['krɛstfɔ:lən] *adj* niedergeschlagen.

**Crete** [kri:t] *n* Kreta *nt*.

**crevasse** [krɪ'væs] *n* Gletscherspalte *f*.

**crevice** ['krɛvɪs] n Spalte f.

**crew** [kru:] n Besatzung f; (TV, CINE) Crew f; (gang) Bande f.

**crew cut** n Bürstenschnitt m.

**crew neck** n runder (Hals)ausschnitt m.

**crib** [krɪb] n Kinderbett nt; (REL) Krippe f ♦ vt (inf: copy) abschreiben.

**cribbage** ['krɪbɪdʒ] n Cribbage nt.

**crib death** (US) n = cot death.

**crick** [krɪk] n Krampf m.

**cricket** ['krɪkɪt] n Kricket nt; (insect) Grille f.

**cricketer** ['krɪkɪtə'] n Kricketspieler(in) m(f).

**crime** [kraɪm] n (no pl: illegal activities) Verbrechen pl; (illegal action, fig) Verbrechen nt; **minor ~** kleinere Vergehen pl.

**crime wave** n Verbrechenswelle f.

**criminal** ['krɪmɪnl] n Kriminelle(r) f(m), Verbrecher(in) m(f) ♦ adj kriminell; **C~ Investigation Department** Kriminalpolizei f.

**criminal code** n Strafgesetzbuch nt.

**crimp** [krɪmp] vt kräuseln; (hair) wellen.

**crimson** ['krɪmzn] adj purpurrot.

**cringe** [krɪndʒ] vi (in fear) zurückweichen; (in embarrassment) zusammenzucken.

**crinkle** ['krɪŋkl] vt (zer)knittern.

**cripple** ['krɪpl] n Krüppel m ♦ vt zum Krüppel machen; (ship, plane) aktionsunfähig machen; (production, exports) lahmlegen, lähmen; **~d with rheumatism** von Rheuma praktisch gelähmt.

**crippling** ['krɪplɪŋ] adj (disease) schwer; (taxation, debts) erdrückend.

**crises** ['kraɪsi:z] npl of crisis.

**crisis** ['kraɪsɪs] (pl crises) n Krise f.

**crisp** [krɪsp] adj (vegetables etc) knackig; (bacon etc) knusprig; (weather) frisch; (manner, tone, reply) knapp.

**crisps** [krɪsps] (BRIT) npl Chips pl.

**crisscross** ['krɪskrɔs] adj (pattern) Kreuz- ♦ vt kreuz und quer durchziehen.

**criteria** [kraɪ'tɪərɪə] npl of criterion.

**criterion** [kraɪ'tɪərɪən] (pl criteria) n Kriterium nt.

**critic** ['krɪtɪk] n Kritiker(in) m(f).

**critical** ['krɪtɪkl] adj kritisch; **to be ~ of sb/sth** jdn/etw kritisieren; **he is in a ~ condition** sein Zustand ist kritisch.

**critically** ['krɪtɪklɪ] adv kritisch; (ill) schwer.

**criticism** ['krɪtɪsɪzəm] n Kritik f.

**criticize** ['krɪtɪsaɪz] vt kritisieren.

**critique** [krɪ'ti:k] n Kritik f.

**croak** [krəuk] vi (frog) quaken; (bird, person) krächzen.

**Croat** n Kroate m, Kroatin f; (LING) Kroatisch nt.

**Croatia** [krəu'eɪʃə] n Kroatien nt.

**Croatian** [krəu'eɪʃən] adj kroatisch.

**crochet** ['krəuʃeɪ] n (activity) Häkeln nt; (result) Häkelei f.

**crock** [krɔk] n Topf m; (inf: also: **old ~**) (vehicle)

Kiste f; (: person) Wrack nt.

**crockery** ['krɔkərɪ] n Geschirr nt.

**crocodile** ['krɔkədaɪl] n Krokodil nt.

**crocus** ['krəukəs] n Krokus m.

**croft** [krɔft] (BRIT) n kleines Pachtgut nt.

**crofter** ['krɔftə'] (BRIT) n Kleinpächter(in) m(f).

**crone** [krəun] n alte Hexe f.

**crony** ['krəunɪ] (inf: pej) n Kumpan(in) m(f).

**crook** [kruk] n (criminal) Gauner m; (of shepherd) Hirtenstab m; (of arm) Beuge f.

**crooked** ['krukɪd] adj krumm; (dishonest) unehrlich.

**crop** [krɔp] n (Feld)frucht f; (amount produced) Ernte f; (riding crop) Reitpeitsche f; (of bird) Kropf m ♦ vt (hair) stutzen; (subj: animal: grass) abfressen.

▶**crop up** vi aufkommen.

**cropper** ['krɔpə'] (inf) n: **to come a ~** hinfallen; (fig: fail) auf die Nase fallen.

**crop spraying** [-'spreɪɪŋ] n Schädlingsbekämpfung f (durch Besprühen).

**croquet** ['krəukeɪ] (BRIT) n Krocket nt.

**croquette** [krə'kɛt] n Krokette f.

**cross** [krɔs] n Kreuz nt; (BIOL, BOT) Kreuzung f ♦ vt (street) überqueren; (room etc) durchqueren; (cheque) zur Verrechnung ausstellen; (arms) verschränken; (legs) übereinanderschlagen; (animal, plant) kreuzen; (thwart: person) verärgern; (: plan) durchkreuzen ♦ adj ärgerlich, böse ♦ vi: **the boat ~es from ... to ...** das Schiff fährt von ... nach ...; **to ~ o.s.** sich bekreuzigen; **we have a ~ed line** (BRIT) es ist jemand in der Leitung; **they've got their lines** or **wires ~ed** (fig) sie reden aneinander vorbei; **to be/get ~ with sb (about sth)** mit jdm or auf jdn (wegen etw) böse sein/werden.

▶**cross out** vt streichen.

▶**cross over** vi hinübergehen.

**crossbar** ['krɔsbɑ:'] n (SPORT) Querlatte f; (of bicycle) Stange f.

**crossbow** n Armbrust f.

**crossbreed** ['krɔsbri:d] n Kreuzung f.

**cross-Channel ferry** ['krɔs'tʃænl-] n Kanalfähre f.

**crosscheck** ['krɔstʃɛk] n Gegenprobe f ♦ vt überprüfen.

**cross-country (race)** ['krɔs'kʌntrɪ-] n Querfeldeinrennen nt.

**cross-dressing** [krɔs'drɛsɪŋ] n (transvestism) Transvestismus m.

**cross-examination** ['krɔsɪgzæmɪ'neɪʃən] n Kreuzverhör nt.

**cross-examine** ['krɔsɪg'zæmɪn] vt ins Kreuzverhör nehmen.

**cross-eyed** ['krɔsaɪd] adj schielend; **to be ~** schielen.

**crossfire** ['krɔsfaɪə'] n Kreuzfeuer nt; **to get caught in the ~** (also fig) ins Kreuzfeuer geraten.

**crossing** ['krɔsɪŋ] n Überfahrt f; (also:

**pedestrian** ~) Fußgängerüberweg m.
**crossing guard** (US) n ≈ Schülerlotse m.
**crossing point** n Übergangsstelle f.
**cross-purposes** ['krɔs'pɔːpəsɪz] npl: **to be at ~ with sb** jdn mißverstehen; **we're (talking) at ~** wir reden aneinander vorbei.
**cross-question** ['krɔs'kwɛstʃən] vt ins Kreuzverhör nehmen.
**cross-reference** ['krɔs'rɛfrəns] n (Quer)verweis m.
**crossroads** ['krɔsrəudz] n Kreuzung f.
**cross section** n Querschnitt m.
**crosswalk** ['krɔswɔːk] (US) n Fußgängerüberweg m.
**crosswind** ['krɔswɪnd] n Seitenwind m.
**crosswise** ['krɔswaɪz] adv quer.
**crossword** ['krɔswɔːd] n (also: ~ **puzzle**) Kreuzworträtsel nt.
**crotch** [krɔtʃ] n Unterleib m; (of garment) Schritt m.
**crotchet** ['krɔtʃɪt] n Viertelnote f.
**crotchety** ['krɔtʃɪtɪ] adj reizbar.
**crouch** [krautʃ] vi kauern.
**croup** [kruːp] n (MED) Krupp m.
**croupier** ['kruːpɪəʳ] n Croupier m.
**crouton** ['kruːtɔn] n Crouton m.
**crow** [krəu] n (bird) Krähe f; (of cock) Krähen nt ♦ vi krähen; (fig) sich brüsten, angeben.
**crowbar** ['krəubɑːʳ] n Brechstange f.
**crowd** [kraud] n (Menschen)menge f ♦ vt (room, stadium) füllen ♦ vi: **to ~ round** sich herumdrängen; ~**s of people** Menschenmassen pl; **the/our ~** (of friends) die/unsere Clique f; **to ~ sb/sth in** jdn/etw hineinstopfen; **to ~ sb/sth into** jdn pferchen/etw stopfen in +acc; **to ~ in** sich hineindrängen.
**crowded** ['kraudɪd] adj überfüllt; (densely populated) dicht besiedelt; ~ **with** voll von.
**crowd scene** n Massenszene f.
**crown** [kraun] n (also of tooth) Krone f; (of head) Wirbel m; (of hill) Kuppe f; (of hat) Kopf m ♦ vt krönen; (tooth) überkronen; **the C~** die Krone; **and to ~ it all ...** (fig) und zur Krönung des Ganzen ...

---

Crown Court ist ein Strafgericht, das in etwa 90 verschiedenen Städten in England und Wales zusammentritt. Schwere Verbrechen wie Mord, Totschlag, Vergewaltigung und Raub werden nur vor dem crown court unter Vorsitz eines Richters mit Geschworenen verhandelt.

---

**crowning** ['kraunɪŋ] adj krönend.
**crown jewels** npl Kronjuwelen pl.
**crown prince** n Kronprinz m.
**crow's-feet** ['krəuzfiːt] npl Krähenfüße pl.
**crow's-nest** ['krəuznɛst] n Krähennest nt, Mastkorb m.
**crucial** ['kruːʃl] adj (decision) äußerst wichtig; (vote) entscheidend; ~ **to** äußerst wichtig für.

**crucifix** ['kruːsɪfɪks] n Kruzifix nt.
**crucifixion** [kruːsɪ'fɪkʃən] n Kreuzigung f.
**crucify** ['kruːsɪfaɪ] vt kreuzigen; (fig) in der Luft zerreißen.
**crude** [kruːd] adj (oil, fibre) Roh-; (fig: basic) primitiv; (: vulgar) ordinär ♦ n = **crude oil.**
**crude oil** n Rohöl nt.
**cruel** ['kruəl] adj grausam.
**cruelty** ['kruəltɪ] n Grausamkeit f.
**cruet** ['kruːɪt] n Gewürzständer m.
**cruise** [kruːz] n Kreuzfahrt f ♦ vi (ship) kreuzen; (car) (mit Dauergeschwindigkeit) fahren; (aircraft) (mit Reisegeschwindigkeit) fliegen; (taxi) gemächlich fahren.
**cruise missile** n Marschflugkörper m.
**cruiser** ['kruːzəʳ] n Motorboot nt; (warship) Kreuzer m.
**cruising speed** n Reisegeschwindigkeit f.
**crumb** [krʌm] n Krümel m; (fig: of information) Brocken m; **a ~ of comfort** ein winziger Trost.
**crumble** ['krʌmbl] vt (bread) zerbröckeln; (biscuit etc) zerkrümeln ♦ vi (building, earth etc) zerbröckeln; (plaster) abbröckeln; (fig: opposition) sich auflösen; (: belief) ins Wanken geraten.
**crumbly** ['krʌmblɪ] adj krümelig.
**crummy** ['krʌmɪ] (inf) adj mies.
**crumpet** ['krʌmpɪt] n Teekuchen m (zum Toasten).
**crumple** ['krʌmpl] vt zerknittern.
**crunch** [krʌntʃ] vt (biscuit, apple etc) knabbern; (underfoot) zertreten ♦ n: **the ~** der große Krach; **if it comes to the ~** wenn es wirklich dahin kommt; **when the ~ comes** wenn es hart auf hart geht.
**crunchy** ['krʌntʃɪ] adj knusprig; (apple etc) knackig; (gravel, snow etc) knirschend.
**crusade** [kruː'seɪd] n Feldzug m ♦ vi: **to ~ for/ against sth** für/gegen etw zu Felde ziehen.
**crusader** [kruː'seɪdəʳ] n Kreuzritter m; (fig): ~ **(for)** Apostel m (+gen).
**crush** [krʌʃ] n (crowd) Gedränge nt ♦ vt quetschen; (grapes) zerquetschen; (paper, clothes) zerknittern; (garlic, ice) (zer)stoßen; (defeat) niederschlagen; (devastate) vernichten; **to have a ~ on sb** (love) für jdn schwärmen; **lemon ~** Zitronensaftgetränk nt.
**crush barrier** (BRIT) n Absperrung f.
**crushing** ['krʌʃɪŋ] adj vernichtend.
**crust** [krʌst] n Kruste f.
**crustacean** [krʌs'teɪʃən] n Schalentier nt, Krustazee f.
**crusty** ['krʌstɪ] adj knusprig.
**crutch** [krʌtʃ] n Krücke f; (support) Stütze f; see also **crotch.**
**crux** [krʌks] n Kern m.
**cry** [kraɪ] vi weinen; (also: ~ **out**) aufschreien ♦ n Schrei m; (shout) Ruf m; **what are you ~ing about?** warum weinst du?; **to ~ for**

help um Hilfe rufen; **she had a good ~** sie hat sich (mal richtig) ausgeweint; **it's a far ~ from** ... *(fig)* das ist etwas ganz anderes als ...

▶**cry off** *(inf) vi* absagen.

**crying** ['kraııŋ] *adj (fig: need)* dringend; **it's a ~ shame** es ist ein Jammer.

**crypt** [krıpt] *n* Krypta *f*.

**cryptic** ['krıptık] *adj* hintergründig, rätselhaft; *(clue)* verschlüsselt.

**crystal** ['krıstl] *n* Kristall *m*; *(glass)* Kristall(glas) *nt*.

**crystal clear** *adj* glasklar.

**crystallize** ['krıstəlaız] *vt (opinion, thoughts)* (feste) Form geben *+dat* ♦ *vi (sugar etc)* kristallisieren; **~d fruits** *(BRIT)* kandierte Früchte *pl*.

**CSA** *n abbr (= Child Support Agency)* Amt zur Regelung von Unterhaltszahlungen für Kinder.

**CSC** *n abbr (= Civil Service Commission)* Einstellungsbehörde für den öffentlichen Dienst.

**CSE** *(BRIT) n abbr (formerly: = Certificate of Secondary Education) Schulabschlußzeugnis,* ≈ mittlere Reife *f*.

**CS gas** *(BRIT) n* ≈ Tränengas *nt*.

**CST** *(US) abbr (= Central Standard Time) mittelamerikanische Standardzeit.*

**CT** *(US) abbr (POST: = Connecticut).*

**ct** *abbr* = **carat.**

**CTC** *(BRIT) n abbr* = **city technology college.**

**CT scanner** *n abbr (MED: = computerized tomography scanner)* CT-Scanner *m*.

**cu.** *abbr* = **cubic.**

**cub** [kʌb] *n* Junge(s) *nt*; *(also:* ~ **scout)** Wölfling *m*.

**Cuba** ['kju:bə] *n* Kuba *nt*.

**Cuban** ['kju:bən] *adj* kubanisch ♦ *n* Kubaner(in) *m(f)*.

**cubbyhole** ['kʌbıhəul] *n (room)* Kabuff *nt*; *(space)* Eckchen *nt*.

**cube** [kju:b] *n* Würfel *m*; *(MATH: of number)* dritte Potenz *f* ♦ *vt (MATH)* in die dritte Potenz erheben, hoch drei nehmen.

**cube root** *n* Kubikwurzel *f*.

**cubic** ['kju:bık] *adj (volume)* Kubik-; **~ metre** *etc* Kubikmeter *m etc*.

**cubic capacity** *n* Hubraum *m*.

**cubicle** ['kju:bıkl] *n* Kabine *f*; *(in hospital)* Bettnische *f*.

**cuckoo** ['kuku:] *n* Kuckuck *m*.

**cuckoo clock** *n* Kuckucksuhr *f*.

**cucumber** ['kju:kʌmbə˙] *n* Gurke *f*.

**cud** [kʌd] *n*: **to chew the ~** *(animal)* wiederkäuen; *(fig: person)* vor sich *acc* hin grübeln.

**cuddle** ['kʌdl] *vt* in den Arm nehmen, drücken ♦ *vi* schmusen.

**cuddly** ['kʌdlı] *adj (toy)* zum Liebhaben *or* Drücken; *(person)* knuddelig *(inf)*.

**cudgel** ['kʌdʒl] *n* Knüppel *m* ♦ *vt*: **to ~ one's**

brains sich *dat* das (Ge)hirn zermartern.

**cue** [kju:] *n (SPORT)* Billardstock *m*, Queue *nt*; *(THEAT: word)* Stichwort *nt*; (: *action)* (Einsatz)zeichen *nt*; *(MUS)* Einsatz *m*.

**cuff** [kʌf] *n (of sleeve)* Manschette *f*; *(US: of trousers)* Aufschlag *m*; *(blow)* Klaps *m* ♦ *vt* einen Klaps geben *+dat*; **off the ~** aus dem Stegreif.

**cuff links** *npl* Manschettenknöpfe *pl*.

**cu. in.** *abbr (= cubic inches)* Kubikzoll.

**cuisine** [kwı'zi:n] *n* Küche *f*.

**cul-de-sac** ['kʌldəsæk] *n* Sackgasse *f*.

**culinary** ['kʌlınərı] *adj (skill)* Koch-; *(delight)* kulinarisch.

**cull** [kʌl] *vt* (zusammen)sammeln; *(animals)* ausmerzen ♦ *n Erlegen überschüssiger Tierbestände.*

**culminate** ['kʌlmıneıt] *vi*: **to ~ in** gipfeln in *+dat*.

**culmination** [kʌlmı'neıʃən] *n* Höhepunkt *m*.

**culottes** [kju:'lɒts] *npl* Hosenrock *m*.

**culpable** ['kʌlpəbl] *adj* schuldig.

**culprit** ['kʌlprıt] *n* Täter(in) *m(f)*.

**cult** [kʌlt] *n* Kult *m*.

**cult figure** *n* Kultfigur *f*.

**cultivate** ['kʌltıveıt] *vt (land)* bebauen, landwirtschaftlich nutzen; *(crop)* anbauen; *(feeling)* entwickeln; *(person)* sich *dat* warmhalten *(inf)*, die Beziehung pflegen zu.

**cultivation** [kʌltı'veıʃən] *n (of land)* Bebauung *f*, landwirtschaftliche Nutzung *f*; *(of crop)* Anbau *m*.

**cultural** ['kʌltʃərəl] *adj* kulturell.

**culture** ['kʌltʃə˙] *n* Kultur *f*.

**cultured** ['kʌltʃəd] *adj* kultiviert; *(pearl)* Zucht-.

**cumbersome** ['kʌmbəsəm] *adj (suitcase etc)* sperrig, unhandlich; *(piece of machinery)* schwer zu handhaben; *(clothing)* hinderlich; *(process)* umständlich.

**cumin** ['kʌmın] *n* Kreuzkümmel *m*.

**cumulative** ['kju:mjulətıv] *adj (effect, result)* Gesamt-.

**cunning** ['kʌnıŋ] *n* Gerissenheit *f* ♦ *adj* gerissen; *(device, idea)* schlau.

**cunt** [kʌnt] *(inf!) n (vagina)* Fotze *f* (*!*); *(term of abuse)* Arsch *m* (*!*).

**cup** [kʌp] *n* Tasse *f*; *(as prize)* Pokal *m*; *(of bra)* Körbchen *nt*; **a ~ of tea** eine Tasse Tee.

**cupboard** ['kʌbəd] *n* Schrank *m*.

**cup final** *(BRIT) n* Pokalendspiel *nt*.

**cupful** ['kʌpful] *n* Tasse *f*.

**Cupid** ['kju:pıd] *n* Amor *m*; *(figurine)* Amorette *f*.

**cupidity** [kju:'pıdıtı] *n* Begierde *f*, Gier *f*.

**cupola** ['kju:pələ] *n* Kuppel *f*.

**cuppa** ['kʌpə] *(BRIT: inf) n* Tasse *f* Tee.

**cup tie** *(BRIT) n* Pokalspiel *nt*.

**curable** ['kjuərəbl] *adj* heilbar.

**curate** ['kjuərıt] *n* Vikar *m*.

**curator** [kjuə'reıtə˙] *n* Kustos *m*.

**curb** [kə:b] *vt* einschränken; *(person)* an die

Kandare nehmen ♦ n Einschränkung f; (US: kerb) Bordstein m.
**curd cheese** n Weißkäse m.
**curdle** ['kɔːdl] vi gerinnen.
**curds** [kɔːdz] npl ≈ Quark m.
**cure** [kjuə*] vt heilen; (CULIN: salt) pökeln; (: smoke) räuchern; (: dry) trocknen; (problem) abhelfen +dat ♦ n (remedy) (Heil)mittel nt; (treatment) Heilverfahren nt; (solution) Abhilfe f; **to be ~d of sth** von etw geheilt sein.
**cure-all** ['kjuərɔːl] n (also fig) Allheilmittel nt.
**curfew** ['kɔːfjuː] n Ausgangssperre f; (time) Sperrstunde f.
**curio** ['kjuərɪəu] n Kuriosität f.
**curiosity** [kjuərɪ'ɒsɪtɪ] n (see adj) Wißbegier(de) f; Neugier f; Merkwürdigkeit f.
**curious** ['kjuərɪəs] adj (interested) wißbegierig; (nosy) neugierig; (strange, unusual) sonderbar, merkwürdig; **I'm ~ about him** ich bin gespannt auf ihn.
**curiously** ['kjuərɪəslɪ] adv neugierig; (inquisitively) wißbegierig; **~ enough, ...** merkwürdigerweise ...
**curl** [kɔːl] n Locke f; (of smoke etc) Kringel m ♦ vt (hair: loosely) locken; (: tightly) kräuseln ♦ vi sich locken; sich kräuseln; (smoke) sich kringeln.
►**curl up** vi sich zusammenrollen.
**curler** ['kɔːlə*] n Lockenwickler m; (SPORT) Curlingspieler(in) m(f).
**curlew** ['kɔːluː] n Brachvogel m.
**curling** ['kɔːlɪŋ] n (SPORT) Curling nt.
**curling tongs,** (US) **curling irons** npl Lockenschere f, Brennschere f.
**curly** ['kɔːlɪ] adj lockig; (tightly curled) kraus.
**currant** ['kʌrnt] n Korinthe f; (blackcurrant, redcurrant) Johannisbeere f.
**currency** ['kʌrnsɪ] n (system) Währung f; (money) Geld nt; **foreign ~** Devisen pl; **to gain ~** (fig) sich verbreiten, um sich greifen.
**current** ['kʌrnt] n Strömung f; (ELEC) Strom m; (of opinion) Tendenz f, Trend m ♦ adj gegenwärtig; (expression) gebräuchlich; (idea, custom) verbreitet; **direct/alternating ~** (ELEC) Gleich-/Wechselstrom m; **the ~ issue of a magazine** die neueste or letzte Nummer einer Zeitschrift; **in ~ use** allgemein gebräuchlich.
**current account** (BRIT) n Girokonto nt.
**current affairs** npl Tagespolitik f.
**current assets** npl (COMM) Umlaufvermögen nt.
**current liabilities** npl (COMM) kurzfristige Verbindlichkeiten pl.
**currently** ['kʌrntlɪ] adv zur Zeit.
**curricula** [kə'rɪkjulə] npl of **curriculum**.
**curriculum** [kə'rɪkjuləm] (pl **~s** or **curricula**) n Lehrplan m.
**curriculum vitae** [-'viːtaɪ] n Lebenslauf m.

**curry** ['kʌrɪ] n (dish) Currygericht nt ♦ vt: **to ~ favour with** sich einschmeicheln bei.
**curry powder** n Curry m or nt, Currypulver nt.
**curse** [kɔːs] vi fluchen ♦ vt verfluchen ♦ n Fluch m.
**cursor** ['kɔːsə*] n (COMPUT) Cursor m.
**cursory** ['kɔːsərɪ] adj flüchtig; (examination) oberflächlich.
**curt** [kɔːt] adj knapp, kurz angebunden.
**curtail** [kɔː'teɪl] vt einschränken; (visit etc) abkürzen.
**curtain** ['kɔːtn] n Vorhang m; (net) Gardine f; **to draw the ~s** (together) die Vorhänge zuziehen; (apart) die Vorhänge aufmachen.
**curtain call** n (THEAT) Vorhang m.
**curts(e)y** ['kɔːtsɪ] vi knicksen ♦ n Knicks m.
**curvature** ['kɔːvətʃə*] n Krümmung f.
**curve** [kɔːv] n Bogen m; (in the road) Kurve f ♦ vi einen Bogen machen; (surface, arch) sich wölben ♦ vt biegen.
**curved** [kɔːvd] adj (line) gebogen; (table legs etc) geschwungen; (surface, arch, sides of ship) gewölbt.
**cushion** ['kuʃən] n Kissen nt ♦ vt dämpfen; (seat) polstern.
**cushy** ['kuʃɪ] (inf) adj: **a ~ job** ein gemütlicher or ruhiger Job; **to have a ~ time** eine ruhige Kugel schieben.
**custard** ['kʌstəd] n (for pouring) Vanillesoße f.
**custard powder** (BRIT) n Vanillesoßenpulver nt.
**custodial** [kʌs'təudɪəl] adj: **~ sentence** Gefängnisstrafe f.
**custodian** [kʌs'təudɪən] n Verwalter(in) m(f); (of museum etc) Aufseher(in) m(f), Wächter(in) m(f).
**custody** ['kʌstədɪ] n (of child) Vormundschaft f; (for offenders) (polizeilicher) Gewahrsam m, Haft f; **to take into ~** verhaften; **in the ~ of** unter der Obhut +gen; **the mother has ~ of the children** die Kinder sind der Mutter zugesprochen worden.
**custom** ['kʌstəm] n Brauch m; (habit) (An)gewohnheit f; (LAW) Gewohnheitsrecht nt; (COMM) Kundschaft f.
**customary** ['kʌstəmərɪ] adj (conventional) üblich; (habitual) gewohnt; **it is ~ to do it** es ist üblich, es zu tun.
**custom-built** ['kʌstəm'bɪlt] adj spezialangefertigt.
**customer** ['kʌstəmə*] n Kunde m, Kundin f; **he's an awkward ~** (inf) er ist ein schwieriger Typ.
**customer profile** n Kundenprofil nt.
**customized** ['kʌstəmaɪzd] adj individuell aufgemacht.
**custom-made** ['kʌstəm'meɪd] adj (shirt etc) maßgefertigt, nach Maß; (car etc) spezialangefertigt.
**customs** ['kʌstəmz] npl Zoll m; **to go through (the) ~** durch den Zoll gehen.

**Customs and Excise** (*BRIT*) *n* die Zollbehörde *f*.

**customs duty** *n* Zoll *m*.

**customs officer** *n* Zollbeamte(r) *m*, Zollbeamtin *f*.

**cut** [kʌt] (*pt, pp* **cut**) *vt* schneiden; (*text, programme, spending*) kürzen; (*prices*) senken, heruntersetzen, herabsetzen; (*supply*) einschränken; (*cloth*) zuschneiden; (*road*) schlagen, hauen; (*inf: lecture, appointment*) schwänzen ♦ *vi* schneiden; (*lines*) sich schneiden ♦ *n* Schnitt *m*; (*in skin*) Schnittwunde *f*; (*in salary, spending etc*) Kürzung *f*; (*of meat*) Stück *nt*; (*of jewel*) Schnitt *m*, Schliff *m*; **to ~ a tooth** zahnen, einen Zahn bekommen; **to ~ one's finger/ hand/knee** sich den Finger/in die Hand/ am Knie schneiden; **to get one's hair ~** sich *dat* die Haare schneiden lassen; **to ~ sth short** etw vorzeitig abbrechen; **to ~ sb dead** jdn wie Luft behandeln; **cold ~s** (*US*) Aufschnitt *m*; **power ~** Stromausfall *m*.

►**cut back** *vt* (*plants*) zurückschneiden; (*production*) zurückschrauben; (*expenditure*) einschränken.

►**cut down** *vt* (*tree*) fällen; (*consumption*) einschränken; **to ~ sb down to size** (*fig*) jdn auf seinen Platz verweisen.

►**cut down on** *vt fus* einschränken.

►**cut in** *vi* (*AUT*) sich direkt vor ein anderes Auto setzen; **to ~ in (on)** (*conversation*) sich einschalten (in +*acc*).

►**cut off** *vt* abschneiden; (*supply*) sperren; (*TEL*) unterbrechen; **we've been ~ off** (*TEL*) wir sind unterbrochen worden.

►**cut out** *vt* ausschneiden; (*an activity etc*) aufhören mit; (*remove*) herausschneiden.

►**cut up** *vt* kleinschneiden; **it really ~ me up** (*inf*) es hat mich ziemlich mitgenommen; **to feel ~ up about sth** (*inf*) betroffen über etw *acc* sein.

**cut and dried** *adj* (*also*: **cut-and-dry**: *answer*) eindeutig; (: *solution*) einfach.

**cutaway** [ˈkʌtəweɪ] *n* (*coat*) Cut(away) *m*; (*drawing*) Schnittdiagramm *m*; (*model*) Schnittmodell *nt*; (*CINE, TV*) Schnitt *m*.

**cutback** [ˈkʌtbæk] *n* Kürzung *f*.

**cute** [kjuːt] *adj* süß, niedlich; (*clever*) schlau.

**cut glass** *n* geschliffenes Glas *nt*.

**cuticle** [ˈkjuːtɪkl] *n* Nagelhaut *f*; **~ remover** Nagelhautentferner *m*.

**cutlery** [ˈkʌtlərɪ] *n* Besteck *nt*.

**cutlet** [ˈkʌtlɪt] *n* Schnitzel *nt*; (*vegetable cutlet, nut cutlet*) Bratling *m*.

**cutoff** [ˈkʌtɔf] *n* (*also*: **~ point**) Trennlinie *f*.

**cutoff switch** *n* Ausschaltmechanismus *m*.

**cutout** [ˈkʌtaut] *n* (*switch*) Unterbrecher *m*; (*shape*) Ausschneidemodell *nt*; (*paper figure*) Ausschneidepuppe *f*.

**cut-price** [ˈkʌtˈpraɪs] *adj* (*goods*) heruntergesetzt; (*offer*) Billig-.

**cut-rate** [ˈkʌtˈreɪt] (*US*) *adj* = **cut-price**.

**cutthroat** [ˈkʌtθrəut] *n* Mörder(in) *m(f)* ♦ *adj* unbarmherzig, mörderisch.

**cutting** [ˈkʌtɪŋ] *adj* (*edge, remark*) scharf ♦ *n* (*BRIT: from newspaper*) Ausschnitt *m*; (: *RAIL*) Durchstich *m*; (*from plant*) Ableger *m*.

**cutting edge** *n* (*fig*) Spitzenstellung *f*; **on the ~ (of)** an der Spitze +*gen*.

**cuttlefish** [ˈkʌtlfɪʃ] *n* Tintenfisch *m*.

**CV** *n abbr* = **curriculum vitae**.

**c.w.o.** *abbr* (*COMM*) = **cash with order**.

**cwt** *abbr* = **hundredweight**.

**cyanide** [ˈsaɪənaɪd] *n* Zyanid *nt*.

**cybernetics** [saɪbəˈnɛtɪks] *n* Kybernetik *f*.

**cyclamen** [ˈsɪkləmən] *n* Alpenveilchen *nt*.

**cycle** [ˈsaɪkl] *n* (*bicycle*) (Fahr)rad *nt*; (*series: of seasons, songs etc*) Zyklus *m*; (: *of events*) Gang *m*; (: *TECH*) Periode *f* ♦ *vi* radfahren.

**cycle race** *n* Radrennen *nt*.

**cycle rack** *n* Fahrradständer *m*.

**cycling** [ˈsaɪklɪŋ] *n* Radfahren *nt*; **to go on a ~ holiday** (*BRIT*) Urlaub mit dem Fahrrad machen.

**cyclist** [ˈsaɪklɪst] *n* (Fahr)radfahrer(in) *m(f)*.

**cyclone** [ˈsaɪkləun] *n* Zyklon *m*.

**cygnet** [ˈsɪgnɪt] *n* Schwanjunge(s) *nt*.

**cylinder** [ˈsɪlɪndə*] *n* Zylinder *m*; (*of gas*) Gasflasche *f*.

**cylinder block** *n* Zylinderblock *m*.

**cylinder head** *n* Zylinderkopf *m*.

**cylinder-head gasket** [ˈsɪlɪndəhɛd-] *n* Zylinderkopfdichtung *f*.

**cymbals** [ˈsɪmblz] *npl* (*MUS*) Becken *nt*.

**cynic** [ˈsɪnɪk] *n* Zyniker(in) *m(f)*.

**cynical** [ˈsɪnɪkl] *adj* zynisch.

**cynicism** [ˈsɪnɪsɪzəm] *n* Zynismus *m*.

**CYO** (*US*) *n abbr* (= *Catholic Youth Organization*) katholische Jugendorganisation.

**cypress** [ˈsaɪprɪs] *n* Zypresse *f*.

**Cypriot** [ˈsɪprɪət] *adj* zypriotisch, zyprisch ♦ *n* Zypriot(in) *m(f)*.

**Cyprus** [ˈsaɪprəs] *n* Zypern *nt*.

**cyst** [sɪst] *n* Zyste *f*.

**cystitis** [sɪsˈtaɪtɪs] *n* Blasenentzündung *f*, Zystitis *f*.

**CZ** (*US*) *n abbr* (= *Canal Zone*) *Bereich des Panamakanals*.

**czar** [zɑː*] *n* = **tsar**.

**Czech** [tʃɛk] *adj* tschechisch ♦ *n* Tscheche *m*, Tschechin *f*; (*language*) Tschechisch *nt*; **the ~ Republic** die Tschechische Republik *f*.

**Czechoslovak** [tʃɛkəˈsləuvæk] *adj, n* = **Czechoslovak(ian)**.

**Czechoslovakia** [tʃɛkəsləˈvækɪə] *n* (*formerly*) die Tschechoslowakei *f*.

**Czechoslovak(ian)** [tʃɛkəˈsləuvæk, tʃɛkəsləˈvækɪən] (*formerly*) *adj* tschechoslowakisch ♦ *n* Tschechoslowake *m*, Tschechoslowakin *f*.

# D, d

**D¹, d¹** [di:] n (letter) D nt, d nt; ~ **for David,** (US) ~ **for Dog** ≈ D wie Dora.

**D²** [di:] n (MUS) D nt, d nt.

**D³** [di:] (US) abbr (POL) = **democrat; democratic.**

**d²** (BRIT: formerly) abbr = **penny.**

**d.** abbr (= died): **Henry Jones,** ~ **1754** Henry Jones, gest. 1754.

**DA** (US) n abbr = **district attorney.**

**dab** [dæb] vt betupfen; (paint, cream) tupfen ♦ n Tupfer m; **to be a** ~ **hand at sth** gut in etw dat sein; **to be a** ~ **hand at doing sth** sich darauf verstehen, etw zu tun.

▶**dab at** vt betupfen.

**dabble** ['dæbl] vi: **to** ~ **in** sich (nebenbei) beschäftigen mit.

**dachshund** ['dækshund] n Dackel m.

**dad** [dæd] (inf) n Papa m, Vati m.

**daddy** ['dædɪ] (inf) n = **dad.**

**daddy-longlegs** [dædɪ'lɒŋlɛgz] (inf) n Schnake f.

**daffodil** ['dæfədɪl] n Osterglocke f, Narzisse f.

**daft** [dɑːft] (inf) adj doof (inf), blöd (inf); **to be** ~ **about sb/sth** verrückt nach jdm/etw sein.

**dagger** ['dægə'] n Dolch m; **to be at** ~**s drawn with sb** mit jdm auf Kriegsfuß stehen; **to look** ~**s at sb** jdn mit Blicken durchbohren.

**dahlia** ['deɪljə] n Dahlie f.

**daily** ['deɪlɪ] adj täglich; (wages) Tages- ♦ n (paper) Tageszeitung f; (BRIT: also: ~ **help**) Putzfrau f ♦ adv täglich; **twice** ~ zweimal täglich or am Tag.

**dainty** ['deɪntɪ] adj zierlich.

**dairy** ['dɛərɪ] n (BRIT: shop) Milchgeschäft nt; (company) Molkerei f; (on farm) Milchkammer f ♦ cpd Milch-; (herd, industry, farming) Milchvieh-.

**dairy farm** n auf Milchviehhaltung spezialisierter Bauernhof.

**dairy products** npl Milchprodukte pl, Molkereiprodukte pl.

**dairy store** (US) n Milchgeschäft nt.

**dais** ['deɪɪs] n Podium nt.

**daisy** ['deɪzɪ] n Gänseblümchen nt.

**daisywheel** ['deɪzɪwiːl] n Typenrad nt.

**daisywheel printer** n Typenraddrucker m.

**Dakar** ['dækə'] n Dakar nt.

**dale** [deɪl] (BRIT) n Tal nt.

**dally** ['dælɪ] vi (herum)trödeln; **to** ~ **with** (plan, idea) spielen mit.

**dalmatian** [dæl'meɪʃən] n Dalmatiner m.

**dam** [dæm] n (Stau)damm m; (reservoir)

Stausee m ♦ vt stauen.

**damage** ['dæmɪdʒ] n Schaden m ♦ vt schaden +dat; (spoil, break) beschädigen; **damages** npl (LAW) Schaden(s)ersatz m; ~ **to property** Sachbeschädigung f; **to pay £5,000 in** ~**s** 5000 Pfund Schaden(s)ersatz (be)zahlen.

**damaging** ['dæmɪdʒɪŋ] adj: ~ **(to)** schädlich (für).

**Damascus** [də'mɑːskəs] n Damaskus nt.

**dame** [deɪm] n Dame f; (US: inf) Weib nt; (THEAT) (komische) Alte f (von einem Mann gespielt).

**damn** [dæm] vt verfluchen; (condemn) verurteilen ♦ adj (inf: also: ~**ed**) verdammt ♦ n (inf): **I don't give a** ~ das ist mir scheißegal (!); ~ **(it)!** verdammt (noch mal)!

**damnable** ['dæmnəbl] adj gräßlich.

**damnation** [dæm'neɪʃən] n Verdammnis f ♦ excl (inf) verdammt.

**damning** ['dæmɪŋ] adj belastend.

**damp** [dæmp] adj feucht ♦ n Feuchtigkeit f ♦ vt (also: ~**en**) befeuchten, anfeuchten; (enthusiasm etc) dämpfen.

**dampcourse** ['dæmpkɔːs] n Dämmschicht f.

**damper** ['dæmpə'] n (MUS) Dämpfer m; (of fire) (Luft)klappe f; **to put a** ~ **on** (fig) einen Dämpfer aufsetzen +dat.

**dampness** ['dæmpnɪs] n Feuchtigkeit f.

**damson** ['dæmzən] n Damaszenerpflaume f.

**dance** [dɑːns] n Tanz m; (social event) Tanz(abend) m ♦ vi tanzen; **to** ~ **about** (herum)tänzeln.

**dance hall** n Tanzsaal m.

**dancer** ['dɑːnsə'] n Tänzer(in) m(f).

**dancing** ['dɑːnsɪŋ] n Tanzen nt ♦ cpd (teacher, school, class etc) Tanz-.

**D and C** n abbr (MED: = dilation and curettage) Ausschabung f.

**dandelion** ['dændɪlaɪən] n Löwenzahn m.

**dandruff** ['dændrəf] n Schuppen pl.

**dandy** ['dændɪ] n Dandy m ♦ adj (US: inf) prima.

**Dane** [deɪn] n Däne m, Dänin f.

**danger** ['deɪndʒə'] n Gefahr f; **there is** ~ **of fire/poisoning** es besteht Feuer-/ Vergiftungsgefahr; **there is a** ~ **of sth happening** es besteht die Gefahr, daß etw geschieht; "~!" „Achtung!"; **in** ~ in Gefahr; **to be in** ~ **of doing sth** Gefahr laufen, etw zu tun; **out of** ~ außer Gefahr.

**danger list** n: **on the** ~ in Lebensgefahr.

**dangerous** ['deɪndʒrəs] adj gefährlich.

**dangerously** ['deɪndʒrəslɪ] adv gefährlich; (close) bedenklich; ~ **ill** schwer krank.

**danger zone** n Gefahrenzone f.

**dangle** ['dæŋgl] vt baumeln lassen ♦ vi baumeln.

**Danish** ['deɪnɪʃ] adj dänisch ♦ n (LING) Dänisch nt.

**Danish pastry** n Plundergebäck nt.

**dank** [dæŋk] adj (unangenehm) feucht.

**Danube** ['dænjuːb] n: **the** ~ die Donau.

**dapper** ['dæpə•] *adj* gepflegt.
**Dardanelles** [dɑːdə'nɛlz] *npl:* **the ~** die Dardanellen *pl.*
**dare** [dɛə•] *vt:* **to ~ sb to do sth** jdn dazu herausfordern, etw zu tun ♦ *vi:* **to ~ (to) do sth** es wagen, etw zu tun; **I ~n't tell him** (*BRIT*) ich wage nicht, es ihm zu sagen; **I ~ say** ich nehme an.
**daredevil** ['dɛədɛvl] *n* Draufgänger *m.*
**Dar-es-Salaam** ['dɑːrɛssə'lɑːm] *n* Daressalam *nt.*
**daring** ['dɛərɪŋ] *adj* kühn, verwegen; (*bold*) gewagt ♦ *n* Kühnheit *f.*
**dark** [dɑːk] *adj* dunkel; (*look*) finster ♦ *n:* **in the ~** im Dunkeln; **to be in the ~ about** (*fig*) keine Ahnung haben von; **after ~** nach Einbruch der Dunkelheit; **it is/is getting ~** es ist/wird dunkel; **~ chocolate** Zartbitterschokolade *f.*
**Dark Ages** *npl:* **the ~** das finstere Mittelalter.
**darken** ['dɑːkn] *vt* dunkel machen ♦ *vi* sich verdunkeln.
**dark glasses** *npl* Sonnenbrille *f.*
**dark horse** *n* (*fig: in competition*) Unbekannte(r) *f(m)* (mit Außenseiterchancen); (*quiet person*) stilles Wasser *nt.*
**darkly** ['dɑːklɪ] *adv* finster.
**darkness** ['dɑːknɪs] *n* Dunkelheit *f,* Finsternis *f.*
**darkroom** ['dɑːkrum] *n* Dunkelkammer *f.*
**darling** ['dɑːlɪŋ] *adj* lieb ♦ *n* Liebling *m;* **to be the ~ of** der Liebling +*gen* sein; **she is a ~** sie ist ein Schatz.
**darn** [dɑːn] *vt* stopfen.
**dart** [dɑːt] *n* (*in game*) (Wurf)pfeil *m;* (*in sewing*) Abnäher *m* ♦ *vi:* **to ~ towards** (*also:* **make a ~ towards**) zustürzen auf +*acc;* **to ~ away/along** davon-/entlangflitzen.
**dartboard** ['dɑːtbɔːd] *n* Dartscheibe *f.*
**darts** [dɑːts] *n* Darts *nt,* Pfeilwurfspiel *nt.*
**dash** [dæʃ] *n* (*sign*) Gedankenstrich *m;* (*rush*) Jagd *f* ♦ *vt* (*throw*) schleudern; (*hopes*) zunichte machen ♦ *vi:* **to ~ towards** zustürzen auf +*acc;* **a ~ of ...** (*small quantity*) etwas ..., ein Schuß *m* ...; **to make a ~ for sth** auf etw *acc* zustürzen; **we'll have to make a ~ for it** wir müssen rennen, so schnell wir können.
▶**dash away** *vi* losstürzen.
▶**dash off** *vi* = **dash away.**
**dashboard** ['dæʃbɔːd] *n* Armaturenbrett *nt.*
**dashing** ['dæʃɪŋ] *adj* flott.
**dastardly** ['dæstədlɪ] *adj* niederträchtig.
**DAT** *n abbr* (= *digital audio tape*) DAT *nt.*
**data** ['deɪtə] *npl* Daten *pl.*
**database** ['deɪtəbeɪs] *n* Datenbank *f.*
**data capture** *n* Datenerfassung *f.*
**data processing** *n* Datenverarbeitung *f.*
**data transmission** *n* Datenübertragung *f.*
**date** [deɪt] *n* Datum *nt;* (*with friend*) Verabredung *f;* (*fruit*) Dattel *f* ♦ *vt* datieren; (*person*) ausgehen mit; **what's the ~ today?**

der Wievielte ist heute?; **~ of birth** Geburtsdatum *nt;* **closing ~** Einsendeschluß *m;* **to ~** bis heute; **out of ~** altmodisch; (*expired*) abgelaufen; **up to ~** auf dem neuesten Stand; **to bring up to ~** auf den neuesten Stand bringen; (*person*) über den neuesten Stand der Dinge informieren; **a letter ~d 5th July** *or* (*US*) **July 5th** ein vom 5. Juli datierter Brief.
**dated** ['deɪtɪd] *adj* altmodisch.
**dateline** ['deɪtlaɪn] *n* (*GEOG*) Datumsgrenze *f;* (*PRESS*) Datumszeile *f.*
**date rape** *n* Vergewaltigung *f* einer Bekannten (*mit der der Täter eine Verabredung hatte*).
**date stamp** *n* Datumsstempel *m.*
**dative** ['deɪtɪv] *n* Dativ *m.*
**daub** [dɔːb] *vt* schmieren; **to ~ with** beschmieren mit.
**daughter** ['dɔːtə•] *n* Tochter *f.*
**daughter-in-law** ['dɔːtərɪnlɔː] *n* Schwiegertochter *f.*
**daunt** [dɔːnt] *vt* entmutigen.
**daunting** ['dɔːntɪŋ] *adj* entmutigend.
**dauntless** ['dɔːntlɪs] *adj* unerschrocken, beherzt.
**dawdle** ['dɔːdl] *vi* trödeln; **to ~ over one's work** bei der Arbeit bummeln *or* trödeln.
**dawn** [dɔːn] *n* Tagesanbruch *m,* Morgengrauen *nt;* (*of period*) Anbruch *m* ♦ *vi* dämmern; (*fig*): **it ~ed on him that ...** es dämmerte ihm, daß ...; **from ~ to dusk** von morgens bis abends.
**dawn chorus** (*BRIT*) *n* Morgenkonzert *nt* der Vögel.
**day** [deɪ] *n* Tag *m;* (*heyday*) Zeit *f;* **the ~ before/after** am Tag zuvor/danach; **the ~ after tomorrow** übermorgen; **the ~ before yesterday** vorgestern; **(on) the following ~** am Tag danach; **the ~ that ...** (am Tag,) als ...; **~ by ~** jeden Tag, täglich; **by ~** tagsüber; **paid by the ~** tageweise bezahlt; **to work an eight hour ~** einen Achtstundentag haben; **these ~s, in the present ~** heute, heutzutage.
**daybook** ['deɪbuk] (*BRIT*) *n* Journal *nt.*
**dayboy** ['deɪbɔɪ] *n* Externe(r) *m.*
**daybreak** ['deɪbreɪk] *n* Tagesanbruch *m.*
**day-care centre** ['deɪkeə-] *n* (*for children*) (Kinder)tagesstätte *f;* (*for old people*) Altentagesstätte *f.*
**daydream** ['deɪdriːm] *vi* (mit offenen Augen) träumen ♦ *n* Tagtraum *m,* Träumerei *f.*
**daygirl** ['deɪgɜːl] *n* Externe *f.*
**daylight** ['deɪlaɪt] *n* Tageslicht *nt.*
**daylight robbery** (*inf*) *n* Halsabschneiderei *f.*
**daylight-saving time** (*US*) *n* Sommerzeit *f.*
**day release** *n:* **to be on ~** tageweise (zur Weiterbildung) freigestellt sein.
**day return** (*BRIT*) *n* Tagesrückfahrkarte *f.*
**day shift** *n* Tagschicht *f.*
**daytime** ['deɪtaɪm] *n* Tag *m;* **in the ~**

tagsüber, bei Tage.

**day-to-day** ['deɪtə'deɪ] *adj* täglich, Alltags-; **on a ~ basis** tageweise.

**day trip** *n* Tagesausflug *m*.

**day-tripper** ['deɪ'trɪpə*] *n* Tagesausflügler(in) *m(f)*.

**daze** [deɪz] *vt* benommen machen ♦ *n*: **in a ~** ganz benommen.

**dazed** [deɪzd] *adj* benommen.

**dazzle** ['dæzl] *vt* blenden.

**dazzling** ['dæzlɪŋ] *adj* (*light*) blendend; (*smile*) strahlend; (*career, achievements*) glänzend.

**DC** *abbr* = **direct current**; (*US: POST*: = *District of Columbia*).

**DCC** *n abbr* (= *digital compact cassette*) DCC *f*.

**DD** *n abbr* (= *Doctor of Divinity*) ≈ Dr. theol.

**D/D** *abbr* = **direct debit**.

**dd.** *abbr* (*COMM*: = *delivered*) geliefert.

**D-day** ['diːdeɪ] *n* der Tag X.

**DDS** (*US*) *n abbr* (= *Doctor of Dental Surgery*) ≈ Dr. med. dent.

**DDT** *n abbr* (= *dichlorodiphenyltrichloroethane*) DDT *nt*.

**DE** (*US*) *abbr* (*POST*: = *Delaware*).

**DEA** (*US*) *n abbr* (= *Drug Enforcement Administration*) *amerikanische Drogenbehörde*.

**deacon** ['diːkən] *n* Diakon *m*.

**dead** [dɛd] *adj* tot; (*flowers*) verwelkt; (*numb*) abgestorben, taub; (*battery*) leer; (*place*) wie ausgestorben ♦ *adv* total, völlig; (*directly, exactly*) genau ♦ *npl*: **the ~** die Toten *pl*; **to shoot sb ~** jdn erschießen; **~ silence** Totenstille *f*; **in the ~ centre (of)** genau in der Mitte +*gen*; **the line has gone ~** (*TEL*) die Leitung ist tot; **~ on time** auf die Minute pünktlich; **~ tired** todmüde; **to stop ~** abrupt stehenbleiben.

**dead beat** (*inf*) *adj* (*tired*) völlig kaputt.

**deaden** [dɛdn] *vt* (*blow*) abschwächen; (*pain*) mildern; (*sound*) dämpfen.

**dead end** *n* Sackgasse *f*.

**dead-end** ['dɛdɛnd] *adj*: **a ~ job** ein Job *m* ohne Aufstiegsmöglichkeiten.

**dead heat** *n*: **to finish in a ~** unentschieden ausgehen.

**dead letter office** *n* Amt *nt* für unzustellbare Briefe.

**deadline** ['dɛdlaɪn] *n* (letzter) Termin *m*; **to work to a ~** auf einen Termin hinarbeiten.

**deadlock** ['dɛdlɔk] *n* Stillstand *m*; **the meeting ended in ~** die Verhandlung war festgefahren.

**dead loss** (*inf*) *n*: **to be a ~** ein hoffnungsloser Fall sein.

**deadly** ['dɛdlɪ] *adj* tödlich ♦ *adv*: **~ dull** tödlich langweilig.

**deadpan** ['dɛdpæn] *adj* (*look*) unbewegt; (*tone*) trocken.

**Dead Sea** *n*: **the ~** das Tote Meer.

**dead season** *n* tote Saison *f*.

**deaf** [dɛf] *adj* taub; (*partially*) schwerhörig; **to**

**turn a ~ ear to sth** sich einer Sache *dat* gegenüber taub stellen.

**deaf aid** (*BRIT*) *n* Hörgerät *nt*.

**deaf-and-dumb** ['dɛfən'dʌm] *adj* taubstumm; **~ alphabet** Taubstummensprache *f*.

**deafen** ['dɛfn] *vt* taub machen.

**deafening** ['dɛfnɪŋ] *adj* ohrenbetäubend.

**deaf-mute** ['dɛfmjuːt] *n* Taubstumme(r) *f(m)*.

**deafness** ['dɛfnɪs] *n* Taubheit *f*.

**deal** [diːl] (*pt, pp* **dealt**) *n* Geschäft *nt*, Handel *m* ♦ *vt* (*blow*) versetzen; (*card*) geben, austeilen; **to strike a ~ with sb** ein Geschäft mit jdm abschließen; **it's a ~!** (*inf*) abgemacht!; **he got a fair/bad ~ from them** er ist von ihnen anständig/schlecht behandelt worden; **a good ~** (*a lot*) ziemlich viel; **a great ~ (of)** ziemlich viel.

▶**deal in** *vt fus* handeln mit.

▶**deal with** *vt fus* (*person*) sich kümmern um; (*problem*) sich befassen mit; (*successfully*) fertigwerden mit; (*subject*) behandeln.

**dealer** ['diːlə*] *n* Händler(in) *m(f)*; (*in drugs*) Dealer *m*; (*CARDS*) Kartengeber(in) *m(f)*.

**dealership** ['diːləʃɪp] *n* (Vertrags)händler *m*.

**dealings** ['diːlɪŋz] *npl* Geschäfte *pl*; (*relations*) Beziehungen *pl*.

**dealt** [dɛlt] *pt, pp of* **deal**.

**dean** [diːn] *n* Dekan *m*; (*US: SCOL: administrator*) Schul- oder Collegeverwalter mit Beratungs- und Disziplinarfunktion.

**dear** [dɪə*] *adj* lieb; (*expensive*) teuer ♦ *n*: **(my) ~** (mein) Liebling *m* ♦ *excl*: **~ me!** (ach) du liebe Zeit!; **D~ Sir/Madam** Sehr geehrte Damen und Herren; **D~ Mr/Mrs X** Sehr geehrter Herr/geehrte Frau X; (*less formal*) Lieber Herr/Liebe Frau X.

**dearly** ['dɪəlɪ] *adv* (*love*) von ganzem Herzen; (*pay*) teuer.

**dear money** *n* (*COMM*) teures Geld *nt*.

**dearth** [dəːθ] *n*: **a ~ of** ein Mangel *m* an +*dat*.

**death** [dɛθ] *n* Tod *m*; (*fatality*) Tote(r) *f(m)*, Todesfall *m*.

**deathbed** ['dɛθbɛd] *n*: **to be on one's ~** auf dem Sterbebett liegen.

**death certificate** *n* Sterbeurkunde *f*, Totenschein *m*.

**deathly** ['dɛθlɪ] *adj* (*silence*) eisig ♦ *adv* (*pale etc*) toten-.

**death penalty** *n* Todesstrafe *f*.

**death rate** *n* Sterbeziffer *f*.

**death row** [-rəu] (*US*) *n* Todestrakt *m*.

**death sentence** *n* Todesurteil *nt*.

**death squad** *n* Todeskommando *nt*.

**death toll** *n* Zahl *f* der Todesopfer *or* Toten.

**deathtrap** ['dɛθtræp] *n* Todesfalle *f*.

**deb** [dɛb] (*inf*) *n abbr* = **debutante**.

**debacle** [deɪ'bɑːkl] *n* Debakel *nt*.

**debar** [dɪ'bɑː*] *vt*: **to ~ sb from doing sth** jdn davon ausschließen, etw zu tun; **to ~ sb from a club** jdn aus einem Klub ausschließen.

**debase** [dɪ'beɪs] *vt* (*value, quality*) mindern,

herabsetzen; (*person*) erniedrigen, entwürdigen.

**debatable** [dɪˈbeɪtəbl] *adj* fraglich.

**debate** [dɪˈbeɪt] *n* Debatte *f* ♦ *vt* debattieren über +*acc*; (*course of action*) überlegen ♦ *vi*: **to** ~ **whether** hin und her überlegen, ob.

**debauchery** [dɪˈbɔːtʃərɪ] *n* Ausschweifungen *pl*.

**debenture** [dɪˈbɛntʃəˈ] *n* Schuldschein *m*.

**debilitate** [dɪˈbɪlɪteɪt] *vt* schwächen.

**debilitating** [dɪˈbɪlɪteɪtɪŋ] *adj* schwächend.

**debit** [ˈdɛbɪt] *n* Schuldposten *m* ♦ *vt*: **to** ~ **a sum to sb/sb's account** jdn/jds Konto mit einer Summe belasten; *see also* **direct**.

**debit balance** *n* Sollsaldo *nt*, Debetsaldo *nt*.

**debit note** *n* Lastschriftanzeige *f*.

**debonair** *adj* flott.

**debrief** [diːˈbriːf] *vt* befragen.

**debriefing** [diːˈbriːfɪŋ] *n* Befragung *f*.

**debris** [ˈdɛbriː] *n* Trümmer *pl*, Schutt *m*.

**debt** [dɛt] *n* Schuld *f*; (*state of owing money*) Schulden *pl*, Verschuldung *f*; **to be in** ~ Schulden haben, verschuldet sein; **bad** ~ uneinbringliche Forderung *f*.

**debt collector** *n* Inkassobeauftragte(r) *f(m)*, Schuldeneintreiber(in) *m(f)*.

**debtor** [ˈdɛtəˈ] *n* Schuldner(in) *m(f)*.

**debug** [diːˈbʌg] *vt* (*COMPUT*) Fehler beseitigen in +*dat*.

**debunk** [diːˈbʌŋk] *vt* (*myths, ideas*) bloßstellen; (*claim*) entlarven; (*person, institution*) vom Sockel stoßen.

**debut** [ˈdeɪbjuː] *n* Debüt *nt*.

**debutante** [ˈdɛbjutænt] *n* Debütantin *f*.

**Dec.** *abbr* = **December.**

**decade** [ˈdɛkeɪd] *n* Jahrzehnt *nt*.

**decadence** [ˈdɛkədəns] *n* Dekadenz *f*.

**decadent** [ˈdɛkədənt] *adj* dekadent.

**decaff** [ˈdiːkæf] *n* koffeinfreier Kaffee *m*.

**decaffeinated** [dɪˈkæfɪneɪtɪd] *adj* koffeinfrei.

**decamp** [dɪˈkæmp] (*inf*) *vi* verschwinden, sich aus dem Staub machen.

**decant** [dɪˈkænt] *vt* umfüllen.

**decanter** [dɪˈkæntəˈ] *n* Karaffe *f*.

**decarbonize** [diːˈkɑːbənaɪz] *vt* entkohlen.

**decathlon** [dɪˈkæθlən] *n* Zehnkampf *m*.

**decay** [dɪˈkeɪ] *n* Verfall *m*; (*of tooth*) Fäule *f* ♦ *vi* (*body*) verwesen; (*teeth*) faulen; (*leaves*) verrotten; (*fig: society etc*) verfallen.

**decease** [dɪˈsiːs] *n* (*LAW*): **upon your** ~ bei Ihrem Ableben.

**deceased** [dɪˈsiːst] *n*: **the** ~ der/die Tote *or* Verstorbene.

**deceit** [dɪˈsiːt] *n* Betrug *m*.

**deceitful** [dɪˈsiːtful] *adj* betrügerisch.

**deceive** [dɪˈsiːv] *vt* täuschen; (*husband, wife etc*) betrügen; **to** ~ **o.s.** sich *dat* etwas vormachen.

**decelerate** [diːˈsɛləreɪt] *vi* (*car etc*) langsamer werden; (*driver*) die Geschwindigkeit herabsetzen.

**December** [dɪˈsɛmbəˈ] *n* Dezember *m*; *see also* July.

**decency** [ˈdiːsənsɪ] *n* (*propriety*) Anstand *m*; (*kindness*) Anständigkeit *f*.

**decent** [ˈdiːsənt] *adj* anständig; **we expect you to do the** ~ **thing** wir erwarten, daß Sie die Konsequenzen ziehen; **they were very** ~ **about it** sie haben sich sehr anständig verhalten; **that was very** ~ **of him** das war sehr anständig von ihm; **are you** ~? (*dressed*) hast du etwas an?

**decently** [ˈdiːsəntlɪ] *adv* anständig.

**decentralization** [ˈdiːsɛntrəlaɪˈzeɪʃən] *n* Dezentralisierung *f*.

**decentralize** [diːˈsɛntrəlaɪz] *vt* dezentralisieren.

**deception** [dɪˈsɛpʃən] *n* Täuschung *f*, Betrug *m*.

**deceptive** [dɪˈsɛptɪv] *adj* irreführend, täuschend.

**decibel** [ˈdɛsɪbɛl] *n* Dezibel *nt*.

**decide** [dɪˈsaɪd] *vt* entscheiden; (*persuade*) veranlassen ♦ *vi* sich entscheiden; **to** ~ **to do sth/that** beschließen, etw zu tun/daß; **to** ~ **on sth** sich für etw entscheiden; **to** ~ **on/against doing sth** sich dafür/dagegen entscheiden, etw zu tun.

**decided** [dɪˈsaɪdɪd] *adj* entschieden; (*character*) entschlossen; (*difference*) deutlich.

**decidedly** [dɪˈsaɪdɪdlɪ] *adv* entschieden; (*emphatically*) entschlossen.

**deciding** [dɪˈsaɪdɪŋ] *adj* entscheidend.

**deciduous** [dɪˈsɪdjuəs] *adj* (*tree, woods*) Laub-.

**decimal** [ˈdɛsɪməl] *adj* (*system, number*) Dezimal- ♦ *n* Dezimalzahl *f*; **to three** ~ **places** auf drei Dezimalstellen.

**decimalize** [ˈdɛsɪməlaɪz] (*BRIT*) *vt* auf das Dezimalsystem umstellen.

**decimal point** *n* Komma *nt*.

**decimate** [ˈdɛsɪmeɪt] *vt* dezimieren.

**decipher** [dɪˈsaɪfəˈ] *vt* entziffern.

**decision** [dɪˈsɪʒən] *n* Entscheidung *f*; (*decisiveness*) Bestimmtheit *f*, Entschlossenheit *f*; **to make a** ~ eine Entscheidung treffen.

**decisive** [dɪˈsaɪsɪv] *adj* (*action etc*) entscheidend; (*person*) entschlußfreudig; (*manner, reply*) bestimmt, entschlossen.

**deck** [dɛk] *n* Deck *nt*; (*record deck*) Plattenspieler *m*; (*of cards*) Spiel *nt*; **to go up on** ~ an Deck gehen; **below** ~ unter Deck; **top** ~ (*of bus*) Oberdeck *nt*; **cassette** ~ Tape-deck *nt*.

**deck chair** *n* Liegestuhl *m*.

**deck hand** *n* Deckshelfer(in) *m(f)*.

**declaration** [dɛkləˈreɪʃən] *n* Erklärung *f*.

**declare** [dɪˈklɛəˈ] *vt* erklären; (*result*) bekanntgeben, veröffentlichen; (*income etc*) angeben; (*goods at customs*) verzollen.

**declassify** [diːˈklæsɪfaɪ] *vt* freigeben.

**decline** [dɪˈklaɪn] *n* Rückgang *m*; (*decay*) Verfall *m* ♦ *vt* ablehnen ♦ *vi* (*strength*) nachlassen; (*business*) zurückgehen; (*old*

*person*) abbauen; ~ **in/of** Rückgang *m* +*gen*;
~ **in living standards** Sinken *nt* des
Lebensstandards.
**declutch** ['diːˈklʌtʃ] *vi* auskuppeln.
**decode** ['diːˈkəud] *vt* entschlüsseln.
**decoder** [diːˈkəudə•] *n* Decoder *m*.
**decompose** [diːkəmˈpəuz] *vi* (*organic matter*)
sich zersetzen; (*corpse*) verwesen.
**decomposition** [diːkɔmpəˈzɪʃən] *n*
Zersetzung *f*.
**decompression** [diːkəmˈprɛʃən] *n*
Dekompression *f*, Druckverminderung *f*.
**decompression chamber** *n*
Dekompressionskammer *f*.
**decongestant** [diːkənˈdʒɛstənt] *n* (*MED*)
abschwellendes Mittel *nt*; (: *drops*)
Nasentropfen *pl*.
**decontaminate** [diːkənˈtæmɪneɪt] *vt*
entgiften.
**decontrol** [diːkənˈtrəul] *vt* freigeben.
**décor** ['deɪkɔː•] *n* Ausstattung *f*; (*THEAT*)
Dekor *m or nt*.
**decorate** ['dɛkəreɪt] *vt*: **to** ~ **(with)** verzieren
(mit); (*tree, building*) schmücken (mit) ♦ *vt*
(*room, house: from bare walls*) anstreichen
und tapezieren; (*redecorate*) renovieren.
**decoration** [dɛkəˈreɪʃən] *n* Verzierung *f*; (*on
tree, building*) Schmuck *m*; (*act: see verb*)
Verzieren *nt*; Schmücken *nt*; (An)streichen
*nt*; Tapezieren *nt*; (*medal*) Auszeichnung *f*.
**decorative** ['dɛkərətɪv] *adj* dekorativ.
**decorator** ['dɛkəreɪtə•] *n* Maler(in) *m(f)*,
Anstreicher(in) *m(f)*.
**decorum** [dɪˈkɔːrəm] *n* Anstand *m*.
**decoy** ['diːkɔɪ] *n* Lockvogel *m*; (*object*) Köder
*m*; **they used him as a** ~ **for the enemy** sie
benutzten ihn dazu, den Feind anzulocken.
**decrease** ['diːkriːs] *vt* verringern, reduzieren
♦ *vi* abnehmen, zurückgehen ♦ *n*: ~ **(in)**
Abnahme *f* (+*gen*); Rückgang *m* (+*gen*); **to be
on the** ~ abnehmen, zurückgehen.
**decreasing** [diːˈkriːsɪŋ] *adj* abnehmend,
zurückgehend.
**decree** [dɪˈkriː] *n* (*ADMIN, LAW*) Verfügung *f*;
(*POL*) Erlaß *m*; (*REL*) Dekret *nt* ♦ *vt*: **to**
~ **(that)** verfügen(, daß), verordnen(, daß).
**decree absolute** *n* endgültiges
Scheidungsurteil *nt*.
**decree nisi** [-ˈnaɪsaɪ] *n* vorläufiges
Scheidungsurteil *nt*.
**decrepit** [dɪˈkrɛpɪt] *adj* (*shack*) baufällig;
(*person*) klapprig (*inf*).
**decry** [dɪˈkraɪ] *vt* schlechtmachen.
**dedicate** ['dɛdɪkeɪt] *vt*: **to** ~ **to** widmen +*dat*.
**dedicated** ['dɛdɪkeɪtɪd] *adj* hingebungsvoll,
engagiert; (*COMPUT*) dediziert; ~ **word
processor** dediziertes
Textverarbeitungssystem *nt*.
**dedication** [dɛdɪˈkeɪʃən] *n* Hingabe *f*; (*in book,
on radio*) Widmung *f*.
**deduce** [dɪˈdjuːs] *vt*: **to** ~ **(that)** schließen(,
daß), folgern(, daß).

**deduct** [dɪˈdʌkt] *vt* abziehen; **to** ~ **sth (from)**
etw abziehen (von); (*esp from wage etc*) etw
einbehalten (von).
**deduction** [dɪˈdʌkʃən] *n* (*act of deducting*)
Abzug *m*; (*act of deducing*) Folgerung *f*.
**deed** [diːd] *n* Tat *f*; (*LAW*) Urkunde *f*; ~ **of
covenant** Vertragsurkunde *f*.
**deem** [diːm] *vt* (*formal*) erachten für, halten
für; **to** ~ **it wise/helpful to do sth** es für
klug/hilfreich halten, etw zu tun.
**deep** [diːp] *adj* tief ♦ *adv*: **the spectators stood
20** ~ die Zuschauer standen in 20 Reihen
hintereinander; **to be 4 metres** ~ 4 Meter
tief sein; **knee-**~ **in water** bis zu den Knien
im Wasser; **he took a** ~ **breath** er holte tief
Luft.
**deepen** ['diːpn] *vt* vertiefen ♦ *vi* (*crisis*) sich
verschärfen; (*mystery*) größer werden.
**deepfreeze** ['diːpˈfriːz] *n* Tiefkühltruhe *f*.
**deep-fry** ['diːpˈfraɪ] *vt* fritieren.
**deeply** ['diːplɪ] *adv* (*breathe*) tief; (*interested*)
höchst; (*moved, grateful*) zutiefst.
**deep-rooted** ['diːpˈruːtɪd] *adj* tief verwurzelt;
(*habit*) fest eingefahren.
**deep-sea** ['diːpˈsiː] *cpd* Tiefsee-; (*fishing*)
Hochsee-.
**deep-seated** ['diːpˈsiːtɪd] *adj* tiefsitzend.
**deep-set** ['diːpsɛt] *adj* tiefliegend.
**deer** [dɪə•] *n inv* Reh *nt*; (*male*) Hirsch *m*; (**red**)
~ Rotwild *nt*; (**roe**) ~ Reh *m*; (**fallow**) ~
Damwild *nt*.
**deerskin** ['dɪəskɪn] *n* Hirschleder *nt*, Rehleder
*nt*.
**deerstalker** ['dɪəstɔːkə•] *n* ≈ Sherlock-
Holmes-Mütze *f*.
**deface** [dɪˈfeɪs] *vt* (*with paint etc*) beschmieren;
(*slash, tear*) zerstören.
**defamation** [dɛfəˈmeɪʃən] *n* Diffamierung *f*,
Verleumdung *f*.
**defamatory** [dɪˈfæmətrɪ] *adj* diffamierend,
verleumderisch.
**default** [dɪˈfɔːlt] *n* (*also*: ~ **value**)
Voreinstellung *f* ♦ *vi*: **to** ~ **on a debt** einer
Zahlungsverpflichtung nicht nachkommen;
**to win by** ~ kampflos gewinnen.
**defaulter** [dɪˈfɔːltə•] *n* säumiger Zahler *m*,
säumige Zahlerin *f*.
**default option** *n* Voreinstellung *f*.
**defeat** [dɪˈfiːt] *vt* besiegen, schlagen ♦ *n*
(*failure*) Niederlage *f*; (*of enemy*): ~ **(of)** Sieg
*m* (über +*acc*).
**defeatism** [dɪˈfiːtɪzəm] *n* Defätismus *m*.
**defeatist** [dɪˈfiːtɪst] *adj* defätistisch ♦ *n*
Defätist(in) *m(f)*.
**defect** [*n* ˈdiːfɛkt, *vi* dɪˈfɛkt] *n* Fehler *m* ♦ *vi*: **to**
~ **to the enemy** zum Feind überlaufen;
**physical/mental** ~ körperlicher/geistiger
Schaden *m or* Defekt *m*; **to** ~ **to the West**
sich in den Westen absetzen.
**defective** [dɪˈfɛktɪv] *adj* fehlerhaft.
**defector** [dɪˈfɛktə•] *n* Überläufer(in) *m(f)*.
**defence,** (*US*) **defense** [dɪˈfɛns] *n*

Verteidigung *f*; (*justification*) Rechtfertigung *f*; **in ~ of** zur Verteidigung +*gen*; **witness for the ~** Zeuge *m*/Zeugin *f* der Verteidigung; **the Ministry of D~**, (*US*) **the Department of Defense** das Verteidigungsministerium.
**defenceless** [dɪ'fɛnslɪs] *adj* schutzlos.
**defend** [dɪ'fɛnd] *vt* verteidigen.
**defendant** [dɪ'fɛndənt] *n* Angeklagte(r) *f(m)*; (*in civil case*) Beklagte(r) *f(m)*.
**defender** [dɪ'fɛndə*] *n* Verteidiger(in) *m(f)*.
**defending champion** [dɪ'fɛndɪŋ-] *n* (*SPORT*) Titelverteidiger(in) *m(f)*.
**defending counsel** [dɪ'fɛndɪŋ-] *n* Verteidiger(in) *m(f)*.
**defense** [dɪ'fɛns] (*US*) *n* = **defence**.
**defensive** [dɪ'fɛnsɪv] *adj* defensiv ♦ *n*: **on the ~** in der Defensive.
**defer** [dɪ'fə:*] *vt* verschieben.
**deference** ['dɛfərəns] *n* Achtung *f*, Respekt *m*; **out of** *or* **in ~ to** aus Rücksicht auf +*acc*.
**deferential** [dɛfə'rɛnʃəl] *adj* ehrerbietig, respektvoll.
**defiance** [dɪ'faɪəns] *n* Trotz *m*; **in ~ of sth** einer Sache *dat* zum Trotz, unter Mißachtung einer Sache *gen*.
**defiant** [dɪ'faɪənt] *adj* trotzig; (*challenging*) herausfordernd.
**defiantly** [dɪ'faɪəntlɪ] *adv* (*see adj*) trotzig; herausfordernd.
**deficiency** [dɪ'fɪʃənsɪ] *n* Mangel *m*; (*defect*) Unzulänglichkeit *f*; (*deficit*) Defizit *nt*.
**deficiency disease** *n* Mangelkrankheit *f*.
**deficient** [dɪ'fɪʃənt] *adj*: **sb/sth is ~ in sth** jdm/etw fehlt es an etw *dat*.
**deficit** ['dɛfɪsɪt] *n* Defizit *nt*.
**defile** [dɪ'faɪl] *vt* (*memory*) beschmutzen; (*statue etc*) schänden ♦ *n* Hohlweg *m*.
**define** [dɪ'faɪn] *vt* (*limits, boundaries*) bestimmen, festlegen; (*word*) definieren.
**definite** ['dɛfɪnɪt] *adj* definitiv; (*date etc*) fest; (*clear, obvious*) klar, eindeutig; (*certain*) bestimmt; **he was ~ about it** er war sich *dat* sehr sicher.
**definite article** *n* bestimmter Artikel *m*.
**definitely** ['dɛfɪnɪtlɪ] *adv* bestimmt; (*decide*) fest, definitiv.
**definition** [dɛfɪ'nɪʃən] *n* (*of word*) Definition *f*; (*of photograph etc*) Schärfe *f*.
**definitive** [dɪ'fɪnɪtɪv] *adj* definitiv; (*version*) maßgeblich.
**deflate** [di:'fleɪt] *vt* (*tyre, balloon*) die Luft ablassen aus; (*person*) einen Dämpfer versetzen +*dat*; (*ECON*) deflationieren.
**deflation** [di:'fleɪʃən] *n* Deflation *f*.
**deflationary** [di:'fleɪʃənrɪ] *adj* deflationistisch.
**deflect** [dɪ'flɛkt] *vt* (*attention*) ablenken; (*criticism*) abwehren; (*shot*) abfälschen; (*light*) brechen, beugen.
**defog** ['di:'fɔg] (*US*) *vt* von Beschlag freimachen.
**defogger** ['di:'fɔgə*] (*US*) *n* Gebläse *nt*.
**deform** [dɪ'fɔ:m] *vt* deformieren,

verunstalten.
**deformed** [dɪ'fɔ:md] *adj* deformiert, mißgebildet.
**deformity** [dɪ'fɔ:mɪtɪ] *n* Deformität *f*, Mißbildung *f*.
**defraud** [dɪ'frɔːd] *vt*: **to ~ sb (of sth)** jdn (um etw) betrügen.
**defray** [dɪ'freɪ] *vt*: **to ~ sb's expenses** jds Unkosten tragen *or* übernehmen.
**defrost** [di:'frɔst] *vt* (*fridge*) abtauen; (*windscreen*) entfrosten; (*food*) auftauen.
**defroster** [di:'frɔstə*] (*US*) *n* (*AUT*) Gebläse *nt*.
**deft** [dɛft] *adj* geschickt.
**defunct** [dɪ'fʌŋkt] *adj* (*industry*) stillgelegt; (*organization*) nicht mehr bestehend.
**defuse** [di:'fjuːz] *vt* entschärfen.
**defy** [dɪ'faɪ] *vt* sich widersetzen +*dat*; (*challenge*) auffordern; **it defies description** es spottet jeder Beschreibung.
**degenerate** [dɪ'dʒɛnəreɪt] *vi* degenerieren ♦ *adj* degeneriert.
**degradation** [dɛgrə'deɪʃən] *n* Erniedrigung *f*.
**degrade** [dɪ'greɪd] *vt* erniedrigen; (*reduce the quality of*) degradieren.
**degrading** [dɪ'greɪdɪŋ] *adj* erniedrigend.
**degree** [dɪ'griː] *n* Grad *m*; (*SCOL*) akademischer Grad *m*; **10 ~s below (zero)** 10 Grad unter Null; **6 ~s of frost** 6 Grad Kälte *or* unter Null; **a considerable ~ of risk** ein gewisses Risiko; **a ~ in maths** ein Hochschulabschluß *m* in Mathematik; **by ~s** nach und nach; **to some ~**, **to a certain ~** einigermaßen, in gewissem Maße.
**dehydrated** [diːhaɪ'dreɪtɪd] *adj* ausgetrocknet, dehydriert; (*milk, eggs*) pulverisiert, Trocken-.
**dehydration** [diːhaɪ'dreɪʃən] *n* Austrocknung *f*, Dehydration *f*.
**de-ice** ['diː'aɪs] *vt* enteisen.
**de-icer** ['diː'aɪsə*] *n* Defroster *m*.
**deign** [deɪn] *vi*: **to ~ to do sth** sich herablassen, etw zu tun.
**deity** ['diːɪtɪ] *n* Gottheit *f*.
**dejected** [dɪ'dʒɛktɪd] *adj* niedergeschlagen, deprimiert.
**dejection** [dɪ'dʒɛkʃən] *n* Niedergeschlagenheit *f*, Depression *f*.
**Del.** (*US*) *abbr* (*POST*: = *Delaware*).
**del.** *abbr* = **delete**.
**delay** [dɪ'leɪ] *vt* (*decision, ceremony*) verschieben, aufschieben; (*person, plane, train*) aufhalten ♦ *vi* zögern ♦ *n* Verzögerung *f*; (*postponement*) Aufschub *m*; **to be ~ed** (*person*) sich verspäten; (*departure etc*) verspätet sein; (*flight etc*) Verspätung haben; **without ~** unverzüglich.
**delayed-action** [dɪ'leɪd'ækʃən] *adj* (*bomb, mine*) mit Zeitzünder; (*PHOT*): **~ shutter release** Selbstauslöser *m*.
**delectable** [dɪ'lɛktəbl] *adj* (*person*) reizend; (*food*) köstlich.
**delegate** ['dɛlɪgɪt] *n* Delegierte(r) *f(m)* ♦ *vt*

delegieren; **to ~ sth to sb** jdm mit etw beauftragen; **to ~ sb to do sth** jdn damit beauftragen, etw zu tun.
**delegation** [dɛlɪˈɡeɪʃən] n Delegation f; (*group*) Abordnung f, Delegation f.
**delete** [dɪˈliːt] vt streichen; (*COMPUT*) löschen.
**Delhi** [ˈdɛlɪ] n Delhi nt.
**deli** [ˈdɛlɪ] n Feinkostgeschäft nt.
**deliberate** [adj dɪˈlɪbərɪt, vi dɪˈlɪbəreɪt] adj absichtlich; (*action, insult*) bewußt; (*slow*) bedächtig ♦ vi überlegen.
**deliberately** [dɪˈlɪbərɪtlɪ] adv absichtlich, bewußt; (*slowly*) bedächtig.
**deliberation** [dɪlɪbəˈreɪʃən] n Überlegung f; (*usu pl: discussions*) Beratungen pl.
**delicacy** [ˈdɛlɪkəsɪ] n Feinheit f, Zartheit f; (*of problem*) Delikatheit f; (*choice food*) Delikatesse f.
**delicate** [ˈdɛlɪkɪt] adj fein; (*colour, health*) zart; (*approach*) feinfühlig; (*problem*) delikat, heikel.
**delicately** [ˈdɛlɪkɪtlɪ] adv zart, fein; (*act, express*) feinfühlig.
**delicatessen** [dɛlɪkəˈtɛsn] n Feinkostgeschäft nt.
**delicious** [dɪˈlɪʃəs] adj köstlich; (*feeling, person*) herrlich.
**delight** [dɪˈlaɪt] n Freude f ♦ vt erfreuen; **sb takes (a) ~ in sth** etw bereitet jdm große Freude; **sb takes (a) ~ in doing sth** es bereitet jdm große Freude, etw zu tun; **to be the ~ of** die Freude +gen sein; **she was a ~ to interview** es war eine Freude, sie zu interviewen; **the ~s of country life** die Freuden des Landlebens.
**delighted** [dɪˈlaɪtɪd] adj: ~ (**at** or **with**) erfreut (über +acc), entzückt (über +acc); **to be ~ to do sth** etw gern tun; **I'd be ~** ich würde mich sehr freuen.
**delightful** [dɪˈlaɪtful] adj reizend, wunderbar.
**delimit** [diːˈlɪmɪt] vt abgrenzen.
**delineate** [dɪˈlɪnɪeɪt] vt (*fig*) beschreiben.
**delinquency** [dɪˈlɪŋkwənsɪ] n Kriminalität f.
**delinquent** [dɪˈlɪŋkwənt] adj straffällig ♦ n Delinquent(in) m(f).
**delirious** [dɪˈlɪrɪəs] adj: **to be ~** (*with fever*) im Delirium sein; (*with excitement*) im Taumel sein.
**delirium** [dɪˈlɪrɪəm] n Delirium nt.
**deliver** [dɪˈlɪvə*] vt liefern; (*letters, papers*) zustellen; (*hand over*) übergeben; (*message*) überbringen; (*speech*) halten; (*blow*) versetzen; (*MED: baby*) zur Welt bringen; (*warning*) geben; (*ultimatum*) stellen; (*free*): **to ~ (from)** befreien (von); **to ~ the goods** (*fig*) halten, was man versprochen hat.
**deliverance** [dɪˈlɪvrəns] n Befreiung f.
**delivery** [dɪˈlɪvərɪ] n Lieferung f; (*of letters, papers*) Zustellung f; (*of speaker*) Vortrag m; (*MED*) Entbindung f; **to take ~ of sth** etw in Empfang nehmen.

**delivery note** n Lieferschein m.
**delivery van,** (*US*) **delivery truck** n Lieferwagen m.
**delouse** [diːˈlaus] vt entlausen.
**delta** [ˈdɛltə] n Delta nt.
**delude** [dɪˈluːd] vt täuschen; **to ~ o.s.** sich dat etwas vormachen.
**deluge** [ˈdɛljuːdʒ] n (*of rain*) Guß m; (*fig: of petitions, requests*) Flut f.
**delusion** [dɪˈluːʒən] n Irrglaube m; **to have ~s of grandeur** größenwahnsinnig sein.
**de luxe** [dəˈlʌks] adj (*hotel, model*) Luxus-.
**delve** [dɛlv] vi: **to ~ into** (*subject*) sich eingehend befassen mit; (*cupboard, handbag*) tief greifen in +acc.
**Dem.** (*US*) abbr (*POL*) = **democrat**; **democratic**.
**demagogue** [ˈdɛməɡɒɡ] n Demagoge m, Demagogin f.
**demand** [dɪˈmɑːnd] vt verlangen; (*rights*) fordern; (*need*) erfordern, verlangen ♦ n Verlangen nt; (*claim*) Forderung f; (*ECON*) Nachfrage f; **to ~ sth (from** or **of sb)** etw (von jdm) verlangen or fordern; **to be in ~** gefragt sein; **on ~** (*available*) auf Verlangen; (*payable*) bei Vorlage or Sicht.
**demand draft** n Sichtwechsel m.
**demanding** [dɪˈmɑːndɪŋ] adj anspruchsvoll; (*work, child*) anstrengend.
**demarcation** [diːmɑːˈkeɪʃən] n (*of area, tasks*) Abgrenzung f.
**demarcation dispute** n Streit m um den Zuständigkeitsbereich.
**demean** [dɪˈmiːn] vt: **to ~ o.s.** sich erniedrigen.
**demeanour,** (*US*) **demeanor** [dɪˈmiːnə*] n Benehmen nt, Auftreten nt.
**demented** [dɪˈmɛntɪd] adj wahnsinnig.
**demilitarized zone** [diːˈmɪlɪtəraɪzd-] n entmilitarisierte Zone f.
**demise** [dɪˈmaɪz] n Ende nt; (*death*) Tod m.
**demist** [diːˈmɪst] (*BRIT*) vt (*AUT: windscreen*) von Beschlag freimachen.
**demister** [diːˈmɪstə*] (*BRIT*) n (*AUT*) Gebläse nt.
**demo** [ˈdɛməu] (*inf*) n abbr = **demonstration**.
**demob** [diːˈmɒb] (*inf*) vt = **demobilize**.
**demobilize** [diːˈməubɪlaɪz] vt aus dem Kriegsdienst entlassen, demobilisieren.
**democracy** [dɪˈmɒkrəsɪ] n Demokratie f.
**democrat** [ˈdɛməkræt] n Demokrat(in) m(f).
**democratic** [dɛməˈkrætɪk] adj demokratisch.
**Democratic Party** (*US*) n: **the ~** die Demokratische Partei.
**demography** [dɪˈmɒɡrəfɪ] n Demographie f.
**demolish** [dɪˈmɒlɪʃ] vt abreißen, abbrechen; (*fig: argument*) widerlegen.
**demolition** [dɛməˈlɪʃən] n Abriß m, Abbruch m; (*of argument*) Widerlegung f.
**demon** [ˈdiːmən] n Dämon m ♦ adj teuflisch gut.
**demonstrate** [ˈdɛmənstreɪt] vt (*theory*)

demonstrieren; (*skill*) zeigen, beweisen; (*appliance*) vorführen ♦ *vi:* to ~ (for/against) demonstrieren (für/gegen).

**demonstration** [dɛmən'streɪʃən] *n* Demonstration *f*; (*of gadget, machine etc*) Vorführung *f*; to hold a ~ eine Demonstration veranstalten *or* durchführen.

**demonstrative** [dɪ'mɔnstrətɪv] *adj* demonstrativ.

**demonstrator** ['dɛmənstreɪtə*] *n* Demonstrant(in) *m(f)*; (*sales person*) Vorführer(in) *m(f)*; (*car*) Vorführwagen *m*; (*computer etc*) Vorführgerät *nt*.

**demoralize** [dɪ'mɔrəlaɪz] *vt* entmutigen.

**demote** [dɪ'məut] *vt* zurückstufen; (*MIL*) degradieren.

**demotion** [dɪ'məuʃən] *n* Zurückstufung *f*; (*MIL*) Degradierung *f*.

**demur** [dɪ'mə:*] (*form*) *vi* Einwände *pl* erheben ♦ *n:* without ~ widerspruchslos; they ~red at the suggestion sie erhoben Einwände gegen den Vorschlag.

**demure** [dɪ'mjuə*] *adj* zurückhaltend; (*smile*) höflich; (*dress*) schlicht.

**demurrage** [dɪ'mʌrɪdʒ] *n* Liegegeld *nt*.

**den** [dɛn] *n* Höhle *f*; (*of fox*) Bau *m*; (*room*) Bude *f*.

**denationalization** ['di:næʃnəlaɪ'zeɪʃən] *n* Privatisierung *f*.

**denationalize** [di:'næʃnəlaɪz] *vt* privatisieren.

**denatured alcohol** [di:'neɪtʃəd-] (*US*) *n* vergällter Alkohol *m*.

**denial** [dɪ'naɪəl] *n* Leugnen *nt*; (*of rights*) Verweigerung *f*.

**denier** ['dɛnɪə*] *n* Denier *nt*.

**denigrate** ['dɛnɪgreɪt] *vt* verunglimpfen.

**denim** ['dɛnɪm] *n* Jeansstoff *m*; denims *npl* (Blue) Jeans *pl*.

**denim jacket** *n* Jeansjacke *f*.

**denizen** ['dɛnɪzn] *n* Bewohner(in) *m(f)*; (*person in town*) Einwohner(in) *m(f)*; (*foreigner*) eingebürgerter Ausländer *m*, eingebürgerte Ausländerin *f*.

**Denmark** ['dɛnmɑ:k] *n* Dänemark *nt*.

**denomination** [dɪnɔmɪ'neɪʃən] *n* (*of money*) Nennwert *m*; (*REL*) Konfession *f*.

**denominator** [dɪ'nɔmɪneɪtə*] *n* Nenner *m*.

**denote** [dɪ'nəut] *vt* (*indicate*) hindeuten auf +*acc*; (*represent*) bezeichnen.

**denounce** [dɪ'nauns] *vt* (*person*) anprangern; (*action*) verurteilen.

**dense** [dɛns] *adj* dicht; (*inf: person*) beschränkt.

**densely** ['dɛnslɪ] *adv* dicht.

**density** ['dɛnsɪtɪ] *n* Dichte *f*; single/double-~ disk (*COMPUT*) Diskette *f* mit einfacher/doppelter Dichte.

**dent** [dɛnt] *n* Beule *f*; (*in pride, ego*) Knacks *m* ♦ *vt* (*also:* make a ~ in) einbeulen; (*pride, ego*) anknacksen.

**dental** ['dɛntl] *adj* (*filling, hygiene etc*) Zahn-;

(*treatment*) zahnärztlich.

**dental floss** [-flɔs] *n* Zahnseide *f*.

**dental surgeon** *n* Zahnarzt *m*, Zahnärztin *f*.

**dentifrice** ['dɛntɪfrɪs] *n* Zahnpasta *f*.

**dentist** ['dɛntɪst] *n* Zahnarzt *m*, Zahnärztin *f*; (*also:* ~'s (surgery)) Zahnarzt *m*, Zahnarztpraxis *f*.

**dentistry** ['dɛntɪstrɪ] *n* Zahnmedizin *f*.

**dentures** ['dɛntʃəz] *npl* Zahnprothese *f*; (*full*) Gebiß *nt*.

**denuded** [di:'nju:dɪd] *adj:* ~ of entblößt von.

**denunciation** [dɪnʌnsɪ'eɪʃən] *n* (*of person*) Anprangerung *f*; (*of action*) Verurteilung *f*.

**deny** [dɪ'naɪ] *vt* leugnen; (*involvement*) abstreiten; (*permission, chance*) verweigern; (*country, religion etc*) verleugnen; he denies having said it er leugnet *or* bestreitet, das gesagt zu haben.

**deodorant** [di:'əudərənt] *n* Deodorant *nt*.

**depart** [dɪ'pɑ:t] *vi* abreisen; (: *on foot*) weggehen; (*bus, train*) abfahren; (*plane*) abfliegen; to ~ from (*fig*) abweichen von.

**departed** [dɪ'pɑ:tɪd] *adj:* the (dear) ~ der/die (liebe) Verstorbene *m/f*; die (lieben) Verstorbenen *pl*.

**department** [dɪ'pɑ:tmənt] *n* Abteilung *f*; (*SCOL*) Fachbereich *m*; (*POL*) Ministerium *nt*; that's not my ~ (*fig*) dafür bin ich nicht zuständig; D~ of State (*US*) Außenministerium *nt*.

**departmental** [di:pɑ:t'mɛntl] *adj* (*budget, costs*) der Abteilung; (*level*) Abteilungs-; ~ manager Abteilungsleiter(in) *m(f)*.

**department store** *n* Warenhaus *nt*.

**departure** [dɪ'pɑ:tʃə*] *n* (*of visitor*) Abreise *f*; (*on foot, of employee etc*) Weggang *m*; (*of bus, train*) Abfahrt *f*; (*of plane*) Abflug *m*; (*fig*): ~ from Abweichen *nt* von; a new ~ ein neuer Weg *m*.

**departure lounge** *n* Abflughalle *f*.

**depend** [dɪ'pɛnd] *vi:* to ~ on abhängen von; (*rely on, trust*) sich verlassen auf +*acc*; (*financially*) abhängig sein von, angewiesen sein auf +*acc*; it ~s es kommt darauf an; ~ing on the result ... je nachdem, wie das Ergebnis ausfällt, ...

**dependable** [dɪ'pɛndəbl] *adj* zuverlässig.

**dependant** [dɪ'pɛndənt] *n* abhängige(r) (Familien)angehörige(r) *f(m)*.

**dependence** [dɪ'pɛndəns] *n* Abhängigkeit *f*.

**dependent** [dɪ'pɛndənt] *adj:* to be ~ on (*person*) abhängig sein von, angewiesen sein auf +*acc*; (*decision*) abhängen von ♦ *n* = dependant.

**depict** [dɪ'pɪkt] *vt* (*in picture*) darstellen; (*describe*) beschreiben.

**depilatory** [dɪ'pɪlətrɪ] *n* (*also:* ~ cream) Enthaarungsmittel *nt*.

**depleted** [dɪ'pli:tɪd] *adj* (*reserves*) aufgebraucht; (*stocks*) erschöpft.

**deplorable** [dɪ'plɔ:rəbl] *adj* bedauerlich.

**deplore** [dɪ'plɔ:*] *vt* verurteilen.

**deploy** [dɪˈplɔɪ] vt einsetzen.
**depopulate** [diːˈpɒpjuleɪt] vt entvölkern.
**depopulation** [ˈdiːpɒpjuˈleɪʃən] n
Entvölkerung f.
**deport** [dɪˈpɔːt] vt (criminal) deportieren;
(illegal immigrant) abschieben.
**deportation** [diːpɔːˈteɪʃən] n (see vb)
Deportation f; Abschiebung f.
**deportation order** n Ausweisung f.
**deportee** [diːpɔːˈtiː] n Deportierte(r) f(m).
**deportment** [dɪˈpɔːtmənt] n Benehmen nt.
**depose** [dɪˈpəʊz] vt absetzen.
**deposit** [dɪˈpɒzɪt] n (in account) Guthaben nt;
(down payment) Anzahlung f; (for hired goods
etc) Sicherheit f, Kaution f; (on bottle etc)
Pfand nt; (CHEM) Ablagerung f; (of ore, oil)
Lagerstätte f ♦ vt deponieren; (subj: river:
sand etc) ablagern; **to put down a ~ of £50**
eine Anzahlung von £50 machen.
**deposit account** n Sparkonto nt.
**depositary** [dɪˈpɒzɪtərɪ] n Treuhänder(in) m(f).
**depositor** [dɪˈpɒzɪtə*] n Deponent(in) m(f),
Einzahler(in) m(f).
**depository** [dɪˈpɒzɪtərɪ] n (person)
Treuhänder(in) m(f); (place) Lager(haus) nt.
**depot** [ˈdɛpəʊ] n Lager(haus) nt; (for vehicles)
Depot nt; (US: station) Bahnhof m; (: bus
station) Busbahnhof m.
**depraved** [dɪˈpreɪvd] adj verworfen.
**depravity** [dɪˈprævɪtɪ] n Verworfenheit f.
**deprecate** [ˈdɛprɪkeɪt] vt mißbilligen.
**deprecating** [ˈdɛprɪkeɪtɪŋ] adj (disapproving)
mißbilligend; (apologetic) entschuldigend.
**depreciate** [dɪˈpriːʃɪeɪt] vi an Wert verlieren;
(currency) an Kaufkraft verlieren; (value)
sinken.
**depreciation** [dɪpriːʃɪˈeɪʃən] n (see vb)
Wertminderung f; Kaufkraftverlust m;
Sinken nt.
**depress** [dɪˈprɛs] vt deprimieren; (price,
wages) drücken; (press down)
herunterdrücken.
**depressant** [dɪˈprɛsnt] n Beruhigungsmittel
nt.
**depressed** [dɪˈprɛst] adj deprimiert,
niedergeschlagen; (price) gesunken;
(industry) geschwächt; (area) Notstands-; **to
get ~** deprimiert werden.
**depressing** [dɪˈprɛsɪŋ] adj deprimierend.
**depression** [dɪˈprɛʃən] n (PSYCH)
Depressionen pl; (ECON) Wirtschaftskrise f;
(MET) Tief(druckgebiet) nt; (hollow)
Vertiefung f.
**deprivation** [dɛprɪˈveɪʃən] n Entbehrung f,
Not f; (of freedom, rights etc) Entzug m.
**deprive** [dɪˈpraɪv] vt: **to ~ sb of sth** (liberty)
jdm etw entziehen; (life) jdm etw nehmen.
**deprived** [dɪˈpraɪvd] adj benachteiligt; (area)
notleidend.
**dept** abbr = **department**.
**depth** [dɛpθ] n Tiefe f; **in the ~s of** in den
Tiefen +gen; **in the ~s of despair** in tiefster

Verzweiflung; **in the ~s of winter** im
tiefsten Winter; **at a ~ of 3 metres** in 3
Meter Tiefe; **to be out of one's ~** (in water)
nicht mehr stehen können; (fig) überfordert
sein; **to study sth in ~** etw gründlich or
eingehend studieren.
**depth charge** n Wasserbombe f.
**deputation** [dɛpjuˈteɪʃən] n Abordnung f.
**deputize** [ˈdɛpjutaɪz] vi: **to ~ for sb** jdn
vertreten.
**deputy** [ˈdɛpjutɪ] cpd stellvertretend ♦ n
(Stell)vertreter(in) m(f); (POL)
Abgeordnete(r) f(m); (US: also: ~ **sheriff**)
Hilfssheriff m; ~ **head** (BRIT: SCOL)
Konrektor(in) m(f).
**derail** [dɪˈreɪl] vt: **to be ~ed** entgleisen.
**derailment** [dɪˈreɪlmənt] n Entgleisung f.
**deranged** [dɪˈreɪndʒd] adj: **to be mentally ~**
geistesgestört sein.
**derby** [ˈdɜːrbɪ] n Derby nt; (US: hat) Melone f.
**Derbys** (BRIT) abbr (POST: = Derbyshire).
**deregulate** [dɪˈrɛgjuleɪt] vt staatliche
Kontrollen aufheben bei.
**deregulation** [dɪˈrɛgjuˈleɪʃən] n Aufhebung f
staatlicher Kontrollen.
**derelict** [ˈdɛrɪlɪkt] adj verfallen.
**deride** [dɪˈraɪd] vt sich lustig machen über
+acc.
**derision** [dɪˈrɪʒən] n Hohn m, Spott m.
**derisive** [dɪˈraɪsɪv] adj spöttisch.
**derisory** [dɪˈraɪsərɪ] adj spöttisch; (sum)
lächerlich.
**derivation** [dɛrɪˈveɪʃən] n Ableitung f.
**derivative** [dɪˈrɪvətɪv] n (LING) Ableitung f;
(CHEM) Derivat nt ♦ adj nachahmend.
**derive** [dɪˈraɪv] vt: **to ~ (from)** gewinnen (aus);
(benefit) ziehen (aus) ♦ vi: **to ~ from**
(originate in) sich herleiten or ableiten von;
**to ~ pleasure from** Freude haben an +dat.
**dermatitis** [dɜːməˈtaɪtɪs] n Hautentzündung f,
Dermatitis f.
**dermatology** [dɜːməˈtɒlədʒɪ] n Dermatologie
f.
**derogatory** [dɪˈrɒgətərɪ] adj abfällig.
**derrick** [ˈdɛrɪk] n (on ship) Derrickkran m; (on
well) Bohrturm m.
**derv** [dɜːv] (BRIT) n (AUT) Diesel(kraftstoff)
m.
**desalination** [diːsælɪˈneɪʃən] n Entsalzung f.
**descend** [dɪˈsɛnd] vt hinuntergehen,
hinuntersteigen; (lift, vehicle)
hinunterfahren; (road) hinunterführen ♦ vi
hinuntergehen; (lift) nach unten fahren; **to
~ from** abstammen von; **to ~ to** sich
erniedrigen zu; **in ~ing order of importance**
nach Wichtigkeit geordnet.
► **descend on** vt fus überfallen; (subj:
misfortune) hereinbrechen über +acc;
(: gloom) befallen; (: silence) sich senken auf
+acc; **visitors ~ed (up)on us** der Besuch hat
uns überfallen.
**descendant** [dɪˈsɛndənt] n Nachkomme m.

**descent** [dɪ'sɛnt] *n* Abstieg *m*; (*origin*) Abstammung *f.*

**describe** [dɪs'kraɪb] *vt* beschreiben.

**description** [dɪs'krɪpʃən] *n* Beschreibung *f*; (*sort*): **of every** ~ aller Art.

**descriptive** [dɪs'krɪptɪv] *adj* (*writing, painting*) deskriptiv.

**desecrate** ['dɛsɪkreɪt] *vt* schänden.

**desegregate** [diː'sɛɡrɪɡeɪt] *vt* die Rassentrennung aufheben in +*dat.*

**desert** [*n* 'dɛzət, *vb* dɪ'zɜːt] *n* Wüste *f* ♦ *vt* verlassen ♦ *vi* desertieren; *see also* **deserts.**

**deserter** [dɪ'zɜːtə*] *n* Deserteur *m.*

**desertion** [dɪ'zɜːʃən] *n* Desertion *f*, Fahnenflucht *f*; (*LAW*) böswilliges Verlassen *nt.*

**desert island** *n* einsame *or* verlassene Insel *f.*

**deserts** [dɪ'zɜːts] *npl*: **to get one's just** ~ bekommen, was man verdient.

**deserve** [dɪ'zɜːv] *vt* verdienen.

**deservedly** [dɪ'zɜːvɪdlɪ] *adv* verdientermaßen.

**deserving** [dɪ'zɜːvɪŋ] *adj* verdienstvoll.

**desiccated** ['dɛsɪkeɪtɪd] *adj* vertrocknet; (*coconut*) getrocknet.

**design** [dɪ'zaɪn] *n* Design *nt*; (*process*) Entwurf *m*, Gestaltung *f*; (*sketch*) Entwurf *m*; (*layout, shape*) Form *f*; (*pattern*) Muster *nt*; (*of car*) Konstruktion *f*; (*intention*) Plan *m*, Absicht *f* ♦ *vt* entwerfen; **to have** ~**s on** es abgesehen haben auf +*acc*; **well-**~**ed** mit gutem Design.

**designate** [*vt* 'dɛzɪɡneɪt, *adj* 'dɛzɪɡnɪt] *vt* bestimmen, ernennen ♦ *adj* designiert.

**designation** [dɛzɪɡ'neɪʃən] *n* Bezeichnung *f.*

**designer** [dɪ'zaɪnə*] *n* Designer(in) *m(f)*; (*TECH*) Konstrukteur(in) *m(f)*; (*fashion designer*) Modeschöpfer(in) *m(f)* ♦ *adj* (*clothes etc*) Designer-.

**desirability** [dɪzaɪərə'bɪlɪtɪ] *n*: **they discussed the** ~ **of the plan** sie besprachen, ob der Plan wünschenswert sei.

**desirable** [dɪ'zaɪərəbl] *adj* (*proper*) wünschenswert; (*attractive*) reizvoll, attraktiv.

**desire** [dɪ'zaɪə*] *n* Wunsch *m*; (*sexual*) Verlangen *nt*, Begehren *nt* ♦ *vt* wünschen; (*lust after*) begehren; **to** ~ **to do sth/that** wünschen, etw zu tun/daß.

**desirous** [dɪ'zaɪərəs] *adj*: **to be** ~ **of doing sth** den Wunsch haben, etw zu tun.

**desist** [dɪ'zɪst] *vi*: **to** ~ **(from)** absehen (von), Abstand nehmen (von).

**desk** [dɛsk] *n* Schreibtisch *m*; (*for pupil*) Pult *nt*; (*in hotel*) Empfang *m*; (*at airport*) Schalter *m*; (*BRIT: in shop, restaurant*) Kasse *f.*

**desk job** *n* Bürojob *m.*

**desktop** ['dɛsktɔp] *n* Arbeitsfläche *f.*

**desktop publishing** *n* Desktop-Publishing *nt.*

**desolate** ['dɛsəlɪt] *adj* trostlos.

**desolation** [dɛsə'leɪʃən] *n* Trostlosigkeit *f.*

**despair** [dɪs'pɛə*] *n* Verzweiflung *f* ♦ *vi*: **to** ~ **of** alle Hoffnung aufgeben auf +*acc*; **to be in** ~ verzweifelt sein.

**despatch** [dɪs'pætʃ] *n*, *vt* = **dispatch.**

**desperate** ['dɛspərɪt] *adj* verzweifelt; (*shortage*) akut; (*criminal*) zum Äußersten entschlossen; **to be** ~ **for sth/to do sth** etw dringend brauchen/unbedingt tun wollen.

**desperately** ['dɛspərɪtlɪ] *adv* (*shout, struggle etc*) verzweifelt; (*ill*) schwer; (*unhappy etc*) äußerst.

**desperation** [dɛspə'reɪʃən] *n* Verzweiflung *f*; **in (sheer)** ~ aus (reiner) Verzweiflung.

**despicable** [dɪs'pɪkəbl] *adj* (*action*) verabscheuungswürdig; (*person*) widerwärtig.

**despise** [dɪs'paɪz] *vt* verachten.

**despite** [dɪs'paɪt] *prep* trotz +*gen.*

**despondent** [dɪs'pɔndənt] *adj* niedergeschlagen, mutlos.

**despot** ['dɛspɔt] *n* Despot *m.*

**dessert** [dɪ'zɜːt] *n* Nachtisch *m*, Dessert *nt.*

**dessertspoon** [dɪ'zɜːtspuːn] *n* Dessertlöffel *m.*

**destabilize** [diː'steɪbɪlaɪz] *vt* destabilisieren.

**destination** [dɛstɪ'neɪʃən] *n* (*Reise*)ziel *nt*; (*of mail*) Bestimmungsort *m.*

**destined** ['dɛstɪnd] *adj*: **to be** ~ **to do sth** dazu bestimmt *or* ausersehen sein, etw zu tun; **to be** ~ **for** bestimmt *or* ausersehen sein für.

**destiny** ['dɛstɪnɪ] *n* Schicksal *nt.*

**destitute** ['dɛstɪtjuːt] *adj* mittellos.

**destroy** [dɪs'trɔɪ] *vt* zerstören; (*animal*) töten.

**destroyer** [dɪs'trɔɪə*] *n* Zerstörer *m.*

**destruction** [dɪs'trʌkʃən] *n* Zerstörung *f.*

**destructive** [dɪs'trʌktɪv] *adj* zerstörerisch; (*child, criticism etc*) destruktiv.

**desultory** ['dɛsəltərɪ] *adj* flüchtig; (*conversation*) zwanglos.

**detach** [dɪ'tætʃ] *vt* (*remove*) entfernen; (*unclip*) abnehmen; (*unstick*) ablösen.

**detachable** [dɪ'tætʃəbl] *adj* abnehmbar.

**detached** [dɪ'tætʃt] *adj* distanziert; (*house*) freistehend, Einzel-.

**detachment** [dɪ'tætʃmənt] *n* Distanz *f*; (*MIL*) Sonderkommando *nt.*

**detail** ['diːteɪl] *n* Einzelheit *f*; (*no pl: in picture, one's work etc*) Detail *nt*; (*trifle*) unwichtige Einzelheit *f* ♦ *vt* (*einzeln*) aufführen; **in** ~ in Einzelheiten; **to go into** ~**s** auf Einzelheiten eingehen, ins Detail gehen.

**detailed** ['diːteɪld] *adj* detailliert, genau.

**detain** [dɪ'teɪn] *vt* aufhalten; (*in captivity*) in Haft halten; (*in hospital*) festhalten.

**detainee** [diːteɪ'niː] *n* Häftling *m.*

**detect** [dɪ'tɛkt] *vt* wahrnehmen; (*MED, TECH*) feststellen; (*MIL*) ausfindig machen.

**detection** [dɪ'tɛkʃən] *n* Entdeckung *f*, Feststellung *f*; **crime** ~ Ermittlungsarbeit *f*; **to escape** ~ (*criminal*) nicht gefaßt werden; (*mistake*) der Aufmerksamkeit *dat* entgehen.

**detective** [dɪ'tɛktɪv] *n* Kriminalbeamte(r) *m*; **private** ~ Privatdetektiv *m.*

**detective story** n Kriminalgeschichte f,
Detektivgeschichte f.
**detector** [dɪ'tɛktə'] n Detektor m.
**détente** [deɪ'tɑːnt] n Entspannung f, Détente f.
**detention** [dɪ'tɛnʃən] n (arrest) Festnahme f;
(captivity) Haft f; (SCOL) Nachsitzen nt.
**deter** [dɪ'təː'] vt (discourage) abschrecken;
(dissuade) abhalten.
**detergent** [dɪ'təːdʒənt] n Reinigungsmittel nt;
(for clothes) Waschmittel nt; (for dishes)
Spülmittel nt.
**deteriorate** [dɪ'tɪərɪəreɪt] vi sich
verschlechtern.
**deterioration** [dɪtɪərɪə'reɪʃən] n
Verschlechterung f.
**determination** [dɪtəːmɪ'neɪʃən] n
Entschlossenheit f; (establishment)
Festsetzung f.
**determine** [dɪ'təːmɪn] vt (facts) feststellen;
(limits etc) festlegen; **to ~ that** beschließen,
daß; **to ~ to do sth** sich entschließen, etw
zu tun.
**determined** [dɪ'təːmɪnd] adj entschlossen;
(quantity) bestimmt; **to be ~ to do sth** (fest)
entschlossen sein, etw zu tun.
**deterrence** [dɪ'tɛrəns] n Abschreckung f.
**deterrent** [dɪ'tɛrənt] n Abschreckungsmittel
nt; **to act as a ~** als Abschreckung(smittel)
dienen.
**detest** [dɪ'tɛst] vt verabscheuen.
**detestable** [dɪ'tɛstəbl] adj abscheulich,
widerwärtig.
**detonate** ['dɛtəneɪt] vi detonieren ♦ vt zur
Explosion bringen.
**detonator** ['dɛtəneɪtə'] n Sprengkapsel f.
**detour** ['diːtuə'] n Umweg m; (US: AUT)
Umleitung f.
**detract** [dɪ'trækt] vi: **to ~ from** schmälern;
(effect) beeinträchtigen.
**detractor** [dɪ'træktə'] n Kritiker(in) m(f).
**detriment** ['dɛtrɪmənt] n: **to the ~ of** zum
Schaden +gen; **without ~ to** ohne Schaden
für.
**detrimental** [dɛtrɪ'mɛntl] adj: **to be ~ to**
schaden +dat.
**deuce** [djuːs] n (TENNIS) Einstand m.
**devaluation** [dɪvælju'eɪʃən] n Abwertung f.
**devalue** ['diː'væljuː] vt abwerten.
**devastate** ['dɛvəsteɪt] vt verwüsten; (fig:
shock): **to be ~d by** niedergeschmettert sein
von.
**devastating** ['dɛvəsteɪtɪŋ] adj verheerend;
(announcement, news) niederschmetternd.
**devastation** [dɛvəs'teɪʃən] n Verwüstung f.
**develop** [dɪ'vɛləp] vt entwickeln; (business)
erweitern, ausbauen; (land, resource)
erschließen; (disease) bekommen ♦ vi sich
entwickeln; (facts) an den Tag kommen;
(symptoms) auftreten; **to ~ a taste for sth**
Geschmack an etw finden; **the machine/car
~ed a fault/engine trouble** an dem Gerät/
dem Wagen trat ein Defekt/ein

Motorschaden auf; **to ~ into** sich
entwickeln zu, werden.
**developer** [dɪ'vɛləpə'] n (also: **property ~**)
Bauunternehmer und Immobilienmakler.
**developing country** [dɪ'vɛləpɪŋ-] n
Entwicklungsland nt.
**development** [dɪ'vɛləpmənt] n Entwicklung f;
(of land) Erschließung f.
**development area** n Entwicklungsgebiet nt.
**deviant** ['diːvɪənt] adj abweichend.
**deviate** ['diːvɪeɪt] vi: **to ~ (from)** abweichen
(von).
**deviation** [diːvɪ'eɪʃən] n Abweichung f.
**device** [dɪ'vaɪs] n Gerät nt; (ploy, stratagem)
Trick m; **explosive ~** Sprengkörper m.
**devil** ['dɛvl] n Teufel m; **go on, be a ~!** nur zu,
riskier mal was!; **talk of the ~!** wenn man
vom Teufel spricht!
**devilish** ['dɛvlɪʃ] adj teuflisch.
**devil's advocate** ['dɛvlz-] n Advocatus
Diaboli m.
**devious** ['diːvɪəs] adj (person) verschlagen;
(route, path) gewunden.
**devise** [dɪ'vaɪz] vt sich dat ausdenken;
(machine) entwerfen.
**devoid** [dɪ'vɔɪd] adj: **~ of** bar +gen, ohne +acc.
**devolution** [diːvə'luːʃən] n Dezentralisierung
f.
**devolve** [dɪ'vɔlv] vt übertragen ♦ vi: **to
~ (up)on** übergehen auf +acc.
**devote** [dɪ'vəut] vt: **to ~ sth/o.s. to** etw/sich
widmen +dat.
**devoted** [dɪ'vəutɪd] adj treu; (admirer) eifrig;
**to be ~ to sb** jdn innig lieben; **the book is
~ to politics** das Buch widmet sich ganz der
Politik dat.
**devotee** [dɛvəu'tiː] n (fan) Liebhaber(in) m(f);
(REL) Anhänger(in) m(f).
**devotion** [dɪ'vəuʃən] n (affection) Ergebenheit
f; (dedication) Hingabe f; (REL) Andacht f.
**devour** [dɪ'vauə'] vt verschlingen.
**devout** [dɪ'vaut] adj fromm.
**dew** [djuː] n Tau m.
**dexterity** [dɛks'tɛrɪtɪ] n Geschicklichkeit f;
(mental) Gewandtheit f.
**dext(e)rous** ['dɛkstrəs] adj geschickt.
**DFE** (BRIT) n abbr (= Department for Education)
≈ Bildungsministerium nt.
**dg** abbr (= decigram) dg.
**DH** (BRIT) n abbr (= Department of Health)
≈ Gesundheitsministerium nt.
**Dhaka** ['dækə] n Dhaka nt.
**DHSS** (BRIT) n abbr (formerly: = Department of
Health and Social Security) Ministerium für
Gesundheit und Sozialfürsorge.
**diabetes** [daɪə'biːtiːz] n Zuckerkrankheit f.
**diabetic** [daɪə'bɛtɪk] adj zuckerkrank;
(chocolate, jam) Diabetiker- ♦ n
Diabetiker(in) m(f).
**diabolical** [daɪə'bɔlɪkl] (inf) adj schrecklich,
fürchterlich.
**diaeresis** [daɪ'ɛrɪsɪs] n Diärese f.

**diagnose** [daɪəg'nəuz] *vt* diagnostizieren.

**diagnoses** [-siːz] *pl of* **diagnosis.**

**diagnosis** [daɪəg'nəusɪs] (*pl* **diagnoses**) *n* Diagnose *f.*

**diagonal** [daɪ'ægənl] *adj* diagonal ♦ *n* Diagonale *f.*

**diagram** ['daɪəgræm] *n* Diagramm *nt,* Schaubild *nt.*

**dial** ['daɪəl] *n* Zifferblatt *nt;* (*on radio set*) Einstellskala *f;* (*of phone*) Wählscheibe *f* ♦ *vt* wählen; **to ~ a wrong number** sich verwählen; **can I ~ London direct?** kann ich nach London durchwählen?

**dial.** *abbr* = **dialect.**

**dialect** ['daɪəlɛkt] *n* Dialekt *m.*

**dialling code** ['daɪəlɪŋ-] *n* Vorwahl(nummer) *f; see also* **area code.**

**dialling tone,** (*US*) **dial tone** *n* Amtszeichen *nt.*

**dialogue,** (*US*) **dialog** ['daɪəlɔg] *n* Dialog *m;* (*conversation*) Gespräch *nt,* Dialog *m.*

**dial tone** (*US*) *n* = **dialling tone.**

**dialysis** [daɪ'ælɪsɪs] *n* Dialyse *f.*

**diameter** [daɪ'æmɪtəʳ] *n* Durchmesser *m.*

**diametrically** [daɪə'mɛtrɪklɪ] *adv:* ~ **opposed (to)** diametral entgegengesetzt (+dat).

**diamond** ['daɪəmənd] *n* Diamant *m;* (*shape*) Raute *f;* **diamonds** *npl* (*CARDS*) Karo *nt.*

**diamond ring** *n* Diamantring *m.*

**diaper** ['daɪəpəʳ] (*US*) *n* Windel *f.*

**diaphragm** ['daɪəfræm] *n* Zwerchfell *nt;* (*contraceptive*) Pessar *nt.*

**diarrhoea,** (*US*) **diarrhea** [daɪə'riːə] *n* Durchfall *m.*

**diary** ['daɪərɪ] *n* (Termin)kalender *m;* (*daily account*) Tagebuch *nt;* **to keep a ~** Tagebuch führen.

**diatribe** ['daɪətraɪb] *n* Schmährede *f;* (*written*) Schmähschrift *f.*

**dice** [daɪs] *n inv* Würfel *m* ♦ *vt* in Würfel schneiden.

**dicey** ['daɪsɪ] (*inf*) *adj* riskant.

**dichotomy** [daɪ'kɔtəmɪ] *n* Dichotomie *f,* Kluft *f.*

**dickhead** ['dɪkhɛd] (*inf*) *n* Knallkopf *m.*

**Dictaphone** ® ['dɪktəfəun] *n* Diktaphon *nt,* Diktiergerät *nt.*

**dictate** [dɪk'teɪt] *vt* diktieren ♦ *n* Diktat *nt;* (*principle*): **the ~s of** die Gebote *+gen* ♦ *vi:* **to ~** diktieren *+dat;* **I won't be ~d to** ich lasse mir keine Vorschriften machen.

**dictation** [dɪk'teɪʃən] *n* Diktat *nt;* **at ~ speed** im Diktiertempo.

**dictator** [dɪk'teɪtəʳ] *n* Diktator *m.*

**dictatorship** [dɪk'teɪtəʃɪp] *n* Diktatur *f.*

**diction** ['dɪkʃən] *n* Diktion *f.*

**dictionary** ['dɪkʃənrɪ] *n* Wörterbuch *nt.*

**did** [dɪd] *pt of* **do.**

**didactic** [daɪ'dæktɪk] *adj* didaktisch.

**diddle** ['dɪdl] (*inf*) *vt* übers Ohr hauen.

**didn't** ['dɪdnt] = **did not.**

**die** [daɪ] *n* (*pl: dice*) Würfel *m;* (: *dies*) Gußform *f* ♦ *vi* sterben; (*plant*) eingehen; (*fig: noise*) aufhören; (: *smile*) vergehen; (*engine*) stehenbleiben; **to ~ of** *or* **from** sterben an +*dat;* **to be dying** im Sterben liegen; **to be dying for sth** etw unbedingt brauchen; **to be dying to do sth** darauf brennen, etw zu tun.

▶**die away** *vi* (*sound*) schwächer werden; (*light*) nachlassen.

▶**die down** *vi* (*wind*) sich legen; (*fire*) herunterbrennen; (*excitement, noise*) nachlassen.

▶**die out** *vi* aussterben.

**die-hard** ['daɪhɑːd] *n* Ewiggestrige(r) *f(m).*

**diesel** ['diːzl] *n* (*vehicle*) Diesel *m;* (*also:* ~ **oil**) Diesel(kraftstoff) *m.*

**diesel engine** *n* Dieselmotor *m.*

**diet** ['daɪət] *n* Ernährung *f;* (*MED*) Diät *f;* (*when slimming*) Schlankheitskur *f* ♦ *vi* (*also:* **be on a ~**) eine Schlankheitskur machen; **to live on a ~ of** sich ernähren von, leben von.

**dietician** [daɪə'tɪʃən] *n* Diätassistent(in) *m(f).*

**differ** ['dɪfəʳ] *vi* (*be different*): **to ~ (from)** sich unterscheiden (von); (*disagree*): **to ~ (about)** anderer Meinung sein (über +*acc*); **to agree to ~** sich *dat* verschiedene Meinungen zugestehen.

**difference** ['dɪfrəns] *n* Unterschied *m;* (*disagreement*) Differenz *f,* Auseinandersetzung *f;* **it makes no ~ to me** das ist mir egal *or* einerlei; **to settle one's ~s** die Differenzen *or* Meinungsverschiedenheiten beilegen.

**different** ['dɪfrənt] *adj* (*various people, things*) verschieden, unterschiedlich; **to be ~ (from)** anders sein (als).

**differential** [dɪfə'rɛnʃəl] *n* (*MATH*) Differential *nt;* (*BRIT: in wages*) (Einkommens)unterschied *m.*

**differentiate** [dɪfə'rɛnʃɪeɪt] *vi:* **to ~ (between)** unterscheiden (zwischen) ♦ *vt:* **to ~ A from B** A von B unterscheiden.

**differently** ['dɪfrəntlɪ] *adv* anders; (*shaped, designed*) verschieden, unterschiedlich.

**difficult** ['dɪfɪkəlt] *adj* schwierig; (*task, problem*) schwer, schwierig; **~ to understand** schwer zu verstehen.

**difficulty** ['dɪfɪkəltɪ] *n* Schwierigkeit *f;* **to be in/get into difficulties** in Schwierigkeiten sein/geraten.

**diffidence** ['dɪfɪdəns] *n* Bescheidenheit *f,* Zurückhaltung *f.*

**diffident** ['dɪfɪdənt] *adj* bescheiden, zurückhaltend.

**diffuse** [dɪ'fjuːs] *adj* diffus ♦ *vt* verbreiten.

**dig** [dɪg] (*pt, pp* **dug**) *vt* graben; (*garden*) umgraben ♦ *n* (*prod*) Stoß *m;* (*archaeological*) (Aus)grabung *f;* (*remark*) Seitenhieb *m,* spitze Bemerkung *f;* **to ~ one's nails into sth** seine Nägel in etw *acc* krallen.

▶**dig in** *vi* (*fig: inf: eat*) reinhauen ♦ *vt* (*compost*) untergraben, eingraben; (*knife*) hineinstoßen; (*claw*) festkrallen; **to ~ one's heels in** (*fig*) sich auf die Hinterbeine stellen (*inf*).

▶**dig into** *vt fus* (*savings*) angreifen; (*snow, soil*) ein Loch graben in +*acc*; **to ~ into one's pockets for sth** in seinen Taschen nach etw suchen *or* wühlen.

▶**dig out** *vt* ausgraben.

▶**dig up** *vt* ausgraben.

**digest** [daɪ'dʒɛst] *vt* verdauen ♦ *n* Digest *m or nt*, Auswahl *f*.

**digestible** [dɪ'dʒɛstəbl] *adj* verdaulich.

**digestion** [dɪ'dʒɛstʃən] *n* Verdauung *f*.

**digestive** [dɪ'dʒɛstɪv] *adj* (*system, upsets*) Verdauungs- ♦ *n* Keks aus Vollkornmehl.

**digit** ['dɪdʒɪt] *n* (*number*) Ziffer *f*; (*finger*) Finger *m*.

**digital** ['dɪdʒɪtl] *adj* (*watch, display etc*) Digital-.

**digital computer** *n* Digitalrechner *m*.

**dignified** ['dɪgnɪfaɪd] *adj* würdevoll.

**dignitary** ['dɪgnɪtərɪ] *n* Würdenträger(in) *m(f)*.

**dignity** ['dɪgnɪtɪ] *n* Würde *f*.

**digress** [daɪ'grɛs] *vi*: **to ~ (from)** abschweifen (von).

**digression** [daɪ'grɛʃən] *n* Abschweifung *f*.

**digs** [dɪgz] (*BRIT: inf*) *npl* Bude *f*.

**dike** [daɪk] *n* = **dyke**.

**dilapidated** [dɪ'læpɪdeɪtɪd] *adj* verfallen.

**dilate** [daɪ'leɪt] *vi* sich weiten ♦ *vt* weiten.

**dilatory** ['dɪlətərɪ] *adj* langsam.

**dilemma** [daɪ'lɛmə] *n* Dilemma *nt*; **to be in a ~** sich in einem Dilemma befinden, in der Klemme sitzen (*inf*).

**diligence** ['dɪlɪdʒəns] *n* Fleiß *m*.

**diligent** ['dɪlɪdʒənt] *adj* fleißig; (*research*) sorgfältig, genau.

**dill** [dɪl] *n* Dill *m*.

**dilly-dally** ['dɪlɪ'dælɪ] *vi* trödeln.

**dilute** [daɪ'lu:t] *vt* verdünnen; (*belief, principle*) schwächen ♦ *adj* verdünnt.

**dim** [dɪm] *adj* schwach; (*outline, figure*) undeutlich, verschwommen; (*room*) dämmerig; (*future*) düster; (*prospects*) schlecht; (*inf: person*) schwer von Begriff ♦ *vt* (*light*) dämpfen; (*US: AUT*) abblenden; **to take a ~ view of sth** wenig *or* nicht viel von etw halten.

**dime** [daɪm] (*US*) *n* Zehncentstück *nt*.

**dimension** [daɪ'mɛnʃən] *n* (*aspect*) Dimension *f*; (*measurement*) Abmessung *f*, Maß *nt*; (*also pl: scale, size*) Ausmaß *nt*.

**-dimensional** [dɪ'mɛnʃənl] *adj suff* -dimensional.

**diminish** [dɪ'mɪnɪʃ] *vi* sich verringern ♦ *vt* verringern.

**diminished responsibility** *n* verminderte Zurechnungsfähigkeit *f*.

**diminutive** [dɪ'mɪnjutɪv] *adj* winzig ♦ *n* Verkleinerungsform *f*.

**dimly** ['dɪmlɪ] *adv* schwach; (*see*) undeutlich, verschwommen.

**dimmer** ['dɪmə*] *n* (*also*: **~ switch**) Dimmer *m*; (*US: AUT*) Abblendschalter *m*.

**dimmers** ['dɪməz] (*US*) *npl* (*AUT: dipped headlights*) Abblendlicht *nt*; (*parking lights*) Parklicht *nt*.

**dimmer (switch)** ['dɪmə-] *n* (*ELEC*) Dimmer *m*; (*US: AUT*) Abblendschalter *m*.

**dimple** ['dɪmpl] *n* Grübchen *nt*.

**dim-witted** ['dɪm'wɪtɪd] (*inf*) *adj* dämlich.

**din** [dɪn] *n* Lärm *m*, Getöse *nt* ♦ *vt* (*inf*): **to ~ sth into sb** jdm etw einbleuen.

**dine** [daɪn] *vi* speisen.

**diner** ['daɪnə*] *n* Gast *m*; (*US: restaurant*) Eßlokal *nt*.

**dinghy** ['dɪŋgɪ] *n* (*also*: **rubber ~**) Schlauchboot *nt*; (*also*: **sailing ~**) Dingi *nt*.

**dingy** ['dɪndʒɪ] *adj* schäbig; (*clothes, curtains etc*) schmuddelig.

**dining car** ['daɪnɪŋ-] (*BRIT*) *n* Speisewagen *m*.

**dining room** *n* Eßzimmer *nt*; (*in hotel*) Speiseraum *m*.

**dinner** ['dɪnə*] *n* (*evening meal*) Abendessen *nt*; (*lunch*) Mittagessen *nt*; (*banquet*) (Fest)essen *nt*.

**dinner jacket** *n* Smokingjackett *nt*.

**dinner party** *n* Abendgesellschaft *f* (mit Essen).

**dinner service** *n* Tafelservice *nt*.

**dinner time** *n* Essenszeit *f*.

**dinosaur** ['daɪnəsɔ:*] *n* Dinosaurier *m*.

**dint** [dɪnt] *n*: **by ~ of** durch +*acc*.

**diocese** ['daɪəsɪs] *n* Diözese *f*.

**dioxide** [daɪ'ɔksaɪd] *n* Dioxyd *nt*.

**Dip.** (*BRIT*) *abbr* = **diploma**.

**dip** [dɪp] *n* Senke *f*; (*in sea*) kurzes Bad *nt*; (*CULIN*) Dip *m*; (*for sheep*) Desinfektionslösung *f* ♦ *vt* eintauchen; (*BRIT: AUT*) abblenden ♦ *vi* abfallen.

**diphtheria** [dɪf'θɪərɪə] *n* Diphtherie *f*.

**diphthong** ['dɪfθɔŋ] *n* Diphthong *m*.

**diploma** [dɪ'pləumə] *n* Diplom *nt*.

**diplomacy** [dɪ'pləuməsɪ] *n* Diplomatie *f*.

**diplomat** ['dɪpləmæt] *n* Diplomat(in) *m(f)*.

**diplomatic** [dɪplə'mætɪk] *adj* diplomatisch; **to break off ~ relations (with)** die diplomatischen Beziehungen abbrechen (mit).

**diplomatic corps** *n* diplomatisches Korps *nt*.

**diplomatic immunity** *n* Immunität *f*.

**dip rod** ['dɪprɔd] (*US*) *n* Ölmeßstab *m*.

**dipstick** ['dɪpstɪk] (*BRIT*) *n* Ölmeßstab *m*.

**dip switch** (*BRIT*) *n* Abblendschalter *m*.

**dire** [daɪə*] *adj* (*consequences, effects*) schrecklich.

**direct** [daɪ'rɛkt] *adj, adv* direkt ♦ *vt* richten; (*company, project, programme etc*) leiten; (*play, film*) Regie führen bei; **to ~ sb to do sth** jdn anweisen, etw zu tun; **can you ~ me to ...?** können Sie mir den Weg nach ... sagen?

**direct access** *n* (*COMPUT*) Direktzugriff *m*.

**direct cost** *n* direkte Kosten *pl*.

**direct current** *n* Gleichstrom *m*.
**direct debit** (*BRIT*) *n* Einzugsauftrag *m*; (*transaction*) automatische Abbuchung *f*.
**direct dialling** *n* Selbstwahl *f*.
**direct hit** *n* Volltreffer *m*.
**direction** [dɪ'rɛkʃən] *n* Richtung *f*; (*TV, RADIO*) Leitung *f*; (*CINE*) Regie *f*; **directions** *npl* (*instructions*) Anweisungen *pl*; **sense of ~** Orientierungssinn *m*; **~s for use** Gebrauchsanweisung *f*, Gebrauchsanleitung *f*; **to ask for ~s** nach dem Weg fragen; **in the ~ of** in Richtung.
**directional** [dɪ'rɛkʃənl] *adj* (*aerial*) Richt-.
**directive** [dɪ'rɛktɪv] *n* Direktive *f*, Weisung *f*; **government ~** Regierungserlaß *m*.
**direct labour** *n* (*COMM*) Produktionsarbeit *f*; (*BRIT*) eigene Arbeitskräfte *pl*.
**directly** [dɪ'rɛktlɪ] *adv* direkt; (*at once*) sofort, gleich.
**direct mail** *n* Werbebriefe *pl*.
**direct mailshot** (*BRIT*) *n* Direktwerbung *f* per Post.
**directness** [daɪ'rɛktnɪs] *n* Direktheit *f*.
**director** [dɪ'rɛktə*] *n* Direktor(in) *m(f)*; (*of project, TV, RADIO*) Leiter(in) *m(f)*; (*CINE*) Regisseur(in) *m(f)*.
**Director of Public Prosecutions** (*BRIT*) *n* ≈ Generalstaatsanwalt *m*, Generalstaatsanwältin *f*.
**directory** [dɪ'rɛktərɪ] *n* (*also:* **telephone ~**) Telefonbuch *nt*; (*also:* **street ~**) Einwohnerverzeichnis *nt*; (*COMPUT*) Verzeichnis *nt*; (*COMM*) Branchenverzeichnis *nt*.
**directory enquiries,** (*US*) **directory assistance** *n* (*Fernsprech*)auskunft *f*.
**dirt** [dəːt] *n* Schmutz *m*; (*earth*) Erde *f*; **to treat sb like ~** jdn wie (den letzten) Dreck behandeln.
**dirt-cheap** ['dəːt't.ʃiːp] *adj* spottbillig.
**dirt road** *n* unbefestigte Straße *f*.
**dirty** ['dəːtɪ] *adj* schmutzig; (*story*) unanständig ♦ *vt* beschmutzen.
**dirty trick** *n* gemeiner Trick *m*.
**disability** [dɪsə'bɪlɪtɪ] *n* Behinderung *f*.
**disability allowance** *n* Behindertenbeihilfe *f*.
**disable** [dɪs'eɪbl] *vt* zum Invaliden machen; (*tank, gun*) unbrauchbar machen.
**disabled** [dɪs'eɪbld] *adj* behindert ♦ *npl:* **the ~** die Behinderten *pl*.
**disabuse** [dɪsə'bjuːz] *vt:* **to ~ sb (of)** jdn befreien (von).
**disadvantage** [dɪsəd'vɑːntɪdʒ] *n* Nachteil *m*; (*detriment*) Schaden *m*; **to be at a ~** benachteiligt *or* im Nachteil sein.
**disadvantaged** [dɪsəd'vɑːntɪdʒd] *adj* benachteiligt.
**disadvantageous** [dɪsædvɑːn'teɪdʒəs] *adj* ungünstig.
**disaffected** [dɪsə'fɛktɪd] *adj* entfremdet.
**disaffection** [dɪsə'fɛkʃən] *n* Entfremdung *f*.

**disagree** [dɪsə'griː] *vi* nicht übereinstimmen; (*to be against, think differently*): **to ~ (with)** nicht einverstanden sein (mit); **I ~ with you** ich bin anderer Meinung; **garlic ~s with me** ich vertrage keinen Knoblauch, Knoblauch bekommt mir nicht.
**disagreeable** [dɪsə'griːəbl] *adj* unangenehm; (*person*) unsympathisch.
**disagreement** [dɪsə'griːmənt] *n* Uneinigkeit *f*; (*argument*) Meinungsverschiedenheit *f*; **to have a ~ with sb** sich mit jdm nicht einig sein.
**disallow** ['dɪsə'lau] *vt* (*appeal*) abweisen; (*goal*) nicht anerkennen, nicht geben.
**disappear** [dɪsə'pɪə*] *vi* verschwinden; (*custom etc*) aussterben.
**disappearance** [dɪsə'pɪərəns] *n* (*see vi*) Verschwinden *nt*; Aussterben *nt*.
**disappoint** [dɪsə'pɔɪnt] *vt* enttäuschen.
**disappointed** [dɪsə'pɔɪntɪd] *adj* enttäuscht.
**disappointing** [dɪsə'pɔɪntɪŋ] *adj* enttäuschend.
**disappointment** [dɪsə'pɔɪntmənt] *n* Enttäuschung *f*.
**disapproval** [dɪsə'pruːvəl] *n* Mißbilligung *f*.
**disapprove** [dɪsə'pruːv] *vi* dagegen sein; **to ~ of** mißbilligen +*acc*.
**disapproving** [dɪsə'pruːvɪŋ] *adj* mißbilligend.
**disarm** [dɪs'ɑːm] *vt* entwaffnen; (*criticism*) zum Verstummen bringen ♦ *vi* abrüsten.
**disarmament** [dɪs'ɑːməmənt] *n* Abrüstung *f*.
**disarming** [dɪs'ɑːmɪŋ] *adj* entwaffnend.
**disarray** [dɪsə'reɪ] *n:* **in ~** (*army, organization*) in Auflösung (begriffen); (*hair, clothes*) unordentlich; (*thoughts*) durcheinander; **to throw into ~** durcheinanderbringen.
**disaster** [dɪ'zɑːstə*] *n* Katastrophe *f*; (*AVIAT etc*) Unglück *nt*; (*fig: mess*) Fiasko *nt*.
**disaster area** *n* Katastrophengebiet *nt*; (*fig: person*) Katastrophe *f*; **my office is a ~** in meinem Büro sieht es katastrophal aus.
**disastrous** [dɪ'zɑːstrəs] *adj* katastrophal.
**disband** [dɪs'bænd] *vt* auflösen ♦ *vi* sich auflösen.
**disbelief** ['dɪsbə'liːf] *n* Ungläubigkeit *f*; **in ~** ungläubig.
**disbelieve** ['dɪsbə'liːv] *vt* (*person*) nicht glauben +*dat*; (*story*) nicht glauben; **I don't ~ you** ich bezweifle nicht, was Sie sagen.
**disc** [dɪsk] *n* (*ANAT*) Bandscheibe *f*; (*record*) Platte *f*; (*COMPUT*) = **disk**.
**disc.** *abbr* (*COMM*) = **discount**.
**discard** [dɪs'kɑːd] *vt* ausrangieren; (*fig: idea, plan*) verwerfen.
**disc brake** *n* Scheibenbremse *f*.
**discern** [dɪ'səːn] *vt* wahrnehmen; (*identify*) erkennen.
**discernible** [dɪ'səːnəbl] *adj* erkennbar; (*object*) wahrnehmbar.
**discerning** [dɪ'səːnɪŋ] *adj* (*judgement*) scharfsinnig; (*look*) kritisch; (*listeners etc*) anspruchsvoll.

**discharge** [dɪs'tʃɑːdʒ] vt (duties) nachkommen +dat; (debt) begleichen; (waste) ablassen; (ELEC) entladen; (MED) ausscheiden, absondern; (patient, employee, soldier) entlassen; (defendant) freisprechen ♦ n (of gas) Ausströmen nt; (of liquid) Ausfließen nt; (ELEC) Entladung f; (MED) Ausfluß m; (of patient, employee, soldier) Entlassung f; (of defendant) Freispruch m; **to ~ a gun** ein Gewehr abfeuern.

**discharged bankrupt** [dɪs'tʃɑːdʒd-] n (LAW) entlasteter Konkursschuldner m, entlastete Konkursschuldnerin f.

**disciple** [dɪ'saɪpl] n Jünger m; (fig: follower) Schüler(in) m(f).

**disciplinary** ['dɪsɪplɪnərɪ] adj (powers etc) Disziplinar-; **to take ~ action against sb** ein Disziplinarverfahren gegen jdn einleiten.

**discipline** ['dɪsɪplɪn] n Disziplin f ♦ vt disziplinieren; (punish) bestrafen; **to ~ o.s. to do sth** sich dazu anhalten or zwingen, etw zu tun.

**disc jockey** n Diskjockey m.

**disclaim** [dɪs'kleɪm] vt (knowledge) abstreiten; (responsibility) von sich weisen.

**disclaimer** [dɪs'kleɪmə*] n Dementi nt; **to issue a ~** eine Gegenerklärung abgeben.

**disclose** [dɪs'kləuz] vt enthüllen, bekanntgeben.

**disclosure** [dɪs'kləuʒə*] n Enthüllung f.

**disco** ['dɪskəu] n abbr = **discotheque**.

**discolor** etc [dɪs'kʌlə*] (US) = **discolour** etc.

**discolour** [dɪs'kʌlə*] vt verfärben ♦ vi sich verfärben.

**discolouration** [dɪskʌlə'reɪʃən] n Verfärbung f.

**discoloured** [dɪs'kʌləd] adj verfärbt.

**discomfort** [dɪs'kʌmfət] n (unease) Unbehagen nt; (physical) Beschwerden pl.

**disconcert** [dɪskən'sɜːt] vt beunruhigen, irritieren.

**disconcerting** [dɪskən'sɜːtɪŋ] adj beunruhigend, irritierend.

**disconnect** [dɪskə'nekt] vt abtrennen; (ELEC, RADIO) abstellen; **I've been ~ed** (TEL) das Gespräch ist unterbrochen worden; (supply, connection) man hat mir das Telefon/den Strom/das Gas etc abgestellt.

**disconnected** [dɪskə'nektɪd] adj unzusammenhängend.

**disconsolate** [dɪs'kɔnsəlɪt] adj niedergeschlagen.

**discontent** [dɪskən'tent] n Unzufriedenheit f.

**discontented** [dɪskən'tentɪd] adj unzufrieden.

**discontinue** [dɪskən'tɪnjuː] vt einstellen; **"~d"** (COMM) „ausgelaufene Serie".

**discord** ['dɪskɔːd] n Zwietracht f; (MUS) Dissonanz f.

**discordant** [dɪs'kɔːdənt] adj unharmonisch.

**discotheque** ['dɪskəutek] n Diskothek f.

**discount** [n 'dɪskaunt, vt dɪs'kaunt] n Rabatt m ♦ vt nachlassen; (idea, fact) unberücksichtigt

lassen; **to give sb a ~ on sth** jdm auf etw acc Rabatt geben; **~ for cash** Skonto nt or m (bei Barzahlung); **at a ~** mit Rabatt.

**discount house** n Diskontbank f; (also: discount store) Diskontgeschäft nt.

**discount rate** n Diskontsatz m.

**discourage** [dɪs'kʌrɪdʒ] vt entmutigen; **to ~ sb from doing sth** jdm davon abraten, etw zu tun.

**discouragement** [dɪs'kʌrɪdʒmənt] n Mutlosigkeit f; **to act as a ~ to sb** entmutigend für jdn sein.

**discouraging** [dɪs'kʌrɪdʒɪŋ] adj entmutigend.

**discourteous** [dɪs'kɜːtɪəs] adj unhöflich.

**discover** [dɪs'kʌvə*] vt entdecken; (missing person) finden; **to ~ that ...** herausfinden, daß ...

**discovery** [dɪs'kʌvərɪ] n Entdeckung f.

**discredit** [dɪs'kredɪt] vt in Mißkredit bringen ♦ n: **to sb's ~** zu jds Schande.

**discreet** [dɪs'kriːt] adj diskret; (unremarkable) dezent.

**discreetly** [dɪs'kriːtlɪ] adv diskret; (unremarkably) dezent.

**discrepancy** [dɪs'krepənsɪ] n Diskrepanz f.

**discretion** [dɪs'kreʃən] n Diskretion f; **at the ~ of** im Ermessen +gen; **use your own ~** Sie müssen nach eigenem Ermessen handeln.

**discretionary** [dɪs'kreʃənrɪ] adj: **~ powers** Ermessensspielraum m; **~ payments** Ermessenszahlungen pl.

**discriminate** [dɪs'krɪmɪneɪt] vi: **to ~ between** unterscheiden zwischen +dat; **to ~ against** diskriminieren +acc.

**discriminating** [dɪs'krɪmɪneɪtɪŋ] adj anspruchsvoll, kritisch; (tax, duty) Differential-.

**discrimination** [dɪskrɪmɪ'neɪʃən] n Diskriminierung f; (discernment) Urteilsvermögen nt; **racial ~** Rassendiskriminierung f; **sexual ~** Diskriminierung aufgrund des Geschlechts.

**discus** ['dɪskəs] n Diskus m; (event) Diskuswerfen nt.

**discuss** [dɪs'kʌs] vt besprechen; (debate) diskutieren; (analyse) erörtern, behandeln.

**discussion** [dɪs'kʌʃən] n Besprechung f; (debate) Diskussion f; **under ~** in der Diskussion.

**disdain** [dɪs'deɪn] n Verachtung f ♦ vt verachten ♦ vi: **to ~ to do sth** es für unter seiner Würde halten, etw zu tun.

**disease** [dɪ'ziːz] n Krankheit f.

**diseased** [dɪ'ziːzd] adj krank; (tree) befallen.

**disembark** [dɪsɪm'bɑːk] vt ausschiffen ♦ vi (passengers) von Bord gehen.

**disembarkation** [dɪsembɑː'keɪʃən] n Ausschiffung f.

**disembodied** ['dɪsɪm'bɔdɪd] adj (voice) geisterhaft; (hand) körperlos.

**disembowel** ['dɪsɪm'bauəl] vt die Eingeweide

herausnehmen +*dat.*
**disenchanted** ['dısın'tʃɑːntıd] *adj:* ~ **(with)** enttäuscht (von).
**disenfranchise** ['dısın'fræntʃaız] *vt* (*POL*) das Wahlrecht entziehen +*dat;* (*COMM*) die Konzession entziehen +*dat.*
**disengage** [dısın'geıdʒ] *vt* (*TECH*) ausrasten; **to** ~ **the clutch** auskuppeln.
**disengagement** [dısın'geıdʒmənt] *n* (*POL*) Disengagement *nt.*
**disentangle** [dısın'tæŋgl] *vt* befreien; (*wool, wire*) entwirren.
**disfavour,** (*US*) **disfavor** [dıs'feıvə*] *n* Mißfallen *nt;* **to fall into** ~ **(with sb)** (bei jdm) in Ungnade fallen.
**disfigure** [dıs'fıgə*] *vt* entstellen; (*object, place*) verunstalten.
**disgorge** [dıs'gɔːdʒ] *vt* (*liquid*) ergießen; (*people*) ausspeien.
**disgrace** [dıs'greıs] *n* Schande *f;* (*scandal*) Skandal *m* ♦ *vt* Schande bringen über +*acc.*
**disgraceful** [dıs'greısful] *adj* skandalös.
**disgruntled** [dıs'grʌntld] *adj* verärgert.
**disguise** [dıs'gaız] *n* Verkleidung *f* ♦ *vt:* **to** ~ **(as)** (*person*) verkleiden (als); (*object*) tarnen (als); **in** ~ (*person*) verkleidet; **there's no disguising the fact that ...** es kann nicht geleugnet werden, daß ...; **to** ~ **o.s. as** sich verkleiden als.
**disgust** [dıs'gʌst] *n* Abscheu *m* ♦ *vt* anwidern; **she walked off in** ~ sie ging voller Empörung weg.
**disgusting** [dıs'gʌstıŋ] *adj* widerlich.
**dish** [dıʃ] *n* Schüssel *f;* (*flat*) Schale *f;* (*recipe, food*) Gericht *nt;* (*also:* **satellite** ~) Parabolantenne *f,* Schüssel (*inf*); **to do or wash the** ~**es** Geschirr spülen, abwaschen.
▶**dish out** *vt* verteilen; (*food, money*) austeilen; (*advice*) erteilen.
▶**dish up** *vt* (*food*) auftragen, servieren; (*facts, statistics*) auftischen (*inf*).
**dishcloth** ['dıʃklɔθ] *n* Spültuch *nt,* Spüllappen *m.*
**dishearten** [dıs'hɑːtn] *vt* entmutigen.
**dishevelled,** (*US*) **disheveled** [dı'ʃevəld] *adj* unordentlich; (*hair*) zerzaust.
**dishonest** [dıs'ɔnıst] *adj* unehrlich; (*means*) unlauter.
**dishonesty** [dıs'ɔnıstı] *n* Unehrlichkeit *f.*
**dishonor** *etc* [dıs'ɔnə*] (*US*) = **dishonour** *etc.*
**dishonour** [dıs'ɔnə*] *n* Schande *f.*
**dishonourable** [dıs'ɔnərəbl] *adj* unehrenhaft.
**dish soap** (*US*) *n* Spülmittel *nt.*
**dishtowel** ['dıʃtauəl] (*US*) *n* Geschirrtuch *nt.*
**dishwasher** ['dıʃwɔʃə*] *n* (*machine*) (Geschirr)spülmaschine *f.*
**dishy** ['dıʃı] (*inf: BRIT*) *adj* attraktiv.
**disillusion** [dısı'luːʒən] *vt* desillusionieren ♦ *n* = **disillusionment; to become** ~**ed (with)** seine Illusionen (über +*acc*) verlieren.
**disillusionment** [dısı'luːʒənmənt] *n* Desillusionierung *f.*

**disincentive** [dısın'sentıv] *n* Entmutigung *f;* **it's a** ~ es hält die Leute ab; **to be a** ~ **to sb** jdm keinen Anreiz bieten.
**disinclined** [dısın'klaınd] *adj:* **to be** ~ **to do sth** abgeneigt sein, etw zu tun.
**disinfect** [dısın'fekt] *vt* desinfizieren.
**disinfectant** [dısın'fektənt] *n* Desinfektionsmittel *nt.*
**disinflation** [dısın'fleıʃən] *n* (*ECON*) Rückgang *m* einer inflationären Entwicklung.
**disinformation** [dısınfə'meıʃən] *n* Desinformation *f.*
**disingenuous** [dısın'dʒenjuəs] *adj* unaufrichtig.
**disinherit** [dısın'herıt] *vt* enterben.
**disintegrate** [dıs'ıntıgreıt] *vi* zerfallen; (*marriage, partnership*) scheitern; (*organization*) sich auflösen.
**disinterested** [dıs'ıntrəstıd] *adj* (*advice*) unparteiisch, unvoreingenommen; (*help*) uneigennützig.
**disjointed** [dıs'dʒɔıntıd] *adj* unzusammenhängend.
**disk** [dısk] *n* Diskette *f;* **single-/double-sided** ~ einseitige/zweiseitige Diskette.
**disk drive** *n* Diskettenlaufwerk *nt.*
**diskette** [dıs'ket] (*US*) *n* = **disk.**
**disk operating system** *n* Betriebssystem *nt.*
**dislike** [dıs'laık] *n* Abneigung *f* ♦ *vt* nicht mögen; **to take a** ~ **to sb/sth** eine Abneigung gegen jdn/etw entwickeln; **I** ~ **the idea** die Idee gefällt mir nicht; **he** ~**s it** er kann es nicht leiden, er mag es nicht.
**dislocate** ['dısləkeıt] *vt* verrenken, ausrenken; **he has** ~**d his shoulder** er hat sich *dat* den Arm ausgekugelt.
**dislodge** [dıs'lɔdʒ] *vt* verschieben.
**disloyal** [dıs'lɔıəl] *adj* illoyal.
**dismal** ['dızml] *adj* trübe, trostlos; (*song, person, mood*) trübsinnig; (*failure*) kläglich.
**dismantle** [dıs'mæntl] *vt* (*machine*) demontieren.
**dismast** [dıs'mɑːst] *vt* (*NAUT*) entmasten.
**dismay** [dıs'meı] *n* Bestürzung *f* ♦ *vt* bestürzen; **much to my** ~ zu meiner Bestürzung; **in** ~ bestürzt.
**dismiss** [dıs'mıs] *vt* entlassen; (*case*) abweisen; (*possibility, idea*) abtun.
**dismissal** [dıs'mısl] *n* Entlassung *f.*
**dismount** [dıs'maunt] *vi* absteigen.
**disobedience** [dısə'biːdıəns] *n* Ungehorsam *m.*
**disobedient** [dısə'biːdıənt] *adj* ungehorsam.
**disobey** [dısə'beı] *vt* nicht gehorchen +*dat;* (*order*) nicht befolgen.
**disorder** [dıs'ɔːdə*] *n* Unordnung *f;* (*rioting*) Unruhen *pl;* (*MED*) (Funktions)störung *f;* **civil** ~ öffentliche Unruhen *pl.*
**disorderly** [dıs'ɔːdəlı] *adj* unordentlich; (*meeting*) undiszipliniert; (*behaviour*) ungehörig.
**disorderly conduct** *n* (*LAW*) ungebührliches

Benehmen nt.

**disorganize** [dɪs'ɔːgənaɪz] vt durcheinanderbringen.

**disorganized** [dɪs'ɔːgənaɪzd] adj chaotisch.

**disorientated** [dɪs'ɔːrɪenteɪtɪd] adj desorientiert, verwirrt.

**disown** [dɪs'əʊn] vt (action) verleugnen; (child) verstoßen.

**disparaging** [dɪs'pærɪdʒɪŋ] adj (remarks) abschätzig, geringschätzig; **to be ~ about sb/sth** (person) abschätzig or geringschätzig über jdn/etw urteilen.

**disparate** ['dɪspərɪt] adj völlig verschieden.

**disparity** [dɪs'pærɪtɪ] n Unterschied m.

**dispassionate** [dɪs'pæʃənət] adj nüchtern.

**dispatch** [dɪs'pætʃ] vt senden, schicken; (deal with) erledigen; (kill) töten ♦ n Senden nt, Schicken nt; (PRESS) Bericht m; (MIL) Depesche f.

**dispatch department** n Versandabteilung f.

**dispatch rider** n (MIL) Meldefahrer m.

**dispel** [dɪs'pel] vt (myths) zerstören; (fears) zerstreuen.

**dispensary** [dɪs'pensərɪ] n Apotheke f; (in chemist's) Raum in einer Apotheke, wo Arzneimittel abgefüllt werden.

**dispensation** [dɪspən'seɪʃən] n (of treatment) Vergabe f; (special permission) Dispens m; **~ of justice** Rechtsprechung f.

**dispense** [dɪs'pens] vt (medicines) abgeben; (charity) austeilen; (advice) erteilen.

▶**dispense with** vt fus verzichten auf +acc.

**dispenser** [dɪs'pensə•] n (machine) Automat m.

**dispensing chemist** [dɪs'pensɪŋ-] (BRIT) n (shop) Apotheke f.

**dispersal** [dɪs'pɜːsl] n (of objects) Verstreuen nt; (of group, crowd) Auflösung f, Zerstreuen nt.

**disperse** [dɪs'pɜːs] vt (objects) verstreuen; (crowd etc) auflösen, zerstreuen; (knowledge, information) verbreiten ♦ vi (crowd) sich auflösen or zerstreuen.

**dispirited** [dɪs'pɪrɪtɪd] adj entmutigt.

**displace** [dɪs'pleɪs] vt ablösen.

**displaced person** [dɪs'pleɪst-] n Verschleppte(r) f(m).

**displacement** [dɪs'pleɪsmənt] n Ablösung f; (of people) Vertreibung f; (PHYS) Verdrängung f.

**display** [dɪs'pleɪ] n (in shop) Auslage f; (exhibition) Ausstellung f; (of feeling) Zeigen nt; (pej) Zurschaustellung f; (COMPUT, TECH) Anzeige f ♦ vt zeigen; (ostentatiously) zur Schau stellen; (results, departure times) aushängen; **on ~** ausgestellt.

**display advertising** n Displaywerbung f.

**displease** [dɪs'pliːz] vt verstimmen, verärgern.

**displeased** [dɪs'pliːzd] adj: **I am very ~ with you** ich bin sehr enttäuscht von dir.

**displeasure** [dɪs'pleʒə•] n Mißfallen nt.

**disposable** [dɪs'pəʊzəbl] adj (lighter) Wegwerf-; (bottle) Einweg-; (income) verfügbar.

**disposable nappy** (BRIT) n Papierwindel f.

**disposal** [dɪs'pəʊzl] n (of goods for sale) Loswerden nt; (of property, belongings: by selling) Verkauf m; (: by giving away) Abgeben nt; (of rubbish) Beseitigung f; **at one's ~** zur Verfügung; **to put sth at sb's ~** jdm etw zur Verfügung stellen.

**dispose** [dɪs'pəʊz]: **~ of** vt fus (body) aus dem Weg schaffen; (unwanted goods) loswerden; (problem, task) erledigen; (stock) verkaufen.

**disposed** [dɪs'pəʊzd] adj: **to be ~ to do sth** (inclined) geneigt sein, etw zu tun; (willing) bereit sein, etw zu tun; **to be well ~ towards sb** jdm wohlwollen.

**disposition** [dɪspə'zɪʃən] n (nature) Veranlagung f; (inclination) Neigung f.

**dispossess** ['dɪspə'zɛs] vt enteignen; **to ~ sb of his/her land** jds Land enteignen.

**disproportion** [dɪsprə'pɔːʃən] n Mißverhältnis nt.

**disproportionate** [dɪsprə'pɔːʃənət] adj unverhältnismäßig; (amount) unverhältnismäßig hoch/niedrig.

**disprove** [dɪs'pruːv] vt widerlegen.

**dispute** [dɪs'pjuːt] n Streit m; (also: **industrial ~**) Auseinandersetzung f zwischen Arbeitgebern und Arbeitnehmern; (POL, MIL) Streitigkeiten pl ♦ vt bestreiten; (ownership etc) anfechten; **to be in** or **under ~** umstritten sein.

**disqualification** [dɪskwɔlɪfɪ'keɪʃən] n: **~ (from)** Ausschluß m (von); (SPORT) Disqualifizierung f (von); **~ (from driving)** (BRIT) Führerscheinentzug m.

**disqualify** [dɪs'kwɔlɪfaɪ] vt disqualifizieren; **to ~ sb for sth** jdn für etw ungeeignet machen; **to ~ sb from doing sth** jdn ungeeignet machen, etw zu tun; **to ~ sb from driving** (BRIT) jdm den Führerschein entziehen.

**disquiet** [dɪs'kwaɪət] n Unruhe f.

**disquieting** [dɪs'kwaɪətɪŋ] adj beunruhigend.

**disregard** [dɪsrɪ'gɑːd] vt nicht beachten, ignorieren ♦ n: **~ (for)** Mißachtung f (+gen); (for danger, money) Geringschätzung f (+gen).

**disrepair** [dɪsrɪ'pɛə•] n: **to fall into ~** (machine) vernachlässigt werden; (building) verfallen.

**disreputable** [dɪs'repjutəbl] adj (person) unehrenhaft; (behaviour) unfein.

**disrepute** ['dɪsrɪ'pjuːt] n schlechter Ruf m; **to bring/fall into ~** in Verruf bringen/kommen.

**disrespectful** [dɪsrɪ'spektful] adj respektlos.

**disrupt** [dɪs'rʌpt] vt (plans) durcheinanderbringen; (conversation, proceedings) unterbrechen.

**disruption** [dɪs'rʌpʃən] n Unterbrechung f; (disturbance) Störung f.

**disruptive** [dɪs'rʌptɪv] adj störend; (action) Stör-.

**dissatisfaction** [dɪssætɪs'fækʃən] *n* Unzufriedenheit *f*.

**dissatisfied** [dɪs'sætɪsfaɪd] *adj:* ~ **(with)** unzufrieden (mit).

**dissect** [dɪ'sɛkt] *vt* sezieren.

**disseminate** [dɪ'sɛmɪneɪt] *vt* verbreiten.

**dissent** [dɪ'sɛnt] *n* abweichende Meinungen *pl*.

**dissenter** [dɪ'sɛntə•] *n* Abweichler(in) *m(f)*.

**dissertation** [dɪsə'teɪʃən] *n* (*speech*) Vortrag *m*; (*piece of writing*) Abhandlung *f*; (*for PhD*) Dissertation *f*.

**disservice** [dɪs'sɔːvɪs] *n:* **to do sb a** ~ jdm einen schlechten Dienst erweisen.

**dissident** ['dɪsɪdnt] *adj* andersdenkend; (*voice*) kritisch ♦ *n* Dissident(in) *m(f)*.

**dissimilar** [dɪ'sɪmɪlə•] *adj:* ~ **(to)** anders (als).

**dissipate** ['dɪsɪpeɪt] *vt* (*heat*) neutralisieren; (*clouds*) auflösen; (*money, effort*) verschwenden.

**dissipated** ['dɪsɪpeɪtɪd] *adj* zügellos, ausschweifend.

**dissociate** [dɪ'səʊʃɪeɪt] *vt* trennen; **to** ~ **o.s. from** sich distanzieren von.

**dissolute** ['dɪsəluːt] *adj* zügellos, ausschweifend.

**dissolution** [dɪsə'luːʃən] *n* Auflösung *f*.

**dissolve** [dɪ'zɒlv] *vt* auflösen ♦ *vi* sich auflösen; **to** ~ **in(to) tears** in Tränen zerfließen.

**dissuade** [dɪ'sweɪd] *vt:* **to** ~ **sb (from sth)** jdn (von etw) abbringen.

**distaff** ['dɪstɑːf] *n:* **the** ~ **side** die mütterliche Seite.

**distance** ['dɪstns] *n* Entfernung *f*; (*in time*) Abstand *m*; (*reserve*) Abstand, Distanz *f* ♦ *vt:* **to** ~ **o.s. (from)** sich distanzieren (von); **in the** ~ in der Ferne; **what's the** ~ **to London?** wie weit ist es nach London?; **it's within walking** ~ es ist zu Fuß erreichbar; **at a** ~ **of 2 metres** in 2 Meter(n) Entfernung; **keep your** ~! halten Sie Abstand!

**distant** ['dɪstnt] *adj* (*place*) weit entfernt, fern; (*time*) weit zurückliegend; (*relative*) entfernt; (*manner*) distanziert, kühl.

**distaste** [dɪs'teɪst] *n* Widerwille *m*.

**distasteful** [dɪs'teɪstful] *adj* widerlich; **to be** ~ **to sb** jdm zuwider sein.

**Dist. Atty.** (*US*) *abbr* = **district attorney**.

**distemper** [dɪs'tɛmpə•] *n* (*paint*) Temperafarbe *f*; (*disease of dogs*) Staupe *f*.

**distend** [dɪs'tɛnd] *vt* blähen ♦ *vi* sich blähen.

**distended** [dɪs'tɛndɪd] *adj* aufgebläht.

**distil,** (*US*) **distill** [dɪs'tɪl] *vt* destillieren; (*fig*) (heraus)destillieren.

**distillery** [dɪs'tɪlərɪ] *n* Brennerei *f*.

**distinct** [dɪs'tɪŋkt] *adj* deutlich, klar; (*possibility*) eindeutig; (*different*) verschieden; **as** ~ **from** im Unterschied zu.

**distinction** [dɪs'tɪŋkʃən] *n* Unterschied *m*; (*honour*) Ehre *f*; (*in exam*) Auszeichnung *f*; **to draw a** ~ **between** einen Unterschied machen zwischen +*dat*; **a writer of** ~ ein Schriftsteller von Rang.

**distinctive** [dɪs'tɪŋktɪv] *adj* unverwechselbar.

**distinctly** [dɪs'tɪŋktlɪ] *adv* deutlich, klar; (*tell*) ausdrücklich; (*unhappy*) ausgesprochen; (*better*) entschieden.

**distinguish** [dɪs'tɪŋgwɪʃ] *vt* unterscheiden; (*details etc*) erkennen, ausmachen; **to** ~ **(between)** unterscheiden (zwischen +*dat*); **to** ~ **o.s.** sich hervortun.

**distinguished** [dɪs'tɪŋgwɪʃt] *adj* von hohem Rang; (*career*) hervorragend; (*in appearance*) distinguiert.

**distinguishing** [dɪs'tɪŋgwɪʃɪŋ] *adj* charakteristisch.

**distort** [dɪs'tɔːt] *vt* verzerren; (*argument*) verdrehen.

**distortion** [dɪs'tɔːʃən] *n* (*see vb*) Verzerrung *f*; Verdrehung *f*.

**distract** [dɪs'trækt] *vt* ablenken.

**distracted** [dɪs'træktɪd] *adj* unaufmerksam; (*anxious*) besorgt, beunruhigt.

**distraction** [dɪs'trækʃən] *n* Unaufmerksamkeit *f*; (*confusion*) Verstörtheit *f*; (*sth which distracts*) Ablenkung *f*; (*amusement*) Zerstreuung *f*; **to drive sb to** ~ jdn zur Verzweiflung treiben.

**distraught** [dɪs'trɔːt] *adj* verzweifelt.

**distress** [dɪs'trɛs] *n* Verzweiflung *f* ♦ *vt* Kummer machen +*dat*; **in** ~ (*ship*) in Seenot; (*person*) verzweifelt; ~**ed area** (*BRIT*) Notstandsgebiet *nt*.

**distressing** [dɪs'trɛsɪŋ] *adj* beunruhigend.

**distress signal** *n* Notsignal *nt*.

**distribute** [dɪs'trɪbjuːt] *vt* verteilen; (*profits*) aufteilen.

**distribution** [dɪstrɪ'bjuːʃən] *n* Vertrieb *m*; (*of profits*) Aufteilung *f*.

**distribution costs** *npl* Vertriebskosten *pl*.

**distributor** [dɪs'trɪbjuːtə•] *n* (*COMM*) Vertreiber(in) *m(f)*; (*AUT, TECH*) Verteiler *m*.

**district** ['dɪstrɪkt] *n* Gebiet *nt*; (*of town*) Stadtteil *m*; (*ADMIN*) (Verwaltungs)bezirk *m*.

**district attorney** (*US*) *n* Bezirksstaatsanwalt *m*, Bezirksstaatsanwältin *f*.

---

**District Council** *heißt der in jedem der britischen* **districts** *(Bezirke) alle vier Jahre neu gewählte Bezirksrat, der für bestimmte Bereiche der Kommunalverwaltung (Gesundheitsschutz, Wohnungsbeschaffung, Baugenehmigungen, Müllabfuhr) zuständig ist. Die district councils werden durch Kommunalabgaben und durch einen Zuschuß von der Regierung finanziert. Ihre Ausgaben werden von einer unabhängigen Prüfungskommission kontrolliert, und bei zu hohen Ausgaben wird der Regierungszuschuß gekürzt.*

---

**district nurse** (*BRIT*) *n* Gemeindeschwester *f*.

**distrust** [dɪs'trʌst] *n* Mißtrauen *nt* ♦ *vt*

mißtrauen +dat.

**distrustful** [dɪs'trʌstful] adj: ~ **(of)** mißtrauisch (gegenüber +dat).

**disturb** [dɪs'tɜːb] vt stören; (upset) beunruhigen; (disorganize) durcheinanderbringen; **sorry to ~ you** entschuldigen Sie bitte die Störung.

**disturbance** [dɪs'tɜːbəns] n Störung f; (political etc) Unruhe f; (violent event) Unruhen pl; (by drunks etc) (Ruhe)störung f; **to cause a ~** Unruhe/eine Ruhestörung verursachen; **~ of the peace** Ruhestörung.

**disturbed** [dɪs'tɜːbd] adj beunruhigt; (childhood) unglücklich; **mentally/emotionally ~** geistig/seelisch gestört.

**disturbing** [dɪs'tɜːbɪŋ] adj beunruhigend.

**disuse** [dɪs'juːs] n: **to fall into ~** nicht mehr benutzt werden.

**disused** [dɪs'juːzd] adj (building) leerstehend; (airfield) stillgelegt.

**ditch** [dɪtʃ] n Graben m ♦ vt (inf: partner) sitzenlassen; (: plan) sausenlassen; (: car etc) loswerden.

**dither** ['dɪðə•] (pej) vi zaudern.

**ditto** ['dɪtəu] adv dito, ebenfalls.

**divan** [dɪ'væn] n (also: ~ **bed**) Polsterbett nt.

**dive** [daɪv] n Sprung m; (underwater) Tauchen nt; (of submarine) Untertauchen nt; (pej: place) Spelunke f (inf) ♦ vi springen; (under water) tauchen; (bird) einen Sturzflug machen; (submarine) untertauchen; **to ~ into** (bag, drawer etc) greifen in +acc; (shop, car etc) sich stürzen in +acc.

**diver** ['daɪvə•] n Taucher(in) m(f); (deep-sea diver) Tiefseetaucher(in) m(f).

**diverge** [daɪ'vɜːdʒ] vi auseinandergehen.

**divergent** [daɪ'vɜːdʒənt] adj unterschiedlich; (views) voneinander abweichend; (interests) auseinandergehend.

**diverse** [daɪ'vɜːs] adj verschiedenartig.

**diversification** [daɪvɜːsɪfɪ'keɪʃən] n Diversifikation f.

**diversify** [daɪ'vɜːsɪfaɪ] vi diversifizieren.

**diversion** [daɪ'vɜːʃən] n (BRIT: AUT) Umleitung f; (distraction) Ablenkung f; (of funds) Umlenkung f.

**diversionary** [daɪ'vɜːʃənrɪ] adj: ~ **tactics** Ablenkungsmanöver pl.

**diversity** [daɪ'vɜːsɪtɪ] n Vielfalt f.

**divert** [daɪ'vɜːt] vt (sb's attention) ablenken; (funds) umlenken; (re-route) umleiten.

**divest** [daɪ'vɛst] vt: **to ~ sb of office/his authority** jdn seines Amtes entkleiden/ seiner Macht entheben.

**divide** [dɪ'vaɪd] vt trennen; (MATH) dividieren, teilen; (share out) verteilen ♦ vi sich teilen; (road) sich gabeln; (people, groups) sich aufteilen ♦ n Kluft f; **to ~ (between or among)** aufteilen (unter +dat); **40 ~d by 5** 40 geteilt or dividiert durch 5.

▶**divide out** vt: **to ~ out (between or among)** aufteilen (unter +dat).

**divided** [dɪ'vaɪdɪd] adj geteilt; **to be ~ about or over sth** geteilter Meinung über etw acc sein.

**divided highway** (US) n ≈ Schnellstraße f.

**dividend** ['dɪvɪdɛnd] n Dividende f; (fig): **to pay ~s** sich bezahlt machen.

**dividend cover** n (COMM) Dividendendeckung f.

**dividers** [dɪ'vaɪdəz] npl (MATH, TECH) Stechzirkel m; (between pages) Register nt.

**divine** [dɪ'vaɪn] adj göttlich ♦ vt (future) weissagen, prophezeien; (truth) erahnen; (water, metal) aufspüren.

**diving** ['daɪvɪŋ] n Tauchen nt; (SPORT) Kunstspringen nt.

**diving board** n Sprungbrett nt.

**diving suit** n Taucheranzug m.

**divinity** [dɪ'vɪnɪtɪ] n Göttlichkeit f; (god or goddess) Gottheit f; (SCOL) Theologie f.

**divisible** [dɪ'vɪzəbl] adj: ~ **(by)** teilbar (durch); **to be ~ into** teilbar sein in +acc.

**division** [dɪ'vɪʒən] n Teilung f; (MATH) Teilen nt, Division f; (sharing out) Verteilung f; (disagreement) Uneinigkeit f; (BRIT: POL) Abstimmung f durch Hammelsprung; (COMM) Abteilung f; (MIL) Division f; (esp FOOTBALL) Liga f; ~ **of labour** Arbeitsteilung f.

**divisive** [dɪ'vaɪsɪv] adj: **to be ~** (tactics) auf Spaltung abzielen; (system) zu Feindseligkeit führen.

**divorce** [dɪ'vɔːs] n Scheidung f ♦ vt sich scheiden lassen von; (dissociate) trennen.

**divorced** [dɪ'vɔːst] adj geschieden.

**divorcee** [dɪvɔː'siː] n Geschiedene(r) f(m).

**divot** ['dɪvət] n vom Golfschläger etc ausgehacktes Rasenstück.

**divulge** [daɪ'vʌldʒ] vt preisgeben.

**DIY** (BRIT) n abbr = **do-it-yourself**.

**dizziness** ['dɪzɪnɪs] n Schwindel m.

**dizzy** ['dɪzɪ] adj schwind(e)lig; (turn, spell) Schwindel-; (height) schwindelerregend; **I feel ~** mir ist or ich bin schwind(e)lig.

**DJ** n abbr = **disc jockey**.

**d.j.** n abbr = **dinner jacket**.

**Djakarta** [dʒə'kɑːtə] n Jakarta nt.

**DJIA** (US) n abbr (= Dow-Jones Industrial Average) Dow-Jones-Index m.

**dl** abbr (= decilitre) dl.

**DLit(t)** n abbr (= Doctor of Literature, Doctor of Letters) akademischer Grad in Literaturwissenschaft.

**DLO** n abbr = **dead letter office**.

**dm** abbr (= decimetre) dm.

**DMus** n abbr (= Doctor of Music) Doktor der Musikwissenschaft.

**DMZ** n abbr = **demilitarized zone**.

**DNA** n abbr (= deoxyribonucleic acid) DNS f.

===================================== KEYWORD

**do** [duː] (*pt* **did**, *pp* **done**) *aux vb* **1** (*in negative constructions*): **I don't understand** ich verstehe nicht

**2** (*to form questions*): **didn't you know?** wußtest du das nicht?; **what ~ you think?** was meinst du?

**3** (*for emphasis*): **she does seem rather upset** sie scheint wirklich recht aufgeregt zu sein; ~ **sit down/help yourself** bitte nehmen Sie Platz/bedienen Sie sich; **oh ~ shut up!** halte endlich den Mund!

**4** (*to avoid repeating vb*): **she swims better than I** ~ sie schwimmt besser als ich; **she lives in Glasgow - so ~ I** sie wohnt in Glasgow - ich auch; **who made this mess? - I did** wer hat dieses Durcheinander gemacht? - ich

**5** (*in question tags*): **you like him, don't you?** du magst ihn, nicht wahr?; **I don't know him, ~ I?** ich kenne ihn nicht, oder?

♦ *vt* **1** (*carry out, perform*) tun, machen; **what are you ~ing tonight?** was machen Sie heute abend?; **what ~ you ~ (for a living)?** was machen Sie beruflich?; **to ~ one's teeth/nails** sich *dat* die Zähne putzen/die Nägel schneiden

**2** (*AUT etc*) fahren; **the car was ~ing 100** das Auto fuhr 100

♦ *vi* **1** (*act, behave*): ~ **as I** ~ mach es wie ich

**2** (*get on, fare*): **he's ~ing well/badly at school** er ist gut/schlecht in der Schule; **the company is ~ing well** der Firma geht es gut; **how ~ you ~?** guten Tag/Morgen/Abend!

**3** (*suit, be sufficient*) reichen; **will that ~?** reicht das?; **will this dress ~ for the party?** ist dieses Kleid gut genug für die Party?; **will £10 ~?** reichen £10?; **that'll ~** das reicht; (*in annoyance*) jetzt reicht's aber!; **to make ~ with** auskommen mit

♦ *n* (*inf: party etc*) Party *f*, Fete *f*; **it was quite a ~** es war ganz schön was los

►**do away with** *vt fus* (*get rid of*) abschaffen.
►**do for** (*inf*) *vt fus*: **to be done for** erledigt sein.
►**do in** (*inf*) *vt* (*kill*) umbringen.
►**do out of** (*inf*) *vt* (*deprive*) bringen um.
►**do up** *vt fus* (*laces, dress, buttons*) zumachen; (*renovate: room, house*) renovieren.
►**do with** *vt fus* **1** (*need*) brauchen; **I could ~ with some help/a drink** ich könnte Hilfe/einen Drink gebrauchen
**2 it has to ~ with money** es hat mit Geld zu tun.
►**do without** *vt fus* auskommen ohne.

**do.** *abbr* = **ditto**.
**DOA** *abbr* (= *dead on arrival*) bei Einlieferung ins Krankenhaus bereits tot.
**d.o.b.** *abbr* = **date of birth**.

**doc** [dɔk] (*inf*) *n* Doktor *m*.
**docile** ['dəusaıl] *adj* sanft(mütig).
**dock** [dɔk] *n* Dock *nt*; (*LAW*) Anklagebank *f*; (*BOT*) Ampfer *m* ♦ *vi* anlegen; (*SPACE*) docken ♦ *vt*: **they ~ed a third of his wages** sie kürzten seinen Lohn um ein Drittel; **docks** *npl* (*NAUT*) Hafen *m*.
**dock dues** [-djuːz] *npl* Hafengebühr *f*.
**docker** ['dɔkə*] *n* Hafenarbeiter *m*, Docker *m*.
**docket** ['dɔkıt] *n* Inhaltserklärung *f*; (*on parcel etc*) Warenbegleitschein *m*, Laufzettel *m*.
**dockyard** ['dɔkjɑːd] *n* Werft *f*.
**doctor** ['dɔktə*] *n* Arzt *m*, Ärztin *f*; (*PhD etc*) Doktor *m* ♦ *vt*: **to ~ a drink** *etc* einem Getränk *etc* etwas beimischen; **~'s office** (*US*) Sprechzimmer *nt*.
**doctorate** ['dɔktərıt] *n* Doktorwürde *f*.

**Doctorate** ist der höchste akademische Grad auf jedem Wissensgebiet und wird nach erfolgreicher Vorlage einer Doktorarbeit verliehen. Die Studienzeit (meist mindestens 3 Jahre) und Länge der Doktorarbeit ist je nach Hochschule verschieden. Am häufigsten wird der Titel **PhD** (Doctor of Philosophy) auf dem Gebiet der Geisteswissenschaften, Naturwissenschaften und des Ingenieurwesens verliehen, obwohl es auch andere Doktortitel (in Musik, Jura usw.) gibt. Siehe auch **bachelor's degree, master's degree**.

**Doctor of Philosophy** *n* Doktor *m* der Philosophie.
**doctrine** ['dɔktrın] *n* Doktrin *f*.
**docudrama** ['dɔkjudrɑːmə] *n* Dokumentarspiel *nt*.
**document** ['dɔkjumənt] *n* Dokument *nt* ♦ *vt* dokumentieren.
**documentary** [dɔkju'mentərı] *adj* dokumentarisch ♦ *n* Dokumentarfilm *m*.
**documentation** [dɔkjumən'teıʃən] *n* Dokumentation *f*.
**DOD** (*US*) *n abbr* (= *Department of Defense*) Verteidigungsministerium *nt*.
**doddering** ['dɔdərıŋ] *adj* (*shaky, unsteady*) zittrig.
**doddery** ['dɔdərı] *adj* = **doddering**.
**doddle** ['dɔdl] (*inf*) *n*: **a ~** ein Kinderspiel *nt*.
**Dodecanese (Islands)** [dəudıkə'niːz ('aıləndz)] *n(pl)*: **the ~** der Dodekanes.
**dodge** [dɔdʒ] *n* Trick *m* ♦ *vt* ausweichen +*dat*; (*tax*) umgehen ♦ *vi* ausweichen; **to ~ out of the way** zur Seite springen; **to ~ through the traffic** sich durch den Verkehr schlängeln.
**dodgems** ['dɔdʒəmz] (*BRIT*) *npl* Autoskooter *pl*.
**dodgy** ['dɔdʒı] (*inf*) *adj* (*person*) zweifelhaft; (*plan etc*) gewagt.
**DOE** *n abbr* (*BRIT*: = *Department of the Environment*) Umweltministerium; (*US*: = *Department of Energy*) Energie-

ministerium.

**doe** [dəu] *n* Reh *nt*, Ricke *f*; (*rabbit*) (Kaninchen)weibchen *nt*.

**does** [dʌz] *vb see* **do**.

**doesn't** ['dʌznt] = **does not**.

**dog** [dɔg] *n* Hund *m* ♦ *vt* (*subj: person*) auf den Fersen bleiben +*dat*; (*: bad luck, memory etc*) verfolgen; **to go to the ~s** (*inf*) vor die Hunde gehen.

**dog biscuits** *npl* Hundekuchen *pl*.

**dog collar** *n* Hundehalsband *nt*; (*REL*) Kragen *m* des Geistlichen.

**dog-eared** ['dɔgɪəd] *adj* mit Eselsohren.

**dog food** *n* Hundefutter *nt*.

**dogged** ['dɔgɪd] *adj* beharrlich.

**doggy** ['dɔgɪ] *n* Hündchen *nt*.

**doggy bag** ['dɔgɪ-] *n* Tüte für Essensreste, die man nach Hause mitnehmen möchte.

**dogma** ['dɔgmə] *n* Dogma *nt*.

**dogmatic** [dɔg'mætɪk] *adj* dogmatisch.

**do-gooder** [du:'gudə•] (*pej*) *n* Weltverbesserer(in) *m(f)*.

**dogsbody** ['dɔgzbɔdɪ] (*BRIT: inf*) *n* Mädchen *nt* für alles.

**doily** ['dɔɪlɪ] *n* Deckchen *nt*.

**doing** ['duɪŋ] *n*: **this is your ~** das ist dein Werk.

**doings** ['duɪŋz] *npl* Treiben *nt*.

**do-it-yourself** ['du:ɪtjɔ:'sɛlf] *n* Heimwerken *nt*, Do-it-yourself *nt*.

**doldrums** ['dɔldrəmz] *npl*: **to be in the ~** (*person*) niedergeschlagen sein; (*business*) in einer Flaute stecken.

**dole** [dəul] (*BRIT*) *n* Arbeitslosenunterstützung *f*; **on the ~** arbeitslos.

♦**dole out** *vt* austeilen, verteilen.

**doleful** ['dəulful] *adj* traurig.

**doll** [dɔl] *n* (*toy, also US: inf: woman*) Puppe *f*.

**dollar** ['dɔlə•] (*US etc*) *n* Dollar *m*.

**dollar area** *n* Dollarblock *m*.

**dolled up** (*inf*) *adj* aufgedonnert.

**dollop** ['dɔləp] (*inf*) *n* Schlag *m*.

**dolly** ['dɔlɪ] (*inf*) *n* (*doll, woman*) Puppe *f*.

**Dolomites** ['dɔləmaɪts] *npl*: **the ~** die Dolomiten *pl*.

**dolphin** ['dɔlfɪn] *n* Delphin *m*.

**domain** [də'meɪn] *n* Bereich *m*; (*empire*) Reich *nt*.

**dome** [dəum] *n* Kuppel *f*.

**domestic** [də'mɛstɪk] *adj* (*trade*) Innen-; (*situation*) innenpolitisch; (*news*) Inland-, aus dem Inland; (*tasks, appliances*) Haushalts-; (*animal*) Haus-; (*duty, happiness*) häuslich.

**domesticated** [də'mɛstɪkeɪtɪd] *adj* (*animal*) zahm; (*person*) häuslich.

**domesticity** [dəumɛs'tɪsɪtɪ] *n* häusliches Leben *nt*.

**domestic servant** *n* Hausangestellte(r) *f(m)*.

**domicile** ['dɔmɪsaɪl] *n* Wohnsitz *m*.

**dominant** ['dɔmɪnənt] *adj* dominierend; (*share*) größte(r, s).

**dominate** ['dɔmɪneɪt] *vt* dominieren, beherrschen.

**domination** [dɔmɪ'neɪʃən] *n* (Vor)herrschaft *f*.

**domineering** [dɔmɪ'nɪərɪŋ] *adj* herrschsüchtig.

**Dominican Republic** [də'mɪnɪkən-] *n*: **the ~** die Dominikanische Republik.

**dominion** [də'mɪnɪən] *n* (*territory*) Herrschaftsgebiet *nt*; (*authority*): **to have ~ over** Macht haben über +*acc*.

**domino** ['dɔmɪnəu] (*pl* **~es**) *n* (*block*) Domino(stein) *m*.

**domino effect** *n* Dominoeffekt *m*.

**dominoes** ['dɔmɪnəuz] *n* (*game*) Domino(spiel) *nt*.

**don** [dɔn] *n* (*BRIT*) (Universitäts)dozent *m* (*besonders in Oxford und Cambridge*) ♦ *vt* anziehen.

**donate** [də'neɪt] *vt*: **to ~ (to)** (*organization, cause*) spenden (für).

**donation** [də'neɪʃən] *n* (*act of donating*) Spenden *nt*; (*contribution*) Spende *f*.

**done** [dʌn] *pp of* **do**.

**donkey** ['dɔŋkɪ] *n* Esel *m*.

**donkey-work** ['dɔŋkɪwɔ:k] (*BRIT: inf*) *n* Dreckarbeit *f*.

**donor** ['dəunə•] *n* Spender(in) *m(f)*.

**donor card** *n* Organspenderausweis *m*.

**don't** [dəunt] = **do not**.

**donut** ['dəunʌt] (*US*) *n* = **doughnut**.

**doodle** ['du:dl] *vi* Männchen malen ♦ *n* Kritzelei *f*.

**doom** [du:m] *n* Unheil *nt* ♦ *vt*: **to be ~ed to failure** zum Scheitern verurteilt sein.

**doomsday** ['du:mzdeɪ] *n* der Jüngste Tag.

**door** [dɔ:•] *n* Tür *f*; **to go from ~ to ~** von Tür zu Tür gehen.

**door bell** *n* Türklingel *f*.

**door handle** *n* Türklinke *f*; (*of car*) Türgriff *m*.

**doorman** ['dɔ:mən] (*irreg: like* **man**) *n* Portier *m*.

**doormat** ['dɔ:mæt] *n* Fußmatte *f*; (*fig*) Fußabtreter *m*.

**doorpost** ['dɔ:pəust] *n* Türpfosten *m*.

**doorstep** ['dɔ:stɛp] *n* Eingangsstufe *f*, Türstufe *f*; **on the ~** vor der Haustür.

**door-to-door** ['dɔ:tə'dɔ:•] *adj* (*selling*) von Haus zu Haus; **~ salesman** Vertreter *m*.

**doorway** ['dɔ:weɪ] *n* Eingang *m*.

**dope** [dəup] *n* (*inf*) Stoff *m*, Drogen *pl*; (*: person*) Esel *m*, Trottel *m*; (*: information*) Informationen *pl* ♦ *vt* dopen.

**dopey** ['dəupɪ] (*inf*) *adj* (*groggy*) benebelt; (*stupid*) blöd, bekloppt.

**dormant** ['dɔ:mənt] *adj* (*plant*) ruhend; (*volcano*) untätig; (*idea, report etc*): **to lie ~** schlummern.

**dormer** ['dɔ:mə•] *n* (*also*: **~ window**) Mansardenfenster *nt*.

**dormice** ['dɔ:maɪs] *npl of* **dormouse**.

**dormitory** ['dɔ:mɪtrɪ] *n* Schlafsaal *m*; (*US:*

*building*) Wohnheim *nt*.
**dormouse** ['dɔːmaus] (*pl* **dormice**) *n* Haselmaus *f*.
**Dors** (*BRIT*) *abbr* (*POST*: = *Dorset*).
**DOS** [dɔs] *n abbr* (*COMPUT*: = *disk operating system*) DOS.
**dosage** ['dəusɪdʒ] *n* Dosis *f*; (*on label*) Dosierung *f*.
**dose** [dəus] *n* Dosis *f*; (*BRIT*: *bout*) Ration *f* ♦ *vt*: **to ~ o.s.** Medikamente nehmen; **a ~ of flu** eine Grippe.
**dosser** ['dɔsəʳ] (*BRIT*: *inf*) *n* Penner(in) *m(f)*.
**dosshouse** ['dɔshaus] (*BRIT*: *inf*) *n* Obdachlosenheim *nt*.
**dossier** ['dɔsɪeɪ] *n* Dossier *nt*.
**DOT** (*US*) *n abbr* (= *Department of Transportation*) ≈ Verkehrsministerium *nt*.
**dot** [dɔt] *n* Punkt *m* ♦ *vt*: **~ted with** übersät mit; **on the ~** (auf die Minute) pünktlich.
**dote** [dəut]: **~ on** *vt fus* abgöttisch lieben.
**dot-matrix printer** [dɔt'meɪtrɪks-] *n* Nadeldrucker *m*.
**dotted line** ['dɔtɪd-] *n* punktierte Linie *f*; **to sign on the ~** (*fig*) seine formelle Zustimmung geben.
**dotty** ['dɔtɪ] (*inf*) *adj* schrullig.
**double** ['dʌbl] *adj* doppelt; (*chin*) Doppel- ♦ *adv* (*cost*) doppelt soviel ♦ *n* Doppelgänger(in) *m(f)* ♦ *vt* verdoppeln; (*paper, blanket*) (einmal) falten ♦ *vi* sich verdoppeln; **~ five two six (5526)** (*BRIT*: *TEL*) fünfundfünfzig sechsundzwanzig; **it's spelt with a ~ "l"** es wird mit zwei l geschrieben; **an egg with a ~ yolk** ein Ei mit zwei Dottern; **on the ~**, (*BRIT*) **at the ~** (*quickly*) schnell; (*immediately*) unverzüglich; **to ~ as ...** (*person*) auch als ... fungieren; (*thing*) auch als ... dienen.
▸**double back** *vi* kehrtmachen, zurückgehen/-fahren.
▸**double up** *vi* sich krümmen; (*share room*) sich ein Zimmer teilen.
**double bass** *n* Kontrabaß *m*.
**double bed** *n* Doppelbett *nt*.
**double bend** (*BRIT*) *n* S-Kurve *f*.
**double-blind** *adj*: **~ experiment** Doppelblindversuch *m*.
**double-breasted** ['dʌbl'brɛstɪd] *adj* (*jacket, coat*) zweireihig.
**double-check** ['dʌbl'tʃɛk] *vt* noch einmal (über)prüfen ♦ *vi* es noch einmal (über)prüfen.
**double-clutch** ['dʌbl'klʌtʃ] (*US*) *vi* mit Zwischengas schalten.
**double cream** (*BRIT*) *n* Sahne *f* mit hohem Fettgehalt, ≈ Schlagsahne *f*.
**double-cross** [dʌbl'krɔs] *vt* ein Doppelspiel treiben mit.
**double-decker** [dʌbl'dɛkəʳ] *n* Doppeldecker *m*.
**double-declutch** ['dʌbldi:'klʌtʃ] (*BRIT*) *vi* mit Zwischengas schalten.

**double exposure** *n* doppelt belichtetes Foto *nt*.
**double glazing** [-'gleɪzɪŋ] (*BRIT*) *n* Doppelverglasung *f*.
**double-page spread** ['dʌblpeɪdʒ-] *n* Doppelseite *f*.
**double-parking** [dʌbl'pɑːkɪŋ] *n* Parken *nt* in der zweiten Reihe.
**double room** *n* Doppelzimmer *nt*.
**doubles** ['dʌblz] *n* (*TENNIS*) Doppel *nt*.
**double time** *n* doppelter Lohn *m*.
**double whammy** [-'wæmɪ] (*inf*) *n* Doppelschlag *m*.
**doubly** ['dʌblɪ] *adv* (ganz) besonders.
**doubt** [daut] *n* Zweifel *m* ♦ *vt* bezweifeln; **without (a) ~** ohne Zweifel; **to ~ sb** jdm nicht glauben; **I ~ it (very much)** das bezweifle ich (sehr), das möchte ich (stark) bezweifeln; **to ~ if** *or* **whether ...** bezweifeln, daß ...; **I don't ~ that ...** ich bezweifle nicht, daß ...
**doubtful** ['dautful] *adj* zweifelhaft; **to be ~ about sth** an etw *dat* zweifeln; **to be ~ about doing sth** Bedenken haben, ob man etw tun soll; **I'm a bit ~** ich bin nicht ganz sicher.
**doubtless** ['dautlɪs] *adv* ohne Zweifel, sicherlich.
**dough** [dəu] *n* Teig *m*; (*inf*: *money*) Kohle *f*, Knete *f*.
**doughnut,** (*US*) **donut** ['dəunʌt] *n* ≈ Berliner (Pfannkuchen) *m*.
**dour** [duəʳ] *adj* mürrisch, verdrießlich.
**douse** [dauz] *vt* Wasser schütten über +*acc*; (*extinguish*) löschen; **to ~ with** übergießen mit.
**dove** [dʌv] *n* Taube *f*.
**Dover** ['dəuvəʳ] *n* Dover *nt*.
**dovetail** ['dʌvteɪl] *vi* übereinstimmen ♦ *n* (*also*: **~ joint**) Schwalbenschwanzverbindung *f*.
**dowager** ['dauədʒəʳ] *n* (adlige) Witwe *f*.
**dowdy** ['daudɪ] *adj* ohne jeden Schick; (*clothes*) unmodern.
**Dow-Jones average** ['dau'dʒəunz-] (*US*) *n* Dow-Jones-Index *m*.
**down** [daun] *n* Daunen *pl* ♦ *adv* hinunter, herunter; (*on the ground*) unten ♦ *prep* hinunter, herunter; (*movement along*) entlang ♦ *vt* (*inf*: *drink*) runterkippen; **~ there/here** da/hier unten; **the price of meat is ~** die Fleischpreise sind gefallen; **I've got it ~ in my diary** ich habe es in meinem Kalender notiert; **to pay £2 ~** £2 anzahlen; **England is two goals ~** England liegt mit zwei Toren zurück; **to ~ tools** (*BRIT*) die Arbeit niederlegen; **~ with ...!** nieder mit ...!
**down-and-out** ['daunəndaut] *n* Penner(in) *m(f)* (*inf*).
**down-at-heel** ['daunət'hi:l] *adj* (*appearance, person*) schäbig, heruntergekommen; (*shoes*) abgetreten.

**downbeat** ['daunbiːt] n (MUS) erster betonter Taktteil m ♦ adj zurückhaltend.

**downcast** ['daunkɑːst] adj niedergeschlagen.

**downer** ['daunə*] (inf) n (drug) Beruhigungsmittel nt; **to be on a ~** deprimiert sein.

**downfall** ['daunfɔːl] n Ruin m; (of dictator etc) Sturz m, Fall m.

**downgrade** ['daungreɪd] vt herunterstufen.

**downhearted** ['daun'hɑːtɪd] adj niedergeschlagen, entmutigt.

**downhill** ['daun'hɪl] adv bergab ♦ n (SKI: also: **~ race**) Abfahrtslauf m; **to go ~** (road) bergab führen; (person) hinuntergehen, heruntergehen; (car) hinunterfahren, herunterfahren; (fig) auf dem absteigenden Ast sein.

> **Downing Street** ist die Straße in London, die von Whitehall zum St James Park führt und in der sich der offizielle Wohnsitz des Premierministers (Nr. 10) und des Finanzministers (Nr. 11) befindet. Im weiteren Sinne bezieht sich der Begriff Downing Street auf die britische Regierung.

**download** ['daunləud] vt laden.

**down-market** ['daun'mɑːkɪt] adj (product) für den Massenmarkt.

**down payment** n Anzahlung f.

**downplay** ['daunpleɪ] (US) vt herunterspielen.

**downpour** ['daunpɔː*] n Wolkenbruch m.

**downright** ['daunraɪt] adj (liar etc) ausgesprochen; (refusal, lie) glatt.

**Downs** [daunz] (BRIT) npl: **the ~** die Downs pl, Hügellandschaft in Südengland.

**downsize** ['daun'saɪz] vi (ECON: company) sich verkleinern.

**Down's syndrome** n (MED) Down-Syndrom nt.

**downstairs** ['daun'stɛəz] adv unten; (downwards) nach unten.

**downstream** ['daunstriːm] adv flußabwärts, stromabwärts.

**downtime** ['dauntaɪm] n Ausfallzeit f.

**down-to-earth** ['dauntu'ɔːθ] adj (person) nüchtern; (solution) praktisch.

**downtown** ['daun'taun] (esp US) adv im Zentrum, in der (Innen)stadt; (go) ins Zentrum, in die (Innen)stadt ♦ adj: **~ Chicago** das Zentrum von Chicago.

**downtrodden** ['dauntrɔdn] adj unterdrückt, geknechtet.

**down under** adv (be) in Australien/ Neuseeland; (go) nach Australien/ Neuseeland.

**downward** ['daunwəd] adj, adv nach unten; **a ~ trend** ein Abwärtstrend m.

**downwards** ['daunwədz] adv = **downward**.

**dowry** ['dauri] n Mitgift f.

**doz.** abbr = **dozen**.

**doze** [dəuz] vi ein Nickerchen machen.

▶**doze off** vi einschlafen, einnicken.

**dozen** ['dʌzn] n Dutzend nt; **a ~ books** ein Dutzend Bücher; **80p a ~** 80 Pence das Dutzend; **~s of** Dutzende von.

**DPh** n abbr (= Doctor of Philosophy) ≈ Dr. phil.

**DPhil** n abbr (= Doctor of Philosophy) ≈ Dr. phil.

**DPP** (BRIT) n abbr = **Director of Public Prosecutions**.

**DPT** n abbr (= diphtheria, pertussis, tetanus) Diphtherie, Keuchhusten und Tetanus.

**DPW** (US) n abbr (= Department of Public Works) Ministerium für öffentliche Bauprojekte.

**Dr** abbr = **doctor**; (in street names: = Drive) ≈ Str.

**dr** abbr (COMM) = **debtor**.

**drab** [dræb] adj trist.

**draft** [drɑːft] n Entwurf m; (bank draft) Tratte f; (US: call-up) Einberufung f ♦ vt entwerfen; see also **draught**.

**draftsman** etc ['drɑːftsmən] (US) n = **draughtsman** etc.

**drag** [dræg] vt schleifen, schleppen; (river) absuchen ♦ vi sich hinziehen ♦ n (AVIAT) Luftwiderstand m; (NAUT) Wasserwiderstand m; (inf): **to be a ~** (boring) langweilig sein; (a nuisance) lästig sein; (women's clothing): **in ~** in Frauenkleidung.

▶**drag away** vt: **to ~ away (from)** wegschleppen or wegziehen (von).

▶**drag on** vi sich hinziehen.

**dragnet** ['drægnet] n Schleppnetz nt; (fig) großangelegte Polizeiaktion f.

**dragon** ['drægn] n Drache m.

**dragonfly** ['drægənflaɪ] n Libelle f.

**dragoon** [drə'guːn] n Dragoner m ♦ vt: **to ~ sb into doing sth** (BRIT) jdn zwingen, etw zu tun.

**drain** [dreɪn] n Belastung f; (in street) Gully m ♦ vt entwässern; (pond) trockenlegen; (vegetables) abgießen; (glass, cup) leeren ♦ vi ablaufen; **to feel ~ed (of energy/emotion)** sich ausgelaugt fühlen.

**drainage** ['dreɪnɪdʒ] n Entwässerungssystem nt; (process) Entwässerung f.

**draining board** ['dreɪnɪŋ-], (US) **drainboard** ['dreɪnbɔːd] n Ablaufbrett nt.

**drainpipe** ['dreɪnpaɪp] n Abflußrohr nt.

**drake** [dreɪk] n Erpel m, Enterich m.

**dram** [dræm] (SCOT) n (drink) Schluck m.

**drama** ['drɑːmə] n Drama nt.

**dramatic** [drə'mætɪk] adj dramatisch; (theatrical) theatralisch.

**dramatically** [drə'mætɪklɪ] adv dramatisch; (say, announce, pause) theatralisch.

**dramatist** ['dræmətɪst] n Dramatiker(in) m(f).

**dramatize** ['dræmətaɪz] vt dramatisieren; (for TV/cinema) für das Fernsehen/den Film bearbeiten.

**drank** [dræŋk] pt of **drink**.

**drape** [dreɪp] vt drapieren.

**drapes** [dreɪps] (*US*) *npl* Vorhänge *pl*.
**drastic** ['dræstɪk] *adj* drastisch.
**drastically** ['dræstɪklɪ] *adv* drastisch.
**draught,** (*US*) **draft** [drɑːft] *n* (Luft)zug *m*;
(*NAUT*) Tiefgang *m*; (*of chimney*) Zug *m*; **on**
~ vom Faß.
**draught beer** *n* Bier *nt* vom Faß.
**draughtboard** ['drɑːftbɔːd] (*BRIT*) *n*
Damebrett *nt*.
**draughts** [drɑːfts] (*BRIT*) *n* Damespiel *nt*.
**draughtsman,** (*US*) **draftsman** ['drɑːftsmən]
(*irreg: like* **man**) *n* Zeichner(in) *m(f)*; (*: as job*)
technischer Zeichner *m*, technische
Zeichnerin *f*.
**draughtsmanship,** (*US*) **draftsmanship**
['drɑːftsmənʃɪp] *n* zeichnerisches Können *nt*;
(*art*) Zeichenkunst *f*.
**draw** [drɔː] (*pt* **drew**, *pp* **drawn**) *vt* zeichnen;
(*cart, gun, tooth, conclusion*) ziehen; (*curtain:
open*) aufziehen; (*: close*) zuziehen;
(*admiration, attention*) erregen; (*money*)
abheben; (*wages*) bekommen ♦ *vi* (*SPORT*)
unentschieden spielen ♦ *n* (*SPORT*)
Unentschieden *nt*; (*lottery*) Lotterie *f*;
(*: picking of ticket*) Ziehung *f*; **to** ~ **a**
**comparison/distinction (between)** einen
Vergleich ziehen/Unterschied machen
(zwischen +*dat*); **to** ~ **near** näherkommen;
(*event*) nahen; **to** ~ **to a close** zu Ende
gehen.
▶**draw back** *vi*: **to** ~ **back (from)**
zurückweichen (von).
▶**draw in** *vi* (*BRIT*: *car*) anhalten; (*: train*)
einfahren; (*nights*) länger werden.
▶**draw on** *vt* (*resources*) zurückgreifen auf
+*acc*; (*imagination*) zu Hilfe nehmen; (*person*)
einsetzen.
▶**draw out** *vi* länger werden ♦ *vt* (*money*)
abheben.
▶**draw up** *vi* (an)halten ♦ *vt* (*chair etc*)
heranziehen; (*document*) aufsetzen.
**drawback** ['drɔːbæk] *n* Nachteil *m*.
**drawbridge** ['drɔːbrɪdʒ] *n* Zugbrücke *f*.
**drawee** [drɔːˈiː] *n* Bezogene(r) *f(m)*.
**drawer** [drɔːʳ] *n* Schublade *f*.
**drawing** ['drɔːɪŋ] *n* Zeichnung *f*; (*skill,
discipline*) Zeichnen *nt*.
**drawing board** *n* Reißbrett *nt*; **back to the** ~
(*fig*) das muß noch einmal neu überdacht
werden.
**drawing pin** (*BRIT*) *n* Reißzwecke *f*.
**drawing room** *n* Salon *m*.
**drawl** [drɔːl] *n* schleppende Sprechweise *f* ♦ *vi*
schleppend sprechen.
**drawn** [drɔːn] *pp of* **draw** ♦ *adj* abgespannt.
**drawstring** ['drɔːstrɪŋ] *n* Kordel *f* zum
Zuziehen.
**dread** [drɛd] *n* Angst *f*, Furcht *f* ♦ *vt* große
Angst haben vor +*dat*.
**dreadful** ['drɛdful] *adj* schrecklich, furchtbar;
**I feel** ~! (*ill*) ich fühle mich schrecklich;
(*ashamed*) es ist mir schrecklich peinlich.

**dream** [driːm] (*pt, pp* **dreamed** *or* **dreamt**) *n*
Traum *m* ♦ *vt, vi* träumen; **to have a** ~ **about**
**sb/sth** von jdm/etw träumen; **sweet** ~**s!**
träume süß!
▶**dream up** *vt* sich *dat* einfallen lassen, sich
*dat* ausdenken.
**dreamer** ['driːməʳ] *n* Träumer(in) *m(f)*.
**dreamt** [drɛmt] *pt, pp of* **dream**.
**dream world** *n* Traumwelt *f*.
**dreamy** ['driːmɪ] *adj* verträumt; (*music*) zum
Träumen.
**dreary** ['drɪərɪ] *adj* langweilig; (*weather*) trüb.
**dredge** [drɛdʒ] *vt* ausbaggern.
▶**dredge up** *vt* ausbaggern; (*fig: unpleasant
facts*) ausgraben.
**dredger** ['drɛdʒəʳ] *n* (*ship*) Schwimmbagger
*m*; (*machine*) Bagger *m*; (*BRIT: also:* **sugar** ~)
Zuckerstreuer *m*.
**dregs** [drɛgz] *npl* Bodensatz *m*; (*of humanity*)
Abschaum *m*.
**drench** [drɛntʃ] *vt* durchnässen; ~**ed to the
skin** naß bis auf die Haut.
**dress** [drɛs] *n* Kleid *nt*; (*no pl: clothing*)
Kleidung *f* ♦ *vt* anziehen; (*wound*) verbinden
♦ *vi* sich anziehen; **she** ~**es very well** sie
kleidet sich sehr gut; **to** ~ **a shop window**
ein Schaufenster dekorieren; **to get** ~**ed**
sich anziehen.
▶**dress up** *vi* sich feinmachen; (*in fancy dress*)
sich verkleiden.
**dress circle** (*BRIT*) *n* (*THEAT*) erster Rang *m*.
**dress designer** *n* Modezeichner(in) *m(f)*.
**dresser** ['drɛsəʳ] *n* (*BRIT*) Anrichte *f*; (*US*)
Kommode *f*; (*also:* **window** ~)
Dekorateur(in) *m(f)*.
**dressing** ['drɛsɪŋ] *n* Verband *m*; (*CULIN*)
(Salat)soße *f*.
**dressing gown** (*BRIT*) *n* Morgenrock *m*.
**dressing room** *n* Umkleidekabine *f*; (*THEAT*)
(Künstler)garderobe *f*.
**dressing table** *n* Frisierkommode *f*.
**dressmaker** ['drɛsmeɪkəʳ] *n*
(Damen)schneider(in) *m(f)*.
**dressmaking** ['drɛsmeɪkɪŋ] *n* Schneidern *nt*.
**dress rehearsal** *n* Generalprobe *f*.
**dressy** ['drɛsɪ] (*inf*) *adj* elegant.
**drew** [druː] *pt of* **draw**.
**dribble** ['drɪbl] *vi* tropfen; (*baby*) sabbern;
(*FOOTBALL*) dribbeln ♦ *vt* (*ball*) dribbeln mit.
**dried** [draɪd] *adj* (*fruit*) getrocknet, Dörr-;
~ **egg** Trockenei *nt*, Eipulver *nt*; ~ **milk**
Trockenmilch *f*, Milchpulver *nt*.
**drier** ['draɪəʳ] *n* = **dryer**.
**drift** [drɪft] *n* Strömung *f*; (*of snow*)
Schneewehe *f*; (*of questions*) Richtung *f* ♦ *vi*
treiben; (*sand*) wehen; **to let things** ~ die
Dinge treiben lassen; **to** ~ **apart** sich
auseinanderleben; **I get** *or* **catch your** ~ ich
verstehe, worauf Sie hinauswollen.
**drifter** ['drɪftəʳ] *n*: **to be a** ~ sich treiben
lassen.
**driftwood** ['drɪftwud] *n* Treibholz *nt*.

**drill** [drɪl] n Bohrer m; (machine) Bohrmaschine f; (MIL) Drill m ♦ vt bohren; (troops) drillen ♦ vi: **to ~ (for)** bohren (nach); **to ~ pupils in grammar** mit den Schülern Grammatik pauken.
**drilling** ['drɪlɪŋ] n Bohrung f.
**drilling rig** n Bohrturm m; (at sea) Bohrinsel f.
**drily** ['draɪlɪ] adv = **dryly**.
**drink** [drɪŋk] (pt **drank**, pp **drunk**) n Getränk nt; (alcoholic) Glas nt, Drink m; (sip) Schluck m ♦ vt, vi trinken; **to have a ~** etwas trinken; **a ~ of water** etwas Wasser; **we had ~s before lunch** vor dem Mittagessen gab es einen Drink; **would you like something to ~?** möchten Sie etwas trinken?
▶**drink in** vt (fresh air) einatmen, einsaugen; (story, sight) (begierig) in sich aufnehmen.
**drinkable** ['drɪŋkəbl] adj trinkbar.
**drink-driving** ['drɪŋk'draɪvɪŋ] n Trunkenheit f am Steuer.
**drinker** ['drɪŋkə*] n Trinker(in) m(f).
**drinking** ['drɪŋkɪŋ] n Trinken nt.
**drinking fountain** n Trinkwasserbrunnen m.
**drinking water** n Trinkwasser nt.
**drip** [drɪp] n Tropfen m; (one drip) Tropfen m; (MED) Tropf m ♦ vi tropfen; (wall) triefnaß sein.
**drip-dry** ['drɪp'draɪ] adj bügelfrei.
**drip-feed** ['drɪpfiːd] vt künstlich ernähren ♦ n: **to be on a ~** künstlich ernährt werden.
**dripping** ['drɪpɪŋ] n Bratenfett nt ♦ adj triefend; **I'm ~** ich bin klatschnaß (inf); **~ wet** triefnaß.
**drive** [draɪv] (pt **drove**, pp **driven**) n Fahrt f; (also: ~**way**) Einfahrt f; (: longer) Auffahrt f; (energy) Schwung m, Elan m; (campaign) Aktion f; (SPORT) Treibschlag m; (COMPUT: also: **disk ~**) Laufwerk nt ♦ vt fahren; (TECH) antreiben ♦ vi fahren; **to go for a ~** ein bißchen (raus)fahren; **it's 3 hours' ~ from London** es ist drei Stunden Fahrt von London (entfernt); **left-/right-hand ~** Links-/Rechtssteuerung f; **front-/rear-wheel ~** Vorderrad-/Hinterradantrieb m; **he ~s a taxi** er ist Taxifahrer; **to ~ sth into sth** (nail, stake etc) etw in etw schlagen acc; (animal) treiben; (ball) weit schlagen; (incite, encourage: also: ~ **on**) antreiben; **to ~ sb home/to the airport** jdn nach Hause/zum Flughafen fahren; **to ~ sb mad** jdn verrückt machen; **to ~ sb to (do) sth** jdn dazu treiben, etw zu tun; **to ~ at 50 km an hour** mit (einer Geschwindigkeit von) 50 Stundenkilometern fahren; **what are you driving at?** worauf wollen Sie hinaus?
▶**drive off** vt vertreiben.
▶**drive out** vt (evil spirit) austreiben; (person) verdrängen.
**drive-by shooting** ['draɪvbaɪ-] n Schußwaffenangriff aus einem vorbeifahrenden Wagen.

**drive-in** ['draɪvɪn] (esp US) adj, n: **~ (cinema)** Autokino nt; **~ (restaurant)** Autorestaurant nt.
**drive-in window** (US) n Autoschalter m.
**drivel** ['drɪvl] (inf) n Blödsinn m.
**driven** ['drɪvn] pp of **drive**.
**driver** ['draɪvə*] n Fahrer(in) m(f); (RAIL) Führer(in) m(f).
**driver's license** ['draɪvəz-] (US) n Führerschein m.
**driveway** ['draɪvweɪ] n Einfahrt f; (longer) Auffahrt f.
**driving** ['draɪvɪŋ] n Fahren nt ♦ adj: **~ rain** strömender Regen m; **~ snow** Schneetreiben nt.
**driving belt** n Treibriemen m.
**driving force** n treibende Kraft f.
**driving instructor** n Fahrlehrer(in) m(f).
**driving lesson** n Fahrstunde f.
**driving licence** (BRIT) n Führerschein m.
**driving mirror** n Rückspiegel m.
**driving school** n Fahrschule f.
**driving test** n Fahrprüfung f.
**drizzle** ['drɪzl] n Nieselregen m ♦ vi nieseln.
**droll** [drəul] adj drollig.
**dromedary** ['drɔmədərɪ] n Dromedar nt.
**drone** [drəun] n Brummen nt; (male bee) Drohne f ♦ vi brummen; (bee) summen; (also: ~ **on**) eintönig sprechen.
**drool** [druːl] vi sabbern; **to ~ over sth/sb** etw/jdn sehnsüchtig anstarren.
**droop** [druːp] vi (flower) den Kopf hängen lassen; **his shoulders/head ~ed** er ließ die Schultern/den Kopf herabhängen.
**drop** [drɔp] n Tropfen m; (lessening) Rückgang m; (distance) Höhenunterschied m; (in salary) Verschlechterung f; (also: **parachute ~**) (Ab)sprung m ♦ vt fallen lassen; (voice, eyes, price) senken; (set down from car) absetzen; (omit) weglassen ♦ vi (herunter)fallen; (wind) sich legen; **drops** npl Tropfen pl; **a 300 ft ~** ein Höhenunterschied von 300 Fuß; **a ~ of 10%** ein Rückgang um 10%; **cough ~s** Hustentropfen pl; **to ~ anchor** ankern, vor Anker gehen; **to ~ sb a line** jdm ein paar Zeilen schreiben.
▶**drop in** (inf) vi: **to ~ in (on sb)** (bei jdm) vorbeikommen.
▶**drop off** vi einschlafen ♦ vt (passenger) absetzen.
▶**drop out** vi (withdraw) ausscheiden; (student) sein Studium abbrechen.
**droplet** ['drɔplɪt] n Tröpfchen nt.
**dropout** ['drɔpaut] n Aussteiger(in) m(f); (SCOL) Studienabbrecher(in) m(f).
**dropper** ['drɔpə*] n Pipette f.
**droppings** ['drɔpɪŋz] npl Kot m.
**dross** [drɔs] n Schlacke f; (fig) Schund m.
**drought** [draut] n Dürre f.
**drove** [drəuv] pt of **drive** ♦ n: **~s of people** Scharen pl von Menschen.
**drown** [draun] vt ertränken; (fig: also: ~ **out**)

übertönen ♦ *vi* ertrinken.
**drowse** [drauz] *vi* (vor sich *acc* hin) dösen *or* dämmern.
**drowsy** ['drauzɪ] *adj* schläfrig.
**drudge** [drʌdʒ] *n* Arbeitstier *nt*.
**drudgery** ['drʌdʒərɪ] *n* (stumpfsinnige) Plackerei *f* (*inf*); **housework is sheer ~** Hausarbeit ist eine einzige Plackerei.
**drug** [drʌg] *n* Medikament *nt*, Arzneimittel *nt*; (*narcotic*) Droge *f*, Rauschgift *nt* ♦ *vt* betäuben; **to be on ~s** drogensüchtig sein; **hard/soft ~s** harte/weiche Drogen *pl*.
**drug addict** *n* Drogensüchtige(r) *f(m)*, Rauschgiftsüchtige(r) *f(m)*.
**druggist** ['drʌgɪst] (*US*) *n* Drogist(in) *m(f)*.
**drug peddler** *n* Drogenhändler(in) *m(f)*, Dealer *m* (*inf*).
**drugstore** ['drʌgstɔː] (*US*) *n* Drogerie *f*.
**drum** [drʌm] *n* Trommel *f*; (*for oil, petrol*) Faß *nt* ♦ *vi* trommeln; **drums** *npl* (*kit*) Schlagzeug *nt*.
▶**drum up** *vt* (*enthusiasm*) erwecken; (*support*) auftreiben.
**drummer** ['drʌmə*] *n* Trommler(in) *m(f)*; (*in band, pop group*) Schlagzeuger(in) *m(f)*.
**drum roll** *n* Trommelwirbel *m*.
**drumstick** ['drʌmstɪk] *n* Trommelstock *m*; (*of chicken*) Keule *f*.
**drunk** [drʌŋk] *pp of* **drink** ♦ *adj* betrunken ♦ *n* (*also:* **~ard**) Trinker(in) *m(f)*; **to get ~** sich betrinken; **a ~ driving offence** Trunkenheit *f* am Steuer.
**drunken** ['drʌŋkən] *adj* betrunken; (*party*) feucht-fröhlich; **~ driving** Trunkenheit *f* am Steuer.
**drunkenness** ['drʌŋkənnɪs] *n* (*state*) Betrunkenheit *f*; (*habit*) Trunksucht *f*.
**dry** [draɪ] *adj* trocken ♦ *vt, vi* trocknen; **on ~ land** auf festem Boden; **to ~ one's hands/hair/eyes** sich *dat* die Hände (ab)trocknen/die Haare trocknen/die Tränen abwischen; **to ~ the dishes** (das Geschirr) abtrocknen.
▶**dry up** *vi* austrocknen; (*in speech*) den Faden verlieren.
**dry-clean** ['draɪ'kliːn] *vt* chemisch reinigen.
**dry-cleaner** ['draɪ'kliːnə*] *n* (*job*) Inhaber(in) *m(f)* einer chemischen Reinigung; (*shop: also:* **~'s**) chemische Reinigung *f*.
**dry-cleaning** ['draɪ'kliːnɪŋ] *n* (*process*) chemische Reinigung *f*.
**dry dock** *n* Trockendock *nt*.
**dryer** ['draɪə*] *n* Wäschetrockner *m*; (*US: spin-dryer*) Wäscheschleuder *f*.
**dry goods** *npl* Kurzwaren *pl*.
**dry ice** *n* Trockeneis *nt*.
**dryly** ['draɪlɪ] *adv* (*say, remark*) trocken.
**dryness** ['draɪnɪs] *n* Trockenheit *f*.
**dry rot** *n* (Haus)schwamm *m*, (Holz)schwamm *m*.
**dry run** *n* (*fig*) Probe *f*.
**dry ski slope** *n* Trockenskipiste *f*.

**DSc** *n abbr* (= *Doctor of Science*) ≈ Dr. rer. nat.
**DSS** (*BRIT*) *n abbr* (= *Department of Social Security*) Ministerium *für* Sozialfürsorge.
**DST** (*US*) *abbr* = **daylight-saving time**.
**DT** *n abbr* (*COMPUT*) = **data transmission**.
**DTI** (*BRIT*) *n abbr* (= *Department of Trade and Industry*) ≈ Wirtschaftsministerium *nt*.
**DTP** *n abbr* (= *desktop publishing*) DTP *nt*; *see also* **desktop publishing**.
**DT's** (*inf*) *npl abbr* (= *delirium tremens*) Delirium tremens *nt*; **to have the ~** vom Trinken den Tatterich haben (*inf*).
**dual** ['djuəl] *adj* doppelt; (*personality*) gespalten.
**dual carriageway** (*BRIT*) *n* ≈ Schnellstraße *f*.
**dual nationality** *n* doppelte Staatsangehörigkeit *f*.
**dual-purpose** ['djuəl'pɜːpəs] *adj* zweifach verwendbar.
**dubbed** [dʌbd] *adj* synchronisiert; (*nicknamed*) getauft.
**dubious** ['djuːbɪəs] *adj* zweifelhaft; **I'm very ~ about it** ich habe da (doch) starke Zweifel.
**Dublin** ['dʌblɪn] *n* Dublin *nt*.
**Dubliner** ['dʌblɪnə*] *n* Dubliner(in) *m(f)*.
**duchess** ['dʌtʃɪs] *n* Herzogin *f*.
**duck** [dʌk] *n* Ente *f* ♦ *vi* (*also:* **~ down**) sich ducken ♦ *vt* (*blow*) ausweichen +*dat*; (*duty, responsibility*) aus dem Weg gehen +*dat*.
**duckling** ['dʌklɪŋ] *n* Entenküken *nt*; (*CULIN*) (junge) Ente *f*.
**duct** [dʌkt] *n* Rohr *nt*; (*ANAT*) Röhre *f*; **tear ~** Tränenkanal *m*.
**dud** [dʌd] *n* Niete *f* (*inf*); (*note*) Blüte *f* (*inf*) ♦ *adj*: **~ cheque** (*BRIT*) ungedeckter Scheck *m*.
**due** [djuː] *adj* fällig; (*attention etc*) gebührend; (*consideration*) reiflich ♦ *n*: **to give sb his/her ~** jdn gerecht behandeln ♦ *adv*: **~ north** direkt nach Norden; **dues** *npl* Beitrag *m*; (*in harbour*) Gebühren *pl*; **in ~ course** zu gegebener Zeit; (*eventually*) im Laufe der Zeit; **~ to** (*owing to*) wegen +*gen*, aufgrund +*gen*; **to be ~ to do sth** etw tun sollen; **the rent is ~ on the 30th** die Miete ist am 30. fällig; **the train is ~ at 8** der Zug soll (laut Fahrplan) um 8 ankommen; **she is ~ back tomorrow** sie müßte morgen zurück sein; **I am ~ 6 days' leave** mir stehen 6 Tage Urlaub zu.
**due date** *n* Fälligkeitsdatum *nt*.
**duel** ['djuəl] *n* Duell *nt*.
**duet** [djuː'et] *n* Duett *nt*.
**duff** [dʌf] (*BRIT: inf*) *adj* kaputt.
▶**duff up** *vt* vermöbeln.
**duffel bag** ['dʌfl-] *n* Matchbeutel *m*.
**duffel coat** *n* Dufflecoat *m*.
**duffer** ['dʌfə*] (*inf*) *n* Versager *m*, Flasche *f*.
**dug** [dʌg] *pt, pp of* **dig**.
**dugout** ['dʌgaut] *n* (*canoe*) Einbaum *m*; (*shelter*) Unterstand *m*.

**duke** [djuːk] *n* Herzog *m*.

**dull** [dʌl] *adj* trüb; (*intelligence, wit*) schwerfällig, langsam; (*event*) langweilig; (*sound, pain*) dumpf ♦ *vt* (*pain, grief*) betäuben; (*mind, senses*) abstumpfen.

**duly** ['djuːlɪ] *adv* (*properly*) gebührend; (*on time*) pünktlich.

**dumb** [dʌm] *adj* stumm; (*pej: stupid*) dumm, doof (*inf*); **he was struck ~** es verschlug ihm die Sprache.

**dumbbell** ['dʌmbɛl] *n* Hantel *f*.

**dumbfounded** [dʌm'faʊndɪd] *adj* verblüfft.

**dummy** ['dʌmɪ] *n* (Schneider)puppe *f*; (*mockup*) Attrappe *f*; (*SPORT*) Finte *f*; (*BRIT: for baby*) Schnuller *m* ♦ *adj* (*firm*) fiktiv; **~ bullets** Übungsmunition *f*.

**dummy run** *n* Probe *f*.

**dump** [dʌmp] *n* (*also*: **rubbish ~**) Abfallhaufen *m*; (*inf: place*) Müllkippe *f*; (*MIL*) Depot *nt* ♦ *vt* fallen lassen; (*get rid of*) abladen; (*car*) abstellen; (*COMPUT: data*) ausgeben; **to be down in the ~s** (*inf*) deprimiert *or* down sein; **"no ~ing"** „Schuttabladen verboten".

**dumpling** ['dʌmplɪŋ] *n* Kloß *m*, Knödel *m*.

**dumpy** ['dʌmpɪ] *adj* pummelig.

**dunce** [dʌns] *n* Niete *f*.

**dune** [djuːn] *n* Düne *f*.

**dung** [dʌŋ] *n* (*AGR*) Dünger *m*, Mist *m*; (*ZOOL*) Dung *m*.

**dungarees** [dʌŋɡə'riːz] *npl* Latzhose *f*.

**dungeon** ['dʌndʒən] *n* Kerker *m*, Verlies *nt*.

**dunk** [dʌŋk] *vt* (ein)tunken.

**Dunkirk** [dʌn'kɜːk] *n* Dünkirchen *nt*.

**duo** ['djuːəʊ] *n* Duo *nt*.

**duodenal** [djuːəʊ'diːnl] *adj* Duodenal-; **~ ulcer** Zwölffingerdarmgeschwür *nt*.

**duodenum** [djuːəʊ'diːnəm] *n* Zwölffingerdarm *m*.

**dupe** [djuːp] *n* Betrogene(r) *f(m)* ♦ *vt* betrügen.

**duplex** ['djuːplɛks] (*US*) *n* Zweifamilienhaus *nt*; (*apartment*) zweistöckige Wohnung *f*.

**duplicate** [*n, adj* 'djuːplɪkət, *vt* 'djuːplɪkeɪt] *n* (*also*: **~ copy**) Duplikat *nt*, Kopie *f*; (*also*: **~ key**) Zweitschlüssel *m* ♦ *adj* doppelt ♦ *vt* kopieren; (*repeat*) wiederholen; **in ~** in doppelter Ausfertigung.

**duplicating machine** ['djuːplɪkeɪtɪŋ-] *n* Vervielfältigungsapparat *m*.

**duplicator** ['djuːplɪkeɪtə*] *n* Vervielfältigungsapparat *m*.

**duplicity** [djuː'plɪsɪtɪ] *n* Doppelspiel *nt*.

**Dur.** (*BRIT*) *abbr* (*POST*: = *Durham*).

**durability** [djuərə'bɪlɪtɪ] *n* Haltbarkeit *f*.

**durable** ['djuərəbl] *adj* haltbar.

**duration** [djuə'reɪʃən] *n* Dauer *f*.

**duress** [djuə'rɛs] *n*: **under ~** unter Zwang.

**Durex** ® ['djuərɛks] (*BRIT*) *n* Gummi *m* (*inf*).

**during** ['djuərɪŋ] *prep* während *+gen*.

**dusk** [dʌsk] *n* (Abend)dämmerung *f*.

**dusky** ['dʌskɪ] *adj* (*room*) dunkel; (*light*) Dämmer-.

**dust** [dʌst] *n* Staub *m* ♦ *vt* abstauben; (*cake etc*): **to ~ with** bestäuben mit.

▶**dust off** *vt* abwischen, wegwischen; (*fig*) hervorkramen.

**dustbin** ['dʌstbɪn] (*BRIT*) *n* Mülltonne *f*.

**dustbin liner** (*BRIT*) *n* Müllsack *m*.

**duster** ['dʌstə*] *n* Staubtuch *nt*.

**dust jacket** *n* (Schutz)umschlag *m*.

**dustman** ['dʌstmən] (*BRIT: irreg: like* **man**) *n* Müllmann *m*.

**dustpan** ['dʌstpæn] *n* Kehrschaufel *f*, Müllschaufel *f*.

**dusty** ['dʌstɪ] *adj* staubig.

**Dutch** [dʌtʃ] *adj* holländisch, niederländisch ♦ *n* Holländisch *nt*, Niederländisch *nt* ♦ *adv*: **to go ~** (*inf*) getrennte Kasse machen; **the Dutch** *npl* die Holländer *pl*, die Niederländer *pl*.

**Dutch auction** *n* Versteigerung mit stufenweise erniedrigtem Ausbietungspreis.

**Dutchman** ['dʌtʃmən] (*irreg: like* **man**) *n* Holländer *m*, Niederländer *m*.

**Dutchwoman** ['dʌtʃwumən] (*irreg: like* **woman**) *n* Holländerin *f*, Niederländerin *f*.

**dutiable** ['djuːtɪəbl] *adj* zollpflichtig.

**dutiful** ['djuːtɪful] *adj* pflichtbewußt; (*son, daughter*) gehorsam.

**duty** ['djuːtɪ] *n* Pflicht *f*; (*tax*) Zoll *m*; **duties** *npl* (*functions*) Aufgaben *pl*; **to make it one's ~ to do sth** es sich *dat* zur Pflicht machen, etw zu tun; **to pay ~ on sth** Zoll auf etw *acc* zahlen; **on/off ~** im/nicht im Dienst.

**duty-free** ['djuːtɪ'friː] *adj* zollfrei; **~ shop** Duty-free-Shop *m*.

**duty officer** *n* Offizier *m* vom Dienst.

**duvet** ['duːveɪ] (*BRIT*) *n* Federbett *nt*.

**DV** *abbr* (= *Deo volente*) so Gott will.

**DVLA** *n abbr* (= *Driver and Vehicle Licensing Authority*) Zulassungsbehörde für Kraftfahrzeuge.

**DVLC** (*BRIT*) *n abbr* (= *Driver and Vehicle Licensing Centre*) Zulassungsstelle für Kraftfahrzeuge.

**DVM** (*US*) *n abbr* (= *Doctor of Veterinary Medicine*) ≈ Dr. med. vet.

**dwarf** [dwɔːf] (*pl* **dwarves**) *n* Zwerg(in) *m(f)* ♦ *vt*: **to be ~ed by sth** neben etw *dat* klein erscheinen.

**dwarves** [dwɔːvz] *npl of* **dwarf**.

**dwell** [dwɛl] (*pt, pp* **dwelt**) *vi* wohnen, leben.

▶**dwell on** *vt fus* (in Gedanken) verweilen bei.

**dweller** ['dwɛlə*] *n* Bewohner(in) *m(f)*; **city ~** Stadtbewohner(in) *m(f)*.

**dwelling** ['dwɛlɪŋ] *n* Wohnhaus *nt*.

**dwelt** [dwɛlt] *pt, pp of* **dwell**.

**dwindle** ['dwɪndl] *vi* abnehmen; (*interest*) schwinden; (*attendance*) zurückgehen.

**dwindling** ['dwɪndlɪŋ] *adj* (*strength, interest*) schwindend; (*resources, supplies*) versiegend.

**dye** [daɪ] *n* Farbstoff *m*; (*for hair*) Färbemittel *nt* ♦ *vt* färben.

**dyestuffs** ['daɪstʌfs] *npl* Farbstoffe *pl.*

**dying** ['daɪɪŋ] *adj* sterbend; (*moments, words*) letzte(r, s).

**dyke** [daɪk] *n* (*BRIT: wall*) Deich *m*, Damm *m*; (*channel*) (Entwässerungs)graben *m*; (*causeway*) Fahrdamm *m.*

**dynamic** [daɪ'næmɪk] *adj* dynamisch.

**dynamics** [daɪ'næmɪks] *n or npl* Dynamik *f.*

**dynamite** ['daɪnəmaɪt] *n* Dynamit *nt* ♦ *vt* sprengen.

**dynamo** ['daɪnəməu] *n* Dynamo *m*; (*AUT*) Lichtmaschine *f.*

**dynasty** ['dɪnəstɪ] *n* Dynastie *f.*

**dysentery** ['dɪsntrɪ] *n* (*MED*) Ruhr *f.*

**dyslexia** [dɪs'lɛksɪə] *n* Legasthenie *f.*

**dyslexic** [dɪs'lɛksɪk] *adj* legasthenisch ♦ *n* Legastheniker(in) *m(f).*

**dyspepsia** [dɪs'pɛpsɪə] *n* Dyspepsie *f*, Verdauungsstörung *f.*

**dystrophy** ['dɪstrəfɪ] *n* Dystrophie *f*, Ernährungsstörung *f*; **muscular** ~ Muskelschwund *m.*

# E, e

**E¹, e** [iː] *n* (*letter*) E *nt*, e *nt*; ~ **for Edward**, (*US*) ~ **for Easy** E wie Emil.

**E²** [iː] *n* (*MUS*) E *nt*, e *nt.*

**E³** [iː] *abbr* (= *east*) O ♦ *n abbr* (*drug:* = *Ecstasy*) Ecstasy *nt.*

**E111** *n abbr* (*also:* **form** ~) E111-Formular *nt.*

**E.A.** (*US*) *n abbr* (= *educational age*) Bildungsstand *m.*

**ea.** *abbr* = **each.**

**each** [iːtʃ] *adj, pron* jede(r, s); ~ **other** sich, einander; **they hate** ~ **other** sie hassen sich *or* einander; **you are jealous of** ~ **other** ihr seid eifersüchtig aufeinander; ~ **day** jeden Tag; **they have 2 books** ~ sie haben je 2 Bücher; **they cost £5** ~ sie kosten 5 Pfund das Stück; ~ **of us** jede(r, s) von uns.

**eager** ['iːgə'] *adj* eifrig; **to be** ~ **to do sth** etw unbedingt tun wollen; **to be** ~ **for sth** auf etw *acc* erpicht *or* aus (*inf*) sein.

**eagerly** ['iːgəlɪ] *adv* eifrig; (*awaited*) gespannt, ungeduldig.

**eagle** ['iːgl] *n* Adler *m.*

**ear** [ɪə'] *n* Ohr *nt*; (*of corn*) Ähre *f*; **to be up to one's** ~**s in debt/work** bis über beide Ohren in Schulden/Arbeit stecken; **to be up to one's** ~**s in paint/baking** mitten im Anstreichen/Backen stecken; **to give sb a thick** ~ jdm ein paar hinter die Ohren geben; **we'll play it by** ~ (*fig*) wir werden es auf uns zukommen lassen.

**earache** ['ɪəreɪk] *n* Ohrenschmerzen *pl.*

**eardrum** ['ɪədrʌm] *n* Trommelfell *nt.*

**earful** ['ɪəful] (*inf*) *n*: **to give sb an** ~ jdm was erzählen; **to get an** ~ was zu hören bekommen.

**earl** [əːl] (*BRIT*) *n* Graf *m.*

**earlier** ['əːlɪə'] *adj, adv* früher; **I can't come any** ~ ich kann nicht früher *or* eher kommen.

**early** ['əːlɪ] *adv* früh; (*ahead of time*) zu früh ♦ *adj* früh; (*Christians*) Ur-; (*death, departure*) vorzeitig; (*reply*) baldig; ~ **in the morning** früh am Morgen; **to have an** ~ **night** früh ins Bett gehen; **in the** ~ **hours** in den frühen Morgenstunden; **in the** ~ *or* ~ **in the spring/19th century** Anfang des Frühjahrs/ des 19. Jahrhunderts; **take the** ~ **train** nimm den früheren Zug; **you're** ~! Sie sind früh dran!; **she's in her** ~ **forties** sie ist Anfang Vierzig; **at your earliest convenience** so bald wie möglich.

**early retirement** *n*: **to take** ~ vorzeitig in den Ruhestand gehen.

**early warning system** *n* Frühwarnsystem *nt.*

**earmark** ['ɪəmɑːk] *vt*: **to** ~ **(for)** bestimmen (für), vorsehen (für).

**earn** [əːn] *vt* verdienen; (*interest*) bringen; **to** ~ **one's living** seinen Lebensunterhalt verdienen; **this** ~**ed him much praise, he** ~**ed much praise for this** das trug ihm viel Lob ein; **he's** ~**ed his rest/reward** er hat sich seine Pause/Belohnung verdient.

**earned income** [əːnd-] *n* Arbeitseinkommen *nt.*

**earnest** ['əːnɪst] *adj* ernsthaft; (*wish, desire*) innig ♦ *n* (*also:* ~ **money**) Angeld *nt*; **in** ~ (*adv*) richtig; (*adj*): **to be in** ~ es ernst meinen; **work on the tunnel soon began in** ~ die Tunnelarbeiten begannen bald richtig; **is the Minister in** ~ **about these proposals?** meint der Minister es mit diesen Vorschlägen ernst?

**earnings** ['əːnɪŋz] *npl* Verdienst *m*; (*of company etc*) Ertrag *m.*

**ear, nose and throat specialist** *n* Hals-Nasen-Ohren-Arzt *m*, Hals-Nasen-Ohren-Ärztin *f.*

**earphones** ['ɪəfəunz] *npl* Kopfhörer *pl.*

**earplugs** ['ɪəplʌgz] *npl* Ohropax ® *nt.*

**earring** ['ɪərɪŋ] *n* Ohrring *m.*

**earshot** ['ɪəʃɔt] *n*: **within/out of** ~ in/außer Hörweite.

**earth** [əːθ] *n* Erde *f*; (*of fox*) Bau *m* ♦ *vt* (*BRIT: ELEC*) erden.

**earthenware** ['əːθnwɛə'] *n* Tongeschirr *nt* ♦ *adj* Ton-.

**earthly** ['əːθlɪ] *adj* irdisch; ~ **paradise** Paradies *nt* auf Erden; **there is no** ~ **reason to think ...** es besteht nicht der geringste Grund für die Annahme ...

**earthquake** ['əːθkweɪk] *n* Erdbeben *nt.*

**earthshattering** ['əːθʃætərɪŋ] *adj* (*fig*) weltbewegend.

**earth tremor** n Erdstoß m.
**earthworks** ['ɔːθwɔːks] npl Erdarbeiten pl.
**earthworm** ['ɔːθwɔːm] n Regenwurm m.
**earthy** ['ɔːθɪ] adj (humour) derb.
**earwig** ['ɪəwɪɡ] n Ohrwurm m.
**ease** [iːz] n Leichtigkeit f; (comfort) Behagen nt ♦ vt (problem) vereinfachen; (pain) lindern; (tension) verringern; (loosen) lockern ♦ vi nachlassen; (situation) sich entspannen; **to ~ sth in/out** (push/pull) etw behutsam hineinschieben/herausziehen; **at ~!** (MIL) rührt euch!; **with ~** mit Leichtigkeit; **life of ~** Leben der Muße; **to ~ in the clutch** die Kupplung behutsam kommen lassen.
▶**ease off** vi nachlassen; (slow down) langsamer werden.
▶**ease up** vi = ease off.
**easel** ['iːzl] n Staffelei f.
**easily** ['iːzɪlɪ] adv (see adj) leicht; ungezwungen; bequem.
**easiness** ['iːzɪnɪs] n Leichtigkeit f; (of manner) Ungezwungenheit f.
**east** [iːst] n Osten m ♦ adj (coast, Asia etc) Ost- ♦ adv ostwärts, nach Osten; **the E~** der Osten.
**Easter** ['iːstə*] n Ostern nt ♦ adj (holidays etc) Oster-.
**Easter egg** n Osterei nt.
**Easter Island** n Osterinsel f.
**easterly** ['iːstəlɪ] adj östlich; (wind) Ost-.
**Easter Monday** n Ostermontag m.
**eastern** ['iːstən] adj östlich; **E~ Europe** Osteuropa nt; **the E~ bloc** (formerly) der Ostblock.
**Easter Sunday** n Ostersonntag m.
**East Germany** n (formerly) die DDR f.
**eastward(s)** ['iːstwəd(z)] adv ostwärts, nach Osten.
**easy** ['iːzɪ] adj leicht; (relaxed) ungezwungen; (comfortable) bequem ♦ adv: **to take it/things ~** (go slowly) sich dat Zeit lassen; (not worry) es nicht so schwer nehmen; (rest) sich schonen; **payment on ~ terms** Zahlung zu günstigen Bedingungen; **that's easier said than done** das ist leichter gesagt als getan; **I'm ~** (inf) mir ist alles recht.
**easy chair** n Sessel m.
**easy-going** ['iːzɪ'ɡəʊɪŋ] adj gelassen.
**easy touch** (inf) n: **to be an ~** (for money etc) leicht anzuzapfen sein.
**eat** [iːt] (pt **ate**, pp **eaten**) vt, vi essen; (animal) fressen.
▶**eat away** vt (subj: sea) auswaschen; (: acid) zerfressen.
▶**eat away at** vt fus (metal) anfressen; (savings) angreifen.
▶**eat into** vt fus = eat away at.
▶**eat out** vi essen gehen.
▶**eat up** vt aufessen; **it ~s up electricity** es verbraucht viel Strom.
**eatable** ['iːtəbl] adj genießbar.

**eau de Cologne** ['əʊdəkə'ləʊn] n Kölnisch Wasser nt, Eau de Cologne nt.
**eaves** [iːvz] npl Dachvorsprung m.
**eavesdrop** ['iːvzdrɒp] vi lauschen; **to ~ on** belauschen +acc.
**ebb** [ɛb] n Ebbe f ♦ vi ebben; (fig: also: ~ **away**) dahinschwinden; (: feeling) abebben; **the ~ and flow** (fig) das Auf und Ab; **to be at a low ~** (fig) auf einem Tiefpunkt angelangt sein.
**ebb tide** n Ebbe f.
**ebony** ['ɛbənɪ] n Ebenholz nt.
**ebullient** [ɪ'bʌlɪənt] adj überschäumend, übersprudelnd.
**EC** n abbr (= European Community) EG f.
**eccentric** [ɪk'sɛntrɪk] adj exzentrisch ♦ n Exzentriker(in) m(f).
**ecclesiastic(al)** [ɪkliːzɪ'æstɪk(l)] adj kirchlich.
**ECG** n abbr (= electrocardiogram) EKG nt.
**echo** ['ɛkəʊ] (pl ~**es**) n Echo nt ♦ vt wiederholen ♦ vi widerhallen; (place) hallen.
**éclair** [eɪ'klɛə*] n Eclair nt.
**eclipse** [ɪ'klɪps] n Finsternis f ♦ vt in den Schatten stellen.
**ECM** (US) n abbr (= European Common Market) EG f.
**eco-** ['iːkəʊ] pref Öko-, öko-.
**ecofriendly** adj umweltfreundlich.
**ecological** [iːkə'lɒdʒɪkəl] adj ökologisch; (damage, disaster) Umwelt-.
**ecologist** [ɪ'kɒlədʒɪst] n Ökologe m, Ökologin f.
**ecology** [ɪ'kɒlədʒɪ] n Ökologie f.
**economic** [iːkə'nɒmɪk] adj (system, policy etc) Wirtschafts-; (profitable) wirtschaftlich.
**economical** [iːkə'nɒmɪkl] adj wirtschaftlich; (person) sparsam.
**economically** [iːkə'nɒmɪklɪ] adv wirtschaftlich; (thriftily) sparsam.
**economics** [iːkə'nɒmɪks] n Wirtschaftswissenschaften pl ♦ npl Wirtschaftlichkeit f; (of situation) wirtschaftliche Seite f.
**economist** [ɪ'kɒnəmɪst] n Wirtschaftswissenschaftler(in) m(f).
**economize** [ɪ'kɒnəmaɪz] vi sparen.
**economy** [ɪ'kɒnəmɪ] n Wirtschaft f; (financial prudence) Sparsamkeit f; **economies of scale** (COMM) Einsparungen pl durch erhöhte Produktion.
**economy class** n Touristenklasse f.
**economy size** n Sparpackung f.
**ecosystem** ['iːkəʊsɪstəm] n Ökosystem nt.
**ecotourism** ['iːkəʊ'tʊərɪzm] n Ökotourismus m.
**ECSC** n abbr (= European Coal and Steel Community) Europäische Gemeinschaft für Kohle und Stahl.
**ecstasy** ['ɛkstəsɪ] n Ekstase f; (drug) Ecstasy nt; **to go into ecstasies over** in Verzückung geraten über +acc; **in ~** verzückt.
**ecstatic** [ɛks'tætɪk] adj ekstatisch.

**ECT** *n abbr* = **electroconvulsive therapy**.
**ECU** ['eɪkjuː] *n abbr* (= *European Currency Unit*) Ecu *m*.
**Ecuador** ['ɛkwədɔː'] *n* Ecuador *nt*, Ekuador *nt*.
**ecumenical** [iːkjuˈmɛnɪkl] *adj* ökumenisch.
**eczema** ['ɛksɪmə] *n* Ekzem *nt*.
**eddy** ['ɛdɪ] *n* Strudel *m*.
**edge** [ɛdʒ] *n* Rand *m*; (*of table, chair*) Kante *f*; (*of lake*) Ufer *nt*; (*of knife etc*) Schneide *f* ♦ *vt* einfassen ♦ *vi*: **to ~ forward** sich nach vorne schieben; **on ~** (*fig*) = **edgy**; **to have the ~ on** überlegen sein +*dat*; **to ~ away from** sich allmählich entfernen von; **to ~ past** sich vorbeischieben, sich vorbeidrücken.
**edgeways** ['ɛdʒweɪz] *adv*: **he couldn't get a word in ~** er kam überhaupt nicht zu Wort.
**edging** ['ɛdʒɪŋ] *n* Einfassung *f*.
**edgy** ['ɛdʒɪ] *adj* nervös.
**edible** ['ɛdɪbl] *adj* eßbar, genießbar.
**edict** ['iːdɪkt] *n* Erlaß *m*.
**edifice** ['ɛdɪfɪs] *n* Gebäude *nt*.
**edifying** ['ɛdɪfaɪɪŋ] *adj* erbaulich.
**Edinburgh** ['ɛdɪnbərə] *n* Edinburg(h) *nt*.
**edit** ['ɛdɪt] *vt* (*text*) redigieren; (*book*) lektorieren; (*film, broadcast*) schneiden, cutten; (*newspaper, magazine*) herausgeben; (*COMPUT*) editieren.
**edition** [ɪˈdɪʃən] *n* Ausgabe *f*.
**editor** ['ɛdɪtəʳ] *n* Redakteur(in) *m(f)*; (*of newspaper, magazine*) Herausgeber(in) *m(f)*; (*of book*) Lektor(in) *m(f)*; (*CINE, RADIO, TV*) Cutter(in) *m(f)*.
**editorial** [ɛdɪˈtɔːrɪəl] *adj* redaktionell; (*staff*) Redaktions- ♦ *n* Leitartikel *m*.
**EDP** *n abbr* (*COMPUT*) (= *electronic data processing*) EDV *f*.
**EDT** (*US*) *abbr* (= *Eastern Daylight Time*) ostamerikanische Sommerzeit.
**educate** ['ɛdjukeɪt] *vt* erziehen; **~d at ...** zur Schule/Universität gegangen in ...
**educated** ['ɛdjukeɪtɪd] *adj* gebildet.
**educated guess** ['ɛdjukeɪtɪd-] *n* wohlbegründete Vermutung *f*.
**education** [ɛdjuˈkeɪʃən] *n* Erziehung *f*; (*schooling*) Ausbildung *f*; (*knowledge, culture*) Bildung *f*; **primary** *or* (*US*) **elementary ~** Grundschul(aus)bildung *f*; **secondary ~** höhere Schul(aus)bildung *f*.
**educational** [ɛdjuˈkeɪʃənl] *adj* pädagogisch; (*experience*) lehrreich; (*toy*) pädagogisch wertvoll; **~ technology** Unterrichtstechnologie *f*.
**Edwardian** [ɛdˈwɔːdɪən] *adj* aus der Zeit Edwards VII.
**EE** *abbr* = **electrical engineer**.
**EEC** *n abbr* (= *European Economic Community*) EWG *f*.
**EEG** *n abbr* (= *electroencephalogram*) EEG *nt*.
**eel** [iːl] *n* Aal *m*.
**EENT** (*US*) *n abbr* (*MED*: = *eye, ear, nose and throat*) Augen und Hals-Nasen-Ohren-.
**EEOC** (*US*) *n abbr* (= *Equal Employment Opportunity Commission*) Kommission *für* Gleichberechtigung am Arbeitsplatz.
**eerie** ['ɪərɪ] *adj* unheimlich.
**EET** *abbr* (= *Eastern European Time*) OEZ *f*.
**efface** [ɪˈfeɪs] *vt* auslöschen; **to ~ o.s.** sich im Hintergrund halten.
**effect** [ɪˈfɛkt] *n* Wirkung *f*, Effekt *m* ♦ *vt* bewirken; (*repairs*) durchführen; **effects** *npl* Effekten *pl*; (*THEAT, CINE etc*) Effekte *pl*; **to take ~** (*law*) in Kraft treten; (*drug*) wirken; **to put into ~** in Kraft setzen; **to have an ~ on sb/sth** eine Wirkung auf jdn/etw haben; **in ~** eigentlich, praktisch; **his letter is to the ~ that ...** sein Brief hat zum Inhalt, daß ...
**effective** [ɪˈfɛktɪv] *adj* effektiv, wirksam; (*actual*) eigentlich, wirklich; **to become ~** in Kraft treten; **~ date** Zeitpunkt *m* des Inkrafttretens.
**effectively** [ɪˈfɛktɪvlɪ] *adv* effektiv.
**effectiveness** [ɪˈfɛktɪvnɪs] *n* Wirksamkeit *f*, Effektivität *f*.
**effeminate** [ɪˈfɛmɪnɪt] *adj* feminin, effeminiert.
**effervescent** [ɛfəˈvɛsnt] *adj* sprudelnd.
**efficacy** ['ɛfɪkəsɪ] *n* Wirksamkeit *f*.
**efficiency** [ɪˈfɪʃənsɪ] *n* (*see adj*) Fähigkeit *f*, Tüchtigkeit *f*; Rationalität *f*; Leistungsfähigkeit *f*.
**efficiency apartment** (*US*) *n* Einzimmerwohnung *f*.
**efficient** [ɪˈfɪʃənt] *adj* fähig, tüchtig; (*organization*) rationell; (*machine*) leistungsfähig.
**efficiently** [ɪˈfɪʃəntlɪ] *adv* gut, effizient.
**effigy** ['ɛfɪdʒɪ] *n* Bildnis *nt*.
**effluent** ['ɛfluənt] *n* Abwasser *nt*.
**effort** ['ɛfət] *n* Anstrengung *f*; (*attempt*) Versuch *m*; **to make an ~ to do sth** sich bemühen, etw zu tun.
**effortless** ['ɛfətlɪs] *adj* mühelos; (*style*) flüssig.
**effrontery** [ɪˈfrʌntərɪ] *n* Unverschämtheit *f*; **to have the ~ to do sth** die Frechheit besitzen, etw zu tun.
**effusive** [ɪˈfjuːsɪv] *adj* überschwenglich.
**EFL** *n abbr* (*SCOL*: = *English as a Foreign Language*) Englisch *nt* als Fremdsprache.
**EFTA** ['ɛftə] *n abbr* (= *European Free Trade Association*) EFTA *f*.
**e.g.** *adv abbr* (= *exempli gratia*) z.B.
**egalitarian** [ɪgælɪˈtɛərɪən] *adj* egalitär; (*principles*) Gleichheits- ♦ *n* Verfechter(in) *m(f)* des Egalitarismus.
**egg** [ɛg] *n* Ei *nt*; **hard-boiled/soft-boiled ~** hart-/weichgekochtes Ei *nt*.
▶**egg on** *vt* anstacheln.
**egg cup** *n* Eierbecher *m*.
**eggplant** ['ɛgplɑːnt] *n* (*esp US*) Aubergine *f*.
**eggshell** ['ɛgʃɛl] *n* Eierschale *f* ♦ *adj* eierschalenfarben.
**egg timer** *n* Eieruhr *f*.
**egg white** *n* Eiweiß *nt*.

**egg yolk** n Eigelb nt.
**ego** ['iːgəu] n (*self-esteem*) Selbstbewußtsein nt.
**egoism** ['ɛgəuɪzəm] n Egoismus m.
**egoist** ['ɛgəuɪst] n Egoist(in) m(f).
**egotism** ['ɛgəutɪzəm] n Ichbezogenheit f, Egotismus m.
**egotist** ['ɛgəutɪst] n ichbezogener Mensch m, Egotist(in) m(f).
**ego trip** (*inf*) n Egotrip m.
**Egypt** ['iːdʒɪpt] n Ägypten nt.
**Egyptian** [ɪ'dʒɪpʃən] adj ägyptisch ♦ n Ägypter(in) m(f).
**eiderdown** ['aɪdədaun] n Federbett nt, Daunendecke f.
**eight** [eɪt] num acht.
**eighteen** [eɪ'tiːn] num achtzehn.
**eighteenth** [eɪ'tiːnθ] num achtzehnte(r, s).
**eighth** [eɪtθ] num achte(r, s) ♦ n Achtel nt.
**eighty** ['eɪtɪ] num achtzig.
**Eire** ['ɛərə] n (Republik f) Irland nt.
**EIS** n abbr (= *Educational Institute of Scotland*) *schottische Lehrergewerkschaft.*
**either** ['aɪðə'] adj (*one or other*) eine(r, s) (von beiden); (*both, each*) beide pl, jede(r, s) ♦ pron: ~ (**of them**) eine(r, s) (davon) ♦ adv auch nicht ♦ conj: ~ **yes or no** entweder ja oder nein; **on** ~ **side** (*on both sides*) auf beiden Seiten; (*on one or other side*) auf einer der beiden Seiten; **I don't like** ~ ich mag beide nicht or keinen von beiden; **no, I don't** ~ nein, ich auch nicht; **I haven't seen** ~ **one or the other** ich habe weder den einen noch den anderen gesehen.
**ejaculation** [ɪdʒækju'leɪʃən] n Ejakulation f, Samenerguß m.
**eject** [ɪ'dʒɛkt] vt ausstoßen; (*tenant, gatecrasher*) hinauswerfen ♦ vi den Schleudersitz betätigen.
**ejector seat** [ɪ'dʒɛktə-] n Schleudersitz m.
**eke out** vt (*make last*) strecken.
**EKG** (*US*) n abbr = **electrocardiogram.**
**el** [ɛl] (*US: inf*) n abbr = **elevated railroad.**
**elaborate** [adj ɪ'læbərɪt, vb ɪ'læbəreɪt] adj kompliziert; (*plan*) ausgefeilt ♦ vt näher ausführen; (*refine*) ausarbeiten ♦ vi mehr ins Detail gehen; **to** ~ **on** näher ausführen.
**elapse** [ɪ'læps] vi vergehen, verstreichen.
**elastic** [ɪ'læstɪk] n Gummi nt ♦ adj elastisch.
**elastic band** (*BRIT*) n Gummiband nt.
**elasticity** [ɪlæs'tɪsɪtɪ] n Elastizität f.
**elated** [ɪ'leɪtɪd] adj: **to be** ~ hocherfreut or in Hochstimmung sein.
**elation** [ɪ'leɪʃən] n große Freude f, Hochstimmung f.
**elbow** ['ɛlbəu] n Ellbogen m ♦ vt: **to** ~ **one's way through the crowd** sich durch die Menge boxen.
**elbow grease** (*inf*) n Muskelkraft f.
**elbowroom** ['ɛlbəurum] n Ellbogenfreiheit f.
**elder** ['ɛldə'] adj älter ♦ n (*BOT*) Holunder m; (*older person: gen pl*) Ältere(r) f(m).

**elderly** ['ɛldəlɪ] adj ältere(r, s) ♦ npl: **the** ~ ältere Leute pl.
**elder statesman** n erfahrener Staatsmann m.
**eldest** ['ɛldɪst] adj älteste(r, s) ♦ n Älteste(r) f(m).
**elect** [ɪ'lɛkt] vt wählen ♦ adj: **the president** ~ der designierte or künftige Präsident; **to** ~ **to do sth** sich dafür entscheiden, etw zu tun.
**election** [ɪ'lɛkʃən] n Wahl f; **to hold an** ~ eine Wahl abhalten.
**election campaign** n Wahlkampf m.
**electioneering** [ɪlɛkʃə'nɪərɪŋ] n Wahlkampf m.
**elector** [ɪ'lɛktə'] n Wähler(in) m(f).
**electoral** [ɪ'lɛktərəl] adj Wahl-.
**electoral college** n Wahlmännergremium nt.
**electorate** [ɪ'lɛktərɪt] n Wähler pl, Wählerschaft f.
**electric** [ɪ'lɛktrɪk] adj elektrisch.
**electrical** [ɪ'lɛktrɪkl] adj elektrisch; (*appliance*) Elektro-; (*failure*) Strom-.
**electrical engineer** n Elektrotechniker m.
**electric blanket** n Heizdecke f.
**electric chair** (*US*) n elektrischer Stuhl m.
**electric cooker** n Elektroherd m.
**electric current** n elektrischer Strom m.
**electric fire** (*BRIT*) n elektrisches Heizgerät nt.
**electrician** [ɪlɛk'trɪʃən] n Elektriker(in) m(f).
**electricity** [ɪlɛk'trɪsɪtɪ] n Elektrizität f; (*supply*) (elektrischer) Strom m ♦ cpd Strom-; **to switch on/off the** ~ den Strom an-/abschalten.
**electricity board** (*BRIT*) n Elektrizitätswerk nt.
**electric light** n elektrisches Licht nt.
**electric shock** n elektrischer Schlag m, Stromschlag m.
**electrify** [ɪ'lɛktrɪfaɪ] vt (*fence*) unter Strom setzen; (*rail network*) elektrifizieren; (*audience*) elektrisieren.
**electro...** [ɪ'lɛktrəu] pref Elektro-.
**electrocardiogram** [ɪ'lɛktrə'kɑːdɪəgræm] n Elektrokardiogramm nt.
**electroconvulsive therapy** [ɪ'lɛktrəkən'vʌlsɪv-] n Elektroschocktherapie f.
**electrocute** [ɪ'lɛktrəkjuːt] vt durch einen Stromschlag töten; (*US: criminal*) auf dem elektrischen Stuhl hinrichten.
**electrode** [ɪ'lɛktrəud] n Elektrode f.
**electroencephalogram** [ɪ'lɛktrəu-ɛn'sɛfələgræm] n Elektroenzephalogramm nt.
**electrolysis** [ɪlɛk'trɒlɪsɪs] n Elektrolyse f.
**electromagnetic** [ɪ'lɛktrəmæg'nɛtɪk] adj elektromagnetisch.
**electron** [ɪ'lɛktrɒn] n Elektron nt.
**electronic** [ɪlɛk'trɒnɪk] adj elektronisch.
**electronic data processing** n elektronische Datenverarbeitung f.
**electronic mail** n elektronische Post f.

**electronics** [ɪlɛk'trɔnɪks] n Elektronik f.
**electron microscope** n
Elektronenmikroskop nt.
**electroplated** [ɪ'lɛktrə'pleɪtɪd] adj
galvanisiert.
**electrotherapy** [ɪ'lɛktrə'θɛrəpɪ] n
Elektrotherapie f.
**elegance** ['ɛlɪgəns] n Eleganz f.
**elegant** ['ɛlɪgənt] adj elegant.
**element** ['ɛlɪmənt] n Element nt; (of heater,
kettle etc) Heizelement nt.
**elementary** [ɛlɪ'mɛntərɪ] adj grundlegend;
~ **school** Grundschule f; ~ **education**
Elementarunterricht m; ~ **maths/French**
Grundbegriffe pl der Mathematik/des
Französischen.

> **Elementary School** ist in den USA und Kanada
> eine Grundschule, an der ein Kind die ersten
> sechs bis acht Schuljahre verbringt. In den
> USA heißt diese Schule auch grade school oder
> grammar school. Siehe auch **high school**.

**elephant** ['ɛlɪfənt] n Elefant m.
**elevate** ['ɛlɪveɪt] vt erheben; (physically)
heben.
**elevated railroad** ['ɛlɪveɪtɪd-] (US) n
Hochbahn f.
**elevation** [ɛlɪ'veɪʃən] n Erhebung f; (height)
Höhe f über dem Meeresspiegel; (ARCHIT)
Aufriß m.
**elevator** ['ɛlɪveɪtə˘] n (US) Aufzug m,
Fahrstuhl m; (in warehouse etc)
Lastenaufzug m.
**eleven** [ɪ'lɛvn] num elf.
**elevenses** [ɪ'lɛvnzɪz] (BRIT) npl zweites
Frühstück nt.
**eleventh** [ɪ'lɛvnθ] num elfte(r, s); **at the**
~ **hour** (fig) in letzter Minute.
**elf** [ɛlf] (pl **elves**) n Elf m, Elfe f; (mischievous)
Kobold m.
**elicit** [ɪ'lɪsɪt] vt: **to** ~ **(from sb)** (information)
(aus jdm) herausbekommen; (reaction,
response) (von jdm) bekommen.
**eligible** ['ɛlɪdʒəbl] adj (marriage partner)
begehrt; **to be** ~ **for sth** für etw in Frage
kommen; **to be** ~ **for a pension**
pensionsberechtigt sein.
**eliminate** [ɪ'lɪmɪneɪt] vt beseitigen; (candidate
etc) ausschließen; (team, contestant) aus dem
Wettbewerb werfen.
**elimination** [ɪlɪmɪ'neɪʃən] n (see vb)
Beseitigung f; Ausschluß m; Ausscheiden nt;
**by process of** ~ durch negative Auslese.
**élite** [eɪ'liːt] n Elite f.
**élitist** [eɪ'liːtɪst] (pej) adj elitär.
**elixir** [ɪ'lɪksə˘] n Elixier nt.
**Elizabethan** [ɪlɪzə'biːθən] adj elisabethanisch.
**ellipse** [ɪ'lɪps] n Ellipse f.
**elliptical** [ɪ'lɪptɪkl] adj elliptisch.
**elm** [ɛlm] n Ulme f.
**elocution** [ɛlə'kjuːʃən] n Sprechtechnik f.

**elongated** ['iːlɔŋgeɪtɪd] adj langgestreckt;
(shadow) verlängert.
**elope** [ɪ'ləup] vi weglaufen.
**elopement** [ɪ'ləupmənt] n Weglaufen nt.
**eloquence** ['ɛləkwəns] n (see adj) Beredtheit f,
Wortgewandtheit f; Ausdrucksfülle f.
**eloquent** ['ɛləkwənt] adj beredt, wort-
gewandt; (speech, description)
ausdrucksvoll.
**else** [ɛls] adv andere(r, s); **something** ~ etwas
anderes; **somewhere** ~ woanders,
anderswo; **everywhere** ~ sonst überall;
**where** ~? wo sonst?; **is there anything** ~ **I
can do?** kann ich sonst noch etwas tun?;
**there was little** ~ **to do** es gab nicht viel
anderes zu tun; **everyone** ~ alle anderen;
**nobody** ~ **spoke** niemand anders sagte
etwas, sonst sagte niemand etwas.
**elsewhere** [ɛls'wɛə˘] adv woanders,
anderswo; (go) woandershin, anderswohin.
**ELT** n abbr (SCOL: = English Language Teaching)
Englisch als Unterrichtsfach.
**elucidate** [ɪ'luːsɪdeɪt] vt erläutern.
**elude** [ɪ'luːd] vt (captor) entkommen +dat;
(capture) sich entziehen +dat; **this fact/idea**
~**d him** diese Tatsache/Idee entging ihm.
**elusive** [ɪ'luːsɪv] adj schwer zu fangen;
(quality) unerreichbar; **he's very** ~ er ist
sehr schwer zu erreichen.
**elves** [ɛlvz] npl of **elf**.
**emaciated** [ɪ'meɪsɪeɪtɪd] adj abgezehrt,
ausgezehrt.
**E-mail** n abbr (= electronic mail) E-Mail f.
**emanate** ['ɛməneɪt] vi: **to** ~ **from** stammen
von; (sound, light etc) ausgehen von.
**emancipate** [ɪ'mænsɪpeɪt] vt (women)
emanzipieren; (poor) befreien; (slave)
freilassen.
**emancipation** [ɪmænsɪ'peɪʃən] n (see vb)
Emanzipation f; Befreiung f; Freilassung f.
**emasculate** [ɪ'mæskjuleɪt] vt schwächen.
**embalm** [ɪm'bɑːm] vt einbalsamieren.
**embankment** [ɪm'bæŋkmənt] n Böschung f;
(of railway) Bahndamm m; (of river) Damm m.
**embargo** [ɪm'bɑːgəu] (pl ~**es**) n Embargo nt
♦ vt mit einem Embargo belegen; **to put** or
**impose** or **place an** ~ **on sth** ein Embargo
über etw acc verhängen; **to lift an** ~ ein
Embargo aufheben.
**embark** [ɪm'bɑːk] vt einschiffen ♦ vi: **to** ~ **(on)**
sich einschiffen (auf); **to** ~ **on** (journey)
beginnen; (task) in Angriff nehmen; (course
of action) einschlagen.
**embarkation** [ɛmbɑː'keɪʃən] n Einschiffung f.
**embarkation card** n Bordkarte f.
**embarrass** [ɪm'bærəs] vt in Verlegenheit
bringen.
**embarrassed** [ɪm'bærəst] adj verlegen.
**embarrassing** [ɪm'bærəsɪŋ] adj peinlich.
**embarrassment** [ɪm'bærəsmənt] n
Verlegenheit f; (embarrassing problem)
Peinlichkeit f.

**embassy** ['ɛmbəsɪ] *n* Botschaft *f*; **the Swiss E~** die Schweizer Botschaft.

**embedded** [ɪm'bɛdɪd] *adj* eingebettet; (*attitude, belief, feeling*) verwurzelt.

**embellish** [ɪm'bɛlɪʃ] *vt* (*account*) ausschmücken; **to be ~ed with** geschmückt sein mit.

**embers** ['ɛmbəz] *npl* Glut *f*.

**embezzle** [ɪm'bɛzl] *vt* unterschlagen.

**embezzlement** [ɪm'bɛzlmənt] *n* Unterschlagung *f*.

**embezzler** [ɪm'bɛzlə*] *n jd, der eine Unterschlagung begangen hat.*

**embitter** [ɪm'bɪtə*] *vt* verbittern.

**embittered** [ɪm'bɪtəd] *adj* verbittert.

**emblem** ['ɛmbləm] *n* Emblem *nt*; (*symbol*) Wahrzeichen *nt*.

**embodiment** [ɪm'bɔdɪmənt] *n* Verkörperung *f*; **to be the ~ of** ... (*subj: thing*) ... verkörpern; (*: person*) ... in Person sein.

**embody** [ɪm'bɔdɪ] *vt* verkörpern; (*include, contain*) enthalten.

**embolden** [ɪm'bəʊldn] *vt* ermutigen.

**embolism** ['ɛmbəlɪzəm] *n* Embolie *f*.

**embossed** [ɪm'bɔst] *adj* geprägt; **~ with a logo** mit geprägtem Logo.

**embrace** [ɪm'breɪs] *vt* umarmen; (*include*) umfassen ♦ *vi* sich umarmen ♦ *n* Umarmung *f*.

**embroider** [ɪm'brɔɪdə*] *vt* (*cloth*) besticken; (*fig: story*) ausschmücken.

**embroidery** [ɪm'brɔɪdərɪ] *n* Stickerei *f*; (*activity*) Sticken *nt*.

**embroil** [ɪm'brɔɪl] *vt*: **to become ~ed (in sth)** (in etw *acc*) verwickelt *or* hineingezogen werden.

**embryo** ['ɛmbrɪəʊ] *n* Embryo *m*; (*fig*) Keim *m*.

**emcee** [ɛm'siː] *n* Conférencier *m*.

**emend** [ɪ'mɛnd] *vt* verbessern, korrigieren.

**emerald** ['ɛmərəld] *n* Smaragd *m*.

**emerge** [ɪ'mɜːdʒ] *vi*: **to ~ (from)** auftauchen (aus); (*from sleep*) erwachen (aus); (*from imprisonment*) entlassen werden (aus); (*from discussion etc*) sich herausstellen (bei); (*new idea, industry, society*) entstehen (aus); **it ~s that** (*BRIT*) es stellt sich heraus, daß.

**emergence** [ɪ'mɜːdʒəns] *n* Entstehung *f*.

**emergency** [ɪ'mɜːdʒənsɪ] *n* Notfall *m* ♦ *cpd* Not-; (*repair*) notdürftig; **in an ~** im Notfall; **state of ~** Notstand *m*.

**emergency cord** (*US*) *n* Notbremse *f*.

**emergency exit** *n* Notausgang *m*.

**emergency landing** *n* Notlandung *f*.

**emergency lane** (*US*) *n* Seitenstreifen *m*.

**emergency road service** (*US*) *n* Pannendienst *m*.

**emergency services** *npl*: **the ~** der Notdienst.

**emergency stop** (*BRIT*) *n* Vollbremsung *f*.

**emergent** [ɪ'mɜːdʒənt] *adj* jung, aufstrebend.

**emeritus** [ɪ'mɛrɪtəs] *adj* emeritiert.

**emery board** ['ɛmərɪ-] *n* Papiernagelfeile *f*.

**emery paper** ['ɛmərɪ-] *n* Schmirgelpapier *nt*.

**emetic** [ɪ'mɛtɪk] *n* Brechmittel *nt*.

**emigrant** ['ɛmɪgrənt] *n* Auswanderer *m*, Auswanderin *f*, Emigrant(in) *m(f)*.

**emigrate** ['ɛmɪgreɪt] *vi* auswandern, emigrieren.

**emigration** [ɛmɪ'greɪʃən] *n* Auswanderung *f*, Emigration *f*.

**émigré** ['ɛmɪgreɪ] *n* Emigrant(in) *m(f)*.

**eminence** ['ɛmɪnəns] *n* Bedeutung *f*.

**eminent** ['ɛmɪnənt] *adj* bedeutend.

**eminently** ['ɛmɪnəntlɪ] *adv* ausgesprochen.

**emirate** ['ɛmɪrɪt] *n* Emirat *nt*.

**emission** [ɪ'mɪʃən] *n* Emission *f*.

**emissions** [ɪ'mɪʃənz] *npl* Emissionen *pl*.

**emit** [ɪ'mɪt] *vt* abgeben; (*smell*) ausströmen; (*light, heat*) ausstrahlen.

**emolument** [ɪ'mɔljumənt] *n* (*often pl*) Vergütung *f*; (*fee*) Honorar *nt*; (*salary*) Bezüge *pl*.

**emotion** [ɪ'məʊʃən] *n* Gefühl *nt*.

**emotional** [ɪ'məʊʃənl] *adj* emotional; (*exhaustion*) seelisch; (*scene*) ergreifend; (*speech*) gefühlsbetont.

**emotionally** [ɪ'məʊʃnəlɪ] *adv* emotional; (*be involved*) gefühlsmäßig; (*speak*) gefühlvoll; **~ disturbed** seelisch gestört.

**emotive** [ɪ'məʊtɪv] *adj* emotional.

**empathy** ['ɛmpəθɪ] *n* Einfühlungsvermögen *nt*; **to feel ~ with sb** sich in jdn einfühlen.

**emperor** ['ɛmpərə*] *n* Kaiser *m*.

**emphases** ['ɛmfəsiːz] *npl of* **emphasis**.

**emphasis** ['ɛmfəsɪs] (*pl* **emphases**) *n* Betonung *f*, (*importance*) (Schwer)gewicht *nt*; **to lay** *or* **place ~ on sth** etw betonen; **the ~ is on reading** das Schwergewicht liegt auf dem Lesen.

**emphasize** ['ɛmfəsaɪz] *vt* betonen; (*feature*) hervorheben; **I must ~ that** ... ich möchte betonen, daß ...

**emphatic** [ɛm'fætɪk] *adj* nachdrücklich; (*denial*) energisch; (*person, manner*) bestimmt, entschieden.

**emphatically** [ɛm'fætɪklɪ] *adv* nachdrücklich; (*certainly*) eindeutig.

**emphysema** [ɛmfɪ'siːmə] *n* Emphysem *nt*.

**empire** ['ɛmpaɪə*] *n* Reich *nt*.

**empirical** [ɛm'pɪrɪkl] *adj* empirisch.

**employ** [ɪm'plɔɪ] *vt* beschäftigen; (*tool, weapon*) verwenden; **he's ~ed in a bank** er ist bei einer Bank angestellt.

**employee** [ɪmplɔɪ'iː] *n* Angestellte(r) *f(m)*.

**employer** [ɪm'plɔɪə*] *n* Arbeitgeber(in) *m(f)*.

**employment** [ɪm'plɔɪmənt] *n* Arbeit *f*; **to find ~** Arbeit *or* eine (An)stellung finden; **without ~** stellungslos; **your place of ~** Ihre Arbeitsstätte *f*.

**employment agency** *n* Stellenvermittlung *f*.

**employment exchange** (*BRIT*) *n* Arbeitsamt *nt*.

**empower** [ɪm'paʊə*] *vt*: **to ~ sb to do sth** jdn ermächtigen, etw zu tun.

**empress** ['ɛmprɪs] n Kaiserin f.

**empties** ['ɛmptɪz] npl Leergut nt.

**emptiness** ['ɛmptɪnɪs] n Leere f.

**empty** ['ɛmptɪ] adj leer; (house, room) leerstehend; (space) frei ♦ vt leeren; (place, house etc) räumen ♦ vi sich leeren; (liquid) abfließen; (river) münden; **on an ~ stomach** auf nüchternen Magen; **to ~ into** (river) münden or sich ergießen in +acc.

**empty-handed** ['ɛmptɪ'hændɪd] adj mit leeren Händen; **he returned ~** er kehrte unverrichteterdinge zurück.

**empty-headed** ['ɛmptɪ'hɛdɪd] adj strohdumm.

**EMS** n abbr (= European Monetary System) EWS nt.

**EMT** (US) n abbr (= emergency medical technician) ≈ Sanitäter(in) m(f).

**EMU** n abbr (= economic and monetary union) EWU f.

**emu** ['iːmjuː] n Emu m.

**emulate** ['ɛmjuleɪt] vt nacheifern +dat.

**emulsion** [ɪ'mʌlʃən] n Emulsion f; (also: ~ paint) Emulsionsfarbe f.

**enable** [ɪ'neɪbl] vt: **to ~ sb to do sth** (permit) es jdm erlauben, etw zu tun; (make possible) es jdm ermöglichen, etw zu tun.

**enact** [ɪ'nækt] vt (law) erlassen; (play) aufführen; (role) darstellen, spielen.

**enamel** [ɪ'næməl] n Email nt, Emaille f; (also: ~ paint) Email(le)lack m; (of tooth) Zahnschmelz m.

**enamoured** [ɪ'næməd] adj: **to be ~ of** (person) verliebt sein in +acc; (pastime, idea, belief) angetan sein von.

**encampment** [ɪn'kæmpmənt] n Lager nt.

**encased** [ɪn'keɪst] adj: **~ in** (shell) umgeben von; **to be ~ in** (limb) in Gips liegen or sein.

**encash** [ɪn'kæʃ] (BRIT) vt einlösen.

**enchant** [ɪn'tʃɑːnt] vt bezaubern.

**enchanted** [ɪn'tʃɑːntɪd] adj verzaubert.

**enchanting** [ɪn'tʃɑːntɪŋ] adj bezaubernd.

**encircle** [ɪn'sɜːkl] vt umgeben; (person) umringen; (building: police etc) umstellen.

**encl.** abbr (on letters etc: = enclosed, enclosure) Anl.

**enclave** ['ɛnkleɪv] n: **an ~ (of)** eine Enklave (+gen).

**enclose** [ɪn'kləuz] vt umgeben; (land, space) begrenzen; (with fence) einzäunen; (letter etc): **to ~ (with)** beilegen (+dat); **please find ~d** als Anlage übersenden wir Ihnen.

**enclosure** [ɪn'kləuʒə'] n eingefriedeter Bereich m; (in letter etc) Anlage f.

**encoder** [ɪn'kəudə'] n Kodierer m.

**encompass** [ɪn'kʌmpəs] vt umfassen.

**encore** [ɔŋ'kɔː'] excl Zugabe! ♦ n Zugabe f.

**encounter** [ɪn'kauntə'] n Begegnung f ♦ vt begegnen +dat; (problem) stoßen auf +acc.

**encourage** [ɪn'kʌrɪdʒ] vt (activity, attitude) unterstützen; (growth, industry) fördern; **to ~ sb (to do sth)** jdn ermutigen(, etw zu tun).

**encouragement** [ɪn'kʌrɪdʒmənt] n (see vb)

Unterstützung f; Förderung f; Ermutigung f.

**encouraging** [ɪn'kʌrɪdʒɪŋ] adj ermutigend.

**encroach** [ɪn'krəutʃ] vi: **to ~ (up)on** (rights) eingreifen in +acc; (property) eindringen in +acc; (time) in Anspruch nehmen.

**encrusted** [ɪn'krʌstɪd] adj: **~ with** (gems) besetzt mit; (snow, dirt) verkrustet mit.

**encumber** [ɪn'kʌmbə'] vt: **to be ~ed with** beladen sein mit; (debts) belastet sein mit.

**encyclop(a)edia** [ɛnsaɪkləu'piːdɪə] n Lexikon nt, Enzyklopädie f.

**end** [ɛnd] n Ende nt; (of film, book) Schluß m, Ende nt; (of table) Schmalseite f; (of pointed object) Spitze f; (aim) Zweck m, Ziel m ♦ vt (also: **bring to an ~, put an ~ to**) beenden ♦ vi enden; **from ~ to ~** von einem Ende zum anderen; **to come to an ~** zu Ende gehen; **to be at an ~** zu Ende sein; **in the ~** schließlich; **on ~** hochkant; **to stand on ~** (hair) zu Berge stehen; **for hours on ~** stundenlang ununterbrochen; **for 5 hours on ~** 5 Stunden ununterbrochen; **at the ~ of the street** am Ende der Straße; **at the ~ of the day** (BRIT, fig) letztlich; **to this ~, with this ~ in view** mit diesem Ziel vor Augen.

▶**end up** vi: **to ~ up in** (place) landen in +dat; **to ~ up in trouble** Ärger bekommen; **to ~ up doing sth** etw schließlich tun.

**endanger** [ɪn'deɪndʒə'] vt gefährden; **an ~ed species** eine vom Aussterben bedrohte Art.

**endear** [ɪn'dɪə'] vt: **to ~ o.s. to sb** sich bei jdm beliebt machen.

**endearing** [ɪn'dɪərɪŋ] adj gewinnend.

**endearment** [ɪn'dɪəmənt] n: **to whisper ~s** zärtliche Worte flüstern; **term of ~** Kosewort nt, Kosename m.

**endeavour**, (US) **endeavor** [ɪn'dɛvə'] n Anstrengung f, Bemühung f; (effort) Bestrebung f ♦ vi: **to ~ to do sth** (attempt) sich anstrengen or bemühen, etw zu tun; (strive) bestrebt sein, etw zu tun.

**endemic** [ɛn'dɛmɪk] adj endemisch, verbreitet.

**ending** ['ɛndɪŋ] n Ende nt, Schluß m; (LING) Endung f.

**endive** ['ɛndaɪv] n Endivie f; (chicory) Chicorée f or m.

**endless** ['ɛndlɪs] adj endlos; (patience, resources, possibilities) unbegrenzt.

**endorse** [ɪn'dɔːs] vt (cheque) indossieren, auf der Rückseite unterzeichnen; (proposal, plan) billigen; (candidate) unterstützen.

**endorsee** [ɪndɔː'siː] n Indossat m.

**endorsement** [ɪn'dɔːsmənt] n Billigung f; (of candidate) Unterstützung f; (BRIT: on driving licence) Strafvermerk m.

**endow** [ɪn'dau] vt (institution) eine Stiftung machen or +acc; **to be ~ed with** besitzen.

**endowment** [ɪn'daumənt] n Stiftung f; (quality) Begabung f.

**endowment assurance** n Versicherung f auf den Erlebensfall, Erlebensversicherung f.

**endowment mortgage** n Hypothek f mit Lebensversicherung.

**end product** n Endprodukt nt; (fig) Produkt nt.

**end result** n Endergebnis nt.

**endurable** [ɪn'djuərəbl] adj erträglich.

**endurance** [ɪn'djuərəns] n Durchhaltevermögen nt; (patience) Geduld f.

**endurance test** n Belastungsprobe f.

**endure** [ɪn'djuə*] vt ertragen ♦ vi Bestand haben.

**enduring** [ɪn'djuərɪŋ] adj dauerhaft.

**end user** n (COMPUT) Endbenutzer m.

**enema** ['ɛnɪmə] n Klistier nt, Einlauf m.

**enemy** ['ɛnəmɪ] adj feindlich; (strategy) des Feindes ♦ n Feind(in) m(f); **to make an ~ of sb** sich dat jdn zum Feind machen.

**energetic** [ɛnə'dʒɛtɪk] adj aktiv.

**energy** ['ɛnədʒɪ] n Energie f; **Department of E~** Energieministerium nt.

**energy crisis** n Energiekrise f.

**energy-saving** ['ɛnədʒɪ'seɪvɪŋ] adj energiesparend; (policy) energiebewußt.

**enervating** ['ɛnəveɪtɪŋ] adj strapazierend.

**enforce** [ɪn'fɔːs] vt (law, rule, decision) Geltung verschaffen +dat.

**enforced** [ɪn'fɔːst] adj erzwungen.

**enfranchise** [ɪn'fræntʃaɪz] vt das Wahlrecht geben or erteilen +dat.

**engage** [ɪn'geɪdʒ] vt in Anspruch nehmen; (employ) einstellen; (lawyer) sich dat nehmen; (MIL) angreifen ♦ vi (TECH) einrasten; **to ~ the clutch** einkuppeln; **to ~ sb in conversation** jdn in ein Gespräch verwickeln; **to ~ in** sich beteiligen an +dat; **to ~ in commerce** kaufmännisch tätig sein; **to ~ in study** studieren.

**engaged** [ɪn'geɪdʒd] adj verlobt; (BRIT: busy, in use) besetzt; **to get ~** sich verloben; **he is ~ in research/a survey** er ist mit Forschungsarbeit/einer Umfrage beschäftigt.

**engaged tone** (BRIT) n Besetztzeichen nt.

**engagement** [ɪn'geɪdʒmənt] n Verabredung f; (booking) Engagement nt; (to marry) Verlobung f; (MIL) Gefecht nt, Kampf m; **I have a previous ~** ich habe schon eine Verabredung.

**engagement ring** n Verlobungsring m.

**engaging** [ɪn'geɪdʒɪŋ] adj einnehmend.

**engender** [ɪn'dʒɛndə*] vt erzeugen.

**engine** ['ɛndʒɪn] n Motor m; (RAIL) Lok(omotive) f.

**engine driver** n (RAIL) Lok(omotiv)-führer(in) m(f).

**engineer** [ɛndʒɪ'nɪə*] n Ingenieur(in) m(f); (BRIT: for repairs) Techniker(in) m(f); (US: RAIL) Lok(omotiv)führer(in) m(f); (on ship) Maschinist(in) m(f); **civil/mechanical ~** Bau-/Maschinenbauingenieur(in) m(f).

**engineering** [ɛndʒɪ'nɪərɪŋ] n Technik f;

(design, construction) Konstruktion f ♦ cpd: **~ works** or **factory** Maschinenfabrik f.

**engine failure** n Maschinenschaden m; (AUT) Motorschaden m.

**engine trouble** n Maschinenschaden m; (AUT) Motorschaden m.

**England** ['ɪŋglənd] n England nt.

**English** ['ɪŋglɪʃ] adj englisch ♦ n Englisch nt; **the English** npl die Engländer pl; **an ~ speaker** jd, der Englisch spricht.

**English Channel** n: **the ~** der Ärmelkanal.

**Englishman** ['ɪŋglɪʃmən] (irreg: like man) n Engländer m.

**English-speaking** ['ɪŋglɪʃ'spiːkɪŋ] adj (country) englischsprachig.

**Englishwoman** ['ɪŋglɪʃwumən] (irreg: like woman) n Engländerin f.

**engrave** [ɪn'greɪv] vt gravieren; (name etc) eingravieren; (fig) einprägen.

**engraving** [ɪn'greɪvɪŋ] n Stich m.

**engrossed** [ɪn'grəust] adj: **~ in** vertieft in +acc.

**engulf** [ɪn'gʌlf] vt verschlingen; (subj: panic, fear) überkommen.

**enhance** [ɪn'hɑːns] vt verbessern; (enjoyment, beauty) erhöhen.

**enigma** [ɪ'nɪgmə] n Rätsel nt.

**enigmatic** [ɛnɪg'mætɪk] adj rätselhaft.

**enjoy** [ɪn'dʒɔɪ] vt genießen; (health, fortune) sich erfreuen +gen; (success) haben; **to ~ o.s.** sich amüsieren; **I ~ dancing** ich tanze gerne.

**enjoyable** [ɪn'dʒɔɪəbl] adj nett, angenehm.

**enjoyment** [ɪn'dʒɔɪmənt] n Vergnügen nt; (activity) Freude f.

**enlarge** [ɪn'lɑːdʒ] vt vergrößern; (scope) erweitern ♦ vi: **to ~ on** weiter ausführen.

**enlarged** [ɪn'lɑːdʒd] adj erweitert; (MED) vergrößert.

**enlargement** [ɪn'lɑːdʒmənt] n Vergrößerung f.

**enlighten** [ɪn'laɪtn] vt aufklären.

**enlightened** [ɪn'laɪtnd] adj aufgeklärt.

**enlightening** [ɪn'laɪtnɪŋ] adj aufschlußreich.

**enlightenment** [ɪn'laɪtnmənt] n (also HIST: Enlightenment) Aufklärung f.

**enlist** [ɪn'lɪst] vt anwerben; (support, help) gewinnen ♦ vi: **to ~ in** eintreten in +acc; **~ed man** (US: MIL) gemeiner Soldat m; (US: in navy) Matrose m.

**enliven** [ɪn'laɪvn] vt beleben.

**enmity** ['ɛnmɪtɪ] n Feindschaft f.

**ennoble** [ɪ'nəubl] vt adeln; (fig: dignify) erheben.

**enormity** [ɪ'nɔːmɪtɪ] n ungeheure Größe f.

**enormous** [ɪ'nɔːməs] adj gewaltig, ungeheuer; (pleasure, success etc) riesig.

**enormously** [ɪ'nɔːməslɪ] adv enorm; (rich) ungeheuer.

**enough** [ɪ'nʌf] adj genug, genügend ♦ pron genug ♦ adv: **big ~** groß genug; **he has not worked ~** er hat nicht genug or genügend gearbeitet; **have you got ~?** haben Sie

genug?; ~ **to eat** genug zu essen; **will 5 be
~?** reichen 5?; **I've had ~!** jetzt reicht's mir
aber!; **it's hot ~ (as it is)** es ist heiß genug;
**he was kind ~ to lend me the money** er war
so gut und hat mir das Geld geliehen; **~!** es
reicht!; **that's ~, thanks** danke, das reicht *or*
ist genug; **I've had ~ of him** ich habe genug
von ihm; **funnily/oddly ~** ... komischerweise ...

**enquire** [ɪn'kwaɪə*] *vt, vi* = **inquire**.

**enrage** [ɪn'reɪdʒ] *vt* wütend machen.

**enrich** [ɪn'rɪtʃ] *vt* bereichern.

**enrol, (US) enroll** [ɪn'rəul] *vt* anmelden; (*at
university*) einschreiben, immatrikulieren
♦ *vi* (*see vt*) sich anmelden; sich
einschreiben, sich immatrikulieren.

**enrolment, (US) enrollment** [ɪn'rəulmənt] *n*
(*v vb*) Anmeldung *f*; Einschreibung *f*,
Immatrikulation *f*.

**en route** [ɒn'ruːt] *adv* unterwegs; ~ **for** auf
dem Weg nach; ~ **from London to Berlin** auf
dem Weg von London nach Berlin.

**ensconced** [ɪn'skɒnst] *adj*: **she is ~ in** ... sie
hat es sich *dat* in ... *dat* gemütlich gemacht.

**ensemble** [ɒn'sɒmbl] *n* Ensemble *nt*.

**enshrine** [ɪn'ʃraɪn] *vt* bewahren; **to be ~d in**
verankert sein in +*dat*.

**ensue** [ɪn'sjuː] *vi* folgen.

**ensuing** [ɪn'sjuːɪŋ] *adj* folgend.

**ensure** [ɪn'ʃuə*] *vt* garantieren; **to ~ that**
sicherstellen, daß.

**ENT** *n abbr* (*MED: = ear, nose and throat*) HNO.

**entail** [ɪn'teɪl] *vt* mit sich bringen.

**entangled** [ɪn'tæŋgld] *adj*: **to become ~ (in)**
sich verfangen (in +*dat*).

**enter** ['entə*] *vt* betreten; (*club*) beitreten +*dat*;
(*army*) gehen zu; (*profession*) ergreifen;
(*race, contest*) sich beteiligen an +*dat*; (*sb for
a competition*) anmelden; (*write down*)
eintragen; (*COMPUT: data*) eingeben ♦ *vi*
(*come in*) hereinkommen; (*go in*)
hineingehen.

►**enter for** *vt fus* anmelden für.

►**enter into** *vt fus* (*discussion, negotiations*)
aufnehmen; (*correspondence*) treten in +*acc*;
(*agreement*) schließen.

►**enter up** *vt* eintragen.

►**enter (up)on** *vt fus* (*career, policy*)
einschlagen.

**enteritis** [entə'raɪtɪs] *n* Dünndarmentzündung
*f*.

**enterprise** ['entəpraɪz] *n* Unternehmen *nt*;
(*initiative*) Initiative *f*; **free ~** freies
Unternehmertum *nt*; **private ~**
Privatunternehmertum *nt*.

**enterprising** ['entəpraɪzɪŋ] *adj* einfallsreich.

**entertain** [entə'teɪn] *vt* unterhalten; (*invite*)
einladen; (*idea, plan*) erwägen.

**entertainer** [entə'teɪnə*] *n* Unterhalter(in)
*m(f)*, Entertainer(in) *m(f)*.

**entertaining** [entə'teɪnɪŋ] *adj* amüsant ♦ *n*: **to
do a lot of ~** sehr oft Gäste haben.

**entertainment** [entə'teɪnmənt] *n*
Unterhaltung *f*; (*show*) Darbietung *f*.

**entertainment allowance** *n*
Aufwandspauschale *f*.

**enthral** [ɪn'θrɔːl] *vt* begeistern; (*story*) fesseln.

**enthralled** [ɪn'θrɔːld] *adj* gefesselt; **he was
~ by** *or* **with the book** das Buch fesselte
ihn.

**enthralling** [ɪn'θrɔːlɪŋ] *adj* fesselnd; (*details*)
spannend.

**enthuse** [ɪn'θuːz] *vi*: **to ~ about** *or* **over**
schwärmen von.

**enthusiasm** [ɪn'θuːzɪæzəm] *n* Begeisterung *f*.

**enthusiast** [ɪn'θuːzɪæst] *n* Enthusiast(in) *m(f)*;
**he's a jazz/sports ~** er begeistert sich für
Jazz/Sport.

**enthusiastic** [ɪnθuːzɪ'æstɪk] *adj* begeistert;
(*response, reception*) enthusiastisch; **to be
~ about** begeistert sein von.

**entice** [ɪn'taɪs] *vt* locken; (*tempt*) verleiten.

**enticing** [ɪn'taɪsɪŋ] *adj* verlockend.

**entire** [ɪn'taɪə*] *adj* ganz.

**entirely** [ɪn'taɪəlɪ] *adv* völlig.

**entirety** [ɪn'taɪərətɪ] *n*: **in its ~** in seiner
Gesamtheit.

**entitle** [ɪn'taɪtl] *vt*: **to ~ sb to sth** jdn zu etw
berechtigen; **to ~ sb to do sth** jdn dazu
berechtigen, etw zu tun.

**entitled** [ɪn'taɪtld] *adj*: **a book/film** *etc* ~ ... ein
Buch/Film *etc* mit dem Titel ...; **to be ~ to
do sth** das Recht haben, etw zu tun.

**entity** ['entɪtɪ] *n* Wesen *nt*.

**entourage** [ɒntu'rɑːʒ] *n* Gefolge *nt*.

**entrails** ['entreɪlz] *npl* Eingeweide *pl*.

**entrance** [*n* 'entrns, *vt* ɪn'trɑːns] *n* Eingang *m*;
(*arrival*) Ankunft *f*; (*on stage*) Auftritt *m* ♦ *vt*
bezaubern; **to gain ~ to** (*building etc*) sich
*dat* Zutritt verschaffen zu; (*university*) die
Zulassung erhalten zu; (*profession etc*)
Zugang erhalten zu.

**entrance examination** *n* Aufnahmeprüfung
*f*.

**entrance fee** *n* Eintrittsgeld *nt*.

**entrance ramp** (*US*) *n* Auffahrt *f*.

**entrancing** [ɪn'trɑːnsɪŋ] *adj* bezaubernd.

**entrant** ['entrnt] *n* Teilnehmer(in) *m(f)*; (*BRIT:
in exam*) Prüfling *m*.

**entreat** [ɛn'triːt] *vt*: **to ~ sb to do sth** jdn
anflehen, etw zu tun.

**entreaty** [ɛn'triːtɪ] *n* (flehentliche) Bitte *f*.

**entrée** ['ɒntreɪ] *n* Hauptgericht *nt*.

**entrenched** [ɛn'trentʃt] *adj* verankert; (*ideas*)
festgesetzt.

**entrepreneur** ['ɒntrəprə'nɜː*] *n*
Unternehmer(in) *m(f)*.

**entrepreneurial** ['ɒntrəprə'nɜːrɪəl] *adj*
unternehmerisch.

**entrust** [ɪn'trʌst] *vt*: **to ~ sth to sb** jdm etw
anvertrauen; **to ~ sb with sth** (*task*) jdn mit
etw betrauen; (*secret, valuables*) jdm etw
anvertrauen.

**entry** ['entrɪ] *n* Eingang *m*; (*in competition*)

Meldung f; (in register, account book, reference book) Eintrag m; (arrival) Eintritt m; (to country) Einreise f; **"no ~"** „Zutritt verboten"; (AUT) „Einfahrt verboten"; **single/double ~ book-keeping** einfache/doppelte Buchführung f.

**entry form** n Anmeldeformular nt.

**entry phone** (BRIT) n Türsprechanlage f.

**entwine** [ɪn'twaɪn] vt verflechten.

**enumerate** [ɪ'njuːməreɪt] vt aufzählen.

**enunciate** [ɪ'nʌnsɪeɪt] vt artikulieren; (principle, plan etc) formulieren.

**envelop** [ɪn'vɛləp] vt einhüllen.

**envelope** ['ɛnvələup] n Umschlag m.

**enviable** ['ɛnvɪəbl] adj beneidenswert.

**envious** ['ɛnvɪəs] adj neidisch; **to be ~ of sth/sb** auf etw/jdn neidisch sein.

**environment** [ɪn'vaɪərnmənt] n Umwelt f; **Department of the E~** (BRIT) Umweltministerium nt.

**environmental** [ɪnvaɪərn'mɛntl] adj (problems, pollution etc) Umwelt-; **~ studies** Umweltkunde f.

**environmentalist** [ɪnvaɪərn'mɛntlɪst] n Umweltschützer(in) m(f).

**Environmental Protection Agency** (US) n staatliche Umweltbehörde der USA.

**environment-friendly** adj umweltfreundlich.

**envisage** [ɪn'vɪzɪdʒ] vt sich dat vorstellen; **I ~ that …** ich stelle mir vor, daß …

**envision** [ɪn'vɪʒən] (US) vt = **envisage**.

**envoy** ['ɛnvɔɪ] n Gesandte(r) f(m).

**envy** ['ɛnvɪ] n Neid m ♦ vt beneiden; **to ~ sb sth** jdn um etw beneiden.

**enzyme** ['ɛnzaɪm] n Enzym nt.

**eon** ['iːən] n Äon m, Ewigkeit f.

**EPA** (US) n abbr = **Environmental Protection Agency**.

**ephemeral** [ɪ'fɛmərl] adj kurzlebig.

**epic** ['ɛpɪk] n Epos nt ♦ adj (journey) lang und abenteuerlich.

**epicentre,** (US) **epicenter** ['ɛpɪsɛntə*] n Epizentrum nt.

**epidemic** [ɛpɪ'dɛmɪk] n Epidemie f.

**epigram** ['ɛpɪgræm] n Epigramm nt.

**epilepsy** ['ɛpɪlɛpsɪ] n Epilepsie f.

**epileptic** [ɛpɪ'lɛptɪk] adj epileptisch ♦ n Epileptiker(in) m(f).

**epilogue** ['ɛpɪlɔg] n Epilog m, Nachwort nt.

**Epiphany** [ɪ'pɪfənɪ] n Dreikönigsfest nt.

**episcopal** [ɪ'pɪskəpl] adj bischöflich; **the E~ Church** die Episkopalkirche.

**episode** ['ɛpɪsəud] n Episode f; (TV, RADIO) Folge f.

**epistle** [ɪ'pɪsl] n Epistel f; (REL) Brief m.

**epitaph** ['ɛpɪtɑːf] n Epitaph nt; (on gravestone etc) Grab(in)schrift f.

**epithet** ['ɛpɪθɛt] n Beiname m.

**epitome** [ɪ'pɪtəmɪ] n Inbegriff m.

**epitomize** [ɪ'pɪtəmaɪz] vt verkörpern.

**epoch** ['iːpɔk] n Epoche f.

**epoch-making** ['iːpɔkmeɪkɪŋ] adj epochal; (discovery) epochemachend.

**eponymous** [ɪ'pɔnɪməs] adj namengebend.

**equable** ['ɛkwəbl] adj ausgeglichen; (reply) sachlich.

**equal** ['iːkwl] adj gleich ♦ n Gleichgestellte(r) f(m) ♦ vt gleichkommen +dat; (number) gleich sein +dat; **they are roughly ~ in size** sie sind ungefähr gleich groß; **the number of exports should be ~ to imports** Export- und Importzahlen sollten gleich sein; **~ opportunities** Chancengleichheit f; **to be ~ to** (task) gewachsen sein +dat; **two times two ~s four** zwei mal zwei ist (gleich) vier.

**equality** [iː'kwɔlɪtɪ] n Gleichheit f; **~ of opportunity** Chancengleichheit f.

**equalize** ['iːkwəlaɪz] vt angleichen ♦ vi (SPORT) ausgleichen.

**equally** ['iːkwəlɪ] adv gleichmäßig; (good, bad etc) gleich; **they are ~ clever** sie sind beide gleich klug.

**Equal Opportunities Commission,** (US) **Equal Employment Opportunity Commission** n Ausschuß m für Chancengleichheit am Arbeitsplatz.

**equal(s) sign** n Gleichheitszeichen nt.

**equanimity** [ɛkwə'nɪmɪtɪ] n Gleichmut m, Gelassenheit f.

**equate** [ɪ'kweɪt] vt: **to ~ sth with** etw gleichsetzen mit ♦ vt (compare) auf die gleiche Stufe stellen; **to ~ A to B** A und B auf die gleiche Stufe stellen.

**equation** [ɪ'kweɪʃən] n Gleichung f.

**equator** [ɪ'kweɪtə*] n Äquator m.

**equatorial** [ɛkwə'tɔːrɪəl] adj äquatorial.

**Equatorial Guinea** n Äquatorial-Guinea nt.

**equestrian** [ɪ'kwɛstrɪən] adj (sport, dress etc) Reit-; (statue) Reiter- ♦ n Reiter(in) m(f).

**equilibrium** [iːkwɪ'lɪbrɪəm] n Gleichgewicht nt.

**equinox** ['iːkwɪnɔks] n Tagundnachtgleiche f; **the spring/autumn ~** die Frühjahrs-/die Herbst-Tagundnachtgleiche f.

**equip** [ɪ'kwɪp] vt: **to ~ (with)** (person, army) ausrüsten (mit); (room, car etc) ausstatten (mit); **to ~ sb for** jdn vorbereiten auf +acc; **to be well ~ped** gut ausgerüstet sein.

**equipment** [ɪ'kwɪpmənt] n Ausrüstung f.

**equitable** ['ɛkwɪtəbl] adj gerecht.

**equities** ['ɛkwɪtɪz] (BRIT) npl Stammaktien pl.

**equity** ['ɛkwɪtɪ] n Gerechtigkeit f.

**equity capital** n Eigenkapital nt.

**equivalent** [ɪ'kwɪvələnt] adj gleich, gleichwertig ♦ n Gegenstück nt; **to be ~ to** or **the ~ of** entsprechen +dat.

**equivocal** [ɪ'kwɪvəkl] adj vieldeutig; (open to suspicion) zweifelhaft.

**equivocate** [ɪ'kwɪvəkeɪt] vi ausweichen, ausweichend antworten.

**equivocation** [ɪkwɪvə'keɪʃən] n Ausflucht f, ausweichende Antwort f.

**ER** (BRIT) abbr (= Elizabeth Regina) offizieller

*Namenszug der Königin.*
**ERA** (*US*) *n abbr* (*POL:* = *Equal Rights Amendment*) *Artikel der amerikanischen Verfassung zur Gleichberechtigung;* (*BASEBALL:* = *earned run average*) *durch Eigenleistung erzielte Läufe.*
**era** ['ɪərə] *n* Ära *f*, Epoche *f*.
**eradicate** [ɪ'rædɪkeɪt] *vt* ausrotten.
**erase** [ɪ'reɪz] *vt* (*tape, COMPUT*) löschen; (*writing*) ausradieren; (*thought, feeling*) auslöschen.
**eraser** [ɪ'reɪzə*] *n* Radiergummi *m*.
**erect** [ɪ'rekt] *adj* aufrecht; (*tail*) hocherhoben; (*ears*) gespitzt ♦ *vt* bauen; (*assemble*) aufstellen.
**erection** [ɪ'rekʃən] *n* Bauen *nt*; (*of statue*) Errichten *nt*; (*of tent, machinery etc*) Aufstellen *nt*; (*PHYSIOL*) Erektion *f*.
**ergonomics** [ɔ:gə'nɔmɪks] *n sing* Ergonomie *f*, Ergonomik *f*.
**ERISA** (*US*) *n abbr* (= *Employee Retirement Income Security Act*) *Gesetz zur Regelung der Rentenversicherung.*
**Eritrea** *n* Eritrea *nt*.
**ERM** *n abbr* (= *Exchange Rate Mechanism*) Wechselkursmechanismus *m*.
**ermine** ['ɔ:mɪn] *n* (*fur*) Hermelin *m*.
**ERNIE, Ernie** ['ɔ:nɪ] (*BRIT*) *n abbr* (= *Electronic Random Number Indicator Equipment*) *Gerät zur Ermittlung von Gewinnummern für Prämiensparer.*
**erode** [ɪ'rəud] *vt* erodieren, auswaschen; (*metal*) zerfressen; (*confidence, power*) untergraben.
**erogenous** [ɪ'rɔdʒənəs] *adj* erogen.
**erosion** [ɪ'rəuʒən] *n* (*see vb*) Erosion *f*, Auswaschen *nt*; Zerfressen *nt*; Untergraben *nt*.
**erotic** [ɪ'rɔtɪk] *adj* erotisch.
**eroticism** [ɪ'rɔtɪsɪzəm] *n* Erotik *f*.
**err** [ɔ:*] *vi* sich irren; **to ~ on the side of caution/simplicity** (im Zweifelsfall) zur Vorsicht/Vereinfachung neigen.
**errand** ['erənd] *n* Besorgung *f*; (*to give a message etc*) Botengang *m*; **to run ~s** Besorgungen/Botengänge machen; **~ of mercy** Rettungsaktion *f*.
**erratic** [ɪ'rætɪk] *adj* unberechenbar; (*attempts*) unkoordiniert; (*noise*) unregelmäßig.
**erroneous** [ɪ'rəunɪəs] *adj* irrig.
**error** ['erə*] *n* Fehler *m*; **typing/spelling ~** Tipp-/Rechtschreibfehler *m*; **in ~** irrtümlicherweise; **~s and omissions excepted** Irrtum vorbehalten.
**error message** *n* Fehlermeldung *f*.
**erstwhile** ['ɔ:stwaɪl] *adj* einstig, vormalig.
**erudite** ['erjudaɪt] *adj* gelehrt.
**erupt** [ɪ'rʌpt] *vi* ausbrechen.
**eruption** [ɪ'rʌpʃən] *n* Ausbruch *m*.
**ESA** *n abbr* (= *European Space Agency*) Europäische Weltraumbehörde *f*.
**escalate** ['eskəleɪt] *vi* eskalieren, sich

ausweiten.
**escalation** [eskə'leɪʃən] *n* Eskalation *f*.
**escalator** ['eskəleɪtə*] *n* Rolltreppe *f*.
**escalator clause** *n* Gleitklausel *f*.
**escapade** [eskə'peɪd] *n* Eskapade *f*.
**escape** [ɪs'keɪp] *n* Flucht *f*; (*TECH: of liquid*) Ausfließen *nt*; (*of gas*) Ausströmen *nt*; (*of air, heat*) Entweichen *nt* ♦ *vi* entkommen; (*from prison*) ausbrechen; (*liquid*) ausfließen; (*gas*) ausströmen; (*air, heat*) entweichen ♦ *vt* (*pursuers etc*) entkommen +*dat*; (*punishment etc*) entgehen +*dat*; **his name ~s me** sein Name ist mir entfallen; **to ~ from** flüchten aus; (*prison*) ausbrechen aus; (*person*) entkommen +*dat*; **to ~ to Peru** nach Peru fliehen; **to ~ to safety** sich in Sicherheit bringen; **to ~ notice** unbemerkt bleiben.
**escape artist** *n* Entfesselungskünstler(in) *m(f)*.
**escape clause** *n* (*in contract*) Befreiungsklausel *f*.
**escapee** [ɪskeɪ'pi:] *n* entwichener Häftling *m*.
**escape hatch** *n* Notluke *f*.
**escape key** *n* (*COMPUT*) Escape-Taste *f*.
**escape route** *n* Fluchtweg *m*.
**escapism** [ɪs'keɪpɪzəm] *n* Wirklichkeitsflucht *f*, Eskapismus *m*.
**escapist** [ɪs'keɪpɪst] *adj* eskapistisch.
**escapologist** [eskə'pɔlədʒɪst] (*BRIT*) *n* = **escape artist**.
**escarpment** [ɪs'kɑ:pmənt] *n* Steilhang *m*.
**eschew** [ɪs'tʃu:] *vt* meiden.
**escort** [*n* 'eskɔ:t, *vt* ɪs'kɔ:t] *n* Eskorte *f*; (*companion*) Begleiter(in) *m(f)* ♦ *vt* begleiten; **his ~** seine Begleiterin; **her ~** ihr Begleiter.
**escort agency** *n* Agentur *f* für Begleiter(innen).
**Eskimo** ['eskɪməu] *n* Eskimo(frau) *m(f)*.
**ESL** *n abbr* (*SCOL:* = *English as a Second Language*) Englisch *nt* als Zweitsprache.
**esophagus** [i:'sɔfəgəs] (*US*) *n* = **oesophagus**.
**esoteric** [esə'terɪk] *adj* esoterisch.
**ESP** *n abbr* = **extrasensory perception**; (*SCOL:* = *English for Special Purposes*) *Englischunterricht für spezielle Fachbereiche.*
**esp.** *abbr* = **especially**.
**especially** [ɪs'peʃlɪ] *adv* besonders.
**espionage** ['espɪənɑːʒ] *n* Spionage *f*.
**esplanade** [esplə'neɪd] *n* Promenade *f*.
**espouse** [ɪs'pauz] *vt* eintreten für.
**Esquire** [ɪs'kwaɪə*] *n* (*abbr Esq.*): **J. Brown, ~** Herrn J. Brown.
**essay** ['eseɪ] *n* Aufsatz *m*; (*LITER*) Essay *m or nt*.
**essence** ['esns] *n* Wesen *nt*; (*CULIN*) Essenz *f*; **in ~** im wesentlichen; **speed is of the ~** Geschwindigkeit ist von entscheidender Bedeutung.
**essential** [ɪ'senʃl] *adj* notwendig; (*basic*) wesentlich ♦ *n* (*see adj*) Notwendigste(s) *nt*; Wesentliche(s) *nt*; **it is ~ that** es ist unbedingt *or* absolut erforderlich, daß.

**essentially** [ɪ'sɛnʃəlɪ] adv im Grunde genommen.

**EST** (US) abbr (= Eastern Standard Time) ostamerikanische Standardzeit.

**est.** abbr = **established; estimate(d).**

**establish** [ɪs'tæblɪʃ] vt gründen; (facts) feststellen; (proof) erstellen; (relations, contact) aufnehmen; (reputation) sich dat verschaffen.

**established** [ɪs'tæblɪʃt] adj üblich; (business) eingeführt.

**establishment** [ɪs'tæblɪʃmənt] n (see vb) Gründung f; Feststellung f; Erstellung f; Aufnahme f; (of reputation) Begründung f; (shop etc) Unternehmen nt; **the E~** das Establishment.

**estate** [ɪs'teɪt] n Gut nt; (BRIT: also: housing ~) Siedlung f; (LAW) Nachlaß m.

**estate agency** (BRIT) n Maklerbüro nt.

**estate agent** (BRIT) n Immobilienmakler(in) m(f).

**estate car** (BRIT) n Kombiwagen m.

**esteem** [ɪs'tiːm] n: **to hold sb in high ~** eine hohe Meinung von jdm haben.

**esthetic** [ɪs'θɛtɪk] (US) adj = **aesthetic.**

**estimate** ['ɛstɪmət] n Schätzung f; (assessment) Einschätzung f; (COMM) (Kosten)voranschlag m ♦ vt schätzen ♦ vi (BRIT: COMM): **to ~ for** einen Kostenvoranschlag machen für; **to give sb an ~ of sth** jdm eine Vorstellung von etw geben; **to ~ for** einen Kostenvoranschlag machen für; **at a rough ~** grob geschätzt, über den Daumen gepeilt (inf); **I ~ that** ich schätze, daß.

**estimation** [ɛstɪ'meɪʃən] n Schätzung f; (opinion) Einschätzung f; **in my ~** meiner Einschätzung nach.

**estimator** ['ɛstɪmeɪtə*] n Schätzer(in) m(f).

**Estonia** [ɛs'təunɪə] n Estland nt.

**Estonian** [ɛs'təunɪən] adj estnisch ♦ n Este m, Estin f; (LING) Estnisch nt.

**estranged** [ɪs'treɪndʒd] adj entfremdet; (from spouse) getrennt; (couple) getrennt lebend.

**estrangement** [ɪs'treɪndʒmənt] n Entfremdung f; (from spouse) Trennung f.

**estrogen** ['iːstrəudʒən] (US) n = **oestrogen.**

**estuary** ['ɛstjuərɪ] n Mündung f.

**ET** (BRIT) n abbr (= Employment Training) Ausbildungsmaßnahmen für Arbeitslose.

**ETA** n abbr (= estimated time of arrival) voraussichtliche Ankunftszeit f.

**et al.** abbr (= et alii) u.a.

**etc.** abbr (= et cetera) etc.

**etch** [ɛtʃ] vt (design, surface: with needle) radieren; (: with acid) ätzen; (: with chisel) meißeln; **it will be ~ed on my memory** es wird sich tief in mein Gedächtnis eingraben.

**etching** ['ɛtʃɪŋ] n Radierung f.

**ETD** n abbr (= estimated time of departure) voraussichtliche Abflugzeit f.

**eternal** [ɪ'təːnl] adj ewig.

**eternity** [ɪ'təːnɪtɪ] n Ewigkeit f.

**ether** ['iːθə*] n Äther m.

**ethereal** [ɪ'θɪərɪəl] adj ätherisch.

**ethical** ['ɛθɪkl] adj ethisch.

**ethics** ['ɛθɪks] n Ethik f ♦ npl (morality) Moral f.

**Ethiopia** [iːθɪ'əupɪə] n Äthiopien nt.

**Ethiopian** [iːθɪ'əupɪən] adj äthiopisch ♦ n Äthiopier(in) m(f).

**ethnic** ['ɛθnɪk] adj ethnisch; (music) folkloristisch; (culture etc) urwüchsig.

**ethnic cleansing** [-'klɛnzɪŋ] n ethnische Säuberung f.

**ethnology** [ɛθ'nɔlədʒɪ] n Ethnologie f, Völkerkunde f.

**ethos** ['iːθɔs] n Ethos nt.

**etiquette** ['ɛtɪkɛt] n Etikette f.

**ETV** (US) n abbr (= educational television) Fernsehsender, der Bildungs- und Kulturprogramme ausstrahlt.

**etymology** [ɛtɪ'mɔlədʒɪ] n Etymologie f; (of word) Herkunft f.

**EU** n abbr (= European Union) EU f.

**eucalyptus** [juːkə'lɪptəs] n Eukalyptus m.

**Eucharist** ['juːkərɪst] n: **the ~** die Eucharistie, das (heilige) Abendmahl.

**eulogy** ['juːlədʒɪ] n Lobrede f.

**euphemism** ['juːfəmɪzəm] n Euphemismus m.

**euphemistic** [juːfə'mɪstɪk] adj euphemistisch, verhüllend.

**euphoria** [juː'fɔːrɪə] n Euphorie f.

**Eurasia** [juə'reɪʃə] n Eurasien nt.

**Eurasian** [juə'reɪʃən] adj eurasisch ♦ n Eurasier(in) m(f).

**Euratom** [juə'rætəm] n abbr (= European Atomic Energy Community) Euratom f.

**Euro-** ['juərəu] pref Euro-.

**Eurocheque** ['juərəutʃɛk] n Euroscheck m.

**Eurocrat** ['juərəukræt] n Eurokrat(in) m(f).

**Eurodollar** ['juərəudɔlə*] n Eurodollar m.

**Europe** ['juərəp] n Europa nt.

**European** [juərə'piːən] adj europäisch ♦ n Europäer(in) m(f).

**European Community** n: **the ~** die Europäische Gemeinschaft.

**European Court of Justice** n: **the ~** der Europäische Gerichtshof.

**European Economic Community** n: **the ~** die Europäische Wirtschaftsgemeinschaft.

**Euro-sceptic** ['juərəuskɛptɪk] n Euroskeptiker(in) m(f).

**euthanasia** [juːθə'neɪzɪə] n Euthanasie f.

**evacuate** [ɪ'vækjueɪt] vt evakuieren; (place) räumen.

**evacuation** [ɪvækju'eɪʃən] n (see verb) Evakuierung f; Räumung f.

**evacuee** [ɪvækju'iː] n Evakuierte(r) f(m).

**evade** [ɪ'veɪd] vt (person, question) ausweichen +dat; (tax) hinterziehen; (duty, responsibility) sich entziehen +dat.

**evaluate** [ɪ'væljueɪt] vt bewerten; (situation) einschätzen.

**evangelical** [iːvænˈdʒɛlɪkl] *adj* evangelisch.
**evangelist** [ɪˈvændʒəlɪst] *n* Evangelist(in) *m(f)*.
**evangelize** [ɪˈvændʒəlaɪz] *vi* evangelisieren.
**evaporate** [ɪˈvæpəreɪt] *vi* verdampfen;
(*feeling, attitude*) dahinschwinden.
**evaporated milk** [ɪˈvæpəreɪtɪd-] *n*
Kondensmilch *f*, Büchsenmilch *f*.
**evaporation** [ɪvæpəˈreɪʃən] *n* Verdampfung *f*.
**evasion** [ɪˈveɪʒən] *n* Ausweichen *nt*; (*of tax*)
Hinterziehung *f*.
**evasive** [ɪˈveɪsɪv] *adj* ausweichend; **to take
~ action** ein Ausweichmanöver machen.
**eve** [iːv] *n*: **on the ~ of** am Tag vor +*dat*;
**Christmas E~** Heiligabend *m*; **New Year's
E~** Silvester *m or nt*.
**even** [ˈiːvn] *adj* (*level*) eben; (*smooth*) glatt;
(*equal*) gleich; (*number*) gerade ♦ *adv* sogar,
selbst; (*introducing a comparison*) sogar noch;
**~ if, ~ though** selbst wenn; **~ more** sogar
noch mehr; **he loves her ~ more** er liebt sie
um so mehr; **it's going ~ faster now** es fährt
jetzt sogar noch schneller; **~ so** (aber)
trotzdem; **not ~** nicht einmal; **~ he was
there** sogar er war da; **to break ~** die
Kosten decken; **to get ~ with sb** es jdm
heimzahlen.
▶**even out** *vi* sich ausgleichen ♦ *vt*
ausgleichen.
**even-handed** [ˈiːvnhændɪd] *adj* gerecht.
**evening** [ˈiːvnɪŋ] *n* Abend *m*; **in the ~** abends,
am Abend; **this ~** heute abend; **tomorrow/
yesterday ~** morgen/gestern abend.
**evening class** *n* Abendkurs *m*.
**evening dress** *n* (*no pl*) Abendkleidung *f*;
(*woman's*) Abendkleid *nt*.
**evenly** [ˈiːvnlɪ] *adv* gleichmäßig.
**evensong** [ˈiːvnsɒŋ] *n* Abendandacht *f*.
**event** [ɪˈvɛnt] *n* Ereignis *nt*; (*SPORT*)
Wettkampf *m*; **in the normal course of ~s**
normalerweise; **in the ~ of** im Falle +*gen*; **in
the ~** schließlich; **at all ~s** (*BRIT*), **in any ~**
auf jeden Fall.
**eventful** [ɪˈvɛntful] *adj* ereignisreich.
**eventing** [ɪˈvɛntɪŋ] *n* (*HORSERIDING*) Military
*f*.
**eventual** [ɪˈvɛntʃuəl] *adj* schließlich; (*goal*)
letztlich.
**eventuality** [ɪvɛntʃuˈælɪtɪ] *n* Eventualität *f*.
**eventually** [ɪˈvɛntʃuəlɪ] *adv* endlich; (*in time*)
schließlich.
**ever** [ˈɛvə*] *adv* immer; (*at any time*) je(mals);
**why ~ not?** warum denn bloß nicht?; **the
best ~** der/die/das Allerbeste; **have you
~ seen it?** haben Sie es schon einmal
gesehen?; **for ~** für immer; **hardly ~** kaum
je(mals); **better than ~** besser als je zuvor;
**~ since** *adv* seitdem ♦ *conj* seit, seitdem; **~ so
pretty** unheimlich hübsch (*inf*); **thank you
~ so much** ganz herzlichen Dank; **yours ~**
(*BRIT: in letters*) alles Liebe.
**Everest** [ˈɛvərɪst] *n* (*also*: **Mount ~**) Mount
Everest *m*.

**evergreen** [ˈɛvəgriːn] *n* (*tree/bush*)
immergrüner Baum/Strauch *m*.
**everlasting** [ɛvəˈlɑːstɪŋ] *adj* ewig.

═══════════════════════════════ *KEYWORD*

**every** [ˈɛvrɪ] *adj* **1** jede(r, s); **~ one of them**
(*persons*) jede(r) (einzelne) von ihnen;
(*objects*) jedes einzelne Stück; **~ day** jeden
Tag; **~ week** jede Woche; **~ other car** jedes
zweite Auto; **~ other/third day** alle zwei/
drei Tage; **~ shop in the town was closed**
alle Geschäfte der Stadt waren
geschlossen; **~ now and then** ab und zu, hin
und wieder

**2** (*all possible*): **I have ~ confidence in him**
ich habe volles Vertrauen in ihn; **we wish
you ~ success** wir wünschen Ihnen alles
Gute.

─────────────────────────────────

**everybody** [ˈɛvrɪbɒdɪ] *pron* jeder, alle *pl*;
**~ knows about it** alle wissen es; **~ else** alle
anderen *pl*.
**everyday** [ˈɛvrɪdeɪ] *adj* täglich; (*usual,
common*) alltäglich; (*life, language*) Alltags-.
**everyone** [ˈɛvrɪwʌn] *pron* = **everybody**.
**everything** [ˈɛvrɪθɪŋ] *pron* alles; **he did
~ possible** er hat sein Möglichstes getan.
**everywhere** [ˈɛvrɪwɛə*] *adv* überall;
(*wherever*) wo auch *or* immer; **~ you go you
meet ...** wo man auch *or* wo immer man
hingeht, trifft man ...
**evict** [ɪˈvɪkt] *vt* zur Räumung zwingen.
**eviction** [ɪˈvɪkʃən] *n* Ausweisung *f*.
**eviction notice** *n* Räumungskündigung *f*.
**eviction order** *n* Räumungsbefehl *m*.
**evidence** [ˈɛvɪdns] *n* Beweis *m*; (*of witness*)
Aussage *f*; (*sign, indication*) Zeichen *nt*, Spur
*f*; **to give ~** (als Zeuge) aussagen; **to show
~ of** zeigen; **in ~** sichtbar.
**evident** [ˈɛvɪdnt] *adj* offensichtlich.
**evidently** [ˈɛvɪdntlɪ] *adv* offensichtlich.
**evil** [ˈiːvl] *adj* böse; (*influence*) schlecht ♦ *n*
Böse(s) *nt*; (*unpleasant situation or activity*)
Übel *nt*.
**evocative** [ɪˈvɒkətɪv] *adj* evokativ.
**evoke** [ɪˈvəuk] *vt* hervorrufen; (*memory*)
wecken.
**evolution** [iːvəˈluːʃən] *n* Evolution *f*;
(*development*) Entwicklung *f*.
**evolve** [ɪˈvɒlv] *vt* entwickeln ♦ *vi* sich
entwickeln.
**ewe** [juː] *n* Mutterschaf *nt*.
**ewer** [ˈjuːə*] *n* (Wasser)krug *m*.
**ex-** [ɛks] *pref* Ex-, frühere(r, s); **the price
~ works** der Preis ab Werk.
**exacerbate** [ɛksˈæsəbeɪt] *vt* verschärfen;
(*pain*) verschlimmern.
**exact** [ɪɡˈzækt] *adj* genau; (*word*) richtig ♦ *vt*:
**to ~ sth (from)** etw verlangen (von);
(*payment*) etw eintreiben (von).
**exacting** [ɪɡˈzæktɪŋ] *adj* anspruchsvoll.
**exactly** [ɪɡˈzæktlɪ] *adv* genau; **~!** (ganz)

genau!; **not** ~ (*hardly*) nicht gerade.
**exaggerate** [ɪɡ'zædʒəreɪt] *vt, vi* übertreiben.
**exaggerated** [ɪɡ'zædʒəreɪtɪd] *adj* übertrieben.
**exaggeration** [ɪɡzædʒə'reɪʃən] *n* Übertreibung *f*.
**exalt** [ɪɡ'zɔːlt] *vt* preisen.
**exalted** [ɪɡ'zɔːltɪd] *adj* hoch; (*elated*) exaltiert.
**exam** [ɪɡ'zæm] *n abbr* = **examination**.
**examination** [ɪɡzæmɪ'neɪʃən] *n* (*see vb*) Untersuchung *f*; Prüfung *f*; Verhör *nt*; **to take** *or* (*BRIT*) **sit an** ~ eine Prüfung machen; **the matter is under** ~ die Angelegenheit wird geprüft *or* untersucht.
**examine** [ɪɡ'zæmɪn] *vt* untersuchen; (*accounts, candidate*) prüfen; (*witness*) verhören.
**examiner** [ɪɡ'zæmɪnə*] *n* Prüfer(in) *m(f)*.
**example** [ɪɡ'zɑːmpl] *n* Beispiel *nt*; **for** ~ zum Beispiel; **to set a good/bad** ~ ein gutes/ schlechtes Beispiel geben.
**exasperate** [ɪɡ'zɑːspəreɪt] *vt* (*annoy*) verärgern; (*frustrate*) zur Verzweiflung bringen; ~**d by** *or* **with** verärgert/ verzweifelt über +*acc*.
**exasperating** [ɪɡ'zɑːspəreɪtɪŋ] *adj* ärgerlich; (*job*) leidig.
**exasperation** [ɪɡzɑːspə'reɪʃən] *n* Verzweiflung *f*; **in** ~ verzweifelt.
**excavate** ['ɛkskəveɪt] *vt* ausgraben; (*hole*) graben ♦ *vi* Ausgrabungen machen.
**excavation** [ɛkskə'veɪʃən] *n* Ausgrabung *f*.
**excavator** ['ɛkskəveɪtə*] *n* Bagger *m*.
**exceed** [ɪk'siːd] *vt* übersteigen; (*hopes*) übertreffen; (*limit, budget, powers*) überschreiten.
**exceedingly** [ɪk'siːdɪŋlɪ] *adv* äußerst.
**excel** [ɪk'sɛl] *vt* übertreffen ♦ *vi*: **to** ~ (**in** *or* **at**) sich auszeichnen (in +*dat*); **to** ~ **o.s.** (*BRIT*) sich selbst übertreffen.
**excellence** ['ɛksələns] *n* hervorragende Leistung *f*.
**Excellency** ['ɛksələnsɪ] *n*: **His** ~ Seine Exzellenz.
**excellent** ['ɛksələnt] *adj* ausgezeichnet, hervorragend.
**except** [ɪk'sɛpt] *prep* (*also*: ~ **for**) außer +*dat* ♦ *vt*: **to** ~ **sb** (**from**) jdn ausnehmen (bei); ~ **if**, ~ **when** außer wenn; ~ **that** nur daß.
**excepting** [ɪk'sɛptɪŋ] *prep* außer +*dat*, mit Ausnahme +*gen*.
**exception** [ɪk'sɛpʃən] *n* Ausnahme *f*; **to take** ~ **to** Anstoß nehmen an +*dat*; **with the** ~ **of** mit Ausnahme von.
**exceptional** [ɪk'sɛpʃənl] *adj* außergewöhnlich.
**excerpt** ['ɛksəːpt] *n* Auszug *m*.
**excess** [ɪk'sɛs] *n* Übermaß *nt*; (*INSURANCE*) Selbstbeteiligung *f*; **excesses** *npl* Exzesse *pl*; **an** ~ **of £15, a £15** ~ eine Selbstbeteiligung von £15; **in** ~ **of** über +*dat*.
**excess baggage** *n* Übergepäck *nt*.
**excess fare** (*BRIT*) *n* Nachlösegebühr *f*.
**excessive** [ɪk'sɛsɪv] *adj* übermäßig.
**excess supply** *n* Überangebot *nt*.

**exchange** [ɪks'tʃeɪndʒ] *n* Austausch *m*; (*conversation*) Wortwechsel *m*; (*also*: **telephone** ~) Fernsprechamt *nt* ♦ *vt*: **to** ~ (**for**) tauschen (gegen); (*in shop*) umtauschen (gegen); **in** ~ **for** für; **foreign** ~ Devisenhandel *m*; (*money*) Devisen *pl*.
**exchange control** *n* Devisenkontrolle *f*.
**exchange market** *n* Devisenmarkt *m*.
**exchange rate** *n* Wechselkurs *m*.
**Exchequer** [ɪks'tʃɛkə*] (*BRIT*) *n*: **the** ~ das Finanzministerium.
**excisable** [ɪk'saɪzəbl] *adj* steuerpflichtig.
**excise** ['ɛksaɪz] *n* Verbrauchssteuer *f* ♦ *vt* entfernen.
**excise duties** *npl* Verbrauchssteuern *pl*.
**excitable** [ɪk'saɪtəbl] *adj* (leicht) erregbar.
**excite** [ɪk'saɪt] *vt* aufregen; (*arouse*) erregen; **to get** ~**d** sich aufregen.
**excitement** [ɪk'saɪtmənt] *n* Aufregung *f*; (*exhilaration*) Hochgefühl *nt*.
**exciting** [ɪk'saɪtɪŋ] *adj* aufregend.
**excl.** *abbr* = **excluding; exclusive (of)**.
**exclaim** [ɪks'kleɪm] *vi* aufschreien.
**exclamation** [ɛksklə'meɪʃən] *n* Ausruf *m*; ~ **of joy** Freudenschrei *m*.
**exclamation mark** *n* Ausrufezeichen *nt*.
**exclude** [ɪks'kluːd] *vt* ausschließen.
**excluding** [ɪks'kluːdɪŋ] *prep*: ~ **VAT** ohne Mehrwertsteuer.
**exclusion** [ɪks'kluːʒən] *n* Ausschluß *m*; **to concentrate on sth to the** ~ **of everything else** sich ausschließlich auf etw *dat* konzentrieren.
**exclusion clause** *n* Freizeichnungsklausel *f*.
**exclusion zone** *n* Sperrzone *f*.
**exclusive** [ɪks'kluːsɪv] *adj* exklusiv; (*story, interview*) Exklusiv–; (*use*) ausschließlich ♦ *n* Exklusivbericht *m* ♦ *adv*: **from 1st to 15th March** ~ vom 1. bis zum 15. März ausschließlich; ~ **of postage** ohne *or* exklusive Porto; ~ **of tax** ausschließlich *or* exklusive Steuern; **to be mutually** ~ sich *or* einander ausschließen.
**exclusively** [ɪks'kluːsɪvlɪ] *adv* ausschließlich.
**exclusive rights** *npl* Exklusivrechte *pl*.
**excommunicate** [ɛkskə'mjuːnɪkeɪt] *vt* exkommunizieren.
**excrement** ['ɛkskrəmənt] *n* Kot *m*, Exkremente *pl*.
**excruciating** [ɪks'kruːʃɪeɪtɪŋ] *adj* gräßlich, fürchterlich; (*noise, embarrassment*) unerträglich.
**excursion** [ɪks'kəːʃən] *n* Ausflug *m*.
**excursion ticket** *n* verbilligte Fahrkarte *f*.
**excusable** [ɪks'kjuːzəbl] *adj* verzeihlich, entschuldbar.
**excuse** [ɪks'kjuːs] *n* Entschuldigung *f* ♦ *vt* entschuldigen; (*forgive*) verzeihen; **to** ~ **sb from sth** jdm etw erlassen; **to** ~ **sb from doing sth** jdn davon befreien, etw zu tum; ~ **me!** entschuldigen Sie!, Entschuldigung!; **if you will** ~ **me** ... entschuldigen Sie mich

bitte ...; **to ~ o.s. for sth** sich für *or* wegen etw entschuldigen; **to ~ o.s. for doing sth** sich entschuldigen, daß man etw tut; **to make ~s for sb** jdn entschuldigen; **that's no ~!** das ist keine Ausrede!

**ex-directory** ['ɛksdɪ'rɛktərɪ] (*BRIT*) *adj* (*number*) geheim; **she's ~** sie steht nicht im Telefonbuch.

**execrable** ['ɛksɪkrəbl] *adj* scheußlich; (*manners*) abscheulich.

**execute** ['ɛksɪkjuːt] *vt* ausführen; (*person*) hinrichten.

**execution** [ɛksɪ'kjuːʃən] *n* (*see vb*) Ausführung *f*; Hinrichtung *f*.

**executioner** [ɛksɪ'kjuːʃnəʳ] *n* Scharfrichter *m*.

**executive** [ɪg'zɛkjutɪv] *n* leitende(r) Angestellte(r) *f(m)*; (*committee*) Vorstand *m* ♦ *adj* geschäftsführend; (*role*) führend; (*secretary*) Chef-; (*car, chair*) für gehobene Ansprüche; (*toys*) Manager-; (*plane*) ≈ Privat-.

**executive director** *n* leitender Direktor *m*, leitende Direktorin *f*.

**executor** [ɪg'zɛkjutəʳ] *n* Testaments-vollstrecker(in) *m(f)*.

**exemplary** [ɪg'zɛmplərɪ] *adj* vorbildlich, beispielhaft; (*punishment*) exemplarisch.

**exemplify** [ɪg'zɛmplɪfaɪ] *vt* verkörpern; (*illustrate*) veranschaulichen.

**exempt** [ɪg'zɛmpt] *adj:* **~ from** befreit von ♦ *vt:* **to ~ sb from** jdn befreien von.

**exemption** [ɪg'zɛmpʃən] *n* Befreiung *f*.

**exercise** ['ɛksəsaɪz] *n* Übung *f*; (*no pl: keep-fit*) Gymnastik *f*; (: *energetic movement*) Bewegung *f*; (: *of authority etc*) Ausübung *f* ♦ *vt* (*patience*) üben; (*right*) ausüben; (*dog*) ausführen; (*mind*) beschäftigen ♦ *vi* (*also:* **to take ~**) Sport treiben.

**exercise book** *n* (Schul)heft *nt*.

**exert** [ɪg'zəːt] *vt* (*influence*) ausüben; (*authority*) einsetzen; **to ~ o.s.** sich anstrengen.

**exertion** [ɪg'zəːʃən] *n* Anstrengung *f*.

**ex gratia** ['ɛks'greɪʃə] *adj:* **~ payment** freiwillige Zahlung *f*.

**exhale** [ɛks'heɪl] *vt, vi* ausatmen.

**exhaust** [ɪg'zɔːst] *n* (*also:* **~ pipe**) Auspuff *m*; (*fumes*) Auspuffgase *pl* ♦ *vt* erschöpfen; (*money*) aufbrauchen; (*topic*) erschöpfend behandeln; **to ~ o.s.** sich verausgaben.

**exhausted** [ɪg'zɔːstɪd] *adj* erschöpft.

**exhausting** [ɪg'zɔːstɪŋ] *adj* anstrengend.

**exhaustion** [ɪg'zɔːstʃən] *n* Erschöpfung *f*; **nervous ~** nervöse Erschöpfung.

**exhaustive** [ɪg'zɔːstɪv] *adj* erschöpfend.

**exhibit** [ɪg'zɪbɪt] *n* Ausstellungsstück *nt*; (*LAW*) Beweisstück *nt* ♦ *vt* zeigen, an den Tag legen; (*paintings*) ausstellen.

**exhibition** [ɛksɪ'bɪʃən] *n* Ausstellung *f*; **to make an ~ of o.s.** sich unmöglich aufführen; **an ~ of bad manners** schlechte Manieren *pl*; **an ~ of draughtsmanship**

zeichnerisches Können *nt*.

**exhibitionist** [ɛksɪ'bɪʃənɪst] *n* Exhibitionist(in) *m(f)*.

**exhibitor** [ɪg'zɪbɪtəʳ] *n* Aussteller(in) *m(f)*.

**exhilarating** [ɪg'zɪləreɪtɪŋ] *adj* erregend, berauschend; (*news*) aufregend.

**exhilaration** [ɪgzɪlə'reɪʃən] *n* Hochgefühl *nt*.

**exhort** [ɪg'zɔːt] *vt:* **to ~ sb to do sth** jdn ermahnen, etw zu tun.

**exile** ['ɛksaɪl] *n* Exil *nt*; (*person*) Verbannte(r) *f(m)* ♦ *vt* verbannen; **in ~** im Exil.

**exist** [ɪg'zɪst] *vi* existieren.

**existence** [ɪg'zɪstəns] *n* Existenz *f*; **to be in ~** existieren.

**existentialism** [ɛgzɪs'tɛnʃlɪzəm] *n* Existentialismus *m*.

**existing** [ɪg'zɪstɪŋ] *adj* bestehend.

**exit** ['ɛksɪt] *n* Ausgang *m*; (*from motorway*) Ausfahrt *f*; (*departure*) Abgang *m* ♦ *vi* (*THEAT*) abgehen; (*COMPUT: from program/ file etc*) das Programm/die Datei *etc* verlassen; **to ~ from** hinausgehen aus; (*motorway etc*) abfahren von.

**exit poll** *n* bei Wählern unmittelbar nach Verlassen der Wahllokale durchgeführte Umfrage.

**exit ramp** (*US*) *n* Ausfahrt *f*.

**exit visa** *n* Ausreisevisum *nt*.

**exodus** ['ɛksədəs] *n* Auszug *m*; **the ~ to the cities** die Abwanderung in die Städte.

**ex officio** ['ɛksə'fɪʃɪəu] *adj* von Amts wegen ♦ *adv* kraft seines Amtes.

**exonerate** [ɪg'zɔnəreɪt] *vt:* **to ~ from** entlasten von.

**exorbitant** [ɪg'zɔːbɪtnt] *adj* (*prices, rents*) astronomisch, unverschämt; (*demands*) maßlos, übertrieben.

**exorcize** ['ɛksɔːsaɪz] *vt* exorzieren; (*spirit*) austreiben.

**exotic** [ɪg'zɔtɪk] *adj* exotisch.

**expand** [ɪks'pænd] *vt* erweitern; (*staff, numbers etc*) vergrößern; (*influence*) ausdehnen ♦ *vi* expandieren; (*population*) wachsen; (*gas, metal*) sich ausdehnen; **to ~ on** weiter ausführen.

**expanse** [ɪks'pæns] *n* Weite *f*.

**expansion** [ɪks'pænʃən] *n* Expansion *f*; (*of population*) Wachstum *nt*; (*of gas, metal*) Ausdehnung *f*.

**expansionism** [ɪks'pænʃənɪzəm] *n* Expansionspolitik *f*.

**expansionist** [ɪks'pænʃənɪst] *adj* Expansions-, expansionistisch.

**expatriate** [ɛks'pætrɪət] *n* im Ausland Lebende(r) *f(m)*.

**expect** [ɪks'pɛkt] *vt* erwarten; (*suppose*) denken, glauben; (*count on*) rechnen mit ♦ *vi:* **to be ~ing** ein Kind erwarten; **to ~ sb to do sth** erwarten, daß jd etw tut; **to ~ to do sth** vorhaben, etw zu tun; **as ~ed** wie erwartet; **I ~ so** ich glaube schon.

**expectancy** [ɪks'pɛktənsɪ] *n* Erwartung *f*; **life**

~ Lebenserwartung *f*.
**expectant** [ɪks'pɛktənt] *adj* erwartungsvoll.
**expectantly** [ɪks'pɛktəntlɪ] *adv*
erwartungsvoll.
**expectant mother** *n* werdende Mutter *f*.
**expectation** [ɛkspɛk'teɪʃən] *n* Erwartung *f*;
(*hope*) Hoffnung *f*; **in** ~ **of** in Erwartung
+*gen*; **against** *or* **contrary to all** ~**(s)** wider
Erwarten; **to come** *or* **live up to sb's** ~**s** jds
Erwartungen *dat* entsprechen.
**expedience** [ɪks'piːdɪəns] *n* = **expediency**.
**expediency** [ɪks'piːdɪənsɪ] *n* Zweckmäßigkeit
*f*; **for the sake of** ~ aus Gründen der
Zweckmäßigkeit.
**expedient** [ɪks'piːdɪənt] *adj* zweckmäßig ♦ *n*
Hilfsmittel *nt*.
**expedite** ['ɛkspədaɪt] *vt* beschleunigen.
**expedition** [ɛkspə'dɪʃən] *n* Expedition *f*; (*for
shopping etc*) Tour *f*.
**expeditionary force** [ɛkspə'dɪʃənrɪ-] *n*
Expeditionskorps *nt*.
**expeditious** [ɛkspə'dɪʃəs] *adj* schnell.
**expel** [ɪks'pɛl] *vt* (*from school*) verweisen;
(*from organization*) ausschließen; (*from place*)
vertreiben; (*gas, liquid*) ausstoßen.
**expend** [ɪks'pɛnd] *vt* ausgeben; (*time, energy*)
aufwenden.
**expendable** [ɪks'pɛndəbl] *adj* entbehrlich.
**expenditure** [ɪks'pɛndɪtʃə*] *n* Ausgaben *pl*; (*of
energy, time*) Aufwand *m*.
**expense** [ɪks'pɛns] *n* Kosten *pl*; (*expenditure*)
Ausgabe *f*; **expenses** *npl* Spesen *pl*; **at the**
~ **of** auf Kosten +*gen*; **to go to the** ~ **of
buying a new car** (viel) Geld für ein neues
Auto anlegen; **at great/little** ~ mit hohen/
geringen Kosten.
**expense account** *n* Spesenkonto *nt*.
**expensive** [ɪks'pɛnsɪv] *adj* teuer; **to have**
~ **tastes** einen teuren Geschmack haben.
**experience** [ɪks'pɪərɪəns] *n* Erfahrung *f*;
(*event, activity*) Erlebnis *nt* ♦ *vt* erleben; **by** *or*
**from** ~ aus Erfahrung; **to learn by** ~ durch
eigene Erfahrung lernen.
**experienced** [ɪks'pɪərɪənst] *adj* erfahren.
**experiment** [ɪks'pɛrɪmənt] *n* Experiment *nt*,
Versuch *m* ♦ *vi:* **to** ~ **(with/on)**
experimentieren (mit/an +*dat*); **to perform** *or*
**carry out an** ~ einen Versuch *or* ein
Experiment durchführen; **as an** ~
versuchsweise.
**experimental** [ɪkspɛrɪ'mɛntl] *adj*
experimentell; **at the** ~ **stage** im
Versuchsstadium.
**expert** ['ɛkspəːt] *adj* ausgezeichnet, geschickt;
(*opinion, help etc*) eines Fachmanns ♦ *n*
Fachmann *m*, Fachfrau *f*, Experte *m*,
Expertin *f*; **to be** ~ **in** *or* **at doing sth** etw
ausgezeichnet können; **an** ~ **on sth/on the
subject of sth** ein Experte für etw/auf dem
Gebiet einer Sache *gen*; ~ **witness** (*LAW*)
sachverständiger Zeuge *m*.
**expertise** [ɛkspəː'tiːz] *n* Sachkenntnis *f*.

**expire** [ɪks'paɪə*] *vi* ablaufen.
**expiry** [ɪks'paɪərɪ] *n* Ablauf *m*.
**expiry date** *n* Ablauftermin *m*; (*of voucher,
special offer etc*) Verfallsdatum *nt*.
**explain** [ɪks'pleɪn] *vt* erklären.
► **explain away** *vt* eine Erklärung finden für.
**explanation** [ɛksplə'neɪʃən] *n* Erklärung *f*; **to
find an** ~ **for sth** eine Erklärung für etw
finden.
**explanatory** [ɪks'plænətrɪ] *adj* erklärend.
**expletive** [ɪks'pliːtɪv] *n* Kraftausdruck *m*.
**explicable** [ɪks'plɪkəbl] *adj* erklärbar; **for no**
~ **reason** aus unerfindlichen Gründen.
**explicit** [ɪks'plɪsɪt] *adj* ausdrücklich; (*sex,
violence*) deutlich, unverhüllt; **to be** ~ (*frank*)
sich deutlich ausdrücken.
**explode** [ɪks'pləud] *vi* explodieren;
(*population*) sprunghaft ansteigen ♦ *vt* zur
Explosion bringen; (*myth, theory*) zu Fall
bringen.
**exploit** ['ɛksplɔɪt] *n* Heldentat *f* ♦ *vt*
ausnutzen; (*workers etc*) ausbeuten;
(*resources*) nutzen.
**exploitation** [ɛksplɔɪ'teɪʃən] *n* (*see vb*)
Ausnutzung *f*; Ausbeutung *f*; Nutzung *f*.
**exploration** [ɛksplə'reɪʃən] *n* (*see vb*)
Erforschung *f*; Erkundung *f*; Untersuchung
*f*.
**exploratory** [ɪks'plɔrətrɪ] *adj* exploratorisch;
(*expedition*) Forschungs-; ~ **operation** (*MED*)
Explorationsoperation *f*; ~ **talks**
Sondierungsgespräche *pl*.
**explore** [ɪks'plɔː*] *vt* erforschen; (*with hands
etc, idea*) untersuchen.
**explorer** [ɪks'plɔːrə*] *n* Forschungsreisende(r)
*f(m)*; (*of place*) Erforscher(in) *m(f)*.
**explosion** [ɪks'pləuʒən] *n* Explosion *f*;
(*outburst*) Ausbruch *m*.
**explosive** [ɪks'pləusɪv] *adj* explosiv; (*device*)
Spreng-; (*temper*) aufbrausend ♦ *n*
Sprengstoff *m*; (*device*) Sprengkörper *m*.
**exponent** [ɪks'pəunənt] *n* Vertreter(in) *m(f)*,
Exponent(in) *m(f)*; (*MATH*) Exponent *m*.
**exponential** [ɛkspəu'nɛnʃl] *adj* exponentiell;
(*MATH: function etc*) Exponential-.
**export** [ɛks'pɔːt] *vt* exportieren, ausführen;
(*ideas, values*) verbreiten ♦ *n* Export *m*,
Ausfuhr *f*; (*product*) Exportgut *nt* ♦ *cpd*
Export-, Ausfuhr-.
**exportation** [ɛkspɔː'teɪʃən] *n* Export *m*,
Ausfuhr *f*.
**exporter** [ɛks'pɔːtə*] *n* Exporteur *m*.
**expose** [ɪks'pəuz] *vt* freilegen; (*to heat,
radiation*) aussetzen; (*unmask*) entlarven; **to**
~ **o.s.** sich entblößen.
**exposé** [ɪk'spəuzeɪ] *n* Enthüllung *f*.
**exposed** [ɪks'pəuzd] *adj* ungeschützt; (*wire*)
bloßliegend; **to be** ~ **to** (*radiation, heat etc*)
ausgesetzt sein +*dat*.
**exposition** [ɛkspə'zɪʃən] *n* Erläuterung *f*;
(*exhibition*) Ausstellung *f*.
**exposure** [ɪks'pəuʒə*] *n* (*to heat, radiation*)

Aussetzung *f*; (*publicity*) Publicity *f*; (*of person*) Entlarvung *f*; (*PHOT*) Belichtung *f*; (: *shot*) Aufnahme *f*; **to be suffering from ~** an Unterkühlung leiden; **to die from ~** erfrieren.

**exposure meter** *n* Belichtungsmesser *m*.

**expound** [ɪks'paʊnd] *vt* darlegen, erläutern.

**express** [ɪks'prɛs] *adj* ausdrücklich; (*intention*) bestimmt; (*BRIT: letter etc*) Expreß-, Eil- ♦ *n* (*train*) Schnellzug *m*; (*bus*) Schnellbus *m* ♦ *adv* (*send*) per Expreß ♦ *vt* ausdrücken; (*view, emotion*) zum Ausdruck bringen; **to ~ o.s.** sich ausdrücken.

**expression** [ɪks'prɛʃən] *n* Ausdruck *m*; (*on face*) (Gesichts)ausdruck *m*.

**expressionism** [ɪks'prɛʃənɪzəm] *n* Expressionismus *m*.

**expressive** [ɪks'prɛsɪv] *adj* ausdrucksvoll; **~ ability** Ausdrucksfähigkeit *f*.

**expressly** [ɪks'prɛslɪ] *adv* ausdrücklich; (*intentionally*) absichtlich.

**expressway** [ɪks'prɛsweɪ] (*US*) *n* Schnellstraße *f*.

**expropriate** [ɛks'prəʊprɪeɪt] *vt* enteignen.

**expulsion** [ɪks'pʌlʃən] *n* (*SCOL*) Verweisung *f*; (*POL*) Ausweisung *f*; (*of gas, liquid etc*) Ausstoßen *nt*.

**expurgate** ['ɛkspə:geɪt] *vt* zensieren; **the ~d version** die zensierte *or* bereinigte Fassung.

**exquisite** [ɛks'kwɪzɪt] *adj* exquisit, erlesen; (*keenly felt*) köstlich.

**exquisitely** [ɛks'kwɪzɪtlɪ] *adv* exquisit; (*carved*) kunstvoll; (*polite, sensitive*) äußerst.

**ex-serviceman** ['ɛks'sə:vɪsmən] (*irreg: like* man) *n* ehemaliger Soldat *m*.

**ext.** *abbr* (*TEL*) = **extension**.

**extemporize** [ɪks'tɛmpəraɪz] *vi* improvisieren.

**extend** [ɪks'tɛnd] *vt* verlängern; (*building*) anbauen an +*acc*; (*offer, invitation*) aussprechen; (*arm, hand*) ausstrecken; (*deadline*) verschieben ♦ *vi* sich erstrecken; (*period*) dauern.

**extension** [ɪks'tɛnʃən] *n* Verlängerung *f*; (*of building*) Anbau *m*; (*of time*) Aufschub *m*; (*of campaign, rights*) Erweiterung *f*; (*TEL*) (Neben)anschluß *m*; **~ 3718** (*TEL*) Apparat 3718.

**extension cable** *n* Verlängerungskabel *nt*.

**extension lead** *n* Verlängerungsschnur *f*.

**extensive** [ɪks'tɛnsɪv] *adj* ausgedehnt; (*effect*) weitreichend; (*damage*) beträchtlich; (*coverage, discussion*) ausführlich; (*inquiries*) umfangreich; (*use*) häufig.

**extensively** [ɪks'tɛnsɪvlɪ] *adv*: **he's travelled ~** er ist viel gereist.

**extent** [ɪks'tɛnt] *n* Ausdehnung *f*; (*of problem, damage, loss etc*) Ausmaß *nt*; **to some ~** bis zu einem gewissen Grade; **to a certain ~** in gewissem Maße; **to a large ~** in hohem Maße; **to the ~ of ...** (*debts*) in Höhe von ...; **to go to the ~ of doing sth** so weit gehen,

etw zu tun; **to such an ~ that ...** dermaßen, daß ...; **to what ~?** inwieweit?

**extenuating** [ɪks'tɛnjʊeɪtɪŋ] *adj*: **~ circumstances** mildernde Umstände *pl*.

**exterior** [ɛks'tɪərɪə*] *adj* (*surface, angle, world*) Außen- ♦ *n* Außenseite *f*; (*appearance*) Äußere(s) *nt*.

**exterminate** [ɪks'tə:mɪneɪt] *vt* ausrotten.

**extermination** [ɪkstə:mɪ'neɪʃən] *n* Ausrottung *f*.

**external** [ɛks'tə:nl] *adj* (*wall etc*) Außen-; (*use*) äußerlich; (*evidence*) unabhängig; (*examiner, auditor*) extern ♦ *n*: **the ~s** die Äußerlichkeiten *pl*; **for ~ use only** nur äußerlich (anzuwenden); **~ affairs** (*POL*) auswärtige Angelegenheiten *pl*.

**externally** [ɛks'tə:nəlɪ] *adv* äußerlich.

**extinct** [ɪks'tɪŋkt] *adj* ausgestorben; (*volcano*) erloschen.

**extinction** [ɪks'tɪŋkʃən] *n* Aussterben *nt*.

**extinguish** [ɪks'tɪŋgwɪʃ] *vt* löschen; (*hope*) zerstören.

**extinguisher** [ɪks'tɪŋgwɪʃə*] *n* (*also:* **fire ~**) Feuerlöscher *m*.

**extol,** (*US*) **extoll** [ɪks'təʊl] *vt* preisen, rühmen.

**extort** [ɪks'tɔ:t] *vt* erpressen; (*confession*) erzwingen.

**extortion** [ɪks'tɔ:ʃən] *n* (*see vb*) Erpressung *f*; Erzwingung *f*.

**extortionate** [ɪks'tɔ:ʃnɪt] *adj* überhöht; (*price*) Wucher-.

**extra** ['ɛkstrə] *adj* zusätzlich ♦ *adv* extra ♦ *n* Extra *nt*; (*surcharge*) zusätzliche Kosten *pl*; (*CINE, THEAT*) Statist(in) *m(f)*; **wine will cost ~** Wein wird extra berechnet.

**extra...** ['ɛkstrə] *pref* außer-, extra-.

**extract** [*vt* ɪks'trækt, *n* 'ɛkstrækt] *vt* (*tooth*) ziehen; (*mineral*) gewinnen ♦ *n* Auszug *m*; (*malt extract, vanilla extract etc*) Extrakt *m*; **to ~ (from)** (*object*) herausziehen (aus); (*money*) herausholen (aus); (*promise*) abringen +*dat*.

**extraction** [ɪks'trækʃən] *n* (*see vb*) Ziehen *nt*; Gewinnung *f*; Herausziehen *nt*; Herausholen *nt*; Abringen *nt*; (*DENTISTRY*) Extraktion *f*; (*descent*) Herkunft *f*, Abstammung *f*; **to be of Scottish ~, to be Scottish by ~** schottischer Herkunft *or* Abstammung sein.

**extractor fan** [ɪks'træktə-] *n* Sauglüfter *m*.

**extracurricular** ['ɛkstrəkə'rɪkjʊlə*] *adj* außerhalb des Lehrplans.

**extradite** ['ɛkstrədaɪt] *vt* ausliefern.

**extradition** [ɛkstrə'dɪʃən] *n* Auslieferung *f* ♦ *cpd* Auslieferungs-.

**extramarital** ['ɛkstrə'mærɪtl] *adj* außerehelich.

**extramural** ['ɛkstrə'mjʊərl] *adj* außerhalb der Universität; **~ classes** von der Universität veranstaltete Teilzeitkurse *pl*.

**extraneous** [ɛks'treɪnɪəs] *adj* unwesentlich.

**extraordinary** [ɪksˈtrɔːdnrɪ] *adj* ungewöhnlich; (*special*) außerordentlich; **the ~ thing is that** ... das Merkwürdige ist, daß ...

**extraordinary general meeting** *n* außerordentliche Hauptversammlung *f*.

**extrapolation** [ɛkstræpəˈleɪʃən] *n* Extrapolation *f*.

**extrasensory perception** [ˈɛkstrəˈsɛnsərɪ-] *n* außersinnliche Wahrnehmung *f*.

**extra time** *n* (*FOOTBALL*) Verlängerung *f*.

**extravagance** [ɪksˈtrævəgəns] *n* (*no pl*) Verschwendungssucht *f*; (*example of spending*) Luxus *m*.

**extravagant** [ɪksˈtrævəgənt] *adj* extravagant; (*tastes, gift*) teuer; (*wasteful*) verschwenderisch; (*praise*) übertrieben; (*ideas*) ausgefallen.

**extreme** [ɪksˈtriːm] *adj* extrem; (*point, edge, poverty*) äußerste(r, s) ♦ *n* Extrem *nt*; **the ~ right/left** (*POL*) die äußerste *or* extreme Rechte/Linke; **~s of temperature** extreme Temperaturen *pl*.

**extremely** [ɪksˈtriːmlɪ] *adv* äußerst, extrem.

**extremist** [ɪksˈtriːmɪst] *n* Extremist(in) *m(f)* ♦ *adj* extremistisch.

**extremities** [ɪksˈtrɛmɪtɪz] *npl* Extremitäten *pl*.

**extremity** [ɪksˈtrɛmɪtɪ] *n* Rand *m*; (*end*) äußerstes Ende *nt*; (*of situation*) Ausmaß *nt*.

**extricate** [ˈɛkstrɪkeɪt] *vt*: **to ~ sb/sth (from)** jdn/etw befreien (aus).

**extrovert** [ˈɛkstrəvɜːt] *n* extravertierter Mensch *m*.

**exuberance** [ɪgˈzjuːbərns] *n* Überschwenglichkeit *f*.

**exuberant** [ɪgˈzjuːbərnt] *adj* überschwenglich; (*imagination etc*) lebhaft.

**exude** [ɪgˈzjuːd] *vt* ausstrahlen; (*liquid*) absondern; (*smell*) ausströmen.

**exult** [ɪgˈzʌlt] *vi*: **to ~ (in)** jubeln (über +*acc*).

**exultant** [ɪgˈzʌltənt] *adj* jubelnd; (*shout*) Jubel-; **to be ~** jubeln.

**exultation** [ɛgzʌlˈteɪʃən] *n* Jubel *m*.

**eye** [aɪ] *n* Auge *nt*; (*of needle*) Öhr *nt* ♦ *vt* betrachten; **to keep an ~ on** aufpassen auf +*acc*; **as far as the ~ can see** soweit das Auge reicht; **in the public ~** im Blickpunkt der Öffentlichkeit; **to have an ~ for sth** einen Blick für etw haben; **with an ~ to doing sth** (*BRIT*) mit der Absicht, etw zu tun; **there's more to this than meets the ~** da steckt mehr dahinter(, als man auf den ersten Blick meint).

**eyeball** [ˈaɪbɔːl] *n* Augapfel *m*.

**eyebath** [ˈaɪbɑːθ] (*BRIT*) *n* Augenbadewanne *f*.

**eyebrow** [ˈaɪbrau] *n* Augenbraue *f*.

**eyebrow pencil** *n* Augenbrauenstift *m*.

**eye-catching** [ˈaɪkætʃɪŋ] *adj* auffallend.

**eyecup** [ˈaɪkʌp] (*US*) *n* = **eyebath**.

**eye drops** *npl* Augentropfen *pl*.

**eyeful** [ˈaɪful] *n*: **to get an ~ of sth** (*lit*) etw ins Auge bekommen; (*fig: have a good look*) einiges von etw zu sehen bekommen; **she's**

**quite an ~** sie hat allerhand zu bieten.

**eyeglass** [ˈaɪglɑːs] *n* Augenglas *nt*.

**eyelash** [ˈaɪlæʃ] *n* Augenwimper *f*.

**eyelet** [ˈaɪlɪt] *n* Öse *f*.

**eye level** *n*: **at ~** in Augenhöhe.

**eyelevel** [ˈaɪlɛvl] *adj* in Augenhöhe.

**eyelid** [ˈaɪlɪd] *n* Augenlid *nt*.

**eyeliner** [ˈaɪlaɪnə*] *n* Eyeliner *m*.

**eye-opener** [ˈaɪəupnə*] *n* Überraschung *f*; **to be an ~ to sb** jdm die Augen öffnen.

**eye shadow** *n* Lidschatten *m*.

**eyesight** [ˈaɪsaɪt] *n* Sehvermögen *nt*.

**eyesore** [ˈaɪsɔː*] *n* Schandfleck *m*.

**eyestrain** [ˈaɪstreɪn] *n*: **to get ~** seine Augen überanstrengen.

**eyetooth** [ˈaɪtuːθ] (*pl* **eyeteeth**) *n* Eckzahn *m*, Augenzahn *m*; **to give one's eyeteeth for sth** alles für etw geben; **to give one's eyeteeth to do sth** alles darum geben, etw zu tun.

**eyewash** [ˈaɪwɔʃ] *n* Augenwasser *nt*; (*fig*) Gewäsch *nt*.

**eyewitness** [ˈaɪwɪtnɪs] *n* Augenzeuge *m*, Augenzeugin *f*.

**eyrie** [ˈɪərɪ] *n* Horst *m*.

# *F, f*

**F¹, f** [ɛf] *n* (*letter*) F *nt*, f *nt*; **~ for Frederick**, (*US*) **~ for Fox** ≈ F wie Friedrich.

**F²** [ɛf] *n* (*MUS*) F *nt*, f *nt*.

**F³** [ɛf] *abbr* (= *Fahrenheit*) F.

**FA** (*BRIT*) *n abbr* (= *Football Association*) englischer Fußball-Dachverband, ≈ DFB *m*.

**FAA** (*US*) *n abbr* (= *Federal Aviation Administration*) amerikanische Luftfahrtbehörde.

**fable** [ˈfeɪbl] *n* Fabel *f*.

**fabric** [ˈfæbrɪk] *n* Stoff *m*; (*of society*) Gefüge *nt*; (*of building*) Bausubstanz *f*.

**fabricate** [ˈfæbrɪkeɪt] *vt* herstellen; (*story*) erfinden; (*evidence*) fälschen.

**fabrication** [fæbrɪˈkeɪʃən] *n* Herstellung *f*; (*lie*) Erfindung *f*.

**fabric ribbon** *n* (*for typewriter*) Gewebefarbband *nt*.

**fabulous** [ˈfæbjuləs] *adj* fabelhaft, toll (*inf*); (*extraordinary*) sagenhaft; (*mythical*) legendär.

**façade** [fəˈsɑːd] *n* Fassade *f*.

**face** [feɪs] *n* Gesicht *nt*; (*expression*) Gesichtsausdruck *m*; (*grimace*) Grimasse *f*; (*of clock*) Zifferblatt *nt*; (*of mountain, cliff*) (Steil)wand *f*; (*of building*) Fassade *f*; (*side, surface*) Seite *f* ♦ *vt* (*subj: person*) gegenübersitzen/-stehen +*dat etc*; (*: building,* street *etc*) liegen zu; (: : *north, south etc*) liegen nach; (*unpleasant situation*) sich gegenübersehen +*dat*; (*facts*) ins Auge sehen +*dat*; ~ **down** mit dem Gesicht nach unten; (*card*) mit der Bildseite nach unten; (*object*) mit der Vorderseite nach unten; **to lose/ save** ~ das Gesicht verlieren/wahren; **to make** *or* **pull a** ~ das Gesicht verziehen; **in the** ~ **of** trotz +*gen*; **on the** ~ **of it** so, wie es aussieht; **to come** ~ **to** ~ **with sb** jdn treffen; **to come** ~ **to** ~ **with a problem** einem Problem gegenüberstehen; **to** ~ **each other** einander gegenüberstehen/ -liegen/-sitzen *etc*; **to** ~ **the fact that** ... der Tatsache ins Auge sehen, daß ...; **the man facing me** der Mann mir gegenüber.

▶**face up to** *vt fus* (*obligations, difficulty*) auf sich *acc* nehmen; (*situation, possibility*) sich abfinden mit; (*danger, fact*) ins Auge sehen +*dat*.

**face cloth** (*BRIT*) *n* Waschlappen *m*.

**face cream** *n* Gesichtscreme *f*.

**faceless** ['feɪslɪs] *adj* (*fig*) anonym.

**face-lift** ['feɪslɪft] *n* Facelifting *nt*; (*of building etc*) Verschönerung *f*.

**face powder** *n* Gesichtspuder *m*.

**face-saving** ['feɪs'seɪvɪŋ] *adj*: **a** ~ **excuse/ tactic** eine Entschuldigung/Taktik, um das Gesicht zu wahren.

**facet** ['fæsɪt] *n* Seite *f*, Aspekt *m*; (*of gem*) Facette *f*.

**facetious** [fə'siːʃəs] *adj* witzelnd.

**face-to-face** [feɪstə'feɪs] *adj* persönlich; (*confrontation*) direkt.

**face value** *n* Nennwert *m*; **to take sth at** ~ (*fig*) etw für bare Münze nehmen.

**facia** ['feɪʃə] *n* = **fascia**.

**facial** ['feɪʃl] *adj* (*expression, massage etc*) Gesichts- ♦ *n* kosmetische Gesichts-behandlung *f*.

**facile** ['fæsaɪl] *adj* oberflächlich; (*comment*) nichtssagend.

**facilitate** [fə'sɪlɪteɪt] *vt* erleichtern.

**facilities** [fə'sɪlɪtɪz] *npl* Einrichtungen *pl*; **cooking** ~ Kochgelegenheit *f*; **credit** ~ Kreditmöglichkeiten *pl*.

**facility** [fə'sɪlɪtɪ] *n* Einrichtung *f*; **to have a** ~ **for** (*skill, aptitude*) eine Begabung haben für.

**facing** ['feɪsɪŋ] *prep* gegenüber +*dat* ♦ *n* (*SEWING*) Besatz *m*.

**facsimile** [fæk'sɪmɪlɪ] *n* Faksimile *nt*; (*also:* ~ **machine**) Fernkopierer *m*, (Tele)faxgerät *nt*; (*transmitted document*) Fernkopie *f*, (Tele)fax *nt*.

**fact** [fækt] *n* Tatsache *f*; (*truth*) Wirklichkeit *f*; **in** ~ eigentlich; (*in reality*) tatsächlich, in Wirklichkeit; **to know for a** ~ **that** ... ganz genau wissen, daß ...; **the** ~ **(of the matter) is that** ... die Sache ist die, daß ...; **it's a** ~ **of life that** ... es ist eine Tatsache, daß ...; **to tell sb the** ~**s of life** (*sex*) jdn aufklären.

**fact-finding** ['fæktfaɪndɪŋ] *adj*: **a** ~ **tour** *or* **mission** eine Informationstour.

**faction** ['fækʃən] *n* Fraktion *f*.

**factional** ['fækʃənl] *adj* (*dispute, system*) Fraktions-.

**factor** ['fæktə*] *n* Faktor *m*; (*COMM*) Kommissionär *m*; (: *agent*) Makler *m*; **safety** ~ Sicherheitsfaktor *m*; **human** ~ menschlicher Faktor.

**factory** ['fæktərɪ] *n* Fabrik *f*.

**factory farming** (*BRIT*) *n* industriell betriebene Viehzucht *f*.

**factory floor** *n*: **the** ~ (*workers*) die Fabrikarbeiter *pl*; **on the** ~ bei *or* unter den Fabrikarbeitern.

**factory ship** *n* Fabrikschiff *nt*.

**factual** ['fæktjuəl] *adj* sachlich; (*information*) Sach-.

**faculty** ['fækəltɪ] *n* Vermögen *nt*, Kraft *f*; (*ability*) Talent *nt*; (*of university*) Fakultät *f*; (*US: teaching staff*) Lehrkörper *m*.

**fad** [fæd] *n* Fimmel *m*, Tick *m*.

**fade** [feɪd] *vi* verblassen; (*light*) nachlassen; (*sound*) schwächer werden; (*flower*) verblühen; (*hope*) zerrinnen; (*smile*) verschwinden.

▶**fade in** *vt sep* allmählich einblenden.

▶**fade out** *vt sep* ausblenden.

**faeces,** (*US*) **feces** ['fiːsiːz] *npl* Kot *m*.

**fag** [fæg] *n* (*BRIT*: *inf*: *cigarette*) Glimmstengel *m*; (: : *chore*) Schinderei *f* (*inf*), Plackerei *f* (*inf*); (*US: inf*: *homosexual*) Schwule(r) *m*.

**fail** [feɪl] *vt* (*exam*) nicht bestehen; (*candidate*) durchfallen lassen; (*subj: courage*) verlassen; (: *leader, memory*) im Stich lassen ♦ *vi* (*candidate*) durchfallen; (*attempt*) fehlschlagen; (*brakes*) versagen; (*also:* be ~**ing**: *health*) sich verschlechtern; (: *eyesight, light*) nachlassen; **to** ~ **to do sth** etw nicht tun; (*neglect*) (es) versäumen, etw zu tun; **without** ~ ganz bestimmt.

**failing** ['feɪlɪŋ] *n* Schwäche *f*, Fehler *m* ♦ *prep* in Ermangelung +*gen*; ~ **that** (oder) sonst, und wenn das nicht möglich ist.

**fail-safe** ['feɪlseɪf] *adj* (ab)gesichert.

**failure** ['feɪljə*] *n* Mißerfolg *m*; (*person*) Versager(in) *m(f)*; (*of brakes, heart*) Versagen *nt*; (*of engine, power*) Ausfall *m*; (*of crops*) Mißernte *f*; (*in exam*) Durchfall *m*; **his** ~ **to turn up meant that we had to** ... weil er nicht kam, mußten wir ...; **it was a complete** ~ es war ein totaler Fehlschlag.

**faint** [feɪnt] *adj* schwach; (*breeze, trace*) leicht ♦ *n* Ohnmacht *f* ♦ *vi* ohnmächtig werden, in Ohnmacht fallen; **she felt** ~ ihr wurde schwach.

**faintest** ['feɪntɪst] *adj, n*: **I haven't the** ~ (*idea*) ich habe keinen blassen Schimmer.

**faint-hearted** ['feɪnt'hɑːtɪd] *adj* zaghaft.

**faintly** ['feɪntlɪ] *adv* schwach.

**fair** [fɛə*] *adj* gerecht, fair; (*size, number*) ansehnlich; (*chance, guess*) recht gut; (*hair*)

blond; (*skin, complexion*) hell; (*weather*)
schön ♦ *adv:* **to play ~ fair** spielen ♦ *n* (*also:*
**trade ~**) Messe *f*; (*BRIT: funfair*) Jahrmarkt
*m*, Rummel *m*; **it's not ~**! das ist nicht fair!;
**a ~ amount of** ziemlich viel.

**fair copy** *n* Reinschrift *f*.

**fair game** *n:* **to be ~ (for)** (*for attack, criticism*)
Freiwild *nt* sein (für).

**fairground** ['fɛəgraund] *n* Rummelplatz *m*.

**fair-haired** [fɛəˈhɛəd] *adj* blond.

**fairly** ['fɛəlɪ] *adv* gerecht; (*quite*) ziemlich; **I'm
~ sure** ich bin (mir) ziemlich sicher.

**fairness** ['fɛənɪs] *n* Gerechtigkeit *f*; **in all ~**
gerechterweise, fairerweise.

**fair play** *n* faires Verhalten *nt*, Fair play *nt*.

**fairway** ['fɛəweɪ] *n* (*GOLF*): **the ~** das
Fairway.

**fairy** ['fɛərɪ] *n* Fee *f*.

**fairy godmother** *n* gute Fee *f*.

**fairy lights** (*BRIT*) *npl* bunte Lichter *pl*.

**fairy tale** *n* Märchen *nt*.

**faith** [feɪθ] *n* Glaube *m*; (*trust*) Vertrauen *nt*; **to
have ~ in sb** jdm vertrauen; **to have ~ in
sth** Vertrauen in etw *acc* haben.

**faithful** ['feɪθful] *adj* (*account*) genau; **~ (to)**
(*person*) treu +*dat*.

**faithfully** ['feɪθfəlɪ] *adv* (*see adj*) genau; treu.

**faith healer** *n* Gesundbeter(in) *m(f)*.

**fake** [feɪk] *n* Fälschung *f*; (*person*)
Schwindler(in) *m(f)* ♦ *adj* gefälscht ♦ *vt*
fälschen; (*illness, emotion*) vortäuschen; **his
illness is a ~** er simuliert seine Krankheit
nur.

**falcon** ['fɔːlkən] *n* Falke *m*.

**Falkland Islands** ['fɔːlklənd-] *npl:* **the ~** die
Falkland-Inseln *pl*.

**fall** [fɔːl] (*pt* fell, *pp* fallen) *n* Fall *m*; (*of price,
temperature*) Sinken *nt*; (*: sudden*) Sturz *m*;
(*US: autumn*) Herbst *m* ♦ *vi* fallen; (*night,
darkness*) hereinbrechen; (*silence*) eintreten;
**falls** *npl* (*waterfall*) Wasserfall *m*; **a ~ of snow**
ein Schneefall *m*; **a ~ of earth** ein Erdrutsch
*m*; **to ~ flat** auf die Nase fallen; (*plan*) ins
Wasser fallen; (*joke*) nicht ankommen; **to
~ in love (with sb/sth)** sich (in jdn/etw)
verlieben; **to ~ short of sb's expectations**
jds Erwartungen nicht erfüllen.

▶**fall apart** *vi* auseinanderfallen,
kaputtgehen; (*inf: emotionally*) durchdrehen.

▶**fall back** *vi* zurückweichen.

▶**fall back on** *vi* zurückgreifen auf +*acc*; **to
have sth to ~ back on** auf etw *acc*
zurückgreifen können.

▶**fall behind** *vi* zurückbleiben; (*fig: with
payment*) in Rückstand geraten.

▶**fall down** *vi* hinfallen; (*building*) einstürzen.

▶**fall for** *vt fus* (*trick, story*) hereinfallen auf
+*acc*; (*person*) sich verlieben in +*acc*.

▶**fall in** *vi* einstürzen; (*MIL*) antreten.

▶**fall in with** *vt fus* eingehen auf +*acc*.

▶**fall off** *vi* herunterfallen; (*takings,
attendance*) zurückgehen.

▶**fall out** *vi* (*hair, teeth*) ausfallen; **to ~ out
with sb** sich mit jdm zerstreiten.

▶**fall over** *vi* hinfallen; (*object*) umfallen ♦ *vt:*
**to ~ over o.s. to do sth** sich *dat* die größte
Mühe geben, etw zu tun.

▶**fall through** *vi* (*plan, project*) ins Wasser
fallen.

**fallacy** ['fæləsɪ] *n* Irrtum *m*.

**fall-back** ['fɔːlbæk] *adj:* **~ position**
Rückzugsbasis *f*.

**fallen** ['fɔːlən] *pp of* **fall**.

**fallible** ['fæləbl] *adj* fehlbar.

**falling** ['fɔːlɪŋ] *adj:* **~ market** (*COMM*)
Baissemarkt *m*.

**falling off** *n* Rückgang *m*.

**falling-out** ['fɔːlɪŋ'aut] *n* (*break-up*) Bruch *m*.

**Fallopian tube** [fəˈləupɪən-] *n* Eileiter *m*.

**fallout** ['fɔːlaut] *n* radioaktiver Niederschlag
*m*.

**fallout shelter** *n* Atombunker *m*.

**fallow** ['fæləu] *adj* brach(liegend).

**false** [fɔːls] *adj* falsch; (*imprisonment*)
widerrechtlich.

**false alarm** *n* falscher *or* blinder Alarm *m*.

**falsehood** ['fɔːlshud] *n* Unwahrheit *f*.

**falsely** ['fɔːlslɪ] *adv* (*accuse*) zu Unrecht.

**false pretences** *npl:* **under ~** unter
Vorspiegelung falscher Tatsachen.

**false teeth** (*BRIT*) *npl* Gebiß *nt*.

**falsify** ['fɔːlsɪfaɪ] *vt* fälschen.

**falter** ['fɔːltə*] *vi* stocken; (*hesitate*) zögern.

**fame** [feɪm] *n* Ruhm *m*.

**familiar** [fəˈmɪlɪə*] *adj* vertraut; (*intimate*)
vertraulich; **to be ~ with** vertraut sein mit;
**to make o.s. ~ with sth** sich mit etw
vertraut machen; **to be on ~ terms with sb**
mit jdm auf vertrautem Fuß stehen.

**familiarity** [fəmɪlɪˈærɪtɪ] *n* (*see adj*)
Vertrautheit *f*; Vertraulichkeit *f*.

**familiarize** [fəˈmɪlɪəraɪz] *vt:* **to ~ o.s. with sth**
sich mit etw vertraut machen.

**family** ['fæmɪlɪ] *n* Familie *f*; (*relations*)
Verwandtschaft *f*.

**family business** *n* Familienbetrieb *m*.

**family credit** *n* Beihilfe für
*einkommensschwache Familien*.

**family doctor** *n* Hausarzt *m*, Hausärztin *f*.

**family life** *n* Familienleben *nt*.

**family man** *n* (*home-loving*) häuslich
veranlagter Mann *m*; (*with a family*)
Familienvater *m*.

**family planning** *n* Familienplanung *f*;
**~ clinic** ≈ Familienberatungsstelle *f*.

**family tree** *n* Stammbaum *m*.

**famine** ['fæmɪn] *n* Hungersnot *f*.

**famished** ['fæmɪʃt] (*inf*) *adj* ausgehungert; **I'm
~** ich sterbe vor Hunger.

**famous** ['feɪməs] *adj* berühmt.

**famously** ['feɪməslɪ] *adv* (*get on*) prächtig.

**fan** [fæn] *n* (*person*) Fan *m*; (*object: folding*)
Fächer *m*; (*: ELEC*) Ventilator *m* ♦ *vt* fächeln;
(*fire*) anfachen; (*quarrel*) schüren.

▶**fan out** vi ausschwärmen; (unfurl) sich fächerförmig ausbreiten.

**fanatic** [fə'nætɪk] n Fanatiker(in) m(f); (enthusiast) Fan m.

**fanatical** [fə'nætɪkl] adj fanatisch.

**fan belt** n (AUT) Keilriemen m.

**fanciful** ['fænsɪful] adj (idea) abstrus, seltsam; (design, name) phantasievoll; (object) reich verziert.

**fan club** n Fanclub m.

**fancy** ['fænsɪ] n Laune f; (imagination) Phantasie f; (fantasy) Phantasievorstellung f ♦ adj (clothes, hat) toll, schick; (hotel) fein, vornehm; (food) ausgefallen ♦ vt mögen; (imagine) sich dat einbilden; (think) glauben; **to take a ~ to sth** Lust auf etw acc bekommen; **when the ~ takes him** wenn ihm gerade danach ist; **it took** or **caught my ~** es gefiel mir; **to ~ that ...** meinen, daß ...; **~ that!** (nein) so was!; **he fancies her** (inf) sie gefällt ihm.

**fancy dress** n Verkleidung f, (Masken)kostüm nt.

**fancy-dress ball** ['fænsɪdrɛs-] n Maskenball m.

**fancy goods** npl Geschenkartikel pl.

**fanfare** ['fænfɛə'] n Fanfare f.

**fanfold paper** ['fænfəuld-] n Endlospapier nt.

**fang** [fæŋ] n (tooth) Fang m; (: of snake) Giftzahn m.

**fan heater** (BRIT) n Heizlüfter m.

**fanlight** ['fænlaɪt] n Oberlicht nt.

**fanny** ['fænɪ] n (US: inf: bottom) Po m; (BRIT: inf!: genitals) Möse f (!).

**fantasize** ['fæntəsaɪz] vi phantasieren.

**fantastic** [fæn'tæstɪk] adj phantastisch.

**fantasy** ['fæntəsɪ] n Phantasie f; (dream) Traum m.

**fanzine** ['fænziːn] n Fanmagazin nt.

**FAO** n abbr (= Food and Agriculture Organization) FAO f.

**f.a.q.** abbr (= free alongside quay) frei Kai.

**far** [fɑː'] adj: **at the ~ side** auf der anderen Seite ♦ adv weit; **at the ~ end** am anderen Ende; **the ~ left/right** die extreme Linke/Rechte; **~ away, ~ off** weit entfernt or weg; **her thoughts were ~ away** sie war mit ihren Gedanken weit weg; **~ from** (fig) alles andere als; **by ~** bei weitem; **is it ~ to London?** ist es weit bis nach London?; **it's not ~ from here** es ist nicht weit von hier; **go as ~ as the church** gehen/fahren Sie bis zur Kirche; **as ~ back as the 13th century** schon im 13. Jahrhundert; **as ~ as I know** soweit ich weiß; **as ~ as possible** soweit wie möglich; **how ~?** wie weit?; **how ~ have you got with your work?** wie weit sind Sie mit Ihrer Arbeit (gekommen)?

**faraway** ['fɑːrəweɪ] adj weit entfernt; (look, voice) abwesend.

**farce** [fɑːs] n Farce f.

**farcical** ['fɑːsɪkl] adj absurd, grotesk.

**fare** [fɛə'] n Fahrpreis m; (money) Fahrgeld nt; (passenger) Fahrgast m; (food) Kost f ♦ vi: **he ~d well/badly** es ging ihm gut/schlecht; **half/full ~** halber/voller Fahrpreis; **how did you ~?** wie ist es Ihnen ergangen?; **they ~d badly in the recent elections** sie haben bei den letzten Wahlen schlecht abgeschnitten.

**Far East** n: **the ~** der Ferne Osten.

**farewell** [fɛə'wɛl] excl lebe/lebt etc wohl! ♦ n Abschied m ♦ cpd Abschieds-.

**far-fetched** ['fɑː'fɛtʃt] adj weit hergeholt.

**farm** [fɑːm] n Bauernhof m ♦ vt bebauen.

▶**farm out** vt (work etc) vergeben.

**farmer** ['fɑːmə'] n Bauer m, Bäu(e)rin f, Landwirt(in) m(f).

**farm hand** n Landarbeiter(in) m(f).

**farmhouse** ['fɑːmhaus] n Bauernhaus nt.

**farming** ['fɑːmɪŋ] n Landwirtschaft f; (of crops) Ackerbau m; (of animals) Viehzucht f; **sheep ~** Schafzucht f; **intensive ~** (of crops) Intensivanbau m; (of animals) Intensivhaltung f.

**farm labourer** n = **farm hand**.

**farmland** ['fɑːmlænd] n Ackerland nt.

**farm produce** n landwirtschaftliche Produkte pl.

**farm worker** n = **farm hand**.

**farmyard** ['fɑːmjɑːd] n Hof m.

**Faroe Islands** ['fɛərəu-] npl: **the ~** die Färöer pl.

**Faroes** ['fɛərəuz] npl = **Faroe Islands**.

**far-reaching** ['fɑː'riːtʃɪŋ] adj weitreichend.

**far-sighted** ['fɑː'saɪtɪd] adj weitsichtig; (fig) weitblickend.

**fart** [fɑːt] vi furzen (inf!) ♦ n Furz m (inf!).

**farther** ['fɑːðə'] adv weiter ♦ adj weiter entfernt.

**farthest** ['fɑːðɪst] superl of **far**.

**FAS, f.a.s.** (BRIT) abbr (= free alongside ship) frei Kai.

**fascia** ['feɪʃə] n (AUT) Armaturenbrett nt.

**fascinate** ['fæsɪneɪt] vt faszinieren.

**fascinating** ['fæsɪneɪtɪŋ] adj faszinierend.

**fascination** [fæsɪ'neɪʃən] n Faszination f.

**fascism** ['fæʃɪzəm] n Faschismus m.

**fascist** ['fæʃɪst] adj faschistisch ♦ n Faschist(in) m(f).

**fashion** ['fæʃən] n Mode f; (manner) Art f ♦ vt formen; **in ~** modern; **out of ~** unmodern; **after a ~** recht und schlecht; **in the Greek ~** im griechischen Stil.

**fashionable** ['fæʃnəbl] adj modisch, modern; (subject) Mode-; (club, writer) in Mode.

**fashion designer** n Modezeichner(in) m(f).

**fashion show** n Modenschau f.

**fast** [fɑːst] adj schnell; (dye, colour) farbecht ♦ adv schnell; (stuck, held) fest ♦ n Fasten nt; (period of fasting) Fastenzeit f ♦ vi fasten; **my watch is (5 minutes) ~** meine Uhr geht (5 Minuten) vor; **to be ~ asleep** tief or fest schlafen; **as ~ as I can** so schnell ich kann; **to make a boat ~** (BRIT) ein Boot

festmachen.
**fasten** ['fɑːsn] vt festmachen; (coat, belt etc) zumachen ♦ vi (see vt) festgemacht werden; zugemacht werden.
▶**fasten (up)on** vt fus sich dat in den Kopf setzen.
**fastener** ['fɑːsnə'] n Verschluß m.
**fastening** ['fɑːsnɪŋ] n = **fastener**.
**fast food** n Fast food nt, Schnellgerichte pl.
**fast-food** ['fɑːstfuːd] cpd (industry, chain) Fast-food-; ~ **restaurant** Schnellimbiß m.
**fastidious** [fæs'tɪdɪəs] adj penibel.
**fast lane** n (AUT): **the** ~ die Überholspur.
**fat** [fæt] adj dick; (person) dick, fett (pej); (animal) fett; (profit) üppig ♦ n Fett nt; **that's a** ~ **lot of use** (inf) das hilft herzlich wenig; **to live off the** ~ **of the land** wie Gott in Frankreich or wie die Made im Speck leben.
**fatal** ['feɪtl] adj tödlich; (mistake) verhängnisvoll.
**fatalistic** [feɪtə'lɪstɪk] adj fatalistisch.
**fatality** [fə'tælɪtɪ] n Todesopfer nt.
**fatally** ['feɪtəlɪ] adv (see adj) tödlich; verhängnisvoll.
**fate** [feɪt] n Schicksal nt; **to meet one's** ~ vom Schicksal ereilt werden.
**fated** ['feɪtɪd] adj (person) unglückselig; (project) zum Scheitern verurteilt; (governed by fate) vorherbestimmt.
**fateful** ['feɪtfʊl] adj schicksalhaft.
**fat-free** ['fæt'friː] adj fettfrei.
**father** ['fɑːðə'] n Vater m.
**Father Christmas** n der Weihnachtsmann.
**fatherhood** ['fɑːðəhʊd] n Vaterschaft f.
**father-in-law** ['fɑːðərənlɔː] n Schwiegervater m.
**fatherland** ['fɑːðəlænd] n Vaterland nt.
**fatherly** ['fɑːðəlɪ] adj väterlich.
**fathom** ['fæðəm] n (NAUT) Faden m ♦ vt (also: ~ out) verstehen.
**fatigue** [fə'tiːg] n Erschöpfung f; **fatigues** npl (MIL) Arbeitsanzug m; **metal** ~ Metallermüdung f.
**fatness** ['fætnɪs] n Dicke f.
**fatten** ['fætn] vt mästen ♦ vi (person) dick werden; (animal) fett werden; **chocolate is** ~**ing** Schokolade macht dick.
**fatty** ['fætɪ] adj fett ♦ n (inf) Dickerchen nt.
**fatuous** ['fætjʊəs] adj albern, töricht.
**faucet** ['fɔːsɪt] (US) n (Wasser)hahn m.
**fault** [fɔːlt] n Fehler m; (blame) Schuld f; (in machine) Defekt m; (GEOG) Verwerfung f ♦ vt (also: **find** ~ **with**) etwas auszusetzen haben an +dat; **it's my** ~ es ist meine Schuld; **at** ~ im Unrecht; **generous to a** ~ übermäßig großzügig.
**faultless** ['fɔːltlɪs] adj fehlerlos.
**faulty** ['fɔːltɪ] adj defekt.
**fauna** ['fɔːnə] n Fauna f.
**faux pas** ['fəʊ'pɑː] n inv Fauxpas m.
**favor** etc (US) = **favour** etc.

**favour,** (US) **favor** ['feɪvə'] n (approval) Wohlwollen nt; (help) Gefallen m ♦ vt bevorzugen; (be favourable for) begünstigen; **to ask a** ~ **of sb** jdn um einen Gefallen bitten; **to do sb a** ~ jdm einen Gefallen tun; **to find** ~ **with sb** bei jdm Anklang finden; **in** ~ **of** (biased) zugunsten von; (rejected) zugunsten +gen; **to be in** ~ **of sth** für etw sein; **to be in** ~ **of doing sth** dafür sein, etw zu tun.
**favourable** ['feɪvrəbl] adj günstig; (reaction) positiv; (comparison) vorteilhaft.
**favourably** ['feɪvrəblɪ] adv (react) positiv; (compare) vorteilhaft.
**favourite** ['feɪvrɪt] adj Lieblings- ♦ n Liebling m; (in race) Favorit(in) m(f).
**favouritism** ['feɪvrɪtɪzəm] n Günstlingswirtschaft f.
**fawn** [fɔːn] n Rehkitz nt ♦ adj (also: ~**-coloured**) hellbraun ♦ vi: **to** ~ **(up)on** sich einschmeicheln bei.
**fax** [fæks] n Fax nt; (machine) Fax(gerät) nt ♦ vt faxen.
**FBI** (US) n abbr (= Federal Bureau of Investigation) FBI nt.
**FCC** (US) n abbr (= Federal Communications Commission) Aufsichtsbehörde im Medienbereich.
**FCO** (BRIT) n abbr (= Foreign and Commonwealth Office) ≈ Auswärtiges Amt nt.
**FD** (US) n abbr = **fire department**.
**FDA** (US) n abbr (= Food and Drug Administration) Nahrungs- und Arzneimittelbehörde.
**FE** n abbr (= further education) Fortbildung f.
**fear** [fɪə'] n Furcht f, Angst f ♦ vt fürchten, Angst haben vor +dat; (be worried about) befürchten ♦ vi sich fürchten; ~ **of heights** Höhenangst f; **for** ~ **of doing sth** aus Angst, etw zu tun; **to** ~ **for** fürchten um; **to** ~ **that** ... befürchten, daß ....
**fearful** ['fɪəfʊl] adj (frightening) furchtbar, schrecklich; (apprehensive) ängstlich; **to be** ~ **of** Angst haben vor +dat.
**fearfully** ['fɪəfəlɪ] adv ängstlich; (inf: very) furchtbar, schrecklich.
**fearless** ['fɪəlɪs] adj furchtlos.
**fearsome** ['fɪəsəm] adj furchterregend.
**feasibility** [fiːzə'bɪlɪtɪ] n Durchführbarkeit f.
**feasibility study** n Durchführbarkeitsstudie f.
**feasible** ['fiːzəbl] adj machbar; (proposal, plan) durchführbar.
**feast** [fiːst] n Festmahl nt; (REL: also: ~ **day**) Festtag m, Feiertag m ♦ vi schlemmen; **to** ~ **on** sich gütlich tun an +dat.
**feat** [fiːt] n Leistung f.
**feather** ['feðə'] n Feder f ♦ cpd Feder-; (mattress) Federkern- ♦ vt: **to** ~ **one's nest** (fig) sein Schäfchen ins trockene bringen.
**featherweight** ['feðəweɪt] n Leichtgewicht nt;

(*BOXING*) Federgewicht *nt*.

**feature** ['fiːtʃə'] *n* Merkmal *nt*; (*PRESS, TV*) Feature *nt* ♦ *vt*: **the film ~s Marlon Brando** Marlon Brando spielt in dem Film mit ♦ *vi*: **to ~ in** vorkommen in +*dat*; (*film*) mitspielen in +*dat*; **features** *npl* (*of face*) (Gesichts)züge *pl*; **it ~d prominently in** es spielte eine große Rolle in +*dat*; **a special ~ on sth/sb** ein Sonderbeitrag *m* über etw/jdn.

**feature film** *n* Spielfilm *m*.

**featureless** ['fiːtʃəlɪs] *adj* (*landscape*) eintönig.

**Feb.** *abbr* (= *February*) Feb.

**February** ['fɛbruərɪ] *n* Februar *m*; *see also* **July**.

**feces** ['fiːsiːz] (*US*) *npl* = **faeces**.

**feckless** ['fɛklɪs] *adj* nutzlos.

**Fed** (*US*) *abbr* = **federal; federation**.

**Fed.** [fɛd] (*US: inf*) *n abbr* = **Federal Reserve Board**.

**fed** [fɛd] *pt, pp of* **feed**.

**federal** ['fɛdərəl] *adj* föderalistisch.

**Federal Republic of Germany** *n* Bundesrepublik *f* Deutschland.

**Federal Reserve Board** (*US*) *n* Kontrollorgan der US-Zentralbank.

**Federal Trade Commission** (*US*) *n* Handels-Kontrollbehörde.

**federation** [fɛdə'reɪʃən] *n* Föderation *f*, Bund *m*.

**fed up** *adj*: **to be ~ with** die Nase voll haben von.

**fee** [fiː] *n* Gebühr *f*; (*of doctor, lawyer*) Honorar *nt*; **school ~s** Schulgeld *nt*; **entrance ~** Eintrittsgebühr *f*; **membership ~** Mitgliedsbeitrag *m*; **for a small ~** eine geringe Gebühr.

**feeble** ['fiːbl] *adj* schwach; (*joke*) lahm.

**feeble-minded** ['fiːbl'maɪndɪd] *adj* dümmlich.

**feed** [fiːd] (*pt, pp* **fed**) *n* Mahlzeit *f*; (*of animal*) Fütterung *f*; (*on printer*) Papiervorschub *m* ♦ *vt* füttern; (*family etc*) ernähren; (*machine*) versorgen; **to ~ sth into sth** etw in etw *acc* einfüllen *or* eingeben; (*data, information*) etw in etw *acc* eingeben; **to ~ material into sth** Material in etw *acc* eingeben.

▶**feed back** *vt* zurückleiten.

▶**feed on** *vt fus* sich nähren von.

**feedback** ['fiːdbæk] *n* Feedback *nt*, Rückmeldung *f*; (*from person*) Reaktion *f*.

**feeder** ['fiːdə'] *n* (*road*) Zubringer *m*; (*railway line, air route*) Zubringerlinie *f*; (*baby's bottle*) Flasche *f*.

**feeding bottle** ['fiːdɪŋ-] (*BRIT*) *n* Flasche *f*.

**feel** [fiːl] (*pt, pp* **felt**) *n* (*sensation, touch*) Gefühl *nt*; (*impression*) Atmosphäre *f* ♦ *vt* (*object*) fühlen; (*desire, anger, grief*) empfinden; (*pain*) spüren; (*cold*) leiden unter +*dat*; (*think, believe*): **I ~ that you ought to do it** ich meine *or* ich bin der Meinung, daß Sie es tun sollten; **it has a soft ~** es fühlt sich weich an; **I ~ hungry** ich habe Hunger; **I ~ cold** mir ist kalt; **to ~ lonely/better** sich einsam/besser fühlen; **I don't ~ well** mir

geht es nicht gut; **I ~ sorry for him** er tut mir leid; **it ~s soft** es fühlt sich weich an; **it ~s colder here** es kommt mir hier kälter vor; **it ~s like velvet** es fühlt sich wie Samt an; **to ~ like** (*desire*) Lust haben auf +*acc*; **to ~ like doing sth** Lust haben, etw zu tun; **to get the ~ of sth** ein Gefühl für etw bekommen; **I'm still ~ing my way** ich versuche noch, mich zu orientieren.

▶**feel about** *vi* umhertasten; **to ~ about** *or* **around in one's pocket for** in seiner Tasche herumsuchen nach.

▶**feel around** *vi* = **feel about**.

**feeler** ['fiːlə'] *n* Fühler *m*; **to put out a ~** *or* **~s** (*fig*) seine Fühler ausstrecken.

**feeling** ['fiːlɪŋ] *n* Gefühl *nt*; (*impression*) Eindruck *m*; **~s ran high about it** man ereiferte sich sehr darüber; **what are your ~s about the matter?** was meinen Sie dazu?; **I have a ~ that ...** ich habe das Gefühl, daß ...; **my ~ is that ...** meine Meinung ist, daß ...; **to hurt sb's ~s** jdn verletzen.

**fee-paying** ['fiːpeɪɪŋ] *adj* (*school*) Privat-; **~ pupils** Schüler, deren Eltern Schulgeld zahlen.

**feet** [fiːt] *npl of* **foot**.

**feign** [feɪn] *vt* vortäuschen.

**feigned** [feɪnd] *adj* vorgetäuscht.

**feint** [feɪnt] *n* fein liniertes Papier *nt*.

**felicitous** [fɪ'lɪsɪtəs] *adj* glücklich.

**feline** ['fiːlaɪn] *adj* (*eyes etc*) Katzen-; (*features, grace*) katzenartig.

**fell** [fɛl] *pt of* **fall** ♦ *vt* fällen; (*opponent*) niederstrecken ♦ *n* (*BRIT: mountain*) Berg *m*; (*: moorland*): **the ~s** das Moor(land) ♦ *adj*: **in one ~ swoop** auf einen Schlag.

**fellow** ['fɛləʊ] *n* Mann *m*, Typ *m* (*inf*); (*comrade*) Kamerad *m*; (*of learned society*) Mitglied *nt*; (*of university*) Fellow *m*; **their ~ prisoners/students** ihre Mitgefangenen/ Kommilitonen (und Kommilitoninnen); **his ~ workers** seine Kollegen (und Kolleginnen).

**fellow citizen** *n* Mitbürger(in) *m(f)*.

**fellow countryman** (*irreg: like* **man**) *n* Landsmann *m*, Landsmännin *f*.

**fellow men** *npl* Mitmenschen *pl*.

**fellowship** ['fɛləʊʃɪp] *n* Kameradschaft *f*; (*society*) Gemeinschaft *f*; (*SCOL*) Forschungsstipendium *nt*.

**fell-walking** ['fɛlwɔːkɪŋ] (*BRIT*) *n* Bergwandern *nt*.

**felon** ['fɛlən] *n* (*LAW*) (Schwer)verbrecher *m*.

**felony** ['fɛlənɪ] *n* (*LAW*) (schweres) Verbrechen *nt*.

**felt** [fɛlt] *pt, pp of* **feel** ♦ *n* Filz *m*.

**felt-tip pen** ['fɛlttɪp-] *n* Filzstift *m*.

**female** ['fiːmeɪl] *n* Weibchen *nt*; (*pej: woman*) Frau *f*, Weib *nt* (*pej*) ♦ *adj* weiblich; (*vote etc*) Frauen-; (*ELEC: connector, plug*) Mutter-, Innen-; **male and ~ students** Studenten und Studentinnen.

**female impersonator** n Damen-Imitator m.
**Femidom** ® ['fɛmɪdɔm] n Kondom nt für die
Frau, Femidom ® nt.
**feminine** ['fɛmɪnɪn] adj weiblich, feminin ♦ n
Femininum nt.
**femininity** [fɛmɪ'nɪnɪtɪ] n Weiblichkeit f.
**feminism** ['fɛmɪnɪzəm] n Feminismus m.
**feminist** ['fɛmɪnɪst] n Feminist(in) m(f).
**fen** [fɛn] (BRIT) n: **the F~s** die Niederungen in
East Anglia.
**fence** [fɛns] n Zaun m; (SPORT) Hindernis nt
♦ vt (also: ~ in) einzäunen ♦ vi (SPORT)
fechten; **to sit on the ~** (fig) neutral bleiben,
nicht Partei ergreifen.
**fencing** ['fɛnsɪŋ] n (SPORT) Fechten nt.
**fend** [fɛnd] vi: **to ~ for o.s.** für sich (selbst)
sorgen, sich allein durchbringen.
▶**fend off** vt abwehren.
**fender** ['fɛndə*] n Kamingitter nt; (on boat)
Fender m; (US: of car) Kotflügel m.
**fennel** ['fɛnl] n Fenchel m.
**ferment** [vi fə'mɛnt, n 'fɜ:mɛnt] vi gären ♦ n (fig:
unrest) Unruhe f.
**fermentation** [fɜ:mɛn'teɪʃən] n Gärung f.
**fern** [fɜ:n] n Farn m.
**ferocious** [fə'rəuʃəs] adj wild; (behaviour)
heftig; (competition) scharf.
**ferocity** [fə'rɔsɪtɪ] n (see adj) Wildheit f;
Heftigkeit f; Schärfe f.
**ferret** ['fɛrɪt] n Frettchen nt.
▶**ferret about** vi herumstöbern.
▶**ferret around** vi = ferret about.
▶**ferret out** vt aufspüren.
**ferry** ['fɛrɪ] n (also: ~boat) Fähre f ♦ vt
transportieren; **to ~ sth/sb across** or **over**
jdn/etw übersetzen.
**ferryman** ['fɛrɪmən] (irreg: like man) n
Fährmann m.
**fertile** ['fɜ:taɪl] adj fruchtbar; ~ **period**
fruchtbare Tage pl.
**fertility** [fə'tɪlɪtɪ] n Fruchtbarkeit f.
**fertility drug** n Fruchtbarkeitsmedikament
nt.
**fertilization** [fɜ:tɪlaɪ'zeɪʃən] n (BIOL)
Befruchtung f.
**fertilize** ['fɜ:tɪlaɪz] vt düngen; (BIOL)
befruchten.
**fertilizer** ['fɜ:tɪlaɪzə*] n Dünger m.
**fervent** ['fɜ:vənt] adj leidenschaftlich;
(admirer) glühend.
**fervour,** (US) **fervor** ['fɜ:və*] n Leidenschaft f.
**fester** ['fɛstə*] vi (wound) eitern; (insult)
nagen; (row) sich verschlimmern.
**festival** ['fɛstɪvəl] n Fest nt; (ART, MUS)
Festival nt, Festspiele pl.
**festive** ['fɛstɪv] adj festlich; **the ~ season**
(BRIT: Christmas and New Year) die Festzeit f.
**festivities** [fɛs'tɪvɪtɪz] npl Feierlichkeiten pl.
**festoon** [fɛs'tu:n] vt: **to ~ with** schmücken
mit.
**fetch** [fɛtʃ] vt holen; (sell for) (ein)bringen;
**would you ~ me a glass of water please?**

kannst du mir bitte ein Glas Wasser
bringen?; **how much did it ~?** wieviel hat es
eingebracht?
▶**fetch up** (inf) vi landen (inf).
**fetching** ['fɛtʃɪŋ] adj bezaubernd, reizend.
**fête** [feɪt] n Fest nt.
**fetid** ['fɛtɪd] adj übelriechend.
**fetish** ['fɛtɪʃ] n Fetisch m.
**fetter** ['fɛtə*] vt fesseln; (horse) anpflocken;
(fig) in Fesseln legen.
**fetters** ['fɛtəz] npl Fesseln pl.
**fettle** ['fɛtl] (BRIT) n: **in fine ~** in bester Form.
**fetus** ['fi:təs] (US) n = **foetus.**
**feud** [fju:d] n Streit m ♦ vi im Streit liegen; **a**
**family ~** ein Familienstreit m.
**feudal** ['fju:dl] adj (society etc) Feudal-.
**feudalism** ['fju:dlɪzəm] n Feudalismus m.
**fever** ['fi:və*] n Fieber nt; **he has a ~** er hat
Fieber.
**feverish** ['fi:vərɪʃ] adj fiebrig; (activity,
emotion) fieberhaft.
**few** [fju:] adj wenige; **a ~** (adj) ein paar,
einige; (pron) ein paar; **a ~ more (days)**
noch ein paar (Tage); **they were ~** sie
waren nur wenige; ~ **succeed** nur wenigen
gelingt es; **very ~ survive** nur sehr wenige
überleben; **I know a ~** ich kenne einige; **a**
**good ~, quite a ~** ziemlich viele; **in the**
**next/past ~ days** in den nächsten/letzten
paar Tagen; **every ~ days/months** alle paar
Tage/Monate.
**fewer** ['fju:ə*] adj weniger; **there are ~ buses**
**on Sundays** Sonntags fahren weniger
Busse.
**fewest** ['fju:ɪst] adj die wenigsten.
**FFA** n abbr (= Future Farmers of America)
Verband von Landwirtschaftsstudenten.
**FH** (BRIT) n abbr = **fire hydrant.**
**FHA** (US) n abbr (= Federal Housing
Administration): ~ **loan** Baudarlehen nt.
**fiancé** [fɪ'ɑ:ŋseɪ] n Verlobte(r) m.
**fiancée** [fɪ'ɑ:ŋseɪ] n Verlobte f.
**fiasco** [fɪ'æskəu] n Fiasko nt.
**fib** [fɪb] n Flunkerei f (inf).
**fibre,** (US) **fiber** ['faɪbə*] n Faser f; (cloth)
(Faser)stoff m; (roughage) Ballaststoffe pl;
(ANAT: tissue) Gewebe nt.
**fibreboard,** (US) **fiberboard** ['faɪbəbɔ:d] n
Faserplatte f.
**fibreglass,** (US) **fiberglass** ['faɪbəglɑ:s] n
Fiberglas nt.
**fibrositis** [faɪbrə'saɪtɪs] n Bindegewebs-
entzündung f.
**FICA** (US) n abbr (= Federal Insurance
Contributions Act) Abgabe zur
Sozialversicherung.
**fickle** ['fɪkl] adj unbeständig; (weather)
wechselhaft.
**fiction** ['fɪkʃən] n Erfindung f; (LITER)
Erzählliteratur f, Prosaliteratur f.
**fictional** ['fɪkʃənl] adj erfunden.
**fictionalize** ['fɪkʃnəlaɪz] vt fiktionalisieren.

**fictitious** [fɪk'tɪʃəs] *adj* (*false*) falsch; (*invented*) fiktiv, frei erfunden.

**fiddle** ['fɪdl] *n* Fiedel *f* (*inf*), Geige *f*; (*fraud, swindle*) Schwindelei *f* ♦ *vt* (*BRIT: accounts*) frisieren (*inf*); **tax** ~ Steuermanipulation *f*; **to work a** ~ ein krummes Ding drehen (*inf*).
▶**fiddle with** *vt fus* herumspielen mit.

**fiddler** ['fɪdlə*] *n* Geiger(in) *m(f)*.

**fiddly** ['fɪdlɪ] *adj* knifflig (*inf*); (*object*) fummelig.

**fidelity** [fɪ'dɛlɪtɪ] *n* Treue *f*; (*accuracy*) Genauigkeit *f*.

**fidget** ['fɪdʒɪt] *vi* zappeln.

**fidgety** ['fɪdʒɪtɪ] *adj* zappelig.

**fiduciary** [fɪ'dju:ʃɪərɪ] *n* (*LAW*) Treuhänder *m*.

**field** [fi:ld] *n* Feld *nt*; (*SPORT: ground*) Platz *m*; (*subject, area of interest*) Gebiet *nt*; (*COMPUT*) Datenfeld *nt* ♦ *cpd* Feld-; **to lead the** ~ das Feld anführen; ~ **trip** Exkursion *f*.

**field day** *n*: **to have a** ~ einen herrlichen Tag haben.

**field glasses** *npl* Feldstecher *m*.

**field hospital** *n* Feldlazarett *nt*.

**field marshal** *n* Feldmarschall *m*.

**field work** *n* Feldforschung *f*; (*ARCHAEOLOGY, GEOG*) Arbeit *f* im Gelände.

**fiend** [fi:nd] *n* Teufel *m*.

**fiendish** ['fi:ndɪʃ] *adj* teuflisch; (*problem*) verzwickt.

**fierce** [fɪəs] *adj* wild; (*look*) böse; (*fighting, wind*) heftig; (*loyalty*) leidenschaftlich; (*enemy*) erbittert; (*heat*) glühend.

**fiery** ['faɪərɪ] *adj* glühend; (*temperament*) feurig, hitzig.

**FIFA** ['fi:fə] *n abbr* (= *Fédération Internationale de Football Association*) FIFA *f*.

**fifteen** [fɪf'ti:n] *num* fünfzehn.

**fifteenth** [fɪf'ti:nθ] *num* fünfzehnte(r, s).

**fifth** [fɪfθ] *num* fünfte(r, s) ♦ *n* Fünftel *nt*.

**fiftieth** ['fɪftɪɪθ] *num* fünfzigste(r, s).

**fifty** ['fɪftɪ] *num* fünfzig.

**fifty-fifty** ['fɪftɪ'fɪftɪ] *adj, adv* halbe-halbe, fifty-fifty; **to go/share** ~ **with sb** mit jdm halbe-halbe *or* fifty-fifty machen; **we have a** ~ **chance (of success)** unsere Chancen stehen fifty-fifty.

**fig** [fɪg] *n* Feige *f*.

**fight** [faɪt] (*pt, pp* **fought**) *n* Kampf *m*; (*quarrel*) Streit *m*; (*punch-up*) Schlägerei *f* ♦ *vt* kämpfen mit *or* gegen; (*prejudice etc*) bekämpfen; (*election*) kandidieren bei; (*emotion*) ankämpfen gegen; (*LAW: case*) durchkämpfen, durchfechten ♦ *vi* kämpfen; (*quarrel*) sich streiten; (*punch-up*) sich schlagen; **to put up a** ~ sich zur Wehr setzen; **to** ~ **one's way through a crowd/the undergrowth** sich *dat* einen Weg durch die Menge/das Unterholz bahnen; **to** ~ **against** bekämpfen; **to** ~ **for one's rights** für seine Rechte kämpfen.
▶**fight back** *vi* zurückschlagen; (*SPORT*) zurückkämpfen; (*after illness*) zu Kräften kommen ♦ *vt fus* unterdrücken.
▶**fight down** *vt* unterdrücken.
▶**fight off** *vt* abwehren; (*sleep, urge*) ankämpfen gegen.
▶**fight out** *vt*: **to** ~ **it out** es untereinander ausfechten.

**fighter** ['faɪtə*] *n* Kämpfer(in) *m(f)*; (*plane*) Jagdflugzeug *nt*; (*fig*) Kämpfernatur *f*.

**fighter pilot** *n* Jagdflieger *m*.

**fighting** ['faɪtɪŋ] *n* Kämpfe *pl*; (*brawl*) Schlägereien *pl*.

**figment** ['fɪgmənt] *n*: **a** ~ **of the imagination** ein Hirngespinst *nt*, pure Einbildung *f*.

**figurative** ['fɪgjurətɪv] *adj* bildlich, übertragen; (*style*) gegensätzlich.

**figure** ['fɪgə*] *n* Figur *f*; (*illustration*) Abbildung *f*; (*number, statistic, cipher*) Zahl *f*; (*person*) Gestalt *f*; (*personality*) Persönlichkeit *f* ♦ *vt* (*esp US*) glauben, schätzen ♦ *vi* eine Rolle spielen; **to put a** ~ **on sth** eine Zahl für etw angeben; **public** ~ Persönlichkeit *f* des öffentlichen Lebens.
▶**figure out** *vt* ausrechnen.

**figurehead** ['fɪgəhed] *n* Galionsfigur *f*.

**figure of speech** *n* Redensart *f*, Redewendung *f*.

**figure skating** *n* Eiskunstlaufen *nt*.

**Fiji (Islands)** ['fi:dʒi:-] *n(pl)* Fidschiinseln *pl*.

**filament** ['fɪləmənt] *n* Glühfaden *m*; (*BOT*) Staubfaden *m*.

**filch** [fɪltʃ] (*inf*) *vt* filzen.

**file** [faɪl] *n* Akte *f*; (*folder*) (Akten)ordner *m*; (*for loose leaf*) (Akten)mappe *f*; (*COMPUT*) Datei *f*; (*row*) Reihe *f*; (*tool*) Feile *f* ♦ *vt* ablegen, abheften; (*claim*) einreichen; (*wood, metal, fingernails*) feilen ♦ *vi*: **to** ~ **in/out** nacheinander hereinkommen/hinausgehen; **to** ~ **a suit against sb** eine Klage gegen jdn erheben; **to** ~ **past** in einer Reihe vorbeigehen; **to** ~ **for divorce** die Scheidung einreichen.

**filename** ['faɪlneɪm] *n* (*COMPUT*) Dateiname *m*.

**filibuster** ['fɪlɪbʌstə*] (*esp US: POL*) *n* (*also*: ~**er**) Dauerredner(in) *m(f)* ♦ *vi* filibustern, Obstruktion betreiben.

**filing** ['faɪlɪŋ] *n* Ablegen *nt*, Abheften *nt*.

**filing cabinet** *n* Aktenschrank *m*.

**filing clerk** *n* Angestellte(r) *f(m)* in der Registratur.

**Filipino** [fɪlɪ'pi:nəu] *n* Filipino *m*, Filipina *f*; (*LING*) Philippinisch *nt*.

**fill** [fɪl] *vt* füllen; (*space, area*) ausfüllen; (*tooth*) plombieren; (*need*) erfüllen ♦ *vi* sich füllen ♦ *n*: **to eat one's** ~ sich satt essen; **we've already** ~**ed that vacancy** wir haben diese Stelle schon besetzt.
▶**fill in** *vt* füllen; (*time*) überbrücken; (*form*) ausfüllen ♦ *vi*: **to** ~ **in for sb** für jdn einspringen; **to** ~ **sb in on sth** (*inf*) jdn über etw *acc* ins Bild setzen.
▶**fill out** *vt* ausfüllen.

▶**fill up** *vt* füllen ♦ *vi* (*AUT*) tanken; ~ **it up, please** (*AUT*) bitte volltanken.
**fillet** ['fɪlɪt] *n* Filet *nt* ♦ *vt* filetieren.
**fillet steak** *n* Filetsteak *nt*.
**filling** ['fɪlɪŋ] *n* Füllung *f*; (*for tooth*) Plombe *f*.
**filling station** *n* Tankstelle *f*.
**fillip** ['fɪlɪp] *n* (*stimulus*) Ansporn *m*.
**filly** ['fɪlɪ] *n* Stutfohlen *nt*.
**film** [fɪlm] *n* Film *m*; (*of powder etc*) Schicht *f*; (*for wrapping*) Plastikfolie *f* ♦ *vt, vi* filmen.
**film star** *n* Filmstar *m*.
**film strip** *n* Filmstreifen *m*.
**film studio** *n* Filmstudio *nt*.
**Filofax ®** ['faɪleufæks] *n* Filofax ® *nt*, Terminplaner *m*.
**filter** ['fɪltə*] *n* Filter *m* ♦ *vt* filtern.
▶**filter in** *vi* durchsickern.
▶**filter through** *vi* = **filter in.**
**filter coffee** *n* Filterkaffee *m*.
**filter lane** (*BRIT*) *n* Abbiegespur *f*.
**filter tip** *n* Filter *m*.
**filter-tipped** ['fɪltə'tɪpt] *adj* (*cigarette*) Filter-.
**filth** [fɪlθ] *n* Dreck *m*, Schmutz *m*.
**filthy** ['fɪlθɪ] *adj* dreckig, schmutzig; (*language*) unflätig.
**fin** [fɪn] *n* Flosse *f*; (*TECH*) Seitenflosse *f*.
**final** ['faɪnl] *adj* letzte(r, s); (*ultimate*) letztendlich; (*definitive*) endgültig ♦ *n* Finale *nt*, Endspiel *nt*; **finals** *npl* (*UNIV*) Abschlußprüfung *f*.
**final demand** *n* letzte Zahlungsaufforderung *f*.
**finale** [fɪ'nɑːlɪ] *n* Finale *nt*; (*THEAT*) Schlußszene *f*.
**finalist** ['faɪnəlɪst] *n* Endrundenteilnehmer(in) *m(f)*, Finalist(in) *m(f)*.
**finality** [faɪ'nælɪtɪ] *n* Endgültigkeit *f*; **with an air of** ~ mit Bestimmtheit.
**finalize** ['faɪnəlaɪz] *vt* endgültig festlegen.
**finally** ['faɪnəlɪ] *adv* endlich, schließlich; (*lastly*) schließlich, zum Schluß; (*irrevocably*) endgültig.
**finance** [faɪ'næns] *n* Geldmittel *pl*; (*money management*) Finanzwesen *nt* ♦ *vt* finanzieren; **finances** *npl* (*personal*) Finanzen *pl*, Finanzlage *f*.
**financial** [faɪ'nænʃəl] *adj* finanziell; ~ **statement** Bilanz *f*.
**financially** [faɪ'nænʃəlɪ] *adv* finanziell.
**financial year** *n* Geschäftsjahr *nt*.
**financier** [faɪ'nænsɪə*] *n* Finanzier *m*.
**find** [faɪnd] (*pt, pp* **found**) *vt* finden; (*discover*) entdecken ♦ *n* Fund *m*; **to** ~ **sb guilty** jdn für schuldig befinden; **to** ~ **(some) difficulty in doing sth** (einige) Schwierigkeiten haben, etw zu tun.
▶**find out** *vt* herausfinden; (*person*) erwischen ♦ *vi:* **to** ~ **out about** etwas herausfinden über +*acc*; (*by chance*) etwas erfahren über +*acc*.
**findings** ['faɪndɪŋz] *npl* (*LAW*) Urteil *nt*; (*of report*) Ergebnis *nt*.

**fine** [faɪn] *adj* fein; (*excellent*) gut; (*thin*) dünn ♦ *adv* gut; (*small*) fein ♦ *n* Geldstrafe *f* ♦ *vt* mit einer Geldstrafe belegen; **he's** ~ es geht ihm gut; **the weather is** ~ das Wetter ist schön; **that's cutting it (a bit)** ~ das ist aber (ein bißchen) knapp; **you're doing** ~ das machen Sie gut.
**fine arts** *npl* schöne Künste *pl*.
**finely** ['faɪnlɪ] *adv* schön; (*chop*) klein; (*slice*) dünn; (*adjust*) fein.
**fine print** *n:* **the** ~ das Kleingedruckte.
**finery** ['faɪnərɪ] *n* (*of dress*) Staat *m*.
**finesse** [fɪ'nɛs] *n* Geschick *nt*.
**fine-tooth comb** ['faɪntuːθ-] *n:* **to go through sth with a** ~ (*fig*) etw genau unter die Lupe nehmen.
**finger** ['fɪŋgə*] *n* Finger *m* ♦ *vt* befühlen; **little** ~ kleiner Finger; **index** ~ Zeigefinger *m*.
**fingernail** ['fɪŋgəneɪl] *n* Fingernagel *m*.
**fingerprint** ['fɪŋgəprɪnt] *n* Fingerabdruck *m* ♦ *vt* Fingerabdrücke abnehmen +*dat*.
**fingerstall** ['fɪŋgəstɔːl] *n* Fingerling *m*.
**fingertip** ['fɪŋgətɪp] *n* Fingerspitze *f*; **to have sth at one's** ~**s** (*to hand*) etw parat haben; (*know well*) etw aus dem Effeff kennen (*inf*).
**finicky** ['fɪnɪkɪ] *adj* pingelig.
**finish** ['fɪnɪʃ] *n* Schluß *m*, Ende *nt*; (*SPORT*) Finish *nt*; (*polish etc*) Verarbeitung *f* ♦ *vt* fertig sein mit; (*work*) erledigen; (*book*) auslesen; (*use up*) aufbrauchen ♦ *vi* enden; (*person*) fertig sein; **to** ~ **doing sth** mit etw fertig werden; **to** ~ **third** als dritter durchs Ziel gehen; **to have** ~**ed with sth** mit etw fertig sein; **she's** ~**ed with him** sie hat mit ihm Schluß gemacht.
▶**finish off** *vt* fertigmachen; (*kill*) den Gnadenstoß geben.
▶**finish up** *vt* (*food*) aufessen; (*drink*) austrinken ♦ *vi* (*end up*) landen.
**finished** ['fɪnɪʃt] *adj* fertig; (*performance*) ausgereift; (*inf: tired*) erledigt.
**finishing line** ['fɪnɪʃɪŋ-] *n* Ziellinie *f*.
**finishing school** *n* höhere Mädchenschule *f* (*in der auch Etikette und gesellschaftliches Verhalten gelehrt wird*).
**finishing touches** *npl:* **the** ~ der letzte Schliff.
**finite** ['faɪnaɪt] *adj* begrenzt; (*verb*) finit.
**Finland** ['fɪnlənd] *n* Finnland *nt*.
**Finn** [fɪn] *n* Finne *m*, Finnin *f*.
**Finnish** ['fɪnɪʃ] *adj* finnisch ♦ *n* (*LING*) Finnisch *nt*.
**fiord** [fjɔːd] *n* = **fjord.**
**fir** [fəː*] *n* Tanne *f*.
**fire** ['faɪə*] *n* Feuer *nt*; (*in hearth*) (Kamin)feuer *nt*; (*accidental fire*) Brand *m* ♦ *vt* abschießen; (*imagination*) beflügeln; (*enthusiasm*) befeuern; (*inf: dismiss*) feuern ♦ *vi* feuern, schießen; **to** ~ **a gun** ein Gewehr abschießen; **to be on** ~ brennen; **to set** ~ **to sth, set sth on** ~ etw anzünden; **insured against** ~ feuerversichert; **electric/gas** ~

Elektro-/Gasofen *m*; **to come/be under**
~ **(from)** unter Beschuß (von) geraten/
stehen.

**fire alarm** *n* Feuermelder *m*.

**firearm** ['faɪərɑːm] *n* Feuerwaffe *f*,
Schußwaffe *f*.

**fire brigade** *n* Feuerwehr *f*.

**fire chief** *n* Branddirektor *m*.

**fire department** (*US*) *n* Feuerwehr *f*.

**fire door** *n* Feuertür *f*.

**fire drill** *n* Probealarm *m*.

**fire engine** *n* Feuerwehrauto *nt*.

**fire escape** *n* Feuertreppe *f*.

**fire-extinguisher** ['faɪərɪk'stɪŋgwɪʃə*] *n*
Feuerlöscher *m*.

**fireguard** ['faɪəgɑːd] (*BRIT*) *n* (Schutz)gitter *nt*
(*vor dem Kamin*).

**fire hazard** *n*: **that's a** ~ das ist
feuergefährlich.

**fire hydrant** *n* Hydrant *m*.

**fire insurance** *n* Feuerversicherung *f*.

**fireman** ['faɪəmən] (*irreg: like* **man**) *n*
Feuerwehrmann *m*.

**fireplace** ['faɪəpleɪs] *n* Kamin *m*.

**fireplug** ['faɪəplʌg] (*US*) *n* = **fire hydrant**.

**fire practice** *n* = **fire drill**.

**fireproof** ['faɪəpruːf] *adj* feuerfest.

**fire regulations** *npl* Brandschutz-
bestimmungen *pl*.

**fire screen** *n* Ofenschirm *m*.

**fireside** ['faɪəsaɪd] *n*: **by the** ~ am Kamin.

**fire station** *n* Feuerwache *f*.

**firewood** ['faɪəwʊd] *n* Brennholz *nt*.

**fireworks** ['faɪəwɜːks] *npl* Feuerwerkskörper
*pl*; (*display*) Feuerwerk *nt*.

**firing line** ['faɪərɪŋ-] *n* Feuerlinie *f*, Schußlinie
*f*; **to be in the** ~ (*fig*) in der Schußlinie sein.

**firing squad** *n* Exekutionskommando *nt*.

**firm** [fɜːm] *adj* fest; (*mattress*) hart; (*measures*)
durchgreifend ♦ *n* Firma *f*; **to be a**
~ **believer in sth** fest von etw überzeugt
sein.

**firmly** ['fɜːmlɪ] *adv* (*see adj*) fest; hart;
(*definitely*) entschlossen.

**firmness** ['fɜːmnɪs] *n* (*see adj*) Festigkeit *f*;
Härte *f*; (*definiteness*) Entschlossenheit *f*.

**first** [fɜːst] *adj* erste(r, s) ♦ *adv* als erste(r, s);
(*before other things*) zuerst; (*when listing
reasons etc*) erstens; (*for the first time*) zum
ersten Mal ♦ *n* Erste(r, s); (*AUT: also:* ~ **gear**)
der erste Gang; (*BRIT: SCOL*) ≈ Eins *f*; **the**
~ **of January** der erste Januar; **at** ~ zuerst,
zunächst; ~ **of all** vor allem; **in the**
~ **instance** zuerst *or* zunächst einmal; **I'll do
it** ~ **thing (tomorrow)** ich werde es
(morgen) als erstes tun; **from the very** ~
gleich von Anfang an.

**first aid** *n* Erste Hilfe *f*.

**first-aid kit** [fɜːst'eɪd-] *n* Erste-Hilfe-
Ausrüstung *f*.

**first-class** ['fɜːst'klɑːs] *adj* erstklassig;
(*carriage, ticket*) Erste(r)-Klasse-; (*post*)

bevorzugt befördert ♦ *adv* (*travel, send*)
erster Klasse.

**first-hand** ['fɜːst'hænd] *adj* aus erster Hand.

**first lady** (*US*) *n* First Lady *f*; **the** ~ **of jazz** die
Königin des Jazz.

**firstly** ['fɜːstlɪ] *adv* erstens, zunächst einmal.

**first name** *n* Vorname *m*.

**first night** *n* Premiere *f*.

**first-rate** ['fɜːst'reɪt] *adj* erstklassig.

**first-time buyer** ['fɜːsttaɪm-] *n* jd, der zum
ersten Mal ein Haus/eine Wohnung kauft.

**fir tree** *n* Tannenbaum *m*.

**FIS** (*BRIT*) *n abbr* (= *Family Income Supplement*)
*Beihilfe für einkommensschwache
Familien.*

**fiscal** ['fɪskl] *adj* (*year*) Steuer-; (*policies*)
Finanz-.

**fish** [fɪʃ] *n inv* Fisch *m* ♦ *vt* (*area*) fischen in
+*dat*; (*river*) angeln in +*dat* ♦ *vi* fischen; (*as
sport, hobby*) angeln; **to go** ~**ing** fischen/
angeln gehen.

▶**fish out** *vt* herausfischen.

**fish bone** *n* (Fisch)gräte *f*.

**fish cake** *n* Fischfrikadelle *f*.

**fisherman** ['fɪʃəmən] (*irreg: like* **man**) *n* Fischer
*m*.

**fishery** ['fɪʃərɪ] *n* Fischereigebiet *nt*.

**fish factory** (*BRIT*) *n* Fischfabrik *f*.

**fish farm** *n* Fischzucht(anlage) *f*.

**fishfingers** [fɪʃ'fɪŋgəz] (*BRIT*) *npl*
Fischstäbchen *pl*.

**fish-hook** ['fɪʃhʊk] *n* Angelhaken *m*.

**fishing boat** ['fɪʃɪŋ-] *n* Fischerboot *nt*.

**fishing line** *n* Angelschnur *f*.

**fishing net** *n* Fischnetz *nt*.

**fishing rod** *n* Angelrute *f*.

**fishing tackle** *n* Angelgeräte *pl*.

**fish market** *n* Fischmarkt *m*.

**fishmonger** ['fɪʃmʌŋgə*] (*esp BRIT*) *n*
Fischhändler(in) *m(f)*.

**fishmonger's (shop)** ['fɪʃmʌŋgəz-] (*esp BRIT*)
*n* Fischgeschäft *nt*.

**fish slice** (*BRIT*) *n* Fischvorlegemesser *nt*.

**fish sticks** (*US*) *npl* = **fishfingers**.

**fishy** ['fɪʃɪ] (*inf*) *adj* verdächtig, faul.

**fission** ['fɪʃən] *n* Spaltung *f*; **atomic** *or* **nuclear**
~ Atomspaltung *f*, Kernspaltung *f*.

**fissure** ['fɪʃə*] *n* Riß *m*, Spalte *f*.

**fist** [fɪst] *n* Faust *f*.

**fist fight** *n* Faustkampf *m*.

**fit** [fɪt] *adj* geeignet; (*healthy*) gesund; (*SPORT*)
fit ♦ *vt* passen +*dat*; (*adjust*) anpassen; (*match*)
entsprechen +*dat*; (*be suitable for*) passen auf
+*acc*; (*put in*) einbauen; (*attach*) anbringen;
(*equip*) ausstatten ♦ *vi* passen; (*parts*)
zusammenpassen; (*in space, gap*)
hineinpassen ♦ *n* (*MED*) Anfall *m*; **to** ~ **the
description** der Beschreibung entsprechen;
~ **to bereit zu**; ~ **to eat** eßbar; ~ **to drink**
trinkbar; **to be** ~ **to keep** es wert sein,
aufbewahrt zu werden; ~ **for** geeignet für;
~ **for work** arbeitsfähig; **to keep** ~ sich fit

halten; **do as you think** *or* **see** ~ tun Sie, was Sie für richtig halten; **a** ~ **of anger** ein Wutanfall *m*; **a** ~ **of pride** eine Anwandlung von Stolz; **to have a** ~ einen Anfall haben; (*inf, fig*) einen Anfall kriegen; **this dress is a good** ~ dieses Kleid sitzt *or* paßt gut; **by** ~**s and starts** unregelmäßig.

▶**fit in** *vi* (*person*) sich einfügen; (*object*) hineinpassen ♦ *vt* (*fig: appointment*) unterbringen, einschieben; (*visitor*) Zeit finden für; **to** ~ **in with sb's plans** sich mit jds Plänen vereinbaren lassen.

**fitful** ['fɪtful] *adj* unruhig.

**fitment** ['fɪtmənt] *n* Einrichtungsgegenstand *m*.

**fitness** ['fɪtnɪs] *n* Gesundheit *f*; (*SPORT*) Fitneß *f*.

**fitted carpet** ['fɪtɪd-] *n* Teppichboden *m*.

**fitted cupboards** *npl* Einbauschränke *pl*.

**fitted kitchen** (*BRIT*) *n* Einbauküche *f*.

**fitter** ['fɪtə*] *n* Monteur *m*; (*for machines*) (Maschinen)schlosser *m*.

**fitting** ['fɪtɪŋ] *adj* passend; (*thanks*) gebührend ♦ *n* (*of dress*) Anprobe *f*; (*of piece of equipment*) Installation *f*; **fittings** *npl* Ausstattung *f*.

**fitting room** *n* Anprobe(kabine) *f*.

**five** [faɪv] *num* fünf.

**five-day week** ['faɪvdeɪ-] *n* Fünftagewoche *f*.

**fiver** ['faɪvə*] (*inf*) *n* (*BRIT*) Fünfpfundschein *m*; (*US*) Fünfdollarschein *m*.

**fix** [fɪks] *vt* (*attach*) befestigen; (*arrange*) festsetzen, festlegen; (*mend*) reparieren; (*meal, drink*) machen; (*inf*) manipulieren ♦ *n*: **to be in a** ~ in der Patsche *or* Klemme sitzen; **to** ~ **sth to/on sth** etw an/auf etw *dat* befestigen; **to** ~ **one's eyes/attention on** seinen Blick/seine Aufmerksamkeit richten auf +*acc*; **the fight was a** ~ (*inf*) der Kampf war eine abgekartete Sache.

▶**fix up** *vt* arrangieren; **to** ~ **sb up with sth** jdm etw besorgen.

**fixation** [fɪk'seɪʃən] *n* Fixierung *f*.

**fixative** ['fɪksətɪv] *n* Fixativ *nt*.

**fixed** [fɪkst] *adj* fest; (*ideas*) fix; (*smile*) starr; ~ **charge** Pauschale *f*; **how are you** ~ **for money?** wie sieht es bei dir mit dem Geld aus?

**fixed assets** *npl* Anlagevermögen *nt*.

**fixture** ['fɪkstʃə*] *n* Ausstattungsgegenstand *m*; (*FOOTBALL etc*) Spiel *nt*; (*ATHLETICS etc*) Veranstaltung *f*.

**fizz** [fɪz] *vi* sprudeln; (*firework*) zischen.

**fizzle out** ['fɪzl-] *vi* (*plan*) im Sande verlaufen; (*interest*) sich verlieren.

**fizzy** ['fɪzɪ] *adj* sprudelnd.

**fjord** [fjɔːd] *n* Fjord *m*.

**FL, Fla.** (*US*) *abbr* (*POST*: = *Florida*).

**flabbergasted** ['flæbəgɑːstɪd] *adj* verblüfft.

**flabby** ['flæbɪ] *adj* schwammig, wabbelig (*inf*).

**flag** [flæg] *n* Fahne *f*; (*of country*) Flagge *f*; (*for signalling*) Signalflagge *f*; (*also:* ~**stone**) (Stein)platte *f* ♦ *vi* erlahmen; ~ **of convenience** Billigflagge *f*; **to** ~ **down** anhalten.

**flagon** ['flægən] *n* Flasche *f*; (*jug*) Krug *m*.

**flagpole** ['flægpəul] *n* Fahnenstange *f*.

**flagrant** ['fleɪgrənt] *adj* flagrant; (*injustice*) himmelschreiend.

**flagship** ['flægʃɪp] *n* Flaggschiff *nt*.

**flagstone** ['flægstəun] *n* (Stein)platte *f*.

**flag stop** (*US*) *n* Bedarfshaltestelle *f*.

**flair** [fleə*] *n* Talent *nt*; (*style*) Flair *nt*.

**flak** [flæk] *n* Flakfeuer *nt*; **to get a lot of** ~ **(for sth)** (*inf: criticism*) (wegen etw) unter Beschuß geraten.

**flake** [fleɪk] *n* Splitter *m*; (*of snow, soap powder*) Flocke *f* ♦ *vi* (*also:* ~ **off**) abblättern, absplittern.

▶**flake out** (*inf*) *vi* aus den Latschen kippen; (*go to sleep*) einschlafen.

**flaky** ['fleɪkɪ] *adj* brüchig; (*skin*) schuppig.

**flaky pastry** *n* Blätterteig *m*.

**flamboyant** [flæm'bɔɪənt] *adj* extravagant.

**flame** [fleɪm] *n* Flamme *f*; **to burst into** ~**s** in Flammen aufgehen; **an old** ~ (*inf*) eine alte Flamme.

**flaming** ['fleɪmɪŋ] (*inf!*) *adj* verdammt.

**flamingo** [flə'mɪŋgəu] *n* Flamingo *m*.

**flammable** ['flæməbl] *adj* leicht entzündbar.

**flan** [flæn] *n* Kuchen *m*; ~ **case** Tortenboden *m*.

**Flanders** ['flɑːndəz] *n* Flandern *nt*.

**flange** [flændʒ] *n* Flansch *m*.

**flank** [flæŋk] *n* Flanke *f* ♦ *vt* flankieren.

**flannel** ['flænl] *n* Flanell *m*; (*BRIT: also:* **face** ~) Waschlappen *m*; (: *inf*) Geschwafel *nt*; **flannels** *npl* (*trousers*) Flanellhose *f*.

**flannelette** [flænə'lɛt] *n* Baumwollflanell *m*, Biber *m or nt*.

**flap** [flæp] *n* Klappe *f*; (*of envelope*) Lasche *f* ♦ *vt* schlagen mit ♦ *vi* flattern; (*inf: also:* **be in a** ~) in heller Aufregung sein.

**flapjack** ['flæpdʒæk] *n* (*US: pancake*) Pfannkuchen *m*; (*BRIT: biscuit*) Haferkeks *m*.

**flare** [fleə*] *n* Leuchtsignal *nt*; (*in skirt etc*) Weite *f*.

▶**flare up** *vi* auflodern; (*person*) aufbrausen; (*fighting, violence, trouble*) ausbrechen; *see also* **flared**.

**flared** ['fleəd] *adj* (*trousers*) mit Schlag; (*skirt*) ausgestellt.

**flash** [flæʃ] *n* Aufblinken *nt*; (*also:* **news**~) Eilmeldung *f*; (*PHOT*) Blitz *m*, Blitzlicht *nt*; (*US: torch*) Taschenlampe *f* ♦ *vt* aufleuchten lassen; (*news, message*) durchgeben; (*look, smile*) zuwerfen ♦ *vi* aufblinken; (*light on ambulance*) blinken; (*eyes*) blitzen; **in a** ~ im Nu; **quick as a** ~ blitzschnell; ~ **of inspiration** Geistesblitz *m*; **to** ~ **one's headlights** die Lichthupe betätigen; **the thought** ~**ed through his mind** der Gedanke schoß ihm durch den Kopf; **to** ~ **by** *or* **past** vorbeiflitzen (*inf*).

**flashback** ['flæʃbæk] n Rückblende f.
**flashbulb** ['flæʃbʌlb] n Blitzbirne f.
**flash card** n Leselernkarte f.
**flashcube** ['flæʃkjuːb] n Blitzwürfel m.
**flasher** ['flæʃə'] n (AUT) Lichthupe f; (inf: man) Exhibitionist m.
**flashlight** ['flæʃlaɪt] n Blitzlicht nt.
**flash point** n (fig): **to be at** ~ auf dem Siedepunkt sein.
**flashy** ['flæʃɪ] (pej) adj auffällig, protzig.
**flask** [flɑːsk] n Flakon m; (CHEM) Glaskolben m; (also: **vacuum** ~) Thermosflasche ® f.
**flat** [flæt] adj flach; (surface) eben; (tyre) platt; (battery) leer; (beer) schal; (refusal, denial) glatt; (note, voice) zu tief; (rate, fee) Pauschal- ♦ n (BRIT: apartment) Wohnung f; (AUT) (Reifen)panne f; (MUS) Erniedrigungszeichen nt; **to work** ~ **out** auf Hochtouren arbeiten; ~ **rate of pay** Pauschallohn m.
**flat-footed** ['flæt'futɪd] adj: **to be** ~ Plattfüße pl haben.
**flatly** ['flætlɪ] adv (refuse, deny) glatt, kategorisch.
**flatmate** ['flætmeɪt] (BRIT) n Mitbewohner(in) m(f).
**flatness** ['flætnɪs] n Flachheit f.
**flat screen** n Flachbildschirm m.
**flatten** ['flætn] vt (also: ~ **out**) (ein)ebnen; (paper, fabric etc) glätten; (building, city) dem Erdboden gleichmachen; (crop) zu Boden drücken; (inf: person) umhauen; **to** ~ **o.s. against a wall/door** etc sich platt gegen or an eine Wand/Tür etc drücken.
**flatter** ['flætə'] vt schmeicheln +dat.
**flatterer** ['flætərə'] n Schmeichler(in) m(f).
**flattering** ['flætərɪŋ] adj schmeichelhaft; (dress etc) vorteilhaft.
**flattery** ['flætərɪ] n Schmeichelei f.
**flatulence** ['flætjuləns] n Blähungen pl.
**flaunt** [flɔːnt] vt zur Schau stellen, protzen mit.
**flavour**, (US) **flavor** ['fleɪvə'] n Geschmack m; (of ice-cream etc) Geschmacksrichtung f ♦ vt Geschmack verleihen +dat; **to give** or **add** ~ **to** Geschmack verleihen +dat; **music with an African** ~ (fig) Musik mit einer afrikanischen Note; **strawberry-~ed** mit Erdbeergeschmack.
**flavouring** ['fleɪvərɪŋ] n Aroma nt.
**flaw** [flɔː] n Fehler m.
**flawless** ['flɔːlɪs] adj (performance) fehlerlos; (complexion) makellos.
**flax** [flæks] n Flachs m.
**flaxen** ['flæksən] adj (hair) flachsblond.
**flea** [fliː] n Floh m.
**flea market** n Flohmarkt m.
**fleck** [flɛk] n Tupfen m, Punkt m; (of dust) Flöckchen nt; (of mud, paint, colour) Fleck(en) m ♦ vt bespritzen; **brown ~ed with white** braun mit weißen Punkten.
**fled** [flɛd] pt, pp of **flee**.

**fledg(e)ling** ['flɛdʒlɪŋ] n Jungvogel m ♦ adj (inexperienced: actor etc) Nachwuchs-; (newly started: business etc) jung.
**flee** [fliː] (pt, pp **fled**) vt fliehen or flüchten vor +dat; (country) fliehen or flüchten aus ♦ vi fliehen, flüchten.
**fleece** [fliːs] n Schafwolle f; (sheep's coat) Schaffell nt, Vlies nt ♦ vt (inf: cheat) schröpfen.
**fleecy** ['fliːsɪ] adj flauschig; (cloud) Schäfchen-.
**fleet** [fliːt] n Flotte f; (of lorries, cars) Fuhrpark m.
**fleeting** ['fliːtɪŋ] adj flüchtig.
**Flemish** ['flɛmɪʃ] adj flämisch ♦ n (LING) Flämisch nt; **the Flemish** npl die Flamen.
**flesh** [flɛʃ] n Fleisch nt; (of fruit) Fruchtfleisch nt.
▶**flesh out** vt ausgestalten.
**flesh wound** [-wuːnd] n Fleischwunde f.
**flew** [fluː] pt of **fly**.
**flex** [flɛks] n Kabel nt ♦ vt beugen; (muscles) spielen lassen.
**flexibility** [flɛksɪ'bɪlɪtɪ] n (see adj) Flexibilität f; Biegsamkeit f.
**flexible** ['flɛksəbl] adj flexibel; (material) biegsam.
**flexitime** ['flɛksɪtaɪm] n gleitende Arbeitszeit f, Gleitzeit f.
**flick** [flɪk] n (of finger) Schnipsen nt; (of hand) Wischen nt; (of whip) Schnalzen nt; (of towel etc) Schlagen nt; (of switch) Knipsen nt ♦ vt schnipsen; (with hand) wischen; (whip) knallen mit; (switch) knipsen; **flicks** (inf) npl Kino nt; **to** ~ **a towel at sb** mit einem Handtuch nach jdm schlagen.
▶**flick through** vt fus durchblättern.
**flicker** ['flɪkə'] vi flackern; (eyelids) zucken ♦ n Flackern nt; (of pain, fear) Aufflackern nt; (of smile) Anflug m; (of eyelid) Zucken nt.
**flick knife** (BRIT) n Klappmesser nt.
**flier** ['flaɪə'] n Flieger(in) m(f).
**flight** [flaɪt] n Flug m; (escape) Flucht f; (also: ~ **of steps**) Treppe f; **to take** ~ die Flucht ergreifen; **to put to** ~ in die Flucht schlagen.
**flight attendant** (US) n Flugbegleiter(in) m(f).
**flight crew** n Flugbesatzung f.
**flight deck** n (AVIAT) Cockpit nt; (NAUT) Flugdeck nt.
**flight path** n Flugbahn f.
**flight recorder** n Flugschreiber m.
**flimsy** ['flɪmzɪ] adj leicht, dünn; (building) leicht gebaut; (excuse) fadenscheinig; (evidence) nicht stichhaltig.
**flinch** [flɪntʃ] vi zusammenzucken; **to** ~ **from** zurückschrecken vor +dat.
**fling** [flɪŋ] (pt, pp **flung**) vt schleudern; (arms) werfen; (oneself) stürzen ♦ n (flüchtige) Affäre f.
**flint** [flɪnt] n Feuerstein m.

**flip** [flɪp] vt (switch) knipsen; (coin) werfen; (US: pancake) umdrehen ♦ vi: **to ~ for sth** (US) um etw mit einer Münze knobeln.
►**flip through** vt fus durchblättern; (records etc) durchgehen.
**flippant** ['flɪpənt] adj leichtfertig.
**flipper** ['flɪpə'] n Flosse f; (for swimming) (Schwimm)flosse f.
**flip side** n (of record) B-Seite f.
**flirt** [flɜːt] vi flirten; (with idea) liebäugeln ♦ n: **he/she is a ~** er/sie flirtet gern.
**flirtation** [flɜː'teɪʃən] n Flirt m.
**flit** [flɪt] vi flitzen; (expression, smile) huschen.
**float** [fləut] n Schwimmkork m; (for fishing) Schwimmer m; (lorry) Festwagen m; (money) Wechselgeld nt ♦ vi schwimmen; (swimmer) treiben; (through air) schweben; (currency) floaten ♦ vt (currency) freigeben, floaten lassen; (company) gründen; (idea, plan) in den Raum stellen.
►**float around** vi im Umlauf sein; (person) herumschweben (inf); (object) herumfliegen (inf).
**flock** [flɔk] n Herde f; (of birds) Schwarm m ♦ vi: **to ~ to** (place) strömen nach; (event) in Scharen kommen zu.
**floe** [fləu] n (also: **ice ~**) Eisscholle f.
**flog** [flɔg] vt auspeitschen; (inf: sell) verscherbeln.
**flood** [flʌd] n Überschwemmung f; (of letters, imports etc) Flut f ♦ vt überschwemmen; (AUT) absaufen lassen (inf) ♦ vi überschwemmt werden; **to be in ~** Hochwasser führen; **to ~ the market** den Markt überschwemmen; **to ~ into Hungary/the square/the palace** nach Ungarn/auf den Platz/in den Palast strömen.
**flooding** ['flʌdɪŋ] n Überschwemmung f.
**floodlight** ['flʌdlaɪt] n Flutlicht nt ♦ vt (mit Flutlicht) beleuchten; (building) anstrahlen.
**floodlit** ['flʌdlɪt] pt, pp of **floodlight** ♦ adj (mit Flutlicht) beleuchtet; (building) angestrahlt.
**flood tide** n Flut f.
**floodwater** ['flʌdwɔːtə'] n Hochwasser nt.
**floor** [flɔː'] n (Fuß)boden m; (storey) Stock nt; (of sea, valley) Boden m ♦ vt (subj: blow) zu Boden werfen; (: question, remark) die Sprache verschlagen +dat; **on the ~** auf dem Boden; **ground** (BRIT) **or first** (US) **~** Erdgeschoß nt; **first** (BRIT) **or second** (US) **~** erster Stock m; **top ~** oberstes Stockwerk nt; **to have the ~** (speaker: at meeting) das Wort haben.
**floorboard** ['flɔːbɔːd] n Diele f.
**flooring** ['flɔːrɪŋ] n (Fuß)boden m; (covering) Fußbodenbelag m.
**floor lamp** (US) n Stehlampe f.
**floor show** n Show f, Vorstellung f.
**floorwalker** ['flɔːwɔːkə'] (esp US) n Ladenaufsicht f.
**floozy** ['fluːzɪ] (inf) n Flittchen nt.

**flop** [flɔp] n Reinfall m ♦ vi (play, book) durchfallen; (fall) sich fallenlassen; (scheme) ein Reinfall sein.
**floppy** ['flɔpɪ] adj schlaff, schlapp ♦ n (also: **~ disk**) Diskette f, Floppy disk f; **~ hat** Schlapphut m.
**floppy disk** n Diskette f, Floppy disk f.
**flora** ['flɔːrə] n Flora f.
**floral** ['flɔːrl] adj geblümt.
**Florence** ['flɔrəns] n Florenz nt.
**Florentine** ['flɔrəntaɪn] adj florentinisch.
**florid** ['flɔrɪd] adj (style) blumig; (complexion) kräftig.
**florist** ['flɔrɪst] n Blumenhändler(in) m(f).
**florist's (shop)** ['flɔrɪsts-] n Blumengeschäft nt.
**flotation** [fləu'teɪʃən] n (of shares) Auflegung f; (of company) Umwandlung f in eine Aktiengesellschaft.
**flotsam** ['flɔtsəm] n (also: **~ and jetsam**) Strandgut nt; (floating) Treibgut nt.
**flounce** [flauns] n Volant m.
►**flounce out** vi hinausstolzieren.
**flounder** ['flaundə'] vi sich abstrampeln; (fig: speaker) ins Schwimmen kommen; (economy) in Schwierigkeiten geraten ♦ n Flunder f.
**flour** ['flauə'] n Mehl nt.
**flourish** ['flʌrɪʃ] vi gedeihen; (business) blühen, florieren ♦ vt schwenken ♦ n (in writing) Schnörkel m; (bold gesture): **with a ~** mit einer schwungvollen Bewegung.
**flourishing** ['flʌrɪʃɪŋ] adj gutgehend, florierend.
**flout** [flaut] vt sich hinwegsetzen über +acc.
**flow** [fləu] n Fluß m; (of sea) Flut f ♦ vi fließen; (clothes, hair) wallen.
**flow chart** n Flußdiagramm nt.
**flow diagram** n = **flow chart**.
**flower** ['flauə'] n Blume f; (blossom) Blüte f ♦ vi blühen; **to be in ~** blühen.
**flowerbed** ['flauəbed] n Blumenbeet nt.
**flowerpot** ['flauəpɔt] n Blumentopf m.
**flowery** ['flauərɪ] adj blumig; (pattern) Blumen-.
**flown** [fləun] pp of **fly**.
**flu** [fluː] n Grippe f.
**fluctuate** ['flʌktjueɪt] vi schwanken; (opinions, attitudes) sich ändern.
**fluctuation** [flʌktju'eɪʃən] n: **~ (in)** Schwankung f (+gen).
**flue** [fluː] n Rauchfang m, Rauchabzug m.
**fluency** ['fluːənsɪ] n Flüssigkeit f; **his ~ in German** sein flüssiges Deutsch.
**fluent** ['fluːənt] adj flüssig; **he speaks ~ German, he's ~ in German** er spricht fließend Deutsch.
**fluently** ['fluːəntlɪ] adv flüssig; (speak a language) fließend.
**fluff** [flʌf] n Fussel m; (fur) Flaum m ♦ vt (inf: do badly) verpatzen; (also: **~ out**) aufplustern.
**fluffy** ['flʌfɪ] adj flaumig; (jacket etc) weich,

kuschelig; ~ **toy** Kuscheltier *nt.*

**fluid** ['fluːɪd] *adj* fließend; (*situation,
arrangement*) unklar ♦ *n* Flüssigkeit *f.*

**fluid ounce** (*BRIT*) *n* flüssige Unze *f* (= *28 ml*).

**fluke** [fluːk] (*inf*) *n* Glücksfall *m*; **by a** ~ durch
einen glücklichen Zufall.

**flummox** ['flʌməks] *vt* verwirren,
durcheinanderbringen.

**flung** [flʌŋ] *pt, pp of* **fling.**

**flunky** ['flʌŋkɪ] *n* Lakai *m.*

**fluorescent** [fluə'rɛsnt] *adj* fluoreszierend;
(*paint*) Leucht-; (*light*) Neon-.

**fluoride** ['fluəraɪd] *n* Fluorid *nt.*

**fluorine** ['fluəriːn] *n* Fluor *nt.*

**flurry** ['flʌrɪ] *n* (*of snow*) Gestöber *nt*; **a** ~ **of
activity/excitement** hektische Aktivität/
Aufregung.

**flush** [flʌʃ] *n* Röte *f*; (*fig: of beauty etc*) Blüte *f*
♦ *vt* (durch)spülen, (aus)spülen ♦ *vi* erröten
♦ *adj:* ~ **with** auf gleicher Ebene mit;
~ **against** direkt an +*dat*; **in the first** ~ **of
youth** in der ersten Jugendblüte; **in the first**
~ **of freedom** im ersten Freiheitstaumel;
**hot** ~**es** (*BRIT*) Hitzewallungen *pl*; **to** ~ **the
toilet** spülen, die Wasserspülung betätigen.
►**flush out** *vt* aufstöbern.

**flushed** [flʌʃt] *adj* rot.

**fluster** ['flʌstə*] *n*: **in a** ~ nervös; (*confused*)
durcheinander ♦ *vt* nervös machen;
(*confuse*) durcheinanderbringen.

**flustered** ['flʌstəd] *adj* nervös; (*confused*)
durcheinander.

**flute** [fluːt] *n* Querflöte *f.*

**fluted** ['fluːtɪd] *adj* gerillt; (*column*) kanneliert.

**flutter** ['flʌtə*] *n* Flattern *nt*; (*of panic, nerves*)
kurzer Anfall *m*; (*of excitement*) Beben *nt* ♦ *vi*
flattern; (*person*) tänzeln; **to have a** ~ (*BRIT:
inf: gamble*) sein Glück (beim Wetten)
versuchen.

**flux** [flʌks] *n*: **in a state of** ~ im Fluß.

**fly** [flaɪ] (*pt* flew, *pp* flown) *n* Fliege *f*; (*on
trousers: also*: **flies**) (Hosen)schlitz *m* ♦ *vt*
fliegen; (*kite*) steigen lassen ♦ *vi* fliegen;
(*escape*) fliehen; (*flag*) wehen; **to** ~ **open**
auffliegen; **to** ~ **off the handle** an die Decke
gehen (*inf*); **pieces of metal went** ~**ing
everywhere** überall flogen Metallteile
herum; **she came** ~**ing into the room** sie
kam ins Zimmer gesaust; **her glasses flew
off** die Brille flog ihr aus dem Gesicht.
►**fly away** *vi* wegfliegen.
►**fly in** *vi* einfliegen; **he flew in yesterday** er
ist gestern mit dem Flugzeug gekommen.
►**fly off** *vi* = **fly away.**
►**fly out** *vi* ausfliegen; **he flew out yesterday**
er ist gestern hingeflogen.

**fly-fishing** ['flaɪfɪʃɪŋ] *n* Fliegenfischen *n.*

**flying** ['flaɪɪŋ] *n* Fliegen *nt* ♦ *adj:* **a** ~ **visit** ein
Blitzbesuch *m*; **he doesn't like** ~ er fliegt
nicht gerne; **with** ~ **colours** mit fliegenden
Fahnen.

**flying buttress** *n* Strebebogen *m.*

**flying picket** *n* mobiler Streikposten *m.*

**flying saucer** *n* fliegende Untertasse *f.*

**flying squad** *n* mobiles Einsatzkommando *nt.*

**flying start** *n*: **to get off to a** ~ (*SPORT*)
hervorragend wegkommen; (*fig*) einen
glänzenden Start haben.

**flyleaf** ['flaɪliːf] *n* Vorsatzblatt *nt.*

**flyover** ['flaɪəuvə*] *n* (*BRIT*) Überführung *f*;
(*US*) Luftparade *f.*

**fly-past** ['flaɪpɑːst] *n* Luftparade *f.*

**flysheet** ['flaɪʃiːt] *n* (*for tent*) Überzelt *nt.*

**flyweight** ['flaɪweɪt] *n* (*BOXING*)
Fliegengewicht *nt.*

**flywheel** ['flaɪwiːl] *n* Schwungrad *nt.*

**FM** *abbr* (*BRIT: MIL*) = **field marshal;** (*RADIO:
* = *frequency modulation*) FM, ≈ UKW.

**FMB** (*US*) *n abbr* (= *Federal Maritime Board*)
*Dachausschuß der Handelsmarine.*

**FMCS** (*US*) *n abbr* (= *Federal Mediation and
Conciliation Service*) *Schlichtungsstelle für
Arbeitskonflikte.*

**FO** (*BRIT*) *n abbr* = **Foreign Office.**

**foal** [fəul] *n* Fohlen *nt.*

**foam** [fəum] *n* Schaum *m*; (*also*: ~ **rubber**)
Schaumgummi *m* ♦ *vi* schäumen.

**fob** [fɔb] *vt*: **to** ~ **sb off** jdn abspeisen ♦ *n* (*also:
* **watch** ~) Uhrkette *f.*

**f.o.b.** *abbr* (*COMM*: = *free on board*) frei Schiff.

**foc** (*BRIT*) *abbr* (*COMM*: = *free of charge*) gratis.

**focal point** ['fəukl-] *n* Mittelpunkt *m*; (*of
camera, telescope etc*) Brennpunkt *m.*

**focus** ['fəukəs] (*pl* ~**es**) *n* Brennpunkt *m*; (*of
storm*) Zentrum *nt* ♦ *vt* einstellen; (*light rays*)
bündeln ♦ *vi*: **to** ~ (**on**) (*with camera*) klar *or*
scharf einstellen +*acc*; (*person*) sich
konzentrieren (auf +*acc*); **in/out of** ~ (*camera
etc*) scharf/unscharf eingestellt;
(*photograph*) scharf/unscharf.

**fodder** ['fɔdə*] *n* Futter *nt.*

**FoE** *n abbr* (= *Friends of the Earth*)
*Umweltschutzorganisation.*

**foe** [fəu] *n* Feind(in) *m(f).*

**foetus,** (*US*) **fetus** ['fiːtəs] *n* Fötus *m.*

**fog** [fɔg] *n* Nebel *m.*

**fogbound** ['fɔgbaund] *adj* (*airport*) wegen
Nebel geschlossen.

**foggy** ['fɔgɪ] *adj* neb(e)lig.

**fog lamp,** (*US*) **fog light** *n* (*AUT*)
Nebelscheinwerfer *m.*

**foible** ['fɔɪbl] *n* Eigenheit *f.*

**foil** [fɔɪl] *vt* vereiteln ♦ *n* Folie *f*; (*complement*)
Kontrast *m*; (*FENCING*) Florett *nt*; **to act as a**
~ **to** einen Kontrast darstellen zu.

**foist** [fɔɪst] *vt*: **to** ~ **sth on sb** (*goods*) jdm etw
andrehen; (*task*) etw an jdn abschieben;
(*ideas, views*) jdm etw aufzwingen.

**fold** [fəuld] *n* Falte *f*; (*AGR*) Pferch *m*; (*fig*)
Schoß *m* ♦ *vt* (zusammen)falten; (*arms*)
verschränken ♦ *vi* (*business*) eingehen (*inf*).
►**fold up** *vi* sich zusammenfalten lassen;
(*bed, table*) sich zusammenklappen lassen;
(*business*) eingehen (*inf*) ♦ *vt*

zusammenfalten.
**folder** ['fəuldə*] n Aktenmappe f; (binder)
Hefter m; (brochure) Informationsblatt nt.
**folding** ['fəuldɪŋ] adj (chair, bed) Klapp-.
**foliage** ['fəulɪdʒ] n Laubwerk nt.
**folk** [fəuk] npl Leute pl ♦ cpd Volks-; **my ~s**
(parents) meine alten Herrschaften.
**folklore** ['fəuklɔ:*] n Folklore f.
**folk music** n Volksmusik f; (contemporary)
Folk m.
**folk song** n Volkslied nt; (contemporary)
Folksong m.
**follow** ['fɒləu] vt folgen +dat; (with eyes)
verfolgen; (advice, instructions) befolgen ♦ vi
folgen; **to ~ in sb's footsteps** in jds
Fußstapfen acc treten; **I don't quite ~ you**
ich kann Ihnen nicht ganz folgen; **it ~s that**
daraus folgt, daß; **to ~ suit** (fig) jds Beispiel
dat folgen.
►**follow on** vi (continue): **to ~ on from**
aufbauen auf +dat.
►**follow out** vt (idea, plan) zu Ende verfolgen.
►**follow through** vt = follow out.
►**follow up** vt nachgehen +dat; (offer)
aufgreifen; (case) weiterverfolgen.
**follower** ['fɒləuə*] n Anhänger(in) m(f).
**following** ['fɒləuɪŋ] adj folgend ♦ n
Anhängerschaft f.
**follow-up** ['fɒləuʌp] n Weiterführung f ♦ adj:
**~ treatment** Nachbehandlung f.
**folly** ['fɒlɪ] n Torheit f; (building) exzentrisches
Bauwerk nt.
**fond** [fɒnd] adj liebevoll; (memory) lieb;
(hopes, dreams) töricht; **to be ~ of** mögen;
**she's ~ of swimming** sie schwimmt gerne.
**fondle** ['fɒndl] vt streicheln.
**fondly** ['fɒndlɪ] adv liebevoll; (naïvely)
törichterweise; **he ~ believed that ...** er war
so naiv zu glauben, daß ...
**fondness** ['fɒndnɪs] n (for things) Vorliebe f;
(for people) Zuneigung f; **a special ~ for** eine
besondere Vorliebe für/Zuneigung zu.
**font** [fɒnt] n Taufbecken nt; (TYP) Schrift f.
**food** [fu:d] n Essen nt; (for animals) Futter nt;
(nourishment) Nahrung f; (groceries)
Lebensmittel pl.
**food chain** n Nahrungskette f.
**food mixer** n Küchenmixer m.
**food poisoning** n Lebensmittelvergiftung f.
**food processor** n Küchenmaschine f.
**food stamp** n Lebensmittelmarke f.
**foodstuffs** ['fu:dstʌfs] npl Lebensmittel pl.
**fool** [fu:l] n Dummkopf m; (CULIN)
Sahnespeise aus Obstpüree ♦ vt
hereinlegen, täuschen ♦ vi herumalbern; **to
make a ~ of sb** jdn lächerlich machen;
(trick) jdn hereinlegen; **to make a ~ of o.s.**
sich blamieren; **you can't ~ me** du kannst
mich nicht zum Narren halten.
►**fool about** (pej) vi herumtrödeln; (behave
foolishly) herumalbern.
►**fool around** vi = fool about.

**foolhardy** ['fu:lhɑ:dɪ] adj tollkühn.
**foolish** ['fu:lɪʃ] adj dumm.
**foolishly** ['fu:lɪʃlɪ] adv dumm; **~, I forgot ...**
dummerweise habe ich ... vergessen.
**foolishness** ['fu:lɪʃnɪs] n Dummheit f.
**foolproof** ['fu:lpru:f] adj idiotensicher.
**foolscap** ['fu:lskæp] n ≈ Kanzleipapier nt.
**foot** [fut] (pl **feet**) n Fuß m; (of animal) Pfote f
♦ vt (bill) bezahlen; **on ~** zu Fuß; **to find
one's feet** sich eingewöhnen; **to put one's
~ down** (AUT) Gas geben; (say no) ein
Machtwort sprechen.
**footage** ['futɪdʒ] n Filmmaterial nt.
**foot-and-mouth (disease)** [futən'mauθ-] n
Maul- und Klauenseuche f.
**football** ['futbɔ:l] n Fußball m; (US) Football
m, amerikanischer Fußball m.
**footballer** ['futbɔ:lə*] (BRIT) n
Fußballspieler(in) m(f).
**football ground** n Fußballplatz m.
**football match** (BRIT) n Fußballspiel nt.
**football player** n (BRIT) Fußballspieler(in)
m(f); (US) Football-Spieler(in) m(f).

---

**Football Pools**, umgangssprachlich auch **the
pools** genannt, ist das in Großbritannien sehr
beliebte Fußballtoto, bei dem auf die
Ergebnisse der samstäglichen Fußballspiele
gewettet wird. Teilnehmer schicken ihren
ausgefüllten Totoschein vor den Spielen an die
Totogesellschaft und vergleichen nach den
Spielen die Ergebnisse mit ihrem Schein. Die
Gewinne können sehr hoch sein und
gelegentlich Millionen von Pfund betragen.

---

**foot brake** n Fußbremse f.
**footbridge** ['futbrɪdʒ] n Fußgängerbrücke f.
**foothills** ['futhɪlz] npl (Gebirgs)ausläufer pl.
**foothold** ['futhəuld] n Halt m; **to get a ~** Fuß
fassen.
**footing** ['futɪŋ] n Stellung f; (relationship)
Verhältnis nt; **to lose one's ~** den Halt
verlieren; **on an equal ~** auf gleicher
Basis.
**footlights** ['futlaɪts] npl Rampenlicht nt.
**footman** ['futmən] (irreg: like man) n Lakai m.
**footnote** ['futnəut] n Fußnote f.
**footpath** ['futpɑ:θ] n Fußweg m; (in street)
Bürgersteig m.
**footprint** ['futprɪnt] n Fußabdruck m; (of
animal) Spur f.
**footrest** ['futrest] n Fußstütze f.
**Footsie** ['futsɪ] (inf) n = **FTSE 100 Index**.
**footsie** ['futsɪ] (inf) n: **to play ~ with sb** mit
jdm füßeln.
**footsore** ['futsɔ:*] adj: **to be ~** wunde Füße
haben.
**footstep** ['futstep] n Schritt m; (footprint)
Fußabdruck m; **to follow in sb's ~s** in jds
Fußstapfen acc treten.
**footwear** ['futwɛə*] n Schuhe pl, Schuhwerk
nt.

===================================== KEYWORD

**for** [fɔːʳ] *prep* **1** für *+acc*; **is this ~ me?** ist das
für mich?; **the train ~ London** der Zug nach
London; **it's time ~ lunch** es ist Zeit zum
Mittagessen; **what's it ~?** wofür ist das?; **he
works ~ the government/a local firm** er
arbeitet für die Regierung/eine Firma am
Ort; **he's mature ~ his age** er ist reif für
sein Alter; **I sold it ~ £20** ich habe es für
£20 verkauft; **I'm all ~ it** ich bin ganz dafür;
**G ~ George** ≈ G wie Gustav
**2** (*because of*): **~ this reason** aus diesem
Grund; **~ fear of being criticised** aus Angst,
kritisiert zu werden
**3** (*referring to distance*): **there are roadworks
~ 5 km** die Straßenbauarbeiten erstrecken
sich über 5 km; **we walked ~ miles** wir sind
meilenweit gelaufen
**4** (*referring to time*): **he was away ~ 2 years**
er war 2 Jahre lang weg; **I have known her
~ years** ich kenne sie bereits seit Jahren
**5** (*with infinitive clause*): **it is not ~ me to
decide** es liegt nicht an mir, das zu
entscheiden; **~ this to be possible ...** um
dies möglich zu machen, ...
**6** (*in spite of*) trotz *+gen or dat*; **~ all his
complaints, he is very fond of her** trotz
seiner vielen Klagen mag er sie sehr
♦ *conj* (*form: since, as*) denn; **she was very
angry, ~ he was late again** sie war sehr
böse, denn er kam wieder zu spät.

**f.o.r.** *abbr* (*COMM: = free on rail*) frei Bahn.
**forage** ['fɔrɪdʒ] *n* Futter *nt* ♦ *vi* herumstöbern;
**to ~** (**for food**) nach Futter suchen.
**forage cap** *n* Schiffmütze *nt*.
**foray** ['fɔreɪ] *n* (Raub)überfall *m*.
**forbad(e)** [fə'bæd] *pt of* **forbid**.
**forbearing** [fɔː'bɛərɪŋ] *adj* geduldig.
**forbid** [fə'bɪd] (*pt* **forbade**, *pp* **forbidden**) *vt*
verbieten; **to ~ sb to do sth** jdm verbieten,
etw zu tun.
**forbidden** [fə'bɪdn] *pp of* **forbid** ♦ *adj* verboten.
**forbidding** [fə'bɪdɪŋ] *adj* (*look*) streng;
(*prospect*) grauenhaft.
**force** [fɔːs] *n* Kraft *f*; (*violence*) Gewalt *f*; (*of
blow, impact*) Wucht *f*; (*influence*) Macht *f* ♦ *vt*
zwingen; (*push*) drücken; (: *person*)
drängen; (*lock, door*) aufbrechen; **the Forces**
(*BRIT*) *npl* die Streitkräfte *pl*; **in ~** (*law etc*)
geltend; (*people: arrive etc*) zahlreich; **to
come into ~** in Kraft treten; **to join ~s** sich
zusammentun; **a ~ 5 wind** Windstärke 5;
**the sales ~** das Verkaufspersonal; **to
~ o.s./sb to do sth** sich/jdn zwingen, etw zu
tun.
►**force back** *vt* zurückdrängen; (*tears*)
unterdrücken.
►**force down** *vt* (*food*) hinunterwürgen (*inf*).
**forced** [fɔːst] *adj* gezwungen; **~ labour**
Zwangsarbeit *f*; **~ landing** Notlandung *f*.

**force-feed** ['fɔːsfiːd] *vt* zwangsernähren;
(*animal*) stopfen.
**forceful** ['fɔːsful] *adj* energisch; (*attack*)
wirkungsvoll; (*point*) überzeugend.
**forceps** ['fɔːsɛps] *npl* Zange *f*.
**forcible** ['fɔːsəbl] *adj* gewaltsam; (*reminder,
lesson*) eindringlich.
**forcibly** ['fɔːsəblɪ] *adv* mit Gewalt; (*express*)
eindringlich.
**ford** [fɔːd] *n* Furt *f* ♦ *vt* durchqueren; (*on foot*)
durchwaten.
**fore** [fɔːʳ] *n:* **to come to the ~** ins Blickfeld
geraten.
**forearm** ['fɔːrɑːm] *n* Unterarm *m*.
**forebear** ['fɔːbɛəʳ] *n* Vorfahr(in) *m(f)*, Ahn(e)
*m(f)*.
**foreboding** [fɔː'bəʊdɪŋ] *n* Vorahnung *f*.
**forecast** ['fɔːkɑːst] *n* Prognose *f*; (*of weather*)
(Wetter)vorhersage *f* ♦ *vt* (*irreg: like* **cast**)
voraussagen.
**foreclose** [fɔː'kləʊz] *vt* (*LAW: also: ~ on*)
kündigen; **to ~ sb** (*on loan/mortgage*) jds
Darlehen/Hypothek kündigen.
**foreclosure** [fɔː'kləʊʒəʳ] *n* Zwangsvoll-
streckung *f*.
**forecourt** ['fɔːkɔːt] *n* Vorplatz *m*.
**forefathers** ['fɔːfɑːðəz] *npl* Vorfahren *pl*.
**forefinger** ['fɔːfɪŋgəʳ] *n* Zeigefinger *m*.
**forefront** ['fɔːfrʌnt] *n:* **in the ~ of** an der
Spitze *+gen*.
**forego** [fɔː'gəʊ] (*irreg: like* **go**) *vt* verzichten auf
*+acc*.
**foregoing** ['fɔːgəʊɪŋ] *adj* vorhergehend ♦ *n:*
**the ~** das Vorhergehende.
**foregone** ['fɔːgɒn] *pp of* **forego** ♦ *adj:* **it's a
~ conclusion** steht von vornherein fest.
**foreground** ['fɔːgraʊnd] *n* Vordergrund *m*.
**forehand** ['fɔːhænd] *n* (*TENNIS*) Vorhand *f*.
**forehead** ['fɔrɪd] *n* Stirn *f*.
**foreign** ['fɔrɪn] *adj* ausländisch; (*holiday*) im
Ausland; (*customs, appearance*) fremdartig;
(*trade, policy*) Außen-; (*correspondent*)
Auslands-; (*object, matter*) fremd; **goods
from ~ countries/a ~ country** Waren aus
dem Ausland.
**foreign body** *n* Fremdkörper *m*.
**foreign currency** *n* Devisen *pl*.
**foreigner** ['fɔrɪnəʳ] *n* Ausländer(in) *m(f)*.
**foreign exchange** *n* Devisenhandel *m*;
(*money*) Devisen *pl*.
**foreign exchange market** *n* Devisenmarkt
*m*.
**foreign exchange rate** *n* Devisenkurs *m*.
**foreign investment** *n* Auslandsinvestition *f*.
**foreign minister** *n* Außenminister(in) *m(f)*.
**Foreign Office** (*BRIT*) *n* Außenministerium *nt*.
**Foreign Secretary** (*BRIT*) *n* Außen-
minister(in) *m(f)*.
**foreleg** ['fɔːlɛg] *n* Vorderbein *nt*.
**foreman** ['fɔːmən] *n* (*irreg: like* **man**) *n*
Vorarbeiter *m*; (*of jury*) Obmann *m*.
**foremost** ['fɔːməʊst] *adj* führend ♦ *adv:* **first**

and ~ zunächst, vor allem.
**forename** ['fɔ:neɪm] n Vorname m.
**forensic** [fə'rensɪk] adj (test) forensisch; (medicine) Gerichts-; (expert) Spurensicherungs-.
**foreplay** ['fɔ:pleɪ] n Vorspiel nt.
**forerunner** ['fɔ:rʌnə*] n Vorläufer m.
**foresee** [fɔ:'si:] (irreg: like see) vt vorhersehen.
**foreseeable** [fɔ:'si:əbl] adj vorhersehbar; **in the ~ future** in absehbarer Zeit.
**foreseen** [fɔ:'si:n] pp of foresee.
**foreshadow** [fɔ:'ʃædəu] vt andeuten.
**foreshore** ['fɔ:ʃɔ:*] n Strand m.
**foreshorten** [fɔ:'ʃɔ:tn] vt perspektivisch verkürzen.
**foresight** ['fɔ:saɪt] n Voraussicht f, Weitblick m.
**foreskin** ['fɔ:skɪn] n (ANAT) Vorhaut f.
**forest** ['fɔrɪst] n Wald m.
**forestall** [fɔ:'stɔ:l] vt zuvorkommen +dat; (discussion) im Keim ersticken.
**forestry** ['fɔrɪstrɪ] n Forstwirtschaft f.
**foretaste** ['fɔ:teɪst] n: **a ~ of** ein Vorgeschmack von.
**foretell** [fɔ:'tel] (irreg: like tell) vt vorhersagen.
**forethought** ['fɔ:θɔ:t] n Vorbedacht m.
**foretold** [fɔ:'təuld] pt, pp of foretell.
**forever** [fə'revə*] adv für immer; (endlessly) ewig; (consistently) dauernd, ständig; **you're ~ finding difficulties** du findest ständig or dauernd neue Schwierigkeiten.
**forewarn** [fɔ:'wɔ:n] vt vorwarnen.
**forewent** [fɔ:'went] pt of forego.
**forewoman** ['fɔ:wumən] (irreg: like woman) n Vorarbeiterin f; (of jury) Obmännin f.
**foreword** ['fɔ:wə:d] n Vorwort nt.
**forfeit** ['fɔ:fɪt] n Strafe f, Buße f ♦ vt (right) verwirken; (friendship etc) verlieren; (one's happiness, health) einbüßen.
**forgave** [fə'geɪv] pt of forgive.
**forge** [fɔ:dʒ] n Schmiede f ♦ vt fälschen; (wrought iron) schmieden.
►**forge ahead** vi große or schnelle Fortschritte machen.
**forger** ['fɔ:dʒə*] n Fälscher(in) m(f).
**forgery** ['fɔ:dʒərɪ] n Fälschung f.
**forget** [fə'get] (pt forgot, pp forgotten) vt vergessen ♦ vi es vergessen; **to ~ o.s.** sich vergessen.
**forgetful** [fə'getful] adj vergeßlich; **~ of sth** (of duties etc) nachlässig gegenüber etw.
**forgetfulness** [fə'getfulnɪs] n Vergeßlichkeit f; (oblivion) Vergessenheit f.
**forget-me-not** [fə'getmɪnɔt] n Vergißmeinnicht nt.
**forgive** [fə'gɪv] (pt forgave, pp forgiven) vt verzeihen +dat, vergeben +dat; **to ~ sb for sth** jdm etw verzeihen or vergeben; **to ~ sb for doing sth** jdm verzeihen or vergeben, daß er etw getan hat; **~ me, but ...** entschuldigen Sie, aber ...; **they could be ~n for thinking that ...** es ist verständlich, wenn

sie denken, daß ...
**forgiveness** [fə'gɪvnɪs] n Verzeihung f.
**forgiving** [fə'gɪvɪŋ] adj versöhnlich.
**forgo** [fɔ:'gəu] (pt forwent, pp forgone) vt = forego.
**forgot** [fə'gɔt] pt of forget.
**forgotten** [fə'gɔtn] pp of forget.
**fork** [fɔ:k] n Gabel f; (in road, river, railway) Gabelung f ♦ vi (road) sich gabeln.
►**fork out** (inf) vt, vi (pay) blechen.
**forked** [fɔ:kt] adj (lightning) zickzackförmig.
**fork-lift truck** ['fɔ:klɪft-] n Gabelstapler m.
**forlorn** [fə'lɔ:n] adj verlassen; (person) einsam und verlassen; (attempt) verzweifelt; (hope) schwach.
**form** [fɔ:m] n Form f; (SCOL) Klasse f; (questionnaire) Formular nt ♦ vt formen, gestalten; (queue, organization, group) bilden; (idea, habit) entwickeln; **in the ~ of** in Form von or +gen; **in the ~ of Peter** in Gestalt von Peter; **to be in good ~** gut in Form sein; **in top ~** in Hochform; **on ~** in Form; **to ~ part of sth** Teil von etw sein.
**formal** ['fɔ:məl] adj offiziell; (person, behaviour) förmlich, formell; (occasion, dinner) feierlich; (clothes) Gesellschafts-; (garden) formell angelegt; (ART, PHILOSOPHY) formal; **~ dress** Gesellschaftskleidung f.
**formalities** [fɔ:'mælɪtɪz] npl Formalitäten pl.
**formality** [fɔ:'mælɪtɪ] n Förmlichkeit f; (procedure) Formalität f.
**formalize** ['fɔ:məlaɪz] vt formell machen.
**formally** ['fɔ:məlɪ] adv (see adj) offiziell; förmlich, formell; feierlich; **to be ~ invited** ausdrücklich eingeladen sein.
**format** ['fɔ:mæt] n Format nt; (form, style) Aufmachung f ♦ vt (COMPUT) formatieren.
**formation** [fɔ:'meɪʃən] n Bildung f; (of theory) Entstehung f; (of business) Gründung f; (pattern: of rocks, clouds) Formation f.
**formative** ['fɔ:mətɪv] adj (influence) prägend; (years) entscheidend.
**former** ['fɔ:mə*] adj früher; **the ~ ... the latter ...** erstere(r, s) ... letztere(r, s); **the ~ president** der ehemalige Präsident; **the ~ East Germany** die ehemalige DDR.
**formerly** ['fɔ:məlɪ] adv früher.
**form feed** n (on printer) Papiervorschub m.
**Formica** ® [fɔ:'maɪkə] n Resopal ® nt.
**formidable** ['fɔ:mɪdəbl] adj (task) gewaltig, enorm; (opponent) furchterregend.
**formula** ['fɔ:mjulə] (pl ~e or ~s) n Formel f; **F~ One** (AUT) Formel Eins.
**formulate** ['fɔ:mjuleɪt] vt formulieren.
**fornicate** ['fɔ:nɪkeɪt] vi Unzucht treiben.
**forsake** [fə'seɪk] (pt forsook, pp forsaken) vt im Stich lassen; (belief) aufgeben.
**forsook** [fə'suk] pt of forsake.
**fort** [fɔ:t] n Fort nt; **to hold the ~** die Stellung halten.
**forte** ['fɔ:tɪ] n Stärke f, starke Seite f.

**forth** [fɔːθ] adv aus; **back and ~** hin und her; **to go back and ~** auf und ab gehen; **to bring ~** hervorbringen; **and so ~** und so weiter.

**forthcoming** [fɔːθ'kʌmɪŋ] adj (event) bevorstehend; (person) mitteilsam; **to be ~** (help) erfolgen; (evidence) geliefert werden.

**forthright** ['fɔːθraɪt] adj offen.

**forthwith** ['fɔːθ'wɪθ] adv umgehend.

**fortieth** ['fɔːtɪɪθ] num vierzigste(r, s).

**fortification** [fɔːtɪfɪ'keɪʃən] n Befestigung f, Festungsanlage f.

**fortified wine** ['fɔːtɪfaɪd-] n weinhaltiges Getränk nt (Sherry, Portwein etc).

**fortify** ['fɔːtɪfaɪ] vt (city) befestigen; (person) bestärken; (: subj: food, drink) stärken.

**fortitude** ['fɔːtɪtjuːd] n innere Kraft or Stärke f.

**fortnight** ['fɔːtnaɪt] (BRIT) n vierzehn Tage pl, zwei Wochen pl; **it's a ~ since** ... es ist vierzehn Tage or zwei Wochen her, daß ...

**fortnightly** ['fɔːtnaɪtlɪ] adj vierzehntägig, zweiwöchentlich ♦ adv alle vierzehn Tage, alle zwei Wochen.

**FORTRAN** ['fɔːtræn] n FORTRAN nt.

**fortress** ['fɔːtrɪs] n Festung f.

**fortuitous** [fɔː'tjuːɪtəs] adj zufällig.

**fortunate** ['fɔːtʃənɪt] adj glücklich; **to be ~** Glück haben; **he is ~ to have** ... er kann sich glücklich schätzen, ... zu haben; **it is ~ that** ... es ist ein Glück, daß ...

**fortunately** ['fɔːtʃənɪtlɪ] adv glücklicherweise, zum Glück.

**fortune** ['fɔːtʃən] n Glück nt; (wealth) Vermögen nt; **to make a ~** ein Vermögen machen; **to tell sb's ~** jdm wahrsagen.

**fortune-teller** ['fɔːtʃəntɛlə'] n Wahrsager(in) m(f).

**forty** ['fɔːtɪ] num vierzig.

**forum** ['fɔːrəm] n Forum nt.

**forward** ['fɔːwəd] adj vordere(r, s); (movement) Vorwärts-; (not shy) dreist; (COMM: buying, price) Termin- ♦ adv nach vorn; (movement) vorwärts; (in time) voraus ♦ n (SPORT) Stürmer m ♦ vt (letter etc) nachsenden; (career, plans) voranbringen; **~ planning** Vorausplanung f; **to move ~** vorwärtskommen; **"please ~"** „bitte nachsenden".

**forwards** ['fɔːwədz] adv nach vorn; (movement) vorwärts; (in time) voraus.

**fossil** ['fɔsl] n Fossil nt.

**fossil fuel** n fossiler Brennstoff m.

**foster** ['fɔstə'] vt (child) in Pflege nehmen; (idea, activity) fördern.

**foster child** n Pflegekind nt.

**foster mother** n Pflegemutter f.

**fought** [fɔːt] pt, pp of **fight**.

**foul** [faul] adj abscheulich; (taste, smell, temper) übel; (water) faulig; (air) schlecht; (language) unflätig ♦ n (SPORT) Foul nt ♦ vt beschmutzen; (SPORT) foulen; (entangle) sich verheddern in +dat.

**foul play** n unnatürlicher or gewaltsamer Tod m; **~ is not suspected** es besteht kein Verdacht auf ein Verbrechen.

**found** [faund] pt, pp of **find** ♦ vt gründen.

**foundation** [faun'deɪʃən] n Gründung f; (base: also fig) Grundlage f; (organization) Stiftung f; (also: ~ cream) Grundierungscreme f; **foundations** npl (of building) Fundament nt; **the rumours are without ~** die Gerüchte entbehren jeder Grundlage; **to lay the ~s** (fig) die Grundlagen schaffen.

**foundation stone** n Grundstein m.

**founder** ['faundə'] n Gründer(in) m(f) ♦ vi (ship) sinken.

**founder member** n Gründungsmitglied nt.

**founding** ['faundɪŋ] adj: **~ fathers** (esp US) Väter pl.

**foundry** ['faundrɪ] n Gießerei f.

**fount** [faunt] n Quelle f; (TYP) Schrift f.

**fountain** ['fauntɪn] n Brunnen m.

**fountain pen** n Füllfederhalter m, Füller m.

**four** [fɔː'] num vier; **on all ~s** auf allen vieren.

**four-letter word** ['fɔːlɛtə-] n Vulgärausdruck m.

**four-poster** ['fɔː'pəustə'] n (also: ~ bed) Himmelbett nt.

**foursome** ['fɔːsəm] n Quartett nt; **in** or **as a ~** zu viert.

**fourteen** ['fɔː'tiːn] num vierzehn.

**fourteenth** ['fɔː'tiːnθ] num vierzehnte(r, s).

**fourth** [fɔːθ] num vierte(r, s) ♦ n (AUT: also: ~ gear) der vierte (Gang).

**four-wheel drive** ['fɔːwiːl-] n (AUT): **with ~** mit Vierradantrieb m.

**fowl** [faul] n Vogel m (besonders Huhn, Gans, Ente etc).

**fox** [fɔks] n Fuchs m ♦ vt verblüffen.

**foxglove** ['fɔksglʌv] n (BOT) Fingerhut m.

**fox-hunting** ['fɔkshʌntɪŋ] n Fuchsjagd f.

**foxtrot** ['fɔkstrɔt] n Foxtrott m.

**foyer** ['fɔɪeɪ] n Foyer nt.

**FPA** (BRIT) n abbr (= Family Planning Association) Organisation für Familienplanung.

**Fr.** abbr (REL) = **father; friar**.

**fr.** abbr (= franc) Fr.

**fracas** ['frækɑː] n Aufruhr m, Tumult m.

**fraction** ['frækʃən] n Bruchteil m; (MATH) Bruch m.

**fractionally** ['frækʃnəlɪ] adv geringfügig.

**fractious** ['frækʃəs] adj verdrießlich.

**fracture** ['fræktʃə'] n Bruch m ♦ vt brechen.

**fragile** ['frædʒaɪl] adj zerbrechlich; (economy) schwach; (health) zart; (person) angeschlagen.

**fragment** [n 'frægmənt, vb fræg'mɛnt] n Stück nt ♦ vt aufsplittern ♦ vi sich aufsplittern.

**fragmentary** ['frægməntərɪ] adj fragmentarisch, bruchstückhaft.

**fragrance** ['freɪgrəns] n Duft m.

**fragrant** ['freɪgrənt] adj duftend.

**frail** [freɪl] adj schwach, gebrechlich;

(*structure*) zerbrechlich.

**frame** [freɪm] *n* Rahmen *m*; (*of building*) (Grund)gerippe *nt*; (*of human, animal*) Gestalt *f*; (*of spectacles: also:* ~**s**) Gestell *nt* ♦ *vt* (*picture*) rahmen; (*reply*) formulieren; (*law, theory*) entwerfen; ~ **of mind** Stimmung *f*, Laune *f*; **to** ~ **sb** (*inf*) jdm etwas anhängen.

**framework** ['freɪmwɔːk] *n* Rahmen *m*.

**France** [frɑːns] *n* Frankreich *nt*.

**franchise** ['fræntʃaɪz] *n* Wahlrecht *nt*; (*COMM*) Konzession *f*, Franchise *f*.

**franchisee** [fræntʃaɪ'ziː] *n* Franchisenehmer(in) *m(f)*.

**franchiser** ['fræntʃaɪzə*] *n* Franchisegeber(in) *m(f)*.

**frank** [fræŋk] *adj* offen ♦ *vt* (*letter*) frankieren.

**Frankfurt** ['fræŋkfət] *n* Frankfurt *nt*.

**frankfurter** ['fræŋkfətə*] *n* (Frankfurter) Würstchen *nt*.

**franking machine** ['fræŋkɪŋ-] *n* Frankiermaschine *f*.

**frankly** ['fræŋklɪ] *adv* ehrlich gesagt; (*candidly*) offen.

**frankness** ['fræŋknɪs] *n* Offenheit *f*.

**frantic** ['fræntɪk] *adj* verzweifelt; (*hectic*) hektisch; (*desperate*) übersteigert.

**frantically** ['fræntɪklɪ] *adv* verzweifelt; (*hectically*) hektisch.

**fraternal** [frə'təːnl] *adj* brüderlich.

**fraternity** [frə'təːnɪtɪ] *n* Brüderlichkeit *f*; (*US: UNIV*) Verbindung *f*; **the legal/medical/ golfing** ~ die Juristen/Mediziner/Golfer *pl*.

**fraternize** ['frætənaɪz] *vi* Umgang haben.

**fraud** [frɔːd] *n* Betrug *m*; (*person*) Betrüger(in) *m(f)*.

**fraudulent** ['frɔːdjulənt] *adj* betrügerisch.

**fraught** [frɔːt] *adj* (*person*) nervös; **to be** ~ **with danger/problems** voller Gefahren/ Probleme sein.

**fray** [freɪ] *n*: **the** ~ der Kampf ♦ *vi* (*cloth*) ausfransen; (*rope*) sich durchscheuern; **to return to the** ~ sich wieder ins Getümmel stürzen; **tempers were** ~**ed** die Gemüter erhitzten sich; **her nerves were** ~**ed** sie war mit den Nerven am Ende.

**FRB** (*US*) *n abbr* = **Federal Reserve Board**.

**FRCM** (*BRIT*) *n abbr* (= *Fellow of the Royal College of Music*) Qualifikationsnachweis in Musik.

**FRCO** (*BRIT*) *n abbr* (= *Fellow of the Royal College of Organists*) Qualifikationsnachweis für Organisten.

**FRCP** (*BRIT*) *n abbr* (= *Fellow of the Royal College of Physicians*) Qualifikationsnachweis für Ärzte.

**FRCS** (*BRIT*) *n abbr* (= *Fellow of the Royal College of Surgeons*) Qualifikationsnachweis für Chirurgen.

**freak** [friːk] *n* Irre(r) *f(m)*; (*in appearance*) Mißgeburt *f*, (*event, accident*) außergewöhnlicher Zufall *m*; (*pej: fanatic*):

**health** ~ Gesundheitsapostel *m*.

▶**freak out** (*inf*) *vi* aussteigen; (*on drugs*) ausflippen.

**freakish** ['friːkɪʃ] *adj* verrückt.

**freckle** ['frɛkl] *n* Sommersprosse *f*.

**freckled** ['frɛkld] *adj* sommersprossig.

**free** [friː] *adj* frei; (*costing nothing*) kostenlos, gratis ♦ *vt* freilassen; (*jammed object*) lösen; **to give sb a** ~ **hand** jdm freie Hand lassen; ~ **and easy** ungezwungen; **admission** ~ Eintritt frei; ~ (**of charge**), **for** ~ umsonst, gratis.

**free agent** *n*: **to be a** ~ sein eigener Herr sein.

**freebie** ['friːbɪ] (*inf*) *n* (*promotional gift*) Werbegeschenk *nt*.

**freedom** ['friːdəm] *n* Freiheit *f*.

**freedom fighter** *n* Freiheitskämpfer(in) *m(f)*.

**free enterprise** *n* freies Unternehmertum *nt*.

**Freefone** ® ['friːfəun] *n*: **call** ~ **0800** rufen Sie gebührenfrei 0800 an.

**free-for-all** ['friːfərɔːl] *n* Gerangel *nt*; **the fight turned into a** ~ schließlich beteiligten sich alle an der Schlägerei.

**free gift** *n* Werbegeschenk *nt*.

**freehold** ['friːhəuld] *n* (*of property*) Besitzrecht *nt*.

**free kick** *n* Freistoß *m*.

**freelance** ['friːlɑːns] *adj* (*journalist etc*) frei(schaffend), freiberuflich tätig.

**freelance work** *n* freiberufliche Arbeit *f*.

**freeloader** ['friːləudə*] *n* (*pej*) Schmarotzer(in) *m(f)*.

**freely** ['friːlɪ] *adv* frei; (*spend*) mit vollen Händen; (*liberally*) großzügig; **drugs are** ~ **available in the city** Drogen sind in der Stadt frei erhältlich.

**free-market economy** ['friːmɑːkɪt-] *n* freie Marktwirtschaft *f*.

**Freemason** ['friːmeɪsn] *n* Freimaurer *m*.

**Freemasonry** ['friːmeɪsnrɪ] *n* Freimaurerei *f*.

**Freepost** ® ['friːpəust] *n* ≈ „Gebühr zahlt Empfänger".

**free-range** ['friː'reɪndʒ] *adj* (*eggs*) von freilaufenden Hühnern.

**free sample** *n* Gratisprobe *f*.

**freesia** ['friːzɪə] *n* Freesie *f*.

**free speech** *n* Redefreiheit *f*.

**freestyle** ['friːstaɪl] *n* Freistil *m*.

**free trade** *n* Freihandel *m*.

**freeway** ['friːweɪ] (*US*) *n* Autobahn *f*.

**freewheel** [friː'wiːl] *vi* im Freilauf fahren.

**free will** *n* freier Wille *m*; **of one's own** ~ aus freien Stücken.

**freeze** [friːz] (*pt* **froze**, *pp* **frozen**) *vi* frieren; (*liquid*) gefrieren; (*pipe*) einfrieren; (*person: stop moving*) erstarren ♦ *vt* einfrieren; (*water, lake*) gefrieren ♦ *n* Frost *m*; (*on arms, wages*) Stopp *m*.

▶**freeze over** *vi* (*river*) überfrieren; (*windscreen, windows*) vereisen.

▶**freeze up** *vi* zufrieren.

**freeze-dried** ['fri:zdraɪd] *adj* gefriergetrocknet.

**freezer** ['fri:zə*] *n* Tiefkühltruhe *f*; (*upright*) Gefrierschrank *m*; (*in fridge: also:* ~ **compartment**) Gefrierfach *nt*.

**freezing** ['fri:zɪŋ] *adj:* ~ **(cold)** eiskalt ♦ *n:* **3 degrees below** ~ 3 Grad unter Null; **I'm** ~ mir ist eiskalt.

**freezing point** *n* Gefrierpunkt *m*.

**freight** [freɪt] *n* Fracht *f*; (*money charged*) Frachtkosten *pl*; ~ **forward** Fracht gegen Nachnahme; ~ **inward** Eingangsfracht *f*.

**freight car** (*US*) *n* Güterwagen *m*.

**freighter** ['freɪtə*] *n* (*NAUT*) Frachter *m*, Frachtschiff *nt*; (*AVIAT*) Frachtflugzeug *nt*.

**freight forwarder** [-'fɔ:wədə*] *n* Spediteur *m*.

**freight train** (*US*) *n* Güterzug *m*.

**French** [frentʃ] *adj* französisch ♦ *n* (*LING*) Französisch *nt*; **the French** *npl* die Franzosen *pl*.

**French bean** (*BRIT*) *n* grüne Bohne *f*.

**French Canadian** *adj* frankokanadisch ♦ *n* Frankokanadier(in) *m(f)*.

**French dressing** *n* Vinaigrette *f*.

**French fried potatoes** *npl* Pommes frites *pl*.

**French fries** [-fraɪz] (*US*) *npl* = **French fried potatoes**.

**French Guiana** [-gaɪ'ænə] *n* Französisch-Guyana *nt*.

**Frenchman** ['frentʃmən] (*irreg: like* **man**) *n* Franzose *m*.

**French Riviera** *n:* **the** ~ die französische Riviera.

**French stick** *n* Stangenbrot *nt*.

**French window** *n* Verandatür *f*.

**Frenchwoman** ['frentʃwumən] (*irreg: like* **woman**) *n* Französin *f*.

**frenetic** [frə'netɪk] *adj* frenetisch, rasend.

**frenzied** ['frenzɪd] *adj* rasend.

**frenzy** ['frenzɪ] *n* Raserei *f*; (*of joy, excitement*) Taumel *m*; **to drive sb into a** ~ jdn zum Rasen bringen; **to be in a** ~ in wilder Aufregung sein.

**frequency** ['fri:kwənsɪ] *n* Häufigkeit *f*; (*RADIO*) Frequenz *f*.

**frequency modulation** *n* Frequenzmodulation *f*.

**frequent** [*adj* 'fri:kwənt, *vt* frɪ'kwent] *adj* häufig ♦ *vt* (*pub, restaurant*) oft *or* häufig besuchen.

**frequently** ['fri:kwəntlɪ] *adv* oft, häufig.

**fresco** ['freskəu] *n* Fresko *nt*.

**fresh** [freʃ] *adj* frisch; (*instructions, approach, start*) neu; (*cheeky*) frech; **to make a** ~ **start** einen neuen Anfang machen.

**freshen** ['freʃən] *vi* (*wind*) auffrischen; (*air*) frisch werden.

▶**freshen up** *vi* sich frisch machen.

**freshener** ['freʃnə*] *n:* **skin** ~ Gesichtswasser *nt*; **air** ~ Raumspray *m or nt*.

**fresher** ['freʃə*] (*BRIT: inf*) *n* Erstsemester(in) *m(f)*.

**freshly** ['freʃlɪ] *adv* frisch.

**freshman** ['freʃmən] (*US: irreg: like* **man**) *n* = **fresher**.

**freshness** ['freʃnɪs] *n* Frische *f*.

**freshwater** ['freʃwɔ:tə*] *adj* (*fish etc*) Süßwasser-.

**fret** [fret] *vi* sich *dat* Sorgen machen.

**fretful** ['fretful] *adj* (*child*) quengelig.

**Freudian** ['frɔɪdɪən] *adj* freudianisch, Freudsch; ~ **slip** Freudscher Versprecher *m*.

**FRG** *n abbr* (= *Federal Republic of Germany*) BRD *f*.

**Fri.** *abbr* (= *Friday*) Fr.

**friar** ['fraɪə*] *n* Mönch *m*, (Ordens)bruder *m*.

**friction** ['frɪkʃən] *n* Reibung *f*; (*between people*) Reibereien *pl*.

**friction feed** *n* (*on printer*) Friktionsvorschub *m*.

**Friday** ['fraɪdɪ] *n* Freitag *m*; *see also* **Tuesday**.

**fridge** [frɪdʒ] (*BRIT*) *n* Kühlschrank *m*.

**fridge-freezer** ['frɪdʒ'fri:zə*] *n* Kühl- und Gefrierkombination *f*.

**fried** [fraɪd] *pt, pp of* **fry** ♦ *adj* gebraten; ~ **egg** Spiegelei *nt*; ~ **fish** Bratfisch *m*.

**friend** [frend] *n* Freund(in) *m(f)*; (*less intimate*) Bekannte(r) *f(m)*; **to make** ~**s with** sich anfreunden mit.

**friendliness** ['frendlɪnɪs] *n* Freundlichkeit *f*.

**friendly** ['frendlɪ] *adj* freundlich; (*government*) befreundet; (*game, match*) Freundschafts- ♦ *n* (*also:* ~ **match**) Freundschaftsspiel *nt*; **to be** ~ **with** befreundet sein mit; **to be** ~ **to** freundlich *or* nett sein zu.

**friendly fire** *n* Beschuß *m* durch die eigene Seite.

**friendly society** *n* Versicherungsverein *m* auf Gegenseitigkeit.

**friendship** ['frendʃɪp] *n* Freundschaft *f*.

**frieze** [fri:z] *n* Fries *m*.

**frigate** ['frɪgɪt] *n* Fregatte *f*.

**fright** [fraɪt] *n* Schreck(en) *m*; **to take** ~ es mit der Angst zu tun bekommen; **she looks a** ~ sie sieht verboten *or* zum Fürchten aus (*inf*).

**frighten** ['fraɪtn] *vt* erschrecken.

▶**frighten away** *or* **off** *vt* verscheuchen.

**frightened** ['fraɪtnd] *adj* ängstlich; **to be** ~ **(of)** Angst haben (vor +*dat*).

**frightening** ['fraɪtnɪŋ] *adj* furchterregend.

**frightful** ['fraɪtful] *adj* schrecklich, furchtbar.

**frightfully** ['fraɪtfəlɪ] *adv* schrecklich, furchtbar; **I'm** ~ **sorry** es tut mir schrecklich leid.

**frigid** ['frɪdʒɪd] *adj* frigide.

**frigidity** [frɪ'dʒɪdɪtɪ] *n* Frigidität *f*.

**frill** [frɪl] *n* Rüsche *f*; **without** ~**s** (*fig*) schlicht.

**fringe** [frɪndʒ] *n* (*BRIT: of hair*) Pony *m*; (*decoration*) Fransen *pl*; (*edge: also fig*) Rand *m*.

**fringe benefits** *npl* zusätzliche Leistungen *pl*.

**fringe theatre** *n* avantgardistisches Theater *nt*.

**Frisbee** ® ['frɪzbɪ] n Frisbee ® nt.
**frisk** [frɪsk] vt durchsuchen, filzen (inf) ♦ vi umhertollen.
**frisky** ['frɪskɪ] adj lebendig, ausgelassen.
**fritter** ['frɪtə*] n Schmalzgebackenes nt no pl mit Füllung.
▶**fritter away** vt vergeuden.
**frivolity** [frɪ'vɔlɪtɪ] n Frivolität f.
**frivolous** ['frɪvələs] adj frivol; (activity) leichtfertig.
**frizzy** ['frɪzɪ] adj kraus.
**fro** [frəu] adv: **to and ~** hin und her; (walk) auf und ab.
**frock** [frɔk] n Kleid nt.
**frog** [frɔg] n Frosch m; **to have a ~ in one's throat** einen Frosch im Hals haben.
**frogman** ['frɔgmən] (irreg: like **man**) n Froschmann m.
**frogmarch** ['frɔgmɑːtʃ] (BRIT) vt: **to ~ sb in/ out** jdn herein-/herausschleppen.
**frolic** ['frɔlɪk] vi umhertollen ♦ n Ausgelassenheit f; (fun) Spaß m.

============================ *KEYWORD*

**from** [frɔm] prep **1** (indicating starting place, origin) von +dat; **where do you come ~?** woher kommen Sie?; **~ London to Glasgow** von London nach Glasgow; **a letter/ telephone call ~ my sister** ein Brief/Anruf von meiner Schwester; **to drink ~ the bottle** aus der Flasche trinken
**2** (indicating time) von (... an); **~ one o'clock to** or **until** or **till now** von ein Uhr bis jetzt; **~ January (on)** von Januar an, ab Januar
**3** (indicating distance) von ... entfernt; **the hotel is 1 km ~ the beach** das Hotel ist 1 km vom Strand entfernt
**4** (indicating price, number etc): **trousers ~ £20** Hosen ab £20; **prices range ~ £10 to £50** die Preise liegen zwischen £10 und £50
**5** (indicating difference): **he can't tell red ~ green** er kann rot und grün nicht unterscheiden; **to be different ~ sb/sth** anders sein als jd/etw
**6** (because of, on the basis of): **~ what he says** nach dem, was er sagt; **to act ~ conviction** aus Überzeugung handeln; **weak ~ hunger** schwach vor Hunger.

**frond** [frɔnd] n Wedel m.
**front** [frʌnt] n Vorderseite f; (of dress) Vorderteil nt; (promenade: also: **sea ~**) Strandpromenade f; (MIL, MET) Front f; (fig: appearances) Fassade f ♦ adj vorderste(r, s); (wheel, tooth, view) Vorder- ♦ vi: **to ~ onto sth** (house) auf etw acc hinausliegen; (window) auf etw acc hinausgehen; **in ~** vorne; **in ~ of** vor; **at the ~ of the coach/ train/car** vorne im Bus/Zug/Auto; **on the political ~, little progress has been made** an der politischen Front sind kaum Fortschritte gemacht worden.

**frontage** ['frʌntɪdʒ] n Vorderseite f, Front f; (of shop) Front.
**frontal** ['frʌntl] adj (attack etc) Frontal-.
**front bench** (BRIT) n (POL) vorderste or erste Reihe f.

Front Bench bezeichnet im britischen Unterhaus die vorderste Bank auf der Regierungs- und Oppositionsseite zur Rechten und Linken des Sprechers. Im weiteren Sinne bezieht sich front bench auf die Spitzenpolitiker der verschiedenen Parteien, die auf dieser Bank sitzen (auch frontbenchers genannt), d.h. die Minister auf der einen Seite und die Mitglieder des Schattenkabinetts auf der anderen.

**front desk** (US) n Rezeption f.
**front door** n Haustür f.
**frontier** ['frʌntɪə*] n Grenze f.
**frontispiece** ['frʌntɪspiːs] n zweite Titelseite f, Frontispiz nt.
**front page** n erste Seite f, Titelseite f.
**front room** (BRIT) n Wohnzimmer nt.
**frontrunner** ['frʌntrʌnə*] n Spitzenreiter m.
**front-wheel drive** ['frʌntwiːl-] n (AUT) Vorderradantrieb m.
**frost** [frɔst] n Frost m; (also: **hoar~**) Rauhreif m.
**frostbite** ['frɔstbaɪt] n Erfrierungen pl.
**frosted** ['frɔstɪd] adj (glass) Milch-; (esp US) glasiert, mit Zuckerguß überzogen.
**frosting** ['frɔstɪŋ] (esp US) n Zuckerguß m.
**frosty** ['frɔstɪ] adj frostig; (look) eisig; (window) bereift.
**froth** [frɔθ] n Schaum m.
**frothy** ['frɔθɪ] adj schäumend.
**frown** [fraun] n Stirnrunzeln nt ♦ vi die Stirn runzeln.
▶**frown on** vt fus mißbilligen.
**froze** [frəuz] pt of **freeze**.
**frozen** ['frəuzn] pp of **freeze** ♦ adj tiefgekühlt; (food) Tiefkühl-; (COMM) eingefroren.
**FRS** n abbr (BRIT: = Fellow of the Royal Society) Auszeichnung für Naturwissenschaftler; (US: = Federal Reserve System) amerikanische Zentralbank.
**frugal** ['fruːgl] adj genügsam; (meal) einfach.
**fruit** [fruːt] n inv Frucht f; (collectively) Obst nt; (fig: results) Früchte pl.
**fruiterer** ['fruːtərə*] (esp BRIT) n Obsthändler(in) m(f).
**fruit fly** n Fruchtfliege f.
**fruitful** ['fruːtful] adj fruchtbar.
**fruition** [fruː'ɪʃən] n: **to come to ~** (plan) Wirklichkeit werden; (efforts) Früchte tragen; (hope) in Erfüllung gehen.
**fruit juice** n Fruchtsaft m.
**fruitless** ['fruːtlɪs] adj fruchtlos, ergebnislos.
**fruit machine** (BRIT) n Spielautomat m.
**fruit salad** n Obstsalat m.
**fruity** ['fruːtɪ] adj (taste, smell etc) Frucht-,

Obst-; (*wine*) fruchtig; (*voice, laugh*) volltönend.

**frump** [frʌmp] *n:* **to feel a** ~ sich *dat* wie eine Vogelscheuche vorkommen.

**frustrate** [frʌs'treɪt] *vt* frustrieren; (*attempt*) vereiteln; (*plan*) durchkreuzen.

**frustrated** [frʌs'treɪtɪd] *adj* frustriert.

**frustrating** [frʌs'treɪtɪŋ] *adj* frustrierend.

**frustration** [frʌs'treɪʃən] *n* Frustration *f*; (*of attempt*) Vereitelung *f*; (*of plan*) Zerschlagung *f*.

**fry** [fraɪ] (*pt, pp* **fried**) *vt* braten; *see also* **small**.

**frying pan** ['fraɪɪŋ-] *n* Bratpfanne *f*.

**FT** (*BRIT*) *n abbr* (= *Financial Times*) Wirtschaftszeitung; **the** ~ **index** der Aktienindex der „Financial Times".

**ft.** *abbr* = **foot; feet.**

**FTC** (*US*) *n abbr* = **Federal Trade Commission.**

**FTSE 100 Index** *n* Aktienindex der „*Financial Times*".

**fuchsia** ['fjuːʃə] *n* Fuchsie *f*.

**fuck** [fʌk] (*inf!*) *vt, vi* ficken (*!*); ~ **off!** (*inf!*) verpiß dich! (*!*).

**fuddled** ['fʌdld] *adj* verwirrt.

**fuddy-duddy** ['fʌdɪdʌdɪ] (*pej*) *n* Langweiler *m*.

**fudge** [fʌdʒ] *n* Fondant *m* ♦ *vt* (*issue, problem*) ausweichen +*dat*, aus dem Weg gehen +*dat*.

**fuel** ['fjuəl] *n* Brennstoff *m*; (*for vehicle*) Kraftstoff *m*; (: *petrol*) Benzin *nt*; (*for aircraft, rocket*) Treibstoff *m* ♦ *vt* (*furnace etc*) betreiben; (*aircraft, ship etc*) antreiben.

**fuel oil** *n* Gasöl *nt*.

**fuel pump** *n* (*AUT*) Benzinpumpe *f*.

**fuel tank** *n* Öltank *m*; (*in vehicle*) (Benzin)tank *m*.

**fug** [fʌg] (*BRIT: inf*) *n* Mief *m* (*inf*).

**fugitive** ['fjuːdʒɪtɪv] *n* Flüchtling *m*.

**fulfil,** (*US*) **fulfill** [ful'fɪl] *vt* erfüllen; (*order*) ausführen.

**fulfilled** [ful'fɪld] *adj* ausgefüllt.

**fulfilment,** (*US*) **fulfillment** [ful'fɪlmənt] *n* Erfüllung *f*.

**full** [ful] *adj* voll; (*complete*) vollständig; (*skirt*) weit; (*life*) ausgefüllt ♦ *adv:* **to know** ~ **well that ...** sehr wohl wissen, daß ...; ~ **up** (*hotel etc*) ausgebucht; **I'm** ~ (**up**) ich bin satt; **a** ~ **two hours** volle zwei Stunden; ~ **marks** die beste Note, ≈ eine Eins; (*fig*) höchstes Lob *nt*; **at** ~ **speed** in voller Fahrt; **in** ~ ganz, vollständig; **to pay in** ~ den vollen Betrag bezahlen; **to write one's name** *etc* **in** ~ seinen Namen *etc* ausschreiben.

**fullback** ['fulbæk] *n* (*RUGBY, FOOTBALL*) Verteidiger *m*.

**full-blooded** ['ful'blʌdɪd] *adj* (*vigorous*) kräftig; (*virile*) vollblütig.

**full board** *n* Vollpension *f*.

**full-cream** ['ful'kriːm] *adj:* ~ **milk** (*BRIT*) Vollmilch *f*.

**full employment** *n* Vollbeschäftigung *f*.

**full grown** *adj* ausgewachsen.

**full-length** ['ful'leŋθ] *adj* (*film*) abendfüllend;

(*coat*) lang; (*portrait*) lebensgroß; (*mirror*) groß; ~ **novel** Roman *m*.

**full moon** *n* Vollmond *m*.

**fullness** ['fulnɪs] *n:* **in the** ~ **of time** zu gegebener Zeit.

**full-page** ['fulpeɪdʒ] *adj* ganzseitig.

**full-scale** ['fulskeɪl] *adj* (*war*) richtig; (*attack*) Groß-; (*model*) in Originalgröße; (*search*) großangelegt.

**full-sized** ['ful'saɪzd] *adj* lebensgroß.

**full stop** *n* Punkt *m*.

**full-time** ['ful'taɪm] *adj* (*work*) Ganztags-; (*study*) Voll- ♦ *adv* ganztags.

**fully** ['fulɪ] *adv* völlig; ~ **as big as** mindestens so groß wie.

**fully fledged** [-'fledʒd] *adj* richtiggehend; (*doctor etc*) voll qualifiziert; (*member*) Voll-; (*bird*) flügge.

**fulsome** ['fulsəm] (*pej*) *adj* übertrieben.

**fumble** ['fʌmbl] *vi:* **to** ~ **with** herumfummeln an +*dat* ♦ *vt* (*ball*) nicht sicher fangen.

**fume** [fjuːm] *vi* wütend sein, kochen (*inf*).

**fumes** [fjuːmz] *npl* (*of fire*) Rauch *m*; (*of fuel*) Dämpfe *pl*; (*of car*) Abgase *pl*.

**fumigate** ['fjuːmɪgeɪt] *vt* ausräuchern.

**fun** [fʌn] *n* Spaß *m*; **he's good** ~ (**to be with**) es macht viel Spaß, mit ihm zusammenzusein; **for** ~ aus *or* zum Spaß; **it's not much** ~ es macht keinen Spaß; **to make** ~ **of, to poke** ~ **at** sich lustig machen über +*acc*.

**function** ['fʌŋkʃən] *n* Funktion *f*; (*social occasion*) Veranstaltung *f*, Feier *f* ♦ *vi* funktionieren; **to** ~ **as** (*thing*) dienen als; (*person*) fungieren als.

**functional** ['fʌŋkʃənl] *adj* (*operational*) funktionsfähig; (*practical*) funktionell, zweckmäßig.

**function key** *n* (*COMPUT*) Funktionstaste *f*.

**fund** [fʌnd] *n* (*of money*) Fonds *m*; (*source, store*) Schatz *m*, Vorrat *m*; **funds** *npl* (*money*) Mittel *pl*, Gelder *pl*.

**fundamental** [fʌndə'mentl] *adj* fundamental, grundlegend.

**fundamentalism** [fʌndə'mentəlɪzəm] *n* Fundamentalismus *m*.

**fundamentalist** [fʌndə'mentəlɪst] *n* Fundamentalist(in) *m(f)*.

**fundamentally** [fʌndə'mentəlɪ] *adv* im Grunde; (*radically*) von Grund auf.

**fundamentals** [fʌndə'mentlz] *npl* Grundbegriffe *pl*.

**funding** ['fʌndɪŋ] *n* Finanzierung *f*.

**fund-raising** ['fʌndreɪzɪŋ] *n* Geldbeschaffung *f*.

**funeral** ['fjuːnərəl] *n* Beerdigung *f*.

**funeral director** *n* Beerdigungs-unternehmer(in) *m(f)*.

**funeral parlour** *n* Leichenhalle *f*.

**funeral service** *n* Trauergottesdienst *m*.

**funereal** [fjuː'nɪərɪəl] *adj* traurig, trübselig.

**funfair** ['fʌnfɛə'] (*BRIT*) *n* Jahrmarkt *m*.

**fungi** ['fʌŋgaɪ] *npl of* **fungus.**

**fungus** ['fʌŋɡəs] (pl fungi) n Pilz m; (mould) Schimmel(pilz) m.

**funicular** [fju:'nɪkjulə°] n (also: ~ **railway**) Seilbahn f.

**funky** ['fʌŋkɪ] adj (music) Funk-.

**funnel** ['fʌnl] n Trichter m; (of ship) Schornstein m.

**funnily** ['fʌnɪlɪ] adv komisch; ~ **enough** komischerweise.

**funny** ['fʌnɪ] adj komisch; (strange) seltsam, komisch.

**funny bone** n Musikantenknochen m.

**fun run** n ≈ Volkslauf m.

**fur** [fə:°] n Fell nt, Pelz m; (BRIT: in kettle etc) Kesselstein m.

**fur coat** n Pelzmantel m.

**furious** ['fjuərɪəs] adj wütend; (exchange, argument) heftig; (effort) riesig; (speed) rasend; **to be** ~ **with sb** wütend auf jdn sein.

**furiously** ['fjuərɪəslɪ] adv (see adj) wütend; (struggle etc) heftig; (run) schnell.

**furl** [fə:l] vt (NAUT) einrollen.

**furlong** ['fə:lɒŋ] n Achtelmeile f (= 201,17 m).

**furlough** ['fə:ləu] n (MIL) Urlaub m.

**furnace** ['fə:nɪs] n (in foundry) Schmelzofen m; (in power plant) Hochofen m.

**furnish** ['fə:nɪʃ] vt einrichten; (room) möblieren; **to** ~ **sb with sth** jdm etw liefern; ~**ed flat** or (US) **apartment** möblierte Wohnung f.

**furnishings** ['fə:nɪʃɪŋz] npl Einrichtung f.

**furniture** ['fə:nɪtʃə°] n Möbel pl; **piece of** ~ Möbelstück nt.

**furniture polish** n Möbelpolitur f.

**furore** [fjuə'rɔːrɪ] n (protests) Proteste pl; (enthusiasm) Furore f or nt.

**furrier** ['fʌrɪə°] n Kürschner(in) m(f).

**furrow** ['fʌrəu] n Furche f, (in skin) Runzel f ♦ vt (brow) runzeln.

**furry** ['fə:rɪ] adj (coat, tail) flauschig; (animal) Pelz-; (toy) Plüsch-.

**further** ['fə:ðə°] adj weitere(r, s) ♦ adv weiter; (moreover) darüber hinaus ♦ vt fördern; **until** ~ **notice** bis auf weiteres; **how much** ~ **is it?** wie weit ist es noch?; ~ **to your letter of** ... (COMM) bezugnehmend auf Ihr Schreiben vom ...

**further education** (BRIT) n Weiterbildung f, Fortbildung f.

**furthermore** [fə:ðə'mɔː°] adv außerdem.

**furthermost** ['fə:ðəməust] adj äußerste(r, s).

**furthest** ['fə:ðɪst] superl of **far**.

**furtive** ['fə:tɪv] adj verstohlen.

**furtively** ['fə:tɪvlɪ] adv verstohlen.

**fury** ['fjuərɪ] n Wut f; **to be in a** ~ in Rage sein.

**fuse,** (US) **fuze** [fju:z] n (ELEC) Sicherung f; (for bomb etc) Zündschnur f ♦ vt (pieces of metal) verschmelzen; (fig) vereinigen ♦ vi (pieces of metal) sich verbinden; (fig) sich vereinigen; **to** ~ **the lights** (BRIT) die Sicherung durchbrennen lassen; **a** ~ **has**

**blown** eine Sicherung ist durchgebrannt.

**fuse box** n Sicherungskasten m.

**fuselage** ['fju:zəlɑːʒ] n Rumpf m.

**fuse wire** n Schmelzdraht m.

**fusillade** [fju:zɪ'leɪd] n Salve f.

**fusion** ['fju:ʒən] n Verschmelzung f; (also: **nuclear** ~) Kernfusion f.

**fuss** [fʌs] n Theater nt (inf) ♦ vi sich (unnötig) aufregen ♦ vt keine Ruhe lassen +dat; **to make a** ~ Krach schlagen (inf); **to make a** ~ **of sb** viel Getue um jdn machen (inf).

▶**fuss over** vt fus bemuttern.

**fusspot** ['fʌspɒt] n Nörgler(in) m(f).

**fussy** ['fʌsɪ] adj kleinlich, pingelig (inf); (clothes, room etc) verspielt; **I'm not** ~ es ist mir egal.

**fusty** ['fʌstɪ] adj muffig.

**futile** ['fju:taɪl] adj vergeblich; (existence) sinnlos; (comment) zwecklos.

**futility** [fju:'tɪlɪtɪ] n (see adj) Vergeblichkeit f; Sinnlosigkeit f; Zwecklosigkeit f.

**futon** ['fu:tɒn] n Futon m.

**future** ['fju:tʃə°] adj zukünftig ♦ n Zukunft f; (LING) Futur nt; **futures** npl (COMM) Termingeschäfte pl; **in (the)** ~ in Zukunft; **in the near** ~ in der nahen Zukunft; **in the immediate** ~ sehr bald.

**futuristic** [fju:tʃə'rɪstɪk] adj futuristisch.

**fuze** [fju:z] (US) n, vt, vi = **fuse.**

**fuzz** [fʌz] (inf) n (police): **the** ~ die Bullen pl.

**fuzzy** ['fʌzɪ] adj verschwommen; (hair) kraus; (thoughts) verworren.

**fwd.** abbr = **forward.**

**fwy** (US) abbr = **freeway.**

**FY** abbr (= fiscal year) Steuerjahr nt.

**FYI** abbr (= for your information) zu Ihrer Information.

# G, g

**G¹, ₲¹** [dʒi:] n (letter) G nt, g nt; ~ **for George** ≈ G wie Gustav.

**G²** [dʒi:] n (MUS) G nt, g nt.

**G³** [dʒi:] n abbr (BRIT: SCOL) = **good**; (US: CINE: = general (audience)) Klassifikation für jugendfreie Filme; (PHYS): ~-**force** g-Druck m.

**G7** n abbr (POL: = Group of Seven) G7 f.

**g²** abbr (= gram(me)) g; (PHYS) = **gravity.**

**GA** (US) n abbr (POST: = Georgia).

**gab** [ɡæb] (inf) n: **to have the gift of the** ~ reden können, nicht auf den Mund gefallen sein.

**gabble** ['ɡæbl] vi brabbeln (inf).

**gaberdine** [ɡæbə'di:n] n Gabardine m.

**gable** ['geɪbl] n Giebel m.
**Gabon** [gə'bɔn] n Gabun nt.
**gad about** [gæd-] (inf) vi herumziehen.
**gadget** ['gædʒɪt] n Gerät nt.
**gadgetry** ['gædʒɪtrɪ] n Geräte pl.
**Gaelic** ['geɪlɪk] adj gälisch ♦ n (LING) Gälisch nt.
**gaffe** [gæf] n Fauxpas m.
**gaffer** ['gæfə*] (BRIT: inf) n (boss) Chef m; (foreman) Vorarbeiter m; (old man) Alte(r) m.
**gag** [gæg] n Knebel m; (joke) Gag m ♦ vt knebeln ♦ vi würgen.
**gaga** ['gɑːgɑː] (inf) adj: **to go** ~ verkalken.
**gage** [geɪdʒ] (US) n, vt = **gauge**.
**gaiety** ['geɪɪtɪ] n Fröhlichkeit f.
**gaily** ['geɪlɪ] adv fröhlich; ~ **coloured** farbenfroh, farbenprächtig.
**gain** [geɪn] n Gewinn m ♦ vt gewinnen ♦ vi (clock, watch) vorgehen; **to do sth for** ~ etw aus Berechnung tun; (for money) etw des Geldes wegen tun; ~ (**in**) (increase) Zunahme f (an +dat); (in rights, conditions) Verbesserung f +gen; **to** ~ **ground** (an) Boden gewinnen; **to** ~ **speed** schneller werden; **to** ~ **weight** zunehmen; **to** ~ **3lbs (in weight)** 3 Pfund zunehmen; **to** ~ (**in**) **confidence** sicherer werden;: **to** ~ **from sth** von etw profitieren; **to** ~ **in strength** stärker werden; **to** ~ **by doing sth** davon profitieren, etw zu tun; **to** ~ **on sb** jdn einholen.
**gainful** ['geɪnful] adj: ~ **employment** Erwerbstätigkeit f.
**gainfully** ['geɪnfəlɪ] adv: ~ **employed** erwerbstätig.
**gainsay** [geɪn'seɪ] (irreg: like say) vt widersprechen +dat; (fact) leugnen.
**gait** [geɪt] n Gang m; **to walk with a slow/confident** ~ mit langsamen Schritten/ selbstbewußt gehen.
**gal.** abbr = **gallon**.
**gala** ['gɑːlə] n Galaveranstaltung f; **swimming** ~ großes Schwimmfest nt.
**Galapagos (Islands)** [gə'læpəgəs-] npl: (**the**) ~ die Galapagosinseln pl.
**galaxy** ['gæləksɪ] n Galaxis f, Sternsystem nt.
**gale** [geɪl] n Sturm m; ~ **force 10** Sturmstärke 10.
**gall** [gɔːl] n Galle f, (fig: impudence) Frechheit f ♦ vt maßlos ärgern.
**gall.** abbr = **gallon**.
**gallant** ['gælənt] adj tapfer; (polite) galant.
**gallantry** ['gæləntrɪ] n (see adj) Tapferkeit f; Galanterie f.
**gall bladder** n Gallenblase f.
**galleon** ['gælɪən] n Galeone f.
**gallery** ['gælərɪ] n (also: **art** ~) Galerie f, Museum nt; (private) (Privat)galerie f; (in hall, church) Galerie f; (in theatre) oberster Rang m, Balkon m.
**galley** ['gælɪ] n Kombüse f; (ship) Galeere f;

(also: ~ **proof**) Fahne f, Fahnenabzug m.
**Gallic** ['gælɪk] adj gallisch; (French) französisch.
**galling** ['gɔːlɪŋ] adj äußerst ärgerlich.
**gallon** ['gælən] n Gallone f (BRIT = 4,5 l, US = 3,8 l).
**gallop** ['gæləp] n Galopp m ♦ vi galoppieren; ~**ing inflation** galoppierende Inflation f.
**gallows** ['gæləuz] n Galgen m.
**gallstone** ['gɔːlstəun] n Gallenstein m.
**Gallup poll** ['gæləp-] n Meinungsumfrage f.
**galore** [gə'lɔː*] adv in Hülle und Fülle.
**galvanize** ['gælvənaɪz] vt (fig) mobilisieren; **to** ~ **sb into action** jdn plötzlich aktiv werden lassen.
**galvanized** ['gælvənaɪzd] adj (metal) galvanisiert.
**Gambia** ['gæmbɪə] n Gambia nt.
**gambit** ['gæmbɪt] n: (**opening**) ~ (einleitender) Schachzug m; (in conversation) (einleitende) Bemerkung f.
**gamble** ['gæmbl] n Risiko nt ♦ vt einsetzen ♦ vi ein Risiko eingehen; (bet) spielen; (on horses etc) wetten; **to** ~ **on the Stock Exchange** an der Börse spekulieren; **to** ~ **on sth** (horses, race) auf etw acc wetten; (success, outcome etc) sich auf etw acc verlassen.
**gambler** ['gæmblə*] n Spieler(in) m(f).
**gambling** ['gæmblɪŋ] n Spielen nt; (on horses etc) Wetten nt.
**gambol** ['gæmbl] vi herumtollen.
**game** [geɪm] n Spiel nt; (sport) Sport m; (strategy, scheme) Vorhaben nt; (CULIN, HUNTING) Wild nt ♦ adj: **to be** ~ (**for**) mitmachen (bei); **games** npl (SCOL) Sport m; **to play a** ~ **of football/tennis** Fußball/(eine Partie) Tennis spielen; **big** ~ Großwild nt.
**game bird** n Federwild nt no pl.
**gamekeeper** ['geɪmkiːpə*] n Wildhüter(in) m(f).
**gamely** ['geɪmlɪ] adv mutig.
**game reserve** n Wildschutzreservat nt.
**games console** ['geɪmz-] n (COMPUT) Gameboy ® m, Konsole f.
**game show** n (TV) Spielshow f.
**gamesmanship** ['geɪmzmənʃɪp] n Gerissenheit f beim Spiel.
**gaming** ['geɪmɪŋ] n (gambling) Spielen nt.
**gammon** ['gæmən] n Schinken m.
**gamut** ['gæmət] n Skala f; **to run the** ~ **of** die ganze Skala +gen durchlaufen.
**gander** ['gændə*] n Gänserich m.
**gang** [gæŋ] n Bande f; (of friends) Haufen m; (of workmen) Kolonne f.
►**gang up** vi: **to** ~ **up on sb** sich gegen jdn zusammentun.
**Ganges** ['gændʒiːz] n: **the** ~ der Ganges.
**gangland** ['gæŋlænd] adj (killer, boss) Unterwelt-.
**gangling** ['gæŋglɪŋ] adj schlaksig, hochaufgeschossen.
**gangly** ['gæŋglɪ] adj schlaksig.

**gangplank** ['gæŋplæŋk] n Laufplanke f.
**gangrene** ['gæŋgriːn] n (MED) Brand m.
**gangster** ['gæŋstə•] n Gangster m.
**gangway** ['gæŋweɪ] n Laufplanke f, Gangway f; (in cinema, bus, plane etc) Gang m.
**gantry** ['gæntrɪ] n (for crane) Portal nt; (for railway signal) Signalbrücke f; (for rocket) Abschußrampe f.
**GAO** (US) n abbr (= General Accounting Office) Rechnungshof der USA.
**gaol** [dʒeɪl] (BRIT) n, vt = **jail**.
**gap** [gæp] n Lücke f; (in time) Pause f; (difference): ~ **(between)** Kluft f (zwischen +dat).
**gape** [geɪp] vi starren, gaffen; (hole) gähnen; (shirt) offenstehen.
**gaping** ['geɪpɪŋ] adj (hole) gähnend; (shirt) offen.
**garage** ['gærɑːʒ] n Garage f; (for car repairs) (Reparatur)werkstatt f; (petrol station) Tankstelle f.
**garb** [gɑːb] n Gewand nt, Kluft f.
**garbage** ['gɑːbɪdʒ] n (US: rubbish) Abfall m, Müll m; (inf: nonsense) Blödsinn m, Quatsch m; (fig: film, book) Schund m.
**garbage can** (US) n Mülleimer m, Abfalleimer m.
**garbage collector** (US) n Müllmann m.
**garbage disposal (unit)** n Müllschlucker m.
**garbage truck** (US) n Müllwagen m.
**garbled** ['gɑːbld] adj (account) wirr; (message) unverständlich.
**garden** ['gɑːdn] n Garten m ♦ vi gärtnern; **gardens** npl (public park) Park m; (private) Gartenanlagen pl; **she was ~ing** sie arbeitete im Garten.
**garden centre** n Gartencenter nt.
**garden city** n Gartenstadt f.
**gardener** ['gɑːdnə•] n Gärtner(in) m(f).
**gardening** ['gɑːdnɪŋ] n Gartenarbeit f.
**gargle** ['gɑːgl] vi gurgeln ♦ n Gurgelwasser nt.
**gargoyle** ['gɑːgɔɪl] n Wasserspeier m.
**garish** ['gɛərɪʃ] adj grell.
**garland** ['gɑːlənd] n Kranz m.
**garlic** ['gɑːlɪk] n Knoblauch m.
**garment** ['gɑːmənt] n Kleidungsstück nt.
**garner** ['gɑːnə•] vt sammeln.
**garnish** ['gɑːnɪʃ] vt garnieren.
**garret** ['gærɪt] n Dachkammer f, Mansarde f.
**garrison** ['gærɪsn] n Garnison f.
**garrulous** ['gærʊləs] adj geschwätzig.
**garter** ['gɑːtə•] n Strumpfband nt; (US: suspender) Strumpfhalter m.
**garter belt** (US) n Strumpfgürtel m, Hüftgürtel m.
**gas** [gæs] n Gas nt; (US: gasoline) Benzin nt ♦ vt mit Gas vergiften; (MIL) vergasen; **to be given** ~ (as anaesthetic) Lachgas bekommen.
**gas cooker** (BRIT) n Gasherd m.
**gas cylinder** n Gasflasche f.
**gaseous** ['gæsɪəs] adj gasförmig.
**gas fire** (BRIT) n Gasofen m.

**gas-fired** ['gæsfaɪəd] adj (heater etc) Gas-.
**gash** [gæʃ] n klaffende Wunde f; (tear) tiefer Schlitz m ♦ vt aufschlitzen.
**gasket** ['gæskɪt] n Dichtung f.
**gas mask** n Gasmaske f.
**gas meter** n Gaszähler m.
**gasoline** ['gæsəliːn] (US) n Benzin nt.
**gasp** [gɑːsp] n tiefer Atemzug m ♦ vi keuchen; (in surprise) nach Luft schnappen; **to give a** ~ **(of shock/horror)** (vor Schreck/Entsetzen) die Luft anhalten; **to be ~ing for** sich sehnen nach +dat.
▶**gasp out** vt hervorstoßen.
**gas permeable** adj (lenses) luftdurchlässig.
**gas ring** n Gasbrenner m.
**gas station** (US) n Tankstelle f.
**gas stove** n (cooker) Gasherd m; (for camping) Gaskocher m.
**gassy** ['gæsɪ] adj (drink) kohlensäurehaltig.
**gas tank** n Benzintank m.
**gastric** ['gæstrɪk] adj (upset, ulcer etc) Magen-.
**gastric flu** n Darmgrippe f.
**gastroenteritis** ['gæstrəʊentə'raɪtɪs] n Magen-Darm-Katarrh m.
**gastronomy** [gæs'trɒnəmɪ] n Gastronomie f.
**gasworks** ['gæswɜːks] n Gaswerk nt.
**gate** [geɪt] n (of garden) Pforte f; (of field) Gatter nt; (of building) Tor nt; (at airport) Flugsteig m; (of level crossing) Schranke f; (of lock) Tor nt.
**gateau** ['gætəʊ] (pl ~x) n Torte f.
**gate-crash** ['geɪtkræʃ] (BRIT) vt (party) ohne Einladung besuchen; (concert) eindringen in +acc ♦ vi ohne Einladung hingehen; eindringen.
**gate-crasher** ['geɪtkræʃə•] n ungeladener Gast m.
**gatehouse** ['geɪthaʊs] n Pförtnerhaus nt.
**gateway** ['geɪtweɪ] n (also fig) Tor nt.
**gather** ['gæðə•] vt sammeln; (flowers, fruit) pflücken; (understand) schließen; (SEWING) kräuseln ♦ vi (assemble) sich versammeln; (dust) sich ansammeln; (clouds) sich zusammenziehen; **to** ~ **(from)** schließen (aus); **to** ~ **(that)** annehmen(, daß); **as far as I can** ~ so wie ich es sehe; **to** ~ **speed** schneller werden.
**gathering** ['gæðərɪŋ] n Versammlung f.
**GATT** [gæt] n abbr (= General Agreement on Tariffs and Trade) GATT nt.
**gauche** [gəʊʃ] adj linkisch.
**gaudy** ['gɔːdɪ] adj knallig.
**gauge,** (US) **gage** [geɪdʒ] n Meßgerät nt, Meßinstrument nt; (RAIL) Spurweite f ♦ vt messen; (fig) beurteilen; **petrol** ~, **fuel** ~, (US) **gas gauge** Benzinuhr f; **to** ~ **the right moment** den richtigen Moment abwägen.
**Gaul** [gɔːl] n Gallien nt; (person) Gallier(in) m(f).
**gaunt** [gɔːnt] adj (haggard) hager; (bare, stark) öde.
**gauntlet** ['gɔːntlɪt] n (Stulpen)handschuh m;

*(fig):* **to run the** ~ Spießruten laufen; **to throw down the** ~ den Fehdehandschuh hinwerfen.

**gauze** [gɔːz] *n* Gaze *f*.

**gave** [geɪv] *pt of* **give**.

**gavel** ['gævl] *n* Hammer *m*.

**gawk** [gɔːk] *(inf) vi* gaffen, glotzen.

**gawky** ['gɔːkɪ] *adj* schlaksig.

**gawp** [gɔːp] *vi:* **to ~ at** angaffen, anglotzen *(inf)*.

**gay** [geɪ] *adj (homosexual)* schwul; *(cheerful)* fröhlich; *(dress)* bunt.

**gaze** [geɪz] *n* Blick *m* ♦ *vi:* **to ~ at sth** etw anstarren.

**gazelle** [gə'zɛl] *n* Gazelle *f*.

**gazette** [gə'zɛt] *n* Zeitung *f*; *(official)* Amtsblatt *nt*.

**gazetteer** [gæzə'tɪə'] *n* alphabetisches Ortsverzeichnis *nt*.

**gazump** [gə'zʌmp] *(BRIT) vt:* **to be ~ed** ein mündlich zugesagtes Haus an einen Höherbietenden verlieren.

**GB** *abbr* (= *Great Britain*) GB.

**GBH** *(BRIT) n abbr (LAW)* = **grievous bodily harm**.

**GC** *(BRIT) n abbr* (= *George Cross*) *britische Tapferkeitsmedaille*.

**GCE** *(BRIT) n abbr* (= *General Certificate of Education*) *Schulabschlußzeugnis*, ≈ Abitur *nt*.

**GCHQ** *(BRIT) n abbr* (= *Government Communications Headquarters*) *Zentralstelle des britischen Nachrichtendienstes*.

**GCSE** *(BRIT) n abbr* (= *General Certificate of Secondary Education*) *Schulabschlußzeugnis*, ≈ mittlere Reife *f*.

**Gdns** *abbr (in street names:* = *Gardens)* ≈ Str.

**GDP** *n abbr* = **gross domestic product**.

**GDR** *n abbr (formerly:* = *German Democratic Republic)* DDR *f*.

**gear** [gɪə'] *n (equipment)* Ausrüstung *f*; *(belongings)* Sachen *pl*; *(TECH)* Getriebe *nt*; *(AUT)* Gang *m*; *(on bicycle)* Gangschaltung *f* ♦ *vt (fig: adapt):* **to ~ sth to** etw ausrichten auf *+acc*; **top** *or (US)* **high/low/bottom ~** hoher/niedriger/erster Gang; **to put a car into ~** einen Gang einlegen; **to leave the car in ~** den Gang eingelegt lassen; **to leave out of ~** im Leerlauf lassen; **our service is ~ed to meet the needs of the disabled** unser Betrieb ist auf die Bedürfnisse von Behinderten eingerichtet.

▶**gear up** *vt, vi:* **to ~ (o.s.) up (to)** sich vorbereiten (auf *+acc*) ♦ *vt:* **to ~ o.s. up to do sth** sich darauf vorbereiten, etw zu tun.

**gearbox** ['gɪəbɔks] *n* Getriebe *nt*.

**gear lever, (***US***) gear shift** *n* Schalthebel *m*.

**GED** *(US) n abbr (SCOL:* = *general educational development)* *allgemeine Lernentwicklung*.

**geese** [giːs] *npl of* **goose**.

**geezer** ['giːzə'] *(inf) n* Kerl *m*, Typ *m*.

**Geiger counter** ['gaɪgə-] *n* Geigerzähler *m*.

**gel** [dʒɛl] *n* Gel *nt*.

**gelatin(e)** ['dʒɛlətiːn] *n* Gelatine *f*.

**gelignite** ['dʒɛlɪgnaɪt] *n* Plastiksprengstoff *m*.

**gem** [dʒɛm] *n* Edelstein *m*; **she/the house is a ~** *(fig)* sie/das Haus ist ein Juwel; **a ~ of an idea** eine ausgezeichnete Idee.

**Gemini** ['dʒɛmɪnaɪ] *n (ASTROL)* Zwillinge *pl*; **to be ~** (ein) Zwilling sein.

**gen** [dʒɛn] *(BRIT: inf) n:* **to give sb the ~ on sth** jdn über etw *acc* informieren.

**Gen.** *abbr (MIL:* = *General)* Gen.

**gen.** *abbr* = **general; generally**.

**gender** ['dʒɛndə'] *n* Geschlecht *nt*.

**gene** [dʒiːn] *n* Gen *nt*.

**genealogy** [dʒiːnɪ'ælədʒɪ] *n* Genealogie *f*, Stammbaumforschung *f*; *(family history)* Stammbaum *m*.

**general** ['dʒɛnərl] *n* General *m* ♦ *adj* allgemein; *(widespread)* weitverbreitet; *(non-specific)* generell; **in ~** im allgemeinen; **the ~ public** die Öffentlichkeit, die Allgemeinheit; **~ audit** *(COMM)* Jahresabschlußprüfung *f*.

**general anaesthetic** *n* Vollnarkose *f*.

**general delivery** *(US) n:* **to send sth ~** etw postlagernd schicken.

**general election** *n* Parlamentswahlen *pl*.

**generalization** ['dʒɛnrəlaɪ'zeɪʃən] *n* Verallgemeinerung *f*.

**generalize** ['dʒɛnrəlaɪz] *vi* verallgemeinern.

**generally** ['dʒɛnrəlɪ] *adv* im allgemeinen.

**general manager** *n* Hauptgeschäfts-führer(in) *m(f)*.

**general practitioner** *n* praktischer Arzt *m*, praktische Ärztin *f*.

**general strike** *n* Generalstreik *m*.

**generate** ['dʒɛnəreɪt] *vt* erzeugen; *(jobs)* schaffen; *(profits)* einbringen.

**generation** [dʒɛnə'reɪʃən] *n* Generation *f*; *(of electricity etc)* Erzeugung *f*.

**generator** ['dʒɛnəreɪtə'] *n* Generator *m*.

**generic** [dʒɪ'nɛrɪk] *adj* allgemein; **~ term** Oberbegriff *m*.

**generosity** [dʒɛnə'rɔsɪtɪ] *n* Großzügigkeit *f*.

**generous** ['dʒɛnərəs] *adj* großzügig; *(measure, remuneration)* reichlich.

**genesis** ['dʒɛnɪsɪs] *n* Entstehung *f*.

**genetic** [dʒɪ'nɛtɪk] *adj* genetisch.

**genetic engineering** *n* Gentechnologie *f*.

**genetic fingerprinting** [-'fɪŋgəprɪntɪŋ] *n* genetische Fingerabdrücke *pl*.

**genetics** [dʒɪ'nɛtɪks] *n* Genetik *f*.

**Geneva** [dʒɪ'niːvə] *n* Genf *nt*.

**genial** ['dʒiːnɪəl] *adj* freundlich; *(climate)* angenehm.

**genitals** ['dʒɛnɪtlz] *npl* Genitalien *pl*, Geschlechtsteile *pl*.

**genitive** ['dʒɛnɪtɪv] *n* Genitiv *m*.

**genius** ['dʒiːnɪəs] *n* Talent *nt*; *(person)* Genie *nt*.

**Genoa** ['dʒɛnəuə] *n* Genua *nt*.

**genocide** ['dʒɛnəusaɪd] *n* Völkermord *m*.

**Genoese** [dʒɛnəu'iːz] *adj* genuesisch ♦ *n inv*

Genuese m, Genuesin f.

**gent** [dʒɛnt] (BRIT: inf) n abbr = **gentleman**.

**genteel** [dʒɛnˈtiːl] adj vornehm, fein.

**gentle** [ˈdʒɛntl] adj sanft; (movement, breeze) leicht; **a ~ hint** ein zarter Hinweis.

**gentleman** [ˈdʒɛntlmən] (irreg: like man) n Herr m; (referring to social position or good manners) Gentleman m; **~'s agreement** Vereinbarung f auf Treu und Glauben.

**gentlemanly** [ˈdʒɛntlmənlɪ] adj zuvorkommend.

**gentleness** [ˈdʒɛntlnɪs] n (see adj) Sanftheit f; Leichtheit f; Zartheit f.

**gently** [ˈdʒɛntlɪ] adv (see adj) sanft; leicht; zart.

**gentry** [ˈdʒɛntrɪ] n inv: **the ~** die Gentry, der niedere Adel.

**gents** [dʒɛnts] n: **the ~** die Herrentoilette.

**genuine** [ˈdʒɛnjuːɪn] adj echt; (person) natürlich, aufrichtig.

**genuinely** [ˈdʒɛnjuːɪnlɪ] adv wirklich.

**geographer** [dʒɪˈɒɡrəfəˈ] n Geograph(in) m(f).

**geographic(al)** [dʒɪəˈɡræfɪk(l)] adj geographisch.

**geography** [dʒɪˈɒɡrəfɪ] n Geographie f; (SCOL) Erdkunde f.

**geological** [dʒɪəˈlɒdʒɪkl] adj geologisch.

**geologist** [dʒɪˈɒlədʒɪst] n Geologe m, Geologin f.

**geology** [dʒɪˈɒlədʒɪ] n Geologie f.

**geometric(al)** [dʒɪəˈmɛtrɪk(l)] adj geometrisch.

**geometry** [dʒɪˈɒmətrɪ] n Geometrie f.

**Geordie** [ˈdʒɔːdɪ] (inf) n aus dem Gebiet von Newcastle stammende oder dort wohnhafte Person.

**Georgia** [ˈdʒɔːdʒə] n (in Eastern Europe) Georgien nt.

**Georgian** [ˈdʒɔːdʒən] adj georgisch ♦ n Georgier(in) m(f); (LING) Georgisch nt.

**geranium** [dʒɪˈreɪnɪəm] n Geranie f.

**geriatric** [dʒɛrɪˈætrɪk] adj geriatrisch ♦ n Greis(in) m(f).

**germ** [dʒɜːm] n Bazillus m; (BIOL, fig) Keim m.

**German** [ˈdʒɜːmən] adj deutsch ♦ n Deutsche(r) f(m); (LING) Deutsch nt.

**German Democratic Republic** n (formerly) Deutsche Demokratische Republik f.

**germane** [dʒɜːˈmeɪn] adj: **~ (to)** von Belang (für).

**German measles** (BRIT) n Röteln pl.

**German Shepherd (dog)** (esp US) n Schäferhund m.

**Germany** [ˈdʒɜːmənɪ] n Deutschland nt.

**germinate** [ˈdʒɜːmɪneɪt] vi keimen; (fig) aufkeimen.

**germination** [dʒɜːmɪˈneɪʃən] n Keimung f.

**germ warfare** n biologische Kriegsführung f, Bakterienkrieg m.

**gerrymandering** [ˈdʒɛrɪmændərɪŋ] n Wahlkreisschiebungen pl.

**gestation** [dʒɛsˈteɪʃən] n (of animals)

Trächtigkeit f; (of humans) Schwangerschaft f.

**gesticulate** [dʒɛsˈtɪkjuleɪt] vi gestikulieren.

**gesture** [ˈdʒɛstjəˈ] n Geste f; **as a ~ of friendship** als Zeichen der Freundschaft.

================================ KEYWORD

**get** [gɛt] (pt, pp **got**, (US) pp **gotten**) vi **1** (become, be) werden; **to ~ old/tired/cold** alt/müde/kalt werden; **to ~ dirty** sich schmutzig machen; **to ~ killed** getötet werden; **to ~ married** heiraten
**2** (go): **to ~ (from ...) to ...** (von ...) nach ... kommen; **how did you ~ here?** wie sind Sie hierhin gekommen?
**3** (begin): **to ~ to know sb** jdn kennenlernen; **let's ~ going** or **started** fangen wir an!
♦ modal aux vb: **you've got to do it** du mußt es tun
♦ vt **1**: **to ~ sth done** (do oneself) etw gemacht bekommen; (have done) etw machen lassen; **to ~ one's hair cut** sich dat die Haare schneiden lassen; **to ~ the car going** or **to go** das Auto in Gang bringen; **to ~ sb to do sth** etw von jdm machen lassen; (persuade) jdn dazu bringen, etw zu tun
**2** (obtain: money, permission, results) erhalten; (find: job, flat) finden; (fetch: person, doctor, object) holen; **to ~ sth for sb** jdm etw besorgen; **can I ~ you a drink?** kann ich Ihnen etwas zu trinken anbieten?
**3** (receive, acquire: present, prize) bekommen; **how much did you ~ for the painting?** wieviel haben Sie für das Bild bekommen?
**4** (catch) bekommen, kriegen (inf); (hit: target etc) treffen; **to ~ sb by the arm/throat** jdn am Arm/Hals packen; **the bullet got him in the leg** die Kugel traf ihn ins Bein
**5** (take, move) bringen; **to ~ sth to sb** jdm etw zukommen lassen
**6** (plane, bus etc: take) nehmen; (: catch) bekommen
**7** (understand: joke etc) verstehen; **I ~ it** ich verstehe
**8** (have, possess): **to have got** haben; **how many have you got?** wie viele hast du?
▶**get about** vi (person) herumkommen; (news, rumour) sich verbreiten.
▶**get across** vt (message, meaning) klarmachen.
▶**get along** vi (be friends) (miteinander) auskommen; (depart) sich auf den Weg machen.
▶**get around** vt fus = **get round**.
▶**get at** vt fus (attack, criticize) angreifen; (reach) herankommen an +acc; **what are you ~ting at?** worauf willst du hinaus?
▶**get away** vi (leave) wegkommen; (on holiday) verreisen; (escape) entkommen.
▶**get away with** vt fus (stolen goods) entkommen mit; **he'll never ~ away with it!**

damit kommt er nicht durch.

▶**get back** vi (*return*) zurückkommen ♦ vt (*regain*) zurückbekommen; ~ **back!** zurück!

▶**get back at** (*inf*) vt fus: **to ~ back at sb for sth** jdm etw heimzahlen.

▶**get back to** vt fus (*return to*) zurückkehren zu; (*contact again*) zurückkommen auf +acc; **to ~ back to sleep** wieder einschlafen.

▶**get by** vi (*pass*) vorbeikommen; (*manage*) zurechtkommen; **I can ~ by in German** ich kann mich auf Deutsch verständlich machen.

▶**get down** vi (*from tree, ladder etc*) heruntersteigen; (*from horse*) absteigen; (*leave table*) aufstehen; (*bend down*) sich bücken; (*duck*) sich ducken ♦ vt (*depress: person*) fertigmachen; (*write*) aufschreiben.

▶**get down to** vt fus: **to ~ down to sth** (*work*) etw in Angriff nehmen; (*find time*) zu etw kommen; **to ~ down to business** (*fig*) zur Sache kommen.

▶**get in** vi (*be elected: candidate, party*) gewählt werden; (*arrive*) ankommen ♦ vt (*bring in: harvest*) einbringen; (: *shopping, supplies*) (herein)holen.

▶**get into** vt fus (*conversation, argument, fight*) geraten in +acc; (*vehicle*) einsteigen in +acc; (*clothes*) hineinkommen in +acc; **to ~ into bed** ins Bett gehen; **to ~ into the habit of doing sth** sich dat angewöhnen, etw zu tun.

▶ **get off** vi (*from train etc*) aussteigen; (*escape punishment*) davonkommen ♦ vt (*remove: clothes*) ausziehen; (: *stain*) herausbekommen ♦ vt fus (*leave: train, bus*) aussteigen aus; **we ~ 3 days off at Christmas** zu Weihnachten bekommen wir 3 Tage frei; **to ~ off to a good start** (*fig*) einen guten Anfang machen.

▶ **get on** vi (*be friends*) (miteinander) auskommen ♦ vt fus (*bus, train*) einsteigen in +acc; **how are you ~ting on?** wie kommst du zurecht?; **time is ~ting on** es wird langsam spät.

▶ **get on to** (*BRIT*) vt fus (*subject, topic*) übergehen zu; (*contact: person*) sich in Verbindung setzen mit.

▶ **get on with** vt fus (*person*) auskommen mit; (*meeting, work etc*) weitermachen mit.

▶ **get out** vi (*leave: on foot*) hinausgehen; (*of vehicle*) aussteigen; (*news etc*) herauskommen ♦ vt (*take out: book etc*) herausholen; (*remove: stain*) herausbekommen.

▶ **get out of** vt fus (*money: bank etc*) abheben von; (*avoid: duty etc*) herumkommen um ♦ vt (*extract: confession etc*) herausbekommen aus; (*derive: pleasure*) haben an +dat; (: *benefit*) haben von.

▶ **get over** vt fus (*overcome*) überwinden; (: *illness*) sich erholen von; (*communicate: idea etc*) verständlich machen ♦ vt: **to ~ it over with** (*finish*) es hinter sich acc bringen.

▶ **get round** vt fus (*law, rule*) umgehen; (*person*) herumkriegen.

▶ **get round to** vt fus: **to ~ round to doing sth** dazu kommen, etw zu tun.

▶ **get through** vi ⟨*TEL*⟩ durchkommen ♦ vt fus (*finish: work*) schaffen; (: *book*) lesen.

▶ **get through to** vt fus (*TEL*) durchkommen zu; (*make o.s. understood*) durchdringen zu.

▶ **get together** vi (*people*) zusammenkommen ♦ vt (*people*) zusammenbringen; (*project, plan etc*) zusammenstellen.

▶ **get up** vi (*rise*) aufstehen ♦ vt: **to ~ up enthusiasm for sth** Begeisterung für etw aufbringen.

▶ **get up to** vt fus (*prank etc*) anstellen.

**getaway** ['gɛtəweɪ] n: **to make a/one's ~** sich davonmachen.

**getaway car** n Fluchtauto nt.

**get-together** ['gɛttəgɛðə*] n Treffen nt; (*party*) Party f.

**get-up** ['gɛtʌp] (*inf*) n Aufmachung f.

**get-well card** [gɛt'wɛl-] n Karte f mit Genesungswünschen.

**geyser** ['giːzə*] n Geiser m; (*BRIT: water heater*) Durchlauferhitzer m.

**Ghana** ['gɑːnə] n Ghana nt.

**Ghanaian** [gɑː'neɪən] adj ghanaisch ♦ n Ghanaer(in) m(f).

**ghastly** ['gɑːstlɪ] adj gräßlich; (*complexion*) totenblaß; **you look ~!** (*ill*) du siehst gräßlich aus!

**gherkin** ['gəːkɪn] n Gewürzgurke f.

**ghetto** ['gɛtəu] n G(h)etto nt.

**ghetto blaster** [-'blɑːstə*] (*inf*) n Ghettoblaster m.

**ghost** [gəust] n Geist m, Gespenst nt ♦ vt für jdn (als Ghostwriter) schreiben; **to give up the ~** den Geist aufgeben.

**ghost town** n Geisterstadt f.

**ghostwriter** ['gəustraɪtə*] n Ghostwriter(in) m(f).

**ghoul** [guːl] n böser Geist m.

**ghoulish** ['guːlɪʃ] adj makaber.

**GHQ** n abbr (*MIL: = general headquarters*) Hauptquartier nt.

**GI** (*US: inf*) n abbr (= *government issue*) GI m.

**giant** ['dʒaɪənt] n (*also fig*) Riese m ♦ adj riesig, riesenhaft; ~ **(size) packet** Riesenpackung f.

**giant killer** n (*fig*) Goliathbezwinger(in) m(f).

**gibber** ['dʒɪbə*] vi brabbeln.

**gibberish** ['dʒɪbərɪʃ] n Quatsch m.

**gibe** [dʒaɪb] n spöttische Bemerkung f ♦ vi: **to ~ at** spöttische Bemerkungen machen über +acc.

**giblets** ['dʒɪblɪts] npl Geflügelinnereien pl.

**Gibraltar** [dʒɪ'brɔːltə*] n Gibraltar nt.

**giddiness** ['gɪdɪnɪs] n Schwindelgefühl nt.

**giddy** ['gɪdɪ] adj: **I am/feel ~** mir ist schwind(e)lig; (*height*) schwindelerregend; ~ **with excitement** vor Aufregung ganz ausgelassen.

**gift** [gɪft] n Geschenk nt; (donation) Spende f; (COMM: also: **free** ~) (Werbe)geschenk nt; (ability) Gabe f; **to have a ~ for sth** ein Talent für etw haben.

**gifted** ['gɪftɪd] adj begabt.

**gift token** n Geschenkgutschein m.

**gift voucher** n = **gift token.**

**gig** [gɪg] (inf) n Konzert nt.

**gigabyte** ['dʒɪgəbaɪt] n (COMPUT) Gigabyte nt.

**gigantic** [dʒaɪ'gæntɪk] adj riesig, riesengroß.

**giggle** ['gɪgl] vi kichern ♦ n Spaß m; **to do sth for a ~** etw aus Spaß tun.

**GIGO** ['gaɪgəu] (inf) abbr (COMPUT: = garbage in, garbage out) GIGO.

**gild** [gɪld] vt vergolden.

**gill** [dʒɪl] n Gill nt (BRIT = 15 cl, US = 12 cl).

**gills** [gɪlz] npl Kiemen pl.

**gilt** [gɪlt] adj vergoldet ♦ n Vergoldung f; **gilts** npl (COMM) mündelsichere Wertpapiere pl.

**gilt-edged** ['gɪltɛdʒd] adj (stocks, securities) mündelsicher.

**gimlet** ['gɪmlɪt] n Handbohrer m.

**gimmick** ['gɪmɪk] n Gag m; **sales ~** Verkaufsmasche f, Verkaufstrick m.

**gin** [dʒɪn] n Gin m.

**ginger** ['dʒɪndʒə*] n Ingwer m ♦ adj (hair) rötlich; (cat) rötlichgelb.

**ginger ale** n Ginger Ale nt.

**ginger beer** n Ingwerbier nt.

**gingerbread** ['dʒɪndʒəbrɛd] n (cake) Ingwerkuchen m; (biscuit) ≈ Pfefferkuchen m.

**ginger group** (BRIT) n Aktionsgruppe f.

**gingerly** ['dʒɪndʒəlɪ] adv vorsichtig.

**gingham** ['gɪŋəm] n Gingan m, Gingham m.

**ginseng** ['dʒɪnsɛŋ] n Ginseng m.

**gipsy** ['dʒɪpsɪ] n Zigeuner(in) m(f).

**gipsy caravan** n Zigeunerwagen m.

**giraffe** [dʒɪ'rɑːf] n Giraffe f.

**girder** ['gəːdə*] n Träger m.

**girdle** ['gəːdl] n Hüftgürtel m, Hüfthalter m ♦ vt (fig) umgeben.

**girl** [gəːl] n Mädchen nt; (young unmarried woman) (junges) Mädchen nt; (daughter) Tochter f; **this is my little ~** das ist mein Töchterchen; **an English ~** eine Engländerin.

**girlfriend** ['gəːlfrɛnd] n Freundin f.

**Girl Guide** n Pfadfinderin f.

**girlish** ['gəːlɪʃ] adj mädchenhaft.

**Girl Scout** (US) n Pfadfinderin f.

**Giro** ['dʒaɪrəu] n: **the National ~** (BRIT) der Postscheckdienst.

**giro** ['dʒaɪrəu] n Giro nt, Giroverkehr m; (post office giro) Postscheckverkehr m; (BRIT: welfare cheque) Sozialhilfescheck m.

**girth** [gəːθ] n Umfang m; (of horse) Sattelgurt m.

**gist** [dʒɪst] n Wesentliche(s) nt.

═══════════════════ KEYWORD

**give** [gɪv] (pt **gave,** pp **given**) vt **1** (hand over): **to ~ sb sth, ~ sth to sb** jdm etw geben; **I'll ~ you £5 for it** ich gebe dir £5 dafür

**2** (used with noun to replace a verb): **to ~ a sigh/cry/laugh** etc seufzen/schreien/lachen etc; **to ~ a speech/a lecture** eine Rede/einen Vortrag halten; **to ~ three cheers** ein dreifaches Hoch ausbringen

**3** (tell, deliver: news, message etc) mitteilen; (: advice, answer) geben

**4** (supply, provide: opportunity, job etc) geben; (: surprise) bereiten; (bestow: title, honour, right) geben, verleihen; **that's given me an idea** dabei kommt mir eine Idee

**5** (devote: time, one's life) geben; (: attention) schenken

**6** (organize: party, dinner etc) geben

♦ vi **1** (also: ~ **way:** break, collapse) nachgeben

**2** (stretch: fabric) sich dehnen.

▶ **give away** vt (money, opportunity) verschenken; (secret, information) verraten; (bride) zum Altar führen; **that immediately gave him away** dadurch verriet er sich sofort.

▶ **give back** vt (money, book etc) zurückgeben.

▶ **give in** vi (yield) nachgeben ♦ vt (essay etc) abgeben.

▶ **give off** vt (heat, smoke) abgeben.

▶ **give out** vt (prizes, books, drinks etc) austeilen ♦ vi (be exhausted: supplies) zu Ende gehen; (fail) versagen.

▶ **give up** vt, vi aufgeben; **to ~ up smoking** das Rauchen aufgeben; **to ~ o.s. up** sich stellen; (after siege etc) sich ergeben.

▶ **give way** vi (yield, collapse) nachgeben; (BRIT: AUT) die Vorfahrt achten.

**give-and-take** ['gɪvənd'teɪk] n (gegenseitiges) Geben und Nehmen nt.

**giveaway** ['gɪvəweɪ] (inf) n: **her expression was a ~** ihr Gesichtsausdruck verriet alles; **the exam was a ~!** die Prüfung war geschenkt!; **~ prices** Schleuderpreise pl.

**given** ['gɪvn] pp of **give** ♦ adj (time, amount) bestimmt ♦ conj: **~ the circumstances ...** unter den Umständen ...; **~ that ...** angesichts der Tatsache, daß ...

**glacial** ['gleɪsɪəl] adj (landscape etc) Gletscher-; (fig) eisig.

**glacier** ['glæsɪə*] n Gletscher m.

**glad** [glæd] adj froh; **to be ~ about sth** sich über etw acc freuen; **to be ~ that** sich freuen, daß; **I was ~ of his help** ich war froh über seine Hilfe.

**gladden** ['glædn] vt erfreuen.

**glade** [gleɪd] n Lichtung f.

**gladioli** [glædɪ'əulaɪ] npl Gladiolen pl.

**gladly** ['glædlɪ] adv gern(e).

**glamorous** ['glæmərəs] adj reizvoll; (model

*etc*) glamourös.

**glamour** ['glæmə*] *n* Glanz *m*, Reiz *m*.

**glance** [glɑːns] *n* Blick *m* ♦ *vi*: **to ~ at** einen Blick werfen auf +*acc*.

▶ **glance off** *vt fus* abprallen von.

**glancing** ['glɑːnsɪŋ] *adj*: **to strike sth a ~ blow** etw streifen.

**gland** [glænd] *n* Drüse *f*.

**glandular fever** ['glændjulə-] (*BRIT*) *n* Drüsenfieber *nt*.

**glare** [glɛə*] *n* wütender Blick *m*; (*of light*) greller Schein *m*; (*of publicity*) grelles Licht *nt* ♦ *vi* (*light*) grell scheinen; **to ~ at** (wütend) anstarren.

**glaring** ['glɛərɪŋ] *adj* eklatant.

**glasnost** ['glæznɔst] *n* Glasnost *f*.

**glass** [glɑːs] *n* Glas *nt*; **glasses** *npl* (*spectacles*) Brille *f*.

**glass-blowing** ['glɑːsbləuɪŋ] *n* Glasbläserei *f*.

**glass ceiling** *n* (*fig*) gläserne Decke *f*.

**glass fibre** *n* Glasfaser *f*.

**glasshouse** ['glɑːshaus] *n* Gewächshaus *nt*.

**glassware** ['glɑːswɛə*] *n* Glaswaren *pl*.

**glassy** ['glɑːsɪ] *adj* glasig.

**Glaswegian** [glæs'wiːdʒən] *adj* Glasgower ♦ *n* Glasgower(in) *m(f)*.

**glaze** [gleɪz] *vt* (*door, window*) verglasen; (*pottery*) glasieren ♦ *n* Glasur *f*.

**glazed** [gleɪzd] *adj* (*eyes*) glasig; (*pottery, tiles*) glasiert.

**glazier** ['gleɪzɪə*] *n* Glaser(in) *m(f)*.

**gleam** [gliːm] *vi* (*light*) schimmern; (*polished surface, eyes*) glänzen ♦ *n*: **a ~ of hope** ein Hoffnungsschimmer *m*.

**gleaming** ['gliːmɪŋ] *adj* schimmernd, glänzend.

**glean** [gliːn] *vt* (*information*) herausbekommen, ausfindig machen.

**glee** [gliː] *n* Freude *f*.

**gleeful** ['gliːful] *adj* fröhlich.

**glen** [glɛn] *n* Tal *nt*.

**glib** [glɪb] *adj* (*person*) glatt; (*promise, response*) leichthin gemacht.

**glibly** ['glɪblɪ] *adv* (*talk*) gewandt; (*answer*) leichthin.

**glide** [glaɪd] *vi* gleiten ♦ *n* Gleiten *nt*.

**glider** ['glaɪdə*] *n* Segelflugzeug *nt*.

**gliding** ['glaɪdɪŋ] *n* Segelfliegen *nt*.

**glimmer** ['glɪmə*] *n* Schimmer *m*; (*of interest, hope*) Funke *m* ♦ *vi* schimmern.

**glimpse** [glɪmps] *n* Blick *m* ♦ *vt* einen Blick werfen auf +*acc*; **to catch a ~ (of)** einen flüchtigen Blick erhaschen (von +*dat*).

**glint** [glɪnt] *vi* glitzern; (*eyes*) funkeln ♦ *n* (*see vb*) Glitzern *nt*; Funkeln *nt*.

**glisten** ['glɪsn] *vi* glänzen.

**glitter** ['glɪtə*] *vi* glitzern; (*eyes*) funkeln ♦ *n* (*see vb*) Glitzern *nt*; Funkeln *nt*.

**glittering** ['glɪtərɪŋ] *adj* glitzernd; (*eyes*) funkelnd; (*career*) glänzend.

**glitz** [glɪts] (*inf*) *n* Glanz *m*.

**gloat** [gləut] *vi*: **to ~ (over)** (*own success*) sich brüsten (mit); (*sb's failure*) sich hämisch freuen (über +*acc*).

**global** ['gləubl] *adj* global.

**global warming** [-'wɔːmɪŋ] *n* Erwärmung *f* der Erdatmosphäre.

**globe** [gləub] *n* Erdball *m*; (*model*) Globus *m*; (*shape*) Kugel *f*.

**globetrotter** ['gləubtrɔtə*] *n* Globetrotter(in) *m(f)*, Weltenbummler(in) *m(f)*.

**globule** ['glɔbjuːl] *n* Tröpfchen *nt*.

**gloom** [gluːm] *n* Düsterkeit *f*; (*sadness*) düstere *or* gedrückte Stimmung *f*.

**gloomily** ['gluːmɪlɪ] *adv* düster.

**gloomy** ['gluːmɪ] *adj* düster; (*person*) bedrückt; (*situation*) bedrückend.

**glorification** [glɔːrɪfɪ'keɪʃən] *n* Verherrlichung *f*.

**glorify** ['glɔːrɪfaɪ] *vt* verherrlichen.

**glorious** ['glɔːrɪəs] *adj* herrlich; (*victory*) ruhmreich; (*future*) glanzvoll.

**glory** ['glɔːrɪ] *n* Ruhm *m*; (*splendour*) Herrlichkeit *f* ♦ *vi*: **to ~ in** sich sonnen in +*dat*.

**glory hole** (*inf*) *n* Rumpelkammer *f*.

**Glos** (*BRIT*) *abbr* (*POST*: = *Gloucestershire*).

**gloss** [glɔs] *n* Glanz *m*; (*also*: ~ **paint**) Lack *m*, Lackfarbe *f*.

▶ **gloss over** *vt fus* vom Tisch wischen.

**glossary** ['glɔsərɪ] *n* Glossar *nt*.

**glossy** ['glɔsɪ] *adj* glänzend; (*photograph, magazine*) Hochglanz- ♦ *n* (*also*: ~ **magazine**) (Hochglanz)magazin *nt*.

**glove** [glʌv] *n* Handschuh *m*.

**glove compartment** *n* Handschuhfach *nt*.

**glow** [gləu] *vi* glühen; (*stars, eyes*) leuchten ♦ *n* (*see vb*) Glühen *nt*; Leuchten *nt*.

**glower** ['glauə*] *vi*: **to ~ at sb** jdn finster ansehen.

**glowing** ['gləuɪŋ] *adj* glühend; (*complexion*) blühend; (*fig: report, description etc*) begeistert.

**glow-worm** ['gləuwəːm] *n* Glühwürmchen *nt*.

**glucose** ['gluːkəus] *n* Traubenzucker *m*.

**glue** [gluː] *n* Klebstoff *m* ♦ *vt*: **to ~ sth onto sth** etw an etw *acc* kleben; **to ~ sth into place** etw festkleben.

**glue-sniffing** ['gluːsnɪfɪŋ] *n* (Klebstoff-)Schnüffeln *nt*.

**glum** [glʌm] *adj* bedrückt, niedergeschlagen.

**glut** [glʌt] *n*: ~ **(of)** Überangebot *nt* (an +*dat*) ♦ *vt*: **to be ~ted (with)** überschwemmt sein (mit); **a ~ of pears** eine Birnenschwemme.

**glutinous** ['gluːtɪnəs] *adj* klebrig.

**glutton** ['glʌtn] *n* Vielfraß *m*; **a ~ for work** ein Arbeitstier *nt*; **a ~ for punishment** ein Masochist *m*.

**gluttonous** ['glʌtənəs] *adj* gefräßig.

**gluttony** ['glʌtənɪ] *n* Völlerei *f*.

**glycerin(e)** ['glɪsəriːn] *n* Glyzerin *nt*.

**gm** *abbr* (= *gram(me)*) g.

**GMAT** (*US*) *n abbr* (= *Graduate Management Admissions Test*) Zulassungsprüfung *für*

*Handelsschulen.*

**GMB** (*BRIT*) *n abbr* (= *General Municipal and Boilermakers (Union)*) *Fabrikarbeiter-gewerkschaft.*

**GMT** *abbr* (= *Greenwich Mean Time*) WEZ *f.*

**gnarled** [nɑːld] *adj* (*tree*) knorrig; (*hand*) knotig.

**gnash** [næʃ] *vt:* **to ~ one's teeth** mit den Zähnen knirschen.

**gnat** [næt] *n* (Stech)mücke *f.*

**gnaw** [nɔː] *vt* nagen an +*dat* ♦ *vi* (*fig*): **to ~ at** quälen.

**gnome** [nəum] *n* Gnom *m*; (*in garden*) Gartenzwerg *m.*

**GNP** *n abbr* (= *gross national product*) BSP *nt.*

━━━━━━━━━━━ *KEYWORD*

**go** [gəu] (*pt* **went**, *pp* **gone**) *vi* **1** gehen; (*travel*) fahren; **a car went by** ein Auto fuhr vorbei **2** (*depart*) gehen; **"I must ~,"** she said „ich muß gehen", sagte sie; **she has gone to Sheffield/Australia** (*permanently*) sie ist nach Sheffield/Australien gegangen **3** (*attend, take part in activity*) gehen; **she went to university in Oxford** sie ist in Oxford zur Universität gegangen; **to ~ for a walk** spazierengehen; **to ~ dancing** tanzen gehen **4** (*work*) funktionieren; **the tape recorder was still ~ing** das Tonband lief noch **5** (*become*): **to ~ pale/mouldy** blaß/ schimmelig werden **6** (*be sold*): **to ~ for £100** für £100 weggehen *or* verkauft werden **7** (*be about to, intend to*): **we're ~ing to stop in an hour** wir hören in einer Stunde auf; **are you ~ing to come?** kommst du?, wirst du kommen? **8** (*time*) vergehen **9** (*event, activity*) ablaufen; **how did it ~?** wie war's? **10** (*be given*): **the job is to ~ to someone else** die Stelle geht an jemand anders **11** (*break etc*) kaputtgehen; **the fuse went** die Sicherung ist durchgebrannt **12** (*be placed*) hingehören; **the milk goes in the fridge** die Milch kommt in den Kühlschrank

♦ *n* **1** (*try*): **to have a ~ at sth** etw versuchen; **I'll have a ~ at mending it** ich will versuchen, es zu reparieren; **to have a ~** es versuchen **2** (*turn*): **whose ~ is it?** wer ist dran *or* an der Reihe? **3** (*move*): **to be on the ~** auf Trab sein.

▶ **go about** *vi* (*also:* **~ around**: *rumour*) herumgehen ♦ *vt fus:* **how do I ~ about this?** wie soll ich vorgehen?; **to ~ about one's business** seinen eigenen Geschäften nachgehen.

▶ **go after** *vt fus* (*pursue: person*) nachgehen +*dat*; (: *job etc*) sich bemühen um; (: *record*) erreichen wollen.

▶ **go against** *vt fus* (*be unfavourable to*) ungünstig verlaufen für; (*disregard: advice, wishes etc*) handeln gegen.

▶ **go ahead** *vi* (*proceed*) weitergehen; **to ~ ahead with** weitermachen mit.

▶ **go along** *vi* gehen.

▶ **go along with** *vt fus* (*agree with*) zustimmen +*dat*; (*accompany*) mitgehen mit.

▶ **go away** *vi* (*leave*) weggehen.

▶ **go back** *vi* zurückgehen.

▶ **go back on** *vt fus* (*promise*) zurücknehmen.

▶ **go by** *vi* (*years, time*) vergehen ♦ *vt fus* (*rule etc*) sich richten nach.

▶ **go down** *vi* (*descend*) hinuntergehen; (*ship, sun*) untergehen; (*price, level*) sinken ♦ *vt fus* (*stairs, ladder*) hinuntergehen; **his speech went down well** seine Rede kam gut an.

▶ **go for** *vt fus* (*fetch*) holen (gehen); (*like*) mögen; (*attack*) losgehen auf +*acc*; (*apply to*) gelten für.

▶ **go in** *vi* (*enter*) hineingehen.

▶ **go in for** *vt fus* (*competition*) teilnehmen an +*dat*; (*favour*) stehen auf +*acc*.

▶ **go into** *vt fus* (*enter*) hineingehen in +*acc*; (*investigate*) sich befassen mit; (*career*) gehen in +*acc*.

▶ **go off** *vi* (*leave*) weggehen; (*food*) schlecht werden; (*bomb, gun*) losgehen; (*event*) verlaufen; (*lights etc*) ausgehen ♦ *vt fus* (*inf*): **I've gone off it/him** ich mache mir nichts mehr daraus/aus ihm; **the gun went off** das Gewehr ging los; **to ~ off to sleep** einschlafen; **the party went off well** die Party verlief gut.

▶ **go on** *vi* (*continue*) weitergehen; (*happen*) vor sich gehen; (*lights*) angehen ♦ *vt fus* (*be guided by*) sich stützen auf +*acc*; **to ~ on doing sth** mit etw weitermachen; **what's ~ing on here?** was geht hier vor?, was ist hier los?

▶ **go on at** (*inf*) *vt fus* (*nag*) herumnörgeln an +*dat*.

▶ **go on with** *vt fus* weitermachen mit.

▶ **go out** *vt fus* (*leave*) hinausgehen ♦ *vi* (*for entertainment*) ausgehen; (*fire, light*) ausgehen; (*couple*): **they went out for 3 years** sie gingen 3 Jahre lang miteinander.

▶ **go over** *vi* hinübergehen ♦ *vt* (*check*) durchgehen; **to ~ over sth in one's mind** etw überdenken.

▶ **go round** *vi* (*circulate: news, rumour*) umgehen; (*revolve*) sich drehen; (*suffice*) ausreichen; (*visit*): **to ~ round (to sb's)** (bei jdm) vorbeigehen; **there's not enough to ~ round** es reicht nicht (für alle).

▶ **go through** *vt fus* (*place*) gehen durch; (*by car*) fahren durch; (*undergo*) durchmachen; (*search through: files, papers*) durchsuchen; (*describe: list, book, story*) durchgehen; (*perform*) durchgehen.

▶ **go through with** *vt fus* (*plan, crime*) durchziehen; **I couldn't ~ through with it** ich brachte es nicht fertig.

▶**go under** *vi* (*sink: person*) untergehen; (*fig: business, project*) scheitern.

▶**go up** *vi* (*ascend*) hinaufgehen; (*price, level*) steigen; **to ~ up in flames** in Flammen aufgehen.

▶**go with** *vt fus* (*suit*) passen zu.

▶**go without** *vt fus* (*food, treats*) verzichten auf *+acc*.

**goad** [gəud] *vt* aufreizen.

▶**goad on** *vt* anstacheln.

**go-ahead** ['gəuəhɛd] *adj* zielstrebig; (*firm*) fortschrittlich ♦ *n* grünes Licht *nt*; **to give sb the ~** jdm grünes Licht geben.

**goal** [gəul] *n* Tor *nt*; (*aim*) Ziel *nt*; **to score a ~** ein Tor schießen *or* erzielen.

**goal difference** *n* Tordifferenz *f*.

**goalie** ['gəulɪ] (*inf*) *n* Tormann *m*.

**goalkeeper** ['gəulkiːpə'] *n* Torwart *m*.

**goal post** *n* Torpfosten *m*.

**goat** [gəut] *n* Ziege *f*.

**gobble** ['gɔbl] *vt* (*also*: ~ **down**, ~ **up**) verschlingen.

**go-between** ['gəubɪtwiːn] *n* Vermittler(in) *m(f)*.

**Gobi Desert** ['gəubɪ-] *n*: **the ~** die Wüste Gobi.

**goblet** ['gɔblɪt] *n* Pokal *m*.

**goblin** ['gɔblɪn] *n* Kobold *m*.

**go-cart** ['gəukɑːt] *n* Seifenkiste *f*.

**God** [gɔd] *n* Gott *m* ♦ *excl* o Gott!

**god** [gɔd] *n* Gott *m*.

**god-awful** [gɔd'ɔːfəl] (*inf*) *adj* beschissen (*!*).

**godchild** ['gɔdtʃaɪld] *n* Patenkind *nt*.

**goddamn(ed)** ['gɔddæm(d)] (*US: inf*) *adj* gottverdammt.

**goddaughter** ['gɔddɔːtə'] *n* Patentochter *f*.

**goddess** ['gɔdɪs] *n* Göttin *f*.

**godfather** ['gɔdfɑːðə'] *n* Pate *m*.

**God-fearing** ['gɔdfɪərɪŋ] *adj* gottesfürchtig.

**godforsaken** ['gɔdfəseɪkən] *adj* gottverlassen.

**godmother** ['gɔdmʌðə'] *n* Patin *f*.

**godparent** ['gɔdpɛərənt] *n* Pate *m*, Patin *f*.

**godsend** ['gɔdsɛnd] *n* Geschenk *nt* des Himmels.

**godson** ['gɔdsʌn] *n* Patensohn *m*.

**goes** [gəuz] *vb see* go.

**gofer** ['gəufə'] (*inf*) *n* Mädchen *nt* für alles.

**go-getter** ['gəugɛtə'] (*inf*) *n* Ellbogentyp (*pej, inf*) *m*.

**goggle** ['gɔgl] (*inf*) *vi*: **to ~ at** anstarren, anglotzen.

**goggles** ['gɔglz] *npl* Schutzbrille *f*.

**going** ['gəuɪŋ] *n*: **it was slow/hard ~** (*fig*) es ging nur langsam/schwer voran ♦ *adj*: **the ~ rate** der gängige Preis; **when the ~ gets tough** wenn es schwierig wird; **a ~ concern** ein gutgehendes Unternehmen.

**going-over** [gəuɪŋ'əuvə'] (*inf*) *n* (*check*) Untersuchung *f*; (*beating-up*) Abreibung *f*; **to give sb a good ~** jdm eine tüchtige

Abreibung verpassen.

**goings-on** ['gəuɪŋz'ɔn] (*inf*) *npl* Vorgänge *pl*, Dinge *pl*.

**go-kart** ['gəukɑːt] *n* = **go-cart**.

**gold** [gəuld] *n* Gold *nt*; (*also*: ~ **medal**) Gold *nt*, Goldmedaille *f* ♦ *adj* golden; (*reserves, jewellery, tooth*) Gold-.

**golden** ['gəuldən] *adj* (*also fig*) golden.

**golden age** *n* Blütezeit *f*.

**golden handshake** (*BRIT*) *n* Abstandssumme *f*.

**golden rule** *n* goldene Regel *f*.

**goldfish** ['gəuldfɪʃ] *n* Goldfisch *m*.

**gold leaf** *n* Blattgold *nt*.

**gold medal** *n* Goldmedaille *f*.

**gold mine** *n* (*also fig*) Goldgrube *f*.

**gold-plated** ['gəuld'pleɪtɪd] *adj* vergoldet.

**goldsmith** ['gəuldsmɪθ] *n* Goldschmied(in) *m(f)*.

**gold standard** *n* Goldstandard *m*.

**golf** [gɔlf] *n* Golf *nt*.

**golf ball** *n* (*for game*) Golfball *m*; (*on typewriter*) Kugelkopf *m*.

**golf club** *n* Golfklub *m*; (*stick*) Golfschläger *m*.

**golf course** *n* Golfplatz *m*.

**golfer** ['gɔlfə'] *n* Golfspieler(in) *m(f)*, Golfer(in) *m(f)*.

**golfing** ['gɔlfɪŋ] *n* Golf(spielen) *nt*; **he does a lot of ~** er spielt viel Golf ♦ *cpd* Golf-.

**gondola** ['gɔndələ] *n* Gondel *f*.

**gondolier** [gɔndə'lɪə'] *n* Gondoliere *m*.

**gone** [gɔn] *pp of* go ♦ *adj* weg; (*days*) vorbei.

**goner** ['gɔnə'] (*inf*) *n*: **to be a ~** hinüber sein.

**gong** [gɔŋ] *n* Gong *m*.

**good** [gud] *adj* gut; (*well-behaved*) brav, lieb ♦ *n* (*virtue, morality*) Gute(s) *nt*; (*benefit*) Wohl *nt*; **goods** *npl* (*COMM*) Güter *pl*; **to have a ~ time** sich (gut) amüsieren; **to be ~ at sth** (*swimming, talking etc*) etw gut können; (*science, sports etc*) gut in etw *dat* sein; **to be ~ for sb/sth** gut für jdn/zu etw *dat* sein; **it's ~ for you** das tut dir gut; **it's a ~ thing you were there** gut, daß Sie da waren; **she is ~ with children** sie kann gut mit Kindern umgehen; **she is ~ with her hands** sie ist geschickt; **to feel ~** sich wohlfühlen; **it's ~ to see you** (es ist) schön, Sie zu sehen; **would you be ~ enough to ...?** könnten Sie bitte ...?; **that's very ~ of you** das ist wirklich nett von Ihnen; **a ~ deal (of)** ziemlich viel; **a ~ many** ziemlich viele; **take a ~ look** sieh dir das genau *or* gut an; **a ~ while ago** vor einiger Zeit; **to make ~** (*damage*) wiedergutmachen; (*loss*) ersetzen; **it's no ~ complaining** es ist sinnlos *or* es nützt nichts, sich zu beklagen; **~ morning/afternoon/evening!** guten Morgen/Tag/Abend!; **~ night!** gute Nacht!; **he's up to no ~** er führt nichts Gutes im Schilde; **for the common ~** zum Wohle aller; **is this any ~?** (*will it help you?*) können Sie das gebrauchen?; (*is it good enough?*) reicht das?; **is the book/film any ~?** was halten Sie von dem Buch/Film?; **for ~** für immer; **~s and chattels** Hab und Gut *nt*.

**goodbye** [gud'baɪ] *excl* auf Wiedersehen!; **to say ~** sich verabschieden.

**good-for-nothing** ['gudfənʌθɪŋ] *adj* nichtsnutzig.

**Good Friday** *n* Karfreitag *m*.

**good-humoured** ['gud'hjuːməd] *adj* gut gelaunt; (*good-natured*) gutmütig; (*remark, joke*) harmlos.

**good-looking** ['gud'lukɪŋ] *adj* gutaussehend.

**good-natured** ['gud'neɪtʃəd] *adj* gutmütig; (*discussion*) freundlich.

**goodness** ['gudnɪs] *n* Güte *f*; **for ~ sake!** um Himmels willen!; **~ gracious!** ach du liebe *or* meine Güte!

**goods train** (*BRIT*) *n* Güterzug *m*.

**goodwill** [gud'wɪl] *n* Wohlwollen *nt*; (*COMM*) Goodwill *m*.

**goody** ['gudɪ] (*inf*) *n* Gute(r) *m*, Held *m*.

**goody-goody** ['gudɪgudɪ] (*pej*) *n* Tugendlamm *nt*, Musterkind (*inf*) *nt*.

**gooey** ['guːɪ] (*inf*) *adj* (*sticky*) klebrig; (*cake*) üppig; (*fig: sentimental*) rührselig.

**goose** [guːs] (*pl* **geese**) *n* Gans *f*.

**gooseberry** ['guzbərɪ] *n* Stachelbeere *f*; **to play ~** (*BRIT*) das fünfte Rad am Wagen sein.

**goose flesh** *n* = **goose pimples.**

**goose pimples** *npl* Gänsehaut *f*.

**goose step** *n* Stechschritt *m*.

**GOP** (*US: inf*) *n abbr* (*POL:* = *Grand Old Party*) Republikanische Partei.

**gopher** ['gəufə*] *n* (*ZOOL*) Taschenratte *f*.

**gore** [gɔː*] *vt* aufspießen ♦ *n* Blut *nt*.

**gorge** [gɔːdʒ] *n* Schlucht *f* ♦ *vt*: **to ~ o.s. (on)** sich vollstopfen (mit).

**gorgeous** ['gɔːdʒəs] *adj* herrlich; (*person*) hinreißend.

**gorilla** [gə'rɪlə] *n* Gorilla *m*.

**gormless** ['gɔːmlɪs] (*BRIT: inf*) *adj* doof.

**gorse** [gɔːs] *n* Stechginster *m*.

**gory** ['gɔːrɪ] *adj* blutig.

**go-slow** ['gəu'sləu] (*BRIT*) *n* Bummelstreik *m*.

**gospel** ['gɔspl] *n* Evangelium *nt*; (*doctrine*) Lehre *f*.

**gossamer** ['gɔsəmə*] *n* Spinnfäden *pl*; (*light fabric*) hauchdünne Gaze *f*.

**gossip** ['gɔsɪp] *n* (*rumours*) Klatsch *m*, Tratsch *m*; (*chat*) Schwatz *m*; (*person*) Klatschbase *f* ♦ *vi* schwatzen; **a piece of ~** eine Neuigkeit.

**gossip column** *n* Klatschkolumne *f*, Klatschspalte *f*.

**got** [gɔt] *pt, pp of* **get.**

**Gothic** ['gɔθɪk] *adj* gotisch.

**gotten** ['gɔtn] (*US*) *pp of* **get.**

**gouge** [gaudʒ] *vt* (*also:* ~ **out:** *hole etc*) bohren; (*: initials*) eingravieren; **to ~ sb's eyes out** jdm die Augen ausstechen.

**gourd** [guəd] *n* (*container*) Kürbisflasche *f*.

**gourmet** ['guəmeɪ] *n* Feinschmecker(in) *m(f)*, Gourmet *m*.

**gout** [gaut] *n* Gicht *f*.

**govern** ['gʌvən] *vt* (*also LING*) regieren; (*event, conduct*) bestimmen.

**governess** ['gʌvənɪs] *n* Gouvernante *f*.

**governing** ['gʌvənɪŋ] *adj* (*POL*) regierend.

**governing body** *n* Vorstand *m*.

**government** ['gʌvnmənt] *n* Regierung *f* ♦ *cpd* Regierungs-; **local ~** Kommunalverwaltung *f*, Gemeindeverwaltung *f*.

**governmental** [gʌvn'mɛntl] *adj* Regierungs-.

**government stocks** *npl* Staatspapiere *pl*, Staatsanleihen *pl*.

**governor** ['gʌvənə*] *n* Gouverneur(in) *m(f)*; (*of bank, hospital, BRIT: of prison*) Direktor(in) *m(f)*; (*of school*) ≈ Mitglied *nt* des Schulbeirats.

**Govt** *abbr* = **government.**

**gown** [gaun] *n* (*Abend*)kleid *nt*; (*of teacher, BRIT: of judge*) Robe *f*.

**GP** *n abbr* = **general practitioner.**

**GPMU** (*BRIT*) *n abbr* (= *Graphical Paper and Media Union*) Grafiker- und Druckergewerkschaft.

**GPO** *n abbr* (*BRIT: formerly:* = *general post office*) Postbehörde *f*; (*US:* = *Government Printing Office*) regierungsamtliche Druckanstalt.

**gr.** *abbr* (*COMM*) = **gross**; (= *gram(me)*) g.

**grab** [græb] *vt* packen; (*chance, opportunity*) (beim Schopf) ergreifen ♦ *vi*: **to ~ at** greifen *or* grapschen nach +*dat*; **to ~ some food** schnell etwas essen; **to ~ a few hours sleep** ein paar Stunden schlafen.

**grace** [greɪs] *n* Gnade *f*; (*gracefulness*) Anmut *f* ♦ *vt* (*honour*) beehren; (*adorn*) zieren; **5 days' ~** 5 Tage Aufschub; **with (a) good ~** anstandslos; **with (a) bad ~** widerwillig; **his sense of humour is his saving ~** was einen mit ihm versöhnt, ist sein Sinn für Humor; **to say ~** das Tischgebet sprechen.

**graceful** ['greɪsful] *adj* anmutig; (*style, shape*) gefällig; (*refusal, behaviour*) charmant.

**gracious** ['greɪʃəs] *adj* (*kind, courteous*) liebenswürdig; (*compassionate*) gnädig; (*smile*) freundlich; (*house, mansion etc*) stilvoll; (*living etc*) kultiviert ♦ *excl*: (**good**) **~!** (ach) du meine Güte!, (ach) du lieber Himmel!

**gradation** [grə'deɪʃən] *n* Abstufung *f*.

**grade** [greɪd] *n* (*COMM*) (*Güte*)klasse *f*; (*in hierarchy*) Rang *m*; (*SCOL: mark*) Note *f*; (*US: school class*) Klasse *f*; (*: gradient: upward*) Neigung *f*, Steigung *f*; (*: : downward*) Neigung *f*, Gefälle *nt* ♦ *vt* klassifizieren; (*work, student*) einstufen; **to make the ~** (*fig*) es schaffen.

**grade crossing** (*US*) *n* Bahnübergang *m*.

**grade school** (*US*) *n* Grundschule *f*.

**gradient** ['greɪdɪənt] *n* (*upward*) Neigung *f*, Steigung *f*; (*downward*) Neigung, Gefälle *nt*;

(*GEOM*) Gradient *m*.
**gradual** ['grædjuǝl] *adj* allmählich.
**gradually** ['grædjuǝlı] *adv* allmählich.
**graduate** [*n* 'grædjuıt, *vi* 'grædjueıt] *n* (*of university*) Hochschulabsolvent(in) *m(f)*; (*US: of high school*) Schulabgänger(in) *m(f)* ♦ *vi* (*from university*) graduieren; (*US*) die (Schul)abschlußprüfung bestehen.
**graduated pension** ['grædjueıtıd-] *n* gestaffelte Rente *f*.
**graduation** [grædjuˈeıʃǝn] *n* (Ab)schlußfeier *f*.
**graffiti** [grǝˈfiːtı] *n, npl* Graffiti *pl*.
**graft** [grɑːft] *n* (*AGR*) (Pfropf)reis *nt*; (*MED*) Transplantat *nt*; (*BRIT: inf: hard work*) Schufterei *f*; (*bribery*) Schiebung *f* ♦ *vt*: **to ~ (onto)** (*AGR*) (auf)pfropfen (auf +*acc*); (*MED*) übertragen (auf +*acc*), einpflanzen (in +*acc*); (*fig*) aufpfropfen +*dat*.
**grain** [greın] *n* Korn *nt*; (*no pl: cereals*) Getreide *nt*; (*US: corn*) Getreide *nt*, Korn; (*of wood*) Maserung *f*; **it goes against the ~** (*fig*) es geht einem gegen den Strich.
**gram** [græm] *n* Gramm *nt*.
**grammar** ['græmǝ*] *n* Grammatik *f*, Sprachlehre *f*.
**grammar school** (*BRIT*) *n* ≈ Gymnasium *nt*.
**grammatical** [grǝˈmætıkl] *adj* grammat(ikal)isch.
**gramme** [græm] *n* = **gram**.
**gramophone** ['græmǝfǝun] (*BRIT*) *n* Grammophon *nt*.
**granary** ['grænǝrı] *n* Kornspeicher *m*; ® (*Granary*): **G~ bread/loaf** Körnerbrot *nt*.
**grand** [grænd] *adj* großartig; (*inf: wonderful*) phantastisch ♦ *n* (*inf*) ≈ Riese *m* (*1000 Pfund/Dollar*).
**grandchild** ['grænt ʃaıld] (*irreg: like* child) *n* Enkelkind *nt*, Enkel(in) *m(f)*.
**granddad** ['grændæd] (*inf*) *n* Opa *m*.
**granddaughter** ['grændɔːtǝ*] *n* Enkelin *f*.
**grandeur** ['grændjǝ*] *n* (*of scenery etc*) Erhabenheit *f*; (*of building*) Vornehmheit *f*.
**grandfather** ['grændfɑːðǝ*] *n* Großvater *m*.
**grandiose** ['grændıǝus] (*also pej*) *adj* grandios.
**grand jury** (*US*) *n* Großes Geschworenengericht *nt*.
**grandma** ['grænmɑː] (*inf*) *n* Oma *f*.
**grandmother** ['grænmʌðǝ*] *n* Großmutter *f*.
**grandpa** ['grænpɑː] (*inf*) *n* Opa *m*.
**grandparents** ['grændpɛǝrǝnts] *npl* Großeltern *pl*.
**grand piano** *n* Flügel *m*.
**Grand Prix** ['grɑ̃ː'priː] *n* (*AUT*) Grand Prix *m*.
**grandson** ['grænsʌn] *n* Enkel *m*.
**grandstand** ['grændstænd] *n* Haupttribüne *f*.
**grand total** *n* Gesamtsumme *f*, Endsumme *f*.
**granite** ['grænıt] *n* Granit *m*.
**granny** ['grænı] (*inf*) *n* Oma *f*.
**grant** [grɑːnt] *vt* (*money*) bewilligen; (*request etc*) gewähren; (*visa*) erteilen; (*admit*) zugeben ♦ *n* Stipendium *nt*; (*subsidy*)

Subvention *f*; **to take sth for ~ed** etw für selbstverständlich halten; **to take sb for ~ed** jdn als selbstverständlich hinnehmen; **to ~ that** zugeben, daß.
**granulated sugar** ['grænjuleıtıd-] *n* (Zucker)raffinade *f*.
**granule** ['grænjuːl] *n* Körnchen *nt*.
**grape** [greıp] *n* (Wein)traube *f*; **a bunch of ~s** eine (ganze) Weintraube.
**grapefruit** ['greıpfruːt] (*pl* ~ *or* ~**s**) *n* Pampelmuse *f*, Grapefruit *f*.
**grapevine** ['greıpvaın] *n* Weinstock *m*; **I heard it on the ~** (*fig*) es ist mir zu Ohren gekommen.
**graph** [grɑːf] *n* (*diagram*) graphische *or* grafische Darstellung *f*, Schaubild *nt*.
**graphic** ['græfık] *adj* plastisch, anschaulich; (*art, design*) graphisch, grafisch; *see also* **graphics**.
**graphic designer** *n* Graphiker(in) *m(f)*, Grafiker(in) *m(f)*.
**graphic equalizer** [-iːkwǝlaızǝ*] *n* (Graphic) Equalizer *m*.
**graphics** ['græfıks] *n* Graphik *f*, Grafik *f* ♦ *npl* (*drawings*) Zeichnungen *pl*, graphische *or* grafische Darstellungen *pl*.
**graphite** ['græfaıt] *n* Graphit *m*.
**graph paper** *n* Millimeterpapier *nt*.
**grapple** ['græpl] *vi*: **to ~ with sb/sth** mit jdm/etw kämpfen; **to ~ with a problem** sich mit einem Problem herumschlagen.
**grasp** [grɑːsp] *vt* (*seize*) ergreifen; (*hold*) festhalten; (*understand*) begreifen ♦ *n* Griff *m*; (*understanding*) Verständnis *nt*; **it slipped from my ~** es entglitt mir; **to have sth within one's ~** etw in greifbarer Nähe haben; **to have a good ~ of sth** (*fig*) etw gut beherrschen.
▶**grasp at** *vt fus* greifen nach; (*fig: opportunity*) ergreifen.
**grasping** ['grɑːspıŋ] *adj* habgierig.
**grass** [grɑːs] *n* Gras *nt*; (*lawn*) Rasen *m*; (*BRIT: inf: informer*) (Polizei)spitzel *m*.
**grasshopper** ['grɑːshɒpǝ*] *n* Grashüpfer *m*, Heuschrecke *f*.
**grass-roots** ['grɑːsruːts] *npl* (*of party etc*) Basis *f* ♦ *adj* (*opinion*) des kleinen Mannes; **at ~ level** an der Basis.
**grass snake** *n* Ringelnatter *f*.
**grassy** ['grɑːsı] *adj* Gras-, grasig.
**grate** [greıt] *n* (Feuer)rost *m* ♦ *vt* reiben; (*carrots etc*) raspeln ♦ *vi*: **to ~ (on)** kratzen (auf +*dat*).
**grateful** ['greıtful] *adj* dankbar; (*thanks*) aufrichtig.
**gratefully** ['greıtfǝlı] *adv* dankbar.
**grater** ['greıtǝ*] *n* Reibe *f*.
**gratification** [grætıfıˈkeıʃǝn] *n* (*pleasure*) Genugtuung *f*; (*satisfaction*) Befriedigung *f*.
**gratify** ['grætıfaı] *vt* (*please*) erfreuen; (*satisfy*) befriedigen.
**gratifying** ['grætıfaıŋ] *adj* (*see vt*) erfreulich;

befriedigend.
**grating** ['greɪtɪŋ] n Gitter nt ♦ adj (noise) knirschend; (voice) schrill.
**gratitude** ['grætɪtjuːd] n Dankbarkeit f.
**gratuitous** [grə'tjuːɪtəs] adj unnötig.
**gratuity** [grə'tjuːɪtɪ] n Trinkgeld nt.
**grave** [greɪv] n Grab nt ♦ adj (decision, mistake) schwer(wiegend); (expression, person) ernst.
**grave digger** n Totengräber m.
**gravel** ['grævl] n Kies m.
**gravely** ['greɪvlɪ] adv (also: see adj) schwer, ernst; ~ **ill** schwerkrank.
**gravestone** ['greɪvstəun] n Grabstein m.
**graveyard** ['greɪvjɑːd] n Friedhof m.
**gravitas** ['grævɪtæs] n Seriosität f.
**gravitate** ['grævɪteɪt] vi: **to ~ towards** angezogen werden von.
**gravity** ['grævɪtɪ] n Schwerkraft f; (seriousness) Ernst m, Schwere f.
**gravy** ['greɪvɪ] n (juice) (Braten)saft m; (sauce) (Braten)soße f.
**gravy boat** n Sauciere f, Soßenschüssel f.
**gravy train** (inf) n: **to ride the ~** leichtes Geld machen.
**gray** [greɪ] (US) adj = **grey**.
**graze** [greɪz] vi grasen, weiden ♦ vt streifen; (scrape) aufschürfen ♦ n (MED) Abschürfung f.
**grazing** ['greɪzɪŋ] n Weideland nt.
**grease** [griːs] n (lubricant) Schmiere f; (fat) Fett nt ♦ vt (see n) schmieren; fetten; **to ~ the skids** (US, fig) die Maschinerie in Gang halten.
**grease gun** n Fettspritze f, Fettpresse f.
**greasepaint** ['griːspeɪnt] n (Fett)schminke f.
**greaseproof paper** ['griːspruːf-] (BRIT) n Pergamentpapier nt.
**greasy** ['griːsɪ] adj fettig; (food: containing grease) fett; (tools) schmierig, ölig; (clothes) speckig; (BRIT: road, surface) glitschig, schlüpfrig.
**great** [greɪt] adj groß; (city) bedeutend; (inf: terrific) prima, toll; **they're ~ friends** sie sind gute Freunde; **we had a ~ time** wir haben uns glänzend amüsiert; **it was ~!** es war toll!; **the ~ thing is that ...** das Wichtigste ist, daß ...
**Great Barrier Reef** n: **the ~** das Große Barriereriff.
**Great Britain** n Großbritannien nt.
**greater** ['greɪtə*] adj see **great**; größer; bedeutender; **people in G~ Calcutta** die Leute in Kalkutta und Umgebung; **G~ Manchester** Groß-Manchester nt.
**great-grandchild** [greɪt'græntʃaɪld] (irreg: like child) n Urenkel(in) m(f).
**great-grandfather** [greɪt'grænfɑːðə*] n Urgroßvater m.
**great-grandmother** [greɪt'grænmʌðə*] n Urgroßmutter f.
**Great Lakes** npl: **the ~** die Großen Seen pl.
**greatly** ['greɪtlɪ] adv sehr; (influenced) stark.

**greatness** ['greɪtnɪs] n Bedeutung f.
**Grecian** ['griːʃən] adj griechisch.
**Greece** [griːs] n Griechenland nt.
**greed** [griːd] n (also: ~iness): ~ **for** Gier f nach; ~ **for power** Machtgier f; ~ **for money** Geldgier f.
**greedily** ['griːdɪlɪ] adv gierig.
**greedy** ['griːdɪ] adj gierig.
**Greek** [griːk] adj griechisch ♦ n Grieche m, Griechin f; (LING) Griechisch nt; **ancient/ modern** ~ Alt-/Neugriechisch nt.
**green** [griːn] adj (also ecological) grün ♦ n (also GOLF) Grün nt; (stretch of grass) Rasen m, Grünfläche f; (also: **village** ~) Dorfwiese f, Anger m; **greens** npl (vegetables) Grüngemüse nt; (POL): **the G~s** die Grünen pl; **to have ~ fingers** or (US) **a ~ thumb** (fig) eine Hand für Pflanzen haben; **to give sb the ~ light** jdm grünes Licht geben.
**green belt** n Grüngürtel m.
**green card** n (AUT) grüne (Versicherungs)karte f; (US) ≈ Aufenthaltserlaubnis f.
**greenery** ['griːnərɪ] n Grün nt.
**greenfly** ['griːnflaɪ] (BRIT) n Blattlaus f.
**greengage** ['griːngeɪdʒ] n Reineclaude f, Reneklode f.
**greengrocer** ['griːngrəusə*] (BRIT) n Obst- und Gemüsehändler(in) m(f).
**greenhouse** ['griːnhaus] n Gewächshaus nt, Treibhaus nt; ~ **effect** Treibhauseffekt m; ~ **gas** Treibhausgas nt.
**greenish** ['griːnɪʃ] adj grünlich.
**Greenland** ['griːnlənd] n Grönland nt.
**Greenlander** ['griːnləndə*] n Grönländer(in) m(f).
**green light** n grünes Licht nt; **to give sb the ~** jdm grünes Licht or freie Fahrt geben.
**Green Party** n (POL): **the ~** die Grünen pl.
**green pepper** n grüne Paprikaschote f.
**green pound** n grünes Pfund nt.
**greet** [griːt] vt begrüßen; (news) aufnehmen.
**greeting** ['griːtɪŋ] n Gruß m; (welcome) Begrüßung f; **Christmas ~s** Weihnachtsgrüße pl; **birthday ~s** Geburtstagsglückwünsche pl; **Season's ~s** Frohe Weihnachten und ein glückliches Neues Jahr.
**greeting(s) card** n Grußkarte f; (congratulating) Glückwunschkarte f.
**gregarious** [grə'gɛərɪəs] adj gesellig.
**grenade** [grə'neɪd] n (also: **hand** ~) (Hand)granate f.
**grew** [gruː] pt of **grow**.
**grey,** (US) **gray** [greɪ] adj grau; (dismal) trüb, grau; **to go ~** grau werden.
**grey-haired** [greɪ'hɛəd] adj grauhaarig.
**greyhound** ['greɪhaund] n Windhund m.
**grid** [grɪd] n Gitter nt; (ELEC) (Verteiler)netz nt; (US: AUT: intersection) Kreuzung f.
**griddle** [grɪdl] n gußeiserne Pfanne zum Braten und Pfannkuchenbacken.

**gridiron** ['grɪdaɪən] n Bratrost m.

**gridlock** ['grɪdlɔk] n (esp US: on road) totaler Stau m; (stalemate) Patt nt ♦ vt: to be ~ed (roads) total verstopft sein; (talks etc) festgefahren sein.

**grief** [griːf] n Kummer m, Trauer f; to come to ~ (plan) scheitern; (person) zu Schaden kommen; good ~! ach du liebe Güte!

**grievance** ['griːvəns] n Beschwerde f; (feeling of resentment) Groll m.

**grieve** [griːv] vi trauern ♦ vt Kummer bereiten +dat, betrüben; to ~ for trauern um.

**grievous** ['griːvəs] adj (mistake) schwer; (situation) beträublich; ~ bodily harm (LAW) schwere Körperverletzung f.

**grill** [grɪl] n Grill m; (grilled food: also: mixed ~) Grillgericht nt; (restaurant) = grillroom ♦ vt (BRIT) grillen; (inf: question) in die Zange nehmen, ausquetschen.

**grille** [grɪl] n (screen) Gitter nt; (AUT) Kühlergrill m.

**grillroom** ['grɪlrum] n Grillrestaurant nt.

**grim** [grɪm] adj trostlos; (serious, stern) grimmig.

**grimace** [grɪ'meɪs] n Grimasse f ♦ vi Grimassen schneiden.

**grime** [graɪm] n Dreck m, Schmutz m.

**grimy** ['graɪmɪ] adj dreckig, schmutzig.

**grin** [grɪn] n Grinsen nt ♦ vi grinsen; to ~ at sb jdn angrinsen.

**grind** [graɪnd] (pt, pp ground) vt zerkleinern; (coffee, pepper etc) mahlen; (US: meat) hacken, durch den Fleischwolf drehen; (knife) schleifen, wetzen; (gem, lens) schleifen ♦ vi (car gears) knirschen ♦ n (work) Schufterei f; to ~ one's teeth mit den Zähnen knirschen; to ~ to a halt (vehicle) quietschend zum Stehen kommen; (fig: talks, scheme) sich festfahren; (work) stocken; (production) zum Erliegen kommen; the daily ~ (inf) der tägliche Trott.

**grinder** ['graɪndə*] n (for coffee) Kaffeemühle f; (for waste disposal etc) Müllzerkleinerungsanlage f.

**grindstone** ['graɪndstəun] n: to keep one's nose to the ~ hart arbeiten.

**grip** [grɪp] n Griff m; (of tyre, shoe) Halt m; (holdall) Reisetasche f ♦ vt packen; (audience, attention) fesseln; to come to ~s with sth etw in den Griff bekommen; to lose one's ~ den Halt verlieren; (fig) nachlassen; to ~ the road (car) gut auf der Straße liegen.

**gripe** [graɪp] (inf) n (complaint) Meckerei f ♦ vi meckern; the ~s (MED) Kolik f, Bauchschmerzen pl.

**gripping** ['grɪpɪŋ] adj fesselnd, packend.

**grisly** ['grɪzlɪ] adj gräßlich, grausig.

**grist** [grɪst] n (fig): it's all ~ to the mill das kann man alles verwerten.

**gristle** ['grɪsl] n Knorpel m.

**grit** [grɪt] n (for icy roads: sand) Sand m;

(crushed stone) Splitt m; (determination, courage) Mut m ♦ vt (road) streuen; **grits** npl (US) Grütze f; **I've got a piece of ~ in my eye** ich habe ein Staubkorn im Auge; **to ~ one's teeth** die Zähne zusammenbeißen.

**grizzle** ['grɪzl] (BRIT) vi quengeln.

**grizzly** ['grɪzlɪ] n (also: ~ bear) Grislybär m, Grizzlybär m.

**groan** [grəun] n Stöhnen nt ♦ vi stöhnen; (tree, floorboard etc) ächzen, knarren.

**grocer** ['grəusə*] n Lebensmittelhändler(in) m(f).

**groceries** ['grəusərɪz] npl Lebensmittel pl.

**grocer's (shop)** n Lebensmittelgeschäft nt.

**grog** [grɔg] n Grog m.

**groggy** ['grɔgɪ] adj angeschlagen.

**groin** [grɔɪn] n Leistengegend f.

**groom** [gruːm] n Stallbursche m; (also: bride~) Bräutigam m ♦ vt (horse) striegeln; (fig): to ~ sb for (job) jdn aufbauen für; well-~ed gepflegt.

**groove** [gruːv] n Rille f.

**grope** [grəup] vi: to ~ for tasten nach; (fig: try to think of) suchen nach.

**grosgrain** ['grəugreɪn] n grob gerippter Stoff m.

**gross** [grəus] adj (neglect) grob; (injustice) kraß; (behaviour, speech) grob, derb; (COMM: income, weight) Brutto- ♦ n inv Gros m ♦ vt: to ~ £500,000 £500 000 brutto einnehmen.

**gross domestic product** n Bruttoinlandsprodukt nt.

**grossly** ['grəuslɪ] adv äußerst; (exaggerated) grob.

**gross national product** n Bruttosozialprodukt nt.

**grotesque** [grə'tɛsk] adj grotesk.

**grotto** ['grɔtəu] n Grotte f.

**grotty** ['grɔtɪ] (inf) adj mies.

**grouch** [grautʃ] (inf) vi schimpfen ♦ n (person) Miesepeter m, Muffel m.

**ground** [graund] pt, pp of grind ♦ n Boden m, Erde f; (land) Land nt; (SPORT) Platz m, Feld nt; (US: ELEC: also: ~ wire) Erde f; (reason: gen pl) Grund m ♦ vt (plane) aus dem Verkehr ziehen; (US: ELEC) erden ♦ adj (coffee etc) gemahlen ♦ vi (ship) auflaufen; **grounds** npl (of coffee etc) Satz m; (gardens etc) Anlagen pl; **below ~** unter der Erde; **to gain/lose ~** Boden gewinnen/verlieren; **common ~** Gemeinsame(s) nt; **on the ~s that** mit der Begründung, daß.

**ground cloth** (US) n = groundsheet.

**ground control** n (AVIAT, SPACE) Bodenkontrolle f.

**ground floor** n Erdgeschoß nt.

**grounding** ['graundɪŋ] n (in education) Grundwissen nt.

**groundless** ['graundlɪs] adj grundlos, unbegründet.

**groundnut** ['graundnʌt] n Erdnuß f.

**ground rent** (BRIT) n Erbbauzins m.

**ground rule** n Grundregel f.
**groundsheet** ['graundʃiːt] (BRIT) n Zeltboden m.
**groundskeeper** ['graundzkiːpə*] (US) n = **groundsman**.
**groundsman** ['graundzmən] (irreg: like man) n (SPORT) Platzwart m.
**ground staff** n (AVIAT) Bodenpersonal nt.
**ground swell** n: **there was a ~ of public opinion against him** die Öffentlichkeit wandte sich gegen ihn.
**ground-to-air missile** ['graundtə'ɛə*-] n Boden-Luft-Rakete f.
**ground-to-ground missile** ['graundtə'graund-] n Boden-Boden-Rakete f.
**groundwork** ['graundwəːk] n Vorarbeit f.
**group** [gruːp] n Gruppe f, (COMM) Konzern m ♦ vt (also: ~ **together**: in one group) zusammentun; (: in several groups) in Gruppen einteilen ♦ vi (also: ~ **together**) sich zusammentun.
**groupie** ['gruːpɪ] (inf) n Groupie nt.
**group therapy** n Gruppentherapie f.
**grouse** [graus] n inv schottisches Moorhuhn nt ♦ vi (complain) schimpfen.
**grove** [grəuv] n Hain m, Wäldchen nt.
**grovel** ['grɔvl] vi (crawl) kriechen; (fig): **to ~ (before)** kriechen (vor +dat).
**grow** [grəu] (pt grew, pp grown) vi wachsen; (increase) zunehmen; (become) werden ♦ vt (roses) züchten; (vegetables) anbauen, ziehen; (beard) sich dat wachsen lassen; **to ~ tired of waiting** das Warten leid sein; **to ~ (out of or from)** (develop) entstehen (aus).
▶**grow apart** vi (fig) sich auseinanderentwickeln.
▶**grow away from** vt fus (fig) sich entfremden +dat.
▶**grow on** vt fus: **that painting is ~ing on me** allmählich finde ich Gefallen an dem Bild.
▶**grow out of** vt fus (clothes) herauswachsen aus; (habit) ablegen; **he'll ~ out of it** diese Phase geht auch vorbei.
▶**grow up** vi aufwachsen; (mature) erwachsen werden; (idea, friendship) entstehen.
**grower** ['grəuə*] n (BOT) Züchter(in) m(f); (AGR) Pflanzer(in) m(f).
**growing** ['grəuɪŋ] adj wachsend; (number) zunehmend; ~ **pains** Wachstumsschmerzen pl; (fig) Kinderkrankheiten pl, Anfangsschwierigkeiten pl.
**growl** [graul] vi knurren.
**grown** [grəun] pp of **grow**.
**grown-up** [grəun'ʌp] n Erwachsene(r) f(m).
**growth** [grəuθ] n Wachstum nt; (what has grown: of weeds, beard etc) Wuchs m; (of person, character) Entwicklung f, (MED) Gewächs nt, Wucherung f.
**growth rate** n Wachstumsrate f, Zuwachsrate f.
**grub** [grʌb] n (larva) Larve f; (inf: food)

Fressalien pl, Futter nt ♦ vi: **to ~ about** or **around (for)** (herum)wühlen (nach).
**grubby** ['grʌbɪ] adj (dirty) schmuddelig; (fig) schmutzig.
**grudge** [grʌdʒ] n Groll m ♦ vt: **to ~ sb sth** jdm etw nicht gönnen; **to bear sb a ~** jdm böse sein, einen Groll gegen jdn hegen.
**grudging** ['grʌdʒɪŋ] adj widerwillig.
**grudgingly** ['grʌdʒɪŋlɪ] adv widerwillig.
**gruelling, (US) grueling** ['gruəlɪŋ] adj (encounter) aufreibend; (trip, journey) äußerst strapaziös.
**gruesome** ['gruːsəm] adj grauenhaft.
**gruff** [grʌf] adj barsch, schroff.
**grumble** ['grʌmbl] vi murren, schimpfen.
**grumpy** ['grʌmpɪ] adj mürrisch, brummig.
**grunge** [grʌndʒ] (inf) n Grunge nt.
**grunt** [grʌnt] vi grunzen ♦ n Grunzen nt.
**G-string** ['dʒiːstrɪŋ] n Minislip m, Tangaslip m.
**GSUSA** n abbr (= Girl Scouts of the United States of America) amerikanische Pfadfinderinnen.
**GT** abbr (AUT: = gran turismo) GT.
**GU** (US) abbr (POST: = Guam).
**guarantee** [gærən'tiː] n Garantie f ♦ vt garantieren; **he can't ~ (that) he'll come** er kann nicht dafür garantieren, daß er kommt.
**guarantor** [gærən'tɔː*] n (COMM) Bürge m.
**guard** [gɑːd] n Wache f, (BOXING, FENCING) Deckung f, (BRIT: RAIL) Schaffner(in) m(f); (on machine) Schutz m, Schutzvorrichtung f; (also: **fire~**) (Schutz)gitter nt ♦ vt (prisoner) bewachen; (protect): **to ~ (against)** (be)schützen (vor +dat); (secret) hüten (vor +dat); **to be on one's ~** auf der Hut sein.
▶**guard against** vt fus (disease) vorbeugen +dat; (damage, accident) verhüten.
**guard dog** n Wachhund m.
**guarded** ['gɑːdɪd] adj vorsichtig, zurückhaltend.
**guardian** ['gɑːdɪən] n Vormund m; (defender) Hüter m.
**guardrail** ['gɑːdreɪl] n (Schutz)geländer nt.
**guard's van** (BRIT) n (RAIL) Schaffnerabteil nt, Dienstwagen m.
**Guatemala** [gwɑːtɪ'mɑːlə] n Guatemala nt.
**Guatemalan** [gwɑːtɪ'mɑːlən] adj guatemaltekisch, aus Guatemala.
**Guernsey** ['gəːnzɪ] n Guernsey nt.
**guerrilla** [gə'rɪlə] n Guerilla m, Guerillakämpfer(in) m(f).
**guerrilla warfare** n Guerillakrieg m.
**guess** [gɛs] vt schätzen; (answer) (er)raten; (US: think) schätzen (inf) ♦ vi (see vt ~) schätzen; raten ♦ n Vermutung f; **I ~ you're right** da haben Sie wohl recht; **to keep sb ~ing** jdn im ungewissen lassen; **to take** or **have a ~** raten; (estimate) schätzen; **my ~ is that ...** ich schätze or vermute, daß ...
**guesstimate** ['gɛstɪmɪt] (inf) n grobe Schätzung f.

**guesswork** ['gɛswɜːk] n Vermutungen pl; **I got the answer by ~** ich habe die Antwort nur geraten.

**guest** [gɛst] n Gast m; **be my ~** (inf) nur zu!

**guesthouse** ['gɛsthaus] n Pension f.

**guest room** n Gästezimmer nt.

**guff** [gʌf] (inf) n Quatsch m, Käse m.

**guffaw** [gʌ'fɔː] vi schallend lachen ♦ n schallendes Lachen nt.

**guidance** ['gaɪdəns] n Rat m, Beratung f; **under the ~ of** unter der Leitung von; **vocational ~** Berufsberatung f; **marriage ~** Eheberatung f.

**guide** [gaɪd] n (person) Führer(in) m(f); (book) Führer m; (BRIT: also: **girl ~**) Pfadfinderin f ♦ vt führen; (direct) lenken; **to be ~d by sb/ sth** sich von jdm/etw leiten lassen.

**guidebook** ['gaɪdbuk] n Führer m.

**guided missile** n Lenkwaffe f.

**guide dog** n Blindenhund m.

**guidelines** ['gaɪdlaɪnz] npl Richtlinien pl.

**guild** [gɪld] n Verein m.

**guildhall** ['gɪldhɔːl] (BRIT) n Gildehaus nt.

**guile** [gaɪl] n Arglist f.

**guileless** ['gaɪllɪs] adj arglos.

**guillotine** ['gɪlətiːn] n Guillotine f, Fallbeil nt; (for paper) (Papier)schneidemaschine f.

**guilt** [gɪlt] n Schuld f; (remorse) Schuldgefühl nt.

**guilty** ['gɪltɪ] adj schuldig; (expression) schuldbewußt; (secret) dunkel; **to plead ~/ not ~** sich schuldig/nicht schuldig bekennen; **to feel ~ about doing sth** ein schlechtes Gewissen haben, etw zu tun.

**Guinea** ['gɪnɪ] n: **Republic of ~** Guinea nt.

**guinea** ['gɪnɪ] (BRIT) n (old) Guinee f.

**guinea pig** n Meerschweinchen nt; (fig: person) Versuchskaninchen nt.

**guise** [gaɪz] n: **in** or **under the ~ of** in der Form +gen, in Gestalt +gen.

**guitar** [gɪ'tɑː] n Gitarre f.

**guitarist** [gɪ'tɑːrɪst] n Gitarrist(in) m(f).

**gulch** [gʌltʃ] (US) n Schlucht f.

**gulf** [gʌlf] n Golf m; (abyss) Abgrund m; (fig: difference) Kluft f; **the (Persian) G~** der (Persische) Golf.

**Gulf States** npl: **the ~** die Golfstaaten pl.

**Gulf Stream** n: **the ~** der Golfstrom.

**Gulf War** n: **the ~** der Golfkrieg.

**gull** [gʌl] n Möwe f.

**gullet** ['gʌlɪt] n Speiseröhre f.

**gullibility** [gʌlɪ'bɪlɪtɪ] n Leichtgläubigkeit f.

**gullible** ['gʌlɪbl] adj leichtgläubig.

**gully** ['gʌlɪ] n Schlucht f.

**gulp** [gʌlp] vi schlucken ♦ vt (also: **~ down**) hinunterschlucken ♦ n: **at one ~** mit einem Schluck.

**gum** [gʌm] n (ANAT) Zahnfleisch nt; (glue) Klebstoff m; (also: **~drop**) Weingummi nt; (also: **chewing-~**) Kaugummi m ♦ vt: **to ~ (together)** (zusammen)kleben.

▶**gum up** vt: **to ~ up the works** (inf) alles

vermasseln.

**gumboots** ['gʌmbuːts] (BRIT) npl Gummistiefel pl.

**gumption** ['gʌmpʃən] n Grips m (inf).

**gumtree** ['gʌmtriː] n: **to be up a ~** (fig: inf) aufgeschmissen sein.

**gun** [gʌn] n (small) Pistole f; (medium-sized) Gewehr nt; (large) Kanone f ♦ vt (also: **~ down**) erschießen; **to stick to one's ~s** (fig) nicht nachgeben, fest bleiben.

**gunboat** ['gʌnbəut] n Kanonenboot nt.

**gun dog** n Jagdhund m.

**gunfire** ['gʌnfaɪə] n Geschützfeuer nt.

**gunge** [gʌndʒ] (inf) n Schmiere f.

**gung ho** [gʌŋ 'həu] (inf) adj übereifrig.

**gunman** ['gʌnmən] (irreg: like **man**) n bewaffneter Verbrecher m.

**gunner** ['gʌnə] n Kanonier m, Artillerist m.

**gunpoint** ['gʌnpɔɪnt] n: **at ~** mit vorgehaltener Pistole; mit vorgehaltenem Gewehr.

**gunpowder** ['gʌnpaudə] n Schießpulver nt.

**gunrunner** ['gʌnrʌnə] n Waffenschmuggler(in) m(f), Waffenschieber(in) m(f).

**gunrunning** ['gʌnrʌnɪŋ] n Waffenschmuggel m, Waffenschieberei f.

**gunshot** ['gʌnʃɔt] n Schuß m.

**gunsmith** ['gʌnsmɪθ] n Büchsenmacher m.

**gurgle** ['gɜːgl] vi (baby) glucksen; (water) gluckern.

**guru** ['guruː] n Guru m.

**gush** [gʌʃ] vi hervorquellen, hervorströmen; (person) schwärmen ♦ n Strahl m.

**gushing** ['gʌʃɪŋ] adj (fig) überschwenglich.

**gusset** ['gʌsɪt] n Keil m, Zwickel m.

**gust** [gʌst] n Windstoß m, Bö(e) f; (of smoke) Wolke f.

**gusto** ['gʌstəu] n: **with ~** mit Genuß, mit Schwung.

**gusty** ['gʌstɪ] adj (wind) böig; (day) stürmisch.

**gut** [gʌt] n (ANAT) Darm m; (for violin, racket) Darmsaiten pl ♦ vt (poultry, fish) ausnehmen; (building) ausräumen; (by fire) ausbrennen; **guts** npl (ANAT) Eingeweide pl; (inf: courage) Mumm m; **to hate sb's ~s** jdn auf den Tod nicht ausstehen können.

**gut reaction** n rein gefühlsmäßige Reaktion f.

**gutsy** ['gʌtsɪ] (inf) adj (vivid) rasant; (courageous) mutig.

**gutter** ['gʌtə] n (in street) Gosse f, Rinnstein m; (of roof) Dachrinne f.

**gutter press** n Boulevardpresse f.

**guttural** ['gʌtərl] adj gutteral.

**guy** [gaɪ] n (inf: man) Typ m, Kerl m; (also: **~rope**) Halteseil nt, Halteseil nt; (for Guy Fawkes' night) (Guy-Fawkes-)Puppe f.

---

**Guy Fawkes' Night**, auch bonfire night genannt, erinnert an den Gunpowder Plot, einen Attentatsversuch auf James I und sein Parlament am 5. November 1605. Einer der

*Verschwörer, Guy Fawkes, wurde auf frischer Tat ertappt, als er das Parlamentsgebäude in die Luft sprengen wollte. Vor der Guy Fawkes' Night basteln Kinder in Großbritannien eine Puppe des Guy Fawkes, mit der sie Geld für Feuerwerkskörper von Passanten erbetteln, und die dann am 5. November auf einem Lagerfeuer mit Feuerwerk verbrannt wird.*

**Guyana** [gaɪˈænə] n Guyana nt.
**guzzle** [ˈgʌzl] vt (food) futtern; (drink) saufen (inf).
**gym** [dʒɪm] n (also: **gymnasium**) Turnhalle f; (also: **gymnastics**) Gymnastik f, Turnen nt.
**gymkhana** [dʒɪmˈkɑːnə] n Reiterfest nt.
**gymnasium** [dʒɪmˈneɪzɪəm] n Turnhalle f.
**gymnast** [ˈdʒɪmnæst] n Turner(in) m(f).
**gymnastics** [dʒɪmˈnæstɪks] n Gymnastik f, Turnen nt.
**gym shoes** npl Turnschuhe pl.
**gymslip** [ˈdʒɪmslɪp] (BRIT) n (Schul)trägerrock m.
**gynaecologist**, (US) **gynecologist** [gaɪnɪˈkɔlədʒɪst] n Gynäkologe m, Gynäkologin f, Frauenarzt m, Frauenärztin f.
**gynaecology**, (US) **gynecology** [gaɪnɪˈkɔlədʒɪ] n Gynäkologie f, Frauenheilkunde f.
**gypsy** [ˈdʒɪpsɪ] n = **gipsy**.
**gyrate** [dʒaɪˈreɪt] vi kreisen, sich drehen.
**gyroscope** [ˈdʒaɪərəskəup] n Gyroskop nt.

# H, h

**H, h** [eɪtʃ] n (letter) H, h nt; ~ **for Harry**, (US) ~ **for How** ≈ H wie Heinrich.
**habeas corpus** [ˈheɪbɪəsˈkɔːpəs] n Habeaskorpusakte f.
**haberdashery** [hæbəˈdæʃərɪ] (BRIT) n Kurzwaren pl.
**habit** [ˈhæbɪt] n Gewohnheit f; (esp undesirable) Angewohnheit f; (addiction) Sucht f; (REL) Habit m or nt; **to get out of/into the** ~ **of doing sth** sich abgewöhnen/ angewöhnen, etw zu tun; **to be in the** ~ **of doing sth** die (An)gewohnheit haben, etw zu tun.
**habitable** [ˈhæbɪtəbl] adj bewohnbar.
**habitat** [ˈhæbɪtæt] n Heimat f; (of animals) Lebensraum m, Heimat f.
**habitation** [hæbɪˈteɪʃən] n Wohnstätte f; **fit for human** ~ für Wohnzwecke geeignet, bewohnbar.
**habitual** [həˈbɪtjuəl] adj (action) gewohnt; (drinker) Gewohnheits-; (liar)

gewohnheitsmäßig.
**habitually** [həˈbɪtjuəlɪ] adv ständig.
**hack** [hæk] vt, vi (also COMPUT) hacken ♦ n (pej: writer) Schreiberling m; (horse) Mietpferd nt.
**hacker** [ˈhækəʳ] n (COMPUT) Hacker m.
**hackles** [ˈhæklz] npl: **to make sb's** ~ **rise** (fig) jdn auf die Palme bringen (inf).
**hackney cab** [ˈhæknɪ-] n Taxi nt.
**hackneyed** [ˈhæknɪd] adj abgedroschen.
**hacksaw** [ˈhæksɔː] n Metallsäge f.
**had** [hæd] pt, pp of **have**.
**haddock** [ˈhædək] (pl ~ or ~s) n Schellfisch m.
**hadn't** [ˈhædnt] = **had not**.
**haematology**, (US) **hematology** [ˈhiːməˈtɔlədʒɪ] n Hämatologie f.
**haemoglobin**, (US) **hemoglobin** [ˈhiːməˈgləubɪn] n Hämoglobin nt.
**haemophilia**, (US) **hemophilia** [ˈhiːməˈfɪlɪə] n Bluterkrankheit f.
**haemorrhage**, (US) **hemorrhage** [ˈhɛmərɪdʒ] n Blutung f.
**haemorrhoids**, (US) **hemorrhoids** [ˈhɛmərɔɪdz] npl Hämorrhoiden pl.
**hag** [hæg] n alte Hexe f; (witch) Hexe f.
**haggard** [ˈhægəd] adj ausgezehrt; (from worry) abgehärmt; (from tiredness) abgespannt.
**haggis** [ˈhægɪs] (SCOT) n Gericht aus gehackten Schafsinnereien und Haferschrot, im Schafsmagen gekocht.
**haggle** [ˈhægl] vi: **to** ~ **(over)** feilschen (um).
**haggling** [ˈhæglɪŋ] n Feilschen nt.
**Hague** [heɪg] n: **The** ~ Den Haag m.
**hail** [heɪl] n Hagel m ♦ vt (person) zurufen +dat; (taxi) herbeiwinken, anhalten; (acclaim: person) zujubeln +dat; (: event etc) bejubeln ♦ vi hageln; **he** ~**s from Scotland** er kommt or stammt aus Schottland.
**hailstone** [ˈheɪlstəun] n Hagelkorn nt.
**hailstorm** [ˈheɪlstɔːm] n Hagelschauer m.
**hair** [hɛəʳ] n (collectively: of person) Haar nt, Haare pl; (: of animal) Fell nt; (single hair) Haar nt; **to do one's** ~ sich frisieren; **by a** ~**'s breadth** um Haaresbreite.
**hairbrush** [ˈhɛəbrʌʃ] n Haarbürste f.
**haircut** [ˈhɛəkʌt] n Haarschnitt m; (style) Frisur f.
**hairdo** [ˈhɛəduː] n Frisur f.
**hairdresser** [ˈhɛədrɛsəʳ] n Friseur m, Friseuse f.
**hairdresser's** [ˈhɛədrɛsəz] n Friseursalon m.
**hair dryer** n Haartrockner m, Fön m.
-**haired** [hɛəd] suff: **fair-**~ blond; **long-**~ langhaarig.
**hairgrip** [ˈhɛəgrɪp] n Haarklemme f.
**hairline** [ˈhɛəlaɪn] n Haaransatz m.
**hairline fracture** n Haarriß m.
**hairnet** [ˈhɛənɛt] n Haarnetz nt.
**hair oil** n Haaröl nt.
**hairpiece** [ˈhɛəpiːs] n Haarteil nt; (for men) Toupet nt.
**hairpin** [ˈhɛəpɪn] n Haarnadel f.

**hairpin bend,** (*US*) **hairpin curve** *n*
Haarnadelkurve *f*.
**hair-raising** ['hɛəreɪzɪŋ] *adj* haarsträubend.
**hair remover** *n* Enthaarungscreme *f*.
**hair slide** *n* Haarspange *f*.
**hair spray** *n* Haarspray *nt*.
**hairstyle** ['hɛəstaɪl] *n* Frisur *f*.
**hairy** ['hɛərɪ] *adj* behaart; (*inf: situation*)
brenzlig, haarig.
**Haiti** ['heɪtɪ] *n* Haiti *nt*.
**hake** [heɪk] (*pl ~ or ~s*) *n* Seehecht *m*.
**halcyon** ['hælsɪən] *adj* glücklich.
**hale** [heɪl] *adj*: ~ **and hearty** gesund und
munter.
**half** [hɑːf] (*pl* **halves**) *n* Hälfte *f*; (*of beer etc*)
kleines Bier *nt etc*; (*RAIL, bus*) Fahrkarte *f*
zum halben Preis ♦ *adj, adv* halb; **first/second**
~ (*SPORT*) erste/zweite Halbzeit *f*; **two and**
**a** ~ zweieinhalb; **~-an-hour** eine halbe
Stunde; ~ **a dozen/pound** ein halbes
Dutzend/Pfund; **a week and a** ~ eineinhalb
*or* anderthalb Wochen; ~ (**of it**) die Hälfte;
~ (**of**) die Hälfte (von *or* +*gen*); ~ **the amount**
**of** die halbe Menge an +*dat*; **to cut sth in** ~
etw halbieren; ~ **past three** halb vier; **to go**
**halves (with sb)** (mit jdm) halbe-halbe
machen; **she never does things by halves** sie
macht keine halben Sachen; **he's too clever**
**by** ~ er ist ein richtiger Schlaumeier;
~ **empty** halbleer; ~ **closed**
halbgeschlossen.
**half-baked** ['hɑːf'beɪkt] *adj* blödsinnig (*inf*).
**half board** *n* Halbpension *f*.
**half-breed** ['hɑːfbriːd] *n* = **half-caste**.
**half-brother** ['hɑːfbrʌðəʳ] *n* Halbbruder *m*.
**half-caste** ['hɑːfkɑːst] *n* Mischling *m*.
**half-day** [hɑːf'deɪ] *n* halber freier Tag *m*.
**half-hearted** ['hɑːf'hɑːtɪd] *adj* halbherzig,
lustlos.
**half-hour** [hɑːf'auəʳ] *n* halbe Stunde *f*.
**half-life** ['hɑːflaɪf] *n* (*TECH*) Halbwertzeit *f*.
**half-mast** ['hɑːf'mɑːst]: **at** ~ *adv* (auf)
halbmast.
**halfpenny** ['heɪpnɪ] (*BRIT*) *n* halber Penny *m*.
**half-price** ['hɑːf'praɪs] *adj, adv* zum halben
Preis.
**half-sister** ['hɑːfsɪstəʳ] *n* Halbschwester *f*.
**half term** (*BRIT*) *n* kleine Ferien *pl* (*in der Mitte*
*des Trimesters*).
**half-timbered** [hɑːf'tɪmbəd] *adj* (*house*)
Fachwerk-.
**half-time** [hɑːf'taɪm] *n* (*SPORT*) Halbzeit *f*.
**halfway** ['hɑːf'weɪ] *adv*: ~ **to** auf halbem
Wege nach; ~ **through** mitten in +*dat*; **to**
**meet sb** ~ (*fig*) jdm auf halbem Wege
entgegenkommen.
**halfway house** *n* (*hostel*) offene Anstalt *f*;
(*fig*) Zwischending *nt*; (: *compromise*)
Kompromiß *m*.
**halfwit** ['hɑːfwɪt] *n* Schwachsinnige(r) *f(m)*;
(*fig: inf*) Schwachkopf *m*.
**half-yearly** [hɑːf'jɪəlɪ] *adv* halbjährlich, jedes

halbe Jahr ♦ *adj* halbjährlich.
**halibut** ['hælɪbət] *n inv* Heilbutt *m*.
**halitosis** [hælɪ'təusɪs] *n* schlechter Atem *m*,
Mundgeruch *m*.
**hall** [hɔːl] *n* Diele *f*, (*Haus*)flur *m*; (*corridor*)
Korridor *m*, Flur *m*; (*mansion*) Herrensitz *m*,
Herrenhaus *nt*; (*for concerts etc*) Halle *f*; **to**
**live in** ~ (*BRIT*) im Wohnheim wohnen.
**hallmark** ['hɔːlmɑːk] *n* (*on gold, silver*)
(Feingehalts)stempel *m*; (*of writer, artist etc*)
Kennzeichen *nt*.
**hallo** [hə'ləu] *excl* = **hello**.
**hall of residence** (*pl* **halls of residence**)
(*BRIT*) *n* Studentenwohnheim *nt*.
**hallowed** ['hæləud] *adj* (*ground*) heilig; (*fig:*
*respected, revered*) geheiligt.
**Hallowe'en** ['hæləu'iːn] *n* der Tag vor
Allerheiligen.

---

**Hallowe'en** *ist der 31. Oktober, der Vorabend*
*von Allerheiligen und nach altem Glauben der*
*Abend, an dem man Geister und Hexen sehen*
*kann. In Großbritannien und vor allem in den*
*USA feiern die Kinder Hallowe'en, indem sie*
*sich verkleiden und mit selbstgemachten*
*Laternen aus Kürbissen von Tür zu Tür ziehen.*

---

**hallucination** [həluːsɪ'neɪʃən] *n* Halluzination
*f*.
**hallucinogenic** [həluːsɪnəu'dʒɛnɪk] *adj* (*drug*)
halluzinogen ♦ *n* Halluzinogen *nt*.
**hallway** ['hɔːlweɪ] *n* Diele *f*, (*Haus*)flur *m*.
**halo** ['heɪləu] *n* Heiligenschein *m*; (*circle of*
*light*) Hof *m*.
**halt** [hɔːlt] *vt* anhalten; (*progress etc*) zum
Stillstand bringen ♦ *vi* anhalten, zum
Stillstand kommen ♦ *n*: **to come to a** ~ zum
Stillstand kommen; **to call a** ~ **to sth** (*fig*)
einer Sache *dat* ein Ende machen.
**halter** ['hɔːltəʳ] *n* Halfter *nt*.
**halter-neck** ['hɔːltənɛk] *adj* (*dress*) rückenfrei
mit Nackenverschluß.
**halve** [hɑːv] *vt* halbieren.
**halves** [hɑːvz] *pl of* **half**.
**ham** [hæm] *n* Schinken *m*; (*inf: also*: **radio** ~)
Funkamateur *m*; (: *actor*)
Schmierenkomödiant(in) *m(f)*.
**Hamburg** ['hæmbɔːg] *n* Hamburg *nt*.
**hamburger** ['hæmbɔːgəʳ] *n* Hamburger *m*.
**ham-fisted** ['hæm'fɪstɪd], (*US*) **ham-handed**
['hæm'hændɪd] *adj* ungeschickt.
**hamlet** ['hæmlɪt] *n* Weiler *m*, kleines Dorf *nt*.
**hammer** ['hæməʳ] *n* Hammer *m* ♦ *vt* hämmern;
(*fig: criticize*) vernichtend kritisieren;
(: *defeat*) vernichtend schlagen ♦ *vi*
hämmern; **to** ~ **sth into sb**, **to** ~ **sth across**
**to sb** jdm etw einhämmern *or* einbleuen.
▶**hammer out** *vt* hämmern; (*solution,*
*agreement*) ausarbeiten.
**hammock** ['hæmɔk] *n* Hängematte *f*.
**hamper** ['hæmpəʳ] *vt* behindern ♦ *n* Korb *m*.
**hamster** ['hæmstəʳ] *n* Hamster *m*.

**hamstring** ['hæmstrɪŋ] n Kniesehne f ♦ vt einengen.

**hand** [hænd] n Hand f; (of clock) Zeiger m; (handwriting) Hand(schrift) f; (worker) Arbeiter(in) m(f); (of cards) Blatt nt; (measurement: of horse) ≈ 10 cm ♦ vt geben, reichen; **to give** or **lend sb a ~** jdm helfen; **at ~** (place) in der Nähe; (time) unmittelbar bevorstehend; **by ~** von Hand; **in ~** (time) zur Verfügung; (job) anstehend; (situation) unter Kontrolle; **we have the matter in ~** wir haben die Sache im Griff; **on ~** zur Verfügung; **out of ~** adj außer Kontrolle ♦ adv (reject etc) rundweg; **to ~** zur Hand; **on the one ~ ...**, **on the other ~ ...** einerseits ... andererseits ...; **to force sb's ~** jdn zwingen; **to have a free ~** freie Hand haben; **to change ~s** den Besitzer wechseln; **to have in one's ~** (also fig) in der Hand halten; **"~s off!"** „Hände weg!".
►**hand down** vt (knowledge) weitergeben; (possessions) vererben; (LAW: judgement, sentence) fällen.
►**hand in** vt abgeben, einreichen.
►**hand out** vt verteilen; (information) austeilen; (punishment) verhängen.
►**hand over** vt übergeben.
►**hand round** vt (BRIT) verteilen; (chocolates etc) herumreichen.

**handbag** ['hændbæg] n Handtasche f.
**hand baggage** n Handgepäck nt.
**handball** ['hændbɔːl] n Handball m.
**hand basin** n Handwaschbecken nt.
**handbook** ['hændbuk] n Handbuch nt.
**handbrake** ['hændbreɪk] n Handbremse f.
**h & c** (BRIT) abbr (= hot and cold (water)) h.u.k.
**hand cream** n Handcreme f.
**handcuff** ['hændkʌf] vt Handschellen anlegen +dat.
**handcuffs** ['hændkʌfs] npl Handschellen pl.
**handful** ['hændful] n Handvoll f.
**hand-held** ['hænd'held] adj (camera) Hand-.
**handicap** ['hændɪkæp] n Behinderung f; (disadvantage) Nachteil m; (SPORT) Handicap nt ♦ vt benachteiligen; **mentally/physically ~ped** geistig/körperlich behindert.
**handicraft** ['hændɪkrɑːft] n Kunsthandwerk nt; (object) Kunsthandwerksarbeit f.
**handiwork** ['hændɪwəːk] n Arbeit f; **this looks like his ~** (pej) das sieht nach seiner Arbeit aus.
**handkerchief** ['hæŋkətʃɪf] n Taschentuch nt.
**handle** ['hændl] n Griff m; (of door) Klinke f; (of cup) Henkel m; (of broom, brush etc) Stiel m; (for winding) Kurbel f; (CB RADIO: name) Sendezeichen nt ♦ vt anfassen, berühren; (problem etc) sich befassen mit; (: successfully) fertigwerden mit; (people) umgehen mit; **"~ with care"** „Vorsicht - zerbrechlich"; **to fly off the ~** an die Decke gehen; **to get a ~ on a problem** (inf) ein

Problem in den Griff bekommen.
**handlebar(s)** ['hændlbɑː(z)] n(pl) Lenkstange f.
**handling** ['hændlɪŋ] n: **~ (of)** (of plant, animal, issue etc) Behandlung f +gen; (of person, tool, machine etc) Umgang m (mit); (ADMIN) Bearbeitung f +gen.
**handling charges** npl Bearbeitungsgebühr f; (BANKING) Kontoführungsgebühr f.
**hand luggage** n Handgepäck nt.
**handmade** ['hænd'meɪd] adj handgearbeitet.
**hand-out** ['hændaut] n (money, food etc) Unterstützung f; (publicity leaflet) Flugblatt nt; (summary) Informationsblatt nt.
**hand-picked** ['hænd'pɪkt] adj von Hand geerntet; (staff etc) handverlesen.
**handrail** ['hændreɪl] n Geländer nt.
**handset** ['hændset] n (TEL) Hörer m.
**handshake** ['hændʃeɪk] n Händedruck m.
**handsome** ['hænsəm] adj gutaussehend; (building) schön; (gift) großzügig; (profit, return) ansehnlich.
**hands-on** ['hændz'ɔn] adj (training) praktisch; (approach etc) aktiv; **~ experience** praktische Erfahrung.
**handstand** ['hændstænd] n: **to do a ~** einen Handstand machen.
**hand-to-mouth** ['hændtə'mauθ] adj: **to lead a ~ existence** von der Hand in den Mund leben.
**handwriting** ['hændraɪtɪŋ] n Handschrift f.
**handwritten** ['hændrɪtn] adj handgeschrieben.
**handy** ['hændɪ] adj praktisch; (skilful) geschickt; (close at hand) in der Nähe; **to come in ~** sich als nützlich erweisen.
**handyman** ['hændɪmæn] (irreg: like **man**) n (at home) Heimwerker m; (in hotel etc) Faktotum nt.
**hang** [hæŋ] (pt, pp **hung**) vt aufhängen; (criminal) (pt, pp **hanged**) hängen; (head) hängen lassen ♦ vi hängen; (hair, drapery) fallen ♦ n: **to get the ~ of sth** (inf) den richtigen Dreh (bei etw) herauskriegen.
►**hang about** vi herumlungern.
►**hang around** vi = **hang about**.
►**hang back** vi: **to ~ back (from doing sth)** zögern(, etw zu tun).
►**hang on** vi warten ♦ vt fus (depend on) abhängen von; **to ~ on to** festhalten; (for protection, support) sich festhalten an +dat; (hope, position) sich klammern an +acc; (ideas) festhalten an +dat; (keep) behalten.
►**hang out** vt draußen aufhängen ♦ vi heraushängen; (inf: live) wohnen.
►**hang together** vi (argument) folgerichtig or zusammenhängend sein; (story, explanation) zusammenhängend sein; (statements) zusammenpassen.
►**hang up** vt aufhängen ♦ vi (TEL): **to ~ up (on sb)** einfach auflegen.
**hangar** ['hæŋəʳ] n Hangar m, Flugzeughalle f.
**hangdog** ['hæŋdɔg] adj zerknirscht.

**hanger** ['hæŋə*] n Bügel m.
**hanger-on** [hæŋər'ɔn] n (parasite) Trabant m (inf); **the ~s-~** der Anhang.
**hang-glide** ['hæŋglaɪd] vi drachenfliegen.
**hang-glider** ['hæŋglaɪdə*] n (Flug)drachen m.
**hang-gliding** ['hæŋglaɪdɪŋ] n Drachenfliegen nt.
**hanging** ['hæŋɪŋ] n (execution) Hinrichtung f durch den Strang; (for wall) Wandbehang m.
**hangman** ['hæŋmən] (irreg: like **man**) n Henker m.
**hangover** ['hæŋəuvə*] n Kater m; (from past) Überbleibsel nt.
**hang-up** ['hæŋʌp] n Komplex m.
**hank** [hæŋk] n Strang m.
**hanker** ['hæŋkə*] vi: **to ~ after** sich sehnen nach.
**hankering** ['hæŋkərɪŋ] n: **~ (for)** Verlangen nt (nach).
**hankie** ['hæŋkɪ] n abbr = **handkerchief**.
**hanky** ['hæŋkɪ] n abbr = **handkerchief**.
**Hants** [hænts] (BRIT) abbr (POST: = Hampshire).
**haphazard** [hæp'hæzəd] adj planlos, wahllos.
**hapless** ['hæplɪs] adj glücklos.
**happen** ['hæpən] vi geschehen; **to ~ to do sth** zufällig(erweise) etw tun; **as it ~s** zufälligerweise; **what's ~ing?** was ist los?; **she ~ed to be free** sie hatte zufällig(erweise) gerade Zeit; **if anything ~ed to him** wenn ihm etwas zustoßen or passieren sollte.
▶**happen (up)on** vt fus zufällig stoßen auf +acc; (person) zufällig treffen.
**happening** ['hæpnɪŋ] n Ereignis nt, Vorfall m.
**happily** ['hæpɪlɪ] adv (luckily) glücklicherweise; (cheerfully) fröhlich.
**happiness** ['hæpɪnɪs] n Glück nt.
**happy** ['hæpɪ] adj glücklich; (cheerful) fröhlich; **to be ~ (with)** zufrieden sein (mit); **to be ~ to do sth** etw gerne tun; **~ birthday!** herzlichen Glückwunsch zum Geburtstag!
**happy-go-lucky** ['hæpɪgəu'lʌkɪ] adj unbekümmert.
**happy hour** n Zeit, in der Bars, Pubs usw Getränke zu ermäßigten Preisen anbieten.
**harangue** [hə'ræŋ] vt predigen +dat (inf).
**harass** ['hærəs] vt schikanieren.
**harassed** ['hærəst] adj geplagt.
**harassment** ['hærəsmənt] n Schikanierung f; **sexual ~** sexuelle Belästigung f.
**harbour,** (US) **harbor** ['hɑːbə*] n Hafen m ♦ vt (hope, fear, grudge etc) hegen; (criminal, fugitive) Unterschlupf gewähren +dat.
**harbour dues** npl Hafengebühren pl.
**harbour master** n Hafenmeister m.
**hard** [hɑːd] adj hart; (question, problem) schwierig; (evidence) gesichert ♦ adv (work) hart, schwer; (think) scharf; (try) sehr; **~ luck!** Pech!; **no ~ feelings!** ich nehme es dir nicht übel; **to be ~ of hearing** schwerhörig sein; **to be ~ done by**

ungerecht behandelt werden; **I find it ~ to believe that ...** ich kann es kaum glauben, daß ...; **to look ~ at sth** (object) sich +dat etw genau ansehen; (idea) etw gründlich prüfen.
**hard-and-fast** ['hɑːdən'fɑːst] adj fest.
**hardback** ['hɑːdbæk] n gebundene Ausgabe f.
**hardboard** ['hɑːdbɔːd] n Hartfaserplatte f.
**hard-boiled egg** ['hɑːd'bɔɪld-] n hartgekochtes Ei nt.
**hard cash** n Bargeld nt.
**hard copy** n (COMPUT) Ausdruck m.
**hard core** n harter Kern m.
**hard-core** ['hɑːd'kɔː*] adj (pornography) hart; (supporters) zum harten Kern gehörend.
**hard court** n (TENNIS) Hartplatz m.
**hard disk** n (COMPUT) Festplatte f.
**harden** ['hɑːdn] vt härten; (attitude, person) verhärten ♦ vi hart werden, sich verhärten.
**hardened** ['hɑːdnd] adj (criminal) Gewohnheits-; **to be ~ to sth** gegen etw abgehärtet sein.
**hardening** ['hɑːdnɪŋ] n Verhärtung f.
**hard graft** n: **by sheer ~** durch harte Arbeit.
**hard-headed** ['hɑːd'hedɪd] adj nüchtern.
**hardhearted** ['hɑːd'hɑːtɪd] adj hartherzig.
**hard-hitting** ['hɑːd'hɪtɪŋ] adj (fig: speech, journalist etc) knallhart.
**hard labour** n Zwangsarbeit f.
**hardliner** [hɑːd'laɪnə*] n Vertreter(in) m(f) der harten Linie.
**hard-luck story** ['hɑːdlʌk-] n Leidensgeschichte f.
**hardly** ['hɑːdlɪ] adv kaum; (harshly) hart, streng; **it's ~ the case** (ironic) das ist wohl kaum der Fall; **I can ~ believe it** ich kann es kaum glauben.
**hard-nosed** [hɑːd'nəuzd] adj abgebrüht.
**hard-pressed** [hɑːd'prest] adj: **to be ~** unter Druck sein; **~ for money** in Geldnot.
**hard sell** n aggressive Verkaufstaktik f.
**hardship** ['hɑːdʃɪp] n Not f.
**hard shoulder** (BRIT) n (AUT) Seitenstreifen m.
**hard up** (inf) adj knapp bei Kasse.
**hardware** ['hɑːdweə*] n Eisenwaren pl; (household goods) Haushaltswaren pl; (COMPUT) Hardware f; (MIL) Waffen pl.
**hardware shop** n Eisenwarenhandlung f.
**hard-wearing** [hɑːd'weərɪŋ] adj strapazierfähig.
**hard-won** [hɑːd'wʌn] adj schwer erkämpft.
**hard-working** [hɑːd'wɜːkɪŋ] adj fleißig.
**hardy** ['hɑːdɪ] adj (animals) zäh; (people) abgehärtet; (plant) winterhart.
**hare** [hɛə*] n Hase m.
**harebrained** ['hɛəbreɪnd] adj verrückt.
**harelip** ['hɛəlɪp] n Hasenscharte f.
**harem** [hɑː'riːm] n Harem m.
**hark back** [hɑːk-] vi: **to ~ to** zurückkommen auf +acc.
**harm** [hɑːm] n Schaden m; (injury) Verletzung f ♦ vt schaden +dat; (person: physically)

verletzen; **to mean no ~** es nicht böse meinen; **out of ~'s way** in Sicherheit; **there's no ~ in trying** es kann nicht schaden, es zu versuchen.

**harmful** ['hɑːmful] *adj* schädlich.

**harmless** ['hɑːmlɪs] *adj* harmlos.

**harmonic** [hɑːˈmɒnɪk] *adj* harmonisch.

**harmonica** [hɑːˈmɒnɪkə] *n* Harmonika *f*.

**harmonics** [hɑːˈmɒnɪks] *npl* Harmonik *f*.

**harmonious** [hɑːˈməʊnɪəs] *adj* harmonisch.

**harmonium** [hɑːˈməʊnɪəm] *n* Harmonium *nt*.

**harmonize** ['hɑːmənaɪz] *vi* (*MUS*) mehrstimmig singen/spielen; (: *one person*) die zweite Stimme singen/spielen; (*colours, ideas*) harmonieren.

**harmony** ['hɑːmənɪ] *n* Einklang *m*; (*MUS*) Harmonie *f*.

**harness** ['hɑːnɪs] *n* (*for horse*) Geschirr *nt*; (*for child*) Laufgurt *m*; (*safety harness*) Sicherheitsgurt *m* ♦ *vt* (*resources, energy etc*) nutzbar machen; (*horse, dog*) anschirren.

**harp** [hɑːp] *n* Harfe *f* ♦ *vi*: **to ~ on about** (*pej*) herumreiten auf +*dat*.

**harpist** ['hɑːpɪst] *n* Harfenspieler(in) *m(f)*.

**harpoon** [hɑːˈpuːn] *n* Harpune *f*.

**harpsichord** ['hɑːpsɪkɔːd] *n* Cembalo *nt*.

**harried** ['hærɪd] *adj* bedrängt.

**harrow** ['hærəʊ] *n* Egge *f*.

**harrowing** ['hærəʊɪŋ] *adj* (*film*) erschütternd; (*experience*) grauenhaft.

**harry** ['hærɪ] *vt* bedrängen, zusetzen +*dat*.

**harsh** [hɑːʃ] *adj* (*sound, light*) grell; (*judge, winter*) streng; (*criticism, life*) hart.

**harshly** ['hɑːʃlɪ] *adv* (*judge*) streng; (*say*) barsch; (*criticize*) hart.

**harshness** ['hɑːʃnɪs] *n* (*see adj*) Grelle *f*; Strenge *f*; Härte *f*.

**harvest** ['hɑːvɪst] *n* Ernte *f* ♦ *vt* ernten.

**harvester** ['hɑːvɪstə*] *n* (*also*: **combine ~**) Mähdrescher *m*.

**has** [hæz] *vb see* **have**.

**has-been** ['hæzbiːn] (*inf*) *n*: **he's/she's a ~** er/sie ist eine vergangene *or* vergessene Größe.

**hash** [hæʃ] *n* (*CULIN*) Haschee *nt*; (*fig*) **to make a ~ of sth** etw verpfuschen (*inf*); ♦ (*inf*) *n abbr* (= *hashish*) Hasch *nt*.

**hashish** ['hæʃɪʃ] *n* Haschisch *nt*.

**hasn't** ['hæznt] = **has not**.

**hassle** ['hæsl] (*inf*) *n* (*bother*) Theater *nt* ♦ *vt* schikanieren.

**haste** [heɪst] *n* Hast *f*; (*speed*) Eile *f*; **in ~** in Eile; **to make ~ (to do sth)** sich beeilen(, etw zu tun).

**hasten** ['heɪsn] *vt* beschleunigen ♦ *vi*: **to ~ to do sth** sich beeilen, etw zu tun; **I ~ to add ...** ich muß allerdings hinzufügen, ...; **she ~ed back to the house** sie eilte zum Haus zurück.

**hastily** ['heɪstɪlɪ] *adv* (*see adj*) hastig, eilig; vorschnell.

**hasty** ['heɪstɪ] *adj* hastig, eilig; (*rash*) vorschnell.

**hat** [hæt] *n* Hut *m*; **to keep sth under one's ~** etw für sich behalten.

**hatbox** ['hætbɒks] *n* Hutschachtel *f*.

**hatch** [hætʃ] *n* (*NAUT: also*: **~way**) Luke *f*; (*also*: **service ~**) Durchreiche *f* ♦ *vi* (*bird*) ausschlüpfen ♦ *vt* ausbrüten; **the eggs ~ed after 10 days** nach 10 Tagen schlüpften die Jungen aus.

**hatchback** ['hætʃbæk] *n* (*AUT: car*) Heckklappenmodell *nt*.

**hatchet** ['hætʃɪt] *n* Beil *nt*; **to bury the ~** das Kriegsbeil begraben.

**hatchet job** (*inf*) *adj*: **to do a ~ on sb** jdn fertigmachen.

**hatchet man** (*inf*) *n* (*fig*) Vollstrecker *m*.

**hate** [heɪt] *vt* hassen ♦ *n* Haß *m*; **I ~ him/milk** ich kann ihn/ Milch nicht ausstehen; **to ~ to do/doing sth** es hassen, etw zu tun; (*weaker*) etw ungern tun; **I ~ to trouble you, but ...** es ist mir sehr unangenehm, daß ich Sie belästigen muß, aber ...

**hateful** ['heɪtful] *adj* abscheulich.

**hatred** ['heɪtrɪd] *n* Haß *m*; (*dislike*) Abneigung *f*.

**hat trick** *n* Hattrick *m*.

**haughty** ['hɔːtɪ] *adj* überheblich.

**haul** [hɔːl] *vt* ziehen; (*by lorry*) transportieren; (*NAUT*) den Kurs ändern +*gen* ♦ *n* Beute *f*; (*of fish*) Fang *m*; **he ~ed himself out of the pool** er stemmte sich aus dem Schwimmbecken.

**haulage** ['hɔːlɪdʒ] *n* (*cost*) Transportkosten *pl*; (*business*) Transport *m*.

**haulage contractor** (*BRIT*) *n* Transportunternehmen *nt*, Spedition *f*; (*person*) Transportunternehmer(in) *m(f)*, Spediteur *m*.

**hauler** ['hɔːlə*] (*US*) *n* Transportunternehmer(in) *m(f)*, Spediteur *m*.

**haulier** ['hɔːlɪə*] (*BRIT*) *n* Transportunternehmer(in) *m(f)*, Spediteur *m*.

**haunch** [hɔːntʃ] *n* Hüftpartie *f*; (*of meat*) Keule *f*.

**haunt** [hɔːnt] *vt* (*place*) spuken in +*dat*, umgehen in +*dat*; (*person, also fig*) verfolgen ♦ *n* Lieblingsplatz *m*; (*of crooks etc*) Treffpunkt *m*.

**haunted** ['hɔːntɪd] *adj* (*expression*) gehetzt, gequält; **this building/room is ~** in diesem Gebäude/Zimmer spukt es.

**haunting** ['hɔːntɪŋ] *adj* (*music*) eindringlich; **a ~ sight** ein Anblick, der einen nicht losläßt.

**Havana** [həˈvænə] *n* Havanna *nt*.

══════════════════════════════ *KEYWORD*

**have** [hæv] (*pt, pp* **had**) *aux vb* **1** haben; (*with verbs of motion*) sein; **to ~ arrived/gone** angekommen/gegangen sein; **to ~ eaten/slept** gegessen/geschlafen haben; **he has been promoted** er ist befördert worden; **having eaten** *or* **when he had eaten, he left** nachdem er gegessen hatte, ging er

**2** (*in tag questions*): **you've done it, ~n't you?** du hast es gemacht, nicht wahr?; **he hasn't done it, has he?** er hat es nicht gemacht, oder?

**3** (*in short answers and questions*): **you've made a mistake - no I ~'t/so I ~** du hast einen Fehler gemacht - nein(, das habe ich nicht)/ja, stimmt; **we ~'t paid - yes we ~!** wir haben nicht bezahlt - doch!; **I've been there before - ~** du warst schon einmal da - wirklich *or* tatsächlich?

♦ *modal aux vb* (*be obliged*): **to ~ (got) to do sth** etw tun müssen; **this has (got) to be a mistake** das muß ein Fehler sein

♦ *vt* **1** (*possess*) haben; **she has (got) blue eyes/dark hair** sie hat blaue Augen/dunkle Haare; **I ~ (got) an idea** ich habe eine Idee

**2** (*referring to meals etc*): **to ~ breakfast** frühstücken; **to ~ lunch/dinner** zu Mittag/ Abend essen; **to ~ a drink** etwas trinken; **to ~ a cigarette** eine Zigarette rauchen

**3** (*receive, obtain etc*) haben; **may I ~ your address?** kann ich Ihre Adresse haben *or* bekommen?; **to ~ a baby** ein Kind bekommen

**4** (*allow*): **I won't ~ this nonsense** dieser Unsinn kommt nicht in Frage!; **we can't ~ that** das kommt nicht in Frage

**5**: **to ~ sth done** etw machen lassen; **to ~ one's hair cut** sich *dat* die Haare schneiden lassen; **to ~ sb do sth** (*order*) jdn etw tun lassen; **he soon had them all laughing/working** bald hatte er alle zum Lachen/Arbeiten gebracht

**6** (*experience, suffer*): **to ~ a cold/flu** eine Erkältung/die Grippe haben; **she had her bag stolen** ihr *dat* wurde die Tasche gestohlen

**7** (*+ noun: take, hold etc*): **to ~ a swim** schwimmen gehen; **to ~ a walk** spazierengehen; **to ~ a rest** sich ausruhen; **to ~ a meeting** eine Besprechung haben; **to ~ a party** eine Party geben

**8** (*inf: dupe*): **you've been had** man hat dich hereingelegt.

▶**have in** (*inf*) *vt*: **to ~ it in for sb** jdn auf dem Kieker haben.

▶**have on** *vt* (*wear*) anhaben; (*BRIT: inf: tease*) auf den Arm nehmen; **I don't ~ any money on me** ich habe kein Geld bei mir; **do you ~ or ~ anything on tomorrow?** haben Sie morgen etwas vor?

▶**have out** *vt*: **to ~ it out with sb** (*settle a problem etc*) ein Wort mit jdm reden.

**haven** ['heɪvn] *n* Hafen *m*; (*safe place*) Zufluchtsort *m*.

**haven't** ['hævnt] = **have not**.

**haversack** ['hævəsæk] *n* Rucksack *m*.

**haves** [hævz] (*inf*) *npl*: **the ~ and the have-nots** die Betuchten und die Habenichtse.

**havoc** ['hævək] *n* Verwüstung *f*; (*confusion*)

Chaos *nt*; **to play ~ with sth** (*disrupt*) etw völlig durcheinanderbringen.

**Hawaii** [hə'waɪiː] *n* Hawaii *nt*.

**Hawaiian** [hə'waɪjən] *adj* hawaiisch ♦ *n* Hawaiianer(in) *m(f)*; (*LING*) Hawaiisch *nt*.

**hawk** [hɔːk] *n* Habicht *m*.

**hawker** ['hɔːkə*] *n* Hausierer(in) *m(f)*.

**hawkish** ['hɔːkɪʃ] *adj* (*person, approach*) knallhart.

**hawthorn** ['hɔːθɔːn] *n* Weißdorn *m*, Rotdorn *m*.

**hay** [heɪ] *n* Heu *nt*.

**hay fever** *n* Heuschnupfen *m*.

**haystack** ['heɪstæk] *n* Heuhaufen *m*; **like looking for a needle in a ~** als ob man eine Stecknadel im Heuhaufen suchte.

**haywire** ['heɪwaɪə*] (*inf*) *adj*: **to go ~** (*machine*) verrückt spielen; (*plans etc*) über den Haufen geworfen werden.

**hazard** ['hæzəd] *n* Gefahr *f* ♦ *vt* riskieren; **to be a health/fire ~** eine Gefahr für die Gesundheit/feuergefährlich sein; **to ~ a guess** (es) wagen, eine Vermutung anzustellen.

**hazardous** ['hæzədəs] *adj* gefährlich.

**hazard pay** (*US*) *n* Gefahrenzulage *f*.

**hazard (warning) lights** *npl* (*AUT*) Warnblinkanlage *f*.

**haze** [heɪz] *n* Dunst *m*.

**hazel** ['heɪzl] *n* Hasel(nuß)strauch *m*, Haselbusch *m* ♦ *adj* haselnußbraun.

**hazelnut** ['heɪzlnʌt] *n* Haselnuß *f*.

**hazy** ['heɪzɪ] *adj* dunstig, diesig; (*idea, memory*) unklar, verschwommen; **I'm rather ~ about the details** kann ich mich nur vage *or* verschwommen erinnern; (*ignorant*) die genauen Einzelheiten sind mir nicht bekannt.

**H-bomb** ['eɪtʃbɔm] *n* H-Bombe *f*.

**HE** *abbr* (*REL, DIPLOMACY:* = *His/Her Excellency*) Seine/Ihre Exzellenz; (= *high explosive*) hochexplosiver Sprengstoff *m*.

**he** [hiː] *pron er* ♦ *pref* männlich; **~ who ...** wer ...

**head** ['hɛd] *n* Kopf *m*; (*of table*) Kopfende *nt*; (*of queue*) Spitze *f*; (*of company, organization*) Leiter(in) *m(f)*; (*of school*) Schulleiter(in) *m(f)*; (*on coin*) Kopfseite *f*; (*on tape recorder*) Tonkopf *m* ♦ *vt* anführen, an der Spitze stehen von; (*group, company*) leiten; (*FOOTBALL: ball*) köpfen; **~s (or tails)** Kopf (oder Zahl); **~ over heels** Hals über Kopf; (*in love*) bis über beide Ohren; **£10 a** *or* **per ~** 10 Pfund pro Kopf; **at the ~ of the list** oben auf der Liste; **to have a ~ for business** einen guten Geschäftssinn haben; **to have no ~ for heights** nicht schwindelfrei sein; **to come to a ~** sich zuspitzen; **they put their ~s together** sie haben sich zusammengesetzt; **off the top of my** *etc* **~** ohne lange zu überlegen; **on your own ~ be it!** auf Ihre eigene Verantwortung *or* Kappe (*inf*)!; **to bite** or **snap sb's** ~ **off** jdn grob anfahren; **he won't bite your** ~ **off** er wird dir schon nicht den Kopf abreißen; **it went to my** ~ es ist mir in den Kopf or zu Kopf gestiegen; **to lose/keep one's** ~ den Kopf verlieren/nicht verlieren; **I can't make** ~ **nor tail of this** hieraus werde ich nicht schlau; **he's off his** ~! (*inf*) er ist nicht (ganz) bei Trost!

▶**head for** vt fus (*on foot*) zusteuern auf +acc; (*by car*) in Richtung … fahren; (*plane, ship*) Kurs nehmen auf +acc; **you are** ~**ing for trouble** du wirst Ärger bekommen.

▶**head off** vt abwenden.

**headache** ['hɛdeɪk] n Kopfschmerzen pl, Kopfweh nt; (*fig*) Problem nt; **to have a** ~ Kopfschmerzen or Kopfweh haben.

**headband** ['hɛdbænd] n Stirnband nt.

**headboard** ['hɛdbɔːd] n Kopfteil nt.

**head cold** n Kopfgrippe f.

**headdress** ['hɛddrɛs] (*BRIT*) n Kopfschmuck m.

**headed notepaper** ['hɛdɪd-] n Schreibpapier nt mit Briefkopf.

**header** ['hɛdə*] (*BRIT: inf*) n (*FOOTBALL*) Kopfball m.

**headfirst** ['hɛd'fəːst] adv (*lit*) kopfüber; (*fig*) Hals über Kopf.

**headgear** ['hɛdɡɪə*] n Kopfbedeckung f.

**head-hunt** ['hɛdhʌnt] vt abwerben.

**head-hunter** ['hɛdhʌntə*] n (*COMM*) Kopfjäger(in) m(f).

**heading** ['hɛdɪŋ] n Überschrift f.

**headlamp** ['hɛdlæmp] (*BRIT*) n = **headlight**.

**headland** ['hɛdlənd] n Landspitze f.

**headlight** ['hɛdlaɪt] n Scheinwerfer m.

**headline** ['hɛdlaɪn] n Schlagzeile f; (*RADIO, TV*): **(news)** ~**s** Nachrichtenüberblick m.

**headlong** ['hɛdlɒŋ] adv kopfüber; (*rush*) Hals über Kopf.

**headmaster** [hɛd'mɑːstə*] n Schulleiter m.

**headmistress** [hɛd'mɪstrɪs] n Schulleiterin f.

**head office** n Zentrale f.

**head of state** (*pl* **heads of state**) n Staatsoberhaupt nt.

**head-on** ['hɛd'ɒn] adj (*collision*) frontal; (*confrontation*) direkt.

**headphones** ['hɛdfəunz] npl Kopfhörer pl.

**headquarters** ['hɛdkwɔːtəz] npl Zentrale f; (*MIL*) Hauptquartier nt.

**headrest** ['hɛdrɛst] n (*AUT*) Kopfstütze f.

**headroom** ['hɛdrum] n (*in car*) Kopfraum m; (*under bridge*) lichte Höhe f.

**headscarf** ['hɛdskɑːf] n Kopftuch nt.

**headset** ['hɛdsɛt] n = **headphones**.

**head start** n Vorsprung m.

**headstone** ['hɛdstəun] n Grabstein m.

**headstrong** ['hɛdstrɒŋ] adj eigensinnig.

**head waiter** n Oberkellner m.

**headway** ['hɛdweɪ] n: **to make** ~ vorankommen.

**headwind** ['hɛdwɪnd] n Gegenwind m.

**heady** ['hɛdɪ] adj (*experience etc*) aufregend; (*drink, atmosphere*) berauschend.

**heal** [hiːl] vt, vi heilen.

**health** [hɛlθ] n Gesundheit f.

**health care** n Gesundheitsfürsorge f.

**health centre** (*BRIT*) n Ärztezentrum nt.

**health food** n Reformkost f, Naturkost f.

**health food shop** n Reformhaus nt, Naturkostladen m.

**health hazard** n Gefahr f für die Gesundheit.

**health service** (*BRIT*) n: **the H**~ **S**~ das Gesundheitswesen.

**healthy** ['hɛlθɪ] adj gesund; (*profit*) ansehnlich.

**heap** [hiːp] n Haufen m ♦ vt: **to** ~ (**up**) (auf)häufen; ~**s of** (*inf*) jede Menge; **to** ~ **sth with** etw beladen mit; **to** ~ **sth on** etw häufen auf +acc; **to** ~ **favours/gifts** etc **on sb** jdn mit Gefälligkeiten/Geschenken etc überhäufen; **to** ~ **praises on sb** jdn mit Lob überschütten.

**hear** [hɪə*] (*pt, pp* **heard**) vt hören; (*LAW: case*) verhandeln; (: *witness*) vernehmen; **to** ~ **about** hören von; **to** ~ **from sb** von jdm hören; **I've never heard of that book** von dem Buch habe ich noch nie etwas gehört; **I wouldn't** ~ **of it!** davon will ich nichts hören.

▶**hear out** vt ausreden lassen.

**heard** [həːd] pt, pp of **hear**.

**hearing** ['hɪərɪŋ] n Gehör nt; (*of facts, by committee*) Anhörung f; (*of witness*) Vernehmung f; (*of a case*) Verhandlung f; **to give sb a** ~ (*BRIT*) jdn anhören.

**hearing aid** n Hörgerät nt.

**hearsay** ['hɪəseɪ] n Gerüchte pl; **by** ~ vom Hörensagen.

**hearse** [həːs] n Leichenwagen m.

**heart** [hɑːt] n Herz nt; (*of problem*) Kern m; **hearts** npl (*CARDS*) Herz nt; **to lose** ~ den Mut verlieren; **to take** ~ Mut fassen; **at** ~ im Grunde; **by** ~ auswendig; **to set one's** ~ **on sth** sein Herz an etw acc hängen; **to set one's** ~ **on doing sth** alles daransetzen, etw zu tun; **the** ~ **of the matter** der Kern der Sache.

**heartache** ['hɑːteɪk] n Kummer m.

**heart attack** n Herzanfall m.

**heartbeat** ['hɑːtbiːt] n Herzschlag m.

**heartbreak** ['hɑːtbreɪk] n großer Kummer m, Leid nt.

**heartbreaking** ['hɑːtbreɪkɪŋ] adj herzzerreißend.

**heartbroken** ['hɑːtbrəukən] adj: **to be** ~ todunglücklich sein.

**heartburn** ['hɑːtbəːn] n Sodbrennen nt.

**-hearted** ['hɑːtɪd] suff: **kind-**~ gutherzig.

**heartening** ['hɑːtnɪŋ] adj ermutigend.

**heart failure** n Herzversagen nt.

**heartfelt** ['hɑːtfɛlt] adj tief empfunden.

**hearth** [hɑːθ] n ≈ Kamin m.

**heartily** ['hɑːtɪlɪ] adv (*see adj*) (laut und)

herzlich; herzhaft; tief; ungeteilt.
**heartland** ['hɑːtlænd] n Herz nt; **Britain's industrial** ~ Großbritanniens Industriezentrum.
**heartless** ['hɑːtlɪs] adj herzlos.
**heartstrings** ['hɑːtstrɪŋz] npl: **to tug at sb's** ~ bei jdm auf die Tränendrüsen drücken.
**heart-throb** ['hɑːtθrɔb] (inf) n Schwarm m.
**heart-to-heart** ['hɑːt'tə'hɑːt] adj, adv ganz im Vertrauen.
**heart transplant** n Herztransplantation f, Herzverpflanzung f.
**heart-warming** ['hɑːtwɔːmɪŋ] adj herzerfreuend.
**hearty** ['hɑːtɪ] adj (person) laut und herzlich; (laugh, appetite) herzhaft; (welcome) herzlich; (dislike) tief; (support) ungeteilt.
**heat** [hiːt] n Hitze f; (warmth) Wärme f; (temperature) Temperatur f; (SPORT: also: **qualifying** ~) Vorrunde f ♦ vt erhitzen, heiß machen; (room, house) heizen; **in** or (BRIT) **on** ~ (ZOOL) brünstig, läufig.
►**heat up** vi sich erwärmen, warm werden ♦ vt aufwärmen; (water, room) erwärmen.
**heated** ['hiːtɪd] adj geheizt; (pool) beheizt; (argument) hitzig.
**heater** ['hiːtə*] n (Heiz)ofen m; (in car) Heizung f.
**heath** [hiːθ] (BRIT) n Heide f.
**heathen** ['hiːðn] n Heide m, Heidin f.
**heather** ['hɛðə*] n Heidekraut nt, Erika f.
**heating** ['hiːtɪŋ] n Heizung f.
**heat-resistant** ['hiːtrɪzɪstənt] adj hitzebeständig.
**heat-seeking** ['hiːtsiːkɪŋ] adj wärmesuchend.
**heatstroke** ['hiːtstrəuk] n Hitzschlag m.
**heat wave** n Hitzewelle f.
**heave** [hiːv] vt (pull) ziehen; (push) schieben; (lift) (hoch)heben ♦ vi sich heben und senken; (retch) sich übergeben ♦ n (see vt) Zug m; Stoß m; Heben nt; **to** ~ **a sigh** einen Seufzer ausstoßen.
►**heave to** (pt, pp hove) vi (NAUT) beidrehen.
**heaven** ['hɛvn] n Himmel m; **thank** ~! Gott sei Dank!; ~ **forbid!** bloß nicht!; **for** ~**'s sake!** um Himmels or Gottes willen!
**heavenly** ['hɛvnlɪ] adj himmlisch.
**heaven-sent** [hɛvn'sɛnt] adj ideal.
**heavily** ['hɛvɪlɪ] adv schwer; (drink, smoke, depend, rely) stark; (sleep, sigh) tief; (say) mit schwerer Stimme.
**heavy** ['hɛvɪ] adj schwer; (clothes) dick; (rain, snow, drinker, smoker) stark; (build, frame) kräftig; (breathing, sleep) tief; (schedule, week) anstrengend; (weather) drückend, schwül; **the conversation was** ~ **going** die Unterhaltung war mühsam; **the book was** ~ **going** das Buch las sich schwer.
**heavy cream** (US) n Sahne mit hohem Fettgehalt, ≈ Schlagsahne f.
**heavy-duty** ['hɛvɪ'djuːtɪ] adj strapazierfähig.
**heavy goods vehicle** n Lastkraftwagen m.

**heavy-handed** ['hɛvɪ'hændɪd] adj schwerfällig, ungeschickt.
**heavy industry** n Schwerindustrie f.
**heavy metal** n (MUS) Heavy metal nt.
**heavyset** ['hɛvɪ'sɛt] (esp US) adj kräftig gebaut.
**heavyweight** ['hɛvɪweɪt] n (SPORT) Schwergewicht nt.
**Hebrew** ['hiːbruː] adj hebräisch ♦ n (LING) Hebräisch nt.
**Hebrides** ['hɛbrɪdiːz] npl: **the** ~ die Hebriden pl.
**heck** [hɛk] (inf) interj: **oh** ~! zum Kuckuck! ♦ n. **a** ~ **of a lot** irrsinnig viel.
**heckle** ['hɛkl] vt durch Zwischenrufe stören.
**heckler** ['hɛklə*] n Zwischenrufer(in) m(f), Störer(in) m(f).
**hectare** ['hɛktɑː*] (BRIT) n Hektar nt or m.
**hectic** ['hɛktɪk] adj hektisch.
**hector** ['hɛktə*] vt tyrannisieren.
**he'd** [hiːd] = **he would; he had.**
**hedge** [hɛdʒ] n Hecke f ♦ vi ausweichen, sich nicht festlegen ♦ vt: **to** ~ **one's bets** (fig) sich absichern; **as a** ~ **against inflation** als Absicherung or Schutz gegen die Inflation.
►**hedge in** vt (person) (in seiner Freiheit) einschränken; (proposals etc) behindern.
**hedgehog** ['hɛdʒhɔg] n Igel m.
**hedgerow** ['hɛdʒrəu] n Hecke f.
**hedonism** ['hiːdənɪzəm] n Hedonismus m.
**heed** [hiːd] vt (also: **take** ~ **of**) beachten ♦ n: **to pay (no)** ~ **to, take (no)** ~ **of** (nicht) beachten.
**heedless** ['hiːdlɪs] adj achtlos; ~ **of sb/sth** ohne auf jdn/etw zu achten.
**heel** [hiːl] n Ferse f; (of shoe) Absatz m ♦ vt (shoe) mit einem neuen Absatz versehen; **to bring to** ~ (dog) bei Fuß gehen lassen; (fig: person) an die Kandare nehmen; **to take to one's** ~**s** (inf) sich aus dem Staub machen.
**hefty** ['hɛftɪ] adj kräftig; (parcel etc) schwer; (profit) ansehnlich.
**heifer** ['hɛfə*] n Färse f.
**height** [haɪt] n Höhe f; (of person) Größe f; (fig of luxury, good taste etc) Gipfel m; **what** ~ **are you?** wie groß bist du?; **of average** ~ durchschnittlich groß; **to be afraid of** ~**s** nicht schwindelfrei sein; **it's the** ~ **of fashion** das ist die neueste Mode; **at the** ~ **of the tourist season** in der Hauptsaison.
**heighten** ['haɪtn] vt erhöhen.
**heinous** ['hiːnəs] adj abscheulich, verabscheuungswürdig.
**heir** [ɛə*] n Erbe m; **the** ~ **to the throne** der Thronfolger.
**heir apparent** n gesetzlicher Erbe m.
**heiress** ['ɛərɛs] n Erbin f.
**heirloom** ['ɛəluːm] n Erbstück nt.
**heist** [haɪst] (US: inf) n Raubüberfall m.
**held** [hɛld] pt, pp of **hold.**
**helicopter** ['hɛlɪkɔptə*] n Hubschrauber m.
**heliport** ['hɛlɪpɔːt] n Hubschrauberflugplatz

*m*, Heliport *m*.

**helium** ['hiːlɪəm] *n* Helium *nt*.

**hell** [hɛl] *n* Hölle *f*; ~! (*inf!*) verdammt! (*inf!*); **a ~ of a lot** (*inf*) verdammt viel (*inf*); **a ~ of a mess** (*inf*) ein wahnsinniges Chaos (*inf*); **a ~ of a noise** (*inf*) ein Höllenlärm *m*; **a ~ of a nice guy** ein wahnsinnig netter Typ.

**he'll** [hiːl] = **he will; he shall.**

**hellbent** [hɛl'bɛnt] *adj:* ~ **(on)** versessen (auf +*acc*).

**hellish** ['hɛlɪʃ] (*inf*) *adj* höllisch.

**hello** [hə'ləu] *excl* hallo; (*expressing surprise*) nanu, he.

**Hell's Angels** *npl* Hell's Angels *pl*.

**helm** [hɛlm] *n* Ruder *nt*, Steuer *nt*; **at the ~** am Ruder.

**helmet** ['hɛlmɪt] *n* Helm *m*.

**helmsman** ['hɛlmzmən] (*irreg: like* **man**) *n* Steuermann *m*.

**help** [hɛlp] *n* Hilfe *f*; (*charwoman*) (Haushalts)hilfe *f* ♦ *vt* helfen +*dat*; **with the ~ of** (*person*) mit (der) Hilfe +*gen*; (*tool etc*) mit Hilfe +*gen*; **to be of ~ to sb** jdm behilflich sein, jdm helfen; **can I ~ you?** (*in shop*) womit kann ich Ihnen dienen?; **~ yourself** bedienen Sie sich; **he can't ~ it** er kann nichts dafür; **I can't ~ thinking that** ... ich kann mir nicht helfen, ich glaube, daß ...

**helper** ['hɛlpə*] *n* Helfer(in) *m(f)*.

**helpful** ['hɛlpful] *adj* hilfsbereit; (*advice, suggestion*) nützlich, hilfreich.

**helping** ['hɛlpɪŋ] *n* Portion *f*.

**helping hand** *n:* **to give** *or* **lend sb a ~** jdm behilflich sein.

**helpless** ['hɛlplɪs] *adj* hilflos.

**helplessly** ['hɛlplɪslɪ] *adv* hilflos.

**helpline** ['hɛlplaɪn] *n* (*for emergencies*) Notruf *m*; (*for information*) Informationsdienst *m*.

**Helsinki** ['hɛlsɪŋkɪ] *n* Helsinki *nt*.

**helter-skelter** ['hɛltə'skɛltə*] (*BRIT*) *n* Rutschbahn *f*.

**hem** [hɛm] *n* Saum *m* ♦ *vt* säumen.

►**hem in** *vt* einschließen, umgeben; **to feel ~med in** (*fig*) sich eingeengt fühlen.

**hematology** ['hiːmə'tɔlədʒɪ] (*US*) *n* = **haematology.**

**hemisphere** ['hɛmɪsfɪə*] *n* Hemisphäre *f*; (*of sphere*) Halbkugel *f*.

**hemlock** ['hɛmlɔk] *n* Schierling *m*.

**hemoglobin** ['hiːmə'gləubɪn] (*US*) *n* = **haemoglobin.**

**hemophilia** ['hiːmə'fɪlɪə] (*US*) *n* = **haemophilia.**

**hemorrhage** ['hɛmərɪdʒ] (*US*) *n* = **haemorrhage.**

**hemorrhoids** ['hɛmərɔɪdz] (*US*) *npl* = **haemorrhoids.**

**hemp** [hɛmp] *n* Hanf *m*.

**hen** [hɛn] *n* Henne *f*, Huhn *nt*; (*female bird*) Weibchen *nt*.

**hence** [hɛns] *adv* daher; **2 years ~** in zwei Jahren.

**henceforth** [hɛns'fɔːθ] *adv* von nun an; (*from that time on*) von da an.

**henchman** ['hɛntʃmən] (*irreg: like* **man**) (*pej*) *n* Spießgeselle *m*.

**henna** ['hɛnə] *n* Henna *nt*.

**hen night, hen party** (*inf*) *n* Damenkränzchen *nt*.

---

Als **hen night** bezeichnet man eine feuchtfröhliche Frauenparty, die kurz vor einer Hochzeit von der Braut und ihren Freundinnen meist in einem Gasthaus oder Nachtklub abgehalten wird, und bei der die Freundinnen dafür sorgen, daß vor allem die Braut große Mengen an Alkohol konsumiert. Siehe auch **stag night**.

---

**henpecked** ['hɛnpɛkt] *adj:* **to be ~** unter dem Pantoffel stehen; **~ husband** Pantoffelheld *m*.

**hepatitis** [hɛpə'taɪtɪs] *n* Hepatitis *f*.

**her** [həː*] *pron* sie; (*indirect*) ihr ♦ *adj* ihr; **I see ~** ich sehe sie; **give ~ a book** gib ihr ein Buch; **after ~** nach ihr; *see also* **me; my.**

**herald** ['hɛrəld] *n* (Vor)bote *m* ♦ *vt* ankündigen.

**heraldic** [hɛ'rældɪk] *adj* heraldisch, Wappen-.

**heraldry** ['hɛrəldrɪ] *n* Wappenkunde *f*, Heraldik *f*; (*coats of arms*) Wappen *pl*.

**herb** [həːb] *n* Kraut *nt*.

**herbaceous** [həː'beɪʃəs] *adj:* ~ **border** Staudenrabatte *f*; ~ **plant** Staude *f*.

**herbal** ['həːbl] *adj* (*tea, medicine*) Kräuter-.

**herbicide** ['həːbɪsaɪd] *n* Unkrautvertilgungsmittel *nt*, Herbizid *nt*.

**herd** [həːd] *n* Herde *f*; (*of wild animals*) Rudel *nt* ♦ *vt* treiben; (*gather*) zusammentreiben; **~ed together** zusammengetrieben.

**here** [hɪə*] *adv* hier; **she left ~ yesterday** sie ist gestern von hier abgereist; ~ **is/are** ... hier ist/sind...; ~ **you are** (*giving*) (hier,) bitte; ~ **we are!** (*finding sth*) da ist es ja!; ~ **she is!** da ist sie ja!; ~ **she comes** da kommt sie ja; **come ~!** komm hierher *or* hierhin!; ~ **and there** hier und da; "~'**s to** ..." „auf ... *acc*".

**hereabouts** ['hɪərə'bauts] *adv* hier.

**hereafter** [hɪər'aːftə*] *adv* künftig.

**hereby** [hɪə'baɪ] *adv* hiermit.

**hereditary** [hɪ'rɛdɪtrɪ] *adj* erblich, Erb-.

**heredity** [hɪ'rɛdɪtɪ] *n* Vererbung *f*.

**heresy** ['hɛrəsɪ] *n* Ketzerei *f*.

**heretic** ['hɛrətɪk] *n* Ketzer(in) *m(f)*.

**heretical** [hɪ'rɛtɪkl] *adj* ketzerisch.

**herewith** [hɪə'wɪð] *adv* hiermit.

**heritage** ['hɛrɪtɪdʒ] *n* Erbe *nt*; **our national ~** unser nationales Erbe.

**hermetically** [həː'mɛtɪklɪ] *adv:* ~ **sealed** hermetisch verschlossen.

**hermit** ['həːmɪt] *n* Einsiedler(in) *m(f)*.

**hernia** ['həːnɪə] *n* Bruch *m*.

**hero** ['hɪərəʊ] (pl ~**es**) n Held m; (idol) Idol nt.
**heroic** [hɪ'rəʊɪk] adj heroisch; (figure, person) heldenhaft.
**heroin** ['hɛrəʊɪn] n Heroin nt.
**heroin addict** n Heroinsüchtige(r) f(m).
**heroine** ['hɛrəʊɪn] n Heldin f; (idol) Idol nt.
**heroism** ['hɛrəʊɪzəm] n Heldentum nt.
**heron** ['hɛrən] n Reiher m.
**hero worship** n Heldenverehrung f.
**herring** ['hɛrɪŋ] n Hering m.
**hers** [hɜːz] pron ihre(r, s); **a friend of** ~ ein Freund von ihr; **this is** ~ das gehört ihr; see also **mine**.
**herself** [hɜː'sɛlf] pron sich; (emphatic) (sie) selbst; see also **oneself**.
**Herts** [hɑːts] (BRIT) abbr (POST: = Hertfordshire).
**he's** [hiːz] = **he is**; **he has**.
**hesitant** ['hɛzɪtənt] adj zögernd; **to be** ~ **about doing sth** zögern, etw zu tun.
**hesitate** ['hɛzɪteɪt] vi zögern; (be unwilling) Bedenken haben; **to** ~ **about** Bedenken haben wegen; **don't** ~ **to see a doctor if you are worried** gehen Sie ruhig zum Arzt, wenn Sie sich Sorgen machen.
**hesitation** [hɛzɪ'teɪʃən] n Zögern nt; Bedenken pl; **to have no** ~ **in saying sth** etw ohne weiteres sagen können.
**hessian** ['hɛsɪən] n Sackleinwand f, Rupfen m.
**heterogenous** [hɛtə'rɔdʒɪnəs] adj heterogen.
**heterosexual** ['hɛtərəʊ'sɛksjuəl] adj heterosexuell ♦ n Heterosexuelle(r) f(m).
**het up** [hɛt-] (inf) adj: **to get** ~ **(about)** sich aufregen (über +acc).
**HEW** (US) n abbr (= Department of Health, Education and Welfare) Ministerium für Gesundheit, Erziehung und Sozialfürsorge.
**hew** [hjuː] (pt, pp **hewed** or **hewn**) vt (stone) behauen; (wood) hacken.
**hex** [hɛks] (US) n Fluch m ♦ vt verhexen.
**hexagon** ['hɛksəgən] n Sechseck nt.
**hexagonal** [hɛk'sægənl] adj sechseckig.
**hey** [heɪ] excl he; (to attract attention) he du/Sie.
**heyday** ['heɪdeɪ] n: **the** ~ **of** (person) die Glanzzeit +gen; (nation, group etc) die Blütezeit +gen.
**HF** n abbr (= high frequency) HF.
**HGV** (BRIT) n abbr (= heavy goods vehicle) LKW m.
**HI** (US) abbr (POST: = Hawaii).
**hi** [haɪ] excl hallo.
**hiatus** [haɪ'eɪtəs] n Unterbrechung f.
**hibernate** ['haɪbəneɪt] vi Winterschlaf halten or machen.
**hibernation** [haɪbə'neɪʃən] n Winterschlaf m.
**hiccough** ['hɪkʌp] vi hicksen.
**hiccoughs** ['hɪkʌps] npl Schluckauf m; **to have (the)** ~ den Schluckauf haben.
**hiccup** ['hɪkʌp] vi = **hiccough**.
**hiccups** ['hɪkʌps] npl = **hiccoughs**.
**hick** [hɪk] (US: inf) n Hinterwäldler m.
**hid** [hɪd] pt of **hide**.

**hidden** ['hɪdn] pp of **hide** ♦ adj (advantage, danger) unsichtbar; (place) versteckt; **there are no** ~ **extras** es gibt keine versteckten Extrakosten.
**hide** [haɪd] (pt **hid**, pp **hidden**) n Haut f, Fell nt; (of birdwatcher etc) Versteck nt ♦ vt verstecken; (feeling, information) verbergen; (obscure) verdecken ♦ vi: **to** ~ **(from sb)** sich (vor jdm) verstecken; **to** ~ **sth (from sb)** etw (vor jdm) verstecken.
**hide-and-seek** ['haɪdən'siːk] n Versteckspiel nt; **to play** ~ Verstecken spielen.
**hideaway** ['haɪdəweɪ] n Zufluchtsort m.
**hideous** ['hɪdɪəs] adj scheußlich; (conditions) furchtbar.
**hideously** ['hɪdɪəslɪ] adv furchtbar.
**hide-out** ['haɪdaʊt] n Versteck nt.
**hiding** ['haɪdɪŋ] n Tracht f Prügel; **to be in** ~ (concealed) sich versteckt halten.
**hiding place** n Versteck nt.
**hierarchy** ['haɪərɑːkɪ] n Hierarchie f.
**hieroglyphic** [haɪərə'glɪfɪk] adj hieroglyphisch.
**hieroglyphics** [haɪərə'glɪfɪks] npl Hieroglyphen pl.
**hi-fi** ['haɪfaɪ] n abbr (= high fidelity) Hi-Fi nt ♦ adj (equipment etc) Hi-Fi-.
**higgledy-piggledy** ['hɪgldɪ'pɪgldɪ] adj durcheinander.
**high** [haɪ] adj hoch; (wind) stark; (risk) groß; (quality) gut; (inf: on drugs) high; (: on drink) blau; (BRIT: food) schlecht; (: game) anbrüchig ♦ adv hoch ♦ n: **exports have reached a new** ~ der Export hat einen neuen Höchststand erreicht; **to pay a** ~ **price for sth** etw teuer bezahlen; **it's** ~ **time you did it** es ist or wird höchste Zeit, daß du es machst; ~ **in the air** hoch oben in der Luft.
**highball** ['haɪbɔːl] (US) n Highball m.
**highboy** ['haɪbɔɪ] (US) n hohe Kommode f.
**highbrow** ['haɪbraʊ] adj intellektuell; (book, discussion etc) anspruchsvoll.
**highchair** ['haɪtʃeə*] n Hochstuhl m.
**high-class** ['haɪ'klɑːs] adj erstklassig; (neighbourhood) vornehm.

---

**High Court** ist in England und Wales die Kurzform für High Court of Justice und bildet zusammen mit dem Berufsgericht den Obersten Gerichtshof. In Schottland ist es die Kurzform für High Court of Justiciary, das höchste Strafgericht in Schottland, das in Edinburgh und anderen Großstädten (immer mit Richter und Geschworenen) zusammentritt und für Verbrechen wie Mord, Vergewaltigung und Hochverrat zuständig ist. Weniger schwere Verbrechen werden vor dem sheriff court verhandelt, und leichtere Vergehen vor dem district court.

---

**higher** ['haɪə*] adj (form of study, life etc) höher

(entwickelt) ♦ *adv* höher.

**higher education** *n* Hochschulbildung *f*.

**highfalutin** [haɪfə'luːtɪn] (*inf*) *adj* (*behaviour, ideas*) hochtrabend.

**high finance** *n* Hochfinanz *f*.

**high-flier, high-flyer** [haɪ'flaɪə•] *n* Senkrechtstarter(in) *m(f)*.

**high-flying** [haɪ'flaɪɪŋ] *adj* (*person*) erfolgreich; (*lifestyle*) exklusiv.

**high-handed** [haɪ'hændɪd] *adj* eigenmächtig.

**high-heeled** [haɪ'hiːld] *adj* hochhackig.

**high heels** *npl* hochhackige Schuhe *pl*.

**high jump** *n* Hochsprung *m*.

**Highlands** ['haɪləndz] *npl*: the ~ das Hochland.

**high-level** ['haɪlɛvl] *adj* (*talks etc*) auf höchster Ebene; ~ **language** (*COMPUT*) höhere Programmiersprache *f*.

**highlight** ['haɪlaɪt] *n* (*of event*) Höhepunkt *m*; (*in hair*) Strähnchen *nt* ♦ *vt* (*problem, need*) ein Schlaglicht werfen auf +*acc*.

**highlighter** ['haɪlaɪtə•] *n* Textmarker *m*.

**highly** ['haɪlɪ] *adv* hoch-; **to speak** ~ **of** sich sehr positiv äußern über +*acc*; **to think** ~ **of** eine hohe Meinung haben von.

**highly strung** *adj* nervös.

**High Mass** *n* Hochamt *nt*.

**highness** ['haɪnɪs] *n*: **Her/His/Your H**~ Ihre/Seine/Eure Hoheit *f*.

**high-pitched** [haɪ'pɪtʃt] *adj* hoch.

**high point** *n* Höhepunkt *m*.

**high-powered** ['haɪ'pauəd] *adj* (*engine*) Hochleistungs-; (*job*) Spitzen-; (*businessman*) dynamisch; (*person*) äußerst fähig; (*course*) anspruchsvoll.

**high-pressure** ['haɪprɛʃə•] *adj* (*area, system*) Hochdruck-; (*inf: sales technique*) aggressiv.

**high-rise** ['haɪraɪz] *adj* (*apartment, block*) Hochhaus-; ~ **building/flats** Hochhaus *nt*.

**high school** *n* ≈ Oberschule *f*.

---

High school *ist eine weiterführende Schule in den USA. Man unterscheidet zwischen* junior high school *(im Anschluß an die Grundschule, umfaßt das 7., 8. und 9. Schuljahr) und* senior high school *(10., 11. und 12. Schuljahr, mit akademischen und berufsbezogenen Fächern). Weiterführende Schulen in Großbritannien werden manchmal auch als* high school *bezeichnet. Siehe auch* elementary school.

---

**high season** (*BRIT*) *n* Hochsaison *f*.

**high spirits** *npl* Hochstimmung *f*.

**high street** (*BRIT*) *n* Hauptstraße *f*.

**high strung** (*US*) *adj* = **highly strung**.

**high tide** *n* Flut *f*.

**highway** ['haɪweɪ] (*US*) *n* Straße *f*; (*between towns, states*) Landstraße *f*; **information** ~ Datenautobahn *f*.

**Highway Code** (*BRIT*) *n* Straßenverkehrsordnung *f*.

**highwayman** ['haɪweɪmən] (*irreg: like* man) *n*

Räuber *m*, Wegelagerer *m*.

**hijack** ['haɪdʒæk] *vt* entführen ♦ *n* (*also:* ~**ing**) Entführung *f*.

**hijacker** ['haɪdʒækə•] *n* Entführer(in) *m(f)*.

**hike** [haɪk] *vi* wandern ♦ *n* Wanderung *f*; (*inf: in prices etc*) Erhöhung *f* ♦ *vt* (*inf*) erhöhen.

**hiker** ['haɪkə•] *n* Wanderer *m*, Wanderin *f*.

**hiking** ['haɪkɪŋ] *n* Wandern *nt*.

**hilarious** [hɪ'lɛərɪəs] *adj* urkomisch.

**hilarity** [hɪ'lærɪtɪ] *n* übermütige Ausgelassenheit *f*.

**hill** [hɪl] *n* Hügel *m*; (*fairly high*) Berg *m*; (*slope*) Hang *m*; (*on road*) Steigung *f*.

**hillbilly** ['hɪlbɪlɪ] (*US*) *n* Hillbilly *m*; (*pej*) Hinterwäldler(in) *m(f)*, Landpomeranze *f*.

**hillock** ['hɪlək] *n* Hügel *m*, Anhöhe *f*.

**hillside** ['hɪlsaɪd] *n* Hang *m*.

**hill start** *n* (*AUT*) Anfahren *nt* am Berg.

**hilltop** ['hɪltɒp] *n* Gipfel *m*.

**hilly** ['hɪlɪ] *adj* hügelig.

**hilt** [hɪlt] *n* (*of sword, knife*) Heft *nt*; **to the** ~ voll und ganz.

**him** [hɪm] *pron* ihn; (*indirect*) ihm; *see also* **me**.

**Himalayas** [hɪmə'leɪəz] *npl*: **the** ~ der Himalaja.

**himself** [hɪm'sɛlf] *pron* sich; (*emphatic*) (er) selbst; *see also* **oneself**.

**hind** [haɪnd] *adj* (*legs*) Hinter- ♦ *n* (*female deer*) Hirschkuh *f*.

**hinder** ['hɪndə•] *vt* behindern; **to** ~ **sb from doing sth** jdn daran hindern, etw zu tun.

**hindquarters** ['haɪnd'kwɔːtəz] *npl* Hinterteil *nt*.

**hindrance** ['hɪndrəns] *n* Behinderung *f*.

**hindsight** ['haɪndsaɪt] *n*: **with** ~ im nachhinein.

**Hindu** ['hɪnduː] *adj* hinduistisch, Hindu-.

**hinge** [hɪndʒ] *n* (*on door*) Angel *f* ♦ *vi*: **to** ~ **on** anhängen von.

**hint** [hɪnt] *n* Andeutung *f*; (*advice*) Tip *m*; (*sign, glimmer*) Spur *f* ♦ *vt*: **to** ~ **that** andeuten, daß ♦ *vi*: **to** ~ **at** andeuten; **to drop a** ~ eine Andeutung machen; **give me a** ~ geben Sie mir einen Hinweis; **white with a** ~ **of pink** weiß mit einem Hauch von Rosa.

**hip** [hɪp] *n* Hüfte *f*.

**hip flask** *n* Taschenflasche *f*, Flachmann *m* (*inf*).

**hip-hop** ['hɪphɒp] *n* Hip-Hop *nt*.

**hippie** ['hɪpɪ] *n* Hippie *m*.

**hippo** ['hɪpəu] *n* Nilpferd *nt*.

**hip pocket** *n* Gesäßtasche *f*.

**hippopotamus** [hɪpə'pɒtəməs] (*pl* ~**es** *or* **hippopotami**) *n* Nilpferd *nt*.

**hippy** ['hɪpɪ] *n* = **hippie**.

**hire** ['haɪə•] *vt* (*BRIT*) mieten; (*worker*) einstellen ♦ *n* (*BRIT*) Mieten *nt*; **for** ~ (*taxi*) frei; (*boat*) zu vermieten; **on** ~ gemietet.

▶**hire out** *vt* vermieten.

**hire(d) car** (*BRIT*) *n* Mietwagen *m*, Leihwagen *m*.

**hire-purchase** [haɪə'pɜːtʃɪs] (*BRIT*) *n*

Ratenkauf *m*; **to buy sth on** ~ etw auf Raten kaufen.

**his** [hɪz] *pron* seine(r, s) ♦ *adj* sein; *see also* **my; mine²**.

**hiss** [hɪs] *vi* zischen; (*cat*) fauchen ♦ *n* Zischen *nt*; (*of cat*) Fauchen *nt*.

**histogram** ['hɪstəgræm] *n* Histogramm *nt*.

**historian** [hɪ'stɔːrɪən] *n* Historiker(in) *m(f)*.

**historic** [hɪ'stɔrɪk] *adj* historisch.

**historical** [hɪ'stɔrɪkl] *adj* historisch.

**history** ['hɪstərɪ] *n* Geschichte *f*; **there's a** ~ **of heart disease in his family** Herzleiden liegen bei ihm in der Familie; **medical** ~ Krankengeschichte *f*.

**hit** [hɪt] (*pt, pp* **hit**) *vt* schlagen; (*reach, affect*) treffen; (*vehicle: another vehicle*) zusammenstoßen mit; (: *wall, tree*) fahren gegen; (: : *more violently*) prallen gegen; (: *person*) anfahren ♦ *n* Schlag *m*; (*success*) Erfolg *m*; (*song*) Hit *m*; **to** ~ **it off with sb** sich gut mit jdm verstehen; **to** ~ **the headlines** Schlagzeilen machen; **to** ~ **the road** (*inf*) sich auf den Weg *or* die Socken (*inf*) machen; **to** ~ **the roof** (*inf*) an die Decke *or* in die Luft gehen.

►**hit back** *vi*: **to** ~ **back at sb** jdn zurückschlagen; (*fig*) jdm Kontra geben.

►**hit out at** *vt fus* auf jdn losschlagen; (*fig*) jdn scharf angreifen.

►**hit (up)on** *vt fus* stoßen auf +*acc*, finden.

**hit-and-miss** ['hɪtən'mɪs] *adj* = **hit-or-miss**.

**hit-and-run driver** ['hɪtən'rʌn-] *n* unfallflüchtiger Fahrer *m*, unfallflüchtige Fahrerin *f*.

**hitch** [hɪtʃ] *vt* festmachen, anbinden; (*also:* ~ **up**: *trousers, skirt*) hochziehen ♦ *n* Schwierigkeit *f*, Problem *nt*; **to** ~ **a lift** trampen, per Anhalter fahren; **technical** ~ technische Panne *f*.

►**hitch up** *vt* anspannen; *see also* **hitch**.

**hitchhike** ['hɪtʃhaɪk] *vi* trampen, per Anhalter fahren.

**hitchhiker** ['hɪtʃhaɪkə*] *n* Tramper(in) *m(f)*, Anhalter(in) *m(f)*.

**hi-tech** ['haɪ'tɛk] *adj* High-Tech-, hochtechnisiert ♦ *n* High-Tech *nt*, Hochtechnologie *f*.

**hitherto** [hɪðə'tuː] *adv* bisher, bis jetzt.

**hit list** *n* Abschußliste *f*.

**hit man** (*inf*) *n* Killer *m*.

**hit-or-miss** ['hɪtə'mɪs] *adj* ungeplant; **to be a** ~ **affair** eine unsichere Sache sein; **it's** ~ **whether ...** es ist nicht zu sagen, ob ...

**hit parade** *n* Hitparade *f*.

**HIV** *n abbr* (= *human immunodeficiency virus*) HIV; ~**-negative** HIV-negativ; ~**-positive** HIV-positiv.

**hive** [haɪv] *n* Bienenkorb *m*; **to be a** ~ **of activity** einem Bienenhaus gleichen.

►**hive off** (*inf*) *vt* ausgliedern, abspalten.

**hl** *abbr* (= *hectolitre*) hl.

**HM** *abbr* (= *His/Her Majesty*) S.*/*I.M.

**HMG** (*BRIT*) *abbr* (= *His/Her Majesty's Government*) die Regierung Seiner*/*Ihrer Majestät.

**HMI** (*BRIT*) *n abbr* (*SCOL*: = *His/Her Majesty's Inspector*) *regierungsamtlicher Schulaufsichtsbeauftragter*.

**HMO** (*US*) *n abbr* (= *health maintenance organization*) Organisation zur Gesundheitsfürsorge.

**HMS** (*BRIT*) *abbr* (= *His* (*or Her*) *Majesty's Ship*) Namensteil von Schiffen der Kriegsmarine.

**HMSO** (*BRIT*) *n abbr* (= *His* (*or Her*) *Majesty's Stationery Office*) *regierungsamtliche Druckerei*.

**HNC** (*BRIT*) *n abbr* (= *Higher National Certificate*) *Berufsschulabschluß*.

**HND** (*BRIT*) *n abbr* (= *Higher National Diploma*) *Qualifikationsnachweis in technischen Fächern*.

**hoard** [hɔːd] *n* (*of food*) Vorrat *m*; (*of money, treasure*) Schatz *m* ♦ *vt* (*food*) hamstern; (*money*) horten.

**hoarding** ['hɔːdɪŋ] (*BRIT*) *n* Plakatwand *f*.

**hoarfrost** ['hɔːfrɔst] *n* (Rauh)reif *m*.

**hoarse** [hɔːs] *adj* heiser.

**hoax** [həʊks] *n* (*false alarm*) blinder Alarm *m*.

**hob** [hɔb] *n* Kochmulde *f*.

**hobble** ['hɔbl] *vi* humpeln.

**hobby** ['hɔbɪ] *n* Hobby *nt*, Steckenpferd *nt*.

**hobbyhorse** ['hɔbɪhɔːs] *n* (*fig*) Lieblingsthema *nt*.

**hobnail boot** ['hɔbneɪl-] *n* Nagelschuh *m*.

**hobnob** ['hɔbnɔb] *vi*: **to** ~ **with** auf du und du stehen mit.

**hobo** ['həʊbəʊ] (*US*) *n* Penner *m* (*inf*).

**hock** [hɔk] *n* (*BRIT*) weißer Rheinwein *m*; (*of animal*) Sprunggelenk *nt*; (*US: CULIN*) Gelenkstück *nt*; (*inf*): **to be in** ~ (*person: in debt*) in Schulden stecken; (*object*) verpfändet *or* im Leihhaus sein.

**hockey** ['hɔkɪ] *n* Hockey *nt*.

**hocus-pocus** ['həʊkəs'pəʊkəs] *n* Hokuspokus *m*; (*trickery*) faule Tricks *pl*; (*jargon*) Jargon *m*.

**hod** [hɔd] *n* (*for bricks etc*) Tragemulde *f*.

**hodgepodge** ['hɔdʒpɔdʒ] (*US*) *n* = **hotchpotch**.

**hoe** [həʊ] *n* Hacke *f* ♦ *vt* hacken.

**hog** [hɔg] *n* (Mast)schwein *nt* ♦ *vt* (*road*) für sich beanspruchen; (*telephone etc*) in Beschlag nehmen; **to go the whole** ~ Nägel mit Köpfen machen.

**Hogmanay** [hɔgmə'neɪ] (*SCOT*) *n* Silvester *nt*.

**hogwash** ['hɔgwɔʃ] (*inf*) *n* (*nonsense*) Quatsch *m*.

**ho hum** ['həʊ'hʌm] *interj* na gut.

**hoist** [hɔɪst] *n* Hebevorrichtung *f* ♦ *vt* hochheben; (*flag, sail*) hissen.

**hoity-toity** [hɔɪtɪ'tɔɪtɪ] (*inf: pej*) *adj* hochnäsig.

**hold** [həʊld] (*pt, pp* **held**) *vt* halten; (*contain*) enthalten; (*power, qualification*) haben; (*opinion*) vertreten; (*meeting*) abhalten;

(*conversation*) führen; (*prisoner, hostage*) festhalten ♦ *vi* halten; (*be valid*) gelten; (*weather*) sich halten ♦ *n* (*grasp*) Griff *m*; (*of ship, plane*) Laderaum *m*; **to ~ one's head up** den Kopf hochhalten; **to ~ sb responsible/ liable etc** jdn verantwortlich/haftbar *etc* machen; **~ the line!** (*TEL*) bleiben Sie am Apparat!; **~ it!** Moment mal!; **to ~ one's own** sich behaupten; **he ~s the view that ...** er ist der Meinung *or* er vertritt die Ansicht, daß ...; **to ~ firm** *or* **fast** halten; **~ still!, ~ steady!** stillhalten!; **his luck held** das Glück blieb ihm treu; **I don't ~ with ...** ich bin gegen ...; **to catch** *or* **get (a) ~ of** sich festhalten an +*dat*; **to get ~ of** (*fig*) finden, auftreiben; **to get ~ of o.s.** sich in den Griff bekommen; **to have a ~ over** in der Hand haben.

► **hold back** *vt* zurückhalten; (*tears, laughter*) unterdrücken; (*secret*) verbergen; (*information*) geheimhalten.

► **hold down** *vt* niederhalten; (*job*) sich halten in +*dat*.

► **hold forth** *vi:* **to ~ forth (about)** sich ergehen *or* sich auslassen (über +*acc*).

► **hold off** *vt* abwehren ♦ *vi:* **if the rain ~s off** wenn es nicht regnet.

► **hold on** *vi* sich festhalten; (*wait*) warten; **~ on!** (*TEL*) einen Moment bitte!

► **hold on to** *vt fus* sich festhalten an; (*keep*) behalten.

► **hold out** *vt* (*hand*) ausstrecken; (*hope*) haben; (*prospect*) bieten ♦ *vi* nicht nachgeben.

► **hold over** *vt* vertagen.

► **hold up** *vt* hochheben; (*support*) stützen; (*delay*) aufhalten; (*rob*) überfallen.

**holdall** ['həuldɔːl] (*BRIT*) *n* Tasche *f*; (*for clothes*) Reisetasche *f*.

**holder** ['həuldə*] *n* Halter *m*; (*of ticket, record, office, title etc*) Inhaber(in) *m(f)*.

**holding** ['həuldɪŋ] *n* (*share*) Anteil *m*; (*small farm*) Gut *nt* ♦ *adj* (*operation, tactic*) zur Schadensbegrenzung.

**holding company** *n* Dachgesellschaft *f*, Holdinggesellschaft *f*.

**hold-up** ['həuldʌp] *n* bewaffneter Raubüberfall *m*; (*delay*) Verzögerung *f*; (*BRIT: in traffic*) Stockung *f*.

**hole** [həul] *n* Loch *nt*; (*unpleasant town*) Kaff *nt* (*inf*) ♦ *vt* (*ship*) leck schlagen; (*building etc*) durchlöchern; **~ in the heart** Loch im Herz(en); **to pick ~s** (*fig*) (über)kritisch sein; **to pick ~s in sth** (*fig*) an etw *dat* herumkritisieren.

► **hole up** *vi* sich verkriechen.

**holiday** ['hɔlɪdeɪ] *n* (*BRIT*) Urlaub *m*; (*SCOL*) Ferien *pl*; (*day off*) freier Tag *m*; (*public holiday*) Feiertag *m*; **on ~** im Urlaub, in den Ferien.

**holiday camp** (*BRIT*) *n* (*also:* **holiday centre**) Feriendorf *nt*.

**holiday-maker** ['hɔlɪdɪmeɪkə*] (*BRIT*) *n* Urlauber(in) *m(f)*.

**holiday pay** *n* Lohn-/Gehaltsfortzahlung während des Urlaubs.

**holiday resort** *n* Ferienort *m*.

**holiday season** *n* Urlaubszeit *f*.

**holiness** ['həulɪnɪs] *n* Heiligkeit *f*.

**holistic** [həu'lɪstɪk] *adj* holistisch.

**Holland** ['hɔlənd] *n* Holland *nt*.

**holler** ['hɔlə*] (*inf*) *vi* brüllen ♦ *n* Schrei *m*.

**hollow** ['hɔləu] *adj* hohl; (*eyes*) tiefliegend; (*laugh*) unecht; (*sound*) dumpf; (*fig*) leer; (*: victory, opinion*) wertlos ♦ *n* Vertiefung *f* ♦ *vt:* **to ~ out** aushöhlen.

**holly** ['hɔlɪ] *n* Stechpalme *f*, Ilex *m*; (*leaves*) Stechpalmenzweige *pl*.

**hollyhock** ['hɔlɪhɔk] *n* Malve *f*.

**holocaust** ['hɔləkɔːst] *n* Inferno *nt*; (*in Third Reich*) Holocaust *m*.

**hologram** ['hɔləgræm] *n* Hologramm *nt*.

**hols** [hɔlz] (*inf*) *npl* Ferien *pl*.

**holster** ['həulstə*] *n* Pistolenhalfter *m or nt*.

**holy** ['həulɪ] *adj* heilig.

**Holy Communion** *n* Heilige Kommunion *f*.

**Holy Father** *n* Heiliger Vater *m*.

**Holy Ghost** *n* Heiliger Geist *m*.

**Holy Land** *n:* **the ~** das Heilige Land.

**holy orders** *npl* Priesterweihe *f*.

**Holy Spirit** *n* Heiliger Geist *m*.

**homage** ['hɔmɪdʒ] *n* Huldigung *f*; **to pay ~ to** huldigen +*dat*.

**home** [həum] *n* Heim *nt*; (*house, flat*) Zuhause *nt*; (*area, country*) Heimat *f*; (*institution*) Anstalt *f* ♦ *cpd* Heim-; (*ECON, POL*) Innen- ♦ *adv* (*go etc*) nach Hause, heim; **at ~** zu Hause; (*in country*) im Inland; **to be** *or* **feel at ~** (*fig*) sich wohl fühlen; **make yourself at ~** machen Sie es sich *dat* gemütlich *or* bequem; **to make one's ~ somewhere** sich irgendwo niederlassen; **the ~ of free enterprise/jazz etc** die Heimat des freien Unternehmertums/Jazz *etc*; **when will you be ~?** wann bist du wieder zu Hause?; **a ~ from ~** ein zweites Zuhause *nt*; **~ and dry** aus dem Schneider; **to drive a nail ~** einen Nagel einschlagen; **to bring sth ~ to sb** jdm etw klarmachen.

► **home in on** *vt fus* (*missiles*) sich ausrichten auf +*acc*.

**home address** *n* Heimatanschrift *f*.

**home-brew** [həum'bruː] *n* selbstgebrautes Bier *nt*.

**homecoming** ['həumkʌmɪŋ] *n* Heimkehr *f*.

**home computer** *n* Heimcomputer *m*.

**Home Counties** (*BRIT*) *npl:* **the ~** die Grafschaften, die an London angrenzen.

**home economics** *n* Hauswirtschaft(slehre) *f*.

**home ground** *n* (*SPORT*) eigener Platz *m*; **to be on ~** (*fig*) sich auf vertrautem Terrain bewegen.

**home-grown** ['həumgrəun] *adj* (*not foreign*)

einheimisch; (*from garden*) selbstgezogen.
**home help** n Haushaltshilfe f.
**homeland** ['həumlænd] n Heimat f,
Heimatland nt.
**homeless** ['həumlɪs] adj obdachlos; (*refugee*)
heimatlos.
**home loan** n Hypothek f.
**homely** ['həumlɪ] adj einfach; (*US: plain*)
unscheinbar.
**home-made** [həum'meɪd] adj selbstgemacht.
**Home Office** (*BRIT*) n Innenministerium nt.
**homeopath** ['həumɪəupæθ] (*US*) n =
**homoeopath**.
**homeopathy** [həumɪ'ɒpəθɪ] (*US*) n
= **homoeopathy**.
**home rule** n Selbstbestimmung f,
Selbstverwaltung f.
**Home Secretary** (*BRIT*) n Innenminister(in)
m(f).
**homesick** ['həumsɪk] adj heimwehkrank; **to
be** ~ Heimweh haben.
**homestead** ['həumstɛd] n Heimstätte f; (*farm*)
Gehöft nt.
**home town** n Heimatstadt f.
**home truth** n bittere Wahrheit f; **to tell sb
some** ~s jdm deutlich die Meinung sagen.
**homeward** ['həumwəd] adj (*journey*) Heim-
♦ adv = **homewards**.
**homewards** ['həumwədz] adv nach Hause,
heim.
**homework** ['həumwɜːk] n Hausaufgaben pl.
**homicidal** [hɒmɪ'saɪdl] adj gemeingefährlich.
**homicide** ['hɒmɪsaɪd] (*US*) n Mord m.
**homily** ['hɒmɪlɪ] n Predigt f.
**homing** ['həumɪŋ] adj (*device, missile*) mit
Zielsucheinrichtung; ~ **pigeon** Brieftaube f.
**homoeopath**, (*US*) **homeopath**
['həumɪəupæθ] n Homöopath(in) m(f).
**homoeopathy**, (*US*) **homeopathy**
[həumɪ'ɒpəθɪ] n Homöopathie f.
**homogeneous** [hɒməu'dʒiːnɪəs] adj homogen.
**homogenize** [hə'mɒdʒənaɪz] vt
homogenisieren.
**homosexual** [hɒməu'sɛksjuəl] adj
homosexuell ♦ n Homosexuelle(r) f(m).
**Hon.** abbr = **honourable; honorary**.
**Honduras** [hɒn'djuərəs] n Honduras nt.
**hone** [həun] n Schleifstein m ♦ vt schleifen;
(*fig: groom*) erziehen.
**honest** ['ɒnɪst] adj ehrlich; (*trustworthy*)
redlich; (*sincere*) aufrichtig; **to be quite**
~ **with you** ... um ehrlich zu sein, ...
**honestly** ['ɒnɪstlɪ] adv (*see adj*) ehrlich;
redlich; aufrichtig.
**honesty** ['ɒnɪstɪ] n (*see adj*) Ehrlichkeit f;
Redlichkeit f; Aufrichtigkeit f.
**honey** ['hʌnɪ] n Honig m; (*US: inf*) Schätzchen
nt.
**honeycomb** ['hʌnɪkəum] n Bienenwabe f;
(*pattern*) Wabe f ♦ vt: **to** ~ **with** durchlöchern
mit.
**honeymoon** ['hʌnɪmuːn] n Flitterwochen pl;

(*trip*) Hochzeitsreise f.
**honeysuckle** ['hʌnɪsʌkl] n Geißblatt nt.
**Hong Kong** ['hɒŋ'kɒŋ] n Hongkong nt.
**honk** [hɒŋk] vi (*AUT*) hupen.
**Honolulu** [hɒnə'luːluː] n Honolulu nt.
**honor** etc ['ɒnə'] (*US*) = **honour** etc.
**honorary** ['ɒnərərɪ] adj ehrenamtlich; (*title,
degree*) Ehren-.
**honour,** (*US*) **honor** ['ɒnə'] vt ehren;
(*commitment, promise*) stehen zu ♦ n Ehre f;
(*tribute*) Auszeichnung f; **in** ~ **of** zu Ehren
von or +gen.
**honourable** ['ɒnərəbl] adj (*person*) ehrenwert;
(*action, defeat*) ehrenvoll.
**honour-bound** ['ɒnə'baund] adj: **to be** ~ **to do
sth** moralisch verpflichtet sein, etw zu tun.
**honours degree** ['ɒnəz-] n akademischer
Grad mit Prüfung im Spezialfach.

---

**Honours Degree** ist ein Universitätsabschluß
mit einer guten Note, also der Note I (*first
class*), II:1 (*upper second class*), II:2 (*lower
second class*) oder III (*third class*). Wer ein
honours degree erhalten hat, darf die
Abkürzung Hons nach seinem Namen und Titel
führen, z.B. Mary Smith BA Hons. Heute sind
fast alle Universitätsabschlüsse in
Großbritannien honours degrees. Siehe auch
**ordinary degree**.

---

**honours list** n Liste verliehener/zu
verleihender Ehrentitel.

---

**Honours List** ist eine Liste von Adelstiteln und
Orden, die der britische Monarch zweimal
jährlich (zu Neujahr und am offiziellen
Geburtstag des Monarchen) an Bürger in
Großbritannien und im Commonwealth
verleiht. Die Liste wird vom Premierminister
zusammengestellt, aber drei Orden (der
Hosenbandorden, der Verdienstorden und der
Victoria-Orden) werden vom Monarchen
persönlich vergeben. Erfolgreiche Geschäfts-
leute, Militärangehörige, Sportler und andere
Prominente, aber auch im sozialen Bereich
besonders aktive Bürger werden auf diese
Weise geehrt.

---

**Hons.** abbr (*UNIV*) = **honours degree**.
**hood** [hud] n (*of coat etc*) Kapuze f; (*of cooker*)
Abzugshaube f; (*AUT: BRIT: folding roof*)
Verdeck nt; (: *US: bonnet*) (Motor)haube f.
**hooded** ['hudɪd] adj maskiert; (*jacket etc*) mit
Kapuze.
**hoodlum** ['huːdləm] n Gangster m.
**hoodwink** ['hudwɪŋk] vt (he)reinlegen.
**hoof** [huːf] (*pl* **hooves**) n Huf m.
**hook** [huk] n Haken m ♦ vt festhaken; (*fish*) an
die Angel bekommen; **by** ~ **or by crook** auf
Biegen und Brechen; **to be** ~**ed on** (*inf: film,
exhibition, etc*) fasziniert sein von; (: *drugs*)
abhängig sein von; (: *person*) stehen auf

+*acc.*

►**hook up** *vt* (*RADIO, TV etc*) anschließen.
**hook and eye** (*pl* **hooks and eyes**) *n* Haken und Öse *pl.*
**hooligan** ['hu:lɪgən] *n* Rowdy *m.*
**hooliganism** ['hu:lɪgənɪzəm] *n* Rowdytum *nt.*
**hoop** [hu:p] *n* Reifen *m*; (*for croquet: arch*) Tor *nt.*
**hooray** [hu:'reɪ] *excl* = **hurrah.**
**hoot** [hu:t] *vi* hupen; (*siren*) heulen; (*owl*) schreien, rufen; (*person*) johlen ♦ *vt* (*horn*) drücken auf +*acc* ♦ *n* (*see vi*) Hupen *nt*; Heulen *nt*; Schreien *nt*, Rufen *nt*; Johlen *nt*; **to ~ with laughter** in johlendes Gelächter ausbrechen.
**hooter** ['hu:tə*] *n* (*BRIT: AUT*) Hupe *f*; (*NAUT, factory*) Sirene *f.*
**Hoover** ® ['hu:və*] (*BRIT*) *n* Staubsauger *m* ♦ *vt*: **h~** (*carpet*) saugen.
**hooves** [hu:vz] *npl of* **hoof.**
**hop** [hɒp] *vi* hüpfen ♦ *n* Hüpfer *m*; *see also* **hops.**
**hope** [həup] *vi* hoffen ♦ *n* Hoffnung *f* ♦ *vt*: **to ~ that** hoffen, daß; **I ~ so** ich hoffe es, hoffentlich; **I ~ not** ich hoffe nicht, hoffentlich nicht; **to ~ for the best** das Beste hoffen; **to have no ~ of sth/doing sth** keine Hoffnung auf etw +*acc* haben/darauf haben, etw zu tun; **in the ~ of/that** in der Hoffnung auf/, daß; **to ~ to do sth** hoffen, etw zu tun.
**hopeful** ['həupful] *adj* hoffnungsvoll; (*situation*) vielversprechend; **I'm ~ that she'll manage** ich hoffe, daß sie es schafft.
**hopefully** ['həupfulɪ] *adv* hoffnungsvoll; (*one hopes*) hoffentlich; **~, he'll come back** hoffentlich kommt er wieder.
**hopeless** ['həuplɪs] *adj* hoffnungslos; (*situation*) aussichtslos; (*useless*): **to be ~ at sth** etw überhaupt nicht können.
**hopper** ['hɒpə*] *n* Einfülltrichter *m.*
**hops** [hɒps] *npl* Hopfen *m.*
**horde** [hɔ:d] *n* Horde *f.*
**horizon** [hə'raɪzn] *n* Horizont *m.*
**horizontal** [hɒrɪ'zɒntl] *adj* horizontal.
**hormone** ['hɔ:məun] *n* Hormon *nt.*
**hormone replacement therapy** *n* Hormonersatztherapie *f.*
**horn** [hɔ:n] *n* Horn *nt*; (*AUT*) Hupe *f.*
**horned** [hɔ:nd] *adj* (*animal*) mit Hörnern.
**hornet** ['hɔ:nɪt] *n* Hornisse *f.*
**horn-rimmed** ['hɔ:n'rɪmd] *adj* (*spectacles*) Horn-.
**horny** ['hɔ:nɪ] (*inf*) *adj* (*aroused*) scharf, geil.
**horoscope** ['hɒrəskəup] *n* Horoskop *nt.*
**horrendous** [hə'rɛndəs] *adj* abscheulich, entsetzlich.
**horrible** ['hɒrɪbl] *adj* fürchterlich, schrecklich; (*scream, dream*) furchtbar.
**horrid** ['hɒrɪd] *adj* entsetzlich, schrecklich.
**horrific** [hɒ'rɪfɪk] *adj* entsetzlich, schrecklich.
**horrify** ['hɒrɪfaɪ] *vt* entsetzen.

**horrifying** ['hɒrɪfaɪɪŋ] *adj* schrecklich, fürchterlich, entsetzlich.
**horror** ['hɒrə*] *n* Entsetzen *nt*, Grauen *nt*; ~ (**of sth**) (*abhorrence*) Abscheu *m* (vor etw *dat*); **the ~s of war** die Schrecken *pl* des Krieges.
**horror film** *n* Horrorfilm *m.*
**horror-stricken** ['hɒrəstrɪkn] *adj* = **horror-struck.**
**horror-struck** ['hɒrəstrʌk] *adj* von Entsetzen *or* Grauen gepackt.
**hors d'oeuvre** [ɔ:'də:vrə] *n* Hors d'oeuvre *nt*, Vorspeise *f.*
**horse** [hɔ:s] *n* Pferd *nt.*
**horseback** ['hɔ:sbæk]: **on ~** *adj, adv* zu Pferd.
**horsebox** ['hɔ:sbɒks] *n* Pferdetransporter *m.*
**horse chestnut** *n* Roßkastanie *f.*
**horse-drawn** ['hɔ:sdrɔ:n] *adj* von Pferden gezogen.
**horsefly** ['hɔ:sflaɪ] *n* (Pferde)bremse *f.*
**horseman** ['hɔ:smən] (*irreg: like* **man**) *n* Reiter *m.*
**horsemanship** ['hɔ:smənʃɪp] *n* Reitkunst *f.*
**horseplay** ['hɔ:spleɪ] *n* Alberei *f*, Balgerei *f.*
**horsepower** ['hɔ:spauə*] *n* Pferdestärke *f.*
**horse racing** *n* Pferderennen *nt.*
**horseradish** ['hɔ:srædɪʃ] *n* Meerrettich *m.*
**horseshoe** ['hɔ:sʃu:] *n* Hufeisen *nt.*
**horse show** *n* Reitturnier *nt.*
**horse trading** *n* Kuhhandel *m.*
**horse trials** *npl* = **horse show.**
**horsewhip** ['hɔ:swɪp] *n* Reitpeitsche *f* ♦ *vt* auspeitschen.
**horsewoman** ['hɔ:swumən] (*irreg: like* **woman**) *n* Reiterin *f.*
**horsey** ['hɔ:sɪ] *adj* pferdenärrisch; (*appearance*) pferdeähnlich.
**horticulture** ['hɔ:tɪkʌltʃə*] *n* Gartenbau *m.*
**hose** [həuz] *n* (*also:* ~ **pipe**) Schlauch *m.*
►**hose down** *vt* abspritzen.
**hosiery** ['həuzɪərɪ] *n* Strumpfwaren *pl.*
**hospice** ['hɒspɪs] *n* Pflegeheim *nt* (*für unheilbar Kranke*).
**hospitable** ['hɒspɪtəbl] *adj* gastfreundlich; (*climate*) freundlich.
**hospital** ['hɒspɪtl] *n* Krankenhaus *nt*; **in ~,** (*US*) **in the ~** im Krankenhaus.
**hospitality** [hɒspɪ'tælɪtɪ] *n* Gastfreundschaft *f.*
**hospitalize** ['hɒspɪtəlaɪz] *vt* ins Krankenhaus einweisen.
**host** [həust] *n* Gastgeber *m*; (*REL*) Hostie *f* ♦ *adj* Gast- ♦ *vt* Gastgeber sein bei; **a ~ of** eine Menge.
**hostage** ['hɒstɪdʒ] *n* Geisel *f*; **to be taken/held ~** als Geisel genommen/festgehalten werden.
**hostel** ['hɒstl] *n* (Wohn)heim *nt*; (*also:* **youth ~**) Jugendherberge *f.*
**hostelling** ['hɒstlɪŋ] *n*: **to go (youth) ~** in Jugendherbergen übernachten.
**hostess** ['həustɪs] *n* Gastgeberin *f*; (*BRIT: air hostess*) Stewardeß *f*; (*in night-club*) Hosteß *f.*

**hostile** ['hɔstaɪl] *adj* (*conditions*) ungünstig; (*environment*) unwirtlich; (*person*): ~ **(to or towards)** feindselig (gegenüber +*dat*).
**hostility** [hɔ'stɪlɪtɪ] *n* Feindseligkeit *f*; **hostilities** *npl* (*fighting*) Feindseligkeiten *pl*.
**hot** [hɔt] *adj* heiß; (*moderately hot*) warm; (*spicy*) scharf; (*temper*) hitzig; **I am** *or* **feel** ~ mir ist heiß; **to be** ~ **on sth** (*knowledgeable etc*) sich gut mit etw auskennen; (*strict*) sehr auf etw *acc* achten.
▶**hot up** (*BRIT: inf*) *vi* (*situation*) sich verschärfen *or* zuspitzen; (*party*) in Schwung kommen ♦ *vt* (*pace*) steigern; (*engine*) frisieren.
**hot air** *n* leeres Gerede *nt*.
**hot-air balloon** [hɔt'ɛə*-] *n* Heißluftballon *m*.
**hotbed** ['hɔtbɛd] *n* (*fig*) Brutstätte *f*.
**hot-blooded** [hɔt'blʌdɪd] *adj* heißblütig.
**hotchpotch** ['hɔtʃpɔtʃ] (*BRIT*) *n* Durcheinander *nt*, Mischmasch *m*.
**hot dog** *n* Hot dog *m or nt*.
**hotel** [həu'tɛl] *n* Hotel *nt*.
**hotelier** [həu'tɛlɪə*] *n* Hotelier(in) *m(f)*.
**hotel industry** *n* Hotelgewerbe *nt*.
**hotel room** *n* Hotelzimmer *nt*.
**hot flash** (*US*) *n* = **hot flush.**
**hot flush** *n* (*MED*) Hitzewallung *f*.
**hotfoot** ['hɔtfut] *adv* eilends.
**hothead** ['hɔthɛd] *n* Hitzkopf *m*.
**hot-headed** [hɔt'hɛdɪd] *adj* hitzköpfig.
**hothouse** ['hɔthaus] *n* Treibhaus *nt*.
**hot line** *n* (*POL*) heißer Draht *m*.
**hotly** ['hɔtlɪ] *adv* (*contest*) heiß; (*speak, deny*) heftig.
**hotplate** ['hɔtpleɪt] *n* Kochplatte *f*.
**hotpot** ['hɔtpɔt] (*BRIT*) *n* Fleischeintopf *m*.
**hot potato** (*fig: inf*) *n* heißes Eisen *nt*; **to drop sb like a** ~ jdn wie eine heiße Kartoffel fallenlassen.
**hot seat** *n*: **to be in the** ~ auf dem Schleudersitz sitzen.
**hot spot** *n* (*fig*) Krisenherd *m*.
**hot spring** *n* heiße Quelle *f*, Thermalquelle *f*.
**hot stuff** *n* große Klasse *f*.
**hot-tempered** ['hɔt'tɛmpəd] *adj* leicht aufbrausend, jähzornig.
**hot-water bottle** [hɔt'wɔːtə*-] *n* Wärmflasche *f*.
**hot-wire** (*inf*) *vt* (*car*) kurzschließen.
**hound** [haund] *vt* hetzen, jagen ♦ *n* Jagdhund *m*; **the ~s** die Meute.
**hour** ['auə*] *n* Stunde *f*; (*time*) Zeit *f*; **at 60 miles an** ~ mit 60 Meilen in der Stunde; **lunch** ~ Mittagspause *f*; **to pay sb by the** ~ jdn stundenweise bezahlen.
**hourly** ['auəlɪ] *adj* stündlich; (*rate*) Stunden-
♦ *adv* stündlich, jede Stunde; (*soon*) jederzeit.
**house** [haus] *n* Haus *nt*; (*household*) Haushalt *m*; (*dynasty*) Geschlecht *nt*, Haus *nt*; (*THEAT: performance*) Vorstellung *f* ♦ *vt* unterbringen; **at my** ~ bei mir (zu Hause);

**to my** ~ zu mir (nach Hause); **on the** ~ (*fig*) auf Kosten des Hauses; **the H~ (of Commons)** (*BRIT*) das Unterhaus; **the H~ (of Lords)** (*BRIT*) das Oberhaus; **the H~ (of Representatives)** (*US*) das Repräsentantenhaus.
**house arrest** *n* Hausarrest *m*.
**houseboat** ['hausbəut] *n* Hausboot *nt*.
**housebound** ['hausbaund] *adj* ans Haus gefesselt.
**housebreaking** ['hausbreɪkɪŋ] *n* Einbruch *m*.
**house-broken** ['hausbrəukn] (*US*) *adj* = **house-trained.**
**housecoat** ['hauskəut] *n* Morgenrock *m*.
**household** ['haushəuld] *n* Haushalt *m*; **to be a** ~ **name** ein Begriff sein.
**householder** ['haushəuldə*] *n* Hausinhaber(in) *m(f)*; (*of flat*) Wohnungsinhaber(in) *m(f)*.
**house-hunting** ['haushʌntɪŋ] *n*: **to go** ~ nach einem Haus suchen.
**housekeeper** ['hauskiːpə*] *n* Haushälterin *f*.
**housekeeping** ['hauskiːpɪŋ] *n* Hauswirtschaft *f*; (*money*) Haushaltsgeld *nt*, Wirtschafts-geld *nt*.
**houseman** ['hausmən] (*BRIT: irreg: like* **man**) *n* (*MED*) Assistenzarzt *m*, Assistenzärztin *f*.

---

*Das* **House of Commons** *ist das Unterhaus des britischen Parlaments, mit 651 Abgeordneten, die in Wahlkreisen in allgemeiner Wahl gewählt werden. Das Unterhaus hat die Regierungsgewalt inne und tagt etwa 175 Tage im Jahr unter Vorsitz des Sprechers.*
*Als* **House of Lords** *wird das Oberhaus des britischen Parlaments bezeichnet. Die Mitglieder sind nicht gewählt, sondern werden auf Lebenszeit ernannt (life peers), oder sie haben ihren Oberhaussitz geerbt (hereditary peers). Das House of Lords setzt sich aus Kirchenmännern und Adeligen zusammen (Lords Spiritual/Temporal). Es hat im Grunde keine Regierungsgewalt, aber kann vom Unterhaus erlassene Gesetze abändern und ist das oberste Berufungsgericht in Großbritannien (außer Schottland).*
*Das* **House of Representatives** *bildet zusammen mit dem Senat die amerikanische gesetzgebende Versammlung (den Kongreß). Es besteht aus 435 Abgeordneten, die entsprechend den Bevölkerungszahlen auf die einzelnen Bundesstaaten verteilt sind und jeweils für 2 Jahre direkt vom Volk gewählt werden. Es tritt im* **Capitol** *in Washington zusammen. Siehe auch* **congress***.*

---

**house owner** *n* Hausbesitzer(in) *m(f)*.
**house party** *n* mehrtägige Einladung *f*; (*people*) Gesellschaft *f*.
**house plant** *n* Zimmerpflanze *f*.
**house-proud** ['hauspraud] *adj* auf Ordnung und Sauberkeit im Haushalt bedacht.

**house-to-house** ['haustə'haus] *adj* von Haus zu Haus.

**house-trained** ['haustreɪnd] (*BRIT*) *adj* (*animal*) stubenrein.

**house-warming (party)** ['hauswɔːmɪŋ-] *n* Einzugsparty *f*.

**housewife** ['hauswaɪf] (*irreg: like* **wife**) *n* Hausfrau *f*.

**housework** ['hauswəːk] *n* Hausarbeit *f*.

**housing** ['hauzɪŋ] *n* Wohnungen *pl*; (*provision*) Wohnungsbeschaffung *f* ♦ *cpd* Wohnungs-.

**housing association** *n* Wohnungsbaugesellschaft *f*.

**housing benefit** *n* ≈ Wohngeld *nt*.

**housing conditions** *npl* Wohnbedingungen *pl*, Wohnverhältnisse *pl*.

**housing development** *n* (Wohn)siedlung *f*.

**housing estate** *n* (Wohn)siedlung *f*.

**hovel** ['hɔvl] *n* (armselige) Hütte *f*.

**hover** ['hɔvə•] *vi* schweben; (*person*) herumstehen; **to ~ round sb** jdm nicht von der Seite weichen.

**hovercraft** ['hɔvəkrɑːft] *n* Hovercraft *nt*, Luftkissenfahrzeug *nt*.

**hoverport** ['hɔvəpɔːt] *n* Anlegestelle *f* für Hovercrafts.

=================== *KEYWORD*

**how** [hau] *adv* **1** (*in what way*) wie; **~ was the film?** wie war der Film?; **~ is school?** was macht die Schule?; **~ are you?** wie geht es Ihnen?

**2** (*to what degree*): **~ much milk?** wieviel Milch?; **~ many people?** wie viele Leute?; **~ long have you been here?** wie lange sind Sie schon hier?; **~ old are you?** wie alt bist du?; **~ lovely/awful!** wie schön/furchtbar!

**however** [hau'εvə•] *conj* jedoch, aber ♦ *adv* wie ... auch; (*in questions*) wie ... bloß *or* nur.

**howl** [haul] *vi* heulen; (*animal*) jaulen; (*baby, person*) schreien ♦ *n* (*see vb*) Heulen *nt*; Jaulen *nt*; Schreien *nt*.

**howler** ['haulə•] (*inf*) *n* (*mistake*) Schnitzer *m*.

**howling** ['haulɪŋ] *adj* (*wind, gale*) heulend.

**HP** (*BRIT*) *n abbr* = **hire-purchase**.

**h.p.** *abbr* (*AUT*: = *horsepower*) PS.

**HQ** *abbr* = **headquarters**.

**HR** (*US*) *n abbr* (*POL*: = *House of Representatives*) Repräsentantenhaus *nt*.

**hr** *abbr* (= *hour*) Std.

**HRH** (*BRIT*) *abbr* (= *His/Her Royal Highness*) Seine/Ihre Königliche Hoheit.

**hrs** *abbr* (= *hours*) Std.

**HS** (*US*) *abbr* = **high school**.

**HST** (*US*) *abbr* (= *Hawaiian Standard Time*) Normalzeit in Hawaii.

**hub** [hʌb] *n* (Rad)nabe *f*; (*fig: centre*) Mittelpunkt *m*, Zentrum *nt*.

**hubbub** ['hʌbʌb] *n* Lärm *m*; (*commotion*) Tumult *m*.

**hubcap** ['hʌbkæp] *n* Radkappe *f*.

**HUD** (*US*) *n abbr* (= *Department of Housing and Urban Development*) Ministerium *für* Wohnungsbau und Stadtentwicklung.

**huddle** ['hʌdl] *vi*: **to ~ together** sich zusammendrängen ♦ *n*: **in a ~** dicht zusammengedrängt.

**hue** [hjuː] *n* Farbton *m*.

**hue and cry** *n* großes Geschrei *nt*.

**huff** [hʌf] *n*: **in a ~** beleidigt, eingeschnappt ♦ *vi*: **to ~ and puff** sich aufregen.

**huffy** ['hʌfɪ] (*inf*) *adj* beleidigt.

**hug** [hʌg] *vt* umarmen; (*thing*) umklammern ♦ *n* Umarmung *f*; **to give sb a ~** jdn umarmen.

**huge** [hjuːdʒ] *adj* riesig.

**hugely** ['hjuːdʒlɪ] *adv* ungeheuer.

**hulk** [hʌlk] *n* (*wrecked ship*) Wrack *nt*; (*person, building etc*) Klotz *m*.

**hulking** ['hʌlkɪŋ] *adj*: **~ great** massig.

**hull** [hʌl] *n* Schiffsrumpf *m*; (*of nuts*) Schale *f*; (*of strawberries etc*) Blättchen *nt* ♦ *vt* (*fruit*) entstielen.

**hullaballoo** [hʌləbə'luː] (*inf*) *n* Spektakel *m*.

**hullo** [hə'ləu] *excl* = **hello**.

**hum** [hʌm] *vt* summen ♦ *vi* summen; (*machine*) brummen ♦ *n* Summen *nt*; (*of traffic*) Brausen *nt*; (*of machines*) Brummen *nt*; (*of voices*) Gemurmel *nt*.

**human** ['hjuːmən] *adj* menschlich ♦ *n* (*also*: **~ being**) Mensch *m*.

**humane** [hjuː'meɪn] *adj* human.

**humanism** ['hjuːmənɪzəm] *n* Humanismus *m*.

**humanitarian** [hjuːmænɪ'tɛərɪən] *adj* humanitär.

**humanity** [hjuː'mænɪtɪ] *n* Menschlichkeit *f*; (*mankind*) Menschheit *f*; (*humaneness*) Humanität *f*; **humanities** *npl* (*SCOL*): **the humanities** die Geisteswissenschaften *pl*.

**humanly** ['hjuːmənlɪ] *adv* menschlich; **if (at all) ~ possible** wenn es irgend möglich ist.

**humanoid** ['hjuːmənɔɪd] *adj* menschenähnlich ♦ *n* menschenähnliches Wesen *nt*.

**human rights** *npl* Menschenrechte *pl*.

**humble** ['hʌmbl] *adj* bescheiden ♦ *vt* demütigen.

**humbly** ['hʌmblɪ] *adv* bescheiden.

**humbug** ['hʌmbʌg] *n* Humbug *m*, Mumpitz *m*; (*BRIT: sweet*) Pfefferminzbonbon *m or nt*.

**humdrum** ['hʌmdrʌm] *adj* eintönig, langweilig.

**humid** ['hjuːmɪd] *adj* feucht.

**humidifier** [hjuː'mɪdɪfaɪə•] *n* Luftbefeuchter *m*.

**humidity** [hjuː'mɪdɪtɪ] *n* Feuchtigkeit *f*.

**humiliate** [hjuː'mɪlɪeɪt] *vt* demütigen.

**humiliating** [hjuː'mɪlɪeɪtɪŋ] *adj* demütigend.

**humiliation** [hjuːmɪlɪ'eɪʃən] *n* Demütigung *f*.

**humility** [hjuː'mɪlɪtɪ] *n* Bescheidenheit *f*.

**humor** *etc* (*US*) = **humour** *etc*.

**humorist** ['hjuːmərɪst] *n* Humorist(in) *m(f)*.

**humorous** ['hjuːmərəs] *adj* (*remark*) witzig; (*book*) lustig; (*person*) humorvoll.

**humour, (US) humor** ['hjuːmə•] *n* Humor *m*;

(*mood*) Stimmung *f* ♦ *vt* seinen Willen lassen +*dat*; **sense of** ~ (Sinn *m* für) Humor; **to be in good/bad** ~ gute/schlechte Laune haben.

**humourless** ['hjuːmələs] *adj* humorlos.

**hump** [hʌmp] *n* Hügel *m*; (*of camel*) Höcker *m*; (*deformity*) Buckel *m*.

**humpbacked** ['hʌmpbækt] *adj*: ~ **bridge** gewölbte Brücke *f*.

**humus** ['hjuːməs] *n* Humus *m*.

**hunch** [hʌntʃ] *n* Gefühl *nt*, Ahnung *f*; **I have a** ~ **that** … ich habe den (leisen) Verdacht, daß …

**hunchback** ['hʌntʃbæk] *n* Bucklige(r) *f(m)*.

**hunched** [hʌntʃt] *adj* gebeugt; (*shoulders*) hochgezogen; (*back*) krumm.

**hundred** ['hʌndrəd] *num* hundert; **a** *or* **one** ~ **books/people/dollars** (ein)hundert Bücher/Personen/Dollar; ~**s of** Hunderte von; **I'm a** ~ **per cent sure** ich bin absolut sicher.

**hundredth** ['hʌndrədθ] *num* hundertste(r, s).

**hundredweight** ['hʌndrɪdweɪt] *n* *Gewichtseinheit* (*BRIT* = 50,8 kg; *US* = 45,3 kg); ≈ Zentner *m*.

**hung** [hʌŋ] *pt, pp of* hang.

**Hungarian** [hʌŋˈgɛərɪən] *adj* ungarisch ♦ *n* Ungar(in) *m(f)*; (*LING*) Ungarisch *nt*.

**Hungary** ['hʌŋɡərɪ] *n* Ungarn *nt*.

**hunger** ['hʌŋɡəˈ] *n* Hunger *m* ♦ *vi*: **to** ~ **for** hungern nach.

**hunger strike** *n* Hungerstreik *m*.

**hung over** (*inf*) *adj* verkatert.

**hungrily** ['hʌŋɡrəlɪ] *adv* hungrig.

**hungry** ['hʌŋɡrɪ] *adj* hungrig; **to be** ~ Hunger haben; **to be** ~ **for** hungern nach; (*news*) sehnsüchtig warten auf; **to go** ~ hungern.

**hung up** (*inf*) *adj*: **to be** ~ **on** (*person*) ein gestörtes Verhältnis haben zu; **to be** ~ **about** nervös sein wegen.

**hunk** [hʌŋk] *n* großes Stück *nt*; (*inf: man*) (großer, gutaussehender) Mann *m*.

**hunt** [hʌnt] *vt* jagen; (*criminal, fugitive*) fahnden nach ♦ *vi* (*SPORT*) jagen ♦ *n* (*see vb*) Jagd *f*; Fahndung *f*; (*search*) Suche *f*; **to** ~ **for** (*search*) suchen (nach).

▶**hunt down** *vt* Jagd machen auf +*acc*.

**hunter** ['hʌntəˈ] *n* Jäger(in) *m(f)*.

**hunting** ['hʌntɪŋ] *n* Jagd *f*, Jagen *nt*.

**hurdle** ['həːdl] *n* Hürde *f*.

**hurl** [həːl] *vt* schleudern; **to** ~ **sth at sb** (*also fig*) jdm etw entgegenschleudern.

**hurling** ['həːlɪŋ] *n* (*SPORT*) Hurling *nt*, *irische Hockeyart*.

**hurly-burly** ['həːlɪ'bəːlɪ] *n* Rummel *m*.

**hurrah** [huˈrɑː] *n* Hurra *nt* ♦ *excl* hurra.

**hurray** [huˈreɪ] *n* = **hurrah**.

**hurricane** ['hʌrɪkən] *n* Orkan *m*.

**hurried** ['hʌrɪd] *adj* eilig; (*departure*) überstürzt.

**hurriedly** ['hʌrɪdlɪ] *adv* eilig.

**hurry** ['hʌrɪ] *n* Eile *f* ♦ *vi* eilen; (*to do sth*) sich beeilen ♦ *vt* (zur Eile) antreiben; (*work*)

beschleunigen; **to be in a** ~ es eilig haben; **to do sth in a** ~ etw schnell tun; **there's no** ~ es eilt nicht; **what's the** ~? warum so eilig?; **they hurried to help him** sie eilten ihm zu Hilfe; **to** ~ **home** nach Hause eilen.

▶**hurry along** *vi* sich beeilen.

▶**hurry away** *vi* schnell weggehen, forteilen.

▶**hurry off** *vi* = hurry away.

▶**hurry up** *vt* (zur Eile) antreiben ♦ *vi* sich beeilen.

**hurt** [həːt] (*pt, pp* **hurt**) *vt* weh tun +*dat*; (*injure, fig*) verletzen ♦ *vi* weh tun ♦ *adj* verletzt; **I've** ~ **my arm** ich habe mir am Arm weh getan; (*injured*) ich habe mir den Arm verletzt; **where does it** ~? wo tut es weh?

**hurtful** ['həːtful] *adj* verletzend.

**hurtle** ['həːtl] *vi*: **to** ~ **past** vorbeisausen; **to** ~ **down** (*fall*) hinunterfallen.

**husband** ['hʌzbənd] *n* (Ehe)mann *m*.

**hush** [hʌʃ] *n* Stille *f* ♦ *vt* zum Schweigen bringen; ~! pst!

▶**hush up** *vt* vertuschen.

**hushed** [hʌʃt] *adj* still; (*voice*) gedämpft.

**hush-hush** [hʌʃˈhʌʃ] (*inf*) *adj* streng geheim.

**husk** [hʌsk] *n* Schale *f*; (*of wheat*) Spelze *f*; (*of maize*) Hüllblatt *nt*.

**husky** ['hʌskɪ] *adj* (*voice*) rauh ♦ *n* Schlittenhund *m*.

**hustings** ['hʌstɪŋz] (*BRIT*) *npl* (*POL*) Wahlkampf *m*.

**hustle** ['hʌsl] *vt* drängen ♦ *n*: ~ **and bustle** Geschäftigkeit *f*.

**hut** [hʌt] *n* Hütte *f*.

**hutch** [hʌtʃ] *n* (Kaninchen)stall *m*.

**hyacinth** ['haɪəsɪnθ] *n* Hyazinthe *f*.

**hybrid** ['haɪbrɪd] *n* (*plant, animal*) Kreuzung *f*; (*mixture*) Mischung *f* ♦ *adj* Misch-.

**hydrant** ['haɪdrənt] *n* (*also*: **fire** ~) Hydrant *m*.

**hydraulic** [haɪˈdrɔːlɪk] *adj* hydraulisch.

**hydraulics** [haɪˈdrɔːlɪks] *n* Hydraulik *f*.

**hydrochloric acid** ['haɪdrəuˈklɔrɪk-] *n* Salzsäure *f*.

**hydroelectric** ['haɪdrəuɪˈlɛktrɪk] *adj* hydroelektrisch.

**hydrofoil** ['haɪdrəfɔɪl] *n* Tragflächenboot *nt*, Tragflügelboot *nt*.

**hydrogen** ['haɪdrədʒən] *n* Wasserstoff *m*.

**hydrogen bomb** *n* Wasserstoffbombe *f*.

**hydrophobia** ['haɪdrəˈfəubɪə] *n* Hydrophobie *f*, Wasserscheu *f*.

**hydroplane** ['haɪdrəpleɪn] *n* Gleitboot *nt*; (*plane*) Wasserflugzeug *nt* ♦ *vi* (*boat*) abheben.

**hyena** [haɪˈiːnə] *n* Hyäne *f*.

**hygiene** ['haɪdʒiːn] *n* Hygiene *f*.

**hygienic** [haɪˈdʒiːnɪk] *adj* hygienisch.

**hymn** [hɪm] *n* Kirchenlied *nt*.

**hype** [haɪp] (*inf*) *n* Rummel *m*.

**hyperactive** ['haɪpərˈæktɪv] *adj* überaktiv.

**hyperinflation** ['haɪpərɪnˈfleɪʃən] *n* galoppierende Inflation *f*.

**hypermarket** ['haɪpəmɑːkɪt] (*BRIT*) *n*

Verbrauchermarkt *m.*
**hypertension** ['haɪpə'tɛnʃən] *n* Hypertonie *f*, Bluthochdruck *m.*
**hyphen** ['haɪfn] *n* Bindestrich *m*; (*at end of line*) Trennungsstrich *m.*
**hyphenated** ['haɪfəneɪtɪd] *adj* mit Bindestrich (geschrieben).
**hypnosis** [hɪp'nəusɪs] *n* Hypnose *f.*
**hypnotic** [hɪp'nɔtɪk] *adj* hypnotisierend; (*trance*) hypnotisch.
**hypnotism** ['hɪpnətɪzəm] *n* Hypnotismus *m.*
**hypnotist** ['hɪpnətɪst] *n* Hypnotiseur *m*, Hypnotiseuse *f.*
**hypnotize** ['hɪpnətaɪz] *vt* hypnotisieren.
**hypoallergenic** ['haɪpəuælə'dʒɛnɪk] *adj* für äußerst empfindliche Haut.
**hypochondriac** [haɪpə'kɔndrɪæk] *n* Hypochonder *m.*
**hypocrisy** [hɪ'pɔkrɪsɪ] *n* Heuchelei *f.*
**hypocrite** ['hɪpəkrɪt] *n* Heuchler(in) *m(f).*
**hypocritical** [hɪpə'krɪtɪkl] *adj* heuchlerisch.
**hypodermic** [haɪpə'dɜːmɪk] *adj* (*injection*) subkutan ♦ *n* (Injektions)spritze *f.*
**hypotenuse** [haɪ'pɔtɪnjuːz] *n* Hypotenuse *f.*
**hypothermia** [haɪpə'θɜːmɪə] *n* Unterkühlung *f.*
**hypothesis** [haɪ'pɔθɪsɪs] (*pl* **hypotheses**) *n* Hypothese *f.*
**hypothesize** [haɪ'pɔθɪsaɪz] *vi* Hypothesen aufstellen ♦ *vt* annehmen.
**hypothetic(al)** [haɪpəu'θɛtɪk(l)] *adj* hypothetisch.
**hysterectomy** [hɪstə'rɛktəmɪ] *n* Hysterektomie *f.*
**hysteria** [hɪ'stɪərɪə] *n* Hysterie *f.*
**hysterical** [hɪ'stɛrɪkl] *adj* hysterisch; (*situation*) wahnsinnig komisch; **to become ~** hysterisch werden.
**hysterically** [hɪ'stɛrɪklɪ] *adv* hysterisch; **~ funny** wahnsinnig komisch.
**hysterics** [hɪ'stɛrɪks] *npl:* **to be in** *or* **to have ~** einen hysterischen Anfall haben; (*laughter*) einen Lachanfall haben.
**Hz** *abbr* (= *hertz*) Hz.

# *I, i*

**I¹, i** [aɪ] *n* (*letter*) I *nt*, i *nt*; **~ for Isaac,** (*US*) **~ for Item** ≈ I wie Ida.
**I²** [aɪ] *pron* ich.
**I.** *abbr* = **island; isle.**
**IA** (*US*) *abbr* (*POST:* = *Iowa*).
**IAEA** *n abbr* = **International Atomic Energy Agency.**
**ib** *abbr* (= *ibidem*) ib(id).

**Iberian** [aɪ'bɪərɪən] *adj:* **the ~ Peninsula** die Iberische Halbinsel.
**IBEW** (*US*) *n abbr* (= *International Brotherhood of Electrical Workers*) Elektrikergewerkschaft.
**ibid** *abbr* (= *ibidem*) ib(id).
**i/c** (*BRIT*) *abbr* (= *in charge (of)*) *see* **charge.**
**ICBM** *n abbr* (= *intercontinental ballistic missile*) Interkontinentalrakete *f.*
**ICC** *n abbr* = **International Chamber of Commerce;** (*US:* = *Interstate Commerce Commission*) Kommission zur Regelung des Warenverkehrs zwischen den US-Bundesstaaten.
**ice** [aɪs] *n* Eis *nt*; (*on road*) Glatteis *nt* ♦ *vt* (*cake*) mit Zuckerguß überziehen, glasieren ♦ *vi* (*also:* **~ over, ~ up**) vereisen; (*puddle etc*) zufrieren; **to put sth on ~** (*fig*) etw auf Eis legen.
**Ice Age** *n* Eiszeit *f.*
**ice axe** *n* Eispickel *m.*
**iceberg** ['aɪsbɜːg] *n* Eisberg *m*; **the tip of the ~** (*fig*) die Spitze des Eisbergs.
**icebox** ['aɪsbɔks] *n* (*US: fridge*) Kühlschrank *m*; (*BRIT: compartment*) Eisfach *nt*; (*insulated box*) Kühltasche *f.*
**icebreaker** ['aɪsbreɪkə'] *n* Eisbrecher *m.*
**ice bucket** *n* Eiskühler *m.*
**icecap** ['aɪskæp] *n* Eisdecke *f*; (*polar*) Eiskappe *f.*
**ice-cold** ['aɪs'kəuld] *adj* eiskalt.
**ice cream** *n* Eis *nt.*
**ice-cream soda** ['aɪskriːm-] *n* Eisbecher mit Sirup und Sodawasser.
**ice cube** *n* Eiswürfel *m.*
**iced** [aɪst] *adj* (*cake*) mit Zuckerguß überzogen, glasiert; (*beer etc*) eisgekühlt; (*tea, coffee*) Eis-.
**ice hockey** *n* Eishockey *nt.*
**Iceland** ['aɪslənd] *n* Island *nt.*
**Icelander** ['aɪsləndə'] *n* Isländer(in) *m(f).*
**Icelandic** [aɪs'lændɪk] *adj* isländisch ♦ *n* (*LING*) Isländisch *nt.*
**ice lolly** (*BRIT*) *n* Eis *nt* am Stiel.
**ice pick** *n* Eispickel *m.*
**ice rink** *n* (Kunst)eisbahn *f*, Schlittschuhbahn *f.*
**ice skate** *n* Schlittschuh *m.*
**ice-skate** ['aɪsskeɪt] *vi* Schlittschuh laufen.
**ice-skating** ['aɪsskeɪtɪŋ] *n* Eislauf *m*, Schlittschuhlaufen *nt.*
**icicle** ['aɪsɪkl] *n* Eiszapfen *m.*
**icing** ['aɪsɪŋ] *n* (*CULIN*) Zuckerguß *m*; (*AVIAT etc*) Vereisung *f.*
**icing sugar** (*BRIT*) *n* Puderzucker *m.*
**ICJ** *n abbr* = **International Court of Justice.**
**icon** ['aɪkɔn] *n* Ikone *f*; (*COMPUT*) Ikon *nt.*
**ICR** (*US*) *n abbr* (= *Institute for Cancer Research*) Krebsforschungsinstitut.
**ICRC** *n abbr* (= *International Committee of the Red Cross*) IKRK *nt.*
**ICU** *n abbr* (*MED*) = **intensive care unit.**

**icy** ['aɪsɪ] adj eisig; (road) vereist.
**ID, Ida.** (US) abbr (POST: = Idaho).
**I'd** [aɪd] = I would; I had.
**ID card** n = identity card.
**IDD** (BRIT) n abbr (TEL: = international direct
dialling) Selbstwählferndienst ins Ausland.
**idea** [aɪ'dɪə] n Idee f; (opinion) Ansicht f;
(notion) Vorstellung f; (objective) Ziel nt;
**good ~!** gute Idee!; **to have a good ~ that**
sich dat ziemlich sicher sein, daß; **I haven't
the least ~** ich habe nicht die leiseste
Ahnung.
**ideal** [aɪ'dɪəl] n Ideal nt ♦ adj ideal.
**idealist** [aɪ'dɪəlɪst] n Idealist(in) m(f).
**ideally** [aɪ'dɪəlɪ] adv ideal; **~ the book should
...** idealerweise or im Idealfall sollte das
Buch ...; **she's ~ suited for ...** sie eignet sich
hervorragend für ...
**identical** [aɪ'dɛntɪkl] adj identisch; (twins)
eineiig.
**identification** [aɪdɛntɪfɪ'keɪʃən] n
Identifizierung f; **(means of) ~**
Ausweispapiere pl.
**identify** [aɪ'dɛntɪfaɪ] vt (recognize) erkennen;
(distinguish) identifizieren; **to ~ sb/sth with**
jdn/etw identifizieren mit.
**Identikit** ® [aɪ'dɛntɪkɪt] n: **~ (picture)**
Phantombild nt.
**identity** [aɪ'dɛntɪtɪ] n Identität f.
**identity card** n (Personal)ausweis m.
**identity papers** npl Ausweispapiere pl.
**identity parade** (BRIT) n Gegenüberstellung
f.
**ideological** [aɪdɪə'lɒdʒɪkl] adj ideologisch,
weltanschaulich.
**ideology** [aɪdɪ'ɒlədʒɪ] n Ideologie f,
Weltanschauung f.
**idiocy** ['ɪdɪəsɪ] n Idiotie f, Dummheit f.
**idiom** ['ɪdɪəm] n (style) Ausdrucksweise f;
(phrase) Redewendung f.
**idiomatic** [ɪdɪə'mætɪk] adj idiomatisch.
**idiosyncrasy** [ɪdɪəu'sɪŋkrəsɪ] n Eigenheit f,
Eigenart f.
**idiosyncratic** [ɪdɪəusɪŋ'krætɪk] adj eigenartig;
(way, method, style) eigen.
**idiot** ['ɪdɪət] n Idiot(in) m(f), Dummkopf m.
**idiotic** [ɪdɪ'ɒtɪk] adj idiotisch, blöd(sinnig).
**idle** ['aɪdl] adj untätig; (lazy) faul; (unemployed)
unbeschäftigt; (machinery, factory)
stillstehend; (question) müßig; (conversation,
pleasure) leer ♦ vi leerlaufen, im Leerlauf
sein; **to lie ~** (machinery) außer Betrieb sein;
(factory) die Arbeit eingestellt haben.
▶**idle away** vt (time) vertrödeln,
verbummeln.
**idleness** ['aɪdlnɪs] n Untätigkeit f; (laziness)
Faulheit f.
**idler** ['aɪdlə*] n Faulenzer(in) m(f).
**idle time** n (COMM) Leerlaufzeit f.
**idly** ['aɪdlɪ] adv untätig; (glance) abwesend.
**idol** ['aɪdl] n Idol nt; (REL) Götzenbild nt.
**idolize** ['aɪdəlaɪz] vt vergöttern.

**idyllic** [ɪ'dɪlɪk] adj idyllisch.
**i.e.** abbr (= id est) d.h.

================= KEYWORD

**if** [ɪf] conj **1** (given that, providing that etc) wenn,
falls; **~ anyone comes in** wenn or falls
jemand hereinkommt; **~ necessary** wenn or
falls nötig; **~ I were you** wenn ich Sie wäre,
an Ihrer Stelle
**2** (whenever) wenn
**3** (although): **(even) ~** auch or selbst wenn; **I
like it, (even) ~ you don't** mir gefällt es,
auch wenn du es nicht magst
**4** (whether) ob; **ask him ~ he can come** frag
ihn, ob er kommen kann
**5**: **~ so/not** falls ja/nein; **~ only** wenn nur;
see also **as**.

**iffy** ['ɪfɪ] (inf) adj (uncertain) unsicher; (plan,
proposal) fragwürdig; **he was a bit ~ about
it** er hat sich sehr vage ausgedrückt.
**igloo** ['ɪgluː] n Iglu m or nt.
**ignite** [ɪg'naɪt] vt entzünden ♦ vi sich
entzünden.
**ignition** [ɪg'nɪʃən] n (AUT) Zündung f.
**ignition key** n (AUT) Zündschlüssel m.
**ignoble** [ɪg'nəubl] adj schändlich,
unehrenhaft.
**ignominious** [ɪgnə'mɪnɪəs] adj schmachvoll.
**ignoramus** [ɪgnə'reɪməs] n Ignorant(in) m(f).
**ignorance** ['ɪgnərəns] n Unwissenheit f,
Ignoranz f; **to keep sb in ~ of sth** jdn in
Unkenntnis über etw acc lassen.
**ignorant** ['ɪgnərənt] adj unwissend, ignorant;
**to be ~ of** (subject) sich nicht auskennen in
+dat; (events) nicht informiert sein über +acc.
**ignore** [ɪg'nɔː*] vt ignorieren; (fact) außer acht
lassen.
**ikon** ['aɪkɒn] n = **icon**.
**IL** (US) abbr (POST: = Illinois).
**ILA** (US) n abbr (= International Longshoremen's
Association) Hafenarbeitergewerkschaft.
**I'll** [aɪl] = I will; I shall.
**ill** [ɪl] adj krank; (effects) schädlich ♦ n Übel nt;
(trouble) Schlechte(s) nt ♦ adv: **to speak ~ of
sb** Schlechtes über jdn sagen; **to be taken ~**
krank werden; **to think ~ of sb** schlecht von
jdm denken.
**ill-advised** [ɪləd'vaɪzd] adj unklug; (person)
schlecht beraten.
**ill at ease** adj unbehaglich.
**ill-considered** [ɪlkən'sɪdəd] adj unüberlegt.
**ill-disposed** [ɪldɪs'pəuzd] adj: **to be ~ toward
sb/sth** jdm/etw nicht wohlgesinnt sein.
**illegal** [ɪ'liːgl] adj illegal.
**illegally** [ɪ'liːgəlɪ] adv illegal.
**illegible** [ɪ'lɛdʒɪbl] adj unleserlich.
**illegitimate** [ɪlɪ'dʒɪtɪmət] adj (child) unehelich;
(activity, treaty) unzulässig.
**ill-fated** [ɪl'feɪtɪd] adj unglückselig.
**ill-favoured,** (US) **ill-favored** [ɪl'feɪvəd] adj
ungestalt (liter), häßlich.

**ill feeling** n Verstimmung f.

**ill-gotten** ['ɪlgɒtn] adj: ~**gains** unrechtmäßig erworbener Gewinn m.

**ill health** n schlechter Gesundheitszustand m.

**illicit** [ɪ'lɪsɪt] adj verboten.

**ill-informed** [ɪlɪn'fɔːmd] adj (judgement) wenig sachkundig; (person) schlecht informiert or unterrichtet.

**illiterate** [ɪ'lɪtərət] adj (person) des Lesens und Schreibens unkundig; (letter) voller Fehler.

**ill-mannered** [ɪl'mænəd] adj unhöflich.

**illness** ['ɪlnɪs] n Krankheit f.

**illogical** [ɪ'lɒdʒɪkl] adj unlogisch.

**ill-suited** [ɪl'suːtɪd] adj nicht zusammen-passend; **he is ~ to the job** er ist für die Stelle ungeeignet.

**ill-timed** [ɪl'taɪmd] adj ungelegen, unpassend.

**ill-treat** [ɪl'triːt] vt mißhandeln.

**ill-treatment** [ɪl'triːtmənt] n Mißhandlung f.

**illuminate** [ɪ'luːmɪneɪt] vt beleuchten.

**illuminated sign** [ɪ'luːmɪneɪtɪd-] n Leuchtzeichen nt.

**illuminating** [ɪ'luːmɪneɪtɪŋ] adj aufschlußreich.

**illumination** [ɪluːmɪ'neɪʃən] n Beleuchtung f; **illuminations** npl (decorative lights) festliche Beleuchtung f, Illumination f.

**illusion** [ɪ'luːʒən] n Illusion f, (trick) (Zauber)trick m; **to be under the ~ that ...** sich dat einbilden, daß ...

**illusive** [ɪ'luːsɪv] adj = **illusory**.

**illusory** [ɪ'luːsərɪ] adj illusorisch, trügerisch.

**illustrate** ['ɪləstreɪt] vt veranschaulichen; (book) illustrieren.

**illustration** [ɪlə'streɪʃən] n Illustration f; (example) Veranschaulichung f.

**illustrator** ['ɪləstreɪtə*] n Illustrator(in) m(f).

**illustrious** [ɪ'lʌstrɪəs] adj (career) glanzvoll; (predecessor) berühmt.

**ill will** n böses Blut nt.

**ILO** n abbr = **International Labour Organization**.

**ILWU** (US) n abbr (= International Longshoremen's and Warehousemen's Union) Hafen- und Lagerarbeitergewerkschaft.

**I'm** [aɪm] = **I am**.

**image** ['ɪmɪdʒ] n Bild nt; (public face) Image nt; (reflection) Abbild nt.

**imagery** ['ɪmɪdʒərɪ] n (in writing) Metaphorik f; (in painting etc) Symbolik f.

**imaginable** [ɪ'mædʒɪnəbl] adj vorstellbar, denkbar; **we've tried every ~ solution** wir haben jede denkbare Lösung ausprobiert; **she had the prettiest hair ~** sie hatte das schönste Haar, das man sich vorstellen kann.

**imaginary** [ɪ'mædʒɪnərɪ] adj erfunden; (being) Phantasie-; (danger) eingebildet.

**imagination** [ɪmædʒɪ'neɪʃən] n Phantasie f; (illusion) Einbildung f; **it's just your ~** das bildest du dir nur ein.

**imaginative** [ɪ'mædʒɪnətɪv] adj phantasievoll;

(solution) einfallsreich.

**imagine** [ɪ'mædʒɪn] vt sich dat vorstellen; (dream) sich dat träumen lassen; (suppose) vermuten.

**imbalance** [ɪm'bæləns] n Unausgeglichenheit f.

**imbecile** ['ɪmbəsiːl] n Schwachkopf m, Idiot m.

**imbue** [ɪm'bjuː] vt: **to ~ sb/sth with** jdn/etw durchdringen mit.

**IMF** n abbr (= International Monetary Fund) IWF m.

**imitate** ['ɪmɪteɪt] vt imitieren; (mimic) nachahmen.

**imitation** [ɪmɪ'teɪʃən] n Imitation f, Nachahmung f.

**imitator** ['ɪmɪteɪtə*] n Imitator(in) m(f), Nachahmer(in) m(f).

**immaculate** [ɪ'mækjulət] adj makellos; (appearance, piece of work) tadellos; (REL) unbefleckt.

**immaterial** [ɪmə'tɪərɪəl] adj unwichtig, unwesentlich.

**immature** [ɪmə'tjuə*] adj unreif; (organism) noch nicht voll entwickelt.

**immaturity** [ɪmə'tjuərɪtɪ] n Unreife f.

**immeasurable** [ɪ'meʒrəbl] adj unermeßlich groß.

**immediacy** [ɪ'miːdɪəsɪ] n Unmittelbarkeit f, Direktheit f; (of needs) Dringlichkeit f.

**immediate** [ɪ'miːdɪət] adj sofortig; (need) dringend; (neighbourhood, family) nächste(r, s).

**immediately** [ɪ'miːdɪətlɪ] adv sofort; (directly) unmittelbar; **~ next to** direkt neben.

**immense** [ɪ'mens] adj riesig, enorm.

**immensely** [ɪ'menslɪ] adv unheimlich; (grateful, complex etc) äußerst.

**immensity** [ɪ'mensɪtɪ] n ungeheure Größe f, Unermeßlichkeit f; (of problems etc) gewaltiges Ausmaß nt.

**immerse** [ɪ'məːs] vt eintauchen; **to ~ sth in** etw tauchen in +acc; **to be ~d in** (fig) vertieft sein in +acc.

**immersion heater** [ɪ'məːʃən-] (BRIT) n elektrischer Heißwasserboiler m.

**immigrant** ['ɪmɪgrənt] n Einwanderer m, Einwanderin f.

**immigration** [ɪmɪ'greɪʃən] n Einwanderung f; (at airport etc) Einwanderungsstelle f ♦ cpd Einwanderungs-.

**imminent** ['ɪmɪnənt] adj bevorstehend.

**immobile** [ɪ'məubaɪl] adj unbeweglich.

**immobilize** [ɪ'məubɪlaɪz] vt (person) handlungsunfähig machen; (machine) zum Stillstand bringen.

**immoderate** [ɪ'mɒdərət] adj unmäßig; (opinion, reaction) extrem; (demand) maßlos.

**immodest** [ɪ'mɒdɪst] adj unanständig; (boasting) unbescheiden.

**immoral** [ɪ'mɒrl] adj unmoralisch; (behaviour) unsittlich.

**immorality** [ɪmə'rælɪtɪ] n (see adj) Unmoral f;

Unsittlichkeit *f*.
**immortal** [ɪ'mɔːtl] *adj* unsterblich.
**immortality** [ɪmɔː'tælɪtɪ] *n* Unsterblichkeit *f*.
**immortalize** [ɪ'mɔːtlaɪz] *vt* unsterblich machen.
**immovable** [ɪ'muːvəbl] *adj* unbeweglich; (*person, opinion*) fest.
**immune** [ɪ'mjuːn] *adj*: ~ **(to)** (*disease*) immun (gegen); (*flattery*) unempfänglich (für); (*criticism*) unempfindlich (gegen); (*attack*) sicher (vor +*dat*).
**immune system** *n* Immunsystem *nt*.
**immunity** [ɪ'mjuːnɪtɪ] *n* (*see adj*) Immunität *f*; Unempfänglichkeit *f*; Unempfindlichkeit *f*; Sicherheit *f*; (*of diplomat, from prosecution*) Immunität *f*.
**immunization** [ɪmjunaɪ'zeɪʃən] *n* Immunisierung *f*.
**immunize** ['ɪmjunaɪz] *vt*: **to** ~ **(against)** immunisieren (gegen).
**imp** [ɪmp] *n* Kobold *m*; (*child*) Racker *m* (*inf*).
**impact** ['ɪmpækt] *n* Aufprall *m*; (*of crash*) Wucht *f*; (*of law, measure*) (Aus)wirkung *f*.
**impair** [ɪm'pɛə*] *vt* beeinträchtigen.
**impaired** [ɪm'pɛəd] *adj* beeinträchtigt; (*hearing*) schlecht; ~ **vision** schlechte Augen *pl*.
**impale** [ɪm'peɪl] *vt*: **to** ~ **sth (on)** etw aufspießen (auf +*dat*).
**impart** [ɪm'paːt] *vt*: **to** ~ **(to)** (*information*) mitteilen +*dat*; (*flavour*) verleihen +*dat*.
**impartial** [ɪm'paːʃl] *adj* unparteiisch.
**impartiality** [ɪmpaːʃɪ'ælɪtɪ] *n* Unparteilichkeit *f*.
**impassable** [ɪm'paːsəbl] *adj* unpassierbar.
**impasse** [æm'paːs] *n* Sackgasse *f*.
**impassive** [ɪm'pæsɪv] *adj* gelassen.
**impatience** [ɪm'peɪʃəns] *n* Ungeduld *f*.
**impatient** [ɪm'peɪʃənt] *adj* ungeduldig; **to get** *or* **grow** ~ ungeduldig werden; **to be** ~ **to do sth** es nicht erwarten können, etw zu tun.
**impatiently** [ɪm'peɪʃəntlɪ] *adv* ungeduldig.
**impeach** [ɪm'piːtʃ] *vt* anklagen; (*public official*) eines Amtsvergehens anklagen.
**impeachment** [ɪm'piːtʃmənt] *n* Anklage *f* wegen eines Amtsvergehens, Impeachment *nt*.
**impeccable** [ɪm'pɛkəbl] *adj* (*dress*) untadelig; (*manners*) tadellos.
**impecunious** [ɪmpɪ'kjuːnɪəs] *adj* mittellos.
**impede** [ɪm'piːd] *vt* behindern.
**impediment** [ɪm'pɛdɪmənt] *n* Hindernis *nt*; (*also*: **speech** ~) Sprachfehler *m*.
**impel** [ɪm'pɛl] *vt*: **to** ~ **sb to do sth** jdn (dazu) nötigen, etw zu tun.
**impending** [ɪm'pɛndɪŋ] *adj* bevorstehend; (*catastrophe*) drohend.
**impenetrable** [ɪm'pɛnɪtrəbl] *adj* undurchdringlich; (*fig*) unergründlich.
**imperative** [ɪm'pɛrətɪv] *adj* dringend; (*tone*) Befehls- ♦ *n* (*LING*) Imperativ *m*,

Befehlsform *f*.
**imperceptible** [ɪmpə'sɛptɪbl] *adj* nicht wahrnehmbar, unmerklich.
**imperfect** [ɪm'pəːfɪkt] *adj* mangelhaft; (*goods*) fehlerhaft ♦ *n* (*LING*: *also*: ~ **tense**) Imperfekt *nt*, Vergangenheit *f*.
**imperfection** [ɪmpə'fɛkʃən] *n* Fehler *m*.
**imperial** [ɪm'pɪərɪəl] *adj* kaiserlich; (*BRIT*: *measure*) britisch.
**imperialism** [ɪm'pɪərɪəlɪzəm] *n* Imperialismus *m*.
**imperil** [ɪm'pɛrɪl] *vt* gefährden.
**imperious** [ɪm'pɪərɪəs] *adj* herrisch, gebieterisch.
**impersonal** [ɪm'pəːsənl] *adj* unpersönlich.
**impersonate** [ɪm'pəːsəneɪt] *vt* sich ausgeben als; (*THEAT*) imitieren.
**impersonation** [ɪmpəːsə'neɪʃən] *n* (*THEAT*) Imitation *f*; ~ **of** (*LAW*) Auftreten *nt* als.
**impertinent** [ɪm'pəːtɪnənt] *adj* unverschämt.
**imperturbable** [ɪmpə'təːbəbl] *adj* unerschütterlich.
**impervious** [ɪm'pəːvɪəs] *adj*: ~ **to** (*criticism, pressure*) unberührt von; (*charm, influence*) unempfänglich für.
**impetuous** [ɪm'pɛtjuəs] *adj* ungestüm, stürmisch; (*act*) impulsiv.
**impetus** ['ɪmpətəs] *n* Schwung *m*; (*fig: driving force*) treibende Kraft *f*.
**impinge** [ɪm'pɪndʒ]: **to** ~ **on** *vt fus* sich auswirken auf +*acc*; (*rights*) einschränken +*acc*.
**impish** ['ɪmpɪʃ] *adj* schelmisch.
**implacable** [ɪm'plækəbl] *adj* unerbittlich, erbittert.
**implant** [ɪm'plaːnt] *vt* (*MED*) einpflanzen; (*fig: idea, principle*) einimpfen.
**implausible** [ɪm'plɔːzɪbl] *adj* unglaubwürdig.
**implement** [*n* 'ɪmplɪmənt, *vt* 'ɪmplɪmɛnt] *n* Gerät *nt*, Werkzeug *nt* ♦ *vt* durchführen.
**implicate** ['ɪmplɪkeɪt] *vt* verwickeln.
**implication** [ɪmplɪ'keɪʃən] *n* Auswirkung *f*; (*involvement*) Verwicklung *f*; **by** ~ implizit.
**implicit** [ɪm'plɪsɪt] *adj* (*inferred*) implizit, unausgesprochen; (*unquestioning*) absolut.
**implicitly** [ɪm'plɪsɪtlɪ] *adv* (*see adj*) implizit; absolut.
**implore** [ɪm'plɔː*] *vt* anflehen.
**imply** [ɪm'plaɪ] *vt* andeuten; (*mean*) bedeuten.
**impolite** [ɪmpə'laɪt] *adj* unhöflich.
**imponderable** [ɪm'pɔndərəbl] *adj* unberechenbar ♦ *n* unberechenbare Größe *f*.
**import** [*vt* ɪm'pɔːt, *n* 'ɪmpɔːt] *vt* importieren, einführen ♦ *n* Import *m*, Einfuhr *f*; (*article*) Importgut *nt* ♦ *cpd* Import-, Einfuhr-.
**importance** [ɪm'pɔːtns] *n* (*see adj*) Wichtigkeit *f*; Bedeutung *f*; **to be of little/ great** ~ nicht besonders wichtig/sehr wichtig sein.
**important** [ɪm'pɔːtnt] *adj* wichtig; (*influential*) bedeutend; **it's not** ~ es ist unwichtig.
**importantly** [ɪm'pɔːtntlɪ] *adv* wichtigtuerisch;

but more ~ ... aber was noch wichtiger ist, ...

**importation** [ɪmpɔːˈteɪʃən] *n* Import *m*, Einfuhr *f*.

**imported** [ɪmˈpɔːtɪd] *adj* importiert, eingeführt.

**importer** [ɪmˈpɔːtə*] *n* Importeur *m*.

**impose** [ɪmˈpəʊz] *vt* auferlegen; (*sanctions*) verhängen ♦ *vi*: **to ~ on sb** jdm zur Last fallen.

**imposing** [ɪmˈpəʊzɪŋ] *adj* eindrucksvoll.

**imposition** [ɪmpəˈzɪʃən] *n* (*of tax etc*) Auferlegung *f*; **to be an ~ on** eine Zumutung sein für.

**impossibility** [ɪmpɒsəˈbɪlɪtɪ] *n* Unmöglichkeit *f*.

**impossible** [ɪmˈpɒsɪbl] *adj* unmöglich; **it's ~ for me to leave now** ich kann jetzt unmöglich gehen.

**impossibly** [ɪmˈpɒsɪblɪ] *adv* unmöglich.

**imposter** [ɪmˈpɒstə*] *n* = **impostor**.

**impostor** [ɪmˈpɒstə*] *n* Hochstapler(in) *m(f)*.

**impotence** [ˈɪmpətns] *n* (*see adj*) Machtlosigkeit *f*; Impotenz *f*.

**impotent** [ˈɪmpətnt] *adj* machtlos; (*MED*) impotent.

**impound** [ɪmˈpaʊnd] *vt* beschlagnahmen.

**impoverished** [ɪmˈpɒvərɪʃt] *adj* verarmt.

**impracticable** [ɪmˈpræktɪkəbl] *adj* (*idea*) undurchführbar; (*solution*) unbrauchbar.

**impractical** [ɪmˈpræktɪkl] *adj* (*plan*) undurchführbar; (*person*) unpraktisch.

**imprecise** [ɪmprɪˈsaɪs] *adj* ungenau.

**impregnable** [ɪmˈpregnəbl] *adj* uneinnehmbar; (*fig*) unerschütterlich.

**impregnate** [ˈɪmpregneɪt] *vt* tränken.

**impresario** [ɪmprɪˈsɑːrɪəʊ] *n* (*THEAT*) Impresario *m*.

**impress** [ɪmˈpres] *vt* beeindrucken; (*mark*) aufdrücken; **to ~ sth on sb** jdm etw einschärfen.

**impression** [ɪmˈpreʃən] *n* Eindruck *m*; (*of stamp, seal*) Abdruck *m*; (*imitation*) Nachahmung *f*, Imitation *f*; **to make a good/bad ~ on sb** einen guten/schlechten Eindruck auf jdn machen; **to be under the ~ that ...** den Eindruck haben, daß ...

**impressionable** [ɪmˈpreʃnəbl] *adj* leicht zu beeindrucken.

**impressionist** [ɪmˈpreʃənɪst] *n* Impressionist(in) *m(f)*; (*entertainer*) Imitator(in) *m(f)*.

**impressive** [ɪmˈpresɪv] *adj* beeindruckend.

**imprint** [ˈɪmprɪnt] *n* (*of hand etc*) Abdruck *m*; (*PUBLISHING*) Impressum *nt*.

**imprinted** [ɪmˈprɪntɪd] *adj*: **it is ~ on my memory/mind** es hat sich mir eingeprägt.

**imprison** [ɪmˈprɪzn] *vt* inhaftieren, einsperren.

**imprisonment** [ɪmˈprɪznmənt] *n* Gefangenschaft *f*; **three years' ~** drei Jahre Gefängnis *or* Freiheitsstrafe.

**improbable** [ɪmˈprɒbəbl] *adj* unwahrscheinlich.

**impromptu** [ɪmˈprɒmptjuː] *adj* improvisiert.

**improper** [ɪmˈprɒpə*] *adj* ungehörig; (*procedure*) unrichtig; (*dishonest*) unlauter.

**impropriety** [ɪmprəˈpraɪətɪ] *n* (*see adj*) Ungehörigkeit *f*; Unrichtigkeit *f*; Unlauterkeit *f*.

**improve** [ɪmˈpruːv] *vt* verbessern ♦ *vi* sich bessern; **the patient is improving** dem Patienten geht es besser.

▶**improve (up)on** *vt fus* verbessern.

**improvement** [ɪmˈpruːvmənt] *n*: **~ (in)** Verbesserung *f* (+*gen*); **to make ~s to** Verbesserungen durchführen an +*dat*.

**improvisation** [ɪmprəvaɪˈzeɪʃən] *n* Improvisation *f*.

**improvise** [ˈɪmprəvaɪz] *vt, vi* improvisieren.

**imprudence** [ɪmˈpruːdns] *n* Unklugheit *f*.

**imprudent** [ɪmˈpruːdnt] *adj* unklug.

**impudent** [ˈɪmpjudnt] *adj* unverschämt.

**impugn** [ɪmˈpjuːn] *vt* angreifen; (*sincerity, motives, reputation*) in Zweifel ziehen.

**impulse** [ˈɪmpʌls] *n* Impuls *m*; (*urge*) Drang *m*; **to act on ~** aus einem Impuls heraus handeln.

**impulse buy** *n* Impulsivkauf *m*.

**impulsive** [ɪmˈpʌlsɪv] *adj* impulsiv, spontan; (*purchase*) Impulsiv-.

**impunity** [ɪmˈpjuːnɪtɪ] *n*: **with ~** ungestraft.

**impure** [ɪmˈpjʊə*] *adj* unrein; (*adulterated*) verunreinigt.

**impurity** [ɪmˈpjʊərɪtɪ] *n* Verunreinigung *f*.

**IN** (*US*) *abbr* (*POST*: = *Indiana*).

═══════════════════════════ *KEYWORD*

**in** [ɪn] *prep* **1** (*indicating place, position*) in +*dat*; (*with motion*) in +*acc*; **~ the house/garden** im Haus/Garten; **~ town** in der Stadt; **~ the country** auf dem Land; **~ here** hierin; **~ there** darin

**2** (*with place names: of town, region, country*) in +*dat*; **~ London/Bavaria** in London/Bayern

**3** (*indicating time*) in +*dat*; **~ spring/summer/May** im Frühling/Sommer/Mai; **~ 1994** 1994; **~ the afternoon** am Nachmittag; **at 4 o'clock ~ the afternoon** um 4 Uhr nachmittags; **I did it ~ 3 hours/days** ich habe es in 3 Stunden/Tagen gemacht; **~ 2 weeks** *or* **2 weeks' time** in 2 Wochen

**4** (*indicating manner, circumstances, state*) in +*dat*; **~ a loud/soft voice** mit lauter/weicher Stimme; **~ English/German** auf Englisch/Deutsch; **~ the sun** in der Sonne; **~ the rain** im Regen; **~ good condition** in guter Verfassung

**5** (*with ratios, numbers*): **1 ~ 10** eine(r, s) von 10; **20 pence ~ the pound** 20 Pence pro Pfund; **they lined up ~ twos** sie stellten sich in Zweierreihen auf

**6** (*referring to people, works*): **the disease is common ~ children** die Krankheit ist bei

Kindern verbreitet; ~ **(the works of)
Dickens** bei Dickens; **they have a good
leader** ~ **him** in ihm haben sie einen guten
Führer
**7** (indicating profession etc) **to be**
~ **teaching/the army** Lehrer(in)/beim
Militär sein
**8** (with present participle): ~ **saying this, I ...**
wenn ich das sage, ...
♦ adv: **to be** ~ (person: at home, work) da sein;
(train, ship, plane) angekommen sein; (in
fashion) in sein; **to ask sb** ~ jdn
hereinbitten; **to run/limp** etc ~
hereinlaufen/-humpeln etc
♦ n: **the ~s and outs** (of proposal, situation etc)
die Einzelheiten pl.

**in.** abbr = **inch.**
**inability** [ɪnə'bɪlɪtɪ] n Unfähigkeit f.
**inaccessible** [ɪnək'sɛsɪbl] adj unzugänglich.
**inaccuracy** [ɪn'ækjurəsɪ] n (see adj)
Ungenauigkeit f; Unrichtigkeit f; (mistake)
Fehler m.
**inaccurate** [ɪn'ækjurət] adj ungenau; (not
correct) unrichtig.
**inaction** [ɪn'ækʃən] n Untätigkeit f.
**inactive** [ɪn'æktɪv] adj untätig.
**inactivity** [ɪnæk'tɪvɪtɪ] n Untätigkeit f.
**inadequacy** [ɪn'ædɪkwəsɪ] n Unzulänglichkeit
f.
**inadequate** [ɪn'ædɪkwət] adj unzulänglich.
**inadmissible** [ɪnəd'mɪsəbl] adj unzulässig.
**inadvertently** [ɪnəd'və:tntlɪ] adv ungewollt.
**inadvisable** [ɪnəd'vaɪzəbl] adj unratsam; **it is**
~ **to** ... es ist nicht ratsam, zu ...
**inane** [ɪ'neɪn] adj dumm.
**inanimate** [ɪn'ænɪmət] adj unbelebt.
**inapplicable** [ɪn'æplɪkəbl] adj unzutreffend.
**inappropriate** [ɪnə'prəuprɪət] adj unpassend;
(word, expression) unangebracht.
**inapt** [ɪn'æpt] adj unpassend.
**inarticulate** [ɪnɑː'tɪkjulət] adj (speech)
unverständlich; **he is** ~ er kann sich nur
schlecht ausdrücken.
**inasmuch as** [ɪnəz'mʌtʃ-] adv da, weil; (in so
far as) insofern als.
**inattention** [ɪnə'tɛnʃən] n Unaufmerksamkeit
f.
**inattentive** [ɪnə'tɛntɪv] adj unaufmerksam.
**inaudible** [ɪn'ɔːdɪbl] adj unhörbar.
**inaugural** [ɪ'nɔːgjurəl] adj (speech, meeting)
Eröffnungs-.
**inaugurate** [ɪ'nɔːgjureɪt] vt einführen;
(president, official) (feierlich) in sein/ihr Amt
einführen.
**inauguration** [ɪnɔːgju'reɪʃən] n (see vb)
Einführung f; (feierliche) Amtseinführung
f.
**inauspicious** [ɪnɔːs'pɪʃəs] adj
unheilverheißend.
**in-between** [ɪnbɪ'twiːn] adj Mittel-,
Zwischen-.

**inborn** [ɪn'bɔːn] adj angeboren.
**inbred** [ɪn'brɛd] adj angeboren; **an** ~ **family**
eine Familie, in der Inzucht herrscht.
**inbreeding** [ɪn'briːdɪŋ] n Inzucht f.
**in-built** ['ɪnbɪlt] adj (quality) ihm/ihr etc eigen;
(feeling etc) angeboren.
**Inc.** abbr = **incorporated company.**
**Inca** ['ɪŋkə] adj (also: ~n) Inka-, inkaisch ♦ n
Inka mf.
**incalculable** [ɪn'kælkjuləbl] adj (effect)
unabsehbar; (loss) unermeßlich.
**incapable** [ɪn'keɪpəbl] adj hilflos; **to be** ~ **of**
sth unfähig zu etw sein; **to be** ~ **of doing sth**
unfähig sein, etw zu tun.
**incapacitate** [ɪnkə'pæsɪteɪt] vt: **to** ~ **sb** jdn
unfähig machen.
**incapacitated** [ɪnkə'pæsɪteɪtɪd] adj (LAW)
entmündigt.
**incapacity** [ɪnkə'pæsɪtɪ] n Hilflosigkeit f;
(inability) Unfähigkeit f.
**incarcerate** [ɪn'kɑːsəreɪt] vt einkerkern.
**incarnate** [ɪn'kɑːnɪt] adj leibhaftig, in Person;
**evil** ~ das leibhaftige Böse.
**incarnation** [ɪnkɑː'neɪʃən] n Inbegriff m; (REL)
Menschwerdung f.
**incendiary** [ɪn'sɛndɪərɪ] adj (bomb) Brand-;
~ **device** Brandsatz m.
**incense** [n 'ɪnsɛns, vt ɪn'sɛns] n Weihrauch m;
(perfume) Duft m ♦ vt wütend machen.
**incense burner** n Weihrauchschwenker m.
**incentive** [ɪn'sɛntɪv] n Anreiz m.
**inception** [ɪn'sɛpʃən] n Beginn m, Anfang m.
**incessant** [ɪn'sɛsnt] adj unablässig.
**incessantly** [ɪn'sɛsntlɪ] adv unablässig.
**incest** ['ɪnsɛst] n Inzest m.
**inch** [ɪntʃ] n Zoll m; **to be within an** ~ **of** sth
kurz vor etw dat stehen; **he didn't give an** ~
(fig) er gab keinen Fingerbreit nach.
▶**inch forward** vi sich millimeterweise or
stückchenweise vorwärtsschieben.
**incidence** ['ɪnsɪdns] n Häufigkeit f.
**incident** ['ɪnsɪdnt] n Vorfall m; (diplomatic etc)
Zwischenfall m.
**incidental** [ɪnsɪ'dɛntl] adj zusätzlich;
(unimportant) nebensächlich; ~ **to**
verbunden mit; ~ **expenses** Nebenkosten pl.
**incidentally** [ɪnsɪ'dɛntəlɪ] adv übrigens.
**incidental music** n Begleitmusik f.
**incident room** n Einsatzzentrale f.
**incinerate** [ɪn'sɪnəreɪt] vt verbrennen.
**incinerator** [ɪn'sɪnəreɪtə*] n (for waste, refuse)
(Müll)verbrennungsanlage f.
**incipient** [ɪn'sɪpɪənt] adj einsetzend.
**incision** [ɪn'sɪʒən] n Einschnitt m.
**incisive** [ɪn'saɪsɪv] adj treffend.
**incisor** [ɪn'saɪzə*] n Schneidezahn m.
**incite** [ɪn'saɪt] vt (rioters) aufhetzen; (violence,
hatred) schüren.
**incl.** abbr = **including; inclusive (of).**
**inclement** [ɪn'klɛmənt] adj (weather) rauh,
unfreundlich.
**inclination** [ɪnklɪ'neɪʃən] n Neigung f.

**incline** [*n* 'ınklaın, *vb* ın'klaın] *n* Abhang *m* ♦ *vt* neigen ♦ *vi* sich neigen; **to be ~d to** neigen zu; **to be well ~d towards sb** jdm geneigt *or* gewogen sein.

**include** [ın'klu:d] *vt* einbeziehen; (*in price*) einschließen; **the tip is not ~d in the price** Trinkgeld ist im Preis nicht inbegriffen.

**including** [ın'klu:dıŋ] *prep* einschließlich; **~ service charge** inklusive Bedienung.

**inclusion** [ın'klu:ʒən] *n* (*see vb*) Einbeziehung *f*; Einschluß *m*.

**inclusive** [ın'klu:sıv] *adj* (*terms*) inklusive; (*price*) Inklusiv-, Pauschal-; **~ of** einschließlich +*gen*.

**incognito** [ınkɔg'ni:təu] *adv* inkognito.

**incoherent** [ınkəu'hıərənt] *adj* zusammenhanglos; (*speech*) wirr; (*person*) sich unklar *or* undeutlich ausdrückend.

**income** ['ınkʌm] *n* Einkommen *nt*; (*from property, investment, pension*) Einkünfte *pl*; **gross/net ~** Brutto-/Nettoeinkommen *nt*; **~ and expenditure account** Gewinn- und Verlustrechnung *f*; **~ bracket** Einkommensklasse *f*.

**income support** *n* ≈ Sozialhilfe *f*.

**income tax** *n* Einkommensteuer *f* ♦ *cpd* Steuer-.

**incoming** ['ınkʌmıŋ] *adj* (*passenger*) ankommend; (*flight*) landend; (*call, mail*) eingehend; (*government, official*) neu; (*wave*) hereinbrechend; **~ tide** Flut *f*.

**incommunicado** ['ınkəmjunı'ka:dəu] *adj*: **to hold sb ~** jdn ohne jede Verbindung zur Außenwelt halten.

**incomparable** [ın'kɔmpərəbl] *adj* unvergleichlich.

**incompatible** [ınkəm'pætıbl] *adj* unvereinbar.

**incompetence** [ın'kɔmpıtns] *n* Unfähigkeit *f*.

**incompetent** [ın'kɔmpıtnt] *adj* unfähig; (*job*) unzulänglich.

**incomplete** [ınkəm'pli:t] *adj* unfertig; (*partial*) unvollständig.

**incomprehensible** [ınkɔmprı'hensıbl] *adj* unverständlich.

**inconceivable** [ınkən'si:vəbl] *adj*: **it is ~ (that ...)** es ist unvorstellbar *or* undenkbar(, daß ...).

**inconclusive** [ınkən'klu:sıv] *adj* (*experiment, discussion*) ergebnislos; (*evidence, argument*) nicht überzeugend; (*result*) unbestimmt.

**incongruous** [ın'kɔŋgruəs] *adj* (*strange*) absurd; (*inappropriate*) unpassend.

**inconsequential** [ınkɔnsı'kwenʃl] *adj* unbedeutend, unwichtig.

**inconsiderable** [ınkən'sıdərəbl] *adj*: **not ~** beachtlich; (*sum*) nicht unerheblich.

**inconsiderate** [ınkən'sıdərət] *adj* rücksichtslos.

**inconsistency** [ınkən'sıstənsı] *n* (*see adj*) Widersprüchlichkeit *f*; Inkonsequenz *f*; Unbeständigkeit *f*.

**inconsistent** [ınkən'sıstnt] *adj* widersprüchlich; (*person*) inkonsequent; (*work*) unbeständig; **to be ~ with** im Widerspruch stehen zu.

**inconsolable** [ınkən'səuləbl] *adj* untröstlich.

**inconspicuous** [ınkən'spıkjuəs] *adj* unauffällig; **to make o.s. ~** sich unauffällig benehmen.

**incontinence** [ın'kɔntınəns] *n* (*MED*) Unfähigkeit *f*, Stuhl und/oder Harn zurückzuhalten, Inkontinenz *f*.

**incontinent** [ın'kɔntınənt] *adj* (*MED*) unfähig, Stuhl und/oder Harn zurückzuhalten, inkontinent.

**inconvenience** [ınkən'vi:njəns] *n* Unannehmlichkeit *f*; (*trouble*) Umstände *pl* ♦ *vt* Umstände bereiten +*dat*; **don't ~ yourself** machen Sie sich keine Umstände.

**inconvenient** [ınkən'vi:njənt] *adj* (*time, place*) ungünstig; (*house*) unbequem, unpraktisch; (*visitor*) ungelegen.

**incorporate** [ın'kɔ:pəreıt] *vt* aufnehmen; (*contain*) enthalten; **safety features have been ~d in the design** in der Konstruktion sind auch Sicherheitsvorkehrungen enthalten.

**incorporated company** [ın'kɔ:pəreıtıd-] (*US*) *n* eingetragene Gesellschaft *f*.

**incorrect** [ınkə'rekt] *adj* falsch.

**incorrigible** [ın'kɔrıdʒıbl] *adj* unverbesserlich.

**incorruptible** [ınkə'rʌptıbl] *adj* unbestechlich.

**increase** [*vb* ın'kri:s, *n* 'ınkri:s] *vi* (*level etc*) zunehmen; (*price*) steigen; (*in size*) sich vergrößern; (*in number, quantity*) sich vermehren ♦ *vt* vergrößern; (*price*) erhöhen ♦ *n*: **~ (in)** Zunahme *f* (+*gen*); (*in wages, spending etc*) Erhöhung *f* (+*gen*); **an ~ of 5%** eine Erhöhung von 5%, eine Zunahme um 5%; **to be on the ~** zunehmen.

**increasing** [ın'kri:sıŋ] *adj* zunehmend.

**increasingly** [ın'kri:sıŋlı] *adv* zunehmend.

**incredible** [ın'kredıbl] *adj* unglaublich; (*amazing, wonderful*) unwahrscheinlich (*inf*), sagenhaft (*inf*).

**incredulity** [ınkrı'dju:lıtı] *n* Ungläubigkeit *f*.

**incredulous** [ın'kredjuləs] *adj* ungläubig.

**increment** ['ınkrımənt] *n* (*in salary*) Erhöhung *f*, Zulage *f*.

**incriminate** [ın'krımıneıt] *vt* belasten.

**incriminating** [ın'krımıneıtıŋ] *adj* belastend.

**incrusted** [ın'krʌstıd] *adj* = **encrusted**.

**incubate** ['ınkjubeıt] *vt* ausbrüten ♦ *vi* ausgebrütet werden; (*disease*) zum Ausbruch kommen.

**incubation** [ınkju'beıʃən] *n* Ausbrüten *nt*; (*of illness*) Inkubation *f*.

**incubation period** *n* Inkubationszeit *f*.

**incubator** ['ınkjubeıtə*] *n* (*for babies*) Brutkasten *m*, Inkubator *m*.

**inculcate** ['ınkʌlkeıt] *vt*: **to ~ sth in(to) sb** jdm etw einprägen.

**incumbent** [ın'kʌmbənt] *n* Amtsinhaber(in)

*m(f)* ♦ *adj*: **it is ~ on him to ...** es obliegt ihm
*or* es ist seine Pflicht, zu ...

**incur** [ɪnˈkɜːʳ] *vt (expenses, debt)* machen;
*(loss)* erleiden; *(disapproval, anger)* sich *dat*
zuziehen.

**incurable** [ɪnˈkjʊərəbl] *adj* unheilbar.

**incursion** [ɪnˈkɜːʃən] *n (MIL)* Einfall *m*.

**Ind.** *(US) abbr (POST:* = *Indiana).*

**indebted** [ɪnˈdɛtɪd] *adj*: **to be ~ to sb** jdm (zu
Dank) verpflichtet sein.

**indecency** [ɪnˈdiːsnsɪ] *n* Unanständigkeit *f*,
Anstößigkeit *f*.

**indecent** [ɪnˈdiːsnt] *adj* unanständig, anstößig;
*(haste)* ungebührlich.

**indecent assault** *(BRIT) n* Sexualverbrechen
*nt*.

**indecent exposure** *n* Erregung *f*
öffentlichen Ärgernisses.

**indecipherable** [ɪndɪˈsaɪfərəbl] *adj* unleserlich; *(expression, glance etc)* unergründlich.

**indecision** [ɪndɪˈsɪʒən] *n* Unentschlossenheit
*f*.

**indecisive** [ɪndɪˈsaɪsɪv] *adj* unentschlossen.

**indeed** [ɪnˈdiːd] *adv* aber sicher; *(in fact)*
tatsächlich, in der Tat; *(furthermore)* sogar;
**yes ~!** oh ja!, das kann man wohl sagen!

**indefatigable** [ɪndɪˈfætɪgəbl] *adj* unermüdlich.

**indefensible** [ɪndɪˈfɛnsɪbl] *adj (conduct)*
unentschuldbar.

**indefinable** [ɪndɪˈfaɪnəbl] *adj* undefinierbar.

**indefinite** [ɪnˈdɛfɪnɪt] *adj* unklar, vage; *(period,
number)* unbestimmt.

**indefinite article** *n (LING)* unbestimmter
Artikel *m*.

**indefinitely** [ɪnˈdɛfɪnɪtlɪ] *adv (continue)* endlos;
*(wait)* unbegrenzt (lange); *(postpone)* auf
unbestimmte Zeit.

**indelible** [ɪnˈdɛlɪbl] *adj (mark, stain)* nicht zu
entfernen; **~ pen** Tintenstift *m*; **~ ink**
Wäschetinte *f*.

**indelicate** [ɪnˈdɛlɪkɪt] *adj* taktlos; *(not polite)*
ungehörig.

**indemnify** [ɪnˈdɛmnɪfaɪ] *vt* entschädigen.

**indemnity** [ɪnˈdɛmnɪtɪ] *n (insurance)*
Versicherung *f*; *(compensation)*
Entschädigung *f*.

**indent** [ɪnˈdɛnt] *vt (text)* einrücken, einziehen.

**indentation** [ɪndɛnˈteɪʃən] *n* Einkerbung *f*;
*(TYP)* Einrückung *f*, Einzug *m*; *(on metal)*
Delle *f*.

**indenture** [ɪnˈdɛntʃəʳ] *n* Ausbildungsvertrag
*m*, Lehrvertrag *m*.

**independence** [ɪndɪˈpɛndns] *n*
Unabhängigkeit *f*.

**Independence Day** *(der 4. Juli) ist in den USA
ein gesetzlicher Feiertag zum Gedenken an die
Unabhängigkeitserklärung am 4. Juli 1776, mit
der die 13 amerikanischen Kolonien ihre
Freiheit und Unabhängigkeit von
Großbritannien erklärten.*

**independent** [ɪndɪˈpɛndnt] *adj* unabhängig.

**independently** [ɪndɪˈpɛndntlɪ] *adv*
unabhängig.

**in-depth** [ˈɪndɛpθ] *adj* eingehend.

**indescribable** [ɪndɪsˈkraɪbəbl] *adj*
unbeschreiblich.

**indestructible** [ɪndɪsˈtrʌktəbl] *adj*
unzerstörbar.

**indeterminate** [ɪndɪˈtəːmɪnɪt] *adj* unbestimmt.

**index** [ˈɪndɛks] *(pl ~es) n (in book)* Register *nt*;
*(in library etc)* Katalog *m*; *(card index)* Kartei
*f*; *(pl indices: ratio)* Index *m*; *(: sign)*
(An)zeichen *nt*.

**index card** *n* Karteikarte *f*.

**indexed** [ˈɪndɛkst] *(US) adj* = **index-linked**.

**index finger** *n* Zeigefinger *m*.

**index-linked** [ˈɪndɛksˈlɪŋkt] *adj* der
Inflationsrate *dat* angeglichen.

**India** [ˈɪndɪə] *n* Indien *nt*.

**Indian** [ˈɪndɪən] *adj* indisch; *(American Indian)*
indianisch ♦ *n* Inder(in) *m(f)*; **American ~**
Indianer(in) *m(f)*.

**Indian Ocean** *n*: **the ~** der Indische Ozean.

**Indian summer** *n* Altweibersommer *m*.

**India paper** *n* Dünndruckpapier *nt*.

**India rubber** *n* Gummi *m*, Kautschuk *m*.

**indicate** [ˈɪndɪkeɪt] *vt* (an)zeigen; *(point to)*
deuten auf +*acc*; *(mention)* andeuten ♦ *vi*
*(BRIT: AUT)*: **to ~ left/right** links/rechts
blinken.

**indication** [ɪndɪˈkeɪʃən] *n* (An)zeichen *nt*.

**indicative** [ɪnˈdɪkətɪv] *n (LING)* Indikativ *m*,
Wirklichkeitsform *f* ♦ *adj*: **to be ~ of sth** auf
etw *acc* schließen lassen.

**indicator** [ˈɪndɪkeɪtəʳ] *n (instrument, gauge)*
Anzeiger *m*; *(fig)* (An)zeichen *nt*; *(AUT)*
Richtungsanzeiger *m*, Blinker *m*.

**indices** [ˈɪndɪsiːz] *npl of* **index**.

**indict** [ɪnˈdaɪt] *vt* anklagen.

**indictable** [ɪnˈdaɪtəbl] *adj (person)*
strafrechtlich verfolgbar; **~ offence**
strafbare Handlung *f*.

**indictment** [ɪnˈdaɪtmənt] *n* Anklage *f*; **to be an
~ of sth** *(fig)* ein Armutszeugnis *nt* für etw
sein.

**indifference** [ɪnˈdɪfrəns] *n* Gleichgültig-
keit *f*.

**indifferent** [ɪnˈdɪfrənt] *adj* gleichgültig;
*(mediocre)* mittelmäßig.

**indigenous** [ɪnˈdɪdʒɪnəs] *adj* einheimisch.

**indigestible** [ɪndɪˈdʒɛstɪbl] *adj* unverdaulich.

**indigestion** [ɪndɪˈdʒɛstʃən] *n*
Magenverstimmung *f*.

**indignant** [ɪnˈdɪgnənt] *adj*: **to be ~ at sth/with
sb** entrüstet über etw/jdn sein.

**indignation** [ɪndɪgˈneɪʃən] *n* Entrüstung *f*.

**indignity** [ɪnˈdɪgnɪtɪ] *n* Demütigung *f*.

**indigo** [ˈɪndɪgəu] *n* Indigo *nt or m*.

**indirect** [ɪndɪˈrɛkt] *adj* indirekt; **~ way** *or*
**route** Umweg *m*.

**indirectly** [ɪndɪˈrɛktlɪ] *adv* indirekt.

**indiscreet** [ɪndɪsˈkriːt] *adj* indiskret.

**indiscretion** [ɪndɪsˈkrɛʃən] n Indiskretion f.
**indiscriminate** [ɪndɪsˈkrɪmɪnət] adj wahllos; (*taste*) unkritisch.
**indispensable** [ɪndɪsˈpɛnsəbl] adj unentbehrlich.
**indisposed** [ɪndɪsˈpəuzd] adj unpäßlich.
**indisputable** [ɪndɪsˈpjuːtəbl] adj unbestreitbar.
**indistinct** [ɪndɪsˈtɪŋkt] adj undeutlich; (*image*) verschwommen; (*noise*) schwach.
**indistinguishable** [ɪndɪsˈtɪŋgwɪʃəbl] adj: ~ **from** nicht zu unterscheiden von.
**individual** [ɪndɪˈvɪdjuəl] n Individuum nt, Einzelne(r) f(m) ♦ adj eigen; (*single*) einzeln; (*case, portion*) Einzel-; (*particular*) individuell.
**individualist** [ɪndɪˈvɪdjuəlɪst] n Individualist(in) m(f).
**individuality** [ɪndɪvɪdjuˈælɪtɪ] n Individualität f.
**individually** [ɪndɪˈvɪdjuəlɪ] adv einzeln, individuell.
**indivisible** [ɪndɪˈvɪzɪbl] adj unteilbar.
**Indochina** [ɪndəʊˈtʃaɪnə] n Indochina nt.
**indoctrinate** [ɪnˈdɔktrɪneɪt] vt indoktrinieren.
**indoctrination** [ɪndɔktrɪˈneɪʃən] n Indoktrination f.
**indolence** [ˈɪndələns] n Trägheit f.
**indolent** [ˈɪndələnt] adj träge.
**Indonesia** [ɪndəˈniːzɪə] n Indonesien nt.
**Indonesian** [ɪndəˈniːzɪən] adj indonesisch ♦ n Indonesier(in) m(f); (*LING*) Indonesisch nt.
**indoor** [ˈɪndɔːʳ] adj (*plant, aerial*) Zimmer-; (*clothes, shoes*) Haus-; (*swimming pool, sport*) Hallen-; (*games*) im Haus.
**indoors** [ɪnˈdɔːz] adv drinnen; **to go** ~ hineingehen.
**indubitable** [ɪnˈdjuːbɪtəbl] adj unzweifelhaft.
**indubitably** [ɪnˈdjuːbɪtəblɪ] adv zweifellos.
**induce** [ɪnˈdjuːs] vt herbeiführen; (*persuade*) dazu bringen; (*MED: birth*) einleiten; **to** ~ **sb to do sth** jdn dazu bewegen *or* bringen, etw zu tun.
**inducement** [ɪnˈdjuːsmənt] n Anreiz m; (*pej: bribe*) Bestechung f.
**induct** [ɪnˈdʌkt] vt (in sein/ihr *etc* Amt) einführen.
**induction** [ɪnˈdʌkʃən] n (*MED: of birth*) Einleitung f.
**induction course** (*BRIT*) n Einführungskurs m.
**indulge** [ɪnˈdʌldʒ] vt nachgeben +dat; (*person, child*) verwöhnen ♦ vi: **to** ~ **in** sich hingeben +dat.
**indulgence** [ɪnˈdʌldʒəns] n (*pleasure*) Luxus m; (*leniency*) Nachgiebigkeit f.
**indulgent** [ɪnˈdʌldʒənt] adj nachsichtig.
**industrial** [ɪnˈdʌstrɪəl] adj industriell; (*accident*) Arbeits-; (*city*) Industrie-.
**industrial action** n Arbeitskampfmaßnahmen pl.
**industrial design** n Industriedesign nt.

**industrial estate** (*BRIT*) n Industriegebiet nt.
**industrialist** [ɪnˈdʌstrɪəlɪst] n Industrielle(r) f(m).
**industrialize** [ɪnˈdʌstrɪəlaɪz] vt industrialisieren.
**industrial park** (*US*) n = **industrial estate**.
**industrial relations** npl Beziehungen zwischen Arbeitgebern, Arbeitnehmern und Gewerkschaften.
**industrial tribunal** (*BRIT*) n Arbeitsgericht nt.
**industrial unrest** (*BRIT*) n Arbeitsunruhen pl.
**industrious** [ɪnˈdʌstrɪəs] adj fleißig.
**industry** [ˈɪndəstrɪ] n Industrie f; (*diligence*) Fleiß m.
**inebriated** [ɪˈniːbrɪeɪtɪd] adj betrunken.
**inedible** [ɪnˈɛdɪbl] adj ungenießbar.
**ineffective** [ɪnɪˈfɛktɪv] adj wirkungslos; (*government*) unfähig.
**ineffectual** [ɪnɪˈfɛktʃuəl] adj = **ineffective**.
**inefficiency** [ɪnɪˈfɪʃənsɪ] n (*see adj*) Ineffizienz f; Leistungsunfähigkeit f.
**inefficient** [ɪnɪˈfɪʃənt] adj ineffizient; (*machine*) leistungsunfähig.
**inelegant** [ɪnˈɛlɪgənt] adj unelegant.
**ineligible** [ɪnˈɛlɪdʒɪbl] adj (*candidate*) nicht wählbar; **to be** ~ **for sth** zu etw nicht berechtigt sein.
**inept** [ɪˈnɛpt] adj (*politician*) unfähig; (*management*) stümperhaft.
**ineptitude** [ɪˈnɛptɪtjuːd] n (*see adj*) Unfähigkeit f; Stümperhaftigkeit f.
**inequality** [ɪnɪˈkwɔlɪtɪ] n Ungleichheit f.
**inequitable** [ɪnˈɛkwɪtəbl] adj ungerecht.
**inert** [ɪˈnɜːt] adj unbeweglich; ~ **gas** Edelgas nt.
**inertia** [ɪˈnɜːʃə] n Trägheit f.
**inertia-reel seat belt** [ɪˈnɜːʃəˈriːl-] n Automatikgurt m.
**inescapable** [ɪnɪsˈkeɪpəbl] adj unvermeidlich; (*conclusion*) zwangsläufig.
**inessential** [ɪnɪˈsɛnʃl] adj unwesentlich; (*furniture etc*) entbehrlich.
**inessentials** [ɪnɪˈsɛnʃlz] npl Nebensächlichkeiten pl.
**inestimable** [ɪnˈɛstɪməbl] adj unschätzbar.
**inevitability** [ɪnɛvɪtəˈbɪlɪtɪ] n Unvermeidlichkeit f; **it is an** ~ es ist nicht zu vermeiden.
**inevitable** [ɪnˈɛvɪtəbl] adj unvermeidlich; (*result*) zwangsläufig.
**inevitably** [ɪnˈɛvɪtəblɪ] adv zwangsläufig; ~, **he was late** es konnte ja nicht ausbleiben, daß er zu spät kam; **as** ~ **happens** ... wie es immer so ist ...
**inexact** [ɪnɪgˈzækt] adj ungenau.
**inexcusable** [ɪnɪksˈkjuːzəbl] adj unentschuldbar, unverzeihlich.
**inexhaustible** [ɪnɪgˈzɔːstɪbl] adj unerschöpflich.
**inexorable** [ɪnˈɛksərəbl] adj unaufhaltsam.
**inexpensive** [ɪnɪksˈpɛnsɪv] adj preisgünstig.

**inexperience** [ɪnɪk'spɪərɪəns] *n*
Unerfahrenheit *f*.
**inexperienced** [ɪnɪk'spɪərɪənst] *adj*
unerfahren; (*swimmer etc*) ungeübt; **to be**
~ **in sth** wenig Erfahrung mit etw haben.
**inexplicable** [ɪnɪk'splɪkəbl] *adj* unerklärlich.
**inexpressible** [ɪnɪk'sprɛsɪbl] *adj*
unbeschreiblich.
**inextricable** [ɪnɪk'strɪkəbl] *adj* unentwirrbar;
(*dilemma*) unlösbar.
**inextricably** [ɪnɪk'strɪkəblɪ] *adv* unentwirrbar;
(*linked*) untrennbar.
**infallibility** [ɪnfælə'bɪlɪtɪ] *n* Unfehlbarkeit *f*.
**infallible** [ɪn'fælɪbl] *adj* unfehlbar.
**infamous** ['ɪnfəməs] *adj* niederträchtig.
**infamy** ['ɪnfəmɪ] *n* Verrufenheit *f*.
**infancy** ['ɪnfənsɪ] *n* frühe Kindheit *f*; (*of
movement, firm*) Anfangsstadium *nt*.
**infant** ['ɪnfənt] *n* Säugling *m*; (*young child*)
Kleinkind *nt* ♦ *cpd* Säuglings-.
**infantile** ['ɪnfəntaɪl] *adj* kindisch, infantil;
(*disease*) Kinder-.
**infantry** ['ɪnfəntrɪ] *n* Infanterie *f*.
**infantryman** ['ɪnfəntrɪmən] (*irreg: like* **man**) *n*
Infanterist *m*.
**infant school** (*BRIT*) *n* Grundschule *f* (*für die
ersten beiden Jahrgänge*).
**infatuated** [ɪn'fætjueɪtɪd] *adj:* ~ **with** vernarrt
in +*acc*; **to become** ~ **with** sich vernarren in
+*acc*.
**infatuation** [ɪnfætju'eɪʃən] *n* Vernarrtheit *f*.
**infect** [ɪn'fɛkt] *vt* anstecken (*also fig*),
infizieren; (*food*) verseuchen; **to become**
~**ed** (*wound*) sich entzünden.
**infection** [ɪn'fɛkʃən] *n* Infektion *f*,
Entzündung *f*; (*contagion*) Ansteckung *f*.
**infectious** [ɪn'fɛkʃəs] *adj* ansteckend.
**infer** [ɪn'fɜːʳ] *vt* schließen; (*imply*) andeuten.
**inference** ['ɪnfərəns] *n* (*see vb*) Schluß *m*;
Andeutung *f*.
**inferior** [ɪn'fɪərɪəʳ] *adj* (*in rank*) untergeordnet,
niedriger; (*in quality*) minderwertig; (*in
quantity, number*) geringer ♦ *n*
Untergebene(r) *f(m)*; **to feel** ~ **(to sb**) sich
(jdm) unterlegen fühlen.
**inferiority** [ɪnfɪərɪ'ɒrɪtɪ] *n* (*see adj*)
untergeordnete Stellung *f*, niedriger Rang
*m*; Minderwertigkeit *f*; geringere Zahl *f*.
**inferiority complex** *n* Minderwertig-
keitskomplex *m*.
**infernal** [ɪn'fɜːnl] *adj* höllisch; (*temper*)
schrecklich.
**inferno** [ɪn'fɜːnəu] *n* (*blaze*) Flammenmeer *nt*.
**infertile** [ɪn'fɜːtaɪl] *adj* unfruchtbar.
**infertility** [ɪnfɜː'tɪlɪtɪ] *n* Unfruchtbarkeit *f*.
**infested** [ɪn'fɛstɪd] *adj:* ~ **(with)** verseucht
(mit).
**infidelity** [ɪnfɪ'dɛlɪtɪ] *n* Untreue *f*.
**infighting** ['ɪnfaɪtɪŋ] *n* interne Machtkämpfe
*pl*.
**infiltrate** ['ɪnfɪltreɪt] *vt* (*organization etc*)
infiltrieren, unterwandern; (*: to spy*)

einschleusen.
**infinite** ['ɪnfɪnɪt] *adj* unendlich; (*time, money*)
unendlich viel.
**infinitely** ['ɪnfɪnɪtlɪ] *adv* unendlich viel.
**infinitesimal** [ɪnfɪnɪ'tɛsɪməl] *adj* unendlich
klein, winzig.
**infinitive** [ɪn'fɪnɪtɪv] *n* (*LING*) Infinitiv *m*,
Grundform *f*.
**infinity** [ɪn'fɪnɪtɪ] *n* Unendlichkeit *f*; (*MATH,
PHOT*) Unendliche *nt*; **an** ~ **of** ... unendlich
viel(e) ...
**infirm** [ɪn'fɜːm] *adj* schwach, gebrechlich.
**infirmary** [ɪn'fɜːmərɪ] *n* Krankenhaus *nt*.
**infirmity** [ɪn'fɜːmɪtɪ] *n* Schwäche *f*,
Gebrechlichkeit *f*.
**inflame** [ɪn'fleɪm] *vt* (*person, crowd*)
aufbringen.
**inflamed** [ɪn'fleɪmd] *adj* entzündet.
**inflammable** [ɪn'flæməbl] *adj* feuergefährlich.
**inflammation** [ɪnflə'meɪʃən] *n* Entzündung *f*.
**inflammatory** [ɪn'flæmətərɪ] *adj* (*speech*)
aufrührerisch, Hetz-.
**inflatable** [ɪn'fleɪtəbl] *adj* aufblasbar; (*dinghy*)
Schlauch-.
**inflate** [ɪn'fleɪt] *vt* aufpumpen; (*balloon*)
aufblasen; (*price*) hochtreiben; (*expectation*)
steigern; (*position, ideas etc*) hochspielen.
**inflated** [ɪn'fleɪtɪd] *adj* (*style*) geschwollen;
(*value, price*) überhöht.
**inflation** [ɪn'fleɪʃən] *n* Inflation *f*.
**inflationary** [ɪn'fleɪʃənərɪ] *adj* inflationär;
(*spiral*) Inflations-.
**inflexible** [ɪn'flɛksɪbl] *adj* inflexibel; (*rule*)
starr.
**inflict** [ɪn'flɪkt] *vt:* **to** ~ **sth on sb** (*damage,
suffering, wound*) jdm etw zufügen;
(*punishment*) jdm etw auferlegen; (*fig:
problems*) jdn mit etw belasten.
**infliction** [ɪn'flɪkʃən] *n* (*see vb*) Zufügen *nt*;
Auferlegung *f*; Belastung *f*.
**in-flight** ['ɪnflaɪt] *adj* während des Fluges.
**inflow** ['ɪnfləu] *n* Zustrom *m*.
**influence** ['ɪnfluəns] *n* Einfluß *m* ♦ *vt*
beeinflussen; **under the** ~ **of alcohol** unter
Alkoholeinfluß.
**influential** [ɪnflu'ɛnʃl] *adj* einflußreich.
**influenza** [ɪnflu'ɛnzə] *n* (*MED*) Grippe *f*.
**influx** ['ɪnflʌks] *n* (*of refugees*) Zustrom *m*; (*of
funds*) Zufuhr *f*.
**inform** [ɪn'fɔːm] *vt:* **to** ~ **sb of sth** jdn von etw
unterrichten, jdn über etw *acc* informieren
♦ *vi:* **to** ~ **on sb** jdn denunzieren.
**informal** [ɪn'fɔːml] *adj* ungezwungen; (*manner,
clothes*) leger; (*unofficial*) inoffiziell;
(*announcement, invitation*) informell.
**informality** [ɪnfɔː'mælɪtɪ] *n* (*see adj*)
Ungezwungenheit *f*; legere Art *f*;
inoffizieller Charakter *m*; informeller
Charakter *m*.
**informally** [ɪn'fɔːməlɪ] *adv* (*see adj*)
ungezwungen; leger; inoffiziell; informell.
**informant** [ɪn'fɔːmənt] *n* Informant(in) *m(f)*.

**information** [ɪnfə'meɪʃən] n Informationen pl,
Auskunft f; (knowledge) Wissen nt; **to get**
~ **on** sich informieren über +acc; **a piece of**
~ eine Auskunft or Information; **for your** ~
zu Ihrer Information.
**information bureau** n Auskunftsbüro nt.
**information desk** n Auskunftsschalter m.
**information office** n Auskunftsbüro nt.
**information processing** n Informations-
verarbeitung f.
**information retrieval** n Informationsabruf
m, Datenabruf m.
**information science** n Informatik f.
**information technology** n
Informationstechnik f.
**informative** [ɪn'fɔ:mətɪv] adj aufschlußreich.
**informed** [ɪn'fɔ:md] adj informiert; (guess,
opinion) wohlbegründet; **to be well/better** ~
gut/besser informiert sein.
**informer** [ɪn'fɔ:mə*] n Informant(in) m(f); (also:
**police** ~) Polizeispitzel m.
**infra dig** ['ɪnfrə'dɪg] (inf) adj abbr (= infra
dignitatem) unter meiner/seiner etc Würde.
**infrared** [ɪnfrə'rɛd] adj infrarot.
**infrastructure** ['ɪnfrəstrʌktʃə*] n
Infrastruktur f.
**infrequent** [ɪn'fri:kwənt] adj selten.
**infringe** [ɪn'frɪndʒ] vt (law) verstoßen gegen,
übertreten ♦ vi: **to** ~ **on** (rights) verletzen.
**infringement** [ɪn'frɪndʒmənt] n (see vb)
Verstoß m, Übertretung f; Verletzung f.
**infuriate** [ɪn'fjuərɪeɪt] vt wütend machen.
**infuriating** [ɪn'fjuərɪeɪtɪŋ] adj äußerst
ärgerlich.
**infuse** [ɪn'fju:z] vt (tea etc) aufgießen; **to** ~ **sb**
**with sth** (fig) jdm etw einflößen.
**infusion** [ɪn'fju:ʒən] n (tea etc) Aufguß m.
**ingenious** [ɪn'dʒi:njəs] adj genial.
**ingenuity** [ɪndʒɪ'nju:ɪtɪ] n Einfallsreichtum m;
(skill) Geschicklichkeit f.
**ingenuous** [ɪn'dʒɛnjuəs] adj offen, aufrichtig;
(innocent) naiv.
**ingot** ['ɪŋgət] n Barren m.
**ingrained** [ɪn'greɪnd] adj (habit) fest; (belief)
unerschütterlich.
**ingratiate** [ɪn'greɪʃɪeɪt] vt: **to** ~ **o.s. with sb**
sich bei jdm einschmeicheln.
**ingratiating** [ɪn'greɪʃɪeɪtɪŋ] adj
schmeichlerisch.
**ingratitude** [ɪn'grætɪtju:d] n Undank m.
**ingredient** [ɪn'gri:dɪənt] n (of cake etc) Zutat f;
(of situation) Bestandteil m.
**ingrowing** ['ɪngrəuɪŋ] adj: ~ **toenail**
eingewachsener Zehennagel m.
**inhabit** [ɪn'hæbɪt] vt bewohnen, wohnen in
+dat.
**inhabitant** [ɪn'hæbɪtnt] n Einwohner(in) m(f);
(of street, house) Bewohner(in) m(f).
**inhale** [ɪn'heɪl] vt einatmen ♦ vi einatmen;
(when smoking) inhalieren.
**inhaler** [ɪn'heɪlə*] n Inhalationsapparat m.
**inherent** [ɪn'hɪərənt] adj: ~ **in** or **to** eigen +dat.

**inherently** [ɪn'hɪərəntlɪ] adv von Natur aus.
**inherit** [ɪn'hɛrɪt] vt erben.
**inheritance** [ɪn'hɛrɪtəns] n Erbe nt.
**inhibit** [ɪn'hɪbɪt] vt hemmen.
**inhibited** [ɪn'hɪbɪtɪd] adj gehemmt.
**inhibiting** [ɪn'hɪbɪtɪŋ] adj hemmend; ~ **factor**
Hemmnis nt.
**inhibition** [ɪnhɪ'bɪʃən] n Hemmung f.
**inhospitable** [ɪnhɒs'pɪtəbl] adj ungastlich;
(place, climate) unwirtlich.
**in-house** ['ɪn'haus] adj, adv hausintern.
**inhuman** [ɪn'hju:mən] adj (behaviour)
unmenschlich; (appearance) nicht
menschlich.
**inhumane** [ɪnhju:'meɪn] adj inhuman;
(treatment) menschenunwürdig.
**inimitable** [ɪ'nɪmɪtəbl] adj unnachahmlich.
**iniquitous** [ɪ'nɪkwɪtəs] adj (unfair) ungerecht.
**iniquity** [ɪ'nɪkwɪtɪ] n Ungerechtigkeit f;
(wickedness) Ungeheuerlichkeit f.
**initial** [ɪ'nɪʃl] adj anfänglich; (stage) Anfangs-
♦ n Initiale f, Anfangsbuchstabe m ♦ vt
(document) abzeichnen; **initials** npl Initialen
pl; (as signature) Namenszeichen nt.
**initialize** [ɪ'nɪʃəlaɪz] vt initialisieren.
**initially** [ɪ'nɪʃəlɪ] adv zu Anfang; (first) zuerst.
**initiate** [ɪ'nɪʃɪeɪt] vt (talks) eröffnen; (process)
einleiten; (new member) feierlich
aufnehmen; **to** ~ **sb into a secret** jdn in ein
Geheimnis einweihen; **to** ~ **proceedings**
**against sb** (LAW) einen Prozeß gegen jdn
anstrengen.
**initiation** [ɪnɪʃɪ'eɪʃən] n (beginning)
Einführung f; (into secret etc) Einweihung f.
**initiative** [ɪ'nɪʃətɪv] n Initiative f; **to take the**
~ die Initiative ergreifen.
**inject** [ɪn'dʒɛkt] vt (ein)spritzen; (fig: funds)
hineinpumpen; **to** ~ **sb with sth** jdm etw
spritzen or injizieren; **to** ~ **money into sth**
(fig) Geld in etw acc pumpen.
**injection** [ɪn'dʒɛkʃən] n Spritze f, Injektion f;
**to give/have an** ~ eine Spritze or Injektion
geben/bekommen; **an** ~ **of money/funds**
(fig) eine Finanzspritze.
**injudicious** [ɪndʒu'dɪʃəs] adj unklug.
**injunction** [ɪn'dʒʌŋkʃən] n (LAW) gerichtliche
Verfügung f.
**injure** ['ɪndʒə*] vt verletzen; (reputation)
schaden +dat; **to** ~ **o.s.** sich verletzen.
**injured** ['ɪndʒəd] adj verletzt; (tone) gekränkt;
~ **party** (LAW) Geschädigte(r) f(m).
**injurious** [ɪn'dʒuərɪəs] adj: **to be** ~ **to** schaden
+dat, schädlich sein +dat.
**injury** ['ɪndʒərɪ] n Verletzung f; **to escape**
**without** ~ unverletzt davonkommen.
**injury time** n (SPORT) Nachspielzeit f; **to play**
~ nachspielen.
**injustice** [ɪn'dʒʌstɪs] n Ungerechtigkeit f; **you**
**do me an** ~ Sie tun mir unrecht.
**ink** [ɪŋk] n Tinte f; (in printing) Druckfarbe f.
**ink-jet printer** ['ɪŋkdʒɛt-] n
Tintenstrahldrucker m.

**inkling** ['ɪŋklɪŋ] *n* (dunkle) Ahnung *f*; **to have an ~ of** ahnen.

**ink pad** *n* Stempelkissen *nt*.

**inky** ['ɪŋkɪ] *adj* tintenschwarz; (*fingers*) tintenbeschmiert.

**inlaid** ['ɪnleɪd] *adj* eingelegt.

**inland** ['ɪnlənd] *adj* (*port, sea, waterway*) Binnen- ♦ *adv* (*travel*) landeinwärts.

**Inland Revenue** (*BRIT*) *n* ≈ Finanzamt *nt*.

**in-laws** ['ɪnlɔːz] *npl* (*parents-in-law*) Schwiegereltern *pl*; (*other relatives*) angeheiratete Verwandte *pl*.

**inlet** ['ɪnlɛt] *n* (schmale) Bucht *f*.

**inlet pipe** *n* Zuleitung *f*, Zuleitungsrohr *nt*.

**inmate** ['ɪnmeɪt] *n* Insasse *m*, Insassin *f*.

**inmost** ['ɪnməʊst] *adj* innerst.

**inn** [ɪn] *n* Gasthaus *nt*.

**innards** ['ɪnədz] (*inf*) *npl* Innereien *pl*.

**innate** [ɪ'neɪt] *adj* angeboren.

**inner** ['ɪnə*] *adj* innere(r, s); (*courtyard*) Innen-.

**inner city** *n* Innenstadt *f*.

**innermost** ['ɪnəməʊst] *adj* = **inmost**.

**inner tube** *n* (*of tyre*) Schlauch *m*.

**innings** ['ɪnɪŋz] *n* (*CRICKET*) Innenrunde *f*; **he's had a good ~** (*fig*) er kann auf ein langes, ausgefülltes Leben zurückblicken.

**innocence** ['ɪnəsns] *n* Unschuld *f*.

**innocent** ['ɪnəsnt] *adj* unschuldig.

**innocuous** [ɪ'nɔkjʊəs] *adj* harmlos.

**innovation** [ɪnəʊ'veɪʃən] *n* Neuerung *f*.

**innuendo** [ɪnjuˈɛndəʊ] (*pl ~es*) *n* versteckte Andeutung *f*.

**innumerable** [ɪ'njuːmrəbl] *adj* unzählig.

**inoculate** [ɪ'nɔkjuleɪt] *vt*: **to ~ sb against sth** jdn gegen etw impfen; **to ~ sb with sth** jdm etw einimpfen.

**inoculation** [ɪnɔkju'leɪʃən] *n* Impfung *f*.

**inoffensive** [ɪnə'fɛnsɪv] *adj* harmlos.

**inopportune** [ɪn'ɔpətjuːn] *adj* unangebracht; (*moment*) ungelegen.

**inordinate** [ɪ'nɔːdɪnət] *adj* (*thirst etc*) unmäßig; (*amount, pleasure*) ungeheuer.

**inordinately** [ɪ'nɔːdɪnətlɪ] *adv* (*proud*) unmäßig; (*long, large etc*) ungeheuer.

**inorganic** [ɪnɔː'gænɪk] *adj* anorganisch.

**inpatient** ['ɪnpeɪʃənt] *n* stationär behandelter Patient *m*, stationär behandelte Patientin *f*.

**input** ['ɪnput] *n* (*of capital, manpower*) Investition *f*; (*of energy*) Zufuhr *f*; (*COMPUT*) Eingabe *f*, Input *m or nt* ♦ *vt* (*COMPUT*) eingeben.

**inquest** ['ɪnkwɛst] *n* gerichtliche Untersuchung *f* der Todesursache.

**inquire** [ɪn'kwaɪə*] *vi*: **to ~ about** sich erkundigen nach, fragen nach ♦ *vt* sich erkundigen nach, fragen nach; **to ~ when/where/whether** fragen *or* sich erkundigen, wann/wo/ob.

▸**inquire after** *vt fus* sich erkundigen nach.

▸**inquire into** *vt fus* untersuchen.

**inquiring** [ɪn'kwaɪərɪŋ] *adj* wissensdurstig.

**inquiry** [ɪn'kwaɪərɪ] *n* Untersuchung *f*;

(*question*) Anfrage *f*; **to hold an ~ into sth** eine Untersuchung +*gen* durchführen.

**inquiry desk** (*BRIT*) *n* Auskunft *f*, Auskunftsschalter *m*.

**inquiry office** (*BRIT*) *n* Auskunft *f*, Auskunftsbüro *nt*.

**inquisition** [ɪnkwɪ'zɪʃən] *n* Untersuchung *f*; (*REL*): **the I~** die Inquisition.

**inquisitive** [ɪn'kwɪzɪtɪv] *adj* neugierig.

**inroads** ['ɪnrəudz] *npl*: **to make ~ into** (*savings, supplies*) angreifen.

**ins** *abbr* (= *inches*) *see* **inch**.

**insane** [ɪn'seɪn] *adj* wahnsinnig; (*MED*) geisteskrank.

**insanitary** [ɪn'sænɪtərɪ] *adj* unhygienisch.

**insanity** [ɪn'sænɪtɪ] *n* Wahnsinn *m*; (*MED*) Geisteskrankheit *f*.

**insatiable** [ɪn'seɪʃəbl] *adj* unersättlich.

**inscribe** [ɪn'skraɪb] *vt* (*on ring*) eingravieren; (*on stone*) einmeißeln; (*on banner*) schreiben; **to ~ a ring/stone/banner with sth** etw in einen Ring eingravieren/in einen Stein einmeißeln/auf ein Spruchband schreiben; **to ~ a book** eine Widmung in ein Buch schreiben.

**inscription** [ɪn'skrɪpʃən] *n* Inschrift *f*; (*in book*) Widmung *f*.

**inscrutable** [ɪn'skruːtəbl] *adj* (*comment*) unergründlich; (*expression*) undurchdringlich.

**inseam measurement** ['ɪnsiːm-] (*US*) *n* innere Beinlänge *f*.

**insect** ['ɪnsɛkt] *n* Insekt *nt*.

**insect bite** *n* Insektenstich *m*.

**insecticide** [ɪn'sɛktɪsaɪd] *n* Insektizid *nt*, Insektengift *nt*.

**insect repellent** *n* Insektenbekämpfungsmittel *nt*.

**insecure** [ɪnsɪ'kjuə*] *adj* unsicher.

**insecurity** [ɪnsɪ'kjuərɪtɪ] *n* Unsicherheit *f*.

**insemination** [ɪnsɛmɪ'neɪʃən] *n*: **artificial ~** künstliche Besamung *f*.

**insensible** [ɪn'sɛnsɪbl] *adj* bewußtlos; **~ to** unempfindlich gegen; **~ of** nicht bewußt +*gen*.

**insensitive** [ɪn'sɛnsɪtɪv] *adj* gefühllos.

**insensitivity** [ɪnsɛnsɪ'tɪvɪtɪ] *n* Gefühllosigkeit *f*.

**inseparable** [ɪn'sɛprəbl] *adj* untrennbar; (*friends*) unzertrennlich.

**insert** [*vt* ɪn'sɔːt, *n* 'ɪnsɔːt] *vt* einfügen; (*into sth*) hineinstecken ♦ *n* (*in newspaper etc*) Beilage *f*; (*in shoe*) Einlage *f*.

**insertion** [ɪn'sɔːʃən] *n* Hineinstecken *nt*; (*of needle*) Einstechen *nt*; (*of comment*) Einfügen *nt*.

**in-service** ['ɪn'sɔːvɪs] *adj*: **~ training** (berufsbegleitende) Fortbildung *f*; **~ course** Fortbildungslehrgang *m*.

**inshore** ['ɪn'ʃɔː*] *adj* (*fishing, waters*) Küsten- ♦ *adv* in Küstennähe; (*move*) auf die Küste zu.

**inside** ['ɪn'saɪd] n Innere(s) nt, Innenseite f; (of road: BRIT) linke Spur f; (: US, Europe etc) rechte Spur f ♦ adj innere(r, s); (pocket, cabin, light) Innen- ♦ adv (go) nach innen, hinein; (be) drinnen ♦ prep (location) in +dat; (motion) in +acc; ~ **10 minutes** innerhalb von 10 Minuten; **insides** npl (inf) Bauch m; (innards) Eingeweide pl.

**inside forward** n (SPORT) Halbstürmer m.

**inside information** n interne Informationen pl.

**inside lane** n (BRIT) linke Spur f; (US, Europe etc) rechte Spur f.

**inside leg measurement** (BRIT) n innere Beinlänge f.

**inside out** adv (know) in- und auswendig; (piece of clothing: be) links or verkehrt herum; (: turn) nach links.

**insider** [ɪn'saɪdə*] n Insider m, Eingeweihte(r) f(m).

**insider dealing** n (STOCK EXCHANGE) Insiderhandel m.

**insider trading** n = **insider dealing**.

**inside story** n Inside-Story f.

**insidious** [ɪn'sɪdɪəs] adj heimtückisch.

**insight** ['ɪnsaɪt] n Verständnis nt; **to gain (an)** ~ **into** einen Einblick gewinnen in +acc.

**insignia** [ɪn'sɪgnɪə] npl Insignien pl.

**insignificant** [ɪnsɪg'nɪfɪknt] adj belanglos.

**insincere** [ɪnsɪn'sɪə*] adj unaufrichtig, falsch.

**insincerity** [ɪnsɪn'serɪtɪ] n Unaufrichtigkeit f, Falschheit f.

**insinuate** [ɪn'sɪnjueɪt] vt anspielen auf +acc.

**insinuation** [ɪnsɪnju'eɪʃən] n Anspielung f.

**insipid** [ɪn'sɪpɪd] adj fad(e); (person) geistlos; (colour) langweilig.

**insist** [ɪn'sɪst] vi bestehen; **to** ~ **on** bestehen auf +dat; **to** ~ **that** darauf bestehen, daß; (claim) behaupten, daß.

**insistence** [ɪn'sɪstəns] n (determination) Bestehen nt.

**insistent** [ɪn'sɪstənt] adj (determined) hartnäckig; (continual) andauernd, penetrant (pej).

**in so far as** adv insofern als.

**insole** ['ɪnsəul] n Einlegesohle f.

**insolence** ['ɪnsələns] n Frechheit f, Unverschämtheit f.

**insolent** ['ɪnsələnt] adj frech, unverschämt.

**insoluble** [ɪn'sɒljubl] adj unlösbar.

**insolvency** [ɪn'sɒlvənsɪ] n Zahlungsunfähigkeit f.

**insolvent** [ɪn'sɒlvənt] adj zahlungsunfähig.

**insomnia** [ɪn'sɒmnɪə] n Schlaflosigkeit f.

**insomniac** [ɪn'sɒmnɪæk] n: **to be an** ~ an Schlaflosigkeit leiden.

**inspect** [ɪn'spɛkt] vt kontrollieren; (examine) prüfen; (troops) inspizieren.

**inspection** [ɪn'spɛkʃən] n (see vb) Kontrolle f; Prüfung f; Inspektion f.

**inspector** [ɪn'spɛktə*] n Inspektor(in) m(f); (BRIT: on buses, trains) Kontrolleur(in) m(f); (: POLICE) Kommissar(in) m(f).

**inspiration** [ɪnspə'reɪʃən] n Inspiration f; (idea) Eingebung f.

**inspire** [ɪn'spaɪə*] vt inspirieren; (confidence, hope etc) (er)wecken.

**inspired** [ɪn'spaɪəd] adj genial; **in an** ~ **moment** in einem Augenblick der Inspiration.

**inspiring** [ɪn'spaɪərɪŋ] adj inspirierend.

**inst.** (BRIT) abbr (COMM: = instant): **of the 16th** ~ vom 16. d.M.

**instability** [ɪnstə'bɪlɪtɪ] n Instabilität f; (of person) Labilität f.

**install** [ɪn'stɔ:l] vt installieren; (telephone) anschließen; (official) einsetzen; **to** ~ **o.s.** sich niederlassen.

**installation** [ɪnstə'leɪʃən] n Installation f; (of telephone) Anschluß m; (INDUSTRY, MIL: plant) Anlage f.

**installment plan** (US) n Ratenzahlung f.

**instalment**, (US) **installment** [ɪn'stɔ:lmənt] n Rate f; (of story) Fortsetzung f; (of TV serial etc) (Sende)folge f; **in** ~**s** in Raten.

**instance** ['ɪnstəns] n Beispiel nt; **for** ~ zum Beispiel; **in that** ~ in diesem Fall; **in many** ~**s** in vielen Fällen; **in the first** ~ zuerst or zunächst (einmal).

**instant** ['ɪnstənt] n Augenblick m ♦ adj (reaction) unmittelbar; (success) sofortig; ~ **food** Schnellgerichte pl; ~ **coffee** Instantkaffee m; **the 10th** ~ (COMM, ADMIN) der 10. dieses Monats.

**instantaneous** [ɪnstən'teɪnɪəs] adj unmittelbar.

**instantly** ['ɪnstəntlɪ] adv sofort.

**instant replay** n (TV) Wiederholung f.

**instead** [ɪn'stɛd] adv statt dessen; ~ **of** +gen; ~ **of sb** an jds Stelle dat; ~ **of doing sth** anstatt or anstelle etw zu tun.

**instep** ['ɪnstɛp] n (of foot) Spann m; (of shoe) Blatt nt.

**instigate** ['ɪnstɪgeɪt] vt anstiften, anzetteln; (talks etc) initiieren.

**instigation** [ɪnstɪ'geɪʃən] n (see vb) Anstiftung f, Anzettelung f; Initiierung f; **at sb's** ~ auf jds Betreiben acc.

**instil** [ɪn'stɪl] vt: **to** ~ **sth into sb** (confidence, fear etc) jdm etw einflößen.

**instinct** ['ɪnstɪŋkt] n Instinkt m; (reaction, inclination) instinktive Reaktion f.

**instinctive** [ɪn'stɪŋktɪv] adj instinktiv.

**instinctively** [ɪn'stɪŋktɪvlɪ] adv instinktiv.

**institute** ['ɪnstɪtjuːt] n Institut nt; (for teaching) Hochschule f; (professional body) Bund m, Verband m ♦ vt einführen; (inquiry, course of action) einleiten; (proceedings) anstrengen.

**institution** [ɪnstɪ'tjuːʃən] n Einführung f; (organization) Institution f, Einrichtung f; (hospital, mental home) Anstalt f, Heim nt.

**institutional** [ɪnstɪ'tjuːʃənl] adj (education) institutionell; (value, quality etc) institutionalisiert; ~ **care** Unterbringung in einem Heim or einer Anstalt; **to be in ~ care** in einem Heim or einer Anstalt sein.

**instruct** [in'strʌkt] vt: **to ~ sb in sth** jdn in etw dat unterrichten; **to ~ sb to do sth** jdn anweisen, etw zu tun.

**instruction** [in'strʌkʃən] n Unterricht m; **instructions** npl (orders) Anweisungen pl; **~s (for use)** Gebrauchsanweisung f, Gebrauchsanleitung f; **~ book/manual/leaflet** etc Bedienungsanleitung f.

**instructive** [in'strʌktiv] adj lehrreich; (response) aufschlußreich.

**instructor** [in'strʌktə*] n Lehrer(in) m(f).

**instrument** ['instrumənt] n Instrument nt; (MUS) (Musik)instrument nt.

**instrumental** [instru'mentl] adj (MUS: music, accompaniment) Instrumental-; **to be ~ in** eine bedeutende Rolle spielen bei.

**instrumentalist** [instru'mentəlist] n Instrumentalist(in) m(f).

**instrument panel** n Armaturenbrett nt.

**insubordination** [insəbɔːdi'neiʃən] n Gehorsamsverweigerung f.

**insufferable** [in'sʌfrəbl] adj unerträglich.

**insufficient** [insə'fiʃənt] adj unzureichend.

**insufficiently** [insə'fiʃəntli] adv unzureichend.

**insular** ['insjulə*] adj engstirnig.

**insulate** ['insjuleit] vt isolieren; (person, group) abschirmen.

**insulating tape** ['insjuleitiŋ-] n Isolierband nt.

**insulation** [insju'leiʃən] n (see vb) Isolierung f; Abschirmung f.

**insulator** ['insjuleitə*] n Isolierstoff m.

**insulin** ['insjulin] n Insulin nt.

**insult** [n 'insʌlt, vt in'sʌlt] n Beleidigung f ♦ vt beleidigen.

**insulting** [in'sʌltiŋ] adj beleidigend.

**insuperable** [in'sjuːprəbl] adj unüberwindlich.

**insurance** [in'ʃuərəns] n Versicherung f; **fire/life ~** Brand-/Lebensversicherung f; **to take out ~ (against)** eine Versicherung abschließen (gegen).

**insurance agent** n Versicherungsvertreter(in) m(f).

**insurance broker** n Versicherungsmakler(in) m(f).

**insurance policy** n Versicherungspolice f.

**insurance premium** n Versicherungsprämie f.

**insure** [in'ʃuə*] vt versichern; **to ~ o.s./sth against sth** sich/etw gegen etw versichern; **to ~ o.s. or one's life** eine Lebensversicherung abschließen; **to ~ (o.s.) against sth** (fig) sich gegen etw absichern; **to be ~d for £5,000** für £5000 versichert sein.

**insured** [in'ʃuəd] n: **the ~** der/die Versicherte.

**insurer** [in'ʃuərə*] n Versicherer m.

**insurgent** [in'sɜːdʒənt] adj aufständisch ♦ n Aufständische(r) f(m).

**insurmountable** [insə'mauntəbl] adj unüberwindlich.

**insurrection** [insə'rekʃən] n Aufstand m.

**intact** [in'tækt] adj intakt; (whole) ganz; (unharmed) unversehrt.

**intake** ['inteik] n (of food) Aufnahme f; (of air) Zufuhr f; (BRIT: SCOL): **an ~ of 200 a year** 200 neue Schüler pro Jahr.

**intangible** [in'tændʒibl] adj unbestimmbar; (idea) vage; (benefit) immateriell.

**integer** ['intidʒə*] n (MATH) ganze Zahl f.

**integral** ['intigrəl] adj wesentlich.

**integrate** ['intigreit] vt integrieren ♦ vi sich integrieren.

**integrated circuit** ['intigreitid-] n (COMPUT) integrierter Schaltkreis m.

**integration** [inti'greiʃən] n Integration f; **racial ~** Rassenintegration f.

**integrity** [in'tegriti] n Integrität f; (of group) Einheit f; (of culture, text) Unversehrtheit f.

**intellect** ['intəlekt] n Intellekt m.

**intellectual** [intə'lektjuəl] adj intellektuell, geistig ♦ n Intellektuelle(r) f(m).

**intelligence** [in'telidʒəns] n Intelligenz f; (information) Informationen pl.

**intelligence quotient** n Intelligenzquotient m.

**intelligence service** n Nachrichtendienst m, Geheimdienst m.

**intelligence test** n Intelligenztest m.

**intelligent** [in'telidʒənt] adj intelligent; (decision) klug.

**intelligently** [in'telidʒəntli] adv intelligent.

**intelligentsia** [inteli'dʒentsiə] n: **the ~** die Intelligenz.

**intelligible** [in'telidʒibl] adj verständlich.

**intemperate** [in'tempərət] adj unmäßig; (remark) überzogen.

**intend** [in'tend] vt: **to be ~ed for sb** für jdn gedacht sein; **to ~ to do sth** beabsichtigen, etw zu tun.

**intended** [in'tendid] adj (effect, victim) beabsichtigt; (journey) geplant; (insult) absichtlich.

**intense** [in'tens] adj intensiv; (anger, joy) äußerst groß; (absorbed) ernsthaft.

**intensely** [in'tensli] adv äußerst; **I dislike him ~** ich verabscheue ihn.

**intensify** [in'tensifai] vt intensivieren, verstärken.

**intensity** [in'tensiti] n Intensität f; (of anger) Heftigkeit f.

**intensive** [in'tensiv] adj intensiv.

**intensive care** n: **to be in ~** auf der Intensivstation sein.

**intensive care unit** n Intensivstation f.

**intent** [in'tent] n Absicht f ♦ adj (attentive) aufmerksam; (absorbed): **~ (on)** versunken (in +acc); **to all ~s and purposes** im Grunde; **to be ~ on doing sth** entschlossen sein, etw zu tun.

**intention** [in'tenʃən] n Absicht f.

**intentional** [in'tenʃnl] adj absichtlich.

**intentionally** [ɪn'tɛnʃnəlɪ] *adv* absichtlich.
**intently** [ɪn'tɛntlɪ] *adv* konzentriert.
**inter** [ɪn'tɜː*] *vt* bestatten.
**interact** [ɪntər'ækt] *vi* (*people*) interagieren; (*things*) aufeinander einwirken; (*ideas*) sich gegenseitig beeinflussen; **to ~ with** interagieren mit; einwirken auf +*acc*; beeinflussen.
**interaction** [ɪntər'ækʃən] *n* (*see vb*) Interaktion *f*; gegenseitige Einwirkung *f*; gegenseitige Beeinflussung *f*.
**interactive** [ɪntər'æktɪv] *adj* (*also COMPUT*) interaktiv.
**intercede** [ɪntə'siːd] *vi*: **to ~ (with sb/on behalf of sb)** sich (bei jdm/für jdn) einsetzen.
**intercept** [ɪntə'sɛpt] *vt* abfangen.
**interception** [ɪntə'sɛpʃən] *n* Abfangen *nt*.
**interchange** ['ɪntətʃeɪndʒ] *n* Austausch *m*; (*on motorway*) (Autobahn)kreuz *nt*.
**interchangeable** [ɪntə'tʃeɪndʒəbl] *adj* austauschbar.
**intercity** [ɪntə'sɪtɪ] *adj*: **~ train** Intercityzug *m*.
**intercom** ['ɪntəkəm] *n* (Gegen)sprechanlage *f*.
**interconnect** [ɪntəkə'nɛkt] *vi* (*rooms*) miteinander verbunden sein.
**intercontinental** ['ɪntəkɔntɪ'nɛntl] *adj* (*flight, missile*) Interkontinental-.
**intercourse** ['ɪntəkɔːs] *n* (*sexual*) (Geschlechts)verkehr *m*; (*social, verbal*) Verkehr *m*.
**interdependence** [ɪntədɪ'pɛndəns] *n* gegenseitige Abhängigkeit *f*.
**interdependent** [ɪntədɪ'pɛndənt] *adj* voneinander abhängig.
**interest** ['ɪntrɪst] *n* Interesse *nt*; (*COMM: in company*) Anteil *m*; (: *sum of money*) Zinsen *pl* ♦ *vt* interessieren; **compound ~** Zinseszins *m*; **simple ~** einfache Zinsen; **British ~s in the Middle East** britische Interessen im Nahen Osten; **his main ~ is ...** er interessiert sich hauptsächlich für ...
**interested** ['ɪntrɪstɪd] *adj* interessiert; (*party, body etc*) beteiligt; **to be ~ in sth** sich für etw interessieren; **to be ~ in doing sth** daran interessiert sein, etw zu tun.
**interest-free** ['ɪntrɪst'friː] *adj, adv* zinslos.
**interesting** ['ɪntrɪstɪŋ] *adj* interessant.
**interest rate** *n* Zinssatz *m*.
**interface** ['ɪntəfeɪs] *n* Verbindung *f*; (*COMPUT*) Schnittstelle *f*.
**interfere** [ɪntə'fɪə*] *vi*: **to ~ in** sich einmischen in +*acc*; **to ~ with** (*object*) sich zu schaffen machen an +*dat*; (*plans*) durchkreuzen; (*career, duty, decision*) beeinträchtigen; **don't ~** misch dich nicht ein.
**interference** [ɪntə'fɪərəns] *n* Einmischung *f*; (*RADIO, TV*) Störung *f*.
**interfering** [ɪntə'fɪərɪŋ] *adj* (*person*) sich ständig einmischend.
**interim** ['ɪntərɪm] *adj* (*agreement, government etc*) Übergangs- ♦ *n*: **in the ~** in der

Zwischenzeit.
**interim dividend** *n* (*COMM*) Abschlagsdividende *f*.
**interior** [ɪn'tɪərɪə*] *n* Innere(s) *nt*; (*decor etc*) Innenausstattung *f* ♦ *adj* Innen-.
**interior decorator** *n* Innenausstatter(in) *m(f)*.
**interior designer** *n* Innenarchitekt(in) *m(f)*.
**interjection** [ɪntə'dʒɛkʃən] *n* Einwurf *m*; (*LING*) Interjektion *f*.
**interlock** [ɪntə'lɔk] *vi* ineinandergreifen.
**interloper** ['ɪntələupə*] *n* Eindringling *m*.
**interlude** ['ɪntəluːd] *n* Unterbrechung *f*, Pause *f*; (*THEAT*) Zwischenspiel *nt*.
**intermarry** [ɪntə'mærɪ] *vi* untereinander heiraten.
**intermediary** [ɪntə'miːdɪərɪ] *n* Vermittler(in) *m(f)*.
**intermediate** [ɪntə'miːdɪət] *adj* (*stage*) Zwischen-; **an ~ student** ein fortgeschrittener Anfänger.
**interment** [ɪn'tɜːmənt] *n* Bestattung *f*.
**interminable** [ɪn'tɜːmɪnəbl] *adj* endlos.
**intermission** [ɪntə'mɪʃən] *n* Pause *f*.
**intermittent** [ɪntə'mɪtnt] *adj* (*noise*) periodisch auftretend; (*publication*) in unregelmäßigen Abständen veröffentlicht.
**intermittently** [ɪntə'mɪtntlɪ] *adv* (*see adj*) periodisch; in unregelmäßigen Abständen.
**intern** [*vt* ɪn'tɜːn, *n* 'ɪntɜːn] *vt* internieren ♦ *n* (*US*) Assistenzarzt *m*, Assistenzärztin *f*.
**internal** [ɪn'tɜːnl] *adj* innere(r, s); (*pipes*) im Haus; (*politics*) Innen-; (*dispute, reform, memo, structure etc*) intern.
**internally** [ɪn'tɜːnəlɪ] *adv*: **"not to be taken ~"** „nicht zum Einnehmen".
**Internal Revenue Service** (*US*) *n* ≈ Finanzamt *nt*.
**international** [ɪntə'næʃənl] *adj* international ♦ *n* (*BRIT: SPORT*) Länderspiel *nt*.
**International Atomic Energy Agency** *n* *Internationale Atomenergiebehörde.*
**International Chamber of Commerce** *n* Internationale Handelskammer *f*.
**International Court of Justice** *n* Internationaler Gerichtshof *m*.
**international date line** *n* Datumsgrenze *f*.
**International Labour Organization** *n* Internationale Arbeitsorganisation *f*.
**internationally** [ɪntə'næʃnəlɪ] *adv* international.
**International Monetary Fund** *n* Internationaler Währungsfonds *m*.
**international relations** *npl* zwischenstaatliche Beziehungen *pl*.
**internecine** [ɪntə'niːsaɪn] *adj* mörderisch; (*war*) Vernichtungs-.
**internee** [ɪntə'niː] *n* Internierte(r) *f(m)*.
**internment** [ɪn'tɜːnmənt] *n* Internierung *f*.
**interplay** ['ɪntəpleɪ] *n*: **~ (of** or **between)** Zusammenspiel *nt* (von).
**Interpol** ['ɪntəpɔl] *n* Interpol *f*.
**interpret** [ɪn'tɜːprɪt] *vt* auslegen,

interpretieren; (*translate*) dolmetschen ♦ *vi* dolmetschen.

**interpretation** [ɪntəːprɪ'teɪʃən] *n* (*see vb*) Auslegung *f*, Interpretation *f*; Dolmetschen *nt*.

**interpreter** [ɪn'təːprɪtə*] *n* Dolmetscher(in) *m(f)*.

**interpreting** [ɪn'təːprɪtɪŋ] *n* Dolmetschen *nt*.

**interrelated** [ɪntərɪ'leɪtɪd] *adj* zusammenhängend.

**interrogate** [ɪn'tɛrəuɡeɪt] *vt* verhören; (*witness*) vernehmen.

**interrogation** [ɪntɛrəu'ɡeɪʃən] *n* (*see vb*) Verhör *nt*; Vernehmung *f*.

**interrogative** [ɪntə'rɔɡətɪv] *adj* (*LING: pronoun*) Interrogativ-, Frage-.

**interrogator** [ɪn'tɛrəɡeɪtə*] *n* (*POLICE*) Vernehmungsbeamte(r) *m*; **the hostage's ~** derjenige, der die Geisel verhörte.

**interrupt** [ɪntə'rʌpt] *vt*, *vi* unterbrechen.

**interruption** [ɪntə'rʌpʃən] *n* Unterbrechung *f*.

**intersect** [ɪntə'sɛkt] *vi* sich kreuzen ♦ *vt* durchziehen; (*MATH*) schneiden.

**intersection** [ɪntə'sɛkʃən] *n* Kreuzung *f*; (*MATH*) Schnittpunkt *m*.

**intersperse** [ɪntə'spəːs] *vt*: **to be ~d with** durchsetzt sein mit; **he ~d his lecture with ...** er spickte seine Rede mit ...

**intertwine** [ɪntə'twaɪn] *vi* sich ineinander verschlingen.

**interval** ['ɪntəvl] *n* Pause *f*; (*MUS*) Intervall *nt*; **bright ~s** (*in weather*) Aufheiterungen *pl*; **at ~s** in Abständen.

**intervene** [ɪntə'viːn] *vi* eingreifen; (*event*) dazwischenkommen; (*time*) dazwischenliegen.

**intervening** [ɪntə'viːnɪŋ] *adj* (*period, years*) dazwischenliegend.

**intervention** [ɪntə'vɛnʃən] *n* Eingreifen *nt*.

**interview** ['ɪntəvjuː] *n* (*for job*) Vorstellungsgespräch *nt*; (*for place at college etc*) Auswahlgespräch *nt*; (*RADIO, TV etc*) Interview *nt* ♦ *vt* (*see n*) ein Vorstellungsgespräch/Auswahlgespräch führen mit; interviewen.

**interviewee** [ɪntəvjuˈiː] *n* (*for job*) Stellenbewerber(in) *m(f)*; (*TV etc*) Interviewgast *m*.

**interviewer** ['ɪntəvjuə*] *n* Leiter(in) *m(f)* des Vorstellungsgesprächs/Auswahlgesprächs; (*RADIO, TV etc*) Interviewer(in) *m(f)*.

**intestate** [ɪn'tɛsteɪt] *adv*: **to die ~** ohne Testament sterben.

**intestinal** [ɪn'tɛstɪnl] *adj* (*infection etc*) Darm-.

**intestine** [ɪn'tɛstɪn] *n* Darm *m*.

**intimacy** ['ɪntɪməsɪ] *n* Vertrautheit *f*.

**intimate** [*adj* 'ɪntɪmət, *vt* 'ɪntɪmeɪt] *adj* eng; (*sexual, also friend, dinner, atmosphere*) intim; (*conversation, matter, detail*) vertraulich; (*knowledge*) gründlich ♦ *vt* andeuten; (*make known*) zu verstehen geben.

**intimately** ['ɪntɪmətlɪ] *adv* (*see adj*) eng; intim; vertraulich; gründlich.

**intimation** [ɪntɪ'meɪʃən] *n* Andeutung *f*.

**intimidate** [ɪn'tɪmɪdeɪt] *vt* einschüchtern.

**intimidation** [ɪntɪmɪ'deɪʃən] *n* Einschüchterung *f*.

═══════════════════════════ KEYWORD

**into** ['ɪntu] *prep* **1** (*indicating motion or direction*) in +*acc*; **to go ~ town** in die Stadt gehen; **he worked late ~ the night** er arbeitete bis spät in die Nacht; **the car bumped ~ the wall** der Wagen fuhr gegen die Mauer **2** (*indicating change of condition, result*): **it broke ~ pieces** es zerbrach in Stücke; **she translated ~ English** sie übersetzte ins Englische; **to change pounds ~ dollars** Pfund in Dollar wechseln; **5 ~ 25** 25 durch 5

**intolerable** [ɪn'tɔlərəbl] *adj* unerträglich.

**intolerance** [ɪn'tɔlərns] *n* Intoleranz *f*.

**intolerant** [ɪn'tɔlərnt] *adj*: **~ (of)** intolerant (gegenüber).

**intonation** [ɪntəu'neɪʃən] *n* Intonation *f*.

**intoxicated** [ɪn'tɔksɪkeɪtɪd] *adj* betrunken; (*fig*) berauscht.

**intoxication** [ɪntɔksɪ'keɪʃən] *n* (Be)trunkenheit *f*; (*fig*) Rausch *m*.

**intractable** [ɪn'træktəbl] *adj* hartnäckig; (*child*) widerspenstig; (*temper*) unbeugsam.

**intransigence** [ɪn'trænsɪdʒəns] *n* Unnachgiebigkeit *f*.

**intransigent** [ɪn'trænsɪdʒənt] *adj* unnachgiebig.

**intransitive** [ɪn'trænsɪtɪv] *adj* (*LING*) intransitiv.

**intrauterine device** ['ɪntrə'juːtəraɪn-] *n* (*MED*) Intrauterinpessar *nt*, Spirale *f* (*inf*).

**intravenous** [ɪntrə'viːnəs] *adj* intravenös.

**in-tray** ['ɪntreɪ] *n* Ablage *f* für Eingänge.

**intrepid** [ɪn'trɛpɪd] *adj* unerschrocken.

**intricacy** ['ɪntrɪkəsɪ] *n* Kompliziertheit *f*.

**intricate** ['ɪntrɪkət] *adj* kompliziert.

**intrigue** [ɪn'triːɡ] *n* Intrigen *pl* ♦ *vt* faszinieren.

**intriguing** [ɪn'triːɡɪŋ] *adj* faszinierend.

**intrinsic** [ɪn'trɪnsɪk] *adj* wesentlich.

**introduce** [ɪntrə'djuːs] *vt* (*sth new*) einführen; (*speaker, TV show etc*) ankündigen; **to ~ sb (to sb)** jdn (jdm) vorstellen; **to ~ sb to** (*pastime, technique*) jdn einführen in +*acc*; **may I ~ ...?** darf ich ... vorstellen?

**introduction** [ɪntrə'dʌkʃən] *n* Einführung *f*; (*of person*) Vorstellung *f*; (*to book*) Einleitung *f*; **a letter of ~** ein Einführungsschreiben *nt*.

**introductory** [ɪntrə'dʌktərɪ] *adj* Einführungs-; **~ remarks** einführende Bemerkungen *pl*; **~ offer** Einführungsangebot *nt*.

**introspection** [ɪntrəu'spɛkʃən] *n* Selbstbeobachtung *f*, Introspektion *f*.

**introspective** [ɪntrəu'spɛktɪv] *adj* in sich

gekehrt.

**introvert** ['ɪntrəʊvɜːt] n Introvertierte(r) f(m)
♦ adj (also: ~ed) introvertiert.

**intrude** [ɪn'truːd] vi eindringen; **to ~ on**
stören; (conversation) sich einmischen in
+acc; **am I intruding?** störe ich?

**intruder** [ɪn'truːdə*] n Eindringling m.

**intrusion** [ɪn'truːʒən] n Eindringen nt.

**intrusive** [ɪn'truːsɪv] adj aufdringlich.

**intuition** [ɪntjuːˈɪʃən] n Intuition f.

**intuitive** [ɪn'tjuːɪtɪv] adj intuitiv; (feeling)
instinktiv.

**inundate** ['ɪnʌndeɪt] vt: **to ~ with**
überschwemmen mit.

**inure** [ɪn'jʊə*] vt: **to ~ o.s. to** sich gewöhnen
an +acc.

**invade** [ɪn'veɪd] vt einfallen in +acc; (fig)
heimsuchen.

**invader** [ɪn'veɪdə*] n Invasor m.

**invalid** [n 'ɪnvəlɪd, adj ɪn'vælɪd] n Kranke(r)
f(m); (disabled) Invalide m ♦ adj ungültig.

**invalidate** [ɪn'vælɪdeɪt] vt entkräften; (law,
marriage, election) ungültig machen.

**invaluable** [ɪn'væljuəbl] adj unschätzbar.

**invariable** [ɪn'vɛəriəbl] adj unveränderlich.

**invariably** [ɪn'vɛəriəblɪ] adv ständig,
unweigerlich; **she is ~ late** sie kommt
immer zu spät.

**invasion** [ɪn'veɪʒən] n Invasion f; **an ~ of
privacy** ein Eingriff m in die Privatsphäre.

**invective** [ɪn'vɛktɪv] n Beschimpfungen pl.

**inveigle** [ɪn'viːgl] vt: **to ~ sb into sth/doing sth**
jdn zu etw verleiten/dazu verleiten, etw zu
tun.

**invent** [ɪn'vɛnt] vt erfinden.

**invention** [ɪn'vɛnʃən] n Erfindung f.

**inventive** [ɪn'vɛntɪv] adj erfinderisch.

**inventiveness** [ɪn'vɛntɪvnɪs] n
Einfallsreichtum m.

**inventor** [ɪn'vɛntə*] n Erfinder(in) m(f).

**inventory** ['ɪnvəntrɪ] n Inventar nt,
Bestandsverzeichnis nt.

**inventory control** n (COMM)
Bestandskontrolle f.

**inverse** [ɪn'vɜːs] adj umgekehrt; **in
~ proportion (to)** im umgekehrten
Verhältnis (zu).

**invert** [ɪn'vɜːt] vt umdrehen.

**invertebrate** [ɪn'vɜːtɪbrət] n wirbelloses Tier
nt.

**inverted commas** [ɪn'vɜːtɪd-] (BRIT) npl
Anführungszeichen pl.

**invest** [ɪn'vɛst] vt investieren ♦ vi: **~ in**
investieren in +acc; (fig) sich dat anschaffen;
**to ~ sb with sth** jdm etw verleihen.

**investigate** [ɪn'vɛstɪgeɪt] vt untersuchen.

**investigation** [ɪnvɛstɪ'geɪʃən] n
Untersuchung f.

**investigative** [ɪn'vɛstɪgeɪtɪv] adj: **~ journalism**
Enthüllungsjournalismus m.

**investigator** [ɪn'vɛstɪgeɪtə*] n Ermittler(in)
m(f); **private ~** Privatdetektiv(in) m(f).

**investiture** [ɪn'vɛstɪtʃə*] n (of chancellor)
Amtseinführung f; (of prince) Investitur f.

**investment** [ɪn'vɛstmənt] n Investition f.

**investment income** n Kapitalerträge pl.

**investment trust** n Investmenttrust m.

**investor** [ɪn'vɛstə*] n (Kapital)anleger(in) m(f).

**inveterate** [ɪn'vɛtərət] adj unverbesserlich.

**invidious** [ɪn'vɪdɪəs] adj (task, job)
unangenehm; (comparison, decision)
ungerecht.

**invigilator** [ɪn'vɪdʒɪleɪtə*] n Aufsicht f.

**invigorating** [ɪn'vɪgəreɪtɪŋ] adj belebend;
(experience etc) anregend.

**invincible** [ɪn'vɪnsɪbl] adj unbesiegbar; (belief,
conviction) unerschütterlich.

**inviolate** [ɪn'vaɪələt] adj sicher; (truth)
unantastbar.

**invisible** [ɪn'vɪzɪbl] adj unsichtbar.

**invisible mending** n Kunststopfen nt.

**invitation** [ɪnvɪ'teɪʃən] n Einladung f; **by
~ only** nur auf Einladung; **at sb's ~** auf jds
Aufforderung acc (hin).

**invite** [ɪn'vaɪt] vt einladen; (discussion)
auffordern zu; (criticism) herausfordern; **to
~ sb to do sth** jdn auffordern, etw zu tun;
**to ~ sb to dinner** jdn zum Abendessen
einladen.

▶**invite out** vt einladen.

**inviting** [ɪn'vaɪtɪŋ] adj einladend; (desirable)
verlockend.

**invoice** ['ɪnvɔɪs] n Rechnung f ♦ vt in
Rechnung stellen; **to ~ sb for goods** jdm
für Waren eine Rechnung ausstellen.

**invoke** [ɪn'vəʊk] vt anrufen; (feelings,
memories etc) heraufbeschwören.

**involuntary** [ɪn'vɒləntrɪ] adj unbeabsichtigt;
(reflex) unwillkürlich.

**involve** [ɪn'vɒlv] vt (person) beteiligen; (thing)
verbunden sein mit; (concern, affect)
betreffen; **to ~ sb in sth** jdn in etw acc
verwickeln.

**involved** [ɪn'vɒlvd] adj kompliziert; **the work/
problems ~** die damit verbundene Arbeit/
verbundenen Schwierigkeiten; **to be ~ in**
beteiligt sein an +dat; (be engrossed)
engagiert sein in +dat; **to become ~ with sb**
Umgang mit jdm haben; (emotionally) mit
jdm eine Beziehung anfangen.

**involvement** [ɪn'vɒlvmənt] n Engagement nt;
(participation) Beteiligung f.

**invulnerable** [ɪn'vʌlnərəbl] adj unverwundbar;
(ship, building etc) uneinnehmbar.

**inward** ['ɪnwəd] adj innerste(r, s); (movement)
nach innen ♦ adv nach innen.

**inwardly** ['ɪnwədlɪ] adv innerlich.

**inwards** ['ɪnwədz] adv nach innen.

**I/O** abbr (COMPUT: = input/output) E/A.

**IOC** n abbr (= International Olympic Committee)
IOC nt, IOK nt.

**iodine** ['aɪəʊdiːn] n Jod nt.

**IOM** (BRIT) abbr (POST: = Isle of Man).

**ion** ['aɪən] n Ion nt.

**Ionian Sea** [aɪˈəʊnɪən-] *n*: **the ~** das Ionische Meer.

**ionizer** [ˈaɪənaɪzə*] *n* Ionisator *m*.

**iota** [aɪˈəʊtə] *n* Jota *nt*.

**IOU** *n abbr* (= *I owe you*) Schuldschein *m*.

**IOW** (*BRIT*) *abbr* (*POST*: = *Isle of Wight*).

**IPA** *n abbr* (= *International Phonetic Alphabet*) internationale Lautschrift *f*.

**IQ** *n abbr* (= *intelligence quotient*) IQ *m*.

**IRA** *n abbr* (= *Irish Republican Army*) IRA *f*; (*US*: = *individual retirement account*) *privates Rentensparkonto*.

**Iran** [ɪˈrɑːn] *n* (der) Iran.

**Iranian** [ɪˈreɪnɪən] *adj* iranisch ♦ *n* Iraner(in) *m(f)*; (*LING*) Iranisch *nt*.

**Iraq** [ɪˈrɑːk] *n* (der) Irak.

**Iraqi** [ɪˈrɑːkɪ] *adj* irakisch ♦ *n* Iraker(in) *m(f)*.

**irascible** [ɪˈræsɪbl] *adj* jähzornig.

**irate** [aɪˈreɪt] *adj* zornig.

**Ireland** [ˈaɪələnd] *n* Irland *nt*; **the Republic of ~** die Republik Irland.

**iris** [ˈaɪrɪs] (*pl* ~**es**) *n* (*ANAT*) Iris *f*, Regenbogenhaut *f*; (*BOT*) Iris, Schwertlilie *f*.

**Irish** [ˈaɪrɪʃ] *adj* irisch ♦ *npl*: **the ~** die Iren *pl*, die Irländer *pl*.

**Irishman** [ˈaɪrɪʃmən] (*irreg: like* **man**) *n* Ire *m*, Irländer *m*.

**Irish Sea** *n*: **the ~** die Irische See.

**Irishwoman** [ˈaɪrɪʃwʊmən] (*irreg: like* **woman**) *n* Irin *f*, Irländerin *f*.

**irk** [ɜːk] *vt* ärgern.

**irksome** [ˈɜːksəm] *adj* lästig.

**IRN** *n abbr* (= *Independent Radio News*) *Nachrichtendienst des kommerziellen Rundfunks*.

**iron** [ˈaɪən] *n* Eisen *nt*; (*for clothes*) Bügeleisen *nt* ♦ *cpd* Eisen-; (*will, discipline etc*) eisern ♦ *vt* bügeln.

▶**iron out** *vt* (*fig: problems*) aus dem Weg räumen.

**Iron Curtain** *n* (*POL*): **the ~** der Eiserne Vorhang.

**iron foundry** *n* (Eisen)gießerei *f*.

**ironic(al)** [aɪˈrɒnɪk(l)] *adj* ironisch; (*situation*) paradox, witzig.

**ironically** [aɪˈrɒnɪklɪ] *adv* ironisch; **~, the intelligence chief was the last to find out** witzigerweise war der Geheimdienstchef der letzte, der es erfuhr.

**ironing** [ˈaɪənɪŋ] *n* Bügeln *nt*; (*clothes*) Bügelwäsche *f*.

**ironing board** *n* Bügelbrett *nt*.

**iron lung** *n* (*MED*) eiserne Lunge *f*.

**ironmonger** [ˈaɪənmʌŋɡə*] (*BRIT*) *n* Eisen- und Haushaltswarenhändler(in) *m(f)*.

**ironmonger's (shop)** [ˈaɪənmʌŋɡəz-] *n* Eisen- und Haushaltswarenhandlung *f*.

**iron ore** *n* Eisenerz *nt*.

**irons** [ˈaɪəns] *npl* Hand- und Fußschellen *pl*; **to clap sb in ~** jdn in Eisen legen.

**ironworks** [ˈaɪənwɜːks] *n* Eisenhütte *f*.

**irony** [ˈaɪrənɪ] *n* Ironie *f*; **the ~ of it is that ...** das Ironische daran ist, daß ...

**irrational** [ɪˈræʃənl] *adj* irrational.

**irreconcilable** [ɪrekənˈsaɪləbl] *adj* unvereinbar.

**irredeemable** [ɪrɪˈdiːməbl] *adj* (*COMM*) nicht einlösbar; (*loan*) unkündbar; (*fault, character*) unverbesserlich.

**irrefutable** [ɪrɪˈfjuːtəbl] *adj* unwiderlegbar.

**irregular** [ɪˈreɡjulə*] *adj* unregelmäßig; (*surface*) uneben; (*behaviour*) ungehörig.

**irregularity** [ɪreɡjuˈlærɪtɪ] *n* (*see adj*) Unregelmäßigkeit *f*; Unebenheit *f*; Ungehörigkeit *f*.

**irrelevance** [ɪˈrɛləvəns] *n* Irrelevanz *f*.

**irrelevant** [ɪˈrɛləvənt] *adj* unwesentlich, irrelevant.

**irreligious** [ɪrɪˈlɪdʒəs] *adj* unreligiös.

**irreparable** [ɪˈrɛprəbl] *adj* nicht wiedergutzumachen.

**irreplaceable** [ɪrɪˈpleɪsəbl] *adj* unersetzlich.

**irrepressible** [ɪrɪˈpresəbl] *adj* (*good humour*) unerschütterlich; (*enthusiasm etc*) unbändig; (*person*) nicht unterzukriegen.

**irreproachable** [ɪrɪˈprəʊtʃəbl] *adj* untadelig.

**irresistible** [ɪrɪˈzɪstɪbl] *adj* unwiderstehlich.

**irresolute** [ɪˈrɛzəluːt] *adj* unentschlossen.

**irrespective** [ɪrɪˈspɛktɪv]: **~ of** *prep* ungeachtet +*gen*.

**irresponsible** [ɪrɪˈspɒnsɪbl] *adj* verantwortungslos; (*action*) unverantwortlich.

**irretrievable** [ɪrɪˈtriːvəbl] *adj* (*object*) nicht mehr wiederzubekommen; (*loss*) unersetzlich; (*damage*) nicht wiedergutzumachen.

**irreverent** [ɪˈrɛvərənt] *adj* respektlos.

**irrevocable** [ɪˈrɛvəkəbl] *adj* unwiderruflich.

**irrigate** [ˈɪrɪɡeɪt] *vt* bewässern.

**irrigation** [ɪrɪˈɡeɪʃən] *n* Bewässerung *f*.

**irritable** [ˈɪrɪtəbl] *adj* reizbar.

**irritant** [ˈɪrɪtənt] *n* Reizerreger *m*; (*situation etc*) Ärgernis *nt*.

**irritate** [ˈɪrɪteɪt] *vt* ärgern, irritieren; (*MED*) reizen.

**irritating** [ˈɪrɪteɪtɪŋ] *adj* ärgerlich, irritierend; **he is ~** er kann einem auf die Nerven gehen.

**irritation** [ɪrɪˈteɪʃən] *n* Ärger *m*; (*MED*) Reizung *f*; (*annoying thing*) Ärgernis *nt*.

**IRS** (*US*) *n abbr* (= *Internal Revenue Service*) *Steuereinzugsbehörde*.

**is** [ɪz] *vb see* **be**.

**ISBN** *n abbr* (= *International Standard Book Number*) ISBN *f*.

**Islam** [ˈɪzlɑːm] *n* der Islam; (*Islamic countries*) die islamischen Länder *pl*.

**Islamic** [ɪzˈlæmɪk] *adj* islamisch.

**island** [ˈaɪlənd] *n* Insel *f*; (*also*: **traffic ~**) Verkehrsinsel *f*.

**islander** [ˈaɪləndə*] *n* Inselbewohner(in) *m(f)*.

**isle** [aɪl] *n* Insel *f*.

**isn't** [ˈɪznt] = **is not**.

**isobar** [ˈaɪsəʊbɑː*] *n* Isobare *f*.

**isolate** ['aısəleıt] vt isolieren.
**isolated** ['aısəleıtıd] adj isoliert; (place)
   abgelegen; ~ **incident** Einzelfall m.
**isolation** [aısə'leıʃən] n Isolierung f.
**isolationism** [aısə'leıʃənızəm] n
   Isolationismus m.
**isotope** ['aısəutəup] n Isotop nt.
**Israel** ['ızreıl] n Israel nt.
**Israeli** [ız'reılı] adj israelisch ♦ n Israeli mf.
**issue** ['ıʃjuː] n Frage f; (subject) Thema nt;
   (problem) Problem nt; (of book, stamps etc)
   Ausgabe f; (offspring) Nachkommenschaft f
   ♦ vt ausgeben; (statement) herausgeben;
   (documents) ausstellen ♦ vi: **to ~ (from)**
   dringen (aus); (liquid) austreten (aus); **the
   point at ~** der Punkt, um den es geht; **to
   avoid the ~** ausweichen; **to confuse** or
   **obscure the ~** es unnötig kompliziert
   machen; **to ~ sth to sb** or **~ sb with sth** jdm
   etw geben; (documents) jdm etw ausstellen;
   (gun etc) jdn mit etw ausstatten; **to take
   ~ with sb (over)** jdm widersprechen (in
   +dat); **to make an ~ of sth** etw aufbauschen.
**Istanbul** [ıstæn'buːl] n Istanbul nt.
**isthmus** ['ısməs] n Landenge f, Isthmus m.
**IT** n abbr = **information technology**.

═══════════════════════════════ *KEYWORD*

**it** [ıt] pron **1** (specific: subject) er/sie/es; (: direct
object) ihn/sie/es; (: indirect object) ihm/ihr/
ihm; **it's on the table** es ist auf dem Tisch; **I
can't find ~** ich kann es nicht finden; **give
~ to me** gib es mir; **about ~** darüber; **from
~ davon; in ~ darin; of ~ davon; what did
you learn from ~?** was hast du daraus
gelernt?; **I'm proud of ~** ich bin stolz darauf
**2** (impersonal) es; **it's raining** es regnet; **it's
Friday tomorrow** morgen ist Freitag; **who is
~? - it's me** wer ist da? - ich bin's.

**ITA,** (BRIT) **i.t.a.** n abbr (= initial teaching
   alphabet) Alphabet zum Lesenlernen.
**Italian** [ı'tæljən] adj italienisch ♦ n
   Italiener(in) m(f); (LING) Italienisch nt; **the
   ~s** die Italiener pl.
**italics** [ı'tælıks] npl Kursivschrift f.
**Italy** ['ıtəlı] n Italien nt.
**ITC** (BRIT) n abbr (= Independent Television
   Commission) Fernseh-Aufsichtsgremium.
**itch** [ıtʃ] n Juckreiz m ♦ vi jucken; **I am ~ing
   all over** mich juckt es überall; **to ~ to do sth**
   darauf brennen, etw zu tun.
**itchy** ['ıtʃı] adj juckend; **my back is ~** mein
   Rücken juckt.
**it'd** ['ıtd] = **it would; it had.**
**item** ['aıtəm] n Punkt m; (of collection) Stück nt;
   (also: **news ~**) Meldung f; (: in newspaper)
   Zeitungsnotiz f; **~s of clothing**
   Kleidungsstücke pl.
**itemize** ['aıtəmaız] vt einzeln aufführen.
**itemized bill** ['aıtəmaızd-] n Rechnung, auf
   der die Posten einzeln aufgeführt sind.

**itinerant** [ı'tınərənt] adj (labourer, priest etc)
   Wander-; (salesman) reisend.
**itinerary** [aı'tınərərı] n Reiseroute f.
**it'll** ['ıtl] = **it will; it shall.**
**ITN** (BRIT) n abbr (TV: = Independent Television
   News) Nachrichtendienst des
   kommerziellen Fernsehens.
**its** [ıts] adj sein(e), ihr(e) ♦ pron seine(r, s),
   ihre(r, s).
**it's** [ıts] = **it is; it has.**
**itself** [ıt'sɛlf] pron sich; (emphatic) selbst.
**ITV** (BRIT) n abbr (TV: = Independent Television)
   kommerzieller Fernsehsender.

> **ITV** steht für Independent Television und ist
> ein landesweiter privater Fernsehsender in
> Großbritannien. Unter der Oberaufsicht einer
> unabhängigen Rundfunkbehörde produzieren
> Privatfirmen die Programme für die
> verschiedenen Sendegebiete. ITV, das seit
> 1955 Programme ausstrahlt, wird ganz durch
> Werbung finanziert und bietet etwa ein Drittel
> Informationssendungen (Nachrichten,
> Dokumentarfilme, Aktuelles) und ansonsten
> Unterhaltung (Sport, Komödien, Drama,
> Spielshows, Filme).

**IUD** n abbr = **intrauterine device.**
**I've** [aıv] = **I have.**
**ivory** ['aıvərı] n Elfenbein nt.
**Ivory Coast** n Elfenbeinküste f.
**ivory tower** n (fig) Elfenbeinturm m.
**ivy** ['aıvı] n Efeu m.
**Ivy League** (US) n Eliteuniversitäten der
   USA.

> Als **Ivy League** bezeichnet man die acht
> renommiertesten Universitäten im Nordosten
> der Vereinigten Staaten (Brown, Columbia,
> Cornell, Dartmouth College, Harvard,
> Princeton, University of Pennsylvania, Yale),
> die untereinander Sportwettkämpfe austragen.
> Der Name bezieht sich auf die
> efeubewachsenen Mauern der
> Universitätsgebäude.

# J, j

**J, j** [dʒeɪ] n (letter) J nt, j nt; ~ **for Jack**, (US) ~ **for Jig** ≈ J wie Julius.
**JA** n abbr = **judge advocate; joint account.**
**J/A** abbr = **joint account.**
**jab** [dʒæb] vt stoßen; (with finger, needle) stechen ♦ n (inf) Spritze f ♦ vi: **to** ~ **at** einstechen auf +acc; **to** ~ **sth into sth** etw in etw acc stoßen/stechen.
**jack** [dʒæk] n (AUT) Wagenheber m; (BOWLS) Zielkugel f; (CARDS) Bube m.
►**jack in** (inf) vt aufgeben.
►**jack up** vt (AUT) aufbocken.
**jackal** ['dʒækl] n Schakal m.
**jackass** ['dʒækæs] (inf) n (person) Esel m.
**jackdaw** ['dʒækdɔː] n Dohle f.
**jacket** ['dʒækɪt] n Jackett nt; (of book) Schutzumschlag m; **potatoes in their** ~**s,** ~ **potatoes** in der Schale gebackene Kartoffeln pl.
**jack-in-the-box** ['dʒækɪndəbɔks] n Schachtelteufel m, Kastenteufel m.
**jack-knife** ['dʒæknaɪf] n Klappmesser nt ♦ vi: **the lorry** ~**d** der Anhänger (des Lastwagens) hat sich quergestellt.
**jack-of-all-trades** ['dʒækəvˈɔːltreɪdz] n Alleskönner m.
**jack plug** n Bananenstecker m.
**jackpot** ['dʒækpɔt] n Hauptgewinn m; **to hit the** ~ (fig) das große Los ziehen.
**jacuzzi** [dʒəˈkuːzɪ] n Whirlpool m.
**jade** [dʒeɪd] n Jade m or f.
**jaded** ['dʒeɪdɪd] adj abgespannt; **to get** ~ die Nase voll haben.
**JAG** n abbr = **Judge Advocate General.**
**jagged** ['dʒægɪd] adj gezackt.
**jaguar** ['dʒægjuə] n Jaguar m.
**jail** [dʒeɪl] n Gefängnis nt ♦ vt einsperren.
**jailbird** ['dʒeɪlbɜːd] n Knastbruder m (inf).
**jailbreak** ['dʒeɪlbreɪk] n (Gefängnis)ausbruch m.
**jalopy** [dʒəˈlɔpɪ] (inf) n alte (Klapper)kiste f or Mühle f.
**jam** [dʒæm] n Marmelade f, Konfitüre f; (also: **traffic** ~) Stau m; (inf: difficulty) Klemme f ♦ vt blockieren; (mechanism, drawer etc) verklemmen; (RADIO) stören ♦ vi klemmen; (gun) Ladehemmung haben; **I'm in a real** ~ (inf) ich stecke wirklich in der Klemme; **to get sb out of a** ~ (inf) jdm aus der Klemme helfen; **to** ~ **sth into sth** etw in etw acc stopfen; **the telephone lines are** ~**med** die Leitungen sind belegt.

**Jamaica** [dʒəˈmeɪkə] n Jamaika nt.
**Jamaican** [dʒəˈmeɪkən] adj jamaikanisch ♦ n Jamaikaner(in) m(f).
**jamb** [dʒæm] n (of door) (Tür)pfosten m; (of window) (Fenster)pfosten m.
**jamboree** [dʒæmbəˈriː] n Fest nt.
**jam-packed** [dʒæmˈpækt] adj: ~ **(with)** vollgestopft (mit).
**jam session** n (MUS) Jam Session f.
**Jan.** abbr (= January) Jan.
**jangle** ['dʒæŋgl] vi klimpern.
**janitor** ['dʒænɪtə] n Hausmeister(in) m(f).
**January** ['dʒænjuərɪ] n Januar m; see also **July.**
**Japan** [dʒəˈpæn] n Japan nt.
**Japanese** [dʒæpəˈniːz] adj japanisch ♦ n inv Japaner(in) m(f); (LING) Japanisch nt.
**jar** [dʒɑː] n Topf m, Gefäß nt; (glass) Glas nt ♦ vi (sound) gellen; (colours) nicht harmonieren, sich beißen ♦ vt erschüttern; **to** ~ **on sb** jdm auf die Nerven gehen.
**jargon** ['dʒɑːgən] n Jargon m.
**jarring** ['dʒɑːrɪŋ] adj (sound) gellend, schrill; (colour) schreiend.
**Jas.** abbr (= James).
**jasmine** ['dʒæzmɪn] n Jasmin m.
**jaundice** ['dʒɔːndɪs] n Gelbsucht f.
**jaundiced** ['dʒɔːndɪst] adj (view, attitude) zynisch.
**jaunt** [dʒɔːnt] n Spritztour f.
**jaunty** ['dʒɔːntɪ] adj munter; (step) schwungvoll.
**Java** ['dʒɑːvə] n Java nt.
**javelin** ['dʒævlɪn] n Speer m.
**jaw** [dʒɔː] n Kiefer m.
**jawbone** ['dʒɔːbəun] n Kieferknochen m.
**jay** [dʒeɪ] n Eichelhäher m.
**jaywalker** ['dʒeɪwɔːkə] n unachtsamer Fußgänger m, unachtsame Fußgängerin f.
**jazz** [dʒæz] n Jazz m.
►**jazz up** vt aufpeppen (inf).
**jazz band** n Jazzband f.
**JCB** ® n Erdräummaschine f.
**JCS** (US) n abbr (= Joint Chiefs of Staff) Stabschefs pl.
**JD** (US) n abbr (= Doctor of Laws) ≈ Dr. jur.; (= Justice Department) ≈ Justizministerium nt.
**jealous** ['dʒeləs] adj eifersüchtig; (envious) neidisch.
**jealously** ['dʒeləslɪ] adv eifersüchtig; (enviously) neidisch; (watchfully) sorgsam.
**jealousy** ['dʒeləsɪ] n Eifersucht f; (envy) Neid m.
**jeans** [dʒiːnz] npl Jeans pl.
**Jeep** ® [dʒiːp] n Jeep ® m.
**jeer** [dʒɪə] vi höhnische Bemerkungen machen; **to** ~ **at** verhöhnen.
**jeering** ['dʒɪərɪŋ] adj höhnisch; (crowd) johlend ♦ n Johlen nt.
**jeers** ['dʒɪəz] npl Buhrufe pl.
**jelly** ['dʒelɪ] n Götterspeise f; (jam) Gelee m or nt.

**jelly baby** (*BRIT*) *n* Gummibärchen *nt*.
**jellyfish** ['dʒɛlɪfɪʃ] *n* Qualle *f*.
**jeopardize** ['dʒɛpədaɪz] *vt* gefährden.
**jeopardy** ['dʒɛpədɪ] *n*: **to be in** ~ gefährdet
  sein.
**jerk** [dʒəːk] *n* Ruck *m*; (*inf: idiot*) Trottel *m* ♦ *vt*
  reißen ♦ *vi* (*vehicle*) ruckeln.
**jerkin** ['dʒəːkɪn] *n* Wams *nt*.
**jerky** ['dʒəːkɪ] *adj* ruckartig.
**jerry-built** ['dʒɛrɪbɪlt] *adj* schlampig gebaut.
**jerry can** ['dʒɛrɪ-] *n* großer Blechkanister *m*.
**Jersey** ['dʒəːzɪ] *n* Jersey *nt*.
**jersey** ['dʒəːzɪ] *n* Pullover *m*; (*fabric*) Jersey *m*.
**Jerusalem** [dʒə'ruːsləm] *n* Jerusalem *nt*.
**jest** [dʒɛst] *n* Scherz *m*.
**jester** ['dʒɛstə*] *n* Narr *m*.
**Jesus** ['dʒiːzəs] *n* Jesus *m*; ~ **Christ** Jesus
  Christus *m*.
**jet** [dʒɛt] *n* Strahl *m*; (*AVIAT*) Düsenflugzeug *nt*;
  (*MINERALOGY, JEWELLERY*) Jett *m or nt*,
  Gagat *m*.
**jet-black** ['dʒɛt'blæk] *adj* pechschwarz.
**jet engine** *n* Düsentriebwerk *nt*.
**jet lag** *n* Jet-lag *nt*.
**jet-propelled** ['dʒɛtprə'pɛld] *adj* Düsen-, mit
  Düsenantrieb.
**jetsam** ['dʒɛtsəm] *n* Strandgut *nt*; (*floating*)
  Treibgut *nt*.
**jet-setter** ['dʒɛtsɛtə*] *n*: **to be a** ~ zum Jet-Set
  gehören.
**jettison** ['dʒɛtɪsn] *vt* abwerfen; (*from ship*)
  über Bord werfen.
**jetty** ['dʒɛtɪ] *n* Landesteg *m*, Pier *m*.
**Jew** [dʒuː] *n* Jude *m*, Jüdin *f*.
**jewel** ['dʒuːəl] *n* Edelstein *m*, Juwel *nt* (*also
  fig*); (*in watch*) Stein *m*.
**jeweller**, (*US*) **jeweler** ['dʒuːələ*] *n* Juwelier
  *m*.
**jeweller's (shop)** *n* Juwelier *m*,
  Juweliergeschäft *nt*.
**jewellery**, (*US*) **jewelry** ['dʒuːəlrɪ] *n* Schmuck
  *m*.
**Jewess** ['dʒuːɪs] *n* Jüdin *f*.
**Jewish** ['dʒuːɪʃ] *adj* jüdisch.
**JFK** (*US*) *n abbr* (= *John Fitzgerald Kennedy
  International Airport*) John-F.-Kennedy-
  Flughafen *m*.
**jib** [dʒɪb] *n* (*NAUT*) Klüver *m*; (*of crane*)
  Ausleger *m* ♦ *vi* (*horse*) scheuen, bocken; **to**
  ~ **at doing sth** sich dagegen sträuben, etw
  zu tun.
**jibe** [dʒaɪb] *n* = **gibe**.
**jiffy** ['dʒɪfɪ] (*inf*) *n*: **in a** ~ sofort.
**jig** [dʒɪg] *n* lebhafter Volkstanz.
**jigsaw** ['dʒɪgsɔː] *n* (*also:* ~ **puzzle**)
  Puzzle(spiel) *nt*; (*tool*) Stichsäge *f*.
**jilt** [dʒɪlt] *vt* sitzenlassen.
**jingle** ['dʒɪŋgl] *n* (*tune*) Jingle *m* ♦ *vi* (*bracelets*)
  klimpern; (*bells*) bimmeln.
**jingoism** ['dʒɪŋgəʊɪzəm] *n* Hurrapatriotismus
  *m*.
**jinx** [dʒɪŋks] (*inf*) *n* Fluch *m*; **there's a** ~ **on it**

  es ist verhext.
**jitters** ['dʒɪtəz] (*inf*) *npl*: **to get the** ~ das große
  Zittern bekommen.
**jittery** ['dʒɪtərɪ] (*inf*) *adj* nervös, rappelig.
**jiujitsu** [dʒuː'dʒɪtsuː] *n* Jiu-Jitsu *nt*.
**job** [dʒɔb] *n* Arbeit *f*; (*post, employment*) Stelle
  *f*, Job *m*; **it's not my** ~ es ist nicht meine
  Aufgabe; **a part-time** ~ eine
  Teilzeitbeschäftigung; **a full-time** ~ eine
  Ganztagsstelle; **he's only doing his** ~ er tut
  nur seine Pflicht; **it's a good** ~ **that** ... nur
  gut, daß ...; **just the** ~! genau das Richtige!
**jobber** ['dʒɔbə*] (*BRIT*) *n* Börsenhändler *m*.
**jobbing** ['dʒɔbɪŋ] (*BRIT*) *adj* Gelegenheits-.
**job centre** (*BRIT*) *n* Arbeitsamt *nt*.
**job creation scheme** *n* Arbeitsbeschaffungsmaßnahmen *pl*.
**job description** *n* Tätigkeitsbeschreibung *f*.
**jobless** ['dʒɔblɪs] *adj* arbeitslos ♦ *npl*: **the** ~ die
  Arbeitslosen *pl*.
**job lot** *n* (Waren)posten *m*.
**job satisfaction** *n* Zufriedenheit *f* am
  Arbeitsplatz.
**job security** *n* Sicherheit *f* des
  Arbeitsplatzes.
**job sharing** *n* Job-sharing *nt*,
  Arbeitsplatzteilung *f*.
**job specification** *n* Tätigkeitsbeschreibung
  *f*.
**Jock** [dʒɔk] (*inf*) *n* Schotte *m*.
**jockey** ['dʒɔkɪ] *n* Jockei *m* ♦ *vi*: **to** ~ **for
  position** um eine gute Position rangeln.
**jockey box** (*US*) *n* (*AUT*) Handschuhfach *nt*.
**jocular** ['dʒɔkjʊlə*] *adj* spaßig, witzig.
**jog** [dʒɔg] *vt* (an)stoßen ♦ *vi* joggen, Dauerlauf
  machen; **to** ~ **sb's memory** jds Gedächtnis
  *dat* nachhelfen.
►**jog along** *vi* entlangzuckeln (*inf*).
**jogger** ['dʒɔgə*] *n* Jogger(in) *m(f)*.
**jogging** ['dʒɔgɪŋ] *n* Jogging *nt*, Joggen *nt*.
**john** [dʒɔn] (*US: inf*) *n* (*toilet*) Klo *nt*.
**join** [dʒɔɪn] *vt* (*club, party*) beitreten +*dat*;
  (*queue*) sich stellen in +*acc*; (*things, places*)
  verbinden; (*group of people*) sich
  anschließen +*dat* ♦ *vi* (*roads*) sich treffen;
  (*rivers*) zusammenfließen ♦ *n*
  Verbindungsstelle *f*; **to** ~ **forces (with)** (*fig*)
  sich zusammentun (mit); **will you** ~ **us for
  dinner?** wollen Sie mit uns zu Abend essen?;
  **I'll** ~ **you later** ich komme später.
►**join in** *vi* mitmachen ♦ *vt fus* sich beteiligen
  an +*dat*.
►**join up** *vi* sich treffen; (*MIL*) zum Militär
  gehen.
**joiner** ['dʒɔɪnə*] (*BRIT*) *n* Schreiner(in) *m(f)*.
**joinery** ['dʒɔɪnərɪ] (*BRIT*) *n* Schreinerei *f*.
**joint** [dʒɔɪnt] *n* (*in woodwork*) Fuge *f*; (*in pipe
  etc*) Verbindungsstelle *f*; (*ANAT*) Gelenk *nt*;
  (*BRIT: CULIN*) Braten *m*; (*inf: place*) Laden *m*;
  (: *of cannabis*) Joint *m* ♦ *adj* gemeinsam;
  (*combined*) vereint.
**joint account** *n* gemeinsames Konto *nt*.

**jointly** ['dʒɔɪntlɪ] *adv* gemeinsam.
**joint ownership** *n* Miteigentum *nt*.
**joint-stock company** ['dʒɔɪnt'stɔk-] *n* Aktiengesellschaft *f*.
**joint venture** *n* Gemeinschaftsunternehmen *nt*, Joint-venture *nt*.
**joist** [dʒɔɪst] *n* Balken *m*, Träger *m*.
**joke** [dʒəʊk] *n* Witz *m*; (*also:* **practical ~**) Streich *m* ♦ *vi* Witze machen; **to play a ~ on sb** jdm einen Streich spielen.
**joker** ['dʒəʊkə*] *n* (*CARDS*) Joker *m*.
**joking** ['dʒəʊkɪŋ] *adj* scherzhaft.
**jokingly** ['dʒəʊkɪŋlɪ] *adv* scherzhaft, im Spaß.
**jollity** ['dʒɔlɪtɪ] *n* Fröhlichkeit *f*.
**jolly** ['dʒɔlɪ] *adj* fröhlich; (*enjoyable*) lustig ♦ *adv* (*BRIT: inf: very*) ganz (schön) ♦ *vt* (*BRIT*): **to ~ sb along** jdm aufmunternd zureden; **~ good!** prima!
**jolt** [dʒəʊlt] *n* Ruck *m*; (*shock*) Schock *m* ♦ *vt* schütteln; (*subj: bus etc*) durchschütteln; (*emotionally*) aufrütteln.
**Jordan** ['dʒɔːdən] *n* Jordanien *nt*; (*river*) Jordan *m*.
**Jordanian** [dʒɔː'deɪnɪən] *adj* jordanisch ♦ *n* Jordanier(in) *m(f)*.
**joss stick** [dʒɔs-] *n* Räucherstäbchen *nt*.
**jostle** ['dʒɔsl] *vt* anrempeln ♦ *vi* drängeln.
**jot** [dʒɔt] *n:* **not one ~** kein bißchen.
▶**jot down** *vt* notieren.
**jotter** ['dʒɔtə*] (*BRIT*) *n* Notizbuch *nt*; (*pad*) Notizblock *m*.
**journal** ['dʒɜːnl] *n* Zeitschrift *f*; (*diary*) Tagebuch *nt*.
**journalese** [dʒɜːnə'liːz] (*pej*) *n* Pressejargon *m*.
**journalism** ['dʒɜːnəlɪzəm] *n* Journalismus *m*.
**journalist** ['dʒɜːnəlɪst] *n* Journalist(in) *m(f)*.
**journey** ['dʒɜːnɪ] *n* Reise *f* ♦ *vi* reisen; **a 5-hour ~** eine Fahrt von 5 Stunden; **return ~** Rückreise *f*; (*both ways*) Hin- und Rückreise *f*.
**jovial** ['dʒəʊvɪəl] *adj* fröhlich; (*atmosphere*) freundlich, herzlich.
**jowl** [dʒaʊl] *n* Backe *f*.
**joy** [dʒɔɪ] *n* Freude *f*.
**joyful** ['dʒɔɪful] *adj* freudig.
**joyride** ['dʒɔɪraɪd] *n* Spritztour in einem gestohlenen Auto.
**joyrider** ['dʒɔɪraɪdə*] *n* Autodieb, der den Wagen nur für eine Spritztour benutzt.
**joystick** ['dʒɔɪstɪk] *n* (*AVIAT*) Steuerknüppel *m*; (*COMPUT*) Joystick *m*.
**JP** *n abbr* = **Justice of the Peace.**
**Jr** *abbr* (*in names:* = *junior*) jun.
**JTPA** (*US*) *n abbr* (= *Job Training Partnership Act*) Arbeitsbeschaffungsprogramm für benachteiligte Bevölkerungsteile und Minderheiten.
**jubilant** ['dʒuːbɪlnt] *adj* überglücklich.
**jubilation** [dʒuːbɪ'leɪʃən] *n* Jubel *m*.
**jubilee** ['dʒuːbɪliː] *n* Jubiläum *nt*; **silver ~**

25jähriges Jubiläum; **golden ~** 50jähriges Jubiläum.
**judge** [dʒʌdʒ] *n* Richter(in) *m(f)*; (*in competition*) Preisrichter(in) *m(f)*; (*fig: expert*) Kenner(in) *m(f)* ♦ *vt* (*LAW: person*) die Verhandlung führen über +*acc*; (: *case*) verhandeln; (*competition*) Preisrichter(in) sein bei; (*person etc*) beurteilen; (*consider*) halten für; (*estimate*) einschätzen ♦ *vi:* **judging by** *or* **to ~ by his expression** seinem Gesichtsausdruck nach zu urteilen; **she's a good ~ of character** sie ist ein guter Menschenkenner; **I'll be the ~ of that** das müssen Sie mich schon selbst beurteilen lassen; **as far as I can ~** soweit ich es beurteilen kann; **I ~d it necessary to inform him** ich hielt es für nötig, ihn zu informieren.
**judge advocate** *n* (*MIL*) Beisitzer(in) *m(f)* bei einem Kriegsgericht.
**Judge Advocate General** *n* (*MIL*) *Vorsitzender des obersten Militärgerichts.*
**judg(e)ment** ['dʒʌdʒmənt] *n* Urteil *nt*; (*REL*) Gericht *nt*; (*view, opinion*) Meinung *f*; (*discernment*) Urteilsvermögen *nt*; **in my ~** meiner Meinung nach; **to pass ~ (on)** (*LAW*) das Urteil sprechen (über +*acc*); (*fig*) ein Urteil fällen (über +*acc*).
**judicial** [dʒuː'dɪʃl] *adj* gerichtlich, Justiz-; (*fig*) kritisch; **~ review** gerichtliche Überprüfung *f*.
**judiciary** [dʒuː'dɪʃɪərɪ] *n:* **the ~** die Gerichtsbehörden *pl*.
**judicious** [dʒuː'dɪʃəs] *adj* klug.
**judo** ['dʒuːdəʊ] *n* Judo *nt*.
**jug** [dʒʌg] *n* Krug *m*.
**jugged hare** ['dʒʌgd-] (*BRIT*) *n* ≈ Hasenpfeffer *m*.
**juggernaut** ['dʒʌgənɔːt] (*BRIT*) *n* Fernlastwagen *m*.
**juggle** ['dʒʌgl] *vi* jonglieren.
**juggler** ['dʒʌglə*] *n* Jongleur *m*.
**Jugoslav** *etc* ['juːgəʊ'slɑːv] = **Yugoslav** etc.
**jugular** ['dʒʌgjulə*] *adj:* **~ (vein)** Drosselvene *f*.
**juice** [dʒuːs] *n* Saft *m*; (*inf: petrol*): **we've run out of ~** wir haben keinen Sprit mehr.
**juicy** ['dʒuːsɪ] *adj* saftig.
**jukebox** ['dʒuːkbɔks] *n* Musikbox *f*.
**Jul.** *abbr* = **July.**
**July** [dʒuː'laɪ] *n* Juli *m*; **the first of ~** der erste Juli; **on the eleventh of ~** am elften Juli; **in the month of ~** im (Monat) Juli; **at the beginning/end of ~** Anfang/Ende Juli; **in the middle of ~** Mitte Juli; **during ~** im Juli; **in ~ of next year** im Juli nächsten Jahres; **each** *or* **every ~** jedes Jahr im Juli; **~ was wet this year** der Juli war dieses Jahr ein nasser Monat.
**jumble** ['dʒʌmbl] *n* Durcheinander *nt*; (*items for sale*) gebrauchte Sachen *pl* ♦ *vt* (*also:* **~ up**) durcheinanderbringen.

**Jumble sale** ist ein Wohltätigkeitsbasar, meist in einer Aula oder einem Gemeindehaus abgehalten, bei dem alle möglichen Gebrauchtwaren (vor allem Kleidung, Spielzeug, Bücher, Geschirr und Möbel) verkauft werden. Der Erlös fließt entweder einer Wohltätigkeitsorganisation zu oder wird für örtliche Zwecke verwendet, z.B. die Pfadfinder, die Grundschule, Reparatur der Kirche usw.

**jumbo (jet)** ['dʒʌmbəu-] n Jumbo(-Jet) m.
**jumbo-size** ['dʒʌmbəusaɪz] adj (packet etc) Riesen-.
**jump** [dʒʌmp] vi springen; (with fear, surprise) zusammenzucken; (increase) sprunghaft ansteigen ♦ vt springen über +acc ♦ n (see vb) Sprung m; Zusammenzucken nt; sprunghafter Anstieg m; **to ~ the queue** (BRIT) sich vordrängeln.
▶**jump about** vi herumspringen.
▶**jump at** vt fus (idea) sofort aufgreifen; (chance) sofort ergreifen; **he ~ed at the offer** er griff bei dem Angebot sofort zu.
▶**jump down** vi herunterspringen.
▶**jump up** vi hochspringen; (from seat) aufspringen.
**jumped-up** ['dʒʌmptʌp] (BRIT: pej) adj eingebildet.
**jumper** ['dʒʌmpə*] n (BRIT) Pullover m; (US: dress) Trägerkleid nt; (SPORT) Springer(in) m(f).
**jumper cables** (US) npl = jump leads.
**jumping jack** n Knallfrosch m.
**jump jet** n Senkrechtstarter m.
**jump leads** (BRIT) npl Starthilfekabel nt.
**jump-start** ['dʒʌmpstɑːt] vt (AUT: engine) durch Anschieben des Wagens in Gang bringen.
**jump suit** n Overall m.
**jumpy** ['dʒʌmpɪ] adj nervös.
**Jun.** abbr = June.
**junction** ['dʒʌŋkʃən] (BRIT) n Kreuzung f; (RAIL) Gleisanschluß m.
**juncture** ['dʒʌŋktʃə*] n: **at this ~** zu diesem Zeitpunkt.
**June** [dʒuːn] n Juni m; see also July.
**jungle** ['dʒʌŋgl] n Urwald m, Dschungel m (also fig).
**junior** ['dʒuːnɪə*] adj jünger; (subordinate) untergeordnet ♦ n Jüngere(r) f(m); (young person) Junior m; **he's ~ to me (by 2 years)**, **he's my ~ (by 2 years)** (younger) er ist (2 Jahre) jünger als ich; **he's ~ to me** (subordinate) er steht unter mir.
**junior executive** n zweiter Geschäftsführer m, zweite Geschäftsführerin f.
**junior high school** (US) n ≈ Mittelschule f.
**junior minister** (BRIT) n Staatssekretär(in) m(f).
**junior partner** n Juniorpartner(in) m(f).

**junior school** (BRIT) n ≈ Grundschule f.
**junior sizes** npl (COMM) Kindergrößen pl.
**juniper** ['dʒuːnɪpə*] n: ~ **berry** Wacholderbeere f.
**junk** [dʒʌŋk] n (rubbish) Gerümpel nt; (cheap goods) Ramsch m; (ship) Dschunke f ♦ vt (inf) ausrangieren.
**junk bond** n (FIN) niedrig eingestuftes Wertpapier mit hohen Ertragschancen bei erhöhtem Risiko.
**junket** ['dʒʌŋkɪt] n Dickmilch f; (inf: pej: free trip): **to go on a ~** eine Reise auf Kosten des Steuerzahlers machen.
**junk food** n ungesundes Essen nt.
**junkie** ['dʒʌŋkɪ] (inf) n Fixer(in) m(f).
**junk mail** n (Post)wurfsendungen pl.
**junk room** n Rumpelkammer f.
**junk shop** n Trödelladen m.
**Junr** abbr (in names: = junior) jun.
**junta** ['dʒʌntə] n Junta f.
**Jupiter** ['dʒuːpɪtə*] n Jupiter m.
**jurisdiction** [dʒuərɪs'dɪkʃən] n Gerichtsbarkeit f; (ADMIN) Zuständigkeit f, Zuständigkeitsbereich m; **it falls within/outside my ~** dafür bin ich zuständig/nicht zuständig.
**jurisprudence** [dʒuərɪs'pruːdəns] n Jura pl, Rechtswissenschaft f.
**juror** ['dʒuərə*] n Schöffe m, Schöffin f; (for capital crimes) Geschworene(r) f(m); (in competition) Preisrichter(in) m(f).
**jury** ['dʒuərɪ] n: **the ~** die Schöffen pl; (for capital crimes) die Geschworenen pl; (for competition) die Jury, das Preisgericht.
**jury box** n Schöffenbank f; Geschworenenbank f.
**juryman** ['dʒuərɪmən] (irreg: like man) n = juror.
**just** [dʒʌst] adj gerecht ♦ adv (exactly) genau; (only) nur; **he's ~ done it/left** er hat es gerade getan/ist gerade gegangen; ~ **as I expected** genau wie ich erwartet habe; ~ **right** genau richtig; ~ **two o'clock** erst zwei Uhr; **we were ~ going** wir wollten gerade gehen; **I was ~ about to phone** ich wollte gerade anrufen; **she's ~ as clever as you** sie ist genauso klug wie du; **it's ~ as well (that ...)** nur gut, daß ...; ~ **as he was leaving** gerade als er gehen wollte; ~ **before** gerade noch; ~ **enough** gerade genug; ~ **here** genau hier, genau an dieser Stelle; **he ~ missed** er hat genau danebengetroffen; **it's ~ me** ich bin's nur; **it's ~ a mistake** es ist nur ein Fehler; ~ **listen** hör mal; ~ **ask someone the way** frage doch einfach jemanden nach dem Weg; **not ~ now** nicht gerade jetzt; ~ **a minute!**, ~ **one moment!** einen Moment, bitte!
**justice** ['dʒʌstɪs] n Justiz f; (of cause, complaint) Berechtigung f; (fairness) Gerechtigkeit f; (US: judge) Richter(in) m(f); **Lord Chief J~** (BRIT) oberster Richter in

*Großbritannien*; **to do ~ to** (*fig*) gerecht werden +*dat*.
**Justice of the Peace** *n* Friedensrichter(in) *m(f)*.
**justifiable** [dʒʌstɪ'faɪəbl] *adj* gerechtfertigt, berechtigt.
**justifiably** [dʒʌstɪ'faɪəblɪ] *adv* zu Recht, berechtigterweise.
**justification** [dʒʌstɪfɪ'keɪʃən] *n* Rechtfertigung *f*; (*TYP*) Justierung *f*.
**justify** ['dʒʌstɪfaɪ] *vt* rechtfertigen; (*text*) justieren; **to be justified in doing sth** etw zu or mit Recht tun.
**justly** ['dʒʌstlɪ] *adv* zu or mit Recht; (*deservedly*) gerecht.
**jut** [dʒʌt] *vi* (*also:* ~ **out**) vorstehen.
**jute** [dʒuːt] *n* Jute *f*.
**juvenile** ['dʒuːvənaɪl] *adj* (*crime, offenders*) Jugend-; (*humour, mentality*) kindisch, unreif ♦ *n* Jugendliche(r) *f(m)*.
**juvenile delinquency** *n* Jugendkriminalität *f*.
**juvenile delinquent** *n* jugendlicher Straftäter *m*, jugendliche Straftäterin *f*.
**juxtapose** ['dʒʌkstəpəuz] *vt* nebeneinanderstellen.
**juxtaposition** ['dʒʌkstəpə'zɪʃən] *n* Nebeneinanderstellung *f*.

# K, k

**K¹, k** [keɪ] *n* (*letter*) K *nt*, k *nt*; ~ **for King** ≈ K wie Kaufmann.
**K²** [keɪ] *abbr* (= *one thousand*) K; (*COMPUT:* = *kilobyte*) KB; (*BRIT: in titles*) = **knight**.
**kaftan** ['kæftæn] *n* Kaftan *m*.
**Kalahari Desert** [kælə'hɑːrɪ-] *n*: **the ~** die Kalahari.
**kale** [keɪl] *n* Grünkohl *m*.
**kaleidoscope** [kə'laɪdəskəup] *n* Kaleidoskop *nt*.
**kamikaze** ['kæmɪ'kɑːzɪ] *adj* (*mission etc*) Kamikaze-, Selbstmord-.
**Kampala** [kæm'pɑːlə] *n* Kampala *nt*.
**Kampuchea** [kæmpu'tʃɪə] *n* Kampuchea *nt*.
**Kampuchean** [kæmpu'tʃɪən] *adj* kampucheanisch.
**kangaroo** [kæŋgə'ruː] *n* Känguruh *nt*.
**Kans.** (*US*) *abbr* (*POST:* = *Kansas*).
**kaput** [kə'put] (*inf*) *adj*: **to be ~** kaputt sein.
**karaoke** [kɑːrə'əukɪ] *n* Karaoke *nt*.
**karate** [kə'rɑːtɪ] *n* Karate *nt*.
**Kashmir** [kæʃ'mɪə*] *n* Kaschmir *nt*.
**kayak** ['kaɪæk] *n* Kajak *m* or *nt*.
**Kazakhstan** [kæzæk'stɑːn] *n* Kasachstan *nt*.

**KC** (*BRIT*) *n* *abbr* (*LAW:* = *King's Counsel*) Kronanwalt *m*.
**kd** (*US*) *abbr* (*COMM:* = *knocked down*) (in Einzelteile) zerlegt.
**kebab** [kə'bæb] *n* Kebab *m*.
**keel** [kiːl] *n* Kiel *m*; **on an even ~** (*fig*) stabil.
►**keel over** *vi* kentern; (*person*) umkippen.
**keen** [kiːn] *adj* begeistert, eifrig; (*interest*) groß; (*desire*) heftig; (*eye, intelligence, competition, edge*) scharf; **to be ~ to do** or **on doing sth** scharf darauf sein, etw zu tun (*inf*); **to be ~ on sth** an etw *dat* sehr interessiert sein; **to be ~ on sb** von jdm sehr angetan sein; **I'm not ~ on going** ich brenne nicht gerade darauf zu gehen.
**keenly** ['kiːnlɪ] *adv* (*enthusiastically*) begeistert; (*feel*) leidenschaftlich; (*look*) aufmerksam.
**keenness** ['kiːnnɪs] *n* Begeisterung *f*, Eifer *m*; **his ~ to go is suspicious** daß er so unbedingt gehen will, ist verdächtig.
**keep** [kiːp] (*pt, pp* **kept**) *vt* behalten; (*preserve, store*) aufbewahren; (*house, shop, accounts, diary*) führen; (*garden etc*) pflegen; (*chickens, bees, fig: promise*) halten; (*family etc*) versorgen, unterhalten; (*detain*) aufhalten; (*prevent*) abhalten ♦ *vi* (*remain*) bleiben; (*food*) sich halten ♦ *n* (*food etc*) Unterhalt *m*; (*of castle*) Bergfried *m*; **to ~ doing sth** etw immer wieder tun; **to ~ sb happy** jdn zufriedenstellen; **to ~ a room tidy** ein Zimmer in Ordnung halten; **to ~ sb waiting** jdn warten lassen; **to ~ an appointment** eine Verabredung einhalten; **to ~ a record of sth** über etw *acc* Buch führen; **to ~ sth to o.s.** etw für sich behalten; **to ~ sth (back) from sb** etw vor jdm geheimhalten; **to ~ sb from doing sth** jdn davon abhalten, etw zu tun; **to ~ sth from happening** etw verhindern; **to ~ time** (*clock*) genau gehen; **enough for his ~** genug für seinen Unterhalt.
►**keep away** *vt* fernhalten ♦ *vi*: **to ~ away (from)** wegbleiben (von).
►**keep back** *vt* zurückhalten; (*tears*) unterdrücken; (*money*) einbehalten ♦ *vi* zurückbleiben.
►**keep down** *vt* (*prices*) niedrig halten; (*spending*) einschränken; (*food*) bei sich behalten ♦ *vi* unten bleiben.
►**keep in** *vt* im Haus behalten; (*at school*) nachsitzen lassen ♦ *vi* (*inf*): **to ~ in with sb** sich mit jdm gut stellen.
►**keep off** *vt* fernhalten ♦ *vi* wegbleiben; "**~ off the grass**" „Betreten des Rasens verboten"; **~ your hands off** Hände weg.
►**keep on** *vi*: **to ~ on doing sth** (*continue*) etw weiter tun; **to ~ on (about sth)** unaufhörlich (von etw) reden.
►**keep out** *vt* fernhalten; "**~ out**" „Zutritt verboten".
►**keep up** *vt* (*payments*) weiterbezahlen; (*standards etc*) aufrechterhalten ♦ *vi*: **to ~ up**

**(with)** mithalten können (mit).
**keeper** ['kiːpə'] n Wärter(in) m(f).
**keep fit** n Fitneßtraining nt.
**keeping** ['kiːpɪŋ] n (care) Obhut f; **in ~ with** in Übereinstimmung mit; **out of ~ with** nicht im Einklang mit; **I'll leave this in your ~** ich vertraue dies deiner Obhut an.
**keeps** [kiːps] n: **for ~** (inf) für immer.
**keepsake** ['kiːpseɪk] n Andenken nt.
**keg** [kɛg] n Fäßchen nt; **~ beer** Bier nt vom Faß.
**Ken.** (US) abbr (POST: = Kentucky).
**kennel** ['kɛnl] n Hundehütte f.
**kennels** ['kɛnlz] n Hundeheim nt; **we had to leave our dog in ~ over Christmas** wir mußten unseren Hund über Weihnachten in ein Heim geben.
**Kenya** ['kɛnjə] n Kenia nt.
**Kenyan** ['kɛnjən] adj kenianisch ♦ n Kenianer(in) m(f).
**kept** [kɛpt] pt, pp of **keep**.
**kerb** [kəːb] (BRIT) n Bordstein m.
**kerb crawler** [-'krɔːlə'] (inf) n Freier m im Autostrich.
**kernel** ['kəːnl] n Kern m.
**kerosene** ['kɛrəsiːn] n Kerosin nt.
**kestrel** ['kɛstrəl] n Turmfalke m.
**ketchup** ['kɛtʃəp] n Ketchup m or nt.
**kettle** ['kɛtl] n Kessel m.
**kettledrum** ['kɛtldrʌm] n (Kessel)pauke f.
**key** [kiː] n Schlüssel m; (MUS) Tonart f; (of piano, computer, typewriter) Taste f ♦ cpd (issue etc) Schlüssel- ♦ vt (also: ~ in) eingeben.
**keyboard** ['kiːbɔːd] n Tastatur f.
**keyboarder** ['kiːbɔːdə'] n Datentypist(in) m(f).
**keyed up** [kiːd-] adj: **to be (all) ~** (ganz) aufgedreht sein (inf).
**keyhole** ['kiːhəul] n Schlüsselloch nt.
**keyhole surgery** n Schlüssellochchirurgie f, minimal invasive Chirurgie f.
**keynote** ['kiːnəut] n Grundton m; (of speech) Leitgedanke m.
**keypad** ['kiːpæd] n Tastenfeld nt.
**key ring** n Schlüsselring m.
**keystroke** ['kiːstrəuk] n Anschlag m.
**kg** abbr (= kilogram) kg.
**KGB** n abbr (POL: formerly) KGB m.
**khaki** ['kɑːkɪ] n K(h)aki nt.
**kHz** abbr (= kilohertz) kHz.
**kibbutz** [kɪ'buts] n Kibbuz m.
**kick** [kɪk] vt treten (table, ball) treten gegen +acc; (inf: habit) ablegen; (: addiction) wegkommen von ♦ vi (horse) ausschlagen ♦ n Tritt m; (to ball) Schuß m; (of rifle) Rückstoß m; (thrill): **he does it for ~s** er macht es zum Spaß.
▶**kick around** (inf) vi (person) rumhängen; (thing) rumliegen.
▶**kick off** vi (SPORT) anstoßen.
**kickoff** ['kɪkɔf] n (SPORT) Anstoß m.
**kick start** n (AUT: also: ~er) Kickstarter m.

**kid** [kɪd] n (inf: child) Kind nt; (animal) Kitz nt; (leather) Ziegenleder nt, Glacéleder nt ♦ vi (inf) Witze machen; **~ brother** kleiner Bruder m; **~ sister** kleine Schwester f.
**kid gloves** npl: **to treat sb with ~** (fig) jdn mit Samthandschuhen anfassen.
**kidnap** ['kɪdnæp] vt entführen, kidnappen.
**kidnapper** ['kɪdnæpə'] n Entführer(in) m(f), Kidnapper(in) m(f).
**kidnapping** ['kɪdnæpɪŋ] n Entführung f, Kidnapping nt.
**kidney** ['kɪdnɪ] n Niere f.
**kidney bean** n Gartenbohne f.
**kidney machine** n (MED) künstliche Niere f.
**Kilimanjaro** [kɪlɪmən'dʒɑːrəu] n: **Mount ~** der Kilimandscharo.
**kill** [kɪl] vt töten; (murder) ermorden, umbringen; (plant) eingehen lassen; (proposal) zu Fall bringen; (rumour) ein Ende machen +dat ♦ n Abschuß m; **to ~ time** die Zeit totschlagen; **to ~ o.s. to do sth** (fig) sich fast umbringen, um etw zu tun; **to ~ o.s. (laughing)** (fig) sich totlachen.
▶**kill off** vt abtöten; (fig: romance) beenden.
**killer** ['kɪlə'] n Mörder(in) m(f).
**killer instinct** n (fig) Tötungsinstinkt m.
**killing** ['kɪlɪŋ] n Töten nt; (instance) Mord m; **to make a ~** (inf) einen Riesengewinn machen.
**killjoy** ['kɪldʒɔɪ] n Spielverderber(in) m(f).
**kiln** [kɪln] n Brennofen m.
**kilo** ['kiːləu] n Kilo nt.
**kilobyte** ['kiːləubaɪt] n Kilobyte nt.
**kilogram(me)** ['kɪləugræm] n Kilogramm nt.
**kilohertz** ['kɪləuhəːts] n inv Kilohertz nt.
**kilometre,** (US) **kilometer** ['kɪləmiːtə'] n Kilometer m.
**kilowatt** ['kɪləuwɔt] n Kilowatt nt.
**kilt** [kɪlt] n Kilt m, Schottenrock m.
**kilter** ['kɪltə'] n: **out of ~** nicht in Ordnung.
**kimono** [kɪ'məunəu] n Kimono m.
**kin** [kɪn] n see **kith, next**.
**kind** [kaɪnd] adj freundlich ♦ n Art f; (sort) Sorte f; **would you be ~ enough to ...?, would you be so ~ as to ...?** wären Sie (vielleicht) so nett und ...?; **it's very ~ of you (to do ...)** es ist wirklich nett von Ihnen(, ... zu tun); **in ~** (COMM) in Naturalien; **a ~ of ...** eine Art ...; **they are two of a ~** sie sind beide von der gleichen Art; (people) sie sind vom gleichen Schlag.
**kindergarten** ['kɪndəgɑːtn] n Kindergarten m.
**kind-hearted** [kaɪnd'hɑːtɪd] adj gutherzig.
**kindle** ['kɪndl] vt anzünden; (emotion) wecken.
**kindling** ['kɪndlɪŋ] n Anzündholz nt.
**kindly** ['kaɪndlɪ] adj, adv freundlich, nett; **will you ~ ...** würden Sie bitte ...; **he didn't take it ~** er konnte sich damit nicht anfreunden.
**kindness** ['kaɪndnɪs] n Freundlichkeit f.
**kindred** ['kɪndrɪd] adj: **~ spirit** Gleichgesinnte(r) f(m).
**kinetic** [kɪ'nɛtɪk] adj kinetisch.
**king** [kɪŋ] n (also fig) König m.

**kingdom** ['kɪŋdəm] *n* Königreich *nt*.
**kingfisher** ['kɪŋfɪʃəʳ] *n* Eisvogel *m*.
**kingpin** ['kɪŋpɪn] *n* (*TECH*) Bolzen *m*; (*AUT*) Achsschenkelbolzen *m*; (*fig*) wichtigste Stütze *f*.
**king-size(d)** ['kɪŋsaɪz(d)] *adj* extra groß; (*cigarette*) King-size-.
**kink** [kɪŋk] *n* Knick *m*; (*in hair*) Welle *f*; (*fig*) Schrulle *f*.
**kinky** ['kɪŋkɪ] (*pej*) *adj* schrullig; (*sexually*) abartig.
**kinship** ['kɪnʃɪp] *n* Verwandtschaft *f*.
**kinsman** ['kɪnzmən] (*irreg: like* **man**) *n* Verwandte(r) *m*.
**kinswoman** ['kɪnzwumən] (*irreg: like* **woman**) *n* Verwandte *f*.
**kiosk** ['kiːɔsk] *n* Kiosk *m*; (*BRIT*) (Telefon)zelle *f*; (*also:* **newspaper** ~) (Zeitungs)kiosk *m*.
**kipper** ['kɪpəʳ] *n* Räucherhering *m*.
**Kirghizia** [kəːˈgɪzɪə] *n* Kirgistan *nt*.
**kiss** [kɪs] *n* Kuß *m* ♦ *vt* küssen ♦ *vi* sich küssen; **to ~ (each other)** sich küssen; **to ~ sb goodbye** jdm einen Abschiedskuß geben.
**kissagram** ['kɪsəgræm] *n durch eine(n) Angestellte(n) einer Agentur persönlich übermittelter Kuß.*
**kiss of life** (*BRIT*) *n:* **the ~** Mund-zu-Mund-Beatmung *f*.
**kit** [kɪt] *n* Zeug *nt*, Sachen *pl*; (*equipment: also MIL*) Ausrüstung *f*; (*set of tools*) Werkzeug *nt*; (*for assembly*) Bausatz *m*.
►**kit out** (*BRIT*) *vt* ausrüsten, ausstatten.
**kitbag** ['kɪtbæg] *n* Seesack *m*.
**kitchen** ['kɪtʃɪn] *n* Küche *f*.
**kitchen garden** *n* Küchengarten *m*.
**kitchen sink** *n* Spüle *f*.
**kitchen unit** (*BRIT*) *n* Küchenschrank *m*.
**kitchenware** ['kɪtʃɪnwɛəʳ] *n* Küchengeräte *pl*.
**kite** [kaɪt] *n* Drachen *m*; (*ZOOL*) Milan *m*.
**kith** [kɪθ] *n:* ~ **and kin** Freunde und Verwandte *pl*.
**kitten** ['kɪtn] *n* Kätzchen *nt*.
**kitty** ['kɪtɪ] *n* (gemeinsame) Kasse *f*.
**kiwi (fruit)** ['kiːwiː] *n* Kiwi(frucht) *f*.
**KKK** (*US*) *n abbr* (= *Ku Klux Klan*) Ku-Klux-Klan *m*.
**Kleenex** ® ['kliːnɛks] *n* Tempo(taschentuch) ® *nt*.
**kleptomaniac** [klɛptəuˈmeɪnɪæk] *n* Kleptomane *m*, Kleptomanin *f*.
**km** *abbr* (= *kilometre*) km.
**km/h** *abbr* (= *kilometres per hour*) km/h.
**knack** [næk] *n:* **to have the ~ of doing sth** es herausnaben, wie man etw macht; **there's a ~ to doing this** da ist ein Trick *or* Kniff dabei.
**knackered** ['nækəd] (*BRIT: inf*) *adj* kaputt.
**knapsack** ['næpsæk] *n* Rucksack *m*.
**knead** [niːd] *vt* kneten.
**knee** [niː] *n* Knie *nt*.
**kneecap** ['niːkæp] *n* Kniescheibe *f*.
**kneecapping** ['niːkæpɪŋ] *n* Durchschießen *nt*

der Kniescheibe.
**knee-deep** ['niːˈdiːp] *adj, adv:* **the water was ~** das Wasser ging mir *etc* bis zum Knie; **~ in mud** knietief *or* bis zu den Knien im Schlamm.
**kneejerk reaction** ['niːˈdʒəːk-] *n* (*fig*) instinktive Reaktion *f*.
**kneel** [niːl] (*pt, pp* **knelt**) *vi* knien; (*also:* ~ **down**) niederknien.
**kneepad** ['niːpæd] *n* Knieschützer *m*.
**knell** [nɛl] *n* Totengeläut(e) *nt*; (*fig*) Ende *nt*.
**knelt** [nɛlt] *pt, pp of* **kneel**.
**knew** [njuː] *pt of* **know**.
**knickers** ['nɪkəz] (*BRIT*) *npl* Schlüpfer *m*.
**knick-knacks** ['nɪknæks] *npl* Nippsachen *pl*.
**knife** [naɪf] (*pl* **knives**) *n* Messer *nt* ♦ *vt* (*injure, attack*) einstechen auf +*acc*; ~, **fork and spoon** Messer, Gabel und Löffel.
**knife edge** *n:* **to be balanced on a ~** (*fig*) auf Messers Schneide stehen.
**knight** [naɪt] *n* (*BRIT*) Ritter *m*; (*CHESS*) Springer *m*, Pferd *nt*.
**knighthood** ['naɪthud] (*BRIT*) *n:* **to get a ~** in den Adelsstand erhoben werden.
**knit** [nɪt] *vt* stricken ♦ *vi* stricken; (*bones*) zusammenwachsen; **to ~ one's brows** die Stirn runzeln.
**knitted** ['nɪtɪd] *adj* gestrickt, Strick-.
**knitting** ['nɪtɪŋ] *n* Stricken *nt*; (*garment being made*) Strickzeug *nt*.
**knitting machine** *n* Strickmaschine *f*.
**knitting needle** *n* Stricknadel *f*.
**knitting pattern** *n* Strickmuster *nt*.
**knitwear** ['nɪtwɛəʳ] *n* Strickwaren *pl*.
**knives** [naɪvz] *npl of* **knife**.
**knob** [nɔb] *n* Griff *m*; (*of stick*) Knauf *m*; (*on radio, TV etc*) Knopf *m*; **a ~ of butter** (*BRIT*) ein Stückchen *nt* Butter.
**knobbly** ['nɔblɪ], **knobby** ['nɔbɪ] (*US*) *adj* (*wood*) knorrig; (*surface*) uneben; ~ **knees** Knubbelknie *pl* (*inf*).
**knock** [nɔk] *vt* schlagen; (*bump into*) stoßen gegen +*acc*; (*inf: criticize*) runtermachen ♦ *vi* klopfen ♦ *n* Schlag *m*; (*bump*) Stoß *m*; (*on door*) Klopfen *nt*; **to ~ a nail into sth** einen Nagel in etw *acc* schlagen; **to ~ some sense into sb** jdn zur Vernunft bringen; **to ~ at/ on** klopfen an/auf +*acc*; **he ~ed at the door** er klopfte an, er klopfte an die Tür.
►**knock about** (*inf*) *vt* schlagen, verprügeln ♦ *vi* rumziehen; ~ **about with** sich rumtreiben mit.
►**knock around** *vt, vi* = **knock about**.
►**knock back** (*inf*) *vt* (*drink*) sich *dat* hinter die Binde kippen.
►**knock down** *vt* anfahren; (*fatally*) überfahren; (*building etc*) abreißen; (*price: buyer*) herunterhandeln; (*: seller*) heruntergehen mit.
►**knock off** *vi* (*inf*) Feierabend machen ♦ *vt* (*from price*) nachlassen; (*inf: steal*) klauen; **to ~ off £10** £10 nachlassen.

▶**knock out** *vt* bewußtlos schlagen; (*subj: drug*) bewußtlos werden lassen; (*BOXING*) k.o. schlagen; (*in game, competition*) besiegen.

▶**knock over** *vt* umstoßen; (*with car*) anfahren.

**knockdown** ['nɔkdaun] *adj:* ~ **price** Schleuderpreis *m*.

**knocker** ['nɔkə*] *n* Türklopfer *m*.

**knock-for-knock** ['nɔkfə'nɔk] (*BRIT*) *adj:* ~ **agreement** Vereinbarung, bei der jede Versicherungsgesellschaft den Schaden am von ihr versicherten Fahrzeug übernimmt.

**knocking** ['nɔkɪŋ] *n* Klopfen *nt*.

**knock-kneed** [nɔk'niːd] *adj* X-beinig; **to be** ~ X-Beine haben.

**knockout** ['nɔkaut] *n* (*BOXING*) K.o.-Schlag *m* ♦ *cpd* (*competition etc*) Ausscheidungs-.

**knock-up** ['nɔkʌp] *n* (*TENNIS*): **to have a** ~ ein paar Bälle schlagen.

**knot** [nɔt] *n* Knoten *m*; (*in wood*) Ast *m* ♦ *vt* einen Knoten machen in +*acc*; (*knot together*) verknoten; **to tie a** ~ einen Knoten machen.

**knotty** ['nɔtɪ] *adj* (*fig: problem*) verwickelt.

**know** [nəu] (*pt* **knew**, *pp* **known**) *vt* kennen; (*facts*) wissen; (*language*) können ♦ *vi*: **to** ~ **about** *or* **of sth/sb** von etw/jdm gehört haben; **to** ~ **how to swim** schwimmen können; **to get to** ~ **sth** etw erfahren; (*place*) etw kennenlernen; **I don't** ~ **him** ich kenne ihn nicht; **to** ~ **right from wrong** Gut und Böse unterscheiden können; **as far as I** ~ soviel ich weiß; **yes, I** ~ ja, ich weiß; **I don't** ~ ich weiß (es) nicht.

**know-all** ['nəuɔːl] (*BRIT: pej*) *n* Alleswisser *m*.

**know-how** ['nəuhau] *n* Know-how *nt*, Sachkenntnis *f*.

**knowing** ['nəuɪŋ] *adj* wissend.

**knowingly** ['nəuɪŋlɪ] *adv* (*purposely*) bewußt; (*smile, look*) wissend.

**know-it-all** ['nəuɪtɔːl] (*US*) *n* = **know-all**.

**knowledge** ['nɔlɪdʒ] *n* Wissen *nt*, Kenntnis *f*; (*learning, things learnt*) Kenntnisse *pl*; **to have no** ~ **of** nichts wissen von; **not to my** ~ nicht, daß ich wüßte; **without my** ~ ohne mein Wissen; **it is common** ~ **that ...** es ist allgemein bekannt, daß ...; **it has come to my** ~ **that ...** ich habe erfahren, daß ...; **to have a working** ~ **of French** Grundkenntnisse in Französisch haben.

**knowledgeable** ['nɔlɪdʒəbl] *adj* informiert.

**known** [nəun] *pp of* **know** ♦ *adj* bekannt; (*expert*) anerkannt.

**knuckle** ['nʌkl] *n* (Finger)knöchel *m*.

▶**knuckle down** (*inf*) *vi* sich dahinterklemmen; **to** ~ **down to work** sich an die Arbeit machen.

▶**knuckle under** (*inf*) *vi* sich fügen, spuren.

**knuckle-duster** ['nʌkl'dʌstə*] *n* Schlagring *m*.

**KO** *n abbr* (= *knockout*) K.o. *m* ♦ *vt* k.o. schlagen.

**koala** [kəu'ɑːlə] *n* (*also:* ~ **bear**) Koala(bär) *m*.

**kook** [kuːk] (*US: inf*) *n* Spinner *m*.

**Koran** [kɔ'rɑːn] *n:* **the** ~ der Koran.

**Korea** [kə'rɪə] *n* Korea *nt*; **North** ~ Nordkorea *nt*; **South** ~ Südkorea *nt*.

**Korean** [kə'rɪən] *adj* koreanisch ♦ *n* Koreaner(in) *m(f)*.

**kosher** ['kəuʃə*] *adj* koscher.

**kowtow** ['kau'tau] *vi:* **to** ~ **to sb** vor jdm dienern *or* einen Kotau machen.

**Kremlin** ['krɛmlɪn] *n:* **the** ~ der Kreml.

**KS** (*US*) *abbr* (*POST:* = *Kansas*).

**Kt** (*BRIT*) *abbr* (*in titles*) = **knight**.

**Kuala Lumpur** ['kwɑːlə'lumpuə*] *n* Kuala Lumpur *nt*.

**kudos** ['kjuːdɔs] *n* Ansehen *nt*, Ehre *f*.

**Kurd** [kəːd] *n* Kurde *m*, Kurdin *f*.

**Kuwait** [ku'weɪt] *n* Kuwait *nt*.

**Kuwaiti** [ku'weɪtɪ] *adj* kuwaitisch ♦ *n* Kuwaiter(in) *m(f)*.

**kW** *abbr* (= *kilowatt*) kW.

**KY** (*US*) *abbr* (*POST:* = *Kentucky*).

# *L, l*

**L¹, l¹** [ɛl] *n* (*letter*) L *nt*, l *nt*; ~ **for Lucy,** (*US*) ~ **for Love** ≈ L wie Ludwig.

**L²** [ɛl] *abbr* (*BRIT: AUT:* = *learner*) am Auto angebrachtes Kennzeichen für Fahrschüler; = *lake*; (= *large*) gr.; (= *left*) l.

**l²** *abbr* (= *litre*) l.

**LA** (*US*) *n abbr* (= *Los Angeles*) ♦ *abbr* (*POST:* = *Louisiana*).

**La.** (*US*) *abbr* (*POST:* = *Louisiana*).

**lab** [læb] *n abbr* = **laboratory.**

**label** ['leɪbl] *n* Etikett *nt*; (*brand: of record*) Label *nt* ♦ *vt* etikettieren; (*fig: person*) abstempeln.

**labor** *etc* ['leɪbə*] (*US*) *n* = **labour** *etc*.

**laboratory** [lə'bɔrətərɪ] *n* Labor *nt*.

> **Labor Day** ist in den USA und Kanada der Name für den Tag der Arbeit. Er wird dort als gesetzlicher Feiertag am ersten Montag im September begangen.

**laborious** [lə'bɔːrɪəs] *adj* mühsam.

**labor union** (*US*) *n* Gewerkschaft *f*.

**labour,** (*US*) **labor** ['leɪbə*] *n* Arbeit *f*; (*work force*) Arbeitskräfte *pl*; (*MED*): **to be in** ~ in den Wehen liegen ♦ *vi:* **to** ~ **(at sth)** sich (mit etw) abmühen ♦ *vt:* **to** ~ **a point** auf einem Thema herumreiten; **L~, the L~ Party** (*BRIT*) die Labour Party; **hard** ~ Zwangsarbeit *f*.

**labour camp** *n* Arbeitslager *nt*.

**labour cost** n Lohnkosten pl.

**labour dispute** n Arbeitskampf m.

**laboured** ['leɪbəd] adj (breathing) schwer; (movement, style) schwerfällig.

**labourer** ['leɪbərə·] n Arbeiter(in) m(f); **farm ~** Landarbeiter(in) m(f).

**labour force** n Arbeiterschaft f.

**labour intensive** adj arbeitsintensiv.

**labour market** n Arbeitsmarkt m.

**labour pains** npl Wehen pl.

**labour relations** npl Beziehungen pl zwischen Arbeitnehmern, Arbeitgebern und Gewerkschaften.

**labour-saving** ['leɪbəseɪvɪŋ] adj arbeitssparend.

**laburnum** [lə'bə:nəm] n (BOT) Goldregen m.

**labyrinth** ['læbɪrɪnθ] n Labyrinth nt.

**lace** [leɪs] n (fabric) Spitze f; (of shoe etc) (Schuh)band nt, Schnürsenkel m ♦ vt (also: ~ **up**) (zu)schnüren; **to ~ a drink** einen Schuß Alkohol in ein Getränk geben.

**lacemaking** ['leɪsmeɪkɪŋ] n Klöppelei f.

**lacerate** ['læsəreɪt] vt zerschneiden.

**laceration** [læsə'reɪʃən] n Schnittwunde f.

**lace-up** ['leɪsʌp] adj (shoes etc) Schnür-.

**lack** [læk] n Mangel m ♦ vt, vi: **sb ~s sth, sb is ~ing in sth** jdm fehlt es an etw dat; **through or for ~ of** aus Mangel an +dat; **to be ~ing** fehlen.

**lackadaisical** [lækə'deɪzɪkl] adj lustlos.

**lackey** ['lækɪ] (pej) n Lakai m.

**lacklustre, (US) lackluster** ['læklʌstə·] adj farblos, langweilig.

**laconic** [lə'kɔnɪk] adj lakonisch.

**lacquer** ['lækə·] n Lack m; (also: **hair ~**) Haarspray nt.

**lacrosse** [lə'krɔs] n Lacrosse nt.

**lacy** ['leɪsɪ] adj Spitzen-; (like lace) spitzenartig.

**lad** [læd] n Junge m.

**ladder** ['lædə·] n (also fig) Leiter f; (BRIT: in tights) Laufmasche f ♦ vt (BRIT) Laufmaschen bekommen in +dat ♦ vi (BRIT) Laufmaschen bekommen.

**laden** ['leɪdn] adj: **~ (with)** beladen (mit); **fully ~** voll beladen.

**ladle** ['leɪdl] n Schöpflöffel m, (Schöpf)kelle f ♦ vt schöpfen.

▸**ladle out** vt (fig) austeilen.

**lady** ['leɪdɪ] n (woman) Frau f; (: dignified, graceful etc) Dame f; (BRIT: title) Lady f; **ladies and gentlemen ...** meine Damen und Herren ...; **young ~** junge Dame; **the ladies' (room)** die Damentoilette.

**ladybird** ['leɪdɪbə:d], **ladybug** ['leɪdɪbʌg] (US) n Marienkäfer m.

**lady-in-waiting** ['leɪdɪɪn'weɪtɪŋ] n Hofdame f.

**lady-killer** ['leɪdɪkɪlə·] n Herzensbrecher m.

**ladylike** ['leɪdɪlaɪk] adj damenhaft.

**ladyship** ['leɪdɪʃɪp] n: **your L~** Ihre Ladyschaft.

**lag** [læg] n (period of time) Zeitabstand m ♦ vi (also: **~ behind**) zurückbleiben; (trade,

investment etc) zurückgehen ♦ vt (pipes etc) isolieren; **old ~** (inf: prisoner) (ehemaliger) Knacki m.

**lager** ['lɑ:gə·] n helles Bier nt.

**lager lout** (BRIT: inf) n betrunkener Rowdy m.

**lagging** ['lægɪŋ] n Isoliermaterial nt.

**lagoon** [lə'gu:n] n Lagune f.

**Lagos** ['leɪgɔs] n Lagos nt.

**laid** [leɪd] pt, pp of **lay**.

**laid-back** [leɪd'bæk] (inf) adj locker.

**laid up** adj: **to be ~ (with)** im Bett liegen (mit).

**lain** [leɪn] pp of **lie**.

**lair** [lɛə·] n Lager nt; (cave) Höhle f; (den) Bau m.

**laissez faire** [lɛseɪ'fɛə·] n Laisser-faire nt.

**laity** ['leɪətɪ] n or npl Laien pl.

**lake** [leɪk] n See m.

**Lake District** (BRIT) n: **the ~** der Lake Distrikt, Seengebiet im NW Englands.

**lamb** [læm] n Lamm nt; (meat) Lammfleisch nt.

**lamb chop** n Lammkotelett nt.

**lambskin** ['læmskɪn] n Lammfell nt.

**lamb's wool** n Lammwolle f.

**lame** [leɪm] adj lahm; (argument, answer) schwach.

**lame duck** n (person) Niete f; (business) unwirtschaftliche Firma f.

**lamely** ['leɪmlɪ] adv lahm.

**lament** [lə'mɛnt] n Klage f ♦ vt beklagen.

**lamentable** ['læməntəbl] adj beklagenswert.

**laminated** ['læmɪneɪtɪd] adj laminiert; (metal) geschichtet; **~ glass** Verbundglas nt; **~ wood** Sperrholz nt.

**lamp** [læmp] n Lampe f.

**lamplight** ['læmplaɪt] n: **by ~** bei Lampenlicht.

**lampoon** [læm'pu:n] n Schmähschrift f ♦ vt verspotten.

**lamppost** ['læmppəʊst] (BRIT) n Laternenpfahl m.

**lampshade** ['læmpʃeɪd] n Lampenschirm m.

**lance** [lɑ:ns] n Lanze f ♦ vt (MED) aufschneiden.

**lance corporal** (BRIT) n Obergefreite(r) m.

**lancet** ['lɑ:nsɪt] n (MED) Lanzette f.

**Lancs** [læŋks] (BRIT) abbr (POST: = Lancashire).

**land** [lænd] n Land nt; (as property) Grund und Boden m ♦ vi (AVIAT, fig) landen; (from ship) an Land gehen ♦ vt (passengers) absetzen; (goods) an Land bringen; **to own ~** Land besitzen; **to go or travel by ~** auf dem Landweg reisen; **to ~ on one's feet** (fig) auf die Füße fallen; **to ~ sb with sth** (inf) jdm etw aufhalsen.

▸**land up** vi: **to ~ up in/at** landen in +dat.

**landed gentry** ['lændɪd-] n Landadel m.

**landfill site** ['lændfɪl-] n ≈ Mülldeponie f.

**landing** ['lændɪŋ] n (of house) Flur m; (outside flat door) Treppenabsatz m; (AVIAT) Landung f.

**landing card** n Einreisekarte f.

**landing craft** n inv Landungsboot nt.
**landing gear** n (AVIAT) Fahrgestell nt.
**landing stage** n Landesteg m.
**landing strip** n Landebahn f.
**landlady** ['lændleɪdɪ] n Vermieterin f; (of pub) Wirtin f.
**landlocked** ['lændlɒkt] adj von Land eingeschlossen; ~ **country** Binnenstaat m.
**landlord** ['lændlɔːd] n Vermieter m; (of pub) Wirt m.
**landlubber** ['lændlʌbəˀ] (old) n Landratte f.
**landmark** ['lændmɑːk] n Orientierungspunkt m; (famous building) Wahrzeichen nt; (fig) Meilenstein m.
**landowner** ['lændəʊnəˀ] n Grundbesitzer(in) m(f).
**landscape** ['lændskeɪp] n Landschaft f ♦ vt landschaftlich or gärtnerisch gestalten.
**landscape architect** n Landschaftsarchitekt(in) m(f).
**landscape gardener** n Landschaftsgärtner(in) m(f).
**landscape painting** n Landschaftsmalerei f.
**landslide** ['lændslaɪd] n Erdrutsch m; (fig: electoral) Erdrutschsieg m.
**lane** [leɪn] n (in country) Weg m; (in town) Gasse f; (of carriageway) Spur f; (of race course, swimming pool) Bahn f; **shipping** ~ Schiffahrtsweg m.
**language** ['læŋgwɪdʒ] n Sprache f; **bad** ~ Kraftausdrücke pl.
**language laboratory** n Sprachlabor nt.
**languid** ['læŋgwɪd] adj träge, matt.
**languish** ['læŋgwɪʃ] vi schmachten; (project, case) erfolglos bleiben.
**lank** [læŋk] adj (hair) strähnig.
**lanky** ['læŋkɪ] adj schlaksig.
**lanolin(e)** ['lænəlɪn] n Lanolin nt.
**lantern** ['læntən] n Laterne f.
**Laos** [laʊs] n Laos nt.
**lap** [læp] n Schoß m; (in race) Runde f ♦ vt (also: ~ **up**) aufschlecken ♦ vi (water) plätschern.
▶**lap up** vt (fig) genießen.
**lapdog** ['læpdɒg] (pej) n (fig) Schoßhund m.
**lapel** [lə'pɛl] n Aufschlag m, Revers nt or m.
**Lapland** ['læplænd] n Lappland nt.
**Lapp** [læp] adj lappländisch ♦ n Lappe m, Lappin f; (LING) Lappländisch nt.
**lapse** [læps] n (bad behaviour) Fehltritt m; (of memory etc) Schwäche f; (of time) Zeitspanne f ♦ vi ablaufen; (law) ungültig werden; **to** ~ **into bad habits** in schlechte Gewohnheiten verfallen.
**laptop** ['læptɒp] (COMPUT) n Laptop m ♦ cpd Laptop-.
**larceny** ['lɑːsənɪ] n Diebstahl m.
**larch** [lɑːtʃ] n Lärche f.
**lard** [lɑːd] n Schweineschmalz nt.
**larder** ['lɑːdəˀ] n Speisekammer f; (cupboard) Speiseschrank m.
**large** [lɑːdʒ] adj groß; (person) korpulent; **to make** ~**r** vergrößern; **a** ~ **number of people**

eine große Anzahl von Menschen; **on a** ~ **scale** im großen Rahmen; (extensive) weitreichend; **at** ~ (as a whole) im allgemeinen; (at liberty) auf freiem Fuß; **by and** ~ im großen und ganzen.
**large goods vehicle** n Lastkraftwagen m.
**largely** ['lɑːdʒlɪ] adv (mostly) zum größten Teil; (mainly) hauptsächlich.
**large-scale** ['lɑːdʒ'skeɪl] adj im großen Rahmen; (extensive) weitreichend; (map, diagram) in einem großen Maßstab.
**largesse** [lɑː'ʒɛs] n Großzügigkeit f.
**lark** [lɑːk] n (bird) Lerche f; (joke) Spaß m, Jux m.
▶**lark about** vi herumalbern.
**larva** ['lɑːvə] (pl ~e) n Larve f.
**larvae** ['lɑːviː] npl of **larva**.
**laryngitis** [lærɪn'dʒaɪtɪs] n Kehlkopfentzündung f.
**larynx** ['lærɪŋks] n Kehlkopf m.
**lasagne** [lə'zænjə] n Lasagne pl.
**lascivious** [lə'sɪvɪəs] adj lüstern.
**laser** ['leɪzəˀ] n Laser m.
**laser beam** n Laserstrahl m.
**laser printer** n Laserdrucker m.
**lash** [læʃ] n (also: **eyelash**) Wimper f; (blow with whip) Peitschenhieb m ♦ vt peitschen; (rain, wind) peitschen gegen; (tie): **to** ~ **to** festbinden an +dat; **to** ~ **together** zusammenbinden.
▶**lash down** vt festbinden ♦ vi (rain) niederprasseln.
▶**lash out** vi um sich schlagen; **to** ~ **out at sb** auf jdn losschlagen; **to** ~ **out at** or **against sb** (criticize) gegen jdn wettern.
**lashing** ['læʃɪŋ] n: ~**s of** (BRIT: inf) massenhaft.
**lass** [læs] (BRIT) n Mädchen nt.
**lasso** [læ'suː] n Lasso nt ♦ vt mit dem Lasso einfangen.
**last** [lɑːst] adj letzte(r, s) ♦ adv (most recently) zuletzt, das letzte Mal; (finally) als letztes ♦ vi (continue) dauern; (: in good condition) sich halten; (money, commodity) reichen; ~ **week** letzte Woche; ~ **night** gestern abend; ~ **but one** vorletzte(r, s); **the** ~ **time** das letzte Mal; **at** ~ endlich; **it** ~**s (for) 2 hours** es dauert 2 Stunden.
**last-ditch** ['lɑːst'dɪtʃ] adj (attempt) allerletzte(r, s).
**lasting** ['lɑːstɪŋ] adj dauerhaft.
**lastly** ['lɑːstlɪ] adv (finally) schließlich; (last of all) zum Schluß.
**last-minute** ['lɑːstmɪnɪt] adj in letzter Minute.
**latch** [lætʃ] n Riegel m; **to be on the** ~ nur eingeklinkt sein.
▶**latch on to** vt fus (person) sich anschließen +dat; (idea) abfahren auf +acc (inf).
**latchkey** ['lætʃkiː] n Hausschlüssel m.
**latchkey child** n Schlüsselkind nt.
**late** [leɪt] adj spät; (not on time) verspätet ♦ adv spät; (behind time) zu spät; (recently): ~ **of Dechmont** bis vor kurzem in Dechmont

wohnhaft; **the** ~ **Mr X** (_deceased_) der verstorbene Herr X; **in** ~ **May** Ende Mai; **to be (10 minutes)** ~ (10 Minuten) zu spät kommen; (_train etc_) (10 Minuten) Verspätung haben; **to work** ~ länger arbeiten; ~ **in life** relativ spät (im Leben); **of** ~ in letzter Zeit.

**latecomer** ['leɪtkʌmə'] _n_ Nachzügler(in) _m(f)_.

**lately** ['leɪtlɪ] _adv_ in letzter Zeit.

**lateness** ['leɪtnɪs] _n_ (_of person_) Zuspätkommen _nt_; (_of train, event_) Verspätung _f_.

**latent** ['leɪtnt] _adj_ (_energy_) ungenutzt; (_skill, ability_) verborgen.

**later** ['leɪtə'] _adj, adv_ später; ~ **on** nachher.

**lateral** ['lætərl] _adj_ seitlich; ~ **thinking** kreatives Denken _nt_.

**latest** ['leɪtɪst] _adj_ neueste(r, s) ♦ _n_: **at the** ~ spätestens.

**latex** ['leɪtɛks] _n_ Latex _m_.

**lathe** [leɪð] _n_ Drehbank _f_.

**lather** ['lɑːðə'] _n_ (Seifen)schaum _m_ ♦ _vt_ einschäumen.

**Latin** ['lætɪn] _n_ Latein _nt_; (_person_) Südländer(in) _m(f)_ ♦ _adj_ lateinisch; (_temperament etc_) südländisch.

**Latin America** _n_ Lateinamerika _nt_.

**Latin American** _adj_ lateinamerikanisch ♦ _n_ Lateinamerikaner(in) _m(f)_.

**Latino** [læ'tiːnəu] (_US_) _adj_ aus Lateinamerika stammend ♦ _n_ Latino _mf_, in den USA lebende(r) Lateinamerikaner(in).

**latitude** ['lætɪtjuːd] _n_ (_GEOG_) Breite _f_; (_fig: freedom_) Freiheit _f_.

**latrine** [lə'triːn] _n_ Latrine _f_.

**latter** ['lætə'] _adj_ (_of two_) letztere(r, s); (_later_) spätere(r, s); (_second part of period_) zweite(r, s); (_recent_) letzte(r, s) ♦ _n_: **the** ~ der/die/das letztere, die letzteren.

**latter-day** ['lætədeɪ] _adj_ modern.

**latterly** ['lætəlɪ] _adv_ in letzter Zeit.

**lattice** ['lætɪs] _n_ Gitter _nt_.

**lattice window** _n_ Gitterfenster _nt_.

**Latvia** ['lætvɪə] _n_ Lettland _nt_.

**Latvian** ['lætvɪən] _adj_ lettisch ♦ _n_ Lette _m_, Lettin _f_; (_LING_) Lettisch _nt_.

**laudable** ['lɔːdəbl] _adj_ lobenswert.

**laudatory** ['lɔːdətrɪ] _adj_ (_comments_) lobend; (_speech_) Lob-.

**laugh** [lɑːf] _n_ Lachen _nt_ ♦ _vi_ lachen; (**to do sth) for a** ~ (etw) aus Spaß (tun).

►**laugh at** _vt fus_ lachen über _+acc_.

►**laugh off** _vt_ mit einem Lachen abtun.

**laughable** ['lɑːfəbl] _adj_ lächerlich, lachhaft.

**laughing gas** ['lɑːfɪŋ-] _n_ Lachgas _nt_.

**laughing matter** _n_: **this is no** ~ das ist nicht zum Lachen.

**laughing stock** _n_: **to be the** ~ **of** zum Gespött +_gen_ werden.

**laughter** ['lɑːftə'] _n_ Lachen _nt_, Gelächter _nt_.

**launch** [lɔːntʃ] _n_ (_of rocket, missile_) Abschuß _m_; (_of satellite_) Start _m_; (_COMM: of product_)

Einführung _f_; (: _with publicity_) Lancierung _f_; (_motorboat_) Barkasse _f_ ♦ _vt_ (_ship_) vom Stapel lassen; (_rocket, missile_) abschießen; (_satellite_) starten; (_fig: start_) beginnen mit; (_COMM_) auf den Markt bringen; (: _with publicity_) lancieren.

►**launch into** _vt fus_ (_speech_) vom Stapel lassen; (_activity_) in Angriff nehmen.

►**launch out** _vi_: **to** ~ **out (into)** beginnen (mit).

**launching** ['lɔːntʃɪŋ] _n_ (_of ship_) Stapellauf _m_; (_of rocket, missile_) Abschuß _m_; (_of satellite_) Start _m_; (_fig: start_) Beginn _m_; (_COMM: of product_) Einführung _f_; (: _with publicity_) Lancierung _f_.

**launch(ing) pad** _n_ Startrampe _f_, Abschußrampe _f_.

**launder** ['lɔːndə'] _vt_ waschen und bügeln; (_pej: money_) waschen.

**Launderette** [lɔːn'drɛt] (_BRIT_) _n_ Waschsalon _m_.

**Laundromat** ® ['lɔːndrəmæt] (_US_) _n_ Waschsalon _m_.

**laundry** ['lɔːndrɪ] _n_ Wäsche _f_; (_dirty_) (schmutzige) Wäsche; (_business_) Wäscherei _f_; (_room_) Waschküche _f_; **to do the** ~ (Wäsche) waschen.

**laureate** ['lɔːrɪət] _adj see_ **poet laureate**.

**laurel** ['lɔrl] _n_ (_tree_) Lorbeer(baum) _m_; **to rest on one's** ~**s** sich auf seinen Lorbeeren ausruhen.

**Lausanne** [ləu'zæn] _n_ Lausanne _nt_.

**lava** ['lɑːvə] _n_ Lava _f_.

**lavatory** ['lævətərɪ] _n_ Toilette _f_.

**lavatory paper** _n_ Toilettenpapier _nt_.

**lavender** ['lævəndə'] _n_ Lavendel _m_.

**lavish** ['lævɪʃ] _adj_ großzügig; (_meal_) üppig; (_surroundings_) feudal; (_wasteful_) verschwenderisch ♦ _vt_: **to** ~ **sth on sb** jdn mit etw überhäufen.

**lavishly** ['lævɪʃlɪ] _adv_ (_generously_) großzügig; (_sumptuously_) aufwendig.

**law** [lɔː] _n_ Recht _nt_; (_a rule: also of nature, science_) Gesetz _nt_; (_professions connected with law_) Rechtswesen _nt_; (_SCOL_) Jura _no art_; **against the** ~ rechtswidrig; **to study** ~ Jura _or_ Recht(swissenschaft) studieren; **to go to** ~ vor Gericht gehen; **to break the** ~ gegen das Gesetz verstoßen.

**law-abiding** ['lɔːəbaɪdɪŋ] _adj_ gesetzestreu.

**law and order** _n_ Ruhe und Ordnung _f_.

**lawbreaker** ['lɔːbreɪkə'] _n_ Rechtsbrecher(in) _m(f)_.

**law court** _n_ Gerichtshof _m_, Gericht _nt_.

**lawful** ['lɔːful] _adj_ rechtmäßig.

**lawfully** ['lɔːfəlɪ] _adv_ rechtmäßig.

**lawless** ['lɔːlɪs] _adj_ gesetzwidrig.

**Law Lord** (_BRIT_) _n_ Mitglied des Oberhauses mit besonderem Verantwortungsbereich in Rechtsfragen.

**lawn** [lɔːn] _n_ Rasen _m_.

**lawn mower** _n_ Rasenmäher _m_.

**lawn tennis** _n_ Rasentennis _nt_.

**law school** (*US*) *n* juristische Hochschule *f*.
**law student** *n* Jurastudent(in) *m(f)*.
**lawsuit** ['lɔːsuːt] *n* Prozeß *m*.
**lawyer** ['lɔːjə*] *n* (Rechts)anwalt *m*,
(Rechts)anwältin *f*.
**lax** [læks] *adj* lax.
**laxative** ['læksətɪv] *n* Abführmittel *nt*.
**laxity** ['læksɪtɪ] *n* Laxheit *f*; **moral** ~ lockere *or*
laxe Moral *f*.
**lay** [leɪ] (*pt, pp* **laid**) *pt of* **lie** ♦ *adj* (*REL: preacher
etc*) Laien- ♦ *vt* legen; (*table*) decken; (*carpet,
cable etc*) verlegen; (*plans*) schmieden; (*trap*)
stellen; **the ~ person** (*not expert*) der Laie;
**to ~ facts/proposals before sb** jdm
Tatsachen vorlegen/Vorschläge
unterbreiten; **to ~ one's hands on sth** (*fig*)
etw in die Finger bekommen; **to get laid**
(*infl*) bumsen (*!*).
►**lay aside** *vt* weglegen, zur Seite legen.
►**lay by** *vt* beiseite *or* auf die Seite legen.
►**lay down** *vt* hinlegen; (*rules, laws etc*)
festlegen; **to ~ down the law** Vorschriften
machen; **to ~ down one's life** sein Leben
geben.
►**lay in** *vt* (*supply*) anlegen.
►**lay into** *vt fus* losgehen auf +*acc*; (*criticize*)
herunterputzen.
►**lay off** *vt* (*workers*) entlassen.
►**lay on** *vt* (*meal*) auftischen; (*entertainment
etc*) sorgen für; (*water, gas*) anschließen;
(*paint*) auftragen.
►**lay out** *vt* ausbreiten; (*inf: spend*) ausgeben.
►**lay up** *vt* (*illness*) außer Gefecht setzen; *see
also* **lay by**.
**layabout** ['leɪəbaut] (*inf: pej*) *n* Faulenzer *m*.
**lay-by** ['leɪbaɪ] (*BRIT*) *n* Parkbucht *f*.
**lay days** *npl* Liegezeit *f*.
**layer** ['leɪə*] *n* Schicht *f*.
**layette** [leɪ'ɛt] *n* Babyausstattung *f*.
**layman** ['leɪmən] (*irreg: like* **man**) *n* Laie *m*.
**lay-off** ['leɪɔf] *n* Entlassung *f*.
**layout** ['leɪaut] *n* (*of garden*) Anlage *f*; (*of
building*) Aufteilung *f*; (*TYP*) Layout *nt*.
**laze** [leɪz] *vi* (*also:* ~ **about**) (herum)faulenzen.
**laziness** ['leɪzɪnɪs] *n* Faulheit *f*.
**lazy** ['leɪzɪ] *adj* faul; (*movement, action*)
langsam, träge.
**LB** (*CANADA*) *abbr* (= *Labrador*).
**lb** *abbr* (= *pound (weight)*) britisches Pfund
(0,45 kg), ≈ Pfd.
**lbw** *abbr* (*CRICKET:* = *leg before wicket*)
Regelverletzung beim Kricket.
**LC** (*US*) *n abbr* (= *Library of Congress*)
Bibliothek des US-Parlaments.
**L/C** *abbr* = **letter of credit**.
**lc** *abbr* (*TYP:* = *lower case*) *see* **case**.
**LCD** *n abbr* (= *liquid-crystal display*) LCD *nt*.
**Ld** (*BRIT*) *abbr* (*in titles*) = **lord**.
**LDS** *n abbr* (*BRIT:* = *Licentiate in Dental Surgery*)
≈ Dr. med. dent. ♦ *n abbr* (= *Latter-day Saints*)
Heilige *pl* der Letzten Tage.
**LEA** (*BRIT*) *n abbr* (= *Local Education Authority*)

örtliche Schulbehörde.
**lead¹** [liːd] (*pt, pp* **led**) *n* (*SPORT, fig*) Führung *f*;
(*clue*) Spur *f*; (*in play, film*) Hauptrolle *f*; (*for
dog*) Leine *f*; (*ELEC*) Kabel *nt* ♦ *vt* anführen;
(*guide*) führen; (*organization, BRIT: orchestra*)
leiten ♦ *vi* führen; **to be in the ~** (*SPORT, fig*)
in Führung liegen; **to take the ~** (*SPORT*) in
Führung gehen; **to ~ the way** vorangehen;
**to ~ sb astray** jdn vom rechten Weg
abführen; (*mislead*) jdn irreführen; **to ~ sb
to believe that ...** jdm den Eindruck
vermitteln, daß ...; **to ~ sb to do sth** jdn
dazu bringen, etw zu tun.
►**lead away** *vt* wegführen; (*prisoner etc*)
abführen.
►**lead back** *vt* zurückführen.
►**lead off** *vi* (*in conversation etc*) den Anfang
machen; (*room, road*) abgehen ♦ *vt fus*
abgehen von.
►**lead on** *vt* (*tease*) aufziehen.
►**lead to** *vt fus* führen zu.
►**lead up to** *vt fus* (*events*) vorangehen +*dat*;
(*in conversation*) hinauswollen auf +*acc*.
**lead²** [lɛd] *n* Blei *nt*; (*in pencil*) Mine *f*.
**leaded** ['lɛdɪd] *adj* (*window*) bleiverglast;
(*petrol*) verbleit.
**leaden** ['lɛdn] *adj* (*sky, sea*) bleiern;
(*movements*) bleischwer.
**leader** ['liːdə*] *n* Führer(in) *m(f)*; (*SPORT*)
Erste(r) *f(m)*; (*in newspaper*) Leitartikel *m*;
**the L~ of the House (of Commons/of Lords)**
(*BRIT*) der Führer des Unterhauses/des
Oberhauses.
**leadership** ['liːdəʃɪp] *n* Führung *f*; (*position*)
Vorsitz *m*; (*quality*) Führungsqualitäten *pl*.
**lead-free** [lɛdˈfriː] (*old*) *adj* bleifrei.
**leading** ['liːdɪŋ] *adj* führend; (*role*) Haupt-;
(*first, front*) vorderste(r, s).
**leading lady** *n* (*THEAT*) Hauptdarstellerin *f*.
**leading light** *n* führende Persönlichkeit *f*.
**leading man** *n* (*THEAT*) Hauptdarsteller *m*.
**leading question** *n* Suggestivfrage *f*.
**lead pencil** [lɛd-] *n* Bleistift *m*.
**lead poisoning** [lɛd-] *n* Bleivergiftung *f*.
**lead singer** [liːd-] *n* Leadsänger(in) *m(f)*.
**lead time** [liːd-] *n* (*COMM: for production*)
Produktionszeit *f*; (*: for delivery*) Lieferzeit *f*.
**lead-up** ['liːdʌp] *n*: **the ~ to sth** die Zeit vor
etw *dat*.
**leaf** [liːf] (*pl* **leaves**) *n* Blatt *nt*; (*of table*)
Ausziehplatte *f*; **to turn over a new ~** einen
neuen Anfang machen; **to take a ~ out of
sb's book** sich *dat* von jdm eine Scheibe
abschneiden.
►**leaf through** *vt fus* durchblättern.
**leaflet** ['liːflɪt] *n* Informationsblatt *nt*.
**leafy** ['liːfɪ] *adj* (*tree, branch*) belaubt; (*lane,
suburb*) grün.
**league** [liːg] *n* (*of people, clubs*) Verband *m*; (*of
countries*) Bund *m*; (*FOOTBALL*) Liga *f*; **to be
in ~ with sb** mit jdm gemeinsame Sache
machen.

**league table** *n* Tabelle *f*.

**leak** [liːk] *n* Leck *nt*; (*in roof, pipe etc*) undichte Stelle *f*; (*piece of information*) zugespielte Information *f* ♦ *vi* (*shoes, roof, pipe*) undicht sein; (*ship*) lecken; (*liquid*) auslaufen; (*gas*) ausströmen ♦ *vt* (*information*) durchsickern lassen; **to ~ sth to sb** jdm etw zuspielen.

▶**leak out** *vi* (*liquid*) auslaufen; (*news, information*) durchsickern.

**leakage** ['liːkɪdʒ] *n* (*of liquid*) Auslaufen *nt*; (*of gas*) Ausströmen *nt*.

**leaky** ['liːkɪ] *adj* (*roof, container*) undicht.

**lean** [liːn] (*pt, pp* **leaned** *or* **leant**) *adj* (*person*) schlank; (*meat, fig: time*) mager ♦ *vt*: **to ~ sth on sth** etw an etw *acc* lehnen; (*rest*) etw auf etw *acc* stützen ♦ *vi* (*slope*) sich neigen; **to ~ against** sich lehnen gegen; **to ~ on** sich stützen auf +*acc*; **to ~ forward/back** sich vorbeugen/zurücklehnen; **to ~ towards** tendieren zu.

▶**lean out** *vi* sich hinauslehnen.

▶**lean over** *vi* sich vorbeugen.

**leaning** ['liːnɪŋ] *n* Hang *m*, Neigung *f*.

**leant** [lɛnt] *pt, pp of* **lean**.

**lean-to** ['liːntuː] *n* Anbau *m*.

**leap** [liːp] (*pt, pp* **leaped** *or* **leapt**) *n* Sprung *m*; (*in price, number etc*) sprunghafter Anstieg *m* ♦ *vi* springen; (*price, number etc*) sprunghaft (an)steigen.

▶**leap at** *vt fus* (*offer*) sich stürzen auf +*acc*; (*opportunity*) beim Schopf ergreifen.

▶**leap up** *vi* aufspringen.

**leapfrog** ['liːpfrɒg] *n* Bockspringen *nt*.

**leapt** [lɛpt] *pt, pp of* **leap**.

**leap year** *n* Schaltjahr *nt*.

**learn** [lɜːn] (*pt, pp* **learned** *or* **learnt**) *vt* lernen; (*facts*) erfahren ♦ *vi* lernen; **to ~ about** *or* **of sth** von etw erfahren; **to ~ about sth** (*study*) etw lernen; **to ~ that ...** (*hear, read*) erfahren, daß ...; **to ~ to do sth** etw lernen.

**learned** ['lɜːnɪd] *adj* gelehrt; (*book, paper*) wissenschaftlich.

**learner** ['lɜːnəʳ] (*BRIT*) *n* (*also:* **~ driver**) Fahrschüler(in) *m(f)*.

**learning** ['lɜːnɪŋ] *n* Gelehrsamkeit *f*.

**learnt** [lɜːnt] *pt, pp of* **learn**.

**lease** [liːs] *n* Pachtvertrag *m* ♦ *vt*: **to ~ sth (to sb)** etw (an jdn) verpachten; **on ~ (to)** verpachtet (an +*acc*); **to ~ sth (from sb)** etw (von jdm) pachten.

▶**lease back** *vt* rückmieten.

**leaseback** ['liːsbæk] *n* Verkauf und Rückmiete *pl*.

**leasehold** ['liːshəuld] *n* Pachtbesitz *m* ♦ *adj* gepachtet.

**leash** [liːʃ] *n* Leine *f*.

**least** [liːst] *adv* am wenigsten ♦ *adj*: **the ~** (+ *noun*) der/die/das wenigste; (: *slightest*) der/die/das geringste; **the ~ expensive car** das billigste Auto; **at ~** mindestens; (*still, rather*) wenigstens; **you could at ~ have written** du hättest wenigstens schreiben

können; **not in the ~** nicht im geringsten; **it was the ~ I could do** das war das wenigste, was ich tun konnte.

**leather** ['lɛðəʳ] *n* Leder *nt*.

**leather goods** *npl* Lederwaren *pl*.

**leave** [liːv] (*pt, pp* **left**) *vt* verlassen; (*leave behind*) zurücklassen; (*mark, stain*) hinterlassen; (*object: accidentally*) liegenlassen, stehenlassen; (*food*) übriglassen; (*space, time etc*) lassen ♦ *vi* (*go away*) (weg)gehen; (*bus, train*) abfahren ♦ *n* Urlaub *m*; **to ~ sth to sb** (*money etc*) jdm etw hinterlassen; **to ~ sb with sth** (*impose*) jdm etw aufhalsen; (*possession*) jdm etw lassen; **they were left with nothing** ihnen blieb nichts; **to be left** übrig sein; **to be left over** (*remain*) übrig(geblieben) sein; **to ~ for** gehen/fahren nach; **to take one's ~ of sb** sich von jdm verabschieden; **on ~** auf Urlaub.

▶**leave behind** *vt* zurücklassen; (*object: accidentally*) liegenlassen, stehenlassen.

▶**leave off** *vt* (*cover, lid*) ablassen; (*heating, light*) auslassen ♦ *vi* (*inf: stop*) aufhören.

▶**leave on** *vt* (*light, heating*) anlassen.

▶**leave out** *vt* auslassen.

**leave of absence** *n* Beurlaubung *f*.

**leaves** [liːvz] *npl of* **leaf**.

**Lebanese** [lɛbəˈniːz] *adj* libanesisch ♦ *n inv* Libanese *m*, Libanesin *f*.

**Lebanon** ['lɛbənən] *n* Libanon *m*.

**lecherous** ['lɛtʃərəs] (*pej*) *adj* lüstern.

**lectern** ['lɛktɜːn] *n* Rednerpult *nt*.

**lecture** ['lɛktʃəʳ] *n* Vortrag *m*; (*UNIV*) Vorlesung *f* ♦ *vi* Vorträge/Vorlesungen halten ♦ *vt* (*scold*): **to ~ sb on** *or* **about sth** jdm wegen einer eine Strafpredigt halten; **to give a ~ on** einen Vortrag/eine Vorlesung halten über +*acc*.

**lecture hall** *n* Hörsaal *m*.

**lecturer** ['lɛktʃərəʳ] (*BRIT*) *n* Dozent(in) *m(f)*; (*speaker*) Redner(in) *m(f)*.

**LED** *n abbr* (*ELEC*: = *light-emitting diode*) LED *f*.

**led** [lɛd] *pt, pp of* **lead¹**.

**ledge** [lɛdʒ] *n* (*of mountain*) (Fels)vorsprung *m*; (*of window*) Fensterbrett *nt*; (*on wall*) Leiste *f*.

**ledger** ['lɛdʒəʳ] *n* (*COMM*) Hauptbuch *nt*.

**lee** [liː] *n* Windschatten *m*; (*NAUT*) Lee *f*.

**leech** [liːtʃ] *n* Blutegel *m*; (*fig: person*) Blutsauger *m*.

**leek** [liːk] *n* Porree *m*, Lauch *m*.

**leer** [lɪəʳ] *vi*: **to ~ at sb** jdm lüsterne Blicke zuwerfen.

**leeward** ['liːwəd] (*NAUT*) *adj* (*side etc*) Lee- ♦ *adv* leewärts ♦ *n*: **to ~** an der Leeseite; (*direction*) nach der Leeseite.

**leeway** ['liːweɪ] *n* (*fig*): **to have some ~** etwas Spielraum haben; **there's a lot of ~ to make up** ein großer Rückstand muß aufgeholt werden.

**left** [lɛft] *pt, pp of* **leave** ♦ *adj* (*remaining*) übrig;

(*of position*) links; (*of direction*) nach links ♦ *n*
linke Seite *f* ♦ *adv* links; nach links; **on the**
**~, to the ~** links; **the L~** (*POL*) die Linke.
**left-hand drive** ['lɛfthænd-] *adj* mit
Linkssteuerung.
**left-handed** [lɛft'hændɪd] *adj* linkshändig.
**left-hand side** ['lɛfthænd-] *n* linke Seite *f*.
**leftie** ['lɛftɪ] (*inf*) *n* Linke(r) *f(m)*.
**leftist** ['lɛftɪst] (*POL*) *n* Linke(r) *f(m)* ♦ *adj*
linke(r, s).
**left-luggage (office)** [lɛft'lʌɡɪdʒ(-)] (*BRIT*) *n*
Gepäckaufbewahrung *f*.
**leftovers** ['lɛftəuvəz] *npl* Reste *pl*.
**left-wing** ['lɛft'wɪŋ] *adj* (*POL*) linke(r, s).
**left-winger** ['lɛft'wɪŋɡə*] *n* (*POL*) Linke(r) *f(m)*.
**lefty** ['lɛftɪ] *n* = **leftie**.
**leg** [lɛɡ] *n* Bein *nt*; (*CULIN*) Keule *f*; (*SPORT*)
Runde *f*; (*: of relay race*) Teilstrecke *f*; (*of*
*journey etc*) Etappe *f*; **to stretch one's ~s**
sich *dat* die Beine vertreten; **to get one's**
**~ over** (*inf*) bumsen.
**legacy** ['lɛɡəsɪ] *n* Erbschaft *f*; (*fig*) Erbe *nt*.
**legal** ['liːɡl] *adj* (*requirement*) rechtlich,
gesetzlich; (*system*) Rechts-; (*allowed by law*)
legal, rechtlich zulässig; **to take ~ action** *or*
**proceedings against sb** jdn verklagen.
**legal adviser** *n* juristischer Berater *m*.
**legal holiday** (*US*) *n* gesetzlicher Feiertag *m*.
**legality** [lɪ'ɡælɪtɪ] *n* Legalität *f*.
**legalize** ['liːɡəlaɪz] *vt* legalisieren.
**legally** ['liːɡəlɪ] *adv* rechtlich, gesetzlich; (*in*
*accordance with the law*) rechtmäßig;
**~ binding** rechtsverbindlich.
**legal tender** *n* gesetzliches Zahlungsmittel
*nt*.
**legation** [lɪ'ɡeɪʃən] *n* Gesandtschaft *f*.
**legend** ['lɛdʒənd] *n* Legende *f*, Sage *f*; (*fig:*
*person*) Legende *f*.
**legendary** ['lɛdʒəndərɪ] *adj* legendär; (*very*
*famous*) berühmt.
**-legged** ['lɛɡɪd] *suff* -beinig.
**leggings** ['lɛɡɪŋz] *npl* Leggings *pl*.
**leggy** ['lɛɡɪ] *adj* langbeinig.
**legibility** [lɛdʒɪ'bɪlɪtɪ] *n* Lesbarkeit *f*.
**legible** ['lɛdʒəbl] *adj* leserlich.
**legibly** ['lɛdʒəblɪ] *adv* leserlich.
**legion** ['liːdʒən] *n* Legion *f* ♦ *adj* zahlreich.
**legionnaire** [liːdʒə'nɛə*] *n* Legionär *m*.
**legionnaire's disease** *n* Legionärskrankheit
*f*.
**legislate** ['lɛdʒɪsleɪt] *vi* Gesetze/ein Gesetz
erlassen.
**legislation** [lɛdʒɪs'leɪʃən] *n* Gesetzgebung *f*;
(*laws*) Gesetze *pl*.
**legislative** ['lɛdʒɪslətɪv] *adj* gesetzgebend;
**~ reforms** Gesetzesreformen *pl*.
**legislator** ['lɛdʒɪsleɪtə*] *n* Gesetzgeber *m*.
**legislature** ['lɛdʒɪslətʃə*] *n* Legislative *f*.
**legitimacy** [lɪ'dʒɪtɪməsɪ] *n* (*validity*)
Berechtigung *f*; (*legality*) Rechtmäßigkeit *f*.
**legitimate** [lɪ'dʒɪtɪmət] *adj* (*reasonable*)
berechtigt; (*excuse*) begründet; (*legal*)

rechtmäßig.
**legitimize** [lɪ'dʒɪtɪmaɪz] *vt* legitimieren.
**legless** ['lɛɡlɪs] (*inf*) *adj* (*drunk*) sternhagelvoll.
**legroom** ['lɛɡruːm] *n* Beinfreiheit *f*.
**Leics** (*BRIT*) *abbr* (*POST: = Leicestershire*).
**leisure** ['lɛʒə*] *n* Freizeit *f*; **at ~** in Ruhe.
**leisure centre** *n* Freizeitzentrum *nt*.
**leisurely** ['lɛʒəlɪ] *adj* geruhsam.
**leisure suit** *n* Freizeitanzug *m*.
**lemon** ['lɛmən] *n* Zitrone *f*; (*colour*)
Zitronengelb *nt*.
**lemonade** [lɛmə'neɪd] *n* Limonade *f*.
**lemon cheese** *n* = **lemon curd**.
**lemon curd** *n* zähflüssiger Brotaufstrich mit
Zitronengeschmack.
**lemon juice** *n* Zitronensaft *m*.
**lemon squeezer** *n* Zitronenpresse *f*.
**lemon tea** *n* Zitronentee *m*.
**lend** [lɛnd] (*pt, pp* **lent**) *vt*: **to ~ sth to sb** jdm
etw leihen; **to ~ sb a hand (with sth)** jdm
(bei etw) helfen; **it ~s itself to ...** es eignet
sich für ...
**lender** ['lɛndə*] *n* Verleiher(in) *m(f)*.
**lending library** ['lɛndɪŋ-] *n* Leihbücherei *f*.
**length** [lɛŋθ] *n* Länge *f*; (*piece*) Stück *nt*;
(*amount of time*) Dauer *f*; **the ~ of the island**
(*all along*) die ganze Insel entlang; **2 metres**
**in ~** 2 Meter lang; **at ~** (*at last*) schließlich;
(*for a long time*) lange; **to go to great ~s to**
**do sth** sich *dat* sehr viel Mühe geben, etw zu
tun; **to fall full-~** lang hinfallen; **to lie full-~**
in voller Länge daliegen.
**lengthen** ['lɛŋθn] *vt* verlängern ♦ *vi* länger
werden.
**lengthways** ['lɛŋθweɪz] *adv* der Länge nach.
**lengthy** ['lɛŋθɪ] *adj* lang.
**leniency** ['liːnɪənsɪ] *n* Nachsicht *f*.
**lenient** ['liːnɪənt] *adj* nachsichtig.
**leniently** ['liːnɪəntlɪ] *adv* nachsichtig.
**lens** [lɛnz] *n* (*of spectacles*) Glas *nt*; (*of camera*)
Objektiv *nt*; (*of telescope*) Linse *f*.
**Lent** [lɛnt] *n* Fastenzeit *f*.
**lent** [lɛnt] *pt, pp of* **lend**.
**lentil** ['lɛntɪl] *n* Linse *f*.
**Leo** ['liːəu] *n* Löwe *m*; **to be ~** Löwe sein.
**leopard** ['lɛpəd] *n* Leopard *m*.
**leotard** ['liːətɑːd] *n* Gymnastikanzug *m*.
**leper** ['lɛpə*] *n* Leprakranke(r) *f(m)*.
**leper colony** *n* Leprasiedlung *f*.
**leprosy** ['lɛprəsɪ] *n* Lepra *f*.
**lesbian** ['lɛzbɪən] *adj* lesbisch ♦ *n* Lesbierin *f*.
**lesion** ['liːʒən] *n* Verletzung *f*.
**Lesotho** [lɪ'suːtuː] *n* Lesotho *nt*.
**less** [lɛs] *adj, pron, adv* weniger ♦ *prep*: **~ tax/**
**10% discount** abzüglich Steuer/10% Rabatt;
**~ than half** weniger als die Hälfte; **~ than**
**ever** weniger denn. je; **~ and ~** immer
weniger; **the ~ he works ...** je weniger er
arbeitet ...; **the Prime Minister, no ~** kein
Geringerer als der Premierminister.
**lessee** [lɛ'siː] *n* Pächter(in) *m(f)*.
**lessen** ['lɛsn] *vi* nachlassen, abnehmen ♦ *vt*

verringern.

**lesser** ['lɛsə'] *adj* geringer; **to a ~ extent** in geringerem Maße.

**lesson** ['lɛsn] *n* (*class*) Stunde *f*; (*example, warning*) Lehre *f*; **to teach sb a ~** (*fig*) jdm eine Lektion erteilen.

**lessor** ['lɛsɔː'] *n* Verpächter(in) *m(f)*.

**lest** [lɛst] *conj* damit ... nicht.

**let** [lɛt] (*pt, pp* **let**) *vt* (*allow*) lassen; (*BRIT: lease*) vermieten; **to ~ sb do sth** jdn etw tun lassen, jdm erlauben, etw zu tun; **to ~ sb know sth** jdn etw wissen lassen; **~'s go** gehen wir!; **~ him come** lassen Sie ihn kommen; **"to ~"** „zu vermieten".

▶**let down** *vt* (*tyre etc*) die Luft herauslassen aus; (*person*) im Stich lassen; (*dress etc*) länger machen; (*hem*) auslassen; **to ~ one's hair down** (*fig*) aus sich herausgehen.

▶**let go** *vi* loslassen ♦ *vt* (*release*) freilassen; **to ~ go of** loslassen; **to ~ o.s. go** aus sich herausgehen; (*neglect o.s.*) sich gehenlassen.

▶**let in** *vt* hereinlassen; (*water*) durchlassen.

▶**let off** *vt* (*culprit*) laufenlassen; (*firework, bomb*) hochgehen lassen; (*gun*) abfeuern; **to ~ sb off sth** (*excuse*) jdm etw erlassen; **to ~ off steam** (*inf, fig*) sich abreagieren.

▶**let on** *vi* verraten.

▶**let out** *vt* herauslassen; (*sound*) ausstoßen; (*house, room*) vermieten.

▶**let up** *vi* (*cease*) aufhören; (*diminish*) nachlassen.

**letdown** ['lɛtdaun] *n* Enttäuschung *f*.

**lethal** ['liːθl] *adj* tödlich.

**lethargic** [lɛ'θɑːdʒɪk] *adj* träge, lethargisch.

**lethargy** ['lɛθədʒɪ] *n* Trägheit *f*, Lethargie *f*.

**letter** ['lɛtə'] *n* Brief *m*; (*of alphabet*) Buchstabe *m*; **small/capital ~** Klein-/ Großbuchstabe *m*.

**letter bomb** *n* Briefbombe *f*.

**letter box** (*BRIT*) *n* Briefkasten *m*.

**letterhead** ['lɛtəhɛd] *n* Briefkopf *m*.

**lettering** ['lɛtərɪŋ] *n* Beschriftung *f*.

**letter of credit** *n* Akkreditiv *nt*.

**letter opener** *n* Brieföffner *m*.

**letterpress** ['lɛtəprɛs] *n* Hochdruck *m*.

**letter-quality printer** ['lɛtəkwɔlɪtɪ-] *n* Schönschreibdrucker *m*.

**letters patent** *npl* Patent *nt*, Patenturkunde *f*.

**lettuce** ['lɛtɪs] *n* Kopfsalat *m*.

**let-up** ['lɛtʌp] *n* Nachlassen *nt*; **there was no ~** es ließ nicht nach.

**leukaemia**, (*US*) **leukemia** [luːˈkiːmɪə] *n* Leukämie *f*.

**level** ['lɛvl] *adj* eben ♦ *n* (*on scale, of liquid*) Stand *m*; (*of lake, river*) Wasserstand *m*; (*height*) Höhe *f*; (*fig: standard*) Niveau *nt*; (*also:* **spirit ~**) Wasserwaage *f* ♦ *vt* (*building*) abreißen; (*forest etc*) einebnen ♦ *vi:* **to ~ with sb** (*inf*) ehrlich mit jdm sein ♦ *adv:* **to draw ~ with** einholen; **to be ~ with** auf gleicher Höhe sein mit; **to do one's ~ best** sein

möglichstes tun; **"A" ~s** (*BRIT*) ≈ Abitur *nt*; **"O" ~s** (*BRIT*) ≈ mittlere Reife *f*; **on the ~** (*fig: honest*) ehrlich, reell; **to ~ a gun at sb** ein Gewehr auf jdn richten; **to ~ an accusation at** *or* **against sb** eine Anschuldigung gegen jdn erheben; **to ~ a criticism at** *or* **against sb** Kritik an jdm üben.

▶**level off** *vi* (*prices etc*) sich beruhigen.

▶**level out** *vi* = **level off**.

**level crossing** (*BRIT*) *n* (beschrankter) Bahnübergang *m*.

**level-headed** [lɛvl'hɛdɪd] *adj* (*calm*) ausgeglichen.

**levelling** ['lɛvlɪŋ] *n* Nivellierung *f*.

**level playing field** *n* Chancengleichheit *f*; **to compete on a ~** unter gleichen Bedingungen antreten.

**lever** ['liːvə'] *n* Hebel *m*; (*bar*) Brechstange *f*; (*fig*) Druckmittel *nt* ♦ *vt:* **to ~ up** hochhieven; **to ~ out** heraushieven.

**leverage** ['liːvərɪdʒ] *n* Hebelkraft *f*; (*fig: influence*) Einfluß *m*.

**levity** ['lɛvɪtɪ] *n* Leichtfertigkeit *f*.

**levy** ['lɛvɪ] *n* (*tax*) Steuer *f*; (*charge*) Gebühr *f* ♦ *vt* erheben.

**lewd** [luːd] *adj* (*look etc*) lüstern; (*remark*) anzüglich.

**lexicographer** [lɛksɪ'kɔgrəfə'] *n* Lexikograph(in) *m(f)*.

**lexicography** [lɛksɪ'kɔgrəfɪ] *n* Lexikographie *f*.

**LGV** (*BRIT*) *n abbr* (= *large goods vehicle*) LKW *m*.

**LI** (*US*) *abbr* (= *Long Island*).

**liability** [laɪə'bɪlətɪ] *n* Belastung *f*; (*LAW*) Haftung *f*; **liabilities** *npl* (*COMM*) Verbindlichkeiten *pl*.

**liable** ['laɪəbl] *adj:* **to be ~ to** (*subject to*) unterliegen +*dat*; (*prone to*) anfällig sein für; **~ for** (*responsible*) haftbar für; **to be ~ to do sth** dazu neigen, etw zu tun.

**liaise** [liː'eɪz] *vi:* **to ~ (with)** sich in Verbindung setzen (mit).

**liaison** [liː'eɪzɔn] *n* Zusammenarbeit *f*; (*sexual relationship*) Liaison *f*.

**liar** ['laɪə'] *n* Lügner(in) *m(f)*.

**libel** ['laɪbl] *n* Verleumdung *f* ♦ *vt* verleumden.

**libellous**, (*US*) **libelous** ['laɪbləs] *adj* verleumderisch.

**liberal** ['lɪbərl] *adj* (*POL*) liberal; (*tolerant*) aufgeschlossen; (*generous: offer*) großzügig; (*: amount etc*) reichlich ♦ *n* (*tolerant person*) liberal eingestellter Mensch *m*; (*POL*): **L~** Liberale(r) *f(m)*; **~ with** großzügig mit.

**Liberal Democrat** *n* Liberaldemokrat(in) *m(f)*.

**liberalize** ['lɪbərəlaɪz] *vt* liberalisieren.

**liberally** ['lɪbrəlɪ] *adv* großzügig.

**liberal-minded** ['lɪbərl'maɪndɪd] *adj* liberal (eingestellt).

**liberate** ['lɪbəreɪt] *vt* befreien.

**liberation** [lɪbə'reɪʃən] n Befreiung f.
**liberation theology** n Befreiungstheologie f.
**Liberia** [laɪ'bɪərɪə] n Liberia nt.
**Liberian** [laɪ'bɪərɪən] adj liberianisch ♦ n
Liberianer(in) m(f).
**liberty** ['lɪbətɪ] n Freiheit f; **to be at ~**
(criminal) auf freiem Fuß sein; **to be at ~ to**
**do sth** etw tun dürfen; **to take the ~ of**
**doing sth** sich dat erlauben, etw zu tun.
**libido** [lɪ'biːdəʊ] n Libido f.
**Libra** ['liːbrə] n Waage f; **to be ~** Waage sein.
**librarian** [laɪ'brɛərɪən] n Bibliothekar(in) m(f).
**library** ['laɪbrərɪ] n Bibliothek f; (institution)
Bücherei f.
**library book** n Buch nt aus der Bücherei.
**libretto** [lɪ'brɛtəʊ] n Libretto nt.
**Libya** ['lɪbɪə] n Libyen nt.
**Libyan** ['lɪbɪən] adj libysch ♦ n Libyer(in) m(f).
**lice** [laɪs] npl of **louse**.
**licence**, (US) **license** ['laɪsns] n (document)
Genehmigung f; (also: **driving ~**)
Führerschein m; (COMM) Lizenz f; (excessive
freedom) Zügellosigkeit f; **to get a TV ~**
≈ Fernsehgebühren bezahlen; **under ~**
(COMM) in Lizenz.
**license** ['laɪsns] n (US) = **licence** ♦ vt (person,
organization) eine Lizenz vergeben an +acc;
(activity) eine Genehmigung erteilen für.
**licensed** ['laɪsnst] adj: **the car is ~** die Kfz-
Steuer für das Auto ist bezahlt; **~ hotel/**
**restaurant** Hotel/Restaurant mit
Schankerlaubnis.
**licensee** [laɪsən'siː] n (of bar) Inhaber(in) m(f)
einer Schankerlaubnis.
**license plate** (US) n Nummernschild nt.
**licensing hours** ['laɪsnsɪŋ-] (BRIT) npl
Ausschankzeiten pl.
**licentious** [laɪ'sɛnʃəs] adj ausschweifend,
zügellos.
**lichen** ['laɪkən] n Flechte f.
**lick** [lɪk] vt lecken; (stamp etc) lecken an +dat;
(inf: defeat) in die Pfanne hauen ♦ n Lecken
nt; **to ~ one's lips** sich dat die Lippen lecken;
(fig) sich dat die Finger lecken; **a ~ of paint**
ein Anstrich m.
**licorice** ['lɪkərɪs] (US) n = **liquorice**.
**lid** [lɪd] n Deckel m; (eyelid) Lid nt; **to take the**
**~ off sth** (fig) etw enthüllen or aufdecken.
**lido** ['laɪdəʊ] (BRIT) n Freibad nt.
**lie¹** [laɪ] (pt, pp **lied**) vi lügen ♦ n Lüge f; **to tell**
**~s** lügen.
**lie²** [laɪ] (pt **lay**, pp **lain**) vi (lit, fig) liegen; **to**
**~ low** (fig) untertauchen.
▶**lie about** vi herumliegen.
▶**lie around** vi = **lie about**.
▶**lie back** vi sich zurücklehnen; (fig: accept the
inevitable) sich fügen.
▶**lie down** vi sich hinlegen.
▶**lie up** vi (hide) untertauchen; (rest) im Bett
bleiben.
**Liechtenstein** ['lɪktənstaɪn] n Liechtenstein
nt.

**lie detector** n Lügendetektor m.
**lie-down** ['laɪdaʊn] (BRIT) n: **to have a ~** ein
Schläfchen machen.
**lie-in** ['laɪɪn] (BRIT) n: **to have a ~** (sich)
ausschlafen.
**lieu** [luː]: **in ~ of** prep an Stelle von, anstatt
+gen.
**Lieut.** abbr (MIL: = lieutenant) Lt.
**lieutenant** [lɛf'tɛnənt, (US) luː'tɛnənt] n
Leutnant m.
**lieutenant colonel** n Oberstleutnant m.
**life** [laɪf] (pl **lives**) n Leben nt; (of machine etc)
Lebensdauer f; **true to ~** lebensecht;
**painted from ~** aus dem Leben gegriffen; **to**
**be sent to prison for ~** zu einer
lebenslänglichen Freiheitsstrafe verurteilt
werden; **such is ~** so ist das Leben; **to come**
**to ~** (fig: person) munter werden; (: party etc)
in Schwung kommen.
**life annuity** n Leibrente f.
**life assurance** (BRIT) n = **life insurance**.
**life belt** (BRIT) n Rettungsgürtel m.
**lifeblood** ['laɪfblʌd] n (fig) Lebensnerv m.
**lifeboat** ['laɪfbəʊt] n Rettungsboot nt.
**life buoy** n Rettungsring m.
**life expectancy** n Lebenserwartung f.
**lifeguard** ['laɪfgɑːd] n (at beach)
Rettungsschwimmer(in) m(f); (at swimming
pool) Bademeister(in) m(f).
**life imprisonment** n lebenslängliche
Freiheitsstrafe f.
**life insurance** n Lebensversicherung f.
**life jacket** n Schwimmweste f.
**lifeless** ['laɪflɪs] adj leblos; (fig: person, party
etc) langweilig.
**lifelike** ['laɪflaɪk] adj lebensecht; (painting)
naturgetreu.
**lifeline** ['laɪflaɪn] n (fig) Rettungsanker m;
(rope) Rettungsleine f.
**lifelong** ['laɪflɒŋ] adj lebenslang.
**life preserver** (US) n = **life belt**; **life jacket**.
**lifer** ['laɪfə*] (inf) n Lebenslängliche(r) f(m).
**life raft** n Rettungsfloß nt.
**life-saver** ['laɪfseɪvə*] n Lebensretter(in) m(f).
**life sciences** npl Biowissenschaften pl.
**life sentence** n lebenslängliche
Freiheitsstrafe f.
**life-size(d)** ['laɪfsaɪz(d)] adj in Lebensgröße.
**life span** n Lebensdauer f; (of person)
Lebenszeit f.
**life style** ['laɪfstaɪl] n Lebensstil m.
**life-support system** ['laɪfsəpɔːt-] n (MED)
Lebenserhaltungssystem nt.
**lifetime** ['laɪftaɪm] n Lebenszeit f; (of thing)
Lebensdauer f; (of parliament)
Legislaturperiode f; **in my ~** während
meines Lebens; **the chance of a ~** eine
einmalige Chance.
**lift** [lɪft] vt (raise) heben; (end: ban etc)
aufheben; (plagiarize) abschreiben; (inf:
steal) mitgehen lassen, klauen ♦ vi (fog) sich
auflösen ♦ n (BRIT) Aufzug m, Fahrstuhl m;

**to take the** ~ mit dem Aufzug *or* Fahrstuhl fahren; **to give sb a** ~ *(BRIT)* jdn (im Auto) mitnehmen.

▶**lift off** *vi* abheben.

▶**lift up** *vt* hochheben.

**liftoff** ['lɪftɔf] *n* Abheben *nt*.

**ligament** ['lɪgəmənt] *n (ANAT)* Band *nt*.

**light** [laɪt] *(pt, pp* lit) *n* Licht *nt* ♦ *vt (candle, cigarette, fire)* anzünden; *(room)* beleuchten ♦ *adj* leicht; *(pale, bright)* hell; *(traffic etc)* gering; *(music)* Unterhaltungs- ♦ *adv:* **to travel** ~ mit leichtem Gepäck reisen; **lights** *npl (AUT: also:* **traffic ~s**) Ampel *f;* **the ~s** *(of car)* die Beleuchtung; **have you got a** ~? haben Sie Feuer?; **to turn the** ~ **on/off** das Licht an-/ausmachen; **to come to** ~ ans Tageslicht kommen; **to cast** *or* **shed** *or* **throw** ~ **on** *(fig)* Licht bringen in *+acc;* **in the** ~ **of** angesichts *+gen;* **to make** ~ **of sth** *(fig)* etw auf die leichte Schulter nehmen; ~ **blue/green** *etc* hellblau/-grün *etc.*

▶**light up** *vi (face)* sich erhellen ♦ *vt (illuminate)* beleuchten, erhellen.

**light bulb** *n* Glühbirne *f.*

**lighten** ['laɪtn] *vt (make less heavy)* leichter machen ♦ *vi (become less dark)* sich aufhellen.

**lighter** ['laɪtə*] *n (also:* **cigarette ~**) Feuerzeug *nt.*

**light-fingered** [laɪt'fɪŋgəd] *(inf) adj* langfingerig.

**light-headed** [laɪt'hɛdɪd] *adj (dizzy)* benommen; *(excited)* ausgelassen.

**light-hearted** [laɪt'hɑːtɪd] *adj* unbeschwert; *(question, remark etc)* scherzhaft.

**lighthouse** ['laɪthaʊs] *n* Leuchtturm *m.*

**lighting** ['laɪtɪŋ] *n* Beleuchtung *f.*

**lighting-up time** [laɪtɪŋ'ʌp-] *n Zeitpunkt, zu dem die Fahrzeugbeleuchtung eingeschaltet werden muß.*

**lightly** ['laɪtlɪ] *adv* leicht; *(not seriously)* leichthin; **to get off** ~ glimpflich davonkommen.

**light meter** *n* Belichtungsmesser *m.*

**lightness** ['laɪtnɪs] *n (in weight)* Leichtigkeit *f.*

**lightning** ['laɪtnɪŋ] *n* Blitz *m* ♦ *adj (attack etc)* Blitz-; **with** ~ **speed** blitzschnell.

**lightning conductor** *n* Blitzableiter *m.*

**lightning rod** *(US) n* = **lightning conductor.**

**light pen** *n* Lichtstift *m,* Lichtgriffel *m.*

**lightship** ['laɪtʃɪp] *n* Feuerschiff *nt.*

**lightweight** ['laɪtweɪt] *adj* leicht ♦ *n (BOXING)* Leichtgewichtler *m.*

**light year** *n* Lichtjahr *nt.*

**like** [laɪk] *vt* mögen ♦ *prep* wie; *(such as)* wie (zum Beispiel); ~ **and the** ~ und dergleichen; **I would** ~, **I'd** ~ ich hätte *or* möchte gern; **would you** ~ **a coffee?** möchten Sie einen Kaffee?; **if you** ~ wenn Sie wollen; **to be/look** ~ **sb/sth** jdm/etw ähnlich sein/sehen; **something** ~ **that** so etwas ähnliches; **what does it look/taste/**

**sound** ~? wie sieht es aus/schmeckt es/hört es sich an?; **what's he/the weather** ~? wie ist er/das Wetter?; **I feel** ~ **a drink** ich möchte gerne etwas trinken; **there's nothing** ~ ... es geht nichts über *+acc;* **that's just** ~ **him** das sieht ihm ähnlich; **do it** ~ **this** mach es so; **it is nothing** ~ *(+noun)* es ist ganz anders als; *(+adj)* es ist alles andere als; **it is nothing** ~ **as** ... es ist bei weitem nicht so ...; **his** ~**s and dislikes** seine Vorlieben und Abneigungen.

**likeable** ['laɪkəbl] *adj* sympathisch.

**likelihood** ['laɪklɪhʊd] *n* Wahrscheinlichkeit *f;* **there is every** ~ **that** ... es ist sehr wahrscheinlich, daß ...; **in all** ~ aller Wahrscheinlichkeit nach.

**likely** ['laɪklɪ] *adj* wahrscheinlich; **to be** ~ **to do sth** wahrscheinlich etw tun; **not** ~! *(inf)* wohl kaum!

**like-minded** ['laɪk'maɪndɪd] *adj* gleichgesinnt.

**liken** ['laɪkən] *vt:* **to** ~ **sth to sth** etw mit etw vergleichen.

**likeness** ['laɪknɪs] *n* Ähnlichkeit *f;* **that's a good** ~ *(photo, portrait)* das ist ein gutes Bild von ihm/ihr *etc.*

**likewise** ['laɪkwaɪz] *adv* ebenso; **to do** ~ das gleiche tun.

**liking** ['laɪkɪŋ] *n:* ~ **(for)** *(person)* Zuneigung *f* (zu); *(thing)* Vorliebe *f* (für); **to be to sb's** ~ nach jds Geschmack sein; **to take a** ~ **to sb** an jdm Gefallen finden.

**lilac** ['laɪlək] *n (BOT)* Flieder *m* ♦ *adj* fliederfarben, (zart)lila.

**Lilo** ® ['laɪləʊ] *n* Luftmatratze *f.*

**lilt** [lɪlt] *n* singender Tonfall *m.*

**lilting** ['lɪltɪŋ] *adj* singend.

**lily** ['lɪlɪ] *n* Lilie *f.*

**lily of the valley** *n* Maiglöckchen *nt.*

**Lima** ['liːmə] *n* Lima *nt.*

**limb** [lɪm] *n* Glied *nt;* *(of tree)* Ast *m;* **to be out on a** ~ *(fig)* (ganz) allein (da)stehen.

**limber up** ['lɪmbə*-] *vi* Lockerungsübungen machen.

**limbo** ['lɪmbəʊ] *n:* **to be in** ~ *(fig: plans etc)* in der Schwebe sein; *(: person)* in der Luft hängen *(inf).*

**lime** [laɪm] *n (fruit)* Limone *f;* *(tree)* Linde *f;* *(also:* ~ **juice)** Limonensaft *m;* *(for soil)* Kalk *m;* *(rock)* Kalkstein *m.*

**limelight** ['laɪmlaɪt] *n:* **to be in the** ~ im Rampenlicht stehen.

**limerick** ['lɪmərɪk] *n* Limerick *m.*

**limestone** ['laɪmstəʊn] *n* Kalkstein *m.*

**limit** ['lɪmɪt] *n* Grenze *f;* *(restriction)* Beschränkung *f* ♦ *vt* begrenzen, einschränken; **within** ~**s** innerhalb gewisser Grenzen.

**limitation** [lɪmɪ'teɪʃən] *n* Einschränkung *f;* **limitations** *npl (shortcomings)* Grenzen *pl.*

**limited** ['lɪmɪtɪd] *adj* begrenzt, beschränkt; **to be** ~ sein beschränkt sein auf *+acc.*

**limited edition** *n* beschränkte Ausgabe *f.*

**limited (liability) company** (*BRIT*) n
≈ Gesellschaft *f* mit beschränkter Haftung.
**limitless** ['lɪmɪtlɪs] *adj* grenzenlos.
**limousine** ['lɪməziːn] n Limousine *f*.
**limp** [lɪmp] *adj* schlaff; (*material etc*) weich ♦ *vi*
hinken ♦ *n*: **to have a ~** hinken.
**limpet** ['lɪmpɪt] n Napfschnecke *f*.
**limpid** ['lɪmpɪd] *adj* klar.
**limply** ['lɪmplɪ] *adv* schlaff.
**linchpin** ['lɪntʃpɪn] n (*fig*) wichtigste Stütze *f*.
**Lincs** [lɪŋks] (*BRIT*) *abbr* (*POST:* = Lincolnshire).
**line** [laɪn] n Linie *f*; (*written, printed*) Zeile *f*;
(*wrinkle*) Falte *f*; (*row: of people*) Schlange *f*;
(: *of things*) Reihe *f*; (*for fishing, washing*)
Leine *f*; (*wire, TEL*) Leitung *f*; (*railway track*)
Gleise *pl*; (*fig: attitude*) Standpunkt *m*;
(: *business*) Branche *f*; (*COMM: of product(s)*)
Art *f* ♦ *vt* (*road*) säumen; (*container*)
auskleiden; (*clothing*) füttern; **hold the
~ please!** (*TEL*) bleiben Sie am Apparat!; **to
cut in ~** (*US*) sich vordrängeln; **in ~** in einer
Reihe; **in ~ with** im Einklang mit, in
Übereinstimmung mit; **to be in ~ for sth**
mit etw an der Reihe sein; **to bring sth into
~ with sth** etw auf die gleiche Linie wie
etw *acc* bringen; **on the right ~s** auf dem
richtigen Weg; **I draw the ~ at that** da
mache ich nicht mehr mit; **to ~ sth with sth**
etw mit etw auskleiden; (*drawers etc*) etw
mit etw auslegen; **to ~ the streets** die
Straßen säumen.
▶**line up** *vi* sich aufstellen ♦ *vt* (*in a row*)
aufstellen; (*engage*) verpflichten; (*prepare*)
arrangieren; **to have sb ~d up** jdn
verpflichtet haben; **to have sth ~d up** etw
geplant haben.
**linear** ['lɪnɪə*] *adj* linear; (*shape, form*) gerade.
**lined** [laɪnd] *adj* (*face*) faltig; (*paper*) liniert;
(*skirt, jacket*) gefüttert.
**line editing** n (*COMPUT*) zeilenweise
Aufbereitung *f*.
**line feed** n (*COMPUT*) Zeilenvorschub *m*.
**lineman** ['laɪnmən] (*US: irreg: like* man) n
(*FOOTBALL*) Stürmer *m*.
**linen** ['lɪnɪn] n (*cloth*) Leinen *nt*; (*tablecloths,
sheets etc*) Wäsche *f*.
**line printer** n (*COMPUT*) Zeilendrucker *m*.
**liner** ['laɪnə*] n (*ship*) Passagierschiff *nt*; (*also:*
**bin ~**) Müllbeutel *m*.
**linesman** ['laɪnzmən] (*irreg: like* man) n (*SPORT*)
Linienrichter *m*.
**line-up** ['laɪnʌp] n (*US: queue*) Schlange *f*;
(*SPORT*) Aufstellung *f*; (*at concert etc*)
Künstleraufgebot *nt*; (*identity parade*)
Gegenüberstellung *f*.
**linger** ['lɪŋgə*] *vi* (*smell*) sich halten; (*tradition
etc*) fortbestehen; (*person*) sich aufhalten.
**lingerie** ['lænʒəriː] n (Damen)unterwäsche *f*.
**lingering** ['lɪŋgərɪŋ] *adj* bleibend.
**lingo** ['lɪŋgəu] (*pl* **~es**) (*inf*) n Sprache *f*.
**linguist** ['lɪŋgwɪst] n (*person who speaks several
languages*) Sprachkundige(r) *f(m)*.

**linguistic** [lɪŋ'gwɪstɪk] *adj* sprachlich.
**linguistics** [lɪŋ'gwɪstɪks] n
Sprachwissenschaft *f*.
**liniment** ['lɪnɪmənt] n Einreibemittel *nt*.
**lining** ['laɪnɪŋ] n (*cloth*) Futter *nt*; (*ANAT: of
stomach*) Magenschleimhaut *f*; (*TECH*)
Auskleidung *f*; (*of brakes*) (Brems)belag *m*.
**link** [lɪŋk] n Verbindung *f*, Beziehung *f*;
(*communications link*) Verbindung; (*of a
chain*) Glied *nt* ♦ *vt* (*join*) verbinden; **links** *npl*
(*GOLF*) Golfplatz *m*; **rail ~** Bahnverbindung
*f*.
▶**link up** *vt* verbinden ♦ *vi* verbunden
werden.
**linkup** ['lɪŋkʌp] n Verbindung *f*; (*of spaceships*)
Koppelung *f*.
**lino** ['laɪnəu] n = **linoleum**.
**linoleum** [lɪ'nəulɪəm] n Linoleum *nt*.
**linseed oil** ['lɪnsiːd-] n Leinöl *nt*.
**lint** [lɪnt] n Mull *m*.
**lintel** ['lɪntl] n (*ARCHIT*) Sturz *m*.
**lion** ['laɪən] n Löwe *m*.
**lion cub** n Löwenjunge(s) *nt*.
**lioness** ['laɪənɪs] n Löwin *f*.
**lip** [lɪp] n (*ANAT*) Lippe *f*; (*of cup etc*) Rand *m*;
(*inf: insolence*) Frechheiten *pl*.
**liposuction** ['lɪpəusʌkʃən] n Liposuktion *f*.
**lip-read** ['lɪpriːd] *vi* von den Lippen ablesen.
**lip salve** n Fettstift *m*.
**lip service** (*pej*) *n*: **to pay ~ to sth** ein
Lippenbekenntnis zu etw ablegen.
**lipstick** ['lɪpstɪk] n Lippenstift *m*.
**liquefy** ['lɪkwɪfaɪ] *vt* verflüssigen ♦ *vi* sich
verflüssigen.
**liqueur** [lɪ'kjuə*] n Likör *m*.
**liquid** ['lɪkwɪd] *adj* flüssig ♦ n Flüssigkeit *f*.
**liquid assets** *npl* flüssige Vermögenswerte *pl*.
**liquidate** ['lɪkwɪdeɪt] *vt* liquidieren.
**liquidation** [lɪkwɪ'deɪʃən] n Liquidation *f*.
**liquidation sale** (*US*) n Verkauf *m* wegen
Geschäftsaufgabe.
**liquidator** ['lɪkwɪdeɪtə*] n Liquidator *m*.
**liquid-crystal display** ['lɪkwɪd'krɪstl-] n
Flüssigkristallanzeige *f*.
**liquidity** [lɪ'kwɪdɪtɪ] n Liquidität *f*.
**liquidize** ['lɪkwɪdaɪz] *vt* (im Mixer) pürieren.
**liquidizer** ['lɪkwɪdaɪzə*] n Mixer *m*.
**liquor** ['lɪkə*] n Spirituosen *pl*, Alkohol *m*; **hard
~** harte Drinks *pl*.
**liquorice** ['lɪkərɪs] (*BRIT*) n Lakritze *f*.
**liquor store** (*US*) n Spirituosengeschäft *nt*.
**Lisbon** ['lɪzbən] n Lissabon *nt*.
**lisp** [lɪsp] n Lispeln *nt* ♦ *vi* lispeln.
**lissom(e)** ['lɪsəm] *adj* geschmeidig.
**list** [lɪst] n Liste *f* ♦ *vt* aufführen; (*COMPUT*)
auflisten; (*write down*) aufschreiben ♦ *vi*
(*ship*) Schlagseite haben.
**listed building** ['lɪstɪd-] (*BRIT*) n unter
Denkmalschutz stehendes Gebäude *nt*.
**listed company** n börsennotierte Firma *f*.
**listen** ['lɪsn] *vi* hören; **to ~ (out) for** horchen
auf +*acc*; **to ~ to sb** jdm zuhören; **to ~ to sth**

etw hören; ~! hör zu!
**listener** ['lɪsnəʳ] n Zuhörer(in) m(f); (RADIO)
Hörer(in) m(f).
**listeria** [lɪs'tɪərɪə] n Listeriose f.
**listing** ['lɪstɪŋ] n Auflistung f; (entry) Eintrag
m.
**listless** ['lɪstlɪs] adj lustlos.
**listlessly** ['lɪstlɪslɪ] adv lustlos.
**list price** n Listenpreis m.
**lit** [lɪt] pt, pp of **light**.
**litany** ['lɪtənɪ] n Litanei f.
**liter** ['liːtəʳ] (US) n = **litre**.
**literacy** ['lɪtərəsɪ] n die Fähigkeit, lesen und
schreiben zu können.
**literacy campaign** n Kampagne f gegen das
Analphabetentum.
**literal** ['lɪtərəl] adj wörtlich, eigentlich;
(translation) (wort)wörtlich.
**literally** ['lɪtrəlɪ] adv buchstäblich.
**literary** ['lɪtərərɪ] adj literarisch.
**literate** ['lɪtərət] adj (educated) gebildet; **to be**
~ lesen und schreiben können.
**literature** ['lɪtrɪtʃəʳ] n Literatur f; (printed
information) Informationsmaterial nt.
**lithe** [laɪð] adj gelenkig; (animal) geschmeidig.
**lithograph** ['lɪθəgraːf] n Lithographie f.
**lithography** [lɪ'θɔgrəfɪ] n Lithographie f.
**Lithuania** [lɪθjuˈeɪnɪə] n Litauen nt.
**Lithuanian** [lɪθjuˈeɪnɪən] adj litauisch ♦ n
Litauer(in) m(f); (LING) Litauisch nt.
**litigation** [lɪtɪˈgeɪʃən] n Prozeß m.
**litmus paper** ['lɪtməs-] n Lackmuspapier nt.
**litre, (**US**) liter** ['liːtəʳ] n Liter m or nt.
**litter** ['lɪtəʳ] n (rubbish) Abfall m; (young
animals) Wurf m.
**litter bin** (BRIT) n Abfalleimer m.
**litterbug** ['lɪtəbʌg] n Dreckspatz m.
**littered** ['lɪtəd] adj: ~ **with** (scattered) übersät
mit.
**litter lout** n Dreckspatz m.
**little** ['lɪtl] adj klein; (short) kurz ♦ adv wenig; **a**
~ ein wenig, ein bißchen; **a** ~ **bit** ein kleines
bißchen; **to have** ~ **time/money** wenig Zeit/
Geld haben; ~ **by** ~ nach und nach.
**little finger** n kleiner Finger m.
**little-known** ['lɪtl'nəʊn] adj wenig bekannt.
**liturgy** ['lɪtədʒɪ] n Liturgie f.
**live** [vi lɪv, adj laɪv] vi leben; (in house, town)
wohnen ♦ adj lebend; (TV, RADIO) live;
(performance, pictures etc) Live-; (ELEC)
stromführend; (bullet, bomb etc) scharf; **to**
~ **with sb** mit jdm zusammenleben.
▶**live down** vt hinwegkommen über +acc.
▶**live for** vt leben für.
▶**live in** vi (student/servant) im Wohnheim/
Haus wohnen.
▶**live off** vt fus leben von; (parents etc) auf
Kosten +gen leben.
▶**live on** vt fus leben von.
▶**live out** vi (BRIT: student/servant) außerhalb
(des Wohnheims/Hauses) wohnen ♦ vt: **to**
~ **out one's days** or **life** sein Leben

verbringen.
▶**live together** vi zusammenleben.
▶**live up** vt: **to** ~ **it up** einen draufmachen
(inf).
▶**live up to** vt fus erfüllen, entsprechen +dat.
**live-in** ['lɪvɪn] adj (cook, maid) im Haus
wohnend; **her** ~ **lover** ihr Freund, der bei
ihr wohnt.
**livelihood** ['laɪvlɪhʊd] n Lebensunterhalt m.
**liveliness** ['laɪvlɪnɪs] n (see adj) Lebhaftigkeit
f; Lebendigkeit f.
**lively** ['laɪvlɪ] adj lebhaft; (place, event, book
etc) lebendig.
**liven up** ['laɪvn-] vt beleben, Leben bringen in
+acc; (person) aufmuntern ♦ vi (person)
aufleben; (discussion, evening etc) in
Schwung kommen.
**liver** ['lɪvəʳ] n (ANAT, CULIN) Leber f.
**liverish** ['lɪvərɪʃ] adj: **to be** ~ sich unwohl
fühlen.
**Liverpudlian** [lɪvəˈpʌdlɪən] adj Liverpooler ♦ n
Liverpooler(in) m(f).
**livery** ['lɪvərɪ] n Livree f.
**lives** [laɪvz] npl of **life**.
**livestock** ['laɪvstɔk] n Vieh nt.
**live wire** (inf) n (person) Energiebündel nt.
**livid** ['lɪvɪd] adj (colour) bleifarben; (inf:
furious) fuchsteufelswild.
**living** ['lɪvɪŋ] adj lebend ♦ n: **to earn** or **make a**
~ sich dat seinen Lebensunterhalt
verdienen; **within** ~ **memory** seit
Menschengedenken; **the cost of** ~ die
Lebenshaltungskosten pl.
**living conditions** npl Wohnverhältnisse pl.
**living expenses** npl Lebenshaltungskosten
pl.
**living room** n Wohnzimmer nt.
**living standards** npl Lebensstandard m.
**living wage** n ausreichender Lohn m.
**lizard** ['lɪzəd] n Eidechse f.
**llama** ['laːmə] n Lama nt.
**LLB** n abbr (= Bachelor of Laws) akademischer
Grad für Juristen.
**LLD** n abbr (= Doctor of Laws) ≈ Dr. jur.
**LMT** (US) abbr (= Local Mean Time) Ortszeit.
**load** [ləʊd] n Last f; (of vehicle) Ladung f;
(weight, ELEC) Belastung f ♦ vt (also: ~ **up**)
beladen; (gun, COMPUT: program, data)
laden; **that's a** ~ **of rubbish** (inf) das ist alles
Blödsinn; ~**s of, a** ~ **of** (fig) jede Menge; **to**
~ **a camera** einen Film einlegen.
**loaded** ['ləʊdɪd] adj (inf: rich) steinreich; (dice)
präpariert; (vehicle): **to be** ~ **with** beladen
sein mit; **a** ~ **question** eine Fangfrage.
**loading bay** ['ləʊdɪŋ-] n Ladeplatz m.
**loaf** [ləʊf] (pl **loaves**) n Brot nt, Laib m ♦ vi (also:
~ **about,** ~ **around**) faulenzen; **use your** ~!
(inf) streng deinen Grips an!
**loam** [ləʊm] n Lehmerde f.
**loan** [ləʊn] n Darlehen nt ♦ vt: **to** ~ **sth to sb**
jdm etw leihen; **on** ~ geliehen.
**loan account** n Darlehenskonto nt.

**loan capital** n Anleihekapital nt.
**loan shark** (inf) n Kreditha¡ m.
**loath** [ləuθ] adj: **to be ~ to do sth** etw ungern tun.
**loathe** [ləuð] vt verabscheuen.
**loathing** ['ləuðɪŋ] n Abscheu m.
**loathsome** ['ləuðsəm] adj abscheulich.
**loaves** [ləuvz] npl of **loaf**.
**lob** [lɔb] vt (ball) lobben.
**lobby** ['lɔbɪ] n (of building) Eingangshalle f; (POL: pressure group) Interessenverband m ♦ vt Einfluß nehmen auf +acc.
**lobbyist** ['lɔbɪɪst] n Lobbyist(in) m(f).
**lobe** [ləub] n Ohrläppchen nt.
**lobster** ['lɔbstə*] n Hummer m.
**lobster pot** n Hummer(fang)korb m.
**local** ['ləukl] adj örtlich; (council) Stadt-, Gemeinde-; (paper) Lokal- ♦ n (pub) Stammkneipe f; **the locals** npl (local inhabitants) die Einheimischen pl.
**local anaesthetic** n örtliche Betäubung f.
**local authority** n Gemeindeverwaltung f, Stadtverwaltung f.
**local call** n Ortsgespräch nt.
**locale** [ləu'kɑːl] n Umgebung f.
**local government** n Kommunalverwaltung f.
**locality** [ləu'kælɪtɪ] n Gegend f.
**localize** ['ləukəlaɪz] vt lokalisieren.
**locally** ['ləukəlɪ] adv am Ort.
**locate** [ləu'keɪt] vt (find) ausfindig machen; **to be ~d in** sich befinden in +dat.
**location** [ləu'keɪʃən] n Ort m; (position) Lage f; (CINE) Drehort m; **he's on ~ in Mexico** er ist bei Außenaufnahmen in Mexiko; **to be filmed on ~** als Außenaufnahme gedreht werden.
**loch** [lɔx] (SCOT) n See m.
**lock** [lɔk] n (of door etc) Schloß nt; (on canal) Schleuse f; (also: ~ **of hair**) Locke f ♦ vt (door etc) abschließen; (steering wheel) sperren; (COMPUT: keyboard) verriegeln ♦ vi (door etc) sich abschließen lassen; (wheels, mechanism etc) blockieren; **on full ~** (AUT) voll eingeschlagen; **~, stock and barrel** mit allem Drum und Dran; **his jaw ~ed** er hatte Mundsperre.
►**lock away** vt wegschließen; (criminal) einsperren.
►**lock in** vt einschließen.
►**lock out** vt aussperren.
►**lock up** vt (criminal etc) einsperren; (house) abschließen ♦ vi abschließen.
**locker** ['lɔkə*] n Schließfach nt.
**locker room** n Umkleideraum m.
**locket** ['lɔkɪt] n Medaillon nt.
**lockjaw** ['lɔkdʒɔː] n Wundstarrkrampf m.
**lockout** ['lɔkaut] n Aussperrung f.
**locksmith** ['lɔksmɪθ] n Schlosser m.
**lockup** ['lɔkʌp] n (US: inf: jail) Gefängnis nt; (also: **lock-up garage**) Garage f.
**locomotive** [ləukə'məutɪv] n Lokomotive f.

**locum** ['ləukəm] n (MED) Vertreter(in) m(f).
**locust** ['ləukəst] n Heuschrecke f.
**lodge** [lɔdʒ] n Pförtnerhaus nt; (hunting lodge) Hütte f; (FREEMASONRY) Loge f ♦ vt (complaint, protest etc) einlegen ♦ vi (bullet) steckenbleiben; (person): **to ~ (with)** zur Untermiete wohnen (bei).
**lodger** ['lɔdʒə*] n Untermieter(in) m(f).
**lodging** ['lɔdʒɪŋ] n Unterkunft f.
**lodging house** n Pension f.
**lodgings** ['lɔdʒɪŋz] npl möbliertes Zimmer nt; (several rooms) Wohnung f.
**loft** [lɔft] n Boden m, Speicher m.
**lofty** ['lɔftɪ] adj (noble) hoch(fliegend); (self-important) hochmütig; (high) hoch.
**log** [lɔg] n (of wood) Holzblock m, Holzklotz m; (written account) Log nt ♦ n abbr (MATH: = logarithm) log ♦ vt (ins Logbuch) eintragen.
►**log in** vi (COMPUT) sich anmelden.
►**log into** vt fus (COMPUT) sich anmelden bei.
►**log off** vi (COMPUT) sich abmelden.
►**log on** vi (COMPUT) = **log in**.
►**log out** vi (COMPUT) = **log off**.
**logarithm** ['lɔgərɪðm] n Logarithmus m.
**logbook** ['lɔgbuk] n (NAUT) Logbuch nt; (AVIAT) Bordbuch nt; (of car) Kraftfahrzeugbrief m; (of lorry driver) Fahrtenbuch nt; (of events) Tagebuch nt; (of movement of goods etc) Dienstbuch nt.
**log fire** n Holzfeuer nt.
**logger** ['lɔgə*] n (lumberjack) Holzfäller m.
**loggerheads** ['lɔgəhedz] npl: **to be at ~** Streit haben.
**logic** ['lɔdʒɪk] n Logik f.
**logical** ['lɔdʒɪkl] adj logisch.
**logically** ['lɔdʒɪkəlɪ] adv logisch; (reasonably) logischerweise.
**logistics** [lɔ'dʒɪstɪks] n Logistik f.
**log jam** n (fig) Blockierung f; **to break the ~** freie Bahn schaffen.
**logo** ['ləugəu] n Logo nt.
**loin** [lɔɪn] n Lende f.
**loincloth** ['lɔɪnklɔθ] n Lendenschurz m.
**loiter** ['lɔɪtə*] vi sich aufhalten.
**loll** [lɔl] vi (also: ~ **about**: person) herumhängen; (head) herunterhängen; (tongue) heraushängen.
**lollipop** ['lɔlɪpɔp] n Lutscher m.
**lollipop lady** (BRIT) n ≈ Schülerlotsin f.
**lollipop man** (BRIT) n ≈ Schülerlotse m.

Lollipop man/lady heißen in Großbritannien die Männer bzw. die Frauen, die mit Hilfe eines runden Stoppschildes den Verkehr anhalten, damit Schulkinder die Straße gefahrlos überqueren können. Der Name bezieht sich auf die Form des Schildes, die an einen Lutscher erinnert.

**lollop** ['lɔləp] vi zockeln.
**lolly** ['lɔlɪ] (inf) n (lollipop) Lutscher m;

(*money*) Mäuse *pl.*
**London** ['lʌndən] *n* London *nt.*
**Londoner** ['lʌndənə*] *n* Londoner(in) *m(f).*
**lone** [ləun] *adj* einzeln, einsam; (*only*) einzig.
**loneliness** ['ləunlɪnɪs] *n* Einsamkeit *f.*
**lonely** ['ləunlɪ] *adj* einsam.
**lonely hearts** *adj:* ~ **ad** Kontaktanzeige *f;* **the** ~ **column** die Kontaktanzeigen *pl.*
**lone parent** *n* Alleinerziehende(r) *f(m).*
**loner** ['ləunə*] *n* Einzelgänger(in) *m(f).*
**long** [lɒŋ] *adj* lang ♦ *adv* lang(e) ♦ *vi:* **to** ~ **for sth** sich nach etw sehnen; **in the** ~ **run** auf die Dauer; **how** ~ **is the lesson?** wie lange dauert die Stunde?; **6 metres/months** ~ 6 Meter/Monate lang; **so** *or* **as** ~ **as** (*on condition that*) solange; (*while*) während; **don't be** ~! bleib nicht so lange!; **all night** ~ die ganze Nacht; **he no** ~**er comes** er kommt nicht mehr; ~ **ago** vor langer Zeit; ~ **before/after** lange vorher/danach; **before** ~ bald; **at** ~ **last** schließlich und endlich; **the** ~ **and the short of it is that** ... kurz gesagt, ...
**long-distance** [lɒŋ'dɪstəns] *adj* (*travel, phone call*) Fern-; (*race*) Langstrecken-.
**longevity** [lɒn'dʒɛvɪtɪ] *n* Langlebigkeit *f.*
**long-haired** ['lɒŋ'hɛəd] *adj* langhaarig; (*animal*) Langhaar-.
**longhand** ['lɒŋhænd] *n* Langschrift *f.*
**longing** ['lɒŋɪŋ] *n* Sehnsucht *f.*
**longingly** ['lɒŋɪŋlɪ] *adv* sehnsüchtig.
**longitude** ['lɒŋɡɪtjuːd] *n* Länge *f.*
**long johns** [-dʒɒnz] *npl* lange Unterhose *f.*
**long jump** *n* Weitsprung *m.*
**long-life** ['lɒŋlaɪf] *adj* (*batteries etc*) mit langer Lebensdauer; ~ **milk** H-Milch *f.*
**long-lost** ['lɒŋlɒst] *adj* verloren geglaubt.
**long-playing record** ['lɒŋpleɪɪŋ-] *n* Langspielplatte *f.*
**long-range** ['lɒŋ'reɪndʒ] *adj* (*plan, forecast*) langfristig; (*missile, plane etc*) Langstrecken-.
**longshoreman** ['lɒŋʃɔːmən] (*US*) (*irreg: like* **man**) *n* Hafenarbeiter *m.*
**long-sighted** ['lɒŋ'saɪtɪd] *adj* weitsichtig.
**long-standing** ['lɒŋ'stændɪŋ] *adj* langjährig.
**long-suffering** [lɒŋ'sʌfərɪŋ] *adj* schwer geprüft.
**long-term** ['lɒŋtəːm] *adj* langfristig.
**long wave** *n* Langwelle *f.*
**long-winded** [lɒŋ'wɪndɪd] *adj* umständlich, langatmig.
**loo** [luː] (*BRIT: inf*) *n* Klo *nt.*
**loofah** ['luːfə] *n* Luffa(schwamm) *m.*
**look** [luk] *vi* sehen, schauen, gucken (*inf*); (*seem, appear*) aussehen ♦ *n* (*glance*) Blick *m;* (*appearance*) Aussehen *nt;* (*expression*) Miene *f;* (*FASHION*) Look *m;* **looks** *npl* (*good looks*) (gutes) Aussehen *f;* **to** ~ (**out**) **onto the sea/ south** (*building etc*) Blick aufs Meer/nach Süden haben; ~ (**here**)! (*expressing annoyance*) hör (mal) zu!; ~! (*expressing*

*surprise*) sieh mal!; **to** ~ **like sb/sth** wie jd/ etw aussehen; **it** ~**s like him** es sieht ihm ähnlich; **it** ~**s about 4 metres long** es scheint etwa 4 Meter lang zu sein; **it** ~**s all right to me** es scheint mir in Ordnung zu sein; **to** ~ **ahead** vorausschauen; **to have a** ~ **at sth** sich *dat* etw ansehen; **let me have a** ~ laß mich mal sehen; **to have a** ~ **for sth** nach etw suchen.
►**look after** *vt fus* sich kümmern um.
►**look at** *vt fus* ansehen; (*read quickly*) durchsehen; (*study, consider*) betrachten.
►**look back** *vi:* **to** ~ **back (on)** zurückblicken (auf +*acc*); **to** ~ **back at sth/sb** sich nach jdm/etw umsehen.
►**look down on** *vt fus* (*fig*) herabsehen auf +*acc.*
►**look for** *vt fus* suchen.
►**look forward to** *vt fus* sich freuen auf +*acc*; **we** ~ **forward to hearing from you** (*in letters*) wir hoffen, bald von Ihnen zu hören.
►**look in** *vi:* **to** ~ **in on sb** bei jdm vorbeikommen.
►**look into** *vt fus* (*investigate*) untersuchen.
►**look on** *vi* (*watch*) zusehen.
►**look out** *vi* (*beware*) aufpassen.
►**look out for** *vt fus* Ausschau halten nach.
►**look over** *vt* (*essay etc*) durchsehen; (*house, town etc*) sich *dat* ansehen; (*person*) mustern.
►**look round** *vi* sich umsehen.
►**look through** *vt fus* durchsehen.
►**look to** *vt fus* (*rely on*) sich verlassen auf +*acc.*
►**look up** *vi* aufsehen; (*situation*) sich bessern ♦ *vt* (*word etc*) nachschlagen; **things are** ~**ing up** es geht bergauf.
►**look up to** *vt fus* aufsehen zu.
**lookalike** ['lukəlaɪk] *n* Doppelgänger(in) *m(f).*
**look-in** ['lukɪn] *n:* **to get a** ~ (*inf*) eine Chance haben.
**lookout** ['lukaut] *n* (*tower etc*) Ausguck *m;* (*person*) Wachtposten *m;* **to be on the** ~ **for sth** nach etw Ausschau halten.
**loom** [luːm] *vi* (*also:* ~ **up**: *object, shape*) sich abzeichnen; (*event*) näherrücken ♦ *n* Webstuhl *m.*
**loony** ['luːnɪ] (*inf*) *adj* verrückt ♦ *n* Verrückte(r) *f(m).*
**loop** [luːp] *n* Schlaufe *f;* (*COMPUT*) Schleife *f* ♦ *vt:* **to** ~ **sth around sth** etw um etw schlingen.
**loophole** ['luːphəul] *n* Hintertürchen *nt;* **a** ~ **in the law** eine Lücke im Gesetz.
**loose** [luːs] *adj* lose, locker; (*clothes etc*) weit; (*long hair*) offen; (*not strictly controlled, promiscuous*) locker; (*definition*) ungenau; (*translation*) frei ♦ *vt* (*animal*) loslassen; (*prisoner*) freilassen; (*set off, unleash*) entfesseln ♦ *n:* **to be on the** ~ frei herumlaufen.
**loose change** *n* Kleingeld *nt.*
**loose chippings** *npl* Schotter *m.*

**loose end** n: **to be at a ~** or (US) **at ~s** nichts mit sich dat anzufangen wissen; **to tie up ~s** die offenstehenden Probleme lösen.

**loose-fitting** ['luːsfɪtɪŋ] adj weit.

**loose-leaf** ['luːsliːf] adj Loseblatt-; **~ binder** Ringbuch nt.

**loose-limbed** [luːs'lɪmd] adj gelenkig, beweglich.

**loosely** ['luːslɪ] adv lose, locker.

**loosely-knit** ['luːslɪ'nɪt] adj (fig) locker.

**loosen** ['luːsn] vt lösen, losmachen; (clothing, belt etc) lockern.

**loosen up** vi (before game) sich auflockern; (relax) auftauen.

**loot** [luːt] n (inf) Beute f ♦ vt plündern.

**looter** ['luːtə*] n Plünderer m.

**looting** ['luːtɪŋ] n Plünderung f.

**lop off** [lɔp-] vt abhacken.

**lopsided** ['lɔp'saɪdɪd] adj schief.

**lord** [lɔːd] n (BRIT) Lord m; **L~ Smith** Lord Smith; **the L~** (REL) der Herr; **my ~** (to bishop) Exzellenz; (to noble) Mylord; (to judge) Euer Ehren; **good L~!** ach, du lieber Himmel!; **the (House of) L~s** (BRIT) das Oberhaus.

**lordly** ['lɔːdlɪ] adj hochmütig.

**lordship** ['lɔːdʃɪp] n: **your L~** Eure Lordschaft.

**lore** [lɔː*] n Überlieferungen pl.

**lorry** ['lɔrɪ] (BRIT) n Lastwagen m, Lkw m.

**lorry driver** (BRIT) n Lastwagenfahrer m.

**lose** [luːz] (pt, pp lost) vt verlieren; (opportunity) verpassen; (pursuers) abschütteln ♦ vi verlieren; **to ~ (time)** (clock) nachgehen; **to ~ weight** abnehmen; **to ~ 5 pounds** 5 Pfund abnehmen; **to ~ sight of sth** (also fig) etw aus den Augen verlieren.

**loser** ['luːzə*] n Verlierer(in) m(f); (inf: failure) Versager m; **to be a good/bad ~** ein guter/ schlechter Verlierer sein.

**loss** [lɔs] n Verlust m; **to make a ~ (of £1,000)** (1000 Pfund) Verlust machen; **to sell sth at a ~** etw mit Verlust verkaufen; **heavy ~es** schwere Verluste pl; **to cut one's ~es** aufgeben, bevor es noch schlimmer wird; **to be at a ~** nicht mehr weiterwissen.

**loss adjuster** n Schadenssachverständige(r) f(m).

**loss leader** n (COMM) Lockvogelangebot nt.

**lost** [lɔst] pt, pp of **lose** ♦ adj (person, animal) vermißt; (object) verloren; **to be ~** sich verlaufen/verfahren haben; **to get ~** sich verlaufen/verfahren; **get ~!** (inf) verschwinde!; **~ in thought** in Gedanken verloren.

**lost and found** (US) n = **lost property**.

**lost cause** n aussichtslose Sache f.

**lost property** (BRIT) n Fundsachen pl; (also: **~ office**) Fundbüro nt.

**lot** [lɔt] n (kind) Art f; (group) Gruppe f; (at auctions, destiny) Los nt; **to draw ~s** losen,

Lose ziehen; **the ~** alles; **a ~ (of)** (a large number (of)) viele; (a great deal (of)) viel; **~s of** viele; **I read a ~** ich lese viel; **this happens a ~** das kommt oft vor.

**loth** [ləʊθ] adj = **loath**.

**lotion** ['ləʊʃən] n Lotion f.

**lottery** ['lɔtərɪ] n Lotterie f.

**loud** [laʊd] adj laut; (clothes) schreiend ♦ adv laut; **to be ~ in one's support of sb/sth** jdn/ etw lautstark unterstützen; **out ~** (read, laugh etc) laut.

**loud-hailer** [laʊd'heɪlə*] (BRIT) n Megaphon nt.

**loudly** ['laʊdlɪ] adv laut.

**loudmouthed** ['laʊdmaʊθt] adj großmäulig.

**loudspeaker** [laʊd'spiːkə*] n Lautsprecher m.

**lounge** [laʊndʒ] n (in house) Wohnzimmer nt; (in hotel) Lounge f; (at airport, station) Wartehalle f; (BRIT: also: **~ bar**) Salon m ♦ vi faulenzen.

▶**lounge about** vi herumliegen, herumsitzen, herumstehen.

▶**lounge around** vi = **lounge about**.

**lounge suit** (BRIT) n Straßenanzug m.

**louse** [laʊs] (pl **lice**) n Laus f.

▶**louse up** (inf) vt vermasseln.

**lousy** ['laʊzɪ] (inf) adj (bad-quality) lausig, mies; (despicable) fies, gemein; (ill): **to feel ~** sich miserabel or elend fühlen.

**lout** [laʊt] n Lümmel m, Flegel m.

**louvre, (US) louver** ['luːvə*] adj (door, window) Lamellen-.

**lovable** ['lʌvəbl] adj liebenswert.

**love** [lʌv] n Liebe f ♦ vt lieben; (thing, activity etc) gern mögen; **" ~ (from) Anne"** (on letter) „mit herzlichen Grüßen, Anne"; **to be in ~ with** verliebt sein in +acc; **to fall in ~ with** sich verlieben in +acc; **to make ~** sich lieben; **~ at first sight** Liebe auf den ersten Blick; **to send one's ~ to sb** jdn grüßen lassen; **"fifteen ~"** (TENNIS) „fünfzehn null"; **to ~ doing sth** etw gern tun; **I'd ~ to come** ich würde sehr gerne kommen; **I ~ chocolate** ich esse Schokolade liebend gern.

**love affair** n Verhältnis nt, Liebschaft f.

**love child** n uneheliches Kind nt, Kind nt der Liebe.

**loved ones** ['lʌvdwʌnz] npl enge Freunde und Verwandte pl.

**love-hate relationship** ['lʌvheɪt-] n Haßliebe f.

**love letter** n Liebesbrief m.

**love life** n Liebesleben nt.

**lovely** ['lʌvlɪ] adj (beautiful) schön; (delightful) herrlich; (person) sehr nett.

**lover** ['lʌvə*] n Geliebte(r) f(m); (person in love) Liebende(r) f(m); **~ of art/music** Kunst-/ Musikliebhaber(in) m(f); **to be ~s** ein Liebespaar sein.

**lovesick** ['lʌvsɪk] adj liebeskrank.

**love song** n Liebeslied nt.

**loving** ['lʌvɪŋ] adj liebend; (actions) liebevoll.

**low** [ləu] *adj* niedrig; (*bow, curtsey*) tief; (*quality*) schlecht; (*sound: deep*) tief; (: *quiet*) leise; (*depressed*) niedergeschlagen, bedrückt ♦ *adv* (*sing*) leise; (*fly*) tief ♦ *n* (*MET*) Tief *nt*; **to be/run** ~ knapp sein/ werden; **sb is running** ~ **on sth** jdm wird etw knapp; **to reach a new** *or* **an all-time** ~ einen neuen Tiefstand erreichen.
**low-alcohol** ['ləu'ælkəhɔl] *adj* alkoholarm.
**lowbrow** ['ləubrau] *adj* (*geistig*) anspruchslos.
**low-calorie** ['ləu'kælərɪ] *adj* kalorienarm.
**low-cut** ['ləukʌt] *adj* (*dress*) tief ausgeschnitten.
**lowdown** ['ləudaun] (*inf*) *n*: **he gave me the** ~ **on it** er hat mich darüber informiert.
**lower** ['ləuə*] *adj* untere(r, s); (*lip, jaw, arm*) Unter- ♦ *vt* senken.
**low-fat** ['ləu'fæt] *adj* fettarm.
**low-key** ['ləu'kiː] *adj* zurückhaltend; (*not obvious*) unaufdringlich.
**lowlands** ['ləuləndz] *npl* Flachland *nt*.
**low-level language** ['ləulevl-] *n* (*COMPUT*) niedere Programmiersprache *f*.
**low-loader** ['ləu'ləudə*] *n* Tieflader *m*.
**lowly** ['ləulɪ] *adj* (*position*) niedrig; (*origin*) bescheiden.
**low-lying** [ləu'laɪŋ] *adj* tiefgelegen.
**low-paid** [ləu'peɪd] *adj* schlechtbezahlt.
**low-rise** ['ləuraɪz] *adj* niedrig (gebaut).
**low-tech** ['ləutɛk] *adj* nicht mit Hi-Tech ausgestattet.
**loyal** ['lɔɪəl] *adj* treu; (*support*) loyal.
**loyalist** ['lɔɪəlɪst] *n* Loyalist(in) *m(f)*.
**loyalty** ['lɔɪəltɪ] *n* (*see adj*) Treue *f*, Loyalität *f*.
**lozenge** ['lɒzɪndʒ] *n* Pastille *f*; (*shape*) Raute *f*.
**LP** *n abbr* (= *long player*) LP *f*; *see also* **long-playing record.**

Als **L-Plates** werden in Großbritannien die weißen Schilder mit einem roten 'L' bezeichnet, die vorne und hinten an jedem von einem Fahrschüler geführten Fahrzeug befestigt werden müssen. Fahrschüler müssen einen vorläufigen Führerschein beantragen und dürfen damit unter der Aufsicht eines erfahrenen Autofahrers auf allen Straßen außer Autobahnen fahren.

**LPN** (*US*) *n abbr* (= *Licensed Practical Nurse*) staatlich anerkannte Krankenschwester *f*, staatlich anerkannter Krankenpfleger *m*.
**LRAM** (*BRIT*) *n abbr* (= *Licentiate of the Royal Academy of Music*) Qualifikationsnachweis in Musik.
**LSAT** (*US*) *n abbr* (= *Law School Admission Test*) Zulassungsprüfung für juristische Hochschulen.
**LSD** *n abbr* (= *lysergic acid diethylamide*) LSD *nt*; (*BRIT: also*: **L.S.D.** = *pounds, shillings and pence*) früheres britisches Währungssystem.
**LSE** (*BRIT*) *n abbr* (= *London School of*

*Economics*) Londoner Wirtschafts-hochschule.
**LT** *abbr* (*ELEC:* = *low-tension*) Niederspannung *f*; (*cable etc*) Niederspannungs-.
**Lt** *abbr* (*MIL:* = *lieutenant*) Lt.
**Ltd** *abbr* (*COMM:* = *limited (liability)*) ≈ GmbH *f*.
**lubricant** ['luːbrɪkənt] *n* Schmiermittel *nt*.
**lubricate** ['luːbrɪkeɪt] *vt* schmieren, ölen.
**lucid** ['luːsɪd] *adj* klar; (*person*) bei klarem Verstand.
**lucidity** [luː'sɪdɪtɪ] *n* Klarheit *f*.
**luck** [lʌk] *n* (*esp good luck*) Glück *nt*; **bad** ~ Unglück *nt*; **good** ~! viel Glück!; **bad** *or* **hard** *or* **tough** ~! so ein Pech!; **hard** *or* **tough** ~! (*showing no sympathy*) Pech gehabt!; **to be in** ~ Glück haben; **to be out of** ~ kein Glück haben.
**luckily** ['lʌkɪlɪ] *adv* glücklicherweise.
**luckless** ['lʌklɪs] *adj* glücklos.
**lucky** ['lʌkɪ] *adj* (*situation, event*) glücklich; (*object*) glücksbringend; (*person*): **to be** ~ Glück haben; **to have a** ~ **escape** noch einmal davonkommen; ~ **charm** Glücksbringer *m*.
**lucrative** ['luːkrətɪv] *adj* einträglich.
**ludicrous** ['luːdɪkrəs] *adj* grotesk.
**ludo** ['luːdəu] *n* Mensch, ärgere dich nicht *nt*.
**lug** [lʌg] (*inf*) *vt* schleppen.
**luggage** ['lʌgɪdʒ] *n* Gepäck *nt*.
**luggage car** (*US*) *n* = **luggage van.**
**luggage rack** *n* Gepäckträger *m*; (*in train*) Gepäckablage *f*.
**luggage van** (*BRIT*) *n* (*RAIL*) Gepäckwagen *m*.
**lugubrious** [lu'guːbrɪəs] *adj* schwermütig.
**lukewarm** ['luːkwɔːm] *adj* lauwarm; (*fig: person, reaction etc*) lau.
**lull** [lʌl] *n* Pause *f* ♦ *vt*: **to** ~ **sb to sleep** jdn einlullen *or* einschläfern; **to be** ~**ed into a false sense of security** in trügerische Sicherheit gewiegt werden.
**lullaby** ['lʌləbaɪ] *n* Schlaflied *nt*.
**lumbago** [lʌm'beɪgəu] *n* Hexenschuß *m*.
**lumber** ['lʌmbə*] *n* (*wood*) Holz *nt*; (*junk*) Gerümpel *nt* ♦ *vi*: **to** ~ **about/along** herum-/entlangtapsen.
▶**lumber with** *vt*: **to be/get** ~**ed with sth** etw am Hals haben/aufgehalst bekommen.
**lumberjack** ['lʌmbədʒæk] *n* Holzfäller *m*.
**lumber room** (*BRIT*) *n* Rumpelkammer *f*.
**lumberyard** ['lʌmbjɑːd] (*US*) *n* Holzlager *nt*.
**luminous** ['luːmɪnəs] *adj* leuchtend, Leucht-.
**lump** [lʌmp] *n* Klumpen *m*; (*on body*) Beule *f*; (*in breast*) Knoten *m*; (*also*: **sugar** ~) Stück *nt* (Zucker) ♦ *vt*: **to** ~ **together** in einen Topf werfen; **a** ~ **sum** eine Pauschalsumme.
**lumpy** ['lʌmpɪ] *adj* klumpig.
**lunacy** ['luːnəsɪ] *n* Wahnsinn *m*.
**lunar** ['luːnə*] *adj* Mond-.
**lunatic** ['luːnətɪk] *adj* wahnsinnig ♦ *n* Wahnsinnige(r) *f(m)*, Irre(r) *f(m)*.
**lunatic asylum** *n* Irrenanstalt *f*.
**lunatic fringe** *n*: **the** ~ die Extremisten *pl*.

**lunch** [lʌntʃ] n Mittagessen nt; (time)
Mittagszeit f ♦ vi zu Mittag essen.
**lunch break** n Mittagspause f.
**luncheon** ['lʌntʃən] n Mittagessen nt.
**luncheon meat** n Frühstücksfleisch nt.
**luncheon voucher** (BRIT) n Essensmarke f.
**lunch hour** n Mittagspause f.
**lunch time** n Mittagszeit f.
**lung** [lʌŋ] n Lunge f.
**lunge** [lʌndʒ] vi (also: ~ forward) sich nach
vorne stürzen; **to ~ at** sich stürzen auf +acc.
**lupin** ['luːpɪn] n Lupine f.
**lurch** [ləːtʃ] vi ruckeln; (person) taumeln ♦ n
Ruck m; (of person) Taumeln nt; **to leave sb
in the ~** jdn im Stich lassen.
**lure** [luə*] n Verlockung f ♦ vt locken.
**lurid** ['luərɪd] adj (story etc) reißerisch; (pej:
brightly coloured) grell, in grellen Farben.
**lurk** [ləːk] vi (also fig) lauern.
**luscious** ['lʌʃəs] adj (attractive) phantastisch;
(food) köstlich, lecker.
**lush** [lʌʃ] adj (fields) saftig; (gardens) üppig;
(luxurious) luxuriös.
**lust** [lʌst] (pej) n (sexual) (sinnliche) Begierde
f; (for money, power etc) Gier f.
▶**lust after** vt fus (sexually) begehren; (crave)
gieren nach.
▶**lust for** vt fus = lust after.
**lustful** ['lʌstful] adj lüstern.
**lustre**, (US) **luster** ['lʌstə*] n Schimmer m,
Glanz m.
**lusty** ['lʌstɪ] adj gesund und munter.
**lute** [luːt] n Laute f.
**luvvie, luvvy** ['lʌvɪ] (inf) n Schätzchen nt.
**Luxembourg** ['lʌksəmbəːg] n Luxemburg nt.
**luxuriant** [lʌg'zjuərɪənt] adj üppig.
**luxuriate** [lʌg'zjuərɪeɪt] vi: **to ~ in sth** sich in
etw dat aalen.
**luxurious** [lʌg'zjuərɪəs] adj luxuriös.
**luxury** ['lʌkʃərɪ] n Luxus m (no pl) ♦ cpd (hotel,
car etc) Luxus-; **little luxuries** kleine
Genüsse.
**LV** n abbr = luncheon voucher.
**LW** abbr (RADIO: = long wave) LW.
**Lycra** ® ['laɪkrə] n Lycra nt.
**lying** ['laɪɪŋ] n Lügen nt ♦ adj verlogen.
**lynch** [lɪntʃ] vt lynchen.
**lynx** [lɪŋks] n Luchs m.
**lyric** ['lɪrɪk] adj lyrisch.
**lyrical** ['lɪrɪkl] adj lyrisch; (fig: praise etc)
schwärmerisch.
**lyricism** ['lɪrɪsɪzəm] n Lyrik f.
**lyrics** ['lɪrɪks] npl (of song) Text m.

# M, m

**M¹, m¹** [ɛm] n (letter) M nt, m nt; **~ for Mary**,
(US) **~ for Mike** ≈ M wie Martha.
**M²** [ɛm] n abbr (BRIT: = motorway): **the M8**
≈ die A8 ♦ abbr = **medium**.
**m²** abbr (= metre) m; = **mile**; (= million) Mio.
**MA** n abbr (= Master of Arts) akademischer
Grad für Geisteswissenschaftler; (= military
academy) Militärakademie f ♦ abbr (US:
POST: = Massachusetts).
**mac** [mæk] (BRIT) n Regenmantel m.
**macabre** [mə'kɑːbrə] adj makaber.
**macaroni** [mækə'rəunɪ] n Makkaroni pl.
**macaroon** [mækə'ruːn] n Makrone f.
**mace** [meɪs] n (weapon) Keule f; (ceremonial)
Amtsstab m; (spice) Muskatblüte f.
**Macedonia** [mæsɪ'dəunɪə] n Makedonien nt.
**Macedonian** [mæsɪ'dəunɪən] adj makedonisch
♦ n Makedonier(in) m(f); (LING)
Makedonisch nt.
**machinations** [mækɪ'neɪʃənz] npl
Machenschaften pl.
**machine** [mə'ʃiːn] n Maschine f; (fig: party
machine etc) Apparat m ♦ vt (TECH)
maschinell herstellen or bearbeiten; (dress
etc) mit der Maschine nähen.
**machine code** n Maschinencode m.
**machine gun** n Maschinengewehr nt.
**machine language** n Maschinensprache f.
**machine-readable** [mə'ʃiːnriːdəbl] adj
maschinenlesbar.
**machinery** [mə'ʃiːnərɪ] n Maschinen pl; (fig:
government) Apparat m.
**machine shop** n Maschinensaal m.
**machine tool** n Werkzeugmaschine f.
**machine washable** adj waschmaschinen-
fest.
**machinist** [mə'ʃiːnɪst] n Maschinist(in) m(f).
**macho** ['mætʃəu] adj Macho-; **a ~ man** ein
Macho m.
**mackerel** ['mækrl] n inv Makrele f.
**mackintosh** ['mækɪntɔʃ] (BRIT) n
Regenmantel m.
**macro...** ['mækrəu] pref Makro-, makro-.
**macroeconomics** ['mækrəuiːkə'nɔmɪks] npl
Makroökonomie f.
**mad** [mæd] adj wahnsinnig, verrückt; (angry)
böse, sauer (inf); **to be ~ about** verrückt
sein auf +acc; **to be ~ at sb** böse or sauer auf
jdn sein; **to go ~** (insane) verrückt or
wahnsinnig werden; (angry) böse or sauer
werden.
**madam** ['mædəm] n gnädige Frau f; **yes, ~**

ja(wohl); **M~ Chairman** Frau Vorsitzende.
**madcap** ['mædkæp] *adj* (*idea*) versponnen;
(*tricks*) toll.
**mad cow disease** *n* Rinderwahn *m*.
**madden** ['mædn] *vt* ärgern, fuchsen (*inf*).
**maddening** ['mædnɪŋ] *adj* unerträglich.
**made** [meɪd] *pt, pp of* **make**.
**Madeira** [mə'dɪərə] *n* Madeira *nt*; (*wine*)
Madeira *m*.
**made-to-measure** ['meɪdtə'mɛʒə*] (*BRIT*) *adj*
maßgeschneidert.
**madhouse** ['mædhaus] *n* (*also fig*) Irrenhaus
*nt*.
**madly** ['mædlɪ] *adv* wie verrückt; ~ **in love** bis
über beide Ohren verliebt.
**madman** ['mædmən] (*irreg: like* **man**) *n*
Verrückte(r) *m*, Irre(r) *m*.
**madness** ['mædnɪs] *n* Wahnsinn *m*.
**Madrid** [mə'drɪd] *n* Madrid *nt*.
**Mafia** ['mæfɪə] *n* Mafia *f*.
**mag** [mæg] (*BRIT: inf*) *n abbr* = **magazine**.
**magazine** [mægə'ziːn] *n* Zeitschrift *f*; (*RADIO,
TV, of firearm*) Magazin *nt*; (*MIL: store*) Depot
*nt*.
**maggot** ['mægət] *n* Made *f*.
**magic** ['mædʒɪk] *n* Magie *f*; (*conjuring*)
Zauberei *f* ♦ *adj* magisch; (*formula*) Zauber-;
(*fig: place, moment etc*) zauberhaft.
**magical** ['mædʒɪkl] *adj* magisch; (*experience,
evening*) zauberhaft.
**magician** [mə'dʒɪʃən] *n* (*wizard*) Magier *m*;
(*conjurer*) Zauberer *m*.
**magistrate** ['mædʒɪstreɪt] *n*
Friedensrichter(in) *m(f)*.
**magnanimous** [mæg'nænɪməs] *adj* großmütig.
**magnate** ['mægneɪt] *n* Magnat *m*.
**magnesium** [mæg'niːzɪəm] *n* Magnesium *nt*.
**magnet** ['mægnɪt] *n* Magnet *m*.
**magnetic** [mæg'nɛtɪk] *adj* magnetisch; (*field,
compass, pole etc*) Magnet-; (*personality*)
anziehend.
**magnetic disk** *n* (*COMPUT*) Magnetplatte *f*.
**magnetic tape** *n* Magnetband *nt*.
**magnetism** ['mægnɪtɪzəm] *n* Magnetismus *m*;
(*of person*) Anziehungskraft *f*.
**magnetize** ['mægnɪtaɪz] *vt* magnetisieren.
**magnification** [mægnɪfɪ'keɪʃən] *n*
Vergrößerung *f*.
**magnificence** [mæg'nɪfɪsns] *n* Großartigkeit *f*;
(*of robes*) Pracht *f*.
**magnificent** [mæg'nɪfɪsnt] *adj* großartig;
(*robes*) prachtvoll.
**magnify** ['mægnɪfaɪ] *vt* vergrößern; (*sound*)
verstärken; (*fig: exaggerate*) aufbauschen.
**magnifying glass** ['mægnɪfaɪɪŋ-] *n*
Vergrößerungsglas *nt*, Lupe *f*.
**magnitude** ['mægnɪtjuːd] *n* (*size*) Ausmaß *nt*,
Größe *f*; (*importance*) Bedeutung *f*.
**magnolia** [mæg'nəʊlɪə] *n* Magnolie *f*.
**magpie** ['mægpaɪ] *n* Elster *f*.
**mahogany** [mə'hɒgənɪ] *n* Mahagoni *nt* ♦ *cpd*
Mahagoni-.

**maid** [meɪd] *n* Dienstmädchen *nt*; **old** ~ (*pej*)
alte Jungfer.
**maiden** ['meɪdn] *n* (*liter*) Mädchen *nt* ♦ *adj*
unverheiratet; (*speech, voyage*) Jungfern-.
**maiden name** *n* Mädchenname *m*.
**mail** [meɪl] *n* Post *f* ♦ *vt* aufgeben; **by** ~ mit
der Post.
**mailbox** ['meɪlbɒks] *n* (*US*) Briefkasten *m*;
(*COMPUT*) Mailbox *f*, elektronischer
Briefkasten *m*.
**mailing list** ['meɪlɪŋ-] *n* Anschriftenliste *f*.
**mailman** ['meɪlmæn] (*US: irreg: like* **man**) *n*
Briefträger *m*, Postbote *m*.
**mail order** *n* (*system*) Versand *m* ♦ *cpd:* **mail-
order firm** *or* **business** Versandhaus *nt*;
**mail-order catalogue** Versandhauskatalog
*m*; **by** ~ durch Bestellung per Post.
**mailshot** ['meɪlʃɒt] (*BRIT*) *n* Werbebrief *m*.
**mail train** *n* Postzug *m*.
**mail truck** (*US*) *n* Postauto *nt*.
**mail van** (*BRIT*) *n* (*AUT*) Postauto *nt*; (*RAIL*)
Postwagen *m*.
**maim** [meɪm] *vt* verstümmeln.
**main** [meɪn] *adj* Haupt-, wichtigste(r, s);
(*door, entrance, meal*) Haupt- ♦ *n*
Hauptleitung *f*; **the mains** *npl* (*ELEC*) das
Stromnetz; (*gas, water*) die Hauptleitung; **in
the** ~ im großen und ganzen.
**main course** *n* (*CULIN*) Hauptgericht *nt*.
**mainframe** ['meɪnfreɪm] *n* (*COMPUT*)
Großrechner *m*.
**mainland** ['meɪnlənd] *n* Festland *nt*.
**mainline** ['meɪnlaɪn] *adj:* ~ **station**
Fernbahnhof *m* ♦ *vt* (*drugs slang*) spritzen
♦ *vi* (*drugs slang*) fixen.
**main line** *n* Hauptstrecke *f*.
**mainly** ['meɪnlɪ] *adv* hauptsächlich.
**main road** *n* Hauptstraße *f*.
**mainstay** ['meɪnsteɪ] *n* (*foundation*)
(wichtigste) Stütze *f*; (*chief constituent*)
Hauptbestandteil *m*.
**mainstream** ['meɪnstriːm] *n* Hauptrichtung *f*
♦ *adj* (*cinema etc*) populär; (*politics*) der
Mitte.
**maintain** [meɪn'teɪn] *vt* (*preserve*)
aufrechterhalten; (*keep up*) beibehalten;
(*provide for*) unterhalten; (*look after: building*)
instand halten; (*: equipment*) warten; (*affirm:
opinion*) vertreten; (*: innocence*) beteuern; **to**
~ **that** ... behaupten, daß ...
**maintenance** ['meɪntənəns] *n* (*of building*)
Instandhaltung *f*; (*of equipment*) Wartung *f*;
(*preservation*) Aufrechterhaltung *f*; (*LAW:
alimony*) Unterhalt *m*.
**maintenance contract** *n* Wartungsvertrag
*m*.
**maintenance order** *n* (*LAW*)
Unterhaltsurteil *nt*.
**maisonette** [meɪzə'nɛt] (*BRIT*) *n*
Maisonettewohnung *f*.
**maize** [meɪz] *n* Mais *m*.
**Maj.** *abbr* (*MIL*) = **major**.

**majestic** [mə'dʒɛstɪk] *adj* erhaben.
**majesty** ['mædʒɪstɪ] *n* (*title*): **Your M~** Eure Majestät; (*splendour*) Erhabenheit *f*.
**major** ['meɪdʒə'] *n* Major *m* ♦ *adj* bedeutend; (*MUS*) Dur ♦ *vi* (*US*): **to ~ in French** Französisch als Hauptfach belegen; **a ~ operation** eine größere Operation.
**Majorca** [mə'jɔːkə] *n* Mallorca *nt*.
**major general** *n* Generalmajor *m*.
**majority** [mə'dʒɒrɪtɪ] *n* Mehrheit *f* ♦ *cpd* (*verdict, holding*) Mehrheits-.
**make** [meɪk] (*pt, pp* **made**) *vt* machen; (*clothes*) nähen; (*cake*) backen; (*speech*) halten; (*manufacture*) herstellen; (*earn*) verdienen; (*cause to be*): **to ~ sb sad** jdn traurig machen; (*force*): **to ~ sb do sth** jdn zwingen, etw zu tun; (*cause*) jdn dazu bringen, etw zu tun; (*equal*): **2 and 2 ~ 4** 2 und 2 ist *or* macht 4 ♦ *n* Marke *f*, Fabrikat *nt*; **to ~ a fool of sb** jdn lächerlich machen; **to ~ a profit/loss** Gewinn/Verlust machen; **to ~ it** (*arrive*) es schaffen; (*succeed*) Erfolg haben; **what time do you ~ it?** wie spät hast du?; **to ~ good** erfolgreich sein; (*threat*) wahrmachen; (*promise*) einlösen; (*damage*) wiedergutmachen; (*loss*) ersetzen; **to ~ do with** auskommen mit.
► **make for** *vt fus* (*place*) zuhalten auf +*acc*.
► **make off** *vi* sich davonmachen.
► **make out** *vt* (*decipher*) entziffern; (*understand*) verstehen; (*see*) ausmachen; (*write: cheque*) ausstellen; (*claim, imply*) behaupten; (*pretend*) so tun, als ob; **to ~ out a case for sth** für etw argumentieren.
► **make over** *vt:* **to ~ over (to)** überschreiben (+*dat*).
► **make up** *vt* (*constitute*) bilden; (*invent*) erfinden; (*prepare: bed*) zurechtmachen; (*: parcel*) zusammenpacken ♦ *vi* (*after quarrel*) sich versöhnen; (*with cosmetics*) sich schminken; **to ~ up one's mind** sich entscheiden; **to be made up of** bestehen aus.
► **make up for** *vt fus* (*loss*) ersetzen; (*disappointment etc*) ausgleichen.
**make-believe** ['meɪkbɪliːv] *n* Phantasie *f*; **a world of ~** eine Phantasiewelt; **it's just ~** es ist nicht wirklich.
**maker** ['meɪkə'] *n* Hersteller *m*; **film ~** Filmemacher(in) *m(f)*.
**makeshift** ['meɪkʃɪft] *adj* behelfsmäßig.
**make-up** ['meɪkʌp] *n* Make-up *nt*, Schminke *f*.
**make-up bag** *n* Kosmetiktasche *f*.
**make-up remover** *n* Make-up-Entferner *m*.
**making** ['meɪkɪŋ] *n* (*fig*): **in the ~** im Entstehen; **to have the ~s of** das Zeug haben zu.
**maladjusted** [mælə'dʒʌstɪd] *adj* verhaltensgestört.
**maladroit** [mælə'drɔɪt] *adj* ungeschickt.
**malaise** [mæ'leɪz] *n* Unbehagen *nt*.
**malaria** [mə'lɛərɪə] *n* Malaria *f*.

**Malawi** [mə'lɑːwɪ] *n* Malawi *nt*.
**Malay** [mə'leɪ] *adj* malaiisch ♦ *n* Malaie *m*, Malaiin *f*; (*LING*) Malaiisch *nt*.
**Malaya** [mə'leɪə] *n* Malaya *nt*.
**Malayan** [mə'leɪən] *adj, n* = **Malay**.
**Malaysia** [mə'leɪzɪə] *n* Malaysia *nt*.
**Malaysian** [mə'leɪzɪən] *adj* malaysisch ♦ *n* Malaysier(in) *m(f)*.
**Maldives** ['mɔːldaɪvz] *npl* Malediven *pl*.
**male** [meɪl] *n* (*animal*) Männchen *nt*; (*man*) Mann *m* ♦ *adj* männlich; (*ELEC*): **~ plug** Stecker *m*; **because he is ~** weil er ein Mann/Junge ist; **~ and female students** Studenten und Studentinnen; **a ~ child** ein Junge.
**male chauvinist** *n* Chauvinist *m*.
**male nurse** *n* Krankenpfleger *m*.
**malevolence** [mə'lɛvələns] *n* Boshaftigkeit *f*; (*of action*) Böswilligkeit *f*.
**malevolent** [mə'lɛvələnt] *adj* boshaft; (*intention*) böswillig.
**malfunction** [mæl'fʌŋkʃən] *n* (*of computer*) Funktionsstörung *f*; (*of machine*) Defekt *m* ♦ *vi* (*computer*) eine Funktionsstörung haben; (*machine*) defekt sein.
**malice** ['mælɪs] *n* Bosheit *f*.
**malicious** [mə'lɪʃəs] *adj* boshaft; (*LAW*) böswillig.
**malign** [mə'laɪn] *vt* verleumden ♦ *adj* (*influence*) schlecht; (*interpretation*) böswillig.
**malignant** [mə'lɪgnənt] *adj* bösartig; (*intention*) böswillig.
**malingerer** [mə'lɪŋgərə'] *n* Simulant(in) *m(f)*.
**mall** [mɔːl] *n* (*also:* **shopping ~**) Einkaufszentrum *nt*.
**malleable** ['mælɪəbl] *adj* (*lit, fig*) formbar.
**mallet** ['mælɪt] *n* Holzhammer *m*.
**malnutrition** [mælnjuː'trɪʃən] *n* Unterernährung *f*.
**malpractice** [mæl'præktɪs] *n* Berufsvergehen *nt*.
**malt** [mɔːlt] *n* Malz *nt*; (*also:* **~ whisky**) Malt Whisky *m*.
**Malta** ['mɔːltə] *n* Malta *nt*.
**Maltese** [mɔːl'tiːz] *adj* maltesisch ♦ *n inv* Malteser(in) *m(f)*; (*LING*) Maltesisch *nt*.
**maltreat** [mæl'triːt] *vt* schlecht behandeln; (*violently*) mißhandeln.
**mammal** ['mæml] *n* Säugetier *nt*.
**mammoth** ['mæməθ] *n* Mammut *nt* ♦ *adj* (*task*) Mammut-.
**man** [mæn] *n* (*pl* **men**) Mann *m*; (*mankind*) der Mensch, die Menschen *pl*; (*CHESS*) Figur *f* ♦ *vt* (*ship*) bemannen; (*gun, machine*) bedienen; (*post*) besetzen; **~ and wife** Mann und Frau.
**manage** ['mænɪdʒ] *vi:* **to ~ to do sth** es schaffen, etw zu tun; (*get by financially*) zurechtkommen ♦ *vt* (*business, organization*) leiten; (*control*) zurechtkommen mit; **to ~ without sb/sth** ohne jdn/etw auskommen;

**well ~d** (*business, shop etc*) gut geführt.
**manageable** ['mænɪdʒəbl] *adj* (*task*) zu bewältigen; (*number*) überschaubar.
**management** ['mænɪdʒmənt] *n* Leitung *f*, Führung *f*; (*persons*) Unternehmensleitung *f*; **"under new ~"** „unter neuer Leitung".
**management accounting** *n* Kosten- und Leistungsrechnung *f*.
**management consultant** *n* Unternehmensberater(in) *m(f)*.
**manager** ['mænɪdʒə*] *n* (*of business*) Geschäftsführer(in) *m(f)*; (*of institution etc*) Direktor(in) *m(f)*; (*of department*) Leiter(in) *m(f)*; (*of pop star*) Manager(in) *m(f)*; (*SPORT*) Trainer(in) *m(f)*; **sales ~** Verkaufsleiter(in) *m(f)*.
**manageress** [mænɪdʒə'rɛs] *n* (*of shop, business*) Geschäftsführerin *f*; (*of office, department etc*) Leiterin *f*.
**managerial** [mænɪ'dʒɪərɪəl] *adj* (*role, post*) leitend; (*decisions*) geschäftlich; **~ staff/ skills** Führungskräfte *pl*/-qualitäten *pl*.
**managing director** ['mænɪdʒɪŋ-] *n* Geschäftsführer(in) *m(f)*.
**Mancunian** [mæŋ'kju:nɪən] *n* Bewohner(in) *m(f)* Manchesters.
**mandarin** ['mændərɪn] *n* (*also:* **~ orange**) Mandarine *f*; (*official: Chinese*) Mandarin *m*; (*: gen*) Funktionär *m*.
**mandate** ['mændeɪt] *n* Mandat *nt*; (*task*) Auftrag *m*.
**mandatory** ['mændətərɪ] *adj* obligatorisch.
**mandolin(e)** ['mændəlɪn] *n* Mandoline *f*.
**mane** [meɪn] *n* Mähne *f*.
**maneuver** *etc* [mə'nu:və*] (*US*) = **manoeuvre** *etc*.
**manfully** ['mænfəlɪ] *adv* mannhaft, beherzt.
**manganese** [mæŋgə'ni:z] *n* Mangan *nt*.
**mangetout** ['mɔnʒ'tu:] (*BRIT*) *n* Zuckererbse *f*.
**mangle** ['mæŋgl] *vt* (übel) zurichten ♦ *n* Mangel *f*.
**mango** ['mæŋgəu] (*pl* **~es**) *n* Mango *f*.
**mangrove** ['mæŋgrəuv] *n* Mangrove(n)baum *m*.
**mangy** ['meɪndʒɪ] *adj* (*animal*) räudig.
**manhandle** ['mænhændl] *vt* (*mistreat*) grob behandeln; (*move by hand*) (von Hand) befördern.
**manhole** ['mænhəul] *n* Kanalschacht *m*.
**manhood** ['mænhud] *n* Mannesalter *nt*.
**man-hour** ['mænauə*] *n* Arbeitsstunde *f*.
**manhunt** ['mænhʌnt] *n* Fahndung *f*.
**mania** ['meɪnɪə] *n* Manie *f*; (*craze*) Sucht *f*; **persecution ~** Verfolgungswahn *m*.
**maniac** ['meɪnɪæk] *n* Wahnsinnige(r) *f(m)*, Verrückte(r) *f(m)*; (*fig*) Fanatiker(in) *m(f)*.
**manic** ['mænɪk] *adj* (*behaviour*) manisch; (*activity*) rasend.
**manic-depressive** ['mænɪkdɪ'presɪv] *n* Manisch-Depressive(r) *f(m)* ♦ *adj* manisch-depressiv.

**manicure** ['mænɪkjuə*] *n* Maniküre *f* ♦ *vt* maniküren.
**manicure set** *n* Nageletui *nt*, Maniküreetui *nt*.
**manifest** ['mænɪfest] *vt* zeigen, bekunden ♦ *adj* offenkundig ♦ *n* Manifest *nt*.
**manifestation** [mænɪfes'teɪʃən] *n* Anzeichen *nt*.
**manifesto** [mænɪ'festəu] *n* Manifest *nt*.
**manifold** ['mænɪfəuld] *adj* vielfältig ♦ *n:* **exhaust ~** Auspuffkrümmer *m*.
**Manila** [mə'nɪlə] *n* Manila *nt*.
**manila** [mə'nɪlə] *adj:* **~ envelope** brauner Briefumschlag *m*.
**manipulate** [mə'nɪpjuleɪt] *vt* manipulieren.
**manipulation** [mənɪpju'leɪʃən] *n* Manipulation *f*.
**mankind** [mæn'kaɪnd] *n* Menschheit *f*.
**manliness** ['mænlɪnɪs] *n* Männlichkeit *f*.
**manly** ['mænlɪ] *adj* männlich.
**man-made** ['mæn'meɪd] *adj* künstlich; (*fibre*) synthetisch.
**manna** ['mænə] *n* Manna *nt*.
**mannequin** ['mænɪkɪn] *n* (*dummy*) Schaufensterpuppe *f*; (*fashion model*) Mannequin *nt*.
**manner** ['mænə*] *n* (*way*) Art *f*, Weise *f*; (*behaviour*) Art *f*; (*type, sort*): **all ~ of things** die verschiedensten Dinge; **manners** *npl* (*conduct*) Manieren *pl*, Umgangsformen *pl*; **bad ~s** schlechte Manieren; **that's bad ~s** das gehört sich nicht.
**mannerism** ['mænərɪzəm] *n* Eigenheit *f*.
**mannerly** ['mænəlɪ] *adj* wohlerzogen.
**manning** ['mænɪŋ] *n* Besatzung *f*.
**manoeuvrable, (US) maneuverable** [mə'nu:vrəbl] *adj* manövrierfähig.
**manoeuvre, (US) maneuver** [mə'nu:və*] *vt* manövrieren; (*situation*) manipulieren ♦ *vi* manövrieren ♦ *n* (*skilful move*) Manöver *nt*; **manoeuvres** *npl* (*MIL*) Manöver *nt*, Truppenübungen *pl*; **to ~ sb into doing sth** jdn dazu bringen, etw zu tun.
**manor** ['mænə*] *n* (*also:* **~ house**) Herrenhaus *nt*.
**manpower** ['mænpauə*] *n* Personal *nt*, Arbeitskräfte *pl*.
**Manpower Services Commission** (*BRIT*) *n* Behörde für Arbeitsbeschaffung, Arbeitsvermittlung und Berufsausbildung.
**manservant** ['mænsə:vənt] (*pl* **menservants**) *n* Diener *m*.
**mansion** ['mænʃən] *n* Villa *f*.
**manslaughter** ['mænslɔ:tə*] *n* Totschlag *m*.
**mantelpiece** ['mæntlpi:s] *n* Kaminsims *nt or m*.
**mantle** ['mæntl] *n* Decke *f*; (*fig*) Deckmantel *m*.
**man-to-man** ['mæntə'mæn] *adj, adv* von Mann zu Mann.
**manual** ['mænjuəl] *adj* manuell, Hand-; (*controls*) von Hand ♦ *n* Handbuch *nt*.
**manufacture** [mænju'fæktʃə*] *vt* herstellen

◆ *n* Herstellung *f*.
**manufactured goods** *npl* Fertigerzeugnisse *pl*.
**manufacturer** [mænju'fækt∫ərə*] *n* Hersteller *m*.
**manufacturing** [mænju'fækt∫ərɪŋ] *n* Herstellung *f*.
**manure** [mə'njuə*] *n* Dung *m*.
**manuscript** ['mænjuskrɪpt] *n* Manuskript *nt*; (*old document*) Handschrift *f*.
**many** ['mɛnɪ] *adj, pron* viele; **a great** ~ eine ganze Reihe; **how** ~**?** wie viele?; **too** ~ **difficulties** zu viele Schwierigkeiten; **twice as** ~ doppelt so viele; ~ **a time** so manches Mal.
**Maori** ['maurɪ] *adj* maorisch ◆ *n* Maori *mf*.
**map** [mæp] *n* (Land)karte *f*; (*of town*) Stadtplan *m* ◆ *vt* eine Karte anfertigen von.
▶**map out** *vt* planen; (*plan*) entwerfen; (*essay*) anlegen.
**maple** ['meɪpl] *n* (*tree, wood*) Ahorn *m*.
**Mar.** *abbr* = **March**.
**mar** [mɑ:*] *vt* (*appearance*) verunstalten; (*day*) verderben; (*event*) stören.
**marathon** ['mærəθən] *n* Marathon *m* ◆ *adj*: **a** ~ **session** eine Marathonsitzung.
**marathon runner** *n* Marathonläufer(in) *m(f)*.
**marauder** [mə'rɔ:də*] *n* (*robber*) Plünderer *m*; (*killer*) Mörder *m*.
**marble** ['mɑ:bl] *n* Marmor *m*; (*toy*) Murmel *f*.
**marbles** ['mɑ:blz] *n* (*game*) Murmeln *pl*.
**March** [mɑ:t∫] *n* März *m*; *see also* **July**.
**march** [mɑ:t∫] *vi* marschieren; (*protesters*) ziehen ◆ *n* Marsch *m*; (*demonstration*) Demonstration *f*; **to** ~ **out of/into** (heraus)marschieren aus +*dat*/ (herein)marschieren in +*acc*.
**marcher** ['mɑ:t∫ə*] *n* Demonstrant(in) *m(f)*.
**marching orders** ['mɑ:t∫ɪŋ-] *npl*: **to give sb his/her** ~ (*employee*) jdn entlassen; (*lover*) jdm den Laufpaß geben.
**march past** *n* Vorbeimarsch *m*.
**mare** [mɛə*] *n* Stute *f*.
**margarine** [mɑ:dʒə'ri:n] *n* Margarine *f*.
**marge** [mɑ:dʒ] (*BRIT: inf*) *n abbr* = **margarine**.
**margin** ['mɑ:dʒɪn] *n* Rand *m*; (*of votes*) Mehrheit *f*; (*for safety, error etc*) Spielraum *m*; (*COMM*) Gewinnspanne *f*.
**marginal** ['mɑ:dʒɪnl] *adj* geringfügig; (*note*) Rand-.
**marginally** ['mɑ:dʒɪnəlɪ] *adv* nur wenig, geringfügig.
**marginal (seat)** *n* (*POL*) *mit knapper Mehrheit gewonnener Wahlkreis*.
**marigold** ['mærɪgəuld] *n* Ringelblume *f*.
**marijuana** [mærɪ'wɑ:nə] *n* Marihuana *nt*.
**marina** [mə'ri:nə] *n* Yachthafen *m*.
**marinade** [mærɪ'neɪd] *n* Marinade *f* ◆ *vt* = **marinate**.
**marinate** ['mærɪneɪt] *vt* marinieren.
**marine** [mə'ri:n] *adj* (*plant, biology*) Meeres- ◆ *n* (*BRIT: soldier*) Marineinfanterist *m*; (*US:*

*sailor*) Marinesoldat *m*; ~ **engineer** Schiff(s)bauingenieur *m*; ~ **engineering** Schiff(s)bau *m*.
**marine insurance** *n* Seeversicherung *f*.
**marital** ['mærɪtl] *adj* ehelich; (*problem*) Ehe-; ~ **status** Familienstand *m*.
**maritime** ['mærɪtaɪm] *adj* (*nation*) Seefahrer-; (*museum*) Seefahrts-; (*law*) See-.
**marjoram** ['mɑ:dʒərəm] *n* Majoran *m*.
**mark** [mɑ:k] *n* Zeichen *nt*; (*stain*) Fleck *m*; (*in snow, mud etc*) Spur *f*; (*level, point*): **the halfway** ~ die Hälfte *f*; (*currency*) Mark *f*; (*BRIT: TECH*): **M~ 2/3** Version *f* 2/3 ◆ *vt* (*with pen*) beschriften; (*with shoes etc*) schmutzig machen; (*with tyres etc*) Spuren hinterlassen auf +*dat*; (*damage*) beschädigen; (*stain*) Flecken machen auf +*dat*; (*indicate*) markieren; (: *price*) auszeichnen; (*commemorate*) begehen; (*characterize*) kennzeichnen; (*BRIT: SCOL*) korrigieren (und benoten); (*SPORT: player*) decken; **punctuation** ~**s** Satzzeichen *pl*; **to be quick off the** ~ (**in doing sth**) (*fig*) blitzschnell reagieren (und etw tun); **to be up to the** ~ den Anforderungen entsprechen; **to** ~ **time** auf der Stelle treten.
▶**mark down** *vt* (*prices, goods*) herabsetzen, heruntersetzen.
▶**mark off** *vt* (*tick off*) abhaken.
▶**mark out** *vt* markieren; (*person*) auszeichnen.
▶**mark up** *vt* (*price*) heraufsetzen.
**marked** [mɑ:kt] *adj* deutlich.
**markedly** ['mɑ:kɪdlɪ] *adv* deutlich.
**marker** ['mɑ:kə*] *n* Markierung *f*; (*bookmark*) Lesezeichen *nt*.
**market** ['mɑ:kɪt] *n* Markt *m* ◆ *vt* (*sell*) vertreiben; (*new product*) auf den Markt bringen; **to be on the** ~ auf dem Markt sein; **on the open** ~ auf dem freien Markt; **to play the** ~ (*STOCK EXCHANGE*) an der Börse spekulieren.
**marketable** ['mɑ:kɪtəbl] *adj* marktfähig.
**market analysis** *n* Marktanalyse *f*.
**market day** *n* Markttag *m*.
**market demand** *n* Marktbedarf *m*.
**market economy** *n* Marktwirtschaft *f*.
**market forces** *npl* Marktkräfte *pl*.
**market garden** (*BRIT*) *n* Gemüseanbaubetrieb *m*.
**marketing** ['mɑ:kɪtɪŋ] *n* Marketing *nt*.
**marketing manager** *n* Marketingmanager(in) *m(f)*.
**marketplace** ['mɑ:kɪtpleɪs] *n* Marktplatz *m*; (*COMM*) Markt *m*.
**market price** *n* Marktpreis *m*.
**market research** *n* Marktforschung *f*.
**market value** *n* Marktwert *m*.
**marking** ['mɑ:kɪŋ] *n* (*on animal*) Zeichnung *f*; (*on road*) Markierung *f*.
**marksman** ['mɑ:ksmən] (*irreg: like* **man**) *n*

Scharfschütze *m*.
**marksmanship** ['mɑːksmənʃɪp] *n*
Treffsicherheit *f*.
**mark-up** ['mɑːkʌp] *n* (*COMM: margin*)
Handelsspanne *f*; (: *increase*)
(Preis)aufschlag *m*.
**marmalade** ['mɑːməleɪd] *n*
Orangenmarmelade *f*.
**maroon** [mə'ruːn] *vt*: **to be ~ed** festsitzen
♦ *adj* kastanienbraun.
**marquee** [mɑː'kiː] *n* Festzelt *nt*.
**marquess, marquis** ['mɑːkwɪs] *n* Marquis *m*.
**Marrakech, Marrakesh** [mærə'kɛʃ] *n* Marra-
kesch *nt*.
**marriage** ['mærɪdʒ] *n* Ehe *f*; (*institution*) die
Ehe; (*wedding*) Hochzeit *f*; **~ of convenience**
Vernunftehe *f*.
**marriage bureau** *n* Ehevermittlung *f*.
**marriage certificate** *n* Heiratsurkunde *f*.
**marriage guidance,** (*US*) **marriage
counseling** *n* Eheberatung *f*.
**married** ['mærɪd] *adj* verheiratet; (*life*) Ehe-;
(*love*) ehelich; **to get ~** heiraten.
**marrow** ['mærəu] *n* (*vegetable*) Kürbis *m*;
(*bone marrow*) (Knochen)mark *nt*.
**marry** ['mærɪ] *vt* heiraten; (*father*)
verheiraten; (*priest*) trauen ♦ *vi* heiraten.
**Mars** [mɑːz] *n* Mars *m*.
**Marseilles** [mɑː'seɪlz] *n* Marseilles *nt*.
**marsh** [mɑːʃ] *n* Sumpf *m*; (*salt marsh*)
Salzsumpf *m*.
**marshal** ['mɑːʃl] *n* (*MIL: also:* **field ~**)
(Feld)marschall *m*; (*official*) Ordner *m*; (*US:
of police*) Bezirkspolizeichef *m* ♦ *vt*
(*thoughts*) ordnen; (*support*) auftreiben;
(*soldiers*) aufstellen.
**marshalling yard** ['mɑːʃlɪŋ-] *n* (*RAIL*)
Rangierbahnhof *m*.
**marshmallow** [mɑːʃ'mæləu] *n* (*BOT*) Eibisch
*m*; (*sweet*) Marshmallow *nt*.
**marshy** ['mɑːʃɪ] *adj* sumpfig.
**marsupial** [mɑː'suːpɪəl] *n* Beuteltier *nt*.
**martial** ['mɑːʃl] *adj* kriegerisch.
**martial arts** *npl* Kampfsport *m*; **the ~** die
Kampfkunst *sing*.
**martial law** *n* Kriegsrecht *nt*.
**Martian** ['mɑːʃən] *n* Marsmensch *m*.
**martin** ['mɑːtɪn] *n* (*also:* **house ~**) Schwalbe *f*.
**martyr** ['mɑːtə'] *n* Märtyrer(in) *m(f)* ♦ *vt*
martern.
**martyrdom** ['mɑːtədəm] *n* Martyrium *nt*.
**marvel** ['mɑːvl] *n* Wunder *nt* ♦ *vi*: **to ~ (at)**
staunen (über +*acc*).
**marvellous,** (*US*) **marvelous** ['mɑːvləs] *adj*
wunderbar.
**Marxism** ['mɑːksɪzəm] *n* Marxismus *m*.
**Marxist** ['mɑːksɪst] *adj* marxistisch ♦ *n*
Marxist(in) *m(f)*.
**marzipan** ['mɑːzɪpæn] *n* Marzipan *nt*.
**mascara** [mæs'kɑːrə] *n* Wimperntusche *f*.
**mascot** ['mæskət] *n* Maskottchen *nt*.
**masculine** ['mæskjulɪn] *adj* männlich;

(*atmosphere, woman*) maskulin; (*LING*)
männlich, maskulin.
**masculinity** [mæskju'lɪnɪtɪ] *n* Männlichkeit *f*.
**MASH** [mæʃ] (*US*) *n abbr* (= *mobile army
surgical hospital*) mobiles Lazarett *nt*.
**mash** [mæʃ] *vt* zerstampfen.
**mashed potatoes** [mæʃt-] *npl*
Kartoffelpüree *nt*, Kartoffelbrei *m*.
**mask** [mɑːsk] *n* Maske *f* ♦ *vt* (*cover*)
verdecken; (*hide*) verbergen; **surgical ~**
Mundschutz *m*.
**masking tape** ['mɑːskɪŋ-] *n* Abdeckband *nt*.
**masochism** ['mæsəukɪzəm] *n* Masochismus *m*.
**masochist** ['mæsəukɪst] *n* Masochist(in) *m(f)*.
**mason** ['meɪsn] *n* (*also:* **stone ~**) Steinmetz *m*;
(*also:* **freemason**) Freimaurer *m*.
**masonic** [mə'sɔnɪk] *adj* (*lodge etc*)
Freimaurer-.
**masonry** ['meɪsnrɪ] *n* Mauerwerk *nt*.
**masquerade** [mæskə'reɪd] *vi*: **to ~ as** sich
ausgeben als ♦ *n* Maskerade *f*.
**Mass.** (*US*) *abbr* (*POST:* = *Massachusetts*).
**mass** [mæs] *n* Masse *f*; (*of people*) Menge *f*;
(*large amount*) Fülle *f*; (*REL*): **M~** Messe *f*
♦ *cpd* Massen- ♦ *vi* (*troops*) sich massieren;
(*protesters*) sich versammeln; **the masses** *npl*
(*ordinary people*) die Masse, die Massen *pl*;
**to go to M~** zur Messe gehen; **~es of** (*inf*)
massenhaft, jede Menge.
**massacre** ['mæsəkə'] *n* Massaker *nt* ♦ *vt*
massakrieren.
**massage** ['mæsɑːʒ] *n* Massage *f* ♦ *vt*
massieren.
**masseur** [mæ'səː'] *n* Masseur *m*.
**masseuse** [mæ'səːz] *n* Masseurin *f*.
**massive** ['mæsɪv] *adj* (*furniture, person*)
wuchtig; (*support*) massiv; (*changes,
increase*) enorm.
**mass market** *n* Massenmarkt *m*.
**mass media** *npl* Massenmedien *pl*.
**mass meeting** *n* Massenveranstaltung *f*; (*of
everyone concerned*) Vollversammlung *f*;
(*POL*) Massenkundgebung *f*.
**mass-produce** ['mæsprə'djuːs] *vt* in
Massenproduktion herstellen.
**mass-production** ['mæsprə'dʌkʃən] *n*
Massenproduktion *f*.
**mast** [mɑːst] *n* (*NAUT*) Mast *m*; (*RADIO etc*)
Sendeturm *m*.
**mastectomy** [mæs'tɛktəmɪ] *n*
Brustamputation *f*.
**master** ['mɑːstə'] *n* Herr *m*; (*teacher*) Lehrer
*m*; (*title*): **M~ X** (der junge) Herr X; (*ART,
MUS, of craft etc*) Meister *m* ♦ *cpd*: **~ baker/
plumber** *etc* Bäcker-/Klempnermeister *etc m*
♦ *vt* meistern; (*feeling*) unter Kontrolle
bringen; (*skill, language*) beherrschen.
**master disk** *n* (*COMPUT*) Stammdiskette *f*.
**masterful** ['mɑːstəful] *adj* gebieterisch;
(*skilful*) meisterhaft.
**master key** *n* Hauptschlüssel *m*.
**masterly** ['mɑːstəlɪ] *adj* meisterhaft.

**mastermind** ['mɑːstəmaɪnd] n (führender) Kopf m ♦ vt planen und ausführen.
**Master of Arts** n Magister m der philosophischen Fakultät.
**Master of Ceremonies** n Zeremonienmeister m; (for variety show etc) Conférencier m.
**Master of Science** n Magister m der naturwissenschaftlichen Fakultät.
**masterpiece** ['mɑːstəpiːs] n Meisterwerk nt.
**master plan** n kluger Plan m.

---

Master's Degree ist ein höherer akademischer Grad, den man in der Regel nach dem bachelor's degree erwerben kann. Je nach Universität erhält man ein master's degree nach einem entsprechenden Studium und/oder einer Dissertation. Die am häufigsten verliehenen Grade sind **MA** (Master of Arts) und **MSc** (Master of Science), die beide Studium und Dissertation erfordern, während für **MLitt** (Master of Letters) und **MPhil** (Master of Philosophy) meist nur eine Dissertation nötig ist. Siehe auch bachelor's degree, doctorate.

---

**masterstroke** ['mɑːstəstrəuk] n Meisterstück nt.
**mastery** ['mɑːstərɪ] n (of language etc) Beherrschung f; (skill) (meisterhaftes) Können nt.
**mastiff** ['mæstɪf] n Dogge f.
**masturbate** ['mæstəbeɪt] vi masturbieren, onanieren.
**masturbation** [mæstə'beɪʃən] n Masturbation f, Onanie f.
**mat** [mæt] n Matte f; (also: **doormat**) Fußmatte f; (also: **table** ~) Untersetzer m; (: of cloth) Deckchen nt ♦ adj = **matt**.
**match** [mætʃ] n Wettkampf m; (team game) Spiel nt; (TENNIS) Match nt; (for lighting fire etc) Streichholz nt; (equivalent): **to be a good/perfect** ~ gut/perfekt zusammenpassen ♦ vt (go well with) passen zu; (equal) gleichkommen +dat; (correspond to) entsprechen +dat; (suit) sich anpassen +dat; (also: ~ **up**: pair) passend zusammenbringen ♦ vi zusammenpassen; **to be a good** ~ gut zusammenpassen; **to be no** ~ **for** sich nicht messen können mit; **with shoes to** ~ mit (dazu) passenden Schuhen.
▶**match up** vi zusammenpassen.
**matchbox** ['mætʃbɒks] n Streichholzschachtel f.
**matching** ['mætʃɪŋ] adj (dazu) passend.
**matchless** ['mætʃlɪs] adj unvergleichlich.
**mate** [meɪt] n (inf: friend) Freund(in) m(f), Kumpel m; (animal) Männchen nt, Weibchen nt; (assistant) Gehilfe m, Gehilfin f; (in merchant navy) Maat m ♦ vi (animals) sich paaren.
**material** [mə'tɪərɪəl] n Material nt; (cloth)

Stoff m ♦ adj (possessions, existence) materiell; (relevant) wesentlich; **materials** npl (equipment) Material nt.
**materialistic** [mətɪərɪə'lɪstɪk] adj materialistisch.
**materialize** [mə'tɪərɪəlaɪz] vi (event) zustande kommen; (plan) verwirklicht werden; (hope) sich verwirklichen; (problem) auftreten; (crisis, difficulty) eintreten.
**maternal** [mə'tɜːnl] adj mütterlich, Mutter-.
**maternity** [mə'tɜːnɪtɪ] n Mutterschaft f ♦ cpd (ward etc) Entbindungs-; (care) für werdende und junge Mütter.
**maternity benefit** n Mutterschaftsgeld nt.
**maternity dress** n Umstandskleid nt.
**maternity hospital** n Entbindungsheim nt.
**maternity leave** n Mutterschaftsurlaub m.
**matey** ['meɪtɪ] (BRIT: inf) adj kumpelhaft.
**math** [mæθ] (US) n abbr = **maths**.
**mathematical** [mæθə'mætɪkl] adj mathematisch.
**mathematician** [mæθəmə'tɪʃən] n Mathematiker(in) m(f).
**mathematics** [mæθə'mætɪks] n Mathematik f.
**maths** [mæθs], (US) **math** [mæθ] n abbr Mathe f.
**matinée** ['mætɪneɪ] n Nachmittagsvorstellung f.
**mating** ['meɪtɪŋ] n Paarung f.
**mating call** n Lockruf m.
**mating season** n Paarungszeit f.
**matriarchal** [meɪtrɪ'ɑːkl] adj matriarchalisch.
**matrices** ['meɪtrɪsiːz] npl of **matrix**.
**matriculation** [mətrɪkju'leɪʃən] n Immatrikulation f.
**matrimonial** [mætrɪ'məunɪəl] adj Ehe-.
**matrimony** ['mætrɪmənɪ] n Ehe f.
**matrix** ['meɪtrɪks] (pl **matrices**) n (MATH) Matrix f; (framework) Gefüge nt.
**matron** ['meɪtrən] n (in hospital) Oberschwester f; (in school) Schwester f.
**matronly** ['meɪtrənlɪ] adj matronenhaft.
**matt** [mæt] adj matt; (paint) Matt-.
**matted** ['mætɪd] adj verfilzt.
**matter** ['mætə'] n (event, situation) Sache f, Angelegenheit f; (PHYS) Materie f; (substance, material) Stoff m; (MED: pus) Eiter m ♦ vi (be important) wichtig sein; **matters** npl (affairs) Angelegenheiten pl, Dinge pl; (situation) Lage f; **what's the** ~**?** was ist los?; **no** ~ **what** egal, was (passiert); **that's another** ~ das ist etwas anderes; **as a** ~ **of course** selbstverständlich; **as a** ~ **of fact** eigentlich; **it's a** ~ **of habit** es ist eine Gewohnheitssache; **vegetable** ~ pflanzliche Stoffe pl; **printed** ~ Drucksachen pl; **reading** ~ (BRIT) Lesestoff m; **it doesn't** ~ es macht nichts.
**matter-of-fact** ['mætərəv'fækt] adj sachlich.
**matting** ['mætɪŋ] n Matten pl; **rush** ~ Binsenmatten pl.
**mattress** ['mætrɪs] n Matratze f.

**mature** [mə'tjuə*] *adj* reif; (*wine*) ausgereift
♦ *vi* reifen; (*COMM*) fällig werden.
**mature student** *n* älterer Student *m*, ältere
Studentin *f*.
**maturity** [mə'tjuərɪtɪ] *n* Reife *f*; **to have
reached** ~ (*person*) erwachsen sein; (*animal*)
ausgewachsen sein.
**maudlin** ['mɔːdlɪn] *adj* gefühlsselig.
**maul** [mɔːl] *vt* (anfallen und) übel zurichten.
**Mauritania** [mɔːrɪ'teɪnɪə] *n* Mauritanien *nt*.
**Mauritius** [mə'rɪfəs] *n* Mauritius *nt*.
**mausoleum** [mɔːsə'lɪəm] *n* Mausoleum *nt*.
**mauve** [məuv] *adj* mauve.
**maverick** ['mævrɪk] *n* (*dissenter*)
Abtrünnige(r) *m*; (*independent thinker*)
Querdenker *m*.
**mawkish** ['mɔːkɪʃ] *adj* rührselig.
**max.** *abbr* = **maximum.**
**maxim** ['mæksɪm] *n* Maxime *f*.
**maxima** ['mæksɪmə] *npl of* **maximum.**
**maximize** ['mæksɪmaɪz] *vt* maximieren.
**maximum** ['mæksɪməm] (*pl* **maxima** *or* ~**s**) *adj*
(*amount, speed etc*) Höchst-; (*efficiency*)
maximal ♦ *n* Maximum *nt*.
**May** [meɪ] *n* Mai *m*; *see also* **July.**
**may** [meɪ] (*conditional* **might**) *vi* (*be possible*)
können; (*have permission*) dürfen; **he**
~ **come** vielleicht kommt er; ~ **I smoke?**
darf ich rauchen?; ~ **God bless you!** (*wish*)
Gott segne dich!; ~ **I sit here?** kann ich
mich hier hinsetzen?; **he might be there** er
könnte da sein; **you might like to try**
vielleicht möchten Sie es mal versuchen;
**you** ~ **as well go** Sie können ruhig gehen.
**maybe** ['meɪbiː] *adv* vielleicht; ~ **he'll** ... es
kann sein, daß er ...; ~ **not** vielleicht nicht.
**Mayday** ['meɪdeɪ] *n* Maydaysignal *nt*, ≈ SOS-
Ruf *m*.
**May Day** *n* der 1. Mai.
**mayhem** ['meɪhɛm] *n* Chaos *nt*.
**mayonnaise** [meɪə'neɪz] *n* Mayonnaise *f*.
**mayor** [mɛə*] *n* Bürgermeister *m*.
**mayoress** ['mɛərɛs] *n* Bürgermeisterin *f*;
(*partner*) Frau *f* des Bürgermeisters.
**maypole** ['meɪpəul] *n* Maibaum *m*.
**maze** [meɪz] *n* Irrgarten *m*; (*fig*) Wirrwarr *m*.
**MB** *abbr* (*COMPUT*: = *megabyte*) MB;
(*CANADA*: = *Manitoba*).
**MBA** *n abbr* (= *Master of Business
Administration*) *akademischer Grad in
Betriebswirtschaft.*
**MBE** (*BRIT*) *n abbr* (= *Member of (the Order of)
the British Empire*) *britischer Ordenstitel.*
**MC** *n abbr* = **Master of Ceremonies.**
**MCAT** (*US*) *n abbr* (= *Medical College
Admissions Test*) *Zulassungsprüfung für
medizinische Fachschulen.*
**MCP** (*BRIT*: *inf*) *n abbr* (= *male chauvinist pig*)
Chauvinistenschwein *nt*.
**MD** *n abbr* (= *Doctor of Medicine*) ≈ Dr. med.;
(*COMM*) = **managing director** ♦ *abbr* (*US:
POST*: = *Maryland*).

**MDT** (*US*) *abbr* (= *Mountain Daylight Time*)
*amerikanische Sommerzeitzone.*
**ME** *n abbr* (*US*) = **medical examiner**; (*MED*:
= *myalgic encephalomyelitis*) *krankhafter
Energiemangel (oft nach Virus-
erkrankungen*) ♦ *abbr* (*US: POST*: = *Maine*).

━━━━━━━━━━━━━━━━━ *KEYWORD*

**me** [miː] *pron* **1** (*direct*) mich; **can you hear** ~?
können Sie mich hören?; **it's** ~ ich bin's
**2** (*indirect*) mir; **he gave the money, he
gave the money to** ~ er gab mir das Geld
**3** (*after prep*): **it's for** ~ es ist für mich; **with**
~ mit mir; **give them to** ~ gib sie mir;
**without** ~ ohne mich.

**meadow** ['mɛdəu] *n* Wiese *f*.
**meagre,** (*US*) **meager** ['miːgə*] *adj* (*amount*)
kläglich; (*meal*) dürftig.
**meal** [miːl] *n* Mahlzeit *f*; (*food*) Essen *nt*; (*flour*)
Schrotmehl *nt*; **to go out for a** ~ essen
gehen; **to make a** ~ **of sth** (*fig*) etw auf sehr
umständliche Art machen.
**meals on wheels** *n sing* Essen *nt* auf Rädern.
**mealtime** ['miːltaɪm] *n* Essenszeit *f*.
**mealy-mouthed** ['miːlɪmauðd] *adj*
unaufrichtig; (*politician*) schönfärberisch.
**mean** [miːn] (*pt, pp* **meant**) *adj* (*with money*)
geizig; (*unkind*) gemein; (*US: inf: animal*)
bösartig; (*shabby*) schäbig; (*average*)
Durchschnitts-, mittlere(r, s) ♦ *vt* (*signify*)
bedeuten; (*refer to*) meinen; (*intend*)
beabsichtigen ♦ *n* (*average*) Durchschnitt *m*;
**means** *npl* (*way*) Möglichkeit *f*; (*money*)
Mittel *pl*; **by** ~**s of** durch; **by all** ~**s!** aber
natürlich *or* selbstverständlich!; **do you**
~ **it?** meinst du das ernst?; **what do you** ~?
was willst du damit sagen?; **to be meant for
sb/sth** für jdn/etw bestimmt sein; **to** ~ **to
do sth** etw tun wollen.
**meander** [mɪ'ændə*] *vi* (*river*) sich schlängeln;
(*person: walking*) schlendern; (: *talking*)
abschweifen.
**meaning** ['miːnɪŋ] *n* Sinn *m*; (*of word, gesture*)
Bedeutung *f*.
**meaningful** ['miːnɪŋful] *adj* sinnvoll; (*glance,
remark*) vielsagend, bedeutsam; (*relationship*)
tiefergehend.
**meaningless** ['miːnɪŋlɪs] *adj* sinnlos; (*word,
song*) bedeutungslos.
**meanness** ['miːnnɪs] *n* (*with money*) Geiz *m*;
(*unkindness*) Gemeinheit *f*; (*shabbiness*)
Schäbigkeit *f*.
**means test** [miːnz-] *n* Überprüfung *f* der
Einkommens- und Vermögensverhältnisse.
**means-tested** ['miːnztestɪd] *adj* von den
Einkommens- und Vermögensverhältnissen
abhängig.
**meant** [mɛnt] *pt, pp of* **mean.**
**meantime** ['miːntaɪm] *adv* (*also*: **in the** ~)
inzwischen.
**meanwhile** ['miːnwaɪl] *adv* = **meantime.**

**measles** ['miːzlz] *n* Masern *pl*.
**measly** ['miːzlɪ] (*inf*) *adj* mick(e)rig.
**measurable** ['mɛʒərəbl] *adj* meßbar.
**measure** ['mɛʒəʳ] *vt, vi* messen ♦ *n* (*amount*)
Menge *f*; (*ruler*) Meßstab *m*; (*of achievement*)
Maßstab *m*; (*action*) Maßnahme *f*; **a litre ~**
ein Meßbecher *m*, der einen Liter faßt; **a/
some ~ of** ein gewisses Maß an +*dat*; **to take
~s to do sth** Maßnahmen ergreifen, um etw
zu tun.
▶**measure up** *vi:* **to ~ up to** herankommen
an +*acc*.
**measured** ['mɛʒəd] *adj* (*tone*) bedächtig;
(*step*) gemessen.
**measurement** ['mɛʒəmənt] *n* (*measure*) Maß
*nt*; (*act*) Messung *f*; **chest/hip ~** Brust-/
Hüftumfang *m*.
**measurements** ['mɛʒəmənts] *npl* Maße *pl*; **to
take sb's ~** bei jdm Maß nehmen.
**meat** [miːt] *n* Fleisch *nt*; **cold ~s** (*BRIT*)
Aufschnitt *m*; **crab ~** Krabbenfleisch *nt*.
**meatball** ['miːtbɔːl] *n* Fleischkloß *m*.
**meat pie** *n* Fleischpastete *f*.
**meaty** ['miːtɪ] *adj* (*meal, dish*) mit viel Fleisch;
(*fig: satisfying: book etc*) gehaltvoll; (: *brawny:
person*) kräftig (gebaut).
**Mecca** ['mɛkə] *n* (*GEOG, fig*) Mekka *nt*.
**mechanic** [mɪ'kænɪk] *n* Mechaniker(in) *m(f)*.
**mechanical** [mɪ'kænɪkl] *adj* mechanisch.
**mechanical engineering** *n* Maschinenbau
*m*.
**mechanics** [mɪ'kænɪks] *n* (*PHYS*) Mechanik *f*
♦ *npl* (*of reading etc*) Technik *f*; (*of
government etc*) Mechanismus *m*.
**mechanism** ['mɛkənɪzəm] *n* Mechanismus *m*.
**mechanization** [mɛkənaɪ'zeɪʃən] *n*
Mechanisierung *f*.
**mechanize** ['mɛkənaɪz] *vt, vi* mechanisieren.
**MEd** *n abbr* (= *Master of Education*)
*akademischer Grad für Lehrer*.
**medal** ['mɛdl] *n* Medaille *f*; (*decoration*) Orden
*m*.
**medallion** [mɪ'dælɪən] *n* Medaillon *nt*.
**medallist**, (*US*) **medalist** ['mɛdlɪst] *n*
Medaillengewinner(in) *m(f)*.
**meddle** ['mɛdl] *vi:* **to ~ (in)** sich einmischen
(in +*acc*); **to ~ with sb** sich mit jdm
einlassen; **to ~ with sth** (*tamper*) sich *dat* an
etw *dat* zu schaffen machen.
**meddlesome** ['mɛdlsəm], **meddling** ['mɛdlɪŋ]
*adj* sich ständig einmischend.
**media** ['miːdɪə] *npl* Medien *pl*.
**media circus** *n* Medienrummel *m*.
**mediaeval** [mɛdɪ'iːvl] *adj* = **medieval**.
**median** ['miːdɪən] (*US*) *n* (*also:* **~ strip**)
Mittelstreifen *m*.
**mediate** ['miːdɪeɪt] *vi* vermitteln.
**mediation** [miːdɪ'eɪʃən] *n* Vermittlung *f*.
**mediator** ['miːdɪeɪtəʳ] *n* Vermittler(in) *m(f)*.
**Medicaid** ['mɛdɪkeɪd] (*US*) *n* staatliche
*Krankenversicherung und Gesundheits-
fürsorge für Einkommensschwache*.

**medical** ['mɛdɪkl] *adj* (*care*) medizinisch;
(*treatment*) ärztlich ♦ *n* (ärztliche)
Untersuchung *f*.
**medical certificate** *n* (*confirming health*)
ärztliches Gesundheitszeugnis *nt*;
(*confirming illness*) ärztliches Attest *nt*.
**medical examiner** (*US*) *n*
≈ Gerichtsmediziner(in) *m(f)*; (*performing
autopsy*) Leichenbeschauer *m*.
**medical student** *n* Medizinstudent(in) *m(f)*.
**Medicare** ['mɛdɪkɛəʳ] (*US*) *n* staatliche
*Krankenversicherung und
Gesundheitsfürsorge für ältere Bürger*.
**medicated** ['mɛdɪkeɪtɪd] *adj* medizinisch.
**medication** [mɛdɪ'keɪʃən] *n* Medikamente *pl*.
**medicinal** [mɛ'dɪsɪnl] *adj* (*substance*) Heil-;
(*qualities*) heilend; (*purposes*) medizinisch.
**medicine** ['mɛdsɪn] *n* Medizin *f*; (*drug*) Arznei
*f*.
**medicine ball** *n* Medizinball *m*.
**medicine chest** *n* Hausapotheke *f*.
**medicine man** *n* Medizinmann *m*.
**medieval** [mɛdɪ'iːvl] *adj* mittelalterlich.
**mediocre** [miːdɪ'əukəʳ] *adj* mittelmäßig.
**mediocrity** [miːdɪ'ɔkrɪtɪ] *n* Mittelmäßigkeit *f*.
**meditate** ['mɛdɪteɪt] *vi* nachdenken; (*REL*)
meditieren.
**meditation** [mɛdɪ'teɪʃən] *n* Nachdenken *nt*;
(*REL*) Meditation *f*.
**Mediterranean** [mɛdɪtə'reɪnɪən] *adj* (*country,
climate etc*) Mittelmeer-; **the ~** (*Sea*) das
Mittelmeer.
**medium** ['miːdɪəm] (*pl* **media** *or* **~s**) *adj*
mittlere(r, s) ♦ *n* (*means*) Mittel *nt*;
(*substance, material*) Medium *nt*; (*pl* **~s**)
(*person*) Medium *nt*; **of ~ height** mittelgroß;
**to strike a happy ~** den goldenen Mittelweg
finden.
**medium-dry** ['miːdɪəm'draɪ] *adj* (*wine, sherry*)
halbtrocken.
**medium-sized** ['miːdɪəm'saɪzd] *adj*
mittelgroß.
**medium wave** *n* (*RADIO*) Mittelwelle *f*.
**medley** ['mɛdlɪ] *n* Gemisch *nt*; (*MUS*) Medley
*nt*.
**meek** [miːk] *adj* sanft(mütig), duldsam.
**meet** [miːt] (*pt, pp* **met**) *vt* (*encounter*) treffen;
(*by arrangement*) sich treffen mit; (*for the
first time*) kennenlernen; (*go and fetch*)
abholen; (*opponent*) treffen auf +*acc*;
(*condition, standard*) erfüllen; (*need,
expenses*) decken; (*problem*) stoßen auf +*acc*;
(*challenge*) begegnen +*dat*; (*bill*) begleichen;
(*join: line*) sich schneiden mit; (: *road etc*)
treffen auf +*acc* ♦ *vi* (*encounter*) sich
begegnen; (*by arrangement*) sich treffen; (*for
the first time*) sich kennenlernen; (*for talks
etc*) zusammenkommen; (*committee*) tagen;
(*join: lines*) sich schneiden; (: *roads etc*)
aufeinandertreffen ♦ *n* (*BRIT: HUNTING*)
Jagd *f*; (*US: SPORT*) Sportfest *nt*; **pleased to
~ you!** (sehr) angenehm!

▶**meet up** vi: **to ~ up with sb** sich mit jdm treffen.

▶**meet with** vt fus (difficulty, success) haben.

**meeting** ['mi:tɪŋ] n (assembly, people assembling) Versammlung f; (COMM, of committee etc) Sitzung f; (also: **business ~**) Besprechung f; (encounter) Begegnung f; (: arranged) Treffen nt; (POL) Gespräch nt; (SPORT) Veranstaltung f; **she's at** or **in a ~** (COMM) sie ist bei einer Besprechung; **to call a ~** eine Sitzung/Versammlung einberufen.

**meeting-place** ['mi:tɪŋpleɪs] n Treffpunkt m.

**megabyte** ['mɛgəbaɪt] n Megabyte nt.

**megalomaniac** [mɛgələ'meɪnɪæk] n Größenwahnsinnige(r) f(m).

**megaphone** ['mɛgəfəʊn] n Megaphon nt.

**megawatt** ['mɛgəwɒt] n Megawatt nt.

**melancholy** ['mɛlənkəlɪ] n Melancholie f, Schwermut f ♦ adj melancholisch, schwermütig.

**mellow** ['mɛləʊ] adj (sound) voll, weich; (light, colour, stone) warm; (weathered) verwittert; (person) gesetzt; (wine) ausgereift ♦ vi (person) gesetzter werden.

**melodious** [mɪ'ləʊdɪəs] adj melodisch.

**melodrama** ['mɛləʊdrɑːmə] n Melodrama nt.

**melodramatic** [mɛlədrə'mætɪk] adj melodramatisch.

**melody** ['mɛlədɪ] n Melodie f.

**melon** ['mɛlən] n Melone f.

**melt** [mɛlt] vi (lit, fig) schmelzen ♦ vt schmelzen; (butter) zerlassen.

▶**melt down** vt einschmelzen.

**meltdown** ['mɛltdaʊn] n (in nuclear reactor) Kernschmelze f.

**melting point** ['mɛltɪŋ-] n Schmelzpunkt m.

**melting pot** n (lit, fig) Schmelztiegel m; **to be in the ~** in der Schwebe sein.

**member** ['mɛmbə*] n Mitglied nt; (ANAT) Glied nt ♦ cpd: **~ country** Mitgliedsland nt; **~ state** Mitgliedsstaat m; **M~ of Parliament** (BRIT) Abgeordnete(r) f(m) (des Unterhauses); **M~ of the European Parliament** (BRIT) Abgeordnete(r) f(m) des Europaparlaments.

**membership** ['mɛmbəʃɪp] n Mitgliedschaft f; (members) Mitglieder pl; (number of members) Mitgliederzahl f.

**membership card** n Mitgliedsausweis m.

**membrane** ['mɛmbreɪn] n Membran(e) f.

**memento** [mə'mɛntəʊ] n Andenken nt.

**memo** ['mɛməʊ] n Memo nt, Mitteilung f.

**memoir** ['mɛmwɑː*] n Kurzbiographie f.

**memoirs** ['mɛmwɑːz] npl Memoiren pl.

**memo pad** n Notizblock m.

**memorable** ['mɛmərəbl] adj denkwürdig; (unforgettable) unvergeßlich.

**memorandum** [mɛmə'rændəm] (pl **memoranda**) n Mitteilung f.

**memorial** [mɪ'mɔːrɪəl] n Denkmal nt ♦ adj (service, prize) Gedenk-.

**Memorial Day** (US) n ≈ Volkstrauertag m.

---

**Memorial Day** ist in den USA ein gesetzlicher Feiertag am letzten Montag im Mai zum Gedenken der in allen Kriegen gefallenen amerikanischen Soldaten. Siehe auch **Remembrance Sunday**.

---

**memorize** ['mɛməraɪz] vt sich dat einprägen.

**memory** ['mɛmərɪ] n Gedächtnis nt; (sth remembered) Erinnerung f; (COMPUT) Speicher m; **in ~ of** zur Erinnerung an +acc; **to have a good/bad ~** ein gutes/schlechtes Gedächtnis haben; **loss of ~** Gedächtnisschwund m.

**men** [mɛn] npl of **man**.

**menace** ['mɛnɪs] n Bedrohung f; (nuisance) (Land)plage f ♦ vt bedrohen; **a public ~** eine Gefahr für die Öffentlichkeit.

**menacing** ['mɛnɪsɪŋ] adj drohend.

**menagerie** [mɪ'nædʒərɪ] n Menagerie f.

**mend** [mɛnd] vt reparieren; (darn) flicken ♦ n: **to be on the ~** auf dem Wege der Besserung sein; **to ~ one's ways** sich bessern.

**mending** ['mɛndɪŋ] n Reparaturen pl; (clothes) Flickarbeiten pl.

**menial** ['mi:nɪəl] (often pej) adj niedrig, untergeordnet.

**meningitis** [mɛnɪn'dʒaɪtɪs] n Hirnhautentzündung f.

**menopause** ['mɛnəʊpɔːz] n: **the ~** die Wechseljahre pl.

**menservants** ['mɛnsəːvənts] npl of **manservant**.

**men's room** (US) n Herrentoilette f.

**menstrual** ['mɛnstruəl] adj (BIOL: cycle etc) Menstruations-; **~ period** Monatsblutung f.

**menstruate** ['mɛnstrueɪt] vi die Menstruation haben.

**menstruation** [mɛnstru'eɪʃən] n Menstruation f.

**menswear** ['mɛnzwɛə*] n Herren(be)kleidung f.

**mental** ['mɛntl] adj geistig; (illness) Geistes-; **~ arithmetic** Kopfrechnen nt.

**mental hospital** n psychiatrische Klinik f.

**mentality** [mɛn'tælɪtɪ] n Mentalität f.

**mentally** ['mɛntlɪ] adv: **to be ~ handicapped** geistig behindert sein.

**menthol** ['mɛnθɒl] n Menthol nt.

**mention** ['mɛnʃən] n Erwähnung f ♦ vt erwähnen; **don't ~ it!** (bitte,) gern geschehen!; **not to ~ ...** von ... ganz zu schweigen.

**mentor** ['mɛntɔː*] n Mentor m.

**menu** ['mɛnjuː] n Menü nt; (printed) Speisekarte f.

**menu-driven** ['mɛnjuːdrɪvn] adj (COMPUT) menügesteuert.

**MEP** (BRIT) n abbr (= Member of the European Parliament) Abgeordnete(r) f(m) des

Europaparlaments.

**mercantile** ['mɜːkəntaɪl] *adj* (*class, society*) handeltreibend; (*law*) Handels-.

**mercenary** ['mɜːsɪnərɪ] *adj* (*person*) geldgierig ♦ *n* Söldner *m*.

**merchandise** ['mɜːtʃəndaɪz] *n* Ware *f*.

**merchandiser** ['mɜːtʃəndaɪzə*] *n* Verkaufsförderungsexperte *m*.

**merchant** ['mɜːtʃənt] *n* Kaufmann *m*; **timber/ wine** ~ Holz-/Weinhändler *m*.

**merchant bank** (*BRIT*) *n* Handelsbank *f*.

**merchantman** ['mɜːtʃəntmən] (*irreg: like* **man**) *n* Handelsschiff *nt*.

**merchant navy**, (*US*) **merchant marine** *n* Handelsmarine *f*.

**merciful** ['mɜːsɪful] *adj* gnädig; **a ~ release** eine Erlösung.

**mercifully** ['mɜːsɪflɪ] *adv* glücklicherweise.

**merciless** ['mɜːsɪlɪs] *adj* erbarmungslos.

**mercurial** [mɜː'kjʊərɪəl] *adj* (*unpredictable*) sprunghaft, wechselhaft; (*lively*) quecksilbrig.

**mercury** ['mɜːkjurɪ] *n* Quecksilber *nt*.

**mercy** ['mɜːsɪ] *n* Gnade *f*; **to have ~ on sb** Erbarmen mit jdm haben; **at the ~ of** ausgeliefert +*dat*.

**mercy killing** *n* Euthanasie *f*.

**mere** [mɪə*] *adj* bloß; **his ~ presence irritates her** schon *or* allein seine Anwesenheit ärgert sie; **she is a ~ child** sie ist noch ein Kind; **it's a ~ trifle** es ist eine Lappalie; **by ~ chance** rein durch Zufall.

**merely** ['mɪəlɪ] *adv* lediglich, bloß.

**merge** [mɜːdʒ] *vt* (*combine*) vereinen; (*COMPUT: files*) mischen ♦ *vi* (*COMM*) fusionieren; (*colours, sounds, shapes*) ineinander übergehen; (*roads*) zusammenlaufen.

**merger** ['mɜːdʒə*] *n* (*COMM*) Fusion *f*.

**meridian** [mə'rɪdɪən] *n* Meridian *m*.

**meringue** [mə'ræŋ] *n* Baiser *nt*.

**merit** ['mɛrɪt] *n* (*worth, value*) Wert *m*; (*advantage*) Vorzug *m*; (*achievement*) Verdienst *nt* ♦ *vt* verdienen.

**meritocracy** [mɛrɪ'tɔkrəsɪ] *n* Leistungsgesellschaft *f*.

**mermaid** ['mɜːmeɪd] *n* Seejungfrau *f*, Meerjungfrau *f*.

**merrily** ['mɛrɪlɪ] *adv* vergnügt.

**merriment** ['mɛrɪmənt] *n* Heiterkeit *f*.

**merry** ['mɛrɪ] *adj* vergnügt; (*music*) fröhlich; **M~ Christmas!** Fröhliche *or* Frohe Weihnachten!

**merry-go-round** ['mɛrɪɡəʊraund] *n* Karussell *nt*.

**mesh** [mɛʃ] *n* Geflecht *nt*; **wire ~** Maschendraht *m*.

**mesmerize** ['mɛzməraɪz] *vt* (*fig*) faszinieren.

**mess** [mɛs] *n* Durcheinander *nt*; (*dirt*) Dreck *m*; (*MIL*) Kasino *nt*; **to be in a ~** (*untidy*) unordentlich sein; (*in difficulty*) in Schwierigkeiten stecken; **to be a ~** (*fig: life*)

verkorkst sein; **to get o.s. in a ~** in Schwierigkeiten geraten.

▶**mess about** (*inf*) *vi* (*fool around*) herumalbern.

▶**mess about with** (*inf*) *vt fus* (*play around with*) herumfummeln an +*dat*.

▶**mess around** (*inf*) *vi* = **mess about**.

▶**mess around with** (*inf*) *vt fus* = **mess about with**.

▶**mess up** *vt* durcheinanderbringen; (*dirty*) verdrecken.

**message** ['mɛsɪdʒ] *n* Mitteilung *f*, Nachricht *f*; (*meaning*) Aussage *f*; **to get the ~** (*inf, fig*) kapieren.

**message switching** [-'swɪtʃɪŋ] *n* (*COMPUT*) Speichervermittlung *f*.

**messenger** ['mɛsɪndʒə*] *n* Bote *m*.

**Messiah** [mɪ'saɪə] *n* Messias *m*.

**Messrs** ['mɛsəz] *abbr* (*on letters: = messieurs*) An (die Herren).

**messy** ['mɛsɪ] *adj* (*dirty*) dreckig; (*untidy*) unordentlich.

**Met** [mɛt] (*US*) *n abbr* (*= Metropolitan Opera*) Met *f*.

**met** [mɛt] *pt, pp of* **meet**.

**met.** *adj abbr* (*= meteorological*): **the M~ Office** das Wetteramt.

**metabolism** [mɛ'tæbəlɪzəm] *n* Stoffwechsel *m*.

**metal** ['mɛtl] *n* Metall *nt*.

**metal fatigue** *n* Metallermüdung *f*.

**metalled** ['mɛtld] *adj* (*road*) asphaltiert.

**metallic** [mɪ'tælɪk] *adj* metallisch; (*made of metal*) aus Metall.

**metallurgy** [mɛ'tælədʒɪ] *n* Metallurgie *f*.

**metalwork** ['mɛtlwɔːk] *n* Metallarbeit *f*.

**metamorphosis** [mɛtə'mɔːfəsɪs] (*pl* **metamorphoses**) *n* Verwandlung *f*.

**metaphor** ['mɛtəfə*] *n* Metapher *f*.

**metaphorical** [mɛtə'fɔrɪkl] *adj* (*speech*) metaphorisch.

**metaphysics** [mɛtə'fɪzɪks] *n* Metaphysik *f*.

**meteor** ['miːtɪə*] *n* Meteor *m*.

**meteoric** [miːtɪ'ɔrɪk] *adj* (*fig*) kometenhaft.

**meteorite** [miːtɪəraɪt] *n* Meteorit *m*.

**meteorological** [miːtɪərə'lɔdʒɪkl] *adj* (*conditions, office etc*) Wetter-.

**meteorology** [miːtɪə'rɔlədʒɪ] *n* Wetterkunde *f*, Meteorologie *f*.

**mete out** [miːt-] *vt* austeilen; **to ~ justice** Recht sprechen.

**meter** ['miːtə*] *n* Zähler *m*; (*water meter*) Wasseruhr *f*; (*parking meter*) Parkuhr *f*; (*US: unit*) = **metre**.

**methane** ['miːθeɪn] *n* Methan *nt*.

**method** ['mɛθəd] *n* Methode *f*; **~ of payment** Zahlungsweise *f*.

**methodical** [mɪ'θɔdɪkl] *adj* methodisch.

**Methodist** ['mɛθədɪst] *n* Methodist(in) *m(f)*.

**methodology** [mɛθə'dɔlədʒɪ] *n* Methodik *f*.

**meths** [mɛθs] (*BRIT*) *n* = **methylated spirit**.

**methylated spirit** ['mɛθɪleɪtɪd-] (*BRIT*) *n* (Brenn)spiritus *m*.

**meticulous** [mɪ'tɪkjuləs] *adj* sorgfältig; (*detail*) genau.

**metre,** (*US*) **meter** ['miːtə'] *n* Meter *m or nt*.

**metric** ['mɛtrɪk] *adj* metrisch; **to go** ~ auf das metrische Maßsystem umstellen.

**metrical** ['mɛtrɪkl] *adj* metrisch.

**metrication** [mɛtrɪ'keɪʃən] *n* Umstellung *f* auf das metrische Maßsystem.

**metric system** *n* metrisches Maßsystem *nt*.

**metric ton** *n* Metertonne *f*.

**metronome** ['mɛtrənəum] *n* Metronom *nt*.

**metropolis** [mɪ'trɔpəlɪs] *n* Metropole *f*.

**metropolitan** [mɛtrə'pɔlɪtn] *adj* großstädtisch.

**Metropolitan Police** (*BRIT*) *n:* **the** ~ die Londoner Polizei.

**mettle** ['mɛtl] *n:* **to be on one's** ~ auf dem Posten sein.

**mew** [mjuː] *vi* miauen.

**mews** [mjuːz] (*BRIT*) *n* Gasse *f* mit ehemaligen Kutscherhäuschen.

**Mexican** ['mɛksɪkən] *adj* mexikanisch ♦ *n* Mexikaner(in) *m(f)*.

**Mexico** ['mɛksɪkəu] *n* Mexiko *nt*.

**Mexico City** *n* Mexico City *f*.

**mezzanine** ['mɛtsəniːn] *n* Mezzanin *nt*.

**MFA** (*US*) *n abbr* (= *Master of Fine Arts*) *akademischer Grad in Kunst.*

**mfr** *abbr* = **manufacture; manufacturer.**

**mg** *abbr* (= *milligram(me)*) mg.

**Mgr** *abbr* (= *Monseigneur, Monsignor*) Mgr.; (*COMM*) = **manager.**

**MHR** (*US, AUSTRALIA*) *n abbr* (= *Member of the House of Representatives*) Abgeordnete(r) *f(m)* des Repräsentantenhauses.

**MHz** *abbr* (= *megahertz*) MHz.

**MI** (*US*) *abbr* (*POST:* = *Michigan*).

**MI5** (*BRIT*) *n abbr* (= *Military Intelligence 5*) *britischer Spionageabwehrdienst.*

**MI6** (*BRIT*) *n abbr* (= *Military Intelligence 6*) *britischer Geheimdienst.*

**MIA** *abbr* (*MIL:* = *missing in action*) vermißt.

**miaow** [miː'au] *vi* miauen.

**mice** [maɪs] *npl of* **mouse.**

**Mich.** (*US*) *abbr* (*POST:* = *Michigan*).

**micro...** ['maɪkrəu] *pref* mikro-, Mikro-.

**microbe** ['maɪkrəub] *n* Mikrobe *f*.

**microbiology** [maɪkrəubaɪ'ɔlədʒɪ] *n* Mikrobiologie *f*.

**microchip** ['maɪkrəutʃɪp] *n* Mikrochip *m*.

**micro(computer)** ['maɪkrəu(kəm'pjuːtə')] *n* Mikrocomputer *m*.

**microcosm** ['maɪkrəukɔzəm] *n* Mikrokosmos *m*.

**microeconomics** ['maɪkrəuiːkə'nɔmɪks] *n* Mikroökonomie *f*.

**microelectronics** ['maɪkrəuɪlɛk'trɔnɪks] *n* Mikroelektronik *f*.

**microfiche** ['maɪkrəufiːʃ] *n* Mikrofiche *m or nt*.

**microfilm** ['maɪkrəufɪlm] *n* Mikrofilm *m*.

**microlight** ['maɪkrəulaɪt] *n* Ultraleichtflugzeug *nt*.

**micrometer** [maɪ'krɔmɪtə'] *n* Meßschraube *f*.

**microphone** ['maɪkrəfəun] *n* Mikrofon *nt*, Mikrophon *nt*.

**microprocessor** ['maɪkrəu'prəusɛsə'] *n* Mikroprozessor *m*.

**microscope** ['maɪkrəskəup] *n* Mikroskop *nt*; **under the** ~ unter dem Mikroskop.

**microscopic** [maɪkrə'skɔpɪk] *adj* mikroskopisch; (*creature*) mikroskopisch klein.

**microwave** ['maɪkrəuweɪv] *n* Mikrowelle *f*; (*also:* ~ **oven**) Mikrowellenherd *m*.

**mid-** [mɪd] *adj:* **in** ~**-May** Mitte Mai; **in** ~**-afternoon** (mitten) am Nachmittag; **in** ~**-air** (mitten) in der Luft; **he's in his** ~**-thirties** er ist Mitte dreißig.

**midday** [mɪd'deɪ] *n* Mittag *m*.

**middle** ['mɪdl] *n* Mitte *f* ♦ *adj* mittlere(r, s); **in the** ~ **of the night** mitten in der Nacht; **I'm in the** ~ **of reading it** ich bin mittendrin; **a** ~ **course** ein Mittelweg *m*.

**middle age** *n* mittleres Lebensalter *nt*.

**middle-aged** [mɪdl'eɪdʒd] *adj* mittleren Alters.

**Middle Ages** *npl* Mittelalter *nt*.

**middle-class** [mɪdl'klɑːs] *adj* mittelständisch.

**middle class(es)** *n(pl)* Mittelstand *m*.

**Middle East** *n* Naher Osten *m*.

**middleman** ['mɪdlmæn] (*irreg: like* **man**) *n* Zwischenhändler *m*.

**middle management** *n* mittleres Management *nt*.

**middle name** *n* zweiter Vorname *m*.

**middle-of-the-road** ['mɪdləvðə'rəud] *adj* gemäßigt; (*politician*) der Mitte; (*MUS*) leicht.

**middleweight** ['mɪdlweɪt] *n* (*BOXING*) Mittelgewicht *nt*.

**middling** ['mɪdlɪŋ] *adj* mittelmäßig.

**Middx** (*BRIT*) *abbr* (*POST:* = *Middlesex*).

**midge** [mɪdʒ] *n* Mücke *f*.

**midget** ['mɪdʒɪt] *n* Liliputaner(in) *m(f)*.

**midi system** ['mɪdɪ-] *n* Midi-System *nt*.

**Midlands** ['mɪdləndz] (*BRIT*) *npl:* **the** ~ Mittelengland *nt*.

**midnight** ['mɪdnaɪt] *n* Mitternacht *f* ♦ *cpd* Mitternachts-; **at** ~ um Mitternacht.

**midriff** ['mɪdrɪf] *n* Taille *f*.

**midst** [mɪdst] *n:* **in the** ~ **of** mitten in +*dat*; **to be in the** ~ **of doing sth** mitten dabei sein, etw zu tun.

**midsummer** [mɪd'sʌmə'] *n* Hochsommer *m*; **M~('s) Day** Sommersonnenwende *f*.

**midway** [mɪd'weɪ] *adj:* **we have reached the** ~ **point** wir haben die Hälfte hinter uns *dat* ♦ *adv* auf halbem Weg; ~ **between** (*in space*) auf halbem Weg zwischen; ~ **through** (*in time*) mitten in +*dat*.

**midweek** [mɪd'wiːk] *adv* mitten in der Woche ♦ *adj* Mitte der Woche.

**midwife** ['mɪdwaɪf] (*pl* **midwives**) *n* Hebamme *f*.

**midwifery** ['mɪdwɪfərɪ] n Geburtshilfe f.
**midwinter** [mɪd'wɪntə*] n: **in** ~ im tiefsten Winter.
**miffed** [mɪft] (inf) adj: **to be** ~ eingeschnappt sein.
**might** [maɪt] vb see **may** ♦ n Macht f; **with all one's** ~ mit aller Kraft.
**mighty** ['maɪtɪ] adj mächtig.
**migraine** ['miːgreɪn] n Migräne f.
**migrant** ['maɪgrənt] adj (bird) Zug-; (worker) Wander- ♦ n (bird) Zugvogel m; (worker) Wanderarbeiter(in) m(f).
**migrate** [maɪ'greɪt] vi (bird) ziehen; (person) abwandern.
**migration** [maɪ'greɪʃən] n Wanderung f; (to cities) Abwanderung f; (of birds) (Vogel)zug m.
**mike** [maɪk] n abbr = **microphone**.
**Milan** [mɪ'læn] n Mailand nt.
**mild** [maɪld] adj mild; (gentle) sanft; (slight: infection etc) leicht; (: interest) gering.
**mildew** ['mɪldjuː] n Schimmel m.
**mildly** ['maɪldlɪ] adv (say) sanft; (slight) leicht; **to put it** ~ gelinde gesagt.
**mildness** ['maɪldnɪs] n Milde f; (gentleness) Sanftheit f; (of infection etc) Leichtigkeit f.
**mile** [maɪl] n Meile f; **to do 30** ~**s per gallon** ≈ 9 Liter auf 100 km verbrauchen.
**mileage** ['maɪlɪdʒ] n Meilenzahl f; (fig) Nutzen m; **to get a lot of** ~ **out of sth** etw gründlich ausnutzen; **there is a lot of** ~ **in the idea** aus der Idee läßt sich viel machen.
**mileage allowance** n ≈ Kilometergeld nt.
**mileometer** [maɪ'lɔmɪtə*] n ≈ Kilometerzähler m.
**milestone** ['maɪlstəun] n (lit, fig) Meilenstein m.
**milieu** ['miːljəː] n Milieu nt.
**militant** ['mɪlɪtnt] adj militant ♦ n Militante(r) f(m).
**militarism** ['mɪlɪtərɪzəm] n Militarismus m.
**militaristic** [mɪlɪtə'rɪstɪk] adj militaristisch.
**military** ['mɪlɪtərɪ] adj (history, leader etc) Militär- ♦ n: **the** ~ das Militär.
**military police** n Militärpolizei f.
**military service** n Militärdienst m.
**militate** ['mɪlɪteɪt] vi: **to** ~ **against** negative Auswirkungen haben auf +acc.
**militia** [mɪ'lɪʃə] n Miliz f.
**milk** [mɪlk] n Milch f ♦ vt (lit, fig) melken.
**milk chocolate** n Vollmilchschokolade f.
**milk float** (BRIT) n Milchwagen m.
**milking** ['mɪlkɪŋ] n Melken nt.
**milkman** ['mɪlkmən] n (irreg: like **man**) n Milchmann m.
**milk shake** n Milchmixgetränk nt.
**milk tooth** n Milchzahn m.
**milk truck** (US) n = **milk float**.
**milky** ['mɪlkɪ] adj milchig; (drink) mit viel Milch; ~ **coffee** Milchkaffee m.
**Milky Way** n Milchstraße f.
**mill** [mɪl] n Mühle f; (factory) Fabrik f; (woollen

mill) Spinnerei f ♦ vt mahlen ♦ vi (also: ~ **about**) umherlaufen.
**millennium** [mɪ'lɛnɪəm] (pl ~**s** or **millennia**) n Jahrtausend nt.
**miller** ['mɪlə*] n Müller m.
**millet** ['mɪlɪt] n Hirse f.
**milli...** ['mɪlɪ] pref Milli-.
**milligram(me)** ['mɪlɪgræm] n Milligramm nt.
**millilitre, (US) milliliter** ['mɪlɪliːtə*] n Milliliter m or nt.
**millimetre, (US) millimeter** ['mɪlɪmiːtə*] n Millimeter m or nt.
**millinery** ['mɪlɪnərɪ] n Hüte pl.
**million** ['mɪljən] n Million f; **a** ~ **times** (fig) tausendmal, x-mal.
**millionaire** [mɪljə'nɛə*] n Millionär m.
**millipede** ['mɪlɪpiːd] n Tausendfüßler m.
**millstone** ['mɪlstəun] n (fig): **it's a** ~ **round his neck** es ist für ihn ein Klotz am Bein.
**millwheel** ['mɪlwiːl] n Mühlrad nt.
**milometer** [maɪ'lɔmɪtə*] n = **mileometer**.
**mime** [maɪm] n Pantomime f; (actor) Pantomime m ♦ vt pantomimisch darstellen.
**mimic** ['mɪmɪk] n Imitator m ♦ vt (for amusement) parodieren; (animal, person) imitieren, nachahmen.
**mimicry** ['mɪmɪkrɪ] n Nachahmung f.
**Min.** (BRIT) abbr (POL) = **ministry**.
**min.** abbr (= minute) Min.; = **minimum**.
**minaret** [mɪnə'rɛt] n Minarett nt.
**mince** [mɪns] vt (meat) durch den Fleischwolf drehen ♦ vi (in walking) trippeln ♦ n (BRIT: meat) Hackfleisch nt; **he does not** ~ (**his**) **words** er nimmt kein Blatt vor den Mund.
**mincemeat** ['mɪnsmiːt] n süße Gebäckfüllung aus Dörrobst und Sirup; (US: meat) Hackfleisch nt; **to make** ~ **of sb** (inf) Hackfleisch aus jdm machen.
**mince pie** n mit Mincemeat gefülltes Gebäck.
**mincer** ['mɪnsə*] n Fleischwolf m.
**mincing** ['mɪnsɪŋ] adj (walk) trippelnd; (voice) geziert.
**mind** [maɪnd] n Geist m, Verstand m; (thoughts) Gedanken pl; (memory) Gedächtnis nt ♦ vt aufpassen auf +acc; (office etc) nach dem Rechten sehen in +dat; (object to) etwas haben gegen; **to my** ~ meiner Meinung nach; **to be out of one's** ~ verrückt sein; **it is on my** ~ es beschäftigt mich; **to keep** or **bear sth in** ~ etw nicht vergessen, an etw denken; **to make up one's** ~ sich entscheiden; **to change one's** ~ es sich dat anders überlegen; **to be in two** ~**s about sth** sich dat über etw acc nicht im klaren sein; **to have it in** ~ **to do sth** die Absicht haben, etw zu tun; **to have sb/sth in** ~ an jdn/etw denken; **it slipped my** ~ ich habe es vergessen; **to bring** or **call sth to** ~ etw in Erinnerung rufen; **I can't get it out of my** ~ es geht mir nicht aus dem Kopf; **his** ~ **was on other things** er war mit den

Gedanken woanders; "~ **the step**"
„Vorsicht Stufe"; **do you** ~ **if ...?** macht es
Ihnen etwas aus, wenn ...?; **I don't** ~ es ist
mir egal; ~ **you,** ... allerdings ...; **never** ~! (*it
makes no odds*) ist doch egal!; (*don't worry*)
macht nichts!

**mind-boggling** ['maɪndbɒglɪŋ] (*inf*) *adj*
atemberaubend.

**-minded** ['maɪndɪd] *adj:* **fair-**~ gerecht; **an
industrially-**~ **nation** ein auf Industrie
ausgerichtetes Land.

**minder** ['maɪndə*] *n* Betreuer(in) *m(f)*; (*inf:
bodyguard*) Aufpasser(in) *m(f)*.

**mindful** ['maɪndful] *adj:* ~ **of** unter
Berücksichtigung +*gen*.

**mindless** ['maɪndlɪs] *adj* (*violence*) sinnlos;
(*work*) geistlos.

**mine¹** [maɪn] *n* (*coal mine, gold mine*)
Bergwerk *nt*; (*bomb*) Mine *f* ♦ *vt* (*coal*)
abbauen; (*beach etc*) verminen; (*ship*) eine
Mine befestigen an +*dat*.

**mine²** [maɪn] *pron* meine(r, s); **that book is** ~
das Buch ist mein(e)s, das Buch gehört
mir; **this is** ~ das ist meins; **a friend of** ~ ein
Freund/eine Freundin von mir.

**mine detector** *n* Minensuchgerät *nt*.

**minefield** ['maɪnfiːld] *n* Minenfeld *nt*; (*fig*)
brisante Situation *f*.

**miner** ['maɪnə*] *n* Bergmann *m*, Bergarbeiter
*m*.

**mineral** ['mɪnərəl] *adj* (*deposit, resources*)
Mineral- ♦ *n* Mineral *nt*; **minerals** *npl* (*BRIT:
soft drinks*) Erfrischungsgetränke *pl*.

**mineralogy** [mɪnə'rælədʒɪ] *n* Mineralogie *f*.

**mineral water** *n* Mineralwasser *nt*.

**minesweeper** ['maɪnswiːpə*] *n*
Minensuchboot *nt*.

**mingle** ['mɪŋgl] *vi:* **to** ~ **(with)** sich
vermischen (mit); **to** ~ **with** (*people*)
Umgang haben mit; (*at party etc*) sich
unterhalten mit; **you should** ~ **a bit** du
solltest dich unter die Leute mischen.

**mingy** ['mɪndʒɪ] (*inf*) *adj* knick(e)rig; (*amount*)
mick(e)rig.

**mini...** ['mɪnɪ] *pref* Mini-.

**miniature** ['mɪnətʃə*] *adj* winzig; (*version etc*)
Miniatur- ♦ *n* Miniatur *f*; **in** ~ im kleinen, im
Kleinformat.

**minibus** ['mɪnɪbʌs] *n* Kleinbus *m*.

**minicab** ['mɪnɪkæb] *n* Kleintaxi *nt*.

**minicomputer** ['mɪnɪkəm'pjuːtə*] *n*
Minicomputer *m*.

**minim** ['mɪnɪm] *n* (*MUS*) halbe Note *f*.

**minima** ['mɪnɪmə] *npl of* **minimum.**

**minimal** ['mɪnɪml] *adj* minimal.

**minimalist** ['mɪnɪməlɪst] *adj* minimalistisch.

**minimize** ['mɪnɪmaɪz] *vt* auf ein Minimum
reduzieren; (*play down*) herunterspielen.

**minimum** ['mɪnɪməm] (*pl* **minima**) *n* Minimum
*nt* ♦ *adj* (*income, speed*) Mindest-; **to reduce
to a** ~ auf ein Mindestmaß reduzieren;
~ **wage** Mindestlohn *m*.

**minimum lending rate** *n* Diskontsatz *m*.

**mining** ['maɪnɪŋ] *n* Bergbau *m* ♦ *cpd* Bergbau-.

**minion** ['mɪnjən] (*pej*) *n* Untergebene(r) *f(m)*.

**miniseries** ['mɪnɪsɪəriːz] *n* Miniserie *f*.

**miniskirt** ['mɪnɪskəːt] *n* Minirock *m*.

**minister** ['mɪnɪstə*] *n* (*BRIT: POL*) Minister(in)
*m(f)*; (*REL*) Pfarrer *m* ♦ *vi:* **to** ~ **to** sich
kümmern um; (*needs*) befriedigen.

**ministerial** [mɪnɪs'tɪərɪəl] (*BRIT*) *adj* (*POL*)
ministeriell.

**ministry** ['mɪnɪstrɪ] *n* (*BRIT: POL*) Ministerium
*nt*; **to join the** ~ (*REL*) Geistliche(r) werden.

**Ministry of Defence** (*BRIT*) *n*
Verteidigungsministerium *nt*.

**mink** [mɪŋk] (*pl* ~**s** *or* ~) *n* Nerz *m*.

**mink coat** *n* Nerzmantel *m*.

**Minn.** (*US*) *abbr* (*POST:* = Minnesota).

**minnow** ['mɪnəu] *n* Elritze *f*.

**minor** ['maɪnə*] *adj* kleinere(r, s); (*poet*)
unbedeutend; (*planet*) klein; (*MUS*) Moll ♦ *n*
Minderjährige(r) *f(m)*.

**Minorca** [mɪ'nɔːkə] *n* Menorca *nt*.

**minority** [maɪ'nɒrɪtɪ] *n* Minderheit *f*; **to be in a**
~ in der Minderheit sein.

**minster** ['mɪnstə*] *n* Münster *nt*.

**minstrel** ['mɪnstrəl] *n* Spielmann *m*.

**mint** [mɪnt] *n* Minze *f*; (*sweet*)
Pfefferminz(bonbon) *nt*; (*place*): **the M**~ die
Münzanstalt ♦ *vt* (*coins*) prägen; **in**
~ **condition** neuwertig.

**mint sauce** *n* Minzsoße *f*.

**minuet** [mɪnju'et] *n* Menuett *nt*.

**minus** ['maɪnəs] *n* (*also:* ~ **sign**) Minuszeichen
*nt* ♦ *prep* minus, weniger; ~ **24ºC** 24 Grad
unter Null.

**minuscule** ['mɪnəskjuːl] *adj* winzig.

**minute¹** [maɪ'njuːt] *adj* winzig; (*search*)
peinlich genau; (*detail*) kleinste(r, s); **in**
~ **detail** in allen Einzelheiten.

**minute²** ['mɪnɪt] *n* Minute *f*; (*fig*) Augenblick
*m*, Moment *m*; **minutes** *npl* (*of meeting*)
Protokoll *nt*; **it is 5** ~**s past 3** es ist 5
Minuten nach 3; **wait a** ~! einen Augenblick
*or* Moment!; **up-to-the-**~ (*news*)
hochaktuell; (*technology*) allerneueste(r, s);
**at the last** ~ in letzter Minute.

**minute book** *n* Protokollbuch *nt*.

**minute hand** *n* Minutenzeiger *m*.

**minutely** [maɪ'njuːtlɪ] *adv* (*in detail*)
genauestens; (*by a small amount*) ganz
geringfügig.

**minutiae** [mɪ'njuːʃiiː] *npl* Einzelheiten *pl*.

**miracle** ['mɪrəkl] *n* (*REL, fig*) Wunder *nt*.

**miraculous** [mɪ'rækjuləs] *adj* wunderbar;
(*powers, effect, cure*) Wunder-; (*success,
change*) unglaublich; **to have a** ~ **escape** wie
durch ein Wunder entkommen.

**mirage** ['mɪrɑːʒ] *n* Fata Morgana *f*; (*fig*)
Trugbild *nt*.

**mire** ['maɪə*] *n* Morast *m*.

**mirror** ['mɪrə*] *n* Spiegel *m* ♦ *vt* (*lit, fig*)
widerspiegeln.

**mirror image** n Spiegelbild nt.

**mirth** [mɜːθ] n Heiterkeit f.

**misadventure** [mɪsəd'vɛntʃəˈ] n Mißgeschick nt; **death by ~** (BRIT) Tod m durch Unfall.

**misanthropist** [mɪ'zænθrəpɪst] n Misanthrop m, Menschenfeind m.

**misapply** [mɪsə'plaɪ] vt (term) falsch verwenden; (rule) falsch anwenden.

**misapprehension** ['mɪsæprɪ'hɛnʃən] n Mißverständnis nt; **you are under a ~** Sie befinden sich im Irrtum.

**misappropriate** [mɪsə'prəuprɪeɪt] vt veruntreuen.

**misappropriation** ['mɪsəprəuprɪ'eɪʃən] n Veruntreuung f.

**misbehave** [mɪsbɪ'heɪv] vi sich schlecht benehmen.

**misbehaviour,** (US) **misbehavior** [mɪsbɪ'heɪvjəˈ] n schlechtes Benehmen nt.

**misc.** abbr = **miscellaneous**.

**miscalculate** [mɪs'kælkjuleɪt] vt falsch berechnen; (misjudge) falsch einschätzen.

**miscalculation** ['mɪskælkju'leɪʃən] n Rechenfehler m; (misjudgement) Fehleinschätzung f.

**miscarriage** ['mɪskærɪdʒ] n (MED) Fehlgeburt f; **~ of justice** (LAW) Justizirrtum m.

**miscarry** [mɪs'kærɪ] vi (MED) eine Fehlgeburt haben; (fail: plans) fehlschlagen.

**miscellaneous** [mɪsɪ'leɪnɪəs] adj verschieden; (subjects, items) divers; **~ expenses** sonstige Unkosten pl.

**mischance** [mɪs'tʃɑːns] n unglücklicher Zufall m.

**mischief** ['mɪstʃɪf] n (bad behaviour) Unfug m; (playfulness) Verschmitztheit f; (harm) Schaden m; (pranks) Streiche pl; **to get into ~** etwas anstellen; **to do sb a ~** jdm etwas antun.

**mischievous** ['mɪstʃɪvəs] adj (naughty) ungezogen; (playful) verschmitzt.

**misconception** ['mɪskən'sɛpʃən] n fälschliche Annahme f.

**misconduct** [mɪs'kɒndʌkt] n Fehlverhalten nt; **professional ~** Berufsvergehen nt.

**misconstrue** [mɪskən'struː] vt mißverstehen.

**miscount** [mɪs'kaunt] vt falsch zählen ♦ vi sich verzählen.

**misdemeanour,** (US) **misdemeanor** [mɪsdɪ'miːnəˈ] n Vergehen nt.

**misdirect** [mɪsdɪ'rɛkt] vt (person) in die falsche Richtung schicken; (talent) vergeuden.

**miser** ['maɪzəˈ] n Geizhals m.

**miserable** ['mɪzərəbl] adj (unhappy) unglücklich; (wretched) erbärmlich, elend; (unpleasant: weather) trostlos; (: person) gemein; (contemptible: offer, donation) armselig; (: failure) kläglich; **to feel ~** sich elend fühlen.

**miserably** ['mɪzərəblɪ] adv (fail) kläglich; (live) elend; (smile, speak) unglücklich; (small)
jämmerlich.

**miserly** ['maɪzəlɪ] adj geizig; (amount) armselig.

**misery** ['mɪzərɪ] n (unhappiness) Kummer m; (wretchedness) Elend nt; (inf: person) Miesepeter m.

**misfire** [mɪs'faɪəˈ] vi (plan) fehlschlagen; (car engine) fehlzünden.

**misfit** ['mɪsfɪt] n Außenseiter(in) m(f).

**misfortune** [mɪs'fɔːtʃən] n Pech nt, Unglück nt.

**misgiving** [mɪs'gɪvɪŋ] n Bedenken pl; **to have ~s about sth** sich bei etw nicht wohl fühlen.

**misguided** [mɪs'gaɪdɪd] adj töricht; (opinion, view) irrig; (misplaced) unangebracht.

**mishandle** [mɪs'hændl] vt falsch handhaben.

**mishap** ['mɪshæp] n Mißgeschick nt.

**mishear** [mɪs'hɪəˈ] (irreg: like **hear**) vt falsch hören ♦ vi sich verhören.

**misheard** [mɪs'hɜːd] pt, pp of **mishear**.

**mishmash** ['mɪʃmæʃ] (inf) n Mischmasch m.

**misinform** [mɪsɪn'fɔːm] vt falsch informieren.

**misinterpret** [mɪsɪn'təːprɪt] vt (gesture, situation) falsch auslegen; (comment) falsch auffassen.

**misinterpretation** ['mɪsɪntəːprɪ'teɪʃən] n falsche Auslegung f.

**misjudge** [mɪs'dʒʌdʒ] vt falsch einschätzen.

**mislay** [mɪs'leɪ] (irreg: like **lay**) vt verlegen.

**mislead** [mɪs'liːd] (irreg: like **lead**) vt irreführen.

**misleading** [mɪs'liːdɪŋ] adj irreführend.

**misled** [mɪs'lɛd] pt, pp of **mislead**.

**mismanage** [mɪs'mænɪdʒ] vt (business) herunterwirtschaften; (institution) schlecht führen.

**mismanagement** [mɪs'mænɪdʒmənt] n Mißwirtschaft f.

**misnomer** [mɪs'nəuməˈ] n unzutreffende Bezeichnung f.

**misogynist** [mɪ'sɒdʒɪnɪst] n Frauenfeind m.

**misplaced** [mɪs'pleɪst] adj (misguided) unangebracht; (wrongly positioned) an der falschen Stelle.

**misprint** ['mɪsprɪnt] n Druckfehler m.

**mispronounce** [mɪsprə'nauns] vt falsch aussprechen.

**misquote** ['mɪs'kwəut] vt falsch zitieren.

**misread** [mɪs'riːd] (irreg: like **read**) vt falsch lesen; (misinterpret) falsch verstehen.

**misrepresent** [mɪsrɛprɪ'zɛnt] vt falsch darstellen; **he was ~ed** seine Worte wurden verfälscht wiedergegeben.

**Miss** [mɪs] n Fräulein nt; **Dear ~ Smith** Liebe Frau Smith.

**miss** [mɪs] vt (train etc, chance, opportunity) verpassen; (target) verfehlen; (notice loss of, regret absence of) vermissen; (class, meeting) fehlen bei ♦ vi danebentreffen; (missile, object) danebengehen ♦ n Fehltreffer m; **you can't ~ it** du kannst es nicht verfehlen; **the bus just ~ed the wall** der Bus wäre um ein Haar gegen die Mauer gefahren; **you're**

~ing the point das geht an der Sache
vorbei.
▶miss out (*BRIT*) *vt* auslassen.
▶miss out on *vt fus* (*party*) verpassen; (*fun*)
zu kurz kommen bei.
missal ['mɪsl] *n* Meßbuch *nt*.
misshapen [mɪs'ʃeɪpən] *adj* mißgebildet.
missile ['mɪsaɪl] *n* (*MIL*) Rakete *f*; (*object
thrown*) (Wurf)geschoß *nt*.
missile base *n* Raketenbasis *f*.
missile launcher [-'lɔːntʃə*] *n* Startrampe *f*.
missing ['mɪsɪŋ] *adj* (*lost: person*) vermißt;
(: *object*) verschwunden; (*absent, removed*)
fehlend; **to be ~** fehlen; **to go ~**
verschwinden; **~ person** Vermißte(r) *f(m)*.
mission ['mɪʃən] *n* (*task*) Mission *f*, Auftrag *m*;
(*representatives*) Gesandtschaft *f*; (*MIL*)
Einsatz *m*; (*REL*) Mission *f*; **on a ~ to** ... (*to
place/people*) im Einsatz in +*dat*/bei ...
missionary ['mɪʃənrɪ] *n* Missionar(in) *m(f)*.
missive ['mɪsɪv] (*form*) *n* Schreiben *nt*.
misspell ['mɪs'spɛl] (*irreg: like spell*) *vt* falsch
schreiben.
misspent ['mɪs'spɛnt] *adj* (*youth*) vergeudet.
mist [mɪst] *n* Nebel *m*; (*light*) Dunst *m* ♦ *vi* (*also:
~ over: eyes*) sich verschleiern; (*BRIT: also:
~ over, ~ up*) (*windows*) beschlagen.
mistake [mɪs'teɪk] (*irreg: like take*) *n* Fehler *m*
♦ *vt* sich irren in +*dat*; (*intentions*) falsch
verstehen; **by ~** aus Versehen; **to make a ~**
(*in writing, calculation*) sich vertun; **to make a
~** (*about sb/sth*) sich (in jdm/etw) irren; **to
~ A for B** A mit B verwechseln.
mistaken [mɪs'teɪkən] *pp of* mistake ♦ *adj*
falsch; **to be ~** sich irren.
mistaken identity *n* Verwechslung *f*.
mistakenly [mɪs'teɪkənlɪ] *adv*
irrtümlicherweise.
mister ['mɪstə*] (*inf*) *n* (*sir*) *not translated; see*
Mr.
mistletoe ['mɪsltəu] *n* Mistel *f*.
mistook [mɪs'tuk] *pt of* mistake.
mistranslation [mɪstræns'leɪʃən] *n* falsche
Übersetzung *f*.
mistreat [mɪs'triːt] *vt* schlecht behandeln.
mistress ['mɪstrɪs] *n* (*lover*) Geliebte *f*; (*of
house, servant, situation*) Herrin *f*; (*BRIT:
teacher*) Lehrerin *f*.
mistrust [mɪs'trʌst] *vt* mißtrauen +*dat* ♦ *n*:
**~ (of)** Mißtrauen *nt* (gegenüber).
mistrustful [mɪs'trʌstful] *adj*: **~ (of)**
mißtrauisch (gegenüber).
misty ['mɪstɪ] *adj* (*day etc*) neblig; (*glasses,
windows*) beschlagen.
misty-eyed ['mɪstɪ'aɪd] *adj* mit
verschleiertem Blick.
misunderstand [mɪsʌndə'stænd] (*irreg: like
understand*) *vt* mißverstehen, falsch
verstehen ♦ *vi* es falsch verstehen.
misunderstanding ['mɪsʌndə'stændɪŋ] *n*
Mißverständnis *nt*; (*disagreement*)
Meinungsverschiedenheit *f*.

misunderstood [mɪsʌndə'stud] *pt, pp of*
misunderstand.
misuse [*n* mɪs'juːs, *vt* mɪs'juːz] *n* Mißbrauch *m*
♦ *vt* mißbrauchen; (*word*) falsch
gebrauchen.
MIT (*US*) *n abbr* (= *Massachusetts Institute of
Technology*) *private technische
Fachhochschule.*
mite [maɪt] *n* (*small quantity*) bißchen *nt*; (*BRIT:
small child*) Würmchen *nt*.
miter ['maɪtə*] (*US*) *n* = mitre.
mitigate ['mɪtɪgeɪt] *vt* mildern; **mitigating
circumstances** mildernde Umstände *pl*.
mitigation [mɪtɪ'geɪʃən] *n* Milderung *f*.
mitre, (*US*) miter ['maɪtə*] *n* (*of bishop*) Mitra
*f*; (*CARPENTRY*) Gehrung *f*.
mitt(en) ['mɪt(n)] *n* Fausthandschuh *m*.
mix [mɪks] *vt* mischen; (*drink*) mixen; (*sauce,
cake*) zubereiten; (*ingredients*) verrühren
♦ *vi*: **to ~ (with)** verkehren (mit) ♦ *n*
Mischung *f*; **to ~ sth with sth** etw mit etw
vermischen; **to ~ business with pleasure**
das Angenehme mit dem Nützlichen
verbinden; **cake ~** Backmischung *f*.
▶mix in *vt* (*eggs etc*) unterrühren.
▶mix up *vt* (*people*) verwechseln; (*things*)
durcheinanderbringen; **to be ~ed up in sth**
in etw *acc* verwickelt sein.
mixed [mɪkst] *adj* gemischt; **~ marriage**
Mischehe *f*.
mixed-ability ['mɪkstə'bɪlɪtɪ] *adj* (*group etc*)
mit unterschiedlichen Fähigkeiten.
mixed bag *n* (*of things, problems*)
Sammelsurium *nt*; (*of people*) gemischter
Haufen *m*.
mixed blessing *n*: **it's a ~** das ist ein
zweischneidiges Schwert.
mixed doubles *npl* gemischtes Doppel *nt*.
mixed economy *n* gemischte
Wirtschaftsform *f*.
mixed grill (*BRIT*) *n* Grillteller *m*.
mixed-up [mɪkst'ʌp] *adj* durcheinander.
mixer ['mɪksə*] *n* (*for food*) Mixer *m*; (*drink*)
Tonic etc zum Auffüllen von alkoholischen
Mixgetränken; **to be a good ~** (*sociable
person*) kontaktfreudig sein.
mixer tap *n* Mischbatterie *f*.
mixture ['mɪkstʃə*] *n* Mischung *f*; (*CULIN*)
Gemisch *nt*; (: *for cake*) Teig *m*; (*MED*)
Mixtur *f*.
mix-up ['mɪksʌp] *n* Durcheinander *nt*.
MK (*BRIT*) *abbr* (*TECH*) = mark.
mk *abbr* (*FIN*) = mark.
mkt *abbr* = market.
MLitt *n abbr* (= *Master of Literature, Master of
Letters*) *akademischer Grad in
Literaturwissenschaft.*
MLR (*BRIT*) *n abbr* = minimum lending rate.
mm *abbr* (= *millimetre*) mm.
MN (*BRIT*) *abbr* = merchant navy; (*US: POST:*)
= Minnesota.
MO *n abbr* (= *medical officer*) Sanitätsoffizier

*m*; (*US: inf*) = **modus operandi** ♦ *abbr* (*US: POST*: = *Missouri*).

**m.o.** *abbr* = **money order.**

**moan** [məun] *n* Stöhnen *nt* ♦ *vi* stöhnen; (*inf: complain*): **to ~ (about)** meckern (über +*acc*).

**moaner** ['məunə'] (*inf*) *n* Miesmacher(in) *m(f)*.

**moat** [məut] *n* Wassergraben *m*.

**mob** [mɔb] *n* Mob *m*; (*organized*) Bande *f* ♦ *vt* herfallen über +*acc.*

**mobile** ['məubaɪl] *adj* beweglich; (*workforce, society*) mobil ♦ *n* (*decoration*) Mobile *nt*; **applicants must be ~** Bewerber müssen motorisiert sein.

**mobile home** *n* Wohnwagen *m*.

**mobile phone** *n* Funktelefon *nt*.

**mobility** [məu'bɪlɪtɪ] *n* Beweglichkeit *f*; (*of workforce etc*) Mobilität *f*.

**mobility allowance** *n* Beihilfe für Gehbehinderte.

**mobilize** ['məubɪlaɪz] *vt* mobilisieren; (*MIL*) mobil machen ♦ *vi* (*MIL*) mobil machen.

**moccasin** ['mɔkəsɪn] *n* Mokassin *m*.

**mock** [mɔk] *vt* sich lustig machen über +*acc* ♦ *adj* (*fake: Elizabethan etc*) Pseudo-; (*exam*) Probe-; (*battle*) Schein-.

**mockery** ['mɔkərɪ] *n* Spott *m*; **to make a ~ of sb** jdn zum Gespött machen; **to make a ~ of sth** etw zur Farce machen.

**mocking** ['mɔkɪŋ] *adj* spöttisch.

**mockingbird** ['mɔkɪŋbə:d] *n* Spottdrossel *f*.

**mock-up** ['mɔkʌp] *n* Modell *nt*.

**MOD** (*BRIT*) *n abbr* = **Ministry of Defence.**

**mod cons** ['mɔd'kɔnz] (*BRIT*) *npl abbr* (= *modern conveniences*) Komfort *m*.

**mode** [məud] *n* Form *f*; (*COMPUT, TECH*) Betriebsart *f*; **~ of life** Lebensweise *f*; **~ of transport** Transportmittel *nt*.

**model** ['mɔdl] *n* Modell *nt*; (*fashion model*) Mannequin *nt*; (*example*) Muster *nt* ♦ *adj* (*excellent*) vorbildlich; (*small scale: railway etc*) Modell- ♦ *vt* (*clothes*) vorführen; (*with clay etc*) modellieren, formen ♦ *vi* (*for designer, photographer etc*) als Modell arbeiten; **to ~ o.s. on sb** sich *dat* jdn zum Vorbild nehmen.

**modeller,** (*US*) **modeler** ['mɔdlə'] *n* Modellbauer *m*.

**model railway** *n* Modelleisenbahn *f*.

**modem** ['məudɛm] *n* Modem *nt*.

**moderate** [*adj* 'mɔdərət, *vb* 'mɔdəreɪt] *adj* gemäßigt; (*amount*) nicht allzu groß; (*change*) leicht ♦ *n* Gemäßigte(r) *f(m)* ♦ *vi* (*storm, wind etc*) nachlassen ♦ *vt* (*tone, demands*) mäßigen.

**moderately** ['mɔdərətlɪ] *adv* mäßig; (*expensive, difficult*) nicht allzu; (*pleased, happy*) einigermaßen; **~ priced** nicht allzu teuer.

**moderation** [mɔdə'reɪʃən] *n* Mäßigung *f*; **in ~** in or mit Maßen.

**moderator** ['mɔdəreɪtə'] *n* (*ECCL*) Synodalpräsident *m*.

**modern** ['mɔdən] *adj* modern; **~ languages** moderne Fremdsprachen *pl*.

**modernization** [mɔdənaɪ'zeɪʃən] *n* Modernisierung *f*.

**modernize** ['mɔdənaɪz] *vt* modernisieren.

**modest** ['mɔdɪst] *adj* bescheiden; (*chaste*) schamhaft.

**modestly** ['mɔdɪstlɪ] *adv* bescheiden; (*behave*) schamhaft; (*to a moderate extent*) mäßig.

**modesty** ['mɔdɪstɪ] *n* Bescheidenheit *f*; (*chastity*) Schamgefühl *nt*.

**modicum** ['mɔdɪkəm] *n*: **a ~ of** ein wenig or bißchen.

**modification** [mɔdɪfɪ'keɪʃən] *n* Änderung *f*; (*to policy etc*) Modifizierung *f*; **to make ~s to** (Ver)änderungen vornehmen an +*dat*, modifizieren.

**modify** ['mɔdɪfaɪ] *vt* (ver)ändern; (*policy etc*) modifizieren.

**modish** ['məudɪʃ] *adj* (*fashionable*) modisch.

**Mods** [mɔdz] (*BRIT*) *n abbr* (*SCOL*: = (*Honour*) *Moderations*) akademische Prüfung an der Universität Oxford.

**modular** ['mɔdjulə'] *adj* (*unit, furniture*) aus Bauelementen (zusammengesetzt); (*COMPUT*) modular.

**modulate** ['mɔdjuleɪt] *vt* modulieren; (*process, activity*) umwandeln.

**modulation** [mɔdju'leɪʃən] *n* Modulation *f*; (*modification*) Veränderung *f*.

**module** ['mɔdju:l] *n* (Bau)element *nt*; (*SPACE*) Raumkapsel *f*; (*SCOL*) Kurs *m*.

**modus operandi** ['məudəsɔpə'rændi:] *n* Modus operandi *m*.

**Mogadishu** [mɔgə'dɪʃu:] *n* Mogadischu *nt*.

**mogul** ['məugl] *n* (*fig*) Mogul *m*.

**MOH** (*BRIT*) *n abbr* (= *Medical Officer of Health*) Amtsarzt *m*, Amtsärztin *f*.

**mohair** ['məuheə'] *n* Mohair *m*.

**Mohammed** [mə'hæmɛd] *n* Mohammed *m*.

**moist** [mɔɪst] *adj* feucht.

**moisten** ['mɔɪsn] *vt* anfeuchten.

**moisture** ['mɔɪstʃə'] *n* Feuchtigkeit *f*.

**moisturize** ['mɔɪstʃəraɪz] *vt* (*skin*) mit einer Feuchtigkeitscreme behandeln.

**moisturizer** ['mɔɪstʃəraɪzə'] *n* Feuchtigkeitscreme *f*.

**molar** ['məulə'] *n* Backenzahn *m*.

**molasses** [mə'læsɪz] *n* Melasse *f*.

**mold** *etc* [məuld] (*US*) *n*, *vt* = **mould** *etc*.

**Moldavia** [mɔl'deɪvɪə] *n* Moldawien *nt*.

**Moldavian** [mɔl'deɪvɪən] *adj* moldawisch.

**Moldova** [mɔl'dəuvə] *n* Moldawien *nt*.

**Moldovan** *adj* moldawisch.

**mole** [məul] *n* (*on skin*) Leberfleck *m*; (*ZOOL*) Maulwurf *m*; (*fig: spy*) Spion(in) *m(f)*.

**molecular** [məu'lɛkjulə'] *adj* molekular; (*biology*) Molekular-.

**molecule** ['mɔlɪkju:l] *n* Molekül *nt*.

**molehill** ['məulhɪl] *n* Maulwurfshaufen *m*.

**molest** [mə'lɛst] *vt* (*assault sexually*) sich vergehen an +*dat*; (*harass*) belästigen.

**mollusc** ['mɔləsk] _n_ Weichtier _nt_.
**mollycoddle** ['mɔlɪkɔdl] _vt_ verhätscheln.
**Molotov cocktail** ['mɔlətɔf-] _n_ Molotowcocktail _m_.
**molt** [məult] (_US_) _vi_ = **moult**.
**molten** ['məultən] _adj_ geschmolzen, flüssig.
**mom** [mɔm] (_US_) _n_ = **mum**.
**moment** ['məumənt] _n_ Moment _m_, Augenblick _m_; (_importance_) Bedeutung _f_; **for a** ~ (für) einen Moment _or_ Augenblick; **at that** ~ in diesem Moment _or_ Augenblick; **at the** ~ momentan; **for the** ~ vorläufig; **in a** ~ gleich; **"one** ~ **please"** (_TEL_) „bleiben Sie am Apparat".
**momentarily** ['məuməntrɪlɪ] _adv_ für einen Augenblick _or_ Moment; (_US: very soon_) jeden Augenblick _or_ Moment.
**momentary** ['məuməntərɪ] _adj_ (_brief_) kurz.
**momentous** [məu'mentəs] _adj_ (_occasion_) bedeutsam; (_decision_) von großer Tragweite.
**momentum** [məu'mentəm] _n_ (_PHYS_) Impuls _m_; (_fig: of movement_) Schwung _m_; (: _of events, change_) Dynamik _f_; **to gather** ~ schneller werden; (_fig_) richtig in Gang kommen.
**mommy** ['mɔmɪ] (_US_) _n_ = **mummy**.
**Mon.** _abbr_ (= _Monday_) Mo.
**Monaco** ['mɔnəkəu] _n_ Monaco _nt_.
**monarch** ['mɔnək] _n_ Monarch(in) _m(f)_.
**monarchist** ['mɔnəkɪst] _n_ Monarchist(in) _m(f)_.
**monarchy** ['mɔnəkɪ] _n_ Monarchie _f_; **the M**~ (_royal family_) die königliche Familie.
**monastery** ['mɔnəstərɪ] _n_ Kloster _nt_.
**monastic** [mə'næstɪk] _adj_ Kloster-, klösterlich; (_fig_) mönchisch, klösterlich einfach.
**Monday** ['mʌndɪ] _n_ Montag _m_; _see also_ **Tuesday**.
**Monegasque** [mɔnə'gæsk] _adj_ monegassisch ♦ _n_ Monegasse _m_, Monegassin _f_.
**monetarist** ['mʌnɪtərɪst] _n_ Monetarist(in) _m(f)_ ♦ _adj_ monetaristisch.
**monetary** ['mʌnɪtərɪ] _adj_ (_system, union_) Währungs-.
**money** ['mʌnɪ] _n_ Geld _nt_; **to make** ~ (_person_) Geld verdienen; (_business_) etwas einbringen; **danger** ~ (_BRIT_) Gefahrenzulage _f_; **I've got no** ~ **left** ich habe kein Geld mehr.
**moneyed** ['mʌnɪd] (_form_) _adj_ begütert.
**moneylender** ['mʌnɪlendə*] _n_ Geldverleiher(in) _m(f)_.
**moneymaker** ['mʌnɪmeɪkə*] _n_ (_person_) Finanzgenie _nt_; (_idea_) einträgliche Sache _f_; (_product_) Verkaufserfolg _m_.
**moneymaking** ['mʌnɪmeɪkɪŋ] _adj_ einträglich.
**money market** _n_ Geldmarkt _m_.
**money order** _n_ Zahlungsanweisung _f_.
**money-spinner** ['mʌnɪspɪnə*] (_inf_) _n_ Verkaufsschlager _m_; (_person, business_) Goldgrube _f_.
**money supply** _n_ Geldvolumen _nt_.

**Mongol** ['mɔŋgəl] _n_ Mongole _m_, Mongolin _f_; (_LING_) Mongolisch _nt_.
**mongol** ['mɔŋgəl] (_offensive_) _n_ Mongoloide(r) _f(m)_.
**Mongolia** [mɔŋ'gəulɪə] _n_ Mongolien _nt_.
**Mongolian** [mɔŋ'gəulɪən] _adj_ mongolisch ♦ _n_ Mongole _m_, Mongolin _f_; (_LING_) Mongolisch _nt_.
**mongoose** ['mɔŋguːs] _n_ Mungo _m_.
**mongrel** ['mʌŋgrəl] _n_ Promenadenmischung _f_.
**monitor** ['mɔnɪtə*] _n_ Monitor _m_ ♦ _vt_ überwachen; (_broadcasts_) mithören.
**monk** [mʌŋk] _n_ Mönch _m_.
**monkey** ['mʌŋkɪ] _n_ Affe _m_.
**monkey business** (_inf_) _n_ faule Sachen _pl_.
**monkey nut** (_BRIT_) _n_ Erdnuß _f_.
**monkey tricks** _npl_ = **monkey business**.
**monkey wrench** _n_ verstellbarer Schraubenschlüssel _m_.
**mono** ['mɔnəu] _adj_ (_recording etc_) Mono-.
**monochrome** ['mɔnəkrəum] _adj_ (_photograph, television_) Schwarzweiß-; (_COMPUT: screen_) Monochrom-.
**monogamous** [mə'nɔgəməs] _adj_ monogam.
**monogamy** [mə'nɔgəmɪ] _n_ Monogamie _f_.
**monogram** ['mɔnəgræm] _n_ Monogramm _nt_.
**monolith** ['mɔnəlɪθ] _n_ Monolith _m_.
**monolithic** [mɔnə'lɪθɪk] _adj_ monolithisch.
**monologue** ['mɔnəlɔg] _n_ Monolog _m_.
**monoplane** ['mɔnəpleɪn] _n_ Eindecker _m_.
**monopolize** [mə'nɔpəlaɪz] _vt_ beherrschen; (_person_) mit Beschlag belegen; (_conversation_) an sich _acc_ reißen.
**monopoly** [mə'nɔpəlɪ] _n_ Monopol _nt_; **to have a** ~ **on** _or_ **of sth** (_fig: domination_) etw für sich gepachtet haben; **Monopolies and Mergers Commission** (_BRIT_) ≈ Kartellamt _nt_.
**monorail** ['mɔnəureɪl] _n_ Einschienenbahn _f_.
**monosodium glutamate** [mɔnə'səudɪəm'gluːtəmeɪt] _n_ Glutamat _nt_.
**monosyllabic** [mɔnəsɪ'læbɪk] _adj_ einsilbig.
**monosyllable** ['mɔnəsɪləbl] _n_ einsilbiges Wort _nt_.
**monotone** ['mɔnətəun] _n_: **in a** ~ monoton.
**monotonous** [mə'nɔtənəs] _adj_ monoton, eintönig.
**monotony** [mə'nɔtənɪ] _n_ Monotonie _f_, Eintönigkeit _f_.
**monsoon** [mɔn'suːn] _n_ Monsun _m_.
**monster** ['mɔnstə*] _n_ Ungetüm _nt_, Monstrum _nt_; (_imaginary creature_) Ungeheuer _nt_, Monster _nt_; (_person_) Unmensch _m_.
**monstrosity** [mɔn'strɔsɪtɪ] _n_ Ungetüm _nt_, Monstrum _nt_.
**monstrous** ['mɔnstrəs] _adj_ (_huge_) riesig; (_ugly_) abscheulich; (_atrocious_) ungeheuerlich.
**Mont.** (_US_) _abbr_ (_POST_: = _Montana_).
**montage** [mɔn'tɑːʒ] _n_ Montage _f_.
**Mont Blanc** [mɔblɑ̃] _n_ Montblanc _m_.
**month** [mʌnθ] _n_ Monat _m_; **every** ~ jeden Monat; **300 dollars a** ~ 300 Dollar im Monat.

**monthly** ['mʌnθlɪ] *adj* monatlich; (*ticket, magazine*) Monats- ♦ *adv* monatlich; **twice ~** zweimal im Monat.

**Montreal** [mɔntrɪ'ɔːl] *n* Montreal *nt*.

**monument** ['mɔnjumənt] *n* Denkmal *nt*.

**monumental** [mɔnju'mɛntl] *adj* (*building, statue*) gewaltig, monumental; (*book, piece of work*) unsterblich; (*storm, row*) ungeheuer.

**moo** [muː] *vi* muhen.

**mood** [muːd] *n* Stimmung *f*; (*of person*) Laune *f*, Stimmung *f*; **to be in a good/bad ~** gut/ schlecht gelaunt sein; **to be in the ~ for** aufgelegt sein zu.

**moodily** ['muːdɪlɪ] *adv* launisch; (*sullenly*) schlecht gelaunt.

**moody** ['muːdɪ] *adj* launisch; (*sullen*) schlecht gelaunt.

**moon** [muːn] *n* Mond *m*.

**moonlight** ['muːnlaɪt] *n* Mondschein *m* ♦ *vi* (*inf*) schwarzarbeiten.

**moonlighting** ['muːnlaɪtɪŋ] (*inf*) *n* Schwarzarbeit *f*.

**moonlit** ['muːnlɪt] *adj* (*night*) mondhell.

**moonshot** ['muːnʃɔt] *n* Mondflug *m*.

**moor** [muə*] *n* (Hoch)moor *nt*, Heide *f* ♦ *vt* vertäuen ♦ *vi* anlegen.

**mooring** ['muərɪŋ] *n* Anlegeplatz *m*; **moorings** *npl* (*chains*) Verankerung *f*.

**Moorish** ['muərɪʃ] *adj* maurisch.

**moorland** ['muələnd] *n* Moorlandschaft *f*, Heidelandschaft *f*.

**moose** [muːs] *n inv* Elch *m*.

**moot** [muːt] *vt*: **to be ~ed** vorgeschlagen werden ♦ *adj*: **it's a ~ point** das ist fraglich.

**mop** [mɔp] *n* (*for floor*) Mop *m*; (*for dishes*) Spülbürste *f*; (*of hair*) Mähne *f* ♦ *vt* (*floor*) wischen; (*face*) abwischen; (*eyes*) sich *dat* wischen; **to ~ the sweat from one's brow** sich *dat* den Schweiß von der Stirn wischen.

▸**mop up** *vt* aufwischen.

**mope** [məup] *vi* Trübsal blasen.

▸**mope about** *vi* mit einer Jammermiene herumlaufen.

▸**mope around** *vi* = **mope about**.

**moped** ['məupɛd] *n* Moped *nt*.

**moquette** [mɔ'kɛt] *n* Mokett *m*.

**MOR** *adj abbr* (*MUS*) = **middle-of-the-road**.

**moral** ['mɔrl] *adj* moralisch; (*welfare, values*) sittlich; (*behaviour*) moralisch einwandfrei ♦ *n* Moral *f*; **morals** *npl* (*principles, values*) Moralvorstellungen *pl*; **~ support** moralische Unterstützung *f*.

**morale** [mɔ'rɑːl] *n* Moral *f*.

**morality** [mə'rælɪtɪ] *n* Sittlichkeit *f*; (*system of morals*) Moral *f*, Ethik *f*; (*correctness*) moralische Richtigkeit *f*.

**moralize** ['mɔrəlaɪz] *vi* moralisieren; **to ~ about** sich moralisch entrüsten über +*acc*.

**morally** ['mɔrəlɪ] *adv* moralisch; (*live, behave*) moralisch einwandfrei.

**moral victory** *n* moralischer Sieg *m*.

**morass** [mə'ræs] *n* Morast *m*, Sumpf *m* (*also* *fig*).

**moratorium** [mɔrə'tɔːrɪəm] *n* Stopp *m*, Moratorium *nt*.

**morbid** ['mɔːbɪd] *adj* (*imagination*) krankhaft; (*interest*) unnatürlich; (*comments, behaviour*) makaber.

═══════════════════════════ *KEYWORD*

**more** [mɔː*] *adj* **1** (*greater in number etc*) mehr; **~ people/work/letters than we expected** mehr Leute/Arbeit/Briefe, als wir erwarteten; **I have ~ wine/money than you** ich habe mehr Wein/Geld als du

**2** (*additional*): **do you want (some) ~ tea?** möchten Sie noch mehr Tee?; **is there any ~ wine?** ist noch Wein da?; **I have no ~ money, I don't have any ~ money** ich habe kein Geld mehr

♦ *pron* **1** (*greater amount*) mehr; **~ than 10** mehr als 10; **it cost ~ than we expected** es kostete mehr, als wir erwarteten

**2** (*further or additional amount*): **is there any ~?** gibt es noch mehr?; **there's no ~** es ist nichts mehr da; **many/much ~** viel mehr

♦ *adv* mehr; **~ dangerous/difficult/easily etc (than)** gefährlicher/schwerer/leichter *etc* (als); **~ and ~** mehr und mehr, immer mehr; **~ and ~ excited/expensive** immer aufgeregter/teurer; **~ or less** mehr oder weniger; **~ than ever** mehr denn je, mehr als jemals zuvor; **~ beautiful than ever** schöner denn je; **no ~, not any ~** nicht mehr.

**moreover** [mɔː'rəuvə*] *adv* außerdem, zudem.

**morgue** [mɔːg] *n* Leichenschauhaus *nt*.

**MORI** ['mɔːrɪ] (*BRIT*) *n abbr* (= *Market and Opinion Research Institute*) Markt- und Meinungsforschungsinstitut.

**moribund** ['mɔrɪbʌnd] *adj* dem Untergang geweiht.

**Mormon** ['mɔːmən] *n* Mormone *m*, Mormonin *f*.

**morning** ['mɔːnɪŋ] *n* Morgen *m*; (*as opposed to afternoon*) Vormittag *m* ♦ *cpd* Morgen-; **in the ~** morgens; vormittags; (*tomorrow*) morgen früh; **7 o'clock in the ~** 7 Uhr morgens; **this ~** heute morgen.

**morning-after pill** ['mɔːnɪŋ'ɑːftə-] *n* Pille *f* danach.

**morning sickness** *n* (Schwangerschafts)übelkeit *f*.

**Moroccan** [mə'rɔkən] *adj* marokkanisch ♦ *n* Marokkaner(in) *m(f)*.

**Morocco** [mə'rɔkəu] *n* Marokko *nt*.

**moron** ['mɔːrɔn] (*inf*) *n* Schwachkopf *m*.

**moronic** [mə'rɔnɪk] (*inf*) *adj* schwachsinnig.

**morose** [mə'rəus] *adj* mißmutig.

**morphine** ['mɔːfiːn] *n* Morphium *nt*.

**morris dancing** ['mɔrɪs-] *n* Moriskentanz *m*, *alter englischer Volkstanz*.

**Morse** [mɔːs] *n* (*also*: **~ code**) Morsealphabet

*nt.*

**morsel** ['mɔːsl] *n* Stückchen *nt.*

**mortal** ['mɔːtl] *adj* sterblich; (*wound, combat*) tödlich; (*danger*) Todes-; (*sin, enemy*) Tod- ♦ *n* (*human being*) Sterbliche(r) *f(m).*

**mortality** [mɔː'tælɪtɪ] *n* Sterblichkeit *f*; (*number of deaths*) Todesfälle *pl.*

**mortality rate** *n* Sterblichkeitsziffer *f.*

**mortar** ['mɔːtə*] *n* (*MIL*) Minenwerfer *m*; (*CONSTR*) Mörtel *m*; (*CULIN*) Mörser *m.*

**mortgage** ['mɔːgɪdʒ] *n* Hypothek *f* ♦ *vt* mit einer Hypothek belasten; **to take out a** ~ eine Hypothek aufnehmen.

**mortgage company** (*US*) *n* Hypotheken-bank *f.*

**mortgagee** [mɔːgə'dʒiː] *n* Hypotheken-gläubiger *m.*

**mortgagor** ['mɔːgədʒə*] *n* Hypotheken-schuldner *m.*

**mortician** [mɔː'tɪʃən] (*US*) *n* Bestattungs-unternehmer *m.*

**mortified** ['mɔːtɪfaɪd] *adj:* **he was** ~ er empfand das als beschämend; (*embarrassed*) es war ihm schrecklich peinlich.

**mortify** ['mɔːtɪfaɪ] *vt* beschämen.

**mortise lock** ['mɔːtɪs-] *n* Einsteckschloß *nt.*

**mortuary** ['mɔːtjuərɪ] *n* Leichenhalle *f.*

**mosaic** [məu'zeɪɪk] *n* Mosaik *nt.*

**Moscow** ['mɔskəu] *n* Moskau *nt.*

**Moslem** ['mɔzləm] *adj, n* = **Muslim.**

**mosque** [mɔsk] *n* Moschee *f.*

**mosquito** [mɔs'kiːtəu] (*pl* ~**es**) *n* Stechmücke *f*; (*in tropics*) Moskito *m.*

**mosquito net** *n* Moskitonetz *nt.*

**moss** [mɔs] *n* Moos *nt.*

**mossy** ['mɔsɪ] *adj* bemoost.

================= *KEYWORD*

**most** [məust] *adj* **1** (*almost all: people, things etc*) meiste(r, s); ~ **people** die meisten Leute

**2** (*largest, greatest: interest, money etc*) meiste(r, s); **who has (the)** ~ **money?** wer hat das meiste Geld?

♦ *pron* (*greatest quantity, number*) der/die/das meiste; ~ **of it** das meiste (davon); ~ **of them** die meisten von ihnen; ~ **of the time/ work** die meiste Zeit/Arbeit; ~ **of the time he's very helpful** er ist meistens sehr hilfsbereit; **to make the** ~ **of sth** das Beste aus etw machen; **at the (very)** ~ (aller)höchstens

♦ *adv* (+ *vb: spend, eat, work etc*) am meisten; (+ *adj*): **the** ~ **intelligent/expensive** *etc* der/ die/das intelligenteste/teuerste *etc*; (+ *adv: carefully, easily etc*) äußerst; (*very: polite, interesting etc*) höchst; **a** ~ **interesting book** ein höchst interessantes Buch.

**mostly** ['məustlɪ] *adv* (*chiefly*) hauptsächlich; (*usually*) meistens.

**MOT** (*BRIT*) *n abbr* (= *Ministry of Transport*):

~ (**test**) ≈ TÜV *m*; **the car failed its** ~ das Auto ist nicht durch den TÜV gekommen.

**motel** [məu'tɛl] *n* Motel *nt.*

**moth** [mɔθ] *n* Nachtfalter *m*; (*clothes moth*) Motte *f.*

**mothball** ['mɔθbɔːl] *n* Mottenkugel *f.*

**moth-eaten** ['mɔθiːtn] (*pej*) *adj* mottenzerfressen.

**mother** ['mʌðə*] *n* Mutter *f* ♦ *adj* (*country*) Heimat-; (*company*) Mutter- ♦ *vt* großziehen; (*pamper, protect*) bemuttern.

**motherboard** ['mʌðəbɔːd] *n* (*COMPUT*) Hauptplatine *f.*

**motherhood** ['mʌðəhud] *n* Mutterschaft *f.*

**mother-in-law** ['mʌðərɪnlɔː] *n* Schwiegermutter *f.*

**motherly** ['mʌðəlɪ] *adj* mütterlich.

**mother-of-pearl** ['mʌðərəv'pɜːl] *n* Perlmutt *nt.*

**mother's help** *n* Haushaltshilfe *f.*

**mother-to-be** ['mʌðətə'biː] *n* werdende Mutter *f.*

**mother tongue** *n* Muttersprache *f.*

**mothproof** ['mɔθpruːf] *adj* mottenfest.

**motif** [məu'tiːf] *n* Motiv *nt.*

**motion** ['məuʃən] *n* Bewegung *f*; (*proposal*) Antrag *m*; (*BRIT: also: bowel* ~) Stuhlgang *m* ♦ *vt, vi:* **to** ~ (**to**) **sb to do sth** jdm ein Zeichen geben, daß er/sie etw tun solle; **to be in** ~ (*vehicle*) fahren; **to set in** ~ in Gang bringen; **to go through the** ~**s (of doing sth)** (*fig*) etw der Form halber tun; (*pretend*) so tun, als ob (man etw täte).

**motionless** ['məuʃənlɪs] *adj* reg(ungs)los.

**motion picture** *n* Film *m.*

**motivate** ['məutɪveɪt] *vt* motivieren.

**motivated** ['məutɪveɪtɪd] *adj* motiviert; ~ **by** getrieben von.

**motivation** [məutɪ'veɪʃən] *n* Motivation *f.*

**motive** ['məutɪv] *n* Motiv *nt*, Beweggrund *m* ♦ *adj* (*power, force*) Antriebs-; **from the best (of)** ~**s** mit den besten Absichten.

**motley** ['mɔtlɪ] *adj* bunt(gemischt).

**motor** ['məutə*] *n* Motor *m*; (*BRIT: inf: car*) Auto *nt* ♦ *cpd* (*industry, trade*) Auto(mobil)-.

**motorbike** ['məutəbaɪk] *n* Motorrad *nt.*

**motorboat** ['məutəbəut] *n* Motorboot *nt.*

**motorcade** ['məutəkeɪd] *n* Fahrzeugkolonne *f.*

**motorcar** ['məutəkaː] (*BRIT*) *n* (Personenkraft)wagen *m.*

**motorcoach** ['məutəkəutʃ] (*BRIT*) *n* Reisebus *m.*

**motorcycle** ['məutəsaɪkl] *n* Motorrad *nt.*

**motorcycle racing** *n* Motorradrennen *nt.*

**motorcyclist** ['məutəsaɪklɪst] *n* Motorradfahrer(in) *m(f).*

**motoring** ['məutərɪŋ] (*BRIT*) *n* Autofahren *nt* ♦ *cpd* Auto-; (*offence, accident*) Verkehrs-.

**motorist** ['məutərɪst] *n* Autofahrer(in) *m(f).*

**motorized** ['məutəraɪzd] *adj* motorisiert.

**motor oil** *n* Motorenöl *nt.*

**motor racing** (*BRIT*) *n* Autorennen *nt.*

**motor scooter** n Motorroller m.
**motor vehicle** n Kraftfahrzeug nt.
**motorway** ['məutəweɪ] (BRIT) n Autobahn f.
**mottled** ['mɔtld] adj gesprenkelt.
**motto** ['mɔtəu] (pl ~es) n Motto nt.
**mould,** (US) **mold** [məuld] n (cast) Form f;
(: for metal) Gußform f; (mildew) Schimmel m
♦ vt (lit, fig) formen.
**moulder** ['məuldə*] vi (decay) vermodern.
**moulding** ['məuldɪŋ] n (ARCHIT) Zierleiste f.
**mouldy** ['məuldɪ] adj schimmelig; (smell)
moderig.
**moult,** (US) **molt** [məult] vi (animal) sich
haaren; (bird) sich mausern.
**mound** [maund] n (of earth) Hügel m; (heap)
Haufen m.
**mount** [maunt] n (in proper names):
**M~ Carmel** der Berg Karmel; (horse) Pferd
nt; (for picture) Passepartout nt ♦ vt (horse)
besteigen; (exhibition etc) vorbereiten;
(jewel) (ein)fassen; (picture) mit einem
Passepartout versehen; (staircase)
hochgehen; (stamp) aufkleben; (attack,
campaign) organisieren ♦ vi (increase)
steigen; (: problems) sich häufen; (on horse)
aufsitzen.
▶**mount up** vi (costs, savings) sich
summieren, sich zusammenläppern (inf).
**mountain** ['mauntɪn] n Berg m ♦ cpd (road,
stream) Gebirgs-; **to make a ~ out of a
molehill** aus einer Mücke einen Elefanten
machen.
**mountain bike** n Mountain-Bike nt.
**mountaineer** [mauntɪ'nɪə*] n Bergsteiger(in)
m(f).
**mountaineering** [mauntɪ'nɪərɪŋ] n
Bergsteigen nt; **to go ~** bergsteigen gehen.
**mountainous** ['mauntɪnəs] adj gebirgig.
**mountain range** n Gebirgskette f.
**mountain rescue team** n Bergwacht f.
**mountainside** ['mauntɪnsaɪd] n (Berg)hang m.
**mounted** ['mauntɪd] adj (police, soldiers)
beritten.
**Mount Everest** n Mount Everest m.
**mourn** [mɔːn] vt betrauern ♦ vi: **to ~ (for)**
trauern (um).
**mourner** ['mɔːnə*] n Trauernde(r) f(m).
**mournful** ['mɔːnful] adj traurig.
**mourning** ['mɔːnɪŋ] n Trauer f; **to be in ~**
trauern; (wear special clothes) Trauer tragen.
**mouse** [maus] (pl **mice**) n (ZOOL, COMPUT)
Maus f; (fig: person) schüchternes Mäuschen
nt.
**mousetrap** ['maustræp] n Mausefalle f.
**moussaka** [mu'saːkə] n Moussaka f.
**mousse** [muːs] n (CULIN) Mousse f; (cosmetic)
Schaumfestiger m.
**moustache,** (US) **mustache** [məs'taːʃ] n
Schnurrbart m.
**mousy** ['mausɪ] adj (hair) mausgrau.
**mouth** [mauθ] (pl ~**s**) n Mund m; (of cave, hole,
bottle) Öffnung f; (of river) Mündung f.

**mouthful** ['mauθful] n (of food) Bissen m; (of
drink) Schluck m.
**mouth organ** n Mundharmonika f.
**mouthpiece** ['mauθpiːs] n Mundstück nt;
(spokesman) Sprachrohr nt.
**mouth-to-mouth** ['mauθtə'mauθ] adj:
**~ resuscitation** Mund-zu-Mund-Beatmung f.
**mouthwash** ['mauθwɔʃ] n Mundwasser nt.
**mouth-watering** ['mauθwɔːtərɪŋ] adj
appetitlich.
**movable** ['muːvəbl] adj beweglich; **~ feast**
beweglicher Feiertag m.
**move** [muːv] n (movement) Bewegung f; (in
game) Zug m; (change: of house) Umzug m;
(: of job) Stellenwechsel m ♦ vt bewegen;
(furniture) (ver)rücken; (car) umstellen; (in
game) ziehen mit; (emotionally) bewegen,
ergreifen; (POL: resolution etc) beantragen
♦ vi sich bewegen; (traffic) vorankommen; (in
game) ziehen; (also: ~ **house**) umziehen;
(develop) sich entwickeln; **it's my ~** ich bin
am Zug; **to get a ~ on** sich beeilen; **to ~ sb
to do sth** jdn (dazu) veranlassen, etw zu
tun; **to ~ towards** sich nähern +dat.
▶**move about** vi sich (hin- und her)bewegen;
(travel) unterwegs sein; (from place to place)
umherziehen; (change residence) umziehen;
(change job) die Stelle wechseln; **I can hear
him moving about** ich höre ihn
herumlaufen.
▶**move along** vi weitergehen.
▶**move around** vi = **move about**.
▶**move away** vi (from town, area) wegziehen.
▶**move back** vi (return) zurückkommen.
▶**move forward** vi (advance) vorrücken.
▶**move in** vi (to house) einziehen; (police,
soldiers) anrücken.
▶**move off** vi (car) abfahren.
▶**move on** vi (leave) weitergehen; (travel)
weiterfahren ♦ vt (onlookers) zum
Weitergehen auffordern.
▶**move out** vi (of house) ausziehen.
▶**move over** vi (to make room) (zur Seite)
rücken.
▶**move up** vi (employee) befördert werden;
(pupil) versetzt werden; (deputy) aufrücken.
**moveable** ['muːvəbl] adj = **movable**.
**movement** ['muːvmənt] n (action, group)
Bewegung f; (freedom to move)
Bewegungsfreiheit f; (transportation)
Beförderung f; (shift) Trend m; (MUS) Satz
m; (MED: also: **bowel ~**) Stuhlgang m.
**mover** ['muːvə*] n (of proposal)
Antragsteller(in) m(f).
**movie** ['muːvɪ] n Film m; **to go to the ~s** ins
Kino gehen.
**movie camera** n Filmkamera f.
**moviegoer** ['muːvɪgəuə*] (US) n
Kinogänger(in) m(f).
**moving** ['muːvɪŋ] adj beweglich; (emotional)
ergreifend; (instigating): **the ~ spirit/force**
die treibende Kraft.

**mow** [məu] (*pt* **mowed,** *pp* **mowed** *or* **mown**) *vt* mähen.

▶**mow down** *vt* (*kill*) niedermähen.

**mower** ['məuə*] *n* (*also:* **lawnmower**) Rasenmäher *m*.

**Mozambique** [məuzəm'bi:k] *n* Mosambik *nt*.

**MP** *n abbr* (= *Member of Parliament*) ≈ MdB; = **military police;** (*CANADA:* = *Mounted Police*) berittene Polizei *f*.

**mpg** *n abbr* (= *miles per gallon*) *see* **mile.**

**mph** *abbr* (= *miles per hour*) Meilen pro Stunde.

**MPhil** *n abbr* (= *Master of Philosophy*) ≈ M.A.

**MPS** (*BRIT*) *n abbr* (= *Member of the Pharmaceutical Society*) *Qualifikationsnachweis für Pharmazeuten.*

**Mr,** (*US*) **Mr.** ['mɪstə*] *n:* ~ **Smith** Herr Smith.

**MRC** (*BRIT*) *n abbr* (= *Medical Research Council*) *medizinischer Forschungsausschuß.*

**MRCP** (*BRIT*) *n abbr* (= *Member of the Royal College of Physicians*) *höchster akademischer Grad in Medizin.*

**MRCS** (*BRIT*) *n abbr* (= *Member of the Royal College of Surgeons*) *höchster akademischer Grad für Chirurgen.*

**MRCVS** (*BRIT*) *n abbr* (= *Member of the Royal College of Veterinary Surgeons*) *höchster akademischer Grad für Tiermediziner.*

**Mrs,** (*US*) **Mrs.** ['mɪsɪz] *n:* ~ **Smith** Frau Smith.

**MS** *n abbr* (= *multiple sclerosis*) MS *f*; (*US:* = *Master of Science*) *akademischer Grad in Naturwissenschaften* ♦ *abbr* (*US: POST:* = *Mississippi*).

**MS.** (*pl* **MSS.**) *n abbr* (= *manuscript*) Ms.

**Ms,** (*US*) **Ms.** [mɪz] *n* (= *Miss or Mrs*): ~ **Smith** Frau Smith.

**MSA** (*US*) *n abbr* (= *Master of Science in Agriculture*) *akademischer Grad in Agronomie.*

**MSc** *n abbr* (= *Master of Science*) *akademischer Grad in Naturwissenschaften.*

**MSG** *n abbr* = **monosodium glutamate.**

**MSS.** *n abbr* (= *manuscripts*) Mss.

**MST** (*US*) *abbr* (= *Mountain Standard Time*) *amerikanische Standardzeitzone.*

**MSW** (*US*) *n abbr* (= *Master of Social Work*) *akademischer Grad in Sozialwissenschaft.*

**MT** *n abbr* (*COMPUT, LING:* = *machine translation*) maschinelle Übersetzung *f* ♦ *abbr* (*US: POST:* = *Montana*).

**Mt** *abbr* (*GEOG*) = **mount.**

**MTV** (*esp US*) *n abbr* (= *music television*) MTV *nt*.

═══════════ *KEYWORD*

**much** [mʌtʃ] *adj* (*time, money, effort*) viel; **how ~ money/time do you need?** wieviel Geld/Zeit brauchen Sie?; **he's done so ~ work for us** er hat so viel für uns gearbeitet; **as ~ as** soviel wie; **I have as ~ money/intelligence as you** ich besitze genauso viel Geld/Intelligenz wie du

♦ *pron* viel; **how ~ is it?** was kostet es?

♦ *adv* **1** (*greatly, a great deal*) sehr; **thank you very ~** vielen Dank, danke sehr; **I read as ~ as I can** ich lese soviel wie ich kann

**2** (*by far*) viel; **I'm ~ better now** mir geht es jetzt viel besser

**3** (*almost*) fast; **how are you feeling? - ~ the same** wie fühlst du dich? - fast genauso; **the two books are ~ the same** die zwei Bücher sind sich sehr ähnlich.

**muck** [mʌk] *n* (*dirt*) Dreck *m*.

▶**muck about** (*inf*) *vi* (*fool about*) herumalbern ♦ *vt:* **to ~ sb about** mit jdm beliebig umspringen.

▶**muck around** *vi* = **muck about.**

▶**muck in** (*BRIT: inf*) *vi* mit anpacken.

▶**muck out** *vt* (*stable*) ausmisten.

▶**muck up** (*inf*) *vt* (*exam etc*) verpfuschen.

**muckraking** ['mʌkreɪkɪŋ] (*fig: inf*) *n* Sensationsmache *f* ♦ *adj* sensationslüstern.

**mucky** ['mʌkɪ] *adj* (*dirty*) dreckig; (*field*) matschig.

**mucus** ['mju:kəs] *n* Schleim *m*.

**mud** [mʌd] *n* Schlamm *m*.

**muddle** ['mʌdl] *n* (*mess*) Durcheinander *nt*; (*confusion*) Verwirrung *f* ♦ *vt* (*person*) verwirren; (*also:* ~ **up**) durcheinanderbringen; **to be in a ~** völlig durcheinander sein; **to get in a ~** (*person*) konfus werden; (*things*) durcheinandergeraten.

▶**muddle along** *vi* vor sich *acc* hinwursteln.

▶**muddle through** *vi* (*get by*) sich durchschlagen.

**muddle-headed** [mʌdl'hɛdɪd] *adj* zerstreut.

**muddy** ['mʌdɪ] *adj* (*floor*) schmutzig; (*field*) schlammig.

**mud flats** *npl* Watt(enmeer) *nt*.

**mudguard** ['mʌdgɑ:d] (*BRIT*) *n* Schutzblech *nt*; (*on old car*) Kotflügel *m*.

**mudpack** ['mʌdpæk] *n* Schlammpackung *f*.

**mud-slinging** ['mʌdslɪŋɪŋ] *n* (*fig*) Schlechtmacherei *f*.

**muesli** ['mju:zlɪ] *n* Müsli *nt*.

**muffin** ['mʌfɪn] *n* (*BRIT*) *weiches, flaches Milchbrötchen, meist warm gegessen*; (*US*) *kleiner runder Rührkuchen.*

**muffle** ['mʌfl] *vt* (*sound*) dämpfen; (*against cold*) einmummeln.

**muffled** ['mʌfld] *adj* (*see vt*) gedämpft; eingemummelt.

**muffler** ['mʌflə*] *n* (*US: AUT*) Auspufftopf *m*; (*scarf*) dicker Schal *m*.

**mufti** ['mʌftɪ] *n:* **in ~** in Zivil.

**mug** [mʌg] *n* (*cup*) Becher *m*; (*for beer*) Krug *m*; (*inf: face*) Visage *f*; (: *fool*) Trottel *m* ♦ *vt* (auf der Straße) überfallen; **it's a ~'s game** (*BRIT*) das ist doch Schwachsinn.

▶**mug up** (*BRIT: inf*) *vt* (*also:* ~ **up on**) pauken.

**mugger** ['mʌgə*] *n* Straßenräuber *m*.

**mugging** ['mʌgɪŋ] n Straßenraub m.
**muggins** ['mʌgɪnz] (BRIT: inf) n Dummkopf m;
... **and ~ does all the work** ... und ich bin mal wieder der/die Dumme und mache die ganze Arbeit.
**muggy** ['mʌgɪ] adj (weather, day) schwül.
**mug shot** (inf) n (of criminal) Verbrecherfoto nt; (for passport) Paßbild nt.
**mulatto** [mjuː'lætəu] (pl ~es) n Mulatte m, Mulattin f.
**mulberry** ['mʌlbrɪ] n (fruit) Maulbeere f; (tree) Maulbeerbaum m.
**mule** [mjuːl] n Maultier nt.
**mulled** [mʌld] adj: ~ **wine** Glühwein m.
**mullioned** ['mʌliənd] adj (windows) längs unterteilt.
**mull over** [mʌl-] vt sich dat durch den Kopf gehen lassen.
**multi...** ['mʌltɪ] pref multi-, Multi-.
**multi-access** ['mʌltɪ'æksɛs] adj (COMPUT: system etc) Mehrplatz-.
**multicoloured, (US) multicolored** ['mʌltɪkʌləd] adj mehrfarbig.
**multifarious** [mʌltɪ'fɛəriəs] adj vielfältig.
**multilateral** [mʌltɪ'lætərl] adj multilateral.
**multi-level** ['mʌltɪlevl] (US) adj = **multistorey**.
**multimillionaire** [mʌltɪmɪljə'nɛə*] n Multimillionär m.
**multinational** [mʌltɪ'næʃənl] adj multinational ♦ n multinationaler Konzern m, Multi m (inf).
**multiple** ['mʌltɪpl] adj (injuries) mehrfach; (interests, causes) vielfältig ♦ n Vielfache(s) nt; ~ **collision** Massenkarambolage f.
**multiple-choice** ['mʌltɪpltʃɔɪs] adj (question etc) Multiple-Choice-.
**multiple sclerosis** n multiple Sklerose f.
**multiplex** ['mʌltɪplɛks] n: ~ **transmitter** Multiplex-Sender m; ~ **cinema** Kinocenter nt.
**multiplication** [mʌltɪplɪ'keɪʃən] n Multiplikation f; (increase) Vervielfachung f.
**multiplication table** n Multiplikationstabelle f.
**multiplicity** [mʌltɪ'plɪsɪtɪ] n: **a ~ of** eine Vielzahl von.
**multiply** ['mʌltɪplaɪ] vt multiplizieren ♦ vi (increase: problems) stark zunehmen; (: number) sich vervielfachen; (breed) sich vermehren.
**multiracial** [mʌltɪ'reɪʃl] adj gemischtrassig; (school) ohne Rassentrennung; ~ **policy** Politik f der Rassenintegration.
**multistorey** [mʌltɪ'stɔːrɪ] (BRIT) adj (building, car park) mehrstöckig.
**multitude** ['mʌltɪtjuːd] n Menge f; **a ~ of** eine Vielzahl von, eine Menge.
**mum** [mʌm] (BRIT: inf) n Mutti f, Mama f ♦ adj: **to keep ~** den Mund halten; **~'s the word** nichts verraten!
**mumble** ['mʌmbl] vt, vi (indistinctly) nuscheln; (quietly) murmeln.
**mumbo jumbo** ['mʌmbəu-] n (nonsense)

Geschwafel nt.
**mummify** ['mʌmɪfaɪ] vt mumifizieren.
**mummy** ['mʌmɪ] n (BRIT: mother) Mami f; (embalmed body) Mumie f.
**mumps** [mʌmps] n Mumps m or f.
**munch** [mʌntʃ] vt, vi mampfen.
**mundane** [mʌn'deɪn] adj (life) banal; (task) stumpfsinnig.
**Munich** ['mjuːnɪk] n München nt.
**municipal** [mjuː'nɪsɪpl] adj städtisch, Stadt-; (elections, administration) Kommunal-.
**municipality** [mjuːnɪsɪ'pælɪtɪ] n Gemeinde f, Stadt f.
**munitions** [mjuː'nɪʃənz] npl Munition f.
**mural** ['mjuərl] n Wandgemälde nt.
**murder** ['mɜːdə*] n Mord m ♦ vt ermorden; (spoil: piece of music, language) verhunzen; **to commit ~** einen Mord begehen.
**murderer** ['mɜːdərə*] n Mörder m.
**murderess** ['mɜːdərɪs] n Mörderin f.
**murderous** ['mɜːdərəs] adj blutrünstig; (attack) Mord-; (fig: look, attack) vernichtend; (: pace, heat) mörderisch.
**murk** [mɜːk] n Düsternis f.
**murky** ['mɜːkɪ] adj düster; (water) trübe.
**murmur** ['mɜːmə*] n (of voices) Murmeln nt; (of wind, waves) Rauschen nt ♦ vt, vi murmeln; **heart ~** Herzgeräusche pl.
**MusB(ac)** n abbr (= Bachelor of Music) akademischer Grad in Musikwissenschaft.
**muscle** ['mʌsl] n Muskel m; (fig: strength) Macht f.
▶**muscle in** vi: **to ~ in (on sth)** (bei etw) mitmischen.
**muscular** ['mʌskjulə*] adj (pain, dystrophy) Muskel-; (person, build) muskulös.
**muscular dystrophy** n Muskeldystrophie f.
**MusD(oc)** n abbr (= Doctor of Music) Doktorat in Musikwissenschaft.
**muse** [mjuːz] vi nachgrübeln ♦ n Muse f.
**museum** [mjuː'zɪəm] n Museum nt.
**mush** [mʌʃ] n Brei m; (pej) Schmalz m.
**mushroom** ['mʌʃrum] n (edible) (eßbarer) Pilz m; (poisonous) Giftpilz m; (button mushroom) Champignon m ♦ vi (fig: buildings etc) aus dem Boden schießen; (: town, organization) explosionsartig wachsen.
**mushroom cloud** n Atompilz m.
**mushy** ['mʌʃɪ] adj matschig; (consistency) breiig; (inf: sentimental) rührselig; ~ **peas** Erbsenbrei m.
**music** ['mjuːzɪk] n Musik f; (written music, score) Noten pl.
**musical** ['mjuːzɪkl] adj musikalisch; (sound, tune) melodisch ♦ n Musical nt.
**music(al) box** n Spieldose f.
**musical chairs** n die Reise f nach Jerusalem.
**musical instrument** n Musikinstrument nt.
**music centre** n Musik-Center nt.
**music hall** n Varieté nt.
**musician** [mjuː'zɪʃən] n Musiker(in) m(f).
**music stand** n Notenständer m.

**musk** [mʌsk] n Moschus m.
**musket** ['mʌskɪt] n Muskete f.
**muskrat** ['mʌskræt] n Bisamratte f.
**musk rose** n Moschusrose f.
**Muslim** ['mʌzlɪm] adj moslemisch ♦ n Moslem m, Moslime f.
**muslin** ['mʌzlɪn] n Musselin m.
**musquash** ['mʌskwɔʃ] n Bisamratte f; (fur) Bisam m.
**mussel** ['mʌsl] n (Mies)muschel f.
**must** [mʌst] aux vb müssen; (in negative) dürfen ♦ n Muß nt; I ~ **do it** ich muß es tun; **you ~ not do that** das darfst du nicht tun; **he ~ be there by now** jetzt müßte er schon dort sein; **you ~ come and see me soon** Sie müssen mich bald besuchen; **why ~ he behave so badly?** warum muß er sich so schlecht benehmen?; I ~ **have made a mistake** ich muß mich geirrt haben; **the film is a ~** den Film muß man unbedingt gesehen haben.
**mustache** ['mʌstæʃ] (US) n = **moustache**.
**mustard** ['mʌstəd] n Senf m.
**mustard gas** n (MIL) Senfgas nt.
**muster** ['mʌstə*] vt (support) zusammenbekommen; (also: ~ **up**: energy, strength, courage) aufbringen; (troops, members) antreten lassen ♦ n: **to pass ~** den Anforderungen genügen.
**mustiness** ['mʌstɪnɪs] n Muffigkeit f.
**mustn't** ['mʌsnt] = **must not**.
**musty** ['mʌstɪ] adj muffig; (building) moderig.
**mutant** ['mjuːtənt] n Mutante f.
**mutate** [mjuː'teɪt] vi (BIOL) mutieren.
**mutation** [mjuː'teɪʃən] n (BIOL) Mutation f; (alteration) Veränderung f.
**mute** [mjuːt] adj stumm.
**muted** ['mjuːtɪd] adj (colour) gedeckt; (reaction, criticism) verhalten; (sound, trumpet, MUS) gedämpft.
**mutilate** ['mjuːtɪleɪt] vt verstümmeln.
**mutilation** [mjuːtɪ'leɪʃən] n Verstümmelung f.
**mutinous** ['mjuːtɪnəs] adj meuterisch; (attitude) rebellisch.
**mutiny** ['mjuːtɪnɪ] n Meuterei f ♦ vi meutern.
**mutter** ['mʌtə*] vt, vi murmeln.
**mutton** ['mʌtn] n Hammelfleisch nt.
**mutual** ['mjuːtʃuəl] adj (feeling, attraction) gegenseitig; (benefit) beiderseitig; (interest, friend) gemeinsam; **the feeling was ~** das beruhte auf Gegenseitigkeit.
**mutually** ['mjuːtʃuəlɪ] adv (beneficial, satisfactory) für beide Seiten; (accepted) von beiden Seiten; **to be ~ exclusive** einander ausschließen; ~ **incompatible** nicht miteinander vereinbar.
**Muzak** ® ['mjuːzæk] n Berieselungsmusik f (inf).
**muzzle** ['mʌzl] n (of dog) Maul nt; (of gun) Mündung f; (guard: for dog) Maulkorb m ♦ vt (dog) einen Maulkorb anlegen +dat; (fig: press, person) mundtot machen.

**MV** abbr (= motor vessel) MS.
**MVP** (US) n abbr (SPORT: = most valuable player) wertvollster Spieler m, wertvollste Spielerin f.
**MW** abbr (RADIO: = medium wave) MW.

━━━━━━━━━━━━━━━━ *KEYWORD*

**my** [maɪ] adj mein(e); **this is ~ brother/sister/ house** das ist mein Bruder/meine Schwester/mein Haus; **I've washed ~ hair/ cut ~ finger** ich habe mir die Haare gewaschen/mir or mich in den Finger geschnitten; **is this ~ pen or yours?** ist das mein Stift oder deiner?

**Myanmar** ['maɪænmɑː] n Myanmar nt.
**myopic** [maɪ'ɔpɪk] adj (MED, fig) kurzsichtig.
**myriad** ['mɪrɪəd] n Unzahl f.
**myrrh** [məː*] n Myrrhe f.
**myself** [maɪ'sɛlf] pron (acc) mich; (dat) mir; (emphatic) selbst; see also **oneself**.
**mysterious** [mɪs'tɪərɪəs] adj geheimnisvoll, mysteriös.
**mysteriously** [mɪs'tɪərɪəslɪ] adv auf mysteriöse Weise; (smile) geheimnisvoll.
**mystery** ['mɪstərɪ] n (puzzle) Rätsel nt; (strangeness) Rätselhaftigkeit f ♦ cpd (guest, voice) mysteriös; ~ **tour** Fahrt f ins Blaue.
**mystery story** n Kriminalgeschichte f.
**mystic** ['mɪstɪk] n Mystiker(in) m(f).
**mystic(al)** ['mɪstɪk(l)] adj mystisch.
**mystify** ['mɪstɪfaɪ] vt vor ein Rätsel stellen.
**mystique** [mɪs'tiːk] n geheimnisvoller Nimbus m.
**myth** [mɪθ] n Mythos m; (fallacy) Märchen nt.
**mythical** ['mɪθɪkl] adj mythisch; (jobs, opportunities etc) fiktiv.
**mythological** [mɪθə'lɔdʒɪkl] adj mythologisch.
**mythology** [mɪ'θɔlədʒɪ] n Mythologie f.

# *N, n*

**N¹, n** [ɛn] n (letter) N nt, n nt; ~ **for Nellie**, (US) ~ **for Nan** ≈ N wie Nordpol.
**N²** [ɛn] abbr (= north) N.
**NA** (US) n abbr (= Narcotics Anonymous) Hilfsorganisation für Drogensüchtige; (= National Academy) Dachverband verschiedener Forschungsunternehmen.
**n/a** abbr (= not applicable) entf.; (COMM etc: = no account) kein Konto.
**NAACP** (US) n abbr (= National Association for the Advancement of Colored People) Vereinigung zur Förderung Farbiger.
**NAAFI** ['næfɪ] (BRIT) n abbr (= Navy, Army and

Air Force Institutes) *Laden für britische Armeeangehörige.*

**NACU** (*US*) *n abbr* (= *National Association of Colleges and Universities*) *Fachhochschul- und Universitätsverband.*

**nadir** ['neɪdɪə'] *n* (*fig*) Tiefstpunkt *m*; (*ASTRON*) Nadir *m*.

**NAFTA** *n abbr* (= *North Atlantic Free Trade Agreement*) *amerikanische Freihandelszone.*

**nag** [næg] *vt* herumnörgeln an +*dat* ♦ *vi* nörgeln ♦ *n* (*pej: horse*) Gaul *m*; (: *person*) Nörgler(in) *m(f)*; **to ~ at sb** jdn plagen, jdm keine Ruhe lassen.

**nagging** ['nægɪŋ] *adj* (*doubt, suspicion*) quälend; (*pain*) dumpf.

**nail** [neɪl] *n* Nagel *m* ♦ *vt* (*inf: thief etc*) drankriegen; (: *fraud*) aufdecken; **to ~ sth to sth** etw an etw *acc* nageln; **to ~ sb down (to sth)** jdn (auf etw *acc*) festnageln.

**nailbrush** ['neɪlbrʌʃ] *n* Nagelbürste *f*.

**nailfile** ['neɪlfaɪl] *n* Nagelfeile *f*.

**nail polish** *n* Nagellack *m*.

**nail polish remover** *n* Nagellackentferner *m*.

**nail scissors** *npl* Nagelschere *f*.

**nail varnish** (*BRIT*) *n* = **nail polish**.

**Nairobi** [naɪˈrəʊbɪ] *n* Nairobi *nt*.

**naive** [naːˈiːv] *adj* naiv.

**naïveté** [naːiːvˈteɪ] *n* = **naivety**.

**naivety** [naɪˈiːvtɪ] *n* Naivität *f*.

**naked** ['neɪkɪd] *adj* nackt; (*flame, light*) offen; **with the ~ eye** mit bloßem Auge; **to the ~ eye** für das bloße Auge.

**nakedness** ['neɪkɪdnɪs] *n* Nacktheit *f*.

**NAM** (*US*) *n abbr* (= *National Association of Manufacturers*) *nationaler Verband der verarbeitenden Industrie.*

**name** [neɪm] *n* Name *m* ♦ *vt* nennen; (*ship*) taufen; (*identify*) (beim Namen) nennen; (*date etc*) bestimmen, festlegen; **what's your ~?** wie heißen Sie?; **my ~ is Peter** ich heiße Peter; **by ~** mit Namen; **in the ~ of** im Namen +*gen*; **to give one's ~ and address** Namen und Adresse angeben; **to make a ~ for o.s.** sich *dat* einen Namen machen; **to give sb a bad ~** jdn in Verruf bringen; **to call sb ~s** jdn beschimpfen; **to be ~d after sb/sth** nach jdm/etw benannt werden.

**name-dropping** ['neɪmdrɒpɪŋ] *n* Angeberei *f* mit berühmten Namen.

**nameless** ['neɪmlɪs] *adj* namenlos; **who/which shall remain ~** der/die/das ungenannt bleiben soll.

**namely** ['neɪmlɪ] *adv* nämlich.

**nameplate** ['neɪmpleɪt] *n* Namensschild *nt*.

**namesake** ['neɪmseɪk] *n* Namensvetter(in) *m(f)*.

**nan bread** [naːn-] *n* Nan-Brot *nt*, fladenförmiges Weißbrot als Beilage zu indischen Gerichten.

**nanny** ['nænɪ] *n* Kindermädchen *nt*.

**nanny-goat** ['nænɪgəʊt] *n* Geiß *f*.

**nap** [næp] *n* Schläfchen *nt*; (*of fabric*) Strich *m* ♦ *vi*: **to be caught ~ping** (*fig*) überrumpelt werden; **to have a ~** ein Schläfchen *or* ein Nickerchen (*inf*) machen.

**NAPA** (*US*) *n abbr* (= *National Association of Performing Artists*) *Künstlergewerkschaft.*

**napalm** ['neɪpɑːm] *n* Napalm *nt*.

**nape** [neɪp] *n*: **the ~ of the neck** der Nacken.

**napkin** ['næpkɪn] *n* (*also*: **table ~**) Serviette *f*.

**Naples** ['neɪplz] *n* Neapel *nt*.

**Napoleonic** [nəpəʊlɪˈɒnɪk] *adj* Napoleonisch.

**nappy** ['næpɪ] (*BRIT*) *n* Windel *f*.

**nappy liner** (*BRIT*) *n* Windeleinlage *f*.

**nappy rash** *n* Wundsein *nt*.

**narcissistic** [nɑːsɪˈsɪstɪk] *adj* narzißtisch.

**narcissus** [nɑːˈsɪsəs] (*pl* **narcissi**) *n* Narzisse *f*.

**narcotic** [nɑːˈkɒtɪk] *adj* narkotisch ♦ *n* Narkotikum *nt*; **narcotics** *npl* (*drugs*) Drogen *pl*; **~ drug** Rauschgift *nt*.

**nark** [nɑːk] (*BRIT: inf*) *vt*: **to be ~ed at sth** sauer über etw *acc* sein.

**narrate** [nəˈreɪt] *vt* erzählen; (*film, programme*) kommentieren.

**narration** [nəˈreɪʃən] *n* Kommentar *m*.

**narrative** ['nærətɪv] *n* Erzählung *f*; (*of journey etc*) Schilderung *f*.

**narrator** [nəˈreɪtə'] *n* Erzähler(in) *m(f)*; (*in film etc*) Kommentator(in) *m(f)*.

**narrow** ['nærəʊ] *adj* eng; (*ledge etc*) schmal; (*majority, advantage, victory, defeat*) knapp; (*ideas, view*) engstirnig ♦ *vi* sich verengen; (*gap, difference*) sich verringern ♦ *vt* (*gap, difference*) verringern; (*eyes*) zusammenkneifen; **to have a ~ escape** mit knapper Not davonkommen; **to ~ sth down (to sth)** etw (auf etw *acc*) beschränken.

**narrow gauge** ['nærəʊgeɪdʒ] *adj* (*RAIL*) Schmalspur-.

**narrowly** ['nærəʊlɪ] *adv* knapp; (*escape*) mit knapper Not.

**narrow-minded** [nærəʊˈmaɪndɪd] *adj* engstirnig.

**NAS** (*US*) *n abbr* (= *National Academy of Sciences*) *Akademie der Wissenschaften.*

**NASA** ['næsə] (*US*) *n abbr* (= *National Aeronautics and Space Administration*) NASA *f*.

**nasal** ['neɪzl] *adj* Nasen-; (*voice*) näselnd.

**Nassau** ['næsɔː] *n* Nassau *nt*.

**nastily** ['nɑːstɪlɪ] *adv* gemein; (*say*) gehässig.

**nastiness** ['nɑːstɪnɪs] *n* Gemeinheit *f*; (*of remark*) Gehässigkeit *f*; (*of smell, taste etc*) Ekelhaftigkeit *f*.

**nasturtium** [nəsˈtəːʃəm] *n* Kapuziner- kresse *f*.

**nasty** ['nɑːstɪ] *adj* (*remark*) gehässig; (*person*) gemein; (*taste, smell*) ekelhaft; (*wound, disease, accident, shock*) schlimm; (*problem, question*) schwierig; (*weather, temper*) abscheulich; **to turn ~** unangenehm werden; **it's a ~ business** es ist schrecklich; **he's got a ~ temper** mit ihm ist nicht gut

Kirschen essen.

**NAS/UWT** (*BRIT*) *n abbr* (= *National Association of Schoolmasters/Union of Women Teachers*) Lehrergewerkschaft.

**nation** ['neɪʃən] *n* Nation *f*; (*people*) Volk *nt*.

**national** ['næʃənl] *adj* (*character, flag*) National-; (*interests*) Staats-; (*newspaper*) überregional ♦ *n* Staatsbürger(in) *m(f)*; **foreign** ~ Ausländer(in) *m(f)*.

**national anthem** *n* Nationalhymne *f*.

**National Curriculum** *n* zentraler Lehrplan *für Schulen in England und Wales*.

**national debt** *n* Staatsverschuldung *f*.

**national dress** *n* Nationaltracht *f*.

**National Guard** (*US*) *n* Nationalgarde *f*.

**National Health Service** (*BRIT*) *n* Staatlicher Gesundheitsdienst *m*.

**National Insurance** (*BRIT*) *n* Sozialversicherung *f*.

**nationalism** ['næʃnəlɪzəm] *n* Nationalismus *m*.

**nationalist** ['næʃnəlɪst] *adj* nationalistisch ♦ *n* Nationalist(in) *m(f)*.

**nationality** [næʃə'nælɪtɪ] *n* Staatsangehörigkeit *f*, Nationalität *f*.

**nationalization** [næʃnəlaɪ'zeɪʃən] *n* Verstaatlichung *f*.

**nationalize** ['næʃnəlaɪz] *vt* verstaatlichen.

**National Lottery** *n* ≈ Lotto *nt*.

**nationally** ['næʃnəlɪ] *adv* landesweit.

**national park** *n* Nationalpark *m*.

**national press** *n* überregionale Presse *f*.

**National Security Council** (*US*) *n* Nationaler Sicherheitsrat *m*.

**national service** *n* Wehrdienst *m*.

**National Trust** (*BRIT*) *n* Organisation zum *Schutz historischer Bauten und Denkmäler sowie zum Landschaftsschutz*.

---

*Der* **National Trust** *ist ein 1895 gegründeter Natur- und Denkmalschutzverband in Großbritannien, der Gebäude und Gelände von besonderem historischem oder ästhetischem Interesse erhält und der Öffentlichkeit zugänglich macht. Viele Gebäude im Besitz des National Trust sind (z.T. gegen ein Eintrittsgeld) zu besichtigen.*

---

**nationwide** ['neɪʃənwaɪd] *adj, adv* landesweit.

**native** ['neɪtɪv] *n* Einheimische(r) *f(m)* ♦ *adj* einheimisch; (*country*) Heimat-; (*language*) Mutter-; (*innate*) angeboren; **a** ~ **of Germany, a** ~ **German** ein gebürtiger Deutscher, eine gebürtige Deutsche; ~ **to** beheimatet in +*dat*.

**Native American** *adj* indianisch, der Ureinwohner Amerikas ♦ *n* Ureinwohner(in) *m(f)* Amerikas.

**native speaker** *n* Muttersprachler(in) *m(f)*.

**Nativity** [nə'tɪvɪtɪ] *n*: **the** ~ Christi Geburt *f*.

**nativity play** *n* Krippenspiel *nt*.

**NATO** ['neɪtəu] *n abbr* (= *North Atlantic Treaty Organization*) NATO *f*.

**natter** ['nætə\*] (*BRIT*) *vi* quatschen (*inf*) ♦ *n*: **to have a** ~ einen Schwatz halten.

**natural** ['nætʃrəl] *adj* natürlich; (*disaster*) Natur-; (*innate*) angeboren; (*born*) geboren; (*MUS*) ohne Vorzeichen; **to die of** ~ **causes** eines natürlichen Todes sterben; ~ **foods** Naturkost *f*; **she played F** ~ **not F sharp** sie spielte f statt fis.

**natural childbirth** *n* natürliche Geburt *f*.

**natural gas** *n* Erdgas *nt*.

**natural history** *n* Naturkunde *f*; **the** ~ **of England** die Naturgeschichte Englands.

**naturalist** ['nætʃrəlɪst] *n* Naturforscher(in) *m(f)*.

**naturalize** ['nætʃrəlaɪz] *vt*: **to become** ~**d** eingebürgert werden.

**naturally** ['nætʃrəlɪ] *adv* natürlich; (*happen*) auf natürlichem Wege; (*die*) eines natürlichen Todes; (*occur: cheerful, talented, blonde*) von Natur aus.

**naturalness** ['nætʃrəlnɪs] *n* Natürlichkeit *f*.

**natural resources** *npl* Naturschätze *pl*.

**natural selection** *n* natürliche Auslese *f*.

**natural wastage** *n* natürliche Personalreduzierung *f*.

**nature** ['neɪtʃə\*] *n* (*also*: **Nature**) Natur *f*; (*kind, sort*) Art *f*; (*character*) Wesen *nt*; **by** ~ von Natur aus; **by its (very)** ~ naturgemäß; **documents of a confidential** ~ Unterlagen vertraulicher Art.

**-natured** ['neɪtʃəd] *suff*: **good-**~ gutmütig; **ill-**~ bösartig.

**nature reserve** (*BRIT*) *n* Naturschutzgebiet *nt*.

**nature trail** *n* Naturlehrpfad *m*.

**naturist** ['neɪtʃərɪst] *n* Anhänger(in) *m(f)* der Freikörperkultur.

**naught** [nɔːt] *n* = **nought**.

**naughtiness** ['nɔːtɪnɪs] *n* (*see adj*) Unartigkeit *f*, Ungezogenheit *f*; Unanständigkeit *f*.

**naughty** ['nɔːtɪ] *adj* (*child*) unartig, ungezogen; (*story, film, words*) unanständig.

**nausea** ['nɔːsɪə] *n* Übelkeit *f*.

**nauseate** ['nɔːsɪeɪt] *vt* Übelkeit verursachen +*dat*; (*fig*) anwidern.

**nauseating** ['nɔːsɪeɪtɪŋ] *adj* ekelerregend; (*fig*) widerlich.

**nauseous** ['nɔːsɪəs] *adj* ekelhaft; **I feel** ~ mir ist übel.

**nautical** ['nɔːtɪkl] *adj* (*chart*) See-; (*uniform*) Seemanns-.

**nautical mile** *n* Seemeile *f*.

**naval** ['neɪvl] *adj* Marine-; (*battle, forces*) See-.

**naval officer** *n* Marineoffizier *m*.

**nave** [neɪv] *n* Hauptschiff *nt*, Mittelschiff *nt*.

**navel** ['neɪvl] *n* Nabel *m*.

**navigable** ['nævɪgəbl] *adj* schiffbar.

**navigate** ['nævɪgeɪt] *vt* (*river*) befahren; (*path*) begehen ♦ *vi* navigieren; (*AUT*) den Fahrer dirigieren.

**navigation** [nævɪ'geɪʃən] *n* Navigation *f*.

**navigator** ['nævɪgeɪtə\*] *n* (*NAUT*) Steuermann

m; (*AVIAT*) Navigator(in) m(f); (*AUT*) Beifahrer(in) m(f).

**navvy** ['nævɪ] (*BRIT*) n Straßenarbeiter m.

**navy** ['neɪvɪ] n (Kriegs)marine f; (*ships*) (Kriegs)flotte f; **Department of the N~** (*US*) Marineministerium nt.

**navy(-blue)** ['neɪvɪ('bluː)] adj marineblau.

**Nazareth** ['næzərɪθ] n Nazareth nt.

**Nazi** ['nɑːtsɪ] n Nazi m.

**NB** abbr (= nota bene) NB; (*CANADA*: = New Brunswick).

**NBA** (*US*) n abbr (= National Basketball Association) Basketball-Dachverband; (= National Boxing Association) Boxsport-Dachverband.

**NBC** (*US*) n abbr (= National Broadcasting Company) Fernsehsender.

**NBS** (*US*) n abbr (= National Bureau of Standards) amerikanischer Normenausschuß.

**NC** abbr (*COMM etc*: = no charge) frei; (*US*: *POST*: = North Carolina).

**NCC** n abbr (*BRIT*: = Nature Conservancy Council) Naturschutzverband; (*US*: = National Council of Churches) Zusammenschluß protestantischer und orthodoxer Kirchen.

**NCCL** (*BRIT*) n abbr (= National Council for Civil Liberties) Organisation zum Schutz von Freiheitsrechten.

**NCO** n abbr (*MIL*: = noncommissioned officer) Uffz.

**ND** (*US*) abbr (*POST*: = North Dakota).

**N.Dak.** (*US*) abbr (*POST*: = North Dakota).

**NE** abbr = **north-east**; (*US*: *POST*: = New England; Nebraska).

**NEA** (*US*) n abbr (= National Education Association) Verband für das Erziehungswesen.

**neap** [niːp] n (*also*: ~ **tide**) Nippflut f.

**Neapolitan** [nɪə'pɒlɪtən] adj neapolitanisch ♦ n Neapolitaner(in) m(f).

**near** [nɪə*] adj nahe ♦ adv nahe; (*almost*) fast, beinahe ♦ prep (*also*: ~ **to**: *in space*) nahe an +dat; (: *in time*) um acc ... herum; (: *in situation, in intimacy*) nahe +dat ♦ vt sich nähern +dat; (*state, situation*) kurz vor +dat stehen; **Christmas is** ~ bald ist Weihnachten; **£25,000 or** ~**est offer** (*BRIT*) £25.000 oder das nächstbeste Angebot; **in the** ~ **future** in naher Zukunft, bald; **in** ~ **darkness** fast im Dunkeln; **a** ~ **tragedy** beinahe eine Tragödie; ~ **here/there** hier/dort in der Nähe; **to be** ~ **(to) doing sth** nahe daran sein, etw zu tun; **the building is** ~**ing completion** der Bau steht kurz vor dem Abschluß.

**nearby** [nɪə'baɪ] adj nahegelegen ♦ adv in der Nähe.

**Near East** n: **the** ~ der Nahe Osten.

**nearer** ['nɪərə*] adj, adv comp of **near**.

**nearest** ['nɪərəst] adj, adv superl of **near**.

**nearly** ['nɪəlɪ] adv fast; **I** ~ **fell** ich wäre beinahe gefallen; **it's not** ~ **big enough** es ist bei weitem nicht groß genug; **she was** ~ **crying** sie war den Tränen nahe.

**near miss** n Beinahezusammenstoß m; **that was a** ~ (*shot*) das war knapp daneben.

**nearness** ['nɪənɪs] n Nähe f.

**nearside** ['nɪəsaɪd] (*AUT*) adj (*when driving on left*) linksseitig; (*when driving on right*) rechtsseitig ♦ n: **the** ~ (*when driving on left*) die linke Seite; (*when driving on right*) die rechte Seite.

**near-sighted** [nɪə'saɪtɪd] adj kurzsichtig.

**neat** [niːt] adj ordentlich; (*handwriting*) sauber; (*plan, solution*) elegant; (*description*) prägnant; (*spirits*) pur; **I drink it** ~ ich trinke es pur.

**neatly** ['niːtlɪ] adv ordentlich; (*conveniently*) sauber.

**neatness** ['niːtnɪs] n Ordentlichkeit f; (*of solution, plan*) Sauberkeit f.

**Nebr.** (*US*) abbr (*POST*: = Nebraska).

**nebulous** ['nɛbjʊləs] adj vage, unklar.

**necessarily** ['nɛsɪsrɪlɪ] adv notwendigerweise; **not** ~ nicht unbedingt.

**necessary** ['nɛsɪsrɪ] adj notwendig, nötig; (*inevitable*) unausweichlich; **if** ~ wenn nötig, nötigenfalls; **it is** ~ **to** ... man muß ...

**necessitate** [nɪ'sɛsɪteɪt] vt erforderlich machen.

**necessity** [nɪ'sɛsɪtɪ] n Notwendigkeit f; **of** ~ notgedrungen; **out of** ~ aus Not; **the necessities (of life)** das Notwendigste (zum Leben).

**neck** [nɛk] n Hals m; (*of shirt, dress, jumper*) Ausschnitt m ♦ vi (*inf*) knutschen; ~ **and** ~ Kopf an Kopf; **to stick one's** ~ **out** (*inf*) seinen Kopf riskieren.

**necklace** ['nɛklɪs] n (Hals)kette f.

**neckline** ['nɛklaɪn] n Ausschnitt m.

**necktie** ['nɛktaɪ] (*esp US*) n Krawatte f.

**nectar** ['nɛktə*] n Nektar m.

**nectarine** ['nɛktərɪn] n Nektarine f.

**NEDC** (*BRIT*) n abbr (= National Economic Development Council) Rat für Wirtschaftsentwicklung.

**Neddy** ['nɛdɪ] (*BRIT*: *inf*) n abbr = **NEDC**.

**née** [neɪ] prep: ~ **Scott** geborene Scott.

**need** [niːd] n Bedarf m; (*necessity*) Notwendigkeit f; (*requirement*) Bedürfnis nt; (*poverty*) Not f ♦ vt brauchen; (*could do with*) nötig haben; **in** ~ bedürftig; **to be in** ~ **of sth** etw nötig haben; **£10 will meet my immediate** ~**s** mit £ 10 komme ich erst einmal aus; (**there's**) **no** ~ (das ist) nicht nötig; **there's no** ~ **to get so worked up about it** du brauchst dich darüber nicht so aufzuregen; **he had no** ~ **to work** er hatte es nicht nötig zu arbeiten; **I** ~ **to do it** ich muß es tun; **you don't** ~ **to go, you** ~**n't go** du brauchst nicht zu gehen; **a signature is** ~**ed** das bedarf einer Unterschrift gen.

**needle** ['ni:dl] n Nadel f ♦ vt (fig: inf: goad) ärgern, piesacken.

**needless** ['ni:dlɪs] adj unnötig; ~ **to say** natürlich.

**needlessly** ['ni:dlɪslɪ] adv unnötig.

**needlework** ['ni:dlwə:k] n Handarbeit f.

**needn't** ['ni:dnt] = **need not.**

**needy** ['ni:dɪ] adj bedürftig ♦ npl: **the** ~ die Bedürftigen pl.

**negation** [nɪ'geɪʃən] n Verweigerung f.

**negative** ['nɛgətɪv] adj negativ; (answer) abschlägig ♦ n (PHOT) Negativ nt; (LING) Verneinungswort nt, Negation f; **to answer in the** ~ eine verneinende Antwort geben.

**negative equity** n Differenz zwischen gefallenem Wert und hypothekarischer Belastung eines Wohnungseigentums.

**neglect** [nɪ'glɛkt] vt vernachlässigen; (writer, artist) unterschätzen ♦ n Vernachlässigung f.

**neglected** [nɪ'glɛktɪd] adj vernachlässigt; (writer, artist) unterschätzt.

**neglectful** [nɪ'glɛktful] adj nachlässig; (father) pflichtvergessen; **to be** ~ **of sth** etw vernachlässigen.

**negligee** ['nɛglɪʒeɪ] n Negligé nt.

**negligence** ['nɛglɪdʒəns] n Nachlässigkeit f; (LAW) Fahrlässigkeit f.

**negligent** ['nɛglɪdʒənt] adj nachlässig; (LAW) fahrlässig; (casual) lässig.

**negligently** ['nɛglɪdʒəntlɪ] adv (see adj) nachlässig; fahrlässig; lässig.

**negligible** ['nɛglɪdʒɪbl] adj geringfügig.

**negotiable** [nɪ'gəuʃɪəbl] adj verhandlungsfähig; (path, river) passierbar; **not** ~ (on cheque etc) nicht übertragbar.

**negotiate** [nɪ'gəuʃɪeɪt] vi verhandeln ♦ vt aushandeln; (obstacle, hill) überwinden; (bend) nehmen; **to** ~ **with sb (for sth)** mit jdm (über etw acc) verhandeln.

**negotiating table** [nɪ'gəuʃɪeɪtɪŋ-] n Verhandlungstisch m.

**negotiation** [nɪgəuʃɪ'eɪʃən] n Verhandlung f; **the matter is still under** ~ über die Sache wird noch verhandelt.

**negotiator** [nɪ'gəuʃɪeɪtə*] n Unterhändler(in) m(f).

**Negress** ['ni:grɪs] n Negerin f.

**Negro** ['ni:grəu] (pl ~**es**) adj (boy, slave) Neger- ♦ n Neger m.

**neigh** [neɪ] vi wiehern.

**neighbour,** (US) **neighbor** ['neɪbə*] n Nachbar(in) m(f).

**neighbourhood** ['neɪbəhud] n (place) Gegend f; (people) Nachbarschaft f; **in the** ~ **of** ... in der Nähe von ...; (sum of money) so um die ...

**neighbourhood watch** n Vereinigung von Bürgern, die Straßenwachen etc zur Unterstützung der Polizei bei der Verbrechensbekämpfung organisiert.

**neighbouring** ['neɪbərɪŋ] adj benachbart, Nachbar-.

**neighbourly** ['neɪbəlɪ] adj nachbarlich.

**neither** ['naɪðə*] conj: **I didn't move and** ~ **did John** ich bewegte mich nicht, und John auch nicht ♦ pron keine(r, s) (von beiden) ♦ adv: ~ ... **nor** ... weder ... noch ...; ~ **story is true** keine der beiden Geschichten stimmt; ~ **is true** beides stimmt nicht; ~ **do I/have I** ich auch nicht.

**neo...** ['ni:əu] pref neo-, Neo-.

**neolithic** [nɪə'lɪθɪk] adv jungsteinzeitlich, neolithisch.

**neologism** [nɪ'ɔlədʒɪzəm] n (Wort)neubildung f, Neologismus m.

**neon** ['ni:ɔn] n Neon nt.

**neon light** n Neonlampe f.

**neon sign** n Neonreklame f.

**Nepal** [nɪ'pɔ:l] n Nepal nt.

**nephew** ['nɛvju:] n Neffe m.

**nepotism** ['nɛpətɪzəm] n Vetternwirtschaft f.

**nerd** [nə:d] (inf) n Schwachkopf m.

**nerve** [nə:v] n (ANAT) Nerv m; (courage) Mut m; (impudence) Frechheit f; **nerves** npl (anxiety) Nervosität f; (emotional strength) Nerven pl; **he gets on my** ~**s** er geht mir auf die Nerven; **to lose one's** ~ die Nerven verlieren.

**nerve-centre,** (US) **nerve-center** ['nə:vsɛntə*] n (fig) Schaltzentrale f.

**nerve gas** n Nervengas nt.

**nerve-racking** ['nə:vrækɪŋ] adj nervenaufreibend.

**nervous** ['nə:vəs] adj Nerven-, nervlich; (anxious) nervös; **to be** ~ **of/about** Angst haben vor +dat.

**nervous breakdown** n Nervenzusammenbruch m.

**nervously** ['nə:vəslɪ] adv nervös.

**nervousness** ['nə:vəsnɪs] n Nervosität f.

**nervous system** n Nervensystem nt.

**nervous wreck** (inf) n Nervenbündel nt; **to be a** ~ mit den Nerven völlig am Ende sein.

**nervy** ['nə:vɪ] (inf) adj (BRIT: tense) nervös; (US: cheeky) dreist.

**nest** [nɛst] n Nest nt ♦ vi nisten; **a** ~ **of tables** ein Satz Tische or von Tischen.

**nest egg** n Notgroschen m.

**nestle** ['nɛsl] vi sich kuscheln; (house) eingebettet sein.

**nestling** ['nɛstlɪŋ] n Nestling m.

**net** [nɛt] n Netz nt; (fabric) Tüll m ♦ adj (COMM) Netto-; (final: result, effect) End- ♦ vt (mit einem Netz) fangen; (profit) einbringen; (deal, sale, fortune) an Land ziehen; ~ **of tax** steuerfrei; **he earns £10,000** ~ **per year** er verdient £ 10.000 netto im Jahr; **it weighs 250g** ~ es wiegt 250 g netto.

**netball** ['nɛtbɔ:l] n Netzball m.

**net curtains** npl Gardinen pl, Stores pl.

**Netherlands** ['nɛðələndz] npl: **the** ~ die Niederlande pl.

**nett** [nɛt] adj = **net.**

**netting** ['nɛtɪŋ] n (for fence etc) Maschendraht m; (fabric) Netzgewebe nt, Tüll m.

**nettle** ['nɛtl] n Nessel f; **to grasp the ~** (fig) in den sauren Apfel beißen.

**network** ['nɛtwəːk] n Netz nt; (TV, RADIO) Sendenetz nt ♦ vt (RADIO, TV) im ganzen Netzbereich ausstrahlen; (computers) in einem Netzwerk zusammenschließen.

**neuralgia** [njuə'rældʒə] n Neuralgie f, Nervenschmerzen pl.

**neurological** [njuərə'lɔdʒɪkl] adj neurologisch.

**neurotic** [njuə'rɔtɪk] adj neurotisch ♦ n Neurotiker(in) m(f).

**neuter** ['njuːtə'] adj (LING) sächlich ♦ vt kastrieren; (female) sterilisieren.

**neutral** ['njuːtrəl] adj neutral ♦ n (AUT) Leerlauf m.

**neutrality** [njuː'trælɪtɪ] n Neutralität f.

**neutralize** ['njuːtrəlaɪz] vt neutralisieren, aufheben.

**neutron** ['njuːtrɔn] n Neutron nt.

**neutron bomb** n Neutronenbombe f.

**Nev.** (US) abbr (POST: = Nevada).

**never** ['nɛvə'] adv nie; (not) nicht; **~ in my life** noch nie; **~ again** nie wieder; **well I ~!** nein, so was!; see also **mind**.

**never-ending** [nɛvər'ɛndɪŋ] adj endlos.

**nevertheless** [nɛvəðə'lɛs] adv trotzdem, dennoch.

**new** [njuː] adj neu; (mother) jung; **as good as ~** so gut wie neu; **to be ~ to sb** jdm neu sein.

**New Age** n New Age nt.

**newborn** ['njuːbɔːn] adj neugeboren.

**newcomer** ['njuːkʌmə'] n Neuankömmling m; (in job) Neuling m.

**new-fangled** ['njuː'fæŋgld] (pej) adj neumodisch.

**new-found** ['njuːfaund] adj neuentdeckt; (confidence) neugeschöpft.

**Newfoundland** ['njuːfənlənd] n Neufundland nt.

**New Guinea** n Neuguinea nt.

**newly** ['njuːlɪ] adv neu.

**newly-weds** ['njuːlɪwɛdz] npl Neuvermählte pl, Frischvermählte pl.

**new moon** n Neumond m.

**newness** ['njuːnɪs] n Neuheit f; (of cheese, bread etc) Frische f.

**New Orleans** [-'ɔːliːənz] n New Orleans nt.

**news** [njuːz] n Nachricht f; **a piece of ~** eine Neuigkeit; **the ~** (RADIO, TV) die Nachrichten pl; **good/bad ~** gute/schlechte Nachrichten.

**news agency** n Nachrichtenagentur f.

**newsagent** ['njuːzeɪdʒənt] (BRIT) n Zeitungshändler(in) m(f).

**news bulletin** n Bulletin nt.

**newscaster** ['njuːzkɑːstə'] n Nachrichten-sprecher(in) m(f).

**newsdealer** ['njuːzdiːlə'] (US) n = **newsagent**.

**newsflash** ['njuːzflæʃ] n Kurzmeldung f.

**newsletter** ['njuːzlɛtə'] n Rundschreiben nt, Mitteilungsblatt nt.

**newspaper** ['njuːzpeɪpə'] n Zeitung f; **daily/weekly ~** Tages-/Wochenzeitung f.

**newsprint** ['njuːzprɪnt] n Zeitungspapier nt.

**newsreader** ['njuːzriːdə'] n = **newscaster**.

**newsreel** ['njuːzriːl] n Wochenschau f.

**newsroom** ['njuːzruːm] n Nachrichten-redaktion f; (RADIO, TV) Nachrichtenstudio nt.

**newsstand** ['njuːzstænd] n Zeitungsstand m.

**newsworthy** ['njuːzwəːðɪ] adj: **to be ~** Neuigkeitswert haben.

**newt** [njuːt] n Wassermolch m.

**new town** (BRIT) n neue, teilweise mit Regierungsgeldern errichtete städtische Siedlung.

**New Year** n neues Jahr nt; (New Year's Day) Neujahr nt; **Happy ~!** (ein) glückliches or frohes neues Jahr!

**New Year's Day** n Neujahr nt, Neujahrstag m.

**New Year's Eve** n Silvester nt.

**New York** [-'jɔːk] n New York nt; (also: **~ State**) der Staat New York.

**New Zealand** [-'ziːlənd] n Neuseeland nt ♦ adj neuseeländisch.

**New Zealander** [-'ziːləndə'] n Neuseeländer(in) m(f).

**next** [nɛkst] adj nächste(r, s); (room) Neben-♦ adv dann; (do, happen) als nächstes; (afterwards) danach; **the ~ day** am nächsten or folgenden Tag; **~ time** das nächste Mal; **~ year** nächstes Jahr; **~ please!** der nächste bitte!; **who's ~?** wer ist der nächste?; **"turn to the ~ page"** „bitte umblättern"; **the week after ~** übernächste Woche; **the ~ on the right/left** der/die/das nächste rechts/ links; **the ~ thing I knew** das nächste, woran ich mich erinnern konnte; **~ to** neben +dat; **~ to nothing** so gut wie nichts; **when do we meet ~?** wann treffen wir uns wieder or das nächste Mal?; **the ~ best** der/ die/das nächstbeste.

**next door** adv nebenan ♦ adj: **next-door** nebenan; **the house ~** das Nebenhaus; **to go ~** nach nebenan gehen; **my next-door neighbour** mein direkter Nachbar.

**next-of-kin** ['nɛkstəv'kɪn] n nächster Verwandter m, nächste Verwandte f.

**NF** n abbr (BRIT: POL: = National Front) rechtsradikale Partei ♦ abbr (CANADA: = Newfoundland).

**NFL** (US) n abbr (= National Football League) Fußball-Nationalliga.

**NG** (US) abbr = **National Guard**.

**NGO** n abbr (= nongovernmental organization) nichtstaatliche Organisation.

**NH** (US) abbr (POST: = New Hampshire).

**NHL** (US) n abbr (= National Hockey League) Hockey-Nationalliga.

**NHS** (BRIT) n abbr = **National Health Service**.

**NI** abbr = **Northern Ireland**; (BRIT) = **National Insurance**.

**Niagara Falls** [naɪˈægərə-] *npl* Niagarafälle *pl.*
**nib** [nɪb] *n* Feder *f.*
**nibble** [ˈnɪbl] *vt* knabbern; *(bite)* knabbern an +*dat* ♦ *vi:* **to ~ at** knabbern an +*dat.*
**Nicaragua** [nɪkəˈrægjuə] *n* Nicaragua *nt.*
**Nicaraguan** [nɪkəˈrægjuən] *adj* nicaraguanisch ♦ *n* Nicaraguaner(in) *m(f).*
**Nice** [niːs] *n* Nizza *nt.*
**nice** [naɪs] *adj* nett; *(holiday, weather, picture etc)* schön; *(taste)* gut; *(person, clothes etc)* hübsch.
**nicely** [ˈnaɪslɪ] *adv (attractively)* hübsch; *(politely)* nett; *(satisfactorily)* gut; **that will do ~** das reicht (vollauf).
**niceties** [ˈnaɪsɪtɪz] *npl:* **the ~** die Feinheiten *pl.*
**niche** [niːʃ] *n* Nische *f;* *(job, position)* Plätzchen *nt.*
**nick** [nɪk] *n* Kratzer *m;* *(in metal, wood etc)* Kerbe *f* ♦ *vt (BRIT: inf: steal)* klauen; *(: : arrest)* einsperren, einlochen; *(cut):* **to ~ o.s.** sich schneiden; **in good ~** *(BRIT: inf)* gut in Schuß; **in the ~** *(BRIT: inf: in prison)* im Knast; **in the ~ of time** gerade noch rechtzeitig.
**nickel** [ˈnɪkl] *n* Nickel *nt;* *(US)* Fünfcentstück *nt.*
**nickname** [ˈnɪkneɪm] *n* Spitzname *m* ♦ *vt* betiteln, taufen *(inf).*
**Nicosia** [nɪkəˈsiːə] *n* Nikosia *nt.*
**nicotine** [ˈnɪkətiːn] *n* Nikotin *nt.*
**nicotine patch** *n* Nikotinpflaster *nt.*
**niece** [niːs] *n* Nichte *f.*
**nifty** [ˈnɪftɪ] *(inf) adj* flott; *(gadget, tool)* schlau.
**Niger** [ˈnaɪdʒə*] *n* Niger *m.*
**Nigeria** [naɪˈdʒɪərɪə] *n* Nigeria *nt.*
**Nigerian** [naɪˈdʒɪərɪən] *adj* nigerianisch ♦ *n* Nigerianer(in) *m(f).*
**niggardly** [ˈnɪgədlɪ] *adj* knauserig; *(allowance, amount)* armselig.
**nigger** [ˈnɪgə*] *(inf) n* Nigger *m (inf!).*
**niggle** [ˈnɪgl] *vt* plagen, zu schaffen machen +*dat* ♦ *vi* herumkritisieren.
**niggling** [ˈnɪglɪŋ] *adj* quälend; *(pain, ache)* bohrend.
**night** [naɪt] *n* Nacht *f;* *(evening)* Abend *m;* **the ~ before last** vorletzte Nacht, vorgestern abend; **at ~, by ~** nachts, abends; **nine o'clock at ~** neun Uhr abends; **in the ~, during the ~** in der Nacht; **~ and day** Tag und Nacht.
**nightcap** [ˈnaɪtkæp] *n* Schlaftrunk *m.*
**nightclub** [ˈnaɪtklʌb] *n* Nachtlokal *nt.*
**nightdress** [ˈnaɪtdrɛs] *n* Nachthemd *nt.*
**nightfall** [ˈnaɪtfɔːl] *n* Einbruch *m* der Dunkelheit.
**nightgown** [ˈnaɪtgaun] *n* = **nightdress.**
**nightie** [ˈnaɪtɪ] *n* = **nightdress.**
**nightingale** [ˈnaɪtɪŋgeɪl] *n* Nachtigall *f.*
**nightlife** [ˈnaɪtlaɪf] *n* Nachtleben *nt.*
**nightly** [ˈnaɪtlɪ] *adj* (all)nächtlich, Nacht-; *(every evening)* (all)abendlich, Abend- ♦ *adv* jede Nacht; *(every evening)* jeden Abend.

**nightmare** [ˈnaɪtmɛə*] *n* Alptraum *m.*
**night porter** *n* Nachtportier *m.*
**night safe** *n* Nachtsafe *m.*
**night school** *n* Abendschule *f.*
**nightshade** [ˈnaɪtʃeɪd] *n:* **deadly ~** Tollkirsche *f.*
**night shift** *n* Nachtschicht *f.*
**night-time** [ˈnaɪttaɪm] *n* Nacht *f.*
**night watchman** *n* Nachtwächter *m.*
**nihilism** [ˈnaɪɪlɪzəm] *n* Nihilismus *m.*
**nil** [nɪl] *n* Nichts *nt;* *(BRIT: SPORT)* Null *f.*
**Nile** [naɪl] *n:* **the ~** der Nil.
**nimble** [ˈnɪmbl] *adj* flink; *(mind)* beweglich.
**nine** [naɪn] *num* neun.
**nineteen** [ˈnaɪnˈtiːn] *num* neunzehn.
**nineteenth** [naɪnˈtiːnθ] *num* neunzehnte(r, s).
**ninety** [ˈnaɪntɪ] *num* neunzig.
**ninth** [naɪnθ] *num* neunte(r, s) ♦ *n* Neuntel *nt.*
**nip** [nɪp] *vt* zwicken ♦ *n* Biß *m;* *(drink)* Schlückchen *nt* ♦ *vi (BRIT: inf):* **to ~ out/down/up** kurz raus-/runter-/raufgehen; **to ~ into a shop** *(BRIT: inf)* kurz in einen Laden gehen.
**nipple** [ˈnɪpl] *n (ANAT)* Brustwarze *f.*
**nippy** [ˈnɪpɪ] *(BRIT) adj (quick: person)* flott; *(: car)* spritzig; *(cold)* frisch.
**nit** [nɪt] *n* Nisse *f;* *(inf: idiot)* Dummkopf *m.*
**nitpicking** [ˈnɪtpɪkɪŋ] *(inf) n* Kleinigkeitskrämerei *f.*
**nitrogen** [ˈnaɪtrədʒən] *n* Stickstoff *m.*
**nitroglycerin(e)** [ˈnaɪtrəʊˈglɪsəriːn] *n* Nitroglyzerin *nt.*
**nitty-gritty** [ˈnɪtɪˈgrɪtɪ] *(inf) n:* **to get down to the ~** zur Sache kommen.
**nitwit** [ˈnɪtwɪt] *(inf) n* Dummkopf *m.*
**NJ** *(US) abbr (POST: = New Jersey).*
**NLF** *n abbr (= National Liberation Front)* vietnamesische Befreiungsbewegung während des Vietnamkrieges.
**NLQ** *abbr (COMPUT, TYP: = near letter quality)* NLQ.
**NLRB** *(US) n abbr (= National Labor Relations Board)* Ausschuß zur Regelung der Beziehungen zwischen Arbeitgebern und Arbeitnehmern.
**NM, N.Mex.** *(US) abbr (POST: = New Mexico).*

━━━━━━━━━━━━━━━━━━━━━ *KEYWORD*

**no** [nəʊ] *(pl* **noes)** *adv (opposite of "yes")* nein; **~ thank you** nein danke
♦ *adj (not any)* kein(e); **I have ~ money/time/books** ich habe kein Geld/keine Zeit/keine Bücher; **"~ entry"** „kein Zutritt"; **"~ smoking"** „Rauchen verboten"
♦ *n* Nein *nt;* **there were 20 noes and one abstention** es gab 20 Neinstimmen und eine Enthaltung; **I won't take ~ for an answer** ich bestehe darauf.

**no.** *abbr (= number)* Nr.
**nobble** [ˈnɔbl] *(BRIT: inf) vt (bribe)* (sich *dat)* kaufen; *(grab)* sich *dat* schnappen; *(RACING:*

*horse, dog*) lahmlegen.

**Nobel Prize** [nəu'bɛl-] n Nobelpreis m.

**nobility** [nəu'bɪlɪtɪ] n Adel m; (*quality*) Edelmut m.

**noble** ['nəubl] adj edel, nobel; (*aristocratic*) ad(e)lig; (*impressive*) prächtig.

**nobleman** ['nəublmən] (*irreg: like* man) n Ad(e)lige(r) f(m).

**nobly** ['nəublɪ] adv edel.

**nobody** ['nəubədɪ] pron niemand, keiner ♦ n: he's a ~ er ist ein Niemand m.

**no-claims bonus** [nəu'kleɪmz-] n Schadenfreiheitsrabatt m.

**nocturnal** [nɔk'təːnl] adj nächtlich; (*animal*) Nacht-.

**nod** [nɔd] vi nicken; (*fig: flowers etc*) wippen ♦ vt: to ~ one's head mit dem Kopf nicken ♦ n Nicken nt; they ~ded their agreement sie nickten zustimmend.

▶**nod off** vi einnicken.

**no-fly zone** [nəu'flaɪ-] n Sperrzone f für den Flugverkehr.

**noise** [nɔɪz] n Geräusch nt; (*din*) Lärm m.

**noiseless** ['nɔɪzlɪs] adj geräuschlos.

**noisily** ['nɔɪzɪlɪ] adv laut.

**noisy** ['nɔɪzɪ] adj laut.

**nomad** ['nəumæd] n Nomade m, Nomadin f.

**nomadic** [nəu'mædɪk] adj Nomaden-, nomadisch.

**no-man's-land** ['nəumænzlænd] n Niemandsland nt.

**nominal** ['nɔmɪnl] adj nominell.

**nominate** ['nɔmɪneɪt] vt nominieren; (*appoint*) ernennen.

**nomination** [nɔmɪ'neɪʃən] n Nominierung f; (*appointment*) Ernennung f.

**nominee** [nɔmɪ'niː] n Kandidat(in) m(f).

**non-** [nɔn] pref nicht-, Nicht-.

**non-alcoholic** [nɔnælkə'hɔlɪk] adj alkoholfrei.

**non-aligned** [nɔnə'laɪnd] adj blockfrei.

**non-breakable** [nɔn'breɪkəbl] adj unzerbrechlich.

**nonce word** ['nɔns-] n Ad-hoc-Bildung f.

**nonchalant** ['nɔnʃələnt] adj lässig, nonchalant.

**noncommissioned officer** [nɔnkə'mɪʃənd-] n Unteroffizier m.

**non-committal** [nɔnkə'mɪtl] adj zurückhaltend; (*answer*) unverbindlich.

**nonconformist** [nɔnkən'fɔːmɪst] n Nonkonformist(in) m(f) ♦ adj nonkonformistisch.

**non-cooperation** ['nɔnkəuɔpə'reɪʃən] n unkooperative Haltung f.

**nondescript** ['nɔndɪskrɪpt] adj unauffällig; (*colour*) unbestimmbar.

**none** [nʌn] pron (*not one*) kein(e, er, es); (*not any*) nichts; ~ of us keiner von uns; I've ~ left (*not any*) ich habe nichts übrig; (*not one*) ich habe kein(e, en, es) übrig; ~ at all (*not any*) überhaupt nicht; (*not one*) überhaupt kein(e, er, es); I was ~ the wiser

ich war auch nicht klüger; **she would have ~ of it** sie wollte nichts davon hören; **it was ~ other than X** es war kein anderer als X.

**nonentity** [nɔ'nɛntɪtɪ] n (*person*) Nichts nt, unbedeutende Figur f.

**non-essential** [nɔnɪ'sɛnʃl] adj unnötig ♦ n: ~s nicht (lebens)notwendige Dinge pl.

**nonetheless** ['nʌnðə'lɛs] adv nichtsdestoweniger, trotzdem.

**nonevent** [nɔnɪ'vɛnt] n Reinfall m.

**non-existent** [nɔnɪg'zɪstənt] adj nicht vorhanden.

**non-fiction** [nɔn'fɪkʃən] n Sachbücher pl ♦ adj (*book*) Sach-; (*prize*) Sachbuch-.

**non-flammable** [nɔn'flæməbl] adj nicht entzündbar.

**non-intervention** ['nɔnɪntə'vɛnʃən] n Nichteinmischung f, Nichteingreifen nt.

**no-no** ['nəunəu] n: it's a ~ (*inf*) das kommt nicht in Frage.

**non obst.** abbr (= *non obstante*) dennoch.

**no-nonsense** [nəu'nɔnsəns] adj (*approach, look*) nüchtern.

**non-payment** [nɔn'peɪmənt] n Nichtzahlung f, Zahlungsverweigerung f.

**nonplussed** [nɔn'plʌst] adj verdutzt, verblüfft.

**non-profit making** ['nɔn'prɔfɪt-] adj (*organization*) gemeinnützig.

**nonreturnable** [nɔnrə'təːnəbl] adj: ~ bottle Einwegflasche f.

**nonsense** ['nɔnsəns] n Unsinn m; ~! Unsinn!, Quatsch!; it is ~ to say that ... es ist dummes Gerede, zu sagen, daß ...; to make (a) ~ of sth etw ad absurdum führen.

**nonsensical** [nɔn'sɛnsɪkl] adj (*idea, action etc*) unsinnig.

**non-shrink** [nɔn'ʃrɪŋk] (*BRIT*) adj nicht einlaufend.

**non-smoker** ['nɔn'sməukəʳ] n Nichtraucher(in) m(f).

**nonstarter** [nɔn'staːtəʳ] n (*fig*): it's a ~ (*idea etc*) es hat keine Erfolgschance.

**non-stick** ['nɔn'stɪk] adj kunststoffbeschichtet, Teflon- ®.

**non-stop** ['nɔn'stɔp] adj ununterbrochen; (*flight*) Nonstop- ♦ adv ununterbrochen; (*fly*) nonstop.

**non-taxable** [nɔn'tæksəbl] adj nichtsteuerpflichtig.

**non-U** [nɔn'juː] (*BRIT: inf*) adj abbr (= *non-upper class*) nicht vornehm.

**non-white** ['nɔn'waɪt] adj farbig ♦ n Farbige(r) f(m).

**noodles** ['nuːdlz] npl Nudeln pl.

**nook** [nuk] n: every ~ and cranny jeder Winkel.

**noon** [nuːn] n Mittag m.

**no-one** ['nəuwʌn] pron = **nobody**.

**noose** [nuːs] n Schlinge f.

**nor** [nɔːʳ] conj, adv = **neither**.

**Norf** (*BRIT*) abbr (*POST*: = Norfolk).

**norm** [nɔːm] *n* Norm *f*.

**normal** ['nɔːml] *adj* normal ♦ *n*: **to return to** ~ sich wieder normalisieren.

**normality** [nɔː'mælɪtɪ] *n* Normalität *f*.

**normally** ['nɔːməlɪ] *adv* normalerweise; (*act, behave*) normal.

**Normandy** ['nɔːməndɪ] *n* Normandie *f*.

**north** [nɔːθ] *n* Norden *m* ♦ *adj* nördlich, Nord- ♦ *adv* nach Norden; ~ **of** nördlich von.

**North Africa** *n* Nordafrika *nt*.

**North African** *adj* nordafrikanisch ♦ *n* Nordafrikaner(in) *m(f)*.

**North America** *n* Nordamerika *nt*.

**North American** *adj* nordamerikanisch ♦ *n* Nordamerikaner(in) *m(f)*.

**Northants** [nɔː'θænts] (*BRIT*) *abbr* (*POST*: = *Northamptonshire*).

**northbound** ['nɔːθbaund] *adj* in Richtung Norden; (*carriageway*) nach Norden (führend).

**Northd** (*BRIT*) *abbr* (*POST*: = *Northumberland*).

**north-east** [nɔːθ'iːst] *n* Nordosten *m* ♦ *adj* nordöstlich, Nordost- ♦ *adv* nach Nordosten; ~ **of** nordöstlich von.

**northerly** ['nɔːðəlɪ] *adj* nördlich.

**northern** ['nɔːðən] *adj* nördlich, Nord-.

**Northern Ireland** *n* Nordirland *nt*.

**North Korea** *n* Nordkorea *nt*.

**North Pole** *n*: **the** ~ der Nordpol.

**North Sea** *n*: **the** ~ die Nordsee *f*.

**North Sea oil** *n* Nordseeöl *nt*.

**northward(s)** ['nɔːθwəd(z)] *adv* nach Norden, nordwärts.

**north-west** [nɔːθ'west] *n* Nordwesten *m* ♦ *adj* nordwestlich, Nordwest- ♦ *adv* nach Nordwesten; ~ **of** nordwestlich von.

**Norway** ['nɔːweɪ] *n* Norwegen *nt*.

**Norwegian** [nɔː'wiːdʒən] *adj* norwegisch ♦ *n* Norweger(in) *m(f)*; (*LING*) Norwegisch *nt*.

**nos.** *abbr* (= *numbers*) Nrn.

**nose** [nəuz] *n* Nase *f*; (*of car*) Schnauze *f* ♦ *vi* (*also*: ~ **one's way**) sich schieben; **to follow one's** ~ immer der Nase nach gehen; **to get up one's** ~ (*inf*) auf die Nerven gehen +*dat*; **to have a (good)** ~ **for sth** eine (gute) Nase für etw haben; **to keep one's** ~ **clean** (*inf*) eine saubere Weste behalten; **to look down one's** ~ **at sb/sth** (*inf*) auf jdn/etw herabsehen; **to pay through the** ~ **(for sth)** (*inf*) (für etw) viel blechen; **to rub sb's** ~ **in sth** (*inf*) jdm etw unter die Nase reiben; **to turn one's** ~ **up at sth** (*inf*) die Nase über etw *acc* rümpfen; **under sb's** ~ vor jds Augen.
▶**nose about** *vi* herumschnüffeln.
▶**nose around** *vi* = **nose about**.

**nosebleed** ['nəuzbliːd] *n* Nasenbluten *nt*.

**nose-dive** ['nəuzdaɪv] *n* (*of plane*) Sturzflug *m* ♦ *vi* (*plane*) im Sturzflug herabgehen.

**nose drops** *npl* Nasentropfen *pl*.

**nosey** ['nəuzɪ] (*inf*) *adj* = **nosy**.

**nostalgia** [nɔs'tældʒɪə] *n* Nostalgie *f*.

**nostalgic** [nɔs'tældʒɪk] *adj* nostalgisch.

**nostril** ['nɔstrɪl] *n* Nasenloch *nt*; (*of animal*) Nüster *f*.

**nosy** ['nəuzɪ] (*inf*) *adj* neugierig.

=========== *KEYWORD*

**not** [nɔt] *adv* nicht; **he is** ~ *or* **isn't here** er ist nicht hier; **you must** ~ *or* **you mustn't do that** das darfst du nicht tun; **it's too late, isn't it?** es ist zu spät, nicht wahr?; ~ **that I don't like him** nicht, daß ich ihn nicht mag; ~ **yet** noch nicht; ~ **now** nicht jetzt; *see also* **all, only**.

**notable** ['nəutəbl] *adj* bemerkenswert.

**notably** ['nəutəblɪ] *adv* hauptsächlich; (*markedly*) bemerkenswert.

**notary** ['nəutərɪ] *n* (*also*: ~ **public**) Notar(in) *m(f)*.

**notation** [nəu'teɪʃən] *n* Notation *f*; (*MUS*) Notenschrift *f*.

**notch** [nɔtʃ] *n* Kerbe *f*; (*in blade, saw*) Scharte *f*; (*fig*) Klasse *f*.
▶**notch up** *vt* erzielen; (*victory*) erringen.

**note** [nəut] *n* Notiz *f*; (*of lecturer*) Manuskript *nt*; (*of student etc*) Aufzeichnung *f*; (*in book etc*) Anmerkung *f*; (*letter*) paar Zeilen *pl*; (*banknote*) Note *f*, Schein *m*; (*MUS: sound*) Ton *m*; (: *symbol*) Note *f*; (*tone*) Ton *m*, Klang *m* ♦ *vt* beachten; (*point out*) anmerken; (*also*: ~ **down**) notieren; **of** ~ bedeutend; **to make a** ~ **of sth** sich *dat* etw notieren; **to take** ~**s** Notizen machen, mitschreiben; **to take** ~ **of sth** etw zur Kenntnis nehmen.

**notebook** ['nəutbuk] *n* Notizbuch *nt*; (*for shorthand*) Stenoblock *m*.

**notecase** ['nəutkeɪs] (*BRIT*) *n* Brieftasche *f*.

**noted** ['nəutɪd] *adj* bekannt.

**notepad** ['nəutpæd] *n* Notizblock *m*.

**notepaper** ['nəutpeɪpə'] *n* Briefpapier *nt*.

**noteworthy** ['nəutwəːðɪ] *adj* beachtenswert.

**nothing** ['nʌθɪŋ] *n* nichts; ~ **new/worse** *etc* nichts Neues/Schlimmeres *etc*; ~ **much** nicht viel; ~ **else** sonst nichts; **for** ~ umsonst; ~ **at all** überhaupt nichts.

**notice** ['nəutɪs] *n* Bekanntmachung *f*; (*sign*) Schild *nt*; (*warning*) Ankündigung *f*; (*dismissal*) Kündigung *f*; (*BRIT: review*) Kritik *f*, Rezension *f* ♦ *vt* bemerken; **to bring sth to sb's** ~ jdn auf etw *acc* aufmerksam machen; **to take no** ~ **of** ignorieren, nicht beachten; **to escape sb's** ~ jdm entgehen; **it has come to my** ~ **that ...** es ist mir zu Ohren gekommen, daß ...; **to give sb** ~ **of sth** jdm von etw Bescheid geben; **without** ~ ohne Ankündigung; **advance** ~ Vorankündigung *f*; **at short/a moment's** ~ kurzfristig/ innerhalb kürzester Zeit; **until further** ~ bis auf weiteres; **to hand in one's** ~ kündigen; **to be given one's** ~ gekündigt werden +*dat*.

**noticeable** ['nəutɪsəbl] *adj* deutlich.

**noticeboard** ['nəutɪsbɔːd] (*BRIT*) *n*

Anschlagbrett *nt.*
**notification** [nəutɪfɪ'keɪʃən] *n*
Benachrichtigung *f.*
**notify** ['nəutɪfaɪ] *vt:* **to ~ sb (of sth)** jdn (von etw) benachrichtigen.
**notion** ['nəuʃən] *n* Vorstellung *f;* **notions** (*US*) *npl* (*haberdashery*) Kurzwaren *pl.*
**notoriety** [nəutə'raɪətɪ] *n* traurige Berühmtheit *f.*
**notorious** [nəu'tɔːrɪəs] *adj* berüchtigt.
**notoriously** [nəu'tɔːrɪəslɪ] *adv* notorisch.
**Notts** [nɔts] (*BRIT*) *abbr* (*POST:* = *Nottinghamshire*).
**notwithstanding** [nɔtwɪθ'stændɪŋ] *adv* trotzdem ♦ *prep* trotz +*dat.*
**nougat** ['nuːgɑː] *n* Nougat *m.*
**nought** [nɔːt] *n* Null *f.*
**noun** [naun] *n* Hauptwort *nt,* Substantiv *nt.*
**nourish** ['nʌrɪʃ] *vt* nähren.
**nourishing** ['nʌrɪʃɪŋ] *adj* nahrhaft.
**nourishment** ['nʌrɪʃmənt] *n* Nahrung *f.*
**Nov.** *abbr* (= *November*) Nov.
**Nova Scotia** ['nəuvə'skəuʃə] *n* Neuschottland *nt.*
**novel** ['nɔvl] *n* Roman *m* ♦ *adj* neu(artig).
**novelist** ['nɔvəlɪst] *n* Romanschriftsteller(in) *m(f).*
**novelty** ['nɔvəltɪ] *n* Neuheit *f;* (*object*) Kleinigkeit *f.*
**November** [nəu'vɛmbə*] *n* November *m; see also* **July.**
**novice** ['nɔvɪs] *n* Neuling *m,* Anfänger(in) *m(f);* (*REL*) Novize *m,* Novizin *f.*
**NOW** [nau] (*US*) *n abbr* (= *National Organization for Women*) Frauenvereinigung.
**now** [nau] *adv* jetzt; (*these days*) heute ♦ *conj:* **~ (that)** jetzt, wo; **right ~** gleich, sofort; **by ~** inzwischen, mittlerweile; **that's the fashion just ~** das ist gerade modern; **I saw her just ~** ich habe sie gerade gesehen; **(every) ~ and then, (every) ~ and again** ab und zu, gelegentlich; **from ~ on** von nun an; **in 3 days from ~** (heute) in 3 Tagen; **between ~ and Monday** bis Montag; **that's all for ~** das ist erst einmal alles; **any day ~** jederzeit; **~ then** also.
**nowadays** ['nauədeɪz] *adv* heute.
**nowhere** ['nəuwɛə*] *adv* (*be*) nirgends, nirgendwo; (*go*) nirgendwohin; **~ else** nirgendwo anders.
**no-win situation** [nəu'wɪn-] *n* aussichtslose Lage *f.*
**noxious** ['nɔkʃəs] *adj* (*gas, fumes*) schädlich; (*smell*) übel.
**nozzle** ['nɔzl] *n* Düse *f.*
**NP** *n abbr* (*LAW*) = **notary public.**
**NS** (*CANADA*) *abbr* (= *Nova Scotia*).
**NSC** (*US*) *n abbr* = **National Security Council.**
**NSF** (*US*) *n abbr* (= *National Science Foundation*) Organisation zur Förderung der Wissenschaft.
**NSPCC** (*BRIT*) *n abbr* (= *National Society for the Prevention of Cruelty to Children*) Kinderschutzbund *m.*

**NSW** (*AUSTRALIA*) *abbr* (*POST:* = *New South Wales*).
**NT** *n abbr* (*BIBLE:* = *New Testament*) NT.
**nth** [ɛnθ] (*inf*) *adj:* **to the ~ degree** in der n-ten Potenz.
**nuance** ['njuːɑːns] *n* Nuance *f.*
**nubile** ['njuːbaɪl] *adj* gut entwickelt.
**nuclear** ['njuːklɪə*] *adj* (*bomb, industry etc*) Atom-; **~ physics** Kernphysik *f;* **~ war** Atomkrieg *m.*
**nuclear disarmament** *n* nukleare *or* atomare Abrüstung *f.*
**nuclear family** *n* Kleinfamilie *f,* Kernfamilie *f.*
**nuclear-free zone** ['njuːklɪə'friː-] *n* atomwaffenfreie Zone *f.*
**nuclei** ['njuːklɪaɪ] *npl of* **nucleus.**
**nucleus** ['njuːklɪəs] (*pl* **nuclei**) *n* Kern *m.*
**NUCPS** (*BRIT*) *n abbr* (= *National Union of Civil and Public Servants*) Gewerkschaft für Beschäftigte im öffentlichen Dienst.
**nude** [njuːd] *adj* nackt ♦ *n* (*ART*) Akt *m;* **in the ~** nackt.
**nudge** [nʌdʒ] *vt* anstoßen.
**nudist** ['njuːdɪst] *n* Nudist(in) *m(f).*
**nudist colony** *n* FKK-Kolonie *f.*
**nudity** ['njuːdɪtɪ] *n* Nacktheit *f.*
**nugget** ['nʌgɪt] *n* (*of gold*) Klumpen *m;* (*fig: of information*) Brocken *m.*
**nuisance** ['njuːsns] *n:* **to be a ~** lästig sein; (*situation*) ärgerlich sein; **he's a ~** er geht einem auf die Nerven; **what a ~!** wie ärgerlich/lästig!
**NUJ** (*BRIT*) *n abbr* (= *National Union of Journalists*) Journalistengewerkschaft.
**null** [nʌl] *adj:* **~ and void** null und nichtig.
**nullify** ['nʌlɪfaɪ] *vt* zunichte machen; (*claim, law*) für null und nichtig erklären.
**NUM** (*BRIT*) *n abbr* (= *National Union of Mineworkers*) Bergarbeitergewerkschaft.
**numb** [nʌm] *adj* taub, gefühllos; (*fig: with fear etc*) wie betäubt ♦ *vt* taub *or* gefühllos machen; (*pain, fig: mind*) betäuben.
**number** ['nʌmbə*] *n* Zahl *f;* (*quantity*) (An)zahl *f;* (*of house, bank account, bus etc*) Nummer *f* ♦ *vt* (*pages etc*) numerieren; (*amount to*) zählen; **a ~ of** einige; **any ~ of** beliebig viele; (*reasons*) alle möglichen; **wrong ~** (*TEL*) falsch verbunden; **to be ~ed among** zählen zu.
**number plate** (*BRIT*) *n* (*AUT*) Nummernschild *nt.*
**Number Ten** (*BRIT*) *n* (*POL:* = *10 Downing Street*) Nummer zehn *f* (Downing Street).
**numbness** ['nʌmnɪs] *n* Taubheit *f,* Starre *f;* (*fig*) Benommenheit *f,* Betäubung *f.*
**numbskull** ['nʌmskʌl] *n* = **numskull.**
**numeral** ['njuːmərəl] *n* Ziffer *f.*
**numerate** ['njuːmərɪt] (*BRIT*) *adj:* **to be ~** rechnen können.

**numerical** [nju:'mɛrɪkl] *adj* numerisch.
**numerous** ['nju:mərəs] *adj* zahlreich.
**numskull** ['nʌmskʌl] (*inf*) *n* Holzkopf *m*.
**nun** [nʌn] *n* Nonne *f*.
**nunnery** ['nʌnərɪ] *n* (Nonnen)kloster *nt*.
**nuptial** ['nʌpʃəl] *adj* (*feast, celebration*)
Hochzeits-; ~ **bliss** Eheglück *nt*.
**nurse** [nə:s] *n* Krankenschwester *f*; (*also:*
~**maid**) Kindermädchen *nt* ♦ *vt* pflegen;
(*cold, toothache etc*) auskurieren; (*baby*)
stillen; (*fig: desire, grudge*) hegen.
**nursery** ['nə:sərɪ] *n* Kindergarten *m*; (*room*)
Kinderzimmer *nt*; (*for plants*) Gärtnerei *f*.
**nursery rhyme** *n* Kinderreim *m*.
**nursery school** *n* Kindergarten *m*.
**nursery slope** (*BRIT*) *n* (*SKI*) Anfängerhügel
*m*.
**nursing** ['nə:sɪŋ] *n* Krankenpflege *f*; (*care*)
Pflege *f*.
**nursing home** *n* Pflegeheim *nt*.
**nursing mother** *n* stillende Mutter *f*.
**nurture** ['nə:tʃə*] *vt* hegen und pflegen; (*fig:
ideas, creativity*) fördern.
**NUS** (*BRIT*) *n abbr* (= *National Union of
Students*) *Studentengewerkschaft*.
**NUT** (*BRIT*) *n abbr* (= *National Union of
Teachers*) *Lehrergewerkschaft*.
**nut** [nʌt] *n* (*TECH*) (Schrauben)mutter *f*; (*BOT*)
Nuß *f*; (*inf: lunatic*) Spinner(in) *m(f)*.
**nutcase** ['nʌtkeɪs] (*inf*) *n* Spinner(in) *m(f)*.
**nutcrackers** ['nʌtkrækəz] *npl* Nußknacker *m*.
**nutmeg** ['nʌtmɛg] *n* Muskat *m*, Muskatnuß *f*.
**nutrient** ['nju:trɪənt] *n* Nährstoff *m*.
**nutrition** [nju:'trɪʃən] *n* Ernährung *f*;
(*nourishment*) Nahrung *f*.
**nutritionist** [nju:'trɪʃənɪst] *n*
Ernährungswissenschaftler(in) *m(f)*.
**nutritious** [nju:'trɪʃəs] *adj* nahrhaft.
**nuts** [nʌts] (*inf*) *adj* verrückt; **he's** ~ er spinnt.
**nutshell** ['nʌtʃɛl] *n* Nußschale *f*; **in a** ~ (*fig*)
kurz gesagt.
**nutty** ['nʌtɪ] *adj* (*flavour*) Nuß-; (*inf: idea etc*)
bekloppt.
**nuzzle** ['nʌzl] *vi:* **to** ~ **up** to sich drücken *or*
schmiegen an +*acc*.
**NV** (*US*) *abbr* (*POST*: = *Nevada*).
**NW** *abbr* = **north-west**.
**NWT** (*CANADA*) *abbr* (= *Northwest Territories*).
**NY** (*US*) *abbr* (*POST*: = *New York*).
**NYC** (*US*) *abbr* (*POST*: = *New York City*).
**nylon** ['naɪlɒn] *n* Nylon *nt* ♦ *adj* Nylon-; **nylons**
*npl* (*stockings*) Nylonstrümpfe *pl*.
**nymph** [nɪmf] *n* Nymphe *f*.
**nymphomaniac** ['nɪmfəʊ'meɪnɪæk] *n*
Nymphomanin *f*.
**NYSE** (*US*) *n abbr* (= *New York Stock Exchange*)
*New Yorker Börse*.
**NZ** *abbr* = **New Zealand**.

# $O, o$

**O, o** [əu] *n* (*letter*) O *nt*, o *nt*; (*US: SCOL:
outstanding*) ≈ Eins *f*; (*TEL etc*) Null *f*; ~ **for
Olive**, (*US*) ~ **for Oboe** ≈ O wie Otto.
**oaf** [əuf] *n* Trottel *m*.
**oak** [əuk] *n* (*tree, wood*) Eiche *f* ♦ *adj* (*furniture,
door*) Eichen-.
**O & M** *n abbr* (= *organization and method*)
Organisation und Arbeitsweise *pl*.
**OAP** (*BRIT*) *n abbr* = **old age pensioner**.
**oar** [ɔ:*] *n* Ruder *nt*; **to put** *or* **shove one's** ~ **in**
(*inf, fig*) mitmischen, sich einmischen.
**oarsman** ['ɔ:zmən] (*irreg: like* **man**) *n* Ruderer
*m*.
**oarswoman** ['ɔ:zwumən] (*irreg: like* **woman**) *n*
Ruderin *f*.
**OAS** *n abbr* (= *Organization of American States*)
OAS *f*.
**oasis** [əu'eɪsɪs] (*pl* **oases**) *n* (*lit, fig*) Oase *f*.
**oath** [əuθ] *n* (*promise*) Eid *m*, Schwur *m*; (*swear
word*) Fluch *m*; **on** (*BRIT*) *or* **under** ~ unter
Eid; **to take the** ~ (*LAW*) vereidigt werden.
**oatmeal** ['əutmi:l] *n* Haferschrot *m*; (*colour*)
Hellbeige *nt*.
**oats** [əuts] *npl* Hafer *m*; **he's getting his** ~
(*BRIT: inf, fig*) er kommt im Bett auf seine
Kosten.
**OAU** *n abbr* (= *Organization of African Unity*)
OAU *f*.
**obdurate** ['ɔbdjurɪt] *adj* unnachgiebig.
**OBE** (*BRIT*) *n abbr* (= *Officer of the order of) the
British Empire*) britischer Ordenstitel.
**obedience** [ə'bi:dɪəns] *n* Gehorsam *m*; **in** ~ **to**
gemäß +*dat*.
**obedient** [ə'bi:dɪənt] *adj* gehorsam; **to be** ~ **to
sb** jdm gehorchen.
**obelisk** ['ɔbɪlɪsk] *n* Obelisk *m*.
**obese** [əu'bi:s] *adj* fettleibig.
**obesity** [əu'bi:sɪtɪ] *n* Fettleibigkeit *f*.
**obey** [ə'beɪ] *vt* (*person*) gehorchen +*dat*, folgen
+*dat*; (*orders, law*) befolgen ♦ *vi* gehorchen.
**obituary** [ə'bɪtjuərɪ] *n* Nachruf *m*.
**object** [*n* 'ɔbdʒɪkt, *vi* əb'dʒɛkt] *n* (*also* LING)
Objekt *nt*; (*aim, purpose*) Ziel *nt*, Zweck *m* ♦ *vi*
dagegen sein; **to be an** ~ **of ridicule** (*person*)
sich lächerlich machen; (*thing*) lächerlich
wirken; **money is no** ~ Geld spielt keine
Rolle; **he** ~**ed that** ... er wandte ein, daß ...;
~**!** ich protestiere!; **do you** ~ **to my
smoking?** haben Sie etwas dagegen, wenn
ich rauche?
**objection** [əb'dʒɛkʃən] *n* (*argument*) Einwand
*m*; **I have no** ~ **to** ... ich habe nichts

dagegen, daß ...; **if you have no** ~ wenn Sie nichts dagegen haben; **to raise** or **voice an** ~ einen Einwand or vorbringen.

**objectionable** [əb'dʒɛkʃənəbl] adj (language, conduct) anstößig; (person) unausstehlich.

**objective** [əb'dʒɛktɪv] adj objektiv ♦ n Ziel nt.

**objectively** [əb'dʒɛktɪvlɪ] adv objektiv.

**objectivity** [ɔbdʒɪk'tɪvɪtɪ] n Objektivität f.

**object lesson** n: **an** ~ **in** ein Paradebeispiel nt für.

**objector** [əb'dʒɛktə*] n Gegner(in) m(f).

**obligation** [ɔblɪ'geɪʃən] n Pflicht f; **to be under an** ~ **to do sth** verpflichtet sein, etw zu tun; **to be under an** ~ **to sb** jdm verpflichtet sein; "**no** ~ **to buy**" (COMM) „kein Kaufzwang".

**obligatory** [ə'blɪgətərɪ] adj obligatorisch.

**oblige** [ə'blaɪdʒ] vt (compel) zwingen; (do a favour for) einen Gefallen tun +dat; **I felt** ~**d to invite him in** ich fühlte mich verpflichtet, ihn hereinzubitten; **to be** ~**d to sb for sth** (grateful) jdm für etw dankbar sein; **anything to** ~! (inf) stets zu Diensten!

**obliging** [ə'blaɪdʒɪŋ] adj entgegenkommend.

**oblique** [ə'bliːk] adj (line, angle) schief; (reference, compliment) indirekt, versteckt ♦ n (BRIT: also: ~ **stroke**) Schrägstrich m.

**obliterate** [ə'blɪtəreɪt] vt (village etc) vernichten; (fig: memory, error) auslöschen.

**oblivion** [ə'blɪvɪən] n (unconsciousness) Bewußtlosigkeit f; (being forgotten) Vergessenheit f; **to sink into** ~ (event etc) in Vergessenheit geraten.

**oblivious** [ə'blɪvɪəs] adj: **he was** ~ **of** or **to it** er war sich dessen nicht bewußt.

**oblong** ['ɔblɔŋ] adj rechteckig ♦ n Rechteck nt.

**obnoxious** [əb'nɔkʃəs] adj widerwärtig, widerlich.

**o.b.o.** (US) abbr (in classified ads: = or best offer) bzw. Höchstgebot.

**oboe** ['əubəu] n Oboe f.

**obscene** [əb'siːn] adj obszön; (fig: wealth) unanständig; (income etc) unverschämt.

**obscenity** [əb'sɛnɪtɪ] n Obszönität f.

**obscure** [əb'skjuə*] adj (little known) unbekannt, obskur; (difficult to understand) unklar ♦ vt (obstruct, conceal) verdecken.

**obscurity** [əb'skjuərɪtɪ] n (of person, book) Unbekanntheit f; (of remark etc) Unklarheit f.

**obsequious** [əb'siːkwɪəs] adj unterwürfig.

**observable** [əb'zəːvəbl] adj wahrnehmbar; (noticeable) erkennbar.

**observance** [əb'zəːvns] n (of law etc) Befolgung f; **religious** ~**s** religiöse Feste pl.

**observant** [əb'zəːvənt] adj aufmerksam.

**observation** [ɔbzə'veɪʃən] n (remark) Bemerkung f; (act of observing, MED) Beobachtung f; **she's in hospital under** ~ sie ist zur Beobachtung im Krankenhaus.

**observation post** n Beobachtungsposten m.

**observatory** [əb'zəːvətrɪ] n Observatorium nt.

**observe** [əb'zəːv] vt (watch) beobachten;

(notice, comment) bemerken; (abide by: rule etc) einhalten.

**observer** [əb'zəːvə*] n Beobachter(in) m(f).

**obsess** [əb'sɛs] vt verfolgen; **to be** ~**ed by** or **with sb/sth** von jdm/etw besessen sein.

**obsession** [əb'sɛʃən] n Besessenheit f.

**obsessive** [əb'sɛsɪv] adj (person) zwanghaft; (interest, hatred, tidiness) krankhaft; **to be** ~ **about cleaning/tidying up** einen Putz-/Ordnungsfimmel haben (inf).

**obsolescence** [ɔbsə'lɛsns] n Veralten nt; **built-in** or **planned** ~ (COMM) geplanter Verschleiß m.

**obsolete** ['ɔbsəliːt] adj veraltet.

**obstacle** ['ɔbstəkl] n (lit, fig) Hindernis nt.

**obstacle race** n Hindernisrennen nt.

**obstetrician** [ɔbstə'trɪʃən] n Geburtshelfer(in) m(f).

**obstetrics** [ɔb'stɛtrɪks] n Geburtshilfe f.

**obstinacy** ['ɔbstɪnəsɪ] n (of person) Starrsinn m.

**obstinate** ['ɔbstɪnɪt] adj (person) starrsinnig, stur; (refusal, cough etc) hartnäckig.

**obstruct** [əb'strʌkt] vt (road, path) blockieren; (traffic, fig) behindern.

**obstruction** [əb'strʌkʃən] n (object) Hindernis nt; (of plan, law) Behinderung f.

**obstructive** [əb'strʌktɪv] adj hinderlich, obstruktiv (esp POL); **she's being** ~ sie macht Schwierigkeiten.

**obtain** [əb'teɪn] vt erhalten, bekommen ♦ vi (form: exist, be the case) gelten.

**obtainable** [əb'teɪnəbl] adj erhältlich.

**obtrusive** [əb'truːsɪv] adj aufdringlich; (conspicuous) auffällig.

**obtuse** [əb'tjuːs] adj (person, remark) einfältig; (MATH) stumpf.

**obverse** ['ɔbvəːs] n (of situation, argument) Kehrseite f.

**obviate** ['ɔbvɪeɪt] vt (need, problem etc) vorbeugen +dat.

**obvious** ['ɔbvɪəs] adj offensichtlich; (lie) klar; (predictable) naheliegend.

**obviously** ['ɔbvɪəslɪ] adv (clearly) offensichtlich; (of course) natürlich; ~! selbstverständlich!; ~ **not** offensichtlich nicht; **he was** ~ **not drunk** er war natürlich nicht betrunken; **he was not** ~ **drunk** offenbar war er nicht betrunken.

**OCAS** n abbr (= Organization of Central American States) mittelamerikanischer Staatenbund.

**occasion** [ə'keɪʒən] n Gelegenheit f; (celebration etc) Ereignis nt ♦ vt (form: cause) verursachen; **on** ~ (sometimes) gelegentlich; **on that** ~ bei der Gelegenheit; **to rise to the** ~ sich der Lage gewachsen zeigen.

**occasional** [ə'keɪʒənl] adj gelegentlich; **he likes the** ~ **cigar** er raucht gelegentlich gern eine Zigarre.

**occasionally** [ə'keɪʒənəlɪ] adv gelegentlich;

**very** ~ sehr selten.
**occasional table** *n* Beistelltisch *m*.
**occult** [ɔ'kʌlt] *n*: **the** ~ der Okkultismus ♦ *adj* okkult.
**occupancy** ['ɔkjupənsɪ] *n* (*of room etc*) Bewohnen *nt*.
**occupant** ['ɔkjupənt] *n* (*of house etc*) Bewohner(in) *m(f)*; (*temporary: of car*) Insasse *m*, Insassin *f*; **the** ~ **of this table/ office** derjenige, der an diesem Tisch sitzt/ in diesem Büro arbeitet.
**occupation** [ɔkju'peɪʃən] *n* (*job*) Beruf *m*; (*pastime*) Beschäftigung *f*; (*of building, country etc*) Besetzung *f*.
**occupational guidance** [ɔkʊ'peɪʃənl-] (*BRIT*) *n* Berufsberatung *f*.
**occupational hazard** *n* Berufsrisiko *nt*.
**occupational pension scheme** *n* betriebliche Altersversorgung *f*.
**occupational therapy** *n* Beschäftigungs-therapie *f*.
**occupier** ['ɔkjupaɪə*] *n* Bewohner(in) *m(f)*.
**occupy** ['ɔkjupaɪ] *vt* (*house, office*) bewohnen; (*place etc*) belegen; (*building, country etc*) besetzen; (*time, attention*) beanspruchen; (*position, space*) einnehmen; **to** ~ **o.s. (in** *or* **with sth)** sich (mit etw) beschäftigen; **to** ~ **o.s. in** *or* **with doing sth** sich damit beschäftigen, etw zu tun; **to be occupied in** *or* **with sth** mit etw beschäftigt sein; **to be occupied in** *or* **with doing sth** damit beschäftigt sein, etw zu tun.
**occur** [ə'kə:*] *vi* (*take place*) geschehen, sich ereignen; (*exist*) vorkommen; **to** ~ **to sb** jdm einfallen.
**occurrence** [ə'kʌrəns] *n* (*event*) Ereignis *nt*; (*incidence*) Auftreten *nt*.
**ocean** ['əuʃən] *n* Ozean *m*, Meer *nt*; ~**s of** (*inf*) jede Menge.
**ocean bed** *n* Meeresgrund *m*.
**ocean-going** ['əuʃəngəuɪŋ] *adj* (*ship, vessel*) Hochsee-.
**Oceania** [əuʃɪ'eɪnɪə] *n* Ozeanien *nt*.
**ocean liner** *n* Ozeandampfer *m*.
**ochre**, (*US*) **ocher** ['əukə*] *adj* ockerfar-ben.
**o'clock** [ə'klɔk] *adv*: **it is 5** ~ es ist 5 Uhr.
**OCR** *n abbr* (*COMPUT*) = **optical character reader**; **optical character recogniton**.
**Oct.** *abbr* (= *October*) Okt.
**octagonal** [ɔk'tægənl] *adj* achteckig.
**octane** ['ɔkteɪn] *n* Oktan *nt*; **high-**~ **petrol** *or* (*US*) **gas** Benzin *nt* mit hoher Oktan-zahl.
**octave** ['ɔktɪv] *n* Oktave *f*.
**October** [ɔk'təubə*] *n* Oktober *m*; *see also* **July**.
**octogenarian** ['ɔktəudʒɪ'nɛərɪən] *n* Achtzigjährige(r) *f(m)*.
**octopus** ['ɔktəpəs] *n* Tintenfisch *m*.
**odd** [ɔd] *adj* (*person*) sonderbar, komisch; (*behaviour, shape*) seltsam; (*number*)

ungerade; (*sock, shoe etc*) einzeln; (*occasional*) gelegentlich; **60-**~ etwa 60; **at** ~ **times** ab und zu; **to be the** ~ **one out** der Außenseiter/die Außenseiterin sein; **add meat or the** ~ **vegetable to the soup** fügen Sie der Suppe Fleisch oder auch etwas Gemüse bei.
**oddball** ['ɔdbɔ:l] (*inf*) *n* komischer Kauz *m*.
**oddity** ['ɔdɪtɪ] *n* (*person*) Sonderling *m*; (*thing*) Merkwürdigkeit *f*.
**odd-job man** [ɔd'dʒɔb-] *n* Mädchen *nt* für alles.
**odd jobs** *npl* Gelegenheitsarbeiten *pl*.
**oddly** ['ɔdlɪ] *adv* (*behave, dress*) seltsam; *see also* **enough**.
**oddments** ['ɔdmənts] *npl* (*COMM*) Restposten *m*.
**odds** [ɔdz] *npl* (*in betting*) Gewinnquote *f*; (*fig*) Chancen *pl*; **the** ~ **are in favour of/against his coming** es sieht so aus, als ob er kommt/nicht kommt; **to succeed against all the** ~ allen Erwartungen zum Trotz erfolgreich sein; **it makes no** ~ es spielt keine Rolle; **to be at** ~ **(with)** (*in disagreement*) uneinig sein (mit); (*at variance*) sich nicht vertragen (mit).
**odds and ends** *npl* Kleinigkeiten *pl*.
**odds-on** [ɔdz'ɔn] *adj*: **the** ~ **favourite** der klare Favorit ♦ *adv*: **it's** ~ **that she'll win** es ist so gut wie sicher, daß sie gewinnt.
**ode** [əud] *n* Ode *f*.
**odious** ['əudɪəs] *adj* widerwärtig.
**odometer** [ɔ'dɔmɪtə*] (*US*) *n* Tacho(meter) *m*.
**odor** *etc* (*US*) = **odour** *etc*.
**odour**, (*US*) **odor** ['əudə*] *n* Geruch *m*.
**odourless** ['əudəlɪs] *adj* geruchlos.
**OECD** *n abbr* (= *Organization for Economic Cooperation and Development*) OECD *f*.
**oesophagus**, (*US*) **esophagus** [i:'sɔfəgəs] *n* Speiseröhre *f*.
**oestrogen**, (*US*) **estrogen** ['i:strəudʒən] *n* Östrogen *nt*.

═══════════════════════════════════ *KEYWORD*

**of** [ɔv] *prep* **1** von; **the history** ~ **Germany** die Geschichte Deutschlands; **a friend** ~ **ours** ein Freund von uns; **a boy** ~ **ten** ein Junge von zehn Jahren, ein zehnjähriger Junge; **that was kind** ~ **you** das war nett von Ihnen; **the city** ~ **New York** die Stadt New York
**2** (*expressing quantity, amount, dates etc*): **a kilo** ~ **flour** ein Kilo Mehl; **how much** ~ **this do you need?** wieviel brauchen Sie davon?; **3** ~ **them** (*people*) 3 von ihnen; (*objects*) 3 davon; **a cup** ~ **tea** eine Tasse Tee; **a vase** ~ **flowers** eine Vase mit Blumen; **the 5th** ~ **July** der 5. Juli
**3** (*from, out of*) aus; **a bracelet** ~ **solid gold** ein Armband aus massivem Gold; **made** ~ **wood** aus Holz (gemacht).

═══════════════════════ KEYWORD

**off** [ɔf] adv **1** (referring to distance, time): **it's a long way** ~ es ist sehr weit weg; **the game is 3 days** ~ es sind noch 3 Tage bis zum Spiel
**2** (departure): **to go** ~ **to Paris/Italy** nach Paris/Italien fahren; **I must be** ~ ich muß gehen
**3** (removal): **to take** ~ **one's coat/clothes** seinen Mantel/sich ausziehen; **the button came** ~ der Knopf ging ab; **10 %** ~ (COMM) 10% Nachlaß
**4**: **to be** ~ (on holiday) im Urlaub sein; (due to sickness) krank sein; **I'm** ~ **on Fridays** freitags habe ich frei; **he was** ~ **on Friday** Freitag war er nicht da; **to have a day** ~ (from work) einen Tag frei haben; **to be** ~ **sick** wegen Krankheit fehlen
♦ adj **1** (not turned on: machine, light, engine etc) aus; (: water, gas) abgedreht; (: tap) zu
**2**: **to be** ~ (meeting, match) ausfallen; (agreement) nicht mehr gelten
**3** (BRIT: not fresh: milk, cheese, meat etc) verdorben, schlecht
**4**: **on the** ~ **chance that ...** für den Fall, daß ...; **to have an** ~ **day** (not as good as usual) nicht in Form sein; **to be badly** ~ sich schlecht stehen
♦ prep **1** (indicating motion, removal etc) von +dat; **to fall** ~ **a cliff** von einer Klippe fallen; **to take a picture** ~ **the wall** ein Bild von der Wand nehmen
**2** (distant from): **5 km** ~ **the main road** 5 km von der Hauptstraße entfernt; **an island** ~ **the coast** eine Insel vor der Küste
**3**: **I'm** ~ **meat/beer** (no longer eat/drink it) ich esse kein Fleisch/trinke kein Bier mehr; (no longer like it) ich kann kein Fleisch/Bier etc mehr sehen

**offal** ['ɔfl] n (CULIN) Innereien pl.
**off-beat** ['ɔfbiːt] adj (clothes, ideas) ausgefallen.
**off-centre**, (US) **off-center** [ɔf'sɛntə*] adj nicht genau in der Mitte, links/rechts von der Mitte ♦ adv asymmetrisch.
**off-colour** ['ɔf'kʌlə*] (BRIT) adj (ill) unpäßlich; **to feel** ~ sich unwohl fühlen.
**offence**, (US) **offense** [ə'fɛns] n (crime) Vergehen nt; (insult) Beleidigung f, Kränkung f; **to commit an** ~ eine Straftat begehen; **to take** ~ (at) Anstoß nehmen (an +dat); **to give** ~ (to) Anstoß erregen (bei); **"no** ~**"** „nichts für ungut".
**offend** [ə'fɛnd] vt (upset) kränken; **to** ~ **against** (law, rule) verstoßen gegen.
**offender** [ə'fɛndə*] n Straftäter(in) m(f).
**offending** [ə'fɛndɪŋ] adj (item etc) Anstoß erregend.
**offense** [ə'fɛns] (US) n = **offence**.
**offensive** [ə'fɛnsɪv] adj (remark, behaviour) verletzend; (smell etc) übel; (weapon) Angriffs- ♦ n (MIL) Offensive f.
**offer** ['ɔfə*] n Angebot nt ♦ vt anbieten; (money, opportunity, service) bieten; (reward) aussetzen; **to make an** ~ **for sth** ein Angebot für etw machen; **on** ~ (COMM: available) erhältlich; (: cheaper) im Angebot; **to** ~ **sth to sb** jdm etw anbieten; **to** ~ **to do sth** anbieten, etw zu tun.
**offering** ['ɔfərɪŋ] n Darbietung f; (REL) Opfergabe f.
**off-hand** [ɔf'hænd] adj (casual) lässig; (impolite) kurz angebunden ♦ adv auf Anhieb; **I can't tell you** ~ das kann ich Ihnen auf Anhieb nicht sagen.
**office** ['ɔfɪs] n Büro nt; (position) Amt nt; **doctor's** ~ (US) Praxis f; **to take** ~ das Amt antreten; **in** ~ (minister etc) im Amt; **through his good** ~**s** durch seine guten Dienste; **O**~ **of Fair Trading** (BRIT) Behörde f gegen unlauteren Wettbewerb.
**office block**, (US) **office building** n Bürogebäude nt.
**office boy** n Bürogehilfe m.
**office holder** n Amtsinhaber(in) m(f).
**office hours** npl (COMM) Bürostunden pl; (US: MED) Sprechstunde f.
**office manager** n Büroleiter(in) m(f).
**officer** ['ɔfɪsə*] n (MIL etc) Offizier m; (also: **police** ~) Polizeibeamte(r) m, Polizeibeamtin f; (of organization) Funktionär m.
**office work** n Büroarbeit f.
**office worker** n Büroangestellte(r) f(m).
**official** [ə'fɪʃl] adj offiziell ♦ n (in government) Beamte(r) m, Beamtin f; (in trade union etc) Funktionär m.
**officialdom** [ə'fɪʃldəm] (pej) n Bürokratie f.
**officially** [ə'fɪʃəlɪ] adv offiziell.
**official receiver** n (COMM) Konkursverwalter m.
**officiate** [ə'fɪʃɪeɪt] vi amtieren; **to** ~ **at a marriage** eine Trauung vornehmen.
**officious** [ə'fɪʃəs] adj übereifrig.
**offing** ['ɔfɪŋ] n: **in the** ~ in Sicht.
**off-key** [ɔf'kiː] adj (MUS: sing, play) falsch; (instrument) verstimmt.
**off-licence** ['ɔflaɪsns] (BRIT) n ≈ Wein- und Spirituosenhandlung f.

┌─────────────────────────────────────┐
**Off-licence** ist ein Geschäft (oder eine Theke in einer Gaststätte), wo man alkoholische Getränke kaufen kann, die aber anderswo konsumiert werden müssen. In solchen Geschäften, die oft von landesweiten Ketten betrieben werden, kann man auch andere Getränke, Süßigkeiten, Zigaretten und Knabbereien kaufen.
└─────────────────────────────────────┘

**off-limits** [ɔf'lɪmɪts] adj verboten.
**off-line** [ɔf'laɪn] (COMPUT) adj Off-line- ♦ adv off line; (switched off) abgetrennt.

**off-load** ['ɒfləʊd] *vt* abladen.
**off-peak** ['ɒf'piːk] *adj* (*heating*)
Nachtspeicher-; (*electricity*) Nacht-; (*train*)
außerhalb der Stoßzeit; ~ **ticket** Fahrkarte *f*
zur Fahrt außerhalb der Stoßzeit.
**off-putting** ['ɒfpʊtɪŋ] (*BRIT*) *adj* (*remark,
behaviour*) abstoßend.
**off-season** ['ɒf'siːzn] *adj*, *adv* außerhalb der
Saison.
**offset** ['ɒfsɛt] (*irreg*: *like* **set**) *vt* (*counteract*)
ausgleichen.
**offshoot** ['ɒfʃuːt] *n* (*BOT, fig*) Ableger *m*.
**offshore** [ɒf'ʃɔː*] *adj* (*breeze*) ablandig; (*oil rig,
fishing*) küstennah.
**offside** ['ɒf'saɪd] *adj* (*SPORT*) im Abseits; (*AUT:
when driving on left*) rechtsseitig; (: *when
driving on right*) linksseitig ♦ *n*: **the ~** (*AUT:
when driving on left*) die rechte Seite; (: *when
driving on right*) die linke Seite.
**offspring** ['ɒfsprɪŋ] *n inv* Nachwuchs *m*.
**offstage** [ɒf'steɪdʒ] *adv* hinter den Kulissen.
**off-the-cuff** [ɒfðə'kʌf] *adj* (*remark*) aus dem
Stegreif.
**off-the-job** ['ɒfðə'dʒɒb] *adj*: ~ **training**
außerbetriebliche Weiterbildung *f*.
**off-the-peg** ['ɒfðə'pɛg], (*US*) **off-the-rack**
['ɒfðə'ræk] *adv* von der Stange.
**off-the-record** ['ɒfðə'rɛkɔːd] *adj* (*conversation,
briefing*) inoffiziell; **that's strictly ~** das ist
ganz im Vertrauen.
**off-white** ['ɒfwaɪt] *adj* gebrochen weiß.
**Ofgas** ['ɒfgæs] *n Überwachungsgremium zum
Verbraucherschutz nach Privatisierung der
Gasindustrie*.
**Oftel** ['ɒftɛl] *n Überwachungsgremium zum
Verbraucherschutz nach Privatisierung der
Telekommunikationsindustrie*.
**often** ['ɒfn] *adv* oft; **how ~?** wie oft?; **more
~ than not** meistens; **as ~ as not** ziemlich
oft; **every so ~** ab und zu.
**Ofwat** ['ɒfwɒt] *n Überwachungsgremium zum
Verbraucherschutz nach Privatisierung der
Wasserindustrie*.
**ogle** ['əʊgl] *vt* schielen nach, begaffen (*pej*).
**ogre** ['əʊgə*] *n* (*monster*) Menschenfresser *m*.
**OH** (*US*) *abbr* (*POST*: = *Ohio*).
**oh** [əʊ] *excl* oh.
**ohm** [əʊm] *n* Ohm *nt*.
**OHMS** (*BRIT*) *abbr* (= *On His/Her Majesty's
Service*) *Aufdruck auf amtlichen
Postsendungen*.
**oil** [ɔɪl] *n* Öl *nt*; (*petroleum*) (Erd)öl *nt* ♦ *vt* ölen.
**oilcan** ['ɔɪlkæn] *n* Ölkanne *f*.
**oil change** *n* Ölwechsel *m*.
**oilcloth** ['ɔɪlklɒθ] *n* Wachstuch *nt*.
**oilfield** ['ɔɪlfiːld] *n* Ölfeld *nt*.
**oil filter** *n* Ölfilter *m*.
**oil-fired** ['ɔɪlfaɪəd] *adj* (*boiler, central heating*)
Öl-.
**oil gauge** *n* Ölstandsmesser *m*.
**oil painting** *n* Ölgemälde *nt*.
**oil refinery** *n* Ölraffinerie *f*.

**oil rig** *n* Ölförderturm *m*; (*at sea*) Bohrinsel *f*.
**oilskins** ['ɔɪlskɪnz] *npl* Ölzeug *nt*.
**oil slick** *n* Ölteppich *m*.
**oil tanker** *n* (*ship*) (Öl)tanker *m*; (*truck*)
Tankwagen *m*.
**oil well** *n* Ölquelle *f*.
**oily** ['ɔɪlɪ] *adj* (*substance*) ölig; (*rag*)
öldurchtränkt; (*food*) fettig.
**ointment** ['ɔɪntmənt] *n* Salbe *f*.
**OK** (*US*) *abbr* (*POST*: = *Oklahoma*).
**O.K.** ['əʊ'keɪ] (*inf*) *excl* okay; (*granted*) gut ♦ *adj*
(*average*) einigermaßen; (*acceptable*) in
Ordnung ♦ *vt* genehmigen ♦ *n*: **to give sb/sth
the ~** jdm/etw seine Zustimmung geben; **is
it ~?** ist es in Ordnung?; **are you ~?** bist du
in Ordnung?; **are you ~ for money?** hast du
(noch) genug Geld?; **it's ~ with** *or* **by me**
mir ist es recht.
**okay** ['əʊ'keɪ] *excl* = **O.K.**
**Okla.** (*US*) *abbr* (*POST*: = *Oklahoma*).
**old** [əʊld] *adj* alt; **how ~ are you?** wie alt bist
du?; **he's 10 years ~** er ist 10 Jahre alt; **~er
brother** ältere(r) Bruder; **any ~ thing will
do** for him ihm ist alles recht.
**old age** *n* Alter *nt*.
**old age pension** *n* Rente *f*.
**old age pensioner** (*BRIT*) *n* Rentner(in) *m(f)*.
**old-fashioned** ['əʊld'fæʃnd] *adj* altmodisch.
**old hand** *n* alter Hase *m*.
**old hat** *adj*: **to be ~** ein alter Hut sein.
**old maid** *n* alte Jungfer *f*.
**old people's home** *n* Altersheim *nt*.
**old-style** ['əʊldstaɪl] *adj* im alten Stil.
**old-time dancing** ['əʊldtaɪm-] *n* Tänze *pl* im
alten Stil.
**old-timer** [əʊld'taɪmə*] (*esp US*) *n* Veteran *m*.
**old wives' tale** *n* Ammenmärchen *nt*.
**oleander** [əʊlɪ'ændə*] *n* Oleander *m*.
**O level** (*BRIT*) *n* (*formerly*) ≈ Abschluß *m* der
Sekundarstufe 1, mittlere Reife *f*.
**olive** ['ɒlɪv] *n* Olive *f*; (*tree*) Olivenbaum *m*
♦ *adj* (*also*: **~-green**) olivgrün; **to offer an
~ branch to sb** (*fig*) jdm ein
Friedensangebot machen.
**olive oil** *n* Olivenöl *nt*.
**Olympic** [əʊ'lɪmpɪk] *adj* olympisch.
**Olympic Games** *npl*: **the ~** (*also*: **the
Olympics**) die Olympischen Spiele *pl*.
**OM** (*BRIT*) *n abbr* (= *Order of Merit*) *britischer
Verdienstorden*.
**Oman** [əʊ'mɑːn] *n* Oman *nt*.
**OMB** (*US*) *n abbr* (= *Office of Management and
Budget*) *Regierungsbehörde für Verwaltung
und Etat*.
**ombudsman** ['ɒmbʊdzmən] *n* Ombudsmann
*m*.
**omelette**, (*US*) **omelet** ['ɒmlɪt] *n* Omelett *nt*;
**ham/cheese omelet(te)** Schinken-/
Käseomelett *nt*.
**omen** ['əʊmən] *n* Omen *nt*.
**ominous** ['ɒmɪnəs] *adj* (*silence, warning*)
ominös; (*clouds, smoke*) bedrohlich.

**omission** [əu'mɪʃən] n (thing omitted)
Auslassung f; (act of omitting) Auslassen nt.
**omit** [əu'mɪt] vt (deliberately) unterlassen; (by
mistake) auslassen ♦ vi: **to ~ to do sth** es
unterlassen, etw zu tun.
**omnivorous** [ɔm'nɪvrəs] adj: **to be ~**
Allesfresser sein.
**ON** (CANADA) abbr (= Ontario).

=========== KEYWORD

**on** [ɔn] prep **1** (indicating position) auf +dat; (with
vb of motion) auf +acc; **it's ~ the table** es ist
auf dem Tisch; **she put the book ~ the table**
sie legte das Buch auf den Tisch; **~ the left**
links; **~ the right** rechts; **the house is ~ the
main road** das Haus liegt an der
Hauptstraße
**2** (indicating means, method, condition etc)
**~ foot** (go, be) zu Fuß; **to be ~ the train/
plane** im Zug/Flugzeug sein; **to go ~ the
train/plane** mit dem Zug/Flugzeug reisen;
(to be wanted) **~ the telephone** am Telefon
(verlangt werden); **~ the radio/television**
im Radio/Fernsehen; **to be ~ drugs** Drogen
nehmen; **to be ~ holiday** im Urlaub sein; **I'm
here ~ business** ich bin geschäftlich hier
**3** (referring to time): **~ Friday** am Freitag;
**~ Fridays** freitags; **~ June 20th** am 20. Juni;
**~ Friday, June 20th** am Freitag, dem 20.
Juni; **a week ~ Friday** Freitag in einer
Woche; **~ (his) arrival he went straight to his
hotel** bei seiner Ankunft ging er direkt in
sein Hotel; **~ seeing this he ...** als er das
sah, ... er ...
**4** (about, concerning) über +acc; **a book
~ physics** ein Buch über Physik
♦ adv **1** (referring to dress): **to have one's coat
~** seinen Mantel anhaben; **what's she got
~?** was hat sie an?
**2** (referring to covering) **screw the lid
~ tightly** dreh den Deckel fest zu
**3** (further, continuously): **to walk/drive/read
~** weitergehen/-fahren/-lesen
♦ adj **1** (functioning, in operation: machine,
radio, TV, light) an; (: tap) auf; (: handbrake)
angezogen; **there's a good film ~ at the
cinema** im Kino läuft ein guter Film
**2: that's not ~!** (inf: of behaviour) das ist
nicht drin!

**ONC** (BRIT) n abbr (= Ordinary National
Certificate) höherer Schulabschluß.
**once** [wʌns] adv (on one occasion) einmal;
(formerly) früher; (a long time ago) früher
einmal ♦ conj (as soon as) sobald; **at ~**
(immediately) sofort; (simultaneously)
gleichzeitig; **~ a week** einmal pro Woche;
**~ more** or **again** noch einmal; **~ and for all**
ein für allemal; **~ upon a time** es war
einmal; **~ in a while** ab und zu; **all at ~**
(suddenly) plötzlich; **for ~** ausnahmsweise
(einmal); **~ or twice** ein paarmal; **~ he had**

left sobald er gegangen war; **~ it was done**
nachdem es getan war.
**oncoming** ['ɔnkʌmɪŋ] adj (traffic etc)
entgegenkommend.
**OND** (BRIT) n abbr (= Ordinary National
Diploma) technisches Diplom.

=========== KEYWORD

**one** [wʌn] num ein(e); (counting) eins;
**~ hundred and fifty** (ein)hundert(und)-
fünfzig; **~ day there was a sudden knock at
the door** eines Tages klopfte es plötzlich an
der Tür; **~ by ~** einzeln
♦ adj **1** (sole) einzige(r, s); **the ~ book which
...** das einzige Buch, das ...
**2** (same): **they came in the ~ car** sie kamen
in demselben Wagen; **they all belong to the
~ family** sie alle gehören zu ein und
demselben Familie
♦ pron **1:** **this ~** diese(r, s); **that ~** der/die/das
(da); **which ~?** welcher/welche/welches?; **he
is ~ of us** er ist einer von uns; **I've already
got ~/a red ~** ich habe schon eins/ein rotes
**2: ~ another** einander; **do you two ever see
~ another?** seht ihr zwei euch jemals?
**3** (impersonal) man; **~ never knows** man
weiß nie; **to cut ~'s finger** sich dat in den
Finger schneiden.

**one-day excursion** ['wʌndeɪ-] (US) n (day
return) Tagesrückfahrkarte f.
**one-man** ['wʌn'mæn] adj (business, show)
Einmann-.
**one-man band** n Einmannkapelle f.
**one-off** [wʌn'ɔf] (BRIT: inf) n einmaliges
Ereignis nt.
**one-parent family** ['wʌnpɛərənt-] n Familie f
mit nur einem Elternteil.
**one-piece** ['wʌnpiːs] adj: **~ swimsuit**
einteiliger Badeanzug m.
**onerous** ['ɔnərəs] adj (duty etc) schwer.

=========== KEYWORD

**oneself** [wʌn'sɛlf] pron (reflexive: after prep)
sich; (emphatic) selbst; **to hurt ~** sich dat
weh tun; **to keep sth for ~** etw für sich
behalten; **to talk to ~** Selbstgespräche
führen.

**one-shot** ['wʌnʃɔt] (US) n = **one-off**.
**one-sided** [wʌn'saɪdɪd] adj einseitig.
**one-time** ['wʌntaɪm] adj ehemalig.
**one-to-one** ['wʌntəwʌn] adj (relationship,
tuition) Einzel-.
**one-upmanship** [wʌn'ʌpmənʃɪp] n: **the art of
~** die Kunst, anderen um einen Schritt
voraus zu sein.
**one-way** ['wʌnweɪ] adj (street, traffic)
Einbahn-; (ticket) Einzel-.
**ongoing** ['ɔngəuɪŋ] adj (project) laufend;
(situation etc) andauernd.
**onion** ['ʌnjən] n Zwiebel f.

**on-line** ['ɔnlaɪn] (*COMPUT*) *adj* (*printer, database*) On-line-; (*switched on*) gekoppelt ♦ *adv* on line.

**onlooker** ['ɔnlukə*] *n* Zuschauer(in) *m(f)*.

**only** ['əunlɪ] *adv* nur ♦ *adj* einzige(r, s) ♦ *conj* nur, bloß; I ~ **took one** ich nahm nur eins; I **saw her** ~ **yesterday** ich habe sie erst gestern gesehen; I'd be ~ **too pleased to help** ich würde allzu gern helfen; **not** ~ ... **but (also)** ... nicht nur ... sondern auch ...; **an** ~ **child** ein Einzelkind *nt*; I **would come**, ~ I'm **too busy** ich würde kommen, wenn ich nicht so viel zu tun hätte.

**ono** (*BRIT*) *abbr* (*in classified ads:* = *or near(est) offer*) *see* **near**.

**onset** ['ɔnsɛt] *n* Beginn *m*.

**onshore** ['ɔnʃɔː*] *adj* (*wind*) auflandig, See-.

**onslaught** ['ɔnslɔːt] *n* Attacke *f*.

**on-the-job** ['ɔnðə'dʒɔb] *adj:* ~ **training** Ausbildung *f* am Arbeitsplatz.

**onto** ['ɔntu] *prep* = **on to**.

**onus** ['əunəs] *n* Last *f*, Pflicht *f*; **the** ~ **is on him to prove it** er trägt die Beweislast.

**onward(s)** ['ɔnwəd(z)] *adv* weiter; **from that time** ~ von der Zeit an ♦ *adj* fortschreitend.

**onyx** ['ɔnɪks] *n* Onyx *m*.

**ooze** [uːz] *vi* (*mud, water etc*) triefen.

**opacity** [əu'pæsɪtɪ] *n* (*of substance*) Undurchsichtigkeit *f*.

**opal** ['əupl] *n* Opal *m*.

**opaque** [əu'peɪk] *adj* (*substance*) undurchsichtig, trüb.

**OPEC** ['əupɛk] *n abbr* (= *Organization of Petroleum-Exporting Countries*) OPEC *f*.

**open** ['əupn] *adj* offen; (*packet, shop, museum*) geöffnet; (*view*) frei; (*meeting, debate*) öffentlich; (*ticket, return*) unbeschränkt; (*vacancy*) verfügbar ♦ *vt* öffnen, aufmachen; (*book, paper etc*) aufschlagen; (*account*) eröffnen; (*blocked road*) freimachen ♦ *vi* (*door, eyes, mouth*) sich öffnen; (*shop, bank etc*) aufmachen; (*commence*) beginnen; (*film, play*) Premiere haben; (*flower*) aufgehen; **in the** ~ (**air**) im Freien; **the** ~ **sea** das offene Meer; **to have an** ~ **mind on sth** etw *dat* aufgeschlossen gegenüberstehen; **to be** ~ **to** (*ideas etc*) offen sein für; **to be** ~ **to criticism** *dat* ausgesetzt sein; **to be** ~ **to the public** für die Öffentlichkeit zugänglich sein; **to** ~ **one's mouth** (*speak*) den Mund aufmachen.

►**open on to** *vt fus* (*room, door*) führen auf +*acc*.

►**open up** *vi* (*unlock*) aufmachen; (*confide*) sich äußern.

**open-air** [əupn'ɛə*] *adj* im Freien; ~ **concert** Open-air-Konzert *nt*; ~ **swimming pool** Freibad *nt*.

**open-and-shut** ['əupənən'ʃʌt] *adj:* ~ **case** klarer Fall *m*.

**open day** *n* Tag *m* der offenen Tür.

**open-ended** [əupn'ɛndɪd] *adj* (*question etc*) mit

offenem Ausgang; (*contract*) unbefristet.

**opener** ['əupnə*] *n* (*also:* **tin** ~, **can** ~) Dosenöffner *m*.

**open-heart** [əupən'hɑːt] *adj:* ~ **surgery** Eingriff *m* am offenen Herzen.

**opening** ['əupnɪŋ] *adj* (*commencing: stages, scene*) erste(r, s); (*remarks, ceremony etc*) Eröffnungs- ♦ *n* (*gap, hole*) Öffnung *f*; (*of play etc*) Anfang *m*; (*of new building etc*) Eröffnung *f*; (*opportunity*) Gelegenheit *f*.

**opening hours** *npl* Öffnungszeiten *pl*.

**opening night** *n* (*THEAT*) Eröffnungsabend *m*.

**open learning** *n* Weiterbildungssystem auf Teilzeitbasis.

**openly** ['əupnlɪ] *adv* offen.

**open-minded** [əupn'maɪndɪd] *adj* aufgeschlossen.

**open-necked** ['əupnnɛkt] *adj* (*shirt*) mit offenem Kragen.

**openness** ['əupnnɪs] *n* (*frankness*) Offenheit *f*.

**open-plan** ['əupn'plæn] *adj* (*office*) Großraum-.

**open prison** *n* offenes Gefängnis *nt*.

**open sandwich** *n* belegtes Brot *nt*.

**open shop** *n* Unternehmen ohne Gewerkschaftszwang.

**Open University** (*BRIT*) *n* ≈ Fernuniversität *f*.

> **Open University** ist eine 1969 in Großbritannien gegründete Fernuniversität für Spätstudierende. Der Unterricht findet durch Fernseh- und Radiosendungen statt, schriftliche Arbeiten werden mit der Post verschickt, und der Besuch von Sommerkursen ist Pflicht. Die Studenten müssen eine bestimmte Anzahl von Unterrichtseinheiten in einem bestimmten Zeitraum absolvieren und für die Verleihung eines akademischen Grades eine Mindestzahl von Scheinen machen.

**open verdict** *n* (*LAW*) Todesfeststellung ohne Angabe der Todesursache.

**opera** ['ɔpərə] *n* Oper *f*.

**opera glasses** *npl* Opernglas *nt*.

**opera house** *n* Opernhaus *nt*.

**opera singer** *n* Opernsänger(in) *m(f)*.

**operate** ['ɔpəreɪt] *vt* (*machine etc*) bedienen ♦ *vi* (*machine etc*) funktionieren; (*company*) arbeiten; (*laws, forces*) wirken; (*MED*) operieren; **to** ~ **on sb** jdn operieren.

**operatic** [ɔpə'rætɪk] *adj* (*singer etc*) Opern-.

**operating room** ['ɔpəreɪtɪŋ-] (*US*) *n* Operationssaal *m*.

**operating system** *n* (*COMPUT*) Betriebssystem *nt*.

**operating table** *n* (*MED*) Operationstisch *m*.

**operating theatre** *n* (*MED*) Operationssaal *m*.

**operation** [ɔpə'reɪʃən] *n* (*activity*) Unternehmung *f*; (*of machine etc*) Betrieb *m*; (*MIL, MED*) Operation *f*; (*COMM*) Geschäft *nt*;

**to be in** ~ (*law, scheme*) in Kraft sein; **to have an** ~ (*MED*) operiert werden; **to perform an** ~ (*MED*) eine Operation vornehmen.

**operational** [ɔpə'reɪʃənl] *adj* (*machine etc*) einsatzfähig.

**operative** ['ɔpərətɪv] *adj* (*measure, system*) wirksam; (*law*) gültig ♦ *n* (*in factory*) Maschinenarbeiter(in) *m(f)*; **the** ~ **word** das entscheidende Wort.

**operator** ['ɔpəreɪtə*] *n* (*TEL*) Vermittlung *f*; (*of machine*) Bediener(in) *m(f)*.

**operetta** [ɔpə'rɛtə] *n* Operette *f*.

**ophthalmic** [ɔf'θælmɪk] *adj* (*department*) Augen-.

**ophthalmic optician** *n* Augenoptiker(in) *m(f)*.

**ophthalmologist** [ɔfθæl'mɔlədʒɪst] *n* Augenarzt *m*, Augenärztin *f*.

**opinion** [ə'pɪnjən] *n* Meinung *f*; **in my** ~ meiner Meinung nach; **to have a good/high** ~ **of sb/o.s.** eine gute/hohe Meinung von jdm/sich haben; **to be of the** ~ **that** ... der Ansicht *or* Meinung sein, daß ...; **to get a second** ~ (*MED etc*) ein zweites Gutachten einholen.

**opinionated** [ə'pɪnjəneɪtɪd] (*pej*) *adj* rechthaberisch.

**opinion poll** *n* Meinungsumfrage *f*.

**opium** ['əupɪəm] *n* Opium *nt*.

**opponent** [ə'pəunənt] *n* Gegner(in) *m(f)*.

**opportune** ['ɔpətjuːn] *adj* (*moment*) günstig.

**opportunism** [ɔpə'tjuːnɪsəm] (*pej*) *n* Opportunismus *m*.

**opportunist** [ɔpə'tjuːnɪst] (*pej*) *n* Opportunist(in) *m(f)*.

**opportunity** [ɔpə'tjuːnɪtɪ] *n* Gelegenheit *f*, Möglichkeit *f*; (*prospects*) Chance *f*; **to take the** ~ **of doing sth** die Gelegenheit ergreifen, etw zu tun.

**oppose** [ə'pəuz] *vt* (*opinion, plan*) ablehnen; **to be** ~**d to sth** gegen etw sein; **as** ~**d to** im Gegensatz zu.

**opposing** [ə'pəuzɪŋ] *adj* (*side, team*) gegnerisch; (*ideas, tendencies*) entgegengesetzt.

**opposite** ['ɔpəzɪt] *adj* (*house, door*) gegenüberliegend; (*end, direction*) entgegengesetzt; (*point of view, effect*) gegenteilig ♦ *adv* gegenüber ♦ *prep* (*in front of*) gegenüber; (*next to: on list, form etc*) neben ♦ *n*: **the** ~ **sex** das andere Geschlecht; **"see** ~ **page"** „siehe gegenüber".

**opposite number** *n* (*person*) Gegenspieler(in) *m(f)*.

**opposition** [ɔpə'zɪʃən] *n* (*resistance*) Widerstand *m*; (*SPORT*) Gegner *pl*; **the O**~ (*POL*) die Opposition.

**oppress** [ə'prɛs] *vt* unterdrücken.

**oppressed** [ə'prɛst] *adj* unterdrückt.

**oppression** [ə'prɛʃən] *n* Unterdrückung *f*.

**oppressive** [ə'prɛsɪv] *adj* (*weather, heat*) bedrückend; (*political regime*) repressiv.

**opprobrium** [ə'prəubrɪəm] *n* (*form*) Schande *f*, Schmach *f*.

**opt** [ɔpt] *vi*: **to** ~ **for** sich entscheiden für; **to** ~ **to do sth** sich entscheiden, etw zu tun.

▶**opt out (of)** *vi* (*not participate*) sich nicht beteiligen (an +*dat*); (*of insurance scheme etc*) kündigen; **to** ~ **out (of local authority control)** (*POL: hospital, school*) aus der Kontrolle der Gemeindeverwaltung austreten.

**optical** ['ɔptɪkl] *adj* optisch.

**optical character reader** *n* optischer Klarschriftleser *m*.

**optical character recognition** *n* optische Zeichenerkennung *f*.

**optical illusion** *n* optische Täuschung *f*.

**optician** [ɔp'tɪʃən] *n* Optiker(in) *m(f)*.

**optics** ['ɔptɪks] *n* Optik *f*.

**optimism** ['ɔptɪmɪzəm] *n* Optimismus *m*.

**optimist** ['ɔptɪmɪst] *n* Optimist(in) *m(f)*.

**optimistic** [ɔptɪ'mɪstɪk] *adj* optimistisch.

**optimum** ['ɔptɪməm] *adj* optimal.

**option** ['ɔpʃən] *n* (*choice*) Möglichkeit *f*; (*SCOL*) Wahlfach *nt*; (*COMM*) Option *f*; **to keep one's** ~**s open** dat alle Möglichkeiten offenhalten; **to have no** ~ keine (andere) Wahl haben.

**optional** ['ɔpʃənl] *adj* freiwillig; ~ **extras** (*COMM*) Extras *pl*.

**opulence** ['ɔpjuləns] *n* Reichtum *m*.

**opulent** ['ɔpjulənt] *adj* (*very wealthy*) reich, wohlhabend.

**OR** (*US*) *abbr* (*POST*: = *Oregon*).

**or** [ɔː*] *conj* oder; **he hasn't seen** ~ **heard anything** er hat weder etwas gesehen noch gehört; ~ **else** (*otherwise*) sonst; **fifty** ~ **sixty people** fünfzig bis sechzig Leute.

**oracle** ['ɔrəkl] *n* Orakel *nt*.

**oral** ['ɔːrəl] *adj* (*test, report*) mündlich; (*MED: vaccine, contraceptive*) zum Einnehmen ♦ *n* (*exam*) mündliche Prüfung *f*.

**orange** ['ɔrɪndʒ] *n* Orange *f*, Apfelsine *f* ♦ *adj* (*colour*) orange.

**orangeade** [ɔrɪndʒ'eɪd] *n* Orangenlimonade *f*.

**oration** [ɔː'reɪʃən] *n* Ansprache *f*.

**orator** ['ɔrətə*] *n* Redner(in) *m(f)*.

**oratorio** [ɔrə'tɔːrɪəu] *n* (*MUS*) Oratorium *nt*.

**orb** [ɔːb] *n* Kugel *f*.

**orbit** ['ɔːbɪt] *n* (*of planet etc*) Umlaufbahn *f* ♦ *vt* umkreisen.

**orbital motorway** ['ɔːbɪtəl-] *n* Ringautobahn *f*.

**orchard** ['ɔːtʃəd] *n* Obstgarten *m*; **apple** ~ Obstgarten mit Apfelbäumen.

**orchestra** ['ɔːkɪstrə] *n* Orchester *nt*; (*US: stalls*) Parkett *nt*.

**orchestral** [ɔː'kɛstrəl] *adj* (*piece, musicians*) Orchester-.

**orchestrate** ['ɔːkɪstreɪt] *vt* orchestrieren.

**orchid** ['ɔːkɪd] *n* Orchidee *f*.

**ordain** [ɔː'deɪn] *vt* (*REL*) ordinieren; (*decree*) verfügen.

**ordeal** [ɔː'diːl] *n* Qual *f*.

**order** ['ɔːdə*] *n* (*command*) Befehl *m*; (*COMM, in restaurant*) Bestellung *f*; (*sequence*) Reihenfolge *f*; (*discipline, organization*) Ordnung *f*; (*REL*) Orden *m* ♦ *vt* (*command*) befehlen; (*COMM, in restaurant*) bestellen; (*also*: **put in ~**) ordnen; **in ~** (*permitted*) in Ordnung; **in (working) ~** betriebsfähig; **in ~ to do sth** um etw zu tun; **in ~ of size** nach Größe (geordnet); **on ~** (*COMM*) bestellt; **out of ~** (*not working*) außer Betrieb; (*in the wrong sequence*) durcheinander; (*motion, proposal*) nicht zulässig; **to place an ~ for sth with sb** eine Bestellung für etw bei jdm aufgeben; **made to ~** (*COMM*) auf Bestellung (gemacht); **to be under ~s to do sth** die Anweisung haben, etw zu tun; **to take ~s** Befehle entgegennehmen; **a point of ~** (*in debate etc*) eine Verfahrensfrage; **"pay to the ~ of ..."** „zahlbar an +*dat* ..."; **of or in the ~ of** in der Größenordnung von; **to ~ sb to do sth** jdn anweisen, etw zu tun.

▶**order around** *vt* (*also*: **order about**) herumkommandieren.

**order book** *n* (*COMM*) Auftragsbuch *nt*.

**order form** *n* Bestellschein *m*.

**orderly** ['ɔːdəlɪ] *n* (*MIL*) Offiziersbursche *m*; (*MED*) Pfleger(in) *m(f)* ♦ *adj* (*manner*) ordentlich; (*sequence, system*) geordnet.

**order number** *n* (*COMM*) Bestellnummer *f*.

**ordinal** ['ɔːdɪnl] *adj*: **~ number** Ordinalzahl *f*.

**ordinarily** ['ɔːdnrɪlɪ] *adv* normalerweise.

**ordinary** ['ɔːdnrɪ] *adj* (*everyday*) gewöhnlich, normal; (*pej: mediocre*) mittelmäßig; **out of the ~** außergewöhnlich.

---

**Ordinary degree** *ist ein Universitätsabschluß, der an Studenten vergeben wird, die entweder die für ein* **honours degree** *nötige Note nicht erreicht haben, aber trotzdem nicht durchgefallen sind, oder die sich nur für ein* ordinary degree *eingeschrieben haben, wobei das Studium meist kürzer ist.*

---

**ordinary seaman** (*BRIT*) *n* Leichtmatrose *m*.

**ordinary shares** *npl* Stammaktien *pl*.

**ordination** [ɔːdɪ'neɪʃən] *n* (*REL*) Ordination *f*.

**ordnance** ['ɔːdnəns] *n* (*unit*) Technische Truppe *f* ♦ *adj* (*factory, supplies*) Munitions-.

**Ordnance Survey** (*BRIT*) *n* Landesvermessung *f*.

**ore** [ɔː*] *n* Erz *nt*.

**Ore.** (*US*) *abbr* (*POST*: = *Oregon*).

**organ** ['ɔːgən] *n* (*ANAT*) Organ *nt*; (*MUS*) Orgel *f*.

**organic** [ɔː'gænɪk] *adj* organisch.

**organism** ['ɔːgənɪzəm] *n* Organismus *m*.

**organist** ['ɔːgənɪst] *n* Organist(in) *m(f)*.

**organization** [ɔːgənaɪ'zeɪʃən] *n* Organisation *f*.

**organization chart** *n* Organisationsplan *m*.

**organize** ['ɔːgənaɪz] *vt* organisieren; **to get ~d** sich fertigmachen.

**organized crime** *n* organisiertes Verbrechen *nt*.

**organized labour** *n* organisierte Arbeiterschaft *f*.

**organizer** ['ɔːgənaɪzə*] *n* (*of conference etc*) Organisator *m*, Veranstalter *m*.

**orgasm** ['ɔːgæzəm] *n* Orgasmus *m*.

**orgy** ['ɔːdʒɪ] *n* Orgie *f*; **an ~ of destruction** eine Zerstörungsorgie.

**Orient** ['ɔːrɪənt] *n*: **the ~** der Orient.

**orient** ['ɔːrɪənt] *vt*: **to ~ o.s. (to)** sich orientieren (in +*dat*); **to be ~ed towards** ausgerichtet sein auf +*acc*.

**oriental** [ɔːrɪ'entl] *adj* orientalisch.

**orientate** ['ɔːrɪənteɪt] *vt*: **to ~ o.s.** sich orientieren; (*fig*) sich zurechtfinden; **to be ~d towards** ausgerichtet sein auf +*acc*.

**orifice** ['ɔrɪfɪs] *n* (*ANAT*) Öffnung *f*.

**origin** ['ɔrɪdʒɪn] *n* Ursprung *m*; (*of person*) Herkunft *f*; **country of ~** Herkunftsland *nt*.

**original** [ə'rɪdʒɪnl] *adj* (*first*) ursprünglich; (*genuine*) original; (*imaginative*) originell ♦ *n* Original *nt*.

**originality** [ərɪdʒɪ'nælɪtɪ] *n* Originalität *f*.

**originally** [ə'rɪdʒɪnəlɪ] *adv* (*at first*) ursprünglich.

**originate** [ə'rɪdʒɪneɪt] *vi*: **to ~ in** (*idea, custom etc*) entstanden sein in +*dat*; **to ~ with** *or* **from** stammen von.

**originator** [ə'rɪdʒɪneɪtə*] *n* (*of idea, custom*) Urheber(in) *m(f)*.

**Orkneys** ['ɔːknɪz] *npl*: **the ~** (*also*: **the Orkney Islands**) die Orkneyinseln *pl*.

**ornament** ['ɔːnəmənt] *n* (*object*) Ziergegenstand *m*; (*decoration*) Verzierungen *pl*.

**ornamental** [ɔːnə'mentl] *adj* (*garden, pond*) Zier-.

**ornamentation** [ɔːnəmen'teɪʃən] *n* Verzierungen *pl*.

**ornate** [ɔː'neɪt] *adj* (*necklace, design*) kunstvoll.

**ornithologist** [ɔːnɪ'θɔlədʒɪst] *n* Ornithologe *m*, Ornithologin *f*.

**ornithology** [ɔːnɪ'θɔlədʒɪ] *n* Ornithologie *f*, Vogelkunde *f*.

**orphan** ['ɔːfn] *n* Waise *f*, Waisenkind *nt* ♦ *vt*: **to be ~ed** zur Waise werden.

**orphanage** ['ɔːfənɪdʒ] *n* Waisenhaus *nt*.

**orthodox** ['ɔːθədɔks] *adj* orthodox; **~ medicine** die konventionelle Medizin.

**orthodoxy** ['ɔːθədɔksɪ] *n* Orthodoxie *f*.

**orthopaedic**, (*US*) **orthopedic** [ɔːθə'piːdɪk] *adj* orthopädisch.

**OS** *abbr* (*BRIT*) = **Ordnance Survey**; (*NAUT*) = **ordinary seaman**; (*DRESS*) = **outsize**.

**O/S** *abbr* (*COMM*: = *out of stock*) nicht auf Lager.

**Oscar** ['ɔskə*] *n* Oscar *m*.

**oscillate** ['ɔsɪleɪt] vi (ELEC, PHYS) schwingen, oszillieren; (fig) schwanken.

**OSHA** (US) n abbr (= Occupational Safety and Health Administration) Regierungsstelle für Arbeitsschutzvorschriften.

**Oslo** ['ɔzləu] n Oslo nt.

**OST** n abbr (= Office of Science and Technology) Ministerium für Wissenschaft und Technologie.

**ostensible** [ɔs'tɛnsɪbl] adj vorgeblich, angeblich.

**ostensibly** [ɔs'tɛnsɪblɪ] adv angeblich.

**ostentation** [ɔstɛn'teɪʃən] n Pomp m, Protz m.

**ostentatious** [ɔstɛn'teɪʃəs] adj (building, car etc) pompös; (person) protzig.

**osteopath** ['ɔstɪəpæθ] n Osteopath(in) m(f).

**ostracize** ['ɔstrəsaɪz] vt ächten.

**ostrich** ['ɔstrɪtʃ] n Strauß m.

**OT** abbr (BIBLE: = Old Testament) AT.

**OTB** (US) n abbr (= offtrack betting) Wetten außerhalb des Rennbahngeländes.

**OTE** abbr (COMM: = on-target earnings) Einkommensziel nt.

**other** ['ʌðə*] adj andere(r, s) ♦ pron: the ~ (one) der/die/das andere; ~s andere pl; the ~s die anderen pl; ~ than (apart from) außer; the ~ day (recently) neulich; some actor or ~ irgendein Schauspieler; somebody or ~ irgend jemand; the car was none ~ than Robert's das Auto gehörte keinem anderen als Robert.

**otherwise** ['ʌðəwaɪz] adv (differently) anders; (apart from that, if not) sonst, ansonsten; an ~ good piece of work eine im übrigen gute Arbeit.

**OTT** (inf) abbr (= over the top) see **top**.

**otter** ['ɔtə*] n Otter m.

**OU** (BRIT) n abbr = **Open University**.

**ouch** [autʃ] excl autsch.

**ought** [ɔːt] (pt ought) aux vb: I ~ to do it ich sollte es tun; this ~ to have been corrected das hätte korrigiert werden müssen; he ~ to win (he probably will win) er dürfte wohl gewinnen; you ~ to go and see it das solltest du dir ansehen.

**ounce** [auns] n Unze f; (fig: small amount) bißchen nt.

**our** ['auə*] adj unsere(r, s); see also **my**.

**ours** [auəz] pron unsere(r, s); see also **mine**¹.

**ourselves** [auə'sɛlvz] pron pl uns (selbst); (emphatic) selbst; we did it (all) by ~ wir haben alles selbst gemacht; see also **oneself**.

**oust** [aust] vt (forcibly remove) verdrängen.

───────── KEYWORD

**out**¹ [aut] adv **1** (not in) draußen; ~ in the rain/snow draußen im Regen/Schnee; ~ here hier; ~ there dort; to go/come etc ~ hinausgehen/-kommen etc; to speak ~ loud laut sprechen

**2** (not at home, absent) nicht da

**3** (indicating distance): the boat was 10 km ~

das Schiff war 10 km weit draußen; **3 days ~ from Plymouth** 3 Tage nach dem Auslaufen von Plymouth

**4** (SPORT) aus; **the ball is ~/has gone ~** der Ball ist aus

♦ adj **1**: **to be ~** (person: unconscious) bewußtlos sein; (: out of game) ausgeschieden sein; (out of fashion: style, singer) out sein

**2** (have appeared: flowers) da; (: news, secret) heraus

**3** (extinguished, finished: fire, light, gas) aus; **before the week was ~** ehe die Woche zu Ende war

**4**: **to be ~ to do sth** (intend) etw tun wollen.

**5** (wrong): **to be ~ in one's calculations** sich in seinen Berechnungen irren.

───────────────

**out²** [aut] vt (inf: expose as homosexual) outen.

**outage** ['autɪdʒ] (esp US) n (power failure) Stromausfall m.

**out-and-out** ['autəndaut] adj (liar, thief etc) ausgemacht.

**outback** ['autbæk] n (in Australia): the ~ das Hinterland.

**outbid** [aut'bɪd] vt überbieten.

**outboard** ['autbɔːd] n (also: ~ motor) Außenbordmotor m.

**outbound** ['autbaund] adj (ship) auslaufend.

**outbreak** ['autbreɪk] n (of war, disease etc) Ausbruch m.

**outbuilding** ['autbɪldɪŋ] n Nebengebäude nt.

**outburst** ['autbəːst] n (of anger etc) Gefühlsausbruch m.

**outcast** ['autkɑːst] n Ausgestoßene(r) f(m).

**outclass** [aut'klɑːs] vt deklassieren.

**outcome** ['autkʌm] n Ergebnis nt, Resultat nt.

**outcrop** ['autkrɔp] n (of rock) Block m.

**outcry** ['autkraɪ] n Aufschrei m.

**outdated** [aut'deɪtɪd] adj (custom, idea) veraltet.

**outdo** [aut'duː] (irreg: like do) vt übertreffen.

**outdoor** [aut'dɔː*] adj (activities) im Freien; (clothes) für draußen; ~ swimming pool Freibad nt; she's an ~ person sie liebt die freie Natur.

**outdoors** [aut'dɔːz] adv (play, sleep) draußen, im Freien.

**outer** ['autə*] adj äußere(r, s); ~ suburbs (äußere) Vorstädte pl; the ~ office das Vorzimmer.

**outer space** n der Weltraum.

**outfit** ['autfɪt] n (clothes) Kleidung f; (inf: team) Verein m.

**outfitter's** ['autfɪtəz] (BRIT) n (shop) Herrenausstatter m.

**outgoing** ['autgəuɪŋ] adj (extrovert) kontaktfreudig; (retiring: president etc) scheidend; (mail etc) ausgehend.

**outgoings** ['autgəuɪŋz] (BRIT) npl Ausgaben pl.

**outgrow** [aut'grəu] (irreg: like grow) vt (clothes) herauswachsen aus; (habits etc) ablegen.

**outhouse** ['authaus] *n* Nebengebäude *nt.*
**outing** ['autɪŋ] *n* Ausflug *m.*
**outlandish** [aut'lændɪʃ] *adj* eigenartig, seltsam.
**outlast** [aut'lɑːst] *vt* überleben.
**outlaw** ['autlɔː] *n* Geächtete(r) *f(m)* ♦ *vt* verbieten.
**outlay** ['autleɪ] *n* Auslagen *pl.*
**outlet** ['autlɛt] *n (hole, pipe)* Abfluß *m; (US: ELEC)* Steckdose *f; (COMM: also:* **retail ~)** Verkaufsstelle *f; (fig: for grief, anger etc)* Ventil *nt.*
**outline** ['autlaɪn] *n (shape)* Umriß *m; (brief explanation)* Abriß *m; (rough sketch)* Skizze *f* ♦ *vt (fig: theory, plan etc)* umreißen, skizzieren.
**outlive** [aut'lɪv] *vt (survive)* überleben.
**outlook** ['autluk] *n (attitude)* Einstellung *f; (prospects)* Aussichten *pl; (for weather)* Vorhersage *f.*
**outlying** ['autlaɪɪŋ] *adj (area, town etc)* entlegen.
**outmanoeuvre,** *(US)* **outmaneuver** [autmə'nuːvə*] *vt* ausmanövrieren.
**outmoded** [aut'məudɪd] *adj* veraltet.
**outnumber** [aut'nʌmbə*] *vt* zahlenmäßig überlegen sein *+dat;* **to be ~ed (by) 5 to 1** im Verhältnis 5 zu 1 in der Minderheit sein

================= *KEYWORD*

**out of** *prep* **1** *(outside, beyond: position)* nicht in *+dat;* (: *motion)* aus *+dat;* **to look ~ the window** aus dem Fenster blicken; **to be ~ danger** außer Gefahr sein
**2** *(cause, origin)* aus *+dat;* **~ curiosity/fear/greed** aus Neugier/Angst/Habgier; **to drink sth ~ a cup** etw aus einer Tasse trinken
**3** *(from among)* von *+dat;* **one ~ every three smokers** einer von drei Rauchern
**4** *(without):* **to be ~ sugar/milk/petrol** *etc* keinen Zucker/keine Milch/kein Benzin *etc* mehr haben.

**out of bounds** *adj:* **to be ~** verboten sein.
**out-of-court** [autəv'kɔːt] *adj (settlement)* außergerichtlich; *see also* **court.**
**out-of-date** [autəv'deɪt] *adj (passport, ticket etc)* abgelaufen; *(clothes, idea)* veraltet.
**out-of-doors** [autəv'dɔːz] *adv (play, stay etc)* im Freien.
**out-of-the-way** ['autəvðə'weɪ] *adj (place)* entlegen; *(pub, restaurant etc)* kaum bekannt.
**out-of-work** ['autəvwəːk] *adj* arbeitslos.
**outpatient** ['autpeɪʃənt] *n* ambulanter Patient *m,* ambulante Patientin *f.*
**outpost** ['autpəust] *n (MIL, COMM)* Vorposten *m.*
**outpouring** ['autpɔːrɪŋ] *n (of emotion etc)* Erguß *m.*
**output** ['autput] *n (production: of factory, writer etc)* Produktion *f; (COMPUT)* Output *m,* Ausgabe *f* ♦ *vt (COMPUT)* ausgeben.

**outrage** ['autreɪdʒ] *n (scandal)* Skandal *m; (atrocity)* Verbrechen *nt,* Ausschreitung *f; (anger)* Empörung *f* ♦ *vt (shock, anger)* empören.
**outrageous** [aut'reɪdʒəs] *adj (remark etc)* empörend; *(clothes)* unmöglich; *(scandalous)* skandalös.
**outrider** ['autraɪdə*] *n (on motorcycle)* Kradbegleiter *m.*
**outright** [aut'raɪt] *adv (kill)* auf der Stelle; *(win)* überlegen; *(buy)* auf einen Schlag; *(ask, refuse)* ohne Umschweife ♦ *adj (winner, victory)* unbestritten; *(refusal, hostility)* total.
**outrun** [aut'rʌn] *(irreg: like* **run)** *vt* schneller laufen als.
**outset** ['autsɛt] *n* Anfang *m,* Beginn *m;* **from the ~** von Anfang an; **at the ~** am Anfang.
**outshine** [aut'ʃaɪn] *(irreg: like* **shine)** *vt (fig)* in den Schatten stellen.
**outside** [aut'saɪd] *n (of building etc)* Außenseite *f* ♦ *adj (wall, lavatory)* Außen- ♦ *adv (be, wait)* draußen; *(go)* nach draußen ♦ *prep* außerhalb *+gen; (door etc)* vor *+dat;* **at the ~** *(at the most)* höchstens; *(at the latest)* spätestens; **an ~ chance** eine geringe Chance.
**outside broadcast** *n* außerhalb des Studios produzierte Sendung *f.*
**outside lane** *n* Überholspur *f.*
**outside line** *n (TEL)* Amtsanschluß *m.*
**outsider** [aut'saɪdə*] *n (stranger)* Außenstehende(r) *f(m); (odd one out, in race etc)* Außenseiter(in) *m(f).*
**outsize** ['autsaɪz] *adj (clothes)* übergroß.
**outskirts** ['autskəːts] *npl (of town)* Stadtrand *m.*
**outsmart** [aut'smɑːt] *vt* austricksen *(inf).*
**outspoken** [aut'spəukən] *adj* offen.
**outspread** [aut'sprɛd] *adj (wings, arms etc)* ausgebreitet.
**outstanding** [aut'stændɪŋ] *adj (exceptional)* hervorragend; *(remaining)* ausstehend; **your account is still ~** Ihr Konto weist noch Außenstände auf.
**outstay** [aut'steɪ] *vt:* **to ~ one's welcome** länger bleiben als erwünscht.
**outstretched** [aut'strɛtʃt] *adj* ausgestreckt.
**outstrip** [aut'strɪp] *vt (competitors, supply):* **to ~ (in)** übertreffen (an *+dat).*
**out tray** *n* Ablage *f* für Ausgänge.
**outvote** [aut'vəut] *vt* überstimmen.
**outward** ['autwəd] *adj (sign, appearances)* äußere(r, s); **~ journey** Hinreise *f.*
**outwardly** ['autwədlɪ] *adv (on the surface)* äußerlich.
**outward(s)** ['autwəd(z)] *adv (move, face)* nach außen.
**outweigh** [aut'weɪ] *vt* schwerer wiegen als.
**outwit** [aut'wɪt] *vt* überlisten.
**ova** ['əuvə] *npl of* **ovum.**
**oval** ['əuvl] *adj* oval ♦ *n* Oval *nt.*

**Oval Office**, *ein großer ovaler Raum im Weißen Haus, ist das private Büro des amerikanischen Präsidenten. Im weiteren Sinne bezieht sich dieser Begriff oft auf die Präsidentschaft selbst.*

**ovarian** [əu'vɛərɪən] *adj (ANAT)* des Eierstocks/der Eierstöcke; **~ cyst** Zyste *f* im Eierstock.
**ovary** ['əuvərɪ] *n (ANAT, MED)* Eierstock *m*.
**ovation** [əu'veɪʃən] *n* Ovation *f*.
**oven** ['ʌvn] *n (CULIN)* Backofen *m*.
**ovenproof** ['ʌvnpruːf] *adj (dish etc)* feuerfest.
**oven-ready** ['ʌvnrɛdɪ] *adj* backfertig.
**ovenware** ['ʌvnwɛə*] *n* feuerfestes Geschirr *nt*.

KEYWORD

**over** ['əuvə*] *adv* **1** *(across: walk, jump, fly etc)* hinüber; **~ here** hier; **~ there** dort (drüben); **to ask sb ~** *(to one's house)* jdn zu sich einladen
**2** *(indicating movement)*: **to fall ~** *(person)* hinfallen; *(object)* umfallen; **to knock sth ~** etw umstoßen; **to turn ~** *(in bed)* sich umdrehen; **to bend ~** sich bücken
**3** *(finished)*: **to be ~** *(game, life, relationship etc)* vorbei sein, zu Ende sein
**4** *(excessively: clever, rich, fat etc)* übermäßig
**5** *(remaining: money, food etc)* übrig; **is there any cake (left) ~?** ist noch Kuchen übrig?
**6**: **all ~** *(everywhere)* überall
**7** *(repeatedly)*: **~ and ~ (again)** immer (und immer) wieder; **five times ~** fünfmal

♦ *prep* **1** *(on top of, above)* über *+dat*; *(with vb of motion)* über *+acc*; **to spread a sheet ~ sth** ein Laken über etw *acc* breiten
**2** *(on the other side of)*: **the pub ~ the road** die Kneipe gegenüber; **he jumped ~ the wall** er sprang über die Mauer
**3** *(more than)* über *+acc*; **~ 200 people** über 200 Leute; **~ and above my normal duties** über meine normalen Pflichten hinaus; **~ and above that** darüber hinaus
**4** *(during)* während; **let's discuss it ~ dinner** wir sollten es beim Abendessen besprechen.

**over...** ['əuvə*] *pref* über-.
**overact** [əuvər'ækt] *vi* übertreiben.
**overall** ['əuvərɔːl] *adj (length, cost etc)* Gesamt-; *(impression, view)* allgemein ♦ *adv (measure, cost)* insgesamt; *(generally)* im allgemeinen ♦ *n (BRIT)* Kittel *m*; **overalls** *npl* Overall *m*.
**overall majority** *n* absolute Mehrheit *f*.
**overanxious** [əuvər'æŋkʃəs] *adj* überängstlich.
**overawe** [əuvər'ɔː] *vt*: **to be ~d (by)** überwältigt sein (von).
**overbalance** [əuvə'bæləns] *vi* das

Gleichgewicht verlieren.
**overbearing** [əuvə'bɛərɪŋ] *adj (person, manner)* aufdringlich.
**overboard** ['əuvəbɔːd] *adv (NAUT)* über Bord; **to go ~** *(fig)* es übertreiben, zu weit gehen.
**overbook** [əuvə'buk] *vt* überbuchen.
**overcame** [əuvə'keɪm] *pt of* **overcome**.
**overcapitalize** [əuvə'kæpɪtəlaɪz] *vt* überkapitalisieren.
**overcast** ['əuvəkɑːst] *adj (day, sky)* bedeckt.
**overcharge** [əuvə'tʃɑːdʒ] *vt* zuviel berechnen *+dat*.
**overcoat** ['əuvəkəut] *n* Mantel *m*.
**overcome** [əuvə'kʌm] *(irreg: like* **come**) *vt (problem, fear)* überwinden ♦ *adj* überwältigt; **she was ~ with grief** der Schmerz übermannte sie.
**overconfident** [əuvə'kɔnfɪdənt] *adj* zu selbstsicher.
**overcrowded** [əuvə'kraudɪd] *adj* überfüllt.
**overcrowding** [əuvə'kraudɪŋ] *n* Überfüllung *f*.
**overdo** [əuvə'duː] *(irreg: like* **do**) *vt* übertreiben; **to ~ it** es übertreiben.
**overdose** ['əuvədəus] *n* Überdosis *f*.
**overdraft** ['əuvədrɑːft] *n* Kontoüberziehung *f*; **to have an ~** sein Konto überziehen.
**overdrawn** [əuvə'drɔːn] *adj (account)* überzogen; **I am ~** ich habe mein Konto überzogen.
**overdrive** ['əuvədraɪv] *n (AUT)* Schongang *m*.
**overdue** [əuvə'djuː] *adj* überfällig; **that change was long ~** diese Änderung war schon lange fällig.
**overemphasis** [əuvər'ɛmfəsɪs] *n*: **~ on** Überbetonung *+gen*.
**overestimate** [əuvər'ɛstɪmeɪt] *vt* überschätzen.
**overexcited** [əuvərɪk'saɪtɪd] *adj* ganz aufgeregt.
**overexertion** [əuvərɪg'zəːʃən] *n* Überanstrengung *f*.
**overexpose** [əuvərɪk'spəuz] *vt (PHOT)* überbelichten.
**overflow** [əuvə'fləu] *vi (river)* über die Ufer treten; *(bath, jar etc)* überlaufen ♦ *n (also:* **~ pipe**) Überlaufrohr *nt*.
**overgenerous** [əuvə'dʒɛnərəs] *adj* allzu großzügig.
**overgrown** [əuvə'grəun] *adj (garden)* verwildert; **he's just an ~ schoolboy** er ist nur ein großes Kind.
**overhang** ['əuvə'hæŋ] *(irreg: like* **hang**) *vt* herausragen über *+acc* ♦ *vi* überhängen ♦ *n* Überhang *m*.
**overhaul** [əuvə'hɔːl] *vt (equipment, car etc)* überholen ♦ *n* Überholung *f*.
**overhead** [əuvə'hɛd] *adv (above)* oben; *(in the sky)* in der Luft ♦ *adj (lighting)* Decken-; *(cables, wires)* Überland- ♦ *n (US)* = **overheads**; **overheads** *npl* allgemeine Unkosten *pl*.
**overhear** [əuvə'hɪə*] *(irreg: like* **hear**) *vt*

(zufällig) mit anhören.

**overheat** [əuvə'hi:t] *vi* (*engine*) heißlaufen.

**overjoyed** [əuvə'dʒɔɪd] *adj* überglücklich; **to be ~ (at)** überglücklich sein (*über +acc*).

**overkill** ['əuvəkɪl] *n* (*fig*): **it would be ~** das wäre zuviel des Guten.

**overland** ['əuvəlænd] *adj* (*journey*) Überland- ♦ *adv* (*travel*) über Land.

**overlap** [əuvə'læp] *vi* (*figures, ideas etc*) sich überschneiden.

**overleaf** [əuvə'li:f] *adv* umseitig, auf der Rückseite.

**overload** [əuvə'ləud] *vt* (*vehicle*) überladen; (*ELEC*) überbelasten; (*fig: with work etc*) überlasten.

**overlook** [əuvə'luk] *vt* (*have view over*) überblicken; (*fail to notice*) übersehen; (*excuse, forgive*) hinwegsehen über *+acc*.

**overlord** ['əuvəlɔ:d] *n* oberster Herr *m*.

**overmanning** [əuvə'mænɪŋ] *n* Überbesetzung *f*.

**overnight** [əuvə'naɪt] *adv* über Nacht ♦ *adj* (*bag, clothes*) Reise-; (*accommodation, stop*) für die Nacht; **to travel ~** nachts reisen; **he'll be away ~** (*tonight*) er kommt erst morgen zurück; **to stay ~** über Nacht bleiben; **~ stay** Übernachtung *f*.

**overpass** ['əuvəpɑ:s] (*esp US*) *n* Überführung *f*.

**overpay** [əuvə'peɪ] *vt*: **to ~ sb by £50** jdm £ 50 zuviel bezahlen.

**overplay** [əuvə'pleɪ] *vt* (*overact*) übertrieben darstellen; **to ~ one's hand** den Bogen überspannen.

**overpower** [əuvə'pauə*] *vt* überwältigen.

**overpowering** [əuvə'pauərɪŋ] *adj* (*heat*) unerträglich; (*stench*) durchdringend; (*feeling, desire*) überwältigend.

**overproduction** ['əuvəprə'dʌkʃən] *n* Überproduktion *f*.

**overrate** [əuvə'reɪt] *vt* überschätzen.

**overreach** [əuvə'ri:tʃ] *vt*: **to ~ o.s.** sich übernehmen.

**overreact** [əuvəri:'ækt] *vi* übertrieben reagieren.

**override** [əuvə'raɪd] (*irreg: like* **ride**) *vt* (*order etc*) sich hinwegsetzen über *+acc*.

**overriding** [əuvə'raɪdɪŋ] *adj* vorrangig.

**overrule** [əuvə'ru:l] *vt* (*claim, person*) zurückweisen; (*decision*) aufheben.

**overrun** [əuvə'rʌn] (*irreg: like* **run**) *vt* (*country, continent*) einfallen in *+acc* ♦ *vi* (*meeting etc*) zu lange dauern; **the town is ~ with tourists** die Stadt ist von Touristen überlaufen.

**overseas** [əuvə'si:z] *adv* (*live, work*) im Ausland; (*travel*) ins Ausland ♦ *adj* (*market, trade*) Übersee-; (*student, visitor*) aus dem Ausland.

**oversee** [əuvə'si:] *vt* (*supervise*) beaufsichtigen, überwachen.

**overseer** ['əuvəsɪə*] *n* Aufseher(in) *m(f)*.

**overshadow** [əuvə'ʃædəu] *vt* (*place, building*

etc) überschatten; (*fig*) in den Schatten stellen.

**overshoot** [əuvə'ʃu:t] (*irreg: like* **shoot**) *vt* (*target, runway*) hinausschießen über *+acc*.

**oversight** ['əuvəsaɪt] *n* Versehen *nt*; **due to an ~** aus Versehen.

**oversimplify** [əuvə'sɪmplɪfaɪ] *vt* zu stark vereinfachen.

**oversleep** [əuvə'sli:p] (*irreg: like* **sleep**) *vi* verschlafen.

**overspend** [əuvə'spɛnd] (*irreg: like* **spend**) *vi* zuviel ausgeben; **we have overspent by 5,000 dollars** wir haben 5000 Dollar zuviel ausgegeben.

**overspill** ['əuvəspɪl] *n* (*excess population*) Bevölkerungsüberschuß *m*.

**overstaffed** [əuvə'stɑ:ft] *adj*: **to be ~** überbesetzt sein.

**overstate** [əuvə'steɪt] *vt* (*exaggerate*) zu sehr betonen.

**overstatement** [əuvə'steɪtmənt] *n* Übertreibung *f*.

**overstay** [əuvə'steɪ] *vt see* **outstay**.

**overstep** [əuvə'stɛp] *vt*: **to ~ the mark** zu weit gehen.

**overstock** [əuvə'stɔk] *vt* zu große Bestände anlegen in *+dat*.

**overstretched** [əuvə'strɛtʃt] *adj* (*person, resources*) überfordert.

**overstrike** ['əuvəstraɪk] (*irreg: like* **strike**) *n* (*on printer*) Mehrfachdruck *m* ♦ *vt* mehrfachdrucken.

**oversubscribed** [əuvəsəb'skraɪbd] *adj* (*COMM etc*) überzeichnet.

**overt** [əu'vɜ:t] *adj* offen.

**overtake** [əuvə'teɪk] (*irreg: like* **take**) *vt* (*AUT*) überholen; (*event, change*) hereinbrechen über *+acc*; (*emotion*) befallen ♦ *vi* (*AUT*) überholen.

**overtaking** [əuvə'teɪkɪŋ] *n* (*AUT*) Überholen *nt*.

**overtax** [əuvə'tæks] *vt* (*ECON*) zu hoch besteuern; (*strength, patience*) überfordern; **to ~ o.s.** sich übernehmen.

**overthrow** [əuvə'θrəu] (*irreg: like* **throw**) *vt* (*government etc*) stürzen.

**overtime** ['əuvətaɪm] *n* Überstunden *pl*; **to do or work ~** Überstunden machen.

**overtime ban** *n* Überstundenverbot *nt*.

**overtone** ['əuvətəun] *n* (*fig: also:* ~s): **~s of** Untertöne *pl* von.

**overture** ['əuvətʃuə*] *n* (*MUS*) Ouvertüre *f*; (*fig*) Annäherungsversuch *m*.

**overturn** [əuvə'tɜ:n] *vt* (*car, chair*) umkippen; (*fig: decision*) aufheben; (: *government*) stürzen ♦ *vi* (*train etc*) umkippen; (*car*) sich überschlagen; (*boat*) kentern.

**overview** ['əuvəvju:] *n* Überblick *m*.

**overweight** [əuvə'weɪt] *adj* (*person*) übergewichtig.

**overwhelm** [əuvə'wɛlm] *vt* überwältigen.

**overwhelming** [əuvə'wɛlmɪŋ] *adj*

überwältigend; one's ~ impression is of
heat/noise man bemerkt vor allem die
Hitze/den Lärm.
**overwhelmingly** [əuvə'wɛlmɪŋlɪ] adv (vote,
reject) mit überwältigender Mehrheit;
(appreciative, generous etc) über alle Maßen;
(opposed etc) überwiegend.
**overwork** [əuvə'wə:k] n Überarbeitung f ♦ vt
(person) (mit Arbeit) überlasten; (cliché etc)
überstrapazieren ♦ vi sich überarbeiten.
**overwrite** [əuvə'raɪt] vt (COMPUT)
überschreiben.
**overwrought** [əuvə'rɔ:t] adj (person)
überreizt.
**ovulate** ['ɔvjuleɪt] vi ovulieren.
**ovulation** [ɔvju'leɪʃən] n Eisprung m,
Ovulation f.
**ovum** ['əuvəm] (pl ova) n Eizelle f.
**owe** [əu] vt: to ~ sb sth, to ~ sth to sb (lit, fig)
jdm etw schulden; (life, talent, good looks etc)
jdm etw verdanken.
**owing to** ['əuɪŋ-] prep (because of) wegen +gen,
aufgrund +gen.
**owl** [aul] n Eule f.
**own** [əun] vt (possess) besitzen ♦ vi (BRIT:
form): to ~ up to sth etw zugeben ♦ adj
eigen; a room of my ~ mein eigenes
Zimmer; to get one's ~ back (take revenge)
sich rächen; on one's ~ allein; to come into
one's ~ sich entfalten.
▶**own up** vi gestehen, es zugeben.
**own brand** n (COMM) Hausmarke f.
**owner** ['əunə'] n Besitzer(in) m(f),
Eigentümer(in) m(f).
**owner-occupier** ['əunər'ɔkjupaɪə'] n (ADMIN,
LAW) Bewohner(in) m(f) im eigenen Haus.
**ownership** ['əunəʃɪp] n Besitz m; under new
~ (shop etc) unter neuer Leitung.
**own goal** n (also fig) Eigentor nt.
**ox** [ɔks] (pl ~en) n Ochse m.

Oxbridge, eine Mischung aus Ox(ford) und
(Cam)bridge, bezieht sich auf die uralten
Universitäten von Oxford und Cambridge.
Dieser Begriff ist oft wertend und bringt das
Prestige und die Privilegien zum Ausdruck, die
traditionellerweise mit diesen Universitäten in
Verbindung gebracht werden.

**OXFAM** (BRIT) n abbr (= Oxford Committee for
Famine Relief) karitative Vereinigung zur
Hungerhilfe.
**oxide** ['ɔksaɪd] n Oxyd nt.
**oxidize** ['ɔksɪdaɪz] vi oxydieren.
**Oxon.** ['ɔksn] (BRIT) abbr (POST:
= Oxfordshire); (in degree titles: = Oxoniensis)
der Universität Oxford.
**oxtail** ['ɔksteɪl] n: ~ soup
Ochsenschwanzsuppe f.
**oxyacetylene** ['ɔksɪə'sɛtɪli:n] adj (flame)
Azetylensauerstoff-; ~ burner
Schweißbrenner m; ~ welding

Autogenschweißen nt.
**oxygen** ['ɔksɪdʒən] n Sauerstoff m.
**oxygen mask** n Sauerstoffmaske f.
**oxygen tent** n Sauerstoffzelt nt.
**oyster** ['ɔɪstə'] n Auster f.
**oz** abbr = **ounce**.
**ozone** ['əuzəun] n Ozon nt.
**ozone hole** n Ozonloch nt.
**ozone layer** n: the ~ die Ozonschicht.

# P, p

**P, p¹** [pi:] n (letter) P nt, p nt; ~ for Peter ≈ P
wie Paula.
**P.** abbr = **president; prince**.
**p²** (BRIT) abbr = **penny; pence**.
**p.** abbr (= page) S.
**PA** n abbr = **personal assistant; public-address
system** ♦ abbr (US: POST: = Pennsylvania).
**pa** [pɑ:] (inf) n Papa m.
**p.a.** abbr (= per annum) p.a.
**PAC** (US) n abbr (= political action committee)
politisches Aktionskomitee.
**pace** [peɪs] n (step) Schritt m; (speed) Tempo
nt ♦ vi: to ~ up and down auf und ab gehen;
to keep ~ with Schritt halten mit; to set the
~ das Tempo angeben; to put sb through
his/her ~s (fig) jdn auf Herz und Nieren
prüfen.
**pacemaker** ['peɪsmeɪkə'] n (MED)
(Herz)schrittmacher m; (SPORT: also:
pacesetter) Schrittmacher m.
**pacesetter** ['peɪssɛtə'] n (SPORT)
= pacemaker.
**Pacific** [pə'sɪfɪk] n (GEOG): the ~ (Ocean) der
Pazifik, der Pazifische Ozean.
**pacific** [pə'sɪfɪk] adj (intentions etc) friedlich.
**pacifier** ['pæsɪfaɪə'] (US) n (dummy) Schnuller
m.
**pacifist** ['pæsɪfɪst] n Pazifist(in) m(f).
**pacify** ['pæsɪfaɪ] vt (person, fears) beruhigen.
**pack** [pæk] n (packet) Packung f; (US: of
cigarettes) Schachtel f; (of people, hounds)
Meute f; (back pack) Rucksack m; (of cards)
(Karten)spiel nt ♦ vt (clothes etc) einpacken;
(suitcase etc, COMPUT) packen; (press down)
pressen ♦ vi packen; to ~ one's bags (fig)
die Koffer packen; to ~ into (cram: people,
objects) hineinstopfen in +acc; to send sb
~ing (inf) jdn kurz abfertigen.
▶**pack in** (BRIT: inf) vt (job) hinschmeißen;
~ it in! hör auf!
▶**pack off** vt schicken.
▶**pack up** vi (BRIT: inf: machine) den Geist
aufgeben; (: : person) Feierabend machen

♦ *vt* (*belongings*) zusammenpacken.
**package** ['pækɪdʒ] *n* (*parcel, COMPUT*) Paket *nt*; (*also*: ~ **deal**) Pauschalangebot *nt* ♦ *vt* verpacken.
**package holiday** (*BRIT*), **package tour** (*US*) *n* Pauschalreise *f*.
**packaging** ['pækɪdʒɪŋ] *n* Verpackung *f*.
**packed** [pækt] *adj* (*crowded*) randvoll.
**packed lunch** (*BRIT*) *n* Lunchpaket *nt*.
**packer** ['pækə'] *n* Packer(in) *m(f)*.
**packet** ['pækɪt] *n* Packung *f*; (*of cigarettes*) Schachtel *m*; **to make a** ~ (*BRIT: inf*) einen Haufen Geld verdienen.
**packet switching** *n* (*COMPUT*) Paketvermittlung *f*.
**pack ice** ['pækaɪs] *n* Packeis *nt*.
**packing** ['pækɪŋ] *n* (*act*) Packen *nt*; (*material*) Verpackung *f*.
**packing case** *n* Kiste *f*.
**pact** [pækt] *n* Pakt *m*.
**pad** [pæd] *n* (*paper*) Block *m*; (*to prevent damage*) Polster *nt*; (*inf: home*) Bude *f* ♦ *vt* (*upholstery etc*) polstern ♦ *vi*: **to** ~ **about/in** herum-/hereintrotten.
**padded cell** ['pædɪd-] *n* Gummizelle *f*.
**padding** ['pædɪŋ] *n* (*material*) Polsterung *f*; (*fig*) Füllwerk *nt*.
**paddle** ['pædl] *n* (*oar*) Paddel *nt*; (*US: for table tennis*) Schläger *m* ♦ *vt* paddeln ♦ *vi* (*at seaside*) planschen.
**paddle steamer** *n* Raddampfer *m*.
**paddling pool** ['pædlɪŋ-] (*BRIT*) *n* Planschbecken *nt*.
**paddock** ['pædək] *n* (*small field*) Koppel *f*; (*at race course*) Sattelplatz *m*.
**paddy field** ['pædɪ-] *n* Reisfeld *nt*.
**padlock** ['pædlɔk] *n* Vorhängeschloß *nt* ♦ *vt* (mit einem Vorhängeschloß) verschließen.
**padre** ['pɑːdrɪ] *n* (*REL*) Feldgeistliche(r) *m*.
**paediatrician** [piːdɪə'trɪʃən] *n* Kinderarzt *m*, Kinderärztin *f*.
**paediatrics,** (*US*) **pediatrics** [piːdɪ'ætrɪks] *n* Kinderheilkunde *f*, Pädiatrie *f*.
**paedophile** ['piːdəʊfaɪl] *n* Pädophile(r) *f(m)* ♦ *adj* pädophil.
**paedophilia** [piːdəʊ'fɪlɪə] *n* Pädophilie *f*.
**pagan** ['peɪɡən] *adj* heidnisch ♦ *n* Heide *m*, Heidin *f*.
**page** [peɪdʒ] *n* (*of book etc*) Seite *f*; (*also*: ~**boy**: *in hotel*) Page *m* ♦ *vt* (*in hotel etc*) ausrufen lassen.
**pageant** ['pædʒənt] *n* (*historical procession*) Festzug *m*; (*show*) Historienspiel *nt*.
**pageantry** ['pædʒəntrɪ] *n* Prunk *m*.
**pageboy** ['peɪdʒbɔɪ] *n see* **page**.
**pager** ['peɪdʒə'] *n* Funkrufempfänger *m*, Piepser *m* (*inf*).
**paginate** ['pædʒɪneɪt] *vt* paginieren.
**pagination** [pædʒɪ'neɪʃən] *n* Paginierung *f*.
**pagoda** [pə'ɡəʊdə] *n* Pagode *f*.
**paid** [peɪd] *pt, pp of* **pay** ♦ *adj* bezahlt; **to put** ~ **to** (*BRIT*) zunichte machen.

**paid-in** ['peɪdɪn] (*US*) *adj* = **paid-up**.
**paid-up** ['peɪdʌp], (*US*) **paid-in** ['peɪdɪn] *adj* (*member*) zahlend; (*COMM: shares*) eingezahlt; ~ **capital** eingezahltes Kapital *nt*.
**pail** [peɪl] *n* Eimer *m*.
**pain** [peɪn] *n* Schmerz *m*; (*also*: ~ **in the neck**: *inf: nuisance*) Plage *f*; **to have a** ~ **in the chest/arm** Schmerzen in der Brust/im Arm haben; **to be in** ~ Schmerzen haben; **to take** ~**s to do sth** (*make an effort*) sich *dat* Mühe geben, etw zu tun; **on** ~ **of death** bei Todesstrafe; **he is/it is a right** ~ (**in the neck**) (*inf*) er/das geht einem auf den Wecker.
**pained** [peɪnd] *adj* (*expression*) gequält.
**painful** ['peɪnful] *adj* (*back, injury etc*) schmerzhaft; (*sight, decision etc*) schmerzlich; (*laborious*) mühsam; (*embarrassing*) peinlich.
**painfully** ['peɪnfəlɪ] *adv* (*fig: extremely*) furchtbar.
**painkiller** ['peɪnkɪlə'] *n* schmerzstillendes Mittel *nt*.
**painless** ['peɪnlɪs] *adj* schmerzlos.
**painstaking** ['peɪnzteɪkɪŋ] *adj* (*work, person*) gewissenhaft.
**paint** [peɪnt] *n* Farbe *f* ♦ *vt* (*door, house etc*) anstreichen; (*person, picture*) malen; (*fig*) zeichnen; **a tin of** ~ eine Dose Farbe; **to** ~ **the door blue** die Tür blau streichen; **to** ~ **in oils** in Öl malen.
**paintbox** ['peɪntbɔks] *n* Farbkasten *m*, Malkasten *m*.
**paintbrush** ['peɪntbrʌʃ] *n* Pinsel *m*.
**painter** ['peɪntə'] *n* (*artist*) Maler(in) *m(f)*; (*decorator*) Anstreicher(in) *m(f)*.
**painting** ['peɪntɪŋ] *n* (*activity: of artist*) Malerei *f*; (: *of decorator*) Anstreichen *nt*; (*picture*) Bild *nt*, Gemälde *nt*.
**paint stripper** *n* Abbeizmittel *nt*.
**paintwork** ['peɪntwɜːk] *n* (*of wall etc*) Anstrich *m*; (*of car*) Lack *m*.
**pair** [pɛə'] *n* Paar *nt*; **a** ~ **of scissors** eine Schere; **a** ~ **of trousers** eine Hose.
►**pair off** *vi*: **to** ~ **off with sb** sich jdm anschließen.
**pajamas** [pə'dʒɑːməz] (*US*) *npl* Schlafanzug *m*, Pyjama *m*.
**Pakistan** [pɑːkɪ'stɑːn] *n* Pakistan *nt*.
**Pakistani** [pɑːkɪ'stɑːnɪ] *adj* pakistanisch ♦ *n* Pakistani *m*, Pakistaner(in) *m(f)*.
**PAL** *n abbr* (*TV*: = *phase alternation line*) PAL *nt*.
**pal** [pæl] (*inf*) *n* (*friend*) Kumpel *m*, Freund(in) *m(f)*.
**palace** ['pæləs] *n* Palast *m*.
**palaeontology** [pælɪɒn'tɔlədʒɪ] *n* Paläontologie *f*.
**palatable** ['pælɪtəbl] *adj* (*food, drink*) genießbar; (*fig: idea, fact etc*) angenehm.
**palate** ['pælɪt] *n* (*ANAT*) Gaumen *m*; (*sense of taste*) Geschmackssinn *m*.

**palatial** [pə'leɪʃəl] *adj* (*residence etc*) prunkvoll.

**palaver** [pə'lɑːvə•] (*inf*) *n* (*fuss*) Theater *nt*.

**pale** [peɪl] *adj* blaß; (*light*) fahl ♦ *vi* erblassen ♦ *n*: **beyond the ~** (*unacceptable: behaviour*) indiskutabel; **to grow** *or* **turn ~** erblassen, blaß werden; **~ blue** zartblau; **to ~ into insignificance (beside)** zur Bedeutungslosigkeit herabsinken (gegenüber +*dat*).

**paleness** ['peɪlnɪs] *n* Blässe *f*.

**Palestine** ['pælɪstaɪn] *n* Palästina *nt*.

**Palestinian** [pælɪs'tɪnɪən] *adj* palästinensisch ♦ *n* Palästinenser(in) *m(f)*.

**palette** ['pælɪt] *n* Palette *f*.

**palings** ['peɪlɪŋz] *npl* (*fence*) Lattenzaun *m*.

**palisade** [pælɪ'seɪd] *n* Palisade *f*.

**pall** [pɔːl] *n* (*cloud of smoke*) (Rauch)wolke *f* ♦ *vi* an Reiz verlieren.

**pallet** ['pælɪt] *n* (*for goods*) Palette *f*.

**palliative** ['pælɪətɪv] *n* (*MED*) Linderungsmittel *nt*; (*fig*) Beschönigung *f*.

**pallid** ['pælɪd] *adj* bleich.

**pallor** ['pælə•] *n* Bleichheit *f*.

**pally** ['pælɪ] (*inf*) *adj*: **they're very ~** sie sind dicke Freunde.

**palm** [pɑːm] *n* (*also*: **~ tree**) Palme *f*; (*of hand*) Handteller *m* ♦ *vt*: **to ~ sth off on sb** (*inf*) jdm etw andrehen.

**palmistry** ['pɑːmɪstrɪ] *n* Handlesekunst *f*.

**Palm Sunday** *n* Palmsonntag *m*.

**palpable** ['pælpəbl] *adj* (*obvious*) offensichtlich.

**palpitations** [pælpɪ'teɪʃənz] *npl* (*MED*) Herzklopfen *nt*.

**paltry** ['pɔːltrɪ] *adj* (*amount, wage*) armselig.

**pamper** ['pæmpə•] *vt* verwöhnen.

**pamphlet** ['pæmflət] *n* Broschüre *f*; (*political*) Flugschrift *f*.

**pan** [pæn] *n* (*also*: **saucepan**) Topf *m*; (*also*: **frying ~**) Pfanne *f* ♦ *vi* (*CINE, TV*) schwenken ♦ *vt* (*inf: book, film*) verreißen; **to ~ for gold** Gold waschen.

**panacea** [pænə'sɪə] *n* Allheilmittel *nt*.

**panache** [pə'næʃ] *n* Elan *m*, Schwung *m*.

**Panama** ['pænəmɑː] *n* Panama *nt*.

**panama** [pænə'mɑː] *n* (*also*: **~ hat**) Panamahut *m*.

**Panama Canal** *n*: **the ~** der Panamakanal.

**Panamanian** [pænə'meɪnɪən] *adj* panamaisch ♦ *n* Panamaer(in) *m(f)*.

**pancake** ['pænkeɪk] *n* Pfannkuchen *m*.

**Pancake Day** (*BRIT*) *n* Fastnachtsdienstag *m*.

**pancake roll** *n* gefüllte Pfannkuchenrolle.

**pancreas** ['pæŋkrɪəs] *n* Bauchspeicheldrüse *f*.

**panda** ['pændə] *n* Panda *m*.

**panda car** (*BRIT*) *n* Streifenwagen *m*.

**pandemonium** [pændɪ'məunɪəm] *n* Chaos *nt*.

**pander** ['pændə•] *vi*: **to ~ to** (*person, desire etc*) sich richten nach, entgegenkommen +*dat*.

**p & h** (*US*) *abbr* (= *postage and handling*) Porto und Bearbeitungsgebühr.

**P & L** *abbr* (= *profit and loss*) Gewinn und Verlust; *see also* **profit**.

**p & p** (*BRIT*) *abbr* (= *postage and packing*) Porto und Verpackung.

**pane** [peɪn] *n* (*of glass*) Scheibe *f*.

**panel** ['pænl] *n* (*wood, metal, glass etc*) Platte *f*, Tafel *f*; (*group of experts etc*) Diskussionsrunde *f*; **~ of judges** Jury *f*.

**panel game** (*BRIT*) *n* Ratespiel *nt*.

**panelling**, (*US*) **paneling** ['pænəlɪŋ] *n* Täfelung *f*.

**panellist**, (*US*) **panelist** ['pænəlɪst] *n* Diskussionsteilnehmer(in) *m(f)*.

**pang** [pæŋ] *n*: **to have** *or* **feel a ~ of regret** Reue empfinden; **hunger ~s** quälender Hunger *m*; **~s of conscience** Gewissensbisse *pl*.

**panhandler** ['pænhændlə•] (*US: inf*) *n* Bettler(in) *m(f)*.

**panic** ['pænɪk] *n* Panik *f* ♦ *vi* in Panik geraten.

**panic buying** [-baɪɪŋ] *n* Panikkäufe *pl*.

**panicky** ['pænɪkɪ] *adj* (*person*) überängstlich; (*feeling*) Angst-; (*reaction*) Kurzschluß-.

**panic-stricken** ['pænɪkstrɪkən] *adj* (*person, face*) von Panik erfaßt.

**pannier** ['pænɪə•] *n* (*on bicycle*) Satteltasche *f*; (*on animal*) (Trage)korb *m*.

**panorama** [pænə'rɑːmə] *n* (*view*) Panorama *nt*.

**panoramic** [pænə'ræmɪk] *adj* (*view*) Panorama-.

**pansy** ['pænzɪ] *n* (*BOT*) Stiefmütterchen *nt*; (*inf: pej: sissy*) Tunte *f*.

**pant** [pænt] *vi* (*person*) keuchen; (*animal*) hecheln.

**pantechnicon** [pæn'tɛknɪkən] (*BRIT*) *n* Möbelwagen *m*.

**panther** ['pænθə•] *n* Panther *m*.

**panties** ['pæntɪz] *npl* Höschen *nt*.

**panto** ['pæntəu] *n see* **pantomime**.

---

**Pantomime** *oder* *umgangssprachlich* **panto** *ist in Großbritannien ein zur Weihnachtszeit aufgeführtes Märchenspiel mit possenhaften Elementen, Musik, Standardrollen (ein als Frau verkleideter Mann, ein Junge, ein Bösewicht) und aktuellen Witzen. Publikumsbeteiligung wird gern gesehen (z.B. warnen die Kinder den Helden mit dem Ruf 'He's behind you' vor einer drohenden Gefahr), und viele der Witze sprechen vor allem Erwachsene an, so daß pantomimes Unterhaltung für die ganze Familie bieten.*

---

**pantry** ['pæntrɪ] *n* (*cupboard*) Vorratsschrank *m*; (*room*) Speisekammer *f*.

**pants** [pænts] *npl* (*BRIT: woman's*) Höschen *nt*; (: *man's*) Unterhose *f*; (*US: trousers*) Hose *f*.

**panty hose** (*US*) *npl* Strumpfhose *f*.

**papacy** ['peɪpəsɪ] *n* Papsttum *nt*; **during the ~ of Paul VI** während der Amtszeit von Papst Paul VI.

**papal** ['peɪpəl] *adj* päpstlich.

**paparazzi** [pæpə'rætsiː] *npl* Pressefotografen

*pl*, Paparazzi *pl*.

**paper** ['peɪpə*] *n* Papier *nt*; (*also*: **newspaper**) Zeitung *f*; (*exam*) Arbeit *f*; (*academic essay*) Referat *nt*; (*document*) Dokument *nt*, Papier, (*wallpaper*) Tapete *f* ♦ *adj* (*made from paper: hat, plane etc*) Papier-, aus Papier ♦ *vt* (*room*) tapezieren; **papers** *npl* (*also*: **identity** ~**s**) Papiere *pl*; **a piece of** ~ (*odd bit*) ein Stück Papier, ein Zettel; (*sheet*) ein Blatt Papier; **to put sth down on** ~ etw schriftlich festhalten.

**paper advance** *n* (*on printer*) Papiervorschub *m*.

**paperback** ['peɪpəbæk] *n* Taschenbuch *nt*, Paperback *nt* ♦ *adj*: ~ **edition** Taschenbuchausgabe *f*.

**paper bag** *n* Tüte *f*.

**paperboy** ['peɪpəbɔɪ] *n* Zeitungsjunge *m*.

**paperclip** ['peɪpəklɪp] *n* Büroklammer *f*.

**paper hankie** *n* Tempotaschentuch ® *nt*.

**paper mill** *n* Papierfabrik *f*.

**paper money** *n* Papiergeld *nt*.

**paper shop** *n* Zeitungsladen *m*.

**paperweight** ['peɪpəweɪt] *n* Briefbeschwerer *m*.

**paperwork** ['peɪpəwɜːk] *n* Schreibarbeit *f*.

**papier-mâché** [pæpjeɪ'mæʃeɪ] *n* Papiermaché *nt*.

**paprika** ['pæprɪkə] *n* Paprika *m*.

**Pap Smear, Pap Test** *n* (*MED*) Abstrich *m*.

**par** [pɑː*] *n* (*GOLF*) Par *nt*; **to be on a** ~ **with** sich messen können mit; **at** ~ (*COMM*) zum Nennwert; **above/below** ~ (*COMM*) über/unter dem Nennwert; **above** *or* **over** ~ (*GOLF*) über dem Par; **below** *or* **under** ~ (*GOLF*) unter dem Par; **to feel below** *or* **under** ~ sich nicht auf der Höhe fühlen; **to be** ~ **for the course** (*fig*) zu erwarten sein.

**parable** ['pærəbl] *n* Gleichnis *nt*.

**parabola** [pə'ræbələ] *n* (*MATH*) Parabel *f*.

**parachute** ['pærəʃuːt] *n* Fallschirm *m*.

**parachute jump** *n* Fallschirmabsprung *m*.

**parachutist** ['pærəʃuːtɪst] *n* Fallschirmspringer(in) *m(f)*.

**parade** [pə'reɪd] *n* (*procession*) Parade *f*; (*ceremony*) Zeremonie *f* ♦ *vt* (*people*) aufmarschieren lassen; (*wealth, knowledge etc*) zur Schau stellen ♦ *vi* (*MIL*) aufmarschieren; **fashion** ~ Modenschau *f*.

**parade ground** *n* Truppenübungsplatz *m*, Exerzierplatz *m*.

**paradise** ['pærədaɪs] *n* (*also fig*) Paradies *nt*.

**paradox** ['pærədɒks] *n* Paradox *nt*.

**paradoxical** [pærə'dɒksɪkl] *adj* (*situation*) paradox.

**paradoxically** [pærə'dɒksɪklɪ] *adv* paradoxerweise.

**paraffin** ['pærəfɪn] (*BRIT*) *n* (*also*: ~ **oil**) Petroleum *nt*; **liquid** ~ Paraffinöl *nt*.

**paraffin heater** (*BRIT*) *n* Petroleumofen *m*.

**paraffin lamp** (*BRIT*) *n* Petroleumlampe *f*.

**paragon** ['pærəgən] *n*: **a** ~ **of** (*honesty, virtue etc*) ein Muster *nt* an +*dat*.

**paragraph** ['pærəgrɑːf] *n* Absatz *m*, Paragraph *m*; **to begin a new** ~ einen neuen Absatz beginnen.

**parallel** ['pærəlɛl] *adj* (*also COMPUT*) parallel; (*fig: similar*) vergleichbar ♦ *n* Parallele *f*; (*GEOG*) Breitenkreis *m*; **to run** ~ (**with** *or* **to**) (*lit, fig*) parallel verlaufen (zu); **to draw** ~**s between/with** Parallelen ziehen zwischen/mit; **in** ~ (*ELEC*) parallel.

**paralyse** ['pærəlaɪz] (*BRIT*) *vt* (*also fig*) lähmen.

**paralysis** [pə'rælɪsɪs] (*pl* **paralyses**) *n* Lähmung *f*.

**paralytic** [pærə'lɪtɪk] *adj* paralytisch, Lähmungs-; (*BRIT: inf: drunk*) sternhagelvoll.

**paralyze** ['pærəlaɪz] (*US*) *vt* = **paralyse**.

**paramedic** [pærə'mɛdɪk] *n* Sanitäter(in) *m(f)*; (*in hospital*) medizinisch-technischer Assistent *m*, medizinisch-technische Assistentin *f*.

**parameter** [pə'ræmɪtə*] *n* (*MATH*) Parameter *m*; (*fig: factor*) Faktor *m*; (: *limit*) Rahmen *m*.

**paramilitary** [pærə'mɪlɪtərɪ] *adj* paramilitärisch.

**paramount** ['pærəmaunt] *adj* vorherrschend; **of** ~ **importance** von höchster *or* größter Wichtigkeit.

**paranoia** [pærə'nɔɪə] *n* Paranoia *f*.

**paranoid** ['pærənɔɪd] *adj* paranoid.

**paranormal** [pærə'nɔːml] *adj* übersinnlich, paranormal ♦ *n*: **the** ~ das Übersinnliche.

**parapet** ['pærəpɪt] *n* Brüstung *f*.

**paraphernalia** [pærəfə'neɪlɪə] *n* Utensilien *pl*.

**paraphrase** ['pærəfreɪz] *vt* umschreiben.

**paraplegic** [pærə'pliːdʒɪk] *n* Paraplegiker(in) *m(f)*, doppelseitig Gelähmte(r) *f(m)*.

**parapsychology** [pærəsaɪ'kɔlədʒɪ] *n* Parapsychologie *f*.

**parasite** ['pærəsaɪt] *n* (*also fig*) Parasit *m*.

**parasol** ['pærəsɔl] *n* Sonnenschirm *m*.

**paratrooper** ['pærətruːpə*] *n* Fallschirmjäger *m*.

**parcel** ['pɑːsl] *n* Paket *nt* ♦ *vt* (*also*: ~ **up**) verpacken.

▶**parcel out** *vt* aufteilen.

**parcel bomb** (*BRIT*) *n* Paketbombe *f*.

**parcel post** *n* Paketpost *f*.

**parch** [pɑːtʃ] *vt* ausdörren, austrocknen.

**parched** [pɑːtʃt] *adj* ausgetrocknet; **I'm** ~ (*inf: thirsty*) ich bin am Verdursten.

**parchment** ['pɑːtʃmənt] *n* Pergament *nt*.

**pardon** ['pɑːdn] *n* (*LAW*) Begnadigung *f* ♦ *vt* (*forgive*) verzeihen +*dat*, vergeben +*dat*; (*LAW*) begnadigen; ~ **me!, I beg your** ~! (*I'm sorry!*) verzeihen Sie bitte!; (**I beg your**) ~?, (*US*) ~ **me?** (*what did you say?*) bitte?

**pare** [pɛə*] *vt* (*BRIT: nails*) schneiden; (*fruit etc*) schälen; (*fig: costs etc*) reduzieren.

**parent** ['pɛərənt] *n* (*mother*) Mutter *f*; (*father*) Vater *m*; **parents** *npl* (*mother and father*) Eltern *pl*.

**parentage** ['pɛərəntɪdʒ] *n* Herkunft *f*; **of**

**unknown** ~ unbekannter Herkunft.
**parental** [pə'rɛntl] adj (love, control etc)
elterlich.
**parent company** n Mutterunternehmen nt.
**parentheses** [pə'rɛnθɪsiːz] npl of **parenthesis**.
**parenthesis** [pə'rɛnθɪsɪs] (pl **parentheses**) n
Klammer f; **in** ~ in Klammern.
**parenthood** ['pɛərənthud] n Elternschaft f.
**parenting** ['pɛərəntɪŋ] n elterliche Pflege f.
**Paris** ['pærɪs] n Paris nt.
**parish** ['pærɪʃ] n Gemeinde f.
**parish council** (BRIT) n Gemeinderat m.
**parishioner** [pə'rɪʃənə*] n Gemeindemitglied
nt.
**Parisian** [pə'rɪzɪən] adj Pariser inv,
paris(er)isch ♦ n Pariser(in) m(f).
**parity** ['pærɪtɪ] n (equality) Gleichstellung f.
**park** [pɑːk] n Park m ♦ vt, vi (AUT) parken.
**parka** ['pɑːkə] n Parka m.
**parking** ['pɑːkɪŋ] n Parken nt; **"no ~"**
„Parken verboten".
**parking lights** npl Parklicht nt.
**parking lot** (US) n Parkplatz m.
**parking meter** n Parkuhr f.
**parking offence** (BRIT) n Parkvergehen nt.
**parking place** n Parkplatz m.
**parking ticket** n Strafzettel m.
**parking violation** (US) n = **parking offence**.
**Parkinson's (disease)** ['pɑːkɪnsənz-] n
Parkinsonsche Krankheit f.
**parkway** ['pɑːkweɪ] (US) n Allee f.
**parlance** ['pɑːləns] n: **in common/modern** ~
im allgemeinen/modernen Sprachgebrauch.
**parliament** ['pɑːləmənt] n Parlament nt.

---
*Parliament ist die höchste gesetzgebende
Versammlung in Großbritannien und tritt im
Parlamentsgebäude in London zusammen. Die
Legislaturperiode beträgt normalerweise 5
Jahre, von einer Wahl zur nächsten. Das
Parlament besteht aus zwei Kammern, dem
Oberhaus (siehe **House of Lords**) und dem
Unterhaus (siehe **House of Commons**).*

---

**parliamentary** [pɑːlə'mɛntərɪ] adj
parlamentarisch.
**parlour**, (US) **parlor** ['pɑːlə*] n Salon m.
**parlous** ['pɑːləs] adj (state) prekär.
**Parmesan** [pɑːmɪ'zæn] n (also: ~ **cheese**)
Parmesan(käse) m.
**parochial** [pə'rəukɪəl] (pej) adj (person,
attitude) engstirnig.
**parody** ['pærədɪ] n Parodie f ♦ vt parodieren.
**parole** [pə'rəul] n (LAW) Bewährung f; **on** ~
auf Bewährung.
**paroxysm** ['pærəksɪzəm] n (also MED) Anfall
m.
**parquet** ['pɑːkeɪ] n (also: ~ **floor(ing)**)
Parkettboden m.
**parrot** ['pærət] n Papagei m.
**parrot-fashion** ['pærətfæʃən] adv (say, learn)
mechanisch; (repeat) wie ein Papagei.

**parry** ['pærɪ] vt (blow, argument) parieren,
abwehren.
**parsimonious** [pɑːsɪ'məunɪəs] adj geizig.
**parsley** ['pɑːslɪ] n Petersilie f.
**parsnip** ['pɑːsnɪp] n Pastinake f.
**parson** ['pɑːsn] n Pfarrer m.
**part** [pɑːt] n Teil m; (TECH) Teil nt; (THEAT,
CINE etc: role) Rolle f; (US: in hair) Scheitel m;
(MUS) Stimme f ♦ adv = **partly** ♦ vt (separate)
trennen; (hair) scheiteln ♦ vi (roads, fig:
people) sich trennen; (crowd) sich teilen; **to
take** ~ **in** teilnehmen an +dat; **to take sth in
good** ~ etw nicht übelnehmen; **to take sb's**
~ (support) sich auf jds Seite acc stellen; **on
his** ~ seinerseits; **for my** ~ für meinen Teil;
**for the most** ~ (generally) zumeist; **for the
better** or **best** ~ **of the day** die meiste Zeit
des Tages; **to be** ~ **and parcel of**
dazugehören zu; ~ **of speech** (LING) Wortart
f.
►**part with** vt fus sich trennen von.
**partake** [pɑː'teɪk] (irreg: like **take**) vi (form): **to**
~ **of sth** etw zu sich nehmen.
**part exchange** (BRIT) n: **to give/take sth in** ~
etw in Zahlung geben/nehmen.
**partial** ['pɑːʃl] adj (victory, solution) Teil-;
(support) teilweise; (biassed) parteiisch; **to
be** ~ **to** (person, drink etc) eine Vorliebe
haben für.
**partially** ['pɑːʃəlɪ] adv (to some extent)
teilweise, zum Teil.
**participant** [pɑː'tɪsɪpənt] n Teilnehmer(in)
m(f).
**participate** [pɑː'tɪsɪpeɪt] vi sich beteiligen; **to**
~ **in** teilnehmen an +dat.
**participation** [pɑːtɪsɪ'peɪʃən] n Teilnahme f.
**participle** ['pɑːtɪsɪpl] n Partizip nt.
**particle** ['pɑːtɪkl] n Teilchen nt, Partikel f.
**particular** [pə'tɪkjulə*] adj (distinct: person,
time, place etc) bestimmt, speziell; (special)
speziell, besondere(r, s) ♦ n: **in** ~ im
besonderen, besonders; **particulars** npl
Einzelheiten pl; (name, address etc)
Personalien pl; **to be very** ~ **about sth**
(fussy) in bezug auf etw acc sehr eigen sein.
**particularly** [pə'tɪkjulərlɪ] adv besonders.
**parting** ['pɑːtɪŋ] n (action) Teilung f; (farewell)
Abschied m; (BRIT: in hair) Scheitel m ♦ adj
(words, gift etc) Abschieds-; **his** ~ **shot was**
... (fig) seine Bemerkung zum Abschied war
...
**partisan** [pɑːtɪ'zæn] adj (politics, views)
voreingenommen ♦ n (supporter)
Anhänger(in) m(f); (fighter) Partisan m.
**partition** [pɑː'tɪʃən] n (wall, screen)
Trennwand f; (of country) Teilung f ♦ vt
(room, office) aufteilen; (country) teilen.
**partly** ['pɑːtlɪ] adv teilweise, zum Teil.
**partner** ['pɑːtnə*] n Partner(in) m(f); (COMM)
Partner(in), Teilhaber(in) m(f) ♦ vt (at dance,
cards etc) als Partner(in) haben.
**partnership** ['pɑːtnəʃɪp] n (POL etc)

Partnerschaft *f*; (*COMM*) Teilhaberschaft *f*;
**to go into ~ (with sb)**, **form a ~ (with sb)**
(mit jdm) eine Partnerschaft eingehen.
**part payment** *n* Anzahlung *f*.
**partridge** ['pɑːtrɪdʒ] *n* Rebhuhn *nt*.
**part-time** ['pɑːt'taɪm] *adj* (*work, staff*) Teilzeit-,
Halbtags- ♦ *adv*: **to work ~** Teilzeit arbeiten;
**to study ~** Teilzeitstudent(in) *m(f)* sein.
**part-timer** [pɑːt'taɪmə\*] *n* (*also*: **part-time**
**worker**) Teilzeitbeschäftigte(r) *f(m)*.
**party** ['pɑːtɪ] *n* (*POL, LAW*) Partei *f*;
(*celebration, social event*) Party *f*, Fete *f*;
(*group of people*) Gruppe *f*, Gesellschaft *f*
♦ *cpd* (*POL*) Partei-; **dinner ~**
Abendgesellschaft *f*; **to give** *or* **throw a ~**
eine Party geben, eine Fete machen; **we're**
**having a ~ next Saturday** bei uns ist
nächsten Samstag eine Party; **our son's**
**birthday ~** die Geburtstagsfeier unseres
Sohnes; **to be a ~ to a crime** an einem
Verbrechen beteiligt sein.
**party dress** *n* Partykleid *nt*.
**party line** *n* (*TEL*) Gemeinschaftsanschluß *m*;
(*POL*) Parteilinie *f*.
**party piece** (*inf*) *n*: **to do one's ~** auf einer
Party etwas zum besten geben.
**party political** *adj* parteipolitisch.
**party political broadcast** *n* parteipolitische
Sendung *f*.
**par value** *n* (*COMM*: *of share, bond*) Nennwert
*m*.
**pass** [pɑːs] *vt* (*spend: time*) verbringen; (*hand*
*over*) reichen, geben; (*go past*)
vorbeikommen an +*dat*; (*: in car*)
vorbeifahren an +*dat*; (*overtake*) überholen;
(*fig: exceed*) übersteigen; (*exam*) bestehen;
(*law, proposal*) genehmigen ♦ *vi* (*go past*)
vorbeigehen; (*: in car*) vorbeifahren; (*in*
*exam*) bestehen ♦ *n* (*permit*) Ausweis *m*; (*in*
*mountains, SPORT*) Paß *m*; **to ~ sth through**
**sth** etw durch etw führen; **to ~ the ball to**
den Ball zuspielen +*dat*; **could you ~ the**
**vegetables round?** könnten Sie das Gemüse
herumreichen?; **to get a ~ in ...** (*SCOL*) die
Prüfung in ... bestehen; **things have come to**
**a pretty ~ when ...** (*BRIT: inf*) so weit ist es
schon gekommen, daß ...; **to make a ~ at sb**
(*inf*) jdn anmachen.
▸**pass away** *vi* (*die*) dahinscheiden.
▸**pass by** *vi* (*go past*) vorbeigehen; (*: in car*)
vorbeifahren ♦ *vt* (*ignore*) vorbeigehen an
+*dat*.
▸**pass down** *vt* (*customs, inheritance*)
weitergeben.
▸**pass for** *vt*: **she could ~ for 25** sie könnte
für 25 durchgehen.
▸**pass on** *vi* (*die*) verscheiden ♦ *vt*: **to ~ on**
(**to**) weitergeben (an +*acc*).
▸**pass out** *vi* (*faint*) ohnmächtig werden;
(*BRIT: MIL*) die Ausbildung beenden.
▸**pass over** *vt* (*ignore*) übergehen ♦ *vi* (*die*)
entschlafen.

▸**pass up** *vt* (*opportunity*) sich *dat* entgehen
lassen.
**passable** ['pɑːsəbl] *adj* (*road*) passierbar;
(*acceptable*) passabel.
**passage** ['pæsɪdʒ] *n* Gang *m*; (*in book*) Passage
*f*; (*way through crowd etc, ANAT*) Weg *m*; (*act*
*of passing: of train etc*) Durchfahrt *f*; (*journey:*
*on boat*) Überfahrt *f*.
**passageway** ['pæsɪdʒweɪ] *n* Gang *m*.
**passenger** ['pæsɪndʒə\*] *n* (*in boat, plane*)
Passagier *m*; (*in car*) Fahrgast *m*.
**passer-by** [pɑːsə'baɪ] (*pl* **~s-~**) *n* Passant(in)
*m(f)*.
**passing** ['pɑːsɪŋ] *adj* (*moment, thought etc*)
flüchtig; **in ~** (*incidentally*) beiläufig,
nebenbei; **to mention sth in ~** etw beiläufig
*or* nebenbei erwähnen.
**passing place** *n* (*AUT*) Ausweichstelle *f*.
**passion** ['pæʃən] *n* Leidenschaft *f*; **to have a**
**~ for sth** eine Leidenschaft für etw haben.
**passionate** ['pæʃənɪt] *adj* leidenschaftlich.
**passion fruit** *n* Passionsfrucht *f*, Maracuja *f*.
**Passion play** *n* Passionsspiel *nt*.
**passive** ['pæsɪv] *adj* passiv; (*LING*) Passiv- ♦ *n*
(*LING*) Passiv *nt*.
**passive smoking** *n* passives Rauchen,
Passivrauchen *nt*.
**passkey** ['pɑːskiː] *n* Hauptschlüssel *m*.
**Passover** ['pɑːsəuvə\*] *n* Passah(fest) *nt*.
**passport** ['pɑːspɔːt] *n* Paß *m*; (*fig: to success*
*etc*) Schlüssel *m*.
**passport control** *n* Paßkontrolle *f*.
**password** ['pɑːswəːd] *n* Kennwort *nt*;
(*COMPUT*) Paßwort *nt*.
**past** [pɑːst] *prep* (*in front of*) vorbei an +*dat*;
(*beyond*) hinter +*dat*; (*later than*) nach ♦ *adj*
(*government etc*) früher, ehemalig; (*week,*
*month etc*) vergangen ♦ *n* Vergangenheit *f*
♦ *adv*: **to run ~** vorbeilaufen; **he's ~ 40** er ist
über 40; **it's ~ midnight** es ist nach
Mitternacht; **ten/quarter ~ eight** zehn/
viertel nach acht; **he ran ~ me** er lief an
mir vorbei; **I'm ~ caring** es kümmert mich
nicht mehr; **to be ~ it** (*BRIT: inf: person*) es
nicht mehr bringen; **for the ~ few/3 days**
während der letzten Tage/3 Tage; **in the ~**
(*also LING*) in der Vergangenheit.
**pasta** ['pæstə] *n* Nudeln *pl*.
**paste** [peɪst] *n* (*wet mixture*) Teig *m*; (*glue*)
Kleister *m*; (*jewellery*) Straß *m*; (*fish, tomato*
*etc paste*) Paste *f* ♦ *vt* (*stick*) kleben.
**pastel** ['pæstl] *adj* (*colour*) Pastell-.
**pasteurized** ['pæstʃəraɪzd] *adj* pasteurisiert.
**pastille** ['pæstɪl] *n* Pastille *f*.
**pastime** ['pɑːstaɪm] *n* Zeitvertreib *m*, Hobby
*nt*.
**past master** (*BRIT*) *n*: **to be a ~ at sth** ein
Experte in etw *dat* sein.
**pastor** ['pɑːstə\*] *n* Pastor(in) *m(f)*.
**pastoral** ['pɑːstərl] *adj* (*REL: duties etc*) als
Pastor.
**pastry** ['peɪstrɪ] *n* (*dough*) Teig *m*; (*cake*)

Gebäckstück nt.

**pasture** ['pɑːstʃə*] n Weide f.

**pasty** [n 'pæstɪ, adj 'peɪstɪ] n (pie) Pastete f
♦ adj (complexion) bläßlich.

**pat** [pæt] vt (with hand) tätscheln ♦ adj (answer,
remark) glatt ♦ n: **to give sb/o.s. a ~ on the
back** (fig) jdm/sich auf die Schulter klopfen;
**he knows it off ~, (US) he has it down ~** er
kennt das in- und auswendig.

**patch** [pætʃ] n (piece of material) Flicken m;
(also: **eye ~**) Augenklappe f; (damp, bald etc)
Fleck m; (of land) Stück nt ♦ (: for growing
vegetables etc) Beet nt ♦ vt (clothes) flicken;
**(to go through) a bad ~** eine schwierige
Zeit (durchmachen).
▶**patch up** vt (clothes etc) flicken; (quarrel)
beilegen.

**patchwork** ['pætʃwəːk] n (SEWING)
Patchwork nt.

**patchy** ['pætʃɪ] adj (colour) ungleichmäßig;
(information, knowledge etc) lückenhaft.

**pate** [peɪt] n: **a bald ~** eine Glatze.

**pâté** ['pæteɪ] n Pastete f.

**patent** ['peɪtnt] n Patent nt ♦ vt patentieren
lassen ♦ adj (obvious) offensichtlich.

**patent leather** n Lackleder nt.

**patently** ['peɪtntlɪ] adv (obvious, wrong)
vollkommen.

**patent medicine** n patentrechtlich
geschütztes Arzneimittel nt.

**Patent Office** n Patentamt nt.

**paternal** [pə'təːnl] adj väterlich; **my
~ grandmother** meine Großmutter
väterlicherseits.

**paternalistic** [pətəːnə'lɪstɪk] adj
patriarchalisch.

**paternity** [pə'təːnɪtɪ] n Vaterschaft f.

**paternity leave** n Vaterschaftsurlaub m.

**paternity suit** n Vaterschaftsprozeß m.

**path** [pɑːθ] n (also fig) Weg m; (trail, track) Pfad
m; (trajectory: of bullet, aircraft, planet) Bahn f.

**pathetic** [pə'θɛtɪk] adj (pitiful)
mitleiderregend; (very bad) erbärmlich.

**pathological** [pæθə'lɔdʒɪkl] adj (liar, hatred)
krankhaft; (MED) pathologisch.

**pathologist** [pə'θɔlədʒɪst] n Pathologe m,
Pathologin f.

**pathology** [pə'θɔlədʒɪ] n Pathologie f.

**pathos** ['peɪθɔs] n Pathos nt.

**pathway** ['pɑːθweɪ] n Pfad m, Weg m; (fig)
Weg.

**patience** ['peɪʃns] n Geduld f; (BRIT: CARDS)
Patience f; **to lose (one's) ~** die Geduld
verlieren.

**patient** ['peɪʃnt] n Patient(in) m(f) ♦ adj
geduldig; **to be ~ with sb** Geduld mit jdm
haben.

**patiently** ['peɪʃntlɪ] adv geduldig.

**patio** ['pætɪəu] n Terrasse f.

**patriot** ['peɪtrɪət] n Patriot(in) m(f).

**patriotic** [pætrɪ'ɔtɪk] adj patriotisch.

**patriotism** ['pætrɪətɪzəm] n Patriotismus m.

**patrol** [pə'trəul] n (MIL) Patrouille f; (POLICE)
Streife f ♦ vt (MIL, POLICE: city, streets etc)
patrouillieren; **to be on ~** (MIL) auf
Patrouille sein; (POLICE) auf Streife sein.

**patrol boat** n Patrouillenboot nt.

**patrol car** n Streifenwagen m.

**patrolman** [pə'trəulmən] (US: irreg: like man) n
(POLICE) (Streifen)polizist m.

**patron** ['peɪtrən] n (customer) Kunde m,
Kundin f; (benefactor) Förderer m; **~ of the
arts** Kunstmäzen m.

**patronage** ['pætrənɪdʒ] n (of artist, charity etc)
Förderung f.

**patronize** ['pætrənaɪz] vt (pej: look down on)
von oben herab behandeln; (artist etc)
fördern; (shop, club) besuchen.

**patronizing** ['pætrənaɪzɪŋ] adj herablassend.

**patron saint** n Schutzheilige(r) f(m).

**patter** ['pætə*] n (of feet) Trappeln nt; (of rain)
Prasseln nt; (sales talk etc) Sprüche pl ♦ vi
(footsteps) trappeln; (rain) prasseln.

**pattern** ['pætən] n Muster nt; (SEWING)
Schnittmuster nt; **behaviour ~s**
Verhaltensmuster pl.

**patterned** ['pætənd] adj gemustert; **~ with
flowers** mit Blumenmuster.

**paucity** ['pɔːsɪtɪ] n: **a ~ of** ein Mangel m an
+dat.

**paunch** [pɔːntʃ] n Bauch m, Wanst m.

**pauper** ['pɔːpə*] n Arme(r) f(m); **~'s grave**
Armengrab nt.

**pause** [pɔːz] n Pause f ♦ vi eine Pause machen;
(hesitate) innehalten; **to ~ for breath** eine
Verschnaufpause einlegen.

**pave** [peɪv] vt (street, yard etc) pflastern; **to
~ the way for** (fig) den Weg bereiten or
bahnen für.

**pavement** ['peɪvmənt] n (BRIT) Bürgersteig
m; (US: roadway) Straße f.

**pavilion** [pə'vɪlɪən] n (SPORT) Klubhaus nt.

**paving** ['peɪvɪŋ] n (material) Straßenbelag m.

**paving stone** n Pflasterstein m.

**paw** [pɔː] n (of cat, dog etc) Pfote f; (of lion,
bear etc) Tatze f, Pranke f ♦ vt (pej: touch)
betatschen; **to ~ the ground** (animal)
scharren.

**pawn** [pɔːn] n (CHESS) Bauer m; (fig)
Schachfigur f ♦ vt versetzen.

**pawnbroker** ['pɔːnbrəukə*] n Pfandleiher m.

**pawnshop** ['pɔːnʃɔp] n Pfandhaus nt.

**pay** [peɪ] (pt, pp paid) n (wage) Lohn m; (salary)
Gehalt nt ♦ vt (sum of money, wage) zahlen;
(bill, person) bezahlen ♦ vi (be profitable) sich
bezahlt machen; (fig) sich lohnen; **how
much did you ~ for it?** wieviel hast du dafür
bezahlt?; **I paid 10 pounds for that book** ich
habe 10 Pfund für das Buch bezahlt, das
Buch hat mich 10 Pfund gekostet; **to
~ one's way** seinen Beitrag leisten; **to
~ dividends** (fig) sich bezahlt machen; **to
~ the price/penalty for sth** (fig) den Preis/
die Strafe für etw zahlen; **to ~ sb a**

**compliment** jdm ein Kompliment machen; **to ~ attention (to)** achtgeben (auf +*acc*); **to ~ sb a visit** jdn besuchen; **to ~ one's respects to sb** jdm seine Aufwartung machen.

▶**pay back** *vt* zurückzahlen; **I'll ~ you back next week** ich gebe dir das Geld nächste Woche zurück.

▶**pay for** *vt fus* (*also fig*) (be)zahlen für.

▶**pay in** *vt* einzahlen.

▶**pay off** *vt* (*debt*) abbezahlen; (*person*) auszahlen; (*creditor*) befriedigen; (*mortgage*) tilgen ♦ *vi* sich auszahlen; **to ~ sth off in instalments** etw in Raten (ab)zahlen.

▶**pay out** *vt* (*money*) ausgeben; (*rope*) ablaufen lassen.

▶**pay up** *vi* zahlen.

**payable** ['peɪəbl] *adj* zahlbar; **to make a cheque ~ to sb** einen Scheck auf jdn ausstellen.

**pay award** *n* Lohn-/Gehaltserhöhung *f*.

**payday** ['peɪdeɪ] *n* Zahltag *m*.

**PAYE** (*BRIT*) *n abbr* (= *pay as you earn*) *Lohnsteuerabzugsverfahren.*

**payee** [peɪ'iː] *n* Zahlungsempfänger *m*.

**pay envelope** (*US*) *n* = **pay packet.**

**paying guest** ['peɪɪŋ-] *n* zahlender Gast *m*.

**payload** ['peɪləʊd] *n* Nutzlast *f*.

**payment** ['peɪmənt] *n* (*act*) Zahlung *f*, Bezahlung *f*; (*of bill*) Begleichung *f*; (*sum of money*) Zahlung *f*; **advance ~** (*part sum*) Anzahlung *f*; (*total sum*) Vorauszahlung *f*; **deferred ~, ~ by instalments** Ratenzahlung *f*; **monthly ~** (*sum of money*) Monatsrate *f*; **on ~ of** gegen Zahlung von.

**pay packet** (*BRIT*) *n* Lohntüte *f*.

**payphone** ['peɪfəʊn] *n* Münztelefon *nt*; (*card phone*) Kartentelefon *nt*.

**payroll** ['peɪrəʊl] *n* Lohnliste *f*; **to be on a firm's ~** bei einer Firma beschäftigt sein.

**pay slip** (*BRIT*) *n* (*see* **pay**) Lohnstreifen *m*; Gehaltsstreifen *m*.

**pay station** (*US*) *n* = **payphone.**

**PBS** (*US*) *n abbr* (= *Public Broadcasting Service*) *öffentliche Rundfunkanstalt.*

**PC** *n abbr* (= *personal computer*) PC *m*; (*BRIT*) = **police constable** ♦ *adj abbr* = **politically correct** ♦ *abbr* (*BRIT*) = **Privy Councillor.**

**pc** *abbr* = **per cent; postcard.**

**p/c** *abbr* = **petty cash.**

**PCB** *n abbr* (*ELEC, COMPUT*) = **printed circuit board**; (= *polychlorinated biphenyl*) PCB *nt*.

**pcm** *abbr* (= *per calendar month*) pro Monat.

**PD** (*US*) *n abbr* = **police department.**

**pd** *abbr* (= *paid*) bez.

**pdq** (*inf*) *adv abbr* (= *pretty damn quick*) verdammt schnell.

**PDSA** (*BRIT*) *n abbr* (= *People's Dispensary for Sick Animals*) *kostenloses Behandlungszentrum für Haustiere.*

**PDT** (*US*) *abbr* = *Pacific Daylight Time*) *pazifische Sommerzeit.*

**PE** *n abbr* (*SCOL*) = **physical education** ♦ *abbr* (*CANADA*: = *Prince Edward Island*).

**pea** [piː] *n* Erbse *f*.

**peace** [piːs] *n* Frieden *m*; **to be at ~ with sb/ sth** mit jdm/etw in Frieden leben; **to keep the ~** (*policeman*) die öffentliche Ordnung aufrechterhalten; (*citizen*) den Frieden wahren.

**peaceable** ['piːsəbl] *adj* friedlich.

**peaceful** ['piːsful] *adj* friedlich.

**peacekeeper** ['piːskiːpə*] *n* Friedenswächter(in) *m(f)*.

**peacekeeping force** ['piːskiːpɪŋ-] *n* Friedenstruppen *pl*.

**peace offering** *n* Friedensangebot *nt*.

**peach** [piːtʃ] *n* Pfirsich *m*.

**peacock** ['piːkɔk] *n* Pfau *m*.

**peak** [piːk] *n* (*of mountain*) Spitze *f*, Gipfel *m*; (*of cap*) Schirm *m*; (*fig*) Höhepunkt *m*.

**peak hours** *npl* Stoßzeit *f*.

**peak period** *n* Spitzenzeit *f*, Stoßzeit *f*.

**peak rate** *n* Höchstrate *f*.

**peaky** ['piːkɪ] (*BRIT: inf*) *adj* blaß.

**peal** [piːl] *n* (*of bells*) Läuten *nt*; **~s of laughter** schallendes Gelächter *nt*.

**peanut** ['piːnʌt] *n* Erdnuß *f*.

**peanut butter** *n* Erdnußbutter *f*.

**pear** [pɛə*] *n* Birne *f*.

**pearl** [pəːl] *n* Perle *f*.

**peasant** ['pɛznt] *n* Bauer *m*.

**peat** [piːt] *n* Torf *m*.

**pebble** ['pɛbl] *n* Kieselstein *m*.

**peck** [pɛk] *vt* (*bird*) picken; (*also*: ~ **at**) picken an +*dat* ♦ *n* (*of bird*) Schnabelhieb *m*; (*kiss*) Küßchen *nt*.

**pecking order** ['pɛkɪŋ-] *n* (*fig*) Hackordnung *f*.

**peckish** ['pɛkɪʃ] (*BRIT: inf*) *adj* (*hungry*) leicht hungrig; **I'm feeling ~** ich könnte was zu essen gebrauchen.

**peculiar** [pɪ'kjuːlɪə*] *adj* (*strange*) seltsam; **~ to** (*exclusive to*) charakteristisch für.

**peculiarity** [pɪkjuːlɪ'ærɪtɪ] *n* (*strange habit*) Eigenart *f*; (*distinctive feature*) Besonderheit *f*, Eigentümlichkeit *f*.

**peculiarly** [pɪ'kjuːlɪəlɪ] *adv* (*oddly*) seltsam; (*distinctively*) unverkennbar.

**pecuniary** [pɪ'kjuːnɪərɪ] *adj* finanziell.

**pedal** ['pɛdl] *n* Pedal *nt* ♦ *vi* in die Pedale treten.

**pedal bin** (*BRIT*) *n* Treteimer *m*.

**pedant** ['pɛdənt] *n* Pedant(in) *m(f)*.

**pedantic** [pɪ'dæntɪk] *adj* pedantisch.

**peddle** ['pɛdl] *vt* (*goods*) feilbieten, verkaufen; (*drugs*) handeln mit; (*gossip*) verbreiten.

**peddler** ['pɛdlə*] *n* (*also*: **drug ~**) Pusher(in) *m(f)*.

**pedestal** ['pɛdəstl] *n* Sockel *m*.

**pedestrian** [pɪ'dɛstrɪən] *n* Fußgänger(in) *m(f)* ♦ *adj* Fußgänger-; (*fig*) langweilig.

**pedestrian crossing** (*BRIT*) *n*

Fußgängerüberweg m.

**pedestrian precinct** (BRIT) n Fußgängerzone f.

**pediatrics** [piːdɪˈætrɪks] (US) n = **paediatrics**.

**pedigree** [ˈpɛdɪɡriː] n (of animal) Stammbaum m; (fig: background) Vorgeschichte f ♦ cpd (dog) Rasse-, reinrassig.

**pee** [piː] (inf) vi pinkeln.

**peek** [piːk] vi: to ~ at/over/into etc gucken nach/über +acc/in +acc etc ♦ n: to have or take a ~ (at) einen (kurzen) Blick werfen (auf +acc).

**peel** [piːl] n Schale f ♦ vt schälen ♦ vi (paint) abblättern; (wallpaper) sich lösen; (skin, back etc) sich schälen.
▶**peel back** vt abziehen.

**peeler** [ˈpiːlə*] n (potato peeler etc) Schälmesser nt.

**peelings** [ˈpiːlɪŋz] npl Schalen pl.

**peep** [piːp] n (look) kurzer Blick m; (sound) Pieps m ♦ vi (look) gucken; to have or take a ~ (at) einen kurzen Blick werfen (auf +acc).
▶**peep out** vi (be visible) hervorgucken.

**peephole** [ˈpiːphəul] n Guckloch nt.

**peer** [pɪə*] n (noble) Peer m; (equal) Gleichrangige(r) f(m); (contemporary) Gleichaltrige(r) f(m) ♦ vi: to ~ at starren auf +acc.

**peerage** [ˈpɪərɪdʒ] n (title) Adelswürde f; (position) Adelsstand m; the ~ (all the peers) der Adel.

**peerless** [ˈpɪəlɪs] adj unvergleichlich.

**peeved** [piːvd] adj verärgert, sauer (inf).

**peevish** [ˈpiːvɪʃ] adj (bad-tempered) mürrisch.

**peg** [pɛg] n (hook, knob) Haken m; (BRIT: also: **clothes** ~) Wäscheklammer f; (also: **tent** ~) Zeltpflock m, Hering m ♦ vt (washing) festklammern; (prices) festsetzen; off the ~ von der Stange.

**pejorative** [pɪˈdʒɔrətɪv] adj abwertend.

**Pekin** [piːˈkɪn] n = **Peking**.

**Pekinese** [piːkɪˈniːz] n = **Pekingese**.

**Peking** [piːˈkɪŋ] n Peking nt.

**Pekingese** [piːkɪˈniːz] n (dog) Pekinese m.

**pelican** [ˈpɛlɪkən] n Pelikan m.

**pelican crossing** (BRIT) n (AUT) Fußgängerüberweg m mit Ampel.

**pellet** [ˈpɛlɪt] n (of paper etc) Kügelchen nt; (of mud etc) Klümpchen nt; (for shotgun) Schrotkugel f.

**pell-mell** [ˈpɛlˈmɛl] adv in heillosem Durcheinander.

**pelmet** [ˈpɛlmɪt] n (wooden) Blende f; (fabric) Querbehang m.

**pelt** [pɛlt] vi (rain: also: ~ **down**) niederprasseln; (inf: run) rasen ♦ n (animal skin) Pelz m, Fell nt ♦ vt: to ~ sb with sth jdn mit etw bewerfen.

**pelvis** [ˈpɛlvɪs] n Becken nt.

**pen** [pɛn] n (also: **fountain** ~) Füller m; (also: **ballpoint** ~) Kugelschreiber m; (also: **felt-tip** ~) Filzstift m; (enclosure: for sheep, pigs etc)

Pferch m; (US: inf: prison) Knast m; **to put** ~ **to paper** zur Feder greifen.

**penal** [ˈpiːnl] adj (LAW: colony, institution) Straf-; (: system, reform) Strafrechts-; ~ **code** Strafgesetzbuch nt.

**penalize** [ˈpiːnəlaɪz] vt (punish) bestrafen; (fig) benachteiligen.

**penal servitude** [-ˈsəːvɪtjuːd] n Zwangsarbeit f.

**penalty** [ˈpɛnltɪ] n Strafe f; (SPORT) Strafstoß m; (: FOOTBALL) Elfmeter m.

**penalty area** (BRIT) n (SPORT) Strafraum m.

**penalty clause** n Strafklausel f.

**penalty kick** n (RUGBY) Strafstoß m; (FOOTBALL) Elfmeter m.

**penalty shoot-out** [-ˈʃuːtaut] n (FOOTBALL) Elfmeterschießen nt.

**penance** [ˈpɛnəns] n (REL): **to do** ~ **for one's sins** für seine Sünden Buße tun.

**pence** [pɛns] npl of **penny**.

**penchant** [ˈpɑ̃ːʃɑ̃ːŋ] n Vorliebe f, Schwäche f; **to have a** ~ **for** eine Schwäche haben für.

**pencil** [ˈpɛnsl] n Bleistift m ♦ vt: **to** ~ **sb/sth in** jdn/etw vormerken.

**pencil case** n Federmäppchen nt.

**pencil sharpener** n Bleistiftspitzer m.

**pendant** [ˈpɛndnt] n Anhänger m.

**pending** [ˈpɛndɪŋ] adj anstehend ♦ prep: ~ **his return** bis zu seiner Rückkehr; ~ **a decision** bis eine Entscheidung getroffen ist.

**pendulum** [ˈpɛndjuləm] n Pendel nt.

**penetrate** [ˈpɛnɪtreɪt] vt (person: territory etc) durchdringen; (light, water, sound) eindringen in +acc.

**penetrating** [ˈpɛnɪtreɪtɪŋ] adj (sound, gaze) durchdringend; (mind, observation) scharf.

**penetration** [pɛnɪˈtreɪʃən] n Durchdringen nt.

**pen friend** (BRIT) n Brieffreund(in) m(f).

**penguin** [ˈpɛŋgwɪn] n Pinguin m.

**penicillin** [pɛnɪˈsɪlɪn] n Penizillin nt.

**peninsula** [pəˈnɪnsjulə] n Halbinsel f.

**penis** [ˈpiːnɪs] n Penis m.

**penitence** [ˈpɛnɪtns] n Reue f.

**penitent** [ˈpɛnɪtnt] adj reuig.

**penitentiary** [pɛnɪˈtɛnʃərɪ] (US) n Gefängnis nt.

**penknife** [ˈpɛnnaɪf] n Taschenmesser nt.

**Penn.** (US) abbr (POST: = Pennsylvania).

**pen name** n Pseudonym nt.

**pennant** [ˈpɛnənt] n (NAUT) Wimpel m.

**penniless** [ˈpɛnɪlɪs] adj mittellos.

**Pennines** [ˈpɛnaɪnz] npl: **the** ~ die Pennines pl.

**penny** [ˈpɛnɪ] (pl **pennies** or (BRIT) **pence**) n Penny m; (US) Cent m; **it was worth every** ~ es war jeden Pfennig wert; **it won't cost you a** ~ es kostet dich keinen Pfennig.

**pen pal** n Brieffreund(in) m(f).

**penpusher** [ˈpɛnpuʃə*] n Schreiberling m.

**pension** [ˈpɛnʃən] n Rente f.
▶**pension off** vt (vorzeitig) pensionieren.

**pensionable** [ˈpɛnʃnəbl] adj (age) Pensions-; (job) mit Pensionsberechtigung.

**pensioner** ['pɛnʃənə•] (*BRIT*) n Rentner(in) m(f).

**pension scheme** n Rentenversicherung f.

**pensive** ['pɛnsɪv] adj nachdenklich.

**pentagon** ['pɛntəgən] (*US*) n: **the P~** das Pentagon.

Pentagon *heißt das fünfeckige Gebäude in Arlington, Virginia, in dem das amerikanische Verteidigungsministerium untergebracht ist. Im weiteren Sinne bezieht sich dieses Wort auf die amerikanische Militärführung.*

**Pentecost** ['pɛntɪkɔst] n (*in Judaism*) Erntefest nt; (*in Christianity*) Pfingsten nt.

**penthouse** ['pɛnthaus] n Penthouse nt.

**pent-up** ['pɛntʌp] adj (*feelings*) aufgestaut.

**penultimate** [pɛ'nʌltɪmət] adj vorletzte(r, s).

**penury** ['pɛnjurɪ] n Armut f, Not f.

**people** ['piːpl] npl (*persons*) Leute pl; (*inhabitants*) Bevölkerung f ♦ n (*nation, race*) Volk nt; old ~ alte Menschen or Leute; **young** ~ junge Leute; **the room was full of** ~ das Zimmer war voller Leute or Menschen; **several** ~ **came** mehrere (Leute) kamen; ~ **say that ...** man sagt, daß ...; **the** ~ (*POL*) das Volk; **a man of the** ~ ein Mann des Volkes.

**PEP** n abbr (= *personal equity plan*) *steuerbegünstigte Kapitalinvestition.*

**pep** [pɛp] (*inf*) n Schwung m, Pep m.

▶**pep up** vt (*person*) aufmöbeln; (*food*) pikanter machen.

**pepper** ['pɛpə•] n (*spice*) Pfeffer m; (*vegetable*) Paprika m ♦ vt: **to** ~ **with** (*fig*) übersäen mit; **two ~s** zwei Paprikaschoten.

**peppercorn** ['pɛpəkɔːn] n Pfefferkorn nt.

**pepper mill** n Pfeffermühle f.

**peppermint** ['pɛpəmɪnt] n (*sweet*) Pfefferminz nt; (*plant*) Pfefferminze f.

**pepperoni** [pɛpə'rəunɪ] n ≈ Pfeffersalami f.

**pepper pot** n Pfefferstreuer m.

**pep talk** (*inf*) n aufmunternde Worte pl.

**per** [pəː•] prep (*for each*) pro; ~ **day/person/ kilo** pro Tag/Person/Kilo; ~ **annum** pro Jahr; **as** ~ **your instructions** gemäß Ihren Anweisungen.

**per capita** [-'kæpɪtə] adj (*income*) Pro-Kopf- ♦ adv pro Kopf.

**perceive** [pə'siːv] vt (*see*) wahrnehmen; (*view, understand*) verstehen.

**per cent** n Prozent nt; **a 20** ~ **discount** 20 Prozent Rabatt.

**percentage** [pə'sɛntɪdʒ] n Prozentsatz m; **on a** ~ **basis** auf Prozentbasis.

**percentage point** n Prozent nt.

**perceptible** [pə'sɛptɪbl] adj (*difference, change*) wahrnehmbar, merklich.

**perception** [pə'sɛpʃən] n (*insight*) Einsicht f; (*opinion, understanding*) Erkenntnis f; (*faculty*) Wahrnehmung f.

**perceptive** [pə'sɛptɪv] adj (*person*)

aufmerksam; (*analysis etc*) erkenntnisreich.

**perch** [pəːtʃ] n (*for bird*) Stange f; (*fish*) Flußbarsch m ♦ vi: **to** ~ **(on)** (*bird*) sitzen (auf +dat); (*person*) hocken (auf +dat).

**percolate** ['pəːkəleɪt] vt (*coffee*) (mit einer Kaffeemaschine) zubereiten ♦ vi (*coffee*) durchlaufen; **to** ~ **through/into** (*idea, light etc*) durchsickern durch/in +acc.

**percolator** ['pəːkəleɪtə•] n (*also:* **coffee** ~) Kaffeemaschine f.

**percussion** [pə'kʌʃən] n (*MUS*) Schlagzeug nt.

**peremptory** [pə'rɛmptərɪ] (*pej*) adj (*person*) herrisch; (*order*) kategorisch.

**perennial** [pə'rɛnɪəl] adj (*plant*) mehrjährig; (*fig: problem, feature etc*) immer wiederkehrend ♦ n (*BOT*) mehrjährige Pflanze f.

**perfect** [adj, n 'pəːfɪkt, vt pə'fɛkt] adj perfekt; (*nonsense, idiot etc*) ausgemacht ♦ vt (*technique*) perfektionieren ♦ n: **the** ~ (*also:* **the** ~ **tense**) das Perfekt; **he's a** ~ **stranger to me** er ist mir vollkommen fremd.

**perfection** [pə'fɛkʃən] n Perfektion f, Vollkommenheit f.

**perfectionist** [pə'fɛkʃənɪst] n Perfektionist(in) m(f).

**perfectly** ['pəːfɪktlɪ] adv vollkommen; (*faultlessly*) perfekt; **I'm** ~ **happy with the situation** ich bin mit der Lage vollkommen zufrieden; **you know** ~ **well that ...** Sie wissen ganz genau, daß ...

**perforate** ['pəːfəreɪt] vt perforieren.

**perforated ulcer** ['pəːfəreɪtəd-] n durchgebrochenes Geschwür nt.

**perforation** [pəːfə'reɪʃən] n (*small hole*) Loch nt; (*line of holes*) Perforation f.

**perform** [pə'fɔːm] vt (*operation, ceremony etc*) durchführen; (*task*) erfüllen; (*piece of music, play etc*) aufführen ♦ vi auftreten; **to** ~ **well/badly** eine gute/schlechte Leistung zeigen.

**performance** [pə'fɔːməns] n Leistung f; (*of play, show*) Vorstellung f; **the team put up a good** ~ die Mannschaft zeigte eine gute Leistung.

**performer** [pə'fɔːmə•] n Künstler(in) m(f).

**performing** [pə'fɔːmɪŋ] adj (*animal*) dressiert.

**performing arts** npl: **the** ~ die darstellenden Künste pl.

**perfume** ['pəːfjuːm] n Parfüm nt; (*fragrance*) Duft m ♦ vt parfümieren.

**perfunctory** [pə'fʌŋktərɪ] adj flüchtig.

**perhaps** [pə'hæps] adv vielleicht; ~ **he'll come** er kommt vielleicht; ~ **not** vielleicht nicht.

**peril** ['pɛrɪl] n Gefahr f.

**perilous** ['pɛrɪləs] adj gefährlich.

**perilously** ['pɛrɪləslɪ] adv: **they came** ~ **close to being caught** sie wären um ein Haar gefangen worden.

**perimeter** [pə'rɪmɪtə•] n Umfang m.

**perimeter fence** n Umzäunung f.

**period** ['pɪərɪəd] n (*length of time*) Zeitraum m,

Periode *f*; (*era*) Zeitalter *nt*; (*SCOL*) Stunde *f*; (*esp US: full stop*) Punkt *m*; (*MED: also:* menstrual ~) Periode ♦ *adj* (*costume etc*) zeitgenössisch; **for a ~ of 3 weeks** für eine Dauer *or* einen Zeitraum von 3 Wochen; **the holiday ~** (*BRIT*) die Urlaubszeit; **I won't do it. P~.** ich mache das nicht, und damit basta!

**periodic** [pɪərɪ'ɔdɪk] *adj* periodisch.

**periodical** [pɪərɪ'ɔdɪkl] *n* Zeitschrift *f* ♦ *adj* periodisch.

**periodically** [pɪərɪ'ɔdɪklɪ] *adv* periodisch.

**period pains** (*BRIT*) *npl* Menstruationsschmerzen *pl*.

**peripatetic** [perɪpə'tetɪk] *adj* (*BRIT: teacher*) an mehreren Schulen tätig; **~ life** Wanderleben *nt*.

**peripheral** [pə'rɪfərəl] *adj* (*feature, issue*) Rand-, nebensächlich; (*vision*) peripher ♦ *n* (*COMPUT*) Peripheriegerät *nt*.

**periphery** [pə'rɪfərɪ] *n* Peripherie *f*.

**periscope** ['perɪskəup] *n* Periskop *nt*.

**perish** ['perɪʃ] *vi* (*die*) umkommen; (*rubber, leather etc*) verschleißen.

**perishable** ['perɪʃəbl] *adj* (*food*) leicht verderblich.

**perishables** ['perɪʃəblz] *npl* leicht verderbliche Waren *pl*.

**perishing** ['perɪʃɪŋ] (*BRIT: inf*) *adj*: **it's ~ (cold)** es ist eisig kalt.

**peritonitis** [perɪtə'naɪtɪs] *n* Bauchfellentzündung *f*.

**perjure** ['pɜːdʒə*] *vt*: **to ~ o.s.** einen Meineid leisten.

**perjury** ['pɜːdʒərɪ] *n* (*in court*) Meineid *m*; (*breach of oath*) Eidesverletzung *f*.

**perks** [pɜːks] (*inf*) *npl* (*extras*) Vergünstigungen *pl*.

**perk up** *vi* (*cheer up*) munter werden.

**perky** ['pɜːkɪ] *adj* (*cheerful*) munter.

**perm** [pɜːm] *n* Dauerwelle *f* ♦ *vt*: **to have one's hair ~ed** sich *dat* eine Dauerwelle machen lassen.

**permanence** ['pɜːmənəns] *n* Dauerhaftigkeit *f*.

**permanent** ['pɜːmənənt] *adj* dauerhaft; (*job, position*) fest; **~ address** ständiger Wohnsitz *m*; **I'm not ~ here** ich bin hier nicht fest angestellt.

**permanently** ['pɜːmənəntlɪ] *adv* (*damage*) dauerhaft; (*stay, live*) ständig; (*locked, open, frozen etc*) dauernd.

**permeable** ['pɜːmɪəbl] *adj* durchlässig.

**permeate** ['pɜːmɪeɪt] *vt* durchdringen ♦ *vi*: **to ~ through** dringen durch.

**permissible** [pə'mɪsɪbl] *adj* zulässig.

**permission** [pə'mɪʃən] *n* Erlaubnis *f*, Genehmigung *f*; **to give sb ~ to do sth** jdm die Erlaubnis geben, etw zu tun.

**permissive** [pə'mɪsɪv] *adj* (*society, age*) permissiv.

**permit** [*n* 'pɜːmɪt, *vt* pə'mɪt] *n* Genehmigung *f*

♦ *vt* (*allow*) erlauben; (*make possible*) gestatten; **fishing ~** Angelschein *m*; **to ~ sb to do sth** jdm erlauben, etw zu tun; **weather ~ting** wenn das Wetter es zuläßt.

**permutation** [pɜːmju'teɪʃən] *n* Permutation *f*; (*fig*) Variation *f*.

**pernicious** [pɜː'nɪʃəs] *adj* (*lie, nonsense*) bösartig; (*effect*) schädlich.

**pernickety** [pə'nɪkɪtɪ] (*inf*) *adj* pingelig.

**perpendicular** [pɜːpən'dɪkjulə*] *adj* senkrecht ♦ *n*: **the ~** die Senkrechte; **~ to** senkrecht zu.

**perpetrate** ['pɜːpɪtreɪt] *vt* (*crime*) begehen.

**perpetual** [pə'petjuəl] *adj* ständig, dauernd.

**perpetuate** [pə'petjueɪt] *vt* (*custom, belief etc*) bewahren; (*situation*) aufrechterhalten.

**perpetuity** [pɜːpɪ'tjuːɪtɪ] *n*: **in ~** auf ewig.

**perplex** [pə'pleks] *vt* verblüffen.

**perplexing** [pə'pleksɪŋ] *adj* verblüffend.

**perquisites** ['pɜːkwɪzɪts] (*form*) *npl* Vergünstigungen *pl*.

**per se** [-seɪ] *adv* an sich.

**persecute** ['pɜːsɪkjuːt] *vt* verfolgen.

**persecution** [pɜːsɪ'kjuːʃən] *n* Verfolgung *f*.

**perseverance** [pɜːsɪ'vɪərns] *n* Beharrlichkeit *f*, Ausdauer *f*.

**persevere** [pɜːsɪ'vɪə*] *vi* durchhalten, beharren.

**Persia** ['pɜːʃə] *n* Persien *nt*.

**Persian** ['pɜːʃən] *adj* persisch ♦ *n* (*LING*) Persisch *nt*; **the (~) Gulf** der (Persische) Golf.

**Persian cat** *n* Perserkatze *f*.

**persist** [pə'sɪst] *vi*: **to ~ (with *or* in)** beharren (auf +*dat*), festhalten (an +*dat*); **to ~ in doing sth** darauf beharren, etw zu tun.

**persistence** [pə'sɪstəns] *n* (*determination*) Beharrlichkeit *f*.

**persistent** [pə'sɪstənt] *adj* (*person, noise*) beharrlich; (*smell, cough etc*) hartnäckig; (*lateness, rain*) andauernd; **~ offender** Wiederholungstäter(in) *m(f)*.

**persnickety** [pə'snɪkɪtɪ] (*US: inf*) *adj* = **pernickety**.

**person** ['pɜːsn] *n* Person *f*, Mensch *m*; **in ~** persönlich; **on *or* about one's ~** bei sich; **~ to ~ call** (*TEL*) Gespräch *nt* mit Voranmeldung.

**personable** ['pɜːsnəbl] *adj* von angenehmer Erscheinung.

**personal** ['pɜːsnl] *adj* persönlich; (*life*) Privat-; **nothing ~!** nehmen Sie es nicht persönlich!

**personal allowance** *n* (*TAX*) persönlicher Steuerfreibetrag *m*.

**personal assistant** *n* persönlicher Referent *m*, persönliche Referentin *f*.

**personal column** *n* private Kleinanzeigen *pl*.

**personal computer** *n* Personalcomputer *m*.

**personal details** *npl* Personalien *pl*.

**personal hygiene** *n* Körperhygiene *f*.

**personal identification number** *n* (*BANKING*) Geheimnummer *f*, PIN-Nummer *f*.

**personality** [pɜːsəˈnælɪtɪ] *n* (*character, person*) Persönlichkeit *f*.

**personal loan** *n* Personaldarlehen *nt*.

**personally** [ˈpɜːsnəlɪ] *adv* persönlich; **to take sth ~** etw persönlich nehmen.

**personal organizer** *n* Terminplaner *m*.

**personal stereo** *n* Walkman ® *m*.

**personify** [pɜːˈsɒnɪfaɪ] *vt* personifizieren; (*embody*) verkörpern.

**personnel** [pɜːsəˈnɛl] *n* Personal *nt*.

**personnel department** *n* Personalabteilung *f*.

**personnel manager** *n* Personalleiter(in) *m(f)*.

**perspective** [pəˈspɛktɪv] *n* (*also fig*) Perspektive *f*; **to get sth into ~** (*fig*) etw in Relation zu anderen Dingen sehen.

**Perspex ®** [ˈpɜːspɛks] *n* Acrylglas *nt*.

**perspicacity** [pɜːspɪˈkæsɪtɪ] *n* Scharfsinn *m*.

**perspiration** [pɜːspɪˈreɪʃən] *n* Transpiration *f*.

**perspire** [pəˈspaɪə⁺] *vi* transpirieren.

**persuade** [pəˈsweɪd] *vt*: **to ~ sb to do sth** jdn dazu überreden, etw zu tun; **to ~ sb that** jdn davon überzeugen, daß; **to be ~d of sth** von etw überzeugt sein.

**persuasion** [pəˈsweɪʒən] *n* (*act*) Überredung *f*; (*creed*) Überzeugung *f*.

**persuasive** [pəˈsweɪsɪv] *adj* (*person, argument*) überzeugend.

**pert** [pɜːt] *adj* (*person*) frech; (*nose, buttocks*) keck; (*hat*) keß.

**pertaining** [pɜːˈteɪnɪŋ]: **~ to** *prep* betreffend *+acc*.

**pertinent** [ˈpɜːtɪnənt] *adj* relevant.

**perturb** [pəˈtɜːb] *vt* beunruhigen.

**Peru** [pəˈruː] *n* Peru *nt*.

**perusal** [pəˈruːzl] *n* Durchsicht *f*.

**peruse** [pəˈruːz] *vt* durchsehen.

**Peruvian** [pəˈruːvjən] *adj* peruanisch ♦ *n* Peruaner(in) *m(f)*.

**pervade** [pəˈveɪd] *vt* (*smell, feeling*) erfüllen.

**pervasive** [pəˈveɪsɪv] *adj* (*smell*) durchdringend; (*influence*) weitreichend; (*mood, atmosphere*) allumfassend.

**perverse** [pəˈvɜːs] *adj* (*person*) borniert; (*behaviour*) widernatürlich, pervers.

**perversion** [pəˈvɜːʃən] *n* (*sexual*) Perversion *f*; (*of truth, justice*) Verzerrung *f*, Pervertierung *f*.

**perversity** [pəˈvɜːsɪtɪ] *n* Widernatürlichkeit *f*.

**pervert** [*n* ˈpɜːvɜːt, *vt* pəˈvɜːt] *n* (*sexual deviant*) perverser Mensch *m* ♦ *vt* (*person, mind*) verderben; (*distort: truth, custom*) verfälschen.

**pessimism** [ˈpɛsɪmɪzəm] *n* Pessimismus *m*.

**pessimist** [ˈpɛsɪmɪst] *n* Pessimist(in) *m(f)*.

**pessimistic** [pɛsɪˈmɪstɪk] *adj* pessimistisch.

**pest** [pɛst] *n* (*insect*) Schädling *m*; (*fig: nuisance*) Plage *f*.

**pest control** *n* Schädlingsbekämpfung *f*.

**pester** [ˈpɛstə⁺] *vt* belästigen.

**pesticide** [ˈpɛstɪsaɪd] *n* Schädlingsbekämpfungsmittel *nt*, Pestizid *nt*.

**pestilence** [ˈpɛstɪləns] *n* Pest *f*.

**pestle** [ˈpɛsl] *n* Stößel *m*.

**pet** [pɛt] *n* (*animal*) Haustier *nt* ♦ *adj* (*theory etc*) Lieblings- ♦ *vt* (*stroke*) streicheln ♦ *vi* (*inf: sexually*) herumknutschen; **teacher's ~** (*favourite*) Lehrers Liebling *m*; **a ~ rabbit/ snake** *etc* ein Kaninchen/eine Schlange *etc* (als Haustier); **that's my ~ hate** das hasse ich besonders.

**petal** [ˈpɛtl] *n* Blütenblatt *nt*.

**peter out** [ˈpiːtə-] *vi* (*road etc*) allmählich aufhören, zu Ende gehen; (*conversation, meeting*) sich totlaufen.

**petite** [pəˈtiːt] *adj* (*woman*) zierlich.

**petition** [pəˈtɪʃən] *n* (*signed document*) Petition *f*; (*LAW*) Klage *f* ♦ *vt* ersuchen ♦ *vi*: **to ~ for divorce** die Scheidung einreichen.

**pet name** (*BRIT*) *n* Kosename *m*.

**petrified** [ˈpɛtrɪfaɪd] *adj* (*fig: terrified*) starr vor Angst.

**petrify** [ˈpɛtrɪfaɪ] *vt* (*fig: terrify*) vor Angst erstarren lassen.

**petrochemical** [pɛtrəˈkɛmɪkl] *adj* petrochemisch.

**petrodollars** [ˈpɛtrəʊdɒləz] *npl* Petrodollar *pl*.

**petrol** [ˈpɛtrəl] (*BRIT*) *n* Benzin *nt*; **two-star ~** Normalbenzin *nt*; **four-star ~** Super(benzin) *nt*; **unleaded ~** bleifreies *or* unverbleites Benzin.

**petrol bomb** *n* Benzinbombe *f*.

**petrol can** (*BRIT*) *n* Benzinkanister *m*.

**petrol engine** (*BRIT*) *n* Benzinmotor *m*.

**petroleum** [pəˈtrəʊlɪəm] *n* Petroleum *nt*.

**petroleum jelly** *n* Vaseline *f*.

**petrol pump** (*BRIT*) *n* (*in garage*) Zapfsäule *f*; (*in engine*) Benzinpumpe *f*.

**petrol station** (*BRIT*) *n* Tankstelle *f*.

**petrol tank** (*BRIT*) *n* Benzintank *m*.

**petticoat** [ˈpɛtɪkəʊt] *n* (*underskirt: full-length*) Unterkleid *nt*; (: *waist*) Unterrock *m*.

**pettifogging** [ˈpɛtɪfɒgɪŋ] *adj* kleinlich.

**pettiness** [ˈpɛtɪnɪs] *n* Kleinlichkeit *f*.

**petty** [ˈpɛtɪ] *adj* (*trivial*) unbedeutend; (*small-minded*) kleinlich; (*crime*) geringfügig; (*official*) untergeordnet; (*excuse*) billig; (*remark*) spitz.

**petty cash** *n* (*in office*) Portokasse *f*.

**petty officer** *n* Maat *m*.

**petulant** [ˈpɛtjulənt] *adj* (*person, expression*) gereizt.

**pew** [pjuː] *n* (*in church*) Kirchenbank *f*.

**pewter** [ˈpjuːtə⁺] *n* Zinn *nt*.

**Pfc** (*US*) *abbr* (*MIL*: = *private first class*) ≈ Obergefreite(r) *m*.

**PG** *n abbr* (*CINE*: = *parental guidance*) Klassifikation für Filme, die Kinder nur in Begleitung Erwachsener sehen dürfen.

**PGA** *n abbr* (= *Professional Golfers' Association*) Golf-Profiverband.

**PH** (*US*) *n abbr* (*MIL*: = *Purple Heart*) Verwundetenauszeichnung.

**pH** n abbr (= potential of hydrogen) pH.
**PHA** (US) n abbr (= Public Housing Administration) Regierungsbehörde für sozialen Wohnungsbau.
**phallic** ['fælık] adj phallisch; (symbol) Phallus-.
**phantom** ['fæntəm] n Phantom nt ♦ adj (fig) Phantom-.
**Pharaoh** ['fɛərəu] n Pharao m.
**pharmaceutical** [fɑːmə'sjuːtɪkl] adj pharmazeutisch.
**pharmaceuticals** [fɑːmə'sjuːtɪklz] npl Arzneimittel pl, Pharmaka pl.
**pharmacist** ['fɑːməsɪst] n Apotheker(in) m(f).
**pharmacy** ['fɑːməsɪ] n (shop) Apotheke f; (science) Pharmazie f.
**phase** [feɪz] n Phase f ♦ vt: to ~ sth in/out etw stufenweise einführen/abschaffen.
**PhD** n abbr (= Doctor of Philosophy) ≈ Dr. phil.
**pheasant** ['fɛznt] n Fasan m.
**phenomena** [fə'nɔmɪnə] npl of **phenomenon**.
**phenomenal** [fə'nɔmɪnl] adj phänomenal.
**phenomenon** [fə'nɔmɪnən] (pl **phenomena**) n Phänomen nt.
**phew** [fjuː] excl puh!
**phial** ['faɪəl] n Fläschchen nt.
**philanderer** [fɪ'lændərə*] n Schwerenöter m.
**philanthropic** [fɪlən'θrɔpɪk] adj philanthropisch.
**philanthropist** [fɪ'lænθrəpɪst] n Philanthrop(in) m(f).
**philatelist** [fɪ'lætəlɪst] n Philatelist(in) m(f).
**philately** [fɪ'lætəlɪ] n Philatelie f.
**Philippines** ['fɪlɪpiːnz] npl: **the ~** die Philippinen pl.
**Philistine** ['fɪlɪstaɪn] n (boor) Banause m.
**philosopher** [fɪ'lɔsəfə*] n Philosoph(in) m(f).
**philosophical** [fɪlə'sɔfɪkl] adj philosophisch; (fig: calm, resigned) gelassen.
**philosophize** [fɪ'lɔsəfaɪz] vi philosophieren.
**philosophy** [fɪ'lɔsəfɪ] n Philosophie f.
**phlegm** [flɛm] n (MED) Schleim m.
**phlegmatic** [flɛg'mætɪk] adj phlegmatisch.
**phobia** ['fəubjə] n Phobie f.
**phone** [fəun] n Telefon nt ♦ vt anrufen ♦ vi anrufen, telefonieren; **to be on the ~** (possess a phone) Telefon haben; (be calling) telefonieren.
▶**phone back** vt, vi zurückrufen.
▶**phone up** vt, vi anrufen.
**phone book** n Telefonbuch nt.
**phone booth** n Telefonzelle f.
**phone box** (BRIT) n Telefonzelle f.
**phone call** n Anruf m.
**phonecard** ['fəunkɑːd] n Telefonkarte f.
**phone-in** ['fəunɪn] (BRIT) n (RADIO, TV) Radio-/Fernsehsendung mit Hörer-/Zuschauerbeteiligung per Telefon, Phone-in nt ♦ adj mit Hörer-/Zuschaueranrufen.
**phone tapping** [-tæpɪŋ] n Abhören nt von Telefonleitungen.
**phonetics** [fə'nɛtɪks] n Phonetik f.

**phoney** ['fəunɪ] adj (address) falsch; (accent) unecht; (person) unaufrichtig.
**phonograph** ['fəunəgrɑːf] (US) n Grammophon nt.
**phony** ['fəunɪ] adj = **phoney**.
**phosphate** ['fɔsfeɪt] n Phosphat nt.
**phosphorus** ['fɔsfərəs] n Phosphor m.
**photo** ['fəutəu] n Foto nt.
**photo...** ['fəutəu] pref Foto-.
**photocopier** ['fəutəukɔpɪə*] n Fotokopierer m.
**photocopy** ['fəutəukɔpɪ] n Fotokopie f ♦ vt fotokopieren.
**photoelectric** [fəutəuɪ'lɛktrɪk] adj (effect) photoelektrisch; (cell) Photo-.
**photo finish** n Fotofinish nt.
**Photofit** ® ['fəutəufɪt] n (also: ~ **picture**) Phantombild nt.
**photogenic** [fəutəu'dʒɛnɪk] adj fotogen.
**photograph** ['fəutəgræf] n Fotografie f ♦ vt fotografieren; **to take a ~ of sb** jdn fotografieren.
**photographer** [fə'tɔgrəfə*] n Fotograf(in) m(f).
**photographic** [fəutə'græfɪk] adj (equipment etc) fotografisch, Foto-.
**photography** [fə'tɔgrəfɪ] n Fotografie f.
**photo opportunity** n Fototermin m; (accidental) Fotogelegenheit f.
**photostat** ['fəutəustæt] n Fotokopie f.
**photosynthesis** [fəutəu'sɪnθəsɪs] n Photosynthese f.
**phrase** [freɪz] n Satz m; (LING) Redewendung f; (MUS) Phrase f ♦ vt ausdrücken; (letter) formulieren.
**phrase book** n Sprachführer m.
**physical** ['fɪzɪkl] adj (bodily) körperlich; (geography, properties) physikalisch; (law, explanation) natürlich; **~ examination** ärztliche Untersuchung f; **the ~ sciences** die Naturwissenschaften.
**physical education** n Sportunterricht m.
**physically** ['fɪzɪklɪ] adv (fit, attractive) körperlich.
**physician** [fɪ'zɪʃən] n Arzt m, Ärztin f.
**physicist** ['fɪzɪsɪst] n Physiker(in) m(f).
**physics** ['fɪzɪks] n Physik f.
**physiological** ['fɪzɪə'lɔdʒɪkl] adj physiologisch.
**physiology** [fɪzɪ'ɔlədʒɪ] n Physiologie f.
**physiotherapist** [fɪzɪəu'θɛrəpɪst] n Physiotherapeut(in) m(f).
**physiotherapy** [fɪzɪəu'θɛrəpɪ] n Physiotherapie f.
**physique** [fɪ'ziːk] n Körperbau m.
**pianist** ['piːənɪst] n Pianist(in) m(f).
**piano** [pɪ'ænəu] n Klavier nt, Piano nt.
**piano accordion** (BRIT) n Akkordeon nt.
**piccolo** ['pɪkələu] n Pikkoloflöte f.
**pick** [pɪk] n (also: **~axe**) Spitzhacke f ♦ vt (select) aussuchen; (gather: fruit, mushrooms) sammeln; (: flowers) pflücken; (remove, take out) herausnehmen; (lock) knacken; (scab,

*spot*) kratzen an +*dat*; **take your ~** (*choose*) Sie haben die Wahl; **the ~ of** (*best*) das Beste +*gen*; **to ~ one's nose** in der Nase bohren; **to ~ one's teeth** in den Zähnen stochern; **to ~ sb's brains** jdn als Informationsquelle nutzen; **to ~ sb's pocket** jdn bestehlen; **to ~ a quarrel (with sb)** einen Streit (mit jdm) anfangen.

▶**pick at** *vt fus* (*food*) herumstochern in +*dat*.

▶**pick off** *vt* (*shoot*) abschießen.

▶**pick on** *vt fus* (*criticize*) herumhacken auf +*dat*.

▶**pick out** *vt* (*distinguish*) ausmachen; (*select*) aussuchen.

▶**pick up** *vi* (*health*) sich verbessern; (*economy*) sich erholen ♦ *vt* (*from floor etc*) aufheben; (*arrest*) festnehmen; (*collect: person, parcel etc*) abholen; (*hitchhiker*) mitnehmen; (*for sexual encounter*) aufreißen; (*learn: skill etc*) mitbekommen; (*RADIO*) empfangen; **to ~ up where one left off** da weitermachen, wo man aufgehört hat; **to ~ up speed** schneller werden; **to ~ o.s. up** (*after falling etc*) sich aufrappeln.

**pickaxe,** (*US*) **pickax** ['pɪkæks] *n* Spitzhacke *f*.

**picket** ['pɪkɪt] *n* (*in strike*) Streikposten *m* ♦ *vt* (*factory etc*) Streikposten aufstellen vor +*dat*.

**picketing** ['pɪkɪtɪŋ] *n* Aufstellen *nt* von Streikposten.

**picket line** *n* Streikpostenkette *f*.

**pickings** ['pɪkɪŋz] *npl*: **there are rich ~ to be had here** hier ist die Ausbeute gut.

**pickle** ['pɪkl] *n* (*also*: **~s**: *as condiment*) Pickles *pl* ♦ *vt* einlegen; **to be in a ~** in der Klemme sitzen; **to get in a ~** in eine Klemme geraten.

**pick-me-up** ['pɪkmiːʌp] *n* Muntermacher *m*.

**pickpocket** ['pɪkpɔkɪt] *n* Taschendieb(in) *m(f)*.

**pick-up** ['pɪkʌp] *n* (*also*: **~ truck**) offener Kleintransporter *m*; (*BRIT: on record player*) Tonabnehmer *m*.

**picnic** ['pɪknɪk] *n* Picknick *nt* ♦ *vi* picknicken.

**picnicker** ['pɪknɪkə*] *n* Picknicker(in) *m(f)*.

**pictorial** [pɪk'tɔːrɪəl] *adj* (*record, coverage etc*) bildlich.

**picture** ['pɪktʃə*] *n* (*also TV, fig*) Bild *nt*; (*film*) Film *m* ♦ *vt* (*imagine*) sich *dat* vorstellen; **the ~s** (*BRIT: inf: the cinema*) das Kino; **to take a ~ of sb** ein Bild von jdm machen; **to put sb in the ~** jdn ins Bild setzen.

**picture book** *n* Bilderbuch *nt*.

**picturesque** [pɪktʃə'rɛsk] *adj* malerisch.

**picture window** *n* Aussichtsfenster *nt*.

**piddling** ['pɪdlɪŋ] (*inf*) *adj* lächerlich.

**pidgin** ['pɪdʒɪn] *adj*: **~ English** Pidgin-Englisch *nt*.

**pie** [paɪ] *n* (*vegetable, meat*) Pastete *f*; (*fruit*) Torte *f*.

**piebald** ['paɪbɔːld] *adj* (*horse*) scheckig.

**piece** [piːs] *n* Stück *nt*; (*DRAUGHTS etc*) Stein *m*; (*CHESS*) Figur *f*; **in ~s** (*broken*) kaputt; (*taken apart*) auseinandergenommen, in

Einzelteilen; **a ~ of clothing/furniture/music** ein Kleidungs-/Möbel-/Musikstück *nt*; **a ~ of machinery** eine Maschine; **a ~ of research** eine Forschungsarbeit; **a ~ of advice** ein Rat *m*; **to take sth to ~s** etw auseinandernehmen; **in one ~** (*object*) unbeschädigt; (*person*) wohlbehalten; **a 10p ~** (*BRIT*) ein 10-Pence-Stück *nt*; **~ by ~** Stück für Stück; **a six-~ band** eine sechsköpfige Band; **let her say her ~** laß sie ausreden.

▶**piece together** *vt* zusammenfügen.

**piecemeal** ['piːsmiːl] *adv* stückweise, Stück für Stück.

**piecework** ['piːswəːk] *n* Akkordarbeit *f*.

**pie chart** *n* Tortendiagramm *nt*.

**pier** [pɪə*] *n* Pier *m*.

**pierce** [pɪəs] *vt* durchstechen; **to have one's ears ~d** sich *dat* die Ohrläppchen durchstechen lassen.

**piercing** ['pɪəsɪŋ] *adj* (*fig: cry, eyes, stare*) durchdringend; (*wind*) schneidend.

**piety** ['paɪətɪ] *n* Frömmigkeit *f*.

**piffling** ['pɪflɪŋ] (*inf*) *adj* lächerlich.

**pig** [pɪg] *n* (*also pej*) Schwein *nt*; (*greedy person*) Vielfraß *m*.

**pigeon** ['pɪdʒən] *n* Taube *f*.

**pigeonhole** ['pɪdʒənhəul] *n* (*for letters etc*) Fach *nt*; (*fig*) Schublade *f* ♦ *vt* (*fig: person*) in eine Schublade stecken.

**pigeon-toed** ['pɪdʒəntəud] *adj* mit einwärts gerichteten Zehen.

**piggy bank** ['pɪgɪ-] *n* Sparschwein *nt*.

**pig-headed** ['pɪg'hɛdɪd] (*pej*) *adj* dickköpfig.

**piglet** ['pɪglɪt] *n* Schweinchen *nt*, Ferkel *nt*.

**pigment** ['pɪgmənt] *n* Pigment *nt*.

**pigmentation** [pɪgmən'teɪʃən] *n* Pigmentierung *f*, Färbung *f*.

**pigmy** ['pɪgmɪ] *n* = **pygmy**.

**pigskin** ['pɪgskɪn] *n* Schweinsleder *nt*.

**pigsty** ['pɪgstaɪ] *n* (*also fig*) Schweinestall *m*.

**pigtail** ['pɪgteɪl] *n* Zopf *m*.

**pike** [paɪk] *n* (*fish*) Hecht *m*; (*spear*) Spieß *m*.

**pilchard** ['pɪltʃəd] *n* Sardine *f*.

**pile** [paɪl] *n* (*heap*) Haufen *m*; (*stack*) Stapel *m*; (*of carpet, velvet*) Flor *m*; (*pillar*) Pfahl *m* ♦ *vt* (*also*: **~ up**) (auf)stapeln; **in a ~** in einem Haufen; **to ~ into/out of** (*vehicle*) sich drängen in +*acc*/aus.

▶**pile on** *vt*: **to ~ it on** (*inf*) zu dick auftragen.

▶**pile up** *vi* (*papers, problems, work*) sich stapeln.

**piles** [paɪlz] *npl* (*MED*) Hämorrhoiden *pl*.

**pile-up** ['paɪlʌp] *n* (*AUT*) Massenkarambolage *f*.

**pilfer** ['pɪlfə*] *vt, vi* stehlen.

**pilfering** ['pɪlfərɪŋ] *n* Diebstahl *m*.

**pilgrim** ['pɪlgrɪm] *n* Pilger(in) *m(f)*.

**pilgrimage** ['pɪlgrɪmɪdʒ] *n* Pilgerfahrt *f*, Wallfahrt *f*.

**pill** [pɪl] *n* Tablette *f*, Pille *f*; **the ~** (*contraceptive*) die Pille; **to be on the ~** die

Pille nehmen.

**pillage** ['pɪlɪdʒ] *n* Plünderung *f* ♦ *vt* plündern.

**pillar** ['pɪlə'] *n* Säule *f*; **a ~ of society** (*fig*) eine Säule *or* Stütze der Gesellschaft.

**pillar box** (*BRIT*) *n* Briefkasten *m*.

**pillion** ['pɪljən] *n*: **to ride ~** (*on motorcycle*) auf dem Soziussitz mitfahren; (*on horse*) hinten auf dem Pferd mitreiten.

**pillory** ['pɪlərɪ] *vt* (*criticize*) anprangern ♦ *n* Pranger *m*.

**pillow** ['pɪləu] *n* (Kopf)kissen *nt*.

**pillowcase** ['pɪləukeɪs] *n* (Kopf)kissenbezug *m*.

**pillowslip** ['pɪləuslɪp] *n* = pillowcase.

**pilot** ['paɪlət] *n* (*AVIAT*) Pilot(in) *m(f)*; (*NAUT*) Lotse *m* ♦ *adj* (*scheme, study etc*) Pilot- ♦ *vt* (*aircraft*) steuern; (*fig: new law, scheme*) sich zum Fürsprecher machen +*gen*.

**pilot boat** *n* Lotsenboot *nt*.

**pilot light** *n* (*on cooker, boiler*) Zündflamme *f*.

**pimento** [pɪ'mentəu] *n* (*spice*) Piment *nt*.

**pimp** [pɪmp] *n* Zuhälter *m*.

**pimple** ['pɪmpl] *n* Pickel *m*.

**pimply** ['pɪmplɪ] *adj* pick(e)lig.

**PIN** *n abbr* (= *personal identification number*) PIN; **~ number** PIN-Nummer *f*.

**pin** [pɪn] *n* (*metal: for clothes, papers*) Stecknadel *f*; (*TECH*) Stift *m*; (*BRIT: also:* **drawing ~**) Heftzwecke *f*; (*in grenade*) Sicherungsstift *m*; (*BRIT: ELEC*) Pol *m* ♦ *vt* (*fasten with pin*) feststecken; **~s and needles** (*in arms, legs etc*) Kribbeln *nt*; **to ~ sb against/to sth** jdn gegen/an etw *acc* pressen; **to ~ sth on sb** (*fig*) jdm etw anhängen.

▶**pin down** *vt* (*fig: person*) festnageln; **there's something strange here but I can't quite ~ it down** hier stimmt etwas nicht, aber ich weiß nicht genau was.

**pinafore** ['pɪnəfɔː'] (*BRIT*) *n* (*also:* **~ dress**) Trägerkleid *nt*.

**pinball** ['pɪnbɔːl] *n* (*game*) Flippern *nt*; (*machine*) Flipper *m*.

**pincers** ['pɪnsəz] *npl* (*tool*) Kneifzange *f*; (*of crab, lobster etc*) Schere *f*.

**pinch** [pɪntʃ] *n* (*of salt etc*) Prise *f* ♦ *vt* (*with finger and thumb*) zwicken, kneifen; (*inf: steal*) klauen ♦ *vi* (*shoe*) drücken; **at a ~** zur Not; **to feel the ~** (*fig*) die schlechte Lage zu spüren bekommen.

**pinched** [pɪntʃt] *adj* (*face*) erschöpft; **~ with cold** verfroren.

**pincushion** ['pɪnkuʃən] *n* Nadelkissen *nt*.

**pine** [paɪn] *n* (*also:* **~ tree**) Kiefer *f*; (*wood*) Kiefernholz *nt* ♦ *vi*: **to ~ for** sich sehnen nach.

▶**pine away** *vi* sich (vor Kummer) verzehren.

**pineapple** ['paɪnæpl] *n* Ananas *f*.

**pine cone** *n* Kiefernzapfen *m*.

**pine needles** *npl* Kiefernnadeln *pl*.

**ping** [pɪŋ] *n* (*noise*) Klingeln *nt*.

**Ping-Pong** ® ['pɪŋpɔŋ] *n* Pingpong *nt*.

**pink** [pɪŋk] *adj* rosa *inv* ♦ *n* (*colour*) Rosa *nt*; (*BOT*) Gartennelke *f*.

**pinking shears** *npl* Zickzackschere *f*.

**pin money** (*BRIT: inf*) *n* Nadelgeld *nt*.

**pinnacle** ['pɪnəkl] *n* (*of building, mountain*) Spitze *f*; (*fig*) Gipfel *m*.

**pinpoint** ['pɪnpɔɪnt] *vt* (*identify*) genau festlegen, identifizieren; (*position of sth*) genau aufzeigen.

**pinstripe** ['pɪnstraɪp] *adj*: **~ suit** Nadelstreifenanzug *m*.

**pint** [paɪnt] *n* (*BRIT: = 568 cc*) (britisches) Pint *nt*; (*US: = 473 cc*) (amerikanisches) Pint; **a ~** (*BRIT: inf: of beer*) ≈ eine Halbe.

**pin-up** ['pɪnʌp] *n* (*picture*) Pin-up-Foto *nt*.

**pioneer** [paɪə'nɪə'] *n* (*lit, fig*) Pionier *m* ♦ *vt* (*invention etc*) Pionierarbeit leisten für.

**pious** ['paɪəs] *adj* fromm.

**pip** [pɪp] *n* (*of apple, orange*) Kern *m* ♦ *vt*: **to be ~ped at the post** (*BRIT, fig*) um Haaresbreite geschlagen werden; **the pips** *npl* (*BRIT: RADIO*) das Zeitzeichen.

**pipe** [paɪp] *n* (*for water, gas*) Rohr *nt*; (*for smoking*) Pfeife *f*; (*MUS*) Flöte *f* ♦ *vt* (*water, gas, oil*) (durch Rohre) leiten; **pipes** *npl* (*also:* **bagpipes**) Dudelsack *m*.

▶**pipe down** (*inf*) *vi* (*be quiet*) ruhig sein.

**pipe cleaner** *n* Pfeifenreiniger *m*.

**piped music** [paɪpt-] *n* Berieselungsmusik *f*.

**pipe dream** *n* Hirngespinst *nt*.

**pipeline** ['paɪplaɪn] *n* Pipeline *f*; **it's in the ~** (*fig*) es ist in Vorbereitung.

**piper** ['paɪpə'] *n* (*bagpipe player*) Dudelsackspieler(in) *m(f)*.

**pipe tobacco** *n* Pfeifentabak *m*.

**piping** ['paɪpɪŋ] *adv*: **~ hot** kochendheiß.

**piquant** ['piːkənt] *adj* (*also fig*) pikant.

**pique** ['piːk] *n*: **in a fit of ~** eingeschnappt, pikiert.

**piracy** ['paɪərəsɪ] *n* Piraterie *f*, Seeräuberei *f*; (*COMM*): **to commit ~** ein Plagiat begehen.

**pirate** ['paɪərət] *n* Pirat *m*, Seeräuber *m* ♦ *vt* (*COMM: video tape, cassette etc*) illegal herstellen.

**pirate radio station** (*BRIT*) *n* Piratensender *m*.

**pirouette** [pɪru'et] *n* Pirouette *f* ♦ *vi* Pirouetten drehen.

**Pisces** ['paɪsiːz] *n* Fische *pl*; **to be ~** Fische *or* (ein) Fisch sein.

**piss** [pɪs] (*inf!*) *vi* pissen ♦ *n* Pisse *f*; **~ off!** verpiß dich!; **to be ~ed off (with sb/sth)** (von jdm/etw) die Schnauze voll haben; **it's ~ing down** (*BRIT: raining*) es schifft; **to take the ~ out of sb** (*BRIT*) jdn verarschen.

**pissed** [pɪst] (*inf!*) *adj* (*drunk*) besoffen.

**pistol** ['pɪstl] *n* Pistole *f*.

**piston** ['pɪstən] *n* Kolben *m*.

**pit** [pɪt] *n* Grube *f*; (*in surface of road*) Schlagloch *nt*; (*coal mine*) Zeche *f*; (*also:* **orchestra ~**) Orchestergraben *m* ♦ *vt*: **to ~ one's wits against sb** seinen Verstand an jdm messen; **the pits** *npl* (*AUT*) die Box; **to ~ o.s. against sth** den Kampf gegen etw aufnehmen; **to ~ sb against sb** jdn gegen jdn antreten lassen; **the ~ of one's stomach** die Magengrube.

**pitapat** ['pɪtə'pæt] (*BRIT*) *adv*: **to go ~** (*heart*) pochen, klopfen; (*rain*) prasseln.

**pitch** [pɪtʃ] *n* (*BRIT: SPORT: field*) Spielfeld *nt*; (*MUS*) Tonhöhe *f*; (*fig: level, degree*) Grad *m*; (*tar*) Pech *nt*; (*also: sales ~*) Verkaufsmasche *f*; (*NAUT*) Stampfen *nt* ♦ *vt* (*throw*) werfen, schleudern; (*set: price, message*) ansetzen ♦ *vi* (*fall forwards*) hinschlagen; (*NAUT*) stampfen; **to ~ a tent** ein Zelt aufschlagen; **to be ~ed forward** vornüber geworfen werden.

**pitch-black** ['pɪtʃ'blæk] *adj* pechschwarz.

**pitched battle** [pɪtʃt-] *n* offene Schlacht *f*.

**pitcher** ['pɪtʃər] *n* (*jug*) Krug *m*; (*US: BASEBALL*) Werfer *m*.

**pitchfork** ['pɪtʃfɔːk] *n* Heugabel *f*.

**piteous** ['pɪtɪəs] *adj* kläglich, erbärmlich.

**pitfall** ['pɪtfɔːl] *n* Falle *f*.

**pith** [pɪθ] *n* (*of orange etc*) weiße Haut *f*; (*of plant*) Mark *nt*; (*fig*) Kern *m*.

**pithead** ['pɪthɛd] *n* Schachtanlagen *pl* über Tage.

**pithy** ['pɪθɪ] *adj* (*comment etc*) prägnant.

**pitiable** ['pɪtɪəbl] *adj* mitleiderregend.

**pitiful** ['pɪtɪful] *adj* (*sight etc*) mitleiderregend; (*excuse, attempt*) jämmerlich, kläglich.

**pitifully** ['pɪtɪfəlɪ] *adv* (*thin, frail*) jämmerlich; (*inadequate, ill-equipped*) fürchterlich.

**pitiless** ['pɪtɪlɪs] *adj* mitleidlos.

**pittance** ['pɪtns] *n* Hungerlohn *m*.

**pitted** ['pɪtɪd] *adj*: **~ with** übersät mit; **~ with rust** voller Rost.

**pity** ['pɪtɪ] *n* Mitleid *nt* ♦ *vt* bemitleiden, bedauern; **what a ~!** wie schade!; **it is a ~ that you can't come** schade, daß du nicht kommen kannst; **to take ~ on sb** Mitleid mit jdm haben.

**pitying** ['pɪtɪɪŋ] *adj* mitleidig.

**pivot** ['pɪvət] *n* (*TECH*) Drehpunkt *m*; (*fig*) Dreh- und Angelpunkt *m* ♦ *vi* sich drehen.

▶**pivot on** (*depend on*) abhängen von.

**pixel** ['pɪksl] *n* (*COMPUT*) Pixel *nt*.

**pixie** ['pɪksɪ] *n* Elf *m*, Elfe *f*.

**pizza** ['piːtsə] *n* Pizza *f*.

**placard** ['plækɑːd] *n* Plakat *nt*, Aushang *m*; (*in march etc*) Transparent *nt*.

**placate** [plə'keɪt] *vt* beschwichtigen, besänftigen.

**placatory** [plə'keɪtərɪ] *adj* beschwichtigend, besänftigend.

**place** [pleɪs] *n* Platz *m*; (*position*) Stelle *f*, Ort *m*; (*seat: on committee etc*) Sitz *m*; (*home*) Wohnung *f*; (*in street names*) ≈ Straße *f* ♦ *vt* (*put: object*) stellen, legen; (*identify: person*) unterbringen; **~ of birth** Geburtsort *m*; **to take ~** (*happen*) geschehen, passieren; **at/to his ~** (*home*) bei/zu ihm; **from ~ to ~** von

Ort zu Ort; **all over the ~** überall; **in ~s** stellenweise; **in sb's/sth's ~** anstelle von jdm/etw; **to take sb's/sth's ~** ~ an die Stelle von jdm/etw treten, jdn/etw ersetzen; **out of ~** (*inappropriate*) unangebracht; **I feel out of ~ here** ich fühle mich hier fehl am Platze; **in the first ~** (*first of all*) erstens; **to change ~s with sb** mit jdm den Platz tauschen; **to put sb in his ~** (*fig*) jdn in seine Schranken weisen; **he's going ~s** er bringt es noch mal weit; **it's not my ~ to do it** es ist nicht an mir, das zu tun; **to be ~d** (*in race, exam*) plaziert sein; **to be ~d third** den dritten Platz belegen; **to ~ an order with sb (for sth)** eine Bestellung bei jdm (für etw) aufgeben; **how are you ~d next week?** wie sieht es bei Ihnen nächste Woche aus?

**placebo** [plə'siːbəu] *n* Placebo *nt*; (*fig*) Beruhigungsmittel *nt*.

**place mat** *n* Set *nt or m*.

**placement** ['pleɪsmənt] *n* Plazierung *f*.

**place name** *n* Ortsname *m*.

**placenta** [plə'sɛntə] *n* Plazenta *f*.

**place setting** *n* Gedeck *nt*.

**placid** ['plæsɪd] *adj* (*person*) ruhig, gelassen; (*place, river etc*) friedvoll.

**plagiarism** ['pleɪdʒərɪzəm] *n* Plagiat *nt*.

**plagiarist** ['pleɪdʒərɪst] *n* Plagiator(in) *m(f)*.

**plagiarize** ['pleɪdʒəraɪz] *vt* (*idea, work*) kopieren, plagiieren.

**plague** [pleɪg] *n* (*MED*) Seuche *f*; (*fig: of locusts etc*) Plage *f* ♦ *vt* (*fig: problems etc*) plagen; **to ~ sb with questions** jdn mit Fragen quälen.

**plaice** [pleɪs] *n inv* Scholle *f*.

**plaid** [plæd] *n* Plaid *nt*.

**plain** [pleɪn] *adj* (*unpatterned*) einfarbig; (*simple*) einfach, schlicht; (*clear, easily understood*) klar; (*not beautiful*) unattraktiv; (*frank*) offen ♦ *adv* (*wrong, stupid etc*) einfach ♦ *n* (*area of land*) Ebene *f*; (*KNITTING*) rechte Masche *f*; **to make sth ~ to sb** jdm etw klarmachen.

**plain chocolate** *n* Bitterschokolade *f*.

**plain-clothes** ['pleɪnkləuðz] *adj* (*police officer*) in Zivil.

**plainly** ['pleɪnlɪ] *adv* (*obviously*) eindeutig; (*clearly*) deutlich, klar.

**plainness** ['pleɪnnɪs] *n* (*of person*) Reizlosigkeit *f*.

**plain speaking** *n* Offenheit *f*; **a bit of ~** ein paar offene Worte.

**plain-spoken** ['pleɪn'spəukən] *adj* offen.

**plaintiff** ['pleɪntɪf] *n* Kläger(in) *m(f)*.

**plaintive** ['pleɪntɪv] *adj* (*cry, voice*) klagend; (*song*) schwermütig; (*look*) traurig.

**plait** [plæt] *n* (*of hair*) Zopf *m*; (*of rope, leather*) Geflecht *nt* ♦ *vt* flechten.

**plan** [plæn] *n* Plan *m* ♦ *vt* planen; (*building, schedule*) entwerfen ♦ *vi* planen; **to ~ to do sth** planen *or* vorhaben, etw zu tun; **how long do you ~ to stay?** wie lange haben Sie vor, zu bleiben?; **to ~ for** *or* **on** (*expect*) sich einstellen auf +acc; **to ~ on doing sth** vorhaben, etw zu tun.

**plane** [pleɪn] n (AVIAT) Flugzeug nt; (MATH) Ebene f; (fig: level) Niveau nt; (tool) Hobel m; (also: ~ **tree**) Platane f ♦ vt (wood) hobeln ♦ vi (NAUT, AUT) gleiten.

**planet** ['plænɪt] n Planet m.

**planetarium** [plænɪ'tɛərɪəm] n Planetarium nt.

**plank** [plæŋk] n (of wood) Brett nt; (fig: of policy etc) Schwerpunkt m.

**plankton** ['plæŋktən] n Plankton nt.

**planned economy** ['plænd-] n Planwirtschaft f.

**planner** ['plænə'] n Planer(in) m(f).

**planning** ['plænɪŋ] n Planung f.

**planning permission** (BRIT) n Baugenehmigung f.

**plant** [plɑ:nt] n (BOT) Pflanze f; (machinery) Maschinen pl; (factory) Anlage f ♦ vt (seed, plant, crops) pflanzen; (field, garden) bepflanzen; (microphone, bomb etc) anbringen; (incriminating evidence) schleusen; (fig: object) stellen; (: kiss) drücken.

**plantation** [plæn'teɪʃən] n Plantage f; (wood) Anpflanzung f.

**plant pot** (BRIT) n Blumentopf m.

**plaque** [plæk] n (on building etc) Tafel f, Plakette f; (on teeth) Zahnbelag m.

**plasma** ['plæzmə] n Plasma nt.

**plaster** ['plɑ:stə'] n (for walls) Putz m; (also: ~ **of Paris**) Gips m; (BRIT: also: **sticking** ~) Pflaster nt ♦ vt (wall, ceiling) verputzen; **in** ~ (BRIT) in Gips; **to** ~ **with** (cover) bepflastern mit.

**plasterboard** ['plɑ:stəbɔ:d] n Gipskarton m.

**plaster cast** n (MED) Gipsverband m; (model, statue) Gipsform f.

**plastered** ['plɑ:stəd] (inf) adj (drunk) sturzbesoffen.

**plasterer** ['plɑ:stərə'] n Gipser m.

**plastic** ['plæstɪk] n Plastik nt ♦ adj (bucket, cup etc) Plastik-; (flexible) formbar; **the ~ arts** die bildende Kunst.

**plastic bag** n Plastiktüte f.

**plastic bullet** n Plastikgeschoß nt.

**plastic explosive** n Plastiksprengstoff m.

**Plasticine** ® ['plæstɪsi:n] n Plastilin nt.

**plastic surgery** n plastische Chirurgie f.

**plate** [pleɪt] n Teller m; (metal cover) Platte f; (TYP) Druckplatte f; (AUT) Nummernschild nt; (in book: picture) Tafel f; (dental plate) Gaumenplatte f; (on door) Schild nt; (gold/silver plate) vergoldeter/versilberter Artikel m; **that necklace is just** ~ die Halskette ist nur vergoldet/versilbert.

**plateau** ['plætəu] (pl ~**s** or ~**x**) n (GEOG) Plateau nt, Hochebene f; (fig) stabiler Zustand m.

**plateful** ['pleɪtful] n Teller m.

**plate glass** n Tafelglas nt.

**platen** ['plætən] n (on typewriter, printer) (Schreib)walze f.

**plate rack** n Geschirrständer m.

**platform** ['plætfɔ:m] n (stage) Podium nt; (for landing, loading on etc, BRIT: of bus) Plattform f; (RAIL) Bahnsteig m; (POL) Programm nt; **the train leaves from** ~ 7 der Zug fährt von Gleis 7 ab.

**platform ticket** (BRIT) n (RAIL) Bahnsteigkarte f.

**platinum** ['plætɪnəm] n Platin nt.

**platitude** ['plætɪtju:d] n Platitüde f, Gemeinplatz m.

**platonic** [plə'tɔnɪk] adj (relationship) platonisch.

**platoon** [plə'tu:n] n Zug m.

**platter** ['plætə'] n Platte f.

**plaudits** ['plɔ:dɪts] npl Ovationen pl.

**plausible** ['plɔ:zɪbl] adj (theory, excuse) plausibel; (liar etc) glaubwürdig.

**play** [pleɪ] n (THEAT) (Theater)stück nt; (TV) Fernsehspiel nt; (RADIO) Hörspiel nt; (activity) Spiel nt ♦ vt spielen; (team, opponent) spielen gegen ♦ vi spielen; **to bring into** ~ ins Spiel bringen; **a** ~ **on words** ein Wortspiel nt; **to** ~ **a trick on sb** jdn hereinlegen; **to** ~ **a part** or **role in sth** (fig) eine Rolle bei etw spielen; **to** ~ **for time** (fig) auf Zeit spielen, Zeit gewinnen wollen; **to** ~ **safe** auf Nummer Sicher gehen; **to** ~ **into sb's hands** jdm in die Hände spielen.

▶**play about with** vt fus = **play around with**.

▶**play along with** vt fus (person) sich richten nach; (plan, idea) eingehen auf +acc.

▶**play around with** vt fus (fiddle with) herumspielen mit.

▶**play at** vt fus (do casually) spielen mit; **to** ~ **at being sb/sth** jdn/etw spielen.

▶**play back** vt (recording) abspielen.

▶**play down** vt herunterspielen.

▶**play on** vt fus (sb's feelings etc) ausnutzen; **to** ~ **on sb's mind** jdm im Kopf herumgehen.

▶**play up** vi (machine, knee etc) Schwierigkeiten machen; (children) frech werden.

**play-act** ['pleɪækt] vi Theater spielen.

**playboy** ['pleɪbɔɪ] n Playboy m.

**player** ['pleɪə'] n (SPORT, MUS) Spieler(in) m(f); (THEAT) Schauspieler(in) m(f).

**playful** ['pleɪful] adj (person, gesture) spielerisch; (animal) verspielt.

**playgoer** ['pleɪɡəuə'] n Theaterbesucher(in) m(f).

**playground** ['pleɪɡraund] n (in park) Spielplatz m; (in school) Schulhof m.

**playgroup** ['pleɪɡru:p] n Spielgruppe f.

**playing card** ['pleɪɪŋ-] n Spielkarte f.

**playing field** n Sportplatz m.

**playmaker** ['pleɪmeɪkə'] n (SPORT) Spielmacher(in) m(f).

**playmate** ['pleɪmeɪt] n Spielkamerad(in) m(f).

**play-off** ['pleɪɔf] n Entscheidungsspiel nt.

**playpen** ['pleɪpɛn] n Laufstall m.

**playroom** ['pleɪruːm] n Spielzimmer nt.
**playschool** ['pleɪskuːl] n = **playgroup**.
**plaything** ['pleɪθɪŋ] n (*also fig*) Spielzeug nt.
**playtime** ['pleɪtaɪm] n (*kleine*) Pause f.
**playwright** ['pleɪraɪt] n Dramatiker(in) m(f).
**plc** (*BRIT*) n abbr (= *public limited company*)
≈ AG f.
**plea** [pliː] n (*request*) Bitte f; (*LAW*): **to enter a
~ of guilty/not guilty** sich schuldig/
unschuldig erklären; (*excuse*) Vorwand m.
**plea bargaining** n Verhandlungen zwischen
*Anklage und Verteidigung mit dem Ziel,
bestimmte Anklagepunkte fallenzulassen,
wenn der Angeklagte sich in anderen
Punkten schuldig bekennt.*
**plead** [pliːd] vi (*LAW*) vor Gericht eine
*Schuld-/Unschuldserklärung abgeben* ♦ vt
(*LAW*): **to ~ sb's case** jdn vertreten; (*give as
excuse: ignorance, ill health etc*) vorgeben,
sich berufen auf +acc; **to ~ with sb** (*beg*) jdn
inständig bitten; **to ~ for sth** um etw
nachsuchen; **to ~ guilty/not guilty** sich
schuldig/nicht schuldig bekennen.
**pleasant** ['plɛznt] adj angenehm; (*smile*)
freundlich.
**pleasantly** ['plɛzntlɪ] adv (*surprised*)
angenehm; (*say, behave*) freundlich.
**pleasantries** ['plɛzntrɪz] npl Höflichkeiten pl,
Nettigkeiten pl.
**please** [pliːz] excl bitte ♦ vt (*satisfy*)
zufriedenstellen ♦ vi (*give pleasure*) gefällig
sein; **~ Miss/Sir!** (*to attract teacher's
attention*) ≈ Frau/Herr X!; **yes, ~** ja, bitte;
**my bill, ~** die Rechnung, bitte; **~ don't cry!**
bitte wein doch nicht!; **~ yourself!** (*inf*) wie
du willst!; **do as you ~** machen Sie, was Sie
für richtig halten.
**pleased** [pliːzd] adj (*happy*) erfreut; (*satisfied*)
zufrieden; **~ to meet you** freut mich(, Sie
kennenzulernen); **~ with** zufrieden mit; **we
are ~ to inform you that ...** wir freuen uns,
Ihnen mitzuteilen, daß ...
**pleasing** ['pliːzɪŋ] adj (*remark, picture etc*)
erfreulich; (*person*) sympathisch.
**pleasurable** ['plɛʒərəbl] adj angenehm.
**pleasure** ['plɛʒə*] n (*happiness, satisfaction*)
Freude f; (*fun, enjoyable experience*)
Vergnügen nt; **it's a ~**, **my ~** gern
geschehen; **with ~** gern, mit Vergnügen; **is
this trip for business or ~?** ist diese Reise
geschäftlich oder zum Vergnügen?
**pleasure boat** n Vergnügungsschiff nt.
**pleasure cruise** n Vergnügungsfahrt f.
**pleat** [pliːt] n Falte f.
**pleb** [plɛb] (*inf: pej*) n Prolet m.
**plebiscite** ['plɛbɪsɪt] n Volksentscheid m,
Plebiszit nt.
**plectrum** ['plɛktrəm] n Plektron nt, Plektrum
nt.
**pledge** [plɛdʒ] n (*promise*) Versprechen nt ♦ vt
(*promise*) versprechen; **to ~ sb to secrecy**
jdn zum Schweigen verpflichten.

**plenary** ['pliːnərɪ] adj (*powers*) unbeschränkt;
**~ session** Plenarsitzung f; **~ meeting**
Vollversammlung f.
**plentiful** ['plɛntɪful] adj reichlich.
**plenty** ['plɛntɪ] n (*lots*) eine Menge; (*sufficient*)
reichlich; **~ of** eine Menge; **we've got ~ of
time to get there** wir haben jede Menge
Zeit, dorthin zu kommen.
**plethora** ['plɛθərə] n: **a ~ of** eine Fülle von,
eine Unmenge an +dat.
**pleurisy** ['pluərɪsɪ] n Rippenfellentzündung f.
**Plexiglas** ® ['plɛksɪglɑːs] (*US*) n Plexiglas ®
nt.
**pliable** ['plaɪəbl] adj (*material*) biegsam; (*fig:
person*) leicht beeinflußbar.
**pliant** ['plaɪənt] adj = **pliable**.
**pliers** ['plaɪəz] npl Zange f.
**plight** [plaɪt] n (*of person, country*) Not f.
**plimsolls** ['plɪmsəlz] (*BRIT*) npl Turnschuhe pl.
**plinth** [plɪnθ] n Sockel m.
**PLO** n abbr (= *Palestine Liberation Organization*)
PLO f.
**plod** [plɒd] vi (*walk*) trotten; (*fig*) sich
abplagen.
**plodder** ['plɒdə*] (*pej*) n (*slow worker*) zäher
Arbeiter m, zähe Arbeiterin f.
**plonk** [plɒŋk] (*inf*) n (*BRIT: wine*) (billiger)
Wein m ♦ vt: **to ~ sth down** etw hinknallen.
**plot** [plɒt] n (*secret plan*) Komplott nt,
Verschwörung f; (*of story, play, film*)
Handlung f ♦ vt (*sb's downfall etc*) planen; (*on
chart, graph*) markieren ♦ vi (*conspire*) sich
verschwören; **a ~ of land** ein Grundstück; **a
vegetable ~** (*BRIT*) ein Gemüsebeet nt.
**plotter** ['plɒtə*] n (*instrument, also COMPUT*)
Plotter m.
**plough, (***US***) plow** [plau] n Pflug m ♦ vt
pflügen; **to ~ money into sth** (*project etc*)
Geld in etw acc stecken.
▶**plough back** vt (*COMM*) reinvestieren.
▶**plough into** vt fus (*crowd*) rasen in +acc.
**ploughman, (***US***) plowman** ['plaumən] (*irreg:
like* **man**) n Pflüger m.
**ploughman's lunch** ['plaumənz-] (*BRIT*) n
Imbiß aus Brot, Käse und Pickles.
**plow** etc (*US*) = **plough** etc.
**ploy** [plɔɪ] n Trick m.
**pluck** [plʌk] vt (*fruit, flower, leaf*) pflücken;
(*musical instrument, eyebrows*) zupfen; (*bird*)
rupfen ♦ n (*courage*) Mut m; **to ~ up courage**
allen Mut zusammennehmen.
**plucky** ['plʌkɪ] (*inf*) adj (*person*) tapfer.
**plug** [plʌg] n (*ELEC*) Stecker m; (*stopper*)
Stöpsel m; (*AUT: also:* **spark(ing) ~**)
Zündkerze f ♦ vt (*hole*) zustopfen; (*inf:
advertise*) Reklame machen für; **to give sb/
sth a ~** für jdn/etw Reklame machen.
▶**plug in** vt (*ELEC*) einstöpseln, anschließen
♦ vi angeschlossen werden.
**plughole** ['plʌghəul] (*BRIT*) n Abfluß m.
**plum** [plʌm] n (*fruit*) Pflaume f ♦ adj (*inf*): **a
~ job** ein Traumjob m.

**plumage** ['plu:mɪdʒ] n Gefieder nt.

**plumb** [plʌm] vt: **to ~ the depths of despair/ humiliation** die tiefste Verzweiflung/ Erniedrigung erleben.

▶**plumb in** vt (washing machine, shower etc) anschließen, installieren.

**plumber** ['plʌmə*] n Installateur m, Klempner m.

**plumbing** ['plʌmɪŋ] n (piping) Installationen pl, Rohrleitungen pl; (trade) Klempnerei f; (work) Installationsarbeiten pl.

**plumb line** n Lot nt, Senkblei nt.

**plume** [plu:m] n (of bird) Feder f; (on helmet, horse's head) Federbusch m; **~ of smoke** Rauchfahne f.

**plummet** ['plʌmɪt] vi (bird, aircraft) (hinunter)stürzen; (price, rate) rapide absacken.

**plump** [plʌmp] adj (person) füllig, mollig.

▶**plump for** (inf) vt fus sich entscheiden für.

▶**plump up** vt (cushion) aufschütteln.

**plunder** ['plʌndə*] n (activity) Plünderung f; (stolen things) Beute f ♦ vt (city, tomb) plündern.

**plunge** [plʌndʒ] n (of bird, person) Sprung m; (fig: of prices, rates etc) Sturz m ♦ vt (hand, knife) stoßen ♦ vi (thing) stürzen; (bird, person) sich stürzen; (fig: prices, rates etc) abfallen, stürzen; **to take the ~** (fig) den Sprung wagen; **the room was ~d into darkness** das Zimmer war in Dunkelheit getaucht.

**plunger** ['plʌndʒə*] n (for sink) Sauger m.

**plunging** ['plʌndʒɪŋ] adj: **~ neckline** tiefer Ausschnitt m.

**pluperfect** [plu:'pə:fɪkt] n: **the ~** das Plusquamperfekt.

**plural** ['pluərl] adj Plural- ♦ n Plural m, Mehrzahl f.

**plus** [plʌs] n (also: **~ sign**) Pluszeichen nt ♦ prep, adj plus; **it's a ~** (fig) es ist ein Vorteil or ein Pluspunkt; **ten/twenty ~** (more than) über zehn/zwanzig; **B ~** (SCOL) ≈ Zwei plus.

**plus fours** npl Überfallhose f.

**plush** [plʌʃ] adj (car, hotel etc) feudal ♦ n (fabric) Plüsch m.

**plutonium** [plu:'təunɪəm] n Plutonium nt.

**ply** [plaɪ] vt (a trade) ausüben, nachgehen +dat; (tool) gebrauchen, anwenden ♦ vi (ship) verkehren ♦ n (of wool, rope) Stärke f; (also: **~wood**) Sperrholz nt; **to ~ sb with drink** jdn ausgiebig bewirten; **to ~ sb with questions** jdm viele Fragen stellen; **two-/three- ~ wool** zwei-/dreifädige Wolle.

**plywood** ['plaɪwud] n Sperrholz nt.

**PM** (BRIT) abbr = **Prime Minister**.

**p.m.** adv abbr (= post meridiem) nachmittags; (later) abends.

**PMT** abbr = **premenstrual tension**.

**pneumatic** [nju:'mætɪk] adj pneumatisch.

**pneumatic drill** n Preßluftbohrer m.

**pneumonia** [nju:'məunɪə] n Lungenentzündung f.

**PO** n abbr = **Post Office**; (MIL) = **petty officer**.

**p.o.** abbr = **postal order**.

**POA** (BRIT) n abbr (= Prison Officers' Association) Gewerkschaft der Gefängnisbeamten.

**poach** [pəutʃ] vt (steal: fish, animals, birds) illegal erbeuten, wildern; (CULIN: egg) pochieren; (: fish) dünsten ♦ vi (steal) wildern.

**poached** [pəutʃt] adj: **~ eggs** verlorene Eier.

**poacher** ['pəutʃə*] n Wilderer m.

**PO Box** n abbr (= Post Office Box) Postf.

**pocket** ['pɔkɪt] n Tasche f; (fig: small area) vereinzelter Bereich m ♦ vt (put in one's pocket, steal) einstecken; **to be out of ~** (BRIT) Verlust machen; **~ of resistance** Widerstandsnest nt.

**pocketbook** ['pɔkɪtbuk] n (notebook) Notizbuch nt; (US: wallet) Brieftasche f; (: handbag) Handtasche f.

**pocket calculator** n Taschenrechner m.

**pocketknife** ['pɔkɪtnaɪf] n Taschenmesser nt.

**pocket money** n Taschengeld nt.

**pocket-sized** ['pɔkɪtsaɪzd] adj im Taschenformat.

**pockmarked** ['pɔkmɑ:kt] adj (face) pockennarbig.

**pod** [pɔd] n Hülse f.

**podgy** ['pɔdʒɪ] (inf) adj rundlich, pummelig.

**podiatrist** [pɔ'di:ətrɪst] (US) n Fußspezialist(in) m(f).

**podiatry** [pɔ'di:ətrɪ] (US) n Fußpflege f.

**podium** ['pəudɪəm] n Podium nt.

**POE** n abbr (= port of embarkation) Ausgangshafen m; (= port of entry) Eingangshafen m.

**poem** ['pəuɪm] n Gedicht nt.

**poet** ['pəuɪt] n Dichter(in) m(f).

**poetic** [pəu'etɪk] adj poetisch, dichterisch; (fig) malerisch.

**poetic justice** n ausgleichende Gerechtigkeit f.

**poetic licence** n dichterische Freiheit f.

**poet laureate** n Hofdichter m.

> **Poet laureate** ist in Großbritannien ein Dichter, der ein Gehalt als Hofdichter bezieht und kraft seines Amtes ein lebenslanges Mitglied des britischen Königshofes ist. Der Poet Laureate schrieb traditionellerweise ausführliche Gedichte zu Staatsanlässen; ein Brauch, der heute kaum noch befolgt wird. Der erste Poet Laureate 1616 war Ben Jonson.

**poetry** ['pəuɪtrɪ] n (poems) Gedichte pl; (writing) Poesie f.

**poignant** ['pɔɪnjənt] adj ergreifend; (situation) herzzerreißend.

**point** [pɔɪnt] n Punkt m; (of needle, knife etc) Spitze f; (purpose) Sinn m, Zweck m; (significant part) Entscheidende(s) nt;

(*moment*) Zeitpunkt *m*; (*ELEC: also:* **power** ~) Steckdose *f*; (*also:* **decimal** ~) ≈ Komma *nt* ♦ *vt* (*show, mark*) deuten auf +*acc* ♦ *vi* (*with finger, stick etc*) zeigen, deuten; **points** *npl* (*AUT*) (Unterbrecher)kontakte *pl*; (*RAIL*) Weichen *pl*; **two** ~ **five** (= 2.5) zwei Komma fünf; **good/bad** ~**s** (*of person*) gute/ schlechte Seiten *or* Eigenschaften; **the train stops at Carlisle and all** ~**s south** der Zug hält in Carlisle und allen Orten weiter südlich; **to be on the** ~ **of doing sth** im Begriff sein, etw zu tun; **to make a** ~ **of doing sth** besonders darauf achten, etw zu tun; (*make a habit of*) Wert darauf legen, etw zu tun; **to get/miss the** ~ verstehen/nicht verstehen, worum es geht; **to come** *or* **get to the** ~ zur Sache kommen; **to make one's** ~ seinen Standpunkt klarmachen; **that's the whole** ~! darum geht es ja gerade!; **what's the** ~? was soll's?; **to be beside the** ~ unwichtig *or* irrelevant sein; **there's no** ~ **talking to you** es ist sinnlos, mit dir zu reden; **you've got a** ~ **there!** da könnten Sie recht haben!; **in** ~ **of fact** in Wirklichkeit; ~ **of sale** (*COMM*) Verkaufsstelle *f*; **to** ~ **sth at sb** (*gun etc*) etw auf jdn richten; (*finger*) mit etw auf jdn *acc* zeigen; **to** ~ **at** zeigen auf +*acc*; **to** ~ **to** zeigen auf +*acc*; (*fig*) hinweisen auf +*acc*.

▶**point out** *vt* hinweisen auf +*acc*.

▶**point to** *vt fus* hindeuten auf +*acc*.

**point-blank** ['pɔɪnt'blæŋk] *adv* (*say, ask*) direkt; (*refuse*) glatt; (*also:* **at** ~ **range**) aus unmittelbarer Entfernung.

**point duty** (*BRIT*) *n:* **to be on** ~ Verkehrsdienst haben.

**pointed** ['pɔɪntɪd] *adj* spitz; (*fig: remark*) spitz, scharf.

**pointedly** ['pɔɪntɪdlɪ] *adv* (*ask, reply etc*) spitz, scharf.

**pointer** ['pɔɪntə\*] *n* (*on chart, machine*) Zeiger *m*; (*fig: piece of information or advice*) Hinweis *m*; (*stick*) Zeigestock *m*; (*dog*) Pointer *m*.

**pointing** ['pɔɪntɪŋ] *n* (*CONSTR*) Ausfugung *f*.

**pointless** ['pɔɪntlɪs] *adj* sinnlos, zwecklos.

**point of view** *n* Ansicht *f*, Standpunkt *m*; **from a practical** ~ von einem praktischen Standpunkt aus.

**poise** [pɔɪz] *n* (*composure*) Selbstsicherheit *f*; (*balance*) Haltung *f* ♦ *vt:* **to be** ~**d for sth** (*fig*) bereit zu etw sein.

**poison** ['pɔɪzn] *n* Gift *nt* ♦ *vt* vergiften.

**poisoning** ['pɔɪznɪŋ] *n* Vergiftung *f*.

**poisonous** ['pɔɪznəs] *adj* (*animal, plant*) Gift-; (*fumes, chemicals etc*) giftig; (*fig: rumours etc*) zersetzend.

**poison-pen letter** [pɔɪzn'pɛn] *n* anonymer Brief *m* (*mit Indiskretionen*).

**poke** [pəʊk] *vt* (*with finger, stick etc*) stoßen; (*fire*) schüren ♦ *n* (*jab*) Stoß *m*, Schubs *m* (*inf*); **to** ~ **sth in(to)** (*put*) etw stecken in +*acc*; **to** ~ **one's head out of the window** seinen

Kopf aus dem Fenster strecken; **to** ~ **fun at sb** sich über jdn lustig machen.

▶**poke about** *vi* (*search*) herumstochern.

▶**poke out** *vi* (*stick out*) vorstehen.

**poker** ['pəʊkə\*] *n* (*metal bar*) Schürhaken *m*; (*CARDS*) Poker *nt*.

**poker-faced** ['pəʊkə'feɪst] *adj* mit unbewegter Miene, mit Pokergesicht.

**poky** ['pəʊkɪ] (*pej*) *adj* (*room, house*) winzig.

**Poland** ['pəʊlənd] *n* Polen *nt*.

**polar** ['pəʊlə\*] *adj* (*icecap*) polar; (*region*) Polar-.

**polar bear** *n* Eisbär *m*.

**polarize** ['pəʊləraɪz] *vt* polarisieren.

**Pole** [pəʊl] *n* Pole *m*, Polin *f*.

**pole** [pəʊl] *n* (*post, stick*) Stange *f*; (*flag pole, telegraph pole etc*) Mast *m*; (*GEOG, ELEC*) Pol *m*; **to be** ~**s apart** (*fig*) durch Welten (voneinander) getrennt sein.

**poleaxe**, (*US*) **poleax** ['pəʊlæks] *vt* (*fig*) umhauen.

**pole bean** (*US*) *n* (*runner bean*) Stangenbohne *f*.

**polecat** ['pəʊlkæt] *n* Iltis *m*.

**Pol. Econ.** ['pɔlɪkɔn] *n abbr* (= *political economy*) Volkswirtschaft *f*.

**polemic** [pɔ'lɛmɪk] *n* Polemik *f*.

**Pole Star** *n* Polarstern *m*.

**pole vault** ['pəʊlvɔːlt] *n* Stabhochsprung *m*.

**police** [pə'liːs] *npl* (*organization*) Polizei *f*; (*members*) Polizisten *pl*, Polizeikräfte *pl* ♦ *vt* (*street, area, town*) kontrollieren; **a large number of** ~ **were hurt** viele Polizeikräfte wurden verletzt.

**police car** *n* Polizeiauto *nt*.

**police constable** (*BRIT*) *n* Polizist(in) *m(f)*, Polizeibeamte(r) *m*, Polizeibeamtin *f*.

**police department** (*US*) *n* Polizei *f*.

**police force** *n* Polizei *f*.

**policeman** [pə'liːsmən] (*irreg: like* **man**) *n* Polizist *m*.

**police officer** *n* = **police constable**.

**police record** *n:* **to have a** ~ vorbestraft sein.

**police state** *n* (*POL*) Polizeistaat *m*.

**police station** *n* Polizeiwache *f*.

**policewoman** [pə'liːswʊmən] (*irreg: like* **woman**) *n* Polizistin *f*.

**policy** ['pɔlɪsɪ] *n* (*POL, ECON*) Politik *f*; (*also:* **insurance** ~) (Versicherungs)police *f*; (*of newspaper*) Grundsatz *m*; **to take out a** ~ (*INSURANCE*) eine Versicherung abschließen.

**policyholder** ['pɔlɪsɪ'həʊldə\*] *n* (*INSURANCE*) Versicherungsnehmer(in) *m(f)*.

**policy making** *n* Strategieplanung *f*.

**polio** ['pəʊlɪəʊ] *n* Kinderlähmung *f*, Polio *f*.

**Polish** ['pəʊlɪʃ] *adj* polnisch ♦ *n* (*LING*) Polnisch *nt*.

**polish** ['pɔlɪʃ] *n* (*for shoes*) Creme *f*; (*for furniture*) Politur *f*; (*for floors*) Bohnerwachs *nt*; (*shine: on shoes, floor etc*) Glanz *m*; (*fig: refinement*) Schliff *m* ♦ *vt* (*shoes*) putzen;

(*floor, furniture etc*) polieren.

▶**polish off** *vt* (*work*) erledigen; (*food*) verputzen.

**polished** ['pɒlɪʃt] *adj* (*fig: person*) mit Schliff; (: *style*) geschliffen.

**polite** [pə'laɪt] *adj* höflich; (*company, society*) fein; **it's not ~ to do that** es gehört sich nicht, das zu tun.

**politely** [pə'laɪtlɪ] *adv* höflich.

**politeness** [pə'laɪtnɪs] *n* Höflichkeit *f*.

**politic** ['pɒlɪtɪk] *adj* klug, vernünftig.

**political** [pə'lɪtɪkl] *adj* politisch.

**political asylum** *n* politisches Asyl *nt*.

**politically** [pə'lɪtɪklɪ] *adv* politisch; **~ correct** politisch korrekt.

**politician** [pɒlɪ'tɪʃən] *n* Politiker(in) *m(f)*.

**politics** ['pɒlɪtɪks] *n* Politik *f* ♦ *npl* (*beliefs, opinions*) politische Ansichten *pl*.

**polka** ['pɒlkə] *n* Polka *f*.

**poll** [pəʊl] *n* (*also:* opinion **~**) (Meinungs)-umfrage *f*; (*election*) Wahl *f* ♦ *vt* (*in opinion poll*) befragen; (*number of votes*) erhalten; **to go to the ~s** (*voters*) zur Wahl gehen; (*government*) sich den Wählern stellen.

**pollen** ['pɒlən] *n* Pollen *m*, Blütenstaub *m*.

**pollen count** *n* Pollenkonzentration *f*.

**pollinate** ['pɒlɪneɪt] *vt* bestäuben.

**polling booth** ['pəʊlɪŋ-] (*BRIT*) *n* Wahlkabine *f*.

**polling day** (*BRIT*) *n* Wahltag *m*.

**polling station** (*BRIT*) *n* Wahllokal *nt*.

**pollster** ['pəʊlstə*] *n* Meinungsforscher(in) *m(f)*.

**poll tax** *n* Kopfsteuer *f*.

**pollutant** [pə'luːtənt] *n* Schadstoff *m*.

**pollute** [pə'luːt] *vt* verschmutzen.

**pollution** [pə'luːʃən] *n* (*process*) Verschmutzung *f*; (*substances*) Schmutz *m*.

**polo** ['pəʊləʊ] *n* Polo *nt*.

**polo neck** *n* (*jumper*) Rollkragenpullover *m*.

**polo-necked** ['pəʊləʊnekt] *adj* (*jumper, sweater*) Rollkragen-.

**poltergeist** ['pɔːltəgaɪst] *n* Poltergeist *m*.

**poly** ['pɒlɪ] (*BRIT*) *n abbr* = **polytechnic**.

**poly bag** (*inf*) *n* Plastiktüte *f*.

**polyester** [pɒlɪ'estə*] *n* Polyester *m*.

**polygamy** [pə'lɪgəmɪ] *n* Polygamie *f*.

**polygraph** ['pɒlɪgrɑːf] (*US*) *n* (*lie detector*) Lügendetektor *m*.

**Polynesia** [pɒlɪ'niːzɪə] *n* Polynesien *nt*.

**Polynesian** [pɒlɪ'niːzɪən] *adj* polynesisch ♦ *n* Polynesier(in) *m(f)*.

**polyp** ['pɒlɪp] *n* Polyp *m*.

**polystyrene** [pɒlɪ'staɪriːn] *n* ≈ Styropor ® *nt*.

**polytechnic** [pɒlɪ'teknɪk] *n* technische Hochschule *f*.

**polythene** ['pɒlɪθiːn] *n* Polyäthylen *nt*.

**polythene bag** *n* Plastiktüte *f*.

**polyurethane** [pɒlɪ'jʊərɪθeɪn] *n* Polyurethan *nt*.

**pomegranate** ['pɒmɪgrænɪt] *n* Granatapfel *m*.

**pommel** ['pɒml] *n* (*on saddle*) Sattelknopf *m*

♦ *vt* (*US*) = **pummel**.

**pomp** [pɒmp] *n* Pomp *m*, Prunk *m*.

**pompom** ['pɒmpɒm] *n* Troddel *f*.

**pompous** ['pɒmpəs] (*pej*) *adj* (*person*) aufgeblasen; (*piece of writing*) geschwollen.

**pond** [pɒnd] *n* Teich *m*.

**ponder** ['pɒndə*] *vt* nachdenken über +*acc* ♦ *vi* nachdenken.

**ponderous** ['pɒndərəs] *adj* (*style, language*) schwerfällig.

**pong** [pɒŋ] (*BRIT: inf*) *n* Gestank *m* ♦ *vi* stinken.

**pontiff** ['pɒntɪf] *n* Papst *m*.

**pontificate** [pɒn'tɪfɪkeɪt] *vi* dozieren.

**pontoon** [pɒn'tuːn] *n* (*floating platform*) Ponton *m*; (*CARDS*) Siebzehnundvier *nt*.

**pony** ['pəʊnɪ] *n* Pony *nt*.

**ponytail** ['pəʊnɪteɪl] *n* Pferdeschwanz *m*; **to have one's hair in a ~** einen Pferdeschwanz tragen.

**pony trekking** (*BRIT*) *n* Ponytrecken *nt*.

**poodle** ['puːdl] *n* Pudel *m*.

**pooh-pooh** ['puː'puː] *vt* verächtlich abtun.

**pool** [puːl] *n* (*pond*) Teich *m*; (*also:* swimming **~**) Schwimmbad *nt*; (*of blood*) Lache *f*; (*SPORT*) Poolbillard *nt*; (*of cash, workers*) Bestand *m*; (*CARDS: kitty*) Kasse *f*; (*COMM: consortium*) Interessengemeinschaft *f* ♦ *vt* (*money*) zusammenlegen; (*knowledge, resources*) vereinigen; **pools** *npl* (*football pools*) ≈ Fußballtoto *nt*; **a ~ of sunlight/shade** eine sonnige/schattige Stelle; **car ~** Fahrgemeinschaft *f*; **typing ~,** (*US*) **secretary ~** Schreibzentrale *f*; **to do the (football) ~s** ≈ im Fußballtoto spielen.

**poor** [pʊə*] *adj* arm; (*bad*) schlecht ♦ *npl*: **the ~** die Armen *pl*; **~ in** (*resources etc*) arm an +*dat*; **~ Bob** der arme Bob.

**poorly** ['pʊəlɪ] *adj* (*ill*) elend, krank ♦ *adv* (*badly: designed, paid, furnished*) schlecht.

**pop** [pɒp] *n* (*MUS*) Pop *m*; (*fizzy drink*) Limonade *f*; (*US: inf: father*) Papa *m*; (*sound*) Knall *m* ♦ *vi* (*balloon*) platzen; (*cork*) knallen ♦ *vt*: **to ~ sth into/onto sth** etw schnell in etw *acc* stecken/auf etw *acc* legen; **his eyes ~ped out of his head** (*inf*) ihm fielen fast die Augen aus dem Kopf; **she ~ped her head out of the window** sie streckte den Kopf aus dem Fenster.

▶**pop in** *vi* vorbeikommen.

▶**pop out** *vi* kurz weggehen.

▶**pop up** *vi* auftauchen.

**popcorn** ['pɒpkɔːn] *n* Popcorn *nt*.

**pope** [pəʊp] *n* Papst *m*.

**poplar** ['pɒplə*] *n* Pappel *f*.

**poplin** ['pɒplɪn] *n* Popeline *f*.

**popper** ['pɒpə*] (*BRIT: inf*) *n* (*for fastening*) Druckknopf *m*.

**poppy** ['pɒpɪ] *n* Mohn *m*.

**poppycock** ['pɒpɪkɒk] (*inf*) *n* Humbug *m*, dummes Zeug *nt*.

**Popsicle** ® ['pɒpsɪkl] (*US*) *n* Eis *nt* am Stiel.

**pop star** n Popstar m.
**populace** ['pɒpjuləs] n: **the** ~ die
Bevölkerung, das Volk.
**popular** ['pɒpjulə*] adj (well-liked, fashionable)
beliebt, populär; (general, non-specialist)
allgemein; (idea) weitverbreitet; (POL:
movement) Volks-; (: cause) des Volkes; **to
be** ~ **with** beliebt sein bei; **the** ~ **press** die
Boulevardpresse.
**popularity** [pɒpju'lærɪtɪ] n Beliebtheit f,
Popularität f.
**popularize** ['pɒpjuləraɪz] vt (sport, music,
fashion) populär machen; (science, ideas)
popularisieren.
**popularly** ['pɒpjuləlɪ] adv (commonly)
allgemein.
**population** [pɒpju'leɪʃən] n Bevölkerung f; (of
a species) Zahl f, Population f; **a prison** ~ **of
44,000** (eine Zahl von) 44.000
Gefängnisinsassen; **the civilian** ~ die
Zivilbevölkerung.
**population explosion** n Bevölkerungs-
explosion f.
**populous** ['pɒpjuləs] adj dicht besiedelt.
**porcelain** ['pɔːslɪn] n Porzellan nt.
**porch** [pɔːtʃ] n (entrance) Vorbau m; (US)
Veranda f.
**porcupine** ['pɔːkjupaɪn] n Stachelschwein nt.
**pore** [pɔː*] n Pore f ♦ vi: **to** ~ **over** (book etc)
gründlich studieren.
**pork** [pɔːk] n Schweinefleisch nt.
**pork chop** n Schweinekotelett nt.
**porn** [pɔːn] (inf) n Porno m; ~ **channel/
magazine/shop** Pornokanal m/-magazin
nt/-laden m.
**pornographic** [pɔːnə'græfɪk] adj
pornographisch.
**pornography** [pɔː'nɒgrəfɪ] n Pornographie f.
**porous** ['pɔːrəs] adj porös.
**porpoise** ['pɔːpəs] n Tümmler m.
**porridge** ['pɒrɪdʒ] n Haferbrei m, Porridge nt.
**port** [pɔːt] n (harbour) Hafen m; (NAUT: left
side) Backbord nt; (wine) Portwein m;
(COMPUT) Port m ♦ adj (NAUT) Backbord-; **to**
~ (NAUT) an Backbord; ~ **of call** (NAUT)
Anlaufhafen nt.
**portable** ['pɔːtəbl] adj (television, typewriter etc)
tragbar, portabel.
**portal** ['pɔːtl] n Portal nt.
**portcullis** [pɔːt'kʌlɪs] n Fallgitter nt.
**portend** [pɔː'tɛnd] vt hindeuten auf +acc.
**portent** ['pɔːtɛnt] n Vorzeichen nt.
**porter** ['pɔːtə*] n (for luggage) Gepäckträger
m; (doorkeeper) Pförtner m; (US: RAIL)
Schlafwagenschaffner(in) m(f).
**portfolio** [pɔːt'fəulɪəu] n (case) Aktenmappe f;
(POL) Geschäftsbereich m; (FIN)
Portefeuille nt; (of artist) Kollektion f.
**porthole** ['pɔːthəul] n Bullauge nt.
**portico** ['pɔːtɪkəu] n Säulenhalle f.
**portion** ['pɔːʃən] n (part) Teil m; (helping of
food) Portion f.

**portly** ['pɔːtlɪ] adj beleibt, korpulent.
**portrait** ['pɔːtreɪt] n Porträt nt.
**portray** [pɔː'treɪ] vt darstellen.
**portrayal** [pɔː'treɪəl] n Darstellung f.
**Portugal** ['pɔːtjugl] n Portugal nt.
**Portuguese** [pɔːtju'giːz] adj portugiesisch ♦ n
inv (person) Portugiese m, Portugiesin f;
(LING) Portugiesisch nt.
**Portuguese man-of-war** [-mænəv'wɔː*] n
(ZOOL) Röhrenqualle f, Portugiesische
Galeere f.
**pose** [pəuz] n Pose f ♦ vt (question, problem)
aufwerfen; (danger) mit sich bringen ♦ vi: **to**
~ **as** (pretend) sich ausgeben als; **to strike a**
~ sich in Positur werfen; **to** ~ **for** (painting
etc) Modell sitzen für, posieren für.
**poser** ['pəuzə*] n (problem, puzzle) harte Nuß f
(inf); (person) = **poseur**.
**poseur** [pəu'zɜː*] (pej) n Angeber(in) m(f).
**posh** [pɒʃ] (inf) adj vornehm; **to talk** ~
vornehm daherreden.
**position** [pə'zɪʃən] n (place: of thing, person)
Position f, Lage f; (of person's body) Stellung
f; (job) Stelle f; (in race etc) Platz m; (attitude)
Haltung f, Standpunkt m; (situation) Lage
♦ vt (person, thing) stellen; **to be in a** ~ **to do
sth** in der Lage sein, etw zu tun.
**positive** ['pɒzɪtɪv] adj positiv; (certain) sicher;
(decisive: action, policy) konstruktiv.
**positively** ['pɒzɪtɪvlɪ] adv (emphatic: rude,
stupid etc) eindeutig; (encouragingly, also
ELEC) positiv; **the body has been**
~ **identified** die Leiche ist eindeutig
identifiziert worden.
**posse** ['pɒsɪ] (US) n (Polizei)truppe f.
**possess** [pə'zɛs] vt besitzen; (subj: feeling,
belief) Besitz ergreifen von; **like a man** ~**ed**
wie besessen; **whatever** ~**ed you to do it?**
was ist in dich gefahren, das zu tun?
**possession** [pə'zɛʃən] n Besitz m; **possessions**
npl (belongings) Besitz m; **to take** ~ **of** Besitz
ergreifen von.
**possessive** [pə'zɛsɪv] adj (nature etc)
besitzergreifend; (LING: pronoun)
Possessiv-; (: adjective) besitzanzeigend; **to
be** ~ **about sb/sth** Besitzansprüche an jdn/
etw acc stellen.
**possessiveness** [pə'zɛsɪvnɪs] n
besitzergreifende Art f.
**possessor** [pə'zɛsə*] n Besitzer(in) m(f).
**possibility** [pɒsɪ'bɪlɪtɪ] n Möglichkeit f.
**possible** ['pɒsɪbl] adj möglich; **it's** ~ (may be
true) es ist möglich, es kann sein; **it's** ~ **to
do it** es ist machbar or zu machen; **as far as**
~ so weit wie möglich; **if** ~ falls or wenn
möglich; **as soon as** ~ so bald wie möglich.
**possibly** ['pɒsɪblɪ] adv (perhaps)
möglicherweise, vielleicht; (conceivably)
überhaupt; **if you** ~ **can** falls überhaupt
möglich; **what could they** ~ **want?** was um
alles in der Welt wollen sie?; **I cannot**
~ **come** ich kann auf keinen Fall kommen.

**post** [pəust] n (BRIT) Post f; (pole, goal post)
Pfosten m; (job) Stelle f; (MIL) Posten m; (also:
**trading** ~) Handelsniederlassung f ♦ vt
(BRIT: letter) aufgeben; (MIL) aufstellen; **by**
~ (BRIT) per Post; **by return of** ~ (BRIT)
postwendend, umgehend; **to keep sb** ~**ed**
(informed) jdn auf dem laufenden halten; **to**
~ **sb to** (town, country) jdn versetzen nach;
(embassy, office) jdn versetzen zu; (MIL) jdn
abkommandieren nach.
▶**post up** vt anschlagen.

**post...** [pəust] pref Post-, post-; ~**-1990** nach
1990.

**postage** ['pəustɪdʒ] n Porto nt.

**postage stamp** n Briefmarke f.

**postal** ['pəustl] adj (charges, service) Post-.

**postal order** (BRIT) n Postanweisung f.

**postbag** ['pəustbæg] (BRIT) n Postsack m;
(letters) Posteingang m.

**postbox** ['pəustbɒks] n Briefkasten m.

**postcard** ['pəustkɑːd] n Postkarte f.

**postcode** ['pəustkəud] (BRIT) n Postleitzahl f.

**postdate** ['pəust'deɪt] vt (cheque) vordatieren.

**poster** ['pəustə*] n Poster nt, Plakat nt.

**poste restante** [pəust'restɑ̃ːnt] (BRIT) n Stelle
f für postlagernde Sendungen ♦ adv
postlagernd.

**posterior** [pɒs'tɪərɪə*] (hum) n
Allerwerteste(r) m.

**posterity** [pɒs'tɛrɪtɪ] n die Nachwelt.

**poster paint** n Plakatfarbe f.

**post exchange** (US) n (MIL) Laden für US-
Militärpersonal.

**post-free** [pəust'friː] (BRIT) adj, adv portofrei.

**postgraduate** ['pəust'grædjuət] n
Graduierte(r) f(m) (im Weiterstudium).

**posthumous** ['pɒstjuməs] adj posthum.

**posthumously** ['pɒstjuməslɪ] adv posthum.

**posting** ['pəustɪŋ] n (job) Stelle f.

**postman** ['pəustmən] (irreg: like **man**) n
Briefträger m, Postbote m.

**postmark** ['pəustmɑːk] n Poststempel m.

**postmaster** ['pəustmɑːstə*] n Postmeister m.

**Postmaster General** n ≈ Postminister(in)
m(f).

**postmistress** ['pəustmɪstrɪs] n Postmeisterin
f.

**postmortem** [pəust'mɔːtəm] n (MED)
Obduktion f; (fig) nachträgliche Erörterung
f.

**postnatal** ['pəust'neɪtl] adj nach der Geburt,
postnatal.

**post office** n (building) Post f, Postamt nt; **the
Post Office** (organization) die Post.

**Post Office Box** n Postfach nt.

**post-paid** ['pəust'peɪd] adj, adv = **post-free**.

**postpone** [pəus'pəun] vt verschieben.

**postponement** [pəus'pəunmənt] n Aufschub
m.

**postscript** ['pəustskrɪpt] n (to letter)
Nachschrift f, PS nt.

**postulate** ['pɒstjuleɪt] vt ausgehen von,

postulieren.

**posture** ['pɒstʃə*] n (also fig) Haltung f ♦ vi
(pej) posieren.

**postwar** [pəust'wɔː*] adj Nachkriegs-.

**posy** ['pəuzɪ] n Blumensträußchen nt.

**pot** [pɒt] n Topf m; (teapot, coffee pot, potful)
Kanne f; (inf: marijuana) Pot nt ♦ vt (plant)
eintopfen; **to go to** ~ (inf) auf den Hund
kommen; ~**s of** (BRIT: inf) jede Menge.

**potash** ['pɒtæʃ] n Pottasche f.

**potassium** [pə'tæsɪəm] n Kalium nt.

**potato** [pə'teɪtəu] (pl ~**es**) n Kartoffel f.

**potato chips** (US) npl = **potato crisps**.

**potato crisps** npl Kartoffelchips pl.

**potato flour** n Kartoffelmehl nt.

**potato peeler** n Kartoffelschäler m.

**potbellied** ['pɒtbelɪd] adj (from overeating)
dickbäuchig; (from malnutrition)
blähbäuchig.

**potency** ['pəutnsɪ] n (sexual) Potenz f; (of drink,
drug) Stärke f.

**potent** ['pəutnt] adj (powerful) stark; (sexually)
potent.

**potentate** ['pəutnteɪt] n Machthaber m,
Potentat m.

**potential** [pə'tɛnʃl] adj potentiell ♦ n Potential
nt; **to have** ~ (person, machine) Fähigkeiten
or Potential haben; (idea, plan) ausbaufähig
sein.

**potentially** [pə'tɛnʃəlɪ] adv potentiell; **it's**
~ **dangerous** es könnte gefährlich sein.

**pothole** ['pɒthəul] n (in road) Schlagloch nt;
(cave) Höhle f.

**potholing** ['pɒthəulɪŋ] (BRIT) n: **to go** ~
Höhlenforschung betreiben.

**potion** ['pəuʃən] n Elixier nt.

**potluck** [pɒt'lʌk] n: **to take** ~ sich
überraschen lassen.

**potpourri** [pəu'puriː] n (dried petals)
Duftsträußchen nt; (fig) Sammelsurium nt.

**pot roast** n Schmorbraten m.

**pot shot** n: **to take a** ~ **at** aufs Geratewohl
schießen auf +acc.

**potted** ['pɒtɪd] adj (food) eingemacht; (plant)
Topf-; (abbreviated: history etc) Kurz-,
kurzgefaßt.

**potter** ['pɒtə*] n Töpfer(in) m(f) ♦ vi: **to**
~ **around,** ~ **about** (BRIT) herumhantieren;
**to** ~ **around the house** im Haus
herumwerkeln.

**potter's wheel** n Töpferscheibe f.

**pottery** ['pɒtərɪ] n (pots, dishes etc) Keramik f,
Töpferwaren pl; (work, hobby) Töpfern nt;
(factory, workshop) Töpferei f; **a piece of** ~
ein Töpferstück nt.

**potty** ['pɒtɪ] adj (inf: mad) verrückt ♦ n (for
child) Töpfchen nt.

**potty-training** ['pɒtɪtreɪnɪŋ] n Entwöhnung f
vom Windeltragen.

**pouch** [pautʃ] n Beutel m (also ZOOL).

**pouf(fe)** [puːf] n (stool) gepolsterter Hocker
m.

**poultice** ['pəultɪs] n Umschlag m.
**poultry** ['pəultrɪ] n Geflügel nt.
**poultry farm** n Geflügelfarm f.
**poultry farmer** n Geflügelzüchter(in) m(f).
**pounce** [pauns] vi: **to ~ on** (also fig) sich stürzen auf +acc.
**pound** [paund] n (unit of money) Pfund nt; (unit of weight) (britisches) Pfund (= 453,6g); (for dogs) Zwinger m; (for cars) Abholstelle f (für abgeschleppte Fahrzeuge) ♦ vt (beat: table, wall etc) herumhämmern auf +dat; (crush: grain, spice etc) zerstoßen; (bombard) beschießen ♦ vi (heart) klopfen, pochen; (head) dröhnen; **half a ~ of butter** ein halbes Pfund Butter; **a five-~ note** ein Fünfpfundschein m.
**pounding** ['paundɪŋ] n: **to take a ~** (fig) schwer angegriffen werden; (team) eine Schlappe einstecken müssen.
**pound sterling** n Pfund nt Sterling.
**pour** [pɔːʳ] vt (tea, wine etc) gießen; (cereal etc) schütten ♦ vi strömen; **to ~ sb a glass of wine/a cup of tea** jdm ein Glas Wein/eine Tasse Tee einschenken; **to ~ with rain** in Strömen gießen.
▶**pour away** vt wegschütten.
▶**pour in** vi (people) hereinströmen; (letters etc) massenweise eintreffen.
▶**pour out** vi (people) herausströmen ♦ vt (tea, wine etc) eingießen; (fig: thoughts, feelings, etc) freien Lauf lassen +dat.
**pouring** ['pɔːrɪŋ] adj: **~ rain** strömender Regen m.
**pout** [paut] vi einen Schmollmund ziehen.
**poverty** ['pɒvətɪ] n Armut f.
**poverty line** n Armutsgrenze f.
**poverty-stricken** ['pɒvətɪstrɪkn] adj verarmt, notleidend.
**poverty trap** (BRIT) n gleichbleibend schlechte wirtschaftliche Situation aufgrund des Wegfalls von Sozialleistungen bei verbessertem Einkommen, Armutsfalle f.
**POW** n abbr = **prisoner of war**.
**powder** ['paudəʳ] n Pulver nt ♦ vt: **to ~ one's face** sich dat das Gesicht pudern; **to ~ one's nose** (euph) kurz mal verschwinden.
**powder compact** n Puderdose f.
**powdered milk** ['paudəd-] n Milchpulver nt.
**powder keg** n (also fig) Pulverfaß nt.
**powder puff** n Puderquaste f.
**powder room** (euph) n Damentoilette f.
**power** ['pauəʳ] n (control, legal right) Macht f; (ability) Fähigkeit f; (of muscles, ideas, words) Kraft f; (of explosion, engine) Gewalt f; (electricity) Strom m; **2 to the ~ (of) 3** (MATH) 2 hoch 3; **to do everything in one's ~ to help** alles in seiner Macht Stehende tun, um zu helfen; **a world ~** eine Weltmacht; **the ~s that be** (authority) diejenigen, die das Sagen haben; **~ of attorney** Vollmacht f; **to be in ~** (POL etc) an der Macht sein.
**powerboat** ['pauəbəut] n schnelles Motorboot

nt, Rennboot nt.
**power cut** n Stromausfall m.
**powered** ['pauəd] adj: **~ by** angetrieben von; **nuclear-~ submarine** atomgetriebenes U-Boot.
**power failure** n Stromausfall m.
**powerful** ['pauəful] adj (person, organization) mächtig; (body, voice, blow etc) kräftig; (engine) stark; (unpleasant: smell) streng; (emotion) überwältigend; (argument, evidence) massiv.
**powerhouse** ['pauəhaus] n: **he is a ~ of ideas** er hat ständig neue Ideen.
**powerless** ['pauəlɪs] adj machtlos; **to be ~ to do sth** nicht die Macht haben, etw zu tun.
**power line** n Stromkabel nt.
**power point** (BRIT) n Steckdose f.
**power station** n Kraftwerk nt.
**power steering** n (AUT) Servolenkung f.
**powwow** ['pauwau] n Besprechung f.
**pp** abbr (= per procurationem) ppa.
**pp.** abbr (= pages) S.
**PPE** (BRIT) n abbr (UNIV: = philosophy, politics and economics) Studiengang bestehend aus Philosophie, Politologie und Volkswirtschaft.
**PPS** n abbr (= post postscriptum) PPS; (BRIT: = parliamentary private secretary) Privatsekretär eines Ministers.
**PQ** (CANADA) abbr (= Province of Quebec).
**PR** n abbr = **public relations**; (POL) = **proportional representation** ♦ abbr (US: POST: = Puerto Rico).
**Pr.** abbr = **prince**.
**practicability** [præktɪkə'bɪlɪtɪ] n Durchführbarkeit f.
**practicable** ['præktɪkəbl] adj (scheme, idea) durchführbar.
**practical** ['præktɪkl] adj praktisch; (person: good with hands) praktisch veranlagt; (ideas, methods) praktikabel.
**practicality** [præktɪ'kælɪtɪ] n (of person) praktische Veranlagung f; **practicalities** npl (of situation etc) praktische Einzelheiten pl.
**practical joke** n Streich m.
**practically** ['præktɪklɪ] adv praktisch.
**practice** ['præktɪs] n (also MED, LAW) Praxis f; (custom) Brauch m; (exercise) Übung f ♦ vt, vi (US) = **practise**; **in ~** in der Praxis; **out of ~** aus der Übung; **2 hours' piano ~** 2 Stunden Klavierübungen; **it's common** or **standard ~** es ist allgemein üblich; **to put sth into ~** etw in die Praxis umsetzen; **target ~** Zielschießen nt.
**practice match** n Übungsspiel nt.
**practise,** (US) **practice** ['præktɪs] vt (train at) üben; (carry out: custom) pflegen; (: activity etc) ausüben; (profession) praktizieren ♦ vi (train) üben; (lawyer, doctor etc) praktizieren.
**practised** ['præktɪst] (BRIT) adj (person, liar) geübt; (performance) gekonnt; **with a ~ eye** mit geschultem Auge.

**practising** ['præktɪsɪŋ] adj praktizierend.
**practitioner** [præk'tɪʃənə•] n: medical ~ praktischer Arzt m, praktische Ärztin f; legal ~ Rechtsanwalt m, Rechtsanwältin f.
**pragmatic** [præg'mætɪk] adj pragmatisch.
**pragmatism** ['prægmətɪzəm] n Pragmatismus m.
**Prague** [prɑːg] n Prag nt.
**prairie** ['prɛərɪ] n (Gras)steppe f; the ~s (US) die Prärien.
**praise** [preɪz] n Lob nt ♦ vt loben; (REL) loben, preisen.
**praiseworthy** ['preɪzwəːðɪ] adj lobenswert.
**pram** [præm] (BRIT) n Kinderwagen m.
**prance** [prɑːns] vi (horse) tänzeln; to ~ about/in/out (person) herum-/hinein-/hinausstolzieren.
**prank** [præŋk] n Streich m.
**prat** [præt] (BRIT: inf) n (idiot) Trottel m.
**prattle** ['prætl] vi: to ~ on (about) pausenlos plappern (über +acc).
**prawn** [prɔːn] n (CULIN, ZOOL) Garnele f, Krabbe f; ~ cocktail n Krabbencocktail m.
**pray** [preɪ] vi beten; to ~ for sb/sth (REL, fig) für jdn/um etw beten.
**prayer** [prɛə•] n Gebet nt; to say one's ~s beten.
**prayer book** n Gebetbuch nt.
**pre...** [priː] pref Prä-, prä-; ~-1970 vor 1970.
**preach** [priːtʃ] vi (REL) predigen; (pej: moralize) Predigten halten ♦ vt (sermon) direkt halten; (fig: advocate) predigen, verkünden; to ~ at sb (fig) jdm Moralpredigten halten; to ~ to the converted (fig) offene Türen einrennen.
**preacher** ['priːtʃə•] n Prediger(in) m(f).
**preamble** [prɪ'æmbl] n Vorbemerkung f.
**prearranged** [priːə'reɪndʒd] adj (vorher) vereinbart.
**precarious** [prɪ'kɛərɪəs] adj prekär.
**precaution** [prɪ'kɔːʃən] n Vorsichtsmaßnahme f; to take ~s Vorsichtsmaßnahmen treffen.
**precautionary** [prɪ'kɔːʃənrɪ] adj (measure) vorbeugend, Vorsichts-.
**precede** [prɪ'siːd] vt (event) vorausgehen +dat; (person) vorangehen +dat; (words, sentences) vorangestellt sein +dat.
**precedence** ['prɛsɪdəns] n (priority) Vorrang m; to take ~ over Vorrang haben vor +dat.
**precedent** ['prɛsɪdənt] n (LAW) Präzedenzfall m; without ~ noch nie dagewesen; to establish or set a ~ einen Präzedenzfall schaffen.
**preceding** [prɪ'siːdɪŋ] adj vorhergehend.
**precept** ['priːsɛpt] n Grundsatz m, Regel f.
**precinct** ['priːsɪŋkt] n (US: part of city) Bezirk m; precincts npl (of cathedral, palace) Gelände nt; shopping ~ (BRIT) Einkaufsviertel nt; (under cover) Einkaufscenter nt.
**precious** ['prɛʃəs] adj wertvoll, kostbar; (pej: person, writing) geziert; (ironic: damned)

heißgeliebt, wundervoll ♦ adv (inf): ~ little/few herzlich wenig/wenige.
**precious stone** n Edelstein m.
**precipice** ['prɛsɪpɪs] n (also fig) Abgrund m.
**precipitate** [vt prɪ'sɪpɪteɪt, adj prɪ'sɪpɪtɪt] vt (event) heraufbeschwören ♦ adj (hasty) überstürzt, übereilt.
**precipitation** [prɪsɪpɪ'teɪʃən] n (rain) Niederschlag m.
**precipitous** [prɪ'sɪpɪtəs] adj (steep) steil; (hasty) übereilt.
**précis** ['preɪsiː] n inv Zusammenfassung f.
**precise** [prɪ'saɪs] adj genau, präzise; at 4 o'clock to be ~ um 4 Uhr, um genau zu sein.
**precisely** [prɪ'saɪslɪ] adv genau, exakt; (emphatic) ganz genau; ~! genau!
**precision** [prɪ'sɪʒən] n Genauigkeit f, Präzision f.
**preclude** [prɪ'kluːd] vt ausschließen; to ~ sb from doing sth jdn daran hindern, etw zu tun.
**precocious** [prɪ'kəuʃəs] adj (child, behaviour) frühreif.
**preconceived** [priːkən'siːvd] adj (idea) vorgefaßt.
**preconception** ['priːkən'sɛpʃən] n vorgefaßte Meinung f.
**precondition** ['priːkən'dɪʃən] n Vorbedingung f.
**precursor** [priː'kəːsə•] n Vorläufer m.
**predate** ['priː'deɪt] vt (precede) vorausgehen +dat.
**predator** ['prɛdətə•] n (ZOOL) Raubtier nt; (fig) Eindringling m.
**predatory** ['prɛdətərɪ] adj (animal) Raub-; (person, organization) auf Beute lauernd.
**predecessor** ['priːdɪsɛsə•] n Vorgänger(in) m(f).
**predestination** [priːdɛstɪ'neɪʃən] n Vorherbestimmung f.
**predetermine** [priːdɪ'təːmɪn] vt vorherbestimmen.
**predicament** [prɪ'dɪkəmənt] n Notlage f, Dilemma nt; to be in a ~ in einer Notlage or einem Dilemma stecken.
**predicate** ['prɛdɪkɪt] n (LING) Prädikat nt.
**predict** [prɪ'dɪkt] vt vorhersagen.
**predictable** [prɪ'dɪktəbl] adj vorhersagbar.
**predictably** [prɪ'dɪktəblɪ] adv (behave, react) wie vorherzusehen; ~ she didn't come wie vorherzusehen war, kam sie nicht.
**prediction** [prɪ'dɪkʃən] n Voraussage f.
**predispose** ['priːdɪs'pəuz] vt: to ~ sb to sth jdn zu etw veranlassen; to be ~d to do sth geneigt sein, etw zu tun.
**predominance** [prɪ'dɔmɪnəns] n Vorherrschaft f.
**predominant** [prɪ'dɔmɪnənt] adj vorherrschend; to become ~ vorherrschend werden.
**predominantly** [prɪ'dɔmɪnəntlɪ] adv überwiegend.

**predominate** [prɪ'dɒmɪneɪt] *vi* (*in number, size*) vorherrschen; (*in strength, influence*) überwiegen.

**pre-eminent** [pri:'ɛmɪnənt] *adj* herausragend.

**pre-empt** [pri:'ɛmt] *vt* zuvorkommen +*dat*.

**pre-emptive** [pri:'ɛmtɪv] *adj:* ~ **strike** Präventivschlag *m*.

**preen** [pri:n] *vt:* **to** ~ **itself** (*bird*) sich putzen; **to** ~ **o.s.** sich herausputzen.

**prefab** ['pri:fæb] *n* Fertighaus *nt*.

**prefabricated** [pri:'fæbrɪkeɪtɪd] *adj* vorgefertigt.

**preface** ['prɛfəs] *n* Vorwort *nt* ♦ *vt:* **to** ~ **with/ by** (*speech, action*) einleiten mit/durch.

**prefect** ['pri:fɛkt] (*BRIT*) *n* (*in school*) Aufsichtsschüler(in) *m(f)*.

**prefer** [prɪ'fə:'] *vt* (*like better*) vorziehen; **to** ~ **charges** (*LAW*) Anklage erheben; **to** ~ **doing** *or* **to do sth** (es) vorziehen, etw zu tun; **I** ~ **tea to coffee** ich mag lieber Tee als Kaffee.

**preferable** ['prɛfrəbl] *adj:* **to be** ~ **(to)** vorzuziehen sein (+*dat*).

**preferably** ['prɛfrəblɪ] *adv* vorzugsweise, am besten.

**preference** ['prɛfrəns] *n:* **to have a** ~ **for** (*liking*) eine Vorliebe haben für; **I drink beer in** ~ **to wine** ich trinke lieber Bier als Wein; **to give** ~ **to** (*priority*) vorziehen, Vorrang einräumen +*dat*.

**preference shares** (*BRIT*) *npl* (*COMM*) Vorzugsaktien *pl*.

**preferential** [prɛfə'rɛnʃəl] *adj:* ~ **treatment** bevorzugte Behandlung *f*; **to give sb** ~ **treatment** jdn bevorzugt behandeln.

**preferred stock** [prɪ'fəd-] (*US*) *npl* = **preference shares**.

**prefix** ['pri:fɪks] *n* (*LING*) Präfix *nt*.

**pregnancy** ['prɛgnənsɪ] *n* (*of woman*) Schwangerschaft *f*; (*of female animal*) Trächtigkeit *f*.

**pregnancy test** *n* Schwangerschaftstest *m*.

**pregnant** ['prɛgnənt] *adj* (*woman*) schwanger; (*female animal*) trächtig; (*fig: pause, remark*) bedeutungsschwer; **3 months** ~ im vierten Monat (schwanger).

**prehistoric** ['pri:hɪs'tɒrɪk] *adj* prähistorisch, vorgeschichtlich.

**prehistory** [pri:'hɪstərɪ] *n* Vorgeschichte *f*.

**prejudge** [pri:'dʒʌdʒ] *vt* vorschnell beurteilen.

**prejudice** ['prɛdʒudɪs] *n* (*bias against*) Vorurteil *nt*; (*bias in favour*) Voreingenommenheit *f* ♦ *vt* beeinträchtigen; **without** ~ **to** (*form*) unbeschadet +*gen*, ohne Beeinträchtigung +*gen*; **to** ~ **sb in favour of/ against sth** jdn für/gegen etw einnehmen.

**prejudiced** ['prɛdʒudɪst] *adj* (*person, view*) voreingenommen.

**prelate** ['prɛlət] *n* Prälat *m*.

**preliminaries** [prɪ'lɪmɪnərɪz] *npl* Vorbereitungen *pl*; (*of competition*) Vorrunde *f*.

**preliminary** [prɪ'lɪmɪnərɪ] *adj* (*step, arrangements*) vorbereitend; (*remarks*) einleitend.

**prelude** ['prɛljuːd] *n* (*MUS*) Präludium *nt*; (: *as introduction*) Vorspiel *nt*; **a** ~ **to** (*fig*) ein Vorspiel *or* ein Auftakt zu.

**premarital** ['pri:'mærɪtl] *adj* vorehelich.

**premature** ['prɛmətʃuə'] *adj* (*earlier than expected*) vorzeitig; (*too early*) verfrüht; **you are being a little** ~ Sie sind etwas voreilig; ~ **baby** Frühgeburt *f*.

**premeditated** [pri:'mɛdɪteɪtɪd] *adj* vorsätzlich.

**premeditation** [pri:mɛdɪ'teɪʃən] *n* Vorsatz *m*.

**premenstrual tension** [pri:'mɛnstruəl-] *n* prämenstruelles Syndrom *nt*.

**premier** ['prɛmɪə'] *adj* (*best*) beste(r, s), bedeutendste(r, s) ♦ *n* (*POL*) Premierminister(in) *m(f)*.

**premiere** ['prɛmɪɛə'] *n* Premiere *f*.

**premise** ['prɛmɪs] *n* (*of argument*) Voraussetzung *f*; **premises** *npl* (*of business etc*) Räumlichkeiten *pl*; **on the** ~**s** im Hause.

**premium** ['pri:mɪəm] *n* (*COMM, INSURANCE*) Prämie *f*; **to be at a** ~ (*expensive*) zum Höchstpreis gehandelt werden; (*hard to get*) Mangelware sein.

**premium bond** (*BRIT*) *n* Prämienanleihe *f*.

---

**Premium Bonds**, eigentlich **Premium Savings Bonds**, sind Lotterieaktien, die seit 1956 vom britischen Finanzministerium ausgegeben werden und keine Zinsen bringen, sondern statt dessen an einer monatlichen Auslosung teilnehmen. Die Gewinnnummern für die verschiedenen Geldpreise werden in Blackpool von einem Computer namens **ERNIE** (**E**lectronic **R**andom **N**umber **I**ndicator **E**quipment) ermittelt.

---

**premium gasoline** (*US*) *n* Super(benzin) *nt*.

**premonition** [prɛmə'nɪʃən] *n* Vorahnung *f*.

**preoccupation** [pri:ɔkju'peɪʃən] *n:* ~ **with** (vorrangige) Beschäftigung mit.

**preoccupied** [pri:'ɔkjupaɪd] *adj* (*thoughtful*) gedankenverloren; (*with work, family*) beschäftigt.

**prep** [prɛp] (*SCOL*) *adj abbr* (= *preparatory*) *see* **preparatory school** ♦ *n abbr* (= *preparation*) Hausaufgaben *pl*.

**prepaid** [pri:'peɪd] *adj* (*paid in advance*) im voraus bezahlt; (*envelope*) frankiert.

**preparation** [prɛpə'reɪʃən] *n* Vorbereitung *f*; (*food, medicine, cosmetic*) Zubereitung *f*; **preparations** *npl* Vorbereitungen *pl*; **in** ~ **for sth** als Vorbereitung für etw.

**preparatory** [prɪ'pærətərɪ] *adj* vorbereitend; ~ **to sth/to doing sth** als Vorbereitung für etw/, um etw zu tun.

**prepare** [prɪ'pɛə'] *vt* vorbereiten; (*food, meal*) zubereiten ♦ *vi:* **to** ~ **for** sich vorbereiten auf +*acc.*

**prepared** [prɪ'pɛəd] *adj*: **to be ~ to do sth** (*willing*) bereit sein, etw zu tun; **to be ~ for sth** (*ready*) auf etw *acc* vorbereitet sein.

**preponderance** [prɪ'pɔndərns] *n* Übergewicht *nt.*

**preposition** [prɛpə'zɪʃən] *n* Präposition *f.*

**prepossessing** [pri:pə'zɛsɪŋ] *adj* von angenehmer Erscheinung.

**preposterous** [prɪ'pɔstərəs] *adj* grotesk, widersinnig.

**prep school** *n* = **preparatory school.**

> **Prep(aratory) school** *ist in Großbritannien eine meist private Schule für Kinder im Alter von 7 bis 13 Jahren, die auf eine weiterführende Privatschule (**public school**) vorbereiten soll.*

**prerecorded** ['pri:rɪ'kɔːdɪd] *adj* (*broadcast*) aufgezeichnet; (*cassette, video*) bespielt.

**prerequisite** [pri:'rɛkwɪzɪt] *n* Vorbedingung *f,* Grundvoraussetzung *f.*

**prerogative** [prɪ'rɔgətɪv] *n* Vorrecht *nt,* Privileg *nt.*

**Presbyterian** [prɛzbɪ'tɪərɪən] *adj* presbyterianisch ♦ *n* Presbyterianer(in) *m(f).*

**presbytery** ['prɛzbɪtərɪ] *n* Pfarrhaus *nt.*

**preschool** ['pri:'sku:l] *adj* (*age, child, education*) Vorschul-.

**prescribe** [prɪ'skraɪb] *vt* (*MED*) verschreiben; (*demand*) anordnen, vorschreiben.

**prescribed** *adj* (*duties, period*) vorgeschrieben.

**prescription** [prɪ'skrɪpʃən] *n* (*MED: slip of paper*) Rezept *nt;* (*: medicine*) Medikament *nt;* **to make up** *or* (*US*) **fill a ~** ein Medikament zubereiten; **"only available on ~"** „rezeptpflichtig".

**prescription charges** (*BRIT*) *npl* Rezeptgebühr *f.*

**prescriptive** [prɪ'skrɪptɪv] *adj* normativ.

**presence** ['prɛzns] *n* Gegenwart *f,* Anwesenheit *f;* (*fig: personality*) Ausstrahlung *f;* (*spirit, invisible influence*) Erscheinung *f;* **in sb's ~** in jds *dat* Gegenwart *or* Beisein; **~ of mind** Geistesgegenwart *f.*

**present** [*adj, n* 'prɛznt, *vt* prɪ'zɛnt] *adj* (*current*) gegenwärtig, derzeitig; (*in attendance*) anwesend ♦ *n* (*gift*) Geschenk *nt;* (*LING: also:* **~ tense**) Präsens *nt,* Gegenwart *f* ♦ *vt* (*give: prize etc*) überreichen; (*plan, report*) vorlegen; (*cause, provide, portray*) darstellen; (*information, view*) darlegen; (*RADIO, TV*) leiten; **to be ~ at** anwesend *or* zugegen sein bei; **those ~** die Anwesenden; **to give sb a ~** jdm ein Geschenk geben; **the ~** (*actuality*) die Gegenwart; **at ~** gegenwärtig, im Augenblick; **to ~ sth to sb, ~ sb with sth** jdm etw übergeben *or* überreichen; **to ~ sb (to)** (*formally: introduce*) jdn vorstellen +*dat;*

**to ~ itself** (*opportunity*) sich bieten.

**presentable** [prɪ'zɛntəbl] *adj* (*person*) präsentabel, ansehnlich.

**presentation** [prɛzn'teɪʃən] *n* (*of prize*) Überreichung *f;* (*of plan, report etc*) Vorlage *f;* (*appearance*) Erscheinungsbild *nt;* (*talk*) Vortrag *m;* **on ~ of** (*voucher etc*) gegen Vorlage +*gen.*

**present-day** ['prɛzntdeɪ] *adj* heutig, gegenwärtig.

**presenter** [prɪ'zɛntə*] *n* (*on radio, TV*) Moderator(in) *m(f).*

**presently** ['prɛzntlɪ] *adv* (*soon after*) gleich darauf; (*soon*) bald, in Kürze; (*currently*) derzeit, gegenwärtig.

**present participle** *n* Partizip *nt* Präsens.

**preservation** [prɛzə'veɪʃən] *n* (*of peace, standards etc*) Erhaltung *f;* (*of furniture, building*) Konservierung *f.*

**preservative** [prɪ'zə:vətɪv] *n* Konservierungsmittel *nt.*

**preserve** [prɪ'zə:v] *vt* erhalten; (*peace*) wahren; (*wood*) schützen; (*food*) konservieren ♦ *n* (*often pl:* jam, chutney etc) Eingemachte(s) *nt;* (*for game, fish*) Revier *nt;* **a male ~** (*fig*) eine männliche Domäne; **a working class ~** (*fig*) eine Domäne der Arbeiterklasse.

**preshrunk** ['pri:'ʃrʌŋk] *adj* (*jeans etc*) vorgewaschen.

**preside** [prɪ'zaɪd] *vi*: **to ~ over** (*meeting etc*) vorsitzen +*dat,* den Vorsitz haben bei.

**presidency** ['prɛzɪdənsɪ] *n* (*POL*) Präsidentschaft *f;* (*US: of company*) Vorsitz *m.*

**president** ['prɛzɪdənt] *n* (*POL*) Präsident(in) *m(f);* (*of organization*) Vorsitzende(r) *f(m).*

**presidential** [prɛzɪ'dɛnʃl] *adj* (*election, campaign etc*) Präsidentschafts-; (*adviser, representative etc*) des Präsidenten.

**press** [prɛs] *n* (*printing press*) Presse *f;* (*of switch, bell*) Druck *m;* (*for wine*) Kelter *f* ♦ *vt* drücken, pressen; (*button, sb's hand etc*) drücken; (*iron: clothes*) bügeln; (*put pressure on: person*) drängen; (*pursue: idea, claim*) vertreten ♦ *vi* (*squeeze*) drücken, pressen; **the P~** (*newspapers, journalists*) die Presse; **to go to ~** (*newspaper*) in Druck gehen; **to be in ~** (*at the printer's*) im Druck sein; **to be in the ~** (*in the newspapers*) in der Zeitung stehen; **at the ~ of a button** auf Knopfdruck; **to ~ sth (up)on sb** (*force*) jdm etw aufdrängen; **we are ~ed for time/ money** wir sind in Geldnot/Zeitnot; **to ~ sb for an answer** auf jds *acc* Antwort drängen; **to ~ sb to do** *or* **into doing sth** jdn drängen, etw zu tun; **to ~ charges (against sb)** (*LAW*) Klage (gegen jdn) erheben; **to ~ for** (*changes etc*) drängen auf +*acc.*

▶**press ahead** *vi* weitermachen; **to ~ ahead with sth** etw durchziehen.

▶**press on** *vi* weitermachen.

**press agency** *n* Presseagentur *f*.
**press clipping** *n* Zeitungsausschnitt *m*.
**press conference** *n* Pressekonferenz *f*.
**press cutting** *n* = **press clipping**.
**press-gang** ['prɛsgæŋ] *vt*: **to ~ sb into doing sth** jdn bedrängen, etw zu tun.
**pressing** ['prɛsɪŋ] *adj* (*urgent*) dringend.
**press officer** *n* Pressesprecher(in) *m(f)*.
**press release** *n* Pressemitteilung *f*.
**press stud** (*BRIT*) *n* Druckknopf *m*.
**press-up** ['prɛsʌp] (*BRIT*) *n* Liegestütz *m*.
**pressure** ['prɛʃə*] *n* (*also fig*) Druck *m* ♦ *vt*: **to ~ sb to do sth** jdn dazu drängen, etw zu tun; **to put ~ on sb (to do sth)** Druck auf jdn ausüben(, etw zu tun); **high/low ~** (*TECH, MET*) Hoch-/Tiefdruck *m*.
**pressure cooker** *n* Schnellkochtopf *m*.
**pressure gauge** *n* Druckmesser *m*, Manometer *nt*.
**pressure group** *n* Interessenverband *m*, Pressure-group *f*.
**pressurize** ['prɛʃəraɪz] *vt*: **to ~ sb (to do sth or into doing sth)** jdn unter Druck setzen(, etw zu tun).
**pressurized** ['prɛʃəraɪzd] *adj* (*cabin, container etc*) Druck-.
**Prestel** ® ['prɛstɛl] *n* ≈ Bildschirmtext *m*, Btx *nt*.
**prestige** [prɛs'tiːʒ] *n* Prestige *nt*.
**prestigious** [prɛs'tɪdʒəs] *adj* (*institution, appointment*) mit hohem Prestigewert.
**presumably** [prɪ'zjuːməblɪ] *adv* vermutlich; **~ he did it** vermutlich *or* wahrscheinlich hat er es getan.
**presume** [prɪ'zjuːm] *vt*: **to ~ (that)** (*assume*) annehmen(, daß); **to ~ to do sth** (*dare*) sich anmaßen, etw zu tun; **I ~ so** das nehme ich an.
**presumption** [prɪ'zʌmpʃən] *n* (*supposition*) Annahme *f*; (*audacity*) Anmaßung *f*.
**presumptuous** [prɪ'zʌmpʃəs] *adj* anmaßend.
**presuppose** [priːsə'pəuz] *vt* voraussetzen.
**presupposition** [priːsʌpə'zɪʃən] *n* Voraussetzung *f*.
**pretax** [priː'tæks] *adj* (*profit*) vor (Abzug der) Steuern.
**pretence,** (*US*) **pretense** [prɪ'tɛns] *n* (*false appearance*) Vortäuschung *f*; **under false ~s** unter Vorspiegelung falscher Tatsachen; **she is devoid of all ~** sie ist völlig natürlich; **to make a ~ of doing sth** vortäuschen, etw zu tun.
**pretend** [prɪ'tɛnd] *vt* (*feign*) vorgeben ♦ *vi* (*feign*) sich verstellen, so tun, als ob; **I don't ~ to understand it** (*claim*) ich erhebe nicht den Anspruch, es zu verstehen.
**pretense** [prɪ'tɛns] (*US*) *n* = **pretence**.
**pretentious** [prɪ'tɛnʃəs] *adj* anmaßend.
**preterite** ['prɛtərɪt] *n* Imperfekt *nt*, Präteritum *nt*.
**pretext** ['priːtɛkst] *n* Vorwand *m*; **on** *or* **under the ~ of doing sth** unter dem Vorwand, etw

zu tun.
**pretty** ['prɪtɪ] *adj* hübsch, nett ♦ *adv*: **~ clever** ganz schön schlau; **~ good** ganz gut.
**prevail** [prɪ'veɪl] *vi* (*be current*) vorherrschen; (*triumph*) siegen; **to ~ (up)on sb to do sth** (*persuade*) jdn dazu bewegen *or* überreden, etw zu tun.
**prevailing** [prɪ'veɪlɪŋ] *adj* (*wind, fashion etc*) vorherrschend.
**prevalent** ['prɛvələnt] *adj* (*belief, custom*) vorherrschend.
**prevaricate** [prɪ'værɪkeɪt] *vi* (*by saying sth*) Ausflüchte machen; (*by doing sth*) Ausweichmanöver machen.
**prevarication** [prɪværɪ'keɪʃən] *n* (*see vi*) Ausflucht *f*; Ausweichmanöver *nt*.
**prevent** [prɪ'vɛnt] *vt* verhindern; **to ~ sb from doing sth** jdn daran hindern, etw zu tun; **to ~ sth from happening** verhindern, daß etw geschieht.
**preventable** [prɪ'vɛntəbl] *adj* verhütbar, vermeidbar.
**preventative** [prɪ'vɛntətɪv] *adj* = **preventive**.
**prevention** [prɪ'vɛnʃən] *n* Verhütung *f*.
**preventive** [prɪ'vɛntɪv] *adj* (*measures, medicine*) vorbeugend.
**preview** ['priːvjuː] *n* (*of film*) Vorpremiere *f*; (*of exhibition*) Vernissage *f*.
**previous** ['priːvɪəs] *adj* (*earlier*) früher; (*preceding*) vorhergehend; **~ to** vor +*dat*.
**previously** ['priːvɪəslɪ] *adv* (*before*) zuvor; (*formerly*) früher.
**prewar** [priː'wɔː*] *adj* (*period*) Vorkriegs-.
**prey** [preɪ] *n* Beute *f*; **to fall ~ to** (*fig*) zum Opfer fallen +*dat*.
▶**prey on** *vt fus* (*animal*) Jagd machen auf +*acc*; **it was ~ing on his mind** es ließ ihn nicht los.
**price** [praɪs] *n* (*also fig*) Preis *m* ♦ *vt* (*goods*) auszeichnen; **what is the ~ of ...?** was kostet ...?; **to go up** *or* **rise in ~** im Preis steigen, teurer werden; **to put a ~ on sth** (*also fig*) einen Preis für etw festsetzen; **what ~ his promises now?** wie steht es jetzt mit seinen Versprechungen?; **he regained his freedom, but at a ~** er hat seine Freiheit wieder, aber zu welchem Preis!; **to be ~d at £30** £30 kosten; **to ~ o.s. out of the market** durch zu hohe Preise konkurrenzunfähig werden.
**price control** *n* Preiskontrolle *f*.
**price-cutting** ['praɪskʌtɪŋ] *n* Preissenkungen *pl*.
**priceless** ['praɪslɪs] *adj* (*diamond, painting*) von unschätzbarem Wert; (*inf: amusing*) unbezahlbar, köstlich.
**price list** *n* Preisliste *f*.
**price range** *n* Preisklasse *f*; **it's within my ~** ich kann es mir leisten.
**price tag** *n* Preisschild *nt*; (*fig*) Preis *m*.
**price war** *n* Preiskrieg *m*.
**pricey** ['praɪsɪ] (*inf*) *adj* kostspielig.
**prick** [prɪk] *n* (*sting*) Stich *m*; (*infl: penis*)

Schwanz m; (: idiot) Arsch m ♦ vt stechen;
(sausage, balloon) einstechen; **to ~ up one's
ears** die Ohren spitzen.
**prickle** ['prɪkl] n (of plant) Dorn m, Stachel m;
(sensation) Prickeln nt.
**prickly** ['prɪklɪ] adj (plant) stachelig; (fabric)
kratzig.
**prickly heat** n Hitzebläschen pl.
**prickly pear** n Feigenkaktus m.
**pride** [praɪd] n Stolz m; (pej: arrogance)
Hochmut m ♦ vt: **to ~ o.s. on** sich rühmen
+gen; **to take (a) ~ in** stolz sein auf +acc; **to
take a ~ in doing sth** etw mit Stolz tun; **to
have** or **take ~ of place** (BRIT) die Krönung
sein.
**priest** [priːst] n Priester m.
**priestess** ['priːstɪs] n Priesterin f.
**priesthood** ['priːsthud] n Priestertum nt.
**prig** [prɪg] n: **he's a ~** er hält sich für ein
Tugendlamm.
**prim** [prɪm] (pej) adj (person) etepetete.
**primacy** ['praɪməsɪ] n (supremacy) Vorrang m;
(position) Vorrangstellung f.
**prima-facie** ['praɪmə'feɪʃɪ] adj: **to have a
~ case** (LAW) eine gute Beweisgrundlage
haben.
**primal** ['praɪməl] adj ursprünglich; **~ scream**
Urschrei m.
**primarily** ['praɪmərɪlɪ] adv in erster Linie,
hauptsächlich.
**primary** ['praɪmərɪ] adj (principal) Haupt-,
hauptsächlich; (education, teacher)
Grundschul- ♦ n (US: election) Vorwahl f.

---

*Als **primary** wird im amerikanischen
Präsidentschaftswahlkampf eine Vorwahl
bezeichnet, die mitentscheidet, welche
Präsidentschaftskandidaten die beiden großen
Parteien aufstellen. Vorwahlen werden nach
komplizierten Regeln von Februar (New
Hampshire) bis Juni in etwa 35 Staaten
abgehalten. Der von den Kandidaten in den
primaries erzielte Stimmenanteil bestimmt,
wie viele Abgeordnete bei der endgültigen
Auswahl der demokratischen bzw.
republikanischen Kandidaten bei den
nationalen Parteitagen im Juli/August für sie
stimmen.*

---

**primary colour** n Primärfarbe f.
**primary school** (BRIT) n Grundschule f.

---

*Primary school* ist in Großbritannien eine
*Grundschule für Kinder im Alter von 5 bis 11
Jahren. Oft wird sie aufgeteilt in **infant school**
(5 bis 7 Jahre) und **junior school** (7 bis 11
Jahre). Siehe auch **secondary school**.*

---

**primate** ['praɪmɪt] n (ZOOL) Primat m; (REL)
Primas m.
**prime** [praɪm] adj (most important) oberste(r,
s); (best quality) erstklassig ♦ n (of person's

life) die besten Jahre pl ♦ vt (wood)
grundieren; (fig: person) informieren; (gun)
schußbereit machen; (pump) auffüllen;
**~ example** erstklassiges Beispiel; **in the
~ of life** im besten Alter.
**Prime Minister** n Premierminister(in) m(f).
**primer** ['praɪmə'] n (paint) Grundierung f;
(book) Einführung f.
**prime time** n (RADIO, TV) Hauptsendezeit f.
**primeval** [praɪ'miːvl] adj (beast) urzeitlich;
(fig: feelings) instinktiv; **~ forest** Urwald m.
**primitive** ['prɪmɪtɪv] adj (tribe, tool, conditions
etc) primitiv; (life form, machine etc)
frühzeitlich; (man) der Urzeit.
**primrose** ['prɪmrəʊz] n Primel f, gelbe
Schlüsselblume f.
**primula** ['prɪmjʊlə] n Primel f.
**Primus (stove)** ® (BRIT) n Primuskocher m.
**prince** [prɪns] n Prinz m.
**Prince Charming** (hum) n Märchenprinz m.
**princess** [prɪn'ses] n Prinzessin f.
**principal** ['prɪnsɪpl] adj (most important)
Haupt-, wichtigste(r, s) ♦ n (of school,
college) Rektor(in) m(f); (THEAT)
Hauptdarsteller(in) m(f); (FIN)
Kapitalsumme f.
**principality** [prɪnsɪ'pælɪtɪ] n Fürstentum nt.
**principally** ['prɪnsɪplɪ] adv vornehmlich.
**principle** ['prɪnsɪpl] n Prinzip nt; **in ~** im
Prinzip, prinzipiell; **on ~** aus Prinzip.
**print** [prɪnt] n (type, ART) Druck m; (PHOT)
Abzug m; (fabric) bedruckter Stoff m ♦ vt
(produce) drucken; (publish)
veröffentlichen; (cloth, pattern) bedrucken;
(write in capitals) in Druckschrift schreiben;
**prints** npl (fingerprints etc) Abdrücke pl; **out
of ~** vergriffen; **in ~** erhältlich; **the fine** or
**small ~** das Kleingedruckte.
▶**print out** vt (COMPUT) ausdrucken.
**printed circuit** ['prɪntɪd-] n gedruckte
Schaltung f.
**printed circuit board** n Leiterplatte f.
**printed matter** n Drucksache f.
**printer** ['prɪntə'] n (person) Drucker(in) m(f);
(firm) Druckerei f; (machine) Drucker m.
**printhead** ['prɪnthed] n Druckkopf m.
**printing** ['prɪntɪŋ] n (activity) Drucken nt.
**printing press** n Druckerpresse f.
**print-out** ['prɪntaʊt] (COMPUT) n Ausdruck m.
**print run** n Auflage f.
**printwheel** ['prɪntwiːl] n (COMPUT) Typenrad
nt.
**prior** ['praɪə'] adj (previous: knowledge, warning)
vorherig; (: engagement) früher; (more
important: claim, duty) vorrangig ♦ n (REL)
Prior m; **without ~ notice** ohne vorherige
Ankündigung; **to have a ~ claim on sth** ein
Vorrecht auf etw acc haben; **~ to** vor +dat.
**priority** [praɪ'ɒrɪtɪ] n vorrangige
Angelegenheit f; **priorities** npl Prioritäten pl;
**to take** or **have ~ (over sth)** Vorrang (vor
etw dat) haben; **to give ~ to sb/sth** jdm/etw

Vorrang einräumen.
**priory** ['praɪərɪ] *n* Kloster *nt*.
**prise** [praɪz] (*BRIT*) *vt*: **to ~ open** aufbrechen.
**prism** ['prɪzəm] *n* Prisma *nt*.
**prison** ['prɪzn] *n* Gefängnis *nt* ♦ *cpd* (*officer, food, cell etc*) Gefängnis-.
**prison camp** *n* Gefangenenlager *nt*.
**prisoner** ['prɪznə\*] *n* Gefangene(r) *f(m)*; **the ~ at the bar** (*LAW*) der/die Angeklagte; **to take sb ~** jdn gefangennehmen.
**prisoner of war** *n* Kriegsgefangene(r) *f(m)*.
**prissy** ['prɪsɪ] (*pej*) *adj* zimperlich.
**pristine** ['prɪstiːn] *adj* makellos; **in ~ condition** in makellosem Zustand.
**privacy** ['prɪvəsɪ] *n* Privatsphäre *f*.
**private** ['praɪvɪt] *adj* privat; (*life*) Privat-; (*thoughts, plans etc*) persönlich; (*place*) abgelegen; (*secretive: person*) verschlossen ♦ *n* (*MIL*) Gefreite(r) *m*; "**~**" (*on envelope*) „vertraulich"; (*on door*) „privat"; **in ~** privat; **in (his) ~ life** in seinem Privatleben; **to be in ~ practice** (*MED*) Privatpatienten haben; **~ hearing** (*LAW*) nichtöffentliche Verhandlung.
**private enterprise** *n* Privatunternehmen *nt*.
**private eye** *n* Privatdetektiv *m*.
**private limited company** (*BRIT*) *n* (*COMM*) ≈ Aktiengesellschaft *f*.
**privately** ['praɪvɪtlɪ] *adv* privat; (*secretly*) insgeheim; **a ~ owned company** eine Firma im Privatbesitz.
**private parts** *npl* (*ANAT*) Geschlechtsteile *pl*.
**private property** *n* Privatbesitz *m*.
**private school** *n* (*fee-paying*) Privatschule *f*.
**privation** [praɪ'veɪʃən] *n* Not *f*.
**privatize** ['praɪvɪtaɪz] *vt* privatisieren.
**privet** ['prɪvɪt] *n* Liguster *m*.
**privilege** ['prɪvɪlɪdʒ] *n* (*advantage*) Privileg *nt*; (*honour*) Ehre *f*.
**privileged** ['prɪvɪlɪdʒd] *adj* privilegiert; **to be ~ to do sth** das Privileg *or* die Ehre haben, etw zu tun.
**privy** ['prɪvɪ] *adj*: **to be ~ to** eingeweiht sein in +*acc*.

---

**Privy Council** *ist eine Gruppe von königlichen Beratern, die ihren Ursprung im normannischen England hat. Heute hat dieser Rat eine rein formale Funktion. Kabinettsmitglieder und andere bedeutende politische, kirchliche oder juristische Persönlichkeiten sind automatisch Mitglieder.*

---

**Privy Councillor** (*BRIT*) *n* Geheimer Rat *m*.
**prize** [praɪz] *n* Preis *m* ♦ *adj* (*prize-winning*) preisgekrönt; (*classic: example*) erstklassig ♦ *vt* schätzen; **~ idiot** (*inf*) Vollidiot *m*.
**prizefighter** ['praɪzfaɪtə\*] *n* Preisboxer *m*.
**prizegiving** ['praɪzgɪvɪŋ] *n* Preisverleihung *f*.
**prize money** *n* Geldpreis *m*.
**prizewinner** ['praɪzwɪnə\*] *n* Preisträger(in) *m(f)*.

**prizewinning** ['praɪzwɪnɪŋ] *adj* preisgekrönt.
**PRO** *n abbr* = **public relations officer**.
**pro** [prəu] *n* (*SPORT*) Profi *m* ♦ *prep* (*in favour of*) pro +*acc*, für +*acc*; **the ~s and cons** das Für und Wider.
**pro-** [prəu] *pref* (*in favour of*) Pro-, pro-; **~-disarmament campaign** Kampagne *f* für Abrüstung.
**proactive** [prəu'æktɪv] *adj* proaktiv.
**probability** [prɔbə'bɪlɪtɪ] *n* Wahrscheinlichkeit *f*; **in all ~** aller Wahrscheinlichkeit nach.
**probable** ['prɔbəbl] *adj* wahrscheinlich; **it seems ~ that ...** es ist wahrscheinlich, daß ...
**probably** ['prɔbəblɪ] *adv* wahrscheinlich.
**probate** ['prəubɪt] *n* gerichtliche Testamentsbestätigung *f*.
**probation** [prə'beɪʃən] *n*: **on ~** (*lawbreaker*) auf Bewährung; (*employee*) auf Probe.
**probationary** [prə'beɪʃənrɪ] *adj* (*period*) Probe-.
**probationer** [prə'beɪʃənə\*] *n* (*nurse: female*) Lernschwester *f*; (: *male*) Lernpfleger *m*.
**probation officer** *n* Bewährungshelfer(in) *m(f)*.
**probe** [prəub] *n* (*MED, SPACE*) Sonde *f*; (*enquiry*) Untersuchung *f* ♦ *vt* (*investigate*) untersuchen; (*poke*) bohren in +*dat*.
**probity** ['prəubɪtɪ] *n* Rechtschaffenheit *f*.
**problem** ['prɔbləm] *n* Problem *nt*; **to have ~s with the car** Probleme *or* Schwierigkeiten mit dem Auto haben; **what's the ~?** wo fehlt's?; **I had no ~ finding her** ich habe sie ohne Schwierigkeiten gefunden; **no ~!** kein Problem!
**problematic(al)** [prɔblə'mætɪk(l)] *adj* problematisch.
**problem-solving** ['prɔbləmsɔlvɪŋ] *adj* (*skills, ability*) zur Problemlösung ♦ *n* Problemlösung *f*.
**procedural** [prə'siːdjurəl] *adj* (*agreement, problem*) verfahrensmäßig.
**procedure** [prə'siːdʒə\*] *n* Verfahren *nt*.
**proceed** [prə'siːd] *vi* (*carry on*) fortfahren; (*person: go*) sich bewegen; **to ~ to do sth** etw tun; **to ~ with** fortfahren mit; **I am not sure how to ~** ich bin nicht sicher über die weitere Vorgehensweise; **to ~ against sb** (*LAW*) gegen jdn gerichtlich vorgehen.
**proceedings** [prə'siːdɪŋz] *npl* (*organized events*) Vorgänge *pl*; (*LAW*) Verfahren *nt*; (*records*) Protokoll *nt*.
**proceeds** ['prəusiːdz] *npl* Erlös *m*.
**process** ['prəuses] *n* (*series of actions*) Verfahren *nt*; (*BIOL, CHEM*) Prozeß *m* ♦ *vt* (*raw materials, food, COMPUT: data*) verarbeiten; (*application*) bearbeiten; (*PHOT*) entwickeln; **in the ~** dabei; **to be in the ~ of doing sth** (*gerade*) dabei sein, etw zu tun.
**processed cheese** ['prəusest-], (*US*) **process cheese** *n* Schmelzkäse *m*.

**processing** ['prəusɛsɪŋ] n (PHOT) Entwickeln nt.

**procession** [prə'sɛʃən] n Umzug m, Prozession f; **wedding/funeral** ~ Hochzeits-/Trauerzug m.

**proclaim** [prə'kleɪm] vt verkünden, proklamieren.

**proclamation** [prɔklə'meɪʃən] n Proklamation f.

**proclivity** [prə'klɪvɪtɪ] (form) n Vorliebe f.

**procrastinate** [prəu'kræstɪneɪt] vi zögern, zaudern.

**procrastination** [prəukræstɪ'neɪʃən] n Zögern nt, Zaudern nt.

**procreation** [prəukrɪ'eɪʃən] n Fortpflanzung f.

**procurator fiscal** ['prɔkjureɪtə-] n (pl **procurators fiscal**) (SCOT) ≈ Staatsanwalt m, Staatsanwältin f.

**procure** [prə'kjuə'] vt (obtain) beschaffen.

**procurement** [prə'kjuəmənt] n (COMM) Beschaffung f.

**prod** [prɔd] vt (push: with finger, stick etc) stoßen, stupsen (inf); (fig: urge) anspornen ♦ n (with finger, stick etc) Stoß m, Stups m (inf); (fig: reminder) mahnender Hinweis m.

**prodigal** ['prɔdɪgl] adj: ~ **son** verlorener Sohn m.

**prodigious** [prə'dɪdʒəs] adj (cost, memory) ungeheuer.

**prodigy** ['prɔdɪdʒɪ] n (person) Naturtalent nt; **child** ~ Wunderkind nt.

**produce** [n 'prɔdjuːs, vt prə'djuːs] n (AGR) (Boden)produkte pl ♦ vt (result etc) hervorbringen; (goods, commodity) produzieren, herstellen; (BIOL, CHEM) erzeugen; (fig: evidence etc) liefern; (: passport etc) vorlegen; (play, film, programme) produzieren.

**producer** [prə'djuːsə'] n (person) Produzent(in) m(f); (country, company) Produzent m, Hersteller m.

**product** ['prɔdʌkt] n Produkt nt.

**production** [prə'dʌkʃən] n Produktion f; (THEAT) Inszenierung f; **to go into** ~ (goods) in Produktion gehen; **on** ~ **of** gegen Vorlage +gen.

**production agreement** (US) n Produktivitätsabkommen nt.

**production line** n Fließband nt, Fertigungsstraße f.

**production manager** n Produktionsleiter(in) m(f).

**productive** [prə'dʌktɪv] adj produktiv.

**productivity** [prɔdʌk'tɪvɪtɪ] n Produktivität f.

**productivity agreement** (BRIT) n Produktivitätsabkommen nt.

**productivity bonus** n Leistungszulage f.

**Prof.** n abbr (= professor) Prof.

**profane** [prə'feɪn] adj (language etc) profan; (secular) weltlich.

**profess** [prə'fɛs] vt (claim) vorgeben, bekunden; (express: feeling, opinion) zeigen, bekunden; **I do not**

~ **to be an expert** ich behaupte nicht, ein Experte zu sein.

**professed** [prə'fɛst] adj (self-declared) erklärt.

**profession** [prə'fɛʃən] n Beruf m; (people) Berufsstand m; **the** ~**s** die gehobenen Berufe.

**professional** [prə'fɛʃənl] adj (organization, musician etc) Berufs-; (misconduct, advice) beruflich; (skilful) professionell ♦ n (doctor, lawyer, teacher etc) Fachmann m, Fachfrau f; (SPORT) Profi m; (skilled person) Experte m, Expertin f; **to seek** ~ **advice** fachmännischen Rat einholen.

**professionalism** [prə'fɛʃnəlɪzəm] n fachliches Können nt.

**professionally** [prə'fɛʃnəlɪ] adv beruflich; (for a living) berufsmäßig; **I only know him** ~ ich kenne ihn nur beruflich.

**professor** [prə'fɛsə'] n (BRIT) Professor(in) m(f); (US, CANADA) Dozent(in) m(f).

**professorship** [prə'fɛsəʃɪp] n Professur f.

**proffer** ['prɔfə'] vt (advice, drink, one's hand) anbieten; (apologies) aussprechen; (plate etc) hinhalten.

**proficiency** [prə'fɪʃənsɪ] n Können nt, Fertigkeiten pl.

**proficient** [prə'fɪʃənt] adj fähig; **to be** ~ **at** or **in** gut sein in +dat.

**profile** ['prəufaɪl] n (of person's face) Profil nt; (fig: biography) Porträt nt; **to keep a low** ~ (fig) sich zurückhalten; **to have a high** ~ (fig) eine große Rolle spielen.

**profit** ['prɔfɪt] n (COMM) Gewinn m, Profit m ♦ vi: **to** ~ **by** or **from** (fig) profitieren von; ~ **and loss account** Gewinn-und-Verlust-Rechnung; **to make a** ~ einen Gewinn machen; **to sell (sth) at a** ~ (etw) mit Gewinn verkaufen.

**profitability** [prɔfɪtə'bɪlɪtɪ] n Rentabilität f.

**profitable** ['prɔfɪtəbl] adj (business, deal) rentabel, einträglich; (fig: useful) nützlich.

**profit centre** n Bilanzabteilung f.

**profiteering** [prɔfɪ'tɪərɪŋ] (pej) n Profitmacherei f.

**profit-making** ['prɔfɪtmeɪkɪŋ] adj (organization) gewinnorientiert.

**profit margin** n Gewinnspanne f.

**profit-sharing** ['prɔfɪtʃɛərɪŋ] n Gewinnbeteiligung f.

**profits tax** (BRIT) n Ertragssteuer f.

**profligate** ['prɔflɪgɪt] adj (person, spending) verschwenderisch; (waste) sinnlos; ~ **with** (extravagant) verschwenderisch mit.

**pro forma** ['prəu'fɔːmə] adj: ~ **invoice** Pro-forma-Rechnung f.

**profound** [prə'faund] adj (shock) schwer, tief; (effect, differences) weitreichend; (idea, book) tiefschürfend.

**profuse** [prə'fjuːs] adj (apologies) überschwenglich.

**profusely** [prə'fjuːslɪ] adv (apologise, thank) vielmals; (sweat, bleed) stark.

**profusion** [prə'fjuːʒən] n Überfülle f.

**progeny** ['prɒdʒɪnɪ] n Nachkommenschaft f.

**prognoses** [prɒg'nəusiːz] npl of **prognosis**.

**prognosis** [prɒg'nəusis] (pl **prognoses**) n (MED, fig) Prognose f.

**program** ['prəugræm] (COMPUT) n Programm nt ♦ vt programmieren.

**programme**, (US) **program** ['prəugræm] n Programm nt ♦ vt (machine, system) programmieren.

**programmer** ['prəugræmə*] n Programmierer(in) m(f).

**programming**, (US) **programing** ['prəugræmɪŋ] n Programmierung f.

**programming language** n Programmiersprache f.

**progress** [n 'prəugres, vi prə'gres] n Fortschritt m; (improvement) Fortschritte pl ♦ vi (advance) vorankommen; (become higher in rank) aufsteigen; (continue) sich fortsetzen; **in** ~ (meeting, battle, match) im Gange; **to make** ~ Fortschritte machen.

**progression** [prə'grɛʃən] n (development) Fortschritt m, Entwicklung f; (series) Folge f.

**progressive** [prə'grɛsɪv] adj (enlightened) progressiv, fortschrittlich; (gradual) fortschreitend.

**progressively** [prə'grɛsɪvlɪ] adv (gradually) zunehmend.

**progress report** n (MED) Fortschrittsbericht m; (ADMIN) Tätigkeitsbericht m.

**prohibit** [prə'hɪbɪt] vt (ban) verbieten; **to** ~ **sb from doing sth** jdm verbieten or untersagen, etw zu tun; **"smoking ~ed"** „Rauchen verboten".

**prohibition** [prəuɪ'bɪʃən] n Verbot nt; **P~** (US) Prohibition f.

**prohibitive** [prə'hɪbɪtɪv] adj (cost etc) untragbar.

**project** [n 'prɒdʒɛkt, vt, vi prə'dʒɛkt] n (plan, scheme) Projekt nt; (SCOL) Referat nt ♦ vt (plan) planen; (estimate) schätzen, voraussagen; (light, film, picture) projizieren ♦ vi (stick out) hervorragen.

**projectile** [prə'dʒɛktaɪl] n Projektil nt, Geschoß nt.

**projection** [prə'dʒɛkʃən] n (estimate) Schätzung f, Voraussage f; (overhang) Vorsprung m; (CINE) Projektion f.

**projectionist** [prə'dʒɛkʃənɪst] n Filmvorführer(in) m(f).

**projection room** n Vorführraum m.

**projector** [prə'dʒɛktə*] n Projektor m.

**proletarian** [prəulɪ'tɛərɪən] adj proletarisch.

**proletariat** [prəulɪ'tɛərɪət] n: **the** ~ das Proletariat.

**proliferate** [prə'lɪfəreɪt] vi sich vermehren.

**proliferation** [prəlɪfə'reɪʃən] n Vermehrung f, Verbreitung f.

**prolific** [prə'lɪfɪk] adj (artist, writer) produktiv.

**prologue**, (US) **prolog** ['prəulɒg] n (of play,

book) Prolog m.

**prolong** [prə'lɒŋ] vt verlängern.

**prom** [prɒm] n abbr = **promenade**; (MUS) = **promenade concert**; (US: college ball) Studentenball m.

---

**Prom** (promenade concert) ist in Großbritannien ein Konzert, bei dem ein Teil der Zuhörer steht (ursprünglich spazierenging). Die seit 1895 alljährlich stattfindenden Proms (seit 1941 immer in der Londoner Royal Albert Hall) zählen zu den bedeutendsten Musikereignissen in England. Der letzte Abend der Proms steht ganz im Zeichen des Patriotismus und gipfelt im Singen des Lieds 'Land of Hope and Glory'. In den USA und Kanada steht das Wort für **promenade**, ein Ball an einer **High School** oder einem **College**.

---

**promenade** [prɒmə'nɑːd] n Promenade f.

**promenade concert** (BRIT) n Promenadenkonzert nt.

**promenade deck** n Promenadendeck nt.

**prominence** ['prɒmɪnəns] n (importance) Bedeutung f; **to rise to** ~ bekannt werden.

**prominent** ['prɒmɪnənt] adj (person) prominent; (thing) bedeutend; (very noticeable) herausragend; **he is** ~ **in the field of science** er ist eine führende Persönlichkeit im naturwissenschaftlichen Bereich.

**prominently** ['prɒmɪnəntlɪ] adv (display, set) deutlich sichtbar; **he figured** ~ **in the case** er spielte in dem Fall eine bedeutende Rolle.

**promiscuity** [prɒmɪs'kjuːɪtɪ] n Promiskuität f.

**promiscuous** [prə'mɪskjuəs] adj promisk.

**promise** ['prɒmɪs] n (vow) Versprechen nt; (potential, hope) Hoffnung f ♦ vi versprechen ♦ vt: **to** ~ **sb sth**, ~ **sth to sb** jdm etw versprechen; **to make/break/keep a** ~ ein Versprechen geben/brechen/halten; **a young man of** ~ ein vielversprechender junger Mann; **she shows** ~ sie gibt zu Hoffnungen Anlaß; **it** ~**s to be lively** es verspricht lebhaft zu werden; **to** ~ (**sb**) **to do sth** (jdm) versprechen, etw zu tun.

**promising** ['prɒmɪsɪŋ] adj vielversprechend.

**promissory note** ['prɒmɪsərɪ-] n Schuldschein m.

**promontory** ['prɒməntrɪ] n Felsvorsprung m.

**promote** [prə'məut] vt (employee) befördern; (advertise) werben für; (encourage: peace etc) fördern; **the team was** ~**d to the first division** (BRIT: FOOTBALL) die Mannschaft stieg in die erste Division auf.

**promoter** [prə'məutə*] n (of concert, event) Veranstalter(in) m(f); (of cause, idea) Förderer m, Förderin f.

**promotion** [prə'məuʃən] n (at work) Beförderung f; (of product, event) Werbung f;

*(of idea)* Förderung *f*; *(publicity campaign)* Werbekampagne *f*.

**prompt** [prɔmpt] *adj* prompt, sofortig ♦ *adv* *(exactly)* pünktlich ♦ *n (COMPUT)* Prompt *m* ♦ *vt (cause)* veranlassen; *(when talking)* auf die Sprünge helfen +*dat*; *(THEAT)* soufflieren +*dat*; **they're very ~ to accept** er nahm unverzüglich an; **at 8 o'clock ~** (um) Punkt 8 Uhr; **to ~ sb to do sth** jdn dazu veranlassen, etw zu tun.

**prompter** ['prɔmptə*'*] *n (THEAT)* Souffleur *m*, Souffleuse *f*.

**promptly** ['prɔmptlı] *adv (immediately)* sofort; *(exactly)* pünktlich.

**promptness** ['prɔmptnıs] *n* Promptheit *f*.

**promulgate** ['prɔmǝlgeıt] *vt (policy)* bekanntmachen, verkünden; *(idea)* verbreiten.

**prone** [prǝun] *adj (face down)* in Bauchlage; **to be ~ to sth** zu etw neigen; **she is ~ to burst into tears if ...** sie neigt dazu, in Tränen auszubrechen, wenn ...

**prong** [prɔŋ] *n (of fork)* Zinke *f*.

**pronoun** ['prǝunaun] *n* Pronomen *nt*, Fürwort *nt*.

**pronounce** [prǝ'nauns] *vt (word)* aussprechen; *(give verdict, opinion)* erklären ♦ *vi:* **to ~ (up)on** sich äußern zu; **they ~d him dead/unfit to drive** sie erklärten ihn für tot/ fahruntüchtig.

**pronounced** [prǝ'naunst] *adj (noticeable)* ausgeprägt, deutlich.

**pronouncement** [prǝ'naunsmǝnt] *n* Erklärung *f*.

**pronto** ['prɔntǝu] *(inf) adv* fix.

**pronunciation** [prǝnʌnsı'eıʃǝn] *n* Aussprache *f*.

**proof** [pruːf] *n (evidence)* Beweis *m*; *(TYP)* (Korrektur)fahne *f* ♦ *adj:* **~ against** sicher vor +*dat*; **to be 70 % ~** *(alcohol)* ≈ einen Alkoholgehalt von 40% haben.

**proofreader** ['pruːfriːdǝ*'*] *n* Korrektor(in) *m(f)*.

**Prop.** *abbr (COMM: = proprietor)* Inh.

**prop** [prɔp] *n (support, also fig)* Stütze *f* ♦ *vt* *(lean):* **to ~ sth against sth** etw an etw *acc* lehnen.

▶**prop up** *vt sep (thing)* (ab)stützen; *(fig: government, industry)* unterstützen.

**propaganda** [prɔpǝ'gændǝ] *n* Propaganda *f*.

**propagate** ['prɔpǝgeıt] *vt (plants)* züchten; *(ideas etc)* propagieren ♦ *vi (plants, animals)* sich fortpflanzen.

**propagation** [prɔpǝ'geıʃǝn] *n (of ideas etc)* Propagierung *f*; *(of plants, animals)* Fortpflanzung *f*.

**propel** [prǝ'pɛl] *vt (vehicle, machine)* antreiben; *(person)* schubsen; *(fig: person)* treiben.

**propeller** [prǝ'pɛlǝ*'*] *n* Propeller *m*.

**propelling pencil** [prǝ'pɛlıŋ-] *(BRIT) n* Drehbleistift *m*.

**propensity** [prǝ'pɛnsıtı] *n:* **a ~ for** *or* **to sth** ein

Hang *m or* eine Neigung zu etw; **to have a ~ to do sth** dazu neigen, etw zu tun.

**proper** ['prɔpǝ*'*] *adj (genuine, correct)* richtig; *(socially acceptable)* schicklich; *(inf: real)* echt; **the town/city ~** die Stadt selbst; **to go through the ~ channels** den Dienstweg einhalten.

**properly** ['prɔpǝlı] *adv (eat, work)* richtig; *(behave)* anständig.

**proper noun** *n* Eigenname *m*.

**property** ['prɔpǝtı] *n (possessions)* Eigentum *nt*; *(building and its land)* Grundstück *nt*; *(quality)* Eigenschaft *f*; **it's their ~** es gehört ihnen.

**property developer** *n* ≈ Grundstücks makler(in) *m(f)*.

**property market** *n* Immobilienmarkt *m*.

**property owner** *n* Grundbesitzer(in) *m(f)*.

**property tax** *n* Vermögenssteuer *f*.

**prophecy** ['prɔfısı] *n* Prophezeiung *f*.

**prophesy** ['prɔfısaı] *vt* prophezeien ♦ *vi* Prophezeiungen machen.

**prophet** ['prɔfıt] *n* Prophet *m*; **~ of doom** Unheilsprophet(in) *m(f)*.

**prophetic** [prǝ'fɛtık] *adj* prophetisch.

**proportion** [prǝ'pɔːʃǝn] *n (part)* Teil *m*; *(number: of people, things)* Anteil *m*; *(ratio)* Verhältnis *nt*; **in ~ to** im Verhältnis zu; **to be out of all ~ to sth** in keinem Verhältnis zu etw stehen; **to get sth in/out of ~** etw im richtigen/falschen Verhältnis sehen; **a sense of ~** *(fig)* ein Sinn für das Wesentliche.

**proportional** [prǝ'pɔːʃǝnl] *adj:* **~ to** proportional zu.

**proportional representation** *n* Verhältniswahlrecht *nt*.

**proportionate** [prǝ'pɔːʃǝnıt] *adj* = **proportional**.

**proposal** [prǝ'pǝuzl] *n (plan)* Vorschlag *m*; **~ (of marriage)** Heiratsantrag *m*.

**propose** [prǝ'pǝuz] *vt (plan, idea)* vorschlagen; *(motion)* einbringen; *(toast)* ausbringen ♦ *vi* *(offer marriage)* einen Heiratsantrag machen; **to ~ to do sth** *or* **doing sth** *(intend)* die Absicht haben, etw zu tun.

**proposer** [prǝ'pǝuzǝ*'*] *n (of motion etc)* Antragsteller(in) *m(f)*.

**proposition** [prɔpǝ'zıʃǝn] *n (statement)* These *f*; *(offer)* Angebot *nt*; **to make sb a ~** jdm ein Angebot machen.

**propound** [prǝ'paund] *vt (idea etc)* darlegen.

**proprietary** [prǝ'praıǝtǝrı] *adj (brand, medicine)* Marken-; *(tone, manner)* besitzergreifend.

**proprietor** [prǝ'praıǝtǝ*'*] *n (of hotel, shop etc)* Inhaber(in) *m(f)*; *(of newspaper)* Besitzer(in) *m(f)*.

**propriety** [prǝ'praıǝtı] *n (seemliness)* Schicklichkeit *f*.

**props** [prɔps] *npl (THEAT)* Requisiten *pl*.

**propulsion** [prǝ'pʌlʃǝn] *n* Antrieb *m*.

**pro rata** [prəu'rɑːtə] *adj, adv* anteilmäßig; **on a ~ basis** anteilmäßig.

**prosaic** [prəu'zeɪɪk] *adj* prosaisch, nüchtern.

**Pros. Atty.** (*US*) *abbr* = **prosecuting attorney**.

**proscribe** [prə'skraɪb] (*form*) *vt* verbieten, untersagen.

**prose** [prəuz] *n* (*not poetry*) Prosa *f*; (*BRIT: SCOL: translation*) Übersetzung *f* in die Fremdsprache.

**prosecute** ['prɔsɪkjuːt] *vt* (*LAW: person*) strafrechtlich verfolgen; (: *case*) die Anklage vertreten in +*dat*.

**prosecuting attorney** ['prɔsɪkjuːtɪŋ-] (*US*) *n* Staatsanwalt *m*, Staatsanwältin *f*.

**prosecution** [prɔsɪ'kjuːʃən] *n* (*LAW: action*) strafrechtliche Verfolgung *f*; (: *accusing side*) Anklage(vertretung) *f*.

**prosecutor** ['prɔsɪkjuːtə*] *n* Anklagevertreter(in) *m(f)*; (*also:* **public ~**) Staatsanwalt *m*, Staatsanwältin *f*.

**prospect** [*n* 'prɔspɛkt, *vi* prə'spɛkt] *n* Aussicht *f* ♦ *vi:* **to ~ (for)** suchen (nach); **prospects** *npl* (*for work etc*) Aussichten *pl*, Chancen *pl*; **we are faced with the ~ of higher unemployment** wir müssen mit der Möglichkeit rechnen, daß die Arbeitslosigkeit steigt.

**prospecting** ['prɔspɛktɪŋ] *n* (*for gold, oil etc*) Suche *f*.

**prospective** [prə'spɛktɪv] *adj* (*son-in-law*) zukünftig; (*customer, candidate*) voraussichtlich.

**prospectus** [prə'spɛktəs] *n* (*of college, company*) Prospekt *m*.

**prosper** ['prɔspə*] *vi* (*person*) Erfolg haben; (*business, city etc*) gedeihen, florieren.

**prosperity** [prɔ'spɛrɪtɪ] *n* Wohlstand *m*.

**prosperous** ['prɔspərəs] *adj* (*person*) wohlhabend; (*business, city etc*) blühend.

**prostate** ['prɔsteɪt] *n* (*also:* **~ gland**) Prostata *f*.

**prostitute** ['prɔstɪtjuːt] *n* (*female*) Prostituierte *f*; (*male*) männliche(r) Prostituierte(r) *m*, Strichjunge *m* (*inf*) ♦ *vt:* **to ~ o.s.** (*fig*) sich prostituieren, sich unter Wert verkaufen.

**prostitution** [prɔstɪ'tjuːʃən] *n* Prostitution *f*.

**prostrate** ['prɔstreɪt] *adj* (*face down*) ausgestreckt (*liegend*); (*fig*) niedergeschmettert ♦ *vt:* **to ~ o.s. before** sich zu Boden werfen vor +*dat*.

**protagonist** [prə'tægənɪst] *n* (*of idea, movement*) Verfechter(in) *m(f)*; (*THEAT, LITER*) Protagonist(in) *m(f)*.

**protect** [prə'tɛkt] *vt* schützen.

**protection** [prə'tɛkʃən] *n* Schutz *m*; **police ~** Polizeischutz *m*.

**protectionism** [prə'tɛkʃənɪzəm] *n* Protektionismus *m*.

**protection racket** *n* Organisation *f* zur Erpressung von Schutzgeld.

**protective** [prə'tɛktɪv] *adj* (*clothing, layer etc*) Schutz-; (*person*) fürsorglich; **~ custody**

Schutzhaft *f*.

**protector** [prə'tɛktə*] *n* (*person*) Beschützer(in) *m(f)*; (*device*) Schutz *m*.

**protégé(e)** ['prɔutɪʒeɪ] *n* Schützling *m*.

**protein** ['prəutiːn] *n* Protein *nt*, Eiweiß *nt*.

**pro tem** [prəu'tɛm] *adv abbr* (= *pro tempore*) vorläufig.

**protest** [*n* 'prəutɛst, *vi, vt* prə'tɛst] *n* Protest *m* ♦ *vi:* **to ~ about** *or* **against** *or* **at sth** gegen etw protestieren ♦ *vt:* **to ~ (that)** (*insist*) beteuern(, daß).

**Protestant** ['prɔtɪstənt] *adj* protestantisch ♦ *n* Protestant(in) *m(f)*.

**protester** [prə'tɛstə*] *n* (*in demonstration*) Demonstrant(in) *m(f)*.

**protest march** *n* Protestmarsch *m*.

**protestor** [prə'tɛstə*] *n* = **protester**.

**protocol** ['prəutəkɔl] *n* Protokoll *nt*.

**prototype** ['prəutətaɪp] *n* Prototyp *m*.

**protracted** [prə'træktɪd] *adj* (*meeting etc*) langwierig, sich hinziehend; (*absence*) länger.

**protractor** [prə'træktə*] *n* (*GEOM*) Winkelmesser *m*.

**protrude** [prə'truːd] *vi* (*rock, ledge, teeth*) vorstehen.

**protuberance** [prə'tjuːbərəns] *n* Auswuchs *m*.

**proud** [praud] *adj* stolz; (*arrogant*) hochmütig; **~ of sb/sth** stolz auf jdn/etw; **to be ~ to do sth** stolz (darauf) sein, etw zu tun; **to do sb/o.s. ~** (*inf*) jdn/sich verwöhnen.

**proudly** ['praudlɪ] *adv* stolz.

**prove** [pruːv] *vt* beweisen ♦ *vi:* **to ~ (to be) correct** sich als richtig herausstellen *or* erweisen; **to ~ (o.s./itself) (to be) useful** sich als nützlich erweisen; **he was ~d right in the end** er hat schließlich recht behalten.

**proverb** ['prɔvəːb] *n* Sprichwort *nt*.

**proverbial** [prə'vəːbɪəl] *adj* sprichwörtlich.

**provide** [prə'vaɪd] *vt* (*food, money, shelter etc*) zur Verfügung stellen; (*answer, example etc*) liefern; **to ~ sb with sth** jdm etw zur Verfügung stellen.

▶**provide for** *vt fus* (*person*) sorgen für; (*future event*) vorsorgen für.

**provided** [prə'vaɪdɪd] *conj:* **~ (that)** vorausgesetzt(, daß).

**Providence** ['prɔvɪdəns] *n* die Vorsehung.

**providing** [prə'vaɪdɪŋ] *conj:* **~ (that)** vorausgesetzt(, daß).

**province** ['prɔvɪns] *n* (*of country*) Provinz *f*; (*responsibility etc*) Bereich *nt*, Gebiet *nt*; **provinces** *npl:* **the ~s** außerhalb der Hauptstadt liegende Landesteile, Provinz *f*.

**provincial** [prə'vɪnʃəl] *adj* (*town, newspaper etc*) Provinz-; (*pej: parochial*) provinziell.

**provision** [prə'vɪʒən] *n* (*supplying*) Bereitstellung *f*; (*preparation*) Vorsorge *f*, Vorkehrungen *pl*; (*stipulation, clause*) Bestimmung *f*; **provisions** *npl* (*food*) Proviant *m*; **to make ~ for** vorsorgen für; (*for people*) sorgen für; **there's no ~ for this in the**

**contract** dies ist im Vertrag nicht vorgesehen.

**provisional** [prə'vɪʒənl] *adj* vorläufig, provisorisch ♦ *n*: **P~** (*IRISH: POL*) Mitglied der provisorischen irisch-republikanischen Armee.

**provisional licence** (*BRIT*) *n* (*AUT*) vorläufige Fahrerlaubnis *f*.

**provisionally** [prə'vɪʒnəlɪ] *adv* vorläufig.

**proviso** [prə'vaɪzəu] *n* Vorbehalt *m*; **with the ~ that** ... unter dem Vorbehalt, daß ...

**Provo** ['prɔvəu] (*IRISH: inf*) *n abbr* (*POL*) = **Provisional**.

**provocation** [prɔvə'keɪʃən] *n* Provokation *f*, Herausforderung *f*; **to be under ~** provoziert werden.

**provocative** [prə'vɔkətɪv] *adj* provozierend, herausfordernd; (*sexually stimulating*) aufreizend.

**provoke** [prə'vəuk] *vt* (*person*) provozieren, herausfordern; (*fight*) herbeiführen; (*reaction etc*) hervorrufen; **to ~ sb to do** *or* **into doing sth** jdn dazu provozieren, etw zu tun.

**provost** ['prɔvəst] *n* (*BRIT: of university*) Dekan *m*; (*SCOT*) Bürgermeister(in) *m(f)*.

**prow** [prau] *n* (*of boat*) Bug *m*.

**prowess** ['prauɪs] *n* Können *nt*, Fähigkeiten *pl*; **his ~ as a footballer** sein fußballerisches Können.

**prowl** [praul] *vi* (*also*: **~ about, ~ around**) schleichen ♦ *n*: **on the ~** (*animal, fig: person*) auf Streifzug.

**prowler** ['praulə*] *n* Herumtreiber *m*.

**proximity** [prɔk'sɪmɪtɪ] *n* Nähe *f*.

**proxy** ['prɔksɪ] *n*: **by ~** durch einen Stellvertreter.

**prude** [pruːd] *n*: **to be a ~** prüde sein.

**prudence** ['pruːdns] *n* Klugheit *f*, Umsicht *f*.

**prudent** ['pruːdnt] *adj* (*sensible*) klug.

**prudish** ['pruːdɪʃ] *adj* prüde.

**prune** [pruːn] *n* Backpflaume *f* ♦ *vt* (*plant*) stutzen, beschneiden.

**pry** [praɪ] *vi*: **to ~ (into)** seine Nase hineinstecken (in *+acc*), herumschnüffeln (in *+dat*).

**PS** *abbr* (= *postscript*) PS.

**psalm** [sɑːm] *n* Psalm *m*.

**PSAT** (*US*) *n abbr* (= *Preliminary Scholastic Aptitude Test*) Schuleignungstest.

**PSBR** (*BRIT*) *n abbr* (*ECON*: = *public sector borrowing requirement*) staatlicher Kreditbedarf *m*.

**pseud** [sjuːd] (*BRIT: inf: pej*) *n* Angeber(in) *m(f)*.

**pseudo-** ['sjuːdəu] *pref* Pseudo-.

**pseudonym** ['sjuːdənɪm] *n* Pseudonym *nt*.

**PST** (*US*) *abbr* (= *Pacific Standard Time*) pazifische Standardzeit.

**PSV** (*BRIT*) *n abbr* = **public-service vehicle**.

**psyche** ['saɪkɪ] *n* Psyche *f*.

**psychedelic** [saɪkə'delɪk] *adj* (*drug*) psychedelisch; (*clothes, colours*) in psychedelischen Farben.

**psychiatric** [saɪkɪ'ætrɪk] *adj* psychiatrisch.

**psychiatrist** [saɪ'kaɪətrɪst] *n* Psychiater(in) *m(f)*.

**psychiatry** [saɪ'kaɪətrɪ] *n* Psychiatrie *f*.

**psychic** ['saɪkɪk] *adj* (*person*) übersinnlich begabt; (*damage, disorder*) psychisch ♦ *n* Mensch *m* mit übersinnlichen Fähigkeiten.

**psycho** ['saɪkəu] (*US: inf*) *n* Verrückte(r) *f(m)*.

**psychoanalyse** [saɪkəu'ænəlaɪz] *vt* psychoanalytisch behandeln, psychoanalysieren.

**psychoanalysis** [saɪkəuə'nælɪsɪs] *n* Psychoanalyse *f*.

**psychoanalyst** [saɪkəu'ænəlɪst] *n* Psychoanalytiker(in) *m(f)*.

**psychological** [saɪkə'lɔdʒɪkl] *adj* psychologisch.

**psychologist** [saɪ'kɔlədʒɪst] *n* Psychologe *m*, Psychologin *f*.

**psychology** [saɪ'kɔlədʒɪ] *n* (*science*) Psychologie *f*; (*character*) Psyche *f*.

**psychopath** ['saɪkəupæθ] *n* Psychopath(in) *m(f)*.

**psychoses** [saɪ'kəusiːz] *npl of* **psychosis**.

**psychosis** [saɪ'kəusɪs] (*pl* **psychoses**) *n* Psychose *f*.

**psychosomatic** ['saɪkəusə'mætɪk] *adj* psychosomatisch.

**psychotherapy** [saɪkəu'θerəpɪ] *n* Psychotherapie *f*.

**psychotic** [saɪ'kɔtɪk] *adj* psychotisch.

**PT** (*BRIT*) *n abbr* (*SCOL*: = *physical training*) Turnen *nt*.

**Pt** *abbr* (*in place names*: = *Point*) Pt.

**pt** *abbr* = **pint; point**.

**PTA** *n abbr* (= *Parent-Teacher Association*) Lehrer- und Elternverband.

**Pte** (*BRIT*) *abbr* (*MIL*) = **private**.

**PTO** *abbr* (= *please turn over*) b.w.

**PTV** (*US*) *n abbr* (= *pay television*) Pay-TV *nt*; (= *public television*) öffentliches Fernsehen *nt*.

**pub** [pʌb] *n* = **public house**.

**Pub** ist ein Gasthaus mit einer Lizenz zum Ausschank von alkoholischen Getränken. Ein Pub besteht meist aus verschiedenen gemütlichen (**lounge, snug**) oder einfacheren Räumen (**public bar**), in der oft auch Spiele wie Darts, Domino und Poolbillard zur Verfügung stehen. In Pubs werden vor allem Mittags oft auch Mahlzeiten angeboten. Pubs sind normalerweise von 11 bis 23 Uhr geöffnet, aber manchmal nachmittags geschlossen.

**pub-crawl** ['pʌbkrɔːl] (*inf*) *n*: **to go on a ~** eine Kneipentour machen.

**puberty** ['pjuːbətɪ] *n* Pubertät *f*.

**pubic** ['pjuːbɪk] *adj* (*hair*) Scham-; **~ bone** Schambein *nt*.

**public** ['pʌblɪk] *adj* öffentlich ♦ *n*: **the ~** (*in* *general)* die Öffentlichkeit; *(particular set of people)* das Publikum; **to be ~ knowledge** allgemein bekannt sein; **to make sth ~** etw bekanntmachen; **to go ~** *(COMM)* in eine Aktiengesellschaft umgewandelt werden; **in ~** in aller Öffentlichkeit; **the general ~** die Allgemeinheit.

**public-address system** [pʌblɪkə'drɛs-] *n* Lautsprecheranlage *f*.

**publican** ['pʌblɪkən] *n* Gastwirt(in) *m(f)*.

**publication** [pʌblɪ'keɪʃən] *n* Veröffentlichung *f*.

**public company** *n* Aktiengesellschaft *f*.

**public convenience** *(BRIT)* *n* öffentliche Toilette *f*.

**public holiday** *n* gesetzlicher Feiertag *m*.

**public house** *(BRIT)* *n* Gaststätte *f*.

**publicity** [pʌb'lɪsɪtɪ] *n* *(information)* Werbung *f*; *(attention)* Publicity *f*.

**publicize** ['pʌblɪsaɪz] *vt* *(fact)* bekanntmachen; *(event)* Publicity machen für.

**public limited company** *n* ≈ Aktiengesellschaft *f*.

**publicly** ['pʌblɪklɪ] *adv* öffentlich; **to be ~ owned** *(COMM)* in Staatsbesitz sein.

**public opinion** *n* die öffentliche Meinung.

**public ownership** *n*: **to be taken into ~** verstaatlicht werden.

**Public Prosecutor** *n* Staatsanwalt *m*, Staatsanwältin *f*.

**public relations** *n* Public Relations *pl*, Öffentlichkeitsarbeit *f*.

**public relations officer** *n* Beauftragte(r) *f(m)* für Öffentlichkeitsarbeit.

**public school** *n* *(BRIT)* Privatschule *f*; *(US)* staatliche Schule *f*.

---

**Public school** *bezeichnet vor allem in England eine weiterführende Privatschule, meist eine Internatsschule mit hohem Prestige, an die oft auch eine* **preparatory school** *angeschlossen ist. Public schools werden von einem Schulbeirat verwaltet und durch Stiftungen und Schulgelder, die an den bekanntesten Schulen wie Eton, Harrow und Westminster sehr hoch sein können, finanziert. Die meisten Schüler einer Public school gehen zur Universität, oft nach Oxford oder Cambridge. Viele Industrielle, Abgeordnete und hohe Beamte haben eine Public school besucht. In Schottland und den USA bedeutet Public school eine öffentliche, vom Steuerzahler finanzierte Schule.*

---

**public sector** *n*: **the ~** der öffentliche Sektor.

**public-service vehicle** [pʌblɪk'sɜːvɪs-] *(BRIT)* *n* öffentliches Verkehrsmittel *nt*.

**public-spirited** [pʌblɪk'spɪrɪtɪd] *adj* gemeinsinnig.

**public transport** *n* öffentliche Verkehrsmittel *pl*.

**public utility** *n* öffentlicher

Versorgungsbetrieb *m*.

**public works** *npl* öffentliche Bauprojekte *pl*.

**publish** ['pʌblɪʃ] *vt* veröffentlichen.

**publisher** ['pʌblɪʃə*] *n* *(person)* Verleger(in) *m(f)*; *(company)* Verlag *m*.

**publishing** ['pʌblɪʃɪŋ] *n* *(profession)* das Verlagswesen.

**publishing company** *n* Verlag *m*, Verlagshaus *nt*.

**puce** [pjuːs] *adj* *(face)* hochrot.

**puck** [pʌk] *n* *(ICE HOCKEY)* Puck *m*.

**pucker** ['pʌkə*] *vi* *(lips, face)* sich verziehen; *(fabric etc)* Falten werfen ♦ *vt* *(lips, face)* verziehen; *(fabric etc)* Falten machen in +*acc*.

**pudding** ['pudɪŋ] *n* *(cooked sweet food)* Süßspeise *f*; *(BRIT: dessert)* Nachtisch *m*; **rice ~** Milchreis *m*; **black ~,** *(US)* **blood ~** ≈ Blutwurst *f*.

**puddle** ['pʌdl] *n* *(of rain)* Pfütze *f*; *(of blood)* Lache *f*.

**puerile** ['pjuəraɪl] *adj* kindisch.

**Puerto Rico** ['pwɔːtəu'riːkəu] *n* Puerto Rico *nt*.

**puff** [pʌf] *n* *(of cigarette, pipe)* Zug *m*; *(gasp)* Schnaufer *m*; *(of air)* Stoß *m*; *(of smoke)* Wolke *f* ♦ *vt* *(also:* **~ on, ~ at:** *cigarette, pipe)* ziehen an +*dat* ♦ *vi* *(gasp)* keuchen, schnaufen.

▶**puff out** *vt* *(one's chest)* herausdrücken; *(one's cheeks)* aufblasen.

**puffed** [pʌft] *(inf)* *adj* außer Puste.

**puffin** ['pʌfɪn] *n* Papageientaucher *m*.

**puff pastry,** *(US)* **puff paste** *n* Blätterteig *m*.

**puffy** ['pʌfɪ] *adj* *(eye)* geschwollen; *(face)* aufgedunsen.

**pugnacious** [pʌg'neɪʃəs] *adj* *(person)* streitsüchtig.

**pull** [pul] *vt* *(rope, handle etc)* ziehen an +*dat*; *(cart etc)* ziehen; *(close: curtain)* zuziehen; *(: blind)* herunterlassen; *(inf: attract: people)* anlocken; *(: sexual partner)* aufreißen; *(pint of beer)* zapfen ♦ *vi* ziehen ♦ *n* *(also fig: attraction)* Anziehungskraft *f*; **to ~ the trigger** abdrücken; **to ~ a face** ein Gesicht schneiden; **to ~ a muscle** sich *dat* einen Muskel zerren; **not to ~ one's** *or* **any punches** *(fig)* sich *dat* keine Zurückhaltung auferlegen; **to ~ to pieces** *(fig)* zerreißen; **to ~ one's weight** *(fig)* sich ins Zeug legen; **to ~ o.s. together** sich zusammenreißen; **to ~ sb's leg** *(fig)* jdn auf den Arm nehmen; **to ~ strings (for sb)** seine Beziehungen (für jdn) spielen lassen; **to give sth a ~** an etw *dat* ziehen.

▶**pull apart** *vt* *(separate)* trennen.

▶**pull away** *vi* *(AUT)* losfahren.

▶**pull back** *vi* *(retreat)* sich zurückziehen; *(fig)* einen Rückzieher machen *(inf)*.

▶**pull down** *vt* *(building)* abreißen.

▶**pull in** *vi* *(AUT: at kerb)* anhalten; *(RAIL)* einfahren ♦ *vt* *(inf: money)* einsacken; *(crowds, people)* anlocken; *(police: suspect)* sich *dat* schnappen *(inf)*.

▶**pull off** vt (clothes etc) ausziehen; (fig: difficult thing) schaffen, bringen (inf).

▶**pull out** vi (AUT: from kerb) losfahren; (: when overtaking) ausscheren; (RAIL) ausfahren; (withdraw) sich zurückziehen ♦ vt (extract) herausziehen.

▶**pull over** vi (AUT) an den Straßenrand fahren.

▶**pull through** vi (MED) durchkommen.

▶**pull up** vi (AUT, RAIL: stop) anhalten ♦ vt (raise) hochziehen; (uproot) herausreißen; (chair) heranrücken.

**pullback** ['pulbæk] n (retreat) Rückzug m.

**pulley** ['pulɪ] n Flaschenzug m.

**pull-out** ['pulaut] n (in magazine) Beilage f (zum Heraustrennen).

**pullover** ['puləuvə'] n Pullover m.

**pulp** [pʌlp] n (of fruit) Fruchtfleisch nt; (for paper) (Papier)brei m; (LITER: pej) Schund m ♦ adj (pej: magazine, novel) Schund-; **to reduce sth to a ~** etw zu Brei machen.

**pulpit** ['pulpɪt] n Kanzel f.

**pulsate** [pʌl'seɪt] vi (heart) klopfen; (music) pulsieren.

**pulse** [pʌls] n (ANAT) Puls m; (rhythm) Rhythmus m; **pulses** npl (BOT) Hülsenfrüchte pl; (TECH) Impuls m; vi pulsieren; **to take** or **feel sb's ~** jdm den Puls fühlen; **to have one's finger on the ~ (of sth)** (fig) den Finger am Puls (einer Sache gen) haben.

**pulverize** ['pʌlvəraɪz] vt pulverisieren; (fig: destroy) vernichten.

**puma** ['pjuːmə] n Puma m.

**pumice** ['pʌmɪs] n (also: ~ **stone**) Bimsstein m.

**pummel** ['pʌml] vt mit Faustschlägen bearbeiten.

**pump** [pʌmp] n Pumpe f; (petrol pump) Zapfsäule f; (shoe) Turnschuh m ♦ vt pumpen; **to ~ sb for information** jdn aushorchen; **she had her stomach ~ed** ihr wurde der Magen ausgepumpt.

▶**pump up** vt (inflate) aufpumpen.

**pumpkin** ['pʌmpkɪn] n Kürbis m.

**pun** [pʌn] n Wortspiel nt.

**punch** [pʌntʃ] n (blow) Schlag m; (fig: force) Schlagkraft f; (tool) Locher m; (drink) Bowle f, Punsch m ♦ vt (hit) schlagen; (make a hole in) lochen; **to ~ a hole in sth** ein Loch in etw acc stanzen.

▶**punch in** (US) vi (bei Arbeitsbeginn) stempeln.

▶**punch out** (US) vi (bei Arbeitsende) stempeln.

**Punch and Judy show** n ≈ Kasper(le)theater nt.

**punch card**, (US) **punched card** [pʌntʃt-] n Lochkarte f.

**punch-drunk** ['pʌntʃdrʌŋk] (BRIT) adj (boxer) angeschlagen.

**punch line** n Pointe f.

**punch-up** ['pʌntʃʌp] (BRIT: inf) n Schlägerei f.

**punctual** ['pʌŋktjuəl] adj pünktlich.

**punctuality** [pʌŋktju'ælɪtɪ] n Pünktlichkeit f.

**punctually** ['pʌŋktjuəlɪ] adv pünktlich; **it will start ~ at 6** es beginnt um Punkt 6 or pünktlich um 6.

**punctuation** [pʌŋktju'eɪʃən] n Zeichensetzung f.

**punctuation mark** n Satzzeichen nt.

**puncture** ['pʌŋktʃə'] n (AUT) Reifenpanne f ♦ vt durchbohren; **I have a ~** ich habe eine Reifenpanne.

**pundit** ['pʌndɪt] n Experte m, Expertin f.

**pungent** ['pʌndʒənt] adj (smell, taste) scharf; (fig: speech, article etc) spitz, scharf.

**punish** ['pʌnɪʃ] vt bestrafen; **to ~ sb for sth** jdn für etw bestrafen; **to ~ sb for doing sth** jdn dafür bestrafen, daß er etw getan hat.

**punishable** ['pʌnɪʃəbl] adj strafbar.

**punishing** ['pʌnɪʃɪŋ] adj (fig: exercise, ordeal) hart.

**punishment** ['pʌnɪʃmənt] n (act) Bestrafung f; (way of punishing) Strafe f; **to take a lot of ~** (fig: car, person etc) viel abbekommen.

**punitive** ['pjuːnɪtɪv] adj (action) Straf-, zur Strafe; (measure) (extrem) hart.

**punk** [pʌŋk] n (also: ~ **rocker**) Punker(in) m(f); (also: ~ **rock**) Punk m; (US: inf: hoodlum) Gangster m.

**punnet** ['pʌnɪt] n (of raspberries etc) Körbchen nt.

**punt¹** [pʌnt] n (boat) Stechkahn m ♦ vi mit dem Stechkahn fahren.

**punt²** [pʌnt] (IRISH) n (currency) irisches Pfund nt.

**punter** ['pʌntə'] (BRIT) n (gambler) Wetter(in) m(f); **the ~s** (inf: customers) die Leute; **the average ~** (inf) Otto Normalverbraucher m.

**puny** ['pjuːnɪ] adj (person, arms etc) schwächlich; (efforts) kläglich, kümmerlich.

**pup** [pʌp] n (young dog) Welpe m, junger Hund m; **seal ~** Welpenjunge(s) nt.

**pupil** ['pjuːpl] n (SCOL) Schüler(in) m(f); (of eye) Pupille f.

**puppet** ['pʌpɪt] n Handpuppe f; (with strings, fig: person) Marionette f.

**puppet government** n Marionettenregierung f.

**puppy** ['pʌpɪ] n (young dog) Welpe m, junger Hund m.

**purchase** ['pɜːtʃɪs] n Kauf m; (grip) Halt m ♦ vt kaufen; **to get** or **gain (a) ~ on** (grip) Halt finden an +dat.

**purchase order** n Bestellung f.

**purchase price** n Kaufpreis m.

**purchaser** ['pɜːtʃɪsə'] n Käufer(in) m(f).

**purchase tax** n Kaufsteuer f.

**purchasing power** ['pɜːtʃɪsɪŋ-] n Kaufkraft f.

**pure** [pjuə'] adj rein; **a ~ wool jumper** ein Pullover aus reiner Wolle; **it's laziness ~ and simple** es ist nichts als reine Faulheit.

**purebred** ['pjuəbred] adj reinrassig.

**puree** ['pjʊəreɪ] *n* Püree *nt*.

**purely** ['pjʊəlɪ] *adv* rein.

**purgatory** ['pɜːgətərɪ] *n* (*REL*) das Fegefeuer; (*fig*) die Hölle.

**purge** [pɜːdʒ] *n* (*POL*) Säuberung *f* ♦ *vt* (*POL: organization*) säubern; (: *extremists etc*) entfernen; (*fig: thoughts, mind etc*) befreien.

**purification** [pjʊərɪfɪ'keɪʃən] *n* Reinigung *f*.

**purify** ['pjʊərɪfaɪ] *vt* reinigen.

**purist** ['pjʊərɪst] *n* Purist(in) *m(f)*.

**puritan** ['pjʊərɪtən] *n* Puritaner(in) *m(f)*.

**puritanical** [pjʊərɪ'tænɪkl] *adj* puritanisch.

**purity** ['pjʊərɪtɪ] *n* Reinheit *f*.

**purl** [pɜːl] (*KNITTING*) *n* linke Masche *f* ♦ *vt* links stricken.

**purloin** [pɜː'lɔɪn] (*form*) *vt* entwenden.

**purple** ['pɜːpl] *adj* violett.

**purport** [pɜː'pɔːt] *vi:* **to ~ to be/do sth** vorgeben, etw zu sein/tun.

**purpose** ['pɜːpəs] *n* (*reason*) Zweck *m*; (*aim*) Ziel *nt*, Absicht *f*; **on ~** absichtlich; **for illustrative ~s** zu Illustrationszwecken; **for all practical ~s** praktisch (gesehen); **for the ~s of this meeting** zum Zweck dieses Treffens; **to little ~** mit wenig Erfolg; **to no ~** ohne Erfolg; **a sense of ~** ein Zielbewußtsein *nt*.

**purpose-built** ['pɜːpəs'bɪlt] (*BRIT*) *adj* speziell angefertigt, Spezial-.

**purposeful** ['pɜːpəsful] *adj* entschlossen.

**purposely** ['pɜːpəslɪ] *adv* absichtlich, bewußt.

**purr** [pɜː*] *vi* (*cat*) schnurren.

**purse** [pɜːs] *n* (*BRIT: for money*) Geldbörse *f*, Portemonnaie *nt*; (*US: handbag*) Handtasche *f* ♦ *vt* (*lips*) kräuseln.

**purser** ['pɜːsə*] *n* (*NAUT*) Zahlmeister *m*.

**purse-snatcher** ['pɜːssnætʃə*] (*US*) *n* Handtaschendieb *m*.

**pursue** [pə'sjuː] *vt* (*person, vehicle, plan, aim*) verfolgen; (*fig: interest etc*) nachgehen +*dat*.

**pursuer** [pə'sjuːə*] *n* Verfolger(in) *m(f)*.

**pursuit** [pə'sjuːt] *n* (*chase*) Verfolgung *f*; (*pastime*) Beschäftigung *f*; (*fig*): **~ of** (*of happiness etc*) Streben *nt* nach; **in ~ of** (*person, car etc*) auf der Jagd nach; (*fig: happiness etc*) im Streben nach.

**purveyor** [pə'veɪə*] (*form*) *n* (*of goods etc*) Lieferant *m*.

**pus** [pʌs] *n* Eiter *m*.

**push** [pʊʃ] *n* Stoß *m*, Schub *m* ♦ *vt* (*press*) drücken; (*shove*) schieben; (*fig: put pressure on: person*) bedrängen; (: *promote: product*) werben für; (*inf: sell: drugs*) pushen ♦ *vi* (*press*) drücken; (*shove*) schieben; **at the ~ of a button** auf Knopfdruck; **at a ~** (*BRIT: inf*) notfalls; **to ~ a door open/shut** eine Tür auf-/zudrücken; **"~"** (*on door*) „drücken"; (*on bell*) „klingeln"; **to be ~ed for time/ money** (*inf*) in Zeitnot/Geldnot sein; **she is ~ing fifty** (*inf*) sie geht auf die Fünfzig zu; **to ~ for** (*demand*) drängen auf +*acc*.

▶**push around** *vt* (*bully*) herumschubsen.

▶**push aside** *vt* beiseite schieben.

▶**push in** *vi* sich dazwischendrängeln.

▶**push off** (*inf*) *vi* abhauen.

▶**push on** *vi* (*continue*) weitermachen.

▶**push over** *vt* umstoßen.

▶**push through** *vt* (*measure etc*) durchdrücken.

▶**push up** *vt* (*total, prices*) hochtreiben.

**push-bike** ['pʊʃbaɪk] (*BRIT*) *n* Fahrrad *nt*.

**push-button** ['pʊʃbʌtn] *adj* (*machine, calculator*) Drucktasten-.

**pushchair** ['pʊʃtʃeə*] (*BRIT*) *n* Sportwagen *m*.

**pusher** ['pʊʃə*] *n* (*drug dealer*) Pusher *m*.

**pushover** ['pʊʃəʊvə*] (*inf*) *n:* **it's a ~** das ist ein Kinderspiel.

**push-up** ['pʊʃʌp] (*US*) *n* Liegestütz *m*.

**pushy** ['pʊʃɪ] (*pej*) *adj* aufdringlich.

**puss** [pʊs] (*inf*) *n* Mieze *f*.

**pussy(cat)** ['pʊsɪ(kæt)] (*inf*) *n* Mieze(katze) *f*.

**put** [pʊt] (*pt, pp* **put**) *vt* (*thing*) tun; (: *upright*) stellen; (: *flat*) legen; (*person: in room, institution etc*) stecken; (: *in state, situation*) versetzen; (*express: idea etc*) ausdrücken; (*present: case, view*) vorbringen; (*ask: question*) stellen; (*classify*) einschätzen; (*write, type*) schreiben; **to ~ sb in a good/ bad mood** jdn gut/schlecht stimmen; **to ~ sb to bed** jdn ins Bett bringen; **to ~ sb to a lot of trouble** jdm viele Umstände machen; **how shall I ~ it?** wie soll ich es sagen *or* ausdrücken?; **to ~ a lot of time into sth** viel Zeit auf etw *acc* verwenden; **to ~ money on a horse** Geld auf ein Pferd setzen; **the cost is now ~ at 2 million pounds** die Kosten werden jetzt auf 2 Millionen Pfund geschätzt; **I ~ it to you that ...** (*BRIT*) ich behaupte, daß ...; **to stay ~** (an Ort und Stelle) bleiben.

▶**put about** *vi* (*NAUT*) den Kurs ändern ♦ *vt* (*rumour*) verbreiten.

▶**put across** *vt* (*ideas etc*) verständlich machen.

▶**put around** *vt* = **put about**.

▶**put aside** *vt* (*work*) zur Seite legen; (*idea, problem*) unbeachtet lassen; (*sum of money*) zurücklegen.

▶**put away** *vt* (*store*) wegräumen; (*inf: consume*) verdrücken; (*save: money*) zurücklegen; (*imprison*) einsperren.

▶**put back** *vt* (*replace*) zurücktun; (: *upright*) zurückstellen; (: *flat*) zurücklegen; (*postpone*) verschieben; (*delay*) zurückwerfen.

▶**put by** *vt* (*money, supplies etc*) zurücklegen.

▶**put down** *vt* (*upright*) hinstellen; (*flat*) hinlegen; (*cup, glass*) absetzen; (*in writing*) aufschreiben; (*riot, rebellion*) niederschlagen; (*humiliate*) demütigen; (*kill*) töten.

▶**put down to** *vt* (*attribute*) zurückführen auf +*acc*.

▶**put forward** *vt* (*ideas etc*) vorbringen;

(*watch, clock*) vorstellen; (*date, meeting*) vorverlegen.

►**put in** *vt* (*application, complaint*) einreichen; (*time, effort*) investieren; (*gas, electricity etc*) installieren ♦ *vi* (*NAUT*) einlaufen.

►**put in for** *vt fus* (*promotion*) sich bewerben um; (*leave*) beantragen.

►**put off** *vt* (*delay*) verschieben; (*distract*) ablenken; **to ~ sb off sth** (*discourage*) jdn von etw abbringen.

►**put on** *vt* (*clothes, brake*) anziehen; (*glasses, kettle*) aufsetzen; (*make-up, ointment etc*) auftragen; (*light, TV*) anmachen; (*play etc*) aufführen; (*record, tape, video*) auflegen; (*dinner etc*) aufsetzen; (*assume: look, behaviour etc*) annehmen; (*inf: tease*) auf den Arm nehmen; (*extra bus, train etc*) einsetzen; **to ~ on airs** sich zieren; **to ~ on weight** zunehmen.

►**put on to** *vt* (*tell about*) vermitteln.

►**put out** *vt* (*fire, light*) ausmachen; (*take out: rubbish*) herausbringen; (: *cat etc*) vor die Tür setzen; (*one's hand*) ausstrecken; (*story, announcement*) verbreiten; (*BRIT: dislocate: shoulder etc*) verrenken; (*inf: inconvenience*) Umstände machen +*dat* ♦ *vi* (*NAUT*): **to ~ out to sea** in See stechen; **to ~ out from Plymouth** von Plymouth auslaufen.

►**put through** *vt* (*TEL: person*) verbinden; (: *call*) durchstellen; (*plan, agreement*) durchbringen; **~ me through to Ms Blair** verbinden Sie mich mit Frau Blair.

►**put together** *vt* (*furniture etc*) zusammenbauen; (*plan, campaign*) ausarbeiten; **more than the rest of them ~ together** mehr als alle anderen zusammen.

►**put up** *vt* (*fence, building*) errichten; (*tent*) aufstellen; (*umbrella*) aufspannen; (*hood*) hochschlagen; (*poster, sign etc*) anbringen; (*price, cost*) erhöhen; (*accommodate*) unterbringen; **to ~ up resistance** Widerstand leisten; **to ~ up a fight** sich zur Wehr setzen; **to ~ sb up to sth** jdn zu etw anstiften; **to ~ sb up to doing sth** jdn dazu anstiften, etw zu tun; **to ~ sth up for sale** etw zum Verkauf anbieten.

►**put upon** *vt fus*: **to be ~ upon** (*imposed on*) ausgenutzt werden.

►**put up with** *vt fus* sich abfinden mit.

**putative** ['pju:tətɪv] *adj* mutmaßlich.

**putrid** ['pju:trɪd] *adj* (*mess, meat*) faul.

**putt** [pʌt] *n* Putt *m*.

**putter** ['pʌtə*] *n* (*GOLF*) Putter *m* ♦ *vi* (*US*) = **potter**.

**putting green** ['pʌtɪŋ-] *n* kleiner Golfplatz *m* zum Putten.

**putty** ['pʌtɪ] *n* Kitt *m*.

**put-up** ['putʌp] *adj*: **a ~ job** ein abgekartetes Spiel *nt*.

**puzzle** ['pʌzl] *n* (*game, toy*) Geschicklichkeitsspiel *nt*; (*mystery*) Rätsel *nt* ♦ *vt*

verwirren ♦ *vi*: **to ~ over sth** sich *dat* über etw *acc* den Kopf zerbrechen; **to be ~d as to why ...** vor einem Rätsel stehen, warum ...

**puzzling** ['pʌzlɪŋ] *adj* verwirrend; (*mysterious*) rätselhaft.

**PVC** *n abbr* (= *polyvinyl chloride*) PVC *nt*.

**Pvt.** (*US*) *abbr* (*MIL*) = **private**.

**PW** (*US*) *n abbr* = **prisoner of war**.

**p.w.** *abbr* (= *per week*) pro Woche.

**PX** (*US*) *n abbr* (*MIL*) = **post exchange**.

**pygmy** ['pɪgmɪ] *n* Pygmäe *m*.

**pyjamas**, (*US*) **pajamas** [pə'dʒɑːməz] *npl* Pyjama *m*, Schlafanzug *m*; **a pair of ~** ein Schlafanzug.

**pylon** ['paɪlən] *n* Mast *m*.

**pyramid** ['pɪrəmɪd] *n* Pyramide *f*.

**Pyrenean** [pɪrə'niːən] *adj* pyrenäisch.

**Pyrenees** [pɪrə'niːz] *npl*: **the ~** die Pyrenäen *pl*.

**Pyrex ®** ['paɪrɛks] *n* ≈ Jenaer Glas ® *nt* ♦ *adj* (*dish, bowl*) aus Jenaer Glas ®.

**python** ['paɪθən] *n* Pythonschlange *f*.

# Q, q

**Q, q** [kju:] *n* (*letter*) Q *nt*, q *nt*; **~ for Queen** ≈ Q wie Quelle.

**Qatar** [kæ'tɑː*] *n* Katar *nt*.

**QC** (*BRIT*) *n abbr* (*LAW:* = *Queen's Counsel*) Kronanwalt *m*.

QC (*kurz für Queen's Counsel, bzw.* KC *für King's Counsel*) ist in Großbritannien ein hochgestellter **barrister**, *der auf Empfehlung des Lordkanzlers ernannt wird und zum Zeichen seines Amtes einen seidenen Umhang trägt und daher auch als* **silk** *bezeichnet wird. Ein QC muß vor Gericht in Begleitung eines rangniedrigeren Anwaltes erscheinen.*

**QED** *abbr* (= *quod erat demonstrandum*) q.e.d.

**QM** *n abbr* (*MIL*) = **quartermaster**.

**q.t.** (*inf*) *n abbr* (= *quiet*): **on the ~** heimlich.

**qty** *abbr* = **quantity**.

**quack** [kwæk] *n* (*of duck*) Schnattern *nt*, Quaken *nt*; (*inf: pej: doctor*) Quacksalber *m* ♦ *vi* schnattern, quaken.

**quad** [kwɔd] *abbr* = **quadrangle**; (= *quadruplet*) Vierling *m*.

**quadrangle** ['kwɔdræŋgl] *n* (*courtyard*) Innenhof *m*.

**quadrilateral** [kwɔdrɪ'lætərəl] *n* Viereck *nt*.

**quadruped** ['kwɔdrupɛd] *n* Vierfüßer *m*.

**quadruple** [kwɔ'dru:pl] *vt* vervierfachen ♦ *vi* sich vervierfachen.

**quadruplets** [kwɔ'dru:plɪts] *npl* Vierlinge *pl*.

**quagmire** ['kwægmaɪəʳ] *n (also fig)* Sumpf *m*.
**quail** [kweɪl] *n* Wachtel *f* ♦ *vi:* **he ~ed at the thought/before her anger** ihm schauderte bei dem Gedanken/vor ihrem Zorn.
**quaint** [kweɪnt] *adj (house, village)* malerisch; *(ideas, customs)* urig, kurios.
**quake** [kweɪk] *vi* beben, zittern ♦ *n* = **earthquake**.
**Quaker** ['kweɪkəʳ] *n* Quäker(in) *m(f)*.
**qualification** [kwɔlɪfɪ'keɪʃən] *n (often pl: degree etc)* Qualifikation *f; (attribute)* Voraussetzung *f; (reservation)* Vorbehalt *m;* **what are your ~s?** welche Qualifikationen haben Sie?
**qualified** ['kwɔlɪfaɪd] *adj (trained: doctor etc)* qualifiziert, ausgebildet; *(limited: agreement, praise)* bedingt; **to be/feel ~ to do sth** *(fit, competent)* qualifiziert sein/sich qualifiziert fühlen, etw zu tun; **it was a ~ success** es war kein voller Erfolg; **he's not ~ for the job** ihm fehlen die Qualifikationen für die Stelle.
**qualify** ['kwɔlɪfaɪ] *vt (entitle)* qualifizieren; *(modify: statement)* einschränken ♦ *vi (pass examination)* sich qualifizieren; **to ~ for** *(be eligible)* die Berechtigung erlangen für; *(in competition)* sich qualifizieren für; **to ~ as an engineer** die Ausbildung zum Ingenieur abschließen.
**qualifying** ['kwɔlɪfaɪɪŋ] *adj:* **~ exam** Auswahlprüfung *f;* **~ round** Qualifikationsrunde *f*.
**qualitative** ['kwɔlɪtətɪv] *adj* qualitativ.
**quality** ['kwɔlɪtɪ] *n* Qualität *f; (characteristic)* Eigenschaft *f* ♦ *cpd* Qualitäts-; **of good/poor ~** von guter/schlechter Qualität; **~ of life** Lebensqualität *f*.
**quality control** *n* Qualitätskontrolle *f*.
**quality papers** *(BRIT) npl:* **the ~** die seriösen Zeitungen *pl*.

> **Quality press** *bezeichnet die auf die seriösen Tages- und Wochenzeitungen, im Gegensatz zu den Massenblättern. Diese Zeitungen sind fast alle großformatig und wenden sich an den anspruchsvolleren Leser, der voll informiert sein möchte und bereit ist, für die Zeitungslektüre viel Zeit aufzuwenden. Siehe auch* **tabloid press**.

**qualm** [kwɑːm] *n* Bedenken *pl;* **to have ~s about sth** Bedenken wegen etw haben.
**quandary** ['kwɔndrɪ] *n:* **to be in a ~** in einem Dilemma sein.
**quango** ['kwæŋgəʊ] *(BRIT) n abbr (= quasi-autonomous nongovernmental organization)* ≈ (regierungsunabhängige) Kommission *f*.
**quantifiable** ['kwɔntɪfaɪəbl] *adj* quantifizierbar.
**quantitative** ['kwɔntɪtətɪv] *adj* quantitativ.

**quantity** ['kwɔntɪtɪ] *n (amount)* Menge *f;* **in large/small quantities** in großen/kleinen Mengen; **in ~** *(in bulk)* in großen Mengen; **an unknown ~** *(fig)* eine unbekannte Größe.
**quantity surveyor** *n* Baukostenkalkulator(in) *m(f)*.
**quantum leap** ['kwɔntəm-] *n (PHYS)* Quantensprung *m; (fig)* Riesenschritt *m*.
**quarantine** ['kwɔrntiːn] *n* Quarantäne *f;* **in ~** in Quarantäne.
**quark** [kwɑːk] *n (cheese)* Quark *m; (PHYS)* Quark *nt*.
**quarrel** ['kwɔrl] *n (argument)* Streit *m* ♦ *vi* sich streiten; **to have a ~ with sb** sich mit jdm streiten; **I've no ~ with him** ich habe nichts gegen ihn; **I can't ~ with that** dagegen kann ich nichts einwenden.
**quarrelsome** ['kwɔrəlsəm] *adj* streitsüchtig.
**quarry** ['kwɔrɪ] *n (for stone)* Steinbruch *m; (prey)* Beute *f* ♦ *vt (marble etc)* brechen.
**quart** [kwɔːt] *n* Quart *nt*.
**quarter** ['kwɔːtəʳ] *n* Viertel *nt; (US: coin)* 25-Cent-Stück *nt; (of year)* Quartal *nt; (district)* Viertel *nt* ♦ *vt (divide)* vierteln; *(MIL: lodge)* einquartieren; **quarters** *npl (MIL)* Quartier *nt; (also: living ~s)* Unterkünfte *pl;* **a ~ of an hour** eine Viertelstunde; **it's a ~ to three,** *(US)* **it's a ~ of three** es ist Viertel vor drei; **it's a ~ past three,** *(US)* **it's a ~ after three** es ist Viertel nach drei; **from all ~s** aus allen Richtungen; **at close ~s** aus unmittelbarer Nähe.
**quarterback** ['kwɔːtəbæk] *n (AMERICAN FOOTBALL)* Quarterback *m*.
**quarterdeck** ['kwɔːtədɛk] *n (NAUT)* Quarterdeck *nt*.
**quarterfinal** ['kwɔːtə'faɪnl] *n* Viertelfinale *nt*.
**quarterly** ['kwɔːtəlɪ] *adj, adv* vierteljährlich ♦ *n* Vierteljahresschrift *f*.
**quartermaster** ['kwɔːtəmɑːstəʳ] *n (MIL)* Quartiermeister *m*.
**quartet** [kwɔː'tɛt] *n (MUS)* Quartett *nt*.
**quarto** ['kwɔːtəʊ] *n (size of paper)* Quartformat *nt; (book)* im Quartformat.
**quartz** [kwɔːts] *n* Quarz *m* ♦ *cpd (watch, clock)* Quarz-.
**quash** [kwɔʃ] *vt (verdict)* aufheben.
**quasi-** ['kweɪzaɪ] *pref* quasi-.
**quaver** ['kweɪvəʳ] *n (BRIT: MUS)* Achtelnote *f* ♦ *vi (voice)* beben, zittern.
**quay** [kiː] *n* Kai *m*.
**quayside** ['kiːsaɪd] *n* Kai *m*.
**queasiness** ['kwiːzɪnɪs] *n* Übelkeit *f*.
**queasy** ['kwiːzɪ] *adj (nauseous)* übel; **I feel ~** mir ist übel *or* schlecht.
**Quebec** [kwɪ'bɛk] *n* Quebec *nt*.
**queen** [kwiːn] *n (also ZOOL)* Königin *f; (CARDS, CHESS)* Dame *f*.
**queen mother** *n* Königinmutter *f*.
**Queen's speech** *(BRIT) n* ≈ Regierungserklärung *f*.

**Queen's Speech** (*bzw* **King's Speech**) *ist eine vom britischen Monarchen bei der feierlichen alljährlichen Parlamentseröffnung im Oberhaus vor dem versammelten Ober- und Unterhaus verlesene Rede. Sie wird vom Premierminister in Zusammenarbeit mit dem Kabinett verfaßt und enthält die Regierungserklärung.*

**queer** [kwɪə'] *adj* (*odd*) sonderbar, seltsam ♦ *n* (*infl: pej: male homosexual*) Schwule(r) *m*; **I feel** ~ (*BRIT: unwell*) mir ist ganz komisch.

**quell** [kwɛl] *vt* (*riot*) niederschlagen; (*fears*) überwinden.

**quench** [kwɛntʃ] *vt:* **to** ~ **one's thirst** seinen Durst stillen.

**querulous** ['kwɛrʊləs] *adj* nörglerisch.

**query** ['kwɪərɪ] *n* Anfrage *f* ♦ *vt* (*check*) nachfragen bezüglich +*gen*; (*express doubt about*) bezweifeln.

**quest** [kwɛst] *n* Suche *f*.

**question** ['kwɛstʃən] *n* Frage *f* ♦ *vt* (*interrogate*) befragen; (*doubt*) bezweifeln; **to ask sb a** ~, **put a** ~ **to sb** jdm eine Frage stellen; **to bring** *or* **call sth into** ~ etw in Frage stellen; **the** ~ **is** ... die Frage ist ...; **there's no** ~ **of him playing for England** es ist ausgeschlossen, daß er für England spielt; **the person/night in** ~ die fragliche Person/Nacht; **to be beyond** ~ außer Frage stehen; **to be out of the** ~ nicht in Frage kommen.

**questionable** ['kwɛstʃənəbl] *adj* fraglich.

**questioner** ['kwɛstʃənə'] *n* Fragesteller(in) *m(f)*.

**questioning** ['kwɛstʃənɪŋ] *adj* (*look*) fragend; (*mind*) forschend ♦ *n* (*POLICE*) Vernehmung *f*.

**question mark** *n* Fragezeichen *nt*.

**questionnaire** [kwɛstʃə'nɛə'] *n* Fragebogen *m*.

**queue** [kjuː] (*BRIT*) *n* Schlange *f* ♦ *vi* (*also:* ~ **up**) Schlange stehen.

**quibble** ['kwɪbl] *vi:* **to** ~ **about** *or* **over** sich streiten über +*acc*; **to** ~ **with** herumnörgeln an +*dat* ♦ *n* Krittelei *f*.

**quiche** [kiːʃ] *n* Quiche *f*.

**quick** [kwɪk] *adj* schnell; (*mind, wit*) wach; (*look, visit*) flüchtig ♦ *adv* schnell ♦ *n:* **to cut sb to the** ~ (*fig*) jdn tief verletzen; **be** ~! mach schnell!; **to be** ~ **to act** schnell handeln; **she was** ~ **to see that** ... sie begriff schnell, daß ...; **she has a** ~ **temper** sie wird leicht hitzig.

**quicken** ['kwɪkən] *vt* beschleunigen ♦ *vi* schneller werden, sich beschleunigen.

**quick-fire** ['kwɪkfaɪə'] *adj* (*questions*) wie aus der Maschinenpistole.

**quick fix** *n* Sofortlösung *f*.

**quicklime** ['kwɪklaɪm] *n* ungelöschter Kalk *m*.

**quickly** ['kwɪklɪ] *adv* schnell.

**quickness** ['kwɪknɪs] *n* Schnelligkeit *f*; ~ **of mind** Scharfsinn *m*.

**quicksand** ['kwɪksænd] *n* Treibsand *m*.

**quickstep** ['kwɪkstɛp] *n* Quickstep *m*.

**quick-tempered** [kwɪk'tɛmpəd] *adj* hitzig, leicht erregbar.

**quick-witted** [kwɪk'wɪtɪd] *adj* schlagfertig.

**quid** [kwɪd] (*BRIT: inf*) *n inv* Pfund *nt*.

**quid pro quo** ['kwɪdprəʊ'kwəʊ] *n* Gegenleistung *f*.

**quiet** ['kwaɪət] *adj* leise; (*place*) ruhig, still; (*silent, reserved*) still; (*business, day*) ruhig; (*without fuss etc: wedding*) in kleinem Rahmen ♦ *n* (*peacefulness*) Stille *f*, Ruhe *f*; (*silence*) Ruhe *f* ♦ *vt, vi* (*US*) = **quieten**; **keep** *or* **be** ~! sei still!; **I'll have a** ~ **word with him** ich werde mal unter vier Augen mit ihm reden; **on the** ~ (*in secret*) heimlich.

**quieten** ['kwaɪətn] (*BRIT: also:* ~ **down**) *vi* ruhiger werden ♦ *vt* (*person, animal*) beruhigen.

**quietly** ['kwaɪətlɪ] *adv* leise; (*silently*) still; (*calmly*) ruhig; ~ **confident** insgeheim sicher.

**quietness** ['kwaɪətnɪs] *n* (*peacefulness*) Ruhe *f*; (*silence*) Stille *f*.

**quill** [kwɪl] *n* (*pen*) Feder *f*; (*of porcupine*) Stachel *m*.

**quilt** [kwɪlt] *n* Decke *f*; (*also:* **continental** ~) Federbett *nt*.

**quin** [kwɪn] (*BRIT*) *n abbr* (= *quintuplet*) Fünfling *m*.

**quince** [kwɪns] *n* Quitte *f*.

**quinine** [kwɪ'niːn] *n* Chinin *nt*.

**quintet** [kwɪn'tɛt] *n* (*MUS*) Quintett *nt*.

**quintuplets** [kwɪn'tjuːplɪts] *npl* Fünflinge *pl*.

**quip** [kwɪp] *n* witzige *or* geistreiche Bemerkung *f* ♦ *vt* witzeln.

**quire** ['kwaɪə'] *n* (*of paper*) 24 Bogen Papier.

**quirk** [kwɔːk] *n* Marotte *f*; **a** ~ **of fate** eine Laune des Schicksals.

**quit** [kwɪt] (*pt, pp* **quit** *or* **quitted**) *vt* (*smoking*) aufgeben; (*job*) kündigen; (*premises*) verlassen ♦ *vi* (*give up*) aufgeben; (*resign*) kündigen; **to** ~ **doing sth** aufhören, etw zu tun; ~ **stalling!** (*US: inf*) weichen Sie nicht ständig aus!; **notice to** ~ (*BRIT*) Kündigung *f*.

**quite** [kwaɪt] *adv* (*rather*) ziemlich; (*entirely*) ganz; **not** ~ nicht ganz; **I** ~ **like it** ich mag es ganz gern; **I** ~ **understand** ich verstehe; **I don't** ~ **remember** ich erinnere mich nicht genau; **not** ~ **as many as the last time** nicht ganz so viele wie das letzte Mal; **that meal was** ~ **something!** das Essen konnte sich sehen lassen!; **it was** ~ **a sight** das war vielleicht ein Anblick; ~ **a few of them** eine ganze Reihe von Ihnen; ~ **(so)!** ganz recht!

**quits** [kwɪts] *adj:* **we're** ~ wir sind quitt; **let's call it** ~ lassen wir's dabei.

**quiver** ['kwɪvə'] *vi* zittern.

**quiz** [kwɪz] *n* (*game*) Quiz *nt* ♦ *vt* (*question*)

befragen.
**quizzical** ['kwɪzɪkl] *adj (look, smile)* wissend.
**quoits** [kwɔɪts] *npl (game)* Wurfspiel mit
Ringen.
**quorum** ['kwɔːrəm] *n* Quorum *nt*.
**quota** ['kwəʊtə] *n (allowance)* Quote *f*.
**quotation** [kwəʊ'teɪʃən] *n (from book etc)* Zitat
*nt; (estimate)* Preisangabe *f; (COMM)*
Kostenvoranschlag *m*.
**quotation marks** *npl* Anführungszeichen *pl*.
**quote** [kwəʊt] *n (from book etc)* Zitat *nt;*
*(estimate)* Kostenvoranschlag *m* ♦ *vt*
zitieren; *(fact, example)* anführen; *(price)*
nennen; **quotes** *npl (quotation marks)*
Anführungszeichen *pl;* **in** ~**s** in
Anführungszeichen; **the figure** ~**d for the**
**repairs** die für die Reparatur genannte
Summe; ~ ... **unquote** Zitat Anfang ... Zitat
Ende.
**quotient** ['kwəʊʃənt] *n* Quotient *m*.
**qv** *abbr (= quod vide)* s.d.
**qwerty keyboard** ['kwə:tɪ-] *n* Qwerty-
Tastatur *f*.

# R, r

**R¹, r** [ɑː*] *n (letter)* R *nt*, r *nt;* ~ **for Robert,** *(US)*
~ **for Roger** ≈ R wie Richard.
**R²** [ɑː*] *abbr (= Réaumur (scale))* R; *(US: CINE:*
*= restricted) Klassifikation für nicht*
*jugendfreie Filme.*
**R.** *abbr (= right)* r.; = **river;** *(US: POL)*
= **republican;** *(BRIT:* = *Rex)* König; *(= Regina)*
*Königin.*
**RA** *abbr (MIL)* = **rear admiral** ♦ *n abbr (BRIT:*
= *Royal Academy) Gesellschaft zur*
*Förderung der Künste;* (= *Royal*
*Academician) Mitglied der Royal Academy.*
**RAAF** *n abbr (MIL:* = *Royal Australian Air Force)*
australische Luftwaffe *f*.
**Rabat** [rə'bɑːt] *n* Rabat *nt*.
**rabbi** ['ræbaɪ] *n* Rabbi *m*.
**rabbit** ['ræbɪt] *n* Kaninchen *nt* ♦ *vi (BRIT: inf:*
*also:* **to** ~ **on)** quatschen, schwafeln.
**rabbit hole** *n* Kaninchenbau *m*.
**rabbit hutch** *n* Kaninchenstall *m*.
**rabble** ['ræbl] *(pej)* Pöbel *m*.
**rabid** ['ræbɪd] *adj (animal)* tollwütig; *(fig:*
*fanatical)* fanatisch.
**rabies** ['reɪbiːz] *n* Tollwut *f*.
**RAC** *(BRIT) n abbr (= Royal Automobile Club)*
*Autofahrerorganisation,* ≈ ADAC *m*.
**raccoon** [rə'kuːn] *n* = **raccoon.**
**race** [reɪs] *n (species)* Rasse *f; (competition)*
Rennen *nt; (for power, control)* Wettlauf *m*

♦ *vt (horse, pigeon)* an Wettbewerben
teilnehmen lassen; *(car etc)* ins Rennen
schicken; *(person)* um die Wette laufen mit
♦ *vi (compete)* antreten; *(hurry)* rennen;
*(pulse, heart)* rasen; *(engine)* durchdrehen;
**the human** ~ die Menschheit; **a** ~ **against**
**time** ein Wettlauf mit der Zeit; **he** ~**d across**
**the road** er raste über die Straße; **to** ~ **in/**
**out** hinein-/hinausstürzen.
**race car** *(US) n* = **racing car.**
**race car driver** *(US) n* = **racing driver.**
**racecourse** ['reɪskɔːs] *n* Rennbahn *f*.
**racehorse** ['reɪshɔːs] *n* Rennpferd *nt*.
**race meeting** *n* Rennveranstaltung *f*.
**race relations** *npl* Beziehungen *pl* zwischen
den Rassen.
**racetrack** ['reɪstræk] *n* Rennbahn *f; (US)*
= **racecourse.**
**racial** ['reɪʃl] *adj* Rassen-.
**racialism** ['reɪʃlɪzəm] *n* Rassismus *m*.
**racialist** ['reɪʃlɪst] *adj* rassistisch ♦ *n (pej)*
Rassist(in) *m(f)*.
**racing** ['reɪsɪŋ] *n (horse racing)* Pferderennen
*nt; (motor racing)* Rennsport *m*.
**racing car** *(BRIT) n* Rennwagen *m*.
**racing driver** *(BRIT) n* Rennfahrer(in) *m(f)*.
**racism** ['reɪsɪzəm] *n* Rassismus *m*.
**racist** ['reɪsɪst] *adj* rassistisch ♦ *n (pej)*
Rassist(in) *m(f)*.
**rack** [ræk] *n (also:* **luggage** ~) Gepäckablage *f;*
*(also:* **roof** ~) Dachgepäckträger *m; (for*
*dresses etc)* Ständer *m; (for dishes)* Gestell *nt*
♦ *vt:* ~**ed by** *(pain etc)* gemartert von;
**magazine/toast** ~ Zeitungs-/Toastständer
*m;* **to** ~ **one's brains** sich *dat* den Kopf
zerbrechen; **to go to** ~ **and ruin** *(building)*
zerfallen; *(business, country)*
herunterkommen.
**racket** ['rækɪt] *n (for tennis etc)* Schläger *m;*
*(noise)* Krach *m*, Radau *m; (swindle)*
Schwindel *m*.
**racketeer** [rækɪ'tɪə*] *(esp US) n* Gangster *m*.
**racoon** [rə'kuːn] *n* = **raccoon.**
**racquet** ['rækɪt] *n (for tennis etc)* Schläger *m*.
**racy** ['reɪsɪ] *adj (book, story)* rasant.
**RADA** [rɑːdə] *(BRIT) n abbr (= Royal Academy of*
*Dramatic Art) Schauspielschule.*
**radar** ['reɪdɑː*] *n* Radar *m* or *nt* ♦ *cpd* Radar-.
**radar trap** *n* Radarfalle *f*.
**radial** ['reɪdɪəl] *adj (roads)* strahlenförmig
verlaufend; *(pattern)* strahlenförmig ♦ *n*
*(also:* ~ **tyre)** Gürtelreifen *m*.
**radiance** ['reɪdɪəns] *n* Glanz *m*.
**radiant** ['reɪdɪənt] *adj* strahlend; *(PHYS: heat)*
Strahlungs-.
**radiate** ['reɪdɪeɪt] *vt (lit, fig)* ausstrahlen ♦ *vi*
*(lines, roads)* strahlenförmig verlaufen.
**radiation** [reɪdɪ'eɪʃən] *n (radioactivity)*
radioaktive Strahlung *f; (from sun etc)*
Strahlung *f*.
**radiation sickness** *n* Strahlenkrankheit *f*.
**radiator** ['reɪdɪeɪtə*] *n (heater)* Heizkörper *m;*

(*AUT*) Kühler m.
**radiator cap** n (*AUT*) Kühlerdeckel m.
**radiator grill** n (*AUT*) Kühlergrill m.
**radical** ['rædɪkl] adj radikal ♦ n (*person*)
Radikale(r) f(m).
**radii** ['reɪdɪaɪ] npl of **radius**.
**radio** ['reɪdɪəʊ] n (*broadcasting*) Radio nt,
Rundfunk m; (*device: for receiving broadcasts*)
Radio nt; (*: for transmitting and receiving*)
Funkgerät nt ♦ vi: **to ~ to sb** mit jdm per
Funk sprechen ♦ vt (*person*) per Funk
verständigen; (*message, position*) per Funk
durchgeben; **on the ~** im Radio.
**radio...** ['reɪdɪəʊ] pref Radio..., radio...
**radioactive** ['reɪdɪəʊ'æktɪv] adj radioaktiv.
**radioactivity** ['reɪdɪəʊæk'tɪvɪtɪ] n
Radioaktivität f.
**radio announcer** n Rundfunksprecher(in)
m(f).
**radio-controlled** ['reɪdɪəʊkən'trəʊld] adj
ferngesteuert.
**radiographer** [reɪdɪ'ɒɡrəfə*] n Röntgenologe
m, Röntgenologin f.
**radiography** [reɪdɪ'ɒɡrəfɪ] n Röntgenographie
f.
**radiologist** [reɪdɪ'ɒlədʒɪst] n Radiologe m,
Radiologin f.
**radiology** [reɪdɪ'ɒlədʒɪ] n Radiologie f.
**radio station** n Radiosender m.
**radio taxi** n Funktaxi nt.
**radiotelephone** ['reɪdɪəʊ'telɪfəʊn] n
Funksprechgerät nt.
**radio telescope** n Radioteleskop nt.
**radiotherapist** ['reɪdɪəʊ'θerəpɪst] n
Strahlentherapeut(in) m(f).
**radiotherapy** ['reɪdɪəʊ'θerəpɪ] n
Strahlentherapie f.
**radish** ['rædɪʃ] n Radieschen nt; (*long white
variety*) Rettich m.
**radium** ['reɪdɪəm] n Radium nt.
**radius** ['reɪdɪəs] (pl **radii**) n Radius m; (*area*)
Umkreis m; **within a ~ of 50 miles** in einem
Umkreis von 50 Meilen.
**RAF** (*BRIT*) n abbr = **Royal Air Force**.
**raffia** ['ræfɪə] n Bast m.
**raffish** ['ræfɪʃ] adj (*person*) verwegen; (*place*)
verkommen.
**raffle** ['ræfl] n Verlosung f, Tombola f ♦ vt
(*prize*) verlosen; **~ ticket** Los nt.
**raft** [rɑːft] n Floß nt; (*also: life ~*) Rettungsfloß
nt.
**rafter** ['rɑːftə*] n Dachsparren m.
**rag** [ræg] n (*piece of cloth*) Lappen m; (*torn
cloth*) Fetzen m; (*pej: newspaper*) Käseblatt
nt; (*BRIT: UNIV*) studentische
Wohltätigkeitsveranstaltung ♦ vt (*BRIT:
tease*) aufziehen; **rags** npl (*torn clothes*)
Lumpen pl; **in ~s** (*person*) zerlumpt; **his was
a ~s-to-riches story** er brachte es vom
Tellerwäscher zum Millionär.
**rag-and-bone man** [rægən'bəʊn-] (*BRIT*) n
Lumpensammler m.

**ragbag** ['rægbæg] n (*assortment*)
Sammelsurium nt.

---

**Rag Day/Week** heißt der Tag bzw. die Woche,
wenn Studenten Geld für wohltätige Zwecke
sammeln. Diverse gesponserte Aktionen wie
Volksläufe, Straßentheater und Kneipentouren
werden zur Unterhaltung der Studenten und
der Bevölkerung organisiert.
Studentenzeitschriften mit schlüpfrigen Witzen
werden auf der Straße verkauft, und fast alle
Universitäten und Colleges halten einen Ball
ab. Der Erlös aller Veranstaltungen fließt
Wohltätigkeitsorganisationen zu.

---

**rag doll** n Stoffpuppe f.
**rage** [reɪdʒ] n (*fury*) Wut f, Zorn m ♦ vi toben,
wüten; **it's all the ~** (*fashionable*) es ist der
letzte Schrei; **to fly into a ~** einen Wutanfall
bekommen.
**ragged** ['rægɪd] adj (*jagged*) zackig; (*clothes,
person*) zerlumpt; (*beard*) ausgefranst.
**raging** ['reɪdʒɪŋ] adj (*sea, storm, torrent*)
tobend, tosend; (*fever*) heftig; (*thirst*)
brennend; (*toothache*) rasend.
**rag trade** (*inf*) n: **the ~** die Modebranche f.
**raid** [reɪd] n (*MIL*) Angriff m, Überfall m; (*by
police*) Razzia f; (*by criminal: forcefully*)
Überfall m; (*: secretly*) Einbruch m ♦ vt (*MIL*)
angreifen, überfallen; (*police*) stürmen;
(*criminal: forcefully*) überfallen; (*: secretly*)
einbrechen in +acc.
**rail** [reɪl] n Geländer nt; (*on deck of ship*) Reling
f; **rails** npl (*for train*) Schienen pl; **by ~** mit der
Bahn.
**railcard** ['reɪlkɑːd] (*BRIT*) n (*for young people*)
≈ Juniorenpaß m; (*for pensioners*)
≈ Seniorenpaß m.
**railing(s)** ['reɪlɪŋ(z)] n(pl) (*fence*) Zaun m.
**railroad** ['reɪlrəʊd] (*US*) n = **railway**.
**railway** ['reɪlweɪ] (*BRIT*) n Eisenbahn f; (*track*)
Gleis nt; (*company*) Bahn f.
**railway engine** (*BRIT*) n Lokomotive f.
**railway line** (*BRIT*) n Bahnlinie f; (*track*) Gleis
nt.
**railwayman** ['reɪlweɪmən] (*irreg: like* **man**)
(*BRIT*) n Eisenbahner m.
**railway station** (*BRIT*) n Bahnhof m.
**rain** [reɪn] n Regen m ♦ vi regnen; **in the ~** im
Regen; **as right as ~** voll auf der Höhe; **it's
~ing** es regnet; **it's ~ing cats and dogs** es
regnet in Strömen.
**rainbow** ['reɪnbəʊ] n Regenbogen m.
**rain check** (*US*) n: **to take a ~ on sth** sich dat
etw noch einmal überlegen.
**raincoat** ['reɪnkəʊt] n Regenmantel m.
**raindrop** ['reɪndrɒp] n Regentropfen m.
**rainfall** ['reɪnfɔːl] n Niederschlag m.
**rainforest** ['reɪnfɒrɪst] n Regenwald m.
**rainproof** ['reɪnpruːf] adj wasserfest.
**rainstorm** ['reɪnstɔːm] n schwere Regenfälle
pl.

**rainwater** ['reɪnwɔːtəˀ] *n* Regenwasser *nt*.

**rainy** ['reɪnɪ] *adj* (*day*) regnerisch, verregnet; (*area*) regenreich; ~ **season** Regenzeit *f*; **to save sth for a** ~ **day** etw für schlechte Zeiten aufheben.

**raise** [reɪz] *n* (*pay rise*) Gehaltserhöhung *f* ♦ *vt* (*lift: hand*) hochheben; (: *window*) hochziehen; (*siege*) beenden; (*embargo*) aufheben; (*increase*) erhöhen; (*improve*) verbessern; (*question etc*) zur Sprache bringen; (*doubts etc*) vorbringen; (*child, cattle*) aufziehen; (*crop*) anbauen; (*army*) aufstellen; (*funds*) aufbringen; (*loan*) aufnehmen; **to** ~ **a glass to sb/sth** das Glas auf jdn/etw erheben; **to** ~ **one's voice** die Stimme erheben; **to** ~ **sb's hopes** jdm Hoffnungen machen; **to** ~ **a laugh/smile** Gelächter/ein Lächeln hervorrufen; **this** ~**s the question...** das wirft die Frage auf...

**raisin** ['reɪzn] *n* Rosine *f*.

**Raj** [rɑːdʒ] *n*: **the** ~ *britische Regierung in Indien vor 1947*.

**rajah** ['rɑːdʒə] *n* Radscha *m*.

**rake** [reɪk] *n* Harke *f*; (*old: person*) Schwerenöter *m* ♦ *vt* harken; (*light, gun: area*) bestreichen; **he's raking it in** (*inf*) er scheffelt das Geld nur so.

**rake-off** ['reɪkɔf] (*inf*) *n* Anteil *m*.

**rally** ['rælɪ] *n* (*POL etc*) Kundgebung *f*; (*AUT*) Rallye *f*; (*TENNIS etc*) Ballwechsel *m* ♦ *vt* (*support*) sammeln ♦ *vi* (*sick person, Stock Exchange*) sich erholen.

▶**rally round** *vi* sich zusammentun ♦ *vt fus* zu Hilfe kommen +*dat*.

**rallying point** ['rælɪɪŋ-] *n* Sammelstelle *f*.

**RAM** [ræm] *n abbr* (*COMPUT: = random access memory*) RAM.

**ram** [ræm] *n* Widder *m* ♦ *vt* rammen.

**ramble** ['ræmbl] *n* Wanderung *f* ♦ *vi* wandern; (*also*: ~ **on**: *talk*) schwafeln.

**rambler** ['ræmbləˀ] *n* Wanderer *m*, Wanderin *f*; (*BOT*) Kletterrose *f*.

**rambling** ['ræmblɪŋ] *adj* (*speech, letter*) weitschweifig; (*house*) weitläufig; (*BOT*) rankend, Kletter-.

**rambunctious** [ræm'bʌŋkʃəs] (*US*) *adj* = **rumbustious**.

**RAMC** (*BRIT*) *n abbr* (= *Royal Army Medical Corps*) *Verband zur Versorgung der Armee mit Stabsärzten und Sanitätern*.

**ramifications** [ræmɪfɪ'keɪʃənz] *npl* Auswirkungen *pl*.

**ramp** [ræmp] *n* Rampe *f*; (*in garage*) Hebebühne *f*; **on** ~ (*US: AUT*) Auffahrt *f*; **off** ~ (*US: AUT*) Ausfahrt *f*.

**rampage** [ræm'peɪdʒ] *n*: **to be/go on the** ~ randalieren ♦ *vi*: **they went rampaging through the town** sie zogen randalierend durch die Stadt.

**rampant** ['ræmpənt] *adj*: **to be** ~ (*crime, disease etc*) wild wuchern.

**rampart** ['ræmpɑːt] *n* Schutzwall *m*.

**ram raiding** [-reɪdɪŋ] *n* Einbruchdiebstahl, *wobei die Diebe mit einem Wagen in die Schaufensterfront eines Ladens eindringen*.

**ramshackle** ['ræmʃækl] *adj* (*house*) baufällig; (*cart*) klapprig; (*table*) altersschwach.

**RAN** *n abbr* (= *Royal Australian Navy*) australische Marine *f*.

**ran** [ræn] *pt of* **run**.

**ranch** [rɑːntʃ] *n* Ranch *f*.

**rancher** ['rɑːntʃəˀ] *n* Rancher(in) *m(f)*; (*worker*) Farmhelfer(in) *m(f)*.

**rancid** ['rænsɪd] *adj* ranzig.

**rancour**, (*US*) **rancor** ['ræŋkəˀ] *n* Verbitterung *f*.

**R & B** *n abbr* (= *rhythm and blues*) R & B.

**R & D** *n abbr* = **research and development**.

**random** ['rændəm] *adj* (*arrangement*) willkürlich; (*selection*) zufällig; (*COMPUT*) wahlfrei; (*MATH*) Zufalls- ♦ *n*: **at** ~ aufs Geratewohl.

**random access** *n* (*COMPUT*) wahlfreier Zugriff *m*.

**random access memory** *n* (*COMPUT*) Schreib-Lese-Speicher *m*.

**R & R** (*US*) *n abbr* (*MIL*: = *rest and recreation*) Urlaub *m*.

**randy** ['rændɪ] (*BRIT: inf*) *adj* geil, scharf.

**rang** [ræŋ] *pt of* **ring**.

**range** [reɪndʒ] *n* (*of mountains*) Kette *f*; (*of missile*) Reichweite *f*; (*of voice*) Umfang *m*; (*series*) Reihe *f*; (*of products*) Auswahl *f*; (*MIL: also: rifle* ~) Schießstand *m*; (*also: kitchen* ~) Herd *m* ♦ *vt* (*place in a line*) anordnen ♦ *vi*: **to** ~ **over** (*extend*) sich erstrecken über +*acc*; **price** ~ Preisspanne *f*; **do you have anything else in this price** ~? haben Sie noch etwas anderes in dieser Preisklasse?; **within (firing)** ~ in Schußweite; **at close** ~ aus unmittelbarer Entfernung; ~**d left/right** (*text*) links-/rechtsbündig; **to** ~ **from ... to ...** sich zwischen ... und ... bewegen.

**ranger** ['reɪndʒəˀ] *n* Förster(in) *m(f)*.

**Rangoon** [ræŋ'guːn] *n* Rangun *nt*.

**rank** [ræŋk] *n* (*row*) Reihe *f*; (*MIL*) Rang *m*; (*social class*) Schicht *f*; (*BRIT: also: taxi* ~) Taxistand *m* ♦ *vi*: **to** ~ **as/among** zählen zu ♦ *vt*: **he is** ~**ed third in the world** er steht weltweit an dritter Stelle ♦ *adj* (*stinking*) stinkend; (*sheer: hypocrisy etc*) rein; **the ranks** *npl* (*MIL*) die Mannschaften *pl*; **the** ~ **and file** (*ordinary members*) die Basis *f*; **to close** ~**s** (*fig, MIL*) die Reihen schließen.

**rankle** ['ræŋkl] *vi* (*insult*) nachwirken; **to** ~ **with sb** jdn wurmen.

**rank outsider** *n* totaler Außenseiter *m*, totale Außenseiterin *f*.

**ransack** ['rænsæk] *vt* (*search*) durchwühlen; (*plunder*) plündern.

**ransom** ['rænsəm] *n* (*money*) Lösegeld *nt*; **to hold sb to** ~ (*hostage*) jdn als Geisel halten; (*fig*) jdn erpressen.

**rant** [rænt] *vi* schimpfen, wettern; **to** ~ **and**

**rave** herumwettern.

**ranting** ['ræntɪŋ] n Geschimpfe nt.

**rap** [ræp] vi klopfen ♦ vt: to ~ **sb's knuckles** jdm auf die Finger klopfen ♦ n (at door) Klopfen nt; (also: ~ **music**) Rap m.

**rape** [reɪp] n Vergewaltigung f; (BOT) Raps m ♦ vt vergewaltigen.

**rape(seed) oil** ['reɪp(siːd)-] n Rapsöl nt.

**rapid** ['ræpɪd] adj schnell; (growth, change) schnell, rapide.

**rapidity** [rə'pɪdɪtɪ] n Schnelligkeit f.

**rapidly** ['ræpɪdlɪ] adv schnell; (grow, change) schnell, rapide.

**rapids** ['ræpɪdz] npl Stromschnellen pl.

**rapist** ['reɪpɪst] n Vergewaltiger m.

**rapport** [ræ'pɔː'] n enges Verhältnis nt.

**rapprochement** [ræ'prɒʃmɑ̃ːŋ] n Annäherung f.

**rapt** [ræpt] adj (attention) gespannt; **to be ~ in thought** in Gedanken versunken sein.

**rapture** ['ræptʃə'] n Entzücken nt; **to go into ~s over** ins Schwärmen geraten über +acc.

**rapturous** ['ræptʃərəs] adj (applause, welcome) stürmisch.

**rare** [reə'] adj selten; (steak) nur angebraten; englisch (gebraten); **it is ~ to find that ...** es kommt nur selten vor, daß ...

**rarebit** ['reəbɪt] n see **Welsh rarebit**.

**rarefied** ['reərɪfaɪd] adj (air, atmosphere) dünn; (fig) exklusiv.

**rarely** ['reəlɪ] adv selten.

**raring** ['reərɪŋ] adj: ~ **to go** (inf) in den Startlöchern.

**rarity** ['reərɪtɪ] n Seltenheit f.

**rascal** ['rɑːskl] n (child) Frechdachs m; (rogue) Schurke m.

**rash** [ræʃ] adj (person) unbesonnen; (promise, act) übereilt ♦ n (MED) Ausschlag m; (of events etc) Flut f; **to come out in a ~** einen Ausschlag bekommen.

**rasher** ['ræʃə'] n (of bacon) Scheibe f.

**rashly** ['ræʃlɪ] adv (promise etc) voreilig.

**rasp** [rɑːsp] n (tool) Raspel f; (sound) Kratzen nt ♦ vt, vi krächzen.

**raspberry** ['rɑːzbərɪ] n Himbeere f; ~ **bush** Himbeerstrauch m; **to blow a ~** (inf) verächtlich schnauben.

**rasping** ['rɑːspɪŋ] adj: **a ~ noise** ein kratzendes Geräusch.

**Rastafarian** n Rastafarier m.

**rat** [ræt] n Ratte f.

**ratable** ['reɪtəbl] adj = **rateable**.

**ratchet** ['rætʃɪt] n Sperrklinke f; ~ **wheel** Sperrad nt.

**rate** [reɪt] n (speed: of change etc) Tempo nt; (of inflation, unemployment etc) Rate f; (of interest, taxation) Satz m; (price) Preis m ♦ vt einschätzen; **rates** npl (BRIT: property tax) Kommunalabgaben pl; **at a ~ of 60 kph** mit einem Tempo von 60 km/h; ~ **of growth** (ECON) Wachstumsrate f; ~ **of return** (FIN) Rendite f; **pulse ~** Pulszahl f; **at this/that ~**

wenn es so weitergeht; **at any ~** auf jeden Fall; **to ~ sb/sth as** jdn/etw einschätzen als; **to ~ sb/sth among** jdn/etw zählen zu; **to ~ sb/sth highly** jdn/etw hoch einschätzen.

**rateable** ['reɪtəbl] adj: ~ **value** (BRIT) steuerbarer Wert m.

**ratepayer** ['reɪtpeɪə'] (BRIT) n Steuerzahler(in) m(f).

**rather** ['rɑːðə'] adv (somewhat) etwas; (very) ziemlich; ~ **a lot** ziemlich or recht viel; **I would ~ go** ich würde lieber gehen; ~ **than** (instead of) anstelle von; **or ~** (more accurately) oder vielmehr; **I'd ~ not say** das möchte ich lieber nicht sagen; **I ~ think he won't come** ich glaube eher, daß er nicht kommt.

**ratification** [rætɪfɪ'keɪʃən] n Ratifikation f.

**ratify** ['rætɪfaɪ] vt (treaty etc) ratifizieren.

**rating** ['reɪtɪŋ] n (score) Rate f; (assessment) Beurteilung f; (NAUT: BRIT: sailor) Matrose m; **ratings** npl (RADIO, TV) Einschaltquote f.

**ratio** ['reɪʃɪəu] n Verhältnis nt; **a ~ of 5 to 1** ein Verhältnis von 5 zu 1.

**ration** ['ræʃən] n Ration f ♦ vt rationieren; **rations** npl (MIL) Rationen pl.

**rational** ['ræʃənl] adj rational, vernünftig.

**rationale** [ræʃə'nɑːl] n Grundlage f.

**rationalization** [ræʃnəlaɪ'zeɪʃən] n (justification) Rechtfertigung f; (of company, system) Rationalisierung f.

**rationalize** ['ræʃnəlaɪz] vt (see n) rechtfertigen, rationalisieren.

**rationally** ['ræʃnəlɪ] adv vernünftig, rational.

**rationing** ['ræʃnɪŋ] n Rationierung f.

**ratpack** (BRIT: inf) n (reporters) Pressemeute f.

**rat poison** n Rattengift nt.

**rat race** n: **the ~** der ständige or tägliche Konkurrenzkampf m.

**rattan** [ræ'tæn] n Rattan nt, Peddigrohr nt.

**rattle** ['rætl] n (of door, window, snake) Klappern nt; (of train, car etc) Rattern nt; (of chain) Rasseln nt; (toy) Rassel f ♦ vi (chains) rasseln; (windows) klappern; (bottles) klirren ♦ vt (shake noisily) rütteln an +dat; (fig: unsettle) nervös machen; **to ~ along** (car, bus) dahinrattern.

**rattlesnake** ['rætlsneɪk] n Klapperschlange f.

**ratty** ['rætɪ] (inf) adj gereizt.

**raucous** ['rɔːkəs] adj (voice etc) rauh.

**raucously** ['rɔːkəslɪ] adv rauh.

**raunchy** ['rɔːntʃɪ] adj (voice, song) lüstern, geil.

**ravage** ['rævɪdʒ] vt verwüsten.

**ravages** ['rævɪdʒɪz] npl (of war) Verwüstungen pl; (of weather) zerstörende Auswirkungen pl; (of time) Spuren pl.

**rave** [reɪv] vi (in anger) toben ♦ adj (inf: review) glänzend; (scene, culture) Rave- ♦ n (BRIT: inf: party) Rave m, Fete f.

▶**rave about** schwärmen von.

**raven** ['reɪvən] n Rabe m.

**ravenous** ['rævənəs] adj (person)

ausgehungert; (*appetite*) unersättlich.
**ravine** [rə'viːn] *n* Schlucht *f*.
**raving** ['reɪvɪŋ] *adj*: **a ~ lunatic** ein total
verrückter Typ.
**ravings** ['reɪvɪŋz] *npl* Phantastereien *pl*.
**ravioli** [rævɪ'əʊlɪ] *n* Ravioli *pl*.
**ravishing** ['rævɪʃɪŋ] *adj* hinreißend.
**raw** [rɔː] *adj* roh; (*sore*) wund; (*inexperienced*)
unerfahren; (*weather, day*) rauh; **to get a
~ deal** ungerecht behandelt werden.
**Rawalpindi** [rɔːl'pɪndɪ] *n* Rawalpindi *nt*.
**raw material** *n* Rohmaterial *nt*.
**ray** [reɪ] *n* Strahl *m*; **~ of hope**
Hoffnungsschimmer *m*.
**rayon** ['reɪɒn] *n* Reyon *nt*.
**raze** [reɪz] *vt* (*also*: **to ~ to the ground**) dem
Erdboden gleichmachen.
**razor** ['reɪzə*] *n* Rasierapparat *m*; (*open ~*)
Rasiermesser *nt*.
**razor blade** *n* Rasierklinge *f*.
**razzle** ['ræzl] (*BRIT: inf*) *n*: **to be/go on the ~**
einen draufmachen.
**razzmatazz** ['ræzmə'tæz] (*inf*) *n* Trubel *m*.
**RC** *abbr* (= *Roman Catholic*) r.-k.
**RCAF** *n abbr* (= *Royal Canadian Air Force*)
kanadische Luftwaffe *f*.
**RCMP** *n abbr* (= *Royal Canadian Mounted Police*)
*kanadische berittene Polizei*.
**RCN** *n abbr* (= *Royal Canadian Navy*)
kanadische Marine.
**RD** (*US*) *abbr* (*POST*: = *rural delivery*)
Landpostzustellung *f*.
**Rd** *abbr* (= *road*) Str.
**RDC** (*BRIT*) *n abbr* = **rural district council**.
**RE** (*BRIT*) *n abbr* (*SCOL*) = **religious education**;
(*MIL*: = *Royal Engineers*) *Königliches
Pionierkorps*.
**re** [riː] *prep* (*with regard to*) bezüglich +*gen*.
**reach** [riːtʃ] *n* (*range*) Reichweite *f* ♦ *vt*
erreichen; (*conclusion, decision*) kommen zu;
(*be able to touch*) kommen an +*acc* ♦ *vi* (*stretch
out one's arm*) langen; **reaches** *npl* (*of river*)
Gebiete *pl*; **within/out of ~** in/außer
Reichweite; **within easy ~ of the
supermarket/station** ganz in der Nähe des
Supermarkts/Bahnhofs; **beyond the ~ of
sb/sth** außerhalb der Reichweite von jdm/
etw; **"keep out of the ~ of children"** „von
Kindern fernhalten"; **can I ~ you at your
hotel?** kann ich Sie in Ihrem Hotel
erreichen?
▶**reach out** *vt* (*hand*) ausstrecken ♦ *vi* die
Hand ausstrecken; **to ~ out for sth** nach
etw greifen.
**react** [riː'ækt] *vi*: **to ~ (to)** (*also MED*)
reagieren (auf +*acc*); (*CHEM*): **to ~ (with)**
reagieren (mit); **to ~ (against)** (*rebel*) sich
wehren (gegen).
**reaction** [riː'ækʃən] *n* Reaktion *f*; **reactions** *npl*
(*reflexes*) Reaktionen *pl*; **a ~ against sth**
Widerstand gegen etw.
**reactionary** [riː'ækʃənrɪ] *adj* reaktionär ♦ *n*

Reaktionär(in) *m(f)*.
**reactor** [riː'æktə*] *n* (*also*: **nuclear ~**)
Kernreaktor *m*.
**read** [riːd] (*pt, pp* **read** [rɛd]) *vi* lesen; (*piece of
writing etc*) sich lesen ♦ *vt* lesen; (*meter,
thermometer etc*) ablesen; (*understand: mood,
thoughts*) sich versetzen in +*acc*; (*meter,
thermometer etc: measurement*) anzeigen;
(*study*) studieren; **to ~ sb's lips** jdm von den
Lippen ablesen; **to ~ sb's mind** jds
Gedanken lesen; **to ~ between the lines**
zwischen den Zeilen lesen; **to take sth as ~**
(*self-evident*) etw für selbstverständlich
halten; **you can take it as ~ that** ... Sie
können davon ausgehen, daß ...; **do you
~ me?** (*TEL*) verstehen Sie mich?; **to ~ sth
into sb's remarks** etw in jds Bemerkungen
hineininterpretieren.
▶**read out** *vt* vorlesen.
▶**read over** *vt* durchlesen.
▶**read through** *vt* durchlesen.
▶**read up on** *vt fus* sich informieren über
+*acc*.
**readable** ['riːdəbl] *adj* (*legible*) lesbar; (*book,
author etc*) lesenswert.
**reader** ['riːdə*] *n* (*person*) Leser(in) *m(f)*; (*book*)
Lesebuch *nt*; (*BRIT: at university*)
≈ Dozent(in) *m(f)*; **to be an avid/slow ~**
eifrig/langsam lesen.
**readership** ['riːdəʃɪp] *n* (*of newspaper etc*)
Leserschaft *f*.
**readily** ['rɛdɪlɪ] *adv* (*without hesitation*)
bereitwillig; (*easily*) ohne weiteres.
**readiness** ['rɛdɪnɪs] *n* Bereitschaft *f*; **in ~ for**
bereit für.
**reading** ['riːdɪŋ] *n* Lesen *nt*; (*understanding*)
Verständnis *nt*; (*from bible, of poetry etc*)
Lesung *f*; (*on meter, thermometer etc*)
Anzeige *f*.
**reading lamp** *n* Leselampe *f*.
**reading matter** *n* Lesestoff *m*.
**reading room** *n* Lesesaal *m*.
**readjust** [riːə'dʒʌst] *vt* (*position, knob,
instrument etc*) neu einstellen ♦ *vi*: **to ~ (to)**
sich anpassen (an +*acc*).
**readjustment** [riːə'dʒʌstmənt] *n* (*fig*)
Neuorientierung *f*.
**ready** ['rɛdɪ] *adj* (*prepared*) bereit, fertig;
(*willing*) bereit; (*easy*) leicht; (*available*)
fertig ♦ *n*: **at the ~** (*MIL*) einsatzbereit; (*fig*)
griffbereit; **~ for use** gebrauchsfertig; **to
be ~ to do sth** bereit sein, etw zu tun; **to get
~** sich fertigmachen; **to get sth ~** etw
bereitmachen.
**ready cash** *n* Bargeld *nt*.
**ready-cooked** ['rɛdɪkʊkt] *adj* vorgekocht.
**ready-made** ['rɛdɪmeɪd] *adj* (*clothes*) von der
Stange, Konfektions-; **~ meal** Fertiggericht
*nt*.
**ready-mix** ['rɛdɪmɪks] *n* (*for cakes etc*)
Backmischung *f*; (*concrete*) Fertigbeton *m*.
**ready money** *n* = **ready cash**.

**ready reckoner** [-'rɛkənə*] (*BRIT*) *n*
Rechentabelle *f*.
**ready-to-wear** ['rɛdɪtə'wɛə*] *adj* (*clothes*) von
der Stange, Konfektions-.
**reaffirm** [riːə'fɜːm] *vt* bestätigen.
**reagent** [riː'eɪdʒənt] *n*: **chemical** ~ Reagens *nt*.
**real** [rɪəl] *adj* (*reason, result etc*) wirklich;
(*leather, gold etc*) echt; (*life, feeling*) wahr; (*for
emphasis*) echt ♦ *adv* (*US: inf: very*) echt; **in
~ life** im wahren *or* wirklichen Leben; **in
~ terms** effektiv.
**real ale** *n* Real Ale *nt*.
**real estate** *n* Immobilien *pl* ♦ *cpd* (*US: agent,
business etc*) Immobilien-.
**realign** *vt* neu ausrichten.
**realism** ['rɪəlɪzəm] *n* (*also ART*) Realismus *m*.
**realist** ['rɪəlɪst] *n* Realist(in) *m(f)*.
**realistic** [rɪə'lɪstɪk] *adj* realistisch.
**reality** [riː'ælɪtɪ] *n* Wirklichkeit *f*, Realität *f*; **in
~** in Wirklichkeit.
**realization** [rɪəlaɪ'zeɪʃən] *n* (*understanding*)
Erkenntnis *f*; (*fulfilment*) Verwirklichung *f*,
Realisierung *f*; (*FIN: of asset*) Realisation *f*.
**realize** ['rɪəlaɪz] *vt* (*understand*) verstehen;
(*fulfil*) verwirklichen, realisieren; (*FIN:
amount, profit*) realisieren; **I ~ that ...** es ist
mir klar, daß ...
**really** ['rɪəlɪ] *adv* wirklich; **what ~ happened**
was wirklich geschah; **~?** wirklich?; **~!**
(*indicating annoyance*) also wirklich!
**realm** [rɛlm] *n* (*fig: field*) Bereich *m*; (*kingdom*)
Reich *nt*.
**real-time** ['rɪːltaɪm] *adj* (*COMPUT: processing
etc*) Echtzeit-.
**Realtor** ® ['rɪəltɔː*] (*US*) *n* Immobilien-
makler(in) *m(f)*.
**ream** [riːm] *n* (*of paper*) Ries *nt*; **reams** (*inf, fig*)
Bände *pl*.
**reap** [riːp] *vt* (*crop*) einbringen, ernten; (*fig:
benefits*) ernten; (: *rewards*) bekommen.
**reaper** ['riːpə*] *n* (*machine*) Mähdrescher *m*.
**reappear** [riːə'pɪə*] *vi* wiederauftauchen.
**reappearance** [riːə'pɪərəns] *n* Wiederauftauchen *nt*.
**reapply** [riːə'plaɪ] *vi*: **to ~ for** sich erneut
bewerben um.
**reappoint** [riːə'pɔɪnt] *vt* (*to job*)
wiedereinstellen.
**reappraisal** [riːə'preɪzl] *n* (*of idea etc*)
Neubeurteilung *f*.
**rear** [rɪə*] *adj* hintere(r, s); (*wheel etc*) Hinter-
♦ *n* Rückseite *f*; (*buttocks*) Hinterteil *nt* ♦ *vt*
(*family, animals*) aufziehen ♦ *vi* (*also: ~ up:
horse*) sich aufbäumen.
**rear admiral** *n* Konteradmiral *m*.
**rear-engined** ['rɪər'ɛndʒɪnd] *adj* mit
Heckmotor.
**rearguard** ['rɪəgɑːd] *n* (*MIL*) Nachhut *f*; **to
fight a ~ action** (*fig*) sich erbittert wehren.
**rearm** [riː'ɑːm] *vi* (*country*) wiederaufrüsten
♦ *vt* wiederbewaffnen.
**rearmament** [riː'ɑːməmənt] *n*
Wiederaufrüstung *f*.
**rearrange** [riːə'reɪndʒ] *vt* (*furniture*) umstellen;
(*meeting*) den Termin ändern +*gen*.
**rear-view mirror** ['rɪəvjuː-] *n* Rückspiegel *m*.
**reason** ['riːzn] *n* (*cause*) Grund *m*; (*rationality*)
Verstand *m*; (*common sense*) Vernunft *f* ♦ *vi*:
**to ~ with sb** vernünftig mit jdm reden; **the
~ for/why** der Grund für/, warum; **we have
~ to believe that ...** wir haben Grund zu der
Annahme, daß ...; **it stands to ~ that ...** es ist
zu erwarten, daß ...; **she claims with good
~ that ...** sie behauptet mit gutem Grund *or*
mit Recht, daß ...; **all the more ~ why ...** ein
Grund mehr, warum ...; **yes, but within ~**
ja, solange es sich im Rahmen hält.
**reasonable** ['riːznəbl] *adj* vernünftig; (*number,
amount*) angemessen; (*not bad*) ganz
ordentlich; **be ~!** sei doch vernünftig!
**reasonably** ['riːznəblɪ] *adv* (*fairly*) ziemlich;
(*sensibly*) vernünftig; **one could ~ assume
that ...** man könnte durchaus annehmen,
daß ...
**reasoned** ['riːznd] *adj* (*argument*) durchdacht.
**reasoning** ['riːznɪŋ] *n* Argumentation *f*.
**reassemble** [riːə'sɛmbl] *vt* (*machine*) wieder
zusammensetzen ♦ *vi* sich wieder
versammeln.
**reassert** [riːə'sɜːt] *vt*: **to ~ oneself/one's
authority** seine Autorität wieder geltend
machen.
**reassurance** [riːə'ʃuərəns] *n* (*comfort*)
Beruhigung *f*; (*guarantee*) Bestätigung *f*.
**reassure** [riːə'ʃuə*] *vt* beruhigen.
**reassuring** [riːə'ʃuərɪŋ] *adj* beruhigend.
**reawakening** [riːə'weɪknɪŋ] *n*
Wiedererwachen *nt*.
**rebate** ['riːbeɪt] *n* (*on tax etc*) Rückerstattung
*f*; (*discount*) Ermäßigung *f*.
**rebel** ['rɛbl] *n* Rebell(in) *m(f)* ♦ *vi* rebellieren.
**rebellion** [rɪ'bɛljən] *n* Rebellion *f*.
**rebellious** [rɪ'bɛljəs] *adj* rebellisch.
**rebirth** [riː'bɜːθ] *n* Wiedergeburt *f*.
**rebound** [rɪ'baund] *vi* (*ball*) zurückprallen ♦ *n*:
**on the ~** (*fig*) als Tröstung *f*.
**rebuff** [rɪ'bʌf] *n* Abfuhr *f* ♦ *vt* zurückweisen.
**rebuild** [riː'bɪld] (*irreg: like* **build**) *vt*
wiederaufbauen; (*confidence*)
wiederherstellen.
**rebuke** [rɪ'bjuːk] *vt* zurechtweisen, tadeln ♦ *n*
Zurechtweisung *f*, Tadel *m*.
**rebut** [rɪ'bʌt] (*form*) *vt* widerlegen.
**rebuttal** [rɪ'bʌtl] (*form*) *n* Widerlegung *f*.
**recalcitrant** [rɪ'kælsɪtrənt] *adj* aufsässig.
**recall** [rɪ'kɔːl] *vt* (*remember*) sich erinnern an
+*acc*; (*ambassador*) abberufen; (*product*)
zurückrufen ♦ *n* (*of memories*) Erinnerung *f*;
(*of ambassador*) Abberufung *f*; (*of product*)
Rückruf *m*; **beyond ~** unwiederbringlich.
**recant** [rɪ'kænt] *vi* widerrufen.
**recap** ['riːkæp] *vt, vi* zusammenfassen ♦ *n*
Zusammenfassung *f*.
**recapitulate** [riːkə'pɪtjuleɪt] *vt, vi* = **recap**.

**recapture** [riː'kæptʃəˣ] *vt* (*town*) wiedereinnehmen; (*prisoner*) wiederergreifen; (*atmosphere etc*) heraufbeschwören.

**rec'd** *abbr* (*COMM:* = *received*) erh.

**recede** [rɪ'siːd] *vi* (*tide*) zurückgehen; (*lights etc*) verschwinden; (*memory, hope*) schwinden; **his hair is beginning to ~** er bekommt eine Stirnglatze.

**receding** [rɪ'siːdɪŋ] *adj* (*hairline*) zurückweichend; (*chin*) fliehend.

**receipt** [rɪ'siːt] *n* (*document*) Quittung *f*; (*act of receiving*) Erhalt *m*; **receipts** *npl* (*COMM*) Einnahmen *pl*; **on ~ of** bei Erhalt +*gen*; **to be in ~ of sth** etw erhalten.

**receivable** [rɪ'siːvəbl] *adj* (*COMM*) zulässig; (*owing*) ausstehend.

**receive** [rɪ'siːv] *vt* erhalten, bekommen; (*injury*) erleiden; (*treatment*) erhalten; (*visitor, guest*) empfangen; **to be on the receiving end of sth** der/die Leidtragende von etw sein; **"~d with thanks"** (*COMM*) „dankend erhalten".

---

Received Pronunciation *oder* RP *ist die hochsprachliche Standardaussprache des britischen Englisch, die bis vor kurzem in der Ober- und Mittelschicht vorherrschte und auch heute noch großes Ansehen unter höheren Beamten genießt.*

---

**receiver** [rɪ'siːvəˣ] *n* (*TEL*) Hörer *m*; (*RADIO, TV*) Empfänger *m*; (*of stolen goods*) Hehler(in) *m(f)*; (*COMM*) Empfänger(in) *m(f)*.

**receivership** [rɪ'siːvəʃɪp] *n*: **to go into ~** in Konkurs gehen.

**recent** [ˈriːsnt] *adj* (*event*) kürzlich; (*times*) letzte(r, s); **in ~ years** in den letzten Jahren.

**recently** [ˈriːsntlɪ] *adv* (*not long ago*) kürzlich; (*lately*) in letzter Zeit; **as ~ as** erst; **until ~** bis vor kurzem.

**receptacle** [rɪ'sɛptɪkl] *n* Behälter *m*.

**reception** [rɪ'sɛpʃən] *n* (*in hotel, office etc*) Rezeption *f*; (*party, RADIO, TV*) Empfang *m*; (*welcome*) Aufnahme *f*.

**reception centre** (*BRIT*) *n* Aufnahmelager *nt*.

**reception desk** *n* Rezeption *f*.

**receptionist** [rɪ'sɛpʃənɪst] *n* (*in hotel*) Empfangschef *m*, Empfangsdame *f*; (*in doctor's surgery*) Sprechstundenhilfe *f*.

**receptive** [rɪ'sɛptɪv] *adj* aufnahmebereit.

**recess** [rɪ'sɛs] *n* (*in room*) Nische *f*; (*secret place*) Winkel *m*; (*POL etc: holiday*) Ferien *pl*; (*US: LAW: short break*) Pause *f*; (*esp US: SCOL*) Pause *f*.

**recession** [rɪ'sɛʃən] *n* (*ECON*) Rezession *f*.

**recharge** [riː'tʃɑːdʒ] *vt* (*battery*) aufladen.

**rechargeable** [riː'tʃɑːdʒəbl] *adj* (*battery*) aufladbar.

**recipe** [ˈrɛsɪpɪ] *n* Rezept *nt*; **a ~ for success** ein Erfolgsrezept *nt*; **to be a ~ for disaster** in die Katastrophe führen.

**recipient** [rɪ'sɪpɪənt] *n* Empfänger(in) *m(f)*.

**reciprocal** [rɪ'sɪprəkl] *adj* gegenseitig.

**reciprocate** [rɪ'sɪprəkeɪt] *vt* (*invitation, feeling*) erwidern ♦ *vi* sich revanchieren.

**recital** [rɪ'saɪtl] *n* (*concert*) Konzert *nt*.

**recitation** [rɛsɪ'teɪʃən] *n* (*of poem etc*) Vortrag *m*.

**recite** [rɪ'saɪt] *vt* (*poem*) vortragen; (*complaints etc*) aufzählen.

**reckless** [ˈrɛkləs] *adj* (*driving, driver*) rücksichtslos; (*spending*) leichtsinnig.

**recklessly** [ˈrɛkləslɪ] *adv* (*drive*) rücksichtslos; (*spend, gamble*) leichtsinnig.

**reckon** [ˈrɛkən] *vt* (*consider*) halten für; (*calculate*) berechnen ♦ *vi*: **he is somebody to be ~ed with** mit ihm muß man rechnen; **I ~ that ...** (*think*) ich schätze, daß ...; **to ~ without sb/sth** nicht mit jdm/etw rechnen.

▶**reckon on** *vt fus* rechnen mit.

**reckoning** [ˈrɛknɪŋ] *n* (*calculation*) Berechnung *f*; **the day of ~** der Tag der Abrechnung.

**reclaim** [rɪ'kleɪm] *vt* (*luggage*) abholen; (*tax etc*) zurückfordern; (*land*) gewinnen; (*waste materials*) zur Wiederverwertung sammeln.

**reclamation** [rɛklə'meɪʃən] *n* (*of land*) Gewinnung *f*.

**recline** [rɪ'klaɪn] *vi* (*sit or lie back*) zurückgelehnt sitzen.

**reclining** [rɪ'klaɪnɪŋ] *adj* (*seat*) Liege-.

**recluse** [rɪ'kluːs] *n* Einsiedler(in) *m(f)*.

**recognition** [rɛkəg'nɪʃən] *n* (*of person, place*) Erkennen *nt*; (*of problem, fact*) Erkenntnis *f*; (*of achievement*) Anerkennung *f*; **in ~ of** in Anerkennung +*gen*; **to gain ~** Anerkennung finden; **she had changed beyond ~** sie war nicht wiederzuerkennen.

**recognizable** [ˈrɛkəgnaɪzəbl] *adj* erkennbar.

**recognize** [ˈrɛkəgnaɪz] *vt* (*person, place, voice*) wiedererkennen; (*sign, problem*) erkennen; (*qualifications, government, achievement*) anerkennen; **to ~ sb by/as** jdn erkennen an +*dat*/als.

**recoil** [rɪ'kɔɪl] *vi* (*person*): **to ~ from** zurückweichen vor +*dat*; (*fig*) zurückschrecken vor +*dat* ♦ *n* (*of gun*) Rückstoß *m*.

**recollect** [rɛkə'lɛkt] *vt* (*remember*) sich erinnern an +*acc*.

**recollection** [rɛkə'lɛkʃən] *n* Erinnerung *f*; **to the best of my ~** soweit ich mich erinnern or entsinnen kann.

**recommend** [rɛkə'mɛnd] *vt* empfehlen; **she has a lot to ~ her** es spricht sehr viel für sie.

**recommendation** [rɛkəmɛn'deɪʃən] *n* Empfehlung *f*; **on the ~ of** auf Empfehlung +*gen*.

**recommended retail price** (*BRIT*) *n* (*COMM*) unverbindlicher Richtpreis *m*.

**recompense** [ˈrɛkəmpɛns] *n* (*reward*)

Belohnung *f*; (*compensation*) Entschädigung *f*.

**reconcilable** ['rɛkənsaɪləbl] *adj* (*ideas*) (miteinander) vereinbar.

**reconcile** ['rɛkənsaɪl] *vt* (*people*) versöhnen; (*facts, beliefs*) (miteinander) vereinbaren, in Einklang bringen; **to ~ o.s. to sth** sich mit etw abfinden.

**reconciliation** [rɛkənsɪlɪ'eɪʃən] *n* (*of people*) Versöhnung *f*; (*of facts, beliefs*) Vereinbarung *f*.

**recondite** [rɪ'kɒndaɪt] *adj* obskur.

**recondition** [riːkən'dɪʃən] *vt* (*machine*) überholen.

**reconditioned** [riːkən'dɪʃənd] *adj* (*engine, TV*) generalüberholt.

**reconnaissance** [rɪ'kɒnɪsns] *n* (*MIL*) Aufklärung *f*.

**reconnoitre**, (*US*) **reconnoiter** [rɛkə'nɔɪtə*] *vt* (*MIL*) erkunden.

**reconsider** [riːkən'sɪdə*] *vt* (noch einmal) überdenken ♦ *vi* es sich *dat* noch einmal überlegen.

**reconstitute** [riː'kɒnstɪtjuːt] *vt* (*organization*) neu bilden; (*food*) wiederherstellen.

**reconstruct** [riːkən'strʌkt] *vt* (*building*) wiederaufbauen; (*policy, system*) neu organisieren; (*event, crime*) rekonstruieren.

**reconstruction** [riːkən'strʌkʃən] *n* Wiederaufbau *m*; (*of crime*) Rekonstruktion *f*.

**reconvene** [riːkən'viːn] *vi* (*meet again*) wieder zusammenkommen ♦ *vt* (*meeting etc*) wieder einberufen.

**record** ['rɛkɔːd] *n* (*written account*) Aufzeichnung *f*; (*of meeting*) Protokoll *nt*; (*of decision*) Beleg *m*; (*COMPUT*) Datensatz *m*; (*file*) Akte *f*; (*MUS: disc*) Schallplatte *f*; (*history*) Vorgeschichte *f*; (*also:* **criminal ~**) Vorstrafen *pl*; (*SPORT*) Rekord *m* ♦ *vt* aufzeichnen; (*song etc*) aufnehmen; (*temperature, speed etc*) registrieren ♦ *adj* (*sales, profits*) Rekord-; **~ of attendance** Anwesenheitsliste *f*; **public ~s** Urkunden *pl* des Nationalarchivs; **to keep a ~ of sth** etw schriftlich festhalten; **to have a good/poor ~** gute/schlechte Leistungen vorzuweisen haben; **to have a (criminal) ~** vorbestraft sein; **to set** *or* **put the ~ straight** (*fig*) Klarheit schaffen; **he is on ~ as saying that** ... er hat nachweislich gesagt, daß ...; **off the ~** (*remark*) inoffiziell ♦ *adv* (*speak*) im Vertrauen; **in ~ time** in Rekordzeit.

**recorded delivery** [rɪ'kɔːdɪd-] (*BRIT*) *n* (*POST*) Einschreiben *nt*; **to send sth (by) ~** etw per Einschreiben senden.

**recorder** [rɪ'kɔːdə*] *n* (*MUS*) Blockflöte *f*; (*LAW*) *nebenamtlich als Richter tätiger Rechtsanwalt*.

**record holder** *n* (*SPORT*) Rekordinhaber(in) *m(f)*.

**recording** [rɪ'kɔːdɪŋ] *n* Aufnahme *f*.

**recording studio** *n* Aufnahmestudio *nt*.

**record library** *n* Schallplattenverleih *m*.

**record player** *n* Plattenspieler *m*.

**recount** [rɪ'kaunt] *vt* (*story etc*) erzählen.

**re-count** ['riːkaunt] *n* (*of votes*) Nachzählung *f* ♦ *vt* (*votes*) nachzählen.

**recoup** [rɪ'kuːp] *vt:* **to ~ one's losses** seine Verluste ausgleichen.

**recourse** [rɪ'kɔːs] *n:* **to have ~ to sth** Zuflucht zu etw nehmen.

**recover** [rɪ'kʌvə*] *vt* (*get back*) zurückbekommen; (*stolen goods*) sicherstellen; (*wreck, body*) bergen; (*financial loss*) ausgleichen ♦ *vi* sich erholen.

**re-cover** [riː'kʌvə*] *vt* (*chair etc*) neu beziehen.

**recovery** [rɪ'kʌvərɪ] *n* (*from illness etc*) Erholung *f*; (*in economy*) Aufschwung *m*; (*of lost items*) Wiederfinden *nt*; (*of stolen goods*) Sicherstellung *f*; (*of wreck, body*) Bergung *f*; (*of financial loss*) Ausgleich *m*.

**re-create** [riːkrɪ'eɪt] *vt* (*atmosphere, situation*) wiederherstellen.

**recreation** [rɛkrɪ'eɪʃən] *n* (*leisure*) Erholung *f*, Entspannung *f*.

**recreational** [rɛkrɪ'eɪʃənl] *adj* (*facilities etc*) Freizeit-.

**recreational drug** *n* Freizeitdroge *f*.

**recreational vehicle** (*US*) *n* Caravan *m*.

**recrimination** [rɪkrɪmɪ'neɪʃən] *n* gegenseitige Anschuldigungen *pl*.

**recruit** [rɪ'kruːt] *n* (*MIL*) Rekrut *m*; (*in company*) neuer Mitarbeiter *m*, neue Mitarbeiterin *f* ♦ *vt* (*MIL*) rekrutieren; (*staff, new members*) anwerben.

**recruiting office** [rɪ'kruːtɪŋ-] *n* (*MIL*) Rekrutierungsbüro *nt*.

**recruitment** [rɪ'kruːtmənt] *n* (*of staff*) Anwerbung *f*.

**rectangle** ['rɛktæŋgl] *n* Rechteck *nt*.

**rectangular** [rɛk'tæŋgjulə*] *adj* (*shape*) rechteckig.

**rectify** ['rɛktɪfaɪ] *vt* (*mistake etc*) korrigieren.

**rector** ['rɛktə*] *n* (*REL*) Pfarrer(in) *m(f)*.

**rectory** ['rɛktərɪ] *n* Pfarrhaus *nt*.

**rectum** ['rɛktəm] *n* Rektum *nt*, Mastdarm *m*.

**recuperate** [rɪ'kjuːpəreɪt] *vi* (*recover*) sich erholen.

**recur** [rɪ'kəː*] *vi* (*error, event*) sich wiederholen; (*pain etc*) wiederholt auftreten.

**recurrence** [rɪ'kəːrns] *n* (*see vi*) Wiederholung *f*; wiederholtes Auftreten *nt*.

**recurrent** [rɪ'kəːrnt] *adj* (*see vi*) sich wiederholend; wiederholt auftretend.

**recurring** [rɪ'kəːrɪŋ] *adj* (*problem, dream*) sich wiederholend; (*MATH*): **six point five four ~** sechs komma fünf Periode vier.

**recycle** [riː'saɪkl] *vt* (*waste, paper etc*) recyceln, wiederverwerten.

**red** [rɛd] *n* Rot *nt*; (*pej: POL*) Rote(r) *f(m)* ♦ *adj* rot; **to be in the ~** (*business etc*) in den roten Zahlen sein.

**red alert** *n:* **to be on** ~ in höchster Alarmbereitschaft sein.
**red-blooded** ['rɛd'blʌdɪd] *adj* heißblütig.

---

*Als* **redbrick university** *werden die jüngeren britischen Universitäten bezeichnet, die im späten 19. und Anfang des 20. Jh. in Städten wie Manchester, Liverpool und Bristol gegründet wurden. Der Name steht im Gegensatz zu Oxford und Cambridge und bezieht sich auf die roten Backsteinmauern der Universitätsgebäude.*

---

**red carpet treatment** *n:* **to give sb the** ~ den roten Teppich für jdn ausrollen.
**Red Cross** *n* Rotes Kreuz *nt*.
**redcurrant** ['rɛdkʌrənt] *n* rote Johannisbeere *f*.
**redden** ['rɛdn] *vt* röten ♦ *vi* (*blush*) erröten.
**reddish** ['rɛdɪʃ] *adj* rötlich.
**redecorate** [riː'dɛkəreɪt] *vt, vi* renovieren.
**redecoration** [riːdɛkə'reɪʃən] *n* Renovierung *f*.
**redeem** [rɪ'diːm] *vt* (*situation etc*) retten; (*voucher, sth in pawn*) einlösen; (*loan*) abzahlen; (*REL*) erlösen; **to** ~ **oneself for sth** etw wiedergutmachen.
**redeemable** [rɪ'diːməbl] *adj* (*voucher etc*) einlösbar.
**redeeming** [rɪ'diːmɪŋ] *adj* (*feature, quality*) versöhnend.
**redefine** [riːdɪ'faɪn] *vt* neu definieren.
**redemption** [rɪ'dɛmpʃən] *n* (*REL*) Erlösung *f*; **past** *or* **beyond** ~ nicht mehr zu retten.
**redeploy** [riːdɪ'plɔɪ] *vt* (*resources, staff*) umverteilen; (*MIL*) verlegen.
**redeployment** [riːdɪ'plɔɪmənt] *n* (*see vt*) Umverteilung *f*; Verlegung *f*.
**redevelop** [riːdɪ'vɛləp] *vt* (*area*) sanieren.
**redevelopment** [riːdɪ'vɛləpmənt] *n* Sanierung *f*.
**red-handed** [rɛd'hændɪd] *adj:* **to be caught** ~ auf frischer Tat ertappt werden.
**redhead** ['rɛdhɛd] *n* Rotschopf *m*.
**red herring** *n* (*fig*) falsche Spur *f*.
**red-hot** [rɛd'hɒt] *adj* (*metal*) rotglühend.
**redirect** [riːdaɪ'rɛkt] *vt* (*mail*) nachsenden; (*traffic*) umleiten.
**rediscover** [riːdɪs'kʌvə*] *vt* wiederentdecken.
**redistribute** [riːdɪs'trɪbjuːt] *vt* umverteilen.
**red-letter day** ['rɛdlɛtə-] *n* besonderer Tag *m*.
**red light** *n* (*AUT*): **to go through a** ~ eine Ampel bei Rot überfahren.
**red-light district** ['rɛdlaɪt-] *n* Rotlichtviertel *nt*.
**red meat** *n* Rind- und *Lammfleisch*.
**redness** ['rɛdnɪs] *n* Röte *f*.
**redo** [riː'duː] *vt* (*irreg: like do*) *vt* noch einmal machen.
**redolent** ['rɛdələnt] *adj:* **to be** ~ **of sth** nach etw riechen; (*fig*) an etw erinnern.
**redouble** [riː'dʌbl] *vt:* **to** ~ **one's efforts** seine Anstrengungen verdoppeln.

**redraft** [riː'drɑːft] *vt* (*agreement*) neu abfassen.
**redraw** [riː'drɔː] *vt* neu zeichnen.
**redress** [rɪ'drɛs] *n* (*compensation*) Wiedergutmachung *f* ♦ *vt* (*error etc*) wiedergutmachen; **to** ~ **the balance** das Gleichgewicht wiederherstellen.
**Red Sea** *n:* **the** ~ das Rote Meer.
**redskin** ['rɛdskɪn] (*old: offensive*) *n* Rothaut *f*.
**red tape** *n* (*fig*) Bürokratie *f*.
**reduce** [rɪ'djuːs] *vt* (*spending, numbers, rates etc*) vermindern, reduzieren; **to** ~ **sth by/to 5%** etw um/auf 5% *acc* reduzieren; **to** ~ **sb to tears/silence** jdn zum Weinen/Schweigen bringen; **to** ~ **sb to begging/stealing** jdn zur Bettelei/zum Diebstahl zwingen; **"~ speed now"** (*AUT*) „langsam fahren".
**reduced** [rɪ'djuːst] *adj* (*goods, ticket etc*) ermäßigt; **"greatly** ~ **prices"** „Preise stark reduziert".
**reduction** [rɪ'dʌkʃən] *n* (*in price etc*) Ermäßigung, Reduzierung *f*; (*in numbers*) Verminderung *f*.
**redundancy** [rɪ'dʌndənsɪ] (*BRIT*) *n* (*dismissal*) Entlassung *f*; (*unemployment*) Arbeitslosigkeit *f*; **compulsory** ~ Entlassung *f*; **voluntary** ~ freiwilliger Verzicht *m* auf den Arbeitsplatz.
**redundancy payment** (*BRIT*) *n* Abfindung *f*.
**redundant** [rɪ'dʌndnt] *adj* (*BRIT: worker*) arbeitslos; (*word, object*) überflüssig; **to be made** ~ (*worker*) den Arbeitsplatz verlieren.
**reed** [riːd] *n* (*BOT*) Schilf *nt*; (*MUS: of clarinet etc*) Rohrblatt *nt*.
**re-educate** [riː'ɛdjukeɪt] *vt* umerziehen.
**reedy** ['riːdɪ] *adj* (*voice*) Fistel-.
**reef** [riːf] *n* (*at sea*) Riff *nt*.
**reek** [riːk] *vi:* **to** ~ **(of)** (*lit, fig*) stinken (nach).
**reel** [riːl] *n* (*of thread etc, on fishing-rod*) Rolle *f*; (*CINE: scene*) Szene *f*; (*of film, tape*) Spule *f*; (*dance*) Reel *m* ♦ *vi* (*sway*) taumeln; **my head is** ~**ing** mir dreht sich der Kopf.
▶**reel in** *vt* (*fish, line*) einholen.
▶**reel off** *vt* (*say*) herunterrasseln.
**re-election** [riːɪ'lɛkʃən] *n* Wiederwahl *f*.
**re-enter** [riː'ɛntə*] *vt* (*country*) wiedereinreisen in +*acc*; (*SPACE*) wiedereintreten in +*acc*.
**re-entry** [riː'ɛntrɪ] *n* Wiedereinreise *f*; (*SPACE*) Wiedereintritt *m*.
**re-examine** [riːɪg'zæmɪn] *vt* (*proposal etc*) nochmals prüfen; (*witness*) nochmals vernehmen.
**re-export** ['riːɪks'pɔːt] *vt* wiederausführen ♦ *n* Wiederausfuhr *f*; (*commodity*) wiederausgeführte Ware *f*.
**ref** [rɛf] (*inf*) *n abbr* (*SPORT*) = **referee**.
**ref.** *abbr* (*COMM:* = **with reference to**) betr.; **your** ~ Ihr Zeichen:.
**refectory** [rɪ'fɛktərɪ] *n* (*in university*) Mensa *f*.
**refer** [rɪ'fəː*] *vt:* **to** ~ **sb to** (*book etc*) jdn verweisen auf +*acc*; (*doctor, hospital*) jdn

überweisen zu; **to ~ sth to** (*task, problem*) etw übergeben an +*acc*; **he ~red me to the manager** er verwies mich an den Geschäftsführer.

▶**refer to** *vt fus* (*mention*) erwähnen; (*relate to*) sich beziehen auf +*acc*; (*consult*) hinzuziehen.

**referee** [rɛfə'riː] *n* (*SPORT*) Schiedsrichter(in) *m(f)*; (*BRIT: for job application*) Referenz *f* ♦ *vt* als Schiedsrichter(in) leiten.

**reference** ['rɛfrəns] *n* (*mention*) Hinweis *m*; (*in book, article*) Quellenangabe *f*; (*for job application, person*) Referenz *f*; **with ~ to** mit Bezug auf +*acc*; **"please quote this ~"** (*COMM*) „bitte dieses Zeichen angeben".

**reference book** *n* Nachschlagewerk *nt*.

**reference library** *n* Präsenzbibliothek *f*.

**reference number** *n* Aktenzeichen *nt*.

**referenda** [rɛfə'rɛndə] *npl of* **referendum**.

**referendum** [rɛfə'rɛndəm] (*pl* **referenda**) *n* Referendum *nt*, Volksentscheid *m*.

**referral** [rɪ'fəːrəl] *n* (*of matter, problem*) Weiterleitung *f*; (*to doctor, specialist*) Überweisung *f*.

**refill** [riː'fɪl] *vt* nachfüllen ♦ *n* (*for pen etc*) Nachfüllmine *f*; (*drink*) Nachfüllung *f*.

**refine** [rɪ'faɪn] *vt* (*sugar, oil*) raffinieren; (*theory, idea*) verfeinern.

**refined** [rɪ'faɪnd] *adj* (*person*) kultiviert; (*taste*) fein, vornehm; (*sugar, oil*) raffiniert.

**refinement** [rɪ'faɪnmənt] *n* (*of person*) Kultiviertheit *f*; (*of system, ideas*) Verfeinerung *f*.

**refinery** [rɪ'faɪnərɪ] *n* (*for oil etc*) Raffinerie *f*.

**refit** [riː'fɪt] (*NAUT*) *n* Überholung *f* ♦ *vt* (*ship*) überholen.

**reflate** [riː'fleɪt] *vt* (*economy*) ankurbeln.

**reflation** [riː'fleɪʃən] *n* (*ECON*) Reflation *f*.

**reflationary** [riː'fleɪʃənrɪ] *adj* (*ECON*) reflationär.

**reflect** [rɪ'flɛkt] *vt* reflektieren; (*fig*) widerspiegeln ♦ *vi* (*think*) nachdenken.

▶**reflect on** *vt fus* (*discredit*) ein schlechtes Licht werfen auf +*acc*.

**reflection** [rɪ'flɛkʃən] *n* (*image*) Spiegelbild *nt*; (*of light, heat*) Reflexion *f*; (*fig*) Widerspiegelung *f*; (*: thought*) Gedanke *m*; **on ~** nach genauerer Überlegung; **this is a ~ on ...** (*criticism*) das sagt einiges über ...

**reflector** [rɪ'flɛktə*] *n* (*AUT etc*) Rückstrahler *m*; (*for light, heat*) Reflektor *m*.

**reflex** ['riːflɛks] *adj* Reflex-; **reflexes** *npl* (*PHYSIOL, PSYCH*) Reflexe *pl*.

**reflexive** [rɪ'flɛksɪv] *adj* (*LING*) reflexiv.

**reform** [rɪ'fɔːm] *n* Reform *f* ♦ *vt* reformieren ♦ *vi* (*criminal etc*) sich bessern.

**reformat** [riː'fɔːmæt] *vt* (*COMPUT*) neu formatieren.

**Reformation** [rɛfə'meɪʃən] *n*: **the ~** die Reformation.

**reformatory** [rɪ'fɔːmətərɪ] (*US*) *n* Besserungsanstalt *f*.

**reformed** [rɪ'fɔːmd] *adj* (*character, alcoholic*) gewandelt.

**refrain** [rɪ'freɪn] *vi*: **to ~ from doing sth** etw unterlassen ♦ *n* (*of song*) Refrain *m*.

**refresh** [rɪ'frɛʃ] *vt* erfrischen; **to ~ one's memory** sein Gedächtnis auffrischen.

**refresher course** [rɪ'frɛʃə-] *n* Auffrischungskurs *m*.

**refreshing** [rɪ'frɛʃɪŋ] *adj* erfrischend; (*sleep*) wohltuend; (*idea etc*) angenehm.

**refreshment** [rɪ'frɛʃmənt] *n* Erfrischung *f*.

**refreshments** [rɪ'frɛʃmənts] *npl* (*food and drink*) Erfrischungen *pl*.

**refrigeration** [rɪfrɪdʒə'reɪʃən] *n* Kühlung *f*.

**refrigerator** [rɪ'frɪdʒəreɪtə*] *n* Kühlschrank *m*.

**refuel** [riː'fjuəl] *vt*, *vi* auftanken.

**refuelling** [riː'fjuəlɪŋ] *n* Auftanken *nt*.

**refuge** ['rɛfjuːdʒ] *n* Zuflucht *f*; **to seek/take ~ in** Zuflucht suchen/nehmen in +*dat*.

**refugee** [rɛfju'dʒiː] *n* Flüchtling *m*; **a political ~** ein politischer Flüchtling.

**refugee camp** *n* Flüchtlingslager *nt*.

**refund** ['riːfʌnd] *n* Rückerstattung *f* ♦ *vt* (*money*) zurückerstatten.

**refurbish** [riː'fəːbɪʃ] *vt* (*shop etc*) renovieren.

**refurbishment** [riːfəːbɪʃmənt] *n* (*of shop etc*) Renovierung *f*.

**refurnish** [riː'fəːnɪʃ] *vt* neu möblieren.

**refusal** [rɪ'fjuːzəl] *n* Ablehnung *f*; **a ~ to do sth** eine Weigerung, etw zu tun; **to give sb first ~ on sth** jdm etw zuerst anbieten.

**refuse¹** [rɪ'fjuːz] *vt* (*request, offer etc*) ablehnen; (*gift*) zurückweisen; (*permission*) verweigern ♦ *vi* ablehnen; (*horse*) verweigern; **to ~ to do sth** sich weigern, etw zu tun.

**refuse²** ['rɛfjuːs] *n* (*rubbish*) Abfall *m*, Müll *m*.

**refuse collection** *n* Müllabfuhr *f*.

**refuse disposal** *n* Müllbeseitigung *f*.

**refusenik** [rɪ'fjuːznɪk] *n* (*inf*) Verweigerer(in) *m(f)*; (*in former USSR*) sowjetischer Jude, dem die Emigration nach Israel verweigert wurde.

**refute** [rɪ'fjuːt] *vt* (*argument*) widerlegen.

**regain** [rɪ'geɪn] *vt* wiedererlangen.

**regal** ['riːgl] *adj* königlich.

**regale** [rɪ'geɪl] *vt*: **to ~ sb with sth** jdn mit etw verwöhnen.

**regalia** [rɪ'geɪlɪə] *n* (*costume*) Amtstracht *f*.

**regard** [rɪ'gɑːd] *n* (*esteem*) Achtung *f* ♦ *vt* (*consider*) ansehen, betrachten; (*view*) betrachten; **to give one's ~s to sb** jdm Grüße bestellen; **"with kindest ~s"** „mit freundlichen Grüßen"; **as ~s, with ~ to** bezüglich +*gen*.

**regarding** [rɪ'gɑːdɪŋ] *prep* bezüglich +*gen*.

**regardless** [rɪ'gɑːdlɪs] *adv* trotzdem ♦ *adj*: **~ of** ohne Rücksicht auf +*acc*.

**regatta** [rɪ'gætə] *n* Regatta *f*.

**regency** ['riːdʒənsɪ] *n* Regentschaft *f* ♦ *adj*: **R~** (*furniture etc*) Regency-.

**regenerate** [rɪ'dʒɛnəreɪt] *vt* (*inner cities, arts*)

erneuern; (*person, feelings*) beleben ♦ *vi*
(*BIOL*) sich regenerieren.
**regent** ['ri:dʒənt] *n* Regent(in) *m(f)*.
**reggae** ['rεgeɪ] *n* Reggae *m*.
**regime** [reɪ'ʒi:m] *n* (*government*) Regime *nt*;
(*diet etc*) Kur *f*.
**regiment** ['rεdʒɪmənt] *n* (*MIL*) Regiment *nt* ♦ *vt*
reglementieren.
**regimental** [rεdʒɪ'mεntl] *adj* Regiments-.
**regimentation** [rεdʒɪmεn'teɪʃən] *n*
Reglementierung *f*.
**region** ['ri:dʒən] *n* (*of land*) Gebiet *nt*; (*of body*)
Bereich *m*; (*administrative division of country*)
Region *f*; **in the** ~ **of** (*approximately*) im
Bereich von.
**regional** ['ri:dʒənl] *adj* regional.
**regional development** *n* regionale
Entwicklung *f*.
**register** ['rεdʒɪstə*] *n* (*list, MUS*) Register *nt*;
(*also*: **electoral** ~) Wählerverzeichnis *nt*;
(*SCOL*) Klassenbuch *nt* ♦ *vt* registrieren;
(*car*) anmelden; (*letter*) als Einschreiben
senden; (*amount, measurement*) verzeichnen
♦ *vi* (*person*) sich anmelden; (: *at doctor's*)
sich (als Patient) eintragen; (*amount etc*)
registriert werden; (*make impression*)
(einen) Eindruck machen; **to** ~ **a protest**
Protest anmelden.
**registered** ['rεdʒɪstəd] *adj* (*letter, parcel*)
eingeschrieben; (*drug addict, childminder etc*)
(offiziell) eingetragen.
**registered company** *n* eingetragene
Gesellschaft *f*.
**registered nurse** (*US*) *n* staatlich geprüfte
Krankenschwester *f*, staatlich geprüfter
Krankenpfleger *m*.
**registered trademark** *n* eingetragenes
Warenzeichen *nt*.
**register office** *n* = **registry office**.
**registrar** ['rεdʒɪstrɑ:*] *n* (*in registry office*)
Standesbeamte(r) *m*, Standesbeamtin *f*; (*in
college etc*) Kanzler *m*; (*BRIT: in hospital*)
Krankenhausarzt *m*, Krankenhausärztin *f*.
**registration** [rεdʒɪs'treɪʃən] *n* Registrierung *f*;
(*of students, unemployed etc*) Anmeldung *f*.
**registration number** (*BRIT*) *n* (*AUT*)
polizeiliches Kennzeichen *nt*.
**registry** ['rεdʒɪstrɪ] *n* Registratur *f*.
**registry office** (*BRIT*) *n* Standesamt *nt*; **to get
married in a** ~ standesamtlich heiraten.
**regret** [rɪ'grεt] *n* Bedauern *nt* ♦ *vt* bedauern;
**with** ~ mit Bedauern; **to have no** ~s nichts
bereuen; **we** ~ **to inform you that** ... wir
müssen Ihnen leider mitteilen, daß ...
**regretfully** [rɪ'grεtfəlɪ] *adv* mit Bedauern.
**regrettable** [rɪ'grεtəbl] *adj* bedauerlich.
**regrettably** [rɪ'grεtəblɪ] *adv*
bedauerlicherweise; ~, **he said** ...
bedauerlicherweise sagte er ...
**Regt** *abbr* (*MIL*: = *regiment*) Rgt.
**regular** ['rεgjulə*] *adj* (*also LING*) regelmäßig;
(*usual: time, doctor*) üblich; (: *customer*)

Stamm-; (*soldier*) Berufs-; (*COMM: size*)
normal ♦ *n* (*client*) Stammkunde *m*,
Stammkundin *f*.
**regularity** [rεgju'lærɪtɪ] *n* Regelmäßigkeit *f*.
**regularly** ['rεgjuləlɪ] *adv* regelmäßig; (*breathe,
beat: evenly*) gleichmäßig.
**regulate** ['rεgjuleɪt] *vt* regulieren.
**regulation** [rεgju'leɪʃən] *n* Regulierung *f*;
(*rule*) Vorschrift *f*.
**regulatory** [rεgju'leɪtrɪ] *adj* (*system*)
Regulierungs-; (*body, agency*)
Überwachungs-.
**rehabilitate** [ri:ə'bɪlɪteɪt] *vt* (*criminal, drug
addict*) (in die Gesellschaft)
wiedereingliedern; (*invalid*) rehabilitieren.
**rehabilitation** ['ri:əbɪlɪ'teɪʃən] *n* (*see vt*)
Wiedereingliederung *f* (in die
Gesellschaft); Rehabilitation *f*.
**rehash** [ri:'hæʃ] (*inf*) *vt* (*idea etc*) aufwärmen.
**rehearsal** [rɪ'hə:səl] *n* (*THEAT*) Probe *f*; **dress**
~ Generalprobe *f*.
**rehearse** [rɪ'hə:s] *vt* (*play, speech etc*) proben.
**rehouse** [ri:'hauz] *vt* neu unterbringen.
**reign** [reɪn] *n* (*lit, fig*) Herrschaft *f* ♦ *vi* (*lit, fig*)
herrschen.
**reigning** ['reɪnɪŋ] *adj* regierend; (*champion*)
amtierend.
**reimburse** [ri:ɪm'bə:s] *vt* die Kosten erstatten
+*dat*.
**rein** [reɪn] *n* Zügel *m*; **to give sb free** ~ (*fig*)
jdm freie Hand lassen; **to keep a tight** ~ **on
sth** (*fig*) bei etw die Zügel kurz halten.
**reincarnation** [ri:ɪnkɑ:'neɪʃən] *n* (*belief*) die
Wiedergeburt *f*; (*person*) Reinkarnation *f*.
**reindeer** ['reɪndɪə*] *n inv* Ren(tier) *nt*.
**reinforce** [ri:ɪn'fɔ:s] *vt* (*strengthen*)
verstärken; (*support: idea etc*) stützen;
(: *prejudice*) stärken.
**reinforced concrete** *n* Stahlbeton *m*.
**reinforcement** [ri:ɪn'fɔ:smənt] *n*
(*strengthening*) Verstärkung *f*; (*of attitude etc*)
Stärkung *f*; **reinforcements** *npl* (*MIL*)
Verstärkung *f*.
**reinstate** [ri:ɪn'steɪt] *vt* (*employee*)
wiedereinstellen; (*tax, law*)
wiedereinführen; (*text*) wiedereinfügen.
**reinstatement** [ri:ɪn'steɪtmənt] *n* (*of
employee*) Wiedereinstellung *f*.
**reissue** [ri:'ɪʃju:] *vt* neu herausgeben.
**reiterate** [ri:'ɪtəreɪt] *vt* wiederholen.
**reject** ['ri:dʒεkt] *n* (*COMM*) Ausschuß *m no pl*
♦ *vt* ablehnen; (*admirer*) abweisen; (*goods*)
zurückweisen; (*machine: coin*) nicht
annehmen; (*MED: heart, kidney*) abstoßen.
**rejection** [rɪ'dʒεkʃən] *n* Ablehnung *f*; (*of
admirer*) Abweisung *f*; (*MED*) Abstoßung *f*.
**rejoice** [rɪ'dʒɔɪs] *vi*: **to** ~ **at** *or* **over** jubeln über
+*acc*.
**rejoinder** [rɪ'dʒɔɪndə*] *n* Erwiderung *f*.
**rejuvenate** [rɪ'dʒu:vəneɪt] *vt* (*person*)
verjüngen; (*organization etc*) beleben.
**rekindle** [ri:'kɪndl] *vt* (*interest, emotion etc*)

wiedererwecken.
**relapse** [rɪˈlæps] n (MED) Rückfall m ♦ vi: **to
~ into** zurückfallen in +acc.

**relate** [rɪˈleɪt] vt (tell) berichten; (connect) in
Verbindung bringen ♦ vi: **to ~ to** (empathize
with: person, subject) eine Beziehung finden
zu; (connect with) zusammenhängen mit.
**related** [rɪˈleɪtɪd] adj: **to be ~** (miteinander)
verwandt sein; (issues etc) zusammen-
hängen.
**relating to** [rɪˈleɪtɪŋ-] prep bezüglich +gen, mit
Bezug auf +acc.
**relation** [rɪˈleɪʃən] n (member of family)
Verwandte(r) f(m); (connection) Beziehung f;
**relations** npl (contact) Beziehungen pl;
**diplomatic/international ~s** diplomatische/
internationale Beziehungen; **in ~ to** im
Verhältnis zu; **to bear no ~ to** in keinem
Verhältnis stehen zu.
**relationship** [rɪˈleɪʃənʃɪp] n Beziehung f,
(between countries) Beziehungen pl; (affair)
Verhältnis nt; **they have a good ~** sie haben
ein gutes Verhältnis zueinander.
**relative** [ˈrɛlətɪv] n Verwandte(r) f(m) ♦ adj
relativ; **all her ~s** ihre ganze
Verwandtschaft; **~ to** im Vergleich zu; **it's
all ~** es ist alles relativ.
**relatively** [ˈrɛlətɪvlɪ] adv relativ.
**relative pronoun** n Relativpronomen nt.
**relax** [rɪˈlæks] vi (person, muscle) sich
entspannen; (calm down) sich beruhigen ♦ vt
(one's grip) lockern; (mind, person)
entspannen; (control etc) lockern.
**relaxation** [riːlækˈseɪʃən] n Entspannung f, (of
control etc) Lockern nt.
**relaxed** [rɪˈlækst] adj (person, atmosphere)
entspannt; (discussion) locker.
**relaxing** [rɪˈlæksɪŋ] adj entspannend.
**relay** [ˈriːleɪ] n (race) Staffel f, Staffellauf m
♦ vt (message etc) übermitteln; (broadcast)
übertragen.
**release** [rɪˈliːs] n (from prison) Entlassung f;
(from obligation, situation) Befreiung f; (of
documents, funds etc) Freigabe f; (of gas etc)
Freisetzung f; (of film, book, record)
Herausgabe f; (record, film) Veröffentlichung f; (TECH: device) Auslöser m ♦ vt
(from prison) entlassen; (person: from
obligation, from wreckage) befreien; (gas etc)
freisetzen; (TECH, AUT: catch, brake etc)
lösen; (record, film) herausbringen; (news,
figures) bekanntgeben; **on general ~** (film)
überall in den Kinos; see also **press release**.
**relegate** [ˈrɛləgeɪt] vt (downgrade)
herunterstufen; (BRIT: SPORT): **to be ~d**
absteigen.
**relent** [rɪˈlɛnt] vi (give in) nachgeben.
**relentless** [rɪˈlɛntlɪs] adj (heat, noise)
erbarmungslos; (enemy etc) unerbittlich.
**relevance** [ˈrɛləvəns] n Relevanz f, Bedeutung
f; **the ~ of religion to society** die Relevanz or
Bedeutung der Religion für die

Gesellschaft.
**relevant** [ˈrɛləvənt] adj relevant; (chapter, area)
entsprechend; **~ to** relevant für.
**reliability** [rɪlaɪəˈbɪlɪtɪ] n Zuverlässigkeit f.
**reliable** [rɪˈlaɪəbl] adj zuverlässig.
**reliably** [rɪˈlaɪəblɪ] adv: **to be ~ informed that**
... zuverlässige Informationen darüber
haben, daß ...
**reliance** [rɪˈlaɪəns] n: **~** (on) (person)
Angewiesenheit f (auf +acc); (drugs, financial
support) Abhängigkeit f (von).
**reliant** [rɪˈlaɪənt] adj: **to be ~ on sth/sb** auf
etw/jdn angewiesen sein.
**relic** [ˈrɛlɪk] n (REL) Reliquie f; (of the past)
Relikt nt.
**relief** [rɪˈliːf] n (from pain etc) Erleichterung f;
(aid) Hilfe f; (ART, GEOG) Relief nt ♦ cpd
(bus) Entlastungs-; (driver) zur Ablösung;
**light ~** leichte Abwechslung f.
**relief map** n Reliefkarte f.
**relief road** (BRIT) n Entlastungsstraße f.
**relieve** [rɪˈliːv] vt (pain) lindern; (fear, worry)
mildern; (take over from) ablösen; **to ~ sb of
sth** (load) jdm etw abnehmen; (duties, post)
jdn einer Sache gen entheben; **to ~ o.s.**
(euphemism) sich erleichtern.
**relieved** [rɪˈliːvd] adj erleichtert; **I'm ~ to hear
it** es erleichtert mich, das zu hören.
**religion** [rɪˈlɪdʒən] n Religion f.
**religious** [rɪˈlɪdʒəs] adj religiös.
**religious education** n Religionsunterricht
m.
**religiously** [rɪˈlɪdʒəslɪ] adv (regularly,
thoroughly) gewissenhaft.
**relinquish** [rɪˈlɪŋkwɪʃ] vt (control etc)
aufgeben; (claim) verzichten auf +acc.
**relish** [ˈrɛlɪʃ] n (CULIN) würzige Soße f, Relish
nt; (enjoyment) Genuß m ♦ vt (enjoy)
genießen; **to ~ doing sth** etw mit Genuß
tun.
**relive** [riːˈlɪv] vt noch einmal durchleben.
**reload** [riːˈləud] vt (gun) neu laden.
**relocate** [riːləuˈkeɪt] vt verlegen ♦ vi den
Standort wechseln; **to ~ in** seinen Standort
verlegen nach.
**reluctance** [rɪˈlʌktəns] n Widerwille m.
**reluctant** [rɪˈlʌktənt] adj unwillig, widerwillig;
**I'm ~ to do that** es widerstrebt mir, das zu
tun.
**reluctantly** [rɪˈlʌktəntlɪ] adv widerwillig, nur
ungern.
**rely on** [rɪˈlaɪ-] vt fus (be dependent on)
abhängen von; (trust) sich verlassen auf
+acc.
**remain** [rɪˈmeɪn] vi bleiben; (survive)
übrigbleiben; **to ~ silent** weiterhin
schweigen; **to ~ in control** die Kontrolle
behalten; **much ~s to be done** es ist noch
viel zu tun; **the fact ~s that ...** Tatsache ist
und bleibt, daß ...; **it ~s to be seen whether**
... es bleibt abzuwarten, ob ...
**remainder** [rɪˈmeɪndə*] n Rest m ♦ vt (COMM)

zu ermäßigtem Preis anbieten.

**remaining** [rɪ'meɪnɪŋ] *adj* übrig.

**remains** [rɪ'meɪnz] *npl* (*of meal*) Überreste *pl*; (*of building etc*) Ruinen *pl*; (*of body*) sterbliche Überreste *pl*.

**remand** [rɪ'mɑːnd] *n*: **to be on** ~ in Untersuchungshaft sein ♦ *vt*: **to be ~ed in custody** in Untersuchungshaft bleiben müssen.

**remand home** (*formerly: BRIT*) *n* Untersuchungsgefängnis *nt* für Jugendliche.

**remark** [rɪ'mɑːk] *n* Bemerkung *f* ♦ *vt* bemerken ♦ *vi*: **to ~ on sth** Bemerkungen über etw *acc* machen; **to ~ that** die Bemerkung machen, daß.

**remarkable** [rɪ'mɑːkəbl] *adj* bemerkenswert.

**remarry** [riː'mærɪ] *vi* wieder heiraten.

**remedial** [rɪ'miːdɪəl] *adj* (*tuition, classes*) Förder-; ~ **exercise** Heilgymnastik *f*.

**remedy** ['rɛmədɪ] *n* (*lit, fig*) (Heil)mittel *nt* ♦ *vt* (*mistake, situation*) abhelfen +*dat*.

**remember** [rɪ'mɛmbə*] *vt* (*call back to mind*) sich erinnern an +*acc*; (*bear in mind*) denken an +*acc*; ~ **me to him** (*send greetings*) grüße ihn von mir; **I ~ seeing it, I ~ having seen it** ich erinnere mich (daran), es gesehen zu haben; **she ~ed to do it** sie hat daran gedacht, es zu tun.

**remembrance** [rɪ'mɛmbrəns] *n* Erinnerung *f*; **in ~ of sb/sth** im Gedenken an +*acc*.

**Remembrance Sunday** (*BRIT*) *n* ≈ Volkstrauertag *m*.

---

**Remembrance Sunday** *oder* **Remembrance Day** *ist der britische Gedenktag für die Gefallenen der beiden Weltkriege und andere Konflikte. Er fällt auf einen Sonntag vor oder nach dem 11. November (am 11. November 1918 endete der erste Weltkrieg) und wird mit einer Schweigeminute, Kranzniederlegungen an Kriegerdenkmälern und dem Tragen von Anstecknadeln in Form einer Mohnblume begangen.*

---

**remind** [rɪ'maɪnd] *vt*: **to ~ sb to do sth** jdn daran erinnern, etw zu tun; **to ~ sb of sth** jdn an etw *acc* erinnern; **to ~ sb that ...** jdn daran erinnern, daß ...; **she ~s me of her mother** sie erinnert mich an ihre Mutter; **that ~s me!** dabei fällt mir etwas ein!

**reminder** [rɪ'maɪndə*] *n* (*of person, place etc*) Erinnerung *f*; (*letter*) Mahnung *f*.

**reminisce** [rɛmɪ'nɪs] *vi*: **to ~ (about)** sich in Erinnerungen ergehen (über +*acc*).

**reminiscences** [rɛmɪ'nɪsnsɪz] *npl* Erinnerungen *pl*.

**reminiscent** [rɛmɪ'nɪsnt] *adj*: **to be ~ of sth** an etw *acc* erinnern.

**remiss** [rɪ'mɪs] *adj* nachlässig; **it was ~ of him** es war nachlässig von ihm.

**remission** [rɪ'mɪʃən] *n* (*of sentence*) Straferlaß *m*; (*MED*) Remission *f*; (*REL*) Erlaß *m*.

**remit** [rɪ'mɪt] *vt* (*money*) überweisen ♦ *n* (*of official etc*) Aufgabenbereich *m*.

**remittance** [rɪ'mɪtns] *n* Überweisung *f*.

**remnant** ['rɛmnənt] *n* Überrest *m*; (*COMM: of cloth*) Rest *m*.

**remonstrate** ['rɛmənstreɪt] *vi*: **to ~ (with sb about sth)** sich beschweren (bei jdm wegen etw).

**remorse** [rɪ'mɔːs] *n* Reue *f*.

**remorseful** [rɪ'mɔːsful] *adj* reumütig.

**remorseless** [rɪ'mɔːslɪs] *adj* (*noise, pain*) unbarmherzig.

**remote** [rɪ'məut] *adj* (*distant: place, time*) weit entfernt; (*aloof*) distanziert; (*slight: chance etc*) entfernt; **there is a ~ possibility that ...** es besteht eventuell die Möglichkeit, daß ...

**remote control** *n* Fernsteuerung *f*; (*TV etc*) Fernbedienung *f*.

**remote-controlled** [rɪ'məutkən'trəuld] *adj* ferngesteuert.

**remotely** [rɪ'məutlɪ] *adv* (*slightly*) entfernt.

**remoteness** [rɪ'məutnɪs] *n* (*of place*) Entlegenheit *f*; (*of person*) Distanziertheit *f*.

**remould** ['riːməuld] (*BRIT*) *n* (*AUT*) runderneuerter Reifen *m*.

**removable** [rɪ'muːvəbl] *adj* (*detachable*) abnehmbar.

**removal** [rɪ'muːvəl] *n* (*of object etc*) Entfernung *f*; (*of threat etc*) Beseitigung *f*; (*BRIT: from house*) Umzug *m*; (*dismissal*) Entlassung *f*; (*MED: of kidney etc*) Entfernung *f*.

**removal man** (*BRIT*) *n* Möbelpacker *m*.

**removal van** (*BRIT*) *n* Möbelwagen *m*.

**remove** [rɪ'muːv] *vt* entfernen; (*clothing*) ausziehen; (*bandage etc*) abnehmen; (*employee*) entlassen; (*name: from list*) streichen; (*doubt, threat, obstacle*) beseitigen; **my first cousin once ~d** mein Vetter ersten Grades.

**remover** [rɪ'muːvə*] *n* (*for paint, varnish*) Entferner *m*; **stain ~** Fleckentferner *m*; **make-up ~** Make-up-Entferner *m*.

**remunerate** [rɪ'mjuːnəreɪt] *vt* vergüten.

**remuneration** [rɪmjuːnə'reɪʃən] *n* Vergütung *f*.

**Renaissance** [rɪ'neɪsɑːs] *n*: **the ~** die Renaissance.

**renal** ['riːnl] *adj* (*MED*) Nieren-.

**renal failure** *n* Nierenversagen *nt*.

**rename** [riː'neɪm] *vt* umbenennen.

**rend** [rɛnd] (*pt, pp* **rent**) *vt* (*air, silence*) zerreißen.

**render** ['rɛndə*] *vt* (*give: assistance, aid*) leisten; (*cause to become: unconscious, harmless, useless*) machen; (*submit*) vorlegen.

**rendering** ['rɛndərɪŋ] (*BRIT*) *n* = **rendition**.

**rendezvous** ['rɔndɪvuː] *n* (*meeting*) Rendezvous *nt*; (*place*) Treffpunkt *m* ♦ *vi* (*people*) sich treffen; (*spacecraft*) ein Rendezvousmanöver durchführen; **to ~ with sb** sich mit jdm treffen.

**rendition** [rɛn'dɪʃən] *n* (*of song etc*) Vortrag *m*.

**renegade** ['rɛnɪgeɪd] *n* Renegat(in) *m(f)*, Überläufer(in) *m(f)*.

**renew** [rɪ'njuː] *vt* erneuern; (*attack, negotiations*) wiederaufnehmen; (*loan, contract etc*) verlängern; (*relationship etc*) wiederaufleben lassen.

**renewables** *npl* erneuerbare Energien *pl*.

**renewal** [rɪ'njuːəl] *n* Erneuerung *f*; (*of conflict*) Wiederaufnahme *f*; (*of contract etc*) Verlängerung *f*.

**renounce** [rɪ'nauns] *vt* verzichten auf +*acc*; (*belief*) aufgeben.

**renovate** ['rɛnəveɪt] *vt* (*building*) restaurieren; (*machine*) überholen.

**renovation** [rɛnə'veɪʃən] *n* (*see vb*) Restaurierung *f*; Überholung *f*.

**renown** [rɪ'naun] *n* Ruf *m*.

**renowned** [rɪ'naund] *adj* berühmt.

**rent** [rɛnt] *pt, pp of* **rend** ♦ *n* (*for house*) Miete *f* ♦ *vt* mieten; (*also: ~ out*) vermieten.

**rental** ['rɛntl] *n* (*for television, car*) Mietgebühr *f*.

**rent boy** (*inf*) *n* Strichjunge *m*.

**rent strike** *n* Mietstreik *m*.

**renunciation** [rɪnʌnsɪ'eɪʃən] *n* Verzicht *m*; (*of belief*) Aufgabe *f*; (*self-denial*) Selbstverleugnung *f*.

**reopen** [riː'əupən] *vt* (*shop etc*) wiedereröffnen; (*negotiations, legal case etc*) wiederaufnehmen.

**reopening** [riː'əupnɪŋ] *n* (*see vt*) Wiedereröffnung *f*; Wiederaufnahme *f*.

**reorder** [riː'ɔːdə•] *vt* (*rearrange*) umordnen.

**reorganization** ['riːɔːgənaɪ'zeɪʃən] *n* Umorganisation *f*.

**reorganize** [riː'ɔːgənaɪz] *vt* umorganisieren.

**Rep.** (*US*) *abbr* (*POL*) = **representative**; **republican**.

**rep** [rɛp] *n abbr* (*COMM*) = **representative**; (*THEAT*) = **repertory**.

**repair** [rɪ'pɛə•] *n* Reparatur *f* ♦ *vt* reparieren; (*clothes, road*) ausbessern; **in good/bad ~** in gutem/schlechtem Zustand; **beyond ~** nicht mehr zu reparieren; **to be under ~** (*road*) ausgebessert werden.

**repair kit** *n* (*for bicycle*) Flickzeug *nt*.

**repair man** *n* Handwerker *m*.

**repair shop** *n* Reparaturwerkstatt *f*.

**repartee** [rɛpɑː'tiː] *n* (*exchange*) Schlagabtausch *m*; (*reply*) schlagfertige Bemerkung *f*.

**repast** [rɪ'pɑːst] (*form*) *n* Mahl *nt*.

**repatriate** [riː'pætrɪeɪt] *vt* repatriieren.

**repay** [riː'peɪ] (*irreg: like* **pay**) *vt* zurückzahlen; (*sb's efforts, attention*) belohnen; (*favour*) erwidern; **I'll ~ you next week** ich zahle es dir nächste Woche zurück.

**repayment** [riː'peɪmənt] *n* Rückzahlung *f*.

**repeal** [rɪ'piːl] *n* (*of law*) Aufhebung *f* ♦ *vt* (*law*) aufheben.

**repeat** [rɪ'piːt] *n* (*RADIO, TV*) Wiederholung *f* ♦ *vt, vi* wiederholen ♦ *cpd* (*performance*) Wiederholungs-; (*order*) Nach-; **to ~ o.s./ itself** sich wiederholen; **to ~ an order for sth** etw nachbestellen.

**repeatedly** [rɪ'piːtɪdlɪ] *adv* wiederholt.

**repel** [rɪ'pɛl] *vt* (*drive away*) zurückschlagen; (*disgust*) abstoßen.

**repellent** [rɪ'pɛlənt] *adj* abstoßend ♦ *n*: **insect ~** Insekten(schutz)mittel *nt*.

**repent** [rɪ'pɛnt] *vi*: **to ~ of sth** etw bereuen.

**repentance** [rɪ'pɛntəns] *n* Reue *f*.

**repercussions** [riːpə'kʌʃənz] *npl* Auswirkungen *pl*.

**repertoire** ['rɛpətwɑː•] *n* (*MUS, THEAT*) Repertoire *nt*; (*fig*) Spektrum *nt*.

**repertory** ['rɛpətərɪ] *n* (*also: ~ theatre*) Repertoiretheater *nt*.

**repertory company** *n* Repertoire-Ensemble *nt*.

**repetition** [rɛpɪ'tɪʃən] *n* (*repeat*) Wiederholung *f*.

**repetitious** [rɛpɪ'tɪʃəs] *adj* (*speech etc*) voller Wiederholungen.

**repetitive** [rɪ'pɛtɪtɪv] *adj* eintönig, monoton.

**replace** [rɪ'pleɪs] *vt* (*put back: upright*) zurückstellen; (: *flat*) zurücklegen; (*take the place of*) ersetzen; **to ~ X with Y** X durch Y ersetzen; **"~ the receiver"** (*TEL*) „Hörer auflegen".

**replacement** [rɪ'pleɪsmənt] *n* Ersatz *m*.

**replacement part** *n* Ersatzteil *nt*.

**replay** ['riːpleɪ] *n* (*of match*) Wiederholungsspiel *nt* ♦ *vt* (*match*) wiederholen; (*track, song: on tape*) nochmals abspielen.

**replenish** [rɪ'plɛnɪʃ] *vt* (*glass, stock etc*) auffüllen.

**replete** [rɪ'pliːt] *adj* (*after meal*) gesättigt; **~ with** reichlich ausgestattet mit.

**replica** ['rɛplɪkə] *n* (*of object*) Nachbildung *f*.

**reply** [rɪ'plaɪ] *n* Antwort *f* ♦ *vi*: **to ~ (to sb/sth)** (jdm/auf etw *acc*) antworten; **in ~ to** als Antwort auf +*acc*; **there's no ~** (*TEL*) es meldet sich niemand.

**reply coupon** *n* Antwortschein *m*.

**report** [rɪ'pɔːt] *n* Bericht *m*; (*BRIT: also:* **school ~**) Zeugnis *nt*; (*of gun*) Knall *m* ♦ *vt* berichten; (*casualties, damage, theft etc*) melden; (*person: to police*) anzeigen ♦ *vi* (*make a report*) Bericht erstatten; **to ~ to sb** (*present o.s. to*) sich bei jdm melden; (*be responsible to*) jdm unterstellt sein; **to ~ on sth** über etw *acc* Bericht erstatten; **to ~ sick** sich krank melden; **it is ~ed that** es wird berichtet *or* gemeldet, daß ...

**report card** (*US, SCOT*) *n* Zeugnis *nt*.

**reportedly** [rɪ'pɔːtɪdlɪ] *adv*: **she is ~ living in Spain** sie lebt angeblich in Spanien.

**reported speech** *n* (*LING*) indirekte Rede *f*.

**reporter** [rɪ'pɔːtə*] *n* Reporter(in) *m(f)*.
**repose** [rɪ'pəuz] *n*: **in ~** in Ruhestellung.
**repository** [rɪ'pɒzɪtərɪ] *n* (*person: of knowledge*) Quelle *f*; (*place: of collection etc*) Lager *nt*.
**repossess** ['riːpə'zɛs] *vt* (wieder) in Besitz nehmen.
**repossession order** [riːpə'zɛʃən-] *n* Beschlagnahmungsverfügung *f*.
**reprehensible** [rɛprɪ'hɛnsɪbl] *adj* verwerflich.
**represent** [rɛprɪ'zɛnt] *vt* (*person, nation*) vertreten; (*show: view, opinion*) darstellen; (*symbolize: idea*) symbolisieren, verkörpern; **to ~ sth as** (*describe*) etw darstellen als.
**representation** [rɛprɪzɛn'teɪʃən] *n* (*state of being represented*) Vertretung *f*; (*picture etc*) Darstellung *f*; **representations** *npl* (*protest*) Proteste *pl*.
**representative** [rɛprɪ'zɛntətɪv] *n* (*also COMM*) Vertreter(in) *m(f)*; (*US: POL*) Abgeordnete(r) *f(m)* des Repräsentantenhauses ♦ *adj* repräsentativ; **~ of** repräsentativ für.
**repress** [rɪ'prɛs] *vt* unterdrücken.
**repression** [rɪ'prɛʃən] *n* Unterdrückung *f*.
**repressive** [rɪ'prɛsɪv] *adj* repressiv.
**reprieve** [rɪ'priːv] *n* (*cancellation*) Begnadigung *f*; (*postponement*) Strafaufschub *m*; (*fig*) Gnadenfrist *f* ♦ *vt*: **he was ~d** (*see n*) er wurde begnadigt; ihm wurde Strafaufschub gewährt.
**reprimand** ['rɛprɪmɑːnd] *n* Tadel *m* ♦ *vt* tadeln.
**reprint** ['riːprɪnt] *n* Nachdruck *m* ♦ *vt* nachdrucken.
**reprisal** [rɪ'praɪzl] *n* Vergeltung *f*; **reprisals** *npl* Repressalien *pl*; (*in war*) Vergeltungsaktionen *pl*; **to take ~s** zu Repressalien greifen; (*in war*) Vergeltungsaktionen durchführen.
**reproach** [rɪ'prəutʃ] *n* (*rebuke*) Vorwurf *m* ♦ *vt*: **to ~ sb for sth** jdm etw zum Vorwurf machen; **beyond ~** über jeden Vorwurf erhaben; **to ~ sb with sth** jdm etw vorwerfen.
**reproachful** [rɪ'prəutʃful] *adj* vorwurfsvoll.
**reproduce** [riːprə'djuːs] *vt* reproduzieren ♦ *vi* (*BIOL*) sich vermehren.
**reproduction** [riːprə'dʌkʃən] *n* Reproduktion *f*; (*BIOL*) Fortpflanzung *f*.
**reproductive** [riːprə'dʌktɪv] *adj* (*system, organs*) Fortpflanzungs-.
**reproof** [rɪ'pruːf] *n* (*rebuke*) Tadel *m*; **with ~** tadelnd.
**reprove** [rɪ'pruːv] *vt* tadeln; **to ~ sb for sth** jdn wegen etw tadeln.
**reproving** [rɪ'pruːvɪŋ] *adj* tadelnd.
**reptile** ['rɛptaɪl] *n* Reptil *nt*.
**Repub.** (*US*) *abbr* (*POL*) = **republican**.
**republic** [rɪ'pʌblɪk] *n* Republik *f*.
**republican** [rɪ'pʌblɪkən] *adj* republikanisch ♦ *n* Republikaner(in) *m(f)*; **the R~s** (*US: POL*) die Republikaner.
**repudiate** [rɪ'pjuːdɪeɪt] *vt* (*accusation*) zurückweisen; (*violence*) ablehnen; (*old: friend, wife etc*) verstoßen.
**repugnance** [rɪ'pʌgnəns] *n* Abscheu *m*.
**repugnant** [rɪ'pʌgnənt] *adj* abstoßend.
**repulse** [rɪ'pʌls] *vt* (*attack etc*) zurückschlagen; (*sight, picture etc*) abstoßen.
**repulsion** [rɪ'pʌlʃən] *n* Abscheu *m*.
**repulsive** [rɪ'pʌlsɪv] *adj* widerwärtig, abstoßend.
**reputable** ['rɛpjutəbl] *adj* (*make, company etc*) angesehen.
**reputation** [rɛpju'teɪʃən] *n* Ruf *m*; **to have a ~ for** einen Ruf haben für; **he has a ~ for being awkward** er gilt als schwierig.
**repute** [rɪ'pjuːt] *n*: **of ~** angesehen; **to be held in high ~** in hohem Ansehen stehen.
**reputed** [rɪ'pjuːtɪd] *adj* angeblich; **he is ~ to be rich** er ist angeblich reich.
**reputedly** [rɪ'pjuːtɪdlɪ] *adv* angeblich.
**request** [rɪ'kwɛst] *n* (*polite*) Bitte *f*; (*formal*) Ersuchen *nt*; (*RADIO*) Musikwunsch *m* ♦ *vt* (*politely*) bitten um; (*formally*) ersuchen; **at the ~ of** auf Wunsch von; **"you are ~ed not to smoke"** „bitte nicht rauchen".
**request stop** (*BRIT*) *n* Bedarfshaltestelle *f*.
**requiem** ['rɛkwɪəm] *n* (*REL: also: ~ mass*) Totenmesse *f*; (*MUS*) Requiem *nt*.
**require** [rɪ'kwaɪə*] *vt* (*need*) benötigen; (*: situation*) erfordern; (*demand*) verlangen; **to ~ sb to do sth** von jdm verlangen, etw zu tun; **if ~d** falls nötig; **what qualifications are ~d?** welche Qualifikationen werden verlangt?; **~d by law** gesetzlich vorgeschrieben.
**required** [rɪ'kwaɪəd] *adj* erforderlich.
**requirement** [rɪ'kwaɪəmənt] *n* (*need*) Bedarf *m*; (*condition*) Anforderung *f*; **to meet sb's ~s** jds Anforderungen erfüllen.
**requisite** ['rɛkwɪzɪt] *adj* erforderlich; **requisites** *npl*: **toilet/travel ~s** Toiletten-/Reiseartikel *pl*.
**requisition** [rɛkwɪ'zɪʃən] *n*: **~ (for)** (*demand*) Anforderung *f* (von) ♦ *vt* (*MIL*) beschlagnahmen.
**reroute** [riː'ruːt] *vt* (*train etc*) umleiten.
**resale** [riː'seɪl] *n* Weiterverkauf *m*; **"not for ~"** „nicht zum Weiterverkauf bestimmt".
**resale price maintenance** *n* Preisbindung *f*.
**rescind** [rɪ'sɪnd] *vt* (*law, order*) aufheben; (*decision*) rückgängig machen; (*agreement*) widerrufen.
**rescue** ['rɛskjuː] *n* Rettung *f* ♦ *vt* retten; **to come to sb's ~** jdm zu Hilfe kommen.
**rescue party** *n* Rettungsmannschaft *f*.
**rescuer** ['rɛskjuə*] *n* Retter(in) *m(f)*.
**research** [rɪ'səːtʃ] *n* Forschung *f* ♦ *vt* erforschen ♦ *vi*: **to ~ into sth** etw erforschen; **to do ~** Forschung betreiben; **a piece of ~** eine Forschungsarbeit; **~ and development** Forschung und Entwicklung.
**researcher** [rɪ'səːtʃə*] *n* Forscher(in) *m(f)*.
**research work** *n* Forschungsarbeit *f*.

**research worker** n = researcher.

**resell** [riː'sɛl] (irreg: like sell) vt
weiterverkaufen.

**resemblance** [rɪ'zɛmbləns] n Ähnlichkeit f; **to
bear a strong** ~ **to** starke Ähnlichkeit haben
mit; **it bears no** ~ **to** ... es hat keine
Ähnlichkeit mit ...

**resemble** [rɪ'zɛmbl] vt ähneln +dat, gleichen
+dat.

**resent** [rɪ'zɛnt] vt (attitude, treatment)
mißbilligen; (person) ablehnen.

**resentful** [rɪ'zɛntful] adj (person) gekränkt;
(attitude) mißbilligend.

**resentment** [rɪ'zɛntmənt] n Verbitterung f.

**reservation** [rɛzə'veɪʃən] n (booking)
Reservierung f; (doubt) Vorbehalt m; (land)
Reservat nt; **to make a** ~ (in hotel etc) eine
Reservierung vornehmen; **with** ~(s)
(doubts) unter Vorbehalt.

**reservation desk** n Reservierungsschalter
m.

**reserve** [rɪ'zəːv] n Reserve f, Vorrat m; (fig: of
talent etc) Reserve f; (SPORT)
Reservespieler(in) m(f); (also: nature ~)
Naturschutzgebiet nt; (restraint)
Zurückhaltung f ♦ vt reservieren; (table,
ticket) reservieren lassen; **reserves** npl (MIL)
Reserve f; **in** ~ in Reserve.

**reserve currency** n Reservewährung f.

**reserved** [rɪ'zəːvd] adj (restrained)
zurückhaltend; (seat) reserviert.

**reserve price** (BRIT) n Mindestpreis m.

**reserve team** (BRIT) n Reservemannschaft f.

**reservist** [rɪ'zəːvɪst] n (MIL) Reservist m.

**reservoir** ['rɛzəvwɑː*] n (lit, fig) Reservoir nt.

**reset** [riː'sɛt] (irreg: like set) vt (watch) neu
stellen; (broken bone) wieder einrichten;
(COMPUT) zurückstellen.

**reshape** [riː'ʃeɪp] vt (policy, view)
umgestalten.

**reshuffle** [riː'ʃʌfl] n: **cabinet** ~
Kabinettsumbildung f.

**reside** [rɪ'zaɪd] vi (live: person) seinen/ihren
Wohnsitz haben.

▶**reside in** vt fus (exist) liegen in +dat.

**residence** ['rɛzɪdəns] n (form: home) Wohnsitz
m; (length of stay) Aufenthalt m; **to take up** ~
sich niederlassen; **in** ~ (queen etc)
anwesend; **writer/artist in** ~ Schriftsteller/
Künstler, der in einer Ausbildungsstätte bei
freier Unterkunft lehrt und arbeitet.

**residence permit** (BRIT) n
Aufenthaltserlaubnis f.

**resident** ['rɛzɪdənt] n (of country, town)
Einwohner(in) m(f); (in hotel) Gast m ♦ adj (in
country, town) wohnhaft; (population)
ansässig; (doctor) hauseigen; (landlord) im
Hause wohnend.

**residential** [rɛzɪ'dɛnʃəl] adj (area) Wohn-;
(course) mit Wohnung am Ort; (staff) im
Hause wohnend.

**residue** ['rɛzɪdjuː] n (CHEM) Rückstand m;

(fig) Überrest m.

**resign** [rɪ'zaɪn] vt (one's post) zurücktreten
von ♦ vi (from post) zurücktreten; **to** ~ **o.s.
to** (situation etc) sich abfinden mit.

**resignation** [rɛzɪg'neɪʃən] n (from post)
Rücktritt m; (state of mind) Resignation f; **to
tender one's** ~ seine Kündigung einreichen.

**resigned** [rɪ'zaɪnd] adj: **to be** ~ **to sth** sich mit
etw abgefunden haben.

**resilience** [rɪ'zɪlɪəns] n (of material)
Widerstandsfähigkeit f; (of person)
Unverwüstlichkeit f.

**resilient** [rɪ'zɪlɪənt] adj (see n)
widerstandsfähig; unverwüstlich.

**resin** ['rɛzɪn] n Harz nt.

**resist** [rɪ'zɪst] vt (change, demand) sich
widersetzen +dat; (attack etc) Widerstand
leisten +dat; (urge etc) widerstehen +dat; **I
couldn't** ~ **(doing)** it ich konnte nicht
widerstehen(, es zu tun).

**resistance** [rɪ'zɪstəns] n (also ELEC)
Widerstand m; (to illness) Widerstandsfähigkeit f.

**resistant** [rɪ'zɪstənt] adj: ~ **(to)** (to change etc)
widerstandsfähig (gegenüber); (to
antibiotics etc) resistent (gegen).

**resolute** ['rɛzəluːt] adj (person) entschlossen,
resolut; (refusal) entschieden.

**resolution** [rɛzə'luːʃən] n (decision) Beschluß
m; (determination) Entschlossenheit f; (of
problem) Lösung f; **to make a** ~ einen
Entschluß fassen.

**resolve** [rɪ'zɔlv] n (determination)
Entschlossenheit f ♦ vt (problem) lösen;
(difficulty) beseitigen ♦ vi: **to** ~ **to do sth**
beschließen, etw zu tun.

**resolved** [rɪ'zɔlvd] adj (determined)
entschlossen.

**resonance** ['rɛzənəns] n Resonanz f.

**resonant** ['rɛzənənt] adj (sound, voice)
volltönend; (place) widerhallend.

**resort** [rɪ'zɔːt] n (town) Urlaubsort m;
(recourse) Zuflucht f ♦ vi: **to** ~ **to** Zuflucht
nehmen zu; **seaside** ~ Seebad nt; **winter
sports** ~ Wintersportort m; **as a last** ~ als
letzter Ausweg; **in the last** ~
schlimmstenfalls.

**resound** [rɪ'zaund] vi: **to** ~ **(with)** widerhallen
(von).

**resounding** [rɪ'zaundɪŋ] adj (noise)
widerhallend; (voice) schallend; (fig: success)
durchschlagend; (: victory) überlegen.

**resource** [rɪ'sɔːs] n (raw material) Bodenschatz
m; **resources** npl (coal, oil etc) Energiequellen
pl; (money) Mittel pl, Ressourcen pl; **natural**
~**s** Naturschätze pl.

**resourceful** [rɪ'sɔːsful] adj einfallsreich.

**resourcefulness** [rɪ'sɔːsfulnɪs] n
Einfallsreichtum m.

**respect** [rɪs'pɛkt] n (consideration, esteem)
Respekt m ♦ vt respektieren; **respects** npl
(greetings) Grüße pl; **to have** ~ **for sb/sth**

Respekt vor jdm/etw haben; **to show sb/sth** ~ Respekt vor jdm/etw zeigen; **out of** ~ **for** aus Rücksicht auf *+acc*; **with** ~ **to, in** ~ **of** in bezug auf *+acc*; **in this** ~ in dieser Hinsicht; **in some/many** ~s in gewisser/vielfacher Hinsicht; **with (all due)** ~ bei allem Respekt.

**respectability** [rɪspɛktə'bɪlɪtɪ] *n* Anständigkeit *f*.

**respectable** [rɪs'pɛktəbl] *adj* anständig; *(amount, income)* ansehnlich; *(standard, mark etc)* ordentlich.

**respected** [rɪs'pɛktɪd] *adj* angesehen.

**respectful** [rɪs'pɛktful] *adj* respektvoll.

**respectfully** [rɪs'pɛktfəlɪ] *adv (behave)* respektvoll.

**respective** [rɪs'pɛktɪv] *adj* jeweilig.

**respectively** [rɪs'pɛktɪvlɪ] *adv* beziehungsweise; **Germany and Britain were 3rd and 4th** ~ Deutschland und Großbritannien belegten den 3. beziehungsweise 4. Platz.

**respiration** [rɛspɪ'reɪʃən] *n see* **artificial**.

**respirator** ['rɛspɪreɪtə*] *n* Respirator *m*, Beatmungsgerät *nt*.

**respiratory** ['rɛspərətərɪ] *adj (system, failure)* Atmungs-.

**respite** ['rɛspaɪt] *n (rest)* Ruhepause *f*.

**resplendent** [rɪs'plɛndənt] *adj (clothes)* prächtig.

**respond** [rɪs'pɒnd] *vi (answer)* antworten; *(react)* reagieren.

**respondent** [rɪs'pɒndənt] *n (LAW)* Beklagte(r) *f(m)*.

**response** [rɪs'pɒns] *n (to question)* Antwort *f*; *(to event etc)* Reaktion *f*; **in** ~ **to** als Antwort/Reaktion auf *+acc*.

**responsibility** [rɪspɒnsɪ'bɪlɪtɪ] *n* Verantwortung *f*; **to take** ~ **for sth/sb** die Verantwortung für etw/jdn übernehmen.

**responsible** [rɪs'pɒnsɪbl] *adj* verantwortlich; *(reliable, important)* verantwortungsvoll; **to be** ~ **for sth** für etw verantwortlich sein; **to be** ~ **for doing sth** dafür verantwortlich sein, etw zu tun; **to be** ~ **to sb** jdm gegenüber verantwortlich sein.

**responsibly** [rɪs'pɒnsɪblɪ] *adv* verantwortungsvoll.

**responsive** [rɪs'pɒnsɪv] *adj (person)* ansprechbar.

**rest** [rɛst] *n (relaxation)* Ruhe *f*; *(pause)* Ruhepause *f*; *(remainder)* Rest *m*; *(support)* Stütze *f*; *(MUS)* Pause *f* ♦ *vi (relax)* sich ausruhen ♦ *vt (eyes, legs etc)* ausruhen; **the** ~ **of them** die übrigen; **to put** *or* **set sb's mind at** ~ jdn beruhigen; **to come to** ~ *(object)* zum Stillstand kommen; **to lay sb to** ~ jdn zur letzten Ruhe betten; **to** ~ **on sth** *(lit, fig)* sich auf etw *acc* stützen; **to let the matter** ~ die Sache auf sich beruhen lassen; ~ **assured that** ... seien Sie versichert, daß ...; **I won't** ~ **until** ... ich werde nicht ruhen,

bis ...; **may he/she** ~ **in peace** möge er/sie in Frieden ruhen; **to** ~ **sth on/against sth** *(lean)* etw an etw *acc*/gegen etw lehnen; **to** ~ **one's eyes** *or* **gaze on sth** den Blick auf etw heften; **I** ~ **my case** mehr brauche ich dazu wohl nicht zu sagen.

**restart** [riː'stɑːt] *vt (engine)* wieder anlassen; *(work)* wiederaufnehmen.

**restaurant** ['rɛstərɒŋ] *n* Restaurant *nt*.

**restaurant car** *(BRIT) n (RAIL)* Speisewagen *m*.

**rest cure** *n* Erholung *f*.

**restful** ['rɛstful] *adj (music)* ruhig; *(lighting)* beruhigend; *(atmosphere)* friedlich.

**rest home** *n* Pflegeheim *nt*.

**restitution** [rɛstɪ'tjuːʃən] *n*: **to make** ~ **to sb of sth** jdm etw zurückerstatten; *(as compensation)* jdn für etw entschädigen.

**restive** ['rɛstɪv] *adj (person, crew)* unruhig; *(horse)* störrisch.

**restless** ['rɛstlɪs] *adj* rastlos; *(audience)* unruhig; **to get** ~ unruhig werden.

**restlessly** ['rɛstlɪslɪ] *adv (walk around)* rastlos; *(turn over)* unruhig.

**restock** [riː'stɒk] *vt (shop, freezer)* wieder auffüllen; *(lake, river: with fish)* wieder besetzen.

**restoration** [rɛstə'reɪʃən] *n (of painting etc)* Restauration *f*; *(of law and order, health, sight etc)* Wiederherstellung *f*; *(of land, rights)* Rückgabe *f*; *(HIST)*: **the R~** die Restauration.

**restorative** [rɪ'stɔːrətɪv] *adj (power, treatment)* stärkend ♦ *n (old: drink)* Stärkungsmittel *nt*.

**restore** [rɪ'stɔː*] *vt (painting etc)* restaurieren; *(law and order, health, faith etc)* wiederherstellen; *(property)* zurückgeben; **to** ~ **sth to** *(to former state)* etw zurückverwandeln in *+acc*; **to** ~ **sb to power** jdn wieder an die Macht bringen.

**restorer** [rɪ'stɔːrə*] *n (ART etc)* Restaurator(in) *m(f)*.

**restrain** [rɪs'treɪn] *vt (person)* zurückhalten; *(feeling)* unterdrücken; *(growth, inflation)* dämpfen; **to** ~ **sb from doing sth** jdn davon abhalten, etw zu tun; **to** ~ **o.s. from doing sth** sich beherrschen, etw nicht zu tun.

**restrained** [rɪs'treɪnd] *adj (person)* beherrscht; *(style etc)* zurückhaltend.

**restraint** [rɪs'treɪnt] *n (restriction)* Einschränkung *f*; *(moderation)* Zurückhaltung *f*; **wage** ~ Zurückhaltung *f* bei Lohnforderungen.

**restrict** [rɪs'trɪkt] *vt* beschränken.

**restricted area** *(BRIT) n (AUT)* Bereich *m* mit Geschwindigkeitsbeschränkung.

**restriction** [rɪs'trɪkʃən] *n* Beschränkung *f*.

**restrictive** [rɪs'trɪktɪv] *adj (law, measure)* restriktiv; *(clothing)* beengend.

**restrictive practices** *(BRIT) npl (INDUSTRY)* wettbewerbshemmende Geschäftspraktiken *pl*.

**rest room** *(US) n* Toilette *f*.

**restructure** [riː'strʌktʃə*] vt umstrukturieren.
**result** [rɪ'zʌlt] n Resultat nt; (of match, election, exam etc) Ergebnis nt ♦ vi: **to ~ in** führen zu; **as a ~ of the accident** als Folge des Unfalls; **he missed the train as a ~ of sleeping in** er verpaßte den Zug, weil er verschlafen hatte; **to ~ from** resultieren or sich ergeben aus; **as a ~ it is too expensive** folglich ist es zu teuer.
**resultant** [rɪ'zʌltənt] adj resultierend, sich ergebend.
**resume** [rɪ'zjuːm] vt (work, journey) wiederaufnehmen; (seat) wieder einnehmen ♦ vi (start again) von neuem beginnen.
**résumé** ['reɪzjuːmeɪ] n Zusammenfassung f; (US: curriculum vitae) Lebenslauf m.
**resumption** [rɪ'zʌmpʃən] n (of work etc) Wiederaufnahme f.
**resurgence** [rɪ'səːdʒəns] n Wiederaufleben nt.
**resurrection** [rezə'rekʃən] n (of hopes, fears) Wiederaufleben nt; (of custom etc) Wiederbelebung f; (REL): **the R~** die Auferstehung f.
**resuscitate** [rɪ'sʌsɪteɪt] vt (MED, fig) wiederbeleben.
**resuscitation** [rɪsʌsɪ'teɪʃən] n Wiederbelebung f.
**retail** ['riːteɪl] adj (trade, department) Verkaufs-; (shop, goods) Einzelhandels- ♦ adv im Einzelhandel ♦ vt (sell) (im Einzelhandel) verkaufen ♦ vi: **to ~ at** (im Einzelhandel) kosten; **this product ~s at £25** dieses Produkt kostet im Laden £25.
**retailer** ['riːteɪlə*] n Einzelhändler(in) m(f).
**retail outlet** n Einzelhandelsverkaufsstelle f.
**retail price** n Einzelhandelspreis m.
**retail price index** n Einzelhandelspreisindex m.
**retain** [rɪ'teɪn] vt (keep) behalten; (: heat, moisture) zurückhalten.
**retainer** [rɪ'teɪnə*] n (fee) Vorauszahlung f.
**retaliate** [rɪ'tælɪeɪt] vi Vergeltung üben.
**retaliation** [rɪtælɪ'eɪʃən] n Vergeltung f; **in ~ for** als Vergeltung für.
**retaliatory** [rɪ'tælɪətərɪ] adj (move, attack) Vergeltungs-.
**retarded** [rɪ'tɑːdɪd] adj zurückgeblieben; **mentally ~** geistig zurückgeblieben.
**retch** [retʃ] vi würgen.
**retention** [rɪ'tenʃən] n (of tradition etc) Beibehaltung f; (of land, memories) Behalten nt; (of heat, fluid etc) Zurückhalten nt.
**retentive** [rɪ'tentɪv] adj (memory) merkfähig.
**rethink** ['riː'θɪŋk] vt noch einmal überdenken.
**reticence** ['retɪsns] n Zurückhaltung f.
**reticent** ['retɪsnt] adj zurückhaltend.
**retina** ['retɪnə] n Netzhaut f.
**retinue** ['retɪnjuː] n Gefolge nt.
**retire** [rɪ'taɪə*] vi (give up work) in den Ruhestand treten; (withdraw, go to bed) sich zurückziehen.
**retired** [rɪ'taɪəd] adj (person) im Ruhestand.

**retirement** [rɪ'taɪəmənt] n (state) Ruhestand m; (act) Pensionierung f.
**retirement age** n Rentenalter nt.
**retiring** [rɪ'taɪərɪŋ] adj (leaving) ausscheidend; (shy) zurückhaltend.
**retort** [rɪ'tɔːt] vi erwidern ♦ n (reply) Erwiderung f.
**retrace** [riː'treɪs] vt: **to ~ one's steps** (lit, fig) seine Schritte zurückverfolgen.
**retract** [rɪ'trækt] vt (promise) zurücknehmen; (confession) zurückziehen; (claws, undercarriage) einziehen.
**retractable** [rɪ'træktəbl] adj (undercarriage, aerial) einziehbar.
**retrain** [riː'treɪn] vt umschulen ♦ vi umgeschult werden.
**retraining** [riː'treɪnɪŋ] n Umschulung f.
**retread** ['riːtred] n (tyre) runderneuerter Reifen m.
**retreat** [rɪ'triːt] n (place) Zufluchtsort m; (withdrawal: also MIL) Rückzug m ♦ vi sich zurückziehen; **to beat a hasty ~** schleunigst den Rückzug antreten.
**retrial** [riː'traɪəl] n erneute Verhandlung f.
**retribution** [retrɪ'bjuːʃən] n Strafe f.
**retrieval** [rɪ'triːvəl] n (of object) Zurückholen nt; (COMPUT) Abruf m.
**retrieve** [rɪ'triːv] vt (object) zurückholen; (situation) retten; (error) wiedergutmachen; (dog) apportieren; (COMPUT) abrufen.
**retriever** [rɪ'triːvə*] n (dog) Apportierhund m.
**retroactive** [retrəu'æktɪv] adj rückwirkend.
**retrograde** ['retrəgreɪd] adj (step) Rück-.
**retrospect** ['retrəspekt] n: **in ~** rückblickend, im Rückblick.
**retrospective** [retrə'spektɪv] adj (opinion etc) im Nachhinein; (law, tax) rückwirkend ♦ n (ART) Retrospektive f.
**return** [rɪ'təːn] n (going or coming back) Rückkehr f; (of sth stolen etc) Rückgabe f; (also: ~ ticket: BRIT) Rückfahrkarte f; (FIN: from investment etc) Ertrag m; (of merchandise) Rücksendung f; (official report) Erklärung f ♦ cpd (journey) Rück- ♦ vi (person etc: come or go back) zurückkehren; (feelings, symptoms etc) wiederkehren ♦ vt (favour, greetings etc) erwidern; (sth stolen etc) zurückgeben; (LAW: verdict) fällen; (POL: candidate) wählen; (ball) zurückspielen; **returns** npl (COMM) Gewinne pl; **in ~ (for)** als Gegenleistung (für); **by ~ of post** postwendend; **many happy ~s (of the day)!** herzlichen Glückwunsch zum Geburtstag!; **~ match** Rückspiel nt.
▶**return to** vt fus (regain: consciousness, power) wiedererlangen.
**returnable** [rɪ'təːnəbl] adj (bottle etc) Mehrweg-.
**returner** n jd, der nach längerer Abwesenheit wieder in die Arbeitswelt zurückkehrt.
**returning officer** [rɪ'təːnɪŋ-] (BRIT) n Wahlleiter(in) m(f).

**return key** *n* (*COMPUT*) Return-Taste *f.*
**reunion** [riː'juːnɪən] *n* Treffen *nt*; (*after long separation*) Wiedervereinigung *f.*
**reunite** [riːju'naɪt] *vt* wiedervereinigen.
**Rev.** *abbr* (*REL*) = **Reverend.**
**rev** [rɛv] *n abbr* (*AUT*: = *revolution per minute*) Umdrehung *f* pro Minute, U/min. ♦ *vt* (*also:* ~ **up:** *engine*) aufheulen lassen.
**revaluation** [riːvælju'eɪʃən] *n* (*of property*) Neuschätzung *f*; (*of currency*) Aufwertung *f*; (*of attitudes*) Neubewertung *f.*
**revamp** [riː'væmp] *vt* (*company, system*) auf Vordermann bringen.
**rev counter** (*BRIT*) *n* (*AUT*) Drehzahlmesser *m.*
**Revd.** *abbr* (*REL*) = **Reverend.**
**reveal** [rɪ'viːl] *vt* (*make known*) enthüllen; (*make visible*) zum Vorschein bringen.
**revealing** [rɪ'viːlɪŋ] *adj* (*comment, action*) aufschlußreich; (*dress*) tief ausgeschnitten.
**reveille** [rɪ'vælɪ] *n* (*MIL*) Wecksignal *nt.*
**revel** ['rɛvl] *vi*: **to** ~ **in sth** in etw schwelgen; **to** ~ **in doing sth** es genießen, etw zu tun.
**revelation** [rɛvə'leɪʃən] *n* (*disclosure*) Enthüllung *f.*
**reveller** ['rɛvlə*] *n* Zecher(in) *m(f).*
**revelry** ['rɛvlrɪ] *n* Gelage *nt.*
**revenge** [rɪ'vɛndʒ] *n* (*for insult etc*) Rache *f* ♦ *vt* rächen; **to get one's** ~ **(for sth)** seine Rache (für etw) bekommen; **to** ~ **o.s.** *or* **take one's** ~ **(on sb)** sich (an jdm) rächen.
**revengeful** [rɪ'vɛndʒful] *adj* rachsüchtig.
**revenue** ['rɛvənjuː] *n* (*of person, company*) Einnahmen *pl*; (*of government*) Staatseinkünfte *pl.*
**reverberate** [rɪ'vəːbəreɪt] *vi* (*sound etc*) widerhallen; (*fig: shock etc*) Nachwirkungen haben.
**reverberation** [rɪvəːbə'reɪʃən] *n* (*of sound*) Widerhall *m*; (*fig: of event etc*) Nachwirkungen *pl.*
**revere** [rɪ'vɪə*] *vt* verehren.
**reverence** ['rɛvərəns] *n* Ehrfurcht *f.*
**Reverend** ['rɛvərənd] *adj* (*in titles*) Pfarrer; **the** ~ **John Smith** Pfarrer John Smith.
**reverent** ['rɛvərənt] *adj* ehrfürchtig.
**reverie** ['rɛvərɪ] *n* Träumerei *f.*
**reversal** [rɪ'vəːsl] *n* (*of policy, trend*) Umkehr *f*; **a** ~ **of roles** ein Rollentausch *m.*
**reverse** [rɪ'vəːs] *n* (*opposite*) Gegenteil *nt*; (*back: of cloth*) linke Seite *f*; (: *of coin, paper*) Rückseite *f*; (*AUT: also:* ~ **gear**) Rückwärtsgang *m*; (*setback*) Rückschlag *m* ♦ *adj* (*side*) Rück-; (*process*) umgekehrt ♦ *vt* (*position, trend etc*) umkehren; (*LAW: verdict*) revidieren; (*roles*) vertauschen; (*car*) zurücksetzen ♦ *vi* (*BRIT: AUT*) zurücksetzen; **in** ~ umgekehrt; **to go into** ~ den Rückwärtsgang einlegen; **in** ~ **order** in umgekehrter Reihenfolge; **to** ~ **direction** sich um 180 Grad drehen.
**reverse-charge call** [rɪ'vəːstʃɑːdʒ-] (*BRIT*) *n*

R-Gespräch *nt.*
**reverse video** *n* (*COMPUT*) invertierte Darstellung *f.*
**reversible** [rɪ'vəːsəbl] *adj* (*garment*) auf beiden Seiten tragbar; (*decision, operation*) umkehrbar.
**reversing lights** [rɪ'vəːsɪŋ-] (*BRIT*) *npl* Rückfahrscheinwerfer *m.*
**reversion** [rɪ'vəːʃən] *n*: ~ **to** Rückfall in +*acc*; (*ZOOL*) Rückentwicklung *f.*
**revert** [rɪ'vəːt] *vi*: **to** ~ **to** (*former state*) zurückkehren zu, zurückfallen in +*acc*; (*LAW: money, property*) zurückfallen an +*acc.*
**review** [rɪ'vjuː] *n* (*magazine*) Zeitschrift *f*; (*MIL*) Inspektion *f*; (*of book, film etc*) Kritik *f*, Besprechung *f*, Rezension *f*; (*of policy etc*) Überprüfung *f* ♦ *vt* (*MIL: troops*) inspizieren; (*book, film etc*) besprechen, rezensieren; (*policy etc*) überprüfen; **to be/come under** ~ überprüft werden.
**reviewer** [rɪ'vjuːə*] *n* Kritiker(in) *m(f)*, Rezensent(in) *m(f).*
**revile** [rɪ'vaɪl] *vt* schmähen.
**revise** [rɪ'vaɪz] *vt* (*manuscript*) überarbeiten, revidieren; (*opinion etc*) ändern; (*price, procedure*) revidieren ♦ *vi* (*study*) wiederholen; ~**d edition** überarbeitete Ausgabe.
**revision** [rɪ'vɪʒən] *n* (*of manuscript, law etc*) Überarbeitung *f*, Revision *f*; (*for exam*) Wiederholung *f.*
**revitalize** [riː'vaɪtəlaɪz] *vt* neu beleben.
**revival** [rɪ'vaɪvl] *n* (*recovery*) Aufschwung *m*; (*of interest, faith*) Wiederaufleben *nt*; (*THEAT*) Wiederaufnahme *f.*
**revive** [rɪ'vaɪv] *vt* (*person*) wiederbeleben; (*economy etc*) Auftrieb geben +*dat*; (*custom*) wiederaufleben lassen; (*hope, interest etc*) neu beleben; (*play*) wiederaufnehmen ♦ *vi* (*person*) wieder zu sich kommen; (*activity, economy etc*) wieder aufblühen; (*hope, interest etc*) wiedererweckt werden.
**revoke** [rɪ'vəuk] *vt* (*law etc*) aufheben; (*title, licence*) entziehen +*dat*; (*promise, decision*) widerrufen.
**revolt** [rɪ'vəult] *n* Revolte *f*, Aufstand *m* ♦ *vi* rebellieren ♦ *vt* abstoßen; **to** ~ **against sb/ sth** gegen jdn/etw rebellieren.
**revolting** [rɪ'vəultɪŋ] *adj* (*disgusting*) abscheulich, ekelhaft.
**revolution** [rɛvə'luːʃən] *n* (*POL etc*) Revolution *f*; (*rotation*) Umdrehung *f.*
**revolutionary** [rɛvə'luːʃənrɪ] *adj* revolutionär; (*leader, army*) Revolutions- ♦ *n* Revolutionär(in) *m(f).*
**revolutionize** [rɛvə'luːʃənaɪz] *vt* revolutionieren.
**revolve** [rɪ'vɔlv] *vi* sich drehen; **to** ~ **(a)round** sich drehen um.
**revolver** [rɪ'vɔlvə*] *n* Revolver *m.*
**revolving** [rɪ'vɔlvɪŋ] *adj* (*chair*) Dreh-; (*sprinkler etc*) drehbar.

**revolving door** n Drehtür f.

**revue** [rɪ'vjuː] n (THEAT) Revue f.

**revulsion** [rɪ'vʌlʃən] n (disgust) Abscheu m, Ekel m.

**reward** [rɪ'wɔːd] n Belohnung f; (satisfaction) Befriedigung f ♦ vt belohnen.

**rewarding** [rɪ'wɔːdɪŋ] adj lohnend; **financially** ~ einträglich.

**rewind** [riː'waɪnd] (irreg: like **wind**) vt (tape etc) zurückspulen.

**rewire** [riː'waɪə*] vt neu verkabeln.

**reword** [riː'wɔːd] vt (message, note) umformulieren.

**rework** [riː'wɔːk] vt (use again: theme etc) wieder verarbeiten; (revise) neu fassen.

**rewrite** [riː'raɪt] (irreg: like **write**) vt neu schreiben.

**Reykjavik** ['reɪkjəviːk] n Reykjavik nt.

**RFD** (US) abbr (POST: = rural free delivery) freie Landpostzustellung.

**RGN** (BRIT) n abbr (= Registered General Nurse) staatlich geprüfte Krankenschwester f, staatlich geprüfter Krankenpfleger m.

**Rh** abbr (MED: = rhesus) Rh.

**rhapsody** ['ræpsədɪ] n (MUS) Rhapsodie f.

**rhesus negative** adj Rhesus negativ.

**rhesus positive** adj Rhesus positiv.

**rhetoric** ['rɛtərɪk] n Rhetorik f.

**rhetorical** [rɪ'tɒrɪkl] adj rhetorisch.

**rheumatic** [ruː'mætɪk] adj rheumatisch.

**rheumatism** ['ruːmətɪzəm] n Rheuma nt, Rheumatismus m.

**rheumatoid arthritis** ['ruːmətɔɪd-] n Gelenkrheumatismus m.

**Rhine** [raɪn] n: **the** ~ der Rhein.

**rhinestone** ['raɪnstəun] n Rheinkiesel m.

**rhinoceros** [raɪ'nɒsərəs] n Rhinozeros nt.

**Rhodes** [rəudz] n Rhodos nt.

**Rhodesia** [rəu'diːʒə] (formerly) n (GEOG) Rhodesien nt.

**rhododendron** [rəudə'dɛndrən] n Rhododendron m or nt.

**Rhone** [rəun] n: **the** ~ die Rhone.

**rhubarb** ['ruːbɑːb] n Rhabarber m.

**rhyme** [raɪm] n Reim m; (verse) Verse pl ♦ vi: **to** ~ **(with)** sich reimen (mit); **without** ~ **or reason** ohne Sinn und Verstand.

**rhythm** ['rɪðm] n Rhythmus m.

**rhythmic(al)** ['rɪðmɪk(l)] adj rhythmisch.

**rhythmically** ['rɪðmɪklɪ] adv (move, beat) rhythmisch, im Rhythmus.

**rhythm method** n Knaus-Ogino-Methode f.

**RI** n abbr (BRIT: SCOL: = religious instruction) Religionsunterricht m ♦ abbr (US: POST: = Rhode Island).

**rib** [rɪb] n Rippe f ♦ vt (mock) aufziehen.

**ribald** ['rɪbəld] adj (laughter, joke) rüde; (person) anzüglich.

**ribbed** [rɪbd] adj (socks, sweater) gerippt.

**ribbon** ['rɪbən] n (for hair, decoration) Band nt; (of typewriter) Farbband nt; **in** ~**s** (torn) in Fetzen.

**rice** [raɪs] n Reis m.

**ricefield** ['raɪsfiːld] n Reisfeld nt.

**rice pudding** n Milchreis m.

**rich** [rɪtʃ] adj reich; (soil) fruchtbar; (food) schwer; (diet) reichhaltig; (colour) satt; (voice) volltönend; (tapestries, silks) prächtig ♦ npl: **the** ~ die Reichen; ~ **in** reich an +dat.

**riches** ['rɪtʃɪz] npl Reichtum m.

**richly** ['rɪtʃlɪ] adv (decorated, carved) reich; (reward, benefit) reichlich; ~ **deserved/ earned** wohlverdient.

**richness** ['rɪtʃnɪs] n (wealth) Reichtum m; (of life, culture, food) Reichhaltigkeit f; (of soil) Fruchtbarkeit f; (of costumes, furnishings) Pracht f.

**rickets** ['rɪkɪts] n Rachitis f.

**rickety** ['rɪkɪtɪ] adj (chair etc) wackelig.

**rickshaw** ['rɪkʃɔː] n Rikscha f.

**ricochet** ['rɪkəʃeɪ] vi abprallen ♦ n Abpraller m.

**rid** [rɪd] (pt, pp **rid**) vt: **to** ~ **sb/sth of** jdn/etw befreien von; **to get** ~ **of** loswerden; (inhibitions, illusions etc) sich befreien von.

**riddance** ['rɪdns] n: **good** ~! gut, daß wir den/ die/das los sind!

**ridden** ['rɪdn] pp of **ride**.

**riddle** ['rɪdl] n Rätsel nt ♦ vt: **to be** ~**d with** (guilt, doubts) geplagt sein von; (holes, corruption) durchsetzt sein von.

**ride** [raɪd] (pt **rode**, pp **ridden**) n (in car, on bicycle) Fahrt f; (on horse) Ritt m; (path) Reitweg m ♦ vi (on horse) reiten; (on bicycle, bus etc) fahren ♦ vt (see vi) reiten; fahren; **car** ~ Autofahrt f; **to go for a** ~ eine Fahrt/ einen Ausritt machen; **to take sb for a** ~ (fig) jdn hereinlegen; **we rode all day/all the way** wir sind den ganzen Tag/den ganzen Weg geritten/gefahren; **to** ~ **at anchor** (NAUT) vor Anker liegen; **can you** ~ **a bike?** kannst du Fahrrad fahren?

►**ride out** vt: **to** ~ **out the storm** (fig) den Sturm überstehen.

**rider** ['raɪdə*] n (on horse) Reiter(in) m(f); (on bicycle etc) Fahrer(in) m(f); (in document etc) Zusatz m.

**ridge** [rɪdʒ] n (of hill) Grat m; (of roof) First m; (in sand etc) Rippelmarke f.

**ridicule** ['rɪdɪkjuːl] n Spott m ♦ vt (person) verspotten; (proposal, system etc) lächerlich machen; **she was the object of** ~ alle machten sich über sie lustig.

**ridiculous** [rɪ'dɪkjuləs] adj lächerlich.

**riding** ['raɪdɪŋ] n Reiten nt.

**riding school** n Reitschule f.

**rife** [raɪf] adj: **to be** ~ (corruption, disease etc) grassieren; **to be** ~ **with** (rumours etc) durchsetzt sein von.

**riffraff** ['rɪfræf] n Gesindel nt.

**rifle** ['raɪfl] n (gun) Gewehr nt ♦ vt (wallet etc) plündern.

►**rifle through** vt fus (papers etc) durchwühlen.

**rifle range** n Schießstand m.
**rift** [rɪft] n Spalt m; (fig) Kluft f.
**rig** [rɪg] n (also: **oil** ~: at sea) Bohrinsel f; (: on land) Bohrturm m ♦ vt (election, game etc) manipulieren.
▶**rig out** (BRIT) vt: **to** ~ **sb out as/in** jdn ausstaffieren als/in +dat.
▶**rig up** vt (device) montieren.
**rigging** ['rɪgɪŋ] n (NAUT) Takelage f.
**right** [raɪt] adj (correct) richtig; (not left) rechte(r, s) ♦ n Recht nt ♦ adv (correctly, properly) richtig; (directly, exactly) genau; (not on the left) rechts ♦ vt (ship, car etc) aufrichten; (fault, situation) korrigieren, berichtigen ♦ excl okay; **the** ~ **time** (exact) die genaue Zeit; (most suitable) die richtige Zeit; **to be** ~ (person) recht haben; (answer, fact) richtig sein; (clock) genau gehen; (reading etc) korrekt sein; **to get sth** ~ etw richtig machen; **let's get it** ~ **this time!** diesmal machen wir es richtig!; **you did the** ~ **thing** du hast das Richtige getan; **to put sth** ~ (mistake etc) etw berichtigen; **on/to the** ~ rechts; **the R~** (POL) die Rechte; **by** ~**s** richtig genommen; **to be in the** ~ im Recht sein; **you're within your** ~**s (to do that)** es ist dein gutes Recht(, das zu tun); **he is a well-known author in his own** ~ er ist selbst auch ein bekannter Autor; **film** ~**s** Filmrechte pl; ~ **now** im Moment; ~ **before/after the party** gleich vor/nach der Party; ~ **against the wall** unmittelbar an der Wand; ~ **ahead** geradeaus; ~ **away** (immediately) sofort; ~ **in the middle** genau in der Mitte; **he went** ~ **to the end of the road** er ging bis ganz ans Ende der Straße.
**right angle** n rechter Winkel m.
**righteous** ['raɪtʃəs] adj (person) rechtschaffen; (indignation) gerecht.
**righteousness** ['raɪtʃəsnɪs] n Rechtschaffenheit f.
**rightful** ['raɪtful] adj rechtmäßig.
**rightfully** ['raɪtfəlɪ] adv von Rechts wegen.
**right-hand drive** adj (vehicle) mit Rechtssteuerung.
**right-handed** [raɪt'hændɪd] adj rechtshändig.
**right-hand man** n rechte Hand f.
**right-hand side** n rechte Seite f.
**rightly** ['raɪtlɪ] adv (with reason) zu Recht; **if I remember** ~ (BRIT) wenn ich mich recht entsinne.
**right-minded** [raɪt'maɪndɪd] adj vernünftig.
**right of way** n (on path etc) Durchgangsrecht f; (AUT) Vorfahrt f.
**rights issue** n (STOCK EXCHANGE) Bezugsrechtsemission f.
**right wing** n (POL, SPORT) rechter Flügel m.
**right-wing** [raɪt'wɪŋ] adj (POL) rechtsgerichtet.
**right-winger** [raɪt'wɪŋə*] n (POL) Rechte(r) f(m); (SPORT) Rechtsaußen m.
**rigid** ['rɪdʒɪd] adj (structure, views) starr;

(principle, control etc) streng.
**rigidity** [rɪ'dʒɪdɪtɪ] n (of structure etc) Starrheit f; (of attitude, views etc) Strenge f.
**rigidly** ['rɪdʒɪdlɪ] adv (hold, fix etc) starr; (control, interpret) streng.
**rigmarole** ['rɪgmərəul] n (procedure) Gedöns nt (inf).
**rigor** ['rɪgə*] (US) n = **rigour**.
**rigor mortis** ['rɪgə'mɔːtɪs] n Totenstarre f.
**rigorous** ['rɪgərəs] adj (control etc) streng; (training) gründlich.
**rigorously** ['rɪgərəslɪ] adv (test, assess etc) streng.
**rigour, (US) rigor** ['rɪgə*] n (of argument, law) Strenge f; (of research) Gründlichkeit f; **the** ~**s of life/winter** die Härten des Lebens/des Winters.
**rig-out** ['rɪgaut] (BRIT: inf) n (clothes) Aufzug m.
**rile** [raɪl] vt ärgern.
**rim** [rɪm] n (of glass, spectacles) Rand m; (of wheel) Felge f, Radkranz m.
**rimless** ['rɪmlɪs] adj (spectacles) randlos.
**rimmed** [rɪmd] adj: ~ **with** umrandet von; **gold-~ spectacles** Brille f mit Goldfassung or Goldrand.
**rind** [raɪnd] n (of bacon) Schwarte f; (of lemon, melon) Schale f; (of cheese) Rinde f.
**ring** [rɪŋ] (pt rang, pp rung) n Ring m; (of people, objects) Kreis m; (of circus) Manege f; (bullring) Arena f; (sound of telephone) Klingeln nt; (sound of bell) Läuten nt; (on cooker) Kochstelle m ♦ vi (TEL: person) anrufen; (telephone, doorbell) klingeln; (bell) läuten; (also: ~ **out**) ertönen ♦ vt (BRIT: TEL) anrufen; (bell etc) läuten; (encircle) einen Kreis machen um; **to give sb a** ~ (BRIT: TEL) jdn anrufen; **that has a** ~ **of truth about it** das können stimmen; **to run** ~**s round sb** (inf, fig) jdn in die Tasche stecken; **to** ~ **true/false** wahr/falsch klingen; **my ears are** ~**ing** mir klingen die Ohren; **to** ~ **the doorbell** klingeln; **the name doesn't** ~ **a bell (with me)** der Name sagt mir nichts.
▶**ring back** (BRIT) vt, vi (TEL) zurückrufen.
▶**ring off** (BRIT) vi (TEL) (den Hörer) auflegen.
▶**ring up** (BRIT) vt (TEL) anrufen.
**ring binder** n Ringbuch nt.
**ring finger** n Ringfinger m.
**ringing** ['rɪŋɪŋ] n (of telephone) Klingeln nt; (of bell) Läuten nt; (in ears) Klingen nt.
**ringing tone** (BRIT) n (TEL) Rufzeichen nt.
**ringleader** ['rɪŋliːdə*] n Rädelsführer(in) m(f).
**ringlets** ['rɪŋlɪts] npl Ringellocken pl; **in** ~ in Ringellocken.
**ring road** (BRIT) n Ringstraße f.
**rink** [rɪŋk] n (also: **ice** ~) Eisbahn f; (also: **roller skating** ~) Rollschuhbahn f.
**rinse** [rɪns] n Spülen nt; (of hands) Abspülen nt; (hair dye) Tönung f ♦ vt spülen; (hands) abspülen; (also: ~ **out**: clothes) auswaschen;

**rissóle** ['rɪsəul] n (of meat, fish etc) Frikadelle f.

**rite** [raɪt] n Ritus m; **last ~s** (REL) Letzte Ölung f.

**ritual** ['rɪtjuəl] adj (law, murder) Ritual-; (dance) rituell ♦ n Ritual nt.

**rival** ['raɪvl] n Rivale m, Rivalin f ♦ adj (firm, newspaper etc) Konkurrenz-; (teams, groups etc) rivalisierend ♦ vt (match) sich messen können mit; **to ~ sth/sb in sth** sich mit etw/jdm in bezug auf etw messen können.

**rivalry** ['raɪvlrɪ] n Rivalität f.

**river** ['rɪvə·] n Fluß m; (fig: of blood etc) Strom m ♦ cpd (port, traffic) Fluß-; **up/down ~** flußaufwärts/-abwärts.

**river bank** n Flußufer nt.

**river bed** n Flußbett nt.

**riverside** ['rɪvəsaɪd] n = **river bank**.

**rivet** ['rɪvɪt] n Niete f ♦ vt (fig: attention) fesseln; (: eyes) heften.

**riveting** ['rɪvɪtɪŋ] adj (fig) fesselnd.

**Riviera** [rɪvɪ'cɑrə] n: **the (French) ~** die (französische) Riviera; **the Italian ~** die italienische Riviera.

**Riyadh** [rɪ'jɑːd] n Riad nt.

**RMT** n abbr (= National Union of Rail, Maritime and Transport Workers) Gewerkschaft der Eisenbahner, Seeleute und Transportarbeiter.

**RN** n abbr (BRIT) = **Royal Navy**; (US) = **registered nurse**.

**RNA** n abbr (= ribonucleic acid) RNS f.

**RNLI** (BRIT) n abbr (= Royal National Lifeboat Institution) durch Spenden finanzierter Seenot-Rettungsdienst, ≈ DLRG f.

**RNZAF** n abbr (= Royal New Zealand Air Force) neuseeländische Luftwaffe f.

**RNZN** n abbr (= Royal New Zealand Navy) neuseeländische Marine f.

**road** [rəud] n Straße f; (fig) Weg m ♦ cpd (accident, sense) Straßen-; **main ~** Hauptstraße f; **it takes four hours by ~** man braucht vier Stunden mit dem Auto; **let's hit the ~** machen wir uns auf den Weg!; **to be on the ~** (salesman etc) unterwegs sein; (pop group etc) auf Tournee sein; **on the ~ to success** auf dem Weg zum Erfolg; **major/minor ~** Haupt-/Nebenstraße f.

**roadblock** ['rəudblɒk] n Straßensperre f.

**road haulage** n Spedition f.

**roadhog** ['rəudhɒg] n Verkehrsrowdy m.

**road map** n Straßenkarte f.

**road safety** n Verkehrssicherheit f.

**roadside** ['rəudsaɪd] n Straßenrand m ♦ cpd (building, sign etc) am Straßenrand; **by the ~** am Straßenrand.

**road sign** n Verkehrszeichen nt.

**roadsweeper** ['rəudswiːpə·] (BRIT) n (person) Straßenkehrer(in) m(f); (vehicle) Straßenkehrmaschine f.

**road user** n Verkehrsteilnehmer(in) m(f).

**roadway** ['rəudweɪ] n Fahrbahn f.

**road works** npl Straßenbauarbeiten pl.

---

(: mouth) ausspülen; **to give sth a ~** etw spülen; (dishes) etw abspülen.

**Rio (de Janeiro)** ['riːəu(dədʒə'nɪərəu)] n Rio (de Janeiro) nt.

**riot** ['raɪət] n (disturbance) Aufruhr m ♦ vi randalieren; **a ~ of colours** ein Farbenmeer nt; **to run ~** randalieren.

**rioter** ['raɪətə·] n Randalierer m.

**riot gear** n Schutzausrüstung f.

**riotous** ['raɪətəs] adj (crowd) randalierend; (nights, party) ausschweifend; (welcome etc) tumultartig.

**riotously** ['raɪətəslɪ] adv: **~ funny** or **comic** urkomisch.

**riot police** n Bereitschaftspolizei f; **hundreds of ~** Hunderte von Bereitschaftspolizisten.

**RIP** abbr (= rest in peace) R.I.P.

**rip** [rɪp] n (tear) Riß m ♦ vt zerreißen ♦ vi reißen.

▶**rip off** vt (clothes) herunterreißen; (inf: swindle) übers Ohr hauen.

▶**rip up** vt zerreißen.

**ripcord** ['rɪpkɔːd] n Reißleine f.

**ripe** [raɪp] adj reif; **to be ~ for sth** (fig) reif für etw sein; **he lived to a ~ old age** er erreichte ein stolzes Alter.

**ripen** ['raɪpn] vt reifen lassen ♦ vi reifen.

**ripeness** ['raɪpnɪs] n Reife f.

**rip-off** ['rɪpɒf] (inf) n: **it's a ~!** das ist Wucher!

**riposte** [rɪ'pɒst] n scharfe Entgegnung f.

**ripple** ['rɪpl] n (wave) kleine Welle f; (of laughter, applause) Welle f ♦ vi (water) sich kräuseln; (muscles) spielen ♦ vt (surface) kräuseln.

**rise** [raɪz] (pt rose, pp risen) n (incline) Steigung f; (BRIT: salary increase) Gehaltserhöhung f; (in prices, temperature etc) Anstieg m; (fig: to fame etc) Aufstieg m ♦ vi (prices, water) steigen; (sun, moon) aufgehen; (wind) aufkommen; (from bed, chair) aufstehen; (sound, voice) ansteigen; (also: ~ up: tower, rebel) sich erheben; (in rank) aufsteigen; **to give ~ to** Anlaß geben zu; **to ~ to power** an die Macht kommen.

**risen** ['rɪzn] pp of **rise**.

**rising** ['raɪzɪŋ] adj (increasing) steigend; (up-and-coming) aufstrebend.

**rising damp** n aufsteigende Feuchtigkeit f.

**rising star** n (fig: person) Aufsteiger(in) m(f).

**risk** [rɪsk] n (danger, chance) Gefahr f; (deliberate) Risiko nt ♦ vt riskieren; **to take a ~** ein Risiko eingehen; **to run the ~ of sth** etw zu fürchten haben; **to run the ~ of doing sth** Gefahr laufen, etw zu tun; **at ~** in Gefahr; **at one's own ~** auf eigene Gefahr; **at the ~ of sounding rude** ... auf die Gefahr hin, unhöflich zu klingen, ...; **it's a fire/health ~** es ist ein Feuer-/Gesundheitsrisiko; **I'll ~ it** ich riskiere es.

**risk capital** n Risikokapital nt.

**risky** ['rɪskɪ] adj riskant.

**risqué** ['riːskeɪ] adj (joke) gewagt.

**roadworthy** ['rəudwə:ðɪ] *adj* verkehrstüchtig.
**roam** [rəum] *vi* wandern, streifen ♦ *vt* (*streets, countryside*) durchstreifen.
**roar** [rɔː'] *n* (*of animal, crowd*) Brüllen *nt*; (*of vehicle*) Getöse *nt*; (*of storm*) Heulen *nt* ♦ *vi* (*animal, person*) brüllen; (*engine, wind etc*) heulen; ~s **of laughter** brüllendes Gelächter; **to** ~ **with laughter** vor Lachen brüllen.
**roaring** ['rɔːrɪŋ] *adj:* **a** ~ **fire** ein prasselndes Feuer; **a** ~ **success** ein Bombenerfolg *m*; **to do a** ~ **trade (in sth)** ein Riesengeschäft (mit etw) machen.
**roast** [rəust] *n* Braten *m* ♦ *vt* (*meat, potatoes*) braten; (*coffee*) rösten.
**roast beef** *n* Roastbeef *nt*.
**roasting** ['rəustɪŋ] (*inf*) *adj* (*hot*) knallheiß ♦ *n* (*criticism*) Verriß *m*; (*telling-off*) Standpauke *f*; **to give sb a** ~ (*criticize*) jdn verreißen; (*scold*) jdm eine Standpauke halten.
**rob** [rɔb] *vt* (*person*) bestehlen; (*house, bank*) ausrauben; **to** ~ **sb of sth** jdm etw rauben; (*fig: deprive*) jdm etw vorenthalten.
**robber** ['rɔbə'] *n* Räuber(in) *m(f)*.
**robbery** ['rɔbərɪ] *n* Raub *m*.
**robe** [rəub] *n* (*for ceremony etc*) Gewand *nt*; (*also:* **bath** ~) Bademantel *m*; (*US*) Morgenrock *m* ♦ *vt:* **to be** ~**d in** (*form*) (festlich) in etw *acc* gekleidet sein.
**robin** ['rɔbɪn] *n* Rotkehlchen *nt*.
**robot** ['rəubɔt] *n* Roboter *m*.
**robotics** [rə'bɔtɪks] *n* Robotik *f*.
**robust** [rəu'bʌst] *adj* robust; (*appetite*) gesund.
**rock** [rɔk] *n* (*substance*) Stein *m*; (*boulder*) Felsen *m*; (*US: small stone*) Stein *m*; (*BRIT: sweet*) ≈ Zuckerstange *f*; (*MUS: also:* ~ **music**) Rock *m*, Rockmusik *f* ♦ *vt* (*swing gently: cradle*) schaukeln; (: *child*) wiegen; (*shake: also fig*) erschüttern ♦ *vi* (*object*) schwanken; (*person*) schaukeln; **on the** ~**s** (*drink*) mit Eis; (*ship*) (auf Felsen) aufgelaufen; (*marriage etc*) gescheitert; **to** ~ **the boat** (*fig*) Unruhe stiften.
**rock and roll** *n* Rock and Roll *m*.
**rock-bottom** ['rɔk'bɔtəm] *adj* (*prices*) Tiefst- ♦ *n:* **to reach** *or* **touch** *or* **hit rock bottom** (*person, prices*) den Tiefpunkt erreichen.
**rock cake** *n* ≈ Rosinenbrötchen *nt*.
**rock climber** *n* Felsenkletterer(in) *m(f)*.
**rock climbing** *n* Felsenklettern *nt*.
**rockery** ['rɔkərɪ] *n* Steingarten *m*.
**rocket** ['rɔkɪt] *n* Rakete *f* ♦ *vi* (*prices*) in die Höhe schießen.
**rocket launcher** *n* Raketenwerfer *m*.
**rock face** *n* Felswand *f*.
**rock fall** *n* Steinschlag *m*.
**rocking chair** ['rɔkɪŋ-] *n* Schaukelstuhl *m*.
**rocking horse** *n* Schaukelpferd *nt*.
**rocky** ['rɔkɪ] *adj* (*path, ground*) felsig; (*fig: business, marriage*) wackelig.
**Rocky Mountains** *npl:* **the** ~ die Rocky Mountains *pl*.

**rod** [rɔd] *n* (*also TECH*) Stange *f*; (*also:* **fishing** ~) Angelrute *f*.
**rode** [rəud] *pt of* ride.
**rodent** ['rəudnt] *n* Nagetier *nt*.
**rodeo** ['rəudɪəu] (*US*) *n* Rodeo *nt*.
**roe** [rəu] *n* (*CULIN*): **hard** ~ Rogen *m*; **soft** ~ Milch *f*.
**roe deer** *n inv* Reh *nt*.
**rogue** [rəug] *n* Gauner *m*.
**roguish** ['rəugɪʃ] *adj* schelmisch.
**role** [rəul] *n* Rolle *f*.
**role model** *n* Rollenmodell *nt*.
**role play** *n* Rollenspiel *nt*.
**roll** [rəul] *n* (*of paper*) Rolle *f*; (*of cloth*) Ballen *m*; (*of banknotes*) Bündel *nt*; (*also:* **bread** ~) Brötchen *nt*; (*register, list*) Verzeichnis *nt*; (*of drums etc*) Wirbel *m* ♦ *vt* rollen; (*also:* ~ **up:** *string*) aufrollen; (: *sleeves*) aufkrempeln; (*cigarette*) drehen; (*also:* ~ **out:** *pastry*) ausrollen; (*flatten: lawn, road*) walzen ♦ *vi* rollen; (*drum*) wirbeln; (*thunder*) grollen; (*ship*) schlingern; (*tears, sweat*) fließen; (*camera, printing press*) laufen; **cheese/ham** ~ Käse-/Schinkenbrötchen *nt*; **he's** ~**ing in it** (*inf: rich*) er schwimmt im Geld.
►**roll about** *vi* sich wälzen.
►**roll around** *vi* = **roll about.**
►**roll in** *vi* (*money, invitations*) hereinströmen.
►**roll over** *vi* sich umdrehen.
►**roll up** *vi* (*inf: arrive*) aufkreuzen ♦ *vt* (*carpet, umbrella etc*) aufrollen; **to** ~ **o.s. up into a ball** sich zusammenrollen.
**roll call** *n* namentlicher Aufruf *m*.
**rolled gold** [rəuld-] *n* Dubleegold *nt*.
**roller** ['rəulə'] *n* Rolle *f*; (*for lawn, road*) Walze *f*; (*for hair*) Lockenwickler *m*.
**roller blind** *n* Rollo *nt*.
**roller coaster** *n* Achterbahn *f*.
**roller skates** *npl* Rollschuhe *pl*.
**rollicking** ['rɔlɪkɪŋ] *adj* toll, Mords-; **to have a** ~ **time** sich ganz toll amüsieren.
**rolling** ['rəulɪŋ] *adj* (*hills*) wellig.
**rolling mill** *n* Walzwerk *nt*.
**rolling pin** *n* Nudelholz *nt*.
**rolling stock** *n* (*RAIL*) Fahrzeuge *pl*.
**roll-on-roll-off** ['rəulɔn'rəulɔf] (*BRIT*) *adj* (*ferry*) Roll-on-roll-off-.
**roly-poly** ['rəulɪ'pəulɪ] (*BRIT*) *n* ≈ Strudel *m*.
**ROM** [rɔm] *n abbr* (*COMPUT:* = *read only memory*) ROM.
**Roman** ['rəumən] *adj* römisch ♦ *n* (*person*) Römer(in) *m(f)*.
**Roman Catholic** *adj* römisch-katholisch ♦ *n* Katholik(in) *m(f)*.
**romance** [rə'mæns] *n* (*love affair*) Romanze *f*; (*romanticism*) Romantik *f*; (*novel*) phantastische Erzählung *f*.
**Romanesque** [rəumə'nɛsk] *adj* romanisch.
**Romania** [rəu'meɪnɪə] *n* Rumänien *nt*.
**Romanian** [rəu'meɪnɪən] *adj* rumänisch ♦ *n* (*person*) Rumäne *m*, Rumänin *f*; (*LING*) Rumänisch *nt*.

**Roman numeral** n römische Ziffer f.
**romantic** [rə'mæntık] adj romantisch.
**romanticism** [rə'mæntısızəm] n (also ART, LITER) Romantik f.
**Romany** ['rɔmənı] adj Roma- ♦ n (person) Roma mf; (LING) Romani nt.
**Rome** [rəum] n Rom nt.
**romp** [rɔmp] n Klamauk m ♦ vi (also: ~ about) herumtollen; **to** ~ **home** (horse) spielend gewinnen.
**rompers** ['rɔmpəz] npl (clothing) einteiliger Spielanzug für Babys.
**rondo** ['rɔndəu] n (MUS) Rondo nt.
**roof** [ru:f] (pl ~s) n Dach nt ♦ vt (house etc) überdachen; **the** ~ **of the mouth** der Gaumen.
**roof garden** n Dachgarten m.
**roofing** ['ru:fıŋ] n Deckung f; ~ **felt** Dachpappe f.
**roof rack** n Dachgepäckträger m.
**rook** [ruk] n (bird) Saatkrähe f; (CHESS) Turm m.
**rookie** ['ruki:] (inf) n (esp MIL) Grünschnabel m.
**room** [ru:m] n (in house, hotel) Zimmer nt; (space) Raum m, Platz m; (scope: for change etc) Raum m ♦ vi: **to** ~ **with sb** (esp US) ein Zimmer mit jdm teilen; **rooms** npl (lodging) Zimmer pl; "~**s to let**", (US) "~**s for rent**" „Zimmer zu vermieten"; **single/double** ~ Einzel-/Doppelzimmer nt; **is there** ~ **for this?** ist dafür Platz vorhanden?; **to make** ~ **for sb** für jdn Platz machen; **there is** ~ **for improvement** es gibt Möglichkeiten zur Verbesserung.
**rooming house** ['ru:mıŋ-] (US) n Mietshaus nt.
**roommate** ['ru:mmeıt] n Zimmergenosse m, Zimmergenossin f.
**room service** n Zimmerservice m.
**room temperature** n Zimmertemperatur f.
**roomy** ['ru:mı] adj (building, car) geräumig.
**roost** [ru:st] vi (birds) sich niederlassen.
**rooster** ['ru:stə·] (esp US) n Hahn m.
**root** [ru:t] n (also MATH) Wurzel f ♦ vi (plant) Wurzeln schlagen ♦ vt: **to be** ~**ed in** verwurzelt sein in +dat; **roots** npl (family origins) Wurzeln pl; **to take** ~ (plant, idea) Wurzeln schlagen; **the** ~ **cause of the problem** die Wurzel des Problems.
▶**root about** vi (search) herumwühlen.
▶**root for** vt fus (support) anfeuern.
▶**root out** vt ausrotten.
**root beer** (US) n kohlensäurehaltiges Getränk aus Wurzel- und Kräuterextrakten.
**rope** [rəup] n Seil nt; (NAUT) Tau nt ♦ vt (tie) festbinden; (also: ~ **together**) zusammenbinden; **to know the** ~**s** (fig) sich auskennen.
▶**rope in** vt (fig: person) einspannen.
▶**rope off** vt (area) mit einem Seil absperren.
**rope ladder** n Strickleiter f.

**rop(e)y** (inf) adj (ill, poor quality) miserabel.
**rosary** ['rəuzərı] n Rosenkranz m.
**rose** [rəuz] pt of **rise** ♦ n (flower) Rose f; (also: ~**bush**) Rosenstrauch m; (on watering can) Brause f ♦ adj rosarot.
**rosé** ['rəuzeı] n (wine) Rosé m.
**rosebed** ['rəuzbɛd] n Rosenbeet nt.
**rosebud** ['rəuzbʌd] n Rosenknospe f.
**rosebush** ['rəuzbuʃ] n Rosenstrauch m.
**rosemary** ['rəuzmərı] n Rosmarin m.
**rosette** [rəu'zɛt] n Rosette f.
**ROSPA** ['rɔspə] (BRIT) n abbr (= Royal Society for the Prevention of Accidents) Verband, der Maßnahmen zur Unfallverhütung propagiert.
**roster** ['rɔstə·] n: **duty** ~ Dienstplan m.
**rostrum** ['rɔstrəm] n Rednerpult nt.
**rosy** ['rəuzı] adj (colour) rosarot; (face, situation) rosig; **a** ~ **future** eine rosige Zukunft.
**rot** [rɔt] n (decay) Fäulnis f; (fig: rubbish) Quatsch m ♦ vt verfaulen lassen ♦ vi (teeth, wood, fruit etc) verfaulen; **to stop the** ~ (BRIT, fig) den Verfall stoppen; **dry** ~ Holzschwamm m; **wet** ~ Naßfäule f.
**rota** ['rəutə] n Dienstplan m; **on a** ~ **basis** reihum nach Plan.
**rotary** ['rəutərı] adj (cutter) rotierend; (motion) Dreh-.
**rotate** [rəu'teıt] vt (spin) drehen, rotieren lassen; (crops) im Wechsel anbauen; (jobs) turnusmäßig wechseln ♦ vi (revolve) rotieren, sich drehen.
**rotating** [rəu'teıtıŋ] adj (revolving) rotierend; (drum, mirror) Dreh-.
**rotation** [rəu'teıʃən] n (of planet, drum etc) Rotation f, Drehung f; (of crops) Wechsel m; (of jobs) turnusmäßiger Wechsel m; **in** ~ der Reihe nach.
**rote** [rəut] n: **by** ~ auswendig.
**rotor** ['rəutə·] n (also: ~ **blade**) Rotor m.
**rotten** ['rɔtn] adj (decayed) faul, verfault; (inf: person, situation) gemein; (: film, weather, driver etc) mies; **to feel** ~ sich elend fühlen.
**rotund** [rəu'tʌnd] adj (person) rundlich.
**rouble,** (US) **ruble** ['ru:bl] n Rubel m.
**rouge** [ru:ʒ] n Rouge nt.
**rough** [rʌf] adj rauh; (terrain, road) uneben; (person, plan, drawing, guess) grob; (life, conditions, journey) hart; (sea, crossing) stürmisch ♦ n (GOLF): **in the** ~ im Rough ♦ vt: **to** ~ **it** primitiv or ohne Komfort leben; **the sea is** ~ **today** die See ist heute stürmisch; **to have a** ~ **time** eine harte Zeit durchmachen; **can you give me a** ~ **idea of the cost?** können Sie mir eine ungefähre Vorstellung von den Kosten geben?; **to feel** ~ (BRIT) sich elend fühlen; **to sleep** ~ (BRIT) im Freien übernachten; **to play** ~ (fig) auf die grobe Tour kommen.
▶**rough out** vt (drawing, idea etc) skizzieren.
**roughage** ['rʌfıdʒ] n Ballaststoffe pl.

**rough-and-ready** ['rʌfən'rɛdɪ] *adj*
provisorisch.

**rough-and-tumble** ['rʌfən'tʌmbl] *n (fighting)*
Balgerei *f*; *(fig)* Schlachtfeld *nt*.

**roughcast** ['rʌfkɑːst] *n* Rauhputz *m*.

**rough copy** *n* Entwurf *m*.

**rough draft** *n* = **rough copy**.

**rough justice** *n* Justizwillkür *f*.

**roughly** ['rʌflɪ] *adv* grob; *(approximately)*
ungefähr; ~ **speaking** grob gesagt.

**roughness** ['rʌfnɪs] *n* Rauheit *f*; *(of manner)*
Grobheit *f*.

**roughshod** ['rʌfʃɔd] *adv:* **to ride** ~ **over** sich
rücksichtslos hinwegsetzen über +*acc*.

**roulette** [ruː'lɛt] *n* Roulette *nt*.

**Roumania** *etc* [ruː'meɪnɪə] *n* = **Romania** *etc*.

**round** [raund] *adj* rund ♦ *n* Runde *f*; *(of
ammunition)* Ladung *f* ♦ *vt (corner)* biegen
um; *(cape)* umrunden ♦ *prep* um ♦ *adv:* **all** ~
rundherum; **in** ~ **figures** rund gerechnet;
**the daily** ~ *(fig)* der tägliche Trott; **a** ~ **of
applause** Beifall *m*; **a** ~ **of (of drinks)** eine
Runde; **a** ~ **of sandwiches** ein Butterbrot; **a**
~ **of toast** *(BRIT)* eine Scheibe Toast; **it's just**
~ **the corner** *(fig)* es steht vor der Tür; **to go**
~ **the back** hinten herum gehen; **to go** ~ **(an
obstacle)** (um ein Hindernis) herumgehen;
~ **the clock** rund um die Uhr; ~ **his neck/
the table** um seinen Hals/den Tisch; **to sail**
~ **the world** die Welt umsegeln; **to walk**
~ **the room/park** im Zimmer/Park
herumgehen; ~ **about 300** *(approximately)*
ungefähr 300; **the long way** ~ auf
Umwegen; **all (the) year** ~ das ganze Jahr
über; **the wrong way** ~ falsch herum; **to ask
sb** ~ **jdn** zu sich einladen; **I'll be** ~ **at 6
o'clock** ich komme um 6 Uhr; **to go** ~
*(rotate)* sich drehen; **to go** ~ **to sb's (house)**
jdn (zu Hause) besuchen; **enough to go** ~
genug für alle.

▶**round off** *vt* abrunden.

▶**round up** *vt (cattle etc)* zusammentreiben;
*(people)* versammeln; *(figure)* aufrunden.

**roundabout** ['raundəbaut] *(BRIT) n (AUT)*
Kreisverkehr *m*; *(at fair)* Karussell *nt* ♦ *adj:*
**by a** ~ **route** auf Umwegen; **in a** ~ **way** auf
Umwegen.

**rounded** ['raundɪd] *adj (hill, figure etc)*
rundlich.

**rounders** ['raundəz] *n* ≈ Schlagball *m*.

**roundly** ['raundlɪ] *adv (fig: criticize etc)*
nachdrücklich.

**round robin** *(esp US) n (SPORT)* Wettkampf,
*bei dem jeder gegen jeden spielt.*

**round-shouldered** ['raund'ʃəuldəd] *adj* mit
runden Schultern.

**round trip** *n* Rundreise *f*.

**roundup** ['raundʌp] *n (of news etc)*
Zusammenfassung *f*; *(of animals)*
Zusammentreiben *nt*; *(of criminals)*
Aufgreifen *nt*; **a** ~ **of the latest news** ein
Nachrichtenüberblick *m*.

**rouse** [rauz] *vt (wake up)* aufwecken; *(stir up)*
reizen.

**rousing** ['rauzɪŋ] *adj (speech)* mitreißend;
*(welcome)* stürmisch.

**rout** [raut] *(MIL) n* totale Niederlage *f* ♦ *vt
(defeat)* vernichtend schlagen.

**route** [ruːt] *n* Strecke *f*; *(of bus, train, shipping)*
Linie *f*; *(of procession, fig)* Weg *m*; **"all ~s"**
*(AUT)* „alle Richtungen"; **the best** ~ **to
London** der beste Weg nach London.

**route map** *(BRIT) n* Streckenkarte *f*.

**routine** [ruː'tiːn] *adj (work, check etc)* Routine-
♦ *n (habits)* Routine *f*; *(drudgery)* Stumpfsinn
*m*; *(THEAT)* Nummer *f*; ~ **procedure**
Routinesache *f*.

**rove** [rəuv] *vt (area, streets)* ziehen durch.

**roving reporter** ['rəuvɪŋ-] *n* Reporter(in) *m(f)*
im Außendienst.

**row¹** [rəu] *n (line)* Reihe *f* ♦ *vi (in boat)* rudern
♦ *vt (boat)* rudern; **three times in a** ~
dreimal hintereinander.

**row²** [rau] *n (din)* Krach *m*, Lärm *m*; *(dispute)*
Streit *m* ♦ *vi (argue)* sich streiten; **to have a**
~ sich streiten.

**rowboat** ['rəubəut] *(US) n* = **rowing boat**.

**rowdiness** ['raudɪnɪs] *n* Rowdytum *nt*.

**rowdy** ['raudɪ] *adj (person)* rüpelhaft; *(party
etc)* lärmend.

**rowdyism** ['raudɪɪzəm] *n* = **rowdiness**.

**rowing** ['rəuɪŋ] *n (sport)* Rudern *nt*.

**rowing boat** *(BRIT) n* Ruderboot *nt*.

**rowlock** ['rɔlək] *(BRIT) n* Dolle *f*.

**royal** ['rɔɪəl] *adj* königlich; **the** ~ **family** die
königliche Familie.

> Die **Royal Academy** *oder* **Royal Academy of
> Arts**, *eine Akademie zur Förderung der
> Malerei, Bildhauerei und Architektur, wurde
> 1768 unter der Schirmherrschaft von George II
> gegründet und befindet sich seit 1869 in
> Burlington House, Piccadilly, London. Jeden
> Sommer findet dort eine Ausstellung mit
> Werken zeitgenössischer Künstler statt. Die
> Royal Academy unterhält auch Schulen, an
> denen Malerei, Bildhauerei und Architektur
> unterrichtet wird.*

**Royal Air Force** *(BRIT) n:* **the** ~ die
Königliche Luftwaffe.

**royal blue** *adj* königsblau.

**royalist** ['rɔɪəlɪst] *n* Royalist(in) *m(f)* ♦ *adj*
royalistisch.

**Royal Navy** *(BRIT) n:* **the** ~ die Königliche
Marine.

**royalty** ['rɔɪəltɪ] *n (royal persons)* die
königliche Familie; **royalties** *npl (to author)*
Tantiemen *pl*; *(to inventor)* Honorar *nt*.

**RP** *(BRIT) n abbr (= received pronunciation)*
*Standardaussprache des Englischen; see also*
**receive**.

**rpm** *abbr (= revolutions per minute)* U/min.

**RR** *(US) abbr* = **railroad**.

**RRP** (*BRIT*) *n abbr* = **recommended retail price.**

**RSA** (*BRIT*) *n abbr* (= *Royal Society of Arts*) akademischer Verband zur Vergabe von Diplomen; (= *Royal Scottish Academy*) Kunstakademie.

**RSI** *n abbr* (*MED*: = *repetitive strain injury*) RSI *nt*, Schmerzempfindung durch ständige Wiederholung bestimmter Bewegungen.

**RSPB** (*BRIT*) *n abbr* (= *Royal Society for the Protection of Birds*) Vogelschutzorganisation.

**RSPCA** (*BRIT*) *n abbr* (= *Royal Society for the Prevention of Cruelty to Animals*) Tierschutzverein *m*.

**RSVP** *abbr* (= *répondez s'il vous plaît*) u.A.w.g.

**RTA** *n abbr* (= *road traffic accident*) Verkehrsunfall *m*.

**Rt Hon.** (*BRIT*) *abbr* (= *Right Honourable*) Titel für Abgeordnete des Unterhauses.

**Rt Rev.** *abbr* (*REL*: = *Right Reverend*) Titel für Bischöfe.

**rub** [rʌb] *vt* reiben ♦ *n*: **to give sth a ~** (*polish*) etw polieren; **he ~bed his hands together** er rieb sich *dat* die Hände; **to ~ sb up** *or* (*US*) **~ sb the wrong way** bei jdm anecken.
▶**rub down** *vt* (*body, horse*) abreiben.
▶**rub in** *vt* (*ointment*) einreiben; **don't ~ it in!** (*fig*) reite nicht so darauf herum!
▶**rub off** *vi* (*paint*) abfärben.
▶**rub off on** *vt fus* abfärben auf +*acc*.
▶**rub out** *vt* (*with eraser*) ausradieren.

**rubber** ['rʌbə*] *n* (*also inf: condom*) Gummi *nt or m*; (*BRIT: eraser*) Radiergummi *m*.

**rubber band** *n* Gummiband *nt*.

**rubber bullet** *n* Gummigeschoß *nt*.

**rubber plant** *n* Gummibaum *m*.

**rubber ring** *n* (*for swimming*) Schwimmreifen *m*.

**rubber stamp** *n* Stempel *m*.

**rubber-stamp** [rʌbə'stæmp] *vt* (*fig: decision*) genehmigen.

**rubbery** ['rʌbəri] *adj* (*material*) gummiartig; (*meat, food*) wie Gummi.

**rubbish** ['rʌbɪʃ] (*BRIT*) *n* (*waste*) Abfall *m*; (*fig: junk*) Schrott *m*; (*: pej: nonsense*) Quatsch *m* ♦ *vt* (*inf*) heruntermachen; **~!** Quatsch!

**rubbish bin** (*BRIT*) *n* Abfalleimer *m*.

**rubbish dump** (*BRIT*) *n* Müllablageplatz *m*.

**rubbishy** ['rʌbɪʃi] (*BRIT: inf*) *adj* miserabel, mies.

**rubble** ['rʌbl] *n* (*debris*) Trümmer *pl*; (*CONSTR*) Schutt *m*.

**ruble** [ru:bl] (*US*) *n* = **rouble.**

**ruby** ['ru:bi] *n* (*gem*) Rubin *m* ♦ *adj* (*red*) rubinrot.

**RUC** (*BRIT*) *n abbr* (= *Royal Ulster Constabulary*) nordirische Polizeibehörde.

**rucksack** ['rʌksæk] *n* Rucksack *m*.

**ructions** ['rʌkʃənz] (*inf*) *npl* Krach *m*, Ärger *m*.

**rudder** ['rʌdə*] *n* (*of ship, plane*) Ruder *nt*.

**ruddy** ['rʌdɪ] *adj* (*complexion etc*) rötlich; (*inf: damned*) verdammt.

**rude** [ru:d] *adj* (*impolite*) unhöflich; (*naughty*) unanständig; (*unexpected: shock etc*) böse; (*crude: table, shelter etc*) primitiv; **to be ~ to sb** unhöflich zu jdm sein; **a ~ awakening** ein böses Erwachen.

**rudely** ['ru:dlɪ] *adv* (*interrupt*) unhöflich; (*say, push*) grob.

**rudeness** ['ru:dnɪs] *n* (*impoliteness*) Unhöflichkeit *f*.

**rudimentary** [ru:dɪ'mɛntərɪ] *adj* (*equipment*) primitiv; (*knowledge*) Grund-.

**rudiments** ['ru:dɪmənts] *npl* Grundlagen *pl*.

**rue** [ru:] *vt* bereuen.

**rueful** ['ru:ful] *adj* (*expression, person*) reuevoll.

**ruff** [rʌf] *n* (*collar*) Halskrause *f*.

**ruffian** ['rʌfɪən] *n* Rüpel *m*.

**ruffle** ['rʌfl] *vt* (*hair, feathers*) zerzausen; (*water*) kräuseln; (*fig: person*) aus der Fassung bringen.

**rug** [rʌg] *n* (*on floor*) Läufer *m*; (*BRIT: blanket*) Decke *f*.

**rugby** ['rʌgbɪ] *n* (*also: ~ football*) Rugby *nt*.

**rugged** ['rʌgɪd] *adj* (*landscape*) rauh; (*man*) robust; (*features, face*) markig; (*determination, independence*) wild.

**rugger** ['rʌgə*] (*BRIT: inf*) *n* Rugby *nt*.

**ruin** ['ru:ɪn] *n* (*destruction, downfall*) Ruin *m*; (*remains*) Ruine *f* ♦ *vt* ruinieren; (*building*) zerstören; (*clothes, carpet etc*) verderben; **ruins** *npl* (*of castle*) Ruinen *pl*; (*of building*) Trümmer *pl*; (*also fig*) in Trümmern.

**ruination** [ru:ɪ'neɪʃən] *n* (*of building etc*) Zerstörung *f*; (*of person, life*) Ruinierung *f*.

**ruinous** ['ru:ɪnəs] *adj* (*expense, interest*) ruinös.

**rule** [ru:l] *n* (*norm*) Regel *f*; (*regulation*) Vorschrift *f*; (*government*) Herrschaft *f*; (*also: ruler*) Lineal *nt* ♦ *vt* (*country, people*) herrschen über +*acc* ♦ *vi* (*monarch etc*) herrschen; **it's against the ~s** das ist nicht gestattet; **as a ~ of thumb** als Faustregel; **under British ~** unter britischer Herrschaft; **as a ~** in der Regel; **to ~ in favour of/against/on sth** (*LAW*) für/gegen/über etw *acc* entscheiden; **to ~ that ...** (*umpire, judge etc*) entscheiden, daß ...
▶**rule out** *vt* (*possibility etc*) ausschließen; **murder cannot be ~d out** Mord ist nicht auszuschließen.

**ruled** [ru:ld] *adj* (*paper*) liniert.

**ruler** ['ru:lə*] *n* (*sovereign*) Herrscher(in) *m(f)*; (*for measuring*) Lineal *nt*.

**ruling** ['ru:lɪŋ] *adj* (*party*) Regierungs-; (*body*) maßgebend ♦ *n* (*LAW*) Entscheidung *f*; **the ~ class** die herrschende Klasse.

**rum** [rʌm] *n* Rum *m* ♦ *adj* (*BRIT: inf: peculiar*) komisch.

**Rumania** *etc n* = **Romania** *etc*.

**rumble** ['rʌmbl] *n* (*of thunder*) Grollen *nt*; (*of traffic*) Rumpeln *nt*; (*of guns*) Donnern *nt*; (*of voices*) Gemurmel *m* ♦ *vi* (*stomach*) knurren; (*thunder*) grollen; (*traffic*) rumpeln; (*guns*) donnern.

**rumbustious** [rʌm'bʌstʃəs] adj (person) ungebärdig.

**ruminate** ['ruːmɪneɪt] vi (person) grübeln; (cow, sheep etc) wiederkäuen.

**rummage** ['rʌmɪdʒ] vi herumstöbern.

**rummage sale** (US) n Trödelmarkt m.

**rumour, (US) rumor** ['ruːmə*] n Gerücht nt ♦ vt: **it is ~ed that** ... man sagt, daß ...

**rump** [rʌmp] n (of animal) Hinterteil nt; (of group etc) Rumpf m.

**rumple** ['rʌmpl] vt (clothes etc) zerknittern; (hair) zerzausen.

**rump steak** n Rumpsteak nt.

**rumpus** ['rʌmpəs] n Krach m; **to kick up a ~** Krach schlagen.

**run** [rʌn] (pt **ran**, pp **run**) n (as exercise, sport) Lauf m; (in car, train etc) Fahrt f; (series) Serie f; (SKI) Abfahrt f; (CRICKET, BASEBALL) Run m; (THEAT) Spielzeit f; (in tights etc) Laufmasche f ♦ vt (race, distance) laufen, rennen; (operate: business) leiten; (: hotel, shop) führen; (: competition, course) durchführen; (COMPUT: program) laufen lassen; (hand, fingers) streichen mit; (water, bath) einlaufen lassen; (PRESS: feature, article) bringen ♦ vi laufen, rennen; (flee) weglaufen; (bus, train) fahren; (river, tears) fließen; (colours) auslaufen; (jumper) färben; (in election) antreten; (road, railway etc) verlaufen; **to go for a ~** (as exercise) einen Dauerlauf machen; **to break into a ~** zu laufen or rennen beginnen; **a ~ of good/bad luck** eine Glücks-/Pechsträhne; **to have the ~ of sb's house** jds Haus zur freien Verfügung haben; **there was a ~ on ...** (meat, tickets) es gab einen Ansturm auf +acc; **in the long ~** langfristig; **in the short ~** kurzfristig; **to make a ~ for it** die Beine in die Hand nehmen; **on the ~** (fugitive) auf der Flucht; **I'll ~ you to the station** ich fahre dich zum Bahnhof; **to ~ the risk of doing sth** Gefahr laufen, etw zu tun; **she ran her finger down the list** sie ging die Liste mit dem Finger durch; **it's very cheap to ~** (car, machine) es ist sehr billig im Verbrauch; **to ~ a bath** das Badewasser einlaufen lassen; **to be ~ off one's feet** (BRIT) ständig auf Trab sein; **the baby's nose was ~ning** dem Baby lief die Nase; **the train ~s between Gatwick and Victoria** der Zug verkehrt zwischen Gatwick und Victoria; **the bus ~s every 20 minutes** der Bus fährt alle 20 Minuten; **to ~ on petrol/off batteries** mit Benzin/auf Batterie laufen; **to ~ for president** für das Amt des Präsidenten kandidieren; **to ~ dry** (well etc) austrocknen; **tempers were ~ning high** alle waren sehr erregt; **unemployment is ~ning at 20 per cent** die Arbeitslosigkeit beträgt 20 Prozent; **blonde hair ~s in the family** blonde Haare liegen in der Familie.

▶**run across** vt fus (find) stoßen auf +acc.

▶**run after** vt fus nachlaufen +dat.

▶**run away** vi weglaufen.

▶**run down** vt (production) verringern; (factory) allmählich stillegen; (AUT: person) überfahren; (criticize) schlechtmachen ♦ vi (battery) leer werden.

▶**run in** (BRIT) vt (car) einfahren.

▶**run into** vt fus (meet: person) begegnen +dat; (: trouble etc) bekommen; (collide with) laufen/fahren gegen; **to ~ into debt** in Schulden geraten; **their losses ran into millions** ihre Schulden gingen in die Millionen.

▶**run off** vt (liquid) ablassen; (copies) machen ♦ vi weglaufen.

▶**run out** vi (time, passport) ablaufen; (money) ausgehen; (luck) zu Ende gehen.

▶**run out of** vt fus: **we're ~ning out of money/petrol** uns geht das Geld/das Benzin aus; **we're ~ning out of time** wir haben keine Zeit mehr.

▶**run over** vt (AUT) überfahren ♦ vt fus (repeat) durchgehen ♦ vi (bath, water) überlaufen.

▶**run through** vt fus (instructions, lines) durchgehen.

▶**run up** vt (debt) anhäufen.

▶**run up against** vt fus (difficulties) stoßen auf +acc.

**runabout** ['rʌnəbaut] n (AUT) Flitzer m.

**run-around** ['rʌnəraund] (inf) n: **to give sb the ~** jdn an der Nase herumführen.

**runaway** ['rʌnəweɪ] adj (horse) ausgerissen; (truck, train) außer Kontrolle geraten; (child, slave) entlaufen; (fig: inflation) unkontrollierbar; (: success) überwältigend.

**rundown** ['rʌndaun] n (of industry etc) allmähliche Stillegung f ♦ adj: **to be run-down** (person) total erschöpft sein; (building, area) heruntergekommen.

**rung** [rʌŋ] pp of **ring** ♦ n (also fig) Sprosse f.

**run-in** ['rʌnɪn] (inf) n Auseinandersetzung f.

**runner** ['rʌnə*] n Läufer(in) m(f); (horse) Rennpferd nt; (on sledge, drawer etc) Kufe f.

**runner bean** (BRIT) n Stangenbohne f.

**runner-up** [rʌnər'ʌp] n Zweitplazierte(r) f(m).

**running** ['rʌnɪŋ] n (sport) Laufen nt; (of business etc) Leitung f; (of machine etc) Betrieb m ♦ adj (water, stream) laufend; **to be in/out of the ~ for sth** bei etw im Rennen liegen/aus dem Rennen sein; **to make the ~** (in race, fig) das Rennen machen; **6 days ~** 6 Tage hintereinander; **to have a ~ battle with sb** ständig im Streit mit jdm liegen; **to give a ~ commentary on sth** etw fortlaufend kommentieren; **a ~ sore** eine nässende Wunde.

**running costs** npl (of car, machine) Unterhaltskosten pl.

**running head** n (TYP, COMPUT) Kolumnentitel m.

**running mate** (US) n (POL)

Vizepräsidentschaftskandidat *m*.

**runny** ['rʌnɪ] *adj* (*egg, butter*) dünnflüssig; (*nose, eyes*) triefend.

**run-off** ['rʌnɔf] *n* (*in contest, election*) Entscheidungsrunde *f*; (*extra race*) Entscheidungsrennen *nt*.

**run-of-the-mill** ['rʌnəvðə'mɪl] *adj* gewöhnlich.

**runt** [rʌnt] *n* (*animal*) kleinstes und schwächstes Tier eines Wurfs; (*pej: person*) Zwerg *m*.

**run-through** ['rʌnθruː] *n* (*rehearsal*) Probe *f*.

**run-up** ['rʌnʌp] *n*: **the ~ to** (*election etc*) die Zeit vor *+dat*.

**runway** ['rʌnweɪ] *n* (*AVIAT*) Start- und Landebahn *f*.

**rupee** [ruː'piː] *n* Rupie *f*.

**rupture** ['rʌptʃə*] *n* (*MED*) Bruch *m*; (*conflict*) Spaltung *f* ♦ *vt*: **to ~ o.s.** (*MED*) sich *dat* einen Bruch zuziehen.

**rural** ['ruərl] *adj* ländlich; (*crime*) auf dem Lande.

**rural district council** (*BRIT*) *n* Landbezirksverwaltung *f*.

**ruse** [ruːz] *n* List *f*.

**rush** [rʌʃ] *n* (*hurry*) Eile *f*, Hetze *f*; (*COMM: sudden demand*) starke Nachfrage *f*; (*of water, air*) Stoß *m*; (*of feeling*) Woge *f* ♦ *vt* (*lunch, job etc*) sich beeilen bei; (*person, supplies etc*) schnellstens bringen ♦ *vi* (*person*) sich beeilen; (*air, water*) strömen; **rushes** *npl* (*BOT*) Schilf *nt*; (*for chair, basket etc*) Binsen *pl*; **is there any ~ for this?** eilt das?; **we've had a ~ of orders** wir hatten einen Zustrom von Bestellungen; **I'm in a ~ (to do sth)** ich habe es eilig (, etw zu tun); **gold ~** Goldrausch *m*; **don't ~ me!** drängen Sie mich nicht!; **to ~ sth off** (*send*) etw schnellstens abschicken; **to ~ sb into doing sth** jdn dazu drängen, etw zu tun.

►**rush through** *vt* (*order, application*) schnellstens erledigen.

**rush hour** *n* Hauptverkehrszeit *f*, Rush-hour *f*.

**rush job** *n* Eilauftrag *m*.

**rush matting** *n* Binsenmatte *f*.

**rusk** [rʌsk] *n* Zwieback *m*.

**Russia** ['rʌʃə] *n* Rußland *nt*.

**Russian** ['rʌʃən] *adj* russisch ♦ *n* (*person*) Russe *m*, Russin *f*; (*LING*) Russisch *nt*.

**rust** [rʌst] *n* Rost *m* ♦ *vi* rosten.

**rustic** ['rʌstɪk] *adj* (*style, furniture*) rustikal ♦ *n* (*pej: person*) Bauer *m*.

**rustle** ['rʌsl] *vi* (*paper, leaves*) rascheln ♦ *vt* (*paper*) rascheln mit; (*US: cattle*) stehlen.

**rustproof** ['rʌstpruːf] *adj* nichtrostend.

**rustproofing** ['rʌstpruːfɪŋ] *n* Rostschutz *m*.

**rusty** ['rʌstɪ] *adj* (*car*) rostig; (*fig: skill etc*) eingerostet.

**rut** [rʌt] *n* (*in path etc*) Furche *f*; (*ZOOL: season*) Brunft *f*, Brunst *f*; **to be in a ~** (*fig*) im Trott stecken.

**rutabaga** [ruːtə'beɪgə] (*US*) *n* Steckrübe *f*.

**ruthless** ['ruːθlɪs] *adj* rücksichtslos.

**ruthlessness** ['ruːθlɪsnɪs] *n* Rücksichtslosigkeit *f*.

**RV** *abbr* (*BIBLE*: = *revised version*) englische Bibelübersetzung von 1885 ♦ *n abbr* (*US*) = **recreational vehicle**.

**Rwanda** [ru'ændə] *n* Ruanda *nt*.

**Rwandan** [ru'ændən] *adj* ruandisch.

**rye** [raɪ] *n* (*cereal*) Roggen *m*.

**rye bread** *n* Roggenbrot *nt*.

# *S, s*

**S¹, s** [ɛs] *n* (*letter*) S *nt*, s *nt*; (*US: SCOL: satisfactory*) ≈ 3; **~ for sugar** ≈ S wie Samuel.

**S²** [ɛs] *abbr* (= *saint*) St.; (= *small*) kl.; (= *south*) S.

**SA** *abbr* = **South Africa, South America**; (= *South Australia*) Südaustralien *nt*.

**Sabbath** ['sæbəθ] *n* (*Jewish*) Sabbat *m*; (*Christian*) Sonntag *m*.

**sabbatical** [sə'bætɪkl] *n* (*also*: ~ **year**) Forschungsjahr *nt*.

**sabotage** ['sæbətɑːʒ] *n* Sabotage *f* ♦ *vt* einen Sabotageakt verüben auf *+acc*; (*plan, meeting*) sabotieren.

**sabre** ['seɪbə*] *n* Säbel *m*.

**sabre-rattling** ['seɪbərætlɪŋ] *n* Säbelrasseln *nt*.

**saccharin(e)** ['sækərɪn] *n* Saccharin *nt* ♦ *adj* (*fig*) zuckersüß.

**sachet** ['sæʃeɪ] *n* (*of shampoo*) Beutel *m*; (*of sugar etc*) Tütchen *nt*.

**sack** [sæk] *n* Sack *m* ♦ *vt* (*dismiss*) entlassen; (*plunder*) plündern; **to get the ~** rausfliegen (*inf*); **to give sb the ~** jdn rausschmeißen (*inf*).

**sackful** ['sækful] *n*: **a ~ of** ein Sack.

**sacking** ['sækɪŋ] *n* (*dismissal*) Entlassung *f*; (*material*) Sackleinen *nt*.

**sacrament** ['sækrəmənt] *n* Sakrament *nt*.

**sacred** ['seɪkrɪd] *adj* heilig; (*music, history*) geistlich; (*memory*) geheiligt; (*building*) sakral.

**sacred cow** *n* (*lit, fig*) heilige Kuh *f*.

**sacrifice** ['sækrɪfaɪs] *n* Opfer *nt* ♦ *vt* opfern; **to make ~s (for sb)** (für jdn) Opfer bringen.

**sacrilege** ['sækrɪlɪdʒ] *n* Sakrileg *nt*; **that would be ~** das wäre ein Sakrileg.

**sacrosanct** ['sækrəusæŋkt] *adj* (*lit, fig*) sakrosankt.

**sad** [sæd] *adj* traurig; **he was ~ to see her go** er war traurig (darüber), daß sie wegging.

**sadden** ['sædn] *vt* betrüben.

**saddle** ['sædl] *n* Sattel *m* ♦ *vt* (*horse*) satteln; **to**

be ~d with sb/sth (*inf*) jdn/etw am Hals
haben.
**saddlebag** ['sædlbæg] *n* Satteltasche *f*.
**sadism** ['seɪdɪzəm] *n* Sadismus *m*.
**sadist** ['seɪdɪst] *n* Sadist(in) *m(f)*.
**sadistic** [sə'dɪstɪk] *adj* sadistisch.
**sadly** ['sædlɪ] *adv* traurig, betrübt;
(*unfortunately*) leider, bedauerlicherweise;
(*seriously*) schwer; **he is ~ lacking in humour**
ihm fehlt leider jeglicher Humor.
**sadness** ['sædnɪs] *n* Traurigkeit *f*.
**sadomasochism** [seɪdəʊ'mæsəkɪzəm] *n*
Sadomasochismus *m*.
**s.a.e.** (*BRIT*) *abbr* (= *stamped addressed
envelope*) *see* **stamp**.
**safari** [sə'fɑːrɪ] *n* Safari *f*; **to go on ~** auf
Safari gehen.
**safari park** *n* Safaripark *m*.
**safe** [seɪf] *adj* sicher; (*out of danger*) in
Sicherheit ♦ *n* Safe *m or nt*, Tresor *m*; **~ from**
sicher vor +*dat*; **~ and sound** gesund und
wohlbehalten; **(just) to be on the ~ side**
(nur) um sicherzugehen; **to play ~** auf
Nummer Sicher gehen (*inf*); **it is ~ to say
that ...** man kann wohl sagen, daß ...;
**~ journey!** gute Fahrt *or* Reise!
**safe bet** *n*: **it's a ~ that ...** es ist sicher,
daß ...
**safe-breaker** ['seɪfbreɪkə*] (*BRIT*) *n*
Safeknacker *m* (*inf*).
**safe-conduct** [seɪf'kɒndʌkt] *n* freies *or*
sicheres Geleit *nt*.
**safe-cracker** ['seɪfkrækə*] *n* = **safe-breaker**.
**safe-deposit** ['seɪfdɪpɒzɪt] *n* (*vault*)
Tresorraum *m*; (*also*: **~ box**) Banksafe *m*.
**safeguard** ['seɪfgɑːd] *n* Schutz *m* ♦ *vt*
schützen; (*interests*) wahren; (*future*)
sichern; **as a ~ against** zum Schutz gegen.
**safe haven** *n* Zufluchtsort *m*.
**safe house** *n* geheimer Unterschlupf *m*.
**safekeeping** ['seɪf'kiːpɪŋ] *n* sichere
Aufbewahrung *f*.
**safely** ['seɪflɪ] *adv* sicher; (*assume, say*) wohl,
ruhig; (*arrive*) wohlbehalten; **I can ~ say ...**
ich kann wohl sagen ...
**safe passage** *n* sichere Durchreise *f*.
**safe sex** *n* geschützter Sex *m*.
**safety** ['seɪftɪ] *n* Sicherheit *f*; **~ first!**
Sicherheit geht vor!
**safety belt** *n* Sicherheitsgurt *m*.
**safety catch** *n* (*on gun*) Sicherung *f*; (*on
window, door*) Sperre *f*.
**safety net** *n* Sprungnetz *nt*, Sicherheitsnetz
*nt*; (*fig*) Sicherheitsvorkehrung *f*.
**safety pin** *n* Sicherheitsnadel *f*.
**safety valve** *n* Sicherheitsventil *nt*.
**saffron** ['sæfrən] *n* Safran *m*.
**sag** [sæg] *vi* durchhängen; (*breasts*) hängen;
(*fig: spirits, demand*) sinken.
**saga** ['sɑːgə] *n* Saga *f*; (*fig*) Geschichte *f*.
**sage** [seɪdʒ] *n* (*herb*) Salbei *m*; (*wise man*)
Weise(r) *m*.

**Sagittarius** [sædʒɪ'tɛərɪəs] *n* Schütze *m*; **to be
~** Schütze sein.
**sago** ['seɪgəʊ] *n* Sago *m*.
**Sahara** [sə'hɑːrə] *n*: **the ~ (Desert)** die (Wüste)
Sahara.
**Sahel** [sæ'hɛl] *n* Sahel *m*, Sahelzone *f*.
**said** [sɛd] *pt, pp of* **say**.
**Saigon** [saɪ'gɒn] *n* Saigon *nt*.
**sail** [seɪl] *n* Segel *nt* ♦ *vt* segeln ♦ *vi* fahren;
(*SPORT*) segeln; (*begin voyage: ship*)
auslaufen; (: *passenger*) abfahren; (*fig: ball
etc*) fliegen, segeln; **to go for a ~** segeln
gehen; **to set ~** losfahren, abfahren.
▶**sail through** *vt fus* (*fig: exam etc*) spielend
schaffen.
**sailboat** ['seɪlbəʊt] (*US*) *n* = **sailing boat**.
**sailing** ['seɪlɪŋ] *n* (*SPORT*) Segeln *nt*; (*voyage*)
Überfahrt *f*; **to go ~** segeln gehen.
**sailing boat** *n* Segelboot *nt*.
**sailing ship** *n* Segelschiff *nt*.
**sailor** ['seɪlə*] *n* Seemann *m*, Matrose *m*.
**saint** [seɪnt] *n* (*lit, fig*) Heilige(r) *f(m)*.
**saintly** ['seɪntlɪ] *adj* heiligmäßig; (*expression*)
fromm.
**sake** [seɪk] *n*: **for the ~ of sb/sth, for sb's/sth's
~** um jds/einer Sache *gen* willen; (*out of
consideration for*) jdm/etw zuliebe; **he enjoys
talking for talking's ~** er redet gerne, nur
damit etwas gesagt wird; **for the ~ of
argument** rein theoretisch; **art for art's ~**
Kunst um der Kunst willen; **for heaven's ~!**
um Gottes willen!
**salad** ['sæləd] *n* Salat *m*; **tomato ~**
Tomatensalat *m*; **green ~** grüner Salat *m*.
**salad bowl** *n* Salatschüssel *f*.
**salad cream** (*BRIT*) *n* ≈ Mayonnaise *f*.
**salad dressing** *n* Salatsoße *f*.
**salami** [sə'lɑːmɪ] *n* Salami *f*.
**salaried** ['sælərɪd] *adj*: **~ staff**
Gehaltsempfänger *pl*.
**salary** ['sælərɪ] *n* Gehalt *nt*.
**salary scale** *n* Gehaltsskala *f*.
**sale** [seɪl] *n* Verkauf *m*; (*at reduced prices*)
Ausverkauf *m*; (*auction*) Auktion *f*; **sales** *npl*
(*total amount sold*) Absatz *m* ♦ *cpd* (*campaign*)
Verkaufs-; (*conference*) Vertreter-; (*figures*)
Absatz-; **"for ~"** „zu verkaufen"; **on ~** im
Handel; **on ~ or return** auf
Kommissionsbasis; **closing-down** *or* (*US*)
**liquidation ~** Räumungsverkauf *m*.
**sale and lease back** *n* (*COMM*) Verkauf *m*
mit Rückmiete.
**saleroom** ['seɪlruːm] *n* Auktionsraum *m*.
**sales assistant**, (*US*) **sales clerk** [seɪlz-] *n*
Verkäufer(in) *m(f)*.
**sales force** *n* Vertreterstab *m*.
**salesman** ['seɪlzmən] (*irreg: like* **man**) *n*
Verkäufer *m*; (*representative*) Vertreter *m*.
**sales manager** *n* Verkaufsleiter *m*.
**salesmanship** ['seɪlzmənʃɪp] *n*
Verkaufstechnik *f*.
**sales tax** (*US*) *n* Verkaufssteuer *f*.

**saleswoman** ['seɪlzwumən] (*irreg: like* **woman**) *n* Verkäuferin *f*; (*representative*) Vertreterin *f*.

**salient** ['seɪlɪənt] *adj* (*features*) hervorstehend; (*points*) Haupt-.

**saline** ['seɪlaɪn] *adj* (*solution etc*) Salz-.

**saliva** [sə'laɪvə] *n* Speichel *m*.

**sallow** ['sæləu] *adj* (*complexion*) fahl.

**sally forth** ['sælɪ-] (*old*) *vi* sich aufmachen.

**sally out** *vi* = **sally forth**.

**salmon** ['sæmən] *n inv* Lachs *m*.

**salmon trout** *n* Lachsforelle *f*.

**salon** ['sælɔn] *n* Salon *m*.

**saloon** [sə'lu:n] *n* (*US: bar*) Saloon *m*; (*BRIT: AUT*) Limousine *f*; (*ship's lounge*) Salon *m*.

**SALT** [sɔ:lt] *n abbr* (= *Strategic Arms Limitation Talks/Treaty*) SALT.

**salt** [sɔ:lt] *n* Salz *nt* ♦ *vt* (*preserve*) einsalzen; (*put salt on*) salzen; (*road*) mit Salz streuen ♦ *cpd* Salz-; (*pork, beef*) gepökelt; **the ~ of the earth** (*fig*) das Salz der Erde; **to take sth with a pinch** *or* **grain of ~** (*fig*) etw nicht ganz so erst nehmen.

**salt cellar** *n* Salzstreuer *m*.

**salt-free** ['sɔ:lt'fri:] *adj* salzlos.

**salt mine** *n* Salzbergwerk *nt*.

**saltwater** ['sɔ:lt'wɔ:tə*] *adj* (*fish, plant*) Meeres-.

**salty** ['sɔ:ltɪ] *adj* salzig.

**salubrious** [sə'lu:brɪəs] *adj* (*district etc*) fein; (*air, living conditions*) gesund.

**salutary** ['sæljutərɪ] *adj* heilsam.

**salute** [sə'lu:t] *n* (*MIL, greeting*) Gruß *m*; (*MIL: with guns*) Salut *m* ♦ *vt* (*MIL*) grüßen, salutieren vor +*dat*; (*fig*) begrüßen.

**salvage** ['sælvɪdʒ] *n* Bergung *f*; (*things saved*) Bergungsgut *nt* ♦ *vt* bergen; (*fig*) retten.

**salvage vessel** *n* Bergungsschiff *nt*.

**salvation** [sæl'veɪʃən] *n* (*REL*) Heil *nt*; (*economic etc*) Rettung *f*.

**Salvation Army** *n* Heilsarmee *f*.

**salver** ['sælvə*] *n* Tablett *nt*.

**salvo** ['sælvəu] (*pl* ~**es**) *n* Salve *f*.

**Samaritan** [sə'mærɪtən] *n*: **the ~s** ≈ die Telefonseelsorge.

**same** [seɪm] *adj* (*similar*) gleiche(r, s); (*identical*) selbe(r, s) ♦ *pron*: **the ~** (*similar*) der/die/das gleiche; (*identical*) derselbe/ dieselbe/dasselbe; **the ~ book as** das gleiche Buch wie; **they are the ~ age** sie sind gleichaltrig; **they are exactly the ~** sie sind genau gleich; **on the ~ day** am gleichen *or* selben Tag; **at the ~ time** (*simultaneously*) gleichzeitig, zur gleichen Zeit; (*yet*) doch; **they're one and the ~** (*person*) das ist doch ein und derselbe/ dieselbe; (*thing*) das ist doch dasselbe; **~ again** (*in bar etc*) das gleiche noch mal; **all** *or* **just the ~** trotzdem; **to do the ~ (as sb)** das gleiche (wie jd) tun; **the ~ to you!** (*danke*) gleichfalls!; **~ here!** ich/wir *etc* auch!; **thanks all the ~** trotzdem vielen

Dank; **it's all the ~ to me** es ist mir egal.

**sample** ['sɑ:mpl] *n* Probe *f*; (*of merchandise*) Probe *f*, Muster *nt* ♦ *vt* probieren; **to take a ~** eine Stichprobe machen; **free ~** kostenlose Probe.

**sanatorium** [sænə'tɔ:rɪəm] (*pl* **sanatoria**) *n* Sanatorium *nt*.

**sanctify** ['sæŋktɪfaɪ] *vt* heiligen.

**sanctimonious** [sæŋktɪ'məunɪəs] *adj* scheinheilig.

**sanction** ['sæŋkʃən] *n* Zustimmung *f* ♦ *vt* sanktionieren; **sanctions** *npl* (*POL*) Sanktionen *pl*; **to impose economic ~s on** *or* **against** Wirtschaftssanktionen verhängen gegen.

**sanctity** ['sæŋktɪtɪ] *n* (*holiness*) Heiligkeit *f*; (*inviolability*) Unantastbarkeit *f*.

**sanctuary** ['sæŋktjuərɪ] *n* (*for birds/animals*) Schutzgebiet *nt*; (*place of refuge*) Zuflucht *f*; (*REL: in church*) Altarraum *m*.

**sand** [sænd] *n* Sand *m* ♦ *vt* (*also*: ~ **down**) abschmirgeln; *see also* **sands**.

**sandal** ['sændl] *n* Sandale *f*.

**sandbag** ['sændbæg] *n* Sandsack *m*.

**sandblast** ['sændblɑ:st] *vt* sandstrahlen.

**sandbox** ['sændbɔks] (*US*) *n* Sandkasten *m*.

**sandcastle** ['sændkɑ:sl] *n* Sandburg *f*.

**sand dune** *n* Sanddüne *f*.

**sander** ['sændə*] *n* (*tool*) Schleifmaschine *f*.

**S & M** (*US*) *n abbr* (= *sadomasochism*) S/M.

**sandpaper** ['sændpeɪpə*] *n* Schmirgelpapier *nt*.

**sandpit** ['sændpɪt] *n* Sandkasten *m*.

**sands** [sændz] *npl* (*beach*) Sandstrand *m*.

**sandstone** ['sændstəun] *n* Sandstein *m*.

**sandstorm** ['sændstɔ:m] *n* Sandsturm *m*.

**sandwich** ['sændwɪtʃ] *n* Sandwich *m* ♦ *vt*: ~**ed between** eingequetscht zwischen; **cheese/ ham ~** Käse-/Schinkenbrot *nt*.

**sandwich board** *n* Reklametafel *f*.

**sandwich course** (*BRIT*) *n* Ausbildungsgang, bei dem sich Theorie und Praxis abwechseln.

**sandwich man** *n* Sandwichmann *m*, Plakatträger *m*.

**sandy** ['sændɪ] *adj* sandig; (*beach*) Sand-; (*hair*) rotblond.

**sane** [seɪn] *adj* geistig gesund; (*sensible*) vernünftig.

**sang** [sæŋ] *pt of* **sing**.

**sanguine** ['sæŋgwɪn] *adj* zuversichtlich.

**sanitarium** [sænɪ'tɛərɪəm] (*US*) (*pl* **sanitaria**) *n* = **sanatorium**.

**sanitary** ['sænɪtərɪ] *adj* hygienisch; (*facilities*) sanitär; (*inspector*) Gesundheits-.

**sanitary towel,** (*US*) **sanitary napkin** *n* Damenbinde *f*.

**sanitation** [sænɪ'teɪʃən] *n* Hygiene *f*; (*toilets etc*) sanitäre Anlagen *pl*; (*drainage*) Kanalisation *f*.

**sanitation department** (*US*) *n* Stadtreinigung *f*.

**sanity** ['sænɪtɪ] *n* geistige Gesundheit *f*; (*common sense*) Vernunft *f*.

**sank** [sæŋk] *pt of* **sink**.

**San Marino** ['sænmə'riːnəu] *n* San Marino *nt*.

**Santa Claus** [sæntə'klɔːz] *n* ≈ der Weihnachtsmann.

**Santiago** [sæntɪ'ɑːgəu] *n* (*also*: ~ **de Chile**) Santiago (de Chile) *nt*.

**sap** [sæp] *n* Saft *m* ♦ *vt* (*strength*) zehren an +*dat*; (*confidence*) untergraben.

**sapling** ['sæplɪŋ] *n* junger Baum *m*.

**sapper** ['sæpə*] *n* (*MIL*) Pionier *m*.

**sapphire** ['sæfaɪə*] *n* Saphir *m*.

**sarcasm** ['sɑːkæzm] *n* Sarkasmus *m*.

**sarcastic** [sɑː'kæstɪk] *adj* sarkastisch.

**sarcophagus** [sɑː'kɔfəgəs] (*pl* **sarcophagi**) *n* Sarkophag *m*.

**sardine** [sɑː'diːn] *n* Sardine *f*.

**Sardinia** [sɑː'dɪnɪə] *n* Sardinien *nt*.

**Sardinian** [sɑː'dɪnɪən] *adj* sardinisch, sardisch ♦ *n* (*person*) Sardinier(in) *m(f)*; (*LING*) Sardinisch *nt*.

**sardonic** [sɑː'dɒnɪk] *adj* (*smile*) süffisant.

**sari** ['sɑːrɪ] *n* Sari *m*.

**sartorial** [sɑː'tɔːrɪəl] *adj*: **his ~ elegance** seine elegante Art, sich zu kleiden.

**SAS** (*BRIT*) *n abbr* (*MIL*: = *Special Air Service*) Spezialeinheit der britischen Armee.

**SASE** (*US*) *n abbr* (= *self-addressed stamped envelope*) frankierter Rückumschlag *m*.

**sash** [sæʃ] *n* Schärpe *f*; (*of window*) Fensterrahmen *m*.

**sash window** *n* Schiebefenster *nt*.

**SAT** (*US*) *n abbr* (= *Scholastic Aptitude Test*) Hochschul-Aufnahmeprüfung.

**Sat.** *abbr* (= *Saturday*) Sa.

**sat** [sæt] *pt, pp of* **sit**.

**Satan** ['seɪtn] *n* Satan *m*.

**satanic** [sə'tænɪk] *adj* satanisch.

**satanism** ['seɪtnɪzəm] *n* Satanismus *m*.

**satchel** ['sætʃl] *n* (*child's*) Schultasche *f*.

**sated** ['seɪtɪd] *adj* gesättigt; **to be ~ with sth** (*fig*) von etw übersättigt sein.

**satellite** ['sætəlaɪt] *n* Satellit *m*; (*also*: ~ **state**) Satellitenstaat *m*.

**satellite dish** *n* Satellitenantenne *f*, Parabolantenne *f*.

**satellite television** *n* Satellitenfernsehen *nt*.

**satiate** ['seɪʃɪeɪt] *vt* (*food*) sättigen; (*fig: pleasure etc*) übersättigen.

**satin** ['sætɪn] *n* Satin *m* ♦ *adj* (*dress etc*) Satin-; **with a ~ finish** mit Seidenglanz.

**satire** ['sætaɪə*] *n* Satire *f*.

**satirical** [sə'tɪrɪkl] *adj* satirisch.

**satirist** ['sætɪrɪst] *n* Satiriker(in) *m(f)*.

**satirize** ['sætɪraɪz] *vt* satirisch darstellen.

**satisfaction** [sætɪs'fækʃən] *n* Befriedigung *f*; **to get ~ from sb** (*refund, apology etc*) Genugtuung von jdm erhalten; **has it been done to your ~?** sind Sie damit zufrieden?

**satisfactorily** [sætɪs'fæktərɪlɪ] *adv* zufriedenstellend.

**satisfactory** [sætɪs'fæktərɪ] *adj* zufriedenstellend.

**satisfied** ['sætɪsfaɪd] *adj* zufrieden.

**satisfy** ['sætɪsfaɪ] *vt* zufriedenstellen; (*needs, demand*) befriedigen; (*requirements, conditions*) erfüllen; **to ~ sb/o.s. that ...** jdn/ sich davon überzeugen, daß ...

**satisfying** ['sætɪsfaɪɪŋ] *adj* befriedigend; (*meal*) sättigend.

**satsuma** [sæt'suːmə] *n* Satsuma *f*.

**saturate** ['sætʃəreɪt] *vt*: **to ~ (with)** durchnässen (mit); (*CHEM, fig: market*) sättigen; (*fig: area etc*) überschwemmen.

**saturated fat** ['sætʃəreɪtɪd-] *n* gesättigtes Fett *nt*.

**saturation** [sætʃə'reɪʃən] *n* (*CHEM, fig*) Sättigung *f*; **~ advertising** flächendeckende Werbung *f*; **~ bombing** Flächenbombardierung *f*.

**Saturday** ['sætədɪ] *n* Samstag *m*; *see also* **Tuesday.**

**sauce** [sɔːs] *n* Soße *f*, Sauce *f*.

**saucepan** ['sɔːspən] *n* Kochtopf *m*.

**saucer** ['sɔːsə*] *n* Untertasse *f*.

**saucy** ['sɔːsɪ] *adj* frech.

**Saudi** ['saudi-] *adj* (*also*: ~ **Arabian**) saudisch, saudiarabisch.

**Saudi Arabia** ['saudɪ-] *n* Saudi-Arabien *nt*.

**sauna** ['sɔːnə] *n* Sauna *f*.

**saunter** ['sɔːntə*] *vi* schlendern.

**sausage** ['sɔsɪdʒ] *n* Wurst *f*.

**sausage roll** *n* Wurst *f* im Schlafrock.

**sauté** ['səuteɪ] *vt* kurz anbraten ♦ *adj*: ~**ed potatoes** Bratkartoffeln *pl*.

**savage** ['sævɪdʒ] *adj* (*attack etc*) brutal; (*dog*) gefährlich; (*criticism*) schonungslos ♦ *n* (*old: pej*) Wilde(r) *f(m)* ♦ *vt* (*maul*) zerfleischen; (*fig: criticize*) verreißen.

**savagely** ['sævɪdʒlɪ] *adv* (*attack etc*) brutal; (*criticize*) schonungslos.

**savagery** ['sævɪdʒrɪ] *n* (*of attack*) Brutalität *f*.

**save** [seɪv] *vt* (*rescue*) retten; (*money, time*) sparen; (*food etc*) aufheben; (*work, trouble*) (er)sparen; (*keep: receipts etc*) aufbewahren; (: *seat etc*) freihalten; (*COMPUT: file*) abspeichern; (*SPORT: shot, ball*) halten ♦ *vi* (*also*: ~ **up**) sparen ♦ *n* (*SPORT*) (Ball)abwehr *f* ♦ *prep* (*form*) außer +*dat*; **it will ~ me an hour** dadurch spare ich eine Stunde; **to ~ face** das Gesicht wahren; **God ~ the Queen!** Gott schütze die Königin!

**saving** ['seɪvɪŋ] *n* (*on price etc*) Ersparnis *f* ♦ *adj*: **the ~ grace of sth** das einzig Gute an etw *dat*; **savings** *npl* (*money*) Ersparnisse *pl*; **to make ~s** sparen.

**savings account** *n* Sparkonto *nt*.

**savings bank** *n* Sparkasse *f*.

**saviour,** (*US*) **savior** ['seɪvjə*] *n* Retter(in) *m(f)*; (*REL*) Erlöser *m*.

**savoir-faire** ['sævwɑːfɛə*] *n* Gewandtheit *f*.

**savour,** (*US*) **savor** ['seɪvə*] *vt* genießen ♦ *n* (*of food*) Geschmack *m*.

**savoury,** (*US*) **savory** ['seɪvərɪ] *adj* pikant.
**savvy** ['sævɪ] (*inf*) *n* Grips *m*; **he hasn't got much** ~ er hat keine Ahnung.
**saw** [sɔ:] (*pt* **sawed**, *pp* **sawed** *or* **sawn**) *vt* sägen ♦ *n* Säge *f* ♦ *pt of* **see**; **to** ~ **sth up** etw zersägen.
**sawdust** ['sɔ:dʌst] *n* Sägemehl *nt*.
**sawmill** ['sɔ:mɪl] *n* Sägewerk *nt*.
**sawn** [sɔ:n] *pp of* **saw**.
**sawn-off** ['sɔ:nɔf], (*US*) **sawed-off** ['sɔ:dɔf] *adj:* ~ **shotgun** Gewehr *nt* mit abgesägtem Lauf.
**saxophone** ['sæksəfəun] *n* Saxophon *nt*.
**say** [seɪ] (*pt, pp* **said**) *vt* sagen ♦ *n:* **to have one's** ~ seine Meinung äußern; **could you** ~ **that again?** können Sie das wiederholen?; **my watch** ~**s 3 o'clock** auf meiner Uhr ist es 3 Uhr; **it** ~**s on the sign "No Smoking"** auf dem Schild steht „Rauchen verboten"; **shall we** ~ **Tuesday?** sagen wir Dienstag?; **come for dinner at,** ~, **8 o'clock** kommt um, sagen wir mal, 8 Uhr, zum Essen; **that doesn't** ~ **much for him** das spricht nicht gerade für ihn; **when all is said and done** letzten Endes; **there is something/a lot to be said for it** es spricht einiges/vieles dafür; **you can** ~ **that again!** das kann man wohl sagen!; **that is to** ~ das heißt; **that goes without** ~**ing** das versteht sich von selbst; **to** ~ **nothing of ...** von ... ganz zu schweigen; ~ **(that) ...** angenommen, (daß) ...; **to have a** *or* **some** ~ **in sth** ein Mitspracherecht bei etw haben.
**saying** ['seɪɪŋ] *n* Redensart *f*.
**say-so** ['seɪsəu] *n* Zustimmung *f*; **to do sth on sb's** ~ etw auf jds Anweisung *acc* hin tun.
**SBA** (*US*) *n abbr* (= *Small Business Administration*) *Regierungsstelle zur Unterstützung kleiner und mittelständischer Betriebe.*
**SC** (*US*) *n abbr* = **Supreme Court** ♦ *abbr* (*POST:* = *South Carolina*).
**s/c** *abbr* = **self-contained**.
**scab** [skæb] *n* (*on wound*) Schorf *m*; (*pej*) Streikbrecher(in) *m(f)*.
**scabby** ['skæbɪ] (*pej*) *adj* (*hands, skin*) schorfig.
**scaffold** ['skæfəld] *n* (*for execution*) Schafott *nt*.
**scaffolding** ['skæfəldɪŋ] *n* Gerüst *nt*.
**scald** [skɔ:ld] *n* Verbrühung *f* ♦ *vt* (*burn*) verbrühen.
**scalding** ['skɔ:ldɪŋ] *adj* (*also:* ~ **hot**) siedend heiß.
**scale** [skeɪl] *n* Skala *f*; (*of fish*) Schuppe *f*; (*MUS*) Tonleiter *f*; (*size, extent*) Ausmaß *nt*, Umfang *m*; (*of map, model*) Maßstab *m* ♦ *vt* (*cliff, tree*) erklettern; **(pair of) scales** *npl* (*for weighing*) Waage *f*; **pay** ~ Lohnskala *f*; **to draw sth to** ~ etw maßstabgetreu zeichnen; **a small-**~ **model** ein Modell in verkleinertem Maßstab; **on a large** ~ im großen Rahmen; ~ **of charges** Gebührenordnung *f*.
▶**scale down** *vt* verkleinern; (*fig*) verringern.
**scaled-down** [skeɪld'daun] *adj* verkleinert; (*project, forecast*) eingeschränkt.
**scale drawing** *n* maßstabgetreue Zeichnung *f*.
**scallion** ['skæljən] *n* Frühlingszwiebel *f*; (*US: shallot*) Schalotte *f*; (: *leek*) Lauch *m*.
**scallop** ['skɔləp] *n* (*ZOOL*) Kammuschel *f*; (*SEWING*) Bogenkante *f*.
**scalp** [skælp] *n* Kopfhaut *f* ♦ *vt* skalpieren.
**scalpel** ['skælpl] *n* Skalpell *nt*.
**scalper** ['skælpə'] (*US: inf*) *n* (*ticket tout*) (Karten)schwarzhändler(in) *m(f)*.
**scam** [skæm] (*inf*) *n* Betrug *m*.
**scamp** [skæmp] (*inf*) *n* Frechdachs *m*.
**scamper** ['skæmpə'] *vi:* **to** ~ **away** *or* **off** verschwinden.
**scampi** ['skæmpɪ] (*BRIT*) *npl* Scampi *pl*.
**scan** [skæn] *vt* (*horizon*) absuchen; (*newspaper etc*) überfliegen; (*TV, RADAR*) abtasten ♦ *vi* (*poetry*) das richtige Versmaß haben ♦ *n* (*MED*) Scan *m*.
**scandal** ['skændl] *n* Skandal *m*; (*gossip*) Skandalgeschichten *pl*.
**scandalize** ['skændəlaɪz] *vt* schockieren.
**scandalous** ['skændələs] *adj* skandalös.
**Scandinavia** [skændɪ'neɪvɪə] *n* Skandinavien *nt*.
**Scandinavian** [skændɪ'neɪvɪən] *adj* skandinavisch ♦ *n* Skandinavier(in) *m(f)*.
**scanner** ['skænə'] *n* (*MED*) Scanner *m*; (*RADAR*) Richtantenne *f*.
**scant** [skænt] *adj* wenig.
**scantily** ['skæntɪlɪ] *adv:* ~ **clad** *or* **dressed** spärlich bekleidet.
**scanty** ['skæntɪ] *adj* (*information*) dürftig; (*meal*) kärglich; (*bikini*) knapp.
**scapegoat** ['skeɪpgəut] *n* Sündenbock *m*.
**scar** [ska:] *n* Narbe *f*; (*fig*) Wunde *f* ♦ *vt* eine Narbe hinterlassen auf +*dat*; (*fig*) zeichnen.
**scarce** [skɛəs] *adj* knapp; **to make o.s.** ~ (*inf*) verschwinden.
**scarcely** ['skɛəslɪ] *adv* kaum; (*certainly not*) wohl kaum; ~ **anybody** kaum jemand; **I can** ~ **believe it** ich kann es kaum glauben.
**scarcity** ['skɛəsɪtɪ] *n* Knappheit *f*; ~ **value** Seltenheitswert *m*.
**scare** [skɛə'] *n* (*fright*) Schreck(en) *m*; (*public fear*) Panik *f* ♦ *vt* (*frighten*) erschrecken; (*worry*) Angst machen +*dat*; **to give sb a** ~ jdm einen Schrecken einjagen; **bomb** ~ Bombendrohung *f*.
▶**scare away** *vt* (*animal*) verscheuchen; (*investor, buyer*) abschrecken.
▶**scare off** *vt* = **scare away**.
**scarecrow** ['skɛəkrəu] *n* Vogelscheuche *f*.
**scared** ['skɛəd] *adj:* **to be** ~ Angst haben; **to be** ~ **stiff** fürchterliche Angst haben.
**scaremonger** ['skɛəmʌngə'] *n* Panikmacher *m*.
**scarf** [ska:f] (*pl* ~**s** *or* **scarves**) *n* Schal *m*; (*headscarf*) Kopftuch *nt*.

**scarlet** ['skɑ:lɪt] *adj* (scharlach)rot.
**scarlet fever** *n* Scharlach *m*.
**scarper** ['skɑ:pə*] (*BRIT: inf*) *vi* abhauen.
**scarred** [skɑ:d] *adj* narbig; (*fig*) gezeichnet.
**scarves** [skɑ:vz] *npl of* **scarf**.
**scary** ['skɛərɪ] (*inf*) *adj* unheimlich; (*film*) gruselig.
**scathing** ['skeɪðɪŋ] *adj* (*comments*) bissig; (*attack*) scharf; **to be ~ about sth** bissige Bemerkungen über etw *acc* machen.
**scatter** ['skætə*] *vt* verstreuen; (*flock of birds*) aufscheuchen; (*crowd*) zerstreuen ♦ *vi* (*crowd*) sich zerstreuen.
**scatterbrained** ['skætəbreɪnd] (*inf*) *adj* schusselig.
**scattered** ['skætəd] *adj* verstreut; **~ showers** vereinzelte Regenschauer *pl*.
**scatty** ['skætɪ] (*BRIT: inf*) *adj* schusselig.
**scavenge** ['skævəndʒ] *vi*: **to ~ for sth** nach etw suchen.
**scavenger** ['skævəndʒə*] *n* (*person*) Aasgeier *m* (*inf*); (*animal, bird*) Aasfresser *m*.
**SCE** *n abbr* (= *Scottish Certificate of Education*) *Schulabschlußzeugnis in Schottland*.
**scenario** [sɪ'nɑ:rɪəu] *n* (*THEAT, CINE*) Szenarium *nt*; (*fig*) Szenario *nt*.
**scene** [si:n] *n* (*lit, fig*) Szene *f*; (*of crime*) Schauplatz *m*; (*of accident*) Ort *m*; (*sight*) Anblick *m*; **behind the ~s** (*fig*) hinter den Kulissen; **to make a ~** (*inf: fuss*) eine Szene machen; **to appear on the ~** (*fig*) auftauchen, auf der Bildfläche erscheinen; **the political ~** die politische Landschaft.
**scenery** ['si:nərɪ] *n* (*THEAT*) Bühnenbild *nt*; (*landscape*) Landschaft *f*.
**scenic** ['si:nɪk] *adj* malerisch, landschaftlich schön.
**scent** [sɛnt] *n* (*fragrance*) Duft *m*; (*track*) Fährte *f*; (*fig*) Spur *f*; (*liquid perfume*) Parfüm *nt*; **to put** *or* **throw sb off the ~** (*fig*) jdn von der Spur abbringen.
**sceptic,** (*US*) **skeptic** ['skɛptɪk] *n* Skeptiker(in) *m(f)*.
**sceptical,** (*US*) **skeptical** ['skɛptɪkl] *adj* skeptisch.
**scepticism,** (*US*) **skepticism** ['skɛptɪsɪzəm] *n* Skepsis *f*.
**sceptre,** (*US*) **scepter** ['sɛptə*] *n* Zepter *nt*.
**schedule** ['ʃɛdju:l, (*US*) 'skɛdju:l] *n* (*of trains, buses*) Fahrplan *m*; (*of events*) Programm *nt*; (*of prices, details etc*) Liste *f* ♦ *vt* planen; (*visit, meeting etc*) ansetzen; **on ~** wie geplant, pünktlich; **we are working to a very tight ~** wir arbeiten nach einem sehr knappen Zeitplan; **everything went according to ~** alles ist planmäßig verlaufen; **to be ahead of/behind ~** dem Zeitplan voraus sein/im Rückstand sein; **he was ~d to leave yesterday** laut Zeitplan hätte er gestern abfahren sollen.
**scheduled** ['ʃɛdju:ld, (*US*) 'skɛdju:ld] *adj* (*date, time*) vorgesehen; (*visit, event*) geplant;

(*train, bus, stop*) planmäßig.
**scheduled flight** *n* Linienflug *m*.
**schematic** [skɪ'mætɪk] *adj* schematisch.
**scheme** [ski:m] *n* (*personal plan*) Plan *m*; (*plot*) raffinierter Plan *m*, Komplott *nt*; (*formal plan*) Programm *nt* ♦ *vi* Pläne schmieden, intrigieren; **colour ~** Farbzusammenstellung *f*; **pension ~** Rentenversicherung *f*.
**scheming** ['ski:mɪŋ] *adj* intrigierend ♦ *n* Machenschaften *pl*.
**schism** ['skɪzəm] *n* Spaltung *f*.
**schizophrenia** [skɪtsə'fri:nɪə] *n* Schizophrenie *f*.
**schizophrenic** [skɪtsə'frɛnɪk] *adj* schizophren ♦ *n* Schizophrene(r) *f(m)*.
**scholar** ['skɒlə*] *n* Gelehrte(r) *f(m)*; (*pupil*) Student(in) *m(f)*, Schüler(in) *m(f)*; (*scholarship holder*) Stipendiat(in) *m(f)*.
**scholarly** ['skɒləlɪ] *adj* gelehrt; (*text, approach*) wissenschaftlich.
**scholarship** ['skɒləʃɪp] *n* Gelehrsamkeit *f*; (*grant*) Stipendium *nt*.
**school** [sku:l] *n* Schule *f*; (*US: inf: university*) Universität *f*; (*of whales, porpoises etc*) Schule *f*, Schwarm *m* ♦ *cpd* Schul-.
**school age** *n* Schulalter *nt*.
**schoolbook** ['sku:lbuk] *n* Schulbuch *nt*.
**schoolboy** ['sku:lbɔɪ] *n* Schuljunge *m*, Schüler *m*.
**schoolchildren** ['sku:ltʃɪldrən] *npl* Schulkinder *pl*, Schüler *pl*.
**schooldays** ['sku:ldeɪz] *npl* Schulzeit *f*.
**schooled** [sku:ld] *adj* geschult; **to be ~ in sth** über etw *acc* gut Bescheid wissen.
**schoolgirl** ['sku:lgɜ:l] *n* Schulmädchen *nt*, Schülerin *f*.
**schooling** ['sku:lɪŋ] *n* Schulbildung *f*.
**school-leaver** [sku:l'li:və*] (*BRIT*) *n* Schulabgänger(in) *m(f)*.
**schoolmaster** ['sku:lmɑ:stə*] *n* Lehrer *m*.
**schoolmistress** ['sku:lmɪstrɪs] *n* Lehrerin *f*.
**school report** (*BRIT*) *n* Zeugnis *nt*.
**schoolroom** ['sku:lru:m] *n* Klassenzimmer *nt*.
**schoolteacher** ['sku:lti:tʃə*] *n* Lehrer(in) *m(f)*.
**schoolyard** ['sku:ljɑ:d] *n* Schulhof *m*.
**schooner** ['sku:nə*] *n* (*ship*) Schoner *m*; (*BRIT: for sherry*) großes Sherryglas *nt*; (*US etc: for beer*) großes Bierglas *nt*.
**sciatica** [saɪ'ætɪkə] *n* Ischias *m or nt*.
**science** ['saɪəns] *n* Naturwissenschaft *f*; (*branch of knowledge*) Wissenschaft *f*; **the ~s** Naturwissenschaften *pl*.
**science fiction** *n* Science-fiction *f*.
**scientific** [saɪən'tɪfɪk] *adj* wissenschaftlich.
**scientist** ['saɪəntɪst] *n* Wissenschaftler(in) *m(f)*.
**sci-fi** ['saɪfaɪ] (*inf*) *n abbr* (= *science fiction*) SF.
**Scillies** ['sɪlɪz] *npl* = **Scilly Isles**.
**Scilly Isles** ['sɪlɪ'aɪlz] *npl*: **the ~** die Scilly-Inseln *pl*.
**scintillating** ['sɪntɪleɪtɪŋ] *adj* (*fig: conversation*)

faszinierend; (*wit*) sprühend.

**scissors** ['sɪzəz] *npl* Schere *f*; **a pair of** ~ eine Schere.

**sclerosis** [sklɪ'rəusɪs] *n* Sklerose *f*.

**scoff** [skɔf] *vt* (*BRIT: inf: eat*) futtern, verputzen ♦ *vi*: **to** ~ **(at)** (*mock*) spotten (über +*acc*), sich lustig machen (über +*acc*).

**scold** [skəuld] *vt* ausschimpfen.

**scolding** ['skəuldɪŋ] *n* Schelte *f*; **to get a** ~ ausgeschimpft werden.

**scone** [skɔn] *n* brötchenartiges Teegebäck.

**scoop** [sku:p] *n* (*for flour etc*) Schaufel *f*; (*for ice cream etc*) Portionierer *m*; (*amount*) Kugel *f*; (*PRESS*) Knüller *m*.

▶**scoop out** *vt* aushöhlen.

▶**scoop up** *vt* aufschaufeln; (*liquid*) aufschöpfen.

**scooter** ['sku:tə*] *n* (*also*: **motor** ~) Motorroller *m*; (*toy*) (Tret)roller *m*.

**scope** [skəup] *n* (*opportunity*) Möglichkeiten *pl*; (*range*) Ausmaß *nt*, Umfang *m*; (*freedom*) Freiheit *f*; **within the** ~ **of** im Rahmen +*gen*; **there is plenty of** ~ **for improvement** (*BRIT*) es könnte noch viel verbessert werden.

**scorch** [skɔ:tʃ] *vt* versengen; (*earth, grass*) verbrennen.

**scorched earth policy** *n* (*MIL*) Politik *f* der verbrannten Erde.

**scorcher** ['skɔ:tʃə*] (*inf*) *n* heißer Tag *m*.

**scorching** ['skɔ:tʃɪŋ] *adj* (*day, weather*) brütend heiß.

**score** [skɔ:*] *n* (*number of points*) (Punkte)stand *m*; (*of game*) Spielstand *m*; (*MUS*) Partitur *f*; (*twenty*) zwanzig ♦ *vt* (*goal*) schießen; (*point, success*) erzielen; (*mark*) einkerben; (*cut*) einritzen ♦ *vi* (*in game*) einen Punkt/Punkte erzielen; (*FOOTBALL etc*) ein Tor schießen; (*keep score*) (Punkte) zählen; **to settle an old** ~ **with sb** (*fig*) eine alte Rechnung mit jdm begleichen; **what's the** ~**?** (*SPORT*) wie steht's?; ~**s of** Hunderte von; **on that** ~ in dieser Hinsicht; **to** ~ **well** gut abschneiden; **to** ~ **6 out of 10** 6 von 10 Punkten erzielen; **to** ~ **(a point) over sb** (*fig*) jdn ausstechen.

▶**score out** *vt* ausstreichen.

**scoreboard** ['skɔ:bɔ:d] *n* Anzeigetafel *f*.

**scorecard** ['skɔ:ka:d] *n* (*SPORT*) Spielprotokoll *nt*.

**score line** *n* (*SPORT*) Spielstand *m*; (: *final score*) Endergebnis *nt*.

**scorer** ['skɔ:rə*] *n* (*FOOTBALL etc*) Torschütze *m*, Torschützin *f*; (*person keeping score*) Anschreiber(in) *m(f)*.

**scorn** [skɔ:n] *n* Verachtung *f* ♦ *vt* verachten; (*reject*) verschmähen.

**scornful** ['skɔ:nful] *adj* verächtlich, höhnisch.

**Scorpio** ['skɔ:pɪəu] *n* Skorpion *m*; **to be** ~ Skorpion sein.

**scorpion** ['skɔ:pɪən] *n* Skorpion *m*.

**Scot** [skɔt] *n* Schotte *m*, Schottin *f*.

**Scotch** [skɔtʃ] *n* Scotch *m*.

**scotch** [skɔtʃ] *vt* (*rumour*) aus der Welt schaffen; (*plan, idea*) unterbinden.

**Scotch tape ®** *n* ≈ Tesafilm ® *m*.

**scot-free** ['skɔt'fri:] *adv*: **to get off** ~ ungeschoren davonkommen.

**Scotland** ['skɔtlənd] *n* Schottland *nt*.

**Scots** [skɔts] *adj* schottisch.

**Scotsman** ['skɔtsmən] (*irreg: like* **man**) *n* Schotte *m*.

**Scotswoman** ['skɔtswumən] (*irreg: like* **woman**) *n* Schottin *f*.

**Scottish** ['skɔtɪʃ] *adj* schottisch.

**Scottish National Party** *n* Partei, die für die Unabhängigkeit Schottlands eintritt.

**scoundrel** ['skaundrl] *n* Schurke *m*.

**scour** ['skauə*] *vt* (*search*) absuchen; (*clean*) scheuern.

**scourer** ['skauərə*] *n* Topfkratzer *m*.

**scourge** [skə:dʒ] *n* (*lit, fig*) Geißel *f*.

**scout** [skaut] *n* (*MIL*) Kundschafter *m*, Späher *m*; (*also*: **boy** ~) Pfadfinder *m*; **girl** ~ (*US*) Pfadfinderin *f*.

▶**scout around** *vi* sich umsehen.

**scowl** [skaul] *vi* ein böses Gesicht machen ♦ *n* böses Gesicht *nt*; **to** ~ **at sb** jdn böse ansehen.

**scrabble** ['skræbl] *vi* (*also*: ~ **around**) herumtasten ♦ *n*: **S**~ ® Scrabble ® *nt*; **to** ~ **at sth** nach etw krallen; **to** ~ **about** *or* **around for sth** nach etw herumsuchen.

**scraggy** ['skrægɪ] *adj* (*animal*) mager; (*body, neck etc*) dürr.

**scram** [skræm] (*inf*) *vi* abhauen, verschwinden.

**scramble** ['skræmbl] *n* (*climb*) Kletterpartie *f*; (*rush*) Hetze *f*; (*struggle*) Gerangel *nt* ♦ *vi*: **to** ~ **up/over** klettern auf/über +*acc*; **to** ~ **for** sich drängeln um; **to go scrambling** (*SPORT*) Querfeldeinrennen fahren.

**scrambled eggs** ['skræmbld-] *n* Rührei *nt*.

**scrap** [skræp] *n* (*bit*) Stückchen *nt*; (*fig: of truth, evidence*) Spur *f*; (*fight*) Balgerei *f*; (*also*: ~ **metal**) Altmetall *nt*, Schrott *m* ♦ *vt* (*machines etc*) verschrotten; (*fig: plans etc*) fallenlassen ♦ *vi* (*fight*) sich balgen; **scraps** *npl* (*leftovers*) Reste *pl*; **to sell sth for** ~ etw als Schrott *or* zum Verschrotten verkaufen.

**scrapbook** ['skræpbuk] *n* Sammelalbum *nt*.

**scrap dealer** *n* Schrotthändler(in) *m(f)*.

**scrape** [skreɪp] *vt* abkratzen; (*hand etc*) abschürfen; (*car*) verschrammen ♦ *n*: **to get into a** ~ (*difficult situation*) in Schwulitäten *pl* kommen (*inf*).

▶**scrape through** *vt* (*exam etc*) durchrutschen durch (*inf*).

▶**scrape together** *vt* (*money*) zusammenkratzen.

**scraper** ['skreɪpə*] *n* Kratzer *m*.

**scrap heap** *n*: **to be on the** ~ (*fig*) zum alten Eisen gehören.

**scrap merchant** (*BRIT*) *n* Schrotthändler(in) *m(f)*.

**scrap metal** n Altmetall nt, Schrott m.
**scrap paper** n Schmierpapier nt.
**scrappy** ['skræpɪ] adj zusammengestoppelt (inf).
**scrap yard** n Schrottplatz m.
**scratch** [skrætʃ] n Kratzer m ♦ vt kratzen; (one's nose etc) sich kratzen an +dat; (paint, car, record) verkratzen; (COMPUT) löschen ♦ vi sich kratzen ♦ cpd (team, side) zusammengewürfelt; **to start from** ~ ganz von vorne anfangen; **to be up to** ~ den Anforderungen entsprechen; **to** ~ **the surface** (fig) an der Oberfläche bleiben.
**scratch pad** (US) n Notizblock m.
**scrawl** [skrɔːl] n Gekritzel nt; (handwriting) Klaue f (inf) ♦ vt hinkritzeln.
**scrawny** ['skrɔːnɪ] adj dürr.
**scream** [skriːm] n Schrei m ♦ vi schreien; **to be a** ~ (inf) zum Schreien sein; **to** ~ **at sb (to do sth)** jdn anschreien(, etw zu tun).
**scree** [skriː] n Geröll nt.
**screech** [skriːtʃ] vi kreischen; (tyres, brakes) quietschen ♦ n Kreischen nt; (of tyres, brakes) Quietschen nt.
**screen** [skriːn] n (CINE) Leinwand f; (TV, COMPUT) Bildschirm m; (movable barrier) Wandschirm m; (fig: cover) Tarnung f, (also: **windscreen**) Windschutzscheibe f ♦ vt (protect) abschirmen; (from the wind etc) schützen; (conceal) verdecken; (film) zeigen, vorführen; (programme) senden; (candidates etc) überprüfen; (for illness): **to** ~ **sb for sth** jdn auf etw acc (hin) untersuchen.
**screen editing** n (COMPUT) Bildschirm-aufbereitung f.
**screening** ['skriːnɪŋ] n (MED) Untersuchung f; (of film) Vorführung f; (TV) Sendung f; (for security) Überprüfung f.
**screen memory** n (COMPUT) Bildschirmspeicher m.
**screenplay** ['skriːnpleɪ] n Drehbuch nt.
**screen test** n Probeaufnahmen pl.
**screw** [skruː] n Schraube f ♦ vt schrauben; (inf!) bumsen (!); **to** ~ **sth in** etw einschrauben; **to** ~ **sth to the wall** etw an der Wand festschrauben; **to have one's head** ~**ed on** (fig) ein vernünftiger Mensch sein.
►**screw up** vt (paper etc) zusammenknüllen; (inf: ruin) vermasseln; **to** ~ **up one's eyes** die Augen zusammenkneifen.
**screwdriver** ['skruːdraɪvəʳ] n Schrauben-zieher m.
**screwed-up** ['skruːd'ʌp] (inf) adj: **to be/get** ~ **about sth** sich wegen etw ganz verrückt machen.
**screwy** ['skruːɪ] (inf) adj verrückt.
**scribble** ['skrɪbl] n Gekritzel nt ♦ vt, vi kritzeln; **to** ~ **sth down** etw hinkritzeln.
**scribe** [skraɪb] n Schreiber m.
**script** [skrɪpt] n (CINE) Drehbuch nt; (of speech, play etc) Text m; (alphabet) Schrift f;

(in exam) schriftliche Arbeit f.
**scripted** ['skrɪptɪd] adj (speech etc) vorbereitet.
**scripture(s)** ['skrɪptʃə(z)] n(pl) (heilige) Schrift f; **the S~(s)** (the Bible) die Heilige Schrift f.
**scriptwriter** ['skrɪptraɪtəʳ] n (RADIO, TV) Autor(in) m(f); (CINE) Drehbuchautor(in) m(f).
**scroll** [skrəul] n Schriftrolle f ♦ vt (COMPUT) scrollen.
**scrotum** ['skrəutəm] n Hodensack m.
**scrounge** [skraundʒ] (inf) vt: **to** ~ **sth off sb** etw bei jdm schnorren ♦ vi schnorren ♦ n: **on the** ~ am Schnorren.
**scrounger** ['skraundʒəʳ] (inf) n Schnorrer(in) m(f).
**scrub** [skrʌb] n Gestrüpp nt ♦ vt (floor etc) schrubben; (inf: idea, plan) fallenlassen.
**scrubbing brush** ['skrʌbɪŋ-] n Scheuerbürste f.
**scruff** [skrʌf] n: **by the** ~ **of the neck** am Genick.
**scruffy** ['skrʌfɪ] adj gammelig, verwahrlost.
**scrum(mage)** ['skrʌm(ɪdʒ)] n (RUGBY) Gedränge nt.
**scruple** ['skruːpl] n (gen pl) Skrupel m, Bedenken nt; **to have no** ~**s about doing sth** keine Skrupel or Bedenken haben, etw zu tun.
**scrupulous** ['skruːpjuləs] adj gewissenhaft; (honesty) unbedingt.
**scrupulously** ['skruːpjuləslɪ] adv gewissenhaft; (honest, fair) äußerst; (clean) peinlich.
**scrutinize** ['skruːtɪnaɪz] vt prüfend ansehen; (data, records etc) genau prüfen or untersuchen.
**scrutiny** ['skruːtɪnɪ] n genaue Untersuchung f; **under the** ~ **of sb** unter jds prüfendem Blick.
**scuba** ['skuːbə] n (Schwimm)tauchgerät nt.
**scuba diving** n Sporttauchen nt.
**scuff** [skʌf] vt (shoes, floor) abwetzen.
**scuffle** ['skʌfl] n Handgemenge nt.
**scull** [skʌl] n Skull nt.
**scullery** ['skʌlərɪ] n (old) Spülküche f.
**sculptor** ['skʌlptəʳ] n Bildhauer(in) m(f).
**sculpture** ['skʌlptʃəʳ] n (art) Bildhauerei f; (object) Skulptur f.
**scum** [skʌm] n (on liquid) Schmutzschicht f; (pej) Abschaum m.
**scupper** ['skʌpəʳ] (BRIT: inf) vt (plan, idea) zerschlagen.
**scurrilous** ['skʌrɪləs] adj verleumderisch.
**scurry** ['skʌrɪ] vi huschen.
►**scurry off** vi forthasten.
**scurvy** ['skɜːvɪ] n Skorbut m.
**scuttle** ['skʌtl] n (also: **coal** ~) Kohleneimer m ♦ vt (ship) versenken ♦ vi: **to** ~ **away** or **off** verschwinden.
**scythe** [saɪð] n Sense f.

**SD, S.Dak.** (US) abbr (POST: = South Dakota).

**SDI** (US) n abbr (MIL: = Strategic Defense Initiative) SDI f.

**SDLP** (BRIT) n abbr (POL: = Social Democratic and Labour Party) sozialdemokratische Partei in Nordirland.

**SDP** (BRIT) n abbr (POL: formerly: = Social Democratic Party) sozialdemokratische Partei.

**SE** abbr (= south-east) SO.

**sea** [si:] n Meer nt, See f; (fig) Meer ♦ cpd See-; **by ~** (travel) mit dem Schiff; **beside** or **by the ~** (holiday) am Meer, an der See; (village) am Meer; **on the ~** (boat) auf See; **at ~** auf See; **to be all at ~** (fig) nicht durchblicken (inf); **out to ~** aufs Meer (hinaus); **to look out to ~** aufs Meer hinausblicken; **heavy/rough ~(s)** schwere/rauhe See f.

**sea anemone** n Seeanemone f.

**sea bed** n Meeresboden m.

**seaboard** ['si:bɔ:d] n Küste f.

**seafarer** ['si:fɛərə*] n Seefahrer m.

**seafaring** ['si:fɛərɪŋ] adj (life, nation) Seefahrer-.

**seafood** ['si:fu:d] n Meeresfrüchte pl.

**seafront** ['si:frʌnt] n Strandpromenade f.

**seagoing** ['si:gəʊɪŋ] adj hochseetüchtig.

**seagull** ['si:gʌl] n Möwe f.

**seal** [si:l] n (animal) Seehund m; (official stamp) Siegel nt; (in machine etc) Dichtung f; (on bottle etc) Verschluß m ♦ vt (envelope) zukleben; (crack, opening) abdichten; (with seal) versiegeln; (agreement, sb's fate) besiegeln; **to give sth one's ~ of approval** einer Sache dat seine offizielle Zustimmung geben.

▶**seal off** vt (place) abriegeln.

**sea level** n Meeresspiegel m; **2,000 ft above/below ~** 2000 Fuß über/unter dem Meeresspiegel.

**sealing wax** ['si:lɪŋ-] n Siegelwachs nt.

**sea lion** n Seelöwe m.

**sealskin** ['si:lskɪn] n Seehundfell nt.

**seam** [si:m] n Naht f; (lit, fig: where edges join) Übergang m; (of coal etc) Flöz nt; **the hall was bursting at the ~s** der Saal platzte aus allen Nähten.

**seaman** ['si:mən] (irreg: like **man**) n Seemann m.

**seamanship** ['si:mənʃɪp] n Seemannschaft f.

**seamless** ['si:mlɪs] adj (lit, fig) nahtlos.

**seamy** ['si:mɪ] adj zwielichtig; **the ~ side of life** die Schattenseite des Lebens.

**séance** ['seɪɒns] n spiritistische Sitzung f.

**seaplane** ['si:pleɪn] n Wasserflugzeug nt.

**seaport** ['si:pɔ:t] n Seehafen m.

**search** [sɜ:tʃ] n Suche f; (inspection) Durchsuchung f; (COMPUT) Suchlauf m ♦ vt durchsuchen; (mind, memory) durchforschen ♦ vi: **to ~ for** suchen nach; **"~ and replace"** (COMPUT) „suchen und ersetzen"; **in ~ of** auf der Suche nach.

▶**search through** vt fus durchsuchen.

**searcher** ['sɜ:tʃə*] n Suchende(r) f(m).

**searching** ['sɜ:tʃɪŋ] adj (question) bohrend; (look) prüfend; (examination) eingehend.

**searchlight** ['sɜ:tʃlaɪt] n Suchscheinwerfer m.

**search party** n Suchtrupp m; **to send out a ~** einen Suchtrupp ausschicken.

**search warrant** n Durchsuchungsbefehl m.

**searing** ['sɪərɪŋ] adj (heat) glühend; (pain) scharf.

**seashore** ['si:ʃɔ:*] n Strand m; **on the ~** am Strand.

**seasick** ['si:sɪk] adj seekrank.

**seasickness** ['si:sɪknɪs] n Seekrankheit f.

**seaside** ['si:saɪd] n Meer nt, See f; **to go to the ~** ans Meer or an die See fahren; **at the ~** am Meer, an der See.

**seaside resort** n Badeort m.

**season** ['si:zn] n Jahreszeit f; (AGR) Zeit f; (SPORT, of films etc) Saison f; (THEAT) Spielzeit f ♦ vt (food) würzen; **strawberries are in ~/out of ~** für Erdbeeren ist jetzt die richtige Zeit/nicht die richtige Zeit; **the busy ~** die Hochsaison f; **the open ~** (HUNTING) die Jagdzeit f.

**seasonal** ['si:znl] adj (work) Saison-.

**seasoned** ['si:znd] adj (fig: traveller) erfahren; (wood) abgelagert; **she's a ~ campaigner** sie ist eine alte Kämpferin.

**seasoning** ['si:znɪŋ] n Gewürz nt.

**season ticket** n (RAIL) Zeitkarte f; (SPORT) Dauerkarte f; (THEAT) Abonnement nt.

**seat** [si:t] n (chair, of government, POL) Sitz m; (place) Platz m; (buttocks) Gesäß nt; (of trousers) Hosenboden m; (of learning) Stätte f ♦ vt setzen; (have room for) Sitzplätze bieten für; **are there any ~s left?** sind noch Plätze frei?; **to take one's ~** sich setzen; **please be ~ed** bitte nehmen Sie Platz; **to be ~ed** sitzen.

**seat belt** n Sicherheitsgurt m.

**seating arrangements** ['si:tɪŋ-] npl Sitzordnung f.

**seating capacity** n Sitzplätze pl.

**SEATO** ['si:təʊ] n abbr (= Southeast Asia Treaty Organization) SEATO f.

**sea urchin** n Seeigel m.

**sea water** n Meerwasser nt.

**seaweed** ['si:wi:d] n Seetang m.

**seaworthy** ['si:wɜ:ðɪ] adj seetüchtig.

**SEC** (US) n abbr (= Securities and Exchange Commission) amerikanische Börsenaufsichtsbehörde.

**sec.** abbr (= second) Sek.

**secateurs** [sɛkə'tɜ:z] npl Gartenschere f.

**secede** [sɪ'si:d] vi (POL): **to ~ (from)** sich abspalten (von).

**secluded** [sɪ'klu:dɪd] adj (place) abgelegen; (life) zurückgezogen.

**seclusion** [sɪ'klu:ʒən] n Abgeschiedenheit f; **in ~** zurückgezogen.

**second¹** [sɪ'kɒnd] (BRIT) vt (employee)

abordnen.
**second²** ['sɛkənd] *adj* zweite(r, s) ♦ *adv* (*come, be placed*) zweite(r, s); (*when listing*) zweitens ♦ *n* (*time*) Sekunde *f*, (*AUT: also:* ~ **gear**) der zweite Gang; (*COMM: imperfect*) zweite Wahl *f* ♦ *vt* (*motion*) unterstützen; **upper/lower** ~ (*BRIT: UNIV*) ≈ Zwei plus/ minus; **Charles the S**~ Karl der Zweite; **just a** ~! einen Augenblick!; ~ **floor** (*BRIT*) zweiter Stock *m*; (*US*) erster Stock *m*; **to ask for a** ~ **opinion** ein zweites Gutachten einholen.
**secondary** ['sɛkəndərɪ] *adj* weniger wichtig.
**secondary education** *n* höhere Schulbildung *f*.
**secondary picketing** *n* *Aufstellung von Streikposten bei nur indirekt beteiligten Firmen.*
**secondary school** *n* höhere Schule *f*.

---

Secondary school *ist in Großbritannien eine weiterführende Schule für Kinder von 11 bis 18 Jahren. Manche Schüler gehen schon mit 16 Jahren, wenn die allgemeine Schulpflicht endet, von der Schule ab. Die meisten secondary schools sind heute Gesamtschulen, obwohl es auch noch selektive Schulen gibt. Siehe auch* **comprehensive school**, **primary school***.*

---

**second-best** [sɛkənd'bɛst] *adj* zweitbeste(r, s) ♦ *n:* **as a** ~ als Ausweichlösung; **don't settle for** ~ gib dich nur mit dem Besten zufrieden.
**second-class** ['sɛkənd'klɑːs] *adj* zweitklassig; (*citizen*) zweiter Klasse; (*RAIL, POST*) Zweite-Klasse- ♦ *adv* (*RAIL, POST*) zweiter Klasse; **to send sth** ~ etw zweiter Klasse schicken; **to travel** ~ zweiter Klasse reisen.
**second cousin** *n* Cousin *m*/Cousine *f* zweiten Grades.
**seconder** ['sɛkəndə*] *n* Befürworter(in) *m(f)*.
**second-guess** ['sɛkənd'gɛs] *vt* vorhersagen; **to** ~ **sb** vorhersagen, was jd machen wird.
**secondhand** ['sɛkənd'hænd] *adj* gebraucht; (*clothing*) getragen ♦ *adv* (*buy*) gebraucht; **to hear sth** ~ etw aus zweiter Hand haben; ~ **car** Gebrauchtwagen *m*.
**second hand** *n* (*on clock*) Sekundenzeiger *m*.
**second-in-command** ['sɛkəndɪnkə'mɑːnd] *n* (*MIL*) stellvertretender Kommandeur *m*; (*ADMIN*) stellvertretender Leiter *m*.
**secondly** ['sɛkəndlɪ] *adv* zweitens.
**secondment** [sɪ'kɒndmənt] (*BRIT*) *n* Abordnung *f*; **to be on** ~ abgeordnet sein.
**second-rate** ['sɛkənd'reɪt] *adj* zweitklassig.
**second thoughts** *npl:* **on** ~ *or* (*US*) **thought** wenn ich es mir (recht) überlege; **to have** ~ (**about doing sth**) es sich *dat* anders überlegen (und etw doch nicht tun).
**Second World War** *n:* **the** ~ der Zweite Weltkrieg.

**secrecy** ['siːkrəsɪ] *n* Geheimhaltung *f*; (*of person*) Verschwiegenheit *f*; **in** ~ heimlich.
**secret** ['siːkrɪt] *adj* geheim; (*admirer*) heimlich ♦ *n* Geheimnis *nt*; **in** ~ heimlich; ~ **passage** Geheimgang *m*; **to keep sth** ~ **from sb** etw vor jdm geheimhalten; **can you keep a** ~? kannst du schweigen?; **to make no** ~ **of sth** kein Geheimnis *or* keinen Hehl aus etw machen.
**secret agent** *n* Geheimagent(in) *m(f)*.
**secretarial** [sɛkrɪ'tɛərɪəl] *adj* (*work*) Büro-; (*course*) Sekretärinnen-; (*staff*) Sekretariats-.
**secretariat** [sɛkrɪ'tɛərɪət] *n* (*POL, ADMIN*) Sekretariat *nt*.
**secretary** ['sɛkrətərɪ] *n* (*COMM*) Sekretär(in) *m(f)*; (*of club*) Schriftführer(in) *m(f)*; **S**~ **of State (for)** (*BRIT: POL*) Minister(in) *m(f)* (für); **S**~ **of State** (*US: POL*) Außenminister(in) *m(f)*.
**secretary-general** ['sɛkrətərɪ'dʒɛnərl] (*pl* **secretaries-general**) *n* Generalsekretär(in) *m(f)*.
**secrete** [sɪ'kriːt] *vt* (*ANAT, BIOL, MED*) absondern; (*hide*) verbergen.
**secretion** [sɪ'kriːʃən] *n* (*substance*) Sekret *nt*.
**secretive** ['siːkrətɪv] *adj* verschlossen; (*pej*) geheimnistuerisch.
**secretly** ['siːkrɪtlɪ] *adv* heimlich; (*hope*) insgeheim.
**secret police** *n* Geheimpolizei *f*.
**secret service** *n* Geheimdienst *m*.
**sect** [sɛkt] *n* Sekte *f*.
**sectarian** [sɛk'tɛərɪən] *adj* (*killing etc*) konfessionell motiviert; ~ **violence** gewalttätige Konfessionsstreitigkeiten *pl*.
**section** ['sɛkʃən] *n* (*part*) Teil *m*; (*department*) Abteilung *f*, (*of document*) Absatz *m*; (*cross-section*) Schnitt *m* ♦ *vt* (*divide*) teilen; **the business/sport** ~ (*PRESS*) der Wirtschafts-/ Sportteil.
**sectional** ['sɛkʃənl] *adj:* ~ **drawing** Darstellung *f* im Schnitt.
**sector** ['sɛktə*] *n* Sektor *m*.
**secular** ['sɛkjulə*] *adj* weltlich.
**secure** [sɪ'kjuə*] *adj* sicher; (*firmly fixed*) fest ♦ *vt* (*fix*) festmachen; (*votes etc*) erhalten; (*contract etc*) (sich *dat*) sichern; (*COMM: loan*) (ab)sichern; **to make sth** ~ etw sichern; **to** ~ **sth for sb** jdm etw sichern.
**secured creditor** [sɪ'kjuəd-] *n* (*COMM*) abgesicherter Gläubiger *m*.
**securely** [sɪ'kjuəlɪ] *adv* (*firmly*) fest; (*safely*) sicher.
**security** [sɪ'kjuərɪtɪ] *n* Sicherheit *f*; (*freedom from anxiety*) Geborgenheit *f*; **securities** *npl* (*STOCK EXCHANGE*) Effekten *pl*, Wertpapiere *pl*; **to increase/tighten** ~ die Sicherheitsvorkehrungen verschärfen; ~ **of tenure** Kündigungsschutz *m*.
**Security Council** *n* Sicherheitsrat *m*.
**security forces** *npl* Sicherheitskräfte *pl*.

**security guard** n Sicherheitsbeamte(r) m; (transporting money) Wachmann m.

**security risk** n Sicherheitsrisiko nt.

**secy.** abbr = **secretary.**

**sedan** [sə'dæn] (US) n (AUT) Limousine f.

**sedate** [sɪ'deɪt] adj (person) ruhig, gesetzt; (life) geruhsam; (pace) gemächlich ♦ vt (MED) Beruhigungsmittel geben +dat.

**sedation** [sɪ'deɪʃən] n (MED) Beruhigungsmittel pl; **to be under** ~ unter dem Einfluß von Beruhigungsmitteln stehen.

**sedative** ['sɛdɪtɪv] n (MED) Beruhigungsmittel nt.

**sedentary** ['sɛdntrɪ] adj (occupation, work) sitzend.

**sediment** ['sɛdɪmənt] n (in bottle) (Boden)satz m; (in lake etc) Ablagerung f.

**sedimentary** [sɛdɪ'mɛntərɪ] adj (GEOG) sedimentär; ~ **rock** Sedimentgestein nt.

**sedition** [sɪ'dɪʃən] n Aufwiegelung f.

**seduce** [sɪ'djuːs] vt verführen; **to** ~ **sb into doing sth** jdn dazu verleiten, etw zu tun.

**seduction** [sɪ'dʌkʃən] n (attraction) Verlockung f; (act of seducing) Verführung f.

**seductive** [sɪ'dʌktɪv] adj verführerisch; (fig: offer) verlockend.

**see** [siː] (pt saw, pp seen) vt sehen; (look at) sich dat ansehen; (understand) verstehen, (ein)sehen; (doctor etc) aufsuchen ♦ vi sehen ♦ n (REL) Bistum nt; **to** ~ **that** (ensure) dafür sorgen, daß; **to** ~ **sb to the door** jdn zur Tür bringen; **there was nobody to be** ~**n** es war niemand zu sehen; **to go and** ~ **sb** jdn besuchen (gehen); **to** ~ **a doctor** zum Arzt gehen; ~ **you!** tschüs! (inf); ~ **you soon!** bis bald!; **let me** ~ (show me) laß mich mal sehen; (let me think) laß mich mal überlegen; **I** ~ ich verstehe, aha; (annoyed) ach so; **you** ~ weißt du, siehst du; ~ **for yourself** überzeug dich doch selbst; **I don't know what she** ~**s in him** ich weiß nicht, was sie an ihm findet; **as far as I can** ~ so wie ich das sehe.

►**see about** vt fus sich kümmern um +acc.

►**see off** vt verabschieden.

►**see through** vt fus durchschauen ♦ vt: **to** ~ **sb through sth** jdm in etw dat beistehen; **to** ~ **sth through to the end** etw zu Ende bringen; **this should** ~ **you through** das müßte dir reichen.

►**see to** vt fus sich kümmern um +acc.

**seed** [siːd] n Samen m; (of fruit) Kern m; (fig: usu pl) Keim m; (TENNIS) gesetzter Spieler m, gesetzte Spielerin f; **to go to** ~ (plant) Samen bilden; (lettuce etc) schießen; (fig: person) herunterkommen.

**seedless** ['siːdlɪs] adj kernlos.

**seedling** ['siːdlɪŋ] n (BOT) Sämling m.

**seedy** ['siːdɪ] adj (person, place) zwielichtig, zweifelhaft.

**seeing** ['siːɪŋ] conj: ~ **as** or **that** da.

**seek** [siːk] (pt, pp sought) vt suchen; **to** ~ **advice from sb** jdn um Rat fragen; **to** ~ **help from sb** jdn um Hilfe bitten.

►**seek out** vt ausfindig machen.

**seem** [siːm] vi scheinen; **there** ~**s to be a mistake** da scheint ein Fehler zu sein; **it** ~**s (that)** es scheint(, daß); **it** ~**s to me that ...** mir scheint, daß ...; **what** ~**s to be the trouble?** worum geht es denn?; (doctor) was fehlt Ihnen denn?

**seemingly** ['siːmɪŋlɪ] adv anscheinend.

**seemly** ['siːmlɪ] adj schicklich.

**seen** [siːn] pp of **see.**

**seep** [siːp] vi sickern.

**seersucker** ['sɪəsʌkə'] n Krepp m, Seersucker m.

**seesaw** ['siːsɔː] n Wippe f.

**seethe** [siːð] vi: **to** ~ **with** (place) wimmeln von; **to** ~ **with anger** vor Wut kochen.

**see-through** ['siːθruː] adj durchsichtig.

**segment** ['sɛgmənt] n Teil m; (of orange) Stück nt.

**segregate** ['sɛgrɪgeɪt] vt trennen, absondern.

**segregation** [sɛgrɪ'geɪʃən] n Trennung f.

**Seine** [seɪn] n: **the** ~ die Seine f.

**seismic shock** n Erdstoß m.

**seize** [siːz] vt packen, ergreifen; (fig: opportunity) ergreifen; (power, control) an sich acc reißen; (territory, airfield) besetzen; (hostage) nehmen; (LAW) beschlagnahmen.

►**seize up** vi (engine) sich festfressen.

►**seize (up)on** vt fus sich stürzen auf +acc.

**seizure** ['siːʒə'] n (MED) Anfall m; (of power) Ergreifung f; (LAW) Beschlagnahmung f.

**seldom** ['sɛldəm] adv selten.

**select** [sɪ'lɛkt] adj exklusiv ♦ vt (aus)wählen; (SPORT) aufstellen; **a** ~ **few** wenige Auserwählte.

**selection** [sɪ'lɛkʃən] n (being chosen) Wahl f; (range) Auswahl f.

**selection committee** n Auswahlkomitee nt.

**selective** [sɪ'lɛktɪv] adj wählerisch; (not general) selektiv.

**selector** [sɪ'lɛktə'] n (SPORT) Mannschaftsaufsteller(in) m(f); (TECH) Wählschalter m; (: button) Taste f.

**self** [sɛlf] (pl selves) n Selbst nt, Ich nt; **she was her normal** ~ **again** sie war wieder ganz die alte.

**self...** [sɛlf] pref selbst-, Selbst-.

**self-addressed** ['sɛlfə'drɛst] adj: ~ **envelope** addressierter Rückumschlag m.

**self-adhesive** [sɛlfəd'hiːzɪv] adj selbstklebend.

**self-appointed** [sɛlfə'pɔɪntɪd] adj selbsternannt.

**self-assertive** [sɛlfə'sɜːtɪv] adj selbstbewußt.

**self-assurance** [sɛlfə'ʃuərəns] n Selbstsicherheit f.

**self-assured** [sɛlfə'ʃuəd] adj selbstsicher.

**self-catering** [sɛlf'keɪtərɪŋ] (BRIT) adj (holiday, flat) für Selbstversorger.

**self-centred, (US) self-centered** [sɛlf'sɛntəd]

*adj* egozentrisch, ichbezogen.
**self-cleaning** [sɛlf'kliːnɪŋ] *adj* selbstreinigend.
**self-confessed** [sɛlfkən'fɛst] *adj* erklärt.
**self-confidence** [sɛlf'kɒnfɪdns] *n*
Selbstbewußtsein *nt*, Selbstvertrauen *nt*.
**self-confident** [sɛlf'kɒnfɪdənt] *adj*
selbstbewußt, selbstsicher.
**self-conscious** [sɛlf'kɒnʃəs] *adj* befangen,
gehemmt.
**self-contained** [sɛlfkən'teɪnd] (*BRIT*) *adj* (*flat*)
abgeschlossen; (*person*) selbständig.
**self-control** [sɛlfkən'trəul] *n*
Selbstbeherrschung *f*.
**self-defeating** [sɛlfdɪ'fiːtɪŋ] *adj* unsinnig.
**self-defence,** (*US*) **self-defense** [sɛlfdɪ'fɛns]
*n* Selbstverteidigung *f*; (*LAW*) Notwehr *f*; **in**
~ zu seiner/ihrer *etc* Verteidigung; (*LAW*) in
Notwehr.
**self-discipline** [sɛlf'dɪsɪplɪn] *n* Selbstdisziplin
*f*.
**self-employed** [sɛlfɪm'plɔɪd] *adj* selbständig.
**self-esteem** [sɛlfɪs'tiːm] *n* Selbstachtung *f*.
**self-evident** [sɛlf'ɛvɪdnt] *adj* offensichtlich.
**self-explanatory** [sɛlfɪks'plænətrɪ] *adj*
unmittelbar verständlich.
**self-financing** [sɛlffaɪ'nænsɪŋ] *adj*
selbstfinanzierend.
**self-governing** [sɛlf'gʌvənɪŋ] *adj*
selbstverwaltet.
**self-help** ['sɛlf'hɛlp] *n* Selbsthilfe *f*.
**self-importance** [sɛlfɪm'pɔːtns] *n*
Aufgeblasenheit *f*.
**self-indulgent** [sɛlfɪn'dʌldʒənt] *adj*
genießerisch; **to be** ~ sich verwöhnen.
**self-inflicted** [sɛlfɪn'flɪktɪd] *adj* selbst
zugefügt.
**self-interest** [sɛlf'ɪntrɪst] *n* Eigennutz *m*.
**selfish** ['sɛlfɪʃ] *adj* egoistisch, selbstsüchtig.
**selfishly** ['sɛlfɪʃlɪ] *adv* egoistisch,
selbstsüchtig.
**selfishness** ['sɛlfɪʃnɪs] *n* Egoismus *m*,
Selbstsucht *f*.
**selfless** ['sɛlflɪs] *adj* selbstlos.
**selflessly** ['sɛlflɪslɪ] *adv* selbstlos.
**selflessness** ['sɛlflɪsnɪs] *n* Selbstlosigkeit *f*.
**self-made** ['sɛlfmeɪd] *adj:* ~ **man**
Selfmademan *m*.
**self-pity** [sɛlf'pɪtɪ] *n* Selbstmitleid *nt*.
**self-portrait** [sɛlf'pɔːtreɪt] *n* Selbstporträt *nt*,
Selbstbildnis *nt*.
**self-possessed** [sɛlfpə'zɛst] *adj*
selbstbeherrscht.
**self-preservation** ['sɛlfprɛzə'veɪʃən] *n*
Selbsterhaltung *f*.
**self-raising** ['sɛlf'reɪzɪŋ], (*US*) **self-rising**
['sɛlf'raɪzɪŋ] *adj:* ~ **flour** Mehl mit bereits
*beigemischtem Backpulver*.
**self-reliant** [sɛlfrɪ'laɪənt] *adj* selbständig.
**self-respect** [sɛlfrɪs'pɛkt] *n* Selbstachtung *f*.
**self-respecting** [sɛlfrɪs'pɛktɪŋ] *adj* mit
Selbstachtung; (*genuine*) der/die/das etwas
auf sich hält.

**self-righteous** [sɛlf'raɪtʃəs] *adj* selbstgerecht.
**self-rising** [sɛlf'raɪzɪŋ] (*US*) *adj* = **self-raising**.
**self-sacrifice** [sɛlf'sækrɪfaɪs] *n*
Selbstaufopferung *f*.
**self-same** ['sɛlfseɪm] *adj:* **the** ~ genau
derselbe/dieselbe/dasselbe.
**self-satisfied** [sɛlf'sætɪsfaɪd] *adj*
selbstzufrieden.
**self-sealing** [sɛlf'siːlɪŋ] *adj* selbstklebend.
**self-service** [sɛlf'səːvɪs] *adj* (*shop, restaurant
etc*) Selbstbedienungs-.
**self-styled** ['sɛlfstaɪld] *adj* selbsternannt.
**self-sufficient** [sɛlfsə'fɪʃənt] *adj* (*country*)
autark; (*person*) selbständig, unabhängig; **to
be** ~ **in coal** seinen Kohlebedarf selbst
decken können.
**self-supporting** [sɛlfsə'pɔːtɪŋ] *adj* (*business*)
sich selbst tragend.
**self-taught** [sɛlf'tɔːt] *adj:* **to be** ~ Autodidakt
sein; **he is a** ~ **pianist** er hat sich das
Klavierspielen selbst beigebracht.
**self-test** ['sɛlftɛst] *n* (*COMPUT*) Selbsttest *m*.
**sell** [sɛl] (*pt, pp* **sold**) *vt* verkaufen; (*shop:
goods*) führen, haben (*inf*); (*fig: idea*)
schmackhaft machen +*dat*, verkaufen (*inf*)
♦ *vi* sich verkaufen (lassen); **to** ~ **at** *or* **for 10
pounds** für 10 Pfund verkauft werden; **to**
~ **sb sth** jdm etw verkaufen; **to** ~ **o.s.** sich
verkaufen.
▶**sell off** *vt* verkaufen.
▶**sell out** *vi:* **we/the tickets are sold out** wir/
die Karten sind ausverkauft; **we have sold
out of ...** wir haben kein ... mehr, ... ist
ausverkauft.
▶**sell up** *vi* sein Haus/seine Firma *etc*
verkaufen.
**sell-by date** ['sɛlbaɪ-] *n* ≈ Haltbarkeitsdatum
*nt*.
**seller** ['sɛlə*] *n* Verkäufer(in) *m(f)*; ~**'s market**
Verkäufermarkt *m*.
**selling price** ['sɛlɪŋ-] *n* Verkaufspreis *m*.
**sellotape ®** ['sɛləuteɪp] (*BRIT*) *n* Klebeband
*nt*, ≈ Tesafilm ® *m*.
**sellout** ['sɛlaut] *n* (*inf: betrayal*) Verrat *m*; **the
match was a** ~ das Spiel war ausverkauft.
**selves** [sɛlvz] *pl of* **self**.
**semantic** [sɪ'mæntɪk] *adj* semantisch.
**semantics** [sɪ'mæntɪks] *n* (*LING*) Semantik *f*.
**semaphore** ['sɛməfɔː*] *n* Flaggenalphabet *nt*.
**semblance** ['sɛmblns] *n* Anschein *m*.
**semen** ['siːmən] *n* Samenflüssigkeit *f*, Sperma
*nt*.
**semester** [sɪ'mɛstə*] (*esp US*) *n* Semester *nt*.
**semi** ['sɛmɪ] *n* = **semidetached (house)**.
**semi...** ['sɛmɪ] *pref* halb-, Halb-.
**semibreve** ['sɛmɪbriːv] (*BRIT*) *n* (*MUS*) ganze
Note *f*.
**semicircle** ['sɛmɪsəːkl] *n* Halbkreis *m*.
**semicircular** ['sɛmɪ'səːkjulə*] *adj*
halbkreisförmig.
**semicolon** [sɛmɪ'kəulən] *n* Strichpunkt *m*,
Semikolon *nt*.

**semiconductor** [sɛmɪkən'dʌktə*] n Halbleiter m.

**semiconscious** [sɛmɪ'kɔnʃəs] adj halb bewußtlos.

**semidetached (house)** (BRIT) n Doppelhaushälfte f.

**semifinal** [sɛmɪ'faɪnl] n Halbfinale nt.

**seminar** ['sɛmɪnɑː*] n Seminar nt.

**seminary** ['sɛmɪnərɪ] n (REL) Priesterseminar nt.

**semi-precious stone** n Halbedelstein m.

**semiquaver** ['sɛmɪkweɪvə*] (BRIT) n (MUS) Sechzehntelnote f.

**semiskilled** [sɛmɪ'skɪld] adj (work) Anlern-; (worker) angelernt.

**semi-skimmed** [sɛmɪ'skɪmd] adj (milk) teilentrahmt, Halbfett-.

**semitone** ['sɛmɪtəun] n (MUS) Halbton m.

**semolina** [sɛmə'liːnə] n Grieß m.

**SEN** (BRIT) n abbr (formerly: = State Enrolled Nurse) staatlich anerkannte Krankenschwester f, staatlich anerkannter Krankenpfleger m.

**Sen., sen.** abbr (US) = **senator**; (in names: = senior) sen.

**senate** ['sɛnɪt] n Senat m.

> **Senate** ist das Oberhaus des amerikanischen Kongresses (das Unterhaus ist das **House of Representatives**). Der Senat besteht aus 100 Senatoren, 2 für jeden Bundesstaat, die für 6 Jahre gewählt werden, wobei ein Drittel alle zwei Jahre neu gewählt wird. Die Senatoren werden in direkter Wahl vom Volk gewählt. Siehe auch **congress**.

**senator** ['sɛnɪtə*] n Senator(in) m(f).

**send** [sɛnd] (pt, pp sent) vt schicken; (transmit) senden; **to ~ sth by post** or (US) **mail** etw mit der Post schicken; **to ~ sb for sth** (for check-up etc) jdn zu etw schicken; **to ~ word that ...** Nachricht geben, daß ...; **she ~s (you) her love** sie läßt dich grüßen; **to ~ sb to Coventry** (BRIT) jdn schneiden (inf); **to ~ sb to sleep** jdn ein einschläfern; **to ~ sth flying** etw umwerfen.

▶**send away** vt wegschicken.

▶**send away for** vt fus (per Post) anfordern.

▶**send back** vt zurückschicken.

▶**send for** vt fus (per Post) anfordern; (doctor, police) rufen.

▶**send in** vt einsenden, einschicken.

▶**send off** vt abschicken; (BRIT: player) vom Platz weisen.

▶**send on** vt (BRIT: letter) nachsenden; (luggage etc) vorausschicken.

▶**send out** vt verschicken; (light, heat) abgeben; (signal) aussenden.

▶**send round** vt schicken; (circulate) zirkulieren lassen.

▶**send up** vt (astronaut) hochschießen; (price, blood pressure) hochtreiben; (BRIT: parody) verulken (inf).

**sender** ['sɛndə*] n Absender(in) m(f).

**sending-off** ['sɛndɪŋɔf] n (SPORT) Platzverweis m.

**send-off** ['sɛndɔf] n: **a good ~** eine große Verabschiedung.

**send-up** ['sɛndʌp] n Verulkung f (inf).

**Senegal** [sɛnɪ'gɔːl] n Senegal nt.

**Senegalese** [sɛnɪgə'liːz] adj senegalesisch ♦ n inv Senegalese m, Senegalesin f.

**senile** ['siːnaɪl] adj senil.

**senility** [sɪ'nɪlɪtɪ] n Senilität f.

**senior** ['siːnɪə*] adj (staff, manager) leitend; (officer) höher; (post, position) leitend ♦ n (SCOL): **the ~s** die Oberstufenschüler pl; **to be ~ to sb** jdm übergeordnet sein; **she is 15 years his ~** sie ist 15 Jahre älter als er; **P. Jones ~** P. Jones senior.

**senior citizen** n Senior(in) m(f).

**senior high school** (US) n Oberstufe f.

**seniority** [siːnɪ'ɔrɪtɪ] n (in service) (längere) Betriebszugehörigkeit f; (in rank) (höhere) Position f.

**sensation** [sɛn'seɪʃən] n (feeling) Gefühl nt; (great success) Sensation f; **to cause a ~** großes Aufsehen erregen.

**sensational** [sɛn'seɪʃənl] adj (wonderful) wunderbar; (result) sensationell; (headlines etc) reißerisch.

**sense** [sɛns] n Sinn m; (feeling) Gefühl nt; (good sense) Verstand m, gesunder Menschenverstand m; (meaning) Bedeutung f, Sinn m ♦ vt spüren; **~ of smell** Geruchssinn m; **it makes ~** (can be understood) es ergibt einen Sinn; (is sensible) es ist vernünftig or sinnvoll; **there's no ~ in that** das hat keinen Sinn; **there is no ~ in doing that** es hat keinen Sinn, das zu tun; **to come to one's ~s** Vernunft annehmen; **to take leave of one's ~s** den Verstand verlieren.

**senseless** ['sɛnslɪs] adj (pointless) sinnlos; (unconscious) besinnungslos, bewußtlos.

**sense of humour** n Sinn m für Humor.

**sensibility** [sɛnsɪ'bɪlɪtɪ] n Empfindsamkeit f; (sensitivity) Empfindlichkeit f; **to offend sb's sensibilities** jds Zartgefühl verletzen.

**sensible** ['sɛnsɪbl] adj vernünftig; (shoes, clothes) praktisch.

**sensitive** ['sɛnsɪtɪv] adj empfindlich; (understanding) einfühlsam; (touchy: person) sensibel; (: issue) heikel; **to be ~ to sth** in bezug auf etw acc empfindlich sein; **he is very ~ about it/to criticism** er reagiert sehr empfindlich darauf/auf Kritik.

**sensitivity** [sɛnsɪ'tɪvɪtɪ] n Empfindlichkeit f; (understanding) Einfühlungsvermögen nt; (of issue etc) heikle Natur f; **an issue of great ~** ein sehr heikles Thema.

**sensual** ['sɛnsjuəl] adj sinnlich; (person, life) sinnenfroh.

**sensuous** ['sɛnsjuəs] adj sinnlich.

**sent** [sɛnt] *pt, pp of* **send**.

**sentence** ['sɛntns] *n* (*LING*) Satz *m*; (*LAW: judgement*) Urteil *nt*; (: *punishment*) Strafe *f* ♦ *vt*: **to ~ sb to death/to 5 years in prison** jdn zum Tode/zu 5 Jahren Haft verurteilen; **to pass ~ on sb** das Urteil über jdn verkünden; (*fig*) jdn verurteilen; **to serve a life ~** eine lebenslängliche Freiheitsstrafe verbüßen.

**sentiment** ['sɛntɪmənt] *n* Sentimentalität *f*; (*also pl: opinion*) Ansicht *f*.

**sentimental** [sɛntɪ'mɛntl] *adj* sentimental.

**sentimentality** [sɛntɪmɛn'tælɪtɪ] *n* Sentimentalität *f*.

**sentry** ['sɛntrɪ] *n* Wachtposten *m*.

**sentry duty** *n*: **to be on ~** auf Wache sein.

**Seoul** [səul] *n* Seoul *nt*.

**separable** ['sɛprəbl] *adj*: **to be ~ from** trennbar sein von.

**separate** ['sɛprɪt] *adj* getrennt; (*occasions*) verschieden; (*rooms*) separat ♦ *vt* trennen ♦ *vi* sich trennen; **~ from** getrennt von; **to go ~ ways** getrennte Wege gehen; **under ~ cover** (*COMM*) mit getrennter Post; **~ into** aufteilen in +*acc*; *see also* **separates**.

**separately** ['sɛprɪtlɪ] *adv* getrennt.

**separates** ['sɛprɪts] *npl* (*clothes*) kombinierbare Einzelteile *pl*.

**separation** [sɛpə'reɪʃən] *n* Trennung *f*.

**sepia** ['si:pjə] *adj* sepiafarben.

**Sept.** *abbr* (= *September*) Sept.

**September** [sɛp'tɛmbə*] *n* September *m*; *see also* **July**.

**septic** ['sɛptɪk] *adj* vereitert, septisch; **to go ~** eitern.

**septicaemia,** (*US*) **septicemia** [sɛptɪ'si:mɪə] *n* Blutvergiftung *f*.

**septic tank** *n* Faulbehälter *m*.

**sequel** ['si:kwl] *n* (*follow-up*) Nachspiel *nt*; (*of film, story*) Fortsetzung *f*.

**sequence** ['si:kwəns] *n* Folge *f*; (*dance/film sequence*) Sequenz *f*; **in ~** der Reihe nach.

**sequential** [sɪ'kwɛnʃəl] *adj* aufeinander-folgend; **~ access** (*COMPUT*) sequentieller Zugriff *m*.

**sequestrate** [sɪ'kwɛstreɪt] *vt* (*LAW, COMM*) sequestrieren, beschlagnahmen.

**sequin** ['si:kwɪn] *n* Paillette *f*.

**Serbia** ['sə:bɪə] *n* Serbien *nt*.

**Serbian** ['sə:bɪən] *adj* serbisch ♦ *n* Serbier(in) *m(f)*; (*LING*) Serbisch *nt*.

**Serbo-Croat** ['sə:bəu'krəuæt] *n* (*LING*) Serbokroatisch *nt*.

**serenade** [sɛrə'neɪd] *n* Serenade *f* ♦ *vt* ein Ständchen *nt* bringen +*dat*.

**serene** [sɪ'ri:n] *adj* (*landscape etc*) friedlich; (*expression*) heiter; (*person*) gelassen.

**serenity** [sə'rɛnɪtɪ] *n* (*of landscape*) Friedlichkeit *f*; (*of expression*) Gelassenheit *f*.

**sergeant** ['sɑ:dʒənt] *n* (*MIL etc*) Feldwebel *m*; (*POLICE*) Polizeimeister *m*.

**sergeant-major** ['sɑ:dʒənt'meɪdʒə*] *n* Oberfeldwebel *m*.

**serial** ['sɪərɪəl] *n* (*TV*) Serie *f*; (*RADIO*) Sendereihe *f*; (*in magazine*) Fortsetzungs-roman *m* ♦ *adj* (*COMPUT*) seriell.

**serialize** ['sɪərɪəlaɪz] *vt* in Fortsetzungen veröffentlichen; (*TV, RADIO*) in Fortsetzungen senden.

**serial killer** *n* Serienmörder(in) *m(f)*.

**serial number** *n* Seriennummer *f*.

**series** ['sɪərɪz] *n inv* (*group*) Serie *f*, Reihe *f*; (*of books*) Reihe *f*; (*TV*) Serie *f*.

**serious** ['sɪərɪəs] *adj* ernst; (*important*) wichtig; (: *illness*) schwer; (: *condition*) bedenklich; **are you ~ (about it)?** meinst du das ernst?

**seriously** ['sɪərɪəslɪ] *adv* ernst; (*talk, interested*) ernsthaft; (*ill, hurt, damaged*) schwer; (*not jokingly*) im Ernst; **to take sb/sth ~** jdn/etw ernst nehmen; **do you ~ believe that ...** glauben Sie ernsthaft *or* im Ernst, daß ...

**seriousness** ['sɪərɪəsnɪs] *n* Ernst *m*, Ernsthaftigkeit *f*; (*of problem*) Bedenklichkeit *f*.

**sermon** ['sə:mən] *n* Predigt *f*; (*fig*) Moralpredigt *f*.

**serrated** [sɪ'reɪtɪd] *adj* gezackt; **~ knife** Sägemesser *nt*.

**serum** ['sɪərəm] *n* Serum *nt*.

**servant** ['sə:vənt] *n* (*lit, fig*) Diener(in) *m(f)*; (*domestic*) Hausangestellte(r) *f(m)*.

**serve** [sə:v] *vt* dienen +*dat*; (*in shop, with food/drink*) bedienen; (*food, meal*) servieren; (*purpose*) haben; (*apprenticeship*) durchmachen; (*prison term*) verbüßen ♦ *vi* (*at table*) auftragen, servieren; (*TENNIS*) aufschlagen; (*soldier*) dienen; (*be useful*): **to ~ as/for** dienen als ♦ *n* (*TENNIS*) Aufschlag *m*; **are you being ~d?** werden Sie schon bedient?; **to ~ its purpose** seinen Zweck erfüllen; **to ~ sb's purpose** jds Zwecken dienen; **it ~s him right** das geschieht ihm recht; **to ~ on a committee** einem Ausschuß angehören; **to ~ on a jury** Geschworene(r) *f(m)* sein; **it's my turn to ~** (*TENNIS*) ich habe Aufschlag; **it ~s to show/explain ...** das zeigt/erklärt ...

►**serve out** *vt* (*food*) auftragen, servieren.

►**serve up** *vt* = **serve out**.

**service** ['sə:vɪs] *n* Dienst *m*; (*commercial*) Dienstleistung *f*; (*in hotel, restaurant*) Bedienung *f*, Service *m*; (*also:* **train ~**) Bahnverbindung *f*; (: *generally*) Zugverkehr *m*; (*REL*) Gottesdienst *m*; (*AUT*) Inspektion *f*; (*TENNIS*) Aufschlag *m*; (*plates etc*) Service *nt* ♦ *vt* (*car, machine*) warten; **the Services** *npl* (*army, navy etc*) die Streitkräfte *pl*; **military/national ~** Militärdienst *m*; **to be of ~ to sb** jdm nützen; **to do sb a ~** jdm einen Dienst erweisen; **to put one's car in for a ~** sein Auto zur Inspektion geben; **dinner ~** Eßservice *nt*.

**serviceable** ['sə:vɪsəbl] *adj* zweckmäßig.
**service area** *n* (*on motorway*) Raststätte *f*.
**service charge** (*BRIT*) *n* Bedienungsgeld *nt*.
**service industry** *n* Dienstleistungsbranche *f*.
**serviceman** ['sə:vɪsmən] (*irreg: like* **man**) *n*
  Militärangehörige(r) *m*.
**service station** *n* Tankstelle *f*.
**serviette** [sə:vɪ'et] (*BRIT*) *n* Serviette *f*.
**servile** ['sə:vaɪl] *adj* unterwürfig.
**session** ['seʃən] *n* Sitzung *f*; (*US, SCOT: SCOL*)
  Studienjahr *nt*; (: : *term*) Semester *nt*;
  **recording** ~ Aufnahme *f*; **to be in** ~ tagen.
**session musician** *n* Session-Musiker(in) *m(f)*.
**set** [set] (*pt, pp* **set**) *n* (*of saucepans, books, keys
  etc*) Satz *m*; (*group*) Reihe *f*; (*of cutlery*)
  Garnitur *f*; (*also:* **radio** ~) Radio(gerät) *nt*;
  (*also:* **TV** ~) Fernsehgerät *nt*; (*TENNIS*) Satz
  *m*; (*group of people*) Kreis *m*; (*MATH*) Menge
  *f*; (*THEAT: stage*) Bühne *f*; (: *scenery*)
  Bühnenbild *nt*; (*CINE*) Drehort *m*;
  (*HAIRDRESSING*) (Ein)legen *nt* ♦ *adj* (*fixed*)
  fest; (*ready*) fertig, bereit ♦ *vt* (*table*)
  decken; (*place*) auflegen; (*time, price, rules
  etc*) festsetzen; (*record*) aufstellen; (*alarm,
  watch, task*) stellen; (*exam*)
  zusammenstellen; (*TYP*) setzen ♦ *vi* (*sun*)
  untergehen; (*jam, jelly, concrete*) fest
  werden; (*bone*) zusammenwachsen; **a** ~ **of
  false teeth** ein Gebiß; **a** ~ **of dining-room
  furniture** eine Eßzimmergarnitur; **a chess** ~
  ein Schachspiel; **to be** ~ **on doing sth** etw
  unbedingt tun wollen; **to be all** ~ **to do sth**
  bereit sein, etw zu tun; **he's** ~ **in his ways** er
  ist in seinen Gewohnheiten festgefahren; **a**
  ~ **phrase** eine feste Redewendung; **a novel**
  ~ **in Rome** ein Roman, der in Rom spielt; **to**
  ~ **to music** vertonen; **to** ~ **on fire**
  anstecken; **to** ~ **free** freilassen; **to** ~ **sail**
  losfahren.
▶**set about** *vt fus* (*task*) anpacken; **to** ~ **about**
  **doing sth** sich daranmachen, etw zu tun.
▶**set aside** *vt* (*money etc*) beiseite legen;
  (*time*) einplanen.
▶**set back** *vt:* **to** ~ **sb back 5 pounds** jdn 5
  Pfund kosten; **to** ~ **sb back (by)** (*in time*) jdn
  zurückwerfen (um); **a house** ~ **back from**
  **the road** ein Haus, das etwas von der
  Straße abliegt.
▶**set in** *vi* (*bad weather*) einsetzen; (*infection*)
  sich einstellen; **the rain has** ~ **in for the day**
  es hat sich für heute eingeregnet.
▶**set off** *vi* (*depart*) aufbrechen ♦ *vt* (*bomb*)
  losgehen lassen; (*alarm, chain of events*)
  auslösen; (*show up well*) hervorheben.
▶**set out** *vi* (*depart*) aufbrechen ♦ *vt* (*goods
  etc*) ausbreiten; (*chairs etc*) aufstellen;
  (*arguments*) darlegen; **to** ~ **out to do sth**
  sich *dat* vornehmen, etw zu tun; **to** ~ **out**
  **from home** zu Hause aufbrechen.
▶**set up** *vt* (*organization*) gründen;
  (*monument*) errichten; **to** ~ **up shop** ein
  Geschäft eröffnen; (*fig*) sich selbständig

machen.
**setback** ['setbæk] *n* Rückschlag *m*.
**set menu** *n* Menü *nt*.
**set square** *n* Zeichendreieck *nt*.
**settee** [se'ti:] *n* Sofa *nt*.
**setting** ['setɪŋ] *n* (*background*) Rahmen *m*;
  (*position*) Einstellung *f*; (*of jewel*) Fassung *f*.
**setting lotion** *n* (Haar)festiger *m*.
**settle** ['setl] *vt* (*matter*) regeln; (*argument*)
  beilegen; (*accounts*) begleichen; (*affairs,
  business*) in Ordnung bringen; (*colonize:
  land*) besiedeln ♦ *vi* (*also:* ~ **down**) sich
  niederlassen; (*sand, dust etc*) sich legen;
  (*sediment*) sich setzen; (*calm down*) sich
  beruhigen; **to** ~ **one's stomach** den Magen
  beruhigen; **that's** ~**d then!** das ist also
  abgemacht!; **to** ~ **down to work** sich an die
  Arbeit setzen; **to** ~ **down to watch TV** es
  sich *dat* vor dem Fernseher gemütlich
  machen.
▶**settle for** *vt fus* sich zufriedengeben mit.
▶**settle in** *vi* sich einleben; (*in job etc*) sich
  eingewöhnen.
▶**settle on** *vt fus* sich entscheiden für.
▶**settle up** *vi:* **to** ~ **up with sb** mit jdm
  abrechnen.
**settlement** ['setlmənt] *n* (*payment*)
  Begleichung *f*; (*LAW*) Vergleich *m*;
  (*agreement*) Übereinkunft *f*; (*of conflict*)
  Beilegung *f*; (*village etc*) Siedlung *f*,
  Niederlassung *f*; (*colonization*) Besiedelung
  *f*; **in** ~ **of our account** (*COMM*) zum
  Ausgleich unseres Kontos.
**settler** ['setlə*] *n* Siedler(in) *m(f)*.
**setup, set-up** ['setʌp] *n* (*organization*)
  Organisation *f*; (*system*) System *nt*.
**seven** ['sevn] *num* sieben.
**seventeen** [sevn'ti:n] *num* siebzehn.
**seventh** ['sevnθ] *num* siebte(r, s).
**seventy** ['sevntɪ] *num* siebzig.
**sever** ['sevə*] *vt* durchtrennen; (*fig: relations*)
  abbrechen; (: *ties*) lösen.
**several** ['sevərl] *adj* einige, mehrere ♦ *pron*
  einige; ~ **of us** einige von uns; ~ **times**
  einige Male, mehrmals.
**severance** ['sevərəns] *n* (*of relations*) Abbruch
  *m*.
**severance pay** *n* Abfindung *f*.
**severe** [sɪ'vɪə*] *adj* (*damage, shortage*) schwer;
  (*pain*) stark; (*person, expression, dress, winter*)
  streng; (*punishment*) hart; (*climate*) rauh.
**severely** [sɪ'vɪəlɪ] *adv* (*damage*) stark; (*punish*)
  hart; (*wounded, ill*) schwer.
**severity** [sɪ'verɪtɪ] *n* (*gravity: of punishment*)
  Härte *f*; (: *of manner, voice, winter*) Strenge *f*;
  (: *of weather*) Rauheit *f*; (*austerity*) Strenge *f*.
**sew** [səu] (*pt* **sewed**, *pp* **sewn**) *vt, vi* nähen.
▶**sew up** *vt* (zusammen)nähen; **it is all** ~**n up**
  (*fig*) es ist unter Dach und Fach.
**sewage** ['su:ɪdʒ] *n* Abwasser *nt*.
**sewage works** *n* Kläranlage *f*.
**sewer** ['su:ə*] *n* Abwasserkanal *m*.

**sewing** ['səʊɪŋ] n Nähen nt; (items) Näharbeit f.

**sewing machine** n Nähmaschine f.

**sewn** [səʊn] pp of **sew**.

**sex** [sɛks] n (gender) Geschlecht nt; (lovemaking) Sex m; **to have ~ with sb** (Geschlechts)verkehr mit jdm haben.

**sex act** n Geschlechtsakt m.

**sex appeal** n Sex-Appeal m.

**sex education** n Sexualerziehung f.

**sexism** ['sɛksɪzəm] n Sexismus m.

**sexist** ['sɛksɪst] adj sexistisch.

**sex life** n Sexualleben nt.

**sex object** n Sexualobjekt nt.

**sextet** [sɛks'tɛt] n Sextett nt.

**sexual** ['sɛksjʊəl] adj sexuell; (reproduction) geschlechtlich; (equality) der Geschlechter.

**sexual assault** n Vergewaltigung f.

**sexual harassment** n sexuelle Belästigung f.

**sexual intercourse** n Geschlechtsverkehr m.

**sexually** ['sɛksjʊəlɪ] adv sexuell; (segregate) nach Geschlechtern; (discriminate) auf Grund des Geschlechts; (reproduce) geschlechtlich.

**sexual orientation** n sexuelle Orientierung f.

**sexy** ['sɛksɪ] adj sexy; (pictures, underwear) sexy, aufreizend.

**Seychelles** [seɪ'ʃɛl(z)] npl: **the ~** die Seychellen pl.

**SF** n abbr (= science fiction) SF.

**SG** (US) n abbr (MIL, MED) = **Surgeon General**.

**Sgt** abbr (POLICE, MIL) = **sergeant**.

**shabbiness** ['ʃæbɪnɪs] n Schäbigkeit f.

**shabby** ['ʃæbɪ] adj schäbig.

**shack** [ʃæk] n Hütte f.

▸**shack up** (inf) vi: **to ~ up (with sb)** (mit jdm) zusammenziehen.

**shackles** ['ʃæklz] npl Ketten pl; (fig) Fesseln pl.

**shade** [ʃeɪd] n Schatten m; (for lamp) (Lampen)schirm m; (of colour) (Farb)ton m; (US: also: **window ~**) Jalousie f, Rollo nt ♦ vt beschatten; (eyes) abschirmen; **shades** npl (inf: sunglasses) Sonnenbrille f; **in the ~** im Schatten; **a ~ of blue** ein Blauton; **a ~ (more/too large)** (small quantity) etwas or eine Spur (mehr/zu groß).

**shadow** ['ʃædəʊ] n Schatten m ♦ vt (follow) beschatten; **without** or **beyond a ~ of a doubt** ohne den geringsten Zweifel.

**shadow cabinet** (BRIT) n Schattenkabinett nt.

**shadowy** ['ʃædəʊɪ] adj schattig; (figure, shape) schattenhaft.

**shady** ['ʃeɪdɪ] adj schattig; (fig: dishonest) zwielichtig; **~ deals** dunkle Geschäfte.

**shaft** [ʃɑːft] n (of arrow, spear) Schaft m; (AUT, TECH) Welle f; (of mine, lift) Schacht m; (of light) Strahl m; **ventilation ~** Luftschacht m.

**shaggy** ['ʃægɪ] adj zottelig; (dog, sheep) struppig.

**shake** [ʃeɪk] (pt **shook**, pp **shaken**) vt schütteln; (weaken, upset, surprise) erschüttern; (weaken: resolve) ins Wanken bringen ♦ vi zittern, beben; (building, table) wackeln; (earth) beben ♦ n Schütteln nt; **to ~ one's head** den Kopf schütteln; **to ~ hands with sb** jdm die Hand schütteln; **to ~ one's fist (at sb)** (jdm) mit der Faust drohen; **give it a good ~** schütteln Sie es gut durch; **a ~ of the head** ein Kopfschütteln.

▸**shake off** vt (lit, fig) abschütteln.

▸**shake up** vt schütteln; (fig: upset) erschüttern.

**shake-out** ['ʃeɪkaʊt] n Freisetzung f von Arbeitskräften.

**shake-up** ['ʃeɪkʌp] n (radikale) Veränderung f.

**shakily** ['ʃeɪkɪlɪ] adv (reply) mit zittriger Stimme; (walk, stand) unsicher, wackelig.

**shaky** ['ʃeɪkɪ] adj (hand, voice) zittrig; (memory) schwach; (knowledge, prospects, future, start) unsicher.

**shale** [ʃeɪl] n Schiefer m.

**shall** [ʃæl] aux vb: **I ~ go** ich werde gehen; **~ I open the door?** soll ich die Tür öffnen?; **I'll go, ~ I?** soll ich gehen?

**shallot** [ʃə'lɒt] (BRIT) n Schalotte f.

**shallow** ['ʃæləʊ] adj flach; (fig) oberflächlich; **the shallows** npl die Untiefen pl.

**sham** [ʃæm] n Heuchelei f; (person) Heuchler(in) m(f); (object) Attrappe f ♦ adj unecht; (fight) Schein- ♦ vt vortäuschen.

**shambles** ['ʃæmblz] n heilloses Durcheinander nt; **the economy is (in) a complete ~** die Wirtschaft befindet sich in einem totalen Chaos.

**shambolic** [ʃæm'bɒlɪk] (inf) adj chaotisch.

**shame** [ʃeɪm] n Scham f; (disgrace) Schande f ♦ vt beschämen; **it is a ~ that ...** es ist eine Schande, daß ...; **what a ~!** wie schade!; **to bring ~ on** Schande bringen über +acc; **to put sb/sth to ~** jdn/etw in den Schatten stellen.

**shamefaced** ['ʃeɪmfeɪst] adj betreten.

**shameful** ['ʃeɪmful] adj schändlich.

**shameless** ['ʃeɪmlɪs] adj schamlos.

**shampoo** [ʃæm'puː] n Shampoo(n) nt ♦ vt waschen.

**shampoo and set** n Waschen und Legen nt.

**shamrock** ['ʃæmrɒk] n (plant) Klee m; (leaf) Kleeblatt nt.

**shandy** ['ʃændɪ] n Bier nt mit Limonade, Radler m.

**shan't** [ʃɑːnt] = **shall not**.

**shantytown** ['ʃæntɪtaʊn] n Elendsviertel nt.

**SHAPE** [ʃeɪp] n abbr (MIL: = Supreme Headquarters Allied Powers, Europe) Hauptquartier der alliierten Streitkräfte in Europa während des 2. Weltkriegs.

**shape** [ʃeɪp] n Form f ♦ vt gestalten; (form) formen; (sb's ideas) prägen; (sb's life) bestimmen; **to take ~** Gestalt annehmen; **in the ~ of a heart** in Herzform; **I can't bear**

**gardening in any ~ or form** ich kann Gartenarbeit absolut nicht ausstehen; **to get (o.s.) into ~** in Form kommen.

►**shape up** vi sich entwickeln.

**-shaped** [ʃeɪpt] suff: **heart-~** herzförmig.

**shapeless** ['ʃeɪplɪs] adj formlos.

**shapely** ['ʃeɪplɪ] adj (woman) wohlproportioniert; (legs) wohlgeformt.

**share** [ʃɛə*] n (part) Anteil m; (contribution) Teil m; (COMM) Aktie f ♦ vt teilen; (room, bed, taxi) sich dat teilen; (have in common) gemeinsam haben; **to ~ in** (joy, sorrow) teilen; (profits) beteiligt sein an +dat; (work) sich beteiligen an +dat.

►**share out** vt aufteilen.

**share capital** n Aktienkapital nt.

**share certificate** n Aktienurkunde f.

**shareholder** ['ʃɛəhəʊldə*] n Aktionär(in) m(f).

**share index** n Aktienindex m; **the 100 Share Index** Aktienindex der Financial Times.

**share issue** n Aktienemission f.

**shark** [ʃɑːk] n Hai(fisch) m.

**sharp** [ʃɑːp] adj scharf; (point, nose, chin) spitz; (pain) heftig; (cold) schneidend; (MUS) zu hoch; (increase) stark; (person: quickwitted) clever; (: dishonest) gerissen ♦ n (MUS) Kreuz nt ♦ adv: **at 2 o'clock ~** um Punkt 2 Uhr; **turn ~ left** biegen Sie scharf nach links ab; **to be ~ with sb** schroff mit jdm sein; **~ practices** (COMM) unsaubere Geschäfte pl; **C ~** (MUS) Cis nt; **look ~!** (ein bißchen) dalli! (inf).

**sharpen** ['ʃɑːpn] vt schleifen, schärfen; (pencil, stick etc) (an)spitzen; (fig: appetite) anregen.

**sharpener** ['ʃɑːpnə*] n (also: **pencil ~**) (Bleistift)spitzer m; (also: **knife ~**) Schleifgerät nt.

**sharp-eyed** [ʃɑːp'aɪd] adj scharfsichtig.

**sharpish** ['ʃɑːpɪʃ] (inf) adj (instantly) auf der Stelle.

**sharply** ['ʃɑːplɪ] adv scharf; (stop) plötzlich; (retort) schroff.

**sharp-tempered** [ʃɑːp'tɛmpəd] adj jähzornig.

**sharp-witted** [ʃɑːp'wɪtɪd] adj scharfsinnig.

**shatter** ['ʃætə*] vt zertrümmern; (fig: hopes, dreams) zunichte machen; (: confidence) zerstören ♦ vi zerbrechen, zerspringen.

**shattered** ['ʃætəd] adj erschüttert; (inf: exhausted) fertig, kaputt.

**shattering** ['ʃætərɪŋ] adj erschütternd, niederschmetternd; (exhausting) äußerst anstrengend.

**shatterproof** ['ʃætəpruːf] adj splitterfest, splitterfrei.

**shave** [ʃeɪv] vt rasieren ♦ vi sich rasieren ♦ n: **to have a ~** sich rasieren.

**shaven** ['ʃeɪvn] adj (head) kahlgeschoren.

**shaver** ['ʃeɪvə*] n (also: **electric ~**) Rasierapparat m.

**shaving** ['ʃeɪvɪŋ] n Rasieren nt; **shavings** npl (of wood etc) Späne pl.

**shaving brush** n Rasierpinsel m.

**shaving cream** n Rasiercreme f.

**shaving foam** n Rasierschaum m.

**shaving point** n Steckdose f für Rasierapparate.

**shaving soap** n Rasierseife f.

**shawl** [ʃɔːl] n (Woll)tuch nt.

**she** [ʃiː] pron sie ♦ pref weiblich; **~-bear** Bärin f; **there ~ is** da ist sie.

**sheaf** [ʃiːf] (pl **sheaves**) n (of corn) Garbe f; (of papers) Bündel nt.

**shear** [ʃɪə*] (pt **sheared**, pp **shorn**) vt scheren.

►**shear off** vi abbrechen.

**shears** ['ʃɪəz] npl (for hedge) Heckenschere f.

**sheath** [ʃiːθ] n (of knife) Scheide f; (contraceptive) Kondom nt.

**sheathe** [ʃiːð] vt ummanteln; (sword) in die Scheide stecken.

**sheath knife** n Fahrtenmesser nt.

**sheaves** [ʃiːvz] npl of **sheaf**.

**shed** [ʃɛd] (pt, pp **shed**) n Schuppen m; (INDUSTRY, RAIL) Halle f ♦ vt (tears, blood) vergießen; (load) verlieren; (workers) entlassen; **to ~ its skin** sich häuten; **to ~ light on** (problem) erhellen.

**she'd** [ʃiːd] = **she had; she would**.

**sheen** [ʃiːn] n Glanz m.

**sheep** [ʃiːp] n inv Schaf nt.

**sheepdog** ['ʃiːpdɔg] n Hütehund m.

**sheep farmer** n Schaffarmer m.

**sheepish** ['ʃiːpɪʃ] adj verlegen.

**sheepskin** ['ʃiːpskɪn] n Schaffell nt ♦ cpd Schaffell-.

**sheer** [ʃɪə*] adj (utter) rein; (steep) steil; (almost transparent) (hauch)dünn ♦ adv (straight up) senkrecht; **by ~ chance** rein zufällig.

**sheet** [ʃiːt] n (on bed) (Bett)laken nt; (of paper) Blatt nt; (of glass, metal) Platte f; (of ice) Fläche f.

**sheet feed** n (on printer) Papiereinzug m.

**sheet lightning** n Wetterleuchten nt.

**sheet metal** n Walzblech nt.

**sheet music** n Notenblätter pl.

**sheik(h)** [ʃeɪk] n Scheich m.

**shelf** [ʃɛlf] (pl **shelves**) n Brett nt, Bord nt; **set of shelves** Regal nt.

**shelf life** n Lagerfähigkeit f.

**shell** [ʃɛl] n (on beach) Muschel f; (of egg, nut etc) Schale f; (explosive) Granate f; (of building) Mauern pl ♦ vt (peas) enthülsen; (MIL: fire on) (mit Granaten) beschießen.

►**shell out** (inf) vt: **to ~ out (for)** blechen (für).

**she'll** [ʃiːl] = **she will; she shall**.

**shellfish** ['ʃɛlfɪʃ] n inv Schalentier nt; (scallop etc) Muschel f; (as food) Meeresfrüchte pl.

**shelter** ['ʃɛltə*] n (building) Unterstand m; (refuge) Schutz m; (also: **bus ~**) Wartehäuschen nt; (also: **night ~**) Obdachlosenasyl nt ♦ vt (protect) schützen; (homeless, refugees) aufnehmen; (wanted

*man*) Unterschlupf gewähren +*dat* ♦ *vi* sich
unterstellen; (*from storm*) Schutz suchen; **to
take ~ (from)** (*from danger*) sich in
Sicherheit bringen (vor +*dat*); (*from storm
etc*) Schutz suchen (vor +*dat*).

**sheltered** ['ʃɛltəd] *adj* (*life*) behütet; (*spot*)
geschützt; **~ housing** (*for old people*)
Altenwohnungen *pl*; (*for handicapped people*)
Behindertenwohnungen *pl*.

**shelve** [ʃɛlv] *vt* (*fig: plan*) ad acta legen.

**shelves** [ʃɛlvz] *npl of* **shelf**.

**shelving** ['ʃɛlvɪŋ] *n* Regale *pl*.

**shepherd** ['ʃɛpəd] *n* Schäfer *m* ♦ *vt* (*guide*)
führen.

**shepherdess** ['ʃɛpədɪs] *n* Schäferin *f*.

**shepherd's pie** (*BRIT*) *n* *Auflauf aus
Hackfleisch und Kartoffelbrei.*

**sherbet** ['ʃɑːbət] *n* (*BRIT: powder*) Brausepulver *nt*; (*US: water ice*) Fruchteis *nt*.

**sheriff** ['ʃɛrɪf] (*US*) *n* Sheriff *m*.

**sherry** ['ʃɛrɪ] *n* Sherry *m*.

**she's** [ʃiːz] = **she is; she has.**

**Shetland** ['ʃɛtlənd] *n* (*also:* **the ~ Islands**) die
Shetlandinseln *pl*.

**Shetland pony** *n* Shetlandpony *nt*.

**shield** [ʃiːld] *n* (*MIL*) Schild *m*; (*trophy*)
Trophäe *f*; (*fig: protection*) Schutz *m* ♦ *vt*: **to
~ (from)** schützen (vor +*dat*).

**shift** [ʃɪft] *n* (*change*) Änderung *f*; (*work-period,
workers*) Schicht *f* ♦ *vt* (*move*) bewegen;
(*furniture*) (ver)rücken; (*stain*)
herausbekommen ♦ *vi* (*move*) sich bewegen;
(*wind*) drehen; **a ~ in demand** (*COMM*) eine
Nachfrageverschiebung.

**shift key** *n* Umschalttaste *f*.

**shiftless** ['ʃɪftlɪs] *adj* träge.

**shift work** *n* Schichtarbeit *f*; **to do ~** Schicht
arbeiten.

**shifty** ['ʃɪftɪ] *adj* verschlagen.

**Shiite** ['ʃiːaɪt] *adj* schiitisch ♦ *n* Schiit(in) *m(f)*.

**shilling** ['ʃɪlɪŋ] (*BRIT: old*) *n* Shilling *m*.

**shilly-shally** ['ʃɪlɪʃælɪ] *vi* unschlüssig sein.

**shimmer** ['ʃɪmə*] *vi* schimmern.

**shimmering** ['ʃɪmərɪŋ] *adj* schimmernd.

**shin** [ʃɪn] *n* Schienbein *nt* ♦ *vi*: **to ~ up a tree**
einen Baum hinaufklettern.

**shindig** ['ʃɪndɪg] (*inf*) *n* Remmidemmi *nt*.

**shine** [ʃaɪn] (*pt, pp* **shone**) *vi* Glanz *m* ♦ *vi* (*sun,
light*) scheinen; (*eyes*) leuchten; (*hair, fig:
person*) glänzen ♦ *vt* (*polish: pt, pp* **shined**)
polieren; **to ~ a torch on sth** etw mit einer
Taschenlampe anleuchten.

**shingle** ['ʃɪŋgl] *n* (*on beach*) Kiesel(steine) *pl*;
(*on roof*) Schindel *f*.

**shingles** ['ʃɪŋglz] *npl* (*MED*) Gürtelrose *f*.

**shining** ['ʃaɪnɪŋ] *adj* glänzend; (*example*)
leuchtend.

**shiny** ['ʃaɪnɪ] *adj* glänzend.

**ship** [ʃɪp] *n* Schiff *nt* ♦ *vt* verschiffen; (*send*)
versenden; (*water*) übernehmen; **on board ~**
an Bord.

**shipbuilder** ['ʃɪpbɪldə*] *n* Schiffbauer *m*.

**shipbuilding** ['ʃɪpbɪldɪŋ] *n* Schiffbau *m*.

**ship canal** *n* Seekanal *m*.

**ship chandler** [-'tʃɑːndlə*] *n* Schiffsausrüster
*m*.

**shipment** ['ʃɪpmənt] *n* (*of goods*) Versand *m*;
(*amount*) Sendung *f*.

**shipowner** ['ʃɪpəunə*] *n* Schiffseigner *m*; (*of
many ships*) Reeder *m*.

**shipper** ['ʃɪpə*] *n* (*person*) Spediteur *m*;
(*company*) Spedition *f*.

**shipping** ['ʃɪpɪŋ] *n* (*transport*) Versand *m*;
(*ships*) Schiffe *pl*.

**shipping agent** *n* Reeder *m*.

**shipping company** *n* Schiffahrtslinie *f*,
Reederei *f*.

**shipping lane** *n* Schiffahrtsstraße *f*.

**shipping line** *n* = **shipping company.**

**shipshape** ['ʃɪpʃeɪp] *adj* tipptopp (*inf*).

**shipwreck** ['ʃɪprɛk] *n* Schiffbruch *m*; (*ship*)
Wrack *nt* ♦ *vt*: **to be ~ed** schiffbrüchig sein.

**shipyard** ['ʃɪpjɑːd] *n* Werft *f*.

**shire** ['ʃaɪə*] (*BRIT*) *n* Grafschaft *f*.

**shirk** [ʃɑːk] *vt* sich drücken vor +*dat*.

**shirt** [ʃɑːt] *n* (Ober)hemd *nt*; (*woman's*)
(Hemd)bluse *f*; **in (one's) ~ sleeves** in
Hemdsärmeln.

**shirty** ['ʃɑːtɪ] (*BRIT: inf*) *adj* sauer (*inf*).

**shit** [ʃɪt] (*inf!*) *excl* Scheiße! (*!*)

**shiver** ['ʃɪvə*] *n* Schauer *m* ♦ *vi* zittern; **to
~ with cold** vor Kälte zittern.

**shoal** [ʃəul] *n* (*of fish*) Schwarm *m*; (*also:* **~s,**
*fig*) Scharen *pl*.

**shock** [ʃɔk] *n* Schock *m*; (*impact*)
Erschütterung *f*; (*also:* **electric ~**) Schlag *m*
♦ *vt* (*upset*) erschüttern; (*offend*)
schockieren; **to be suffering from ~** (*MED*)
einen Schock haben; **to be in ~** unter
Schock stehen; **it gave us a ~** es hat uns
erschreckt; **it came as a ~ to hear that ...**
wir hörten mit Bestürzung, daß ...

**shock absorber** *n* (*AUT*) Stoßdämpfer *m*.

**shocker** ['ʃɔkə*] (*inf*) *n* (*film etc*) Schocker *m*,
Reißer *m*; **that's a real ~** (*event etc*) das haut
einen echt um.

**shocking** ['ʃɔkɪŋ] *adj* schrecklich,
fürchterlich; (*outrageous*) schockierend.

**shockproof** ['ʃɔkpruːf] *adj* stoßfest.

**shock therapy** *n* Schocktherapie *f*.

**shock treatment** *n* = **shock therapy.**

**shock wave** *n* (*lit*) Druckwelle *f*; (*fig*)
Schockwelle *f*.

**shod** [ʃɔd] *pt, pp of* **shoe.**

**shoddy** ['ʃɔdɪ] *adj* minderwertig.

**shoe** [ʃuː] (*pt, pp* **shod**) *n* Schuh *m*; (*for horse*)
Hufeisen *nt*; (*also:* **brake ~**) Bremsbacke *f*
♦ *vt* (*horse*) beschlagen.

**shoebrush** ['ʃuːbrʌʃ] *n* Schuhbürste *f*.

**shoehorn** ['ʃuːhɔːn] *n* Schuhanzieher *m*.

**shoelace** ['ʃuːleɪs] *n* Schnürsenkel *m*.

**shoemaker** ['ʃuːmeɪkə*] *n* Schuhmacher *m*,
Schuster *m*.

**shoe polish** *n* Schuhcreme *f*.

**shoe shop** n Schuhgeschäft nt.

**shoestring** ['ʃuːstrɪŋ] n (fig): **on a ~** mit ganz wenig Geld.

**shoetree** ['ʃuːtriː] n Schuhspanner m.

**shone** [ʃɒn] pt, pp of **shine**.

**shoo** [ʃuː] excl (to dog etc) pfui ♦ vt (also: **~ away, ~ off,** etc) verscheuchen; (somewhere) scheuchen.

**shook** [ʃʊk] pt of **shake**.

**shoot** [ʃuːt] (pt, pp **shot**) n (on branch) Trieb m; (seedling) Sämling m; (SPORT) Jagd f ♦ vt (gun) abfeuern; (arrow, goal) schießen; (kill, execute) erschießen; (wound) anschießen; (BRIT: game birds) schießen; (film) drehen ♦ vi: **to ~ (at)** schießen (auf +acc); **to ~ past (sb/sth)** (an jdm/etw) vorbeischießen.

▶**shoot down** vt abschießen.

▶**shoot in** vi hereingeschossen kommen.

▶**shoot out (of)** vi herausgeschossen kommen (aus +dat).

▶**shoot up** vi (fig: increase) in die Höhe schnellen.

**shooting** ['ʃuːtɪŋ] n Schießen nt, Schüsse pl; (attack) Schießerei f; (murder) Erschießung f; (CINE) Drehen nt; (HUNTING) Jagen nt.

**shooting range** n Schießplatz m.

**shooting star** n Sternschnuppe f.

**shop** [ʃɒp] n Geschäft nt, Laden m; (workshop) Werkstatt f ♦ vi (also: **go ~ping**) einkaufen (gehen); **repair ~** Reparaturwerkstatt f; **to talk ~** (fig) über die Arbeit reden.

▶**shop around** vi Preise vergleichen; (fig) sich umsehen.

**shopaholic** ['ʃɒpə'hɒlɪk] (inf) n: **to be a ~** einen Einkaufsfimmel haben.

**shop assistant** (BRIT) n Verkäufer(in) m(f).

**shop floor** (BRIT) n (workers) Arbeiter pl; **on the ~** bei or unter den Arbeitern.

**shopkeeper** ['ʃɒpkiːpə'] n Geschäftsinhaber(in) m(f), Ladenbesitzer(in) m(f).

**shoplifter** ['ʃɒplɪftə'] n Ladendieb(in) m(f).

**shoplifting** ['ʃɒplɪftɪŋ] n Ladendiebstahl m.

**shopper** ['ʃɒpə'] n Käufer(in) m(f).

**shopping** ['ʃɒpɪŋ] n (goods) Einkäufe pl.

**shopping bag** n Einkaufstasche f.

**shopping centre,** (US) **shopping center** n Einkaufszentrum nt.

**shopping mall** n Shopping-Center nt.

**shop-soiled** ['ʃɒpsɔɪld] adj angeschmutzt.

**shop steward** (BRIT) n gewerkschaftlicher Vertrauensmann m.

**shop window** n Schaufenster nt.

**shore** [ʃɔː'] n Ufer nt; (beach) Strand m ♦ vt: **to ~ (up)** abstützen; **on ~** an Land.

**shore leave** n (NAUT) Landurlaub m.

**shorn** [ʃɔːn] pp of **shear**; **to be ~ of** (power etc) entkleidet sein +gen.

**short** [ʃɔːt] adj kurz; (person) klein; (curt) schroff, kurz angebunden (inf); (scarce) knapp ♦ n (also: **~ film**) Kurzfilm m; **to be ~ of** ... zuwenig ... haben; **I'm 3 ~** ich habe 3 zu wenig, mir fehlen 3; **in ~** kurz gesagt; **to**

**be in ~ supply** knapp sein; **it is ~ for** ... es ist die Kurzform von ...; **a ~ time ago** vor kurzem; **in the ~ term** auf kurze Sicht; **~ of doing sth** außer etw zu tun; **to cut ~** abbrechen; **everything ~ of** ... alles außer ... +dat; **to fall ~ of sth** etw nicht erreichen; (expectations) etw nicht erfüllen; **to run ~ of** ... nicht mehr viel ... haben; **to stop ~** plötzlich innehalten; **to stop ~ of** haltmachen vor +dat; see also **shorts**.

**shortage** ['ʃɔːtɪdʒ] n: **a ~ of** ein Mangel m an +dat.

**shortbread** ['ʃɔːtbred] n Mürbegebäck nt.

**short-change** [ʃɔːt'tʃeɪndʒ] vt: **to ~ sb** jdm zuwenig Wechselgeld geben.

**short circuit** n Kurzschluß m.

**shortcoming** ['ʃɔːtkʌmɪŋ] n Fehler m, Mangel m.

**shortcrust pastry** (BRIT) n Mürbeteig m.

**short cut** n Abkürzung f; (fig) Schnellverfahren nt.

**shorten** ['ʃɔːtn] vt verkürzen.

**shortening** ['ʃɔːtnɪŋ] n (Back)fett nt.

**shortfall** ['ʃɔːtfɔːl] n Defizit nt.

**shorthand** ['ʃɔːthænd] n Kurzschrift f, Stenographie f; (fig) Kurzform f; **to take sth down in ~** etw stenographieren.

**shorthand notebook** (BRIT) n Stenoblock m.

**shorthand typist** (BRIT) n Stenotypist(in) m(f).

**short list** (BRIT) n Auswahlliste f; **to be on the ~** in der engeren Wahl sein.

**short-list** ['ʃɔːtlɪst] (BRIT) vt in die engere Wahl ziehen; **to be ~ed** in die engere Wahl kommen.

**short-lived** ['ʃɔːt'lɪvd] adj kurzlebig; **to be ~** nicht von Dauer sein.

**shortly** ['ʃɔːtlɪ] adv bald.

**shorts** [ʃɔːts] npl: **(a pair of) ~** Shorts pl.

**short-sighted** [ʃɔːt'saɪtɪd] (BRIT) adj (lit, fig) kurzsichtig.

**short-sightedness** [ʃɔːt'saɪtɪdnɪs] n Kurzsichtigkeit f.

**short-staffed** [ʃɔːt'stɑːft] adj: **to be ~** zuwenig Personal haben.

**short story** n Kurzgeschichte f.

**short-tempered** [ʃɔːt'tempəd] adj gereizt.

**short-term** ['ʃɔːttəːm] adj kurzfristig.

**short time** n: **to work ~, to be on ~** kurzarbeiten, Kurzarbeit haben.

**short-wave** ['ʃɔːtweɪv] (RADIO) adj auf Kurzwelle ♦ n Kurzwelle f.

**shot** [ʃɒt] pt, pp of **shoot** ♦ n Schuß m; (shotgun pellets) Schrot m; (injection) Spritze f; (PHOT) Aufnahme f; **to fire a ~ at sb/sth** einen Schuß auf jdn/etw abgeben; **to have a ~ at (doing) sth** etw mal versuchen; **to get ~ of sb/sth** (inf) jdn/etw loswerden; **a big ~** (inf) ein hohes Tier; **a good/poor ~** (person) ein guter/schlechter Schütze; **like a ~** sofort.

**shotgun** ['ʃɒtɡʌn] n Schrotflinte f.

**should** [ʃʊd] aux vb: **I ~ go now** ich sollte jetzt

gehen; **he ~ be there now** er müßte eigentlich schon da sein; **I ~ go if I were you** an deiner Stelle würde ich gehen; **I ~ like to** ich möchte gerne, ich würde gerne; **~ he phone ...** falls er anruft ...

**shoulder** ['ʃəʊldə*] n Schulter f ♦ vt (fig) auf sich acc nehmen; **to rub ~s with sb** (fig) mit jdm in Berührung kommen; **to give sb the cold ~** (fig) jdm die kalte Schulter zeigen.

**shoulder bag** n Umhängetasche f.

**shoulder blade** n Schulterblatt nt.

**shoulder strap** n (on clothing) Träger m; (on bag) Schulterriemen m.

**shouldn't** ['ʃʊdnt] = should not.

**shout** [ʃaʊt] n Schrei m, Ruf m ♦ vt schreien, rufen ♦ vi (also: ~ out) aufschreien; **to give sb a ~** jdn rufen.

▶**shout down** vt niederbrüllen.

**shouting** ['ʃaʊtɪŋ] n Geschrei nt.

**shouting match** (inf) n: **to have a ~** sich gegenseitig anschreien.

**shove** [ʃʌv] vt schieben; (with one push) stoßen, schubsen (inf) ♦ n: **to give sb a ~** jdn stoßen or schubsen (inf); **to give sth a ~** etw verrücken; (door) gegen etw stoßen; **to ~ sth in sth** (inf: put) etw in etw acc stecken; **he ~d me out of the way** er stieß mich zur Seite.

▶**shove off** (inf) vi abschieben.

**shovel** ['ʃʌvl] n Schaufel f; (mechanical) Bagger m ♦ vt schaufeln.

**show** [ʃəʊ] (pt showed, pp shown) n (exhibition) Ausstellung f, Schau f; (THEAT) Aufführung f; (TV) Show f; (CINE) Vorstellung f ♦ vt zeigen; (exhibit) ausstellen ♦ vi: **it ~s** man sieht es; (is evident) man merkt es; **to ask for a ~ of hands** um Handzeichen bitten; **without any ~ of emotion** ohne jede Gefühlsregung; **it's just for ~** es ist nur zur Schau; **on ~** ausgestellt, zu sehen; **who's running the ~ here?** (inf) wer ist hier verantwortlich?; **to ~ sb to his seat/to the door** jdn an seinen Platz/zur Tür bringen; **to ~ a profit/loss** Gewinn/Verlust aufweisen; **it just goes to ~ that ...** da sieht man's mal wieder, daß ...

▶**show in** vt hereinführen.

▶**show off** (pej) vi angeben ♦ vt vorführen.

▶**show out** vt hinausbegleiten.

▶**show up** vi (stand out) sich abheben; (inf: turn up) auftauchen ♦ vt (uncover) deutlich erkennen lassen; (shame) blamieren.

**show biz** n = show business.

**show business** n Showgeschäft nt.

**showcase** ['ʃəʊkeɪs] n Schaukasten m; (fig) Werbung f.

**showdown** ['ʃəʊdaʊn] n Kraftprobe f.

**shower** ['ʃaʊə*] n (of rain) Schauer m; (of stones etc) Hagel m; (for bathing in) Dusche f; (US: party) Party, bei der jeder ein Geschenk für den Ehrengast mitbringt ♦ vi duschen ♦ vt: **to ~ sb with** (gifts etc) jdn

überschütten mit; (missiles, abuse etc) auf jdn niederhageln lassen; **to have** or **take a ~** duschen; **a ~ of sparks** ein Funkenregen.

**showercap** ['ʃaʊəkæp] n Duschhaube f.

**showerproof** ['ʃaʊəpruːf] adj regenfest.

**showery** ['ʃaʊərɪ] adj regnerisch.

**showground** ['ʃəʊgraʊnd] n Ausstellungsgelände nt.

**showing** ['ʃəʊɪŋ] n (of film) Vorführung f.

**show jumping** n Springreiten nt.

**showman** ['ʃəʊmən] (irreg: like man) n (at fair) Schausteller m; (at circus) Artist m; (fig) Schauspieler m.

**showmanship** ['ʃəʊmənʃɪp] n Talent nt für effektvolle Darbietung.

**shown** [ʃəʊn] pp of show.

**show-off** ['ʃəʊɒf] (inf) n Angeber(in) m(f).

**showpiece** ['ʃəʊpiːs] n (of exhibition etc) Schaustück nt; (best example) Paradestück nt; (prime example) Musterbeispiel nt.

**showroom** ['ʃəʊrʊm] n Ausstellungsraum m.

**show trial** n Schauprozeß m.

**showy** ['ʃəʊɪ] adj auffallend.

**shrank** [ʃræŋk] pt of shrink.

**shrapnel** ['ʃræpnl] n Schrapnell nt.

**shred** [ʃred] n (gen pl) Fetzen m; (fig): **not a ~ of truth** kein Fünkchen Wahrheit; **not a ~ of evidence** keine Spur eines Beweises ♦ vt zerfetzen; (CULIN) raspeln.

**shredder** ['ʃredə*] n (vegetable shredder) Raspel f; (document shredder) Reißwolf m; (garden shredder) Häcksler m.

**shrew** [ʃruː] n (ZOOL) Spitzmaus f; (pej: woman) Xanthippe f.

**shrewd** [ʃruːd] adj klug.

**shrewdness** ['ʃruːdnɪs] n Klugheit f.

**shriek** [ʃriːk] n schriller Schrei m ♦ vi schreien; **to ~ with laughter** vor Lachen quietschen.

**shrift** [ʃrɪft] n: **to give sb short ~** jdn kurz abfertigen.

**shrill** [ʃrɪl] adj schrill.

**shrimp** [ʃrɪmp] n Garnele f.

**shrine** [ʃraɪn] n Schrein m; (fig) Gedenkstätte f.

**shrink** [ʃrɪŋk] (pt shrank, pp shrunk) vi (cloth) einlaufen; (profits, audiences) schrumpfen; (forests) schwinden; (also: ~ away) zurückweichen ♦ vt (cloth) einlaufen lassen ♦ n (inf: pej) Klappsdoktor m; **to ~ from sth** vor etw dat zurückschrecken; **to ~ from doing sth** davor zurückschrecken, etw zu tun.

**shrinkage** ['ʃrɪŋkɪdʒ] n (of clothes) Einlaufen nt.

**shrink-wrap** ['ʃrɪŋkræp] vt einschweißen.

**shrivel** ['ʃrɪvl] (also: ~ up) vt austrocknen ♦ vi austrocknen, verschrumpeln.

**shroud** [ʃraʊd] n Leichentuch nt ♦ vt: **~ed in mystery** von einem Geheimnis umgeben.

**Shrove Tuesday** ['ʃrəʊv-] n Fastnachtsdienstag m.

**shrub** [ʃrʌb] n Strauch m, Busch m.
**shrubbery** ['ʃrʌbərɪ] n Gebüsch nt.
**shrug** [ʃrʌg] n: ~ **(of the shoulders)**
Achselzucken nt ♦ vi, vt: **to ~ (one's
shoulders)** mit den Achseln zucken.
▶**shrug off** vt (criticism) auf die leichte
Schulter nehmen; (illness) abschütteln.
**shrunk** [ʃrʌŋk] pp of **shrink**.
**shrunken** ['ʃrʌŋkn] adj (ein)geschrumpft.
**shudder** ['ʃʌdə*] n Schauder m ♦ vi schaudern;
**I ~ to think of it** (fig) mir graut, wenn ich
nur daran denke.
**shuffle** ['ʃʌfl] vt (cards) mischen ♦ vi
schlurfen; **to ~ (one's feet)** mit den Füßen
scharren.
**shun** [ʃʌn] vt meiden; (publicity) scheuen.
**shunt** [ʃʌnt] vt rangieren.
**shunting yard** ['ʃʌntɪŋ-] n Rangierbahnhof m.
**shush** [ʃuʃ] excl pst!, sch!
**shut** [ʃʌt] (pt, pp **shut**) vt schließen, zumachen
(inf) ♦ vi sich schließen, zugehen; (shop)
schließen, zumachen (inf).
▶**shut down** vt (factory etc) schließen;
(machine) abschalten ♦ vi schließen,
zumachen (inf).
▶**shut off** vt (gas, electricity) abstellen; (oil
supplies etc) abschneiden.
▶**shut out** vt (person) aussperren; (cold,
noise) nicht hereinlassen; (view)
versperren; (memory, thought) verdrängen.
▶**shut up** vi (inf: keep quiet) den Mund halten
♦ vt (silence) zum Schweigen bringen.
**shutdown** ['ʃʌtdaun] n Schließung f.
**shutter** ['ʃʌtə*] n Fensterladen m; (PHOT)
Verschluß m.
**shuttle** ['ʃʌtl] n (plane) Pendelflugzeug nt;
(train) Pendelzug m; (space shuttle)
Raumtransporter m; (also: ~ **service**)
Pendelverkehr m; (for weaving) Schiffchen
nt ♦ vi: **to ~ to and fro** pendeln; **to ~
between** pendeln zwischen ♦ vt
(passengers) transportieren.
**shuttlecock** ['ʃʌtlkɔk] n Federball m.
**shuttle diplomacy** n Reisediplomatie f.
**shy** [ʃaɪ] adj schüchtern; (animal) scheu ♦ vi: **to
~ away from doing sth** (fig) davor
zurückschrecken, etw zu tun; **to fight ~ of**
aus dem Weg gehen +dat; **to be ~ of doing
sth** Hemmungen haben, etw zu tun.
**shyly** ['ʃaɪlɪ] adv schüchtern, scheu.
**shyness** ['ʃaɪnɪs] n Schüchternheit f, Scheu f.
**Siam** [saɪ'æm] n Siam nt.
**Siamese** [saɪə'miːz] adj: ~ **cat** Siamkatze f;
~ **twins** siamesische Zwillinge pl.
**Siberia** [saɪ'bɪərɪə] n Sibirien nt.
**sibling** ['sɪblɪŋ] n Geschwister nt.
**Sicilian** [sɪ'sɪlɪən] adj sizilianisch ♦ n
Sizilianer(in) m(f).
**Sicily** ['sɪsɪlɪ] n Sizilien nt.
**sick** [sɪk] adj krank; (humour, joke) makaber;
**to be ~** (vomit) brechen, sich übergeben; **I
feel ~** mir ist schlecht; **to fall ~** krank

werden; **to be (off) ~** wegen Krankheit
fehlen; **a ~ person** ein Kranker, eine
Kranke; **to be ~ of** (fig) satt haben +acc.
**sickbag** ['sɪkbæg] n Spucktüte f.
**sickbay** ['sɪkbeɪ] n Krankenrevier nt.
**sickbed** ['sɪkbɛd] n Krankenbett nt.
**sick building syndrome** n Kopfschmerzen,
Allergien etc, die in modernen,
vollklimatisierten Bürogebäuden
entstehen.
**sicken** ['sɪkn] vt (disgust) anwidern ♦ vi: **to be
~ing for a cold/flu** eine Erkältung/Grippe
bekommen.
**sickening** ['sɪknɪŋ] adj (fig) widerlich,
ekelhaft.
**sickle** ['sɪkl] n Sichel f.
**sick leave** n: **to be on ~** krank geschrieben
sein.
**sickle-cell anaemia** n Sichelzellenanämie f.
**sick list** n: **to be on the ~** auf der
Krankenliste stehen.
**sickly** ['sɪklɪ] adj kränklich; (causing nausea)
widerlich, ekelhaft.
**sickness** ['sɪknɪs] n Krankheit f; (vomiting)
Erbrechen nt.
**sickness benefit** n Krankengeld nt.
**sick note** n Krankmeldung f.
**sick pay** n Lohnfortzahlung f im
Krankheitsfall; (paid by insurance)
Krankengeld nt.
**sickroom** ['sɪkruːm] n Krankenzimmer nt.
**side** [saɪd] n Seite f; (team) Mannschaft f; (in
conflict etc) Partei f, Seite f; (of hill) Hang m
♦ adj (door, entrance) Seiten-, Neben- ♦ vi: **to
~ with sb** jds Partei ergreifen; **by the ~ of**
neben +dat; ~ **by** ~ Seite an Seite; **the right/
wrong ~** (of cloth) die rechte/linke Seite;
**they are on our ~** sie stehen auf unserer
Seite; **she never left my ~** sie wich mir
nicht von der Seite; **to put sth to one ~** etw
beiseite legen; **from ~ to ~** von einer Seite
zur anderen; **to take ~s (with)** Partei
ergreifen (für); **a ~ of beef** ein halbes Rind;
**a ~ of bacon** eine Seite Speckseite.
**sideboard** ['saɪdbɔːd] n Sideboard nt;
**sideboards** (BRIT) npl = **sideburns**.
**sideburns** ['saɪdbəːnz] npl Koteletten pl.
**sidecar** ['saɪdkɑː*] n Beiwagen m.
**side dish** n Beilage f.
**side drum** n kleine Trommel f.
**side effect** n (MED, fig) Nebenwirkung f.
**sidekick** ['saɪdkɪk] (inf) n Handlanger m.
**sidelight** ['saɪdlaɪt] n (AUT)
Begrenzungsleuchte f.
**sideline** ['saɪdlaɪn] n (SPORT) Seitenlinie f; (fig:
job) Nebenerwerb m; **to stand on the ~s**
(fig) unbeteiligter Zuschauer sein; **to wait
on the ~s** (fig) in den Kulissen warten.
**sidelong** ['saɪdlɔŋ] adj (glance) Seiten-;
(: surreptitious) verstohlen; **to give sb a
~ glance** jdn kurz aus den Augenwinkeln
ansehen.

**side plate** *n* kleiner Teller *m*.
**side road** *n* Nebenstraße *f*.
**side-saddle** ['saɪdsædl] *adv* (*ride*) im Damensitz.
**sideshow** ['saɪdʃəu] *n* Nebenattraktion *f*.
**sidestep** ['saɪdstɛp] *vt* (*problem*) umgehen; (*question*) ausweichen +*dat* ♦ *vi* (*BOXING etc*) seitwärts ausweichen.
**side street** *n* Seitenstraße *f*.
**sidetrack** ['saɪdtræk] *vt* (*fig*) ablenken.
**sidewalk** ['saɪdwɔːk] (*US*) *n* Bürgersteig *m*.
**sideways** ['saɪdweɪz] *adv* seitwärts; (*lean, look*) zur Seite.
**siding** ['saɪdɪŋ] *n* Abstellgleis *nt*.
**sidle** ['saɪdl] *vi*: **to ~ up (to)** sich heranschleichen (an +*acc*).
**SIDS** *n abbr* (*MED*: = *sudden infant death syndrome*) plötzlicher Kindstod *m*.
**siege** [siːdʒ] *n* Belagerung *f*; **to be under ~** belagert sein; **to lay ~ to** belagern.
**siege economy** *n* Belagerungswirtschaft *f*.
**siege mentality** *n* Belagerungsmentalität *f*.
**Sierra Leone** [sɪˈɛrəliˈəun] *n* Sierra Leone *f*.
**siesta** [sɪˈɛstə] *n* Siesta *f*.
**sieve** [sɪv] *n* Sieb *nt* ♦ *vt* sieben.
**sift** [sɪft] *vt* sieben; (*also*: **~ through**) durchgehen.
**sigh** [saɪ] *n* Seufzer *m* ♦ *vi* seufzen; **to breathe a ~ of relief** erleichtert aufseufzen.
**sight** [saɪt] *n* (*faculty*) Sehvermögen *nt*, Augenlicht *nt*; (*spectacle*) Anblick *m*; (*on gun*) Visier *nt* ♦ *vt* sichten; **in ~** in Sicht; **on ~** (*shoot*) sofort; **out of ~** außer Sicht; **at ~** (*COMM*) bei Sicht; **at first ~** auf den ersten Blick; **I knew her by ~** ich kenne sie vom Sehen; **to catch ~ of sb/sth** jdn/etw sehen; **to lose ~ of sth** (*fig*) etw aus den Augen verlieren; **to set one's ~s on sth** ein Auge auf etw werfen.
**sighted** ['saɪtɪd] *adj* sehend; **partially ~** sehbehindert.
**sightseeing** ['saɪtsiːɪŋ] *n* Besichtigungen *pl*; **to go ~** auf Besichtigungstour gehen.
**sightseer** ['saɪtsiːə*] *n* Tourist(in) *m(f)*.
**sign** [saɪn] *n* Zeichen *nt*; (*notice*) Schild *nt*; (*evidence*) Anzeichen *nt*; (*also*: **road ~**) Verkehrsschild *nt* ♦ *vt* unterschreiben; (*player*) verpflichten; **a ~ of the times** ein Zeichen unserer Zeit; **it's a good/bad ~** es ist ein gutes/schlechtes Zeichen; **plus/minus ~** Plus-/Minuszeichen *nt*; **there's no ~ of her changing her mind** nichts deutet darauf hin, daß sie es sich anders überlegen wird; **he was showing ~s of improvement** er ließ Anzeichen einer Verbesserung erkennen; **to ~ one's name** unterschreiben; **to ~ sth over to sb** jdm etw überschreiben.
▶**sign away** *vt* (*rights etc*) verzichten auf +*acc*.
▶**sign in** *vi* sich eintragen.
▶**sign off** *vi* (*RADIO, TV*) sich verabschieden; (*in letter*) Schluß machen.

▶**sign on** *vi* (*MIL*) sich verpflichten; (*BRIT: as unemployed*) sich arbeitslos melden; (*for course*) sich einschreiben ♦ *vt* (*MIL*) verpflichten; (*employee*) anstellen.
▶**sign out** *vi* (*from hotel etc*) sich (aus dem Hotelgästebuch *etc*) austragen.
▶**sign up** *vi* (*MIL*) sich verpflichten; (*for course*) sich einschreiben ♦ *vt* (*player, recruit*) verpflichten.
**signal** ['sɪgnl] *n* Zeichen *nt*; (*RAIL*) Signal *nt* ♦ *vi* (*AUT*) Zeichen/ein Zeichen geben ♦ *vt* ein Zeichen geben +*dat*; **to ~ a right/left turn** (*AUT*) rechts/links blinken.
**signal box** *n* Stellwerk *nt*.
**signalman** ['sɪgnlmən] (*irreg: like* **man**) *n* Stellwerkswärter *m*.
**signatory** ['sɪgnətərɪ] *n* Unterzeichner *m*; (*state*) Signatarstaat *m*.
**signature** ['sɪgnətʃə*] *n* Unterschrift *f*; (*ZOOL, BIOL*) Kennzeichen *nt*.
**signature tune** *n* Erkennungsmelodie *f*.
**signet ring** ['sɪgnət-] *n* Siegelring *m*.
**significance** [sɪgˈnɪfɪkəns] *n* Bedeutung *f*; **that is of no ~** das ist belanglos *or* bedeutungslos.
**significant** [sɪgˈnɪfɪkənt] *adj* bedeutend, wichtig; (*look, smile*) vielsagend, bedeutsam; **it is ~ that** ... es ist bezeichnend, daß ...
**significantly** [sɪgˈnɪfɪkəntlɪ] *adv* bedeutend; (*smile*) vielsagend, bedeutsam.
**signify** ['sɪgnɪfaɪ] *vt* bedeuten; (*person*) zu erkennen geben.
**sign language** *n* Zeichensprache *f*.
**signpost** ['saɪnpəust] *n* (*lit, fig*) Wegweiser *m*.
**Sikh** [siːk] *n* Sikh *mf* ♦ *adj* (*province etc*) Sikh-.
**silage** ['saɪlɪdʒ] *n* Silage *f*, Silofutter *nt*.
**silence** ['saɪləns] *n* Stille *f*; (*of person*) Schweigen *nt* ♦ *vt* zum Schweigen bringen; **in ~** still; (*not talking*) schweigend.
**silencer** ['saɪlənsə*] *n* (*on gun*) Schalldämpfer *m*; (*BRIT: AUT*) Auspufftopf *m*.
**silent** ['saɪlənt] *adj* still; (*machine*) ruhig; **~ film** Stummfilm *m*; **to remain ~** still bleiben; (*about sth*) sich nicht äußern.
**silently** ['saɪləntlɪ] *adv* lautlos; (*not talking*) schweigend.
**silent partner** *n* stiller Teilhaber *m*.
**silhouette** [sɪluːˈɛt] *n* Silhouette *f*, Umriß *m* ♦ *vt*: **to be ~d against sth** sich als Silhouette gegen etw abheben.
**silicon** ['sɪlɪkən] *n* Silizium *nt*.
**silicon chip** *n* Silikonchip *m*.
**silicone** ['sɪlɪkəun] *n* Silikon *nt*.
**Silicon Valley** *n* Silicon Valley *nt*.
**silk** [sɪlk] *n* Seide *f* ♦ *adj* (*dress etc*) Seiden-.
**silky** ['sɪlkɪ] *adj* seidig.
**sill** [sɪl] *n* (*also*: **window ~**) (Fenster)sims *m or nt*; (*of door*) Schwelle *f*; (*AUT*) Türleiste *f*.
**silly** ['sɪlɪ] *adj* (*person*) dumm; **to do something ~** etwas Dummes tun.
**silo** ['saɪləu] *n* Silo *nt*; (*for missile*) Raketensilo

nt.
**silt** [sɪlt] n Schlamm m, Schlick m.
▶**silt up** vi verschlammen ♦ vt
verschlämmen.
**silver** ['sɪlvə*] n Silber nt; (coins) Silbergeld nt
♦ adj silbern.
**silver foil** (BRIT) n Alufolie f.
**silver paper** (BRIT) n Silberpapier nt.
**silver-plated** [sɪlvə'pleɪtɪd] adj versilbert.
**silversmith** ['sɪlvəsmɪθ] n Silberschmied(in)
m(f).
**silverware** ['sɪlvəwɛə*] n Silber nt.
**silver wedding (anniversary)** n
Silberhochzeit f.
**silvery** ['sɪlvrɪ] adj silbern; (sound) silberhell.
**similar** ['sɪmɪlə*] adj: ~ **(to)** ähnlich (wie or
+dat).
**similarity** [sɪmɪ'lærɪtɪ] n Ähnlichkeit f.
**similarly** ['sɪmɪləlɪ] adv ähnlich; (likewise)
genauso.
**simile** ['sɪmɪlɪ] n (LING) Vergleich m.
**simmer** ['sɪmə*] vi auf kleiner Flamme
kochen.
▶**simmer down** (inf) vi (fig) sich abregen.
**simper** ['sɪmpə*] vi geziert lächeln.
**simpering** ['sɪmprɪŋ] adj geziert.
**simple** ['sɪmpl] adj einfach; (dress) einfach,
schlicht; (foolish) einfältig; **the ~ truth
is that ...** es ist einfach so, daß ...
**simple interest** n Kapitalzinsen pl.
**simple-minded** [sɪmpl'maɪndɪd] (pej) adj
einfältig.
**simpleton** ['sɪmpltən] (pej) n Einfaltspinsel m.
**simplicity** [sɪm'plɪsɪtɪ] n Einfachheit f; (of
dress) Schlichtheit f.
**simplification** [sɪmplɪfɪ'keɪʃən] n
Vereinfachung f.
**simplify** ['sɪmplɪfaɪ] vt vereinfachen.
**simply** ['sɪmplɪ] adv (just, merely) nur, bloß; (in
a simple way) einfach.
**simulate** ['sɪmjuleɪt] vt vortäuschen, spielen;
(illness) simulieren.
**simulated** ['sɪmjuleɪtɪd] adj (hair, fur) imitiert;
(TECH) simuliert.
**simulation** [sɪmju'leɪʃən] n Vortäuschung f;
(simulated object) Imitation f; (TECH)
Simulation f.
**simultaneous** [sɪməl'teɪnɪəs] adj gleichzeitig;
(translation, interpreting) Simultan-.
**simultaneously** [sɪməl'teɪnɪəslɪ] adv
gleichzeitig.
**sin** [sɪn] n Sünde f ♦ vi sündigen.
**Sinai** ['saɪneɪaɪ] n Sinai m.
**since** [sɪns] adv inzwischen, seitdem ♦ prep seit
♦ conj (time) seit(dem); (because) da; ~ **then,
ever** ~ seitdem.
**sincere** [sɪn'sɪə*] adj aufrichtig, offen;
(apology, belief) aufrichtig.
**sincerely** [sɪn'sɪəlɪ] adv aufrichtig, offen;
**yours** ~ (in letter) mit freundlichen Grüßen.
**sincerity** [sɪn'sɛrɪtɪ] n Aufrichtigkeit f.
**sine** [saɪn] n Sinus m.

**sine qua non** [sɪnɪkwɑː'nɔn] n unerläßliche
Voraussetzung f.
**sinew** ['sɪnjuː] n Sehne f.
**sinful** ['sɪnful] adj sündig, sündhaft.
**sing** [sɪŋ] (pt sang, pp sung) vt, vi singen.
**Singapore** [sɪŋgə'pɔː*] n Singapur nt.
**singe** [sɪndʒ] vt versengen; (lightly) ansengen.
**singer** ['sɪŋə*] n Sänger(in) m(f).
**Singhalese** [sɪŋə'liːz] adj = **Sinhalese**.
**singing** ['sɪŋɪŋ] n Singen nt, Gesang m; **a ~ in
the ears** ein Dröhnen in den Ohren.
**single** ['sɪŋgl] adj (solitary) einzige(r, s);
(individual) einzeln; (unmarried) ledig,
unverheiratet; (not double) einfach ♦ n
(BRIT: also: ~ **ticket**) Einzelfahrschein m;
(record) Single f; **not a ~ one was left** es war
kein einziges mehr übrig; **every ~ day**
jeden Tag; ~ **spacing** einfacher
Zeilenabstand m.
▶**single out** vt auswählen; **to ~ out for praise**
lobend erwähnen.
**single bed** n Einzelbett nt.
**single-breasted** ['sɪŋglbrɛstɪd] adj einreihig.
**Single European Market** n: **the** ~ der
Europäische Binnenmarkt.
**single file** n: **in** ~ im Gänsemarsch.
**single-handed** [sɪŋgl'hændɪd] adv ganz allein.
**single-minded** [sɪŋgl'maɪndɪd] adj zielstrebig.
**single parent** n Alleinerziehende(r) f(m).
**single room** n Einzelzimmer nt.
**singles** ['sɪŋglz] npl (TENNIS) Einzel nt.
**singles bar** n Singles-Bar f.
**single-sex school** n reine Jungen-/
Mädchenschule f; **education in** ~s nach
Geschlechtern getrennte Schulerziehung.
**singly** ['sɪŋglɪ] adv einzeln.
**singsong** ['sɪŋsɔŋ] adj (tone) singend ♦ n: **to
have a** ~ zusammen singen.
**singular** ['sɪŋgjulə*] adj (odd) eigenartig;
(outstanding) einzigartig; (LING: form etc)
Singular- ♦ n (LING) Singular m, Einzahl f; **in
the** ~ im Singular.
**singularly** ['sɪŋgjuləlɪ] adv außerordentlich.
**Sinhalese** [sɪnhə'liːz] adj singhalesisch.
**sinister** ['sɪnɪstə*] adj unheimlich.
**sink** [sɪŋk] (pt sank, pp sunk) n Spülbecken nt
♦ vt (ship) versenken; (well) bohren;
(foundations) absenken ♦ vi (ship) sinken,
untergehen; (ground) sich senken; (person)
sinken; **to ~ one's teeth/claws into sth** die
Zähne/seine Klauen in etw acc schlagen; **his
heart/spirits sank at the thought** bei dem
Gedanken verließ ihn der Mut; **he sank into
the mud/a chair** er sank in den Schlamm
ein/in einen Sessel.
▶**sink back** vi (zurück)sinken.
▶**sink down** vi (nieder)sinken.
▶**sink in** vi (fig) verstanden werden; **it's only
just sunk in** ich begreife es erst jetzt.
**sinking** ['sɪŋkɪŋ] n (of ship) Untergang m;
(: deliberate) Versenkung f ♦ adj: ~ **feeling**
flaues Gefühl nt (im Magen).

**sinking fund** n Tilgungsfonds m.
**sink unit** n Spüle f.
**sinner** ['sɪnə*] n Sünder(in) m(f).
**Sinn Féin** [ʃɪn'feɪn] n republikanisch-nationalistische irische Partei.
**Sino-** ['saɪnəu] pref chinesisch-.
**sinuous** ['sɪnjuəs] adj (snake) gewunden; (dance) geschmeidig.
**sinus** ['saɪnəs] n (Nasen)nebenhöhle f.
**sip** [sɪp] n Schlückchen nt ♦ vt nippen an +dat.
**siphon** ['saɪfən] n Heber m; (also: **soda** ~) Siphon m.
▶**siphon off** vt absaugen; (petrol) abzapfen.
**SIPS** n abbr (= side impact protection system) Seitenaufprallschutz m.
**sir** [sə*] n mein Herr, Herr X; **S**~ **John Smith** Sir John Smith; **yes,** ~ ja(, Herr X); **Dear S**~ **(or Madam)** (in letter) Sehr geehrte (Damen und) Herren!
**siren** ['saɪərn] n Sirene f.
**sirloin** ['sɜːlɔɪn] n (also: ~ **steak**) Filetsteak nt.
**sirocco** [sɪ'rɒkəu] n Schirokko m.
**sisal** ['saɪsəl] n Sisal m.
**sissy** ['sɪsɪ] (inf: pej) n Waschlappen m ♦ adj weichlich.
**sister** ['sɪstə*] n Schwester f; (nun) (Ordens)schwester f; (BRIT: nurse) Oberschwester f ♦ cpd: ~ **organization** Schwesterorganisation f; ~ **ship** Schwesterschiff nt.
**sister-in-law** ['sɪstərɪnlɔː] n Schwägerin f.
**sit** [sɪt] (pt, pp **sat**) vi (sit down) sich setzen; (be sitting) sitzen; (assembly) tagen; (for painter) Modell sitzen ♦ vt (exam) machen; **to** ~ **on a committee** in einem Ausschuß sitzen; **to** ~ **tight** abwarten.
▶**sit about** vi herumsitzen.
▶**sit around** vi = **sit about**.
▶**sit back** vi sich zurücklehnen.
▶**sit down** vi sich (hin)setzen; **to be** ~**ting down** sitzen.
▶**sit in on** vt fus dabeisein bei.
▶**sit up** vi sich aufsetzen; (straight) sich gerade hinsetzen; (not go to bed) aufbleiben.
**sitcom** ['sɪtkɒm] n abbr (TV) = **situation comedy**.
**sit-down** ['sɪtdaun] adj: **a** ~ **strike** ein Sitzstreik m; **a** ~ **meal** eine richtige Mahlzeit.
**site** [saɪt] n (place) Platz m; (of crime) Ort m; (also: **building** ~) Baustelle f ♦ vt (factory) legen; (missiles) stationieren.
**sit-in** ['sɪtɪn] n Sit-in nt.
**siting** ['saɪtɪŋ] n (location) Lage f.
**sitter** ['sɪtə*] n (for painter) Modell nt; (also: **baby-**~) Babysitter m.
**sitting** ['sɪtɪŋ] n Sitzung f; **we have two** ~**s for lunch** bei uns wird das Mittagessen in zwei Schüben serviert; **at a single** ~ auf einmal.
**sitting member** n (POL) (derzeitiger) Abgeordnete(r) m, (derzeitige) Abgeordnete f.

**sitting room** n Wohnzimmer nt.
**sitting tenant** (BRIT) n (derzeitiger) Mieter m.
**situate** ['sɪtjueɪt] vt legen.
**situated** ['sɪtjueɪtɪd] adj gelegen; **to be** ~ liegen.
**situation** [sɪtju'eɪʃən] n Situation f, Lage f; (job) Stelle f; (location) Lage f; **"~s vacant"** (BRIT) „Stellenangebote“.
**situation comedy** n (TV) Situationskomödie f.
**six** [sɪks] num sechs.
**six-pack** ['sɪkspæk] n Sechserpack m.
**sixteen** [sɪks'tiːn] num sechzehn.
**sixth** [sɪksθ] num sechste(r, s); **the upper/lower** ~ (BRIT: SCOL) ≈ die Ober-/Unterprima.
**sixty** ['sɪkstɪ] num sechzig.
**size** [saɪz] n Größe f; (extent) Ausmaß nt; **I take** ~ **14** ich habe Größe 14; **the small/large** ~ (of soap powder etc) die kleine/große Packung; **it's the** ~ **of ...** es ist so groß wie ...; **cut to** ~ auf die richtige Größe zurechtgeschnitten.
▶**size up** vt einschätzen.
**sizeable** ['saɪzəbl] adj ziemlich groß; (income etc) ansehnlich.
**sizzle** ['sɪzl] vi brutzeln.
**SK** (CANADA) abbr (= Saskatchewan).
**skate** [skeɪt] n (ice skate) Schlittschuh m; (roller skate) Rollschuh m; (fish: pl inv) Rochen m ♦ vi Schlittschuh laufen.
▶**skate around** vt fus (problem, issue) einfach übergehen.
▶**skate over** vt fus = **skate around**.
**skateboard** ['skeɪtbɔːd] n Skateboard nt.
**skater** ['skeɪtə*] n Schlittschuhläufer(in) m(f).
**skating** ['skeɪtɪŋ] n Eislauf m.
**skating rink** n Eisbahn f.
**skeleton** ['skɛlɪtn] n Skelett nt ♦ attrib (plan, outline) skizzenhaft.
**skeleton key** n Dietrich m, Nachschlüssel m.
**skeleton staff** n Minimalbesetzung f.
**skeptic** etc ['skɛptɪk] (US) = **sceptic** etc.
**sketch** [skɛtʃ] n Skizze f; (THEAT, TV) Sketch m ♦ vt skizzieren; (also: ~ **out**: ideas) umreißen.
**sketchbook** ['skɛtʃbuk] n Skizzenbuch nt.
**sketchpad** ['skɛtʃpæd] n Skizzenblock m.
**sketchy** ['skɛtʃɪ] adj (coverage) oberflächlich; (notes etc) bruchstückhaft.
**skew** [skjuː] adj schief.
**skewed** [skjuːd] adj (distorted) verzerrt.
**skewer** ['skjuːə*] n Spieß m.
**ski** [skiː] n Ski m, Schi m ♦ vi Ski laufen or fahren.
**ski boot** n Skistiefel m.
**skid** [skɪd] n (AUT) Schleudern nt ♦ vi rutschen; (AUT) schleudern; **to go into a** ~ ins Schleudern geraten or kommen.
**skid marks** npl Reifenspuren pl; (from braking) Bremsspuren pl.
**skier** ['skiːə*] n Skiläufer(in) m(f),

Skifahrer(in) m(f).
**skiing** ['ski:ɪŋ] n Skilaufen nt, Skifahren nt; **to go ~** Skilaufen or Skifahren gehen.
**ski instructor** n Skilehrer(in) m(f).
**ski jump** n (event) Skispringen nt; (ramp) Sprungschanze f.
**skilful**, (US) **skillful** ['skɪlful] adj geschickt.
**skilfully** adv geschickt.
**ski lift** n Skilift m.
**skill** [skɪl] n (ability) Können nt; (dexterity) Geschicklichkeit f; **skills** (acquired abilities) Fähigkeiten pl; **computer/language ~s** Computer-/Sprachkenntnisse pl; **to learn a new ~** etwas Neues lernen.
**skilled** [skɪld] adj (skilful) geschickt; (trained) ausgebildet; (work) qualifiziert.
**skillet** ['skɪlɪt] n Bratpfanne f.
**skillful** etc ['skɪlful] (US) = **skilful** etc.
**skim** [skɪm] vt (also: ~ **off**: cream, fat) abschöpfen; (glide over) gleiten über +acc ♦ vi: **to ~ through** (book etc) überfliegen.
**skimmed milk** [skɪmd-] n Magermilch f.
**skimp** [skɪmp] (also: ~ **on**) vt (work etc) nachlässig machen; (cloth etc) sparen an +dat.
**skimpy** ['skɪmpɪ] adj (meagre) dürftig; (too small) knapp.
**skin** [skɪn] n Haut f; (fur) Fell nt; (of fruit) Schale f ♦ vt (animal) häuten; **wet** or **soaked to the ~** naß bis auf die Haut.
**skin cancer** n Hautkrebs m.
**skin-deep** ['skɪn'di:p] adj oberflächlich.
**skin diver** n Sporttaucher(in) m(f).
**skin diving** n Sporttauchen nt.
**skinflint** ['skɪnflɪnt] n Geizkragen m.
**skin graft** n Hautverpflanzung f.
**skinhead** ['skɪnhɛd] n Skinhead m.
**skinny** ['skɪnɪ] adj dünn.
**skin test** n Hauttest m.
**skintight** ['skɪntaɪt] adj hauteng.
**skip** [skɪp] n Sprung m, Hüpfer m; (BRIT: container) (Müll)container m ♦ vi springen, hüpfen; (with rope) seilspringen ♦ vt überspringen; (miss: lunch, lecture) ausfallen lassen; **to ~ school** (esp US) die Schule schwänzen.
**ski pants** npl Skihose f.
**ski pole** n Skistock m.
**skipper** ['skɪpə*] n (NAUT) Kapitän m; (inf: SPORT) Mannschaftskapitän m ♦ vt: **to ~ a boat/team** Kapitän eines Schiffes/einer Mannschaft sein.
**skipping rope** ['skɪpɪŋ-] (BRIT) n Sprungseil nt.
**ski resort** n Wintersportort m.
**skirmish** ['skə:mɪʃ] n (MIL) Geplänkel nt; (political etc) Zusammenstoß m.
**skirt** [skə:t] n Rock m ♦ vt (fig) umgehen.
**skirting board** ['skə:tɪŋ-] (BRIT) n Fußleiste f.
**ski run** n Skipiste f.
**ski slope** n Skipiste f.
**ski suit** n Skianzug m.

**skit** [skɪt] n Parodie f.
**ski tow** n Schlepplift m.
**skittle** ['skɪtl] n Kegel m.
**skittles** ['skɪtlz] n (game) Kegeln nt.
**skive** [skaɪv] (BRIT: inf) vi blaumachen; (from school) schwänzen.
**skulk** [skʌlk] vi sich herumdrücken.
**skull** [skʌl] n Schädel m.
**skullcap** ['skʌlkæp] n Scheitelkäppchen nt.
**skunk** [skʌŋk] n Skunk m, Stinktier nt; (fur) Skunk m.
**sky** [skaɪ] n Himmel m; **to praise sb to the skies** jdn in den Himmel heben.
**sky-blue** [skaɪ'blu:] adj himmelblau.
**skydiving** ['skaɪdaɪvɪŋ] n Fallschirmspringen nt.
**sky-high** ['skaɪ'haɪ] adj (prices, confidence) himmelhoch ♦ adv: **to blow a bridge ~** eine Brücke in die Luft sprengen.
**skylark** ['skaɪlɑ:k] n Feldlerche f.
**skylight** ['skaɪlaɪt] n Dachfenster nt.
**skyline** ['skaɪlaɪn] n (horizon) Horizont m; (of city) Skyline f, Silhouette f.
**skyscraper** ['skaɪskreɪpə*] n Wolkenkratzer m.
**slab** [slæb] n (stone) Platte f; (of wood) Tafel f; (of cake, cheese) großes Stück nt.
**slack** [slæk] adj (loose) locker; (rope) durchhängend; (skin) schlaff; (careless) nachlässig; (COMM: market) flau; (: demand) schwach; (period) ruhig ♦ n (in rope etc) durchhängendes Teil nt; **slacks** npl (trousers) Hose f; **business is ~** das Geschäft geht schlecht.
**slacken** ['slækn] vi (also: ~ **off**: speed, rain) nachlassen; (: pace) langsamer werden; (: demand) zurückgehen ♦ vt (grip) lockern; (speed) verringern; (pace) verlangsamen.
**slag heap** [slæg-] n Schlackenhalde f.
**slag off** (BRIT: inf) vt (criticize) (he)runtermachen.
**slain** [sleɪn] pp of **slay**.
**slake** [sleɪk] vt (thirst) stillen.
**slalom** ['slɑ:ləm] n Slalom m.
**slam** [slæm] vt (door) zuschlagen, zuknallen (inf); (throw) knallen (inf); (criticize) verreißen ♦ vi (door) zuschlagen, zuknallen (inf); **to ~ on the brakes** (AUT) auf die Bremse steigen (inf).
**slammer** ['slæmə*] (inf) n (prison) Knast m.
**slander** ['slɑ:ndə*] n (LAW) Verleumdung f; (insult) Beleidigung f ♦ vt verleumden.
**slanderous** ['slɑ:ndrəs] adj verleumderisch.
**slang** [slæŋ] n Slang m; (jargon) Jargon m.
**slanging match** ['slæŋɪŋ-] n gegenseitige Beschimpfungen pl.
**slant** [slɑ:nt] n Neigung f, Schräge f; (fig: approach) Perspektive f ♦ vi (floor) sich neigen; (ceiling) schräg sein.
**slanted** ['slɑ:ntɪd] adj (roof) schräg; (eyes) schräggestellt.
**slanting** ['slɑ:ntɪŋ] adj = **slanted**.
**slap** [slæp] n Schlag m, Klaps m ♦ vt schlagen

♦ *adv* (*inf: directly*) direkt; **to ~ sth on sth** etw auf etw *acc* klatschen; **it fell ~(-bang) in the middle** es fiel genau in die Mitte.

**slapdash** ['slæpdæʃ] *adj* nachlässig, schludrig (*inf*).

**slapstick** ['slæpstɪk] *n* Klamauk *m*.

**slap-up** ['slæpʌp] *adj:* **a ~ meal** (*BRIT*) ein Essen mit allem Drum und Dran.

**slash** [slæʃ] *vt* aufschlitzen; (*fig: prices*) radikal senken; **to ~ one's wrists** sich *dat* die Pulsadern aufschneiden.

**slat** [slæt] *n* Leiste *f*, Latte *f*.

**slate** [sleɪt] *n* Schiefer *m*; (*piece*) Schieferplatte *f* ♦ *vt* (*criticize*) verreißen.

**slaughter** ['slɔːtə*] *n* (*of animals*) Schlachten *nt*; (*of people*) Gemetzel *nt* ♦ *vt* (*animals*) schlachten; (*people*) abschlachten.

**slaughterhouse** ['slɔːtəhaus] *n* Schlachthof *m*.

**Slav** [slɑːv] *adj* slawisch ♦ *n* Slawe *m*, Slawin *f*.

**slave** [sleɪv] *n* Sklave *m*, Sklavin *f* ♦ *vi* (*also:* **~ away**) sich abplagen, schuften (*inf*); **to ~ (away) at sth** sich mit etw herumschlagen.

**slave-driver** ['sleɪvdraɪvə*] *n* Sklaventreiber(in) *m(f)*.

**slave labour** *n* Sklavenarbeit *f*; **it's just ~** (*fig*) es ist die reinste Sklavenarbeit.

**slaver** ['slævə*] *vi* (*dribble*) geifern.

**slavery** ['sleɪvərɪ] *n* Sklaverei *f*.

**Slavic** ['slævɪk] *adj* slawisch.

**slavish** ['sleɪvɪʃ] *adj* sklavisch.

**slavishly** ['sleɪvɪʃlɪ] *adv* sklavisch.

**Slavonic** [slə'vɒnɪk] *adj* slawisch.

**slay** [sleɪ] (*pt* **slew,** *pp* **slain**) *vt* (*liter*) erschlagen.

**SLD** (*BRIT*) *n abbr* (*POL:* = *Social and Liberal Democratic Party*) *sozialliberale Partei.*

**sleazy** ['sliːzɪ] *adj* schäbig.

**sledge** [slɛdʒ] *n* Schlitten *m*.

**sledgehammer** ['slɛdʒhæmə*] *n* Vorschlaghammer *m*.

**sleek** [sliːk] *adj* glatt, glänzend; (*car, boat etc*) schnittig.

**sleep** [sliːp] (*pt, pp* **slept**) *n* Schlaf *m* ♦ *vi* schlafen ♦ *vt:* **we can ~ 4** bei uns können 4 Leute schlafen; **to go to ~** einschlafen; **to have a good night's ~** sich richtig ausschlafen; **to put to ~** (*euph: kill*) einschläfern; **to ~ lightly** einen leichten Schlaf haben; **to ~ with sb** (*euph: have sex*) mit jdm schlafen.

▶**sleep around** *vi* mit jedem/jeder schlafen.

▶**sleep in** *vi* (*oversleep*) verschlafen; (*rise late*) lange schlafen.

**sleeper** ['sliːpə*] *n* (*train*) Schlafwagenzug *m*; (*berth*) Platz *m* im Schlafwagen; (*BRIT: on track*) Schwelle *f*; (*person*) Schläfer(in) *m(f)*.

**sleepily** ['sliːpɪlɪ] *adv* müde, schläfrig.

**sleeping accommodation** *n* (*beds etc*) Schlafgelegenheiten *pl.*

**sleeping arrangements** *npl*

Bettenverteilung *f.*

**sleeping bag** *n* Schlafsack *m*.

**sleeping car** *n* Schlafwagen *m*.

**sleeping partner** (*BRIT*) = **silent partner.**

**sleeping pill** *n* Schlaftablette *f.*

**sleeping sickness** *n* Schlafkrankheit *f.*

**sleepless** ['sliːplɪs] *adj* (*night*) schlaflos.

**sleeplessness** ['sliːplɪsnɪs] *n* Schlaflosigkeit *f.*

**sleepwalk** ['sliːpwɔːk] *vi* schlafwandeln.

**sleepwalker** ['sliːpwɔːkə*] *n* Schlafwandler(in) *m(f)*.

**sleepy** ['sliːpɪ] *adj* müde, schläfrig; (*fig: village etc*) verschlafen; **to be** *or* **feel ~** müde sein.

**sleet** [sliːt] *n* Schneeregen *m*.

**sleeve** [sliːv] *n* Ärmel *m*; (*of record*) Hülle *f*; **to have sth up one's ~** (*fig*) etw in petto haben.

**sleeveless** ['sliːvlɪs] *adj* (*garment*) ärmellos.

**sleigh** [sleɪ] *n* (Pferde)schlitten *m*.

**sleight** [slaɪt] *n:* **~ of hand** Fingerfertigkeit *f.*

**slender** ['slɛndə*] *adj* schlank, schmal; (*small*) knapp.

**slept** [slɛpt] *pt, pp of* **sleep.**

**sleuth** [sluːθ] *n* Detektiv *m*.

**slew** [sluː] *vi* (*BRIT: also: ~* **round**) herumschwenken; **the bus ~ed across the road** der Bus rutschte über die Straße ♦ *pt of* **slay.**

**slice** [slaɪs] *n* Scheibe *f*; (*utensil*) Wender *m* ♦ *vt* (in Scheiben) schneiden; **~d bread** aufgeschnittenes Brot *nt*; **the best thing since ~d bread** der/die/das Allerbeste.

**slick** [slɪk] *adj* professionell; (*pej*) glatt ♦ *n* (*also:* **oil ~**) Ölteppich *m*.

**slid** [slɪd] *pt, pp of* **slide.**

**slide** [slaɪd] (*pt, pp* **slid**) *n* (*on ice etc*) Rutschen *nt*; (*fig: to ruin etc*) Abgleiten *nt*; (*in playground*) Rutschbahn *f*; (*PHOT*) Dia *nt*; (*BRIT: also:* **hair ~**) Spange *f*; (*microscope slide*) Objektträger *m*; (*in prices*) Preisrutsch *m* ♦ *vt* schieben ♦ *vi* (*slip*) rutschen; (*glide*) gleiten; **to let things ~** (*fig*) die Dinge schleifen lassen.

**slide projector** *n* Diaprojektor *m*.

**slide rule** *n* Rechenschieber *m*.

**sliding** ['slaɪdɪŋ] *adj* (*door, window etc*) Schiebe-.

**sliding roof** *n* (*AUT*) Schiebedach *nt*.

**sliding scale** *n* gleitende Skala *f.*

**slight** [slaɪt] *adj* zierlich; (*small*) gering; (*error, accent, pain etc*) leicht; (*trivial*) leicht ♦ *n:* **a ~ (on sb/sth)** ein Affront *m* (gegen jdn/etw); **the ~est noise** der geringste Lärm; **the ~est problem** das kleinste Problem; **I haven't the ~est idea** ich habe nicht die geringste Ahnung; **not in the ~est** nicht im geringsten.

**slightly** ['slaɪtlɪ] *adv* etwas, ein bißchen; **~ built** zierlich.

**slim** [slɪm] *adj* schlank; (*chance*) gering ♦ *vi* eine Schlankheitskur machen, abnehmen.

**slime** [slaɪm] *n* Schleim *m*.

**slimming** ['slɪmɪŋ] *n* Abnehmen *nt*.

**slimy** ['slaɪmɪ] *adj* (*lit, fig*) schleimig.

**sling** [slɪŋ] (pt, pp **slung**) n Schlinge f; (for baby) Tragetuch nt; (weapon) Schleuder f ♦ vt schleudern; **to have one's arm in a ~** den Arm in der Schlinge tragen.

**slingshot** ['slɪŋʃɒt] n Steinschleuder f.

**slink** [slɪŋk] (pt, pp **slunk**) vi: **to ~ away** or **off** sich davonschleichen.

**slinky** ['slɪŋkɪ] adj (dress) enganliegend.

**slip** [slɪp] n (fall) Ausrutschen nt; (mistake) Fehler m, Schnitzer m; (underskirt) Unterrock m; (also: **~ of paper**) Zettel m ♦ vt (slide) stecken ♦ vi ausrutschen; (decline) fallen; **he had a nasty ~** er ist ausgerutscht und böse gefallen; **to give sb the ~** jdm entwischen; **a ~ of the tongue** ein Versprecher m; **to ~ into/out of sth, to ~ sth on/off** in etw acc/aus etw schlüpfen; **to let a chance ~ by** eine Gelegenheit ungenutzt lassen; **it ~ped from her hand** es rutschte ihr aus der Hand.

▶**slip away** vi sich davonschleichen.

▶**slip in** vt stecken in +acc.

▶**slip out** vi kurz weggehen.

▶**slip up** vi sich vertun (inf).

**slip-on** ['slɪpɒn] adj zum Überziehen; **~ shoes** Slipper pl.

**slipped disc** [slɪpt-] n Bandscheibenschaden m.

**slipper** ['slɪpə*] n Pantoffel m, Hausschuh m.

**slippery** ['slɪpərɪ] adj (lit, fig) glatt; (fish etc) schlüpfrig.

**slippy** ['slɪpɪ] adj (slippery) glatt.

**slip road** (BRIT) n (to motorway etc) Auffahrt f; (from motorway etc) Ausfahrt f.

**slipshod** ['slɪpʃɒd] adj schludrig (inf).

**slipstream** ['slɪpstriːm] n (TECH) Sog m; (AUT) Windschatten m.

**slip-up** ['slɪpʌp] n Fehler m, Schnitzer m.

**slipway** ['slɪpweɪ] n (NAUT) Ablaufbahn f.

**slit** [slɪt] (pt, pp **slit**) n Schlitz m; (tear) Riß m ♦ vt aufschlitzen; **to ~ sb's throat** jdm die Kehle aufschlitzen.

**slither** ['slɪðə*] vi rutschen; (snake etc) gleiten.

**sliver** ['slɪvə*] n (of glass, wood) Splitter m; (of cheese etc) Scheibchen nt.

**slob** [slɒb] (inf) n Drecksau f (!).

**slog** [slɒg] (BRIT) vi (work hard) schuften ♦ n: **it was a hard ~** es war eine ganz schöne Schufterei; **to ~ away at sth** sich mit etw abrackern.

**slogan** ['sləʊgən] n Slogan m.

**slop** [slɒp] vi schwappen ♦ vt verschütten.

▶**slop out** vi (in prison etc) den Toiletteneimer ausleeren.

**slope** [sləʊp] n Hügel m; (side of mountain) Hang m; (ski slope) Piste f; (slant) Neigung f ♦ vi: **to ~ down** abfallen; **to ~ up** ansteigen.

**sloping** ['sləʊpɪŋ] adj (upwards) ansteigend; (downwards) abfallend; (roof, handwriting) schräg.

**sloppy** ['slɒpɪ] adj (work) nachlässig; (appearance) schlampig; (sentimental) rührselig.

**slops** [slɒps] npl Abfallbrühe f.

**slosh** [slɒʃ] (inf) vi: **to ~ around** or **about** (person) herumplanschen; (liquid) herumschwappen.

**sloshed** [slɒʃt] (inf) adj (drunk) blau.

**slot** [slɒt] n Schlitz m; (fig: in timetable) Termin m; (: RADIO, TV) Sendezeit f ♦ vt: **to ~ sth in** etw hineinstecken ♦ vi: **to ~ into** sich einfügen lassen in +acc.

**sloth** [sləʊθ] n (laziness) Trägheit f, Faulheit f; (ZOOL) Faultier nt.

**slot machine** n (BRIT) Münzautomat m; (for gambling) Spielautomat m.

**slot meter** (BRIT) n Münzzähler m.

**slouch** [slaʊtʃ] vi eine krumme Haltung haben; (when walking) krumm gehen ♦ n: **he's no ~** er hat etwas los (inf); **she was ~ed in a chair** sie hing auf einem Stuhl.

**Slovak** ['sləʊvæk] adj slowakisch ♦ n Slowake m, Slowakin f; (LING) Slowakisch nt; **the ~ Republic** die Slowakische Republik.

**Slovakia** [sləʊ'vækɪə] n die Slowakei.

**Slovakian** [sləʊ'vækɪən] adj, n = **Slovak**.

**Slovene** ['sləʊviːn] n Slowene m, Slowenin f; (LING) Slowenisch nt ♦ adj slowenisch.

**Slovenia** [sləʊ'viːnɪə] n Slowenien nt.

**Slovenian** [sləʊ'viːnɪən] adj, n = **Slovene**.

**slovenly** ['slʌvənlɪ] adj schlampig; (careless) nachlässig, schludrig (inf).

**slow** [sləʊ] adj langsam; (not clever) langsam, begriffsstutzig ♦ adv langsam ♦ vt (also: **~ down, ~ up**) verlangsamen; (business) verschlechtern ♦ vi (also: **~ down, ~ up**) sich verlangsamen; (business) schlechter gehen; **to be ~** (watch, clock) nachgehen; **"~"** „langsam fahren"; **at a ~ speed** langsam; **to be ~ to act** sich dat Zeit lassen; **to be ~ to decide** lange brauchen, um sich zu entscheiden; **my watch is 20 minutes ~** meine Uhr geht 20 Minuten nach; **business is ~** das Geschäft geht schlecht; **to go ~** (driver) langsam fahren; (BRIT: in industrial dispute) einen Bummelstreik machen.

**slow-acting** [sləʊ'æktɪŋ] adj mit Langzeitwirkung.

**slowly** ['sləʊlɪ] adv langsam.

**slow motion** n: **in ~** in Zeitlupe.

**slow-moving** [sləʊ'muːvɪŋ] adj langsam; (traffic) kriechend.

**slowness** ['sləʊnɪs] n Langsamkeit f.

**sludge** [slʌdʒ] n Schlamm m.

**slue** [sluː] (US) vi = **slew**.

**slug** [slʌg] n Nacktschnecke f; (US: inf: bullet) Kugel f.

**sluggish** ['slʌgɪʃ] adj träge; (engine) lahm; (COMM) flau.

**sluice** [sluːs] n Schleuse f; (channel) (Wasch)rinne f ♦ vt: **to ~ down** or **out** abspritzen.

**slum** [slʌm] n Slum m, Elendsviertel nt.

**slumber** ['slʌmbə*] n Schlaf m.

**slump** [slʌmp] *n* Rezession *f* ♦ *vi* fallen; ~ **in sales** Absatzflaute *f*; ~ **in prices** Preissturz *m*; **he was ~ed over the wheel** er war über dem Steuer zusammengesackt.

**slung** [slʌŋ] *pt, pp of* **sling**.

**slunk** [slʌŋk] *pt, pp of* **slink**.

**slur** [sləː'] *n* (*fig*): ~ **(on)** Beleidigung *f* (für) ♦ *vt* (*words*) undeutlich aussprechen; **to cast a ~ on** verunglimpfen.

**slurp** [sləːp] (*inf*) *vt, vi* schlürfen.

**slurred** [sləːd] *adj* (*speech, voice*) undeutlich.

**slush** [slʌʃ] *n* (*melted snow*) Schneematsch *m*.

**slush fund** *n* Schmiergelder *pl*, Schmiergeldfonds *m*.

**slushy** ['slʌʃɪ] *adj* matschig; (*BRIT, fig*) schmalzig.

**slut** [slʌt] (*pej*) *n* Schlampe *f*.

**sly** [slaɪ] *adj* (*smile, expression*) wissend; (*remark*) vielsagend; (*person*) schlau, gerissen; **on the ~** heimlich.

**S/M** *n abbr* (= *sadomasochism*) S/M.

**smack** [smæk] *n* Klaps *m*; (*on face*) Ohrfeige *f* ♦ *vt* (*hit*) schlagen; (: *child*) einen Klaps geben +*dat*; (: *on face*) ohrfeigen ♦ *vi*: **to ~ of** riechen nach ♦ *adv*: **it fell ~ in the middle** (*inf*) es fiel genau in die Mitte; **to ~ one's lips** schmatzen.

**smacker** ['smækə'] (*inf*) *n* (*kiss*) Schmatzer *m*.

**small** [smɔːl] *adj* klein ♦ *n*: **the ~ of the back** das Kreuz; **to get** *or* **grow ~er** (*thing*) kleiner werden; (*numbers*) zurückgehen; **to make ~er** (*amount, income*) kürzen; (*object, garment*) kleiner machen; **a ~ shopkeeper** der Inhaber eines kleinen Geschäfts; **a ~ business** ein Kleinunternehmen *nt*.

**small ads** (*BRIT*) *npl* Kleinanzeigen *pl*.

**small arms** *n* Handfeuerwaffen *pl*.

**small business** *n* Kleinunternehmen *nt*.

**small change** *n* Kleingeld *nt*.

**small fry** *npl* (*unimportant people*) kleine Fische *pl*.

**smallholder** ['smɔːlhəʊldə'] (*BRIT*) *n* Kleinbauer *m*.

**smallholding** ['smɔːlhəʊldɪŋ] (*BRIT*) *n* kleiner Landbesitz *m*.

**small hours** *npl*: **in the ~** in den frühen Morgenstunden.

**smallish** ['smɔːlɪʃ] *adj* ziemlich klein.

**small-minded** [smɔːl'maɪndɪd] *adj* engstirnig.

**smallpox** ['smɔːlpɒks] *n* Pocken *pl*.

**small print** *n*: **the ~** das Kleingedruckte.

**small-scale** ['smɔːlskeɪl] *adj* (*map, model*) in verkleinertem Maßstab; (*business, farming*) kleinangelegt.

**small talk** *n* (oberflächliche) Konversation *f*.

**small-time** ['smɔːltaɪm] *adj* (*farmer etc*) klein; **a ~ thief** ein kleiner Ganove.

**small-town** ['smɔːltaʊn] *adj* kleinstädtisch.

**smarmy** ['smɑːmɪ] (*BRIT: pej*) *adj* schmierig.

**smart** [smɑːt] *adj* (*neat*) ordentlich, gepflegt; (*fashionable*) schick, elegant; (*clever*) intelligent, clever (*inf*); (*quick*) schnell ♦ *vi*

(*sting*) brennen; (*suffer*) leiden; **the ~ set** die Schickeria (*inf*); **and look ~ (about it)!** und zwar ein bißchen plötzlich! (*inf*).

**smart card** *n* Chipkarte *f*.

**smarten up** ['smɑːtn-] *vi* sich feinmachen ♦ *vt* verschönern.

**smash** [smæʃ] *n* (*also*: ~-**up**) Unfall *m*; (*sound*) Krachen *nt*; (*song, play, film*) Superhit *m*; (*TENNIS*) Schmetterball *m* ♦ *vt* (*break*) zerbrechen; (*car etc*) kaputtfahren; (*hopes*) zerschlagen; (*SPORT: record*) haushoch schlagen ♦ *vi* (*break*) zerbrechen; (*against wall, into sth etc*) krachen.

▶**smash up** *vt* (*car*) kaputtfahren; (*room*) kurz und klein schlagen (*inf*).

**smash hit** *n* Superhit *m*.

**smashing** ['smæʃɪŋ] (*inf*) *adj* super, toll.

**smattering** ['smætərɪŋ] *n*: **a ~ of Greek** *etc* ein paar Brocken Griechisch *etc*.

**smear** [smɪə'] *n* (*trace*) verschmierter Fleck *m*; (*insult*) Verleumdung *f*; (*MED*) Abstrich *m* ♦ *vt* (*spread*) verschmieren; (*make dirty*) beschmieren; **his hands were ~ed with oil/ink** seine Hände waren mit Öl/Tinte beschmiert.

**smear campaign** *n* Verleumdungs-kampagne *f*.

**smear test** *n* Abstrich *m*.

**smell** [smel] (*pt, pp* **smelt** *or* **smelled**) *n* Geruch *m*; (*sense*) Geruchssinn *m* ♦ *vt* riechen ♦ *vi* riechen; (*pej*) stinken; (*pleasantly*) duften; **to ~ of** riechen nach.

**smelly** ['smelɪ] (*pej*) *adj* stinkend.

**smelt** [smelt] *pt, pp of* **smell** ♦ *vt* schmelzen.

**smile** [smaɪl] *n* Lächeln *nt* ♦ *vi* lächeln.

**smiling** ['smaɪlɪŋ] *adj* lächelnd.

**smirk** [sməːk] (*pej*) *n* Grinsen *nt*.

**smithy** ['smɪðɪ] *n* Schmiede *f*.

**smitten** ['smɪtn] *adj*: ~ **with** vernarrt in +*acc*.

**smock** [smɒk] *n* Kittel *m*; (*US: overall*) Overall *m*.

**smog** [smɒg] *n* Smog *m*.

**smoke** [sməʊk] *n* Rauch *m* ♦ *vi, vt* rauchen; **to have a ~** eine rauchen; **to go up in ~** in Rauch (und Flammen) aufgehen; (*fig*) sich in Rauch auflösen; **do you ~?** rauchen Sie?

**smoked** [sməʊkt] *adj* geräuchert, Räucher-; ~ **glass** Rauchglas *nt*.

**smokeless fuel** ['sməʊklɪs-] *n* rauchlose Kohle *f*.

**smokeless zone** (*BRIT*) *n* rauchfreie Zone *f*.

**smoker** ['sməʊkə'] *n* Raucher(in) *m(f)*; (*RAIL*) Raucherabteil *m*.

**smoke screen** *n* Rauchvorhang *m*; (*fig*) Deckmantel *m*.

**smoke shop** (*US*) *n* Tabakladen *m*.

**smoking** ['sməʊkɪŋ] *n* Rauchen *nt*; "**no ~**" „Rauchen verboten".

**smoking compartment**, (*US*) **smoking car** *n* Raucherabteil *nt*.

**smoking room** *n* Raucherzimmer *nt*.

**smoky** ['sməʊkɪ] *adj* verraucht; (*taste*)

rauchig.

**smolder** ['sməʊldə*] (*US*) *vi* = **smoulder**.

**smoochy** ['smu:tʃɪ] *adj* (*music, tape*) zum Schmusen.

**smooth** [smu:ð] *adj* (*lit, fig: pej*) glatt; (*flavour, whisky*) weich; (*movement*) geschmeidig; (*flight*) ruhig.

▶**smooth out** *vt* glätten; (*fig: difficulties*) aus dem Weg räumen.

▶**smooth over** *vt:* **to ~ things over** (*fig*) die Sache bereinigen.

**smoothly** ['smu:ðlɪ] *adv* reibungslos, glatt; **everything went ~** alles ging glatt über die Bühne.

**smoothness** ['smu:ðnɪs] *n* Glätte *f*; (*of flight*) Ruhe *f*.

**smother** ['smʌðə*] *vt* (*fire, person*) ersticken; (*repress*) unterdrücken.

**smoulder**, (*US*) **smolder** ['sməʊldə*] *vi* (*lit, fig*) glimmen, schwelen.

**smudge** [smʌdʒ] *n* Schmutzfleck *m* ♦ *vt* verwischen.

**smug** [smʌg] (*pej*) *adj* selbstgefällig.

**smuggle** ['smʌgl] *vt* schmuggeln; **to ~ in/out** einschmuggeln/herausschmuggeln.

**smuggler** ['smʌglə*] *n* Schmuggler(in) *m(f)*.

**smuggling** ['smʌglɪŋ] *n* Schmuggel *m*.

**smut** [smʌt] *n* (*grain of soot*) Rußflocke *f*; (*in conversation etc*) Schmutz *m*.

**smutty** ['smʌtɪ] *adj* (*fig: joke, book*) schmutzig.

**snack** [snæk] *n* Kleinigkeit *f* (zu essen); **to have a ~** eine Kleinigkeit essen.

**snack bar** *n* Imbißstube *f*.

**snag** [snæg] *n* Haken *m*, Schwierigkeit *f*.

**snail** [sneɪl] *n* Schnecke *f*.

**snake** [sneɪk] *n* Schlange *f*.

**snap** [snæp] *n* Knacken *nt*; (*photograph*) Schnappschuß *m*; (*card game*) ≈ Schnippschnapp *nt* ♦ *adj* (*decision*) plötzlich, spontan ♦ *vt* (*break*) (zer)brechen ♦ *vi* (*break*) (zer)brechen; (*rope, thread etc*) reißen; **a cold ~** ein Kälteeinbruch *m*; **his patience ~ped** ihm riß der Geduldsfaden; **his temper ~ped** er verlor die Beherrschung; **to ~ one's fingers** mit den Fingern schnipsen *or* schnalzen; **to ~ open/shut** auf-/zuschnappen.

▶**snap at** *vt fus* (*dog*) schnappen nach; (*fig: person*) anschnauzen (*inf*).

▶**snap off** *vt* (*break*) abbrechen.

▶**snap up** *vt* (*bargains*) wegschnappen.

**snap fastener** *n* Druckknopf *m*.

**snappy** ['snæpɪ] (*inf*) *adj* (*answer*) kurz und treffend; (*slogan*) zündend; **make it ~** ein bißchen dalli!; **he is a ~ dresser** er zieht sich flott an.

**snapshot** ['snæpʃɔt] *n* Schnappschuß *m*.

**snare** [snɛə*] *n* Falle *f* ♦ *vt* (*lit, fig*) fangen.

**snarl** [snɑ:l] *vi* knurren ♦ *vt:* **to get ~ed up** (*plans*) durcheinanderkommen; (*traffic*) stocken.

**snarl-up** ['snɑ:lʌp] *n* Verkehrschaos *nt*.

**snatch** [snætʃ] *n* (*of conversation*) Fetzen *m*; (*of song*) paar Takte *pl* ♦ *vt* (*grab*) greifen; (*steal*) stehlen, klauen (*inf*); (*child*) entführen; (*fig: opportunity*) ergreifen; (: *look*) werfen ♦ *vi:* **don't ~!** nicht grapschen!; **to ~ a sandwich** schnell ein Butterbrot essen; **to ~ some sleep** etwas Schlaf ergattern.

▶**snatch up** *vt* schnappen.

**snazzy** ['snæzɪ] (*inf*) *adj* flott.

**sneak** [sni:k] (*pt US also* **snuck**) *vi:* **to ~ in/out** sich einschleichen/sich hinausschleichen ♦ *vt:* **to ~ a look at sth** heimlich auf etw *acc* schielen ♦ *n* (*inf: pej*) Petze *f*.

▶**sneak up** *vi:* **to ~ up on sb** sich an jdn heranschleichen.

**sneakers** ['sni:kəz] *npl* Freizeitschuhe *pl*.

**sneaking** ['sni:kɪŋ] *adj:* **to have a ~ feeling/ suspicion that …** das ungute Gefühl/den leisen Verdacht haben, daß …

**sneaky** ['sni:kɪ] (*pej*) *adj* raffiniert.

**sneer** [snɪə*] *vi* (*smile nastily*) spöttisch lächeln; (*mock*): **to ~ at** verspotten ♦ *n* (*smile*) spöttisches Lächeln *nt*; (*remark*) spöttische Bemerkung *f*.

**sneeze** [sni:z] *n* Niesen *nt* ♦ *vi* niesen.

▶**sneeze at** *vt fus:* **it's not to be ~d at** es ist nicht zu verachten.

**snicker** ['snɪkə*] *vi see* **snigger**.

**snide** [snaɪd] (*pej*) *adj* abfällig.

**sniff** [snɪf] *n* Schniefen *nt*; (*smell*) Schnüffeln *nt* ♦ *vi* schniefen ♦ *vt* riechen, schnuppern an +*dat*; (*glue*) schnüffeln.

**sniffer dog** ['snɪfə-] *n* Spürhund *m*.

**snigger** ['snɪgə*] *vi* kichern.

**snip** [snɪp] *n* Schnitt *m*; (*BRIT: inf: bargain*) Schnäppchen *nt* ♦ *vt* schnippeln; **to ~ sth off/through sth** etw abschnippeln/ durchschnippeln.

**sniper** ['snaɪpə*] *n* Heckenschütze *m*.

**snippet** ['snɪpɪt] *n* (*of information*) Bruchstück *nt*; (*of conversation*) Fetzen *m*.

**snivelling**, (*US*) **sniveling** ['snɪvlɪŋ] *adj* heulend.

**snob** [snɔb] *n* Snob *m*.

**snobbery** ['snɔbərɪ] *n* Snobismus *m*.

**snobbish** ['snɔbɪʃ] *adj* snobistisch, versnobt (*inf*).

**snog** [snɔg] (*BRIT: inf*) *n* Knutscherei *f*; **to have a ~ with sb** mit jdm (rum)knutschen ♦ *vi* (rum)knutschen.

**snooker** ['snu:kə*] *n* Snooker *nt* ♦ *vt* (*BRIT: inf*): **to be ~ed** festsitzen.

**snoop** [snu:p] *vi:* **to ~ about** herumschnüffeln; **to ~ on sb** jdm nachschnüffeln.

**snooper** ['snu:pə*] *n* Schnüffler(in) *m(f)*.

**snooty** ['snu:tɪ] *adj* hochnäsig.

**snooze** [snu:z] *n* Schläfchen *nt* ♦ *vi* ein Schläfchen machen.

**snore** [snɔ:*] *n* Schnarchen *nt* ♦ *vi* schnarchen.

**snoring** ['snɔ:rɪŋ] *n* Schnarchen *nt*.

**snorkel** ['snɔːkl] *n* Schnorchel *m*.
**snort** [snɔːt] *n* Schnauben *nt* ♦ *vi* (*animal*) schnauben; (*person*) prusten ♦ *vt* (*inf: cocaine*) schnüffeln.
**snotty** ['snɒtɪ] (*inf*) *adj* (*handkerchief, nose*) Rotz-; (*pej: snobbish*) hochnäsig.
**snout** [snaut] *n* Schnauze *f*.
**snow** [snəu] *n* Schnee *m* ♦ *vi* schneien ♦ *vt*: **to be ~ed under with work** mit Arbeit reichlich eingedeckt sein; **it's ~ing** es schneit.
**snowball** ['snəubɔːl] *n* Schneeball *m* ♦ *vi* (*fig: problem*) eskalieren; (: *campaign*) ins Rollen kommen.
**snowbound** ['snəubaund] *adj* eingeschneit.
**snow-capped** ['snəukæpt] *adj* schneebedeckt.
**snowdrift** ['snəudrɪft] *n* Schneewehe *f*.
**snowdrop** ['snəudrɒp] *n* Schneeglöckchen *nt*.
**snowfall** ['snəufɔːl] *n* Schneefall *m*.
**snowflake** ['snəufleɪk] *n* Schneeflocke *f*.
**snowline** ['snəulaɪn] *n* Schneegrenze *f*.
**snowman** ['snəumæn] (*irreg: like* **man**) *n* Schneemann *m*.
**snowplough**, (*US*) **snowplow** ['snəuplau] *n* Schneepflug *m*.
**snowshoe** ['snəuʃuː] *n* Schneeschuh *m*.
**snowstorm** ['snəustɔːm] *n* Schneesturm *m*.
**snowy** ['snəuɪ] *adj* schneeweiß; (*covered with snow*) verschneit.
**SNP** (*BRIT*) *n abbr* (*POL*) = **Scottish National Party**.
**snub** [snʌb] *vt* (*person*) vor den Kopf stoßen ♦ *n* Abfuhr *f*.
**snub-nosed** [snʌb'nəuzd] *adj* stupsnasig.
**snuff** [snʌf] *n* Schnupftabak *m* ♦ *vt* (*also*: ~ **out**: *candle*) auslöschen.
**snuff movie** *n* Pornofilm, in dem jemand tatsächlich stirbt.
**snug** [snʌg] *adj* behaglich, gemütlich; (*well-fitting*) gutsitzend; **it's a ~ fit** es paßt genau.
**snuggle** ['snʌgl] *vi*: **to ~ up to sb** sich an jdn kuscheln; **to ~ down in bed** sich ins Bett kuscheln.
**snugly** ['snʌglɪ] *adv* behaglich; **it fits ~** (*object in pocket etc*) es paßt genau hinein; (*garment*) es paßt wie angegossen.
**SO** *n abbr* (*BANKING*) = **standing order**.

===================== *KEYWORD* ======================

**so** [səu] *adv* **1** (*thus, likewise*) so; ~ **saying he walked away** mit diesen Worten ging er weg; **if** ~ **falls ja; I didn't do it - you did** ~! ich hab es nicht getan - hast du wohl!; ~ **do I,** ~ **am I** *etc* ich auch; **it's 5 o'clock -** ~ **it is!** es ist 5 Uhr - tatsächlich!; **I hope/think** ~ ich hoffe/glaube ja; ~ **far** bis jetzt
**2** (*in comparisons etc: to such a degree*) so; ~ **big/quickly (that)** so groß/schnell(, daß); **I'm** ~ **glad to see you** ich bin ja so froh, dich zu sehen
**3**: ~ **much** so viel; **I've got** ~ **much work** ich habe so viel Arbeit; **I love you** ~ **much** ich

liebe dich so sehr; ~ **many** so viele
**4** (*phrases*): **10 or** ~ 10 oder so; ~ **long!** (*inf: goodbye*) tschüs!
♦ *conj* **1** (*expressing purpose*): ~ **as to do sth** um etw zu tun; ~ **(that)** damit
**2** (*expressing result*) also; ~ **I was right after all** ich hatte also doch recht; ~ **you see, I could have gone** wie Sie sehen, hätte ich gehen können; ~ **(what?)** na und?

**soak** [səuk] *vt* (*drench*) durchnässen; (*steep*) einweichen ♦ *vi* einweichen; **to be ~ed through** völlig durchnäßt sein.
▶**soak in** *vi* einziehen.
▶**soak up** *vt* aufsaugen.
**soaking** ['səukɪŋ] *adj* (*also*: ~ **wet**) patschnaß.
**so-and-so** ['səuənsəu] *n* (*somebody*) Soundso *no art*; **Mr/Mrs** ~ Herr/Frau Soundso; **the little** ~! (*pej*) das Biest!
**soap** [səup] *n* Seife *f*; (*TV: also*: ~ **opera**) Fernsehserie *f*, Seifenoper *f* (*inf*).
**soapbox** ['səupbɒks] *n* (*lit*) Seifenkiste *f*; (*fig: platform*) Apfelsinenkiste *f*.
**soapflakes** ['səupfleɪks] *npl* Seifenflocken *pl*.
**soap opera** *n* (*TV*) Fernsehserie *f*, Seifenoper *f* (*inf*).
**soap powder** *n* Seifenpulver *nt*.
**soapsuds** ['səupsʌds] *npl* Seifenschaum *m*.
**soapy** ['səupɪ] *adj* seifig; ~ **water** Seifenwasser *nt*.
**soar** [sɔː] *vi* aufsteigen; (*price, temperature*) hochschnellen; (*building etc*) aufragen.
**soaring** ['sɔːrɪŋ] *adj* (*prices*) in die Höhe schnellend; (*inflation*) unaufhaltsam.
**sob** [sɒb] *n* Schluchzer *m* ♦ *vi* schluchzen.
**s.o.b.** (*US: inf!*) *n abbr* (= *son of a bitch*) Scheißkerl *m*.
**sober** ['səubə] *adj* nüchtern; (*serious*) ernst; (*colour*) gedeckt; (*style*) schlicht.
▶**sober up** *vt* nüchtern machen ♦ *vi* nüchtern werden.
**sobriety** [sə'braɪətɪ] *n* Nüchternheit *f*; (*seriousness*) Ernst *m*.
**sobriquet** ['səubrɪkeɪ] *n* Spitzname *m*.
**sob story** *n* rührselige Geschichte *f*.
**Soc.** *abbr* (= *society*) Ges.
**so-called** ['səu'kɔːld] *adj* sogenannt.
**soccer** ['sɒkə] *n* Fußball *m*.
**soccer pitch** *n* Fußballplatz *m*.
**soccer player** *n* Fußballspieler(in) *m(f)*.
**sociable** ['səuʃəbl] *adj* gesellig.
**social** ['səuʃl] *adj* sozial; (*history*) Sozial-; (*structure*) Gesellschafts-; (*event, contact*) gesellschaftlich; (*person*) gesellig; (*animal*) gesellig lebend ♦ *n* (*party*) geselliger Abend *m*; ~ **life** gesellschaftliches Leben *nt*; **to have no** ~ **life** nicht mit anderen Leuten zusammenkommen.
**social class** *n* Gesellschaftsklasse *f*.
**social climber** (*pej*) *n* Emporkömmling *m*, sozialer Aufsteiger *m*.
**social club** *n* Klub *m* für geselliges

Beisammensein.

**Social Democrat** n Sozialdemokrat(in) m(f).

**social insurance** (US) n Sozialversicherung f.

**socialism** ['səʊʃəlɪzəm] n Sozialismus m.

**socialist** ['səʊʃəlɪst] adj sozialistisch ♦ n Sozialist(in) m(f).

**socialite** ['səʊʃəlaɪt] n Angehörige(r) f(m) der Schickeria.

**socialize** ['səʊʃəlaɪz] vi unter die Leute kommen; **to** ~ **with** (meet socially) gesellschaftlich verkehren mit; (chat to) sich unterhalten mit.

**socially** ['səʊʃəlɪ] adv (visit) privat; (acceptable) in Gesellschaft.

**social science** n Sozialwissenschaft f.

**social security** (BRIT) n Sozialhilfe f; **Department of Social Security** Ministerium nt für Soziales.

**social services** npl soziale Einrichtungen pl.

**social welfare** n soziales Wohl nt.

**social work** n Sozialarbeit f.

**social worker** n Sozialarbeiter(in) m(f).

**society** [sə'saɪətɪ] n Gesellschaft f; (people, their lifestyle) die Gesellschaft; (club) Verein m; (also: **high** ~) High-Society f ♦ cpd (party, lady) Gesellschafts-.

**socioeconomic** ['səʊsɪəʊiːkə'nɒmɪk] adj sozioökonomisch.

**sociological** [səʊsɪə'lɒdʒɪkl] adj soziologisch.

**sociologist** [səʊsɪ'ɒlədʒɪst] n Soziologe m, Soziologin f.

**sociology** [səʊsɪ'ɒlədʒɪ] n Soziologie f.

**sock** [sɒk] n Socke f ♦ vt (inf: hit) hauen; **to pull one's ~s up** (fig) sich am Riemen reißen.

**socket** ['sɒkɪt] n (of eye) Augenhöhle f; (of joint) Gelenkpfanne f; (BRIT: ELEC: wall socket) Steckdose f; (: : for light bulb) Fassung f.

**sod** [sɒd] n (earth) Sode f; (BRIT: inf!) Sau f (!); **the poor** ~ das arme Schwein.

▶**sod off** (BRIT: inf!) vi: **sod off!** verpiß dich!

**soda** ['səʊdə] n Soda nt; (also: ~ **water**) Soda(wasser) nt; (US: also: ~ **pop**) Brause f.

**sodden** ['sɒdn] adj durchnäßt.

**sodium** ['səʊdɪəm] n Natrium nt.

**sodium chloride** n Natriumchlorid nt, Kochsalz nt.

**sofa** ['səʊfə] n Sofa nt.

**Sofia** ['səʊfɪə] n Sofia nt.

**soft** [sɒft] adj weich; (not rough) zart; (voice, music, light, colour) gedämpft; (lenient) nachsichtig; ~ **in the head** (inf) nicht ganz richtig im Kopf.

**soft-boiled** ['sɒftbɔɪld] adj (egg) weich(gekocht).

**soft drink** n alkoholfreies Getränk nt.

**soft drugs** npl weiche Drogen pl.

**soften** ['sɒfn] vt weich machen; (effect, blow) mildern ♦ vi weich werden; (voice, expression) sanfter werden.

**softener** ['sɒfnə'] n (water softener)

Enthärtungsmittel nt; (fabric softener) Weichspüler m.

**soft fruit** (BRIT) n Beerenobst nt.

**soft furnishings** npl Raumtextilien pl.

**soft-hearted** [sɒft'hɑːtɪd] adj weichherzig.

**softly** ['sɒftlɪ] adv (gently) sanft; (quietly) leise.

**softness** ['sɒftnɪs] n Weichheit f; (gentleness) Sanftheit f.

**soft option** n Weg m des geringsten Widerstandes.

**soft sell** n weiche Verkaufstaktik f.

**soft spot** n: **to have a** ~ **for sb** eine Schwäche für jdn haben.

**soft target** n leicht verwundbares Ziel nt.

**soft toy** n Stofftier nt.

**software** ['sɒftwɛə'] n (COMPUT) Software f.

**software package** n (COMPUT) Softwarepaket nt.

**soft water** n weiches Wasser nt.

**soggy** ['sɒgɪ] adj (ground) durchweicht; (sandwiches etc) matschig.

**soil** [sɔɪl] n Erde f, Boden m ♦ vt beschmutzen.

**soiled** [sɔɪld] adj schmutzig.

**sojourn** ['sɒdʒɜːn] (form) n Aufenthalt m.

**solace** ['sɒlɪs] n Trost m.

**solar** ['səʊlə'] adj (eclipse, power station etc) Sonnen-.

**solarium** [sə'lɛərɪəm] (pl **solaria**) n Solarium nt.

**solar panel** n Sonnenkollektor m.

**solar plexus** [-'plɛksəs] n (ANAT) Solarplexus m, Magengrube f.

**solar power** n Sonnenenergie f.

**solar system** n Sonnensystem nt.

**solar wind** n Sonnenwind m.

**sold** [səʊld] pt, pp of **sell**.

**solder** ['səʊldə'] vt löten ♦ n Lötmittel nt.

**soldier** ['səʊldʒə'] n Soldat m ♦ vi: **to** ~ **on** unermüdlich weitermachen; **toy** ~ Spielzeugsoldat m.

**sold out** adj ausverkauft.

**sole** [səʊl] n Sohle f; (fish: pl inv) Seezunge f ♦ adj einzig, Allein-; (exclusive) alleinig; **the** ~ **reason** der einzige Grund.

**solely** ['səʊllɪ] adv nur, ausschließlich; **I will hold you** ~ **responsible** ich mache Sie allein dafür verantwortlich.

**solemn** ['sɒləm] adj feierlich; (person) ernst.

**sole trader** n (COMM) Einzelunternehmer m.

**solicit** [sə'lɪsɪt] vt (request) erbitten, bitten um ♦ vi (prostitute) Kunden anwerben.

**solicitor** [sə'lɪsɪtə'] (BRIT) n Rechtsanwalt m, Rechtsanwältin f.

**solid** ['sɒlɪd] adj (not hollow, pure) massiv; (not liquid) fest; (reliable) zuverlässig; (strong: structure) stabil; (: foundations) solide; (substantial: advice) gut; (: experience) solide; (unbroken) ununterbrochen ♦ n (solid object) Festkörper m; **solids** npl (food) feste Nahrung f; **to be on** ~ **ground** (fig) sich auf festem Boden befinden; **I read for 2 hours** ~ ich habe 2 Stunden ununterbrochen gelesen.

**solidarity** [sɔlɪ'dærɪtɪ] *n* Solidarität *f*.
**solid fuel** *n* fester Brennstoff *m*.
**solidify** [sə'lɪdɪfaɪ] *vi* fest werden ♦ *vt* fest werden lassen.
**solidity** [sə'lɪdɪtɪ] *n* (*of structure*) Stabilität *f*; (*of foundations*) Solidität *f*.
**solidly** ['sɔlɪdlɪ] *adv* (*built*) solide; (*in favour*) geschlossen, einmütig; **a ~ respectable family** eine durch und durch respektable Familie.
**solid-state** ['sɔlɪdsteɪt] *adj* (*ELEC: equipment*) Halbleiter-.
**soliloquy** [sə'lɪləkwɪ] *n* Monolog *m*.
**solitaire** [sɔlɪ'tɛə•] *n* (*gem*) Solitär *m*; (*game*) Patience *f*.
**solitary** ['sɔlɪtərɪ] *adj* einsam; (*single*) einzeln.
**solitary confinement** *n* Einzelhaft *f*.
**solitude** ['sɔlɪtjuːd] *n* Einsamkeit *f*; **to live in ~** einsam leben.
**solo** ['səuləu] *n* Solo *nt* ♦ *adv* (*fly*) allein; (*play, perform*) solo; **~ flight** Alleinflug *m*.
**soloist** ['səuləuɪst] *n* Solist(in) *m(f)*.
**Solomon Islands** ['sɔləmən-] *npl*: **the ~** die Salomoninseln *pl*.
**solstice** ['sɔlstɪs] *n* Sonnenwende *f*.
**soluble** ['sɔljubl] *adj* löslich.
**solution** [sə'luːʃən] *n* (*answer, liquid*) Lösung *f*; (*to crossword*) Auflösung *f*.
**solve** [sɔlv] *vt* lösen; (*mystery*) enträtseln.
**solvency** ['sɔlvənsɪ] *n* (*COMM*) Zahlungsfähigkeit *f*.
**solvent** ['sɔlvənt] *adj* (*COMM*) zahlungsfähig ♦ *n* (*CHEM*) Lösungsmittel *nt*.
**solvent abuse** *n* Lösungsmittelmißbrauch *m*.
**Som.** (*BRIT*) *abbr* (*POST: = Somerset*).
**Somali** [sə'mɑːlɪ] *adj* somalisch ♦ *n* Somalier(in) *m(f)*.
**Somalia** [sə'mɑːlɪə] *n* Somalia *nt*.
**Somaliland** *n* (*formerly*) Somaliland *nt*.
**sombre,** (*US*) **somber** ['sɔmbə•] *adj* (*dark*) dunkel, düster; (*serious*) finster.

========================= *KEYWORD*

**some** [sʌm] *adj* **1** (*a certain amount or number of*) einige; **~ tea/water/money** etwas Tee/Wasser/Geld; **~ biscuits** ein paar Plätzchen; **~ children came** einige Kinder kamen; **he asked me ~ questions** er stellte mir ein paar Fragen
**2** (*certain: in contrasts*) manche(r, s); **~ people say that …** manche Leute sagen, daß …; **~ films were excellent** einige *or* manche Filme waren ausgezeichnet
**3** (*unspecified*) irgendein(e); **~ woman was asking for you** eine Frau hat nach Ihnen gefragt; **~ day** eines Tages; **~ day next week** irgendwann nächste Woche; **that's ~ house!** das ist vielleicht ein Haus!
♦ *pron* **1** (*a certain number*) einige; **I've got ~** (*books etc*) ich habe welche
**2** (*a certain amount*) etwas; **I've got ~** (*money, milk*) ich habe welche(s); **I've read ~ of the**

**book** ich habe das Buch teilweise gelesen
♦ *adv*: **~ 10 people** etwa 10 Leute.

**somebody** ['sʌmbədɪ] *pron* = **someone**.
**someday** ['sʌmdeɪ] *adv* irgendwann.
**somehow** ['sʌmhau] *adv* irgendwie.
**someone** ['sʌmwʌn] *pron* (*irgend*) jemand; **there's ~ coming** es kommt jemand; **I saw ~ in the garden** ich habe jemanden im Garten gesehen.
**someplace** ['sʌmpleɪs] (*US*) *adv* = **somewhere**.
**somersault** ['sʌməsɔːlt] *n* Salto *m* ♦ *vi* einen Salto machen; (*vehicle*) sich überschlagen.
**something** ['sʌmθɪŋ] *pron* etwas; **~ nice** etwas Schönes; **there's ~ wrong** da stimmt etwas nicht; **would you like ~ to eat/drink?** möchten Sie etwas zu essen/trinken?
**sometime** ['sʌmtaɪm] *adv* irgendwann; **~ last month** irgendwann letzten Monat; **I'll finish it ~** ich werde es irgendwann fertigmachen.
**sometimes** ['sʌmtaɪmz] *adv* manchmal.
**somewhat** ['sʌmwɔt] *adv* etwas, ein wenig; **~ to my surprise** ziemlich zu meiner Überraschung.
**somewhere** ['sʌmwɛə•] *adv* (*be*) irgendwo; (*go*) irgendwohin; **~ (or other) in Scotland** irgendwo in Schottland; **~ else** (*be*) woanders; (*go*) woandershin.
**son** [sʌn] *n* Sohn *m*.
**sonar** ['səunɑː•] *n* Sonar(gerät) *nt*, Echolot *nt*.
**sonata** [sə'nɑːtə] *n* Sonate *f*.
**song** [sɔŋ] *n* Lied *nt*; (*of bird*) Gesang *m*.
**songbook** ['sɔŋbuk] *n* Liederbuch *nt*.
**songwriter** ['sɔŋraɪtə•] *n* Liedermacher *m*.
**sonic** ['sɔnɪk] *adj* (*speed*) Schall-; **~ boom** Überschallknall *m*.
**son-in-law** ['sʌnɪnlɔː] *n* Schwiegersohn *m*.
**sonnet** ['sɔnɪt] *n* Sonett *nt*.
**sonny** ['sʌnɪ] (*inf*) *n* Junge *m*.
**soon** [suːn] *adv* bald; (*a short time after*) bald, schnell; (*early*) früh; **~ afterwards** kurz *or* bald danach; **quite ~** ziemlich bald; **how ~ can you finish it?** bis wann haben Sie es fertig?; **how ~ can you come back?** wann können Sie frühestens wiederkommen?; **see you ~!** bis bald!; *see also* **as**.
**sooner** ['suːnə•] *adv* (*time*) früher, eher; (*preference*) lieber; **I would ~ do that** das würde ich lieber tun; **~ or later** früher oder später; **the ~ the better** je eher, desto besser; **no ~ said than done** gesagt, getan; **no ~ had we left than …** wir waren gerade gegangen, da …
**soot** [sut] *n* Ruß *m*.
**soothe** [suːð] *vt* beruhigen; (*pain*) lindern.
**soothing** ['suːðɪŋ] *adj* beruhigend; (*ointment etc*) schmerzlindernd; (*drink*) wohltuend; (*bath*) entspannend.
**SOP** *n abbr* (= *standard operating procedure*) normale Vorgehensweise *f*.
**sop** [sɔp] *n*: **that's only a ~** das soll nur zur

Beschwichtigung dienen.

**sophisticated** [səˈfɪstɪkeɪtɪd] adj (woman, lifestyle) kultiviert; (audience) anspruchsvoll; (machinery) hochentwickelt; (arguments) differenziert.

**sophistication** [səfɪstɪˈkeɪʃən] n (of person) Kultiviertheit f; (of machine) hoher Entwicklungsstand m; (of argument etc) Differenziertheit f.

**sophomore** [ˈsɔfəmɔːˈ] (US) n Student(in) im 2. Studienjahr.

**soporific** [sɔpəˈrɪfɪk] adj einschläfernd ♦ n Schlafmittel nt.

**sopping** [ˈsɔpɪŋ] adj: ~ **(wet)** völlig durchnäßt.

**soppy** [ˈsɔpɪ] (pej) adj (person) sentimental; (film) schmalzig.

**soprano** [səˈprɑːnəu] n Sopranist(in) m(f).

**sorbet** [ˈsɔːbeɪ] n Sorbet nt or m, Fruchteis nt.

**sorcerer** [ˈsɔːsərəˈ] n Hexenmeister m.

**sordid** [ˈsɔːdɪd] adj (dirty) verkommen; (wretched) elend.

**sore** [sɔːˈ] adj wund; (esp US: offended) verärgert, sauer (inf) ♦ n wunde Stelle f; **to have a ~ throat** Halsschmerzen haben; **it's a ~ point** (fig) es ist ein wunder Punkt.

**sorely** [ˈsɔːlɪ] adv: **I am ~ tempted (to)** ich bin sehr in Versuchung(, zu).

**soreness** [ˈsɔːnɪs] n (pain) Schmerz m.

**sorrel** [ˈsɔrəl] n (BOT) (großer) Sauerampfer m.

**sorrow** [ˈsɔrəu] n Trauer f; **sorrows** npl (troubles) Sorgen und Nöte pl.

**sorrowful** [ˈsɔrəuful] adj traurig.

**sorry** [ˈsɔrɪ] adj traurig; (excuse) faul; (sight) jämmerlich; ~**!** Entschuldigung!, Verzeihung!; ~**?** wie bitte?; **I feel ~ for him** er tut mir leid; **I'm ~ to hear that ...** es tut mir leid, daß ...; **I'm ~ about ...** es tut mir leid wegen ...

**sort** [sɔːt] n Sorte f; (make: of car etc) Marke f ♦ vt (also: ~ **out**) sortieren; (: problems) ins reine bringen; (COMPUT) sortieren; **all ~s of reasons** alle möglichen Gründe; **what ~ do you want?** welche Sorte möchten Sie?; **what ~ of car?** was für ein Auto?; **I'll do nothing of the ~!** das kommt überhaupt nicht in Frage!; **it's ~ of awkward** (inf) es ist irgendwie schwierig; **to ~ sth out** etw in Ordnung bringen.

**sort code** n Bankleitzahl f.

**sortie** [ˈsɔːtɪ] n (MIL) Ausfall m; (fig) Ausflug m.

**sorting office** [ˈsɔːtɪŋ-] n Postverteilstelle f.

**SOS** n abbr (= save our souls) SOS nt.

**so-so** [ˈsəusəu] adv, adj so lala.

**soufflé** [ˈsuːfleɪ] n Soufflé nt.

**sought** [sɔːt] pt, pp of **seek**.

**sought-after** [ˈsɔːtɑːftəˈ] adj begehrt, gesucht; **a much ~ item** ein vielbegehrtes Stück.

**soul** [səul] n Seele f; (MUS) Soul m; **the poor ~ had nowhere to sleep** der Ärmste hatte

keine Unterkunft; **I didn't see a ~** ich habe keine Menschenseele gesehen.

**soul-destroying** [ˈsəuldɪstrɔɪŋ] adj geisttötend.

**soulful** [ˈsəulful] adj (eyes) seelenvoll; (music) gefühlvoll.

**soulless** [ˈsəullɪs] adj (place) seelenlos; (job) eintönig.

**soul mate** n Seelenfreund(in) m(f).

**soul-searching** [ˈsəulsɜːtʃɪŋ] n: **after much ~** nach reiflicher Überlegung.

**sound** [saund] adj (healthy) gesund; (safe, secure) sicher; (not damaged) einwandfrei; (reliable) solide; (thorough) gründlich; (sensible, valid) vernünftig ♦ adv: **to be ~ asleep** tief und fest schlafen ♦ n Geräusch nt; (MUS) Klang m; (on TV etc) Ton m; (GEOG) Meerenge f, Sund m ♦ vt: **to ~ the alarm** Alarm schlagen ♦ vi (alarm, horn) ertönen; (fig: seem) sich anhören, klingen; **to be of ~ mind** bei klarem Verstand sein; **I don't like the ~ of it** das klingt gar nicht gut; **to ~ one's horn** (AUT) hupen; **to ~ like** sich anhören wie; **that ~s like them arriving** das hört sich so an, als ob sie ankommen; **it ~s as if ...** es klingt or es hört sich so an, als ob ...

▶**sound off** (inf) vi: **to ~ off (about)** sich auslassen (über +acc).

▶**sound out** vt (person) aushorchen; (opinion) herausbekommen.

**sound barrier** n Schallmauer f.

**sound bite** n prägnantes Zitat nt.

**sound effects** npl Toneffekte pl.

**sound engineer** n Toningenieur(in) m(f).

**sounding** [ˈsaundɪŋ] n (NAUT) Loten nt, Peilung f.

**sounding board** n (MUS) Resonanzboden m; (fig): **to use sb as a ~ for one's ideas** seine Ideen an jdm testen.

**soundly** [ˈsaundlɪ] adv (sleep) tief und fest; (beat) tüchtig.

**soundproof** [ˈsaundpruːf] adj schalldicht ♦ vt schalldicht machen.

**sound system** n Verstärkersystem nt.

**soundtrack** [ˈsaundtræk] n Filmmusik f.

**sound wave** n Schallwelle f.

**soup** [suːp] n Suppe f; **to be in the ~** (fig) in der Tinte sitzen.

**soup course** n Vorsuppe f.

**soup kitchen** n Suppenküche f.

**soup plate** n Suppenteller m.

**soupspoon** [ˈsuːpspuːn] n Suppenlöffel m.

**sour** [ˈsauəˈ] adj sauer; (fig: bad-tempered) säuerlich; **to go** or **turn ~** (milk, wine) sauer werden; (fig: relationship) sich trüben; **it's ~ grapes** (fig) die Trauben hängen ihm zu hoch.

**source** [sɔːs] n Quelle f; (fig: of problem, anxiety) Ursache f; **I have it from a reliable ~ that ...** ich habe es aus sicherer Quelle, daß ...

**south** [sauθ] n Süden m ♦ adj südlich, Süd-

♦ *adv* nach Süden; **(to the)** ~ **of** im Süden *or* südlich von; **to travel** ~ nach Süden fahren; **the S**~ **of France** Südfrankreich *nt*.

**South Africa** *n* Südafrika *nt*.

**South African** *adj* südafrikanisch ♦ *n* Südafrikaner(in) *m(f)*.

**South America** *n* Südamerika *nt*.

**South American** *adj* südamerikanisch ♦ *n* Südamerikaner(in) *m(f)*.

**southbound** ['sauθbaund] *adj* in Richtung Süden; (*carriageway*) Richtung Süden.

**south-east** [sauθ'i:st] *n* Südosten *m*.

**South-East Asia** *n* Südostasien *nt*.

**southerly** ['sʌðəlɪ] *adj* südlich; (*wind*) aus südlicher Richtung.

**southern** ['sʌðən] *adj* südlich, Süd-; **the** ~ **hemisphere** die südliche Halbkugel *or* Hemisphäre.

**South Korea** *n* Südkorea *nt*.

**South Pole** *n* Südpol *m*.

**South Sea Islands** *npl* Südseeinseln *pl*.

**South Seas** *npl* Südsee *f*.

**southward(s)** ['sauθwəd(z)] *adv* nach Süden, in Richtung Süden.

**south-west** [sauθ'west] *n* Südwesten *m*.

**souvenir** [su:və'nɪə*] *n* Andenken *nt*, Souvenir *nt*.

**sovereign** ['sɔvrɪn] *n* Herrscher(in) *m(f)*.

**sovereignty** ['sɔvrɪntɪ] *n* Oberhoheit *f*, Souveränität *f*.

**soviet** ['səuvɪət] (*formerly*) *adj* sowjetisch ♦ *n* Sowjetbürger(in) *m(f)*; **the S~ Union** die Sowjetunion *f*.

**sow**[1] [sau] *n* Sau *f*.

**sow**[2] [səu] (*pt* **sowed**, *pp* **sown**) *vt* (*lit, fig*) säen.

**soya** ['sɔɪə], (*US*) **soy** [sɔɪ] *n*: ~ **bean** Sojabohne *f*; ~ **sauce** Sojasoße *f*.

**sozzled** ['sɔzld] (*BRIT: inf*) *adj* besoffen.

**spa** [spa:] *n* (*town*) Heilbad *nt*; (*US: also:* **health** ~) Fitneßzentrum *nt*.

**space** [speɪs] *n* Platz *m*, Raum *m*; (*gap*) Lücke *f*; (*beyond Earth*) der Weltraum; (*interval, period*) Zeitraum *m* ♦ *cpd* Raum- ♦ *vt* (*also:* ~ **out**) verteilen; **to clear a** ~ **for sth** für etw Platz schaffen; **in a confined** ~ auf engem Raum; **in a short** ~ **of time** in kurzer Zeit; **(with)in the** ~ **of an hour** innerhalb einer Stunde.

**space bar** *n* (*on keyboard*) Leertaste *f*.

**spacecraft** ['speɪskrɑ:ft] *n* Raumfahrzeug *nt*.

**spaceman** ['speɪsmæn] (*irreg: like* **man**) *n* Raumfahrer *m*.

**spaceship** ['speɪsʃɪp] *n* Raumschiff *nt*.

**space shuttle** *n* Raumtransporter *m*.

**spacesuit** ['speɪssu:t] *n* Raumanzug *m*.

**spacewoman** ['speɪswumən] (*irreg: like* **woman**) *n* Raumfahrerin *f*.

**spacing** ['speɪsɪŋ] *n* Abstand *m*; **single/double** ~ einfacher/doppelter Zeilenabstand.

**spacious** ['speɪʃəs] *adj* geräumig.

**spade** [speɪd] *n* Spaten *m*; (*child's*) Schaufel *f*;

**spades** *npl* (*CARDS*) Pik *nt*.

**spadework** ['speɪdwɜ:k] *n* (*fig*) Vorarbeit *f*.

**spaghetti** [spə'getɪ] *n* Spaghetti *pl*.

**Spain** [speɪn] *n* Spanien *nt*.

**span** [spæn] *n* (*of bird, plane, arch*) Spannweite *f*; (*in time*) Zeitspanne *f* ♦ *vt* überspannen; (*fig: time*) sich erstrecken über +*acc*.

**Spaniard** ['spænjəd] *n* Spanier(in) *m(f)*.

**spaniel** ['spænjəl] *n* Spaniel *m*.

**Spanish** ['spænɪʃ] *adj* spanisch ♦ *n* (*LING*) Spanisch *nt*; **the Spanish** *npl* die Spanier *pl*; ~ **omelette** *Omelett mit Paprikaschoten, Zwiebeln, Tomaten etc*.

**spank** [spæŋk] *vt*: **to** ~ **sb's bottom** jdm den Hintern versohlen (*inf*).

**spanner** ['spænə*] (*BRIT*) *n* Schraubenschlüssel *m*.

**spar** [spɑ:*] *n* (*NAUT*) Sparren *m* ♦ *vi* (*BOXING*) ein Sparring *nt* machen.

**spare** [speə*] *adj* (*free*) frei; (*extra: part, fuse etc*) Ersatz- ♦ *n* = **spare part** ♦ *vt* (*save: trouble etc*) (er)sparen; (*make available*) erübrigen; (*afford to give*) (übrig) haben; (*refrain from hurting*) verschonen; **these 2 are going** ~ diese beiden sind noch übrig; **to** ~ (*surplus*) übrig; **to** ~ **no expense** keine Kosten scheuen, an nichts sparen; **can you** ~ **the time?** haben Sie Zeit?; **I've a few minutes to** ~ ich habe ein paar Minuten Zeit; **there is no time to** ~ es ist keine Zeit; ~ **me the details** verschone mich mit den Einzelheiten.

**spare part** *n* Ersatzteil *nt*.

**spare room** *n* Gästezimmer *nt*.

**spare time** *n* Freizeit *f*.

**spare tyre** *n* Reservereifen *m*.

**spare wheel** *n* Reserverad *nt*.

**sparing** ['speərɪŋ] *adj*: **to be** ~ **with** sparsam umgehen mit.

**sparingly** ['speərɪŋlɪ] *adv* sparsam.

**spark** [spɑ:k] *n* (*lit, fig*) Funke *m*.

**spark(ing) plug** ['spɑ:k(ɪŋ)-] *n* Zündkerze *f*.

**sparkle** ['spɑ:kl] *n* Funkeln *nt*, Glitzern *nt* ♦ *vi* funkeln, glitzern.

**sparkler** ['spɑ:klə*] *n* (*firework*) Wunderkerze *f*.

**sparkling** ['spɑ:klɪŋ] *adj* (*water*) mit Kohlensäure; (*conversation*) vor Geist sprühend; (*performance*) glänzend; ~ **wine** Schaumwein *m*.

**sparring partner** ['spɑ:rɪŋ-] *n* (*also fig*) Sparringspartner *m*.

**sparrow** ['spærəu] *n* Spatz *m*.

**sparse** [spɑ:s] *adj* spärlich; (*population*) dünn.

**spartan** ['spɑ:tən] *adj* (*fig*) spartanisch.

**spasm** ['spæzəm] *n* (*MED*) Krampf *m*; (*fig: of anger etc*) Anfall *m*.

**spasmodic** [spæz'mɔdɪk] *adj* (*fig*) sporadisch.

**spastic** ['spæstɪk] (*old*) *n* Spastiker(in) *m(f)* ♦ *adj* spastisch.

**spat** [spæt] *pt, pp of* **spit** ♦ *n* (*US: quarrel*) Krach *m*.

**spate** [speɪt] n (fig): **a ~ of** eine Flut von; **to be in full ~** (river) Hochwasser führen.

**spatial** ['speɪʃl] adj räumlich.

**spatter** ['spætə*] vt (liquid) verspritzen; (surface) bespritzen ♦ vi spritzen.

**spatula** ['spætjulə] n (CULIN) Spachtel m; (MED) Spatel m.

**spawn** [spɔːn] vi laichen ♦ vt hervorbringen, erzeugen ♦ n Laich m.

**SPCA** (US) n abbr (= Society for the Prevention of Cruelty to Animals) Tierschutzverein m.

**SPCC** (US) n abbr (= Society for the Prevention of Cruelty to Children) Kinderschutzbund m.

**speak** [spiːk] (pt **spoke**, pp **spoken**) vt (say) sagen; (language) sprechen ♦ vi sprechen, reden; (make a speech) sprechen; **to ~ one's mind** seine Meinung sagen; **to ~ to sb/of or about sth** mit jdm/über etw acc sprechen or reden; **~ up!** sprich lauter!; **to ~ at a conference** bei einer Tagung einen Vortrag halten; **to ~ in a debate** in einer Debatte sprechen; **he has no money to ~ of** er hat so gut wie kein Geld; **so to ~** sozusagen.
► **speak for** vt fus: **to ~ for sb** (on behalf of) in jds Namen dat or für jdn sprechen; **that picture is already spoken for** (in shop) das Bild ist schon verkauft or vergeben; **~ for yourself!** das meinst auch nur du!

**speaker** ['spiːkə*] n (in public) Redner(in) m(f); (also: **loudspeaker**) Lautsprecher m; (POL): **the S~** (BRIT, US) der Sprecher, die Sprecherin; **are you a Welsh ~?** sprechen Sie Walisisch?

**speaking** ['spiːkɪŋ] adj sprechend; **Italian-~ people** Italienischsprechende pl; **to be on ~ terms** miteinander reden or sprechen; **~ clock** telefonische Zeitansage.

**spear** [spɪə*] n Speer m ♦ vt aufspießen.

**spearhead** ['spɪəhɛd] vt (MIL, fig) anführen.

**spearmint** ['spɪəmɪnt] n grüne Minze f.

**spec** [spɛk] (inf) n: **on ~** auf Verdacht, auf gut Glück; **to buy/go on ~** auf gut Glück kaufen/hingehen.

**spec.** n abbr (TECH) = **specification**.

**special** ['spɛʃl] adj besondere(r, s); (service, performance, adviser, permission, school) Sonder- ♦ n (train) Sonderzug m; **take ~ care** paß besonders gut auf; **nothing ~** nichts Besonderes; **today's ~** (at restaurant) Tagesgericht nt.

**special agent** n Agent(in) m(f).

**special correspondent** n Sonderbericht-erstatter(in) m(f).

**special delivery** n (POST): **by ~** durch Eilzustellung.

**special effects** npl Spezialeffekte pl.

**specialist** ['spɛʃəlɪst] n Spezialist(in) m(f); (MED) Facharzt m, Fachärztin f; **heart ~** Facharzt m/Fachärztin f für Herzkrankheiten.

**speciality** [spɛʃɪ'ælɪtɪ] n Spezialität f; (study) Spezialgebiet nt.

**specialize** ['spɛʃəlaɪz] vi: **to ~ (in)** sich spezialisieren (auf +acc).

**specially** ['spɛʃəlɪ] adv besonders, extra.

**special offer** n Sonderangebot nt.

**specialty** ['spɛʃəltɪ] (esp US) = **speciality**.

**species** ['spiːʃiːz] n inv Art f.

**specific** [spə'sɪfɪk] adj (fixed) bestimmt; (exact) genau; **to be ~ to** eigentümlich sein für.

**specifically** [spə'sɪfɪklɪ] adv (specially) speziell; (exactly) genau; **more ~** und zwar.

**specification** [spɛsɪfɪ'keɪʃən] n genaue Angabe f; (requirement) Bedingung f; **specifications** npl (TECH) technische Daten pl.

**specify** ['spɛsɪfaɪ] vt angeben; **unless otherwise specified** wenn nicht anders angegeben.

**specimen** ['spɛsɪmən] n Exemplar nt; (MED) Probe f.

**specimen copy** n Belegexemplar nt, Probeexemplar nt.

**specimen signature** n Unterschriftsprobe f.

**speck** [spɛk] n Fleckchen nt; (of dust) Körnchen nt.

**speckled** ['spɛkld] adj gesprenkelt.

**specs** [spɛks] (inf) npl Brille f.

**spectacle** ['spɛktəkl] n (scene) Schauspiel nt; (sight) Anblick m; (grand event) Spektakel nt; **spectacles** npl (glasses) Brille f.

**spectacle case** (BRIT) n Brillenetui nt.

**spectacular** [spɛk'tækjulə*] adj sensationell; (success) spektakulär ♦ n (THEAT etc) Show f.

**spectator** [spɛk'teɪtə*] n Zuschauer(in) m(f); **~ sport** Publikumssport m.

**spectra** ['spɛktrə] npl of **spectrum**.

**spectre**, (US) **specter** ['spɛktə*] n Gespenst nt; (fig) (Schreck)gespenst nt.

**spectrum** ['spɛktrəm] (pl **spectra**) n (lit, fig) Spektrum nt.

**speculate** ['spɛkjuleɪt] vi (FIN) spekulieren; **to ~ about** spekulieren or Vermutungen anstellen über +acc.

**speculation** [spɛkju'leɪʃən] n Spekulation f.

**speculative** ['spɛkjulətɪv] adj spekulativ.

**speculator** ['spɛkjuleɪtə*] n Spekulant(in) m(f).

**sped** [spɛd] pt, pp of **speed**.

**speech** [spiːtʃ] n Sprache f; (manner of speaking) Sprechweise f; (enunciation) (Aus)sprache f; (formal talk: THEAT) Rede f.

**speech day** (BRIT) n (SCOL) ≈ Schulfeier f.

**speech impediment** n Sprachfehler m.

**speechless** ['spiːtʃlɪs] adj sprachlos.

**speech therapist** n Logopäde m, Logopädin f, Sprachtherapeut(in) m(f).

**speech therapy** n Logopädie f, Sprachtherapie f.

**speed** [spiːd] (pt, pp **sped**) n Geschwindigkeit f, Schnelligkeit f ♦ vi (exceed speed limit) zu schnell fahren; **to ~ along** dahinsausen; **to ~ by** (car etc) vorbeischießen; (years) verfliegen; **at ~** (BRIT) mit hoher Geschwindigkeit; **at full** or **top ~** mit

Höchstgeschwindigkeit; **at a ~ of 70km/h** mit (einer Geschwindigkeit *or* einem Tempo von) 70 km/h; **shorthand/typing ~s** Silben/Anschläge pro Minute; **a five- ~ gearbox** ein Fünfganggetriebe *nt*.

▶**speed up** (*pt, pp* **speeded up**) *vi* beschleunigen; (*fig*) sich beschleunigen ♦ *vt* beschleunigen.

**speedboat** ['spiːdbəut] *n* Rennboot *nt*.

**speedily** ['spiːdɪlɪ] *adv* schnell.

**speeding** ['spiːdɪŋ] *n* Geschwindigkeits-überschreitung *f*.

**speed limit** *n* Tempolimit *nt*, Geschwindigkeitsbegrenzung *f*.

**speedometer** [spɪ'dɔmɪtə*] *n* Tachometer *m*.

**speed trap** *n* Radarfalle *f*.

**speedway** ['spiːdweɪ] *n* (*also: ~ racing*) Speedwayrennen *nt*.

**speedy** ['spiːdɪ] *adj* schnell; (*reply, settlement*) prompt.

**speleologist** [spɛlɪ'ɔlədʒɪst] *n* Höhlenkundler(in) *m(f)*.

**spell** [spɛl] (*pt, pp* **spelt** (*BRIT*) *or* **spelled**) *n* (*also: magic ~*) Zauber *m*; (*incantation*) Zauberspruch *m*; (*period of time*) Zeit *f*, Weile *f* ♦ *vt* schreiben; (*also: ~ out: aloud*) buchstabieren; (*signify*) bedeuten; **to cast a ~ on sb** jdn verzaubern; **cold ~** Kältewelle *f*; **how do you ~ your name?** wie schreibt sich Ihr Name?; **can you ~ it for me?** können Sie das bitte buchstabieren?; **he can't ~** er kann keine Rechtschreibung.

**spellbound** ['spɛlbaund] *adj* gebannt.

**spelling** ['spɛlɪŋ] *n* Schreibweise *f*; (*ability*) Rechtschreibung *f*; **~ mistake** Rechtschreibfehler *m*.

**spelt** [spɛlt] *pt, pp of* **spell**.

**spend** [spɛnd] (*pt, pp* **spent**) *vt* (*money*) ausgeben; (*time, life*) verbringen; **to ~ time/money/effort on sth** Zeit/Geld/Mühe für etw aufbringen.

**spending** ['spɛndɪŋ] *n* Ausgaben *pl*; **government ~** öffentliche Ausgaben *pl*.

**spending money** *n* Taschengeld *nt*.

**spending power** *n* Kaufkraft *f*.

**spendthrift** ['spɛndθrɪft] *n* Verschwender(in) *m(f)*.

**spent** [spɛnt] *pt, pp of* **spend** ♦ *adj* (*patience*) erschöpft; (*cartridge, bullets*) verbraucht; (*match*) abgebrannt.

**sperm** [spəːm] *n* Samenzelle *f*, Spermium *nt*.

**sperm bank** *n* Samenbank *f*.

**sperm whale** *n* Pottwal *m*.

**spew** [spjuː] *vt* (*also: ~ up*) erbrechen; (*fig*) ausspucken.

**sphere** [sfɪə*] *n* Kugel *f*; (*area*) Gebiet *nt*, Bereich *m*.

**spherical** ['sfɛrɪkl] *adj* kugelförmig.

**sphinx** [sfɪŋks] *n* Sphinx *f*.

**spice** [spaɪs] *n* Gewürz *nt* ♦ *vt* würzen.

**spick-and-span** ['spɪkən'spæn] *adj* blitzsauber.

**spicy** ['spaɪsɪ] *adj* stark gewürzt.

**spider** ['spaɪdə*] *n* Spinne *f*; **~'s web** Spinnengewebe *nt*, Spinnennetz *nt*.

**spidery** ['spaɪdərɪ] *adj* (*handwriting*) krakelig.

**spiel** [spiːl] (*inf*) *n* Sermon *m*.

**spike** [spaɪk] *n* (*point*) Spitze *f*; (*BOT*) Ähre *f*; (*ELEC*) Spannungsspitze *f*; **spikes** *npl* (*SPORT*) Spikes *pl*.

**spike heel** (*US*) *n* Pfennigabsatz *m*.

**spiky** ['spaɪkɪ] *adj* stachelig; (*branch*) dornig.

**spill** [spɪl] (*pt, pp* **spilt** *or* **spilled**) *vt* verschütten ♦ *vi* verschüttet werden; **to ~ the beans** (*inf, fig*) alles ausplaudern.

▶**spill out** *vi* (*people*) herausströmen.

▶**spill over** *vi* überlaufen; (*fig: spread*) sich ausbreiten; **to ~ over into** sich auswirken auf +*acc*.

**spillage** ['spɪlɪdʒ] *n* (*act*) Verschütten *nt*; (*quantity*) verschüttete Menge *f*.

**spin** [spɪn] (*pt* **spun, span**, *pp* **spun**) *n* (*trip*) Spritztour *f*; (*revolution*) Drehung *f*; (*AVIAT*) Trudeln *nt*; (*on ball*) Drall *m* ♦ *vt* (*wool etc*) spinnen; (*ball, coin*) (hoch)werfen; (*wheel*) drehen; (*BRIT: also: ~-dry*) schleudern ♦ *vi* (*make thread*) spinnen; (*person*) sich drehen; (*car etc*) schleudern; **to ~ a yarn** Seemannsgarn spinnen; **to ~ a coin** (*BRIT*) eine Münze werfen; **my head is ~ning** mir dreht sich alles.

▶**spin out** *vt* (*talk*) ausspinnen; (*job, holiday*) in die Länge ziehen; (*money*) strecken.

**spina bifida** ['spaɪnə'bɪfɪdə] *n* offene Wirbelsäule *f*, Spina bifida *f*.

**spinach** ['spɪnɪtʃ] *n* Spinat *m*.

**spinal** ['spaɪnl] *adj* (*injury etc*) Rückgrat-.

**spinal column** *n* Wirbelsäule *f*.

**spinal cord** *n* Rückenmark *nt*.

**spindly** ['spɪndlɪ] *adj* spindeldürr.

**spin doctor** *n* PR-Fachmann *m*, PR-Fachfrau *f*.

**spin-dry** ['spɪn'draɪ] *vt* schleudern.

**spin-dryer** [spɪn'draɪə*] (*BRIT*) *n* (Wäsche)schleuder *f*.

**spine** [spaɪn] *n* (*ANAT*) Rückgrat *nt*; (*thorn*) Stachel *m*.

**spine-chilling** ['spaɪntʃɪlɪŋ] *adj* schaurig, gruselig.

**spineless** ['spaɪnlɪs] *adj* (*fig*) rückgratlos.

**spinner** ['spɪnə*] *n* (*of thread*) Spinner(in) *m(f)*.

**spinning** ['spɪnɪŋ] *n* (*art*) Spinnen *nt*.

**spinning top** *n* Kreisel *m*.

**spinning wheel** *n* Spinnrad *nt*.

**spin-off** ['spɪnɔf] *n* (*fig*) Nebenprodukt *nt*.

**spinster** ['spɪnstə*] *n* unverheiratete Frau; (*pej*) alte Jungfer.

**spiral** ['spaɪərl] *n* Spirale *f* ♦ *vi* (*fig: prices etc*) in die Höhe klettern; **the inflationary ~** die Inflationsspirale.

**spiral staircase** *n* Wendeltreppe *f*.

**spire** ['spaɪə*] *n* Turmspitze *f*.

**spirit** ['spɪrɪt] *n* Geist *m*; (*soul*) Seele *f*; (*energy*) Elan *m*, Schwung *m*; (*courage*) Mut *m*; (*sense*)

Geist m, Sinn m; (*frame of mind*) Stimmung f; **spirits** npl (*drink*) Spirituosen pl; **in good ~s** guter Laune; **community ~** Gemeinschaftssinn m.

**spirited** ['spɪrɪtɪd] adj (*resistance, defence*) mutig; (*performance*) lebendig.

**spirit level** n Wasserwaage f.

**spiritual** ['spɪrɪtjuəl] adj geistig, seelisch; (*religious*) geistlich ♦ n (*also:* **Negro ~**) Spiritual nt.

**spiritualism** ['spɪrɪtjuəlɪzəm] n Spiritismus m.

**spit** [spɪt] (*pt, pp* **spat**) n (*for roasting*) Spieß m; (*saliva*) Spucke f ♦ vi spucken; (*fire*) Funken sprühen; (*cooking*) spritzen; (*inf: rain*) tröpfeln.

**spite** [spaɪt] n Boshaftigkeit f ♦ vt ärgern; **in ~ of** trotz +*gen*.

**spiteful** ['spaɪtful] adj boshaft, gemein.

**spitroast** ['spɪtrəust] n Spießbraten m.

**spitting** ['spɪtɪŋ] n: "**~ prohibited**" „Spucken verboten" ♦ adj: **to be the ~ image of sb** jdm wie aus dem Gesicht geschnitten sein.

**spittle** ['spɪtl] n Speichel m, Spucke f.

**spiv** [spɪv] (*BRIT: inf: pej*) n schmieriger Typ m.

**splash** [splæʃ] n (*sound*) Platschen nt; (*of colour*) Tupfer m ♦ excl platsch! ♦ vt bespritzen ♦ vi (*also:* **~ about**) herumplanschen; (*water, rain*) spritzen; **to ~ paint on the floor** den Fußboden mit Farbe bespritzen.

**splashdown** ['splæʃdaun] n (*SPACE*) Wasserung f.

**splayfooted** ['spleɪfutɪd] adj mit nach außen gestellten Füßen.

**spleen** [spliːn] n Milz f.

**splendid** ['splɛndɪd] adj hervorragend, ausgezeichnet; (*impressive*) prächtig.

**splendour,** (*US*) **splendor** ['splɛndə*] n Pracht f; **splendours** npl Pracht f.

**splice** [splaɪs] vt spleißen, kleben.

**splint** [splɪnt] n Schiene f.

**splinter** ['splɪntə*] n Splitter m ♦ vi (zer)splittern.

**splinter group** n Splittergruppe f.

**split** [splɪt] (*pt, pp* **split**) n (*tear*) Riß m; (*fig: division*) Aufteilung f; (: *difference*) Kluft f; (*POL*) Spaltung f ♦ vt (*divide*) aufteilen; (*party*) spalten; (*share equally*) teilen ♦ vi (*divide*) sich aufteilen; (*tear*) reißen; **to do the ~s** (einen) Spagat machen; **let's ~ the difference** teilen wir uns die Differenz.

▶**split up** vi sich trennen; (*meeting*) sich auflösen.

**split-level** ['splɪtlɛvl] adj mit versetzten Geschossen.

**split peas** npl getrocknete (halbe) Erbsen pl.

**split personality** n gespaltene Persönlichkeit f.

**split second** n Bruchteil m einer Sekunde.

**splitting** ['splɪtɪŋ] adj: **a ~ headache** rasende Kopfschmerzen pl.

**splutter** ['splʌtə*] vi (*engine etc*) stottern;

(*person*) prusten.

**spoil** [spɔɪl] (*pt, pp* **spoilt** *or* **spoiled**) vt verderben; (*child*) verwöhnen; (*ballot paper, vote*) ungültig machen ♦ vi: **to be ~ing for a fight** Streit suchen.

**spoils** [spɔɪlz] npl Beute f; (*fig*) Gewinn m.

**spoilsport** ['spɔɪlspɔːt] (*pej*) n Spielverderber m.

**spoilt** [spɔɪlt] pt, pp of **spoil** ♦ adj (*child*) verwöhnt; (*ballot paper*) ungültig.

**spoke** [spəuk] pt of **speak** ♦ n Speiche f.

**spoken** ['spəukn] pp of **speak**.

**spokesman** ['spəuksmən] (*irreg: like* **man**) n Sprecher m.

**spokesperson** ['spəukspəːsn] n Sprecher(in) m(f).

**spokeswoman** ['spəukswumən] (*irreg: like* **woman**) n Sprecherin f.

**sponge** [spʌndʒ] n Schwamm m; (*also:* **~ cake**) Biskuit(kuchen) m ♦ vt mit einem Schwamm waschen ♦ vi: **to ~ off** or **on sb** jdm auf der Tasche liegen.

**sponge bag** (*BRIT*) n Waschbeutel m, Kulturbeutel m.

**sponger** ['spʌndʒə*] (*pej*) n Schmarotzer m.

**spongy** ['spʌndʒɪ] adj schwammig.

**sponsor** ['spɔnsə*] n Sponsor(in) m(f), Geldgeber(in) m(f); (*BRIT: for charitable event*) Sponsor(in) m(f); (*for application, bill etc*) Befürworter(in) m(f) ♦ vt sponsern, finanziell unterstützen; (*fund-raiser*) sponsern; (*applicant*) unterstützen; (*proposal, bill etc*) befürworten; **I ~ed him at 3p a mile** (*in fund-raising race*) ich habe mich verpflichtet, ihm 3 Pence pro Meile zu geben.

**sponsorship** ['spɔnsəʃɪp] n finanzielle Unterstützung f.

**spontaneity** [spɔntə'neɪɪtɪ] n Spontaneität f.

**spontaneous** [spɔn'teɪnɪəs] adj spontan; **~ combustion** Selbstentzündung f.

**spoof** [spuːf] n (*parody*) Parodie f; (*hoax*) Ulk m.

**spooky** ['spuːkɪ] (*inf*) adj gruselig.

**spool** [spuːl] n Spule f.

**spoon** [spuːn] n Löffel m.

**spoon-feed** ['spuːnfiːd] vt (mit dem Löffel) füttern; (*fig*) gängeln.

**spoonful** ['spuːnful] n Löffel m.

**sporadic** [spə'rædɪk] adj sporadisch, vereinzelt.

**sport** [spɔːt] n Sport m; (*type*) Sportart f; (*also:* **good ~**: *person*) feiner Kerl m ♦ vt (*wear*) tragen; **indoor ~s** Hallensport m; **outdoor ~s** Sport m im Freien.

**sporting** ['spɔːtɪŋ] adj (*event etc*) Sport-; (*generous*) großzügig; **to give sb a ~ chance** jdm eine faire Chance geben.

**sport jacket** (*US*) n = **sports jacket**.

**sports car** n Sportwagen m.

**sports centre** n Sportzentrum nt.

**sports ground** n Sportplatz m.

**sports jacket** (*BRIT*) *n* Sakko *m*.
**sportsman** ['spɔːtsmən] (*irreg: like* **man**) *n* Sportler *m*.
**sportsmanship** ['spɔːtsmənʃɪp] *n* Sportlichkeit *f*.
**sports page** *n* Sportseite *f*.
**sportswear** ['spɔːtsweəˀ] *n* Sportkleidung *f*.
**sportswoman** ['spɔːtswumən] (*irreg: like* **woman**) *n* Sportlerin *f*.
**sporty** ['spɔːtɪ] *adj* sportlich.
**spot** [spɔt] *n* (*mark*) Fleck *m*; (*dot*) Punkt *m*; (*on skin*) Pickel *m*; (*place*) Stelle *f*, Platz *m*; (*RADIO, TV*) Nummer *f*, Auftritt *m*; (*also:* ~ **advertisement**) Werbespot *m*; (*small amount*): **a** ~ **of** ein bißchen ♦ *vt* entdecken; **on the** ~ (*in that place*) an Ort und Stelle; (*immediately*) auf der Stelle; **to be in a** ~ in der Klemme sitzen; **to put sb on the** ~ jdn in Verlegenheit bringen; **to come out in** ~**s** Pickel bekommen.
**spot check** *n* Stichprobe *f*.
**spotless** ['spɔtlɪs] *adj* makellos sauber.
**spotlight** ['spɔtlaɪt] *n* Scheinwerfer *m*; (*in room*) Strahler *m*.
**spot-on** [spɔt'ɔn] (*BRIT: inf*) *adj* genau richtig.
**spot price** *n* Kassapreis *m*.
**spotted** ['spɔtɪd] *adj* gepunktet.
**spotty** ['spɔtɪ] *adj* pickelig.
**spouse** [spaus] *n* (*male*) Gatte *m*; (*female*) Gattin *f*.
**spout** [spaut] *n* (*of jug, teapot*) Tülle *f*; (*of pipe*) Ausfluß *m*; (*of liquid*) Strahl *m* ♦ *vi* spritzen; (*flames*) sprühen.
**sprain** [spreɪn] *n* Verstauchung *f* ♦ *vt*: **to** ~ **one's ankle/wrist** sich *dat* den Knöchel/das Handgelenk verstauchen.
**sprang** [spræŋ] *pt of* **spring**.
**sprawl** [sprɔːl] *vi* (*person*) sich ausstrecken; (*place*) wild wuchern ♦ *n*: **urban** ~ wildwuchernde Ausbreitung des Stadtgebietes; **to send sb** ~**ing** jdn zu Boden werfen.
**spray** [spreɪ] *n* (*small drops*) Sprühnebel *m*; (*sea spray*) Gischt *m or f*; (*container*) Sprühdose *f*; (*garden spray*) Sprühgerät *nt*; (*of flowers*) Strauß *m* ♦ *vt* sprühen, spritzen; (*crops*) spritzen ♦ *cpd* (*deodorant*) Sprüh-; ~ **can** Sprühdose *f*.
**spread** [sprɛd] (*pt, pp* **spread**) *n* (*range*) Spektrum *nt*; (*selection*) Auswahl *f*; (*distribution*) Verteilung *f*; (*for bread*) (Brot)aufstrich *m*; (*inf: food*) Festessen *nt*; (*PRESS, TYP: two pages*) Doppelseite *f* ♦ *vt* ausbreiten; (*butter*) streichen; (*workload, wealth, repayments etc*) verteilen; (*scatter*) verstreuen; (*rumour, disease*) verbreiten ♦ *vi* (*disease, news*) sich verbreiten; (*also:* ~ **out:** *stain*) sich ausbreiten; **to get a middle-age** ~ in den mittleren Jahren Speck ansetzen.
▶**spread out** *vi* (*move apart*) sich verteilen.
**spread-eagled** ['sprɛdiːgld] *adj* mit ausgestreckten Armen und Beinen; **to be or**

**lie** ~ mit ausgestreckten Armen und Beinen daliegen.
**spreadsheet** ['sprɛdʃiːt] *n* (*COMPUT*) Tabellenkalkulation *f*.
**spree** [spriː] *n*: **to go on a** ~ (*drinking*) eine Zechtour machen; (*spending*) groß einkaufen gehen.
**sprig** [sprɪg] *n* Zweig *m*.
**sprightly** ['spraɪtlɪ] *adj* rüstig.
**spring** [sprɪŋ] (*pt* **sprang**, *pp* **sprung**) *n* (*coiled metal*) Sprungfeder *f*; (*season*) Frühling *m*, Frühjahr *nt*; (*of water*) Quelle *f* ♦ *vi* (*leap*) springen ♦ *vt*: **to** ~ **a leak** (*pipe etc*) undicht werden; **in** ~ im Frühling *or* Frühjahr; **to walk with a** ~ **in one's step** mit federnden Schritten gehen; **to** ~ **from** (*result*) herrühren von; **to** ~ **into action** aktiv werden; **he sprang the news on me** er hat mich mit der Nachricht überrascht.
▶**spring up** *vi* (*building, plant*) aus dem Boden schießen.
**springboard** ['sprɪŋbɔːd] *n* (*SPORT, fig*) Sprungbrett *nt*.
**spring-clean(ing)** [sprɪŋ'kliːn(ɪŋ)] *n* Frühjahrsputz *m*.
**spring onion** (*BRIT*) *n* Frühlingszwiebel *f*.
**spring roll** *n* Frühlingsrolle *f*.
**springtime** ['sprɪŋtaɪm] *n* Frühling *m*.
**springy** ['sprɪŋɪ] *adj* federnd; (*mattress*) weich gefedert.
**sprinkle** ['sprɪŋkl] *vt* (*liquid*) sprenkeln; (*salt, sugar*) streuen; **to** ~ **water on,** ~ **with water** mit Wasser besprengen; **to** ~ **sugar** *etc* **on,** ~ **with sugar** *etc* mit Zucker *etc* bestreuen.
**sprinkler** ['sprɪŋkləˀ] *n* (*for lawn*) Rasensprenger *m*; (*to put out fire*) Sprinkler *m*.
**sprinkling** ['sprɪŋklɪŋ] *n*: **a** ~ **of** (*water*) ein paar Tropfen; (*salt, sugar*) eine Prise; (*fig*) ein paar.
**sprint** [sprɪnt] *n* Sprint *m* ♦ *vi* rennen; (*SPORT*) sprinten; **the 200 metres** ~ der 200-Meter-Lauf.
**sprinter** ['sprɪntəˀ] *n* Sprinter(in) *m(f)*.
**sprite** [spraɪt] *n* Kobold *m*.
**spritzer** ['sprɪtsəˀ] *n* Schorle *f*.
**sprocket** ['sprɔkɪt] *n* Kettenzahnrad *nt*.
**sprout** [spraut] *vi* sprießen; (*vegetable*) keimen.
**sprouts** [sprauts] *npl* (*also:* **Brussels** ~) Rosenkohl *m*.
**spruce** [spruːs] *n inv* Fichte *f* ♦ *adj* gepflegt, adrett.
▶**spruce up** *vt* auf Vordermann bringen (*inf*); **to** ~ **o.s. up** sein Äußeres pflegen.
**sprung** [sprʌŋ] *pp of* **spring**.
**spry** [spraɪ] *adj* rüstig.
**SPUC** *n abbr* (= *Society for the Protection of the Unborn Child*) *Gesellschaft zum Schutz des ungeborenen Lebens*.
**spud** [spʌd] (*inf*) *n* Kartoffel *f*.
**spun** [spʌn] *pt, pp of* **spin**.
**spur** [spɜːˀ] *n* Sporn *m*; (*fig*) Ansporn *m* ♦ *vt*

(*also:* ~ **on**, *fig*) anspornen; **on the ~ of the moment** ganz spontan.
**spurious** ['spjʊərɪəs] *adj* falsch.
**spurn** [spɜːn] *vt* verschmähen.
**spurt** [spɜːt] *n* (*of blood etc*) Strahl *m*; (*of energy*) Anwandlung *f* ♦ *vi* (*blood*) (heraus)spritzen; **to put on a ~** (*lit, fig*) einen Spurt einlegen.
**sputter** ['spʌtə*] *vi* = **splutter**.
**spy** [spaɪ] *n* Spion(in) *m(f)* ♦ *vi:* **to ~ on** nachspionieren +*dat* ♦ *vt* sehen ♦ *cpd* (*film, story*) Spionage-.
**spying** ['spaɪɪŋ] *n* Spionage *f*.
**Sq.** *abbr* (*in address:* = *square*) ≈ Pl.
**sq.** *abbr* = **square**.
**squabble** ['skwɔbl] *vi* (sich) zanken ♦ *n* Streit *m*.
**squad** [skwɔd] *n* (*MIL*) Trupp *m*; (*POLICE*) Kommando *nt*; (: *drug/fraud squad*) Dezernat *nt*; (*SPORT*) Mannschaft *f*; **flying ~** (*POLICE*) Überfallkommando *nt*.
**squad car** (*BRIT*) *n* (*POLICE*) Streifenwagen *m*.
**squaddie** ['skwɔdɪ] (*BRIT*) *n* (*private soldier*) Gefreite(r) *m*.
**squadron** ['skwɔdrn] *n* (*MIL*) Schwadron *f*; (*AVIAT*) Staffel *f*; (*NAUT*) Geschwader *nt*.
**squalid** ['skwɔlɪd] *adj* verkommen; (*conditions*) elend; (*sordid*) erbärmlich.
**squall** [skwɔːl] *n* Bö(e) *f*.
**squalor** ['skwɔlə*] *n* Elend *nt*.
**squander** ['skwɔndə*] *vt* verschwenden; (*chances*) vertun.
**square** [skwɛə*] *n* Quadrat *nt*; (*in town*) Platz *m*; (*US: block of houses*) Block *m*; (*also:* **set ~**) Zeichendreieck *nt*; (*inf: person*) Spießer *m* ♦ *adj* quadratisch; (*inf: ideas, person*) spießig ♦ *vt* (*arrange*) ausrichten; (*MATH*) quadrieren; (*reconcile*) in Einklang bringen ♦ *vi* (*accord*) übereinstimmen; **we're back to ~ one** jetzt sind wir wieder da, wo wir angefangen haben; **all ~** (*SPORT*) unentschieden; (*fig*) quitt; **a ~ meal** eine ordentliche Mahlzeit; **2 metres ~** 2 Meter im Quadrat; **2 ~ metres** 2 Quadratmeter; **I'll ~ it with him** (*inf*) ich mache das mit ihm ab; **can you ~ it with your conscience?** können Sie das mit Ihrem Gewissen vereinbaren?
►**square up** (*BRIT*) *vi* abrechnen.
**square bracket** *n* eckige Klammer *f*.
**squarely** ['skwɛəlɪ] *adv* (*directly*) direkt, genau; (*firmly*) fest; (*honestly*) ehrlich; (*fairly*) gerecht, fair.
**square root** *n* Quadratwurzel *f*.
**squash** [skwɔʃ] *n* (*BRIT*): **lemon/orange ~** Zitronen-/Orangensaftgetränk *nt*; (*US: marrow etc*) Kürbis *m*; (*SPORT*) Squash *nt* ♦ *vt* zerquetschen.
**squat** [skwɔt] *adj* gedrungen ♦ *vi* (*also:* **~ down**) sich (hin)hocken; (*on property*): **to ~ (in a house)** ein Haus besetzen.
**squatter** ['skwɔtə*] *n* Hausbesetzer(in) *m(f)*.

**squawk** [skwɔːk] *vi* kreischen.
**squeak** [skwiːk] *vi* quietschen; (*mouse etc*) piepsen ♦ *n* Quietschen *nt*; (*of mouse etc*) Piepsen *nt*.
**squeaky-clean** [skwiːkɪ'kliːn] (*inf*) *adj* blitzsauber.
**squeal** [skwiːl] *vi* quietschen.
**squeamish** ['skwiːmɪʃ] *adj* empfindlich.
**squeeze** [skwiːz] *n* Drücken *nt*; (*ECON*) Beschränkung *f*; (*also:* **credit ~**) Kreditbeschränkung *f* ♦ *vt* drücken; (*lemon etc*) auspressen ♦ *vi:* **to ~ past sth** sich an etw *dat* vorbeidrücken; **to ~ under sth** sich unter etw *dat* durchzwängen; **to give sth a ~** etw drücken; **a ~ of lemon** ein Spritzer Zitronensaft.
►**squeeze out** *vt* (*juice etc*) (her)auspressen; (*fig: exclude*) hinausdrängen.
**squelch** [skwɛltʃ] *vi* (*mud etc*) quatschen.
**squib** [skwɪb] *n* Knallfrosch *m*.
**squid** [skwɪd] *n* Tintenfisch *m*.
**squiggle** ['skwɪgl] *n* Schnörkel *m*.
**squint** [skwɪnt] *vi* (*in the sunlight*) blinzeln ♦ *n* (*MED*) Schielen *nt*; **he has a ~** er schielt.
**squire** ['skwaɪə*] (*BRIT*) *n* Gutsherr *m*; (*inf*) Chef *m*.
**squirm** [skwɜːm] *vi* (*lit, fig*) sich winden.
**squirrel** ['skwɪrəl] *n* Eichhörnchen *nt*.
**squirt** [skwɜːt] *vi, vt* spritzen.
**Sr** *abbr* (*in names:* = *senior*) sen.; (*REL*) = **sister**.
**SRC** (*BRIT*) *n abbr* (= *Students' Representative Council*) *studentische Vertretung.*
**Sri Lanka** [srɪ'læŋkə] *n* Sri Lanka *nt*.
**SRN** (*BRIT*) *n abbr* (*formerly:* = *State Registered Nurse*) staatlich geprüfte Krankenschwester *f*, staatlich geprüfter Krankenpfleger *m*.
**SRO** (*US*) *abbr* (= *standing room only*) nur Stehplätze.
**SS** *abbr* = **steamship**.
**SSA** (*US*) *n abbr* (= *Social Security Administration*) Sozialversicherungsbehörde.
**SST** (*US*) *n abbr* (= *supersonic transport*) Überschallverkehr *m*.
**ST** (*US*) *abbr* = **standard time**.
**St** *abbr* (= *saint*) St.; (= *street*) Str.
**stab** [stæb] *n* Stich *m*, Stoß *m*; (*inf: try*): **to have a ~ at sth** etw probieren ♦ *vt* (*person*) niederstechen; (*body*) einstechen auf +*acc*; **a ~ of pain** ein stechender Schmerz; **to ~ sb to death** jdn erstechen.
**stabbing** ['stæbɪŋ] *n* Messerstecherei *f* ♦ *adj* (*pain*) stechend.
**stability** [stə'bɪlɪtɪ] *n* Stabilität *f*.
**stabilization** [steɪbəlaɪ'zeɪʃən] *n* Stabilisierung *f*.
**stabilize** ['steɪbəlaɪz] *vt* stabilisieren ♦ *vi* sich stabilisieren.
**stabilizer** ['steɪbəlaɪzə*] *n* (*AVIAT*) Stabilisierungsfläche *f*; (*NAUT, food additive*) Stabilisator *m*.
**stable** ['steɪbl] *adj* stabil; (*marriage*) dauerhaft

♦ *n* Stall *m*; **riding** ~**s** Reitstall *m*.
**staccato** [stə'kɑːtəu] *adv* (*MUS*) stakkato ♦ *adj* abgehackt.
**stack** [stæk] *n* Stapel *m*; (*of books etc*) Stoß *m* ♦ *vt* (*also:* ~ **up**) aufstapeln; ~**s of time** (*BRIT: inf*) jede Menge Zeit; **to** ~ **with** vollstapeln mit.
**stadia** ['steɪdɪə] *npl of* **stadium**.
**stadium** ['steɪdɪəm] (*pl* **stadia** *or* ~**s**) *n* Stadion *nt*.
**staff** [stɑːf] *n* (*workforce, servants*) Personal *nt*; (*BRIT: also:* **teaching** ~) (Lehrer)kollegium *nt*; (*stick: MIL*) Stab *m* ♦ *vt* (mit Personal) besetzen; **one of his** ~ einer seiner Mitarbeiter; **a member of** ~ ein(e) Mitarbeiter(in) *m(f)*; (*SCOL*) ein(e) Lehrer(in) *m(f)*.
**staffroom** ['stɑːfruːm] *n* (*SCOL*) Lehrerzimmer *nt*.
**Staffs** (*BRIT*) *abbr* (*POST:* = *Staffordshire*).
**stag** [stæg] *n* Hirsch *m*; (*BRIT: STOCK EXCHANGE*) Spekulant *m* (*der junge Aktien aufkauft*); ~ **market** (*BRIT: STOCK EXCHANGE*) Spekulantenmarkt *m*.
**stage** [steɪdʒ] *n* Bühne *f*; (*platform*) Podium *nt*; (*point, period*) Stadium *nt* ♦ *vt* (*play*) aufführen; (*demonstration*) organisieren; (*perform: recovery etc*) schaffen; **the** ~ das Theater, die Bühne; **in** ~**s** etappenweise; **to go through a difficult** ~ eine schwierige Phase durchmachen; **in the early/final** ~**s** im Anfangs-/Endstadium.
**stagecoach** ['steɪdʒkəutʃ] *n* Postkutsche *f*.
**stage door** *n* Bühneneingang *m*.
**stage fright** *n* Lampenfieber *nt*.
**stagehand** ['steɪdʒhænd] *n* Bühnenarbeiter(in) *m(f)*.
**stage-manage** ['steɪdʒmænɪdʒ] *vt* (*fig*) inszenieren.
**stage manager** *n* Inspizient(in) *m(f)*.
**stagger** ['stægə'] *vi* schwanken, taumeln ♦ *vt* (*amaze*) die Sprache verschlagen +*dat*; (*hours, holidays*) staffeln.
**staggering** ['stægərɪŋ] *adj* (*amazing*) atemberaubend.
**staging post** ['steɪdʒɪŋ-] *n* Zwischenstation *f*.
**stagnant** ['stægnənt] *adj* (*water*) stehend; (*economy etc*) stagnierend.
**stagnate** [stæg'neɪt] *vi* (*economy etc*) stagnieren; (*person*) verdummen.
**stagnation** [stæg'neɪʃən] *n* Stagnation *f*.
**stag night, stag party** *n* Herrenabend *m*.

> *Als* **stag night** *bezeichnet man eine feucht-fröhliche Männerparty, die kurz vor einer Hochzeit vom Bräutigam und seinen Freunden meist in einem Gasthaus oder Nachtklub abgehalten wird. Diese Feiern sind oft sehr ausgelassen und können manchmal auch zu weit gehen (wenn dem betrunkenen Bräutigam ein Streich gespielt wird). Siehe auch* **hen night**.

**staid** [steɪd] *adj* gesetzt.
**stain** [steɪn] *n* Fleck *m*; (*colouring*) Beize *f* ♦ *vt* beflecken; (*wood*) beizen.
**stained glass window** [steɪnd-] *n* buntes Glasfenster *nt*.
**stainless steel** ['steɪnlɪs-] *n* (rostfreier) Edelstahl *m*.
**stain remover** *n* Fleckentferner *m*.
**stair** [steə'] *n* (*step*) Stufe *f*; **stairs** *npl* (*flight of steps*) Treppe *f*; **on the** ~**s** auf der Treppe.
**staircase** ['steəkeɪs] *n* Treppe *f*.
**stairway** ['steəweɪ] *n* = **staircase**.
**stairwell** ['steəwel] *n* Treppenhaus *nt*.
**stake** [steɪk] *n* (*post*) Pfahl *m*, Pfosten *m*; (*COMM*) Anteil *m*; (*BETTING: gen pl*) Einsatz *m* ♦ *vt* (*money*) setzen; (*also:* ~ **out:** *area*) abstecken; **to be at** ~ auf dem Spiel stehen; **to have a** ~ **in sth** einen Anteil an etw *dat* haben; **to** ~ **a claim (to sth)** sich *dat* ein Anrecht (auf etw *acc*) sichern; **to** ~ **one's life on sth** seinen Kopf auf etw *acc* wetten; **to** ~ **one's reputation on sth** sich für etw verbürgen.
**stakeout** ['steɪkaut] *n* (*surveillance*) Überwachung *f*.
**stalactite** ['stæləktaɪt] *n* Stalaktit *m*.
**stalagmite** ['stæləgmaɪt] *n* Stalagmit *m*.
**stale** [steɪl] *adj* (*bread*) altbacken; (*food*) alt; (*smell*) muffig; (*air*) verbraucht; (*beer*) schal.
**stalemate** ['steɪlmeɪt] *n* (*CHESS*) Patt *nt*; (*fig*) Sackgasse *f*.
**stalk** [stɔːk] *n* Stiel *m* ♦ *vt* sich heranpirschen an +*acc* ♦ *vi*: **to** ~ **out/off** hinaus-/davonstolzieren.
**stall** [stɔːl] *n* (*BRIT: in market etc*) Stand *m*; (*in stable*) Box *f* ♦ *vt* (*engine, car*) abwürgen; (*fig: person*) hinhalten; (: *decision etc*) hinauszögern ♦ *vi* (*engine*) absterben; (*car*) stehenbleiben; (*fig: person*) ausweichen; **stalls** *npl* (*BRIT: in cinema, theatre*) Parkett *nt*; **a seat in the** ~**s** ein Platz im Parkett; **a clothes/flower** ~ ein Kleidungs-/Blumenstand *m*; **to** ~ **for time** versuchen, Zeit zu gewinnen.
**stallholder** ['stɔːlhəuldə'] (*BRIT*) *n* Standbesitzer(in) *m(f)*.
**stallion** ['stæljən] *n* Hengst *m*.
**stalwart** ['stɔːlwət] *adj* treu.
**stamen** ['steɪmen] *n* Staubgefäß *nt*.
**stamina** ['stæmɪnə] *n* Ausdauer *f*.
**stammer** ['stæmə'] *n* Stottern *nt* ♦ *vi* stottern; **to have a** ~ stottern.
**stamp** [stæmp] *n* (*lit, fig*) Stempel *m*; (*postage stamp*) Briefmarke *f* ♦ *vi* stampfen; (*also:* ~ **one's foot**) (mit dem Fuß) aufstampfen ♦ *vt* stempeln; (*with postage stamp*) frankieren; ~**ed addressed envelope** frankierter Rückumschlag.
▶**stamp out** *vt* (*fire*) austreten; (*fig: crime*) ausrotten; (: *opposition*) unterdrücken.
**stamp album** *n* Briefmarkenalbum *nt*.

**stamp collecting** *n* Briefmarkensammeln *nt*.
**stamp duty** (*BRIT*) *n* (Stempel)gebühr *f*.
**stampede** [stæm'pi:d] *n* (*of animals*) wilde Flucht *f*; (*fig*) Massenandrang *m*.
**stamp machine** *n* Briefmarkenautomat *m*.
**stance** [stæns] *n* Haltung *f*; (*fig*) Einstellung *f*.
**stand** [stænd] (*pt, pp stood*) *n* (*COMM*) Stand *m*; (*SPORT*) Tribüne *f*; (*piece of furniture*) Ständer *m* ♦ *vi* stehen; (*rise*) aufstehen; (*remain*) bestehenbleiben; (*in election etc*) kandidieren ♦ *vt* stellen; (*tolerate, withstand*) ertragen; **to make a ~ against sth** Widerstand gegen etw leisten; **to take a ~ on sth** einen Standpunkt zu etw vertreten; **to take the ~** (*US: LAW*) in den Zeugenstand treten; **to ~ at** (*value, score etc*) betragen; (*level*) liegen bei; **to ~ for parliament** (*BRIT*) in den Parlamentswahlen kandidieren; **to ~ to gain/lose sth** etw gewinnen/verlieren können; **it ~s to reason** es ist einleuchtend; **as things ~** nach Lage der Dinge; **to ~ sb a drink/meal** jdm einen Drink/ein Essen spendieren; **I can't ~ him** ich kann ihn nicht leiden *or* ausstehen; **we don't ~ a chance** wir haben keine Chance; **to ~ trial** vor Gericht stehen.
▶**stand by** *vi* (*be ready*) sich bereithalten; (*fail to help*) (unbeteiligt) danebenstehen ♦ *vt fus* (*opinion, decision*) stehen zu; (*person*) halten zu.
▶**stand down** *vi* zurücktreten.
▶**stand for** *vt fus* (*signify*) bedeuten; (*represent*) stehen für; (*tolerate*) sich *dat* gefallen lassen.
▶**stand in for** *vt fus* vertreten.
▶**stand out** *vi* hervorstechen.
▶**stand up** *vi* aufstehen.
▶**stand up for** *vt fus* eintreten für.
▶**stand up to** *vt fus* standhalten +*dat*; (*person*) sich behaupten gegenüber +*dat*.
**stand-alone** ['stændələun] *adj* (*COMPUT*) selbständig.
**standard** ['stændəd] *n* (*level*) Niveau *nt*; (*norm*) Norm *f*; (*criterion*) Maßstab *m*; (*flag*) Standarte *f* ♦ *adj* (*size, model, value etc*) Standard-; (*normal*) normal; **standards** *npl* (*morals*) (sittliche) Maßstäbe *pl*; **to be** *or* **to come up to ~** den Anforderungen genügen; **to apply a double ~** mit zweierlei Maß messen.
**standardization** [stændədaɪ'zeɪʃən] *n* Vereinheitlichung *f*.
**standardize** ['stændədaɪz] *vt* vereinheitlichen.
**standard lamp** (*BRIT*) *n* Stehlampe *f*.
**standard of living** *n* Lebensstandard *m*.
**standard time** *n* Normalzeit *f*.
**stand-by, standby** ['stændbaɪ] *n* Reserve *f*; (*also:* **standby ticket**) Standby-Ticket *nt* ♦ *adj* (*generator*) Reserve-, Ersatz-; **to be on ~** (*doctor*) Bereitschaftsdienst haben; (*crew, firemen etc*) in Bereitschaft sein, einsatzbereit sein.

**stand-by ticket** *n* Standby-Ticket *nt*.
**stand-in** ['stændɪn] *n* Ersatz *m*.
**standing** ['stændɪŋ] *adj* (*permanent*) ständig; (*army*) stehend ♦ *n* (*status*) Rang *m*, Stellung *f*; **a ~ ovation** stürmischer Beifall; **of many years' ~** von langjähriger Dauer; **a relationship of 6 months' ~** eine seit 6 Monaten bestehende Beziehung; **a man of some ~** ein angesehener Mann.
**standing committee** *n* ständiger Ausschuß *m*.
**standing joke** *n* Standardwitz *m*.
**standing order** (*BRIT*) *n* (*at bank*) Dauerauftrag *m*.
**standing room** *n* Stehplätze *pl*.
**standoff** *n* (*situation*) ausweglose *or* verfahrene Situation *f*.
**stand-offish** [stænd'ɔfɪʃ] *adj* distanziert.
**standpat** ['stændpæt] (*US*) *adj* konservativ.
**standpipe** ['stændpaɪp] *n* Steigrohr *nt*.
**standpoint** ['stændpɔɪnt] *n* Standpunkt *m*.
**standstill** ['stændstɪl] *n*: **to be at a ~** stillstehen; (*fig: negotiations*) in eine Sackgasse geraten sein; **to come to a ~** (*traffic*) zum Stillstand kommen.
**stank** [stæŋk] *pt of* **stink**.
**stanza** ['stænzə] *n* Strophe *f*.
**staple** ['steɪpl] *n* (*for papers*) Heftklammer *f*; (*chief product*) Hauptartikel *m* ♦ *adj* (*food, diet*) Grund-, Haupt- ♦ *vt* heften.
**stapler** ['steɪplə'] *n* Hefter *m*.
**star** [stɑ:'] *n* Stern *m*; (*celebrity*) Star *m* ♦ *vt* (*THEAT, CINE*) in der Hauptrolle zeigen ♦ *vi*: **to ~ in** die Hauptrolle haben in; **the stars** *npl* (*horoscope*) das Horoskop; **4-~ hotel** 4-Sterne-Hotel *nt*; **2-~ petrol** (*BRIT*) Normal(benzin) *nt*; **4-~ petrol** (*BRIT*) Super(benzin) *nt*.
**star attraction** *n* Hauptattraktion *f*.
**starboard** ['stɑ:bɔːd] *adj* (*side*) Steuerbord-; **to ~** (nach) Steuerbord.
**starch** [stɑ:tʃ] *n* Stärke *f*.
**starched** [stɑ:tʃt] *adj* gestärkt.
**starchy** ['stɑ:tʃɪ] *adj* (*food*) stärkehaltig; (*pej: person*) steif.
**stardom** ['stɑ:dəm] *n* Berühmtheit *f*.
**stare** [stɛə'] *n* starrer Blick *m* ♦ *vi*: **to ~ at** anstarren.
**starfish** ['stɑ:fɪʃ] *n* Seestern *m*.
**stark** [stɑ:k] *adj* (*bleak*) kahl; (*simplicity*) schlicht; (*colour*) eintönig; (*reality, poverty*) nackt ♦ *adv*: **~ naked** splitternackt.
**starkers** ['stɑ:kəz] (*inf*) *adj* splitter(faser)nackt.
**starlet** ['stɑ:lɪt] *n* (Film)sternchen *nt*, Starlet *nt*.
**starlight** ['stɑ:laɪt] *n* Sternenlicht *nt*.
**starling** ['stɑ:lɪŋ] *n* Star *m*.
**starlit** ['stɑ:lɪt] *adj* sternklar.
**starry** ['stɑ:rɪ] *adj* sternklar; **~ sky** Sternenhimmel *m*.
**starry-eyed** [stɑ:rɪ'aɪd] *adj* (*innocent*) arglos,

blauäugig; (*from wonder*) verzückt.

**Stars and Stripes** *n sing* Sternenbanner *nt*.

**star sign** *n* Sternzeichen *nt*.

**star-studded** ['stɑːstʌdɪd] *adj:* **a ~ cast** eine Starbesetzung *f*.

**START** *n abbr* (*MIL:* = *Strategic Arms Reduction Talks*) START.

**start** [stɑːt] *n* Beginn *m*, Anfang *m*; (*departure*) Aufbruch *m* ♦ *vt* anfangen mit; (*panic*) auslösen; (*fire*) anzünden; (*found*) gründen; (: *restaurant etc*) eröffnen; (*engine*) anlassen; (*car*) starten ♦ *vi* anfangen; (*with fright*) zusammenfahren; (*engine etc*) anspringen; **at the ~** am Anfang, zu Beginn; **for a ~** erstens; **to make an early ~** frühzeitig aufbrechen; **to give a ~** zusammenfahren; **to wake up with a ~** aus dem Schlaf hochschrecken; **to ~ doing** *or* **to do sth** anfangen, etw zu tun; **to ~ (off) with ...** (*firstly*) erstens; (*at the beginning*) zunächst.

▶**start off** *vi* (*begin*) anfangen; (*begin moving*) losgehen/-fahren.

▶**start out** *vi* (*leave*) sich aufmachen.

▶**start over** (*US*) *vi* noch einmal von vorn anfangen.

▶**start up** *vt* (*business*) gründen; (*restaurant etc*) eröffnen; (*car*) starten; (*engine*) anlassen.

**starter** ['stɑːtə*] *n* (*AUT*) Anlasser *m*; (*SPORT: official, runner, horse*) Starter *m*; (*BRIT: CULIN*) Vorspeise *f*; **for ~s** (*inf*) für den Anfang.

**starting point** ['stɑːtɪŋ-] *n* (*lit, fig*) Ausgangspunkt *m*.

**starting price** *n* (*at auction*) Ausgangsangebot *nt*.

**startle** ['stɑːtl] *vt* erschrecken.

**startling** ['stɑːtlɪŋ] *adj* (*news etc*) überraschend.

**star turn** (*BRIT*) *n* Sensation *f*, Hauptattraktion *f*.

**starvation** [stɑː'veɪʃən] *n* Hunger *m*; **to die of/from ~** verhungern.

**starve** [stɑːv] *vi* hungern; (*to death*) verhungern ♦ *vt* hungern lassen; (*fig: deprive*): **to ~ sb of sth** jdm etw vorenthalten; **I'm starving** ich sterbe vor Hunger.

**Star Wars** *n* Krieg *m* der Sterne.

**stash** [stæʃ] *vi* (*also:* **~ away**) beiseite schaffen ♦ *n* (*secret store*) geheimes Lager *nt*.

**state** [steɪt] *n* (*condition*) Zustand *m*; (*POL*) Staat *m* ♦ *vt* (*say*) feststellen; (*declare*) erklären; **the States** *npl* (*GEOG*) die (Vereinigten) Staaten *pl*; **to be in a ~** aufgeregt sein; (*on edge*) nervös sein; (*in a mess*) in einem schrecklichen Zustand sein; **to get into a ~** durchdrehen (*inf*); **in ~** feierlich; **to lie in ~** (feierlich) aufgebahrt sein; **~ of emergency** Notstand *m*; **~ of mind** Verfassung *f*.

**state control** *n* staatliche Kontrolle *f*.

**stated** ['steɪtɪd] *adj* erklärt.

**State Department** (*US*) *n* Außenministerium *nt*.

**state education** (*BRIT*) *n* staatliche Erziehung *f*; (*system*) staatliches Bildungswesen *nt*.

**stateless** ['steɪtlɪs] *adj* staatenlos.

**stately** ['steɪtlɪ] *adj* würdevoll; (*walk*) gemessen; **~ home** Schloß *nt*.

**statement** ['steɪtmənt] *n* (*thing said*) Feststellung *f*; (*declaration*) Erklärung *f*; (*FIN*) (Konto)auszug *m*; **official ~** (amtliche) Erklärung *f*; **bank ~** Kontoauszug *m*.

**state of the art** *n:* **the ~** der neueste Stand der Technik ♦ *adj:* **state-of-the-art** auf dem neuesten Stand der Technik; (*technology*) Spitzen-.

**state-owned** ['steɪtəund] *adj* staatseigen.

**state school** *n* öffentliche Schule *f*.

**state secret** *n* Staatsgeheimnis *nt*.

**statesman** ['steɪtsmən] (*irreg: like* **man**) *n* Staatsmann *m*.

**statesmanship** ['steɪtsmənʃɪp] *n* Staatskunst *f*.

**static** ['stætɪk] *n* (*RADIO, TV*) atmosphärische Störungen *pl* ♦ *adj* (*not moving*) konstant.

**static electricity** *n* Reibungselektrizität *f*.

**station** ['steɪʃən] *n* (*RAIL*) Bahnhof *m*; (*also:* **bus ~**) Busbahnhof *m*; (*also:* **police ~**) (Polizei)wache *f*; (*RADIO*) Sender *m* ♦ *vt* (*guards etc*) postieren; (*soldiers etc*) stationieren; **action ~s** (*MIL*) Stellung *f*; **above one's ~** über seinem Stand.

**stationary** ['steɪʃnərɪ] *adj* (*vehicle*) haltend; **to be ~** stehen.

**stationer** ['steɪʃənə*] *n* Schreibwaren-händler(in) *m(f)*.

**stationer's (shop)** *n* Schreibwarenhandlung *f*.

**stationery** ['steɪʃnərɪ] *n* Schreibwaren *pl*; (*writing paper*) Briefpapier *nt*.

**stationmaster** ['steɪʃənmɑːstə*] *n* Bahnhofsvorsteher *m*.

**station wagon** (*US*) *n* Kombi(wagen) *m*.

**statistic** [stə'tɪstɪk] *n* Statistik *f*.

**statistical** [stə'tɪstɪkl] *adj* statistisch.

**statistics** [stə'tɪstɪks] *n* (*science*) Statistik *f*.

**statue** ['stætjuː] *n* Statue *f*.

**statuesque** [stætju'esk] *adj* stattlich.

**statuette** [stætju'et] *n* Statuette *f*.

**stature** ['stætʃə*] *n* Wuchs *m*, Statur *f*; (*fig: reputation*) Format *nt*.

**status** ['steɪtəs] *n* Status *m*; (*position*) Stellung *f*; **the ~ quo** der Status quo.

**status line** *n* (*COMPUT*) Statuszeile *f*.

**status symbol** *n* Statussymbol *nt*.

**statute** ['stætjuːt] *n* Gesetz *nt*; **statutes** *npl* (*of club etc*) Satzung *f*.

**statute book** *n:* **to be on the ~** geltendes Recht sein.

**statutory** ['stætjutrɪ] *adj* gesetzlich;

~ **declaration** eidesstattliche Erklärung *f*.

**staunch** [stɔ:ntʃ] *adj* treu ♦ *vt* (*flow*) stauen; (*blood*) stillen.

**stave** [steɪv] *n* (*MUS*) Notensystem *nt*.

▶**stave off** *vt* (*attack*) abwehren; (*threat*) abwenden.

**stay** [steɪ] *n* Aufenthalt *m* ♦ *vi* bleiben; (*with sb, as guest*) wohnen; (*in hotel*) übernachten; ~ **of execution** (*LAW*) Aussetzung *f*; **to ~ put** bleiben; **to ~ with friends** bei Freunden untergebracht sein; **to ~ the night** übernachten.

▶**stay behind** *vi* zurückbleiben.

▶**stay in** *vi* (*at home*) zu Hause bleiben.

▶**stay on** *vi* bleiben.

▶**stay out** *vi* (*of house*) wegbleiben; (*remain on strike*) weiterstreiken.

▶**stay up** *vi* (*at night*) aufbleiben.

**staying power** ['steɪɪŋ-] *n* Stehvermögen *nt*, Durchhaltevermögen *nt*.

**STD** *n abbr* (*BRIT: TEL: = subscriber trunk dialling*) Selbstwählferndienst *m*; (*MED: = sexually transmitted disease*) durch Geschlechtsverkehr übertragene Krankheit *f*.

**stead** [sted] *n:* **in sb's ~** an jds Stelle; **to stand sb in good ~** jdm zugute *or* zustatten kommen.

**steadfast** ['stedfa:st] *adj* standhaft.

**steadily** ['stedɪlɪ] *adv* (*regularly*) regelmäßig; (*constantly*) stetig; (*fixedly*) fest, unverwandt.

**steady** ['stedɪ] *adj* (*job, boyfriend, girlfriend, look*) fest; (*income*) regelmäßig; (*speed*) gleichmäßig; (*rise*) stetig; (*person, character*) zuverlässig, solide; (*voice, hand etc*) ruhig ♦ *vt* (*stabilize*) ruhig halten; (*nerves*) beruhigen; **to ~ o.s. on sth** sich auf etw *acc* stützen; **to ~ o.s. against sth** sich an etw *dat* abstützen.

**steak** [steɪk] *n* Steak *nt*; (*fish*) Filet *nt*.

**steakhouse** ['steɪkhaus] *n* Steakrestaurant *nt*.

**steal** [sti:l] (*pt* **stole**, *pp* **stolen**) *vt* stehlen ♦ *vi* stehlen; (*move secretly*) sich stehlen, schleichen.

▶**steal away** *vi* sich davonschleichen.

**stealth** [stelθ] *n:* **by ~** heimlich.

**stealthy** ['stelθɪ] *adj* heimlich, verstohlen.

**steam** [sti:m] *n* Dampf *m* ♦ *vt* (*CULIN*) dämpfen, dünsten ♦ *vi* dampfen; **covered with ~** (*window etc*) beschlagen; **under one's own ~** (*fig*) allein, ohne Hilfe; **to run out of ~** (*fig*) den Schwung verlieren; **to let off ~** (*inf, fig*) Dampf ablassen.

▶**steam up** *vi* (*window*) beschlagen; **to get ~ed up about sth** (*inf, fig*) sich über etw *acc* aufregen.

**steam engine** *n* (*RAIL*) Dampflok(omotive) *f*.

**steamer** ['sti:mə*] *n* Dampfer *m*; (*CULIN*) Dämpfer *m*.

**steam iron** *n* Dampfbügeleisen *nt*.

**steamroller** ['sti:mrəulə*] *n* Dampfwalze *f*.

**steamship** ['sti:mʃɪp] *n* = **steamer**.

**steamy** ['sti:mɪ] *adj* (*room*) dampfig; (*window*) beschlagen; (*book, film*) heiß.

**steed** [sti:d] (*liter*) *n* Roß *nt*.

**steel** [sti:l] *n* Stahl *m* ♦ *adj* (*girder, wool etc*) Stahl-.

**steel band** *n* (*MUS*) Steelband *f*.

**steel industry** *n* Stahlindustrie *f*.

**steel mill** *n* Stahlwalzwerk *nt*.

**steelworks** ['sti:lwɜ:ks] *n* Stahlwerk *nt*.

**steely** ['sti:lɪ] *adj* (*determination*) eisern; (*eyes, gaze*) hart, stählern.

**steep** [sti:p] *adj* steil; (*increase, rise*) stark; (*price, fees*) gepfeffert ♦ *vt* einweichen; **to be ~ed in history** geschichtsträchtig sein.

**steeple** ['sti:pl] *n* Kirchturm *m*.

**steeplechase** ['sti:pltʃeɪs] *n* (*for horses*) Hindernisrennen *nt*; (*for runners*) Hindernislauf *m*.

**steeplejack** ['sti:pldʒæk] *n* Turmarbeiter *m*.

**steeply** ['sti:plɪ] *adv* steil.

**steer** [stɪə*] *vt* steuern; (*car etc*) lenken; (*person*) lotsen ♦ *vi* steuern; (*in car etc*) lenken; **to ~ for** zusteuern auf +*acc*; **to ~ clear of sb** (*fig*) jdm aus dem Weg gehen; **to ~ clear of sth** (*fig*) etw meiden.

**steering** ['stɪərɪŋ] *n* (*AUT*) Lenkung *f*.

**steering column** *n* (*AUT*) Lenksäule *f*.

**steering committee** *n* Lenkungsausschuß *m*.

**steering wheel** *n* (*AUT*) Lenkrad *nt*, Steuer *nt*.

**stellar** ['stelə*] *adj* stellar.

**stem** [stem] *n* Stiel *m*; (*of pipe*) Hals *m* ♦ *vt* aufhalten; (*flow*) eindämmen; (*bleeding*) zum Stillstand bringen.

▶**stem from** *vt fus* zurückgehen auf +*acc*.

**stench** [stentʃ] (*pej*) *n* Gestank *m*.

**stencil** ['stensl] *n* Schablone *f* ♦ *vt* mit Schablone zeichnen.

**stenographer** [ste'nɔgrəfə*] (*US*) *n* Stenograph(in) *m(f)*.

**stenography** [ste'nɔgrəfɪ] (*US*) *n* Stenographie *f*.

**step** [step] *n* (*lit, fig*) Schritt *m*; (*of stairs*) Stufe *f* ♦ *vi*: **to ~ forward/back** vor-/zurücktreten; **steps** *npl* (*BRIT*) = **stepladder**; ~ **by ~** (*fig*) Schritt für Schritt; **in/out of ~** (**with**) im/ nicht im Tritt (mit); (*fig*) im/nicht im Gleichklang (mit).

▶**step down** *vi* (*fig: resign*) zurücktreten.

▶**step in** *vi* (*fig*) eingreifen.

▶**step off** *vt fus* aussteigen aus +*dat*.

▶**step on** *vt fus* treten auf +*acc*.

▶**step over** *vt fus* steigen über +*acc*.

▶**step up** *vt* (*efforts*) steigern; (*pace etc*) beschleunigen.

**stepbrother** ['stepbrʌðə*] *n* Stiefbruder *m*.

**stepchild** ['steptʃaɪld] *n* Stiefkind *nt*.

**stepdaughter** ['stepdɔ:tə*] *n* Stieftochter *f*.

**stepfather** ['stepfa:ðə*] *n* Stiefvater *m*.

**stepladder** ['steplædə*] (*BRIT*) *n* Trittleiter *f*.

**stepmother** ['stɛpmʌðə*] n Stiefmutter f.

**stepping stone** ['stɛpɪŋ-] n Trittstein m; (fig) Sprungbrett nt.

**stepsister** ['stɛpsɪstə*] n Stiefschwester f.

**stepson** ['stɛpsʌn] n Stiefsohn m.

**stereo** ['stɛrɪəu] n (system) Stereoanlage f ♦ adj (sound etc) Stereo-; **in ~** in Stereo.

**stereotype** ['stɪərɪətaɪp] n Klischee nt, Klischeevorstellung f ♦ vt in ein Klischee zwängen; **~d** stereotyp.

**sterile** ['stɛraɪl] adj steril, keimfrei; (barren) unfruchtbar; (fig: debate) fruchtlos.

**sterility** [stɛ'rɪlɪtɪ] n Unfruchtbarkeit f.

**sterilization** [stɛrɪlaɪ'zeɪʃən] n Sterilisation f, Sterilisierung f.

**sterilize** ['stɛrɪlaɪz] vt sterilisieren.

**sterling** ['stə:lɪŋ] adj (silver) Sterling-; (fig) gediegen ♦ n (ECON) das Pfund Sterling, das englische Pfund; **one pound ~** ein Pfund Sterling.

**sterling area** n (ECON) Sterlingländer pl.

**stern** [stə:n] adj streng ♦ n Heck nt.

**sternum** ['stə:nəm] n Brustbein nt.

**steroid** ['stɪərɔɪd] n Steroid nt.

**stethoscope** ['stɛθəskəup] n Stethoskop nt.

**stevedore** ['sti:vədɔ:*] n Stauer m, Schauermann m.

**stew** [stju:] n Eintopf m ♦ vt schmoren; (fruit, vegetables) dünsten ♦ vi schmoren; **~ed tea** bitterer Tee m; **~ed fruit** (Obst)kompott nt.

**steward** ['stju:əd] n Steward m; (at public event) Ordner(in) m(f); (also: **shop ~**) gewerkschaftliche Vertrauensperson f.

**stewardess** ['stjuədɛs] n Stewardeß f.

**stewardship** ['stjuədʃɪp] n Verwaltung f.

**stewing steak**, (US) **stew meat** ['stju:ɪŋ-] n (Rinder)schmorfleisch nt.

**St. Ex.** abbr = **stock exchange**.

**stg** abbr = **sterling**.

**stick** [stɪk] (pt, pp **stuck**) n Zweig m; (of dynamite) Stange f, (of chalk etc) Stück nt; (as weapon) Stock m; (also: **walking ~**) (Spazier)stock m ♦ vt (with glue etc) kleben; (inf: put) tun, stecken; (: tolerate) aushalten; (thrust) stoßen ♦ vi: **to ~ (to)** kleben (an +dat); (remain) (hängen)bleiben; (door etc) klemmen; (lift) steckenbleiben; **to get hold of the wrong end of the ~** (BRIT, fig) es falsch verstehen; **to ~ in sb's mind** jdm im Gedächtnis (haften)bleiben.

▶**stick around** (inf) vi hier-/dableiben.

▶**stick out** vi (ears etc) abstehen ♦ vt: **to ~ it out** (inf) durchhalten.

▶**stick to** vt fus (one's word, promise) halten; (agreement, rules) sich halten an +acc; (the truth, facts) bleiben bei.

▶**stick up** vi hochstehen.

▶**stick up for** vt fus eintreten für.

**sticker** ['stɪkə*] n Aufkleber m.

**sticking plaster** ['stɪkɪŋ-] n Heftpflaster nt.

**sticking point** n Hindernis nt; (in discussion etc) strittiger Punkt m.

**stickleback** ['stɪklbæk] n Stichling m.

**stickler** ['stɪklə*] n: **to be a ~ for sth** es mit etw peinlich genau nehmen.

**stick shift** (US) n Schaltknüppel m; (car) Wagen m mit Handschaltung.

**stick-up** ['stɪkʌp] n (inf) n Überfall m.

**sticky** ['stɪkɪ] adj klebrig; (label, tape) Klebe-; (weather, day) schwül.

**stiff** [stɪf] adj steif; (hard, firm) hart; (paste, egg-white) fest; (door, zip etc) schwer gehend; (competition) hart; (sentence) schwer; (drink) stark ♦ adv (bored, worried, scared) zu Tode; **to be** or **feel ~** steif sein; **to have a ~ neck** einen steifen Hals haben; **to keep a ~ upper lip** (BRIT, fig) die Haltung bewahren.

**stiffen** ['stɪfn] vi steif werden; (body) erstarren.

**stiffness** ['stɪfnɪs] n Steifheit f.

**stifle** ['staɪfl] vt unterdrücken; (heat) erdrücken.

**stifling** ['staɪflɪŋ] adj (heat) drückend.

**stigma** ['stɪgmə] n Stigma nt; (BOT) Narbe f, Stigma nt; **stigmata** npl (MED) Wundmal nt.

**stile** [staɪl] n Zaunübertritt m.

**stiletto** [stɪ'lɛtəu] (BRIT) n (also: **~ heel**) Bleistiftabsatz m.

**still** [stɪl] adj (motionless) bewegungslos; (tranquil) ruhig; (air, water) still; (BRIT: drink) ohne Kohlensäure ♦ adv (immer) noch; (yet, even) noch; (nonetheless) trotzdem ♦ n (CINE) Standfoto nt; **to stand ~** stillstehen; **keep ~!** halte still!; **he ~ hasn't arrived** er ist immer noch nicht angekommen.

**stillborn** ['stɪlbɔ:n] adj totgeboren.

**still life** n Stilleben nt.

**stilt** [stɪlt] n (pile) Pfahl m; (for walking on) Stelze f.

**stilted** ['stɪltɪd] adj gestelzt.

**stimulant** ['stɪmjulənt] n Anregungsmittel nt.

**stimulate** ['stɪmjuleɪt] vt anregen, stimulieren; (demand) ankurbeln.

**stimulating** ['stɪmjuleɪtɪŋ] adj anregend, stimulierend.

**stimulation** [stɪmju'leɪʃən] n Anregung f, Stimulation f.

**stimuli** ['stɪmjulaɪ] npl of **stimulus**.

**stimulus** ['stɪmjuləs] (pl **stimuli**) n (incentive) Anreiz m; (BIOL) Reiz m; (PSYCH) Stimulus m.

**sting** [stɪŋ] (pt, pp **stung**) n Stich m; (pain) Stechen nt; (organ: of insect) Stachel m; (inf: confidence trick) Ding nt ♦ vt stechen; (fig) treffen, verletzen ♦ vi stechen; (eyes, ointment, plant etc) brennen; **my eyes are ~ing** mir brennen die Augen.

**stingy** ['stɪndʒɪ] (pej) adj geizig, knauserig.

**stink** [stɪŋk] (pt **stank**, pp **stunk**) n Gestank m ♦ vi stinken.

**stinker** ['stɪŋkə*] (inf) n (problem) harter Brocken m; (person) Ekel nt.

**stinking** ['stɪŋkɪŋ] (inf) adj (fig) beschissen (!);

a ~ **cold** eine scheußliche Erkältung; ~ **rich** stinkreich.

**stint** [stɪnt] n (*period*) Zeit f; (*batch of work*) Pensum nt; (*share*) Teil m ♦ vi: **to ~ on** sparen mit.

**stipend** ['staɪpɛnd] n Gehalt nt.

**stipendiary** [staɪ'pɛndɪərɪ] adj: ~ **magistrate** bezahlter Friedensrichter m.

**stipulate** ['stɪpjuleɪt] vt festsetzen; (*condition*) stellen.

**stipulation** [stɪpju'leɪʃən] n Bedingung f, Auflage f.

**stir** [stɜːʳ] n (*fig*) Aufsehen nt ♦ vt umrühren; (*fig: emotions*) aufwühlen; (: *person*) bewegen ♦ vi sich bewegen; **to give sth a ~** etw umrühren; **to cause a ~** Aufsehen erregen.

▶**stir up** vt: **to ~ up trouble** Unruhe stiften; **to ~ things up** stänkern.

**stir-fry** ['stɜː'fraɪ] vt unter Rühren kurz anbraten ♦ n Pfannengericht nt (*das unter Rühren kurz angebraten wurde*).

**stirring** ['stɜːrɪŋ] adj bewegend.

**stirrup** ['stɪrəp] n Steigbügel m.

**stitch** [stɪtʃ] n (*SEWING*) Stich m; (*KNITTING*) Masche f; (*MED*) Faden m; (*pain*) Seitenstiche pl ♦ vt nähen; **he had to have ~es** er mußte genäht werden.

**stoat** [stəʊt] n Wiesel nt.

**stock** [stɔk] n Vorrat m; (*COMM*) Bestand m; (*AGR*) Vieh nt; (*CULIN*) Brühe f; (*descent, origin*) Abstammung f, Herkunft f; (*FIN*) Wertpapiere pl; (*RAIL: also: rolling* ~) rollendes Material nt ♦ adj (*reply, excuse etc*) Standard- ♦ vt (*in shop*) führen; **in/out of ~** vorrätig/nicht vorrätig; ~**s and shares** (Aktien und) Wertpapiere pl; **government ~** Staatsanleihe f; **to take ~ of** (*fig*) Bilanz ziehen über +acc; **well-~ed** (*shop*) mit gutem Sortiment.

▶**stock up** vi: **to ~ up (with)** sich eindecken (mit).

**stockade** [stɔ'keɪd] n Palisade f.

**stockbroker** ['stɔkbrəʊkəʳ] n Börsenmakler m.

**stock control** n Bestandsüberwachung f.

**stock cube** (*BRIT*) n Brühwürfel m.

**stock exchange** n Börse f.

**stockholder** ['stɔkhəʊldəʳ] (*esp US*) n Aktionär(in) m(f).

**Stockholm** ['stɔkhəʊm] n Stockholm nt.

**stocking** ['stɔkɪŋ] n Strumpf m.

**stock-in-trade** ['stɔkɪn'treɪd] n (*fig*): **it's his ~** es gehört zu seinem festen Repertoire.

**stockist** ['stɔkɪst] (*BRIT*) n Händler m.

**stock market** (*BRIT*) n Börse f.

**stock phrase** n Standardsatz m.

**stockpile** ['stɔkpaɪl] n Vorrat m; (*of weapons*) Lager nt ♦ vt horten.

**stockroom** ['stɔkruːm] n Lager nt, Lagerraum m.

**stocktaking** ['stɔkteɪkɪŋ] (*BRIT*) n Inventur f.

**stocky** ['stɔkɪ] adj stämmig.

**stodgy** ['stɔdʒɪ] adj (*food*) pampig (*inf*), schwer.

**stoic** ['stəʊɪk] n Stoiker(in) m(f).

**stoic(al)** ['stəʊɪk(l)] adj stoisch.

**stoke** [stəʊk] vt (*fire*) schüren; (*furnace, boiler*) heizen.

**stoker** ['stəʊkəʳ] n Heizer m.

**stole** [stəʊl] pt of **steal** ♦ n Stola f.

**stolen** ['stəʊln] pp of **steal**.

**stolid** ['stɔlɪd] adj phlegmatisch, stur (*inf*).

**stomach** ['stʌmək] n Magen m; (*belly*) Bauch m ♦ vt (*fig*) vertragen.

**stomach ache** n Magenschmerzen pl.

**stomach pump** n Magenpumpe f.

**stomach ulcer** n Magengeschwür nt.

**stomp** [stɔmp] vi stapfen.

**stone** [stəʊn] n Stein m; (*BRIT: weight*) Gewichtseinheit (= 6,35 kg) ♦ adj (*wall, jar etc*) Stein-, steinern ♦ vt (*person*) mit Steinen bewerfen; (*fruit*) entkernen, entsteinen; **within a ~'s throw of the station** nur einen Katzensprung vom Bahnhof entfernt.

**Stone Age** n Steinzeit f.

**stone-cold** ['stəʊn'kəʊld] adj eiskalt.

**stoned** [stəʊnd] (*inf*) adj (*on drugs*) stoned; (*drunk*) total zu.

**stone-deaf** ['stəʊn'dɛf] adj stocktaub.

**stonemason** ['stəʊnmeɪsn] n Steinmetz m.

**stonewall** [stəʊn'wɔːl] vi mauern; (*in answering questions*) ausweichen.

**stonework** ['stəʊnwɜːk] n Mauerwerk nt.

**stony** ['stəʊnɪ] adj steinig; (*fig: silence etc*) steinern.

**stood** [stʊd] pt, pp of **stand**.

**stooge** [stuːdʒ] n (*inf*) Handlanger(in) m(f); (*THEAT*) Stichwortgeber(in) m(f).

**stool** [stuːl] n Hocker m.

**stoop** [stuːp] vi (*also:* ~ **down**) sich bücken; (*walk*) gebeugt gehen; **to ~ to sth** (*fig*) sich zu etw herablassen; **to ~ to doing sth** sich dazu herablassen, etw zu tun.

**stop** [stɔp] n Halt m; (*short stay*) Aufenthalt m; (*in punctuation: also: full* ~) Punkt m; (*bus stop etc*) Haltestelle f ♦ vt stoppen; (*car etc*) anhalten; (*block*) sperren; (*prevent*) verhindern ♦ vi (*car etc*) anhalten; (*train*) halten; (*pedestrian, watch, clock*) stehenbleiben; (*end*) aufhören; **to come to a ~** anhalten; **to put a ~ to** einen Riegel vorschieben +dat; **to ~ doing sth** aufhören, etw zu tun; **to ~ sb (from) doing sth** jdn davon abhalten, etw zu tun; ~ **it!** laß das!, hör auf!

▶**stop by** vi kurz vorbeikommen.

▶**stop off** vi kurz haltmachen, Zwischenstation machen.

▶**stop up** vt (*hole*) zustopfen.

**stopcock** ['stɔpkɔk] n Absperrhahn m.

**stopgap** ['stɔpgæp] n (*person*) Lückenbüßer m; (*thing*) Notbehelf m; ~ **measure** Überbrückungsmaßnahme f.

**stop-go** [stɔp'gəʊ] adj (*economic cycle etc*) mit

ständigem Auf und Ab.
**stoplights** ['stɔplaɪts] *npl* (*AUT*) Bremslichter
*pl*.
**stopover** ['stɔpəuvə'] *n* Zwischenaufenthalt
*m*; (*AVIAT*) Zwischenlandung *f*.
**stoppage** ['stɔpɪdʒ] *n* (*strike*) Streik *m*;
(*blockage*) Unterbrechung *f*; (*of pay, cheque*)
Sperrung *f*; (*deduction*) Abzug *m*.
**stopper** ['stɔpə'] *n* Stöpsel *m*.
**stop press** *n* letzte Meldungen *pl*.
**stopwatch** ['stɔpwɔtʃ] *n* Stoppuhr *f*.
**storage** ['stɔːrɪdʒ] *n* Lagerung *f*; (*also:*
~ **space**) Stauraum *m*; (*COMPUT*)
Speicherung *f*.
**storage capacity** *n* (*COMPUT*)
Speicherkapazität *f*.
**storage heater** (*BRIT*) *n* (Nacht)speicherofen
*m*.
**store** [stɔː'] *n* Vorrat *m*; (*depot*) Lager *nt*;
(*BRIT: large shop*) Geschäft *nt*, Kaufhaus *nt*;
(*US: shop*) Laden *m*; (*fig*): **a** ~ **of** eine Fülle
an +*dat* ♦ *vt* lagern; (*information etc, COMPUT*)
speichern; (*food, medicines etc*)
aufbewahren; (*in filing system*) ablegen;
**stores** *npl* (*provisions*) Vorräte *pl*; **in** ~
eingelagert; **who knows what's in** ~ **for us?**
wer weiß, was uns bevorsteht?; **to set**
**great/little** ~ **by sth** viel/wenig von etw
halten.
▶**store up** *vt* einen Vorrat anlegen von;
(*memories*) im Gedächtnis bewahren.
**storehouse** ['stɔːhaus] *n* (*US: COMM*)
Lager(haus) *nt*; (*fig*) Fundgrube *f*.
**storekeeper** ['stɔːkiːpə'] (*US*) *n*
Ladenbesitzer(in) *m(f)*.
**storeroom** ['stɔːruːm] *n* Lagerraum *m*.
**storey,** (*US*) **story** ['stɔːrɪ] *n* Stock *m*,
Stockwerk *nt*.
**stork** [stɔːk] *n* Storch *m*.
**storm** [stɔːm] *n* (*lit, fig*) Sturm *m*; (*bad weather*)
Unwetter *nt*; (*also:* **electrical** ~) Gewitter *nt*
♦ *vi* (*fig*) toben ♦ *vt* (*attack*) stürmen.
**storm cloud** *n* Gewitterwolke *f*.
**storm door** *n* äußere Windfangtür *f*.
**stormy** ['stɔːmɪ] *adj* (*lit, fig*) stürmisch.
**story** ['stɔːrɪ] *n* Geschichte *f*; (*PRESS*) Artikel
*m*; (*lie*) Märchen *nt*; (*US*) = **storey**.
**storybook** ['stɔːrɪbuk] *n* Geschichtenbuch *nt*.
**storyteller** ['stɔːrɪtelə'] *n* Geschichten-
erzähler(in) *m(f)*.
**stout** [staut] *adj* (*strong*) stark; (*fat*)
untersetzt; (*resolute*) energisch ♦ *n*
Starkbier *nt*.
**stove** [stəuv] *n* Herd *m*; (*small*) Kocher *m*; (*for*
*heating*) (Heiz)ofen *m*; **gas** ~ Gasherd *m*.
**stow** [stəu] *vt* (*also:* ~ **away**) verstauen.
**stowaway** ['stəuəweɪ] *n* blinder Passagier *m*.
**straddle** ['strædl] *vt* (*sitting*) rittlings sitzen
auf +*dat*; (*standing*) breitbeinig stehen über
+*dat*; (*jumping*) grätschen über +*acc*; (*fig*)
überspannen.
**strafe** [strɑːf] *vt* beschießen.

**straggle** ['strægl] *vi* (*houses etc*) verstreut
liegen; (*people etc*) zurückbleiben.
**straggler** ['stræglə'] *n* Nachzügler *m*.
**straggly** ['stræglɪ] *adj* (*hair*) unordentlich.
**straight** [streɪt] *adj* gerade; (*hair*) glatt;
(*honest*) offen, direkt; (*simple*) einfach;
(: *fight*) direkt; (*THEAT*) ernst; (*inf:*
*heterosexual*) hetero; (*whisky etc*) pur ♦ *adv*
(*in time*) sofort; (*in direction*) direkt; (*drink*)
pur ♦ *n* (*SPORT*) Gerade *f*; **to put** *or* **get sth** ~
(*make clear*) etw klären; (*make tidy*) etw in
Ordnung bringen; **let's get this** ~ das
wollen wir mal klarstellen; **10** ~ **wins** 10
Siege hintereinander; **to win in** ~ **sets**
(*TENNIS*) ohne Satzverlust gewinnen; **to go**
~ **home** direkt nach Hause gehen; ~ **out**
rundheraus; ~ **away,** ~ **off** sofort, gleich.
**straighten** ['streɪtn] *vt* (*skirt, sheet etc*)
geradeziehen.
▶**straighten out** *vt* (*fig*) klären.
**straight-faced** [streɪt'feɪst] *adj*: **to be/remain**
~ ernst bleiben ♦ *adv* ohne zu lachen.
**straightforward** [streɪt'fɔːwəd] *adj* (*simple*)
einfach; (*honest*) offen.
**straight sets** *npl* (*TENNIS*): **to win in** ~ ohne
Satzverlust gewinnen.
**strain** [streɪn] *n* Belastung *f*; (*MED: also:* **back**
~) überanstrengter Rücken *m*; (: *tension*)
Überlastung *f*; (*of virus*) Art *f*; (*breed*) Sorte *f*
♦ *vt* (*back etc*) überanstrengen; (*resources*)
belasten; (*CULIN*) abgießen ♦ *vi:* **to** ~ **to do**
**sth** sich anstrengen, etw zu tun; **strains** *npl*
(*MUS*) Klänge *pl*; **he's been under a lot of** ~
er hat unter großem Streß gestanden.
**strained** [streɪnd] *adj* (*back*) überanstrengt;
(*muscle*) gezerrt; (*forced*) gezwungen;
(*relations*) gespannt.
**strainer** ['streɪnə'] *n* Sieb *nt*.
**strait** [streɪt] *n* Meerenge *f*, Straße *f*; **straits** *npl*
(*fig*): **to be in dire** ~**s** in großen Nöten sein.
**straitjacket** ['streɪtdʒækɪt] *n* Zwangsjacke *f*.
**strait-laced** [streɪt'leɪst] *adj* prüde,
puritanisch.
**strand** [strænd] *n* (*lit, fig*) Faden *m*; (*of wire*)
Litze *f*; (*of hair*) Strähne *f*.
**stranded** ['strændɪd] *adj*: **to be** ~ (*traveller*)
festsitzen; (*ship, sea creature*) gestrandet.
**strange** [streɪndʒ] *adj* fremd; (*odd*) seltsam,
merkwürdig.
**strangely** ['streɪndʒlɪ] *adv* seltsam,
merkwürdig; *see also* **enough**.
**stranger** ['streɪndʒə'] *n* Fremde(r) *f(m)*; **I'm a**
~ **here** ich bin hier fremd.
**strangle** ['stræŋgl] *vt* erwürgen, erdrosseln;
(*fig: economy etc*) ersticken.
**stranglehold** ['stræŋglhəuld] *n* (*fig*) absolute
Machtposition *f*.
**strangulation** [stræŋgju'leɪʃən] *n* Erwürgen
*nt*, Erdrosseln *nt*.
**strap** [stræp] *n* Riemen *m*; (*of dress etc*) Träger
*m* ♦ *vt* (*also:* ~ **in**) anschnallen; (*also:* ~ **on**)
umschnallen.

**straphanging** ['stræphæŋɪŋ] n Pendeln nt (als stehender Fahrgast).

**strapless** ['stræplɪs] adj trägerlos, schulterfrei.

**strapped** [stræpt] (inf) adj: ~ **(for cash)** pleite.

**strapping** ['stræpɪŋ] adj stramm.

**Strasbourg** ['stræzbɔːg] n Straßburg nt.

**strata** ['strɑːtə] npl of **stratum**.

**stratagem** ['strætɪdʒəm] n List f.

**strategic** [strə'tiːdʒɪk] adj strategisch; (error) taktisch.

**strategist** ['strætɪdʒɪst] n Stratege m, Strategin f.

**strategy** ['strætɪdʒɪ] n Strategie f.

**stratosphere** ['strætəsfɪə'] n Stratosphäre f.

**stratum** ['strɑːtəm] (pl **strata**) n Schicht f.

**straw** [strɔː] n Stroh nt; (drinking straw) Strohhalm m; **that's the last ~!** das ist der Gipfel!

**strawberry** ['strɔːbərɪ] n Erdbeere f.

**stray** [streɪ] adj (animal) streunend; (bullet) verirrt; (scattered) einzeln, vereinzelt ♦ vi (children) sich verirren; (animals) streunen; (thoughts) abschweifen.

**streak** [striːk] n Streifen m; (in hair) Strähne f; (fig: of madness etc) Zug m ♦ vt streifen ♦ vi: **to ~ past** vorbeiflitzen; **a winning/losing ~** eine Glücks-/Pechsträhne.

**streaker** ['striːkə'] (inf) n Blitzer(in) m(f).

**streaky** ['striːkɪ] adj (bacon) durchwachsen.

**stream** [striːm] n (small river) Bach m; (current) Strömung f; (of people, vehicles) Strom m; (of questions, insults etc) Flut f, Schwall m; (of smoke) Schwaden m; (SCOL) Leistungsgruppe f ♦ vt (SCOL) in Leistungsgruppen einteilen ♦ vi strömen; **against the ~** gegen den Strom; **to come on ~** (new power plant etc) in Betrieb genommen werden.

**streamer** ['striːmə'] n Luftschlange f.

**stream feed** n automatischer Papiereinzug m.

**streamline** ['striːmlaɪn] vt Stromlinienform geben +dat; (fig) rationalisieren.

**streamlined** ['striːmlaɪnd] adj stromlinienförmig; (AVIAT, AUT) windschlüpfrig; (fig) rationalisiert.

**street** [striːt] n Straße f; **the back ~s** die Seitensträßchen pl; **to be on the ~s** (homeless) obdachlos sein; (as prostitute) auf den Strich gehen.

**streetcar** ['striːtkɑː'] (US) n Straßenbahn f.

**street cred** [-krɛd] (inf) n Glaubwürdigkeit f.

**street lamp** n Straßenlaterne f.

**street lighting** n Straßenbeleuchtung f.

**street map** n Stadtplan m.

**street market** n Straßenmarkt m.

**street plan** n Stadtplan m.

**streetwise** ['striːtwaɪz] (inf) adj: **to be ~** wissen, wo's langgeht.

**strength** [strɛŋθ] n (lit, fig) Stärke f; (physical) Kraft f, Stärke f; (of girder etc) Stabilität f; (of knot etc) Festigkeit f; (of chemical solution) Konzentration f; (of wine) Schwere f; **on the ~ of** auf Grund +gen; **at full ~** vollzählig; **to be below ~** nicht die volle Stärke haben.

**strengthen** ['strɛŋθn] vt (lit, fig) verstärken; (muscle) kräftigen; (economy, currency, relationship) festigen.

**strenuous** ['strɛnjuəs] adj anstrengend; (determined) unermüdlich.

**strenuously** ['strɛnjuəslɪ] adv energisch; **she ~ denied the rumour** sie leugnete das Gerücht hartnäckig.

**stress** [strɛs] n Druck m; (mental) Belastung f, Streß m; (LING) Betonung f; (emphasis) Akzent m, Gewicht nt ♦ vt betonen; **to lay great ~ on sth** großen Wert auf etw acc legen; **to be under ~** großen Belastungen ausgesetzt sein, unter Streß stehen.

**stressful** ['strɛsful] adj anstrengend, stressig; (situation) angespannt.

**stretch** [strɛtʃ] n (of sand, water etc) Stück nt; (of time) Zeit f ♦ vi (person, animal) sich strecken; (land, area) sich erstrecken ♦ vt (pull) spannen; (fig: job, task) fordern; **at a ~** an einem Stück, ohne Unterbrechung; **by no ~ of the imagination** beim besten Willen nicht; **to ~ to** or **as far as the frontier** (extend) sich bis zur Grenze erstrecken; **to ~ one's legs** sich dat die Beine vertreten.

▶**stretch out** vi sich ausstrecken ♦ vt ausstrecken.

▶**stretch to** vt fus (be enough) reichen für.

**stretcher** ['strɛtʃə'] n (Trag)bahre f.

**stretcher-bearer** ['strɛtʃəbɛərə'] n Krankenträger m.

**stretch marks** npl Dehnungsstreifen pl; (through pregnancy) Schwangerschafts-streifen pl.

**strewn** [struːn] adj: ~ **with** übersät mit.

**stricken** ['strɪkən] adj (person) leidend; (city, industry etc) notleidend; ~ **with** (disease) geschlagen mit; (fear etc) erfüllt von.

**strict** [strɪkt] adj streng; (precise) genau; **in the ~est confidence** streng vertraulich; **in the ~ sense of the word** streng genommen.

**strictly** ['strɪktlɪ] adv streng; (exactly) genau; (solely) ausschließlich; ~ **confidential** streng vertraulich; ~ **speaking** genau genommen; **not ~ true** nicht ganz richtig; ~ **between ourselves** ganz unter uns.

**strictness** ['strɪktnɪs] n Strenge f.

**stridden** ['strɪdn] pp of **stride**.

**stride** [straɪd] (pt **strode**, pp **stridden**) n Schritt m ♦ vi schreiten; **to take sth in one's ~** (fig) mit etw spielend fertig werden.

**strident** ['straɪdnt] adj schrill, durchdringend; (demands) lautstark.

**strife** [straɪf] n Streit m, Zwietracht f.

**strike** [straɪk] (pt, pp **struck**) n Streik m, Ausstand m; (MIL) Angriff m ♦ vt (hit) schlagen; (fig: idea, thought) in den Sinn kommmen +dat; (oil etc) finden, stoßen auf

+*acc*; (*bargain, deal*) aushandeln; (*coin, medal*) prägen ♦ *vi* streiken; (*illness, killer*) zuschlagen; (*disaster*) hereinbrechen; (*clock*) schlagen; **on ~** streikend; **to be on ~** streiken; **to ~ a balance** einen Mittelweg finden; **to be struck by lightning** vom Blitz getroffen werden; **to ~ a match** ein Streichholz anzünden.

▶**strike back** *vi* (*MIL*) zurückschlagen; (*fig*) sich wehren.

▶**strike down** *vt* niederschlagen.

▶**strike off** *vt* (*from list*) (aus)streichen; (*doctor etc*) die Zulassung entziehen +*dat*.

▶**strike out** *vi* losziehen, sich aufmachen ♦ *vt* (*word, sentence*) (aus)streichen.

▶**strike up** *vt* (*MUS*) anstimmen; (*conversation*) anknüpfen; (*friendship*) schließen.

**strikebreaker** ['straɪkbreɪkə*] *n* Streikbrecher *m*.

**strike pay** *n* Streikgeld *nt*.

**striker** ['straɪkə*] *n* Streikende(r) *f(m)*; (*SPORT*) Stürmer *m*.

**striking** ['straɪkɪŋ] *adj* auffallend; (*attractive*) attraktiv.

**strimmer** ['strɪmə*] *n* Rasentrimmer *m*.

**string** [strɪŋ] (*pt, pp* **strung**) *n* Schnur *f*; (*of islands*) Kette *f*; (*of people, cars*) Schlange *f*; (*series*) Serie *f*; (*COMPUT*) Zeichenfolge *f*; (*MUS*) Saite *f* ♦ *vt*: **to ~ together** aneinanderreihen; **the strings** *npl* (*MUS*) die Streichinstrumente *pl*; **to pull ~s** (*fig*) Beziehungen spielen lassen; **with no ~s attached** (*fig*) ohne Bedingungen; **to ~ sth out** etw verteilen.

**string bean** *n* grüne Bohne *f*.

**stringed instrument** *n* Saiteninstrument *nt*.

**stringent** ['strɪndʒənt] *adj* streng; (*measures*) drastisch.

**string quartet** *n* Streichquartett *nt*.

**strip** [strɪp] *n* Streifen *m*; (*of metal*) Band *nt*; (*SPORT*) Trikot *nt*, Dreß *m* ♦ *vt* (*undress*) ausziehen; (*paint*) abbeizen; (*also:* ~ **down**: *machine etc*) auseinandernehmen ♦ *vi* (*undress*) sich ausziehen.

**strip cartoon** *n* Comic(strip) *m*.

**stripe** [straɪp] *n* Streifen *m*; **stripes** *npl* (*MIL, POLICE*) (Ärmel)streifen *pl*.

**striped** [straɪpt] *adj* gestreift.

**strip lighting** (*BRIT*) *n* Neonlicht *nt*.

**stripper** ['strɪpə*] *n* Stripper(in) *m(f)*, Stripteasetänzer(in) *m(f)*.

**strip-search** ['strɪpsɜːtʃ] *n* Leibesvisitation *f* (*bei der man sich ausziehen muß*) ♦ *vt*: **to be ~ed** sich ausziehen müssen und durchsucht werden.

**striptease** ['strɪptiːz] *n* Striptease *m or nt*.

**strive** [straɪv] (*pt* **strove**, *pp* **striven**) *vi*: **to ~ for sth** nach etw streben; **to ~ to do sth** danach streben, etw zu tun.

**striven** ['strɪvn] *pp of* **strive**.

**strobe** [strəʊb] *n* (*also:* ~ **lights**)

Stroboskoplicht *nt*.

**strode** [strəʊd] *pt of* **stride**.

**stroke** [strəʊk] *n* Schlag *m*, Hieb *m*; (*SWIMMING: style*) Stil *m*; (*MED*) Schlaganfall *m*; (*of clock*) Schlag *m*; (*of paintbrush*) Strich *m* ♦ *vt* (*caress*) streicheln; **at a ~** mit einem Schlag; **on the ~ of 5** Punkt 5 (Uhr); **a ~ of luck** ein Glücksfall *m*; **a 2-~ engine** ein Zweitaktmotor *m*.

**stroll** [strəʊl] *n* Spaziergang *m* ♦ *vi* spazieren; **to go for a ~, have** *or* **take a ~** einen Spaziergang machen.

**stroller** ['strəʊlə*] (*US*) *n* (*pushchair*) Sportwagen *m*.

**strong** [strɔŋ] *adj* stark; (*person, arms, grip*) stark, kräftig; (*healthy*) kräftig; (*object, material*) solide, stabil; (*letter*) geharnischt; (*measure*) drastisch; (*language*) derb; (*nerves*) gut; (*taste, smell*) streng ♦ *adv*: **to be going ~** (*company*) sehr erfolgreich sein; (*person*) gut in Schuß sein; **I have no ~ feelings about it** es ist mir ziemlich egal; **they are 50 ~** sie sind insgesamt 50.

**strong-arm** ['strɔŋɑːm] *adj* brutal.

**strongbox** ['strɔŋbɔks] *n* (Geld)kassette *f*.

**stronghold** ['strɔŋhəʊld] *n* Festung *f*; (*fig*) Hochburg *f*.

**strongly** ['strɔŋlɪ] *adv* (*solidly*) stabil; (*forcefully*) entschieden; (*deeply*) fest; **to feel ~ that ...** fest davon überzeugt sein, daß ...; **I feel ~ about it** mir liegt sehr viel daran; (*negatively*) ich bin sehr dagegen.

**strongman** ['strɔŋmæn] (*irreg: like* **man**) *n* (*lit, fig*) starker Mann *m*.

**strongroom** ['strɔŋruːm] *n* Tresorraum *m*.

**stroppy** ['strɔpɪ] (*BRIT: inf*) *adj* pampig; (*obstinate*) stur.

**strove** [strəʊv] *pt of* **strive**.

**struck** [strʌk] *pt, pp of* **strike**.

**structural** ['strʌktʃrəl] *adj* strukturell; (*damage*) baulich; (*defect*) Konstruktions-.

**structurally** ['strʌktʃrəlɪ] *adv*: **~ sound** mit guter Bausubstanz.

**structure** ['strʌktʃə*] *n* Struktur *f*, Aufbau *m*; (*building*) Gebäude *nt*.

**struggle** ['strʌgl] *n* Kampf *m*; (*difficulty*) Anstrengung *f* ♦ *vi* (*try hard*) sich abmühen; (*fight*) kämpfen; (*in self-defence*) sich wehren; **to have a ~ to do sth** Mühe haben, etw zu tun; **to be a ~ for sb** jdm große Schwierigkeiten bereiten.

**strum** [strʌm] *vt* (*guitar*) klimpern auf +*dat*.

**strung** [strʌŋ] *pt, pp of* **string**.

**strut** [strʌt] *n* Strebe *f*, Stütze *f* ♦ *vi* stolzieren.

**strychnine** ['strɪkniːn] *n* Strychnin *nt*.

**stub** [stʌb] *n* (*of cheque, ticket etc*) Abschnitt *m*; (*of cigarette*) Kippe *f* ♦ *vt*: **to ~ one's toe** sich *dat* den Zeh stoßen.

▶**stub out** *vt* (*cigarette*) ausdrücken.

**stubble** ['stʌbl] *n* Stoppeln *pl*.

**stubborn** ['stʌbən] *adj* hartnäckig; (*child*) störrisch.

**stubby** ['stʌbɪ] *adj* kurz und dick.

**stucco** ['stʌkəu] *n* Stuck *m*.

**stuck** [stʌk] *pt, pp of* **stick** ♦ *adj:* **to be ~** (*jammed*) klemmen; (*unable to answer*) nicht klarkommen; **to get ~** steckenbleiben; (*fig*) nicht weiterkommen.

**stuck-up** [stʌk'ʌp] (*inf*) *adj* hochnäsig.

**stud** [stʌd] *n* (*on clothing etc*) Niete *f*; (*on collar*) Kragenknopf *m*; (*earring*) Ohrstecker *m*; (*on boot*) Stollen *m*; (*also:* ~ **farm**) Gestüt *nt*; (*also:* ~ **horse**) Zuchthengst *m* ♦ *vt* (*fig*): **~ded with** übersät mit; (*with jewels*) dicht besetzt mit.

**student** ['stju:dənt] *n* Student(in) *m(f)*; (*at school*) Schüler(in) *m(f)* ♦ *cpd* Studenten-; **law/medical** ~ Jura-/Medizinstudent(in) *m(f)*; ~ **nurse** Krankenpflegeschüler(in) *m(f)*; ~ **teacher** Referendar(in) *m(f)*.

**student driver** (*US*) *n* Fahrschüler(in) *m(f)*.

**students' union** ['stju:dənts-] (*BRIT*) *n* Studentenvereinigung *f*, ≈ AStA *m*; (*building*) Gebäude *nt* der Studentenvereinigung.

**studied** ['stʌdɪd] *adj* (*expression*) einstudiert; (*attitude*) berechnet.

**studio** ['stju:dɪəu] *n* Studio *nt*; (*sculptor's etc*) Atelier *nt*.

**studio flat,** (*US*) **studio apartment** *n* Einzimmerwohnung *f*.

**studious** ['stju:dɪəs] *adj* lernbegierig.

**studiously** ['stju:dɪəslɪ] *adv* (*carefully*) sorgsam.

**study** ['stʌdɪ] *n* Studium *nt*, Lernen *nt*; (*room*) Arbeitszimmer *nt* ♦ *vt* studieren; (*face*) prüfend ansehen; (*evidence*) prüfen ♦ *vi* studieren, lernen; **studies** *npl* (*studying*) Studien *pl*; **to make a ~ of sth** etw untersuchen; (*academic*) etw studieren; **to ~ for an exam** sich auf eine Prüfung vorbereiten.

**stuff** [stʌf] *n* Zeug *nt* ♦ *vt* ausstopfen; (*CULIN*) füllen; (*inf: push*) stopfen; **my nose is ~ed up** ich habe eine verstopfte Nase; **get ~ed!** (*inf!*) du kannst mich mal!

**stuffed toy** [stʌft-] *n* Stofftier *nt*.

**stuffing** ['stʌfɪŋ] *n* Füllung *f*; (*in sofa etc*) Polstermaterial *nt*.

**stuffy** ['stʌfɪ] *adj* (*room*) stickig; (*person, ideas*) spießig.

**stumble** ['stʌmbl] *vi* stolpern; **to ~ across or on** (*fig*) (zufällig) stoßen auf +*acc*.

**stumbling block** ['stʌmblɪŋ-] *n* Hürde *f*, Hindernis *nt*.

**stump** [stʌmp] *n* Stumpf *m* ♦ *vt*: **to be ~ed** überfragt sein.

**stun** [stʌn] *vt* betäuben; (*news*) fassungslos machen.

**stung** [stʌŋ] *pt, pp of* **sting**.

**stunk** [stʌŋk] *pp of* **stink**.

**stunning** ['stʌnɪŋ] *adj* (*news, event*) sensationell; (*girl, dress*) hinreißend.

**stunt** [stʌnt] *n* (*in film*) Stunt *m*; (*publicity stunt*) (Werbe)gag *m*.

**stunted** ['stʌntɪd] *adj* verkümmert.

**stuntman** ['stʌntmæn] (*irreg: like* **man**) *n* Stuntman *m*.

**stupefaction** [stju:pɪ'fækʃən] *n* Verblüffung *f*.

**stupefy** ['stju:pɪfaɪ] *vt* benommen machen; (*fig*) verblüffen.

**stupendous** [stju:'pɛndəs] *adj* enorm.

**stupid** ['stju:pɪd] *adj* dumm.

**stupidity** [stju:'pɪdɪtɪ] *n* Dummheit *f*.

**stupidly** ['stju:pɪdlɪ] *adv* dumm.

**stupor** ['stju:pə*'*] *n* Benommenheit *f*; **in a ~** benommen.

**sturdily** ['stɜːdɪlɪ] *adv*: ~ **built** (*person*) kräftig gebaut; (*thing*) stabil gebaut.

**sturdy** ['stɜːdɪ] *adj* (*person*) kräftig; (*thing*) stabil.

**sturgeon** ['stɜːdʒən] *n* Stör *m*.

**stutter** ['stʌtə*'*] *n* Stottern *nt* ♦ *vi* stottern; **to have a ~** stottern.

**Stuttgart** ['stutgɑːt] *n* Stuttgart *nt*.

**sty** [staɪ] *n* Schweinestall *m*.

**stye** [staɪ] *n* Gerstenkorn *nt*.

**style** [staɪl] *n* Stil *m*; (*design*) Modell *nt*; **in the latest ~** nach der neuesten Mode; **hair ~** Frisur *f*.

**styli** ['staɪlaɪ] *npl of* **stylus**.

**stylish** ['staɪlɪʃ] *adj* elegant.

**stylist** ['staɪlɪst] *n* (*hair stylist*) Friseur *m*, Friseuse *f*; (*literary stylist*) Stilist(in) *m(f)*.

**stylized** ['staɪlaɪzd] *adj* stilisiert.

**stylus** ['staɪləs] (*pl* **styli** *or* ~**es**) *n* Nadel *f*.

**Styrofoam** ® ['staɪrəfəum] *n* ≈ Styropor *nt* ®.

**suave** [swɑːv] *adj* zuvorkommend.

**sub** [sʌb] *n abbr* (*NAUT*) = **submarine**; (*ADMIN*) = **subscription**; (*BRIT: PRESS*) = **subeditor**.

**sub...** [sʌb] *pref* Unter-, unter-.

**subcommittee** ['sʌbkəmɪtɪ] *n* Unterausschuß *m*.

**subconscious** [sʌb'kɒnʃəs] *adj* unterbewußt.

**subcontinent** [sʌb'kɒntɪnənt] *n*: **the (Indian) ~** der (indische) Subkontinent.

**subcontract** [*vt* sʌbkən'trækt, *n* 'sʌb'kɒntrækt] *vt* (vertraglich) weitervergeben ♦ *n* Nebenvertrag *m*.

**subcontractor** ['sʌbkən'træktə*'*] *n* Subunternehmer *m*.

**subdivide** [sʌbdɪ'vaɪd] *vt* unterteilen.

**subdivision** ['sʌbdɪvɪʒən] *n* Unterteilung *f*.

**subdue** [səb'dju:] *vt* unterwerfen; (*emotions*) dämpfen.

**subdued** [səb'dju:d] *adj* (*light*) gedämpft; (*person*) bedrückt.

**subeditor** [sʌb'ɛdɪtə*'*] (*BRIT*) *n* Redakteur(in) *m(f)*.

**subject** [*n* 'sʌbdʒɪkt, *vt* səb'dʒɛkt] *n* (*matter*) Thema *nt*; (*SCOL*) Fach *nt*; (*of country*) Staatsbürger(in) *m(f)*; (*GRAM*) Subjekt *nt* ♦ *vt*: **to ~ sb to sth** jdn einer Sache *dat* unterziehen; (*expose*) jdn einer Sache *dat* aussetzen; **to change the ~** das Thema wechseln; **to be ~ to** (*law, tax*) unterworfen sein +*dat*; (*heart attacks etc*) anfällig sein für;

~ **to confirmation in writing** vorausgesetzt, es wird schriftlich bestätigt.

**subjection** [səb'dʒekʃən] n Unterwerfung f.

**subjective** [səb'dʒektɪv] adj subjektiv.

**subject matter** n Stoff m; (content) Inhalt m.

**sub judice** [sʌb'dju:dɪsɪ] adj (LAW): **to be ~** verhandelt werden.

**subjugate** ['sʌbdʒugeɪt] vt unterwerfen.

**subjunctive** [səb'dʒʌŋktɪv] n Konjunktiv m; **in the ~** im Konjunktiv.

**sublet** [sʌb'let] vt untervermieten.

**sublime** [sə'blaɪm] adj erhaben, vollendet; **that's going from the ~ to the ridiculous** das ist ein Abstieg ins Profane.

**subliminal** [sʌb'lɪmɪnl] adj unterschwellig.

**submachine gun** ['sʌbməˈʃiːn-] n Maschinenpistole f.

**submarine** [sʌbmə'riːn] n Unterseeboot nt, U-Boot nt.

**submerge** [səb'mɜːdʒ] vt untertauchen; (flood) überschwemmen ♦ vi tauchen; **~d** unter Wasser.

**submersion** [səb'mɜːʃən] n Untertauchen nt; (of submarine) Tauchen nt; (by flood) Überschwemmung f.

**submission** [səb'mɪʃən] n (subjection) Unterwerfung f; (of plan, application etc) Einreichung f; (proposal) Vorlage f.

**submissive** [səb'mɪsɪv] adj gehorsam; (gesture) demütig.

**submit** [səb'mɪt] vt (proposal) vorlegen; (application etc) einreichen ♦ vi: **to ~ to sth** sich einer Sache dat unterwerfen.

**subnormal** [sʌb'nɔːml] adj (below average) unterdurchschnittlich; (old: child etc) minderbegabt; **educationally ~** lernbehindert.

**subordinate** [sə'bɔːdɪnət] n Untergebene(r) f(m); (LING): **~ clause** Nebensatz m ♦ adj untergeordnet; **to be ~ to sb** jdm untergeordnet sein.

**subpoena** [səb'piːnə] n (LAW) Vorladung f ♦ vt vorladen.

**subroutine** [sʌbruːˈtiːn] n (COMPUT) Unterprogramm nt.

**subscribe** [səb'skraɪb] vi spenden; **to ~ to** (opinion, theory) sich anschließen +dat; (fund, charity) regelmäßig spenden an +acc; (magazine etc) abonnieren.

**subscriber** [səb'skraɪbə*] n (to magazine) Abonnent(in) m(f); (TEL) Teilnehmer(in) m(f).

**subscript** ['sʌbskrɪpt] n tiefgestelltes Zeichen nt.

**subscription** [səb'skrɪpʃən] n (to magazine etc) Abonnement nt; (membership dues) (Mitglieds)beitrag m; **to take out a ~ to** (magazine etc) abonnieren.

**subsequent** ['sʌbsɪkwənt] adj später, nachfolgend; (further) weiter; **~ to** im Anschluß an +acc.

**subsequently** ['sʌbsɪkwəntlɪ] adv später.

**subservient** [səb'sɜːvɪənt] adj unterwürfig;

(less important) untergeordnet; **to be ~ to** untergeordnet sein +dat.

**subside** [səb'saɪd] vi (feeling, pain) nachlassen; (flood) sinken; (earth) sich senken.

**subsidence** [səb'saɪdns] n Senkung f.

**subsidiarity** [səbsɪdɪ'ærɪtɪ] n Subsidiarität f.

**subsidiary** [səb'sɪdɪərɪ] adj (question, role, BRIT: SCOL: subject) Neben- ♦ n (also: ~ **company**) Tochtergesellschaft f.

**subsidize** ['sʌbsɪdaɪz] vt subventionieren.

**subsidy** ['sʌbsɪdɪ] n Subvention f.

**subsist** [səb'sɪst] vi: **to ~ on sth** sich von etw ernähren.

**subsistence** [səb'sɪstəns] n Existenz f; **enough for ~** genug zum (Über)leben.

**subsistence allowance** n Unterhaltszuschuß m.

**subsistence level** n Existenzminimum nt.

**substance** ['sʌbstəns] n Substanz f, Stoff m; (fig: essence) Kern m; **a man of ~** ein vermögender Mann; **to lack ~** (book) keine Substanz haben; (argument) keine Durchschlagskraft haben.

**substance abuse** n Mißbrauch von Alkohol, Drogen, Arzneimitteln etc.

**substandard** [sʌb'stændəd] adj minderwertig; (housing) unzulänglich.

**substantial** [səb'stænʃl] adj (solid) solide; (considerable) beträchtlich, größere(r, s); (meal) kräftig.

**substantially** [səb'stænʃəlɪ] adv erheblich; (in essence) im wesentlichen.

**substantiate** [səb'stænʃɪeɪt] vt erhärten, untermauern.

**substitute** ['sʌbstɪtjuːt] n Ersatz m ♦ vt: **to ~ A for B** B durch A ersetzen.

**substitute teacher** (US) n Vertretung f.

**substitution** [sʌbstɪ'tjuːʃən] n Ersetzen nt; (FOOTBALL) Auswechseln nt.

**subterfuge** ['sʌbtəfjuːdʒ] n Tricks pl; (trickery) Täuschung f.

**subterranean** [sʌbtə'reɪnɪən] adj unterirdisch.

**subtitle** ['sʌbtaɪtl] n Untertitel m.

**subtle** ['sʌtl] adj fein; (indirect) raffiniert.

**subtlety** ['sʌtltɪ] n Feinheit f; (art of being subtle) Finesse f.

**subtly** ['sʌtlɪ] adv (change, vary) leicht; (different) auf subtile Weise; (persuade) raffiniert.

**subtotal** [sʌb'təutl] n Zwischensumme f.

**subtract** [səb'trækt] vt abziehen, subtrahieren.

**subtraction** [səb'trækʃən] n Abziehen nt, Subtraktion f.

**subtropical** [sʌb'trɒpɪkl] adj subtropisch.

**suburb** ['sʌbɜːb] n Vorort m.

**suburban** [sə'bɜːbən] adj (train etc) Vorort-; (lifestyle etc) spießig, kleinbürgerlich.

**suburbia** [sə'bɜːbɪə] n die Vororte pl.

**subvention** [səb'vɛnʃən] n Subvention f.

**subversion** [səb'vɜːʃən] n Subversion f.

**subversive** [səb'vɜːsɪv] adj subversiv.

**subway** ['sʌbweɪ] *n (US)* Untergrundbahn *f*, U-Bahn *f*; (*BRIT: underpass*) Unterführung *f*.

**sub-zero** [sʌb'zɪərəʊ] *adj*: ~ **temperatures** Temperaturen unter Null.

**succeed** [sək'siːd] *vi (plan etc)* gelingen, erfolgreich sein; (*person*) erfolgreich sein, Erfolg haben ♦ *vt (in job)* Nachfolger werden +*gen*; (*in order*) folgen +*dat*; **sb ~s in doing sth** es gelingt jdm, etw zu tun.

**succeeding** [sək'siːdɪŋ] *adj* folgend; ~ **generations** spätere *or* nachfolgende Generationen *pl*.

**success** [sək'sɛs] *n* Erfolg *m*; **without** ~ ohne Erfolg, erfolglos.

**successful** [sək'sɛsful] *adj* erfolgreich; **to be** ~ erfolgreich sein, Erfolg haben; **sb is** ~ **in doing sth** es gelingt jdm, etw zu tun.

**successfully** [sək'sɛsfəlɪ] *adv* erfolgreich, mit Erfolg.

**succession** [sək'sɛʃən] *n* Folge *f*, Serie *f*; (*to throne etc*) Nachfolge *f*; **3 years in** ~ 3 Jahre nacheinander *or* hintereinander.

**successive** [sək'sɛsɪv] *adj* aufeinander-folgend; **on 3** ~ **days** 3 Tage nacheinander *or* hintereinander.

**successor** [sək'sɛsə*] *n* Nachfolger(in) *m(f)*.

**succinct** [sək'sɪŋkt] *adj* knapp, prägnant.

**succulent** ['sʌkjulənt] *adj* saftig ♦ *n* Fettpflanze *f*, Sukkulente *f*.

**succumb** [sə'kʌm] *vi*: **to ~ to** (*temptation*) erliegen +*dat*; (*illness: become affected by*) bekommen; (: *die of*) erliegen +*dat*.

**such** [sʌtʃ] *adj (of that kind)*: ~ **a book** so ein Buch; (*so much*): ~ **courage** so viel Mut; (*emphasizing similarity*): **or some** ~ **place/ name** *etc* oder so ähnlich ♦ *adv* so; ~ **books** solche Bücher; ~ **a lot of** so viel; **she made** ~ **a noise that** ... sie machte so einen Lärm, daß ...; ~ **books as I have** was ich an Büchern habe; **I said no** ~ **thing** das habe ich nie gesagt; ~ **a long trip** so eine lange Reise; ~ **as** wie (zum Beispiel); **as** ~ an sich.

**such-and-such** ['sʌtʃənsʌtʃ] *adj* die und die, der und der, das und das.

**suchlike** ['sʌtʃlaɪk] (*inf*) *pron*: **and** ~ und dergleichen.

**suck** [sʌk] *vt (sweet etc)* lutschen; (*ice-lolly*) lutschen an +*dat*; (*baby*) saugen an +*dat*; (*pump, machine*) saugen.

**sucker** ['sʌkə*] *n (ZOOL)* Saugnapf *m*; (*TECH*) Saugfuß *m*; (*BOT*) unterirdischer Ausläufer *m*; (*inf*) Dummkopf *m*.

**suckle** ['sʌkl] *vt (baby)* stillen; (*animal*) säugen.

**sucrose** ['suːkrəʊz] *n (pflanzlicher)* Zucker *m*.

**suction** ['sʌkʃən] *n* Saugwirkung *f*.

**suction pump** *n* Saugpumpe *f*.

**Sudan** [su'dɑːn] *n* der Sudan.

**Sudanese** [suːdə'niːz] *adj* sudanesisch ♦ *n* Sudanese *m*, Sudanesin *f*.

**sudden** ['sʌdn] *adj* plötzlich; **all of a** ~ ganz plötzlich.

**sudden death** *n (also:* **sudden-death play-off**) Stichkampf *m*.

**suddenly** ['sʌdnlɪ] *adv* plötzlich.

**suds** [sʌdz] *npl* Seifenschaum *m*.

**sue** [suː] *vt* verklagen ♦ *vi* klagen, vor Gericht gehen; **to ~ sb for damages** jdn auf Schadenersatz verklagen; **to ~ for divorce** die Scheidung einreichen.

**suede** [sweɪd] *n* Wildleder *nt* ♦ *cpd* Wildleder-.

**suet** ['suːɪt] *n* Nierenfett *nt*.

**Suez** ['suːɪz] *n*: **the** ~ **Canal** der Suezkanal.

**Suff.** (*BRIT*) *abbr* (*POST:* = *Suffolk*).

**suffer** ['sʌfə*] *vt* erleiden; (*rudeness etc*) ertragen ♦ *vi* leiden; **to ~ from** leiden an +*dat*; **to ~ the effects of sth** an den Folgen von etw leiden.

**sufferance** ['sʌfərns] *n*: **he was only there on** ~ er wurde dort nur geduldet.

**sufferer** ['sʌfərə*] *n* Leidende(r) *f(m)*.

**suffering** ['sʌfərɪŋ] *n* Leid *nt*.

**suffice** [sə'faɪs] *vi* genügen.

**sufficient** [sə'fɪʃənt] *adj* ausreichend; ~ **money** genug Geld.

**sufficiently** [sə'fɪʃəntlɪ] *adv* genug, ausreichend; ~ **powerful/enthusiastic** mächtig/begeistert genug.

**suffix** ['sʌfɪks] *n* Suffix *nt*, Nachsilbe *f*.

**suffocate** ['sʌfəkeɪt] *vi (lit, fig)* ersticken.

**suffocation** [sʌfə'keɪʃən] *n* Ersticken *nt*.

**suffrage** ['sʌfrɪdʒ] *n* Wahlrecht *nt*.

**suffragette** [sʌfrə'dʒɛt] *n* Suffragette *f*.

**suffused** [sə'fjuːzd] *adj*: ~ **with** erfüllt von; ~ **with light** lichtdurchflutet.

**sugar** ['ʃugə*] *n* Zucker *m* ♦ *vt* zuckern.

**sugar beet** *n* Zuckerrübe *f*.

**sugar bowl** *n* Zuckerdose *f*.

**sugar cane** *n* Zuckerrohr *nt*.

**sugar-coated** ['ʃugə'kəʊtɪd] *adj* mit Zucker überzogen.

**sugar lump** *n* Zuckerstück *nt*.

**sugar refinery** *n* Zuckerraffinerie *f*.

**sugary** ['ʃugərɪ] *adj* süß; (*fig: smile, phrase*) süßlich.

**suggest** [sə'dʒɛst] *vt* vorschlagen; (*indicate*) andeuten, hindeuten auf +*acc*; **what do you** ~ **I do?** was schlagen Sie vor?

**suggestion** [sə'dʒɛstʃən] *n* Vorschlag *m*; (*indication*) Anflug *m*; (*trace*) Spur *f*.

**suggestive** [sə'dʒɛstɪv] (*pej*) *adj* anzüglich.

**suicidal** [suɪ'saɪdl] *adj* selbstmörderisch; (*person*) selbstmordgefährdet; **to be** *or* **feel** ~ Selbstmordgedanken haben.

**suicide** ['suɪsaɪd] *n (lit, fig)* Selbstmord *m*; (*person*) Selbstmörder(in) *m(f)*; *see also* **commit**.

**suicide attempt, suicide bid** *n* Selbstmordversuch *m*.

**suit** [suːt] *n (man's)* Anzug *m*; (*woman's*) Kostüm *nt*; (*LAW*) Prozeß *m*, Verfahren *nt*; (*CARDS*) Farbe *f* ♦ *vt* passen +*dat*; (*colour, clothes*) stehen +*dat*; **to bring a** ~ **against sb**

(*LAW*) gegen jdn Klage erheben *or* einen
Prozeß anstrengen; **to follow** ~ (*fig*) das
Gleiche tun; **to** ~ **sth to** etw anpassen an
+*acc*; **to be** ~**ed to do sth** sich dafür eignen,
etw zu tun; ~ **yourself!** wie du willst!; **well**
~**ed** (*couple*) gut zusammenpassend.

**suitability** [suːtə'bɪlɪtɪ] *n* Eignung *f*.

**suitable** ['suːtəbl] *adj* (*convenient*) passend;
(*appropriate*) geeignet; **would tomorrow be**
~**?** würde Ihnen morgen passen?; **Monday
isn't** ~ Montag paßt nicht; **we found
somebody** ~ wir haben jemand Passenden
gefunden.

**suitably** ['suːtəblɪ] *adv* passend; (*impressed*)
gebührend.

**suitcase** ['suːtkeɪs] *n* Koffer *m*.

**suite** [swiːt] *n* (*of rooms*) Suite *f*, Zimmerflucht
*f*; (*MUS*) Suite *f*; **bedroom/dining room** ~
Schlafzimmer-/Eßzimmereinrichtung *f*; **a
three-piece** ~ eine dreiteilige
Polstergarnitur.

**suitor** ['suːtə*] *n* Kläger(in) *m(f)*.

**sulfate** ['sʌlfeɪt] (*US*) *n* = **sulphate.**

**sulfur** ['sʌlfə*] (*US*) *n* = **sulphur.**

**sulfuric** [sʌl'fjuərɪk] (*US*) *adj* = **sulphuric.**

**sulk** [sʌlk] *vi* schmollen.

**sulky** ['sʌlkɪ] *adj* schmollend.

**sullen** ['sʌlən] *adj* mürrisch, verdrossen.

**sulphate,** (*US*) **sulfate** ['sʌlfeɪt] *n* Sulfat *nt*,
schwefelsaures Salz *nt*.

**sulphur,** (*US*) **sulfur** ['sʌlfə*] *n* Schwefel *m*.

**sulphur dioxide** *n* Schwefeldioxid *nt*.

**sulphuric,** (*US*) **sulfuric** [sʌl'fjuərɪk] *adj*:
~ **acid** Schwefelsäure *f*.

**sultan** ['sʌltən] *n* Sultan *m*.

**sultana** [sʌl'tɑːnə] *n* Sultanine *f*.

**sultry** ['sʌltrɪ] *adj* schwül.

**sum** [sʌm] *n* (*calculation*) Rechenaufgabe *f*;
(*amount*) Summe *f*, Betrag *m*.

▶**sum up** *vt* zusammenfassen; (*evaluate
rapidly*) einschätzen ♦ *vi* zusammenfassen.

**Sumatra** [suˈmɑːtrə] *n* Sumatra *nt*.

**summarize** ['sʌməraɪz] *vt* zusammenfassen.

**summary** ['sʌmərɪ] *n* Zusammenfassung *f*
♦ *adj* (*justice, executions*) im
Schnellverfahren.

**summer** ['sʌmə*] *n* Sommer *m* ♦ *cpd* Sommer-;
**in** ~ im Sommer.

**summer camp** (*US*) *n* Ferienlager *nt*.

**summer holidays** *npl* Sommerferien *pl*.

**summerhouse** ['sʌməhaus] *n* (*in garden*)
Gartenhaus *nt*, Gartenlaube *f*.

**summertime** ['sʌmətaɪm] *n* Sommer *m*,
Sommerszeit *f*.

**summer time** *n* Sommerzeit *f*.

**summery** ['sʌmərɪ] *adj* sommerlich.

**summing-up** [sʌmɪŋ'ʌp] *n* (*LAW*) Resümee *nt*.

**summit** ['sʌmɪt] *n* Gipfel *m*; (*also:*
~ **conference/meeting**) Gipfelkonferenz *f*
/-treffen *nt*.

**summon** ['sʌmən] *vt* rufen, kommen lassen;
(*help*) holen; (*meeting*) einberufen; (*LAW:*
*witness*) vorladen.

▶**summon up** *vt* aufbringen.

**summons** ['sʌmənz] *n* (*LAW*) Vorladung *f*;
(*fig*) Aufruf *m* ♦ *vt* (*LAW*) vorladen; **to serve
a** ~ **on sb** jdn vor Gericht laden.

**sumo (wrestling)** ['suːməu] *n*
Sumo(-Ringen) *nt*.

**sump** [sʌmp] (*BRIT*) *n* Ölwanne *f*.

**sumptuous** ['sʌmptjuəs] *adj* (*meal*) üppig;
(*costume*) aufwendig.

**Sun.** *abbr* (= *Sunday*) So.

**sun** [sʌn] *n* Sonne *f*; **to catch the** ~ einen
Sonnenbrand bekommen; **everything under
the** ~ alles Mögliche.

**sunbathe** ['sʌnbeɪð] *vi* sich sonnen.

**sunbeam** ['sʌnbiːm] *n* Sonnenstrahl *m*.

**sunbed** ['sʌnbed] *n* (*with sun lamp*)
Sonnenbank *f*.

**sunburn** ['sʌnbəːn] *n* Sonnenbrand *m*.

**sunburned** ['sʌnbəːnd] *adj* = **sunburnt.**

**sunburnt** ['sʌnbəːnt] *adj* sonnenverbrannt,
sonnengebräunt; **to be** ~ (*painfully*) einen
Sonnenbrand haben.

**sun-cream** ['sʌnkriːm] *n* Sonnencreme *f*.

**sundae** ['sʌndeɪ] *n* Eisbecher *m*.

**Sunday** ['sʌndɪ] *n* Sonntag *m*; *see also* **Tuesday.**

**Sunday paper** *n* Sonntagszeitung *f*.

---

*Die* **Sunday papers** *umfassen sowohl
Massenblätter als auch seriöse Zeitungen. The
Observer ist die älteste überregionale
Sonntagszeitung der Welt. Die Sonntags-
zeitungen sind alle sehr umfangreich mit
vielen Farb- und Sonderbeilagen. Zu den
meisten Tageszeitungen gibt es parallele
Sonntagsblätter, die aber separate
Redaktionen haben.*

---

**Sunday school** *n* Sonntagsschule *f*.

**sundial** ['sʌndaɪəl] *n* Sonnenuhr *f*.

**sundown** ['sʌndaun] (*esp US*) *n*
Sonnenuntergang *m*.

**sundries** ['sʌndrɪz] *npl* Verschiedenes *nt*.

**sundry** ['sʌndrɪ] *adj* verschiedene; **all and** ~
jedermann.

**sunflower** ['sʌnflauə*] *n* Sonnenblume *f*.

**sunflower oil** *n* Sonnenblumenöl *nt*.

**sung** [sʌŋ] *pp of* **sing.**

**sunglasses** ['sʌnglɑːsɪz] *npl* Sonnenbrille *f*.

**sunk** [sʌŋk] *pp of* **sink.**

**sunken** ['sʌŋkn] *adj* versunken; (*eyes*)
tiefliegend; (*cheeks*) eingefallen; (*bath*)
eingelassen.

**sunlamp** ['sʌnlæmp] *n* Höhensonne *f*.

**sunlight** ['sʌnlaɪt] *n* Sonnenlicht *nt*.

**sunlit** ['sʌnlɪt] *adj* sonnig, sonnenbeschienen.

**sunny** ['sʌnɪ] *adj* sonnig; (*fig*) heiter.

**sunrise** ['sʌnraɪz] *n* Sonnenaufgang *m*.

**sun roof** *n* (*AUT*) Schiebedach *nt*; (*on building*)
Sonnenterrasse *f*.

**sun screen** *n* Sonnenschutzmittel *nt*.

**sunset** ['sʌnset] *n* Sonnenuntergang *m*.

**sunshade** ['sʌnʃeɪd] n Sonnenschirm m.
**sunshine** ['sʌnʃaɪn] n Sonnenschein m.
**sunspot** ['sʌnspɒt] n Sonnenfleck m.
**sunstroke** ['sʌnstrəuk] n Sonnenstich m.
**suntan** ['sʌntæn] n (Sonnen)bräune f; **to get a**
~ braun werden.
**suntan lotion** n Sonnenmilch f.
**suntanned** ['sʌntænd] adj braun(gebrannt).
**suntan oil** n Sonnenöl nt.
**suntrap** ['sʌntræp] n sonniges Eckchen nt.
**super** ['su:pə*] (inf) adj phantastisch, toll.
**superannuation** [su:pərænjuˈeɪʃən] n Beitrag
m zur Rentenversicherung.
**superb** [su:ˈpə:b] adj ausgezeichnet,
großartig; (meal) vorzüglich.
**Super Bowl** n Super Bowl m, American-
Football-Turnier zwischen den
Spitzenreitern der Nationalligen.
**supercilious** [su:pəˈsɪlɪəs] adj herablassend.
**superconductor** [su:pəkənˈdʌktə*] n (PHYS)
Superleiter m.
**superficial** [su:pəˈfɪʃəl] adj oberflächlich.
**superficially** [su:pəˈfɪʃəlɪ] adv oberflächlich;
(from a superficial point of view) oberflächlich
gesehen.
**superfluous** [suˈpə:fluəs] adj überflüssig.
**superglue** ['su:pəglu:] n Sekundenkleber m.
**superhighway** (US) n ≈ Autobahn f;
**information** ~ Datenautobahn f.
**superhuman** [su:pəˈhju:mən] adj
übermenschlich.
**superimpose** ['su:pərɪmˈpəuz] vt (two things)
übereinanderlegen; **to** ~ **on** legen auf +acc;
**to** ~ **with** überlagern mit.
**superintend** [su:pərɪnˈtɛnd] vt beaufsichtigen,
überwachen.
**superintendent** [su:pərɪnˈtɛndənt] n
Aufseher(in) m(f); (POLICE) Kommissar(in)
m(f).
**superior** [suˈpɪərɪə*] adj besser, überlegen
+dat; (more senior) höhergestellt; (smug)
überheblich; (: smile) überlegen ♦ n
Vorgesetzte(r) f(m); **Mother S**~ (REL) Mutter
Oberin.
**superiority** [supɪərɪˈɒrɪtɪ] n Überlegenheit f.
**superlative** [suˈpə:lətɪv] n Superlativ m ♦ adj
überragend.
**superman** ['su:pəmæn] (irreg: like **man**) n
Übermensch m.
**supermarket** ['su:pəmɑ:kɪt] n Supermarkt m.
**supermodel** ['su:pəmɒdl] n Supermodell nt.
**supernatural** [su:pəˈnætʃərəl] adj
übernatürlich ♦ n: **the** ~ das
Übernatürliche.
**supernova** [su:pəˈnəuvə] n Supernova f.
**superpower** ['su:pəpauə*] n Supermacht f.
**superscript** ['su:pəskrɪpt] n hochgestelltes
Zeichen nt.
**supersede** [su:pəˈsi:d] vt ablösen, ersetzen.
**supersonic** ['su:pəˈsɒnɪk] adj (aircraft etc)
Überschall-.
**superstar** ['su:pəstɑ:*] n Superstar m.

**superstition** [su:pəˈstɪʃən] n Aberglaube m.
**superstitious** [su:pəˈstɪʃəs] adj abergläubisch.
**superstore** ['su:pəstɔ:*] (BRIT) n Großmarkt
m.
**supertanker** ['su:pətæŋkə*] n Supertanker m.
**supertax** ['su:pətæks] n Höchststeuer f.
**supervise** ['su:pəvaɪz] vt beaufsichtigen.
**supervision** [su:pəˈvɪʒən] n Beaufsichtigung f;
**under medical** ~ unter ärztlicher Aufsicht.
**supervisor** ['su:pəvaɪzə*] n Aufseher(in) m(f);
(of students) Tutor(in) m(f).
**supervisory** ['su:pəvaɪzərɪ] adj
beaufsichtigend, Aufsichts-.
**supine** ['su:paɪn] adj: **to be** ~ auf dem Rücken
liegen ♦ adv auf dem Rücken.
**supper** ['sʌpə*] n Abendessen nt; **to have** ~ zu
Abend essen.
**supplant** [səˈplɑ:nt] vt ablösen, ersetzen.
**supple** ['sʌpl] adj geschmeidig; (person)
gelenkig.
**supplement** ['sʌplɪmənt] n Zusatz m; (of book)
Ergänzungsband m; (of newspaper etc)
Beilage f ♦ vt ergänzen.
**supplementary** [sʌplɪˈmɛntərɪ] adj zusätzlich,
ergänzend.
**supplementary benefit** (BRIT: old) n
≈ Sozialhilfe f.
**supplier** [səˈplaɪə*] n Lieferant(in) m(f).
**supply** [səˈplaɪ] vt liefern; (provide) sorgen
für; (a need) befriedigen ♦ n Vorrat m;
(supplying) Lieferung f, **supplies** npl (food)
Vorräte pl; (MIL) Nachschub m; **to** ~ **sth to**
**sb** jdm etw liefern; **to** ~ **sth with sth** etw
mit etw versorgen; **it comes supplied with**
**an adaptor** es wird mit einem Adapter
geliefert; **office supplies** Bürobedarf m; **to**
**be in short** ~ knapp sein; **the electricity/**
**water/gas** ~ die Strom-/Wasser-/
Gasversorgung f; ~ **and demand** Angebot nt
und Nachfrage.
**supply teacher** (BRIT) n Vertretung f.
**support** [səˈpɔ:t] n Unterstützung f; (TECH)
Stütze f ♦ vt unterstützen, eintreten für;
(financially: family etc) unterhalten; (: party
etc) finanziell unterstützen; (TECH)
(ab)stützen; (theory etc) untermauern; **they**
**stopped work in** ~ **of ...** sie sind in den
Streik getreten, um für ... einzutreten; **to**
~ **o.s.** (financially) finanziell unabhängig
sein; **to** ~ **Arsenal** Arsenal-Fan sein.
**supporter** [səˈpɔ:tə*] n (POL etc) Anhänger(in)
m(f); (SPORT) Fan m.
**supporting** [səˈpɔ:tɪŋ] adj: ~ **role** Nebenrolle f;
~ **actor** Schauspieler m in einer Nebenrolle;
~ **film** Vorfilm m.
**supportive** [səˈpɔ:tɪv] adj hilfreich; **to be** ~ **of**
**sb/sth** jdn/etw unterstützen.
**suppose** [səˈpəuz] vt annehmen, glauben;
(imagine) sich dat vorstellen; **to be** ~**d to do**
**sth** etw tun sollen; **it was worse than she'd**
~**d** es war schlimmer, als sie es sich
vorgestellt hatte; **I don't** ~ **she'll come** ich

glaube kaum, daß sie kommt; **he's about sixty, I** ~ er muß wohl so um die Sechzig sein; **he's ~d to be an expert** er ist angeblich ein Experte; **I** ~ **so/not** ich glaube schon/nicht.

**supposedly** [sə'pəuzɪdlɪ] *adv* angeblich.

**supposing** [sə'pəuzɪŋ] *conj* angenommen.

**supposition** [sʌpə'zɪʃən] *n* Annahme *f*.

**suppository** [sə'pɒzɪtrɪ] *n* Zäpfchen *nt*.

**suppress** [sə'prɛs] *vt* unterdrücken; (*publication*) verbieten.

**suppression** [sə'prɛʃən] *n* Unterdrückung *f*.

**suppressor** [sə'prɛsə*] *n* (*ELEC etc*) Entstörungselement *nt*.

**supremacy** [su'prɛməsɪ] *n* Vormachtstellung *f*.

**supreme** [su'pri:m] *adj* Ober-, oberste(r, s); (*effort*) äußerste(r, s); (*achievement*) höchste(r, s).

**Supreme Court** (*US*) *n* Oberster Gerichtshof *m*.

**supremo** [su'pri:məu] (*BRIT: inf*) *n* Boß *m*.

**Supt** *abbr* (*POLICE*) = **superintendent**.

**surcharge** ['sə:tʃɑ:dʒ] *n* Zuschlag *m*.

**sure** [ʃuə*] *adj* sicher; (*reliable*) zuverlässig, sicher ♦ *adv* (*inf: esp US*): **that** ~ **is pretty, that's** ~ **pretty** das ist aber schön; **to make** ~ **of sth** sich einer Sache *gen* vergewissern; **to make** ~ **that** sich vergewissern, daß; **I'm** ~ **of it** ich bin mir da sicher; **I'm not** ~ **how/why/when** ich bin mir nicht sicher *or* ich weiß nicht genau, wie/warum/wann; **to be** ~ **of o.s.** selbstsicher sein; ~! klar!; ~ **enough** tatsächlich.

**sure-fire** ['ʃuəfaɪə*] (*inf*) *adj* todsicher.

**sure-footed** [ʃuə'futɪd] *adj* trittsicher.

**surely** ['ʃuəlɪ] *adv* sicherlich, bestimmt; ~ **you don't mean that!** das meinen Sie doch bestimmt *or* sicher nicht (so)!

**surety** ['ʃuərətɪ] *n* Bürgschaft *f*, Sicherheit *f*; **to go** *or* **stand** ~ **for sb** für jdn bürgen.

**surf** [sə:f] *n* Brandung *f*.

**surface** ['sə:fɪs] *n* Oberfläche *f* ♦ *vt* (*road*) mit einem Belag versehen ♦ *vi* (*lit, fig*) auftauchen; (*feeling*) hochkommen; (*rise from bed*) hochkommen; **on the** ~ (*fig*) oberflächlich betrachtet.

**surface area** *n* Fläche *f*.

**surface mail** *n* Post *f* auf dem Land-/Seeweg.

**surface-to-surface** ['sə:fɪstə'sə:fɪs] *adj* (*missile*) Boden-Boden-.

**surfboard** ['sə:fbɔ:d] *n* Surfbrett *nt*.

**surfeit** ['sə:fɪt] *n*: **a** ~ **of** ein Übermaß an +*dat*.

**surfer** ['sə:fə*] *n* Surfer(in) *m(f)*.

**surfing** ['sə:fɪŋ] *n* Surfen *nt*; **to go** ~ Surfen gehen.

**surge** [sə:dʒ] *n* Anstieg *m*; (*fig: of emotion*) Woge *f*; (*ELEC*) Spannungsstoß *m* ♦ *vi* (*water*) branden; (*people*) sich drängen; (*vehicles*) sich wälzen; (*emotion*) aufwallen; (*ELEC: power*) ansteigen; **to** ~ **forward** nach vorne drängen.

**surgeon** ['sə:dʒən] *n* Chirurg(in) *m(f)*.

**Surgeon General** (*US*) *n* (*MED*) ≈ Gesundheitsminister(in) *m(f)*; (*MIL*) Sanitätsinspekteur(in) *m(f)*.

**surgery** ['sə:dʒərɪ] *n* Chirurgie *f*, (*BRIT: room*) Sprechzimmer *nt*; (: *building*) Praxis *f*; (*also*: ~ **hours**: *of doctor, MP etc*) Sprechstunde *f*; **to have** ~ operiert werden; **to need** ~ operiert werden müssen.

**surgical** ['sə:dʒɪkl] *adj* chirurgisch; (*treatment*) operativ.

**surgical spirit** (*BRIT*) *n* Wundbenzin *nt*.

**surly** ['sə:lɪ] *adj* verdrießlich, mürrisch.

**surmise** [sə:'maɪz] *vt* vermuten, mutmaßen.

**surmount** [sə:'maunt] *vt* (*fig*) überwinden.

**surname** ['sə:neɪm] *n* Nachname *m*.

**surpass** [sə:'pɑ:s] *vt* übertreffen.

**surplus** ['sə:pləs] *n* Überschuß *m* ♦ *adj* überschüssig; **it is** ~ **to our requirements** das benötigen wir nicht.

**surprise** [sə'praɪz] *n* Überraschung *f* ♦ *vt* überraschen; (*astonish*) erstaunen; (*army*) überrumpeln; (*thief*) ertappen; **to take sb by** ~ jdn überraschen.

**surprising** [sə'praɪzɪŋ] *adj* überraschend; (*situation*) erstaunlich; **it is** ~ **how/that** es ist erstaunlich, wie/daß.

**surprisingly** [sə'praɪzɪŋlɪ] *adv* überraschend, erstaunlich; **(somewhat)** ~, **he agreed** erstaunlicherweise war er damit einverstanden.

**surrealism** [sə'rɪəlɪzəm] *n* Surrealismus *m*.

**surrealist** [sə'rɪəlɪst] *adj* surrealistisch.

**surrender** [sə'rɛndə*] *n* Kapitulation *f* ♦ *vi* sich ergeben ♦ *vt* aufgeben.

**surrender value** *n* Rückkaufswert *m*.

**surreptitious** [sʌrəp'tɪʃəs] *adj* heimlich, verstohlen.

**surrogate** ['sʌrəgɪt] *n* Ersatz *m* ♦ *adj* (*parents*) Ersatz-.

**surrogate mother** *n* Leihmutter *f*.

**surround** [sə'raund] *vt* umgeben; (*MIL, POLICE etc*) umstellen.

**surrounding** [sə'raundɪŋ] *adj* umliegend; **the** ~ **area** die Umgebung.

**surroundings** [sə'raundɪŋz] *npl* Umgebung *f*.

**surtax** ['sə:tæks] *n* Steuerzuschlag *m*.

**surveillance** [sə:'veɪləns] *n* Überwachung *f*; **to be under** ~ überwacht werden.

**survey** ['sə:veɪ] *n* (*of land*) Vermessung *f*; (*of house*) Begutachtung *f*, (*investigation*) Untersuchung *f*; (*report*) Gutachten *nt*; (*comprehensive view*) Überblick *m* ♦ *vt* (*land*) vermessen; (*house*) inspizieren; (*look at*) betrachten.

**surveying** [sə'veɪɪŋ] *n* (*of land*) Vermessung *f*.

**surveyor** [sə'veɪə*] *n* (*of land*) Landvermesser(in) *m(f)*; (*of house*) Baugutachter(in) *m(f)*.

**survival** [sə'vaɪvl] *n* Überleben *nt*; (*relic*) Überbleibsel *nt*; ~ **course/kit** Überlebenstraining *nt*/-ausrüstung *f*; ~ **bag**

Expeditionsschlafsack m.

**survive** [sə'vaɪv] vi überleben; (custom etc) weiterbestehen ♦ vt überleben.

**survivor** [sə'vaɪvə·] n Überlebende(r) f(m).

**susceptible** [sə'sɛptəbl] adj: ~ **(to)** anfällig (für); (influenced by) empfänglich (für).

**suspect** ['sʌspɛkt] adj verdächtig ♦ n Verdächtige(r) f(m) ♦ vt: **to ~ sb of** jdn verdächtigen +gen; (think) vermuten; (doubt) bezweifeln.

**suspected** [sə'pɛktɪd] adj (terrorist etc) mutmaßlich; **he is a ~ member of this organization** er steht im Verdacht, Mitglied dieser Organisation zu sein.

**suspend** [sə'pɛnd] vt (hang) (auf)hängen; (delay, stop) einstellen; (from employment) suspendieren; **to be ~ed (from)** (hang) hängen (an +dat).

**suspended animation** [sə'pɛndɪd-] n vorübergehender Stillstand aller Körperfunktionen.

**suspended sentence** n (LAW) zur Bewährung ausgesetzte Strafe f.

**suspender belt** [sə'pɛndə·-] n Strumpfhaltergürtel m.

**suspenders** [sə'pɛndəz] npl (BRIT) Strumpfhalter pl; (US) Hosenträger pl.

**suspense** [sə'pɛns] n Spannung f; (uncertainty) Ungewißheit f; **to keep sb in ~** jdn auf die Folter spannen.

**suspension** [sə'pɛnʃən] n (from job) Suspendierung f; (from team) Sperrung f; (AUT) Federung f; (of driving licence) zeitweiliger Entzug m; (of payment) zeitweilige Einstellung f.

**suspension bridge** n Hängebrücke f.

**suspicion** [sə'pɪʃən] n Verdacht m; (distrust) Mißtrauen nt; (trace) Spur f; **to be under ~** unter Verdacht stehen; **arrested on ~ of murder** wegen Mordverdachts festgenommen.

**suspicious** [sə'pɪʃəs] adj (suspecting) mißtrauisch; (causing suspicion) verdächtig; **to be ~ of** or **about sb/sth** jdn/etw mit Mißtrauen betrachten.

**suss out** [sʌs-] (BRIT: inf) vt (discover) rauskriegen; (understand) durchschauen.

**sustain** [sə'teɪn] vt (continue) aufrechterhalten; (food, drink) bei Kräften halten; (suffer: injury) erleiden.

**sustainable** [sə'teɪnəbl] adj: **to be ~** aufrechtzuerhalten sein; ~ **growth** stetiges Wachstum nt.

**sustained** [sə'teɪnd] adj (effort) ausdauernd; (attack) anhaltend.

**sustenance** ['sʌstɪnəns] n Nahrung f.

**suture** ['suːtʃə·] n Naht f.

**SW** abbr (= south-west) SW; (RADIO: = short-wave) KW.

**swab** [swɔb] n (MED) Tupfer m ♦ vt (NAUT: also: ~ **down**) wischen.

**swagger** ['swægə·] vi stolzieren.

**swallow** ['swɔləu] n (bird) Schwalbe f; (of food, drink etc) Schluck m ♦ vt (herunter)schlucken; (fig: story, insult, one's pride) schlucken; **to ~ one's words** (speak indistinctly) seine Worte verschlucken; (retract) alles zurücknehmen.

▶**swallow up** vt verschlingen.

**swam** [swæm] pt of **swim**.

**swamp** [swɔmp] n Sumpf m ♦ vt (lit, fig) überschwemmen.

**swampy** ['swɔmpɪ] adj sumpfig.

**swan** [swɔn] n Schwan m.

**swank** [swæŋk] (inf) vi angeben.

**swan song** n (fig) Schwanengesang m.

**swap** [swɔp] n Tausch m ♦ vt: **to ~ (for)** (ein)tauschen (gegen).

**SWAPO** ['swɑːpəu] n abbr (= South-West Africa People's Organization) SWAPO f.

**swarm** [swɔːm] n Schwarm m; (of people) Schar f ♦ vi (bees, people) schwärmen; **to be ~ing with** wimmeln von.

**swarthy** ['swɔːðɪ] adj (person, face) dunkelhäutig; (complexion) dunkel.

**swashbuckling** ['swɔʃbʌklɪŋ] adj draufgängerisch; (hero) verwegen.

**swastika** ['swɔstɪkə] n Hakenkreuz nt.

**SWAT** (US) n abbr (= Special Weapons and Tactics): ~ **team** ≈ schnelle Eingreiftruppe f.

**swat** [swɔt] vt totschlagen ♦ n (BRIT: also: **fly** ~) Fliegenklatsche f.

**swathe** [sweɪð] vt: **to ~ in** wickeln in +acc.

**swatter** ['swɔtə·] n (also: **fly** ~) Fliegenklatsche f.

**sway** [sweɪ] vi schwanken ♦ vt (influence) beeinflussen ♦ n: **to hold ~** herrschen; **to hold ~ over sb** jdn beherrschen or in seiner Macht haben.

**Swaziland** ['swɑːzɪlænd] n Swasiland nt.

**swear** [swɛə·] (pt **swore**, pp **sworn**) vi (curse) fluchen ♦ vt (promise) schwören; **to ~ an oath** einen Eid ablegen.

▶**swear in** vt vereidigen.

**swearword** ['swɛəwɔːd] n Fluch m, Kraftausdruck m.

**sweat** [swɛt] n Schweiß m ♦ vi schwitzen; **to be in a ~** schwitzen.

**sweatband** ['swɛtbænd] n Schweißband nt.

**sweater** ['swɛtə·] n Pullover m.

**sweatshirt** ['swɛtʃəːt] n Sweatshirt nt.

**sweatshop** ['swɛtʃɔp] (pej) n Ausbeuterbetrieb m.

**sweaty** ['swɛtɪ] adj verschwitzt; (hands) schweißig.

**Swede** [swiːd] n Schwede m, Schwedin f.

**swede** [swiːd] (BRIT) n Steckrübe f.

**Sweden** ['swiːdn] n Schweden nt.

**Swedish** ['swiːdɪʃ] adj schwedisch ♦ n Schwedisch nt.

**sweep** [swiːp] (pt, pp **swept**) n: **to give sth a ~** etw fegen or kehren; (curve) Bogen m; (range) Bereich m; (also: **chimney** ~)

Kaminkehrer *m*, Schornsteinfeger *m* ♦ *vt*
fegen, kehren; (*current*) reißen ♦ *vi* (*through
air*) gleiten; (*wind*) fegen.
▶**sweep away** *vt* hinwegfegen.
▶**sweep past** *vi* vorbeirauschen.
▶**sweep up** *vi* zusammenfegen,
zusammenkehren.
**sweeper** ['swi:pə*] *n* (*FOOTBALL*) Ausputzer
*m*.
**sweeping** ['swi:pɪŋ] *adj* (*gesture*) weit
ausholend; (*changes, reforms*) weitreichend;
(*statement*) verallgemeinernd.
**sweepstake** ['swi:psteɪk] *n Pferdewette, bei
der der Preis aus der Summe der Einsätze
besteht*.
**sweet** [swi:t] *n* (*candy*) Bonbon *nt or m*; (*BRIT:
CULIN*) Nachtisch *m* ♦ *adj* süß; (*air, water*)
frisch; (*kind*) lieb ♦ *adv*: **to smell/taste ~** süß
duften/schmecken; **~ and sour** süß-sauer.
**sweetbread** ['swi:tbred] *n* Bries *nt*.
**sweetcorn** ['swi:tkɔ:n] *n* Mais *m*.
**sweeten** ['swi:tn] *vt* süßen; (*temper*) bessern;
(*person*) gnädig stimmen.
**sweetener** ['swi:tnə*] *n* Süßstoff *m*; (*fig*)
Anreiz *m*.
**sweetheart** ['swi:thɑ:t] *n* Freund(in) *m(f)*; (*in
speech, writing*) Schatz *m*, Liebling *m*.
**sweetness** ['swi:tnɪs] *n* Süße *f*; (*kindness*)
Liebenswürdigkeit *f*.
**sweet pea** *n* (Garten)wicke *f*.
**sweet potato** *n* Süßkartoffel *f*, Batate *f*.
**sweet shop** (*BRIT*) *n* Süßwarengeschäft *nt*.
**sweet tooth** *n*: **to have a ~** gern Süßes
essen.
**swell** [swel] (*pt* **swelled**, *pp* **swollen** *or* **swelled**)
*n* Seegang *m* ♦ *adj* (*US: inf*) toll, prima ♦ *vi*
(*increase*) anwachsen; (*sound*) anschwellen;
(*feeling*) stärker werden; (*also*: **~ up**)
anschwellen.
**swelling** ['swelɪŋ] *n* Schwellung *f*.
**sweltering** ['sweltərɪŋ] *adj* (*heat*) glühend;
(*weather, day*) glühend heiß.
**swept** [swept] *pt, pp of* **sweep**.
**swerve** [swə:v] *vi* (*animal*) ausbrechen; (*driver,
vehicle*) ausschwenken; **to ~ off the road**
ausschwenken und von der Straße
abkommen.
**swift** [swɪft] *n* Mauersegler *m* ♦ *adj* schnell.
**swiftly** ['swɪftlɪ] *adv* schnell.
**swiftness** ['swɪftnɪs] *n* Schnelligkeit *f*.
**swig** [swɪg] (*inf*) *n* Schluck *m* ♦ *vt*
herunterkippen.
**swill** [swɪl] *vt* (*also*: **~ out**) ausspülen; (*also*:
**~ down**) abspülen ♦ *n* (*for pigs*)
Schweinefutter *nt*.
**swim** [swɪm] (*pt* **swam**, *pp* **swum**) *vi*
schwimmen; (*before one's eyes*)
verschwimmen ♦ *vt* (*the Channel etc*)
durchschwimmen; (*a length*) schwimmen
♦ *n*: **to go for a ~** schwimmen gehen; **to go
~ming** schwimmen gehen; **my head is
~ming** mir dreht sich der Kopf.

**swimmer** ['swɪmə*] *n* Schwimmer(in) *m(f)*.
**swimming** ['swɪmɪŋ] *n* Schwimmen *nt*.
**swimming baths** (*BRIT*) *npl* Schwimmbad *nt*.
**swimming cap** *n* Badekappe *f*, Bademütze *f*.
**swimming costume** (*BRIT*) *n* Badeanzug *m*.
**swimmingly** ['swɪmɪŋlɪ] (*inf*) *adv* glänzend.
**swimming pool** *n* Schwimmbad *nt*.
**swimming trunks** *npl* Badehose *f*.
**swimsuit** ['swɪmsu:t] *n* Badeanzug *m*.
**swindle** ['swɪndl] *n* Schwindel *m*, Betrug *m*
♦ *vt*: **to ~ sb (out of sth)** jdn (um etw)
betrügen *or* beschwindeln.
**swindler** ['swɪndlə*] *n* Schwindler(in) *m(f)*.
**swine** [swaɪn] (*inf!*) *n* Schwein *nt*.
**swing** [swɪŋ] (*pt, pp* **swung**) *n* (*in playground*)
Schaukel *f*; (*movement*) Schwung *m*; (*change*)
Umschwung *m*; (*MUS*) Swing *m* ♦ *vt* (*arms,
legs*) schwingen (mit); (*also*: **~ round**)
herumschwenken ♦ *vi* schwingen; (*also*:
**~ round**) sich umdrehen; (*vehicle*)
herumschwenken; **a ~ to the left** (*POL*) ein
Linksruck *m*; **to get into the ~ of things**
richtig reinkommen; **to be in full ~** (*party
etc*) in vollem Gang sein.
**swing bridge** *n* Drehbrücke *f*.
**swing door,** (*US*) **swinging door** *n*
Pendeltür *f*.
**swingeing** ['swɪndʒɪŋ] (*BRIT*) *adj* (*blow*) hart;
(*attack*) scharf; (*cuts, increases*) extrem.
**swinging** ['swɪŋɪŋ] *adj* (*music*) schwungvoll;
(*movement*) schaukelnd.
**swipe** [swaɪp] *vt* (*also*: **~ at**) schlagen nach;
(*inf: steal*) klauen ♦ *n* Schlag *m*.
**swirl** [swə:l] *vi* wirbeln ♦ *n* Wirbeln *nt*.
**swish** [swɪʃ] *vi* rauschen; (*tail*) schlagen ♦ *n*
Rauschen *nt*; (*of tail*) Schlagen *nt* ♦ *adj* (*inf*)
schick.
**Swiss** [swɪs] *adj* schweizerisch, Schweizer ♦ *n
inv* Schweizer(in) *m(f)*.
**Swiss French** *adj* französischschweizerisch.
**Swiss German** *adj* deutschschweizerisch.
**Swiss roll** *n* Biskuitrolle *f*.
**switch** [swɪtʃ] *n* Schalter *m*; (*change*)
Änderung *f* ♦ *vt* (*change*) ändern; (*exchange*)
tauschen, wechseln; **to ~ (round or over)**
vertauschen.
▶**switch off** *vt* abschalten; (*light*) ausschalten
♦ *vi* (*fig*) abschalten.
▶**switch on** *vt* einschalten; (*radio*) anstellen;
(*engine*) anlassen.
**switchback** ['swɪtʃbæk] (*BRIT*) *n* (*road*) auf
und ab führende Straße *f*; (*roller-coaster*)
Achterbahn *f*.
**switchblade** ['swɪtʃbleɪd] *n* Schnappmesser
*nt*.
**switchboard** ['swɪtʃbɔ:d] *n* Vermittlung *f*,
Zentrale *f*.
**switchboard operator** *n* Telefonist(in) *m(f)*.
**Switzerland** ['swɪtsələnd] *n* die Schweiz *f*.
**swivel** ['swɪvl] *vi* (*also*: **~ round**) sich
(herum)drehen.
**swollen** ['swəʊlən] *pp of* **swell** ♦ *adj*

geschwollen; (*lake etc*) angeschwollen.
**swoon** [swuːn] *vi* beinahe ohnmächtig
werden ♦ *n* Ohnmacht *f*.
**swoop** [swuːp] *n* (*by police etc*) Razzia *f*; (*of
bird etc*) Sturzflug *m* ♦ *vi* (*also*: ~ **down**: *bird*)
herabstoßen; (*plane*) einen Sturzflug
machen.
**swop** [swɔp] = **swap.**
**sword** [sɔːd] *n* Schwert *nt*.
**swordfish** ['sɔːdfɪʃ] *n* Schwertfisch *m*.
**swore** [swɔː°] *pt of* **swear.**
**sworn** [swɔːn] *pp of* **swear** ♦ *adj* (*statement*)
eidlich; (*evidence*) unter Eid; (*enemy*)
geschworen.
**swot** [swɔt] *vi* pauken ♦ *n* (*pej*) Streber(in)
*m(f)*.
▶**swot up** *vt:* to ~ **up** (**on**) pauken (*+acc*).
**swum** [swʌm] *pp of* **swim.**
**swung** [swʌŋ] *pt, pp of* **swing.**
**sycamore** ['sɪkəmɔː°] *n* Bergahorn *m*.
**sycophant** ['sɪkəfænt] *n* Kriecher *m*,
Speichellecker *m*.
**sycophantic** [sɪkə'fæntɪk] *adj* kriecherisch.
**Sydney** ['sɪdnɪ] *n* Sydney *nt*.
**syllable** ['sɪləbl] *n* Silbe *f*.
**syllabus** ['sɪləbəs] *n* Lehrplan *m*; **on the** ~ im
Lehrplan.
**symbol** ['sɪmbl] *n* Symbol *nt*.
**symbolic(al)** [sɪm'bɔlɪk(l)] *adj* symbolisch; **to
be** ~ **of sth** etw symbolisieren, ein Symbol
für etw sein.
**symbolism** ['sɪmbəlɪzəm] *n* Symbolismus *m*.
**symbolize** ['sɪmbəlaɪz] *vt* symbolisieren.
**symmetrical** [sɪ'mɛtrɪkl] *adj* symmetrisch.
**symmetry** ['sɪmɪtrɪ] *n* Symmetrie *f*.
**sympathetic** [sɪmpə'θɛtɪk] *adj* (*understanding*)
verständnisvoll; (*showing pity*) mitfühlend;
(*likeable*) sympathisch; (*supportive*)
wohlwollend; **to be** ~ **to a cause** (*well-
disposed*) einer Sache wohlwollend
gegenüberstehen.
**sympathetically** [sɪmpə'θɛtɪklɪ] *adv* (*showing
understanding*) verständnisvoll; (*showing
support*) wohlwollend.
**sympathize** ['sɪmpəθaɪz] *vi:* **to** ~ **with** (*person*)
Mitleid haben mit; (*feelings*) Verständnis
haben für; (*cause*) sympathisieren mit.
**sympathizer** ['sɪmpəθaɪzə°] *n* (*POL*)
Sympathisant(in) *m(f)*.
**sympathy** ['sɪmpəθɪ] *n* Mitgefühl *nt*;
**sympathies** *npl* (*support, tendencies*)
Sympathien *pl*; **with our deepest** ~ mit
aufrichtigem *or* herzlichem Beileid; **to
come out in** ~ (*workers*) in einen
Sympathiestreik treten.
**symphonic** [sɪm'fɔnɪk] *adj* sinfonisch.
**symphony** ['sɪmfənɪ] *n* Sinfonie *f*.
**symphony orchestra** *n* Sinfonieorchester
*nt*.
**symposia** [sɪm'pəuzɪə] *npl of* **symposium.**
**symposium** [sɪm'pəuzɪəm] (*pl* ~**s** *or*
**symposia**) *n* Symposium *nt*.

**symptom** ['sɪmptəm] *n* (*MED, fig*) Symptom *nt*,
Anzeichen *nt*.
**symptomatic** [sɪmptə'mætɪk] *adj:* ~ **of**
symptomatisch für.
**synagogue** ['sɪnəgɔg] *n* Synagoge *f*.
**sync** [sɪŋk] *n abbr* (= *synchronization*): **in** ~
synchron; **out of** ~ nicht synchron.
**synchromesh** [sɪŋkrəu'mɛʃ] *n*
Synchrongetriebe *nt*.
**synchronize** ['sɪŋkrənaɪz] *vt* (*watches*)
gleichstellen; (*movements*) aufeinander
abstimmen; (*sound*) synchronisieren ♦ *vi:* **to**
~ **with** (*sound*) synchron sein mit.
**synchronized swimming** ['sɪŋkrənaɪzd-] *n*
Synchronschwimmen *nt*.
**syncopated** ['sɪŋkəpeɪtɪd] *adj* synkopiert.
**syndicate** ['sɪndɪkɪt] *n* Interessengemeinschaft *f*; (*of businesses*) Verband *m*;
(*of newspapers*) Pressezentrale *f*.
**syndrome** ['sɪndrəum] *n* Syndrom *nt*; (*fig*)
Phänomen *nt*.
**synonym** ['sɪnənɪm] *n* Synonym *nt*.
**synonymous** [sɪ'nɔnɪməs] *adj* (*fig*): ~ (**with**)
gleichbedeutend (mit).
**synopses** [sɪ'nɔpsiːz] *npl of* **synopsis.**
**synopsis** [sɪ'nɔpsɪs] (*pl* **synopses**) *n* Abriß *m*,
Zusammenfassung *f*.
**syntactic** [sɪn'tæktɪk] *adj* syntaktisch.
**syntax** ['sɪntæks] *n* Syntax *f*.
**syntax error** *n* (*COMPUT*) Syntaxfehler *m*.
**syntheses** ['sɪnθəsiːz] *npl of* **synthesis.**
**synthesis** ['sɪnθəsɪs] (*pl* **syntheses**) *n* Synthese
*f*.
**synthesizer** ['sɪnθəsaɪzə°] *n* Synthesizer *m*.
**synthetic** [sɪn'θɛtɪk] *adj* synthetisch; (*speech*)
künstlich; **synthetics** *npl* (*man-made fabrics*)
Synthetik *f*.
**syphilis** ['sɪfɪlɪs] *n* Syphilis *f*.
**syphon** ['saɪfən] = **siphon.**
**Syria** ['sɪrɪə] *n* Syrien *nt*.
**Syrian** ['sɪrɪən] *adj* syrisch ♦ *n* Syrer(in) *m(f)*.
**syringe** [sɪ'rɪndʒ] *n* Spritze *f*.
**syrup** ['sɪrəp] *n* Sirup *m*; (*also*: **golden** ~)
(gelber) Sirup *m*.
**syrupy** ['sɪrəpɪ] *adj* sirupartig; (*pej, fig:
sentimental*) schmalzig.
**system** ['sɪstəm] *n* System *nt*; (*body*) Körper
*m*; (*ANAT*) Apparat *m*, System *nt*; **it was a
shock to his** ~ er hatte schwer damit zu
schaffen.
**systematic** [sɪstə'mætɪk] *adj* systematisch.
**system disk** *n* (*COMPUT*) Systemdiskette *f*.
**systems analyst** ['sɪstəmz-] *n*
Systemanalytiker(in) *m(f)*.

# *T, t*

**T, t** [tiː] *n* (*letter*) T *nt*, t *nt*; ~ **for Tommy** ≈ T wie Theodor.

**TA** (*BRIT*) *n abbr* = **Territorial Army**.

**ta** [tɑː] (*BRIT: inf*) *interj* danke.

**tab** [tæb] *n abbr* = **tabulator** ♦ *n* (*on drinks can*) Ring *m*; (*on garment*) Etikett *nt*; **to keep ~s on sb/sth** (*fig*) jdn/etw im Auge behalten.

**tabby** ['tæbɪ] *n* (*also:* ~ **cat**) getigerte Katze *f*.

**tabernacle** ['tæbənækl] *n* Tabernakel *nt*.

**table** ['teɪbl] *n* Tisch *m*; (*MATH, CHEM etc*) Tabelle *f* ♦ *vt* (*BRIT: PARL: motion etc*) einbringen; **to lay** *or* **set the** ~ den Tisch decken; **to clear the** ~ den Tisch abräumen; **league** ~ (*BRIT: SPORT*) Tabelle *f*.

**tablecloth** ['teɪblklɔθ] *n* Tischdecke *f*.

**table d'hôte** [tɑːblˈdəʊt] *adj* (*menu, meal*) Tagesmenü *nt*.

**table lamp** *n* Tischlampe *f*.

**tablemat** ['teɪblmæt] *n* (*of cloth*) Set *nt* or *m*; (*for hot dish*) Untersatz *m*.

**table of contents** *n* Inhaltsverzeichnis *nt*.

**table salt** *n* Tafelsalz *nt*.

**tablespoon** ['teɪblspuːn] *n* Eßlöffel *m*; (*also:* ~**ful**) Eßlöffel(voll) *m*.

**tablet** ['tæblɪt] *n* (*MED*) Tablette *f*; (*HIST: for writing*) Tafel *f*; (*plaque*) Plakette *f*; ~ **of soap** (*BRIT*) Stück *nt* Seife.

**table tennis** *n* Tischtennis *nt*.

**table wine** *n* Tafelwein *m*.

**tabloid** ['tæblɔɪd] *n* (*newspaper*) Boulevard-zeitung *f*; **the** ~**s** die Boulevardpresse.

> *Der Ausdruck* **tabloid press** *bezieht sich auf kleinformatige Zeitungen (ca 30 × 40cm); die sind in Großbritannien fast ausschließlich Massenblätter. Im Gegensatz zur* **quality press** *verwenden diese Massenblätter viele Fotos und einen knappen, oft reißerischen Stil. Sie kommen den Lesern entgegen, die mehr Wert auf Unterhaltung legen.*

**taboo** [təˈbuː] *n* Tabu *nt* ♦ *adj* tabu; **a** ~ **subject/word** ein Tabuthema/Tabuwort.

**tabulate** ['tæbjuleɪt] *vt* tabellarisieren.

**tabulator** ['tæbjuleɪtə*] *n* (*on typewriter*) Tabulator *m*.

**tachograph** ['tækəgrɑːf] *n* Fahrtenschreiber *m*.

**tachometer** [tæˈkɔmɪtə*] *n* Tachometer *m*.

**tacit** ['tæsɪt] *adj* stillschweigend.

**taciturn** ['tæsɪtəːn] *adj* schweigsam.

**tack** [tæk] *n* (*nail*) Stift *m* ♦ *vt* (*nail*) anheften;

(*stitch*) heften ♦ *vi* (*NAUT*) kreuzen; **to change** ~ (*fig*) den Kurs ändern; **to** ~ **sth on to (the end of) sth** etw (hinten) an etw *acc* anheften.

**tackle** ['tækl] *n* (*for fishing*) Ausrüstung *f*; (*for lifting*) Flaschenzug *m*; (*FOOTBALL, RUGBY*) Angriff *m* ♦ *vt* (*deal with: difficulty*) in Angriff nehmen; (*challenge: person*) zur Rede stellen; (*physically, also SPORT*) angreifen.

**tacky** ['tækɪ] *adj* (*sticky*) klebrig; (*pej: cheap-looking*) schäbig.

**tact** [tækt] *n* Takt *m*.

**tactful** ['tæktful] *adj* taktvoll; **to be** ~ taktvoll sein.

**tactfully** ['tæktfəlɪ] *adv* taktvoll.

**tactical** ['tæktɪkl] *adj* taktisch; ~ **error** taktischer Fehler; ~ **voting** taktische Stimmabgabe.

**tactician** [tækˈtɪʃən] *n* Taktiker(in) *m(f)*.

**tactics** ['tæktɪks] *npl* Taktik *f*.

**tactless** ['tæktlɪs] *adj* taktlos.

**tactlessly** ['tæktlɪslɪ] *adv* taktlos.

**tadpole** ['tædpəʊl] *n* Kaulquappe *f*.

**taffy** ['tæfɪ] (*US*) *n* (*toffee*) Toffee *nt*, Sahnebonbon *nt*.

**tag** [tæg] *n* (*label*) Anhänger *m*; **price/name** ~ Preis-/Namensschild *nt*.

►**tag along** *vi* sich anschließen.

**Tahiti** [tɑːˈhiːtɪ] *n* Tahiti *nt*.

**tail** [teɪl] *n* (*of animal*) Schwanz *m*; (*of plane*) Heck *nt*; (*of shirt, coat*) Schoß *m* ♦ *vt* (*follow*) folgen +*dat*; **tails** *npl* (*formal suit*) Frack *m*; **to turn** ~ die Flucht ergreifen; *see also* **head**.

►**tail off** *vi* (*in size etc*) abnehmen; (*voice*) schwächer werden.

**tailback** ['teɪlbæk] (*BRIT*) *n* (*AUT*) Stau *m*.

**tail coat** *n* = **tails**.

**tail end** *n* Ende *nt*.

**tailgate** ['teɪlgeɪt] *n* (*AUT*) Heckklappe *f*.

**taillight** ['teɪllaɪt] *n* (*AUT*) Rücklicht *nt*.

**tailor** ['teɪlə*] *n* Schneider(in) *m(f)* ♦ *vt*: **to** ~ **sth (to)** etw abstimmen (auf +*acc*); ~**'s shop** Schneiderei *f*.

**tailoring** ['teɪlərɪŋ] *n* (*craft*) Schneiderei *f*; (*cut*) Verarbeitung *f*.

**tailor-made** ['teɪlə'meɪd] *adj* (*also fig*) maßgeschneidert.

**tailwind** ['teɪlwɪnd] *n* Rückenwind *m*.

**taint** [teɪnt] *vt* (*meat, food*) verderben; (*fig: reputation etc*) beschmutzen.

**tainted** ['teɪntɪd] *adj* (*food, water, air*) verdorben; (*fig: profits, reputation etc*): ~ **with** behaftet mit.

**Taiwan** ['taɪ'wɑːn] *n* Taiwan *nt*.

**Tajikistan** [tɑːdʒɪkɪ'stɑːn] *n* Tadschikistan *nt*.

**take** [teɪk] (*pt* **took**, *pp* **taken**) *vt* nehmen; (*photo, notes*) machen; (*decision*) fällen; (*require: courage, time*) erfordern; (*tolerate: pain etc*) ertragen; (*hold: passengers etc*) fassen; (*accompany: person*) begleiten; (*carry, bring*) mitnehmen; (*exam, test*) machen; (*conduct: meeting*) leiten; (: *class*) unterrichten ♦ vi (*have effect: drug*) wirken; (: *dye*) angenommen werden ♦ n (*CINE*) Aufnahme *f*; **to ~ sth from** (*drawer etc*) etw nehmen aus +*dat*; **I ~ it (that)** ich nehme an(, daß); **I took him for a doctor** (*mistake*) ich hielt ihn für einen Arzt; **to ~ sb's hand** jds Hand nehmen; **to ~ sb for a walk** mit jdm spazierengehen; **to be ~n ill** krank werden; **to ~ it upon o.s. to do sth** es auf sich nehmen, etw zu tun; **~ the first (street) on the left** nehmen Sie die erste Straße links; **to ~ Russian at university** Russisch studieren; **it won't ~ long** es dauert nicht lange; **I was quite ~n with her/it** (*attracted to*) ich war von ihr/davon recht angetan.

►**take after** *vt fus* (*resemble*) ähneln +*dat*, ähnlich sein +*dat*.

►**take apart** *vt* auseinandernehmen.

►**take away** *vt* wegnehmen; (*carry off*) wegbringen; (*MATH*) abziehen ♦ *vi*: **to ~ away from** (*detract from*) schmälern, beeinträchtigen.

►**take back** *vt* (*return*) zurückbringen; (*one's words*) zurücknehmen.

►**take down** *vt* (*write down*) aufschreiben; (*dismantle*) abreißen.

►**take in** *vt* (*deceive: person*) hereinlegen, täuschen; (*understand*) begreifen; (*include*) einschließen; (*lodger*) aufnehmen; (*orphan, stray dog*) zu sich nehmen; (*dress, waistband*) enger machen.

►**take off** *vi* (*AVIAT*) starten; (*go away*) sich absetzen ♦ *vt* (*clothes*) ausziehen; (*glasses*) abnehmen; (*make-up*) entfernen; (*time*) frei nehmen; (*imitate: person*) nachmachen.

►**take on** *vt* (*work, responsibility*) übernehmen; (*employee*) einstellen; (*compete against*) antreten gegen.

►**take out** *vt* (*invite*) ausgehen mit; (*remove: tooth*) herausnehmen; (*licence*) erwerben; **to ~ sth out of sth** (*drawer, pocket etc*) etw aus etw nehmen; **don't ~ it out on me!** laß es nicht an mir aus!

►**take over** *vt* (*business*) übernehmen; (*country*) Besitz ergreifen von ♦ *vi* (*replace*): **to ~ over from sb** jdn ablösen.

►**take to** *vt fus* (*person, thing*) mögen; (*activity*) Gefallen finden an +*dat*; (*form habit of*): **to ~ to doing sth** sich *dat* angewöhnen, etw zu tun.

►**take up** *vt* (*hobby, sport*) anfangen mit; (*job*) antreten; (*idea etc*) annehmen; (*time, space*) beanspruchen; (*continue: task, story*) fortfahren mit; (*shorten: hem, garment*) kürzer machen ♦ *vi* (*befriend*): **to ~ up with sb** sich mit jdm anfreunden; **to ~ sb up on an offer/a suggestion** auf jds Angebot/ Vorschlag eingehen.

**takeaway** ['teɪkəweɪ] (*BRIT*) n (*shop, restaurant*) ≈ Schnellimbiß *m*; (*food*) Imbiß *m* (*zum Mitnehmen*).

**take-home pay** ['teɪkhəum-] n Nettolohn *m*.

**taken** ['teɪkən] *pp of* **take**.

**takeoff** ['teɪkɔf] n (*AVIAT*) Start *m*.

**takeout** ['teɪkaut] (*US*) n = **takeaway**.

**takeover** ['teɪkəuvə*] n (*COMM*) Übernahme *f*; (*of country*) Inbesitznahme *f*.

**takeover bid** n Übernahmeangebot *nt*.

**takings** ['teɪkɪŋz] *npl* Einnahmen *pl*.

**talc** [tælk] n (*also*: **talcum powder**) Talkumpuder *nt*.

**tale** [teɪl] n Geschichte *f*; **to tell ~s (to sb)** (*child*) (jdm) Geschichten erzählen.

**talent** ['tælnt] n Talent *nt*.

**talented** ['tæləntɪd] *adj* talentiert, begabt.

**talent scout** n Talentsucher(in) *m(f)*.

**talisman** ['tælɪzmən] n Talisman *m*.

**talk** [tɔːk] n (*speech*) Vortrag *m*; (*conversation, discussion*) Gespräch *nt*; (*gossip*) Gerede *nt* ♦ *vi* (*speak*) sprechen; (*chat*) reden; (*gossip*) klatschen; **talks** *npl* (*POL etc*) Gespräche *pl*; **to give a ~** einen Vortrag halten; **to ~ about** (*discuss*) sprechen *or* reden über; **~ing of films, have you seen …?** da wir gerade von Filmen sprechen: hast du … gesehen?; **to ~ sb into doing sth** jdn zu etw überreden; **to ~ sb out of doing sth** jdm etw ausreden.

►**talk over** *vt* (*problem etc*) besprechen, bereden.

**talkative** ['tɔːkətɪv] *adj* gesprächig.

**talker** ['tɔːkə*] n: **to be a good/entertaining/ fast** *etc* **~** gut/amüsant/schnell *etc* reden können.

**talking point** ['tɔːkɪŋ-] n Gesprächsthema *nt*.

**talking-to** ['tɔːkɪŋtu] n: **to give sb a (good) ~** jdm eine (ordentliche) Standpauke halten (*inf*).

**talk show** n Talkshow *f*.

**tall** [tɔːl] *adj* (*person*) groß; (*glass, bookcase, tree, building*) hoch; (*ladder*) lang; **to be 6 feet ~** (*person*) ≈ 1,80m groß sein; **how ~ are you?** wie groß bist du?

**tallboy** ['tɔːlbɔɪ] (*BRIT*) n Kommode *f*.

**tallness** ['tɔːlnɪs] n (*of person*) Größe *f*; (*of tree, building etc*) Höhe *f*.

**tall story** n unglaubliche Geschichte *f*.

**tally** ['tælɪ] n (*of marks, amounts etc*) aktueller Stand *m* ♦ *vi*: **to ~ (with)** (*figures, stories etc*) übereinstimmen mit; **to keep a ~ of sth** über etw *acc* Buch führen.

**talon** ['tælən] n Kralle *f*.

**tambourine** [tæmbə'riːn] n Tamburin *nt*.

**tame** [teɪm] *adj* (*animal, bird*) zahm; (*fig: story, party, performance*) lustlos, lahm (*inf*).

**Tamil** ['tæmɪl] *adj* tamilisch ♦ n Tamile *m*, Tamilin *f*; (*LING*) Tamil *nt*.

**tamper** ['tæmpə*] *vi*: **to ~ with sth** an etw *dat* herumpfuschen (*inf*).

**tampon** ['tæmpɔn] n Tampon *m*.

**tan** [tæn] n (*also*: **suntan**) (Sonnen)bräune *f* ♦ *vi* (*person, skin*) braun werden ♦ *vt* (*hide*) gerben; (*skin*) bräunen ♦ *adj* (*colour*) hellbraun; **to get a ~** braun werden.

**tandem** ['tændəm] n Tandem *nt*; (*together*): **in**

~ (*fig*) zusammen.

**tandoori** [tæn'duəri] *n*: ~ **oven** Tandoori-Ofen *m*; ~ **chicken** *im Tandoori-Ofen gebratenes Huhn*.

**tang** [tæŋ] *n* (*smell*) Geruch *m*; (*taste*) Geschmack *m*.

**tangent** ['tændʒənt] *n* (*MATH*) Tangente *f*; **to go off at a** ~ (*fig*) vom Thema abschweifen.

**tangerine** [tændʒə'riːn] *n* (*fruit*) Mandarine *f*; (*colour*) Orangerot *nt*.

**tangible** ['tændʒəbl] *adj* greifbar; ~ **assets** (*COMM*) Sachanlagevermögen *nt*.

**Tangier** [tæn'dʒɪə*] *n* Tanger *nt*.

**tangle** ['tæŋgl] *n* (*of branches, wire etc*) Gewirr *nt*; **to be in a** ~ verheddert sein; (*fig*) durcheinander sein; **to get in a** ~ sich verheddern; (*fig*) durcheinandergeraten.

**tango** ['tæŋgəu] *n* Tango *m*.

**tank** [tæŋk] *n* Tank *m*; (*for photographic processing*) Wanne *f*; (*also*: **fish** ~) Aquarium *nt*; (*MIL*) Panzer *m*.

**tankard** ['tæŋkəd] *n* Bierkrug *m*.

**tanker** ['tæŋkə*] *n* (*ship*) Tanker *m*; (*truck*) Tankwagen *m*.

**tanned** [tænd] *adj* (*person*) braungebrannt; (*hide*) gegerbt.

**tannin** ['tænɪn] *n* Tannin *nt*.

**tanning** ['tænɪŋ] *n* (*of leather*) Gerben *nt*.

**Tannoy** ® ['tænɔɪ] (*BRIT*) *n* Lautsprechersystem *nt*; **over the** ~ über Lautsprecher.

**tantalizing** ['tæntəlaɪzɪŋ] *adj* (*smell*) verführerisch; (*possibility*) verlockend.

**tantamount** ['tæntəmaunt] *adj*: ~ **to** gleichbedeutend mit.

**tantrum** ['tæntrəm] *n* Wutanfall *m*; **to throw a** ~ einen Wutanfall bekommen.

**Tanzania** [tænzə'nɪə] *n* Tansania *nt*.

**Tanzanian** [tænzə'nɪən] *adj* tansanisch ♦ *n* (*person*) Tansanier(in) *m(f)*.

**tap** [tæp] *n* (*on sink, gas tap*) Hahn *m*; (*gentle blow*) leichter Schlag *m*, Klaps *m* ♦ *vt* (*hit gently*) klopfen; (*exploit: resources, energy*) nutzen; (*telephone*) abhören, anzapfen; **on** ~ (*fig: resources, information*) zur Verfügung; (*beer*) vom Faß.

**tap-dancing** ['tæpdɑːnsɪŋ] *n* Steptanz *m*.

**tape** [teɪp] *n* (*also*: **magnetic** ~) Tonband *nt*; (*cassette*) Kassette *f*; (*also*: **sticky** ~) Klebeband *nt*; (*for tying*) Band *nt* ♦ *vt* (*record, conversation*) aufnehmen, aufzeichnen; (*stick with tape*) mit Klebeband befestigen; **on** ~ (*song etc*) auf Band.

**tape deck** *n* Tapedeck *nt*.

**tape measure** *n* Bandmaß *nt*.

**taper** ['teɪpə*] *n* (*candle*) lange, dünne Kerze ♦ *vi* sich verjüngen.

**tape recorder** *n* Tonband(gerät) *nt*.

**tape recording** *n* Tonbandaufnahme *f*.

**tapered** ['teɪpəd] *adj* (*skirt, jacket*) nach unten enger werdend.

**tapering** ['teɪpərɪŋ] *adj* spitz zulaufend.

**tapestry** ['tæpɪstrɪ] *n* (*on wall*) Wandteppich

*m*; (*fig*) Kaleidoskop *nt*.

**tapeworm** ['teɪpwɜːm] *n* Bandwurm *m*.

**tapioca** [tæpɪ'əukə] *n* Tapioka *f*.

**tappet** ['tæpɪt] *n* (*AUT*) Stößel *m*.

**tar** [tɑː] *n* Teer *m*; **low/middle** ~ **cigarettes** Zigaretten mit niedrigem/mittlerem Teergehalt.

**tarantula** [tə'ræntjulə] *n* Tarantel *f*.

**tardy** ['tɑːdɪ] *adj* (*reply, letter*) verspätet; (*progress*) langsam.

**target** ['tɑːgɪt] *n* Ziel *nt*; (*fig: of joke, criticism etc*) Zielscheibe *f*; **to be on** ~ (*project, work*) nach Plan verlaufen.

**target practice** *n* Zielschießen *nt*.

**tariff** ['tærɪf] *n* (*tax on goods*) Zoll *m*; (*BRIT: in hotels etc*) Preisliste *f*.

**tariff barrier** *n* Zollschranke *f*.

**tarmac** ® ['tɑːmæk] *n* (*BRIT: on road*) Asphalt *m*; (*AVIAT*): **on the** ~ auf dem Rollfeld ♦ *vt* (*BRIT: road etc*) asphaltieren.

**tarn** [tɑːn] *n* Bergsee *m*.

**tarnish** ['tɑːnɪʃ] *vt* (*silver, brass etc*) stumpf werden lassen; (*fig: reputation etc*) beflecken, in Mitleidenschaft ziehen.

**tarot** ['tærəu] *n* Tarot *nt or m*.

**tarpaulin** [tɑː'pɔːlɪn] *n* Plane *f*.

**tarragon** ['tærəgən] *n* Estragon *m*.

**tart** [tɑːt] *n* (*CULIN*) Torte *f*; (*: small*) Törtchen *nt*; (*BRIT: inf: prostitute*) Nutte *f* ♦ *adj* (*apple, grapefruit etc*) säuerlich.

▶**tart up** (*BRIT: inf*) *vt* (*room, building*) aufmotzen; **to** ~ **o.s. up** sich feinmachen; (*pej*) sich auftakeln.

**tartan** ['tɑːtn] *n* Tartan *m*, Schottenstoff *m* ♦ *adj* (*scarf etc*) mit Schottenmuster.

**tartar** ['tɑːtə*] *n* (*on teeth*) Zahnstein *m*; (*pej: person*) Tyrann(in) *m(f)*.

**tartar(e) sauce** ['tɑːtə-] *n* Remouladensoße *f*.

**task** [tɑːsk] *n* Aufgabe *f*; **to take sb to** ~ jdn ins Gebet nehmen.

**task force** *n* (*MIL*) Sonderkommando *nt*; (*POLICE*) Spezialeinheit *f*.

**taskmaster** ['tɑːskmɑːstə*] *n*: **a hard** ~ ein strenger Lehrmeister.

**Tasmania** [tæz'meɪnɪə] *n* Tasmanien *nt*.

**tassel** ['tæsl] *n* Quaste *f*.

**taste** [teɪst] *n* Geschmack *m*; (*sample*) Kostprobe *f*; (*fig: of suffering, freedom etc*) Vorgeschmack *m* ♦ *vt* (*get flavour of*) schmecken; (*test*) probieren, versuchen ♦ *vi*: **to** ~ **of/like sth** nach/wie etw schmecken; **sense of** ~ Geschmackssinn *m*; **to have a** ~ **of sth** (*sample*) etw probieren; **to acquire a** ~ **for sth** (*liking*) Geschmack an etw *dat* finden; **to be in good/bad** ~ (*joke etc*) geschmackvoll/geschmacklos sein; **you can** ~ **the garlic (in it)** (*detect*) man schmeckt den Knoblauch durch; **what does it** ~ **like?** wie schmeckt es?

**taste buds** *npl* Geschmacksknospen *pl*.

**tasteful** ['teɪstful] *adj* geschmackvoll.

**tastefully** ['teɪstfəlɪ] *adv* geschmackvoll.

**tasteless** ['teɪstlɪs] adj geschmacklos.

**tasty** ['teɪstɪ] adj schmackhaft.

**tattered** ['tætəd] adj (clothes, paper etc) zerrissen; (fig: hopes etc) angeschlagen.

**tatters** ['tætəz] npl: **to be in ~** (clothes) in Fetzen sein.

**tattoo** [tə'tuː] n (on skin) Tätowierung f; (spectacle) Zapfenstreich m ♦ vt: **to ~ sth on sth** etw auf etw acc tätowieren.

**tatty** ['tætɪ] (BRIT: inf) adj schäbig.

**taught** [tɔːt] pt, pp of **teach**.

**taunt** [tɔːnt] n höhnische Bemerkung f ♦ vt (person) verhöhnen.

**Taurus** ['tɔːrəs] n Stier m; **to be ~** (ein) Stier sein.

**taut** [tɔːt] adj (skin, thread etc) straff.

**tavern** ['tævən] n Taverne f.

**tawdry** ['tɔːdrɪ] adj (jewellery, clothes etc) billig.

**tawny** ['tɔːnɪ] adj gelbbraun.

**tawny owl** n Waldkauz m.

**tax** [tæks] n Steuer f ♦ vt (earnings, goods etc) besteuern; (fig: memory, knowledge) strapazieren; (: patience etc) auf die Probe stellen; **before/after ~** vor/nach Abzug der Steuern; **free of ~** steuerfrei.

**taxable** ['tæksəbl] adj steuerpflichtig; (income) steuerbar.

**tax allowance** n Steuerfreibetrag m.

**taxation** [tæk'seɪʃən] n (system) Besteuerung f; (money paid) Steuern pl.

**tax avoidance** n Steuerumgehung f.

**tax collector** n Steuerbeamte(r) m, Steuerbeamtin f.

**tax disc** (BRIT) n (AUT) Steuerplakette f.

**tax evasion** n Steuerhinterziehung f.

**tax exemption** n Steuerbefreiung f.

**tax exile** (person) n Steuerflüchtling m.

**tax-free** ['tæksfriː] adj steuerfrei.

**tax haven** n Steuerparadies nt.

**taxi** ['tæksɪ] n Taxi nt ♦ vi (AVIAT: plane) rollen.

**taxidermist** ['tæksɪdəːmɪst] n Taxidermist(in) m(f), Tierpräparator(in) m(f).

**taxi driver** n Taxifahrer(in) m(f).

**tax inspector** (BRIT) n Steuerinspektor(in) m(f).

**taxi rank** (BRIT) n Taxistand m.

**taxi stand** n = **taxi rank**.

**taxpayer** ['tækspeɪə'] n Steuerzahler(in) m(f).

**tax rebate** n Steuerrückvergütung f.

**tax relief** n Steuernachlaß m.

**tax return** n Steuererklärung f.

**tax shelter** n (COMM) System zur Verhinderung von Steuerbelastung.

**tax year** n Steuerjahr nt.

**TB** n abbr (= tuberculosis) Tb f, Tbc f.

**TD** (US) n abbr = **Treasury Department**; (FOOTBALL) = **touchdown**.

**tea** [tiː] n (drink) Tee m; (BRIT: evening meal) Abendessen nt; **afternoon ~** (BRIT) Nachmittagstee m.

**tea bag** n Teebeutel m.

**tea break** (BRIT) n Teepause f.

**teacake** ['tiːkeɪk] (BRIT) n Rosinenbrötchen nt.

**teach** [tiːtʃ] (pt, pp taught) vt: **to ~ sb sth, ~ sth to sb** (instruct) jdm etw beibringen; (in school) jdn in etw dat unterrichten ♦ vi unterrichten; **it taught him a lesson** (fig) er hat seine Lektion gelernt.

**teacher** ['tiːtʃə'] n Lehrer(in) m(f); **German ~** Deutschlehrer(in) m(f).

**teacher training college** n (for primary schools) ≈ pädagogische Hochschule f; (for secondary schools) ≈ Studienseminar nt.

**teaching** ['tiːtʃɪŋ] n (work of teacher) Unterricht m.

**teaching aids** npl Lehrmittel pl.

**teaching hospital** (BRIT) n Ausbildungskrankenhaus nt.

**teaching staff** (BRIT) n Lehrerkollegium nt.

**tea cosy** n Teewärmer m.

**teacup** ['tiːkʌp] n Teetasse f.

**teak** [tiːk] n Teak nt.

**tea leaves** npl Teeblätter pl.

**team** [tiːm] n (of experts etc) Team nt; (SPORT) Mannschaft f, Team nt; (of horses, oxen) Gespann nt.

▶**team up** vi: **to ~ up (with)** sich zusammentun (mit).

**team game** n Mannschaftsspiel nt.

**team spirit** n Teamgeist m.

**teamwork** ['tiːmwəːk] n Teamwork nt, Teamarbeit f.

**tea party** n Teegesellschaft f.

**teapot** ['tiːpɒt] n Teekanne f.

**tear¹** [tɛə'] (pt tore, pp torn) n (hole) Riß m ♦ vt (rip) zerreißen ♦ vi (become torn) reißen; **to ~ sth to pieces or bits or shreds** (lit, fig) etw in Stücke reißen; **to ~ sb to pieces** jdn fertigmachen.

▶**tear along** vi (rush: driver, car) entlanggrasen.

▶**tear apart** vt (book, clothes, people) auseinanderreißen; (upset: person) hin- und herreißen.

▶**tear away** vt: **to ~ o.s. away (from sth)** (fig) sich (von etw) losreißen.

▶**tear out** vt (sheet of paper etc) herausreißen.

▶**tear up** vt (sheet of paper etc) zerreißen.

**tear²** [tɪə'] n (in eye) Träne f; **in ~s** in Tränen; **to burst into ~s** in Tränen ausbrechen.

**tearaway** ['tɛərəweɪ] (BRIT: inf) n Rabauke m.

**teardrop** ['tɪədrɒp] n Träne f.

**tearful** ['tɪəful] adj (person) weinend; (face) tränenüberströmt.

**tear gas** n Tränengas nt.

**tearing** ['tɛərɪŋ] adj: **to be in a ~ hurry** es unheimlich eilig haben.

**tearoom** ['tiːruːm] n = **teashop**.

**tease** [tiːz] vt necken; (unkindly) aufziehen ♦ n: **she's a real ~** sie zieht einen ständig auf.

**tea set** n Teeservice nt.

**teashop** ['tiːʃɒp] (BRIT) n Teestube f.

**Teasmade ®** ['tiːzmeɪd] n Teemaschine f (mit Zeiteinstellung).

**teaspoon** ['tiːspuːn] n Teelöffel m; (also: ~**ful**: measure) Teelöffel(voll) m.

**tea strainer** n Teesieb nt.

**teat** [tiːt] n (on bottle) Sauger m.

**teatime** ['tiːtaɪm] n Teestunde f.

**tea towel** (BRIT) n Geschirrtuch nt.

**tea urn** n Teespender m.

**tech** [tɛk] (inf) n abbr = **technical college; technology.**

**technical** ['tɛknɪkl] adj technisch; (terms, language) Fach-.

**technical college** (BRIT) n Technische Fachschule f.

**technicality** [tɛknɪ'kælɪtɪ] n (point of law) Formalität f; (detail) technische Einzelheit f; **on a (legal)** ~ aufgrund einer (juristischen) Formalität.

**technically** ['tɛknɪklɪ] adv (strictly speaking) genau genommen; (regarding technique) technisch (gesehen).

**technician** [tɛk'nɪʃən] n Techniker(in) m(f).

**technique** [tɛk'niːk] n Technik f.

**techno** ['tɛknəʊ] n (MUS) Techno nt.

**technocrat** ['tɛknəkræt] n Technokrat(in) m(f).

**technological** [tɛknə'lɔdʒɪkl] adj technologisch.

**technologist** [tɛk'nɔlədʒɪst] n Technologe m, Technologin f.

**technology** [tɛk'nɔlədʒɪ] n Technologie f.

**technology college** n Oberstufenkolleg mit technischem Schwerpunkt.

**teddy (bear)** ['tɛdɪ(-)] n Teddy(bär) m.

**tedious** ['tiːdɪəs] adj langweilig.

**tedium** ['tiːdɪəm] n Langeweile f.

**tee** [tiː] n (GOLF) Tee nt.

▶**tee off** vi (vom Tee) abschlagen.

**teem** [tiːm] vi: **to** ~ **with** (tourists etc) wimmeln von; **it is** ~**ing down** es gießt in Strömen.

**teenage** ['tiːneɪdʒ] adj (fashions etc) Jugend-; (children) im Teenageralter.

**teenager** ['tiːneɪdʒə*] n Teenager m, Jugendliche(r) f(m).

**teens** [tiːnz] npl: **to be in one's** ~ im Teenageralter sein.

**tee shirt** n = T-shirt.

**teeter** ['tiːtə*] vi (also fig) schwanken, taumeln.

**teeth** [tiːθ] npl of **tooth.**

**teethe** [tiːð] vi Zähne bekommen, zahnen.

**teething ring** ['tiːðɪŋ-] n Beißring m.

**teething troubles** npl (fig) Kinderkrankheiten pl.

**teetotal** ['tiː'təʊtl] adj (person) abstinent.

**teetotaller,** (US) **teetotaler** ['tiː'təʊtlə*] n Abstinenzler(in) m(f), Antialkoholiker(in) m(f).

**TEFL** ['tɛfl] n abbr (= Teaching of English as a Foreign Language) Unterricht in Englisch als Fremdsprache.

**Teflon** ® ['tɛflɔn] n Teflon ® nt.

**Teheran** [tɛə'rɑːn] n Teheran nt.

**tel.** abbr (= telephone) Tel.

**Tel Aviv** ['tɛlə'viːv] n Tel Aviv nt.

**telecast** ['tɛlɪkɑːst] n Fernsehsendung f.

**telecommunications** ['tɛlɪkəmjuːnɪ'keɪʃənz] n Nachrichtentechnik f.

**telegram** ['tɛlɪgræm] n Telegramm nt.

**telegraph** ['tɛlɪgrɑːf] n (system) Telegraf m.

**telegraphic** [tɛlɪ'græfɪk] adj (equipment) telegrafisch.

**telegraph pole** n Telegrafenmast m.

**telegraph wire** n Telegrafenleitung f.

**telepathic** [tɛlɪ'pæθɪk] adj telepathisch.

**telepathy** [tə'lɛpəθɪ] n Telepathie f.

**telephone** ['tɛlɪfəʊn] n Telefon nt ♦ vt (person) anrufen ♦ vi anrufen, telefonieren; **to be on the** ~ (talking) telefonieren; (possessing phone) ein Telefon haben.

**telephone box,** (US) **telephone booth** n Telefonzelle f.

**telephone call** n Anruf m.

**telephone directory** n Telefonbuch nt.

**telephone exchange** n Telefonzentrale f.

**telephone number** n Telefonnummer f.

**telephone operator** n Telefonist(in) m(f).

**telephone tapping** n Abhören nt von Telefonleitungen.

**telephonist** [tə'lɛfənɪst] (BRIT) n Telefonist(in) m(f).

**telephoto** ['tɛlɪ'fəʊtəʊ] adj: ~ **lens** Teleobjektiv nt.

**teleprinter** ['tɛlɪprɪntə*] n Fernschreiber m.

**Teleprompter** ® ['tɛlɪprɔmptə*] (US) n Teleprompter m.

**telesales** ['tɛlɪseɪlz] n Verkauf m per Telefon.

**telescope** ['tɛlɪskəʊp] n Teleskop nt ♦ vi (fig: bus, lorry) sich ineinanderschieben ♦ vt (make shorter) zusammenschieben.

**telescopic** [tɛlɪ'skɔpɪk] adj (legs, aerial) ausziehbar; ~ **lens** Fernrohrlinse f.

**Teletext** ® ['tɛlɪtɛkst] n Videotext m.

**telethon** ['tɛlɪθɔn] n Spendenaktion für wohltätige Zwecke in Form einer vielstündigen Fernsehsendung.

**televise** ['tɛlɪvaɪz] vt (im Fernsehen) übertragen.

**television** ['tɛlɪvɪʒən] n Fernsehen nt; (set) Fernseher m, Fernsehapparat m; **to be on** ~ im Fernsehen sein.

**television licence** (BRIT) n Fernsehgenehmigung f.

**television programme** n Fernsehprogramm nt.

**television set** n Fernseher m, Fernsehapparat m.

**telex** ['tɛlɛks] n (system, machine, message) Telex nt ♦ vt (message) telexen; (person) ein Telex schicken +dat ♦ vi telexen.

**tell** [tɛl] (pt, pp **told**) vt (say) sagen; (relate: story) erzählen; (distinguish): **to** ~ **sth from** etw unterscheiden von; (be sure) wissen ♦ vi (have an effect) sich auswirken; **to** ~ **sb to do sth** jdm sagen, etw zu tun; **to** ~ **sb of** or about sth jdm von etw erzählen; **to be able to ~ the time** (*know how to*) die Uhr kennen; **can you ~ me the time?** können Sie mir sagen, wie spät es ist?; **(I) ~ you what, let's go to the cinema** weißt du was? Laß uns ins Kino gehen!; **I can't ~ them apart** ich kann sie nicht unterscheiden.

►**tell off** *vt*: **to ~ sb off** jdn ausschimpfen.

►**tell on** *vt fus* (*inform against*) verpetzen.

**teller** ['tɛlə'] *n* (*in bank*) Kassierer(in) *m(f)*.

**telling** ['tɛlɪŋ] *adj* (*remark etc*) verräterisch.

**telltale** ['tɛlteɪl] *adj* verräterisch ♦ *n* (*pej*) Petzer *m*, Petze *f*.

**telly** ['tɛlɪ] (*BRIT: inf*) *n abbr* = **television**.

**temerity** [tə'mɛrɪtɪ] *n* Unverschämtheit *f*.

**temp** [tɛmp] (*BRIT: inf*) *n abbr* (= *temporary office worker*) Zeitarbeitskraft *f* ♦ *vi* als Zeitarbeitskraft arbeiten.

**temper** ['tɛmpə'] *n* (*nature*) Naturell *nt*; (*mood*) Laune *f* ♦ *vt* (*moderate*) mildern; **a (fit of) ~** ein Wutanfall; **to be in a ~** gereizt sein; **to lose one's ~** die Beherrschung verlieren.

**temperament** ['tɛmprəmənt] *n* Temperament *nt*.

**temperamental** [tɛmprə'mɛntl] *adj* (*person, car*) launisch.

**temperate** ['tɛmprət] *adj* gemäßigt.

**temperature** ['tɛmprətʃə'] *n* Temperatur *f*; **to have** *or* **run a ~** Fieber haben; **to take sb's ~** bei jdm Fieber messen.

**temperature chart** *n* (*MED*) Fiebertabelle *f*.

**tempered** ['tɛmpəd] *adj* (*steel*) gehärtet.

**tempest** ['tɛmpɪst] *n* Sturm *m*.

**tempestuous** [tɛm'pɛstjuəs] *adj* (*also fig*) stürmisch; (*person*) leidenschaftlich.

**tempi** ['tɛmpiː] *npl of* **tempo**.

**template** ['tɛmplɪt] *n* Schablone *f*.

**temple** ['tɛmpl] *n* (*building*) Tempel *m*; (*ANAT*) Schläfe *f*.

**tempo** ['tɛmpəu] (*pl* ~**s** *or* **tempi**) *n* (*MUS, fig*) Tempo *nt*.

**temporal** ['tɛmpərl] *adj* (*non-religious*) weltlich; (*relating to time*) zeitlich.

**temporarily** ['tɛmpərərɪlɪ] *adv* vorübergehend; (*unavailable, alone etc*) zeitweilig.

**temporary** ['tɛmpərərɪ] *adj* (*arrangement*) provisorisch; (*worker, job*) Aushilfs-; **~ secretary** Sekretärin zur Aushilfe; **~ teacher** Aushilfslehrer(in) *m(f)*.

**temporize** ['tɛmpəraɪz] *vi* ausweichen.

**tempt** [tɛmpt] *vt* in Versuchung führen; **to ~ sb into doing sth** jdn dazu verleiten, etw zu tun; **to be ~ed to do sth** versucht sein, etw zu tun.

**temptation** [tɛmp'teɪʃən] *n* Versuchung *f*.

**tempting** ['tɛmptɪŋ] *adj* (*offer*) verlockend; (*food*) verführerisch.

**ten** [tɛn] *num* zehn ♦ *n*: **~s of thousands** Zehntausende *pl*.

**tenable** ['tɛnəbl] *adj* (*argument, position*) haltbar.

**tenacious** [tə'neɪʃəs] *adj* zäh, hartnäckig.

**tenacity** [tə'næsɪtɪ] *n* Zähigkeit *f*, Hartnäckigkeit *f*.

**tenancy** ['tɛnənsɪ] *n* (*of room*) Mietverhältnis *nt*; (*of land*) Pachtverhältnis *nt*.

**tenant** ['tɛnənt] *n* (*of room*) Mieter(in) *m(f)*; (*of land*) Pächter(in) *m(f)*.

**tend** [tɛnd] *vt* (*crops, sick person*) sich kümmern um ♦ *vi*: **to ~ to do sth** dazu neigen *or* tendieren, etw zu tun.

**tendency** ['tɛndənsɪ] *n* (*of person*) Neigung *f*; (*of thing*) Tendenz *f*.

**tender** ['tɛndə'] *adj* (*person, care*) zärtlich; (*heart*) gut; (*sore*) empfindlich; (*meat, age*) zart ♦ *n* (*COMM*) Angebot *nt*; (*money*): **legal ~** gesetzliches Zahlungsmittel *nt* ♦ *vt* (*offer*) vorlegen; (*resignation*) einreichen; (*apology*) anbieten; **to put in a ~ (for)** ein Angebot vorlegen (für); **to put work out to ~** (*BRIT*) Arbeiten ausschreiben.

**tenderize** ['tɛndəraɪz] *vt* (*meat*) zart machen.

**tenderly** ['tɛndəlɪ] *adv* zärtlich, liebevoll.

**tenderness** ['tɛndənɪs] *n* (*affection*) Zärtlichkeit *f*; (*of meat*) Zartheit *f*.

**tendon** ['tɛndən] *n* Sehne *f*.

**tendril** ['tɛndrɪl] *n* (*BOT*) Ranke *f*; (*of hair etc*) Strähne *f*.

**tenement** ['tɛnəmənt] *n* Mietshaus *nt*.

**Tenerife** [tɛnə'riːf] *n* Teneriffa *nt*.

**tenet** ['tɛnət] *n* Prinzip *nt*.

**Tenn.** (*US*) *abbr* (*POST*: = *Tennessee*).

**tenner** ['tɛnə'] (*BRIT: inf*) *n* Zehner *m*.

**tennis** ['tɛnɪs] *n* Tennis *nt*.

**tennis ball** *n* Tennisball *m*.

**tennis club** *n* Tennisclub *m*.

**tennis court** *n* Tennisplatz *m*.

**tennis elbow** *n* (*MED*) Tennisell(en)bogen *m*.

**tennis match** *n* Tennismatch *nt*.

**tennis player** *n* Tennisspieler(in) *m(f)*.

**tennis racket** *n* Tennisschläger *m*.

**tennis shoes** *npl* Tennisschuhe *pl*.

**tenor** ['tɛnə'] *n* (*MUS*) Tenor *m*; (*of speech etc*) wesentlicher Gehalt *m*.

**tenpin bowling** ['tɛnpɪn-] (*BRIT*) *n* Bowling *nt*.

**tense** [tɛns] *adj* (*person, muscle*) angespannt; (*smile*) verkrampft; (*period, situation*) gespannt ♦ *n* (*LING*) Zeit *f*, Tempus *nt* ♦ *vt* (*muscles*) anspannen.

**tenseness** ['tɛnsnɪs] *n* Gespanntheit *f*.

**tension** ['tɛnʃən] *n* (*nervousness*) Angespanntheit *f*; (*between ropes etc*) Spannung *f*.

**tent** [tɛnt] *n* Zelt *nt*.

**tentacle** ['tɛntəkl] *n* (*ZOOL*) Fangarm *m*; (*fig*) Klaue *f*.

**tentative** ['tɛntətɪv] *adj* (*person, smile*) zögernd; (*step*) unsicher; (*conclusion, plans*) vorläufig.

**tentatively** ['tɛntətɪvlɪ] *adv* (*suggest*) versuchsweise; (*wave etc*) zögernd.

**tenterhooks** ['tɛntəhuks] *npl*: **to be on ~** wie auf glühenden Kohlen sitzen.

**tenth** [tɛnθ] *num* zehnte(r, s) ♦ *n* Zehntel *nt*.
**tent peg** *n* Hering *m*.
**tent pole** *n* Zeltstange *f*.
**tenuous** ['tɛnjʊəs] *adj* (*hold, links etc*) schwach.
**tenure** ['tɛnjʊəʳ] *n* (*of land etc*) Nutzungsrecht *nt*; (*of office*) Amtszeit *f*; (*UNIV*): **to have ~** eine Dauerstellung haben.
**tepid** ['tɛpɪd] *adj* (*also fig*) lauwarm.
**Ter.** *abbr* (*in street names:* = *terrace*) ≈ Str.
**term** [tɜːm] *n* (*word*) Ausdruck *m*; (*period in power etc*) Amtszeit *f*; (*SCOL: three per year*) Trimester *nt* ♦ *vt* (*call*) nennen; **terms** *npl* (*also COMM*) Bedingungen *pl*; **in economic/ political ~s** wirtschaftlich/politisch gesehen; **in ~s of business** was das Geschäft angeht *or* betrifft; **~ of imprisonment** Gefängnisstrafe *f*; **"easy ~s"** (*COMM*) „günstige Bedingungen"; **in the short/long ~** auf kurze/lange Sicht; **to be on good ~s with sb** sich mit jdm gut verstehen; **to come to ~s with** (*problem*) sich abfinden mit.
**terminal** ['tɜːmɪnl] *adj* (*disease, patient*) unheilbar ♦ *n* (*AVIAT, COMM, COMPUT*) Terminal *nt*; (*ELEC*) Anschluß *m*; (*BRIT: also:* **bus ~**) Endstation *f*.
**terminate** ['tɜːmɪneɪt] *vt* beenden ♦ *vi*: **to ~ in** enden in *+dat*.
**termination** [tɜːmɪ'neɪʃən] *n* Beendigung *f*; (*expiry: of contract*) Ablauf *m*; (*MED: of pregnancy*) Abbruch *m*.
**termini** ['tɜːmɪnaɪ] *npl of* **terminus**.
**terminology** [tɜːmɪ'nɒlədʒɪ] *n* Terminologie *f*.
**terminus** ['tɜːmɪnəs] (*pl* **termini**) *n* (*for buses, trains*) Endstation *f*.
**termite** ['tɜːmaɪt] *n* Termite *f*.
**term paper** (*US*) *n* (*UNIV*) ≈ Semesterarbeit *f*.
**Terr.** *abbr* (*in street names:* = *terrace*) ≈ Str.
**terrace** ['tɛrəs] *n* (*BRIT: row of houses*) Häuserreihe *f*; (*AGR, patio*) Terrasse *f*; **the terraces** *npl* (*BRIT: SPORT*) die Ränge *pl*.
**terraced** ['tɛrəst] *adj* (*house*) Reihen-; (*garden*) terrassenförmig angelegt.
**terracotta** ['tɛrə'kɒtə] *n* (*clay*) Terrakotta *f*; (*colour*) Braunrot *nt* ♦ *adj* (*pot, roof etc*) Terrakotta-.
**terrain** [tɛ'reɪn] *n* Gelände *nt*, Terrain *nt*.
**terrible** ['tɛrɪbl] *adj* schrecklich, furchtbar.
**terribly** ['tɛrɪblɪ] *adv* (*very*) furchtbar; (*very badly*) entsetzlich.
**terrier** ['tɛrɪəʳ] *n* Terrier *m*.
**terrific** [tə'rɪfɪk] *adj* (*very great: thunderstorm, speed*) unheimlich; (*time, party*) sagenhaft.
**terrify** ['tɛrɪfaɪ] *vt* erschrecken; **to be terrified** schreckliche Angst haben.
**terrifying** ['tɛrɪfaɪɪŋ] *adj* entsetzlich, grauenvoll.
**territorial** [tɛrɪ'tɔːrɪəl] *adj* (*boundaries, dispute*) territorial, Gebiets-; (*waters*) Hoheits- ♦ *n* (*MIL*) Soldat *m* der Territorialarmee.

**Territorial Army** (*BRIT*) *n* (*MIL*): **the ~** die Territorialarmee.
**territorial waters** *npl* Hoheitsgewässer *pl*.
**territory** ['tɛrɪtərɪ] *n* (*also fig*) Gebiet *nt*.
**terror** ['tɛrəʳ] *n* (*great fear*) panische Angst *f*.
**terrorism** ['tɛrərɪzəm] *n* Terrorismus *m*.
**terrorist** ['tɛrərɪst] *n* Terrorist(in) *m(f)*.
**terrorize** ['tɛrəraɪz] *vt* terrorisieren.
**terse** [tɜːs] *adj* knapp.
**tertiary** ['tɜːʃərɪ] *adj* tertiär; **~ education** (*BRIT*) Universitätsausbildung *f*.
**Terylene** ® ['tɛrɪliːn] *n* Terylen ® *nt* ♦ *adj* Terylen-.
**TESL** ['tɛsl] *n abbr* (= *Teaching of English as a Second Language*) Unterricht in Englisch als Zweitsprache.
**TESSA** ['tɛsə] (*BRIT*) *n abbr* (= *Tax Exempt Special Savings Account*) steuerfreies Sparsystem mit begrenzter Einlagehöhe.
**test** [tɛst] *n* Test *m*; (*of courage etc*) Probe *f*; (*SCOL*) Prüfung *f*; (*also:* **driving ~**) Fahrprüfung *f* ♦ *vt* testen; (*check, SCOL*) prüfen; **to put sth to the ~** etw auf die Probe stellen; **to ~ sth for sth** etw auf etw *acc* prüfen.
**testament** ['tɛstəmənt] *n* Zeugnis *nt*; **the Old/ New T~** das Alte/Neue Testament; **last will and ~** Testament *nt*.
**test ban** *n* (*also:* **nuclear ~**) Teststopp *m*.
**test card** *n* (*TV*) Testbild *nt*.
**test case** *n* (*LAW*) Musterfall *m*; (*fig*) Musterbeispiel *nt*.
**testes** ['tɛstiːz] *npl* Testikel *pl*, Hoden *pl*.
**test flight** *n* Testflug *m*.
**testicle** ['tɛstɪkl] *n* Hoden *m*.
**testify** ['tɛstɪfaɪ] *vi* (*LAW*) aussagen; **to ~ to sth** (*LAW, fig*) etw bezeugen.
**testimonial** [tɛstɪ'məʊnɪəl] *n* (*BRIT: reference*) Referenz *f*; (*SPORT: also:* **~ match**) Benefizspiel, dessen Erlös einem verdienten Spieler zugute kommt.
**testimony** ['tɛstɪmənɪ] *n* (*statement*) Aussage *f*; (*clear proof*): **to be (a) ~ to** ein Zeugnis sein für.
**testing** ['tɛstɪŋ] *adj* schwierig.
**test match** *n* (*CRICKET, RUGBY*) Test Match *nt*, Länderspiel *nt*.
**testosterone** [tɛs'tɒstərəʊn] *n* Testosteron *nt*.
**test paper** *n* (*SCOL*) Klassenarbeit *f*.
**test pilot** *n* Testpilot(in) *m(f)*.
**test tube** *n* Reagenzglas *nt*.
**test-tube baby** ['tɛsttjuːb-] *n* Retortenbaby *nt*.
**testy** ['tɛstɪ] *adj* gereizt.
**tetanus** ['tɛtənəs] *n* Tetanus *m*, Wundstarrkrampf *m*.
**tetchy** ['tɛtʃɪ] *adj* gereizt.
**tether** ['tɛðəʳ] *vt* (*animal*) festbinden ♦ *n*: **to be at the end of one's ~** völlig am Ende sein.
**Tex.** (*US*) *abbr* (*POST:* = *Texas*).
**text** [tɛkst] *n* Text *m*.
**textbook** ['tɛkstbʊk] *n* Lehrbuch *nt*.

**textiles** ['tɛkstaɪlz] *npl* Textilien *pl*.
**textual** ['tɛkstjuəl] *adj* (*analysis etc*) Text-.
**texture** ['tɛkstʃə*] *n* Beschaffenheit *f*,
Struktur *f*.
**TGWU** (*BRIT*) *n abbr* (= *Transport and General
Workers' Union*) Transportarbeitergewerk-
schaft.
**Thai** [taɪ] *adj* thailändisch ♦ *n* Thailänder(in)
*m(f)*.
**Thailand** ['taɪlænd] *n* Thailand *nt*.
**thalidomide** ® [θə'lɪdəmaɪd] *n* Contergan ®
*nt*.
**Thames** [tɛmz] *n*: **the ~** die Themse.
**than** [ðæn] *conj* (*in comparisons*) als; **more ~ 10**
mehr als 10; **she is older ~ you think** sie ist
älter als Sie denken; **more ~ once** mehr als
einmal.
**thank** [θæŋk] *vt* danken +*dat*; **~ you** danke;
**~ you very much** vielen Dank; **~ God!** Gott
sei Dank!
**thankful** ['θæŋkful] *adj*: **~ (for/that)** dankbar
(für/, daß).
**thankfully** ['θæŋkfəlɪ] *adv* dankbar; **~ there
were few victims** zum Glück gab es nur
wenige Opfer.
**thankless** ['θæŋklɪs] *adj* undankbar.
**thanks** [θæŋks] *npl* Dank *m* ♦ *excl* (*also*: **many
~**, **~ a lot**) danke, vielen Dank; **~ to** dank
+*gen*.
**Thanksgiving (Day)** ['θæŋksgɪvɪŋ(-)] (*US*) *n*
Thanksgiving Day *m*.

---

**Thanksgiving (Day)** ist ein Feiertag in den USA,
der auf den vierten Donnerstag im November
fällt. Er soll daran erinnern, wie die
Pilgerväter die gute Ernte im Jahre 1621
feierten. In Kanada gibt es einen ähnlichen
Erntedanktag (der aber nichts mit den
Pilgervätern zu tun hat) am zweiten Montag im
Oktober.

---

===================================== *KEYWORD*

**that** [ðæt, ðət] (*pl* **those**) *adj* (*demonstrative*)
der/die/das; **~ man** der Mann; **~ woman** die
Frau; **~ book** das Buch; **~ one** der/die/das
da; **I want this one, not ~ one** ich will dieses
(hier), nicht das (da)
♦ *pron* **1** (*demonstrative*) das; **who's/what's
~?** wer/was ist das?; **is ~ you?** bist du das?;
**will you eat all ~?** ißt du das alles?; **that's
what he said** das hat er gesagt; **what
happened after ~?** was geschah danach?;
**~ is (to say)** das heißt; **and that's that!** und
damit Schluß!
**2** (*relative: subject*) der/die/das; (: : *pl*) die;
(: *direct object*) den/die/das; (: : *pl*) die;
(: *indirect object*) dem/der/dem; (: : *pl*) denen;
**the man ~ I saw** der Mann, den ich gesehen
habe; **all ~ I have** alles, was ich habe; **the
people ~ I spoke to** die Leute, mit denen ich
geredet habe

**3** (*relative: of time*) **the day ~** he came der
Tag, an dem er kam; **the winter ~ he came
to see us** der Winter, in dem er uns
besuchte
♦ *conj* daß; **he thought ~ I was ill** er dachte,
daß ich krank sei, er dachte, ich sei krank
♦ *adv* (*demonstrative*) so; **I can't work ~ much**
ich kann nicht so viel arbeiten; **~ high** so
hoch.

---

**thatched** [θætʃt] *adj* (*roof, cottage*)
strohgedeckt.
**Thatcherism** ['θætʃərɪzəm] *n* Thatcherismus
*m*.
**Thatcherite** ['θætʃəraɪt] *adj* thatcheristisch
♦ *n* Thatcher-Anhänger(in) *m(f)*.
**thaw** [θɔː] *n* Tauwetter *nt* ♦ *vi* (*ice*) tauen;
(*food*) auftauen ♦ *vt* (*also*: **~ out**) auftauen;
**it's ~ing** es taut.

===================================== *KEYWORD*

**the** [ðiː, ðə] *def art* **1** (*before masculine noun*)
der; (*before feminine noun*) die; (*before neuter
noun*) das; (*before plural noun*) die; **to play
~ piano/violin** Klavier/Geige spielen; **I'm
going to ~ butcher's/the cinema** ich gehe
zum Metzger/ins Kino
**2** (+ *adj to form noun*): **~ rich and ~ poor** die
Reichen und die Armen; **to attempt
~ impossible** das Unmögliche versuchen
**3** (*in titles*): **Elizabeth ~ First** Elisabeth die
Erste; **Peter ~ Great** Peter der Große
**4** (*in comparisons*): **~ more he works ~ more
he earns** je mehr er arbeitet, desto mehr
verdient er; **~ sooner ~ better** je eher,
desto besser.

---

**theatre**, (*US*) **theater** ['θɪətə*] *n* Theater *nt*;
(*also*: **lecture ~**) Hörsaal *m*; (*also*: **operating
~**) Operationsaal *m*.
**theatre-goer** ['θɪətəgəʊə*] *n* Theater-
besucher(in) *m(f)*.
**theatrical** [θɪ'ætrɪkl] *adj* (*event, production*)
Theater-; (*gestures etc*) theatralisch.
**theft** [θɛft] *n* Diebstahl *m*.
**their** [ðɛə*] *adj* ihr.
**theirs** [ðɛəz] *pron* ihre(r, s); **it is ~** es gehört
ihnen; **a friend of ~** ein Freund/eine
Freundin von ihnen; *see also* **my**, **mine**[1].
**them** [ðɛm] *pron* (*direct*) sie; (*indirect*) ihnen; **I
see ~** ich sehe sie; **give ~ the book** gib
ihnen das Buch; **give me a few of ~** geben
Sie mir ein paar davon; **with ~** mit ihnen;
**without ~** ohne sie; *see also* **me**.
**theme** [θiːm] *n* (*also MUS*) Thema *nt*.
**theme park** *n* Themenpark *m*.
**theme song** *n* Titelmusik *f*.
**theme tune** *n* Titelmelodie *f*.
**themselves** [ðəm'sɛlvz] *pl pron* (*reflexive, after
prep*) sich; (*emphatic, alone*) selbst; **between
~** unter sich.
**then** [ðɛn] *adv* (*at that time*) damals; (*next,*

*later*) dann ♦ *conj* (*therefore*) also ♦ *adj:* **the ~ president** der damalige Präsident; **by ~** (*past*) bis dahin; (*future*) bis dann; **from ~ on** von da an; **before ~** davor; **until ~** bis dann; **and ~ what?** und was dann?; **what do you want me to do ~?** was soll ich dann machen?; **... but ~** (**again**) **he's the boss ...** aber er ist ja der Chef.

**theologian** [θɪəˈləʊdʒən] *n* Theologe *m*, Theologin *f*.

**theological** [θɪəˈlɒdʒɪkl] *adj* theologisch.

**theology** [θɪˈɒlədʒɪ] *n* Theologie *f*.

**theorem** [ˈθɪərəm] *n* Lehrsatz *m*.

**theoretical** [θɪəˈrɛtɪkl] *adj* theoretisch.

**theorize** [ˈθɪəraɪz] *vi* theoretisieren.

**theory** [ˈθɪərɪ] *n* Theorie *f*; **in ~** theoretisch.

**therapeutic** [θɛrəˈpjuːtɪk] *adj* therapeutisch.

**therapist** [ˈθɛrəpɪst] *n* Therapeut(in) *m(f)*.

**therapy** [ˈθɛrəpɪ] *n* Therapie *f*.

═══════════════════ *KEYWORD*

**there** [ðɛəˈ] *adv* **1: ~ is/are** da ist/sind; (*there exist(s)*) es gibt; **~ are 3 of them** es gibt 3 davon; **~ has been an accident** da war ein Unfall; **~ will be a meeting tomorrow** morgen findet ein Treffen statt
**2** (*referring to place*) da, dort; **down/over ~** da unten/drüben; **put it in/on ~** leg es dort hinein/hinauf; **I want that book ~** ich möchte das Buch da; **~ he is!** da ist er ja!
**3: ~, ~** (*esp to child*) ist ja gut.

**thereabouts** [ˈðɛərəˈbaʊts] *adv:* **or ~** (*place*) oder dortherum; (*amount, time*) oder so.

**thereafter** [ðɛərˈɑːftəˈ] *adv* danach.

**thereby** [ˈðɛəbaɪ] *adv* dadurch.

**therefore** [ˈðɛəfɔːˈ] *adv* daher, deshalb.

**there's** [ˈðɛəz] = **there is; there has.**

**thereupon** [ˈðɛərəˈpɒn] *adv* (*at that point*) darauf(hin).

**thermal** [ˈθəːml] *adj* (*springs*) Thermal-; (*underwear, paper, printer*) Thermo-.

**thermodynamics** [ˈθəːmədaɪˈnæmɪks] *n* Thermodynamik *f*.

**thermometer** [θəˈmɒmɪtəˈ] *n* Thermometer *nt*.

**thermonuclear** [ˈθəːməʊˈnjuːklɪəˈ] *adj* thermonuklear.

**Thermos®** [ˈθəːməs] *n* (*also:* **~ flask**) Thermosflasche ® *f*.

**thermostat** [ˈθəːməʊstæt] *n* Thermostat *m*.

**thesaurus** [θɪˈsɔːrəs] *n* Synonymwörterbuch *nt*.

**these** [ðiːz] *pl adj, pl pron* diese.

**theses** [ˈθiːsiːz] *npl of* **thesis.**

**thesis** [ˈθiːsɪs] (*pl* **theses**) *n* These *f*; (*for doctorate etc*) Dissertation *f*, Doktorarbeit *f*.

**they** [ðeɪ] *pl pron* sie; **~ say that ...** (*it is said that*) man sagt, daß ...

**they'd** [ðeɪd] = **they had; they would.**

**they'll** [ðeɪl] = **they shall; they will.**

**they're** [ðɛəˈ] = **they are.**

**they've** [ðeɪv] = **they have.**

**thick** [θɪk] *adj* dick; (*sauce etc*) dickflüssig; (*fog, forest, hair etc*) dicht; (*inf: stupid*) blöd ♦ *n:* **in the ~ of the battle** mitten im Gefecht; **it's 20 cm ~** es ist 20 cm dick.

**thicken** [ˈθɪkn] *vi* (*fog etc*) sich verdichten ♦ *vt* (*sauce etc*) eindicken; **the plot ~s** die Sache wird immer verwickelter.

**thicket** [ˈθɪkɪt] *n* Dickicht *nt*.

**thickly** [ˈθɪklɪ] *adv* (*spread, cut*) dick; **~ populated** dicht bevölkert.

**thickness** [ˈθɪknɪs] *n* (*of rope, wire*) Dicke *f*; (*layer*) Lage *f*.

**thickset** [θɪkˈsɛt] *adj* (*person, body*) gedrungen.

**thick-skinned** [θɪkˈskɪnd] *adj* (*also fig*) dickhäutig.

**thief** [θiːf] (*pl* **thieves**) *n* Dieb(in) *m(f)*.

**thieves** [θiːvz] *npl of* **thief.**

**thieving** [ˈθiːvɪŋ] *n* Stehlen *nt*.

**thigh** [θaɪ] *n* Oberschenkel *m*.

**thighbone** [ˈθaɪbəʊn] *n* Oberschenkelknochen *m*.

**thimble** [ˈθɪmbl] *n* Fingerhut *m*.

**thin** [θɪn] *adj* dünn; (*fog*) leicht; (*hair, crowd*) spärlich ♦ *vt:* **to ~** (**down**) (*sauce, paint*) verdünnen ♦ *vi* (*fog, crowd*) sich lichten; **his hair is ~ning** sein Haar lichtet sich.

**thing** [θɪŋ] *n* Ding *nt*; (*matter*) Sache *f*; (*inf*): **to have a ~ about sth** (*be fascinated by*) wie besessen sein von etw; (*hate*) etw nicht ausstehen können; **things** *npl* (*belongings*) Sachen *pl*; **to do sth first ~** (**every morning/tomorrow morning**) etw (morgens/morgen früh) als erstes tun; **I look awful first ~ in the morning** ich sehe frühmorgens immer furchtbar aus; **to do sth last ~** (**at night**) etw als letztes (am Abend) tun; **the ~ is ...** die Sache ist die: ...; **for one ~** zunächst mal; **don't worry about a ~** du brauchst dir überhaupt keine Sorgen zu machen; **you'll do no such ~!** das läßt du schön bleiben!; **poor ~** armes Ding; **the best ~ would be to ...** das Beste wäre, zu ...; **how are ~s?** wie geht's?

**think** [θɪŋk] (*pt, pp* **thought**) *vi* (*reflect*) nachdenken; (*reason*) denken ♦ *vt* (*be of the opinion*) denken; (*believe*) glauben; **to ~ of** denken an +*acc*; (*recall*) sich erinnern an +*acc*; **what did you ~ of them?** was hielten Sie von ihnen?; **to ~ about sth/sb** (*ponder*) über etw/jdn nachdenken; **I'll ~ about it** ich werde es mir überlegen; **to ~ of doing sth** daran denken, etw zu tun; **to ~ highly of sb** viel von jdm halten; **to ~ aloud** laut nachdenken; **~ again!** denk noch mal nach!; **I ~ so/not** ich glaube ja/nein.

▶**think over** *vt* (*offer, suggestion*) überdenken; **I'd like to ~ things over** ich möchte mir die Sache noch einmal überlegen.

▶**think through** *vt* durchdenken.

▶**think up** *vt* sich *dat* ausdenken.

**thinking** ['θɪŋkɪŋ] n Denken nt; **to my (way of)** ~ meiner Meinung or Ansicht nach.

**think-tank** ['θɪŋktæŋk] n Expertengremium nt.

**thinly** ['θɪnlɪ] adv dünn; (disguised, veiled) kaum.

**thinness** ['θɪnnɪs] n Dünne f.

**third** [θɜːd] num dritte(r, s) ♦ n (fraction) Drittel nt; (AUT: also: ~ gear) dritter Gang m; (BRIT: SCOL: degree) ≈ Ausreichend nt; **a** ~ **of** ein Drittel +gen.

**third-degree burns** ['θɜːddɪgriː-] npl Verbrennungen pl dritten Grades.

**thirdly** ['θɜːdlɪ] adv drittens.

**third party insurance** (BRIT) n ≈ Haftpflichtversicherung f.

**third-rate** ['θɜːd'reɪt] (pej) adj drittklassig.

**Third World** n: **the** ~ die Dritte Welt ♦ adj der Dritten Welt.

**thirst** [θɜːst] n Durst m.

**thirsty** ['θɜːstɪ] adj durstig; **to be** ~ Durst haben; **gardening is** ~ **work** Gartenarbeit macht durstig.

**thirteen** [θɜː'tiːn] num dreizehn.

**thirteenth** ['θɜː'tiːnθ] num dreizehnte(r, s).

**thirtieth** ['θɜːtɪɪθ] num dreißigste(r, s).

**thirty** ['θɜːtɪ] num dreißig.

========================= KEYWORD

**this** [ðɪs] (pl **these**) adj (demonstrative) diese(r, s); ~ **man** dieser Mann; ~ **woman** diese Frau; ~ **book** dieses Buch; ~ **one** diese(r, s) (hier)

♦ pron (demonstrative) dies, das; **who/what is** ~? wer/was ist das?; ~ **is where I live** hier wohne ich; ~ **is what he said** das hat er gesagt; ~ **is Mr Brown** (in introductions, photo) das ist Herr Brown; (on telephone) hier ist Herr Brown

♦ adv (demonstrative): ~ **high/long** etc so hoch/lang etc.

**thistle** ['θɪsl] n Distel f.

**thong** [θɒŋ] n Riemen m.

**thorn** [θɔːn] n Dorn m.

**thorny** ['θɔːnɪ] adj dornig; (fig: problem) heikel.

**thorough** ['θʌrə] adj gründlich.

**thoroughbred** ['θʌrəbrɛd] n (horse) Vollblüter m.

**thoroughfare** ['θʌrəfɛəʳ] n (road) Durchgangsstraße f; **"no** ~**"** (BRIT) „Durchfahrt verboten".

**thoroughgoing** ['θʌrəgəʊɪŋ] adj (changes, reform) grundlegend; (investigation) gründlich.

**thoroughly** ['θʌrəlɪ] adv gründlich; (very) äußerst; **I** ~ **agree** ich stimme vollkommen zu.

**thoroughness** ['θʌrənɪs] n Gründlichkeit f.

**those** [ðəʊz] pl adj, pl pron die (da); ~ **(of you) who ...** diejenigen (von Ihnen), die ...

**though** [ðəʊ] conj obwohl ♦ adv aber; **even** ~ obwohl; **it's not easy,** ~ es ist aber nicht einfach.

**thought** [θɔːt] pt, pp of **think** ♦ n Gedanke m; **thoughts** npl (opinion) Gedanken pl; **after much** ~ nach langer Überlegung; **I've just had a** ~ mir ist gerade etwas eingefallen; **to give sth some** ~ sich dat Gedanken über etw acc machen.

**thoughtful** ['θɔːtful] adj (deep in thought) nachdenklich; (considerate) aufmerksam.

**thoughtfully** ['θɔːtfəlɪ] adv (look etc) nachdenklich; (behave etc) rücksichtsvoll; (provide) rücksichtsvollerweise.

**thoughtless** ['θɔːtlɪs] adj gedankenlos.

**thoughtlessly** ['θɔːtlɪslɪ] adv gedankenlos.

**thoughtlessness** ['θɔːtlɪsnɪs] n Gedankenlosigkeit f.

**thought-out** [θɔːt'aut] adj durchdacht.

**thought-provoking** ['θɔːtprəvəukɪŋ] adj: **to be** ~ Denkanstöße geben.

**thousand** ['θauzənd] num (ein)tausend; **two** ~ zweitausend; ~**s of** Tausende von.

**thousandth** ['θauzəntθ] num tausendste(r, s).

**thrash** [θræʃ] vt (beat) verprügeln; (defeat) (vernichtend) schlagen.

▶**thrash about** vi um sich schlagen.

▶**thrash around** vi = **thrash about**.

▶**thrash out** vt (problem) ausdiskutieren.

**thrashing** ['θræʃɪŋ] n: **to give sb a** ~ jdn verprügeln.

**thread** [θrɛd] n (yarn) Faden m; (of screw) Gewinde nt ♦ vt (needle) einfädeln; **to** ~ **one's way between** sich hindurchschlängeln zwischen.

**threadbare** ['θrɛdbɛəʳ] adj (clothes) abgetragen; (carpet) abgelaufen.

**threat** [θrɛt] n Drohung f; (fig): ~ **(to)** Gefahr f (für); **to be under** ~ **of** (closure etc) bedroht sein von.

**threaten** ['θrɛtn] vi bedrohen ♦ vt: **to** ~ **sb with sth** jdm mit etw drohen; **to** ~ **to do sth** (damit) drohen, etw zu tun.

**threatening** ['θrɛtnɪŋ] adj drohend, bedrohlich.

**three** [θriː] num drei.

**three-dimensional** [θriːdɪ'mɛnʃənl] adj dreidimensional.

**threefold** ['θriːfəuld] adv: **to increase** ~ dreifach or um das Dreifache ansteigen.

**three-piece suit** ['θriːpiːs-] n dreiteiliger Anzug m.

**three-piece suite** n dreiteilige Polstergarnitur f.

**three-ply** [θriː'plaɪ] adj (wool) dreifädig; (wood) dreilagig.

**three-quarters** [θriː'kwɔːtəz] npl Dreiviertel nt; ~ **full** dreiviertel voll.

**three-wheeler** ['θriː'wiːləʳ] n (car) Dreiradwagen m.

**thresh** [θrɛʃ] vt dreschen.

**threshing machine** ['θrɛʃɪŋ-] n

Dreschmaschine f.

**threshold** ['θreʃhəuld] n Schwelle f; **to be on the ~ of sth** (fig) an der Schwelle zu etw sein or stehen.

**threshold agreement** n (ECON) Tarifvereinbarung über der Inflationsrate angeglichene Lohnerhöhungen.

**threw** [θruː] pt of **throw.**

**thrift** [θrɪft] n Sparsamkeit f.

**thrifty** ['θrɪftɪ] adj sparsam.

**thrill** [θrɪl] n (excitement) Aufregung f; (shudder) Erregung f ♦ vi zittern ♦ vt (person, audience) erregen; **to be ~ed** (with gift etc) sich riesig freuen.

**thriller** ['θrɪlə*] n Thriller m.

**thrilling** ['θrɪlɪŋ] adj (ride, performance etc) erregend; (news) aufregend.

**thrive** [θraɪv] (pt **thrived** or **throve**, pp **thrived**) vi gedeihen; **to ~ on sth** von etw leben.

**thriving** ['θraɪvɪŋ] adj (business, community) blühend, florierend.

**throat** [θrəut] n Kehle f; **to have a sore ~** Halsschmerzen haben.

**throb** [θrɔb] n (of heart) Klopfen nt; (pain) Pochen nt; (of engine) Dröhnen nt ♦ vi (heart) klopfen; (pain) pochen; (machine) dröhnen; **my head is ~bing** ich habe rasende Kopfschmerzen.

**throes** [θrəuz] npl: **in the ~ of** (war, moving house etc) mitten in +dat; **death ~** Todeskampf m.

**thrombosis** [θrɔm'bəusɪs] n Thrombose f.

**throne** [θrəun] n Thron m; **on the ~** auf dem Thron.

**throng** ['θrɔŋ] n Masse f ♦ vt (streets etc) sich drängen in +dat ♦ vi: **to ~ to** strömen zu; **a ~ of people** eine Menschenmenge; **to be ~ed with** wimmeln von.

**throttle** ['θrɔtl] n (in car) Gaspedal nt; (on motorcycle) Gashebel m ♦ vt (strangle) erdrosseln.

**through** [θruː] prep durch; (time) während; (owing to) infolge +gen ♦ adj (ticket, train) durchgehend ♦ adv durch; **(from) Monday ~ Friday** (US) von Montag bis Freitag; **to be ~** (TEL) verbunden sein; **to be ~ with sb/sth** mit jdm/etw fertig sein; **we're ~!** es ist aus zwischen uns!; **"no ~ road** or (US) **traffic"** „keine Durchfahrt"; **to let sb ~** jdn durchlassen; **to put sb ~ to sb** (TEL) jdn mit jdm verbinden.

**throughout** [θruː'aut] adv (everywhere) überall; (the whole time) die ganze Zeit über ♦ prep (place) überall in +dat; (time): **~ the morning/afternoon** während des ganzen Morgens/Nachmittags; **~ her life** ihr ganzes Leben lang.

**throughput** ['θruːput] n (also COMPUT) Durchsatz m.

**throve** [θrəuv] pt of **thrive.**

**throw** [θrəu] (pt **threw**, pp **thrown**) n Wurf m ♦ vt werfen; (rider) abwerfen; (fig: confuse)

aus der Fassung bringen; (pottery) töpfern; **to ~ a party** eine Party geben; **to ~ open** (doors, windows) aufreißen; (debate) öffnen.

▶**throw about** vt (money) herumwerfen mit.

▶**throw around** vt = **throw about.**

▶**throw away** vt wegwerfen; (waste) verschwenden.

▶**throw off** vt (get rid of: burden) abwerfen.

▶**throw out** vt (rubbish) wegwerfen; (idea) verwerfen; (person) hinauswerfen.

▶**throw together** vt (meal) hinhauen; (clothes) zusammenpacken.

▶**throw up** vi (vomit) sich übergeben.

**throwaway** ['θrəuəweɪ] adj (cutlery etc) Einweg-; (line, remark) beiläufig.

**throwback** ['θrəubæk] n: **it's a ~ to** (reminder) es erinnert an +acc.

**throw-in** ['θrəuɪn] n (FOOTBALL) Einwurf m.

**thrown** [θrəun] pp of **throw.**

**thru** [θruː] (US) prep, adj, adv = **through.**

**thrush** [θrʌʃ] n (bird) Drossel f; (MED: esp in children) Soor m; (: BRIT: in women) vaginale Pilzerkrankung f.

**thrust** [θrʌst] (pt, pp **thrust**) n (TECH) Schubkraft f; (push) Stoß m; (fig: impetus) Stoßkraft f ♦ vt stoßen.

**thud** [θʌd] n dumpfes Geräusch nt.

**thug** [θʌg] n Schlägertyp m.

**thumb** [θʌm] n Daumen m ♦ vt: **to ~ a lift** per Anhalter fahren; **to give sb/sth the ~s up** (approve) jdm/etw zur Genüge Licht geben; **to give sb/sth the ~s down** (disapprove) jdn/ etw ablehnen.

▶**thumb through** vt fus (book) durchblättern.

**thumb index** n Daumenregister nt.

**thumbnail** ['θʌmneɪl] n Daumennagel m.

**thumbnail sketch** n kurze Darstellung f.

**thumbtack** ['θʌmtæk] (US) n Heftzwecke f.

**thump** [θʌmp] n (blow) Schlag m; (sound) dumpfer Schlag m ♦ vt schlagen auf +acc ♦ vi (heart etc) heftig pochen.

**thumping** ['θʌmpɪŋ] adj (majority, victory etc) Riesen-; (headache, cold) fürchterlich.

**thunder** ['θʌndə*] n Donner m ♦ vi donnern; (shout angrily) brüllen; **to ~ past** (train etc) vorbeidonnern.

**thunderbolt** ['θʌndəbəult] n Blitzschlag m.

**thunderclap** ['θʌndəklæp] n Donnerschlag m.

**thunderous** ['θʌndrəs] adj donnernd.

**thunderstorm** ['θʌndəstɔːm] n Gewitter nt.

**thunderstruck** ['θʌndəstrʌk] adj: **to be ~** (shocked) wie von Donner gerührt sein.

**thundery** ['θʌndərɪ] adj (weather) gewitterig.

**Thur(s).** abbr (= Thursday) Do.

**Thursday** ['θɜːzdɪ] n Donnerstag m; see also **Tuesday.**

**thus** [ðʌs] adv (in this way) so; (consequently) somit.

**thwart** [θwɔːt] vt (person) einen Strich durch die Rechnung machen +dat; (plans) vereiteln.

**thyme** [taɪm] n Thymian m.

**thyroid** ['θaɪrɔɪd] n (also: ~ **gland**) Schilddrüse f.

**tiara** [tɪ'ɑːrə] n Diadem nt.

**Tiber** ['taɪbə*] n: **the** ~ der Tiber.

**Tibet** [tɪ'bɛt] n Tibet nt.

**Tibetan** [tɪ'bɛtən] adj tibetanisch ♦ n (person) Tibetaner(in) m(f); (LING) Tibetisch nt.

**tibia** ['tɪbɪə] n Schienbein nt.

**tic** [tɪk] n nervöse Zuckung f, Tic m.

**tick** [tɪk] n (sound) Ticken nt; (mark) Häkchen nt; (ZOOL) Zecke f; (BRIT: inf: moment) Augenblick m; (: credit): **to buy sth on** ~ etw auf Pump kaufen ♦ vi (clock, watch) ticken ♦ vt (item on list) abhaken; **to put a** ~ **against sth** etw abhaken; **what makes him** ~? was ist er für ein Mensch?

▶**tick off** vt (item on list) abhaken; (person) rüffeln.

▶**tick over** vi (engine) im Leerlauf sein; (fig: business etc) sich über Wasser halten.

**ticker tape** ['tɪkəteɪp] n Lochstreifen m; (US: in celebrations) ≈ Luftschlangen pl.

**ticket** ['tɪkɪt] n (for public transport) Fahrkarte f; (for theatre etc) Eintrittskarte f; (in shop: on goods) Preisschild nt; (: from cash register) Kassenbon m; (for raffle) Los nt; (for library) Ausweis m; (also: **parking** ~: fine) Strafzettel m; (US: POL) Wahlliste f; **to get a (parking)** ~ (AUT) einen Strafzettel bekommen.

**ticket agency** n (THEAT) Vorverkaufsstelle f.

**ticket collector** n (RAIL: at station) Fahrkartenkontrolleur(in) m(f); (on train) Schaffner(in) m(f).

**ticket holder** n Karteninhaber(in) m(f).

**ticket inspector** n Fahrkartenkontrolleur(in) m(f).

**ticket office** n (RAIL) Fahrkartenschalter m; (THEAT) Theaterkasse f.

**tickle** ['tɪkl] vt kitzeln; (fig: amuse) amüsieren ♦ vi kitzeln; **it ~s!** das kitzelt!

**ticklish** ['tɪklɪʃ] adj (person, situation) kitzlig.

**tidal** ['taɪdl] adj (force) Gezeiten-, der Gezeiten; (river) Tide-.

**tidal wave** n Flutwelle f.

**tidbit** ['tɪdbɪt] (US) n = **titbit**.

**tiddlywinks** ['tɪdlɪwɪŋks] n Flohhüpfen nt.

**tide** [taɪd] n (in sea) Gezeiten pl; (fig: of events, opinion etc) Trend m; **high** ~ Flut f; **low** ~ Ebbe f; **the** ~ **is in/out** es ist Flut/Ebbe; **the** ~ **is coming in** die Flut kommt.

▶**tide over** vt über die Runden helfen +dat.

**tidily** ['taɪdɪlɪ] adv ordentlich.

**tidiness** ['taɪdɪnɪs] n Ordentlichkeit f.

**tidy** ['taɪdɪ] adj (room, desk) ordentlich, aufgeräumt; (person) ordnungsliebend; (sum, income) ordentlich ♦ vt (also: ~ **up**) aufräumen.

**tie** [taɪ] n (BRIT: also: **necktie**) Krawatte f; (string etc) Band nt; (fig: link) Verbindung f; (SPORT: match) Spiel nt; (in competition: draw) Unentschieden nt ♦ vt (parcel) verschnüren; (shoelaces) zubinden; (ribbon) binden ♦ vi (SPORT etc): **to** ~ **with sb for first place** sich mit jdm den ersten Platz teilen; "**black** ~" „Abendanzug"; "**white** ~" „Frackzwang"; **family** ~**s** familiäre Bindungen; **to** ~ **sth in a bow** etw zu einer Schleife binden; **to** ~ **a knot in sth** einen Knoten in etw acc machen.

▶**tie down** vt (fig: restrict) binden; (: : to date, price etc) festlegen.

▶**tie in** vi: **to** ~ **in with** zusammenpassen mit.

▶**tie on** vt (BRIT) anbinden.

▶**tie up** vt (parcel) verschnüren; (dog) anbinden; (boat) festmachen; (person) fesseln; (arrangements) unter Dach und Fach bringen; **to be** ~**d up** (busy) zu tun haben, beschäftigt sein.

**tie-break(er)** ['taɪbreɪk(ə*)] n (TENNIS) Tie-break m; (in quiz) Entscheidungsfrage f.

**tie-on** ['taɪɒn] (BRIT) adj (label) Anhänge-.

**tiepin** ['taɪpɪn] (BRIT) n Krawattennadel f.

**tier** [tɪə*] n (of stadium etc) Rang m; (of cake) Lage f.

**tie-tack** ['taɪtæk] (US) n = **tiepin**.

**tiff** [tɪf] n Krach m.

**tiger** ['taɪgə*] n Tiger m.

**tight** [taɪt] adj (screw, knot, grip) fest; (shoes, clothes, bend) eng; (security) streng; (budget, money) knapp; (schedule) gedrängt; (inf: drunk) voll; (: stingy) knickerig ♦ adv fest; **to be packed** ~ (suitcase) prallvoll sein; (room) gerammelt voll sein; **everybody hold** ~! alle festhalten!

**tighten** ['taɪtn] vt (rope, strap) straffen; (screw, bolt) anziehen; (grip) festigen; (security) verschärfen ♦ vi (grip) sich festigen; (rope etc) sich spannen.

**tightfisted** [taɪt'fɪstɪd] adj knickerig (inf).

**tight-lipped** ['taɪt'lɪpt] adj (fig: silence) eisern; **to be** ~ **about sth** über etw acc schweigen.

**tightly** ['taɪtlɪ] adv fest.

**tightrope** ['taɪtrəʊp] n Seil nt; **to be on** or **walking a** ~ (fig) einen Balanceakt vollführen.

**tightrope walker** n Seiltänzer(in) m(f).

**tights** [taɪts] (BRIT) npl Strumpfhose f.

**tigress** ['taɪgrɪs] n Tigerin f.

**tilde** ['tɪldə] n Tilde f.

**tile** [taɪl] n (on roof) Ziegel m; (on floor) Fliese f; (on wall) Kachel f ♦ vt (floor) mit Fliesen auslegen; (bathroom) kacheln.

**tiled** [taɪld] adj (floor) mit Fliesen ausgelegt; (wall) gekachelt.

**till** [tɪl] n (in shop etc) Kasse f ♦ vt (land) bestellen ♦ prep, conj = **until**.

**tiller** ['tɪlə*] n (NAUT) Ruderpinne f.

**tilt** [tɪlt] vt neigen ♦ vi sich neigen ♦ n (slope) Neigung f; **to wear one's hat at a** ~ den Hut schief aufhaben; **(at) full** ~ mit Volldampf.

**timber** ['tɪmbə*] n (material) Holz nt; (trees) Nutzholz nt.

**time** [taɪm] n Zeit f; (occasion) Gelegenheit f, Mal nt; (MUS) Takt m ♦ vt (measure time of) die Zeit messen bei; (runner) stoppen; (fix *moment for: visit etc)* den Zeitpunkt festlegen für; **a long** ~ eine lange Zeit; **for the** ~ **being** vorläufig; **4 at a** ~ 4 auf einmal; **from** ~ **to** ~ von Zeit zu Zeit; ~ **after** ~, ~ **and again** immer (und immer) wieder; **at** ~**s** manchmal, zuweilen; **in** ~ *(soon enough)* rechtzeitig; *(eventually)* mit der Zeit; *(MUS)* im Takt; **in a week's** ~ in einer Woche; **in no** ~ im Handumdrehen; **any** ~ jederzeit; **on** ~ rechtzeitig; **to be 30 minutes behind/ahead of** ~ 30 Minuten zurück/voraus sein; **by the** ~ **he arrived** als er ankam; **5** ~**s 5** 5 mal 5; **what** ~ **is it?** wie spät ist es?; **to have a good** ~ sich amüsieren; **we/they** *etc* **had a hard** ~ wir/sie *etc* hatten es schwer; ~**'s up!** die Zeit ist um!; **I've no** ~ **for it** *(fig)* dafür habe ich nichts übrig; **he'll do it in his own (good)** ~ *(without being hurried)* er macht es, ohne sich hetzen zu lassen; **he'll do it in** *or (US)* **on his own** ~ *(out of working hours)* er macht es in seiner Freizeit; **to be behind the** ~**s** rückständig sein; **to** ~ **sth well/badly** den richtigen/falschen Zeitpunkt für etw wählen; **the bomb was** ~**d to go off 5 minutes later** die Bombe war so eingestellt, daß sie 5 Minuten später explodieren sollte.

**time-and-motion study** ['taɪmənd'məuʃən-] *n* Arbeitsstudie *f.*

**time bomb** *n (also fig)* Zeitbombe *f.*

**time card** *n* Stechkarte *f.*

**time clock** *n (in factory etc)* Stechuhr *f.*

**time-consuming** ['taɪmkənsju:mɪŋ] *adj* zeitraubend.

**time difference** *n* Zeitunterschied *m.*

**time frame** *n* zeitlicher Rahmen *m.*

**time-honoured,** *(US)* **time-honored** ['taɪmɔnəd] *adj* althergebracht.

**timekeeper** ['taɪmki:pə*] *n:* **she's a good** ~ sie erfüllt ihr Zeitsoll.

**time-lag** ['taɪmlæg] *n* Verzögerung *f.*

**timeless** ['taɪmlɪs] *adj* zeitlos.

**time limit** *n* zeitliche Grenze *f.*

**timely** ['taɪmlɪ] *adj (arrival)* rechtzeitig; *(reminder)* zur rechten Zeit.

**time off** *n:* **to take** ~ sich *dat* frei nehmen.

**timer** ['taɪmə*] *n (time switch)* Schaltuhr *f; (on cooker)* Zeitmesser *m; (on video)* Timer *m.*

**time-saving** ['taɪmseɪvɪŋ] *adj* zeitsparend.

**timescale** ['taɪmskeɪl] *(BRIT) n* Zeitspanne *f.*

**time-share** ['taɪmʃɛə*] *n* Ferienwohnung *f* auf Timesharing-Basis.

**time-sharing** ['taɪmʃɛərɪŋ] *n (of property, COMPUT)* Timesharing *nt.*

**time sheet** *n* = **time card.**

**time signal** *n (RADIO)* Zeitzeichen *nt.*

**time switch** *n* Zeitschalter *m.*

**timetable** ['taɪmteɪbl] *n (RAIL etc)* Fahrplan *m; (SCOL)* Stundenplan *m; (programme of events)* Programm *nt.*

**time zone** *n* Zeitzone *f.*

**timid** ['tɪmɪd] *adj (person)* schüchtern; *(animal)* scheu.

**timidity** [tɪ'mɪdɪtɪ] *n (shyness)* Schüchternheit *f.*

**timing** ['taɪmɪŋ] *n (SPORT)* Timing *nt;* **the** ~ **of his resignation** der Zeitpunkt seines Rücktritts.

**timing device** *n (on bomb)* Zeitzünder *m.*

**timpani** ['tɪmpənɪ] *npl* Kesselpauken *pl.*

**tin** [tɪn] *n (metal)* Blech *nt; (container)* Dose *f;* (: *for baking)* Form *f;* (: *BRIT: can)* Büchse *f,* Dose *f;* **two** ~**s of paint** zwei Dosen Farbe.

**tinfoil** ['tɪnfɔɪl] *n* Alufolie *f.*

**tinge** [tɪndʒ] *n (of colour)* Färbung *f; (fig: of emotion etc)* Anflug *m,* Anstrich *m* ♦ *vt:* ~**d with blue/red** leicht blau/rot gefärbt; **to be** ~**d with sth** *(fig: emotion etc)* einen Anstrich von etw haben.

**tingle** ['tɪŋgl] *vi* prickeln; *(from cold)* kribbeln; **I was tingling with excitement** ich zitterte vor Aufregung.

**tinker** ['tɪŋkə*] *n (gipsy)* Kesselflicker *m.*

▶**tinker with** *vt fus* herumbasteln an +*dat.*

**tinkle** ['tɪŋkl] *vi* klingeln ♦ *n (inf):* **to give sb a** ~ *(TEL)* bei jdm anklingeln.

**tin mine** *n* Zinnbergwerk *nt.*

**tinned** [tɪnd] *(BRIT) adj (food, peas)* Dosen-, in Dosen.

**tinnitus** ['tɪnɪtəs] *n* Tinnitus *m,* Ohrensummen *nt.*

**tinny** ['tɪnɪ] *(pej) adj (sound)* blechern; *(car etc)* Schrott-.

**tin-opener** ['tɪnəupnə*] *(BRIT) n* Dosenöffner *m.*

**tinsel** ['tɪnsl] *n* Rauschgoldgirlanden *pl.*

**tint** [tɪnt] *n (colour)* Ton *m; (for hair)* Tönung *f* ♦ *vt (hair)* tönen.

**tinted** ['tɪntɪd] *adj* getönt.

**tiny** ['taɪnɪ] *adj* winzig.

**tip** [tɪp] *n (end)* Spitze *f; (gratuity)* Trinkgeld *nt; (BRIT: for rubbish)* Müllkippe *f;* (: *for coal)* Halde *f; (advice)* Tip *m,* Hinweis *m* ♦ *vt (waiter)* ein Trinkgeld geben +*dat; (tilt)* kippen; *(also:* ~ **over:** *overturn)* umkippen; *(also:* ~ **out:** *empty)* leeren; *(predict: winner etc)* tippen *or* setzen auf +*acc;* **he** ~**ped out the contents of the box** er kippte den Inhalt der Kiste aus.

▶**tip off** *vt* einen Tip *or* Hinweis geben +*dat.*

**tip-off** ['tɪpɔf] *n* Hinweis *m.*

**tipped** ['tɪpt] *adj (BRIT: cigarette)* Filter-; **steel-** ~ mit Stahlspitze.

**Tipp-Ex** ® ['tɪpɛks] *n* Tipp-Ex ® *nt.*

**tipple** ['tɪpl] *(BRIT) vi* picheln ♦ *n:* **to have a** ~ einen trinken.

**tipster** ['tɪpstə*] *n* jd, der bei Pferderennen, Börsengeschäften etc Tips gegen Bezahlung weitergibt.

**tipsy** ['tɪpsɪ] *(inf) adj* beschwipst.

**tiptoe** ['tɪptəu] *n:* **on** ~ auf Zehenspitzen.

**tip-top** ['tɪp'tɔp] *adj:* **in** ~ **condition** tipptopp.

**tirade** [taɪ'reɪd] *n* Tirade *f.*

**tire** ['taɪə*] *n (US)* = **tyre** ♦ *vt* müde machen, ermüden ♦ *vi (become tired)* müde werden;

to ~ of sth genug von etw haben.
▶tire out vt erschöpfen.

**tired** ['taɪəd] adj müde; to be/look ~ müde
sein/aussehen; to feel ~ sich müde fühlen;
to be ~ of sth etw satt haben; to be ~ of
doing sth es satt haben, etw zu tun.

**tiredness** ['taɪədnɪs] n Müdigkeit f.

**tireless** ['taɪəlɪs] adj unermüdlich.

**tiresome** ['taɪəsəm] adj lästig.

**tiring** ['taɪərɪŋ] adj ermüdend, anstrengend.

**tissue** ['tɪʃuː] n (ANAT, BIOL) Gewebe nt;
(paper handkerchief) Papiertaschentuch nt.

**tissue paper** n Seidenpapier nt.

**tit** [tɪt] n (bird) Meise f; (inf: breast) Titte f;
~ **for tat** wie du mir, so ich dir.

**titanium** [tɪ'teɪnɪəm] n Titan nt.

**titbit,** (US) **tidbit** ['tɪtbɪt] n (food, news)
Leckerbissen m.

**titillate** ['tɪtɪleɪt] vt erregen, reizen.

**titivate** ['tɪtɪveɪt] vt feinmachen.

**title** ['taɪtl] n Titel m; (LAW): ~ **to** Anspruch
auf +acc.

**title deed** n Eigentumsurkunde f.

**title page** n Titelseite f.

**title role** n Titelrolle f.

**title track** n Titelstück nt.

**titter** ['tɪtə*] vi kichern.

**tittle-tattle** ['tɪtltætl] (inf) n Klatsch m,
Gerede nt.

**tizzy** ['tɪzɪ] n: to be in a ~ aufgeregt sein; to
get in a ~ sich aufregen.

**T-junction** ['tiː'dʒʌŋkʃən] n T-Kreuzung f.

**TM** abbr (= trademark) Wz; = **transcendental
meditation**.

**TN** (US) abbr (POST: = Tennessee).

**TNT** n abbr (= trinitrotoluene) TNT nt.

════════════════════ KEYWORD

**to** [tuː] prep **1** (direction) nach +dat, zu +dat; to
go ~ **France/London/school/the station**
nach Frankreich/nach London/zur Schule/
zum Bahnhof gehen; ~ **the left/right** nach
links/rechts; **I have never been** ~ **Germany**
ich war noch nie in Deutschland
**2** (as far as) bis; **to count** ~ **10** bis 10 zählen
**3** (with expressions of time) vor +dat; **a quarter**
~ **5** (BRIT) Viertel vor 5
**4** (for, of): **the key** ~ **the front door** der
Schlüssel für die Haustür; **a letter** ~ **his
wife** ein Brief an seine Frau
**5** (expressing indirect object): **to give sth** ~ **sb**
jdm etw geben; **to talk** ~ **sb** mit jdm
sprechen; **I sold it** ~ **a friend** ich habe es an
einen Freund verkauft; **you've done
something** ~ **your hair** du hast etwas mit
deinem Haar gemacht
**6** (in relation to) zu; **A is** ~ **B as C is** ~ **D** A
verhält sich zu B wie C zu D; **3 goals** ~ **2** 3
zu 2 Tore; **40 miles** ~ **the gallon** 40 Meilen
pro Gallone
**7** (purpose, result) zu; **to sentence sb to death**
jdn zum Tode verurteilen; ~ **my surprise** zu

meiner Überraschung
♦ with vb **1** (simple infinitive): ~ **go** gehen; ~
**eat** essen
**2** (following another vb): **to want** ~ **do sth**
etw tun wollen; **to try/start** ~ **do sth**
versuchen/anfangen, etw zu tun
**3** (with vb omitted): **I don't want** ~ ich will
nicht; **you ought** ~ du solltest es tun
**4** (purpose, result) (um ...) zu; **I did it** ~ **help
you** ich habe es getan, um dir zu helfen
**5** (equivalent to relative clause): **he has a lot**
~ **lose** er hat viel zu verlieren; **the main
thing is** ~ **try** die Hauptsache ist, es zu
versuchen
**6** (after adjective etc): **ready** ~ **use**
gebrauchsfertig; **too old/young** ~ ... zu alt/
jung, um zu ...; **it's too heavy** ~ **lift** es ist zu
schwer zu heben
♦ adv: **to push/pull the door** ~ die Tür
zudrücken/zuziehen; ~ **and fro** hin und her.

**toad** [təud] n Kröte f.

**toadstool** ['təudstuːl] n Giftpilz m.

**toady** ['təudɪ] (pej) vi: **to** ~ **to sb** vor jdm
kriechen.

**toast** [təust] n (CULIN, drink) Toast m ♦ vt
(bread etc) toasten; (drink to) einen Toast or
Trinkspruch ausbringen auf +acc; **a piece** or
**slice of** ~ eine Scheibe Toast.

**toaster** ['təustə*] n Toaster m.

**toastmaster** ['təustmɑːstə*] n
Zeremonienmeister m.

**toast rack** n Toastständer m.

**tobacco** [tə'bækəu] n Tabak m; **pipe** ~
Pfeifentabak m.

**tobacconist** [tə'bækənɪst] n Tabakhändler(in)
m(f).

**tobacconist's (shop)** [tə'bækənɪsts-] n
Tabakwarenladen m.

**Tobago** [tə'beɪgəu] n see **Trinidad**.

**toboggan** [tə'bɔgən] n Schlitten m.

**today** [tə'deɪ] adv, n heute; **what day is it** ~?
welcher Tag ist heute?; **what date is it** ~?
der wievielte ist heute?; ~ **is the 4th of
March** heute ist der 4. März; **a week ago** ~
heute vor einer Woche; ~'s **paper** die
Zeitung von heute.

**toddle** ['tɔdl] (inf) vi: **to** ~ **in/off/along**
herein-/davon-/entlangwatscheln.

**toddler** ['tɔdlə*] n Kleinkind nt.

**to-do** [tə'duː] n Aufregung f, Theater nt.

**toe** [təu] n Zehe f, Zeh m; (of shoe, sock) Spitze
f; **to** ~ **the line** (fig) auf Linie bleiben; **big/
little** ~ großer/kleiner Zeh.

**toehold** ['təuhəuld] n (in climbing) Halt m für
die Fußspitzen; (fig): **to get/gain a** ~ (in)
einen Einstieg bekommen/sich dat einen
Einstieg verschaffen (in +dat).

**toenail** ['təuneɪl] n Zehennagel m.

**toffee** ['tɔfɪ] n Toffee m.

**toffee apple** (BRIT) n ≈ kandierter Apfel m.

**tofu** ['təufuː] n Tofu m.

**toga** ['təʊgə] *n* Toga *f*.

**together** [tə'gɛðəʳ] *adv* zusammen; (*at the same time*) gleichzeitig; ~ **with** gemeinsam mit.

**togetherness** [tə'gɛðənɪs] *n* Beisammensein *nt*.

**toggle switch** ['tɔgl-] *n* (*COMPUT*) Toggle-Schalter *m*.

**Togo** ['təʊgəʊ] *n* Togo *nt*.

**togs** [tɔgz] (*inf*) *npl* Klamotten *pl*.

**toil** [tɔɪl] *n* Mühe *f* ♦ *vi* sich abmühen.

**toilet** ['tɔɪlət] *n* Toilette *f* ♦ *cpd* (*kit, accessories etc*) Toiletten-; **to go to the** ~ auf die Toilette gehen.

**toilet bag** (*BRIT*) *n* Kulturbeutel *m*.

**toilet bowl** *n* Toilettenbecken *nt*.

**toilet paper** *n* Toilettenpapier *nt*.

**toiletries** ['tɔɪlətrɪz] *npl* Toilettenartikel *pl*.

**toilet roll** *n* Rolle *f* Toilettenpapier.

**toilet soap** *n* Toilettenseife *f*.

**toilet water** *n* Toilettenwasser *nt*.

**to-ing and fro-ing** ['tu:ɪŋən'frəʊɪŋ] (*BRIT*) *n* Hin und Her *nt*.

**token** ['təʊkən] *n* (*sign, souvenir*) Zeichen *nt*; (*substitute coin*) Wertmarke *f* ♦ *adj* (*strike, payment etc*) symbolisch; **by the same** ~ (*fig*) in gleicher Weise; **book/record/gift** ~ (*BRIT*) Bücher-/Platten-/Geschenkgutschein *m*.

**tokenism** ['təʊkənɪzəm] *n*: **to be (pure)** ~ (nur) eine Alibifunktion haben.

**Tokyo** ['təʊkjəʊ] *n* Tokio *nt*.

**told** [təʊld] *pt, pp of* **tell**.

**tolerable** ['tɔlərəbl] *adj* (*bearable*) erträglich; (*fairly good*) passabel.

**tolerably** ['tɔlərəblɪ] *adv*: ~ **good** ganz annehmbar *or* passabel.

**tolerance** ['tɔlərns] *n* Toleranz *f*.

**tolerant** ['tɔlərnt] *adj* tolerant; **to be** ~ **of sth** tolerant gegenüber etw sein.

**tolerate** ['tɔləreɪt] *vt* (*pain, noise*) erdulden, ertragen; (*injustice*) tolerieren.

**toleration** [tɔlə'reɪʃən] *n* (*of person, pain etc*) Duldung *f*; (*REL, POL*) Toleranz *f*.

**toll** [təʊl] *n* (*of casualties, deaths*) (Gesamt)zahl *f*; (*tax, charge*) Gebühr *f* ♦ *vi* (*bell*) läuten; **the work took its** ~ **on us** die Arbeit blieb nicht ohne Auswirkungen auf uns.

**tollbridge** ['təʊlbrɪdʒ] *n* gebührenpflichtige Brücke *f*, Mautbrücke *f*.

**toll call** (*US*) *n* Ferngespräch *nt*.

**toll-free** ['təʊlfri:] (*US*) *adj* gebührenfrei.

**toll road** *n* gebührenpflichtige Straße *f*, Mautstraße *f*.

**tomato** [tə'mɑːtəʊ] (*pl* ~**es**) *n* Tomate *f*.

**tomato purée** *n* Tomatenmark *nt*.

**tomb** [tuːm] *n* Grab *nt*.

**tombola** [tɔm'bəʊlə] *n* Tombola *f*.

**tomboy** ['tɔmbɔɪ] *n* Wildfang *m*.

**tombstone** ['tuːmstəʊn] *n* Grabstein *m*.

**tomcat** ['tɔmkæt] *n* Kater *m*.

**tome** [təʊm] *n* (*form*) Band *m*.

**tomorrow** [tə'mɔrəʊ] *adv* morgen ♦ *n* morgen; (*future*) Zukunft *f*; **the day after** ~ übermorgen; **a week** ~ morgen in einer Woche; ~ **morning** morgen früh.

**ton** [tʌn] *n* (*BRIT*) (britische) Tonne *f*; (*US: also: short* ~) (US-)Tonne *f* (*ca. 907 kg*); (*metric ton*) (metrische) Tonne *f*; ~**s of** (*inf*) Unmengen von.

**tonal** ['təʊnl] *adj* (*MUS*) klanglich, tonal.

**tone** [təʊn] *n* Ton *m* ♦ *vi* (*also:* ~ **in:** *colours*) (farblich) passen.

▶**tone down** *vt* (*also fig*) abschwächen.

▶**tone up** *vt* (*muscles*) kräftigen.

**tone-deaf** [təʊn'dɛf] *adj* ohne Gefühl für Tonhöhen.

**toner** ['təʊnəʳ] *n* (*for photocopier*) Toner *m*.

**Tonga** [tɔŋə] *n* Tonga *nt*.

**tongs** [tɔŋz] *npl* Zange *f*; (*also:* **curling** ~) Lockenstab *m*.

**tongue** [tʌŋ] *n* Zunge *f*; (*form: language*) Sprache *f*; ~**-in-cheek** (*speak, say*) ironisch.

**tongue-tied** ['tʌŋtaɪd] *adj* (*fig*) sprachlos.

**tongue-twister** ['tʌŋtwɪstəʳ] *n* Zungenbrecher *m*.

**tonic** ['tɔnɪk] *n* (*MED*) Tonikum *nt*; (*fig*) Wohltat *f*; (*also:* ~ **water**) Tonic *nt*; (*MUS*) Tonika *f*, Grundton *m*.

**tonight** [tə'naɪt] *adv* (*this evening*) heute abend; (*this night*) heute nacht ♦ *n* (*this evening*) der heutige Abend; (*this night*) die kommende Nacht; (**I'll) see you** ~! bis heute abend!

**tonnage** ['tʌnɪdʒ] *n* Tonnage *f*.

**tonne** [tʌn] (*BRIT*) *n* (*metric ton*) Tonne *f*.

**tonsil** ['tɔnsl] *n* Mandel *f*; **to have one's** ~**s out** sich *dat* die Mandeln herausnehmen lassen.

**tonsillitis** [tɔnsɪ'laɪtɪs] *n* Mandelentzündung *f*.

**too** [tuː] *adv* (*excessively*) zu; (*also*) auch; **it's** ~ **sweet** es ist zu süß; **I went** ~ ich bin auch mitgegangen; ~ **much** (*adj*) zuviel; (*adv*) zu sehr; ~ **many** zu viele; ~ **bad!** das ist eben Pech!

**took** [tuk] *pt of* **take**.

**tool** [tuːl] *n* (*also fig*) Werkzeug *nt*.

**tool box** *n* Werkzeugkasten *m*.

**tool kit** *n* Werkzeugsatz *m*.

**toot** [tuːt] *n* (*of horn*) Hupton *m*; (*of whistle*) Pfeifton *m* ♦ *vi* (*with car-horn*) hupen.

**tooth** [tuːθ] (*pl* **teeth**) *n* (*also TECH*) Zahn *m*; **to have a** ~ **out** *or* (*US*) **pulled** sich *dat* einen Zahn ziehen lassen; **to brush one's teeth** sich *dat* die Zähne putzen; **by the skin of one's teeth** (*fig*) mit knapper Not.

**toothache** ['tuːθeɪk] *n* Zahnschmerzen *pl*; **to have** ~ Zahnschmerzen haben.

**toothbrush** ['tuːθbrʌʃ] *n* Zahnbürste *f*.

**toothpaste** ['tuːθpeɪst] *n* Zahnpasta *f*.

**toothpick** ['tuːθpɪk] *n* Zahnstocher *m*.

**tooth powder** *n* Zahnpulver *nt*.

**top** [tɔp] *n* (*of mountain, tree, ladder*) Spitze *f*; (*of cupboard, table, box*) Oberseite *f*; (*of street*) Ende *nt*; (*lid*) Verschluß *m*; (*AUT: also:* ~ **gear**) höchster Gang *m*; (*also:* **spinning** ~:

*toy*) Kreisel *m*; (*blouse etc*) Oberteil *nt*; (*of pyjamas*) Jacke *f* ♦ *adj* höchste(r, s); (*highest in rank*) oberste(r, s); (: *golfer etc*) Top- ♦ *vt* (*poll, vote, list*) anführen; (*estimate etc*) übersteigen; **at the ~ of the stairs/page** oben auf der Treppe/Seite; **at the ~ of the street** am Ende der Straße; **on ~ of** (*above*) auf +*dat*; (*in addition to*) zusätzlich zu; **from ~ to bottom** von oben bis unten; **from ~ to toe** (*BRIT*) von Kopf bis Fuß; **at the ~ of the list** oben auf der Liste; **at the ~ of his voice** so laut er konnte; **over the ~** (*inf: behaviour etc*) übertrieben; **to go over the ~** (*inf*) übertreiben; **at ~ speed** bei Höchstgeschwindigkeit.

►**top up** , (*US*) **top off** *vt* (*drink*) nachfüllen; (*salary*) aufbessern.

**topaz** ['təupæz] *n* Topas *m*.

**top-class** ['tɔp'klɑːs] *adj* erstklassig; (*hotel, player etc*) Spitzen-.

**topcoat** ['tɔpkəut] *n* (*overcoat*) Mantel *m*; (*of paint*) Deckanstrich *m*.

**top floor** *n* oberster Stock *m*.

**top hat** *n* Zylinder *m*.

**top-heavy** [tɔp'hɛvɪ] *adj* (*also fig*) kopflastig.

**topic** ['tɔpɪk] *n* Thema *nt*.

**topical** ['tɔpɪkl] *adj* (*issue etc*) aktuell.

**topless** ['tɔplɪs] *adj* (*waitress*) Oben-ohne-; (*bather*) barbusig ♦ *adv* oben ohne.

**top-level** ['tɔplɛvl] *adj* auf höchster Ebene.

**topmost** ['tɔpməust] *adj* oberste(r, s).

**top-notch** ['tɔp'nɔtʃ] *adj* erstklassig.

**topography** [tə'pɔgrəfɪ] *n* Topographie *f*.

**topping** ['tɔpɪŋ] *n* (*CULIN*) Überzug *m*.

**topple** ['tɔpl] *vt* (*government etc*) stürzen ♦ *vi* (*person*) stürzen; (*object*) fallen.

**top-ranking** ['tɔpræŋkɪŋ] *adj* (*official*) hochgestellt.

**top-secret** ['tɔp'siːkrɪt] *adj* streng geheim.

**top-security** ['tɔpsə'kjuərɪtɪ] (*BRIT*) *adj* (*prison, wing*) Hochsicherheits-.

**topsy-turvy** ['tɔpsɪ'təːvɪ] *adj* auf den Kopf gestellt ♦ *adv* durcheinander; (*fall, land*) verkehrt herum.

**top-up** ['tɔpʌp] *n:* **would you like a ~?** darf ich Ihnen nachschenken?

**top-up loan** *n* Ergänzungsdarlehen *nt*.

**torch** [tɔːtʃ] *n* Fackel *f*; (*BRIT: electric*) Taschenlampe *f*.

**tore** [tɔːʳ] *pt of* **tear**.

**torment** [*n* tɔːmɛnt, *vt* tɔːˈmɛnt] *n* Qual *f* ♦ *vt* quälen; (*annoy*) ärgern.

**torn** [tɔːn] *pp of* **tear¹** ♦ *adj:* **~ between** (*fig*) hin- und hergerissen zwischen.

**tornado** [tɔːˈneɪdəu] (*pl* **~es**) *n* (*storm*) Tornado *m*.

**torpedo** [tɔːˈpiːdəu] (*pl* **~es**) *n* Torpedo *m*.

**torpedo boat** *n* Torpedoboot *nt*.

**torpor** ['tɔːpəʳ] *n* Trägheit *f*.

**torrent** ['tɔrnt] *n* (*flood*) Strom *m*; (*fig*) Flut *f*.

**torrential** [tɔ'rɛnʃl] *adj* (*rain*) wolkenbruchartig.

**torrid** ['tɔrɪd] *adj* (*weather, love affair*) heiß.

**torso** ['tɔːsəu] *n* Torso *m*.

**tortoise** ['tɔːtəs] *n* Schildkröte *f*.

**tortoiseshell** ['tɔːtəʃɛl] *adj* (*jewellery, ornaments*) aus Schildpatt; (*cat*) braun-gelb-schwarz.

**tortuous** ['tɔːtjuəs] *adj* (*path*) gewunden; (*argument, mind*) umständlich.

**torture** ['tɔːtʃəʳ] *n* Folter *f*; (*fig*) Qual *f* ♦ *vt* foltern; (*fig: torment*) quälen; **it was ~** (*fig*) es war eine Qual.

**torturer** ['tɔːtʃərəʳ] *n* Folterer *m*.

**Tory** ['tɔːrɪ] (*BRIT: POL*) *adj* konservativ ♦ *n* Tory *m*, Konservative(r) *f(m)*.

**toss** [tɔs] *vt* (*throw*) werfen; (*one's head*) zurückwerfen; (*salad*) anmachen; (*pancake*) wenden ♦ *n:* **with a ~ of her head** mit einer Kopfbewegung; **to ~ a coin** eine Münze werfen; **to win/lose the ~** die Entscheidung per Münzwurf gewinnen/verlieren; **to ~ up for sth** etw per Münzwurf entscheiden; **to ~ and turn** (*in bed*) sich hin und her wälzen.

**tot** [tɔt] *n* (*BRIT: drink*) Schluck *m*; (*child*) Knirps *m*.

►**tot up** (*BRIT*) *vt* (*figures*) zusammenzählen.

**total** ['təutl] *adj* (*number etc*) gesamt; (*failure, wreck etc*) völlig, total ♦ *n* Gesamtzahl *f* ♦ *vt* (*add up*) zusammenzählen; (*add up to*) sich belaufen auf; **in ~** insgesamt.

**totalitarian** [təutælɪ'tɛərɪən] *adj* totalitär.

**totality** [təu'tælɪtɪ] *n* Gesamtheit *f*.

**totally** ['təutəlɪ] *adv* völlig.

**totem pole** ['təutəm-] *n* Totempfahl *m*.

**totter** ['tɔtəʳ] *vi* (*person*) wanken, taumeln; (*fig: government*) im Wanken sein.

**touch** [tʌtʃ] *n* (*sense of touch*) Gefühl *nt*; (*contact*) Berührung *f*; (*skill: of pianist etc*) Hand *f* ♦ *vt* berühren; (*tamper with*) anrühren; (*emotionally*) rühren ♦ *vi* (*make contact*) sich berühren; **the personal ~** die persönliche Note; **to put the finishing ~es to sth** letzte Hand an etw *acc* legen; **a ~ of** (*fig: frost etc*) etwas, ein Hauch von; **in ~ with** (*person, group*) in Verbindung mit; **to get in ~ with sb** mit jdm in Verbindung treten; **I'll be in ~** ich melde mich; **to lose ~** (*friends*) den Kontakt verlieren; **to be out of ~ with sb** keine Verbindung mehr zu jdm haben; **to be out of ~ with events** nicht auf dem laufenden sein; **~ wood!** hoffen wir das Beste!

►**touch on** *vt fus* (*topic*) berühren.

►**touch up** *vt* (*car etc*) ausbessern.

**touch-and-go** ['tʌtʃən'gəu] *adj* (*situation*) auf der Kippe; **it was ~ whether we'd succeed** es war völlig offen, ob wir Erfolg haben würden.

**touchdown** ['tʌtʃdaun] *n* (*of rocket, plane*) Landung *f*; (*US: FOOTBALL*) Touchdown *m*.

**touched** [tʌtʃt] *adj* (*moved*) gerührt; (*inf: mad*) plemplem.

**touching** ['tʌtʃɪŋ] *adj* rührend.

**touchline** ['tʌtʃlaɪn] n (SPORT) Seitenlinie f.
**touch-sensitive** ['tʌtʃ'sɛnsɪtɪv] adj berührungsempfindlich; (switch) Kontakt-.
**touch-type** ['tʌtʃtaɪp] vi blindschreiben.
**touchy** ['tʌtʃɪ] adj (person, subject) empfindlich.
**tough** [tʌf] adj (strong, firm, difficult) hart; (resistant) widerstandsfähig; (meat, animal, person) zäh; (rough) rauh; ~ **luck!** Pech!
**toughen** ['tʌfn] vt (sb's character) hart machen; (glass etc) härten.
**toughness** ['tʌfnɪs] n Härte f.
**toupee** ['tuːpeɪ] n Toupet nt.
**tour** ['tuə*] n (journey) Reise f, Tour f; (of factory, museum etc) Rundgang m; (: also: **guided** ~) Führung f; (by pop group etc) Tournee f ♦ vt (country, factory etc: on foot) ziehen durch; (: in car) fahren durch; **to go on a ~ of a museum/castle** an einer Museums-/Schloßführung teilnehmen; **to go on a ~ of the Highlands** die Highlands bereisen; **to go/be on ~** (pop group, theatre company etc) auf Tournee gehen/sein.
**touring** ['tuərɪŋ] n Umherreisen nt.
**tourism** ['tuərɪzm] n Tourismus m.
**tourist** ['tuərɪst] n Tourist(in) m(f) ♦ cpd (attractions, season) Touristen-; **the ~ trade** die Tourismusbranche.
**tourist class** n Touristenklasse f.
**tourist information centre** (BRIT) n Touristen-Informationszentrum nt.
**tourist office** n Verkehrsamt nt.
**tournament** ['tuənəmənt] n Turnier nt.
**tourniquet** ['tuənɪkeɪ] n Aderpresse f.
**tour operator** (BRIT) n Reiseveranstalter m.
**tousled** ['tauzld] adj (hair) zerzaust.
**tout** [taut] vi: **to ~ for business** die Reklametrommel schlagen; **to ~ for custom** auf Kundenfang gehen ♦ n (also: **ticket** ~) Schwarzhändler, der Eintrittskarten zu überhöhten Preisen verkauft.
**tow** [təu] vt (vehicle) abschleppen; (caravan, trailer) ziehen ♦ n: **to give sb a ~** (AUT) jdn abschleppen; **"on** or (US) **in~"** „Fahrzeug wird abgeschleppt".
▶ **tow away** vt (vehicle) abschleppen.
**toward(s)** [tə'wɔːd(z)] prep (direction) zu; (attitude) gegenüber +dat; (purpose) für; (in time) gegen; **~ noon/the end of the year** gegen Mittag/Ende des Jahres; **to feel friendly ~ sb** jdm freundlich gesinnt sein.
**towel** ['tauəl] n Handtuch nt; **to throw in the ~** (fig) das Handtuch werfen.
**towelling** ['tauəlɪŋ] n Frottee nt or m.
**towel rail,** (US) **towel rack** n Handtuchstange f.
**tower** ['tauə*] n Turm m ♦ vi aufragen; **to ~ above** or **over sb/sth** über jdm/etw aufragen.
**tower block** (BRIT) n Hochhaus nt.
**towering** ['tauərɪŋ] adj hoch aufragend.
**towline** ['təulaɪn] n Abschleppseil nt.

**town** [taun] n Stadt f; **to go (in)to ~** in die Stadt gehen; **to go to ~ on sth** (fig) sich bei etw ins Zeug legen; **in ~** in der Stadt; **to be out of ~** (person) nicht in der Stadt sein.
**town centre** n Stadtzentrum nt.
**town clerk** n Stadtdirektor(in) m(f).
**town council** n Stadtrat m.
**town crier** [-'kraɪə*] n Ausrufer m.
**town hall** n Rathaus nt.
**town house** n (städtisches) Wohnhaus nt; (US: in a complex) Reihenhaus nt.
**townie** ['taunɪ] (inf) n (town-dweller) Städter(in) m(f).
**town plan** n Stadtplan m.
**town planner** n Stadtplaner(in) m(f).
**town planning** n Stadtplanung f.
**township** ['taunʃɪp] n Stadt(gemeinde) f; (formerly: in South Africa) Township f.
**townspeople** ['taunzpiːpl] npl Stadtbewohner pl.
**towpath** ['təupɑːθ] n Leinpfad m.
**towrope** ['təurəup] n Abschleppseil nt.
**tow truck** (US) n Abschleppwagen m.
**toxic** ['tɔksɪk] adj giftig, toxisch.
**toxin** ['tɔksɪn] n Gift nt, Giftstoff m.
**toy** [tɔɪ] n Spielzeug nt.
▶ **toy with** vt fus (object, idea) spielen mit.
**toyshop** ['tɔɪʃɔp] n Spielzeugladen m.
**trace** [treɪs] n (sign, small amount) Spur f ♦ vt (draw) nachzeichnen; (follow) verfolgen; (locate) aufspüren; **without ~** (disappear) spurlos; **there was no ~ of it** es war spurlos verschwunden.
**trace element** n Spurenelement nt.
**tracer** ['treɪsə*] n (MIL: also: ~ **bullet**) Leuchtspurgeschoß nt; (MED) Indikator m.
**trachea** [trə'kɪə] n Luftröhre f.
**tracing paper** ['treɪsɪŋ-] n Pauspapier nt.
**track** [træk] n Weg m; (of comet, SPORT) Bahn f; (of suspect, animal) Spur f; (RAIL) Gleis nt; (on tape, record) Stück nt, Track m ♦ vt (follow) verfolgen; **to keep ~ of sb/sth** (fig) jdn/etw im Auge behalten; **to be on the right ~** (fig) auf der richtigen Spur sein.
▶ **track down** vt aufspüren.
**tracker dog** ['trækə-] (BRIT) n Spürhund m.
**track events** npl Laufwettbewerbe f.
**tracking station** ['trækɪŋ-] n Bodenstation f.
**track meet** (US) n (SPORT) Leichtathletik-wettkampf m.
**track record** n: **to have a good ~** (fig) gute Leistungen vorzuweisen haben.
**tracksuit** ['træksuːt] n Trainingsanzug m.
**tract** [trækt] n (GEOG) Gebiet nt; (pamphlet) Traktat m or nt; **respiratory ~** Atemwege pl.
**traction** ['trækʃən] n (power) Zugkraft f; (AUT: grip) Bodenhaftung f; (MED): **in ~** im Streckverband.
**traction engine** n Zugmaschine f.
**tractor** ['træktə*] n Traktor m.
**trade** [treɪd] n (activity) Handel m; (skill, job) Handwerk nt ♦ vi (do business) handeln ♦ vt:

to ~ **sth (for sth)** etw (gegen etw)
eintauschen; **foreign** ~ Außenhandel m;
**Department of T**~ **and Industry** (BRIT)
≈ Wirtschaftsministerium nt; **to** ~ **with**
Handel treiben mit; **to** ~ **in** (merchandise)
handeln in +dat.
▶**trade in** vt in Zahlung geben.
**trade barrier** n Handelsschranke f.
**trade deficit** n Handelsdefizit nt.
**Trade Descriptions Act** (BRIT) n Gesetz über
korrekte Warenbeschreibungen.
**trade discount** n Händlerrabatt m.
**trade fair** n Handelsmesse f.
**trade figures** npl Handelsziffern pl.
**trade-in** ['treɪdɪn] n: **to take sth as a** ~ etw in
Zahlung nehmen.
**trade-in value** n Gebrauchtwert m.
**trademark** ['treɪdmɑːk] n Warenzeichen nt.
**trade mission** n Handelsmission f.
**trade name** n Handelsname m.
**trade-off** ['treɪdɔf] n Handel m; **there's bound
to be a** ~ **between speed and quality** es gibt
entweder Einbußen bei der Schnelligkeit
oder bei der Qualität.
**trader** ['treɪdə*] n Händler(in) m(f).
**trade secret** n (also fig) Betriebsgeheimnis
nt.
**tradesman** ['treɪdzmən] (irreg: like **man**) n
(shopkeeper) Händler m.
**trade union** n Gewerkschaft f.
**trade unionist** [-'juːnjənɪst] n
Gewerkschaftler(in) m(f).
**trade wind** n Passat m.
**trading** ['treɪdɪŋ] n Handel m.
**trading estate** (BRIT) n Industriegelände nt.
**trading stamp** n Rabattmarke f.
**tradition** [trə'dɪʃən] n Tradition f.
**traditional** [trə'dɪʃənl] adj traditionell.
**traditionally** [trə'dɪʃnəlɪ] adv traditionell.
**traffic** ['træfɪk] n Verkehr m; (in drugs etc)
Handel m ♦ vi: **to** ~ **in** handeln mit.
**traffic calming** n Verkehrsberuhigung f.
**traffic circle** (US) n Kreisverkehr m.
**traffic island** n Verkehrsinsel f.
**traffic jam** n Verkehrsstauung f, Stau m.
**trafficker** ['træfɪkə*] n Händler(in) m(f).
**traffic lights** npl Ampel f.
**traffic offence** (BRIT) n Verkehrsdelikt nt.
**traffic sign** n Verkehrszeichen nt.
**traffic violation** (US) n = **traffic offence**.
**traffic warden** n Verkehrspolizist für
Parkvergehen; (woman) ≈ Politesse f.
**tragedy** ['trædʒədɪ] n Tragödie f.
**tragic** ['trædʒɪk] adj tragisch.
**tragically** ['trædʒɪkəlɪ] adv tragisch.
**trail** [treɪl] n (path) Weg m; (track) Spur f; (of
smoke, dust) Wolke f ♦ vt (drag) schleifen;
(follow) folgen +dat ♦ vi (hang loosely)
schleifen; (in game, contest) zurückliegen; **to
be on sb's** ~ jdm auf der Spur sein.
▶**trail away** vi (sound, voice) sich verlieren.
▶**trail behind** vi hinterhertrotten.

▶**trail off** vi = **trail away**.
**trailer** ['treɪlə*] n (AUT) Anhänger m; (US:
caravan) Caravan m, Wohnwagen m; (CINE,
TV) Trailer m.
**trailer truck** (US) n Sattelschlepper m.
**train** [treɪn] n (RAIL) Zug m; (of dress)
Schleppe f ♦ vt (apprentice etc) ausbilden;
(dog) abrichten; (athlete) trainieren; (mind)
schulen; (plant) ziehen; (point: camera, gun
etc): **to** ~ **on** richten auf +acc ♦ vi (learn a
skill) ausgebildet werden; (SPORT)
trainieren; ~ **of thought** Gedankengang m;
**to go by** ~ mit dem Zug fahren; ~ **of events**
Ereignisfolge f; **to** ~ **sb to do sth** jdn dazu
ausbilden, etw zu tun.
**train attendant** (US) n Schlafwagen-
schaffner m.
**trained** [treɪnd] adj (worker) gelernt; (teacher)
ausgebildet; (animal) dressiert; (eye)
geschult.
**trainee** [treɪ'niː] n Auszubildende(r) f(m).
**trainer** ['treɪnə*] n (SPORT: coach) Trainer(in)
m(f); (: shoe) Trainingsschuh m; (of animals)
Dresseur(in) m(f).
**training** ['treɪnɪŋ] n (for occupation)
Ausbildung f; (SPORT) Training nt; **in** ~
(SPORT) im Training.
**training college** n (for teachers)
≈ Pädagogische Hochschule f.
**training course** n Ausbildungskurs m.
**traipse** [treɪps] vi: **to** ~ **in/out** hinein-/
herauslatschen.
**trait** [treɪt] n Zug m, Eigenschaft f.
**traitor** ['treɪtə*] n Verräter(in) m(f).
**trajectory** [trə'dʒɛktərɪ] n Flugbahn f.
**tram** [træm] (BRIT) n (also: ~**car**) Straßenbahn
f.
**tramline** ['træmlaɪn] n Straßenbahnschiene f.
**tramp** [træmp] n Landstreicher m; (pej:
woman) Flittchen nt ♦ vi stapfen ♦ vt (walk
through: town, streets) latschen durch.
**trample** ['træmpl] vt: **to** ~ **(underfoot)**
niedertrampeln ♦ vi (also fig): **to** ~ **on**
herumtrampeln auf +dat.
**trampoline** ['træmpəliːn] n Trampolin nt.
**trance** [trɑːns] n Trance f; **to go into a** ~ in
Trance verfallen.
**tranquil** ['træŋkwɪl] adj ruhig, friedlich.
**tranquillity,** (US) **tranquility** [træŋ'kwɪlɪtɪ] n
Ruhe f.
**tranquillizer,** (US) **tranquilizer**
['træŋkwɪlaɪzə*] n Beruhigungsmittel nt.
**transact** [træn'zækt] vt (business) abwickeln.
**transaction** [træn'zækʃən] n Geschäft nt; **cash**
~ Bargeldtransaktion f.
**transatlantic** ['trænzət'læntɪk] adj
transatlantisch; (phone-call) über den
Atlantik.
**transcend** [træn'sɛnd] vt überschreiten.
**transcendental** [trænsɛn'dɛntl] adj:
~ **meditation** transzendentale Meditation f.
**transcribe** [træn'skraɪb] vt transkribieren.

**transcript** ['trænskrɪpt] n Niederschrift f, Transkription f.

**transcription** [træn'skrɪpʃən] n Transkription f.

**transept** ['trænsɛpt] n Querschiff nt.

**transfer** ['trænsfə*] n (of employees) Versetzung f; (of money) Überweisung f; (of power) Übertragung f; (SPORT) Transfer m; (picture, design) Abziehbild nt ♦ vt (employees) versetzen; (money) überweisen; (power, ownership) übertragen; **by bank** ~ per Banküberweisung; **to ~ the charges** (BRIT: TEL) ein R-Gespräch führen.

**transferable** [træns'fə:rəbl] adj übertragbar; **"not ~"** „nicht übertragbar".

**transfix** [træns'fɪks] vt aufspießen; ~**ed with fear** (fig) starr vor Angst.

**transform** [træns'fɔ:m] vt umwandeln.

**transformation** [trænsfə'meɪʃən] n Umwandlung f.

**transformer** [træns'fɔ:mə*] n (ELEC) Transformator m.

**transfusion** [træns'fju:ʒən] n (also: **blood** ~) Bluttransfusion f.

**transgress** [træns'grɛs] vt (go beyond) überschreiten; (violate: rules, law) verletzen.

**transient** ['trænzɪənt] adj vorübergehend.

**transistor** [træn'zɪstə*] n (ELEC) Transistor m; (also: ~ **radio**) Transistorradio nt.

**transit** ['trænzɪt] n: **in** ~ unterwegs.

**transit camp** n Durchgangslager nt.

**transition** [træn'zɪʃən] n Übergang m.

**transitional** [træn'zɪʃənl] adj (period, stage) Übergangs-.

**transitive** ['trænzɪtɪv] adj (verb) transitiv.

**transit lounge** n Transithalle f.

**transitory** ['trænzɪtərɪ] adj (emotion, arrangement etc) vorübergehend.

**transit visa** n Transitvisum nt.

**translate** [trænz'leɪt] vt übersetzen; **to ~ (from/into)** übersetzen (aus/in +acc).

**translation** [trænz'leɪʃən] n Übersetzung f; **in** ~ als Übersetzung.

**translator** [trænz'leɪtə*] n Übersetzer(in) m(f).

**translucent** [trænz'lu:snt] adj (object) lichtdurchlässig.

**transmission** [trænz'mɪʃən] n (also TV) Übertragung f; (of information) Übermittlung f; (AUT) Getriebe nt.

**transmit** [trænz'mɪt] vt (also TV) übertragen; (message, signal) übermitteln.

**transmitter** [trænz'mɪtə*] n (TV, RADIO) Sender m.

**transparency** [træns'pɛərnsɪ] n (of glass etc) Durchsichtigkeit f; (BRIT: PHOT) Dia nt.

**transparent** [træns'pærnt] adj durchsichtig; (fig: obvious) offensichtlich.

**transpire** [træns'paɪə*] vi (turn out) bekannt werden; (happen) passieren; **it finally ~d that ...** schließlich sickerte durch, daß ...

**transplant** [vt trænsˈplɑ:nt, n 'trɑ:nsplɑ:nt] vt (organ, seedlings) verpflanzen ♦ n (MED)

Transplantation f; **to have a heart** ~ sich einer Herztransplantation unterziehen.

**transport** ['trænspɔ:t] n Transport m, Beförderung f ♦ vt transportieren; **do you have your own ~?** haben Sie ein Auto?; **public** ~ öffentliche Verkehrsmittel pl; **Department of T~** (BRIT) Verkehrsministerium nt.

**transportation** ['trænspɔ:'teɪʃən] n Transport m, Beförderung f; (means of transport) Beförderungsmittel nt; **Department of T~** (US) Verkehrsministerium nt.

**transport café** (BRIT) n Fernfahrerlokal nt.

**transpose** [træns'pəuz] vt versetzen.

**transsexual** [trænz'sɛksuəl] adj transsexuell ♦ n Transsexuelle(r) f(m).

**transverse** ['trænzvɔ:s] adj (beam etc) Quer-.

**transvestite** [trænz'vɛstaɪt] n Transvestit m.

**trap** [træp] n (also fig) Falle f; (carriage) zweirädriger Pferdewagen m ♦ vt (animal) (mit einer Falle) fangen; (person: trick) in die Falle locken; (: confine) gefangen halten; (immobilize) festsetzen; (capture: energy) stauen; **to set** or **lay a** ~ **(for sb)** (jdm) eine Falle stellen; **to shut one's** ~ (inf) die Klappe halten; **to** ~ **one's finger in the door** sich dat den Finger in der Tür einklemmen.

**trap door** n Falltür f.

**trapeze** [trə'pi:z] n Trapez nt.

**trapper** ['træpə*] n Fallensteller m, Trapper m.

**trappings** ['træpɪŋz] npl äußere Zeichen pl; (of power) Insignien pl.

**trash** [træʃ] n (rubbish) Abfall m, Müll m; (pej: nonsense) Schund m, Mist m.

**trash can** (US) n Mülleimer m.

**trashy** ['træʃɪ] adj (goods) minderwertig, wertlos; (novel etc) Schund-.

**trauma** ['trɔ:mə] n Trauma nt.

**traumatic** [trɔ:'mætɪk] adj traumatisch.

**traumatize** ['trɔ:mətaɪz] vt traumatisieren.

**travel** ['trævl] n (travelling) Reisen nt ♦ vi reisen; (short distance) fahren; (move: car, aeroplane) sich bewegen; (sound etc) sich fortpflanzen; (news) sich verbreiten ♦ vt (distance) zurücklegen; **travels** npl (journeys) Reisen pl; **this wine doesn't** ~ **well** dieser Wein verträgt den Transport nicht.

**travel agency** n Reisebüro nt.

**travel agent** n Reisebürokaufmann m, Reisebürokauffrau f.

**travel brochure** n Reiseprospekt m.

**traveling** etc (US) = **travelling** etc.

**traveller,** (US) **traveler** ['trævlə*] n Reisende(r) f(m); (COMM) Vertreter(in) m(f).

**traveller's cheque,** (US) **traveler's check** n Reisescheck m.

**travelling,** (US) **traveling** ['trævlɪŋ] n Reisen nt ♦ cpd (circus, exhibition) Wander-; (bag, clock) Reise-; ~ **expenses** Reisespesen pl.

**travelling salesman** n Vertreter m.

**travelogue** ['trævəlɒg] n Reisebericht m.

**travel sickness** n Reisekrankheit f.

**traverse** ['trævəs] *vt* durchqueren.

**travesty** ['trævəstɪ] *n* Travestie *f*.

**trawler** ['trɔːlə*] *n* Fischdampfer *m*.

**tray** [treɪ] *n* (*for carrying*) Tablett *nt*; (*also:* **in-~/out-~**: *on desk*) Ablage *f* für Eingänge/Ausgänge.

**treacherous** ['tretʃərəs] *adj* (*person, look*) verräterisch; (*ground, tide*) tückisch; **road conditions are ~** die Straßen sind in gefährlichem Zustand.

**treachery** ['tretʃərɪ] *n* Verrat *m*.

**treacle** ['triːkl] *n* Sirup *m*.

**tread** [tred] (*pt* **trod**, *pp* **trodden**) *n* (*of tyre*) Profil *nt*; (*footstep*) Schritt *m*; (*of stair*) Stufe *f* ♦ *vi* gehen.

▶**tread on** *vt fus* treten auf *+acc*.

**treadle** ['tredl] *n* Pedal *nt*.

**treas.** *abbr* = **treasurer**.

**treason** ['triːzn] *n* Verrat *m*.

**treasure** ['treʒə*] *n* (*also fig*) Schatz *m* ♦ *vt* schätzen; **treasures** *npl* (*art treasures etc*) Schätze *pl*, Kostbarkeiten *pl*.

**treasure hunt** *n* Schatzsuche *f*.

**treasurer** ['treʒərə*] *n* Schatzmeister(in) *m(f)*.

**treasury** ['treʒərɪ] *n*: **the T~**, (*US*) **the T~ Department** das Finanzministerium.

**treasury bill** *n* kurzfristiger Schatzwechsel *m*.

**treat** [triːt] *n* (*present*) (besonderes) Vergnügen *nt* ♦ *vt* (*also MED, TECH*) behandeln; **it came as a ~** es war eine besondere Freude; **to ~ sth as a joke** etw als Witz ansehen; **to ~ sb to sth** jdm etw spendieren.

**treatment** ['triːtmənt] *n* Behandlung *f*, **to have ~ for sth** wegen etw in Behandlung sein.

**treaty** ['triːtɪ] *n* Vertrag *m*.

**treble** ['trebl] *adj* (*triple*) dreifach; (*MUS: voice, part*) (Knaben)sopran-; (*instrument*) Diskant- ♦ *n* (*singer*) (Knaben)sopran *m*; (*on hi-fi, radio etc*) Höhen *pl* ♦ *vt* verdreifachen ♦ *vi* sich verdreifachen; **to be ~ the amount/size of sth** dreimal soviel/so groß wie etw sein.

**treble clef** *n* Violinschlüssel *m*.

**tree** [triː] *n* Baum *m*.

**tree-lined** ['triːlaɪnd] *adj* baumbestanden.

**treetop** ['triːtɔp] *n* Baumkrone *f*.

**tree trunk** *n* Baumstamm *m*.

**trek** [trek] *n* Treck *m*; (*tiring walk*) Marsch *m* ♦ *vi* trecken.

**trellis** ['trelɪs] *n* Gitter *nt*.

**tremble** ['trembl] *vi* (*voice, body, trees*) zittern; (*ground*) beben.

**trembling** ['tremblɪŋ] *n* (*of ground*) Beben *nt*, Erschütterung *f*; (*of trees*) Zittern *nt* ♦ *adj* (*hand, voice etc*) zitternd.

**tremendous** [trɪ'mendəs] *adj* (*amount, success etc*) gewaltig, enorm; (*holiday, view etc*) phantastisch.

**tremendously** [trɪ'mendəslɪ] *adv* (*difficult, exciting*) ungeheuer; **he enjoyed it ~** es hat ihm ausgezeichnet gefallen.

**tremor** ['tremə*] *n* Zittern *nt*; (*also:* **earth ~**) Beben *nt*, Erschütterung *f*.

**trench** [trentʃ] *n* Graben *m*.

**trench coat** *n* Trenchcoat *m*.

**trench warfare** *n* Stellungskrieg *m*.

**trend** [trend] *n* Tendenz *f*; (*fashion*) Trend *m*; **a ~ towards/away from sth** eine Tendenz zu/weg von etw; **to set a/the ~** richtungsweisend sein.

**trendy** ['trendɪ] *adj* modisch.

**trepidation** [trepɪ'deɪʃən] *n* (*apprehension*) Beklommenheit *f*; **in ~** beklommen.

**trespass** ['trespəs] *vi*: **to ~ on** (*private property*) unbefugt betreten; **"no ~ing"** „Betreten verboten".

**trespasser** ['trespəsə*] *n* Unbefugte(r) *f(m)*; **"~s will be prosecuted"** „widerrechtliches Betreten wird strafrechtlich verfolgt".

**tress** [tres] *n* (*of hair*) Locke *f*.

**trestle** ['tresl] *n* Bock *m*.

**trestle table** *n* Klapptisch *m*.

**trial** ['traɪəl] *n* (*LAW*) Prozeß *m*; (*test: of machine, drug etc*) Versuch *m*; (*worry*) Plage *f*; **trials** *npl* (*unpleasant experiences*) Schwierigkeiten *pl*; **~ by jury** Schwurgerichtsverfahren *nt*; **to be sent for ~** vor Gericht gestellt werden; **to be/go on ~** (*LAW*) angeklagt sein/werden; **by ~ and error** durch Ausprobieren.

**trial balance** *n* Probebilanz *f*.

**trial basis** *n*: **on a ~** probeweise.

**trial period** *n* Probezeit *f*.

**trial run** *n* Versuch *m*.

**triangle** ['traɪæŋgl] *n* Dreieck *nt*; (*US: set square*) (Zeichen)dreieck *nt*; (*MUS*) Triangel *f*.

**triangular** [traɪ'æŋgjulə*] *adj* dreieckig.

**triathlon** [traɪ'æθlən] *n* Triathlon *nt*.

**tribal** ['traɪbl] *adj* (*warrior, warfare, dance*) Stammes-.

**tribe** [traɪb] *n* Stamm *m*.

**tribesman** ['traɪbzmən] (*irreg: like* **man**) *n* Stammesangehörige(r) *m*.

**tribulations** [trɪbju'leɪʃənz] *npl* Kümmernisse *pl*.

**tribunal** [traɪ'bjuːnl] *n* Gericht *nt*.

**tributary** ['trɪbjutərɪ] *n* (*of river*) Nebenfluß *m*.

**tribute** ['trɪbjuːt] *n* Tribut *m*; **to pay ~** Tribut zollen *+dat*.

**trice** [traɪs] *n*: **in a ~** im Handumdrehen.

**trick** [trɪk] *n* Trick *m*; (*CARDS*) Stich *m* ♦ *vt* hereinlegen; **to play a ~ on sb** jdm einen Streich spielen; **it's a ~ of the light** das Licht täuscht; **that should do the ~** das müßte hinhauen; **to ~ sb into doing sth** jdn (mit einem Trick) dazu bringen, etw zu tun; **to ~ sb out of sth** jdn um etw prellen.

**trickery** ['trɪkərɪ] *n* Tricks *pl*, Betrügerei *f*.

**trickle** ['trɪkl] *n* (*of water etc*) Rinnsal *nt* ♦ *vi* (*water, rain etc*) rinnen; (*people*) sich langsam bewegen.

**trick photography** *n* Trickfotografie *f*.

**trick question** *n* Fangfrage *f*.
**trickster** ['trɪkstə*] *n* Betrüger(in) *m(f)*.
**tricky** ['trɪkɪ] *adj* (*job, problem*) schwierig.
**tricycle** ['traɪsɪkl] *n* Dreirad *nt*.
**trifle** ['traɪfl] *n* (*detail*) Kleinigkeit *f*; (*CULIN*)
Trifle *nt* ♦ *adv:* **a** ~ **long** ein bißchen lang ♦ *vi:*
**to** ~ **with sb/sth** jdn/etw nicht ernst
nehmen; **he is not (someone) to be** ~**d with**
mit ihm ist nicht zu spaßen.
**trifling** ['traɪflɪŋ] *adj* (*detail*) unbedeutend.
**trigger** ['trɪgə*] *n* Abzug *m*.
▶**trigger off** *vt fus* auslösen.
**trigonometry** [trɪgə'nɒmətrɪ] *n*
Trigonometrie *f*.
**trilby** ['trɪlbɪ] (*BRIT*) *n* (*also:* ~ **hat**) Filzhut *m*.
**trill** [trɪl] *n* (*MUS*) Triller *m*; (*of birds*) Trillern
*nt*.
**trilogy** ['trɪlədʒɪ] *n* Trilogie *f*.
**trim** [trɪm] *adj* (*house, garden*) gepflegt; (*figure,
person*) schlank ♦ *n* (*haircut etc*): **to have a** ~
sich *dat* die Haare nachschneiden lassen;
(*on clothes, car*) Besatz *m* ♦ *vt* (*hair, beard*)
nachschneiden; (*decorate*): **to** ~ (**with**)
besetzen (mit); (*NAUT: a sail*) trimmen mit;
**to keep o.s. in (good)** ~ (gut) in Form
bleiben.
**trimmings** ['trɪmɪŋz] *npl* (*CULIN*): **with all the**
~ mit allem Drum und Dran; (*cuttings: of
pastry etc*) Reste *pl*.
**Trinidad and Tobago** ['trɪnɪdæd-] *n* Trinidad
und Tobago *nt*.
**trinity** ['trɪnɪtɪ] *n* (*REL*) Dreieinigkeit *f*.
**trinket** ['trɪŋkɪt] *n* (*ornament*) Schmuckgegen-
stand *m*; (*piece of jewellery*) Schmuckstück
*nt*.
**trio** ['triːəu] *n* Trio *nt*.
**trip** [trɪp] *n* (*journey*) Reise *f*; (*outing*) Ausflug
*m* ♦ *vi* (*stumble*) stolpern; (*go lightly*)
trippeln; **on a** ~ auf Reisen.
▶**trip over** *vt fus* stolpern über +*acc*.
▶**trip up** *vi* stolpern ♦ *vt* (*person*) zu Fall
bringen.
**tripartite** [traɪ'pɑːtaɪt] *adj* (*agreement, talks*)
dreiseitig.
**tripe** [traɪp] *n* (*CULIN*) Kaldaunen *pl*; (*pej:
rubbish*) Stuß *m*.
**triple** ['trɪpl] *adj* dreifach ♦ *adv:* ~ **the
distance/the speed** dreimal so weit/schnell;
~ **the amount** dreimal soviel.
**triple jump** *n* Dreisprung *m*.
**triplets** ['trɪplɪts] *npl* Drillinge *pl*.
**triplicate** ['trɪplɪkət] *n:* **in** ~ in dreifacher
Ausfertigung.
**tripod** ['traɪpɒd] *n* (*PHOT*) Stativ *nt*.
**Tripoli** ['trɪpəlɪ] *n* Tripolis *nt*.
**tripper** ['trɪpə*] (*BRIT*) *n* Ausflügler(in) *m(f)*.
**tripwire** ['trɪpwaɪə*] *n* Stolperdraht *m*.
**trite** [traɪt] (*pej*) *adj* (*comment, idea etc*) banal.
**triumph** ['traɪʌmf] *n* Triumph *m* ♦ *vi:* **to**
~ (**over**) triumphieren (über +*acc*).
**triumphal** [traɪ'ʌmfl] *adj* (*return*) triumphal.
**triumphant** [traɪ'ʌmfənt] *adj* triumphierend;

(*victorious*) siegreich.
**triumphantly** [traɪ'ʌmfəntlɪ] *adv*
triumphierend.
**trivia** ['trɪvɪə] (*pej*) *npl* Trivialitäten *pl*.
**trivial** ['trɪvɪəl] *adj* trivial.
**triviality** [trɪvɪ'ælɪtɪ] *n* Trivialität *f*.
**trivialize** ['trɪvɪəlaɪz] *vt* trivialisieren.
**trod** [trɒd] *pt of* **tread**.
**trodden** [trɒdn] *pp of* **tread**.
**trolley** ['trɒlɪ] *n* (*for luggage*) Kofferkuli *m*; (*for
shopping*) Einkaufswagen *m*; (*table on
wheels*) Teewagen *m*; (*also:* ~ **bus**)
Oberleitungsomnibus *m*, Obus *m*.
**trollop** ['trɒləp] (*pej*) *n* (*woman*) Schlampe *f*.
**trombone** [trɒm'bəun] *n* Posaune *f*.
**troop** [truːp] *n* (*of people, monkeys etc*) Gruppe
*f* ♦ *vi:* **to** ~ **in/out** hinein-/hinausströmen;
**troops** *npl* (*MIL*) Truppen *pl*.
**troop carrier** *n* Truppentransporter *m*;
(*NAUT: also:* **troopship**) Truppentransport-
schiff *nt*.
**trooper** ['truːpə*] *n* (*MIL*) Kavallerist *m*; (*US:
policeman*) Polizist *m*.
**trooping the colour** ['truːpɪŋ-] (*BRIT*) *n*
(*ceremony*) Fahnenparade *f*.
**troopship** ['truːpʃɪp] *n* Truppentransport-
schiff *nt*.
**trophy** ['trəufɪ] *n* Trophäe *f*.
**tropic** ['trɒpɪk] *n* Wendekreis *m*; **the tropics** *npl*
die Tropen *pl*; **T~ of Cancer/Capricorn**
Wendekreis des Krebses/Steinbocks.
**tropical** ['trɒpɪkl] *adj* tropisch.
**trot** [trɒt] *n* (*fast pace*) Trott *m*; (*of horse*) Trab
*m* ♦ *vi* (*horse*) traben; (*person*) trotten; **on the**
~ (*BRIT, fig*) hintereinander.
▶**trot out** *vt* (*facts, excuse etc*) vorbringen.
**trouble** ['trʌbl] *n* Schwierigkeiten *pl*; (*bother,
effort*) Umstände *pl*; (*unrest*) Unruhen *pl* ♦ *vt*
(*worry*) beunruhigen; (*disturb: person*)
belästigen ♦ *vi:* **to** ~ **to do sth** sich *dat* die
Mühe machen, etw zu tun; **troubles** *npl*
(*personal*) Probleme *pl*; (*POL etc*) Unruhen *pl*;
**to be in** ~ in Schwierigkeiten sein; **to have**
~ **doing sth** Schwierigkeiten *or* Probleme
haben, etw zu tun; **to go to the** ~ **of doing
sth** sich *dat* die Mühe machen, etw zu tun;
**it's no** ~! das macht mir nichts aus!; **the**
~ **is ...** das Problem ist ...; **what's the** ~? wo
fehlt's?; **stomach** *etc* ~ Probleme mit dem
Magen *etc*; **please don't** ~ **yourself** bitte
bemühen Sie sich nicht.
**troubled** ['trʌbld] *adj* (*person*) besorgt;
(*country, life, era*) von Problemen
geschüttelt.
**trouble-free** ['trʌblfriː] *adj* problemlos.
**troublemaker** ['trʌblmeɪkə*] *n*
Unruhestifter(in) *m(f)*.
**troubleshooter** ['trʌblʃuːtə*] *n* Vermittler(in)
*m(f)*.
**troublesome** ['trʌblsəm] *adj* (*child*) schwierig;
(*cough etc*) lästig.
**trouble spot** *n* (*MIL*) Unruheherd *m*.

**troubling** ['trʌblɪŋ] adj (question etc) beunruhigend.

**trough** [trɔf] n (also: **drinking** ~) Wassertrog m; (also: **feeding** ~) Futtertrog m; (channel) Rinne f; (low point) Tief nt; **a** ~ **of low pressure** ein Tiefdruckkeil m.

**trounce** [trauns] vt (defeat) vernichtend schlagen.

**troupe** [tru:p] n Truppe f.

**trouser press** ['trauzə-] n Hosenpresse f.

**trousers** ['trauzəz] npl Hose f; **short** ~ kurze Hose; **a pair of** ~ eine Hose.

**trouser suit** (BRIT) n Hosenanzug m.

**trousseau** ['tru:səu] (pl ~x or ~s) n Aussteuer f.

**trout** [traut] n inv Forelle f.

**trowel** ['trauəl] n (garden tool) Pflanzkelle f; (builder's tool) (Maurer)kelle f.

**truant** ['truənt] (BRIT) n: **to play** ~ die Schule schwänzen.

**truce** [tru:s] n Waffenstillstand m.

**truck** [trʌk] n (lorry) Lastwagen m; (RAIL) Güterwagen m; (for luggage) Gepäckwagen m; **to have no** ~ **with sb** nichts mit jdm zu tun haben.

**truck driver** n Lkw-Fahrer(in) m(f).

**trucker** ['trʌkə-] (US) n Lkw-Fahrer(in) m(f).

**truck farm** (US) n Gemüsefarm f.

**trucking** ['trʌkɪŋ] (US) n Transport m.

**trucking company** (US) n Spedition f.

**truculent** ['trʌkjulənt] adj aufsässig.

**trudge** [trʌdʒ] vi (also: ~ **along**) sich dahinschleppen.

**true** [tru:] adj wahr; (accurate) genau; (genuine) echt; (faithful: friend) treu; (wall, beam) gerade; (circle) rund; **to come** ~ wahr werden; ~ **to life** lebensecht.

**truffle** ['trʌfl] n (fungus, sweet) Trüffel f.

**truly** ['tru:lɪ] adv wahrhaft, wirklich; (truthfully) wirklich; **yours** ~ (in letter) mit freundlichen Grüßen.

**trump** [trʌmp] n (also: ~ **card**, also fig) Trumpf m; **to turn up** ~**s** (fig) sich als Retter in der Not erweisen.

**trumped-up** adj: **a** ~ **charge** eine erfundene Anschuldigung.

**trumpet** ['trʌmpɪt] n Trompete f.

**truncated** [trʌŋ'keɪtɪd] adj (message, object) verstümmelt.

**truncheon** ['trʌntʃən] (BRIT) n Gummiknüppel m.

**trundle** ['trʌndl] vt (trolley etc) rollen ♦ vi: **to** ~ **along** (person) dahinschlendern; (vehicle) dahinrollen.

**trunk** [trʌŋk] n (of tree) Stamm m; (of person) Rumpf m; (of elephant) Rüssel m; (case) Schrankkoffer m; (US: AUT) Kofferraum m; **trunks** npl (also: **swimming** ~**s**) Badehose f.

**trunk call** (BRIT) n Ferngespräch nt.

**trunk road** (BRIT) n Fernstraße f.

**truss** [trʌs] n (MED) Bruchband nt.

▶**truss (up)** vt (CULIN) dressieren; (person) fesseln.

**trust** [trʌst] n Vertrauen nt; (COMM: for charity etc) Stiftung f ♦ vt vertrauen +dat; **to take sth on** ~ (advice etc) etw einfach glauben; **to be in** ~ (LAW) treuhänderisch verwaltet werden; **to** ~ (**that**) (hope) hoffen(, daß).

**trust company** n Trust m.

**trusted** ['trʌstɪd] adj (friend, servant) treu.

**trustee** [trʌs'ti:] n (LAW) Treuhänder(in) m(f); (of school etc) Aufsichtsratsmitglied nt.

**trustful** ['trʌstful] adj vertrauensvoll.

**trust fund** n Treuhandvermögen nt.

**trusting** ['trʌstɪŋ] adj vertrauensvoll.

**trustworthy** ['trʌstwə:ðɪ] adj (person) vertrauenswürdig.

**trusty** ['trʌstɪ] adj getreu.

**truth** [tru:θ] (pl ~**s**) n: **the** ~ die Wahrheit f.

**truthful** ['tru:θful] adj (person) ehrlich; (answer etc) wahrheitsgemäß.

**truthfully** ['tru:θfəlɪ] adv (answer) wahrheitsgemäß.

**truthfulness** ['tru:θfəlnɪs] n Ehrlichkeit f.

**try** [traɪ] n (also RUGBY) Versuch m ♦ vt (attempt) versuchen; (test) probieren; (LAW) vor Gericht stellen; (strain: patience) auf die Probe stellen ♦ vi es versuchen; **to have a** ~ es versuchen, einen Versuch machen; **to** ~ **to do sth** versuchen, etw zu tun; **to** ~ **one's (very) best** or **hardest** sein Bestes versuchen or tun.

▶**try on** vt (clothes) anprobieren; **she's** ~**ing it on** (fig) sie probiert, wie weit sie gehen kann.

▶**try out** vt ausprobieren.

**trying** ['traɪɪŋ] adj (person) schwierig; (experience) schwer.

**tsar** [zɑ:-] n Zar m.

**T-shirt** ['ti:ʃɜ:t] n T-Shirt nt.

**T-square** ['ti:skwɛə-] n (TECH) Reißschiene f.

**TT** adj abbr (BRIT: inf) = **teetotal** ♦ abbr (US: POST: = Trust Territories) der UN-Verwaltungshoheit unterstellte Gebiete.

**tub** [tʌb] n (container) Kübel m; (bath) Wanne f.

**tuba** ['tju:bə] n Tuba f.

**tubby** ['tʌbɪ] adj rundlich.

**tube** [tju:b] n (pipe) Rohr nt; (container) Tube f; (BRIT: underground) U-Bahn f; (US: inf): **the** ~ (television) die Röhre.

**tubeless** ['tju:blɪs] adj (tyre) schlauchlos.

**tuber** ['tju:bə-] n (BOT) Knolle f.

**tuberculosis** [tjubə:kju'ləusɪs] n Tuberkulose f.

**tube station** (BRIT) n U-Bahn-Station f.

**tubing** ['tju:bɪŋ] n Schlauch m; **a piece of** ~ ein Schlauch.

**tubular** ['tju:bjulə-] adj röhrenförmig.

**TUC** (BRIT) n abbr (= Trades Union Congress) britischer Gewerkschafts-Dachverband.

**tuck** [tʌk] vt (put) stecken ♦ n (SEWING) Biese f.

▶**tuck away** vt (money) wegstecken; **to be** ~**ed away** (building) versteckt liegen.

▶**tuck in** *vt* (*clothing*) feststecken; (*child*)
zudecken ♦ *vi* (*eat*) zulangen.
▶**tuck up** *vt* (*invalid, child*) zudecken.
**tuck shop** *n* Süßwarenladen *m.*
**Tue(s).** *abbr* (= *Tuesday*) Di.
**Tuesday** ['tjuːzdɪ] *n* Dienstag *m*; **it is ~ 23rd
March** heute ist Dienstag, der 23. März; **on
~ am Dienstag; on ~s** dienstags; **every ~**
jeden Dienstag; **every other ~** jeden
zweiten Dienstag; **last/next ~** letzten/
nächsten Dienstag; **the following ~** am
Dienstag darauf; **~'s newspaper** die
Zeitung von Dienstag; **a week/fortnight on
~** Dienstag in einer Woche/in vierzehn
Tagen; **the ~ before last** der vorletzte
Dienstag; **the ~ after next** der übernächste
Dienstag; **~ morning/lunchtime/afternoon/
evening** Dienstag morgen/mittag/
nachmittag/abend; **~ night** (*overnight*)
Dienstag nacht.
**tuft** [tʌft] *n* Büschel *nt.*
**tug** [tʌg] *n* (*ship*) Schlepper *m* ♦ *vt* zerren.
**tug of love** *n* Tauziehen *nt* (*um das Sorgerecht
für Kinder*).
**tug-of-war** [tʌgəvˈwɔːˈ] *n* (*also fig*) Tauziehen
*nt.*
**tuition** [tjuːˈɪʃən] *n* (*BRIT*) Unterricht *m*; (*US:
school fees*) Schulgeld *nt.*
**tulip** ['tjuːlɪp] *n* Tulpe *f.*
**tumble** ['tʌmbl] *n* (*fall*) Sturz *m* ♦ *vi* (*fall*)
stürzen.
▶**tumble to** (*inf*) *vt fus* kapieren.
**tumbledown** ['tʌmbldaun] *adj* (*building*)
baufällig.
**tumble dryer** (*BRIT*) *n* Wäschetrockner *m.*
**tumbler** ['tʌmbləˈ] *n* (*glass*) Trinkglas *nt.*
**tummy** ['tʌmɪ] (*inf*) *n* Bauch *m.*
**tumour,** (*US*) **tumor** ['tjuːməˈ] *n* (*MED*)
Tumor *m*, Geschwulst *f.*
**tumult** ['tjuːmʌlt] *n* Tumult *m.*
**tumultuous** [tjuːˈmʌltjuəs] *adj* (*welcome,
applause etc*) stürmisch.
**tuna** ['tjuːnə] *n inv* (*also:* **~ fish**) Thunfisch *m.*
**tune** [tjuːn] *n* (*melody*) Melodie *f* ♦ *vt* (*MUS*)
stimmen; (*RADIO, TV, AUT*) einstellen; **to be
in/out of ~** (*instrument*) richtig gestimmt/
verstimmt sein; (*singer*) richtig/falsch
singen; **to be in/out of ~ with** (*fig*) in
Einklang/nicht in Einklang stehen mit; **she
was robbed to the ~ of 10,000 pounds** sie
wurde um einen Betrag in Höhe von 10.000
Pfund beraubt.
▶**tune in** *vi* (*RADIO, TV*) einschalten; **to ~ in
to BBC1** BBC1 einschalten.
▶**tune up** *vi* (*MUS*) (das Instrument/die
Instrumente) stimmen.
**tuneful** ['tjuːnful] *adj* melodisch.
**tuner** ['tjuːnəˈ] *n:* **piano ~** Klavierstimmer(in)
*m(f)*; (*radio set*) Tuner *m.*
**tuner amplifier** *n* Steuergerät *nt.*
**tungsten** ['tʌŋstən] *n* Wolfram *nt.*
**tunic** ['tjuːnɪk] *n* Hemdbluse *f.*

**tuning fork** ['tjuːnɪŋ-] *n* Stimmgabel *f.*
**Tunis** ['tjuːnɪs] *n* Tunis *nt.*
**Tunisia** [tjuːˈnɪzɪə] *n* Tunesien *nt.*
**Tunisian** [tjuːˈnɪzɪən] *adj* tunesisch ♦ *n*
(*person*) Tunesier(in) *m(f).*
**tunnel** ['tʌnl] *n* Tunnel *m*; (*in mine*) Stollen *m*
♦ *vi* einen Tunnel bauen.
**tunnel vision** *n* (*MED*) Gesichtsfeld-
einengung *f*; (*fig*) Engstirnigkeit *f.*
**tunny** ['tʌnɪ] *n* Thunfisch *m.*
**turban** ['tɜːbən] *n* Turban *m.*
**turbid** ['tɜːbɪd] *adj* (*water*) trüb; (*air*)
schmutzig.
**turbine** ['tɜːbaɪn] *n* Turbine *f.*
**turbo** ['tɜːbəu] *n* Turbo *m*; **~ engine**
Turbomotor *m.*
**turbojet** [tɜːbəuˈdʒɛt] *n* Düsenflugzeug *nt.*
**turboprop** [tɜːbəuˈprɔp] *n* (*engine*) Turbo-
Prop-Turbine *f.*
**turbot** ['tɜːbət] *n inv* Steinbutt *m.*
**turbulence** ['tɜːbjuləns] *n* (*AVIAT*) Turbulenz
*f.*
**turbulent** ['tɜːbjulənt] *adj* (*water, seas*)
stürmisch; (*fig: career, period*) turbulent.
**tureen** [təˈriːn] *n* Terrine *f.*
**turf** [tɜːf] *n* (*grass*) Rasen *m*; (*clod*) Sode *f* ♦ *vt*
(*area*) mit Grassoden bedecken; **the T~**
(*horse-racing*) der Pferderennsport.
▶**turf out** (*inf*) *vt* (*person*) rausschmeißen.
**turf accountant** (*BRIT*) *n* Buchmacher *m.*
**turgid** ['tɜːdʒɪd] *adj* geschwollen.
**Turin** ['tjuəˈrɪn] *n* Turin *nt.*
**Turk** [tɜːk] *n* Türke *m*, Türkin *f.*
**Turkey** ['tɜːkɪ] *n* die Türkei *f.*
**turkey** ['tɜːkɪ] *n* (*bird*) Truthahn *m*, Truthenne
*f*; (*meat*) Puter *m.*
**Turkish** ['tɜːkɪʃ] *adj* türkisch ♦ *n* (*LING*)
Türkisch *nt.*
**Turkish bath** *n* türkisches Bad *nt.*
**Turkish delight** *n geleeartige Süßigkeit, mit
Puderzucker oder Schokolade überzogen.*
**turmeric** ['tɜːmərɪk] *n* Kurkuma *f.*
**turmoil** ['tɜːmɔɪl] *n* Aufruhr *m*; **in ~** in
Aufruhr.
**turn** [tɜːn] *n* (*change*) Wende *f*; (*in road*) Kurve
*f*; (*rotation*) Drehung *f*; (*performance*)
Nummer *f*; (*inf: MED*) Anfall *m* ♦ *vt* (*handle,
key*) drehen; (*collar, steak*) wenden; (*page*)
umblättern; (*shape: wood*) drechseln;
(*: metal*) drehen ♦ *vi* (*object*) sich drehen;
(*person*) sich umdrehen; (*change direction*)
abbiegen; (*milk*) sauer werden; **to do sb a
good ~** jdm einen guten Dienst erweisen; **a
~ of events** eine Wendung der Dinge; **it
gave me quite a ~** (*inf*) das hat mir einen
schönen Schrecken eingejagt; **"no left ~"**
(*AUT*) „Linksabbiegen verboten"; **it's your ~**
du bist dran; **in ~** der Reihe nach; **to take
~s (at)** sich abwechseln (bei); **at the ~ of
the century/year** zur Jahrhundertwende/
Jahreswende; **to take a ~ for the worse**
(*events*) sich zum Schlechten wenden; **his**

**health** or **he has taken a ~ for the worse** sein Befinden hat sich verschlechtert; **to ~ nasty/forty/grey** unangenehm/vierzig/grau werden.

►**turn against** vt fus sich wenden gegen.

►**turn around** vi sich umdrehen; (in car) wenden.

►**turn away** vi sich abwenden ♦ vt (applicants) abweisen; (business) zurückweisen.

►**turn back** vi umkehren ♦ vt (person, vehicle) zurückweisen.

►**turn down** vt (request) ablehnen; (heating) kleiner stellen; (radio etc) leiser stellen; (bedclothes) aufschlagen.

►**turn in** vi (inf: go to bed) sich hinhauen ♦ vt (to police) anzeigen; **to ~ o.s.** in sich stellen.

►**turn into** vt fus (change) sich verwandeln in +acc ♦ vt machen zu.

►**turn off** vi (from road) abbiegen ♦ vt (light, radio etc) ausmachen; (tap) zudrehen; (engine) abstellen.

►**turn on** vt (light, radio etc) anmachen; (tap) aufdrehen; (engine) anstellen.

►**turn out** vt (light) ausmachen; (gas) abstellen ♦ vi (appear, attend) erscheinen; **to ~ out to be** (prove to be) sich erweisen als; **to ~ out well/badly** (situation) gut/schlecht enden.

►**turn over** vi (person) sich umdrehen ♦ vt (object) umdrehen, wenden; (page) umblättern; **to ~ sth over to** (to sb) etw übertragen +dat; (to sth) etw verlagern zu.

►**turn round** vi sich umdrehen; (vehicle) wenden.

►**turn up** vi (person) erscheinen; (lost object) wieder auftauchen ♦ vt (collar) hochklappen; (heater) höher stellen; (radio etc) lauter stellen.

**turnabout** ['tə:nəbaut] n (fig) Kehrtwendung f.

**turnaround** ['tə:nəraund] n = **turnabout**.

**turncoat** ['tə:nkəut] n Überläufer(in) m(f).

**turned-up** ['tə:ndʌp] adj: ~ **nose** Stupsnase f.

**turning** ['tə:nɪŋ] n (in road) Abzweigung f; **the first ~ on the right** die erste Straße rechts.

**turning circle** (BRIT) n (AUT) Wendekreis m.

**turning point** n (fig) Wendepunkt m.

**turning radius** (US) n = **turning circle**.

**turnip** ['tə:nɪp] n Rübe f.

**turnout** ['tə:naut] n (of voters etc) Beteiligung f.

**turnover** ['tə:nəuvə*] n (COMM: amount of money) Umsatz m; (: of staff) Fluktuation f; (CULIN): **apple ~** Apfeltasche f; **there is a rapid ~ in staff** der Personalbestand wechselt ständig.

**turnpike** ['tə:npaɪk] (US) n gebührenpflichtige Autobahn f.

**turnstile** ['tə:nstaɪl] n Drehkreuz nt.

**turntable** ['tə:nteɪbl] n (on record player) Plattenteller m.

**turn-up** ['tə:nʌp] (BRIT) n (on trousers) Aufschlag m; **that's a ~ for the books!** (inf) das ist eine echte Überraschung!

**turpentine** ['tə:pəntaɪn] n (also: **turps**) Terpentin nt.

**turquoise** ['tə:kwɔɪz] n (stone) Türkis m ♦ adj (colour) türkis.

**turret** ['tʌrɪt] n Turm m.

**turtle** ['tə:tl] n Schildkröte f.

**turtleneck (sweater)** ['tə:tlnɛk(-)] n Pullover m mit rundem Kragen.

**Tuscan** ['tʌskən] adj toskanisch ♦ n (person) Toskaner(in) m(f).

**Tuscany** ['tʌskənɪ] n die Toskana.

**tusk** [tʌsk] n (of elephant) Stoßzahn m.

**tussle** ['tʌsl] n Gerangel nt.

**tutor** ['tju:tə*] n Tutor(in) m(f); (private tutor) Privatlehrer(in) m(f).

**tutorial** [tju:'tɔ:rɪəl] n Kolloquium nt.

**tuxedo** [tʌk'si:dəu] (US) n Smoking m.

**TV** [ti:'vi:] n abbr (= television) TV nt.

**TV dinner** n Fertiggericht nt.

**twaddle** ['twɔdl] (inf) n dummes Zeug nt.

**twang** [twæŋ] n (of instrument) singender Ton m; (of voice) näselnder Ton m ♦ vi einen singenden Ton von sich geben ♦ vt (guitar) zupfen.

**tweak** [twi:k] vt kneifen.

**tweed** [twi:d] n Tweed m ♦ adj (jacket, skirt) Tweed-.

**tweezers** ['twi:zəz] npl Pinzette f.

**twelfth** [twelfθ] num zwölfte(r, s) ♦ n Zwölftel nt.

**Twelfth Night** n ≈ Dreikönige nt.

**twelve** [twelv] num zwölf; **at ~** (o'clock) (midday) um zwölf Uhr (mittags); (midnight) um zwölf Uhr nachts.

**twentieth** ['twentɪɪθ] num zwanzigste(r, s).

**twenty** ['twentɪ] num zwanzig.

**twerp** [twə:p] (inf) n Schwachkopf m.

**twice** [twaɪs] adv zweimal; ~ **as much** zweimal soviel; ~ **a week** zweimal die Woche; **she is ~ your age** sie ist doppelt so alt wie du.

**twiddle** ['twɪdl] vt drehen an +dat ♦ vi: **to ~ (with)** herumdrehen (an +dat); **to ~ one's thumbs** (fig) Däumchen drehen.

**twig** [twɪg] n Zweig m ♦ vi, vt (BRIT: inf: realize) kapieren.

**twilight** ['twaɪlaɪt] n Dämmerung f; **in the ~** in der Dämmerung.

**twill** [twɪl] n (cloth) Köper m.

**twin** [twɪn] adj (sister, brother) Zwillings-; (towers) Doppel- ♦ n Zwilling m; (room in hotel etc) Zweibettzimmer nt ♦ vt (towns etc): **to be ~ned with ... ...** als Partnerstadt haben.

**twin-bedded room** ['twɪn'bɛdɪd-] n Zweibettzimmer nt.

**twin beds** npl zwei (gleiche) Einzelbetten pl.

**twin-carburettor** ['twɪnkɑ:bju'rɛtə*] adj Doppelvergaser-.

**twine** [twaɪn] *n* Bindfaden *m* ♦ *vi* sich winden.
**twin-engined** [twɪn'ɛndʒɪnd] *adj* zweimotorig.
**twinge** [twɪndʒ] *n* (*of pain*) Stechen *nt*; **a ~ of conscience** Gewissensbisse *pl*; **a ~ of fear/ guilt** ein Angst-/Schuldgefühl *nt*.
**twinkle** ['twɪŋkl] *vi* funkeln ♦ *n* Funkeln *nt*.
**twin town** *n* Partnerstadt *f*.
**twirl** [twəːl] *vt* herumwirbeln ♦ *vi* wirbeln ♦ *n* Wirbel *m*.
**twist** [twɪst] *n* (*action*) Drehung *f*; (*in road*) Kurve; (*in coil, flex*) Biegung *f*; (*in story*) Wendung *f* ♦ *vt* (*turn*) drehen; (*injure: ankle etc*) verrenken; (*twine*) wickeln; (*fig: meaning etc*) verdrehen ♦ *vi* (*road, river*) sich winden; **~ my arm!** (*inf*) überreden Sie mich einfach!
**twisted** ['twɪstɪd] *adj* (*wire, rope*) gedreht; (*ankle*) verrenkt; (*fig: logic, mind*) verdreht.
**twit** [twɪt] (*inf*) *n* Trottel *m*.
**twitch** [twɪtʃ] *n* (*jerky movement*) Zucken *nt* ♦ *vi* zucken.
**two** [tuː] *num* zwei; **~ by ~**, **in ~s** zu zweit; **to put ~ and ~ together** (*fig*) zwei und zwei zusammenzählen.
**two-bit** [tuː'bɪt] (*inf*) *adj* (*worthless*) mies.
**two-door** [tuː'dɔː] *adj* zweitürig.
**two-faced** [tuː'feɪst] (*pej*) *adj* scheinheilig.
**twofold** ['tuːfəʊld] *adv*: **to increase ~** um das Doppelte ansteigen ♦ *adj* (*increase*) um das Doppelte; (*aim, value etc*) zweifach.
**two-piece (suit)** ['tuːpiːs-] *n* Zweiteiler *m*.
**two-piece (swimsuit)** *n* zweiteiliger Badeanzug *m*.
**two-ply** ['tuːplaɪ] *adj* (*wool*) zweifädig; (*tissues*) zweilagig.
**two-seater** ['tuː'siːtə] *n* (*car*) Zweisitzer *m*.
**twosome** ['tuːsəm] *n* (*people*) Paar *nt*.
**two-stroke** ['tuːstrəʊk] *n* (*also:* **~ engine**) Zweitakter *m* ♦ *adj* (*engine*) Zweitakt-.
**two-tone** ['tuːtəʊn] *adj* (*in colour*) zweifarbig.
**two-way** ['tuːweɪ] *adj*: **~ traffic** Verkehr *m* in beiden Richtungen; **~ radio** Funksprechgerät *nt*.
**TX** (*US*) *abbr* (*POST:* = *Texas*).
**tycoon** [taɪ'kuːn] *n* Magnat *m*.
**type** [taɪp] *n* (*category, model, example*) Typ *m*; (*TYP*) Schrift *f* ♦ *vt* (*letter etc*) tippen, mit der Maschine schreiben; **a ~ of** eine Art von; **what ~ do you want?** welche Sorte möchten Sie?; **in bold/italic ~** in Fett-/ Kursivdruck.
**typecast** ['taɪpkɑːst] (*irreg: like* **cast**) *vt* (*actor*) (auf eine Rolle) festlegen.
**typeface** ['taɪpfeɪs] *n* Schrift *f*, Schriftbild *nt*.
**typescript** ['taɪpskrɪpt] *n* (*maschinen- geschriebenes*) Manuskript *nt*.
**typeset** ['taɪpsɛt] (*irreg: like* **set**) *vt* setzen.
**typesetter** ['taɪpsɛtə] *n* Setzer(in) *m(f)*.
**typewriter** ['taɪpraɪtə] *n* Schreibmaschine *f*.
**typewritten** ['taɪprɪtn] *adj* maschine(n)- geschrieben.
**typhoid** ['taɪfɔɪd] *n* Typhus *m*.

**typhoon** [taɪ'fuːn] *n* Taifun *m*.
**typhus** ['taɪfəs] *n* Fleckfieber *nt*.
**typical** ['tɪpɪkl] *adj* typisch; **~ (of)** typisch (für); **that's ~!** das ist typisch!
**typify** ['tɪpɪfaɪ] *vt* typisch sein für.
**typing** ['taɪpɪŋ] *n* Maschine(n)schreiben *nt*.
**typing error** *n* Tippfehler *m*.
**typing pool** *n* Schreibzentrale *f*.
**typist** ['taɪpɪst] *n* Schreibkraft *f*.
**typo** ['taɪpəʊ] (*inf*) *n abbr* (= *typographical error*) Druckfehler *m*.
**typography** [tɪ'pɒɡrəfɪ] *n* Typographie *f*.
**tyranny** ['tɪrənɪ] *n* Tyrannei *f*.
**tyrant** ['taɪərnt] *n* Tyrann(in) *m(f)*.
**tyre**, (*US*) **tire** ['taɪə] *n* Reifen *m*.
**tyre pressure** *n* Reifendruck *m*.
**Tyrol** [tɪ'rəʊl] *n* Tirol *nt*.
**Tyrolean** [tɪrə'liːən] *adj* Tiroler ♦ *n* (*person*) Tiroler(in) *m(f)*.
**Tyrolese** [tɪrə'liːz] = **Tyrolean**.
**Tyrrhenian Sea** [tɪ'riːnɪən-] *n*: **the ~** das Tyrrhenische Meer.
**tzar** [zɑː] *n* = **tsar**.

# U, u

**U¹, u** [juː] *n* (*letter*) U *nt*, u *nt*; **~ for Uncle** ≈ U wie Ulrich.
**U²** [juː] (*BRIT*) *n abbr* (*CINE:* = *universal*) *Klassifikation für jugendfreie Filme.*
**UAW** (*US*) *n abbr* (= *United Automobile Workers*) *Automobilarbeitergewerkschaft.*
**UB40** (*BRIT*) *n abbr* (= *unemployment benefit form 40*) Arbeitslosenausweis *m*.
**U-bend** ['juːbɛnd] *n* (*in pipe*) U-Krümmung *f*.
**ubiquitous** [juː'bɪkwɪtəs] *adj* allgegenwärtig.
**UCCA** ['ʌkə] (*BRIT*) *n abbr* (= *Universities Central Council on Admissions*) *akademische Zulassungsstelle,* ≈ ZVS *f*.
**UDA** (*BRIT*) *n abbr* (= *Ulster Defence Association*) *paramilitärische protestantische Organisation in Nordirland.*
**UDC** (*BRIT*) *n abbr* (= *Urban District Council*) Stadtverwaltung *f*.
**udder** ['ʌdə] *n* Euter *nt*.
**UDI** (*BRIT*) *n abbr* (*POL:* = *unilateral declaration of independence*) einseitige Unabhängig- keitserklärung *f*.
**UDR** (*BRIT*) *n abbr* (= *Ulster Defence Regiment*) *Regiment aus Teilzeitsoldaten zur Unterstützung der britischen Armee und Polizei in Nordirland.*
**UEFA** [juː'eɪfə] *n abbr* (= *Union of European Football Associations*) UEFA *f*.
**UFO** ['juːfəʊ] *n abbr* (= *unidentified flying object*)

Ufo nt.

**Uganda** [juːˈgændə] n Uganda nt.

**Ugandan** [juːˈgændən] adj ugandisch ♦ n Ugander(in) m(f).

**UGC** (BRIT) n abbr (= University Grants Committee) Ausschuß zur Verteilung von Geldern an Universitäten.

**ugh** [əːh] excl igitt.

**ugliness** [ˈʌglɪnɪs] n Häßlichkeit f.

**ugly** [ˈʌglɪ] adj häßlich; (nasty) schlimm.

**UHF** abbr (= ultrahigh frequency) UHF.

**UHT** abbr (= ultra heat treated): ~ **milk** H-Milch f.

**UK** n abbr = **United Kingdom**.

**Ukraine** [juːˈkreɪn] n Ukraine f.

**Ukrainian** [juːˈkreɪnɪən] adj ukrainisch ♦ n Ukrainer(in) m(f); (LING) Ukrainisch nt.

**ulcer** [ˈʌlsəˀ] n (stomach ulcer etc) Geschwür nt; (also: mouth ~) Abszeß m im Mund.

**Ulster** [ˈʌlstəˀ] n Ulster nt.

**ulterior** [ʌlˈtɪərɪəˀ] adj: ~ **motive** Hintergedanke m.

**ultimata** [ʌltɪˈmeɪtə] npl of **ultimatum.**

**ultimate** [ˈʌltɪmət] adj (final) letztendlich; (greatest) größte(r, s); (: deterrent) äußerste(r, s); (: authority) höchste(r, s) ♦ n: **the ~ in luxury** das Äußerste or Höchste an Luxus.

**ultimately** [ˈʌltɪmətlɪ] adv (in the end) schließlich, letzten Endes; (basically) im Grunde (genommen).

**ultimatum** [ʌltɪˈmeɪtəm] (pl ~s or **ultimata**) n Ultimatum nt.

**ultrasonic** [ʌltrəˈsɔnɪk] adj (sound) Ultraschall-.

**ultrasound** [ˈʌltrəsaund] n Ultraschall m.

**ultraviolet** [ˈʌltrəˈvaɪəlɪt] adj ultraviolett.

**umbilical cord** [ʌmˈbɪlɪkl-] n Nabelschnur f.

**umbrage** [ˈʌmbrɪdʒ] n: **to take ~ at** Anstoß nehmen an +dat.

**umbrella** [ʌmˈbrɛlə] n (for rain) (Regen)schirm m; (for sun) Sonnenschirm m; (fig): **under the ~ of** unter der Leitung von.

**umlaut** [ˈumlaut] n Umlaut m; (mark) Umlautzeichen nt.

**umpire** [ˈʌmpaɪəˀ] n Schiedsrichter(in) m(f) ♦ vt (game) als Schiedsrichter leiten.

**umpteen** [ʌmpˈtiːn] adj zig.

**umpteenth** [ʌmpˈtiːnθ] adj: **for the ~ time** zum x-ten Mal.

**UMWA** n abbr (= United Mineworkers of America) amerikanische Bergarbeitergewerkschaft.

**UN** n abbr (= United Nations) UNO f.

**unabashed** [ʌnəˈbæʃt] adj: **to be/seem ~** unbeeindruckt sein/scheinen.

**unabated** [ʌnəˈbeɪtɪd] adj unvermindert ♦ adv: **to continue ~** nicht nachlassen.

**unable** [ʌnˈeɪbl] adj: **to be ~ to do sth** etw nicht tun können.

**unabridged** [ʌnəˈbrɪdʒd] adj ungekürzt.

**unacceptable** [ʌnəkˈsɛptəbl] adj unannehmbar, nicht akzeptabel.

**unaccompanied** [ʌnəˈkʌmpənɪd] adj (child, song) ohne Begleitung; (luggage) unbegleitet.

**unaccountably** [ʌnəˈkauntəblɪ] adv unerklärlich.

**unaccounted** [ʌnəˈkauntɪd] adj: **to be ~ for** (passengers, money etc) (noch) fehlen.

**unaccustomed** [ʌnəˈkʌstəmd] adj: **to be ~ to** nicht gewöhnt sein an +acc.

**unacquainted** [ʌnəˈkweɪntɪd] adj: **to be ~ with** nicht vertraut sein mit.

**unadulterated** [ʌnəˈdʌltəreɪtɪd] adj rein.

**unaffected** [ʌnəˈfɛktɪd] adj (person, behaviour) natürlich, ungekünstelt; **to be ~ by sth** von etw nicht berührt werden.

**unafraid** [ʌnəˈfreɪd] adj: **to be ~** keine Angst haben.

**unaided** [ʌnˈeɪdɪd] adv ohne fremde Hilfe.

**unanimity** [juːnəˈnɪmɪtɪ] n Einstimmigkeit f.

**unanimous** [juːˈnænɪməs] adj einstimmig.

**unanimously** [juːˈnænɪməslɪ] adv einstimmig.

**unanswered** [ʌnˈɑːnsəd] adj unbeantwortet.

**unappetizing** [ʌnˈæpɪtaɪzɪŋ] adj (food) unappetitlich.

**unappreciative** [ʌnəˈpriːʃɪətɪv] adj (person) undankbar; (audience) verständnislos.

**unarmed** [ʌnˈɑːmd] adj unbewaffnet; ~ **combat** Nahkampf m ohne Waffen.

**unashamed** [ʌnəˈʃeɪmd] adj (pleasure, greed etc) unverhohlen.

**unassisted** [ʌnəˈsɪstɪd] adv ohne fremde Hilfe.

**unassuming** [ʌnəˈsjuːmɪŋ] adj bescheiden.

**unattached** [ʌnəˈtætʃt] adj (single: person) ungebunden; (unconnected) ohne Verbindung.

**unattended** [ʌnəˈtɛndɪd] adj (car, luggage, child) unbeaufsichtigt.

**unattractive** [ʌnəˈtræktɪv] adj unattraktiv.

**unauthorized** [ʌnˈɔːθəraɪzd] adj (visit, use) unbefugt; (version) nicht unautorisiert.

**unavailable** [ʌnəˈveɪləbl] adj (article, room) nicht verfügbar; (person) nicht zu erreichen; ~ **for comment** nicht zu sprechen.

**unavoidable** [ʌnəˈvɔɪdəbl] adj unvermeidlich.

**unavoidably** [ʌnəˈvɔɪdəblɪ] adv (delayed etc) auf unvermeidliche Weise.

**unaware** [ʌnəˈwɛəˀ] adj: **he was ~ of it** er war sich dat dessen nicht bewußt.

**unawares** [ʌnəˈwɛəz] adv (catch, take) unerwartet.

**unbalanced** [ʌnˈbælənst] adj (report) unausgewogen; (mentally) ~ geistig gestört.

**unbearable** [ʌnˈbɛərəbl] adj unerträglich.

**unbeatable** [ʌnˈbiːtəbl] adj unschlagbar.

**unbeaten** [ʌnˈbiːtn] adj ungeschlagen.

**unbecoming** [ʌnbɪˈkʌmɪŋ] adj (language, behaviour) unpassend; (garment) unvorteilhaft.

**unbeknown(st)** [ʌnbɪˈnəun(st)] adv: ~ **to me/**

**Peter** ohne mein/Peters Wissen.
**unbelief** [ʌnbɪ'liːf] *n* Ungläubigkeit *f*.
**unbelievable** [ʌnbɪ'liːvəbl] *adj* unglaublich.
**unbelievably** [ʌnbɪ'liːvəblɪ] *adv* unglaublich.
**unbend** [ʌn'bɛnd] (*irreg: like* bend) *vi* (*relax*) aus sich herausgehen ♦ *vt* (*wire etc*) geradebiegen.
**unbending** [ʌn'bɛndɪŋ] *adj* (*person, attitude*) unnachgiebig.
**unbias(s)ed** [ʌn'baɪəst] *adj* unvoreingenommen.
**unblemished** [ʌn'blɛmɪʃt] *adj* (*also fig*) makellos.
**unblock** [ʌn'blɔk] *vt* (*pipe*) frei machen.
**unborn** [ʌn'bɔːn] *adj* ungeboren.
**unbounded** [ʌn'baundɪd] *adj* grenzenlos.
**unbreakable** [ʌn'breɪkəbl] *adj* (*object*) unzerbrechlich.
**unbridled** [ʌn'braɪdld] *adj* ungezügelt.
**unbroken** [ʌn'brəukən] *adj* (*seal*) unversehrt; (*silence*) ununterbrochen; (*record, series*) ungebrochen.
**unbuckle** [ʌn'bʌkl] *vt* aufschnallen.
**unburden** [ʌn'bəːdn] *vt:* **to ~ o.s. (to sb)** (jdm) sein Herz ausschütten.
**unbusinesslike** [ʌn'bɪznɪslaɪk] *adj* ungeschäftsmäßig.
**unbutton** [ʌn'bʌtn] *vt* aufknöpfen.
**uncalled-for** [ʌn'kɔːldfɔː*] *adj* (*remark etc*) unnötig.
**uncanny** [ʌn'kænɪ] *adj* unheimlich.
**unceasing** [ʌn'siːsɪŋ] *adj* (*search, flow etc*) unaufhörlich; (*loyalty*) unermüdlich.
**unceremonious** [ʌnsɛrɪ'məunɪəs] *adj* (*abrupt, rude*) brüsk, barsch.
**uncertain** [ʌn'səːtn] *adj* (*person*) unsicher; (*future, outcome*) ungewiß; **to be ~ about sth** unsicher über etw *acc* sein; **in no ~ terms** unzweideutig.
**uncertainty** [ʌn'səːtntɪ] *n* Ungewißheit *f*; **uncertainties** *npl* (*doubts*) Unsicherheiten *pl.*
**unchallenged** [ʌn'tʃælɪndʒd] *adj* unbestritten ♦ *adv* (*walk, enter*) ungehindert; **to go ~** unangefochten bleiben.
**unchanged** [ʌn'tʃeɪndʒd] *adj* unverändert.
**uncharitable** [ʌn'tʃærɪtəbl] *adj* (*remark, behaviour etc*) unfreundlich.
**uncharted** [ʌn'tʃɑːtɪd] *adj* (*land, sea*) unverzeichnet.
**unchecked** [ʌn'tʃɛkt] *adv* (*grow, continue*) ungehindert.
**uncivil** [ʌn'sɪvɪl] *adj* (*person*) grob.
**uncivilized** [ʌn'sɪvɪlaɪzd] *adj* unzivilisiert.
**uncle** ['ʌŋkl] *n* Onkel *m.*
**unclear** [ʌn'klɪə*] *adj* unklar; **I'm still ~ about what I'm supposed to do** mir ist immer noch nicht klar, was ich tun soll.
**uncoil** [ʌn'kɔɪl] *vt* (*rope, wire*) abwickeln ♦ *vi* (*snake*) sich strecken.
**uncomfortable** [ʌn'kʌmfətəbl] *adj* (*person, chair*) unbequem; (*room*) ungemütlich; (*nervous*) unbehaglich; (*unpleasant: situation,*

*fact*) unerfreulich.
**uncomfortably** [ʌn'kʌmfətəblɪ] *adv* (*sit*) unbequem; (*smile*) unbehaglich.
**uncommitted** [ʌnkə'mɪtɪd] *adj* nicht engagiert; **~ to** nicht festgelegt auf +*acc.*
**uncommon** [ʌn'kɔmən] *adj* ungewöhnlich.
**uncommunicative** [ʌnkə'mjuːnɪkətɪv] *adj* (*person*) schweigsam.
**uncomplicated** [ʌn'kɔmplɪkeɪtɪd] *adj* unkompliziert.
**uncompromising** [ʌn'kɔmprəmaɪzɪŋ] *adj* (*person, belief*) kompromißlos.
**unconcerned** [ʌnkən'səːnd] *adj* (*person*) unbekümmert; **to be ~ about sth** sich nicht um etw kümmern.
**unconditional** [ʌnkən'dɪʃənl] *adj* bedingungslos; (*acceptance*) vorbehaltlos.
**uncongenial** [ʌnkən'dʒiːnɪəl] *adj* (*surroundings*) unangenehm.
**unconnected** [ʌnkə'nɛktɪd] *adj* (*unrelated*) ohne Verbindung; **to be ~ with sth** nicht mit etw in Beziehung stehen.
**unconscious** [ʌn'kɔnʃəs] *adj* (*in faint*) bewußtlos; (*unaware*): **~ of** nicht bewußt +*gen* ♦ *n:* **the ~** das Unbewußte; **to knock sb ~** jdn bewußtlos schlagen.
**unconsciously** [ʌn'kɔnʃəslɪ] *adv* unbewußt.
**unconsciousness** [ʌn'kɔnʃəsnɪs] *n* Bewußtlosigkeit *f.*
**unconstitutional** ['ʌnkɔnstɪ'tjuːʃənl] *adj* verfassungswidrig.
**uncontested** [ʌnkən'tɛstɪd] *adj* (*POL: seat, election*) ohne Gegenkandidat; (*divorce*) ohne Einwände der Gegenseite.
**uncontrollable** [ʌnkən'trəuləbl] *adj* unkontrollierbar; (*laughter*) unbändig.
**uncontrolled** [ʌnkən'trəuld] *adj* (*behaviour*) ungezähmt; (*price rises etc*) ungehindert.
**unconventional** [ʌnkən'vɛnʃənl] *adj* unkonventionell.
**unconvinced** [ʌnkən'vɪnst] *adj:* **to be/remain ~** nicht überzeugt sein/bleiben.
**unconvincing** [ʌnkən'vɪnsɪŋ] *adj* nicht überzeugend.
**uncork** [ʌn'kɔːk] *vt* (*bottle*) entkorken.
**uncorroborated** [ʌnkə'rɔbəreɪtɪd] *adj* (*evidence*) unbestätigt.
**uncouth** [ʌn'kuːθ] *adj* (*person, behaviour*) ungehobelt.
**uncover** [ʌn'kʌvə*] *vt* aufdecken.
**unctuous** ['ʌŋktjuəs] (*form*) *adj* (*person, behaviour*) salbungsvoll.
**undamaged** [ʌn'dæmɪdʒd] *adj* unbeschädigt.
**undaunted** [ʌn'dɔːntɪd] *adj* (*person*) unverzagt; **~, she struggled on** sie kämpfte unverzagt weiter.
**undecided** [ʌndɪ'saɪdɪd] *adj* (*person*) unentschlossen; (*question*) unentschieden.
**undelivered** [ʌndɪ'lɪvəd] *adj* (*goods*) nicht geliefert; (*letters*) nicht zugestellt; **if ~ return to sender** (*on envelope*) falls unzustellbar, zurück an Absender.

**undeniable** [ʌndɪ'naɪəbl] *adj* unbestreitbar.
**undeniably** [ʌndɪ'naɪəblɪ] *adv* (*true*) zweifellos; (*handsome*) unbestreitbar.
**under** ['ʌndə*] *prep* (*position*) unter +*dat*; (*motion*) unter +*acc*; (*according to: law etc*) nach, gemäß +*dat* ♦ *adv* (*go, fly etc*) darunter; **to come from ~ sth** unter etw *dat* hervorkommen; **~ there** darunter; **in ~ 2 hours** in weniger als 2 Stunden; **~ anaesthetic** unter Narkose; **to be ~ discussion** diskutiert werden; **~ repair** in Reparatur; **~ the circumstances** unter den Umständen.
**under...** ['ʌndə*] *pref* Unter-, unter-.
**underage** [ʌndər'eɪdʒ] *adj* (*person*) minderjährig; **~ drinking** Alkoholgenuß durch Minderjährige.
**underarm** ['ʌndərɑːm] *adv* (*bowl, throw*) von unten ♦ *adj* (*throw, shot*) von unten; (*deodorant*) Achselhöhlen-.
**undercapitalized** ['ʌndə'kæpɪtəlaɪzd] *adj* unterkapitalisiert.
**undercarriage** ['ʌndəkærɪdʒ] *n* (*AVIAT*) Fahrgestell *nt*.
**undercharge** [ʌndə'tʃɑːdʒ] *vt* zu wenig berechnen +*dat*.
**underclass** ['ʌndəklɑːs] *n* Unterklasse *f*.
**underclothes** ['ʌndəkləuðz] *npl* Unterwäsche *f*.
**undercoat** ['ʌndəkəut] *n* (*paint*) Grundierung *f*.
**undercover** [ʌndə'kʌvə*] *adj* (*duty, agent*) Geheim- ♦ *adv* (*work*) insgeheim.
**undercurrent** ['ʌndəkʌrnt] *n* (*also fig*) Unterströmung *f*.
**undercut** [ʌndə'kʌt] (*irreg: like cut*) *vt* (*person, prices*) unterbieten.
**underdeveloped** ['ʌndədɪ'vɛləpt] *adj* unterentwickelt.
**underdog** ['ʌndədɒg] *n*: **the ~** der/die Benachteiligte.
**underdone** [ʌndə'dʌn] *adj* (*food*) nicht gar; (: *meat*) nicht durchgebraten.
**underemployment** ['ʌndərɪm'plɔɪmənt] *n* Unterbeschäftigung *f*.
**underestimate** ['ʌndər'ɛstɪmeɪt] *vt* unterschätzen.
**underexposed** ['ʌndərɪks'pəuzd] *adj* (*PHOT*) unterbelichtet.
**underfed** [ʌndə'fɛd] *adj* unterernährt.
**underfoot** [ʌndə'fut] *adv*: **to crush sth ~** etw am Boden zerdrücken; **to trample sth ~** auf etw *dat* herumtrampeln.
**underfunded** ['ʌndə'fʌndɪd] *adj* unterfinanziert.
**undergo** [ʌndə'gəu] (*irreg: like go*) *vt* (*change*) durchmachen; (*test, operation*) sich unterziehen; **the car is ~ing repairs** das Auto wird gerade repariert.
**undergraduate** [ʌndə'grædjuɪt] *n* Student(in) *m(f)* ♦ *cpd*: **~ courses** Kurse *pl* für nichtgraduierte Studenten.

**underground** ['ʌndəgraund] *adj* unterirdisch; (*POL: newspaper, activities*) Untergrund- ♦ *adv* (*work*) unterirdisch; (: *miners*) unter Tage; (*POL*): **to go ~** untertauchen ♦ *n*: **the ~** (*BRIT*) die U-Bahn; (*POL*) die Untergrundbewegung; **~ car park** Tiefgarage *f*.
**undergrowth** ['ʌndəgrəuθ] *n* Unterholz *nt*.
**underhand(ed)** [ʌndə'hænd(ɪd)] *adj* (*fig: behaviour, person*) hinterhältig.
**underinsured** [ʌndərɪn'ʃuəd] *adj* unterversichert.
**underlay** [ʌndə'leɪ] *n* Unterlage *f*.
**underlie** [ʌndə'laɪ] (*irreg: like lie*) *vt* (*fig: be basis of*) zugrunde liegen +*dat*; **the underlying cause** der eigentliche Grund.
**underline** [ʌndə'laɪn] *vt* unterstreichen; (*fig: emphasize*) betonen.
**underling** ['ʌndəlɪŋ] (*pej*) *n* Befehlsempfänger(in) *m(f)*.
**undermanning** [ʌndə'mænɪŋ] *n* Personalmangel *m*.
**undermentioned** [ʌndə'mɛnʃənd] *adj* untengenannt.
**undermine** [ʌndə'maɪn] *vt* unterminieren, unterhöhlen.
**underneath** [ʌndə'niːθ] *adv* darunter ♦ *prep* (*position*) unter +*dat*; (*motion*) unter +*acc*.
**undernourished** [ʌndə'nʌrɪʃt] *adj* unterernährt.
**underpaid** [ʌndə'peɪd] *adj* unterbezahlt.
**underpants** ['ʌndəpænts] *npl* Unterhose *f*.
**underpass** ['ʌndəpɑːs] (*BRIT*) *n* Unterführung *f*.
**underpin** [ʌndə'pɪn] *vt* (*argument*) untermauern.
**underplay** [ʌndə'pleɪ] (*BRIT*) *vt* herunterspielen.
**underpopulated** [ʌndə'pɒpjuleɪtɪd] *adj* unterbevölkert.
**underprice** [ʌndə'praɪs] *vt* (*goods*) zu billig anbieten.
**underprivileged** [ʌndə'prɪvɪlɪdʒd] *adj* unterprivilegiert.
**underrate** [ʌndə'reɪt] *vt* unterschätzen.
**underscore** [ʌndə'skɔː*] *vt* unterstreichen.
**underseal** [ʌndə'siːl] (*BRIT*) *vt* (*car*) mit Unterbodenschutz versehen ♦ *n* (*of car*) Unterbodenschutz *m*.
**undersecretary** ['ʌndə'sɛkrətərɪ] *n* (*POL*) Staatssekretär(in) *m(f)*.
**undersell** [ʌndə'sɛl] (*irreg: like sell*) *vt* (*competitors*) unterbieten.
**undershirt** ['ʌndəʃəːt] (*US*) *n* Unterhemd *nt*.
**undershorts** ['ʌndəʃɔːts] (*US*) *npl* Unterhose *f*.
**underside** ['ʌndəsaɪd] *n* Unterseite *f*.
**undersigned** ['ʌndə'saɪnd] *adj* unterzeichnet ♦ *n*: **the ~** der/die Unterzeichnete; **we the ~ agree that ...** wir, die Unterzeichneten, kommen überein, daß ...
**underskirt** ['ʌndəskəːt] (*BRIT*) *n* Unterrock *m*.
**understaffed** [ʌndə'stɑːft] *adj* unterbesetzt.

**understand** [ʌndə'stænd] (*irreg: like* stand) *vt, vi* verstehen; **I ~ (that) you have ...** (*believe*) soweit ich weiß, haben Sie ...; **to make o.s. understood** sich verständlich machen.

**understandable** [ʌndə'stændəbl] *adj* verständlich.

**understanding** [ʌndə'stændɪŋ] *adj* verständnisvoll ♦ *n* Verständnis *nt*; **to come to an ~ with sb** mit jdm übereinkommen; **on the ~ that ...** unter der Voraussetzung, daß ...

**understate** [ʌndə'steɪt] *vt* herunterspielen.

**understatement** ['ʌndəsteɪtmənt] *n* Understatement *nt*, Untertreibung *f*; **that's an ~!** das ist untertrieben!

**understood** [ʌndə'stud] *pt, pp of* **understand** ♦ *adj* (*agreed*) abgemacht; (*implied*) impliziert.

**understudy** ['ʌndəstʌdɪ] *n* zweite Besetzung *f*.

**undertake** [ʌndə'teɪk] (*irreg: like* take) *vt* (*task*) übernehmen ♦ *vi*: **to ~ to do sth** es übernehmen, etw zu tun.

**undertaker** ['ʌndəteɪkə•] *n* (Leichen)bestatter *m*.

**undertaking** ['ʌndəteɪkɪŋ] *n* (*job*) Unternehmen *nt*; (*promise*) Zusicherung *f*.

**undertone** ['ʌndətəun] *n* (*of criticism etc*) Unterton *m*; **in an ~** mit gedämpfter Stimme.

**undervalue** [ʌndə'vælju:] *vt* (*person, work etc*) unterbewerten.

**underwater** ['ʌndə'wɔːtə•] *adv* (*swim etc*) unter Wasser ♦ *adj* (*exploration, camera etc*) Unterwasser-.

**underwear** ['ʌndəwɛə•] *n* Unterwäsche *f*.

**underweight** [ʌndə'weɪt] *adj*: **to be ~** Untergewicht haben.

**underworld** ['ʌndəwɜːld] *n* Unterwelt *f*.

**underwrite** [ʌndə'raɪt] *vt* (*FIN*) garantieren; (*INSURANCE*) versichern.

**underwriter** ['ʌndəraɪtə•] *n* (*INSURANCE*) Versicherer(in) *m(f)*.

**undeserved** [ʌndɪ'zɜːvd] *adj* unverdient.

**undesirable** [ʌndɪ'zaɪərəbl] *adj* unerwünscht.

**undeveloped** [ʌndɪ'vɛləpt] *adj* (*land*) unentwickelt; (*resources*) ungenutzt.

**undies** ['ʌndɪz] (*inf*) *npl* Unterwäsche *f*.

**undiluted** ['ʌndaɪ'luːtɪd] *adj* (*substance*) unverdünnt; (*emotion*) unverfälscht.

**undiplomatic** ['ʌndɪplə'mætɪk] *adj* undiplomatisch.

**undischarged** ['ʌndɪs'tʃɑːdʒd] *adj*: **~ bankrupt** nicht entlasteter Konkursschuldner *m*, nicht entlastete Konkursschuldnerin *f*.

**undisciplined** [ʌn'dɪsɪplɪnd] *adj* undiszipliniert.

**undiscovered** ['ʌndɪs'kʌvəd] *adj* unentdeckt.

**undisguised** ['ʌndɪs'gaɪzd] *adj* (*dislike, amusement etc*) unverhohlen.

**undisputed** ['ʌndɪs'pjuːtɪd] *adj* unbestritten.

**undistinguished** ['ʌndɪs'tɪŋgwɪʃt] *adj* (*career, person*) mittelmäßig; (*appearance*) durchschnittlich.

**undisturbed** [ʌndɪs'tɜːbd] *adj* ungestört; **to leave sth ~** etw unberührt lassen.

**undivided** [ʌndɪ'vaɪdɪd] *adj*: **you have my ~ attention** Sie haben meine ungeteilte Aufmerksamkeit.

**undo** [ʌn'duː] (*irreg: like* do) *vt* (*unfasten*) aufmachen; (*spoil*) zunichte machen.

**undoing** [ʌn'duːɪŋ] *n* Verderben *nt*.

**undone** [ʌn'dʌn] *pp of* **undo** ♦ *adj*: **to come ~** (*shoelaces etc*) aufgehen.

**undoubted** [ʌn'dautɪd] *adj* unzweifelhaft.

**undoubtedly** [ʌn'dautɪdlɪ] *adv* zweifellos.

**undress** [ʌn'drɛs] *vi* sich ausziehen ♦ *vt* ausziehen.

**undrinkable** [ʌn'drɪŋkəbl] *adj* (*unpalatable*) ungenießbar; (*poisonous*) nicht trinkbar.

**undue** [ʌn'djuː] *adj* (*excessive*) übertrieben.

**undulating** ['ʌndjuleɪtɪŋ] *adj* (*movement*) Wellen-; (*hills*) sanft.

**unduly** [ʌn'djuːlɪ] *adv* (*excessively*) übermäßig.

**undying** [ʌn'daɪɪŋ] *adj* (*love, loyalty etc*) ewig.

**unearned** [ʌn'ɜːnd] *adj* (*praise*) unverdient; **~ income** Kapitaleinkommen *nt*.

**unearth** [ʌn'ɜːθ] *vt* (*skeleton etc*) ausgraben; (*fig: secrets etc*) ausfindig machen.

**unearthly** [ʌn'ɜːθlɪ] *adj* (*eerie*) unheimlich; **at some ~ hour** zu nachtschlafender Zeit.

**unease** [ʌn'iːz] *n* Unbehagen *nt*.

**uneasy** [ʌn'iːzɪ] *adj* (*person*) unruhig; (*feeling*) unbehaglich; (*peace, truce*) unsicher; **to feel ~ about doing sth** ein ungutes Gefühl dabei haben, etw zu tun.

**uneconomic** ['ʌniːkə'nɔmɪk] *adj* unwirtschaftlich.

**uneconomical** ['ʌniːkə'nɔmɪkl] *adj* unwirtschaftlich.

**uneducated** [ʌn'ɛdjukeɪtɪd] *adj* ungebildet.

**unemployed** [ʌnɪm'plɔɪd] *adj* arbeitslos ♦ *npl*: **the ~** die Arbeitslosen *pl*.

**unemployment** [ʌnɪm'plɔɪmənt] *n* Arbeitslosigkeit *f*.

**unemployment benefit** (*BRIT*) *n* Arbeitslosenunterstützung *f*.

**unemployment compensation** (*US*) *n* = **unemployment benefit**.

**unending** [ʌn'ɛndɪŋ] *adj* endlos.

**unenviable** [ʌn'ɛnvɪəbl] *adj* (*task, conditions etc*) wenig beneidenswert.

**unequal** [ʌn'iːkwəl] *adj* ungleich; **to feel ~ to** sich nicht gewachsen fühlen +*dat*.

**unequalled**, (*US*) **unequaled** [ʌn'iːkwəld] *adj* unübertroffen.

**unequivocal** [ʌnɪ'kwɪvəkl] *adj* (*answer*) unzweideutig; **to be ~ about sth** eine klare Haltung zu etw haben.

**unerring** [ʌn'ɜːrɪŋ] *adj* unfehlbar.

**UNESCO** [juː'nɛskəu] *n abbr* (= *United Nations Educational, Scientific and Cultural Organization*) UNESCO *f*.

**unethical** [ʌn'ɛθɪkl] *adj* (*methods*) unlauter; (*doctor's behaviour*) unethisch.

**uneven** [ʌn'iːvn] *adj* (*teeth, road etc*) uneben; (*performance*) ungleichmäßig.

**uneventful** [ʌnɪ'vɛntfl] *adj* ereignislos.

**unexceptional** [ʌnɪk'sɛpʃənl] *adj* durchschnittlich.

**unexciting** [ʌnɪk'saɪtɪŋ] *adj* (*film, news*) wenig aufregend.

**unexpected** [ʌnɪks'pɛktɪd] *adj* unerwartet.

**unexpectedly** [ʌnɪks'pɛktɪdlɪ] *adv* unerwartet.

**unexplained** [ʌnɪks'pleɪnd] *adj* (*mystery, failure*) ungeklärt.

**unexploded** [ʌnɪks'pləʊdɪd] *adj* nicht explodiert.

**unfailing** [ʌn'feɪlɪŋ] *adj* (*support, energy*) unerschöpflich.

**unfair** [ʌn'fɛə*] *adj* unfair, ungerecht; (*advantage*) ungerechtfertigt; ~ **to** unfair *or* ungerecht zu.

**unfair dismissal** *n* ungerechtfertigte Entlassung *f*.

**unfairly** [ʌn'fɛəlɪ] *adv* (*treat*) unfair, ungerecht; (*dismiss*) ungerechtfertigt.

**unfaithful** [ʌn'feɪθful] *adj* (*lover, spouse*) untreu.

**unfamiliar** [ʌnfə'mɪlɪə*] *adj* ungewohnt; (*person*) fremd; **to be ~ with sth** mit etw nicht vertraut sein.

**unfashionable** [ʌn'fæʃnəbl] *adj* (*clothes, ideas*) unmodern; (*place*) unbeliebt.

**unfasten** [ʌn'fɑːsn] *vt* (*seat belt, strap*) lösen.

**unfathomable** [ʌn'fæðəməbl] *adj* unergründlich.

**unfavourable**, (*US*) **unfavorable** [ʌn'feɪvrəbl] *adj* (*circumstances, weather*) ungünstig; (*opinion, report*) negativ.

**unfavourably**, (*US*) **unfavorably** [ʌn'feɪvrəblɪ] *adv*: **to compare ~ (with sth)** im Vergleich (mit etw) ungünstig sein; **to compare ~ (with sb)** im Vergleich (mit jdm) schlechter abschneiden; **to look ~ on** (*suggestion etc*) ablehnend gegenüberstehen +*dat*.

**unfeeling** [ʌn'fiːlɪŋ] *adj* gefühllos.

**unfinished** [ʌn'fɪnɪʃt] *adj* unvollendet.

**unfit** [ʌn'fɪt] *adj* (*physically*) nicht fit; (*incompetent*) unfähig; ~ **for work** arbeitsunfähig; ~ **for human consumption** zum Verzehr ungeeignet.

**unflagging** [ʌn'flægɪŋ] *adj* (*attention, energy*) unermüdlich.

**unflappable** [ʌn'flæpəbl] *adj* unerschütterlich.

**unflattering** [ʌn'flætərɪŋ] *adj* (*dress, hairstyle*) unvorteilhaft; (*remark*) wenig schmeichelhaft.

**unflinching** [ʌn'flɪntʃɪŋ] *adj* unerschrocken.

**unfold** [ʌn'fəʊld] *vt* (*sheets, map*) auseinanderfalten ♦ *vi* (*situation, story*) sich entfalten.

**unforeseeable** [ʌnfɔː'siːəbl] *adj* unvorhersehbar.

**unforeseen** ['ʌnfɔː'siːn] *adj* unvorhergesehen.

**unforgettable** [ʌnfə'gɛtəbl] *adj* unvergeßlich.

**unforgivable** [ʌnfə'gɪvəbl] *adj* unverzeihlich.

**unformatted** [ʌn'fɔːmætɪd] *adj* (*disk, text*) unformatiert.

**unfortunate** [ʌn'fɔːtʃənət] *adj* (*unlucky*) unglücklich; (*regrettable*) bedauerlich; **it is ~ that** ... es ist bedauerlich, daß ...

**unfortunately** [ʌn'fɔːtʃənətlɪ] *adv* leider.

**unfounded** [ʌn'faʊndɪd] *adj* (*allegations, fears*) unbegründet.

**unfriendly** [ʌn'frɛndlɪ] *adj* unfreundlich.

**unfulfilled** [ʌnful'fɪld] *adj* (*ambition, prophecy*) unerfüllt; (*person*) unausgefüllt.

**unfurl** [ʌn'fəːl] *vt* (*flag etc*) entrollen.

**unfurnished** [ʌn'fəːnɪʃt] *adj* unmöbliert.

**ungainly** [ʌn'geɪnlɪ] *adj* (*person*) unbeholfen.

**ungodly** [ʌn'gɒdlɪ] *adj* (*annoying*) heillos; **at some ~ hour** zu nachtschlafender Zeit.

**ungrateful** [ʌn'greɪtful] *adj* undankbar.

**unguarded** [ʌn'gɑːdɪd] *adj*: **in an ~ moment** in einem unbedachten Augenblick.

**unhappily** [ʌn'hæpɪlɪ] *adv* (*miserably*) unglücklich; (*unfortunately*) leider.

**unhappiness** [ʌn'hæpɪnɪs] *n* Traurigkeit *f*.

**unhappy** [ʌn'hæpɪ] *adj* unglücklich; ~ **about/with** (*dissatisfied*) unzufrieden über +*acc*/mit.

**unharmed** [ʌn'hɑːmd] *adj* (*person, animal*) unversehrt.

**UNHCR** *n abbr* (= *United Nations High Commission for Refugees*) *Flüchtlingskommission der Vereinten Nationen.*

**unhealthy** [ʌn'hɛlθɪ] *adj* (*person*) nicht gesund; (*place*) ungesund; (*fig: interest*) krankhaft.

**unheard-of** [ʌn'həːdɒv] *adj* (*unknown*) unbekannt; (*outrageous*) unerhört.

**unhelpful** [ʌn'hɛlpful] *adj* (*person*) nicht hilfreich; (*advice*) nutzlos.

**unhesitating** [ʌn'hɛzɪteɪtɪŋ] *adj* (*loyalty*) bereitwillig; (*reply, offer*) prompt.

**unholy** [ʌn'həʊlɪ] *adj* (*inf*) *adj* (*fig: alliance*) übel; (: *mess*) heillos; (: *row*) furchtbar.

**unhook** [ʌn'huk] *vt* (*unfasten*) losmachen.

**unhurt** [ʌn'həːt] *adj* unverletzt.

**unhygienic** ['ʌnhaɪ'dʒiːnɪk] *adj* unhygienisch.

**UNICEF** ['juːnɪsɛf] *n abbr* (= *United Nations International Children's Emergency Fund*) UNICEF *f*.

**unicorn** ['juːnɪkɔːn] *n* Einhorn *nt*.

**unidentified** [ʌnaɪ'dɛntɪfaɪd] *adj* (*unknown*) unbekannt; (*unnamed*) ungenannt; *see also* **UFO.**

**unification** [juːnɪfɪ'keɪʃən] *n* Vereinigung *f*.

**uniform** ['juːnɪfɔːm] *n* Uniform *f* ♦ *adj* (*length, width etc*) einheitlich.

**uniformity** [juːnɪ'fɔːmɪtɪ] *n* Einheitlichkeit *f*.

**unify** ['juːnɪfaɪ] *vt* vereinigen.

**unilateral** [juːnɪ'lætərəl] *adj* einseitig.

**unimaginable** [ʌnɪ'mædʒɪnəbl] *adj* unvorstellbar.

**unimaginative** [ʌnɪ'mædʒɪnətɪv] *adj* phantasielos.

**unimpaired** [ʌnɪm'pɛəd] *adj* unbeeinträchtigt.

**unimportant** [ʌnɪm'pɔːtənt] *adj* unwichtig.

**unimpressed** [ʌnɪm'prɛst] *adj* unbeeindruckt.

**uninhabited** [ʌnɪn'hæbɪtɪd] *adj* unbewohnt.

**uninhibited** [ʌnɪn'hɪbɪtɪd] *adj* (*person*) ohne Hemmungen; (*behaviour*) hemmungslos.

**uninjured** [ʌn'ɪndʒəd] *adj* unverletzt.

**uninspiring** [ʌnɪn'spaɪərɪŋ] *adj* wenig aufregend; (*person*) trocken, nüchtern.

**unintelligent** [ʌnɪn'tɛlɪdʒənt] *adj* unintelligent.

**unintentional** [ʌnɪn'tɛnʃənəl] *adj* unbeabsichtigt.

**unintentionally** [ʌnɪn'tɛnʃnəlɪ] *adv* unabsichtlich.

**uninvited** [ʌnɪn'vaɪtɪd] *adj* (*guest*) ungeladen.

**uninviting** [ʌnɪn'vaɪtɪŋ] *adj* (*food*) unappetitlich; (*place*) wenig einladend.

**union** ['juːnjən] *n* (*unification*) Vereinigung *f*; (*also:* **trade** ~) Gewerkschaft *f* ♦ *cpd* (*activities, leader etc*) Gewerkschafts-; **the U~** (*US*) die Vereinigten Staaten.

**unionize** ['juːnjənaɪz] *vt* (*employees*) gewerkschaftlich organisieren.

**Union Jack** *n* Union Jack *m*.

**union shop** *n* gewerkschaftspflichtiger Betrieb *m*.

**unique** [juː'niːk] *adj* (*object etc*) einmalig; (*ability, skill*) einzigartig; **to be ~ to** charakteristisch sein für.

**unisex** ['juːnɪsɛks] *adj* (*clothes*) Unisex-; (*hairdresser*) für Damen und Herren.

**UNISON** ['juːnɪsn] *n Gewerkschaft der Angestellten im öffentlichen Dienst.*

**unison** ['juːnɪsn] *n:* **in ~** (*say, sing*) einstimmig; (*act*) in Übereinstimmung.

**unit** ['juːnɪt] *n* Einheit *f*; **production ~** Produktionsabteilung *f*; **kitchen ~** Küchen-Einbauelement *nt*.

**unitary** ['juːnɪtrɪ] *adj* (*state, system etc*) einheitlich.

**unit cost** *n* (*COMM*) Stückkosten *pl*.

**unite** [juː'naɪt] *vt* vereinigen ♦ *vi* sich zusammenschließen.

**united** [juː'naɪtɪd] *adj* (*agreed*) einig; (*country, party*) vereinigt.

**United Arab Emirates** *npl:* **the ~** die Vereinigten Arabischen Emirate *pl*.

**United Kingdom** *n:* **the ~** das Vereinigte Königreich.

**United Nations** *npl:* **the ~** die Vereinten Nationen *pl*.

**United States (of America)** *n:* **the ~** die Vereinigten Staaten *pl* (von Amerika).

**unit price** *n* (*COMM*) Einzelpreis *m*.

**unit trust** (*BRIT*) *n* (*COMM*) Investmenttrust *m*.

**unity** ['juːnɪtɪ] *n* Einheit *f*.

**Univ.** *abbr* = **university**.

**universal** [juːnɪ'vəːsl] *adj* allgemein.

**universe** ['juːnɪvəːs] *n* Universum *nt*.

**university** [juːnɪ'vəːsɪtɪ] *n* Universität *f* ♦ *cpd*

(*student, professor*) Universitäts-; (*education, year*) akademisch.

**university degree** *n* Universitätsabschluß *m*.

**unjust** [ʌn'dʒʌst] *adj* ungerecht; (*society*) unfair.

**unjustifiable** ['ʌndʒʌstɪ'faɪəbl] *adj* nicht zu rechtfertigen.

**unjustified** [ʌn'dʒʌstɪfaɪd] *adj* (*belief, action*) ungerechtfertigt; (*text*) nicht bündig.

**unkempt** [ʌn'kɛmpt] *adj* ungepflegt.

**unkind** [ʌn'kaɪnd] *adj* (*person, comment etc*) unfreundlich.

**unkindly** [ʌn'kaɪndlɪ] *adv* unfreundlich.

**unknown** [ʌn'nəʊn] *adj* unbekannt; **~ to me,** ... ohne daß ich es wußte, ...; **~ quantity** (*fig*) unbekannte Größe.

**unladen** [ʌn'leɪdn] *adj* (*ship*) ohne Ladung; (*weight*) Leer-.

**unlawful** [ʌn'lɔːful] *adj* gesetzwidrig.

**unleaded** ['ʌn'lɛdɪd] *adj* (*petrol*) bleifrei, unverbleit; **I use ~** ich fahre bleifrei.

**unleash** [ʌn'liːʃ] *vt* (*fig: feeling, forces etc*) entfesseln.

**unleavened** [ʌn'lɛvnd] *adj* (*bread*) ungesäuert.

**unless** [ʌn'lɛs] *conj* es sei denn; **~ he comes** wenn er nicht kommt; **~ otherwise stated** wenn nicht anders angegeben; **~ I am mistaken** wenn ich mich nicht irre; **there will be a strike ~** ... es wird zum Streik kommen, es sei denn, ...

**unlicensed** [ʌn'laɪsnst] (*BRIT*) *adj* (*restaurant*) ohne Schankkonzession.

**unlike** [ʌn'laɪk] *adj* (*not alike*) unähnlich ♦ *prep* (*different from*) verschieden von; **~ me, she is very tidy** im Gegensatz zu mir ist sie sehr ordentlich.

**unlikelihood** [ʌn'laɪklɪhud] *n* Unwahrscheinlichkeit *f*.

**unlikely** [ʌn'laɪklɪ] *adj* unwahrscheinlich; (*combination etc*) merkwürdig; **in the ~ event of/that** ... im unwahrscheinlichen Fall +*gen*/daß ....

**unlimited** [ʌn'lɪmɪtɪd] *adj* unbeschränkt.

**unlisted** ['ʌn'lɪstɪd] *adj* (*STOCK EXCHANGE*) nicht notiert; (*US: TEL*): **to be ~** nicht im Telefonbuch stehen.

**unlit** [ʌn'lɪt] *adj* (*room etc*) unbeleuchtet.

**unload** [ʌn'ləʊd] *vt* (*box etc*) ausladen; (*car etc*) entladen.

**unlock** [ʌn'lɔk] *vt* aufschließen.

**unlucky** [ʌn'lʌkɪ] *adj* (*object*) unglückbringend; (*number*) Unglücks-; **to be ~** (*person*) Pech haben.

**unmanageable** [ʌn'mænɪdʒəbl] *adj* (*tool, vehicle*) kaum zu handhaben; (*person, hair*) widerspenstig; (*situation*) unkontrollierbar.

**unmanned** [ʌn'mænd] *adj* (*station, spacecraft etc*) unbemannt.

**unmarked** [ʌn'mɑːkt] *adj* (*unstained*) fleckenlos; (*unscarred*) nicht gezeichnet; (*unblemished*) makellos; **~ police car** nicht gekennzeichneter Streifenwagen *m*.

**unmarried** [ʌn'mærɪd] *adj* unverheiratet.
**unmarried mother** *n* ledige Mutter *f*.
**unmask** [ʌn'mɑːsk] *vt* (*reveal*) enthüllen.
**unmatched** [ʌn'mætʃt] *adj* unübertroffen.
**unmentionable** [ʌn'menʃnəbl] *adj* (*topic, word*) Tabu-; **to be ~** tabu sein.
**unmerciful** [ʌn'məːsɪful] *adj* erbarmungslos.
**unmistak(e)able** [ʌnmɪs'teɪkəbl] *adj* unverkennbar.
**unmistak(e)ably** [ʌnmɪs'teɪkəblɪ] *adv* unverkennbar.
**unmitigated** [ʌn'mɪtɪgeɪtɪd] *adj* (*disaster etc*) total.
**unnamed** [ʌn'neɪmd] *adj* (*nameless*) namenlos; (*anonymous*) ungenannt.
**unnatural** [ʌn'nætʃrəl] *adj* unnatürlich; (*against nature: habit*) widernatürlich.
**unnecessarily** [ʌn'nesəsərɪlɪ] *adv* (*worry etc*) unnötigerweise; (*severe etc*) übertrieben.
**unnecessary** [ʌn'nesəsərɪ] *adj* unnötig.
**unnerve** [ʌn'nɔːv] *vt* entnerven.
**unnoticed** [ʌn'nəʊtɪst] *adj*: **to go** *or* **pass ~** unbemerkt bleiben.
**UNO** ['juːnəʊ] *n abbr* (= *United Nations Organization*) UNO *f*.
**unobservant** [ʌnəb'zɔːvnt] *adj* unaufmerksam.
**unobtainable** [ʌnəb'teɪnəbl] *adj* (*item*) nicht erhältlich; **this number is ~** (*TEL*) kein Anschluß unter dieser Nummer.
**unobtrusive** [ʌnəb'truːsɪv] *adj* unauffällig.
**unoccupied** [ʌn'ɔkjupaɪd] *adj* (*seat*) frei; (*house*) leer(stehend).
**unofficial** [ʌnə'fɪʃl] *adj* inoffiziell.
**unopened** [ʌn'əʊpənd] *adj* ungeöffnet.
**unopposed** [ʌnə'pəʊzd] *adj*: **to be ~** (*suggestion*) nicht auf Widerstand treffen; (*motion, bill*) ohne Gegenstimmen angenommen werden.
**unorthodox** [ʌn'ɔːθədɔks] *adj* (*also REL*) unorthodox.
**unpack** [ʌn'pæk] *vt, vi* auspacken.
**unpaid** [ʌn'peɪd] *adj* unbezahlt.
**unpalatable** [ʌn'pælətəbl] *adj* (*meal*) ungenießbar; (*truth*) bitter.
**unparalleled** [ʌn'pærəleld] *adj* beispiellos.
**unpatriotic** ['ʌnpætrɪ'ɔtɪk] *adj* unpatriotisch.
**unplanned** [ʌn'plænd] *adj* ungeplant.
**unpleasant** [ʌn'pleznt] *adj* unangenehm; (*person, manner*) unfreundlich.
**unplug** [ʌn'plʌg] *vt* (*iron, record player etc*) den Stecker herausziehen +*gen*.
**unpolluted** [ʌnpə'luːtɪd] *adj* unverschmutzt.
**unpopular** [ʌn'pɔpjulə*] *adj* unpopulär; **to make o.s. ~ (with)** sich unbeliebt machen (bei).
**unprecedented** [ʌn'presɪdentɪd] *adj* noch nie dagewesen; (*decision*) einmalig.
**unpredictable** [ʌnprɪ'dɪktəbl] *adj* (*person, weather*) unberechenbar; (*reaction*) unvorhersehbar.
**unprejudiced** [ʌn'predʒudɪst] *adj*

unvoreingenommen.
**unprepared** [ʌnprɪ'peəd] *adj* unvorbereitet.
**unprepossessing** ['ʌnpriːpə'zesɪŋ] *adj* (*person, place*) unattraktiv.
**unpretentious** [ʌnprɪ'tenʃəs] *adj* (*building, person*) schlicht.
**unprincipled** [ʌn'prɪnsɪpld] *adj* (*person*) charakterlos.
**unproductive** [ʌnprə'dʌktɪv] *adj* (*land*) unfruchtbar, ertragsarm; (*discussion*) unproduktiv.
**unprofessional** [ʌnprə'feʃənl] *adj* unprofessionell.
**unprofitable** [ʌn'prɔfɪtəbl] *adj* nicht profitabel, unrentabel.
**UNPROFOR** *n abbr* (= *United Nations Protection Force*) UNPROFOR *f*; **~ troops** UNPROFOR-Truppen, UNO-Schutztruppen.
**unprotected** ['ʌnprə'tektɪd] *adj* ungeschützt.
**unprovoked** [ʌnprə'vəʊkt] *adj* (*attack*) grundlos.
**unpunished** [ʌn'pʌnɪʃt] *adj*: **to go ~** straflos bleiben.
**unqualified** [ʌn'kwɔlɪfaɪd] *adj* unqualifiziert; (*disaster, success*) vollkommen.
**unquestionably** [ʌn'kwestʃənəblɪ] *adv* fraglos.
**unquestioning** [ʌn'kwestʃənɪŋ] *adj* bedingungslos.
**unravel** [ʌn'rævl] *vt* (*also fig*) entwirren.
**unreal** [ʌn'rɪəl] *adj* (*artificial*) unecht; (*peculiar*) unwirklich.
**unrealistic** ['ʌnrɪə'lɪstɪk] *adj* unrealistisch.
**unreasonable** [ʌn'riːznəbl] *adj* (*person, attitude*) unvernünftig; (*demand, length of time*) unzumutbar.
**unrecognizable** [ʌn'rekəgnaɪzəbl] *adj* nicht zu erkennen.
**unrecognized** [ʌn'rekəgnaɪzd] *adj* (*talent etc*) unerkannt; (*POL: regime*) nicht anerkannt.
**unreconstructed** ['ʌnriːkən'strʌktɪd] (*esp US*) *adj* (*unwilling to accept change*) unverbesserlich.
**unrecorded** [ʌnrə'kɔːdɪd] *adj* (*piece of music etc*) nicht aufgenommen; (*incident, statement*) nicht schriftlich festgehalten.
**unrefined** [ʌnrə'faɪnd] *adj* (*sugar, petroleum*) nicht raffiniert.
**unrehearsed** [ʌnrɪ'həːst] *adj* (*THEAT etc*) nicht geprobt; (*spontaneous*) spontan.
**unrelated** [ʌnrɪ'leɪtɪd] *adj* (*incidents*) ohne Beziehung; (*people*) nicht verwandt.
**unrelenting** [ʌnrɪ'lentɪŋ] *adj* (*person, behaviour etc*) unnachgiebig.
**unreliable** [ʌnrɪ'laɪəbl] *adj* unzuverlässig.
**unrelieved** [ʌnrɪ'liːvd] *adj* ungemindert.
**unremitting** [ʌnrɪ'mɪtɪŋ] *adj* (*efforts, attempts*) unermüdlich.
**unrepeatable** [ʌnrɪ'piːtəbl] *adj* (*offer*) einmalig; (*comment*) nicht wiederholbar.
**unrepentant** [ʌnrɪ'pentənt] *adj*: **to be ~ about**

**sth** etw nicht bereuen; **he's an ~ Marxist** er bereut es nicht, nach wie vor Marxist zu sein.

**unrepresentative** ['ʌnrɛprɪ'zɛntətɪv] *adj:* **~ (of)** nicht repräsentativ (für).

**unrepresented** ['ʌnrɛprɪ'zɛntɪd] *adj* nicht vertreten.

**unreserved** [ʌnrɪ'zəːvd] *adj* (*seat*) unreserviert; (*approval etc*) uneingeschränkt, vorbehaltlos.

**unreservedly** [ʌnrɪ'zəːvɪdlɪ] *adv* ohne Vorbehalt.

**unresponsive** [ʌnrɪs'pɒnsɪv] *adj* unempfänglich.

**unrest** [ʌn'rɛst] *n* Unruhen *pl*.

**unrestricted** [ʌnrɪ'strɪktɪd] *adj* unbeschränkt; **to have ~ access to** ungehinderten Zugang haben zu.

**unrewarded** [ʌnrɪ'wɔːdɪd] *adj* unbelohnt.

**unripe** [ʌn'raɪp] *adj* unreif.

**unrivalled,** (*US*) **unrivaled** [ʌn'raɪvəld] *adj* unübertroffen.

**unroll** [ʌn'rəul] *vt* entrollen ♦ *vi* sich entrollen.

**unruffled** [ʌn'rʌfld] *adj* unbewegt; (*hair*) unzerzaust.

**unruly** [ʌn'ruːlɪ] *adj* (*child, behaviour*) ungebärdig; (*hair*) widerspenstig.

**unsafe** [ʌn'seɪf] *adj* unsicher; (*machine, bridge, car etc*) gefährlich; **~ to eat/drink** ungenießbar.

**unsaid** [ʌn'sɛd] *adj:* **to leave sth ~** etw ungesagt lassen.

**unsaleable,** (*US*) **unsalable** [ʌn'seɪləbl] *adj* unverkäuflich.

**unsatisfactory** ['ʌnsætɪs'fæktərɪ] *adj* unbefriedigend.

**unsatisfied** [ʌn'sætɪsfaɪd] *adj* unzufrieden.

**unsavoury,** (*US*) **unsavory** [ʌn'seɪvərɪ] *adj* (*fig: person, place*) widerwärtig.

**unscathed** [ʌn'skeɪðd] *adj* unversehrt.

**unscientific** ['ʌnsaɪən'tɪfɪk] *adj* unwissenschaftlich.

**unscrew** [ʌn'skruː] *vt* losschrauben.

**unscrupulous** [ʌn'skruːpjuləs] *adj* skrupellos.

**unseat** [ʌn'siːt] *vt* (*rider*) abwerfen; (*from office*) aus dem Amt drängen.

**unsecured** ['ʌnsɪ'kjuəd] *adj:* **~ creditor** nicht gesicherter Gläubiger *m*; **~ loan** Blankokredit *m*.

**unseeded** [ʌn'siːdɪd] *adj* (*player*) nicht gesetzt.

**unseemly** [ʌn'siːmlɪ] *adj* unschicklich.

**unseen** [ʌn'siːn] *adj* (*person, danger*) unsichtbar.

**unselfish** [ʌn'sɛlfɪʃ] *adj* selbstlos.

**unsettled** [ʌn'sɛtld] *adj* (*person*) unruhig; (*future*) unsicher; (*question*) ungeklärt; (*weather*) unbeständig.

**unsettling** [ʌn'sɛtlɪŋ] *adj* beunruhigend.

**unshak(e)able** [ʌn'ʃeɪkəbl] *adj* unerschütterlich.

**unshaven** [ʌn'ʃeɪvn] *adj* unrasiert.

**unsightly** [ʌn'saɪtlɪ] *adj* unansehnlich.

**unskilled** [ʌn'skɪld] *adj* (*work, worker*) ungelernt.

**unsociable** [ʌn'səuʃəbl] *adj* ungesellig.

**unsocial** [ʌn'səuʃl] *adj:* **to work ~ hours** außerhalb der normalen Arbeitszeit arbeiten.

**unsold** [ʌn'səuld] *adj* unverkauft.

**unsolicited** [ʌnsə'lɪsɪtɪd] *adj* unerbeten.

**unsophisticated** [ʌnsə'fɪstɪkeɪtɪd] *adj* (*person*) anspruchslos; (*method, device*) simpel.

**unsound** [ʌn'saund] *adj* (*floor, foundations*) unsicher; (*policy, advice*) unklug; **of ~ mind** unzurechnungsfähig.

**unspeakable** [ʌn'spiːkəbl] *adj* (*indescribable*) unsagbar; (*awful*) abscheulich.

**unspoken** [ʌn'spəukn] *adj* (*word*) unausgesprochen; (*agreement etc*) stillschweigend.

**unstable** [ʌn'steɪbl] *adj* (*piece of furniture*) nicht stabil; (*government*) instabil; (*person: mentally*) labil.

**unsteady** [ʌn'stɛdɪ] *adj* (*step, voice, legs*) unsicher; (*ladder*) wack(e)lig.

**unstinting** [ʌn'stɪntɪŋ] *adj* (*support*) vorbehaltlos; (*generosity*) unbegrenzt.

**unstuck** [ʌn'stʌk] *adj:* **to come ~** (*label etc*) sich lösen; (*fig: plan, idea etc*) versagen.

**unsubstantiated** ['ʌnsəb'stænʃɪeɪtɪd] *adj* (*rumour*) unbestätigt; (*accusation*) unbegründet.

**unsuccessful** [ʌnsək'sɛsful] *adj* erfolglos; (*marriage*) gescheitert; **to be ~** keinen Erfolg haben.

**unsuccessfully** [ʌnsək'sɛsfəlɪ] *adv* ohne Erfolg, vergeblich.

**unsuitable** [ʌn'suːtəbl] *adj* (*time*) unpassend; (*clothes, person*) ungeeignet.

**unsuited** [ʌn'suːtɪd] *adj:* **to be ~ for** *or* **to sth** für etw ungeeignet sein.

**unsung** ['ʌnsʌŋ] *adj:* **an ~ hero** ein unbesungener Held.

**unsure** [ʌn'ʃuə•] *adj* unsicher; **to be ~ of o.s.** unsicher sein.

**unsuspecting** [ʌnsəs'pɛktɪŋ] *adj* ahnungslos.

**unsweetened** [ʌn'swiːtnd] *adj* ungesüßt.

**unswerving** [ʌn'swəːvɪŋ] *adj* unerschütterlich.

**unsympathetic** ['ʌnsɪmpə'θɛtɪk] *adj* (*showing little understanding*) abweisend; (*unlikeable*) unsympathisch; **to be ~ to(wards) sth** einer Sache *dat* ablehnend gegenüberstehen.

**untangle** [ʌn'tæŋgl] *vt* entwirren.

**untapped** [ʌn'tæpt] *adj* (*resources*) ungenutzt.

**untaxed** [ʌn'tækst] *adj* (*goods, income*) steuerfrei.

**unthinkable** [ʌn'θɪŋkəbl] *adj* undenkbar.

**unthinking** [ʌn'θɪŋkɪŋ] *adj* (*uncritical*) bedenkenlos; (*thoughtless*) gedankenlos.

**untidy** [ʌn'taɪdɪ] *adj* unordentlich.

**untie** [ʌn'taɪ] *vt* (*knot, parcel*) aufschnüren; (*prisoner, dog*) losbinden.

**until** [ən'tɪl] *prep* bis +*acc*; (*after negative*) vor

+dat ♦ conj bis; (after negative) bevor; ~ **now**
bis jetzt; ~ **then** bis dann; **from morning**
~ **night** von morgens bis abends; ~ **he**
**comes** bis er kommt.

**untimely** [ʌn'taɪmlɪ] adj (moment) unpassend;
(arrival) ungelegen; (death) vorzeitig.

**untold** [ʌn'təʊld] adj (joy, suffering, wealth)
unermeßlich; **the** ~ **story** die Hintergründe.

**untouched** [ʌn'tʌtʃt] adj unberührt;
(undamaged) unversehrt; ~ **by** (unaffected)
unberührt von.

**untoward** [ʌntə'wɔːd] adj (events, effects etc)
ungünstig.

**untrained** ['ʌn'treɪnd] adj unausgebildet; (eye,
hands) ungeschult.

**untrammelled** [ʌn'træmld] adj (person)
ungebunden; (behaviour) unbeschränkt.

**untranslatable** [ʌntrænz'leɪtəbl] adj
unübersetzbar.

**untried** [ʌn'traɪd] adj (policy, remedy)
unerprobt; (prisoner) noch nicht vor Gericht
gestellt.

**untrue** [ʌn'truː] adj unwahr.

**untrustworthy** [ʌn'trʌstwɜːðɪ] adj
unzuverlässig.

**unusable** [ʌn'juːzəbl] adj (object)
unbrauchbar; (room) nicht benutzbar.

**unused**[1] [ʌn'juːzd] adj (new) unbenutzt.

**unused**[2] [ʌn'juːst] adj: **to be** ~ **to sth** an etw
acc nicht gewöhnt sein; **to be** ~ **to doing sth**
nicht daran gewöhnt sein, etw zu tun.

**unusual** [ʌn'juːʒʊəl] adj ungewöhnlich;
(exceptional) außergewöhnlich.

**unusually** [ʌn'juːʒʊəlɪ] adv (large, high etc)
ungewöhnlich.

**unveil** [ʌn'veɪl] vt (also fig) enthüllen.

**unwanted** [ʌn'wɒntɪd] adj unerwünscht.

**unwarranted** [ʌn'wɒrəntɪd] adj
ungerechtfertigt.

**unwary** [ʌn'wɛərɪ] adj unachtsam.

**unwavering** [ʌn'weɪvərɪŋ] adj (faith, support)
unerschütterlich; (gaze) fest.

**unwelcome** [ʌn'wɛlkəm] adj (guest)
unwillkommen; (news) unerfreulich; **to feel**
~ sich nicht willkommen fühlen.

**unwell** [ʌn'wɛl] adj: **to be** ~, **to feel** ~ sich
nicht wohl fühlen.

**unwieldy** [ʌn'wiːldɪ] adj (object) unhandlich;
(system) schwerfällig.

**unwilling** [ʌn'wɪlɪŋ] adj: **to be** ~ **to do sth** etw
nicht tun wollen.

**unwillingly** [ʌn'wɪlɪŋlɪ] adv widerwillig.

**unwind** [ʌn'waɪnd] (irreg: like **wind**) vt
abwickeln ♦ vi sich abwickeln; (relax) sich
entspannen.

**unwise** [ʌn'waɪz] adj unklug.

**unwitting** [ʌn'wɪtɪŋ] adj (accomplice)
unwissentlich; (victim) ahnungslos.

**unworkable** [ʌn'wəːkəbl] adj (plan)
undurchführbar.

**unworthy** [ʌn'wəːðɪ] adj unwürdig; **to be** ~ **of**
**sth** einer Sache gen nicht wert or würdig

sein; **to be** ~ **to do sth** es nicht wert sein,
etw zu tun; **that remark is** ~ **of you** diese
Bemerkung ist unter deiner Würde.

**unwrap** [ʌn'ræp] vt auspacken.

**unwritten** [ʌn'rɪtn] adj (law) ungeschrieben;
(agreement) stillschweigend.

**unzip** [ʌn'zɪp] vt aufmachen.

=================================== *KEYWORD*

**up** [ʌp] prep: **to be** ~ **sth** (oben) auf etw dat
sein; **to go** ~ **sth** (auf) etw acc hinaufgehen;
**go** ~ **that road and turn left** gehen Sie die
Straße hinauf und biegen Sie links ab
♦ adv **1** (upwards, higher) oben; **put it a bit**
**higher** ~ stelle es etwas höher; ~ **there** dort
oben; ~ **above** hoch oben
**2**: **to be** ~ (out of bed) auf sein; (prices, level)
gestiegen sein; (building, tent) stehen; **time's**
~ die Zeit ist um or vorbei
**3**: ~ **to** (as far as) bis; ~ **to now** bis jetzt
**4**: **to be** ~ **to** (depending on) abhängen von;
**it's** ~ **to you** das hängt von dir ab; **it's not**
~ **to me to decide** es liegt nicht bei mir, das
zu entscheiden
**5**: **to be** ~ **to** (equal to) gewachsen sein +dat;
**he's not** ~ **to it** (job, task etc) er ist dem
nicht gewachsen; **his work is not** ~ **to the**
**required standard** seine Arbeit entspricht
nicht dem gewünschten Niveau
**6**: **to be** ~ **to** (inf: be doing) vorhaben; **what**
**is he** ~ **to?** (showing disapproval, suspicion)
was führt er im Schilde?
♦ n: ~**s and downs** (in life, career) Höhen und
Tiefen pl ♦ vi (inf): **she** ~**ped and left** sie
sprang auf und rannte davon
♦ vt (inf: price) heraufsetzen.

**up-and-coming** [ʌpənd'kʌmɪŋ] adj (actor,
company etc) kommend.

**upbeat** ['ʌpbiːt] n (MUS) Auftakt m; (in
economy etc) Aufschwung m ♦ adj (optimistic)
optimistisch.

**upbraid** [ʌp'breɪd] vt tadeln.

**upbringing** ['ʌpbrɪŋɪŋ] n Erziehung f.

**upcoming** ['ʌpkʌmɪŋ] adj (esp US) kommend.

**update** [ʌp'deɪt] vt aktualisieren.

**upend** [ʌp'ɛnd] vt auf den Kopf stellen.

**upfront** [ʌp'frʌnt] adj (person) offen ♦ adv:
**20%** ~ 20% (als) Vorschuß, 20% im voraus.

**upgrade** [ʌp'greɪd] vt (house)
Verbesserungen durchführen in +dat; (job)
verbessern; (employee) befördern;
(COMPUT) nachrüsten.

**upheaval** [ʌp'hiːvl] n Unruhe f.

**uphill** ['ʌp'hɪl] adj bergaufwärts (führend);
(fig: task) mühsam ♦ adv (push, move)
bergaufwärts; (go) bergauf.

**uphold** [ʌp'həʊld] (irreg: like **hold**) vt (law,
principle) wahren; (decision) unterstützen.

**upholstery** [ʌp'həʊlstərɪ] n Polsterung f.

**upkeep** ['ʌpkiːp] n (maintenance)
Instandhaltung f.

**up-market** [ʌp'mɑːkɪt] *adj* anspruchsvoll.
**upon** [ə'pɒn] *prep* (*position*) auf +*dat*; (*motion*) auf +*acc*.
**upper** ['ʌpə'] *adj* obere(r, s) ♦ *n* (*of shoe*) Oberleder *nt*.
**upper class** *n*: **the** ~ die Oberschicht.
**upper-class** ['ʌpə'klɑːs] *adj* vornehm.
**uppercut** ['ʌpəkʌt] *n* Uppercut *m*.
**upper hand** *n*: **to have the** ~ die Oberhand haben.
**Upper House** *n* (*POL*) Oberhaus *nt*.
**uppermost** ['ʌpəməust] *adj* oberste(r, s); **what was** ~ **in my mind** woran ich in erster Linie dachte.
**Upper Volta** [-'vɒltə] *n* Obervolta *nt*.
**upright** ['ʌpraɪt] *adj* (*vertical*) vertikal; (*fig: honest*) rechtschaffen ♦ *adv* (*sit, stand*) aufrecht ♦ *n* (*CONSTR*) Pfosten *m*.
**uprising** ['ʌpraɪzɪŋ] *n* Aufstand *m*.
**uproar** ['ʌprɔː'] *n* Aufruhr *m*.
**uproarious** [ʌp'rɔːrɪəs] *adj* (*laughter*) brüllend; (*joke*) brüllend komisch; (*mirth*) überwältigend.
**uproot** [ʌp'ruːt] *vt* (*tree*) entwurzeln; (*fig: people*) aus der gewohnten Umgebung reißen; (: *in war etc*) entwurzeln.
**upset** [*vt, adj* ʌp'sɛt, *n* 'ʌpsɛt] (*irreg: like* **set**) *vt* (*knock over*) umstoßen; (*person: offend, make unhappy*) verletzen; (*routine, plan*) durcheinanderbringen ♦ *adj* (*unhappy*) aufgebracht; (*stomach*) verstimmt ♦ *n*: **to have/get a stomach** ~ (*BRIT*) eine Magenverstimmung haben/bekommen; **to get** ~ sich aufregen.
**upset price** ['ʌpsɛt-] (*US, SCOT*) *n* Mindestpreis *m*.
**upsetting** [ʌp'sɛtɪŋ] *adj* (*distressing*) erschütternd.
**upshot** ['ʌpʃɒt] *n* Ergebnis *nt*; **the** ~ **of it all was that** ... es lief schließlich darauf hinaus, daß ...
**upside down** ['ʌpsaɪd-] *adv* verkehrt herum; **to turn a room** ~ (*fig*) ein Zimmer auf den Kopf stellen.
**upstage** ['ʌp'steɪdʒ] *adv* (*THEAT*) im Bühnenhintergrund ♦ *vt*: **to** ~ **sb** (*fig*) jdn ausstechen, jdm die Schau stehlen (*inf*).
**upstairs** [ʌp'stɛəz] *adv* (*be*) oben; (*go*) nach oben ♦ *adj* (*room*) obere(r, s); (*window*) im oberen Stock ♦ *n* oberes Stockwerk *nt*; **there's no** ~ das Haus hat kein Obergeschoß.
**upstart** ['ʌpstɑːt] (*pej*) *n* Emporkömmling *m*.
**upstream** [ʌp'striːm] *adv, adj* flußaufwärts.
**upsurge** ['ʌpsəːdʒ] *n* (*of enthusiasm etc*) Schwall *m*.
**uptake** ['ʌpteɪk] *n*: **to be quick on the** ~ schnell kapieren; **to be slow on the** ~ schwer von Begriff sein.
**uptight** [ʌp'taɪt] (*inf*) *adj* nervös.
**up-to-date** ['ʌptə'deɪt] *adj* (*modern*) modern; (*person*) up to date.

**upturn** ['ʌptəːn] *n* (*in economy*) Aufschwung *m*.
**upturned** ['ʌptəːnd] *adj*: ~ **nose** Stupsnase *f*.
**upward** ['ʌpwəd] *adj* (*movement*) Aufwärts-; (*glance*) nach oben gerichtet.
**upwardly mobile** ['ʌpwədlɪ-] *adj*: **to be** ~ ein Aufsteigertyp *m* sein.
**upwards** ['ʌpwədz] *adv* (*move*) aufwärts; (*glance*) nach oben; **upward(s) of** (*more than*) über +*acc*.
**URA** (*US*) *n abbr* (= *Urban Renewal Administration*) Stadtsanierungsbehörde.
**Ural Mountains** ['juərəl-] *npl*: **the** ~ (*also*: **the Urals**) der Ural.
**uranium** [juə'reɪnɪəm] *n* Uran *nt*.
**Uranus** [juə'reɪnəs] *n* Uranus *m*.
**urban** ['əːbən] *adj* städtisch; (*unemployment*) in den Städten.
**urbane** [əː'beɪn] *adj* weltgewandt.
**urbanization** ['əːbənaɪ'zeɪʃən] *n* Urbanisierung *f*, Verstädterung *f*.
**urchin** ['əːtʃɪn] (*pej*) *n* Gassenkind *nt*.
**Urdu** ['uəduː] *n* Urdu *nt*.
**urge** [əːdʒ] *n* (*need, desire*) Verlangen *nt* ♦ *vt*: **to** ~ **sb to do sth** jdn eindringlich bitten, etw zu tun; **to** ~ **caution** zur Vorsicht mahnen.
▶**urge on** *vt* antreiben.
**urgency** ['əːdʒənsɪ] *n* Dringlichkeit *f*.
**urgent** ['əːdʒənt] *adj* dringend; (*voice*) eindringend.
**urgently** ['əːdʒəntlɪ] *adv* dringend.
**urinal** ['juərɪnl] *n* (*building*) Pissoir *nt*; (*vessel*) Urinal *nt*.
**urinate** ['juərɪneɪt] *vi* urinieren.
**urine** ['juərɪn] *n* Urin *m*.
**urn** [əːn] *n* Urne *f*; (*also*: **tea** ~) Teekessel *m*.
**Uruguay** ['juərəgwaɪ] *n* Uruguay *nt*.
**Uruguayan** [juərə'gwaɪən] *adj* uruguayisch ♦ *n* (*person*) Uruguayer(in) *m(f)*.
**US** *n abbr* (= *United States*) USA *pl*.
**us** [ʌs] *pl pron* uns; (*emphatic*) wir; *see also* **me**.
**USA** *n abbr* (= *United States of America*) USA *f*; (*MIL*: = *United States Army*) US-Armee *f*.
**usable** ['juːzəbl] *adj* brauchbar.
**USAF** *n abbr* (= *United States Air Force*) US-Luftwaffe *f*.
**usage** ['juːzɪdʒ] *n* (*LING*) (Sprach)gebrauch *m*.
**USCG** *n abbr* (= *United States Coast Guard*) Küstenwache der USA.
**USDA** *n abbr* (= *United States Department of Agriculture*) US-Landwirtschafts-ministerium.
**USDAW** ['ʌzdɔː] (*BRIT*) *n abbr* (= *Union of Shop, Distributive and Allied Workers*) Einzelhandelsgewerkschaft.
**USDI** *n abbr* (= *United States Department of the Interior*) US-Innenministerium.
**use** [*n* juːs, *vt* juːz] *n* (*using*) Gebrauch *m*, Verwendung *f*; (*usefulness, purpose*) Nutzen *m* ♦ *vt* benutzen, gebrauchen; (*phrase*) verwenden; **in** ~ in Gebrauch; **out of** ~

außer Gebrauch; **to be of ~** nützlich *or* von Nutzen sein; **to make ~ of sth** Gebrauch von etw machen; **it's no ~** es hat keinen Zweck; **to have the ~ of sth** über etw *acc* verfügen können; **what's this ~d for?** wofür wird das gebraucht?; **to be ~d to sth** etw gewohnt sein; **to get ~d to sth** sich an etw *acc* gewöhnen; **she ~d to do it** sie hat es früher gemacht.

▶**use up** *vt* (*food, leftovers*) aufbrauchen; (*money*) verbrauchen.

**used** [ju:zd] *adj* gebraucht; (*car*) Gebraucht-.

**useful** ['ju:sful] *adj* nützlich; **to come in ~** sich als nützlich erweisen.

**usefulness** ['ju:sfəlnɪs] *n* Nützlichkeit *f*.

**useless** ['ju:slɪs] *adj* nutzlos; (*person: hopeless*) hoffnungslos.

**user** ['ju:zə*] *n* Benutzer(in) *m(f)*; (*of petrol, gas etc*) Verbraucher(in) *m(f)*.

**user-friendly** ['ju:zə'frɛndlɪ] *adj* benutzerfreundlich.

**usher** ['ʌʃə*] *n* (*at wedding*) Platzanweiser *m* ♦ *vt:* **to ~ sb in** jdn hineinführen.

**usherette** [ʌʃə'rɛt] *n* Platzanweiserin *f*.

**USIA** *n abbr* (= *United States Information Agency*) US-Informations- und Kulturinstitut.

**USM** *n abbr* (= *United States Mint*) US-Münzanstalt; (= *United States Mail*) US-Postbehörde.

**USN** *n abbr* (= *United States Navy*) US-Marine *f*.

**USPHS** *n abbr* (= *United States Public Health Service*) US-Gesundheitsbehörde.

**USPO** *n abbr* (= *United States Post Office*) US-Postbehörde.

**USS** *abbr* (= *United States Ship*) Namensteil von Schiffen der Kriegsmarine.

**USSR** *n abbr* (*formerly:* = *Union of Soviet Socialist Republics*) UdSSR *f*.

**usu.** *abbr* = **usually.**

**usual** ['ju:ʒuəl] *adj* üblich, gewöhnlich; **as ~** wie gewöhnlich.

**usually** ['ju:ʒuəlɪ] *adv* gewöhnlich.

**usurer** ['ju:ʒərə*] *n* Wucherer *m*.

**usurp** [ju:'zə:p] *vt* (*title, position*) an sich *acc* reißen.

**usury** ['ju:ʒurɪ] *n* Wucher *m*.

**UT** (*US*) *abbr* (*POST:* = *Utah*).

**utensil** [ju:'tɛnsl] *n* Gerät *nt*; **kitchen ~s** Küchengeräte *pl*.

**uterus** ['ju:tərəs] *n* Gebärmutter *f*, Uterus *m*.

**utilitarian** [ju:tɪlɪ'tɛərɪən] *adj* (*building, object*) praktisch; (*PHILOSOPHY*) utilitaristisch.

**utility** [ju:'tɪlɪtɪ] *n* (*usefulness*) Nützlichkeit *f*; (*public utility*) Versorgungsbetrieb *m*.

**utility room** *n* ≈ Hauswirtschaftsraum *m*.

**utilization** [ju:tɪlaɪ'zeɪʃən] *n* Verwendung *f*.

**utilize** ['ju:tɪlaɪz] *vt* verwenden.

**utmost** ['ʌtməʊst] *adj* äußerste(r, s) ♦ *n:* **to do one's ~** sein möglichstes tun; **of the ~ importance** von äußerster Wichtigkeit.

**utter** ['ʌtə*] *adj* (*amazement*) äußerste(r, s); (*rubbish, fool*) total ♦ *vt* (*sounds, words*) äußern.

**utterance** ['ʌtərəns] *n* Äußerung *f*.

**utterly** ['ʌtəlɪ] *adv* (*totally*) vollkommen.

**U-turn** ['ju:'tə:n] *n* (*also fig*) Kehrtwendung *f*.

**Uzbekistan** [ʌzbɛkɪ'sta:n] *n* Usbekistan *nt*.

# V, v

**V¹, v** [vi:] *n* (*letter*) V *nt*, v *nt*; **~ for Victor** ≈ V wie Viktor.

**V²** *abbr* (= *volt*) V.

**v.** *abbr* = **verse;** (= *versus*) vs.; (= *vide*) s.

**VA** (*US*) *abbr* (*POST:* = *Virginia*).

**vac** [væk] (*BRIT: inf*) *n abbr* = **vacation.**

**vacancy** ['veɪkənsɪ] *n* (*BRIT: job*) freie Stelle *f*; (*room in hotel etc*) freies Zimmer *nt*; **"no vacancies"** „belegt"; **have you any vacancies?** (*hotel*) haben Sie Zimmer frei?; (*office*) haben Sie freie Stellen?

**vacant** ['veɪkənt] *adj* (*room, seat, job*) frei; (*look*) leer.

**vacant lot** (*US*) *n* unbebautes Grundstück *nt*.

**vacate** [və'keɪt] *vt* (*house*) räumen; (*one's seat*) frei machen; (*job*) aufgeben.

**vacation** [və'keɪʃən] (*esp US*) *n* (*holiday*) Urlaub *m*; (*SCOL*) Ferien *pl*; **to take a ~** Urlaub machen; **on ~** im Urlaub.

**vacation course** *n* Ferienkurs *m*.

**vaccinate** ['væksɪneɪt] *vt:* **to ~ sb (against sth)** jdn (gegen etw) impfen.

**vaccination** [væksɪ'neɪʃən] *n* Impfung *f*.

**vaccine** ['væksi:n] *n* Impfstoff *m*.

**vacuum** ['vækjum] *n* (*empty space*) Vakuum *nt*.

**vacuum cleaner** *n* Staubsauger *m*.

**vacuum flask** (*BRIT*) *n* Thermosflasche ® *f*.

**vacuum-packed** ['vækjum'pækt] *adj* vakuumverpackt.

**vagabond** ['vægəbɒnd] *n* Vagabund *m*.

**vagary** ['veɪgərɪ] *n:* **the vagaries of** die Launen +*gen*.

**vagina** [və'dʒaɪnə] *n* Scheide *f*, Vagina *f*.

**vagrancy** ['veɪgrənsɪ] *n* Landstreicherei *f*; (*in towns, cities*) Stadtstreicherei *f*.

**vagrant** ['veɪgrənt] *n* Landstreicher(in) *m(f)*; (*in town, city*) Stadtstreicher(in) *m(f)*.

**vague** [veɪg] *adj* (*memory*) vage; (*outline*) undeutlich; (*look, idea, instructions*) unbestimmt; (*person: not precise*) unsicher; (: *evasive*) unbestimmt; **to look ~** (*absent-minded*) zerstreut aussehen; **I haven't the ~st idea** ich habe nicht die leiseste Ahnung.

**vaguely** ['veɪglɪ] *adv* (*unclearly*) vage,

unbestimmt; (*slightly*) in etwa.
**vagueness** ['veɪgnɪs] n Unbestimmtheit f.
**vain** [veɪn] adj (*person*) eitel; (*attempt, action*) vergeblich; **in** ~ vergebens; **to die in** ~ umsonst sterben.
**vainly** ['veɪnlɪ] adv vergebens.
**valance** ['væləns] n (*of bed*) Volant m.
**valedictorian** [vælɪdɪk'tɔːrɪən] (*US*) n (*SCOL*) Abschiedsredner(in) bei der Schulentlassungsfeier.
**valedictory** [vælɪ'dɪktərɪ] adj (*speech*) Abschieds-; (*remarks*) zum Abschied.
**valentine** ['væləntaɪn] n (*also:* ~ **card**) Valentinsgruß m; (*person*) Freund/Freundin, dem/der man am Valentinstag einen Gruß schickt.
**valet** ['vælɪt] n Kammerdiener m.
**valet parking** n Einparken nt (*durch Hotelangestellte etc*).
**valet service** n Reinigungsdienst m.
**valiant** ['vælɪənt] adj (*effort*) tapfer.
**valid** ['vælɪd] adj (*ticket, document*) gültig; (*argument, reason*) stichhaltig.
**validate** ['vælɪdeɪt] vt (*contract, document*) für gültig erklären; (*argument, claim*) bestätigen.
**validity** [və'lɪdɪtɪ] n (*soundness*) Gültigkeit f.
**valise** [və'liːz] n kleiner Koffer m.
**valley** ['vælɪ] n Tal nt.
**valour,** (*US*) **valor** ['vælə*] n Tapferkeit f.
**valuable** ['væljuəbl] adj wertvoll; (*time*) kostbar.
**valuables** ['væljuəblz] npl Wertsachen pl.
**valuation** [vælju'eɪʃən] n (*of house etc*) Schätzung f; (*judgement of quality*) Einschätzung f.
**value** ['væljuː] n Wert m; (*usefulness*) Nutzen m ♦ vt schätzen; **values** npl (*principles, beliefs*) Werte pl; **you get good** ~ (**for money**) **in that shop** in dem Laden bekommt man etwas für sein Geld; **to lose (in)** ~ an Wert verlieren; **to gain (in)** ~ im Wert steigen; **to be of great** ~ (**to sb**) (*fig*) von großem Wert (für jdn) sein.
**value-added tax** [vælju:'ædɪd-] (*BRIT*) n Mehrwertsteuer f.
**valued** ['vælju:d] adj (*customer, advice*) geschätzt.
**valuer** ['væljuə*] n Schätzer(in) m(f).
**valve** [vælv] n Ventil nt; (*MED*) Klappe f.
**vampire** ['væmpaɪə*] n Vampir m.
**van** [væn] n (*AUT*) Lieferwagen m; (*BRIT: RAIL*) Waggon m.
**V and A** (*BRIT*) n abbr (= *Victoria and Albert Museum*) Londoner Museum.
**vandal** ['vændl] n Rowdy m.
**vandalism** ['vændəlɪzəm] n Vandalismus m.
**vandalize** ['vændəlaɪz] vt mutwillig zerstören.
**vanguard** ['vænɡɑːd] n (*fig*): **in the** ~ **of** an der Spitze +gen.
**vanilla** [və'nɪlə] n Vanille f.
**vanilla ice cream** n Vanilleeis nt.

**vanish** ['vænɪʃ] vi verschwinden.
**vanity** ['vænɪtɪ] n (*of person*) Eitelkeit f.
**vanity case** n Kosmetikkoffer m.
**vantage point** ['vɑːntɪdʒ-] n Aussichtspunkt m; (*fig*): **from our** ~ aus unserer Sicht.
**vaporize** ['veɪpəraɪz] vt verdampfen ♦ vi verdunsten.
**vapour,** (*US*) **vapor** ['veɪpə*] n (*gas, steam*) Dampf m; (*mist*) Dunst m.
**vapour trail** n (*AVIAT*) Kondensstreifen m.
**variable** ['vɛərɪəbl] adj (*likely to change: mood, quality, weather*) veränderlich, wechselhaft; (*able to be changed: temperature, height, speed*) variabel ♦ n veränderlicher Faktor m; (*MATH*) Variable f.
**variance** ['vɛərɪəns] n: **to be at** ~ (**with**) nicht übereinstimmen (mit).
**variant** ['vɛərɪənt] n Variante f.
**variation** [vɛərɪ'eɪʃən] n (*change*) Veränderung f; (*different form: of plot, theme etc*) Variation f.
**varicose** ['værɪkəus] adj: ~ **veins** Krampfadern pl.
**varied** ['vɛərɪd] adj (*diverse*) unterschiedlich; (*full of changes*) abwechslungsreich.
**variety** [və'raɪətɪ] n (*diversity*) Vielfalt f; (*varied collection*) Auswahl f; (*type*) Sorte f; **a wide** ~ **of** ... eine Vielfalt an *+acc* ...; **for a** ~ **of reasons** aus verschiedenen Gründen.
**variety show** n Varietévorführung f.
**various** ['vɛərɪəs] adj (*reasons, people*) verschiedene; **at** ~ **times** (*different*) zu verschiedenen Zeiten; (*several*) mehrmals, mehrfach.
**varnish** ['vɑːnɪʃ] n Lack m ♦ vt (*wood, one's nails*) lackieren.
**vary** ['vɛərɪ] vt verändern ♦ vi (*be different*) variieren; **to** ~ **with** (*weather, season etc*) sich ändern mit.
**varying** ['vɛərɪɪŋ] adj unterschiedlich.
**vase** [vɑːz] n Vase f.
**vasectomy** [væ'sɛktəmɪ] n Vasektomie f.
**Vaseline** ® ['væsɪliːn] n Vaseline f.
**vast** [vɑːst] adj (*knowledge*) enorm; (*expense, area*) riesig.
**vastly** ['vɑːstlɪ] adv (*superior, improved*) erheblich.
**vastness** ['vɑːstnɪs] n ungeheure Größe f.
**VAT** [væt] (*BRIT*) n abbr (= *value-added tax*) MWSt f.
**vat** [væt] n Faß nt.
**Vatican** ['vætɪkən] n: **the** ~ der Vatikan.
**vatman** ['vætmæn] (*inf: irreg: like* **man**) n ≈ Fiskus m (*bezüglich Einbehaltung der Mehrwertsteuer*).
**vaudeville** ['vəudəvɪl] n Varieté nt.
**vault** [vɔːlt] n (*of roof*) Gewölbe nt; (*tomb*) Gruft f; (*in bank*) Tresorraum m; (*jump*) Sprung m ♦ vt (*also:* ~ **over**) überspringen.
**vaunted** ['vɔːntɪd] adj: **much-**~ vielgepriesen.
**VC** n abbr = **vice-chairman**; (*BRIT:* = *Victoria Cross*) Viktoriakreuz nt, *höchste britische*

*Tapferkeitsauszeichnung.*
**VCR** *n abbr* = **video cassette recorder.**
**VD** *n abbr* = **venereal disease.**
**VDU** *n abbr* (*COMPUT*) = **visual display unit.**
**veal** [viːl] *n* Kalbfleisch *nt.*
**veer** [vɪə*] *vi* (*wind*) sich drehen; (*vehicle*) ausscheren.
**veg** (*BRIT: inf*) *n abbr* = **vegetable(s).**
**vegan** ['viːɡən] *n* Veganer(in) *m(f)* ♦ *adj* radikal vegetarisch.
**vegeburger** ['vɛdʒɪbəːɡə*] *n* vegetarischer Hamburger *m.*
**vegetable** ['vɛdʒtəbl] *n* (*plant*) Gemüse *nt*; (*plant life*) Pflanzen *pl* ♦ *cpd* (*oil etc*) Pflanzen-; (*garden, plot*) Gemüse-.
**vegetarian** [vɛdʒɪ'tɛərɪən] *n* Vegetarier(in) *m(f)* ♦ *adj* vegetarisch.
**vegetate** ['vɛdʒɪteɪt] *vi* (*fig: person*) dahinvegetieren.
**vegetation** [vɛdʒɪ'teɪʃən] *n* (*plants*) Vegetation *f.*
**vegetative** ['vɛdʒɪtətɪv] *adj* vegetativ.
**veggieburger** ['vɛdʒɪbəːɡə*] *n* = **vegeburger.**
**vehemence** ['viːɪməns] *n* Vehemenz *f*, Heftigkeit *f.*
**vehement** ['viːɪmənt] *adj* heftig.
**vehicle** ['viːɪkl] *n* (*machine*) Fahrzeug *nt*; (*fig: means*) Mittel *nt.*
**vehicular** [vɪ'hɪkjulə*] *adj:* **"no ~ traffic"** „kein Fahrzeugverkehr".
**veil** [veɪl] *n* Schleier *m* ♦ *vt* (*also fig*) verschleiern; **under a ~ of secrecy** unter einem Schleier von Geheimnissen.
**veiled** [veɪld] *adj* (*also fig: threat*) verschleiert.
**vein** [veɪn] *n* Ader *f*; (*fig: mood, style*) Stimmung *f.*
**Velcro** ® ['vɛlkrəu] *n* (*also: ~ **fastener** or **fastening**) Klettverschluß *m.*
**vellum** ['vɛləm] *n* (*writing paper*) Pergament *nt.*
**velocity** [vɪ'lɔsɪtɪ] *n* Geschwindigkeit *f.*
**velours** *n* Velours *m.*
**velvet** ['vɛlvɪt] *n* Samt *m* ♦ *adj* (*skirt, jacket*) Samt-.
**vendetta** [vɛn'dɛtə] *n* Vendetta *f*; (*between families*) Blutrache *f.*
**vending machine** ['vɛndɪŋ-] *n* Automat *m.*
**vendor** ['vɛndə*] *n* Verkäufer(in) *m(f)*; **street ~** Straßenhändler(in) *m(f).*
**veneer** [və'nɪə*] *n* (*on furniture*) Furnier *nt*; (*fig*) Anstrich *m.*
**venerable** ['vɛnərəbl] *adj* ehrwürdig; (*REL*) hochwürdig.
**venereal** [vɪ'nɪərɪəl] *adj:* **~ disease** Geschlechtskrankheit *f.*
**Venetian** [vɪ'niːʃən] *adj* (*also GEOG*) venezianisch ♦ *n* (*person*) Venezianer(in) *m(f).*
**Venetian blind** *n* Jalousie *f.*
**Venezuela** [vɛnɛ'zweɪlə] *n* Venezuela *nt.*
**Venezuelan** [vɛnɛ'zweɪlən] *adj* venezolanisch ♦ *n* (*person*) Venezolaner(in) *m(f).*
**vengeance** ['vɛndʒəns] *n* Rache *f*; **with a ~**

(*fig: fiercely*) gewaltig; **he broke the rules with a ~** er verstieß die Regeln - und nicht zu knapp.
**vengeful** ['vɛndʒful] *adj* rachsüchtig.
**Venice** ['vɛnɪs] *n* Venedig *nt.*
**venison** ['vɛnɪsn] *n* Rehfleisch *nt.*
**venom** ['vɛnəm] *n* (*poison*) Gift *nt*; (*bitterness, anger*) Gehässigkeit *f.*
**venomous** ['vɛnəməs] *adj* (*snake, insect*) giftig; (*look*) gehässig.
**vent** [vɛnt] *n* (*also:* **air ~**) Abzug *m*; (*in jacket*) Schlitz *m* ♦ *vt* (*fig: feelings*) abreagieren.
**ventilate** ['vɛntɪleɪt] *vt* (*building*) belüften; (*room*) lüften.
**ventilation** [vɛntɪ'leɪʃən] *n* Belüftung *f.*
**ventilation shaft** *n* Luftschacht *m.*
**ventilator** ['vɛntɪleɪtə*] *n* (*TECH*) Ventilator *m*; (*MED*) Beatmungsgerät *nt.*
**ventriloquist** [vɛn'trɪləkwɪst] *n* Bauchredner(in) *m(f).*
**venture** ['vɛntʃə*] *n* Unternehmung *f* ♦ *vt* (*opinion*) zu äußern wagen ♦ *vi* (*dare to go*) sich wagen; **a business ~** ein geschäftliches Unternehmen; **to ~ to do sth** es wagen, etw zu tun.
**venture capital** *n* Risikokapital *nt.*
**venue** ['vɛnjuː] *n* (*for meeting*) Treffpunkt *m*; (*for big events*) Austragungsort *m.*
**Venus** ['viːnəs] *n* Venus *f.*
**veracity** [və'ræsɪtɪ] *n* (*of person*) Aufrichtigkeit *f*; (*of evidence etc*) Richtigkeit *f.*
**veranda(h)** [və'rændə] *n* Veranda *f.*
**verb** [vəːb] *n* Verb *nt.*
**verbal** ['vəːbl] *adj* verbal; (*skills*) sprachlich; (*translation*) wörtlich.
**verbally** ['vəːbəlɪ] *adv* (*communicate etc*) mündlich, verbal.
**verbatim** [vəː'beɪtɪm] *adj* wörtlich ♦ *adv* Wort für Wort.
**verbose** [vəː'bəus] *adj* (*person*) wortreich; (*writing*) weitschweifig.
**verdict** ['vəːdɪkt] *n* (*LAW, fig*) Urteil *nt*; **~ of guilty/not guilty** Schuld-/Freispruch *m.*
**verge** [vəːdʒ] (*BRIT*) *n* (*of road*) Rand *m*, Bankett *nt*; **"soft ~s"** (*BRIT: AUT*) „Seitenstreifen nicht befahrbar"; **to be on the ~ of doing sth** im Begriff sein, etw zu tun.
▶**verge on** *vt fus* grenzen an *+acc.*
**verger** ['vəːdʒə*] *n* (*REL*) Küster *m.*
**verification** [vɛrɪfɪ'keɪʃən] *n* (*see vt*) Bestätigung *f*; Überprüfung *f.*
**verify** ['vɛrɪfaɪ] *vt* (*confirm*) bestätigen; (*check*) überprüfen.
**veritable** ['vɛrɪtəbl] *adj* (*real*) wahr.
**vermin** ['vəːmɪn] *npl* Ungeziefer *nt.*
**vermouth** ['vəːməθ] *n* Wermut *m.*
**vernacular** [və'nækjulə*] *n* (*of country*) Landessprache *f*; (*of region*) Dialekt *m.*
**versatile** ['vəːsətaɪl] *adj* vielseitig.
**versatility** [vəːsə'tɪlɪtɪ] *n* Vielseitigkeit *f.*

**verse** [vəːs] n (poetry) Poesie f; (stanza) Strophe f; (in bible) Vers m; **in ~** in Versform.

**versed** [vəːst] adj: **(well-)~ in** (gut) bewandert in +dat.

**version** ['vəːʃən] n Version f.

**versus** ['vəːsəs] prep gegen.

**vertebra** ['vəːtɪbrə] (pl ~e) n Rückenwirbel m.

**vertebrae** ['vəːtɪbriː] npl of **vertebra**.

**vertebrate** ['vəːtɪbrɪt] n Wirbeltier nt.

**vertical** ['vəːtɪkl] adj vertikal, senkrecht ♦ n Vertikale f.

**vertically** ['vəːtɪklɪ] adv vertikal.

**vertigo** ['vəːtɪgəu] n Schwindelgefühle pl; **to suffer from ~** leicht schwindlig werden.

**verve** [vəːv] n Schwung m.

**very** ['vɛrɪ] adv sehr ♦ adj: **the ~ book which ...** genau das Buch, das ...; **the ~ last** der/die/ das allerletzte; **at the ~ least** allerwenigstens; **~ well/little** sehr gut/ wenig; **~ much** sehr viel; (like, hope) sehr; **the ~ thought (of it) alarms me** der bloße Gedanke (daran) beunruhigt mich; **at the ~ end** ganz am Ende.

**vespers** ['vɛspəz] npl (REL) Vesper f.

**vessel** ['vɛsl] n Gefäß nt; (NAUT) Schiff nt; see **blood**.

**vest** [vɛst] n (BRIT: underwear) Unterhemd nt; (US: waistcoat) Weste f ♦ vt: **to ~ sb with sth, ~ sth in sb** jdm etw verleihen.

**vested interest** ['vɛstɪd-] n (COMM) finanzielles Interesse nt; **to have a ~ in doing sth** ein besonderes Interesse daran haben, etw zu tun.

**vestibule** ['vɛstɪbjuːl] n Vorhalle f.

**vestige** ['vɛstɪdʒ] n Spur f.

**vestment** ['vɛstmənt] n (REL) Ornat nt.

**vestry** ['vɛstrɪ] n Sakristei f.

**Vesuvius** [vɪ'suːvɪəs] n Vesuv m.

**vet** [vɛt] (BRIT) n abbr = **veterinary surgeon** ♦ vt (examine) überprüfen.

**veteran** ['vɛtərn] n Veteran(in) m(f) ♦ adj: **she's a ~ campaigner for ...** sie ist eine altgediente Kämpferin für ...

**veteran car** n Oldtimer m (vor 1919 gebaut).

**veterinarian** [vɛtrɪ'nɛərɪən] (US) n = **veterinary surgeon**.

**veterinary** ['vɛtrɪnərɪ] adj (practice, medicine) Veterinär-; (care, training) tierärztlich.

**veterinary surgeon** (BRIT) n Tierarzt m, Tierärztin f.

**veto** ['viːtəu] (pl ~es) n Veto nt ♦ vt ein Veto einlegen gegen; **to put a ~ on sth** gegen etw ein Veto einlegen.

**vetting** ['vɛtɪŋ] n Überprüfung f.

**vex** [vɛks] vt (irritate, annoy) ärgern.

**vexed** [vɛkst] adj (upset) verärgert; (question) umstritten.

**VFD** (US) n abbr (= volunteer fire department) ≈ freiwillige Feuerwehr f.

**VG** (BRIT) n abbr (SCOL etc: = very good) ≈ Sehr Gut nt.

**VHF** abbr (RADIO: = very high frequency) VHF.

**VI** (US) abbr (POST: = Virgin Islands).

**via** ['vaɪə] prep über +acc.

**viability** [vaɪə'bɪlɪtɪ] n (see adj) Durchführbarkeit f; Rentabilität f.

**viable** ['vaɪəbl] adj (project) durchführbar; (company) rentabel.

**viaduct** ['vaɪədʌkt] n Viadukt m.

**vial** ['vaɪəl] n Fläschchen nt.

**vibes** [vaɪbz] npl (MUS) see **vibraphone**; (inf: vibrations): **I get good/bad ~ from it/him** das/er/macht mich an/nicht an.

**vibrant** ['vaɪbrnt] adj (lively) dynamisch; (bright) lebendig; (full of emotion: voice) volltönend.

**vibraphone** ['vaɪbrəfəun] n Vibraphon nt.

**vibrate** [vaɪ'breɪt] vi (house) zittern, beben; (machine, sound etc) vibrieren.

**vibration** [vaɪ'breɪʃən] n (act of vibrating) Vibrieren nt; (instance) Vibration f.

**vibrator** [vaɪ'breɪtə*] n Vibrator m.

**vicar** ['vɪkə*] n Pfarrer m.

**vicarage** ['vɪkərɪdʒ] n Pfarrhaus nt.

**vicarious** [vɪ'kɛərɪəs] adj (pleasure, experience) indirekt.

**vice** [vaɪs] n (moral fault) Laster nt; (TECH) Schraubstock m.

**vice-** [vaɪs] pref Vize-.

**vice-chairman** [vaɪs'tʃɛəmən] n stellvertretender Vorsitzender m.

**vice chancellor** (BRIT) n (of university) ≈ Rektor m.

**vice president** n Vizepräsident(in) m(f).

**viceroy** ['vaɪsrɔɪ] n Vizekönig m.

**vice squad** n (POLICE) Sittendezernat nt.

**vice versa** ['vaɪsɪ'vəːsə] adv umgekehrt.

**vicinity** [vɪ'sɪnɪtɪ] n: **in the ~ (of)** in der Nähe or Umgebung (+gen).

**vicious** ['vɪʃəs] adj (attack, blow) brutal; (words, look) gemein; (horse, dog) bösartig.

**vicious circle** n Teufelskreis m.

**viciousness** ['vɪʃəsnɪs] n Bösartigkeit f, Gemeinheit f.

**vicissitudes** [vɪ'sɪsɪtjuːdz] npl Wechselfälle pl.

**victim** ['vɪktɪm] n Opfer nt; **to be the ~ of an attack** einem Angriff zum Opfer fallen.

**victimization** ['vɪktɪmaɪ'zeɪʃən] n Schikanierung f.

**victimize** ['vɪktɪmaɪz] vt schikanieren.

**victor** ['vɪktə*] n Sieger(in) m(f).

**Victorian** [vɪk'tɔːrɪən] adj viktorianisch.

**victorious** [vɪk'tɔːrɪəs] adj (team) siegreich; (shout) triumphierend.

**victory** ['vɪktərɪ] n Sieg m; **to win a ~ over sb** einen Sieg über jdn erringen.

**video** ['vɪdɪəu] n (film, cassette, recorder) Video nt ♦ vt auf Video aufnehmen ♦ cpd Video-.

**video camera** n Videokamera f.

**video cassette** n Videokassette f.

**video cassette recorder** n Videorekorder m.

**videodisc, videodisk** ['vɪdɪəudɪsk] n Bildplatte f.

**video game** n Videospiel nt, Telespiel nt.
**video nasty** n Video mit übertriebenen Gewaltszenen und/oder pornographischem Inhalt.
**videophone** ['vɪdɪəufəun] n Bildtelefon nt.
**video recorder** n Videorekorder m.
**video recording** n Videoaufnahme f.
**video tape** n Videoband nt.
**vie** [vaɪ] vi: **to ~ with sb/for sth** mit jdm/um etw wetteifern.
**Vienna** [vɪ'enə] n Wien nt.
**Viennese** [vɪə'niːz] adj Wiener.
**Vietnam** ['vjet'næm] n Vietnam nt.
**Viet Nam** ['vjet'næm] n = **Vietnam**.
**Vietnamese** [vjetnə'miːz] adj vietnamesisch ♦ n inv (person) Vietnamese m, Vietnamesin f; (LING) Vietnamesisch nt.
**view** [vjuː] n (from window etc) Aussicht f; (sight) Blick m; (outlook) Sicht f; (opinion) Ansicht f ♦ vt betrachten; (house) besichtigen; **to be on ~** (in museum etc) ausgestellt sein; **in full ~ of** vor den Augen +gen; **to take the ~ that ...** der Ansicht sein, daß ...; **in ~ of the weather/the fact that** in Anbetracht des Wetters/der Tatsache, daß ...; **in my ~** meiner Ansicht nach; **an overall ~ of the situation** ein allgemeiner Überblick über die Lage; **with a ~ to doing sth** mit der Absicht, etw zu tun.
**viewdata** ® ['vjuːdeɪtə] (BRIT) n Bildschirmtext m.
**viewer** ['vjuːə'] n (person) Zuschauer(in) m(f); (viewfinder) Sucher m.
**viewfinder** ['vjuːfaɪndə'] n Sucher m.
**viewpoint** ['vjuːpɔɪnt] n (attitude) Standpunkt m; (place) Aussichtspunkt m.
**vigil** ['vɪdʒɪl] n Wache f; **to keep ~** Wache halten.
**vigilance** ['vɪdʒɪləns] n Wachsamkeit f.
**vigilance committee** (US) n Bürgerwehr f.
**vigilant** ['vɪdʒɪlənt] adj wachsam.
**vigilante** [vɪdʒɪ'læntɪ] n Mitglied einer Selbstschutzorganisation oder Bürgerwehr ♦ adj (group, patrol) Bürgerwehr-, Selbstschutz-.
**vigorous** ['vɪgərəs] adj (action, campaign) energisch, dynamisch; (plant) kräftig.
**vigour,** (US) **vigor** ['vɪgə'] n (of person, campaign) Energie f, Dynamik f.
**vile** [vaɪl] adj abscheulich.
**vilify** ['vɪlɪfaɪ] vt diffamieren.
**villa** ['vɪlə] n Villa f.
**village** ['vɪlɪdʒ] n Dorf nt.
**villager** ['vɪlɪdʒə'] n Dorfbewohner(in) m(f).
**villain** ['vɪlən] n (scoundrel) Schurke m; (in novel etc) Bösewicht m; (BRIT: criminal) Verbrecher(in) m(f).
**VIN** (US) n abbr (= vehicle identification number) amtliches Kennzeichen nt.
**vinaigrette** [vɪneɪ'gret] n Vinaigrette f.
**vindicate** ['vɪndɪkeɪt] vt (person) rehabilitieren; (action) rechtfertigen.

**vindication** [vɪndɪ'keɪʃən] n Rechtfertigung f.
**vindictive** [vɪn'dɪktɪv] adj (person) nachtragend; (action) aus Rache.
**vine** [vaɪn] n (BOT: producing grapes) Weinrebe f; (: in jungle) Rebengewächs nt.
**vinegar** ['vɪnɪgə'] n Essig m.
**vine grower** n Weinbauer m.
**vine-growing** ['vaɪngrəuɪŋ] adj (region) Weinbau- ♦ n Weinbau m.
**vineyard** ['vɪnjɑːd] n Weinberg m.
**vintage** ['vɪntɪdʒ] n (of wine) Jahrgang m ♦ cpd (classic) klassisch; **the 1980 ~** (of wine) der Jahrgang 1980.
**vintage car** n Oldtimer m (zwischen 1919 und 1930 gebaut).
**vintage wine** n erlesener Wein m.
**vinyl** ['vaɪnl] n Vinyl nt; (records) Schallplatten pl.
**viola** [vɪ'əulə] n Bratsche f.
**violate** ['vaɪəleɪt] vt (agreement) verletzen; (peace) stören; (graveyard) schänden.
**violation** [vaɪə'leɪʃən] n (of agreement etc) Verletzung f; **in ~ of** (rule, law) unter Verletzung +gen.
**violence** ['vaɪələns] n Gewalt f; (strength) Heftigkeit f.
**violent** ['vaɪələnt] adj (behaviour) gewalttätig; (death) gewaltsam; (explosion, criticism, emotion) heftig; **a ~ dislike of sb/sth** eine heftige Abneigung gegen jdn/etw.
**violently** ['vaɪələntlɪ] adv heftig; (ill) schwer; (angry) äußerst.
**violet** ['vaɪələt] adj violett ♦ n (colour) Violett nt; (plant) Veilchen nt.
**violin** [vaɪə'lɪn] n Geige f, Violine f.
**violinist** [vaɪə'lɪnɪst] n Violinist(in) m(f), Geiger(in) m(f).
**VIP** n abbr (= very important person) VIP m.
**viper** ['vaɪpə'] n Viper f.
**viral** ['vaɪərəl] adj (disease, infection) Virus-.
**virgin** ['vəːdʒɪn] n Jungfrau f ♦ adj (snow, forest etc) unberührt; **she is a ~** sie ist Jungfrau; **the Blessed V~** die Heilige Jungfrau.
**virgin birth** n unbefleckte Empfängnis f; (BIOL) Jungfernzeugung f.
**virginity** [vəː'dʒɪnɪtɪ] n (of person) Jungfräulichkeit f.
**Virgo** ['vəːgəu] n (sign) Jungfrau f; **to be ~** Jungfrau sein.
**virile** ['vɪraɪl] adj (person) männlich.
**virility** [vɪ'rɪlɪtɪ] n (masculine qualities) Männlichkeit f.
**virtual** ['vəːtjuəl] adj (COMPUT, PHYS) virtuell; **it's a ~ impossibility** es ist so gut wie unmöglich; **to be the ~ leader** eigentlich or praktisch der Führer sein.
**virtually** ['vəːtjuəlɪ] adv praktisch, nahezu; **it is ~ impossible** es ist so gut wie unmöglich.
**virtual reality** n virtuelle Realität f.
**virtue** ['vəːtjuː] n Tugend f; (advantage) Vorzug m; **by ~ of** aufgrund +gen.
**virtuosi** [vəːtju'əuzɪ] npl of virtuoso.

**virtuosity** [vəːtjuˈɔsɪtɪ] n Virtuosität f.
**virtuoso** [vəːtjuˈəuzəu] (pl ~s or **virtuosi**) n Virtuose m.
**virtuous** [ˈvəːtjuəs] adj tugendhaft.
**virulence** [ˈvɪruləns] n (of disease) Bösartigkeit f; (hatred) Feindseligkeit f.
**virulent** [ˈvɪrulənt] adj (disease) bösartig; (actions, feelings) feindselig.
**virus** [ˈvaɪərəs] n (MED, COMPUT) Virus m or nt.
**visa** [ˈviːzə] n Visum nt.
**vis-à-vis** [viːzəˈviː] prep gegenüber.
**viscose** [ˈvɪskəus] n (also CHEM) Viskose f.
**viscount** [ˈvaɪkaunt] n Viscount m.
**viscous** [ˈvɪskəs] adj zähflüssig.
**vise** [vaɪs] (US) n (TECH) = vice.
**visibility** [vɪzɪˈbɪlɪtɪ] n (range of vision) Sicht(weite) f.
**visible** [ˈvɪzəbl] adj sichtbar; ~ **exports/imports** sichtbare Ausfuhren/Einfuhren.
**visibly** [ˈvɪzəblɪ] adv sichtlich.
**vision** [ˈvɪʒən] n (sight) Sicht f; (foresight) Weitblick m; (in dream) Vision f.
**visionary** [ˈvɪʒənrɪ] adj (with foresight) vorausblickend.
**visit** [ˈvɪzɪt] n Besuch m ♦ vt besuchen; **a private/official** ~ ein privater/offizieller Besuch.
**visiting** [ˈvɪzɪtɪŋ] adj (speaker, team) Gast-.
**visiting card** n Visitenkarte f.
**visiting hours** npl Besuchszeiten pl.
**visiting professor** n Gastprofessor(in) m(f).
**visitor** [ˈvɪzɪtə*] n Besucher(in) m(f).
**visitors' book** [ˈvɪzɪtəz-] n Gästebuch nt.
**visor** [ˈvaɪzə*] n (of helmet etc) Visier nt.
**VISTA** [ˈvɪstə] (US) n abbr (= Volunteers in Service to America) staatliches Förderprogramm für strukturschwache Gebiete.
**vista** [ˈvɪstə] n Aussicht f.
**visual** [ˈvɪzjuəl] adj (image etc) visuell; **the** ~ **arts** die darstellenden Künste.
**visual aid** n Anschauungsmaterial nt.
**visual display unit** n (Daten)sichtgerät nt.
**visualize** [ˈvɪzjuəlaɪz] vt sich dat vorstellen.
**visually** [ˈvɪzjuəlɪ] adv visuell; ~ **appealing** optisch ansprechend; ~ **handicapped** sehbehindert.
**vital** [ˈvaɪtl] adj (essential) unerläßlich; (organ) lebenswichtig; (full of life) vital; **of** ~ **importance (to sb/sth)** von größter Wichtigkeit (für jdn/etw).
**vitality** [vaɪˈtælɪtɪ] n (liveliness) Vitalität f.
**vitally** [ˈvaɪtəlɪ] adv: ~ **important** äußerst wichtig.
**vital statistics** npl (fig: of woman) Körpermaße pl; (of population) Bevölkerungsstatistik f.
**vitamin** [ˈvɪtəmɪn] n Vitamin nt ♦ cpd (pill, deficiencies) Vitamin-.
**vitiate** [ˈvɪʃɪeɪt] vt (spoil) verunreinigen.
**vitreous** [ˈvɪtrɪəs] adj: ~ **china** Porzellanemail nt; ~ **enamel** Glasemail nt.

**vitriolic** [vɪtrɪˈɔlɪk] adj (fig: language, behaviour) haßerfüllt.
**viva** [ˈvaɪvə] n (SCOL: also: ~ **voce** [-ˈvəutʃɪ]) mündliche Prüfung f.
**vivacious** [vɪˈveɪʃəs] adj lebhaft.
**vivacity** [vɪˈvæsɪtɪ] n Lebendigkeit f.
**vivid** [ˈvɪvɪd] adj (description) lebendig; (memory, imagination) lebhaft; (colour) leuchtend; (light) hell.
**vividly** [ˈvɪvɪdlɪ] adv (describe) lebendig; (remember) lebhaft.
**vivisection** [vɪvɪˈsɛkʃən] n Vivisektion f.
**vixen** [ˈvɪksn] n (ZOOL) Füchsin f; (pej: woman) Drachen m.
**viz** [vɪz] abbr (= videlicet) nämlich.
**VLF** abbr (RADIO: = very low frequency) VLF.
**V-neck** [ˈviːnɛk] n (also: ~ **jumper** or **pullover**) Pullover m mit V-Ausschnitt.
**VOA** n abbr (= Voice of America) Stimme f Amerikas.
**vocabulary** [vəuˈkæbjulərɪ] n (words known) Vokabular nt, Wortschatz m.
**vocal** [ˈvəukl] adj (of the voice) stimmlich; (articulate) lautstark.
**vocal cords** npl Stimmbänder pl.
**vocalist** [ˈvəukəlɪst] n Sänger(in) m(f).
**vocals** [ˈvəuklz] npl (MUS) Gesang m, Vocals pl.
**vocation** [vəuˈkeɪʃən] n (calling) Berufung f; (profession) Beruf m.
**vocational** [vəuˈkeɪʃənl] adj (training, guidance etc) Berufs-.
**vociferous** [vəˈsɪfərəs] adj (protesters, demands) lautstark.
**vodka** [ˈvɔdkə] n Wodka m.
**vogue** [vəug] n (fashion) Mode f; (popularity) Popularität f; **in** ~ in Mode.
**voice** [vɔɪs] n (also fig) Stimme f ♦ vt (opinion) zum Ausdruck bringen; **in a loud/soft** ~ mit lauter/leiser Stimme; **to give** ~ **to** Ausdruck verleihen +dat.
**voice-over** [ˈvɔɪsəuvə*] n (Film)kommentar m.
**void** [vɔɪd] n (hole) Loch nt; (fig: emptiness) Leere f ♦ adj (invalid) ungültig; ~ **of** (empty) ohne.
**voile** [vɔɪl] n Voile m.
**vol.** abbr (= volume) Bd.
**volatile** [ˈvɔlətaɪl] adj (person) impulsiv; (situation) unsicher; (liquid etc) flüchtig.
**volcanic** [vɔlˈkænɪk] adj (rock, eruption) vulkanisch, Vulkan-.
**volcano** [vɔlˈkeɪnəu] (pl ~**es**) n Vulkan m.
**volition** [vəˈlɪʃən] n: **of one's own** ~ aus freiem Willen.
**volley** [ˈvɔlɪ] n (of gunfire) Salve f; (of stones, questions) Hagel m; (TENNIS etc) Volley m.
**volleyball** [ˈvɔlɪbɔːl] n Volleyball m.
**volt** [vəult] n Volt nt.
**voltage** [ˈvəultɪdʒ] n Spannung f; **high/low** ~ Hoch-/Niederspannung f.
**volte-face** [ˈvɔltˈfɑːs] n Kehrtwendung f.
**voluble** [ˈvɔljubl] adj (person) redselig;

(*speech*) wortreich.

**volume** ['vɔljuːm] n (*space*) Volumen nt; (*amount*) Umfang m, Ausmaß nt; (*book*) Band m; (*sound level*) Lautstärke f; ~ **one/two** (*of book*) Band eins/zwei; **his expression spoke** ~**s** sein Gesichtsausdruck sprach Bände.

**volume control** n (*RADIO, TV*) Lautstärkeregler m.

**volume discount** n (*COMM*) Mengenrabatt m.

**voluminous** [və'luːmɪnəs] adj (*clothes*) sehr weit; (*correspondence, notes*) umfangreich.

**voluntarily** ['vɔləntrɪlɪ] adv freiwillig.

**voluntary** ['vɔləntərɪ] adj freiwillig.

**voluntary liquidation** n freiwillige Liquidation f.

**volunteer** [vɔlən'tɪə*] n Freiwillige(r) f(m) ♦ vt (*information*) vorbringen ♦ vi (*for army etc*) sich freiwillig melden; **to** ~ **to do sth** sich anbieten, etw zu tun.

**voluptuous** [və'lʌptjuəs] adj sinnlich, wollüstig.

**vomit** ['vɔmɪt] n Erbrochene(s) nt ♦ vt erbrechen ♦ vi sich übergeben.

**voracious** [və'reɪʃəs] adj (*person*) gefräßig; ~ **appetite** Riesenappetit m.

**vote** [vəut] n Stimme f; (*votes cast*) Stimmen pl; (*right to vote*) Wahlrecht nt; (*ballot*) Abstimmung f ♦ vt (*elect*): **to be** ~**d chairman** etc zum Vorsitzenden etc gewählt werden; (*propose*): **to** ~ **that** vorschlagen, daß ♦ vi (*in election etc*) wählen; **to put sth to the** ~, **(take a)** ~ **on sth** über etw acc abstimmen; ~ **of censure** Tadelsantrag m; **to pass a** ~ **of confidence/no confidence** ein Vertrauens-/Mißtrauensvotum annehmen; **to** ~ **to do sth** dafür stimmen, etw zu tun; **to** ~ **yes/no** mit Ja/Nein stimmen; **to** ~ **Labour/Green** etc Labour/die Grünen etc wählen; **to** ~ **for** or **in favour of sth/against sth** für/gegen etw stimmen.

**vote of thanks** n Danksagung f.

**voter** ['vəutə*] n Wähler(in) m(f).

**voting** ['vəutɪŋ] n Wahl f.

**voting paper** (*BRIT*) n Stimmzettel m.

**voting right** n Stimmrecht nt.

**vouch** [vautʃ]: ~ **for** vt fus bürgen für.

**voucher** ['vautʃə*] n (*receipt*) Beleg m; **gift** ~ Geschenkgutschein m; **luncheon** ~ Essensmarke f; **travel** ~ Reisegutschein m.

**vow** [vau] n Versprechen nt ♦ vt: **to** ~ **to do sth/that** geloben, etw zu tun/daß; **to take** or **make a** ~ **to do sth** geloben, etw zu tun.

**vowel** ['vauəl] n Vokal m.

**voyage** ['vɔɪɪdʒ] n Reise f.

**voyeur** [vwaː'jəː*] n Voyeur(in) m(f).

**voyeurism** [vwaː'jəːrɪzəm] n Voyeurismus m.

**VP** n abbr = **vice president**.

**vs** abbr (= *versus*) vs.

**V-sign** ['viːsaɪn] (*BRIT*) n: **to give sb the** ~ ≈ jdm den Vogel zeigen.

**VSO** (*BRIT*) n abbr (= *Voluntary Service Overseas*) britischer Entwicklungsdienst.

**VT** (*US*) abbr (*POST:* = *Vermont*).

**vulgar** ['vʌlgə*] adj (*remarks, gestures*) vulgär; (*decor, ostentation*) geschmacklos.

**vulgarity** [vʌl'gærɪtɪ] n (*see adj*) Vulgarität f; Geschmacklosigkeit f.

**vulnerability** [vʌlnərə'bɪlɪtɪ] n Verletzlichkeit f.

**vulnerable** ['vʌlnərəbl] adj (*person, position*) verletzlich.

**vulture** ['vʌltʃə*] n (*also fig*) Geier m.

**vulva** ['vʌlvə] n Vulva f.

# W, w

**W¹, w** ['dʌbljuː] n (*letter*) W nt, w nt; ~ **for William** ≈ W wie Wilhelm.

**W²** ['dʌbljuː] abbr (*ELEC:* = *watt*) W; (= *west*) W.

**WA** abbr (*US: POST:* = *Washington*); (*AUSTRALIA:* = *Western Australia*).

**wad** [wɔd] n (*of cotton wool*) Bausch m; (*of paper, banknotes*) Bündel nt.

**wadding** ['wɔdɪŋ] n Füllmaterial nt.

**waddle** ['wɔdl] vi watscheln.

**wade** [weɪd] vi: **to** ~ **across** (*a river, stream*) waten durch; **to** ~ **through** (*fig: a book*) sich durchkämpfen durch.

**wafer** ['weɪfə*] n (*biscuit*) Waffel f.

**wafer-thin** ['weɪfə'θɪn] adj hauchdünn.

**waffle** ['wɔfl] n (*CULIN*) Waffel f; (*inf: empty talk*) Geschwafel nt ♦ vi (*in speech etc*) schwafeln.

**waffle iron** n Waffeleisen nt.

**waft** [wɔft] vt, vi wehen.

**wag** [wæg] vt (*tail*) wedeln mit; (*finger*) drohen mit ♦ vi (*tail*) wedeln; **the dog** ~**ged its tail** der Hund wedelte mit dem Schwanz.

**wage** [weɪdʒ] n (*also:* ~**s**) Lohn m ♦ vt: **to** ~ **war** Krieg führen; **a day's** ~**s** ein Tageslohn.

**wage claim** n Lohnforderung f.

**wage differential** n Lohnunterschied m.

**wage earner** [-əːnə*] n Lohnempfänger(in) m(f).

**wage freeze** n Lohnstopp m.

**wage packet** n Lohntüte f.

**wager** ['weɪdʒə*] n Wette f ♦ vt wetten.

**waggle** ['wægl] vt (*ears etc*) wackeln mit ♦ vi wackeln.

**wag(g)on** ['wægən] n (*horse-drawn*) Fuhrwerk nt; (*BRIT: RAIL*) Waggon m.

**wail** [weɪl] n (*of person*) Jammern nt; (*of siren*) Heulen nt ♦ vi (*person*) jammern; (*siren*) heulen.

**waist** [weɪst] n (*ANAT, of clothing*) Taille f.
**waistcoat** ['weɪskəut] (*BRIT*) n Weste f.
**waistline** ['weɪstlaɪn] n Taille f.
**wait** [weɪt] n Wartezeit f ♦ vi warten; **to lie in ~ for sb** jdm auflauern; **to keep sb ~ing** jdn warten lassen; **I can't ~ to** ... (*fig*) ich kann es kaum erwarten, zu ...; **to ~ for sb/sth** auf jdn/etw warten; **~ a minute!** Moment mal!; **"repairs while you ~"** „Reparaturen sofort".
▶**wait behind** vi zurückbleiben.
▶**wait on** vt fus (*serve*) bedienen.
▶**wait up** vi aufbleiben; **don't ~ up for me** warte nicht auf mich.
**waiter** ['weɪtə'] n Kellner m.
**waiting** ['weɪtɪŋ] n: **"no ~"** (*BRIT: AUT*) „Halten verboten".
**waiting list** n Warteliste f.
**waiting room** n (*in surgery*) Wartezimmer nt; (*in railway station*) Wartesaal m.
**waitress** ['weɪtrɪs] n Kellnerin f.
**waive** [weɪv] vt (*rule*) verzichten auf +acc.
**waiver** ['weɪvə'] n Verzicht m.
**wake** [weɪk] (*pt* woke, waked, *pp* woken, waked) vt (*also: ~ up*) wecken ♦ vi (*also: ~ up*) aufwachen ♦ n (*for dead person*) Totenwache f; (*NAUT*) Kielwasser nt; **to ~ up to** (*fig*) sich *dat* bewußt werden +gen; **in the ~ of** (*fig*) unmittelbar nach, im Gefolge +gen; **to follow in sb's ~** (*fig*) hinter jdm herziehen.
**waken** ['weɪkn] vt = **wake**.
**Wales** [weɪlz] n Wales nt; **the Prince of ~** der Prinz von Wales.
**walk** [wɔːk] n (*hike*) Wanderung f; (*shorter*) Spaziergang m; (*gait*) Gang m; (*path*) Weg m; (*in park, along coast etc*) (Spazier)weg m ♦ vi gehen; (*instead of driving*) zu Fuß gehen; (*for pleasure, exercise*) spazierengehen ♦ vt (*distance*) gehen, laufen; (*dog*) ausführen; **it's 10 minutes' ~ from here** es ist 10 Minuten zu Fuß von hier; **to go for a ~** spazierengehen; **to slow to a ~** im Schrittempo weitergehen; **people from all ~s of life** Leute aus allen Gesellschaftsschichten; **to ~ in one's sleep** schlafwandeln; **I'd rather ~ than take the bus** ich gehe lieber zu Fuß, als mit dem Bus zu fahren; **I'll ~ you home** ich bringe dich nach Hause.
▶**walk out** vi (*audience*) den Saal verlassen; (*workers*) in Streik treten.
▶**walk out on** (*inf*) vt fus (*family etc*) verlassen.
**walkabout** ['wɔːkəbaut] n: **the Queen/president went on a ~** die Königin/der Präsident mischte sich unters Volk or nahm ein Bad in der Menge.
**walker** ['wɔːkə'] n (*person*) Spaziergänger(in) m(f).
**walkie-talkie** ['wɔːkɪ'tɔːkɪ] n Walkie-talkie nt.
**walking** ['wɔːkɪŋ] n Wandern nt; **it's within**

**~ distance** es ist zu Fuß erreichbar.
**walking holiday** n Wanderurlaub m.
**walking shoes** npl Wanderschuhe pl.
**walking stick** n Spazierstock m.
**Walkman** ® ['wɔːkmən] n Walkman ® m.
**walk-on** ['wɔːkɔn] adj (*THEAT*): **~ part** Statistenrolle f.
**walkout** ['wɔːkaut] n (*of workers*) Streik m.
**walkover** ['wɔːkəuvə'] (*inf*) n (*competition, exam etc*) Kinderspiel nt.
**walkway** ['wɔːkweɪ] n Fußweg m.
**wall** [wɔːl] n Wand f; (*exterior, city wall etc*) Mauer f; **to go to the ~** (*fig: firm etc*) kaputtgehen.
▶**wall in** vt (*enclose*) ummauern.
**wall cupboard** n Wandschrank m.
**walled** [wɔːld] adj von Mauern umgeben.
**wallet** ['wɔlɪt] n Brieftasche f.
**wallflower** ['wɔːlflauə'] n (*BOT*) Goldlack m; **to be a ~** (*fig*) ein Mauerblümchen sein.
**wall hanging** n Wandbehang m.
**wallop** ['wɔləp] (*BRIT: inf*) vt verprügeln.
**wallow** ['wɔləu] vi (*in mud, water*) sich wälzen; (*in guilt, grief*) schwelgen.
**wallpaper** ['wɔːlpeɪpə'] n Tapete f ♦ vt tapezieren.
**wall-to-wall** ['wɔːltə'wɔːl] adj: **~ carpeting** Teppichboden m.
**wally** ['wɔlɪ] (*inf*) n Trottel m.
**walnut** ['wɔːlnʌt] n (*nut*) Walnuß f; (*tree*) Walnußbaum m; (*wood*) Nußbaumholz nt.
**walrus** ['wɔːlrəs] (*pl* ~ *or* ~**es**) n Walroß nt.
**waltz** [wɔːlts] n Walzer m ♦ vi Walzer tanzen.
**wan** [wɔn] adj bleich; (*smile*) matt.
**wand** [wɔnd] n (*also: magic ~*) Zauberstab m.
**wander** ['wɔndə'] vi (*person*) herumlaufen; (*mind, thoughts*) wandern ♦ vt (*the streets, the hills etc*) durchstreifen.
**wanderer** ['wɔndərə'] n Wandervogel m.
**wandering** ['wɔndrɪŋ] adj (*tribe*) umherziehend; (*minstrel, actor*) fahrend.
**wane** [weɪn] vi (*moon*) abnehmen; (*influence etc*) schwinden.
**wangle** ['wæŋgl] (*BRIT: inf*) vt sich *dat* verschaffen.
**wanker** ['wæŋkə'] (*inf!*) n Wichser m.
**wannabe(e)** ['wɔnəbiː] (*inf*) n Möchtegern m; **James Bond ~** Möchtegern-James-Bond m.
**want** [wɔnt] vt (*wish for*) wollen; (*need*) brauchen ♦ n (*lack*): **for ~ of** aus Mangel an +dat; **wants** npl (*needs*) Bedürfnisse pl; **to ~ to do sth** etw tun wollen; **to ~ sb to do sth** wollen, daß jd etw tut; **to ~ in/out** herein-/hinauswollen; **you're ~ed on the phone** Sie werden am Telefon verlangt; **he is ~ed by the police** er wird von der Polizei gesucht; **a ~ of foresight** ein Mangel an Voraussicht.
**want ads** (*US*) npl Kaufgesuche pl.
**wanted** ['wɔntɪd] adj (*criminal etc*) gesucht; **"cook ~"** „Koch/Köchin gesucht".
**wanting** ['wɔntɪŋ] adj: **to be found ~** sich als

unzulänglich erweisen.

**wanton** ['wɒntn] *adj* (*violence*) mutwillig; (*promiscuous: woman*) schamlos.

**war** [wɔː*] *n* Krieg *m*; **to go to ~** (*start*) einen Krieg anfangen; **to be at ~ (with)** sich im Kriegszustand befinden (mit); **to make ~ (on)** Krieg führen (gegen); **a ~ on drugs/ crime** ein Feldzug gegen Drogen/das Verbrechen.

**warble** ['wɔːbl] *n* Trällern *nt* ♦ *vi* trällern.

**war cry** *n* Kriegsruf *m*; (*fig: slogan*) Schlachtruf *m*.

**ward** [wɔːd] *n* (*in hospital*) Station *f*; (*POL*) Wahlbezirk *m*; (*LAW: also:* **~ of court**) Mündel *nt* unter Amtsvormundschaft.

▶**ward off** *vt* (*attack, enemy, illness*) abwehren.

**warden** ['wɔːdn] *n* (*of park etc*) Aufseher(in) *m(f)*; (*of jail*) Wärter(in) *m(f)*; (*BRIT: of youth hostel*) Herbergsvater *m*, Herbergsmutter *f*; (*: in university*) Wohnheimleiter(in) *m(f)*; (*:also:* **traffic ~**) Verkehrspolizist(in) *m(f)*.

**warder** ['wɔːdə*] (*BRIT*) *n* Gefängniswärter(in) *m(f)*.

**wardrobe** ['wɔːdrəub] *n* (*for clothes*) Kleiderschrank *m*; (*collection of clothes*) Garderobe *f*; (*CINE, THEAT*) Kostüme *pl*.

**warehouse** ['wɛəhaus] *n* Lager *nt*.

**wares** [wɛəz] *npl* Waren *pl*.

**warfare** ['wɔːfɛə*] *n* Krieg *m*.

**war game** *n* Kriegsspiel *nt*.

**warhead** ['wɔːhɛd] *n* Sprengkopf *m*.

**warily** ['wɛərɪlɪ] *adv* vorsichtig.

**Warks** (*BRIT*) *abbr* (*POST:* = *Warwickshire*).

**warlike** ['wɔːlaɪk] *adj* kriegerisch.

**warm** [wɔːm] *adj* warm; (*thanks, applause, welcome, person*) herzlich; **it's ~** es ist warm; **I'm ~** mir ist warm; **to keep sth ~** etw warm halten; **with my ~est thanks/ congratulations** mit meinem herzlichsten Dank/meinen herzlichsten Glückwünschen.

▶**warm up** *vi* warm werden; (*athlete*) sich aufwärmen ♦ *vt* aufwärmen.

**warm-blooded** ['wɔːm'blʌdɪd] *adj* warmblütig.

**war memorial** *n* Kriegerdenkmal *nt*.

**warm-hearted** [wɔːm'hɑːtɪd] *adj* warmherzig.

**warmly** ['wɔːmlɪ] *adv* (*applaud, welcome*) herzlich; (*dress*) warm.

**warmonger** ['wɔːmʌŋgə*] (*pej*) *n* Kriegshetzer *m*.

**warmongering** ['wɔːmʌŋgrɪŋ] (*pej*) *n* Kriegshetze *f*.

**warmth** [wɔːmθ] *n* Wärme *f*; (*friendliness*) Herzlichkeit *f*.

**warm-up** ['wɔːmʌp] *n* Aufwärmen *nt*; **~ exercise** Aufwärmübung *f*.

**warn** [wɔːn] *vt*: **to ~ sb that** ... jdn warnen, daß ...; **to ~ sb of sth** jdn vor etw *dat* warnen; **to ~ sb not to do sth** *or* **against doing sth** jdn davor warnen, etw zu tun.

**warning** ['wɔːnɪŋ] *n* Warnung *f*; **without (any) ~** (*suddenly*) unerwartet; (*without notifying*) ohne Vorwarnung; **gale ~** Sturmwarnung *f*.

**warning light** *n* Warnlicht *nt*.

**warning triangle** *n* (*AUT*) Warndreieck *nt*.

**warp** [wɔːp] *vi* (*wood etc*) sich verziehen ♦ *vt* (*fig: character*) entstellen ♦ *n* (*TEXTILES*) Kette *f*.

**warpath** ['wɔːpɑːθ] *n*: **to be on the ~** auf dem Kriegspfad sein.

**warped** [wɔːpt] *adj* (*wood*) verzogen; (*fig: character, sense of humour etc*) abartig.

**warrant** ['wɒrnt] *n* (*LAW: for arrest*) Haftbefehl *m*; (*:also:* **search ~**) Durchsuchungsbefehl *m* ♦ *vt* (*justify, merit*) rechtfertigen.

**warrant officer** *n* (*MIL*) Dienstgrad *zwischen Offizier und Unteroffizier*.

**warranty** ['wɒrəntɪ] *n* Garantie *f*; **under ~** (*COMM*) unter Garantie.

**warren** ['wɒrən] *n* (*of rabbits*) Bau *m*; (*fig: of passages, streets*) Labyrinth *nt*.

**warring** ['wɔːrɪŋ] *adj* (*nations*) kriegführend; (*interests*) gegensätzlich; (*factions*) verfeindet.

**warrior** ['wɒrɪə*] *n* Krieger *m*.

**Warsaw** ['wɔːsɔː] *n* Warschau *nt*.

**warship** ['wɔːʃɪp] *n* Kriegsschiff *nt*.

**wart** [wɔːt] *n* Warze *f*.

**wartime** ['wɔːtaɪm] *n*: **in ~** im Krieg.

**wary** ['wɛərɪ] *adj* (*person*) vorsichtig; **to be ~ about** *or* **of doing sth** Bedenken haben, etw zu tun.

**was** [wɒz] *pt of* **be**.

**wash** [wɒʃ] *vt* waschen; (*dishes*) spülen, abwaschen; (*remove grease, paint etc*) ausspülen ♦ *vi* (*person*) sich waschen ♦ *n* (*clothes etc*) Wäsche *f*; (*washing programme*) Waschgang *m*; (*of ship*) Kielwasser *nt*; **he was ~ed overboard** er wurde über Bord gespült; **to ~ over/against sth** (*sea etc*) über/gegen etw *acc* spülen; **to have a ~** sich waschen; **to give sth a ~** etw waschen.

▶**wash away** *vt* wegspülen.

▶**wash down** *vt* (*wall, car*) abwaschen; (*food: with wine etc*) hinunterspülen.

▶**wash off** *vi* sich herauswaschen ♦ *vt* abwaschen.

▶**wash out** *vt* (*stain*) herauswaschen.

▶**wash up** *vi* (*BRIT: wash dishes*) spülen, abwaschen; (*US: have a wash*) sich waschen.

**Wash.** (*US*) *abbr* (*POST:* = *Washington*).

**washable** ['wɒʃəbl] *adj* (*fabric*) waschbar; (*wallpaper*) abwaschbar.

**washbasin** ['wɒʃbeɪsn], (*US*) **washbowl** ['wɒʃbəul] *n* Waschbecken *nt*.

**washcloth** ['wɒʃklɒθ] (*US*) *n* Waschlappen *m*.

**washer** ['wɒʃə*] *n* (*on tap etc*) Dichtungsring *m*.

**washing** ['wɒʃɪŋ] *n* Wäsche *f*.

**washing line** (*BRIT*) *n* Wäscheleine *f*.

**washing machine** *n* Waschmaschine *f*.

**washing powder** (*BRIT*) *n* Waschpulver *nt*.

**Washington** ['wɒʃɪŋtən] *n* Washington *nt*.

**washing-up** [wɔʃɪŋ'ʌp] n Abwasch m; **to do the ~** spülen, abwaschen.
**washing-up liquid** (*BRIT*) n (Geschirr)spülmittel nt.
**wash-out** ['wɔʃaut] (*inf*) n (*failed event*) Reinfall m.
**washroom** ['wɔʃrum] (*US*) n Waschraum m.
**wasn't** ['wɔznt] = **was not**.
**WASP, Wasp** [wɔsp] (*US: inf*) n abbr (= *White Anglo-Saxon Protestant*) weißer angelsächsischer Protestant m.
**wasp** [wɔsp] n Wespe f.
**waspish** ['wɔspɪʃ] adj giftig.
**wastage** ['weɪstɪdʒ] n Verlust m; **natural ~** natürliche Personalreduzierung.
**waste** [weɪst] n Verschwendung f; (*rubbish*) Abfall m ♦ adj (*material*) Abfall-; (*left over: paper etc*) ungenutzt ♦ vt verschwenden; (*opportunity*) vertun; **wastes** npl (*area of land*) Wildnis f; **it's a ~ of money** das ist Geldverschwendung; **to go to ~** umkommen; **to lay ~** (*area, town*) verwüsten.
▶**waste away** vi verkümmern.
**wastebasket** ['weɪstbɑːskɪt] (*US*) n = **wastepaper basket**.
**waste disposal unit** (*BRIT*) n Müllschlucker m.
**wasteful** ['weɪstful] adj (*person*) verschwenderisch; (*process*) aufwendig.
**waste ground** (*BRIT*) n unbebautes Grundstück nt.
**wasteland** ['weɪstlənd] n Ödland nt; (*in town*) ödes Gebiet nt; (*fig*) Einöde f.
**wastepaper basket** ['weɪstpeɪpə-] (*BRIT*) n Papierkorb m.
**waste pipe** n Abflußrohr nt.
**waste products** npl Abfallprodukte pl.
**waster** ['weɪstə*] n Verschwender(in) m(f); (*good-for-nothing*) Taugenichts m.
**watch** [wɔtʃ] n (*also: wristwatch*) (Armband)uhr f; (*surveillance*) Bewachung f; (*MIL, NAUT: group of guards*) Wachmannschaft f; (*NAUT: spell of duty*) Wache f ♦ vt (*look at*) betrachten; (: *match, programme*) sich dat ansehen; (*spy on, guard*) beobachten; (*be careful of*) aufpassen auf +acc ♦ vi (*look*) zusehen; **to be on ~** Wache halten; **to keep a close ~ on sb/sth** jdn/etw genau im Auge behalten; **to ~ TV** fernsehen; **~ what you're doing!** paß auf!; **~ how you drive!** fahr vorsichtig!
▶**watch out** vi aufpassen; **~ out!** Vorsicht!
**watchband** ['wɔtʃbænd] (*US*) n = **watchstrap**.
**watchdog** ['wɔtʃdɔg] n (*dog*) Wachhund m; (*fig*) Aufpasser(in) m(f).
**watchful** ['wɔtʃful] adj wachsam.
**watchmaker** ['wɔtʃmeɪkə*] n Uhrmacher(in) m(f).
**watchman** ['wɔtʃmən] (*irreg: like* **man**) n *see* **night watchman**.
**watch stem** (*US*) n (*winder*) Krone f,

Aufziehrädchen nt.
**watchstrap** ['wɔtʃstræp] n Uhrarmband nt.
**watchword** ['wɔtʃwɜːd] n Parole f.
**water** ['wɔːtə*] n Wasser nt ♦ vt (*plant*) gießen; (*garden*) bewässern ♦ vi (*eyes*) tränen; **a drink of ~** ein Schluck Wasser; **in British ~s** in britischen (Hoheits)gewässern; **to pass ~** (*urinate*) Wasser lassen; **my mouth is ~ing** mir läuft das Wasser im Mund zusammen; **to make sb's mouth ~** jdm den Mund wäßrig machen.
▶**water down** vt (*also fig*) verwässern.
**water biscuit** n Kräcker m.
**water cannon** n Wasserwerfer m.
**water closet** (*BRIT: old*) n Wasserklosett nt.
**watercolour,** (*US*) **watercolor** ['wɔːtəkʌlə*] n (*picture*) Aquarell nt; **watercolours** npl (*paints*) Wasserfarben pl.
**water-cooled** ['wɔːtəkuːld] adj wassergekühlt.
**watercress** ['wɔːtəkres] n Brunnenkresse f.
**waterfall** ['wɔːtəfɔːl] n Wasserfall m.
**waterfront** ['wɔːtəfrʌnt] n (*at seaside*) Ufer nt; (*at docks*) Hafengegend f.
**water heater** n Heißwassergerät nt.
**water hole** n Wasserloch nt.
**water ice** n Fruchteis nt (*auf Wasserbasis*).
**watering can** ['wɔːtərɪŋ-] n Gießkanne f.
**water level** n Wasserstand m; (*of flood*) Pegelstand m.
**water lily** n Seerose f.
**water line** n Wasserlinie f.
**waterlogged** ['wɔːtəlɔgd] adj (*ground*) unter Wasser.
**water main** n Hauptwasserleitung f.
**watermark** ['wɔːtəmɑːk] n (*on paper*) Wasserzeichen nt.
**watermelon** ['wɔːtəmelən] n Wassermelone f.
**waterproof** ['wɔːtəpruːf] adj (*trousers, jacket etc*) wasserdicht.
**water-repellent** ['wɔːtərɪ'pelnt] adj wasserabstoßend.
**watershed** ['wɔːtəʃed] n (*GEOG*) Wasserscheide f; (*fig*) Wendepunkt m.
**water-skiing** ['wɔːtəskiːɪŋ] n Wasserski nt.
**water softener** n Wasserenthärter m.
**water tank** n Wassertank m.
**watertight** ['wɔːtətaɪt] adj wasserdicht; (*fig: excuse, case, agreement etc*) hieb- und stichfest.
**water vapour** n Wasserdampf m.
**waterway** ['wɔːtəweɪ] n Wasserstraße f.
**waterworks** ['wɔːtəwɜːks] n Wasserwerk nt; (*inf, fig: bladder*) Blase f.
**watery** ['wɔːtərɪ] adj (*coffee, soup etc*) wäßrig; (*eyes*) tränend.
**watt** [wɔt] n Watt nt.
**wattage** ['wɔtɪdʒ] n Wattleistung f.
**wattle** ['wɔtl] n Flechtwerk nt.
**wattle and daub** n Lehmgeflecht nt.
**wave** [weɪv] n (*also fig*) Welle f; (*of hand*) Winken nt ♦ vi (*signal*) winken; (*branches*)

sich hin- und herbewegen; (*grass*) wogen; (*flag*) wehen ♦ *vt* (*hand, flag etc*) winken mit; (*gun, stick*) schwenken; (*hair*) wellen; **short/ medium/long** ~ (*RADIO*) Kurz-/Mittel-/ Langwelle *f*; **the new** ~ (*CINE, MUS*) die Neue Welle *f*; **he ~d us over to his table** er winkte uns zu seinem Tisch hinüber; **to** ~ **goodbye to sb** jdm zum Abschied winken.

▶**wave aside** *vt* (*fig: suggestion etc*) zurückweisen.

**waveband** ['weɪvbænd] *n* (*RADIO*) Wellenbereich *m*.

**wavelength** ['weɪvlɛŋθ] *n* (*RADIO*) Wellenlänge *f*; **on the same** ~ (*fig*) auf derselben Wellenlänge.

**waver** ['weɪvəʳ] *vi* (*voice*) schwanken; (*eyes*) zucken; (*love, person*) wanken.

**wavy** ['weɪvɪ] *adj* (*line*) wellenförmig; (*hair*) wellig.

**wax** [wæks] *n* Wachs *nt*; (*for sealing*) Siegellack *m*; (*in ear*) Ohrenschmalz *nt* ♦ *vt* (*floor*) bohnern; (*car, skis*) wachsen ♦ *vi* (*moon*) zunehmen.

**waxed** [wækst] *adj* (*jacket*) gewachst.

**waxen** [wæksn] *adj* (*face*) wachsbleich.

**waxworks** ['wækswəːks] *npl* (*models*) Wachsfiguren *pl* ♦ *n* (*place*) Wachsfigurenkabinett *nt*.

**way** [weɪ] *n* Weg *m*; (*distance*) Strecke *f*; (*direction*) Richtung *f*; (*manner*) Art *f*; (*method*) Art und Weise *f*; (*habit*) Gewohnheit *f*; **which** ~ **to ...?** wo geht es zu ...?; **this** ~, **please** hier entlang, bitte; **on the** ~ (*en route*) auf dem Weg, unterwegs; **to be on one's** ~ auf dem Weg sein; **to fight one's** ~ **through a crowd** sich *acc* durch die Menge kämpfen; **to lie one's** ~ **out of sth** sich aus etw herauslügen; **to keep out of sb's** ~ jdm aus dem Weg gehen; **it's a long** ~ **away** es ist weit entfernt; (*event*) das ist noch lange hin; **the village is rather out of the** ~ das Dorf ist recht abgelegen; **to go out of one's** ~ **to do sth** sich sehr bemühen, etw zu tun; **to be in the** ~ im Weg sein; **to lose one's** ~ sich verirren; **under** ~ (*project etc*) im Gang; **the** ~ **back** der Rückweg; **to make** ~ **(for sb/sth)** (für jdn/etw) Platz machen; **to get one's own** ~ seinen Willen bekommen; **put it the right** ~ **up** (*BRIT*) stell es richtig herum hin; **to be the wrong** ~ **round** verkehrt herum sein; **he's in a bad** ~ ihm geht es schlecht; **in a** ~ in gewisser Weise; **in some** ~**s** in mancher Hinsicht; **no** ~! (*inf*) kommt nicht in Frage!; **by the** ~ ... übrigens ...; "~ **in**" (*BRIT*) „Eingang"; "~ **out**" (*BRIT*) „Ausgang"; "**give** ~" (*BRIT: AUT*) „Vorfahrt beachten"; ~ **of life** Lebensstil *m*.

**waybill** ['weɪbɪl] *n* Frachtbrief *m*.

**waylay** [weɪˈleɪ] (*irreg: like* lay) *vt* auflauern +*dat*; **to get waylaid** (*fig*) abgefangen

werden.

**wayside** ['weɪsaɪd] *adj* am Straßenrand ♦ *n* Straßenrand *m*; **to fall by the** ~ (*fig*) auf der Strecke bleiben.

**way station** (*US*) *n* (*RAIL*) kleiner Bahnhof *m*; (*fig*) Zwischenstation *f*.

**wayward** ['weɪwəd] *adj* (*behaviour*) eigenwillig; (*child*) eigensinnig.

**WC** (*BRIT*) *n abbr* (= *water closet*) WC *nt*.

**WCC** *n abbr* (= *World Council of Churches*) Weltkirchenrat *m*.

**we** [wiː] *pl pron* wir; **here** ~ **are** (*arriving*) da sind wir; (*finding sth*) na bitte.

**weak** [wiːk] *adj* schwach; (*tea, coffee*) dünn; **to grow** ~**(er)** schwächer werden.

**weaken** ['wiːkn] *vi* (*resolve, person*) schwächer werden; (*influence, power*) nachlassen ♦ *vt* schwächen.

**weak-kneed** [wiːkˈniːd] *adj* (*fig*) schwächlich.

**weakling** ['wiːklɪŋ] *n* Schwächling *m*.

**weakly** [ˈwiːklɪ] *adv* schwach.

**weakness** ['wiːknɪs] *n* Schwäche *f*; **to have a** ~ **for** eine Schwäche haben für.

**wealth** [wɛlθ] *n* Reichtum *m*; (*of details, knowledge etc*) Fülle *f*.

**wealth tax** *n* Vermögenssteuer *f*.

**wealthy** ['wɛlθɪ] *adj* wohlhabend, reich.

**wean** [wiːn] *vt* (*also fig*) entwöhnen.

**weapon** ['wɛpən] *n* Waffe *f*.

**wear** [wɛəʳ] (*pt* **wore**, *pp* **worn**) *vt* (*clothes, shoes, beard*) tragen; (*put on*) anziehen ♦ *vi* (*last*) halten; (*become old: carpet, jeans*) sich abnutzen ♦ *n* (*damage*) Verschleiß *m*; (*use*): **I got a lot of/very little** ~ **out of the coat** der Mantel hat lange/nicht sehr lange gehalten; **baby**~ Babykleidung *f*; **sports**~ Sportkleidung *f*; **town/evening** ~ Kleidung für die Stadt/den Abend; **to** ~ **a hole in sth** (*coat etc*) etw durchwetzen.

▶**wear away** *vt* verschleißen ♦ *vi* (*inscription etc*) verwittern.

▶**wear down** *vt* (*heels*) abnutzen; (*person, strength*) zermürben.

▶**wear off** *vi* (*pain etc*) nachlassen.

▶**wear on** *vi* sich hinziehen.

▶**wear out** *vt* (*shoes, clothing*) verschleißen; (*person, strength*) erschöpfen.

**wearable** ['wɛərəbl] *adj* tragbar.

**wear and tear** [-tɛəʳ] *n* Verschleiß *m*.

**wearer** ['wɛərəʳ] *n* Träger(in) *m(f)*.

**wearily** ['wɪərɪlɪ] *adv* (*say, sit*) lustlos, müde.

**weariness** ['wɪərɪnɪs] *n* (*tiredness*) Müdigkeit *f*.

**wearisome** ['wɪərɪsəm] *adj* (*boring*) langweilig; (*tiring*) ermüdend.

**weary** ['wɪərɪ] *adj* (*tired*) müde; (*dispirited*) lustlos ♦ *vi*: **to** ~ **of sb/sth** jds/etw *gen* überdrüssig werden.

**weasel** ['wiːzl] *n* Wiesel *nt*.

**weather** ['wɛðəʳ] *n* Wetter *nt* ♦ *vt* (*storm, crisis*) überstehen; (*rock, wood*) verwittern; **what's the** ~ **like?** wie ist das Wetter?; **under the** ~

*(fig: ill)* angeschlagen.
**weather-beaten** ['wɛðəbiːtn] *adj (face)* vom
Wetter gegerbt; *(building, stone)* verwittert.
**weathercock** ['wɛðəkɔk] *n* Wetterhahn *m*.
**weather forecast** *n* Wettervorhersage *f*.
**weatherman** ['wɛðəmæn] *(irreg: like* **man***) n*
Mann *m* vom Wetteramt, Wetterfrosch *m*
*(hum inf)*.
**weatherproof** ['wɛðəpruːf] *adj* wetterfest.
**weather report** *n* Wetterbericht *m*.
**weather vane** [-veɪn] *n* = **weathercock**.
**weave** [wiːv] *(pt* **wove***, pp* **woven***) vt (cloth)*
weben; *(basket)* flechten ♦ *vi (fig: pt, pp*
**weaved***: move in and out)* sich schlängeln.
**weaver** ['wiːvə*] n* Weber(in) *m(f)*.
**weaving** ['wiːvɪŋ] *n* Weberei *f*.
**web** [wɛb] *n (also fig)* Netz *nt*; *(on duck's foot)*
Schwimmhaut *f*.
**webbed** ['wɛbd] *adj (foot)* Schwimm-.
**webbing** ['wɛbɪŋ] *n (on chair)* Gewebe *nt*.
**wed** [wɛd] *(pt, pp* **wedded***) vt, vi* heiraten ♦ *n:*
**the newly-~s** die Jungvermählten *pl*.
**Wed.** *abbr* (= *Wednesday*) Mi.
**we'd** [wiːd] = **we had; we would.**
**wedded** ['wɛdɪd] *pt, pp of* **wed** ♦ *adj:* **to be ~ to
sth** *(idea etc)* mit etw eng verbunden sein.
**wedding** [wɛdɪŋ] *n* Hochzeit *f*; **silver/golden
~** silberne/goldene Hochzeit.
**wedding day** *n* Hochzeitstag *m*.
**wedding dress** *n* Hochzeitskleid *nt*.
**wedding present** *n* Hochzeitsgeschenk *nt*.
**wedding ring** *n* Trauring *m*.
**wedge** [wɛdʒ] *n* Keil *m*; *(of cake)* Stück *nt* ♦ *vt*
*(fasten)* festklemmen; *(pack tightly)*
einkeilen.
**wedge-heeled shoes** ['wɛdʒhiːld-] *npl*
Schuhe *pl* mit Keilabsätzen.
**wedlock** ['wɛdlɔk] *n* Ehe *f*.
**Wednesday** ['wɛdnzdɪ] *n* Mittwoch *m*; *see also*
**Tuesday.**
**wee** [wiː] *(SCOT) adj* klein.
**weed** [wiːd] *n (BOT)* Unkraut *nt*; *(pej: person)*
Schwächling *m* ♦ *vt (garden)* jäten.
▶**weed out** *vt (fig)* aussondern.
**weedkiller** ['wiːdkɪlə*] n* Unkrautvertilger *m*.
**weedy** ['wiːdɪ] *adj (person)* schwächlich.
**week** [wiːk] *n* Woche *f*; **once/twice a ~**
einmal/zweimal die Woche; **in two ~s' time**
in zwei Wochen; **a ~ today/on Friday** heute/
Freitag in einer Woche.
**weekday** ['wiːkdeɪ] *n* Wochentag *m*; *(COMM:
Monday to Saturday)* Werktag *m*; **on ~s** an
Wochentagen/Werktagen.
**weekend** [wiːk'ɛnd] *n* Wochenende *nt*; **this/
next/last ~** an diesem/am nächsten/am
letzten Wochenende; **what are you doing at
the ~?** was machen Sie am Wochenende?;
**open at ~s** an Wochenenden geöffnet.
**weekly** ['wiːklɪ] *adv* wöchentlich ♦ *adj
(newspaper)* Wochen- ♦ *n (newspaper)*
Wochenzeitung *f*; *(magazine)*
Wochenzeitschrift *f*.

**weep** [wiːp] *(pt, pp* **wept***) vi (person)* weinen;
*(wound)* nässen.
**weeping willow** ['wiːpɪŋ-] *n (tree)*
Trauerweide *f*.
**weepy** ['wiːpɪ] *adj (person)* weinerlich; *(film)*
rührselig ♦ *n (film etc)* Schmachtfetzen *m*.
**weft** [wɛft] *n* Schußfaden *m*.
**weigh** [weɪ] *vt* wiegen; *(fig: evidence, risks)*
abwägen ♦ *vi* wiegen; **to ~ anchor** den
Anker lichten.
▶**weigh down** *vt* niederdrücken.
▶**weigh out** *vt (goods)* auswiegen.
▶**weigh up** *vt (person, offer, risk)* abschätzen.
**weighbridge** ['weɪbrɪdʒ] *n* Brückenwaage *f*.
**weighing machine** ['weɪɪŋ-] *n* Waage *f*.
**weight** [weɪt] *n* Gewicht *nt* ♦ *vt (fig):* **to be
~ed in favour of sb/sth** jdn/etw
begünstigen; **to be sold by ~** nach Gewicht
verkauft werden; **to lose ~** abnehmen; **to
put on ~** zunehmen; **~s and measures** Maße
und Gewichte.
**weighting** ['weɪtɪŋ] *n (allowance)* Zulage *f*.
**weightlessness** ['weɪtlɪsnɪs] *n*
Schwerelosigkeit *f*.
**weightlifter** ['weɪtlɪftə*] n* Gewichtheber *m*.
**weight limit** *n* Gewichtsbeschränkung *f*.
**weight training** *n* Krafttraining *nt*.
**weighty** ['weɪtɪ] *adj* schwer; *(fig: important)*
gewichtig.
**weir** [wɪə*] n (in river)* Wehr *nt*.
**weird** [wɪəd] *adj (object, situation, effect)*
komisch; *(person)* seltsam.
**weirdo** ['wɪədəu] *(inf) n* verrückter Typ *m*.
**welcome** ['wɛlkəm] *adj* willkommen ♦ *n*
Willkommen *nt* ♦ *vt* begrüßen, willkommen
heißen; **~ to London!** willkommen in
London!; **to make sb ~** jdn freundlich
aufnehmen; **you're ~ to try** du kannst es
gern versuchen; **thank you - you're ~!**
danke - nichts zu danken!
**welcoming** ['wɛlkəmɪŋ] *adj (smile, room)*
einladend; *(person)* freundlich.
**weld** [wɛld] *n* Schweißnaht *f* ♦ *vt* schweißen.
**welder** ['wɛldə*] n (person)* Schweißer(in) *m(f)*.
**welding** ['wɛldɪŋ] *n* Schweißen *nt*.
**welfare** ['wɛlfɛə*] n (well-being)* Wohl *nt*;
*(social aid)* Sozialhilfe *f*.
**welfare state** *n* Wohlfahrtsstaat *m*.
**welfare work** *n* Fürsorgearbeit *f*.
**well** [wɛl] *n (for water)* Brunnen *m*; *(oil well)*
Quelle *f* ♦ *adv* gut; *(for emphasis with adj)*
durchaus ♦ *adj:* **to be ~** *(person)* gesund sein
♦ *excl* nun!, na!; **as ~** *(in addition)* ebenfalls;
**you might as ~ tell me** sag es mir ruhig; **he
did as ~ as he could** er machte es so gut er
konnte; **pretty as ~ as rich** sowohl hübsch
als auch reich; **~ done!** gut gemacht!; **to do
~** *(person)* gut vorankommen; *(business)* gut
gehen; **~ before dawn** lange vor
Tagesanbruch; **~ over 40** weit über 40; **I
don't feel ~** ich fühle mich nicht gut *or*
wohl; **get ~ soon!** gute Besserung!; **~, as I**

**was saying** ... also, wie ich bereits sagte, ...
▶**well up** vi (*tears, emotions*) aufsteigen.
**we'll** [wiːl] = **we will; we shall.**
**well-behaved** ['wɛlbɪ'heɪvd] adj wohlerzogen.
**well-being** ['wɛl'biːɪŋ] n Wohl(ergehen) nt.
**well-bred** ['wɛl'brɛd] adj (*person*) gut erzogen.
**well-built** ['wɛl'bɪlt] adj gut gebaut.
**well-chosen** ['wɛl'tʃəuzn] adj gut gewählt.
**well-deserved** ['wɛldɪ'zəːvd] adj
  wohlverdient.
**well-developed** ['wɛldɪ'vɛləpt] adj gut
  entwickelt.
**well-disposed** ['wɛl'dɪspəuzd] adj: ~
  **to(wards)** freundlich gesonnen +dat.
**well-dressed** ['wɛl'drɛst] adj gut gekleidet.
**well-earned** ['wɛl'əːnd] adj (*rest*)
  wohlverdient.
**well-groomed** ['wɛl'gruːmd] adj gepflegt.
**well-heeled** ['wɛl'hiːld] (*inf*) adj betucht.
**well-informed** ['wɛlɪn'fɔːmd] adj gut
  informiert.
**Wellington** ['wɛlɪŋtən] n (GEOG) Wellington
  nt.
**wellingtons** ['wɛlɪŋtənz] npl (*also:* **wellington
  boots**) Gummistiefel pl.
**well-kept** ['wɛl'kɛpt] adj (*house, grounds*)
  gepflegt; (*secret*) gut gehütet.
**well-known** ['wɛl'nəun] adj wohlbekannt.
**well-mannered** ['wɛl'mænəd] adj
  wohlerzogen.
**well-meaning** ['wɛl'miːnɪŋ] adj (*person*)
  wohlmeinend; (*offer etc*) gutgemeint.
**well-nigh** ['wɛl'naɪ] adv: ~ **impossible**
  geradezu unmöglich.
**well-off** ['wɛl'ɔf] adj (*rich*) begütert.
**well-read** ['wɛl'rɛd] adj belesen.
**well-spoken** ['wɛl'spəukn] adj: **to be** ~ sich
  gut or gewandt ausdrücken.
**well-stocked** ['wɛl'stɔkt] adj gut bestückt.
**well-timed** ['wɛl'taɪmd] adj gut abgepaßt.
**well-to-do** ['wɛltə'duː] adj wohlhabend.
**well-wisher** ['wɛlwɪʃə*] n (*friend, admirer*)
  wohlmeinender Mensch m; **scores of** ~**s had
  gathered** eine große Gefolgschaft hatte
  sich versammelt; **letters from** ~**s** Briefe
  von Leuten, die es gut meinen.
**well-woman clinic** ['wɛlwumən-] n
  ≈ Frauensprechstunde f.
**Welsh** [wɛlʃ] adj walisisch ♦ n (LING)
  Walisisch nt; **the Welsh** npl die Waliser pl.
**Welshman** ['wɛlʃmən] (*irreg: like* **man**) n
  Waliser m.
**Welsh rarebit** n überbackenes Käsebrot nt.
**Welshwoman** ['wɛlʃwumən] (*irreg: like*
  **woman**) n Waliserin f.
**welter** ['wɛltə*] n: **a** ~ **of** eine Flut von.
**went** [wɛnt] pt of **go.**
**wept** [wɛpt] pt, pp of **weep.**
**were** [wəː*] pt of **be.**
**we're** [wɪə*] = **we are.**
**weren't** [wəːnt] = **were not.**
**werewolf** ['wɪəwulf] (*pl* **werewolves**) n

Werwolf m.
**werewolves** ['wɪəwulvz] npl of **werewolf.**
**west** [wɛst] n Westen m ♦ adj (*wind, side, coast*)
  West-, westlich ♦ adv (*to or towards the west*)
  westwärts; **the W**~ (POL) der Westen.
**westbound** ['wɛstbaund] adj (*traffic,
  carriageway*) in Richtung Westen.
**West Country** (BRIT) n: **the** ~
  Südwestengland nt.
**westerly** ['wɛstəlɪ] adj westlich.
**western** ['wɛstən] adj westlich ♦ n (CINE)
  Western m.
**westerner** ['wɛstənə*] n Abendländer(in) m(f).
**westernized** ['wɛstənaɪzd] adj (*society etc*)
  verwestlicht.
**West German** adj westdeutsch ♦ n (*person*)
  Westdeutsche(r) f(m).
**West Germany** n (*formerly*) Bundesrepublik
  f Deutschland.
**West Indian** adj westindisch ♦ n (*person*)
  Westinder(in) m(f).
**West Indies** [-'ɪndɪz] npl: **the** ~ Westindien nt.
**Westminster** ['wɛstmɪnstə*] n Westminster
  nt; (*parliament*) das britische Parlament.
**westward(s)** ['wɛstwəd(z)] adv westwärts.
**wet** [wɛt] adj naß ♦ n (BRIT: POL)
  Gemäßigte(r) f(m), Waschlappen m (pej); **to
  get** ~ naß werden; "~ **paint**" „frisch
  gestrichen"; **to be a** ~ **blanket** (*fig: pej:
  person*) ein(e) Spielverderber(in) m(f) sein;
  **to** ~ **one's pants/o.s.** sich dat in die Hosen
  machen.
**wetness** ['wɛtnɪs] n Nässe f; (*of climate*)
  Feuchtigkeit f.
**wet suit** n Taucheranzug m.
**we've** [wiːv] = **we have.**
**whack** [wæk] vt schlagen.
**whacked** [wækt] (BRIT: inf) adj (*exhausted*)
  erschlagen.
**whale** [weɪl] n Wal m.
**whaler** ['weɪlə*] n Walfänger m.
**whaling** ['weɪlɪŋ] n Walfang m.
**wharf** [wɔːf] (*pl* **wharves**) n Kai m.
**wharves** [wɔːvz] npl of **wharf.**

═══════════════════════════ KEYWORD

**what** [wɔt] adj **1** (*in direct/indirect questions*)
  welche(r, s); ~ **colour/shape is it?** welche
  Farbe/Form hat es?; **for** ~ **reason?** aus
  welchem Grund?
  **2** (*in exclamations*) was für ein(e); ~ **a mess!**
  was für ein Durcheinander!; ~ **a fool I am!**
  was bin ich doch (für) ein Idiot! ♦ pron
  (*interrogative, relative*) was; ~ **are you doing?**
  was machst du?; ~ **are you talking about?**
  wovon redest du?; ~ **is it called?** wie heißt
  das?; ~ **about me?** und ich?; ~ **about a cup
  of tea?** wie wär's mit einer Tasse Tee?;
  ~ **about going to the cinema?** sollen wir ins
  Kino gehen?; **I saw** ~ **you did/what was on
  the table** ich habe gesehen, was du getan
  hast/was auf dem Tisch war; **tell me**

~ **you're thinking about** sag mir, woran du denkst
♦ *excl (disbelieving)* was, wie; ~, **no coffee!** was *or* wie, kein Kaffee?

**whatever** [wɒt'ɛvə*] *adj:* ~ **book** welches Buch auch immer ♦ *pron:* **do** ~ **is necessary/ you want** tun Sie, was nötig ist/was immer Sie wollen; ~ **happens** was auch passiert; **no reason** ~ *or* **whatsoever** überhaupt kein Grund; **nothing** ~ *or* **whatsoever** überhaupt nichts.

**whatsoever** [wɒtsəu'ɛvə*] *adj* = **whatever**.

**wheat** [wiːt] *n* Weizen *m*.

**wheatgerm** ['wiːtdʒɜːm] *n* Weizenkeim *m*.

**wheatmeal** ['wiːtmiːl] *n* Weizenmehl *nt*.

**wheedle** ['wiːdl] *vt:* **to** ~ **sb into doing sth** jdn beschwatzen, etw zu tun; **to** ~ **sth out of sb** jdm etw abluchsen.

**wheel** [wiːl] *n* Rad *nt*; (*also:* **steering** ~) Lenkrad *nt*; (*NAUT*) Steuer *nt* ♦ *vt* (*pram etc*) schieben ♦ *vi* (*birds*) kreisen; (*also:* ~ **round:** *person*) sich herumdrehen.

**wheelbarrow** ['wiːlbærəu] *n* Schubkarre *f*.

**wheelbase** ['wiːlbeɪs] *n* Radstand *m*.

**wheelchair** ['wiːltʃɛə*] *n* Rollstuhl *m*.

**wheel clamp** *n* Parkkralle *f*.

**wheeler-dealer** ['wiːlə'diːlə*] (*pej*) *n* Geschäftemacher(in) *m(f)*.

**wheelie-bin** ['wiːlɪbɪn] *n* Mülltonne *f* auf Rädern.

**wheeling** ['wiːlɪŋ] *n:* ~ **and dealing** (*pej*) Geschäftemacherei *f*.

**wheeze** [wiːz] *vi* (*person*) keuchen ♦ *n* (*idea, joke etc*) Scherz *m*.

**wheezy** ['wiːzɪ] *adj* (*person*) mit pfeifendem Atem; (*cough*) keuchend; (*breath*) pfeifend; (*laugh*) asthmatisch.

============ *KEYWORD*

**when** [wɛn] *adv* wann
♦ *conj* **1** (*at, during, after the time that*) wenn; **she was reading** ~ **I came in** als ich hereinkam, las sie gerade; **be careful** ~ **you cross the road** sei vorsichtig, wenn du die Straße überquerst
**2** (*on, at which*) als; **on the day** ~ **I met him** am Tag, als ich ihn traf
**3** (*whereas*) wo ... doch, obwohl; **why did you buy that** ~ **you can't afford it?** warum hast du das gekauft, obwohl du es dir nicht leisten kannst?

**whenever** [wɛn'ɛvə*] *adv, conj* (*any time that*) wann immer; (*every time that*) (jedesmal,) wenn; **I go** ~ **I can** ich gehe, wann immer ich kann.

**where** [wɛə*] *adv, conj* wo; **this is** ~ ... hier ...; ~ **possible** soweit möglich; ~ **are you from?** woher kommen Sie?

**whereabouts** [wɛərə'bauts] *adv* wo ♦ *n:* **nobody knows his** ~ keiner weiß, wo er ist.

**whereas** [wɛər'æz] *conj* während.

**whereby** [wɛə'baɪ] (*form*) *adv* wonach.

**whereupon** [wɛərə'pɒn] *conj* worauf.

**wherever** [wɛər'ɛvə*] *conj* (*position*) wo (auch) immer; (*motion*) wohin (auch) immer ♦ *adv* (*surprise*) wo (um alles in der Welt); **sit** ~ **you like** nehmen Sie Platz, wo immer Sie wollen.

**wherewithal** ['wɛəwɪðɔːl] *n:* **the** ~ **(to do sth)** (*money*) das nötige Kleingeld(, um etw zu tun).

**whet** [wɛt] *vt* (*appetite*) anregen; (*tool*) schleifen.

**whether** ['wɛðə*] *conj* ob; **I don't know** ~ **to accept or not** ich weiß nicht, ob ich annehmen soll oder nicht; ~ **you go or not** ob du gehst oder nicht; **it's doubtful** ~ ... es ist zweifelhaft, ob ...

**whey** ['weɪ] *n* Molke *f*.

============ *KEYWORD*

**which** [wɪtʃ] *adj* **1** (*interrogative: direct, indirect*) welche(r, s); ~ **picture?** welches Bild?; ~ **books?** welche Bücher?; ~ **one?** welche(r,s)?
**2:** **in** ~ **case** in diesem Fall; **by** ~ **time** zu dieser Zeit
♦ *pron* **1** (*interrogative*) welche(r, s); ~ **of you are coming?** wer von Ihnen kommt?; **I don't mind** ~ mir ist gleich, welche(r,s)
**2** (*relative*) der/die/das; **the apple** ~ **you ate/ which is on the table** der Apfel, den du gegessen hast/der auf dem Tisch liegt; **the chair on** ~ **you are sitting** der Stuhl, auf dem Sie sitzen; **the book of** ~ **you spoke** das Buch, wovon *or* von dem Sie sprachen; **he said he saw her,** ~ **is true** er sagte, er habe sie gesehen, was auch stimmt; **after** ~ wonach.

**whichever** [wɪtʃ'ɛvə*] *adj:* **take** ~ **book you want** nehmen Sie irgendein *or* ein beliebiges Buch; ~ **book you take** welches Buch Sie auch nehmen.

**whiff** [wɪf] *n* (*of perfume*) Hauch *m*; (*of petrol, smoke*) Geruch *m*; **to catch a** ~ **of sth** den Geruch von etw wahrnehmen.

**while** [waɪl] *n* Weile *f* ♦ *conj* während; **for a** ~ eine Weile (lang); **in a** ~ gleich; **all the** ~ die ganze Zeit (über); **I'll/we'll** *etc* **make it worth your** ~ es wird sich für Sie lohnen.

▶**while away** *vt* (*time*) sich *dat* vertreiben.

**whilst** [waɪlst] *conj* = **while**.

**whim** [wɪm] *n* Laune *f*.

**whimper** ['wɪmpə*] *n* (*cry, moan*) Wimmern *nt* ♦ *vi* wimmern.

**whimsical** ['wɪmzɪkəl] *adj* wunderlich, seltsam; (*story*) kurios.

**whine** [waɪn] *n* (*of pain*) Jammern *nt*; (*of engine, siren*) Heulen *nt* ♦ *vi* (*person*) jammern; (*dog*) jaulen; (*engine, siren*) heulen.

**whip** [wɪp] n Peitsche f; (POL)
≈ Fraktionsführer m ♦ vt (person, animal)
peitschen; (cream, eggs) schlagen; (move
quickly): **to ~ sth out/off** etw blitzschnell
hervorholen/wegbringen.

---

*Der Ausdruck **whip** bezieht sich in der Politik
auf einen Abgeordneten, der für die Einhaltung
der Parteidisziplin zuständig ist, besonders für
die Anwesenheit und das Wahlverhalten der
Abgeordneten im Unterhaus. Die whips
fordern die Abgeordneten ihrer Partei
schriftlich zur Anwesenheit auf und deuten die
Wichtigkeit der Abstimmungen durch ein-,
zwei-, oder dreimaliges Unterstreichen an,
wobei dreimaliges Unterstreichen (3-line whip)
strengsten Fraktionszwang bedeutet.*

---

▶**whip up** vt (cream) schlagen; (inf: meal)
hinzaubern; (arouse: support) anheizen;
(: people) mitreißen.

**whiplash** ['wɪplæʃ] n Peitschenhieb m; (MED:
also: ~ **injury**) Schleudertrauma nt.

**whipped cream** [wɪpt-] n Schlagsahne f.

**whipping boy** ['wɪpɪŋ-] n (fig) Prügelknabe
m.

**whip-round** ['wɪpraund] (BRIT: inf) n
(Geld)sammlung f.

**whirl** [wə:l] vt (arms, sword etc) herumwirbeln
♦ vi wirbeln ♦ n (of activity, pleasure) Wirbel
m; **to be in a ~** (mind, person) völlig verwirrt
sein.

**whirlpool** ['wə:lpu:l] n (lit) Strudel m.

**whirlwind** ['wə:lwɪnd] n (lit) Wirbelwind m.

**whirr** [wə:] vi (motor etc) surren.

**whisk** [wɪsk] n (CULIN) Schneebesen m ♦ vt
(cream, eggs) schlagen; **to ~ sb away** or **off**
jdn in Windeseile wegbringen.

**whiskers** ['wɪskəz] npl (of animal) Barthaare
pl; (of man) Backenbart m.

**whisky,** (US, Ireland) **whiskey** ['wɪskɪ] n
Whisky m.

**whisper** ['wɪspə] n Flüstern nt; (fig: of wind)
Wispern nt ♦ vt, vi flüstern; **to ~ sth to sb**
jdm etw zuflüstern.

**whispering** ['wɪspərɪŋ] n Geflüster nt.

**whist** [wɪst] (BRIT) n Whist nt.

**whistle** ['wɪsl] n (sound) Pfiff m; (object)
Pfeife f ♦ vi pfeifen ♦ vt **to ~ a tune** eine
Melodie pfeifen.

**whistle-stop** ['wɪslstɔp] adj: **to make a ~ tour
of** (fig) eine Rundreise machen durch; (POL)
eine Wahlkampfreise machen durch.

**Whit** [wɪt] n = **Whitsun.**

**white** [waɪt] adj weiß ♦ n (colour) Weiß nt;
(person) Weiße(r) f(m); (of egg, eye) Weiße(s)
nt; **to turn** or **go ~** (person: with fear) weiß or
bleich werden; (: with age) weiße Haare
bekommen; (hair) weiß werden; **the ~s**
(washing) die Weißwäsche f; **tennis/cricket
~s** weiße Tennis-/Krickettrikots.

**whitebait** ['waɪtbeɪt] n eßbare Jungfische

(Heringe, Sprotten etc).

**white coffee** (BRIT) n Kaffee m mit Milch.

**white-collar worker** ['waɪtkɔlə-] n
Schreibtischarbeiter(in) m(f).

**white elephant** n (fig: venture)
Fehlinvestition f.

**white goods** npl (appliances) große
Haushaltsgeräte pl; (linen etc) Weißwaren pl.

**white-hot** [waɪt'hɔt] adj (metal) weißglühend.

---

*White House, eine weiß gestrichene Villa in
Washington, ist der offizielle Wohnsitz des
amerikanischen Präsidenten. Im weiteren
Sinne bezieht sich dieser Begriff auf die
Exekutive der amerikanischen Regierung.*

---

**white lie** n Notlüge f.

**whiteness** ['waɪtnɪs] n Weiß nt.

**white noise** n weißes Rauschen nt.

**whiteout** ['waɪtaut] n starkes
Schneegestöber nt.

**white paper** n (POL) Weißbuch nt.

**whitewash** ['waɪtwɔʃ] n (paint) Tünche f; (inf:
SPORT) totale Niederlage f ♦ vt (building)
tünchen; (fig: incident, reputation)
reinwaschen.

**white water** n: **white-water rafting**
Wildwasserflößen nt.

**whiting** ['waɪtɪŋ] n inv (fish) Weißling m.

**Whit Monday** n Pfingstmontag m.

**Whitsun** ['wɪtsn] n Pfingsten nt.

**whittle** ['wɪtl] vt: **to ~ away** or **down** (costs
etc) verringern.

**whizz** [wɪz] vi: **to ~ past** or **by** vorbeisausen.

**whizz kid** (inf) n Senkrechtstarter(in) m(f).

**WHO** n abbr (= World Health Organization)
Weltgesundheitsorganisation f, WHO f.

=========================================== KEYWORD

**who** [hu:] pron **1** (interrogative) wer; (: acc)
wen; (: dat) wem; **~ is it?, who's there?** wer
ist da?; **~ did you give it to?** wem hast du es
gegeben?

**2** (relative) der/die/das; **the man/woman
~ spoke to me** der Mann, der/die Frau, die
mit mir gesprochen hat.

---

**whodunit, whodunnit** [hu:'dʌnɪt] (inf) n
Krimi m.

**whoever** [hu:'ɛvə] pron: **~ finds it** wer (auch
immer) es findet; **ask ~ you like** fragen Sie,
wen Sie wollen; **~ he marries** ganz gleich or
egal, wen er heiratet; **~ told you that?** wer
um alles in der Welt hat dir das erzählt?

**whole** [həul] adj (entire) ganz; (not broken) heil
♦ n Ganze(s) nt; **the ~ lot (of it)** alles; **the
~ lot (of them)** alle; **the ~ (of the) time** die
ganze Zeit; **~ villages were destroyed** ganze
Dörfer wurden zerstört; **the ~ of** der/die/
das ganze; **the ~ of Glasgow/Europe** ganz
Glasgow/Europa; **the ~ of the town** die
ganze Stadt; **on the ~** im ganzen (gesehen).

**wholefood(s)** ['həulfu:d(z)] *n(pl)* Vollwertkost *f*.

**wholefood shop** *n* ≈ Reformhaus *nt*.

**wholehearted** [həul'hɑ:tɪd] *adj* (*agreement etc*) rückhaltlos.

**wholeheartedly** [həul'hɑ:tɪdlɪ] *adv* (*agree etc*) rückhaltlos.

**wholemeal** ['həulmi:l] (*BRIT*) *adj* (*bread, flour*) Vollkorn-.

**whole note** (*US*) *n* ganze Note *f*.

**wholesale** ['həulseɪl] *n* (*business*) Großhandel *m* ♦ *adj* (*price*) Großhandels-; (*destruction etc*) umfassend ♦ *adv* (*buy, sell*) im Großhandel.

**wholesaler** ['həulseɪlə*] *n* Großhändler *m*.

**wholesome** ['həulsəm] *adj* (*food*) gesund; (*effect*) zuträglich; (*attitude*) positiv.

**wholewheat** ['həulwi:t] *adj* = **wholemeal**.

**wholly** ['həulɪ] *adv* ganz und gar.

================ *KEYWORD*

**whom** [hu:m] *pron* **1** (*interrogative: acc*) wen; (: *dat*) wem; ~ **did you see?** wen hast du gesehen?; **to** ~ **did you give it?** wem hast du es gegeben?
**2** (*relative: acc*) den/die/das; (: *dat*) dem/der/dem; **the man** ~ **I saw/to** ~ **I spoke** der Mann, den ich gesehen habe/mit dem ich gesprochen habe.

**whooping cough** ['hu:pɪŋ-] *n* Keuchhusten *m*.

**whoosh** [wuʃ] *vi*: **to** ~ **along/past/down** entlang-/vorbei-/hinuntersausen ♦ *n* Sausen *nt*; **the skiers** ~**ed past, skiers came by with a** ~ die Skifahrer sausten vorbei.

**whopper** ['wɒpə*] (*inf*) *n* (*lie*) faustdicke Lüge *f*; (*large thing*) Mordsding *nt*.

**whopping** ['wɒpɪŋ] (*inf*) *adj* Riesen-, riesig.

**whore** [hɔ:*] (*inf: pej*) *n* Hure *f*.

================ *KEYWORD*

**whose** [hu:z] *adj* **1** (*possessive: interrogative*) wessen; ~ **book is this?**, ~ **is this book?** wessen Buch ist das?, wem gehört das Buch?; **I don't know** ~ **it is** ich weiß nicht, wem es gehört
**2** (*possessive: relative*) dessen/deren/dessen; **the man** ~ **son you rescued** der Mann, dessen Sohn du gerettet hast; **the woman** ~ **car was stolen** die Frau, deren Auto gestohlen worden war
♦ *pron* ~ **is this?** wem gehört das?; **I know** ~ **it is** ich weiß, wem es gehört.

**Who's Who** ['hu:z'hu:] *n* (*book*) Who's Who *nt*.

================ *KEYWORD*

**why** [waɪ] *adv* warum; ~ **not?** warum nicht?
♦ *conj* warum; **I wonder** ~ **he said that** ich frage mich, warum er das gesagt hat; **that's not** ~ **I'm here** ich bin nicht deswegen hier; **the reason** ~ der Grund, warum *or* weshalb

♦ *excl* (*expressing surprise, shock*) na so was; (*expressing annoyance*) ach; ~, **yes (of course)** aber ja doch; ~, **it's you!** na so was, du bist's!

**WI** *n abbr* (*BRIT:* = *Women's Institute*) britischer *Frauenverband* ♦ *abbr* = **West Indies**; (*US: POST:* = *Wisconsin*).

**wick** [wɪk] *n* Docht *m*; **he gets on my** ~ (*BRIT: inf*) er geht mir auf den Geist.

**wicked** ['wɪkɪd] *adj* (*crime, person*) böse; (*smile, wit*) frech; (*inf: prices*) unverschämt; (: *weather*) schrecklich.

**wicker** ['wɪkə*] *adj* (*chair etc*) Korb-; (*basket*) Weiden-.

**wickerwork** ['wɪkə*wə:k] *adj* (*chair etc*) Korb-; (*basket*) Weiden- ♦ *n* (*objects*) Korbwaren *pl*.

**wicket** ['wɪkɪt] *n* (*CRICKET: stumps*) Tor *nt*, Wicket *nt*; (: *grass area*) Spielbahn *f*.

**wicket-keeper** ['wɪkɪtki:pə*] *n* Torwächter *m*.

**wide** [waɪd] *adj* breit; (*area*) weit; (*publicity*) umfassend ♦ *adv*: **to open sth** ~ etw weit öffnen; **it is 3 metres** ~ es ist 3 Meter breit; **to go** ~ vorbeigehen.

**wide-angle lens** ['waɪdæŋgl-] *n* Weitwinkelobjektiv *nt*.

**wide-awake** [waɪdə'weɪk] *adj* hellwach.

**wide-eyed** [waɪd'aɪd] *adj* mit großen Augen; (*fig*) unschuldig, naiv.

**widely** ['waɪdlɪ] *adv* (*differ, vary*) erheblich; (*travel*) ausgiebig, viel; (*spaced*) weit; (*believed, known*) allgemein; **to be** ~ **read** (*reader*) sehr belesen sein.

**widen** ['waɪdn] *vt* (*road, river*) verbreitern; (*one's experience*) erweitern ♦ *vi* sich verbreitern.

**wideness** ['waɪdnɪs] *n* (*of road, river, gap*) Breite *f*.

**wide open** *adj* (*window, eyes, mouth*) weit geöffnet.

**wide-ranging** [waɪd'reɪndʒɪŋ] *adj* (*effects*) weitreichend; (*interview, survey*) umfassend.

**widespread** ['waɪdspred] *adj* weitverbreitet.

**widow** ['wɪdəu] *n* Witwe *f*.

**widowed** ['wɪdəud] *adj* verwitwet.

**widower** ['wɪdəuə*] *n* Witwer *m*.

**width** [wɪdθ] *n* Breite *f*; (*in swimming pool*) (Quer)bahn *f*; **it's 7 metres in** ~ es ist 7 Meter breit.

**widthways** ['wɪdθweɪz] *adv* der Breite nach.

**wield** [wi:ld] *vt* (*sword*) schwingen; (*power*) ausüben.

**wife** [waɪf] (*pl* **wives**) *n* Frau *f*.

**wig** [wɪg] *n* Perücke *f*.

**wigging** ['wɪgɪŋ] (*BRIT: inf*) *n* Standpauke *f*.

**wiggle** ['wɪgl] *vt* wackeln mit.

**wiggly** ['wɪglɪ] *adj*: ~ **line** Schlangenlinie *f*.

**wigwam** ['wɪgwæm] *n* Wigwam *m*.

**wild** [waɪld] *adj* wild; (*weather*) rauh, stürmisch; (*person, behaviour*) ungestüm; (*idea*) weithergeholt; (*applause*) stürmisch ♦ *n*: **the** ~ (*natural surroundings*) die freie

Natur f; **the wilds** npl die Wildnis; **I'm not
~ about it** ich bin nicht versessen or scharf
darauf.
**wild card** n (COMPUT) Wildcard f,
Ersatzzeichen nt.
**wildcat** ['waɪldkæt] n Wildkatze f.
**wildcat strike** n wilder Streik m.
**wilderness** ['wɪldənɪs] n Wildnis f.
**wildfire** ['waɪldfaɪə'] n: **to spread like ~** sich
wie ein Lauffeuer ausbreiten.
**wild-goose chase** [waɪld'guːs-] n
aussichtslose Suche f.
**wildlife** ['waɪldlaɪf] n (animals) die Tierwelt f.
**wildly** ['waɪldlɪ] adv wild; (very: romantic)
wild-; (: inefficient) furchtbar.
**wiles** [waɪlz] npl List f.
**wilful**, (US) **willful** ['wɪlful] adj (obstinate)
eigensinnig; (deliberate) vorsätzlich.

================================= KEYWORD

**will** [wɪl] (vt: pt, pp willed) aux vb **1** (forming
future tense): **I ~ finish it tomorrow** ich
werde es morgen fertigmachen, ich mache
es morgen fertig; **~ you do it? - yes I ~/no I
won't** machst du es? - ja/nein
**2** (in conjectures, predictions): **that ~ be the
postman** das ist bestimmt der Briefträger
**3** (in commands, requests, offers): **~ you sit
down** (politely) bitte nehmen Sie Platz;
(angrily) nun setz dich doch; **~ you be quiet!**
seid jetzt still!; **~ you help me?** hilfst du
mir?; **~ you have a cup of tea?** möchten Sie
eine Tasse Tee?; **I won't put up with it!** das
lasse ich mir nicht gefallen! ♦ vt: **to ~ sb to
do sth** jdn durch Willenskraft dazu
bewegen, etw zu tun; **he ~ed himself to go
on** er zwang sich dazu, weiterzumachen
♦ n (volition) Wille m; (testament) Testament
nt; **he did it against his ~** er tat es gegen
seinen Willen.

**willful** ['wɪlful] (US) adj = **wilful**.
**willing** ['wɪlɪŋ] adj (having no objection)
gewillt; (enthusiastic) bereitwillig; **he's ~ to
do it** er ist bereit, es zu tun; **to show ~**
guten Willen zeigen.
**willingly** ['wɪlɪŋlɪ] adv bereitwillig.
**willingness** ['wɪlɪŋnɪs] n (readiness)
Bereitschaft f; (enthusiasm) Bereitwilligkeit
f.
**will-o'-the-wisp** ['wɪlədð'wɪsp] n Irrlicht nt;
(fig) Trugbild nt.
**willow** ['wɪləu] n (tree) Weide f; (wood)
Weidenholz nt.
**willpower** ['wɪl'pauə'] n Willenskraft f.
**willy-nilly** ['wɪlɪ'nɪlɪ] adv (willingly or not) wohl
oder übel.
**wilt** [wɪlt] vi (plant) welken.
**Wilts** [wɪlts] (BRIT) abbr (POST: = Wiltshire).
**wily** ['waɪlɪ] adj listig, raffiniert.
**wimp** [wɪmp] (inf: pej) n Waschlappen m.
**wimpish** ['wɪmpɪʃ] (inf) adj weichlich.

**win** [wɪn] (pt, pp won) n Sieg m ♦ vt gewinnen
♦ vi siegen, gewinnen.
▶**win over** vt (persuade) gewinnen.
▶**win round** (BRIT) vt = **win over**.
**wince** [wɪns] vi zusammenzucken.
**winch** [wɪntʃ] n Winde f.
**Winchester disk** ['wɪntʃɪstə-] n
Winchesterplatte f.
**wind¹** [wɪnd] n (air) Wind m; (MED)
Blähungen pl; (breath) Atem m ♦ vt (take
breath away from) den Atem nehmen +dat;
**the winds** npl (MUS) die Bläser pl; **into** or
**against the ~** gegen den Wind; **to get ~ of
sth** (fig) von etw Wind bekommen; **to break
~** Darmwind entweichen lassen.
**wind²** [waɪnd] (pt, pp wound) vt (thread, rope,
bandage) wickeln; (clock, toy) aufziehen ♦ vi
(road, river) sich winden.
▶**wind down** vt (car window) herunter-
drehen; (fig: production) zurückschrauben.
▶**wind up** vt (clock, toy) aufziehen; (debate)
abschließen.
**windbreak** ['wɪndbreɪk] n Windschutz m.
**windbreaker** ['wɪndbreɪkə'] (US) n
= **windcheater**.
**windcheater** ['wɪndtʃiːtə'] n Windjacke f.
**winder** ['waɪndə'] (BRIT) n (on watch) Krone f,
Aufziehrädchen nt.
**windfall** ['wɪndfɔːl] n (money) unverhoffter
Glücksfall m; (apple) Fallobst nt.
**winding** ['waɪndɪŋ] adj gewunden.
**wind instrument** ['wɪnd-] n Blasinstrument
nt.
**windmill** ['wɪndmɪl] n Windmühle f.
**window** ['wɪndəu] n (also COMPUT) Fenster
nt; (in shop) Schaufenster nt.
**window box** n Blumenkasten m.
**window cleaner** n Fensterputzer(in) m(f).
**window dresser** n Schaufenster-
dekorateur(in) m(f).
**window envelope** n Fensterumschlag m.
**window frame** n Fensterrahmen m.
**window ledge** n Fenstersims m.
**window-shopping** ['wɪndəuʃɒpɪŋ] n
Schaufensterbummel m; **to go ~** einen
Schaufensterbummel machen.
**windowsill** ['wɪndəusɪl] n Fensterbank f.
**windpipe** ['wɪndpaɪp] n Luftröhre f.
**wind power** ['wɪnd-] n Windkraft f,
Windenergie f.
**windscreen** ['wɪndskriːn] n
Windschutzscheibe f.
**windscreen washer** n Scheibenwasch-
anlage f.
**windscreen wiper** [-waɪpə'] n
Scheibenwischer m.
**windshield** ['wɪndʃiːld] (US) n = **windscreen**.
**windsurfing** ['wɪndsɜːfɪŋ] n Windsurfen nt.
**windswept** ['wɪndswɛpt] adj (place) vom
Wind gepeitscht; (person) vom Wind
zerzaust.

**wind tunnel** ['wɪnd-] *n* Windkanal *m*.
**windy** ['wɪndɪ] *adj* windig; **it's ~** es ist windig.
**wine** [waɪn] *n* Wein *m* ♦ *vt*: **to ~ and dine sb** jdm zu einem guten Essen ausführen.
**wine bar** *n* Weinlokal *nt*.
**wine cellar** *n* Weinkeller *m*.
**wine glass** *n* Weinglas *nt*.
**wine list** *n* Weinkarte *f*.
**wine merchant** *n* Weinhändler(in) *m(f)*.
**wine tasting** [-teɪstɪŋ] *n* Weinprobe *f*.
**wine waiter** *n* Weinkellner *m*.
**wing** [wɪŋ] *n* (*of bird, insect, plane*) Flügel *m*; (*of building*) Trakt *m*; (*of car*) Kotflügel *m*; **the wings** *npl* (*THEAT*) die Kulissen *pl*.
**winger** ['wɪŋə*] *n* (*SPORT*) Flügelspieler(in) *m(f)*.
**wing mirror** (*BRIT*) *n* Seitenspiegel *m*.
**wing nut** *n* Flügelmutter *f*.
**wingspan** ['wɪŋspæn] *n* Flügelspannweite *f*.
**wingspread** ['wɪŋspred] *n* = **wingspan**.
**wink** [wɪŋk] *n* (*of eye*) Zwinkern *m* ♦ *vi* (*with eye*) zwinkern; (*light etc*) blinken.
**winkle** [wɪŋkl] *n* Strandschnecke *f*.
**winner** ['wɪnə*] *n* (*of race, competition*) Sieger(in) *m(f)*; (*of prize*) Gewinner(in) *m(f)*.
**winning** ['wɪnɪŋ] *adj* (*team, entry*) siegreich; (*shot, goal*) entscheidend; (*smile*) einnehmend; *see also* **winnings**.
**winning post** *n* (*lit*) Zielpfosten *m*; (*fig*) Ziel *nt*.
**winnings** ['wɪnɪŋz] *npl* Gewinn *m*.
**winsome** ['wɪnsəm] *adj* (*expression*) gewinnend; (*person*) reizend.
**winter** ['wɪntə*] *n* Winter *m* ♦ *vi* (*birds*) überwintern; **in ~** im Winter.
**winter sports** *npl* Wintersport *m*.
**wintry** ['wɪntrɪ] *adj* (*weather, day*) winterlich, Winter-.
**wipe** [waɪp] *vt* wischen; (*dry*) abtrocknen; (*clean*) abwischen; (*erase: tape*) löschen; **to ~ one's nose** sich *dat* die Nase putzen ♦ *n*: **to give sth a ~** etw abwischen.
▶**wipe off** *vt* abwischen.
▶**wipe out** *vt* (*destroy: city etc*) auslöschen.
▶**wipe up** *vt* (*mess*) aufwischen.
**wire** ['waɪə*] *n* Draht *m*; (*US: telegram*) Telegramm *nt* ♦ *vt* (*US*): **to ~ sb** jdm telegrafieren; (*also: ~ up: electrical fitting*) anschließen.
**wire brush** *n* Drahtbürste *f*.
**wire cutters** *npl* Drahtschere *f*.
**wireless** ['waɪəlɪs] (*BRIT: old*) *n* Funk *m*; (*set*) Rundfunkgerät *nt*.
**wire netting** *n* Maschendraht *m*.
**wire service** (*US*) *n* Nachrichtenagentur *f*.
**wire-tapping** ['waɪə'tæpɪŋ] *n* Anzapfen *nt* von Leitungen.
**wiring** ['waɪərɪŋ] *n* elektrische Leitungen *pl*.
**wiry** ['waɪərɪ] *adj* (*person*) drahtig; (*hair*) borstig.
**Wis.** (*US*) *abbr* (*POST: = Wisconsin*).
**wisdom** ['wɪzdəm] *n* (*of person*) Weisheit *f*; (*of action, remark*) Klugheit *f*.
**wisdom tooth** *n* Weisheitszahn *m*.
**wise** *adj* (*person*) weise; (*action, remark*) klug; **I'm none the ~r** ich bin genauso klug wie vorher.
▶**wise up** (*inf*) *vi*: **to ~ up to sth** hinter etw *acc* kommen.
**...wise** [waɪz] *suff*: **timewise/moneywise** *etc* zeitmäßig/geldmäßig *etc*.
**wisecrack** ['waɪzkræk] *n* Witzelei *f*.
**wisely** ['waɪzlɪ] *adv* klug, weise.
**wish** [wɪʃ] *n* Wunsch *m* ♦ *vt* wünschen; **best ~es** (*for birthday etc*) herzliche Grüße, alle guten Wünsche; **with best ~es** (*in letter*) mit den besten Wünschen *or* Grüßen; **give her my best ~es** grüßen Sie sie herzlich von mir; **to make a ~** sich *dat* etw wünschen; **to ~ sb goodbye** jdm auf Wiedersehen sagen; **he ~ed me well** er wünschte mir alles Gute; **to ~ to do sth** etw tun wollen; **to ~ sth on sb** jdm etw wünschen; **to ~ for sth** sich *dat* etw wünschen.
**wishbone** ['wɪʃbəʊn] *n* Gabelbein *nt*.
**wishful** ['wɪʃful] *adj*: **it's ~ thinking** das ist reines Wunschdenken.
**wishy-washy** ['wɪʃɪ'wɒʃɪ] (*inf*) *adj* (*colour*) verwaschen; (*person*) farblos; (*ideas*) nichtssagend.
**wisp** [wɪsp] *n* (*of grass*) Büschel *nt*; (*of hair*) Strähne *f*; (*of smoke*) Fahne *f*.
**wistful** ['wɪstful] *adj* wehmütig.
**wit** [wɪt] *n* (*wittiness*) geistreiche Art *f*; (*person*) geistreicher Mensch *m*; (*presence of mind*) Verstand *m*; **wits** *npl* (*intelligence*) Verstand *m*; **to be at one's ~s' end** mit seinem Latein am Ende sein; **to have one's ~s about one** einen klaren Kopf haben; **to ~** (*namely*) und zwar.
**witch** [wɪtʃ] *n* Hexe *f*.
**witchcraft** ['wɪtʃkrɑːft] *n* Hexerei *f*.
**witch doctor** *n* Medizinmann *m*.
**witch-hunt** ['wɪtʃhʌnt] *n* (*fig*) Hexenjagd *f*.

=================================== *KEYWORD*

**with** [wɪð] *prep* **1** (*accompanying, in the company of*) mit; **we stayed ~ friends** wir wohnten bei Freunden; **I'll be ~ you in a minute** einen Augenblick, ich bin sofort da; **I'm ~ you** (*I understand*) ich verstehe; **to be ~ it** (*inf: up-to-date*) auf dem laufenden sein; (*: alert*) da sein
**2** (*descriptive, indicating manner*) mit; **the man ~ the grey hat/blue eyes** der Mann mit dem grauen Hut/den blauen Augen; **~ tears in her eyes** mit Tränen in den Augen; **red ~ anger** rot vor Wut.

**withdraw** [wɪθ'drɔː] (*irreg: like draw*) *vt* (*object, offer*) zurückziehen; (*remark*) zurücknehmen ♦ *vi* (*troops*) abziehen; (*person*) sich zurückziehen; **to ~ money** (*from bank*) Geld abheben; **to ~ into o.s.** sich in sich *acc* selbst zurückziehen.

**withdrawal** [wɪθ'drɔːəl] n (of offer, remark) Zurücknahme f; (of troops) Abzug m; (of participation) Ausstieg m; (of services) Streichung f; (of money) Abhebung f.

**withdrawal symptoms** npl Entzugserscheinungen pl.

**withdrawn** [wɪθ'drɔːn] pp of **withdraw ♦** adj (person) verschlossen.

**wither** ['wɪðə*] vi (plant) verwelken.

**withered** ['wɪðəd] adj (plant) verwelkt; (limb) verkümmert.

**withhold** [wɪθ'həuld] (irreg: like **hold**) vt vorenthalten.

**within** [wɪð'ɪn] prep (place) innerhalb +gen; (time, distance) innerhalb von ♦ adv innen; ~ **reach** in Reichweite; ~ **sight (of)** in Sichtweite (+gen); ~ **the week** vor Ende der Woche; ~ **a mile of** weniger als eine Meile entfernt von; ~ **an hour** innerhalb einer Stunde; ~ **the law** im Rahmen des Gesetzes.

**without** [wɪð'aut] prep ohne; ~ **a coat** ohne Mantel; ~ **speaking** ohne zu sprechen; **it goes** ~ **saying** das versteht sich von selbst; ~ **anyone knowing** ohne daß jemand davon wußte.

**withstand** [wɪθ'stænd] (irreg: like **stand**) vt widerstehen +dat.

**witness** ['wɪtnɪs] n Zeuge m, Zeugin f ♦ vt (event) sehen, Zeuge/Zeugin sein +gen; (fig) miterleben; **to bear** ~ **to sth** Zeugnis für etw ablegen; ~ **for the prosecution/defence** Zeuge/Zeugin der Anklage/Verteidigung; **to** ~ **to sth** etw bezeugen; **to** ~ **having seen sth** bezeugen, etw gesehen zu haben.

**witness box** n Zeugenstand m.

**witness stand** (US) n = **witness box**.

**witticism** ['wɪtɪsɪzəm] n geistreiche Bemerkung f.

**witty** ['wɪtɪ] adj geistreich.

**wives** [waɪvz] npl of **wife**.

**wizard** ['wɪzəd] n Zauberer m.

**wizened** ['wɪznd] adj (person) verhutzelt; (fruit, vegetable) verschrumpelt.

**wk** abbr = **week**.

**Wm.** abbr (= William).

**WO** n abbr (MIL) = **warrant officer**.

**wobble** ['wɔbl] vi wackeln; (legs) zittern.

**wobbly** ['wɔblɪ] adj (hand, voice) zitt(e)rig; (table, chair) wack(e)lig; **to feel** ~ sich wack(e)lig fühlen.

**woe** [wəu] n (sorrow) Jammer m; (misfortune) Kummer m.

**woeful** ['wəuful] adj traurig.

**wok** [wɔk] n Wok m.

**woke** [wəuk] pt of **wake**.

**woken** ['wəukn] pp of **wake**.

**wolf** [wulf] (pl **wolves**) n Wolf m.

**wolves** [wulvz] npl of **wolf**.

**woman** ['wumən] (pl **women**) n Frau f; ~ **friend** Freundin f; ~ **teacher** Lehrerin f; **young** ~ junge Frau; **women's page**

**Frauenseite** f.

**woman doctor** n Ärztin f.

**womanize** ['wumənaɪz] (pej) vi hinter Frauen her sein.

**womanly** ['wumənlɪ] adj (virtues etc) weiblich.

**womb** [wuːm] n Mutterleib m; (MED) Gebärmutter f.

**women** ['wɪmɪn] npl of **woman**.

**women's lib** ['wɪmɪnz-] (inf) n Frauenbefreiung f.

**Women's (Liberation) Movement** n Frauenbewegung f.

**won** [wʌn] pt, pp of **win**.

**wonder** ['wʌndə*] n (miracle) Wunder nt; (awe) Verwunderung f ♦ vi: **to** ~ **whether/why** etc sich fragen, ob/warum etc; **it's no** ~ **(that)** es ist kein Wunder(, daß); **to** ~ **at** (marvel at) staunen über +acc; **to** ~ **about** sich dat Gedanken machen über +acc; **I** ~ **if you could help me** könnten Sie mir vielleicht helfen.

**wonderful** ['wʌndəful] adj wunderbar.

**wonderfully** ['wʌndəfəlɪ] adv wunderbar.

**wonky** ['wɔŋkɪ] (BRIT: inf) adj wack(e)lig.

**wont** [wəunt] n: **as is his** ~ wie er zu tun pflegt.

**won't** [wəunt] = **will not**.

**woo** [wuː] vt (woman, audience) umwerben.

**wood** [wud] n (timber) Holz nt; (forest) Wald m ♦ cpd Holz-.

**woodcarving** ['wudkɑːvɪŋ] n (act, object) Holzschnitzerei f.

**wooded** ['wudɪd] adj bewaldet.

**wooden** ['wudn] adj (also fig) hölzern.

**woodland** ['wudlənd] n Waldland nt.

**woodpecker** ['wudpɛkə*] n Specht m.

**wood pigeon** n Ringeltaube f.

**woodwind** ['wudwɪnd] adj (instrument) Holzblasinstrument nt; **the** ~ die Holzbläser pl.

**woodwork** ['wudwɜːk] n (skill) Holzarbeiten pl.

**woodworm** ['wudwɜːm] n Holzwurm m.

**woof** [wuf] n (of dog) Wau nt ♦ vi kläffen; ~, ~! wau, wau!

**wool** [wul] n Wolle f; **to pull the** ~ **over sb's eyes** (fig) jdn hinters Licht führen.

**woollen**, (US) **woolen** ['wulən] adj (hat) Woll-, wollen.

**woollens** ['wulənz] npl Wollsachen pl.

**woolly**, (US) **wooly** ['wulɪ] adj (socks, hat etc) Woll-; (fig: ideas) schwammig; (person) verworren ♦ n (pullover) Wollpullover m.

**woozy** ['wuːzɪ] (inf) adj duselig.

**Worcs** (BRIT) abbr (POST: = Worcestershire).

**word** [wɜːd] n Wort nt; (news) Nachricht f ♦ vt (letter, message) formulieren; ~ **for** ~ Wort für Wort, (wort)wörtlich; **what's the** ~ **for "pen" in German?** was heißt „pen" auf deutsch?; **to put sth into** ~s etw in Worte fassen; **in other** ~s mit anderen Worten; **to break/keep one's** ~ sein Wort brechen/

halten; **to have ~s with sb** eine Auseinandersetzung mit jdm haben; **to have a ~ with sb** mit jdm sprechen; **I'll take your ~ for it** ich verlasse mich auf Sie; **to send ~ of sth** etw verlauten lassen; **to leave ~ (with sb/for sb) that ...** (bei jdm/für jdn) die Nachricht hinterlassen, daß ...; **by ~ of mouth** durch mündliche Überlieferung.

**wording** ['wə:dıŋ] *n* (*of message, contract etc*) Wortlaut *m*, Formulierung *f*.

**word-perfect** ['wə:d'pə:fıkt] *adj*: **to be ~** den Text perfekt beherrschen.

**word processing** *n* Textverarbeitung *f*.

**word processor** [-prəusesə*] *n* Textverarbeitungssystem *nt*.

**wordwrap** ['wə:dræp] *n* (*COMPUT*) (automatischer) Zeilenumbruch *m*.

**wordy** ['wə:dı] *adj* (*book*) langatmig; (*person*) wortreich.

**wore** [wɔ:*] *pt of* **wear**.

**work** [wə:k] *n* Arbeit *f*; (*ART, LITER*) Werk *nt* ♦ *vi* arbeiten; (*mechanism*) funktionieren; (*be successful: medicine etc*) wirken ♦ *vt* (*clay, wood, land*) bearbeiten; (*mine*) arbeiten in; (*machine*) bedienen; (*create: effect, miracle*) bewirken; **to go to ~** zur Arbeit gehen; **to set to ~, to start ~** sich an die Arbeit machen; **to be at ~ (on sth)** (an etw *dat*) arbeiten; **to be out of ~** arbeitslos sein; **to be in ~** eine Stelle haben; **to ~ hard** hart arbeiten; **to ~ loose** (*part, knot*) sich lösen; **to ~ on the assumption that ...** von der Annahme ausgehen, daß ...

▶**work on** *vt fus* (*task*) arbeiten an +*dat*; (*person: influence*) bearbeiten; **he's ~ing on his car** er arbeitet an seinem Auto.

▶**work out** *vi* (*plans etc*) klappen; (*SPORT*) trainieren ♦ *vt* (*problem*) lösen; (*plan*) ausarbeiten; **it ~s out at 100 pounds** es ergibt 100 Pfund.

▶**work up** *vt*: **to get ~ed up** sich aufregen.

**workable** ['wə:kəbl] *adj* (*system*) durchführbar; (*solution*) brauchbar.

**workaholic** [wə:kə'hɔlık] *n* Arbeitstier *nt*.

**workbench** ['wə:kbɛntʃ] *n* Werkbank *f*.

**worker** ['wə:kə*] *n* Arbeiter(in) *m(f)*; **office ~** Büroarbeiter(in) *m(f)*.

**workforce** ['wə:kfɔ:s] *n* Arbeiterschaft *f*.

**work-in** ['wə:kın] (*BRIT*) *n* Fabrikbesetzung *f*.

**working** ['wə:kıŋ] *adj* (*day, conditions*) Arbeits-; (*population*) arbeitend; (*mother*) berufstätig; **a ~ knowledge of English** (*adequate*) Grundkenntnisse in Englisch.

**working capital** *n* Betriebskapital *nt*.

**working class** *n* Arbeiterklasse *f*.

**working-class** ['wə:kıŋ'klɑ:s] *adj* (*family, town*) Arbeiter-.

**working man** *n* Arbeiter *m*.

**working order** *n*: **in ~** in betriebsfähigem Zustand.

**working party** (*BRIT*) *n* Ausschuß *m*.

**working relationship** *n* Arbeitsbeziehung *f*.

**working week** *n* Arbeitswoche *f*.

**work-in-progress** ['wə:kın'prəugres] *n* laufende Arbeiten *pl*.

**workload** ['wə:kləud] *n* Arbeitsbelastung *f*.

**workman** ['wə:kmən] (*irreg: like* **man**) *n* Arbeiter *m*.

**workmanship** ['wə:kmənʃıp] *n* Arbeitsqualität *f*.

**workmate** ['wə:kmeıt] *n* Arbeitskollege *m*, Arbeitskollegin *f*.

**workout** ['wə:kaut] *n* Fitneßtraining *nt*.

**work permit** *n* Arbeitserlaubnis *f*.

**works** [wə:ks] (*BRIT*) *n* (*factory*) Fabrik *f*, Werk *nt* ♦ *npl* (*of clock*) Uhrwerk *nt*; (*of machine*) Getriebe *nt*.

**work sheet** *n* Arbeitsblatt *nt*.

**workshop** ['wə:kʃɔp] *n* (*building*) Werkstatt *f*; (*practical session*) Workshop *nt*.

**work station** *n* Arbeitsplatz *m*; (*COMPUT*) Workstation *f*.

**work-study** ['wə:kstʌdı] *n* Arbeitsstudie *f*.

**worktop** ['wə:ktɔp] *n* Arbeitsfläche *f*.

**work-to-rule** ['wə:ktə'ru:l] (*BRIT*) *n* Dienst *m* nach Vorschrift.

**world** [wə:ld] *n* Welt *f* ♦ *cpd* (*champion, power, war*) Welt-; **all over the ~** auf der ganzen Welt; **to think the ~ of sb** große Stücke auf jdn halten; **what in the ~ is he doing?** was um alles in der Welt macht er?; **to do sb a** *or* **the ~ of good** jdm unwahrscheinlich gut tun; **W~ War One/Two** der Erste/Zweite Weltkrieg; **out of this ~** phantastisch.

**World Cup** *n*: **the ~** (*FOOTBALL*) die Fußballweltmeisterschaft *f*.

**world-famous** [wə:ld'feıməs] *adj* weltberühmt.

**worldly** ['wə:ldlı] *adj* weltlich; (*knowledgeable*) weltgewandt.

**world music** *n* World Music *f*, Richtung der Popmusik, die musikalische Stilelemente der Dritten Welt verwendet.

**World Series** (*US*) *n* Endrunde der Baseball-Weltmeisterschaft zwischen den Tabellenführern der Spitzenligen.

**worldwide** ['wə:ld'waıd] *adj, adv* weltweit.

**worm** [wə:m] *n* Wurm *m*.

▶**worm out** *vt*: **to ~ sth out of sb** jdm etw entlocken.

**worn** [wɔ:n] *pp of* **wear** ♦ *adj* (*carpet*) abgenutzt; (*shoe*) abgetragen.

**worn-out** ['wɔ:naut] *adj* (*object*) abgenutzt; (*person*) erschöpft.

**worried** ['wʌrıd] *adj* besorgt; **to be ~ about sth** sich wegen etw Sorgen machen.

**worrier** ['wʌrıə*] *n*: **to be a ~** sich ständig Sorgen machen.

**worrisome** ['wʌrısəm] *adj* besorgniserregend.

**worry** ['wʌrı] *n* Sorge *f* ♦ *vt* beunruhigen ♦ *vi* sich *dat* Sorgen machen; **to ~ about** *or* **over sth/sb** sich um etw/jdn Sorgen machen.

**worrying** ['wʌrııŋ] *adj* beunruhigend.

**worse** [wə:s] *adj* schlechter, schlimmer ♦ *adv*

schlechter ♦ n Schlechtere(s) nt, Schlimmere(s) nt; **to get ~** (*situation etc*) sich verschlechtern *or* verschlimmern; **he is none the ~ for it** er hat keinen Schaden dabei erlitten; **so much the ~ for you!** um so schlimmer für dich!; **a change for the ~** eine Wendung zum Schlechten.

**worsen** ['wəːsn] *vt* verschlimmern ♦ *vi* sich verschlechtern.

**worse off** *adj* (*also fig*) schlechter dran; **he is now ~ than before** er ist jetzt schlechter dran als zuvor.

**worship** ['wəːʃɪp] *n* (*act*) Verehrung *f* ♦ *vt* (*god*) anbeten; (*person, thing*) verehren; **Your W~** (*BRIT: to mayor*) verehrter Herr Bürgermeister; (: *to judge*) Euer Ehren.

**worshipper** ['wəːʃɪpə\*] *n* (*in church etc*) Kirchgänger(in) *m(f)*; (*fig*) Anbeter(in) *m(f)*, Verehrer(in) *m(f)*.

**worst** [wəːst] *adj* schlechteste(r, s), schlimmste(r, s) ♦ *adv* am schlimmsten ♦ *n* Schlimmste(s) *nt*; **at ~** schlimmstenfalls; **if the ~ comes to the ~** wenn alle Stricke reißen.

**worst-case scenario** ['wəːstkeɪs-] *n* Schlimmstfallszenario *nt*.

**worsted** ['wustɪd] *n* Kammgarn *nt*.

**worth** [wəːθ] *n* Wert *m* ♦ *adj*: **to be ~** wert sein; **£2 ~ of apples** Äpfel für £ 2; **how much is it ~?** was *or* wieviel ist es wert?; **it's ~ it** (*effort, time*) es lohnt sich; **it's ~ every penny** es ist sein Geld wert.

**worthless** ['wəːθlɪs] *adj* wertlos.

**worthwhile** ['wəːθ'waɪl] *adj* lohnend.

**worthy** [wəːðɪ] *adj* (*person*) würdig; (*motive*) ehrenwert; **~ of** wert +*gen*.

―――――――――― *KEYWORD*

**would** [wud] *aux vb* **1** (*conditional tense*): **if you asked him he ~ do it** wenn du ihn fragtest, würde er es tun; **if you had asked him he ~ have done it** wenn du ihn gefragt hättest, hätte er es getan

**2** (*in offers, invitations, requests*): **~ you like a biscuit?** möchten Sie ein Plätzchen?; **~ you ask him to come in?** würden Sie ihn bitten, hereinzukommen?

**3** (*in indirect speech*): **I said I ~ do it** ich sagte, ich würde es tun

**4** (*emphatic*): **it WOULD have to snow today!** ausgerechnet heute mußte es schneien!

**5** (*insistence*): **she ~n't behave** sie wollte sich partout nicht benehmen

**6** (*conjecture*): **it ~ have been midnight** es mochte etwa Mitternacht gewesen sein; **it ~ seem so** so scheint es wohl

**7** (*indicating habit*): **he ~ go there on Mondays** er ging montags immer dorthin; **he ~ spend every day on the beach** er verbrachte jeden Tag am Strand.

**would-be** ['wudbiː] *adj* (*singer, writer*) Möchtegern-.

**wouldn't** ['wudnt] = **would not**.

**wound¹** [waund] *pt, pp of* **wind²**.

**wound²** [wuːnd] *n* Wunde *f* ♦ *vt* verwunden; **~ed in the leg** am Bein verletzt.

**wove** [wəuv] *pt of* **weave**.

**woven** ['wəuvn] *pp of* **weave**.

**WP** *n abbr* = **word processing; word processor** ♦ *abbr* (*BRIT: inf: = weather permitting*) bei günstiger Witterung.

**WPC** *n abbr* (= *woman police constable*) Polizistin *f*.

**wpm** *abbr* (= *words per minute*) Worte pro Minute (*beim Maschineschreiben*).

**WRAC** (*BRIT*) *n abbr* (= *Women's Royal Army Corps*) Frauenkorps der Armee.

**WRAF** (*BRIT*) *n abbr* (= *Women's Royal Air Force*) Frauenkorps der Luftwaffe.

**wrangle** ['ræŋgl] *n* Gerangel *nt* ♦ *vi*: **to ~ with sb over sth** sich mit jdm um etw zanken.

**wrap** [ræp] *n* (*shawl*) Umhang *m*; (*cape*) Cape *nt* ♦ *vt* einwickeln; (*also: ~ up: pack*) einpacken; (*wind: tape etc*) wickeln; **under ~s** (*fig: plan*) geheim.

**wrapper** ['ræpə\*] *n* (*on chocolate*) Papier *nt*; (*BRIT: of book*) Umschlag *m*.

**wrapping paper** ['ræpɪŋ-] *n* (*brown*) Packpapier *nt*; (*fancy*) Geschenkpapier *nt*.

**wrath** [rɔθ] *n* Zorn *m*.

**wreak** [riːk] *vt*: **to ~ havoc (on)** verheerenden Schaden anrichten (bei); **to ~ vengeance** *or* **revenge on sb** Rache an jdm üben.

**wreath** [riːθ] (*pl ~s*) *n* Kranz *m*.

**wreck** [rɛk] *n* Wrack *nt*; (*vehicle*) Schrotthaufen *m* ♦ *vt* kaputtmachen; (*car*) zu Schrott fahren; (*chances*) zerstören.

**wreckage** ['rɛkɪdʒ] *n* (*of car, plane, building*) Trümmer *pl*; (*of ship*) Wrackteile *pl*.

**wrecker** ['rɛkə\*] (*US*) *n* (*breakdown van*) Abschleppwagen *m*.

**Wren** (*BRIT*) *n abbr* weibliches Mitglied der britischen Marine.

**wren** [rɛn] *n* (*ZOOL*) Zaunkönig *m*.

**wrench** [rɛntʃ] *n* (*TECH*) Schraubenschlüssel *m*; (*tug*) Ruck *m*; (*fig*) schmerzhaftes Erlebnis *nt* ♦ *vt* (*pull*) reißen; (*injure: arm, back*) verrenken; **to ~ sth from sb** jdm etw entreißen.

**wrest** [rɛst] *vt*: **to ~ sth from sb** jdm etw abringen.

**wrestle** ['rɛsl] *vi*: **to ~ (with sb)** (mit jdm) ringen; **to ~ with a problem** mit einem Problem kämpfen.

**wrestler** ['rɛslə\*] *n* Ringer(in) *m(f)*.

**wrestling** ['rɛslɪŋ] *n* Ringen *nt*; (*also: all-in ~*) Freistilringen *nt*.

**wrestling match** *n* Ringkampf *m*.

**wretch** [rɛtʃ] *n*: **poor ~** (*man*) armer Schlucker *m*; (*woman*) armes Ding *nt*; **little ~!** (*often humorous*) kleiner Schlingel!

**wretched** ['rɛtʃɪd] *adj* (*poor*) erbärmlich; (*unhappy*) unglücklich; (*inf: damned*) elend.

**wriggle** ['rɪgl] *vi (also:* ~ **about:** *person)* zappeln; *(fish)* sich winden; *(snake etc)* sich schlängeln ♦ *n* Zappeln *nt.*

**wring** [rɪŋ] *(pt, pp* **wrung)** *vt (wet clothes)* auswringen; *(hands)* wringen; *(neck)* umdrehen; **to** ~ **sth out of sth/sb** *(fig)* etw/ jdm etw abringen.

**wringer** ['rɪŋəʳ] *n* Mangel *f.*

**wringing** ['rɪŋɪŋ] *adj (also:* ~ **wet)** tropfnaß.

**wrinkle** ['rɪŋkl] *n* Falte *f* ♦ *vt (nose, forehead etc)* runzeln ♦ *vi (skin, paint etc)* sich runzeln.

**wrinkled** ['rɪŋkld] *adj (fabric, paper)* zerknittert; *(surface)* gekräuselt; *(skin)* runzlig.

**wrinkly** ['rɪŋklɪ] *adj* = **wrinkled.**

**wrist** [rɪst] *n* Handgelenk *nt.*

**wristband** ['rɪstbænd] *(BRIT) n (of shirt)* Manschette *f*; *(of watch)* Armband *nt.*

**wristwatch** ['rɪstwɔtʃ] *n* Armbanduhr *f.*

**writ** [rɪt] *n (LAW)* (gerichtliche) Verfügung *f*; **to issue a** ~ **against sb, serve a** ~ **on sb** eine Verfügung gegen jdn erlassen.

**write** [raɪt] *(pt* **wrote,** *pp* **written)** *vt* schreiben; *(cheque)* ausstellen ♦ *vi* schreiben; **to** ~ **to sb** jdm schreiben.

▶**write away** *vi:* **to** ~ **away for sth** etw anfordern.

▶**write down** *vt* aufschreiben.

▶**write off** *vt (debt, project)* abschreiben; *(wreck: car etc)* zu Schrott fahren ♦ *vi* = **write away.**

▶**write out** *vt (put in writing)* schreiben; *(cheque, receipt etc)* ausstellen.

▶**write up** *vt (report etc)* schreiben.

**write-off** ['raɪtɔf] *n (AUT)* Totalschaden *m.*

**write-protected** ['raɪtprə'tɛktɪd] *adj (COMPUT)* schreibgeschützt.

**writer** ['raɪtəʳ] *n (author)* Schriftsteller(in) *m(f)*; *(of report, document etc)* Verfasser(in) *m(f).*

**write-up** ['raɪtʌp] *n (review)* Kritik *f.*

**writhe** [raɪð] *vi* sich krümmen.

**writing** ['raɪtɪŋ] *n* Schrift *f*; *(of author)* Arbeiten *pl*; *(activity)* Schreiben *nt*; **in** ~ schriftlich; **in my own** ~ in meiner eigenen Handschrift.

**writing case** *n* Schreibmappe *f.*

**writing desk** *n* Schreibtisch *m.*

**writing paper** *n* Schreibpapier *nt.*

**written** ['rɪtn] *pp of* **write.**

**WRNS** *(BRIT) n abbr* (= *Women's Royal Naval Service)* Frauenkorps der Marine.

**wrong** [rɔŋ] *adj* falsch; *(morally bad)* unrecht; *(unfair)* ungerecht ♦ *adv* falsch ♦ *n (injustice)* Unrecht *nt*; *(evil):* **right and** ~ Gut und Böse ♦ *vt (treat unfairly)* Unrecht tun *+dat*; **to be** ~ *(answer)* falsch sein; *(in doing, saying sth)* unrecht haben; **you are** ~ **to do it** es ist ein Fehler von dir, das zu tun; **it's** ~ **to steal, stealing is** ~ Stehlen ist unrecht; **you are** ~ **about that, you've got it** ~ da hast du unrecht; **what's** ~**?** wo fehlt's?; **there's**

**nothing** ~ es ist alles in Ordnung; **to go** ~ *(person)* einen Fehler machen; *(plan)* schiefgehen; *(machine)* versagen; **to be in the** ~ im Unrecht sein.

**wrongdoer** ['rɔŋduːəʳ] *n* Übeltäter(in) *m(f).*

**wrong-foot** [rɔŋ'fut] *vt:* **to** ~ **sb** *(SPORT)* jdn auf dem falschen Fuß erwischen; *(fig)* jdn im falschen Moment erwischen.

**wrongful** ['rɔŋful] *adj* unrechtmäßig.

**wrongly** ['rɔŋlɪ] *adv* falsch; *(unjustly)* zu Unrecht.

**wrong number** *n (TEL):* **you've got the** ~ Sie sind falsch verbunden.

**wrong side** *n:* **the** ~ *(of material)* die linke Seite.

**wrote** [rəut] *pt of* **write.**

**wrought** [rɔːt] *adj:* ~ **iron** Schmiedeeisen *nt.*

**wrung** [rʌŋ] *pt, pp of* **wring.**

**WRVS** *(BRIT) n abbr* (= *Women's Royal Voluntary Service) karitativer Frauenverband.*

**wry** [raɪ] *adj (smile, humour)* trocken.

**wt.** *abbr* = **weight.**

**WV** *(US) abbr (POST:* = *West Virginia).*

**W.Va.** *(US) abbr (POST:* = *West Virginia).*

**WY, Wyo.** *(US) abbr (POST:* = *Wyoming).*

**WYSIWYG** ['wɪzɪwɪg] *abbr (COMPUT:* = *what you see is what you get)* WYSIWYG *nt.*

# X, x

**X, x** [ɛks] *n (letter)* X *nt,* x *nt*; *(BRIT: CINE: formerly) Klassifikation für nicht jugendfreie Filme;* ~ **for Xmas** ≈ X wie Xanthippe.

**Xerox** ® ['zɪərɔks] *n (also:* ~ **machine)** Xerokopierer *m*; *(photocopy)* Xerokopie *f* ♦ *vt* xerokopieren.

**XL** *abbr* (= *extra large)* XL.

**Xmas** ['ɛksməs] *n abbr* = **Christmas.**

**X-rated** ['ɛks'reɪtɪd] *(US) adj (film)* nicht jugendfrei.

**X-ray** ['ɛksreɪ] *n* Röntgenstrahl *m*; *(photo)* Röntgenbild *nt* ♦ *vt* röntgen; **to have an** ~ sich röntgen lassen.

**xylophone** ['zaɪləfəun] *n* Xylophon *nt.*

# Y, y

**Y, y** [waɪ] n (letter) Y nt, y nt; ~ **for Yellow**, (US) ~ **for Yoke** ≈ Y wie Ypsilon.

**yacht** [jɔt] n Jacht f.

**yachting** ['jɔtɪŋ] n Segeln nt.

**yachtsman** ['jɔtsmən] (irreg: like **man**) n Segler m.

**yam** [jæm] n Yamswurzel f.

**Yank** [jæŋk] (pej) n Ami m.

**yank** [jæŋk] vt reißen ♦ n Ruck m; **to give sth a** ~ mit einem Ruck an etw dat ziehen.

**Yankee** ['jæŋkɪ] (pej) n = **Yank**.

**yap** [jæp] vi (dog) kläffen.

**yard** [jɑːd] n (of house etc) Hof m; (US: garden) Garten m; (measure) Yard nt (= 0,91 m); **builder's** ~ Bauhof m.

**yardstick** ['jɑːdstɪk] n (fig) Maßstab m.

**yarn** [jɑːn] n (thread) Garn nt; (tale) Geschichte f.

**yawn** [jɔːn] n Gähnen nt ♦ vi gähnen.

**yawning** ['jɔːnɪŋ] adj (gap) gähnend.

**yd** abbr = **yard**.

**yeah** [jɛə] (inf) adv ja.

**year** [jɪə*] n Jahr nt; (referring to wine) Jahrgang m; **every** ~ jedes Jahr; **this** ~ dieses Jahr; **a** or **per** ~ pro Jahr; ~ **in**, ~ **out** jahrein, jahraus; **to be 8** ~**s old** 8 Jahre alt sein; **an eight-~-old child** ein achtjähriges Kind.

**yearbook** ['jɪəbuk] n Jahrbuch nt.

**yearling** ['jɪəlɪŋ] n (horse) Jährling m.

**yearly** ['jɪəlɪ] adj, adv (once a year) jährlich; **twice** ~ zweimal jährlich or im Jahr.

**yearn** [jəːn] vi: **to** ~ **for sth** sich nach etwas sehnen; **to** ~ **to do sth** sich danach sehnen, etw zu tun.

**yearning** ['jəːnɪŋ] n: **to have a** ~ **for sth** ein Verlangen nach etw haben; **to have a** ~ **to do sth** ein Verlangen danach haben, etw zu tun.

**yeast** [jiːst] n Hefe f.

**yell** [jɛl] n Schrei m ♦ vi schreien.

**yellow** ['jɛləu] adj gelb ♦ n Gelb nt.

**yellow fever** n Gelbfieber nt.

**yellowish** ['jɛləuɪʃ] adj gelblich.

**Yellow Pages** ® npl: **the** ~ die Gelben Seiten pl, das Branchenverzeichnis.

**Yellow Sea** n: **the** ~ das Gelbe Meer.

**yelp** [jɛlp] n Jaulen nt ♦ vi jaulen.

**Yemen** ['jɛmən] n: **(the)** ~ (der) Jemen.

**Yemeni** ['jɛmənɪ] adj jemenitisch ♦ n Jemenit(in) m(f).

**yen** [jɛn] n (currency) Yen m; (craving): **to have**

**a** ~ **for** Lust auf etw haben; **to have a** ~ **to do sth** Lust darauf haben, etw zu tun.

**yeoman** ['jəumən] (irreg: like **man**) n: **Y~ of the Guard** (königlicher) Leibgardist m.

**yes** [jɛs] adv ja; (in reply to negative) doch ♦ n Ja nt; **to say** ~ ja sagen; **to answer** ~ mit ja antworten.

**yes-man** ['jɛsmæn] (irreg: like **man**) (pej) n Jasager m.

**yesterday** ['jɛstədɪ] adv gestern ♦ n Gestern nt; ~ **morning/evening** gestern morgen/abend; ~**'s paper** die Zeitung von gestern; **the day before** ~ vorgestern; **all day** ~ gestern den ganzen Tag (lang).

**yet** [jɛt] adv noch ♦ conj jedoch; **it is not finished** ~ es ist noch nicht fertig; **must you go just** ~? mußt du schon gehen?; **the best** ~ der/die/das bisher beste; **as** ~ bisher; **it'll be a few days** ~ es wird noch ein paar Tage dauern; **not for a few days** ~ nicht in den nächsten paar Tagen; ~ **again** wiederum.

**yew** [juː] n (tree) Eibe f; (wood) Eibenholz nt.

**Y-fronts** ® ['waɪfrʌnts] npl (Herren-)Slip m (mit Y-förmiger Vorderseite).

**YHA** (BRIT) n abbr (= Youth Hostels Association) britischer Jugendherbergsverband.

**Yiddish** ['jɪdɪʃ] n Jiddisch nt.

**yield** [jiːld] n (AGR) Ertrag m; (COMM) Gewinn m ♦ vt (surrender: control etc) abtreten; (produce: results, profit) hervorbringen ♦ vi (surrender, give way) nachgeben; (US: AUT) die Vorfahrt achten; **a** ~ **of 5%** ein Ertrag or Gewinn von 5%.

**YMCA** n abbr (organization: = Young Men's Christian Association) CVJM m.

**yob(bo)** ['jɔb(əu)] (BRIT: inf: pej) n Rowdy m.

**yodel** ['jəudl] vi jodeln.

**yoga** ['jəugə] n Yoga m or nt.

**yog(h)ourt** ['jəugət] n Joghurt m or nt.

**yog(h)urt** ['jəugət] n = **yog(h)ourt**.

**yoke** [jəuk] n (also fig) Joch nt ♦ vt (also: ~ **together**: oxen) einspannen.

**yolk** [jəuk] n (of egg) Dotter m, Eigelb nt.

**yonder** ['jɔndə*] adv: **(over)** ~ dort drüben ♦ adj: **from** ~ **house** von dem Haus dort drüben.

**yonks** [jɔŋks] (inf) n: **for** ~ seit einer Ewigkeit.

**Yorks** [jɔːks] (BRIT) abbr (POST: = Yorkshire).

————————————— KEYWORD

**you** [juː] pron **1** (subject: familiar: singular) du; (: : plural) ihr; (: polite) Sie; ~ **Germans enjoy your food** ihr Deutschen eßt gern gut **2** (object: direct: familiar: singular) dich; (: : : plural) euch; (: : polite) Sie; (: indirect: familiar: singular) dir; (: : : plural) euch; (: : polite) Ihnen; **I know** ~ ich kenne dich/euch/Sie; **I gave it to** ~ ich habe es dir/euch/Ihnen gegeben; **if I were** ~ **I would** ... an deiner/eurer/Ihrer Stelle würde ich ...

**3** (after prep, in comparisons): **it's for** ~ es ist

für dich/euch/Sie; **she's younger than** ~ sie ist jünger als du/ihr/Sie
**4** (*impersonal: one*) man; ~ **never know** man weiß nie.

**you'd** [juːd] = **you had; you would.**

**you'll** [juːl] = **you will; you shall.**

**young** [jʌŋ] *adj* jung; **the young** *npl* (*of animal*) die Jungen *pl*; (*people*) die jungen Leute *pl*; **a** ~ **man** ein junger Mann; **a** ~ **lady** eine junge Dame.

**younger** [ˈjʌŋgə*] *adj* jünger; **the** ~ **generation** die jüngere Generation.

**youngish** [ˈjʌŋɪʃ] *adj* recht jung.

**youngster** [ˈjʌŋstə*] *n* Kind *nt*.

**your** [jɔː*] *adj* (*familiar: sing*) dein/deine/dein; (: *pl*) euer/eure/euer; (*polite*) Ihr/Ihre/Ihr; (*one's*) sein; **you mustn't eat with** ~ **fingers** man darf nicht mit den Fingern essen; *see also* **my.**

**you're** [juə*] = **you are.**

**yours** [jɔːz] *pron* (*familiar: sing*) deiner/deine/dein(e)s; (: *pl*) eurer/eure/eures; (*polite*) Ihrer/Ihre/Ihres; **a friend of** ~ ein Freund von dir/Ihnen; **is it** ~**?** gehört es dir/Ihnen?; ~ **sincerely/faithfully** mit freundlichen Grüßen; *see also* **mine**[1].

**yourself** [jɔːˈsɛlf] *pron* (*reflexive: familiar: sing: acc*) dich; (: : : *dat*) dir; (: : *pl*) euch; (: *polite*) sich; (*emphatic*) selbst; **you** ~ **told me** das haben Sie mir selbst gesagt.

**yourselves** [jɔːˈsɛlvz] *pl pron* (*reflexive: familiar*) euch; (: *polite*) sich; (*emphatic*) selbst; *see also* **oneself.**

**youth** [juːθ] *n* Jugend *f*; (*young man: pl* youths) Jugendliche(r) *m*; **in my** ~ in meiner Jugend.

**youth club** *n* Jugendklub *m*.

**youthful** [ˈjuːθful] *adj* jugendlich.

**youthfulness** [ˈjuːθfəlnɪs] *n* Jugendlichkeit *f*.

**youth hostel** *n* Jugendherberge *f*.

**youth movement** *n* Jugendbewegung *f*.

**you've** [juːv] = **you have.**

**yowl** [jaul] *n* (*of animal*) Jaulen *nt*; (*of person*) Heulen *nt*.

**yr** *abbr* (= *year*) J.

**YT** (*CANADA*) *abbr* (= *Yukon Territory*).

**Yugoslav** [ˈjuːgəuslɑːv] (*formerly*) *adj* jugoslawisch ♦ *n* Jugoslawe *m*, Jugoslawin *f*.

**Yugoslavia** [ˈjuːgəuˈslɑːvɪə] (*formerly*) *n* Jugoslawien *nt*.

**Yugoslavian** [ˈjuːgəuˈslɑːvɪən] (*formerly*) *adj* jugoslawisch.

**Yule log** [juːl-] *n* Biskuitrolle mit Überzug, die zu Weihnachten gegessen wird.

**yuppie** [ˈjʌpɪ] (*inf*) *n* Yuppie *m* ♦ *adj* yuppiehaft; (*job, car*) Yuppie-.

**YWCA** *n abbr* (*organization*: = *Young Women's Christian Association*) CVJF *m*.

# Z, z

**Z, z** [zɛd, (*US*) ziː] *n* (*letter*) Z *nt*, z *nt*; ~ **for Zebra** ≈ Z wie Zacharias.

**Zaire** [zɑːˈiːə*] *n* Zaire *nt*.

**Zambia** [ˈzæmbɪə] *n* Sambia *nt*.

**Zambian** [ˈzæmbɪən] *adj* sambisch ♦ *n* Sambier(in) *m(f)*.

**zany** [ˈzeɪnɪ] *adj* verrückt.

**zap** [zæp] *vt* (*COMPUT: delete*) löschen.

**zeal** [ziːl] *n* Eifer *m*.

**zealot** [ˈzɛlət] *n* Fanatiker(in) *m(f)*.

**zealous** [ˈzɛləs] *adj* eifrig.

**zebra** [ˈziːbrə] *n* Zebra *nt*.

**zebra crossing** (*BRIT*) *n* Zebrastreifen *m*.

**zenith** [ˈzɛnɪθ] *n* (*also fig*) Zenit *m*.

**zero** [ˈzɪərəu] *n* (*number*) Null *f* ♦ *vi*: **to** ~ **in on sth** (*target*) etw einkreisen; **5 degrees below** ~ 5 Grad unter Null.

**zero hour** *n* die Stunde X.

**zero option** *n* (*esp POL*) Nullösung *f*.

**zero-rated** [ˈziːrəureɪtɪd] (*BRIT*) *adj* (*TAX*) mehrwertsteuerfrei.

**zest** [zɛst] *n* (*for life*) Begeisterung *f*; (*of orange*) Orangenschale *f*.

**zigzag** [ˈzɪgzæg] *n* Zickzack *m* ♦ *vi* sich im Zickzack bewegen.

**Zimbabwe** [zɪmˈbɑːbwɪ] *n* Zimbabwe *nt*.

**Zimbabwean** [zɪmˈbɑːbwɪən] *adj* zimbabwisch.

**zimmer** ® [ˈzɪmə*] *n* (*also:* ~ **frame**) Laufgestell *nt*.

**zinc** [zɪŋk] *n* Zink *nt*.

**Zionism** [ˈzaɪənɪzəm] *n* Zionismus *m*.

**Zionist** [ˈzaɪənɪst] *adj* zionistisch ♦ *n* Zionist(in) *m(f)*.

**zip** [zɪp] *n* (*also:* ~ **fastener**) Reißverschluß *m* ♦ *vt* (*also:* ~ **up**: *dress etc*) den Reißverschluß zumachen an +*dat*.

**zip code** (*US*) *n* Postleitzahl *f*.

**zipper** [ˈzɪpə*] (*US*) *n* = **zip.**

**zither** [ˈzɪðə*] *n* Zither *f*.

**zodiac** [ˈzəudɪæk] *n* Tierkreis *m*.

**zombie** [ˈzɔmbɪ] *n* (*fig*) Schwachkopf *m*.

**zone** [zəun] *n* (*also MIL*) Zone *f*, Gebiet *nt*; (*in town*) Bezirk *m*.

**zonked** [zɔŋkt] (*inf*) *adj* (*tired*) total geschafft; (*high on drugs*) high; (*drunk*) voll.

**zoo** [zuː] *n* Zoo *m*.

**zoological** [zuəˈlɔdʒɪkl] *adj* zoologisch.

**zoologist** [zuˈɔlədʒɪst] *n* Zoologe *m*, Zoologin *f*.

**zoology** [zuːˈɔlədʒɪ] *n* Zoologie *f*.

**zoom** [zuːm] *vi*: **to** ~ **past** vorbeisausen; **to** ~ **in (on sth/sb)** (*PHOT, CINE*) (etw/jdn)

näher heranholen.
**zoom lens** n Zoomobjektiv nt.
**zucchini** [zuːˈkiːnɪ] (US) n(pl) Zucchini pl.

**Zulu** [ˈzuːluː] adj (tribe, culture) Zulu- ♦ n (person) Zulu m/f; (LING) Zulu nt.
**Zürich** [ˈzjuərɪk] n Zürich nt.

# *Grammar*
# *Grammatik*

# Using the Grammar

The Grammar section deals systematically and comprehensively with all the information you will need in order to communicate accurately in German. The user-friendly layout explains the grammar point on a left-hand page, leaving the facing page free for illustrative examples. The bracketed numbers (→1) direct you to the relevant example in every case.

The Grammar section also provides invaluable guidance on the danger of translating English structure by identical structures in German. Use of Numbers and Punctuation are important areas covered towards the end of this section. Finally, the index lists the main words and grammatical terms in both English and German.

# Abbreviations

| | | | |
|---|---|---|---|
| **acc** | accusative | **gen** | genitive |
| **ctd** | continued | **masc** | masculine |
| **dat** | dative | **neut** | neuter |
| **fem** | feminine | **nom** | nominative |
| **ff** | and following pages | **p(p)** | page(s) |

# 4  CONTENTS

# CONTENTS 5

## Tense Formation

Tenses are either **simple** or **compound**. Once you know how to form the past participle, compound tenses are similar for all verbs (see pp 22 to 29). To form simple tenses you need to know whether a verb is **weak, strong** or **mixed**.

## Simple Tenses

In German these are:

| | |
|---|---|
| Present indicative | (→**1**) |
| Imperfect indicative | (→**2**) |
| Present subjunctive | (→**3**) |
| Imperfect subjunctive | (→**4**) |

Subjunctive forms are widely used in German, especially for indirect or reported speech (see pp 66 and 67).

The simple tenses are formed by adding endings to a verb **stem**. The endings show the number, person and tense of the subject of the verb (→**5**)

The types of verb you need to know to form simple tenses are:
- **Strong verbs** (pp 12 to 15), those whose vowel usually changes in forming the imperfect indicative (→**6**)

- **Weak verbs** (pp 8 to 11), which are usually completely regular and have no vowel changes. Their endings differ from those of strong verbs (→**7**)

- **Mixed verbs** (pp 16 and 17), which have a vowel change like strong verbs, but the endings of weak verbs (→**8**)

*Continued*

**1 ich hole**
I fetch, I am fetching, I do fetch

**2 ich holte**
I fetched, I was fetching, I used to fetch

**3 (daß) ich hole**
(that) I fetch/I fetched

**4 (daß) ich holte**
(that) I fetched

| | |
|---|---|
| **5 ich hole** | I fetch |
| **wir holen** | we fetch |
| **du holtest** | you fetched |
| | |
| **6 singen** | to sing |
| **er singt** | he sings |
| **er sang** | he sang |
| | |
| **7 holen** | to fetch |
| **er holt** | he fetches |
| **er holte** | he fetched |
| | |
| **8 nennen** | to name |
| **er nennt** | he names |
| **er nannte** | he named |

## Weak Verbs

Weak verbs are usually **regular** in conjugation. Their simple tenses are formed as follows:

- **Present** and **imperfect** tenses are formed by adding the endings shown below to the verb **stem**. This stem is formed by removing the **-en** ending of the infinitive (the form found in the dictionary) (→**1**)

- Where the infinitive of a weak verb ends in **-eln** or **-ern**, only the **-n** is removed to form the verb stem (→**2**)

- The endings are as follows (→**3**):

|  | PRESENT INDICATIVE | PRESENT SUBJUNCTIVE |
|---|---|---|
| 1st singular | **-e** | **-e** |
| 2nd | **-st** | **-est** |
| 3rd | **-t** | **-e** |
| 1st plural | **-en** | **-en** |
| 2nd | **-t** | **-et** |
| 3rd | **-en** | **-en** |

|  | IMPERFECT INDICATIVE | IMPERFECT SUBJUNCTIVE |
|---|---|---|
| 1st singular | **-te** | **-te** |
| 2nd | **-test** | **-test** |
| 3rd | **-te** | **-te** |
| 1st plural | **-ten** | **-ten** |
| 2nd | **-tet** | **-tet** |
| 3rd | **-ten** | **-ten** |

*Continued*

**1** *INFINITIVE*                                        *STEM*
**holen**          to fetch                          **hol-**
**machen**         to make                           **mach-**
**kauen**          to chew                           **kau-**

**2 wandern**      to roam                           **wander-**
**handeln**        to trade,                         **handel-**
                   to act

**3 holen**        to fetch

*PRESENT*              *PRESENT*
*INDICATIVE*           *SUBJUNCTIVE*
ich hole              ich hole              I fetch
du holst             du holest             you fetch
er/sie/es holt       er/sie/es hole        he/she/it fetches
wir holen            wir holen             we fetch
ihr holt             ihr holet             you (*plural*) fetch
sie/Sie holen        sie/Sie holen         they/you (*polite*) fetch

*IMPERFECT INDICATIVE AND SUBJUNCTIVE*
(*These tenses are identical for weak verbs*)

ich holte            I fetched
du holtest           you fetched
er/sie/es holte      he/she/it fetched
wir holten           we fetched
ihr holtet           you (*plural*) fetched
sie/Sie holten       they/you (*polite*) fetched

## Weak Verbs (contd)

- Where the stem of a weak verb ends in **-d** or **-t**, an extra **-e-** is inserted before those endings where this will ease pronunciation (→**1**)

- Weak verbs whose stems end in **-m** or **-n** may take this extra **-e-**, or not, depending on whether its addition is necessary for pronunciation. If the **-m** or **-n** is preceded by a consonant *other than* **l, r** or **h**, the **-e-** is inserted (→**2**)

- Weak (and strong) verbs whose stem ends in a sibilant sound (**-s, -z, -ß**) normally lose the **-s-** of the second person singular ending (the **du** form) in the present indicative (→**3**)

  *NOTE*: When this sibilant is **-sch**, the **-s-** of the ending remains (→**4**)

**1  reden**  to speak

| PRESENT | IMPERFECT |
|---------|-----------|
| ich rede | ich redete |
| du redest | du redetest |
| er redet | er redete |
| wir reden | wir redeten |
| ihr redet | ihr redetet |
| sie reden | sie redeten |

**arbeiten**  to work

| PRESENT | IMPERFECT |
|---------|-----------|
| ich arbeite | ich arbeitete |
| du arbeitest | du arbeitetest |
| er arbeitet | er arbeitete |
| wir arbeiten | wir arbeiteten |
| ihr arbeitet | ihr arbeitetet |
| sie arbeiten | sie arbeiteten |

**2  atmen**  to breathe

| PRESENT | IMPERFECT |
|---------|-----------|
| ich atme | ich atmete |
| du atmest | du atmetest |
| er atmet | er atmete |
| wir atmen | wir atmeten |
| ihr atmet | ihr atmetet |
| sie atmen | sie atmeten |

**segnen**  to bless

| PRESENT | IMPERFECT |
|---------|-----------|
| ich segne | ich segnete |
| du segnest | du segnetest |
| er segnet | er segnete |
| wir segnen | wir segneten |
| ihr segnet | ihr segnetet |
| sie segnen | sie segneten |

*BUT*:

**umarmen**  to embrace

| PRESENT | IMPERFECT |
|---------|-----------|
| ich umarme | ich umarmte |
| du umarmst | du umarmtest |
| er umarmt | er umarmte |
| wir umarmen | wir umarmten |
| ihr umarmt | ihr umarmtet |
| sie umarmen | sie umarmten |

**lernen**  to learn

| PRESENT | IMPERFECT |
|---------|-----------|
| ich lerne | ich lernte |
| du lernst | du lerntest |
| er lernt | er lernte |
| wir lernen | wir lernten |
| ihr lernt | ihr lerntet |
| sie lernen | sie lernten |

**3  grüßen**  to greet

PRESENT
ich grüße
du **grüßt**
er grüßt
wir grüßen
ihr grüßt
sie grüßen

**4  löschen**  to extinguish

PRESENT
ich lösche
du löschst
er löscht
wir löschen
ihr löscht
sie löschen

## Strong Verbs

A list of the most useful strong verbs is given on pp 86 to 97.

● What differentiates strong verbs from weak ones is that when forming their **imperfect indicative** tense, strong verbs undergo a vowel change and have a different set of endings (→**1**)

  Their past participles are also formed differently (see p 24).

● To form the **imperfect subjunctive** of strong verbs, the endings from the appropriate table below are added to the stem of the imperfect indicative, but the vowel is modified by an umlaut where this is possible, i.e. **a → ä, o → ö, u → ü**. Exceptions to this are clearly shown in the table of strong verbs (→**2**)

The endings for the simple tenses of strong verbs are as follows (→**3**)

|  | PRESENT INDICATIVE | PRESENT SUBJUNCTIVE |
|---|---|---|
| 1st singular | -e | -e |
| 2nd | -st | -est |
| 3rd | -t | -e |
| 1st plural | -en | -en |
| 2nd | -t | -et |
| 3rd | -en | -en |
|  | IMPERFECT INDICATIVE | IMPERFECT SUBJUNCTIVE |
| 1st singular | — | -e |
| 2nd | -st | -(e)st |
| 3rd | — | -e |
| 1st plural | -en | -en |
| 2nd | -t | -(e)t |
| 3rd | -en | -en |

*Continued*

**1** Compare:

|          | INFINITIVE        | PRESENT   | IMPERFECT  |
|----------|-------------------|-----------|------------|
| WEAK     | **sagen** to say  | **er sagt** | **er sagte** |
| STRONG   | **rufen** to shout| **er ruft** | **er rief** |

**2**

|        | IMPERFECT INDICATIVE        | IMPERFECT SUBJUNCTIVE            |
|--------|-----------------------------|---------------------------------|
|        | **er gab** he gave          | **er gäbe** (*umlaut added*)     |
| BUT    | **er rief** he shouted      | **er riefe** (*no umlaut possible*) |

**3 singen** to sing

| PRESENT INDICATIVE | PRESENT SUBJUNCTIVE |
|--------------------|---------------------|
| ich singe          | ich singe           |
| du singst          | du singest          |
| er singt           | er singe            |
| wir singen         | wir singen          |
| ihr singt          | ihr singet          |
| sie singen         | sie singen          |
| Sie singen         | Sie singen          |

| IMPERFECT INDICATIVE | IMPERFECT SUBJUNCTIVE |
|----------------------|-----------------------|
| ich sang             | ich sänge             |
| du sangst            | du säng(e)st          |
| er sang              | er sänge              |
| wir sangen           | wir sängen            |
| ihr sangt            | ihr säng(e)t          |
| sie sangen           | sie sängen            |
| Sie sangen           | Sie sängen            |

## Strong Verbs (contd)

- In the present tense of strong verbs, the vowel also often changes for the second and third persons singular (the **du** and **er/sie/es** forms).
  The pattern of possible changes is as follows:

  long **e** → **ie**
  short **e** → **i**
  **a** → **ä**
  **au** → **äu**
  **o** → **ö**

  Verbs which undergo these changes are clearly shown in the table on p 86 (→**1**)

- Strong (and weak) verbs whose stem ends with a sibilant sound (**-s, -z, -ß**) normally lose the **-s-** of the second person singular ending (the **du** form) in the *present indicative*, unless the sibilant is **-sch**, when it remains (→**2**)

- In the second person singular of the *imperfect* tense of strong verbs whose stem ends in a sibilant sound (including **-sch**) the sibilant remains, and an **-e-** is inserted between it and the appropriate ending (→**3**)

**1**  **sehen** to see            **helfen** to help
    ich sehe                ich helfe
    du siehst               du hilfst
    er/sie/es sieht         er/sie/es hilft
    wir sehen               wir helfen
    ihr seht                ihr helft
    sie sehen               sie helfen

    **fahren** to drive       **saufen** to booze     **stoßen** to push
    ich fahre               ich saufe               ich stoße
    du fährst               du säufst               du stößt
    er fährt                er säuft                er stößt
    wir fahren              wir saufen              wir stoßen
    ihr fahrt               ihr sauft               ihr stoßt
    sie fahren              sie saufen              sie stoßen

**2**  **wachsen** to grow        **waschen** to wash
    ich wachse              ich wasche
    du wächst               du wäschst
    er wächst               er wäscht
    wir wachsen             wir waschen
    ihr wachst              ihr wascht
    sie wachsen             sie waschen

**3**  **lesen** to read         **schließen** to close  **waschen** to wash
    ich las                 ich schloß              ich wusch
    du lasest               du schlossest           du wuschest
    er las                  er schloß               er wusch
    wir lasen               wir schlossen           wir wuschen
    ihr last                ihr schloßt             ihr wuscht
    sie lasen               sie schlossen           sie wuschen

# Mixed Verbs

There are nine **mixed** verbs in German, and, as their name implies, they are formed according to a mixture of the rules already outlined for weak and strong verbs.

The mixed verbs are:

| | | |
|---|---|---|
| **denken** to think | **kennen** to know | **nennen** to name |
| **rennen** to run | **senden** to send | **bringen** to bring |
| **brennen** to burn | **wenden** to turn | **wissen** to know |

Full details of their principal parts are given in the verb list beginning on p 86.

- Mixed verbs form their **imperfect** tense by adding the weak verb endings to a stem whose vowel has been changed as for a strong verb (→**1**)

  *NOTE*: **bringen** and **denken** have a consonant change too in their imperfect forms (→**2**)

- The **imperfect subjunctive** forms of mixed verbs are unusual and should be noted (→**3**)

- Other tenses of mixed verbs are formed as for strong verbs.

- The past participle of mixed verbs has characteristics of both weak and strong verbs, as shown on p 24.

**1**  *IMPERFECT INDICATIVE*

| **kennen** to know | **wissen** to know | **senden** to send |
|---|---|---|
| ich kannte | ich wußte | ich sandte |
| du kanntest | du wußtest | du sandtest |
| er kannte | er wußte | er sandte |
| wir kannten | wir wußten | wir sandten |
| ihr kanntet | ihr wußtet | ihr sandtet |
| sie kannten | sie wußten | sie sandten |

**2**  *IMPERFECT INDICATIVE*

| **denken** to think | **bringen** to bring |
|---|---|
| ich dachte | ich brachte |
| du dachtest | du brachtest |
| er dachte | er brachte |
| wir dachten | wir brachten |
| ihr dachtet | ihr brachtet |
| sie dachten | sie brachten |

**3**  *IMPERFECT SUBJUNCTIVE*

| **kennen** | **rennen** | **senden** |
|---|---|---|
| ich kennte | ich rennte | ich sendete |
| du kenntest | du renntest | du sendetest |
| er kennte *etc* | er rennte *etc* | er sendete *etc* |
| **brennen** | **wissen** | **wenden** |
| ich brennte | ich wüßte | ich wendete |
| du brenntest | du wüßtest | du wendetest |
| er brennte *etc* | er wüßte etc | er wendete *etc* |
| **denken** | **bringen** | **nennen** |
| ich dächte | ich brächte | ich nennte |
| du dächtest | du brächtest | du nenntest |
| er dächte *etc* | er brächte *etc* | er nennte *etc* |

# The Imperative

This is the form of a verb used to give an order or a command, or to make a request:

*Come here/stand up/please bring me a beer* ( $\rightarrow$ **1**)

- German has three main imperative forms. These go with the three ways of addressing people **Sie**, **du** and **ihr** (see p 160)

|  | FORMATION | EXAMPLES | |
|---|---|---|---|
| SINGULAR | stem (+ **e**) | **hol(e)!** | *fetch!* |
| PLURAL | stem + **t** | **holt!** | *fetch!* |
| POLITE (*sing and pl*) | stem + **en Sie** | **holen Sie!** | *fetch!* |

- The **-e** of the singular form is often dropped, BUT NOT where the verb stem ends in **-chn**, **-ckn**, **-dn**, **-fn**, **-gn** or **-tm** ( $\rightarrow$ **2**)

- **Weak verbs** ending in **-eln** or **-ern** take the **-e** ending in the singular form, but the additional **-e-** within the stem may be dropped ( $\rightarrow$ **3**)

- Any vowel change in the present tense of a **strong verb** (see p 14) occurs also in its singular imperative form and no **-e** is added ( $\rightarrow$ **4**)

  BUT if the vowel modification in the present tense of a **strong verb** is the addition of an umlaut, this is not added in the singular form of the imperative ( $\rightarrow$ **5**)

- In the imperative form of a **reflexive verb** (see p 30) the pronoun is placed immediately after the verb ( $\rightarrow$ **6**)

- **Separable prefixes** (see p 72) are placed at the end of an imperative statement ( $\rightarrow$ **7**)

*Continued*

**1**  *SINGULAR*:   **Komm mal her!**        Come here!
       *PLURAL*:     **Steht auf!**           Stand up!
       *POLITE*:     **Kommen Sie herein!**   Do come in

**2**  **Hör zu!** Listen!
       **Hol es!** Fetch it!
       *BUT*:
       **Öffne die Tür!** Open the door!

**3**  **wandern**     to walk        **handeln**      to act
       **wand(e)re!**  walk!          **hand(e)le!**   act!

**4**  **nehmen**      to take        **helfen**       to help
       **du nimmst**   you take       **du hilfst**    you help
       **nimm!**       take!          **hilf!**        help!

       *EXCEPTION*:
       **sehen**       to see
       **sieh(e)!**    see!

**5**  **laufen**      to run         **stoßen**       to push
       **du läufst**   you run        **du stößt**     you push
       **lauf(e)!**    run!           **stoß(e)!**     push!

**6**  **sich setzen** to sit down:
       **Setz dich!**
       **Setzt euch!**
       **Setzen Sie sich!**

**7**  **zumachen** to close:          **aufhören** to stop:
       **Mach die Tür zu!**            **Hör aber endlich auf!**
       Close the door!                 Do stop it!

# The Imperative (contd)

- Imperatives are followed in German by an exclamation mark, unless the imperative is not intended as a command (→**1**)

- **du** and **ihr**, though not normally present in imperative forms, may be included for emphasis (→**2**)

- An imperative form also exists for the **wir** form of the verb. It consists of the normal present tense form, but with the pronoun **wir** *following* the verb. It is used for making suggestions (→**3**)

- The imperative forms of **sein** (*to be*) are irregular (→**4**)

- The particles **auch, nur, mal, doch** are frequently used with imperatives. They heighten or soften the imperative effect, or add a note of encouragement to a request or command. Often they have no direct equivalent in English and are therefore not always translated (→**5**)

## Some Alternatives to the Imperative in German

- Infinitives are often used instead of the imperative in written instructions or public announcements (→**6**)

- The impersonal passive (see p 34) may be used (→**7**)

- Nouns, adjectives or adverbs can also be used with imperative effect (→**8**)
  Some of these have become set expressions (→**9**)

**1 Laß ihn in Ruhe!** Leave him alone
**Sagen Sie mir bitte, wie spät es ist** What's the time please?

**2 Geht ihr voran!** You go on ahead
**Sag du ihm, was los ist** You tell him what's wrong

**3 Nehmen wir an, daß ...**
Let's assume that ...
**Sagen wir mal, es habe 4,000 DM gekostet**
Let's just say it cost 4,000 marks

**4 sein** to be
**sei!**
**seid!**
**seien wir!**
**seien Sie!**

**5 Geh doch!** Go on!/Get going!
**Sag mal, ...** Tell me ...
**Versuchen Sie es mal!** Do give it a try!
**Komm schon!** Do come/Please come
**Mach es auch richtig!** Be sure to do it properly

**6 Einsteigen!**
All aboard!
**Zwiebeln abziehen und in Ringe schneiden**
Peel the onions and slice them

**7 Jetzt wird aufgeräumt!**
You're going to clear up now!

**8 Ruhe!** Be quiet! Silence!
**Vorsicht!** Careful! Look out!

**9 Achtung!** Listen!/Attention!
**Rauchen verboten!** No smoking

# Compound Tenses

The present and imperfect tenses in German are **simple** tenses, as described on pp 6 to 17.

All other tenses, called **compound tenses**, are formed for all types of verb by using the appropriate tense of an **auxiliary verb** plus a part of the main verb.

There are three auxiliary verbs:
> **haben** for past tenses
> **sein** also for past tenses
> **werden** for future and conditional tenses

The **compound past tenses** in German are:

| | |
|---|---|
| Perfect indicative | (→**1**) |
| Perfect subjunctive | (→**2**) |
| Pluperfect indicative | (→**3**) |
| Pluperfect subjunctive | (→**4**) |

These are dealt with on pp 26 ff.

The **future** and **conditional tenses** in German are all compound tenses. They are:

| | |
|---|---|
| Future indicative | (→**5**) |
| Future subjunctive | (→**6**) |
| Future perfect | (→**7**) |
| Conditional | (→**8**) |
| Conditional perfect | (→**9**) |

These are dealt with on pp 28 ff.

|  | with **haben** | with **sein** |
|---|---|---|
| 1 | **er hat geholt**<br>he (has) fetched | **er ist gereist**<br>he (has) travelled |
| 2 | **er habe geholt**<br>he (has) fetched | **er sei gereist**<br>he (has) travelled |
| 3 | **er hatte geholt**<br>he had fetched | **er war gereist**<br>he had travelled |
| 4 | **er hätte geholt**<br>he had fetched | **er wäre gereist**<br>he had travelled |
| 5 | **er wird holen**<br>he will fetch | **er wird reisen**<br>he will travel |
| 6 | **er werde holen**<br>he will fetch | **er werde reisen**<br>he will travel |
| 7 | **er wird geholt haben**<br>he will have fetched | **er wird gereist sein**<br>he will have travelled |
| 8 | **er würde holen**<br>he would fetch | **er würde reisen**<br>he would travel |
| 9 | **er würde geholt haben**<br>he would have fetched | **er würde gereist sein**<br>he would have travelled |

# Compound Past Tenses: Formation

- Compound past tenses are normally formed by using the auxiliary verb **haben**, plus the past participle of the main verb (see below) (→**1**)

- Certain types of verb take **sein** instead of **haben**, and this is clearly indicated in the verb tables starting on p 86. They fall into three main types:
  1. intransitive verbs (those that take no direct object, often showing a change of state or place)          (→**2**)
  2. certain verbs meaning "to happen"          (→**3**)
  3. miscellaneous others, including:
     **bleiben** to remain, **gelingen** to succeed
     **begegnen** to meet, **sein** to be
     **werden** to become          (→**4**)

- In some cases the verb can be conjugated with either **haben** or **sein**, depending on whether it is used transitively (with a direct object) or intransitively (where no direct object is possible) (→**5**)

## The Past Participle: Formation *(see also p 50)*

- **Weak** verbs add the prefix **ge-** and the suffix **-t** to the verb stem (→**6**)

  Verbs ending in **-ieren** or **-eien** omit the **ge-** (→**7**)

- **Strong** verbs add the prefix **ge-** and the suffix **-en** to the verb stem (→**8**). The vowel of the stem may be modified (see verb list, p 86) (→**9**)

- **Mixed** verbs add the prefix **ge-** and the "weak" suffix **-t** to the stem. The stem vowel is modified as for many strong verbs (→**10**)

*Continued*

**1 Haben Sie gut geschlafen?**
Did you sleep well?
**Die Kinder hatten fleißig gearbeitet**
The children had worked hard

**2 Wir sind nach Bonn gefahren**
We went to Bonn
**Er ist schnell eingeschlafen**
He quickly fell asleep

**3 Was ist geschehen?**
What happened?

**4 Er ist zu Hause geblieben**      **Er ist krank gewesen**
He stayed at home      He has been ill
**Es ist uns nicht gelungen**      **Sie ist krank geworden**
We did not succeed      She became ill
**Er ist einem Freund begegnet**
He met a friend

**5 Er hat den Wagen nach Köln gefahren**
He drove the car to Cologne
**Er ist nach Köln gefahren**
He went to Cologne

**6 holen** to fetch      **9 singen** to sing
  **geholt** fetched        **gesungen** sung

**7 studieren** to study      **10 senden** to send
  **studiert** studied        **gesandt** sent
  **prophezeien** to prophesy        **bringen** to bring
  **prophezeit** prophesied        **gebracht** brought

**8 laufen** to run
  **gelaufen** run

*For a full list of strong and mixed verbs see p 86*

# Compound Past Tenses: Formation (contd)

The formation of past participles for weak, strong and mixed verbs is described on p 24, and a comprehensive list of the principal parts of the most commonly used strong and mixed verbs is provided for reference on pp 86 to 97.

## How to form the compound past tenses:

| | |
|---|---|
| Perfect indicative | the present tense of **haben** or **sein** plus the past participle of the verb (→**1**) |
| Perfect subjunctive | (used in indirect or reported speech) the present subjunctive of **haben** or **sein** plus the past participle (→**2**) |
| Pluperfect indicative | imperfect indicative of **haben** or **sein** plus the past participle (→**3**) |
| Pluperfect subjunctive | (for indirect or reported speech) imperfect subjunctive of **haben** or **sein** plus the past participle (→**4**) |
| | *NOTE*: The pluperfect subjunctive is a frequently used tense in German, since it can replace the much clumsier conditional perfect tense shown on p 28 |

| with **haben** | with **sein** |
|---|---|
| **1** *PERFECT INDICATIVE* | |
| ich habe geholt | ich bin gereist |
| du hast geholt | du bist gereist |
| er/sie/es hat geholt | er/sie/es ist gereist |
| wir haben geholt | wir sind gereist |
| ihr habt geholt | ihr seid gereist |
| sie/Sie haben geholt | sie/Sie sind gereist |
| | |
| **2** *PERFECT SUBJUNCTIVE* | |
| ich habe geholt | ich sei gereist |
| du habest geholt | du sei(e)st gereist |
| er/sie/es habe geholt | er/sie/es sei gereist |
| wir haben geholt | wir seien gereist |
| ihr habet geholt | ihr seiet gereist |
| sie/Sie haben geholt | sie/Sie seien gereist |
| | |
| **3** *PLUPERFECT INDICATIVE* | |
| ich hatte geholt | ich war gereist |
| du hattest geholt | du warst gereist |
| er/sie/es hatte geholt | er/sie/es war gereist |
| wir hatten geholt | wir waren gereist |
| ihr hattet geholt | ihr wart gereist |
| sie/Sie hatten geholt | sie/Sie waren gereist |
| | |
| **4** *PLUPERFECT SUBJUNCTIVE* | |
| ich hätte geholt | ich wäre gereist |
| du hättest geholt | du wär(e)st gereist |
| er/sie/es hätte geholt | er/sie/es wäre gereist |
| wir hätten geholt | wir wären gereist |
| ihr hättet geholt | ihr wär(e)t gereist |
| sie/Sie hätten geholt | sie/Sie wären gereist |

# Future and Conditional Tenses: Formation

- The **future** and **conditional** tenses are formed in the same way for all verbs, whether weak, strong or mixed.

- The auxiliary **werden** is used for all verbs together with the infinitive of the main verb.

- The infinitive is usually placed at the end of the clause (see p 224).

## How to form the future and conditional tenses:

| | |
|---|---|
| Future indicative | present tense of **werden** plus the infinitive of the verb   (→1) |
| Future subjunctive | present subjunctive of **werden** plus the infinitive   (→2) |
| Future perfect | present indicative of **werden** plus the **perfect infinitive** (see below)   (→3) |
| Conditional | imperfect subjunctive of **werden** plus the infinitive   (→4) |
| Conditional perfect | imperfect subjunctive of **werden** plus the perfect infinitive (see below)   (→5) |
| | *NOTE*: often replaced by the pluperfect subjunctive |

- The **perfect infinitive** consists of the infinitive of **haben/sein** plus the past participle of the verb.

# Examples

**1** *FUTURE INDICATIVE*
| | |
|---|---|
| ich werde holen | wir werden holen |
| du wirst holen | ihr werdet holen |
| er/sie/es wird holen | sie/Sie werden holen |

**2** *FUTURE SUBJUNCTIVE*
| | |
|---|---|
| ich werde holen | wir werden holen |
| du werdest holen | ihr werdet holen |
| er/sie/es werde holen | sie/Sie werden holen |

**3** *FUTURE PERFECT*
| | |
|---|---|
| ich werde geholt haben | wir werden geholt haben |
| du wirst geholt haben | ihr werdet geholt haben |
| er wird geholt haben | sie/Sie werden geholt haben |

**4** *CONDITIONAL*
| | |
|---|---|
| ich würde holen | wir würden holen |
| du würdest holen | ihr würdet holen |
| er/sie/es würde holen | sie/Sie würden holen |

**5** *CONDITIONAL PERFECT*[1]
| | |
|---|---|
| ich würde geholt haben | wir würden geholt haben |
| du würdest geholt haben | ihr würdet geholt haben |
| er würde geholt haben | sie/Sie würden geholt haben |

1. *NB Often replaced by the pluperfect subjunctive (see p 26)*

# Reflexive Verbs

A verb whose action is reflected back to its subject may be termed reflexive: *she* washes *herself*.

Reflexive verbs in German are recognized in the infinitive by the preceding reflexive pronoun **sich** (→**1**)

German has many reflexive verbs, a great number of which are not reflexive in English (→**1**)

- Reflexive verbs are composed of the verb and a reflexive pronoun (see p 170).
  This pronoun may be either the direct object (and therefore in the accusative case) or the indirect object (and therefore in the dative case) (→**2**)

- Many verbs in German which are not essentially reflexive may become reflexive by the addition of a reflexive pronoun (→**3**)
  When a verb with an indirect object is made reflexive (see p 170) the pronoun is usually dative (→**4**)

- A direct object reflexive pronoun changes to the dative if another direct object is present (→**5**)

- In a main clause the reflexive pronoun follows the verb (→**6**)
  After inversion (see p 226), or in a subordinate clause, the reflexive pronoun must come after the subject if the subject is a personal pronoun (→**7**)
  It may precede or follow a noun subject (→**8**)

- Reflexive verbs are always conjugated with **haben** *except* where the pronoun is used to mean *each other*. Then the verb is normally conjugated with **sein**.

- The imperative forms are show on p 19.

*Continued*

**1** sich beeilen to hurry
wir beeilen uns we are hurrying

**2** sich (*accusative*) erinnern
to remember
ich erinnere mich
du erinnerst dich
er/sie/es erinnert sich
wir erinnern uns
ihr erinnert euch
sie/Sie erinnern sich

sich (*dative*) erlauben
to allow oneself
ich erlaube mir
du erlaubst dir
er/sie/es erlaubt sich
wir erlauben uns
ihr erlaubt euch
sie/Sie erlauben sich

**3** etwas melden to report something
  sich melden to report for/to volunteer for
  Ich habe mich gemeldet I volunteered
**4** weh tun to hurt
  sich weh tun to get hurt
  Hast du dir weh getan? Have you hurt yourself?
kaufen to buy
  Er kaufte ihr einen Mantel He bought her a coat
  Er kaufte sich (*dative*) einen neuen Mantel
  He bought himself a new coat
**5** Ich wasche mich I am having a wash
  Ich wasche mir die Hände I am washing my hands
**6** Er wird sich darüber freuen
  He'll be pleased about that
**7** Darüber wird er sich freuen
  Ich frage mich, ob er sich darüber freuen wird
  I wonder if he'll be pleased about that
**8** Langsam drehten sich die Kinder um
  *OR*
  Langsam drehten die Kinder sich um
  The children slowly turned around

## Reflexive Verbs (contd)

Some examples of verbs which can be used with a reflexive pronoun in the accusative case:

**sich anziehen** to get dressed (→**1**)
**sich aufregen** to get excited (→**2**)
**sich beeilen** to hurry (→**3**)
**sich beschäftigen mit**[1] to be occupied with (→**4**)
**sich bewerben um**[1] to apply for (→**5**)
**sich erinnern an**[1] to remember (→**6**)
**sich freuen auf**[1] to look forward to (→**7**)
**sich interessieren für**[1] to be interested in (→**8**)
**sich irren** to be wrong (→**9**)
**sich melden** to report (for duty etc)
**sich rasieren** to shave
**sich (hin)setzen** to sit down (→**10**)
**sich trauen**[2] to trust oneself
**sich umsehen** to look around (→**11**)

Some examples of verbs which can be used with a reflexive pronoun in the dative case:

**sich abgewöhnen** to give up (something) (→**12**)
**sich aneignen** to appropriate
**sich ansehen** to have a look at
**sich einbilden** to imagine (wrongly) (→**13**)
**sich erlauben** to allow oneself (→**14**)
**sich leisten** to treat oneself (→**15**)
**sich nähern** to get close to
**sich vornehmen** to plan to do (→**16**)
**sich vorstellen** to imagine (→**17**)
**sich wünschen** to want (→**18**)

1. For verbs normally followed by a preposition, the reader is referred to p 76 ff.
2. **trauen** when non-reflexive takes the dative case.

**1 Du sollst dich sofort anziehen**
You are to get dressed immediately

**2 Reg dich doch nicht so auf!**
Calm down!

**3 Wir müssen uns beeilen**
We must hurry

**4 Sie beschäftigen sich sehr mit den Kindern**
They spend a lot of time with the children

**5 Hast du dich um diese Stelle beworben?**
Have you applied for this post?

**6 Ich erinnere mich nicht daran**
I can't remember it

**7 Ich freue mich auf die Fahrt**
I am looking forward to the journey

**8 Interessierst du dich für Musik?**
Are you interested in music?

**9 Er hat sich geirrt**
He was wrong

**10 Bitte, setzt euch hin!**
Please sit down

**11 Die Kinder sahen sich erstaunt um**
The children looked around in amazement

**12 Eigentlich müßte man sich das Rauchen abgewöhnen**
One really ought to give up smoking

**13 Bilde dir doch nichts ein!**
Don't kid yourself!

**14 Eins könntest du dir doch erlauben**
You could surely allow yourself one

**15 Wenn ich mir nur einen Mercedes leisten könnte!**
If only I could afford a Mercedes!

**16 Du hast dir wieder zuviel vorgenommen!**
You've taken on too much again!

**17 So hatte ich es mir oft vorgestellt**
I had often imagined it like this

**18 Was wünscht ihr euch zu Weihnachten?**
What do you want for Christmas?

# The Passive

In active tenses, the subject of a verb carries out the action of the verb, but in passive tenses the subject of the verb has something done to it.
Compare the following:

> *Peter kicked the cat* (subject: *Peter*)
> *The cat was kicked by Peter* (subject: *the cat*)

- English uses the verb "to be" to form its passive tenses. German uses **werden** (→**1**)
  A sample verb is conjugated in the passive on pp 39 to 41.

- In English, the word "by" usually introduces the agent through which the action of a passive tense is performed. In German this agent is introduced by:
  **von** for the performer of the action
  **durch** for an inanimate cause (→**2**)

- The passive can be used to add impersonality or distance to an event (→**3**)
  It may also be used where the identity of the cause of the deed is unknown or not important (→**4**)

- In general however the passive is used less in German than in English. The following are common replacements for the passive:

  1. an active tense with the impersonal pronoun **man** as subject (meaning *they/one*). This resembles the use of *on* in French, and **man** is not always translated as *one* or *they* (→**5**)

  2. **sich lassen** plus a verb in the infinitive (→**6**)

*Continued*

**1 Das Auto wurde gekauft**
The car was bought

**2 Das ist von seinem Onkel geschickt worden**
It was sent by his uncle
**Das Kind wurde von einem Hund gebissen**
The child was bitten by a dog
**Seine Bewerbung ist von der Firma abgelehnt worden**
(*the firm is viewed as a human agent*)
His application was turned down by the firm

**Die Tür wurde durch den Wind geöffnet**
The door was opened by the wind
**Das Getreide wurde durch den Sturm niedergeschlagen**
The crop was flattened by the storm

**3 Die Praxis ist von Dr. Disselkamp übernommen worden**
The practice has been taken over by Dr Disselkamp
**Anfang 1993 wurde ein weiterer Anschlag auf sein Leben gemacht**
Another attempt was made on his life early in 1993

**4 In letzter Zeit sind neue Gesetze eingeführt worden**
New laws have recently been introduced

**5 Man hatte es schon verkauft**
It had already been sold
**Man wird es verkauft haben**
It will have been sold

**6 Das läßt sich schnell herausfinden**
We'll/You'll/One will be able to find that out quickly

## The Passive (contd)

- In English the indirect object of an active tense can become the subject of a passive statement e.g.
  
  Peter gave *him* a car (*him* = to him)
  
  *He* was given a car by Peter

  This is not possible in German, where the indirect object (*him*) must remain in the dative case (see p 110). There are two ways of handling this in German:
  1. with the direct object (*car*) as the subject of a passive verb (→**1**)
  2. by means of an impersonal passive construction, with or without the impersonal subject **es** (→**1**)

  These constructions would however normally be avoided in favour of an active tense, when the agent of the action is known (→**2**)

- Verbs which are normally followed by the dative case in German and so have only an indirect object (see p 80) should therefore be especially noted, as they can only adopt the impersonal or **man**-forms of the passive (→**3**)

- Some passive tenses are avoided in German, as they are inelegant (and difficult to use!). For instance, the future perfect passives should be replaced by an active tense or a **man**-construction (→**4**)

  The conditional perfect passives are also rarely used, past conditional being shown by the pluperfect subjunctives, either passive or active (→**5**)

- English passive constructions such as
  *he was heard whistling/they were thought to be dying*
  are not possible in German (→**6**)

*Continued*

**1 Ein Auto wurde ihm von Peter geschenkt**
*OR*:
**Es wurde ihm von Peter ein Auto geschenkt**
*OR*:
**Ihm wurde von Peter ein Auto geschenkt**
He was given a car by Peter

**2 Peter schenkte ihm ein Auto**
Peter gave him a car

**3 helfen** (+ *dative*)          to help:
  **Sie half mir**              **Mir wurde von ihr geholfen**
  She helped me      →    *OR*:
                          **Es wurde mir von ihr geholfen**
                          I was helped by her

**4 Er meint, es werde schon gesehen worden sein**
He thinks that it will already have been seen

  *BETTER*: **Er meint, man werde es schon gesehen haben**

**5 Es würde geholt worden sein / Man würde es geholt haben**
It would have been fetched

  *BETTER*: **Es wäre geholt worden / Man hätte es geholt**

**6 Man hörte ihn singen**
He was heard singing
**Man sah sie ankommen**
She was seen arriving
**Man glaubte, er sei betrunken**
He was thought to be drunk

# Passive Tenses: Conjugation

## Simple Tenses

| | |
|---|---|
| Present passive indicative<br>e.g. *it is seen* | present indicative of **werden** + past participle of the verb (→**1**) |
| Present passive subjunctive | present subjunctive of **werden** + past participle of the verb (→**2**) |
| Imperfect passive indicative<br>e.g. *it was seen* | imperfect indicative of **werden** + past participle of the verb (→**3**) |
| Imperfect passive subjunctive | imperfect subjunctive of **werden** + past participle of the verb (→**4**) |

## Compound Tenses

| | |
|---|---|
| Perfect passive indicative<br>e.g. *it has been seen* | present indicative of **sein** + past participle of the verb + **worden** (→**5**) |
| Perfect passive subjunctive | present subjunctive of **sein** + past participle of the verb + **worden** (→**6**) |
| Pluperfect passive indicative<br>e.g. *it had been seen* | imperfect indicative of **sein** + past participle + **worden** (→**7**) |

*Continued*

**1** *PRESENT PASSIVE INDICATIVE*

| | |
|---|---|
| ich werde gesehen | wir werden gesehen |
| du wirst gesehen | ihr werdet gesehen |
| er/sie/es wird gesehen | sie/Sie werden gesehen |

*OR:* **man sieht mich/man sieht dich** *etc*

**2** *PRESENT PASSIVE SUBJUNCTIVE*

| | |
|---|---|
| ich werde gesehen | wir werden gesehen |
| du werdest gesehen | ihr werdet gesehen |
| er/sie/es werde gesehen | sie/Sie werden gesehen |

*OR:* **man sehe mich/man sehe dich** *etc*

**3** *IMPERFECT PASSIVE INDICATIVE*
**ich wurde gesehen/wir wurden gesehen** *etc*

*OR:* **man sah mich/man sah uns** *etc*

**4** *IMPERFECT PASSIVE SUBJUNCTIVE*
**ich würde gesehen/wir würden gesehen** *etc*

*OR:* **man sähe mich/man sähe uns** *etc*

**5** *PERFECT PASSIVE INDICATIVE*
**ich bin gesehen worden/wir sind gesehen worden** *etc*

*OR:* **man hat mich/uns gesehen** *etc*

**6** *PERFECT PASSIVE SUBJUNCTIVE*
**ich sei gesehen worden/wir seien gesehen worden** *etc*

*OR:* **man habe mich/uns gesehen** *etc*

**7** *PLUPERFECT PASSIVE INDICATIVE*
**ich war gesehen worden/wir waren gesehen worden** *etc*

*OR:* **man hatte mich/uns gesehen** *etc*

## Passive Tenses: Conjugation (contd)

| | |
|---|---|
| Pluperfect passive subjunctive | imperfect subjunctive of **sein** + past participle of the verb + **worden** (→**1**) |
| Present passive infinitive<br>e.g. *to be seen* | infinitive of **werden** + past participle of the verb (→**2**) |
| Future passive indicative<br>e.g. *it will be seen* | present indicative of **werden** + present passive infinitive of the verb (→**3**) |
| Future passive subjunctive | present subjunctive of **werden** + present passive infinitive (→**4**) |
| Perfect passive infinitive<br>e.g. *to have been seen* | past participle of the verb + **worden sein** (→**5**) |
| Future perfect passive<br>e.g. *it will have been seen* | present indicative of **werden** + perfect passive infinitive of the verb (→**6**) |
| Conditional passive<br>e.g. *it would be seen* | imperfect subjunctive of **werden** + present passive infinitive of the verb (→**7**) |
| Conditional perfect passive<br>e.g. *it would have been seen* | imperfect subjunctive of **werden** + perfect passive infinitive of the verb (→**8**) |

**1** *PLUPERFECT PASSIVE SUBJUNCTIVE*
**ich wäre gesehen worden/wir wären gesehen worden** *etc*

*OR*: **man hätte mich/uns gesehen** *etc*

**2** *PRESENT PASSIVE INFINITIVE*
**gesehen werden**

**3** *FUTURE PASSIVE INDICATIVE*
**ich werde gesehen werden/wir werden gesehen werden** *etc*

*OR*: **man wird mich/uns sehen** *etc*

**4** *FUTURE PASSIVE SUBJUNCTIVE*
**ich werde gesehen werden/wir werden gesehen werden** *etc*

*OR*: **man werde mich/uns sehen** *etc*

**5** *PERFECT PASSIVE INFINITIVE*
**gesehen worden sein**

**6** *FUTURE PERFECT PASSIVE*
**ich werde/wir werden gesehen worden sein** *etc*

*OR*: **man wird mich/uns gesehen haben** *etc*

**7** *CONDITIONAL PASSIVE*
**ich würde gesehen werden/wir würden gesehen werden**

*OR*: **man würde mich/uns sehen** *etc*

**8** *CONDITIONAL PERFECT PASSIVE*
**ich würde/wir würden gesehen worden sein**

*OR*: **man würde mich/uns gesehen haben** *etc*
*OR*: pluperfect subjunctive: **man hätte mich/uns gesehen** *etc*

## Impersonal Verbs

These verbs are used only in the third person singular, usually with the subject **es** meaning *it* (→**1**)

- Intransitive verbs (verbs with no direct object) are often made impersonal in the passive to describe activity of a general nature (→**2**)
  When the verb and subject are inverted (see p 226), the **es** is omitted (→**3**)
  Impersonal verbs in the passive can also be used as an imperative form (see p 20) (→**4**)

- In certain expressions in the active, the impersonal pronoun **es** can be omitted. In this case, a personal pronoun object begins the clause (→**5**)
  In the following lists * indicates that **es** may be omitted in this way:

### Some common impersonal verbs and expressions

**es donnert** *it's thundering*
**es fällt mir ein, daß/zu\*** *it occurs to me that/to* (→**6**)
**es fragt sich, ob** *one wonders whether* (→**7**)
**es freut mich, daß/zu** *I am glad that/to* (→**8**)
**es friert** *it is freezing* (→**9**)
**es gefällt mir** *I like it* (→**10**)
**es geht mir gut/schlecht** *I'm fine/not too good*
**es geht nicht** *it's not possible*
**es geht um** *it's about*
**es gelingt mir (, zu)** *I succeed (in)* (→**11**)
**es geschieht** *it happens* (→**12**)
**es gießt** *it's pouring*
**es handelt sich um** *it's a question of*

*Continued*

**1 Es regnet** It's raining

**2 Es wurde viel gegessen und getrunken**
There was a lot of eating and drinking

**3 Auf der Hochzeit wurde viel gegessen und getrunken**
There was a lot of eating and drinking at the wedding

**4 Jetzt wird gearbeitet!** Now you're/we're going to work

**5 Mir ist warm** I'm warm

**6 Nachher fiel (es) mir ein, daß der Mann ziemlich komisch angezogen war**
Afterwards it occurred to me that the man was rather oddly dressed

**7 Es fragt sich, ob es sich lohnt, das zu machen**
One wonders if that's worth doing

**8 Es freut mich sehr, daß du gekommen bist**
I'm so pleased that you have come

**9 Heute nacht hat es gefroren**
It was below freezing last night

**10 Ihm hat es gar nicht gefallen**
He didn't like it at all

**11 Es war ihnen gelungen, die letzten Karten zu kriegen**
They had succeeded in getting the last tickets

**12 Und so geschah es, daß ...**
And so it came about that ...

## Impersonal Verbs and Expressions (contd)

**es hängt davon ab** *it depends*
**es hat keinen Zweck (zu)** *there's no point (in)* (→**1**)
**es interessiert mich, daß/zu*** *I am interested that/to*
**es ist mir egal (ob)*** *it's all the same to me (if)* (→**2**)
**es ist möglich (, daß)** *it's possible (that)* (→**3**)
**es ist nötig** *it's necessary* (→**4**)
**es ist mir, als ob*** *I feel as if*
**es ist mir gut/schlecht** *etc* **zumute*** *I feel good/bad etc*
   (→**5**)
**es ist schade (, daß)** *it's a pity (that)*
**es ist (mir) wichtig*** *it's important (to me)*
**es ist mir warm/kalt*** *I'm hot/cold*
**es ist warm/kalt** *it's (the weather is) warm/cold*
**es ist zu hoffen/bedauern** *etc* * *it is to be hoped/regretted*
   *etc*
**es klingelt** *someone is ringing the bell* (→**6**)
**es klopft** *someone's knocking*
**es kommt darauf an (, ob)** *it all depends (whether)*
**es kommt mir vor (, als ob)** *it seems to me (as if)*
**es läutet** *the bell is ringing* (→**7**)
**es liegt an** *it is because of* (→**8**)
**es lohnt sich (nicht)** *it's (not) worth it* (→**9**)
**es macht nichts** *it doesn't matter*
**es macht nichts aus** *it makes no difference* (→**10**)
**es macht mir (keinen) Spaß (, zu)** *it's (no) fun (to)* (→**11**)
**es passiert** *it happens* (→**12**)
**es regnet** *it's raining* (→**13**)
**es scheint mir, daß/als ob*** *it seems to me that/as if*
**es schneit** *it's snowing*
**es stellt sich heraus, daß** *it turns out that*
**es stimmt (nicht), daß** *it's (not) true, that*
**es tut mir leid (, daß)** *I'm sorry (that)*
**wie geht es (dir)?** *how are you?* (→**14**)
**mir wird schlecht** *I feel sick*

**1 Es hat keinen Zweck, weiter darüber zu diskutieren**
There's no point in discussing this any further

**2 Es ist mir egal, ob du kommst oder nicht**
I don't care if you come or not

**3 Es ist doch möglich, daß der Zug Verspätung hat**
It's always possible the train has been delayed

**4 Es wird nicht nötig sein, uns darüber zu informieren**
It won't be necessary to inform us of it

**5 Mir ist heute seltsam zumute** I feel strange today

**6 Es hat gerade geklingelt**
The bell just went/The phone just rang

**7 Es hat schon geläutet** The bell has gone

**8 Woran liegt es?** Why is that?

**9 Ich weiß nicht, ob es sich lohnt oder nicht**
I don't know if it's worth it or not

**10 Mir macht es nichts aus** It makes no difference to me
**Macht es Ihnen etwas aus, wenn ...** Would you mind if ...

**11 Hauptsache, es macht Spaß**
The main thing is to enjoy yourself

**12 Ihm ist bestimmt etwas passiert**
Something must have happened to him

**13 Es hat den ganzen Tag geregnet** It rained the whole day

**14 Wie geht's denn? – Danke, es geht**
How are things? – All right thank you

## The Infinitive

### Forms

There are four forms of the infinitive (→**1**). These forms are used in certain compound tenses (see p 28). The present active infinitive is the most widely used and is the form found in dictionaries.

### Uses

● Preceded by **zu** (*to*)

1. as in English, after other verbs ("I tried *to come*") (→**2**)
2. as in English, after adjectives ("it was easy *to see*") (→**3**)
3. where the English equivalent is not always an infinitive:
   - after nouns, where English may use an "-ing" form (→**4**)
   - after **sein**, where the English equivalent may be a passive tense (→**5**)

● Without **zu**, the infinitive is used after the following:

modal verbs (→**6**)
**lassen** (→**7**)
**heißen** (→**8**)
**bleiben** (→**9**)
**gehen** (→**10**)
verbs of perception (→**11**)
*NOTE*: verbs of perception can also be followed by a subordinate clause beginning with **wie** or **daß**, especially if the sentence is long or involved (→**12**)

*Continued*

**1** *INFINITIVES*:

| *PRESENT ACTIVE* | *PERFECT ACTIVE* |
|---|---|
| **holen** | **geholt haben** |
| to fetch | to have fetched |
| *PRESENT PASSIVE* | *PERFECT PASSIVE* |
| **geholt werden** | **geholt worden sein** |
| to be fetched | to have been fetched |

**2 Ich versuchte zu kommen** I tried to come

**3 Es war leicht zu sehen** It was easy to see

**4 Ich habe nur wenig Gelegenheit, Musik zu hören**
I have little opportunity to listen to music

**5 Er ist zu bedauern** He is to be pitied

**6 Er kann schwimmen** He can swim

**7 Sie ließen uns warten** They kept us waiting

**8 Er hieß ihn kommen** He bade him come

**9 Er blieb sitzen** He remained seated

**10 Sie ging einkaufen** She went shopping

**11 Ich sah ihn kommen** I saw him coming
**Er hörte sie singen** He heard her singing

**12 Er sah, wie sie langsam auf und ab schlenderte**
He watched her strolling slowly up and down

## The Infinitive (contd)

### Used as an imperative
- The infinitive can be used as an imperative (see p 20) (→**1**)

### Used as a noun
- The infinitive can be made into a noun by giving it a capital letter. Its gender is always neuter (→**2**)

### Used with modal verbs (see p 52)
- An infinitive used with a modal verb is always placed at the end of a clause (see p 56) (→**3**)

- If the modal verb is in a compound tense, its auxiliary will follow the subject in a main clause in the normal way, and the modal participle comes after the infinitive. *BUT* in a subordinate clause, the auxiliary immediately precedes the infinitive and the modal participle, instead of coming at the end (→**4**)

- An infinitive expressing change of place may be omitted entirely after a modal verb (see p 56) (→**5**)

### Used in infinitive phrases

Infinitive phrases can be formed with:

| | |
|---|---|
| **zu** | **ohne ... zu** |
| **um ... zu** | **anstatt ... zu** (→**6**) |

- The infinitive comes at the end of its phrase (→**7**)

- In separable verbs, **zu** is inserted *between* the verb and its prefix in the present infinitive (→**8**)

- A reflexive pronoun comes first, immediately following an introductory word if there is one (→**9**)

**1 Einsteigen und Türen schließen!**
All aboard! Close the doors!

**2 rauchen** to smoke:
**Er hat das Rauchen aufgegeben**
He's given up smoking

**3 Wir müssen morgen einkaufen gehen**
We have to go shopping tomorrow

**4 Sie haben gestern aufräumen müssen**
They had to tidy up yesterday
*BUT*
**Da sie gestern haben aufräumen müssen, durften sie nicht kommen**
They couldn't come as they had to tidy up yesterday

**5 Er will jetzt nach Hause** He wants to go home now

**6 es zu tun** to do it
**es getan zu haben** to have done it
**um es zu tun** in order to do it
**um es getan zu haben** in order to have done it
**ohne es zu tun** without doing it
**ohne es getan zu haben** without having done it
**anstatt es zu tun** instead of doing it
**anstatt es getan zu haben** instead of having done it

**7 Ohne ein Wort zu sagen, verließ er das Haus**
He left the house without saying a word
**Er ging nach Hause, ohne mit ihr gesprochen zu haben**
He went home without having spoken to her

**8 aufgeben** to give up:
**um es aufzugeben** in order to give it up

**9 Sie gingen weg, ohne sich zu verabschieden**
They left without saying goodbye

# The Present Participle

- The present participle for all verbs is formed by adding **-d** to the infinitive form (→**1**)

- The present participle may be used as an adjective.
  As with all adjectives, it is declined if used attributively (see p 140) (→**2**)

- The present participle may also be used as an adjectival noun (see p 148) (→**3**)

## The Past Participle

- For weak verbs, the past participle is formed by prefixing **ge-** and adding **-t** to the verb stem (→**4**)

- For strong verbs, the past participle is formed by adding the prefix **ge-** and the ending **-en** to the verb stem (→**5**)
  The vowel is often modified too (→**6**)
  (See list of strong and mixed verbs beginning on p 86)

- Mixed verbs form their past participle by adding the **ge-** and **-t** of weak verbs, but they change their vowel as for strong verbs. (See list, p 86) (→**7**)

- The past participles of *separable* verbs are formed according to the above rules and are joined on to the separable prefix (→**8**)

- For *inseparable* verbs, past participles are formed without the **ge-** prefix (→**9**)

- Many past participles can also be used as adjectives and adjectival nouns (→**10**)

**1**  **lachen** to laugh
    **lachend** laughing

    **singen** to sing
    **singend** singing

**2**  **ein lachendes Kind** a laughing child
    **mit klopfendem Herzen** with beating heart

**3**  **der Vorsitzende/ein Vorsitzender** the/a chairman

**4**  **machen** to do/make
    **gemacht** done/made

**5**  **sehen** to see
    **gesehen** seen

**6**  **singen** to sing
    **gesungen** sung

**7**  **wissen** to know
    **gewußt** known

**8**  **aufstehen** to get up
    **aufgestanden** got up

    **nachmachen** to copy/imitate
    **nachgemacht** imitated

**9**  **bestellen** to order
    **bestellt** ordered

    **entscheiden** to decide
    **entschieden** decided

**10**  **seine verlorene Brille** his lost spectacles
    **Wir aßen Gebratenes** We ate fried food

## Modal Auxiliary Verbs

Modal verbs, sometimes called modal auxiliaries, are used to *modify* other verbs (to show e.g. possibility, ability, willingness, permission, necessity) much as in English:

> he *can* swim; *may* I come?; we *shouldn't* go

- In German the modal auxiliary verbs are: **dürfen, können, mögen, müssen, sollen** and **wollen**.

- Modal verbs have some important differences in their uses and in their conjugation from other verbs, and these are clearly shown on pp 86 to 97.

- Modal verbs have the following meanings:

**dürfen**        *to be allowed to/may* (→**1**)
used negatively: *must not/may not* (→**2**)
to show probability (→**3**)
also used in some polite expressions (→**4**)

**können**        *to be able to, can* (→**5**)
in its subjunctive forms:
*would be able to/could* (→**6**)
as an informal alternative to **dürfen** with the meaning: *allowed to/can* (→**7**)
to show possibility (→**8**)

**mögen**        *to like/to like to* (→**9**)
most common in its imperfect subjunctive form which expresses polite inquiry or request: *should like to/would like to* (→**10**)
to show possibility or probability (→**11**)

*Continued*

1 **Darfst du mit ins Kino kommen?**
   Are you allowed to (can you) come with us to the cinema?
   **Darf ich bitte mitkommen?**
   May I come with you please?
   **Ich dürfte schon, aber ich will nicht**
   I could (would be allowed to), but I don't want to
2 **Hier darf man nicht rauchen**
   Smoking is prohibited here
3 **Das dürfte wohl das beste sein**
   That's probably the best thing
4 **Was darf es sein?**
   Can I help you?/What would you like?
5 **Wir konnten es nicht schaffen**
   We couldn't (weren't able to) do it
6 **Er könnte noch früher kommen**
   He could (would be able to) come even earlier
   **Er meinte, er könne noch früher kommen**
   He thought he could come earlier
   **Wir könnten vielleicht morgen hinfahren?**
   Perhaps we could go there tomorrow?
7 **Kann ich (darf ich) ein Eishaben?**
   Can I (may I) have an ice-cream?
8 **Wer könnte es gewesen sein?**
   Who could it have been?
   **Das kann sein**
   That may be so
   *BUT*: **Das kann nicht sein** That cannot be so
9 **Magst du Butter?**
   Do you like butter?
10 **Wir möchten bitte etwas trinken**
   We should like something to drink
   **Möchtest du sie besuchen?**
   Would you like to visit her?
11 **Wie alt mag sie sein?**
   How old might she be?

# Modal Auxiliary Verbs (contd)

**müssen**    *to have to/must/need to* (→**1**)
                 certain idiomatic uses (→**2**)

                 NOTE: for *must have ...*, use the relevant tense of
                 **müssen** + past participle of main verb + the
                 auxiliary **haben** or **sein** (→**3**)
                 for *don't have to/need not*, a negative form of
                 **brauchen** (*to need*) may be used instead of
                 **müssen** (→**4**)

**sollen**    *ought to/should* (→**5**)
                 *to be (supposed) to* where the demand is not self-
                 imposed (→**6**)
                 *to be said to be* (→**7**)
                 as a command, either direct or indirect (→**8**)

**wollen**    *to want/want to* (→**9**)
                 used as a less formal version of **mögen** to mean:
                 *want/wish* (→**10**)
                 *to be willing to* (→**11**)
                 to show previous intention (→**12**)
                 to claim or pretend (→**13**)

*Continued*

**1  Er hatte jeden Tag um sechs aufstehen müssen**
He had to get up at six o'clock every day
**Man mußte lachen**
One had to laugh/couldn't help laughing

**2  Muß das sein?** Is that really necessary?
**Ein Millionär müßte man sein!**
Oh to be a millionaire!
**Den Film muß man gesehen haben**
That film is worth seeing

**3  Es muß geregnet haben** It must have been raining
**Er meinte, es müsse am vorigen Abend passiert sein**
He thought it must have happened the previous evening

**4  Das brauchtest du nicht zu sagen**
You didn't have to say that

**5  Man sollte immer die Wahrheit sagen**
One should always tell the truth
**Er wußte nicht, was er tun sollte**
He didn't know what to do (*what he should do*)

**6  Ich soll dir helfen**
I am to help you (*I have been told to help you*)
**Du sollst sofort deine Frau anrufen**
You are to phone your wife at once (*She has left a message asking you to ring*)

**7  Er soll sehr reich sein**
I've heard he's very rich/He is said to be very rich

**8  Es soll niemand sagen, daß die Schotten geizig sind!**
Let no-one say the Scots are mean!
**Sie sagte mir, ich solle damit aufhören**
She told me to stop it

**9  Das Kind will LKW-Fahrer werden**
The child wants to become a lorry driver

**10  Willst du eins?** Do you want one?
**Willst du (möchtest du) etwas trinken?**
Do you want (would you like) something to drink?

**11  Er wollte nichts sagen** He refused to say anything

**12  Ich wollte gerade anrufen** I was just about to phone

**13  Keiner will es gewesen sein** No-one admits to doing it

## Modal Auxiliary Verbs (contd)

### Conjugation and Use

- Modal verbs have unusual present tenses (→**1**)
  Their principal parts are given on pp 86 to 97.

- Each modal verb has two past participles.
  The first, which is the more common, is the same as the infinitive form and is used where the modal is modifying a verb (→**2**)
  The second resembles a normal weak past participle and is used only where no verb is being modified (see the verb list, p 86) (→**3**)

- The verb modified by the modal is placed in its infinitive form at the end of a clause (→**4**)

- Where the modal is used in a compound tense, its past participle in the form of the infinitive is also placed at the end of a clause, immediately after the modified verb (→**5**)

- If the modal verb is modifying a verb, and if the modal is used in a compound tense in a subordinate clause, then the normal word order for subordinate clauses (see p 228) does not apply. The auxiliary used to form the compound tense of the modal is not placed right at the end of the subordinate clause, but instead comes before both infinitives (→**6**)
  Such constructions are usually avoided in German, by using a simple tense in place of a compound. (For notes on the use of tenses in German, see p 58ff) (→**7**)

- A modified verb which expresses motion may be omitted entirely if an adverb or adverbial phrase is present to indicate the movement or destination (→**8**)

**1 dürfen**
ich/er/sie/es darf
du darfst
wir/sie/Sie dürfen
ihr dürft

**können**
ich/er/sie/es kann
du kannst
wir/sie/Sie können
ihr könnt

**mögen**
ich/er/sie/es mag
du magst
wir/sie/Sie mögen
ihr mögt

**müssen**
ich/er/sie/es muß
du mußt
wir/sie/Sie müssen
ihr müßt

**sollen**
ich/er/sie/es soll
du sollst
wir/sie/Sie sollen
ihr sollt

**wollen**
ich/er/sie/es will
du willst
wir/sie/Sie wollen
ihr wollt

**2 wollen**: Past participle **wollen**
**Er hat kommen wollen** he wanted to come
**3 wollen**: Past participle **gewollt**
**Hast du es gewollt?** Did you want it?
**4 Er kann gut schwimmen** He can swim well
**5 Wir haben das Haus nicht kaufen wollen**
We didn't want to buy the house
**Sie wird dich bald sehen wollen**
She will want to see you soon
**6 *Compare***:
**Obwohl wir das Haus gekauft haben, ...**
Although we bought the house ...
**Obwohl wir das Haus haben kaufen wollen, ...**
Although we wanted to buy the house ...
**7 Obwohl wir das Haus kaufen wollten ...**
Although we wanted to buy the house ...
**8 Ich muß nach Hause** I must go home
**Die Kinder sollen jetzt ins Bett**
The children have to go to bed now

## 58   VERBS

## Use of Tenses

### Continuous Forms
- Unlike English, the German verb does not distinguish between its simple and continuous forms (→**1**)
- To emphasize continuity, the following may be used:
  - simple tense plus an adverb or adverbial phrase (→**2**)
  - **am** or **beim** plus an infinitive used as a noun (→**3**)
  - **eben/gerade dabei sein zu** plus an infinitive (→**4**)

### The Present
- The present tense is used in German with **seit** or **seitdem** where English uses a past tense to show an action which began in the past and still continues (→**5**)
  If the action is finished, or does not continue, a past tense is used (→**6**)
- The present is commonly used with future meaning (→**7**)

### The Future
- The present is often used as a future tense (→**7**)
- The future tense is used however to:
  - emphasize the future (→**8**)
  - express doubt or supposition about the future (→**9**)
  - express future intention (→**10**)

### The Future Perfect
- Used as in English to mean *shall/will have done* (→**11**)
- It is used in German to express a supposition (→**12**)
- In conversation it is replaced by the perfect (→**13**)

### The Conditional
- May be used in place of the imperfect subjunctive to express improbable condition (see p 62) (→**14**)
- Is used in indirect statements or questions to replace the future subjunctive in conversation or where the subjunctive form is not distinctive (→**15**)

*Continued*

**1 ich tue** I do (*simple form*) OR I am doing (*continuous*)
  **er rauchte** he smoked OR he was smoking
  **sie hat gelesen** she has read OR she has been reading
  **es ist geschickt worden** it is sent OR it is being sent

**2 Er kochte gerade das Abendessen**
  He was cooking the supper
  **Nun spricht sie mit ihm** Now she's talking to him

**3 Ich bin am Bügeln** I am ironing

**4 Wir waren eben dabei, einige Briefe zu schreiben**
  We were just writing a few letters

**5 Ich wohne seit drei Jahren hier**
  I have been living here for three years
  **Seit ich hier wohne, fühle ich mich wohl**
  I've been feeling at home since I've lived here

**6 Seit er krank ist, hat er uns nicht besucht**
  He hasn't visited us since he's been ill
  **Seit seiner Verlobung habe ich ihn nicht gesehen**
  I haven't seen him since his engagement

**7 Wir fahren nächstes Jahr nach Griechenland**
  We're going to Greece next year

**8 Das werde ich erst nächstes Jahr machen können**
  I won't be able to do that until next year

**9 Wenn er zurückkommt, wird er mir bestimmt helfen**
  He's sure to help me when he returns

**10 Ich werde ihm helfen** I'm going to help him

**11 Bis Sonntag wird er es gelesen haben**
  He will have read it by Sunday

**12 Das wird Herr Keute gewesen sein**
  That must have been Herr Keute

**13 Bis du zurückkommst, haben wir alles aufgeräumt**
  We'll have tidied up by the time you get back

**14 Wenn ich eins hätte, würde ich es dir geben**
  If I had one I would give it to you
  **Wenn er jetzt bloß kommen würde!**
  If only he would get here!

**15 Er fragte, ob wir fahren würden**
  He asked if we were going to go

## Use of Tenses (contd)

### The Conditional Perfect

- May be used in place of the pluperfect subjunctive in a sentence containing a **wenn**-clause (→**1**)
- But the pluperfect subjunctive is preferred (→**2**)

### The Imperfect

- Is used in German with **seit** or **seitdem** where the pluperfect is used in English to show an action which began in the remote past and continued to a point in the more recent past (→**3**)
  For discontinued actions the pluperfect is used (→**4**)
- Used to describe past actions which have no link with the present as far as the speaker is concerned (→**5**)
  for narrative purposes (→**6**)
  for repeated, habitual or prolonged past action (→**7**)

See also the note on the **Perfect** (below).

### The Perfect

- Is used to translate the English perfect tense *I have spoken, he has been reading* (→**8**)
- Describes past actions or events which still have a link with the present or the speaker (→**9**)
- Is used in conversation and similar communication (→**10**)

*NOTE*: In practice however the perfect and imperfect are often interchangeable in German usage and in spoken German a mixture of both is common.

### The Pluperfect

- Is used to translate *had done/had been doing*, except in conjunction with **seit/seitdem** (see **Imperfect**) (→**11**)

### The Subjunctive

For uses of the subjunctive tenses, see pp 62 to 67.

1 **Wenn du es gesehen hättest, würdest du's geglaubt haben**
You would have believed it if you'd seen it

2 **Hättest du es gesehen, so hättest du es geglaubt**
If you had seen it, you'd have believed it
**Wenn ich das nur nicht gemacht hätte!**
If only I hadn't done it!
**Wäre ich nur da gewesen!** If I'd only been there

3 **Sie war seit ihrer Heirat als Lehrerin beschäftigt**
She had been working as a teacher since her marriage

4 **Ihren Sohn hatten sie seit zwölf Jahren nicht gesehen**
They hadn't seen their son for twelve years

5 **Er kam zu spät, um teilnehmen zu können**
He arrived too late to take part

6 **Das Mädchen stand auf, wusch sich das Gesicht, und verließ das Haus**
The girl got up, washed her face and went out

7 **Wir machten jeden Tag einen kleinen Spaziergang**
We went (used to go) for a little walk every day

8 **Ich habe ihn heute nicht gesehen**
I haven't seen him today

9 **Ich habe ihr nichts davon erzählt**
I didn't tell her anything about it
**Gestern sind wir in die Stadt gefahren und haben uns ein paar Sachen gekauft**
Yesterday we went into town and bought ourselves a few things

10 **Hast du den Krimi gestern abend im Fernsehen gesehen?**
Did you see the thriller on television last night?

11 **Sie waren schon weggefahren**
They had already left
**Diese Bücher hatten sie schon gelesen**
They had already read these books

## The Subjunctive: when to use it

The subjunctive form in English has almost died out, leaving only a few examples such as:

if I *were* rich/if only he *were* to come/so *be* it

German however makes much wider use of subjunctive forms, especially in formal, educated or literary contexts. Although there is a growing tendency to use indicatives in spoken German, subjunctives are still very common.

- The indicative tenses in German display fact or certainty. The subjunctives show unreality, uncertainty, speculation about a situation or any doubt in the speaker's mind (→1)
  Subjunctives are also used in indirect speech, as shown on pp 66 and 67.

- For how to form all tenses of the subjunctive, the reader is referred to the relevant sections on Simple Tenses (pp 6 to 17) and Compound Tenses (pp 22 to 29). See also the Subjunctive in Reported Speech (p 66).

- The **imperfect subjunctive** is very common. It is important to note that the imperfect subjunctive form does not always represent actions performed in the past (→2)

## Uses of the Subjunctive in German

- To show improbable condition (e.g. if he *came*, he would ...)
  The *if*-clause (**wenn** in German) has a verb in the imperfect subjunctive and the main clause can have either an imperfect subjunctive or a conditional (→3)

*Continued*

**1** *INDICATIVE*
**Das stimmt**
That's true
**Es ist eine Unverschämtheit**
It's a scandal

*SUBJUNCTIVE*
**Es könnte doch wahr sein**
It could well be true
**Sie meint, es sei eine Unverschämtheit**
She thinks it's a scandal   (*speaker not necessarily in
                                agreement with her*)

**2** *imperfect subjunctive expressing the future*
**Wenn ich morgen nur da sein könnte!**
If only I could be there tomorrow!

*expressing the present/immediate future*
**Wenn er jetzt nur käme!**
If only he would come now!

*speaker's opinion, referring to present or future*
**Sie wäre die Beste**
She's the best

**3 Wenn du kämest, wäre ich froh**
*OR*
**Wenn du kämest, würde ich froh sein**
I should be happy if you came

**Wenn es mir nicht gefiele, würde ich es nicht bezahlen**
*OR*
**Wenn es mir nicht gefiele, bezahlte ich es nicht**
If I wasn't happy with it, I wouldn't pay for it
(*The second form is less likely, as the imperfect subjunctive
and imperfect indicative forms of* **bezahlen** *are identical*)

## The Subjunctive: when to use it (contd)

- The imperfect of **sollen** or **wollen**, or a conditional tense might be used in the **wenn**-clause to replace an uncommon imperfect subjunctive, or a subjunctive which is not distinct from the same tense of the indicative (→**1**)

- To show unfulfilled condition (if he *had come*, he would have…)
  The **wenn**-clause requires a pluperfect subjunctive, the main clause a pluperfect subjunctive or conditional perfect (→**2**)
  *NOTE*: The indicative is used to express a *probable* condition, as in English (→**3**)
  **wenn** can be omitted from conditional clauses. The verb must then follow the subject and **dann** or **so** usually begins the main clause (→**4**)

- With **selbst wenn** (*even if/even though*) (→**5**)

- With **wenn … nur** (*if only …*) (→**6**)

- To speculate or make assumptions (→**7**)

- After **als** (*as if/as though*) (→**8**)

- Where there is uncertainty or doubt (→**9**)

- To make a polite enquiry (→**10**)

- To indicate theoretical possibility or unreality (→**11**)

- As an alternative to the conditional perfect (→**12**)

1 **Wenn er mich so sehen würde, würde er mich für verrückt halten!**
*OR*
**Wenn er mich so sehen würde, hielte er mich für verrückt!**
*OR*
**Wenn er mich so sehen sollte, würde er mich für verrückt halten!**
If he saw me like this, he would think I was mad!
**(Wenn er mich so sähe** *would sound rather stilted*)

2 **Wenn du pünktlich gekommen wärest, hättest du ihn gesehen**
*OR*
**Wenn du pünktlich gekommen wärest, würdest du ihn gesehen haben**
If you had been on time, you would have seen him

3 **Wenn ich ihn sehe, gebe ich es ihm**
If I see him I'll give him it

4 **Hättest du mich nicht gesehen, so wäre ich schon weg**
If you hadn't seen me, I would have been gone by now

5 **Selbst wenn er etwas wüßte, würde er nichts sagen**
Even if he knew about it, he wouldn't say anything

6 **Wenn wir nur erfolgreich wären!** If only we were successful!

7 **Und wenn er recht hätte?** What if he were right?
**Eine Frau, die das sagen würde** (*or* **die das sagte**)**, müßte Feministin sein!**
Any woman who would say that must be a feminist!

8 **Er sah aus, als sei er krank**
He looked as if he were ill

9 **Er wußte nicht, wie es ihr jetzt ginge**
He didn't know how she was

10 **Wäre da sonst noch etwas?** Will there be anything else?

11 **Er stellte sich vor, wie gut er in dem Anzug aussähe**
He imagined how good he would look in the suit

12 **Ich hätte ihn gesehen = Ich würde ihn gesehen haben**
I would have seen him

# The Subjunctive in Indirect Speech

What a person asks or thinks can be reported in one of two ways,
either **directly**:

*Tom said, "I have been on holiday"*
OR **indirectly**:
*Tom said (that) he had been on holiday*

- In English, indirect, or reported, speech can be indicated by a
change in tense of what has been reported:
    He said, "*I know* your sister"
    He said (that) *he knew* my sister
In German the change is not in tense, but from indicative to
subjunctive (→**1**)

- These are two ways of introducing indirect speech in German,
similar to the parallel English constructions:
    1. The clause which reports what is said may be introduced by
    **daß** (*that*). The finite verb or auxiliary comes at the end of
    the clause (→**2**)
    2. **daß** may be omitted. The verb in this case must stand in
    second position in the clause, instead of being placed at the
    end (→**3**)

## Forms of the Subjunctive in Indirect Speech

See the conjugation of verbs in the subjunctive (pp 8 to 15 and 26
to 31). In indirect (or reported) speech, wherever the present
subjunctive is identical to the present indicative form, the
imperfect subjunctive is used instead (→**4**)

**1 Er sagte: "Sie kennt deine Schwester"**
He said, "She knows your sister"
**Er sagte, sie kenne meine Schwester**
He said she knew my sister
**"Habe ich zu viel gesagt?", fragte er**
"Did I say too much?", he asked
**Er fragte, ob er zuviel gesagt habe**
He asked if he had said too much

**2 Er hat uns gesagt, daß er Italienisch spreche**
He told us that he spoke Italian

**3 Er hat uns gesagt, er spreche Italienisch**
He told us he spoke Italian

**4** *PRESENT SUBJUNCTIVE IN INDIRECT SPEECH*

   *WEAK VERBS* e.g. **holen** to fetch:

| | |
|---|---|
| **ich holte** | **wir holten** |
| du holest | ihr holet |
| er hole | **sie holten** |

   *STRONG VERBS* e.g. **singen** to sing:

| | |
|---|---|
| **ich sänge** | **wir sängen** |
| du singest | ihr singet |
| er singe | **sie sängen** |

## Verbs with Prefixes

Many verbs in German begin with a prefix. A prefix is a word or part of a word which precedes the verb stem (→**1**)

- Often the addition of a prefix changes the meaning of the basic verb (→**2**)

- Prefixes may be found in strong, weak or mixed verbs. Adding a prefix may occasionally change the verb conjugation (→**3**)

- There are four kinds of prefix and each behaves in a slightly different way, as shown on the following pages. Prefixes may be:

  inseparable (→**4**)

  separable (→**5**)

  double (→**6**)

  variable, i.e. either separable or inseparable, depending on the verb (→**7**)

*Continued*

**1** zu   +   **geben**   =   **zugeben**
   an   +   **ziehen**   =   **anziehen**

**2 nehmen** to take
   **zunehmen** to put on weight, to increase
   **sich benehmen** to behave

**3** *WEAK*:                          *STRONG*:

| | | | |
|---|---|---|---|
| **suchen** | to look for | **stehen** | to stand |
| **versuchen** | to try | **verstehen** | to understand |
| **besuchen** | to visit | **aufstehen** | to get up |

   *WEAK*:                          *WEAK*:

| | | | |
|---|---|---|---|
| **löschen** | to extinguish | **fehlen** | to be missing |

   *STRONG*:                       *STRONG*:

| | | | |
|---|---|---|---|
| **erlöschen** | to go out | **empfehlen** | to recommend |

**4 entdecken** to discover
   **er entdeckt, er entdeckte, er hat entdeckt**

**5 mitmachen** to join in
   **er macht mit, er machte mit, er hat mitgemacht**

**6 ausverkaufen** to sell off
   **er verkauft aus, er verkaufte aus, er hat ausverkauft**

**7 wiederholen** to repeat
   **er wiederholt, er wiederholte, er hat wiederholt**

   **wieder(-)holen** to fetch back
   **er holt wieder, er holte wieder, er hat wiedergeholt**

## Verbs with Prefixes (contd)

### Inseparable Prefixes

● The eight inseparable prefixes are:

| | |
|---|---|
| **be-** | **emp-** |
| **ge-** | **ent-** |
| **er-** | **miß-** |
| **ver-** | **zer-** (→**1**) |

● These exist only as prefixes, and cannot be words in their own right.

● They are never separated from the verb stem, whatever tense of the verb is used (→**2**)

● Inseparable prefixes are always unstressed (→**3**)

● They have no **ge-** in their past participles (see p 50) (→**4**)

*Continued*

**1 beschreiben**    to describe
   **gehören**        to belong
   **erhalten**        to contain
   **verlieren**        to lose
   **empfangen**        to receive
   **enttäuschen**        to disappoint
   **mißtrauen**        to mistrust
   **zerlegen**        to dismantle

**2 besuchen**        to visit:

   **Er besucht uns regelmäßig**
   He visits us regularly
   **Er besuchte uns jeden Tag**
   He used to visit us every day
   **Er hat uns jeden Tag besucht**
   He visited us every day
   **Er wird uns morgen besuchen**
   He will visit us tomorrow
   **Besuche sofort deine Tante!**
   Visit your aunt at once

**3** er**lau**ben, ver**steh**en, emp**fang**en, ver**gess**en

**4** *COMPARE*:
   **verstehen: wir haben verstanden** we understood
   **stehen: wir haben gestanden** we stood

   **empfangen: wir haben empfangen** we received
   **fangen: wir haben gefangen** we caught

# Verbs with Prefixes (contd)

## Separable Prefixes

Some common examples are:

| ab | empor | herbei | hinauf | nieder |
|----|-------|--------|--------|--------|
| an | entgegen | herein | hinaus | vor |
| auf | fest | herüber | hindurch | vorbei |
| aus | frei | herum | hinein | vorüber |
| bei | her | herunter | hinüber | weg |
| da(r) | herab | hervor | hinunter | zu |
| davon | heran | hierher | los | zurecht |
| dazu | herauf | hin | mit | zurück |
| ein | heraus | hinab | nach | zusammen |

- Unlike inseparable prefixes, separable prefixes may be words in their own right. Indeed, nouns, adjectives, adverbs and even other verbs are often used as separable prefixes (→1)

- The past participle of a verb with a separable prefix is formed with **ge-**. It comes between the verb and the prefix (→2)

- In main clauses, the prefix is placed at the end of the clause if the verb is in a simple tense (i.e. present, imperfect or imperative form) (→3)

- In subordinate clauses, whatever the tense of the verb, the prefix is attached to the verb and the resulting whole placed at the end of the clause (→4)

- Where an infinitive construction requiring **zu** is used (see p 46), the **zu** is placed between the infinitive and prefix to form one word (→5)

**1** *noun + verb*: **teilnehmen** to take part
*verb + verb*: **kennenlernen** to get to know
*adjective + verb*: **loswerden** to get free of
*adverb + verb*: **niederlegen** to lay down

**2** **Er ist gestern spazierengegangen**
He went for a walk yesterday
**Wir sind an der Grenze zurückgewiesen worden**
We were turned back at the border

**3** **wegbringen**: to take for repair, to take away
*PRESENT*: **Wir bringen das Auto weg**
*IMPERFECT*: **Wir brachten das Auto weg**
*IMPERATIVE*: **Bringt das Auto weg!**

*CONDITIONAL*: **Wir würden das Auto wegbringen**
*FUTURE*: **Wir werden das Auto wegbringen**
*PERFECT*: **Wir haben das Auto weggebracht**
*PERFECT PASSIVE*: **Das Auto ist weggebracht worden**
*PLUPERFECT SUBJUNCTIVE*: **Wir hätten das Auto weggebracht**

**4** *PRESENT*: **Weil wir das Auto wegbringen, ...**
*IMPERFECT*: **Daß wir das Auto wegbrachten, ...**
*PERFECT*: **Nachdem wir das Auto weggebracht haben, ...**
*PLUPERFECT SUBJUNCTIVE*: **Wenn wir das Auto weggebracht hätten, ...**
*FUTURE*: **Obwohl wir das Auto wegbringen werden, ...**

**5** **Um das Auto rechtzeitig wegzubringen, müssen wir morgen früh aufstehen**
In order to take the car in on time, we shall have to get up early tomorrow

## Verbs with Prefixes (contd)

### Variable Prefixes

These are:   **über**           **um**
            **unter**         **voll**
            **durch**         **wider**
            **hinter**        **wieder**

- These can be separable or inseparable (→**1**)

- Often they are used separably and inseparably with the same verb. In such cases the verb and prefix will tend to retain their basic meanings if the prefix is used separably, but adopt figurative meanings when the prefix is used inseparably (→**2**)

- Variable prefixes behave as separable prefixes when used separably, and as inseparable prefixes when used inseparably (→**3**)

### Double Prefixes

These occur where a verb with an inseparable prefix is preceded by a separable prefix (→**4**)

- The separable prefix behaves as described on p 72, the verb plus inseparable prefix representing the basic verb to which the separable prefix is attached (→**5**)

- Unlike other separable verbs, however, verbs with double prefixes have no **ge-** in their past participles (→**6**)

**1 unternehmen** (*inseparable*) to undertake, take on:

**Wir haben in den Ferien vieles unternommen**
We did a great deal in the holidays
**Du unternimmst zuviel**
You take on too much

**untergehen** (*separable*) to sink, go down:

**Die Sonne ist untergegangen**
The sun has gone down/has set
**Die Sonne geht unter**
The sun is going down/is setting

**2 etwas wiederholen** (*separable*) to retrieve something
**etwas wiederholen** (*inseparable*) to repeat something

**3 Er holte ihr die Tasche wieder**
He brought her back her bag
**Er wiederholte den Satz**
He repeated the sentence

**4 ausverkaufen** to sell off

**5 Er verkauft alles aus**
He's selling everything off
**Um alles auszuverkaufen ...**
In order to sell everything off ...
**Er wird alles ausverkaufen**
He'll be selling everything off

**6 Aber er hat doch alles ausverkauft**
But he's sold everything off

## Verbs followed by Prepositions

• Some verbs in English usage require a preposition (*for/with/by* etc) for their completion.
 This also happens in German, though the prepositions used with German verbs may not be those expected from their English counterparts (→**1**)

• The preposition used may significantly alter the meaning of a verb in German (→**2**)

• Occasionally German verbs use a preposition where their English equivalents do not (→**3**)

• Prepositions used with verbs behave as normal prepositions and affect the *case* of the following noun (see p 198).

• A verb plus preposition may be followed by a clause containing another verb rather than by a noun or pronoun. This often corresponds to an *-ing* construction in English:
   Thank you for *coming*
 In German, this is dealt with in two ways:
 1.   Where the "verb-plus-preposition" construction has the same subject as the following verb, the preposition is preceded by **da-** or **dar-** and the following verb becomes an infinitive used with **zu** (→**4**)
 2.   Where the subject of the "verb-plus-preposition" is not the same as for the following verb, a **daß** clause is used (→**5**)

• Following clauses may also be introduced by interrogatives (**ob, wie** etc) if the meaning demands them (→**6**)

*Continued*

**1**  Compare:

| GERMAN | ENGLISH |
|---|---|
| sich sehnen **nach** | to long *for* |
| warten **auf** | to wait *for* |
| bitten **um** | to ask *for* |

**2  bestehen** to pass (an examination/a test *etc*)
**bestehen aus** to consist of
**bestehen auf** to insist on

**sich freuen auf** to look forward to
**sich freuen über** to be pleased about

**3  diskutieren über** to discuss

**4  Ich freue mich sehr darauf, mal wieder mit ihm zu arbeiten**
I am looking forward to working with him again

**5  Ich freue mich sehr darauf, daß du morgen kommst**
I am looking forward to your coming tomorrow
**Er sorgte dafür, daß die Kinder immer gut gepflegt waren**
He saw to it that the children were always well cared for

**6  Er dachte lange darüber nach, ob er es wirklich kaufen wollte**
He thought for ages about whether he really wanted to buy it
**Sie freut sich darüber, wie schnell ihre Schüler gelernt haben**
She is pleased at how quickly her students have learned

## Verbs followed by Prepositions (contd)

*Common verbs followed by preposition + accusative case*:
**achten auf** to pay attention to, keep an eye on (→**1**)
**sich amüsieren über** to laugh at, smile about
**sich ärgern über** to get annoyed about/with
**sich bewerben um** to apply for (→**2**)
**bitten um** to ask for (→**3**)
**denken an** to be thinking of (→**4**)
**denken über** to hold an opinion of, think about (→**5**)
**sich erinnern an** to remember
**sich freuen auf** to look forward to
**sich freuen über** to be pleased about (→**6**)
**sich gewöhnen an** to get used to (→**7**)
**sich interessieren für** to be interested in (→**8**)
**kämpfen um** to fight for
**sich kümmern um** to take care of, see to
**nachdenken über** to ponder, reflect on (→**9**)
**sich unterhalten über** to talk about
**sich verlassen auf** to rely on, depend on (→**10**)
**warten auf** to wait for

*Common verbs followed by preposition + dative case*:
**abhängen von** to be dependent on (→**11**)
**sich beschäftigen mit** to occupy oneself with (→**12**)
**bestehen aus** to consist of (→**13**)
**leiden an/unter** to suffer from (→**14**)
**neigen zu** to be inclined to
**riechen nach** to smell of (→**15**)
**schmecken nach** to taste of
**sich sehnen nach** to long for
**sterben an** to die of
**teilnehmen an** to take part in (→**16**)
**träumen von** to dream of (→**17**)
**sich verabschieden von** to say goodbye to
**sich verstehen mit** to get along with, get on with
**zittern vor** to tremble with (→**18**)

1 **Er mußte auf die Kinder achten**
  He had to keep an eye on the children
2 **Sie hat sich um die Stelle als Sekretärin beworben**
  She applied for the post of secretary
3 **Die Kinder baten ihre Mutter um Plätzchen**
  The children asked their mother for some biscuits
4 **Woran denkst du?** What are you thinking about?
  **Daran habe ich gar nicht mehr gedacht**
  I'd forgotten about that
5 **Wie denkt ihr darüber?** What do you think about it?
6 **Ich freute mich sehr darüber, Johannes besucht zu haben**
  I was very glad I had visited Johannes
7 **Man gewöhnt sich an alles** One gets used to anything
8 **Sie interessiert sich sehr für Politik**
  She is very interested in politics
9 **Er hatte schon lange darüber nachgedacht**
  He had been thinking about it for a long time
10 **Er verläßt sich darauf, daß seine Frau alles tut**
  He relies on his wife to do everything
11 **Das hängt davon ab** It all depends
12 **Sie sind im Moment sehr damit beschäftigt, ihr neues Haus
   in Ordnung zu bringen**
   They are very busy sorting out their new house at the moment
13 **Dieser Kuchen besteht aus Eiern, Mehl und Zucker**
   This cake consists of eggs, flour and sugar
14 **Sie hat lange an dieser Krankheit gelitten**
   She suffered from this illness for a long time
   **Alte Leute können sehr unter der Einsamkeit leiden**
   Old people can suffer dreadful loneliness
15 **Der Kuchen roch nach Zimt**
   The cake smelled of cinnamon
16 **Sie hat an der Bonner Tagung teilnehmen müssen**
   She had to attend the Bonn conference
17 **Er hat von seinem Urlaub geträumt**
   He dreamt of his holiday
18 **Er zitterte vor Freude** He was trembling with joy

## Verbs followed by the Dative

Some verbs have a direct object and an indirect object. In the English sentence *He gave me a book, me* (= *to me*) is the indirect object and would appear in the dative case in German; *a book* is the direct object of *gave* and would be in the accusative (→**1**)

- In German, as in English, this type of verb is usually concerned with giving or telling something to someone, or with performing an action for someone (→**2**)

- The normal word order after such verbs is for the direct object to follow the indirect, *except* where the direct object is a personal pronoun (see p 224) (→**2**)
  This order may be reversed for emphasis (→**3**)

- Some examples of verbs followed by the dative in this way:

| | | |
|---|---|---|
| anbieten | bringen | beweisen |
| erzählen | geben | gönnen |
| kaufen | leihen | mitteilen |
| schenken | schicken | schreiben |
| schulden | verkaufen | zeigen (→**4**) |

- Certain verbs in German however can be followed *only* by an indirect object in the dative case. These should be noted especially, since most of them are quite different from their English equivalents:

| | | |
|---|---|---|
| begegnen | danken | fehlen |
| gefallen | gehören | gelingen |
| gleichen | gratulieren | helfen |
| imponieren | mißtrauen | nachgehen |
| schaden | schmecken | schmeicheln |
| trauen | trotzen | vorangehen |
| weh tun | widersprechen | widerstehen (→**5**) |

- For how to form the passive of such verbs, see p 36.

**1 Er gab mir ein Buch** He gave me a book

**2 Er wusch dem Kind** (*indirect*) **das Gesicht** (*direct*)
He washed the child's face
**Er erzählte ihm** (*indirect*) **eine Geschichte** (*direct*)
He told him a story
*BUT*
**Er hat sie** (*direct*) **meiner Mutter** (*indirect*) **gezeigt**
He showed it to my mother
**Kaufst du es** (*direct*) **mir** (*indirect*)**?**
Will you buy it for me?

**3 Er wollte das Buch** (*direct*) **seiner Mutter** (*indirect*) **geben**
(*This emphasises* **seiner Mutter**)
He wanted to give the book to his mother

**4 Er bot ihr die Arbeitsstelle an** He offered her the job
**Bringst du mir eins?** Will you bring me one?
**Ich gönne dir das neue Kleid**
I want you to have the new dress
**Er hat ihr mitgeteilt, daß ...** He told her that ...
**Ich schenke meiner Mutter Parfüm zum Geburtstag**
I am giving my mother perfume for her birthday
**Das schulde ich ihm** I owe him that
**Zeig es mir!** Show me it!

**5 Er ist seinem Freund in der Stadt begegnet**
He bumped into his friend in town
**Mir fehlt der Mut dazu** I don't have the courage
**Es ist ihnen gelungen** They succeeded
**Wem gehört dieses Buch?** Whose book is this?
**Er wollte ihr nicht helfen** He refused to help her
**Ich gratuliere dir!** Congratulations!
**Rauchen schadet der Gesundheit**
Smoking is bad for your health
**Das Essen hat ihnen gut geschmeckt**
They enjoyed the meal

# There is/There are

There are three ways of expressing this in German:

## es gibt

- This is always used in the singular form, and is followed by an accusative object which may be either singular or plural (→**1**)
- **es gibt** is used to refer to things of a general nature or location (→**2**)
- It also has some idiomatic usages (→**3**)

## es ist/es sind

- The **es** here merely introduces the real subject. The verb therefore becomes plural where the real subject is plural. The real subject is in the nominative case (→**4**)
- The **es** is not required and is therefore omitted when the verb and real subject come together. This happens when inversion of subject and verb occurs (see p 226) and in subordinate clauses (→**5**)
- **es ist** or **es sind** are used to refer to
  1. subjects with a specific and confined location.
     This location must always be mentioned either by name or by **da, darauf, darin** etc (→**6**)
  2. temporary existence (→**7**)
  3. as a beginning to a story (→**8**)

## The Passive Voice

Often *there is/there are* in English will be rendered by a verb in the passive voice in German (→**9**)

1 **Es gibt zu viele Probleme dabei**
There are too many problems involved
**Es gibt kein besseres Bier** There's no better beer

2 **Es gibt bestimmt Regen**
It's definitely going to rain
**Ruhe hat es bei uns nie gegeben**
There has never been any peace here

3 **Was gibt's (= gibt es) zum Essen?** What's there to eat?
**Was gibt's?** What's wrong? What's up?
**So was gibt's doch nicht!** That's impossible!

4 **Es waren zwei ältere Leute unten im Hof**
There were two elderly people down in the yard
**Es sind so viele Touristen da**
There are so many tourists there

5 **Unten im Hof waren zwei ältere Leute**
Down in the yard were two elderly people
**Wenn so viele Touristen da sind ...**
If there are so many tourists there ...

6 **Es waren viele Flaschen Sekt im Keller**
There were a lot of bottles of champagne in the cellar
**Ein Brief lag auf dem Tisch. Es waren auch zwei Bücher
darauf**
A letter lay on the table. There were also two books on it

7 **Es war niemand da** There was no-one there

8 **Es war einmal ein König ...**
Once upon a time there was a king ...

9 **Es wurde auf der Party viel getrunken**
There was a lot of drinking at the party

## Use of "es" as an anticipatory object

Many verbs can have as their object a **daß** clause or an infinitive with **zu** (→**1**)

- With some verbs **es** is used as an object to anticipate this clause or infinitive phrase (→**2**)
- When the clause or infinitive phrase begins the sentence, **es** is not used in the main clause but its place may be taken by an optional **das** (→**3**)

### Common verbs which usually have the "es" object

**es ablehnen, zu** to refuse to
**es aushalten, zu tun/daß** to stand doing (→**4**)
**es ertragen, zu tun/daß** to endure doing
**es leicht haben, zu** to find it easy to (→**5**)
**es nötig haben, zu** to need to (→**6**)
**es satt haben, zu** to have had enough of (doing)
**es verstehen, zu** to know how to (→**7**)

### Common verbs which often have the "es" object

**es jemandem anhören/ansehen, daß** to tell by listening to/looking at someone that (→**8**)
**es begreifen, daß/warum/wie** to understand that/why/how
**es bereuen, zu tun/daß** to regret having done/that
**es leugnen, daß** to deny that (→**9**)
**es unternehmen, zu** to undertake to
**es jemandem verbieten, zu** to forbid someone to
**es jemandem vergeben, daß** to forgive someone for (doing)
**es jemandem verschweigen, daß** not to tell someone that
**es jemandem verzeihen, daß** to forgive someone for (doing)
**es wagen zu** to dare to

**1 Er wußte, daß wir pünktlich kommen würden**
He knew that we would come on time
**Sie fing an zu lachen**
She began to laugh

**2 Er hatte es abgelehnt mitzufahren**
He had refused to come

**3 Daß es Wolfgang war, das haben wir ihr verschwiegen**
*OR*: **Daß es Wolfgang war, haben wir ihr verschwiegen**
We didn't tell her that it was Wolfgang

**4 Ich halte es nicht mehr aus, bei ihnen zu arbeiten**
I can't stand working for them any longer

**5 Er hatte es nicht leicht, sie zu überreden**
He didn't have an easy job persuading them

**6 Ich habe es nicht nötig, mit dir darüber zu reden**
I don't have to talk to you about it

**7 Er versteht es, Autos zu reparieren**
He knows about repairing cars

**8 Man hörte es ihm sofort an, daß er kein Deutscher war**
*OR*: **Daß er kein Deutscher war, (das) hörte man ihm sofort an**
One could tell immediately (from the way he spoke) that he wasn't German

**Man sieht es ihm sofort an, daß er dein Bruder ist**
*OR*: **Daß er dein Bruder ist, (das) sieht man ihm sofort an**
One can tell at a glance that he's your brother

**9 Er hat es nie geleugnet, das Geld genommen zu haben**
He has never denied taking the money

## Strong and Mixed Verbs - Principal Parts

| INFINITIVE | | 3RD PERSON PRESENT |
|---|---|---|
| backen | to bake | er bäckt |
| befehlen | to command | er befiehlt |
| beginnen | to begin | er beginnt |
| beißen | to bite | er beißt |
| bergen | to rescue | er birgt |
| bersten | to burst *intr* | er birst |
| betrügen | to deceive | er betrügt |
| biegen | to bend *tr*/to turn *intr* | er biegt |
| bieten | to offer | er bietet |
| binden | to tie | er bindet |
| bitten | to ask for | er bittet |
| blasen | to blow | er bläst |
| bleiben | to remain | er bleibt |
| braten | to fry | er brät |
| brechen | to break | er bricht |
| brennen | to burn | er brennt |
| bringen | to bring | er bringt |
| denken | to think | er denkt |
| dreschen | to thresh | er drischt |
| dringen | to penetrate | er dringt |
| dürfen | to be allowed to | er darf |
| empfehlen | to recommend | er empfiehlt |
| erlöschen | to go out (*fire, light*) | er erlischt |
| erschallen | to resound | er erschallt |
| erschrecken | to be startled[1] | er erschrickt |
| erwägen | to weigh up | er erwägt |
| essen | to eat | er ißt |
| fahren | to travel | er fährt |

1. **erschrecken** meaning "to frighten" is **weak**:
   **erschrecken, erschreckt, erschreckte, hat erschreckt**

| 3RD PERSON IMPERFECT | PERFECT | IMPERFECT SUBJUNCTIVE |
|---|---|---|
| er backte | er hat gebacken | er backte |
| er befahl | er hat befohlen | er befähle |
| er begann | er hat begonnen | er begänne |
| er biß | er hat gebissen | er bisse |
| er barg | er hat geborgen | er bärge |
| er barst | er ist geborsten | er bärste |
| er betrog | er hat betrogen | er betröge |
| er bog | er hat/ist gebogen | er böge |
| er bot | er hat geboten | er böte |
| er band | er hat gebunden | er bände |
| er bat | er hat gebeten | er bäte |
| er blies | er hat geblasen | er bliese |
| er blieb | er ist geblieben | er bliebe |
| er briet | er hat gebraten | er briete |
| er brach | er hat/ist gebrochen | er bräche |
| er brannte | er hat gebrannt | er brennte |
| er brachte | er hat gebracht | er brächte |
| er dachte | er hat gedacht | er dächte |
| er drosch | er hat gedroschen | er drösche |
| er drang | er ist gedrungen | er dränge |
| er durfte | er hat gedurft/dürfen[1] | er dürfte |
| er empfahl | er hat empfohlen | er empfähle |
| er erlosch | er ist erloschen | er erlösche |
| er erschallte | er ist erschollen | er erschölle |
| er erschrak | er ist erschrocken | er erschräke |
| er erwog | er hat erwogen | er erwöge |
| er aß | er hat gegessen | er äße |
| er fuhr | er ist gefahren | er führe |

1.  The second (infinitive) form is used when combined with an infinitive construction (see p 56).

Continued

| INFINITIVE | | 3RD PERSON PRESENT |
|---|---|---|
| **fallen** | to fall | **er fällt** |
| **fangen** | to catch | **er fängt** |
| **fechten** | to fight | **er ficht** |
| **finden** | to find | **er findet** |
| **fliegen** | to fly | **er fliegt** |
| **fliehen** | to flee *tr/intr* | **er flieht** |
| **fließen** | to flow | **er fließt** |
| **fressen** | to eat (*of animals*) | **er frißt** |
| **frieren** | to be cold; freeze over | **er friert** |
| **gebären** | to give birth to | **sie gebärt** |
| **geben** | to give | **er gibt** |
| **gedeihen** | to thrive | **er gedeiht** |
| **gehen** | to go | **er geht** |
| **gelingen** | to succeed | **es gelingt** |
| **gelten** | to be valid | **er gilt** |
| **genesen** | to get well | **er genest** |
| **genießen** | to enjoy | **er genießt** |
| **geraten** | to get into (*a state etc*) | **er gerät** |
| **geschehen** | to happen | **es geschieht** |
| **gewinnen** | to win | **er gewinnt** |
| **gießen** | to pour | **er gießt** |
| **gleichen** | to resemble; equal | **er gleicht** |
| **gleiten** | to glide | **er gleitet** |
| **glimmen** | to glimmer | **er glimmt** |
| **graben** | to dig | **er gräbt** |
| **greifen** | to grip | **er greift** |
| **haben** | to have | **er hat** |
| **halten** | to hold, stop | **er hält** |
| **hängen** | to hang *intr*[1] | **er hängt** |
| **heben** | to lift | **er hebt** |
| **heißen** | to be called | **er heißt** |

1. **hängen** is **weak** when used transitively.

| 3RD PERSON IMPERFECT | PERFECT | IMPERFECT SUBJUNCTIVE |
|---|---|---|
| er fiel | er ist gefallen | er fiele |
| er fing | er hat gefangen | er finge |
| er focht | er hat gefochten | er föchte |
| er fand | er hat gefunden | er fände |
| er flog | er hat/ist geflogen | er flöge |
| er floh | er hat/ist geflohen | er flöhe |
| er floß | er ist geflossen | er flösse |
| er fraß | er hat gefressen | er fräße |
| er fror | er hat/ist gefroren | er fröre |
| sie gebar | sie hat geboren | sie gebäre |
| er gab | er hat gegeben | er gäbe |
| er gedieh | er ist gediehen | er gediehe |
| er ging | er ist gegangen | er ginge |
| es gelang | es ist gelungen | es gelänge |
| er galt | er hat gegolten | er gälte |
| er genas | er ist genesen | er genäse |
| er genoß | er hat genossen | er genösse |
| er geriet | er ist geraten | er geriete |
| es geschah | es ist geschehen | es geschähe |
| er gewann | er ist gewonnen | er gewönne |
| er goß | er hat gegossen | er gösse |
| er glich | er hat geglichen | er gliche |
| er glitt | er ist geglitten | er glitte |
| er glomm | er hat geglommen | er glömme |
| er grub | er hat gegraben | er grübe |
| er griff | er hat gegriffen | er griffe |
| er hatte | er hat gehabt | er hätte |
| er hielt | er hat gehalten | er hielte |
| er hing | er hat gehangen | er hinge |
| er hob | er hat gehoben | er höbe |
| er hieß | er hat geheißen | er hieße |

Continued

| INFINITIVE | | 3RD PERSON PRESENT |
|---|---|---|
| **helfen** | to help | **er hilft** |
| **kennen** | to know (*someone etc*) | **er kennt** |
| **klingen** | to sound | **er klingt** |
| **kommen** | to come | **er kommt** |
| **kneifen** | to pinch | **er kneift** |
| **können** | to be able to | **er kann** |
| **kriechen** | to crawl | **er kriecht** |
| **laden** | to load | **er lädt** |
| **lassen** | to allow | **er läßt** |
| **laufen** | to walk; run | **er läuft** |
| **leiden** | to suffer | **er leidet** |
| **leihen** | to lend | **er leiht** |
| **lesen** | to read | **er liest** |
| **liegen** | to lie | **er liegt** |
| **lügen** | to tell a lie | **er lügt** |
| **mahlen** | to grind | **er mahlt** |
| **messen** | to measure | **er mißt** |
| **mißlingen** | to fail | **es mißlingt** |
| **mögen** | to like to | **er mag** |
| **müssen** | to have to | **er muß** |
| **nehmen** | to take | **er nimmt** |
| **nennen** | to call | **er nennt** |
| **pfeifen** | to whistle | **er pfeift** |
| **preisen** | to praise | **er preist** |
| **quellen** | to gush | **er quillt** |
| **raten** | to advise; guess | **er rät** |
| **reiben** | to rub | **er reibt** |
| **reißen** | to tear *tr/intr* | **er reißt** |
| **reiten** | to ride *tr/intr* | **er reitet** |

| 3RD PERSON IMPERFECT | PERFECT | IMPERFECT SUBJUNCTIVE |
|---|---|---|
| er half | er hat geholfen | er hülfe |
| er kannte | er hat gekannt | er kennte |
| er klang | er hat geklungen | er klänge |
| er kam | er ist gekommen | er käme |
| er kniff | er hat gekniffen | er kniffe |
| er konnte | er hat gekonnt/können[1] | er könnte |
| er kroch | er ist gekrochen | er kröche |
| er lud | er hat geladen | er lüde |
| er ließ | er hat gelassen | er ließe |
| er lief | er ist gelaufen | er liefe |
| er litt | er hat gelitten | er litte |
| er lieh | er hat geliehen | er liehe |
| er las | er hat gelesen | er läse |
| er lag | er hat gelegen | er läge |
| er log | er hat gelogen | er löge |
| er mahlte | er hat gemahlen | er mahlte |
| er maß | er hat gemessen | er mäße |
| es mißlang | es ist mißlungen | es mißlänge |
| er mochte | er hat gemocht/mögen[1] | er möchte |
| er mußte | er hat gemußt/müssen[1] | er müßte |
| er nahm | er hat genommen | er nähme |
| er nannte | er hat gennant | er nennte |
| er pfiff | er hat gepfiffen | er pfiffe |
| er pries | er hat gepriesen | er priese |
| er quoll | er ist gequollen | er quölle |
| er riet | er hat geraten | er riete |
| er rieb | er hat gerieben | er riebe |
| er riß | er hat/ist gerissen | er risse |
| er ritt | er hat/ist geritten | er ritte |

1. The second (infinitive) form is used when combined with an infinitive construction (see p 56).

Continued

| *INFINITIVE* | | *3RD PERSON PRESENT* |
|---|---|---|
| **rennen** | to run | **er rennt** |
| **riechen** | to smell | **er riecht** |
| **ringen** | to wrestle | **er ringt** |
| **rinnen** | to flow | **er rinnt** |
| **rufen** | to shout | **er ruft** |
| **salzen** | to salt | **er salzt** |
| **saufen** | to booze; drink | **er säuft** |
| **saugen** | to suck | **er saugt** |
| **schaffen** | to create[1] | **er schafft** |
| **scheiden** | to separate *tr/intr* | **er scheidet** |
| **scheinen** | to seem; shine | **er scheint** |
| **schelten** | to scold | **er schilt** |
| **scheren** | to shear | **er schert** |
| **schieben** | to shove | **er schiebt** |
| **schießen** | to shoot | **er schießt** |
| **schlafen** | to sleep | **er schläft** |
| **schlagen** | to hit | **er schlägt** |
| **schleichen** | to creep | **er schleicht** |
| **schleifen** | to grind | **er schleift** |
| **schließen** | to close | **er schließt** |
| **schlingen** | to wind | **er schlingt** |
| **schmeißen** | to fling | **er schmeißt** |
| **schmelzen** | to melt *tr/intr* | **er schmilzt** |
| **schneiden** | to cut | **er schneidet** |
| **schreiben** | to write | **er schreibt** |
| **schreien** | to shout | **er schreit** |
| **schreiten** | to stride | **er schreitet** |
| **schweigen** | to be silent | **er schweigt** |

1.  **schaffen** meaning "to work hard/manage" is **weak**:
    **schaffen, schafft, schaffte, hat geschafft**

| 3RD PERSON IMPERFECT | PERFECT | IMPERFECT SUBJUNCTIVE |
|---|---|---|
| er rannte | er ist gerannt | er rennte |
| er roch | er hat gerochen | er röche |
| er rang | er hat gerungen | er ränge |
| er rann | er ist geronnen | er ränne |
| er rief | er hat gerufen | er riefe |
| er salzte | er hat gesalzen | er salzte |
| er soff | er hat gesoffen | er söffe |
| er sog | er hat gesogen | er söge |
| er schuf | er hat geschaffen | er schüfe |
| er schied | er hat/ist geschieden | er schiede |
| er schien | er hat geschienen | er schiene |
| er schalt | er hat gescholten | er schölte |
| er schor | er hat geschoren | er schöre |
| er schob | er hat geschoben | er schöbe |
| er schoß | er hat geschossen | er schösse |
| er schlief | er hat geschlafen | er schliefe |
| er schlug | er hat geschlagen | er schlüge |
| er schlich | er ist geschlichen | er schliche |
| er schliff | er hat geschliffen | er schliffe |
| er schloß | er hat geschlossen | er schlösse |
| er schlang | er hat geschlungen | er schlänge |
| er schmiß | er hat geschmissen | er schmisse |
| er schmolz | er hat/ist geschmolzen | er schmölze |
| er schnitt | er hat geschnitten | er schnitte |
| er schrieb | er hat geschrieben | er schriebe |
| er schrie | er hat geschrie(e)n | er schriee |
| er schritt | er ist geschritten | er schritte |
| er schwieg | er hat geschwiegen | er schwiege |

Continued

| INFINITIVE | | 3RD PERSON PRESENT |
|---|---|---|
| **schwellen** | to swell *intr*[1] | **er schwillt** |
| **schwimmen** | to swim | **er schwimmt** |
| **schwingen** | to swing | **er schwingt** |
| **schwören** | to vow | **er schwört** |
| **sehen** | to see | **er sieht** |
| **sein** | to be | **er ist** |
| **senden** | to send[2] | **er sendet** |
| **singen** | to sing | **er singt** |
| **sinken** | to sink | **er sinkt** |
| **sinnen** | to ponder | **er sinnt** |
| **sitzen** | to sit | **er sitzt** |
| **sollen** | to be supposed to be | **er soll** |
| **spalten** | to split *tr/intr* | **er spaltet** |
| **speien** | to spew | **er speit** |
| **spinnen** | to spin | **er spinnt** |
| **sprechen** | to speak | **er spricht** |
| **sprießen** | to sprout | **er sprießt** |
| **springen** | to jump | **er springt** |
| **stechen** | to sting/prick | **er sticht** |
| **stehen** | to stand | **er steht** |
| **stehlen** | to steal | **er stiehlt** |
| **steigen** | to climb | **er steigt** |
| **sterben** | to die | **er stirbt** |
| **stinken** | to stink | **er stinkt** |
| **stoßen** | to knock/come across | **er stößt** |
| **streichen** | to stroke/wander | **er streicht** |
| **streiten** | to quarrel | **er streitet** |

1. **schwellen** is **weak** when used transitively:
   **schwellen, schwellt, schwellte, hat geschwellt**
2. **senden** meaning "to broadcast" is **weak**:
   **senden, sendet, sendete, hat gesendet**

| 3RD PERSON IMPERFECT | PERFECT | IMPERFECT SUBJUNCTIVE |
|---|---|---|
| er schwoll | er ist geschwollen | er schwölle |
| er schwamm | er ist geschwommen | er schwömme |
| er schwang | er hat geschwungen | er schwänge |
| er schwor | er hat geschworen | er schwüre |
| er sah | er hat gesehen | er sähe |
| er war | er ist gewesen | er wäre |
| er sandte | er hat gesandt | er sendete |
| er sang | er hat gesungen | er sänge |
| er sank | er ist gesunken | er sänke |
| er sann | er hat gesonnen | er sänne |
| er saß | er hat gesessen | er säße |
| er sollte | er hat gesollt/sollen[1] | er sollte |
| er spaltete | er hat/ist gespalten | er spaltete |
| er spie | er hat gespie(e)n | er spiee |
| er spann | er hat gesponnen | er spönne |
| er sprach | er hat gesprochen | er spräche |
| er sproß | er ist gesprossen | er sprösse |
| er sprang | er ist gesprungen | er spränge |
| er stach | er hat gestochen | er stäche |
| er stand | er hat gestanden | er stünde |
| er stahl | er hat gestohlen | er stähle |
| er stieg | er ist gestiegen | er stiege |
| er starb | er ist gestorben | er stürbe |
| er stank | er hat gestunken | er stänke |
| er stieß | er hat/ist gestoßen | er stieße |
| er strich | er hat/ist gestrichen | er striche |
| er stritt | er hat gestritten | er stritte |

1. The second (infinitive) form is used when combined with an infinitive construction (see p 56).

Continued

| *INFINITIVE* | | *3RD PERSON PRESENT* |
|---|---|---|
| **tragen** | to carry; wear | **er trägt** |
| **treffen** | to meet | **er trifft** |
| **treiben** | to drive; engage in | **er treibt** |
| **treten** | to kick/step | **er tritt** |
| **trinken** | to drink | **er trinkt** |
| **tun** | to do | **er tut** |
| **verderben** | to spoil/go bad | **er verdirbt** |
| **verdrießen** | to irritate | **er verdrießt** |
| **vergessen** | to forget | **er vergißt** |
| **verlieren** | to lose | **er verliert** |
| **vermeiden** | to avoid | **er vermeidet** |
| **verschwinden** | to disappear | **er verschwindet** |
| **verzeihen** | to pardon | **er verzeiht** |
| **wachsen** | to grow | **er wächst** |
| **waschen** | to wash | **er wäscht** |
| **weichen** | to yield | **er weicht** |
| **weisen** | to point | **er weist** |
| **wenden** | to turn | **er wendet** |
| **werben** | to recruit | **er wirbt** |
| **werden** | to become | **er wird** |
| **werfen** | to throw | **er wirft** |
| **wiegen** | to weigh[1] | **er wiegt** |
| **winden** | to wind | **er windet** |
| **wissen** | to know | **er weiß** |
| **wollen** | to want to | **er will** |
| **ziehen** | to pull | **er zieht** |
| **zwingen** | to force | **er zwingt** |

1.  **wiegen** meaning "to rock" is **weak**

| 3RD PERSON IMPERFECT | PERFECT | IMPERFECT SUBJUNCTIVE |
|---|---|---|
| er trug | er hat getragen | er trüge |
| er traf | er hat getroffen | er träfe |
| er trieb | er hat getrieben | er triebe |
| er trat | er hat/ist getreten | er träte |
| er trank | er hat getrunken | er tränke |
| er tat | er hat getan | er täte |
| er verdarb | er hat/ist verdorben | er verdürbe |
| er verdroß | er hat verdrossen | er verdrösse |
| er vergaß | er hat vergessen | er vergäße |
| er verlor | er hat verloren | er verlöre |
| er vermied | er hat vermieden | er vermiede |
| er verschwand | er ist verschwunden | er verschwände |
| er verzieh | er hat verziehen | er verziehe |
| er wuchs | er ist gewachsen | er wüchse |
| er wusch | er hat gewaschen | er wüsche |
| er wich | er ist gewichen | er wiche |
| er wies | er hat gewiesen | er wiese |
| er wandte | er hat gewandt | er wendete |
| er warb | er hat geworben | er würbe |
| er wurde | er ist geworden | er würde |
| er warf | er hat geworfen | er würfe |
| er wog | er hat gewogen | er wöge |
| er wand | er hat gewunden | er wände |
| er wußte | er hat gewußt | er wüßte |
| er wollte | er hat gewollt/wollen[1] | er wollte |
| er zog | er hat gezogen | er zöge |
| er zwang | er hat gezwungen | er zwänge |

1. The second (infinitive) form is used when combined with an infinitive construction (see p 56).

# The Declension of Nouns

In German, all nouns may be declined. This means that they may change their form according to their

*gender* (i.e. masculine, feminine or neuter) (→**1**)

*case* (i.e. their function in the sentence) (→**2**)

*number* (i.e. singular or plural) (→**3**)

- Nearly all *feminine* nouns change in the *plural* form by adding -**n** or -**en**. Many *masculine* and *neuter* nouns also change (→**4**)

- *Masculine* and *neuter* nouns, with a few exceptions, add -**s** (-**s** or -**es** for nouns of one syllable) in the *genitive singular* (but see p 110) (→**5**)

- All nouns end in -**n** or -**en** in the *dative plural*. This is added to the nominative plural form, where this does not already end in -**n** (→**6**)

- A good dictionary will provide guidance on how to decline a noun:
  The nominative singular form is given in full, followed by the gender of the noun, then the genitive singular and nominative plural endings are shown where appropriate (→**7**)

- Adjectives used as nouns are declined as adjectives rather than nouns. Their declension endings are therefore dictated by the preceding article, as well as by number, case and gender (see p 140) (→**8**)

*Continued*

1  **der Tisch** (*masculine*) the table
   **die Gabel** (*feminine*) the fork
   **das Mädchen** (*neuter*) the girl

2  **des Tisches** of the table
   **auf den Tischen** on the tables

3  **die Tische** the tables
   **die Gabeln** the forks
   **die Mädchen** the girls

4 |  | NOM SING | NOM PLURAL |
|---|---|---|
| MASC | **der Apfel** | **die Äpfel** |
| FEM | **die Schule** | **die Schulen** |
| NEUT | **das Kind** | **die Kinder** |

5 |  | NOM SING | GEN SING |
|---|---|---|
| MASC | **der Apfel** | **des Apfels** |
| FEM | **die Schule** | **der Schule** |
| NEUT | **das Kind** | **des Kind(e)s** |

6  **den Äpfeln**
   **den Schulen**
   **den Kindern**

7  **Tiger** *m* -s, -

| NOM SING | **der Tiger** | the tiger |
|---|---|---|
| GEN SING | **des Tigers** | of the tiger, the tiger's |
| NOM PL | **die Tiger** | the tigers |

8  **der Angestellte**        the employee
   **ein Angestellter**       an employee
   **(die) Angestellten**     (the) employees

# The Gender of Nouns

In German a noun may be masculine, feminine or neuter. Gender is relatively unpredictable and has to be learned for each noun. This is best done by learning each noun with its definite article, i.e.

**der Teppich, die Zeit, das Bild**

The following are intended therefore only as guidelines in helping decide the gender of a word.

- Nouns denoting male people and animals are masculine (→**1**)

- Nouns denoting the female of the species, as shown on p 104 are of course feminine (→**2**)

- But nouns denoting an entire species can be of any gender (→**3**)

- Makes of cars identify with **der Wagen** and so are usually masculine (→**4**)

- Makes of aeroplane usually identify with **die Maschine** and so are feminine (→**5**)

- Seasons, months, days of the week, weather features and north, south, east, and west are masculine (→**6**)

- Names of objects that perform an action are usually masculine (→**7**)

- Foreign nouns ending in **-ant, -ast, -ismus, -or** are masculine (→**8**) (But see the list of exceptions below)

- Nouns ending in **-ich, -ig, -ing, -ling** are masculine (→**9**)

*Continued*

1 **der Hörer** (male) listener
  **der Löwe** (male) lion
  **der Onkel** uncle
  **der Vetter** (male) cousin

2 **die Hörerin** (female) listener
  **die Löwin** lioness
  **die Tante** aunt
  **die Kusine** (female) cousin

3 **der Hund** dog
  **die Schlange** snake
  **das Vieh** cattle

4 **der Mercedes** Mercedes
  **der VW** Volkswagen

5 **die Boeing** Boeing
  **die Concorde** Concorde

6 **der Sommer** summer
  **der Winter** winter
  **der August** August
  **der Freitag** Friday
  **der Wind** wind
  **der Schnee** snow
  **der Norden** north
  **der Osten** east

7 **der Wecker** alarm clock
  **der Computer** computer

8 **der Ballast** ballast
  **der Chauvinismus** chauvinism

9 **der Essig** vinegar
  **der Schmetterling** butterfly

## The Gender of Nouns (contd)

- Cardinal numbers are mostly feminine, but fractions are neuter (→**1**)

- Most nouns ending in **-e** are feminine (→**2**)
  *EXCEPTIONS*:    male people or animals are masculine (→**3**)
  nouns beginning with **Ge-** are normally neuter (*see below*)

- Nouns ending in **-heit, -keit, -schaft, -ung, -ei** are feminine (→**4**)

- Foreign nouns ending in **-anz, -enz, -ie, -ik, -ion, -tät, -ur** are generally feminine (→**5**)

- Nouns denoting the young of a species are neuter (→**6**)

- Infinitives used as nouns are neuter (→**7**)

- Most nouns beginning with **Ge-** are neuter (→**8**)

- **-chen** or **-lein** may be added to many words to give a diminutive form. These words are then neuter (→**9**)
  Note that the vowel adds an umlaut where possible (i.e. on **a, o, u** or **au**) and a final **-e** is dropped before these endings (→**10**)

- Nouns ending in **-nis** or **-tum** are neuter (→**11**)

- Foreign nouns ending in **-at, -ett, -fon, -ma, -ment, -um, -ium** are mainly neuter (→**12**)

- Adjectives and participles may be used as masculine, feminine or neuter nouns (see p 148) (→**13**)

*Continued*

1 **Er hat eine Drei gekriegt** He got a three (*mark*)
  **ein Drittel davon** a third of it
2 **die Falte** crease, wrinkle
  **die Brücke** bridge
3 **der Löwe** lion
  **der Matrose** sailor
4 **die Eitelkeit** vanity
  **die Gewerkschaft** trade union
  **die Scheidung** divorce
  **die Druckerei** printing works
5 **die Distanz** distance
  **die Konkurrenz** rivalry
  **die Theorie** theory
  **die Panik** panic
  **die Union** union
  **die Elektrizität** electricity
  **die Partitur** score (*musical*)
6 **das Baby** baby
  **das Kind** child
7 **das Schwimmen** swimming
8 **das Geschirr** crockery, dishes
  **das Geschöpf** creature
  **das Getreide** crop
9 **das Kindlein** child
10 **das Bächlein** (small) stream (*from* **der Bach**)
   **das Kätzchen** kitten (*from* **die Katze**)
11 **das Ereignis** event
   **das Altertum** antiquity
12 **das Tablett** tray
   **das Telefon** telephone
   **das Testament** will
   **das Podium** platform, podium
13 **der Verwandte** male relative
   **die Verwandte** female relative
   **das Gehackte** minced meat

# The Gender of Nouns

The following are some common exceptions to the gender guidelines shown on pp 100 to 103

**das Weib** woman, wife
**die Person** person
**die Waise** orphan
**das Mitglied** member
**das Genie** genius
**die Wache** sentry, guard
**das Restaurant** restaurant

## The Formation of Feminine Nouns

As in English, male and female forms are sometimes shown by two completely different words, e.g.
*mother/father, uncle/aunt etc* (→**1**)
Where such separate forms do not exist, however, German often differentiates between male and female forms in one of two ways:

- The masculine form may sometimes be made feminine by the addition of **-in** in the singular and **-innen** in the plural (→**2**)

- An adjective may be used as a feminine noun (see p 148). It has feminine adjective endings which change according to the article which precedes it (see p 140) (→**3**)

*Continued*

1 **der Vater**                 **die Mutter**
  father                        mother
  **der Bulle**                 **die Kuh**
  bull                          cow
  **der Mann**                  **die Frau**
  man                           woman

2 **der Lehrer**                **die Lehrerin**
  (male) teacher                (female) teacher
  **der König**                 **die Königin**
  king                          queen
  **der Hörer**                 **die Hörerin**
  (male) listener               (female) listener

*HENCE*:
**Liebe Hörer und Hörerinnen!** Dear listeners!
**unsere Leser und Leserinnen** our readers

3 **eine Deutsche** a German woman
  **Er ist mit einer Deutschen verheiratet**
  He is married to a German
  **die Abgeordnete** the female MP
  **Nur Abgeordnete durften dabeisein**
  Only MPs were allowed in

# The Gender of Nouns: miscellaneous points

## Compound Nouns

Compound nouns, i.e. nouns composed of two or more nouns put together, are a regular feature of German.

- They normally take their gender and declension from the last noun of the compound word (→**1**)

- Exceptions to this are compounds ending in **-mut, -scheu** and **-wort**, which do not always have the same gender as the last word when it stands alone (→**2**)

## Nouns with more than one gender

- A few nouns have two genders, one of which may only be used in certain regions (→**3**)

- Other nouns have two genders, each of which gives the noun a different meaning (→**4**)

## Abbreviations

- These take the gender of their principal noun (→**5**)

1  **die Armbanduhr** wristwatch (*from* **die Uhr**)
   **der Tomatensalat** tomato salad (*from* **der Salat**)
   **der Fußballspieler** footballer (*from* **der Spieler**)

2  **der Mut** courage
   **die Armut** poverty
   **die Demut** humility

   **die Scheu** fear, shyness, timidity
   **der Abscheu** repugnance, abhorrence

   **das Wort** word
   **die Antwort** reply

3  **das/der Radio** radio
   **das/der Keks** biscuit

4  **der Band** volume, book
   **das Band** ribbon, band, tape, bond
   **der See** lake
   **die See** sea
   **der Leiter** leader, manager
   **die Leiter** ladder
   **der Tau** dew
   **das Tau** rope, hawser

5  **der DGB** the Federation of German Trade Unions (*from* **der Deutsche Gewerkschaftsbund**)
   **die EG** the EC (*from* **die Europäische Gemeinschaft**)
   **das AKW** nuclear power station (*from* **das Atomkraftwerk**)

# The Cases

There are four grammatical *cases*, which are generally shown by the form of the article used before the noun (see p 118).

## The nominative case

- The nominative singular is the form shown in full in dictionary entries. The nominative plural is formed as described on p 98.

- The nominative case is used for:
  - the subject of a verb (→**1**)
  - the complement of **sein** or **werden** (→**2**)

## The accusative case

- The noun in the accusative case usually has the same form as in the nominative (→**3**)
  Exceptions to this are "weak" masculine nouns (see p 115) and adjectives used as nouns (see p 148).

- It is used:
  - for the direct object of the verb (→**4**)
  - after those prepositions which always take the accusative case (see p 206 ff) (→**5**)
  - to show change of location after prepositions of place (see p 210) (→**6**)
  - in many expressions of time and place which do not contain a preposition (→**7**)
  - in certain fixed expressions (→**8**)

*Continued*

**1  Das Mädchen singt** The girl is singing

**2  Er ist ein guter Lehrer** He's a good teacher
   **Das wird ein Pullover** It's going to be a jumper

**3  das Lied** the song (*nominative*)
   **das Lied** the song (*accusative*)
   **der Wagen** the car (*nominative*)
   **den Wagen** the car (*accusative*)
   **die Dose** the tin (*nominative*)
   **die Dose** the tin (*accusative*)

**4  Er hat ein Lied gesungen** He sang a song

**5  für seine Freundin** for his girlfriend
   **ohne diesen Wagen** without this car
   **durch das Rauchen** through smoking

**6  in die Stadt** (*accusative*) into town
   *BUT*:
   **in der Stadt** (*dative*) in town

**7  Das macht sie jeden Donnerstag**
   She does that every Thursday
   **Die Schule ist einen Kilometer entfernt**
   The school is a kilometre away

**8  Guten Abend!** Good evening!
   **Vielen Dank!** Thank you very much!

## The Cases (contd)

### The genitive case

- In the genitive singular, *masculine* and *neuter* nouns take endings as follows:
  1) **-s** is added to nouns ending in **-en, -el, -er** (→**1**)
  2) **-es** is added to nouns ending in **-tz, -sch, -st** or **-ß** (→**2**)
  3) For nouns of one syllable, either **-s** or **-es** may be added (→**3**)
- *Feminine singular* and all *plural* nouns have the same form as their nominative.
- The genitive is used:
  - to show possession (→**3**)
  - after prepositions taking the genitive (see p 212) (→**4**)
  - in expressions of time when the exact occasion is not specified (→**5**)

### The dative case

- Singular nouns in the dative have the same form as in the nominative (→**6**)
- **-e** may be added to the dative singular of *masculine* and *neuter* nouns if the sentence rhythm needs it (→**7**)
  This **-e** is always used in certain set phrases (→**8**)
- Dative plural forms for all genders end in **-n** (→**9**)
  The only exceptions to this are some nouns of foreign origin that end in **-s** in all plural forms, including the dative plural (see p 114) (→**10**)
- The dative is used:
  - as the indirect object (→**11**)
  - after verbs taking the dative (see p 80) (→**12**)
  - after prepositions taking the dative (see p 202) (→**13**)
  - in certain idiomatic expressions (→**14**)
  - instead of the possessive adjective to refer to parts of the body and items of clothing (see p 122) (→**15**)

1 der Wagen car → des Wagens of the car
  das Rauchen smoking → des Rauchens of smoking
  der Computer computer → des Computers of the computer
  der Reiter rider → des Reiters of the rider
2 der Sitz seat; residence → des Sitzes of the seat/residence
  der Arzt doctor → des Arztes of the doctor
  das Schloß castle → des Schlosses of the castle
3 das Kind →
  Die Zähne des Kindes waren faul geworden
  The child's teeth had decayed
  Der Name des Kinds war ihm unbekannt
  The child's name was not known to him
4 wegen seiner Krankheit because of his illness
  trotz ihrer Bemühungen despite her efforts
5 eines Tages one day
6 dem Wagen to the car
  der Frau to the woman
  dem Mädchen to the girl
7 zu welchem Zwecke? to what purpose?
8 nach Hause home
  sich zu Tode trinken/arbeiten
  to drink/work oneself to death
9 mit den Anwälten with the lawyers
  nach den Kindern after the children
10 SINGULAR      PLURAL
   das Auto      die Autos
   das Auto      die Autos
   des Autos     der Autos
   dem Auto      den Autos
11 Er gab dem Mann das Buch He gave the man the book
12 Sie half ihrer Mutter She helped her mother
13 Nach dem Essen … After eating …
14 Mir ist kalt I'm cold
15 Ich habe mir die Hände gewaschen I've washed my hands

## The Formation of Plurals

The following pages show full noun declensions in all their singular and plural forms.

Those nouns shown represent the most common types of plural.

- Most feminine nouns add -n, -en or -nen to form their plurals:

|  | SINGULAR | PLURAL |
|---|---|---|
| NOM | die Frau | die Frauen |
| ACC | die Frau | die Frauen |
| GEN | der Frau | der Frauen |
| DAT | der Frau | den Frauen |

- Many nouns have no plural ending.
  These are mainly masculine or neuter nouns ending in -en, -er, -el.
  An umlaut is sometimes added to the vowel in the plural forms.

|  | SINGULAR | PLURAL |
|---|---|---|
| NOM | der Onkel | die Onkel |
| ACC | den Onkel | die Onkel |
| GEN | des Onkels | der Onkel |
| DAT | dem Onkel | den Onkeln |

|  | SINGULAR | PLURAL |
|---|---|---|
| NOM | der Apfel | die Äpfel |
| ACC | den Apfel | die Äpfel |
| GEN | des Apfels | der Äpfel |
| DAT | dem Apfel | den Äpfeln |

*Continued*

## The Formation of Plurals (contd)

• Many nouns form their plurals by adding ̈-e

| | SINGULAR | PLURAL |
|---|---|---|
| NOM | der Stuhl | die Stühle |
| ACC | den Stuhl | die Stühle |
| GEN | des Stuhl(e)s | der Stühle |
| DAT | dem Stuhl(e) | den Stühlen |

| | SINGULAR | PLURAL |
|---|---|---|
| NOM | die Angst | die Ängste |
| ACC | die Angst | die Ängste |
| GEN | der Angst | der Ängste |
| DAT | der Angst | den Ängsten |

• Masculine and neuter nouns often add -e in the plural

| | SINGULAR | PLURAL |
|---|---|---|
| NOM | das Schicksal | die Schicksale |
| ACC | das Schicksal | die Schicksale |
| GEN | des Schicksals | der Schicksale |
| DAT | dem Schicksal(e) | den Schicksalen |

• Masculine and neuter nouns sometimes add ̈-er or -er

| | SINGULAR | PLURAL |
|---|---|---|
| NOM | das Dach | die Dächer |
| ACC | das Dach | die Dächer |
| GEN | des Dach(e)s | der Dächer |
| DAT | dem Dach(e) | den Dächern |

*Continued*

## The Formation of Plurals (contd)

### Some Unusual Plurals

**das Ministerium, die Ministerien** department(s)
**das Prinzip, die Prinzipien** principle(s)
**das Thema, die Themen** theme(s), topic(s), subject(s)
**das Drama, die Dramen** drama(s)
**die Firma, die Firmen** firm(s)
**das Konto, die Konten** bank account(s)
**das Risiko, die Risiken** risk(s)
**das Komma, die Kommas** *or* **Kommata** comma(s); decimal point(s)
**das Baby, die Babys** baby (babies)
**der Klub, die Klubs** club(s)
**der Streik, die Streiks** strike(s)
**der Park, die Parks** park(s)
**der Chef, die Chefs** boss(es), chief(s), head(s)
**der Israeli, die Israelis** Israeli(s)
**das Restaurant, die Restaurants** restaurant(s)
**das Bonbon, die Bonbons** sweet(s)
**das Hotel, die Hotels** hotel(s)
**das Niveau, die Niveaus** standard(s), level(s)

### German singular/English plural nouns

Some nouns are always plural in English, but singular in German:
• Some of the most common examples are:

   **eine Brille** glasses, spectacles
   **eine Schere** scissors
   **eine Hose** trousers

• They are only used in the plural in German to mean more than one pair, e.g. **zwei Hosen** *two pairs of trousers*

## The Declension of Nouns (contd)

### "Weak" Masculine nouns

Some masculine nouns have a weak declension, which means that in all cases apart from the nominative singular, they end in **-en** or, if the word ends in a vowel, in **-n**

- The dictionary will often show such nouns as
  **Junge** *m* **-n, -n** boy
  **Held** *m* **-en, -en** hero

- Weak masculine nouns are declined as follows:

|       | SINGULAR    | PLURAL      |
|-------|-------------|-------------|
| NOM   | **der Junge** | **die Jungen** |
| ACC   | **den Jungen** | **die Jungen** |
| GEN   | **des Jungen** | **der Jungen** |
| DAT   | **dem Jungen** | **den Jungen** |

- Masculine nouns falling into this category include:
  - those ending in **-og(e)** referring to males:
    **der Psychologe, der Geologe, der Astrologe**
  - those ending in **-aph** or **-oph**:
    **der Paragraph, der Philosoph**
  - those ending in **-nom** referring to males:
    **der Astronom, der Gastronom**
  - those ending in **-ant**:
    **der Elefant, der Diamant**
  - those ending in **-t** which refer to males:
    **der Astronaut, der Komponist, der Architekt**
  - miscellaneous others:
    **der Chirurg, der Bauer, der Ochse, der Kollege, der Spatz, der Mensch, der Katholik, der Franzose**

- **der Name** (*name*) has a different ending in the genitive singular, **-ns**: **des Namens**. Otherwise it is the same as **der Junge** shown above. Others in this category are: **der Buchstabe, der Glaube, der Gedanke, der Haufe, der Funke**.

## The Declension of Proper Nouns

- Names of people and places add **-s** in the genitive singular unless they are preceded by the definite article or a demonstrative (→**1**)

- Where proper names end in a sibilant (**-s, -sch, -ß, -x, -z, -tz**) and this makes the genitive form with **-s** almost impossible to pronounce, they are best avoided altogether by using **von** followed by the dative case (→**2**)

- Personal names can be given diminutive forms if desired. These may be used as a sign of affection as well as with diminutive meaning (→**3**)

- **Herr** (*Mr*) is always declined where it occurs as part of a proper name (→**4**)

- When articles or adjectives form part of a proper name (e.g. in the names of books, plays, hotels, restaurants *etc*), these are declined in the normal way (see pp 118 and 140) (→**5**)

- Surnames usually form their plurals by adding **-s**, unless they end in a sibilant, in which case they sometimes add **-ens**. They are often preceded by the definite article (→**6**)

## Nouns of Measurement and Quantity

- These usually remain singular, even if preceded by a plural number (→**7**)

- The substance which they measure follows in the same case as the noun of quantity, and not in the genitive case as in English (→**8**)

**1 Annas Buch** Anna's book
   **Klaras Mantel** Klara's coat
   **die Werke Goethes** Goethe's works
   *BUT:* **die Versenkung der Bismarck**
   the sinking of the Bismarck

**2 das Buch von Hans** Hans' book
   **die Werke von Marx** the works of Marx
   **die Freundin von Klaus** Klaus's girlfriend

**3 von Deinem Sabinchen** from your Sabine
   **das kleine Kläuschen hat uns dann ein Lied gesungen**
   Then little Klaus sang us a song

**4 an Herrn Schmidt** to Mr Schmidt
   **Sehr geehrte Herren** Dear Sirs

**5 im Weißen Schwan** in the White Swan
   **Er hat den "Zauberberg" schon gelesen**
   He has already read "The Magic Mountain"
   **nach Karl dem Großen** after Charlemagne

**6 Die Schmidts haben uns eingeladen**
   The Schmidts have invited us
   **Die Zeißens haben uns eingeladen**
   Mr and Mrs Zeiß have invited us

**7 Möchten Sie zwei Stück?**
   Would you like two?

**8 Er wollte zwei Kilo Kartoffeln**
   He wanted two kilos of potatoes
   **Sie hat drei Tassen Kaffee getrunken**
   She drank three cups of coffee
   **Drei Glas Weißwein, bitte!**
   Three glasses of white wine please

# The Definite Article

In English the definite article *the* always keeps the same form
    *the* book/*the* books/with *the* books
In German, however, the definite article has many forms:

- In its singular form it changes for masculine, feminine and neuter nouns (→**1**)

- In its plural forms, it is the same for all genders (→**2**)

- The definite article is also used to show the function of the noun in the sentence by showing which case it is.
  There are four cases, as explained more fully on p 108:
  *nominative* for the subject or complement of the verb (→**3**)
  *accusative* for the object of the verb and after some prepositions (→**4**)
  *genitive* to show possession and after some prepositions (→**5**)
  *dative* for an indirect object (*to* or *for*) and after some prepositions and certain verbs (→**6**)

- The forms of the definite article are as follows:

|  | SINGULAR | | | PLURAL |
|---|---|---|---|---|
|  | *MASC* | *FEM* | *NEUT* | *ALL GENDERS* |
| *NOM* | **der** | **die** | **das** | **die** |
| *ACC* | **den** | **die** | **das** | **die** |
| *GEN* | **des** | **der** | **des** | **der** |
| *DAT* | **dem** | **der** | **dem** | **den** (→**7**) |

*Continued*

**1** *MASCULINE*:   **der Mann** the man
                    **der Wagen** the car
  *FEMININE*:       **die Frau** the wife/woman
                    **die Blume** the flower
  *NEUTER*:         **das Ding** the thing
                    **das Mädchen** the girl

**2 die Männer/die Frauen/die Dinge**
  the men/the women/the things

**3 Der Mann ist jung** The man is young
  **Die Frau/das Kind ist jung** The woman/the child is young

**4 Ich kenne den Mann/die Frau/das Kind**
  I know the man/the woman/the child

**5 der Kopf des Mannes/der Frau/des Kindes**
  the man's/woman's/child's head
  **wegen des Mannes/der Frau/des Kindes**
  because of the man/the woman/the child

**6 Ich gab es dem Mann/der Frau/dem Kind**
  I gave it to the man/to the woman/to the child

**7**

|  | SINGULAR | | |
|---|---|---|---|
|  | MASC | FEM | NEUT |
| *NOM* | **der Mann** | **die Frau** | **das Kind** |
| *ACC* | **den Mann** | **die Frau** | **das Kind** |
| *GEN* | **des Mann(e)s** | **der Frau** | **des Kind(e)s** |
| *DAT* | **dem Mann(e)** | **der Frau** | **dem Kind(e)** |

|  | PLURAL | | |
|---|---|---|---|
|  | MASC | FEM | NEUT |
| *NOM* | **die Männer** | **die Frauen** | **die Kinder** |
| *ACC* | **die Männer** | **die Frauen** | **die Kinder** |
| *GEN* | **der Männer** | **der Frauen** | **der Kinder** |
| *DAT* | **den Männern** | **den Frauen** | **den Kindern** |

# Uses of the Definite Article

When to use and when not to use the definite article in German is one of the most difficult areas for the learner. The following guidelines show where German practice varies from English.

The definite article is used with:

- abstract and other nouns where something is being referred to as a whole or as a general idea (→**1**)
  Where these nouns are quantified or modified, the article is not used (→**2**)

- the genitive, unless the noun is a proper name or is acting as a proper name (→**3**)

- occasionally with proper names to make the sex or case clearer (→**4**)

- always with proper names preceded by an adjective (→**5**)

- sometimes with proper names in familiar contexts or for slight emphasis (→**6**)

- with masculine and feminine countries and districts (→**7**)

- with geographical names preceded by an adjective (→**8**)

- with names of seasons (→**9**)

- often with meals (→**10**)

- with the names of roads (→**11**)

*Continued*

**1** **Das Leben ist schön** Life is wonderful
**2** **Es braucht Mut** It needs (some) courage
  **Gibt es dort Leben?** Is there (any) life there?
**3** **das Auto des Lehrers** the teacher's car
  **Günters Auto** Günter's car
  **Muttis Auto** Mummy's car
**4** **Er hat es Frau Lehmann gegeben**
  **Er hat es der Frau Lehmann gegeben**
  He gave it to Frau Lehmann
**5** **Der alte Herr Brockhaus ist gestorben**
  Old Mr Brockhaus has died
**6** **Ich habe heute den Christoph gesehen**
  I saw Christoph today
  **Du hast es aber nicht der Petra geschenkt!**
  You haven't given it to *Petra*!
**7** **Deutschland ist sehr schön** Germany is very beautiful
  **Die Schweiz ist auch schön** Switzerland is also lovely
**8** **im (= in dem) heutigen Deutschland**
  in today's Germany
**9** **Im (= in dem) Sommer gehen wir schwimmen**
  We go swimming in summer
  **Der Winter kommt bald**
  Soon it will be winter
**10** **Das Abendessen wird ab acht Uhr serviert**
  Dinner is served from eight o'clock
  **Was gibt's zum (= zu dem) Mittagessen?**
  What's for lunch?
  *BUT*:
  **Um 8 Uhr ist Frühstück**
  Breakfast is at 8 o'clock
**11** **Sie wohnt jetzt in der Geisenerstraße**
  She lives in Geisener Road now

## Uses of the Definite Article (contd)

• with months of the year except after **seit/nach/vor** (→**1**)

• instead of the possessive adjective to refer to parts of the body and items of clothing (→**2**)
A reflexive pronoun or noun in the dative case is used if it is necessary to clarify to whom the parts of the body belong (→**3**)

• in expressions of price, to mean *each/per/a* (→**4**)

• with certain common expressions (→**5**)

## Others Uses

• The definite article can be used with demonstrative meaning (→**6**)

• After certain prepositions, forms of the definite article can be shortened (see p 198 ff).
Some of these forms are best used in informal situations (→**7**)
Others are commonly and correctly used in formal contexts (→**8, 1, 5**)

## The definite article may be omitted in German:

• in certain set expressions (→**9**)

• in *preposition* + *adjective* + *noun* combinations (→**10**)
For the declension of adjectives without the article see p 142.

1 **Wir fahren im (= in dem) September weg**
We are going away in September
**Wir sind seit September hier**
We have been here since September

2 **Er legte den Hut auf den Tisch**
He laid his hat on the table
**Ich drücke Ihnen die Daumen** I'm keeping my fingers crossed for you

3 **Er hat sich die Hände schon gewaschen**
He has already washed his hands
**Er hat dem Kind schon die Hände gewaschen**
He has already washed the child's hands

4 **Die kosten ...**          They cost ...
   **... fünf Mark das Pfund**      ... five marks a pound
   **... sechs Mark das Stück**      ... six marks each

5 **in die Stadt fahren** to go into town
   **zur (= zu der) Schule gehen** to go to school
   **mit der Post** by post
   **mit dem Zug/Bus/Auto** by train/bus/car
   **im (= in dem) Gefängnis** in prison

6 **Du willst das Buch lesen!**
You want to read *that* book!

7 **für das → fürs; vor dem → vorm; um das → ums** *etc*

8 **an dem → am; zu dem → zum; zu der → zur** *etc*

9 **von Beruf** by profession
   **nach Wunsch** as desired
   **Nachrichten hören** to listen to the news

10 **Mit gebeugtem Rücken ...** Bending his back, ...

# The Indefinite Article

Like the definite article, the form of the indefinite article varies depending on the gender and case of the noun (→**1**). It has no plural forms (→**2**)

The indefinite article is declined as follows:

|      | MASC   | FEM    | NEUT              |
|------|--------|--------|-------------------|
| NOM  | ein    | eine   | ein               |
| ACC  | einen  | eine   | ein               |
| GEN  | eines  | einer  | eines             |
| DAT  | einem  | einer  | einem (→**3**)    |

* The indefinite article is omitted in the following:

  − descriptions of people by profession, religion, nationality *etc* (→**4**)
    But note that the article is included when an adjective precedes the noun (→**5**)

  − in certain fixed expressions (→**6**)

  − after **als** *as a* (→**7**)

*Continued*

**1 Da ist ein Auto** There's a car
  **Er hat eine Wohnung** He has a flat
  **Sie gab es einem Kind** She gave it to a child

**2 Autos sind in letzter Zeit teurer geworden**
  Cars have become more expensive recently

**3**

|        | MASC | SINGULAR FEM | NEUT |
|--------|------|-----|------|
| NOM | ein Mann | eine Frau | ein Kind |
| ACC | einen Mann | eine Frau | ein Kind |
| GEN | eines Mann(e)s | einer Frau | eines Kind(e)s |
| DAT | einem Mann(e) | einer Frau | einem Kind(e) |

**4 Sie ist Kinderärztin** She's a paediatrician
  **Sie ist Deutsche** She's (a) German

**5 Sie ist eine sehr geschickte Kinderärztin**
  She's a very clever paediatrician

**6 Es ist Geschmacksache** It's a question of taste
  **Tatsache ist ...** It's a fact ...
  **Ich habe Kopfschmerzen** I've got a headache

**7 Als Ausländer ist er hier nicht wahlberechtigt**
  As a foreigner he doesn't have the vote here
  **... und ich rede nun als Vater von vier Kindern**
  ... and I'm talking now as a father of four

# The Indefinite Article (contd)

In German, a separate negative form of the indefinite article exists. It is declined exactly like **ein** in the singular and also has plural forms:

|      |        | SINGULAR |       | PLURAL      |
|------|--------|----------|-------|-------------|
|      | MASC   | FEM      | NEUT  | ALL GENDERS |
| NOM  | **kein**   | **keine**    | **kein**  | **keine**       |
| ACC  | **keinen** | **keine**    | **kein**  | **keine**       |
| GEN  | **keines** | **keiner**   | **keines** | **keiner**      |
| DAT  | **keinem** | **keiner**   | **keinem** | **keinen** (→**1**) |

- It has the meaning *no/not a/not one/not any* (→**2**)

- It is used even where the equivalent *positive* phrase has no article (→**3**)

- It is also used in many idiomatic expressions (→**4**)

- **nicht ein** may be used instead of **kein** where the **ein** is to be emphasized (→**5**)

**1**

| | MASC | SINGULAR<br>FEM | NEUT |
|---|---|---|---|
| NOM | kein Mann | keine Frau | kein Kind |
| ACC | keinen Mann | keine Frau | kein Kind |
| GEN | keines Mann(e)s | keiner Frau | keines Kind(e)s |
| DAT | keinem Mann(e) | keiner Frau | keinem Kind(e) |

| | | PLURAL | |
|---|---|---|---|
| NOM | keine Männer | keine Frauen | keine Kinder |
| ACC | keine Männer | keine Frauen | keine Kinder |
| GEN | keiner Männer | keiner Frauen | keiner Kinder |
| DAT | keinen Männern | keinen Frauen | keinen Kindern |

**2 Er hatte keine Geschwister**
He had no brothers or sisters
**Ich sehe keinen Unterschied** I don't see any difference
**Das ist keine richtige Antwort** That's no answer
**Kein Mensch hat es gesehen** Not one person has seen it

**3 Er hatte Angst davor** He was frightened
**Er hatte keine Angst davor** He wasn't frightened

**4 Er hatte kein Geld mehr** All his money was gone
**Es waren keine drei Monate vergangen, als ...**
It was less than three months later that ...
**Es hat mich keine zehn Mark gekostet**
It cost me less than ten marks

**5 Nicht ein Kind hat es singen können**
Not *one* child could sing it

## Words declined like the Definite Article

The following have endings similar to those of the definite article shown on p 118:

> **jeder, jede, jedes** each, each one, every
> **jener, jene, jenes** that, that one, those
> **dieser, diese, dieses** this, this one, these
> **solcher, solche, solches** such/such a
> **sämtliche** all, entire (*usually plural*)
> **mancher, manche, manches** many a/some
> **einiger, einige, einiges** some, a few, a little
> **welcher, welche, welches** which, which one
> **aller, alle, alles** all, all of them
> **irgendwelcher, -e, -es** some or other
> **beide** both (*plural only*)

- These words can be used as:  articles (→**1**)
                                 pronouns (→**2**)

- They have the following endings:

|  | SINGULAR | | | PLURAL |
|  | MASC | FEM | NEUT | ALL GENDERS |
|---|---|---|---|---|
| NOM | -er | -e | -es | -e |
| ACC | -en | -e | -es | -e |
| GEN | -es/-en | -er | -es/-en | -er |
| DAT | -em | -er | -em | -en |

Example declensions are shown on p 134 ff.

- **einiger** and **irgendwelcher** use the **-en** genitive ending before masculine or neuter nouns ending in **-s** (→**3**)
  **jeder, welcher, mancher** and **solcher** may also do so (→**4**)

*Continued*

1 **Dieser Mann kommt aus Südamerika**
  This man comes from South America
  **Er geht jeden Tag ins Büro**
  He goes to the office every day
  **Manche Leute können das nicht**
  A good many people can't do it

2 **Willst du diesen?** Do you want this one?
  **In manchem hat er recht** He's right about some things
  **Mann kann ja nicht alles wissen**
  You can't know everything
  **Es gibt manche, die keinen Alkohol mögen**
  There are some people who don't like alcohol

3 **wegen irgendwelchen Geredes**
  on account of some gossip

4 **der Besitz solchen Reichtums**
  the possession of such wealth
  **trozt jeden Versuchs**
  despite all attempts

# Words declined like the Definite Article
(contd)

- Adjectives following these words have the weak declension (see p 140) (→**1**)
  Exceptions are the plural forms of **einige**, which are followed by the strong declension (see p 142) (→**2**)

## Further points

- **solcher, beide, sämtliche** may be used after another article or possessive adjective. They then take weak (see p 140) or mixed (see p 142) adjectival endings, as appropriate (→**3**)

- Although **beide** generally has plural forms only, one singular form does exist. This is in the neuter nominative and accusative: **beides** (→**4**)

- **dies** often replaces the nominative and accusative **dieses** and **diese** when used as a pronoun (→**5**)

- A fixed form **all** exists which is used together with other articles or possessive pronouns (→**6**)

- **ganz** can also be used to replace both the inflected form **aller/ alle/alles** and the uninflected **all das/dieses/sein** *etc.*
  It is declined as a normal adjective (see p 140) (→**7**)
  It must be used with collective nouns, in time phrases and geographical references (→**8**)

*Continued*

**1 dieses alte Auto** this old car
**aus irgendwelchem dummen Grund**
for some stupid reason or other
**welche neuen Waren?** which new goods?

**2 Dies sind einige gute Freunde von mir**
These are some good friends of mine

**3 Ein solches Kleid habe ich früher auch getragen**
I used to wear a dress like that too
**Diese beiden Männer haben es gesehen**
Both of these men have seen it

**4 Beides ist richtig** Both are right
**Sie hat beides genommen** She took both

**5 Hast du dies schon gelesen?**
Have you already read this?
**Dies sind meine neuen Sachen**
These are my new things

**6 All sein Mut war verschwunden**
All his courage had vanished
**mit all diesem Geld** with all this money

**7 mit dem ganzen Geld** with all this money

**8 die ganze Gesellschaft** the entire company
**Es hat den ganzen Tag geschneit**
It snowed the whole day long
**Im ganzen Land gab es kein besseres**
There wasn't a better one in the whole country

# Words declined like the Definite Article
(contd)

- **derjenige/diejenige/dasjenige** (*the one, those*) is declined exactly as the definite article plus an adjective in the weak declension (see p 140) (→**1**)

- **derselbe/dieselbe/dasselbe** (*the same, the same one*) is declined in the same way as **derjenige** (→**2**)

After prepositions, however, the normal contracted forms of the definite article are used for the appropriate parts of **derselbe** (→**3**)

*Continued*

**1**

| | SINGULAR | |
|---|---|---|
| *MASC* | *FEM* | *NEUT* |
| derjenige Mann | diejenige Frau | dasjenige Kind |
| denjenigen Mann | diejenige Frau | dasjenige Kind |
| desjenigen Mann(e)s | derjenigen Frau | desjenigen Kind(e)s |
| demjenigen Mann(e) | derjenigen Frau | demjenigen Kind(e) |

| | PLURAL | |
|---|---|---|
| *MASC* | *FEM* | *NEUT* |
| diejenigen Männer | diejenigen Frauen | diejenigen Kinder |
| diejenigen Männer | diejenigen Frauen | diejenigen Kinder |
| derjenigen Männer | derjenigen Frauen | derjenigen Kinder |
| denjenigen Männern | denjenigen Frauen | denjenigen Kindern |

**2**

| | SINGULAR | |
|---|---|---|
| *MASC* | *FEM* | *NEUT* |
| derselbe Mann | dieselbe Frau | dasselbe Kind |
| denselben Mann | dieselbe Frau | dasselbe Kind |
| desselben Mann(e)s | derselben Frau | desselben Kind(e)s |
| demselben Mann(e) | derselben Frau | demselben Kind(e) |

| | PLURAL | |
|---|---|---|
| *MASC* | *FEM* | *NEUT* |
| dieselben Männer | dieselben Frauen | dieselben Kinder |
| dieselben Männer | dieselben Frauen | dieselben Kinder |
| derselben Männer | derselben Frauen | derselben Kinder |
| denselben Männern | denselben Frauen | denselben Kindern |

**3 zur selben** (= **zu derselben**) **Zeit** at the same time
**im selben** (= **in demselben**) **Zimmer** in the same room

# Words declined like the Definite Article
(contd)

## Sample Declensions in full

**dieser, diese, dieses** this, this one

|  | SINGULAR |  |  |
|---|---|---|---|
|  | *MASC* | *FEM* | *NEUT* |
| *NOM* | dieser Mann | diese Frau | dieses Kind |
| *ACC* | diesen Mann | diese Frau | dieses Kind |
| *GEN* | dieses Mann(e)s | dieser Frau | dieses Kind(e)s |
| *DAT* | diesem Mann(e) | dieser Frau | diesem Kind(e) |

|  | PLURAL |  |  |
|---|---|---|---|
|  | *MASC* | *FEM* | *NEUT* |
| *NOM* | diese Männer | diese Frauen | diese Kinder |
| *ACC* | diese Männer | diese Frauen | diese Kinder |
| *GEN* | dieser Männer | dieser Frauen | dieser Kinder |
| *DAT* | diesen Männern | diesen Frauen | diesen Kindern |

**jener, jene, jenes** that, that one

|  | SINGULAR |  |  |
|---|---|---|---|
|  | *MASC* | *FEM* | *NEUT* |
| *NOM* | jener Mann | jene Frau | jenes Kind |
| *ACC* | jenen Mann | jene Frau | jenes Kind |
| *GEN* | jenes Mann(e)s | jener Frau | jenes Kind(e)s |
| *DAT* | jenem Mann(e) | jener Frau | jenem Kind(e) |

|  | PLURAL |  |  |
|---|---|---|---|
|  | *MASC* | *FEM* | *NEUT* |
| *NOM* | jene Männer | jene Frauen | jene Kinder |
| *ACC* | jene Männer | jene Frauen | jene Kinder |
| *GEN* | jener Männer | jener Frauen | jener Kinder |
| *DAT* | jenen Männern | jenen Frauen | jenen Kindern |

**jeder, jede, jedes** each, every, everybody

|  | MASC | SINGULAR<br>FEM | NEUT |
|---|---|---|---|
| NOM | jed**er** Wagen | jed**e** Minute | jed**es** Bild |
| ACC | jed**en** Wagen | jed**e** Minute | jed**es** Bild |
| GEN | jed**es** Wagens<br>(jed**en** Wagens) | jed**er** Minute | jed**es** Bild(e)s<br>(jed**en** Bild(e)s) |
| DAT | jed**em** Wagen | jed**er** Minute | jed**em** Bild(e) |

**welcher, welche, welches** which?, which

|  | MASC | SINGULAR<br>FEM | NEUT |
|---|---|---|---|
| NOM | welch**er** Preis | welch**e** Sorte | welch**es** Mädchen |
| ACC | welch**en** Preis | welch**e** Sorte | welch**es** Mädchen |
| GEN | welch**es** Preises<br>(welch**en** Preises) | welch**er** Sorte | welch**es** Mädchens<br>(welch**en** Mädchens) |
| DAT | welch**em** Preis | welch**er** Sorte | welch**em** Mädchen |

|  | MASC | PLURAL<br>FEM | NEUT |
|---|---|---|---|
| NOM | welch**e** Preise | welch**e** Sorten | welch**e** Mädchen |
| ACC | welch**e** Preise | welch**e** Sorten | welch**e** Mädchen |
| GEN | welch**er** Preise | welch**er** Sorten | welch**er** Mädchen |
| DAT | welch**en** Preisen | welch**en** Sorten | welch**en** Mädchen |

# Words declined like the Indefinite Article

The following have the same declension pattern as the indefinite
articles **ein** and **kein** (see pp 124 and 126):

## The possessive adjectives

**mein** my (→**1**)
**dein** your (*singular familiar*)
**sein** his/its
**ihr** her/its (→**2**)
**unser** our
**euer** your (*plural familiar*)
**ihr** their (→**2**)
**Ihr** your (*polite singular and plural*)

These words are declined as follows:

|       | SINGULAR |      |      | PLURAL |
|-------|------|------|------|--------------|
|       | MASC | FEM  | NEUT | ALL GENDERS  |
| NOM   | —    | -e   | —    | -e           |
| ACC   | -en  | -e   | —    | -e           |
| GEN   | -es  | -er  | -es  | -er          |
| DAT   | -em  | -er  | -em  | -en          |

• Adjectives following these determiners have the mixed
declension forms (see p 142), e.g.:

**sein altes Auto**  his old car

• **irgendein** *some ... or other* also follows this declension pattern
in the singular.
Its plural form is **irgendwelche** (see p 128).

**1 mein, meine, mein** my

SINGULAR

|  | MASC | FEM | NEUT |
|---|---|---|---|
| NOM | mein Bruder | meine Schwester | mein Kind |
| ACC | meinen Bruder | meine Schwester | mein Kind |
| GEN | meines Bruders | meiner Schwester | meines Kind(e)s |
| DAT | meinem Bruder | meiner Schwester | meinem Kind(e) |

PLURAL

|  | MASC | FEM | NEUT |
|---|---|---|---|
| NOM | meine Brüder | meine Schwestern | meine Kinder |
| ACC | meine Brüder | meine Schwestern | meine Kinder |
| GEN | meiner Brüder | meiner Schwestern | meiner Kinder |
| DAT | meinen Brüdern | meinen Schwestern | meinen Kindern |

**2 ihr, ihre, ihr** her/its/their

SINGULAR

|  | MASC | FEM | NEUT |
|---|---|---|---|
| NOM | ihr Bruder | ihre Schwester | ihr Kind |
| ACC | ihren Bruder | ihre Schwester | ihr Kind |
| GEN | ihres Bruders | ihrer Schwester | ihres Kind(e)s |
| DAT | ihrem Bruder | ihrer Schwester | ihrem Kind(e) |

PLURAL

|  | MASC | FEM | NEUT |
|---|---|---|---|
| NOM | ihre Brüder | ihre Schwestern | ihre Kinder |
| ACC | ihre Brüder | ihre Schwestern | ihre Kinder |
| GEN | ihrer Brüder | ihrer Schwestern | ihrer Kinder |
| DAT | ihren Brüdern | ihren Schwestern | ihren Kindern |

# Indefinite Adjectives

These are adjectives used in place of, or together with, an article:
**mehrere** (*plural only*) several
**viel** much, a lot, many
**wenig** little, a little, few
**ander** other, different

● After the definite article and words declined like it (see p 128) these adjectives have weak declension endings (→**1**)
Adjectives following the indefinite adjectives are also weak (→**2**)

● After **ein, kein, irgendein** or the possessive adjectives, they have mixed declension endings (→**3**)
Adjectives following the indefinite adjectives are also mixed in declension (→**4**)

● When used without a preceding article, **ander** and **mehrere** have strong declension endings (→**5**)

● When used without a preceding article, **viel** and **wenig** may be declined as follows, though in the singular they are usually undeclined (→**6**):

|  | SINGULAR | | | PLURAL |
|  | MASC | FEM | NEUT | ALL GENDERS |
|---|---|---|---|---|
| NOM | **viel** | **viel** | **viel** | **viele** |
| ACC | **viel** | **viel** | **viel** | **viele** |
| GEN | **vielen** | **vieler** | **vielen** | **vieler** |
| DAT | **viel(em)** | **vieler** | **viel(em)** | **vielen** |

● Any adjective following **viel** or **wenig** has strong endings (→**7**)

**1 Die wenigen Kuchen, die übriggeblieben waren ...**
The few cakes which were left over ...

**2 Die vielen interessanten Ideen, die ans Licht kamen**
The many interesting ideas which came to light

**3 Ihr anderes Auto ist in der Werkstatt**
Their other car is in for repair

**4 Mehrere gute Freunde waren gekommen**
Several good friends had come

**5 Mehrere prominente Gäste sind eingeladen**
Various prominent guests are invited

**Er war anderer Meinung**
He was of a different opinion

**6 Es wurde viel Bier getrunken**
They drank a lot of beer

**Sie essen nur wenig Obst**
They don't eat a lot of fruit

**7 Er kaufte viele billige Sachen**
He bought a lot of cheap things

**Es wurde viel gutes Bier getrunken**
They drank a lot of good beer

**Sie essen wenig frisches Obst**
They don't eat a lot of fresh fruit

# The Declension of Adjectives

There are two ways of using adjectives.

- They can be used **attributively**, where the adjective comes before the noun: *the new book*

- They can be used **non-attributively**, where the adjective comes after the verb: *the book is new*

- In English the adjective does not change its form no matter how it is used.
  In German, however, adjectives remain unchanged only when used the second way (non-attributively) (→**1**)
  Used attributively, adjectives change to show the number, gender and case of the noun they precede (→**2**)
  The endings also depend on the nature of the article which precedes them (→**3**)

There are three sets of endings:

### 1 The weak declension

These are the endings used after **der** and those words declined like it as shown on p 128 (→**4**)

|      | SINGULAR | | | PLURAL |
|------|------|-----|------|-------------|
|      | MASC | FEM | NEUT | ALL GENDERS |
| NOM  | -e   | -e  | -e   | -en         |
| ACC  | -en  | -e  | -e   | -en         |
| GEN  | -en  | -en | -en  | -en         |
| DAT  | -en  | -en | -en  | -en         |

*Continued*

**1 Das Buch ist neu** The book is new
  **Der Vortrag war sehr langweilig**
  The lecture was very boring

**2 Das neue Buch ist da** The new book has arrived
  **Während des langweiligen Vortrags sind wir alle einge-
  schlafen**
  We all fell asleep during the boring lecture

**3 der junge Rechtsanwalt** the young lawyer
  **ein junger Rechtsanwalt** a young lawyer
  **manch junger Rechtsanwalt** many a young lawyer

**4**

|  | MASC | FEM | NEUT |
|---|---|---|---|
|  |  | *SINGULAR* |  |
| *NOM* | der alte Mann | die alte Frau | das alte Haus |
| *ACC* | den alten Mann | die alte Frau | das alte Haus |
| *GEN* | des alten Mann(e)s | der alten Frau | des alten Hauses |
| *DAT* | dem alten Mann(e) | der alten Frau | dem alten Haus(e) |

|  | MASC | FEM | NEUT |
|---|---|---|---|
|  |  | *PLURAL* |  |
| *NOM* | die alten Männer | die alten Frauen | die alten Häuser |
| *ACC* | die alten Männer | die alten Frauen | die alten Häuser |
| *GEN* | der alten Männer | der alten Frauen | der alten Häuser |
| *DAT* | den alten Männern | den alten Frauen | den alten Häusern |

# The Declension of Adjectives (contd)

### 2 The mixed declension

These are the endings used after **ein, kein, irgendein** and the possessive adjectives (see p 136) (→**1**):

|      |        | SINGULAR |      | PLURAL      |
| ---- | ------ | -------- | ---- | ----------- |
|      | *MASC* | *FEM*    | *NEUT* | *ALL GENDERS* |
| *NOM* | -er   | -e      | -es  | -en         |
| *ACC* | -en   | -e      | -es  | -en         |
| *GEN* | -en   | -en     | -en  | -en         |
| *DAT* | -en   | -en     | -en  | -en    (→**2**) |

### 3 The strong declension

Strong declension endings:

|      |        | SINGULAR |      | PLURAL      |
| ---- | ------ | -------- | ---- | ----------- |
|      | *MASC* | *FEM*    | *NEUT* | *ALL GENDERS* |
| *NOM* | -er   | -e      | -es  | -e          |
| *ACC* | -en   | -e      | -es  | -e          |
| *GEN* | -en   | -er     | -en  | -er         |
| *DAT* | -em   | -er     | -em  | -en    (→**3**) |

These endings are used where there is no preceding article. The article is omitted more frequently in German than in English, especially in combinations "preposition + adjective + noun" (see p 122).

These endings enable the adjective to do the work of the missing article by showing case, number and gender (→**4**)

*Continued*

**1  Meine neue Stelle ist bei einer großen Druckerei**
My new job is with a large printing works
**Ihre frühere Theorie ist jetzt bestätigt worden**
Her earlier theory has now been proved true

**2**                                      *SINGULAR*

|  *MASC*            | *FEM*              | *NEUT*                 |
|--------------------|--------------------|------------------------|
| ein langer Weg     | eine lange Reise   | ein langes Spiel       |
| einen langen Weg   | eine lange Reise   | ein langes Spiel       |
| eines langen Wegs  | einer langen Reise | eines langen Spieles   |
| einem langen Weg   | einer langen Reise | einem langen Spiel     |

*PLURAL*
*ALL GENDERS*

| | |
|---|---|
| *NOM* | ihre langen Wege / Reisen / Spiele |
| *ACC* | ihre langen Wege / Reisen /Spiele |
| *GEN* | ihrer langen Wege / Reisen /Spiele |
| *DAT* | ihren langen Wegen / Reisen / Spielen |

**3**                                      *SINGULAR*

|        | *MASC*       | *FEM*          | *NEUT*      |
|--------|--------------|----------------|-------------|
| *NOM*  | guter Käse   | gute Marmelade | gutes Bier  |
| *ACC*  | guten Käse   | gute Marmelade | gutes Bier  |
| *GEN*  | guten Käses  | guter Marmelade| guten Biers |
| *DAT*  | gutem Käse   | guter Marmelade| gutem Bier  |

*PLURAL*
*ALL GENDERS*

| | |
|---|---|
| *NOM* | gute Käse / Marmeladen / Biere |
| *ACC* | gute Käse / Marmeladen / Biere |
| *GEN* | guter Käse / Marmeladen / Biere |
| *DAT* | guten Käsen / Marmeladen / Bieren |

**4  nach kurzer Fahrt** after a short journey
   **mit gleichem Gehalt** with the same salary

# The Declension of Adjectives (contd)

- Strong declension endings are also used after any of the following where they are not preceded by an article or other determiner:

  **ein bißchen** a little, a bit of
  **ein wenig** a little
  **ein paar** a few, a couple (→**1**)
  **weniger** fewer, less
  **einige** (*plural forms only*) some
  **allerlei/allerhand** all kinds of, all sorts of
  **keinerlei** no ... whatsoever, no ... at all
  **mancherlei** various, a number of
  **etwas** some, any (*singular*) (→**2**)
  **mehr** more
  **lauter** nothing but, sheer, pure
  **solch** such
  **vielerlei** various, all sorts of, many different
  **mehrerlei** several kinds of
  **was für** what, what kind of
  (*note that* **was für ein** *takes the mixed declension*)
  **welcherlei** what kind of, what sort of
  **viel** much, many, a lot of
  **wievielerlei** how many kinds of
  **welch!** what! what a! (→**3**)
  **manch** many a
  **wenig** little, few, not much (→**4**)
  **zweierlei/dreierlei** *etc* two/three *etc* kinds of
  **zwei, drei** *etc* two, three *etc* (→**5**)
  (*but note that the mixed declension is used after* **ein**)

- The strong declension is also required after possessives where no other word indicates the case, gender and number (→**6**)

*Continued*

**1 ein paar gute Tips** (*strong declension*)
a couple of good tips

**2 Etwas starken Pfeffer zugeben** (*strong*)
Add a little strong pepper

**3 Welch herrliches Wetter!** (*strong*)
What splendid weather!

**4 Es gab damals nur wenig frisches Obst** (*strong*)
At that time there was little fresh fruit
*BUT*:
**Das wenige frische Obst, das es damals gab ...** (*weak*)
The little fresh fruit that was then available ...

**5 Zwei große Jungen waren gekommen** (*strong*)
Two big boys had come along
*BUT*:
**Die zwei großen Jungen, die gekommen waren** (*weak*)
The two big boys who had come along
**Meine zwei großen Jungen** (*mixed*)
My two big sons

**6 Herberts altes Buch** (*strong*)
Herbert's old book

**Muttis neues Auto** (*strong*)
Mum's new car

## The Declension of Adjectives (contd)

### Some spelling changes when adjectives are declined

- When the adjective **hoch** (*high*) is declined, its stem changes to **hoh-** (→**1**)

- Adjectives ending in **-el** lose the **-e-** of their stem when inflected, i.e. when endings are added (→**2**)

- Adjectives with an **-er** ending often lose the **-e-** from the ending when inflected (→**3**)

### The participles as adjectives

- The present participle can be used as an adjective with normal adjectival endings (pp 140 to 143) (→**4**)
  The present participles of **sein** and **haben** cannot be used in this way

- The past participle can also be used as an adjective in this way (→**5**)

## Adjectives followed by the dative case

A *dative case* is required after many adjectives e.g. (→**6**):
  **ähnlich** similar to
  **bekannt** familiar to
  **dankbar** grateful to
  **fremd** alien to
  **gleich** all the same to; like
  **leicht** easy for
  **nah** close to
  **peinlich** painful for
  **unbekannt** unknown to

1 **Das Gebäude ist hoch** The building is high
*BUT*:
**ein hohes Gebäude** a high building

2 **Das Zimmer ist dunkel** The room is dark
*BUT*:
**in dem dunklen Zimmer** in the dark room

3 **Das Auto war teuer** The car was expensive
*BUT*:
**Er kaufte ein teures Auto** He bought an expensive car

4 **die werdende Mutter** the mother-to-be
**ein lachendes Kind** a laughing child

5 **meine verlorenen Sachen** my lost things
**die ausgebeuteten Arbeiter**
the exploited workers

6 **Ist dir das bekannt?** Do you know about it?
**Ich wäre Ihnen dankbar, wenn ...**
I should be grateful to you if ...
**Diese Sache ist mir etwas peinlich**
This matter is somewhat embarrassing for me
**Solche Gedanken waren ihm fremd**
Such thoughts were alien to him

## Adjectives used as nouns

All adjectives in German, and those participles used as adjectives, can also be used as nouns. These are often called **adjectival nouns**.

- Adjectives and participles used as nouns have:
  a capital letter like other nouns (→**1**)
  declension endings like other adjectives, depending on the preceding article, if any (see below) (→**2**)

## Declension endings for adjectives used as nouns:

- after **der, dieser** and words like it shown on p 128, the normal *weak* adjective endings apply (see p 140) (→**3**)
  **Der Junge** (*the boy*) is an exception and is declined like a weak masculine noun, as shown on p 115.

- after **ein, kein, irgendein** and the possessive adjectives shown on p 136, the *mixed* adjective endings apply (see p 142) (→**4**)

- where no article is present, or after those words shown on p 144, the *strong* adjective endings are used (see p 142) (→**5**)
  When another adjective precedes the adjectival noun, the *strong* endings become *weak* in two instances:

  in the *dative singular* (→**6**)

  in the *nominative and accusative plural* after a possessive, where the strong endings might cause confusion with the singular feminine form (→**7**)

- Some adjectival nouns have become part of set expressions, and these tend to be written without the capital letter (→**8**)

**1 der Angestellte** the employee

**2 die Angestellte** the female employee
**das Neue daran ist** ... the new thing about it is ...

**3 für den Angeklagten** for the accused
**mit dieser Bekannten** with this (*female*) friend

**4 Kein Angestellter darf hier rauchen**
No employee may smoke here
**Sie machten einen Ausflug mit ihren Bekannten zusammen**
They went on a trip with their friends

**5 Etwas Besonderes ist geschehen**
Something special has happened

**6 Ich hatte es Rudis jüngerem Verwandten versprochen**
I had promised it to Rudi's young relative

**7 Rudis jüngere Verwandten wollten es haben**
Rudi's young relatives wanted to have it

**8 Es bleibt beim alten** Things remain as they were
**Er hat den ersten besten genommen**
He took the first that came to hand

## Miscellaneous points

### Adjectives of nationality

- These are not spelt with a capital letter in German except in public or official names (→**1**)

- However, when used as a noun to refer to the language, a capital is used (→**2**)

- In German, for expressions like *he is English/he is German etc* a noun or adjectival noun is used instead of an adjective (→**3**)

### Adjectives derived from place names

- These are formed by adding **-er** to names of towns (→**4**)

- They are never inflected (→**5**)

- Adjectives from **die Schweiz** and from certain regions can also be formed in this way (→**6**)

- Such adjectives may be used as nouns denoting the inhabitants of a town.
  They are then declined as normal nouns (see p 98ff) (→**7**) The feminine form is made by adding **-in** in the singular and **-innen** in the plural (→**8**)

- Certain names ending in **-en** drop the **-e-** or the **-en** of their ending before adding **-er** (→**9**)

- A second type of adjective formed from place names exists, ending in **-isch** and spelt with a small letter. It is inflected as a normal adjective (see p 140).
  It is used mainly where the speaker is referring to the mood of, or something typical of, that place (→**10**)

1 **die deutsche Sprache** the German language
  **das französische Volk** the French people
  *BUT* **die Deutsche Bundesbahn**

2 **Sie sprechen kein Englisch** They don't speak English

3 **Er ist Deutscher** He is German
  **Sie ist Deutsche** She is German

4 **Kölner, Frankfurter, Leipziger** *etc*

5 **der Kölner Dom** Cologne cathedral
  **ein Frankfurter Würstchen** a frankfurter sausage

6 **Schweizer Käse** Swiss cheese

7 **Die Sprache des Kölners heißt Kölsch**
  **von den Frankfurtern**

8 **Die Kölnerin, die Kölnerinnen**
  **Die Londonerin, die Londonerinnen**

9 **München**   →   **der Münchner**
  **Bremen**   →   **der Bremer**
  **Göttingen**   →   **der Göttinger**

10 **ein echt frankfurterischer Ausdruck**
   a real Frankfurt expression
   **Er spricht etwas münchnerisch**
   He has something of a Munich accent

# The Comparison of Adjectives

Adjectives have three basic forms of comparison:

## A simple form used to describe something or someone:

e.g. a *little* house/the house is *little*

- This form is fully dealt with on pp 140 to 147.

- Simple forms are used in *as ... as / not as ... as* comparisons (→**1**)

## A comparative form used to compare two things or persons:

e.g. he is *bigger* than his brother

- In German, comparatives are formed by adding -**er** to the simple form (→**2**)

- *than* in comparative statements is translated by **als** (→**3**)

- Unlike English, the vast majority of German adjectives, including those of several syllables, form their comparatives in this way (→**4**)

- Many adjectives modify the stem vowel when forming their comparatives, as in the common examples shown opposite (→**5**)

*Continued*

**1 so ... wie** as ... as:
**Er ist so gut wie sein Bruder**
He is as good as his brother

**ebenso ... wie** just as ... as:
**Er war ebenso glücklich wie ich**
He was just as happy as I was

**zwei-/dreimal** etc **so ... wie**
twice/three etc times as ... as:
**Er war zweimal so groß wie sein Bruder**
He was twice as big as his brother

**nicht so ... wie** not as ... as:
**Er ist nicht so alt wie du**
He is not as old as you

**2 klein / kleiner**     small / smaller
  **schön / schöner**    lovely / lovelier

**3 Er ist kleiner als seine Schwester**
He is smaller than his sister

**4 bequem / bequemer**       comfortable / more comfortable
  **gebildet / gebildeter**       educated / more educated
  **effektiv / effektiver**        effective / more effective

**5 alt / älter**    old / older
  **stark / stärker**    strong / stronger
  **schwach / schwächer**    weak / weaker
  **scharf / schärfer**    sharp / sharper
  **lang / länger**    long / longer
  **kurz / kürzer**    short / shorter
  **warm / wärmer**    warm / warmer
  **kalt / kälter**    cold / colder
  **hart / härter**    hard / harder
  **groß / größer**    big / bigger

## Comparison of Adjectives (contd)

- Adjectives whose simple form ends in **-el** lose the **-e-** before adding the comparative ending **-er** (→**1**)

- Adjectives with a diphthong followed by **-er** in their simple forms also drop the **-e-** before adding **-er** (→**2**)

- Adjectives whose simple form ends in **-en** or **-er** may drop the **-e-** of the simple form when adjectival endings are added to their comparative forms (→**3**)

- With a few adjectives, comparative forms may be used not only for comparison, but also to render the idea of "-ish" or "rather …"
  Some common examples are:

  | | |
  |---|---|
  | **älter** elderly | **dünner** thinnish |
  | **größer** largish | **kürzer** shortish |
  | **kleiner** smallish | **jünger** youngish |
  | **dicker** fattish | **neuer** newish (→**4**) |

- When used attributively (*before* the noun), comparative forms are declined in exactly the same way as simple adjectives (see pp 140 to 147) (→**4, 5**)

## A superlative form used to compare three or more persons or things:

e.g. he is *the biggest/the best*

- Superlatives are formed by adding **-st** to the simple adjective. The vowel is modified, as for comparative forms, where applicable.
  Superlative forms are generally used with an article and take endings accordingly (see p 140) (→**6**)

*Continued*

1 **eitel / eitler** vain / vainer
**dunkel / dunkler** dark / darker

2 **sauer / saurer** sour / more sour
**die saurere Zitrone** the sourer lemon
**Der Wein ist saurer geworden**
The wine has grown more sour
**teuer / teurer** expensive / more expensive
**Das ist eine teurere Sorte**
That is a more expensive kind
**Die Neuen sind teurer**
The new ones are more expensive

3 **finster / finsterer** dark / darker
**ein finstreres Gesicht**
*OR*
**ein finstereres Gesicht**
a grimmer face

4 **ein älterer Herr** an elderly gentleman
**eine größere Summe** a rather large sum
**von jüngerem Aussehen** of youngish appearance

5 **Die jüngere Schwester ist größer als die ältere**
The younger sister is bigger than the older one
**Mein kleinerer Bruder geht jetzt zur Schule**
My younger brother goes to school now

6 **Er ist der Jüngste** He is the youngest
**Ihr erfolgreichster Versuch war im Herbst 1990**
Her most successful attempt was in the autumn of 1990

## Comparison of Adjectives (contd)

• Many adjectives form their superlative forms by adding **-est** instead of **-st** where pronunciation would otherwise be difficult or unaesthetic (→**1**)

• The English superlative *most* meaning *very* can be shown in German by any of the following (→**2**):

**äußerst**
**sehr**
**besonders**
**außerordentlich**
**höchst** (not with monosyllabic words)
**furchtbar** (conversational only)
**richtig** (conversational only)

## Some irregular comparative and superlative forms

| SIMPLE FORM | COMPARATIVE | SUPERLATIVE |
|---|---|---|
| gut | besser | der beste |
| hoch | höher | der höchste |
| viel | mehr | der meiste |
| nah | näher | der nächste |

**1** **der/die/das schlechteste** the worst
  **der/die/das schmerzhafteste** the most painful
  **der/die/das süßeste** the sweetest
  **der/die/das neueste** the newest
  **der/die/das stolzeste** the proudest
  **der/die/das frischeste** the freshest

**2** **Er ist ein äußerst begabter Mensch**
  He is a most gifted person

  **Das Essen war besonders schlecht**
  The food was really/most dreadful

  **Der Wein war furchtbar teuer!**
  The wine was dreadfully/most expensive!

  **Das sieht richtig komisch aus**
  That looks really/most funny

# Personal Pronouns

As in English, personal pronouns change their form depending on their function in the sentence:
*I* saw *him* / *He* saw *me* / *We* saw *her* (→**1**)

The personal pronouns are declined as follows (→**2**):

| NOMINATIVE | ACCUSATIVE | DATIVE |
|---|---|---|
| **ich** I | **mich** me | **mir** to/for me |
| **du** you | **dich** you | **dir** to/for you |
| **er** he/it | **ihn** him/it | **ihm** to/for him/it |
| **sie** she/it | **sie** her/it | **ihr** to/for her/it |
| **es** it/he/she | **es** it/him/her | **ihm** to/for it/him/her |
| **wir** we | **uns** us | **uns** to/for us |
| **ihr** you (*plural*) | **euch** you | **euch** to/for you |
| **sie** they | **sie** them | **ihnen** to/for them |
| **Sie** you (*polite*) | **Sie** you | **Ihnen** to/for you |
| **man** one | **einen** one | **einem** to/for one |

- As can be seen from the above table, there are three ways of addressing people in German, by **du, ihr** or **Sie**.
  All three forms are illustrated overleaf.

- Personal pronouns in the dative require no preposition when acting as indirect object, i.e. *to* me, *to* him *etc* (→**3**)

*Continued*

1 **Ich sah ihn** I saw him
  **Er sah mich** He saw me
  **Wir sahen sie** We saw her

2 **Wir sind mit ihnen spazierengegangen**
  We went for a walk with them
  **Sie haben uns eine tolle Geschichte erzählt**
  They told us a great story
  **Soll ich Ihnen etwas mitbringen?**
  Shall I bring something back for you?

3 **Er hat es ihr gegeben**
  He gave it to her
  **Ich habe ihm ein neues Buch gekauft**
  I bought a new book for him/I bought him a new book

## Personal Pronouns (contd)

- **du** is a singular form, used only when speaking to one person. It is used to talk to children, close friends and relatives, animals and objects of affection such as a toy, one's car etc.
  When in doubt it is always best to use the more formal **Sie** form.

- **ihr** is simply the plural form of **du** and is used in exactly the same situations wherever more than one person is to be addressed (→**1**)

- The familiar forms and their possessives are usually written with a small letter (→**2**)
  In letters, however, they must begin with a capital letter (→**3**)

- **Sie** is the polite, or formal, way of addressing people. It is written in all its declined forms with a capital letter, including the possessive (→**4**)

  **Sie** is used:
  a)  by children talking to adults outside their immediate family
  b)  by adults talking to older children from mid-teens onwards. Teachers use it to their senior classes and bosses to their trainees etc.
  c)  among adult strangers meeting for the first time
  d)  among colleagues, friends and acquaintances unless a suggestion has been formally made by one party and accepted by the other that the familiar forms should be used. Familiar forms must then continue to be used at all times, as a reversion to the formal might be considered insulting.

*Continued*

**1 Kinder, was wollt ihr essen?**
Children, what do you want to eat?

**2 Er hat mir gesagt, du sollst deine Frau mitbringen**
He told me you were to bring your wife

**3 Liebe Elke,**
**Gestern bin ich Deinem Bruder begegnet. Er wollte wissen,**
**warum Du nichts von Dir hören läßt!**
Dear Elke,
I met your brother yesterday. He was wondering why you
haven't been in touch!

**4 Was haben Sie gesagt?**
What did you say?

**Ich habe es Ihnen schon gegeben**
I have already given it to you

**Ja, Ihre Sachen sind jetzt fertig**
Yes, your things are ready now

## Personal Pronouns (contd)

### er/sie/es

All German nouns are masculine, feminine or neuter (→**1**)
The personal pronoun must agree in number and in gender with
the noun which it represents.

> **es** is used only for neuter nouns, and not for all inanimate
> objects (→**2**)
> Inanimate objects which are masculine use the pronoun **er**
> (→**3**)
> Feminine inanimate objects use the pronoun **sie** (→**4**)
> Neuter nouns referring to people have the neuter pronoun
> **es** (→**5**)

A common error for English speakers is to call all objects **es**.

### man

This is used in much the same way as the pronoun **one** in English,
but it is much more commonly used in German (→**6**)
It is also used to make an alternative passive form (see p 34) (→**7**)

### The genitive personal pronoun

Genitive forms of the personal pronouns do exist (→**8**)
In practice, however, these are rarely used. Wherever possible,
alternative expressions are found which do not require the genitive
personal pronoun.

Special genitive forms exist for use with the prepositions **wegen**
and **willen** (→**9**)

*Continued*

**1 der Tisch** the table (*masculine*)
  **die Gardine** the curtain (*feminine*)
  **das Baby** the baby (*neuter*)

**2 Das Bild ist schön**          →   **Es ist schön**
  The picture is beautiful    →   It is beautiful

**3 Der Tisch ist groß**          →   **Er ist groß**
  The table is large          →   It is large

**4 Die Gardine ist weiß**        →   **Sie ist weiß**
  The curtain is white        →   It is white

**5 Das Kind stand auf**          →   **Es stand auf**
  The child stood up          →   He/she stood up

**6 Es tut einem gut** It does one good

**7 Man holt mich um sieben ab**
  I am being picked up at seven

**8 meiner**  of me              **unser**  of us
  **deiner**  of you             **euer**   of you (*plural*)
  **seiner**  of him/of it       **ihrer**  of them
  **ihrer**   of her/it          **Ihrer**  of you (*polite*)

**9 meinetwegen** because of me, on my account
  **deinetwegen** because of you, on your account *etc*
  **seinetwegen**
  **ihretwegen**
  **unsertwegen**
  **euretwegen**
  **Ihretwegen**

  **meinetwillen** for my sake, for me *etc*
  **deinetwillen**
  **ihretwillen** *etc*

## Personal Pronouns (contd)

### The use of pronouns after prepositions

- Personal pronouns used after prepositions and referring to a person are in the *case* required by the preposition in question (see p 198 ff) (→**1**)

- When, however, a *thing* rather than a person is referred to, the construction:

  *preposition + pronoun*

  becomes:

  **da-** + *preposition* (→**2**) Before a preposition beginning with a vowel, the form: **dar-** + *preposition* is used (→**3**)

  This affects the following prepositions:

  | | | |
  |---|---|---|
  | **an** | **auf** | **aus** |
  | **bei** | **durch** | **für** |
  | **in** | **mit** | **nach** |
  | **neben** | **über** | **unter** |
  | **zwischen** | | |

- These contracted forms are used after verbs followed by a preposition (see p 76 ff) (→**4**)

- After prepositions used to express motion the form with **da(r)-** is not felt to be sufficiently strong. Forms with **hin** and **her** are used as follows:

  **aus** : heraus / hinaus
  **auf** : herauf / hinauf
  **in**  : herein / hinein (→**5**)

**1 Ich bin mit ihm spazierengegangen**
I went for a walk with him

**2 Klaus hatte ein Messer geholt und wollte damit den Kuchen schneiden**
Klaus had brought a knife and was about to cut the cake with it

**3 Lege es bitte darauf**
Put it there please

**4 Der Unterschied liegt darin, daß ...**
The difference is that ...
**Ich erinnere mich nicht daran**
I don't remember (it)

**5 Er sah eine Treppe und ging leise hinauf**
He saw some stairs and climbed them quietly
**Endlich fand er unser Zelt und kam herein**
He finally found our tent and came in
**Er öffnete den Koffer und legte das Hemd hinein**
He opened his suitcase and put in his shirt

## Possessive Pronouns

> **meiner** mine
> **deiner** yours
> **seiner** his/its
> **ihrer** hers/its
> **uns(e)rer** ours
> **eu(e)rer** yours (*plural*)
> **ihrer** theirs
> **Ihrer** yours (*polite form*)

These have the same endings as **dieser**. Their declension is therefore the same as for possessive adjectives (see p 136) except in the masculine nominative singular and the neuter nominative and accusative singular:

|  | SINGULAR | | | PLURAL |
|  | MASC | FEM | NEUT | ALL GENDERS |
|---|---|---|---|---|
| NOM | **-er** | **-e** | **-(e)s** | **-e** |
| ACC | **-en** | **-e** | **-(e)s** | **-e** |
| GEN | **-es** | **-er** | **-es** | **-er** |
| DAT | **-em** | **-er** | **-em** | **-en** |

- The bracketed (**e**) is often omitted, especially in spoken German

- Possessive pronouns must agree in number, gender and case with the noun they replace (→**1**)

- Note the translation of *of mine, of yours* etc (→**2**)

- **meiner** is declined in full opposite (→**3**)
  Like **meiner** are **deiner, seiner** and **ihrer**.
  **Unserer** and **euerer** are shown in full, since they have slightly different forms with an optional **-e-** (→**4**)

*Continued*

**1 Der Wagen da drüben ist meiner. Er ist kleiner als deiner**
The car over there is mine. It is smaller than yours

**2 Er ist ein Bekannter von mir**
He is an acquaintance of mine

**3 meiner** mine

|  | SINGULAR | | | PLURAL |
|---|---|---|---|---|
|  | MASC | FEM | NEUT | ALL GENDERS |
| NOM | meiner | meine | mein(e)s | meine |
| ACC | meinen | meine | mein(e)s | meine |
| GEN | meines | meiner | meines | meiner |
| DAT | meinem | meiner | meinem | meinen |

**4 uns(e)rer** ours

|  | SINGULAR | | | PLURAL |
|---|---|---|---|---|
|  | MASC | FEM | NEUT | ALL GENDERS |
| NOM | uns(e)rer | uns(e)re | uns(e)res | uns(e)re |
| ACC | uns(e)ren | uns(e)re | uns(e)res | uns(e)re |
| GEN | uns(e)res | uns(e)rer | uns(e)res | uns(e)rer |
| DAT | uns(e)rem | uns(e)rer | uns(e)rem | uns(e)ren |

**eu(e)rer** yours (*plural*)

|  | SINGULAR | | | PLURAL |
|---|---|---|---|---|
|  | MASC | FEM | NEUT | ALL GENDERS |
| NOM | eu(e)rer | eu(e)re | eu(e)res | eu(e)re |
| ACC | eu(e)ren | eu(e)re | eu(e)res | eu(e)re |
| GEN | eu(e)res | eu(e)rer | eu(e)res | eu(e)rer |
| DAT | eu(e)rem | eu(e)rer | eu(e)rem | eu(e)ren |

## Possessive Pronouns (contd)

### Alternative forms

There are two alternatives to the **meiner/deiner** *etc* forms shown on p 167:

- **der, die, das meinige** mine
  **der, die, das deinige** yours
  **der, die, das seinige** his/its
  **der, die, das ihrige** hers/its
  **der, die, das uns(e)rige** ours
  **der, die, das eu(e)rige** yours (*plural*)
  **der, die, das ihrige** theirs
  **der, die, das Ihrige** yours (*polite form*)

  These are not as common as the **meiner/deiner** *etc* forms (→**1**)

  These forms are declined as the definite article plus a weak adjective (see p 140) (→**2**)

  The bracketed (**e**) of the first and second person plural is often omitted in spoken German.

- **der, die, das meine** mine
  **der, die, das deine** yours
  **der, die, das seine** his/its
  **der, die, das ihre** hers/its
  **der, die, das uns(e)re** ours
  **der, die, das eu(e)re** yours (*plural*)
  **der, die, das ihre** theirs
  **der, die, das Ihre** yours (*polite form*)

  These forms are also less common than the **meiner/deiner** *etc* forms. They are declined as the definite article followed by a weak adjective (→**3**)

**1 Ihr Auto ist aber neuer als das meinige**
Your car is newer than mine
**Paul hat seiner Freundin Blumen gekauft. Ich habe der meinigen Parfüm geschenkt**
Paul bought his girlfriend some flowers. I bought mine perfume

**2**

|  | SINGULAR | | |
|---|---|---|---|
|  | *MASC* | *FEM* | *NEUT* |
| *NOM* | **der meinige** | **die meinige** | **das meinige** |
| *ACC* | **den meinigen** | **die meinige** | **das meinige** |
| *GEN* | **des meinigen** | **der meinigen** | **des meinigen** |
| *DAT* | **dem meinigen** | **der meinigen** | **dem meinigen** |

| | PLURAL |
|---|---|
| | *ALL GENDERS* |
| *NOM* | **die meinigen** |
| *ACC* | **die meinigen** |
| *GEN* | **der meinigen** |
| *DAT* | **den meinigen** |

**3**

|  | SINGULAR | | |
|---|---|---|---|
|  | *MASC* | *FEM* | *NEUT* |
| *NOM* | **der meine** | **die meine** | **das meine** |
| *ACC* | **den meinen** | **die meine** | **das meine** |
| *GEN* | **des meinen** | **der meinen** | **des meinen** |
| *DAT* | **dem meinen** | **der meinen** | **dem meinen** |

| | PLURAL |
|---|---|
| | *ALL GENDERS* |
| *NOM* | **die meinen** |
| *ACC* | **die meinen** |
| *GEN* | **der meinen** |
| *DAT* | **den meinen** |

# Reflexive Pronouns

Reflexive pronouns, used to form reflexive verbs, have two forms, accusative and dative, as follows (→**1**)

| ACCUSATIVE | DATIVE | |
|---|---|---|
| **mich** | **mir** | myself |
| **dich** | **dir** | yourself |
| **sich** | **sich** | himself/herself/itself/ themselves |
| **uns** | **uns** | ourselves |
| **euch** | **euch** | yourselves |
| **sich** | **sich** | yourself/yourselves (*polite forms*) |

• Unlike personal pronouns and possessives, the polite forms have no capital letter (→**2**)

• For the position of reflexive pronouns within a sentence see p 30 (reflexive verbs) and pp 224 to 235 (sentence structure).

• Reflexive pronouns are also used after prepositions when the pronoun has the function of "reflecting back" to the subject of the sentence (→**3**)

• A further use of reflexive pronouns in German is with transitive verbs where the action is performed for the benefit of the subject, as in the English phrase:

I bought *myself* a new hat

The pronoun is not always translated in English (→**4**)

*Continued*

**1  Er hat sich rasiert** He had a shave
   **Du hast dich gebadet** You had a bath
   **Ich will es mir zuerst überlegen**
   I'll have to think about it first

**2  Setzen Sie sich bitte** Please take a seat

**3  Er hatte nicht genug Geld bei sich** (*NOT* **bei ihm**)
   He didn't have enough money on him

**4  Ich hole mir ein Bier**
   I'm going to get a beer (for myself)
   **Er hat sich einen neuen Anzug gekauft**
   He bought (himself) a new suit

## Reflexive Pronouns (contd)

- Reflexive pronouns may be used for *reciprocal* actions, usually rendered by "each other" in English (→**1**)

  Reciprocal actions may also be expressed by **einander**. This does not change in form (→**2**)

  **einander** is always used in place of the reflexive pronoun after prepositions. Note that the preposition and **einander** come together to form one word (→**3**)

### Emphatic reflexive pronouns

In English, these have the same forms as the normal reflexive pronouns:

>   The queen *herself* has given the order
>   I haven't read it *myself*, but …

In German, this idea is expressed not by the reflexive pronouns, but by **selbst** or (in colloquial speech) **selber** placed at some point in the sentence after the noun or pronoun to which they refer (→**4**)

- **selbst/selber** do not change their form, regardless of number and gender of the noun to which they refer (→**4**)

- They are always stressed, regardless of their position in the sentence.

1 **Wir sind uns letzte Woche begegnet**
  We met (each other) last week
  **Sie hatten sich auf einer Tagung kennengelernt**
  They had got to know each other at a conference

2 **Wir kennen uns schon**
  *OR*:
  **Wir kennen einander schon**
  We already know each other

  **Sie kennen sich schon**
  *OR*:
  **Sie kennen einander schon**
  They already know each other

3 **Sie redeten miteinander**
  They were talking to each other

4 **Die Königin selbst hat es befohlen**
  The queen herself has given the order
  **Ich selbst habe es nicht gelesen, aber ...**
  I haven't read it myself, but ...

## Relative Pronouns

These have the same forms as the definite article, except in the dative plural and genitive cases.

They are declined as follows:

|  | SINGULAR | | | PLURAL |
| --- | --- | --- | --- | --- |
|  | MASC | FEM | NEUT | ALL GENDERS |
| NOM | der | die | das | die |
| ACC | den | die | das | die |
| GEN | dessen | deren | dessen | deren |
| DAT | dem | der | dem | denen |

- Relative pronouns must agree in gender and number with the noun to which they refer. They take their case however from the function they have in their own relative clause (→1)

- The relative pronoun cannot be omitted in German as it sometimes is in English (→2)

- The genitive forms are used in relative clauses in much the same way as in English (→3)
  Note however the translation of certain phrases (→4)

- When a preposition introduces the relative clause, the relative pronoun may be replaced by **wo-** or **wor-** if the noun or pronoun it stands for refers to an inanimate object or abstract concept (→5)
  The full form of relative pronoun plus preposition is however stylistically better.

- Relative clauses are always divided off by commas from the rest of the sentence (→1-5)

*Continued*

1 **Der Mann, den ich gestern gesehen habe, kommt aus Hamburg**
The man whom I saw yesterday comes from Hamburg

2 **Die Frau, mit der ich gestern gesprochen habe, kennt deine Mutter**
The woman I spoke to yesterday knows your mother

3 **Das Kind, dessen Fahrrad gestohlen worden war, ...**
The child whose bicycle had been stolen ...

4 **Die Kinder, von denen einige schon lesen konnten, ...**
The children, some of whom could read, ...
**Meine Freunde, von denen einer ...**
My friends, one of whom ...

5 **Das Buch, woraus ich vorgelesen habe, ...**
*OR:*
**Das Buch, aus dem ich vorgelesen habe, ...**
The book I read aloud from ...

## Relative Pronouns (contd)

### welcher

A second relative pronoun exists. This has the same forms as the interrogative adjective **welcher** without the genitive forms:

|  | | SINGULAR | | PLURAL |
|  | MASC | FEM | NEUT | ALL GENDERS |
|---|---|---|---|---|
| NOM | welcher | welche | welches | welche |
| ACC | welchen | welche | welches | welche |
| GEN | — | — | — | — |
| DAT | welchem | welcher | welchem | welchen |

- These forms are used only infrequently as relative pronouns, where sentence rhythm might benefit.

- They are also useful used as articles or adjectives to connect a noun in the relative clause with the contents of the main clause (→1)

### wer, was

These are normally used as interrogative pronouns meaning *who?, what?* and are declined as such on p 178.

- They may, however, also be used without interrogative meaning to replace both subject and relative pronoun in English:
  *he who, a woman who, anyone who, those who* etc (→2)

- **was** is the relative pronoun used in set expressions with certain neuter forms (→3)

**1 Er glaubte, mit der Hausarbeit nicht helfen zu brauchen, mit welcher Idee seine Mutter nicht einverstanden war!**
He thought he didn't have to help in the house, an idea with which his mother was not in agreement!

**2 Wer das glaubt, ist verrückt**
Anyone who believes that is mad
**Was mich angeht, ...** For my part ...
**Was du gestern gekauft hast, steht dir ganz gut**
The things you bought yesterday suit you very well

**3 nichts, was** ... nothing that
  **vieles, was** ... a lot that
  **einiges, was** ... some that
  **dasselbe, was** ... the same one that
  **wenig, was** ... little that
  **dasjenige, was** ... that which
  **folgendes, was** ... the following which
  **manches, was** ... some which
  **allerlei, was** ... all kinds of things that
  **alles, was** ... everything which
  **das, was** ... that which

  **Nichts, was er sagte, hat gestimmt**
  Nothing that he said was right
  **Das, was du jetzt machst, ist reiner Unsinn!**
  What you are doing now is sheer nonsense!
  **Mit allem, was du gesagt hast, sind wir einverstanden**
  We agree with everything you said

## Interrogative Pronouns

These are the pronouns used to ask questions.

As in English, they have few forms, singular and plural being the same.

They are declined as follows:

|  | PERSONS | THINGS |
|---|---|---|
| NOM | wer? | was? |
| ACC | wen? | was? |
| GEN | wessen? | wessen? |
| DAT | wem? | — |

- They are used in direct questions    (→1)
  or in indirect questions    (→2)

- When used as the subject of a sentence, they are always followed by a singular verb (→3)
  EXCEPTION:
  When followed by a verb and taking a noun complement, the verb may be plural if the sense demands it (→4)

- The interrogative pronouns can be used in rhetorical questions or in exclamations (→5)

Continued

**1 Wer hat es gemacht?** Who did it?
**Mit wem bist du gekommen?**
Who did you come with?

**2 Ich weiß nicht, wer es gemacht hat**
I don't know who did it
**Er wollte wissen, mit wem er fahren sollte**
He wanted to know who he was to travel with

**3 Wer kommt heute?** Who's coming today?

**4 Wer sind diese Leute?** Who are these people?

**5 Was haben wir gelacht!** How we laughed!

## Interrogative Pronouns (contd)

- When used with prepositions, **was** usually becomes **wo-** and is placed in front of the preposition to form one word with it (→**1**) Where the preposition begins with a vowel, **wor-** is used instead (→**2**) This construction is similar to **da(r)-** + *preposition* shown on p 164

  As with **da(r)-** + *preposition,* this construction is not used when the preposition is intended to convey movement. **Wohin** (*where to*) and **woher** (*where from*) are used instead (→**3**)

## was für ein?, welcher?

- These are used to mean *what kind of one?* and *which one?*

- They are declined as shown on pp 124 and 128.

- They are used to form either direct or indirect questions (→**4**)

- They may refer either to persons or to things with the appropriate declension endings (→**5**)

**1 Wonach sehnst du dich?** What do you long for?
**Wodurch ist es zerstört worden?**
How was it destroyed?

**2 Worauf kann man sich heutzutage noch verlassen?**
What is there left to rely on these days?

**3 Wohin fährst du?** Where are you going?
**Woher kommt das?**
Where has this come from?/How has this come about?

**4 Was für eins hat er?**
What kind (of one) does he have?
**Welches hast du gewollt?**
Which one did you want?

**5 Für welchen hat sie sich entschieden?**
Which one (*man/hat etc*) did she choose?

## Indefinite Pronouns

**jemand** someone, somebody

| | |
|---|---|
| *NOM* | **jemand** |
| *ACC* | **jemanden, jemand** |
| *GEN* | **jemand(e)s** |
| *DAT* | **jemandem, jemand** (→**1**) |

**niemand** no-one, nobody

| | |
|---|---|
| *NOM* | **niemand** |
| *ACC* | **niemanden, niemand** |
| *GEN* | **niemand(e)s** |
| *DAT* | **niemandem, niemand** (→**2**) |

- The forms without endings are used in conversational German, but the inflected forms are preferred in literary and written styles.

- When **niemand** and **jemand** are used with a following adjective, they are usually not declined, but the adjective takes a capital letter and is declined as follows:

| | |
|---|---|
| *NOM* | **jemand/niemand Neues** |
| *ACC* | **jemand/niemand Neues** |
| *GEN* | **—** |
| *DAT* | **jemand/niemand Neuem** (→**3**) |

- When **jemand** and **niemand** are followed by **ander(e)s**, this is written with a small letter, e.g. **jemand/niemand ander(e)s.**

*Continued*

**1 Ich habe es jemandem** (*dat*) **gegeben**
I gave it to someone

**Irgend jemand** (*nom*) **hat es genommen**
Someone or other has stolen it

**2 Er hat niemanden** (*acc*) **gesehen**
He didn't see anyone

**Er ist unterwegs niemandem** (*dat*) **begegnet**
He encountered no-one on the way

**3 Diese Aufgabe erfordert jemand Intelligentes**
Someone intelligent is needed for this task

## 184   PRONOUNS

## Indefinite Pronouns (contd)

**keiner** none

| | | SINGULAR | | PLURAL |
|---|---|---|---|---|
| | MASC | FEM | NEUT | ALL GENDERS |
| NOM | keiner | keine | keins | keine |
| ACC | keinen | keine | keins | keine |
| GEN | keines | keiner | keines | keiner |
| DAT | keinem | keiner | keinem | keinen |

- It is declined like the article **kein, keine, kein** (see p 126) except in the nominative masculine and nominative and accusative neuter forms (→**1**)

- It may be used to refer to people or things (→**1**)

**einer** one

| | | SINGULAR | |
|---|---|---|---|
| | MASC | FEM | NEUT |
| NOM | einer | eine | ein(e)s |
| ACC | einen | eine | ein(e)s |
| GEN | eines | einer | eines |
| DAT | einem | einer | einem |

- This pronoun may be used to refer to either persons or things (→**2**)

- It exists only in the singular forms.

*Continued*

**1 Keiner von ihnen hat es tun können**
Not one of them was able to do it

  **Gibst du mir eine Zigarette? — Tut mir leid, ich habe keine**
  Will you give me a cigarette? — Sorry, I haven't got any

**2 Sie ist mit einem meiner Verwandten verlobt**
She is engaged to one of my relatives

  **Wo sind die anderen Kinder? Ich sehe hier nur eins**
  Where are the rest of the children? I can only see one here

  **Gibst du mir einen?** (e.g. **einen Whisky, einen Zehner** *etc*)
  **Gibst du mir eine?** (e.g. **eine Zigarette, eine Blume** *etc*)
  **Gibst du mir eins?** (e.g. **ein Buch, ein Butterbrot** *etc*)
  Will you give me one?

# Indefinite Pronouns (contd)

- Certain adjectives and articles can be used as pronouns.

- The following are all declined to agree in gender and number with the noun or pronoun they represent (→**1**):

  **mehrere** several
  **ander** other

  **derjenige** that one
  **derselbe** the same one

  **mancher** some
  **jeder** each (one), every one
  **jener** that one
  **dieser** this one
  **solcher** such as that, such a one
  **mancher** some, quite a few
  **einiger** some
  **welcher** which one
  **aller** all
  **irgendwelcher** someone or other; something or other
  **beide** both
  **sämtliche** all, the lot

- The following do not change whatever the gender or number of the noun or pronoun they represent (→**2**):

  | | |
  |---|---|
  | **etwas** some, something | **nichts** nothing, none |
  | **ein paar** a few | **ein wenig** a little, a few |
  | **mehr** more | **ein bißchen** a bit, a little |

- When an adjective follows **etwas** or **nichts**, it takes a capital letter and declension endings: **etwas/nichts Gutes** something/ nothing good.

**1 Andere machen es besser** (e.g. **Leute, Waschmaschinen** *etc*)
Others do it better

**Mit einem solchen kommst du nicht bis nach Hause** (e.g.
**Wagen** *etc*)
You won't make it home in one like that

**Alles, was er ihr schenkte, schickte sie sofort zurück**
Everything that he gave her she sent back at once

**Er war mit beiden zufrieden** (e.g. **Computern, Autos** *etc*)
He was satisfied with both

**2 Ich muß dir etwas sagen**
I must tell you something

**Etwas ist herausgefallen**
Something fell out

**Nichts ist geschehen**
Nothing happened

**Er ist mit nichts zufrieden**
He is content with nothing

**Gibst du mir bitte ein paar?**
Will you give me a few?

**Er hatte ein wenig bei sich**
He had a little with him

**Er braucht immer mehr, um zu überleben**
He needs more and more to survive

## Use of Adverbs

- Adverbs, or phrases which are used as adverbs, may:

  a) modify a verb (→**1**)

  b) modify an adjective (→**2**)

  c) modify another adverb (→**3**)

  d) modify a conjunction (→**4**)

  e) ask a question (→**5**)

  f) form verb prefixes (see p 72) (→**6**)

- Adverbs are also used, in much the same way as in English, to make the meaning of certain tenses more precise e.g.

  a) with continuous tenses (→**7**)

  b) to show a future meaning where the tense used is not future (→**8**)

*Continued*

**1 Er ging langsam über die Brücke**
He walked slowly over the bridge

**2 Er ist ein ziemlich großer Kerl**
He's quite a big chap

**3 Sie arbeitet heute besonders tüchtig**
She's working exceptionally well today

**4 Wenn er es nur aufgeben wollte!**
If only he would give it up!

**5 Wann kommt er an?**
When does he arrive?

**6 falsch spielen** to cheat (*at cards*)
**hintragen** to carry (*to a place*)

**7 Er liest gerade die Zeitung**
He's just reading the paper

**8 Er wollte gerade aufstehen, als ...**
He was just about to get up when ...

**Wir fahren morgen nach Köln**
We're driving to Cologne tomorrow

# The Formation of Adverbs

- Many adverbs are simply adjectives used as adverbs. Used in this way, unlike adjectives, they are not declined (→**1**)

- Some adverbs are formed by adding **-weise** or **-sweise** to a noun (→**2**)

- Some adverbs are also formed by adding **-erweise** to an uninflected adjective.
  Such adverbs are used mainly to show the speaker's opinion (→**3**)

- There is also a class of adverbs which are not formed from other parts of speech e.g.
  **unten, oben, leider** (→**4**)
  and those shown in the paragraphs below.

- For the position of adverbs within a clause or sentence, see the section on sentence structure, pp 224 to 235.

- The following are some common adverbs of time:
  **morgen** tomorrow
  **morgens** in the mornings
  **heute** today
  **endlich** finally
  **sofort** at once
  **immer** always                          (→**5**)

- The following are some common adverbs of degree:
  **äußerst** extremely
  **besonders** especially
  **ziemlich** fairly
  **beträchtlich** considerably              (→**6**)

*Continued*

**1 Habe ich das richtig gehört?**
Is it true what I've heard?

**Sie war modern angezogen**
She was fashionably dressed

**2 beispielsweise** for example
**beziehungsweise** or; or rather; that is to say
**schrittweise** step by step
**zeitweise** at times
**zwangsweise** compulsorily

**3 glücklicherweise** fortunately
**komischerweise** strangely enough
**erstaunlicherweise** astonishingly enough

**4 Unten wohnte Frau Schmidt**
Mrs Schmidt lived downstairs

**Leider können wir nicht kommen**
Unfortunately we cannot come

**5 Ich kann erst morgen kommen**
I can't come till tomorrow

**Das Kind hat immer Hunger**
The child is always hungry

**6 Das Paket war besonders schwer**
The parcel was unusually heavy

**Diese Übung ist ziemlich leicht**
This exercise is quite easy

## Adverbs of place

In certain respects German adverbs of place behave very differently from their English counterparts:

- Where no movement, or movement within the same place, is involved, the adverb is used in its simple dictionary form (→**1**)

- Movement *away from the speaker* is shown by the presence of **hin** (→**2**)
  The following compound adverbs are therefore often used when movement away from the original position is concerned, even though a simple adverb would be used in English:

  **wohin?** where (to)?
  **irgendwohin** (to) somewhere or other
  **überallhin** everywhere
  **dahin** (to) there
  **hierhin** here
  **dorthin** there                                    (→**3**)

- Movement *towards the speaker* or central person is shown by the presence of **her**.
  The following compound adverbs are therefore often used to show movement towards a person:

  **woher?** where from?
  **hierher** here
  **irgendwoher** from somewhere or other
  **daher** from there
  **überallher** from all over                         (→**4**)

*Continued*

**1 Wo ist er?** Where is he?
**Er is nicht da** He isn't there

**Hier darf man nicht parken**
You can't park here

**2 Klaus und Ulli geben heute eine Party. Gehen wir hin?**
Klaus and Ulli are giving a party today. Shall we go?

**3 Wohin fährst du?** Where are you going?

**Sie liefen überallhin** They ran everywhere

**4 Woher kommst du?** Where do you come from?

**Woher hast du das?** Where did you get that from?

**Das habe ich irgendwoher gekriegt**
I got that from somewhere or other

## Comparison of Adverbs

- The **comparative** form of the adverb is obtained in exactly the same way as that of adjectives, i.e. by adding **-er** (→**1**)

- The **superlative** form is formed as follows:
    **am** + *adverb* + **-sten/-esten**
    It is not declined (→**2**)

- Note the use of the comparative adverb with **immer** to show progression (→**3**)

- *the more ... the more ...* is expressed in German by **je ... desto ...** or **je ... um so ...** (→**4**)

- Some adverbial superlatives are used to show the extent of a quality rather than a comparison with others. These are as follows:
    **spätestens** at the latest
    **höchstens** at the most; at best
    **wenigstens** at least
    **meistens** mostly; most often
    **strengstens** strictly, absolutely
    **bestens** very well; very warmly        (→**5**)

- Two irregular comparatives and superlatives:
    **gern → lieber → am liebsten** (used with **haben**)
    well → better → best

    **bald → eher → am ehesten**
    soon → sooner → soonest        (→**6**)

**1 Er läuft schneller als seine Schwester**
He runs faster than his sister

**Ich sehe ihn seltener als früher**
I see him less often than before

**2 Wer von ihnen arbeitet am schnellsten?**
Which of them works fastest?

**Er ißt am meisten** He eats most

**3 Die Mädchen sprachen immer lauter**
The girls were talking more and more loudly

**Er fuhr immer langsamer**
He drove more and more slowly

**4 Je eher, desto besser** The sooner the better

**5 Er kommt meistens zu spät an**
He usually arrives late

**Rauchen strengstens verboten!**
Smoking strictly prohibited

**6 Welches hast du am liebsten?**
Which do you like best?

# Emphasizers

These are words commonly used in German, as indeed in English, especially in the spoken language, to emphasize or modify in some way the meaning of the sentence. The following are some of the most common:

**aber**
Used to lend emphasis to a statement (→**1**)

**denn**
As well as its uses as a conjunction (see p 214), **denn** is widely used to emphasize the meaning. It often cannot be directly translated (→**2**)

**doch**
Is used as a positive reply in order to correct negative assumptions or impressions (→**3**)

It can strengthen an imperative (→**4**)

It can make a question out of a statement (→**5**)

**mal**
May be used with imperatives (→**6**)

It also has several idiomatic uses (→**7**)

**ja**
Strengthens a statement (→**8**)

It also has several idiomatic uses (→**9**)

**schon**
Is used familiarly with an imperative (→**10**)

It is also used in various idiomatic ways (→**11**)

**1 Das ist aber schön!** Oh that's pretty!
**Aber ja!** Yes indeed!

**2 Was ist denn hier los?**
What's going on here then?
**Wo denn?** Where?

**3 Hat es dir nicht gefallen? – Doch!**
Didn't you like it? – Oh yes, I did!

**4 Laß ihn doch!** Just leave him

**5 Das schaffst du doch?**
You'll manage it, won't you?

**6 Komm mal her!** Come here!
**Moment mal!** Just a minute!

**7 Mal sehen** We'll see
**Er soll es nur mal versuchen!**
Just let him try it!
**Hören Sie mal** ... Look here now ...

**8 Er sieht ja wie seine Mutter aus**
He looks like his mother
**Das kann ja sein** That may well be

**9 Ja und?** So what?/What then?
**Das ist ja lächerlich** That's ridiculous
**Das ist es ja** That's just it

**10 Mach schon!** Get on with it!

**11 Wenn schon!** What of it?/So what?
**Schon gut** Okay/Very well

# Prepositions

In English, a preposition does not affect the word or phrase which it introduces e.g.

the women / a large meal / these events

*with* the women / *after* a large meal / *before* these events

In German, however, the noun following a preposition must be put in a certain *case*:   *accusative*   (→**1**)
*dative*   (→**2**)
*genitive*   (→**3**)

It is therefore important to learn each preposition with the case, or cases, it governs.

The following guidelines will help you:

- Prepositions which take the accusative or dative cases are much more common than those taking the genitive case.

- Certain prepositions may take a dative or accusative case, depending on whether *movement* is involved or not. This is explained further on pp 202 ff (→**4**)

- Prepositions are often used to complete the sense of certain verbs, as shown on p 76 ff (→**5**)

- After many prepositions, a shortened or *contracted* form of the definite article may be merged with the preposition to form one word, e.g.

| | |
|---|---|
| **auf** + **das** | becomes **aufs** |
| **bei** + **dem** | becomes **beim** |
| **zu** + **der** | becomes **zur** |

*Continued*

**1 Es ist für dich**
It's for you
**Wir sind durch die ganze Welt gereist**
We travelled all over the world

**2 Er ist mit seiner Frau gekommen**
He came with his wife

**3 Es ist ihm trotz seiner Bemühungen nicht gelungen**
Despite his efforts, he still didn't succeed

**4 Es liegt auf dem Tisch**
It's on the table (*dative*: no movement implied)
**Lege es bitte auf den Tisch** Please put it on the table
(*accusative*: movement *onto* the table)

**5 Ich warte auf meinen Mann**
I'm waiting for my husband

## Prepositions: contracted forms (contd)

Such contractions are possible with the following prepositions:

| preposition | + **das** | + **den** | + **dem** | + **der** |
|---|---|---|---|---|
| hinter | hinters* | hintern* | hinterm* | |
| über | übers* | übern* | überm* | |
| unter | unters* | untern* | unterm* | |
| zu | | | zum | zur |
| an | ans | | am | |
| vor | vors* | | vorm* | |
| in | ins | | im | |
| bei | | | beim | |
| von | | | vom | |
| durch | durchs* | | | |
| für | fürs* | | | |
| auf | aufs* | | | |
| um | ums* | | | |

- Those forms marked with an asterisk are suitable only for use in colloquial, spoken German.
  All other forms (not marked with an asterisk) may be safely used in any context, formal or informal (→**1**)

- Contracted forms are obviously not used where the article is to be stressed (→**2**)

- Other contracted forms involving prepositions, as shown on pp 164 and 174, occur:
  1) in the introduction to relative clauses (→**3**)
  2) with personal pronouns representing inanimate objects (→**4**)

*Continued*

1 **Wir gehen heute Abend ins Theater**
We are going to the theatre this evening

**Er geht zur Schule**
He goes to school

**Das kommt vom Trinken**
That comes from drinking

2 **In dem Anzug kann ich mich nicht sehen lassen!**
I can't go out in that suit!

3 **Die Bank, worauf wir saßen, war etwas wackelig**
The bench we were sitting on was rather wobbly

4 **Er war damit zufrieden**
He was satisfied with that

**Er hat es darauf gesetzt**
He put it on it

# Prepositions followed by the Dative Case

Some of the most common prepositions taking the dative case are:

| | | |
|---|---|---|
| aus | gegenüber | seit |
| außer | mit | von |
| bei | nach | zu |

**aus**
- as a preposition meaning *out of/from* (→**1**)
- as a separable verbal prefix (see p 72) (→**2**)

**außer**
- as a preposition meaning:  *out of*  (→**3**)
  *except*  (→**4**)

**bei**
- as a preposition meaning:  *at the home/shop/work (etc) of* (→**5**)
  *near* (→**6**)
  *in the course of/during* (→**7**)
- as a separable verbal prefix (see p 72) (→**8**)

**gegenüber**
- as a preposition meaning:  *opposite* (→**9**)
  *to(wards)* (→**10**)
  - *NOTE*:   when used as a preposition, **gegenüber** is placed *after a pronoun*, but may be placed *before or after a noun*
- as a separable verbal prefix (→**11**)

*Continued*

**1 Er trinkt aus der Flasche**
He is drinking out of the bottle
**Er kommt aus Essen** He comes from Essen

**2 aushalten** to endure →
**Ich halte es nicht mehr aus**
I can't stand it any longer

**3 außer Gefahr/Betrieb** out of danger/order

**4 alle außer mir** all except me

**5 Bei uns in Schottland**
At home in Scotland
**Er wohnt immer noch bei seinen Eltern**
He still lives with his parents

**6 Er saß bei mir**
He was sitting next to me

**7 Ich singe immer beim Arbeiten**
I always sing when I'm working
**Bei unserer Ankunft ...**
On our arrival ...

**8 Er stand seinem Freund bei**
He stood by his friend

**9 Er wohnt uns gegenüber**
He lives opposite us

**10 Er ist mir gegenüber immer sehr freundlich gewesen**
He has always been very friendly towards me

**11 gegenüberstehen** to face/to have an attitude towards →
**Er steht ihnen kritisch gegenüber**
He takes a critical view of them

# Prepositions followed by the Dative Case
(contd)

### mit
- as a preposition meaning *with* (→**1**)
- as a separable verbal prefix (see p 72) (→**2**)

### nach
- as a preposition meaning:   *after* (→**3**)

                                 *to* (→**4**)

                                 *according to* (it can be placed after the noun with this meaning) (→**5**)
- as a separable verbal prefix (see p 72) (→**6**)

### seit
- as a preposition meaning: *since* (→**7**)

                                 *for* (of time; note the tense!) (→**8**)

### von
- as a preposition meaning:   *from* (→**9**)

                                 *about* (→**10**)
- as an alternative, often preferred, to the genitive case (→**11**)
- meaning *by*, to introduce the agent of a passive action (see p 34) (→**12**)

### zu
- as a preposition meaning:   *to* (→**13**)

                                 *for* (→**14**)
- as a separable verbal prefix (see p 72) (→**15**)

*Continued*

1 **Er ging mit seinen Freunden spazieren**
He went walking with his friends
2 **jemanden mitnehmen** to give someone a lift →
**Nimmst du mich bitte mit?**
Will you give me a lift please?
3 **Nach zwei Stunden kam er wieder**
He returned two hours later
4 **Er ist nach London gereist**
He went to London
5 **Ihrer Sprache nach ist sie Süddeutsche**
From the way she spoke I would say she is from southern
Germany
6 **nachmachen** to copy →
**Sie macht mir alles nach**
She copies everything I do
7 **Seit der Zeit** ...
Since then ...
8 **Ich wohne seit zwei Jahren in Frankfurt**
I've been living in Frankfurt for two years
9 **Von Frankfurt sind wir weiter nach München gefahren**
From Frankfurt we went on to Munich
10 **Ich weiß nichts von ihm**
I know nothing about him
11 **Die Mutter von diesen Mädchen** ...
The mother of these girls ...
**Sie ist eine Freundin von Horst**
She is a friend of Horst's
12 **Er ist von unseren Argumenten überzeugt worden**
He was convinced by our arguments
13 **Er ging zum Arzt**
He went to the doctor's
14 **Wir sind zum Essen eingeladen**
We're invited for dinner
15 **zumachen** to shut →
**Mach die Tür zu**
Shut the door

# Prepositions followed by the Accusative Case

The most common of these are:

> durch    für    ohne    wider
> entlang    gegen    um

## durch

- as a preposition meaning *through* (→**1**)
- preceding the inanimate agent of a passive action (see p 34) (→**2**)
- as a separable verbal prefix

## entlang

- as a preposition meaning *along*, in which case it follows the noun (→**3**)
- as a separable verbal prefix (→**4**)

## für

- as a preposition meaning:    *for*    (→**5**)
                               *to*    (→**6**)
- in **was für/was für ein** *what kind of/what*, as shown on p 144 and p 180 (→**7**)

## gegen

- as a preposition meaning:    *against* (→**8**)
                               *towards/getting on for* (→**9**)
- as a separable verbal prefix

*Continued*

**1  durch das Fenster blicken**
to look through the window

**2  Durch seine Bemühungen wurden alle gerettet**
Everyone was saved through his efforts

**3  die Straße entlang**
along the street

**4  Wir gingen die Straße entlang**
We went along the street

**5  Ich habe es für dich getan**
I did it for you

**6  Das ist für ihn sehr wichtig**
That is very important to him

**7  Was für Äpfel sind das?**
What kind of apples are they?

**8  Stelle es gegen die Mauer**
Put it against the wall
**Haben Sie ein Mittel gegen Schnupfen?**
Have you something for (= against) colds?
**Ich habe nichts dagegen**
I've got nothing against it

**9  Wir sind gegen vier angekommen**
We arrived at getting on for/around four o'clock

# Prepositions followed by the Accusative Case (contd)

**ohne**

● as a preposition meaning *without* (→**1**)


**um**

● as a preposition meaning:   *(a)round/round about* (→**2**)
                              *at* (in time expressions) (→**3**)
                              *for* (after certain verbs) (→**4**)
                              *about* (after certain verbs) (→**5**)
                              *by* (in expressions of quantity) (→**6**)
● as a variable verbal prefix (see p 74) (→**7**)


**wider**

● as a preposition meaning *contrary to/against* (→**8**)
● as a variable verbal prefix (see p 74) (→**9**)


*Continued*

**1 Ohne ihn geht's nicht**
It won't work without him

**2 um die Ecke** (a)round the corner

**3 Es fängt um neun Uhr an** It begins at nine

**4 Sie baten ihre Mutter um Kekse**
They asked their mother for some biscuits

**5 Es handelt sich um dein Benehmen**
It's a question of your behaviour

**6 Es ist um zehn Mark billiger**
It is cheaper by ten marks

**7 umarmen** to embrace (*inseparable*) →
**Er hat sie umarmt**
He gave her a hug

**umfallen** to fall over (*separable*) →
**Er ist umgefallen**
He fell over

**8 Das geht mir wider die Natur**
That's against my nature

**9 widersprechen** to go against (*inseparable*) →
**Das hat meinen Wünschen widersprochen**
That went against my wishes

**(sich) widerspiegeln** to reflect (*separable*) →
**Der Baum spiegelt sich im Wasser wider**
The tree is reflected in the water

# Prepositions followed by the Dative or the Accusative

These prepositions are followed by:

the **accusative** when *movement towards* a different place is involved

the **dative** when *position* is described as opposed to movement, or when the movement is *within* the same place.

- The most common prepositions in this category are:

**in** *in/into/to* (→**1**)
**an** *on/at/to*
**auf** *on/in/to/at*
**unter** *under/among* (→**2**)
**über** *over/across/above*
**vor** *in front of/before*
**hinter** *behind*
**neben** *next to/beside*
**zwischen** *between* (→**3**)

- These prepositions may also be used with figurative meanings as part of a *verb + preposition* construction (see p 76).
The case following **auf** or **an** is then not the same after all verbs (→**4**)
It is therefore best to learn such constructions together with the case which follows them.

- Many of these prepositions are also used as verb prefixes in the same way as the prepositions described on pp 202 to 209 (→**5**)

*Continued*

**1 Er ging ins Zimmer** (*acc*)
He entered the room

**Im Zimmer** (*dat*) **warteten viele Leute auf ihn**
A lot of people were waiting for him in the room

**2 Er stellte sich unter den Baum** (*acc*)
He (came and) stood under the tree

**Er lebte dort unter Freunden** (*dat*)
There he lived among friends

**3 Er legte es zwischen die beiden Teller** (*acc*)
He put it between the two plates

**Das Dorf liegt zwischen den Bergen** (*dat*)
The village lies between the mountains

**4 sich verlassen auf** (+ *acc*) to depend on
**bestehen auf** (+ *dat*) to insist on

**glauben an** (+ *acc*) to believe in
**leiden an** (+ *dat*) to suffer from

**5 anrechnen** to charge for (*separable*) →
**Das wird Ihnen später angerechnet**
You'll be charged for that later

**aufsetzen** to put on (*separable*) →
**Sie setzte sich den Hut auf**
She put her hat on

**überqueren** to cross (*inseparable*) →
**Sie hat die Straße überquert**
She crossed the street

# Prepositions followed by the Genitive Case

The following are some of the more common prepositions which take the genitive case:

**diesseits** *on this side of*
**jenseits** *on the other side of* (→**1**)
**beiderseits** *on both sides of*
**innerhalb** *within/inside* (→**2**)
**außerhalb** *outside*
**während*** *during* (→**3**)
**statt*** *instead of*
**trotz*** *in spite of* (→**4**)
**wegen*** *on account of* (→**5**)
**infolge** *as a result of*
**hinsichtlich** *with regard to*
... **halber** *for ... sake/because of ...*
**um ... willen** *for ... sake/because of ...*

- Those prepositions marked with an asterisk may also be followed by the dative case (→**6**)

- Note that special forms of the possessive and relative pronouns are used with **wegen, halber** and **willen** (→**7**)

**1 jenseits der Grenze**
on the other side of the frontier

**2 innerhalb dieses Zeitraums**
within this period of time

**3 während der Vorstellung**
during the performance

**4 trotz seiner Befürchtungen**
despite his fears

**5 wegen der neuen Stelle**
because of the new job

**6 trotz allem** in spite of everything
**wegen mir** because of me

**7 meinetwegen** on my account, because of me
**deinetwegen** on your account, because of you
**seinetwegen** on his account, because of him
**ihretwegen** on her/their account, because of her/them
**unsertwegen** on our account, because of us
**euertwegen** on your account, because of you
**Ihretwegen** on your account, because of you (*polite*)
**derentwegen** for whose sake, for her/their/its sake
**dessentwegen** for whose sake, for his/its sake

**meinethalben** *etc* on my *etc* account
**derenthalben** on whose account, on her/their/its account
**dessenthalben** on whose account, on his/its account

**meinetwillen** *etc* for my *etc* sake
**derentwillen** for whose sake, for her/its/their sake
**dessentwillen** for whose sake, for his/its sake

# Co-ordinating Conjunctions

These are used to link words, phrases or clauses (→**1**)

• These are the main co-ordinating conjunctions:

| | |
|---|---|
| **und** | and (→**1**) |
| **oder** | or (→**2**) |
| **aber** | but (→**3**) |
| | however (→**4**) |
| **denn** | for (→**5**) |
| **sondern** | but (after a negative construction) (→**6**) |

• These do not cause subject-verb inversion, i.e. the verb follows the subject in the normal way (see p 224) (→**1-6**)

• Inversion may however be caused by something other than the co-ordinating conjunction, e.g. **dann, trotzdem, montags** in the examples opposite (→**7**)

• When used with the meaning of *however*, **aber** is placed within the clause, and not at the beginning (→**4**)

• When linked by co-ordinating conjunctions, no comma is required between clauses (cf p 240).

*Continued*

**1 Horst und Veronika** Horst and Veronika
**Er ging in die Stadt und kaufte sich ein neues Hemd**
He went into town and bought himself a new shirt

**2 Er hatte noch nie Whisky oder Schnaps getrunken**
He had never drunk whisky or schnapps
**Willst du eins, oder hast du vielleicht keinen Hunger?**
Do you want one or aren't you hungry?

**3 Wir wollten ins Kino, aber wir hatten kein Geld**
We wanted to go to the cinema but we had no money

**4 Ich wollte ins Theater; er aber wollte nicht mit**
I wanted to go the theatre; however he wouldn't come

**5 Wir wollten heute fahren, denn montags ist weniger Verkehr**
We wanted to travel today because the traffic is lighter on
Mondays

**6 Er ist nicht alt, sondern jung**
He isn't old, but young

**7 Er hat sie besucht, und dann ist er wieder nach Hause
gegangen**
He paid her a visit and then went home again
**Wir wollten doch ins Kino, aber trotzdem sind wir zu Hause
geblieben**
We wanted to go to the cinema, but even so we stayed at home
**Wir wollten heute fahren, denn montags ist der Verkehr
geringer**
We wanted to travel today because there is less traffic on
Mondays

## Double Co-ordinating Conjunctions

These conjunctions consist of two separate elements, like their English counterparts e.g.

*not only ... but also ...*

The following are widely used:

**sowohl ... als (auch)** *both ... and*

• This may link words or phrases (→**1**)

• The verb is usually plural, whether the subjects are singular or plural (→**1**)

**weder ... noch** *neither ... nor*

• This may link words or phrases (→**2**)

• It may also link clauses, and inversion of subject and verb then takes place in both clauses (→**3**)

• The verb is plural unless both subjects are singular (→**4**)

*Continued*

**1 Sowohl sein Vater als auch seine Mutter haben sich darüber gefreut**
Both his father and his mother were pleased about it
**Sowohl unser Lehrkörper als auch unsere Schüler haben teilgenommen**
Both our staff and our pupils took part

**2 Weder Georg noch sein Bruder kannte das Mädchen**
Neither Georg nor his brother knew the girl

**3 Weder mag ich ihn, noch respektiere ich ihn**
I neither like nor respect him

**4 Weder die Befürworter noch die Gegner haben recht**
Neither the supporters nor the opponents are right
**Weder du noch ich würde es schaffen**
Neither you nor I would be able to do it

## Double Co-ordinating Conjunctions (contd)

**nicht nur ... sondern auch** *not only ... but also*

• This is used to link clauses as well as words and phrases (→**1**)

• The word order is: inversion of subject and verb in the first clause, and normal order in the second (→**2**)
However, if **nicht nur** does not begin the clause, normal order prevails (→**3**)

• The verb agrees in number with the subject nearest to it (→**4**)

**entweder ... oder** *either ... or*

• The verb agrees with the subject nearest it (→**5**)

• The normal word order is: inversion in the first clause, and normal order in the second (→**6**)
However, it is possible to use normal order in the first clause, and this may lend a more threatening tone to the statement (→**7**)

**teils ... teils** *partly ... partly*

• The verb is normally plural unless both subjects are singular (→**8**)

• Inversion of subject and verb takes place in both clauses (→**9**)

1  **Er ist nicht nur geschickt, sondern auch intelligent**
   **Nicht nur ist er geschickt, sondern er ist auch intelligent**
   He is not only skilful but also intelligent

2  **Nicht nur hat es die ganze Zeit geregnet, sondern ich habe**
   **mir auch noch das Bein gebrochen**
   Not only did it rain the whole time, but I also broke my leg

3  **Es hat nicht nur die ganze Zeit geregnet, sondern ich habe**
   **mir auch noch das Bein gebrochen**
   Not only did it rain the whole time, but I also broke my leg

4  **Nicht nur ich, sondern auch die Mädchen sind dafür**
   **verantwortlich**
   Not just me, but the girls too are responsible
   **Nicht nur sie, sondern auch ich habe es gehört**
   It wasn't only they who heard it − I heard it too

5  **Entweder du oder Georg muß es getan haben**
   It must have been either you or Georg who did it

6  **Entweder komme ich morgen vorbei, oder ich rufe dich an**
   I'll either drop in tomorrow or I'll give you a ring

7  **Entweder du gibst das sofort auf, oder du kriegst kein**
   **Taschengeld mehr**
   Either you give it up immediately, or you get no more pocket
   money

8  **Die Studenten waren teils Deutsche, teils Ausländer**
   The students were partly German and partly from abroad

9  **Teils bin ich überzeugt, teils bleibe ich skeptisch**
   A bit of me is convinced, and a bit remains sceptical

## Subordinating Conjunctions

These are used to link clauses in such a way as to make one clause dependent on another for its meaning. The dependent clause is called a **subordinate clause** and the other a **main clause**.

• The subordinate clause is always separated from the rest of the sentence by commas (→**1**)

• The subordinate clause may precede the main clause. When this happens, the verb and subject of the main clause are inverted, i.e. they swap places, as shown as p 226 (→**2**)

• The finite part of the verb (i.e. the conjugated part) is always at the end of a subordinate clause (see p 228) (→**3**)

• For compound tenses in subordinate clauses, it is the **auxiliary** (the main part of the verb) which comes last, after the participle or infinitive used to form the compound tense (see the section on compound tenses) (→**4**)

• Any **modal verb** (**mögen, können** etc — p 52 ff) used in a subordinate clause is placed last in the clause (→**5**)

*EXCEPTION:* when the modal verb is in a compound tense, the order is as shown (→**6**)

*Continued*

*MAIN CLAUSE*      *SUBORDINATE CLAUSE*

1 **Er ist zu Fuß gekommen, weil der Bus zu teuer ist**
He came on foot because the bus is too dear
**Ich trinke viel Bier, obwohl es nicht gesund ist**
I drink a lot of beer although it isn't good for me
**Wir haben weiter gefeiert, nachdem sie gegangen waren**
We carried on the party after they went

*SUBORDINATE CLAUSE*      *MAIN CLAUSE*

2 **Weil der Bus zu teuer ist, geht er zu Fuß**
**Obwohl es nicht gesund ist, trinke ich viel Bier**
**Nachdem sie gegangen waren, haben wir weiter gefeiert**

3 **Als er uns sah, ist er davongelaufen**
**Er ist davongelaufen, als er uns sah**
He ran away when he saw us

4 **Nachdem er gegessen hatte, ging er hinaus**
He went out after he had eaten

5 **Da er nicht mit uns sprechen wollte, ist er davongelaufen**
Since he didn't want to speak to us he ran away

6 **Da er nicht mit uns hat sprechen wollen, ist er davongelaufen**
Since he didn't want to speak to us, he ran away

## Subordinating conjunctions (contd)

• Here are some common examples of subordinating conjunctions and their uses:

**nachdem** after (→**1**)
**indem** while
**wenn** when/whenever; if (→**2**)
**als** when (→**3**)
**wann** when (*interrogative*) (→**4**)
**während** while (→**5**)
**bevor** before
**sobald** as soon as
**wohin** to where
**worin** in which
**inwiefern** to what extent
**soweit** as far as
**worauf** whereupon; on which
**als ob** as if/as though
**weil** because (→**6**)
**seitdem** since
**bis** until (→**7**)
**wo** where
**wie** as/like
**da** as/since (→**8**)
**obwohl** although
**damit** so (that)
**so daß** such that, so that
**ob** whether, if

*Continued*

1 **Er wird uns Bescheid sagen können, nachdem er angerufen hat**
  **Nachdem er angerufen hat, wird er uns Bescheid sagen können**
  He will be able to let us know for certain, once he has phoned

2 **Wenn ich ins Kino gehe ...**
  When(ever) I go to the cinema ...
  **Ich komme, wenn du willst**
  I'll come if you like

3 **Es regnete, als ich in Köln ankam**
  **Als ich in Köln ankam, regnete es**
  It was raining when I arrived in Cologne

4 **Er möchte wissen, wann der Zug ankommt**
  He would like to know when the train is due to arrive

5 **Während seine Frau die Koffer auspackte, machte er das Abendessen**
  **Er machte das Abendessen, während seine Frau die Koffer auspackte**
  He made the supper while his wife unpacked the cases

6 **Wir haben den Hund nicht mitgenommen, weil im Auto nicht genug Platz war**
  **Weil im Auto nicht genug Platz war, haben wir den Hund nicht mitgenommen**
  We didn't take the dog because there wasn't enough room in the car

7 **Ich warte, bis du zurückkommst**
  I'll wait till you get back

8 **Da er nicht kommen wollte, ...**
  Since he didn't want to come ...

# Word Order: Main Clauses

- In a main clause the subject comes first and is followed by the verb, as in English:

    His mother (*subject*) drinks (*verb*) whisky (→**1**)

- If the verb is in a compound or passive tense, the auxiliary follows the subject and the past participle or infinitive goes to the end of the clause (→**2**)

- The verb is the second concept in a main clause. The first concept may be a word, phrase or clause (→**3**)

- Any reflexive pronoun *follows* the main verb in simple tenses and the auxiliary in compound tenses (→**4**)

- The order for articles, adjectives and nouns is as in English: "a/the/this/that" + *adjective(s)* + *noun* (→**5**)

- A direct object usually follows an indirect, except where the direct object is a personal pronoun.
    But the indirect object can be placed last for emphasis, providing it is not a pronoun (→**6**)

- The position of adverbial expressions (see p 188) is not fixed. As a general rule they are placed close to the words to which they refer. Adverbial items of *time* often come first in the clause, but this is flexible (→**7**)
    Adverbials of *place* can be placed at the beginning of a clause when emphasis is required (→**8**)
    Adverbial items of *manner* are more likely to be within the clause, close to the word to which they refer (→**9**)

- Where there is more than one adverb, a useful rule of thumb is "time, manner, place" (→**10**)

*Continued*

**1 Seine Mutter trinkt Whisky**
His mother drinks whisky

**2 Sie wird dir etwas sagen** She will tell you something
**Sie hat mir nichts gesagt** She told me nothing
**Es ist für ihn gekauft worden** It was bought for him

|  | 1 | 2 |
|---|---|---|
| **3** | **Die neuen Waren** | **kommen** | **morgen** |
|  | The new goods | are coming | tomorrow |

|  | 1 | 2 |
|---|---|---|
|  | **Was du gesagt hast,** | **stimmt nicht** |
|  | What you said | isn't true |

**4 Er rasierte sich** He shaved
**Er hat sich rasiert** He (has) shaved

**5 ein alter Mann** an old man
**diese alten Sachen** these old things

**6 Ich gab dem Mann das Geld** I gave the man the money
**Ich gab ihm das Geld** I gave him the money
**Ich gab es ihm** I gave him it/I gave it to him
**Ich gab es dem Mann** I gave it to the man
**Er gab das Geld seiner Schwester**
He gave the money to his sister (*not his brother*)

**7 Gestern gingen wir ins Theater** ⎫   We went to the theatre
**Wir gingen gestern ins Theater** ⎬        yesterday

**8 Dort haben sie Fußball gespielt** ⎫   They played football
**Sie haben dort Fußball gespielt** ⎬        there

**9 Sie spielen gut Fußball** They play football well
**Das war furchtbar teuer** It was terribly expensive

**10 Wir haben gestern gut hierhin gefunden**
We found our way here all right yesterday

## Word Order: Main Clauses (contd)

- A pronoun object precedes all adverbs (→**1**)
- While the main verb must normally remain the second concept, the first concept need not always be the subject. Main clauses can begin with many things, including:

  an adverb (→**2**)
  a direct or indirect object (→**3**)
  an infinitive phrase (→**4**)
  a complement (→**5**)
  a past participle (→**6**)
  a prepositional phrase (→**7**)
  a clause acting as the object of the verb (→**8**)
  a subordinate clause (→**9**)

- If the subject does not begin a main clause, the verb and subject must be turned around or "inverted" (→**2-9**)
- Beginning a sentence with something other than the subject is frequent in German.

  It may however also be used for special effect to:
  *highlight* whatever is placed first in the clause (→**10**)
  *emphasize* the subject of the clause by forcing it from its initial position to the end of the clause (→**11**)

- After inversion, any reflexive pronoun precedes the subject, unless the subject is a pronoun (→**12**)
- The following do not cause inversion when placed at the beginning of a main clause, although inversion may be caused by something else placed after them:

  **und, allein, oder, sondern, denn** (→**13**)
  **ja** and **nein** (→**14**)
  certain exclamations: **ach, also, nun** *etc* (→**15**)
  words or phrases qualifying the subject: **nur, sogar, auch** *etc* (→**16**)

1 **Sie haben es gestern sehr billig gekauft**
They bought it very cheaply yesterday

2 **Gestern sind wir ins Theater gegangen**
We went to the theatre yesterday

3 **So ein Kind habe ich noch nie gesehen!**
I've never seen such a child!
**Seinen Freunden wollte er es nicht zeigen**
He wouldn't show it to his friends

4 **Seinen Freunden zu helfen, hat er nicht versucht**
He didn't try to help his friends

5 **Deine Schwester war es** It was your sister

6 **Geraucht hatte er nie** He had never smoked

7 **In diesem Haus ist Mozart auf die Welt gekommen**
Mozart was born in this house

8 **Was mit ihm los war, haben wir nicht herausgefunden**
We never discovered what was wrong with him

9 **Nachdem ich ihn gesehen hatte, ging ich nach Hause**
I went home after seeing him

10 **Dem würde ich nichts sagen!** I wouldn't tell *him* anything

11 **An der Ecke stand eine riesengroße Fabrik**
A huge factory stood on the corner

12 **Daran erinnerten sich die Zeugen nicht**
The witnesses didn't remember that
**Daran erinnerten sie sich nicht** They didn't remember that

13 **Peter ging nach Hause, und Elsa blieb auf der Party**
Peter went home and Elsa stayed at the party
*BUT*   **Peter ging nach Hause, und unterwegs sah er Kurt**
Peter went home and on the way he saw Kurt

14 **Nein, ich will nicht** No, I don't want to
*BUT*   **Nein, das tue ich nicht** No I won't do that

15 **Also, wir fahren nach Hamburg** So we'll go to Hamburg
*BUT*   **Also, nach Hamburg wollt ihr fahren**
So you want to go to Hamburg

16 **Sogar seine Mutter wollte es ihm nicht glauben**
Even his mother wouldn't believe him
*BUT*   **Sogar mit dem Zug ginge es nicht schneller**
It would be no faster even by train

# Word Order: Subordinate Clauses

- A subordinate clause may be introduced by:
  a relative pronoun (see p 174) (→**1**)
  a subordinating conjunction (see p 222) (→**2-3**)

- The subject follows the opening conjunction or relative pronoun
  — **wir** and **er** in examples **1-3**

- The main verb almost always goes to the end of a subordinate
  clause (→**1-3**)

The exceptions to this are:

1. in a **wenn** clause where **wenn** is omitted (see p 64) (→**4**)
2. in an indirect statement without **daß** (see p 64) (→**5**)

- The order for articles, nouns, adjectives, adverbs, direct and
  indirect objects is the same as for main clauses (see
  p 224), but they are all placed between the subject of the clause
  and the verb (→**6**)

- If the subject of a reflexive verb in a subordinate clause is a
  pronoun, the order is *subject pronoun + reflexive pronoun*
  (→**7**) If the subject is a noun, the reflexive pronoun may follow
  or precede it (→**8**)

- Where one subordinate clause lies inside another, both still obey
  the order rule for subordinate clauses (→**9**)

**1 Die Kinder, die wir gesehen haben …**
The children whom we saw …

**2 Da er nicht schwimmen wollte, ist er nicht mitgekommen**
As he didn't want to swim he didn't come

**3 Ich weiß, daß er zur Zeit in London wohnt**
I know he's living in London at the moment
**Ich weiß nicht, ob er kommt**
I don't know if he's coming

**4 Findest du meine Uhr, so ruf mich bitte an**
**(= Wenn du meine Uhr findest, ruf mich bitte an)**
If you find my watch, please give me a ring

**5 Er meint, er werde es innerhalb einer Stunde schaffen**
**(= Er meint, daß er es innerhalb einer Stunde schaffen werde)**
He thinks (that) he would manage it inside an hour

**6** *main clause:*
**Er ist gestern mit seiner Mutter in die Stadt gefahren**
He went to town with his mother yesterday
*subordinate clauses:*
**Da er gestern mit seiner Mutter in die Stadt gefahren ist …**
Since he went to town with his mother yesterday …
**Der Junge, der gestern mit seiner Mutter in die Stadt gefahren ist …**
The boy who went to town with his mother yesterday …
**Ich weiß, daß er gestern mit seiner Mutter in die Stadt gefahren ist**
I know that he went to town with his mother yesterday

**7 Weil er sich nicht setzen wollte …**
Because he wouldn't sit down …

**8 Weil das Kind sich nicht setzen wollte, …**
*OR*     **Weil sich das Kind nicht setzen wollte, …**
Because the child wouldn't sit down …

**9 Er wußte, daß der Mann, mit dem er gesprochen hatte, bei einer Baufirma arbeitete**
He knew that the man he had been speaking to worked for a construction company

## Word Order (contd)

### In the Imperative

- normal order (→**1**)

- with reflexive verbs (→**2**)

- with separable verbs (→**3**)

- with separable reflexive verbs (→**4**)

### In Direct and Indirect speech

- the verb of saying ("he replied/he said") must be inverted if it is placed within a quotation (→**5**)

- the position of the verb in indirect speech depends on whether or not **daß** (see p 66) is used (→**6**)

### Verbs with Separable Prefixes (see pp 72 to 75)

- in main clauses the verb and prefix are separated in simple tenses and imperative forms (→**7**)

- for compound tenses of main clauses and all tenses of subordinate clauses, the verb and its prefix are united at the end of the clause (→**8**)

- in a present infinitive phrase (see p 46), the verb and prefix are joined together by **zu** and placed at the end of the phrase (→**9**)

1 **Hol mir das Buch!** (*singular*)
  **Holt mir das Buch!** (*plural*)      } Fetch me that book!
  **Holen Sie mir das Buch!** (*polite*)

2 **Wasch dich sofort!** Wash yourself at once!
  **Wascht euch sofort!** Wash yourselves at once!
  **Waschen Sie sich sofort!** (*polite*)

3 **Hör jetzt auf!** (*singular*)
  **Hört jetzt auf!** (*plural*)      } Stop it!
  **Hören Sie jetzt auf!** (*polite*)

4 **Dreh dich um!** (*singular*)
  **Dreht euch um!** (*plural*)      } Turn round!
  **Drehen Sie sich um!** (*polite*)

5 **"Meine Mutter" sagte er, "kommt erst morgen an"**
  "My mother", he said, "won't arrive till tomorrow"

6 **Er sagte, daß sie erst am nächsten Tag ankomme**
  He said that she would not arrive until the next day
  **Er sagte, sie komme erst am nächsten Tag an**
  He said she would not arrive until the next day

7 **Er machte die Tür zu** He closed the door
  **Ich räume zuerst auf** I'll clean up first
  **Hol mich um 7 ab!** Pick me up at 7 o'clock!

8 **Er hat die Tür zugemacht** He closed the door
  **Ich werde zuerst aufräumen** I'll clean up first
  **Er wurde um 7 abgeholt** He was picked up at 7
  **Wenn du mich um 7 abholst, ...** If you pick me up at 7 ...
  **Nachdem du mich abgeholt hast, ...**
  After you've picked me up ...

9 **Um frühzeitig anzukommen, fuhren wir sofort ab**
  In order to arrive early we left immediately

# Question Forms

## Direct Questions

- In German, a direct question is formed by simply inverting the verb and subject (→**1**)

- In compound tenses (see pp 22 ff), the past participle or infinitive goes to the end of the clause (→**2**)

- A statement can be made into a question by the addition of **nicht, nicht wahr** or **doch**, as with "isn't it" in English (→**3**) Questions formed in this way normally expect the answer to be "yes".

- When a question is put in the negative, **doch** can be used to answer it more positively than **ja** (→**4**)

## Questions Formed Using Interrogative Words

- When questions are formed with **interrogative adverbs**, the subject and verb are inverted (→**5**)

- When questions are formed with **interrogative pronouns** and **adjectives** (see pp 144 and 176 to 178), the word order is that of direct statements:
  1. as the subject of the verb at the beginning of the clause they do not cause inversion (→**6**)
  2. if *not* the subject of the verb *and* at the beginning of the clause they do cause inversion (→**7**)

## Indirect Questions

These are questions following verbs of asking and wondering etc. The verb comes at the end of an indirect question (→**8**)

**1 Magst du ihn?**
Do you like him?
**Gehst du ins Kino?**
Do you go to the cinema? Are you going to the cinema?

**2 Hast du ihn gesehen?**
Did you see him? Have you seen him?
**Wird sie mit ihm kommen?**
Will she come with him?

**3 Das stimmt, nicht (wahr)?** That's true, isn't it?
**Das schaffst du doch?** You'll manage, won't you?

**4 Glaubst du mir nicht? — Doch!**
Don't you believe me? — Yes I do!

**5 Wann ist er gekommen?** When did he come?
**Wo willst du hin?** Where are you off to?

**6 Wer hat das gemacht?** Who did this?

**7 Wem hast du es geschenkt?** Who did you give it to?

**8 Er fragte, ob du mitkommen wolltest**
He asked if you wanted to come
**Er möchte wissen, warum du nicht gekommen bist**
He would like to know why you didn't come

# Negatives

A statement or question is made negative by adding:

**nicht** (*not*) or **nie** (*never*)

- The negative may be placed next to the phrase or word to which it refers. The negative meaning can be shifted from one element of the sentence to another in this way (→**1**)

- **nie** can be placed at the beginning of a sentence for added emphasis, in which case subject-verb inversion occurs (→**2**)

- **nicht** comes at the end of a negative imperative, except when the verb is separable, in which case **nicht** *precedes* the separable prefix (→**3**)

- The combination **nicht ein** is usually replaced by forms of **kein** (see p 126) (→**4**)

- **doch** (see p 196) is used in place of **ja** to contradict a negative statement (→**5**)

- Negative comparison is made with **nicht ... sondern** (*not ... but*). This construction is used to correct a previous false impression or idea (→**6**)

1 **Mit ihr wollte er nicht sprechen**
   He didn't want to speak to *her*
   **Er wollte nicht mit ihr sprechen**
   He didn't *want* to speak to her

   **Er will nicht morgen nach Hause**
   *OR* **Morgen will er nicht nach Hause**
   He doesn't want to go home *tomorrow*
   **Er will morgen nicht nach Hause**
   He doesn't want to go *home* tomorrow

   **Wohnen Sie nicht in Dortmund?**
   Don't you live in Dortmund?
   **Warum ist er nicht mitgekommen?**
   Why didn't he come with you?
   **Waren Sie nie in Dortmund?**
   Have you never been to Dortmund?

2 **Nie war sie glücklicher gewesen**
   She had never been happier

3 **Iß das nicht!** Don't eat that!
   **Beeilen Sie sich nicht!** Don't hurry!
   *BUT* **Geh nicht weg!** Don't go away!

4 **Gibt es keine Plätzchen?** Aren't there any biscuits?
   **Kein einziges Kind hatte die Arbeit geschrieben**
   Not a single child had done the work

5 **Du kommst nicht mit — Doch, ich komme mit**
   You're not coming — Yes I am

6 **Nicht Joachim, sondern sein Bruder war es**
   It wasn't Joachim, but his brother

# Numbers

| Cardinal (*one, two etc*) | | Ordinal (*first, second etc*) | |
|---|---|---|---|
| null | 0 | | |
| eins | 1 | der erste[2] | 1. |
| zwei[1] | 2 | der zweite[1] | 2. |
| drei | 3 | der dritte | 3. |
| vier | 4 | der vierte | 4. |
| fünf | 5 | der fünfte | 5. |
| sechs | 6 | der sechste | 6. |
| sieben | 7 | der siebte | 7. |
| acht | 8 | der achte | 8. |
| neun | 9 | der neunte | 9. |
| zehn | 10 | der zehnte | 10. |
| elf | 11 | der elfte | 11. |
| zwölf | 12 | der zwölfte | 12. |
| dreizehn | 13 | der dreizehnte | 13. |
| vierzehn | 14 | der vierzehnte | 14. |
| fünfzehn | 15 | der fünfzehnte | 15. |
| sechzehn | 16 | der sechzehnte | 16. |
| siebzehn | 17 | der siebzehnte | 17. |
| achtzehn | 18 | der achtzehnte | 18. |
| neunzehn | 19 | der neunzehnte | 19. |
| zwanzig | 20 | der zwanzigste | 20. |
| einundzwanzig | 21 | der einundzwanzigste | 21. |
| zweiundzwanzig[1] | 22 | der zweiundzwanzigste[1] | 22. |
| dreißig | 30 | der dreißigste | 30. |
| vierzig | 40 | der vierzigste | 40. |

1. **zwo** often replaces **zwei** in speech, to distinguish it clearly from **drei: zwo, zwoundzwanzig** *etc.*

2. The ordinal number and the preceding definite article (and adjective if there is one) are declined e.g.:
   **sie ist die zehnte** *she's the tenth*
   **bei seinem dritten Versuch** *at his third attempt*

| | | | |
|---|---|---|---|
| **fünfzig** | 50 | **der fünfzigste** | 50. |
| **sechzig** | 60 | **der sechzigste** | 60. |
| **siebzig** | 70 | **der siebzigste** | 70. |
| **achtzig** | 80 | **der achtzigste** | 80. |
| **neunzig** | 90 | **der neunzigste** | 90. |
| **hundert** | *a hundred* | **der hundertste** | 100. |
| **einhundert** | *one hundred* | | |
| **hunderteins** | 101 | **der hunderterste** | 101. |
| **hundertzwei** | 102 | **der hundertzweite** | 102. |
| **hunderteinundzwanzig** | 121 | **der hunderteinundzwanzigste** | 121. |
| **zweihundert** | 200 | **der zweihundertste** | 200. |
| **tausend** | *a thousand* | **der tausendste** | 1000. |
| **eintausend** | *one thousand* | | |
| **tausendeins** | 1001 | **der tausenderste** | 1001. |
| **zweitausend** | 2000 | **der zweitausendste** | 2000. |
| **hunderttausend** | 100 000 | **der hunderttausendste** | 100 000. |
| **eine Million** | 1 000 000 | **der millionste** | 1 000 000. |

- With large numbers, spaces or full stops are used where English uses a comma e.g.:
  1.000.000 or 1 000 000 for 1,000,000 (*a million*).

- Decimals are written with a comma instead of a full stop e.g.:
  7,5 (**sieben Komma fünf**) for 7.5 (*seven point five*).

## Fractions

| | |
|---|---|
| **halb** | half (a) |
| **die Hälfte** | half (the) |
| **eine halbe Stunde** | half an hour |
| **das Drittel** | third |
| **das Viertel** | quarter |
| **zwei Drittel** | two thirds |
| **dreiviertel** | three quarters |
| **anderthalb/eineinhalb** | one and a half |
| **zweieinhalb** | two and a half |

# Time

**Wie spät ist es?**     What time is it?
**Wieviel Uhr ist es?**

**Es ist …**     It's …

| | |
|---|---|
| 00.00 | **Mitternacht / null Uhr / vierundzwanzig Uhr / zwölf Uhr** |
| 00.10 | **zehn (Minuten) nach zwölf / null Uhr zehn** |
| 00.15 | **Viertel nach zwölf / null Uhr fünfzehn** |
| 00.30 | **halb eins / null Uhr dreißig** |
| 00.40 | **zwanzig (Minuten) vor eins / null Uhr vierzig** |
| 00.45 | **viertel vor eins / dreiviertel eins / null Uhr fünfundvierzig** |
| 01.00 | **ein Uhr** |
| 01.10 | **zehn (Minuten) nach eins / ein Uhr zehn** |
| 01.15 | **Viertel nach eins / ein Uhr fünfzehn** |
| 01.30 | **halb zwei / ein Uhr dreißig** |
| 01.40 | **zwanzig (Minuten) vor zwei / ein Uhr vierzig** |
| 01.45 | **viertel vor zwei / dreiviertel zwei / ein Uhr fünfundvierzig** |
| 01.50 | **zehn (Minuten) vor zwei / ein Uhr fünfzig** |
| 12.00 | **zwölf Uhr** |
| 12.30 | **halb eins / zwölf Uhr dreißig** |
| 13.00 | **ein Uhr / dreizehn Uhr** |
| 16.30 | **halb fünf / sechzehn Uhr dreißig** |
| 22.00 | **zehn Uhr / zweiundzwanzig Uhr / zwoundzwanzig Uhr** |

**morgen um halb drei** at half past two tomorrow
**um drei Uhr (nachmittags)** at three (pm)
**kurz vor zehn Uhr** just before ten
**gegen vier Uhr (nachmittags)** towards four (in the afternoon)
**erst um halb neun** not until half past eight
**ab neun Uhr** from nine o'clock onwards
**morgen früh/abend** tomorrow morning/evening

## The Calendar

### Dates

| | |
|---|---|
| **Der wievielte ist heute?** | What's the date today? |
| **Welches Datum haben wir heute?** | |

| | |
|---|---|
| **Heute ist ...** | It's ... |
| **der zwanzigste März** | the twentieth of March |
| **der Zwanzigste** | the twentieth |

| | |
|---|---|
| **Heute haben wir ...** | It's ... |
| **den zwanzigsten März** | the twentieth of March |
| **den Zwanzigsten** | the twentieth |

| | |
|---|---|
| **Am wievielten findet es statt?** | When does it take place? |
| **Es findet am ersten April statt** | ... on the first of April |
| **Es findet am Ersten statt** | ... on the first |

**Es findet (am) Montag, den ersten April statt**
**Es findet Montag, den 1. April statt**
It takes place on Monday, the first of April/April 1st

### Years

**(im Jahre) 1994 (neunzehnhundertvierundneunzig)** in 1994
**Er wurde 1970 (neunzehnhundertsiebzig) geboren**
He was born in 1970

### Other Expressions

**Im Dezember/Januar** *etc* in December/January *etc*
**im Winter/Sommer/Herbst/Frühling**
in winter/summer/autumn/spring
**Anfang September** at the beginning of September
**nächstes Jahr** next year

# Punctuation

German punctuation differs from English in the following cases:

## Commas

- Decimal places are always shown by a comma (→**1**)

- Large numbers are separated off by means of a space or a full stop (→**2**)

- Subordinate clauses are always marked off from the rest of the sentence by a comma (→**3**)
  This applies to all types of subordinate clause e.g.:

  clauses with an adverbial function (→**3**)

  relative clauses (→**4**)

  clauses containing indirect speech (→**5**)

- A comma is not required between two main clauses linked by a co-ordinating conjunction (→**6**)

## Exclamation Marks

- An exclamation mark is occasionally used after the name at the beginning of a letter, but this tends to be rather old-fashioned (→**7**)

- Exclamation marks are used after imperative forms unless these are not intended as commands (→**8**)

**1** **3,4 (drei Komma vier)** 3.4 (three point four)

**2** **20 000** *OR* **20.000 (zwanzigtausend)**
20,000 (twenty thousand)

**3** **Als er nach Hause kam, war sie schon weg**
She had already gone when he came home
**Er bleibt gesund, obwohl er zuviel trinkt**
He stays healthy, even though he drinks too much

**4** **Der Mann, mit dem sie verheiratet ist, soll sehr reich sein**
The man she is married to is said to be very rich

**5** **Er sagt, es gefällt ihm nicht**
He says he doesn't like it

**6** **Ich möchte hin aber ich darf nicht**
I would love to go but I can't

**7** **Liebe Elke!** ... Dear Elke, ...
**Sehr geehrter Herr Braun!** ... Dear Mr. Braun, ...

**8** **Steh auf!** Get up
**Bitte nehmen Sie doch Platz**
Do please sit down

The following index lists comprehensively both grammatical terms and key words in German and English contained in this book.